ANNUAL REGISTER OF
GRANT SUPPORT™
A DIRECTORY OF FUNDING SOURCES

Annual Register of Grant Support™
54th Edition

Publisher
Thomas H. Hogan

Director, ITI Reference Group
Owen O'Donnell

Managing Editor
Debra James

Consulting Editor
Stephen L. Torpie

ANNUAL REGISTER OF GRANT SUPPORT™

A DIRECTORY OF FUNDING SOURCES

54th EDITION | 2021

Published by

Information Today, Inc.
143 Old Marlton Pike
Medford, NJ 08055-8750
Phone: (609) 654-6266
Fax: (609) 654-4309
E-mail (Orders): **custserv@infotoday.com**
Web site: http://www.infotoday.com

ISSN 0066-4049
ISBN 978-1-57387-566-0
Library of Congress Catalog Card Number: 69-18307

Information Today, Inc.
143 Old Marlton Pike
Medford, NJ 08055-8750
Phone: 800-300-9868 (Customer Service)
             800-409-4929 (Editorial)
Fax: 609-654-6098
E-mail (orders): custserv@infotoday.com
Web Site: www.infotoday.com

Printed and bound in the United States of America

US $389.50
ISBN 13: 978-1-57387-566-0
38950>

9 781573 875660

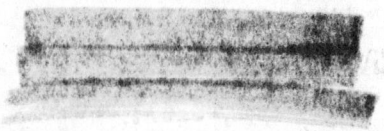

Contents

Continued

Preface

Now in its 54th edition, the *Annual Register of Grant Support™: A Directory of Funding Sources* has achieved a deserved reputation as an authoritative standard reference source on financial support. Known and relied upon by academic scholars and researchers, *Grant Support* also responds to the needs of those in the fields of business, civic improvement, and social welfare. Recognized for its value to the individual, *Grant Support* assists hospitals, arts organizations, community service groups, medical research facilities, and other institutional applicants as well.

The 2021 edition includes details of 2,467 grant support programs of government agencies, public and private foundations, corporations, community trusts, unions, educational and professional associations, and special interest organizations. These organizations support a total of 3,894 grant programs and cover a broad spectrum of interests from academic and scientific research, project development, travel and exchange programs, and publication support to equipment and construction grants, in-service training, and competitive awards and prizes in a variety of fields. Please see the "Key to entry information" and associated definitions on pages xiv and xv. This feature illustrates a sample listing with all the data elements defined.

Grant Support attempts to be as comprehensive as possible by including the following forms of financial aid: programs that offer non-repayable financial assistance directly to the grantee or indirectly through payment to the sponsoring institution; programs that accept applicants from the United States or Canada or directly benefit the United States or Canada; study grants and fellowships aimed principally though not exclusively at the graduate or postgraduate levels; grants for construction, facilities, or project costs for education, medical research, health care, civic improvement, etc.; and programs donating consulting services in lieu of a direct monetary grant.

Funding sources are given the opportunity annually to update entry data. Staff research continues to within weeks of *Grant Support*'s publication date to assure information is as current and complete as possible and to identify new funding sources for inclusion. Essential programs for which no updated information has been returned are included, either as they appeared in the last edition, revised where possible, or compiled entirely through secondary research.

Support programs are divided into eleven major areas, further subdivided into more specific subject fields. Each entry contained in *Grant Support* has been placed in the section that reflects its principal interest. If program interests equally emphasize diverse fields, such as communications and business and economics, one full entry and a cross-reference will appear in the respective sections. Similarly, a program for minority political scientists will appear in either "Special Populations" or "Political Science," with a cross-reference in the appropriate section. However, organizations with broad support purposes or interests in three or more well-defined areas are listed in the "Multiple Special Purpose" section.

Four helpful indexes conclude the volume: Subject, Organization and Program, Geographic, and Personnel. Please note: *References in each index point to the entry number visible in the listing—not to a page number.*

In the Subject Index, each grant has been indexed in terms of the specific areas to which it may be applied (e.g., Cartography, Mathematics), the type of grant (e.g., Medical Research, Theology), and the individuals or organizations eligible for support, if limitations are specified (e.g., Religious Institutions, Women). The Organization and Program Index lists grant programs in upper/lower case and funding organizations in all upper case. Programs are also listed following the organizations that sponsor them. The Geographic Index groups grantmaking organizations according to the state or country in which they are located. In the Personnel Index, officers of the organizations, trustees, directors, and awards committee members are listed with their program entry number.

While consulting the Subject Index, should the reader wish to know in which chapter a particular entry appears, he or she may consult the Emtry Listing by Chapter Index, a one page outline that precedes the Subject Index.

The editorial staff of *Annual Register of Grant Support* strives continually to provide the professional community with the most comprehensive information on existing forms of financial aid from as wide a variety of sources as possible. The staff urges the users of this edition to inform us of any corrections or additions to existing entries and of funding sources not included, and cordially invites suggestions for improvement of future editions.

Introduction

In the United States today, the support of human services through grants, awards, fellowships, and private gifts is a multibillion-dollar enterprise. Private foundations, corporations, individuals, charitable organizations, and agencies gave an estimated $449.64 billion to charity in 2019, an increase of 4.9 percent compared with the revised estimate of $427.71 billion given in 2018, according to the Giving USA Foundation.

Of the total $449.61 billion given in 2019, $309.66 billion came from individuals and accounts for 69 percent of all estimated giving. Grants from foundations, excluding those affiliated with business enterprises, totalled $75.69 billion, an increase of 17.0 percent. Gifts received through bequests increased an estimated 10.0 percent to $43.21 billion; corporations contributed $21.09 billion, a decrease of 5.0 percent.

When total charitable giving is analyzed by recipient fields, religion received the largest share of 2019 dollars—$128.17 billion—followed by education ($64.11 billion); human services ($55.99 billion); foundations ($53.51 billion); health ($41.46 billion); public-society benefit ($37.16 billion); international affairs ($28.89 billion); arts, culture, and humanities ($21.64 billion); environment and animals ($14.16billion); and individuals ($10.11 billion).

The entries listed in this edition of *Annual Register of Grant Support*™ represent billions of dollars in financial assistance to potential grant seekers.

Part of the success in using the *Annual Register of Grant Support*™ will depend on an understanding of the various types of grantmaking entities, how they differ in their objectives and grantmaking procedures, what they look for in the grant applicant, and how they are approached. It is hoped that the following descriptions of grant supporting organizations will increase the usability of *Grant Support* to the potential grant seeker.

PRIVATE FOUNDATIONS

Probably no area of philanthropy is so misunderstood and misused as that of private foundations. According to studies, as many as 80 percent of all applications to private foundations are incorrect, inappropriate, or misdirected. While at least part of the blame for this error must be attributed to private foundations themselves, grant seekers often compound the error by tending to lump all private foundations together as if they shared a common purpose.

Not only do private foundations differ greatly from public funding sources, but there is a wide diversity among private foundations themselves. What may be an appropriate application to The Ford Foundation, for example, may be totally inappropriate to the San Francisco Foundation.

There are more than 75,000 grantmaking foundations in the United States. The reason that an approximate figure must be used is that the federal government defines private foundations more by exclusion than by anything else. If an organization cannot qualify as a charitable, religious, educational, scientific, or governmental organization, it may be classified as a private foundation even if it has never made a grant nor intends to make one. Potential grant seekers should be aware that the mere use of the word "foundation" in the title of an organization is not evidence that the organization will make grants.

Of particular interest to the potential grant seeker is a requirement that every private foundation with assets of $5,000 or more (virtually all of them) must submit an annual report that is available for public inspection. These annual reports, printed on special Internal Revenue Service form 990-PF (Private Foundation), include the names and addresses of all principal officers of the foundation, the total assets and investments of the foundation and, most important, a complete listing of every grant made during the year of record. Users of *Grant Support* may wish to review selected 990-PFs of those foundations included in this edition in order to supplement information on current grants.

These 990-PF forms may be obtained directly from the private foundations themselves, or they may be found in over 400 Foundation Center Funding Information Network locations. To obtain a list of participating Network organizations near you, visit the Foundation Center web site at: http://network..foundationcenter.org/directory.

A substantial number of private foundations publish their own annual reports, over and above the 990-PF requirement mentioned earlier. Copies of these annual reports may be obtained by writing the foundation directly.

TYPES OF FOUNDATIONS

There are certain aspects common to all private foundations in the United States. However, foundations can be broken down into five types, which will assist the grant seeker in understanding their current objectives and grant distribution patterns.

1. National Foundations

Most of the foundations listed in Grant Support are national foundations, meaning that they are not limited to any geographic area in their grant support. National foundations are usually quite large, with assets of $25 million or more. They include all the better-known foundations, such as The Ford Foundation, the Lilly Endowment, The Rockefeller Foundation, and the Carnegie Corporation of New York. Because national foundations may make grants anywhere in the country, it is important to remember that these foundations are usually more attracted to programs and proposals with national, or at least regional, implications. Most of the national foundations are staffed with professional grantmakers, publish their own annual reports, and often have well-defined philanthropic goals.

While national foundations are large enough to fund projects of almost any size—and have been known to make grants of a million dollars or more—it should be remembered that competition for these national foundation grants is extremely fierce. The Ford Foundation, for example, will receive as many as 30,000 proposals every year and will fund only about 2,000.

2. Special-Interest Foundations

Many foundations listed in this edition of Grant Support devote their entire grant efforts to programs within a single field of interest. These special-interest foundations, just as the national foundations, often make grants without any geographic limitations so long as the projects relate to the specific areas. Special-interest foundations range from the massive Robert Wood Johnson Foundation (health) to the Joseph P. Kennedy Foundation (mental retardation) to those supporting research on a single disease.

Some of the larger special-interest foundations employ staff whose purpose is not only to review grants but to stay abreast of information being gathered about that special field of interest. Potential grant seekers, then, should consider special-interest foundations as a potential source of information about a given subject as well as a potential source of funds.

3. Corporate Foundations

During the 1950s, many major corporations created private foundations to serve as the corporate philanthropic arm, although the Tax Reform Act of 1969 greatly slowed the increase in their number. The ExxonMobil Foundation, Inc. is an example. Readers should be alerted to the fact that while many foundations carry names of large corporations, they are not corporate foundations. The Ford Foundation, for example, is not a corporate foundation; it was created by the Ford family.

Most corporate foundations, while "independent," are very much creatures of the corporations that founded them and fund them. Corporate foundations will, therefore, often be more receptive to proposals that are in line with their corporate interest. Historically, corporate foundations more often have made grants in the fields of education, federated giving (United Way, etc.), minority enterprises, and local social services that demonstrate a benefit to the company employees as well as the community at large. Most corporate foundations will have relatively small assets in comparison with the amount of grants. This is because once the money has moved from the corporation to the corporate foundation, it can never go back to the corporation. Usually corporations will keep only enough funds in the corporate foundation to sustain the foundation's grant efforts without harming the corporate financial position.

4. Family Foundations

By far, the largest number of private foundations are family foundations. They range in assets from hundreds of millions of dollars, such as those of the several Rockefeller Foundations, to a few thousand dollars.

The grant support pattern of family foundations is very often a personal matter. Often the family foundation will be controlled entirely by family members, and even when these family members have died, the family foundation will often continue to reflect their wishes. Unlike special interest foundations, family foundations seldom have set fields of interest. Grants more probably will reflect areas of current family interest rather than any recognizable pattern of traditional philanthropy.

Most family foundations are small, and few will have staff or guidelines for submitting proposals. A vast majority of family foundations limit their grants to the city or locality in which the family resides and accumulated its wealth. Unlike national foundations, family foundations are best approached as if they were individual donors, not private foundations.

Because most family foundations are relatively small and have such a limited geographic giving pattern, few are included in Grant Support. These foundations should be explored, however, for modest gifts of a local nature. While the average gift of small family foundations is less than $5,000, the sheer volume of family foundations makes them an important factor in grant support.

5. Community Foundations

In a strictly legal sense, community foundations are not really foundations at all but, rather, public charities. Community foundations maintain this favored tax status by collecting money from the public and directing grants within the community for which they are named. Because community foundations are not private foundations, they have no minimum giving requirements and pay no excise taxes on their net investment income. This is partly responsible for their rapid growth during the past decade, for hundreds of foundations (including some with assets in the many millions of dollars) have given all their money to community foundations.

A number of the larger community foundations, such as The Cleveland Foundation and The New York Community Trust, are listed in Grant Support. It is easy to distinguish a community foundation, for it will always be named for the community it serves. The San Francisco Foundation serves San Francisco, The Chicago Community Trust serves Chicago, and so forth. Readers of Grant Support should bear in mind that community foundations cannot, by law, make grants outside the geographic regions they serve. The San Francisco Foundation, for example, is not likely to fund a project in Texas, regardless of the merit of the proposal.

For more information about the existence of a community foundation in a given city, readers may wish to consult the local trust bank in that city. (Information can also be obtained by writing the Council on Foundations, Inc., 2121 Crystal Drive, Suite 700, Arlington, VA 22202 or via their web site at *www.cof.org*.)

CORPORATE GIVING

Although the practice of corporations making grants and gifts to charity is now largely accepted, it was not until 1935 that the Internal Revenue Service allowed a charitable deduction for corporate gifts. In 1982, changes in the tax law enhanced the value of donations of company products, and increased the deduction of corporate contributions from 5 to 10 percent of net income. Yet while this modest federal government incentive has spurred corporate philanthropy, approximately only one-third of all corporations in the United States make corporate gifts. Corporations made the largest percentage of their donations to education over the last several years, with health and human services receiving the second largest amounts. Cultural and arts groups, civic and community activities, and various other recipients received the balance of corporate dollars. Most corporations do not have professional grant reviewers but will often have grant guidelines, specific philanthropic objectives, or well-defined procedures for grant applicants.

An important consideration when approaching corporations is to introduce a benefit, either directly to the company or indirectly through its employees, that grant support can make. A proposal for support of an alcoholism program may be received more readily if the corporation feels alcoholism is a problem among its employees.

Many corporations are willing to provide volunteer service and specific expert assistance as well as money. Corporations also make in-kind contributions, such as free printing, equipment, etc., and will sometimes match gifts made by individual employees.

FEDERATED GIVING

Grant Support lists many grant opportunities from funding sources which, though neither foundations nor corporations, provide many millions of dollars of grant support every year. These funding sources can best be described as federated giving organizations, in that a number of small organizations combine their funding efforts for maximum effect.

The largest and best known federated agency is, of course, United Way. Most United Ways, however, do not make grants so much as they support existing agencies.

There are a number of other federated agencies that do make grants. The Catholic Campaign for Human Development, which is the federated arm of the Catholic Church in America, provides some $18 million in grant support annually. Other federated agencies include the United Negro College Fund, the United Jewish Appeal, and the American Association of University Women.

PUBLIC MONEY

Government funding is as complex and confusing as it is big, and the special terms and language of government grants make the subject seem more confusing than it really is. An understanding of the various types of grants and some of the most often used terms may help readers break through the perplexing language of government grants.

Types of Grants

The federal government makes grants in many forms, some of which allow the independent grant seeker an opportunity to be funded, and some which do not. Below are some of the most common types of government grants.

Block Grants: Sometimes called "bloc" grants, these are made from the federal government directly to states or local units of government, such as counties and municipalities. The grant most often comes to the state in a "block," and the state may spend the money as it wishes as long as the funds are being used to fulfill the basic purposes for which they were authorized. Many of the more recent federal grants under what is called "new federalism" have been block grants such as the Housing and Community Development Act money, the Comprehensive Employment and Training Act money, and funds to support programs for older Americans. Under the rules of most block grants, the state must submit an annual "state plan" to the federal government explaining how and where the funds are to be used. This state plan is public information, and potential grant seekers may wish to review it for programs under which they wish to seek grant support. One important aspect of block grants is that while the money is federal, the authority to spend it is local, and the recipients of block grant funds are allowed great flexibility in how they use the money.

Capitation Grants: Stemming from a concept of providing funds per capita of service, capitation grants are awarded based on the actual number of people served, rather than on the task to be performed. For example, an organization may be providing housing for runaway youths. This organization's annual budget is $100,000, and last year it provided housing for 1,000 youths. A capitation grant would provide $100 for each youth housed during the coming year ($100,000 divided by 1,000 youths). Capitation grants are most often used for training grants where payment is based on enrollment, rather than training outcome.

Categorical Grants: Simply stated, funds under a certain "category" must be expended within a certain field of interest, such as mental health, services for the handicapped, or maternity and child care. Although the number of categorical grants provided by the federal government has decreased in the past few years because of an increase in block grants, there are still more than 850 federal grant programs active within the federal government.

Construction Grants: Unless specifically stated, most federal grants will not provide funds for capital purposes, requiring instead that the grantee rent or lease the appropriate facility. Special construction grants, especially in the fields of health and mental health, have been made in the past for construction, renovation, and expansion. Many more important construction grant programs have been severely cut in the past few years, however, and it appears that the federal government is less enamored with this type of grant than in the past.

Demonstration Grants: Among the most common types of grants made in the human services field, demonstration grants, as opposed to basic research grants, are made to agencies in order to illustrate the effectiveness of a certain procedure or methodology, while at the same time providing a direct benefit to a group of clients. Unlike research grants, there is usually a large amount of evidence that the methodology to be demonstrated should prove effective before the grant is awarded. Often, demonstration grants are the second step of research grants, attempting to show that the success of a research grant may have greater applicability or a wider target population than originally envisioned.

Formula Grants: Not so much a type of grant as a method of determining the amount of funds to be made available, formula grants are based most often on the population, income, taxation, and special need of a given area.

The formula for grants will be written into the legislation or regulation that established the fund. The capitation grant mentioned earlier is one type of formula.

Matching Grants: Often confused with formula grants in that there is usually a "formula" for establishing the matching grant requirement, a matching grant means that the agency or individual who is receiving the grant guarantees to provide a certain portion of the total grant funds from sources other than the government. This "match" may be as small as one percent to as much as 50 percent with organizations such as the National Endowment for the Arts and National Endowment for the Humanities. Often there is a "sliding match" requirement, which means that the agency receiving the grant will provide a greater share of the total costs in the second and subsequent years of the award. Matching requirements may be for a "hard" or "soft" match. A "hard" match means that actual dollar matches must be secured, whereas a "soft" match allowed for such donated services as volunteer time and goods or equipment to be counted in lieu of "hard" dollars.

Project Grants: The grants allow the granting agency, usually a department or agency of the federal government, to determine funding based solely on the merits of the project of an individual or organization, rather than by formula requirements mentioned earlier. This is one of the most flexible types of grants in that the granting agency may have complete control in selecting the project, the grant recipient, and the amount of the award.

Research Grants: As opposed to demonstration grants and project grants, research grants are provided to test theories and hypotheses, develop or interpret new information, or revise accepted theories without the requirement that some benefit be immediately passed on to the clients. In fact the term "client" is often replaced with the term "subject" in research grants. There are two types, basic and applied. Basic research, which enjoyed great favor in the 1960s, has found funding harder to obtain lately, while applied research funds have continued to grow, especially in environmental programs.

Staffing Grants: As the phrase implies, these grants are provided for support of salaries of professional and technical staff members, plus in-service training in many cases. Most staffing grants come with a sliding match requirement.

Training Grants: These are awarded to organizations, corporations, or individuals to support the costs of training existing staff, students, or potential staff in the techniques or procedures needed to develop skills in a particular field, such as nursing, paramedical training and legal aid.

Seeking Governmental Sources

In addition to the *Annual Register of Grant Support*™, there are several places potential grant seekers can look for information about federal grants.

Catalog of Federal Domestic Assistance

The most important index for identifying federal resources can be found on *beta.SAM.gov* (formerly the *Catalog of Federal Domestic Assistance* whose web site, www.cfda.gov, has since been retired). The resources on *beta.SAM.gov* give you access to a database of all Federal programs available to state and local governments (including the District of Columbia); federally-recognized Native American tribal governments; territories (and possessions) of the United States; domestic public, quasi-public, and private profit and nonprofit organizations and institutions; specialized groups; and individuals.

Federal Register

Another valuable source is the *Federal Register*, available at *www.federalregister.gov*. Published by the Office of the Federal Register, National Archives and Records Administration (NARA), the Federal Register is the official daily publication for rules, proposed rules, and notices of Federal agencies and organizations. It includes such items as presidential orders, advisory meetings, program announcements, requests for applications and deadline dates.

Grants.gov

Grants.gov is a central storehouse for information on over 1,000 grant programs and provides access to approximately $500 billion in annual awards. The Department of Health and Human Services is the Grants.gov program's managing partner, and allows access to 26 federal grant-making agencies through the *www.grants.gov* web site.

Clearinghouses

Begun in the 1960s on a limited basis, a coordinated grant support process known as clearinghouse review was once required on hundreds of government grants.

As part of this review process, an applicant submits a brief description of the project or activity for which federal support is sought. Some clearinghouses have developed special forms for this "notification of intent," while others ask for a simple program description, along with the name and location of the applicant agency. Clearinghouses then notify the government agencies and elected officials of local governments that might be interested in the project, in order for the departments and agencies to comment.

If the clearinghouse does not identify any problems or possible conflicts, the applicant may complete and submit the proposal to the funding agency unless the clearinghouse specifies that it wants to review the completed proposal.

If there are concerns or unresolved issues, the clearinghouse may arrange a meeting between the applicant and the various departments that have expressed the concern. After any issues have been addressed, the applicant may wish to rewrite the proposal, continue discussions with the departments that are expressing concern, or submit the proposal to the funding source with the comments of the clearinghouse attached.

Key to entry information

(1) **XYZ FOUNDATION**   (2) **[101]**

(3) One Central Commerce Building
Main and Division Streets
Anytown, IL 60009

(4) (312) 555-5555
Fax: (312) 555-1234
E-Mail Address: abcd@xyzfdn.edu
Web Site Address: www.xyzfdn.edu

(5) FOUNDED: 1950

(6) AREAS OF INTEREST:
Education, medical research, the
environment, youth groups, law and
social welfare.

(7) CONSULTING OR VOLUNTEER
SERVICES:
Technical assistance to community
groups, particularly to those providing
cultural activities.

(8) NAME OF PROGRAM
John Doe Project Grants Fund

(9) TYPE:
Project/Program grants. Support for a
variety of activities in the areas of
education, medical research, desert
research, atmospheric, earth, and
oceanographic sciences, youth
organizations, libraries, conservation
projects, water pollution studies, fish
and game management, preservation,
parks and recreation, environmental
studies, law, judicial education, crime
delinquency, law enforcement, relief and
social agencies, museums and historical
projects, health, hospitals, and
community improvement organizations.
Awards are not available for
endowment, contingency or reserve
purposes.

(10) YEAR PROGRAM STARTED: 1990

(11) PURPOSE:
To support endeavors for the benefit of
mankind.

(12) LEGAL BASIS:
Private foundation; tax-exempt under
statute 501(c)(3) of the Internal
Revenue Code.

(13) ELIGIBILITY: U.S. tax-exempt
nonprofit organizations with
appropriate interests are eligible to
apply. Grants are not made, however,
to organizations   which distribute them
to beneficiaries of their own selection.
Priority is given to projects which are
not normally financed by public tax
funds.

(14) GEOGRAPHIC RESTRICTIONS:
United States.

(15) FINANCIAL DATA:
Grants vary in amount depending upon
the needs and nature of the request.

(16) *Amount of support per award:*
$1,000 to $500,000.

(17) *Total amount of support:*
$6,005,000 for the year ended May 31,
2019.

(18) *Matching fund requirements:* Grants
exceeding $25,000 must be matched by
an amount not less than one-third the
total amount of the grant.

(19) COOPERATIVE FUNDING PRO-
GRAMS: The Foundation prefers joint
funding whenever possible.

(20) NUMBER OF APPLICANTS MOST
RECENT YEAR: 512

(21) NUMBER OF AWARDS: 92 for the
year ended May 31, 2019.

(22) REPRESENTATIVE AWARDS:
$75,000 to Anytown Hospital, toward
facilities and equipment for its new
Community Health Center; $25,000 to
State University, for development of an
interdisciplinary studies program;
$15,000 to City Youth Center, toward
purchase of equipment for its model
reading laboratory program for youths.

(23) APPLICATION INFORMATION:
No official application forms are issued.
Interested applicants should submit an
informal proposal which briefly
includes: (1) amount requested and an
explanation of the necessity or purpose
therefore; (2) aid sought and amounts
received from other foundations and
sources (include names) during the
preceding three years; (3) aid presently
being sought from other sources (or
whether such solicitation is contem-
plated) and, if so, from whom; (4) copy
of tax-exempt letter from the U.S.
Treasury and Section 509 classification
determination; (5) latest audited balance
sheet and detailed income account and;
(6) signature and approval of the
overall head of the applicant institution
or organization. Seven copies of
application proposals and covering
letters should be submitted. Letters of
support from appropriate authorities
and/or organizations are also encouraged.

(24) *Duration:* Varies according to length
of project. Grants may be renewed if
continued support can be shown to be
beneficial and vital to project success.

(25) *Deadline:* Formal proposals and
supporting documents must be received
two months prior to board meetings,
held in June and December.

(26) PUBLICATIONS:
Annual report; application guidelines.

(27) IRS IDENTIFICATION NUMBER:
00-1234567

(28) BOARD OF TRUSTEES:
John Doe III, Chairman
Margaret Lee, Vice Chairman
Samuel Smith, Treasurer
Robert Johnson, Secretary
Arthur Boyle
Anthony Cates
Phillip Sevoy

(29) OFFICERS:
Phyllis Hartley, Executive Director
David Lisle, President
Susan Banks, Vice President
John Quincy Smith, Project Grants
Coordinator

(30) ADDRESS INQUIRIES TO:
John Quincy Smith, Project Grants
Coordinator
P.O. Box 777
Neartown, IL 60008

(31) * PLEASE NOTE:
If an applicant is unclear as to the
Foundation's current fields of interest,
an inquiry directed to it describing the
applicant's project may save the trouble
or expense of preparing and submitting
a formal application.

(1)   Grantmaking organization.

(2)   Entry number, reference corresponding to numbers used in the indexes.

(3)   Address.

(4)   Telephone and fax numbers. E-mail, Web Site addresses, and TDD numbers when available.

(5)   Date organization was founded.

(6)   Major fields of organizational interest.

(7)   Fields in which the organization donates consulting, volunteer, or similar services, if applicable; nature of the service.

(8)   Name(s) of grant program(s).

(9)   Nature of support available under the program(s), e.g., fellowships, project grants, research grants, technical assistance, etc.

(10)   Date program was established.

(11)   Objective of the grant program and/or sponsoring institution.

(12)   Organization's legal status or type (e.g., IRS ruling, state statute, corporate giving program, etc.); legal authority for expenditure of government funds, etc.

(13)   Qualifications required of the applicant individual or project and/or sponsoring institution.

(14)   Restrictions or preferences as to geographic location of the applicant individual or project and/or sponsoring institution.

(15)   Fiscal nature of the grant, including expenses to which it may be applied, restrictions on its use and non-cash benefits.

(16)   Fixed sum, average amount, or range of funds offered for each award.

(17)   Total funding available for the program or, when indicated, for all programs of a grantmaking organization, and the year in question.

(18)   Cost-sharing stipulations.

(19)   Nature of participation with other donors for project support.

(20)   Total applicants, for the most recent year statistics are available.

(21)   Total recipients, and the year in question.

(22)   Representative awards made under the program for the most recent year, including the amount, recipient, and project title or purpose of the award.

(23)   Application requirements and procedures, or references for further information.

(24)   Period for which support is provided; renewal possibilities.

(25)   Closing date(s) for application submission; award announcement date(s).

(26)   Publications that are available from the organization, e.g., annual report, application guidelines, program announcements, etc.

(27)   Internal Revenue Service tax identification number, if applicable.

(28)   Names and titles of principal personnel, e.g., Trustees, Directors, Awards Committee members, etc.

(29)   Names and titles of organization and/or program officers.

(30)   Source of further information and/or recipient of applications.

(31)   Unusual specifications or conditions concerning the program.

An asterisk (*) following an organization name indicates no or incomplete data was received from the source to update or compile the entry. The program listing is then reprinted from the last edition of *Grant Support*, revised where possible, or compiled entirely through staff research.

New listings in 2021 edition

The following is a list of foundations that are offering new grant programs. Bulleted items (•) reflect new program names for the foundation listed.

HUMANITIES
Literature
Asian American Writers' Workshop, New York, NY
- (•) Margins Fellowship
- (•) Open City Fellowship

PEN America, New York, NY
- (•) PEN/Diamonstein Spielvogel Award for the Art of the Essay
- (•) PEN/E. O. Wilson Prize for Literary Science Writing
- (•) PEN/Heim Translation Fund Grant
- (•) PEN/Jacqueline Bograd Weld Award for Biography
- (•) PEN/Jean Stein Grant for Literary Oral History
- (•) PEN/Robert J. Dau Short Story Prize for Emerging Writers

INTERNATIONAL AFFAIRS AND AREA STUDIES
International studies and research abroad
Cyprus American Archaeological Research Institute, Alexandria, VA
- (•) CAARI/CAORC Research Fellowships
- (•) Edgar J. Peltenburg Postdoctoral Research Fellowship in Cypriot Prehistory

Villa I Tatti: The Harvard University Center for Italian Renaissance Studies, Florence, Italy
- (•) I Tatti/Museo Nacional del Prado Joint Fellowship
- (•) Villa I Tatti Bogazici University Joint Fellowship

SOCIAL SCIENCES
Social sciences (general)
The Phi Beta Kappa Society, Washington, DC
- (•) Dr. Martin R. Lebowitz and Eve Lewellis Lebowitz Prize for Philosophical Achievement and Contribution

The Society for the Psychological Study of Social Issues (SPSSI), Washington, DC
- (•) SPSSI Action Teaching Grants

Business and economics
American Institute of Certified Public Accountants (AICPA), Durham, NC
- (•) AICPA Foundation Scholarship for Future CPAs

Communications
Broadcast Education Association, Washington, DC
- (•) PILOT Media Technology and Innovation Scholarships

LIFE SCIENCES
Medicine (multiple disciplines)
The Educational and Research Foundation for the American Academy of Facial Plastic and Reconstructive Surgery (AAFPRS Foundation), Alexandria, VA
- (•) AAFPRS Clinical Research Scholarship
- (•) AAFPRS Research Scholar Award
- (•) AAFPRS Wally K. Dyer Award

Pharmaceutical Research and Manufacturers of America Foundation, Inc., Washington, DC
- (•) Value Assessment Challenge Awards
- (•) Value Assessment Research Award

Metabolism, gastroenterology, nephrology
American Gastroenterological Association (AGA), Bethesda, MD
- (•) AGA Medtronic Pilot Research Award in Technology Innovation
- (•) AGA Pfizer Pilot Research Award in Inflammatory Bowel Disease
- (•) AGA Takeda Pharmaceuticals Research Scholar Awards in Celiac Disease

Canadian Liver Foundation, Markham, ON
- (•) Graduate Studentships

TECHNOLOGY AND INDUSTRY
Engineering
National Action Council for Minorities in Engineering, Inc. (NACME), New York, NY
- (•) Americas Styrenics Scholarship
- (•) Autodesk Scholarship
- (•) Bechtel Undergraduate Scholarship Award
- (•) Bechtel Undergraduate Women in Engineering Scholarship
- (•) Bridge Scholarship
- (•) Chevron Scholarship Program

- (•) Collegiate Scholarship
- (•) Sidney and Katherine Friend Scholarship
- (•) William Randolph Hearst Endowment Scholarship
- (•) Phillip D. Reed Undergraduate Endowment Fellowship

EDUCATION
Scholar aid programs (all disciplines)
State of Idaho Board of Education, Boise, ID
- (•) Idaho Governor's Cup Scholarship

MULTIPLE SPECIAL PURPOSE

Multiple special purpose

ABBOTT FUND [1]

100 Abbott Park Road, D379/AP6D
Abbott Park, IL 60064-3500
(224) 667-6100
Web Site: www.abbottfund.org

FOUNDED: 1951

AREAS OF INTEREST:
Health and welfare, education, culture and arts, civic and public policy.

NAME(S) OF PROGRAMS:
- **General Grant Program**

TYPE:
General operating grants; Project/program grants. Primary interest in the fields of higher education and human health and welfare. In addition, support of appropriate programs in culture, the arts and civic activities will continue to be a portion of Abbott's program.

YEAR PROGRAM STARTED: 1951

PURPOSE:
To provide support through cash grants to U.S.-based recipients whose areas of interest are consistent with Abbott's basic philanthropic policies and objectives.

LEGAL BASIS:
Corporate nonprofit giving program.

ELIGIBILITY:
Grants will be made only to associations and organizations and not directly to individuals. Grantees must be able to provide evidence of nonprofit, tax-exempt status and must complete the eligibility test to ensure that the organization or program falls within the funding criteria.

Preference is given to requests for one-time contributions and for programmatic and operating purposes. However, grants extending over a defined period of years or directed towards the support of specific building or other capital projects will be considered on an exception basis.

Priority will be given to organizations serving communities in which Abbott has significant operations or employee populations, to organizations whose activities are directed towards the support of professions which provide, directly or indirectly, health care or other services related to Abbott's primary areas of operation.

Grants will not be made to individuals, purely social organizations, political parties or candidates, religious organizations, advertising journals, booklets, symposiums or conferences, social events, for ticket purchases, memberships, business-related purposes or for-profit entities.

FINANCIAL DATA:
Grants vary in amount, depending upon the needs and nature of the request.

APPLICATION INFO:
During periods when the Fund is accepting unsolicited grant applications, requests must be made online.
Duration: One year. Possible multiyear.

ADDRESS INQUIRIES TO:
Grant Program
(See address above.)

THE ABELL FOUNDATION, INC. [2]

111 South Calvert Street
Suite 2300
Baltimore, MD 21202-6174
(410) 547-1300
Fax: (410) 539-6579
E-mail: abell@abell.org
Web Site: www.abell.org

FOUNDED: 1953

AREAS OF INTEREST:
Arts and culture, community development, education, conservation and environment, health and human services, workforce development, criminal justice and addiction.

TYPE:
Capital grants; Challenge/matching grants; Demonstration grants; Development grants; General operating grants; Matching gifts; Project/program grants; Seed money grants.

YEAR PROGRAM STARTED: 1953

PURPOSE:
To improve the quality of life in the area around Baltimore, MD.

LEGAL BASIS:
Private foundation.

ELIGIBILITY:
Individuals are not eligible for grants. Qualifying organizations must have IRS 509(a) and 501(c)(3) not-for-profit status. Religious organizations are eligible.

GEOG. RESTRICTIONS: Maryland, with a focus on Baltimore.

FINANCIAL DATA:
Amount of support per award: $500 to $1,000,000.
Total amount of support: $13,731,857 in grants approved for the year 2019.

NO. AWARDS: 223 for the year 2019.

APPLICATION INFO:
Foundation application form must be completed and submitted. Applicant organizations must provide IRS 501(c)(3) and 509(a) documentation, the most recently audited financial statement, operating budget, projected budget for each year funding is requested, a list of the board of directors as well as pertinent information regarding the program. Application needs to be preceded by a two-page letter of inquiry.
Duration: Primarily one-year grants; few multiyear awards.
Deadline: Grants will be awarded five times a year: February, April, July, September and December.

PUBLICATIONS:
Annual Report; *Abell Report*, newsletter; periodic research reports.

IRS I.D.: 52-6036106

OFFICER:
Robert C. Embry, Jr., President
Frances M. Keenan, Senior Vice President

ADDRESS INQUIRIES TO:
Robert C. Embry, Jr., President
(See address above.)

THE ABNEY FOUNDATION [3]

100 Vine Street
Anderson, SC 29621
(864) 964-9201
Fax: (864) 964-9209
E-mail: info@abneyfoundation.org
Web Site: www.abneyfoundation.org

FOUNDED: 1957

AREAS OF INTEREST:
Religious, charitable, scientific, literary or educational, including encouragement of art and music.

TYPE:
Capital grants; Development grants; Endowments; Project/program grants; Research grants.

YEAR PROGRAM STARTED: 1957

PURPOSE:
To make grants for innovative and creative projects and to programs which are responsive to changing community needs in the areas of education, health, social service and cultural affairs.

LEGAL BASIS:
Tax-exempt, private foundation.

ELIGIBILITY:
Applicants must be tax-exempt organizations. No grants to individuals.

GEOG. RESTRICTIONS: South Carolina.

FINANCIAL DATA:
Amount of support per award: $1,000 to $250,000.
Total amount of support: $1,855,000 for the year 2019.

NO. MOST RECENT APPLICANTS: 200.

NO. AWARDS: 38.

APPLICATION INFO:
Applicants may submit a Letter of Intent briefly describing the project before submitting a proposal in order to find out if their ideas are potentially fundable by the Foundation.
Duration: No grants on a continuing basis.
Deadline: November 15.

PUBLICATIONS:
Application guidelines.

IRS I.D.: 57-6019445

TRUSTEES AND OFFICERS:
John R. Fulp, Jr., Chairman
Dr. Lisa C. McWherter, Vice Chairman and Executive Director
Johnnye K. Palmer, Treasurer
Bonnie Nash, Secretary
Lebrena Fulp Campbell
Carl T. Edwards
John R. Fulp, III
Dr. John T. Meehan
Edd Sheriff

ADDRESS INQUIRIES TO:
Dr. Lisa C. McWherter
Vice Chairman and Executive Director
(See address above.)

ACADIA UNIVERSITY [4]

18 University Avenue
Wolfville NS B4P 2R6 Canada
(902) 585-1914
Fax: (902) 585-1096
E-mail: theresa.starratt@acadiau.ca
Web Site: www.acadiau.ca

AREAS OF INTEREST:
English, political science, sociology, biology, chemistry, computer science, geology, psychology, education, community development, mathematics, statistics and applied geomatics, and social and political thought.

NAME(S) OF PROGRAMS:
- **Acadia Graduate Scholarships/Acadia Graduate Teaching Assistantships**

TYPE:
Assistantships; Awards/prizes.

PURPOSE:
To financially support graduate students.

ELIGIBILITY:
Open to registered full-time graduate students at Acadia University. Candidates must possess a 3.0/4.3 grade point average in each of the last two years of undergraduate study in their major.

FINANCIAL DATA:
Amount of support per award: Varies depending on budget and decision of department or school.

APPLICATION INFO:
Consult the University for guidelines.
Duration: One or two years.
Deadline: February.

ADDRESS INQUIRIES TO:
Theresa Starratt, Graduate Studies Officer (See address above.)

*SPECIAL STIPULATIONS:
Acadia Graduate Teaching Assistantship recipients should expect to undertake certain duties during the academic year (up to maximum of 12 hours per week and to a maximum of 144 hours per semester) as a condition of tenure. Specific duties will be established by agreement at the beginning of each academic year. An Acadia Graduate Scholarship does not require students to do any work.

THE ACHELIS AND BODMAN FOUNDATION   [5]
420 Lexington Avenue
Suite 2803
New York, NY 10170
(212) 644-0322
E-mail: info@achelisbodman.org
Web Site: achelisbodman.org

FOUNDED: 2015

AREAS OF INTEREST:
Primarily arts and culture, education, employment, health, public policy and youth and families.

TYPE:
Challenge/matching grants; Conferences/seminars; Development grants; General operating grants; Internships; Matching gifts; Project/program grants; Research grants; Scholarships; Technical assistance; Training grants. Over 90% of the Foundation's grants fall into its six program areas.

PURPOSE:
To impact the greater New York City region and enhance the quality of life for its people, especially the disadvantaged; to advance human dignity, inspire personal achievement and foster self-reliance.

LEGAL BASIS:
Private foundation under Section 501(c)(3) of the Internal Revenue Code.

ELIGIBILITY:
Nonprofit organizations based in New York City and northern New Jersey that are tax-exempt under Section 501(c)(3) of the Internal Revenue Code and fall within the program areas of the Foundation are welcome to submit an inquiry or proposal letter.

The Foundation generally does not make grants to nonprofit organizations outside of New York and New Jersey; annual appeals, dinner functions and fund-raising events; endowments and capital campaigns; loans and deficit financing; direct grants to individuals (such as scholarships and financial aid); individual day-care and after-school programs; housing; international projects; films and travel; projects for the elderly; small art, dance, music and theater groups; independent or public K-12 schools (except charter schools); national health and mental health organizations and; government agencies and nonprofit programs and services significantly funded or substantially reimbursed by government.

GEOG. RESTRICTIONS: Primarily New York City and northern New Jersey.

FINANCIAL DATA:
Amount of support per award: $5,000 to $300,000 for the year 2019.
Total amount of support: $5,455,000 for the year 2019.

NO. AWARDS: 131 for the year 2019.

APPLICATION INFO:
It is recommended that an organization's initial contact with the Foundation include only the following items:
(1) an inquiry or proposal letter briefly summarizing the history of the project, need, research, objectives, time period, key staff, project budget, and evaluation plan emphasizing measurable outcomes and specific program results;
(2) latest annual report;
(3) current and complete audited financial statements and;
(4) copy of the organization's IRS 501(c)(3) tax-exemption letter.
Duration: One year. Renewal does not generally follow the year of a grant.

OFFICERS:
John N. Irwin, III, Chairman
Russell P. Pennoyer, President
Tatiana Pouschine, Vice President
Horace I. Crary, Jr., Treasurer
John B. Krieger, Executive Director, Secretary and Assistant Treasurer

BOARD OF TRUSTEES:
Horace I. Crary, Jr.
Oliver Grace
John N. Irwin, III
Leslie Lenkowsky
George McCabe
Russell P. Pennoyer
Tatiana Pouschine
Magdalena Zavalia de Miguens

ADDRESS INQUIRIES TO:
John B. Krieger, Executive Director (See address above.)

AETNA FOUNDATION, INC.   [6]
151 Farmington Avenue
Hartford, CT 06156-3180
(860) 273-6382
Fax: (860) 273-4764
E-mail: aetnafoundation@aetna.com
Web Site: www.aetna-foundation.org

FOUNDED: 1972

AREAS OF INTEREST:
Social determinants of health.

NAME(S) OF PROGRAMS:
● **Cultivating Healthy Communities**
● **Healthiest Cities and Counties Challenge**

TYPE:
Matching gifts; Project/program grants; Research grants.

YEAR PROGRAM STARTED: 1972

PURPOSE:
To promote wellness, health and access to high-quality health care for everyone, while supporting the communities Aetna serves.

LEGAL BASIS:
Corporate giving program.

ELIGIBILITY:
Nonprofit organizations with evidence of IRS 501(c)(3) designation of de facto tax-exempt status may apply for a grant. Complete details are available on the Foundation web site.

FINANCIAL DATA:
Amount of support per award: Varies.

APPLICATION INFO:
Unsolicited requests for funding are not accepted. Requests for proposals are posted online when opportunities are available.
Duration: Varies.
Deadline: Varies.

PUBLICATIONS:
Aetna Annual Giving Report.

IRS I.D.: 23-7241940

STAFF:
Garth N. Graham, M.D., M.P.H., President
Patti MacRae, Executive Director
Amy Aparicio Clark, Managing Director, Community Impact and Strategy
Sharon R. Ions, Corporate Relations Director
Lamond Daniels, Program Officer
Kate Lincoln, Program Officer
Cheryl A. Tourigny, Program Associate
Alan C. Eversley, Program Consultant
Juanita Galvis Rueda, Program Consultant

BOARD OF DIRECTORS:
Mark T. Bertolini
Shawn Guertin
Steven B. Kelmar
Harold Paz, M.D., M.S.

ADDRESS INQUIRIES TO:
See e-mail address above.

THE AHMANSON FOUNDATION   [7]
9215 Wilshire Boulevard
Beverly Hills, CA 90210
(310) 278-0770
E-mail: info@theahmansonfoundation.org
Web Site: www.theahmansonfoundation.org

FOUNDED: 1952

AREAS OF INTEREST:
Arts and humanities, education, human services, medicine and health.

TYPE:
Capital grants; Endowments; Matching gifts; Project/program grants; Scholarships.

PURPOSE:
To support programs that improve the quality of life in Los Angeles County.

LEGAL BASIS:
Private family foundation.

ELIGIBILITY:
Grants are made to organizations that have tax-exempt status under Section 501(c)(3) of the Internal Revenue Code. No grants are made to individuals. Nonsectarian religious programs may apply.

GEOG. RESTRICTIONS: Los Angeles County, California.

FINANCIAL DATA:
Amount of support per award: Varies.

NO. AWARDS: Approximately 400 to 500.

APPLICATION INFO:
Send letter of inquiry to the Grants Administrator.
Duration: Varies.

ADDRESS INQUIRIES TO:
Grants Administrator
(See address above.)

ALABAMA POWER FOUNDATION [8]

600 North 18th Street
Birmingham, AL 35291
(205) 257-2508
Web Site: powerofgood.com

FOUNDED: 1989

AREAS OF INTEREST:
Education, arts and culture, civic and community, health and human services, and environment.

NAME(S) OF PROGRAMS:
- **Brighter Minds Grant**
- **Educational Grant Program**
- **Elevate Grant**
- **Foundation Grants**
- **Gateway Grant**
- **Good Roots Grant**
- **Students to Stewards Program**

TYPE:
Capital grants; Challenge/matching grants; Endowments; General operating grants; Project/program grants; Scholarships; Seed money grants.

PURPOSE:
To improve the quality of life of Alabamians and to strengthen the communities in which they live.

LEGAL BASIS:
Corporate foundation.

ELIGIBILITY:
Applicant must be a 501(c)(3) tax-exempt, nonprofit Alabama organization. No grants to individuals, religious or political groups.

GEOG. RESTRICTIONS: Alabama.

FINANCIAL DATA:
Amount of support per award: Elevate Grant: $10,000, plus $5,000 challenge grant the following year; Foundation Grants: Varies; Gateway: Up to $2,000; Good Roots: Up to $1,000; Students to Stewards: Up to $7,500.
Total amount of support: $137,660,000 for the year 2017.

NO. AWARDS: Brighter Minds: Over 180; Elevate: 7; Gateway: 21; Good Roots: 41 for the year 2017.

APPLICATION INFO:
All grant applications are received online. Applicants will be asked for specific information about their organization. On the last page, applicants will be prompted to attach the following:
(1) actual grant request with cover letter outlining goals, objectives and specific needs addressed, including an implementation plan and timeline with an outline for any activities planned in the near future and achievements thus far (no more than four pages);
(2) project budget with an evaluation plan with specific criteria for judging the effectiveness;
(3) a copy of the program's most recent audited financial statement;
(4) a copy of the program's current operating budget and;
(5) a copy of the program's Section 501(c)(3) IRS determination letter.

Attachments must be in MS Word, MS Excel or Adobe Acrobat file formats to be accepted.
Duration: One-time funding.
Deadline: Elevate Grant: September 1. Foundation Grant: February, April, July and October. Gateway: Late June. Good Roots: May. Students to Stewards: March.

PUBLICATIONS:
Annual report; information and guidelines.

ADDRESS INQUIRIES TO:
President
(See address above.)

ALCOA FOUNDATION [9]

201 Isabella Street
Suite 500
Pittsburgh, PA 15212-5858
E-mail: alcoafoundation@alcoa.com
Web Site: www.alcoa.com/foundation

FOUNDED: 1952

AREAS OF INTEREST:
Community enhancement, climate change and biodiversity.

TYPE:
Project/program grants.

YEAR PROGRAM STARTED: 1964

PURPOSE:
To promote the prevention of and resilience to climate change; to promote the restoration and preservation of biodiversity.

LEGAL BASIS:
Nonprofit foundation.

ELIGIBILITY:
Organizations and programs must meet the following basic requirements in order to be considered for funding:
(1) must serve communities where Alcoa has operating plants or offices;
(2) U.S. organizations must be classified as not-for-profit public charities and tax-exempt under Section 501(c)(3) of the U.S. Internal Revenue Code. Public educational institutions and government entities, while not classified as 501(c)(3) public charities, may be eligible for grant funds provided that funds are used for charitable purposes;
(3) non-U.S. organizations must operate as the equivalent of a U.S. 501(c)(3) public charity, public educational institution or government entity and must complete the required Equivalency Determination process and;
(4) organizations must demonstrate a commitment to diversity and nondiscrimination and sign the Alcoa Foundation inclusivity statement.

FINANCIAL DATA:
Amount of support per award: Varies.
Total amount of support: Varies.

APPLICATION INFO:
Applications are accepted on an invitation-only basis.
Duration: Varies.
Deadline: Generally July 31.

GEORGE I. ALDEN TRUST [10]

c/o Fletcher Tilton P.C.
370 Main Street, 11th Floor
Worcester, MA 01608
(508) 459-8005
Fax: (508) 459-8305
E-mail: trustees@aldentrust.org
Web Site: www.aldentrust.org

FOUNDED: 1912

AREAS OF INTEREST:
Higher education.

TYPE:
Capital grants; Challenge/matching grants. Capital projects related to teaching and learning technology, in general, and to the sciences, in particular; some support for need-based scholarship endowment and faculty development.

YEAR PROGRAM STARTED: 1912

LEGAL BASIS:
Probate Trust.

ELIGIBILITY:
Principal focus is on independent colleges and universities with full-time traditional undergraduate enrollments of at least 1,000 students and with a total undergraduate and graduate student population (full-time equivalents) of under 5,000. Also, educationally related entities in the Worcester (MA) area and at YMCAs in Massachusetts.

GEOG. RESTRICTIONS: New Jersey, New York, Pennsylvania and the six New England states.

FINANCIAL DATA:
Total amount of support: $10,452,000 for the year 2019.
Matching fund requirements: Usually 1:2 or 1:3 (Alden Trust:matching dollars), with 18-month challenge period. The Trust only pays when the challenge is met in full. The Trust makes no interim or partial payments.

APPLICATION INFO:
Guidelines are available on the web site.
Deadline: Completed proposals received for March, June, September and December meetings must be received by the 15th of the month prior to the meeting.

IRS I.D.: 04-6023784

TRUSTEES:
Warner S. Fletcher, Chairperson
James E. Collins
Douglas Q. Meystre
Gail T. Randall

ADDRESS INQUIRIES TO:
Warner S. Fletcher, Chairperson
(See address above.)

ALLEGHENY FOUNDATION [11]

One Oxford Centre
301 Grant Street, Suite 3900
Pittsburgh, PA 15219-6402
(412) 392-2900
Web Site: www.scaife.com

AREAS OF INTEREST:
Education, civic development and historic preservation.

TYPE:
General operating grants.

ELIGIBILITY:
Applicant must be a 501(c)(3) nonprofit organization.

GEOG. RESTRICTIONS: Western Pennsylvania.

FINANCIAL DATA:
Amount of support per award: Varies.
Total amount of support: $50,699,100 for the year 2019.

APPLICATION INFO:
Initial inquiries to the Foundation should be in letter form signed by the organization's President, or authorized representative, and have the approval of the Board of Directors. The letter should include a concise description of the specific program for which funds are requested. Additional information must include a budget for the program and for the organization, the latest audited financial statement and annual report. A copy of the organization's current ruling letter evidencing tax exemption under Section 501(c)(3) of the Internal Revenue Code is required.
Duration: Typically one year.
Deadline: The Foundation considers grants on a quarterly basis. Requests may be submitted at any time and will be acted upon as expeditiously as possible.

ADDRESS INQUIRIES TO:
Matthew A. Groll, Chairman
(See address above.)

AMERICAN PHILOSOPHICAL SOCIETY [12]
104 South Fifth Street
Philadelphia, PA 19106-3387
(215) 440-3429
E-mail: lmusumeci@amphilsoc.org
Web Site: www.amphilsoc.org/grants/franklin-research-grants

FOUNDED: 1743

AREAS OF INTEREST:
Scholarly research.

NAME(S) OF PROGRAMS:
● **Franklin Research Grants**

TYPE:
Grants-in-aid; Research grants. Postdoctoral grants toward the cost of scholarly research in all areas of knowledge except those in which support by government or corporate enterprise is more appropriate. Scholarly research covers most kinds of scholarly inquiry by individuals. It does not include journalistic or other writing for general readership; the preparation of textbooks, casebooks, anthologies, or other materials for classroom use by students; or the work of creative and performing artists.

The Society does not have fellowships or scholarships for study, nor does it give grants for travel to conferences.

YEAR PROGRAM STARTED: 1933

PURPOSE:
To support scholarly research by individual scholars.

LEGAL BASIS:
Nonprofit learned society.

ELIGIBILITY:
Applications may be made by residents of the U.S., by American citizens resident abroad and by foreign nationals. American citizens and foreign nationals employed by an American institution may apply for support to carry out work anywhere in the world. Foreign nationals not employed by an American institution may apply for funding to work in the U.S. Applicants expecting to use materials or conduct interviews in a

foreign language must possess the necessary competence in the language or languages involved. Grants are never made for predoctoral study or research.

It is the Society's long-standing practice to encourage research by younger and less well-established scholars.

FINANCIAL DATA:
Grants are made payable to the applicant.

The Society offers no funds for conference support, fellowships and scholarships, maintenance work already done, or costs of publication.
Amount of support per award: Funding is offered up to a maximum of $6,000.
Total amount of support: $525,800 for the year 2019-20.

CO-OP FUNDING PROGRAMS: If an applicant receives an award for the same project from another granting insititution, the Society will consider limiting its award to costs that are not covered by the other grant.

NO. MOST RECENT APPLICANTS: 339.

NO. AWARDS: 98 for the year 2019-20.

APPLICATION INFO:
Applications are submitted through the Society's online application portal. Two letters of support are required.
Duration: One year.
Deadline: October 1 and December 3.

ADDRESS INQUIRIES TO:
Linda Musumeci
Director of Grants and Fellowships
(See address above.)

AMERICAN PHILOSOPHICAL SOCIETY [13]
The Lewis and Clark Fund
104 South Fifth Street
Philadelphia, PA 19106-3387
(215) 440-3429
E-mail: lmusumeci@amphilsoc.org
Web Site: amphilsoc.org/grants/lewis-and-clark-fund-exploration-and-field-research

FOUNDED: 1743

AREAS OF INTEREST:
Scholarly research.

NAME(S) OF PROGRAMS:
● **The Lewis and Clark Fund for Exploration and Field Research**

TYPE:
Research grants. The Lewis and Clark Fund for Exploration and Field Research (initially supported by the Stanford Ascherman/Baruch Blumberg Fund for Basic Science, established by a benefaction from the late Stanford Ascherman, M.D., of San Francisco) encourages exploratory field studies for the collection of specimens and data and to provide the imaginative stimulus that accompanies direct observation. Applications are invited from disciplines with a large dependence on field studies, such as archeology, anthropology, biology, ecology, geography, geology, linguistics, paleontology and population genetics, but grants will not be restricted to these fields.

YEAR PROGRAM STARTED: 2005

PURPOSE:
To support scholarly research by individual scholars.

LEGAL BASIS:
Nonprofit learned society.

ELIGIBILITY:
Grants will be available to doctoral students. Postdoctoral fellows, Master's degree candidates, and undergraduates are not eligible. Applicants who have received Lewis and Clark Fund grants may reapply after an interval of two years.

The competition is open to U.S. residents wishing to carry out research anywhere in the world. Foreign applicants must either be based at a U.S. institution or plan to carry out their work in the U.S.

Funding is contingent on successful applicants demonstrating that required permits and permissions have been secured.

FINANCIAL DATA:
Amount of support per award: Up to $5,000.
Total amount of support: $255,300 for the year 2019-20.

NO. MOST RECENT APPLICANTS: 339.

NO. AWARDS: 58 for the year 2019-20.

APPLICATION INFO:
Applications must be submitted electronically through the Society's online portal. The applicant should ask his or her academic adviser to write one of the two letters of recommendation, specifying the student's qualifications to carry out the proposed work and the educational content of the trip. Budgets should be limited to travel and related expenses, including personal field equipment.

When appropriate, the applicant should provide assurances that safety measures will be taken for potentially hazardous projects. When necessary, the applicant and his or her supervisor should discuss the field training that will be provided and the provisions for experienced supervision.
Duration: Preferably one year.
Deadline: Letters of Support: November 13. Application: November 16. Notification in March, for work in May and beyond.

ADDRESS INQUIRIES TO:
Linda Musumeci
Director of Grants and Fellowships
(See address above.)

AMERICAN SCHLAFHORST FOUNDATION [14]
8801 South Boulevard
Charlotte, NC 28273
(704) 554-0800
Fax: (704) 556-1643

AREAS OF INTEREST:
Arts, children, education, health care, sciences, senior citizens and social services.

TYPE:
Capital grants; Endowments; General operating grants; Research grants; Scholarships; Seed money grants.

PURPOSE:
To improve the quality of life in the community.

LEGAL BASIS:
Corporate foundation.

ELIGIBILITY:
Grants are made to organizations that have tax-exempt status under Section 501(c)(3) of the Internal Revenue Code. No grants are made to individuals.

GEOG. RESTRICTIONS: Greater Charlotte, North Carolina.

FINANCIAL DATA:
Amount of support per award: Varies.
Total amount of support: Varies.

APPLICATION INFO:
Applicants should submit a Letter of Inquiry to the Foundation at the address above.
Duration: Varies.
Deadline: October.

ADDRESS INQUIRIES TO:
Dan Loftis, Grant Administrator
(See address above.)

AMGEN FOUNDATION, INC. [15]
One Amgen Center Drive, M/S 28-4-C
Thousand Oaks, CA 91320-1799
(805) 447-1000
E-mail: amgenfoundation@amgen.com
Web Site: www.amgen.
com/responsibility/amgen-foundation

FOUNDED: 1991

AREAS OF INTEREST:
Science education, human services and community life including arts and culture, social services and environment.

TYPE:
Challenge/matching grants; General operating grants; Grants-in-aid; Matching gifts; Project/program grants. The Foundation funds national-level science education programs.

YEAR PROGRAM STARTED: 1991

PURPOSE:
To advance excellence in science education to inspire the next generation of innovators; to invest in strengthening communities where Amgen staff members live and work.

LEGAL BASIS:
Company-sponsored foundation.

ELIGIBILITY:
The Foundation will consider grant requests from nonprofit organizations that are recognized by the IRS as tax-exempt public charities under Sections 501(c)(3) and 509(a)(1), (2) or (3) of the Internal Revenue Code, located in the U.S. and Puerto Rico. In addition, the Foundation will consider requests for funding from governmental organizations located in the U.S. where the purpose of the grant is to support a charitable, educational, scientific or literary purpose. Thus, eligible grantees may include public elementary and secondary schools, as well as public colleges and universities, public libraries and public hospitals. Successful requests will fall within both the current eligibility guidelines and funding priority areas established by the Foundation. The Foundation has established a grantmaking partnership with United Way Worldwide (UWW) to manage donations to organizations chartered in Europe.

GEOG. RESTRICTIONS: California, Florida, Massachusetts, Puerto Rico, Rhode Island, and parts of Europe.

FINANCIAL DATA:
Amount of support per award: Varies.
Total amount of support: Varies.

APPLICATION INFO:
Letter of intent must first be submitted online.

Duration: Typically one year. Possible multiyear funding.

ADDRESS INQUIRIES TO:
Jennifer Egglin, Manager
(See address above.)

THE ANNENBERG FOUNDATION [16]
2000 Avenue of the Stars
Suite 1000 S
Los Angeles, CA 90067
(310) 209-4560
Fax: (310) 209-1631
E-mail: info@annenberg.org
requests@annenberg.org
Web Site: www.annenberg.org

FOUNDED: 1989

AREAS OF INTEREST:
Arts, culture and humanities; animal welfare; civic and community; environment; education; human health and wellness; military veterans.

TYPE:
General operating grants; Grants-in-aid; Project/program grants; Technical assistance.

PURPOSE:
To provide funding and support to nonprofit organizations in the U.S. and globally; to advance the public well-being through improved communication; to encourage the development of effective ways to share ideas and knowledge.

ELIGIBILITY:
The Foundation seeks to fund organizations that have a deep level of community involvement, are led by effective leaders and tackle challenging and timely problems. The Foundation values the following organizational attributes: visionary leadership, impact, sustainability, innovation, organizational strength, network of partnerships, plus the population being served (hence the acronym VISION).

Only organizations that have 501(c)(3) not-for-profit status are eligible.

GEOG. RESTRICTIONS: Greater Los Angeles, California area (five-county region including Los Angeles, Orange, Riverside, San Bernardino and Ventura).

FINANCIAL DATA:
Total assets of $1.6 billion for year ended December 31, 2017.
Amount of support per award: Varies.
Total amount of support: Varies.

APPLICATION INFO:
Application guidelines are available on the Foundation web site.
Duration: One year. Grants are renewable, but applicant must reapply.

APPLIED MATERIALS, INC. [17]
3050 Bowers Avenue
Mail Stop 0106
Santa Clara, CA 95052-3299
(408) 727-5555
E-mail: community_affairs@amat.com
Web Site: www.appliedmaterials.com

FOUNDED: 1967

AREAS OF INTEREST:
Arts and culture, community development, education and the environment.

NAME(S) OF PROGRAMS:
• **Applied Materials Corporate Philanthropy Program**

TYPE:
Project/program grants.

YEAR PROGRAM STARTED: 1990

PURPOSE:
To support the arts and culture, education, community development and the environment.

LEGAL BASIS:
Corporate giving program.

ELIGIBILITY:
Organizations classified as 501(c)(3) by the IRS can apply. Preference is given to areas of company operation. Individuals and religious organizations are ineligible.

FINANCIAL DATA:
Amount of support per award: Varies.
Total amount of support: Varies.

APPLICATION INFO:
Application procedures are available online.
Duration: One year. May be renewed for up to two additional years based on results.
Deadline: January 15 and June 15.

PUBLICATIONS:
Annual report; community report; guidelines.

ADDRESS INQUIRIES TO:
See e-mail address above.

*SPECIAL STIPULATIONS:
Progress is requested to be shared in writing with the Corporate Contribution Committee at least once a year.

APS CORPORATE GIVING PROGRAM [18]
Arizona Public Service Company
400 North 5th Street, 10th Floor
Phoenix, AZ 85004
(602) 250-2702
Fax: (602) 250-2113
E-mail: corporategiving@aps.com
Web Site: aps.com/corporategiving

FOUNDED: 1888

AREAS OF INTEREST:
Education, most specifically STEM engineering; community vitality; community and economic development in APS service territories.

TYPE:
Challenge/matching grants; Development grants; Project/program grants. Primary focus is on program support.

YEAR PROGRAM STARTED: 1981

PURPOSE:
To enhance the quality of life in Arizona.

LEGAL BASIS:
Corporate giving program.

ELIGIBILITY:
Applicants must be 501(c)(3) nonprofit organizations for a minimum of three years. Preference is given to organizations within the APS service territory, although there are exceptions. No funds for individuals, individual scholarships, religious, political, fraternal, legislative or lobbying efforts, travel or hotel expenses. The program will not fund any organization that discriminates.

GEOG. RESTRICTIONS: Arizona.

FINANCIAL DATA:
Amount of support per award: $2,500 to $250,000.

Total amount of support: Approximately $9,000,000 for the year 2017.

NO. AWARDS: Varies.

APPLICATION INFO:
Applications must be submitted online and will require the following documentation:
(1) 501(c)(3) IRS letter of determination;
(2) current list of board members;
(3) list of sponsorship levels (if applicable);
(4) line-item budget;
(5) list of other funders and dollar amounts and;
(6) grant evaluation form (if applicable).
Duration: One year. Renewable by reapplication.
Deadline: APS Foundation: March 1 and September 1. Corporate Funding is on a rolling basis.

PUBLICATIONS:
Community Investment Report.

IRS I.D.: 95-3735903

THE ARCA FOUNDATION [19]
1308 19th Street, N.W.
Washington, DC 20036
(202) 822-9193
E-mail: proposals@arcafoundation.org
Web Site: www.arcafoundation.org

FOUNDED: 1952

AREAS OF INTEREST:
Wall Street reform, financial regulation, corporate accountability, and advocating for a U.S. foreign policy approach that increases peace and security.

TYPE:
General operating grants; Project/program grants.

YEAR PROGRAM STARTED: 1952

PURPOSE:
To provide funding for nonprofit organizations working on ways to engage citizens in social change, promote democracy, and reform unjust practices in public policy.

LEGAL BASIS:
Private foundation.

ELIGIBILITY:
Nonprofit organizations.

GEOG. RESTRICTIONS: United States.

FINANCIAL DATA:
Amount of support per award: $50,000.
Total amount of support: Approximately $2,500,000 annually.

NO. MOST RECENT APPLICANTS: 500.

NO. AWARDS: Approximately 60 to 70 annually.

APPLICATION INFO:
Applications must be submitted online. Applications submitted by any other method will not be considered.

The Foundation highly recommends the applicant review the instructions on using the system and online application system FAQs before beginning the application process. The Proposal FAQs outlines the information to be included in the narrative of the proposal, as well as the list of documents that the organization should be prepared to submit/upload electronically. Documents include the organization's IRS 501(c)(3) letter and Arca's Lobbying Expenditure Form. As always, the Foundation only considers full proposals and does not accept letters of inquiry.

Duration: One year, or the program period.
Deadline: February 1 or August 1 by 5 P.M., or first business day following if the first falls on a weekend.

STAFF:
Anna Lefer Kuhn, Executive Director
Stacie Posie, Grants Officer

BOARD OF DIRECTORS AND OFFICERS:
Nancy R. Bagley, President
Nicole Bagley, Vice President
Mike Lux, Treasurer
Mary E. King, Secretary
Austin Belali
Rev. Joseph Elderidge
Amaha Kassa
Janet Shenk
Margery Tabankin

ASSISI FOUNDATION OF MEMPHIS INC. [20]
515 Erin Drive
Memphis, TN 38117
(901) 684-1564
Fax: (901) 684-1997
E-mail: twamble@assisifoundation.org
Web Site: www.assisifoundation.org

AREAS OF INTEREST:
Education and life long learning, health and human services, social justice and ethics, and cultural enrichment and the arts.

TYPE:
Challenge/matching grants; Endowments; General operating grants; Matching gifts; Project/program grants; Research grants; Technical assistance. Capacity building.

YEAR PROGRAM STARTED: 1994

PURPOSE:
To address pressing challenges while also searching for root causes with the goal of creating community-wide transformation.

ELIGIBILITY:
Grants are made to organizations that already have tax-exempt status under Section 501(c)(3) of the Internal Revenue Code.

GEOG. RESTRICTIONS: Crittenden County, Arkansas; Desoto County, Mississippi; Fayette, Shelby and Tipton counties, Tennessee.

FINANCIAL DATA:
Amount of support per award: Varies.
Total amount of support: Varies.

APPLICATION INFO:
Grant application process and required forms are available to download from the Foundation's web site.
Duration: Varies.
Deadline: Dates are posted online.

ADDRESS INQUIRIES TO:
Dr. Jan Young, Executive Director
(See address above.)

ATHWIN FOUNDATION [21]
Center for Organizational Development
7101 York Avenue South, Suite 306
Edina, MN 55435
(612) 616-0256
E-mail: jstormcod1@aol.com
Web Site: www.catchcod.com

FOUNDED: 1956

AREAS OF INTEREST:
Arts and humanities, education, human services, environmental enhancement and organizational capacity building.

TYPE:
Capital grants; General operating grants; Project/program grants.

YEAR PROGRAM STARTED: 1956

PURPOSE:
To provide funds for charitable, scientific, literary or educational purposes.

LEGAL BASIS:
Tax-exempt private foundation.

ELIGIBILITY:
Only tax-exempt organizations may apply. No grants are awarded to individuals.

GEOG. RESTRICTIONS: Primarily greater Minnesota.

FINANCIAL DATA:
Amount of support per award: Varies.

NO. MOST RECENT APPLICANTS: 100.

NO. AWARDS: Varies.

REPRESENTATIVE AWARDS:
$1,000 to American Indian OIC for program support; $25,000 to the American Red Cross-Minneapolis Chapter for a capital campaign; $100,000 to Blake School for a two-year capital campaign.

APPLICATION INFO:
The Foundation will initiate communication with those organizations it selects for potential funding. All organizations receiving notification will complete the application process and submit material by the date identified by the Foundation.
Duration: Varies.

PUBLICATIONS:
Annual report.

IRS I.D.: 41-6021773

TRUSTEES:
Andrew Bean
Bruce W. Bean
Glen Bean
Mary F. Bean

ADDRESS INQUIRIES TO:
Jim Storm, Administrator
(See address above.)

ATKINSON FOUNDATION [22]
c/o Pacific Foundation Services
1600 Bush Street, Suite 300
San Francisco, CA 94019
(415) 561-6540
Web Site: www.atkinsonfdn.org
www.pfs-llc.net

FOUNDED: 1939

AREAS OF INTEREST:
Social services and education in San Mateo County, CA, as well as American private volunteer organizations.

NAME(S) OF PROGRAMS:
● **Community**
● **Education and Youth Development**

TYPE:
General operating grants; Project/program grants.

YEAR PROGRAM STARTED: 1939

PURPOSE:
To foster the efforts of individuals and families to become socially, economically and physically self-sufficient, and to increase their economic and social welfare.

LEGAL BASIS:
Private foundation.

ELIGIBILITY:
Applicants must be organizations with Internal Revenue Code 501(c)(3) status.

No loans or grants to individuals or for doctoral study or research. The Foundation does not sponsor nor contribute to one-time events or nationwide appeals from organizations and does not fund publications, films or conferences.

GEOG. RESTRICTIONS: San Mateo County, California.

FINANCIAL DATA:
Amount of support per award: Generally $5,000 to $20,000.

Total amount of support: $1,200,000 for the year 2019.

NO. MOST RECENT APPLICANTS: 160.

NO. AWARDS: 110 for the year 2019.

REPRESENTATIVE AWARDS:
$200,000 to Boys & Girls Club of the Coastside; $7,500 to Second Harvest Food Bank; $10,000 to Marine Science Institute.

APPLICATION INFO:
Application information is available on the Foundation web site.
Duration: Usually one year.
Deadline: February 1, May 1, August 1 and November 1.

IRS I.D.: 94-6075613

ATRAN FOUNDATION, INC.   [23]
155 North Dean Street, Suite 3-D
Englewood, NJ 07631
(201) 569-9677
Fax: (201) 569-2290
E-mail: foundatran@gmail.com

FOUNDED: 1948

AREAS OF INTEREST:
Civic, medical, charitable and educational organizations aligned with the Foundation's principles.

TYPE:
General operating grants; Project/program grants.

YEAR PROGRAM STARTED: 1948

PURPOSE:
To support worthy civic, medical, charitable, or educational organizations that align with the founding philanthropic principles of the Foundation.

LEGAL BASIS:
Tax-exempt under Section 501(c)(3) of the Internal Revenue Code.

ELIGIBILITY:
Grants are made only to 501(c)(3) tax-exempt organizations. No grants to individuals.

GEOG. RESTRICTIONS: United States.

FINANCIAL DATA:
Amount of support per award: Varies.
Total amount of support: Varies.

NO. MOST RECENT APPLICANTS: 50.

NO. AWARDS: Approximately 35 per year.

APPLICATION INFO:
No formal application form is required. Application guidelines may be requested from the Foundation.

Duration: One year.
Deadline: September 30.

PUBLICATIONS:
Guideline for application procedure.

IRS I.D.: 13-5566548

OFFICERS:
Allison Fischer, President
Robert Kaplan, Vice President
Samuel Norich, Treasurer
Harris Atran, Secretary

ADDRESS INQUIRIES TO:
Judah Fischer, Executive Director
(See address above.)

MARY REYNOLDS BABCOCK FOUNDATION   [24]
2920 Reynolda Road
Winston-Salem, NC 27106
(336) 748-9222
Fax: (336) 777-0095
E-mail: info@mrbf.org
Web Site: www.mrbf.org

FOUNDED: 1953

AREAS OF INTEREST:
Racism and poverty in the southeastern U.S.

NAME(S) OF PROGRAMS:
● **Moving People and Places Out of Poverty**

TYPE:
Challenge/matching grants; Development grants; General operating grants; Travel grants. Program-related investments.

YEAR PROGRAM STARTED: 2005

PURPOSE:
To help to move people and places out of poverty.

LEGAL BASIS:
Private foundation.

ELIGIBILITY:
Applicants must be nonprofit tax-exempt organizations with appropriate interests, located or working in the Southeast.

GEOG. RESTRICTIONS: Southeastern United States.

FINANCIAL DATA:
Amount of support per award: Varies.
Total amount of support: Approximately $7,000,000.
Matching fund requirements: Varies.

NO. AWARDS: Varies.

APPLICATION INFO:
Applications must be submitted electronically.
Duration: One to three years depending on the grant.
Deadline: Applications are accepted on a rolling basis.

PUBLICATIONS:
Application form.

IRS I.D.: 56-0690140

BOARD OF DIRECTORS:
Laura Mountcastle, President
Ken Mountcastle, Treasurer
Karama Neal, Secretary
LaVeeda Battle
Chad Berry
Ashleigh Gardere
Micah Gilmer
Jerry Gonzalez
Zachary Lassiter

James Mitchell
Holt Mountcastle
Kara Mountcastle
Kathy Mountcastle
Mary Mountcastle
Stephanie Tyree

ADDRESS INQUIRIES TO:
Program Officers
(See address above.)

BADER PHILANTHROPIES, INC.   [25]
3300 North Dr. Martin Luther King Jr. Drive
Milwaukee, WI 53212
(414) 224-6464
Fax: (414) 224-1441
E-mail: baderphilanthropies@bader.org
Web Site: www.bader.org

FOUNDED: 1991

AREAS OF INTEREST:
Alzheimer's disease and dementia, workforce development, Jewish education, program-related investments, and youth development.

TYPE:
Capital grants; Challenge/matching grants; Conferences/seminars; General operating grants; Matching gifts; Project/program grants; Technical assistance; Training grants.

YEAR PROGRAM STARTED: 1991

PURPOSE:
To fund innovative projects and programs in four primary areas including Alzheimer's disease and dementia, workforce development, children and youth, and Jewish education.

LEGAL BASIS:
Family foundation.

ELIGIBILITY:
U.S. organizations must be tax-exempt under Section 501(c)(3) of the IRS or governmental entities. Grants will only be approved for foreign entities which meet specific charitable status requirements.

GEOG. RESTRICTIONS: Milwaukee, Wisconsin.

FINANCIAL DATA:
Amount of support per award: $500 to $180,000. Median is $10,000.
Total amount of support: Average $14,000,000 annually.

CO-OP FUNDING PROGRAMS: Milwaukee Area Workforce Funding Alliance.

NO. AWARDS: 446 grants awarded for the year 2019-20.

REPRESENTATIVE AWARDS:
Above the Clouds, Inc.; City Year, Inc.; Wisconsin Humane Society, Inc.

APPLICATION INFO:
Application information is available on the Foundation web site.
Duration: Varies. Renewal possible.
Deadline: Applications are accepted at any time.

IRS I.D.: 39-1710914

BOARD OF DIRECTORS:
Jere D. McGaffey, Chairman and Treasurer
Daniel J. Bader, President
David M. Bader, Vice President
Deirdre Britt, Secretary
Linda C. Bader
Michelle Berrong Bader
Margaret Foster

Adina Shapiro
Frances Wolff

ADDRESS INQUIRIES TO:
Kristen Lie, Grants Manager
(See address above.)

R.C. BAKER FOUNDATION   [26]
330 Encinitas Boulevard
Suite 101
Encinitas, CA 92024-8705
(760) 632-8322

FOUNDED: 1952

AREAS OF INTEREST:
Education, health, cultural, scientific research, social services for youth and elderly, and crime prevention.

TYPE:
Capital grants; Fellowships; General operating grants; Project/program grants; Scholarships; Technical assistance; Training grants; Work-study programs.

LEGAL BASIS:
Private foundation.

ELIGIBILITY:
Applicant organizations must have IRS tax-exempt status. No grants are made to individuals, endowments or loans. No grants to capital programs of tax-supported institutions.

GEOG. RESTRICTIONS: United States.

FINANCIAL DATA:
Amount of support per award: Varies.
Total amount of support: $737,820 for the year 2017.

APPLICATION INFO:
Applications should include a description of the proposed project and goals, a recently audited financial statement, amount requested, and a list of other sources of support. In addition, the applicant should include its IRS statement of tax-exempt status. The Foundation does not grant personal interviews.
Duration: Typically, one-time grants.
Deadline: May 1 and October 1.

IRS I.D.: 95-1742283

BOARD OF TRUSTEES:
Frank L. Scott, Chairman
James Benedict
Dennis Cronin
F. Laurence Scott, Jr.

ADDRESS INQUIRIES TO:
F. Laurence Scott, Jr., Board of Trustees
(See address above.)

BALL BROTHERS FOUNDATION   [27]
222 South Mulberry
Muncie, IN 47305
(765) 741-5500
Fax: (765) 741-5518
E-mail: info@ballfdn.org
Web Site: www.ballfdn.org

FOUNDED: 1926

AREAS OF INTEREST:
Education, arts, culture and humanities, human services, public/society benefit, health and environment.

TYPE:
Awards/prizes; Challenge/matching grants; General operating grants; Project/program grants; Seed money grants; Technical assistance; Training grants.

YEAR PROGRAM STARTED: 1926

PURPOSE:
To promote recreational, educational or charitable purposes within the state of Indiana.

LEGAL BASIS:
Private foundation.

ELIGIBILITY:
Indiana not-for-profit organizations or institutions are eligible to apply. No grants to individuals.

GEOG. RESTRICTIONS: Indiana.

FINANCIAL DATA:
Amount of support per award: $1,000 to $1,000,000.
Total amount of support: $7,600,000 for the year 2018.

NO. MOST RECENT APPLICANTS: 200 for the year 2018.

NO. AWARDS: 94 for the year 2018.

REPRESENTATIVE AWARDS:
$25,000 to Indiana Historical Society; $34,000 to Motivate Our Minds; $50,000 to Second Harvest Food Bank; $62,000 to Indiana Youth Institute; $155,000 to Ivy Tech Community College.

APPLICATION INFO:
Application must include a description of the project, project staff and budget, IRS determination letter, objective of the proposal, plan of development, expected results and method of evaluation.
Duration: One year.
Deadline: February 15 and July 15.

PUBLICATIONS:
Guidelines; annual report.

IRS I.D.: 35-0882856

OFFICERS:
James A. Fisher, Chairman
Frank B. Petty, Vice Chairman
Tamara S. Phillips, Treasurer
Terry L. Walker, Secretary

DIRECTORS:
Charles Ball
Elizabeth Bracken
William Bracken
Stephanie Duckmann
Jud Fisher
Nancy B. Keilty
Terri Matchett
Stacy McHenry
Judy Oetinger
Scott E. Shockley

ADDRESS INQUIRIES TO:
Donna Munchel, Grant Process and Program Manager
(See address above.)

GEORGE AND FRANCES BALL FOUNDATION   [28]
222 South Mulberry
Muncie, IN 47305
(765) 741-5500
Fax: (765) 741-5518
Web Site: gfballfdn.org

FOUNDED: 1937

AREAS OF INTEREST:
Education, arts and culture, civic community projects, health and human services, environment and conservation.

TYPE:
Challenge/matching grants; Endowments; General operating grants; Matching gifts; Professorships; Project/program grants.

LEGAL BASIS:
Family foundation.

ELIGIBILITY:
Applicants must be 501(c)(3) organizations or institutes.

GEOG. RESTRICTIONS: East central Indiana, primarily Delaware County.

FINANCIAL DATA:
Amount of support per award: $25,000 median.
Total amount of support: $4,800,000 for the year ended December 31, 2017.
Matching fund requirements: Usually 1:1.

NO. MOST RECENT APPLICANTS: 50.

NO. AWARDS: 50 for the year 2017.

APPLICATION INFO:
General grant guidelines are available on the Foundation web site.
Deadline: Mid-February, mid-May, mid-August and mid-November.

OFFICERS AND DIRECTORS:
Stefan S. Anderson, Chairman
Jon H. Moll, First Vice Chairman
Thomas C. Bracken, Second Vice Chairman
Thomas J. Kinghorn, President and Chief Executive Officer
Tamara S. Phillips, Treasurer
Carol E. Seals, Assistant Treasurer
Joan H. McKee, Secretary
Shannon Cline, Assistant Secretary
Norman E. Beck
Ronald K. Fauquher
Mike Galliher
Robert M. Smitson
Joseph F. Wiese, III

ADDRESS INQUIRIES TO:
Shannon Cline, Executive Assistant
(See address above.)

BALTIMORE COMMUNITY FOUNDATION   [29]
2 East Read Street, 9th Floor
Baltimore, MD 21202
(410) 332-4171
Fax: (410) 837-4701
E-mail: info@bcf.org
Web Site: www.bcf.org

FOUNDED: 1972

AREAS OF INTEREST:
Education and neighborhoods.

TYPE:
Scholarships. Neighborhood grants. Education grants.

YEAR PROGRAM STARTED: 1972

PURPOSE:
To work for a healthy productive Baltimore region and to provide a flexible effective way for charitable individuals, corporations and foundations to invest in those efforts.

LEGAL BASIS:
Community foundation.

ELIGIBILITY:
The Foundation welcomes grant applications from organizations in the Greater Baltimore region that are tax-exempt under Section 501(c)(3) of the Internal Revenue Code.

The Foundation will be most likely to fund programs that:
(1) address underlying causes of specific problems and seek long-term systemic solutions;
(2) are preventive rather than remedial;
(3) reach a broad segment of the community;
(4) increase individual access and opportunity;
(5) attract financial or volunteer resources or involve collaboration;
(6) build the capacity of grantee organizations and;
(7) strengthen the private, nonprofit sector.

The Foundation does not make grants for annual fund campaigns, operating support except for start-up, religious or sectarian purposes, capital campaigns, or individuals (including scholarships and fellowships).

GEOG. RESTRICTIONS: Baltimore city and Baltimore County, Maryland.

FINANCIAL DATA:
Amount of support per award: Varies.
Total amount of support: Approximately $23,000,000 for the year 2016.

APPLICATION INFO:
Contact the Foundation for guidelines and application form.
Duration: Typically one year; multiyear grants are dependent upon funds available and is at the discretion of the board committee.
Deadline: Letters of inquiry are welcomed throughout the year. Proposal deadlines vary by grant program.

PUBLICATIONS:
The BCF Edge, newsletter; annual report.

OFFICERS:
Laura L. Gamble, Chairman
Shanaysha M. Sauls, President
Tedd Alexander, III, Treasurer
Marsha Y. Reeves, Secretary

STAFF:
Shanaysha M. Sauls, President and Chief Executive Officer
Patricia Chandler, C.P.A., Vice President, Finance and Administration

BARRA FOUNDATION [30]

200 West Lancaster Avenue
Suite 202
Wayne, PA 19087-4046
(610) 964-7601
Fax: (610) 964-0155
E-mail: info@barrafoundation.org
Web Site: www.barrafoundation.org

FOUNDED: 1963

AREAS OF INTEREST:
Arts and culture, human services, education and health.

TYPE:
Project/program grants.

LEGAL BASIS:
Private foundation.

ELIGIBILITY:
501(c)(3) nonprofit organizations only.

GEOG. RESTRICTIONS: Philadelphia, Pennsylvania metropolitan area.

FINANCIAL DATA:
Amount of support per award: $25,000 to $100,000.
Total amount of support: Approximately $3,500,000.

APPLICATION INFO:
Applications are accepted online only.
Duration: Varies.
Deadline: Applications accepted on a continuous basis.

PUBLICATIONS:
Policy statement.

STAFF:
Kristina L. Wahl, President

ADDRESS INQUIRIES TO:
Kristina L. Wahl, President
(See address above.)

*SPECIAL STIPULATIONS:
No grants for environmental programs, exhibitions, publications or religious organizations.

BATTLE CREEK COMMUNITY FOUNDATION [31]

32 West Michigan Avenue
Suite 1
Battle Creek, MI 49017-3505
(269) 962-2181
Fax: (269) 962-2182
E-mail: bccf@bccfoundation.org
Web Site: www.bccfoundation.org

FOUNDED: 1974

AREAS OF INTEREST:
Education, health, and liveable communities.

TYPE:
Challenge/matching grants; Conferences/seminars; Demonstration grants; Development grants; Endowments; Exchange programs; Internships; Matching gifts; Project/program grants; Research grants; Scholarships; Technical assistance; Training grants; Travel grants. Emerging needs grants.

YEAR PROGRAM STARTED: 1974

PURPOSE:
To promote philanthropic giving and the use of endowment funds; to serve as a leader in coordinating local resources to meet the current and future needs of the Battle Creek community.

LEGAL BASIS:
Community foundation.

ELIGIBILITY:
Applicants must be nonprofit organizations whose programs will benefit residents or students of the greater Battle Creek community.

No grants for general operating support, endowments, annual fund-raising programs, or projects outside of the Battle Creek area which do not benefit the local community.

General operating support is only given for arts and culture initiatives.

GEOG. RESTRICTIONS: Battle Creek, Michigan area.

FINANCIAL DATA:
Amount of support per award: Average: $10,000 to $15,000.
Total amount of support: $8,500,000.

NO. MOST RECENT APPLICANTS: Approximately 2,400.

NO. AWARDS: Approximately 165.

APPLICATION INFO:
Prospective grant applicants must attend a grantseeker orientation and should contact Foundation staff to gather information on upcoming orientations, dates/times, etc.
Duration: One year.
Deadline: Varies by program.

PUBLICATIONS:
Guidelines; annual report.

ADDRESS INQUIRIES TO:
Annette Chapman, Vice President of Grantmaking and Scholarships
(See address above.)

THE BAXTER INTERNATIONAL FOUNDATION [32]

One Baxter Parkway
Deerfield, IL 60015
(847) 948-4605
E-mail: fdninfo@baxter.com
Web Site: www.baxter.com

FOUNDED: 1981

AREAS OF INTEREST:
Health care and its enhancement.

TYPE:
Matching gifts; Project/program grants. The Foundation supports health care awards programs, including the Foster G. McGaw Prize, a $100,000 grant awarded annually to a U.S. hospital that has distinguished itself in community service, the William Graham Health Services Research Award, a $50,000 award made annually to an individual who has made significant contributions to the improved delivery of medical care through innovative health-services research, and the Episteme Award, a $15,000 award given once every two years to recognize outstanding research conducted by a nurse.

YEAR PROGRAM STARTED: 1982

PURPOSE:
To increase access to health care services for the disadvantaged; to improve the quality and cost-effectiveness of health care.

LEGAL BASIS:
Corporate foundation.

ELIGIBILITY:
Grants are made to nonprofit 501(c)(3) organizations with new or expanded programs or direct health care services proposals consistent with the Foundation's priorities. In evaluating a grant application, the Foundation looks for eligibility under Foundation guidelines, including geographies where Baxter employees work and live, evidence that the project is a response to a valid need and is superior to other competing projects, and evidence of the agency's capacity to accomplish its goals.

In general, the Foundation does not make grants to capital and endowment campaigns, hospitals, disease-specific organizations, educational institutions, individuals, organizations with a limited constituency such as fraternal, veterans' or religious organizations, organizations soliciting contributions for advertising space, tickets to dinners and fund-raising events and promotional materials.

FINANCIAL DATA:
Amount of support per award: Varies.
Total amount of support: $1,390,000 in Community Grants for the year 2017.

NO. AWARDS: More than 30 grants for the year 2017.

REPRESENTATIVE AWARDS:
$50,000 to Health and Medicine Policy Research Group; $87,027 to Irish Hospice Foundation; $98,175 to The Trevor Project, Inc.

APPLICATION INFO:
All grants must utilize the Foundation's online application process. Requirements of the application include:
(1) organization's full legal name, complete mailing address, phone number, fax number, contact person's name and e-mail address;
(2) if applicable, a description of the organization's relationship with the local Baxter facility;
(3) a brief but complete description of the organization, its purpose, history, governance, programs and achievements;
(4) a statement describing the specific purpose of the grant requested, including how the project meets the priorities of the Foundation;
(5) a statement of the amount of money requested in U.S. dollars and over what period of time;
(6) a plan for how the program or services will be sustained after the conclusion of funding;
(7) a plan for measuring results and reporting periodic progress, as well as for a final evaluation;
(8) financial information, including the organization's current operating full budget and the budget for the proposed project;
(9) a list of sources of income and amounts, including support from corporate donors, foundations, the United Way and the government - committed and approaching - for both the organization and the proposed project;
(10) audited financial statements for the most recent fiscal year and the two previous years (total of three);
(11) a copy of the organization's certificate of tax exemption for the IRS as a 501(c)(3) or equivalent organization. For organizations outside the U.S., a copy of the charitable certificate and exemption from taxes from the local or national government;
(12) a list of officers and board members, with their home addresses and their affiliations and;
(13) a list of the names and home addresses of the five highest paid employees.

Duration: Typically one to two years.

Deadline: Periodically. Dates will be published online.

ADDRESS INQUIRIES TO:
See e-mail address above.

ADELAIDE BREED BAYRD FOUNDATION [33]
350 Main Street
Suite 13
Malden, MA 02148
(781) 324-1231
Fax: (781) 397-0531
E-mail: kezer@kezer.com
Web Site: bayrd.org

FOUNDED: 1927

AREAS OF INTEREST:
Community services, education and cultural projects, health-related projects and youth-related projects.

TYPE:
Capital grants; Project/program grants; Scholarships; Seed money grants.

PURPOSE:
To support organizations whose activities are centered in the Malden, MA, area, and to support organizations elsewhere, whose activities give substantial benefit to the citizens of Malden.

LEGAL BASIS:
Private foundation.

ELIGIBILITY:
Grants are made to nonprofit, 501(c)(3) organizations in the Foundation's areas of interest. Requests from individuals, endowment funds, performing arts (excepting educational projects and programs) and research will generally be excluded.

In general, the Foundation favors grants toward project services over operational expenditures.

GEOG. RESTRICTIONS: Boston area, with emphasis on Malden and vicinity.

FINANCIAL DATA:
Amount of support per award: Varies.
Total amount of support: Average $1,000,000 annually.

REPRESENTATIVE AWARDS:
$33,000 to ABBF New Scholarships; $5,000 to Agassiz Village.

APPLICATION INFO:
No particular form of request is required. A letter stating the need, the purpose of the organization and other salient matters will suffice. Copies of summaries of current budget or recent financial statements may be helpful. Organizations should be prepared to furnish a copy of IRS tax form 501(c)(3) or another tax-exempt certificate.
Duration: Typically one year.
Deadline: Second Tuesday in February.

PUBLICATIONS:
Annual report.

IRS I.D.: 04-6051258

TRUSTEES:
C. Henry Kezer, President
Susan C. Mansur, Treasurer
Francis K. Brown, II
Richard R. Burns, Jr.
Laura L. Hodgin
Rev. Paul C. McPheeters
Robert M. Wallask
Dorothy Whittier

ADDRESS INQUIRIES TO:
C. Henry Kezer, President
(See address above.)

BEMIS COMPANY FOUNDATION [34]
One Neenah Center
P.O. Box 669
Neenah, WI 54957
E-mail: kim.wetzel@bemis.com
Web Site: www.bemis.com/about-bemis/citizenship/bemis-company-foundation

FOUNDED: 1959

AREAS OF INTEREST:
Basic needs, education, arts and culture, and STEM.

NAME(S) OF PROGRAMS:
- **Bemis Scholarship Program**
- **Community Enrichment Grant Program**
- **Community Support Grant Program**
- **Nonprofit/Educational Gift Matching Program**
- **United Way Program**

TYPE:
Capital grants; Challenge/matching grants; General operating grants; Matching gifts; Project/program grants. Grants to tax-exempt organizations in the communities in which the Bemis Company operates in the U.S. Scholarships, matching educational and matching nonprofit gifts are for employees only.

The Bemis Scholarship Program provides financial aid to sons and daughters of employees of the company and its subsidiaries. The Program is open to the sons and daughters under age 25 who wish to attend community colleges, four-year colleges, universities or vocational schools.

The Educational Gift Matching program gives employees an opportunity to have their personal contributions to eligible secondary schools, vocational/technical schools, colleges and universities double-matched by the Bemis Company.

In the United Way program, Bemis contributes to the United Way in communities where the company has facilities.

YEAR PROGRAM STARTED: 1959

PURPOSE:
To match available funds with those public needs where the interests of the company and its employees are inseparable; to support communities where Bemis has operations in the U.S.

LEGAL BASIS:
Corporate foundation.

ELIGIBILITY:
Nonprofits and schools must be located or serve U.S. Bemis facility communities. Grants are made to tax-exempt, U.S.-based organizations only. Priorities in grants will be given to those organizations and/or programs that will contribute the most to advancing the quality of life for all peoples in the communities in which the Bemis Company operates. Emphasis will be on those programs that encourage the development of our human resources, education programs and, in a lesser degree, civic and art institutions that encourage participation by the general public. Special consideration will be given to those programs in which the company's employees actively participate or are directly benefited.

The Foundation will not make grants to individuals or to organizations for religious purposes or for political purposes, either for lobbying efforts or campaigns. The Foundation prefers not to make grants for educational capital funds programs, endowment purposes or to support trips or tours.

Bemis Scholarship Program is only open to the children of full-time Bemis employees.

GEOG. RESTRICTIONS: United States.

FINANCIAL DATA:
Amount of support per award: Community Enrichment Grant Program: Up to $1,000; Community Support Grant Program: $1,000 and up; All others: Varies.
Total amount of support: Approximately $2,500,000 for the year 2017.

Matching fund requirements: The Plan provides that the employee's contribution be to an eligible 501(c)(3) nonprofit or accredited educational institution and will be matched dollar-for-dollar. Under this Plan, employee volunteer hours are matched $10 per hour. Each employee has up to $2,500 per year for matching.

APPLICATION INFO:
Complete application information may be obtained online. Grant proposals need not follow a specific format, but all proposals should include:
(1) name of the organization and amount requested;
(2) brief description of the objectives for which the grant is sought;
(3) details as to how the objectives are to be attained;
(4) budget, including information about existing and other possible sources of income;
(5) officers and board members and;
(6) statement that the organization has tax-exempt status under Section 501(c)(3) of the Internal Revenue Code and that contributions to it are tax-deductible.
It is preferred that all initial inquiries be by e-mail and not by telephone or personal visits.
Duration: Varies.
Deadline: Community Support Grant Program: March, June and December.

PUBLICATIONS:
Application guidelines.

IRS I.D.: 41-6038616

ADDRESS INQUIRIES TO:
See e-mail address above.

*SPECIAL STIPULATIONS:
All initial inquiries should be made by e-mail.

H.N. AND FRANCES C. BERGER FOUNDATION [35]
P.O. Box 13390
Palm Desert, CA 92255
(760) 341-5293
Fax: (760) 341-3518
Web Site: www.hnberger.org

FOUNDED: 1961

AREAS OF INTEREST:
Arts, culture, children, education, environment, health, human services and youth.

TYPE:
Project/program grants.

PURPOSE:
To provide people with the opportunity to improve their own situations.

LEGAL BASIS:
Private family foundation.

ELIGIBILITY:
Grants are made to organizations that have tax-exempt status under Section 501(c)(3) of the Internal Revenue Code. No grants are made to individuals. Nonsectarian religious programs may apply.

GEOG. RESTRICTIONS: United States, primarily southern California.

FINANCIAL DATA:
Amount of support per award: Grants vary in amount, depending upon the needs and nature of the request.

Total amount of support: Varies.

APPLICATION INFO:
Submit a one- to two-page request for consideration. This should include a concise statement of intent as well as a brief history of the organization and its activities.
Duration: Typically one year.

ADDRESS INQUIRIES TO:
Christopher McGuire
Vice President of Programs
(See address above.)

THE GRACE AND FRANKLIN BERNSEN FOUNDATION [36]
15 West 6th Street, Suite 1308
Tulsa, OK 74119-5407
(918) 584-4711
E-mail: info@bernsen.org
Web Site: www.bernsen.org

FOUNDED: 1968

AREAS OF INTEREST:
Arts, civic, education, medical, religious, United Way, and children.

TYPE:
Capital grants; Challenge/matching grants; Project/program grants.

YEAR PROGRAM STARTED: 1968

PURPOSE:
To provide grants in support of religious, charitable, scientific, literary or educational purposes, or for the prevention of cruelty to children.

LEGAL BASIS:
Private family foundation.

ELIGIBILITY:
The Foundation gives priority to applications from nonprofit organizations with clearly defined benefits, such as those for building and capital funding purposes, and other special program needs. Education programs, including those in the arts, higher education, human services and community programs, religious causes and youth programs are eligible for support.

Grants may require matching funds to be raised by the recipient.

No grants are made to elementary or secondary education institutions unless they involve programs for at-risk, handicapped or learning-disabled children. No grants are made to individuals, or for the benefit of specific individuals.

GEOG. RESTRICTIONS: Tulsa, Oklahoma area.

FINANCIAL DATA:
Amount of support per award: Average: $10,000.
Total amount of support: $1,500,000.

NO. MOST RECENT APPLICANTS: 200.

NO. AWARDS: 50 to 75.

APPLICATION INFO:
Applicants are urged to review the grant guidelines before submitting a proposal. Applications that do not conform to the required format will not be considered. The Foundation welcomes questions about the Foundation and potential applications.
Deadline: Grant applications are accepted monthly.

IRS I.D.: 23-7009414

TRUSTEES:
Melissa P. Easterling

Barbara H. Pray
Donald E. Pray
W. Bland Williamson

ADDRESS INQUIRIES TO:
David M. Zemel, Director
(See address above.)

*PLEASE NOTE:
Applicants are urged to review the grant guidelines before submitting a proposal.

BERRIEN COMMUNITY FOUNDATION [37]
2900 South State Street
Suite 2 East
St. Joseph, MI 49085
(269) 983-3486
E-mail: bcf@berriencommunity.org
Web Site: www.berriencommunity.org

FOUNDED: 1952

AREAS OF INTEREST:
Building spirit of community/arts and culture, nurturing our children, encouraging youth leadership and development.

TYPE:
Development grants; General operating grants; Project/program grants; Scholarships; Seed money grants; Technical assistance.

PURPOSE:
To promote philanthropy, build a spirit of community and enhance the quality of life in Berrien County, MI.

ELIGIBILITY:
501(c)(3) or equivalent.

GEOG. RESTRICTIONS: Berrien County, Michigan.

FINANCIAL DATA:
Amount of support per award: Varies.
Total amount of support: More than $4,800,000 for the year 2016.

APPLICATION INFO:
Contact the Foundation.
Duration: Typically one year.

ADDRESS INQUIRIES TO:
Program Manager
(See address or e-mail above.)

BERWIND CORPORATION [38]
3000 Centre Square West
1500 Market Street
Philadelphia, PA 19102
(215) 575-2350
(215) 575-2420
E-mail: mlarue@berwind.com
jgreen@berwind.com
Web Site: www.berwind.com

FOUNDED: 1886

AREAS OF INTEREST:
Education and community development.

TYPE:
Matching gifts.

LEGAL BASIS:
Nonprofit 501(c)(3) philanthropic organization.

ELIGIBILITY:
Applicants must be 501(c)(3) organizations within Berwind operating areas. Matching gift program is for employees or retired employees only.

GEOG. RESTRICTIONS: Primarily Philadelphia area, Pennsylvania.

FINANCIAL DATA:
Amount of support per award: Varies.
Matching fund requirements: $50 to $10,000 for employee grants only.

APPLICATION INFO:
Contact the Corporation.
Duration: One year.
Deadline: Must receive completed form no later than 90 days from the eligible participant's gift.

ADDRESS INQUIRIES TO:
Mary A. LaRue
Human Resources Department
Matching Gift Officer
(See address above.)

BINC FOUNDATION   **[39]**
3135 South State Street
Suite 203
Ann Arbor, MI 48108
(866) 733-9064
Fax: (734) 477-2806
E-mail: info@bincfoundation.org
Web Site: www.bincfoundation.org

FOUNDED: 1996

AREAS OF INTEREST:
Book industry.

NAME(S) OF PROGRAMS:
● **Binc Foundation Scholarship Program**
● **Financial Assistance Grants**

TYPE:
Challenge/matching grants; Grants-in-aid; Scholarships.

PURPOSE:
To strengthen the bookselling community through charitable programs that support employees and their families.

LEGAL BASIS:
501(c)(3) nonprofit organization.

ELIGIBILITY:
To apply for a Financial Assistance Grant, a bookseller must be a regular full-time or part-time bookseller, currently employed for a minimum of 90 days at a bricks-and-mortar bookstore in the U.S., Puerto Rico, the U.S. Virgin Islands or Guam.

Scholarships are awarded to bookstore employees and their dependents for full-time or part-time study at any accredited institution in the U.S. Awards are based on financial need, academic performance and community involvement.

FINANCIAL DATA:
Scholarship awards may be used for tuition, fees, books, supplies, and room and board.
Amount of support per award: Matching Grants: Up to $2,000; Scholarships: $3,500.
Total amount of support: Scholarships: $109,000 for the year 2018.

NO. AWARDS: Scholarships: Up to 27.

APPLICATION INFO:
Details on applying for a Binc Scholarship can be found at www.scholarsapply.org/binc in January.

Applications for financial assistance are available online under the Request Assistance menu.
Deadline: Scholarship Program: March 5.

THE WILLIAM BINGHAM FOUNDATION   **[40]**
1375 East 9th Street, Suite 900
Cleveland, OH 44114
(216) 759-9142
E-mail: info@wbinghamfoundation.org
Web Site: wbinghamfoundation.org

FOUNDED: 1955

AREAS OF INTEREST:
Education, science, health and human services, and the arts.

TYPE:
Capital grants; Challenge/matching grants; Endowments; General operating grants; Project/program grants.

YEAR PROGRAM STARTED: 1955

PURPOSE:
To provide funding to nonprofit organizations that sponsor programs in the areas of education, science, health and human services, and the arts; to strengthen civil society and its institutions.

LEGAL BASIS:
Private family foundation.

ELIGIBILITY:
Grants are made only to public charities. Grants are not made to individuals or to organizations located outside of the U.S.

GEOG. RESTRICTIONS: United States.

FINANCIAL DATA:
Amount of support per award: Varies.
Total amount of support: $615,000 for the year 2018.

NO. AWARDS: 17 for the year 2018.

APPLICATION INFO:
The majority of grantmaking is by invitation only.
Duration: Generally one year.

IRS I.D.: 34-6513791

ADDRESS INQUIRIES TO:
Daniel L. Horn, Administrator
(See address above.)

THE BLUESCOPE FOUNDATION NORTH AMERICA   **[41]**
1540 Genessee Street
Kansas City, MO 64102
(816) 968-3208
Fax: (816) 627-8993
E-mail: jill.harmon@bluescope.com
Web Site: www.bluescopebuildings.com

FOUNDED: 1952

AREAS OF INTEREST:
United charities, scholarship program, aid to education, community needs, youth and civic cultural activities, hospitals and health, and minorities.

TYPE:
Capital grants; General operating grants; Matching gifts; Project/program grants; Scholarships. Scholarship program available to children of Company employees only. Matching gift program for employee contributions to eligible educational or cultural institutions.

In the area of community needs, support is given to organizations which serve broadly the communities in which the Company has employees and significant capital investment. Programs falling within this category include United Way organizations in Company plant cities, minority assistance limited to nonprofit agencies that help provide jobs or job training for the disadvantaged, foster the movement of minorities into the mainstream of economic life and enable minorities to improve their level of educational attainment, and neighborhood and nonresidential building programs utilizing the company's products.

In the area of education, grants are made to colleges and universities which supply significant numbers of employees to the Company and/or which provide opportunities for continuing education to employees, help disadvantaged students who demonstrate ability and desire to prepare for and remain in colleges and universities, have programs which have the objective of providing education to residents of Company plant locations and provide educational opportunities which advance minorities, women and individuals with disabilities.

In the area of culture, the Foundation considers programs which help broaden the cultural experience of the residents of local communities through the support of visual and performing arts organizations, demonstrate concern for excellence and innovation in the arts, and bring cultural opportunity to the economically disadvantaged.

In the area of public affairs, the Foundation helps promote strong relationships between the public and private sectors to assist in the solution to urban problems, reinforce the efforts of groups formed to gather and disseminate information that is in the general public interest, encourage community volunteerism, and promote economic education and the merits of the free enterprise system.

YEAR PROGRAM STARTED: 1952

PURPOSE:
To provide sustained financial assistance to worthy charitable, educational, health and welfare programs in the U.S.; to enhance the quality of life in those communities where employees of BlueScope Steel reside.

LEGAL BASIS:
A nonprofit, benevolent and charitable corporation under the laws of the State of Missouri. A 501(c)(3) private foundation under IRS code.

ELIGIBILITY:
Grants are made only to nonprofit organizations located in areas where the company has facilities. Organizations must have a clear statement of purpose in the public interest, a program consistent with the organization's stated purpose, evidence of interagency cooperation to avoid duplication of services, an active and responsive governing body of volunteers holding regular meetings, evidence of professional program management and reasonable fund-raising expenses, maintenance of ethical publicity and promotion of the program that excludes exaggerated or misleading claims, and fund solicitation policies which prohibit the payment of commission or other compensation based on total funds raised or undue pressures.

Grants are not normally made to individuals, political organizations, religious organizations for sectarian purposes, pre-school, primary and secondary educational institutions, fraternal or veteran's organizations, organizations receiving United Way support for operating expenses, national health organizations, including local or regional chapters, hospitals (except those providing unique services, burn centers or children's services), tours, conferences, seminars, workshops, testimonial dinners, tables, tickets, advertisements, walk-a-thons, endowment funds, and other foundations of any type providing grants to not-for-profits or programs beyond the Foundation's stated geographic areas of interest.

GEOG. RESTRICTIONS: Rainsville, Alabama; Pine Bluff, Arkansas; Sacramento and Visalia, California; Kansas City and St. Joseph, Missouri; Greensboro, North Carolina; Annville, Pennsylvania; Jackson and Memphis, Tennessee; Kalama, Washington; and Evansville, Wisconsin.

FINANCIAL DATA:
Amount of support per award: $1,000 to $10,000.

Total amount of support: $450,000 annually.

Matching fund requirements: The minimum single gift the Foundation will match per eligible donor is $25. The maximum single gift or total of annual gifts to be matched per eligible donor for full-time employees is $2,000 per calendar year.

NO. MOST RECENT APPLICANTS: 100.

NO. AWARDS: Approximately 100, excluding matching gifts.

REPRESENTATIVE AWARDS:
$10,000 to Harvesters, Kansas City, MO; $5,000 to Genesis School, Kansas City, MO.

APPLICATION INFO:
Initial contact should be made by phone, e-mail or letter addressed to the Foundation Administrator or, in non-Kansas City locations, to the plant or division manager describing the need, purpose and general activities of the requesting charitable organization. The letter will be reviewed by the plant or division manager to assure compliance with the policies established by the Foundation Trustees with a recommendation and forwarded to the Foundation Administrator.

Applicants must provide evidence of compliance with eligibility requirements, plus an annual report describing program activities and supporting services including financial statements, detailed annual budget and copy of IRS not-for-profit determination.

Duration: One year.

Deadline: Announcements are made after quarterly Trustee meetings.

PUBLICATIONS:
Annual report; contributions policy; application guidelines.

IRS I.D.: 44-0663648

ADDRESS INQUIRIES TO:
Jill Harmon, Foundation Director
(See address above.)

THE BOOTH-BRICKER FUND [42]
826 Union Street
Suite 300
New Orleans, LA 70112
(504) 581-2430
Fax: (504) 566-4785
E-mail: heather@boo-ker.com

FOUNDED: 1966

AREAS OF INTEREST:
The Fund focuses exclusively on taking advantage of the historic opportunity to reform public education in New Orleans.

TYPE:
Capital grants; Development grants; Project/program grants.

PURPOSE:
To promote, develop and foster religious, charitable, scientific, literary and educational nonprofit organizations.

ELIGIBILITY:
The Fund generally does not provide sustaining (operations and maintenance) funding. Requests are welcomed for capital needs, special projects and other one-time requirements. No grants are made to individuals or supporting organizations (i.e., a Section 501(c)(3) organization with further designation under Section 509(a)(3)).

GEOG. RESTRICTIONS: Louisiana, with priority given to the New Orleans area.

FINANCIAL DATA:
Market value of assets as of December 31, 2018: $50,850,000.

Amount of support per award: Varies.

Total amount of support: Charitable distributions of $2,393,000 for the year ended December 31, 2018. Since its inception, the Fund has made charitable contributions exceeding $40,000,000.

NO. AWARDS: 83 for the year 2018.

APPLICATION INFO:
Applications, which should be made by letter, are considered by the board of trustees at its quarterly meetings. There are no forms or deadlines. Requests should include complete information about the applicant organization, including its history, purpose, finances, current operations, governing board and tax status. A detailed explanation of the proposed use of the funds must be provided. Videotapes or DVDs should not be submitted.

Duration: Varies.

BOARD OF TRUSTEES:
Charles B. Mayer
Gray S. Parker
Mary Kay Parker
Nathaniel P. Phillips, Jr.
Nathaniel P. Phillips, III
Elizabeth S. Raindre
H. Hunter White, Jr.

OFFICERS:
Gray S. Parker, Chairman
Ingrid C. Laffont, Treasurer
Heather A. Travland, Secretary

ADDRESS INQUIRIES TO:
Gray S. Parker, Chairman
(See address above.)

JAMES GRAHAM BROWN FOUNDATION, INC. [43]
4350 Brownsboro Road
Suite 200
Louisville, KY 40207
(502) 896-2440
Fax: (502) 896-1774
E-mail: grants@jgbf.org
Web Site: www.jgbf.org

FOUNDED: 1954

AREAS OF INTEREST:
Education and workforce, community and economic prosperity, and quality of life.

TYPE:
General operating grants; Grants-in-aid.

YEAR PROGRAM STARTED: 1954

PURPOSE:
To establish the commonwealth as a national leader; to create a public image of Louisville and Kentucky of which we can all be proud.

LEGAL BASIS:
Private foundation.

ELIGIBILITY:
Only Kentucky organizations that have a tax-exempt designation under Section 501(c)(3) of the IRS Code can apply.

GEOG. RESTRICTIONS: Kentucky, with emphasis on Louisville.

FINANCIAL DATA:
Amount of support per award: $500 and up.
Total amount of support: $15,971,708 for the year 2018.

NO. MOST RECENT APPLICANTS: Approximately 100 for the year 2018.

NO. AWARDS: 54 for the year 2018.

REPRESENTATIVE AWARDS:
$3,000,000 to Louisville Urban League for the Sports and Learning Complex; $1,000,000 to Metro United Way for improving developmental, educational and life outcomes for Louisville citizens; $500,000 to Gilda's Club Louisville for the Red Door Campaign in order to establish a Shared Services Group among local nonprofits with similar goals and operations to FCP.

APPLICATION INFO:
Contact the Foundation for details.
Duration: One year.
Deadline: Varies.

PUBLICATIONS:
Annual report.

ADDRESS INQUIRIES TO:
Mason Rummel, President and Chief Executive Officer
(See address above.)

THE JOE W. AND DOROTHY DORSETT BROWN FOUNDATION [44]
320 Metairie Hammond Highway
Suite 500
Metairie, LA 70005
(504) 834-3433
Fax: (504) 834-3441
E-mail: bethbuscher@thebrownfoundation.org
Web Site: www.thebrownfoundation.org

FOUNDED: 1959

AREAS OF INTEREST:
Human services; medical, health and science; education; community benefit; and conservation and environment.

TYPE:
General operating grants; Project/program grants; Research grants; Training grants.

PURPOSE:
To alleviate human suffering.

ELIGIBILITY:
Applicants must be nonprofit 501(c)(3). The Foundation favors requests for funds where funds are generally unavailable from most other sources. Within the five focus areas, the focus is primarily on relieving human suffering; secondary interest includes cultural, spiritual, educational or scientific initiatives. No grants are made to individuals.

GEOG. RESTRICTIONS: Louisiana and Mississippi. Preference is given to the greater New Orleans area and Mississippi gulf coast.

FINANCIAL DATA:
Amount of support per award: Varies.
Total amount of support: Varies.

APPLICATION INFO:
Contact the Foundation.
Duration: One year. Must reapply.
Deadline: August 30.

THE MARGARET E. BURNHAM CHARITABLE TRUST   [45]

c/o H.M. Payson & Co.
P.O. Box 31
Portland, ME 04112-0031
(207) 772-3761
Fax: (207) 871-7508
E-mail: jbe@hmpayson.com
Web Site: www.margaretburnham.org

AREAS OF INTEREST:
Community/social services, medical, educational, arts and culture, and environment.

TYPE:
Grants-in-aid; Project/program grants. Annual grant dedicated to responding to the needs of the Maine communities served.

PURPOSE:
To benefit nonprofit organizations located or operating in the state of Maine.

ELIGIBILITY:
Organizations must be 501(c)(3) and must operate in and serve the state of Maine. Individuals, private foundations under Section 509, and religious organizations are not eligible.

GEOG. RESTRICTIONS: Maine.

FINANCIAL DATA:
Amount of support per award: $1,000 to $20,000.
Total amount of support: Varies.

APPLICATION INFO:
A completed application consists of the following:
(1) certification, application, project description, and budget pages;
(2) copy of the organization's most recent 501(c)(3) IRS ruling;
(3) copy of the organization's most recent financial statement or tax return and;
(4) list of the organization's officers and directors.
Duration: One year.
Deadline: October 1.

ADDRESS INQUIRIES TO:
Thomas M. Pierce, Trustee
(See address above.)

EDYTH BUSH CHARITABLE FOUNDATION, INC.   [46]

199 East Welbourne Avenue, Suite 100
Winter Park, FL 32789
(407) 647-4322
Fax: (407) 647-7716
E-mail: pcorkum@edythbush.org
Web Site: www.edythbush.org

FOUNDED: 1973

AREAS OF INTEREST:
Children, youth and families, education, health care, limited interest in the arts, improvement of nonprofit organizations, and human services.

TYPE:
Capital grants; Challenge/matching grants; Demonstration grants; Development grants; Matching gifts; Project/program grants; Technical assistance; Training grants. Capacity building grants.

PURPOSE:
To create innovative civic solutions to help people help themselves.

LEGAL BASIS:
Private foundation.

ELIGIBILITY:
The Foundation welcomes grant applications from nonprofit organizations that have secured their 501(c)(3) and 509(a) IRS rulings. The Foundation has elected to focus its resources within Lake, Orange, Osceola and Seminole counties, FL. The Foundation will not fund organizations that are chiefly tax-supported, nor does it fund individual scholarships, individual research (even if through an exempt or otherwise qualified educational organization), alcoholism or drug abuse programs or facilities, routine operating expenses, the pay-off of deficits or pre-existing debt, foreign organizations or foreign expenditures, travel projects or fellowships, chiefly church, sacramental, denominational or interdenominational purposes (except those outreach programs for elderly, indigents, needy, youth or homeless, regardless of belief, race, color, creed, or sex), endowment funds, advocacy organizations, or organizations that have receipts or revenues from memberships and/or contributions of less than $25,000.

GEOG. RESTRICTIONS: Lake, Orange, Osceola and Seminole counties, Florida.

FINANCIAL DATA:
Amount of support per award: Typically $5,000 to $50,000. Maximum grant has been $1,000,000 spread over five years. Large grants are typically spread over two or three years.
Total amount of support: Varies.
Matching fund requirements: Must be new or increased cash contributions or pledges.

APPLICATION INFO:
Detailed information is available on the web site.
Duration: One year.
Deadline: Applications are accepted year-round.

PUBLICATIONS:
Guidelines.

IRS I.D.: 23-7318041

OFFICERS:
David A. Odahowski, President and Chief Executive Officer
Mary Ellen Hutcheson, CPA, Vice President and Treasurer
Matthew W. Certo, Corporate Secretary

BOARD OF DIRECTORS:
Richard J. Walsh, Chairman
Matthew W. Certo, Vice Chairman and Corporate Secretary
Elizabeth Dvorak
Patricia Engfer
Anne B. Kerr, Ph.D.
David A. Odahowski
John A. Riley

ADDRESS INQUIRIES TO:
Phyllis Corkum, Grants Manager
(See address above.)

CABOT FAMILY CHARITABLE TRUST   [47]

22 Batterymarch Street
Boston, MA 02109
(617) 226-7505
Fax: (617) 451-1733
E-mail: kmchugh@cabotwellington.com
Web Site: www.cabotfamilytrust.org

FOUNDED: 1942

AREAS OF INTEREST:
Arts and culture, education and youth development, environment and conservation, health and human services, and for the public benefit.

TYPE:
Capital grants; General operating grants; Project/program grants. Capital campaigns.

YEAR PROGRAM STARTED: 1942

PURPOSE:
To provide funding for nonprofit organizations working in the arts, environment, youth development, education, health and human services.

LEGAL BASIS:
Charitable trust.

ELIGIBILITY:
The Trust supports only nonprofit organizations holding active 501(c)(3) status under the IRS code. The Trust does not make contributions to individuals, political organizations, religious institutions, advertising, sponsorship or fraternal organizations.

Applicants must meet the following criteria:
(1) extend important services to individuals and groups not served adequately through other programs and institutions;
(2) manage change by assessing community needs and developing programs to meet emerging needs;
(3) promote productive cooperation and full use of resources by nonprofit organizations and community groups and;
(4) test new approaches to problems or adapt solutions that have been successful elsewhere.

GEOG. RESTRICTIONS: Boston and other contiguous communities.

FINANCIAL DATA:
Assets of $48,000,000.
Amount of support per award: $5,000 to $50,000 per year.
Total amount of support: $2,000,000.

NO. MOST RECENT APPLICANTS: 380 for the year 2017.

NO. AWARDS: Approximately 80.

REPRESENTATIVE AWARDS:
$25,000 to Reach Out and Read for an early reading program for infants in the Neonatal Intensive Care Unit at Boston Medical Center; $40,000 to Urban Farming Institute to train inner city residents interested in careers in agriculture and farming; $100,000 (over two years) to Artists for Humanity for expansion of facilities serving teen entrepreneurs in the arts and design.

APPLICATION INFO:
Applicants should submit a concept paper of three pages plus cover sheet and budget. Application form is available on the web site.
Duration: Usually, one year; multiyear considered.

Deadline: February 1 and September 1.

PUBLICATIONS:
Annual report.

IRS I.D.: 04-6035446

TRUSTEES:
Shoma Aditya
Frank Bradley
Laura C. Carrigan
Mary Schneider Enriquez
Greenfield Sluder
Hendrika Sluder

EXECUTIVE DIRECTOR:
Katherine S. McHugh

ADDRESS INQUIRIES TO:
Katherine S. McHugh, Executive Director
(See address above.)

THE MORRIS AND GWENDOLYN CAFRITZ FOUNDATION [48]

1825 K Street, N.W.
Suite 1400
Washington, DC 20006
(202) 223-3100
Fax: (202) 296-7567
E-mail: info@cafritzfoundation.org
Web Site: www.cafritzfoundation.org

FOUNDED: 1948

AREAS OF INTEREST:
Community services, arts and humanities, education, health and the environment.

TYPE:
Challenge/matching grants; General operating grants; Project/program grants; Scholarships; Technical assistance.

YEAR PROGRAM STARTED: 1948

PURPOSE:
To build a stronger community for residents of the Washington, DC area through support of programs in arts and humanities, community services, education, health and the environment.

LEGAL BASIS:
Private foundation.

ELIGIBILITY:
Grants are made only to charitable, educational and cultural institutions exempt from taxation under the Internal Revenue Code. IRS-registered, tax-exempt, 501(c)(3) organizations with a public charity status of 509(a)(1) or 509(a)(2) only. The general policy is to concentrate grants to organizations, operating within the greater Washington metropolitan area, with projects of direct assistance to the District of Columbia and its environs. Grants are not made for capital purposes, endowments or to individuals.

GEOG. RESTRICTIONS: Montgomery and Prince George's counties in Maryland; Arlington and Fairfax counties, and the cities of Alexandria and Falls Church in Virginia; and Washington, DC.

FINANCIAL DATA:
Amount of support per award: Varies.
Total amount of support: Approximately $7,500,000.

NO. MOST RECENT APPLICANTS: Approximately 700.

NO. AWARDS: Approximately 425.

APPLICATION INFO:
To be considered for funding, an organization must submit a complete proposal, not a Letter of Inquiry (LOI). LOIs are not required. Organizations may submit a proposal for only one deadline within a 12-month period.
Duration: One year.
Deadline: November 1, March 1 and July 1.

PUBLICATIONS:
Annual report; application guidelines.

OFFICERS:
Calvin Cafritz, President and Chief Executive Officer
John E. Chapoton, Vice Chairman

STAFF:
Mardell Moffett, Executive Director
Mary Mulcahy, Associate Director
Tobi Printz-Platnick, Associate Director
Miyesha Perry, Associate Director, Grants and Administration
Messay Derebe, Program Officer
Hannah Hahn, Program Officer
Debbi Lindenberg, Program Officer
Jessica Plocher, Program Officer
Mike Schwartz, Program Officer
Nailah Hart, Program Associate
Connie Sun, Grants Assistant

DIRECTORS:
Calvin Cafritz, Chairman of the Board
Michael F. Brewer
Jane Lipton Cafritz
John E. Chapoton
Dorothy Kosinski
Patricia McGuire
Earl A. Powell, III
Robert Sloan

ADVISORY BOARD:
Anthony W. Cafritz
Elliot S. Cafritz
The Hon. Constance A. Morella
Elizabeth M. Peltekian

ADDRESS INQUIRIES TO:
Mardell Moffett, Executive Director
(See address above.)

THE CALERES CARES CHARITABLE TRUST [49]

8300 Maryland Avenue
St. Louis, MO 63105
(314) 854-4000
E-mail: charitablegiving@caleres.com
Web Site: www.caleres.com/c/about/community

FOUNDED: 1951

AREAS OF INTEREST:
Family, healthy living/wellness, arts and culture, local community, and footwear industry.

TYPE:
Project/program grants.

YEAR PROGRAM STARTED: 1951

PURPOSE:
To help develop stronger families by providing opportunities for enrichment; to encourage individuals to live better lives through health and wellness efforts; to provide occasions for families and individuals to step feet-first into the arts and cultural opportunities in the community.

LEGAL BASIS:
Corporate contributions program.

ELIGIBILITY:
The Caleres Trust encourages tax-exempt, nonprofit organizations who meet the Trust's

funding priorities to apply. Organization must be located in St. Louis, MO, or in communities around the world where the company operates.

The Trust supports charitable organizations which are either strategically aligned with the Trust's mission, vision and values, focused on advancing the footwear industry or benefit the overall St. Louis community in growing and attracting new businesses and residents.

Grants are not made to individuals. In general, the Trust does not support galas, walks, golf outings, trivia nights, etc.

FINANCIAL DATA:
To date, Caleres has donated more than $20,000,000 to 501(c)(3) organizations.

APPLICATION INFO:
Applications must be submitted through the Trust's online system. The online application requires the following attachments:
(1) current year's operating budget;
(2) list of board members and;
(3) program or project budget (if applicable).
Attachments can be in Microsoft Word, Excel or Adobe PDF format. Compressed ZIP files must not be included.
Deadline: Grant proposals: March 31, June 30, September 30 and December 31.

*PLEASE NOTE:
The Caleres Cares Charitable Trust was formerly known as the Brown Shoe Company, Inc. Charitable Trust.

CAMPBELL SOUP FOUNDATION [50]

One Campbell Place
Camden, NJ 08103
(856) 342-5264
Web Site: www.campbellsoupcompany.com

FOUNDED: 1953

AREAS OF INTEREST:
Increasing access to healthy food, encouraging healthy living and nurturing Campbell neighborhoods.

NAME(S) OF PROGRAMS:
● **Dollars for Doers Fund**
● **Matching Gift Program**
● **United Way Match Program**

TYPE:
Matching gifts. Dollars for Doers Program provides financial support to nonprofit organizations where Campbell employees volunteer in Campbell communities.

Matching Gift Program supports employee's gifts to higher education and to six pre-selected nonprofit organizations whose mission closely meets the Foundation's CSR goals.

The Campbell Soup Foundation also supports 15 separate United Way campaigns hosted at Campbell and Pepperidge Farm operating facilities throughout the U.S.

YEAR PROGRAM STARTED: 1954

PURPOSE:
To provide financial support to local champions that inspire positive change in communities throughout the U.S. where Campbell Soup Company employees live and work.

LEGAL BASIS:
Tax-exempt private foundation.

ELIGIBILITY:
Grants are made to tax-exempt organizations providing service consistent with Foundation's goals. Grants are not directed at supporting individuals.

GEOG. RESTRICTIONS: United States.

FINANCIAL DATA:
Amount of support per award: Varies.
Total amount of support: Approximately $1,900,000 each fiscal year.

NO. MOST RECENT APPLICANTS: 90 grant applications for the year 2018.

NO. AWARDS: 33 grants awarded for the year 2018.

APPLICATION INFO:
Grants are offered by invitation only.
Duration: Usually one-time grants.
Deadline: Two funding cycles per year, one in the fall and one in the spring, typically four months in length. Fall cycle runs September through December and Spring cycle runs January through April.

OFFICERS:
Kim Fortunato, President
Ashok Madhavan, Treasurer
Andrew Kupchik, Secretary
Stanley Polomski, Controller

TRUSTEES:
Gary Biscoll
Mark Cacciatore
Kim Fortunato
Richard Landers
Helen Le Du
Karen Lewis
Anthony Sanzio
Dave Stangis
Emily Waldorf

ADDRESS INQUIRIES TO:
Kate Barrett
Senior Manager Community Affairs
(See address above.)

THE CANNON FOUNDATION, INC.   [51]
52 Spring Street, N.W.
Concord, NC 28025
(704) 786-8216
Fax: (704) 782-2812
E-mail: vskahen@cannonfoundation.org
info@cannonfoundation.org
Web Site: www.cannonfoundation.org

FOUNDED: 1943

AREAS OF INTEREST:
Primarily health care, higher education and human services. Limited grants to arts, historical preservation and environment.

TYPE:
Capital grants.

YEAR PROGRAM STARTED: 1943

LEGAL BASIS:
Private foundation.

ELIGIBILITY:
Applicant must be 501(c)(3) nonprofit organization. No grants to individuals.

GEOG. RESTRICTIONS: North Carolina.

FINANCIAL DATA:
Amount of support per award: $5,000 to $200,000.

APPLICATION INFO:
Applications are requested through the web site. Links to the online application are sent

to the applying organization's chief executive officer/executive director, not to grant writers or consultants.
Duration: One year.
Deadline: January 10, May 10 and September 10. Notification approximately 12 weeks after deadline.

STAFF:
Venetia Skahen, Executive Director

ADDRESS INQUIRIES TO:
Venetia Skahen, Executive Director
(See address above.)

CARNEGIE CORPORATION OF NEW YORK   [52]
437 Madison Avenue
New York, NY 10022
(212) 371-3200
Fax: (212) 754-4073
E-mail: grantsinfo@carnegie.org
Web Site: www.carnegie.org/grants

FOUNDED: 1911

AREAS OF INTEREST:
Education, democracy, international peace and security, and higher education and research in Africa.

TYPE:
Conferences/seminars; Development grants; Project/program grants; Research grants; Seed money grants.

YEAR PROGRAM STARTED: 1911

PURPOSE:
To promote the advancement and diffusion of knowledge and understanding.

LEGAL BASIS:
Private foundation.

ELIGIBILITY:
Grants are made primarily to academic institutions and national or regional organizations.

FINANCIAL DATA:
Amount of support per award: Approximately $550,000.
Total amount of support: Approximately $120,000,000 for the year 2017.

NO. AWARDS: Varies.

APPLICATION INFO:
Only Letters of Inquiry submitted via the Corporation's online system will be considered.
Duration: Varies.

PUBLICATIONS:
Program guidelines; pamphlet; meeting and occasional papers; *Carnegie Reporter*, magazine; annual report.

IRS I.D.: 13-1628151

ADDRESS INQUIRIES TO:
See e-mail address above.

AMON G. CARTER FOUNDATION   [53]
201 Main Street, Suite 1945
Fort Worth, TX 76102
(817) 332-2783
Fax: (817) 332-2787
E-mail: mwallace@agcf.org
Web Site: www.agcf.org

FOUNDED: 1945

AREAS OF INTEREST:
Education, arts, health and medical services, and human and social services.

TYPE:
Capital grants; Challenge/matching grants; Seed money grants. Program expansion.

PURPOSE:
To support arts, education, health and medical services, programs benefiting youth and elderly, and civic and community endeavors that enhance quality of life.

LEGAL BASIS:
Private foundation.

ELIGIBILITY:
Applicants must be 501(c)(3) organizations. Board focus on Fort Worth and Tarrant County, TX.

No loans. No grants to individuals.

GEOG. RESTRICTIONS: Texas.

FINANCIAL DATA:
Amount of support per award: $1,000 to $500,000.
Total amount of support: $35,000,000.

NO. MOST RECENT APPLICANTS: 400.

NO. AWARDS: 200.

REPRESENTATIVE AWARDS:
$500,000 to All Saints Health Foundation; $3,000,000 to Texas Christian University; $150,000 to University of Texas Medical Branch; $175,000 to Communities in Schools of Greater Tarrant County.

APPLICATION INFO:
Send brief letter request supplemented with project budget and/or other pertinent information in support of request.
Duration: Most grants are for one year.
Deadline: February, May and November.

PUBLICATIONS:
Grant policy and guideline statement.

OFFICERS:
W. Patrick Harris, Executive Vice President-Investments
John H. Robinson, Executive Vice President, Grant Administration
Tamara Dean, Controller

BOARD OF DIRECTORS:
Robert W. Brown, M.D.
Kate L. Johnson
Mark L. Johnson
Sheila B. Johnson

ADDRESS INQUIRIES TO:
John H. Robinson
Executive Vice President
Grant Administration
(See address above.)

HAROLD K.L. CASTLE FOUNDATION   [54]
1197 Auloa Road
Kailua, HI 96734-4606
(808) 263-7073
Fax: (808) 261-6918
E-mail: amatsukado@castlefoundation.org
Web Site: www.castlefoundation.org

FOUNDED: 1962

AREAS OF INTEREST:
Hawaii's public education redesign and enhancement, Hawaii's nearshore marine resource conservation, strengthening the communities of Windward Oahu, and other areas of focus when the Foundation sees a special opportunity to make a difference with limited resources.

TYPE:
Capital grants; Project/program grants; Seed money grants.

PURPOSE:
To benefit the people of Hawaii.

LEGAL BASIS:
Family foundation.

ELIGIBILITY:
Nonprofit organizations serving the state of Hawaii with Internal Revenue Code Sections 501(c)(3) and 509(a) public charity status and public schools in Hawaii.

GEOG. RESTRICTIONS: Hawaii.

CO-OP FUNDING PROGRAMS: Hawaii Community Stabilization Initiative.

NO. MOST RECENT APPLICANTS: 125.

NO. AWARDS: 74.

REPRESENTATIVE AWARDS:
$1,049,983 to University of Hawaii Foundation; $1,045,002 to Teach for America; $1,200,000 to The Nature Conservancy of Hawaii.

APPLICATION INFO:
Prospective grant applicants must submit an Online Inquiry Form, which is the first step in requesting funds from the Foundation. The Foundation will contact applicants within one month to request more information, invite the submission of a full proposal, or to inform applicant that the Foundation will be unable to consider a full proposal due to limited resources and/or a mismatch with Foundation priorities.
Duration: Program grants: Up to five years.
Deadline: Applications accepted on a rolling basis. Capital support requests due each year by October 1.

PUBLICATIONS:
Application guidelines; annual report.

IRS I.D.: 99-6005445

STAFF:
Terrence R. George, President and Chief Executive Officer
Carlton K.C. Au, Vice President, Chief Financial Officer and Treasurer
Eric Co, Senior Program Officer for Ocean Resiliency
Georgianna DeCosta, Program Officer for Windward Oahu
Ann Matsukado, Controller/Grants Manager
Susan Sumida, Corporate Secretary
Linda Mekaru, Accountant
Alex Harris, Advisor

BOARD OF DIRECTORS:
H. Mitchell D'Olier, Chairman of the Board
Dr. Claire L. Asam, Director
Dr. Kittredge A. Baldwin, Director
Corbett A.K. Kalama, Director
Dee Jay Mailer, Director
James C. McIntosh, Director
Eric K. Yeaman, Director

ADDRESS INQUIRIES TO:
Ann Matsukado, Controller/Grants Manager
(See address above.)

CENTRAL MAINE POWER COMPANY [55]
83 Edison Drive
Augusta, ME 04336
Fax: (207) 629-4819
E-mail: kathleen.newman@cmpco.com
Web Site: www.cmpco.com

AREAS OF INTEREST:
Education, civic, science, technology education and economic development.

NAME(S) OF PROGRAMS:
● **Central Maine Power Company Corporate Contributions Program**

TYPE:
Capital grants; Challenge/matching grants; Demonstration grants; General operating grants; Project/program grants; Research grants.

LEGAL BASIS:
Corporation giving program.

ELIGIBILITY:
Applicants must be nonprofit organizations, limited to the area serviced by Central Maine Power.

GEOG. RESTRICTIONS: Maine.

FINANCIAL DATA:
Amount of support per award: $100 to $1,000.

NO. MOST RECENT APPLICANTS: 500.

NO. AWARDS: 100.

APPLICATION INFO:
Applicants should send a proposal letter.
Duration: Typically one year. Some multiyear funding.
Deadline: Applications accepted throughout the year. Grants announced monthly.

ADDRESS INQUIRIES TO:
Government Relations
(See address above.)

*SPECIAL STIPULATIONS:
Only available to schools and nonprofits within company's service territory in Maine.

CENTRAL VALLEY COMMUNITY FOUNDATION [56]
5260 North Palm Avenue
Suite 122
Fresno, CA 93704
(559) 226-5600
Fax: (559) 230-2078
E-mail: info@centralvalleycf.org
Web Site: www.centralvalleycf.org

FOUNDED: 1966

AREAS OF INTEREST:
Primarily arts and culture, health and human services, and youth services, environment, high impact with a lesser emphasis on parks and music.

NAME(S) OF PROGRAMS:
● **Arts and Culture**
● **Environment**
● **High Impact**
● **Regional Sustainability**
● **Teen Pregnancy Prevention Initiative**
● **Youth Grants**

TYPE:
General operating grants; Project/program grants.

PURPOSE:
To improve the quality of life for the people of the Central San Joaquin Valley.

LEGAL BASIS:
Community foundation.

ELIGIBILITY:
To apply, an organization should be a 501(c)(3) nonprofit, government agency, community group with fiscal agent, public agency, or educational institution.

The Foundation does not consider requests for previously incurred expenses, fund-raising by one agency on behalf of another, endowments, individuals, or institutions limiting their services to persons of a single religious sect or denomination.

GEOG. RESTRICTIONS: Central San Joaquin Valley, California; primarily the counties of Fresno, Kings, Madera, Mariposa, Merced, and Tulare.

FINANCIAL DATA:
Amount of support per award: Varies.
Total amount of support: Varies.

APPLICATION INFO:
There is an online application process; the beginning step is to complete the organization card.
Duration: One year. Renewal possible. High Impact grants: Multiyear. Teen Pregnancy Prevention Initiative: Two-year grants.
Deadline: Varies.

STAFF:
Ashley Swearengin, President and Chief Executive Officer
Yen Kilday, Director of Programs and Evaluation

ADDRESS INQUIRIES TO:
Yen Kilday, Director of Programs and Evaluation
(See address above.)

THE CHAMPLIN FOUNDATION [57]
2000 Chapel View Boulevard, Suite 350
Cranston, RI 02920
(401) 944-9200
Fax: (401) 944-9299
E-mail: office@champlinfoundation.org
Web Site: champlinfoundation.org

FOUNDED: 1932

AREAS OF INTEREST:
Conservation, environment, education, health, cultural programs, youth, social services, historic preservation and libraries.

TYPE:
Capital grants; Challenge/matching grants; Scholarships. Direct grants for capital needs including the purchase of equipment, real estate, renovations, construction and reduction of mortgage indebtedness.

Other grants are made only in certain circumstances.

Challenge grants are made at the Foundations' discretion.

Scholarships are only to Brown University for graduates of Rhode Island public high schools.

YEAR PROGRAM STARTED: 1932

PURPOSE:
To make grants to qualified charitable organizations to promote the general well-being of humanity, with preference to Rhode Island.

LEGAL BASIS:
Tax-exempt private foundation.

ELIGIBILITY:
Tax-exempt organizations, preferably in Rhode Island, may apply. No grants are awarded to individuals. Scholarships are limited to Rhode Island public high school graduates accepted at Brown University.

GEOG. RESTRICTIONS: Rhode Island.

FINANCIAL DATA:
  Amount of support per award: Average:
  $25,000 to $65,000.

  Total amount of support: $18,523,000 for the
  year 2017.

NO. MOST RECENT APPLICANTS: Approximately
400.

NO. AWARDS: 175 for the year 2017.

REPRESENTATIVE AWARDS:
  Health Care: $80,000 to Bethany Home;
  Education: $525,000 to Brown University;
  Libraries: $54,400 to Cranston Public
  Library; Youth/Fitness: $67,150 to Boys and
  Girls Club of Cumberland-Lincoln; Social
  Services: $250,000 to Oasis International;
  The Arts: $18,000 to Newport Art Museum;
  Conservation and Parks: $114,000 to
  Audubon Society of Rhode Island.

APPLICATION INFO:
  Applicants must submit a brief letter
  concisely describing the project and its
  intended purpose, status of any fund-raising
  effort and other sources of funds available.
  Copies of IRS 501(c)(3) tax-exemption and
  509(a) letters must be furnished. Audited
  financial statements may be required on
  request.

  Duration: No grants are awarded on a
  continuing basis. Applicants may apply
  annually.

  Deadline: April 30. Grants awarded in
  November; checks issued in December.
  Invited public schools: June 30.

PUBLICATIONS:
  Annual report; guidelines; Report on Open
  Space and Recreation Grants.

IRS I.D.: 51-0165988

EXECUTIVE COMMITTEE:
  R. Kelly Sheridan, Chairman
  Nina Stack, Executive Director
  Timothy N. Gorham, Director of Grants
  Administration

ADDRESS INQUIRIES TO:
  Nina Stack, Executive Director
  (See address above.)

*SPECIAL STIPULATIONS:
  Preference is given to Rhode Island
  tax-exempt organizations.

  All initial inquiries must be made by mail.

BEN B. CHENEY
FOUNDATION   [58]
3110 Ruston Way, Suite A
Tacoma, WA 98402
(253) 572-2442
E-mail: info@benbcheneyfoundation.org
Web Site: www.benbcheneyfoundation.org

AREAS OF INTEREST:
  Charity, civic affairs, culture, education, the
  elderly, health, social services and youth.

TYPE:
  Capital grants.

PURPOSE:
  To improve the quality of life in communities
  where the Cheney Lumber Company
  operated.

LEGAL BASIS:
  Foundation.

ELIGIBILITY:
  Applicants must be 501(c)(3) tax-exempt
  organizations.

GEOG. RESTRICTIONS: Tacoma and Pierce
County, Washington; Medford and Jackson
County, Oregon and the seven northernmost
counties in California.

FINANCIAL DATA:
  Amount of support per award: $1,000 to
  $15,000 for small grants; $16,000 to
  $125,000 for regular grants.

  Total amount of support: Varies.

NO. MOST RECENT APPLICANTS: Approximately
300.

NO. AWARDS: 110.

APPLICATION INFO:
  Details are available on the Foundation web
  site. Application must be submitted
  electronically.

  Duration: Typically one to two years. No
  renewals.

ADDRESS INQUIRIES TO:
  Brad Cheney, Executive Director
  (See address above.)

THE CHRISTENSEN FUND   [59]
487 Bryant Street
Second Floor
San Francisco, CA 94107
(415) 644-1600
Fax: (415) 644-1601
E-mail: info@christensenfund.org
Web Site: www.christensenfund.org

FOUNDED: 1957

AREAS OF INTEREST:
  Supporting organizations working on
  biological and cultural diversity.

NAME(S) OF PROGRAMS:
  ● **African Rift Valley**
  ● **Central Asia**
  ● **Global**
  ● **Melanesia**
  ● **Northern Australia**
  ● **Northwest Mexico**
  ● **San Francisco-Bay Area**
  ● **Southwest U.S.**

TYPE:
  General operating grants; Project/program
  grants; Research grants.

YEAR PROGRAM STARTED: 2004

PURPOSE:
  To buttress the efforts of people and
  institutions who believe in a biodiverse world
  infused with artistic expression and who
  work to secure ways of life and landscapes
  that are beautiful, bountiful and resilient.

LEGAL BASIS:
  Private, independent foundation.

ELIGIBILITY:
  Must have nonprofit 501(c)(3) status or
  similar not-for-profit organization based
  either in the U.S. or another country.

GEOG. RESTRICTIONS: Southwest United States,
northwest Mexico, Central Asia, Northern
Australia, Melanesia, and the Africa Rift
Valley (Southwest Ethiopia/Northern Kenya).

FINANCIAL DATA:
  Amount of support per award: $50,000 to
  $100,000.

  Total amount of support: Approximately
  $10,000,000 for the year 2018.

NO. MOST RECENT APPLICANTS: 250.

NO. AWARDS: 90 on average.

APPLICATION INFO:
  Unsolicited requests are not accepted.
  Duration: Typically one to two years.
  Deadline: Varies.

ADDRESS INQUIRIES TO:
  See e-mail address above.

EDNA MCCONNELL CLARK
FOUNDATION   [60]
415 Madison Avenue, 10th Floor
New York, NY 10017
(212) 551-9100
Fax: (212) 421-9325
E-mail: info@bluemeridian.org
Web Site: www.emcf.org

FOUNDED: 1970

AREAS OF INTEREST:
  Youth development.

NAME(S) OF PROGRAMS:
  ● **Blue Meridian Partners**
  ● **PropelNext**
  ● **Youth Development Fund**

TYPE:
  General operating grants. Business planning
  grants. Blue Meridian Partners, a
  collaboration of 12 philanthropic institutions
  and individuals, invests up to $100 to $200
  million to scale individual high-performing
  nonprofits poised to have a national impact
  on children and young people, ages 0 to 30.

  PropelNext helps promising nonprofits, often
  at an earlier stage of organizational
  development, improve their collection and
  use of data to produce better outcomes for
  youth.

  Youth Development Fund concentrates on
  helping high-performing youth-serving
  nonprofits achieve greater impact.

PURPOSE:
  To help nonprofits make a real difference in
  the lives of economically disadvantaged
  young people in the U.S.

LEGAL BASIS:
  Private foundation.

GEOG. RESTRICTIONS: United States.

FINANCIAL DATA:
  Amount of support per award: Varies.

  Total amount of support: $125,863,816 for
  the year 2018.

CO-OP FUNDING PROGRAMS: When Foundation
interests are shared with other organizations.

NO. AWARDS: 58.

APPLICATION INFO:
  Organizations need to complete survey
  online.

  Duration: Varies.

  Deadline: No official deadlines. Board meets
  four times a year, plus standing committee
  meetings.

PUBLICATIONS:
  Annual report.

IRS I.D.: 23-7047034

TRUSTEES AND OFFICERS:
  H. Lawrence Clark, Chairman
  Ralph Stefano, Chief Financial Officer
  Nancy Roob, President
  James McConnell Clark, Jr.

ADDRESS INQUIRIES TO:
  Albert Chung
  Chief, Strategic Initiatives
  (See address above.)

*PLEASE NOTE:
The Foundation does not accept unsolicited proposals.

THE CLEVELAND-CLIFFS FOUNDATION [61]
200 Public Square
Suite 3300
Cleveland, OH 44114-2589
(216) 694-5700
Fax: (216) 694-4880
E-mail: clevelandcliffsfoundation_ohio@
clevelandcliffs.com
Web Site: www.clevelandcliffs.com

FOUNDED: 1962

AREAS OF INTEREST:
Education and community building.

TYPE:
Capital grants; General operating grants.

PURPOSE:
To enhance the quality of life of the Company's employees and communities in which the Company operates.

ELIGIBILITY:
501(c)(3) organizations, as defined by the IRS, may apply. Request must address Cliffs Foundation funding priorities, including geographical and cause areas of interest. Organizations and their proposed programs must address specific community needs.

GEOG. RESTRICTIONS: Upper Peninsula of Michigan; northeastern Minnesota and Cleveland, Ohio.

FINANCIAL DATA:
Amount of support per award: $250 minimum.

APPLICATION INFO:
A brief project summary must be e-mailed to the regional public affairs contact listed online. Summary must be no greater than two paragraphs in length.
Duration: One year.
Deadline: Applications accepted throughout the year.

PUBLICATIONS:
Guidelines.

ADDRESS INQUIRIES TO:
Anna Ediger, Manager of Government Relations
(See address above.)

COASTAL BEND COMMUNITY FOUNDATION [62]
555 North Carancahua Street
Suite 900
Corpus Christi, TX 78401
(361) 882-9745
Fax: (361) 882-2865
E-mail: kselim@cbcfoundation.org
Web Site: www.cbcfoundation.org

FOUNDED: 1981

AREAS OF INTEREST:
Arts, children and youth, community development, crime prevention, elderly, environment, health, social welfare, education and human services.

TYPE:
Project/program grants; Scholarships.

YEAR PROGRAM STARTED: 1981

PURPOSE:
To improve the quality of life in the Coastal Bend area.

LEGAL BASIS:
Community foundation.

ELIGIBILITY:
Grants are made to organizations that have tax-exempt status under Section 501(c)(3) of the Internal Revenue Code. No grants are made to individuals.

GEOG. RESTRICTIONS: Aransas, Bee, Jim Wells, Kleberg, Nueces, Refugio and San Patricio counties, Texas.

FINANCIAL DATA:
Amount of support per award: Varies.
Total amount of support: $11,079,883 for the year 2018.
Matching fund requirements: Determined on individual basis.

CO-OP FUNDING PROGRAMS: Coastal Bend Day of Giving.

NO. AWARDS: Varies.

APPLICATION INFO:
Applications accepted online between May 1 and June 15. Organizations should submit application with requested documentation by the application deadline. Applications that do not conform to the required format will not be considered.
Duration: Grants must be completed by the following September 30.
Deadline: Posted online.

PUBLICATIONS:
Annual report.

IRS I.D.: 74-2190039

ADDRESS INQUIRIES TO:
Karen W. Selim, President and Chief Executive Officer
(See address above.)

THE COCKRELL FOUNDATION [63]
3737 Buffalo Speedway
Suite 1100
Houston, TX 77098
(713) 209-7500
E-mail: foundation@cockrellfoundation.org
Web Site: www.cockrellfoundation.org

FOUNDED: 1957

AREAS OF INTEREST:
Education, health, culture and community.

TYPE:
Endowments; Professorships; Project/program grants; Scholarships. Endowments, fellowships, professorships and scholarships at University of Texas, Cockrell School of Engineering.

YEAR PROGRAM STARTED: 1966

PURPOSE:
To provide financial support for charitable organizations in the Houston area in support of education, health, civic, religious and social services.

LEGAL BASIS:
Private foundation.

ELIGIBILITY:
Endowments, fellowships, professorships and scholarships to the University of Texas Cockrell School of Engineering only.

In general, the Foundation gives support for annual and capital campaigns, building funds, endowment funds, general purposes, matching funds, and special projects. Grants are made only to nonprofit, tax-exempt

organizations. To be eligible, an organization must have a determination letter from the IRS indicating that it is an organization described in Section 501(c)(3) of the Internal Revenue Code and is not a private foundation within the meaning of Section 509(a) of the Code.

GEOG. RESTRICTIONS: Primarily Houston, Texas.

FINANCIAL DATA:
Amount of support per award: Varies.
Total amount of support: $8,722,728 in grants for the year 2019.

NO. AWARDS: 33 grants for the year 2018.

APPLICATION INFO:
The Foundation accepts online grant applications only. The following materials must be uploaded to the online application:
(1) name and address of tax-exempt organization which will be the recipient if a donation is made and a copy of the exemption letter from the U.S. Treasury Department;
(2) specific sum being requested;
(3) an Executive Summary sheet (one page) describing the need or problem with an explanation of how the grant money will be used and what is hoped to be accomplished;
(4) budget for the project or program giving the total cost;
(5) amount raised to date toward the project or program and the souces from which it has come, including private, religious organizations and/or government sources and, in particular, the total amount contributed by the individuals on the Board of Directors;
(6) plans for raising any uncovered balance;
(7) an explanation of why it is necessary to seek outside support;
(8) current status of the project;
(9) plans for putting continuing projects on a self-sustaining basis and an estimate of when this will occur;
(10) copy of the organization's current annual budget;
(11) copy of the organization's latest IRS-990;
(12) copy of the organization's latest audited financials;
(13) list of the members of the Board of Directors and;
(14) list of the officers of the organization.
Duration: One year.

IRS I.D.: 74-6076993

OFFICERS AND DIRECTORS:
Ernest H. Cockrell, President and Director
M. Nancy Williams, Executive Vice President
Sherrie J. Reinhackel, Vice President
Stacy L. White, Secretary/Treasurer
David A. Cockrell, Director
Ernest D. Cockrell, Director
Janet S. Cockrell, Director
Richard B. Curran, Director
Milton T. Graves, Director
J. Webb Jennings, III, Director
Ronald T. Nixon, Director
Laura Jennings Turner, Director

ADDRESS INQUIRIES TO:
M. Nancy Williams
Executive Vice President
(See address above.)

THE OGDEN CODMAN TRUST [64]

c/o Rackemann, Sawyer & Brewster
160 Federal Street, 15th Floor
Boston, MA 02110-1700
(617) 951-1108
Fax: (617) 542-7437
E-mail: smonahan@rackemann.com
Web Site: www.codmantrust.org

FOUNDED: 1968

AREAS OF INTEREST:
Environment, conservation, historic preservation, cultural, health and social services in the town of Lincoln, MA.

TYPE:
Project/program grants. Support for special programs.

YEAR PROGRAM STARTED: 1972

PURPOSE:
To improve the quality of life in Lincoln.

LEGAL BASIS:
Private independent foundation.

ELIGIBILITY:
Organizations must be IRS 501(c)(3) tax-exempt.

GEOG. RESTRICTIONS: Lincoln, Massachusetts.

FINANCIAL DATA:
Amount of support per award: $2,000 to $50,000.
Total amount of support: Approximately $250,000 for the year 2019.
Matching fund requirements: Case-by-case basis.

NO. MOST RECENT APPLICANTS: 16 for the year 2019.

NO. AWARDS: 14 for the year 2019.

REPRESENTATIVE AWARDS:
Town of Lincoln; Codman Community Farm; Lincoln School Foundation.

APPLICATION INFO:
Contact Grants Coordinator prior to submitting an application.
Duration: Varies.
Deadline: Applications are reviewed on a rolling basis.

PUBLICATIONS:
Application guidelines.

TRUSTEES:
Susan T. Monahan
Maura E. Murphy, Esq.
Michael F. O'Connell, Esq.

ADDRESS INQUIRIES TO:
Susan T. Monahan
Grants Coordinator and Trustee
(See e-mail address above.)

THE GEORGE W. CODRINGTON CHARITABLE FOUNDATION [65]

c/o Thompson Hine LLP
3900 Key Center, 127 Public Square
Cleveland, OH 44114-1291
(216) 566-5699
Fax: (216) 566-5800
E-mail: craig.martahus@thompsonhine.com
tommie.robertson@thompsonhine.com

FOUNDED: 1955

AREAS OF INTEREST:
Greater Cleveland area community projects, with an emphasis on contributions to diversity, equity and inclusion.

TYPE:
Capital grants; Challenge/matching grants; Endowments; General operating grants; Matching gifts. Annual grants to public charitable or educational projects.

YEAR PROGRAM STARTED: 1955

PURPOSE:
To assist, encourage and promote the well-being of mankind, regardless of race, color or creed.

LEGAL BASIS:
Private foundation.

ELIGIBILITY:
The Foundation's supportive services are limited to public charitable or educational projects. No grants are made to individuals.

GEOG. RESTRICTIONS: Cuyahoga County, Ohio and immediately adjacent areas.

FINANCIAL DATA:
Amount of support per award: $5,000 to $50,000.
Total amount of support: Varies.

NO. MOST RECENT APPLICANTS: 130.

NO. AWARDS: 55.

REPRESENTATIVE AWARDS:
$50,000 to Musical Arts Association; $10,000 to YWCA Greater Cleveland; $5,000 to Cleveland Public Theatre.

APPLICATION INFO:
Applications should be directed to the Supervisory Board of the Foundation. The application should state fully but briefly the amount requested, the need for the grant, the area served by the applicant, a brief history of the applicant's organization, description of the applicant's contributions to the area and listing of the applicant's officers and trustees. Original plus three copies should be submitted. Must also include IRS letter as evidence of Section 501(c)(3) status.
Duration: One year.
Deadline: Pending applications are considered at meetings of the Supervisory Board held in April, June, September and December.

IRS I.D.: 34-6507457

SUPERVISORY BOARD:
Craig R. Martahus, Esq., Chairman
William R. Seelbach, Vice Chairman
Raymond T. Sawyer, Esq., Secretary
Robyn Minter Smyers

ADDRESS INQUIRIES TO:
Tommie Robertson, Legal Secretary
E-mail:
tommie.robertson@thompsonhine.com or
Craig Martahus, Esq., Chairman
(See address above.)

THE COLEMAN FOUNDATION, INC. [66]

651 West Washington Boulevard
Suite 306
Chicago, IL 60661-2134
(312) 902-7120
Fax: (312) 902-7124
E-mail: info@colemanfoundation.org
Web Site: www.colemanfoundation.org

FOUNDED: 1951

AREAS OF INTEREST:
Entrepreneurship education, cancer care, and developmental disability services.

TYPE:
Capital grants; Challenge/matching grants; Conferences/seminars; Project/program grants. The major areas of grantmaking include:
(1) education, with a strong emphasis on entrepreneurship education (national in scope, with focus in Chicago);
(2) cancer care and treatment in the Chicago metropolitan area and;
(3) services for the disabled in the Chicago metropolitan area, with a strong emphasis on developmental disabilities.

ELIGIBILITY:
Grants are only made to IRS-certified tax-exempt nonprofit organizations, 501(c)(3) or 509(a)(1) and that are not supporting foundations. Funding is prohibited to individuals, for-profit businesses, advertising books and tickets. General solicitations and annual appeals will not be considered.

Only programs within the Foundation's region of focus will be considered.

GEOG. RESTRICTIONS: Primarily metropolitan Chicago and other select parts of the Midwest.

FINANCIAL DATA:
Amount of support per award: Varies.
Total amount of support: Varies.

NO. AWARDS: Approximately 100.

APPLICATION INFO:
A two-page letter of inquiry should be sent by the applicant which includes the following:
(1) brief description of the organization;
(2) synopsis of the program to be proposed;
(3) clear statement of program/grant objectives and how they will be evaluated;
(4) estimate of the size grant to be proposed or range of proposed funding;
(5) statement of how the program/project will be sustained following the grant period and;
(6) contact name and information, including e-mail address of the project manager, for further communication.

Brochures, video tapes, CDs and other attachments should not be sent with the letter of inquiry. Any such attachments will not be considered at this stage of review.
Duration: Typically one year.
Deadline: Letters of Inquiry are accepted on a continuing basis.

ADDRESS INQUIRIES TO:
Michael Hennessy
President and Chief Executive Officer
(See address above.)

THE COLLINS FOUNDATION [67]

1618 S.W. First Avenue
Suite 505
Portland, OR 97201
(503) 227-7171
Fax: (503) 295-3794
E-mail: information@collinsfoundation.org
Web Site: www.collinsfoundation.org

FOUNDED: 1947

AREAS OF INTEREST:
Arts, children and youth, community welfare, education, environment, health and science, humanities, and religion.

TYPE:
Challenge/matching grants; Project/program grants. Grants made to agencies exclusively

in the state of Oregon to improve, enrich and give greater expression to its religious, educational, cultural and scientific endeavors. Also, to assist in improving the quality of life in the state.

YEAR PROGRAM STARTED: 1947

PURPOSE:
To help fund programs or projects that will make life better in the community.

LEGAL BASIS:
Private, nonprofit foundation.

ELIGIBILITY:
The Foundation is organized in the state of Oregon for projects within the state. All applicant agencies must be tax-exempt, as established by the Treasury Department of the United States. No support is given to individuals.

GEOG. RESTRICTIONS: Oregon.

FINANCIAL DATA:
Amount of support per award: Varies.
Total amount of support: Approximately $10,000,000 annually.
Matching fund requirements: The Foundation looks favorably on grants which must be matched.

NO. AWARDS: 241 for the year 2019.

APPLICATION INFO:
Application information is available online.
Duration: Varies.
Deadline: Not specified. Awards are announced periodically throughout the year.

OFFICERS:
Truman W. Collins, Jr., President
Cynthia G. Addams, Chief Executive Officer

BOARD OF TRUSTEES:
Jaime Arredondo
Truman W. Collins, Jr.
Serena Cruz
Ryan Luria
Cherida Collins Smith
Lee Diane Collins Vest

ADDRESS INQUIRIES TO:
Cynthia G. Addams, Chief Executive Officer
(See address above.)

COMMUNITIES FOUNDATION OF TEXAS, INC. [68]
Grants Department
5500 Caruth Haven Lane
Dallas, TX 75225
(214) 750-4222
Fax: (214) 750-4210
E-mail: eliser@cftexas.org
Web Site: www.cftexas.org

AREAS OF INTEREST:
Arts, community improvement, disaster relief, education, health, housing, religion, scientific research, social services and youth.

NAME(S) OF PROGRAMS:
● **CFT for Business**
● **Community Impact Grants**
● **Donor-Advised Grants**
● **Educate Texas**

TYPE:
Project/program grants.

YEAR PROGRAM STARTED: 1953

LEGAL BASIS:
Public charity.

ELIGIBILITY:
Organizations with IRS 501(c)(3) tax-exempt designation.

GEOG. RESTRICTIONS: Primarily Dallas, Denton, Colin, Rockwell and Tarrant counties in Texas.

FINANCIAL DATA:
Amount of support per award: Varies.
Total amount of support: Varies.

APPLICATION INFO:
Requests must be submitted using the Foundation Letter of Inquiry checklist and form, which can be downloaded from the web site above.
Duration: Varies.
Deadline: Letter of Intent: March 1, April 1 and May 1.

ADDRESS INQUIRIES TO:
Grants Processing
(See address above.)

COMMUNITY FOUNDATION FOR A GREATER RICHMOND [69]
3409 Moore Street
Richmond, VA 23230
(804) 330-7400
Fax: (804) 330-5992
E-mail: sblackwell@cfrichmond.org
info@cfrichmond.org
Web Site: www.cfrichmond.org

FOUNDED: 1968

AREAS OF INTEREST:
Community vibrancy, economic prosperity, educational success, and health and wellness.

TYPE:
Awards/prizes; Capital grants; Challenge/matching grants; Conferences/seminars; Development grants; General operating grants; Project/program grants; Research grants; Scholarships; Seed money grants; Technical assistance; Training grants. Community grants programs.

YEAR PROGRAM STARTED: 1995

PURPOSE:
To develop a healthy, thriving community.

LEGAL BASIS:
Community foundation.

ELIGIBILITY:
Proposals will be accepted from 501(c)(3) charitable organizations which serve the city of Richmond, outlying counties or the Tri-Cities.

GEOG. RESTRICTIONS: Richmond, Virginia metropolitan area and the Tri-Cities, Colonial Heights, Goochland, Hopewell and Petersburg.

FINANCIAL DATA:
Amount of support per award: Typically $10,000 to $50,000.
Total amount of support: Over $50,000,000 annually.

APPLICATION INFO:
Instructions for submitting preliminary proposals are available on the Foundation's web site.
Duration: Usually one year. Renewal possible.
Deadline: Varies.

PUBLICATIONS:
Annual report; policy and guidelines for grant requests.

IRS I.D.: 23-7009135

OFFICERS:
Pamela J. Royal, M.D., Chairperson
Austin Brockenbrough, IV, Vice Chairperson
Sherrie Armstrong, President and Chief Executive Officer
Philip H. Goodpasture, Treasurer
Kristen Hager, Secretary

ADDRESS INQUIRIES TO:
Charles Dyson, Director of Data and Customer Support
(See address above.)

COMMUNITY FOUNDATION FOR SOUTHEAST MICHIGAN [70]
333 West Fort Street
Suite 2010
Detroit, MI 48226
(313) 961-6675
Fax: (313) 961-2886
E-mail: cfsem@cfsem.org
Web Site: www.cfsem.org

FOUNDED: 1984

AREAS OF INTEREST:
Environment, health, arts and culture, education, economic development, human services and civic affairs.

TYPE:
Development grants; Endowments; Project/program grants; Seed money grants.

LEGAL BASIS:
Public Foundation.

ELIGIBILITY:
The Foundation grants to federal 501(c)(3) tax-exempt organizations, government entities, school districts and universities. No grants for buildings, equipment, religious programs, fund-raising, individuals, conferences or annual meetings.

GEOG. RESTRICTIONS: The seven counties of southeast Michigan: Livingston, Macomb, Monroe, Oakland, St. Clair, Washtenaw and Wayne.

FINANCIAL DATA:
Amount of support per award: Varies.

NO. AWARDS: 3,900 grants were awarded for the year 2018.

APPLICATION INFO:
Guidelines are available on the Foundation web site. Interested organizations should call a program officer before applying.
Duration: One year.
Deadline: Quarterly.

PUBLICATIONS:
Annual report; newsletters.

STAFF:
Mariam C. Noland, President
Karen L. Leppanen, Vice President, Finance and Administration
Sheryl G. Arb, Vice President, Marketing and Communications
Katie G. Brisson, Vice President, Programs

OFFICERS OF THE TRUSTEES:
James B. Nicholson, Chairman
Penny B. Blumenstein, Vice Chairman
David M. Hempstead, Vice Chairman
Reginald M. Turner, Vice Chairman
Michael T. Monahan, Treasurer
Mary M. Weiser, Secretary

ADDRESS INQUIRIES TO:
Mariam C. Noland, President
(See address above.)

COMMUNITY FOUNDATION OF EASTERN CONNECTICUT

68 Federal Street
New London, CT 06320
(860) 442-3572
Fax: (860) 442-0584
E-mail: jennob@cfect.org
Web Site: www.cfect.org

TYPE:
General operating grants; Project/program grants; Scholarships.

See entry 1119 for full listing.

COMMUNITY FOUNDATION OF GREATER MEMPHIS   [71]

1900 Union Avenue
Memphis, TN 38104
(901) 728-4600
Fax: (901) 722-0010
E-mail: ewarren@cfgm.org
Web Site: www.cfgm.org

FOUNDED: 1969

AREAS OF INTEREST:
Grants administered for charitable purposes in metropolitan Memphis.

NAME(S) OF PROGRAMS:
● **Nonprofit Capacity Building Grants**
● **Scholarship Funds**

TYPE:
Challenge/matching grants; Project/program grants; Scholarships; Technical assistance.

YEAR PROGRAM STARTED: 1969

PURPOSE:
To provide support for the benefit of the geographic area that the Foundation serves; to strengthen the community through philanthropy.

LEGAL BASIS:
Community foundation.

ELIGIBILITY:
Applicants must be charitable and nonprofit under IRS regulations, holding a 501(c)(3) tax-exempt status. Applicants must be located in the geographic area that the Foundation serves.

GEOG. RESTRICTIONS: Eastern Arkansas, northern Mississippi and West Tennessee.

FINANCIAL DATA:
Amount of support per award: Varies.
Total amount of support: Varies.
Matching fund requirements: Stipulated with some grant awards.

NO. MOST RECENT APPLICANTS: Varies.

APPLICATION INFO:
Grant guidelines and application forms are available online.
Duration: One year.
Deadline: Varies.

PUBLICATIONS:
Newsletters; annual report.

IRS I.D.: 58-1723645

ADDRESS INQUIRIES TO:
Elizabeth Warren
Director of Grants and Initiatives
(See address above.)

COMMUNITY FOUNDATION OF THE EASTERN SHORE

1324 Belmont Avenue, Suite 401
Salisbury, MD 21804
(410) 742-9911
Fax: (410) 742-6638
E-mail: hmahler@cfes.org
Web Site: www.cfes.org

TYPE:
Awards/prizes; Challenge/matching grants; Demonstration grants; Project/program grants; Scholarships; Seed money grants; Technical assistance; Training grants.

See entry 1132 for full listing.

THE COMMUNITY FOUNDATION OF THE HOLLAND/ZEELAND AREA   [72]

85 East Eighth Street
Suite 110
Holland, MI 49423
(616) 396-6590
Fax: (616) 396-3573
E-mail: info@cfhz.org
Web Site: www.cfhz.org

FOUNDED: 1951

AREAS OF INTEREST:
Education, arts and culture, recreation, community and economic development, the needs of youth and the elderly, health and human services, environment and housing.

TYPE:
Research grants; Scholarships; Technical assistance.

YEAR PROGRAM STARTED: 1951

PURPOSE:
To ensure the community thrives today, tomorrow and forever by building our community's endowment to support high-impact charitable projects, helping donors achieve their charitable goals, and leading and partnering in community-level initiatives.

LEGAL BASIS:
Corporation and public charity, 501(c)(3).

ELIGIBILITY:
Grants are made to organizations that have tax-exempt status under Section 501(c)(3) of the Internal Revenue Code or governmental agencies. No grants are made to individuals. Nonsectarian religious programs may apply.

GEOG. RESTRICTIONS: Holland and Zeeland, Michigan area only.

FINANCIAL DATA:
Amount of support per award: $500 to $75,000.
Total amount of support: Varies.

NO. MOST RECENT APPLICANTS: 521.

NO. AWARDS: 318.

APPLICATION INFO:
Grant applicants must contact the Foundation to discuss a proposal prior to submitting an application.

Scholarship applications must be completed on the Foundation web site.
Duration: One year.
Deadline: Varies.

PUBLICATIONS:
Annual report; application guidelines.

IRS I.D.: 38-6095283

STAFF:
Elizabeth Kidd, Vice President of Community Impact
Stacy Timmerman, Director of Scholarships

ADDRESS INQUIRIES TO:
Vice President of Community Impact
(See address above.)

THE COMMUNITY FOUNDATION OF WESTERN NORTH CAROLINA   [73]

4 Vanderbilt Park Drive
Suite 300
Asheville, NC 28803
(828) 254-4960
Fax: (828) 251-2258
E-mail: info@cfwnc.org
Web Site: www.cfwnc.org

FOUNDED: 1978

AREAS OF INTEREST:
Food and farming, people in need, early childhood development, and natural and cultural resources.

TYPE:
Project/program grants; Scholarships.

YEAR PROGRAM STARTED: 1978

PURPOSE:
To inspire philanthropy and mobilize resources to enrich lives and communities in western North Carolina.

ELIGIBILITY:
Grants are awarded to tax-exempt organizations. Eligibility varies by program.

GEOG. RESTRICTIONS: Western North Carolina.

FINANCIAL DATA:
Amount of support per award: Varies.
Total amount of support: Approximately $20,000,000 in grants and scholarships for the fiscal year 2019.

NO. AWARDS: Varies.

APPLICATION INFO:
Application information is available on the web site.
Duration: Varies.
Deadline: Varies.

PUBLICATIONS:
Quarterly newsletter; annual report.

IRS I.D.: 56-1223384

ADDRESS INQUIRIES TO:
Diane Crisp, Grants Manager
(See address above.)

COMPTON FOUNDATION, INC.   [74]

44 Montgomery Street
Floor 3
San Francisco, CA 94104
(415) 391-9001
Fax: (415) 391-9007
Web Site: www.comptonfoundation.org

FOUNDED: 1946

AREAS OF INTEREST:
Climate change, peace and national security, and reproductive rights and justice.

TYPE:
Project/program grants.

PURPOSE:
To ignite change; to support transformative leadership and courageous storytelling, inspiring action toward a peaceful, just, sustainable future.

ELIGIBILITY:
501(c)(3) nonprofit organizations in the U.S. that are working domestically may apply.

The Foundation does not support organizations that work solely in one city or state.

FINANCIAL DATA:
Amount of support per award: Varies.
Total amount of support: $1,900,000 for the year 2019.

NO. AWARDS: Varies.

APPLICATION INFO:
Proposals are by invitation only. Unsolicited proposals are not accepted.

PUBLICATIONS:
Grant Highlights (available on web site).

STAFF:
Ellen Friedman, Executive Director
Jennifer Turnage, Director of Finance
Deborah K. Daughtry, Director of Operations
Johanna Hanson, Senior Program Officer

BOARD OF DIRECTORS:
Vanessa Davenport, President
Ian Compton, Vice President
Emilie Cortes, Treasurer
Jakada Imani, Secretary

ADDRESS INQUIRIES TO:
Deborah K. Daughtry, Director of Operations
(See address above.)

THE CONNELLY FOUNDATION   [75]

One Tower Bridge
100 Front Street, Suite 1450
West Conshohocken, PA 19428
(610) 834-3222
Fax: (610) 834-0866
E-mail: info@connellyfdn.org
Web Site: www.connellyfdn.org

FOUNDED: 1955

AREAS OF INTEREST:
Educational, civic and cultural institutions, health with emphasis on human services. A significant portion of funding is directed toward organizations affiliated with the Catholic Church.

TYPE:
Capital grants; General operating grants; Project/program grants.

PURPOSE:
To enhance the quality of life in the Delaware Valley.

LEGAL BASIS:
Private foundation.

ELIGIBILITY:
No grants to individuals, political or national organizations or other foundations, nor does the Foundation respond to annual appeals or general letters of solicitation. Foundation guidelines restrict funding any organization more than once during a 12-month period. Applicants who have received previous grants from the Foundation should submit final reports under separate cover.

GEOG. RESTRICTIONS: Camden, New Jersey; Bucks, Chester, Delaware and Montgomery counties and city of Philadelphia, Pennsylvania.

FINANCIAL DATA:
Amount of support per award: $5,000 to $50,000.
Total amount of support: $12,110,204 for the year 2019.

NO. AWARDS: 549 for the year 2017.

APPLICATION INFO:
The Foundation requires prospective grantees that choose not to apply online to use the Philanthropy Network Greater Philadelphia Common Grant Application Form. The Foundation does not accept applications via e-mail, but does accept grant proposals online and by mail.
Duration: Varies.
Deadline: Written proposals are accepted and reviewed by the Foundation throughout the year. With the exception of Foundation initiatives, there are no deadlines. Applicants receive a response within approximately three months.

PUBLICATIONS:
Application guidelines.

OFFICERS:
Thomas A. Riley, President
Emily C. Riley, Executive Vice President
Valerie Martin, Chief Financial Officer
Fran Burns, Chief Operating Officer

ADDRESS INQUIRIES TO:
Program Officer
(See address above.)

*PLEASE NOTE:
Visits to the Foundation office or contacts with its staff initiated by applicants during the proposal review process are discouraged.

CONSUMERS ENERGY FOUNDATION   [76]

One Energy Plaza, Room EP8-210
Jackson, MI 49201-2276
(517) 788-0432
(877) 501-4952
Fax: (517) 788-2281
E-mail: foundation@consumersenergy.com
Web Site: www.consumersenergy.com/foundation

FOUNDED: 1989

AREAS OF INTEREST:
Social welfare, education, culture and arts, community and civic affairs, and environment.

CONSULTING OR VOLUNTEER SERVICES:
Employee volunteer program.

NAME(S) OF PROGRAMS:
● **Caring for Community**
● **Volunteer Investment Program**

TYPE:
Capital grants; Challenge/matching grants; General operating grants; Matching gifts; Project/program grants; Scholarships; Seed money grants; Technical assistance. Volunteer grants.

YEAR PROGRAM STARTED: 1990

PURPOSE:
To support the charitable interest of Consumers Energy.

LEGAL BASIS:
Corporate program.

ELIGIBILITY:
501(c)(3) tax-exempt status, nonprofit organizations are eligible for support. The Foundation will not fund individuals, political, religious, labor or veteran's organizations.

Requests will be considered from organizations elsewhere for programs or projects that significantly benefit the state of Michigan.

GEOG. RESTRICTIONS: Michigan.

FINANCIAL DATA:
Amount of support per award: Typically $1,000 to $10,000.
Total amount of support: $6,000,000 for the year 2018.
Matching fund requirements: Foundation will match employee and retiree contributions to Michigan higher education, food banks, homeless shelters and community foundations. Minimum $25 and maximum $1,000 per year per employee and retiree. Retirees eligible for 50% match.

REPRESENTATIVE AWARDS:
$250,000 to Detroit Zoological Society; $100,000 to Food Bank of Eastern Michigan; $50,000 to Great Start Collaborative of Traverse Bay; $75,000 to Impression 5 Science Center; $150,000 to Michigan State University, College of Engineering.

APPLICATION INFO:
Cover letter and completed grant application required by mail only.
Duration: Varies. Renewal unlikely.

PUBLICATIONS:
Guidelines brochure.

DIRECTORS:
Patricia K. Poppe, Chairman
Brandon J. Hofmeister, President
Carolyn A. Bloodworth, Secretary and Treasurer
Jean-Francois Brossoit
Reiji P. Hayes
Catherine A. Hendrian
Venkat Dhenuvakonda Rao
Catherine Reynolds
Brian F. Rich
Garrick J. Rochow

ADDRESS INQUIRIES TO:
Carolyn A. Bloodworth
Secretary and Treasurer
(See address above.)

V.V. COOKE FOUNDATION   [77]

P.O. Box 7664
Louisville, KY 40257-0664
(502) 901-3179
E-mail: carl.vvcooke@att.net

FOUNDED: 1947

AREAS OF INTEREST:
Civic affairs, education, religion and humanitarianism.

TYPE:
Capital grants; Endowments; General operating grants; Scholarships; Seed money grants.

LEGAL BASIS:
Private foundation.

ELIGIBILITY:
Grants are made to organizations that have tax-exempt status under Section 501(c)(3) and are not described in Section 509(a)(3) of the Internal Revenue Code. Grants are made for religious, educational, humanitarian and civic purposes. No grants are made to individuals.

GEOG. RESTRICTIONS: Metropolitan Louisville, Kentucky and the Commonwealth of Kentucky.

FINANCIAL DATA:
Amount of support per award: $250 to $25,000.

Total amount of support: $330,960 for the year ended August 31, 2018.

NO. MOST RECENT APPLICANTS: 87.

NO. AWARDS: 50.

REPRESENTATIVE AWARDS:
$1,000 to Lighthouse Promise; $25,000 to Baptist Healthcare Foundation.

APPLICATION INFO:
Applications should be in letter form. Applicants must:
(1) outline the organization's goals and purposes, and the intended use and amount of the grant requested;
(2) list other organizations that serve the needs addressed by this application and what distinguishes this organization and;
(3) identify the percentage of the organization's budget that is used for fund-raising and for administrative expenses.

Eight copies of the application with a single copy of the applicant's IRS 501(c)(3) letter are required.

Deadline: Mid-January, April, July and October for consideration in mid-February, May, August and November, respectively.

PUBLICATIONS:
Application guidelines.

IRS I.D.: 61-6033714

STAFF:
Carl M. Thomas, Executive Director

ADDRESS INQUIRIES TO:
Carl M. Thomas, Executive Director
(See address above.)

COOPER FOUNDATION   [78]
1248 O Street, Suite 870
Lincoln, NE 68508-1493
(402) 476-7571
E-mail: info@cooperfoundation.org
Web Site: cooperfoundation.org

FOUNDED: 1934

AREAS OF INTEREST:
Education, human services, arts and humanities, and the environment.

TYPE:
Challenge/matching grants; Demonstration grants.

PURPOSE:
To support the operations and core programs of strong, well-managed and effective nonprofit organizations located in and working in Lancaster and Lincoln counties, NE.

LEGAL BASIS:
Private foundation.

ELIGIBILITY:
Most grants are made to organizations located in and impacting residents of Lancaster and Lincoln counties, NE.

The Foundation does not fund individuals, businesses, health organizations or issues, churches, religious organizations or issues, travel, memberships, endowments, non-501(c)(3) organizations, 509(a)(3) supporting organizations, fiscal agents, or private foundations.

GEOG. RESTRICTIONS: Nebraska.

FINANCIAL DATA:
Amount of support per award: Varies.
Total amount of support: $669,568 for the year 2017.

NO. MOST RECENT APPLICANTS: 60.

NO. AWARDS: 60.

APPLICATION INFO:
The online grant process consists of two phases:
(1) invited applicants must submit a Letter of Inquiry by the deadline;
(2) Cooper Foundation staff will review the Letter of Inquiry and determine to advance it to the application state. Applicants will be notified to submit a full application.

To be invited to submit a Letter of Inquiry, submit information about your organization, project and budget to the e-mail address listed above.
Duration: One year. Must reapply annually.
Deadline: January 15, April 1, July 1 and October 1.

ADDRESS INQUIRIES TO:
Victoria Grasso, President
(See address above.)

THE MARY S. AND DAVID C. CORBIN FOUNDATION   [79]
Akron Centre Plaza
50 South Main Street, Suite 703
Akron, OH 44308-1830
(330) 762-6427
Fax: (330) 762-6428
E-mail: info@corbinfdn.org
Web Site: corbinfdn.org

FOUNDED: 1968

AREAS OF INTEREST:
Arts, culture, environment, health, housing, human services, education, youth and medical research.

TYPE:
Project grants.

PURPOSE:
To benefit charities in the Akron and Summit County, OH areas and national charities that have a presence in the Akron and Summit County areas of Ohio.

ELIGIBILITY:
Organizations classified as 501(c)(3) by the IRS can apply. The Foundation gives primary consideration to the City of Akron and Summit County, OH charitable organizations and/or local chapters of national charities located in the Akron, Summit County area of Ohio.

The Foundation does not fund individuals, annual fund-raising campaigns, ongoing requests for general operating support, operating deficits, or organizations which in turn make grants to others. The Foundation generally does not fund endowments, faith-based or religious organizations, nor does it support schools.

GEOG. RESTRICTIONS: City of Akron and Summit County, Ohio.

FINANCIAL DATA:
Amount of support per award: $500 to $50,000.
Total amount of support: $599,000 for the year 2019.

NO. AWARDS: 68 for the year 2019.

APPLICATION INFO:
Guidelines are available on the Foundation web site. Applications must be submitted through the online application portal system.
Duration: One year.
Deadline: March 1 and September 1, for consideration in May and November respectively.

ADDRESS INQUIRIES TO:
Erika J. May, Grants Administrator
(See address above.)

MARION STEDMAN COVINGTON FOUNDATION   [80]
P.O. Box 29304
Greensboro, NC 27429-9304
(336) 282-0480
E-mail: info@mscovingtonfoundation.org
Web Site: www.mscovingtonfoundation.org

AREAS OF INTEREST:
Historic preservation.

TYPE:
Capital grants; Challenge/matching grants; Conferences/seminars; General operating grants; Project/program grants; Research grants; Seed money grants.

YEAR PROGRAM STARTED: 1986

PURPOSE:
To provide grants to nonprofit organizations operating in the area of historic preservation.

ELIGIBILITY:
Grants are made to federally tax-exempt, nonprofit organizations.

GEOG. RESTRICTIONS: Primarily North Carolina.

FINANCIAL DATA:
Amount of support per award: $10,000 average.
Total amount of support: Approximately $350,000.

NO. AWARDS: Varies.

APPLICATION INFO:
Application procedures are available on the web site.
Duration: Varies.
Deadline: August 1 and March 1. Announcements in mid-October and mid-May.

PUBLICATIONS:
Annual report; guidelines.

IRS I.D.: 56-6286555

ADDRESS INQUIRIES TO:
Alexa S. Aycock, Executive Director
(See address above.)

*PLEASE NOTE:
Challenge grants may be requested or the Foundation may designate a grant as such. In either event, there will be a specified time period in which the matching funds are to be raised.

S.H. COWELL FOUNDATION [81]
595 Market Street, Suite 950
San Francisco, CA 94105
(415) 397-0285
Fax: (415) 986-6786
E-mail: farley@shcowell.org
Web Site: shcowell.org

FOUNDED: 1955

AREAS OF INTEREST:
Family resource centers, public education, youth development, and improving the quality of life of low-income children and families in neighborhoods that meet the Foundation's place-based criteria.

TYPE:
Capital grants; Challenge/matching grants; Project/program grants; Technical assistance; Training grants. Community building. Operating support.

YEAR PROGRAM STARTED: 1955

PURPOSE:
To improve the quality of life of children living in poverty in northern California by making grants that support and strengthen their families and the neighborhoods where they live.

LEGAL BASIS:
Independent nonprofit foundation.

ELIGIBILITY:
Organization must be tax-exempt and must submit evidence that a grant would qualify under the Tax Reform Act of 1969. Grants are restricted to organizations, projects and programs in northern California, except by invitation of the Foundation.

As a matter of policy, the Foundation typically does not make grants to hospitals for construction or research, sectarian religious groups, individuals for scholarships or financial aid.

GEOG. RESTRICTIONS: Northern and central California.

FINANCIAL DATA:
Amount of support per award: $1,000 to over $500,000.

APPLICATION INFO:
The application process is rigorous, and prospective grantees should expect to work with Cowell staff before, during, and after a formal proposal is submitted. There are five steps to the process:
(1) make sure that your project meets Foundation funding criteria;
(2) call the Foundation;
(3) if asked to do so, submit a letter of inquiry;
(4) if asked to do so, submit a full proposal. Please do not send a formal proposal unless a program officer requests one. If you are asked to submit a proposal, staff will give you a list of required information and;
(5) plan on at least one site visit.
Duration: Varies.
Deadline: The Directors meet regularly and review only those proposals recommended by staff.

STAFF:
Anu Cairo, Program Director

OFFICERS AND BOARD OF DIRECTORS:
Ann Alpers, President
Ken Doane, Executive Vice President and Chief Program Officer
Nina Washburne, Vice President, Administration
Dr. Lisa Backus
Charles E. Ellwein
Charles A. Higueras
Dr. Mikiko Huang
Scott Mosher
Lydia Tan
Kim Thompson

ADDRESS INQUIRIES TO:
Cynthia Farley, Administrative Assistant
(See e-mail address above.)

*SPECIAL STIPULATIONS:
No grants to individuals, for media projects, conferences, seminars, to sectarian organizations, hospitals or public/governmental agencies.

HENRY P. AND SUSAN C. CROWELL TRUST [82]
102 North Cascade Avenue
Suite 300
Colorado Springs, CO 80903
(719) 645-8119
Fax: (719) 418-2695
E-mail: info@crowelltrust.org
Web Site: www.crowelltrust.org

FOUNDED: 1927

AREAS OF INTEREST:
Evangelical foreign missions.

TYPE:
General operating grants; Project/program grants.

YEAR PROGRAM STARTED: 1927

PURPOSE:
To aid evangelical Christianity by support to organizations having for their purposes its teaching, advancement and active extension at home and abroad.

LEGAL BASIS:
Private foundation.

ELIGIBILITY:
No grants to churches, individuals or for endowment funds or research. No loans.

GEOG. RESTRICTIONS: United States.

FINANCIAL DATA:
Amount of support per award: Average $35,000.
Total amount of support: $3,500,000.

NO. MOST RECENT APPLICANTS: 375.

NO. AWARDS: 100.

APPLICATION INFO:
Applicants must ensure the project fits the guidelines of the Trust by completing the online Self-Screening Aid to determine eligibility and begin the application process. If the organization and project fit the minimum requirements, applicants should proceed to the online grant management system. No proposals will be accepted in hard copy or through e-mail.
Duration: One year. May resubmit annually.
Deadline: Proposals should be submitted by February 28 for spring and July 31 for fall consideration.

PUBLICATIONS:
Application guidelines.

IRS I.D.: 36-6038028

STAFF:
Candace Sparks, Chief Executive Officer

ADDRESS INQUIRIES TO:
Angela Hunter
Assistant to the Executive Director
(See address above.)

THE CULLEN FOUNDATION [83]
2727 Allen Parkway
Suite 1050
Houston, TX 77019
(713) 651-8837
E-mail: gina@cullenfdn.org
Web Site: www.cullenfdn.org

FOUNDED: 1947

AREAS OF INTEREST:
Cultural, education, health care and public service.

TYPE:
Capital grants; Challenge/matching grants; Development grants; Endowments; Fellowships; Professorships; Project/program grants.

PURPOSE:
To provide charitable grants to cultural, educational, health care and public service organizations.

LEGAL BASIS:
Tax-exempt, private foundation.

ELIGIBILITY:
Grants are limited to the state of Texas by indenture. No grants are made to individuals or businesses.

GEOG. RESTRICTIONS: Texas, primarily Houston.

FINANCIAL DATA:
Amount of support per award: Minimum $10,000.

NO. MOST RECENT APPLICANTS: 117.

NO. AWARDS: 31 new grants.

APPLICATION INFO:
Applications are accepted online only through the link on the Foundation web site.
Duration: No grants are awarded on a continuing basis.

IRS I.D.: 76-0647361

OFFICERS:
Isaac Arnold, Jr., Chairman
Wilhemina E. Robertson, Vice Chairman, Assistant Treasurer and Secretary
Scott W. Wise, President and Treasurer
Meredith T. Cullen, Assistant Secretary

DIRECTORS:
Isaac Arnold, Jr.
Bert L. Campbell
Meredith T. Cullen
Carla Knobloch
Wilhemina E. Robertson

ADDRESS INQUIRIES TO:
Gina McEvily, Grant Administrator
(See address above.)

*SPECIAL STIPULATIONS:
Grants are made to qualified charities in the state of Texas, primarily in the Houston area. No grants to individuals or businesses.

THE NATHAN CUMMINGS FOUNDATION, INC. [84]
475 10th Avenue, 14th Floor
New York, NY 10018
(212) 787-7300
Fax: (212) 787-7377
E-mail: contact@nathancummings.org
Web Site: nathancummings.org

FOUNDED: 1949

AREAS OF INTEREST:
Inequality and climate change.

NAME(S) OF PROGRAMS:
- **Corporate and Political Accountability**
- **Inclusive Clean Economy**
- **Racial and Economic Justice**
- **Voice, Creativity and Culture**

TYPE:
General operating grants; Project/program grants.

YEAR PROGRAM STARTED: 1989

PURPOSE:
To promote democratic values and social justice, including fairness, diversity and community; to build a socially and economically just society that values and protects the ecological balance for future generations; to promote humane health care; to foster arts and culture that enrich communities.

LEGAL BASIS:
Private foundation.

ELIGIBILITY:
Applying organizations must be recognized as 501(c)(3) tax-exempt public charities, as defined by the IRS. Projects that are not recognized as tax-exempt public charities must have a fiscal sponsor.

GEOG. RESTRICTIONS: United States.

FINANCIAL DATA:
Amount of support per award: Varies.

APPLICATION INFO:
To apply for a grant, applicant must take the eligibility quiz. Those projects which align with the Foundation goals will be prompted to complete the registration process.
Duration: Varies.
Deadline: Letters of Inquiry are accepted on a rolling basis.

IRS I.D.: 23-7093201

STAFF:
Nealon DeVore, Chief of Staff
Leticia Peguero, Vice President of Programs
Laura Campos, Director, Corporate and Political Accountability
Danielle Deane-Ryan, Director, Inclusive Clean Economy
Lavastian Glenn, Director, Racial and Economic Justice
Isaac Luria, Director, Voice, Creativity and Culture
Janet Disla, Senior Grants Manager

ADDRESS INQUIRIES TO:
Program Associate
E-mail: gadmin@nathancummings.org

THE CUMMINS FOUNDATION, INC.   [85]
500 Jackson Street, MC 60633
Columbus, IN 47201
Fax: (812) 377-7897
E-mail: cummins.foundation@cummins.com
Web Site: www.cummins.com

FOUNDED: 1954

AREAS OF INTEREST:
Focus on environment, education and equality of opportunity.

TYPE:
Development grants. Incubator grants. Matching grants.

YEAR PROGRAM STARTED: 1954

PURPOSE:
To improve the quality of life in communities where Cummins has manufacturing operations and subsidiaries; to promote the Foundation's philanthropic objectives through grants in priority areas as well as projects of special interest in Columbus and subsidiary communities.

LEGAL BASIS:
Corporate foundation.

ELIGIBILITY:
Grantees must be tax-exempt organizations or institutions located in areas where Cummins has a presence. Organizations must have proof of past Cummins employee engagement.

No grants are made to individuals or for denominational religious organizations. No scholarships are granted.

FINANCIAL DATA:
Amount of support per award: Varies.
Total amount of support: Varies.

APPLICATION INFO:
The Foundation requires initial contact via e-mail.

PUBLICATIONS:
Sustainability report.

IRS I.D.: 35-6042373

ADDRESS INQUIRIES TO:
See e-mail address above.

DANIELS FUND   [86]
101 Monroe Street
Denver, CO 80206-4467
(303) 393-7220
E-mail: info@danielsfund.org
grantsinfo@danielsfund.org
Web Site: www.danielsfund.org

FOUNDED: 2000

AREAS OF INTEREST:
Daniels Fund Grants Program: Aging, amateur sports, disabilities, drug and alcohol addiction, early childhood education, K-12 education reform, ethics and integrity in education, homeless and disadvantaged, youth development.

NAME(S) OF PROGRAMS:
- **Daniels Fund Ethics Initiative**
- **Daniels Fund Grants Program**
- **Daniels Fund Scholarship Program**

TYPE:
Capital grants; General operating grants; Project/program grants; Scholarships. Daniels Fund Ethics Initiative delivers principle-based ethics education and reinforces the value of ethical business and personal conduct. The Ethics Initiative consists of a Collegiate Program, High School Program, Middle School Program, Community College Program, Elementary School Program, Law Enforcement Program, Business Program, and an online Case Bank. Each of the Ethics Initiative's components utilizes a specific approach to reach its target audience. Funding is provided through the Daniels Fund Grants Program.

Daniels Fund Grants Program supports highly effective nonprofit organizations in Colorado, New Mexico, Utah and Wyoming.

Daniels Fund Scholarship Program consists of the Daniels Scholarship Program and the Boundless Opportunity Scholarship Program. The Daniels Scholarship Program provides a comprehensive, four-year annually-renewable college scholarship for highly motivated students to earn a Bachelor's degree that helps them build a successful career and rewarding life. Daniels Scholars are honest, respectful, self-reliant, and compassionate. They are proud Americans who value our free enterprise system and are prepared to give the world their very best shot. The scholarship applies toward the expense of attaining a Bachelor's degree at any

nonprofit, accredited college or university in the U.S. The Boundless Opportunity Scholarship Program provides college scholarships for non-traditional students of all ages, awarded by select colleges and universities using funds provided by the Daniels Fund.

YEAR PROGRAM STARTED: 2000

PURPOSE:
To help excellent nonprofits achieve a high level of effectiveness and impact; to help Daniels Scholars succeed in college and ultimately become independent, successful in a rewarding career, and actively engaged in their community.

ELIGIBILITY:
Daniels Grants Program: Applying organizations must have 501(c)(3) not-for-profit status or government equivalent.

Daniels Scholarship Program: High school seniors seeking to obtain a Bachelor's degree. Applicants must meet the core values of character, leadership and service, and demonstrate financial need.

Boundless Opportunity Scholarship: Applicants must demonstrate financial need and be:
(1) an adult entering or returning to college;
(2) a GED recipient;
(3) a former foster care youth;
(4) a former juvenile justice youth or;
(5) a veteran entering or returning to college.

GEOG. RESTRICTIONS: Colorado, New Mexico, Utah and Wyoming.

FINANCIAL DATA:
Total assets of $1,594,000,000 for the year ended December 31, 2019.
Amount of support per award: Varies.
Total amount of support: $58,800,000 in grants, scholarships and ethics funding for the year ended December 31, 2019.

NO. AWARDS: Daniels Fund Grants Program and Boundless Opportunity Scholarship: Varies. Daniels Scholarship Program: Approximately 200.

APPLICATION INFO:
Online application process. Daniels Scholarship Program application process opens in September.
Duration: Grants: Typically one year. Must reapply. Daniels Scholarship Program: Four years. Boundless Opportunity Scholarship: Varies.
Deadline: Daniels Scholarship Program: November 15.

IRS I.D.: 84-1393308

ADDRESS INQUIRIES TO:
E-mail: grantsinfo@danielsfund.org

MARGARET A. DARRIN CHARITABLE TRUST   [87]
120 Columbia Turnpike
Florham Park, NJ 07932
(973) 822-2905

FOUNDED: 2015

AREAS OF INTEREST:
Arts, humanities, civic affairs, education, health, social services and women's issues.

TYPE:
General operating grants.

ELIGIBILITY:
No restrictions or limitations on funding. Grants made to nonprofit 501(c)(3) organizations only.

GEOG. RESTRICTIONS: Northeastern United States.

FINANCIAL DATA:
Amount of support per award: Varies.
Total amount of support: $1,661,000 for the year 2018.

APPLICATION INFO:
Applications should take the form of a brief letter describing the charity, its background and the purpose of the contribution. Applicant must include a copy of their 501(c)(3) status.

Applicant will be notified only if approved.
Duration: One year. Must reapply for additional funding.

IRS I.D.: 47-6723443

STAFF:
Michael Hanifin, Trustee
Kevin J. O'Donnell, Trustee

ADDRESS INQUIRIES TO:
Charitable Contributions
(See address above.)

THE ARTHUR VINING DAVIS FOUNDATIONS [88]
814 North Highway A1A
Suite 300
Ponte Vedra Beach, FL 32082
(904) 359-0670
E-mail: office@avdf.org
Web Site: www.avdf.org

FOUNDED: 1952

AREAS OF INTEREST:
Private higher education, public educational media, interfaith leadership and religious literacy, environmental engagement, and palliative care.

TYPE:
Project/program grants.

LEGAL BASIS:
Privately endowed foundation established by the will of Arthur Vining Davis.

ELIGIBILITY:
Grants are limited to institutions in the U.S. and its territories. Activities and functions not supported include assistance to individuals, capital projects, scholarships, endowments, indirect costs associated with projects, voter registration drives and voter education, efforts to influence elections or legislation, and expenditures for noncharitable purposes.

GEOG. RESTRICTIONS: United States.

FINANCIAL DATA:
Amount of support per award: Varies by grant award type.
Total amount of support: Approximately $9,706,532 approved for the year 2019.

CO-OP FUNDING PROGRAMS: As a policy, the Foundations' support increased cooperation among foundations and expanded communication with the public. The staff has taken an active part in national and regional efforts in this direction.

NO. MOST RECENT APPLICANTS: 226 for the year 2019.

NO. AWARDS: 42 program grants for the year 2019.

APPLICATION INFO:
Application information is available online.
Duration: Two to three years.

Deadline: November 1.

PUBLICATIONS:
65th Anniversary brochure.

OFFICERS:
Michael J. Murray, Ph.D., President
Timothy Michel, Chief Financial Officer
Doreen A. Gross, Chief Operating Officer

TRUSTEES:
Serena Davis Hall, Chairperson
James Cote
Christopher Davis
Jonathan P. Davis
Sarah Davis
Tamara Davis
Dorothy Davis Kee
John L. Kee, III
Haley Davis Madole

ADDRESS INQUIRIES TO:
See e-mail address above.

DELAWARE COUNTY FOUNDATION
737 Enterprise Drive
Suite A
Lewis Center, OH 43035
(614) 764-2332
Fax: (614) 764-2333
E-mail: foundation@delawarecf.org
Web Site: www.delawarecf.org

TYPE:
Scholarships.

See entry 1147 for full listing.

DELUXE CORPORATION FOUNDATION [89]
3680 Victoria Street North
Shoreview, MN 55126-2966
(651) 787-5124
(651) 483-7842
E-mail: pam.bridger@deluxe.com
Web Site: community.deluxe.com

FOUNDED: 1952

AREAS OF INTEREST:
K-12 economic education programs, employment programs, small business coaching and arts.

TYPE:
Capital grants; General operating grants; Project/program grants. Volunteer match on behalf of employee volunteerism at 501(c)(3) nonprofits.

LEGAL BASIS:
Corporate foundation.

ELIGIBILITY:
Nonprofit organizations that meet the grant focus areas are encouraged to apply. The Foundation accepts grant proposals from qualifying nonprofit organizations that serve the general communities in which Deluxe facilities are located. In addition, nonprofits must:
(1) have obtained tax-exempt status under section 501(c)(3) or 509(a)(1), (2), or (3);
(2) have operated as a nonprofit for at least two years;
(3) have secured support from other corporate funders and;
(4) be located in the general community of a Deluxe facility.

GEOG. RESTRICTIONS: United States.

FINANCIAL DATA:
Amount of support per award: $5,000 to $10,000 average.

Total amount of support: Varies.
Matching fund requirements: Qualifying organizations for matching funds: Accredited educational institutions; public television and radio; professional arts; historical societies; museums.

CO-OP FUNDING PROGRAMS: United Way.

NO. MOST RECENT APPLICANTS: 367 for the year 2018.

NO. AWARDS: 129 for the year 2018.

APPLICATION INFO:
Applications are submitted online.
Duration: One year.
Deadline: Varies according to geographic area.

BOARD OF DIRECTORS:
Barry McCarthy, President
Jennifer A. Anderson, Director of Foundations and Community Affairs
Amanda K. Brinkman
Keith Bush
Jeffrey Cotter
Edward A. Merritt

ADDRESS INQUIRIES TO:
Pamela G. Bridger, Grants Administrator
(See address above.)

GERALDINE R. DODGE FOUNDATION [90]
14 Maple Avenue, Suite 400
Morristown, NJ 07960
(973) 540-8442
Fax: (973) 540-1211
E-mail: info@grdodge.org
Web Site: www.grdodge.org

FOUNDED: 1974

AREAS OF INTEREST:
The arts, environment, education, Morris County projects, informed communities, and poetry.

TYPE:
General operating grants; Project/program grants. Grants in four key areas:
(1) Art grants enhance the cultural richness of the community in which citizens reside and contribute to New Jersey's creative economy;
(2) Educational grants provide transformational experiential educational opportunities both inside and outside of the classroom for young people who have limited access to educational excellence;
(3) Environmental grants help to achieve ecosystem resilience and sustainable community solutions and;
(4) Media grants support traditional and innovative uses of media to educate and engage the public around issues of importance to New Jersey and its citizens, as well as efforts to uncover the abuses of power by the institutions in which citizens have placed their trust.

PURPOSE:
To support and encourage those educational, cultural, social and environmental values that contribute to making our society more humane and our world more livable.

LEGAL BASIS:
Private foundation.

ELIGIBILITY:
Applicants must be nonprofit, 501(c)(3) tax-exempt organizations located in or providing benefits to the residents of the state of New Jersey. No grants in areas of higher

education, health and religion. No support for capital programs, endowments, equipment purchases, scholarships, indirect costs or deficit reduction. No direct awards to individuals nor grants to conduit organizations, nor is funding made for lobbying efforts.

GEOG. RESTRICTIONS: New Jersey.

FINANCIAL DATA:
Total amount of support: Approximately $8,000,000 annually.

APPLICATION INFO:
Unsolicited requests for scholarships and grants are not accepted. New applicants should submit a one-page letter of inquiry to determine if a project falls within the Foundation's guidelines. Letters of inquiry may be submitted throughout the year, but must be received at least two weeks prior to the corresponding submission deadline. Letters of inquiry must be submitted online or e-mailed, without attachments. Following staff review of initial inquiries, applicants will be notified whether or not to submit a full proposal.

Applicants invited to apply are then required to submit an electronic copy of their proposal.
Duration: Typically 12 months.
Deadline: Arts: December 3 and March 4. Notification April and July, respectively. Education: March 4 and September 3. Notification July and December, respectively. Environment: December 3 and September 4. Notification April and December, respectively. Informed Communities: March 4. Notification in July.

PUBLICATIONS:
Application guidelines; biannual report.

IRS I.D.: 23-7406010

STAFF:
Cynthia Evans, Interim President and Chief Executive Officer

ADDRESS INQUIRIES TO:
Marisa Benson, Grants Manager
Tel: (973) 695-1187
E-mail: mbenson@grdodge.org

*SPECIAL STIPULATIONS:
The Foundation does not accept fax proposals or proposals sent via express mail carriers.

DOMINION ENERGY CHARITABLE FOUNDATION [91]
120 Tredegar Street
Richmond, VA 23219
E-mail: dominionfoundation@dominionenergy. com
Web Site: www.dominionenergy.com/foundation

FOUNDED: 1985

AREAS OF INTEREST:
Human needs, environmental stewardship, education and community vitality.

NAME(S) OF PROGRAMS:
● **ArtStars Awards**
● **Community Impact Awards**
● **Critical Community Needs Grants**
● **Dollars for Doers Grants**
● **Environmental Education and Stewardship Grants**
● **Solar for Students Program**

TYPE:
Matching gifts; Project/program grants.

PURPOSE:
To improve the physical, social and economic well-being of the communities served by Dominion companies.

ELIGIBILITY:
Applicants must be 501(c)(3) organizations. No grants to individuals, sectarian purposes, fraternal, political, advocacy or labor organizations, religious programs of churches, or operating funds of individual United Way agencies.

GEOG. RESTRICTIONS: ArtStars Awards and Solar for Students Program: Virginia; Community Impact Awards: Ohio.

FINANCIAL DATA:
Amount of support per award: Generally $1,000 to $15,000.
Total amount of support: Approximately $21,000,000 annually.
Matching fund requirements: Must be employee or retiree of Dominion Energy.

NO. MOST RECENT APPLICANTS: 2,490.

NO. AWARDS: 1,433.

APPLICATION INFO:
Grant applications are accepted online. Before applying for a grant, it is recommended to review the Grant Guidelines and Restrictions, as well as the Frequently Asked Questions. Those organizations meeting the eligibility requirements can begin the application process by completing the eligibility quiz.
Deadline: Year-round on a calendar year, except competitive programs.

PUBLICATIONS:
Grant guidelines.

IRS I.D.: 47-2746460

OFFICER:
Hunter A. Applewhite, President

GAYLORD AND DOROTHY DONNELLEY FOUNDATION [92]
35 East Wacker Drive, Suite 2600
Chicago, IL 60601
(312) 977-2700
Fax: (312) 977-1686
E-mail: info@gddf.org
Web Site: gddf.org

FOUNDED: 1952

AREAS OF INTEREST:
Artistic vitality, land conservation and collections in Chicago or the Lowcountry of South Carolina.

TYPE:
Challenge/matching grants; Development grants; General operating grants; Matching gifts; Project/program grants; Technical assistance.

YEAR PROGRAM STARTED: 1952

PURPOSE:
To promote artistic vitality and land conservation.

LEGAL BASIS:
Tax-exempt, private foundation.

ELIGIBILITY:
Grants are made to tax-exempt, nonprofit 501(c)(3) organizations. Grants are not made to individuals, for community welfare, education, benefits, conferences, loans or pledges.

GEOG. RESTRICTIONS: Chicago region and South Carolina's Lowcountry.

FINANCIAL DATA:
Amount of support per award: Varies.
Total amount of support: Varies.

NO. AWARDS: 178 for the year 2018.

APPLICATION INFO:
Proposals should be submitted in response to guidelines, if projects are applicable.
Duration: Typically two years.
Deadline: Varies.

OFFICERS AND DIRECTORS:
David Farren, Executive Director
Brian Bannon, Director
Betsy Chaffin, Director
Inanna Donnelly, Director
Laura Donnelley, Director
Shawn M. Donnelley, Director
Rick Lowe, Director
Alex Shuford, Director
Alaka Wali, Director
Trenyholm Walker, Director
Mimi Wheeler, Director
Tom Trinley, Director of Finance and Administration

ADDRESS INQUIRIES TO:
Program Director
(See address above.)

THE DOUTY FOUNDATION [93]
P.O. Box 1437
Philadelphia, PA 19105
(215) 620-1869
E-mail: jennifer@doutyfoundation.org
Web Site: www.doutyfoundation.org

FOUNDED: 1968

AREAS OF INTEREST:
Economic and educational opportunities to disadvantaged people, especially children.

TYPE:
General operating grants; Project/program grants. Projects with social impact, innovative projects and general operations.

YEAR PROGRAM STARTED: 1969

PURPOSE:
To support programs that provide either educational opportunities for the disadvantaged or local innovative social services.

LEGAL BASIS:
Tax-exempt private foundation.

ELIGIBILITY:
Qualifying tax-exempt organizations are eligible. Grants are not made for capital expenditures, agency promotions, annual reports, renovations or to organizations with annual budgets of more than $1,000,000. Grants are not made to individuals or for religious or political purposes.

GEOG. RESTRICTIONS: Greater Philadelphia, Pennsylvania area with preference to Montgomery and Philadelphia counties.

FINANCIAL DATA:
Amount of support per award: First-time applicants: Up to $5,000; Previously funded applicants: Up to $7,500.
Total amount of support: $240,600 for the year 2017.

NO. AWARDS: 48 for the year 2017.

APPLICATION INFO:
Applications may be submitted online via the Foundation web site.
Duration: One year. Renewals are usually limited to six years.

Deadline: March 15 and September 15.

IRS I.D.: 46-3309525

TRUSTEES:
Judith L. Bardes
Carrolle Perry Devonish
Peter Gonzales, Esq.
Thomas B. Harvey, Esq.
Nancy J. Kirby
Elbert Sampson
Ludy Soderman

STAFF:
Jennifer Leith, Executive Director

ADDRESS INQUIRIES TO:
Jennifer Leith, Executive Director
(See address above.)

*SPECIAL STIPULATIONS:
Organizations that have been funded for a six-year period may not reapply until at least two years have passed.

DOW JONES FOUNDATION [94]
1211 Avenue of the Americas, 7th Floor
New York, NY 10036
(212) 416-3202
E-mail: brad.rolston@dowjones.com

FOUNDED: 1954

AREAS OF INTEREST:
Journalism, free press, literacy and education, and diversity and inclusion.

TYPE:
General operating grants. Program support.

PURPOSE:
To support causes engaged in the promotion and protection of journalism and free press, as well as causes devoted specifically to literacy and education or diversity and inclusion.

LEGAL BASIS:
Corporate foundation.

ELIGIBILITY:
Applicant must be a U.S. 501(c)(3) organization.

FINANCIAL DATA:
Amount of support per award: Varies.

APPLICATION INFO:
All requests for Foundation support must be submitted in writing. Each request must indicate IRS tax-exemption certificate number.
Deadline: Normally, requests received will be considered by the board of directors only at their annual meeting in June for distribution in the next fiscal year.

PUBLICATIONS:
Application guidelines.

IRS I.D.: 13-6070158

STAFF:
Bradley P. Rolston, Esq., President and Director

ADDRESS INQUIRIES TO:
Bradley P. Rolston, Esq.
President and Director
(See address above.)

JOSEPH DROWN FOUNDATION [95]
1999 Avenue of the Stars, Suite 2330
Los Angeles, CA 90067
(310) 277-4488
Fax: (310) 277-4573
E-mail: alyssa@jdrown.org
Web Site: www.jdrown.org

FOUNDED: 1953

AREAS OF INTEREST:
Education.

TYPE:
General operating grants; Project/program grants.

YEAR PROGRAM STARTED: 1953

PURPOSE:
To assist individuals in becoming successful, self-sustaining and contributing members of society.

ELIGIBILITY:
No funds to individuals, endowments, capital campaigns or building funds. The Foundation will not underwrite annual meeting or conferences. No funding for religious programs and special events.

In the area of medical research, the Foundation does not accept unsolicited requests.

GEOG. RESTRICTIONS: Los Angeles, California.

FINANCIAL DATA:
Amount of support per award: $5,000 to $50,000.

Total amount of support: Approximately $4,000,000 for the fiscal year ended March 31, 2018.

NO. MOST RECENT APPLICANTS: 1,200.

NO. AWARDS: 150.

APPLICATION INFO:
Applications are accepted online only.
Duration: One year.
Deadline: January 15, April 15, July 15 and October 15.

PUBLICATIONS:
Application guidelines.

OFFICERS AND STAFF:
Wendy Wachtell, President
Ann T. Miller, Chief Financial Officer
Alyssa Santino, Program Officer

ADDRESS INQUIRIES TO:
Alyssa Santino, Program Officer
(See address above.)

*SPECIAL STIPULATIONS:
In the area of medical research, the Foundation does not accept unsolicited requests.

DORIS DUKE CHARITABLE FOUNDATION [96]
650 Fifth Avenue, 19th Floor
New York, NY 10019
(212) 974-7000
Fax: (212) 974-7590
Web Site: www.ddcf.org

FOUNDED: 1996

AREAS OF INTEREST:
Environment, performing arts, child abuse prevention and clinical research.

NAME(S) OF PROGRAMS:
- **Arts Program**
- **Child Well-being Program**
- **Environment Program**
- **Medical Research Program**

TYPE:
Grants-in-aid. The Arts Program supports performing artists with the creation and public performance of their work. The Program focuses its support on contemporary dance, jazz and theatre, and the organizations that nurture, present and produce them.

The Child Well-being Program promotes children's healthy development and protects them from abuse and neglect. The Program favors a public health approach and is especially interested in place-based, whole-community approaches that seek to engage a range of participants from various disciplines to ensure that family well-being is supported by strong communities.

The Environment Program enables communities to protect and manage wildlife habitat and create efficient built environments. The Program's awareness of climate change as the greatest emerging threat to biodiversity - and the need to aggressively mitigate it without unnecessarily sacrificing wildlife habitat - shapes the Program's grantmaking priorities.

The Medical Research Program supports the prevention, treatment and cure of human disease. The goal of the Program is to strengthen and support clinical research to help advance the translation of basic biomedical discoveries into new treatments, preventions and cures for human diseases.

YEAR PROGRAM STARTED: 1997

PURPOSE:
To improve the quality of people's lives through grants supporting the performing arts, environmental conservation, medical research and the prevention of child abuse, and through the preservation of the cultural and environmental legacy of Doris Duke's properties.

LEGAL BASIS:
Nonprofit foundation.

ELIGIBILITY:
While all Foundation programs require that grantee organizations be publicly supported 501(c)(3) tax-exempt organizations based in the U.S., each program has a customized approach to its grantmaking strategy.

FINANCIAL DATA:
Amount of support per award: $315,000 average.

Total amount of support: Approximately $76,000,000.

APPLICATION INFO:
The majority of the Foundation's grants are awarded through competitive (request-for-proposal) processes or by invitation. Open competitions and funding opportunities for grants are listed on the Foundation's web site. Foundation staff also welcome letters of inquiry from qualifying organizations.

To submit a letter of inquiry, the Foundation requests that organizations visit its web site and submit letters of inquiry through the online form. To do so, applicant will need a nonprofit tax ID as well as the title of the proposed project, a brief description of the specific project for which funding is sought, the requested funding amount, a description of how the objectives of the proposed project relate to those of the Foundation, the organization's mission and strategies, and a primary contact for the organization. Staff will respond to the letters of inquiry within two months and will notify the writer if additional information is desired.

Duration: Short-term or multiyear grants are awarded.

THE DUKE ENDOWMENT   [97]
800 East Morehead Street
Charlotte, NC 28202
(704) 376-0291
Fax: (704) 376-9336
E-mail: cperkins@tde.org
Web Site: www.dukeendowment.org

FOUNDED: 1924

AREAS OF INTEREST:
Not-for-profit hospitals in North Carolina and
South Carolina; children's welfare and
adoption assistance institutions in North
Carolina and South Carolina; rural United
Methodist churches and retired ministers in
North Carolina and four colleges: Duke,
Furman and Johnson C. Smith universities
and Davidson College.

TYPE:
Capital grants; General operating grants;
Project/program grants.

YEAR PROGRAM STARTED: 1924

PURPOSE:
To carry out the terms of the Trust Indenture,
as written by James B. Duke, by supporting
four institutions in higher education,
not-for-profit hospitals and children's homes
in North Carolina and South Carolina, retired
pastors of the United Methodist Church and
programs and projects of rural United
Methodist Churches in North Carolina.

LEGAL BASIS:
Charitable trust.

ELIGIBILITY:
North and South Carolina organizations and
institutions with appropriate interests and
activities are eligible.

GEOG. RESTRICTIONS: North Carolina and South
Carolina.

FINANCIAL DATA:
Amount of support per award: Varies.
Total amount of support: $221,314,460 in
new grants for the year 2018.
Matching fund requirements: Varies with
grant.

NO. MOST RECENT APPLICANTS: Varies.

NO. AWARDS: Varies.

REPRESENTATIVE AWARDS:
$750,000 to support the integration of
behavioral health treatment and therapeutic
child care services; $5,700,000 to use data to
reduce opioid prescriptions and increase
alternative treatments for pain management;
$25,000,000 to increase capacity in the
sciences by recruiting outstanding faculty for
Duke University's Health System; $2,793,000
to pilot stress interventions for clergy.

APPLICATION INFO:
Applicants must check the eligibility criteria
before applying. Complete guidelines and
application form are available on the web
site.
Duration: Varies. All eligible beneficiaries
may request continued and renewed support.
Deadline: Varies.

PUBLICATIONS:
Annual report; e-newsletter, occasional
papers and reports on projects and programs.

IRS I.D.: 56-0529965

OFFICERS:
Rhett N. Mabry, President
Karen H. Rogers, Chief Financial
Officer/Treasurer
K. Todd Walker, Managing Director,
Investments

TRUSTEES:
Minor M. Shaw, Chairperson
Dennis M. Campbell, Ph.D., Vice
Chairperson
Jean G. Spaulding, M.D., Vice Chairperson
William Barnet, III
John F.A.V. Cecil
Ravenel B. Curry, III
Harris E, DeLoach, Jr.
Constance F. Gray
J. Trent Jones
Thomas S. Kenan, III
Charles C. Lucas, III
Clarence G. Newsome
Wilhelmina M. Reuben-Cooke, J.D.
Kenneth D. Weeks, Jr., M.D.
Judy Woodruff

ADDRESS INQUIRIES TO:
Charity L. Perkins
Director of Communications
(See address above.)

DUNSPAUGH DALTON
FOUNDATION   [98]
1501 Venera Avenue, Suite 312
Coral Gables, FL 33146
(305) 668-4192
Fax: (305) 668-4247
E-mail: ddf@dunspaughdalton.org
Web Site: dunspaughdalton.org

AREAS OF INTEREST:
Higher, secondary, and elementary education;
social services; youth; health associations and
hospitals; cultural programs; and civic affairs.

TYPE:
Capital grants; General operating grants;
Project/program grants.

ELIGIBILITY:
Grants are made to organizations that have
tax-exempt status under Section 501(c)(3) of
the Internal Revenue Code. No grants are
made to individuals.

GEOG. RESTRICTIONS: Monterey County,
California; Miami-Dade County, Florida;
Charlotte and Mecklenburg County, North
Carolina.

FINANCIAL DATA:
Amount of support per award: $5,000
average.

APPLICATION INFO:
Applicant must submit:
(1) proposal summary (not to exceed one-half
page) explaining why the grant is requested,
what outcomes are hoped to be achieved and
how funds will be spent;
(2) narrative including background, funding

requirements and evaluation (not to exceed
five pages);
(3) completed Grant Application Form and;
(4) the most recent financial statements used
as the basis for filing IRS Form 990.

Submit all application documents to the
office listed on the Grant Application Form.
Duration: One year. Can reapply.

OFFICERS:
Alexina H. Lane, President
Robert C. Bonner, III, Vice
President/Treasurer
Leslie W. Buchanan, Vice President/Secretary

ADDRESS INQUIRIES TO:
Leslie W. Buchanan, Secretary or
Alexina Lane, President
(See address above.)

JESSIE BALL DUPONT
FUND   [99]
40 East Adams Street
Suite 300
Jacksonville, FL 32202-3302
(904) 353-0890
Web Site: www.dupontfund.org

FOUNDED: 1976

AREAS OF INTEREST:
Education, religion, health and human
services, arts and culture, juvenile justice,
environment, housing, community and
economic development, historic preservation,
nonprofit capacity building and financial asset
building.

TYPE:
Challenge/matching grants; General operating
grants; Project/program grants; Technical
assistance. Organizational capacity building.

Geared to nonprofit, religious organizations
and educational institutions.

YEAR PROGRAM STARTED: 1976

PURPOSE:
To expand access and create opportunity
through investing in people, organizations
and communities that were important to
Jessie Ball duPont.

LEGAL BASIS:
Private foundation.

ELIGIBILITY:
The Fund makes grants only to a defined
universe of organizations. An organization is
eligible if it received a contribution from
Mrs. duPont between January 1, 1960 and
December 31, 1964. Proof of eligibility is
determined by examining Mrs. duPont's
personal or tax records or by the applicant
presenting written, verifiable evidence of
having received a contribution during the
eligibility period.

GEOG. RESTRICTIONS: Primarily the South,
especially Delaware, Florida, and Virginia.

FINANCIAL DATA:
Amount of support per award: Feasibility
Grants: Up to $5,000; Technical Assistance
Grants: Up to $4,000.
Total amount of support: $10,177,544 in
grants awarded for the year 2016.

NO. MOST RECENT APPLICANTS: Varies.

NO. AWARDS: Varies.

APPLICATION INFO:
Grants are made by invitation only. The
trustees do not entertain unsolicited
proposals.
Duration: One year.

Deadline: Trustees meet at the end of January, June and November to consider grant applications. Awards are announced immediately after the meetings.

PUBLICATIONS:
Annual report; policy briefings; *Notes from the Field.*

IRS I.D.: 59-6368632

TRUSTEES:
Marty Lanahan, Chairperson
Rev. Eddie E. Jones, Jr., Vice Chairperson and Clerical Trustee
David Llewellyn, Representing Corporate Trustee, Northern Trust
Anna Cabral
Leroy Davis
Thomas H. Jeavons
Elizabeth Kiss

STAFF:
Mari Kuraishi, President
Chris Crothers, Senior Program Officer
Katie Ensign, Senior Program Officer
Barbara Roole, Senior Program Officer
Mark Walker, Knowledge Management and Technology Officer

*PLEASE NOTE:
Guidelines must be followed carefully when submitting proposal.

EASTERN BANK CHARITABLE FOUNDATION   [100]
195 Market Street
Lynn, MA 01901
(781) 598-7595
Fax: (781) 598-7640
E-mail: l.kurzrok@easternbank.com
Web Site: www.easternbank.com

FOUNDED: 1994

AREAS OF INTEREST:
Human services, family and children, affordable housing, health care, education, social justice, and workforce development.

NAME(S) OF PROGRAMS:
● **Community Grants**
● **Partnership Grants**
● **Targeted Grants**

TYPE:
Capital grants; Endowments; General operating grants; Project/program grants. Community grants; Partnership grants.

YEAR PROGRAM STARTED: 1994

PURPOSE:
To contribute, in a meaningful way, to the health and vitality of the various communities which are served by Eastern Bank, by providing financial support to selected nonprofit organizations operating within those communities; to support organizations providing services to the underserved and neediest members of our community; to ensure all our neighbors have equal access to food, shelter, education, employment, child care and other basic human needs.

LEGAL BASIS:
Corporate foundation.

ELIGIBILITY:
Applicants must be nonprofit 501(c)(3) organizations and be located in the market area served by Eastern Bank. The Foundation does not accept applications from organizations with 509(a)(3) designation or private foundations.

GEOG. RESTRICTIONS: Eastern Massachusetts and southern and coastal New Hampshire.

FINANCIAL DATA:
Amount of support per award: Community Grants: $100 to $10,000.
Total amount of support: $11,000,000 for the year 2018.
Matching fund requirements: Full-time employees, trustees and directors: Minimum $50, maximum $1,000 per year.

NO. MOST RECENT APPLICANTS: 3,000.

NO. AWARDS: 2,000.

APPLICATION INFO:
Applications are only accepted through the online application site.
Deadline: Ongoing for requests up to $10,000.

PUBLICATIONS:
Annual report, available online.

IRS I.D.: 22-3317340

ADDRESS INQUIRIES TO:
Laura Kurzrok, Executive Director
(See address above.)

EATON CHARITABLE FUND   [101]
Eaton Center
1000 Eaton Boulevard
Cleveland, OH 44122
(440) 523-4502
(440) 523-4905
Web Site: www.eaton.com

FOUNDED: 1953

AREAS OF INTEREST:
Health and human services, education, arts and culture, community improvement and neighborhood development.

TYPE:
Capital grants; Challenge/matching grants; Matching gifts; Product donations; Project/program grants. The Corporation places a priority on contributing to those organizations in which Eaton employees are personally involved and which serve their needs. Contributions are made to health, human service, civic, arts and cultural organizations and educational institutions.

Support of capital campaigns at educational institutions is generally limited to programs of direct interest to Eaton, which prefers to invest in engineering, scientific, technological and business-related projects.

YEAR PROGRAM STARTED: 1953

PURPOSE:
To contribute to the betterment of life in communities where Eaton employees live and work; to support employee involvement and investment; to promote self-sufficiency; to sustain arts and cultural institutions; to enhance education.

LEGAL BASIS:
Corporate foundation.

ELIGIBILITY:
501(c)(3) organizations within the Corporation's areas of interest are eligible for support. Grants are not made to religious, fraternal or labor organizations; to individuals or individual endeavors; debt retirement; medical research; endowment funds; fund-raising benefits, sponsorships or other events; or annual operating budgets of United Way agencies or hospitals.

Grants are only made in communities where Eaton has operations.

FINANCIAL DATA:
Cash grants are mainly from the Charitable Fund, but also from the company.
Amount of support per award: Typically, $1,000 to $100,000. Average: $5,000 to $15,000.
Total amount of support: Approximately $11,400,000 for the year 2017.
Matching fund requirements: Donations are matched fifty cents on the dollar to most 501(c)(3) nonprofits, including arts, cultural, educational, and health and human services organizations. Religious, political and fraternal organizations are ineligible. U.S. employees are eligible to participate. Match maximum per employee per year is $5,000.

APPLICATION INFO:
Contact the nearest Eaton facility for more information on charitable grants. Each facility determines the organizations and interests they wish to support and will provide the link to the online application and more information on the application and approval processes.
Duration: Grants are typically given for one year. Multiyear commitments are usually capital grants.
Deadline: Grant requests are accepted and reviewed throughout the year.

PUBLICATIONS:
Annual report; guidelines.

STAFF:
Lisa Durst, Manager, Community Affairs

CONTRIBUTIONS COMMITTEE:
Taras Szmagala, Jr., Chairman
Revathi Advaithi
Bill Blausey
Cynthia Brabander
Ken Semelsberger
Uday Yadav

ADDRESS INQUIRIES TO:
Taras Szmagala, Jr., Senior Vice President Public and Community Affairs
(See address above.)

EDISON INTERNATIONAL   [102]
2244 Walnut Grove Avenue
Rosemead, CA 91770
(626) 302-2222
Web Site: edison.com/community

FOUNDED: 1996

AREAS OF INTEREST:
Education (science, technology, engineering, arts and math), environment, public safety and emergency preparedness, and civic engagement.

CONSULTING OR VOLUNTEER SERVICES:
Volunteer Program, Energy in Action.

NAME(S) OF PROGRAMS:
● **Corporate Contributions Program**
● **Edison Scholars Program**
● **Employee Matching Gifts Program**
● **Volunteer Program**

TYPE:
Challenge/matching grants; General operating grants; Matching gifts; Project/program grants; Scholarships. Matching gifts and employees for education only: private and public schools (K-University).

YEAR PROGRAM STARTED: 1986

PURPOSE:
To promote the economic prosperity and overall quality of life in the areas where its employees live and work by supporting numerous community initiatives and historically supporting a variety of effective educational, civic and charitable activities.

ELIGIBILITY:
Organization must have 501(c)(3) status. Primary focus on Southern California and other areas where Edison International operates.

No grants to individuals, political organizations or candidates, veterans organizations, fraternal orders, labor groups, commercial profit-making enterprises, religious or sectarian organizations or any group whose activities are not in the best interests of Edison International, its employees, shareholders, customers or the communities it serves.

FINANCIAL DATA:
Amount of support per award: Edison Scholars: $40,000 over four years.
Total amount of support: Varies.
Matching fund requirements: Equal match to $2,000 for accredited public and private educational institutions; Up to $2,000 for Energy Assistance Fund.

NO. AWARDS: Edison Scholars: 30 annually; Grants: Varies.

APPLICATION INFO:
Applications for Edison grants and sponsorships must be submitted online during Edison's funding cycles. Application links are active only during funding cycles.

PUBLICATIONS:
Annual report; contributions policy; application guidelines.

ADDRESS INQUIRIES TO:
Lisa Woon, Corporate Philanthropy
(See address above.)

EL POMAR FOUNDATION   [103]
10 Lake Circle
Colorado Springs, CO 80906
(719) 633-7733
E-mail: grants@elpomar.org
Web Site: www.elpomar.org

FOUNDED: 1937

AREAS OF INTEREST:
Health, education, welfare, arts and culture, humanities, civic and community, and leadership.

NAME(S) OF PROGRAMS:
● **Grants Program**

TYPE:
Capital grants; General operating grants; Matching gifts; Project/program grants.

PURPOSE:
To support general-purpose grantmaking, civic collaboration, projects of major community importance and initiatives that provide various kinds of assistance to nonprofit organizations; to provide leadership development opportunities for a range of individuals, from those just out of college to those responsible for the state's most important nonprofits; to help those least able to help themselves.

LEGAL BASIS:
Private nonprofit charitable foundation.

ELIGIBILITY:
Priority consideration will be provided to projects and organizations that have received local community and other support. The Foundation does not accept grant applications for grant support to:
(1) other foundations or nonprofits that distribute money to recipients of its own selection;
(2) endowments;
(3) organizations that practice discrimination of any kind;
(4) organizations that do not have fiscal responsibility for the proposed project;
(5) organizations that do not have an active 501(c)(3) nonprofit IRS determination letter;
(6) camps, camp programs, or other seasonal activities;
(7) religious organizations for support of religious programs;
(8) cover deficits or debt elimination;
(9) cover travel, conferences, conventions, group meetings, or seminars;
(10) influence legislation or support candidates for political office;
(11) produce videos or other media projects;
(12) fund research projects or studies and;
(13) primary or secondary schools (K-12).
The Foundation will consider, on a limited basis, capital requests from nonpublicly funded secondary schools.

Capital grant requests exceeding $100,000, unless initiated by the Foundation, will not be considered.

GEOG. RESTRICTIONS: Colorado.

FINANCIAL DATA:
Amount of support per award: Capital Grants: $10,000 to $25,000; General Operating Grants and Program Grants: $2,500 to $10,000.
Total amount of support: $22,000,000 in grants approved for the year 2019.

NO. MOST RECENT APPLICANTS: Over 1,300 per year.

NO. AWARDS: Over 1,000 grants approved for the year 2019.

APPLICATION INFO:
Online grant application includes a concise narrative and three years of financial documents. Fellowship and grant guidelines are available on the Foundation web site.
Duration: Typically one year.
Deadline: Proposals are accepted on a rolling basis.

PUBLICATIONS:
Annual report; application guidelines.

IRS I.D.: 84-6002373

OFFICERS:
William J. Hybl, Executive Chairman
R. Thayer Tutt, Jr., Vice Chairman and Chief Investment Officer
Kyle H. Hybl, President and Chief Executive Officer
Matt Carpenter, Executive Vice President and Chief Operating Officer
Elaine Martinez, Chief Financial Officer

TRUSTEES:
Andrea Aragon
Judy Bell
Matt Carpenter
Erik Estrada
Nechie Hall
Kyle H. Hybl
William J. Hybl, Jr.
Charles H. Jacoby
David J. Palenchar

R. Thayer Tutt, Jr.
William R. Ward

ADDRESS INQUIRIES TO:
See e-mail address above.

EMERSON   [104]
8000 West Florissant Avenue
St. Louis, MO 63136
(314) 553-2000
(314) 553-3621
Web Site: www.emerson.com

FOUNDED: 1944

AREAS OF INTEREST:
Education; youth, culture and the arts; health, welfare and civic needs.

TYPE:
Capital grants; Challenge/matching grants; Development grants; Endowments; General operating grants; Matching gifts; Project/program grants.

YEAR PROGRAM STARTED: 1950

PURPOSE:
To encourage sound, innovative programs that enrich human lives, promote volunteerism, provide services directly to those in need and increase the overall impact of contributed funds.

LEGAL BASIS:
Corporate contributions program.

ELIGIBILITY:
Grants are made to organizations having IRS 501(c)(3) tax-exempt status, located in areas where Emerson has facilities. The Trust does not contribute to organizations that practice discrimination by race, color, creed, sex, age or national origin, religious or politically partisan organizations, projects requiring funding directly to an organization located outside the U.S. or its territories, loans or investment funds, fraternal, veterans' or labor groups unless they furnish services benefiting the general public, aid to individuals, underwriting of deficits or post-event funding.

FINANCIAL DATA:
Amount of support per award: Varies.
Total amount of support: $28,600,000 for the year 2019.
Matching fund requirements: Dollar-for-dollar match of employee donations to institutions of higher learning (up to $10,000 annual maximum) and cultural arts organizations (up to $5,000 annually to any one organization, up to $10,000 maximum).

APPLICATION INFO:
Proposals should be submitted in writing and include the following information:
(1) brief description and history of the organization submitting the proposal;
(2) a clear statement of the purpose and objectives of the project or program (including expected results), the program budget, the amount requested, a statement of how the funds will be used and a timetable of project completion;
(3) statement of the relationship of the project's goals to the priorities of the Emerson Charitable Trust;
(4) annual report or audited financial statement of the requesting organization showing income and expenses, operational budget and which may include a copy of the most recent IRS 990 report;
(5) supporting factual information that may be useful as a basis of evaluation, such as a

list of sources providing support to the organization;
(6) copy of the organization's IRS 501(c)(3) tax-exemption determination letter;
(7) listing of the organization's Board of Directors and a statement regarding staff who will manage the project and;
(8) statement of general plans for sustaining activities and post-grant evaluation of the project.
Applicants should expect a 30- to 60-day turnaround on all written proposals.
Duration: One year. Must reapply, unless multiyear funding at outset.

PUBLICATIONS:
Annual report; guidelines.

ADDRESS INQUIRIES TO:
David J. Rabe, Vice President
Corporate Social Responsibility
(See address above.)

ERION FOUNDATION   [105]
P.O. Box 732
Loveland, CO 80539
(970) 667-4549
Fax: (970) 663-6187
E-mail: erionfoundationorg@gmail.com
Web Site: www.erionfoundation.org

FOUNDED: 1986

AREAS OF INTEREST:
Education, health, welfare, and culture.

TYPE:
Capital grants; Challenge/matching grants; Development grants.

YEAR PROGRAM STARTED: 1986

PURPOSE:
To support the Loveland, CO community.

LEGAL BASIS:
Private foundation.

ELIGIBILITY:
Eligible organizations must be IRS 501(c)(3) tax-exempt.

GEOG. RESTRICTIONS: Loveland, Colorado and the immediate surrounding area.

FINANCIAL DATA:
Amount of support per award: Varies.

APPLICATION INFO:
Organization must submit an application packet that includes the following:
(1) completed application form;
(2) a copy of the organization's 501(c)(3) designation letter and;
(3) page one of the organization's most recent IRS Form 990.

Additional information is included in the Grant Guidelines section.

The Foundation prefers that grant requests be submitted via e-mail to GrantRequest@erionfoundation.org. Organization may also submit the application and attachments online.

Duration: Varies.

ADDRESS INQUIRIES TO:
Doug Erion, President
(See address above.)

*PLEASE NOTE:
Due to numerous large capital projects, the Foundation is not currently accepting grant applications.

EVERSOURCE ENERGY FOUNDATION   [106]
P.O. Box 270
Hartford, CT 06103
(888) 682-4639
E-mail: responsibleenergy@eversource.com
Web Site: www.eversource.com

FOUNDED: 1981

AREAS OF INTEREST:
Health and well-being of youth and advancement and promotion of clean energy and related technologies.

TYPE:
Challenge/matching grants; Development grants; Matching gifts; Project/program grants; Research grants; Scholarships; Technical assistance. Grants to nonprofit charitable organizations in the Foundation's service territory.

YEAR PROGRAM STARTED: 1981

PURPOSE:
To make a positive difference in the lives of Eversource customers.

LEGAL BASIS:
Corporate foundation.

ELIGIBILITY:
Applicants must be institutions and organizations with a 501(c)(3) tax-exempt designation.

The Foundation does not support personal expenses related to events, conferences or travel, corporations that do not qualify as charitable organizations as defined by the IRS Code, projects benefiting limited groups (religious, fraternal or political), private foundations or endowments, requests aimed at reducing or eliminating a pre-existing debt, golf outings, organizations located outside the Foundation areas served and whose services do not benefit Eversource customers, and advertising. Generally speaking, grants are not provided to organizations that receive direct support from United Way or other federated funds, as these umbrella agencies are supported through Eversource direct giving and employee giving campaigns.

FINANCIAL DATA:
Amount of support per award: $1,000 to $100,000. $2,500 average.
Total amount of support: $1,000,000 to $1,500,000.
Matching fund requirements: The Foundation matches dollar-for-dollar employee gifts to approved educational or cultural organizations and homeless shelters. Minimum of $100 and maximum of $2,500 in any calendar year.

APPLICATION INFO:
Applications for support must be submitted through the online application form. Requests by e-mail or other means will not be considered.
Duration: Usually one year.
Deadline: November 15.

PUBLICATIONS:
Guidelines; matching grants program brochure.

EXELON CORPORATION   [107]
Corporate Relations
10 South Dearborn Street
Chicago, IL 60603
(312) 394-4361
E-mail: steve.solomon@exeloncorp.com
Web Site: www.exeloncorp.com

FOUNDED: 1888

AREAS OF INTEREST:
Math and science, environmental education, arts and culture, neighborhood development, and environmental conservation.

NAME(S) OF PROGRAMS:
● **Corporate Giving Program**

TYPE:
General operating grants; Matching gifts; Project/program grants. Sponsorship for events.

PURPOSE:
To strengthen customer and community relations by promoting the advancement of math, science and energy education, contributing to charitable organizations that promote efficiency and renewable energy, promoting economic and community development, and contributing to organizations that promote diversity in the workplace and community.

LEGAL BASIS:
Corporate contributions program.

ELIGIBILITY:
Grants are made to institutions, organizations and agencies located in Exelon's service area (District of Columbia, northern Illinois, central Maryland and southeastern Pennsylvania). The company does not purchase ads in benefit programs. No contributions are made to religious organizations for religious purposes, political organizations, or to individuals.

GEOG. RESTRICTIONS: District of Columbia, northern Illinois, central Maryland and southeastern Pennsylvania.

FINANCIAL DATA:
Total amount of support: $51,000,000 to nonprofit organizations for the year 2018.

NO. AWARDS: Approximately 16,000.

APPLICATION INFO:
Application must be submitted online.
Duration: One year.
Deadline: Applications are reviewed on an ongoing basis.

PUBLICATIONS:
Guidelines.

STAFF:
Christopher M. Crane, President and Chief Executive Officer of Exelon Corporation

ADDRESS INQUIRIES TO:
Steve Solomon
Vice President, Corporate Relations
(See address above.)

FAIRFIELD COUNTY'S COMMUNITY FOUNDATION   [108]
40 Richards Avenue
Norwalk, CT 06854
(203) 750-3200
Fax: (203) 750-3232
E-mail: info@fccfoundation.org
Web Site: fccfoundation.org

FOUNDED: 1992

AREAS OF INTEREST:
Community development, housing, education, youth development, health and human services, and arts and culture.

NAME(S) OF PROGRAMS:
● **Competitive Grantmaking Program**

TYPE:
  General operating grants; Project/program
  grants. Capacity building grants. Scholarships
  are for high school students pursuing college
  or postsecondary training.

YEAR PROGRAM STARTED: 1992

PURPOSE:
  To promote philanthropy as a means to create
  change in Fairfield County, CT, focusing on
  innovative and collaborative solutions to
  critical issues impacting the community.

ELIGIBILITY:
  Grants are made to organizations that have
  tax-exempt status under Section 501(c)(3) of
  the Internal Revenue Code. No grants are
  made to individuals.

  Competitive grants are awarded to nonprofit
  organizations benefitting residents of Fairfield
  County, CT.

  Discretionary grants are only made to
  organizations serving Fairfield County, CT.

  Donor-advised grants can be awarded to
  nonprofits throughout the U.S. and also
  abroad.

FINANCIAL DATA:
  Assets over $230,000,000 for the year ended
  June 30, 2018.

  Amount of support per award: Grants vary in
  amount, depending upon the needs and
  nature of the request.

  Total amount of support: Approximately
  $19,000,000 in grants and scholarships for
  fiscal year 2019.

NO. AWARDS: Varies.

APPLICATION INFO:
  Application information is available on the
  web site.
  Duration: One year. Renewal possible.

STAFF:
  Juanita T. James, President and Chief
  Executive Officer

ADDRESS INQUIRIES TO:
  Sharon Jones, Community Impact Associate
  E-mail: sjones@fccfoundation.org
  (See address above.)

FARGO-MOORHEAD AREA
FOUNDATION   [109]
409 7th Street South
Fargo, ND 58103
(701) 234-0756
Fax: (701) 234-9724
E-mail: lexi@areafoundation.org
Web Site: www.areafoundation.org

FOUNDED: 1960

AREAS OF INTEREST:
  Basic human needs, education, community
  building, arts, culture and creativity.

TYPE:
  Project/program grants; Scholarships.

PURPOSE:
  To encourage philanthropy; to develop a
  permanent endowment to assess and respond
  to emerging and changing community needs;
  to provide a permanent charitable trust to
  donors with varied interests and giving
  capacities.

ELIGIBILITY:
  Must be 501(c)(3) nonprofit organization.

GEOG. RESTRICTIONS: Clay County, Minnesota
  and Cass County, North Dakota.

FINANCIAL DATA:
  Amount of support per award: Varies per
  award.

  Total amount of support: Approximately
  $2,300,000 annually.

NO. AWARDS: Varies.

APPLICATION INFO:
  Organizations applying for funds are required
  to use the Foundation Grant Proposal Forms
  available online.
  Duration: One year.

ADDRESS INQUIRIES TO:
  Lexi Oestreich, Program Officer
  (See address above.)

FIELD FOUNDATION OF
ILLINOIS   [110]
200 South Wacker Drive, Suite 3860
Chicago, IL 60606
(312) 831-0910
Fax: (312) 831-0961
E-mail: mgoldberg@fieldfoundation.org
Web Site: www.fieldfoundation.org

FOUNDED: 1960

AREAS OF INTEREST:
  Justice, art, leadership investment, and media
  and storytelling.

TYPE:
  Capital grants; Challenge/matching grants;
  Conferences/seminars; General operating
  grants; Matching gifts; Project/program
  grants.

YEAR PROGRAM STARTED: 1960

PURPOSE:
  To provide support to organizations serving
  the people of Chicago, with a focus on
  communities commonly divested in.

LEGAL BASIS:
  Private foundation.

ELIGIBILITY:
  Support is limited to programs primarily
  serving Chicago residents. Grants are made
  to nonprofit institutions. Grants are not made
  directly to individuals.

GEOG. RESTRICTIONS: Chicago, Illinois.

FINANCIAL DATA:
  Amount of support per award:
  Programs/projects: $10,000 to $50,000.
  Grants to individual schools do not exceed
  $20,000 a year.

  Total amount of support: Approximately
  $3,000,000 annually.

  Matching fund requirements: Only Board of
  Directors and staff can submit matching gift
  applications.

NO. MOST RECENT APPLICANTS: 400.

NO. AWARDS: 110.

APPLICATION INFO:
  All organizations must create an account on
  the Foundation's online portal. Applicants
  must submit an online Letter of Inquiry
  (LOI) outlining the proposed project. All
  fields must be completed for the LOI to be
  considered. If invited, applicants will be
  asked to submit a full application.

  Duration: Programs/projects and capital
  funding: One year. Possible renewal up to
  three years.

  Deadline: Grants are awarded three times per
  year. Deadlines are listed on the Foundation
  web site.

PUBLICATIONS:
  Biennial reports; information brochure
  (including application guidelines).

IRS I.D.: 36-6059408

ADDRESS INQUIRIES TO:
  Operations/Grants Manager
  (See address above.)

FIRMAN FUND   [111]
1422 Euclid Avenue
Hanna Building, Suite 1150
Cleveland, OH 44115
(216) 303-8060
Fax: (216) 862-2737

FOUNDED: 1953

AREAS OF INTEREST:
  Medicine, education, culture, youth, welfare,
  conservation and community funds.

TYPE:
  Capital grants; Endowments; General
  operating grants; Project/program grants;
  Research grants.

LEGAL BASIS:
  Tax-exempt, private foundation.

ELIGIBILITY:
  No grants are awarded to individuals. No
  unsolicited requests accepted.

GEOG. RESTRICTIONS: Denver, Colorado;
  Thomasville, Georgia and Cleveland, Ohio.

FINANCIAL DATA:
  Amount of support per award: $1,000 to
  $250,000.

  Total amount of support: Approximately
  $400,000.

NO. AWARDS: Approximately 25.

APPLICATION INFO:
  The Fund does not accept unsolicited
  requests for funds.

  Duration: Grants awarded are not to be
  considered on a continuing basis.

TRUSTEES:
  Royal Firman, III, President
  Stephanie Firman
  Pamela Murphy
  Robert C. Webster, III

FIRST COMMUNITY
FOUNDATION PARTNERSHIP OF
PENNSYLVANIA   [112]
201 West Fourth Street
Williamsport, PA 17701
(570) 321-1500
Fax: (570) 321-6434
E-mail: FCFP@fcfpartnership.org
Web Site: www.fcfpartnership.org

FOUNDED: 1916

AREAS OF INTEREST:
  Arts and culture, education, recreation and
  environment, health, human services,
  economic and community development.

CONSULTING OR VOLUNTEER SERVICES:
  Estate planning seminars, grant applicant
  training.

TYPE:
  Project/program grants; Scholarships.

PURPOSE:
  To improve the quality of life in northcentral
  Pennsylvania.

LEGAL BASIS:
  Community foundation.

ELIGIBILITY:
Central and northcentral Pennsylvania qualified 501(c)(3) organizations only.

GEOG. RESTRICTIONS: Bradford, Clinton, Columbia, Lycoming, Montour, Northumberland, Potter, Snyder, Sullivan, Tioga and Union counties, Pennsylvania.

FINANCIAL DATA:
Amount of support per award: Varies.
Total amount of support: Approximately $5,271,000 for the year ended December 31, 2019.

CO-OP FUNDING PROGRAMS: Scholarships in combination with donor-advised, designated, organizational endowment and unrestricted funds.

NO. MOST RECENT APPLICANTS: 170.

NO. AWARDS: 591 (including grants processed through a 30-hour fund-raising event).

APPLICATION INFO:
Application information is available on the web site. Application must include a copy of the IRS tax determination letter.
Duration: Typically one year.
Deadline: Varies.

PUBLICATIONS:
Annual report; grants and loans policy; *Insights in Estate and Financial Planning*; other tax and estate planning brochures.

IRS I.D.: 24-6013117

ADDRESS INQUIRIES TO:
Betty Gilmour
Director of Grantmaking
E-mail: bettyg@fcfpartnership.org

FIRSTENERGY FOUNDATION   [113]

76 South Main Street
Akron, OH 44308-1890
(330) 384-5022
Fax: (330) 245-5566
E-mail: fe_comm_involve@firstenergycorp.com
Web Site: www.firstenergycorp.com/community/firstenergy_foundation.html

FOUNDED: 1961

AREAS OF INTEREST:
Principally education, the arts, community improvements, professional development and literacy, and overall health of the community.

TYPE:
Capital grants; General operating grants; Matching gifts; Project/program grants.

PURPOSE:
To improve the vitality of our communities and support key safety initiatives; to promote local and regional economic development and revitalization efforts; to support FirstEnergy employees' community leadership and volunteer interests; to advance an educated workforce by supporting professional development and literacy, and science, technology, engineering and mathematics (STEM) education initiatives.

LEGAL BASIS:
Corporate foundation.

ELIGIBILITY:
The Foundation supports nonprofit, tax-exempt organizations within the FirstEnergy operating companies' service area including Ohio Edison, The Illuminating Company and Toledo Edison in Ohio; Met-Ed, Penelec, Penn Power and West Penn

Power in Pennsylvania; Jersey Central Power and Light in New Jersey; Mon Power and Potomac Edison in West Virginia and Maryland; and where FirstEnergy Solutions Corp., FirstEnergy Generation and FirstEnergy Nuclear Operations conduct business.

Generally, no grants are made to individuals or for political organizations, endowment funds, deficit financing, research, scholarships or fellowships. No loans.

FINANCIAL DATA:
Amount of support per award: Grants vary in amount, depending upon the needs and nature of the request.
Matching fund requirements: Employees only.

NO. AWARDS: Varies.

APPLICATION INFO:
The Foundation does not accept unsolicited grant applications. Applicants are encouraged to discuss grant inquiries with the local management of FirstEnergy companies and the staff of FirstEnergy's Community Involvement Department.

ADDRESS INQUIRIES TO:
Lorna Wisham, President
(See address above.)

*SPECIAL STIPULATIONS:
Unsolicited grant applications are not accepted.

A.J. FLETCHER FOUNDATION   [114]

909 Glenwood Avenue
Raleigh, NC 27605
(919) 322-2580
Fax: (919) 322-2581
E-mail: natalie@ajf.org
contact@ajf.org
Web Site: ajf.org

AREAS OF INTEREST:
Artistic endeavors, education, elderly, infirm and indigent, media and communication, public recreation, and religious faith.

TYPE:
General operating grants; Project/program grants.

PURPOSE:
To support nonprofit organizations in their endeavors to improve the quality of life in North Carolina.

ELIGIBILITY:
Eligible organizations must be IRS 501(c)(3) tax-exempt.

GEOG. RESTRICTIONS: North Carolina.

FINANCIAL DATA:
Amount of support per award: Varies.
Total amount of support: Varies.

APPLICATION INFO:
Applications for funding are by request only.
Duration: One-time to multiyear funding.
Deadline: Varies.

ADDRESS INQUIRIES TO:
Natalie Fogg, Director of Operations and Grants Administration
(See address above.)

THE FLINN FOUNDATION   [115]

1802 North Central Avenue
Phoenix, AZ 85004
(602) 744-6800
E-mail: info@flinn.org
Web Site: flinn.org

FOUNDED: 1965

AREAS OF INTEREST:
Biosciences, education, arts and culture, and civic leadership in Arizona.

NAME(S) OF PROGRAMS:
- **Arizona Center for Civic Leadership**
- **Flinn Scholars Program**

TYPE:
Demonstration grants; Fellowships; Project/program grants; Scholarships; Seed money grants. The arts and culture grants program assists Arizona's large arts and culture organizations in generating capital through creative programming and fiscal planning.

The Foundation's biosciences grant projects aim to strengthen Arizona's biosciences infrastructure and thereby improve the state's capacity to compete nationally and internationally in the biosciences economy.

The Arizona Center for Civic Leadership seeks to strengthen civic leadership in Arizona.

The Flinn Scholars Program annually awards top Arizona high school graduates full scholarship support.

YEAR PROGRAM STARTED: 1981

PURPOSE:
To improve the quality of life in Arizona to benefit future generations through support of the biosciences, arts and culture, the Flinn Scholars and civic leadership.

LEGAL BASIS:
Tax-exempt private foundation.

ELIGIBILITY:
Flinn Scholarship applicant must be a U.S. citizen or lawful permanent resident and be an Arizona resident for two full years immediately preceding entry to the university.

Grant applicants must be tax-exempt, nonprofit organizations which have qualified for exemption under Section 501(c)(3) of the IRS code and, generally, are not those classified as private foundations.

Grants are made only for charitable purposes that support organizations and activities in Arizona. The Foundation generally does not make grants to support individuals, building and equipment projects, endowment or annual fund-raising campaigns or to meet ongoing operating costs or deficits.

GEOG. RESTRICTIONS: Arizona.

FINANCIAL DATA:
Foundation assets of approximately $220,000,000.
Amount of support per award: Varies.
Total amount of support: Varies.

CO-OP FUNDING PROGRAMS: The Flinn-Brown Civic Leadership Academy, a component of the Arizona Center for Civic Leadership, is co-funded by the Thomas R. Brown Foundations.

NO. AWARDS: Flinn Scholars: Approximately 20 annually.

REPRESENTATIVE AWARDS:
$504,000 to Arizona State University for Flinn Scholarship awards; $1,500,000 to

Translational Genomics Research Institute for support of three genomic-based research projects in collaboration with Arizona institutions; $100,000 to Mesa Arts Center to choose and expand programming that connects to the Center's audiences and donors under age 40.

APPLICATION INFO:
No unsolicited applications accepted. There is no standard application form, except for those proposals submitted in response to a Foundation-initiated program.

Duration: Varies.

PUBLICATIONS:
Annual report; special reports; electronic newsletters.

STAFF:
Dawn Wallace, Vice President, Arizona Center for Civic Leadership
Sara Larsen, Program Manager, Arizona Center for Civic Leadership
Linda Kissel, Program Coordinator, Arizona Center for Civic Leadership

*SPECIAL STIPULATIONS:
No unsolicited applications accepted.

THE FORD FOUNDATION [116]
320 East 43rd Street
New York, NY 10017
(212) 573-5000
Fax: (212) 351-3677
Web Site: www.fordfoundation.org

FOUNDED: 1936

NAME(S) OF PROGRAMS:
- **Cities and States Program**
- **Civic Engagement and Government Program**
- **Creativity and Free Expression Program**
- **Future of Work(ers) Program**
- **Gender, Racial and Ethnic Justice Program**
- **Natural Resources and Climate Change Program**
- **Technology and Society Program**

TYPE:
Conferences/seminars; Endowments; Fellowships; General operating grants; Matching gifts; Project/program grants; Research grants; Seed money grants; Technical assistance. General purposes, publications, program-related investments, special projects, individual grants.

Cities and States Program addresses geographic disparities across the nation.

Civic Engagement and Government Program deals with the issues of expanding participation, engaging government and equitable resources.

Creativity and Free Expression Program deals with the issues of social justice storytelling and 21st century arts infrastructure.

Future of Work(ers) Program deals with the opportunity for decent work and fair reward, which is key to reducing inequality.

Gender, Racial and Ethnic Justice Program deals with the issues of freedom and dignity and rights of race, gender and ethnicity, and to recognize they are deeply connected.

Natural Resources and Climate Change Program aims to address inequality as it relates to the climate crisis.

Technology and Society Program supports the growth of technically sophisticated, diverse organizations dedicated to advancing equitable and more inclusive digital spaces and systems.

PURPOSE:
To reduce poverty and injustice and to promote democratic values, free expression and human achievement.

LEGAL BASIS:
Private foundation.

ELIGIBILITY:
Qualified institutions, individuals and communities with appropriate interests are eligible to apply. Most of the Foundation's grant funds are given to organizations. Although the Foundation also makes grants to individuals, such grants are few in number relative to demand. These are limited to research, training and other activities related to the Foundation's program interests and subject to certain limitations and procedural requirements under the U.S. Internal Revenue Code.

The Foundation does not award undergraduate scholarships or make grants for purely personal or local needs. Support for graduate fellowships is generally funneled through grants to universities and other organizations, which are responsible for the selection of recipients. Support is not normally given for routine operating costs of institutions or for religious activities. Except in rare cases, funding is not available for the construction or maintenance of buildings.

FINANCIAL DATA:
Amount of support per award: Grants vary in amount, depending upon the needs and nature of the request. Average grant to organizations: $230,000.

Total amount of support: Approximately $8,000,000 in total grants, program-related investments and Foundation-administered projects annually.

NO. MOST RECENT APPLICANTS: Approximately 40,000 grant proposals annually.

NO. AWARDS: Approximately 1,500 grants annually.

APPLICATION INFO:
Prospective applicants should, as a first step, submit a brief letter of inquiry in order to determine whether the Foundation's present interests and funds permit consideration as a proposal.

There is no application form. Proposals should set forth objectives, the proposed program for pursuing objectives, qualifications of persons engaged in the work, a detailed budget, present means of support and status of applications to other funding sources and legal and tax status.

Duration: Varies.

Deadline: Applications are considered throughout the year.

PUBLICATIONS:
Annual report; program policy statement including application guidelines; *Ford Foundation Report*, issued quarterly.

IRS I.D.: 13-1684331

OFFICERS:
Darren Walker, President
Depelsha McGruder, Chief Operating Officer and Treasurer
Hilary Pennington, Executive Vice President of Programs

Nishka Chandrasoma, Vice President, Secretary and General Counsel
Eric W. Doppstadt, Vice President and Chief Investment Officer
Michele Moore, Vice President, Global Communications
Martin Abregu, Vice President, International Programs
Diane Samuels, Vice President, People and Culture
Maria Torres-Springer, Vice President, U.S. Programs

ADDRESS INQUIRIES TO:
Office of the Secretary
E-mail: secretary@fordfoundation.org

FORD MOTOR COMPANY FUND AND COMMUNITY SERVICES [117]
One American Road
Dearborn, MI 48126-2701
(888) 313-0102
E-mail: fordfund@ford.com
Web Site: www.fordfund.org

FOUNDED: 1949

AREAS OF INTEREST:
Education, community development and auto-related safety.

NAME(S) OF PROGRAMS:
- **Community Grants Program**

TYPE:
Capital grants; Project/program grants; Scholarships. Support largely for education, including basic research grants, community funds and urban affairs, and civic and cultural programs.

PURPOSE:
To support initiatives and institutions that enhance and/or improve opportunities for those who live in communities where Ford Motor Company operates.

LEGAL BASIS:
Corporate foundation.

ELIGIBILITY:
No grants are made directly to individuals. Not-for-profit organizations with 501(c)(3) tax-exempt status may apply.

GEOG. RESTRICTIONS: United States.

FINANCIAL DATA:
Amount of support per award: Varies.
Total amount of support: Varies.

APPLICATION INFO:
Organization must complete a grant application online.

Duration: Varies.

Deadline: Requests for support are accepted and reviewed throughout the year.

FREEMAN FOUNDATION   [118]

c/o The Rockefeller Trust Company, N.A.
45 Rockefeller Plaza, Fifth Floor
New York, NY 10111
(212) 549-5270
Fax: (212) 549-5524

FOUNDED: 1993

AREAS OF INTEREST:
Asian studies, environmental conservation
and preservation, and Hawaii and Vermont
programs.

TYPE:
Challenge/matching grants; Exchange
programs; Fellowships; General operating
grants; Professorships; Project/program
grants; Research grants; Scholarships; Seed
money grants; Technical assistance; Training
grants; Travel grants; Visiting scholars.

PURPOSE:
To support a range of charitable
organizations; to strengthen the bonds of
friendship between the U.S. and the countries
of East Asia; to preserve and protect the
forests, lands and natural resources of the
U.S. for future generations; to contribute to
and enhance the development of a vibrant,
international free enterprise system.

ELIGIBILITY:
Eligible organizations must be IRS 501(c)(3)
tax-exempt.

GEOG. RESTRICTIONS: Hawaii, Vermont and
Asia.

FINANCIAL DATA:
Foundation grants since inception now total
over $800,000,000.
Amount of support per award: Generally,
$5,000 to $750,000.
Total amount of support: $19,613,048 in total
grants for the year 2019.

APPLICATION INFO:
Letters of Inquiry: Applicants should submit
a letter describing the program and financial
needs.

A grant proposal should:
(1) include a cover letter for the grant
request;
(2) provide a brief history of one's
organization, its mission and leadership;
(3) provide financial information for the most
recent fiscal year as well as financials for the
next fiscal year, if available, and;
(4) provide a list of current funding sources,
including amounts.
Six sets of the proposal should be mailed.
Two of the six sets should include the
organization's IRS Form 990, the IRS
501(c)(3) determination letter and the most
recent audit. The length of the proposal,
including cover letter and project budget
sheet, should not exceed six pages.
Mail proposals to Mr. Graeme Freeman;
President; The Freeman Foundation; 1601
East-West Road; Honolulu, HI 96848-1601.
Duration: Varies by the program. Renewal
possible.
Deadline: Applications must be received at
least one month prior to Trustees' meetings,
which occur three times yearly.

PUBLICATIONS:
Annual report.

IRS I.D.: 13-2965090

TRUSTEES AND OFFICERS:
Graeme Freeman, President
David Stack, Trustee
George Tsandikos, Trustee

ADDRESS INQUIRIES TO:
The Rockefeller Trust Company
George S. Tsandikos, Managing Director
(See address above.)

FREEPORT-MCMORAN
FOUNDATION   [119]

333 North Central Avenue
Phoenix, AZ 85004
(602) 366-8116
Fax: (602) 366-7368
E-mail: foundation@fmi.com
communitydevelopment@fmi.com
Web Site: www.fcx.com
www.freeportinmycommunity.com

FOUNDED: 1953

AREAS OF INTEREST:
Education and workforce development,
economic opportunity, and capacity,
resiliency and leadership.

NAME(S) OF PROGRAMS:
● **Matching Gifts Program**
● **Social Investment Program**

TYPE:
Matching gifts; Project/program grants. In the
area of capacity, resiliency and leadership,
the Foundation supports programs that
engage citizens, activate community leaders,
improve financial well-being, and strengthen
organizational effectiveness and efficiency to
steward and amplify investments.

In the area of economic opportunity, the
Foundation supports programs that create
diverse jobs, strengthen local businesses,
ensure attainable housing, enable accessible
health resources, protect land and waterways,
and increase food security.

In the area of education and workforce
development, the Foundation supports
programs that improve academic
performance, enable reskilling, up-skilling
and transferable skills for jobs of the future,
facilitate completion of postsecondary
education, and create pathways to jobs with a
living wage or better.

YEAR PROGRAM STARTED: 1932

PURPOSE:
To serve as a catalyst of positive change in
the communities where the company has
major facilities and update the quality of life.

LEGAL BASIS:
Corporate foundation.

ELIGIBILITY:
Nonprofit programs and organizations aligned
with the core values of the company. Must be
located in communities where the company
has a presence.

GEOG. RESTRICTIONS: United States.

FINANCIAL DATA:
Amount of support per award: Varies.
Total amount of support: Varies.
Matching fund requirements: Minimum $25.
First $1,000 is matched 2:1; above $1,000 is
matched dollar-for-dollar.

NO. MOST RECENT APPLICANTS: Varies.

NO. AWARDS: Varies.

APPLICATION INFO:
Guidelines and application are available on
the Foundation web site.
Duration: Social Investment Program: One
year. Renewable.

Deadline: Social Investment Program: August
30 for grant award the following year.

OFFICERS:
Tracy Bame, President and Director of Social
Responsibility and Community Development

ADDRESS INQUIRIES TO:
Contributions Administrator
(See address above.)

FREY FOUNDATION   [120]

40 Pearl Street, N.W.
Suite 1100
Grand Rapids, MI 49503-3028
(616) 451-0303
Fax: (616) 451-8481
E-mail: contact@freyfdn.org
Web Site: freyfdn.org

FOUNDED: 1974

AREAS OF INTEREST:
Children and their families, environment,
community arts, civic progress, and
philanthropy.

NAME(S) OF PROGRAMS:
● **Building Community**
● **Children and Families**
● **Community Arts**
● **Environment**

TYPE:
Capital grants; Demonstration grants;
Project/program grants; Seed money grants;
Technical assistance. Grants are available for
special one-time only or time-limited
purposes, such as "start-up" or program
expansion, demonstration projects, planning
or other forms of technical assistance,
evaluation, advocacy, and applied research.
Capital is available in some program areas.

YEAR PROGRAM STARTED: 1974

PURPOSE:
To promote healthy development of children
and their families, particularly infants and
children under the age of six and their
parents, with special attention to traditionally
disadvantaged populations; to protect,
preserve and improve the ecological health of
natural resources; to stimulate vitality,
effectiveness and growth of community-based
arts; to encourage civic action to improve the
livability of cities and communities; to
improve the effectiveness of organized
philanthropy and stimulate its growth.

LEGAL BASIS:
Private family foundation.

ELIGIBILITY:
Applicants must be public institutions and
501(c)(3) nonprofit organizations. No grants
to individuals, endowment funds, debt
retirement, general operating expenses,
scholarships, travel, to cover routine, current
or emergency expenses and/or sectarian
charitable activities.

GEOG. RESTRICTIONS: Charlevoix, Emmet or
Kent counties and lower western Michigan.

FINANCIAL DATA:
Amount of support per award: Varies upon
nature of request.
Total amount of support: Over $5,000,000
for the year 2018.

NO. AWARDS: Approximately 50 to 60 per year.

APPLICATION INFO:
Applicants must submit a brief inquiry using
the online system.
Duration: One year.

Deadline: February 15, May 15, August 15 and November 15.

PUBLICATIONS:
Annual report; *Taking Care of Civic Business*; *Charting the Course*; *Today's Winners, Tomorrow's Losers*.

STAFF:
Holly Johnson, President
Randy A. VanAntwerp, Chief Financial Officer
Lynne J. Ferrell, Program Director
Sarah Hockin, Program and Accounting Associate
Bryana Hopkins, Program and Communication Associate

BOARD OF TRUSTEES:
Mary Frey Bennett, Chairperson
Ellie Frey Zagel, Vice Chairperson
Tripp Frey, Treasurer
Sarah Frey, Secretary
Campbell W. Frey
Katrine E. Frey
Laura D. Frey

ADDRESS INQUIRIES TO:
Holly Johnson, President
(See address above.)

THE FROST FOUNDATION, LTD.   [121]
511 Armijo Street, Suite A
Santa Fe, NM 87501
(505) 986-0208
Fax: (505) 986-0430
E-mail: info@frostfound.org
Web Site: www.frostfound.org

FOUNDED: 1959

AREAS OF INTEREST:
Social service and humanitarian needs, the environment and education.

CONSULTING OR VOLUNTEER SERVICES:
Professional services of staff are offered for special projects.

TYPE:
Project/program grants; Research grants.

YEAR PROGRAM STARTED: 1959

PURPOSE:
To seek and assist innovative projects that will have positive impact beyond the boundaries of a single state.

LEGAL BASIS:
Tax-exempt private foundation.

ELIGIBILITY:
The Foundation encourages self-reliance, creativity and ingenuity on the part of prospective recipients.

Its efforts are directed primarily to support exemplary organizations and programs which can generate positive change beyond traditional boundaries, to encourage creativity which recognizes emerging needs, and to assist innovation which addresses current urgent problems.

Within these parameters, it provides initial impetus to exemplary organizations and programs, to operating funds, to pioneering organizations and programs which other institutions might similarly use, and to programs which have potential for wider service or educational exposure than an individual community.

The Foundation encourages collaborations, mergers and the formation of alliances among agencies within the community to reduce duplication of effort and to promote a maximum effective use of funds. The Foundation also considers requests for operating. It is prepared to review applications of human service needs, environmental and education programs in New Mexico and Louisiana from organizations which have an IRS 501(c)(3) determination.

GEOG. RESTRICTIONS: Louisiana and New Mexico.

FINANCIAL DATA:
Amount of support per award: $15,000 average.
Total amount of support: Approximately $2,000,000 annually.

NO. MOST RECENT APPLICANTS: Approximately 500.

NO. AWARDS: Approximately 65.

APPLICATION INFO:
A brief description of the institution/organization, including its mission, must be submitted along with evidence of tax-exempt status, the amount requested, a statement of the specific need(s) to be met by the project, a budget projection with the time frame expected and the qualifications of the staff members selected to serve the project. Faxed summaries are not accepted.
Duration: Typically one year. On rare occasions, because of special circumstances, applicant can reapply.
Deadline: December 1 for March Board meeting and June 1 for September Board meeting.

PUBLICATIONS:
Annual report; application guidelines.

OFFICERS:
Mary Amelia Whited-Howell, President
Philip B. Howell, Executive Vice-President
Taylor F. Moore, Secretary/Treasurer

BOARD OF DIRECTORS:
Ann Rogers Gerber
Amelia Reid Howell
Philip B. Howell
Philip Carter Howell
Taylor F. Moore
Mary Amelia Whited-Howell

ADDRESS INQUIRIES TO:
Mary Amelia Whited-Howell, President
(See address above.)

LLOYD A. FRY FOUNDATION   [122]
120 South LaSalle Street
Suite 1950
Chicago, IL 60603
(312) 580-0310
Fax: (312) 580-0980
E-mail: info@fryfoundation.org
Web Site: www.fryfoundation.org

FOUNDED: 1983

AREAS OF INTEREST:
Education, arts and culture education, access to health care, and employment, with special emphasis on support of inner-city projects.

TYPE:
Project/program grants.

PURPOSE:
To address persistent problems of urban Chicago resulting from poverty, violence, ignorance and despair.

LEGAL BASIS:
Private foundation.

ELIGIBILITY:
501(c)(3).

GEOG. RESTRICTIONS: Inner-city Chicago, Illinois.

FINANCIAL DATA:
Amount of support per award: $15,000 to $50,000 average.
Total amount of support: Over $7,000,000 in grants and awards annually.

NO. MOST RECENT APPLICANTS: 355 for fiscal year 2020.

NO. AWARDS: 306 for fiscal year 2020.

APPLICATION INFO:
Application guidelines are available at the Foundation web site.
Duration: One to two years.
Deadline: Letters of Intent are accepted year-round. Proposals: March 1, June 1, September 1 and December 1.

PUBLICATIONS:
Annual report.

IRS I.D.: 36-6108775

STAFF:
Unmi Song, President
Merril Prager, Controller
Sydney Sidell, Director of Education and Arts Learning
Sabrina Greig, Program Officer, Art
Kristie Conklin, Program Officer, Employment
Brian Bragg, Program Officer, Health
Lisa Brock, Program Assistant
Jessica Thompson, Program Assistant

ADDRESS INQUIRIES TO:
Ms. Unmi Song, President
(See e-mail address above.)

GANNETT FOUNDATION   [123]
7950 Jones Branch Drive
McLean, VA 22107-0150
(703) 854-3780
(703) 854-6000
E-mail: foundation@gannett.com
Web Site: www.gannettfoundation.org

FOUNDED: 1991

AREAS OF INTEREST:
Education and neighborhood improvement, economic development, youth development, community problem-solving, assistance to disadvantaged people, environmental conservation and cultural enrichment.

TYPE:
General operating grants; Matching gifts; Project/program grants.

PURPOSE:
To improve the education, health and advancement of the people who live in Gannett communities.

LEGAL BASIS:
Corporate foundation.

ELIGIBILITY:
Local organizations determined by the IRS to be tax-exempt under 501(c)(3) in communities where the Gannett Company, Inc. owns a daily newspaper.

FINANCIAL DATA:
Amount of support per award: Average $1,000 to $5,000.
Total amount of support: Approximately $4,500,000 in grants for the year 2018.

Matching fund requirements: Gifts for programs or initiatives where the primary purpose is the promotion of religious doctrine or tenets are excluded.

NO. MOST RECENT APPLICANTS: 1,000.

NO. AWARDS: 700.

APPLICATION INFO:
Application form and guidelines are available online.

Duration: One year. Renewal possible.

ADDRESS INQUIRIES TO:
Sue Madden, Manager
(See address above.)

THE CARL GELLERT AND CELIA BERTA GELLERT FOUNDATION [124]

455 Hickey Boulevard
Suite 509
Daly City, CA 94015
(650) 985-2080
Fax: (650) 985-2084
E-mail: info@gellertfoundation.org
Web Site: www.gellertfoundation.org

FOUNDED: 1958

AREAS OF INTEREST:
Religious, charitable, scientific, literary or educational purposes.

TYPE:
Capital grants; Development grants; Endowments; General operating grants; Project/program grants; Scholarships; Technical assistance.

YEAR PROGRAM STARTED: 1958

LEGAL BASIS:
Private foundation.

ELIGIBILITY:
Organization must have proof of current IRS 501(c)(3) tax-exempt status and classification as a public charity under Sections 509(a)(1) and 170(b)(1)(A) of the Internal Revenue Code, or 509(a)(2), or 509(a)(3), types I or II.

The Foundation does not fund individuals or private foundations, sponsorships or fund-raising events such as dinners, walk-a-thons, tournaments and fashion shows, or lobbying and attempts to influence legislation.

GEOG. RESTRICTIONS: Alameda, Contra Costa, Marin, Napa, San Francisco, San Mateo, Santa Clara, Solano and Sonoma, the nine counties of the Greater San Francisco Bay area, California.

FINANCIAL DATA:
Amount of support per award: Varies.
Total amount of support: $2,396,875 for the year 2019.

NO. AWARDS: 116 for the year 2019.

APPLICATION INFO:
Application information can be found at the Foundation's web site. Application must be submitted online.

Deadline: August 15, annually or following Monday if 15th falls on a weekend.

IRS I.D.: 94-6062858

DIRECTORS:
Carol Conroy
Andrew A. Cresci
Jack Fitzpatrick
Kevin Flynn

Robert J. Grassilli, Jr.
Michael J. King
J. Malcolm Visbal
Christine Whelan

ADDRESS INQUIRIES TO:
Jack Fitzpatrick, Executive Director
(See address above.)

THE FRED GELLERT FAMILY FOUNDATION [125]

1038 Redwood Highway
Building B, Suite 2
Mill Valley, CA 94941
(415) 381-7570
Fax: (415) 381-8526
E-mail: FGFamilyFoundation@gmail.com
Web Site: www.FGFamilyFoundation.com

FOUNDED: 1958

AREAS OF INTEREST:
Long-term sustainability planning, advanced and specialized education, local community support through social service organizations, and reproductive health.

TYPE:
Challenge/matching grants; Endowments; Fellowships; General operating grants; Matching gifts; Professorships; Project/program grants; Research grants; Seed money grants.

YEAR PROGRAM STARTED: 1958

PURPOSE:
To advance positive forces for social change to ensure quality of life for future generations.

LEGAL BASIS:
Private family foundation.

ELIGIBILITY:
Applicants must be 501(c)(3) organizations. No grants to individuals or for purchasing development rights or land.

GEOG. RESTRICTIONS: Primarily the Greater Bay area, Marin and San Francisco, California.

FINANCIAL DATA:
Amount of support per award: $1,000 to $25,000; Average: $5,000.
Total amount of support: Approximately $300,000 for the year 2018.
Matching fund requirements: Provide information on challenge grant.

NO. AWARDS: 35 for the year 2018.

REPRESENTATIVE AWARDS:
$20,000 to Marin General Hospital; $10,000 to Slide Ranch; $10,000 to Huckleberry Youth Services; $1,000 to Education Outside; $7,000 to Sustainable Conservation.

APPLICATION INFO:
The Foundation does not accept unsolicited letters of inquiry or grant proposals.
Duration: Typically one year.

IRS I.D.: 94-6062859

STAFF:
Patty O'Day, Controller
Heather Wyatt, Grant Manager
Serena Lim, Accountant

BOARD OFFICERS:
Annette Gellert, Co-Chairperson and Trustee
Fred Gellert, Jr., Co-Chairperson and Trustee

*PLEASE NOTE:
Grant monies awarded September to November.

GENERAL SERVICE FOUNDATION [126]

2120 University Avenue
Berkeley, CA 94704
(510) 679-3876
E-mail: info@generalservice.org
Web Site: www.generalservice.org

FOUNDED: 1946

NAME(S) OF PROGRAMS:
● **Building Voice and Power**

TYPE:
General operating grants.

YEAR PROGRAM STARTED: 1946

PURPOSE:
To build a more just and sustainable world.

LEGAL BASIS:
Private foundation, tax-exempt under IRS statute 501(c)(3).

ELIGIBILITY:
Organizations must be tax-exempt under U.S. law.

In general, the Foundation does not contribute to annual campaigns, nor to capital campaigns, to individuals or for relief.

Because the Foundation's areas of concern are broad, the Board has determined guidelines within each area. All applicants are urged only to submit applications falling within the Foundation's Contribution Policy and Guidelines.

GEOG. RESTRICTIONS: United States.

FINANCIAL DATA:
Amount of support per award: $45,000 to $150,000.

NO. MOST RECENT APPLICANTS: Approximately 165.

NO. AWARDS: 66.

APPLICATION INFO:
The Foundation requests that applications for contributions be in line with the approved guidelines and be submitted online.

Duration: One to three years.

IRS I.D.: 36-6018535

OFFICERS:
Robin Snidow, Board Chairperson
Griff Foxley, Vice Chairperson
Peter Halby, Treasurer
Marcie J. Musser, Secretary
William M. Repplinger, Assistant Treasurer

DIRECTORS:
Eliot Estrin
Jesse Estrin
Mary Lloyd Estrin
Griff Foxley
Zoe L. Foxley
Peter Halby
Will Halby
Kierra Johnson
Marcie J. Musser
Robert W. Musser
Carmen Rojas
Robin Snidow

ADDRESS INQUIRIES TO:
Elaine Mui, Grants and Operations Manager
E-mail: elaine@generalservice.org

*PLEASE NOTE:
GSF has allocated its grants through 2020 and will not be taking on any new grants through open intake. The process will be reopened in 2021 if new funds are available.

GEORGIA-PACIFIC FOUNDATION [127]

133 Peachtree Street, N.E.
12th Floor
Atlanta, GA 30303
(404) 652-4182
Fax: (404) 749-2754
E-mail: gpfoundation@gapac.com
Web Site: www.gp.
com/company/community/foundation

FOUNDED: 1958

AREAS OF INTEREST:
Education, environment, entrepreneurship, community enrichment and employee involvement.

TYPE:
Project/program grants; Scholarships.

PURPOSE:
To fund and support community-based programs, volunteer service projects, disaster relief and other initiatives that improve the quality of life in communities where Georgia-Pacific employees live and work.

LEGAL BASIS:
Corporate foundation.

ELIGIBILITY:
Organizations must have 501(c)(3) tax-exemption status from the IRS.

The Foundation does not support organizations that discriminate on the basis of race, color, creed, national origin or gender; private organizations; "bail-out" funds given to provide emergency assistance to organizations for general operating purposes; individuals, other than through scholarship and community service programs; political causes, candidates and legislative lobbying or advocacy efforts of any type; churches or religious denominations, religious or theological schools; general operating support for United Way member agencies; operating support for colleges and universities; fund-raising events such as raffles, telethons, walk-a-thons and auctions; and for trips and tours.

FINANCIAL DATA:
Amount of support per award: Minimum $1,000.

APPLICATION INFO:
Prospective applicants must first complete the Eligibility Quiz. If their program meets the initial criteria for funding, the applicant will be invited to submit a full proposal.

Only one copy of the proposal is required. Proposals must be sent via mail. E-mails or faxes will not be accepted.

Deadline: Charitable contribution requests are reviewed on a rolling cycle. Within 60 days of receipt of the request with the appropriate documentation, the Foundation will respond with written notification as to whether the grant is accepted.

THE GHEENS FOUNDATION, INC. [128]

401 West Main Street
Suite 705
Louisville, KY 40202
(502) 584-4650
E-mail: barry@gheensfoundation.org
Web Site: gheensfoundation.org

FOUNDED: 1957

AREAS OF INTEREST:
Culture, education and health.

TYPE:
Capital grants; Challenge/matching grants; Development grants; General operating grants; Project/program grants; Technical assistance.

YEAR PROGRAM STARTED: 1957

PURPOSE:
To support programs that meet the needs of society and improve the quality of life in the community.

LEGAL BASIS:
501(c)(3), private foundation.

ELIGIBILITY:
Grants are made to organizations that have tax-exempt status under Section 501(c)(3) of the Internal Revenue Code. No grants are made to individuals.

GEOG. RESTRICTIONS: Metropolitan Louisville, Kentucky.

FINANCIAL DATA:
Amount of support per award: Varies depending on the nature of the request.
Total amount of support: Approximately $6,500,000 annually.

NO. MOST RECENT APPLICANTS: 250.

NO. AWARDS: Approximately 125 per year.

APPLICATION INFO:
Application is available on the Foundation web site.
Duration: One year. May reapply.
Deadline: Prior to meetings in March, June, September and December.

ADDRESS INQUIRIES TO:
Barry G. Allen, President
(See address above.)

HERMAN GOLDMAN FOUNDATION [129]

14 Wall Street, 20th Floor
New York, NY 10005
(212) 461-2132
Fax: (212) 461-2223
E-mail: rbaron@hermangoldman.com

FOUNDED: 1942

AREAS OF INTEREST:
Arts, health, social justice and education.

TYPE:
General operating grants; Grants-in-aid; Project/program grants.

YEAR PROGRAM STARTED: 1943

PURPOSE:
To benefit those in need.

LEGAL BASIS:
Private foundation.

ELIGIBILITY:
Grants for individuals are not considered. It is not possible to respond to emergency requests, nor to financial needs of crash programs because of the time the Foundation requires to study grant proposals. Applicants must be tax-exempt organizations.

GEOG. RESTRICTIONS: Primarily, New York City metropolitan area.

FINANCIAL DATA:
Amount of support per award: $1,000 to $50,000.
Total amount of support: Varies.

APPLICATION INFO:
Applicants should submit one copy only of a written proposal and/or can use the New

York-New Jersey area Common Grant Application Form. No letter of inquiry required. Applicants must provide IRS tax-exempt documentation.
Duration: One year.
Deadline: Applications accepted throughout the year.

PUBLICATIONS:
Annual report.

ADDRESS INQUIRIES TO:
Richard K. Baron, Executive Director
(See e-mail address above.)

THE GOODYEAR TIRE & RUBBER COMPANY [130]

200 Innovation Way
Akron, OH 44316-0001
(330) 796-2244
Web Site: www.goodyear.com
corporate.goodyear.com/en-US/responsibility/community/community-support.html

FOUNDED: 1898

AREAS OF INTEREST:
Safety, health and human services, culture and the arts, education, civic and community improvement.

TYPE:
Project/program grants.

PURPOSE:
To promote healthy, high-functioning communities in locations where Company major plants and offices reside; to be a socially aware and responsive global citizen wherever the Company operates or does business.

LEGAL BASIS:
Corporate contributions program.

ELIGIBILITY:
Grants are made to nonprofit, tax-exempt organizations in communities where Goodyear plants and headquarters offices are located. No grants are made to individuals.

Requests are required to meet guidelines of strategic giving based on safety by focusing on safety programs plus at least one additional category noted below and/or provide volunteer opportunities for Company associates which are appropriately aligned with Company strategy:
(1) Civic and Community and Other: Grant awards will depend on local needs and customs in the communities in which the Company operates;
(2) Culture and the Arts: Requests from organizations and institutions serving plant communities and selected national arts organizations will be considered provided they comply with the connection to safety;
(3) Education: Requests for support from colleges, universities, and other educational institutions serving the areas in which Company plants and principal offices are located must demonstrate a connection with safety and/or must be a source of subsidized educational opportunities for Company associates and their families; a limited number of private and public universities of national or regional significance whose programs are of special interest or those that provide a continuing source of associates to the Company may also receive priority and;
(4) Health and Human Services: Highest priority is given to United Way campaigns in communities where Company plants and

principal offices are located; organizations receiving United Way support may not be eligible for additional funding.

A limited number of traditional grants will be honored at the Company's discretion.

FINANCIAL DATA:
Amount of support per award: Typically $5,000 to $25,000.
Total amount of support: Varies.

APPLICATION INFO:
All requests for community grants must be submitted through the online application system. If a proposal meets specific guidelines and strategic goals and objectives, it will be considered for funding.
Applications that are faxed or mailed will be returned to the organization with an invitation to the online application system.

PUBLICATIONS:
Overview.

ADDRESS INQUIRIES TO:
Community Affairs
(See address above.)

*PLEASE NOTE:
The Company does not accept grant requests by telephone.

W.R. GRACE FOUNDATION, INC. [131]
7500 Grace Drive
Columbia, MD 21044
(410) 531-4000
Fax: (410) 531-8372
E-mail: shirley.h.hewitt@grace.com
Web Site: www.grace.com

FOUNDED: 1961

AREAS OF INTEREST:
Higher education, civic, youth development, cultural programs, community funds, health and human services, and science, technology, engineering and mathematics education (STEM).

TYPE:
Challenge/matching grants; Matching gifts; Project/program grants.

YEAR PROGRAM STARTED: 1961

PURPOSE:
To provide primary support for education, particularly programs emphasizing math, sciences and chemistry.

LEGAL BASIS:
Company-sponsored foundation.

ELIGIBILITY:
Nonprofit, tax-exempt organizations with a 501(c)(3) tax-exempt status are eligible for support. The Foundation will not support individuals, political or religious organizations.

Grants to organizations in communities where W.R. Grace & Co. has significant employee population.

GEOG. RESTRICTIONS: United States and Canada.

FINANCIAL DATA:
Amount of support per award: Grants vary in amount based on the needs and nature of the request; Average: $1,000.

NO. AWARDS: Approximately 200 each year.

APPLICATION INFO:
Applications accepted online only. Complete details available at the web site.

Duration: Usually one year. Multiyear commitments possible.
Deadline: November 30.

DIRECTORS:
Mark A. Shelnitz, Chairman

ADDRESS INQUIRIES TO:
Shirley Hewitt, Deputy Executive Director
(See address above.)

GRAHAM HOLDINGS COMPANY [132]
1300 North 17th Street
Suite 1700
Arlington, VA 22209
(703) 345-6450
E-mail: pinkie.mayfield@ghco.com
Web Site: www.ghco.com

FOUNDED: 1947

AREAS OF INTEREST:
Civic and community, health and human services, education and cultural programs.

TYPE:
General operating grants. Employee Matching Gifts Program.

PURPOSE:
To support communities where Graham Holdings Company operates.

ELIGIBILITY:
Applicants must be nonprofit 501(c)(3) organizations.

GEOG. RESTRICTIONS: Metropolitan Washington, DC area.

FINANCIAL DATA:
Amount of support per award: Average $500 to $2,500.
Total amount of support: Varies.
Matching fund requirements: $25 minimum, $2,000 per year/per employee maximum. 1:1 or 1:2 for schools or where employee is an active volunteer.

REPRESENTATIVE AWARDS:
The Phillips Collection; Martha's Table; Capital Area Food Bank; Inner City-Inner Child; Northern Virginia Family Services.

APPLICATION INFO:
Send a short letter describing proposed program and budget.
Duration: One year. Renewal possible.
Deadline: Proposals are accepted on an ongoing basis.

ADDRESS INQUIRIES TO:
Pinkie Mayfield
Vice President-Corporate Affairs
Special Assistant to the Chairman
(See address above.)

PHILIP L. GRAHAM FUND [133]
c/o Graham Holdings Company
1300 North 17th Street, Suite 1700
Arlington, VA 22209
(703) 345-6515
E-mail: plgfund@ghco.com
Web Site: www.plgrahamfund.org

FOUNDED: 1963

AREAS OF INTEREST:
Primarily health and human services, education, arts and humanities, and community endeavors in the Washington, DC metropolitan area.

TYPE:
Capital grants.

YEAR PROGRAM STARTED: 1963

PURPOSE:
To use resources for the betterment of the Washington, DC metropolitan area.

LEGAL BASIS:
General interest foundation.

ELIGIBILITY:
Applicants must be 501(c)(3) organizations located in the Washington, DC metropolitan area.

No grants to individuals, for religious or political purposes, research, conferences, travel, fund-raising, event sponsorships, hospitals or publications.

GEOG. RESTRICTIONS: Primarily Washington, DC metropolitan area.

FINANCIAL DATA:
Amount of support per award: $25,000 to $35,000 average grant.
Total amount of support: $4,125,000 for the year 2017.

NO. AWARDS: 138 for the year 2017.

APPLICATION INFO:
Organizations interested in applying for funding must first submit a letter of inquiry (LOI) through the online application system prior to one of the three deadlines each year.
Duration: Typically one year.
Deadline: Varies each year. Refer to web site for annual application deadlines.

IRS I.D.: 52-6051781

TRUSTEES:
Richard Bynum
Theodore C. Lutz
Pinkie Mayfield
Carol Melamed
Laura O'Shaughnessy
Katharine Weymouth

ADDRESS INQUIRIES TO:
Eileen Daly, President
(See address above.)

*PLEASE NOTE:
Proposals accepted only through the Fund web site.

GRAND RAPIDS COMMUNITY FOUNDATION [134]
185 Oakes Street, S.W.
Grand Rapids, MI 49503
(616) 454-1751
Fax: (616) 454-6455
E-mail: grfound@grfoundation.org
Web Site: www.grfoundation.org

FOUNDED: 1922

AREAS OF INTEREST:
Education, environment, engagement, health, neighborhoods and prosperity.

NAME(S) OF PROGRAMS:
● **Access Camps**

TYPE:
Capital grants; Challenge/matching grants; Demonstration grants; Development grants; Project/program grants; Scholarships; Technical assistance.

YEAR PROGRAM STARTED: 1922

PURPOSE:
To build and manage our community's permanent endowment and lead the community to strengthen the lives of its people.

LEGAL BASIS:
Nonprofit organization established by resolution and declaration of trust. Incorporated in 1989.

ELIGIBILITY:
Applicant must have a current 501(c)(3) nonprofit designation from the IRS or be a governmental organization located in Kent County and serve local residents. No grants to individuals except through the scholarship program.

GEOG. RESTRICTIONS: Grand Rapids, Michigan and surrounding communities.

FINANCIAL DATA:
Amount of support per award: General grants vary by fund; typically $2,000 to $250,000.
Total amount of support: $12,454,868 in grants and scholarships authorized for fiscal year ended June 30, 2018.

REPRESENTATIVE AWARDS:
$5,000 to Dwelling Place for the development of a collaborative plan to integrate behavioral health and economic development solutions in the Heartside Neighborhood; $40,000 to Spectrum Health Foundation for continuation of the Youth Tobacco Prevention Program, a classroom-based tobacco prevention education for K-12 students, including education, advocacy and refusal skill development; $100,000 to Kids' Food Basket to preserve historical farmland within Grand Rapids' urban core.

APPLICATION INFO:
For the general fund, applicants fill out an online pre-application on the Foundation's web site. After committee review, applicants may be asked to submit a Full Proposal, with final grant disposition determined by the Board of Trustees.
Duration: Generally, one-time grants. Foundation will, under certain circumstances, award multiyear grants.
Deadline: Varies by Fund. No deadline for the General Fund; pre-applications are reviewed every two weeks.

PUBLICATIONS:
Annual report; quarterly newsletter.

IRS I.D.: 38-2877959

OFFICERS:
Diana R. Sieger, President
Stan Vander Roest, Chief Financial Officer
Laurie Craft, Vice President of Community Investment
Marilyn Zack, Vice President of Development
Kate Schmid, Vice President of Program
Ashley Lee, Vice President of Public Relations and Marketing

ADDRESS INQUIRIES TO:
Keri Jaynes, Grants Manager
(See address above.)

JOHN SIMON GUGGENHEIM MEMORIAL FOUNDATION   [135]
90 Park Avenue
New York, NY 10016
(212) 687-4470
Fax: (212) 697-3248
E-mail: fellowships@gf.org
Web Site: www.gf.org

FOUNDED: 1925

AREAS OF INTEREST:
Sciences, social sciences, humanities and the creative arts.

NAME(S) OF PROGRAMS:
● **Guggenheim Fellowships**

TYPE:
Fellowships.

YEAR PROGRAM STARTED: 1925

PURPOSE:
To further the development of scholars and artists by assisting them to engage in research in any field of knowledge and creation in any of the arts.

LEGAL BASIS:
Private foundation.

ELIGIBILITY:
The Fellowships are awarded to men and women who have already demonstrated exceptional capacity for productive scholarship or exceptional creative ability in the arts.

Fellowships are awarded through two annual competitions: one open to citizens and permanent residents of the U.S. and Canada, and the other open to citizens and permanent residents of Latin America and the Caribbean. The Fellowships will be awarded by the Trustees upon nominations made by a Committee of Selection.

FINANCIAL DATA:
The amounts of the grants will be adjusted to the needs of the Fellows, considering their other resources and the purpose and scope of their plans, in accord with the Foundation's annual fellowship budget.
Amount of support per award: Varies.
Total amount of support: Approximately $9,000,000 annually.

NO. AWARDS: Approximately 180 annually.

APPLICATION INFO:
Online application is available at the Foundation web site.
Duration: Appointments must be from six to 12 months. Fellows of the Foundation, until further notice from the Board of Trustees, may no longer seek renewed assistance.
Deadline: Applications must be submitted on or before September 17 for U.S. and Canadian competition. Fellowships to be announced the following April for U.S. competition.

PUBLICATIONS:
Annual report; announcement of Fellowship competition and recipients; application guidelines.

IRS I.D.: 13-5673173

OFFICERS:
Edward Hirsch, President
Andre Bernard, Vice President and Secretary

TRUSTEES:
Dwight E. Lee, Chairman
Emery Brown
Robert A. Caro
Joel Conarroe
Dorothy Tapper Goldman
Edward Hirsch
William P. Kelly
Steven Lavine
Lily Lynton
Eric S. Maskin
E. Wayne Nordberg
Stacy Schiff
Eric Schwartz
Cindy Sherman
Benjamin Taylor
Sandra Wijnberg
Ellen Taaffe Zwilich

ADDRESS INQUIRIES TO:
Keith Lewis, Program Officer
Fellowships Program
(See address above.)

*PLEASE NOTE:
Latin American and Caribbean Competition has been suspended pending examination of the program. The U.S. and Canadian competition is unaffected.

THE GEORGE GUND FOUNDATION   [136]
1845 Guildhall Building
45 Prospect Avenue West
Cleveland, OH 44115
(216) 241-3114
Fax: (216) 241-6560
E-mail: info@gundfdn.org
Web Site: gundfoundation.org

FOUNDED: 1952

AREAS OF INTEREST:
Education, economic development and community revitalization, human services, arts and environment.

TYPE:
General operating grants; Project/program grants.

YEAR PROGRAM STARTED: 1952

PURPOSE:
To enhance the quality of life, particularly for those living in the greater Cleveland area; to solve community problems; to improve living conditions, particularly for the poor and underprivileged; to provide opportunities for all people to live constructive lives in a peaceful world.

LEGAL BASIS:
Private foundation.

ELIGIBILITY:
Grants are made only to nonprofit, tax-exempt educational and philanthropic organizations. No awards are made to individuals. Grants for operating budget support will be considered only if the need is for limited duration and will accomplish some important purpose which will strengthen the future position of the institution. Preference will be given to pilot projects, innovative programs and research which hold promise of significant benefits of broad applicability.

GEOG. RESTRICTIONS: Primarily greater Cleveland and Cuyahoga County, Ohio.

FINANCIAL DATA:
Amount of support per award: Varies.
Total amount of support: $38,623,250 for the year 2018.

NO. MOST RECENT APPLICANTS: 287.

NO. AWARDS: 259 grants for the year 2018.

APPLICATION INFO:
Foundation requires that all applications for grants be submitted online at the Foundation's web site. Application materials to be uploaded with application include:
(1) organizational background;
(2) project description;
(3) project budget;
(4) organizational budget;
(5) list of current trustees;
(6) most recent audited financial statements and;
(7) climate change statement.
Duration: One year.

Deadline: March 15, July 15 and November 15, for board meetings to be held in July, November and February, respectively.

PUBLICATIONS:
Annual report; Guidelines for Grant Applicants (on Foundation web site).

TRUSTEES:
Geoffrey Gund, President and Treasurer
Ann L. Gund, Vice President
Catherine Gund, Secretary
Susanna Bien-Gund
Lara Gund
Zachary Gund
Mark Joseph
Randell McShepard
Anna Traggio

ADMINISTRATIVE STAFF:
David T. Abbott, Executive Director
Robert B. Jaquay, Associate Director and Senior Program Officer for Economic Development and Community Revitalization
Jennifer Coleman, Senior Program Officer, Arts
Ann K. Mullin, Senior Program Officer, Education
John Mitterholzer, Senior Program Officer, Environment
Marcia Egbert, Senior Program Officer, Human Services

ADDRESS INQUIRIES TO:
David T. Abbott, Executive Director or Cynthia Gasparro
Grants and Office Administrator
(See address above.)

HALL FAMILY FOUNDATION   [137]
P.O. Box 419580
Mail Drop 323
Kansas City, MO 64141-6580
(816) 274-8516
Fax: (816) 274-8547
E-mail: hff@hallmark.com
Web Site: www.hallfamilyfoundation.org

FOUNDED: 1943

AREAS OF INTEREST:
Early and K-12th-grade education, higher education, children, youth and families, community development, the arts, and support of community-wide efforts that seek to provide long-term solutions to high-priority local issues.

TYPE:
Capital grants; Project/program grants; Training grants.

YEAR PROGRAM STARTED: 1943

PURPOSE:
To promote the health, welfare and happiness of school-age children; to promote the advancement and diffusion of knowledge; to fund activities for the improvement of public health; to advance social welfare.

ELIGIBILITY:
Applying nonprofit organizations must be 501(c)(3) and must have been in operation for at least five years. No grants are made to individuals. Grants are made to a religious organization only if its program is of a nonsectarian nature.

GEOG. RESTRICTIONS: Usually, organizations in the greater Kansas City, Missouri area.

FINANCIAL DATA:
Amount of support per award: Varies.
Total amount of support: Varies.

APPLICATION INFO:
Prospective grant recipients should first submit a brief letter of inquiry. Those applicants whose request appears to fall within the Foundation's areas of interest and to meet its guidelines will be asked to submit a full proposal.
Duration: Two to five years, depending on the type of project.

HARDEN FOUNDATION   [138]
1636 Ercia Street
Salinas, CA 93906
(831) 442-3005
Fax: (831) 443-1429
E-mail: joe@hardenfoundation.org
Web Site: www.hardenfoundation.org

FOUNDED: 1963

AREAS OF INTEREST:
Children, youth and family, senior citizens, animal welfare and the environment, agriculture, education, arts and culture, and health.

TYPE:
Capital grants; General operating grants; Project/program grants.

YEAR PROGRAM STARTED: 1963

PURPOSE:
To fund groups working in the Foundation's areas of interest.

LEGAL BASIS:
Private foundation.

ELIGIBILITY:
The Foundation does not fund schools, churches or religious activities, or individuals for endowments or fund-raising. Eligible organizations must be of a 501(c)(3), not-for-profit character.

GEOG. RESTRICTIONS: Monterey County, California.

FINANCIAL DATA:
Amount of support per award: Typically $5,000 to $100,000.
Total amount of support: $1,857,200 in grants awarded for the year 2018.

APPLICATION INFO:
Guidelines and application forms are available online.
Duration: Operating grants for start-up programs: Generally up to two years.
Deadline: March 1 and September 1.

ADDRESS INQUIRIES TO:
Joseph C. Grainger, Executive Director
(See address above.)

THE JOHN A. HARTFORD FOUNDATION, INC.   [139]
55 East 59th Street, 16th Floor
New York, NY 10022
(212) 832-7788
Fax: (212) 593-4913
E-mail: mark.barreiro@johnahartford.org
Web Site: johnahartford.org

FOUNDED: 1929

AREAS OF INTEREST:
Age-friendly health systems, family caregiving, and serious illness and end of life.

TYPE:
Demonstration grants; Matching gifts; Project/program grants; Research grants; Technical assistance.

YEAR PROGRAM STARTED: 1983

PURPOSE:
To improve the care of older adults.

LEGAL BASIS:
Private foundation.

ELIGIBILITY:
Grantee organizations must be located in the U.S. and must have 501(c)(3) IRS tax-exempt designation.

The Foundation's prior grantmaking related to enhancing geriatric research and training, and integrating and improving health-related services to the elderly. Currently, the Foundation makes grants that will put geriatrics expertise to work in all health care settings by:
(1) advancing practice change and innovation;
(2) supporting team-based care through interdisciplinary education of all health care providers;
(3) supporting policies and regulations that promote better care and;
(4) developing and disseminating new, evidence-based models that deliver better, more cost-effective health care.

The Foundation awards both single and multiple-year grants. No support for general purposes, endowment funds or capital budgets.

GEOG. RESTRICTIONS: United States.

FINANCIAL DATA:
Amount of support per award: Varies.
Total amount of support: $28,949,667 in grants awarded for the year 2019.

NO. AWARDS: 17 for the year 2019.

APPLICATION INFO:
All proposals are by invitation only from one of the Foundation's program officers, the program director, or the president.
Duration: One to three years.

PUBLICATIONS:
Annual report.

TRUSTEES:
Margaret L. Wolff, Chairperson
Christopher T.H. Pell, Co-Vice Chairperson
Earl A. Samson, III, Co-Vice Chairperson
John H. Allen
David Di Martino
William Donohue
Charles M. Farkas
John R. Mach, Jr., M.D.
Audrey A. McNiff
Elizabeth A. Palmer
Nirav R. Shah

STAFF:
Terry Fulmer, Ph.D., R.N., President
Marcus R. Escobedo, M.P.A., Vice President, Communications and Senior Program Officer
Eva Cheng, Vice President, Finance
Rani E. Synder, M.P.A., Vice President, Program
Mark Barreiro, Senior Grants Officer
Amy J. Berman, R.N., Senior Program Officer
Scott Bane, Program Officer
Jane Carmody, Program Officer
Rutuma M. Gandhi, Accounting Manager
Melida Galvez, Senior Accountant
Julianne N. McLean, Program Secretary

ADDRESS INQUIRIES TO:
Mark Barreiro, Senior Grants Officer
(See address above.)

HENDERSON FOUNDATION [140]

P.O. Box 420
Sudbury, MA 01776-0420
(978) 443-4646
Fax: (978) 443-9510
E-mail: rhenderson@sudburypines.com

FOUNDED: 1947

AREAS OF INTEREST:
Charitable, educational, religious, health, political, environmental, and community outreach.

TYPE:
General operating grants.

PURPOSE:
To continue support to general operations of those organizations now supported.

LEGAL BASIS:
Nonprofit foundation.

ELIGIBILITY:
Funding limited to public charities with a nonprofit 501(c)(3) tax-exempt status. The Foundation does not support activities for which the IRS requires grantor's responsibility and reports.

GEOG. RESTRICTIONS: United States.

FINANCIAL DATA:
Amount of support per award: Minimum $500.
Total amount of support: Varies.

NO. MOST RECENT APPLICANTS: 150.

NO. AWARDS: 100.

APPLICATION INFO:
Send letter of inquiry with documentation of nonprofit 501(c)(3) tax-exempt status.
Duration: Varies.
Deadline: December 31.

TRUSTEES:
Barclay G. Henderson
Roberta Henderson
Mrs. Joseph C. Petrone

ADDRESS INQUIRIES TO:
Roberta Henderson, Trustee
(See address above.)

B. KEITH & NORMA F. HEUERMANN FOUNDATION [141]

Whitney, Newman, Mersch and Otto
1228 L Street
Aurora, NE 68818
(402) 694-3161

FOUNDED: 1994

AREAS OF INTEREST:
Children, the aged, the developmentally challenged, disabled, physically impaired, youth education and agriculturally related activities.

TYPE:
Capital grants; Matching gifts; Project/program grants; Research grants; Technical assistance.

YEAR PROGRAM STARTED: 1994

PURPOSE:
To support programs that meet the needs of society and improve the quality of life preferably in communities in rural Nebraska.

LEGAL BASIS:
Private foundation.

ELIGIBILITY:
Grants are made to organizations that have tax-exempt status under Section 501(c)(3) of the Internal Revenue Code. No grants are made to individuals. The Foundation does not loan funds to grant applicants.

GEOG. RESTRICTIONS: Rural areas in Nebraska.

FINANCIAL DATA:
Amount of support per award: $1,000 to $25,000.
Total amount of support: Varies.

APPLICATION INFO:
The Foundation does not have an application form. The Grant Proposal should identify a special need or project to which funds will be applied including the objectives to be attained, people or groups who will benefit, work plans or timetables for achieving the stated objectives, and any other means of support. A copy of the 501(c)(3) letter from the IRS should accompany the application. Provide the grant applicant's federal ID number.

Grant Proposal should be limited to two pages. Supporting documents such as project budget, other resources, names of supporters, and background information about the organization may be attached to the proposal. Stapled proposals are favored over bound ones. Brevity is appreciated.

Applicants must submit five original copies of the proposal.
Duration: Proposal may be for a project which extends over several years; however, the Foundation may review and make grants only on an annual basis.
Deadline: Proposals may be submitted at any time. The Directors convene at least three times per year at meetings to be scheduled in its discretion to review requests for grants.

PUBLICATIONS:
Guidelines.

IRS I.D.: 47-0748466

ADDRESS INQUIRIES TO:
Timothy J. Otto
(See address above.)

THE WILLIAM AND FLORA HEWLETT FOUNDATION [142]

2121 Sand Hill Road
Menlo Park, CA 94025
(650) 234-4500
Fax: (650) 234-4501
E-mail: communications@hewlett.org
Web Site: hewlett.org

FOUNDED: 1966

AREAS OF INTEREST:
Education, the environment, performing arts, philanthropy, global development and population, democracy, and cybersecurity.

NAME(S) OF PROGRAMS:
• **Education**
• **Environment**
• **Global Development and Population**
• **Performing Arts**
• **Philanthropy**

TYPE:
Capital grants; Challenge/matching grants; Conferences/seminars; Development grants; Endowments; General operating grants; Project/program grants; Research grants; Seed money grants; Technical assistance; Training grants; Travel grants.

YEAR PROGRAM STARTED: 1966

PURPOSE:
To help people build measurably better lives.

LEGAL BASIS:
Private foundation.

ELIGIBILITY:
The Foundation does not fund individuals and generally does not fund scholarships, building construction, or unincorporated associations or groups.

Requirements vary by area of interest and are available on the Foundation web site.

FINANCIAL DATA:
Total assets of $10.8 billion as of December 31, 2019.
Amount of support per award: $436,406 average for the year 2019.
Total amount of support: $454,458,000 in grants awarded for the year ended December 31, 2019.
Matching fund requirements: Foundation matches eligible employees' contributions to qualifying organizations.

NO. AWARDS: 1,043 for the year 2019.

APPLICATION INFO:
Information may be obtained at the Foundation web site.
Duration: Generally, one to three years.
Deadline: Varies according to program.

PUBLICATIONS:
Annual report; application guidelines.

BOARD OF DIRECTORS:
Stephen C. Neal, Chairman
Larry Kramer, President
Mariano-Florentino Cuellar
Alecia A. DeCoudreaux
Persis S. Drell
Nathalie Farman-Farma
Eric Gimon
Billy Hewlett
Patricia A. House
Koh Boon Hwee
Brian Jaffe
James Manyika
Rakesh Rajani
Sarah Singh

ADDRESS INQUIRIES TO:
Vidya Krishnamurthy
Director of Communications
(See address above.)

HILLSDALE FUND, INC. [143]

600 Green Valley Road
Suite 200
Greensboro, NC 27408
(336) 574-8696

FOUNDED: 1963

TYPE:
Project/program grants.

LEGAL BASIS:
Family foundation.

ELIGIBILITY:
Must have 501(c)(3) status of Internal Revenue Code to be eligible. Grants will not be made available for indirect costs or overhead as opposed to direct funding, routine, recurring operating expenses, conferences and seminars, travel and study, or individuals for any purpose.

FINANCIAL DATA:
Amount of support per award: Varies.
Total amount of support: Approximately $1,400,000 for the year 2018.

APPLICATION INFO:
Applicants should contact the Foundation for guidelines and application form.
Duration: Varies.
Deadline: Varies. Contact Fund for specific deadlines.

ADDRESS INQUIRIES TO:
Mary Scott, Executive Director
(See address above.)

HOBLITZELLE FOUNDATION [144]

5556 Caruth Haven Lane, Suite 200
Dallas, TX 75225
(214) 373-0462
Fax: (214) 750-7412
E-mail: krobbins@hoblitzelle.org
Web Site: www.hoblitzelle.org

FOUNDED: 1942

AREAS OF INTEREST:
Education, cultural affairs, social welfare and health.

TYPE:
Capital grants; Challenge/matching grants; Matching gifts.

YEAR PROGRAM STARTED: 1942

LEGAL BASIS:
Private foundation.

ELIGIBILITY:
Educational institutions, hospitals, community agencies, youth and other welfare programs and organizations with appropriate interests are eligible.

GEOG. RESTRICTIONS: Texas, primarily Dallas.

FINANCIAL DATA:
Amount of support per award: $25,000 to $500,000.
Total amount of support: Approximately $6,500,000 annually.

NO. MOST RECENT APPLICANTS: 200.

NO. AWARDS: 70.

APPLICATION INFO:
Grant applications should be submitted online. Formal oral presentations to the Board are not allowed.
Duration: One year and multiyear.
Deadline: April 15 for May meeting, August 15 for September meeting and December 15 for January meeting. If holiday or weekend, next business day.

PUBLICATIONS:
Annual report; application guidelines.

IRS I.D.: 75-6003984

BOARD OF DIRECTORS AND OFFICERS:
John W. Dayton, Chairman
Karen L. Shuford, Vice Chairman
Katie H. Robbins, President and Chief Executive Officer
Jere W. Thompson, Jr., Treasurer
Raphael M. Anchia
Holland P. Gary
Lydia H. Novakov
Daniel K. Podolsky, M.D.
Catherine Rose

ADDRESS INQUIRIES TO:
Katie H. Robbins, President and Chief Executive Officer
(See address above.)

HOUSTON ENDOWMENT INC. [145]

600 Travis, Suite 6400
Houston, TX 77002-3000
(713) 238-8100
Fax: (713) 238-8101
E-mail: connect@houstonendowment.org
Web Site: www.houstonendowment.org

FOUNDED: 1937

AREAS OF INTEREST:
Arts, education, environment, health and human services.

TYPE:
Capital grants; General operating grants; Project/program grants. Program support. Building completion.

LEGAL BASIS:
Private foundation.

ELIGIBILITY:
Organizations exempt under Section 501(c)(3). No grants are made directly to individuals. All scholarship funds are disbursed through recipient institutions. No grants made outside the U.S.

GEOG. RESTRICTIONS: Harris County and contiguous counties (Brazoria, Chambers, Fort Bend, Galveston, Liberty, Montgomery and Waller).

FINANCIAL DATA:
Amount of support per award: Varies.
Total amount of support: $76,885,080 in grants approved for the year 2017.

NO. AWARDS: Grants to over 130 organizations for the year 2017.

APPLICATION INFO:
Application must be made online. Written applications will not be considered. Scholarships are never awarded directly on the basis of personal inquiry but are administered by colleges and universities.
Duration: One year to multiyear.

PUBLICATIONS:
Annual report.

MABEL Y. HUGHES CHARITABLE TRUST [146]

Wells Fargo Wealth Management
100 North Main Street, 6th Floor
MAC-D4001-065
Winston-Salem, NC 27101
(888) 235-4351 ext. 241539
E-mail: grantadministration@wellsfargo.com
Web Site: www.wellsfargo.com/private-foundations/hughes-charitable-trust

FOUNDED: 1969

AREAS OF INTEREST:
Arts, animals, environment, humanities, religion, health, education, culture and human services in the state of Colorado, with emphasis on Denver metropolitan area.

TYPE:
General operating grants; Project/program grants.

PURPOSE:
To provide funding to nonprofit and educational institutions that address vital community needs especially, but not limited to, human services.

LEGAL BASIS:
Private tax-exempt foundation.

ELIGIBILITY:
501(c)(3) tax-exempt organizations in Colorado only may apply. No grants are awarded to individuals.

GEOG. RESTRICTIONS: Colorado.

FINANCIAL DATA:
Amount of support per award: $5,000 to $25,000.
Total amount of support: Approximately $500,000 per year.

NO. MOST RECENT APPLICANTS: Approximately 300.

NO. AWARDS: 50.

APPLICATION INFO:
Submit a brief letter describing project, why needed, population to be served, brief line-item budget, information about organization seeking funds and its accomplishments to date, starting and ending dates, plans for postgrant funding and project evaluation, and a copy of latest 501(c)(3) exemption.
Duration: No grants awarded on a continuing basis.
Deadline: March 1, July 1 and November 1.

TRUSTEES:
W.R. Alexander

ADDRESS INQUIRIES TO:
Chris Poplin, Administrator
(See address above.)

THE HYDE AND WATSON FOUNDATION [147]

31-F Mountain Boulevard
Warren, NJ 07059-5617
(908) 753-3700
Fax: (908) 753-0004
E-mail: info@hydeandwatson.org
Web Site: www.hydeandwatson.org

FOUNDED: 1983

AREAS OF INTEREST:
Broad fields include education, social services, arts, health, religion and humanities.

TYPE:
Capital grants; Challenge/matching grants. The Foundation supports capital projects such as hard costs related to purchase and relocation of facilities and/or building improvements, purchase of capital equipment and furnishings, and other one-time capital needs.

LEGAL BASIS:
Private.

ELIGIBILITY:
Grants are made to nonprofit organizations that have received 501(c)(3) and 509(a)(1) or 509(a)(2) status from the IRS. In general, the Foundation does not accept applications for endowment, operating support, benefit fund-raisers, annual fund appeals, or from fiscal agents.

GEOG. RESTRICTIONS: Primarily the five boroughs of New York City, and Essex, Morris and Union counties in New Jersey.

FINANCIAL DATA:
Amount of support per award: Average grant: $5,000 to $10,000.
Total amount of support: $5,709,400 for the year ended December 31, 2018.

NO. MOST RECENT APPLICANTS: 804 for the year 2018.

NO. AWARDS: 540 for the year 2018.

APPLICATION INFO:
Applicants must submit the following:
(1) a completed Grant Application Form
(entered online or in paper form); document
is available at the Foundation web site;
(2) a brief narrative (no longer than three
pages), signed by an authorized official,
summarizing the background of the
organization and constituency served, the
purpose of the appeal, project total and
amount requested, anticipated time frame for
the project and how the equipment/capital
improvement will benefit the organization;
(3) a project budget with line items;
(4) an operating budget for the current fiscal
year;
(5) a list of corporate and foundation
supporters for the most recent fiscal year;
(6) a list of the Board of Directors/Trustees
and their business affiliations;
(7) an audited financial report for the most
recent fiscal year. If an audit is not
performed, the most recent Form 990 will be
accepted;
(8) a copy of the organization's annual report
(optional) and;
(9) a copy of the organization's most recent
501(c)(3) and 509(a) IRS ruling letter(s).

If one's organization is a former grantee,
please note that the Foundation will not
consider any future proposals from one's
organization until a report is provided for any
previous grants received from the
Foundation. The "Grant Report Form" is
available on the Foundation web site.

Duration: Typically one year.

Deadline: Spring grant applications are
accepted between November 15 and February
15. Fall grant applications are accepted
between June 15 and September 15. There is
an ongoing review of proposals during the
application period.

PUBLICATIONS:
Program policy statement and grant
application guidelines.

IRS I.D.: 22-2425725

OFFICERS:
William V. Engel, Chairman
Brunilda Moriarty, President
Hans Dekker, Secretary
Thomas W. Berry, Treasurer
Sarah A. Kalra, Assistant Secretary
Allison J. Pena, Assistant Secretary
John W. Holman, III, Assistant Treasurer
Thomas H. MacCowatt, Assistant Treasurer
Maureen T. McCutcheon, Assistant Treasurer

DIRECTORS:
Deborah J. Barker
Thomas W. Berry
Hunter W. Corbin
Hans Dekker
William V. Engel
John W. Holman, Jr.
John W. Holman, III
Anne-Marie Kim
Thomas H. MacCowatt
Brunilda Moriarty
Robert W. Parsons, Jr.
Andrew J. Thompson

ADDRESS INQUIRIES TO:
Brunilda Moriarty, President
(See address above.)

*PLEASE NOTE:
Because there is a finite amount of funds
budgeted for each grants cycle, it is strongly
suggested that applicants submit proposals
early in the application period.

Appeals or inquiries submitted by e-mail will
not be considered.

IDAHO COMMUNITY FOUNDATION   [148]

210 West State Street
Boise, ID 83702
(208) 342-3535
Fax: (208) 342-3577
E-mail: elly@idahocf.org
Web Site: www.idahocf.org

FOUNDED: 1988

AREAS OF INTEREST:
Arts, civic affairs, community, conservation,
culture, education, environment, health and
human services.

NAME(S) OF PROGRAMS:
- **Bonner County Fund for Arts
  Enhancement**
- **Bonner County Human Rights Task
  Force Fund**
- **The F.M., Anne G., and Beverly B.
  Bistline Foundation Fund**
- **CenturyLink Middle School
  Philanthropy Program**
- **Junior Garnier and Bud Ashford
  Military Veterans Fund**
- **Idaho Future Fund**
- **lfft Foundation Fund**
- **Lassahn-Worrell Fund for Community
  Support Services**
- **North Idaho Action Fund**
- **Perc H. Shelton and Gladys A. Pospisil
  Shelton Foundation Advised Fund**
- **Regional Grant**

TYPE:
Capital grants; General operating grants;
Scholarships.

YEAR PROGRAM STARTED: 1988

PURPOSE:
To enrich the quality of life throughout
Idaho.

LEGAL BASIS:
Community foundation; 501(c)(3) public
charity.

ELIGIBILITY:
Grants are made to organizations that are
nonprofit. Nonsectarian religious programs
and government entities may apply. No
grants are made to individuals.

GEOG. RESTRICTIONS: Idaho.

FINANCIAL DATA:
Amount of support per award: Regional
Grants: Up to $5,000. Others unlimited.
Total amount of support: Varies.

APPLICATION INFO:
Form can be downloaded from the
Foundation web site.
Duration: Varies.
Deadline: Varies per grant or scholarship.

IRS I.D.: 82-0425063

ADMINISTRATION:
Karen Belowith, Chief Executive Officer
Elly Davis, Community Impact Officer

ADDRESS INQUIRIES TO:
Elly Davis, Community Impact Officer
(See address above.)

INDEPENDENCE FOUNDATION   [149]

Offices at the Bellevue
200 South Broad Street, Suite 1101
Philadelphia, PA 19102
(215) 985-4009
Fax: (215) 985-3989
E-mail: ssherman@independencefoundation.org
Web Site: www.independencefoundation.org

FOUNDED: 1932

AREAS OF INTEREST:
Community-based care, health promotion,
family planning and comprehensive health
care services where issues of quality, access
and cost are taken into consideration; culture,
arts and legal aid and assistance to the
disadvantaged; visual and performing arts.

NAME(S) OF PROGRAMS:
- **Individual Artists
  Fellowship/Performing and Visual Arts**
- **New Theater Works Initiative**
- **Public Interest Law Fellowships**

TYPE:
Challenge/matching grants; Fellowships;
General operating grants; Project/program
grants.

YEAR PROGRAM STARTED: 1993

PURPOSE:
To encourage and support health services; to
have a valuable impact on the quality of
health care services; to strengthen nursing
education's focus on community-based care
in both Philadelphia and surrounding
Pennsylvania counties.

LEGAL BASIS:
Private foundation.

ELIGIBILITY:
No grants to individuals.

GEOG. RESTRICTIONS: Philadelphia and four
surrounding counties of Bucks, Chester,
Delaware and Montgomery.

FINANCIAL DATA:
Amount of support per award: Average:
$3,000 to $10,000; Multiyear: Up to $50,000.

Matching fund requirements: Match of
contributions by individual new donors or
increase in contributions by current
individual donors
(nongovernmental/nonfoundation funds).

APPLICATION INFO:
Each year the Foundation sends out a limited
number of Requests for Proposals (RFP) in
each of the funding initiatives. Organizations
not previously funded by the Foundation are
encouraged to send a two-page Letter of
Inquiry including organizational background
information, amount being requested, and a
description of the program/services for which
the funds will be used.

Duration: Varies.

Deadline: Letters of Inquiry are accepted
January 1 to January 31. Deadlines vary.

PUBLICATIONS:
Annual report; application guidelines.

IRS I.D.: 23-1352110

ADDRESS INQUIRIES TO:
Susan E. Sherman
President and Chief Executive Officer
(See address above.)

ANN JACKSON FAMILY FOUNDATION [150]

P.O. Box 5580
Santa Barbara, CA 93150-5580
(805) 455-0505
Web Site: www.annjacksonfamilyfoundation.org

FOUNDED: 1978

AREAS OF INTEREST:
Community infrastructure, art, human services and health.

TYPE:
Capital grants; General operating grants.

PURPOSE:
To enhance the community.

LEGAL BASIS:
Private foundation.

ELIGIBILITY:
Grants are made to organizations that have tax-exempt status under Section 501(c)(3) of the Internal Revenue Code. No grants are made to individuals.

GEOG. RESTRICTIONS: Primarily Santa Barbara County, California.

FINANCIAL DATA:
Amount of support per award: Typically $1,000 to $10,000 for general operating grants.
Total amount of support: Varies.

NO. AWARDS: Over 100 annually.

APPLICATION INFO:
For grants of $10,000 or more and all capital requests, the Foundation encourages applicants to use the Common Grant Application form, a link to which is available on the web site. For grants under $10,000, organizations may also put their request in the form of a one- to two-page letter which clearly states the compelling nature of the request.

If an organization has not previously been funded by the Foundation, a one-page letter of intent will be accepted.
Duration: One year, with occasional multiyear. Renewal by reapplication.

ADDRESS INQUIRIES TO:
Palmer G. Jackson, Jr., Trustee
(See address above.)

THE JACKSON FOUNDATION [151]

c/o U.S. Bank, NA
111 S.W. 5th Avenue, Suite 600
Portland, OR 97204
(503) 464-4920
E-mail: march.voyles@usbank.com
Web Site: www.thejacksonfoundation.com

FOUNDED: 1960

AREAS OF INTEREST:
Arts/performing arts, economic development, substance abuse, human services, minorities, housing, disabilities, humanities, education, environment, health, children/youth, aged and women.

TYPE:
Capital grants; Challenge/matching grants; Development grants; General operating grants; Matching gifts; Project/program grants; Research grants.

YEAR PROGRAM STARTED: 1963

PURPOSE:
To support new programs that will enhance and expand the well-being of individuals, with a focus on people in the Portland metropolitan area, by granting funds for the purpose of health and education.

LEGAL BASIS:
Private foundation.

ELIGIBILITY:
Grants are made to 501(c)(3) organizations.

GEOG. RESTRICTIONS: Oregon.

FINANCIAL DATA:
Amount of support per award: $1,000 to $50,000; average $3,370.

NO. MOST RECENT APPLICANTS: 250.

NO. AWARDS: 125.

APPLICATION INFO:
Guidelines and application forms are available online.
Duration: One year.
Deadline: March 31, June 30, September 30 and December 31.

ADDRESS INQUIRIES TO:
Trustees, Jackson Foundation
(See address or e-mail above.)

HENRY M. JACKSON FOUNDATION [152]

1200 Fifth Avenue
Suite 1450
Seattle, WA 98101
(206) 682-8565
E-mail: foundation@hmjackson.org
Web Site: www.hmjackson.org

FOUNDED: 1983

AREAS OF INTEREST:
International affairs, public service, environment/natural resources and human rights.

NAME(S) OF PROGRAMS:
- **Environmental and Natural Resources Management Program**
- **Human Rights Program**
- **International Affairs Education Program**
- **Public Service Program**

TYPE:
Challenge/matching grants; Conferences/seminars; Internships; Professorships; Project/program grants; Seed money grants.

YEAR PROGRAM STARTED: 1983

PURPOSE:
To advance education and public understanding of critical public policy issues in the four priority areas above.

LEGAL BASIS:
Publicly supported foundation.

ELIGIBILITY:
Grants are made to private, nonprofit, tax-exempt organizations under 501(c)(3) and public, tax-exempt entities under 170(c). No grants are made to individuals.

No grants for capital or general operating expenses.

FINANCIAL DATA:
Amount of support per award: $1,000 to $50,000.
Total amount of support: Average: $250,000 per year.

NO. AWARDS: 10 to 15 per year.

REPRESENTATIVE AWARDS:
$71,000 to support guest faculty on topics of current foreign policy concerns for senior-level courses at the University of Washington's Jackson School of International Studies; $15,000 to support the publication and dissemination of a report on urban sprawl's toll on open space and farmland; $10,000 to create two new exhibits representing gulag life during different epochs of Soviet history on the site of a former prison labor camp; $34,536 for a program that places young adults on city boards and commissions.

APPLICATION INFO:
Proposals should include:
(1) a cover letter summarizing the project and amount requested;
(2) a detailed budget, implementation strategy, identification of board and/or those responsible for the project and plans for evaluation and;
(3) IRS tax-exempt status determination letter.
Duration: Varies.
Deadline: January 1, April 1, July 1 and October 1, for awards announced in March, June, September and December, respectively.

PUBLICATIONS:
Application guidelines; annual report; newsletter.

IRS I.D.: 52-1313011

OFFICERS:
Craig Gannett, President
Susan Wickwire, Vice President
Linda Mason Wilgis, Vice President
David Rostov, Treasurer
Anna Marie Laurence, Secretary
Joel C. Merkel, General Counsel

JACKSONVILLE JAGUARS FOUNDATION [153]

One TIAA Bank Field Drive
Jacksonville, FL 32202
(904) 633-5437
Fax: (904) 633-5683
Web Site: www.jaguars.com/community

FOUNDED: 1993

AREAS OF INTEREST:
Social welfare for disadvantaged youths.

TYPE:
General operating grants; Project/program grants. Limited capital grants that target economically and socially "at-risk" youths in northeast Florida.

YEAR PROGRAM STARTED: 1994

PURPOSE:
To support programs benefiting economically and socially disadvantaged youth, families and other NFL and team charitable initiatives.

LEGAL BASIS:
Corporation foundation.

ELIGIBILITY:
Organizations in northeast Florida that work for disadvantaged youths on a nonsectarian basis. Must have 501(c)(3) IRS documentation.

No grants to individuals, schools or single-disease organizations.

GEOG. RESTRICTIONS: Baker, Clay, Duval, Nassau, and Saint Johns counties, Florida.

FINANCIAL DATA:
Amount of support per award: Varies.

Total amount of support: Over $2,000,000 for the year 2017.

CO-OP FUNDING PROGRAMS: Youth Anti-Obesity Grants with Baptist Health; Teen Pregnancy Prevention Grants with Blue Cross Blue Shield of Florida.

NO. MOST RECENT APPLICANTS: Over 50.

NO. AWARDS: Over 50.

APPLICATION INFO:
Submit a one-page summary that includes the specific goals, objectives, proposed activities and results expected to the Foundation.

Duration: One year. Renewal by reapplication.

Deadline: July and February.

ADDRESS INQUIRIES TO:
Peter Racine, President
(See address above.)

JOHNSON & JOHNSON FAMILY OF COMPANIES   [154]
One Johnson & Johnson Plaza
New Brunswick, NJ 08933
(732) 524-0400
Web Site: www.jnj.com

FOUNDED: 1953

AREAS OF INTEREST:
Health care and education.

TYPE:
Matching gifts; Project/program grants; Research grants. International programs, product donation, cash grants. Emphasis on health care, with a special interest in maternal and child health care issues. The Company administers major programs in partnership with selected nonprofit organizations. Grants largely extended through these programs on a Request for Proposal basis.

The Corporation conducts extensive product giving program but only through established partnerships with selected nonprofit organizations. No unsolicited requests accepted.

The Corporation also conducts large matching gifts program in areas of higher education, hospitals, disease-specific organizations, cultural organizations and prevention and treatment of substance abuse.

PURPOSE:
To make life-changing, long-term differences in human health by targeting the world's major health-related issues through community-based partnerships.

ELIGIBILITY:
Grants are made to organizations with 501(c)(3) status. Grants are not made for endowments, appeals for unrestricted funds, tours, fund-raising galas and sporting events, political, fraternal or athletic groups, sectarian or religious organizations, capital expenditures, individuals or loans. Priority is given to activities and needs in locations where the company has a presence in the U.S. and Puerto Rico.

FINANCIAL DATA:
Amount of support per award: Varies.
Total amount of support: Varies.

NO. AWARDS: More than 600 grants.

APPLICATION INFO:
No unsolicited requests are accepted.

PUBLICATIONS:
Corporate Contributions report; application guidelines, policy statement.

STAFF:
Frank Welvaert, Vice President, Global Community Impact
Ben Davies, Executive Director, Trust EMEA Team

ADDRESS INQUIRIES TO:
Charitable Contributions
(See address above.)

JOHNSON CONTROLS FOUNDATION   [155]
5757 North Green Bay Avenue
Milwaukee, WI 53209-4408
(414) 524-2296
Web Site: www.johnsoncontrols.com

FOUNDED: 1952

AREAS OF INTEREST:
Higher education, health and social services, civic activities, culture and arts.

TYPE:
Matching gifts; Project/program grants. The Foundation matches the personal gifts of employees, retirees and directors to accredited colleges and universities, community arts and cultural organizations and to United Way in the aggregate from its U.S. company units.

PURPOSE:
To be operated for charitable purposes which include the distribution and application of financial support to soundly managed and operated organizations or causes which are fundamentally philanthropic.

LEGAL BASIS:
Corporate foundation.

ELIGIBILITY:
Contributions are limited to organizations which are exempt from taxation under the Internal Revenue Code. Applicant must meet one or more of the Foundation's funding priorities and benefit communities where Johnson Controls, Inc. has operations and employees work and live. Special consideration is given to those requests which impact the Milwaukee community.

No gifts will be made to any municipal, state, federal agency or department or to any organization established to influence legislation. No distribution will be made to a private individual. No gifts will be made to sectarian institutions or programs whose services are limited to members of any one religious group or whose funds are used primarily for the propagation of a religion. Grants are not usually given to public or private pre-schools, elementary or secondary institutions, but are limited to colleges and universities.

GEOG. RESTRICTIONS: United States.

FINANCIAL DATA:
Amount of support per award: Varies.
Total amount of support: Grants of more than $7,000,000 annually.
Matching fund requirements: $50 to $3,000 on a 1:1 basis per individual, per organization, per year to U.S. educational institutions, U.S. arts and cultural organizations and U.S. civic organizations.

NO. AWARDS: Up to 40.

REPRESENTATIVE AWARDS:
$300,000 to Discovery World at Pier Wisconsin; $19,525 to Milwaukee Symphony Orchestra; $21,000 to Milwaukee Film; $10,000 to the University of Wisconsin, Madison.

APPLICATION INFO:
Grant proposals must be submitted online.

Duration: Most grants are one-time only.

Deadline: Proposals submitted after October 1 will be reviewed the following calendar year.

ADDRESS INQUIRIES TO:
Johnson Controls Foundation
P.O. Box 591
Milwaukee, WI 53201-0591

MAGIC JOHNSON FOUNDATION   [156]
9100 Wilshire Boulevard
Suite 700, East Tower
Beverly Hills, CA 90212
(310) 246-4400
Fax: (310) 786-8796
Web Site: magicjohnson.org

FOUNDED: 1991

AREAS OF INTEREST:
Youth; HIV/AIDS education, prevention and care.

NAME(S) OF PROGRAMS:
● **Magic Johnson Foundation HIV/AIDS Grant**

TYPE:
Project/program grants; Technical assistance.

PURPOSE:
To support organizations and programs specializing in HIV/AIDS education, prevention and care, and in the areas of education, social needs and health issues of young people.

LEGAL BASIS:
National public charity.

ELIGIBILITY:
Organizations classified as 501(c)(3) by the IRS can apply. Funding will not be considered for projects by individuals and families. Advertising or sponsorship for other funding events are not eligible to receive funds. Research grants, conferences, travel, videos and capital acquisitions are also excluded.

GEOG. RESTRICTIONS: Northern and southern California; Washington, DC; Atlanta, Georgia; Chicago, Illinois; Baltimore, Maryland; New York, New York; Cleveland, Ohio; Houston, Texas.

FINANCIAL DATA:
Amount of support per award: Grants: $5,000 to $10,000.
Total amount of support: Varies.

APPLICATION INFO:
Grants are awarded by invitation only, without exception.

Duration: Grants: One year.

PUBLICATIONS:
Annual report; grant guidelines.

ADDRESS INQUIRIES TO:
Shane Jenkins, Vice President
(See address above.)

DAISY MARQUIS JONES FOUNDATION [157]

1600 South Avenue
Suite 250
Rochester, NY 14620-3921
(585) 461-4950
E-mail: mail@dmjf.org
Web Site: www.dmjf.org

FOUNDED: 1968

AREAS OF INTEREST:
Disadvantaged children and families, access to health care, assistance to senior citizens and economic security for families.

TYPE:
Capital grants; Challenge/matching grants; Development grants; General operating grants; Matching gifts; Project/program grants.

YEAR PROGRAM STARTED: 1968

PURPOSE:
To improve the well-being of residents of Monroe and Yates counties, NY, particularly within the city of Rochester; to meet the needs of the disadvantaged, focusing on prevention; to develop children and families to their maximum potential.

LEGAL BASIS:
Not-for-profit, private foundation.

ELIGIBILITY:
Applicants must be nonprofit, tax-exempt organizations in Monroe and Yates counties, NY. The Foundation does not consider requests for aid for basic research, private schools, the arts, or religious purposes. The Foundation does not make grants to individuals.

GEOG. RESTRICTIONS: Monroe and Yates counties, New York.

FINANCIAL DATA:
Amount of support per award: Varies.

Total amount of support: $1,902,676 in grants committed in 2018.

Matching fund requirements: Stipulated with specific programs.

NO. AWARDS: 107 grants in 2018.

REPRESENTATIVE AWARDS:
$125,000 to Center for Youth Services to support the Alternative to Out-of-School Suspension Program and New Beginnings School; $50,000 to Greater Rochester Summer Learning Association for PreK-3rd grade reading skills; $45,000 to Seneca Park Zoo Society to support the Butterfly Beltway Program; $50,000 to Lifespan of Greater Rochester to support senior citizens; $25,000 to Neighborworks Rochester to support the neighborhood reviltalization program.

APPLICATION INFO:
Applicant must complete the inquiry form that is available on the Foundation web site. The Foundation will reply by e-mail.

Duration: Typically one year.

PUBLICATIONS:
Annual report.

TRUSTEES AND OFFICERS:
Donald W. Whitney, President
Roger L. Gardner

ADDRESS INQUIRIES TO:
Donald W. Whitney, President
(See address above.)

THE JOYCE FOUNDATION [158]

321 North Clark Street
Suite 1500
Chicago, IL 60654
(312) 782-2464
Fax: (312) 595-1350
E-mail: info@joycefdn.org
Web Site: www.joycefdn.org

FOUNDED: 1948

AREAS OF INTEREST:
Education and economic mobility, environment, gun violence prevention and justice reform, democracy, and culture.

TYPE:
Awards/prizes; Challenge/matching grants; Demonstration grants; Development grants; General operating grants; Research grants; Technical assistance.

YEAR PROGRAM STARTED: 1948

PURPOSE:
To support efforts to protect the natural environment of the Great Lakes; to reduce poverty and violence in the region; to ensure that its people have access to good schools, decent jobs, and a diverse and thriving culture; to reform the system of financing elections campaigns to ensure that public policies truly reflect public rather than private interests.

LEGAL BASIS:
Private foundation.

ELIGIBILITY:
Applicants must be tax-exempt, charitable organizations that are based or have a program in the Midwest, which the Foundation defines as including Illinois, Indiana, Michigan, Minnesota, Ohio and Wisconsin. A limited number of environment grants are made to organizations in Canada. The Foundation generally does not support capital proposals, endowment campaigns, religious activities, commercial ventures, direct service programs or scholarships.

GEOG. RESTRICTIONS: Great Lakes region, including Illinois, Indiana, Michigan, Minnesota, Ohio and Wisconsin.

FINANCIAL DATA:
Amount of support per award: Up to $1,000,000 over three years; average grant: $250,000.

Total amount of support: $36,440,380 for the year 2017.

NO. MOST RECENT APPLICANTS: 713.

NO. AWARDS: 280.

REPRESENTATIVE AWARDS:
$75,000 to World Business Chicago, Chicago, IL, to support the development and dissemination of the ChicagoMade economic impact study of the local arts and creative industry sector; $178,500 to Urban Institute, Washington, DC, to conduct research on segregation in higher education; $200,000 to CeaseFire Pennsylvania Education Fund, Philadelphia, PA, for education and advocacy to reduce gun violence in Pennsylvania.

APPLICATION INFO:
Letters of inquiry must precede any formal grant proposal. Formal proposals are accepted by invitation of the Foundation after review. Applicants are encouraged to download the formal grant proposal before completing it online and refer to the How to Submit a Grant Proposal Reference Sheet. E-mail applications@joycefdn.org for questions regarding the application process.

Duration: The majority of awards are for one year, although multiyear grants are also considered. Renewal of funding is primarily based on grantee's fulfillment of terms and goals of the previous grant and the program's continued advancement of Foundation priorities.

Deadline: April 10 for July; August 7 for November; December 5 for the following April.

PUBLICATIONS:
Program and Grant Proposal Guidelines (online); newsletters; annual report.

IRS I.D.: 36-6079185

STAFF:
Ellen S. Alberding, President
Deborah Gillespie, Vice President of Finance and Administration, Secretary and Treasurer
Nickol Hackett, Chief Investment Officer
Kayce Ataiyo, Director of Communications
Tracie D. Hall, Program Director, Culture
Carrie L. Davis, Program Director, Democracy
Stephanie Banchero, Program Director, Education
Edmund Miller, Program Director, Environment
Nina Vinik, Program Director, Gun Violence Prevention
Sameer Gadkaree, Senior Program Officer, Education and Economic Mobility
Elizabeth Cisar, Senior Program Officer, Environment
Tim Daly, Senior Program Officer, Gun Violence Prevention
Soledad A. McGrath, Senior Program Officer, Gun Violence Prevention
Jason Quiara, Program Officer, Education and Economic Mobility
Kerry M. Goese, Controller

BOARD OF DIRECTORS:
Jose B. Alvarez, Chairman
Margot M. Rogers, Vice Chairman
Ellen S. Alberding
Sally Blount
Robert G. Bottoms
Michael F. Brewer
Piyush Chaudhari
Charles U. Daly
Anthony S. Earl
Roger R. Fross
Carlton L. Guthrie
Tracey L. Meares
Carter Stewart
Paula Wolff

ADDRESS INQUIRIES TO:
E-mail: applications@joycefdn.org

THE J.M. KAPLAN FUND, INC. [159]

71 West 23rd Street
9th Floor
New York, NY 10010
(212) 767-0630
Fax: (212) 767-0639
E-mail: acarabine@jmkfund.org
Web Site: www.jmkfund.org

FOUNDED: 1945

AREAS OF INTEREST:
Environment, social justice, and cultural heritage.

NAME(S) OF PROGRAMS:
● **Discretionary Grants**
● **Environment Program Grant**
● **Furthermore Grant**
● **Heritage Conservation Grant**

- The J.M.K. Innovation Prize
- Social Justice Grant

TYPE:
General operating grants; Project/program grants.

YEAR PROGRAM STARTED: 1945

PURPOSE:
To champion inventive giving that supports transformative social, environmental and cultural causes.

LEGAL BASIS:
Family foundation.

ELIGIBILITY:
No grants are made to individuals. Unsolicited requests are not accepted.

FINANCIAL DATA:
Amount of support per award: $30,000 to $200,000 for program grants; $2,500 to $50,000 for discretionary grants.

NO. MOST RECENT APPLICANTS: Over 750.

APPLICATION INFO:
Application is by invitation only, except for the J.M.K. Innovation Prize.
Duration: 12 to 24 months.

TRUSTEES:
Peter W. Davidson, Chairman
Betsy Davidson
Bradford Davidson
Joan K. Davidson
J. Matthew Davidson
Caio Fonseca
Isabel Fonseca
Quina Fonseca
Mary E. Kaplan

STAFF:
Amy L. Freitag, Executive Director
William P. Falahee, Director of Finance and Administration
Angela D. Carabine, Grants Manager
Elizabeth Barthelmes Wolff, Program Director, Environment
Will Raynolds, Program Director, Heritage Conservation
Prachi Patankar, Program Director, Social Justice
Justin Goldbach, Program Director, The J.M.K. Innovation Prize
Ann Birckmayer, Administrator, Furthermore Grants in Publishing

ADDRESS INQUIRIES TO:
Angela D. Carabine, Grants Manager
(See address above.)

KATE SPADE NEW YORK FOUNDATION [160]
2 Park Avenue, 12th Floor
New York, NY 10016
(800) 519-3778
E-mail: foundation@katespade.com
Web Site: www.katespade.com

FOUNDED: 1981

AREAS OF INTEREST:
Women's programs only, specifically economic empowerment.

TYPE:
Challenge/matching grants; General operating grants; Matching gifts; Project/program grants; Seed money grants; Technical assistance.

YEAR PROGRAM STARTED: 1981

PURPOSE:
To support multidimensional programs that transition women from underserved communities into successful individuals that inspire the people around them.

LEGAL BASIS:
Corporate foundation.

ELIGIBILITY:
Organizations classified as 501(c)(3) by the IRS can apply. Individuals and religious, political and fraternal organizations are ineligible.

GEOG. RESTRICTIONS: Hudson County, New Jersey and New York, New York.

FINANCIAL DATA:
Amount of support per award: $15,000 to $120,000.
Total amount of support: Approximately $1,200,000 annually.
Matching fund requirements: 1:1; $25 minimum and $10,000 annual total per employee; includes arts, education, health, human services and the environment.

REPRESENTATIVE AWARDS:
$95,000 to Per Scholas, Women in Tech Training, New York, NY; $90,000 to International Rescue Committee, New York, NY; $75,000 to New, Inc., New York, NY.

APPLICATION INFO:
Guidelines and application form are available online.
Duration: One year. Grants are renewable.
Deadline: Applications are accepted throughout the year.

PUBLICATIONS:
Application guidelines.

IRS I.D.: 13-3060673

ADDRESS INQUIRIES TO:
Valerie Biberaj, Director
(See address above.)

MAY GORDON LATHAM KELLENBERGER HISTORICAL FOUNDATION [161]
529 South Front Street
New Bern, NC 28562
(252) 639-3500
Fax: (252) 514-4876

FOUNDED: 1978

AREAS OF INTEREST:
Historic preservation in the city of New Bern and Craven County, NC.

TYPE:
Project/program grants.

YEAR PROGRAM STARTED: 1978

PURPOSE:
To aid in the preservation of significant structures in New Bern as well as to assist in historical research and study pertaining to the city of New Bern and Craven County, NC.

LEGAL BASIS:
Special-interest foundation.

ELIGIBILITY:
Applicants must be organizations, agencies and institutions which are tax-exempt under the provisions of the U.S. Internal Revenue Code.

GEOG. RESTRICTIONS: Craven County and New Bern, North Carolina.

FINANCIAL DATA:
Amount of support per award: Varies.

Total amount of support: Varies.

APPLICATION INFO:
Contact Foundation for application form and guidelines.
Duration: One year. Can be renewed for one additional year.
Deadline: June 10 and December 10. Announcement on August 1 and February 1.

PUBLICATIONS:
Application guidelines.

OFFICERS:
John A.J. Ward, Chairperson
Dr. Kevin Cherry, Vice Chairperson
William C. Cannon, Secretary and Treasurer
Joe M. Hunt, III, Project Review Committee Chairperson

ADDRESS INQUIRIES TO:
Laurie Bowles, Administrative Support
(See address above.)

W.K. KELLOGG FOUNDATION [162]
One Michigan Avenue East
Battle Creek, MI 49017-4012
(269) 968-1611
(269) 969-2307
Fax: (269) 968-0413
E-mail: communications@wkkf.org
Web Site: www.wkkf.org

FOUNDED: 1930

AREAS OF INTEREST:
Equitable communities, thriving children and working families.

TYPE:
Challenge/matching grants; Development grants; Endowments; Fellowships; General operating grants; Matching gifts; Project/program grants; Seed money grants. Grants for pilot projects to improve human well-being are made in the U.S., Mexico, Haiti, northeastern Brazil, and with sovereign tribes. Up to two-thirds of grantmaking falls under priority places: New Orleans, Louisiana; Michigan; Mississippi; New Mexico; Chiapas and the Yucatan Peninsula, Mexico; and in Central and South Haiti. The Foundation is committed to working in each of these priority places for at least a generation.

The Foundation encourages grant seekers to review the latest information on its web site regarding its focus areas of thriving children, working families, and equitable communities.

YEAR PROGRAM STARTED: 1930

PURPOSE:
To support children, families and communities as they strengthen and create conditions that propel vulnerable children to achieve success as individuals and as contributors to the larger community and society.

LEGAL BASIS:
Independent private foundation.

ELIGIBILITY:
To be eligible for support, applying organization or institution, as well as the purpose of the proposed project, must qualify under the regulations of the U.S. IRS. Grantees must have the financial potential to sustain the project on a continuing basis after Foundation funding is ended. The Foundation is not able to provide funding directly to individuals.

GEOG. RESTRICTIONS: Haiti, Mexico and United States, with priority in Michigan, Mississippi, New Mexico and New Orleans, Louisiana.

FINANCIAL DATA:
Total assets of $7,806,078,755 for the year ended August 31, 2019.

Amount of support per award: Varies.

Total amount of support: $213,275,136 for the year ended August 31, 2019.

NO. MOST RECENT APPLICANTS: 957 for fiscal year 2018-19.

NO. AWARDS: 445 new commitments for fiscal year 2018-19.

REPRESENTATIVE AWARDS:
$3,600,000 to National Congress of American Indians; $510,000 to Food Security Network.

APPLICATION INFO:
The preferred method for grant submissions is the Foundation's online application. The Foundation will give prompt consideration to all preproposal submissions. The initial review may take up to three months to complete. If the proposed project falls within the Foundation's priorities and available resources, applicants may be asked to develop a more detailed proposal.

Duration: Varies.

Deadline: The Foundation accepts proposals on an ongoing basis, and staff members review them as they are received.

PUBLICATIONS:
Annual report.

BOARD OF TRUSTEES:
Celeste Clark, Chairman
Milton Chen
Roderick Gillum
Christina Hanger
Cathann Kress
Ramón Murguía
Khan Nedd
Richard Tsoumas

EXECUTIVE STAFF:
La June Montgomery Tabron, President and Chief Executive Officer
Joel Wittenburg, Vice President and Chief Investment Officer
Mary B. Cohen, Vice President for Communications
Donald Williamson, Vice President for Finance and Treasurer
Ross Comstock, Vice President for Information Systems and Technology
Cindy Smith, Vice President for Integrated Services
Joseph Scantlebury, Vice President for Place-Based Programs
Carla Thompson, Vice President for Program Strategy
Dianna Langenburg, Vice President for Talent and Human Resources
Alandra Washington, Vice President for Transformation and Organizational Effectiveness
Paul Martinez, Chief Leadership and Human Capital Strategist
Kathryn Krecke, General Counsel and Corporate Secretary

ADDRESS INQUIRIES TO:
See e-mail address above.

HARRIS AND ELIZA KEMPNER FUND   [163]
2201 Market Street, Suite 1250
Galveston, TX 77550-1529
(409) 762-1603
Fax: (409) 762-5435
E-mail: information@kempnerfund.org
Web Site: www.kempnerfund.org

FOUNDED: 1946

AREAS OF INTEREST:
Arts, historic preservation, community development, education, environment, and health and human services.

NAME(S) OF PROGRAMS:
- **Matching Gifts Program**
- **Primary Grant Program**
- **Program Related Investments**

TYPE:
Capital grants; Challenge/matching grants; Conferences/seminars; Demonstration grants; Endowments; General operating grants; Matching gifts; Project/program grants; Seed money grants. Primary Grant Program provides grants to qualifying organizations in the greater Galveston, TX area in the arts and historic preservation, community development, education, environment, and health and human services.

Program Related Investments are recommended by Fund trustees for Galveston projects.

YEAR PROGRAM STARTED: 1946

PURPOSE:
To support a wide range of innovative as well as traditional programs for the enhancement of the local community.

LEGAL BASIS:
Independent private foundation.

ELIGIBILITY:
Primary Grant Program: Preferred applicants are programs/projects that benefit the greater Galveston, TX community. Seed money, operating funds, small capital needs and special projects, and partnering with other funding sources are supported. Proposals will not be considered for fund-raising benefits, direct-mail solicitations, grants to individuals, or grants to non-U.S.-based organizations.

Matching Gifts Program: Restricted to Kempner family members and trustees of the Kempner Fund.

GEOG. RESTRICTIONS: Galveston, Texas.

FINANCIAL DATA:
Amount of support per award: Grants: $1,000 to $45,000 for the year ended December 31, 2019.

Total amount of support: $1,585,808 in grants and $192,636 in matching gifts for the year ended December 31, 2019.

Matching fund requirements: Restricted to descendants of Harris and Eliza Kempner.

NO. AWARDS: 115 for the year 2019.

REPRESENTATIVE AWARDS:
$50,000 to the Grand 1894 Opera House; $60,000 to the Family Service Center; $125,000 to the City of Galveston for a community swimming pool.

APPLICATION INFO:
Applicants should submit a brief cover letter, signed by the Executive Director and Board Chairman, stating the need and amount being requested. Complete guidelines and forms are available at the web site.

The following project/program information also needs to be submitted:
(1) name and telephone number of contact person;
(2) description;
(3) timeline;
(4) budget (income and expenses);
(5) list of sources and amounts being solicited and/or received or pledged;
(6) future funding plans (for new and continuing programs) and;
(7) plans for evaluating program's progress and/or results.

The following organization information should be attached:
(1) statement of purpose and brief history;
(2) names of present officers and board members;
(3) operating budget (revenue and expenses) for year for which funds are sought;
(4) financial statements (year-to-date), audit, and/or Tax Form 990 for most recent fiscal year;
(5) copy of post-1969 IRS determination letter to document tax-exempt status and;
(6) statement on organization letterhead that there has been no change in IRS status since issuance of ruling letter.

Duration: Varies.

Deadline: Health or Human Services: March 15. Arts, Community Development, Environment, Historic Preservation or Education: October 15.

IRS I.D.: 74-6042458

STAFF:
Lauren E. Scott, Executive Director

DIRECTORS:
Robert K. Lynch, Honorary Director
Barbara W. Sasser, Honorary Director
Lisa Allen, Director
Armin Cantini, Director
Mary K. Daniel, Director
Carroll Goldstone, Director
Hetta T. Kempner, Director
Randall Kempner, Director
Andrew Mytelka, Director
Emily Sasser, Director
Brooke Thompson, Director
Stephanie Thompson, Director

OFFICERS AND TRUSTEES:
Eliza Quigley, President
Lisa Allen, Vice President
Andrew Mytelka, Treasurer
Carroll Goldstone, Secretary

ADDRESS INQUIRIES TO:
See e-mail address above.

*SPECIAL STIPULATIONS:
Funding is limited to Galveston, TX area only.

JOHN F. KENNEDY LIBRARY FOUNDATION   [164]
220 Morrissey Boulevard
Columbia Point
Boston, MA 02125-3313
(617) 514-1630
Fax: (617) 514-1625
E-mail: kennedy.fellowships@nara.gov
Web Site: www.jfklibrary.org/archives/research-fellowships-grants

FOUNDED: 1964

AREAS OF INTEREST:
History, political science, journalism, and other academic disciplines.

NAME(S) OF PROGRAMS:
- **Marjorie Kovler Fellowship**
- **Arthur M. Schlesinger, Jr. Fellowship**
- **Abba T. Schwartz Fellowship**
- **Theodore C. Sorensen Fellowship**

TYPE:
Fellowships. Fellowships are strictly intended to support research in the holdings of the John F. Kennedy Presidential Library.

PURPOSE:
To support scholars who need to use the archival holdings of the John F. Kennedy Presidential Library.

FINANCIAL DATA:
Amount of support per award: Kovler Fellowship: Up to $2,500; Schlesinger Fellowship: Up to $5,000; Schwartz Fellowship: Up to $3,100; Sorensen Fellowship: Up to $3,600.

NO. MOST RECENT APPLICANTS: 22.

NO. AWARDS: Varies.

APPLICATION INFO:
Applicants are encouraged to contact an archivist at the Library for information about relevant archival holdings before applying. Candidates can apply for only one fellowship per year. The Fellowship Committee will access each application with the most relevant fellowship opportunity in mind.
Deadline: Varies.

ADDRESS INQUIRIES TO:
Fellowships Coordinator
(See address above.)

JOHN F. KENNEDY PRESIDENTIAL LIBRARY   [165]
220 Morrissey Boulevard
Columbia Point
Boston, MA 02125-3313
(617) 514-1630
Fax: (617) 514-1625
E-mail: kennedy.library@nara.gov
Web Site: www.jfklibrary.org

FOUNDED: 1964

AREAS OF INTEREST:
Archival administration and library science, history, government, journalism, communications and other related disciplines.

NAME(S) OF PROGRAMS:
- **Kennedy Library Archival Internships**

TYPE:
Internships. Awarded to undergraduate and graduate students majoring in history, government, archival administration, library science, journalism, communications and related disciplines for on-site work with the archives staff at the Kennedy Library.

YEAR PROGRAM STARTED: 1970

LEGAL BASIS:
Private foundation in cooperation with a U.S. government agency.

FINANCIAL DATA:
Amount of support per award: Monthly stipend of $750 for part-time interns.

NO. AWARDS: Varies according to archivists' needs and capability.

APPLICATION INFO:
Candidate must complete application form, submit a copy of current college transcript, and a letter of reference.
Duration: Varies.
Deadline: Varies.

ADDRESS INQUIRIES TO:
Internship Coordinator
(See address above.)

THE KERR FOUNDATION, INC.   [166]
12501 North May Avenue
Oklahoma City, OK 73120
(405) 749-7991
Fax: (405) 749-2877
Web Site: www.thekerrfoundation.org

FOUNDED: 1963

AREAS OF INTEREST:
Education, cultural activities, and health and human services.

TYPE:
Capital grants; General operating grants; Project/program grants.

YEAR PROGRAM STARTED: 1986

PURPOSE:
To support programs of interest to the Foundation in the areas of health, education, youth services and cultural activities.

LEGAL BASIS:
Private, charitable foundation.

ELIGIBILITY:
Application is limited to nonprofit, 501(c)(3) tax-exempt organizations. No grants to individuals.

GEOG. RESTRICTIONS: Arkansas, Colorado, Kansas, Missouri, New Mexico, Oklahoma, Texas, and Washington, D.C.

FINANCIAL DATA:
Grant-seeking organizations must first raise a specified amount in actual new dollars donations or up-to-three-year pledges. The grant will be paid upon successful raising of the funds or pledges, which must occur within one year or a mutually agreed-upon time limit.
Amount of support per award: $5,000 to $50,000.

CO-OP FUNDING PROGRAMS: All Oklahoma foundations.

NO. AWARDS: 45 for the year 2018.

APPLICATION INFO:
A letter of inquiry is required before a formal grant application can be submitted. Forms and guidelines are available online.
Duration: Most grants awarded on a one-time basis. The Foundation does not give back-to-back grants. Organizations must allow one full year before reapplying.

OFFICERS AND TRUSTEES:
Mrs. Robert S. Kerr, Jr., President and Chairperson
Laura D. Kerr, Vice President
Steven Kerr, Treasurer
Laura Kerr Ogle, Secretary
Cody T. Kerr

ADDRESS INQUIRIES TO:
Laura D. Kerr, Vice President
E-mail: lauradkerr@thekerrfoundation.org

GRAYCE B. KERR FUND, INC.   [167]
117 Bay Street
Easton, MD 21601
(410) 822-6652
Fax: (410) 822-4546
E-mail: office@gbkf.org
Web Site: www.gbkf.org

FOUNDED: 1986

AREAS OF INTEREST:
Education, cultural programs, and public policy research, with major emphasis on education.

TYPE:
Project/program grants. Grants to nonprofit organizations. Grants are not limited to any one specific area of interest or geographical location. Currently, the Fund's principal areas of interest include nurturing educational achievement and excellence, fostering life skills critical to self-sufficiency, and encouraging cultural growth. The Fund supports research and other activities directed toward improving the information base available to the public.

YEAR PROGRAM STARTED: 1986

PURPOSE:
To provide financial support to worthy nonprofit organizations that enhance the quality of life, significantly impact and sustain long-term change and growth in organizations and institutions.

LEGAL BASIS:
Private, charitable foundation.

ELIGIBILITY:
Applicants must be nonprofit, 501(c)(3) tax-exempt organizations. No grants to individuals.

GEOG. RESTRICTIONS: United States.

FINANCIAL DATA:
Grant minimums and maximums are not designated. Preference may be given, in some years, to large grants where a genuine impact may be accomplished.
Amount of support per award: Varies.
Total amount of support: Varies.

APPLICATION INFO:
The Foundation self-selects grantees based on the interests of the family and Trustees. Unsolicited proposals are not accepted.

PUBLICATIONS:
Annual report; application.

IRS I.D.: 73-1256124

BOARD OF TRUSTEES:
Marcy Kerr Yuknat, Chairperson
John R. Valliant, President and Trustee
David A. Yuknat, Secretary and Treasurer

ADDRESS INQUIRIES TO:
John R. Valliant, President
(See address above.)

KIMBERLY-CLARK FOUNDATION, INC.   [168]
P.O. Box 619100
Dallas, TX 75261-9100
(972) 281-1200
E-mail: kcfoundation@kcc.com
Web Site: www.kimberly-clark.com

FOUNDED: 1952

AREAS OF INTEREST:
Social welfare, medicine and health.

TYPE:
Project/program grants.

YEAR PROGRAM STARTED: 1952

PURPOSE:
To support organizations that strengthen today's families.

LEGAL BASIS:
Corporate foundation.

ELIGIBILITY:
Grants are made to tax-exempt, charitable, 501(c)(3) nonprofit organizations in communities where Kimberly-Clark has operations. There are a limited number of contributions to national organizations.

FINANCIAL DATA:
Amount of support per award: Varies.
Total amount of support: Varies.

REPRESENTATIVE AWARDS:
$1,300,000 to Boys and Girls Clubs of America; $20,000 to Susan G. Komen Foundation; $50,000 to Catalyst for Women; $200,000 to American Red Cross.

APPLICATION INFO:
Applicants are required to e-mail the Foundation before sending requests.
Duration: One to five years.

PUBLICATIONS:
Annual report.

OFFICERS:
Flavio Costa, Vice President and Treasurer
Jenny Lewis, Vice President

ADDRESS INQUIRIES TO:
Jenny Lewis, Vice President
(See address above.)

STEPHEN AND TABITHA KING FOUNDATION   [169]
P.O. Box 855
Bangor, ME 04402
(207) 990-2910
Fax: (207) 990-2975
E-mail: info@stkfoundation.org
Web Site: stkfoundation.org

FOUNDED: 1986

AREAS OF INTEREST:
Arts, children/youth, health, education, libraries, recovery, women's issues, human rights, literacy, public safety, and conservation.

TYPE:
Awards/prizes; Capital grants; Challenge/matching grants; Demonstration grants; Development grants; Matching gifts; Project/program grants; Seed money grants; Training grants.

PURPOSE:
To improve the quality of life in Maine.

LEGAL BASIS:
Private family foundation.

ELIGIBILITY:
Organizations classified as 501(c)(3) by the IRS and located in Maine can apply. Grants are only awarded to nonprofit organizations operating in the state of Maine. Individuals and religious organizations are ineligible.

GEOG. RESTRICTIONS: Maine.

FINANCIAL DATA:
Amount of support per award: Grants: $500 to $50,000.
Total amount of support: Varies, dependent on investment revenue.
Matching fund requirements: Must be met through grassroots local community funding.

NO. MOST RECENT APPLICANTS: 1,200 to 1,500 annually.

NO. AWARDS: Approximately 250.

APPLICATION INFO:
Applications are submitted online.
Duration: Foundation prefers one-time grants. Multiyear commitments occasionally.
Deadline: April 15 and October 15. Decisions on grants may take as long as eight weeks.

IRS I.D.: 13-3364647

STAFF:
Stephanie Leonard, Administrator

ADDRESS INQUIRIES TO:
Stephanie Leonard, Administrator
(See address above.)

*SPECIAL STIPULATIONS:
Applicants should apply only once per year and those that receive funding should wait two full years before reapplying.

F.M. KIRBY FOUNDATION, INC.   [170]
17 DeHart Street
Morristown, NJ 07963
(973) 538-4800
Fax: (973) 538-4801
Web Site: fmkirbyfoundation.org

FOUNDED: 1931

AREAS OF INTEREST:
General charitable support.

TYPE:
Capital grants; Challenge/matching grants; Endowments; Fellowships; General operating grants; Professorships; Project/program grants; Research grants; Scholarships. Grants usually are reflective of personal interest by one or more members of the Kirby family who are, or have been, active in the affairs of the Foundation.

YEAR PROGRAM STARTED: 1931

LEGAL BASIS:
Private foundation.

ELIGIBILITY:
Organizations must be tax-exempt under applicable provisions of the IRS code and not private foundations. No grants are made to individuals. No grants are made to public foundations which would, as a result thereof, become private foundations. No grants for fund-raising activities such as benefits, charitable dinners, sports or theater events, etc. No loans are made.

GEOG. RESTRICTIONS: Morris County, New Jersey; Adirondack Park, New York area, Raleigh-Durham, North Carolina area, and Wilkes-Barre, Pennsylvania area.

FINANCIAL DATA:
Amount of support per award: Varies.
Total amount of support: $13,194,500 for the year 2019.
Matching fund requirements: Determined on a case-by-case basis.

NO. AWARDS: 227 for the year 2019.

APPLICATION INFO:
The preferred method of initial contact is a full proposal with a cover letter. The Foundation provides no formal application forms and sets down no specific guidelines. Proposals should include:
(1) a report on the use of previous grants if applicable;
(2) a description of the organization, its purpose and the project, if any;
(3) an indication of the budget for which

financial support is requested;
(4) roster of directors and principal officers;
(5) copy of the current audited financial statement;
(6) copy of the valid IRS tax determination letter and;
(7) copy of current annual budget.
Duration: One year. Renewal possible.
Deadline: October 31. Solicitations received after deadline will be held over to following year.

PUBLICATIONS:
Application guidelines.

IRS I.D.: 51-6017929

STAFF:
JoAnn F. Tiefau, Program Officer
Erin Clifford, Communications and Program Associate

OFFICERS AND DIRECTORS:
S. Dillard Kirby, President and Director
Justin J. Kiczek, Executive Vice President
Jefferson W. Kirby, Vice President and Director
Diana L. Kostas, Treasurer and Secretary
Alice K. Horton, Assistant Secretary and Director
Wilson M. Compton, Director
Ashley Horton Freeman, Director
Leigh Kirby Klein, Director
Sandra Brown Sherman, Director

ADDRESS INQUIRIES TO:
S. Dillard Kirby, President
(See address above.)

KITSAP COMMUNITY FOUNDATION
9657 Levin Road, N.W.
Suite 220
Silverdale, WA 98383
(360) 698-3622
E-mail: kcf@kitsapfoundation.org
Web Site: www.kitsapfoundation.org

TYPE:
General operating grants; Project/program grants; Scholarships.

See entry 1200 for full listing.

ROBERT J. KLEBERG, JR. AND HELEN C. KLEBERG FOUNDATION   [171]
112 East Pecan Street
Suite 1020
San Antonio, TX 78205
(210) 271-3691 ext. 116
Fax: (210) 299-1541
E-mail: margretb@alexventures.com
Web Site: www.klebergfoundation.org

FOUNDED: 1950

AREAS OF INTEREST:
Basic biological sciences and translational medicine; community services in Kleberg and surrounding counties; arts and humanities; and wildlife, conservation and animal sciences.

TYPE:
Capital grants; Project/program grants; Research grants.

PURPOSE:
To provide financial support for research projects or actual programs in the area of biomedical research, the arts, wildlife and habitat stewardship, and community services in Kleberg and surrounding counties.

LEGAL BASIS:
Private foundation.

ELIGIBILITY:
Applicants must be IRS 501(c)(3) organizations or public universities under Section 170(c) of the Internal Revenue Code. No grants to individuals. No grants for endowments, deficit financing, community organizations outside of South Texas, indirect costs or overhead for research projects.

Funding is highly competitive and priority is given to organizations with whom the Foundation has a previous relationship.

GEOG. RESTRICTIONS: United States; Kleberg and surrounding counties only for community services.

FINANCIAL DATA:
The Foundation has awarded nearly $318,000,000 since its founding.

Amount of support per award: Varies.

Total amount of support: Approximately $11,000,000 annually.

NO. MOST RECENT APPLICANTS: 120.

NO. AWARDS: 32 new grants for the year 2019.

APPLICATION INFO:
Only online grant applications will be accepted.

Duration: Project support can be up to three years.

Deadline: March 31 and September 30. Decision early June and early December, respectively.

PUBLICATIONS:
Guidelines.

STAFF:
Margret Bamford, Grants Administrator

ADDRESS INQUIRIES TO:
Margret Bamford, Grants Administrator (See address above.)

JOSIAH W. AND BESSIE H. KLINE FOUNDATION, INC. [172]

515 South 29th Street
Harrisburg, PA 17104
(717) 561-4373
Fax: (717) 561-0826
E-mail: info@kline-foundation.org
Web Site: www.kline-foundation.org

FOUNDED: 1952

AREAS OF INTEREST:
Medical, academic, benevolent, community and cultural.

NAME(S) OF PROGRAMS:
• **Kline Foundation Grants**

TYPE:
Project/program grants; Research grants.

YEAR PROGRAM STARTED: 1952

PURPOSE:
To aid blind or incapacitated persons or crippled children in need of financial assistance; to make grants to Pennsylvania colleges and universities, to hospitals and institutions for crippled children or to any other benevolent or charitable institution; to make grants for scientific or medical research to be performed by scientific persons or by colleges, universities or research institutions.

LEGAL BASIS:
Community foundation.

ELIGIBILITY:
The Foundation does not make loans and does not make grants to individuals and generally does not make grants for normal operational phases of established programs or to national organizations or religious programs.

Normally grants are not made to state-affiliated schools, colleges, or universities.

GEOG. RESTRICTIONS: South central Pennsylvania, with emphasis on Cumberland and Dauphin counties.

FINANCIAL DATA:
Amount of support per award: $500 to $250,000.

Total amount of support: Varies.

APPLICATION INFO:
Application information is available on the web site. To be considered for Foundation aid, a copy of the Foundation's completed application form must be submitted and the following information must be fully stated:
(1) a description of the need and purpose, the qualifications of the requesting organization and the location as to where and how the support will be used;
(2) a budget for the project and any support that will be received from other sources;
(3) the amount of the request from the Foundation and the dates the funds are needed and;
(4) a copy of a letter from the IRS showing that the organization is exempt from federal income tax under Section 501(c)(3) of the Internal Revenue Code and that the organization is not a private foundation under Section 509(a).

Application may be submitted online.

Deadline: April and October. Some grants are awarded in June, while others are generally awarded after December 1 of each year.

PUBLICATIONS:
Annual report; application guidelines; application.

ADDRESS INQUIRIES TO:
John A. Obrock, C.P.A.
(See address above.)

*SPECIAL STIPULATIONS:
One grant per year per organization.

JOHN S. AND JAMES L. KNIGHT FOUNDATION [173]

200 South Biscayne Boulevard
Suite 3300
Miami, FL 33131-2349
(305) 908-2600
Fax: (305) 908-2698
E-mail: grants@knightfoundation.org
Web Site: www.knightfoundation.org

FOUNDED: 1950

AREAS OF INTEREST:
Journalism and engaged and informed communities.

NAME(S) OF PROGRAMS:
• **Arts Program**
• **Communities Program**
• **Journalism Program**
• **National Program**

TYPE:
Capital grants; Challenge/matching grants; Development grants; Endowments; Matching gifts; Project/program grants; Seed money

grants; Technical assistance. The Foundation promotes excellence in journalism worldwide and invests in the vitality of 26 U.S. communities.

The Foundation focuses on three areas:
(1) Innovating Media and Journalism: The Foundation aims to help sustain democracy by leading journalism to its best possible future in the 21st century;
(2) Engaging Communities: To sustain healthy communities in a democracy, the Foundation's community engagement initiatives aim to give all residents a strong sense of belonging and caring, timely access to relevant information, the ability to understand that information, and the motivation to take sustainable action on the issues that matter most to them and;
(3) Fostering the Arts: Through its national arts program, the Foundation seeks to weave the arts into the fabric of the Knight resident communities to engage and inspire their residents; the Foundation believes that the arts are a catalyst for public dialogue, and that shared cultural experiences contribute to a sense of place and communal identity.

YEAR PROGRAM STARTED: 1950

PURPOSE:
To sustain democracy in the digital age by fostering informed and engaged communities; to back transformational ideas at the intersection of media, journalism, community engagement and the arts; to advance media innovation with a wide range of initiatives; to support projects, including in the arts, that increase community engagement through the use of technology and other innovative approaches.

LEGAL BASIS:
Private non-operating foundation.

ELIGIBILITY:
A segment of the Foundation's activities focuses on 26 communities where the Knight brothers owned newspapers, with donor-advised programs in 18 and program director-led programs in the eight "resident Knight communities."

An applicant organization must have received a letter of determination from the IRS granting it 501(c)(3) tax-exempt status and stating that it is not a private foundation according to the definition in Section 509(a) of the Internal Revenue Code.

The Knight News Challenge permits for-profit entities and individuals to apply from anywhere in the world.

The Knight Community Information Challenge accepts applications from community and place-based foundations in the U.S. and its territories, as well as Mexico and Canada.

The Knight Arts Challenge accepts applications from South Florida, Detroit (MI), and Greater Philadelphia individuals, for-profit and nonprofit organizations.

FINANCIAL DATA:
Amount of support per award: Varies.

Total amount of support: Approximately $1,500,000 for the year 2017.

NO. AWARDS: Approximately 600 grants for the year 2017.

APPLICATION INFO:
Applicants must submit an online letter of inquiry. If the inquiry is determined to fall into Knight Foundation funding priorities, applicants are asked to submit a full proposal.

Duration: Varies per project; usually from one to five years.

PUBLICATIONS:
Evaluation and Assessment publications; Reporter Analysis evaluation articles; KnightBlog posts.

IRS I.D.: 65-0464177

STAFF:
Terese Coudreaut Curiel, Vice President/Administration
Juan Martinez, Vice President and Chief Financial Officer
Jorge Martinez, Vice President and Chief Technology Officer
Victoria Rogers, Vice President/Arts
Andrew Sherry, Vice President/Communications
Jennifer Preston, Vice President/Journalism Program

TRUSTEES AND OFFICERS:
Francisco L. Borges, Chairman
Alberto Ibarguen, President and Chief Executive Officer
Christopher M. Austen
Martin Baron
Stephanie Bell-Rose
Shana L. Brown
Adriana Cisneros
William H. Considine
Susan D. Kronick
Christine Amer Mayer
Anna Spangler Nelson
Beverly Knight Olson
John Palfrey
Ray Rodriguez

ADDRESS INQUIRIES TO:
Grants Administrator
(See address above.)

MARION I. AND HENRY J. KNOTT FOUNDATION, INC. [174]

3904 Hickory Avenue
Baltimore, MD 21211
(410) 235-7068
Fax: (410) 889-2577
E-mail: knott@knottfoundation.org
Web Site: www.knottfoundation.org

FOUNDED: 1977

AREAS OF INTEREST:
Education (private and Catholic schools only), health care, human and social services, arts and humanities.

TYPE:
Challenge/matching grants; Development grants; General operating grants; Matching gifts.

YEAR PROGRAM STARTED: 1977

PURPOSE:
To further Roman Catholic activities and other charitable, cultural, educational, health care and human service activities within the meaning of Section 501(c)(3) of the Internal Revenue Code.

LEGAL BASIS:
Private family foundation.

ELIGIBILITY:
Applicants must be nonprofit, charitable organizations with evidence of tax-exemption ruling under Section 501(c)(3) of the Internal Revenue Code. No grants pertaining to scholarships, individuals, annual giving, pro-choice causes, public education or institutions, or politically oriented activities.

The Foundation does not favor multiyear requests.

GEOG. RESTRICTIONS: Central and western Maryland, including the Archdiocese of Baltimore.

FINANCIAL DATA:
Amount of support per award: $10,000 to $50,000. Average $45,000.
Total amount of support: Approximately $2,200,000 for the year 2017.
Matching fund requirements: Specific to grantee. Usually matched within a six-month period.

NO. MOST RECENT APPLICANTS: 75 discretionary grant applications.

NO. AWARDS: 42 discretionary grants.

APPLICATION INFO:
Details are available on the Foundation web site.
Duration: Usually one year.
Deadline: Letters of Inquiry and Financials: February, June and October. Full Proposal: March, July and November, respectively.

IRS I.D.: 52-1517876

TRUSTEES AND OFFICERS:
Mary Lindsay Gallagher, President
Daniel Gallagher
David Gallagher
Michael Gallagher
Emily Hanssen
E.B. Harris
Kelly L. Harris
Thomas Harris
Carlisle Hashim
Marion Hashim
Erin Knott
Marion I. Knott
Martin G. Knott, Sr.
Martin G. Knott, Jr.
Owen M. Knott
Teresa A. Knott
Brian McDonald
Meghan McDonald
Peter McGill
David L. Porter
Joanna O. Porter
Laurel Porter
Martin Porter
John H. Riehl, IV
Margie Riehl
Michael Riehl
Brooke Rodgers
Michael Rodgers
Patrick Rodgers
Geralynn D. Smyth
John Smyth
Jamie Stodd
Emmett Voelkel
Ryan Voelkel

ADDRESS INQUIRIES TO:
Kelly Medinger, Executive Director
(See e-mail address above.)

KNOX COUNTY FOUNDATION [175]

101 East Gambier Street
Mount Vernon, OH 43050
(740) 392-3270
E-mail: marc@knoxcf.org
Web Site: knoxcf.org

FOUNDED: 1944

AREAS OF INTEREST:
New projects in educational, charitable and civic fields.

TYPE:
Capital grants; Challenge/matching grants; Matching gifts; Project/program grants; Scholarships; Seed money grants.

YEAR PROGRAM STARTED: 1944

PURPOSE:
To improve the quality of life for the people of Mount Vernon and Knox County, OH.

LEGAL BASIS:
Nonprofit, community foundation.

ELIGIBILITY:
Grants from unrestricted funds generally limited to projects in Knox County, OH.

GEOG. RESTRICTIONS: Knox County, Ohio.

FINANCIAL DATA:
Amount of support per award: Varies.
Total amount of support: $4,000,000 annually.

APPLICATION INFO:
Application forms are available online. Personal presentations only at invitation of Distribution Committee.

PUBLICATIONS:
Annual report.

IRS I.D.: 23-7002871

BOARD OF DIRECTORS:
Richard K. Mavis, Chairman
Marsha K. Rinehart, Vice Chairman
Kurt E. Schisler, Treasurer
Kim Rose, Secretary
Jeffrey L. Boucher
Chris Cordle, Ph.D.
Kathy Daniels
Sean Decatur, Ph.D.
John D. Lambert
Jan Reynolds
Vickie A. Sant
Susan Sukys
Dr. Michael Sullivan

ADDRESS INQUIRIES TO:
Marc Odenweller, Finance Director
(See address above.)

KORET FOUNDATION [176]

611 Front Street
San Francisco, CA 94111-1963
(415) 882-7740
Fax: (415) 882-7775
E-mail: koret@koretfoundation.org
Web Site: koret.org

FOUNDED: 1979

AREAS OF INTEREST:
Arts, community service and volunteerism, Jewish community services, education and employment for youth, elderly, hunger and homelessness.

TYPE:
Capital grants; General operating grants; Project/program grants; Seed money grants.

YEAR PROGRAM STARTED: 1979

PURPOSE:
To address societal challenges and strengthen Bay Area life; to invest in strategic, local solutions that help to inspire a multiplier effect, encouraging collaborative funding and developing model initiatives.

LEGAL BASIS:
Private foundation.

ELIGIBILITY:
Grant applicants must be 501(c)(3) organizations. Private foundations are not eligible to apply.

Although the majority of funding is granted to six of nine bay area counties, the Foundation will consider national and Israeli projects.

GEOG. RESTRICTIONS: Alameda, Contra Costa, Marin, San Francisco, San Mateo and Santa Clara counties, California.

FINANCIAL DATA:
Amount of support per award: Grants vary in amount, depending upon the needs and nature of the request.

APPLICATION INFO:
The Foundation considers grant requests by invitation only.
Duration: Varies.

PUBLICATIONS:
Annual report; application guidelines.

IRS I.D.: 94-1624987

OFFICERS:
Jeffrey A. Farber, Chief Executive Officer

THE KRAFT HEINZ COMPANY FOUNDATION   [177]

200 East Randolph
Suite 7600
Chicago, IL 60601
Web Site: www.kraftheinzcompany.
com/community-involvement.html

FOUNDED: 1951

AREAS OF INTEREST:
Eliminating global hunger.

TYPE:
Project/program grants.

YEAR PROGRAM STARTED: 1951

PURPOSE:
To eliminate global hunger through the support of organizations and initiatives dedicated to increasing food access and security; to seek sustainable solutions to hunger; to promote hunger prevention programs; to feed families in times of disaster.

LEGAL BASIS:
Corporate foundation.

ELIGIBILITY:
All organizations seeking funding must be tax-exempt under Section 501(c)(3) of the Internal Revenue Code.

The Foundation does not make grants for loans or assistance to individuals, general scholarships, fellowships, travel grants, political campaigns either local or national and/or sectarian religious purposes.

FINANCIAL DATA:
Amount of support per award: Varies.
Total amount of support: Varies.

REPRESENTATIVE AWARDS:
Extra Mile Education Foundation;
Make-A-Wish Foundation of Western Pennsylvania.

APPLICATION INFO:
A written project summary may be sent including the goals of the applying organization, the specific purpose for which funds are requested, how the objective will be accomplished, to whom and where the program will be offered and whether the project is a single project or one that requires additional phases. A letter of intent is recommended to approach the Foundation.
Duration: Mostly one year. Renewal requests are considered.

TRUSTEES:
Tammy B. Aupperle, Chairperson
Ted Bobby
Kristen Clark
Beth Eckenrode
Michael Mullen
Michael Okoroafer

ADDRESS INQUIRIES TO:
Jenece Upton, Manager
(See address above.)

THE KRESGE FOUNDATION   [178]

3215 West Big Beaver Road
Troy, MI 48084
(248) 643-9630
Fax: (248) 643-0588
E-mail: info@kresge.org
Web Site: kresge.org

FOUNDED: 1924

AREAS OF INTEREST:
Arts and culture, Detroit/community development, education, environment, and health and human services.

TYPE:
General operating grants; Project/program grants. Program-related investments.

YEAR PROGRAM STARTED: 1924

PURPOSE:
To expand opportunity for low-income people so they can gain the tools and support needed to lead self-determined lives and join the economic mainstream.

LEGAL BASIS:
Independent private foundation.

ELIGIBILITY:
Tax-exempt charitable organizations operating in the fields of higher education (including community colleges), health care and long-term care, human services, science and the environment, arts and humanities and public affairs. Governmental agencies are also eligible to apply. Full accreditation is required for higher education and hospital applicants and preferred in all other fields that offer it. Evidence of initial funding for the requested project is considered essential.

The following projects are eligible:
(1) construction of facilities;
(2) renovation of facilities;
(3) purchase of major equipment or an integrated system at a cost of at least $300,000; equipment costs may include computer software expenses, if applicable and;
(4) purchase of real estate.

Religious organizations, elementary and secondary schools, private foundations and individuals are not eligible to apply. However, accredited seminaries are eligible to apply. Also, agencies operated by religious organizations that serve secular needs may be eligible if the programs have financial and governing autonomy separate from the parent organization. They must also have space formally dedicated to their programs.

Some elementary and secondary schools may be eligible in the Foundation's Human Services category, if they predominantly serve individuals with physical and/or developmental disabilities.

FINANCIAL DATA:
Amount of support per award: Varies.

Total amount of support: $120,000,000 to $150,000,000 annually.

NO. AWARDS: 521 for the year 2019.

REPRESENTATIVE AWARDS:
$205,000 to Community Catalyst Inc.;
$436,015 to Michigan Public Health Institute;
$250,000 to Dorothy Day House.

APPLICATION INFO:
Grant and social investment opportunities are announced online. Only electronic application is accepted.
Duration: Varies.

PUBLICATIONS:
Annual report.

ADDRESS INQUIRIES TO:
Grants Inquiry Coordinator
(See address above.)

ALBERT AND BESSIE MAE KRONKOSKY CHARITABLE FOUNDATION   [179]

112 East Pecan, Suite 830
San Antonio, TX 78205
(210) 475-9000
Fax: (210) 354-2204
E-mail: kronfndn@kronkosky.org
Web Site: www.kronkosky.org

FOUNDED: 1991

AREAS OF INTEREST:
Elderly, youth, child abuse and neglect, persons with disabilities, culture and the arts, museums, libraries, prevention of cruelty to animals, health, parks, zoos and wildlife sanctuaries.

TYPE:
Capital grants; Challenge/matching grants; Endowments; General operating grants; Matching gifts; Project/program grants; Research grants; Seed money grants; Technical assistance; Training grants; Research contracts.

YEAR PROGRAM STARTED: 1999

PURPOSE:
To produce profound good that is tangible and measurable in Bandera, Bexar, Comal, and Kendall counties in Texas by implementing the Kronkoskys' charitable purposes.

LEGAL BASIS:
Private foundation.

ELIGIBILITY:
Corporate organizations that are exempt under Section 501(c)(3) of the Internal Revenue Code. The Foundation will not make grants to individuals or for-profit organizations. In addition, the Foundation has a geographic limitation that requires that grant funds be used in the specific counties listed below.

GEOG. RESTRICTIONS: Bandera, Bexar, Comal and Kendall counties, Texas.

FINANCIAL DATA:
Amount of support per award: $10,000 to $1,000,000 for the year 2019. Average grant: $147,000.

Total amount of support: $14,873,175 for the year 2019.

NO. MOST RECENT APPLICANTS: 186 for the year 2019.

NO. AWARDS: 101 grants for the year 2019.

APPLICATION INFO:
Letter of Inquiry may be submitted online or mailed to the address above. If the Letter of Inquiry meets requirements, it will be reviewed by Foundation's staff within 10 days of receipt. If the proposal is accepted, an application package as well as a timeline for submission of the grant proposal will be forwarded. If proposal is not accepted, notification in writing will be sent. Please note geographic requirement.

Duration: Usually one year.

Deadline: Letters of Inquiry will be accepted throughout the year and reviewed on a rolling basis.

PUBLICATIONS:
Program guidelines; annual report (online only).

IRS I.D.: 74-6385152

ADDRESS INQUIRIES TO:
Tullos Wells, Managing Director
(See address above.)

THE JEAN AND E. FLOYD KVAMME FOUNDATION

P.O. Box 2494
Saratoga, CA 95070
(408) 395-2829
Fax: (408) 354-0804

TYPE:
Capital grants; Development grants; General operating grants; Project/program grants. Medical grants are given primarily in the areas of Alzheimers, leukemia, arthritis, and spondylitis; however, grants for research in other areas are considered.

See entry 1421 for full listing.

LAIDLAW FOUNDATION   [180]

2 St. Clair Avenue East
3rd Floor
Toronto ON M4T 2T5 Canada
(416) 964-3614 ext. 301
Fax: (416) 975-1428
E-mail: voctive@laidlawfdn.org
Web Site: laidlawfdn.org

FOUNDED: 1949

AREAS OF INTEREST:
Youth engagement, youth social infrastructure and policy development.

NAME(S) OF PROGRAMS:
● Youth Action Fund

TYPE:
General operating grants; Project/program grants. The Youth Action Fund offers grants to grassroots initiatives working with youth who are underserved by the education system and overrepresented in the justice and child welfare systems.

YEAR PROGRAM STARTED: 1949

PURPOSE:
To tackle barriers facing young people in the justice, education and child welfare systems.

LEGAL BASIS:
Private family foundation.

ELIGIBILITY:
Initiatives must be Ontario-based, demonstrate youth leadership, and be based within the communities they are serving and/or with a proven history of working with the communities they identify. Distant programming with First Nations must be

welcomed by invitation and/or in partnership with the youth and supported by their community-based allies.

GEOG. RESTRICTIONS: Ontario, Canada.

FINANCIAL DATA:
Amount of support per award: Up to $100,000 per year.
Total amount of support: Varies.

APPLICATION INFO:
E-mail info@laidlawfdn.org for information regarding this grant program.
Duration: Up to three years.
Deadline: Varies.

ADDRESS INQUIRIES TO:
Veanna Octive, Grants Manager
(See address and e-mail above.)

LAMB FOUNDATION   [181]

P.O. Box 1705
Lake Oswego, OR 97035
(503) 635-8010
E-mail: lambfdn@lambfoundation.org
Web Site: www.lambfoundation.org

FOUNDED: 1971

AREAS OF INTEREST:
Social services for youth and children, arts, and environment.

TYPE:
Challenge/matching grants; General operating grants; Project/program grants.

LEGAL BASIS:
Private foundation.

ELIGIBILITY:
Applicants must be nonprofit 501(c)(3) public charity organizations.

GEOG. RESTRICTIONS: Pacific Northwest.

FINANCIAL DATA:
Amount of support per award: Typical grants: $5,000 to $15,000.
Total amount of support: Approximately $280,000.

NO. MOST RECENT APPLICANTS: 22 for the year 2018.

NO. AWARDS: 46.

REPRESENTATIVE AWARDS:
$15,000 to p:ear for an arts and culture program; $15,000 to The Freshwater Trust for the Scalable Tools for Freshwater Restoration Project; $15,000 to Mountain Star Family Relief Nursery for the expansion of services in Prineville, OR.

APPLICATION INFO:
The Foundation does not accept unsolicited applications. Upon invitation, application information will be sent to the prospective applicant.
Duration: One year.
Deadline: Included in application materials sent to invited applicants.

PUBLICATIONS:
Brochure.

IRS I.D.: 23-7120564

STAFF:
Debra Iguchi, Administrator

ADDRESS INQUIRIES TO:
Debra Iguchi, Administrator
(See address above.)

*PLEASE NOTE:
Prospective applicants are encouraged to contact the office or web site periodically for changes.

LAND O'LAKES FOUNDATION   [182]

4001 Lexington Avenue North
Arden Hills, MN 55126
(651) 375-2470
E-mail: landolakesfoundation@landolakes.com
Web Site: www.landolakesinc.com/responsibility

FOUNDED: 1997

AREAS OF INTEREST:
Hunger, education and community.

CONSULTING OR VOLUNTEER SERVICES:
Group projects.

NAME(S) OF PROGRAMS:
● California Regions Grant Program
● Community Grants Program
● Dollars for Doers Program
● Matching Gifts to Education Program
● Member Co-op Match Program
● Mid-Atlantic Grant Program

TYPE:
Capital grants; Endowments; General operating grants; Matching gifts; Project/program grants. Major support is in the form of cash contributions, supplemented with food and product donations to Feeding America National Food Bank Network only.

California Regions Grant Program funds community projects in three areas of California: Orland, Tulare/Kings/Bakersfield and Ontario, initiated by Land O'Lakes dairy member-leaders.

Community Grants Program provides support through cash grants to nonprofit organizations that are working to improve communities where Land O'Lakes has a significant concentration of members or employees. Foundation's primary focus area is hunger and hunger-related issues.

Dollars for Doers Program recognizes employee and retiree volunteerism with financial contributions to 501(c)(3) nonprofit organizations based on volunteer hours.

Matching Gifts to Education Program matches gifts by full- and part-time employees, Board of Directors members and Leadership Council members to grades K-12, postsecondary education, and public radio and public television stations.

Member Co-op Match Program matches dollar-for-dollar the cash donations of member cooperatives, thus doubling the funds available for hometown projects.

Mid-Atlantic Grant Program funds community projects in Maryland, New York, Pennsylvania and Virginia, initiated by Land O'Lakes dairy member-leaders.

YEAR PROGRAM STARTED: 1981

PURPOSE:
To demonstrate a commitment to improving and enhancing the quality of life in communities where Land O'Lakes has facilities, plants, members and employees; to invest and participate in community programs that strengthen and preserve the quality of rural life; to encourage and support employee volunteerism.

LEGAL BASIS:
Corporate foundation.

ELIGIBILITY:
Contributions are generally restricted to organizations which have been granted

501(c)(3) tax-exempt status and are working to improve communities where Land O'Lakes has a significant concentration of members or employees. Contributions are focused in the western, north central and eastern states. Of our donations, 85% will be made in rural areas and 15% in urban areas within those states.

Funds generally will not be used for lobbying, political and religious organizations, veteran, fraternal and labor organizations, fund-raising events, benefits or advertising, national groups, individuals, scholarships, private colleges and universities, disease/medical research or treatment or racing/sports sponsorships.

Matching Gift recipient organizations must be located in the U.S. and be tax-exempt under Section 501(c)(3) of the Internal Revenue Code. Eligible institutions include the following:
(1) elementary and secondary schools that are fully accredited by the Department of Education;
(2) public or private colleges, universities, junior colleges, technical/vocational institutes, community colleges and graduate professional schools with appropriate regional or professional accreditation, or tax-exempt alumni funds, foundations or associations that collect funds exclusively for the direct benefit of an eligible institution and;
(3) public radio and television stations that meet the criteria established by the Corporation for Public Broadcasting.

Organizations are eligible for only one grant per calendar year.

FINANCIAL DATA:
Amount of support per award: Varies.
Total amount of support: Approximately $13,200,000 for the year 2017.
Matching fund requirements: Cash only.

CO-OP FUNDING PROGRAMS: Through the Member Co-op Match Program, Land O'Lakes member cooperatives may request that the Foundation match their donations to local nonprofits, within the parameters of the program.

REPRESENTATIVE AWARDS:
Feeding America National Food Bank Network.

APPLICATION INFO:
Grant applications are by invitation only.
Duration: Varies.

PUBLICATIONS:
Contributions program guidelines.

IRS I.D.: 41-1864977

ADDRESS INQUIRIES TO:
Vice President
Land O'Lakes Foundation
P.O. Box 64101
St. Paul, MN 55164-0101

LAND O'LAKES FOUNDATION   [183]
4001 Lexington Avenue North
Arden Hills, MN 55126
(651) 375-2470
E-mail: landolakesfoundation@landolakes.com
Web Site: www.landolakesinc.
com/responsibility

AREAS OF INTEREST:
Dairy science or dairy manufacturing/marketing.

NAME(S) OF PROGRAMS:
● **John Brandt Memorial Scholarship Fund**

TYPE:
Scholarships. John Brandt Memorial Scholarship Program is a $5,000 scholarship available to graduate students pursuing dairy-related degrees. One or two scholarships are awarded annually to deserving candidates who have demonstrated exceptional commitment and aptitude toward their field of study.

PURPOSE:
To encourage graduate study in dairy science or dairy marketing/manufacturing.

LEGAL BASIS:
Corporate foundation.

ELIGIBILITY:
Applicants must be pursuing a program of study leading to a Master's or Doctorate degree in dairy cattle nutrition, genetics, physiology or management, or the manufacturing, processing or marketing of milk and dairy products at one of the four following institutions: University of Minnesota, University of Wisconsin, Iowa State University and South Dakota State University. Such factors as personal recommendations, scholastic record, planned program of study and research and future plans for working in the dairy industry or closely related fields shall be considered in making the award.

FINANCIAL DATA:
Total amount of support: Up to $25,000, depending on need and endowment market performance.

NO. AWARDS: Up to 2 annually.

APPLICATION INFO:
The Foundation sends out Requests for Proposals (RFPs) to the qualifying schools to begin the application process. Those with recommendations should send an application form including personal history, transcripts of scholastic record, and a plan of study and research to be followed in pursuit of an advanced degree. Applications should be sent to the Land O'Lakes Foundation, P.O. Box 64101, MS 2018, St. Paul, MN 55164-0101.
Duration: One academic year. No renewals.
Deadline: June 15.

ADDRESS INQUIRIES TO:
Land O'Lakes Foundation
P.O. Box 64101
MS 2018
St. Paul, MN 55164-0101

*SPECIAL STIPULATIONS:
Scholarships for graduate-level studies.

HERBERT AND GERTRUDE LATKIN CHARITABLE FOUNDATION   [184]
445 South Figueroa Street
MC G02-053
Los Angeles, CA 90071
(800) 227-6468
E-mail: premier.california@unionbank.com

FOUNDED: 1991

AREAS OF INTEREST:
Animal cruelty, child abuse, emergency medical services, health and welfare to elderly and needy people, scholarships to deserving college students.

TYPE:
Project/program grants; Scholarships.

YEAR PROGRAM STARTED: 1991

PURPOSE:
To promote the health and welfare of the elderly; to prevent cruelty to animals; to provide emergency medical service for persons suffering as a result of calamity or disaster; to prevent child abuse; to provide assistance to the needy; to provide scholarships to college students.

LEGAL BASIS:
Private family foundation.

ELIGIBILITY:
Grants are made to organizations that have tax-exempt status under Section 501(c)(3) of the Internal Revenue Code. No grants are made to individuals or religious organizations.

GEOG. RESTRICTIONS: Santa Barbara County, California.

FINANCIAL DATA:
Amount of support per award: Varies.
Total amount of support: $213,500 for the year 2017.

NO. MOST RECENT APPLICANTS: 65.

NO. AWARDS: 57.

APPLICATION INFO:
Send a letter of inquiry outlining the organization's goal and purposes, the intended use and amount of the grant requested and 501(c)(3) letter.
Duration: One year. Renewal possible.
Deadline: April 1 and October 1.

IRS I.D.: 77-6070540

ADDRESS INQUIRIES TO:
Stephanie Eubanks, Trust Officer
(See address above.)

THE BLANCHE AND IRVING LAURIE FOUNDATION   [185]
P.O. Box 53
Roseland, NJ 07068-5788
(973) 993-1743
Fax: (973) 993-3146

AREAS OF INTEREST:
Arts, children, needs of the elderly, education, medical care and needs of the Jewish community.

TYPE:
Capital grants; Project/program grants.

LEGAL BASIS:
Private foundation.

ELIGIBILITY:
Funds given for specific projects only. No funds for general organization endowments, nor to meet general operating expenses or budget deficits.

GEOG. RESTRICTIONS: Social service programs: New Jersey.

FINANCIAL DATA:
Amount of support per award: $25,000 to $50,000.

APPLICATION INFO:
Submit seven copies of proposal including statement of program objectives, project budget, plans for publicizing the project, background information about the organization and copy of IRS tax-exemption letter.
Duration: Varies.
Deadline: Proposals accepted year-round.

PUBLICATIONS:
Informational brochure.

ADDRESS INQUIRIES TO:
Gene R. Korf, Esq., Executive Director
(See address above.)

LIBRA FOUNDATION [186]
Three Canal Plaza, Suite 500
Portland, ME 04101
(207) 879-6280
Fax: (207) 879-6281
E-mail: kathi@librafoundation.org
Web Site: www.librafoundation.org

FOUNDED: 1989

AREAS OF INTEREST:
Arts, culture and humanities, education,
environment, health, human services,
public/society benefit and religion.

TYPE:
Grants-in-aid; Project/program grants.

YEAR PROGRAM STARTED: 1989

PURPOSE:
To strive for innovative ways to enrich
Maine, empower communities, and enhance
the quality of life of all Maine citizens.

ELIGIBILITY:
Charitable nonprofit organizations whose
activities, operations, or purposes take place
only within the state of Maine. Religious
organizations are eligible. Organizations must
supply a copy of tax-exempt 501(c)(3) letter.
Grants are not made to individuals.

GEOG. RESTRICTIONS: Maine.

FINANCIAL DATA:
Amount of support per award: Up to
$25,000.
Total amount of support: Approximately
$5,331,594 for the year 2018.

NO. MOST RECENT APPLICANTS: 317.

NO. AWARDS: 48.

APPLICATION INFO:
Applicants are asked to complete a
two-paged application in accordance with the
Foundation's guidelines, both of which may
be obtained from the Foundation web site.
Duration: One-time grant. May reapply after
expiration of one year.
Deadline: February 15, May 15, August 15
and November 15.

ADDRESS INQUIRIES TO:
Kathi Giedris, Administrative Assistant
(See address above.)

LILLY ENDOWMENT INC. [187]
2801 North Meridian Street
Indianapolis, IN 46208
(317) 924-5471
Fax: (317) 926-4431
E-mail: cebulaj@lei.org
Web Site: www.lillyendowment.org

FOUNDED: 1937

AREAS OF INTEREST:
Community development, education and
religion.

TYPE:
Awards/prizes; Challenge/matching grants;
Conferences/seminars; Development grants;
Fellowships; General operating grants;
Matching gifts; Project/program grants;
Research grants. In the area of community
development, grantmaking focuses primarily
on enhancing the quality of life in
Indianapolis and Indiana. Grants support
human and social needs, central-city and
neighborhood revitalization, low- and
moderate-income housing, and arts and
culture in Indianapolis. On a statewide level,
grants are made through initiatives to support
community foundations and United Ways.
Nationally, Lilly Endowment provides
support on an invitational basis for
compelling other causes that are consistent
with areas of interest, such as disaster relief
and recovery efforts and programs for
veterans' affairs and their families.

In the area of education, grantmaking
revolves primarily around objectives to
enhance and increase the educational
attainment and meaningful economic
opportunities of residents in Indiana and the
overall aim of improving the quality of life
of the state's residents. Lilly Endowment
supports efforts in Indiana on an invitational
basis that promote high-quality early
childhood education, strengthen K-12
education, prepare students for education and
careers beyond high school, connect college
students and graduates with meaningful
employment opportunities in Indiana,
enhance the effectiveness of Indiana colleges
and universities to prepare their students for
successful lives and careers, and build the
state's intellectual capital. Nationally, Lilly
Endowment supports on an invitational basis
programs that expand and enhance higher
education opportunities for African
Americans, Native Americans and Latino
Americans.

In the area of religion, support for programs
that enrich the religious lives of American
Christians, mainly by supporting efforts to
call, support and educate a new generation of
talented pastors and to strengthen current
pastors in their capacities for excellence in
ministry; support for programs that seek to
help congregations be healthy communities
of faith; support for theological seminaries
and other educational and religious
institutions that share these aims; and support
for projects which strengthen the
contributions that religious ideas, practices,
values and institutions make to the common
good. In addition, through grants to major
cultural institutions and 501(c)(3) news and
media organizations, Lilly Endowment seeks
to foster public understanding about religious
and lift up in fair and accurate ways the
contributions that people of all faiths and
diverse religious communities make to our
greater civic well-being.

In the area of youth, support for
direct-service organizations in central
Indiana; support for building capacity of
intermediary organizations throughout the
state; and support for professional
development for the staff and volunteer
leadership of these organizations.

In the area of fund-raising and philanthropy,
support for programs (nationally and in
Indiana) to increase the charitable giving
among Americans; support for efforts to
create a body of reliable knowledge about
giving and fund-raising; and support for
scholarly pursuit of the subject.

YEAR PROGRAM STARTED: 1937

PURPOSE:
To support the causes of community
development, education and religion.

LEGAL BASIS:
Private foundation.

ELIGIBILITY:
Applicants must be 501(c)(3) tax-exempt
public organizations and institutions with
appropriate interests in targeted areas.
Grantmaking prohibitions generally include
loans or cash to individuals, health care
projects, mass media projects, endowments,
libraries outside Indianapolis, and general
operating support/capital campaigns for
organizations outside of Indiana.

GEOG. RESTRICTIONS: Primarily Indianapolis
and the state of Indiana.

FINANCIAL DATA:
Grants vary in amount depending on the
needs and nature of the request.
Amount of support per award: Varies.
Total amount of support: $527,700,000 in
grants paid (excluding employee incentive
matching program) for the year 2019.
Matching fund requirements: Varies.

NO. MOST RECENT APPLICANTS: 2,121
(excluding employee incentive matching
program requests) for the year 2018.

APPLICATION INFO:
Except for specialized programs, no official
application forms are required. Guidelines for
applicants are found on the web site. The
usual first step is a two-page letter outlining
the project and budget and a description of
the applicant organization, including a
statement of federal tax-exempt status.
Duration: One to three years; typically, one
year.
Deadline: Applications accepted on an
ongoing basis.

PUBLICATIONS:
Application guidelines; annual report.

IRS I.D.: 35-0868122

ADDRESS INQUIRIES TO:
Program Office
(See address above.)

*SPECIAL STIPULATIONS:
Awards are made to 501(c)(3) groups only.

LINCOLN FINANCIAL
FOUNDATION   [188]
1300 South Clinton Street
Fort Wayne, IN 46802
(260) 455-3868
Fax: (260) 455-4004
E-mail: allison.sandsdrinkwater@lfg.com
Web Site: www.lfg.com

FOUNDED: 1962

AREAS OF INTEREST:
Arts, youth education, human services and
workforce/economic development.

CONSULTING OR VOLUNTEER SERVICES:
Volunteer Involvement Program for
employees of Lincoln Financial Group.

TYPE:
Matching gifts; Project/program grants.

YEAR PROGRAM STARTED: 1962

PURPOSE:
To enhance the quality of life and help
individuals face their futures with confidence
in communities where employees work.

LEGAL BASIS:
Corporate Foundation.

ELIGIBILITY:
Applicants must be 501(c)(3) organizations.

No grants to individuals, for endowments, for
sponsorship of sporting events or for the
purchase of tickets.

GEOG. RESTRICTIONS: Hartford, Connecticut;
Fort Wayne, Indiana; Omaha, Nebraska;
Concord, New Hampshire; Greensboro, North
Carolina; Philadelphia, Pennsylvania.

FINANCIAL DATA:
Amount of support per award: Varies.

NO. MOST RECENT APPLICANTS: 420.

NO. AWARDS: Over 300 annually.

APPLICATION INFO:
Online application form required. Some
attachments requested.
Deadline: Varies.

PUBLICATIONS:
Guidelines.

IRS I.D.: 35-6042099

ADDRESS INQUIRIES TO:
Program Officer
(See address above.)

THE LOATS FOUNDATION,
INC.   [189]
35 East Church Street
Frederick, MD 21701
(301) 663-6361
Fax: (301) 663-7747

FOUNDED: 1979

AREAS OF INTEREST:
Scholarship for Frederick County residents
only and charitable organizations of
Frederick County, MD.

TYPE:
Scholarships.

YEAR PROGRAM STARTED: 1979

PURPOSE:
To help residents of Frederick County, MD
go on to higher education by providing
financial aid.

LEGAL BASIS:
Nonprofit foundation.

ELIGIBILITY:
Applicant must be a resident of Frederick
County, MD. Scholarships are distributed by
colleges on a need basis.

GEOG. RESTRICTIONS: Frederick County,
Maryland.

FINANCIAL DATA:
Amount of support per award: $3,000 cap.
Total amount of support: Varies.

APPLICATION INFO:
Applications for scholarships are available at
all Maryland colleges and universities.
Duration: One year. Renewable on need
basis.

ADDRESS INQUIRIES TO:
Helen Hahn, Secretary
(See address above.)

THE LUBRIZOL
FOUNDATION   [190]
29400 Lakeland Boulevard, Mail Drop 054B
Wickliffe, OH 44092-2298
(440) 347-1797
Fax: (440) 347-1858
E-mail: karen.lerchbacher@lubrizol.com
Web Site: www.lubrizol.com

FOUNDED: 1952

AREAS OF INTEREST:
Education, health and human services, civic,
cultural, environmental and youth activities.

NAME(S) OF PROGRAMS:
- **Community Connection Employee
  Volunteer Gift Program**
- **Matching Gift Program**

TYPE:
Capital grants; Fellowships; General
operating grants; Matching gifts;
Project/program grants; Scholarships. The
Foundation has scholarship programs at 22
selected colleges and universities. It also
matches gifts of Lubrizol employees to most
charitable organizations on a dollar-for-dollar
basis.

In the area of education, support is given for
scholarships, fellowships and awards in
selected fields of study through selected
colleges and universities, with major
emphasis on the study of chemistry and
chemical and mechanical engineering, capital
and operating grants to colleges, universities,
schools, educational programs and combined
educational funds.

In the area of health and human services,
support is provided for combined funds,
direct grants to health and human service
activities.

In the area of civic and cultural, support is
provided for public television stations,
performing arts organizations, schools of fine
arts and museums.

In the area of youth activities, support is
given to programs that contribute to
character-building, such as those which
promote good citizenship, self-reliance, an
understanding of free enterprise and an
appreciation of nature and the environment.

In the environmental area, support is given to
parks, nature centers, conservancies and local
environmental education efforts.

YEAR PROGRAM STARTED: 1952

PURPOSE:
To support educational, youth, health, human
services, civic and cultural and environmental
activities of a tax-exempt, charitable nature.

LEGAL BASIS:
Private, tax-exempt foundation.

ELIGIBILITY:
Grants are made to U.S. nonprofit,
educational or other charitable tax-exempt
organizations. Grants are not generally made
to endowments, religious or political
purposes or individuals.

GEOG. RESTRICTIONS: Primarily Greater
Cleveland, Ohio and Houston, Texas.

FINANCIAL DATA:
Amount of support per award: Grants vary in
amount, depending upon the needs and
nature of the request.
Total amount of support: $3,897,132,
including matching gifts, for the year 2019.
Matching fund requirements: 1:1 match; $100
minimum; $5,000 maximum, and five gifts
maximum.

NO. AWARDS: 187 grants for the year 2019.

REPRESENTATIVE AWARDS:
$25,000 to Cleveland Zoological Society in
support of the Zoo Education and Workforce
Development Initiative; $100,000 to
Vocational Guidance Services for ACHIEVE
Capital Campaign; $50,000 to University
Hospital Rainbow Babies & Children's
Hospital for support of the Education
Program providing equipment, technology
and supplies; $25,000 to The Literacy
Cooperative to support three years of
implementation of the Imagination.

APPLICATION INFO:
Grant proposals should include the following:
(1) a cover letter that summarizes the
purpose of the request signed by the
executive officer of the organization;
(2) a narrative of specific information related
to the subject of the request;
(3) current audited financial statements and a
specific project budget, if applicable and;
(4) documentation of the organization's
Federal tax-exempt status.

Additional descriptive literature (annual
report, brochures, etc.) that accurately
characterizes the overall activities of the
organization is appreciated. Upon review,
further information may be requested
including an interview or site visit.

Applicants will receive written notification of
the decision on their proposal. An
organization whose request has been declined
should not submit another proposal for at
least 12 months after such notification.
Duration: One year, with possible renewal.
Some grants are ongoing.

PUBLICATIONS:
Annual report.

IRS I.D.: 34-6500595

OFFICERS:
Eric R. Schnur, Chairman
E.A. Grove, President
J. Bryan Pitts, Treasurer
K.A. Lerchbacher, Secretary

TRUSTEES:
J.A. Edgar
R.T. Graf

E.A. Grove
K.L. Jethrow
K.A. Lerchbacher
Eric R. Schnur

ADDRESS INQUIRIES TO:
Karen A. Lerchbacher, Program Officer
(See address above.)

THE HENRY LUCE FOUNDATION, INC. [191]

51 Madison Avenue, 30th Floor
New York, NY 10010
(212) 489-7700
Fax: (212) 581-9541
E-mail: hlf1@hluce.org
Web Site: www.hluce.org

FOUNDED: 1936

AREAS OF INTEREST:
Interdisciplinary exploration of higher education, increased understanding between Asia and the U.S., the study of religion and theology, scholarship in American art, advancement of women in science and engineering, and environmental and public policy programs.

NAME(S) OF PROGRAMS:
- **American Art Program**
- **Asia Program**
- **Clare Boothe Luce Program**
- **Higher Education Program**
- **HRL Initiative on Religion in International Affairs**
- **Luce Foundation Theology Program**
- **Luce Scholars Program**
- **Public Policy Program**

TYPE:
Fellowships; Project/program grants; Scholarships. American Art Program focuses on the American fine and decorative arts and is committed to scholarship and the overall enhancement of this field. The program is national in scope and provides support for all periods and genres of American art history.

The Clare Boothe Luce Program promotes the advancement of American women through higher education in the sciences, engineering and mathematics.

The Luce Foundation's Theology program encourages the development of leadership for religious communities through theological education, and fosters scholarship that links the academy to churches and the wider public. The program provides funding for seminary education, leadership, ecumenical and interreligious programs, and religion and the arts.

The Luce Scholars Program provides stipends and internships for young Americans to live and work in Asia each year.

PURPOSE:
To promote interdisciplinary exploration of higher education, increased understanding between Asia and the U.S., the study of religion and theology, scholarship in American art, opportunities for women in science, mathematics and engineering, and public policy programs.

ELIGIBILITY:
The Foundation does not support health care or medical projects and does not fund development assistance work overseas. It does not normally assist journalism, media and film projects or the performing arts. The Foundation does not offer funding for individuals.

FINANCIAL DATA:
Amount of support per award: Varies.
Total amount of support: Varies.

APPLICATION INFO:
The Foundation receives inquiries through its web site portal. There is an eligibility quiz to perform prior to being able to submit an inquiry. Applicants must review the program guidelines before taking the eligibility quiz. If successfully completed, the applicant will be directed to create an account. Once registration is approved, applicant may begin the inquiry process.
Duration: Varies.
Deadline: Varies.

LYNDHURST FOUNDATION [192]

517 East Fifth Street
Chattanooga, TN 37403-1826
(423) 756-0767
Fax: (423) 756-0770
E-mail: bclark@lyndhurstfoundation.org
Web Site: www.lyndhurstfoundation.org

FOUNDED: 1938

AREAS OF INTEREST:
Education, conservation, arts, culture, economy, urban design and development, neighborhood revitalization and physical health.

Enhancing the quality of Chattanooga's public gathering places in downtown and along the riverfront, plus its public schools, its diverse arts and cultural organizations and its natural environment. Beyond the city's boundaries, the Foundation wants to be involved in projects that protect and enhance the natural environment of the southern Appalachian region.

TYPE:
Matching gifts; Project/program grants. The Foundation intends to focus upon continued development of the Tennessee Riverpark, redevelopment of the Southside as a live-and-work urban neighborhood, facilitation of historic preservation, stimulation of downtown housing development, strengthening of the city's arts and cultural life, protection and enhancement of the community's natural environment, the reform of the community's public schools, the continued development of improved housing opportunities for people of modest means and innovations in social service programs that provide genuine progress against social problems and genuine enhancement of community strengths in Chattanooga.

YEAR PROGRAM STARTED: 1978

PURPOSE:
To identify and invest in initiatives, institutions, people and programs that contribute to the long-term livability and resilience of the greater Chattanooga, TN region.

LEGAL BASIS:
Private foundation.

ELIGIBILITY:
Applicants must be 501(c)(3) organizations.

Grants are distributed primarily at the initiative of the Foundation through the cultivation of strategic partnerships with nonprofit organizations which have the demonstrated capacity and leadership to engender positive and measurable outcomes within the Foundation's declared areas of interest.

Unsolicited proposals will not be eligible for consideration.

GEOG. RESTRICTIONS: The greater Chattanooga, Tennessee region.

FINANCIAL DATA:
Amount of support per award:
Approximately $96,000 average grant for the year 2018.
Total amount of support: Grants of $5,915,386 for the year 2018.

NO. AWARDS: Varies.

REPRESENTATIVE AWARDS:
$50,000 to Georgia Alabama Land Trust; $40,000 to Tennessee Valley Railroad Museum.

APPLICATION INFO:
Potential partners will be invited to submit grant proposals that:
(1) describe the program of work to be undertaken;
(2) indicate the desired level of funding;
(3) list the results that should be achieved and;
(4) define the means by which the project outcomes will be evaluated.

The narrative section of the proposal should be limited to three pages and include the following attachments:
(1) a description of the sponsoring organization;
(2) a list of the board of directors and staff;
(3) a copy of the organization's annual budget (both income and expenditures);
(4) an estimated project budget with line items and;
(5) a copy of the organization's tax-exempt ruling from the IRS.
Duration: One year. Renewal possible for up to three years.
Deadline: Proposals are due six weeks in advance of the Foundation's quarterly board meeting dates, which typically occur in February, May, August and November. Program staff will be available to work with applicants to ensure that materials are delivered on a timely basis and in the required format.

OFFICERS:
Alison G. Lebovitz, Chairman of the Board
Benic M. Clark, III, President/Treasurer
Katherine N. Currin, Secretary

TRUSTEES:
Stephen A. Culp
Katherine N. Currin
Kathleen S. Hunt, M.D.
James O. Kennedy
Alison G. Lebovitz
James J. McGinness
Robert K. Mills
Robert C. Taylor, Jr.
Margaret W. Townsend

STAFF:
Benic M. Clark, III, President/Treasurer
Macon C. Toledano, Associate Director
Nena Powell, Controller
Kathleen Nolte, Program Officer

ADDRESS INQUIRIES TO:
Catherine C. Cox
(See phone number above.)

*PLEASE NOTE:
Funding is limited to a 16-county, tri-state area surrounding Chattanooga.

M & M AREA COMMUNITY FOUNDATION

1110 10th Avenue, Suite L-1
Menominee, MI 49858
(906) 864-3599
E-mail: info@mmacf.org
Web Site: www.mmacf.org

TYPE:
Project/program grants; Scholarships.

See entry 1206 for full listing.

JOHN D. AND CATHERINE T. MACARTHUR FOUNDATION   [193]

140 South Dearborn Street
Chicago, IL 60603-5285
(312) 726-8000
E-mail: 4answers@macfound.org
Web Site: www.macfound.org

FOUNDED: 1978

NAME(S) OF PROGRAMS:
- **Awards**
- **Big Bets**
- **Enduring Commitments**
- **Field Support**

TYPE:
Fellowships; General operating grants; Project/program grants. The following specific programs are found under the above general program areas:

Awards & Special Projects: 100 & Change; MacArthur Award for Creative & Effective Institutions; MacArthur Fellows.

Big Bets: Climate Solutions; Criminal Justice; Nuclear Challenges; On Nigeria.

Enduring Commitments: Chicago Commitment; Journalism & Media.

Field Support: Impact Investments; Philanthropy; Technology in the Public Interest.

YEAR PROGRAM STARTED: 1978

PURPOSE:
To build a more just, verdant and peaceful world.

LEGAL BASIS:
Private, independent foundation.

ELIGIBILITY:
The Foundation develops grantmaking strategies designed to meet very specific goals. Please consult the Foundation's web site regarding the grantmaking guidelines for each program.

The Foundation does not support political activities or attempts to influence action on specific legislation, and does not provide the following:
(1) scholarships/tuition assistance for undergraduate, graduate or postgraduate studies;
(2) annual fund-raising drives;
(3) institutional benefits;
(4) honorary functions or similar projects and;
(5) unsolicited grants to individuals (except for the MacArthur Fellows, which operates through a separate nominating process that is not open to public nominations).

FINANCIAL DATA:
Amount of support per award: Varies.
Total amount of support: $283,820,733 for the year 2019.

NO. MOST RECENT APPLICANTS: Over 1,100 for the year 2019.

NO. AWARDS: 387 for the year 2019.

APPLICATION INFO:
Complete details are available on the Foundation web site.
Duration: One to five years. Renewals by reapplication.
Deadline: Varies.

PUBLICATIONS:
Annual report.

IRS I.D.: 23-7093598

ADDRESS INQUIRIES TO:
Web site: macfound.fluxx.io

*PLEASE NOTE:
The Foundation awards the majority of its grants to organizations identified by its staff. Each year it also awards grants to individuals through the MacArthur Fellows program, which does not accept applications or nominations.

MARBROOK FOUNDATION [194]

730 Second Avenue South
Suite 1400
Minneapolis, MN 55402
(612) 752-1783
Fax: (612) 752-1780
E-mail: mbrooks@marbrookfoundation.org
Web Site: www.marbrookfoundation.org

FOUNDED: 1948

AREAS OF INTEREST:
Arts, environment, immigrants and refugees, and body, mind and spirit.

TYPE:
Capital grants; General operating grants; Project/program grants.

YEAR PROGRAM STARTED: 1948

PURPOSE:
To promote the values of the Brooks Family by making grants and focusing involvement in designated charitable areas and causes that reflect those values.

LEGAL BASIS:
Tax-exempt, private foundation.

ELIGIBILITY:
The Foundation's priorities in the area of arts are projects and programs that foster cultural awareness and understanding and projects and programs that encourage cross-cultural collaboration, community integration, and inclusion.

In the area of environment, the Foundation only makes grants to 501(c)(3) charitable organizations. The Foundation does not fund health clinics and medical treatment, food shelves or food stamp programs, conferences and events, individual college and academic scholarships or affordable housing.

In the area of immigrants and refugees, the Foundation will consider proposals for programs that provide support in the following areas:
(1) Culturally safe and conducive learning environments for children and youth. These programs may include a focus on mindfulness;
(2) Intentional intercultural learning and cross-cultural experiences;
(3) Healthy development, life-skill development, and well-being for youth and families;
(4) The development of skills for financial

independence;
(5) Leadership development and empowerment in the community and;
(6) Cultural preservation.

GEOG. RESTRICTIONS: Seven county metropolitan area of Minneapolis, Minnesota.

FINANCIAL DATA:
Amount of support per award: Minimum $5,000, except Environmental Grants.
Total amount of support: $652,500 for the year 2019.

NO. AWARDS: Varies.

REPRESENTATIVE AWARDS:
$12,000 to World Savvy for empowering schools to engage immigrant learners; $10,000 to Wilderness Inquiry for introductory outdoor adventures for underserved immigrant youth; $10,000 to Minnesota Museum of American Art for an exhibit called Choice of Weapons, Honor and Glory: The Visions of Gordon Parks and Jamel Shabazz; $30,000 to Fresh Energy for public policy work toward a more equitable clean energy future.

APPLICATION INFO:
Applications must be submitted online.
Deadline: March 1 for Immigrants and Refugees. September 1 for Arts and Environment.

TRUSTEES:
Markell Kiefer, Chairperson
Edward Brooks
Katherine Werner Brooks
Markell Hapka
Bill King
John Larsen

EXECUTIVE DIRECTOR:
Minna K. Brooks

MARIN COMMUNITY FOUNDATION   [195]

5 Hamilton Landing, Suite 200
Novato, CA 94949
(415) 464-2500
Fax: (415) 464-2555
E-mail: info@marincf.org
Web Site: www.marincf.org

FOUNDED: 1986

AREAS OF INTEREST:
Education, economic opportunity, health and environment.

TYPE:
Capital grants; Challenge/matching grants; General operating grants; Project/program grants; Scholarships; Technical assistance.

YEAR PROGRAM STARTED: 1987

PURPOSE:
To encourage and apply philanthropic contributions to help improve the human condition, embrace diversity, promote a humane and democratic society, and enhance the community's quality of life, now and for future generations.

LEGAL BASIS:
Community foundation.

ELIGIBILITY:
Proposals must be consistent with the Foundation's program goals and must meet two additional requirements. First, the applicant must be a public or nonprofit organization and, second, the proposed project must be conducted in and/or benefit the residents of Marin County, CA. Projects with a regional or multi-county benefit may

be funded only in proportion to the extent that they benefit the Marin County community.

Ineligible activities include for-profit purposes, basic research, the start-up of new nonprofit organizations that will unnecessarily duplicate existing programs or services or undertake services that can be more effectively provided by other organizations and grants to individuals. Other limitations specific to each program area are outlined in the funding guidelines. No grants are made to individuals.

Buck Trust grants are limited to Marin County.

GEOG. RESTRICTIONS: Grants from the Buck Trust are restricted to Marin County, California.The Foundation's donor-advised funds support efforts locally and in communities around the world.

FINANCIAL DATA:
The Foundation manages more than $2.18 billion in total assets.
Amount of support per award: Varies.
Total amount of support: Over $244,400,000 in grants annually.

NO. AWARDS: 345.

APPLICATION INFO:
The following procedures apply:
(1) The Foundation issues a Request for Proposals (RFP);
(2) If interested, a representative from a nonprofit organization can register on the Foundation's online Grant Center;
(3) The nonprofit representative can then submit an online Letter of Intent (LOI) for the RFP and;
(4) Following the Foundation's review of the LOIs, selected applicants are invited to submit a full proposal through the Grant Center.
Consult the web site address above for further details.
Duration: Varies. Renewal possible.

PUBLICATIONS:
General information brochure.

IRS I.D.: 94-3007979

OFFICERS:
Thomas Peters, Ph.D., President and Chief Executive Officer
Sid Hartman, Chief Financial and Operating Officer

BOARD OF DIRECTORS:
Mark Buell, Chairperson
Mitch Cohen
Peter Hamilton
Saul Pena
Robert J. Reynolds
Roxanne Richards
Maureen Sedonaen
Daniel Skaff
Debra Wetherby

MARRIOTT INTERNATIONAL, INC. [196]

10400 Fernwood Road
Bethesda, MD 20817
E-mail: community.engagement@marriott.com
Web Site: serve360.marriott.com

FOUNDED: 1927

AREAS OF INTEREST:
Shelter and food, environment, readiness for hotel careers, vitality of children, and embracing diversity and people with disabilities.

TYPE:
Project/program grants. Support to national and global nonprofits that address help, support readiness for jobs, diversity and inclusion, poverty alleviation, and the environment.

LEGAL BASIS:
Corporate contributions program.

ELIGIBILITY:
Grants are made to tax-exempt 501(c)(3) organizations which fulfill important community needs.

FINANCIAL DATA:
Amount of support per award: Varies.
Total amount of support: Varies.

APPLICATION INFO:
The Corporation only accepts requests online via its web site.
Duration: Varies.
Deadline: Before end of October.

PUBLICATIONS:
Application guidelines.

ROBERT R. MCCORMICK FOUNDATION [197]

205 North Michigan Avenue
Suite 4300
Chicago, IL 60601-5927
(312) 445-5000
Fax: (312) 445-5001
E-mail: info@mccormickfoundation.org
Web Site: www.mccormickfoundation.org

FOUNDED: 1955

AREAS OF INTEREST:
Community strengthening, community justice, democracy, youth media, early childhood education, and veterans affairs.

NAME(S) OF PROGRAMS:
- **Communities Program**
- **Community Justice Initiative**
- **Democracy Program**
- **Education Program**
- **Veterans Program**

TYPE:
General operating grants; Project/program grants.

YEAR PROGRAM STARTED: 1955

PURPOSE:
To foster communities of educated, informed and engaged citizens.

ELIGIBILITY:
The Foundation only makes grants to 501(c)(3) organizations that serve charitable purposes and meet the Foundation's program guidelines. Programs that advance a particular religious or sectarian purpose, partisan political or electoral activities, endowments, or individual scholarships or personal research projects are not funded.

FINANCIAL DATA:
Total amount of support: $77,000,000 in total grants approved for the year ended December 31, 2018.

NO. AWARDS: 460 total grants approved for the year ended December 31, 2018.

PUBLICATIONS:
Annual report; program brochures; conference reports.

J.M. MCDONALD FOUNDATION, INC. [198]

P.O. Box 3219
Evergreen, CO 80437-3219
(303) 674-9300
Fax: (303) 674-9216
E-mail: info@jmmcdonaldfoundation.org
Web Site: jmmcdonaldfoundation.org

FOUNDED: 1952

AREAS OF INTEREST:
Education, humanities, health, and a variety of social and human services.

TYPE:
Capital grants; Development grants; Project/program grants.

YEAR PROGRAM STARTED: 1952

LEGAL BASIS:
Private foundation.

ELIGIBILITY:
Nonprofit organizations with appropriate interests are eligible for support. Applicants must be located in the U.S. and have IRS-509A and 501(c)(3) letter. No grants are made to individuals, for projects to influence legislation or elections, or solely for conferences, seminars, workshops, travel or exhibits.

GEOG. RESTRICTIONS: Primarily upstate New York.

FINANCIAL DATA:
Amount of support per award: Grants vary in amount, depending upon the needs and nature of the request.

APPLICATION INFO:
Application for funding through online granting process is available at the Foundation web site.
Duration: One year.
Deadline: April 15 and September 15, with responses in May and October, respectively.

PUBLICATIONS:
Application guidelines.

OFFICERS AND TRUSTEES:
Donald R. McJunkin, President
Nancy J. Palmer, Vice President and Director
Janet E. Stanton, Vice President and Director
Pamela Criswell, Treasurer and Director
Dana Amundson, Secretary and Director
Scott Palmer, Director

JAMES S. MCDONNELL FOUNDATION [199]

1034 South Brentwood Boulevard
Suite 1850
St. Louis, MO 63117
(314) 721-1532
E-mail: info@jsmf.org
Web Site: www.jsmf.org

FOUNDED: 1950

AREAS OF INTEREST:
Understanding human cognition, teacher learning and teacher change in K-12 classrooms; understanding dynamic and multi-scale systems.

NAME(S) OF PROGRAMS:
- **Special Initiatives**
- **Understanding Dynamic and Multi-Scale Systems**
- **Understanding Human Cognition**

TYPE:
Fellowships; Research grants. Collaborative Activity Awards are to initiate interdisciplinary discussions on problems or issues, to help launch interdisciplinary

research networks, or to fund communities of researchers dedicated to developing new methods, tools and applications of basic research.

Postdoctoral Fellowship Awards are intended to provide students in the final stages of completing a Ph.D. degree more leeway in identifying and securing postdoctoral training opportunities in dynamic and multi-scale systems.

Scholar Awards provide funding in the area of Understanding Human Cognition.

Teachers as Learners focuses on research that builds from a cognitive science perspective on teachers as learners.

YEAR PROGRAM STARTED: 2000

PURPOSE:
To encourage investigators to engage difficult problems; to support ideas and approaches departing from conventional wisdom; to fund novel or interdisciplinary proposals.

LEGAL BASIS:
Private foundation.

FINANCIAL DATA:
Amount of support per award: Collaborative Activity Awards: Varies; Postdoctoral Fellowship: $200,000; Scholar Awards: Up to $600,000, depending on award; Teachers as Learners: Maximum $2,500,000 over five years.

NO. MOST RECENT APPLICANTS: Approximately 150 for the year 2019.

NO. AWARDS: 25.

APPLICATION INFO:
Guidelines and all program applications are available on the Foundation's web site. Letters of inquiry are accepted by invitation only for collaborative fund-seekers.
Duration: Varies.
Deadline: Postdoctoral Fellowship and Teachers as Learners: Varies. There are no deadlines for Collaborative Activity Awards.

IRS I.D.: 54-2074788

OFFICERS:
Dr. Susan Fitzpatrick, President

BOARD OF DIRECTORS:
Jeanne M. Champer
Holly M. James
Alicia S. McDonnell
James S. McDonnell, III
Jeffrey M. McDonnell
John F. McDonnell
Katherine Pipoli
Marcella M. Stevens

ADDRESS INQUIRIES TO:
See e-mail address above.

MCGREGOR FUND   [200]
333 West Fort Street, Suite 2090
Detroit, MI 48226-3134
(313) 963-3495
Fax: (313) 963-3512
E-mail: heidi@mcgregorfund.org
Web Site: www.mcgregorfund.org

FOUNDED: 1925

AREAS OF INTEREST:
Basic needs, recovery and restoration, and skill building in metropolitan Detroit.

TYPE:
General operating grants; Project/program grants. Limited capital grants; program and operational support.

YEAR PROGRAM STARTED: 1925

PURPOSE:
To relieve misfortunes and promote the well-being of mankind.

LEGAL BASIS:
Tax-exempt private foundation.

ELIGIBILITY:
Tax-exempt, Internal Revenue Code 501(c)(3) organizations in the Detroit metropolitan area.

The Fund does not provide loan funds, make direct grants to students for scholarships, make grants for travel, conferences, seminars or workshops, or make grants to individuals.

GEOG. RESTRICTIONS: Tri-county area of Detroit, Michigan.

FINANCIAL DATA:
Amount of support per award: $30,000 to $1,000,000.
Total amount of support: Varies.

NO. AWARDS: Approximately 80 for the year 2019.

APPLICATION INFO:
Guidelines are available on the Fund web site.
Duration: No grants are made on a continuing basis.
Deadline: Submit applications three months prior to Board meeting dates in March, June, September and December.

PUBLICATIONS:
Annual report; guidelines; application procedures.

IRS I.D.: 38-0808800

OFFICERS AND TRUSTEES:
Richard L. Rogers, Chairman
Cynthia N. Ford, Vice Chairman
Kate Levin Markel, President and Secretary
William W. Shelden, Jr., Treasurer
Gerard M. Anderson
Joyce Jenereaux
Leslie A. Murphy
Susan Schooley, M.D.

ADDRESS INQUIRIES TO:
See e-mail address above.

THE MCLEAN CONTRIBUTIONSHIP   [201]
230 Sugartown Road
Suite 30
Wayne, PA 19087
(610) 989-8090
Web Site: fdnweb.org/mclean

FOUNDED: 1951

AREAS OF INTEREST:
Education, environment, health and hospitals, care of the elderly and youth development.

TYPE:
Capital grants; Endowments. The Contributionship makes a relatively limited number of grants for projects of long-term benefit. Its trustees focus on capital projects: bricks and mortar and endowment; they may make grants in ways to encourage the successful funding of projects.

PURPOSE:
To support understanding and preserving the environment; to encourage compassionate and cost-effective health care; to improve the quality of life through education and through support of the communities' cultural assets usually in the form of capital projects.

LEGAL BASIS:
Private foundation.

ELIGIBILITY:
Organizations, including some religious, classified as 501(c)(3) by the IRS can apply. Individuals are ineligible.

The Contributionship favors projects that:
(1) stimulate a better understanding of the natural environment, and encourage the preservation of its important features;
(2) encourage more compassionate and cost-effective care for the ill and aging, in an atmosphere of dignity and self-respect and;
(3) promote education, or medical, scientific or (on occasion) cultural developments enhancing the quality of life.

In addition, the trustees from time to time support projects which:
(1) motivate promising young people to assess and develop their talents despite social and economic obstacles and;
(2) encourage those in newspaper and related fields to become more effective and responsible in helping people understand better how events in their communities and around the world affect them.

GEOG. RESTRICTIONS: Mainly in the Greater Philadelphia area.

FINANCIAL DATA:
Amount of support per award: $1,000 to $150,000.
Total amount of support: $2,700,000 for the year 2019.

NO. MOST RECENT APPLICANTS: 170 for the year 2019.

NO. AWARDS: 117 for the year 2019.

REPRESENTATIVE AWARDS:
$12,000 to Bernardine Center, Chester, PA, towards making essential repairs and improvements to Bernardine Center's Food Pantry and West Side Branch; $38,075,000 to Eastern University, St. Davids, PA, towards equipment for the Nursing Clinical Resource and Simulation Center Expansion Project; $25,000 to Kencrest Centers, Blue Bell, PA, towards the renovation of the facility for KenCrest Day Program for Adults with Disabilities.

APPLICATION INFO:
The Contributionship accepts the common grant application form of the Philanthropy Network Greater Philadelphia. Application should include:
(1) a letter, which describes and justifies the project;
(2) a budget and timetable, strategy for securing funding and latest financial statement;
(3) interim operating statements or budgets for future periods if appropriate;
(4) evidence of tax-exempt status and;
(5) a list of officers and directors.

Application can be submitted online (preferred) or mailed to Sandra L. McLean, Executive Director, at the address above.
Duration: One to three years.
Deadline: Applications must be received six weeks prior to meeting date.

IRS I.D.: 23-6396940

TRUSTEES:
John F. Bales, Chairman
Sandra L. McLean, Executive Director and Trustee
Otis Bullock, Jr.

Diana McLean Liefer
Wendy McLean
Stephen Holt, Advisory Trustee
Martha Morris, Advisory Trustee
Marrea D. Walker-Smith, Advisory Trustee

ADDRESS INQUIRIES TO:
Sandra L. McLean
Executive Director and Trustee
(See address above.)

*PLEASE NOTE:
No grants to individuals.

THE JOSEPH AND MERCEDES MCMICKING FOUNDATION [202]

1004B O'Reilly Avenue
San Francisco, CA 94129
(415) 474-1784
Fax: (415) 474-1754
E-mail: miriam@mcmickingfoundation.org
Web Site: mcmickingfoundation.org

AREAS OF INTEREST:
Arts, computer science, education and
science.

TYPE:
Project/program grants.

PURPOSE:
To improve the quality of life for San
Francisco Bay Area residents through grants
and scholarships for the education and
welfare of children and their families.

LEGAL BASIS:
501(c)(3) nonprofit corporation.

ELIGIBILITY:
The Foundation makes grants only to
organizations that are exempt from federal
tax under Section 501(c)(3) of the Internal
Revenue Code and are not classified as
private foundations under Section 509(a) of
the Code.

The Foundation does not provide support for
grants to individuals or loans.

GEOG. RESTRICTIONS: San Francisco Bay area,
California.

FINANCIAL DATA:
Amount of support per award: Varies.
Total amount of support: $602,915 in total
grants for the year 2019.

APPLICATION INFO:
Organizations seeking information should
mail a letter and application to the Executive
Director. Calls of inquiry are strongly
encouraged. The Foundation will not accept
proposals sent by facsimile.

Complete guidelines and application form are
available on the web site.

Duration: One year.

Deadline: Proposals are accepted throughout
the year.

ADDRESS INQUIRIES TO:
Miriam deQuadros, Executive Director
(See address or phone number above.)

THE MARGARET MCNAMARA EDUCATION GRANTS (MMEG) [203]

The World Bank Family Network
1818 H Street, N.W.
MSN J2-202
Washington, DC 20433
(202) 473-8751
E-mail: info@mmeg.org
Web Site: www.mmeg.org

FOUNDED: 1981

AREAS OF INTEREST:
Agriculture, architecture and urban planning,
civil engineering, education, forestry,
journalism, nursing, nutrition, pediatrics,
public administration, public health, social
sciences, social work and others.

TYPE:
Scholarships. Education grants are awarded
to women from developing and
middle-income countries who, upon
obtainment of their degree, intend to return
to or remain in their countries or other
developing countries, and work to improve
the lives of women and/or children.

YEAR PROGRAM STARTED: 1981

PURPOSE:
To support the education of women from
developing countries and underserved
communities in the U.S. who are committed
to improving the lives of women and children
in their home countries.

LEGAL BASIS:
501(c)(3) public charity.

ELIGIBILITY:
Applicants must meet the following
eligibility criteria:
(1) be at least 25 years of age at time of
application deadline;
(2) be a national of a country listed on the
MMEG Country Eligibility List;
(3) be enrolled at an accredited academic
institution when submitting application and
plan to be enrolled for a full academic term
after award of the grant by the Board and;
(4) not be related to a World Bank Group,
International Monetary Fund or
Inter-American Development Bank staff
member or spouse.

Additional criteria vary by country.

GEOG. RESTRICTIONS: United States, Canada,
South Africa and Latin America.

FINANCIAL DATA:
Amount of support per award: Up to $15,000
in U.S./Canada; $7,000 in South Africa and
Latin America.

NO. AWARDS: 29 for the year 2020.

APPLICATION INFO:
Complete application information is available
on the web site.

Duration: One year. Nonrenewable.

Deadline: U.S. and Canada: January 15.
Latin America: August 15. South Africa:
September 14.

IRS I.D.: 52-1655741

ADDRESS INQUIRIES TO:
MMEG Coordinator
(See address above.)

MEADOWS FOUNDATION, INC. [204]

Wilson Historic District
3003 Swiss Avenue
Dallas, TX 75204-6049
(214) 826-9431
(800) 826-9431
Fax: (214) 827-7042
E-mail: webgrants3003@mfi.org
Web Site: www.mfi.org

FOUNDED: 1948

AREAS OF INTEREST:
Arts and culture, civic and public affairs
(including the natural environment),
education, health (including mental health),
and human services.

TYPE:
Awards/prizes; Capital grants;
Challenge/matching grants; Demonstration
grants; Development grants; Endowments;
General operating grants; Matching gifts;
Project/program grants; Research grants;
Seed money grants; Technical assistance;
Training grants; Loan forgiveness programs.
Program-related investments. Support for
organizations, agencies, programs and
projects within the areas of the Foundation's
interest. Areas of high interest: environment,
mental health and public education.

YEAR PROGRAM STARTED: 1948

PURPOSE:
To assist people and institutions of Texas
improve the quality and circumstances of life
for themselves and future generations.

LEGAL BASIS:
Tax-exempt, private foundation.

ELIGIBILITY:
Applicants must be tax-exempt organizations,
benefitting Texas. No grants are awarded to
individuals. Generally, no contributions for
church or seminary construction, annual
fund-raising drives, out-of-state travel, or
professional conferences/symposia.

GEOG. RESTRICTIONS: Texas.

FINANCIAL DATA:
Amount of support per award: $120,800
average grant for the year 2018.
Total amount of support: Approximately
$35,400,000 for the year 2018.
Matching fund requirements: Stipulated with
specific grants.

NO. MOST RECENT APPLICANTS: 700 to 800.

NO. AWARDS: 195 for the year 2018.

APPLICATION INFO:
Application/proposal should include:
(1) a brief history of the organization, its
current focus and recent accomplishments;
(2) a copy of the latest verification of
tax-exempt status from the IRS;
(3) certified audits for the last three years,
current operating budget and year-to-date
financial statements;
(4) statement of need for the proposed
project, to include population served, and
how project will address need;
(5) a list of trustees or directors, corporate
officers and key staff;
(6) the specific dollar amount requested and
the date payment is needed;
(7) a list of all entities asked to give financial
support and their responses;
(8) project line-item budget (include income
and expenses);
(9) plans to evaluate the project (include
measurable, time-specific goals) and;
(10) support for the project after the grant
period.

Duration: Grants are seldom awarded on a
continuing basis.

Deadline: Proposals are accepted throughout
the year.

PUBLICATIONS:
Annual report; guidelines.

IRS I.D.: 75-6015322

STAFF:
Charles Glover, Senior Program Officer
Michael K. McCoy, Senior Program Officer

Cindy M. Patrick, Senior Program Officer
Kathy Smith, Senior Program Officer

OFFICERS AND DIRECTORS:
Robert A. Meadows, Chairman, Board of
Trustees, Director and Vice President
Linda Perryman Evans, President and Chief
Executive Officer, Trustee and Director
Paula Herring, Vice President and Treasurer
Tom Gale, Vice President and Chief
Investment Officer
Bruce H. Esterline, Senior Vice President for
Strategic Initiatives and Grants
Deborah Fitzpatrick, Vice President for
Human Resources and Administration
Milly Ritzen Crawford, Director
Eric Meadows, Trustee and Director
John Meadows, Director
Mark A. Meadows, Trustee and Director
Kimberly Morris, Director
Dawn Culbertson Peterson, Trustee and
Director
George Ritzen, Director
Joel T. Williams, III, Trustee and Director
Andrew Wilson, Trustee and Director

ADDRESS INQUIRIES TO:
Bruce H. Esterline
Senior Vice President for
Strategic Initiatives and Grants
(See address above.)

MEDICAL LIBRARY ASSOCIATION [205]

225 West Wacker Drive
Suite 650
Chicago, IL 60606
(312) 419-9094
E-mail: awards@mail.mlahq.org
Web Site: www.mlanet.org

FOUNDED: 1898

AREAS OF INTEREST:
Health sciences librarianship.

NAME(S) OF PROGRAMS:
● **MLA Continuing Education Grants**

TYPE:
Grants-in-aid. The Continuing Education
Grants are designed to aid in the study of the
theoretical, administrative and technical
aspects of library and information science.

PURPOSE:
To provide professional health science
librarians with the opportunity to continue
their education.

ELIGIBILITY:
Candidates must be U.S. or Canadian
citizens, or permanent residents who are
mid-level librarians with a graduate degree in
library science and a practicing health
sciences librarian with at least two years of
work experience at the professional level.
Membership in MLA is required. In
exceptional cases, consideration will be given
to an outstanding candidate not meeting the
above eligibility criteria.

FINANCIAL DATA:
Amount of support per award: $100 to $500.

NO. AWARDS: 1 to 2.

APPLICATION INFO:
Applicants must complete and submit an
application form which is available online.
Candidates should also identify a continuing
education program.
Duration: One year.
Deadline: December 1.

STAFF:
Maria Lopez, Grants, Scholarships and
Awards Coordinator

ADDRESS INQUIRIES TO:
Coordinator
Grants, Scholarships and Awards
(See address above.)

*PLEASE NOTE:
The award is not to support work towards a
degree or certificate.

MEDTRONIC FOUNDATION [206]

710 Medtronic Parkway
Minneapolis, MN 55432-5604
(763) 505-2647
(800) 633-8766
E-mail: rs.medtronicfoundation@medtronic.com
Web Site: foundation.medtronic.com

FOUNDED: 1979

AREAS OF INTEREST:
Health.

NAME(S) OF PROGRAMS:
● **Community Education**
● **HealthRise**
● **HeartRescue**
● **Strengthening Health Systems**

TYPE:
Challenge/matching grants; General operating
grants; Matching gifts; Project/program
grants. Sponsorships.

YEAR PROGRAM STARTED: 1979

PURPOSE:
To expand access to health care for the
underserved worldwide in supporting healthy
communities where we live and give.

LEGAL BASIS:
Corporate foundation.

ELIGIBILITY:
Grants are made to 501(c)(3) tax-exempt
organizations, schools or government
agencies by invitation only.

FINANCIAL DATA:
Amount of support per award: Varies
depending on need and nature of request.
Total amount of support: $29,300,000 for
fiscal year 2019.

APPLICATION INFO:
Applications are by invitation only.
Duration: Varies.

IRS I.D.: 41-1306950

ADDRESS INQUIRIES TO:
See e-mail address above.

THE ANDREW W. MELLON FOUNDATION [207]

140 East 62nd Street
New York, NY 10065
(212) 838-8400
Fax: (212) 888-4172
E-mail: inquiries@mellon.org
Web Site: www.mellon.org

FOUNDED: 1969

AREAS OF INTEREST:
Higher education and scholarship in the
humanities, scholarly communications, arts
and cultural heritage, diversity, and
international higher education and strategic
projects.

TYPE:
Challenge/matching grants; Endowments;
General operating grants; Project/program
grants; Research grants. Grants on a selective
basis to institutions in the Foundation's areas
of interest.

PURPOSE:
To build, strengthen and sustain institutions
and their core capacities, rather than be a
source for narrowly defined projects.

LEGAL BASIS:
Not-for-profit corporation.

ELIGIBILITY:
Organizations and institutions with
appropriate interests are eligible. The
Foundation does not award fellowships or
grants to individuals or make grants to
primarily local organizations.

FINANCIAL DATA:
Amount of support per award: Varies.

APPLICATION INFO:
Prospective grantees should review program
area guidelines before inquiring about grant
support. Inquiries concerning a proposed
grant should be made through the
Foundation's grantee portal Fluxx, located at
mellon.fluxx.io. If Foundation staff find that
the proposed grant fits within the
Foundation's grantmaking priorities, staff will
invite a grant proposal through the portal.
Duration: Varies.

PUBLICATIONS:
Annual report.

OFFICERS:
Elizabeth Alexander, President
Michele S. Warman, Chief Operating Officer,
Executive Vice President and Secretary
Mariet Westermann, Executive Vice President
for Programs and Research
Scott Taylor, Financial Vice President and
Chief Investment Officer

TRUSTEES:
Kathryn A. Hall, Chairperson
Elizabeth Alexander
Richard H. Brodhead
Katherine Farley
Joshua S. Friedman
Heather Gerken
Thelma Golden
Jonathan Holloway
Glenn D. Lowry
Jane L. Mendillo
Eric Mindich
Alondra Nelson
Sarah E. Thomas

ADDRESS INQUIRIES TO:
Michele S. Warman, Chief Operating Officer,
Executive Vice President and Secretary
(See address above.)

*PLEASE NOTE:
The Foundation rarely funds unsolicited
proposals.

MERCK FAMILY FUND [208]

P.O. Box 870245
Milton Village, MA 02187
(617) 696-3580
Fax: (617) 696-7262
E-mail: merck@merckff.org
Web Site: www.merckff.org

FOUNDED: 1954

AREAS OF INTEREST:
Protecting the natural environment, meeting
human needs and addressing the root causes
of problems faced by social and
economically disadvantaged people.

NAME(S) OF PROGRAMS:
● **Conserving Ecologically Valuable Land**

- **Promoting a Price on Carbon**
- **Promoting Energy Efficiency**
- **Promoting Sustainable Paper Production**
- **Urban Agriculture and Youth Leadership**

TYPE:
General operating grants; Project/program grants; Seed money grants.

YEAR PROGRAM STARTED: 1993

PURPOSE:
To protect and restore vital eastern ecosystems and promote economic practices for a sustainable environment.

LEGAL BASIS:
Tax-exempt corporation.

GEOG. RESTRICTIONS: Northeastern and southeastern United States.

FINANCIAL DATA:
Amount of support per award: $10,000 to $150,000.

Total amount of support: $2,852,550 for the year 2019.

NO. MOST RECENT APPLICANTS: 109.

NO. AWARDS: 86.

APPLICATION INFO:
New requests for support should be made through the online application system rather than with a full proposal or a request for a personal meeting. Applicants will be contacted if a full proposal is warranted. Unsolicited proposals will not be acknowledged.

Duration: Grants may be from one to two years. Progress reports must be received before continuation or renewal support will be considered.

Deadline: Letter of Intent: January 10 for spring and July 10 for fall. Full Proposal: January 31 for spring and July 31 for fall.

PUBLICATIONS:
Annual report; grants list; guidelines.

IRS I.D.: 22-6063382

STAFF:
Jenny Russell, Executive Director
James Maguire, Chief Financial Officer
Ruth Goldman, Consulting Program Officer

OFFICERS AND TRUSTEES:
Oona Coy, President
Eliza Hatch, Vice President
Patience Chamberlin, Secretary
Katie Chamberlin
Nat Chamberlin
Olivia Farr
Susannah Hatch
Friedrike Merck
Wil Merck
Morgan Whitridge

ADDRESS INQUIRIES TO:
Jenny Russell, Executive Director
(See address above.)

METLIFE FOUNDATION   [209]

200 Park Avenue, 6th Floor
New York, NY 10166
E-mail: metlifefoundation@metlife.com
Web Site: www.metlife.com/corporate-responsibility/metlife-foundation

FOUNDED: 1976

AREAS OF INTEREST:
Financial health and program-related investments.

CONSULTING OR VOLUNTEER SERVICES:
Employee volunteer programs.

TYPE:
Matching gifts; Project/program grants; Scholarships. Program-related investments. Grants are made in the areas of financial empowerment.

MetLife Foundation has a new global focus - financial inclusion - and it has committed $200,000,000 over a five-year period to this initiative. These grants are focused in the following three categories:
(1) Access and Knowledge: Grants to partners with the ability to reach large numbers of underserved households around the world and work with them to develop financial strategies and capabilities to improve lives;
(2) Access to Services: Partnering with experts in financial inclusion to deliver high-quality services like savings, microinsurance and credit to individuals in need and ensure they are prepared, incentivized and motivated to improve the lives of their families and communities and;
(3) Access to Insights: Sharing what the Foundation learns by gathering knowledge from its partners and the communities with which it works; the Foundation offers its insights to the financial inclusion community to help enhance the approach and advance the goals they share in common.

MetLife and the Foundation make below-market-rate investments with groups and projects working to improve communities across the country. Either directly or through relending with nonprofit intermediaries, social investments reach every major city in the nation and over 30 states. Loans support affordable housing developments with social services, organizations serving the homeless and mentally ill, health care services and community-based economic development.

YEAR PROGRAM STARTED: 1976

PURPOSE:
To advance financial inclusion, helping to build a secure future for individuals and communities around the world.

LEGAL BASIS:
The Foundation is a tax-exempt organization under Section 501(c)(3) and is classified as a private foundation as defined by Section 509(a) of the Internal Revenue Code.

ELIGIBILITY:
Applicants must be 501(c)(3) tax-exempt organizations in the Foundation's areas of interest.

No grants are made to private foundations or religious, fraternal, political, athletic, or social organizations, capital fund campaigns, local chapters of national organizations, labor groups, organizations primarily engaged in patient care or direct treatment, drug treatment centers and community health clinics, elementary and secondary schools, courtesy advertising or festival participation or individuals. Generally, no support is given for endowment funds.

FINANCIAL DATA:
Total amount of support: $39,939,177 for the year 2019.

Matching fund requirements: Employee contributions to colleges and universities.

NO. AWARDS: Varies.

APPLICATION INFO:
The Foundation does not accept unsolicited proposals.
Duration: Varies.

PUBLICATIONS:
Annual report of contributions; guidelines (available online).

BOARD OF DIRECTORS:
Michael Zarcone, Chairman
A. Dennis White, President and Chief Executive Officer
Steven Goulart, Treasurer
Michel Khalaf
Esther Lee
Martin Lippert
Susan Podlogar
Oscar Schmidt

ADDRESS INQUIRIES TO:
A. Dennis White
President and Chief Executive Officer
(See address above.)

MEYER MEMORIAL TRUST   [210]

425 N.W. 10th Avenue, Suite 400
Portland, OR 97209
(503) 228-5512
E-mail: questions@mmt.org
Web Site: www.mmt.org

FOUNDED: 1978

AREAS OF INTEREST:
Education, environment, affordable housing and building community.

YEAR PROGRAM STARTED: 1982

PURPOSE:
To work with and invest in organizations, communities, ideas and efforts that contribute to a flourishing and equitable Oregon.

LEGAL BASIS:
Private, independent foundation.

ELIGIBILITY:
Applicants must:
(1) be an IRS-sanctioned tax-exempt organization;
(2) be requesting support for a program that operates in Oregon and;
(3) provide equal opportunity in leadership, staffing and service regardless of age, gender, race, ethnicity, sexual orientation, disability, national origin, political affiliation or religious belief.

GEOG. RESTRICTIONS: Oregon.

FINANCIAL DATA:
Amount of support per award: Varies.

APPLICATION INFO:
Organizations must register on the Trust's online system to complete and submit the application.
Duration: Varies.

TRUSTEES:
Toya Fick, Chairperson
April Cuprill-Comas
Janet Hamada
Mitch Hornecker
Charles Wilhoite

STAFF:
Michelle DePass, President and Chief Executive Officer
Rukaiyah Adams, Chief Investment Officer

ADDRESS INQUIRIES TO:
Phoebe O'Leary
Director of Operations
(See address above.)

*SPECIAL STIPULATIONS:
No grants given to individuals or for businesses.

ROBERT R. MEYER FOUNDATION [211]

1900 5th Avenue North, Suite 2600
Birmingham, AL 35203
(205) 264-7881
E-mail: marcie.braswell@regions.com

FOUNDED: 1942

AREAS OF INTEREST:
Arts, education, humanities, civic affairs, health and human services, and charitable work.

TYPE:
Challenge/matching grants; Matching gifts; Project/program grants; Research grants; Technical assistance; Training grants.

YEAR PROGRAM STARTED: 1942

PURPOSE:
To help in community affairs.

LEGAL BASIS:
Private foundation.

ELIGIBILITY:
Grants restricted to organizations that benefit the Birmingham, AL area, or to Birmingham, AL nonprofit organizations. No grants to individuals or corporations.

GEOG. RESTRICTIONS: Birmingham, Alabama area.

FINANCIAL DATA:
Amount of support per award: $2,500 to $200,000; Average: $30,000.
Total amount of support: Approximately $2,000,000 for the year 2018.

NO. AWARDS: Approximately 70.

APPLICATION INFO:
Call for grant guidelines and application.
Duration: One year.
Deadline: March 1 and September 1.

PUBLICATIONS:
Application form.

ADVISORY COMMITTEE:
Beverly Baker, Esq.
Sharon L. Blackburn
Raymond J. Harbert, Jr.
Elmer B. Harris

ADDRESS INQUIRIES TO:
Marcie P. Braswell, Senior Vice President
(See address above.)

THE MIAMI FOUNDATION [212]

40 N.W. 3rd Street
Suite 305
Miami, FL 33128
(305) 371-2711
Fax: (305) 371-5342
E-mail: info@miamifoundation.org
Web Site: www.miamifoundation.org

FOUNDED: 1967

AREAS OF INTEREST:
Arts and culture, healthy lifestyles, housing and affordability, well-being of children and youth, LGBTQ issues, crime prevention/deterrence, victim assistance, public spaces, transportation, and sea level rise.

NAME(S) OF PROGRAMS:
● **Community Grants Program**
● **LGBTQ Community Fund**
● **Denise Moon Memorial Fund**
● **Public Space Challenge**

TYPE:
Fellowships; Project/program grants; Scholarships; Training grants. Special initiative grants.

YEAR PROGRAM STARTED: 1967

PURPOSE:
To enhance the quality of life for all the residents of Greater Miami.

LEGAL BASIS:
Community foundation.

ELIGIBILITY:
Applicants must be 501(c)(3) organizations as well as some grassroots organizations.

No grants to individuals. No grants for memberships, fund-raising events or memorials.

GEOG. RESTRICTIONS: Miami-Dade County, Florida.

FINANCIAL DATA:
Amount of support per award: Varies.
Total amount of support: Varies.

NO. MOST RECENT APPLICANTS: 600.

NO. AWARDS: 130.

APPLICATION INFO:
Responsive grant applications must be made through the Foundation's online portal. Application includes cover letter with the purpose of the grant and the amount requested as well as a narrative about the applicant organization and budget. Attachments should include board list and current fiscal year operating budget. Slight variations per grant program may apply.
Duration: Typically one year.
Deadline: Varies.

PUBLICATIONS:
Annual report; monthly newsletter; grant guidelines; professional advisors guides.

IRS I.D.: 65-0350357

STAFF:
Rebecca Fishman Lipsey, President and Chief Executive Officer
Charisse Grant, Senior Vice President for Programs and Grants
Gloria Ortega Rex, Vice President for Finance and Chief Financial Officer
Julie Vives, Chief Operating Officer
Lindsey Linzer, Senior Director of Programs and Grants
Kamilah Wallen, Grants Administration Manager
Valerie Crum, Senior Programs Associate
Chelsea Clark, Programs Associate
Alex Rosales, Programs Associate

ADDRESS INQUIRIES TO:
See e-mail address above.

MICROSOFT PHILANTHROPIES [213]

One Microsoft Way
Redmond, WA 98052-6399
(425) 882-8080
(425) 706-8185
Fax: (425) 706-7329
Web Site: www.microsoft.com/en-us/philanthropies

FOUNDED: 1983

AREAS OF INTEREST:
Internet access, digital skills development, and computer science education.

NAME(S) OF PROGRAMS:
● **Disaster Response and Humanitarian Relief**
● **Employee Giving and Volunteer Programs**
● **Microsoft YouthSpark**
● **Nongovernmental Organization Capacity Building**
● **Product Donations Program**

TYPE:
Grants-in-aid; Matching gifts; Product donations; Scholarships; Technical assistance.

YEAR PROGRAM STARTED: 1983

PURPOSE:
To invest in programs and partnerships that advance digital inclusion by bringing greater social and economic opportunity to people in underserved populations around the world; to support Microsoft employees taking an active role in their community through volunteer and matching gift programs.

LEGAL BASIS:
Corporate giving program.

ELIGIBILITY:
Cash grants are awarded to nonprofit organizations identified by Microsoft staff. Eligible nonprofits can benefit from the Product Donations Program.

FINANCIAL DATA:
Matching fund requirements: Employee donations of money and time to eligible organizations are matched up to $15,000 per employee per year.

APPLICATION INFO:
Microsoft does not respond to unsolicited grant proposals or letters of inquiry.

PUBLICATIONS:
Program brochure; annual report of giving.

ADDRESS INQUIRIES TO:
Community Affairs
(See address above.)

*SPECIAL STIPULATIONS:
Proposals submitted by e-mail, fax or phone will not be accepted.

MID-NEBRASKA COMMUNITY FOUNDATION, INC. [214]

121 North Dewey Street, Suite 112
North Platte, NE 69101
(308) 534-3315
Fax: (308) 534-6117
E-mail: mncf@hamilton.net
Web Site: www.midnebraskafoundation.org

FOUNDED: 1978

AREAS OF INTEREST:
Arts, education, civic development, environment, health and welfare.

TYPE:
Capital grants; Demonstration grants; Development grants; Endowments; Project/program grants; Scholarships.

PURPOSE:
To serve charitable people and nonprofit causes in North Platte and the surrounding area.

GEOG. RESTRICTIONS: Custer, Dawson, Frontier, Hayes, Keith, Lincoln, Logan, McPherson, and Perkins counties, Nebraska.

FINANCIAL DATA:
Amount of support per award: Varies.

Total amount of support: Average: $1,000,000 to $1,500,000.

APPLICATION INFO:
Application form required. Initial approach by letter or telephone.
Duration: Varies.
Deadline: April 15, July 15, October 15 and January 15.

IRS I.D.: 47-0604965

ADDRESS INQUIRIES TO:
Eric Seacrest, Executive Director
(See address above.)

ADAH K. MILLARD CHARITABLE TRUST [215]
Northern Trust Company
One Oakbrook Terrace, Suite 200
Oakbrook Terrace, IL 60181
(630) 932-6981
Fax: (630) 932-6968
E-mail: kwm1@ntrs.com

FOUNDED: 1976

AREAS OF INTEREST:
Youth agencies, arts, cultural programs and hospitals.

TYPE:
Capital grants; Project/program grants. Project grants in areas of the Foundation's interest.

YEAR PROGRAM STARTED: 1976

PURPOSE:
To make grants to charitable agencies in Omaha and Douglas County, NE.

LEGAL BASIS:
Tax-exempt.

ELIGIBILITY:
Tax-exempt organizations in Omaha and Douglas County, NE. No grants are awarded to individuals.

GEOG. RESTRICTIONS: Douglas County and Omaha, Nebraska.

FINANCIAL DATA:
Amount of support per award: $1,000 to $35,000.
Matching fund requirements: Stipulated with specific programs.

NO. AWARDS: 35 annually.

REPRESENTATIVE AWARDS:
Salvation Army; United Way; Nebraska Food Bank.

APPLICATION INFO:
A request should be made for guidelines to submit grant applications. Six copies of the application are required.
Duration: No grants are awarded on a continuing basis. May reapply after two years.
Deadline: March 20 and October 1. Announcements in May and November.

PUBLICATIONS:
Application guidelines.

IRS I.D.: 36-6629069

ADDRESS INQUIRIES TO:
Kristin Weaver, Senior Vice President
(See address above.)

MILLIPORESIGMA [216]
400 Summit Drive
Burlington, MA 01803
(781) 533-6000
Web Site: www.emdmillipore.com

FOUNDED: 1985

AREAS OF INTEREST:
Science, education (K-12), sustainability, and health care.

TYPE:
Capital grants; Challenge/matching grants; Matching gifts; Project/program grants; Research grants; Scholarships.

YEAR PROGRAM STARTED: 1985

PURPOSE:
To serve the public interest in ways that are meaningful to the company and its employees.

ELIGIBILITY:
Organizations, excluding religious and political, classified as 501(c)(3) by the IRS can apply.

FINANCIAL DATA:
Since inception, over $20,000,000 has been distributed to deserving nonprofit programs on a local and national level.
Amount of support per award: Grants: $5,000 to $10,000; Scholarships: $5,000.
Matching fund requirements: 1:1 up to $1,000 per employee per year.

NO. AWARDS: Scholarships: 2.

APPLICATION INFO:
Eligible programs may submit a copy of the 501(c)(3) certificate, tax identification number, and a letter of inquiry no more than two pages in length briefly describing the organization, the program for which funding is sought, and the amount of funding requested. Those organizations whose programs are of interest to Millipore will be invited to submit full proposals.

Millipore also accepts the Associated Grant Makers Common Proposal Form.
Duration: One year. Grants are renewable. Scholarship is renewable for an additional three years.
Deadline: Proposals are considered quarterly at Review Committee meetings.

ADDRESS INQUIRIES TO:
Director of Corporate Responsibility
(See address above.)

THE MOODY FOUNDATION [217]
2302 Post Office Street, Suite 704
Galveston, TX 77550
(409) 797-1500
Fax: (409) 763-5564
E-mail: info@moodyf.org
Web Site: www.moodyf.org

FOUNDED: 1942

AREAS OF INTEREST:
Arts, education, medical research, community and economic development, environment and youth programs.

TYPE:
Capital grants; Challenge/matching grants; Endowments; Grants-in-aid; Project/program grants; Research grants; Scholarships. Capital campaigns; Equipment; Matching funds; Building/renovation; Program development and research.

YEAR PROGRAM STARTED: 1942

PURPOSE:
To assist in supporting activities that are directed toward improving the general well-being of the citizens of the state of Texas, especially Galveston.

LEGAL BASIS:
Private family foundation.

ELIGIBILITY:
Tax-exempt 501(c)(3) organizations in the state of Texas only are eligible to apply. The Foundation generally does not make grant awards for deficit financing, operational expenses of established organizations, or grants for any activities considered a taxable expenditure under the 1969 Tax Reform Act. No grants to individuals (except for one scholarship program). No loans.

GEOG. RESTRICTIONS: Texas.

FINANCIAL DATA:
Amount of support per award: Varies.
Total amount of support: Varies.

NO. AWARDS: 20 to 30.

REPRESENTATIVE AWARDS:
$30,000 to American Cancer Society Inc./Cattle Baron's Ball, Dallas, TX; $15,000 to Community Schools in Dallas; $5,000 to Garland Family Outreach, Inc., Garland, TX.

APPLICATION INFO:
Prospective candidates should consult the Foundation's web site for an online inquiry to ascertain if appropriate to request guidelines for making application.
Duration: Generally, grants are awarded for one year at a time.

PUBLICATIONS:
Annual report; application guidelines.

IRS I.D.: 74-1403105

STAFF:
Frances Anne Moody-Dahlberg, Executive Director
Garrik Addison, Chief Financial Officer
Angela Blair, Education Director
Allan Matthews, Grants Director
Bernice C. Torregrossa, Regional Grants Director for Central Texas and Grants Analyst
Jamie Williams, Regional Grants Director for North Texas and Human Resources
Erica Tovar, Scholarship Director
Gerald Smith, Program Officer

BOARD OF TRUSTEES:
Frances Anne Moody-Dahlberg, Chairperson
Elizabeth Moody
Ross R. Moody

FOUNDERS:
Libbie Shearn Moody
W.L. Moody, Jr.

ADDRESS INQUIRIES TO:
See e-mail address above.

THE CLARENCE E. MULFORD TRUST [218]
P.O. Box 290
Fryeburg, ME 04037
(207) 935-2061
Fax: (866) 225-8160

AREAS OF INTEREST:
Animals, education, literature, religion, science and youth.

TYPE:
Project/program grants.

PURPOSE:
To support charitable organizations that are working to improve the quality of life for Maine residents.

LEGAL BASIS:
Trust fund.

ELIGIBILITY:
Grants are made to organizations that have tax-exempt status under Section 501(c)(3) of the Internal Revenue Code. No grants are made to individuals. Religious organizations may apply.

GEOG. RESTRICTIONS: Fryeburg, Maine and adjoining towns.

FINANCIAL DATA:
Amount of support per award: $500 to $10,000.

Total amount of support: Approximately $500,000 for the year 2017.

APPLICATION INFO:
Organizations should submit IRS tax exemption letter under 501(c)(3) of the Internal Revenue Code.
Duration: One year. Renewal by reapplication.
Deadline: January 10 and July 10.

TRUSTEES:
David R. Hastings, III
Peter Hastings

ADDRESS INQUIRIES TO:
Peter Hastings, Trustee
(See address above.)

M.J. MURDOCK CHARITABLE TRUST   [219]
655 West Columbia Way
Suite 700
Vancouver, WA 98660
(360) 694-8415
Fax: (360) 694-1819
E-mail: stevem@murdocktrust.org
Web Site: murdocktrust.org

FOUNDED: 1975

AREAS OF INTEREST:
Education, science, health and human services, arts and culture.

TYPE:
Capital grants; Challenge/matching grants; Development grants; Project/program grants; Research grants. Equipment grants. In addition to a special interest in education and scientific research, the Trust partners with a wide variety of organizations that serve the arts, public affairs, health and medicine, human services, leadership development and persons with disabilities.

PURPOSE:
To enrich the quality of life in the Pacific Northwest by providing grants and enrichment programs to organizations seeking to strengthen the region's educational, spiritual and cultural base in creative and sustainable ways.

LEGAL BASIS:
Private foundation.

ELIGIBILITY:
Applications for grants are considered only from organizations which have been ruled to be tax-exempt under Section 501(c)(3) of the Internal Revenue Code and are not private foundations. Primary attention is given to applications for the support of projects and programs conducted by qualified institutions within five states of the Pacific Northwest, including Alaska, Idaho, Montana, Oregon and Washington. Priority is given to

organizations and projects which are not primarily or normally financed by public tax funds.

Applications are not considered for loans, endowment, debt retirement, operational deficits, contributions to general fund drives or annual charitable appeals, continuation of programs previously financed from external sources or emergency funding.

GEOG. RESTRICTIONS: Pacific Northwest.

FINANCIAL DATA:
Amount of support per award: Varies.
Total amount of support: Varies.

NO. MOST RECENT APPLICANTS: 450.

APPLICATION INFO:
Submit a letter of inquiry through the Trust's Grants Portal.
Duration: One year to multiyear.
Deadline: Varies.

PUBLICATIONS:
Annual report; *Grants Proposal Guidelines*; proposal form.

TRUSTEES:
John W. Castles
Jeffrey T. Grubb
Jeff Pinneo

OFFICERS AND STAFF:
Steven G.W. Moore, Executive Director
Mike True, Chief Financial Officer
Moses Lee, Senior Director, Scientific Research and Enrichment Programs
Terry Stokesbary, Senior Program Director for Enrichment Initiatives
Dana L. Miller, Senior Program Director for Grant Programs
Rudy Carrasco, Program Director
Lorin Dunlop, Program Director
Pauline Fong, Program Director
John Frankin, Program Director
Jill Lemke, Program Director
Kim Newman, Program Director
Jan Kennedy Ferguson, Program Advisor
Romanita Hairston-Overstreet, Program Advisor

ADDRESS INQUIRIES TO:
E-mail: info@murdocktrust.org

NATIONWIDE FOUNDATION   [220]
One Nationwide Plaza
Mail Drop 1.2.16
Columbus, OH 43215-2220
(614) 249-4310
Fax: (866) 212-7960
E-mail: corpcit@nationwide.com
Web Site: www.nationwide.com/foundation

FOUNDED: 1959

AREAS OF INTEREST:
Health and welfare, education, culture and the arts, and civic and community affairs. Highest priorities are emergency and basic needs and crisis stabilization.

TYPE:
Capital grants; Challenge/matching grants; General operating grants; Project/program grants.

YEAR PROGRAM STARTED: 1959

PURPOSE:
To provide financial support for qualified tax-exempt organizations whose programs address basic human needs.

LEGAL BASIS:
Corporate foundation.

ELIGIBILITY:
Qualified, tax-exempt organizations in Columbus, OH and locations with a large number of Nationwide associates are eligible.

GEOG. RESTRICTIONS: Primarily Scottsdale, Arizona; Des Moines, Iowa and Columbus, Ohio. Tiers One and Two funding considered in Sacramento, California; Denver, Colorado; Gainesville, Florida; Raleigh/Durham, North Carolina; Harrisburg, Pennsylvania; San Antonio, Texas; and Wausau, Wisconsin.

FINANCIAL DATA:
Total amount of support: Varies.

APPLICATION INFO:
Guidelines and application form are available at the Foundation web site.
Duration: One year. Renewal possible.
Deadline: September 1. Announcement in mid-March.

PUBLICATIONS:
Contributions guidelines.

ADDRESS INQUIRIES TO:
Karen H. Blickley, Vice President
(See address above.)

NEW ENGLAND BIOLABS FOUNDATION   [221]
240 County Road
Ipswich, MA 01938
(978) 998-7990
E-mail: info@nebf.org
Web Site: www.nebf.org

FOUNDED: 1982

AREAS OF INTEREST:
Environmental issues: landscapes and seascapes, and the associated biocultural diversity, ecosystem services and foodways.

TYPE:
Grants-in-aid; Project/program grants; Seed money grants. The Foundation prefers to help organizations start their projects with the understanding that once they are established, funding from other sources will be sought.

YEAR PROGRAM STARTED: 1982

PURPOSE:
To support grassroots organizations working with the environment.

ELIGIBILITY:
The Foundation prefers to fund grassroots organizations and/or projects (i.e., those conceived, developed and managed by the community). Grassroots organizations, emerging support groups and charitable organizations may apply. Grants are not made to religious organizations.

FINANCIAL DATA:
Amount of support per award: International grants: Maximum $12,000; Local grants: Maximum $8,000.

Total amount of support: Approximately $500,000 annually.

NO. MOST RECENT APPLICANTS: 200.

NO. AWARDS: 70.

APPLICATION INFO:
Letters of Inquiry and Proposals should be submitted electronically through the NEBF online portal.
Duration: Typically one year.

ADDRESS INQUIRIES TO:
Deborah Fraize, Associate Director
(See address above.)

THE NEW YORK COMMUNITY TRUST [222]

909 Third Avenue, 22nd Floor
New York, NY 10022
(212) 686-0010
Fax: (212) 532-8528
E-mail: info@nyct-cfi.org
Web Site: www.nycommunitytrust.org

FOUNDED: 1924

AREAS OF INTEREST:
Health, behavioral health, older adults, the
blind or visually impaired, children and
youth with disabilities, people with
developmental disabilities, education, arts,
human justice, human services, jobs and
workforce development, youth development,
community development, civic affairs, the
environment, historic preservation, and
technical assistance.

TYPE:
Project/program grants; Technical assistance.
The Trust is a grantmaking foundation
dedicated to improving the lives of residents
of New York City and its suburbs. It brings
together individuals, families, foundations,
and businesses to build a better community
and support nonprofits that make a
difference.

The competitive grants are supported by
hundreds of funds. Some can be used at the
Trust's discretion, while others were created
for particular purposes and range from
specific (helping injured, needy, classical
ballet dancers) to broad (improving
opportunities for poor girls and women). The
Trust funds programs that promote change in
policy or systems, build capacity of
organizations, and expand and/or improve
direct service.

The Trust seeks to promote healthy lives,
expand opportunities, strengthen families,
develop children and youth, and create
strong, vital communities. The governing
board has identified three categories of
activity to carry out these objectives:
Healthy Lives - The Trust helps providers
deliver efficient, patient-focused, equitable,
and cost-effective health and behavioral
health services to all New Yorkers. Projects
that develop the skills and independence of
four groups of people with special needs:
older adults, the blind or visually impaired,
children and youth with disabilities, and
people with developmental disabilities are
supported. The Trust also supports
biomedical research and projects for animal
welfare.
Promising Futures - These grants build
promising futures by helping young people
prosper; providing job training and
placement; making the educational and
justice systems work for everyone; alleviating
hunger and homelessness; improving family
and child welfare services; and advancing the
practice of social work.
Thriving Communities - Grants are made to
groups that protect and create affordable
housing, promote equity in the arts, improve
civic engagement, and protect our
environment. Agencies working on these
issues at the neighborhood level, as well as
government and nonprofit institutions
developing strategies, are supported. The
Trust also supports efforts to improve the
functioning of nonprofits and government.

YEAR PROGRAM STARTED: 1924

PURPOSE:
To support the nonprofits that make New
York City a vital and secure place to live and
work.

LEGAL BASIS:
Public nonprofit community foundation.

ELIGIBILITY:
Priority is given to grant proposals from
nonprofit organizations that deal with the
problems of the New York metropolitan
region. Preference is given to proposals that
support specific programs or projects.

Grants also are available to support
endowments, building fund campaigns, deficit
financing, annual giving, religious purposes,
financial assistance and to individual
applicants.

GEOG. RESTRICTIONS: Primarily New York, New
York.

FINANCIAL DATA:
Amount of support per award: $5,000 to
$200,000.
Total amount of support: Competitive grants:
Approximately $50,000,000 annually.

NO. MOST RECENT APPLICANTS: 952.

NO. AWARDS: 436.

APPLICATION INFO:
Applicants should begin by going to the
Grantee Application Hub on the Trust's web
site.
Duration: One year or multiyear.
Deadline: Grant applications are accepted
throughout the year. Trust's Board reviews
grants five times per year.

PUBLICATIONS:
Annual report; application and individual
program guidelines; proposal cover sheet;
newsletter.

OFFICERS:
Lorie A. Slutsky, President
Mercedes Leon, Vice President,
Administration
Gay Young, Vice President, Donor Services
Shawn Morehead, Vice President, Grants
Kerry McCarthy, Vice President,
Philanthropic Initiatives
Carolyn M. Weiss, C.P.A., Chief Financial
Officer
Mary Z. Greenebaum, Chief Investment
Officer
Jane Wilton, General Counsel

DISTRIBUTION COMMITTEE:
Valerie Peltier, Chairman
Jamie Drake
Mali Sananikone Gaw
Obaid Z. Khan
Roger J. Maldonado
Anne Moore, M.D.
Stephen C. Robinson
Judith O. Rubin
Lorie A. Slutsky
Barron Tenny
Ann Unterberg
Jason H. Wright

THE NORCLIFFE FOUNDATION [223]

600 University Street
Suite 2003
Seattle, WA 98101
(206) 682-4820
E-mail: info@norcliffefoundation.org
Web Site: www.norcliffefoundation.org

FOUNDED: 1952

AREAS OF INTEREST:
Human services, health care, civic and
community projects, education, and arts and
culture.

TYPE:
Capital grants; General operating grants;
Project/program grants.

YEAR PROGRAM STARTED: 1952

PURPOSE:
To improve the quality of life for all people.

LEGAL BASIS:
Private foundation.

ELIGIBILITY:
Eligible organizations must be of IRS
501(c)(3), not-for-profit status. Projects must
impact the Puget Sound region of
Washington state.

Grants are not given to individuals.

GEOG. RESTRICTIONS: Puget Sound area of
Washington state.

FINANCIAL DATA:
Amount of support per award: Varies.
Total amount of support: $24,388,877 for the
year 2017.

NO. AWARDS: Over 370 for the year 2017.

APPLICATION INFO:
Application details can be found on the
Foundation web site.
Duration: Varies by project. Grants are
generally not renewable.
Deadline: Applications are accepted
throughout the year.

ADDRESS INQUIRIES TO:
Jennifer Beatty, Foundation Manager
(See address above.)

THE NORDSON CORPORATION FOUNDATION [224]

28601 Clemens Road
Westlake, OH 44145-1148
(440) 892-1580
E-mail: crender@nordson.com
Web Site: www.nordson.com

FOUNDED: 1952

AREAS OF INTEREST:
Education, human welfare, civic, arts and
culture.

CONSULTING OR VOLUNTEER SERVICES:
Corporate volunteer program.

NAME(S) OF PROGRAMS:
● **Time and Talent**

TYPE:
Capital grants; Challenge/matching grants;
General operating grants; Matching gifts;
Project/program grants; Technical assistance.

YEAR PROGRAM STARTED: 1988

PURPOSE:
To improve the quality of life in our
communities by improving educational
outcomes that enable individuals to become
self-sufficient, active participants in the
community.

LEGAL BASIS:
Corporate foundation.

ELIGIBILITY:
Grants are made to tax-exempt organizations,
as defined in Section 501(c)(3) of the Internal
Revenue Code. No grants to religious
organizations.

GEOG. RESTRICTIONS: North San Diego and
Santa Clara counties, California; Larimer
County, Colorado; New London and

Windham counties, Connecticut; Emanuel and Gwinnett counties, Georgia; Worcester County and the cities of Billerica, Chelmsford, Dracut, Framingham, Haverhill, Lawrence, Lowell, Marlborough and Tewksbury, Massachusetts; Minneapolis, Minnesota; Manchester, Nashua and Salem, New Hampshire; Mercer County, New Jersey; Mahoning Valley and Lorain County, Ohio; Providence County, Rhode Island; and Chippewa Valley, Wisconsin.

FINANCIAL DATA:
Amount of support per award: Varies.
Total amount of support: $9,000,000 for the year 2018.
Matching fund requirements: Foundation will match minimum contributions of $25 to a maximum of $10,000 for any calendar year.

NO. MOST RECENT APPLICANTS: Approximately 500 for the year 2018.

NO. AWARDS: Approximately 200 for the year 2018.

APPLICATION INFO:
Application forms are available online.
Duration: Typically one year.
Deadline: February 15, May 15, August 15 and November 15 for meetings held in January, April, July and October, respectively.

STAFF:
Sara Vaz, Community Relations Manager/California and Colorado
Cindy Baumgardner, Community Relations Manager/Georgia, Minnesota and Wisconsin
Joan Szczepanik, Community Relations Manager
Amonica Davis, Manager, Student Outreach

DIRECTORS:
Michael Hilton
John Keane
Stephen Lovass
Greg Merk
Shelly Peet
Jeff Pembroke
Joseph Stockunas
Greg Thaxton

ADDRESS INQUIRIES TO:
Cindy Baumgardner, Tel: (770) 497-3672 (GA, MN and WI)
Amonica Davis, Tel: (440) 414-5444
Cecilia H. Render, Tel: (440) 892-1580
Joan Szczepanik, Tel: (440) 414-5440
Sara Vaz, Tel: (760) 930-7246 (CA and CO)

KENNETH T. AND EILEEN L. NORRIS FOUNDATION   [225]
11 Golden Shore, Suite 450
Long Beach, CA 90802
(562) 435-8444
Fax: (562) 436-0584
E-mail: grants@norrisfoundation.org
Web Site: norrisfoundation.org

FOUNDED: 1963

AREAS OF INTEREST:
Funding categories include medicine, education and science, youth, community and culture.

TYPE:
Capital grants; Challenge/matching grants; Endowments; General operating grants; Project/program grants; Research grants.

YEAR PROGRAM STARTED: 1963

PURPOSE:
To support programs that advance better health and intellectual enlightenment through education, cultivation of the arts, individual responsibility, freedom and dignity.

LEGAL BASIS:
Family foundation.

ELIGIBILITY:
Applicants must be nonprofit, tax-exempt organizations. The Foundation does not support individuals and/or political or religious organizations.

GEOG. RESTRICTIONS: Southern California.

FINANCIAL DATA:
Amount of support per award: Grants vary in amount, depending upon the needs and nature of the request.
Total amount of support: Varies.

APPLICATION INFO:
Applications are accepted by invitation only.
Duration: Most grants are for one year.
Deadline: Education/Science and Medical: May 1 to June 30. Decision in October; Youth: February 15 to March 31. Decision in August; Community and Cultural: December 1 to January 31. Decision in May.

PUBLICATIONS:
Biannual report.

IRS I.D.: 95-6080374

TRUSTEES AND OFFICERS:
Lisa D. Hansen, Chairman
James R. Martin
Bradley K. Norris
Brooks B. Norris
Kimberley D. Presley
Walter J. Zanino

ADDRESS INQUIRIES TO:
Walter J. Zanino, Executive Director
(See address above.)

NORTH CAROLINA COMMUNITY FOUNDATION   [226]
3737 Glenwood Avenue
Suite 460
Raleigh, NC 27612
(919) 828-4387
(800) 532-1349
Fax: (919) 827-0749
E-mail: info@nccommunityfoundation.org
Web Site: www.nccommunityfoundation.org

FOUNDED: 1988

AREAS OF INTEREST:
Arts and conservation, education, health, historical and culture resources, preservation of environmental and social services.

TYPE:
General operating grants; Project/program grants; Scholarships.

YEAR PROGRAM STARTED: 1988

PURPOSE:
To inspire North Carolinians to make lasting and meaningful contributions to their communities.

LEGAL BASIS:
501(c)(3).

ELIGIBILITY:
Nonprofit, tax-exempt organizations. No grants are made to individuals.

GEOG. RESTRICTIONS: North Carolina.

FINANCIAL DATA:
Amount of support per award: Varies.
Total amount of support: $15,122,226 for the year 2018.

APPLICATION INFO:
Details regarding eligibility criteria, program guidelines, and application process can be found on the Foundation web site.

ADDRESS INQUIRIES TO:
Grants and Scholarships
North Carolina Community Foundation
(See address above.)

THE NORTHWEST MINNESOTA FOUNDATION
201 Third Street, N.W.
Bemidji, MN 56601
(218) 759-2057
Fax: (218) 759-2328
E-mail: info@nwmf.org
Web Site: www.nwmf.org

TYPE:
Challenge/matching grants; Demonstration grants; Project/program grants; Research grants; Scholarships; Seed money grants; Technical assistance.

See entry 1223 for full listing.

WILLIAM J. AND DOROTHY K. O'NEILL FOUNDATION   [227]
2529 Detroit Avenue
Suite 126
Cleveland, OH 44113
(216) 831-4134
Fax: (216) 378-0594
E-mail: info@oneill-foundation.org
Web Site: oneill-foundation.org

FOUNDED: 1987

AREAS OF INTEREST:
Capacity building - all program areas.

TYPE:
General operating grants; Matching gifts; Project/program grants. Capacity building; Proactive grants; Gifts in recognition of service; Youth Philanthropy grants; Responsive grants; Special initiative grants; Rapid responsive grants. In the area of capacity building, the Foundation funds projects that create and implement strategic plans, governance and board development, leadership succession planning, planning and implementing technology systems, fund development, and communications and marketing strategies.

Matching gifts and gifts in recognition of service are directed by O'Neill Family members.

Youth Philanthropy grants are made by O'Neill Family youth.

YEAR PROGRAM STARTED: 1987

PURPOSE:
To fund programs that address root causes of family strength and family disintegration, capacity building for nonprofits and areas of interest to individual family members.

LEGAL BASIS:
Family foundation.

ELIGIBILITY:
Nonprofit organizations with IRS 501(c)(3) tax-exempt status are eligible for support. No grants to individuals or to organizations which operate wholly outside the U.S. No grants in response to annual appeal form letters.

In order to be eligible, you must have either received a grant from the Foundation already and/or be notified that you are eligible.

GEOG. RESTRICTIONS: Washington, DC; Greater Orlando, Florida; Big Island, Hawaii; Annapolis and Baltimore, Maryland; New York, New York; Cleveland, Ohio; Houston, Texas; and Dorset, Manchester, Pawlet and Rupert, Vermont.

FINANCIAL DATA:
Amount of support per award: $5,000 to $50,000.
Total amount of support: $2,060,938 for the year 2018.

NO. AWARDS: 75 Responsive Grants for the year 2018.

REPRESENTATIVE AWARDS:
$23,312 to Cleveland Clinic Foundation, Cleveland, OH; $25,000 to University Settlement Society of New York, Inc., New York, NY; $30,000 to The Fishing School, Washington, DC.

APPLICATION INFO:
Proposal, budget and activity plan must be submitted through the Foundation's grants management system.
Duration: One year.
Deadline: February 21 and August 21.

PUBLICATIONS:
Annual report; application guidelines.

IRS I.D.: 34-1560893

OFFICERS:
Leslie Perkul, President and Chief Executive Officer
David Donahey, Treasurer
Timothy M. O'Neill, Secretary

TRUSTEES:
Robert W. Donahey, Chairperson
Leslie Perkul, President and Chief Executive Officer
Laura Bower
Linda France Clifford
David Donahey
Timothy M. O'Neill
Brian Sweeney

ADDRESS INQUIRIES TO:
For DC, MD, NY and VT:
Marci Lu, Senior Program Officer
E-mail: mlu@oneill-foundation.org

For FL, HI, OH and TX:
Leslie Perkul, President and Chief Executive Officer
E-mail: lperkul@oneill-foundation.org

THE JOHN R. OISHEI FOUNDATION [228]

726 Exchange Street
Suite 510
Buffalo, NY 14210
(716) 856-9490
E-mail: info@oishei.org
Web Site: www.oishei.org

FOUNDED: 1940

AREAS OF INTEREST:
Strengthening the P-20 education continuum; enhancing options for self-sufficiency; building livable, stable neighborhoods; promoting health and improving systems; expanding the role of arts, culture and heritage in regional development.

TYPE:
Capital grants; Challenge/matching grants; General operating grants; Project/program grants; Seed money grants; Technical assistance; Training grants. Education grants.

PURPOSE:
To be a catalyst for change; to enhance the economic vitality and the quality of life for the Buffalo Niagara region through grantmaking, leadership and network building.

LEGAL BASIS:
Private foundation.

ELIGIBILITY:
An organization seeking support must be determined by the Internal Revenue Code to be tax-exempt under Section 501(c)(3). Private foundations, as defined in Section 509(a) of the Internal Revenue Code, will not be eligible for Foundation support. To receive Foundation support, an organization must be well managed, including an active board drawn from a cross section of the community. It must have a consistent record of sound fiscal management and a demonstrated track record of efficient operations and effective programming. The Foundation does not make grants to governmental institutions, agencies or projects. Organizations that rely heavily on government funding are eligible to apply, but must be able to demonstrate that a grant from the Foundation would supplement rather than supplant public funding.

GEOG. RESTRICTIONS: Erie and Niagara counties and the remaining six counties in western New York.

FINANCIAL DATA:
Amount of support per award: $750 to $1,000,000.
Total amount of support: More than $11,900,000 for the year 2018.

NO. AWARDS: 178 for the year 2018.

REPRESENTATIVE AWARDS:
$1,000,000 to National Comedy Center; $777,000 to Education Collaborative of Western New York.

APPLICATION INFO:
Letters of Inquiry (LOIs) and applications for general funding requests must be submitted online.
Duration: One to four years.
Deadline: The Foundation accepts and processes applications throughout the year. Notification generally within three months.

PUBLICATIONS:
Community reports; annual report; grantmaking reports; research briefs.

OFFICERS:
William G. Gisel, Jr., Chairman
Florence M. Conti, Vice Chairman
Robert D. Gioia, President
Edward F. Walsh, Jr., Treasurer
Gayle L. Houck, Secretary
Jackie Reisdorf, Recording Secretary

DIRECTORS:
Donald K. Boswell
Florence M. Conti
William G. Gisel, Jr.
Maureen Hurley
Luke T. Jacobs
Yvonne Minor-Ragan, Ph.D.
Francisco M. Vasquez, Ph.D.
Melva D. Visher
Edward F. Walsh, Jr.

ADDRESS INQUIRIES TO:
Robert D. Gioia, President
(See address above.)

OMAHA COMMUNITY FOUNDATION [229]

3555 Farnam Street
Suite 222
Omaha, NE 68131
(402) 342-3458
Fax: (402) 342-3582
E-mail: info@omahafoundation.org
Web Site: www.omahafoundation.org

FOUNDED: 1982

AREAS OF INTEREST:
General philanthropy.

CONSULTING OR VOLUNTEER SERVICES:
Nonprofit Capacity Building Program.

NAME(S) OF PROGRAMS:
- **African American Unity Fund**
- **Endowment Funds of Southwest Iowa**
- **Equality Fund for LGBTQIA**
- **Fund for Omaha**
- **Futuro Latino Fund**
- **Omaha Neighborhood Grants Program**

TYPE:
Capital grants; General operating grants; Project/program grants; Technical assistance. Donors can contribute through the Omaha Community Foundation to any nonprofit agency. The OCF also has 10 discretionary grant programs.

PURPOSE:
To facilitate charitable giving and serve as a vehicle for community improvement; to improve the quality of life in Greater Omaha by supporting needs not being met in the areas of civic, cultural, health, education and social service.

LEGAL BASIS:
Public foundation.

ELIGIBILITY:
Organizations applying for grants must be tax-exempt as defined by IRS 501(c)(3) status. Except under unusual circumstances, no grants for endowments, capital campaigns, deficit financing, annual fund drives or fund-raising activities. The grant request must have the approval of the governing board of the requesting organization.

GEOG. RESTRICTIONS: Nine counties in southwestern Iowa and the greater Omaha, Nebraska area.

FINANCIAL DATA:
Amount of support per award: Up to $50,000.
Total amount of support: Varies.

NO. MOST RECENT APPLICANTS: Varies.

NO. AWARDS: Varies.

APPLICATION INFO:
Contact the Foundation for details.
Duration: Varies.
Deadline: Varies.

PUBLICATIONS:
Newsletter.

IRS I.D.: 47-0645958

ADDRESS INQUIRIES TO:
Program Manager or
Director of Community Investment
(See address above.)

ORANGE COUNTY COMMUNITY FOUNDATION [230]

4041 MacArthur Boulevard
Suite 510
Newport Beach, CA 92660-2503
(949) 553-4202
Fax: (949) 553-4211
E-mail: info@oc-cf.org
Web Site: www.oc-cf.org

FOUNDED: 1989

AREAS OF INTEREST:
Children and youth, family relationships, diverse communities, music education and performance, classical music and education, health, environment and education.

TYPE:
Endowments; General operating grants; Project/program grants; Scholarships. The Foundation offers several grant programs throughout the year in human services, education, health, arts and culture, veterans, citizenship, and the environment. Other special grant competitions also occur throughout the year.

YEAR PROGRAM STARTED: 1990

PURPOSE:
To encourage, support and facilitate philanthropy in Orange County.

LEGAL BASIS:
Community foundation.

ELIGIBILITY:
Applicant agencies must be tax-exempt, serve its residents, and operate without discrimination on the basis of race, religion, gender, sexual orientation, age, national origin or disability.

GEOG. RESTRICTIONS: Primarily Orange County, California.

FINANCIAL DATA:
Amount of support per award: Average grant: $5,000 to $25,000.
Total amount of support: $58,979,000 for fiscal year ending June 30, 2017.

CO-OP FUNDING PROGRAMS: Accelerate Change Together Anaheim; OC Veterans Initiative; I Heart OC Giving Day; OC Grantmakers.

APPLICATION INFO:
All applications and transcripts must be submitted through the online application system. Guidelines are available on the web site.
Duration: Generally one year for unrestricted grants. Renewal occasionally possible for scholarships.
Deadline: Varies.

PUBLICATIONS:
Annual report; newsletters; guidelines.

IRS I.D.: 33-0378778

ADDRESS INQUIRIES TO:
Cathleen Otero, Vice President
Donor Relations and Programs
(See address above.)

THE BERNARD OSHER FOUNDATION [231]

One Market Plaza
Spear Tower, Suite 4025
San Francisco, CA 94105
(415) 861-5587
E-mail: info@osherfoundation.org
Web Site: www.osherfoundation.org

FOUNDED: 1977

AREAS OF INTEREST:
Scholarship funding to selected colleges and universities, integrative medicine, lifelong learning for seasoned adults, arts and humanities.

TYPE:
Project/program grants; Scholarships. The Foundation provides scholarship funding nationally to selected colleges and universities and funds integrative medicine centers at Harvard University, Northwestern University, Vanderbilt University, the University of California at San Francisco, and the Karolinska Institute in Stockholm. It also supports a growing network of lifelong learning institutes for seasoned adults located at 121 colleges and universities from Maine to Hawaii. Arts and humanities grants are made to nonprofit organizations principally in the Greater San Francisco Bay Area, specifically Alameda and San Francisco counties, as well as the state of Maine.

YEAR PROGRAM STARTED: 1977

PURPOSE:
To provide scholarship funding nationally to selected colleges and universities and to fund integrative medicine centers; to support a network of lifelong learning institutes for seasoned adults; to support the arts and humanities.

ELIGIBILITY:
Requests will be accepted only from organizations which are classified by the IRS as nonprofit and designated as IRS 501(c)(3). Organizations seeking funds should have experience which is relevant to the proposed project.

The Foundation is precluded by its policies from making direct grants to individuals.

FINANCIAL DATA:
Amount of support per award: Varies.
Total amount of support: Varies.

APPLICATION INFO:
A letter of inquiry is invited as the first step in communicating with the Foundation. Details can be found on the Foundation web site.
Duration: Generally one year.

STAFF:
Mary G.F. Bitterman, President
Thomas Moffett, Chief Financial Officer/Chief Investment Officer
David Blazevich, Senior Program Director
Eric Gillespie, Program Director
Jeanie Hirokane, Corporate Secretary and Program Director

BOARD OF DIRECTORS:
Barbro Osher, Chairman
Bernard Osher, Founder and Treasurer
Mary G.F. Bitterman, President
David Agger
Phyllis Cook
Robert Friend
John Gallo
Laura Lauder
John Pritzker

ADDRESS INQUIRIES TO:
Jeanie Hirokane, Corporate Secretary and Program Director
(See address above.)

PACCAR FOUNDATION [232]

777 106th Avenue, N.E.
Bellevue, WA 98004
(425) 468-7400
Fax: (425) 468-8216
E-mail: ken.hastings@paccar.com
Web Site: www.paccar.com

FOUNDED: 1951

AREAS OF INTEREST:
Education, science, arts and humanities.

TYPE:
Capital grants.

LEGAL BASIS:
Private foundation.

ELIGIBILITY:
No grants to individuals, political or lobbying groups, fraternal organizations or religious organizations for sectarian purposes.

GEOG. RESTRICTIONS: Columbus, Mississippi; Chillicothe, Ohio; Broken Arrow, Oklahoma; Denton, Texas; Bellevue, Kirkland, Renton, Seattle and Skagit, Washington.

FINANCIAL DATA:
Amount of support per award: $10,000 to $250,000.
Total amount of support: Average $5,000,000 per year.

APPLICATION INFO:
Guidelines and application procedures are available on the Foundation web site.
Duration: One year. Must reapply for continued funding.
Deadline: Applications accepted throughout the year. Decisions made semiannually.

STAFF:
Ken Hastings, Vice President and General Manager

ADDRESS INQUIRIES TO:
Ken Hastings
Vice President and General Manager
(See address above.)

PACIFIC GAS AND ELECTRIC COMPANY [233]

77 Beale Street
San Francisco, CA 94105
(415) 973-1150
E-mail: pmm2@pge.com
communityrelations@pge.com
Web Site: www.pge.com/giving

AREAS OF INTEREST:
Emergency preparedness and safety.

CONSULTING OR VOLUNTEER SERVICES:
Volunteer program.

TYPE:
Project/program grants; Scholarships. Signature programs.

YEAR PROGRAM STARTED: 2001

LEGAL BASIS:
Corporate contributions program.

ELIGIBILITY:
Applicants must have tax-deductible status from the IRS under Section 501(c)(3) or be a unit of government (including a public school). Contributions are not made to individuals, for tickets for contests, raffles or other prize-oriented activities, to religious organizations (unless for a program offered to the public on a nondiscriminatory basis and without regard to the recipient's religious affiliation), endowments, debt-reduction campaigns, films, or to political or partisan organizations or events.

The most successful grant applications are those that:
(1) address a demonstrated community need;
(2) link a nonprofit or government program to the Company's business goals and employee presence in the community and;
(3) can provide the grantee and the Company with recognition in the community.

GEOG. RESTRICTIONS: Northern and central California.

FINANCIAL DATA:
Amount of support per award: $1,000 to $25,000. Most grants are under $5,000.

Total amount of support: $17,500,000 in grants for the year 2019.

Matching fund requirements: 1:1 basis: $25 to $1,000 per calendar year, per employee.

NO. AWARDS: 735 grants for the year 2019.

APPLICATION INFO:
Prior to applying for a grant, applicants should contact the local PG&E representative in their project area to discuss the grant proposal. All applicants must use the online grant application. PG&E will neither accept nor process grant proposals in any other format. Please submit only a fully completed application. Incomplete applications will not be considered.

Duration: Generally one year.

Deadline: Applications are preferred before September 30 of each year.

ADDRESS INQUIRIES TO:
Pat Mora, Executive Administrator
(See address above.)

PACIFIC LIFE
FOUNDATION   [234]
700 Newport Center Drive
Newport Beach, CA 92660-6397
(949) 219-3214
E-mail: plfoundation@pacificlife.com
Web Site: www.pacificlifefoundation.com

FOUNDED: 1984

AREAS OF INTEREST:
Broad spectrum of social issues.

NAME(S) OF PROGRAMS:
- **Arts and Culture**
- **Civic, Community, and Environment**
- **Education**
- **Health and Human Services**

TYPE:
Capital grants; General operating grants; Matching gifts; Project/program grants. Arts and Culture: Funds nonprofit agencies that provide the public with a broad spectrum of arts and cultural initiatives (e.g., workshops, performances) to help build the public's appreciation of and participation in dance, music, and theater.

Civic, Community, and Environment: Funding is directed to a wide range of programs that enhance communities through leadership development and environmental protection, as well as fund research to learn more about marine mammals.

Education: Funds nonprofit agencies committed to providing quality educational programs for youth and adults (e.g., mentoring, tutoring, literacy) to help them excel academically and in life.

Health and Human Services: Contributions are allocated to agencies that seek to improve the quality of life of those in need, including

the working poor, the homeless, and individuals with physical or developmental disabilities.

PURPOSE:
To recognize and support employees' varied interests and community involvement and, through focus programs, to identify and respond to particular community needs so that, whenever possible, funds may be channeled to those areas in which the most good can be accomplished with the funds available.

LEGAL BASIS:
Corporate foundation and corporate contributions program.

ELIGIBILITY:
Grants are made to nonprofit, tax-exempt, 501(c)(3) organizations. The Foundation does not provide support for individuals, for political parties, candidates or partisan political organizations, for labor organizations, fraternal organizations, athletic clubs or social clubs, for K-12 schools, school districts, or school foundations (contact Foundation for exceptions), for sectarian or denominational religious organizations, except for programs which are broadly promoted, available to anyone, and free from religious orientation, for fund-raising events (e.g., membership drives, luncheons/dinners, tournaments and benefits), or for advertising sponsorships.

GEOG. RESTRICTIONS: The Greater Orange County, California area and other areas, such as Omaha, Nebraska and Lynchburg, VA.

FINANCIAL DATA:
Amount of support per award: General grants: $5,000 to $15,000 for a one-year period of funding; Capital grants: $20,000 to $100,000, paid out over multiple years; Matching Gift Program for Higher Education: Up to $2,000; Matching Gift Program to Nonprofits: Up to $500.

Total amount of support: $7,000,000 in grants and $363,842 in matching gifts for the year 2018.

APPLICATION INFO:
Grant guidelines and application form are available online.

Duration: Agencies may reapply annually for funding; however, grants are made to any one agency for no more than three consecutive years. Support may again be requested after a two-year interim period.

Deadline: Submissions accepted July 15 to August 15.

PUBLICATIONS:
Annual report.

OFFICERS:
James T. Morris, Chairman and Chief Executive Officer
Carol R. Sudbeck, Vice Chairman
Tennyson S. Oyler, President
Tere Segarra, Vice President
Joshua Scott, Chief Financial Officer
Joseph J. Tortorelli, General Counsel
Jane M. Guon, Secretary
Marryn D. Santucci, Assistant Secretary
Starla C. Yamauchi, Assistant Secretary

BOARD OF DIRECTORS:
Ray Dinstel
Laurie Fitzgerald
Charles Jernigan
Lori Johnstone
David Leutenachlager
James T. Morris

Tennyson S. Oyler
Tere Segarra
Tim N. Shaheen
David Spencer
Janine C. Stallings
Carol R. Sudbeck
Brian T. Woolfolk
Christina Wu

ADDRESS INQUIRIES TO:
Tennyson S. Oyler, President
(See address above.)

THE DAVID AND LUCILE
PACKARD FOUNDATION   [235]
343 Second Street
Los Altos, CA 94022
(650) 948-7658
E-mail: inquiries@packard.org
Web Site: www.packard.org

FOUNDED: 1964

AREAS OF INTEREST:
Arts; children and youth, families and communities, food and shelter; conservation and sciences; organizational effectiveness; philanthropy; and Pueblo, CO.

NAME(S) OF PROGRAMS:
- **Children, Families and Communities**
- **Conservation and Science**
- **Local Grantmaking Program**
- **Reproductive Health**

TYPE:
Capital grants; Challenge/matching grants; Conferences/seminars; Demonstration grants; Development grants; Fellowships; General operating grants; Matching gifts; Project/program grants; Research grants; Scholarships; Seed money grants; Technical assistance. Grants are made to provide support in the local five-county area for organizational development, arts education and traditional performing arts, as well as for areas of wetlands preservation and restoration, marine fisheries protection and restoration.

Funds are also provided to support fellowships for 20 young professors in science and engineering.

In addition, the Foundation supports children's health programs through children, families, and communities programs, population and family planning services.

Support is given for research of the deep ocean in the Monterey, CA area and community grants in Pueblo County, CO.

YEAR PROGRAM STARTED: 1964

PURPOSE:
To support private, voluntary charities.

LEGAL BASIS:
Private foundation incorporated under California law.

ELIGIBILITY:
Applicants must be qualified tax-exempt charitable organizations. Most community-oriented grants are made to organizations that serve the people of Monterey, San Benito, San Mateo, Santa Clara and Santa Cruz counties. Requests for support of community and local activities outside of these geographical areas will rarely be considered. Grants are also made in Pueblo (CO) and for national and international programs in conservation, population, public policy and children's health. No proposals may be accepted that benefit individuals or that are for religious purposes.

APPLICATION INFO:
Contact the Foundation for guidelines.

Duration: Grants are made for one year, with occasional multiyear grants.

PUBLICATIONS:
Annual report; guideline brochures.

OFFICERS:
David Orr, Chairperson
Nancy Packard Burnett, Vice Chairperson
Julie E. Packard, Vice Chairperson
Craig Neyman, President and Chief Executive Officer
Alisa E. Mulligan, Chief Financial Officer and Controller
Chris DeCardy, Vice President and Director of Programs
Mary Anne Rodgers, General Counsel

BOARD OF TRUSTEES:
Ned Barnholt
Jason K. Burnett
Nancy Packard Burnett
Michael C. Camunez
Sierra Clark
Michael J. Klag
Dr. Stephen H. Lockhart
Jane Lubchenco
Linda A. Mason
Craig Neyman
David Orr
Katherine Orr
Susan Packard Orr
Julie E. Packard
Louise Stephens

ADDRESS INQUIRIES TO:
See e-mail address above.

THE PARKER FOUNDATION [236]

2604-B El Camino Real
Suite 244
Carlsbad, CA 92008
(760) 720-0630
E-mail: mail@theparkerfoundation.org
Web Site: www.theparkerfoundation.org

FOUNDED: 1971

AREAS OF INTEREST:
Adult and youth services, visual and performing arts, museums and zoos, education, medical purposes, environment and community activities.

TYPE:
Capital grants; Challenge/matching grants; Matching gifts; Project/program grants. Programs and capital funding.

YEAR PROGRAM STARTED: 1971

PURPOSE:
To improve all aspects of life of the people of San Diego County, CA.

LEGAL BASIS:
Tax-exempt, independent private foundation.

ELIGIBILITY:
Applicants must be organizations operating in San Diego County, CA, qualified under IRS 501(c)(3). No grants to individuals or for support of conferences or symposia. No support provided for any project to the extent that it becomes dependent on the Foundation for continued existence.

GEOG. RESTRICTIONS: San Diego County, California.

FINANCIAL DATA:
Amount of support per award: Varies.
Total amount of support: $1,927,950 for fiscal year 2019.

NO. MOST RECENT APPLICANTS: 247 for the year 2019.

NO. AWARDS: 67 for the year 2019.

APPLICATION INFO:
Prior to submitting a proposal, an applicant should review the Application Process. Proposals may be submitted electronically through the Foundation's online process. Written proposals are also accepted.

Deadline: May, July and September for Board meetings held in June, July and September, respectively. Exact dates are posted online.

ADDRESS INQUIRIES TO:
Robbin C. Powell
Chief Administrative Officer
(See address above.)

*SPECIAL STIPULATIONS:
Limited by governing documents to San Diego County, CA.

PARKER HANNIFIN FOUNDATION [237]

6035 Parkland Boulevard
Cleveland, OH 44124
(216) 896-3000
E-mail: parkerfoundation@parker.com
Web Site: www.parker.com

FOUNDED: 1953

AREAS OF INTEREST:
Education, disaster relief, energy and water conservation, and other charitable organizations.

TYPE:
Capital grants; Matching gifts; Project/program grants. Through the National Merit Scholarship for Parker employee children only. Matching gifts are for education.

LEGAL BASIS:
Corporate foundation.

ELIGIBILITY:
Grants are made to nonprofit organizations. Emphasis will be placed on organizations that benefit Parker employees and shareholders by improving services in communities with Parker operations and educational opportunities for current and potential employees. Organization must have a Parker sponsor.

Contributions will not be made to fraternal or labor organizations. Donations to religious organizations are limited to organizations serving the general public on a nondenominational basis, such as the Y's, Salvation Army, educational institutions, hospitals, etc.

GEOG. RESTRICTIONS: United States.

FINANCIAL DATA:
Amount of support per award: $500 minimum.
Total amount of support: Over $6,000,000 annually.

APPLICATION INFO:
Applicants should submit a proposal stating needs and what the grant will be used for, to the Parker division in their locality.

Duration: One-time award.

Deadline: June 30.

IRS I.D.: 34-6555686

THE RALPH M. PARSONS FOUNDATION [238]

888 West 6th Street, 7th Floor
Los Angeles, CA 90017
(213) 362-7600
Web Site: www.rmpf.org

FOUNDED: 1961

AREAS OF INTEREST:
Civic and cultural, education, health, and human services.

TYPE:
Capital grants; General operating grants. Program support grants.

YEAR PROGRAM STARTED: 1978

LEGAL BASIS:
Not-for-profit corporation.

ELIGIBILITY:
Applicants must be 501(c)(3) organizations not classified under 509(a). Grants limited to organizations providing services in Los Angeles County.

No funding for mass mailings, fund-raisers, individuals, conferences, religious or political activities and/or dinners or endowments.

GEOG. RESTRICTIONS: Los Angeles County, California.

FINANCIAL DATA:
Amount of support per award: Varies.
Total amount of support: $18,500,000 for the year 2019.

NO. AWARDS: 311 for the year 2019.

REPRESENTATIVE AWARDS:
$100,000 to A Community of Friends for general support of housing with supportive services; $250,000 to Boys and Girls Club of Metro Los Angeles for general support of youth development programs; $500,000 over two years to Excellent Education Development for general support to expand and sustain the capacity of charter schools in Los Angeles County.

APPLICATION INFO:
Submit preliminary letter outlining project and amount requested. Program staff will determine whether applicant is qualified and may request additional information. Applicants are encouraged to visit the Foundation web site prior to submitting Letter of Inquiry.

Duration: Generally, one year.

Deadline: Applications are accepted on a rolling basis.

STAFF:
Wendy Garen, President and Chief Executive Officer
E. Thomas Brewer, Director, Finance and Administration
Nicole Larsen, Director, Grants Administration
Jennifer Price-Letscher, Director, Programs and Special Projects

BOARD OF DIRECTORS:
Peter J. Taylor, Chairperson
Paul G. Haaga, Jr., Vice Chairperson
Manuel A. Abascal
Karen Hill Scott
Elizabeth Lowe
Steven A. Nissen
Nina Revoyr
James A. Thomas
Gayle Wilson

ADDRESS INQUIRIES TO:
Wendy Garen
President and Chief Executive Officer
(See address above.)

AMELIA PEABODY CHARITABLE FUND [239]

185 Devonshire Street
Suite 600
Boston, MA 02110
(617) 451-6178
Web Site: apcfund.org

FOUNDED: 1984

AREAS OF INTEREST:
Medicine (human and animal), social welfare, visual arts, historic preservation and land conservation.

TYPE:
Capital grants; Challenge/matching grants. Grants to qualified nonprofit organizations existing and operating in Massachusetts.

PURPOSE:
To continue Amelia Peabody's philanthropy in perpetuity through grants.

LEGAL BASIS:
Private foundation.

ELIGIBILITY:
Eligible organizations must be IRS 501(c)(3) tax-exempt and classified as a public charity under Section 509(a)(1) or 509(a)(2) of the Internal Revenue Code.

No grants to individuals, religious organizations, education, startups, operating, administrative overhead, emergencies, scholarships, fellowships, endowments, organizations located outside of Massachusetts, or Section 509(a)(3) organizations funded principally with tax dollars.

GEOG. RESTRICTIONS: Massachusetts.

FINANCIAL DATA:
Amount of support per award: Varies per project.
Total amount of support: Approximately $8,000,000 annually.

NO. MOST RECENT APPLICANTS: Approximately 300.

NO. AWARDS: 100.

APPLICATION INFO:
All proposals are submitted online through the Fund web site.
Duration: May reapply after three years.
Deadline: February 1 and July 1.

PUBLICATIONS:
Guidelines.

IRS I.D.: 23-7364949

STAFF:
Bethany B. Kendall, Executive Director
Cheryl Gideon, Business and Grants Coordinator

ADDRESS INQUIRIES TO:
Cheryl Gideon
Business and Grants Coordinator
(See address above.)

PEACOCK FOUNDATION, INC. [240]

4000 Ponce De Leon Boulevard
Suite 450
Coral Gables, FL 33146
(305) 373-1386
Fax: (305) 375-0660
Web Site: peacockfoundationinc.org

AREAS OF INTEREST:
Elderly, children, youth, art for educational purposes, environmental education, disabilities, health and hospitals, medical research and human services.

TYPE:
General operating grants; Project/program grants. Support is provided for projects/programs and limited operating funds.

ELIGIBILITY:
Organizations classified as 501(c)(3) by the IRS can apply. Individuals are ineligible.

GEOG. RESTRICTIONS: Miami-Dade County, Florida.

FINANCIAL DATA:
Amount of support per award: Average $25,000.

NO. AWARDS: 51 for the year 2019.

APPLICATION INFO:
Applicants must initially submit letter of inquiry.
Duration: One year.

ADDRESS INQUIRIES TO:
Joelle Allen, Executive Director
(See address above.)

THE WILLIAM PENN FOUNDATION [241]

Two Logan Square, 11th Floor
100 North 18th Street
Philadelphia, PA 19103-2757
(215) 988-1830
Fax: (215) 988-1823
E-mail: grants@williampennfoundation.org
Web Site: www.williampennfoundation.org

FOUNDED: 1945

AREAS OF INTEREST:
Art, communities, culture, environment, children, youth and families.

NAME(S) OF PROGRAMS:
● **Creative Communities**
● **Great Learning**
● **Watershed Protection**

TYPE:
Capital grants; Challenge/matching grants; Demonstration grants; Development grants; General operating grants; Project/program grants; Research grants; Seed money grants; Technical assistance. Planning grants; Implementation grants.

In the areas of children, youth and families, grants are made to promote a better early care and education system, more effective and equitable education policies, networks of developmental opportunities for older youth, and improvements to the systems supporting families. The program focuses on critical transitions in the lives of children as they progress from birth, through early childhood, and into young adulthood.

In the area of environment and communities, grants are made to foster greater cross-sector collaborations that build on the assets of our region through revitalization of its urban core and protection and restoration of watersheds, with a focus on key waterways. Investments are intended to catalyze innovation and leadership in the region.

In the area of arts and culture, the Foundation provides various types of core operating support for arts groups and cultural institutions, enabling them to pursue their

creative missions. Work is also funded that broadly advances the region's cultural sector. General operating grants are made only for arts funding.

YEAR PROGRAM STARTED: 1945

PURPOSE:
To improve the quality of life in the Greater Philadelphia area, particularly for its economically disadvantaged residents; to serve nonprofit organizations that help people improve their lives within a more just and caring society.

LEGAL BASIS:
Private foundation.

ELIGIBILITY:
Applicants must be organizations which are defined as tax-exempt under Section 501(c)(3) of the Internal Revenue Code and which are not private foundations. Grants may be made to religious institutions for nonsectarian purposes, to governments and national organizations in support of policy and advocacy projects.

The Foundation does not fund scholarships, fellowships, or grants to individuals; loans or investment programs; debt reduction; sectarian religious activities; housing capital projects; exempt organizations that pass funds to nonexempt groups; profit-making enterprises; nonpublic schools; programs for rehabilitation or research; programs to replace discontinued government support or national or international grants.

GEOG. RESTRICTIONS: Philadelphia area (Bucks, Chester, Delaware, Montgomery and Philadelphia counties), Pennsylvania and Camden, New Jersey.

FINANCIAL DATA:
Amount of support per award: Varies.
Total amount of support: $115,163,860 in total grants for year ended December 31, 2018.

CO-OP FUNDING PROGRAMS: The Foundation regularly joins with other foundations and institutions to fund projects.

NO. AWARDS: 256 for the year 2019.

APPLICATION INFO:
All applicants must first submit a letter of inquiry. Guidelines and inquiry form are available on the Foundation web site.

PUBLICATIONS:
Annual report.

IRS I.D.: 23-1503488

BOARD OF DIRECTORS:
Janet Haas, M.D., Chairperson
Katherine Christiano, Vice Chairperson
Christina Haas, Vice Chairperson
Sarah Haas Block
Andrew Haas
Leonard C. Haas
Peter Haas
Thomas Haas
Don Kimelman
Claire Lomax
Howard Meyers
Michael Pearson
Robert Victor
Suzanne Welsh

OFFICERS AND STAFF:
Shawn McCaney, Executive Director
Bryan Ulishney, Director, Finance and Administration
Barbara Scace, Director, Grants Management

ADDRESS INQUIRIES TO:
See e-mail address above.

PEPSICO FOUNDATION [242]
700 Anderson Hill Road
Purchase, NY 10577
(914) 253-2000
Web Site: www.pepsico.
com/sustainability/philanthropy

FOUNDED: 1962

AREAS OF INTEREST:
Nutrition, water, women, and waste.

TYPE:
Capital grants.

PURPOSE:
To support programs that encourage healthy
lifestyles, improve availability of affordable
nutrition, expand access to clean water,
enhance sustainable agriculture capability,
enable job readiness, and empower women
and girls.

LEGAL BASIS:
Nonprofit under 501(c)(3).

ELIGIBILITY:
Organizations seeking a grant must be
registered and have an official tax-exemption
under Section 501(c)(3) of the Internal
Revenue Code, or the equivalent. The
Foundation does not make grants to
individuals, religious organizations or
political causes.

FINANCIAL DATA:
Amount of support per award: Varies.

APPLICATION INFO:
Submit a brief Letter of Interest. Complete
details are available on the Foundation web
site.

ADDRESS INQUIRIES TO:
Grants Manager
(See address above.)

THE CARL AND LILY PFORZHEIMER FOUNDATION, INC. [243]
122 East 42nd Street
Suite 4305
New York, NY 10168
(212) 223-6500
Fax: (212) 223-2222

FOUNDED: 1942

AREAS OF INTEREST:
Education, primarily early 19th century
English literature.

TYPE:
Grants-in-aid; Project/program grants.

PURPOSE:
To provide resources for the in-depth study
of 19th century English literature.

LEGAL BASIS:
Private foundation.

ELIGIBILITY:
Grants are awarded only to IRS 501(c)(3)
tax-exempt organizations. No grants are made
directly to individuals.

GEOG. RESTRICTIONS: Primarily United States.

FINANCIAL DATA:
Amount of support per award: Average:
$25,000 to $50,000.

APPLICATION INFO:
Organizations may submit a proposal.

Duration: Varies.

ADDRESS INQUIRIES TO:
Carl H. Pforzheimer III, President
(See address above.)

THE ALBERT PICK, JR. FUND [244]
70 East Lake Street
Suite 1120
Chicago, IL 60601
(312) 236-1192
E-mail: bettyjo@albertpickjrfund.org
Web Site: www.albertpickjrfund.org

FOUNDED: 1947

AREAS OF INTEREST:
Education, health and human services.

TYPE:
Challenge/matching grants; Demonstration
grants; Development grants; General
operating grants; Project/program grants.

YEAR PROGRAM STARTED: 1947

PURPOSE:
To offer a hand when help is needed.

LEGAL BASIS:
Private family foundation.

ELIGIBILITY:
Nonprofits with offices and separately
budgeted programs operating within the city
of Chicago.

GEOG. RESTRICTIONS: Chicago, Illinois.

FINANCIAL DATA:
Amount of support per award: $15,000 to
$35,000.
Total amount of support: Approximately
$1,330,189 for the year 2018.

NO. MOST RECENT APPLICANTS: Approximately
200.

NO. AWARDS: 80.

APPLICATION INFO:
Eligible nonprofits are requested to complete
an application form, available on the Fund
web site. Only those proposals which
completely meet the requirements outlined in
the guidelines will be reviewed.
Duration: Generally, one year.
Deadline: December 15 for the Spring
quarter, March 21 for the Summer quarter,
June 15 for Fall quarter and September 14
for Winter quarter.

PUBLICATIONS:
Guidelines; grant application form.

IRS I.D.: 36-6071402

OFFICERS AND BOARD OF DIRECTORS:
Shelly A. Davis, President
Mark A. Rosenberg, Treasurer
Rachel Lindsey, Secretary

ADDRESS INQUIRIES TO:
Betty Jo Joy, Grants Manager
(See address above.)

IRWIN ANDREW PORTER FOUNDATION [245]
3817 Thomas Avenue South
Minneapolis, MN 55410
E-mail: iapfound@gmail.com
Web Site: www.iapfoundation.org

FOUNDED: 1996

AREAS OF INTEREST:
Arts, education, environment and social
programs.

TYPE:
Challenge/matching grants; Grants-in-aid;
Project/program grants.

PURPOSE:
To fund innovative projects that foster
connections between individuals,
communities, the environment and the world
at large.

ELIGIBILITY:
The Foundation provides funding for a
variety of interest areas. The quality,
innovation, thoughtfulness and effectiveness
of a project are of more importance than the
specific interest area. However, its areas of
interest are the arts, education, environment
and social programs.

International projects should be applicable to,
and repeatable in, other regions. The
Foundation gives funding to nonprofit
organizations with U.S. IRS tax-exempt
status only. International organizations must
have a fiscal agent incorporated in the U.S.
with an appropriate U.S. IRS tax-exempt
designation.

The Foundation does not provide financial
support for:
(1) general operating expenses;
(2) capital projects;
(3) endowments;
(4) scholarships;
(5) fund-raising events or activities, social
events, goodwill advertising or marketing;
(6) lobbying, political, fraternal, athletic,
social or veterans organizations;
(7) religious programs;
(8) travel for individuals or groups;
(9) individuals or;
(10) ordinary school funding.

GEOG. RESTRICTIONS: Illinois, Iowa, Michigan,
Minnesota, North Dakota, South Dakota and
Wisconsin.

FINANCIAL DATA:
Amount of support per award: Grants: $1,000
to $30,000 annually.
Total amount of support: Approximately
$135,000 annually.

APPLICATION INFO:
Organizations are selected for an invitation to
apply from a group of secret nominators.
Duration: Generally, one year.

ADDRESS INQUIRIES TO:
Amy L. Hubbard, Chairman
(See address above.)

*PLEASE NOTE:
Foundation grantmaking is by invitation only;
unsolicited proposals will not be considered.

PPG INDUSTRIES FOUNDATION [246]
One PPG Place
Pittsburgh, PA 15272
(412) 434-2962
E-mail: foundation@ppg.com
Web Site: communities.ppg.com

FOUNDED: 1951

AREAS OF INTEREST:
Education and community sustainability.

TYPE:
Grants are provided to select organizations
and programs that advance the priority giving
areas of Education and Community
Sustainability. The PPG Foundation may be
able to provide in-kind support in the form of

product donations or employee volunteers (mentors, guest speakers etc.) in addition to its grants.

In the area of education, the Foundation is committed to supporting science, technology, engineering and math education programs that lead to academic and career achievement in fields such as Collision Repair Training, Color Science, Ceramic Engineering, Chemistry and Material Science. These investments help communities meet today's demands for a skilled workforce in research and development, manufacturing, information technology and other industry related professions, and develop a generation of innovators for tomorrow.

The Foundation also aims to stimulate interest and achievement in subjects related to science, technology, engineering and math as well as to help young people envision a future in a related career. In addition, limited funds are available to support initiatives designed to advance key industry and STEM-related topics central to the long-term needs of the industry.

In the area of community sustainability, the Foundation aims to strengthen local communities by supporting organizations and programs that meet critical needs, promote environmental sustainability, foster economic development and support disaster relief efforts. Priority funding within this area varies by location, based on the specific needs of PPG communities.

YEAR PROGRAM STARTED: 1951

PURPOSE:
To create brighter and more colorful communities where PPG has a presence around the world.

LEGAL BASIS:
Corporate, nonprofit foundation.

ELIGIBILITY:
All grants recipients must be nonprofit, charitable organizations tax-exempt under section 501(c)(3) of the Internal Revenue Code, if U.S.-based, or must be equivalent organizations, if outside of the U.S., with registered charitable status if available.

Funding priority is with organizations that are located in PPG or wholly-owned subsidiary locations.

FINANCIAL DATA:
Amount of support per award: Varies.
Total amount of support: $11,800,000 in support paid for the year 2019.
Matching fund requirements: Contributions by PPG employees and members of the board of directors of the company are matched on a 1:1 basis by the Foundation; $25 minimum, $10,000 maximum per year per donor.

APPLICATION INFO:
Applications are accepted on an invitation-only basis.
Duration: Varies.
Deadline: Requests for funding are accepted year-round.

BOARD OF DIRECTORS:
Michael H. McGarry, Chairman and Chief Executive Officer
Vince Morales, Senior Vice President and Chief Financial Officer
Anne M. Foulkes, Senior Vice President and General Counsel
Kevin Walling, Vice President and Chief Human Resources Officer

PRINCIPAL FINANCIAL GROUP FOUNDATION INC. [247]
711 High Street
Des Moines, IA 50392-0150
(515) 247-7227
E-mail: mcreynolds.mandi@principal.com
Web Site: www.principal.com/about-us/corporate-citizenship

FOUNDED: 1987

AREAS OF INTEREST:
Civic and community, arts and culture, higher education, K-12 education, STEM education, job readiness and job training, financial security, financial literacy, and disaster relief.

CONSULTING OR VOLUNTEER SERVICES:
The mission of the Principal Volunteer Network is to be the primary volunteer network for community service to educate and recruit employees, agents and retirees of the Principal Financial Group; thus enhancing the company's social responsibility goals and business objectives.

NAME(S) OF PROGRAMS:
● **Charitable Giving Program**

TYPE:
Capital grants; General operating grants; Project/program grants.

YEAR PROGRAM STARTED: 1987

LEGAL BASIS:
Corporate foundation.

ELIGIBILITY:
Applicants must be nonprofit IRS 501(c)(3) organizations located in communities with significant employee presence.

Grants are generally not made to athletes or athletic organizations, conference or seminar attendance, goodwill advertising, endowments or memorials, festival participation, fraternal organizations, hospital or health care facility capital fund drives, individuals, K-12 schools, libraries, partisan political organizations, private foundations, sectarian, religious or denominational organizations, social organizations, tax-supported organizations, or United Way organizations seeking funds for United Way-funded programs.

Grants to global locations are by invitation only.

GEOG. RESTRICTIONS: Folsom, California; Wilmington, Delaware; Cedar Falls, Greater Des Moines, Mason City and Waterloo, Iowa; Grand Island, Nebraska; Spokane, Washington; Appleton, Wisconsin.

FINANCIAL DATA:
Amount of support per award: $10,000 minimum.
Total amount of support: Varies.

NO. MOST RECENT APPLICANTS: 125.

NO. AWARDS: 110.

APPLICATION INFO:
Applications are submitted through the Foundation's web site. Paper or e-mail applications are no longer accepted.
Duration: One to two years, depending on funding area.
Deadline: March 15, June 15 and September 15, depending on funding area.

PUBLICATIONS:
Guidelines.

ADDRESS INQUIRIES TO:
Rachel Woodhouse, Program Manager
(See address above.)

PUBLIC WELFARE FOUNDATION, INC. [248]
1200 U Street, N.W.
Washington, DC 20009-4443
(202) 965-1800
Fax: (202) 265-8851
E-mail: info@publicwelfare.org
Web Site: www.publicwelfare.org

FOUNDED: 1947

AREAS OF INTEREST:
Criminal justice and youth justice.

NAME(S) OF PROGRAMS:
● **Criminal Justice**
● **Special Opportunities**
● **Youth Justice**

TYPE:
General operating grants; Project/program grants.

YEAR PROGRAM STARTED: 1947

PURPOSE:
To support efforts to ensure fundamental rights and opportunities for people in need; to look for carefully defined points where the Foundation's funds can make a difference in bringing about systemic changes that can improve the lives of countless people.

LEGAL BASIS:
Private foundation.

ELIGIBILITY:
Applicants' requests must adhere to the Foundation's funding guidelines.

GEOG. RESTRICTIONS: United States.

FINANCIAL DATA:
Amount of support per award: Varies.
Total amount of support: $1,372,000 for fiscal year 2018.

NO. AWARDS: 175 approved grants for fiscal year 2018.

APPLICATION INFO:
Applicants should submit letters of inquiry using the online application system. This letter should contain facts and figures about the organization, describe its mission and explain the purpose of the request, including the Program under which a grant is being requested. Applicants will be invited by e-mail to submit full proposals. The Foundation cannot consider full proposals which have not been invited.
Duration: Usually one to two years. Renewal possible.
Deadline: Varies.

IRS I.D.: 54-0597601

BOARD OF DIRECTORS AND OFFICERS:
Cliff Sloan, Chairperson
Craig Aase
Stephanie Bell-Rose
Colin Diver
David Dodson
Christopher Graham
Gumersindo Oliveros
Maria Otero
Shirley Sagawa
Kim Taylor-Thompson
Eric Washington

ADDRESS INQUIRIES TO:
Grants Management
(See address above.)

THE QUAKER CHEMICAL FOUNDATION [249]

901 East Hector Street
Conshohocken, PA 19428-2380
(610) 832-8659
Fax: (610) 832-4496
E-mail: foundation@quakerchem.com
Web Site: www.quakerchem.com

FOUNDED: 1959

AREAS OF INTEREST:
Civic and community; cultural, health and welfare; and education.

NAME(S) OF PROGRAMS:
- **Grant Program**
- **Matching Gift Program**
- **Scholarship Program**

TYPE:
Matching gifts; Project/program grants; Scholarships. The Foundation matches employee gifts to qualified educational institutions, health and welfare organizations, civic and community, and arts or cultural institutions which are operated for the benefit of the general public.

YEAR PROGRAM STARTED: 1959

PURPOSE:
To help community projects where the company has domestic operations.

LEGAL BASIS:
Corporate foundation.

ELIGIBILITY:
Applicants must be IRS 501(c)(3) tax-exempt organizations. As a general rule, the Foundation does not support national organizations, limiting its interest to those organizations that are active in the areas in which the Quaker Chemical Corporation has operations, generally located within a five-mile radius of company facilities and locations.

FINANCIAL DATA:
Amount of support per award: $1,000 to $5,000; average: $1,500.

Matching fund requirements: Minimum $25 and maximum $1,000 per employee, retiree, director or spouse thereof per fiscal year.

REPRESENTATIVE AWARDS:
Conshohocken Fellowship House; Delaware Valley Science Fairs.

APPLICATION INFO:
In addition to a completed grant application, the grant request should include the following:
(1) cover letter on the organization's stationery, providing a brief history of the organization and its objectives;
(2) description of the program or activity for which funds are being requested, including the amount of funds being requested and the benefits realized by the local community;
(3) current operating budget and latest audited financial statements;
(4) list of funding sources for the organization, including past major contributors with amounts, recent applications with results, and anticipated future funding sources;
(5) list of directors and officers and their affiliations and;
(6) copy of organization's tax-exempt ruling under Section 501(c)(3) of the Internal Revenue Code.
Duration: One year.
Deadline: April 30.

PUBLICATIONS:
Grant application guidelines.

IRS I.D.: 23-6245803

TRUSTEES:
Cindy Cetnar
James Gabriel
Paul Gorman
Jennifer Hill
Jessica Sabedra

ADDRESS INQUIRIES TO:
Quaker Chemical Foundation Secretary
(See address above.)

THE NELL J. REDFIELD FOUNDATION [250]

P.O. Box 61
Reno, NV 89504
(775) 323-1373
Fax: (775) 323-4476
E-mail: gsmith@redfieldfoundation.org

FOUNDED: 1974

AREAS OF INTEREST:
Education, health care, and care for the needy.

TYPE:
Capital grants; Challenge/matching grants; Development grants; Matching gifts; Project/program grants. Grants for higher education. Medical and social welfare for disadvantaged children and seniors.

PURPOSE:
To promote education, health care and care for the homeless poor.

LEGAL BASIS:
Nonprofit foundation.

ELIGIBILITY:
Grants are made to organizations that have tax-exempt status under Section 501(c)(3) of the Internal Revenue Code. Nonsectarian religious programs may apply. No grants are made to individuals or private foundations.

Grants are restricted to organizations in Washoe County, Nevada.

GEOG. RESTRICTIONS: Washoe County, Nevada.

FINANCIAL DATA:
Amount of support per award: Varies.
Total amount of support: Varies.

NO. MOST RECENT APPLICANTS: 125.

NO. AWARDS: 75.

APPLICATION INFO:
Initially, contact the fund with a two-page summary that includes the specific goals, objectives, proposed activities and results expected.
Duration: One year. Renewal possible.
Deadline: Quarterly during each calendar year.

ADDRESS INQUIRIES TO:
Gerald C. Smith, Director
(See address above.)

THE REEBOK FOUNDATION [251]

25 Drydock Avenue
Boston, MA 02210
(857) 443-2000

FOUNDED: 1986

AREAS OF INTEREST:
Sport and fitness.

TYPE:
General operating grants; Matching gifts.

YEAR PROGRAM STARTED: 1986

PURPOSE:
To improve health outcomes of disadvantaged women and children through increased fitness access and inspiration.

LEGAL BASIS:
Corporate foundation.

ELIGIBILITY:
Grant applicants must be nonprofit organizations that provide equal access to funding and equal opportunity, and do not discriminate based on race, religion or sex. Grants are not made to individuals, political or fraternal organizations, or for advertising in program books or medical research.

GEOG. RESTRICTIONS: United States.

FINANCIAL DATA:
Amount of support per award; Grants: Up to $15,000.

Matching fund requirements: Employees of Reebok International Ltd, its subsidiaries and divisions. Organizations must be IRS 501(c)(3). Employee contributions to qualified organizations are matched dollar-for-dollar, up to $1,500 maximum.

APPLICATION INFO:
All requests for community support must be submitted online.
Deadline: Letters of Intent are accepted March 15 to April 15. Full Application: June 1. Decision by July 1.

PUBLICATIONS:
Guidelines.

IRS I.D.: 04-3073548

THE REGENSTEIN FOUNDATION [252]

225 West Wacker Drive
Suite 1500
Chicago, IL 60606
(312) 917-1833
Fax: (312) 917-1822

FOUNDED: 1950

AREAS OF INTEREST:
Education, community services, medicine and health, urban affairs, arts and music.

TYPE:
Capital grants; Endowments. Most grants are made to organizations located in and directly serving the residents of Illinois, basically in the metropolitan Chicago area.

YEAR PROGRAM STARTED: 1950

PURPOSE:
To help improve life and the community in and around Chicago.

LEGAL BASIS:
Private foundation.

ELIGIBILITY:
Any charitable organization other than private foundations for exempt purposes. No grants are made to individuals or for the benefit of designated individuals.

GEOG. RESTRICTIONS: Chicago, Illinois.

FINANCIAL DATA:
Amount of support per award: Varies.
Total amount of support: Varies.

NO. AWARDS: 35.

APPLICATION INFO:
Contact the Foundation in writing for an application.

Duration: One year. Renewable.

Deadline: March 31 and September 30.

OFFICERS:
Susan Regenstein, Chairperson

EXECUTIVE DIRECTOR:
Patricia Wallies

ADDRESS INQUIRIES TO:
Susan Regenstein, Chairperson
(See address above.)

*PLEASE NOTE:
Only a small number of applicants will
receive funds due to the relatively limited
amount available and the number of
organizations funded on trustee initiative.

THE CHARLES H. REVSON FOUNDATION [253]

55 East 59th Street
23rd Floor
New York, NY 10022
(212) 935-3340
Fax: (212) 688-0633
E-mail: info@revsonfoundation.org
Web Site: revsonfoundation.org

FOUNDED: 1956

AREAS OF INTEREST:
Urban affairs, with emphasis on New York
City, education, biomedical research policy
and Jewish philanthropy and education.

TYPE:
Fellowships; Project/program grants;
Research grants. The Foundation supports a
number of ongoing fellowship programs in
public policy, biomedical research and Jewish
education.

YEAR PROGRAM STARTED: 1978

PURPOSE:
To make a commitment to spread knowledge
and to improve human life.

LEGAL BASIS:
Private foundation.

ELIGIBILITY:
Grants are made to nonprofit, tax-exempt
organizations. The Foundation does not make
grants to individuals or for endowments,
local health appeals, direct-service programs,
building or construction funds, or routine
budgetary support.

GEOG. RESTRICTIONS: New York, New York and
Israel.

FINANCIAL DATA:
Amount of support per award: Varies.

APPLICATION INFO:
The Foundation welcomes e-mails from
prospective grantees. Applicant should send a
very brief description of the project including
the following information:
(1) organization name;
(2) name of contact, including e-mail, phone
number and mailing address;
(3) project title;
(4) project budget;
(5) amount sought and;
(6) description of project.
Do not include any attachments.

The Foundation is unable to accept inquiries
by mail or phone.
Duration: Varies.

IRS I.D.: 13-6126105

STAFF:
Julie Sandorf, President

Azade Ardali, Chief Financial and
Administrative Officer
Maria Marcantonio, Senior Program Officer
Elizabeth Leiman Kraiem, Program Officer
Rebecca Furth, Assistant Program Officer
Katie Shragge, Grants Manager
Karen Yu, Controller

BOARD OF DIRECTORS:
Cheryl Cohen Effron, Chairman
Stacy Dick, Treasurer
Sharon Greenberger, Secretary
Steven E. Hyman, M.D.
Dr. Robert Kingston
Reynold Levy
Errol Louis
David Resnick
Charles H. Revson, Jr.
Marcia Lynn Sells
Pam Wasserstein

ADDRESS INQUIRIES TO:
See e-mail address above.

Z. SMITH REYNOLDS FOUNDATION, INC. [254]

102 West Third Street
Suite 1110
Winston-Salem, NC 27101-3940
(336) 725-7541
(800) 443-8319
Fax: (336) 725-6069
E-mail: shaheens@zsr.org
Web Site: www.zsr.org

FOUNDED: 1936

AREAS OF INTEREST:
Civic participation, collaboration, dignity and
equity, fairness and justice, excellence,
integrity, stewardship, and sustainability.

NAME(S) OF PROGRAMS:
* **All for NC**

TYPE:
Challenge/matching grants; Fellowships;
General operating grants; Project/program
grants; Seed money grants. Sabbatical
Program. All for NC aligns with the
Foundation's mission and core values through
three key strategies: support a network of
organizations that are working to affect
change through a State-Level Systemic
Change Strategy; create more connections
between people, places, organizations and
sectors who are working to impact the
communities in which they live through a
Community-Based Strategy; and remain open
to bold, unconventional or higher-risk ideas
that have transformative potential through an
Exploratory, Visionary Ideas Strategy.

Alongside these three main strategies, the
Foundation also has expressed its
commitment to augment its participation in
its hometown of Winston-Salem/Forsyth
County, NC; use a racial equity lens to
underpin all of its work; and continue to be a
learning organization.

YEAR PROGRAM STARTED: 1936

PURPOSE:
To support charitable causes within the state
of North Carolina.

LEGAL BASIS:
Private foundation.

ELIGIBILITY:
North Carolina public and nonprofit private
institutions and organizations are eligible. No
grants are made to individuals for any
purpose.

GEOG. RESTRICTIONS: North Carolina.

FINANCIAL DATA:
Total amount of support: Approximately
$17,055,945 for the year ended December
31, 2018.

APPLICATION INFO:
Application information can be downloaded
from the web site.
Deadline: Application deadlines are posted
on the Foundation web site.

PUBLICATIONS:
Annual report (online).

IRS I.D.: 58-6038145

OFFICERS:
W. Noah Reynolds, President
Daniel G. Clodfelter, Vice President
Piper Neal Beveridge, Treasurer
Terry Lockamy, Assistant Treasurer
Maurice O. Green, Secretary
Chapel Thompson, Assistant Secretary

TRUSTEES:
Nancy R. Bagley
Piper Neal Beveridge
Anita Brown-Graham
Angela R. Bryant
Daniel G. Clodfelter
Ilana Dubester
Mary Mountcastle
Anna Warburton Munroe
David L. Neal
Jane S. Patterson
W. Noah Reynolds
Virgil L. Smith
Lloyd P. Tate, Jr.

ADDRESS INQUIRIES TO:
Maurice O. Green, Secretary
(See address above.)

THE RHODE ISLAND FOUNDATION/RHODE ISLAND COMMUNITY FOUNDATION [255]

One Union Station
Providence, RI 02903-1746
(401) 274-4564
Fax: (401) 331-8085
E-mail: info@rifoundation.org
Web Site: www.rifoundation.org

FOUNDED: 1916

AREAS OF INTEREST:
Economic security, educational success,
healthy lives, arts and culture, children and
families, environment, housing and human
basic needs.

TYPE:
Challenge/matching grants;
Conferences/seminars; Demonstration grants;
Development grants; Fellowships; General
operating grants; Project/program grants;
Research grants; Scholarships; Technical
assistance; Loan forgiveness programs.
Strategy grants; Small grants; Basic human
needs grants; Regional grants.

YEAR PROGRAM STARTED: 1916

PURPOSE:
To support projects that address significant
community challenges, aim for lasting
impact, and serve disadvantaged Rhode
Islanders.

LEGAL BASIS:
Community foundation.

ELIGIBILITY:
Grants are not generally made directly to
individuals. Programs must primarily benefit
Rhode Island.

GEOG. RESTRICTIONS: Rhode Island.

FINANCIAL DATA:
Amount of support per award: Varies.
Total amount of support: $54,987,010 for the
year 2018.

APPLICATION INFO:
Guidelines are available at the Foundation
web site.

PUBLICATIONS:
Annual report; newsletter; guidelines; reports.

BOARD OF DIRECTORS:
Marie Brooks Wall, Chairman
Michael K. Allio
Jonathan D. Fain
Carrie Bridges Feliz
Ann-Marie Harrington
Meghan Hughes, Ph.D
G. Alan Kurose, MD., MBA, FACP
Marie J. Langlois
Tony Mendez
Theresa Moore
Janet Robinson
Hon. Ernst C. Torres
James Wright

ADDRESS INQUIRIES TO:
Donna Sowden, Administrative Assistant of
Grant Programs
(See address above.)

SID W. RICHARDSON FOUNDATION [256]

309 Main Street
Fort Worth, TX 76102
(817) 336-0494
E-mail: sranelle@sidrichardson.org
Web Site: www.sidrichardson.org

FOUNDED: 1947

AREAS OF INTEREST:
Education, health, human service, and the
arts.

TYPE:
Capital grants; Challenge/matching grants;
Development grants; General operating
grants; Matching gifts; Project/program
grants; Research grants.

PURPOSE:
To support organizations that serve the
people of Texas.

LEGAL BASIS:
Private foundation.

ELIGIBILITY:
All funds must be limited to the state of
Texas for IRS 501(c)(3) tax-exempt
institutions and organizations or 509(a)
organizations (other than a private foundation
under the latter code). An organization also
may qualify if it falls within the terms of
Section 170(c)(1) and the contribution
requested is to be used exclusively for public
purposes. No grants are made to individuals.

GEOG. RESTRICTIONS: Texas.

FINANCIAL DATA:
Amount of support per award: $1,000 to
$5,000,000.
Matching fund requirements: Varies.

NO. MOST RECENT APPLICANTS: Approximately
500 to 600.

NO. AWARDS: Approximately 145 to 160.

REPRESENTATIVE AWARDS:
Education: $150,000 to Communities in
Schools, Fort Worth, Inc. for the program to
place counselors in public schools across
Tarrant County; Health: $75,000 to Child
Study Center for diagnostic and treatment
services for children with disabilities; Human
Services: $110,000 to Catholic Charities
Diocese of Fort Worth for the transportation
program; Cultural: $50,000 to National
Cowgirl Museum and Hall of Fame, Inc. for
operational support.

APPLICATION INFO:
Initial contact should be by letter briefly
explaining project or program. If the project
is within areas of current activity, an
application will be provided.
Duration: Typically one year.
Deadline: January 15.

PUBLICATIONS:
Annual report.

IRS I.D.: 75-6015828

BOARD OF DIRECTORS:
Edward P. Bass, Chairman
Lee M. Bass, Vice President
Sid R. Bass, Vice President

ADDRESS INQUIRIES TO:
Pete Geren, President
(See address above.)

ROCKEFELLER FAMILY FUND [257]

475 Riverside Drive
Suite 900
New York, NY 10115-0066
(212) 812-4252
Fax: (212) 812-4299
E-mail: ccaddle-steele@rffund.org
Web Site: www.rffund.org

FOUNDED: 1967

NAME(S) OF PROGRAMS:
● **Economic Justice for Women**
● **Environment**
● **Institutional Accountability and
  Individual Liberty**

TYPE:
Challenge/matching grants; General operating
grants. Economic Justice for Women program
seeks to improve the quality of life for
working women and their families by
advocating for equitable employment
opportunities and updated employment
standards.

Initiatives under the Environment program
are designed to enact aggressive policies at
the state and national levels to reduce carbon
emissions, highlight the risks of coal-burning
power plants and mountaintop removal
coal-mining, and sound climate science,
while exposing those who distort it.

The Institutional Accountability and
Individual Liberty program encourages the
active participation of citizens in government,
seeks to make government and private
institutions more accountable and responsive,
and supports efforts to ensure that
individuals' rights and liberties under the
Constitution are protected.

YEAR PROGRAM STARTED: 1967

PURPOSE:
To make grants to nonprofit organizations in
the areas of economic justice for women, the
environment, and institutional accountability
and individual liberty.

LEGAL BASIS:
A not-for-profit charitable corporation
existing under the New York state
not-for-profit corporation law.

ELIGIBILITY:
Tax-exempt organizations engaged in
educational and charitable activities of
national significance are eligible for support.

The Fund does not ordinarily consider
projects that pertain to a single community,
except in the rare instance where a project is
unique, strategically placed to advance a
national issue, or is likely to serve as a
national model. Grants are rarely made to
organizations which traditionally enjoy
popular support, such as universities,
museums, hospitals or endowed institutions.

The Family Fund does not make grants for
academic or scholarly research or social or
human service programs. Grants are also not
made to support individuals, scholarships,
international programs, domestic programs
dealing with international issues,
profit-making businesses, construction or
restoration projects, or to reduce an
organization's debt. Instead, support is
offered for advocacy efforts that are
action-oriented and likely to yield tangible
public policy results.

GEOG. RESTRICTIONS: United States.

FINANCIAL DATA:
Amount of support per award: $25,000 to
$75,000.
Total amount of support: Approximately
$2,500,000 annually.
Matching fund requirements: Fund will
match employee contributions.

REPRESENTATIVE AWARDS:
Citizen Participation and Government
Accountability: $50,000 to the William J.
Brennan Jr. Center for Justice, Inc., New
York, NY, to support the Center's work to
restore voting rights to citizens with criminal
convictions; Economic Justice for Women:
$50,000 to the National Partnership for
Women & Families, Washington, DC, to
support the Partnership's state and local paid
sick days campaigns; Environment: $50,000
to CommunityWise Bellingham, Bellingham,
WA, to support work on anti-coal issues;
Institutional Responsiveness: $55,000 to
MAPLight.org, Berkeley, CA, to continue
publishing data on the connections between
political contributions and votes.

APPLICATION INFO:
The Fund has implemented an initial online
inquiry system as part of its grantmaking
process. The initial inquiry system consists of
an eligibility quiz followed by an online
letter of inquiry. Before taking the eligibility
quiz, applicants are urged to review the
Frequently Asked Questions section, which
details the funding guidelines.
Duration: One year. Limited multiyear
funding for select projects.
Deadline: Letters of inquiry are accepted
throughout the year.

PUBLICATIONS:
Annual report.

TRUSTEES:
Miranda Kaiser, President
Alexandra Chasin, Vice President
Clare M. Pierson, Vice President
Tara Rockefeller, Vice President
Lucia Gill Case
Peter Gill Case

Adam Growald
Michael Lambert
Rebecca Lambert
Fran Rodgers
Tracy Toon Spencer
Naomi Waletzky
Liam Wang

ADDRESS INQUIRIES TO:
Carolyn Caddle-Steele, Grants Manager
(See address above.)

ROCKWELL FUND, INC.   [258]
770 South Post Oak Lane
Suite 525
Houston, TX 77056
(713) 629-9022
Fax: (713) 629-7702
E-mail: grantsinfo@rockfund.org
Web Site: www.rockfund.org

FOUNDED: 1931

AREAS OF INTEREST:
Education, health and housing.

NAME(S) OF PROGRAMS:
- **Capacity Building Grants**
- **Operating Funds**
- **Program/Project Support**

TYPE:
Challenge/matching grants; Development grants; General operating grants; Matching gifts; Project/program grants; Seed money grants; Technical assistance. Capacity building grants.

YEAR PROGRAM STARTED: 1949

PURPOSE:
To improve the quality of life in the greater Houston area; to pursue change through cooperative philanthropy.

LEGAL BASIS:
Nonprofit organization.

ELIGIBILITY:
Eligible organizations must have IRS 501(c)(3) not-for-profit status. A church or political subdivision that is not required to obtain a Section 501(c)(3) designation in order to be a permitted donee of a private foundation is also eligible. Grants are not made to individuals. The Fund does not provide financial support to programs or organizations outside of its stated issue areas.

GEOG. RESTRICTIONS: Greater Houston, Texas area.

FINANCIAL DATA:
Amount of support per award: Varies.
Total amount of support: $3,653,873 in total grants for the year 2018.

CO-OP FUNDING PROGRAMS: Yes.

NO. AWARDS: 54 for the year 2018.

APPLICATION INFO:
Applying organizations must have IRS Form 990 and Internal Revenue Code 501(c)(3) documentation. Consult the web site for application details. The Fund only accepts electronic submission of completed applications via e-mail. It does not accept applications sent via fax, mail or hand delivery.
Duration: One year. Renewable by reapplication.
Deadline: Varies.

IRS I.D.: 74-6040258

STAFF:
R. Terry Bell, President and Chief Executive Officer

Margaret E. McConn, C.P.A., Vice President, Chief Financial Officer and Chief Investment Officer
Don A. Titcombe, M.S.S.W., Senior Program Officer
Judy A. Ahlgrim, Grants Administrator
Michelle Sealey, Controller

ADDRESS INQUIRIES TO:
Judy A. Ahlgrim, Grants Administrator
(See address above.)

ROLEX SA   [259]
P.O. Box 1311
1211 Geneva 26 Switzerland
(41) 22 302 7269
(41) 22 302 2200
E-mail: rae@rolex.com
Web Site: www.rolex.org

FOUNDED: 1976

AREAS OF INTEREST:
Environment, applied technology, exploration, health and science, and cultural heritage.

NAME(S) OF PROGRAMS:
- **Rolex Awards for Enterprise Program**

TYPE:
Awards/prizes; Project/program grants. For more than 40 years, Rolex has biennially honored extraordinary individuals who possess the courage and conviction to take on major challenges. Each Rolex Award for Enterprise is given for a new or ongoing project anywhere in the world - one that deserves support for its capacity to improve lives, or protect the world's natural and cultural heritage. These projects have touched all aspects of humanity by expanding knowledge or improving life on the planet.

YEAR PROGRAM STARTED: 1976

PURPOSE:
To honor individuals who possess the courage and conviction to take on major challenges.

ELIGIBILITY:
Open to candidates over the age of 18 at the time of application.

An application may be submitted only by an individual. No institutional or collective applications are allowed. Only one application per person is allowed.

The application must be completed in English by the person who plays a leading role in the project or organization.

NO. MOST RECENT APPLICANTS: 1,500 to 2,500.

NO. AWARDS: 5.

APPLICATION INFO:
Complete application information is available on the web site.
Duration: One time per project.
Deadline: Varies.

ST. CROIX VALLEY FOUNDATION
516 Second Street, Suite 214
Hudson, WI 54016
(715) 386-9490
Fax: (715) 386-1250
E-mail: info@scvfoundation.org
Web Site: www.scvfoundation.org

TYPE:
Project/program grants; Scholarships. Environmental and humane grants.

See entry 1246 for full listing.

SALISBURY-ROWAN COMMUNITY FOUNDATION   [260]
220 North Tryon Street
Charlotte, NC 28202
(704) 973-4568
Fax: (704) 973-4959
E-mail: aowens@fftc.org
Web Site: www.salisbury-cf.org

FOUNDED: 1944

AREAS OF INTEREST:
Arts and culture, public education K-12, higher education, environment and human services.

TYPE:
Project/program grants.

YEAR PROGRAM STARTED: 1944

PURPOSE:
To support charitable organizations in the Salisbury and Rowan County areas.

LEGAL BASIS:
Community foundation.

ELIGIBILITY:
Applicants must be 501(c)(3) nonprofit organizations. Priority will be given to requests for projects and programs that address a community need.

GEOG. RESTRICTIONS: Salisbury and Rowan County, North Carolina.

FINANCIAL DATA:
Amount of support per award: Up to $10,000. Typically, $2,500 to $8,000.

APPLICATION INFO:
Grantseekers are invited to visit the Online Grants Center at fftcgrants.communityforce.com and search for Salisbury-Rowan Community Foundation to access the online application.
Duration: One year.
Deadline: September 13.

PUBLICATIONS:
Annual report.

IRS I.D.: 56-0772117

BOARD OF TRUSTEES:
Kathleen S. Boyd, Chairperson
Richard L. Huffman, Vice Chairperson
Karen Alexander
Greg Edds
Shari M. Graham
Darrell Hancock
Alvena Heggins
William Kennedy
April Kuhn
Vergel L. Lattimore
Laura Lewis
Eva Nelson
Edward P. Norvell
Bryan Overcash
Bill Wagoner
LaSheka Walker
Lee Wallace
Lauren Whaley

ADDRESS INQUIRIES TO:
Daavonia Womack-Lee, Administrative Assistant
Foundation for the Carolinas
E-mail: dwomack-lee@fftc.org or
Alexis Owens, Board and Grant Specialist
(See address above.)

THE FAN FOX AND LESLIE R. SAMUELS FOUNDATION, INC. [261]

275 Madison Avenue, 31st Floor
New York, NY 10016
(212) 239-3030
Fax: (212) 239-3039
E-mail: info@samuels.org
Web Site: www.samuels.org

FOUNDED: 1959

AREAS OF INTEREST:
Performing arts, health care, and quality of life for the elderly.

NAME(S) OF PROGRAMS:
- **Healthy Aging Program**
- **Performing Arts**

TYPE:
Development grants; Project/program grants. General operating grants for performing artists only.

In the area of health care, the Foundation will consider funding direct health care and social service programs to improve quality of life for New York City elderly.

The Foundation realizes that it cannot support an organization indefinitely and expects the programs it funds to become self-supporting within a few years.

YEAR PROGRAM STARTED: 1959

PURPOSE:
To provide funding for the performing arts in New York, NY; to improve the health care and quality of life of the elderly in New York, NY.

LEGAL BASIS:
Private foundation.

ELIGIBILITY:
Grants are made to organizations that are tax-exempt under Section 501(c)(3) of the Internal Revenue Code. The Foundation does not give grants to individuals or for scholarships. General operating support is for performing arts only.

GEOG. RESTRICTIONS: New York, New York.

FINANCIAL DATA:
Amount of support per award: $5,000 to $300,000.
Total amount of support: Varies.

NO. MOST RECENT APPLICANTS: 275.

NO. AWARDS: 190.

APPLICATION INFO:
A letter (not to exceed three typewritten pages) should briefly summarize the proposal and state the amount of the grant being requested. A copy of the organization's tax exemption letter issued by the IRS, most recent audited financial report, organization brochure (if available), Board of Directors list, project budget and current contributors list should be included. Specific guidelines on the application process can be found on the Foundation web site.
Duration: Health Care: One to two years; Performing Arts: One year.

IRS I.D.: 13-3124818

STAFF:
Alexandra Francis, Program Associate

OFFICERS AND DIRECTORS:
Joseph Mitchell, Chairman
Robert Marx, President
Julio Urbina, Vice President

ADDRESS INQUIRIES TO:
Alexandra Francis, Program Associate
(See address above.)

SAN FRANCISCO FOUNDATION [262]

One Embarcadero Center
Suite 1400
San Francisco, CA 94111
(415) 733-8500
Fax: (415) 477-2783
E-mail: info@sff.org
Web Site: sff.org

FOUNDED: 1948

AREAS OF INTEREST:
Community health, education, arts and culture, community development, and the environment.

NAME(S) OF PROGRAMS:
- **Koshland Young Leader Awards**

TYPE:
Scholarships. The Koshland Young Leader Awards recognize the next generation of leadership in the local community. This scholarship program provides financial assistance to college-bound San Francisco public high school students from economically disadvantaged backgrounds.

PURPOSE:
To promote change in the areas of community health, education, arts and culture, community development, and the environment.

LEGAL BASIS:
Community foundation.

ELIGIBILITY:
Nominee must have 3.25 cumulative or continually improving grade point average, be college-bound, and embrace a commitment to strengthening their families and communities despite facing formidable life challenges.

GEOG. RESTRICTIONS: San Francisco, California.

FINANCIAL DATA:
Award to be used for education-related expenses such as academic test fees, computers, books and supplies for classes.
Amount of support per award: $10,000.

NO. AWARDS: Up to 11 each year.

APPLICATION INFO:
Contact the Foundation.
Duration: Two years.

ADDRESS INQUIRIES TO:
Amanda Katz
E-mail: akatz@sff.org

SARKEYS FOUNDATION [263]

530 East Main Street
Norman, OK 73071
(405) 364-3703
Fax: (405) 364-8191
E-mail: sarkeys@sarkeys.org
Web Site: www.sarkeys.org

FOUNDED: 1962

AREAS OF INTEREST:
Education, health care and medical research, cultural and humanitarian programs of regional interest.

TYPE:
Capital grants; Challenge/matching grants; Development grants; Endowments; Matching gifts; Professorships; Project/program grants; Research grants; Technical assistance; Training grants.

YEAR PROGRAM STARTED: 1962

PURPOSE:
To improve the quality of life in Oklahoma.

LEGAL BASIS:
Private charitable foundation.

ELIGIBILITY:
Applicants must be 501(c)(3) organizations which are not private foundations under 509(a) of the Internal Revenue Code. Organization must be headquartered and operating within the state of Oklahoma.

GEOG. RESTRICTIONS: Oklahoma.

FINANCIAL DATA:
Amount of support per award: Varies.
Total amount of support: Approximately $3,200,000 for the year 2018.

NO. AWARDS: Approximately 125.

APPLICATION INFO:
Organizations are required to submit a Letter of Inquiry to determine whether they meet the criteria and priorities for funding. Form and instructions are posted on the Foundation web site. Letter of Inquiry and grant application must be submitted electronically.

Representatives are required to speak with a program officer for a pre-grant interview.
Duration: Varies.
Deadline: Letter of Inquiry: December 1 and June 1.

PUBLICATIONS:
Application guidelines; annual report.

BOARD MEMBERS:
Teresa B. Adwan
Elizabeth Base
Dr. John Bell
Dan Little
Joseph W. Morris
The Hon. Kris Steele
Blake Virgin
Terry W. West

ADDRESS INQUIRIES TO:
Kim Henry, Executive Director
Susan Frantz, Senior Program Officer
Linda English Weeks, Senior Program Officer
or
Natalie Carns, Program Officer
(See address above.)

*SPECIAL STIPULATIONS:
The recipient must sign an agreement outlining the terms of the award and provide reports as requested. Outside independent audit required for organizations whose assets or operating budget exceeds $500,000.

DR. SCHOLL FOUNDATION [264]

1033 Skokie Boulevard
Suite 230
Northbrook, IL 60062-4109
(847) 559-7430
Web Site: www.drschollfoundation.com

FOUNDED: 1947

AREAS OF INTEREST:
Private education at all levels, including elementary and secondary schools, colleges and universities, and medical and nursing institutions; general charitable programs, including grants to hospitals and programs for children, developmentally disabled and senior citizens, civic, cultural, social services, health care, economic and religious activities.

TYPE:
Project/program grants.

YEAR PROGRAM STARTED: 1947

PURPOSE:
To help support worthwhile projects and activities.

LEGAL BASIS:
Private foundation.

ELIGIBILITY:
Organization must submit copy of tax-exemption letter from the IRS identifying that the applicant is a tax-exempt organization under Internal Revenue Code 501(c)(3), but is not a private foundation under 509(a) of the Internal Revenue Code. All grant requests should be in the form of a special project or program.

GEOG. RESTRICTIONS: United States.

FINANCIAL DATA:
Amount of support per award: Average $5,000 to $25,000.
Total amount of support: Varies.

NO. MOST RECENT APPLICANTS: 1,300.

NO. AWARDS: 250.

APPLICATION INFO:
Procedures are available on the Foundation web site.
Duration: Usually one year.
Deadline: March 1. Notification in November and distribution in December.

OFFICER:
Pamela Scholl, President

ADDRESS INQUIRIES TO:
Pamela Scholl, President
(See address above.)

CHARLES AND HELEN SCHWAB FOUNDATION [265]
201 Mission Street, Suite 1950
San Francisco, CA 94105
(415) 795-4920
Fax: (415) 795-4921
E-mail: info@schwabfoundation.org
Web Site: www.schwabfoundation.org

FOUNDED: 1987

AREAS OF INTEREST:
K-12 education reform, community needs, human services and health, and trustee grants.

NAME(S) OF PROGRAMS:
● **Foundation Initiative Grants**

TYPE:
General operating grants; Project/program grants; Technical assistance. Capacity building and human services programs.

YEAR PROGRAM STARTED: 2001

PURPOSE:
To improve education and student learning for children in the San Francisco Bay area, the state of California, and the nation more broadly.

LEGAL BASIS:
Private foundation.

ELIGIBILITY:
The Foundation supports organizations characterized by strong leadership, a compelling track record and future potential.

GEOG. RESTRICTIONS: Primarily California.

FINANCIAL DATA:
Amount of support per award: Varies.

Total amount of support: $19,805,339 in total grants for the year ended December 31, 2018.

APPLICATION INFO:
The Foundation does not accept unsolicited grant applications, grant proposals or letters of inquiry.
Duration: Varies.

PUBLICATIONS:
Foundation brochure; program reports.

IRS I.D.: 94-3374170

STAFF:
Kristi Kimball, Executive Director
Erin Gilbert, Program Officer and Administrative Director

BOARD OF DIRECTORS AND OFFICERS:
Helen O. Schwab, President
Charles R. Schwab, Chairman
Nancy Bechtle, Director
Katie Schwab Paige, Director
Matt Wilsey, Director

ADDRESS INQUIRIES TO:
Human Services Program
(See address above.)

THE ELLEN BROWNING SCRIPPS FOUNDATION [266]
6121 Terryhill Drive
La Jolla, CA 92037
(858) 212-3311
Fax: (858) 459-4809
E-mail: dougdawson46@yahoo.com

FOUNDED: 1935

AREAS OF INTEREST:
Health care, medical research, education, conservation, recreation, family, youth and child welfare agencies, wildlife and animals, libraries and literacy.

TYPE:
Project/program grants; Research grants; Scholarships; Technical assistance.

YEAR PROGRAM STARTED: 1935

PURPOSE:
To provide funding for a number of social causes including medical research, health care, the arts, conservation and programs to help children.

LEGAL BASIS:
Private foundation.

ELIGIBILITY:
Applicant must be a tax-exempt, 501(c)(3) organization within San Diego County, CA.

GEOG. RESTRICTIONS: San Diego County, California.

FINANCIAL DATA:
Amount of support per award: $5,000 to $110,000.
Total amount of support: $1,200,000 for the fiscal year ended June 30, 2020.

NO. AWARDS: 42.

APPLICATION INFO:
Information is available from the Foundation.
Deadline: May 1.

ADDRESS INQUIRIES TO:
E. Douglas Dawson, Executive Director
(See address above.)

SEATTLE FOUNDATION [267]
1601 Fifth Avenue, Suite 1900
Seattle, WA 98101
(206) 515-2131
(206) 515-2109
Fax: (206) 622-7673
E-mail: c.erickson@seattlefoundation.org
grantmaking@seattlefoundation.org
Web Site: www.seattlefoundation.org

FOUNDED: 1946

AREAS OF INTEREST:
Racial and economic equity.

NAME(S) OF PROGRAMS:
● **Center for Community Partnerships**

TYPE:
General operating grants.

YEAR PROGRAM STARTED: 1946

PURPOSE:
To improve the quality of life in the Puget Sound area.

LEGAL BASIS:
Community foundation.

ELIGIBILITY:
Organizations must be IRS 501(c)(3) tax-exempt. No grants to individuals.

GEOG. RESTRICTIONS: King County, Washington.

FINANCIAL DATA:
Amount of support per award: Average $100,000.
Total amount of support: $4,000,000.

NO. MOST RECENT APPLICANTS: 500.

NO. AWARDS: 250.

APPLICATION INFO:
Application form and guidelines are available on the web site.
Duration: Varies.
Deadline: Varies by program.

PUBLICATIONS:
Annual report; *Heart & Science Magazine*.

STAFF:
Ceil Erickson, Director, Nonprofit Relations

ADDRESS INQUIRIES TO:
Ceil Erickson
Director, Nonprofit Relations
(See address above.)

THE SEAVER INSTITUTE [268]
12400 Wilshire Boulevard
Suite 1240
Los Angeles, CA 90025
(310) 979-0298
Fax: (310) 979-0297
E-mail: vsd@theseaverinstitute.org

FOUNDED: 1955

AREAS OF INTEREST:
Arts and the sciences.

TYPE:
Project/program grants; Research grants; Seed money grants.

YEAR PROGRAM STARTED: 1955

PURPOSE:
To provide seed money to highly regarded organizations for particular projects which offer the potential for significant advancement in their fields.

LEGAL BASIS:
Tax-exempt private foundation.

ELIGIBILITY:
Applicant must be a legally tax-exempt organization. The Institute does not support endowments, scholarships, construction, ongoing projects or deficit grants.

GEOG. RESTRICTIONS: United States.

FINANCIAL DATA:
Amount of support per award: $75,000 to $400,000.

NO. MOST RECENT APPLICANTS: 30.

NO. AWARDS: 20.

REPRESENTATIVE AWARDS:
University of Hawaii for foundation reefs; National Geographic for Timur's Garrison at Lake Issyk Kul; Massachusetts Institute of Technology for music21: a toolkit for computer-aided musicology; Sustainable Conservation for ecosystem services.

APPLICATION INFO:
A written request is required. No formal guidelines.
Duration: One year. Renewal is possible.
Deadline: Early April and early October.

PUBLICATIONS:
Official guidelines letter; annual report.

BOARD OF TRUSTEES:
Nancy Bekavac
Lynne Brickner
Kyle Dean
Nathan Dean
Victoria Seaver Dean
Robert Flick
Margaret Keene
Marie Knowles
Thomas Pfister
Carlton Seaver
Christopher Seaver
Martha Seaver
Patrick Seaver
Barbara Wagner
Roxanne Wilson

ADDRESS INQUIRIES TO:
Victoria Seaver Dean, President
(See address above.)

SIMMONS FAMILY FOUNDATION [269]

722 West Shepard Lane
Suite 103
Farmington, UT 84025
(801) 550-5026
E-mail: elizabeth@simmonsfoundation.org
Web Site: www.simmonsfoundation.org

FOUNDED: 1986

AREAS OF INTEREST:
Religion, community enhancement, education, art and medicine.

TYPE:
Challenge/matching grants; Development grants; General operating grants; Matching gifts; Project/program grants; Research grants; Scholarships; Seed money grants.

PURPOSE:
To foster virtues of good citizenship through religious, medical, community, art and educational purposes.

LEGAL BASIS:
Private family foundation.

ELIGIBILITY:
Grants to nonprofit organizations that are tax-exempt under Section 501(c)(3) or Section 170(c) of the Internal Revenue Code. No grants to individuals.

GEOG. RESTRICTIONS: Utah.

FINANCIAL DATA:
Amount of support per award: Varies.
Total amount of support: $770,000 for the year 2018.

NO. MOST RECENT APPLICANTS: 150.

NO. AWARDS: 27.

APPLICATION INFO:
E-mail a one-page letter of intent summarizing the organization and project to the address posted. Organizations will then be invited to submit a formal application. Additional information is available on the Foundation web site.
Duration: Usually one year.
Deadline: August 15.

PUBLICATIONS:
Application guidelines.

IRS I.D.: 13-3420599

ADDRESS INQUIRIES TO:
Elizabeth W. Gerner
Executive Director
(See address above.)

J. MARION SIMS FOUNDATION, INC. [270]

800 North White Street
Lancaster, SC 29720
(803) 286-8772
E-mail: sdevenny@jmsims.org
Web Site: www.jmsims.org

FOUNDED: 1995

AREAS OF INTEREST:
Building a healthy community.

YEAR PROGRAM STARTED: 1995

PURPOSE:
To provide community support.

LEGAL BASIS:
Private foundation.

ELIGIBILITY:
Organizations and agencies classified as 501(c)(3) by the IRS can apply. Individuals are ineligible.

GEOG. RESTRICTIONS: Fort Lawn, Great Falls and Lancaster County, South Carolina.

FINANCIAL DATA:
Amount of support per award: Varies.

NO. MOST RECENT APPLICANTS: Varies.

APPLICATION INFO:
Application guidelines are available on the Foundation web site.
Duration: Typically one year.

PUBLICATIONS:
Annual report.

IRS I.D.: 57-0355295

STAFF:
Susan W. DeVenny, President and Chief Executive Officer
Cynthia Curtis, Community Investment Officer
Donna Ortega, Community Investment Officer
Karen Ormond, Grants Administrator

ADDRESS INQUIRIES TO:
Susan W. DeVenny, President and Chief Executive Officer
(See address above.)

THE SIRAGUSA FAMILY FOUNDATION [271]

One East Wacker Drive
Suite 1850
Chicago, IL 60601
(312) 755-0064
Fax: (312) 755-0069
E-mail: info@siragusa.org
Web Site: www.siragusa.org

FOUNDED: 1950

AREAS OF INTEREST:
Arts learning, education and health.

TYPE:
General operating grants; Project/program grants; Scholarships; Technical assistance. Project grants or unrestricted support.

YEAR PROGRAM STARTED: 1950

PURPOSE:
To help people help themselves with the ultimate goal of improving their quality of life.

LEGAL BASIS:
Tax-exempt private foundation, incorporated in Illinois.

ELIGIBILITY:
Tax-exempt organizations are eligible. No grants are made to individuals.

GEOG. RESTRICTIONS: Greater Chicago, Illinois area.

FINANCIAL DATA:
Amount of support per award: $5,000 to $20,000.

NO. AWARDS: Approximately 120 annually.

APPLICATION INFO:
Unsolicited letters of inquiry and proposals are not currently accepted.
Duration: Varies.

PUBLICATIONS:
Annual report; guidelines.

BOARD OF DIRECTORS:
Ross D. Siragusa, III, President and Chairperson
John R. Siragusa, III, Vice President and Treasurer
James Durkan
Noah Ginsburg
Caitlyn Hicks
John Ross Hicks
Andrew Perrotte
Irene S. Phelps
Alexander C. Siragusa
Isabel Siragusa
Marco Siragusa
Philip Siragusa
Sinclair C. Siragusa

ADDRESS INQUIRIES TO:
John E. Hicks, Executive Director
(See address above.)

THE SKILLMAN FOUNDATION [272]

100 Talon Centre Drive
Suite 100
Detroit, MI 48207
(313) 393-1185
E-mail: grants@skillman.org
Web Site: www.skillman.org

FOUNDED: 1960

AREAS OF INTEREST:
Education and economic well-being.

TYPE:
Project/program grants.

YEAR PROGRAM STARTED: 1960

PURPOSE:
To improve the lives of children in metropolitan Detroit by improving their homes, schools and neighborhoods.

LEGAL BASIS:
Private foundation.

ELIGIBILITY:
Foundation grantseekers and grantees must: (1) be a nonprofit 501(c)(3) tax-exempt organization and provide its tax identification (EIN) number or be a government or public agency (city, county, state, public school district); (2) be a publicly supported charity as defined in Section 509(a) of the Internal Revenue Code; (3) have total revenues of at least $100,000 for its preceding fiscal year and be able to provide a copy of a current financial audit conducted by an independent certified public accountant and; (4) in policy and practice, offer opportunity and service to all, regardless of age, race, creed, gender, religion, disability, sexual orientation and ethnicity.

Multiyear grants are awarded on a case-by-case basis in special situations and may only be submitted at the invitation of a program officer.

GEOG. RESTRICTIONS: Detroit, Michigan.

FINANCIAL DATA:
Amount of support per award: Generally $20,000 to $200,000.
Total amount of support: Annual grants budget of approximately $17,000,000.

NO. MOST RECENT APPLICANTS: Over 400.

NO. AWARDS: Over 200.

APPLICATION INFO:
Consult the Foundation web site.
Duration: Generally one year.
Deadline: New grant inquiries should be submitted approximately two months in advance of Trustee meetings in March, June, September and December.

PUBLICATIONS:
Annual report; application guidelines.

IRS I.D.: 38-1675780

TRUSTEES:
Bill Emerson, Chairperson
Mary L. Kramer, Vice Chairperson
Tonya Allen
Lizabeth Ardisana
Herman B. Gray, Dr.
Ronald Hall, Jr.
Denise Ilitch
Eddie R. Munson
Jerry Norcia
Mark Reuss
Suzanne Shank

OFFICERS AND STAFF:
Tonya Allen, President and Chief Executive Officer
Maria Woodruff Jordan, Vice President, Operations and Chief Financial Officer
Punita Dani Thurman, Vice President, Program and Strategy
David McGhee, Associate Vice President, Organizational Excellence and Impact
Natalie Fotias, Director of Communications
Andrea Anderson, Director of Evaluation, Learning and Impact
Kumar Raj, Senior Program Officer, Economic Well-Being

Carmen Kennedy-Rogers, Senior Program Officer, Education
Ashley Aidenbaum, Program Officer, Economic Well-Being
Terry Whitfield, Program Officer, Education
Matthew Hoerauf, Associate Program Officer, Education
Mary Beth Baumeister, Grants Manager
Simonne Searles, Human Resource/Operations Manager
Jessica Eiland, Special Projects Manager
Lauren Hawkins, Controller

ADDRESS INQUIRIES TO:
Mary Beth Baumeister, Grants Manager
(See address above.)

ALFRED P. SLOAN FOUNDATION [273]

630 Fifth Avenue
Suite 2200
New York, NY 10111
(212) 649-1649
Fax: (212) 757-5117
E-mail: lin@sloan.org
grantsadmin@sloan.org
Web Site: sloan.org

FOUNDED: 1934

AREAS OF INTEREST:
Research and related programs in science and technology, education in science, technology, and economic growth.

TYPE:
Fellowships; Project/program grants; Research grants.

YEAR PROGRAM STARTED: 1934

PURPOSE:
To support imaginative and constructive approaches to problems of domestic needs and uses.

LEGAL BASIS:
Private foundation.

ELIGIBILITY:
Recognized tax-exempt educational and research institutions with appropriate interests are eligible to apply. The Foundation's activities do not extend to primary or secondary education, religion, the creative or performing arts, medical research, health care or to the humanities. Grants are not made for endowments, buildings or equipment and are very rarely made for general support or for activities outside the U.S.

GEOG. RESTRICTIONS: United States.

FINANCIAL DATA:
Amount of support per award: Varies.
Total amount of support: Approximately $80,000,000 in grants annually.

NO. AWARDS: Approximately 400 annually.

APPLICATION INFO:
A brief letter of inquiry, rather than a fully developed proposal, is an advisable first step for an applicant, conserving his or her time and allowing the Foundation to make a preliminary response as to the possibility of support.
Duration: One to three years. Extensions or renewals are possible.

PUBLICATIONS:
Annual report.

BOARD OF TRUSTEES:
Marta Tienda, Chairperson
Cynthia Barnhart
Bonnie Bassler

Francine Berman
Richard Bernstein
Kevin Burke
Mary Schmidt Campbell
Adam F. Falk
Frederick Henderson
Freeman A. Hrabowski, III
Robert Litterman
James Poterba
Michael Purugganan

ADMINISTRATIVE OFFICERS AND STAFF:
Adam F. Falk, President
Leisle Lin, Senior Vice President, Finance and Operations/Treasurer
Anne McKissick, Director, Grants Management and Information Services
Lauren von Eckartsberg, Grants Coordinator

ADDRESS INQUIRIES TO:
Anne McKissick
Director, Grants Management and Information Services
(See address above.)

A.O. SMITH FOUNDATION [274]

11270 West Park Place
Suite 170
Milwaukee, WI 53224
(414) 359-4107
E-mail: foundation@aosmith.com
Web Site: www.aosmith.com

FOUNDED: 1955

AREAS OF INTEREST:
Education, civic and cultural affairs, human services, health and hospital, and United Way.

TYPE:
Project/program grants. Employee Education Matching Gift to secondary, four-year colleges and universities, junior colleges, community colleges, graduate and professional schools, technical and specialized schools.

YEAR PROGRAM STARTED: 1955

PURPOSE:
To strengthen higher education throughout the country; to promote the civic, cultural and social welfare of communities; to advance medical research and improve local health services where A.O. Smith plants are located.

LEGAL BASIS:
Corporate foundation.

ELIGIBILITY:
Organization must be located where A.O. Smith has operating facilities. The Foundation does not make contributions to politically active organizations or any other organization whose chief purpose is to influence legislation.

FINANCIAL DATA:
Amount of support per award: $500 minimum.
Total amount of support: $1,600,000.

NO. AWARDS: Over 180 annually.

APPLICATION INFO:
No specific application form is required. Inquiries should be made on organization's letterhead and include the following information:
(1) the exact name and location of the organization;
(2) a description of the organization, including its objectives and purpose;
(3) verification of IRS 501(c)(3) tax-exempt status;

(4) the geographic area served by the organization;
(5) an explanation of the activity for which support is being requested;
(6) the amount of support being requested;
(7) a description of the benefits to be achieved and who will receive them;
(8) budget information about the organization, including other sources of income and;
(9) plans for reporting results.

Duration: Varies.

Deadline: October 30.

PUBLICATIONS:
Annual report.

ADDRESS INQUIRIES TO:
Rita Schwalbach, Foundation Manager
(See address above.)

THE ETHEL SERGEANT CLARK SMITH MEMORIAL FUND   [275]

Wells Fargo Philanthropic Services
123 South Broad Street
Philadelphia, PA 19109
(888) 235-4351
E-mail: grantadministration@wellsfargo.com
Web Site: www.wellsfargo.com/private-foundations/smith-memorial-fund-ethel-sergeant-clark

FOUNDED: 1977

AREAS OF INTEREST:
Arts, culture, education, health and human services, and medicine.

TYPE:
Capital grants; Challenge/matching grants; Development grants; Project/program grants. Grants and challenge grants to community interest organizations in southeastern Pennsylvania. Grants to hospitals, colleges and schools for program and capital projects. Grants for social services, arts/cultural events and centers.

YEAR PROGRAM STARTED: 1977

PURPOSE:
To promote the public welfare in Delaware County, PA.

LEGAL BASIS:
Private foundation.

ELIGIBILITY:
Organizations must be tax-exempt and not classified as private foundations or private operating foundations within the terms of the Tax Reform Act of 1969. Primary emphasis is on those serving community needs in Delaware County, the former home of Ethel Sergeant Clark Smith. Grants will be made for capital projects, operating expenses and special programs that are meaningful to the success of the individual endeavors of the organizations. As a general rule, requests for funds on a long-term basis or for deficit financing will not be considered.

GEOG. RESTRICTIONS: Southeastern Pennsylvania.

FINANCIAL DATA:
Amount of support per award: $5,000 to $25,000.

Total amount of support: Approximately $540,000 annually.

Matching fund requirements: Varies.

NO. MOST RECENT APPLICANTS: Approximately 200.

NO. AWARDS: Approximately 60 annually.

APPLICATION INFO:
Application process is online only.
Duration: Three consecutive years maximum.
Deadline: March 1 and September 1.

PUBLICATIONS:
Biennial report.

IRS I.D.: 23-6648857

ADVISORY COMMITTEE:
Diane R. Bricker
Jack Holefelder
Dr. Joseph E. Pappano, Jr.
Hon. Dominic F. Pileggi
Alice Strine, Esq.

ADDRESS INQUIRIES TO:
Grant Administrator
(See address above.)

THE W.W. SMITH CHARITABLE TRUST   [276]

200 Four Falls Corporate Center
Suite 300
West Conshohocken, PA 19428
(610) 397-1844
Fax: (610) 397-1680
E-mail: info@wwsmithcharitabletrust.org
Web Site: www.wwsmithcharitabletrust.org

FOUNDED: 1976

AREAS OF INTEREST:
Basic medical research protocols dealing with cancer, AIDS and heart disease; financial aid programs for qualified needy full-time undergraduate students; and programs providing shelter, food and clothing for children and needy families with children, and the elderly.

NAME(S) OF PROGRAMS:
● **College Scholarships**
● **Food, Clothing and Shelter**
● **Maritime Education**
● **Medical Research**

TYPE:
Project/program grants; Research grants; Scholarships.

YEAR PROGRAM STARTED: 1978

PURPOSE:
To enhance medical excellence; to enable children, families and the elderly to improve their lives; to assure students of a college education.

LEGAL BASIS:
Private foundation.

ELIGIBILITY:
Grants are limited to nonprofit organizations within the Delaware Valley area: Bucks, Chester, Delaware, Montgomery and Philadelphia counties (PA), as well as the city of Camden (NJ). Grants are made only to tax-exempt, 501(c)(3) organizations, not classified as private foundations or private operating foundations within the terms of the Tax Reform Act of 1969.

Grants will be made for programs or organizations with proven or prudently predictable records of performance; never directly to individuals. Renovation projects, special programs that deal with food, clothing and shelter for children and the elderly may be funded, but requests for general operating expenses, deficit financing and capital campaigns are not considered.

As a rule, under the Basic Needs Grants, the further away any request is from direct provision of literal food, clothing or shelter, the less likely funding may be granted.

Financial aid programs are for qualified needy full-time undergraduate students attending MSCHE accredited colleges and universities, as well as two-year community colleges, technical colleges, and trade schools located in, and serving students from the same geographic areas defined by the existing program for MSCHE accredited colleges and universities.

The Trust budgets no funds to purchase charity tables, program advertisements, golf tournament sponsorships, organizational memberships or analogous fund-raising events.

GEOG. RESTRICTIONS: With few exceptions, grants are limited to organizations within Bucks, Chester, Delaware, Montgomery and Philadelphia counties, Pennsylvania and Camden, New Jersey.

FINANCIAL DATA:
Amount of support per award: $5,000 to $229,000 for fiscal year 2018-19.

Total amount of support: $8,204,708 for fiscal year 2018-19.

NO. AWARDS: 198 for the year 2018-19.

APPLICATION INFO:
Complete application information is available online. Proposals will be considered only for the following purposes:
(1) specific, basic medical research projects dealing with cancer, heart disease or AIDS;
(2) by invitation of the Trust only, accredited, four-year university and college financial aid programs for needy, worthy, full-time undergraduate students (no requests ever accepted directly from individual students) and;
(3) providing shelter, food or clothing for children age 18 or under (including needy families with dependent children) or the elderly age 60 and above.

The trustees endeavor to keep abreast of the needs and conditions in the area served by the Trust and variations from these policies may be made at their discretion.

Grants are offered by invitation only.

Duration: Scholarship and Food, Clothing and Shelter grants: One year; Medical Research grant: Typically one year.

Deadline: Heart, Cancer and AIDS Research: July 15; Food, Clothing, and Shelter: December 15 and June 15; Scholarships: April 1.

PUBLICATIONS:
Biennial report (includes application guidelines).

IRS I.D.: 23-6648841

TRUSTEES:
Louise A. Havens

ADMINISTRATORS:
Brian Jones, Grant Administrator, Food, Clothing and Shelter/Scholarships
Louise A. Havens, Grant Administrator, Medical Research
Deborah J. McKenna, Advisor

ADDRESS INQUIRIES TO:
Brian Jones, Grant Administrator
(See address above.)

*SPECIAL STIPULATIONS:
Grants only in the Philadelphia, PA area and surrounding five counties, plus the city of Camden, NJ.

THE JOHN BEN SNOW FOUNDATION, INC. [277]

50 Presidential Plaza
Suite 106
Syracuse, NY 13202
(315) 471-5256
Fax: (315) 471-5256
E-mail: info@johnbensnow.org
Web Site: johnbensnow.org

FOUNDED: 1948

AREAS OF INTEREST:
Arts and culture, community initiatives, disabilities and universal access, education, environment, youth programs and historic preservation.

TYPE:
Capital grants; Challenge/matching grants; Development grants; Fellowships; Project/program grants; Scholarships; Seed money grants; Technical assistance.

YEAR PROGRAM STARTED: 1948

PURPOSE:
To grant funds for educational, cultural and humanitarian purposes.

LEGAL BASIS:
Private foundation.

ELIGIBILITY:
Applicants must be IRS 501(c)(3) organizations primarily in central and northern New York state. Grants are made to qualified organizations for educational and humanitarian purposes.

The general policy of the Board of Directors gives preference to proposals seeking one-year funding of program-related grants, matching grants, startup grants and capital grants and to reject proposals from individuals, religious organizations, government agencies, or for endowments, contingency funding, or general operating support.

GEOG. RESTRICTIONS: Central New York state, primarily Cayuga, Cortland, Madison, Onondaga and Oswego counties.

FINANCIAL DATA:
Amount of support per award: Typically $5,000 to $10,000.

Total amount of support: $244,000 in total grants for the year ended December 31, 2019.

NO. MOST RECENT APPLICANTS: More than 60.

NO. AWARDS: 41 for the year 2019.

REPRESENTATIVE AWARDS:
Arts and Culture: $4,500 to Front Row Players; Community Initiatives: $10,000 to Syracuse Area Landmark Theatre; Education: $10,000 to Mercy Works; Youth Programs: $7,500 to Purpose Farm, Inc.

APPLICATION INFO:
An initial letter of inquiry must be submitted through the Foundation's online grant management system. If the proposal meets the stated guidelines and priorities of the Foundation, grant application instructions will be sent to the applicant.
Duration: One year. Renewals depend on the project.
Deadline: Letter of inquiry: No later than January 31 of the year in which the grant is requested. Grant application: April 1. Notification by July 1.

PUBLICATIONS:
Guidelines; annual report.

STAFF:
Elizabeth Snow, Grants Manager

BOARD MEMBERS:
Jonathan L. Snow, President
David H. Snow, Vice President and Treasurer
Emelie M. Williams, Secretary
Angus M. Burton
Marion Hancock Fish
Valerie MacFie
Keegan Snow

ADDRESS INQUIRIES TO:
Jonathan L. Snow, President
(See address above.)

SOUTHWEST FLORIDA COMMUNITY FOUNDATION

2031 Jackson Street
Suite 100
Fort Myers, FL 33901
(239) 274-5900
Fax: (239) 274-5930
E-mail: info@floridacommunity.com
bkelly@floridacommunity.com
Web Site: www.floridacommunity.com

TYPE:
Demonstration grants; Project/program grants; Scholarships.

See entry 1258 for full listing.

SOWERS CLUB OF NEBRASKA FOUNDATION [278]

1701 South 17th Street
Suite 1H
Lincoln, NE 68502
(402) 438-2244
E-mail: info@thesowersclub.com
Web Site: www.thesowersclub.com

FOUNDED: 1986

AREAS OF INTEREST:
Charity and education.

TYPE:
Project/program grants; Scholarships.

PURPOSE:
To offer assistance to organizations that serve and educate the community.

ELIGIBILITY:
Agency must have been in existence for a minimum of five years and must qualify as exempt under Section 501(c)(3) of the Internal Revenue Code. Grant requests will not be considered for individuals, promoting religious purposes or for political purposes.

GEOG. RESTRICTIONS: Lincoln, Nebraska and surrounding communities.

FINANCIAL DATA:
Total amount of support: $50,000 per year.

APPLICATION INFO:
Grant request must include eight copies of the following:
(1) Letter of Determination from the IRS regarding 501(c)(3) status and;
(2) annual report or current balance sheet outlining the organization's administrative costs. All information will be treated with strict confidentiality.

All blanks on the grant request form must be completed. Do not answer a question on the request form by reference to another question, document or party.
Deadline: February 15, June 15 and September 15.

BOARD OF DIRECTORS AND OFFICERS:
Dick Stevenson, President
Michael Fiene, Vice President
Roger Zajicek, Treasurer
Robby Robinson, Secretary
Bob Flynn
Ed Packer
John Trayer

ADDRESS INQUIRIES TO:
Wendy Rieck, Executive Director
(See address above.)

SETH SPRAGUE EDUCATIONAL AND CHARITABLE FOUNDATION [279]

c/o Bank of America Private Bank
114 West 47th Street, 10th Floor
New York, NY 10036
(646) 855-1011

AREAS OF INTEREST:
Hospitals, educational institutions and social agencies.

TYPE:
Project/program grants.

ELIGIBILITY:
The Foundation makes grants to hospitals, educational institutions, social agencies and other charitable organizations. No grants to individuals.

GEOG. RESTRICTIONS: San Diego, California; Maine; Boston area, Massachusetts; and New York City, New York.

FINANCIAL DATA:
Amount of support per award: $10,000 to $20,000.

Total amount of support: $3,000,000 for the year 2019.

NO. MOST RECENT APPLICANTS: 450.

NO. AWARDS: 100.

APPLICATION INFO:
Application must be submitted online. The Foundation does not accept Letters of Inquiry.
Duration: One year.
Deadline: April 1 and September 1. Award announcement in June and December.

ADDRESS INQUIRIES TO:
Christine O'Donnell, Senior Vice President
E-mail: christine.i.odonnell@bofa.com
(See address above.)

THE STATE STREET FOUNDATION [280]

State Street Financial Center
One Lincoln Street
Boston, MA 02111-2900
(617) 664-8720
E-mail: wyoung@statestreet.com
Web Site: www.statestreet.com

FOUNDED: 1804

AREAS OF INTEREST:
Assisting disadvantaged populations in gaining the skills and educational qualifications needed to secure sustainable employment.

NAME(S) OF PROGRAMS:
● **Strategic Grantmaking Program**

TYPE:
General operating grants; Project/program grants. State Street Foundation's Strategic Grantmaking Program considers two types of grants:
(1) Project Support Grants are intended to

support specific projects or programs aligned with the Program's primary investment focus. These requests may include some funds earmarked for the overhead costs associated with running a project, including staff costs. (2) General Operating Support Grants are intended to provide general operating support for the core business functions of organizations whose missions and activities are highly aligned with the Program's primary investment focus. These grants will often help the grantee build organizational, programmatic and fund-raising capacity. Operating support is not intended to help organizations in fiscal crisis.

YEAR PROGRAM STARTED: 1977

PURPOSE:
To promote economic opportunity in communities where State Street operates.

LEGAL BASIS:
Corporate foundation.

ELIGIBILITY:
Grant applicants must be tax-exempt, 501(c)(3) organizations located in communities where State Street has a presence.

The Foundation does not make individual scholarship grants, nor does it fund research, having a preference for programs emphasizing direct delivery of services. It does not support organizations by purchasing advertisements, tables or tickets at dinners or other functions.

General Operating Support Grant applicants must have a current strategic or business plan that clearly outlines the organization's goals and presents a plan for achieving results. Operating support grants must not exceed 10 to 15% of an organization's total agency budget.

FINANCIAL DATA:
Amount of support per award: $25,000 to $100,000.

Total amount of support: Approximately $13,100,000.

NO. AWARDS: 246 for the year 2017.

APPLICATION INFO:
Grant Proposal Summary Form and instructions are available at the Foundation web site.

Duration: One year.

Deadline: Applications are accepted on a rolling basis.

PUBLICATIONS:
Contributions guidelines.

ADDRESS INQUIRIES TO:
Wayne Young, Strategic Grants Manager (See address above.)

JOHN STAUFFER CHARITABLE TRUST   [281]
301 North Lake Avenue, Suite 1000
Pasadena, CA 91101-4108
(626) 793-9400
Fax: (626) 793-5900
E-mail: dfederico@lagerlof.com

FOUNDED: 1974

AREAS OF INTEREST:
Colleges, universities and hospitals within California.

TYPE:
Capital grants; Challenge/matching grants; Endowments; Fellowships; Matching gifts; Professorships; Project/program grants; Scholarships.

YEAR PROGRAM STARTED: 1974

PURPOSE:
To support universities and colleges located in the U.S. in acquiring land, erecting buildings and other facilities, obtaining equipment, instruments, books, furnishings, and providing scholarships, fellowships and professorships; to support hospitals located in the U.S. which are organized and operated for charitable purposes in acquiring land, erecting buildings and other facilities, and obtaining equipment, instruments and furnishings.

LEGAL BASIS:
Tax-exempt private foundation founded in 1974 as a Testamentary Trust under will of John Stauffer by Order of the Superior Court of the State of California in and for the County of Los Angeles.

ELIGIBILITY:
Each university, college or hospital that receives funds from the Trust must be, at the time of the receipt of the funds:
(1) an exempt organization under Section 501(c)(3) of the Internal Revenue Code;
(2) an organization described in Section 170(c) of the Internal Revenue Code (or the corresponding provisions of any subsequent federal tax law) and;
(3) an organization meeting the qualifications of Sections 13842 and 23701(d) of the Revenue and Taxation Code of the state of California (or the corresponding provisions of any subsequent California tax law).
The organization must not be a private foundation.

Because of the Trust's finite resources, its Trustees must focus their attention on a few fields of activity and on certain priorities. The Trustees will favor:
(1) projects or programs of private nonprofit universities, colleges and hospitals within southern California;
(2) grants for facilities, educational or medical equipment, scholarships, professorships and fellowships;
(3) projects and programs that link science and medicine in education, research and treatment;
(4) projects and programs that emphasize chemistry as an integral component of education or treatment;
(5) institutions and organizations that as a matter of policy and practice maintain balanced operating budgets and avoid deficit financing and;
(6) projects and programs supported by matching funds from other donors.

GEOG. RESTRICTIONS: California, with a focus on southern California.

FINANCIAL DATA:
Amount of support per award: $100,000 to $3,000,000.

Total amount of support: Varies.

NO. MOST RECENT APPLICANTS: Approximately 200.

REPRESENTATIVE AWARDS:
$3,000,000 to Huntington Hospital; $300,000 to Claremont McKenna College; $500,000 to Stanford University; $2,500,000 to California Institute of Technology.

APPLICATION INFO:
All applications must be presented to the Trustees in writing and in digital format, with proposals clear and concise. Each application should include:
(1) a brief summary that sets forth the exact amount requested, an explanation of the need for the subject of the grant, the objectives to be achieved and the manner in which John Stauffer's name will be memorialized;
(2) full financial information, including a detailed budget for the project to be assisted by the grant;
(3) a statement indicating whether a grant for the same or similar purpose is presently being sought from other foundations or other sources, and, if so, which ones;
(4) the application's being executed by an officer of the applicant institution;
(5) (preferably) accompanying letters of support from board members or authorities and/or organizations in the applicant's field and;
(6) where applicable, copies of the latest exemption determination letter from the IRS and the corresponding state tax authorities in the state in which the applicant is located; the IRS determination that the applicant is not a private foundation; the latest audited balance sheet; and the latest audited statement of income and expenditures.

Duration: For large grants, up to two or more years.

PUBLICATIONS:
Application guidelines.

IRS I.D.: 23-7434707

TRUSTEES:
John F. Bradley, Sr., Esq.
Timothy J. Gosney, Esq.
Michael R. Whalen, Esq.

ADDRESS INQUIRIES TO:
John Stauffer Charitable Trust
c/o Timothy J. Gosney, Esq.
(See address above.)

*SPECIAL STIPULATIONS:
Each grantee is required to make a report on the use of the funds granted by the Trustees, including a certification that the funds have been used for the purpose(s) for which the grant was made. In addition, grantees shall comply with all reporting requirements contained in conditions of the grant, which will be set forth in writing by the Trustees. The Trustees reserve the right to require a reasonable audit of the use of grant funds conducted by their representative at the Trust's expense.

STEELCASE FOUNDATION   [282]
P.O. Box 1967 GH-2E
Grand Rapids, MI 49501-1967
(616) 246-4695
E-mail: jridenou@steelcase.com
Web Site: www.steelcasefoundation.org

FOUNDED: 1951

AREAS OF INTEREST:
Education and social justice.

TYPE:
Demonstration grants; Development grants; General operating grants; Matching gifts; Project/program grants; Seed money grants. Special projects, startup, capital and capacity building.

YEAR PROGRAM STARTED: 1951

PURPOSE:
To improve the quality of life in the communities where Steelcase employees live; to empower people to reach their full potential.

LEGAL BASIS:
Corporate foundation.

ELIGIBILITY:
The Foundation makes grants to IRS-certified nonprofit organizations in areas where Steelcase manufacturing plants are located.

GEOG. RESTRICTIONS: Athens, Alabama and Grand Rapids, Michigan.

FINANCIAL DATA:
Amount of support per award: $5,000 to $250,000.

Total amount of support: $5,258,767 for the year 2018.

NO. MOST RECENT APPLICANTS: 100.

NO. AWARDS: 40.

APPLICATION INFO:
To obtain a grant application, send a Letter of Inquiry through the Foundation's online portal. The request should be on the organization's letterhead and signed by the Chief Executive Officer. Include the following items with the letter:
(1) description of organization or project;
(2) expected results of the project;
(3) amount of grant funds requested and;
(4) copy of IRS 501(c)(3) nonprofit certification.

If the proposal meets the Foundation criteria, a detailed application form will be sent to the organization.
Duration: Varies.
Deadline: Grant requests are reviewed quarterly.

PUBLICATIONS:
Annual report; application; guidelines.

IRS I.D.: 38-6050470

TRUSTEES:
Kate Pew Wolters, Chairperson
Brian Cloyd
Mary Anne Hunting
James Keane
Craig Niemann
Cary Pew
Robert C. Pew, III
Elizabeth Welch

ADDRESS INQUIRIES TO:
Julie Ridenour, President
(See address above.)

THE WILLIAM B. STOKELY, JR. FOUNDATION [283]

620 Campbell Station Road, Station West
Suite 27
Knoxville, TN 37934
(865) 966-4878
Fax: (865) 675-5095

FOUNDED: 1951

AREAS OF INTEREST:
College and university scholarship programs and cultural, educational, religious and health service organizations.

TYPE:
General operating grants; Matching gifts; Scholarships.

YEAR PROGRAM STARTED: 1951

PURPOSE:
To provide funds for colleges and universities for scholarships.

LEGAL BASIS:
Tax-exempt private foundation.

ELIGIBILITY:
The Foundation does not extend funds to individuals but rather to colleges and universities in the form of scholarships to disburse under the guidelines of their particular program. Also considered are the needs of cultural, educational, religious (Christian) and health service organizations in areas where the Stokely family has ties. Regional priority is given to the southeastern U.S. and eastern Tennessee.

Organizations requesting funds must be approved, listed nonprofit organizations with 501(c)(3) status. All proposals must be submitted in writing for review by the Board of Directors.

GEOG. RESTRICTIONS: Southeastern United States and Eastern Tennessee.

FINANCIAL DATA:
Amount of support per award: $25 to $100,000.

APPLICATION INFO:
All proposals must be submitted in writing for review by the Board of Directors.
Duration: Varies.
Deadline: Proposals are reviewed on an ongoing basis.

IRS I.D.: 35-6016402

BOARD OF DIRECTORS:
William B. Stokely, III, President
Kay H. Stokely, Executive Vice President
Andrea White, Vice President, Treasurer and Secretary
Stacy S. Byerly
Shelley S. Przewrocki
Clayton F. Stokely
William B. Stokely, IV

ADDRESS INQUIRIES TO:
William B. Stokely, III, President
(See address above.)

ROY AND CHRISTINE STURGIS CHARITABLE AND EDUCATIONAL TRUST [284]

c/o Bank of America, N.A.
901 Main Street, 19th Floor
Dallas, TX 75202-3714
E-mail: tx.philanthropic@ustrust.com
Web Site: www.bankofamerica.com/philanthropic/grantmaking.go

FOUNDED: 1981

AREAS OF INTEREST:
Arts, culture and humanities, education, health, and human services.

TYPE:
Capital grants; Challenge/matching grants; Matching gifts; Project/program grants.

PURPOSE:
To support and promote quality educational, cultural, human services and health care programming for all people.

LEGAL BASIS:
Private foundation (charitable trust).

ELIGIBILITY:
Applicants must have a 501(c)(3) exempt status from federal income tax as determined by the IRS before applying for a grant.

Charitable organizations which receive a one-payment grant must skip a year before applying again. Charitable organizations which receive multiyear payments cannot apply again while receiving payments and must skip a year after the last payment is received.

Trustee will consider grant requests for supplements for capital improvements, special projects, medical research and equipment, grants to meet challenges, endowments, start-up funds (extraordinary review), limited general operating expenses and construction or renovation of facilities.

The Trustee may favorably consider proposals which are unique, necessary and of high priority for the charitable organizations and which do not duplicate other services which are available, proposals for which funding may not be readily available from other sources and essential projects which are sufficiently described as worthwhile, important and of a substantive nature.

The Trustee will not consider providing support for political organizations, loans, scholarships for individuals, tuition for individuals or for seminars. No grants to individuals or for mass appeals for funding.

GEOG. RESTRICTIONS: Arkansas and Dallas area in Texas.

FINANCIAL DATA:
Amount of support per award: $5,000 to $200,000 for multiyear payments. Average: $23,500.

APPLICATION INFO:
Guidelines and application forms are available on the Trust web site.
Duration: One year; occasional multiyear.
Deadline: March 1. Notification on or before June 30.

PUBLICATIONS:
Guidelines.

IRS I.D.: 75-6331832

SUNTRUST FOUNDATION [285]

303 Peachtree Street, 33rd Floor
Atlanta, GA 30308
(804) 782-7907
E-mail: jane.markins@suntrust.com
Web Site: www.suntrust.com/about-us/community-commitment/philanthropy/suntrust-foundation

AREAS OF INTEREST:
Education, health and human services, culture and art, civic and community, and financial education.

TYPE:
General operating grants; Matching gifts; Project/program grants. Employee matching gifts program is designed to encourage SunTrust employees to support educational institutions and cultural organizations.

PURPOSE:
To support not-for-profit organizations that help advance financial education and counseling, career-readiness/workforce development training and entrepreneurship; to support the unique needs of SunTrust communities, including education, health and human services, and civic and cultural development.

LEGAL BASIS:
Corporate giving program.

ELIGIBILITY:
Support is limited to 501(c)(3) organizations. The following criteria are considered with each grant request:
(1) Does the grant request support one of the four Financial Well-Being areas of interest?
(2) Will the grant support programs and activities for the improvement of the quality of life in the community served?
(3) Will the grant have an impact on communities located primarily within the Southeastern and Mid-Atlantic states? and;
(4) Does the organization requesting the grant have good management and active involvement of community leaders? Evaluation of each grant request will also be based on such factors as program management and budget, sources of income, population served, distinctive features, and community impact.

Neither SunTrust Bank teammates nor SunTrust Bank can receive direct or indirect benefits from the grant. No grants are made to:
(1) nonreligious organizations that have a written policy of discrimination on the basis of sexual orientation and/or gender identity;
(2) individuals;
(3) political parties or candidates;
(4) religious, veteran or fraternal organizations, unless involved in a project benefiting the general community or involving economic education;
(5) individual agencies already receiving SunTrust Bank support through general service organizations such as United Way; a grant may be made if the agency has permission from the general service organization to solicit funds;
(6) organizations that foster or encourage racial, religious, class or other prejudices and;
(7) any organization that does not qualify as a tax-exempt organization under section 501(c)(3) of the U.S. Internal Revenue Code.

GEOG. RESTRICTIONS: Florida, Georgia, Maryland, North Carolina, South Carolina, Tennessee, Texas, Virginia and Washington, DC.

FINANCIAL DATA:
Amount of support per award: Varies.
Total amount of support: $16,900,000 for the year 2017.
Matching fund requirements: SunTrust will match employee contributions to eligible educational institutions and arts/cultural enrichment programs.

APPLICATION INFO:
Grant applications must be submitted through the online portal. Proposals must include appropriate documentation, including:
(1) project and/or operating budgets;
(2) full description of the area of need and;
(3) reasons for the request.

Special attention should be paid to the points covered under "Program Guidelines."
Duration: Varies. Renewal possible.
Deadline: September 1 for the next year's budget.

PUBLICATIONS:
Guidelines.

ADDRESS INQUIRIES TO:
Regional Headquarters or
SunTrust Foundation
(See address above.)

SURDNA FOUNDATION INC.   [286]
200 Madison Avenue, 25th Floor
New York, NY 10016
(212) 557-0010 ext. 237
Fax: (212) 557-0003
E-mail: grants@surdna.org
Web Site: www.surdna.org

FOUNDED: 1917

AREAS OF INTEREST:
Sustainable environments, strong local economies, and thriving cultures.

NAME(S) OF PROGRAMS:
● **The Inclusive Economies**
● **Sustainable Environments**
● **Thriving Cultures**

TYPE:
General operating grants; Project/program grants; Research grants; Technical assistance.

YEAR PROGRAM STARTED: 1917

PURPOSE:
To foster catalytic, entrepreneurial programs which offer viable solutions to difficult systemic problems.

ELIGIBILITY:
Grant applicants must be 501(c)(3) nonprofits located within the U.S.

No grants to individuals. No grants for capital support.

GEOG. RESTRICTIONS: United States.

FINANCIAL DATA:
Amount of support per award: Varies.
Total amount of support: $36,466,835 in grants approved in fiscal year 2017.

NO. MOST RECENT APPLICANTS: Approximately 1,300 per year.

NO. AWARDS: 159 approved in fiscal year 2017.

APPLICATION INFO:
Letters of Inquiry should be submitted on the Foundation web site. Application guidelines are available online.
Duration: One to three years. Grants are renewable.
Deadline: Letters of Inquiry are reviewed on a rolling basis.

PUBLICATIONS:
Annual report.

ADDRESS INQUIRIES TO:
See e-mail address above.

TAHOE TRUCKEE COMMUNITY FOUNDATION   [287]
11071 Donner Pass Road
Truckee, CA 96161
(530) 587-1776 ext. 106
Fax: (530) 550-7985
E-mail: phyllis@ttcf.net
Web Site: www.ttcf.net

FOUNDED: 1998

AREAS OF INTEREST:
Education, environment, arts and culture, civic benefits, health, human services, youth development, recreation and animal welfare.

TYPE:
Block grants; Challenge/matching grants; Demonstration grants; General operating grants; Project/program grants; Scholarships. Capacity building.

YEAR PROGRAM STARTED: 1998

PURPOSE:
To enhance the quality of life in the Truckee Tahoe community.

ELIGIBILITY:
Grants are made to organizations that have tax-exempt status under Section 501(c)(3) of the Internal Revenue Code. No grants are made to individuals.

GEOG. RESTRICTIONS: Truckee and Tahoe region, California.

FINANCIAL DATA:
Amount of support per award: $5,000 to $10,000.
Total amount of support: $1,500,000 for the year 2017.

NO. MOST RECENT APPLICANTS: 109.

NO. AWARDS: 48.

APPLICATION INFO:
Guidelines are available on the Foundation web site.
Duration: One year.
Deadline: Varies.

IRS I.D.: 68-0416404

ADMINISTRATIVE STAFF:
Phyllis McConn, Community Impact Officer

EXECUTIVE OFFICERS:
Stacy Caldwell, Chief Executive Officer

ADDRESS INQUIRIES TO:
Phyllis McConn, Community Impact Officer
(See address above.)

S. MARK TAPER FOUNDATION   [288]
12011 San Vicente Boulevard, Suite 400
Los Angeles, CA 90049
(310) 476-5413
E-mail: questions@smtfoundation.org
Web Site: www.smtfoundation.org

FOUNDED: 1989

AREAS OF INTEREST:
Including, but not limited to, environment, independent living for the disabled, children, hunger, AIDS, teenage pregnancy prevention, economic revitalization, the arts, public education and civic affairs.

TYPE:
Capital grants; Challenge/matching grants; Demonstration grants; Development grants; Endowments; General operating grants; Matching gifts; Project/program grants; Scholarships; Seed money grants; Technical assistance; Training grants. Specific project grants.

YEAR PROGRAM STARTED: 1989

PURPOSE:
To enhance the quality of people's lives.

LEGAL BASIS:
Independent foundation.

ELIGIBILITY:
No grants to individuals. Applicants must be certified tax-exempt under Section 501(c)(3) of the Internal Revenue Code.

Previously funded nonprofit organizations are not eligible for another grant until after three full cycles have elapsed following the grant cycle during which previous grant was made.

GEOG. RESTRICTIONS: Southern California, primarily Los Angeles County.

FINANCIAL DATA:
Amount of support per award: Small grants: Up to $50,000; medium grants: $50,001 to $249,999; large grants: Over $250,000.

Total amount of support: Varies.

NO. MOST RECENT APPLICANTS: 400.

NO. AWARDS: 80.

APPLICATION INFO:
Application form required. Make initial contact by way of Letter of Inquiry. Letter must include organization background information, purpose of project, amount requested and anticipated results. Documentation of 501(c)(3) status required. Letters of Inquiry submitted by e-mail or fax will not be accepted.

Duration: One year unless paid in installments.

Deadline: Letters of Inquiry are accepted December through February 15. Applications are mailed in May through July. Notification in September.

PUBLICATIONS:
Letter of Inquiry Guidelines.

OFFICERS:
Janice Taper Lazarof, President

ADDRESS INQUIRIES TO:
Adrienne Wittenberg, Executive Director (See address above.)

JOHN TEMPLETON FOUNDATION [289]

300 Conshohocken State Road
Suite 500
West Conshohocken, PA 19428
(610) 941-2828
Fax: (610) 825-1730
E-mail: info@templeton.org
Web Site: www.templeton.org

FOUNDED: 1987

AREAS OF INTEREST:
Higher education, science and religion, theology, medicine, philosophy, spirituality and health, character development and free enterprise education.

TYPE:
Awards/prizes; Challenge/matching grants; Project/program grants; Research grants. Awards are financial in nature.

PURPOSE:
To promote and support relationships and progress between science and religion.

LEGAL BASIS:
Private foundation.

ELIGIBILITY:
Organizations classified as 501(c)(3) by the IRS can apply.

FINANCIAL DATA:
Amount of support per award: Varies.
Total amount of support: Varies.
Matching fund requirements: Defined on an individual grant basis.

NO. AWARDS: 110 new grants for the year 2017.

APPLICATION INFO:
Online Funding Inquiry must be submitted through the Templeton Portal.

Duration: Up to three years. In rare instances, up to five years.

Deadline: August 31.

PUBLICATIONS:
Brochures; newsletter; articles.

IRS I.D.: 62-1322826

TEXAS INSTRUMENTS FOUNDATION [290]

12500 TI Boulevard
Dallas, TX 75243
(972) 995-2011
E-mail: giving@ti.com
Web Site: www.ti.com/giving

FOUNDED: 1964

AREAS OF INTEREST:
Human services and STEM education arts.

TYPE:
Matching gifts; Project/program grants.

YEAR PROGRAM STARTED: 1965

PURPOSE:
To better the communities in which Texas Instruments operates.

LEGAL BASIS:
Nonprofit foundation.

ELIGIBILITY:
Organization must be 501(c)(3) and tax-exempt. No grants to individuals, student scholarships, good will advertising or for contributions of Texas Instruments products.

GEOG. RESTRICTIONS: Texas. STEM education arts in Dallas only.

FINANCIAL DATA:
Matching fund requirements: Up to $30,000 per person per category each year for most U.S.-based nonprofits.

APPLICATION INFO:
All requests for funding should be submitted online.

Duration: Varies. Renewals possible.

PUBLICATIONS:
Guidelines.

IRS I.D.: 75-6038519

STAFF:
Andy Smith, Executive Director

3M FOUNDATION, INC. [291]

Community Affairs
3M Center Building 225-01-S-23
St. Paul, MN 55144-1000
(651) 733-0144
Fax: (651) 737-3061
E-mail: mstroik@mmm.com
Web Site: www.3Mgives.com

FOUNDED: 1953

AREAS OF INTEREST:
Education, arts and culture, human services and environment.

TYPE:
Capital grants; General operating grants; Matching gifts; Product donations; Project/program grants. 3Mgives consists of gifts by the 3M Foundation, cash and product donations by 3M and employee/retiree volunteerism.

YEAR PROGRAM STARTED: 1953

PURPOSE:
To improve every life.

LEGAL BASIS:
Corporate contributions program.

ELIGIBILITY:
Grants are made in the program areas of interest to established, well-managed organizations which have an IRS 501(c)(3) nonprofit status, and which are located in and serving 3M communities. Essential qualities are programs with broad-based community support, a reputation for leadership and high-quality service delivery and measurable results.

The 3M Foundation will not fund organizations in non-3M communities, individuals, for-profit organizations, disease-related organizations, hospitals, (in general) individual K-12 schools, organizations with a limited constituency, such as religious, fraternal, social, veterans or military organizations, and scholarship funds or organizations.

Grants are not awarded for advocacy and lobbying efforts to influence legislation; conferences, seminars, workshops or publications of their proceedings; endowments; film/video production; fund-raising, testimonial, athletic and special events; purchase of equipment that has not been manufactured by 3M; and travel for individuals or groups.

3Mgives generally will not consider organizations or causes that do not impact 3M communities, lease, conferences, seminars, workshops, symposia, publication of proceedings and all aspects relating to conferences, fund-raising and testimonial events/dinners, grants to individual K-12 schools, including tickets, silent auctions, raffles, telethons, etc., not more than 10% of the organization's campaign goal or annual budget, whichever is smaller, programs or projects beyond three years.

FINANCIAL DATA:
Amount of support per award: Varies.
Total amount of support: $73,513,396 cash and in-kind contributions for the year 2017.
Matching fund requirements: Limited to 3M employees and retirees.

NO. MOST RECENT APPLICANTS: 10,000.

NO. AWARDS: Approximately 3,000.

APPLICATION INFO:
Applications are by invitation only.
Duration: Generally one year, and not more than three years.
Deadline: Varies according to focus area.

PUBLICATIONS:
Annual report; contributions guidelines.

IRS I.D.: 41-6038262

JOHN H. AND H. NAOMI TOMFOHRDE FOUNDATION [292]

c/o Rackemann, Sawyer & Brewster
160 Federal Street, 15th Floor
Boston, MA 02110-1700
(617) 951-1108
Fax: (617) 542-7437
E-mail: smonahan@rackemann.com
Web Site: www.cybergrants.com/tomfohrde

FOUNDED: 1996

AREAS OF INTEREST:
Cultural, social and civic betterment, community health, higher education, scientific research within the New England area with a special focus on Greater Boston.

TYPE:
Capital grants; Conferences/seminars; Matching gifts; Product donations; Project/program grants; Seed money grants; Technical assistance. The Foundation's particular focus is on supporting the work of charitable institutions, organizations and agencies in the New England area and particularly in Greater Boston, which are

dedicated to the cultural, social and civic betterment of the community and particularly which foster the advancement of higher education, the classic arts, scientific research in biomedicine and the improvement of community health. Each year the trustees identify a specific funding priority.

PURPOSE:
To bring about the cultural, social and civic betterment of the community and particularly to foster the advancement of higher education, the classic arts, scientific research in biomedicine and the improvement of community health.

LEGAL BASIS:
Private, independent foundation.

ELIGIBILITY:
The Foundation supports nonprofit 501(c)(3) organizations only.

GEOG. RESTRICTIONS: New England, with a preference for Greater Boston.

FINANCIAL DATA:
Amount of support per award: $5,000 to $15,000.
Total amount of support: $250,000.
Matching fund requirements: Determined on a case-by-case basis.

NO. MOST RECENT APPLICANTS: 45 for the year 2018.

NO. AWARDS: 20 for the year 2018.

REPRESENTATIVE AWARDS:
Julie's Family Learning Program.

APPLICATION INFO:
Applicants are required to submit a Preliminary Application-Concept Cover Letter. Only applicants whose preliminary application has been approved will be invited to submit a full proposal.
Deadline: January, April and August for trustees meetings in February, June and October, respectively.

IRS I.D.: 04-3338742

TRUSTEES:
Maura E. Murphy, Esq.
Michael F. O'Connell, Esq.

STAFF:
Susan T. Monahan, Grants Coordinator

ADDRESS INQUIRIES TO:
Susan T. Monahan, Grants Coordinator
(See e-mail address above.)

*PLEASE NOTE:
Applicants should check web site annually to learn of the Foundation's current funding priority.

TOPFER FAMILY FOUNDATION   [293]
3600 North Capital of Texas Highway
Building B, Suite 310
Austin, TX 78746
(512) 329-0009
(866) 897-0298
Fax: (512) 329-6462
E-mail: info@topferfoundation.org
Web Site: www.topferfoundation.org

FOUNDED: 2000

AREAS OF INTEREST:
Child abuse prevention and treatment, youth enrichment, job training and support services, children's health, and aging in place.

TYPE:
Project/program grants.

PURPOSE:
To help people connect to the tools and resources needed to build self-sufficient and fulfilling lives; to address the needs of the communities in which the Topfer family resides.

ELIGIBILITY:
Organizations must be nonprofit, classified 501(c)(3). No grants to individuals.

GEOG. RESTRICTIONS: Greater Chicago, Illinois and greater Austin, Texas metropolitan areas. In Illinois, preference is given to Cook and DuPage counties.

FINANCIAL DATA:
Amount of support per award: $2,500 to $300,000.
Total amount of support: $66,000,000.

NO. MOST RECENT APPLICANTS: 150.

NO. AWARDS: 100.

APPLICATION INFO:
Application should be submitted online.
Duration: One year. Must reapply.
Deadline: Varies.

ADDRESS INQUIRIES TO:
Melanie Cazier, Program Officer
(See address above.)

*PLEASE NOTE:
Unsolicited requests are not accepted in the greater Chicago, IL area. Must be by invitation only.

TOTAL USA FOUNDATION   [294]
1201 Lousiana, Suite 1800
Houston, TX 77002
(713) 483-5000
Web Site: us.total.com

FOUNDED: 1974

AREAS OF INTEREST:
Education.

TYPE:
Development grants; Matching gifts; Project/program grants.

LEGAL BASIS:
Corporate foundation.

ELIGIBILITY:
The Foundation supports the efforts of its employees to nominate potential organizations. Requested donations are submitted and reviewed by the Board to determine if the grant will be made, which in turn will decide amount of allocation. Due diligence is required for qualification.

GEOG. RESTRICTIONS: Louisiana and Texas.

FINANCIAL DATA:
Amount of support per award: Varies.
Total amount of support: Varies.
Matching fund requirements: All gifts from Total Petrochemicals & Refining USA, Inc. full-time employees are matched to four-year educational institutions from which the donor received a degree. The minimum gift that will be matched is $25 and the maximum gift per person per calendar year is $5,000. The contribution must be a personal gift of the eligible donor and cannot include resources from other people or institutions.

NO. MOST RECENT APPLICANTS: Approximately 500.

NO. AWARDS: Varies.

APPLICATION INFO:
No form is prescribed for submitting grant applications; however, budgets and statements of financial condition will assist the Foundation in acting upon any request for funds. A categorized statement regarding the expected sources of funds, excluding individual contributors and specifically whether the organization is supported by the United Way, are also of interest. Prior to issuance of a grant, an organization will be requested to furnish documentation of its status under the Code and a statement regarding its present operation and sources of support.
Duration: Varies.

OFFICERS:
Vincent Stoquart, Chief Executive Officer
Tricia Fuller, Secretary

ADDRESS INQUIRIES TO:
Tricia Fuller, Manager, Communications
(See address above.)

THE HARRY A. AND MARGARET D. TOWSLEY FOUNDATION   [295]
P.O. Box 349
Midland, MI 48640-0349
(989) 837-1100
E-mail: chatland@towsleyfoundation.org
Web Site: www.towsleyfoundation.org

FOUNDED: 1959

AREAS OF INTEREST:
Education, cultural arts, health and community service.

TYPE:
Capital grants; Challenge/matching grants; Endowments; General operating grants; Project/program grants; Research grants.

YEAR PROGRAM STARTED: 1959

PURPOSE:
To assist religious, educational, charitable and scientific organizations with their programs; to prevent cruelty to children.

LEGAL BASIS:
Private foundation.

ELIGIBILITY:
The Foundation does not make direct grants to individuals, provide loan funds, fund travel or conferences, or make grants to students for scholarships, books or other media. Grants are not made to institutions which in policy or practice unfairly discriminate against age, race, color, creed or sex.

GEOG. RESTRICTIONS: Primarily Michigan.

FINANCIAL DATA:
Amount of support per award: $5,000 to $1,000,000.
Total amount of support: Varies.

APPLICATION INFO:
Organizations seeking aid should complete the Grant Application located on the Foundation web site. All required fields, including relevant attachments, must be completed.
Duration: Varies. Renewal possible.

PUBLICATIONS:
Brochure; annual report.

IRS I.D.: 38-6091798

OFFICERS:
Lynn T. White, Chairperson
Wendell Dunbar, President
Judith D. Rumelhart, Vice President

Mary Ivers, Treasurer
Margaret E. Thompson, M.D., Secretary

ADDRESS INQUIRIES TO:
See e-mail address above.

TRUST FUNDS INCORPORATED [296]

1104 Corporate Way
Sacramento, CA 95831-3875
(916) 395-4472

FOUNDED: 1934

AREAS OF INTEREST:
Elementary, secondary and graduate Catholic education, Catholic religious and social service organizations and programs, and religious arts.

TYPE:
General operating grants; Grants-in-aid.

YEAR PROGRAM STARTED: 1934

PURPOSE:
To support worthwhile projects and programs that share the interests of the Foundation.

LEGAL BASIS:
Private foundation.

ELIGIBILITY:
Grants are usually limited to the San Francisco Bay area. No grants to individuals. No grants for buildings or endowments, annual campaigns, or to organizations which draw substantial public support.

GEOG. RESTRICTIONS: San Francisco, California and surrounding area.

FINANCIAL DATA:
Amount of support per award: $1,000 to $15,000.

APPLICATION INFO:
Application forms provided for all grant proposals complying with guidelines. Write or call first.

PUBLICATIONS:
Applications and guidelines.

IRS I.D.: 94-6062952

DIRECTORS:
James T. Healy, President
Thomas F. Kubasak, Chief Financial Officer
John Strain, Secretary
Liz Kelley, Director
Joan C. O'Rourke, Director

ADDRESS INQUIRIES TO:
James T. Healy, President
(See address above.)

TULL CHARITABLE FOUNDATION, INC. [297]

191 Peachtree Street, N.E.
Suite 3950
Atlanta, GA 30303
(404) 659-7079
Fax: (404) 659-1223
E-mail: carol@tullfoundation.org
Web Site: www.tullfoundation.org

FOUNDED: 1952

AREAS OF INTEREST:
Education, health and human services, youth development and the arts.

TYPE:
Capital grants.

YEAR PROGRAM STARTED: 1952

PURPOSE:
To respond to charitable and community needs in the Atlanta metropolitan area and in Georgia.

LEGAL BASIS:
Converted from Trust to Nonprofit Corporation of Georgia.

ELIGIBILITY:
Nonprofit 501(c)(3) organizations located within Georgia are eligible for support.

The Foundation does not make grants to individuals or churches and does not participate in the operation of a project other than that of providing start-up funds.

The Foundation's trustees prefer to make grants that will have a significant and lasting impact on an organization, as well as the community. Priority is given to grant requests that:
(1) are strategically important to an organization's growth and capacity;
(2) enable the organization to more effectively address important community needs and;
(3) are cost-effective.

Proposals that address education, health and human services, youth development, and the arts are given priority by Foundation trustees.

GEOG. RESTRICTIONS: Georgia.

FINANCIAL DATA:
Amount of support per award: Average: $50,000.

Total amount of support: Varies.

APPLICATION INFO:
Prior to receiving a full proposal, the Foundation prefers a concise letter-of-intent providing a brief description of the applicant organization, the project for which funding is being requested, the total cost of the project and the amount being requested and a copy of the organization's 501(c)(3) certification. If the Foundation determines that further consideration is to be given to the proposed project, additional information will be requested.

Duration: Typically one year.

Deadline: December 1, April 1, June 4 and August 1.

PUBLICATIONS:
Guidelines; policies.

ADDRESS INQUIRIES TO:
Barbara T. Cleveland, Executive Director or Carol Aiken, Assistant
(See address above.)

UNION PACIFIC FOUNDATION [298]

1400 Douglas, Stop 1560
Omaha, NE 68179
(402) 544-5600
Fax: (402) 501-0011
E-mail: upf@up.com
Web Site: www.up.com/foundation

FOUNDED: 1955

AREAS OF INTEREST:
Safety, workforce development and community spaces.

TYPE:
Capital grants; Project/program grants. Support generally for capital campaigns, building funds, equipment and materials, and renovation.

YEAR PROGRAM STARTED: 1959

PURPOSE:
To improve the quality of life in the communities served by Union Pacific and where its employees live and work.

LEGAL BASIS:
Incorporated in Utah, May 13, 1955.

ELIGIBILITY:
Organization must be a public charity, 501(c)(3) tax-exempt and located in a community served by Union Pacific.

GEOG. RESTRICTIONS: Arizona, Arkansas, California, Colorado, Idaho, Illinois, Iowa, Kansas, Louisiana, Minnesota, Missouri, Montana, Nebraska, Nevada, New Mexico, Oklahoma, Oregon, Tennessee, Texas, Utah, Washington, Wisconsin and Wyoming.

FINANCIAL DATA:
Amount of support per award: Typically, $2,500 to $25,000.

Total amount of support: $8,300,000 for fiscal year 2018.

NO. MOST RECENT APPLICANTS: 2,100.

NO. AWARDS: 615 for fiscal year 2018.

APPLICATION INFO:
Any organization interested in receiving a Local Grant must complete a survey to determine eligibility. The Foundation will provide immediate access to those invited to submit a full grant application.

Duration: Most grants are awarded annually.

Deadline: May 31. Notification in September.

TRUSTEES:
R.S. Ferguson
L.M. Fritz
R.M. Knight, Jr.
S.D. Moore
E.F. Whited

ADDRESS INQUIRIES TO:
Ranae Keckeisen, Director
(See address above.)

*PLEASE NOTE:
Due to the Foundation undergoing a strategic plan, some of this information is subject to change.

USG FOUNDATION, INC. [299]

550 West Adams Street
Chicago, IL 60661
(312) 436-4021
(312) 436-4000
Fax: (312) 672-4021
Web Site: www.usg.com

FOUNDED: 1978

AREAS OF INTEREST:
Community, arts and culture, health and welfare, and education.

TYPE:
Project/program grants.

YEAR PROGRAM STARTED: 1978

PURPOSE:
To provide assistance to nonprofit organizations seeking solutions to educational, social or health problems or whose work contributes to cultural enrichment.

LEGAL BASIS:
Tax-exempt, corporate foundation.

ELIGIBILITY:
Applicants must be tax-exempt 501(c)(3) organizations. The Foundation supports the creation of economic opportunity through grants to organizations that provide

affordable housing/shelter, encourage self-sufficiency and assist economic development.

The Foundation does not contribute to organizations without IRS tax-exempt 501(c)(3) status, sectarian organizations having an exclusively religious nature, individuals, political parties, offices or candidates, fraternal organizations, primary or secondary schools, organizations that cannot provide adequate accounting records, procedures or courtesy advertising.

GEOG. RESTRICTIONS: Primarily Chicago, Illinois.

FINANCIAL DATA:
Amount of support per award: Varies.
Total amount of support: Varies.

APPLICATION INFO:
Grant proposals should be submitted in writing to receive consideration. Application form is available on the Foundation web site.
Duration: One year. Renewal possible upon reapplication.

PUBLICATIONS:
Guidelines.

OFFICER:
Brian Cook, President

ADDRESS INQUIRIES TO:
Margaret Clark, Assistant Secretary
(See address above.)

VERIZON FOUNDATION   [300]
One Verizon Way
Basking Ridge, NJ 07920
(866) 247-2687 (volunteers program)
Fax: (908) 630-2660
E-mail: verizon.foundation@verizon.com
Web Site: www.verizon.com/about/responsibility/giving-and-grants

FOUNDED: 2001

AREAS OF INTEREST:
STEM education for K-12 youth and domestic violence education for youth, women and older adults.

TYPE:
Matching gifts; Project/program grants.

PURPOSE:
To address critical disparities among targeted segments in education, family, safety, health care and sustainability.

LEGAL BASIS:
Private, nonprofit organization.

ELIGIBILITY:
To be considered for an invitation, an organization must be classified as tax-exempt under Section 501(c)(3) of the Internal Revenue Code and further classified as a public charity under Section 509(a)(1)-(3).

Proposals will also be considered from elementary and secondary schools (public and private) that are registered with the National Center for Education Statistics (NCES), providing that the grant is not for the sponsorship of a field trip.

GEOG. RESTRICTIONS: United States.

FINANCIAL DATA:
Amount of support per award: Varies.
Total amount of support: Varies.

APPLICATION INFO:
Grants applications are by invitation only.

IRS I.D.: 13-3319048

THE WALLACE FOUNDATION   [301]
5 Penn Plaza, 7th Floor
New York, NY 10001
(212) 251-9700
Fax: (212) 679-6990
Web Site: www.wallacefoundation.org

FOUNDED: 1965

AREAS OF INTEREST:
Education leadership, arts education, building audiences for the arts, summer and expanded learning, afterschool learning, and social and emotional learning.

NAME(S) OF PROGRAMS:
- **Building Audiences for Sustainability**
- **Partnerships for Social and Emotional Learning**
- **Principal Supervisor Initiative**
- **University Principal Preparation Initiative**

TYPE:
Project/program grants; Research grants; Technical assistance; Research contracts.

YEAR PROGRAM STARTED: 2003

PURPOSE:
To foster improvements in learning and enrichment for disadvantaged children and the vitality of the arts for everyone.

LEGAL BASIS:
Private foundation.

ELIGIBILITY:
Grant applicants must be 501(c)(3) tax-exempt organizations. No grants are made to individuals.

Unsolicited proposals are rarely funded.

GEOG. RESTRICTIONS: United States.

FINANCIAL DATA:
Estimated assets of $1.574 billion as of December 31, 2017.
Amount of support per award: Varies depending on needs and nature of request.
Total amount of support: Approximately $57,131,810 in grants paid for fiscal year 2017.

NO. MOST RECENT APPLICANTS: 258.

NO. AWARDS: 159.

APPLICATION INFO:
Virtually all of the grants the Foundation awards are made through a competitive process. In most cases, the Foundation identifies and evaluates prospective grantees through the issuance of Requests for Proposals or other careful screening processes.
Duration: Varies.
Deadline: Varies.

IRS I.D.: 13-6183757

OFFICERS AND BOARD OF DIRECTORS:
Will Miller, President
Stacy J. Martin, Chief Financial Officer and Treasurer
Rob D. Nagel, Chief Investment Officer and Assistant Treasurer
Kenneth W. Austin, Corporate Secretary
Candace K. Beinecke
Anne Dinneen
Richard L. Kauffman
Kent McGuire
Jorge Ruiz de Velasco
Amor H. Towles
Daniel H. Weiss
Mary Beth West

*PLEASE NOTE:
Grants are rarely made to unsolicited projects, especially from local organizations.

THE WASIE FOUNDATION   [302]
230 Manitoba Avenue South
Suite 110
Wayzata, MN 55391-1612
(952) 955-8500
Fax: (952) 955-8509
Web Site: www.wasie.org

FOUNDED: 1966

AREAS OF INTEREST:
Care, treatment and research regarding schizophrenia and arthritis; children's health; and organizations providing services and programs to people living with cancer.

NAME(S) OF PROGRAMS:
- **Arthritis Grants**
- **Cancer Grants**
- **Children's Medical Health Grants**
- **Schizophrenia Grants**

TYPE:
Capital grants; Challenge/matching grants; Conferences/seminars; Development grants; General operating grants; Matching gifts; Project/program grants; Research grants. The grant program provides funding in four health areas, specifically: schizophrenia, arthritis, cancer, and children with medical problems.

YEAR PROGRAM STARTED: 1966

LEGAL BASIS:
Private foundation.

ELIGIBILITY:
Grants are made to 501(c)(3) nonprofit organizations.

GEOG. RESTRICTIONS: Minnesota, primarily the Twin Cities, and South Florida (Broward, Miami-Dade, and Palm Beach counties).

FINANCIAL DATA:
Amount of support per award: Varies.
Total amount of support: $668,370 in grants paid for the year 2017.

NO. AWARDS: 34 grants paid for the year 2017.

REPRESENTATIVE AWARDS:
$75,000 to Joe DiMaggio Children's Hospital Foundation; $5,000 to Vail Place; $20,000 to Ridgeview Foundation; $75,000 to 4Kids of South Florida.

APPLICATION INFO:
The Foundation encourages organizations which believe they fall within their funding guidelines to initiate contact through a telephone call to one of the program staff who will gather information and assist with the proposal process.

Proposal submission is by invitation only.
Duration: One to three years. Renewal possible.
Deadline: Submissions are invited throughout the year.

STAFF:
Gregg D. Sjoquist, President and Chief Executive Officer
Dani Mathison, Chief Operating Officer
Jan Preble, Vice President of Programs

ADDRESS INQUIRIES TO:
Jan Preble
Vice President of Programs
(See address above.)

*SPECIAL STIPULATIONS:
Grant proposals are by invitation only.
Inquiries open to any organization falling
within funding areas and within demographic
areas noted.

EDWIN S. WEBSTER FOUNDATION [303]

c/o GMA Foundations
2 Liberty Square, Suite 500
Boston, MA 02109
(617) 399-1852
Fax: (617) 426-7087
E-mail: pcappello@gmafoundations.com
Web Site: www.gmafoundations.com
websterfoundation.grantsmanagement08.com

FOUNDED: 1948

AREAS OF INTEREST:
Charitable purposes, with emphasis on
hospitals, medical research and education,
youth agencies, cultural activities and
programs addressing the needs of minorities.

TYPE:
Capital grants; Challenge/matching grants;
Endowments; General operating grants.

YEAR PROGRAM STARTED: 1982

PURPOSE:
To work towards a better society by giving
grants to organizations trying to help people
with serious needs not otherwise being
addressed.

LEGAL BASIS:
Nonprofit foundation.

ELIGIBILITY:
No grants are given to individuals or
organizations outside the U.S. The majority
of contributions are made to organizations in
the New England area. It is the policy of the
Foundation to support charitable
organizations that are well known to the
Trustees, with emphasis on hospitals, medical
research, education, youth agencies, cultural
activities and programs addressing the needs
of minorities. Grantees must have tax-exempt
status.

GEOG. RESTRICTIONS: Primarily New England.

FINANCIAL DATA:
Amount of support per award: $10,000 to
$25,000. Average $15,000.
Total amount of support: $1,470,000 for the
year 2018.

NO. MOST RECENT APPLICANTS: 75 to 80 per
grant cycle.

NO. AWARDS: 61 for the year 2018.

APPLICATION INFO:
Proposals are submitted by using the online
application form.
Duration: One year.
Deadline: For consideration at spring
meeting, proposals should arrive by May 1.
For consideration at the fall meeting,
proposals should arrive by November 1.

PUBLICATIONS:
Guidelines.

TRUSTEES:
Henry U. Harris, III
Alexander Hiam
Suzanne Harte Sears

WEINGART FOUNDATION [304]

700 South Flower Street
Suite 1900
Los Angeles, CA 90017
(213) 688-7799
Fax: (213) 688-1515
E-mail: info@weingartfnd.org
Web Site: www.weingartfnd.org

FOUNDED: 1951

AREAS OF INTEREST:
Human services, health, education, immigrant
integration, homelessness, 2020 census, youth
organizing, leadership for movement
building, and capacity building.

TYPE:
General operating grants.

PURPOSE:
To support historically under-resourced
individuals and communities in reaching their
full potential.

ELIGIBILITY:
An organization that is certified as
tax-exempt under Section 501(c)(3) of the
U.S. Internal Revenue Code and is not a
private foundation as defined in Section
509(a) of that Code is eligible for
consideration. The Foundation does not fund
Section 509(a)(3) Type III nonfunctionally
integrated supporting organizations.

Grants are not made:
(1) to organizations that discriminate against
certain groups or individuals in the delivery
of programs and services on the basis of
race, religion, national origin, gender, age,
sexual orientation or disability;
(2) for elections, political candidates or
political campaigns;
(3) for social or political issues outside the
U.S.;
(4) to individuals;
(5) for temporary exhibits, travel, surveys,
films or publishing activities;
(6) for endowment funds;
(7) for fund-raising dinners or events or;
(8) for animal welfare.

Grants generally are not approved for:
(1) research;
(2) national organizations that do not have
local chapters operating in the geographic
area of grant focus;
(3) religious programs or consumer interest
or;
(4) feasibility studies.

GEOG. RESTRICTIONS: Southern California, with
priority given to Los Angeles County and
South Los Angeles.

FINANCIAL DATA:
Assets of $830,894,039 for the year ended
June 30, 2019.
Amount of support per award: Varies.
Total amount of support: $39,288,493 in
grants approved for the fiscal year ended
June 30, 2019.
Matching fund requirements: Organization
matches 1:1.

CO-OP FUNDING PROGRAMS: Nonprofit
Sustainability Initiative, Home for Good.

NO. MOST RECENT APPLICANTS: 407.

NO. AWARDS: 170.

APPLICATION INFO:
Applications are accepted by invitation only.
Duration: Multi-year.
Deadline: The Foundation accepts
applications throughout the year.

PUBLICATIONS:
Annual report, only available on web site.

IRS I.D.: 95-6054814

OFFICERS:
Fred J. Ali, President and Chief Executive
Officer
Tim Ortez, Vice President and Chief
Financial Officer

BOARD OF DIRECTORS:
Aileen Adams, Chairman
Fred J. Ali
William C. Allen
Monica C. Lozano
Miriam Muscarolas
Linda Oubre
Dr. Robert K. Ross
Miguel A. Santana
Steven L. Soboroff

ADDRESS INQUIRIES TO:
President and Chief Executive Officer
Weingart Foundation
(See address above.)

HERMAN O. WEST FOUNDATION [305]

530 Herman O. West Drive
Exton, PA 19341
(610) 594-2900
Web Site: www.westpharma.com

FOUNDED: 1972

AREAS OF INTEREST:
Funding of nonprofit organizations serving
cultural, health and public service needs of
the areas/communities where West
Pharmaceutical Services maintains
operations.

TYPE:
Matching gifts; Scholarships. Emergency
grants.

YEAR PROGRAM STARTED: 1972

PURPOSE:
To provide employee emergency grants,
scholarship programs and employee matching
gifts program.

LEGAL BASIS:
Corporate contributions program; private
foundation.

ELIGIBILITY:
Employees of West Pharmaceutical Services
may participate in the Employee Emergency
Grants Program, Employee Matching Gifts
Program and Matching Gifts Program.

Scholarships are available to children of West
Pharmaceutical Services employees.

GEOG. RESTRICTIONS: United States.

FINANCIAL DATA:
Amount of support per award: $500 to
$150,000.
Total amount of support: $400,000 annually.

APPLICATION INFO:
Application information is available on the
Foundation web site.
Duration: Varies. Renewal possible.

PUBLICATIONS:
Application guidelines.

TRUSTEES:
Annette Favorite
Paula Johnson, M.D.

ADDRESS INQUIRIES TO:
Laura Pitt
(See address above.)

WESTERN INTERSTATE COMMISSION FOR HIGHER EDUCATION [306]

3035 Center Green Drive
Suite 200
Boulder, CO 80301
(303) 541-0270
E-mail: info-sep@wiche.edu
Web Site: www.wiche.edu/psep

FOUNDED: 1953

AREAS OF INTEREST:
Allopathic medicine, dentistry, physical and occupational therapy, optometry, podiatry, osteopathic medicine, veterinary medicine, physician assistant and pharmacy.

NAME(S) OF PROGRAMS:
● **Professional Student Exchange Program (PSEP)**

TYPE:
Scholarships. Tuition assistance/loan for service.

YEAR PROGRAM STARTED: 1953

PURPOSE:
To provide affordable access to professional health care education.

ELIGIBILITY:
Must be a resident of a state listed below. Rules vary by state.

GEOG. RESTRICTIONS: Alaska, Arizona, Colorado, Hawaii, Montana, Nevada, New Mexico, North Dakota, Utah, Wyoming and the Commonwealth of the Mariana Islands.

FINANCIAL DATA:
Amount of support per award: Varies.
Total amount of support: Varies.

NO. AWARDS: 611 for the year 2019-20.

APPLICATION INFO:
Applicants should contact their state certifying officers, listed on the web site above, for more information.
Duration: One year. Grants are renewable for course of study; subject to available funding.
Deadline: October 15 of the year prior to enrollment.

ADDRESS INQUIRIES TO:
Director of Student Access Programs
(See address above.)

*PLEASE NOTE:
Grant is for residents of one western state making applications to participating schools in another western state.

E. L. WIEGAND FOUNDATION [307]

Wiegand Center
165 West Liberty Street, Suite 200
Reno, NV 89501
(775) 333-0310 ext. 112
Fax: (775) 333-0314

FOUNDED: 1982

AREAS OF INTEREST:
Education, medical research, civic and community affairs, arts and cultural affairs, and public affairs.

TYPE:
Capital grants; Project/program grants.

YEAR PROGRAM STARTED: 1982

PURPOSE:
To support charitable organizations and Roman Catholic charitable institutions.

LEGAL BASIS:
Private charitable trust.

ELIGIBILITY:
The Foundation will consider applications from institutions that are tax-exempt under Section 501(c)(3) of the IRS, and which are not private foundations as defined in Section 509.

The review process by the Foundation will consider institutions that:
(1) are exemplary in their field;
(2) have a history of high achievement and sound management;
(3) demonstrate a stable financial condition;
(4) have the potential to be self-supporting after the stage of initial funding by the Foundation;
(5) focus on strengthening traditional values essential to the preservation of a democratic society nurtured by free market principles (in the area of public affairs) and;
(6) are developing programs and projects that have a significant impact in the area for which the grant is requested.

GEOG. RESTRICTIONS: Arizona, Hawaii, Idaho, Montana, Nevada, Oregon, Utah, Washington, and New York City/Washington, DC (public policy).

FINANCIAL DATA:
Amount of support per award: $1,000 to $1,750,000.
Total amount of support: $4,647,300 for the year 2018.

NO. AWARDS: 34 for the year 2018.

APPLICATION INFO:
A prospective applicant should describe the highlights of the proposal (including data regarding the organization, sources of funding, a brief description of the project or program, estimated budget and timeline) in a letter addressed to the Foundation. If, after staff consideration, it is determined that the program or project complies with the preliminary review, a prospective applicant shall receive an application for grant form which shall be assigned numerically to such applicant. The Foundation is only able to support a small percentage of the proposals it receives.
Deadline: Letters of Inquiry accepted throughout the year.

IRS I.D.: 94-2839372

ADDRESS INQUIRIES TO:
Kristen A. Avansino
President and Executive Director
Grants Program
(See address above.)

*PLEASE NOTE:
Written communications to the Foundation are preferred.

MATILDA R. WILSON FUND [308]

6th Floor at Ford Field
1901 St. Antoine Street
Detroit, MI 48226
(313) 259-7777
Fax: (313) 393-7579
E-mail: roosterveen@bodmanlaw.com

FOUNDED: 1944

AREAS OF INTEREST:
Arts, education, health and human services.

TYPE:
Capital grants; Project/program grants.

PURPOSE:
To primarily fund pre-selected organizations supported by Matilda R. Wilson during her lifetime.

ELIGIBILITY:
Applicants must be 501(c)(3) organizations. No grants to individuals.

GEOG. RESTRICTIONS: Primarily southeast Michigan.

FINANCIAL DATA:
Amount of support per award: $500 to $1,000,000.
Total amount of support: Varies.

NO. MOST RECENT APPLICANTS: 60.

NO. AWARDS: 35.

APPLICATION INFO:
No application form. Applicants must submit tax-exempt documentation.
Duration: One year; some multiyear.
Deadline: January, April and August.

IRS I.D.: 38-6087665

STAFF:
Robin L. Oosterveen, Program Director

ADDRESS INQUIRIES TO:
Robin L. Oosterveen, Program Director
(See address above.)

*PLEASE NOTE:
Priority given to organizations that Mrs. Wilson supported during her lifetime, or with which the Fund has a long-standing commitment.

THE ROBERT W. WOODRUFF FOUNDATION [309]

191 Peachtree Street, N.E.
Suite 3540
Atlanta, GA 30303
(404) 522-6755
Fax: (404) 522-7026
E-mail: fdns@woodruff.org
Web Site: woodruff.org

FOUNDED: 1937

AREAS OF INTEREST:
K-12th-grade and higher education; health care and health outreach; human services, particularly for children and youth; community development in metropolitan Atlanta; major Atlanta arts and cultural institutions; large-scale conservation projects; and Atlanta parks and greenspaces.

TYPE:
Capital grants; Project/program grants.

YEAR PROGRAM STARTED: 1937

PURPOSE:
To improve the quality of life in Georgia by investing in health, education, economic opportunity and the vitality of the community.

LEGAL BASIS:
Independent, private foundation with a broad charter to support charitable activities in the areas of health, education, environment, human services, arts and culture, and community development.

ELIGIBILITY:
Grants generally are limited to 501(c)(3) public charities located and operating in metropolitan Atlanta, GA, although grants are occasionally considered for significant institutions and initiatives in communities throughout Georgia. Grants are typically awarded for one-time capital or capacity

needs of well-established charitable organizations with strong leadership, sustainable operations, a broad base of financial support, and proven program effectiveness.

Grants for ongoing operating support or endowments are avoided. No grants are made for individuals, loans, churches, conferences, startup organizations, debt relief, political activities, professional associations, festivals, performances, exhibits, fund-raising events or sponsorships.

GEOG. RESTRICTIONS: Georgia, with a focus on metropolitan Atlanta.

FINANCIAL DATA:
Amount of support per award:
Approximately $150,000 to $30,000,000.
Total amount of support: $131,240,121 for the year 2019.

NO. MOST RECENT APPLICANTS: Approximately 350.

NO. AWARDS: Approximately 18 for the year 2019.

REPRESENTATIVE AWARDS:
$250,000 to Historic Westville for relocation of history museum to Columbus, GA; $1,000,000 to friends of the Jimmy Carter National Historic Site for expansion and development; $5,000,000 to the University of Georgia for Phase II construction of the Business Learning Community campus for the Terry College of Business; $200,000 to National Families in Action for a program to educate the public about the effects of marijuana use.

APPLICATION INFO:
Application form not required. Proposal (one copy) should be made in letter form and should briefly describe the organization (its mission, history and programs) and the proposed project or initiative, including the challenge it addresses, project goals and/or expected outcomes. Proposals that are concise and to the point are preferred. Applicant must include these attachments: (1) itemized project budget, including other

sources of support in-hand or anticipated; (2) a list of executive staff and board members, including an address for the board chairperson; (3) financial statements, including most recent audit report and; (4) the current IRS determination letter.
Deadline: August 15 and February 1.

PUBLICATIONS:
Application guidelines.

OFFICERS:
P. Russell Hardin, President
Erik S. Johnson, Treasurer and Secretary

TRUSTEES:
James B. Williams, Chairman
E. Jenner Wood, III, Vice Chairman
Lawrence L. Gellerstedt, III
Thomas J. Lawley, M.D.
David P. Stockert

ADDRESS INQUIRIES TO:
P. Russell Hardin, President
(See address above.)

XCEL ENERGY FOUNDATION [310]

414 Nicollet Mall
Minneapolis, MN 55401
(612) 330-6200
E-mail: foundation@xcelenergy.com
Web Site: www.xcelenergy.com

FOUNDED: 2001

AREAS OF INTEREST:
Education, economic sustainability, environmental stewardship, and access to the arts.

TYPE:
Project/program grants. Employee/retiree matching gifts program.

YEAR PROGRAM STARTED: 2001

PURPOSE:
To help promote a desirable, healthy environment in those areas served by Xcel Energy.

ELIGIBILITY:
Applicants must be 501(c)(3) nonprofit organizations in the service area. Grants will not be made to individuals, political parties, national organizations, research programs or government agencies.

GEOG. RESTRICTIONS: Cities within Xcel Energy service areas.

FINANCIAL DATA:
Amount of support per award: $1,000 to $30,000.

Total amount of support: Grants: Approximately $4,000,000 annually; Employee matching gifts: Approximately $3,000,000 annually.

Matching fund requirements: 501(c)(3) nonprofits. Employee and retiree matching gifts program: Minimum donation $50, maximum $500.

NO. MOST RECENT APPLICANTS: 400.

NO. AWARDS: 380.

APPLICATION INFO:
Grant applications are accepted by invitation only. Organizations that are deemed eligible may be contacted by a regional corporate giving representative for further discussion.
Deadline: April 1.

STAFF:
Liz Gardner, Representative, Colorado
Jennifer Prochnow, Representative, Michigan and Wisconsin
Elisa Rasmussen, Representative, Minnesota
Terry Price, Representative, New Mexico and Texas
Mark Nisbet, Representative, Fargo, North Dakota
Judith Paukert, Representative, Grand Forks, North Dakota
Kathleen Aas, Representative, Minot, North Dakota

ADDRESS INQUIRIES TO:
Veronica Hayden
Corporate Giving Representative
(See address above.)

HUMANITIES

Humanities (general)

AMERICAN ACADEMY IN ROME [311]

7 East 60th Street
New York, NY 10022-1001
(212) 751-7200
Fax: (212) 751-7220
E-mail: info@aarome.org
Web Site: www.aarome.org

FOUNDED: 1894

AREAS OF INTEREST:
Arts and humanities.

NAME(S) OF PROGRAMS:
● **Rome Prize Fellowships**

TYPE:
Awards/prizes; Fellowships; Residencies.
Fellowships for independent work in
architecture, landscape architecture, design,
musical composition, visual arts, historic
preservation/conservation, literature, ancient
studies, medieval studies, renaissance and
early modern studies, and modern Italian
studies. Supported projects must be
conducted at American Academy in Rome
facilities.

YEAR PROGRAM STARTED: 1894

PURPOSE:
To support emerging artists and scholars in
the early or middle stages of their careers; to
refine and expand their professional, artistic
or scholarly aptitudes, drawing on their
colleagues' erudition and experience, as well
as on the inestimable resources of the Italian
capital of Rome, Europe and the
Mediterranean.

LEGAL BASIS:
Private, not-for-profit.

ELIGIBILITY:
Must be U.S. citizen at the time of
application. Graduate students in the
humanities may apply only for Predoctoral
Fellowships. Previous winners of the Rome
Prize are not eligible to reapply.
Undergraduate students are not eligible for
Rome Prize Fellowships.

U.S. citizens and foreign nationals who have
lived in the U.S. for three years immediately
preceding the application deadline may apply
for the NEH Postdoctoral Fellowships.

FINANCIAL DATA:
Rome Prize includes stipend, meals, a
bedroom with private bath, and a study or
studio.
Amount of support per award: Fellowships
provide stipends of $16,000 (half-term) and
$28,000 (full-term).
Total amount of support: $2,700,000.

CO-OP FUNDING PROGRAMS: National
Endowment for the Arts, National
Endowment for the Humanities, Andrew W.
Mellon Foundation and Samuel Kress
Foundation.

NO. MOST RECENT APPLICANTS: 928.

NO. AWARDS: 29.

APPLICATION INFO:
Application forms are available online.
Duration: Five and one-half months for
half-term fellowships. 11 months for
full-term fellowships. Two-year fellowships
are also available for predoctoral candidates
studying art history.
Deadline: November 1.

PUBLICATIONS:
AAR Magazine, biannually.

STAFF:
Shawn Miller, Program Director

ADDRESS INQUIRIES TO:
Programs Department
(See address above.)

AMERICAN ANTIQUARIAN SOCIETY (AAS) [312]

185 Salisbury Street
Worcester, MA 01609-1634
(508) 755-5221
Fax: (508) 754-9069
E-mail: nwolverton@mwa.org
Web Site: www.americanantiquarian.org

FOUNDED: 1812

AREAS OF INTEREST:
American history and culture through 1876.

NAME(S) OF PROGRAMS:
● **AAS American Society for Eighteenth Century Studies Fellowship**
● **AAS National Endowment for the Humanities Fellowships**
● **American Historical Print Collectors Fellowship**
● **Stephen Botein Fellowships**
● **The "Drawn to Art" Fellowship**
● **David Jaffee Fellowship**
● **Kate Van Winkle Keller Fellowship**
● **Linda F. and Julian L. Lapides Fellowship**
● **Jay and Deborah Last Fellowship**
● **The Legacy Fellowship**
● **Alstott Morgan Fellowship**
● **Barbara Packer Fellowship**
● **Kate B. and Hall J. Peterson Fellowships**
● **The Reese Fellowship**
● **Justin G. Schiller Fellowship**
● **Joyce A. Tracy Fellowship**

TYPE:
Conferences/seminars; Fellowships.
Fellowships provide support for residence at
the Society's library for research on any topic
supported by the collections. All awards are
for research and writing using the library's
resources.

YEAR PROGRAM STARTED: 1972

PURPOSE:
To enable scholars to come to Worcester for
an extended period to do research in the
Society's collections.

LEGAL BASIS:
AAS was incorporated by the legislature of
Massachusetts, October 24, 1812.

ELIGIBILITY:
Fellows are selected on the basis of the
applicant's scholarly qualifications, the
scholarly significance of the project, and the
appropriateness of the proposed study to the
Society's collections.

The National Endowment for the Humanities
Fellowships are intended for scholars beyond
the Doctorate, for which senior and
midcareer scholars are encouraged to apply.
Applicant must be a U.S. citizen.

Short-term fellowships are available for
scholars holding Ph.D. and for doctoral
candidates engaged in dissertation research.

FINANCIAL DATA:
Amount of support per award: Long-term
fellowships carry stipends up to $5,000 per
month. Short-term fellowships are $1,850 per
month.

Total amount of support: Varies.

APPLICATION INFO:
Application information is available online.
Duration: One month for short-term
fellowships. Four to 12 months for long-term
fellowships.
Deadline: January 15. Announcement by
March 30.

ADDRESS INQUIRIES TO:
Nan Wolverton, Director of Fellowships
(See e-mail address above.)

*SPECIAL STIPULATIONS:
Recipient must maintain regular and
continuous residence at the Society during
his or her period of tenure.

AMERICAN ANTIQUARIAN SOCIETY (AAS) [313]

185 Salisbury Street
Worcester, MA 01609-1634
(508) 755-5221
Fax: (508) 754-9069
E-mail: nwolverton@mwa.org
Web Site: www.americanantiquarian.org

AREAS OF INTEREST:
American history, literature and culture
through 1876.

NAME(S) OF PROGRAMS:
● **AAS Fellowship for Creative and Performing Artists and Writers**

TYPE:
Fellowships. Visiting fellowship for historical
research by creative and performing artists,
writers, filmmakers and journalists.

YEAR PROGRAM STARTED: 1995

PURPOSE:
To multiply and improve ways in which an
understanding of history is communicated to
the American people.

ELIGIBILITY:
Creative and performing artists, writers,
filmmakers, journalists, and others whose
goals are to produce imaginative,
non-formulaic works dealing with pre-20th
century American history. Works are for the
general public, rather than for academic or
educational audiences.

FINANCIAL DATA:
Amount of support per award: Stipend of
$1,850.
Total amount of support: Varies.

NO. MOST RECENT APPLICANTS: 40.

NO. AWARDS: Minimum 5.

APPLICATION INFO:
Instructions are included in the online
application.
Duration: Four-week residency.
Deadline: October 5, with notification on or
about December 5.

ADDRESS INQUIRIES TO:
Nan Wolverton, Director of Fellowships
(See e-mail address above.)

AMERICAN COUNCIL OF LEARNED SOCIETIES [314]

633 Third Avenue, 8th Floor
New York, NY 10017-6795
E-mail: fellowships@acls.org
Web Site: www.acls.org

FOUNDED: 1919

AREAS OF INTEREST:
The humanities and related social sciences.

NAME(S) OF PROGRAMS:
- **ACLS Fellowship**

TYPE:
Fellowships. Postdoctoral fellowships to support research in the humanities or research projects with a predominantly humanities-related emphasis in the social sciences.

PURPOSE:
To provide opportunities for scholars to engage in humanities research.

LEGAL BASIS:
Nonprofit.

ELIGIBILITY:
U.S. citizens or permanent residents holding a Ph.D. degree conferred two years before application deadline or its equivalent (taken to mean scholarly maturity as demonstrated by professional experience and publications) may apply.

FINANCIAL DATA:
Amount of support per award: Fellowships are up to $70,000 for full professor (and career equivalent), up to $50,000 for associate professor (and career equivalent), and up to $40,000 for assistant professor (and career equivalent).
Total amount of support: Varies.

NO. MOST RECENT APPLICANTS: 1,100.

NO. AWARDS: 81.

APPLICATION INFO:
Applications must be submitted through the ACLS Online Fellowship Application system, located at ofa.acls.org.
Duration: Fellows must devote six to 12 continuous months to full-time work on supported projects.
Deadline: September. Notification by early March.

THE AMERICAN NUMISMATIC SOCIETY   [315]
75 Varick Street, Floor 11
New York, NY 10013
(212) 571-4470 ext. 153
Fax: (212) 571-4479
E-mail: vanalfen@numismatics.org
Web Site: numismatics.org

FOUNDED: 1858

AREAS OF INTEREST:
Numismatics (coins and medals), history and archeology.

NAME(S) OF PROGRAMS:
- **The Eric P. Newman Graduate Summer Seminar**

TYPE:
Grants-in-aid. Grants for graduate students and junior faculty to attend the Society's summer seminar held at its museum in New York. The Graduate Seminar in Numismatics is an intensive program of study including lectures and conferences conducted by specialists in various fields, preparation and oral delivery of a research paper and actual contact with the coinage in the Society's collection. Curatorial staff and other experts from the U.S. and abroad will participate in the seminar.

YEAR PROGRAM STARTED: 1952

PURPOSE:
To familiarize students with numismatic methodology and scholarship; to provide a deeper understanding of the contributions made by numismatics to other fields of study.

ELIGIBILITY:
Applications are accepted from students of demonstrated competence who will have completed at least one year of graduate work in history, art history, classical studies, economics, economic history or other related fields. Applications are encouraged from junior faculty members with an advanced degree in one of these fields.

Applications are also accepted from outstanding students from foreign institutions who have completed at least one year of graduate work and are able to demonstrate fluency in English; however, no financial aid for them is offered.

FINANCIAL DATA:
Stipends are available to qualified applicants who are citizens or permanent residents of the U.S.
Amount of support per award: Varies.
Total amount of support: Varies.

CO-OP FUNDING PROGRAMS: Support of attendance at the Seminar is made possible by a generous donation from Mr. and Mrs. Eric P. Newman.

NO. MOST RECENT APPLICANTS: 50.

NO. AWARDS: Up to 8.

APPLICATION INFO:
Details are available on the Society's web site.
Duration: Seven to eight weeks, June through July.
Deadline: Usually February. Specific date is posted online.

OFFICERS:
Dr. Peter Van Alfen, Director

ADDRESS INQUIRIES TO:
Dr. Peter Van Alfen, Director
(See address above.)

AMERICAN PHILOSOPHICAL SOCIETY   [316]
c/o American Philosophical Society Library
104 South Fifth Street
Philadelphia, PA 19106-3387
(215) 440-3400
Fax: (215) 440-3423
E-mail: libfellows@amphilsoc.org
Web Site: www.amphilsoc.
org/grants/fellowships

FOUNDED: 1743

AREAS OF INTEREST:
Scholarly research.

NAME(S) OF PROGRAMS:
- **The Library Resident Research Fellowships**

TYPE:
Fellowships; Grants-in-aid; Research grants. Short-term residential fellowships for conducting research in the Library's collections.

YEAR PROGRAM STARTED: 1991

PURPOSE:
To encourage research by scholars in the Library's collections.

LEGAL BASIS:
Nonprofit learned society.

ELIGIBILITY:
Open to both U.S. citizens and foreign nationals who are holders of a Ph.D. or the equivalent, Ph.D. candidates who have passed their preliminary exams and degreed independent scholars. Applicants in any relevant field of scholarship may apply.

FINANCIAL DATA:
Amount of support per award: $3,000 per month.

NO. AWARDS: 25 to 30 annually.

APPLICATION INFO:
All application materials will be submitted online. This includes:
(1) cover letter;
(2) curriculum vitae;
(3) research proposal (two pages) that outlines the status of the applicant's work and what applicant will research at the American Philosophical Society Library. Special attention must be made to specific collections that will be of use during the fellowship; and
(4) two confidential letters of reference.
Duration: One to three months, taken between June 1 and May 31.
Deadline: March 6. Notification in late April.

PUBLICATIONS:
Program announcement; list of guides to the Society's collections.

ADDRESS INQUIRIES TO:
See e-mail address above.

*SPECIAL STIPULATIONS:
Fellows are expected to be in residence during the period of their award.

AMERICAN SCHOOL OF CLASSICAL STUDIES AT ATHENS
6-8 Charlton Street
Princeton, NJ 08540-5232
(609) 683-0800
Fax: (609) 924-0578
E-mail: application@ascsa.org
Web Site: www.ascsa.edu.gr

TYPE:
Fellowships. Fellowships for postdoctoral scholars and professionals in the humanities.

See entry 819 for full listing.

AMERICAN SCHOOL OF CLASSICAL STUDIES AT ATHENS
6-8 Charlton Street
Princeton, NJ 08540-5232
(609) 683-0800
Fax: (609) 924-0578
E-mail: application@ascsa.org
Web Site: www.ascsa.edu.gr

TYPE:
Fellowships. The M. Alison Frantz Fellowship is part of the Student Associate Program, which is open to advanced graduate students in the same fields as the Regular Academic Program (classical studies and ancient Mediterranean studies and related fields such as history of art, anthropology, prehistory, studies in postclassical Greece, etc.), who plan to pursue independent research projects and who do not wish to commit to the full Regular Academic Program.

See entry 820 for full listing.

AMERICAN SCHOOL OF CLASSICAL STUDIES AT ATHENS

6-8 Charlton Street
Princeton, NJ 08540-5232
(609) 683-0800
Fax: (609) 924-0578
E-mail: application@ascsa.org
Web Site: www.ascsa.edu.gr

TYPE:
Fellowships.

See entry 826 for full listing.

AMERICAN SCHOOL OF CLASSICAL STUDIES AT ATHENS

6-8 Charlton Street
Princeton, NJ 08540-5232
(609) 683-0800
Fax: (609) 924-0578
E-mail: application@ascsa.org
Web Site: www.ascsa.edu.gr

TYPE:
Fellowships. The Heinrich Schliemann and the John Williams White Fellowships in Archaeology are awarded based on the student's performance on the archaeology examination.

The Thomas Day Seymour Fellowship in History and Literature is awarded based on the student's combined performance on the history and literature examination.

Nine fellowships are unrestricted to field. These are the Virginia Grace, the Michael Jameson, the Philip Lockhart, the Lucy Shoe Meritt, the Fowler Merle-Smith, the Martin Ostwald, and the James Rignall Wheeler Fellowships. The Bert Hodge Hill Fellowship is unrestricted, but with a preference for a student in art history. The Emily Townsend Vermeule Fellowship is unrestricted, but with a preference for Bronze Age archaeology.

See entry 827 for full listing.

AMERICAN SCHOOL OF CLASSICAL STUDIES AT ATHENS

6-8 Charlton Street
Princeton, NJ 08540-5232
(609) 683-0800
Fax: (609) 924-0578
E-mail: application@ascsa.org
Web Site: www.ascsa.edu.gr

TYPE:
Fellowships. Several Fellowships awarded by the School for the full academic year: the Gorham Phillips Stevens Fellowship in the history of architecture; the Ione Mylonas Shear Fellowship in Mycenaean archaeology or Athenian architecture and/or archaeology; the Homer A. and Dorothy B. Thompson Fellowship in the study of pottery. Additionally, three Fellowships are unrestricted as to field: the Edward Capps, the Doreen Canaday Spitzer, and the Eugene Vanderpool Fellowships.

See entry 821 for full listing.

ARCHAEOLOGICAL INSTITUTE OF AMERICA   [317]

44 Beacon Street
Boston, MA 02108
(857) 305-9358
Fax: (857) 233-4270
E-mail: saustin@archaeological.org
Web Site: www.archaeological.org/grants/16811

FOUNDED: 1879

AREAS OF INTEREST:
Archaeology or related fields.

NAME(S) OF PROGRAMS:
● **Elizabeth Bartman Museum Internship**

TYPE:
Internships. Established in honor of AIA Honorary President Elizabeth Bartman, this internship assists graduate students or those who have recently completed a Master's degree with the expenses associated with participating in a museum internship either in the U.S. or abroad.

PURPOSE:
To assist graduate students with expenses associated with participating in a museum internship.

ELIGIBILITY:
Applicants must have been members of the AIA for at least one year at the time of application. The recipient should remain a member until the end of the internship period. Applicants must be enrolled in a graduate program in archaeology or a related field, or have recently completed a Master's degree in archaeology or a related field.

FINANCIAL DATA:
Amount of support per award: $1,250 to $2,500.

NO. MOST RECENT APPLICANTS: 1.

NO. AWARDS: 1.

APPLICATION INFO:
Applicants must complete the online application form that asks for the following:
(1) Project Proposal - The Fellowships Committee attaches the greatest importance to the summary statement of the applicant's interest in museum work and how the proposed internship will help achieve the applicant's larger goals. It is helpful to include background information outlining any past museum experience, field experience, and the reasons for pursuing museum work in general, and this internship project in particular. Proposal must include information about the internship and the anticipated length of stay.
(2) Budget - An outline of anticipated expenses associated with participation in the project and a statement from the applicant indicating any other financial resources available or applied for, if any, to help cover these expenses.
(3) Transcripts - Applicants must include completed undergraduate transcripts and transcripts for completed postgraduate work. Transcripts may be mailed to the attention of Samantha Austin or sent digitally to saustin@archaeological.org and;
(4) Letters of Recommendation - The names and e-mails of two professors or academic advisors at the applicant's college or university who know the applicant's work and who are willing to provide letters of recommendation. These references will receive further instructions from the AIA. A recommendation from the prospective supervisor of the internship is encouraged.

Duration: Minimum eight weeks or a semester. Nonrenewable.
Deadline: April 1.

ADDRESS INQUIRIES TO:
Samantha Austin
Manager of Membership and Governance
(See address and e-mail above.)

*SPECIAL STIPULATIONS:
At the conclusion of the internship tenure, the recipient is required to submit a report on the use of the award to AIA Headquarters.

ARCHAEOLOGICAL INSTITUTE OF AMERICA   [318]

44 Beacon Street
Boston, MA 02108
(857) 305-9360
Fax: (857) 233-4270
E-mail: fellowships@archaeological.org
Web Site: www.archaeological.org

FOUNDED: 1879

AREAS OF INTEREST:
Archaeological research and publication.

NAME(S) OF PROGRAMS:
● **John R. Coleman Traveling Fellowship**
● **Olivia James Traveling Fellowship**

TYPE:
Fellowships. John R. Coleman Traveling Fellowship: Awarded to be used for travel and study in Italy, the western Mediterranean, or North Africa. Applicants must be engaged in dissertation research in a U.S. graduate program.

Olivia James Traveling Fellowship: Awarded, preferably, to individuals engaged in dissertation research or to recent recipients of the Ph.D. (within five years of the application deadline) for travel and study in Greece, the Aegean Islands, Cyprus, Sicily, Southern Italy, Asia Minor or Mesopotamia to conduct a project in (most suitably) classics, sculpture, architecture, archaeology or history.

YEAR PROGRAM STARTED: 1961

PURPOSE:
John R. Coleman Traveling Fellowship: To encourage the continued study of archaeological sites; to provide funding for travel and study in Italy, the western Mediterranean or North Africa.

Olivia James Traveling Fellowship: To encourage the continued study of archaeological sites; to provide fellowships for travel and study in Greece, the Aegean Islands, Cyprus, Sicily, Southern Italy, Asia Minor or Mesopotamia.

LEGAL BASIS:
Nonprofit, scientific and educational organization.

ELIGIBILITY:
Applicants must have been AIA members in good standing for at least two consecutive years before the application deadline.

John R. Coleman Traveling Fellowship: Applicants must be members of the AIA at the time of application. The recipient should remain a member until the end of the fellowship term and subsequent submission of an abstract and/or presentation at the AIA annual meeting. Applicants must be engaged in dissertation research in a U.S. graduate program.

Olivia James Traveling Fellowship: Applicants must be U.S. citizens. Preference is given to individuals engaged in dissertation research or to recent Ph.D. recipients (within five years of application deadline). Preference is also given to projects of at least a half-year's duration. The award is for travel and study in Greece, the Aegean Islands, Cyprus, Sicily, Southern Italy, Asia Minor or Mesopotamia and is not intended to support field excavation projects. Recipients may not hold other major fellowships during the requested tenure.

FINANCIAL DATA:
Amount of support per award: John R. Coleman Traveling Fellowship: $10,000. Olivia James Traveling Fellowship: $24,000.

Total amount of support: John R. Coleman Traveling Fellowship: $10,000. Olivia James Traveling Fellowship: $24,000.

NO. MOST RECENT APPLICANTS: John R. Coleman Traveling Fellowship: 5. Olivia James Traveling Fellowship: 13.

NO. AWARDS: 1 per award.

APPLICATION INFO:
Official application materials are available August of each year on the Institute's web site. Graduate transcripts, two letters of reference and a summary statement of proposed project are required. Applications for the fellowship can be submitted electronically.

Duration: Single fellowship for work to be conducted between July 1 of the award year and the following June 30.

Deadline: November 1. Announcement by February 1.

ADDRESS INQUIRIES TO:
Laurel Nilsen Sparks
Lecture and Fellowship Coordinator
(See address above.)

ARCHAEOLOGICAL INSTITUTE OF AMERICA   [319]
44 Beacon Street
Boston, MA 02108
(857) 305-9360
Fax: (857) 233-4270
E-mail: fellowships@archaeological.org
Web Site: www.archaeological.org

FOUNDED: 1879

AREAS OF INTEREST:
Archaeological research and publication.

NAME(S) OF PROGRAMS:
● **Harriet and Leon Pomerance Fellowship**

TYPE:
Fellowships. Awarded to support a person on an individual project of a scholarly nature relating to Aegean Bronze Age Archaeology. Preference will be given to candidates whose project requires travel to the Mediterranean for the purpose stated above.

YEAR PROGRAM STARTED: 1972

PURPOSE:
To promote serious scholarly study of Aegean Bronze Age Archaeology.

LEGAL BASIS:
Nonprofit, scientific and educational organization.

ELIGIBILITY:
Applicants must be citizens or permanent residents of the U.S. or Canada, or be

actively pursuing an advanced degree at a North American college or university. Applicants must have been AIA members in good standing for at least two consecutive years before the application deadline. Previous Harriet Pomerance Fellows are not eligible.

At the conclusion of the fellowship tenure, the recipient must submit a report on the use of the stipend to the president of the Institute.

FINANCIAL DATA:
Amount of support per award: $5,000.
Total amount of support: $5,000.

NO. MOST RECENT APPLICANTS: 5.

NO. AWARDS: 1.

APPLICATION INFO:
Official application materials are available online in August of each year. Graduate transcript(s), two letters of reference, and a summary statement of proposed project are required. Applications for the fellowship can be submitted electronically.

Duration: Work to be conducted between July 1 of the award year and the following June 30.

Deadline: November 1. Announcement by February 1.

ADDRESS INQUIRIES TO:
Laurel Nilsen Sparks
Lecture and Fellowship Coordinator
(See address above.)

ARCHAEOLOGICAL INSTITUTE OF AMERICA   [320]
44 Beacon Street
Boston, MA 02108
(857) 305-9360
Fax: (857) 233-4270
E-mail: fellowships@archaeological.org
Web Site: www.archaeological.org

FOUNDED: 1879

AREAS OF INTEREST:
Archaeological research and publication.

NAME(S) OF PROGRAMS:
● **Jane C. Waldbaum Archaeological Field School Scholarship**

TYPE:
Scholarships. Award to support participation in an archaeological excavation or survey project.

YEAR PROGRAM STARTED: 2006

ELIGIBILITY:
Open to junior and senior undergraduates or first-year graduate students. Applicants cannot previously have participated in archaeological excavation and must be at least a junior at the time of application. Applicants must be enrolled in a college or university in the U.S. or Canada, but do not have to be U.S. citizens or residents.

FINANCIAL DATA:
Amount of support per award: $1,000.
Total amount of support: Varies.

NO. MOST RECENT APPLICANTS: Over 80.

NO. AWARDS: 8 for the year 2019.

APPLICATION INFO:
All applications must be submitted electronically through the AIA web site. Required materials include the application form, two letters of reference, official

transcript(s) and a letter of acceptance from the field school. All application materials must be received by the deadline.

Duration: Minimum one-month stay at the field school. Nonrenewable.

Deadline: March 1.

ADDRESS INQUIRIES TO:
Laurel Nilsen Sparks
Lecture and Fellowship Coordinator
(See address above.)

ARCHAEOLOGICAL INSTITUTE OF AMERICA   [321]
44 Beacon Street
Boston, MA 02108
(857) 305-9360
Fax: (857) 233-4270
E-mail: fellowships@archaeological.org
Web Site: www.archaeological.org

FOUNDED: 1879

AREAS OF INTEREST:
Archaeological research and publication.

NAME(S) OF PROGRAMS:
● **Anna C. and Oliver C. Colburn Fellowship**

TYPE:
Fellowships. Awarded to an applicant every other year contingent upon his or her acceptance as an incoming Associate Member or Student Associate Member of the American School of Classical Studies at Athens, Greece.

YEAR PROGRAM STARTED: 1991

PURPOSE:
To support studies at the American School of Classical Studies at Athens, Greece.

LEGAL BASIS:
Nonprofit, scientific and educational organization.

ELIGIBILITY:
Applicants must be U.S. or Canadian citizens or permanent residents, or those who are actively pursuing an advanced degree at a North American college or university, who are at the predoctoral stage or who have recently received the Ph.D. degree (within five years of the date of application). They must apply concurrently to the American School for Senior Associate Membership or Student Associate Membership. Applicants may not be Members of the American School during the year of application.

Applicants must have been AIA members in good standing for at least two consecutive years (one year for graduate students) before the application deadline.

The fellowship recipient is required to submit a report on the use of the stipend both to the President of the Archaeological Institute of America and to the Director of the American School of Classical Studies at Athens at the conclusion of the tenure of the fellowship.

FINANCIAL DATA:
Amount of support per award: $5,500.
Total amount of support: $11,000.

NO. MOST RECENT APPLICANTS: 8.

NO. AWARDS: 2.

APPLICATION INFO:
Official application materials are available on the web site. Graduate transcript(s), three letters of reference, and a summary statement of the proposed project are required. Candidates must apply concurrently to the

American School for Senior Associate Membership or Student Associate Membership.

Duration: Work to be conducted between July 1 of the award year and the following June 30.

Deadline: January 15, 2020 and every other year thereafter.

ADDRESS INQUIRIES TO:
Laurel Nilsen Sparks
Lecture and Fellowship Coordinator
(See address above.)

*SPECIAL STIPULATIONS:
After the tenure of their fellowship, all fellows are expected to submit an abstract to the Program Committee within two years, in accordance with that committee's guidelines, in order to present a paper on their research at the Institute annual meeting.

THE AUSTRALIAN NATIONAL UNIVERSITY [322]
Humanities Research Centre
Sir Roland Wilson Building
120 McCoy Circuit
Acton A.C.T. 2601 Australia
(61) 02 6125 4357
E-mail: hrc@anu.edu.au
Web Site: hrc.cass.anu.edu.au

FOUNDED: 1973

AREAS OF INTEREST:
European thought and culture, their influence overseas, any area of research in the humanities (broadly interpreted), and human rights.

NAME(S) OF PROGRAMS:
● **Visiting Fellows Program**

TYPE:
Conferences/seminars; Fellowships. Visiting Fellowships are offered with a grant, without a grant or with a partial grant.

YEAR PROGRAM STARTED: 1973

PURPOSE:
To stimulate research in the humanities throughout Australia.

LEGAL BASIS:
Integral part of the Australian National University, Research School of Humanities.

ELIGIBILITY:
Applicants must have an institutional affiliation to a university or equivalent research or cultural organization, and generally have at least a higher research degree, research experience, and publications.

FINANCIAL DATA:
Visiting Fellowships provide accommodation for up to 12 weeks plus airfare.
Total amount of support: Up to $150,000 (AUD) annually.

NO. AWARDS: Approximately 12 to 18.

APPLICATION INFO:
Applicants should submit a completed application form, curriculum vitae, and a list of publications and/or professional activities. A one- to two-page description of the proposed project must be submitted, along with the title of the research project. Applicants need to identify and provide the Referees' Comments Form to two or three referees who will support the application. Referees should submit their confidential comments separately to the Senior Administrator on the form provided no later than May 31.

Duration: Six to 12 weeks.
Deadline: May 31. Award announcement by June 30.

PUBLICATIONS:
Annual report; descriptive brochure; journal; application guidelines; forms and HRC bulletin.

ADDRESS INQUIRIES TO:
Professor Will Christie
Head, Humanities Research Centre
Tel: (61) 02 6125 0151
E-mail: william.christie@anu.edu.au

JOHN CARTER BROWN LIBRARY
Brown University
94 George Street
Providence, RI 02906
(401) 863-2725
Fax: (401) 863-3477
E-mail: jcb-fellowships@brown.edu
Web Site: www.jcbl.org

TYPE:
Fellowships. The John Carter Brown Library (JCB), an independently funded institution for advanced research at Brown University, contains one of the world's premier collections of primary materials related to the discovery, exploration, and settlement of the New World to 1825, including books, maps, newspapers and other printed objects.

The Library offers both Short-term and Long-term Fellowships.

See entry 537 for full listing.

CANADIAN FEDERATION FOR THE HUMANITIES AND SOCIAL SCIENCES
141 Laurier Avenue West
Suite 200
Ottawa ON K1P 5J3 Canada
(613) 238-6112 ext. 319
Fax: (613) 238-6114
E-mail: aspp-paes@ideas-idees.ca
Web Site: www.ideas-idees.ca

TYPE:
Grants-in-aid. Grants to support the publication of scholarly books in the social sciences and humanities.

See entry 1679 for full listing.

CANADIAN INSTITUTE IN GREECE/L'INSTITUT CANADIEN EN GRECE [323]
Brock University, Department of Classics
1812 Sir Isaac Brock Way
St. Catharines ON L2S 3A1 Canada
(905) 688-5550 ext. 3798
Fax: (905) 984-4859
E-mail: rsmith@brocku.ca
Web Site: www.cig-icg.gr

FOUNDED: 1974

AREAS OF INTEREST:
Modern Greek, classical languages and literatures, history, archaeology, history of art and music.

NAME(S) OF PROGRAMS:
● **Elizabeth Alfoldi-Rosenbaum Fellowship**
● **Neda and Franz Leipen Fellowship**
● **Schaus Internship Bursary**

● **Homer and Dorothy Thompson Fellowship**
● **Frederick E. and Joan Winter Student Travel Bursary**

TYPE:
Fellowships; Internships; Travel grants. Intended to support the graduate work of a person who needs to study in Greece.

YEAR PROGRAM STARTED: 1974

PURPOSE:
To promote the study of classical languages and literatures, history, archaeology, history of art and music in Greece.

LEGAL BASIS:
Incorporated in Canada and Greece.

ELIGIBILITY:
Open to Canadian citizens or landed immigrants.

FINANCIAL DATA:
Amount of support per award: Fellowships: $9,000 (CAN) plus housing at the Institute; Bursaries: $2,000 (CAN).
Total amount of support: Varies each year.

NO. MOST RECENT APPLICANTS: 2 to 3.

NO. AWARDS: Bursaries: 2; Fellowships: 1.

APPLICATION INFO:
Applicants must write, enclosing a curriculum vitae and an outline of the proposed research. Applicants must also arrange for three referees to send letters to the chair of the Fellowships Committee.
Duration: Bursaries: Three months. Fellowships: Nine months.
Deadline: March 1. All fellowships are not offered every year.

PUBLICATIONS:
CIG Bulletin, semi-annually.

STAFF:
Prof. Jacques Y. Perreault, Director
Dr. Jonathan E. Tomlinson, Assistant Director

ADDRESS INQUIRIES TO:
E-mail: info@cig-icg.gr

CENTER FOR HELLENIC STUDIES [324]
3100 Whitehaven Street, N.W.
Washington, DC 20008
(202) 745-4400
Fax: (202) 797-8650
E-mail: fellowships@chs.harvard.edu
Web Site: www.chs.harvard.edu

FOUNDED: 1961

AREAS OF INTEREST:
Postdoctoral ancient Greek studies.

TYPE:
Fellowships; Residencies; Visiting scholars. The Center offers Residential Fellowships to scholars working on various aspects of ancient Greek civilization. Eligible fields of research include archaeology, art history, epigraphy, history, literary criticism, philology, philosophy, pedagogical applications and interdisciplinary research.

YEAR PROGRAM STARTED: 1961

PURPOSE:
To encourage research in Hellenic studies.

LEGAL BASIS:
A unit of Harvard University.

ELIGIBILITY:
Investigators holding a Ph.D. degree or equivalent are eligible to apply. Professional competence in ancient Greek, as evidenced by publication, is essential.

FINANCIAL DATA:
Residential fellowships provide a stipend (maximum $17,000) plus lodging.

NO. MOST RECENT APPLICANTS: 75.

NO. AWARDS: Varies.

APPLICATION INFO:
Official application materials are available on the web site.

Duration: Support is available for a nine-month period beginning September 1 and ending May 31. Fellowships are available for varying periods (four to 16 weeks) in the spring or the fall.

Deadline: October.

PUBLICATIONS:
Application form and guidelines.

STAFF:
Gregory Nagy, Director

ADDRESS INQUIRIES TO:
Lanah Koelle
Fellowship Program Manager
(See address above.)

CENTER FOR MEDIEVAL AND RENAISSANCE STUDIES   [325]
University of California, Los Angeles
302 Royce Hall
Box 951485
Los Angeles, CA 90095-1485
(310) 825-1880
Fax: (310) 825-0655
E-mail: cmrs@humnet.ucla.edu
Web Site: www.cmrs.ucla.edu

FOUNDED: 1963

AREAS OF INTEREST:
All aspects related to the Medieval and Renaissance periods.

NAME(S) OF PROGRAMS:
- **Ahmanson Research Fellowships for the Study of Medieval and Renaissance Books and Manuscripts**
- **CMRS Conference Travel Grants**
- **CMRS Research and Study Travel Grants**
- **The George T. and Margaret W. Romani Fellowship**
- **Lynn and Maude White Fellowship**

TYPE:
Fellowships; Research grants; Travel grants.

PURPOSE:
To promote interdisciplinary and cross-cultural studies of modern civilization in its formative period between the fourth and mid-17th centuries and to provide added research opportunities, facilities and assistance.

LEGAL BASIS:
Nonprofit university research organization.

ELIGIBILITY:
Requirements vary by program. Applicants are advised to consult the CMRS web site for specific details.

FINANCIAL DATA:
Amount of support per award: Ahmanson Research Fellowships: A stipend of $2,500 per month for fellowships lasting up to three

months; CMRS Travel Grants: Varies; Romani Fellowship: $20,000 per year; Lynn and Maude White Fellowship: $20,000.

CO-OP FUNDING PROGRAMS: Ahmanson Research Fellowships are offered through the generosity of the Ahmanson Foundation, the UCLA Center for Medieval and Renaissance Studies (CMRS) and the UCLA Library Special Collections (LSC).

NO. AWARDS: Ahmanson Research Fellowships and CMRS Travel Grants: Varies; Romani Fellowship and Lynn and Maude White Fellowship: 1 every other year.

APPLICATION INFO:
Instructions vary by program. Applicants are advised to review the CMRS web site for specific details.

Duration: Ahmanson Research Fellowships: Up to three months. Lynn and Maude White Fellowship and Romani Fellowship: One year.

Deadline: Varies by program. Applicants are advised to review the CMRS web site for specific details.

PUBLICATIONS:
Viator, annual journal; *Comitatus*, graduate journal; *Cursor Mundi*, book series.

STAFF:
Zrinka Stahuljak, Director
Karen E. Burgess, Assistant Director
Benay Furtivo, Financial Analyst
Brett Landenberger, Programmer Analyst
Heather Sottong, Publications Manager
Erin Romo, Program Coordinator

ADDRESS INQUIRIES TO:
Karen E. Burgess, Assistant Director
(See address above.)

CENTER FOR 17TH AND 18TH CENTURY STUDIES   [326]
University of California, Los Angeles
10745 Dickson Plaza, 302 Royce Hall
Los Angeles, CA 90095-1404
(310) 206-8552
Fax: (310) 206-8577
E-mail: c1718cs@humnet.ucla.edu
Web Site: www.1718.ucla.edu/research/

FOUNDED: 1985

AREAS OF INTEREST:
England between 1640 and 1830 (history, language and literature, religion and theology), Oscar Wilde and the 1890s, and modern fine printing.

NAME(S) OF PROGRAMS:
- **Short-Term Research Fellowships**

TYPE:
Fellowships. Short-term (one to three months) postdoctoral fellowships for research in residence for any period of the year (July 1 through June 30) at the William Andrews Clark Memorial Library on specific subjects relevant to the collections and interests of the Library.

YEAR PROGRAM STARTED: 1985

PURPOSE:
To provide support for research in the humanities.

LEGAL BASIS:
University.

ELIGIBILITY:
Candidates must have received the Doctorate prior to appointment.

FINANCIAL DATA:
Amount of support per award: $3,000 per month.
Total amount of support: Varies.

NO. AWARDS: Varies.

APPLICATION INFO:
Applicants must submit:
(1) a curriculum vitae (maximum of three pages, including bibliography of published and unpublished scholarly work) and;
(2) a project proposal (maximum 1,000 words, double-spaced, including bibliography of Clark materials relevant to the project).

In addition to the information provided on the application form, applicants must arrange for three scholarly references to be submitted directly to the Center.

Duration: One to three months. Nonrenewable.

Deadline: February 1 of each year.

PUBLICATIONS:
Application guidelines; brochure on the Center and Library and its holdings; biennial newsletters; proceedings of conferences.

OFFICERS:
Candis Snoddy, Assistant Director

ADDRESS INQUIRIES TO:
Myrna Ortiz, Fellowship Coordinator
(See address above.)

CENTER FOR 17TH AND 18TH CENTURY STUDIES   [327]
University of California, Los Angeles
10745 Dickson Plaza, 302 Royce Hall
Los Angeles, CA 90095-1404
(310) 206-8552
Fax: (310) 206-8577
E-mail: c1718cs@humnet.ucla.edu
Web Site: www.1718.ucla.edu/research/

FOUNDED: 1985

AREAS OF INTEREST:
England between 1640 and 1830 (history, language and literature, religion and theology), Oscar Wilde and the 1890s, and modern fine printing.

NAME(S) OF PROGRAMS:
- **Clark Predoctoral Fellowships**

TYPE:
Fellowships. Offered for one to three consecutive months during the period July 1 through June 30 to registered University of California doctoral candidates whose dissertation project is on a specific subject relevant to the collections and interests of the Clark Library.

YEAR PROGRAM STARTED: 1990

PURPOSE:
To provide support for research in the humanities.

LEGAL BASIS:
University.

ELIGIBILITY:
Advanced, registered University of California doctoral candidates are eligible.

GEOG. RESTRICTIONS: California.

FINANCIAL DATA:
Amount of support per award: $3,000 per month for one to three months.

APPLICATION INFO:
Applicants must submit:
(1) a curriculum vitae (maximum of three

pages, including a bibliography of published and unpublished scholarly work) and;
(2) a project proposal (maximum 1,000 words, double-spaced, including a bibliography of Clark materials relevant to the project).

In addition to the information provided on the application form, applicants must arrange for three scholarly references to be submitted directly to the Center.

Duration: One to three months. Nonrenewable.

Deadline: February 1 of each year.

PUBLICATIONS:
Application guidelines; brochure on the Center and Library and its holdings; biennial newsletters; proceedings of conferences.

OFFICERS:
Candis Snoddy, Assistant Director

ADDRESS INQUIRIES TO:
Myrna Ortiz, Fellowship Coordinator (See address above.)

CENTER FOR 17TH AND 18TH CENTURY STUDIES   [328]
University of California, Los Angeles
10745 Dickson Plaza, 302 Royce Hall
Los Angeles, CA 90095-1404
(310) 206-8552
Fax: (310) 206-8577
E-mail: c1718cs@humnet.ucla.edu
Web Site: www.1718.ucla.edu/research/

FOUNDED: 1985

AREAS OF INTEREST:
England between 1640 and 1750 (history, language and literature, religion and theology), Oscar Wilde and the 1890s, and modern fine printing.

NAME(S) OF PROGRAMS:
● **ASECS/Clark Library Fellowships**

TYPE:
Fellowships. Postdoctoral fellowships for research in residence for a period of one month any time from July 1 through June 30 at the William Andrews Clark Memorial Library on a project in The Restoration or 18th century.

YEAR PROGRAM STARTED: 1985

PURPOSE:
To provide support for research in the humanities.

LEGAL BASIS:
University.

ELIGIBILITY:
Candidates must:
(1) have received the Doctorate prior to appointment;
(2) be members in good standing of the American Society for Eighteenth-Century Studies and;
(3) be working on a project in The Restoration or the eighteenth century.

FINANCIAL DATA:
Amount of support per award: $3,000 for one month.

APPLICATION INFO:
Applicants must submit:
(1) a curriculum vitae (maximum of three pages, including a bibliography of published and unpublished scholarly work) and;
(2) a project proposal (maximum 1,000

words, double-spaced, including a bibliography of Clark materials relevant to the project).

In addition to the information provided on the application form, applicants must arrange for three scholarly references to be submitted directly to the Center.

Duration: One month. Nonrenewable.

Deadline: February 1 of each year.

PUBLICATIONS:
Application guidelines; brochure on the Center and Library and its holdings; biennial newsletters; proceedings of conferences.

OFFICERS:
Candis Snoddy, Assistant Director

ADDRESS INQUIRIES TO:
Myrna Ortiz, Fellowship Coordinator (See address above.)

CENTER FOR 17TH AND 18TH CENTURY STUDIES   [329]
University of California, Los Angeles
10745 Dickson Plaza, 302 Royce Hall
Los Angeles, CA 90095-1404
(310) 206-8552
Fax: (310) 206-8577
E-mail: c1718cs@humnet.ucla.edu
Web Site: www.1718.ucla.edu/research/

FOUNDED: 1985

AREAS OF INTEREST:
England between 1640 and 1830 (history, language and literature, religion and theology), Oscar Wilde and the 1890s, and modern fine printing.

NAME(S) OF PROGRAMS:
● **Ahmanson and Getty Postdoctoral Fellowships**

TYPE:
Fellowships. With the support of the Ahmanson Foundation of Los Angeles and the J. Paul Getty Trust, the UCLA Center for 17th- and 18th-Century Studies and the William Andrews Clark Memorial Library have a theme-based fellowship program to encourage the participation of junior scholars in the Center's cross-disciplinary, comparative research projects. The major theme for a given year is announced the preceding fall.

Participating fellows will be expected to make a substantive contribution to program seminars.

YEAR PROGRAM STARTED: 1992

PURPOSE:
To provide support for research in the humanities.

LEGAL BASIS:
University.

ELIGIBILITY:
Candidates must have received their Ph.D. in the last six years prior to application and be engaged in research pertaining to the theme.

FINANCIAL DATA:
Amount of support per award: Stipend of $50,760 plus paid medical benefits for scholar and dependents for the academic year.

APPLICATION INFO:
Applicants must submit:
(1) a curriculum vitae (maximum of three pages, including bibliography of published and unpublished scholarly work) and;

(2) a project proposal (maximum 1,000 words, double-spaced, including a bibliography of Clark materials relevant to the project).

In addition to the information provided on the application form, applicants must arrange for three scholarly references to be submitted directly to the Center.

Duration: Three academic quarters. Nonrenewable.

Deadline: February 1 of each year preceding the award.

PUBLICATIONS:
Application guidelines; brochure on the Center and Library and its holdings; fellowships brochure; biennial newsletters; proceedings of conferences.

OFFICERS:
Candis Snoddy, Assistant Director

ADDRESS INQUIRIES TO:
Myrna Ortiz, Fellowship Coordinator (See address above.)

CENTER FOR THE HUMANITIES   [330]
Mellon Postdoctoral Fellowship Program
Wesleyan University
95 Pearl Street
Middletown, CT 06459-0069
(860) 685-3044
Fax: (860) 685-2171
E-mail: esavage@wesleyan.edu
Web Site: www.wesleyan.edu/humanities

FOUNDED: 1959

AREAS OF INTEREST:
The Center aims to explore fresh and vital aspects of the humanities, to realize an interdisciplinary response to human problems and to generate new possibilities for curricular reform. In fulfilling these aims, the Center must also examine the assumptions that underlie academic disciplines and humanistic theories. It must encourage research as well as the fundamental discourse of teachers and students.

NAME(S) OF PROGRAMS:
● **Andrew W. Mellon Postdoctoral Fellowship**

TYPE:
Fellowships. The aims of the Center are reflected in its constituency which includes scholars, artists, public figures and students. Fellows range in age and achievement from undergraduates to the most eminent humanists. Departments at Wesleyan University participating in the Center include Classics, Modern Languages and Literatures, English, the College of Letters, Philosophy, History, Religion, Anthropology, Psychology and the Fine Arts.

PURPOSE:
To promote advanced study and research in the humanities, arts and qualitative social sciences; to provide scholars who have lately completed their Ph.Ds. with free time to further their own work in a cross-disciplinary setting, and to associate them with a distinguished faculty.

LEGAL BASIS:
Grant from Andrew W. Mellon Foundation to Wesleyan University.

ELIGIBILITY:
Scholars who have received their Ph.D. degree after June 2015 in any field of inquiry

in the humanities or humanistic social sciences - broadly conceived - are invited to apply.

Fellows will be expected to participate in the lectures, colloquia and discussion groups that are organized each semester around a specific theme chosen for its theoretical interest and its pertinence to crucial problems in related disciplines of the humanities, the qualitative social sciences or the arts. Additional duties of the fellows will be to teach one course and to give one public lecture.

Fellow must reside in Middletown, CT for tenure of fellowship.

FINANCIAL DATA:
Amount of support per award: $55,000.

CO-OP FUNDING PROGRAMS: Andrew W. Mellon Foundation.

NO. MOST RECENT APPLICANTS: Over 600.

NO. AWARDS: 1 to 2 each year.

APPLICATION INFO:
There is no official application form. Applications should include:
(1) a letter from the applicant, including a statement of current research interests and a brief proposal for a one-semester undergraduate course related to the Center for the Humanities theme;
(2) a full curriculum vitae;
(3) three letters of recommendation and;
(4) copies of published work, extracts from the dissertation, or drafts of work in progress (not to exceed 25 pages).
Duration: Two years.

PUBLICATIONS:
Brochure.

ADDRESS INQUIRIES TO:
Natasha Korda, Director
(See address above.)

CONNECTICUT HUMANITIES   [331]
100 Riverview Center, Suite 270
292 Main Street
Middletown, CT 06457
(860) 937-6535
E-mail: swands@cthumanities.org
Web Site: cthumanities.org

FOUNDED: 1973

AREAS OF INTEREST:
Humanities in Connecticut, heritage and reading.

NAME(S) OF PROGRAMS:
• **Connecticut Humanities Fund**

TYPE:
Project/program grants. Capacity building grants.

YEAR PROGRAM STARTED: 1973

PURPOSE:
To create opportunities to think, learn and understand more about ourselves, our communities and our state.

ELIGIBILITY:
Applicants must be incorporated as private, nonprofit organizations or municipalities in Connecticut, and must regularly provide service to the public.

GEOG. RESTRICTIONS: Connecticut.

FINANCIAL DATA:
Amount of support per award: $250 to $35,000.

Total amount of support: $700,000 for the year 2019.

Matching fund requirements: All Connecticut Humanities Fund grants must be matched dollar for dollar through a combination of in-kind contributions and/or cash offered by applicants, partners, and/or third parties, i.e., grants or bequests. Funds from the State of Connecticut may not be used for matching purposes.

CO-OP FUNDING PROGRAMS: Hartford Foundation for Public Giving.

NO. MOST RECENT APPLICANTS: 142 for the year 2019.

NO. AWARDS: 76 for the year 2019.

REPRESENTATIVE AWARDS:
$20,000 to Lockwood Mathews Mansion Museum for implementing an exhibition entitled "What Is It? Technologies and Discoveries of the Victorian Era;" $13,700 to Noah Webster House to develop an electronic tablet-guided tour that combines storytelling, interpretive illustrations and new technologies to tell the story of Noah Webster's life and times.

APPLICATION INFO:
Preapplication discussion with CTH staff is required two months before submission of formal application. Specify the grant line and program category when submitting proposal.
Duration: Nine months to two years.
Deadline: For quick grants: Every other month; For grants over $5,000: November and April.

STAFF:
Scott Wands, Manager, Grants and Programs

ADDRESS INQUIRIES TO:
Scott Wands, Manager
Grants and Programs
(See address above.)

CORNELL UNIVERSITY   [332]
Society for the Humanities
A.D. White House
121 Presidents Drive
Ithaca, NY 14853-1101
(607) 255-9274
(607) 255-4086
Fax: (607) 255-1422
E-mail: humctr@cornell.edu
Web Site: societyhumanities.as.cornell.edu/fellowships

FOUNDED: 1966

AREAS OF INTEREST:
Postdoctoral fellowships in the humanities.

NAME(S) OF PROGRAMS:
• **Mellon Postdoctoral Fellowships**

TYPE:
Fellowships. Postdoctoral teaching-research fellowships in the humanities, each awarded for a two-year period. While in residence at Cornell, postdoctoral fellows hold department affiliation and have limited teaching duties and the opportunity for scholarly work.

PURPOSE:
To encourage the academic growth of promising humanists with recent Ph.D. degrees.

LEGAL BASIS:
University.

ELIGIBILITY:
Applicants who will receive the Ph.D. degree by June 30 of the beginning program year are eligible to apply. Such applicants must include a letter of confirmation.

International scholars are welcome to apply.

FINANCIAL DATA:
Fellows receive stipend while in residence.
Amount of support per award: $53,000 per year.
Total amount of support: Varies.

CO-OP FUNDING PROGRAMS: Funded by a grant from the Andrew W. Mellon Foundation.

NO. MOST RECENT APPLICANTS: 150.

NO. AWARDS: 2 per year.

APPLICATION INFO:
Application procedures are found on the web site. Application materials must be uploaded to Academic Jobs Online.

If the applicant does not have a Ph.D. in hand at the time of application, a letter of confirmation must be received from applicant's committee chair or department stating that applicant will have the Ph.D. degree before the term of the fellowship begins on August 1 of the beginning program year.
Duration: Two years.
Deadline: Varies.

ADDRESS INQUIRIES TO:
Emily Parsons, Program Manager
Mellon Postdoctoral Fellowships
(See address above.)

CORNELL UNIVERSITY   [333]
Society for the Humanities
A.D. White House
121 Presidents Drive
Ithaca, NY 14853-1101
(607) 255-9274
(607) 255-4086
Fax: (607) 255-1422
E-mail: humctr@cornell.edu
Web Site: societyhumanities.as.cornell.edu/fellowships

FOUNDED: 1966

AREAS OF INTEREST:
Humanities studies.

NAME(S) OF PROGRAMS:
• **Society for the Humanities Fellowships**

TYPE:
Fellowships. Yearly fellowships with a new focal theme each year. Fellows include scholars from other universities and members of the Cornell faculty released from regular duties. Fellows spend most of their time in research and offer one course related to their research.

YEAR PROGRAM STARTED: 1966

PURPOSE:
To support research and encourage imaginative teaching in the humanities.

LEGAL BASIS:
University.

ELIGIBILITY:
Applicants must have received the Ph.D. degree before January 1 of the year of their application. They must have one or more years of teaching experience, which may include teaching as a graduate student. Fellows should be working on topics related to the year's theme. Their approach to the

humanities should be broad enough to appeal to students and scholars in several humanistic disciplines.

International scholars are welcome to apply.

FINANCIAL DATA:
Amount of support per award: $52,000 stipend.
Total amount of support: Varies.

NO. MOST RECENT APPLICANTS: 200.

NO. AWARDS: 6 to 8 each year.

APPLICATION INFO:
Application guidelines are available on the Society's web site. All application materials, including letters of recommendation, must be submitted via Academic Jobs Online.
Duration: One academic year.
Deadline: October 1 of the year prior to the beginning of the fellowship. Awards are announced by the end of December of that year of application.

PUBLICATIONS:
Brochure.

ADDRESS INQUIRIES TO:
Kina Viola, Program Coordinator
Society for the Humanities
(See address above.)

*SPECIAL STIPULATIONS:
Fellows spend their time in research and writing, participate in the weekly Fellows Seminar, and offer one seminar related to their research.

GLADYS KRIEBLE DELMAS FOUNDATION   [334]

275 Madison Avenue
Suite 2102
New York, NY 10016-1101
(212) 687-0011
Fax: (212) 687-1470
E-mail: info@delmas.org
Web Site: www.delmas.org

FOUNDED: 1976

AREAS OF INTEREST:
Humanities, research libraries, performing arts and research in the history and culture of Venice and the Veneto.

NAME(S) OF PROGRAMS:
● **Humanities Program**
● **Performing Arts Program**
● **Research Library Program**
● **Venetian Research Program**

TYPE:
Fellowships; General operating grants; Project/program grants; Research grants.

YEAR PROGRAM STARTED: 1977

PURPOSE:
To provide grants for research projects in Venice and the Veneto; to support performing arts organizations in New York and research libraries and humanities projects.

LEGAL BASIS:
Private foundation.

ELIGIBILITY:
For Venetian Research Program, applicants must be U.S. citizens or permanent residents at the predoctoral and postdoctoral levels. If graduate students, applicants must have fulfilled all doctoral requirements except for completion of the dissertation at the time of application.

GEOG. RESTRICTIONS: Performing Arts Grants to New York City only.

FINANCIAL DATA:
Amount of support per award: Up to $20,000.

NO. MOST RECENT APPLICANTS: 300.

NO. AWARDS: 150.

REPRESENTATIVE AWARDS:
$17,000 to the American Academy in Rome, New York, NY, for the preservation, cataloging and stabilization of material in the Photographic Archive; $15,000 to the Brooklyn Academy of Music, Brooklyn, NY, for BAM Hamm Archives in 2016; $15,000 to The New School, New York, NY, for the Journal Donation Project; $5,000 to Words Without Borders, New York, NY, for expansion and promotion of campus.

APPLICATION INFO:
Applications are submitted using the Foundation's online portal.
Duration: Varies.
Deadline: Venetian Research Program: December 15.

TRUSTEES:
James S. Grub
Joseph C. Mitchell
Deirdre C. Stam

DISTRICT OF COLUMBIA COMMISSION ON THE ARTS AND HUMANITIES

200 I Street, S.E.
Washington, DC 20003
(202) 724-5613
Fax: (202) 727-4135
TDD: (202) 727-3148
E-mail: heran.sereke-brhan2@dc.gov
Web Site: dcarts.dc.gov

TYPE:
Awards/prizes; Capital grants; Challenge/matching grants; Conferences/seminars; Exchange programs; Fellowships; General operating grants; Grants-in-aid; Project/program grants; Research grants; Residencies. Services provided to arts institutions and individual artists including inquiry services, technical assistance and funding.

See entry 409 for full listing.

DUMBARTON OAKS   [335]

1703 32nd Street, N.W.
Washington, DC 20007
(202) 339-6400
(202) 339-6413
Fax: (202) 339-6416
E-mail: FellowshipPrograms@doaks.org
Web Site: www.doaks.org

FOUNDED: 1940

AREAS OF INTEREST:
Archaeology, gardens, history, history of art, philosophy, landscape, language, literature, religion and theology.

NAME(S) OF PROGRAMS:
● **Fellowships and Project Grants in Byzantine Studies, Pre-Columbian Studies and Garden and Landscape Studies**

TYPE:
Awards/prizes; Fellowships; Internships; Project/program grants; Residencies. Residential fellowships and project support in the area of Byzantine studies (including related aspects of late Roman, early

Christian, western medieval, Slavic and Near Eastern studies), Pre-Columbian studies (of Mexico, Central America and Andean South America), and Garden and Landscape studies (including garden history, landscape architecture and related disciplines).

YEAR PROGRAM STARTED: 1941

PURPOSE:
To promote research in the Humanities, with a focus on Byzantine studies, Pre-Columbian studies, and Garden and Landscape studies.

LEGAL BASIS:
Research institute affiliated with Harvard University.

ELIGIBILITY:
Fellowships are awarded on the basis of demonstrated scholarly ability and preparation of the candidate, including knowledge of the requisite languages, interest and value of the study or project and the project's relevance to the resources of Dumbarton Oaks.

Junior Fellowships are awarded to degree candidates who at the time of application have fulfilled all preliminary requirements for a Ph.D. or appropriate final degree and plan to work on a dissertation or final project at Dumbarton Oaks under the direction of a faculty member from their own university.

Fellowships are awarded to scholars who hold a Ph.D. or appropriate final degree or have established themselves in their field and wish to pursue their own research. Graduate students who expect to have a Ph.D. prior to taking up residence at Dumbarton Oaks may also apply.

Summer Fellowships are awarded to Byzantine, Pre-Columbian, or Garden and Landscape scholars on any level beyond the first year of graduate (post-Baccalaureate) study.

FINANCIAL DATA:
Fellowships and Junior Fellowships: Award includes stipend, housing (with the exception of residents from the greater Washington, DC metropolitan area), a research expense allowance, lunch on weekdays, and a health insurance contribution from Dumbarton Oaks. Travel expense reimbursement may be provided for Fellows and Junior Fellows if support cannot be obtained from other sources.

Summer Fellowships: Besides maintenance allowance, support includes housing in a Dumbarton Oaks apartment, lunch on weekdays, Dumbarton Oaks's health insurance contribution, and travel expense reimbursement if other travel support cannot be obtained. No housing allowances or dependents' allowances for families are available in the summer.

Amount of support per award: Support includes a stipend of approximately $21,000 for a Junior Fellow; $35,000 stipend for a Fellow for the full academic year.

A maintenance allowance of $250 per week for Summer Fellowships.

NO. MOST RECENT APPLICANTS: 252.

NO. AWARDS: 42 Fellowships (20 in Byzantine Studies, 11 in Garden and Landscape Studies, including the Mellon Fellowship in Urban Landscape Studies, and 11 in Pre-Columbian Studies); 7 Project Grants for the year 2018-19.

APPLICATION INFO:
Applications must be submitted electronically. A brochure is available upon request to the Director's office. Additional information can be found online.

Duration: Fellowships are usually awarded for a full academic year (mid-September to mid-May); however, requests for a single term of support (mid-September to early January or mid-January to mid-May) are also considered. Summer Fellowships are awarded for periods of seven to nine weeks, beginning early June and ending early August.

Deadline: Varies. Contact Dumbarton Oaks for detailed information.

PUBLICATIONS:
Fellowship and Project award brochure; application guidelines.

OFFICERS:
Jan Ziolkowski, Director

ADDRESS INQUIRIES TO:
E-mail specific program:
Byzantine@doaks.org
Pre-Columbian@doaks.org or
Landscape@doaks.org

*SPECIAL STIPULATIONS:
Fellowships are tenable only for full-time resident work.

DUQUESNE UNIVERSITY, DEPARTMENT OF PHILOSOPHY   [336]
600 Forbes Avenue
Pittsburgh, PA 15282
(412) 396-6500
Fax: (412) 396-5353
E-mail: polansky@duq.edu
Web Site: www.duq.
edu/academics/schools/liberal-arts/graduate-school/programs/philosophy

FOUNDED: 1878

AREAS OF INTEREST:
The Ph.D. program in the Department of Philosophy at Duquesne University emphasizes continental philosophy, i.e., phenomenology and 20th century French and German philosophy, as well as the history of philosophy.

NAME(S) OF PROGRAMS:
● **Duquesne University Graduate Assistantship**

TYPE:
Assistantships; Conferences/seminars; Exchange programs. Philosophy assistantship.

PURPOSE:
To provide a stipend to enable students to obtain a Ph.D. in philosophy.

ELIGIBILITY:
Open to holders of a Bachelor's degree in philosophy, or its equivalent, who have a grade point average of at least 3.7 and an excellent graduate record examination score. Candidates should have knowledge of a second language.

FINANCIAL DATA:
Amount of support per award: Stipend of $18,000 plus all tuition for coursework.

NO. MOST RECENT APPLICANTS: 188 for the year 2019.

NO. AWARDS: 14 Ph.D. and 10 M.A. for the year 2019.

APPLICATION INFO:
Applicants must complete an application including a statement of intent and three letters of recommendation, Graduate Record Examination scores and application form and fee, plus test of English as a Foreign Language scores.

Duration: Ph.D.: Six years; M.A.: Two years.

Deadline: Ph.D. January 15; M.A. March 1.

ADDRESS INQUIRIES TO:
Ronald Polansky, Chairperson
(See address above.)

EARTHWATCH INSTITUTE
1380 Soldiers Field Road
2nd Floor
Boston, MA 02135
(800) 776-0188
E-mail: fellowshipawards@earthwatch.org
Web Site: www.earthwatch.org/education

TYPE:
Fellowships. Teachers in grades K-12 apply for seven- to 14-day Earthwatch expedition fellowships that take place during the summer. Earthwatch selects teachers from all subject areas across the U.S. to assist scientists on expeditions by collecting data on climate change and sustainable resource management. Funding for these fellowships comes from a variety of donors, e.g., individuals, corporations, family foundations, community organizations and nonprofits. On their return from the field, these teachers must develop a lesson or action plan that ties their experience back to their classroom or community.

See entry 1649 for full listing.

THE HARRY FRANK GUGGENHEIM FOUNDATION
42 West 54th Street
16th Floor
New York, NY 10019
(646) 428-0971
Fax: (646) 428-0981
E-mail: info@hfg.org
Web Site: www.hfg.org

TYPE:
Research grants. Support for projects which seek to advance and coordinate creative breakthroughs in the social and biological sciences relating to the study of violence and aggression.

See entry 1682 for full listing.

THE GWATHMEY MEMORIAL TRUST   [337]
Bank of America–Philanthropic Solutions
1800 K Street, N.W., Fifth Floor
Washington, DC 20006
(202) 442-7460
E-mail: dc.grantmaking@ustrust.com
Web Site: www.bankofamerica.com/philanthropic

FOUNDED: 1982

AREAS OF INTEREST:
Arts, culture and humanities, education, and human services.

TYPE:
Development grants; Project/program grants.

YEAR PROGRAM STARTED: 1982

ELIGIBILITY:
Grants are made to Virginia institutions and organizations which are tax-exempt 501(c)(3) organizations and operate for charitable, scientific, literary, or educational purposes. Preference is given to specific, well-defined projects and programs whose results can be evaluated.

Grants are not made to private foundations, national or community organizations, or to individuals.

GEOG. RESTRICTIONS: Virginia.

FINANCIAL DATA:
Amount of support per award: $5,000 to $60,000; Average: $15,000 to $20,000.

Total amount of support: Average $650,000 annually.

NO. AWARDS: 30 to 40.

APPLICATION INFO:
All applicants must submit a description of the organization, evidence of the organization's tax-exempt and private foundation status, financial statements, and names and affiliations of the organization's trustees, directors, advisors and principal staff. In addition, a concise description of the project including the needs and anticipated benefits to be met, detailed financial plan, brief biographical background of the person who will conduct or supervise the proposed program, plans for evaluation of the project's results, and covering letter from an official of the organization stating that the organization has formally approved the proposed program are required.

Duration: One year.

Deadline: March 1 and September 1.

PUBLICATIONS:
Guidelines for applicants.

ADDRESS INQUIRIES TO:
Lee Parker, Vice President
Philanthropic Client Manager
(See address above.)

THE HASTINGS CENTER
21 Malcolm Gordon Road
Garrison, NY 10524
(845) 424-4040
Fax: (845) 424-4545
E-mail: visitors@thehastingscenter.org
Web Site: www.thehastingscenter.org

TYPE:
Residencies; Visiting scholars. Independent study.

See entry 1923 for full listing.

HAWAII STATE FOUNDATION ON CULTURE AND THE ARTS
250 South Hotel Street
Second Floor
Honolulu, HI 96813
(808) 586-0301
Fax: (808) 586-0308
TTY: (808) 586-0740
E-mail: jonathan.johnson@hawaii.gov
Web Site: hawaii.gov/sfca

TYPE:
Project/program grants.

See entry 418 for full listing.

THE GEORGE A. AND ELIZA GARDNER HOWARD FOUNDATION

University Hall, Room 406
Brown University
One Prospect Street
Providence, RI 02912
(401) 863-2429
Fax: (401) 863-1339
E-mail: howard_foundation@brown.edu
Web Site: www.brown.edu/howard-foundation

TYPE:
Fellowships. The Foundation awards a limited number of fellowships each year for independent projects in fields selected on a rotational basis.

See entry 1475 for full listing.

HUMANITIES NEW YORK   [338]

150 Broadway
Suite 1700
New York, NY 10038
(212) 233-1131
Fax: (212) 233-4607
E-mail: info@humanitiesny.org
Web Site: humanitiesny.org

FOUNDED: 1975

AREAS OF INTEREST:
Humanities, public programs and education.

NAME(S) OF PROGRAMS:
● **Action Grants**
● **Community Conversations Program**
● **Reading and Discussion Program**
● **Vision Grants**

TYPE:
Challenge/matching grants; Project/program grants; Seed money grants. Action Grants help launch public programs that use the humanities to activate conversations within a community. Projects that encourage participants to reflect on their values, explore new ideas, and connect with others across New York state are encouraged. These grants require matching funds to demonstrate your community's investment in the project.

Community Conversations Program promotes thoughtful, engaged community dialogue, using a short text and a facilitator from the local community.

Reading and Discussion Programs are awarded to involve community members in ongoing discussions of books and ideas.

Vision Grants help groups brainstorm, connect, research, strategize, and design engaging public humanities programs. Innovation is welcomed, and projects that use the tools of the humanities (civic engagement, critical inquiry, debate, discussion, historical framing, etc.) to address contemporary issues are encouraged.

YEAR PROGRAM STARTED: 1975

PURPOSE:
To help all New Yorkers become thoughtful participants in our communities by promoting critical inquiry, cultural understanding, and civic engagement.

LEGAL BASIS:
State humanities council, nonprofit under Internal Revenue Code 501(c)(3).

ELIGIBILITY:
Tax-exempt, nonprofit 501(c)(3) organizations in New York state.

GEOG. RESTRICTIONS: New York state.

FINANCIAL DATA:
Amount of support per award: Action Grants: Typically $1,501 to $5,000; Vision Grants: Typically $500 to $1,500.

Total amount of support: $430,000.

Matching fund requirements: All Action Grants must be matched (at least dollar-for-dollar) with cash and/or in-kind contributions. Vision Grants do not require a match.

NO. MOST RECENT APPLICANTS: Action Grants: 268; Vision Grants: 50.

NO. AWARDS: Action Grants: 75; Vision Grants: 25.

APPLICATION INFO:
All applications are available online.

PUBLICATIONS:
Application guidelines.

IRS I.D.: 51-0152266

ADDRESS INQUIRIES TO:
Scarlett Rebman, Grants Officer
E-mail: grants@humanitiesny.org

Michael Washburn, Director of Programs
E-mail: programs@humanitiesny.org

*SPECIAL STIPULATIONS:
Grants available only to New York-based, tax-exempt organizations, but fiscal sponsorship is permitted.

HENRY E. HUNTINGTON LIBRARY AND ART GALLERY   [339]

1151 Oxford Road
San Marino, CA 91108
(626) 405-2194
Fax: (626) 449-5703
E-mail: cwehrey@huntington.org
Web Site: www.huntington.org

FOUNDED: 1919

AREAS OF INTEREST:
British and American history, British and American literature, art history, and the history of science, technology and medicine.

NAME(S) OF PROGRAMS:
● **Research Awards at the Huntington Library and Art Gallery**

TYPE:
Fellowships; Travel grants; Visiting scholars. Awards support scholarship in British and American history, British and American literature, art history, and the history of science, technology and medicine.

YEAR PROGRAM STARTED: 1927

PURPOSE:
To encourage, facilitate and disseminate high-quality humanities scholarship on the basis of the Huntington Library and art collections.

LEGAL BASIS:
Private, nonprofit.

ELIGIBILITY:
Humanities scholars in the fields of history, literature and art history at the doctoral and postdoctoral level are encouraged to apply. Consideration is given to the value of the candidate's project and the degree to which the Huntington Library collections will be used. Proposals from postgraduate students who have advanced to doctoral candidacy are particularly welcome.

FINANCIAL DATA:
Amount of support per award: Short-term fellowships: $3,500 per month; Long-term fellowships: $50,000 for the academic year.

Total amount of support: $2,100,000 for fiscal year 2019-20.

CO-OP FUNDING PROGRAMS: Caltech.

NO. MOST RECENT APPLICANTS: Short-term: 306; Long-term: 111.

NO. AWARDS: Short-term: 124; Long-term: 13.

APPLICATION INFO:
Contact the Library.

Duration: Short-term grants: One to five months. Long-term awards: Minimum of nine months.

Deadline: November 15 for commencement on July 1.

IRS I.D.: 95-1644589

ADDRESS INQUIRIES TO:
Steve Hindle, Director of Research
(See address above.)

*SPECIAL STIPULATIONS:
Recipients of all fellowships are expected to be in continuous residence at the Huntington.

THE INSTITUTE FOR ADVANCED STUDIES IN THE HUMANITIES   [340]

The University of Edinburgh
2 Hope Park Square
Edinburgh EH8 9NW Scotland
(44) 0131 650 4671
E-mail: iash@ed.ac.uk
Web Site: www.iash.ed.ac.uk

FOUNDED: 1969

AREAS OF INTEREST:
Humanities and social science.

CONSULTING OR VOLUNTEER SERVICES:
Institute has connections with and is within easy reach of the National Library of Scotland, the National Archives of Scotland, the Royal Museum of Scotland and the Edinburgh University Library.

NAME(S) OF PROGRAMS:
● **Visiting Research Fellowships**

TYPE:
Fellowships. Visiting Research Fellowships with the use of a private office in the Institute with all the usual research facilities. Recipients of the Fellowships are expected to play a full part in the activities of the Institute.

YEAR PROGRAM STARTED: 1970

PURPOSE:
To further advanced studies in the humanities, broadly conceived.

LEGAL BASIS:
Institution of University of Edinburgh.

ELIGIBILITY:
Applicants should be scholars of established reputation or younger scholars holding a Doctorate or offering equivalent evidence of aptitude for advanced study.

The Election Committee will consider the academic record and the publications of all applicants, their capacity to disseminate their views effectively in public and the likelihood of completing the proposed research by task by the end of the fellowship or shortly afterwards. Students who have not completed their studies for a particular degree are not eligible.

No teaching is required of Fellows in the project, but each Fellow will be expected to make at least one public presentation of his or her research activities.

NO. MOST RECENT APPLICANTS: 21.

NO. AWARDS: Up to 20.

APPLICATION INFO:
Apply online through the Institute web site. The Election Committee will only consider applications accompanied by full documentation and supported by a minimum of two and a maximum of three references. It is the responsibility of each applicant to ensure that their referees submit their reports directly to Edinburgh. Candidates may like to submit a copy of an article or publication relevant to their application. The Institute will not return any documents to applicants.
Duration: Fellowships are tenable for two to six months. Nonrenewable.
Deadline: February 28. Notification by e-mail by end of April.

PUBLICATIONS:
Application guidelines.

OFFICERS:
Prof. Steve Yearley, Director

ADDRESS INQUIRIES TO:
Prof. Steve Yearley, Director
(See address above.)

*SPECIAL STIPULATIONS:
Fellows, as well as carrying out research, are required to live in or near Edinburgh and will be asked to give one seminar.

INSTITUTE FOR ADVANCED STUDY
One Einstein Drive
Princeton, NJ 08540
(609) 734-8250
Fax: (609) 951-4457
E-mail: donne@ias.edu
Web Site: www.sss.ias.edu

TYPE:
Fellowships. Postdoctoral research fellowships at the School of Social Science.

See entry 1685 for full listing.

INSTITUTE FOR HUMANE STUDIES (IHS)
3434 Washington Boulevard, MS 1C5
Arlington, VA 22201
(703) 993-4880
Fax: (703) 993-4890
E-mail: funding@theihs.org
Web Site: www.theihs.org

TYPE:
Fellowships; Research grants. Humane Studies Fellowships cover the fields of the social sciences and humanities.

See entry 1823 for full listing.

MASS HUMANITIES   [341]
66 Bridge Street
Northampton, MA 01060-2406
(413) 584-8440
Fax: (413) 584-8454
E-mail: info@masshumanities.org
Web Site: masshumanities.org

FOUNDED: 1974

AREAS OF INTEREST:
Humanities and areas of special concern in Massachusetts, historic societies and libraries.

NAME(S) OF PROGRAMS:
● **Discussion Grants**
● **Local History Grants**
● **Project Grants**

TYPE:
Project/program grants.

PURPOSE:
To identify and develop major initiatives in areas of special interest or concern.

LEGAL BASIS:
Private, nonprofit corporation.

ELIGIBILITY:
Each grant type has its own goals and guidelines. Applicants must be nonprofit or government organizations that serve Massachusetts residents.

GEOG. RESTRICTIONS: Massachusetts.

FINANCIAL DATA:
Amount of support per award: Varies.
Total amount of support: $522,000 in grants awarded for the year 2019.
Matching fund requirements: Outright Funds must be matched equally by your organization through cost-sharing.

NO. AWARDS: 78 for the year 2019.

REPRESENTATIVE AWARDS:
$58,750 to Center for Independent Documentary, Walpole, MA, for a documentary focused on the life of a Jewish teen living in Germany in the 1930s who was gradually targeted by the Nazis and eventually escaped to Britain and then to Massachusetts; $15,000 to Filmmakers Collaborative, Melrose, MA, for a documentary on the experience of four women from Voices From Inside, a Greenfield-based organization that facilitates writing groups for incarcerated and formerly incarcerated women; $3,500 to Barrington Stage Company, Pittsfield, MA, for a free symposium in connection with a performance of "Fall Springs," a dark musical comedy about environmental disaster.

APPLICATION INFO:
Applicants should submit the Foundation's web-based Letter of Inquiry form six weeks before final proposal deadline. Application is an online process.
Duration: Typically one year.
Deadline: Varies.

PUBLICATIONS:
Newsletter; application guidelines; brochure.

STAFF:
Brian Boyles, Executive Director

John Sieracki, Director of Development and Communications
Katherine Stevens, Director of Grants
Michelle Wilson, Associate Director of Development
Jennifer Hall-Witt, Program Officer

ALLETTA MORRIS MCBEAN CHARITABLE TRUST   [342]
78140 Calle Tampico
Suite 104
La Quinta, CA 92253
(760) 564-3000
Fax: (760) 564-3030
E-mail: mcbeanproperties@att.net
Web Site: allettamcbeancharitabletrust.org

FOUNDED: 1986

AREAS OF INTEREST:
Historic and land preservation in and around Newport, RI.

TYPE:
Capital grants; Challenge/matching grants; Endowments; Project/program grants.

YEAR PROGRAM STARTED: 1986

PURPOSE:
To enhance the quality of life in and around Newport and Aquidneck Island, RI.

LEGAL BASIS:
Private charitable trust.

ELIGIBILITY:
Applicants must be tax-exempt organizations.

GEOG. RESTRICTIONS: Aquidneck Island, Rhode Island.

FINANCIAL DATA:
Amount of support per award: $25,000 to $100,000.
Total amount of support: Approximately $3,000,000 per year.
Matching fund requirements: Varies.

NO. MOST RECENT APPLICANTS: 20 to 25.

REPRESENTATIVE AWARDS:
$50,000 to American Red Cross for Hurricane Florence disaster relief; $250,000 to Newport Performing Arts Center Task Group for continued restoration of the Newport Opera House; $56,000 to Bradley Hospital Foundation for the Outdoor Learning Program.

APPLICATION INFO:
Five formal proposals with budgets are preferred, as well as other sources of funding for project, tax-exempt status and other background material.
Deadline: February 28 and July 31.

IRS I.D.: 94-3019660

OFFICERS:
Donald C. Christ, Chairman
Walter G.D. Reed, Acting Secretary
Charlene C. Kleiner, Assistant Secretary
Dorienne Farzan
Gladys V. Szapary

ADDRESS INQUIRIES TO:
Donald C. Christ, Chairman
Charlene C. Kleiner, Assistant Secretary
(See address above.)

MICHIGAN SOCIETY OF FELLOWS [343]

University of Michigan
0540 Rackham Building
915 East Washington Street
Ann Arbor, MI 48109-1070
(734) 763-1259
E-mail: society.of.fellows@umich.edu
Web Site: www.societyoffellows.umich.edu

FOUNDED: 1970

AREAS OF INTEREST:
All schools and colleges at the University of Michigan.

NAME(S) OF PROGRAMS:
- **Postdoctoral Fellowships in the Humanities and the Arts, Sciences and Professions**

TYPE:
Fellowships. Fellows are appointed as Assistant Professors in appropriate departments and as Postdoctoral Scholars in the Michigan Society of Fellows. They are expected to be in residence in Ann Arbor during the academic years of the fellowship, to teach for the equivalent of one academic year, to participate in the informal intellectual life of the Society, and to devote time to their independent research or artistic projects.

YEAR PROGRAM STARTED: 1970

PURPOSE:
To recognize and support academic and creative excellence in humanities and the arts, the social, physical, and life sciences, and the professions.

LEGAL BASIS:
Nonprofit, tax-exempt organization.

ELIGIBILITY:
Candidates should be near the beginning of their professional careers, but not more than three years beyond completion of their degrees. The Ph.D. degree or comparable professional or artistic degree, received prior to appointment, is required.

Applications from degree candidates and recipients of the Ph.D. from the University of Michigan will not be considered.

FINANCIAL DATA:
Amount of support per award: $60,000 annually plus health benefits for fellowships. $1,500 per year allowance toward travel and research expenses.

CO-OP FUNDING PROGRAMS: Mellon Foundation.

NO. MOST RECENT APPLICANTS: Approximately 900 annually.

NO. AWARDS: 6 each year.

APPLICATION INFO:
Only online applications will be considered. Applications will be reviewed by members of the Society of Fellows and by faculty in appropriate University of Michigan departments. Final selection of candidates will be made by the senior fellows of the Society.
Duration: Three years.
Deadline: September 24. Final selections made end of February.

PUBLICATIONS:
Application guidelines.

OFFICERS:
Donald S. Lopez, Jr., Chairperson of Society

ADDRESS INQUIRIES TO:
See e-mail address above.

*SPECIAL STIPULATIONS:
Fellows are expected to reside in Ann Arbor during the academic years of the fellowship.

NATIONAL ENDOWMENT FOR THE HUMANITIES [344]

The Constitution Center
400 7th Street, S.W.
Washington, DC 20506
(202) 606-8424
Fax: (202) 606-8240
E-mail: communications@neh.gov
Web Site: www.neh.gov

FOUNDED: 1965

AREAS OF INTEREST:
Scholarship, research, education and public programs in the humanities. In the act that established the Endowment, the term humanities includes, but is not limited to, the study of history, philosophy, languages, linguistics, literature, archaeology, jurisprudence, the history, theory and criticism of the arts, ethics, comparative religion and those aspects of the social sciences that employ historical or philosophical approaches.

NAME(S) OF PROGRAMS:
- **Research Program**

TYPE:
Research grants. Grants provide support for collaborative research in the preparation of publication of editions, translations and other important works in the humanities and in the conduct of large or complex interpretive studies including archaeology projects and the humanities studies of science and technology. Grants also support research opportunities offered through independent research centers and scholarly organizations and international research centers.

YEAR PROGRAM STARTED: 1967

PURPOSE:
To provide funding for research and the publication of that research. The work must be in a field of interest to the National Endowment.

LEGAL BASIS:
Federal agency, established by act of Congress: The National Foundation on the Arts and Humanities Act of 1965, Public Law 89-209, as amended.

ELIGIBILITY:
Applicants can be individuals, institutions of higher education, nonprofit professional associations, scholarly societies and other nonprofit organizations.

GEOG. RESTRICTIONS: United States.

FINANCIAL DATA:
Amount of support per award: Varies.
Total amount of support: Varies.

APPLICATION INFO:
Application can be downloaded from the web site.
Duration: Varies.
Deadline: Varies.

PUBLICATIONS:
Annual report; *Grant Programs*; *Humanities Magazine*.

IRS I.D.: 52-1098584

ADDRESS INQUIRIES TO:
Paula Wasley
Senior Public Affairs Specialist
(See address above.)

NATIONAL ENDOWMENT FOR THE HUMANITIES [345]

The Constitution Center
400 7th Street, S.W.
Washington, DC 20506
(202) 606-8424
Fax: (202) 606-8240
E-mail: communications@neh.gov
Web Site: www.neh.gov

FOUNDED: 1965

AREAS OF INTEREST:
Scholarship, research, education and public programs in the humanities. In the act that established the Endowment, the term humanities includes, but is not limited to, the study of history, philosophy, languages, linguistics, literature, archaeology, jurisprudence, the history, theory and criticism of the arts, ethics, comparative religion and those aspects of the social sciences that employ historical or philosophical approaches.

NAME(S) OF PROGRAMS:
- **Challenge Grants Program**

TYPE:
Capital grants; Challenge/matching grants; Professorships; Residencies; Visiting scholars. The Office of Challenge Grants offers grants that "challenge" local, state and national institutions to respond to opportunities that exist in this country's humanities ecosystem.

YEAR PROGRAM STARTED: 1977

PURPOSE:
To encourage long-range financial and program planning within humanities institutions and organizations; to provide means for humanities organizations and institutions to increase levels and kinds of continuing financial support; to sustain or develop high-quality work within the humanities; to join federal with nonfederal support so that those institutions in which teaching, learning and research of the humanities occur may achieve greater financial stability.

LEGAL BASIS:
Federal agency, established by act of Congress: The National Foundation on the Arts and Humanities Act of 1965, Public Law 89-209, as amended.

ELIGIBILITY:
Nonprofit postsecondary, educational, research or cultural institutions and organizations working within the humanities are eligible for support.

GEOG. RESTRICTIONS: United States.

FINANCIAL DATA:
Amount of support per award: Varies.
Total amount of support: Varies.

APPLICATION INFO:
Applications can be downloaded from the above web site.
Duration: Varies.
Deadline: Varies.

PUBLICATIONS:
Annual report; *Grant Programs*; *Humanities Magazine*.

IRS I.D.: 52-1098584

ADDRESS INQUIRIES TO:
Paula Wasley
Senior Public Affairs Specialist
(See address above.)

NATIONAL ENDOWMENT FOR THE HUMANITIES   [346]

The Constitution Center
400 7th Street, S.W.
Washington, DC 20506
(202) 606-8424
Fax: (202) 606-8240
E-mail: communications@neh.gov
Web Site: www.neh.gov

FOUNDED: 1965

AREAS OF INTEREST:
Scholarship, research, education and public programs in the humanities.

NAME(S) OF PROGRAMS:
● **Fellowships**
● **Summer Stipends**

TYPE:
Awards/prizes; Fellowships. Grants provide support for scholars to undertake full-time independent research and writing in the humanities. Grants are available for a maximum of one year and a minimum of six weeks to two months of summer study.

Grants also provide support for historically Black college and university faculty to undertake one year of full-time study leading to a doctoral degree in the humanities with preference given to those individuals who are at the dissertation stage of their work.

YEAR PROGRAM STARTED: 1967

PURPOSE:
To encourage continued research and study in the humanities discipline.

LEGAL BASIS:
Federal agency, established by act of Congress: The National Foundation on the Arts and Humanities Act of 1965, Public Law 89-209, as amended.

GEOG. RESTRICTIONS: United States.

FINANCIAL DATA:
Amount of support per award: Fellowship: $5,000 per month; Summer Stipend: Up to $6,000.
Total amount of support: Varies.

APPLICATION INFO:
Application can be downloaded from the web site.
Duration: Fellowship: Six to 12 months; Summer Stipend: Two months.
Deadline: Fellowships: April 8; Summer Stipends: Late September.

PUBLICATIONS:
Annual report; *Grant Programs*; *Humanities Magazine*.

IRS I.D.: 52-1098584

ADDRESS INQUIRIES TO:
Paula Wasley
Senior Public Affairs Specialist
(See address above.)

NATIONAL ENDOWMENT FOR THE HUMANITIES   [347]

The Constitution Center
400 7th Street, S.W.
Washington, DC 20506
(202) 606-8424
Fax: (202) 606-8240
E-mail: communications@neh.gov
Web Site: www.neh.gov

FOUNDED: 1965

AREAS OF INTEREST:
Scholarship, research, education and public programs in the humanities. In the act that established the Endowment, the term humanities includes, but is not limited to, the study of history, philosophy, languages, linguistics, literature, archaeology, jurisprudence, the history, theory and criticism of the arts, ethics, comparative religion and those aspects of the social sciences that employ historical or philosophical approaches.

NAME(S) OF PROGRAMS:
● **Seminars and Institutes Program**

TYPE:
Conferences/seminars. Grants support summer seminars and national institutes in the humanities for college and school teachers. These faculty development activities are conducted at colleges and universities across the country. Lists of pending seminars and institutes are available from the program.

YEAR PROGRAM STARTED: 1983

PURPOSE:
To provide opportunities for teachers to study under the direction of a master teacher and distinguished scholar in an area of mutual interest at a college or university during the summer.

LEGAL BASIS:
Federal agency, established by act of Congress: The National Foundation on the Arts and Humanities Act of 1965, Public Law 89-209, as amended.

ELIGIBILITY:
Applicants can be individuals or institutions of higher learning.

GEOG. RESTRICTIONS: United States.

FINANCIAL DATA:
Amount of support per award: Varies.
Total amount of support: Varies.

APPLICATION INFO:
Complete application information can be found online. Participant application forms and instructions can be obtained from seminar directors at the host institutions. Those wishing to participate in seminars should submit their applications to the seminar director. Information about the program is publicized in the fall preceding the summer in question.
Duration: Seminars last one to four weeks, depending on the choice of the director.
Deadline: February 14.

PUBLICATIONS:
Annual report; *Grant Programs*; *Humanities Magazine*.

IRS I.D.: 52-1098584

ADDRESS INQUIRIES TO:
Paula Wasley
Senior Public Affairs Specialist
(See address above.)

NATIONAL ENDOWMENT FOR THE HUMANITIES   [348]

The Constitution Center
400 7th Street, S.W.
Washington, DC 20506
(202) 606-8424
Fax: (202) 606-8240
E-mail: communications@neh.gov
Web Site: www.neh.gov

FOUNDED: 1965

AREAS OF INTEREST:
Scholarship, research, education and public programs in the humanities. In the act that established the Endowment, the term humanities includes, but is not limited to, the study of history, philosophy, languages, linguistics, literature, archaeology, jurisprudence, the history, theory and criticism of the arts, ethics, comparative religion and those aspects of the social sciences that employ historical or philosophical approaches.

NAME(S) OF PROGRAMS:
● **Preservation and Access**

TYPE:
Project/program grants. Support may be sought to preserve the intellectual content and aid bibliographic control of collections, to compile bibliographies, descriptive catalogs and guides to cultural holdings, to create dictionaries, encyclopedias, databases and other types of research tools and reference works and to stabilize material culture collections through the appropriate housing and storing of objects, improved environmental control and the installation of security, lighting and fire-prevention systems.

Applications may also be submitted for national and regional education and training projects, regional preservation field service programs and research and demonstration projects that are intended to enhance institutional practice and the use of technology for preservation and access.

YEAR PROGRAM STARTED: 1985

PURPOSE:
To advance study in the area indicated.

LEGAL BASIS:
Federal agency, established by act of Congress: The National Foundation on the Arts and Humanities Act of 1965, Public Law 89-209, as amended.

GEOG. RESTRICTIONS: United States.

FINANCIAL DATA:
Amount of support per award: Varies.
Total amount of support: Varies.

APPLICATION INFO:
Application can be downloaded from the web site.
Duration: Varies.
Deadline: Varies.

PUBLICATIONS:
Annual report; *Grant Programs*; *Humanities Magazine*.

IRS I.D.: 52-1098584

ADDRESS INQUIRIES TO:
Paula Wasley
Senior Public Affairs Specialist
(See address above.)

NATIONAL ENDOWMENT FOR THE HUMANITIES

The Constitution Center
400 7th Street, S.W.
Washington, DC 20506
(202) 606-8269
Fax: (202) 606-8557
E-mail: publicpgms@neh.gov
Web Site: www.neh.gov

TYPE:
Project/program grants. Public Humanities Projects grants support projects that bring the ideas and insights of the humanities to life for general audiences. Projects must engage humanities scholarship to illuminate

significant themes in disciplines such as history, literature, ethics and art, or to address challenging issues in contemporary life. NEH encourages projects that involve members of the public in collaboration with humanities scholars or that invite contributions from the community in the development and delivery of humanities programming. The grant program supports a variety of forms of audience engagement: Community Conversations: This format supports one- to three-year-long series of community-wide public discussions in which diverse residents creatively address community challenges, guided by the perspectives of the humanities; Exhibitions: This format supports permanent exhibitions that will be on view for at least three years, or traveling exhibitions that will be available to public audiences in at least two venues in the U.S. (including the originating location) and; Historic Places: This format supports the interpretation of historic sites, houses, neighborhoods and regions, which might include living history presentations, guided tours, exhibitions and public programs.

See entry 1775 for full listing.

NATIONAL HUMANITIES CENTER   [349]
7 T.W. Alexander Drive
Research Triangle Park, NC 27709
(919) 549-0661
Fax: (919) 990-8535
E-mail: fellowships@nationalhumanitiescenter.org
Web Site: www.nationalhumanitiescenter.org

FOUNDED: 1976

AREAS OF INTEREST:
History, literature, philosophy, classics, political theory, law, religion, anthropology, art history, folklore and other humanistic fields.

NAME(S) OF PROGRAMS:
- **National Humanities Center Fellowships**

TYPE:
Fellowships; Visiting scholars. Awards for advanced study in the humanities in residence at the Center.

YEAR PROGRAM STARTED: 1978

PURPOSE:
To support advanced study in the humanities; to encourage the exchange of ideas among humanist scholars; to enhance the influence of the humanities in the U.S.

LEGAL BASIS:
Privately incorporated nonprofit institute for advanced study.

ELIGIBILITY:
Open to scholars in the humanities. As a rule, the Center does not consider applications from candidates who have not yet completed the Doctorate. Fellowships for younger scholars are not intended for an immediate postdoctoral year but are awarded to individuals who have begun their professional careers and are undertaking research significantly beyond their dissertations.

FINANCIAL DATA:
Fellows receive travel expenses to and from the Center for themselves and their families.

Amount of support per award: Individually determined based on need.
Total amount of support: Varies.
Matching fund requirements: Stipulated with specific grants.

CO-OP FUNDING PROGRAMS: Scholars who have financial support from university or other funding agencies are welcome to apply and receive from the Center the difference between that support and their normal academic salaries.

NO. MOST RECENT APPLICANTS: 647.

NO. AWARDS: 40.

APPLICATION INFO:
Applications accepted online only.
Duration: One academic year, September through May.
Deadline: October 10. Announcement in February.

PUBLICATIONS:
Annual report; application guidelines; semiannual newsletter.

IRS I.D.: 59-1735367

OFFICERS:
Ben Vinson, III, Chairman
Joshua Ruch, Vice Chairman
Raymond J. Wiacek, Treasurer
Thomas Scherer, Secretary

STAFF:
Tania Munz, Vice President for Scholarly Programs

ADDRESS INQUIRIES TO:
Lynn Miller, Program Coordinator
Fellowship Program
(See address above.)

THE NEWBERRY LIBRARY [350]
Newberry Institute for Research and Education
60 West Walton Street
Chicago, IL 60610
(312) 255-3666
E-mail: research@newberry.org
Web Site: www.newberry.org/fellowships

FOUNDED: 1887

AREAS OF INTEREST:
Late Medieval and Renaissance studies.

NAME(S) OF PROGRAMS:
- **The Audrey Lumsden-Kouvel Fellowship**

TYPE:
Fellowships. The Audrey Lumsden-Kouvel Fellowship is for postdoctoral scholars conducting extended research in residence at the Newberry Library in the areas of late medieval and early modern history and literature.

LEGAL BASIS:
Private research library.

ELIGIBILITY:
Preference will be given to projects focusing on Romance cultures, including work that draws on sources from the colonial Americas. Topics in Portuguese, Spanish and Latin American Studies are especially welcome, as are translation projects. Recent recipients of Ph.Ds. are encouraged to apply.

FINANCIAL DATA:
Awardees may combine this fellowship with sabbatical or other stipendiary support.
Amount of support per award: $4,200 per month.

NO. MOST RECENT APPLICANTS: 40.

NO. AWARDS: 1 to 2.

APPLICATION INFO:
Applications must be submitted through the online webform.
Duration: Four to six months.
Deadline: November 1. Notification in mid-February.

STAFF:
D. Bradford Hunt, Vice President for Research and Academic Programs

ADDRESS INQUIRIES TO:
See e-mail address above.

THE NEWBERRY LIBRARY [351]
Newberry Institute for Research and Education
60 West Walton Street
Chicago, IL 60610
(312) 255-3666
E-mail: research@newberry.org
Web Site: www.newberry.org/fellowships

FOUNDED: 1887

AREAS OF INTEREST:
The humanities of Western Europe, England and the Americas from the late Middle Ages to the early 20th century.

NAME(S) OF PROGRAMS:
- **Newberry Short-Term Resident Fellowships for Individual Research**

TYPE:
Fellowships; Residencies. Fellowships of one month for advanced research, including doctoral dissertations, in history and the humanities. Fellowships provide access to the Newberry's collections for those who live and work beyond commuting distance from Chicago.

YEAR PROGRAM STARTED: 1942

PURPOSE:
To give scholars engaged in research in the fields listed above the opportunity to utilize the specialized collections of the Newberry Library.

LEGAL BASIS:
Private research library.

ELIGIBILITY:
Applicants must have the Ph.D. or terminal degree in their field, or have completed all requirements except the dissertation. Preference will be given to applicants from outside the greater Chicago area whose research particularly requires study at the Newberry. Applicants must live and work outside of the Chicago area.

FINANCIAL DATA:
Amount of support per award: $2,500 per month.

NO. MOST RECENT APPLICANTS: Varies.

NO. AWARDS: 5.

APPLICATION INFO:
Applications must be submitted through the online webform.
Duration: One month.
Deadline: December 15.

STAFF:
D. Bradford Hunt, Vice President for Research and Academic Programs

ADDRESS INQUIRIES TO:
See e-mail address above.

THE NEWBERRY LIBRARY [352]

Newberry Institute for Research and Education
60 West Walton Street
Chicago, IL 60610
(312) 255-3666
E-mail: research@newberry.org
Web Site: www.newberry.org/fellowships

FOUNDED: 1887

AREAS OF INTEREST:
The humanities of Western Europe, England
and the Americas from the late Middle Ages
to the early 20th century.

NAME(S) OF PROGRAMS:
- **National Endowment for the
  Humanities (NEH) Fellowships**

TYPE:
Fellowships; Residencies. Support for
projects in any field appropriate to the
Library's collections.

YEAR PROGRAM STARTED: 1975

PURPOSE:
To encourage the individual scholar's
research and to deepen and enrich the
opportunities for serious intellectual
exchange.

LEGAL BASIS:
Private research library.

ELIGIBILITY:
Established scholars at the postdoctoral level
or its equivalent may apply. Awards are open
to U.S. citizens and foreign nationals who
have been living in the U.S. for at least three
continuous years of residence. Preference is
given to applicants who have not held major
fellowships for three years preceding the
proposed period of residency.

Projects must be appropriate for research in
the Newberry collection.

FINANCIAL DATA:
Awardees may combine grants with
sabbaticals or other stipendiary support.
Amount of support per award: $4,200 per
month.

NO. MOST RECENT APPLICANTS: 100.

NO. AWARDS: 4 to 6.

APPLICATION INFO:
Applications must be submitted through the
online webform.
Duration: Four to nine months.
Deadline: November 1. Notification in
mid-February.

STAFF:
D. Bradford Hunt, Vice President for
Research and Academic Programs

ADDRESS INQUIRIES TO:
See e-mail address above.

THE NEWBERRY LIBRARY [353]

Newberry Institute for Research and Education
60 West Walton Street
Chicago, IL 60610
(312) 255-3666
E-mail: research@newberry.org
Web Site: www.newberry.org/fellowships

FOUNDED: 1887

AREAS OF INTEREST:
The humanities of Western Europe, England
and the Americas from the late Middle Ages
to the early 20th century.

NAME(S) OF PROGRAMS:
- **Arthur and Lila Weinberg Fellowship
  for Independent Scholars and
  Researchers**

TYPE:
Fellowships; Residencies. Weinberg
Fellowship is for scholars working outside
traditional acedemic settings. The program
seeks scholars, journalists, writers,
filmmakers, visual and performing artists and
other humanists. Preference is given to
scholars working on historical issues related
to social justice or reform.

LEGAL BASIS:
Private research library.

ELIGIBILITY:
Candidates are those working in a field
appropriate to the Newberry collections.
Preference is given to scholars working on
historical issues related to social justice or
reform. Applicants must be individuals
working outside of traditional academic
settings who are not employed, or seeking to
be employed, as full-time academic faculty.

FINANCIAL DATA:
Amount of support per award: $2,500 total
stipend.

NO. MOST RECENT APPLICANTS: 10.

NO. AWARDS: 1.

APPLICATION INFO:
Applications must be submitted through the
online webform.
Duration: One to 12 months.
Deadline: December 15.

STAFF:
D. Bradford Hunt, Vice President for
Research and Academic Programs

ADDRESS INQUIRIES TO:
See e-mail address above.

THE NEWBERRY LIBRARY

Newberry Institute for Research and Education
60 West Walton Street
Chicago, IL 60610
(312) 255-3666
E-mail: research@newberry.org
Web Site: www.newberry.org/fellowships

TYPE:
Fellowships. For scholars wishing to use the
Newberry's collections to study the period
1660 to 1815.

See entry 577 for full listing.

THE NEWBERRY LIBRARY [354]

Newberry Institute for Research and Education
60 West Walton Street
Chicago, IL 60610
(312) 255-3666
E-mail: research@newberry.org
Web Site: www.newberry.org/fellowships

FOUNDED: 1887

AREAS OF INTEREST:
The humanities of Western Europe, England
and the Americas from the late Middle Ages
to the early 20th century.

NAME(S) OF PROGRAMS:
- **Lloyd Lewis Fellowship in American
  History**

TYPE:
Fellowships. The Lloyd Lewis Fellowship in
American History is awarded to postdoctoral

scholars pursuing projects in any area of
American history appropriate to the
Newberry's collections.

PURPOSE:
To further research in American history.

ELIGIBILITY:
Applicants must hold a Ph.D. at the time of
application and be pursuing projects in any
area of American history that are applicable
to the Newberry Collection.

FINANCIAL DATA:
Awardees may combine these fellowship
awards with sabbatical or other stipendiary
support.
Amount of support per award: Monthly
stipend of $4,200.

NO. MOST RECENT APPLICANTS: Varies.

NO. AWARDS: 1 to 2.

APPLICATION INFO:
Applications must be submitted through the
online webform.
Duration: Four to nine months.
Deadline: November 1. Notification in
mid-February.

STAFF:
D. Bradford Hunt, Vice President for
Research and Academic Programs

ADDRESS INQUIRIES TO:
See e-mail address above.

*PLEASE NOTE:
The Newberry's long-term fellowship grants
support individual research and promote
serious intellectual exchange through active
participation in the Newberry's scholarly
activities, including fellows' seminars and a
weekly colloquium.

THE NEWBERRY LIBRARY [355]

Newberry Institute for Research and Education
60 West Walton Street
Chicago, IL 60610
(312) 255-3666
E-mail: research@newberry.org
Web Site: www.newberry.org/fellowships

FOUNDED: 1887

AREAS OF INTEREST:
The humanities of Western Europe, England
and the Americas from the late Middle Ages
to the early 20th century.

NAME(S) OF PROGRAMS:
- **Monticello College Foundation
  Fellowship for Women**

TYPE:
Fellowships. The Monticello College
Foundation Fellowship for Women is
intended to help a postdoctoral woman
scholar at an early stage (pre-tenure) of her
academic career.

PURPOSE:
To provide assistance to postdoctoral woman
scholars at an early stage of their academic
careers.

ELIGIBILITY:
Applicants must hold a Ph.D. at the time of
application. This award is intended for a
postdoctoral woman scholar at an early stage
(pre-tenure) of her academic career.
Preference will be given to proposals
particularly concerned with the study of
women.

FINANCIAL DATA:
Awardees may combine this fellowship
awards with sabbatical or other stipendiary
support.

Amount of support per award: Monthly stipend of $4,200 per month.

NO. MOST RECENT APPLICANTS: Varies.

NO. AWARDS: 1 to 2.

APPLICATION INFO:
Applications must be submitted through the online webform.
Duration: Four to six months.
Deadline: November 1. Notification in mid-February.

ADDRESS INQUIRIES TO:
See e-mail address above.

*PLEASE NOTE:
The Newberry's long-term fellowship grants support individual research and promote serious intellectual exchange through active participation in the Newberry's scholarly activities, including fellows' seminars and a weekly colloquium.

THE NEWBERRY LIBRARY [356]
Newberry Institute for Research and Education
60 West Walton Street
Chicago, IL 60610
(312) 255-3666
E-mail: research@newberry.org
Web Site: www.newberry.org/fellowships

FOUNDED: 1887

AREAS OF INTEREST:
The humanities of Western Europe, England and the Americas from the late Middle Ages to the early 20th century.

NAME(S) OF PROGRAMS:
● **Newberry Consortium of American Indian and Indigenous Studies (NCAIS) Faculty Fellowship**

TYPE:
Fellowships.

PURPOSE:
To promote research in American Indian studies.

ELIGIBILITY:
This award is intended for faculty members at institutions participating in the Consortium. Preference is given to scholars at an early career stage.

FINANCIAL DATA:
Awardees may combine these fellowship awards with sabbatical or other stipendiary support.
Amount of support per award: Monthly stipend of $4,200.

NO. MOST RECENT APPLICANTS: Varies.

NO. AWARDS: 1.

APPLICATION INFO:
Awardees must indicate in their applications how many months they intend to be in residence at the Newberry. Applications must be submitted through the online webform.
Duration: Four to six months.
Deadline: November 1. Notification in mid-February.

ADDRESS INQUIRIES TO:
See e-mail address above.

*PLEASE NOTE:
The Newberry's long-term fellowship grants support individual research and promote serious intellectual exchange through active participation in the Newberry's scholarly activities, including fellows' seminars and a weekly colloquium.

THE NEWBERRY LIBRARY [357]
Newberry Institute for Research and Education
60 West Walton Street
Chicago, IL 60610
(312) 255-3666
E-mail: research@newberry.org
Web Site: www.newberry.org/fellowships

FOUNDED: 1887

AREAS OF INTEREST:
The humanities of Western Europe, England and the Americas from the late Middle Ages to the early 20th century.

NAME(S) OF PROGRAMS:
● **Newberry Library - Jack Miller Center Fellowship**

TYPE:
Fellowships; Residencies. Support for projects in any field appropriate to the Library's collection.

PURPOSE:
To advance scholarship in those fields of study that will contribute to a deeper understanding of America's founding principles and history and wider traditions that influenced its development.

LEGAL BASIS:
Private research library.

ELIGIBILITY:
Applicants must have the Ph.D. or terminal degree in their field, or have completed all doctoral requirements except the dissertation. Preference will be given to applicants whose research particularly requires study at the Newberry.

Applicants must live and work outside the greater Chicago area.

FINANCIAL DATA:
Amount of support per award: $2,500 per month in residence.

NO. MOST RECENT APPLICANTS: Varies.

NO. AWARDS: 4.

APPLICATION INFO:
Applications may be submitted through the online webform.
Duration: One month.
Deadline: December 15.

EXECUTIVE STAFF:
D. Bradford Hunt, Vice President for Research and Academic Programs

ADDRESS INQUIRIES TO:
See e-mail address above.

THE NEWBERRY LIBRARY [358]
Newberry Institute for Research and Education
60 West Walton Street
Chicago, IL 60610
(312) 255-3666
E-mail: research@newberry.org
Web Site: www.newberry.org/fellowships

FOUNDED: 1887

AREAS OF INTEREST:
The humanities of Western Europe, England and the Americas from the late Middle Ages to the early 20th century.

NAME(S) OF PROGRAMS:
● **Susan Kelly Power and Helen Hornbeck Tanner Fellowship**

TYPE:
Fellowships; Residencies. Support for projects in any field appropriate to the Library's collection.

PURPOSE:
To support Ph.D. candidates and postdoctoral scholars of American Indian heritage for one or two months of residential research in any field in the humanities using the Newberry collection.

LEGAL BASIS:
Private research library.

ELIGIBILITY:
Applicants must have the Ph.D. or be a postdoctoral scholar of American Indian heritage.

Applicants this fellowship need not be from outside the Chicago area.

FINANCIAL DATA:
Amount of support per award: $2,500 per month in residence.

NO. MOST RECENT APPLICANTS: 5.

NO. AWARDS: 1.

APPLICATION INFO:
Applications must be submitted through the online webform.
Duration: One to two months of residential research.
Deadline: December 15.

EXECUTIVE STAFF:
D. Bradford Hunt, Vice President for Research and Academic Programs

ADDRESS INQUIRIES TO:
See e-mail address above.

THE NEWBERRY LIBRARY [359]
Newberry Institute for Research and Education
60 West Walton Street
Chicago, IL 60610
(312) 255-3666
E-mail: research@newberry.org
Web Site: www.newberry.org/fellowships

FOUNDED: 1887

AREAS OF INTEREST:
The humanities of Western Europe, England and the Americas from the late Middle Ages to the early 20th century.

NAME(S) OF PROGRAMS:
● **Society of Mayflower Descendants in the State of Illinois Fellowship**

TYPE:
Fellowships; Residencies. Support for projects in any field appropriate to the Library's collection.

PURPOSE:
To encourage research work, especially those working in early American or transatlantic history.

LEGAL BASIS:
Private research library.

ELIGIBILITY:
Applicants must have the Ph.D. or terminal degree in their field, or have completed all doctoral requirements except the dissertation. Preference will be given to applicants whose research particularly requires study at the Newberry, and whose research work is in early American or Trans-Atlantic history.

Applicants must live and work outside the greater Chicago area.

FINANCIAL DATA:
Amount of support per award: $2,500 for one month in residence.

NO. MOST RECENT APPLICANTS: Varies.

NO. AWARDS: 2.

APPLICATION INFO:
Applications must be submitted through the online webform.

Duration: One month.

Deadline: December 15.

EXECUTIVE STAFF:
D. Bradford Hunt, Vice President for Research and Academic Programs

ADDRESS INQUIRIES TO:
See e-mail address above.

THE NEWBERRY LIBRARY [360]

Newberry Institute for Research and Education
60 West Walton Street
Chicago, IL 60610
(312) 255-3666
E-mail: research@newberry.org
Web Site: www.newberry.org/fellowships

FOUNDED: 1887

AREAS OF INTEREST:
The humanities of Western Europe, England and the Americas from the late Middle Ages to the early 20th century.

NAME(S) OF PROGRAMS:
● **Charles Montgomery Gray Fellowship**

TYPE:
Fellowships; Residencies. Support for projects in any field appropriate to the Library's collection.

PURPOSE:
To encourage the individual scholar's research and to deepen and enrich the opportunities for serious intellectual exchange.

LEGAL BASIS:
Private research library.

ELIGIBILITY:
Applicants must have the Ph.D. or terminal degree in their field, or have completed all doctoral requirements except the dissertation. Projects must be appropriate for research in residence, within the Newberry's collection. Preference will be given to applicants whose research particularly requires study at the Newberry. Preference may be given to those working in the early modern period or Renaissance, as well as English history, legal history or European history.

Applicants must live and work outside the greater Chicago area.

FINANCIAL DATA:
Amount of support per award: $2,500 per month of residency.

NO. MOST RECENT APPLICANTS: Varies.

NO. AWARDS: 3.

APPLICATION INFO:
Applications must be submitted through the online webform.

Duration: One month.

Deadline: December 15.

EXECUTIVE STAFF:
D. Bradford Hunt, Vice President for Research and Academic Programs

ADDRESS INQUIRIES TO:
See e-mail address above.

THE NEWBERRY LIBRARY [361]

Newberry Institute for Research and Education
60 West Walton Street
Chicago, IL 60610
(312) 255-3666
E-mail: research@newberry.org
Web Site: www.newberry.org/fellowships

FOUNDED: 1887

AREAS OF INTEREST:
The humanities of Western Europe, England and the Americas from the late Middle Ages to the early 20th century.

NAME(S) OF PROGRAMS:
● **Andrew W. Mellon Foundation Fellowship**

TYPE:
Fellowships; Residencies. Support for projects in any field appropriate to the Library's collection.

PURPOSE:
To encourage the individual scholar's research and to deepen and enrich the opportunities for serious intellectual exchange.

LEGAL BASIS:
Private research library.

ELIGIBILITY:
Established scholars at the postdoctoral level may apply. An established scholar, as defined by the Awards Committee, is generally someone who has at least two published articles in refereed journals or the equivalent at the time of application. Projects must be appropriate for research in residence, within the Newberry's collection. There may be preference given for scholars who live and work outside of the Chicago area.

FINANCIAL DATA:
Awardees may combine this fellowship award with sabbatical or other stipendiary support.

Amount of support per award: $4,200 per month of residency.

NO. MOST RECENT APPLICANTS: Varies.

NO. AWARDS: 1 to 2.

APPLICATION INFO:
Applications may be submitted through the online webform.

Duration: Four to nine months.

Deadline: November 1. Notification in mid-February.

EXECUTIVE STAFF:
D. Bradford Hunt, Vice President for Research and Academic Programs

ADDRESS INQUIRIES TO:
See e-mail address above.

THE PHI BETA KAPPA SOCIETY

1606 New Hampshire Avenue, N.W.
Washington, DC 20009
(202) 745-3287
Fax: (202) 986-1601
E-mail: awards@pbk.org
Web Site: www.pbk.org

TYPE:
Fellowships. Grant to women scholars made in alternate years for advanced research dealing with Greek language, literature, history or archaeology (odd-numbered years) or with French language or literature (even-numbered years).

See entry 995 for full listing.

THE ROYAL SOCIETY OF CANADA

Walter House
282 Somerset Street West
Ottawa ON K2P 0J6 Canada
(613) 991-6990 ext. 106
Fax: (613) 991-6996
E-mail: nominations@rsc-src.ca
Web Site: www.rsc-src.ca

TYPE:
Awards/prizes. The Yvan Allaire Medal is awarded in recognition of outstanding research in governance of public and private organizations.

The Bancroft Award is given for publication, instruction and research in the earth sciences that have conspicuously contributed to public understanding and appreciation of the subject.

The Pierre Chauveau Medal is awarded for a distinguished contribution to knowledge in the humanities.

The Sir John William Dawson Medal is awarded for important contributions of knowledge in multiple domains.

The Flavelle Medal is awarded for an outstanding contribution to biological science during the preceding 10 years or for significant additions to a previous outstanding contribution to biological science.

The Ursula Franklin Award in Gender Studies is intended to recognize significant contributions by a Canadian scholar in the humanities and social sciences to furthering our understanding of issues concerning gender.

The Jason A. Hannah Medal is awarded for an important publication in the history of medicine.

The Innis-Gérin Medal is presented for a distinguished and sustained contribution to the literature of the social sciences.

The McLaughlin Medal is awarded for important research of sustained excellence in any branch of the medical sciences.

The Willet G. Miller Medal is given for outstanding research in any branch of earth sciences.

The Lorne Pierce Medal is awarded for an achievement of special significance and conspicuous merit in imaginative or critical literature written in either English or French (critical literature dealing with Canadian subjects has priority over critical literature of equal merit that does not deal with Canadian subjects).

The Miroslaw Romanowski Medal is awarded for significant contributions to the resolution of scientific aspects of environmental problems or for important improvements to the quality of an ecosystem in all aspects - terrestrial, atmospheric and aqueous - brought about by scientific means.

The Rutherford Memorial Medals are awarded for outstanding research in any branch of physics and chemistry.

The John L. Synge Award is given to acknowledge outstanding research in any of the branches of the mathematical sciences.

The Henry Marshall Tory Medal is given for outstanding research in any branch of astronomy, chemistry, mathematics, physics or an allied science.

The J.B. Tyrrell Historical Medal is awarded for outstanding work in the history of Canada.

See entry 1669 for full listing.

THE SCHOMBURG CENTER FOR RESEARCH IN BLACK CULTURE [362]

515 Malcolm X Boulevard
New York, NY 10037-1801
(212) 491-2228
E-mail: sir@nypl.org
Web Site: www.nypl.org/about/locations/schomburg/fellowships

FOUNDED: 1925

AREAS OF INTEREST:
African, African-American and Afro-Caribbean history and culture.

NAME(S) OF PROGRAMS:
● **Scholars-in-Residence**

TYPE:
Fellowships. Awarded to scholars and professionals whose research in African diasporic studies can benefit from extended access to the Center's collections. Seminars, colloquia, forums, symposia and conferences complement the residency program.

YEAR PROGRAM STARTED: 1983

PURPOSE:
To encourage research and writing in African diasporic studies; to facilitate interaction among the participants, including fellows funded by other sources; to provide for widespread dissemination of findings through lectures, publications and the Schomburg Center Seminars.

ELIGIBILITY:
Applicants must be professionals and/or scholars in the humanities studying African diaspora and fields related to the Schomburg Center's collections and program activities, including librarianship, archives and museum administration, special collections, photographs, audiovisual materials and publications. Studies in the social sciences, the arts, science and technology, psychology, education and religion are also eligible if they utilize a humanistic approach and contribute to humanistic knowledge. Creative writing projects (works of poetry and fiction) and projects that result in a performance are not eligible.

Persons seeking support for research leading to degrees are not eligible under this program. Candidates for advanced degrees must have received the degree or completed all requirements for it by the application deadline. Foreign nationals are ineligible unless they will have resided in the U.S. for three years immediately preceding the award date of the fellowship.

FINANCIAL DATA:
Amount of support per award: Long-term Fellowship: Stipend of $35,000; Short-term Fellowship: Stipend of $3,000 per month.

CO-OP FUNDING PROGRAMS: Funding support for the program has been provided by the National Endowment for the Humanities, the Ford Foundation, the Samuel I. Newhouse Foundation, the Andrew W. Mellon Foundation, the Rockefeller Foundation, the Pitts Foundation, the Aaron Diamond Foundation, and the Irene Diamond Foundation.

NO. AWARDS: 9 Long-term and 5 Short-term for the year 2019-20.

APPLICATION INFO:
Applications are accepted electronically only.
Duration: Long-term Fellowship: Six consecutive months; Short-term Fellowship: One to three months.
Deadline: December 1.

PUBLICATIONS:
Program announcement.

STAFF:
Kevin Young, Director

ADDRESS INQUIRIES TO:
Scholars-in-Residence Program
(See address or e-mail above.)

*PLEASE NOTE:
The Center will assist scholars in locating housing.

*SPECIAL STIPULATIONS:
Fellows may not be employed or hold other major fellowships or grants during period of residency.

SOCIAL SCIENCES AND HUMANITIES RESEARCH COUNCIL OF CANADA

350 Albert Street
Ottawa ON K1P 6G4 Canada
(613) 943-7777
Fax: (613) 943-1329
E-mail: vanier@cihr-irsc.gc.ca
Web Site: www.vanier.gc.ca

TYPE:
Awards/prizes; Fellowships; Scholarships. For doctoral students in the humanities and social sciences. Administered by the Canadian Institutes of Health Research, the Natural Sciences and Engineering Research Council and the Social Sciences Research Council.

See entry 1701 for full listing.

SOCIAL SCIENCES AND HUMANITIES RESEARCH COUNCIL OF CANADA

350 Albert Street
Ottawa ON K1P 6G4 Canada
(613) 943-7777
Fax: (613) 943-1329
E-mail: fellowships@sshrc-crsh.gc.ca
Web Site: www.sshrc-crsh.gc.ca

TYPE:
Fellowships. For Canadian citizens, permanent residents of Canada and foreign citizens to support postdoctoral research in the humanities and social sciences.

See entry 1702 for full listing.

SOCIAL SCIENCES AND HUMANITIES RESEARCH COUNCIL OF CANADA

350 Albert Street
Ottawa ON K1P 6G4 Canada
(613) 943-7777
Fax: (613) 943-1329
E-mail: fellowships@sshrc-crsh.gc.ca
Web Site: www.sshrc-crsh.gc.ca

TYPE:
Awards/prizes; Fellowships; Scholarships.

See entry 1700 for full listing.

SOCIAL SCIENCES AND HUMANITIES RESEARCH COUNCIL OF CANADA

350 Albert Street
Ottawa ON K1P 6G4 Canada
(613) 943-7777
Fax: (613) 943-1329
E-mail: fellowships@sshrc-crsh.gc.ca
Web Site: www.sshrc-crsh.gc.ca

TYPE:
Awards/prizes; Fellowships; Scholarships. Through its Doctoral Awards program, SSHRC offers two types of funding for doctoral students:
(1) SSHRC Doctoral Fellowships and;
(2) Joseph-Armand Bombardier (JAB) Canada Graduate Scholarships (CGS) program - Doctoral Scholarships.

See entry 1698 for full listing.

SOCIAL SCIENCES AND HUMANITIES RESEARCH COUNCIL OF CANADA

350 Albert Street
Ottawa ON K1P 6G4 Canada
(613) 943-7777
Fax: (613) 943-1329
E-mail: fellowships@sshrc-crsh.gc.ca
Web Site: www.sshrc-crsh.gc.ca

TYPE:
Fellowships. For Canadian citizens or permanent residents of Canada, to support postdoctoral research in the humanities and social sciences.

See entry 1699 for full listing.

STANFORD HUMANITIES CENTER [363]

Stanford University
424 Santa Teresa Street
Stanford, CA 94305
(650) 724-8106
(650) 723-3052
Fax: (650) 723-1895
E-mail: shc-fellowships@stanford.edu
Web Site: shc.stanford.edu

FOUNDED: 1980

AREAS OF INTEREST:
History, literature, philosophy, classics, languages, social theory, political theory, law, religion, anthropology, art history, archeology and other areas of the humanities.

NAME(S) OF PROGRAMS:
● **External Faculty Fellowships**

TYPE:
Fellowships. Fellowships are awarded to support research projects in the humanities; creative arts projects are not eligible. The Humanities Center seeks candidates whose research is likely to contribute to intellectual exchange among a diverse group of scholars within the disciplines of the humanities. The Center is open to projects employing information technology in humanities research.

YEAR PROGRAM STARTED: 1982

PURPOSE:
To promote the humanities and humanistic study at Stanford and nationally, primarily through a research fellowship program.

LEGAL BASIS:
Private, nonprofit research center at Stanford University.

ELIGIBILITY:
Postdoctoral level research in the humanities. Applicants must be at least three years beyond receipt of their Ph.D. at the start of their fellowship year.

External Faculty Fellowships are offered only once. Former External Faculty Fellows are not eligible to reapply.

FINANCIAL DATA:
Amount of support per award: Up to $70,000, plus a moving and housing allowance of up to $40,000.
Matching fund requirements: Applicants are encouraged to seek supplementary financial support.

NO. MOST RECENT APPLICANTS: 350.

NO. AWARDS: Up to 10.

APPLICATION INFO:
Online application is required and may be obtained directly from the Humanities Center web site. Access to the system opens in August.
Duration: Academic year. Normally September 15 to June 15. No renewals.
Deadline: October. Award announcement by late March.

ADVISORY COUNCIL:
R. Lanier Anderson
William Atkins
Giovanna Ceserani
Kristin Kennedy Clark
Susan Dackerman
Andrea Davies
Fred Donner
Paula Findlen
Roland Greene
Mark Greif
Niloofar Haeri
Roberta Katz
Regina Kunzel
Linda R. Meier
Kathryn Moler
Serena Rao
Mary Anne Rothberg Rowen
Peter Seymour
Dafna Zur

ADDRESS INQUIRIES TO:
See e-mail address above.

STIFTELSEN RIKSBANKENS JUBILEUMSFOND   [364]
Regeringsgatan 67
111 56 Stockholm Sweden
(46) 08-50 62 64 00
E-mail: rj@rj.se
Web Site: www.rj.se

FOUNDED: 1964

AREAS OF INTEREST:
Scientific research in humanities and social sciences.

NAME(S) OF PROGRAMS:
● **Europe and Global Challenges**
● **Flexit**
● **Pro Futura**
● **Research Grants**

TYPE:
Conferences/seminars; Research grants.

YEAR PROGRAM STARTED: 1965

PURPOSE:
To support and promote scientific research in humanities and social sciences.

LEGAL BASIS:
Independent, non-governmental foundation.

ELIGIBILITY:
Open to single researchers or research groups. The Foundation is interested in supporting multidisciplinary or interdisciplinary research projects in which researchers from different disciplines, faculties, localities or countries collaborate with Swedish scholars.

FINANCIAL DATA:
Amount of support per award: Average Project Grant: SEK 3,600,000; Average Program Grant: SEK 35,000,000.
Total amount of support: Approximately SEK 435,385,000 for the year 2018.

CO-OP FUNDING PROGRAMS: Occasional co-financing for large projects.

NO. MOST RECENT APPLICANTS: 647 for the year 2018.

NO. AWARDS: 42 projects for the year 2018.

APPLICATION INFO:
Applicants should first submit a short outline sketch and a publication list. If the preliminary proposal is accepted, applicants will be required to send a complete application.
Duration: Three years average for projects; six to eight years for programs.
Deadline: March 15.

PUBLICATIONS:
Annual report; program publications; yearbook.

STAFF:
Marika Hedin, Chief Executive Officer
Bjorn Olsson, Chief Investment Officer
Hanna Kollerstrom, Head of Communications
Elisabeth Hong, Administrative Director
AnnaLena Hallner, Research Manager, Art, Languages, and Literature
Dr. Robert Hamren, Research Manager, Economics, Law, and Political Science
Dr. Eva Stenskold, Research Manager, Humanities
Dr. Torbjorn Eng, Research Manager, Social Science
Dr. Fredrik Lundmark, Research Manager, Social Science

ADDRESS INQUIRIES TO:
Hanna Kollerstrom
Head of Communications
(See address above.)

SWANN FOUNDATION FOR CARICATURE AND CARTOON   [365]
Prints and Photographs Division
Library of Congress
101 Independence Avenue, S.E.
Washington, DC 20540-4730
(202) 707-9115
Fax: (202) 707-6647
E-mail: swann@loc.gov
Web Site: www.loc.gov/rr/print/swann/swann-fellow.html

FOUNDED: 1967

AREAS OF INTEREST:
Caricature and cartoons.

NAME(S) OF PROGRAMS:
● **Swann Foundation Fellowship**

TYPE:
Conferences/seminars; Fellowships; Internships; Project/program grants; Visiting scholars. Small grants. Annual fellowship awarded to candidate for a Ph.D. or Master's degree.

YEAR PROGRAM STARTED: 1995

PURPOSE:
To support the documentation and understanding of caricature and cartoon as art.

LEGAL BASIS:
Nonprofit, federal agency.

ELIGIBILITY:
Fellowships are awarded to active Ph.D. candidates, M.A. candidates and those people who have received an advanced degree within the last three years.

GEOG. RESTRICTIONS: North America.

FINANCIAL DATA:
Amount of support per award: Up to $5,000.
Total amount of support: Varies.

NO. MOST RECENT APPLICANTS: Approximately 15.

NO. AWARDS: Varies.

APPLICATION INFO:
Applicants should submit a project proposal and budget.
Duration: One academic year, generally fall through following late spring.
Deadline: February 15.

STAFF:
Martha H. Kennedy, Curator, Popular and Applied Graphic Art
Helena Zinkham, Swann Fund Administrator

ADDRESS INQUIRIES TO:
Martha Kennedy
Curator, Popular and Applied Graphic Art
(See address above.)

*SPECIAL STIPULATIONS:
Must be a graduate student or a postgraduate within three years of receiving an M.A. or Ph.D. from a university in the U.S., Canada, or Mexico.

UCLA CHICANO STUDIES RESEARCH CENTER
193 Haines Hall
Box 951544
Los Angeles, CA 90095
(310) 825-2363
Fax: (310) 206-1784
E-mail: csrcinfo@chicano.ucla.edu
Web Site: www.chicano.ucla.edu
www.iac.ucla.edu

TYPE:
Fellowships; Visiting scholars.

See entry 976 for full listing.

UKRAINIAN RESEARCH INSTITUTE AT HARVARD UNIVERSITY   [366]
34 Kirkland Street
Cambridge, MA 02138
(617) 495-4053
Fax: (617) 495-8097
E-mail: huri@fas.harvard.edu
Web Site: www.huri.harvard.edu

AREAS OF INTEREST:
Ukrainian history, literature, philology, culture, and related areas of study.

NAME(S) OF PROGRAMS:
● **Petro Jacyk Distinguished Fellowship in Ukrainian Studies**

TYPE:
Fellowships. The Jacyk Distinguished Fellowship is designed to bring senior scholars to Harvard University for focused research in Ukrainian history, literature, philology, culture, and other related areas of study in the humanities and social sciences fields. This fellowship is awarded biennially.

PURPOSE:
To further professional development in the field of Ukrainian studies.

ELIGIBILITY:
All senior scholars in the field of Ukrainian studies are eligible to apply.

FINANCIAL DATA:
Stipend covers the cost of housing, health insurance, and other living expenses. In addition to the stipend, the award provides for the cost of direct round-trip travel to Harvard University.
Amount of support per award: $5,000 per month stipend.

APPLICATION INFO:
Application is available online. Nominations may also be submitted. Individuals submitting nominations should submit a letter stating the nominees name, current position, field of study, and basis for nomination.
Duration: Five months.
Deadline: January 2022.

ADDRESS INQUIRIES TO:
Tymish Holowinsky, HURI Executive Director
(See address above.)

*SPECIAL STIPULATIONS:
Jacyk Distinguished Fellow will preside over the Petro Jacyk Seminar in Ukrainian Studies, a forum presented as part of the HURI Seminar Series in Ukrainian Studies.

UKRAINIAN RESEARCH INSTITUTE AT HARVARD UNIVERSITY [367]
34 Kirkland Street
Cambridge, MA 02138
(617) 495-4053
Fax: (617) 495-8097
E-mail: huri@fas.harvard.edu
Web Site: www.huri.harvard.edu

AREAS OF INTEREST:
Ukrainian history, literature, philology, culture, and other related areas of study.

NAME(S) OF PROGRAMS:
● **The HURI Research Fellowships in Ukrainian Studies**
● **The Jaroslaw and Nadia Mihaychuk Postdoctoral Research Fellowships in Ukrainian Studies**

TYPE:
Fellowships.

PURPOSE:
To bring scholars from the international academic community to Harvard for focused research on projects in Ukrainian history, literature, philology, culture, and other related areas of study in the humanities and social sciences fields.

ELIGIBILITY:
Individuals who hold a doctorate in one of the above-mentioned fields of study and who have demonstrated a commitment to Ukrainian studies are eligible to apply.

Applicants who have received their Ph.D. or its academic equivalent within the past eight to 10 years are especially encouraged to apply for the HURI Research Fellowship. Those individuals who are more recent Ph.Ds. or have completed or defended their dissertation by the time they submit their application are encouraged to apply for the Mihaychuk Postdoctoral Research Fellowship.

Applicants must be eligible to receive and maintain a short-term J-1 visa to carry out research on an Institute fellowship.

FINANCIAL DATA:
Stipend covers cost of housing, health insurance, and other living expenses. In addition to the stipend, the awards provide for the cost of direct round-trip travel to Harvard University.
Amount of support per award: Stipend of $4,400 per month.

APPLICATION INFO:
Application is available online.
Duration: Three to eight months.
Deadline: January.

ADDRESS INQUIRIES TO:
The HURI Fellowships in Ukrainian Studies
Tymish Holowinsky, HURI Executive Director
(See address above.)

*SPECIAL STIPULATIONS:
Fellows are expected to participate in the scholarly life of the University during Harvard's academic year and offer a formal presentation based on original research.

VILLA I TATTI: THE HARVARD UNIVERSITY CENTER FOR ITALIAN RENAISSANCE STUDIES
Via di Vincigliata, 26
50135 Florence Italy
E-mail: fellowships@itatti.harvard.edu
Web Site: itatti.harvard.edu/fellowships

TYPE:
Fellowships. Villa I Tatti - The Harvard University Center for Italian Renaissance Studies in Florence, Italy, and the Warburg Institute School of Advanced Study at the University of London offer a joint, residential fellowship. Fellows will spend the fall term (September to December) in London and the spring term (January to June) in Florence. The fellowship is designed for early and midcareer scholars in the field of history, with preference given to advanced research projects that address the history of science and knowledge related to early modern Italy, including transnational connections between Italy and other cultures. Scholars can also apply to work on the transmission and circulation of ideas, objects, and people during the Renaissance, into and beyond the Italian peninsula, or on the historiography of the Italian Renaissance, including the rebirth of interest in the Renaissance in later periods.

See entry 872 for full listing.

VILLA I TATTI: THE HARVARD UNIVERSITY CENTER FOR ITALIAN RENAISSANCE STUDIES
Via di Vincigliata, 26
50135 Florence Italy
E-mail: fellowships@itatti.harvard.edu
Web Site: itatti.harvard.edu/fellowships
byzantinestudies.boun.edu.tr

TYPE:
Fellowships. Villa I Tatti: The Harvard University Center for Italian Renaissance Studies and the Byzantine Studies Research Center of Bogazici University offer a joint, residential fellowship to support research on the interaction between Italy and the Byzantine Empire (ca. 1300 to ca. 1700). This collaboration aims to foster the development of research on Late Byzantine-Italian relations by supporting early-career scholars whose work explores Byzantium's cross-cultural contacts in the late medieval and early modern Mediterranean world through the study of art, architecture, archaeology, history, literature, material culture, music, philosophy, religion, or science.

See entry 873 for full listing.

VILLA I TATTI: THE HARVARD UNIVERSITY CENTER FOR ITALIAN RENAISSANCE STUDIES
Via di Vincigliata, 26
50135 Florence Italy
E-mail: fellowships@itatti.harvard.edu
Web Site: itatti.harvard.edu/fellowships

TYPE:
Fellowships. Joint fellowship designed to support early and midcareer scholars in the field of art history.

See entry 874 for full listing.

VILLA I TATTI: THE HARVARD UNIVERSITY CENTER FOR ITALIAN RENAISSANCE STUDIES
Via di Vincigliata, 26
50135 Florence Italy
E-mail: fellowships@itatti.harvard.edu
Web Site: itatti.harvard.edu/fellowships

TYPE:
Fellowships. Berenson Fellowship supports postdoctoral research of scholars who explore "Italy in the World." Projects should address the transnational dialogues between Italy and other cultures during the Renaissance, broadly understood historically to include the period from the 14th to the 17th century.

Fellowship in the Digital Humanities supports research of scholars in the humanities or social sciences, librarians, archivists, and data science professionals whose research interests or practice cut across traditional disciplinary boundaries and actively employ technology in their work.

I Tatti Fellowship supports postdoctoral research in any aspect of the Italian Renaissance.

Craig Hugh Smyth Fellowship is designed for curators and conservators pursuing advanced research in any aspect of the Italian Renaissance.

David and Julie Tobey Fellowship supports postdoctoral research on drawings, prints, and illustrated manuscripts from the Italian Renaissance, and especially the role that these works played in the creative process, the history of taste and collecting, and questions of connoisseurship.

Wallace Fellowship supports postdoctoral research on the historiography and impact of the Italian Renaissance in the modern era, namely the 19th to 21st centuries.

See entry 871 for full listing.

LEWIS WALPOLE LIBRARY [368]

Yale University
154 Main Street
Farmington, CT 06032
(860) 677-2140
Fax: (860) 677-6369
E-mail: walpole@yale.edu
Web Site: www.library.yale.edu/walpole

FOUNDED: 1979

AREAS OF INTEREST:
18th century studies (mainly British), the study of Horace Walpole and Strawberry Hill, 18th century British satirical prints.

NAME(S) OF PROGRAMS:
- **Visiting Research Fellowship Program**

TYPE:
Conferences/seminars; Fellowships; Travel grants. 18th century studies (mainly British), including history, literature, theatre, drama, art, architecture, politics, philosophy or social history.

YEAR PROGRAM STARTED: 1979

PURPOSE:
To fund study into any aspect of British 18th century studies in the Library's collection of 18th century British prints, paintings, books and manuscripts.

ELIGIBILITY:
Applicants should normally be pursuing an advanced degree or must be engaged in postdoctoral research or equivalent research. Study is at doctoral, postdoctoral, postgraduate and research levels.

FINANCIAL DATA:
Amount of support per award: Research Fellowship: Includes round-trip travel to the Library from the fellow's home location, a per diem for days in residence at the Library, and free accommodation in the fellows' quarters on the Lewis Walpole Library campus.

Travel Grant: Includes round-trip travel to the Library from the fellow's home location and free accommodation in the fellows' quarters on the Lewis Walpole Library campus but not the per diem.

Total amount of support: Varies.

CO-OP FUNDING PROGRAMS: ASECS Library fellowship; Lewis Walpole Library/Beinecke Rare Book & Manuscript Library joint eight-week fellowship.

NO. MOST RECENT APPLICANTS: 63.

NO. AWARDS: Up to 26.

APPLICATION INFO:
Applicants must submit a curriculum vitae, a brief outline of research proposal of up to three pages and two confidential letters of recommendation.

Duration: Four-week and eight-week Visiting Research Fellowship; two-week travel grants.

Deadline: Second Monday in January.

ADDRESS INQUIRIES TO:
Nicole L. Bouché
W.S. Lewis Librarian
and Executive Director
Lewis Walpole Library
Yale University
P.O. Box 1408
Farmington, CT 06034

WOODROW WILSON INTERNATIONAL CENTER FOR SCHOLARS [369]

One Woodrow Wilson Plaza
1300 Pennsylvania Avenue, N.W.
Washington, DC 20004-3027
(202) 691-4170
Fax: (202) 691-4001
E-mail: fellowships@wilsoncenter.org
Web Site: www.wilsoncenter.org

FOUNDED: 1968

AREAS OF INTEREST:
Social sciences, humanities and public policy.

NAME(S) OF PROGRAMS:
- **Fellowship Program at the Woodrow Wilson International Center for Scholars**

TYPE:
Fellowships; Research grants; Residencies; Scholarships; Visiting scholars. The Center seeks to commemorate, through its residential fellowship program of advanced research, both the scholarly depth and the public concerns of Woodrow Wilson. The Center welcomes outstanding project proposals in the social sciences and humanities on global issues - topics that intersect with questions of public policy or provide the historical framework to illume policy issues of contemporary importance. The Center especially welcomes projects likely to foster communication between the world of ideas and the world of public affairs.

Projects should have relevance to the world of public policy. Fellows should be prepared to interact with policymakers in Washington and with the Center's staff working on similar areas.

Fellowships are tenable in residence only at the Woodrow Wilson International Center for Scholars. The Center will not provide support for research to be carried out elsewhere. Fellows devote their full time to research and writing.

YEAR PROGRAM STARTED: 1970

LEGAL BASIS:
Government agency.

ELIGIBILITY:
The Center seeks individuals from throughout the world with superior projects representing diverse scholarly interests in the social sciences and humanities - topics that intersect with questions of public policy.

Academic participants are normally established scholars at the postdoctoral level but cannot be currently working on a Ph.D.

For nonacademic participants, namely those from careers in government, journalism, business, diplomacy and other professions, an equivalent degree of professional achievement is required.

Criteria for selection include scholarly capabilities, promise and achievements, the importance and originality of the proposed research, and the likelihood of the applicant being able to accomplish what he or she proposes.

Applicants should have a very good command of spoken English, since the Center is designed to encourage the exchange of ideas among its Fellows.

FINANCIAL DATA:
The Center tries to ensure that the stipend provided under the fellowship, together with fellow's other sources of funding (e.g., grants secured by applicant and sabbatical allowances), approximate a fellow's regular salary.

Amount of support per award: Varies.
Total amount of support: $1,000,000 (appropriated) for the year 2017.

NO. MOST RECENT APPLICANTS: 320.

NO. AWARDS: 15 to 20.

REPRESENTATIVE AWARDS:
"Technology and the Rise of the U.S. Global Security State: How Can History Inform Policy?;" " The Organizational Roots of Persistent Electoral Violence in Africa;" "Rule of Law and Open Governance Reforms in China: Implications for China, U.S.-China Relations and International Relations."

APPLICATION INFO:
A complete application must include the following:
(1) the Fellowship Application Form;
(2) a current curriculum vitae (not to exceed three pages);
(3) a list of publications that includes exact titles, names of publishers, dates of publication and status of forthcoming publications (not to exceed three pages);
(4) a project proposal (not to exceed five single-spaced typed pages, using 12-point type);
(5) a bibliography for the project that includes primary sources and relevant secondary sources (not to exceed three pages);
(6) the Financial Information Form and;
(7) two letters of reference.

All application materials must be submitted in English.

Duration: Fellowships of usually nine months are tenable September 1 of the fellowship year.

Deadline: October 1 for receipt of applications. Decisions announced by March of the following year.

PUBLICATIONS:
Annual report; application guidelines.

OFFICERS:
Jane Harman, Director, President and Chief Executive Officer

ADDRESS INQUIRIES TO:
Kim Conner, Fellowship Specialist
(See address above.)

WINTERTHUR MUSEUM, GARDEN & LIBRARY [370]

5105 Kennett Pike
Winterthur, DE 19735
(302) 888-4876
Fax: (302) 888-4870
E-mail: croeber@winterthur.org
Web Site: www.winterthur.org

FOUNDED: 1951

AREAS OF INTEREST:
American decorative arts, American art, American cultural and social history and horticulture.

NAME(S) OF PROGRAMS:
- **Dissertation Fellowships**
- **Maker-Creator Fellowships**
- **Postdoctoral Fellowship**
- **Short-term Fellowship**

TYPE:
Fellowships. Long-term and short-term fellowships to be held in residence at Winterthur Museum, Garden & Library.

The Dissertation Fellowships are for doctoral candidates. The award is a four- to nine-month fellowship.

Maker-Creator Fellowships are one- to three-month fellowships designed for artists, writers, filmmakers, horticulturalists, craftspeople and others who wish to examine, study and immerse themselves in Winterthur's vast collections in order to inspire creative and artistic works.

Short-term Fellowship consists of one- to three-month fellowships designed to promote research and study in topics of relevance to Winterthur's collections.

All fellowships are residential, requiring study to be done at Winterthur.

PURPOSE:
To promote research in any humanistic field related to Winterthur's collections (museum, library, garden), work of an interdisciplinary nature and/or research with both objects and documents.

LEGAL BASIS:
Tax-exempt, public charitable organization.

ELIGIBILITY:
Applicants for a Dissertation Fellowship must have completed coursework, passed qualifying exams, fulfilled language requirements, and have an approved prospectus. The fellowship is open to students in departments of history, anthropology, folklore, material culture, art history, American studies, African-American history, historic preservation, and related fields.

Maker-Creator Fellowships are available to artists, writers, filmmakers, horticulturalists, craftspeople, and those in related fields.

Short-term Fellowships are available to academic, museum and independent scholars and to support dissertation research.

FINANCIAL DATA:
Applicants may hold sabbaticals and grants from their own institutions, but may not simultaneously hold other major fellowships. Housing is available in a cottage on the museum grounds (full housekeeping facilities and furnished rooms).
Amount of support per award: Dissertation Fellowships: $7,000 per semester; Postdoctoral Fellowships: $16,800 over four months; Short-term Fellowships: $1,750 per month.
Total amount of support: Varies.

REPRESENTATIVE AWARDS:
John Lardas Modern, Professor of Religious Studies, Franklin & Marshall College, Lancaster, PA, "Haunted Modernity; or, the Metaphysics of Secularism in Antebellum America;" Julia A. Sienkewicz, University of Illinois, "Citizenship by Design: the Creation of Identity through Art, Architecture and

Landscape in the Early Republic;" Sarah Carter, Harvard University, "A Basket, A Needle, A Penknife: Object Lessons in Nineteenth-Century American Material and Visual Culture;" Nicole Belolan, Ph.D. candidate, University of Delaware, Newark, DE, "Navigating the World: The Material Culture of Physical Mobility Impairment in the Early American North, 1700-1861."

APPLICATION INFO:
Application instructions and materials are available online at the Winterthur web site. Applicants for each fellowship should submit a three- to five-page statement of purpose, a curriculum vitae and two letters of recommendation. Supporting materials for dissertation research must include a letter from the dissertation advisor.
Duration: Dissertation Fellowships: Four to nine months; Maker-Creator Fellowships and Short-term Fellowships: One to three months; Postdoctoral Fellowships: Four months.
Deadline: January 15. Announcement by April 30.

IRS I.D.: 51-0066038

STAFF:
Thomas A. Guiler, Ph.D., Assistant Professor of History and Public Humanities

ADDRESS INQUIRIES TO:
Research Fellowship Program
Academic Programs Department
E-mail: academicprograms@winterthur.org
(See address above.)

WOLF HUMANITIES CENTER [371]

619 Williams Hall
255 South 36th Street
Philadelphia, PA 19104-6305
(215) 746-5940
E-mail: wolfhumanities@upenn.edu
Web Site: www.wolfhumanities.upenn.edu

FOUNDED: 1999

AREAS OF INTEREST:
Humanities.

NAME(S) OF PROGRAMS:
- **Andrew W. Mellon Postdoctoral Fellowships in the Humanities**

TYPE:
Fellowships. Fellows conduct research and teach one course.

YEAR PROGRAM STARTED: 1999

PURPOSE:
To support and encourage the intellectual development of untenured scholars in the humanities.

LEGAL BASIS:
Nonprofit, non-taxable university.

ELIGIBILITY:
Candidates must have research interests that relate to the Wolf Humanities Center topic of study for the year of the fellowship. Preference is given to proposals that are interdisciplinary and to candidates who have not previously used the resources of the University of Pennsylvania and whose work would allow them to take advantage of the research strengths of the institution and to make a contribution to its intellectual life. Research proposals are invited in all areas of humanistic studies except educational curriculum-building and performing arts.

FINANCIAL DATA:
Fellowships include health insurance and a $3,000 research fund.
Amount of support per award: $59,300.

NO. AWARDS: 5.

APPLICATION INFO:
Applications are available, commencing in May, on the web site. Applicants are expected to submit the application online, which includes a description of their proposed project, as well as recommendations.
Duration: One year in residence at University of Pennsylvania.
Deadline: October 15 of the year preceding the fellowship. Announcement in December.

STAFF:
Karen Redrob, Director
Sara Varney, Associate Director
Sarah Miliniski, Program Manager
Dru Baker, Program Coordinator

ADDRESS INQUIRIES TO:
Sara Varney, Associate Director
(See address above.)

CARTER G. WOODSON INSTITUTE FOR AFRICAN-AMERICAN AND AFRICAN STUDIES [372]

University of Virginia
McCormick Road, 108 Minor Hall
Charlottesville, VA 22903
(434) 924-3109
Fax: (434) 924-8820
E-mail: woodson@virginia.edu
Web Site: woodson.virginia.edu

FOUNDED: 1981

AREAS OF INTEREST:
Those disciplines of the humanities and social sciences which concern themselves with Afro-American and African Studies.

NAME(S) OF PROGRAMS:
- **African-American and African Studies Fellowships**

TYPE:
Fellowships. The Woodson Institute offers residential fellowships to predoctoral and postdoctoral scholars. These fellowships are designed to facilitate the completion of works in progress by providing scholars with unencumbered leave.

Afro-American and African Studies is considered to cover Africa, Africans and peoples of African descent in North, Central and South America and the Caribbean, past and present.

YEAR PROGRAM STARTED: 1981

PURPOSE:
To help researchers complete dissertations, books and other research projects focusing on the Black experience.

LEGAL BASIS:
University.

ELIGIBILITY:
Applicants for the predoctoral fellowships must have completed all requirements for the Ph.D. except the dissertation prior to August 1. Applicants for the postdoctoral fellowship must have been awarded their Ph.D. by the time of application or furnish proof that it will have been received prior to July. There are no restrictions as to citizenship or current residence. Employees of the University of Virginia may not apply.

Postdoctoral applicants must have received their Ph.D. no earlier than six years prior to the application deadline.

Proposals will be judged on the basis of the significance of the proposed work, the applicant's qualifications, familiarity with existing relevant research literature, the research design of the project and the promise of completion within the award period. Preference will be given to projects whose field research is already substantially completed.

Fellowship recipients must be in residence at the University of Virginia for the duration of the award period and must agree to teach one course per year in the African-American Studies Program during the fall or spring semester. In pursuit of these goals, predoctoral fellows will become visiting graduate students attached to their respective disciplinary departments, and postdoctoral fellows will receive the status of visiting scholars in their respective fields.

FINANCIAL DATA:
Amount of support per award: Predoctoral Fellowship: $24,000 per year; Postdoctoral Fellowship: $47,476.

NO. AWARDS: 6 per year.

APPLICATION INFO:
Complete guidelines are available on the Institute web site.
Duration: Two years.
Deadline: December 1. Notification by mail early March.

PUBLICATIONS:
Program guidelines.

STAFF:
Deborah E. McDowell, Director

ADDRESS INQUIRIES TO:
Program Administrator
(See address above.)

*SPECIAL STIPULATIONS:
Fellows are required to present a formal paper to the University community at least once a year.

YALE CENTER FOR BRITISH ART [373]
1080 Chapel Street
New Haven, CT 06520
(203) 432-9805
Fax: (203) 432-4538
E-mail: ycba.research@yale.edu
Web Site: british.yale.edu/research/residential-scholar-awards

FOUNDED: 1977

AREAS OF INTEREST:
British art, history and literature.

NAME(S) OF PROGRAMS:
● Visiting Scholar Awards

TYPE:
Fellowships; Research grants; Residencies; Visiting scholars. Short-term resident fellowships for scholars of literature, history, the history of art or related fields.

YEAR PROGRAM STARTED: 1978

PURPOSE:
To allow scholars of literature, history, the history of art or related fields to study the Center's holdings of paintings, sculpture, drawings, prints and rare books and to make use of its research facilities (photograph archive and reference library).

LEGAL BASIS:
University-affiliated museum and research center.

ELIGIBILITY:
Open to scholars engaged in predoctoral and postdoctoral or equivalent research related to British art and to museum professionals whose responsibilities and research interests include British art.

FINANCIAL DATA:
Fellowships include the cost of travel to and from New Haven and also provide accommodation and a living allowance. Recipients will be required to be in residence in New Haven during the Fellowship period.
Amount of support per award: Varies.

CO-OP FUNDING PROGRAMS: One fellowship per annum is reserved for members of the American Society for Eighteenth-Century Studies; by arrangement with the Huntington Library and the Delaware Art Museum, scholars may apply for tandem awards.

NO. MOST RECENT APPLICANTS: 22.

NO. AWARDS: Approximately 20.

REPRESENTATIVE AWARDS:
Sria Chatterjee, Ph.D. candidate, Princeton University, "Colonial Weather;" Elena Korotkikh, Assistant Curator, Department for 19th and 20th century European and American Art, State Pushkin Museum of Fine Art.

APPLICATION INFO:
Application must be submitted online. Complete application information is available on the web site.
Duration: One to four months.
Deadline: January.

PUBLICATIONS:
Brochure.

STAFF:
Courtney J. Martin, Director
Martina Droth, Deputy Director of Research
Dr. Jemma Field, Associate Director of Research

ADDRESS INQUIRIES TO:
Dr. Jemma Field
Associate Director of Research
P.O. Box 208280
New Haven, CT 06520
E-mail: jemma.field@yale.edu

*SPECIAL STIPULATIONS:
Inquiries by e-mail only.

Architecture

THE AMERICAN INSTITUTE OF ARCHITECTS [374]
1735 New York Avenue, N.W.
Washington, DC 20006-5292
(202) 626-7358
Fax: (202) 626-7399
E-mail: aah@aia.org
Web Site: www.aia.org

FOUNDED: 1952

AREAS OF INTEREST:
Health care, facility planning, design and construction, facilities management, clinical engineering, and safety and security.

NAME(S) OF PROGRAMS:
● AIA Arthur N. Tuttle, Jr. Graduate Fellowship in Health Facility Planning and Design

TYPE:
Fellowships; Research grants. The American Institute of Architects and the Academy of Architecture for Health sponsor this program with additional support from the Steris Corporation, which offers one or more graduate fellowships.

YEAR PROGRAM STARTED: 1952

PURPOSE:
To increase the amount of research being done in the area of health care facility design and planning.

LEGAL BASIS:
Nonprofit organization.

ELIGIBILITY:
Open to graduate and postgraduate students enrolled at an accredited school of architecture. Applicants must be citizens of Canada, Mexico or the U.S.

FINANCIAL DATA:
Amount of support per award: Typically $2,000 to $10,000.

NO. AWARDS: 2 for the year 2017.

APPLICATION INFO:
Guidelines and application forms are available on the Institute web site.
Duration: One to two years depending on proposal.
Deadline: February.

PUBLICATIONS:
Guidelines.

THE AMERICAN INSTITUTE OF ARCHITECTS [375]
1735 New York Avenue, N.W.
Washington, DC 20006-5292
(202) 626-7529
Fax: (202) 626-7399
E-mail: scholarships@aia.org
Web Site: www.aia.org

FOUNDED: 1943

AREAS OF INTEREST:
Architecture.

NAME(S) OF PROGRAMS:
● AIA/F Diversity Advancement Scholarship

TYPE:
Scholarships. Awards to provide an opportunity for financially disadvantaged and/or minority groups to pursue a professional degree in architecture.

YEAR PROGRAM STARTED: 1973

PURPOSE:
To provide scholarships for those who would not otherwise have the opportunity to be enrolled in professional architecture studies.

ELIGIBILITY:
Student must be a U.S. citizen, have a minimum 3.0 grade point average, and be:
(1) a high school student planning to enroll in an NAAB-accredited architecture degree program;
(2) a rising second-year college student in an NAAB-accredited architecture degree program or;
(3) a technical school or community college student who has completed high school or its equivalent and intends to transfer to an NAAB-accredited architecture program.

GEOG. RESTRICTIONS: United States.

FINANCIAL DATA:
Scholarship awards vary according to financial need. The amount of the award is determined based on the financial information and consultation with the Director of Financial Aid at the student's school.
Amount of support per award: $4,000 per year (up to $20,000 total award).

NO. MOST RECENT APPLICANTS: 120.

NO. AWARDS: Approximately 5.

APPLICATION INFO:
Candidates must submit:
(1) a resume;
(2) a personal essay;
(3) two letters of recommendation;
(4) two examples of their creative work and;
(5) estimated college expenses (FAFSA required).
Duration: One academic year. Renewable up to five years.
Deadline: January.

OFFICERS:
Robert Ivey, Executive Vice President and Chief Executive Officer, American Institute of Architects

ADDRESS INQUIRIES TO:
Jamie Yeung, Manager
Professional Development and Resources
(See address above.)

AMERICAN SCHOOL OF CLASSICAL STUDIES AT ATHENS
6-8 Charlton Street
Princeton, NJ 08540-5232
(609) 683-0800
Fax: (609) 924-0578
E-mail: application@ascsa.org
Web Site: www.ascsa.edu.gr

TYPE:
Fellowships.

See entry 395 for full listing.

AMERICAN SOCIETY OF INTERIOR DESIGNERS EDUCATIONAL FOUNDATION, INC. [376]
1152 15th Street, N.W.
Suite 910
Washington, DC 20005
(202) 675-2345
Fax: (202) 546-3240
E-mail: foundation@asid.org
Web Site: www.asid.org/foundation

FOUNDED: 1975

AREAS OF INTEREST:
Interior design (commercial and residential) and interior design-related industry.

NAME(S) OF PROGRAMS:
• **ASID Foundation Legacy Scholarships for Graduate Students**
• **ASID Foundation Legacy Scholarships for Undergraduates**
• **ASID Foundation Transform Grant**
• **Irene Winifred Eno Grant**
• **Joel Polsky Academic Achievement Award**
• **Joel Polsky Prize**

TYPE:
Awards/prizes; Research grants; Scholarships; Seed money grants. The ASID Foundation

Legacy Scholarships for Graduate Students are awarded on the basis of academic/creative accomplishment.

The ASID Foundation Legacy Scholarships for Undergraduates are given to creatively outstanding students as demonstrated through their portfolio.

The ASID Foundation Transform Grant is a research grant to address critical gaps in industry knowledge, advance design understanding, and transform the practice of interior design for the benefit of everyone. The grant provides funding for seed/start-up projects and research projects.

Irene Winifred Eno Grant provides financial assistance to individuals or groups engaged in the creation of an educational program(s) or an interior design research project dedicated to health, safety and welfare.

The Polsky Academic Achievement Award is given annually to recognize an outstanding undergraduate or graduate student's interior design research or thesis project.

The Joel Polsky Prize recognizes outstanding academic contributions to the discipline of interior design through literature or visual communication.

PURPOSE:
To encourage excellence in the field of interior design.

LEGAL BASIS:
Nonprofit foundation.

ELIGIBILITY:
The ASID Foundation Legacy Scholarships for Graduate Students are open to students who are enrolled in or have been accepted to a graduate-level interior design program at a degree-granting institution.

The ASID Foundation Legacy Scholarships for Undergraduates are open to all students in their junior or senior year of undergraduate study and enrolled in at least a three-year program of interior design.

The ASID Foundation Transform Grant is open to graduate students, educators, researchers, interior design practitioners, institutions or other research-related groups.

The Irene Winifred Eno Grant is open to students, educators, interior design practitioners, institutions or other interior design-related groups.

The Joel Polsky Academic Achievement Award judges interior design research or doctoral and Master's thesis projects.

The Joel Polsky Prize entrants should address the needs of the public, designers and students on such topics as educational research, behavioral science, business practice, design process, theory or other technical subjects.

High school students and college freshmen are not eligible.

GEOG. RESTRICTIONS: United States.

FINANCIAL DATA:
Amount of support per award: Irene Winifred Eno Grant, Joel Polsky Academic Achievement Award and Joel Polsky Prize: $5,000; Legacy Scholarship for graduate and undergraduate students: $4,000.

APPLICATION INFO:
Complete details are available online.
Duration: One-time award.

PUBLICATIONS:
ASID ICON, magazine; application guidelines.

OFFICERS:
Valerie O'Keefe, Foundation Manager

ADDRESS INQUIRIES TO:
Valerie O'Keefe, Foundation Manager
(See address above.)

ARCHITECTURAL LEAGUE OF NEW YORK [377]
594 Broadway, Suite 607
New York, NY 10012
(212) 753-1722
Fax: (212) 486-9173
E-mail: info@archleague.org
Web Site: archleague.org

FOUNDED: 1881

AREAS OF INTEREST:
Architecture, architectural history and urban studies.

NAME(S) OF PROGRAMS:
• **Deborah J. Norden Fund**

TYPE:
Travel grants. The Deborah J. Norden Fund, established in 1995 in memory of architect and arts administrator Deborah Norden, awards travel/study grants to students and recent graduates in the field of architecture, architectural history, and urban studies.

YEAR PROGRAM STARTED: 1995

PURPOSE:
To support genuinely independent projects that require travel.

ELIGIBILITY:
Open to full-time residents of the U.S., Canada and Mexico. Applicants need not be citizens.

While requests for support of dissertation research will be considered, they are not a priority of the fund. Preference will be given to strong proposals from applicants who have not had this sort of opportunity before.

Architectural League board members or staff members, firms or immediate family of board or staff members, and firms or immediate family of jury members are not eligible to participate.

FINANCIAL DATA:
Amount of support per award: Up to $5,000.
Total amount of support: $5,000.

NO. MOST RECENT APPLICANTS: 110.

NO. AWARDS: 2.

APPLICATION INFO:
Applicants should submit a maximum three-page proposal which succinctly describes the objectives of the grant request and how it will assist the applicant's intellectual and creative development. The grant amount requested must be specified. The submission should also include a resume of not more than two pages, project schedule, and budget for travel and other project costs. Two letters of recommendation must be requested from individuals who are knowledgeable about the applicant's ability and project. The applicant's name and brief project title must appear on the first page of the proposal.
Deadline: Mid-April. Announcement in early June.

ADDRESS INQUIRIES TO:
E-mail: norden@archleague.org

ARCHITECTURAL LEAGUE OF NEW YORK [378]
594 Broadway, Suite 607
New York, NY 10012
(212) 753-1722
E-mail: info@archleague.org
Web Site: archleague.org

FOUNDED: 1881

AREAS OF INTEREST:
Young architects.

NAME(S) OF PROGRAMS:
- **The League Prize for Young Architects and Designers**

TYPE:
Awards/prizes; Conferences/seminars.

YEAR PROGRAM STARTED: 1982

PURPOSE:
To recognize specific works of high quality and to encourage the exchange of ideas among young architects and designers who might otherwise not have a forum; to focus on the aesthetic, cultural, and social concerns of architecture and the allied arts; to help architects, artists, and the public enrich their understanding of the purposes and importance of the art of architecture.

ELIGIBILITY:
Entrants may submit work done independently. Entrants must be 10 years or less out of graduate or undergraduate school; students are not eligible for this competition. Work completed for fulfillment of course requirements at academic institutions is not eligible.

FINANCIAL DATA:
Amount of support per award: $2,000.

NO. MOST RECENT APPLICANTS: 100.

NO. AWARDS: 6 per year.

APPLICATION INFO:
A call for entries is issued each fall. A written statement (not to exceed 250 words) is required, which defines and considers the work under the rubric of the competition theme. Significant weight is given to how an applicant's work addresses the theme. A single portfolio, which may include several projects, must be bound and no larger than 11x14 inches. The portfolio may not contain more than 30 double-sided pages. CDs, models, slides and transparencies will not be accepted.

Each submission must include a $25 entry fee. Each entrant must submit one digital form and one hard copy form. Insert form, intact, into an unsealed envelope attached to the inside back cover of the submission. To maintain anonymity, no identification of the entrant may appear on any part of the submission, except on the entry form and return envelope.

Portfolios will be returned by mail only if a self-addressed envelope with postage is also enclosed. The Architectural League assumes no liability for original drawings. The League will take every precaution to return submissions intact, but can assume no responsibility for loss or damage. Portfolios may be discarded after six months if no return envelope is provided.

Deadline: Varies.

ADDRESS INQUIRIES TO:
Anne Rieselbach, Program Director
(See address above.)

THE COMMUNITY FOUNDATION OF LOUISVILLE, INC.
325 West Main Street, Suite 1110
Louisville, KY 40202
(502) 585-4649
Fax: (502) 587-7484
E-mail: info@cflouisville.org
Web Site: www.cflouisville.org

TYPE:
Endowments; General operating grants; Scholarships.

See entry 403 for full listing.

ENTERPRISE COMMUNITY PARTNERS [379]
334 Boylston Street, Suite 400
Boston, MA 02116
(781) 235-2006
E-mail: rosefellowship@enterprisecommunity.org
Web Site: www.enterprisecommunity.org/rose

AREAS OF INTEREST:
Architecture and community development.

NAME(S) OF PROGRAMS:
- **Enterprise Rose Fellowship**

TYPE:
Fellowships. The Rose Fellowship partners community-engaged architects and artists with local community development organizations. Architectural fellows are designers with an accredited degree in architecture and a passion for applying their skills in a community development context. Artists are defined as socially-engaged creative practitioners, teaching artists, and culture bearers working in all disciplines.

YEAR PROGRAM STARTED: 2000

PURPOSE:
To promote architectural and community design in low-income communities and to encourage architects to become lifelong leaders in public service and community development.

ELIGIBILITY:
Applicants for architectural fellowships must have an NAAB-accredited Professional Architecture Degree (B.Arch or M.Arch) or an equivalent level of professional experience.

Applicants for the arts fellowships must demonstrate experience in applying their artistic or cultural practice in a community-engaged context. Applicant must have a minimum of either a Bachelor's degree or an equivalent level of professional experience.

Applicants must be eligible to work in the U.S. for the entire fellowship period.

GEOG. RESTRICTIONS: United States.

FINANCIAL DATA:
Fellows are placed with a host organization for a two-year period in which they receive the standard employee benefits and insurance package offered to all employees. In joining, fellows are also provided with annual fellowship retreats and networking opportunities and a professional development stipend.
Amount of support per award: $62,000 per year.

Matching fund requirements:
Community-based organizations are most often required to match the grant funds received for the fellow's stipend.

NO. MOST RECENT APPLICANTS: 150.

NO. AWARDS: 8 for the 2019-21 term.

APPLICATION INFO:
Applicant must submit:
(1) resume or curriculum vitae demonstrating relevant academic and community experience;
(2) essays and response to work plan;
(3) portfolio and;
(4) references.

In-person interview is required.
Duration: Two years.
Deadline: Midsummer.

ADDRESS INQUIRIES TO:
Mark Matel, Program Director
Enterprise Rose Fellowship
(See address above.)

THE JAMES MARSTON FITCH CHARITABLE FOUNDATION [380]
c/o The Neighborhood Preservation Center
232 East 11th Street
New York, NY 10003
(212) 252-6809
Fax: (212) 471-9987
E-mail: cpena@fitchfoundation.org
Web Site: fitchfoundation.org

FOUNDED: 1989

AREAS OF INTEREST:
Architecture, engineering, environmental planning, and historic preservation.

NAME(S) OF PROGRAMS:
- **Richard L. Blinder Award**
- **Mid-Career Fellowship**

TYPE:
Research grants. Richard L. Blinder Award was created to promote studies that explore the architecture of cultural buildings which integrate historic preservation and new construction - past, present and future; presented biennially.

Mid-Career Fellowship: This grant is the primary mission and the signature grant of this Foundation. The grants are intended to support projects of innovative original research or creative design that advance the practice of historic preservation in the U.S.

PURPOSE:
To support professionals in the field of historic preservation by providing midcareer grants to those working in preservation, landscape architecture, urban design, environmental planning, decorative arts, and architectural design and history.

ELIGIBILITY:
Richard L. Blinder Award proposal must demonstrate that it fosters architectural preservation in the U.S. Applicant must be an architect holding a professional degree or a valid license to practice architecture with at least 10 years experience in architecture, historic preservation or related fields. Grants are awarded only to individuals, not organizations or university-sponsored research projects. Grants are not awarded for professional fees.

Mid-Career Fellowships are awarded only to individuals, not organizations. Applicants must be midcareer professionals with at least ten years experience in historic preservation or related fields, including architecture, landscape architecture, architectural conservation, urban design, environment planning, archaeology, architectural history, and the decorative arts. Applicants must be legal residents or citizens of the U.S.

GEOG. RESTRICTIONS: United States.

FINANCIAL DATA:
Amount of support per award: Up to $15,000.

NO. AWARDS: Richard Blinder Award: 1 biennially; Mid-Career Fellowship: 1 to 2.

APPLICATION INFO:
Applications must be submitted electronically in PDF format. Applicants are required to submit the following materials:
(1) cover page, including project title, primary contact person, and applicant address, telephone number and e-mail address. Also specify which award and the amount of money requested;
(2) brief description of the project (up to three pages), including how the final work product will be disseminated;
(3) detailed work schedule and project budget;
(4) curriculum vita, including professional and academic background, and past and present grants received and;
(5) two letters of support.
Duration: One year.
Deadline: Blinder Award: October 22.

ADDRESS INQUIRIES TO:
See e-mail address above.

GRAHAM FOUNDATION FOR ADVANCED STUDIES IN THE FINE ARTS [381]
Madlener House
4 West Burton Place
Chicago, IL 60610
(312) 787-4071
E-mail: grantprograms@grahamfoundation.org
Web Site: www.grahamfoundation.org

FOUNDED: 1956

AREAS OF INTEREST:
Architecture and related spatial practices that engage a wide range of cultural, social, political, technological, environmental and aesthetic issues. The Foundation is interested in projects that investigate the contemporary condition, expand historical perspectives, or explore the future of architecture and the designed environment.

NAME(S) OF PROGRAMS:
● **Carter Manny Award**
● **Production and Presentation Grants**
● **Research and Development Grants**

TYPE:
Awards/prizes; Project/program grants; Research grants. Grants to organizations, individuals and public programs.

Carter Manny Award: To support research for academic dissertations by promising scholars who are presently candidates for a doctoral degree, and whose dissertations focus on areas traditionally supported by the Foundation. Students must be nominated by their department to apply for this Award.

Production and Presentation Grants: To assist individuals and organizations with the production-related expenses that are necessary to take a project from

conceptualization to realization and public presentation. These projects may include, but are not limited to, publications, exhibitions, installations, conferences, films, new-media projects, and other public programs.

Research and Development Grants: To assist individuals with seed money for research-related expenses such as travel, documentation, materials, supplies and other development costs.

YEAR PROGRAM STARTED: 1956

PURPOSE:
To make project-based grants to individuals and organizations and to produce public programs to foster the development and exchange of diverse and challenging ideas about architecture and its role in the arts, culture and society.

LEGAL BASIS:
Private foundation.

ELIGIBILITY:
Individuals and institutions may apply. No grants for endowments, general operating expenses, capital projects, scholarship aid or for work in pursuit of an academic degree (except for the Carter Manny Award), debt or expenses incurred prior to the date of grant request.

NO. AWARDS: 116 for the year 2017.

APPLICATION INFO:
Application to the Foundation involves a two-stage process and is open submission.

Stage One/Inquiry Form: Eligible candidates interested in applying for a grant must first submit an Inquiry Form. The Inquiry Form is available on the Foundation web site with each grant cycle and must be submitted online.

Stage Two/Proposal Form: Applicants whose projects best match the Foundation's priorities and interests are invited to submit a Proposal Form and supplementary materials. Applicants not invited to submit a Proposal Form are sent a decline letter at this stage. An invitation to submit a Proposal Form does not guarantee eventual funding.

Award Decision: Funding recommendations are presented to the Board of Trustees for consideration. If a grant is awarded, applicant will be asked to sign a Grant Agreement that outlines the conditions of the award, such as annual reporting. Funding decisions at all stages of the review are based on the priority of the proposed project as related to the Foundation's mission and interests, the project's fulfillment of the Foundation's criteria for evaluation, and availability of Foundation funds.

Duration: Varies.

Deadline: February 25 for organizations; September 15 for individuals.

PUBLICATIONS:
Annual report; guidelines.

OFFICERS:
Sarah Herda, Director
Ellen Hartwell Alderman, Deputy Director
Carolyn T. Kelly, Grants Manager

ADDRESS INQUIRIES TO:
See e-mail address above.

THE LEF FOUNDATION [382]
P.O. Box 382066
Cambridge, MA 02238-2066
(617) 492-5333
Fax: (617) 868-5603
E-mail: gen@lef-foundation.org
Web Site: lef-foundation.org

FOUNDED: 1985

AREAS OF INTEREST:
Nonfiction film and video.

NAME(S) OF PROGRAMS:
● **Moving Image Fund**

TYPE:
The Foundation gives grants for preproduction, production and post production of nonfiction film and video.

YEAR PROGRAM STARTED: 2002

PURPOSE:
To fund the work of independent documentary film and video artists in the region; to broaden recognition and support for the artist's work both locally and nationally.

ELIGIBILITY:
Projects must be long format, with running times of 40 minutes or more. The primary creative personnel (director and/or producer) must reside in New England. Priority will be given to smaller scale projects with budgets under $400,000.

Applicants must have a fiscal sponsor, namely a nonprofit with a 501(c)(3) designation from the federal government, that has agreed to manage the fiscal activity of the grant.

Students enrolled in degree-granting programs may not apply. Multichannel or installation work will not be considered.

Selection will be based on the following criteria:
(1) quality of cinematic form and technique;
(2) originality of filmmaker's voice, vision and point of view;
(3) resonance and power of the film's core idea or story and;
(4) feasibility of production.

GEOG. RESTRICTIONS: New England.

FINANCIAL DATA:
Amount of support per award:
Pre-Production: $5,000; Production: $15,000; Post-Production: $25,000.
Total amount of support: $200,000 annually.

NO. AWARDS: Pre-Production: 4 to 6; Production: Up to 6; Post-Production: Up to 3.

APPLICATION INFO:
Application form and guidelines are available on the Foundation web site.
Duration: Varies.
Deadline: Varies.

ADDRESS INQUIRIES TO:
Genevieve Carmel, Program Officer
(See address above.)

THE PAUL MELLON CENTRE FOR STUDIES IN BRITISH ART [383]
16 Bedford Square
London WC1B 3JA England
(44) 020 7580 0311
Fax: (44) 020 7636 6730
E-mail: info@paul-mellon-centre.ac.uk
Web Site: www.paul-mellon-centre.ac.uk

FOUNDED: 1970

AREAS OF INTEREST:
British art and architectural history.

NAME(S) OF PROGRAMS:
- **Educational Programme Grants**
- **Junior Fellowships**
- **Paul Mellon Centre Rome Fellowship**
- **Mid-Career Fellowships**
- **Postdoctoral Fellowships**
- **Research Support Grants**
- **Senior Fellowships**
- **Terra-PMC Fellowship**

TYPE:
Conferences/seminars; Fellowships; Project/program grants; Research grants. Educational Programme Grants for lectures, symposia, seminars or conferences on British art or architectural history.

The Junior Fellowship is to pursue ongoing doctoral research at an American or British university.

The Paul Mellon Centre Rome Fellowship offers fellowships to scholars working on Grand Tour subjects or in the field of Anglo-Italian cultural and artistic relations.

Mid-Career Fellowships are offered for research in the field of British art and architectural history.

The Postdoctoral Fellowship works to transform doctoral research into publishable form such as a book, series of articles, or exhibition catalogues.

Research Support Grants are for expenses in pursuit of research.

The Senior Fellowship supports an established scholar in the field of British art and architectural history to complete a manuscript or book for immediate publication.

Terra-PMC Fellowship is designed to facilitate original, rigorous and exciting scholarship that investigates an aspect of the artistic dialogue between Britain and the U.S. from any period up to 1980.

YEAR PROGRAM STARTED: 1998

PURPOSE:
To promote scholarship and publications.

LEGAL BASIS:
University-affiliated research center.

ELIGIBILITY:
Candidates for the Junior Fellowship may be of any nationality but must be enrolled in a graduate program at an American or other non-British university for study in the U.K. or at a non-American university for study in the U.S.

Candidates for Mid-Career Fellowships are academics or scholars at universities, museums, galleries or other institutions who are established in their careers and were awarded their Doctorates over six years previously. Applications are also welcome from independent and freelance scholars, and from individuals who do not hold a Doctorate. All applicants must have an established scholarly profile.

The Postdoctoral Fellowship is awarded within four years of an applicant's doctoral award. Applicants must have had their doctoral theses successfully examined.

Applicants for the Rome Fellowship should, preferably, be competent in spoken and written Italian.

Candidates for the Terra-PMC Fellowship may be of any nationality, although U.S. citizens are not eligible. The applicant must be employed at a college, university, museum or archive, or for an independent scholar. The award is open to a range of individuals, from early-career postdoctoral scholars to those who are internationally recognized in their field of expertise. The Centre will make allowance for applicants who have had a career break or who are established scholars without Doctorates.

FINANCIAL DATA:
Amount of support per award: Varies.

NO. MOST RECENT APPLICANTS: 182 spring applicants and 185 autumn applicants for the year 2019.

NO. AWARDS: Junior Fellowships: 8; Mid-Career Fellowships: 7; Postdoctoral Fellowships: 11; Rome Fellowship: 1; Senior Fellowships: 3.

APPLICATION INFO:
Applications are submitted through the online system at grants.paul-mellon-centre.ac.uk.
Duration: Junior Fellowship and Rome Fellowship: Three months. Mid-Career Fellowship and Terra-PMC Fellowship: Four months. Postdoctoral Fellowship: Six months. Senior Fellowship: Nine months.
Deadline: September 30 for autumn grant season. January 31 for spring grant season.

ADDRESS INQUIRIES TO:
Fellowships and Grants Manager
E-mail: grants@paul-mellon-centre.ac.uk

NATIONAL SOCIETY DAUGHTERS OF THE AMERICAN REVOLUTION   [384]
1776 D Street, N.W.
Washington, DC 20006-5303
(202) 879-3263
E-mail: nsdarscholarships@nsdar.org
Web Site: www.dar.org

FOUNDED: 1895

AREAS OF INTEREST:
Historic preservation.

NAME(S) OF PROGRAMS:
- **DAR Centennial Scholarship**

TYPE:
Scholarships.

YEAR PROGRAM STARTED: 1985

PURPOSE:
To provide ways and means to aid students in attaining higher education.

LEGAL BASIS:
Incorporated historical society.

ELIGIBILITY:
Applicants must be enrolled in the junior or senior year of a fully accredited college or university in the U.S. and pursuing a degree in the field of historic preservation, may reside in any state, and must be a U.S. citizen.

GEOG. RESTRICTIONS: United States.

FINANCIAL DATA:
Amount of support per award: $2,500.
Total amount of support: $5,000.

NO. AWARDS: 2.

APPLICATION INFO:
Applicants must use the DAR Scholarship Committee's online submission process found on the DAR public web site. Once applicants

have set up their scholarship profile, they will be able to complete the application. If necessary, applicants will be able to provide access to individuals wishing to submit confidential letters of recommendations or school transcripts.
Duration: One year. Nonrenewable.
Deadline: February 15.

PUBLICATIONS:
American Spirit, magazine.

ADDRESS INQUIRIES TO:
National Vice Chairman
E-mail: darcentennialscholarship@nsdar.org

ROTCH TRAVELLING SCHOLARSHIP IN ARCHITECTURE   [385]
Boston Society of Architects
290 Congress Street, Suite 200
Boston, MA 02210
(617) 391-4000
E-mail: chart@architects.org
Web Site: www.rotch.org

FOUNDED: 1883

AREAS OF INTEREST:
Architecture.

NAME(S) OF PROGRAMS:
- **Rotch Travelling Scholarship**

TYPE:
Awards/prizes; Fellowships; Travel grants. Traveling Fellowships. Rotch Travelling Scholarship awards a minimum of six months of foreign travel and study in the field of architecture and allied subjects.

YEAR PROGRAM STARTED: 1883

PURPOSE:
To provide young architects with the opportunity to gain experience with other cultures; to augment the architectural education of students of architecture at the highest level of scholarship within a studio format.

LEGAL BASIS:
Private trust.

ELIGIBILITY:
Candidates must be U.S. citizens who have obtained a professional degree (B.Arch./M.Arch.) from an accredited school in the last 10 years. Candidates must have one year full-time professional experience in a Massachusetts architecture firm as of January 1 of the competition year, or have obtained an accredited degree from an accredited Massachusetts school of architecture as of January 1 of the competition year.

GEOG. RESTRICTIONS: United States.

FINANCIAL DATA:
Amount of support per award: Minimum $40,000.

APPLICATION INFO:
Official application forms are available online.
Duration: Minimum six months.
Deadline: January.

ROYAL INSTITUTE OF BRITISH ARCHITECTS [386]

RIBA Research Fund
Education Department
66 Portland Place
London W1B 1AD England
(44) 020 7307 3625
E-mail: education@riba.org
Web Site: www.architecture.com

FOUNDED: 1834

AREAS OF INTEREST:
Architecture, and the arts and sciences connected therewith, in the U.K.

NAME(S) OF PROGRAMS:
- **RIBA Research Fund**

TYPE:
Research grants. Grants to support independent research conducted by academics or practitioners in the field of architecture.

PURPOSE:
To support individuals who wish to conduct research in the field of architecture, with the anticipation that the final output will contribute towards the development of architecture as a discipline and a profession.

ELIGIBILITY:
Open to applicants interested in a wide range of subjects relevant to the advancement of architecture, and connected arts and sciences, in the U.K.

Grants from the RIBA Research Fund are for closely defined pieces of architectural research and support practice-led or academic research, but will not support course fees and subsistence costs for Ph.D./M.Phil. or Master's programmes. Grants are given only to named individuals, not organisations.

Applicants based outside the U.K. are also eligible to apply; however, the research work must in the main be undertaken within the U.K.

GEOG. RESTRICTIONS: United Kingdom.

FINANCIAL DATA:
Grants will be determined by the estimated requirements of the project.
Amount of support per award: Maximum award not to exceed GBP 10,000.

CO-OP FUNDING PROGRAMS: A candidate may have funding from other sources.

NO. AWARDS: 4 for the year 2019.

APPLICATION INFO:
Application forms are available from the RIBA web site. Only requests up to GBP 10,000 will be considered.
Duration: Up to two years.
Deadline: Varies.

OFFICER:
Alan Vallance, Chief Executive

ADDRESS INQUIRIES TO:
Gillian Harrison
E-mail: gillian.harrison@riba.org

SNAME THE INTERNATIONAL COMMUNITY FOR MARITIME AND OCEAN PROFESSIONALS

99 Canal Center Plaza, Suite 310
Alexandria, VA 22314
(703) 997-6701
E-mail: sname@sname.org
Web Site: www.sname.org

TYPE:
Scholarships. SNAME annually awards both graduate and undergraduate scholarships to encourage study in naval architecture, marine engineering, ocean engineering, ship hydrodynamics and wave theory, ship and offshore structures, or marine industry-related fields.

Graduate Scholarships are made for one year of study leading to a Master's in naval architecture, marine engineering, ocean engineering or in fields directly related to the marine industry.

Undergraduate Scholarships are made for one year of study leading to a Bachelor of Science degree in naval architecture, marine engineering, ocean engineering, or in other fields directly related to the marine industry.

See entry 2447 for full listing.

SIR JOHN SOANE MUSEUM FOUNDATION [387]

120 Broadway, 20th Floor
New York, NY 10271
(646) 740-1976
E-mail: fellowships@soanefoundation.org
Web Site: www.soanefoundation.org

AREAS OF INTEREST:
Education of the public in architecture and the fine and decorative arts.

NAME(S) OF PROGRAMS:
- **Sir John Soane's Museum Foundation Graduate Fellowship**

TYPE:
Fellowships. Designed to help graduate students and scholars pursue research projects related to the work of Sir John Soane's Museum and its collections.

PURPOSE:
To educate and inspire the general public and professionals in architecture and the fine and decorative arts.

ELIGIBILITY:
Applicants must be enrolled in a graduate degree program in a field appropriate to the Foundation's purpose. Level of study is postgraduate.

FINANCIAL DATA:
Total amount of support: $6,000.

NO. MOST RECENT APPLICANTS: 20.

NO. AWARDS: 2.

APPLICATION INFO:
Applicants must submit a formal proposal of not more than one page describing the goal, scope and purpose of the research project, in addition to three letters of recommendation.
Duration: One year.
Deadline: Posted on the Foundation web site.

ADDRESS INQUIRIES TO:
Michael Diaz-Griffith, Executive Director
(See address above.)

SOCIETY OF ARCHITECTURAL HISTORIANS [388]

1365 North Astor Street
Chicago, IL 60610-2144
(312) 573-1365
Fax: (312) 573-1141
E-mail: fellowships@sah.org
Web Site: www.sah.org

FOUNDED: 1940

AREAS OF INTEREST:
Architecture and its related arts.

NAME(S) OF PROGRAMS:
- **Sally Kress Tompkins Fellowship**

TYPE:
Fellowships; Internships; Travel grants. The Sally Kress Tompkins Fellowship, a joint program of the Society of Architectural Historians and the National Park Service's Historic American Buildings Survey, permits an architectural historian to work on a 12-week project during the summer. The Fellow will prepare a written history to become part of the permanent collection focusing on either a specific nationally significant building/site, or a broader architectural history topic. The Fellow will be stationed in the field working in conjunction with a measured drawings team, or in the Washington, DC office. The Fellow will be selected by a jury of two SAH members and one HABS representative.

PURPOSE:
To advance the knowledge and understanding of architecture, design, landscape and urbanism worldwide.

LEGAL BASIS:
Nonprofit professional organization.

ELIGIBILITY:
Graduate students and member of SAH.

FINANCIAL DATA:
Amount of support per award: $500 to $9,200.
Total amount of support: $10,000.

CO-OP FUNDING PROGRAMS: National Park Service's Historic American Buildings Survey (HABS).

NO. MOST RECENT APPLICANTS: 5.

NO. AWARDS: 1.

APPLICATION INFO:
Details are available online, for members.
Duration: One year.
Deadline: October 1.

PUBLICATIONS:
Newsletter; *Journal of the Society of Architectural Historians.*

ADDRESS INQUIRIES TO:
Beth Eifrig, Comptroller
(See address above.)

VIRGINIA POLYTECHNIC INSTITUTE AND STATE UNIVERSITY

MAOP Office
280 Stanger Street
Blacksburg, VA 24061
(540) 231-5023
Fax: (540) 231-2618
E-mail: maop@vt.edu
Web Site: www.maop.vt.edu

TYPE:
Assistantships; Fellowships; Internships; Scholarships. The program assists with graduate school financing in exchange for assistance to MAOP administration. Graduate students assist with programming implementation such as mentoring to undergraduate students.

See entry 935 for full listing.

WASHINGTON UNIVERSITY [389]

School of Architecture
Campus Box 1079
One Brookings Drive
St. Louis, MO 63130-4899
(314) 935-4636
E-mail: treece.audrey@wustl.edu
Web Site: www.samfoxschool.wustl.
edu/steedman

FOUNDED: 1926

AREAS OF INTEREST:
Architectural education.

NAME(S) OF PROGRAMS:
- **James Harrison Steedman Memorial Fellowship in Architecture**

TYPE:
Awards/prizes; Fellowships; Travel grants. An award made on the basis of a design competition that requires the recipient to travel and study abroad for six to 12 months. Not to be used towards tuition.

YEAR PROGRAM STARTED: 1926

PURPOSE:
To assist well-qualified architectural graduates to benefit by travel and study of architecture in foreign countries.

ELIGIBILITY:
Open to graduates of an accredited school of architecture, regardless of age, for a period up to eight years after the receipt of their first professional degree. Candidates must have at least one year of practical experience in the office of a practicing architect. Citizens of all countries are eligible.

FINANCIAL DATA:
Amount of support per award: $50,000 stipend for six to 12 months of travel abroad.
Total amount of support: $50,000.

NO. MOST RECENT APPLICANTS: 125.

NO. AWARDS: 1 awarded biennially.

APPLICATION INFO:
Registration forms are available online. Applications are available in August every odd year and fellowships are awarded in the spring every even year.
Duration: Six to 12 months.

PUBLICATIONS:
Application guidelines.

GOVERNING BOARD:
William Wischmeyer

ADDRESS INQUIRIES TO:
Audrey Treece, Programs Manager
(See address above.)

Arts (multiple disciplines)

ACADEMY FOUNDATION OF THE ACADEMY OF MOTION PICTURE ARTS AND SCIENCES

1313 North Vine Street
Los Angeles, CA 90028
(310) 247-3000
E-mail: sguthrie@oscars.org
Web Site: www.oscars.org

TYPE:
Awards/prizes.

See entry 502 for full listing.

ALABAMA STATE COUNCIL ON THE ARTS [390]

201 Monroe Street
Suite 110
Montgomery, AL 36104-3721
(334) 242-4076
Fax: (334) 240-3269
E-mail: staff@arts.alabama.gov
Web Site: www.arts.alabama.gov

FOUNDED: 1966

AREAS OF INTEREST:
Architecture, literature, fine arts, arts in education, museums and libraries, music, and creative and performing arts.

CONSULTING OR VOLUNTEER SERVICES:
Strengthens cultural activities already in existence, assists in formation of new cultural activities, works towards improving the quality of presentations by both professional and amateur organizations and offers assistance to culturally oriented groups.

NAME(S) OF PROGRAMS:
- **Art and Cultural Facilities**
- **Arts-in-Education**
- **Community Arts Development**
- **Folk Arts**
- **Literary Art**
- **Performing Arts**
- **Visual Arts and Crafts**

TYPE:
Awards/prizes; Challenge/matching grants; Conferences/seminars; Development grants; Fellowships; General operating grants; Internships; Project/program grants; Residencies; Technical assistance. Grants to various disciplines comprising technical and financial assistance to local organizations in sponsoring activities of quality and promise in the various arts disciplines of the visual and performing arts within communities throughout Alabama.

YEAR PROGRAM STARTED: 1967

PURPOSE:
To increase interest, participation and support in the arts by supplementing local initiatives and local funds in order to enable a greater number of quality activities to be seen or heard throughout the state.

LEGAL BASIS:
Alabama Law, Act No. 551, Regular Session 1967 and Act No. 1065, Regular Session, 1969.

ELIGIBILITY:
Applicants must be qualified organizations sponsoring arts events or programs for communities. Such groups include local arts councils, arts associations, museums, literary associations, colleges and universities, dance and theatre groups. Evidence of nonprofit status is required.

GEOG. RESTRICTIONS: Alabama.

FINANCIAL DATA:
Amount of support per award: $500 to $250,000.
Matching fund requirements: Equal amounts from other sources with exception of Artists Fellowships.

APPLICATION INFO:
A special application form can be obtained and submitted by using the Council eGRANT system which is available on their web site.
Duration: One year. Renewal by reapplication.
Deadline: March 1, June 1 and September 1.

PUBLICATIONS:
Guide to Programs; *Alabama Arts*, magazine; *Touring & Presenting Guide.*

IRS I.D.: 63-6000619

EXECUTIVE COUNCIL:
James Harrison, Chairman
Dr. Henry Panion, III, Vice Chairman
Lisa Weil, Secretary

ADDRESS INQUIRIES TO:
Elliot A. Knight, Ph.D., Executive Director
(See address above.)

ALASKA STATE COUNCIL ON THE ARTS [391]

161 Klevin Street
Suite 102
Anchorage, AK 99508-1506
(907) 269-6610
Fax: (907) 269-6601
E-mail: aksca.info@alaska.gov
Web Site: arts.alaska.gov

FOUNDED: 1966

AREAS OF INTEREST:
Alaska arts and culture.

CONSULTING OR VOLUNTEER SERVICES:
Technical assistance for grantees.

TYPE:
General operating grants; Project/program grants; Residencies. Grants in 16 categories for organizations and individuals based in Alaska.

YEAR PROGRAM STARTED: 1966

PURPOSE:
To foster the development of the arts for all Alaskans through education, partnerships, grants and services.

LEGAL BASIS:
State agency.

GEOG. RESTRICTIONS: Alaska.

FINANCIAL DATA:
Amount of support per award: Varies according to program.
Matching fund requirements: All organizational grants require at least 1:1 match (cash).

APPLICATION INFO:
Specific guidelines and applications are available online.
Duration: One year.
Deadline: Varies according to program.

PUBLICATIONS:
Annual report; individual grant program guidelines.

ADDRESS INQUIRIES TO:
Executive Director
(See address above.)

THE ALLIANCE FOR YOUNG ARTISTS & WRITERS [392]

557 Broadway
New York, NY 10012
Fax: (212) 389-3939
E-mail: info@artandwriting.org
Web Site: www.artandwriting.org

FOUNDED: 1923

AREAS OF INTEREST:
Art and writing.

NAME(S) OF PROGRAMS:
- **The Scholastic Art and Writing Awards**

TYPE:
Awards/prizes; Scholarships. The Alliance for Young Artists & Writers identifies teenagers with exceptional artistic and literary talent and brings their remarkable work to a national audience through The Scholastic Art and Writing Awards.

YEAR PROGRAM STARTED: 1923

PURPOSE:
To provide guidance and support for the next generation of artists and writers and reward outstanding achievement in the creative arts.

LEGAL BASIS:
501(c)(3) organization.

ELIGIBILITY:
Public, private, or home-school students (grades 7 to 12) in the U.S., Canada, or American schools abroad, regardless of citizenship, may submit work. Foreign exchange students who are temporarily residing in the U.S. may also participate.

FINANCIAL DATA:
Scholarship recipients are additionally eligible for school-specific, tuition scholarships at more than 50 colleges.
Amount of support per award: $1,000 to $10,000.
Total amount of support: More than $250,000 given annually through the Scholastic Awards program in awards and scholarships to top Awards recipients and their educators.

NO. AWARDS: Approximately 100.

APPLICATION INFO:
Guidelines vary by region. Contact Affiliate Partner for information.
Duration: One year.
Deadline: Varies by geographic location, approximately December 15 to January 15.

IRS I.D.: 13-3780998

ADDRESS INQUIRIES TO:
Daniel Embree, Director
National Programs
(See address above.)

AMERICA-ISRAEL CULTURAL FOUNDATION

322 Eighth Avenue
Suite 1702
New York, NY 10001
(212) 557-1600
Fax: (212) 557-1611
E-mail: admin@aicf.org
Web Site: www.aicf.org

TYPE:
Awards/prizes; Endowments; Fellowships; Project/program grants; Scholarships. For study in the arts of music, painting and sculpture, dance and drama, film and television, to be pursued either in Israel or in other countries.

See entry 877 for full listing.

THE AMERICAN CERAMIC SOCIETY [393]

550 Polaris Parkway
Suite 510
Westerville, OH 43082
(614) 794-5827
(866) 721-3322
Fax: (614) 794-5817
E-mail: ynatividad@ceramics.org
Web Site: ceramics.org

FOUNDED: 1898

AREAS OF INTEREST:
Ceramic education and glass.

NAME(S) OF PROGRAMS:
- **Graduate Student Poster Contest**
- **Student Speaking Contest**
- **Undergraduate Student Poster Contest**

TYPE:
Awards/prizes.

PURPOSE:
To promote and encourage materials science and engineering studies in the discipline of glass and ceramics.

FINANCIAL DATA:
Amount of support per award: Varies.

APPLICATION INFO:
Contact the Society.
Duration: One-time awards.
Deadline: Graduate Student Poster Contest: March; Student Speaking and Undergraduate Student Poster Contests: September.

ADDRESS INQUIRIES TO:
Yolanda Natividad, Membership Engagement Manager
(See address and e-mail above.)

AMERICAN FIDELITY FOUNDATION [394]

9000 Cameron Parkway
Oklahoma City, OK 73114
(405) 523-5008
E-mail: joella.ramsey@americanfidelity.com
Web Site: americanfidelityfoundation.org

AREAS OF INTEREST:
Education, arts, culture, health and human services, and civic and economic development.

TYPE:
Endowments; General operating grants; Research grants. Employment Matching Gifts.

ELIGIBILITY:
Organization must be tax-exempt with 501(c)(3) status. No grants to individuals.

FINANCIAL DATA:
Amount of support per award: Grants to a single charity are typically $500 to $5,000.
Total amount of support: Varies.

NO. AWARDS: 177 for the year 2018.

APPLICATION INFO:
Organizations that wish to be considered for a grant are asked to submit a letter of interest. If the Foundation chooses to pursue the project or program described, a formal application will be sent for completion to the organization within two weeks.
Duration: One year.

ADDRESS INQUIRIES TO:
Jo Ella Ramsey, Administrator
(See address above.)

AMERICAN SCHOOL OF CLASSICAL STUDIES AT ATHENS [395]

6-8 Charlton Street
Princeton, NJ 08540-5232
(609) 683-0800
Fax: (609) 924-0578
E-mail: application@ascsa.org
Web Site: www.ascsa.edu.gr

FOUNDED: 1881

AREAS OF INTEREST:
Financial support for individuals involved in research.

NAME(S) OF PROGRAMS:
- **CAORC Multi-Country Research Fellowships**

TYPE:
Fellowships.

PURPOSE:
To provide support for individuals whose research has regional significance and requires travel to multiple countries, at least one of which hosts an American overseas research center such as the American School.

ELIGIBILITY:
Fellowship is limited to U.S. citizens. Open to U.S. doctoral candidates who have completed all Ph.D. requirements except the dissertation and U.S. postdoctoral scholars at all levels with research requiring travel to several countries with an American overseas research center.

School programs are generally open to qualified students and scholars at colleges or universities in the U.S. or Canada; restrictions may apply for specific fellowships and programs. The American School of Classical Studies at Athens does not discriminate on the basis of race, age, sex, sexual orientation, color, religion, ethnic origin, or disability when considering admission to any form of membership.

FINANCIAL DATA:
School fees are to be paid out of the fellowship stipend by the recipient. Fellowship does not include travel costs, housing, board, and other living expenses.
Amount of support per award: Stipend up to $10,500.

CO-OP FUNDING PROGRAMS: Fellowships for Multi-Country Research are funded by the Bureau of Educational and Cultural Affairs of the U.S. Department of State through a grant to the Council of American Overseas Research Centers.

NO. MOST RECENT APPLICANTS: 15.

NO. AWARDS: 1.

APPLICATION INFO:
Application guidelines are available at CAORC's web site (www.caorc.org). Upon notice from CAORC, successful applicants must immediately submit the ASCSA Visiting Associate Member application with a copy of the CAORC application online.
Duration: Doctoral and postdoctoral scholars: Minimum of 90 days.
Deadline: January 31.

STAFF:
Jenifer Neils, Director

ADDRESS INQUIRIES TO:
See e-mail address above.

*SPECIAL STIPULATIONS:
Recipients may not hold any other federally funded grant at the same time, such as a Fulbright or NEH Fellowship.

Membership application to the ASCSA must be made online on the web site at the same time one applies to any outside funding organization for work at the School.

A final report is due at the end of the award period, and the ASCSA expects that copies of all publications that result from research conducted as a Fellow of the ASCSA be contributed to the relevant library of the School.

ARIZONA COMMISSION ON THE ARTS [396]

417 West Roosevelt Street
Phoenix, AZ 85003
(602) 771-6502
Fax: (602) 256-0282
E-mail: info@azarts.gov
Web Site: www.azarts.gov

FOUNDED: 1967

AREAS OF INTEREST:
Performing arts, visual arts and literary arts.

TYPE:
Challenge/matching grants; Conferences/seminars; Development grants; General operating grants; Internships; Project/program grants; Research grants; Technical assistance. Specialized library services to artists and arts organizations. Dedicated to making quality arts opportunities available to its citizens, the Arts Commission takes a leadership role in broadening the support systems for the arts and demonstrating how the arts are integral to the vitality of our communities and citizens.

YEAR PROGRAM STARTED: 1967

PURPOSE:
To stimulate and encourage public interest in the arts; to increase opportunities for all residents of Arizona to experience the arts; to assist individual artists and arts organizations in Arizona; to stimulate support and visibility for the arts in Arizona; to foster the preservation, promotion and availability of Arizona's diverse ethnic arts; to make the arts fundamental to education.

LEGAL BASIS:
State agency.

GEOG. RESTRICTIONS: Arizona.

FINANCIAL DATA:
Amount of support per award: Varies.
Total amount of support: Varies.

APPLICATION INFO:
Call for application or access from web site.
Duration: Varies.
Deadline: Varies.

ASIAN CULTURAL COUNCIL [397]

333 West 39th Street
Suite 1502
New York, NY 10018
(212) 843-0403
Fax: (212) 843-0343
E-mail: acc@accny.org
Web Site: www.asianculturalcouncil.org

FOUNDED: 1980

AREAS OF INTEREST:
Visual and performing arts of Asia.

NAME(S) OF PROGRAMS:
● **Graduate Scholarship**

● **Individual Fellowship Program**
● **New York Fellowship Program**
● **Organization and Project Grant**
● **Travel Grant**

TYPE:
Fellowships; Project/program grants; Scholarships; Travel grants. Support of cultural exchange in the visual and performing arts between the U.S. and those countries of Asia extending from Afghanistan through Japan.

Graduate Scholarships support students pursuing graduate degrees in the U.S., with priority given to students who do not have access to comparable programs at home, and to those studying in fields that are underrepresented in their home country.

Individual Fellowships provide support to individuals or two collaborators undertaking self-directed research trips. Partial funding for dissertation research projects of up to one year are also available in this category.

New York Fellowships provide support to individuals who wish to participate in a fellowship program based in New York City. Fellowships may involve targeted research, but open-ended exploration is also allowed and encouraged.

Organization and Project Grants are for organizations that are facilitating a cultural exchange opportunity for individual project participants, or for collaborations involving three or more individuals.

Travel Grants provide support to individuals or two collaborators who need modest financial support for travel.

YEAR PROGRAM STARTED: 1980

PURPOSE:
To award fellowships to individuals and grants to organizations to support projects that foster exchange between Asia and the U.S.; to fund regional travel within Asia.

LEGAL BASIS:
Public foundation organized under Section 501(c)(3).

ELIGIBILITY:
Grants are open to citizens and permanent residents of the countries of Asia from Afghanistan eastward through Japan and Indonesia, and citizens and permanent residents of the U.S. Individuals pursuing projects in their home countries are not supported. Priority consideration is generally given to individuals who have not previously received funding support from the Council.

FINANCIAL DATA:
The Asian Cultural Council's grant programs are supported by endowment income and annual contributions from foundations, corporations, and individuals in the U.S. and Asia. Levels of grant activity are based on financial resources available.
Amount of support per award: Varies.
Total amount of support: Varies.

NO. MOST RECENT APPLICANTS: 500 annually.

NO. AWARDS: 50.

APPLICATION INFO:
Grant applicants must first submit the appropriate online Individual or Organization Inquiry form. Applications are available through the web site September 1 through October 31 of each calendar year for grants in the following year.

Duration: Graduate Scholarship: One year. Individual Fellowship: One to six months. New York Fellowship: Six months. Organization and Project Grant: Varies. Travel Grant: Up to one month.
Deadline: Fall. Check web site for exact date.

PUBLICATIONS:
Annual report.

IRS I.D.: 13-3018822

OFFICERS:
Wendy O'Neill, Chairman
Hans Michael Jebsen, Vice Chairman
Josie Cruz Natori, Vice Chairman
Jonathan Fanton, Treasurer
Valerie Rockefeller Wayne, Secretary

TRUSTEES:
Kazuko Aso
Ernest de Leon Escaler
Jonathan Fanton
Douglas Tong Hsu
Tonia Hsu
Hans Michael Jebsen
Julie Ann Kohn
Richard S. Lanier
Yi Ling Mao
Elizabeth J. McCormack
Josie Cruz Natori
Wendy O'Neill
Carol Rattray
Missie Rennie
Charles Rockefeller
David Rockefeller, Jr.
Valerie Rockefeller
Ruby Shang
Dan Swift
Yuji Tsutsumi
John R. Witt
Mercedes Zobel

ADDRESS INQUIRIES TO:
E-mail: applications@accny.org

ASTRAEA LESBIAN FOUNDATION FOR JUSTICE

116 East 16th Street, 7th Floor
New York, NY 10003
(212) 529-8021
Fax: (212) 982-3321
E-mail: info@astraeafoundation.org
Web Site: www.astraeafoundation.org

TYPE:
Awards/prizes.

See entry 899 for full listing.

THE WILLIAM G. BAKER, JR. MEMORIAL FUND [398]

2 East Read Street, Ninth Floor
Baltimore, MD 21202
(410) 332-4172 ext. 150
Fax: (410) 837-4701
E-mail: mwarlow@bcf.org
Web Site: www.bcf.org/baker

FOUNDED: 1964

AREAS OF INTEREST:
Arts and culture.

NAME(S) OF PROGRAMS:
● **Baker Artist Portfolios**

TYPE:
Technical assistance.

YEAR PROGRAM STARTED: 1964

PURPOSE:
To strengthen Baltimore's arts and culture sector.

LEGAL BASIS:
Private, nonprofit foundation.

ELIGIBILITY:
Cultural organizations (or their fiscal agents) serving the Baltimore area that qualify as public charities under Section 501(c)(3) of the Internal Revenue Code.

The fund does not normally make grants to endowment campaigns, annual appeals, event sponsorships, services outside the greater Baltimore area, or art programs and projects that use the arts as a mechanism to achieve other ends such as community development, health, social justice, arts education or youth development objectives.

GEOG. RESTRICTIONS: Greater Baltimore area.

FINANCIAL DATA:
Amount of support per award: $1,500 to $40,000.
Total amount of support: $1,254,615 for the year 2018.

NO. MOST RECENT APPLICANTS: 51.

NO. AWARDS: 49 for the year 2018.

APPLICATION INFO:
Applicants must complete the online application and evaluation chart. Data Arts Cultural Data Profile is required.
Duration: One year.
Deadline: September 27.

IRS I.D.: 52-6057178

GOVERNING BOARD:
Connie E. Imboden, President
Gwen Davidson
Laura L. Gamble
Steven G. Ziger

ADDRESS INQUIRIES TO:
Melissa Warlow, Director
(See address above.)

BATON ROUGE AREA FOUNDATION [399]

100 North Street
Suite 900
Baton Rouge, LA 70802
(225) 387-6126
E-mail: rschutte@braf.org
Web Site: www.braf.org

AREAS OF INTEREST:
Arts, cultural programs, education, community development, human services, environment, scholarships, medical and health.

TYPE:
Capital grants; Challenge/matching grants; Conferences/seminars; Demonstration grants; Development grants; Matching gifts; Project/program grants; Scholarships; Seed money grants; Technical assistance; Training grants; Visiting scholars.

PURPOSE:
To connect philanthropists with capable nonprofits to make sure the needs of the community are met; to invest in and manage pivotal projects that can change the community.

ELIGIBILITY:
Eligible organizations must be IRS 501(c)(3) tax-exempt.

FINANCIAL DATA:
Amount of support per award: Varies.
Total amount of support: Varies.

APPLICATION INFO:
Application details are available online. All applications must include a copy of the IRS tax determination letter.
Duration: One year. Must reapply for additional funding.

ADDRESS INQUIRIES TO:
Rebecca Schutte, Director of Donor Services (See address above.)

CALIFORNIA ARTS COUNCIL [400]

1300 I Street, Suite 930
Sacramento, CA 95814
(916) 322-6555
(800) 201-6201
Fax: (916) 322-6575
E-mail: kimberly.brown@arts.ca.gov
Web Site: www.arts.ca.gov

FOUNDED: 1976

AREAS OF INTEREST:
Operating and creative support to art organizations, artists, visual and performing arts programs in schools and after-school programs.

CONSULTING OR VOLUNTEER SERVICES:
Sponsor conferences and technical assistance to art organizations.

NAME(S) OF PROGRAMS:
• **Artists in Communities**
• **Artists in Schools**
• **Arts and Accessibility**
• **Arts and Public Media**
• **Arts Education Exposure**
• **Arts Integration Training**
• **Creative California Communities**
• **Cultural Pathways**
• **JUMP StArts**
• **Local Impact**
• **Organizational Development**
• **Professional Development**
• **Reentry Through the Arts**
• **Research in the Arts**
• **State-Local Partners**
• **Statewide and Regional Networks**
• **Veterans in the Arts**
• **Youth Arts Action**

TYPE:
Challenge/matching grants; Project/program grants.

YEAR PROGRAM STARTED: 1976

PURPOSE:
To advance California in the arts and creativity.

LEGAL BASIS:
State arts agency, funded by state budget and other sources.

ELIGIBILITY:
To be eligible for funding, a California-based group or organization should be an incorporated nonprofit and have been in existence at least two years and be able to demonstrate fiscal and managerial responsibility. Grants are given to provide in-school and after-school arts educational activities, assistance for specific artistic services such as events, exhibitions and publications, to expand participation by segments of the public who have had limited access to cultural events, and to encourage and enhance communication among artists, organizations and the general public.

GEOG. RESTRICTIONS: California.

FINANCIAL DATA:
Amount of support per award: Varies according to program.
Total amount of support: Varies.
Matching fund requirements: Varies.

NO. MOST RECENT APPLICANTS: Approximately 1,400.

NO. AWARDS: Approximately 1,100.

APPLICATION INFO:
Contact the Council.
Duration: Six months to two years.
Deadline: Varies according to program.

PUBLICATIONS:
Guide to programs; applications; newsletters.

COUNCIL MEMBERS:
Nashormeh Lindo, Chairperson
Larry Baza, Vice Chairperson
Juan Devis
Jodie Evans
Kathleen Gallegos
Jaime Galli
Donn K. Harris
Louise McGuinness

ADDRESS INQUIRIES TO:
Kimberly Brown
Public Affairs Specialist
(See address above.)

CINTAS FOUNDATION [401]

8724 Sunset Drive
P.M.B. 528
Miami, FL 33173
E-mail: info@cintasfoundation.org
Web Site: www.cintasfoundation.org

FOUNDED: 1981

AREAS OF INTEREST:
Architecture and design, creative writing, music composition and the visual arts.

NAME(S) OF PROGRAMS:
• **Cintas Fellowships in the Arts**

TYPE:
Awards/prizes; Fellowships. Awarded to persons of Cuban citizenship or lineage residing outside Cuba for achievement of a creative nature in architecture, painting, sculpture, printmaking, music composition and literature.

PURPOSE:
To recognize outstanding creative work done by a person from Cuba or a person of Cuban descent.

LEGAL BASIS:
Private, not-for-profit agency.

ELIGIBILITY:
Applications are open to professionals in the creative arts, of Cuban citizenship or lineage, who can give evidence of their creative production by records of exhibitions, performances or (when appropriate) by published books or scores. Students wishing to pursue academic programs are not eligible for awards nor are performing artists as opposed to creative artists. Although there is no fixed age limit, the Fellowships are intended for young professionals in the arts who have completed their academic and technical training.

FINANCIAL DATA:
Amount of support per award: $20,000, paid in four equal quarterly stipends.
Total amount of support: Varies.

NO. MOST RECENT APPLICANTS: 150.

NO. AWARDS: 3 to 4 annually.

APPLICATION INFO:
Eligible candidates may request application forms and letter of reference forms from the Foundation. Applications should be in English or Spanish and should be accompanied by supporting documentation of an appropriate nature, such as published books or music scores or photographs and reproductions of paintings or sculpture.

Duration: 12 consecutive months beginning October 10.

Deadline: June 1.

COLORADO CREATIVE INDUSTRIES   [402]

1600 Broadway, Suite 2500
Denver, CO 80202
(303) 892-3802
Fax: (303) 892-3848
TDD: (303) 894-2664
E-mail: oedit_creativeindustries@state.co.us
Web Site: www.coloradocreativeindustries.org

FOUNDED: 1967

AREAS OF INTEREST:
Visual arts, literature, performing arts, folk arts and media arts, youth-at-risk and economic benefits.

NAME(S) OF PROGRAMS:
- **Arts in Society**
- **Career Advancement**
- **Colorado Creates**
- **Creative Districts**

TYPE:
Project/program grants.

PURPOSE:
To promote, support and expand the creative industries to drive Colorado's economy, grow jobs and enhance the quality of life.

LEGAL BASIS:
State government agency.

ELIGIBILITY:
Colorado artists, creative small business and nonprofit tax-exempt organizations and municipalities.

GEOG. RESTRICTIONS: Colorado.

FINANCIAL DATA:
Amount of support per award: Arts in Society: $5,000 to $35,000; Career Advancement: Up to $2,500; Colorado Creates: $4,000 to $10,000.

Total amount of support: Varies.

Matching fund requirements: Career Advancement: 1:1 cash match; Colorado Creates: Based on cash operating income. Creative Districts: 1:1 match.

NO. MOST RECENT APPLICANTS: 380.

NO. AWARDS: 300.

APPLICATION INFO:
Contact Colorado Creative Industries.
Duration: Colorado Creates: Two years on, one year off. Other programs: Generally one year.

PUBLICATIONS:
Annual report; guidelines; press releases; news clips; strategic plan.

OFFICERS:
Jared Polis, Governor
Timothy Schultz, Chairperson
Margaret Hunt, Executive Director

ADDRESS INQUIRIES TO:
Christy Costello, Deputy Director
(See address above.)

THE COMMUNITY FOUNDATION OF LOUISVILLE, INC.   [403]

325 West Main Street, Suite 1110
Louisville, KY 40202
(502) 585-4649
Fax: (502) 587-7484
E-mail: info@cflouisville.org
Web Site: www.cflouisville.org

AREAS OF INTEREST:
Visual arts, crafts, theatre, historic preservation, environment, education, religion and humanities.

TYPE:
Endowments; General operating grants; Scholarships.

PURPOSE:
To enrich the quality of life for all citizens in the Louisville area and to serve as a catalyst for promoting philanthropy within the local community.

ELIGIBILITY:
Grants are made to organizations that have tax-exempt status under Section 501(c)(3) of the Internal Revenue Code.

GEOG. RESTRICTIONS: United States.

FINANCIAL DATA:
Amount of support per award: Varies.
Total amount of support: Varies.

APPLICATION INFO:
Contact the Foundation.
Duration: One year.
Deadline: Details are available on the web site.

ADDRESS INQUIRIES TO:
For Scholarships:
Emory Williamson
E-mail: emoryw@cflouisville.org

For Grants:
Program Officer
E-mail: grants@cflouisville.org

CONGRESSIONAL BLACK CAUCUS FOUNDATION, INC.

1720 Massachusetts Avenue, N.W.
Washington, DC 20036
(202) 263-2800
Fax: (202) 263-0846
E-mail: scholarships@cbcfinc.org
Web Site: www.cbcfinc.org

TYPE:
Scholarships. CBC Spouses Performing Arts Scholarship, developed in honor of the late Curtis Mayfield, is intended to ensure that students pursuing a career in the performing arts receive the financial assistance to achieve their goals.

CBC Spouses Visual Arts Scholarship was established for students who are pursuing a career in the visual arts.

See entry 939 for full listing.

CONSEIL DES ARTS DE MONTREAL   [404]

1210 East Sherbrooke Street
First Floor
Montreal QC H2L 2L9 Canada
(514) 280-3582
E-mail: nathalie.maille@montreal.ca
Web Site: www.artsmontreal.org

FOUNDED: 1956

AREAS OF INTEREST:
Visual arts, dance, theatre, music, literature, cinema, new artistic practices, video and electronic arts.

NAME(S) OF PROGRAMS:
- **Programme de tournees**
- **Programme General**

TYPE:
Awards/prizes; Development grants; Exchange programs; General operating grants; Project/program grants; Technical assistance. Grants to nonprofit professional organizations having their head offices in Montreal.

YEAR PROGRAM STARTED: 1956

PURPOSE:
To assist Montreal's artistic and cultural organizations.

LEGAL BASIS:
Regional organization.

ELIGIBILITY:
Professional, nonprofit organizations in Montreal.

GEOG. RESTRICTIONS: Montreal, Quebec.

FINANCIAL DATA:
Amount of support per award: Varies.
Total amount of support: $14,405,216 (CAN) for the year 2018.

NO. AWARDS: 525 for the year 2018.

APPLICATION INFO:
Contact the Conseil des Arts.
Duration: One fiscal year.
Deadline: Programme de tournees: September. Programme General: Varies by type of grant.

PUBLICATIONS:
Annual report.

STAFF:
Sylviane Martineau, Cultural Advisor, Dance
Marie-Anne Raulet, Cultural Advisor, Literature, Cinema
Claire Metras, Cultural Advisor, Music
Salome Viguier, Cultural Advisor, New Artistic Practices
Frederic Cote, Cultural Advisor, Theatre
Marie-Michele Cron, Cultural Advisor, Visual Arts, Media Arts

ADDRESS INQUIRIES TO:
Cultural Advisor
(See address above.)

THE CORPORATION OF YADDO   [405]

312 Union Avenue
Saratoga Springs, NY 12866
(518) 584-0746
Fax: (518) 584-1312
E-mail: cwilliams@yaddo.org
Web Site: www.yaddo.org

FOUNDED: 1900

AREAS OF INTEREST:
Literature, visual arts, music composition, filmmaking, choreography, performance art and other creative arts.

NAME(S) OF PROGRAMS:
- **Artist Residencies**

TYPE:
Residencies; Travel grants.

YEAR PROGRAM STARTED: 1926

PURPOSE:
To enable artists to work in a quiet, protected and supportive environment.

LEGAL BASIS:
A publicly supported charity.

ELIGIBILITY:
For creative artists working at a professional level in their field. Artists of all backgrounds are encouraged to apply.

FINANCIAL DATA:
No cash grants. The award covers room, board and studio costs. A small fund exists to provide limited help towards the expenses of travel or renting equipment to invited guests of any discipline who otherwise might not be able to visit.

NO. MOST RECENT APPLICANTS: Approximately 1,500 annually.

APPLICATION INFO:
Applicants should apply to the Admissions Panel that best represents the project they wish to undertake should they be invited for a residency. Applicants may apply to only one admissions panel, in one genre, at a time. Applicants with concerns about choice of panel should contact the Program Director.

All application materials, including contact information, resume, work sample, and reference letters must be submitted electronically.

Duration: Up to two months.

Deadline: January 5 and August 1.

PUBLICATIONS:
Annual report; newsletter; case statement.

IRS I.D.: 14-1343055

OFFICERS:
A.M. Homes, Chairperson
Susan Unterberg, Chairperson
Jaime Wolf, Vice Chairperson
Elaina Richardson, President
Christine Holle, Vice President, Finance and Assistant Treasurer
Candace Weir, Treasurer
Peter Cameron, Corporate Secretary
Susan Brynteson, Recording Secretary

ADDRESS INQUIRIES TO:
Christy Williams, Program Manager
(See address above.)

COSTUME SOCIETY OF AMERICA [406]

P.O. Box 852
Columbus, GA 31902-0852
(706) 615-2851
(800) 272-9447 (U.S.)
E-mail: national.office@costumesocietyamerica.com
Web Site: www.costumesocietyamerica.com

FOUNDED: 1973

AREAS OF INTEREST:
Costume, art history, research, textile and fashion design, museum studies and anthropology.

NAME(S) OF PROGRAMS:
● **Stella Blum Research Grant**
● **CSA Travel Research Grant**
● **Adele Filene Student Presenter Grant**

TYPE:
Awards/prizes; Conferences/seminars; Development grants; Fellowships; Project/program grants; Research grants;

Scholarships; Travel grants. Stella Blum Research Grant is a merit award for a student researching a North American costume topic.

CSA Travel Research Grant aids in travel to collections to any library, archive, museum or site for research to further an ongoing project.

Adele Filene Student Presenter Grant assists the travel of a CSA student member to that year's CSA national symposium to present either a juried paper or poster.

YEAR PROGRAM STARTED: 1987

PURPOSE:
To advance the global understanding of all aspects of dress and appearance.

ELIGIBILITY:
Must be a Costume Society of America member for all awards.

CSA Travel Research Grant: Must be a CSA nonstudent member. Proof must be given that work on the project is already underway.

Adele Filene Student Presenter Grant: Must be currently enrolled as a student with a juried paper or poster accepted by the CSA symposium.

FINANCIAL DATA:
Amount of support per award: Stella Blum Research Grant: $3,000, plus up to $600 to present completed research at the National Symposium and one day presentation registration fee; CSA Travel Research Grant: $2,100; Adele Filene Student Presenter Grant: Up to $600, plus one day presentation registration fee.

Total amount of support: Varies.

NO. MOST RECENT APPLICANTS: 12.

NO. AWARDS: 3.

APPLICATION INFO:
Information is available, under "Resources/Grants, Awards and Honors," on the Society's web site.

Duration: One year.

Deadline: Grant deadlines are posted online.

ADDRESS INQUIRIES TO:
Executive Director
(See e-mail address above.)

DELAWARE DIVISION OF THE ARTS [407]

Carvel State Office Building
820 North French Street
Wilmington, DE 19801
(302) 577-8278
Fax: (302) 577-6561
E-mail: delarts@delaware.gov
Web Site: arts.delaware.gov

FOUNDED: 1969

AREAS OF INTEREST:
Performing arts, visual arts, literature and media.

CONSULTING OR VOLUNTEER SERVICES:
Technical assistance to community groups and arts organizations.

NAME(S) OF PROGRAMS:
● **Arts in Education**
● **Arts Organizations Grants**
● **Community Based Organizations Grants**
● **Gallery Program**
● **Individual Artist Fellowships**
● **Opportunity Grants**

TYPE:
Challenge/matching grants; Conferences/seminars; Fellowships; General operating grants; Project/program grants; Residencies; Technical assistance. Grants to Delaware nonprofit, tax-exempt organizations for projects in the arts. Fellowships program for individual creative artists who reside in Delaware.

YEAR PROGRAM STARTED: 1970

PURPOSE:
To nurture and support the arts to enhance the quality of life for all Delawareans.

LEGAL BASIS:
State agency.

ELIGIBILITY:
Applicants must be nonprofit, tax-exempt organizations in the state of Delaware. Fellowship applicants are individual creative artists who reside in Delaware.

GEOG. RESTRICTIONS: Delaware.

FINANCIAL DATA:
Amount of funds available is determined by state appropriation and funding from the National Endowment for the Arts.

Amount of support per award: Variable according to program.

Total amount of support: $3,275,000 for fiscal year 2019.

Matching fund requirements: Organization grants matching requirements vary according to program.

NO. MOST RECENT APPLICANTS: 411 for fiscal year 2019.

NO. AWARDS: 226 for fiscal year 2019.

APPLICATION INFO:
Application must be made on forms available on the web site.

Duration: Varies.

Deadline: March 1 for most grants. Announcement July 1 for most grants.

ADDRESS INQUIRIES TO:
Paul Weagraff, Director
(See address above.)

DEPARTMENT OF ECONOMIC AND COMMUNITY DEVELOPMENT/CONNECTICUT OFFICE OF THE ARTS [408]

450 Columbus Boulevard, 4th Floor
Hartford, CT 06103
(860) 500-2300
E-mail: elizabeth.shapiro@ct.gov
Web Site: www.cultureandtourism.org

FOUNDED: 1965

AREAS OF INTEREST:
Arts, program services, and infrastructure.

CONSULTING OR VOLUNTEER SERVICES:
Volunteer Lawyers for the Arts program.

TYPE:
Challenge/matching grants; Conferences/seminars; Endowments; Fellowships; General operating grants; Internships; Project/program grants; Technical assistance. Grants are available to Connecticut artists, arts institutions, arts organizations and nonprofit arts-sponsoring organizations for program support and technical assistance.

Project grants are available to non-arts organizations using arts or conducting arts programming, as well as schools, libraries and PTOs.

YEAR PROGRAM STARTED: 1965

PURPOSE:
To invest in the state's art-based cultural activities and infrastructure in ways that will advance the attractiveness and competitiveness of Connecticut cities, towns and villages as meaningful communities in which to live, work, learn and play.

LEGAL BASIS:
The State of Connecticut Enabling Legislation, Public Act No. 78-187 created the original Connecticut Commission on the Arts.

ELIGIBILITY:
Connecticut artists, art institutions, units of state or local government, art organizations and nonprofit arts-sponsoring associations whose principle residence is in Connecticut. Ineligible programs are those which take place out of state, student projects, fund-raising benefits, social activities, membership activities, scholarships, underwriting of past deficits or capital expenditures.

GEOG. RESTRICTIONS: Connecticut.

FINANCIAL DATA:
Amount of support per award: Varies.
Total amount of support: Varies.

CO-OP FUNDING PROGRAMS: Matching funds, Federal-state partnership and designated regional service organizations.

NO. AWARDS: 445.

APPLICATION INFO:
A guidelines brochure may be requested from the Commission three to four months in advance to the project.
Duration: Varies.
Deadline: Varies.

PUBLICATIONS:
Copyright Law; *Non-Profit Incorporation-A Guide for Artists and Organizations*; *Contract Law for Artists and Organizations*; *Culture and Tourism Newsletter*; Bi-Monthly Bulletin; *Art in Public Spaces Program Guide*; *Hot Schools Transform Education*; *Economic Impact of the Nonprofit Arts Industry in Connecticut*; *Performing Artists*, online directories.

ADDRESS INQUIRIES TO:
Rhonda Olisky, Special Projects Coordinator
(See address above.)

DISTRICT OF COLUMBIA COMMISSION ON THE ARTS AND HUMANITIES   [409]
200 I Street, S.E.
Washington, DC 20003
(202) 724-5613
Fax: (202) 727-4135
TDD: (202) 727-3148
E-mail: heran.sereke-brhan2@dc.gov
Web Site: dcarts.dc.gov

FOUNDED: 1968

AREAS OF INTEREST:
The arts and humanities in the District of Columbia.

NAME(S) OF PROGRAMS:
● **Art Bank Program**

● **Arts and Humanities Education Projects**
● **Arts and Humanities Fellowship Program**
● **Curatorial Grant Program**
● **East of the River Program**
● **Facilities and Buildings**
● **Field Trip Experiences**
● **General Operating Support**
● **Projects, Events and Festivals**
● **Public Art Building Communities**
● **Sister Cities Grant**
● **UPSTART Program**

TYPE:
Awards/prizes; Capital grants; Challenge/matching grants; Conferences/seminars; Exchange programs; Fellowships; General operating grants; Grants-in-aid; Project/program grants; Research grants; Residencies. Services provided to arts institutions and individual artists including inquiry services, technical assistance and funding.

YEAR PROGRAM STARTED: 1968

PURPOSE:
To administer funds to arts organizations, community organizations and individual artists to support arts endeavors within the District of Columbia.

LEGAL BASIS:
State arts agency authorized by executive order.

ELIGIBILITY:
Applicants must be artists or arts professionals (e.g., presenters, producers, and educators) aged 18 or older and residents of Washington, DC.

Organizations must be located in Washington, DC and be nonprofit IRS 501(c)(3) arts organizations within the District of Columbia at least two years prior to application in some programs and one year in most others. Organizations are also required to participate in the DC Cultural Data Project.

Grant funds cannot be used for scholarships, reserve funds, or any food/receptions. Fiscal agents are strictly prohibited.

GEOG. RESTRICTIONS: Washington, DC.

FINANCIAL DATA:
Amount of support per award: Varies by program.
Total amount of support: Varies.
Matching fund requirements: Most grants require organizations to have matching funds.

CO-OP FUNDING PROGRAMS: National Endowment for the Arts.

REPRESENTATIVE AWARDS:
$27,800 to Thomas Circle Singers for general operating support; $150,000 to National Museum of Women in the Arts; $1,000,000 to the Washington Ballet.

APPLICATION INFO:
Applications must be submitted through the online grants portal. The Commission will not accept mailed, e-mailed or hand-delivered copies of grant applications.
Duration: All expenses must be paid within the District's fiscal year of October 1 to September 30.
Deadline: Varies per grant cycle.

PUBLICATIONS:
Guide to Grants.

ADDRESS INQUIRIES TO:
Heran Sereke-Brhan, Senior Grants Officer
(See address above.)

EAST TENNESSEE FOUNDATION
520 West Summit Hill Drive
Suite 1101
Knoxville, TN 37902
(865) 524-1223
(877) 524-1223
Fax: (865) 637-6039
E-mail: etf@etf.org
Web Site: www.easttennesseefoundation.org

TYPE:
Project/program grants; Scholarships; Seed money grants; Technical assistance. The Foundation is comprised of 400 philanthropic funds and nine supporting organizations.

See entry 1022 for full listing.

FENIMORE ART MUSEUM   [410]
5798 State Highway 80
Cooperstown, NY 13326
(607) 547-1416
Fax: (607) 547-1404
E-mail: publications@fenimoreart.org
Web Site: www.fenimoreartmuseum.org

FOUNDED: 1899

AREAS OF INTEREST:
New York state and culture.

NAME(S) OF PROGRAMS:
● **Henry Allen Moe Prize**

TYPE:
Awards/prizes. Prizes for published catalogues treating collections located or exhibited in New York state.

YEAR PROGRAM STARTED: 1983

PURPOSE:
To foster and recognize scholarship in art history and decorative arts studies in the form of published catalogues located or exhibited in New York state.

LEGAL BASIS:
Private.

ELIGIBILITY:
Entries should add new information to what is known about the subject and may completely document an exhibition. Only catalogues treating collections located or exhibited in New York state qualify.

FINANCIAL DATA:
Amount of support per award: $250 to $1,000.

NO. MOST RECENT APPLICANTS: Approximately 8.

NO. AWARDS: 1 for the year 2017.

APPLICATION INFO:
Entries must have been published in the previous year. Submit four copies, accompanied by a letter of transmittal stating intent to enter the contest.
Deadline: On or before February 28 for awards in the current year.

PUBLICATIONS:
New York History; *Heritage Magazine.*

OFFICERS AND TRUSTEES:
Jeffrey H. Pressman, M.D., Chairman of the Board
Thomas O. Putnam, Vice Chairman
Stephen M. Duff
Douglas E. Evelyn
Kathleen Flanagan
Nellie Gipson

Shelley Graham
Robert S. Hanft
Josef E. Jelinek
Charles B. Kieler
Doris Fischer Malesardi
Erna Morgan McReynolds
Anne G. Older
Ellen Tillapaugh
Richard C. Vanison

ADDRESS INQUIRIES TO:
Cynthia G. Falk
Assistant Professor of Material Culture
(See address above.)

FLORIDA DEPARTMENT OF STATE, DIVISION OF CULTURAL AFFAIRS   [411]

500 South Bronough Street
Tallahassee, FL 32399-0250
(850) 245-6470
E-mail: dcainfo@dos.myflorida.com
Web Site: dos.myflorida.com/cultural

FOUNDED: 1969

AREAS OF INTEREST:
The Division of Cultural Affairs administers the cultural grant programs of the Department of State and is responsible for planning and implementing arts programs statewide, providing technical assistance to artists and arts organizations, awarding, administering, monitoring and evaluating the grants program, disseminating arts-related information and encouraging cultural development in Florida.

CONSULTING OR VOLUNTEER SERVICES:
Facilitative services in all areas are available.

NAME(S) OF PROGRAMS:
● **Cultural Facilities Program**
● **Florida Cultural Endowment Program**
● **General Program Support Grants Program**
● **Specific Cultural Projects Grants Program**

TYPE:
Capital grants; Conferences/seminars; Endowments; Formula grants; General operating grants; Grants-in-aid; Internships; Project/program grants. Cultural facilities grants.

YEAR PROGRAM STARTED: 1969

PURPOSE:
To encourage the creation of projects that promote excellence in the arts and that strive to bring arts to a communitywide audience.

LEGAL BASIS:
State government agency.

ELIGIBILITY:
To apply for a grant, an organization must qualify as a political subdivision of a municipal, county or state government in Florida or be a not-for-profit, tax-exempt Florida corporation, meet specific budgetary and program requirements as outlined for the appropriate artistic disciplines, special programs and funding categories, match dollar-for-dollar, in most cases, the grant amount requested from the Division and meet all legal and financial requirements described in the *Guide to Cultural Programs*.

An individual artist living and working in the state of Florida may apply.

GEOG. RESTRICTIONS: Florida.

FINANCIAL DATA:
Cash grants are for program expenses rather than for capital improvements.
Amount of support per award: Varies depending upon grant program and specific eligibility.
Total amount of support: Varies by program.
Matching fund requirements: In most cases, grants are matched 1:1.

NO. MOST RECENT APPLICANTS: 682 for the year 2018-19.

NO. AWARDS: 444 for the year 2018-19.

APPLICATION INFO:
Program guidelines can be downloaded from the web site.
Duration: One year or up to two years.
Deadline: June for General Program Support, Cultural Facilities and Specific Cultural Projects grants.

OFFICERS:
Sandy Shaughnessy, Director, Division of Cultural Affairs

STAFF:
Geri Abstein, Chief of Grants Administration

ADDRESS INQUIRIES TO:
Geri Abstein
Chief of Grants Administration or
Curtis Young
Operations Management Consultant
(See address above.)

FORECAST PUBLIC ART   [412]

2300 Myrtle Avenue
Suite 160
St. Paul, MN 55114
(651) 641-1128
E-mail: grants@forecastpublicart.org
Web Site: www.forecastpublicart.org

FOUNDED: 1978

AREAS OF INTEREST:
Public art.

CONSULTING OR VOLUNTEER SERVICES:
Provide consulting for public artists and communities.

NAME(S) OF PROGRAMS:
● **Early-Career Artist Project Grant**
● **Early-Career Artist Research and Development Grant**
● **Mid-Career Professional Development Grant**
● **Mid-Career Project Grant**

TYPE:
Awards/prizes; Project/program grants; Research grants.

YEAR PROGRAM STARTED: 1988

PURPOSE:
To fund emerging and midcareer artists of all disciplines to develop and/or produce public art projects.

LEGAL BASIS:
Private nonprofit corporation.

ELIGIBILITY:
Open to emerging and midcareer artists of all disciplines. Applicant must be a Minnesota resident.

Mid-Career Project Grant applicants must be midcareer public artists.

GEOG. RESTRICTIONS: Minnesota.

FINANCIAL DATA:
Amount of support per award: Early-Career Artist Project Grant: $8,000; Early-Career

Artist Research and Development Grant: $2,500; Mid-Career Professional Development Grant: $5,000; Mid-Career Project Grant: $10,000.

NO. MOST RECENT APPLICANTS: 50 to 100 per competition.

NO. AWARDS: Early-Career Artist Project Grant: 2; Early-Career Artist Research and Development Grant: 4; Mid-Career Professional Development Grant: 2; Mid-Career Project Grant: 5.

APPLICATION INFO:
Application information is available online.
Duration: 11 months.
Deadline: Mid-Career Project Grant: July. Early-Career Artist Project Grant, Early-Career Artist Research and Development Grant, and Mid-Career Professional Development Grant: October.

PUBLICATIONS:
Public Art Review, a semiannual publication focusing on public art projects and issues.

IRS I.D.: 41-1361351

STAFF:
Theresa Sweetland, Executive Director
Jen Krava, Director of Programming
Karen Olson, Editor, *Public Art Review*

ADDRESS INQUIRIES TO:
Jen Krava, Director of Programming
(See address above.)

CARL M. FREEMAN FOUNDATION   [413]

31556 Winterberry Parkway
Selbyville, DE 19975
(302) 483-7639
Fax: (302) 483-7639
E-mail: grantsmanager@freemanfoundation.org
Web Site: www.carlfreemanfoundation.org

FOUNDED: 1960

AREAS OF INTEREST:
Facilitating, supporting and promoting innovative community-based leadership and giving.

NAME(S) OF PROGRAMS:
● **FACES Grant**

TYPE:
Capital grants; Challenge/matching grants; General operating grants.

YEAR PROGRAM STARTED: 2000

PURPOSE:
To provide funding and capacity-building support to nonprofit organizations in the communities served by the Carl M. Freeman Companies.

ELIGIBILITY:
Must be IRS-recognized 501(c)(3) tax-exempt, nonprofit organizations or public agencies serving the residents of the Companies' funding areas.

GEOG. RESTRICTIONS: Sussex County, Delaware and Montgomery County, Maryland.

FINANCIAL DATA:
Amount of support per award: $2,500 or $5,000.
Total amount of support: $100,000 annually ($50,000 per geographic area).

APPLICATION INFO:
Guidelines are available on the web site.
Duration: Six months; possible several-month renewal.
Deadline: Varies.

ADDRESS INQUIRIES TO:
Lindsay Richard, Grants Manager
(See address above.)

FREER GALLERY OF ART AND ARTHUR M. SACKLER GALLERY [414]

Smithsonian Institution, MRC 707
1050 Independence Avenue, S.W.
Washington, DC 20560
(202) 633-0401
E-mail: mirzas@si.edu
Web Site: www.freersackler.si.
edu/research/fellowships-internships

FOUNDED: 1923

AREAS OF INTEREST:
Asian art, 19th and early 20th century American art.

CONSULTING OR VOLUNTEER SERVICES:
Docent tours for the public through Freer Gallery of Art and Arthur M. Sackler Gallery.

NAME(S) OF PROGRAMS:
- **The J.S. Lee Memorial Fellowship**
- **Smithsonian Institution Fellowship**
- **Anne van Biema Fellowship**

TYPE:
Awards/prizes; Fellowships; Internships; Project/program grants; Research grants; Technical assistance; Visiting scholars. The J.S. Lee Memorial Fellowship facilitates the international exchange of curatorial expertise and contributes to the professional development of Chinese art curators and academics.

Anne van Biema Fellowship is established to promote excellence in research and publication on the Japanese visual arts. One award is made each year to support a scholar at the postdoctoral level for a period of two to nine months.

YEAR PROGRAM STARTED: 1923

PURPOSE:
To advance scholarship of Asian art and 19th and early 20th century American art.

LEGAL BASIS:
U.S. government agency.

ELIGIBILITY:
Varies with each fellowship.

FINANCIAL DATA:
Amount of support per award: Varies.
Total amount of support: Varies.

CO-OP FUNDING PROGRAMS: Smithsonian Office of Fellowships and Grants, University of Michigan.

APPLICATION INFO:
For Smithsonian Fellowship, write to Office of Fellowships and Internships in the Smithsonian. For the J.S. Lee Memorial Fellowship, visit the fellowship page at www.jsleefellowship.org. Van Biema Fellowship information is available on the web site.
Duration: Varies.
Deadline: Varies.

PUBLICATIONS:
Annual report.

OFFICERS:
Chase F. Robinson, Director

ADDRESS INQUIRIES TO:
Sana Mirza
Scholarly Programs and Publications
(See address above.)

THE DAVID GEFFEN FOUNDATION

12011 San Vicente Boulevard
Suite 606
Los Angeles, CA 90049
(310) 581-5955
E-mail: ddishman@geffenco.com

TYPE:
General operating grants; Project/program grants.
See entry 1308 for full listing.

GEORGIA COUNCIL FOR THE ARTS [415]

75 Fifth Street, N.W.
Suite 1200
Atlanta, GA 30308
(404) 962-4827
E-mail: gaarts@gaarts.org
Web Site: gaarts.org

FOUNDED: 1968

AREAS OF INTEREST:
The arts.

CONSULTING OR VOLUNTEER SERVICES:
Extensive technical assistance to nonprofit arts organizations in all disciplines on matters of artistic, administrative or technical concern.

NAME(S) OF PROGRAMS:
- **Arts Education Grants**
- **Partner Grants**
- **Project Grants**
- **Vibrant Communities Grants**

TYPE:
General operating grants; Project/program grants.

YEAR PROGRAM STARTED: 1968

PURPOSE:
To cultivate the growth of Georgia communities through the arts.

LEGAL BASIS:
Government agency.

ELIGIBILITY:
Grants are made to nonprofit, tax-exempt arts organizations or units of government which are incorporated in the state of Georgia.

GEOG. RESTRICTIONS: Georgia.

FINANCIAL DATA:
Amount of support per award: $1,000 to $20,000.
Total amount of support: Over $1,000,000 for the year 2019.
Matching fund requirements: Varies.

NO. AWARDS: 132 for the year 2019.

APPLICATION INFO:
Grant applications are available online.
Duration: One year. Must reapply for additional funding.
Deadline: Varies.

PUBLICATIONS:
Application guidelines; quarterly newsletter.

ADDRESS INQUIRIES TO:
Tina Lilly, Grants Program Director
(See address above.)

NANCY GRAVES FOUNDATION [416]

33-20 48th Avenue, 2nd Floor
Long Island City, NY 11101
(718) 482-1100
E-mail: mail@nancygravesfoundation.org
Web Site: www.nancygravesfoundation.org

FOUNDED: 1996

AREAS OF INTEREST:
Visual arts.

NAME(S) OF PROGRAMS:
- **Nancy Graves Grant for Visual Artists**

TYPE:
Grant for nominated visual artists for work in any medium other than their own.

YEAR PROGRAM STARTED: 2000

PURPOSE:
To give assistance to individual artists; to maintain an archive of the Founder's life and work and organize exhibitions of her art.

ELIGIBILITY:
Grantees must be residents of the U.S. who have been working as artists for at least five years beyond his or her schooling. Grants will not be awarded to students. Applications will be solicited from nominated visual artists who wish to have the opportunity to master a technique, medium or discipline that is different from the one in which he or she is primarily recognized.

GEOG. RESTRICTIONS: United States.

FINANCIAL DATA:
Amount of support per award: $12,500 for the year 2018.

NO. AWARDS: 4 for the year 2018.

APPLICATION INFO:
Artist applicants must be nominated by Foundation nominators and will subsequently receive an application for consideration by a second panel of jurors.
Duration: One year.
Deadline: Varies.

STAFF:
Christina Hunter, Director

ADDRESS INQUIRIES TO:
Christina Hunter, Director
(See address above.)

HAMBIDGE [417]

P.O. Box 339
Rabun Gap, GA 30568
(706) 746-5718
Fax: (706) 746-9933
E-mail: center@hambidge.org
Web Site: www.hambidge.org

FOUNDED: 1934

AREAS OF INTEREST:
Artist residency program.

NAME(S) OF PROGRAMS:
- **Hambidge Residency Program Fellowships**

TYPE:
Fellowships; Residencies. The Hambidge Center awards residency fellowships to distinguished artists and scientists at its 600-acre creative sanctuary in the Blue Ridge Mountains. Fellowships apply to any field or discipline of creative work.

PURPOSE:
To provide applicants with an environment for creative work in the arts and sciences.

ELIGIBILITY:

Open to qualified applicants in all disciplines who can demonstrate seriousness, dedication and professionalism. International residents are welcome.

FINANCIAL DATA:

Each of the individuals in residence has private accommodations and studio space, and shares communal dinners prepared by an in-residence chef. Eight individuals are in residence at any given time.

Amount of support per award: Each artist receives a two-week residency with no fees, a $700 stipend, and the honor of a Distinguished Fellowship.

APPLICATION INFO:

Application information is available on the web site.

Duration: Two weeks.

Deadline: January 15, April 15 and September 15.

ADDRESS INQUIRIES TO:

Christine Jason, Operations Manager (See e-mail address above.)

HAWAII STATE FOUNDATION ON CULTURE AND THE ARTS [418]

250 South Hotel Street
Second Floor
Honolulu, HI 96813
(808) 586-0301
Fax: (808) 586-0308
TTY: (808) 586-0740
E-mail: jonathan.johnson@hawaii.gov
Web Site: hawaii.gov/sfca

FOUNDED: 1965

AREAS OF INTEREST:

Arts education, community arts, heritage and preservation, presentation, and community arts.

NAME(S) OF PROGRAMS:
- **Biennium Grants Program**

TYPE:

Project/program grants.

YEAR PROGRAM STARTED: 1965

PURPOSE:

To promote, perpetuate, preserve, and encourage culture and the arts as central to the quality of life of the people of Hawaii.

LEGAL BASIS:

State arts agency.

ELIGIBILITY:

Hawaii Revised Statutes for organizations and individuals as defined in Section 9-11.

GEOG. RESTRICTIONS: Hawaii.

FINANCIAL DATA:

Limits on the amount of funding for any one project are established by the SFCA Board. Certain costs are not allowable for SFCA funding.

Amount of support per award: $5,000 to $15,000.

Total amount of support: Over $500,000 for fiscal year 2019.

Matching fund requirements: 1:1 match required.

NO. MOST RECENT APPLICANTS: 74.

NO. AWARDS: 37 for the year 2019.

APPLICATION INFO:

Applicants must complete the required application forms and attachments.

Duration: Funds are awarded on a biennial basis. No funds are awarded on a continuing basis.

Deadline: Grant applications are received and reviewed during the State budgetary process.

PUBLICATIONS:

Annual Report; application guidelines.

BOARD MEMBERS:

Susan Browne
Nalani Brun
Jane Clement
Ronald Michioka
Karen Tiller Polivka
Dr. Clyde M. Sakamoto
Lloyd Unebasami
Sherman Warner
Allison Wong

ADDRESS INQUIRIES TO:

Jonathan Johnson, Executive Director (See address above.)

HAYSTACK MOUNTAIN SCHOOL OF CRAFTS [419]

89 Haystack School Drive
Deer Isle, ME 04627
(207) 348-2306
Fax: (207) 348-2307
E-mail: haystack@haystack-mtn.org
Web Site: www.haystack-mtn.org

FOUNDED: 1950

AREAS OF INTEREST:

Craft education and exploration in ceramics, metals, wood, fibers, graphics, glass and blacksmithing.

NAME(S) OF PROGRAMS:
- **Conferences/Seminars**
- **Exhibitions**
- **Maine Programs**
- **Open Studio Residency**
- **Summer Conference**
- **Summer Workshops**

TYPE:

Conferences/seminars; Fellowships; Residencies; Scholarships; Visiting scholars; Work-study programs. Minority scholarships; Technical Assistant and Work Study Scholarships. Awards for study in diverse craft media and workshops in six studios including ceramics, metals, wood, fibers, graphics, glass and blacksmithing.

YEAR PROGRAM STARTED: 1950

PURPOSE:

To offer professional instruction and demonstration in crafts.

LEGAL BASIS:

Nonprofit educational organization.

ELIGIBILITY:

U.S. and foreign citizens who are capable of doing graduate-level work are eligible for technical assistant scholarships. Candidates must be at least 18 years of age.

FINANCIAL DATA:

Annual scholarships cover the cost of tuition, or tuition and room and board.

Amount of support per award: $1,650.

Total amount of support: $325,000.

NO. MOST RECENT APPLICANTS: 625 (250 scholarship applicants; 375 non-scholarship applicants).

NO. AWARDS: 152 (56 work-study students; 50 technical assistants; 21 fellowships; 25 current-year scholarships).

APPLICATION INFO:

Guidelines and application form are available at the web site.

Duration: One- to two-week sessions.

Deadline: Scholarship applications: March 1; Regular applications: April 1.

PUBLICATIONS:

Catalog; newsletter; scholarly monographs; regional program brochures; eNewsletters.

IRS I.D.: 01-0243548

TRUSTEES:

Susan Haas Bralove, President
Ayumi Horie, Vice President
Laura Galaida, Treasurer

ADDRESS INQUIRIES TO:

Haystack Mountain School of Crafts
22 Church Street (November to April)
89 Haystack School Drive (May to October)
Deer Isle, ME 04627

THE MAXIMILIAN E. & MARION O. HOFFMAN FOUNDATION, INC.

970 Farmington Avenue, Suite 203
West Hartford, CT 06107
(860) 521-2949
Fax: (860) 561-5082

TYPE:

Project/program grants.

See entry 2071 for full listing.

HUTCHINSON COMMUNITY FOUNDATION [420]

One North Main Street
Suite 501
Hutchinson, KS 67501
(620) 663-5293
Fax: (620) 663-9277
E-mail: info@hutchcf.org
Web Site: hutchcf.org

FOUNDED: 1989

AREAS OF INTEREST:

Arts, civic improvements, education, health and human services.

TYPE:

Project/program grants; Seed money grants.

YEAR PROGRAM STARTED: 1989

PURPOSE:

To make Hutchinson area a better place to work and live.

LEGAL BASIS:

501(c)(3) public foundation.

ELIGIBILITY:

Organizations that support innovative projects located in Reno County, KS, and government units that work in the Foundation's objective.

GEOG. RESTRICTIONS: Reno County, Kansas.

FINANCIAL DATA:

Amount of support per award: Varies.

Total amount of support: Varies.

NO. MOST RECENT APPLICANTS: 50.

NO. AWARDS: 27 for the year 2018.

APPLICATION INFO:

One copy of the applicant's current IRS determination letter Section 501(c)(3) or 509(a) is required. Contact the Foundation for application procedures.

Duration: One year. Reapplication possible.

Deadline: Mid-February and late August. Contact Foundation for exact date.

PUBLICATIONS:
Annual report; application guidelines.

OFFICERS AND STAFF:
Aubrey A. Patterson, President and Executive Director
Kari Jackson Mailloux, Program Officer

ADDRESS INQUIRIES TO:
Aubrey A. Patterson
President and Executive Director
(See address above.)

IDAHO COMMISSION ON THE ARTS   [421]
2410 Old Penitentiary Road
Boise, ID 83712
(208) 334-2119
Fax: (208) 334-2488
E-mail: info@arts.idaho.gov
Web Site: arts.idaho.gov

FOUNDED: 1966

AREAS OF INTEREST:
All disciplines in the arts.

CONSULTING OR VOLUNTEER SERVICES:
Technical assistance in arts management.

NAME(S) OF PROGRAMS:
- **Arts Education Projects**
- **Directory of Teaching Artists**
- **Entry Track**
- **Fellowships**
- **Public Programs in the Arts**
- **Quick Funds**
- **Traditional Arts Apprenticeship Program**
- **Writer-in-Residence Program**

TYPE:
Conferences/seminars; Fellowships; General operating grants; Project/program grants; Residencies; Technical assistance. Fellowship/apprenticeship, touring/sponsorship, immediate assistance.

YEAR PROGRAM STARTED: 1966

PURPOSE:
To develop the artistic and cultural life of Idaho.

LEGAL BASIS:
State agency.

ELIGIBILITY:
Applicants must be nonprofit, tax-exempt organizations or artists living in Idaho.

GEOG. RESTRICTIONS: Idaho.

FINANCIAL DATA:
Fiscal restrictions, non-cash benefits.
Amount of support per award: Up to $25,000.
Total amount of support: $693,704 in grants and services for fiscal year 2018.
Matching fund requirements: 50:50, cash or in-kind.

NO. MOST RECENT APPLICANTS: 347 for fiscal year 2018.

NO. AWARDS: 302 for fiscal year 2018.

APPLICATION INFO:
Applicants must register online. Application cannot be submitted until all sections are completed.
Duration: 12 months.
Deadline: Varies. Consult the Commission.

PUBLICATIONS:
Application guidelines.

IRS I.D.: 82-6000952

OFFICERS:
Steve Allred, Chairperson
Michael Faison, Executive Director
Stuart Weiser, Deputy Director
John McMahon, Artist Services Director
Rebecca Martin, Arts Education Director
Juta Geurtsen, Community Development Director
Steven Hatcher, Folk and Traditional Arts Director
Jocelyn Robertson, Literature Director and Public Information Officer
Jadee Carson, Grants Manager

ADDRESS INQUIRIES TO:
Jadee Carson
Grants Manager or
Stuart Weiser
Deputy Director
(See address or phone number above.)

ILLINOIS ARTS COUNCIL AGENCY   [422]
James R. Thompson Center
100 West Randolph Street, Suite 10-500
Chicago, IL 60601
(312) 814-6750
Fax: (312) 814-1471
E-mail: iac.info@illinois.gov
Web Site: www.arts.illinois.gov

FOUNDED: 1965

AREAS OF INTEREST:
The arts.

TYPE:
General operating grants; Project/program grants.

PURPOSE:
To make the arts more widely available to Illinois residents; to promote an environment that is beneficial to artistic activities; to aid the continuing development of the state's cultural resources.

ELIGIBILITY:
Applicants must be tax-exempt 501(c)(3) organizations registered as not-for-profit corporations in good standing with the Illinois Secretary of State, or units of government (i.e., school, school district, park district, library district), or institutions of higher education. Applicant organizations must have been in active service to the public for at least one year prior to the date of application.

GEOG. RESTRICTIONS: Illinois.

FINANCIAL DATA:
Amount of support per award: Varies depending on needs and nature of the request.
Matching fund requirements: Varies per application type.

NO. MOST RECENT APPLICANTS: 1,724 for the year 2019.

NO. AWARDS: 1,024 for the year 2019.

APPLICATION INFO:
Guidelines are available on the Council web site.
Duration: Up to one year.

OFFICERS:
Shirley R. Madigan, Chairperson
Rhoda A. Pierce, Vice Chairperson

ADDRESS INQUIRIES TO:
See e-mail address above.

INDIANA ARTS COMMISSION   [423]
100 North Senate Avenue
Room N505
Indianapolis, IN 46204
(317) 232-1278
Fax: (317) 232-5595
TDD: (317) 233-3001
E-mail: GrantsAdmin@iac.in.gov
Web Site: www.in.gov/arts

FOUNDED: 1969

AREAS OF INTEREST:
The arts including crafts, dance, design, education, expansion arts, folk, literature, media, multiarts, museums, music, presenters, statewide arts service organizations, theatre and visual and local arts agencies.

CONSULTING OR VOLUNTEER SERVICES:
Consultation on a limited basis to Indiana organizations and artists.

TYPE:
Block grants; Conferences/seminars; Development grants; General operating grants; Project/program grants; Technical assistance. Arts in education; Arts organizations and services; Capacity building; Individual artist projects. Most grants are awarded through a network of regional partners which serve all 92 counties.

YEAR PROGRAM STARTED: 1969

PURPOSE:
To act as public catalyst, partner and investor that serves the citizens of Indiana by funding, encouraging, promoting and expanding all the arts.

LEGAL BASIS:
State agency.

ELIGIBILITY:
Applicants must be private tax-exempt, not-for-profit arts organizations or public agencies or individual artists. Eligible organizations without tax-exempt status should submit a fiscal year budget. IAC does not fund capital improvements, purchase of permanent equipment, costs of receptions, foods or beverages or agents fees for programs contracted through commercial agencies.

Must have impact on the state of Indiana.

GEOG. RESTRICTIONS: Indiana.

FINANCIAL DATA:
Amount of support per award: Varies.
Total amount of support: $3,600,000.
Matching fund requirements: Matching funds may include in-kind as well as cash.

NO. MOST RECENT APPLICANTS: 520.

NO. AWARDS: 410.

APPLICATION INFO:
Applicants must complete an application, grant agreement and any reporting required by the program guidelines. Program guidelines are available from the Commission. Potential applicants should contact the agency before applying.
Duration: July 1 through June 30, fiscal year.

PUBLICATIONS:
Monthy newsletters; press releases; grant/program guidelines.

IRS I.D.: 35-6000158

COMMISSION MEMBERS:
Kathy Ziliak Anderson, Chairperson

Allen C. Platt, III, Vice Chairperson
Jennifer Perry, Secretary
Alberta Barker
Libby Chiu
Ruth Ann Cowling
M. Susan Hardwick
Laurie Burns McRobbie
Micah L. Smith
Sherry Stark
Yolanda Stemer
Nancy P. Stewart
Anne Penny Valentine

ADDRESS INQUIRIES TO:
Paige Sharp, Deputy Director of Programs or
Miah Michaelsen, Deputy Director
(See address above.)

INTERNATIONAL DOCUMENTARY ASSOCIATION [424]

3600 Wilshire Boulevard
Suite 1810
Los Angeles, CA 90010
(213) 232-1660
Fax: (213) 232-1669
E-mail: grants@documentary.org
Web Site: www.documentary.org

FOUNDED: 1982

AREAS OF INTEREST:
Documentary film.

NAME(S) OF PROGRAMS:
● **IDA Documentary Awards**
● **IDA/David L. Wolper Student Documentary Achievement Award**
● **Pare Lorentz Award**
● **Pare Lorentz Documentary Fund**
● **Los Angeles County Arts Commission Internships**

TYPE:
Awards/prizes; Internships. IDA Documentary Awards celebrate the best nonfiction films and programs of the year. Prize awarded in seven categories: feature, short, episodic series, curated series, short film series, limited series, and the David L. Wolper Student Documentary Award.

IDA/David L. Wolper Student Documentary Achievement Award recognizes exceptional achievement in nonfiction film and video production at the university level and brings greater public and industry awareness to the work of students in the documentary field.

The Pare Lorentz Award is awarded for films that reflect the spirit and tradition of Pare Lorentz's work. The film should demonstrate one or more of Lorentz's central concerns (the appropriate use of the natural environment, justice for all, and the illumination of pressing social problems) presented as a compelling story by skillful filmmaking.

Pare Lorentz Documentary Fund supports full-length documentary films that reflect the spirit and nature of Pare Lorentz's work, exhibiting objective research, artful storytelling, strong visual style, high production values, artistic writing and outstanding music composition, as well as skillful direction, camerawork and editing.

Los Angeles County Arts Commission Internships are offered to undergraduate students who currently reside or are enrolled in a college or university located in Los Angeles County, CA. Those interested should consult the Association web site for up-to-date details.

YEAR PROGRAM STARTED: 1984

PURPOSE:
To provide resources, create community, and defend rights and freedoms for documentary artists, activists, and journalists.

LEGAL BASIS:
501(c)(3).

ELIGIBILITY:
Varies by program or award.

FINANCIAL DATA:
Amount of support per award: IDA Enterprise Documentary Fund: $50,000 to $100,000 for Production Grant and $15,000 for Development Grant; Pare Lorentz Documentary Fund: $15,000 to $25,000.
Total amount of support: IDA Enterprise Documentary Fund: $1,000,000; Pare Lorentz Documentary Fund: $95,000 for the year 2019.

NO. AWARDS: IDA Enterprise Documentary Fund: 21; Pare Lorentz: 4 for the year 2017.

APPLICATION INFO:
Pare Lorentz Documentary Fund: Guidelines are available on the Association web site.
Deadline: Varies by program or award.

IRS I.D.: 95-3911227

EXECUTIVE DIRECTOR:
Simon Kilmurry

ADDRESS INQUIRIES TO:
Dana Merwin, Program Officer
(See e-mail address above.)

IOWA ARTS COUNCIL [425]

600 East Locust Street
Des Moines, IA 50319-0290
(515) 281-4641
Fax: (515) 242-6498
E-mail: iowa.arts@iowa.gov
Web Site: www.iowaculture.gov/arts

FOUNDED: 1967

AREAS OF INTEREST:
All arts disciplines, primarily in Iowa.

CONSULTING OR VOLUNTEER SERVICES:
Technical assistance in a variety of disciplines and subject areas, including information.

NAME(S) OF PROGRAMS:
● **Arts Resources and Artists Programs**
● **Funding and Arts in Education Programs**
● **Technical Assistance and Community Development Programs**

TYPE:
Awards/prizes; Capital grants; Challenge/matching grants; Conferences/seminars; Development grants; Fellowships; General operating grants; Internships; Project/program grants; Scholarships. Seminars, technical assistance and funding. Services provided to institutions and individuals statewide.

YEAR PROGRAM STARTED: 1967

PURPOSE:
To cultivate creativity, learning and participation of the arts in Iowa.

LEGAL BASIS:
State agency established under Chapter 304A, Code of Iowa.

ELIGIBILITY:
Applicants must be nonprofit, tax-exempt 501(c)(3) organizations incorporated and

located in Iowa, schools or institutions of higher education located in Iowa, units of local, county or federally recognized tribal government located in Iowa, or Iowa resident artists, age 18 or older.

GEOG. RESTRICTIONS: Iowa.

FINANCIAL DATA:
Amount of support per award: Varies.
Total amount of support: Varies by program.
Matching fund requirements: One-to-one cash or in-kind match for most grant programs.

NO. MOST RECENT APPLICANTS: 403.

NO. AWARDS: 173.

APPLICATION INFO:
Refer to the Council web site.
Duration: 12 months or less.
Deadline: May 1 annually.

PUBLICATIONS:
Online e-newsletter (bimonthly).

IRS I.D.: 42-6004812

STAFF:
Veronica O'Hern, Grants and Artist Program Manager

ADDRESS INQUIRIES TO:
Veronica O'Hern
Grants and Artist Program Manager
(See address above.)

JEROME FOUNDATION, INC. [426]

550 Vandalia Street
Suite 109
St. Paul, MN 55114
(651) 224-9431
E-mail: info@jeromefdn.org
Web Site: www.jeromefdn.org

FOUNDED: 1964

AREAS OF INTEREST:
Arts with a focus on film and video, literature, dance, music, theater and visual arts. Emphasis is on creation of new works by early career artists.

TYPE:
Fellowships; Project/program grants; Residencies.

YEAR PROGRAM STARTED: 1964

PURPOSE:
To contribute to a dynamic and evolving culture by supporting the creation, development and production of new works by early career artists.

LEGAL BASIS:
Tax-exempt, private foundation.

ELIGIBILITY:
Foundation grants are made primarily to not-for-profit arts organizations and to individual professional artists through specific programs. The Foundation accepts requests from new organizations.

The Foundation does not support capital (building and endowment) campaigns.

Foundation support is restricted to emerging artists who are legal residents of Minnesota and/or New York City, NY.

GEOG. RESTRICTIONS: Minnesota and the five boroughs of New York City, New York.

FINANCIAL DATA:
Amount of support per award: Individual artists: $38,000 average; Organizations: $36,200 average.

Total amount of support: Individual artists: $1,850,000; Organizations: Average $2,100,000 annually.

APPLICATION INFO:
Guidelines and application forms are available on the web site.
Duration: Two years.

PUBLICATIONS:
Annual report.

STAFF:
Ben Cameron, President
Eleanor Savage, Program Director
Lann Briel, Program Officer
Andrea Brown, Grants and Program Administrator

DIRECTORS:
Kate Barr
Sarah Bellamy
Linda Earle
Daniel Alexander Jones
Lori Pourier
Rick Scott
Elizabeth Streb
Mark Tribe
Ryan Lee Wong

ADDRESS INQUIRIES TO:
Ben Cameron, President
(See address above.)

KENTUCKY ARTS COUNCIL   [427]
1025 Capital Center Drive, 3rd Floor
Frankfort, KY 40601
(502) 892-3118
Fax: (502) 564-2839
E-mail: kyarts@ky.gov
Web Site: artscouncil.ky.gov

FOUNDED: 1966

AREAS OF INTEREST:
Arts development (visual arts, performing arts, literature and media), community development, arts-in-education and individual artists.

CONSULTING OR VOLUNTEER SERVICES:
Staff available for assistance in planning in above areas and in applying for grants.

NAME(S) OF PROGRAMS:
● **Arts Education Programs**
● **Arts Organizations**
● **Community Arts**
● **Individual Artists**

TYPE:
Awards/prizes; Fellowships; General operating grants; Project/program grants; Residencies; Technical assistance. Arts development and artist support.

YEAR PROGRAM STARTED: 1966

PURPOSE:
To help sponsoring organizations and artists reach and develop new audiences or strengthen themselves artistically or managerially; to act as the funding and program coordinating organization for the arts in Kentucky.

LEGAL BASIS:
State Arts Agency of the Commonwealth of Kentucky.

ELIGIBILITY:
Nonprofit organizations incorporated in the state of Kentucky or Kentucky artists. Most grant programs require IRS tax-exempt status.

GEOG. RESTRICTIONS: Kentucky.

FINANCIAL DATA:
Amount of support per award: $200 to $135,000.
Total amount of support: $1,500,000 annually.
Matching fund requirements: Varies by program.

NO. MOST RECENT APPLICANTS: 500.

NO. AWARDS: 175.

APPLICATION INFO:
Guidelines and applications are found on the Council web site.
Duration: One fiscal year, July 1 through June 30.
Deadline: Varies.

PUBLICATIONS:
Bimonthly newsletter; annual report.

IRS I.D.: 61-0600439

OFFICERS:
Christopher Cathers, Executive Director

ADDRESS INQUIRIES TO:
Christopher Cathers, Executive Director
(See address above.)

THE LEEWAY FOUNDATION
1315 Walnut Street
Suite 832
Philadelphia, PA 19107
(215) 545-4078
Fax: (215) 545-4021
E-mail: info@leeway.org
Web Site: www.leeway.org

TYPE:
Awards/prizes; Project/program grants. Art and Change Grants provide project-based grants to fund art for social change projects.

Leeway Transformation Award is an unrestricted award (not project-based) for women and trans people demonstrating a commitment of five years or more to art for social change work.

See entry 990 for full listing.

LEHIGH VALLEY COMMUNITY FOUNDATION   [428]
840 West Hamilton Street
Suite 310
Allentown, PA 18101
(610) 351-5353
Fax: (610) 351-9353
E-mail: lvcfoundation@lvcfoundation.org
Web Site: www.lehighvalleyfoundation.org

FOUNDED: 1967

AREAS OF INTEREST:
Arts and culture, community development, education, environment, health care, history and heritage, human services and science.

TYPE:
Endowments; Scholarships. Community investment grants.

YEAR PROGRAM STARTED: 1967

PURPOSE:
To promote philanthropy in order to improve the quality of life in the Foundation's region.

LEGAL BASIS:
Nonprofit, tax-exempt 501(c)(3) organization.

ELIGIBILITY:
Limited to nonprofit, tax-exempt organizations serving citizens within the geographic limits of its outreach.

GEOG. RESTRICTIONS: Lehigh and Northampton counties, Pennsylvania.

FINANCIAL DATA:
Amount of support per award: Average discretionary grant: $5,000.
Total amount of support: $5,600,000 in grants for fiscal year 2018-19.

NO. AWARDS: 600 grants for fiscal year 2017-18.

APPLICATION INFO:
Application can be downloaded from the Foundation's web site. Financial sheet must be submitted with grant application.
Deadline: July 1. Notification December 15. Grants: Varies.

IRS I.D.: 23-1686634

STAFF:
Bernard Story, President and Chief Executive Officer

ADDRESS INQUIRIES TO:
Bernard Story
President and Chief Executive Officer
(See address above.)

THE JOHN J. LEIDY FOUNDATION
305 West Chesapeake Avenue
Suite 308
Towson, MD 21204
(410) 821-3006
Fax: (410) 821-3007
E-mail: info@leidyfoundation.org
Web Site: www.leidyfoundation.org

TYPE:
General operating grants; Project/program grants.

See entry 1203 for full listing.

LOUISIANA DIVISION OF THE ARTS, DEPARTMENT OF CULTURE, RECREATION AND TOURISM   [429]
1051 North Third Street, Room 420
Baton Rouge, LA 70802
(225) 342-8200
Fax: (225) 342-8173
E-mail: arts@crt.la.gov
Web Site: www.crt.state.la.us/cultural-development/arts

FOUNDED: 1976

AREAS OF INTEREST:
Dance, design, folklife, literature, media, music, theater, visual arts and crafts, arts-in-education, and arts service organizations.

CONSULTING OR VOLUNTEER SERVICES:
Grants writing, program development, community development, and alternate funding sources.

NAME(S) OF PROGRAMS:
● **Decentralized Arts Funding Program**
● **Statewide Arts Grants Programs**

TYPE:
General operating grants; Technical assistance. Grants in a variety of programs are offered to arts organizations across the state.

General operating support grants are offered in three levels of operating support to nonprofit arts organizations.

YEAR PROGRAM STARTED: 1977

PURPOSE:
To support established and emerging arts organizations; to stimulate public participation in the arts.

LEGAL BASIS:
Government agency (the official state arts agency of Louisiana).

ELIGIBILITY:
Grants are available for nonprofit arts organizations. Organizations domiciled in Louisiana are eligible to apply for grants to support arts activities taking place in Louisiana.

Eligible applicants generally fall into one of the following categories: nonprofit 501(c)(3) organizations, public or private educational institutions, colleges or universities sponsoring arts activities intended for community participation (not academic, credit-producing, or curriculum-oriented projects), agencies of local, parish, or state government such as state or parish libraries, units of municipal government, parish police juries and agencies of state government.

GEOG. RESTRICTIONS: Louisiana.

FINANCIAL DATA:
Amount of support per award: Decentralized Arts Funding Program: $500 to $15,000; General Operating Support: $1,000 to $20,000; Local Arts Agencies: $1,000 to $100,000.

Matching fund requirements: Decentralized Arts Funding Program: No minimum match requirement; Stabilization and Local Arts Agencies: Dollar-for-dollar or as high as 3:1.

APPLICATION INFO:
Applications are available online.

Duration: Decentralized Arts Funding Program: One year. Statewide Arts Grants Program: Two years.

Deadline: Decentralized Arts Funding Program: Varies by region. Statewide Arts Grants Program: First business day in March.

ADDRESS INQUIRIES TO:
Grants Director
Tel: (225) 342-8175
(See e-mail address above.)

MACDOWELL   [430]
100 High Street
Peterborough, NH 03458
(603) 924-3886
(212) 535-9690
Fax: (603) 924-9142
E-mail: info@macdowellcolony.org
admissions@macdowellcolony.org
Web Site: www.macdowellcolony.org

FOUNDED: 1907

AREAS OF INTEREST:
Writing, theatre, visual art, music composition, filmmaking, architecture and interdisciplinary art.

NAME(S) OF PROGRAMS:
● **Artist Residency Program**

TYPE:
Fellowships; Residencies; Travel grants. Residency fellowships awarded to emerging and established artists across a spectrum of disciplines - architecture, film, interdisciplinary practices, literature, music, visual art, and theatre - to support studio time and artistic exchange in an ideal environment for the creative process.

YEAR PROGRAM STARTED: 1907

PURPOSE:
To nurture the arts by offering creative individuals of the highest talent an inspiring environment in which they can produce enduring works of the imagination.

LEGAL BASIS:
Nonprofit corporation, certified by IRS as falling under Code Section 509(a)(2).

ELIGIBILITY:
Talent is the sole criterion for acceptance. Established artists as well as emerging artists of promising talent are encouraged to apply.

FINANCIAL DATA:
No residency fees. Fellowships cover costs of living accommodations, all meals, and use of an individual studio building. Travel reimbursement and stipends are available for artists who demonstrate need.

Amount of support per award: Stipends and travel grants up to $2,500.

Total amount of support: $4,000,000.

NO. MOST RECENT APPLICANTS: Approximately 2,700.

NO. AWARDS: Approximately 300 artists-in-residence.

APPLICATION INFO:
Application forms are available on the web site. There is a $30 application fee. Work samples must be submitted digitally with the application. Read guidelines before applying.

Duration: Residence periods are from two weeks to two months. No more than one application per 24-month period.

Deadline: January 15, April 15 and September 15.

PUBLICATIONS:
Application guidelines.

OFFICERS AND STAFF:
Nell Painter, Chairman
Andrew Senchak, President
Philip Himberg, Executive Director

ADDRESS INQUIRIES TO:
Courtney Bethel, Admissions Director
(See address above.)

MAINE ARTS COMMISSION   [431]
193 State Street
25 State House Station
Augusta, ME 04333-0025
(207) 287-2724
Fax: (207) 287-2725
TTY: (877) 887-3878
E-mail: arts.grants@maine.gov
Web Site: mainearts.maine.gov

FOUNDED: 1966

AREAS OF INTEREST:
Arts.

CONSULTING OR VOLUNTEER SERVICES:
Opportunities for artists and arts organization.

NAME(S) OF PROGRAMS:
● **Arts and Humanities Grants**
● **Arts Learning**
● **CCED Grant**
● **Creative Aging Grant**
● **Creative Communities = Economic Development Cultural Planning**
● **Maine Artist Fellowship**
● **Jane Morrison Film Fund**
● **Organizational Development**
● **Partnership Grant**
● **Project Grant for Artists**

● **Project Grant for Organizations**
● **Traditional Arts Apprenticeship**

TYPE:
Awards/prizes; Conferences/seminars; Fellowships; General operating grants; Matching gifts; Project/program grants; Residencies; Technical assistance.

YEAR PROGRAM STARTED: 1966

PURPOSE:
To encourage and stimulate public interest and participation in the cultural heritage and cultural programs of our state; to expand the state's cultural resources; to encourage and assist freedom of artistic expression for the well-being of the arts; to meet the needs and aspirations of persons in all parts of the state.

LEGAL BASIS:
Government agency.

ELIGIBILITY:
Applicants must be nonprofit Maine arts organizations, individual artists, schools and/or certain units of city/state or tribal government.

GEOG. RESTRICTIONS: Maine.

FINANCIAL DATA:
Amount of support per award: $1,500 to $75,000; average grant $2,400.

Total amount of support: $480,800 for the year 2018.

Matching fund requirements: 1:1, cash or in-kind for most grants. No matching requirement for grants to individual artists.

CO-OP FUNDING PROGRAMS: Maine Community Foundation; Maine Humanities Council.

NO. MOST RECENT APPLICANTS: 417 for the year 2017.

NO. AWARDS: 302 for the year 2018.

APPLICATION INFO:
Applicant may speak with a staff member about the project before submitting an application.

Application forms must be submitted electronically.

Duration: Varies from 30 days to a full fiscal year period.

Deadline: Varies for all programs.

IRS I.D.: 01-6000001

COMMISSION MEMBERS:
David Greenham, Chairperson
Cynthia Orcutt, Vice Chairperson

ADDRESS INQUIRIES TO:
Darren Henry, Operations Director
(See address above.)

ROBERT MAPPLETHORPE FOUNDATION, INC.   [432]
477 Madison Avenue, 15th Floor
New York, NY 10022-5835
(212) 755-3025
Fax: (212) 941-4764
E-mail: joree@mapplethorpe.org
info@mapplethorpe.org
Web Site: www.mapplethorpe.org

FOUNDED: 1988

AREAS OF INTEREST:
Photography as an art form; scientific study of AIDS and AIDS-related research in order to help find a cure, and education prevention.

NAME(S) OF PROGRAMS:
● **Photography Program**

TYPE:
Project/program grants. Funds medical research in the fight against AIDS and HIV infection and supports the promotion of photography as a fine art, embracing exhibitions, acquisitions, and publications.

YEAR PROGRAM STARTED: 1988

ELIGIBILITY:
The Foundation will not provide grants or scholarships to individual photographers. The Foundation will supply museums and other public institutions by assisting in the creation or expansion of photographic departments.

GEOG. RESTRICTIONS: United States.

FINANCIAL DATA:
Amount of support per award: Varies.
Total amount of support: Varies.

APPLICATION INFO:
There is no formal application form.
Duration: Varies.
Deadline: Proposals are accepted on a continuing basis.

ADDRESS INQUIRIES TO:
Joree Adilman, Managing Director
(See address above.)

MARYLAND STATE ARTS COUNCIL   [433]
175 West Ostend Street
Suite E
Baltimore, MD 21230
(410) 767-6555
Fax: (410) 333-1062
TDD/TTY: (410) 333-4519
E-mail: msac.commerce@maryland.gov
Web Site: www.msac.org

FOUNDED: 1967

AREAS OF INTEREST:
Arts.

NAME(S) OF PROGRAMS:
- **Arts and Entertainment Districts General Operating Support**
- **Arts and Entertainment Districts Technical Assistance**
- **Arts in Education**
- **Community Arts Development**
- **Creativity Grant Program**
- **Grants for Organizations**
- **Individual Artist Awards**
- **Maryland Traditions**
- **Professional Development Program**
- **Public Art Program**

TYPE:
Awards/prizes; Block grants; General operating grants; Project/program grants; Residencies; Technical assistance. Arts program, arts project grants. Individual artist awards. The Council awards grants to county arts councils in Maryland through its Community Arts Development program.

The Arts in Education program is designed to increase access to a range of artistic disciplines and to assist schools in integrating the arts into the curriculum. Projects vary in length from one-day visits to four-week residencies.

The Grants for Organizations Program provides support to those who produce or present the arts to the public.

The Maryland Traditions program is dedicated to the identification, documentation and presentation of Maryland traditional artists to general audiences through public life and educational activities.

Grant program information by type can be found on the "Programs" page on the Council web site.

YEAR PROGRAM STARTED: 1967

PURPOSE:
To make the arts more widely available to all Maryland residents, to strengthen the state's cultural institutions and to encourage the development of resident artistic activity throughout the state.

LEGAL BASIS:
Article 41 of the Annotated Code of Maryland as amended, Sections 387 to 395, inclusive.

ELIGIBILITY:
Applying organizations must be not-for-profit, tax-exempt and incorporated in the state of Maryland. Individuals must be 18 years of age or older and a Maryland resident.

Funding is not provided for acquisition of capital assets, capital improvements, depreciation, deficits, capital debt reduction and contributions to endowments.

GEOG. RESTRICTIONS: Maryland.

FINANCIAL DATA:
Amount of support per award: Varies by program.
Total amount of support: Varies by program.

NO. MOST RECENT APPLICANTS: Varies.

NO. AWARDS: Varies.

APPLICATION INFO:
Guidelines and grant application forms may be acquired by writing to the Council office.
Duration: Varies by program.
Deadline: Varies by program.

EXECUTIVE DIRECTOR:
Ken Skrzesz

ADDRESS INQUIRIES TO:
Dana Parsons, Director of Grants and Professional Development
(See address above.)

MICHIGAN COUNCIL FOR ARTS AND CULTURAL AFFAIRS   [434]
Michigan Economic Development Corporation
300 North Washington Square
Lansing, MI 48913
(517) 241-4011
Fax: (517) 241-3979
E-mail: watsona11@michigan.org
Web Site: www.michigan.gov/arts

FOUNDED: 1966

AREAS OF INTEREST:
Arts.

NAME(S) OF PROGRAMS:
- **Arts in Education Grants**
- **Capital Improvement Grants**
- **Operational Support Grants**
- **Project Support Grants**

TYPE:
General operating grants; Project/program grants.

PURPOSE:
To develop and encourage programs and projects that make music, painting, literature, cinema, dance, sculpture, crafts, architecture and all the arts available to the people of Michigan, regardless of their age, location, background or economic status; to support activities of Michigan artists.

LEGAL BASIS:
State agency.

ELIGIBILITY:
Generally, grants will be awarded only for activities within the state of Michigan. For most programs, applicants should be Michigan-based nonprofit tax-exempt organizations residing in Michigan. The Council ordinarily does not finance an existing deficit, capital improvements, curriculum-oriented activities or permanent equipment.

GEOG. RESTRICTIONS: Michigan.

FINANCIAL DATA:
Amount of support per award: Varies.
Total amount of support: $10,700,000 for the year 2019.
Matching fund requirements: Varies with program.

CO-OP FUNDING PROGRAMS: Re-Granting and Partnership programs.

NO. MOST RECENT APPLICANTS: 648.

NO. AWARDS: 530.

APPLICATION INFO:
Applicants are required to use the Council's online eGrant system.
Duration: One year, October 1 through September 30.
Deadline: Primary programs: June 1. All other programs: Varies.

PUBLICATIONS:
Program guidelines; factsheet.

IRS I.D.: 38-6000134

OFFICERS:
W. Omari Rush, Chairman

STAFF:
Alison Watson, Director

ADDRESS INQUIRIES TO:
Alison Watson, Director
(See address above.)

MID-AMERICA ARTS ALLIANCE   [435]
2018 Baltimore Avenue
Kansas City, MO 64108
(816) 421-1388
Fax: (816) 421-3918
E-mail: christine@maaa.org
Web Site: www.maaa.org

FOUNDED: 1972

AREAS OF INTEREST:
All artistic disciplines.

NAME(S) OF PROGRAMS:
- **Artistic Innovations Grant Program**
- **Regional Touring Program**
- **Touring Exhibits through ExhibitsUSA**

TYPE:
Project/program grants; Technical assistance. Support and project/program grants for community arts projects and touring performing arts.

YEAR PROGRAM STARTED: 1973

PURPOSE:
To increase the access to high-quality arts programs and to sponsor competency.

LEGAL BASIS:
Missouri corporation, 501(c)(3).

ELIGIBILITY:
Nonprofit organizations presenting M-AAA touring programs in Arkansas, Kansas, Missouri, Nebraska, Oklahoma and Texas may apply. Visual arts exhibitors throughout the country may request traveling exhibits.

GEOG. RESTRICTIONS: Arkansas, Kansas, Missouri, Nebraska, Oklahoma and Texas.

FINANCIAL DATA:
Amount of support per award: $500 to $15,000.

Total amount of support: Varies.

Matching fund requirements: Most grants require a dollar-for-dollar match.

CO-OP FUNDING PROGRAMS: State arts agencies of Arkansas, Kansas, Missouri, Nebraska, Oklahoma, Texas, corporations and foundations, and the National Endowment for the Arts.

NO. MOST RECENT APPLICANTS: Approximately 190.

NO. AWARDS: 21.

APPLICATION INFO:
Application information is available on the web site.

Duration: Varies.

Deadline: Varies.

PUBLICATIONS:
Annual report; exhibit catalogs.

IRS I.D.: 23-7303693

OFFICERS:
Todd Stein, President and Chief Executive Officer

ADDRESS INQUIRIES TO:
Christine Bial, Director of Arts and Humanities Grant Programs
(See address above.)

MID ATLANTIC ARTS FOUNDATION [436]

201 North Charles Street
Suite 401
Baltimore, MD 21201
(410) 539-6656 ext. 104
Fax: (410) 837-5517
E-mail: info@midatlanticarts.org
Web Site: www.midatlanticarts.org

FOUNDED: 1979

AREAS OF INTEREST:
Regional arts activities crossing state lines in Delaware, District of Columbia, Maryland, New Jersey, New York, Pennsylvania, Virginia, West Virginia and the U.S. Virgin Islands; national and international funding through Southern Exposure and USArtists International.

NAME(S) OF PROGRAMS:
- **ArtsCONNECT**
- **Alan Cooper Leadership in the Arts Award**
- **Folk and Traditional Arts Touring Network**
- **Jazz Touring Network**
- **Living Legacy Jazz Award**
- **Mid Atlantic Creative Fellowships**
- **Mid Atlantic Tours**
- **On Screen/In Person**
- **Southern Exposure**
- **Special Presenter Initiatives**
- **USArtists International**

TYPE:
Fellowships; Project/program grants; Residencies.

YEAR PROGRAM STARTED: 1979

PURPOSE:
To promote the sharing of arts resources among the Foundation's partner states, regionally, nationally and internationally.

LEGAL BASIS:
Private, not-for-profit organization.

ELIGIBILITY:
Individuals and organizations must be based in the region for most programs. Other requirements vary according to the specific program.

ArtsCONNECT provides artist fee support to not-for-profit presenting networks comprised of at least three Mid Atlantic-based organizations.

Mid Atlantic Creative Fellowships places an artist from each member state in residence at selected organizations. A different artistic discipline is selected each year for foundation support.

Mid Atlantic Tours provide fee support for foundation-initiated performing arts tours.

On Screen/In Person provides fee subsidy to film series host sites.

Southern Exposure provides support to U.S. presenters for foundation-initiated tours of artists from Latin America.

USArtists International supports U.S. music, dance, and theatre artists at international festivals and performing arts markets.

GEOG. RESTRICTIONS: Delaware, District of Columbia, Maryland, New Jersey, New York, Pennsylvania, Virginia, West Virginia and the United States Virgin Islands for all programs except Southern Exposure and USArtists International.

FINANCIAL DATA:
Amount of support per award: $1,000 to $15,000.

Total amount of support: $1,900,000 in direct grants for the year 2019.

Matching fund requirements: Varies according to program.

NO. AWARDS: 420 grants for the year 2019.

APPLICATION INFO:
Guidelines are available on the web site. The Foundation utilizes an electronic application process.

Duration: Varies.

Deadline: Varies.

PUBLICATIONS:
Guidelines; monthly e-mail newsletter; biennial report.

IRS I.D.: 52-1169382

STAFF:
Theresa M. Colvin, Executive Director

THE MILLAY COLONY FOR THE ARTS, INC. [437]

454 East Hill Road
Austerlitz, NY 12017-0003
(518) 392-3103
E-mail: residency@millaycolony.org
Web Site: www.millaycolony.org

FOUNDED: 1973

AREAS OF INTEREST:
Writing, composing, music and visual arts.

NAME(S) OF PROGRAMS:
- **Artist Residencies**

TYPE:
Residencies. The Millay Colony offers a variety of residencies from the months of April through November for visual artists, writers and composers in order to immerse themselves in creative work. The Colony accommodates a multidisciplinary group of six to seven artists each month and offers special residencies to collaborating groups of artists. It also offers free arts education programs in local schools.

YEAR PROGRAM STARTED: 1973

PURPOSE:
To provide space, studio and time for writers and composers to immerse themselves in their work.

ELIGIBILITY:
Residents are selected after undergoing an application and juried process. Juries make selections anonymously.

FINANCIAL DATA:
No cash award is made. No residency fee is required. If invited, room, studio and meals are provided at no cost.

Amount of support per award: Approximate value $4,000 per resident.

NO. MOST RECENT APPLICANTS: 1,600 for the year 2019.

NO. AWARDS: 60 for the year 2019.

APPLICATION INFO:
Online application process is available. An application form may also be requested by sending a self-addressed, stamped envelope to the address above.

An application fee of $40 is required.

Duration: Approximately three and one-half weeks. Two-week residencies are available in June and September.

Deadline: October 1 for the following April through July. March 1 for the following August through November.

ADDRESS INQUIRIES TO:
Calliope Nicholas, Director
Residencies and Facilities
(See address above.)

JOAN MITCHELL FOUNDATION [438]

137 West 25th Street
2nd Floor
New York, NY 10001
(212) 524-0100
Fax: (212) 524-0101
E-mail: info@joanmitchellfoundation.org
Web Site: www.joanmitchellfoundation.org

AREAS OF INTEREST:
Art: painting, sculpture and/or drawing.

NAME(S) OF PROGRAMS:
- **Emergency Grant Program**

TYPE:
Grants-in-aid. The Foundation provides emergency support to U.S.-based visual artists working in the mediums of painting, sculpture and/or drawing, who have suffered significant losses after natural or manmade disasters that have affected their community. Artists who have been negatively impacted due to catastrophic situations of this nature can apply to the Foundation for funding.

Information on the full range of Foundation programs can be found online.

PURPOSE:
To provide emergency support to visual
artists in need.

GEOG. RESTRICTIONS: United States.

FINANCIAL DATA:
Amount of support per award: Up to $6,000.
Total amount of support: Varies yearly.

NO. AWARDS: Varies.

APPLICATION INFO:
Contact the Foundation.

ADDRESS INQUIRIES TO:
Grants Program Director
(See e-mail address above.)

THE MOODY FOUNDATION
2302 Post Office Street, Suite 704
Galveston, TX 77550
(409) 797-1500
Fax: (409) 763-5564
E-mail: info@moodyf.org
Web Site: www.moodyf.org

TYPE:
Capital grants; Challenge/matching grants;
Endowments; Grants-in-aid; Project/program
grants; Research grants; Scholarships. Capital
campaigns; Equipment; Matching funds;
Building/renovation; Program development
and research.

See entry 217 for full listing.

MARIETTA MCNEILL MORGAN AND SAMUEL TATE MORGAN, JR. TRUST
Bank of America Private Bank
1800 K Street, N.W., Mail Code
DC1-842-05-01
Washington, DC 20006
(202) 442-7460
E-mail: dc.grantmaking@ustrust.com
Web Site: www.bankofamerica.
com/grantmaking

TYPE:
Capital grants.

See entry 1365 for full listing.

WILLIAM MORRIS SOCIETY IN THE U.S. [439]
P.O. Box 53263
Washington, DC 20009
E-mail: wmsusmembership@gmail.com
Web Site: www.morrissociety.org

FOUNDED: 1957

AREAS OF INTEREST:
The life and work of William Morris as a
craftsman, designer and writer.

NAME(S) OF PROGRAMS:
● **Joseph R. Dunlap Memorial Fellowship**

TYPE:
Fellowships; Research grants; Scholarships;
Travel grants; Visiting scholars; Research
contracts. Supports scholarly, creative, and
translation projects about William Morris and
his designs, writings and other work.

YEAR PROGRAM STARTED: 1995

PURPOSE:
To support research projects that deal with
any subject relating to William Morris.

LEGAL BASIS:
Society.

ELIGIBILITY:
Projects may deal with any subject -
biographical, literary, historical, social,
artistic, political, typographical - relating to
Morris. They may be scholarly or creative,
and may include translations or the
preparation of educational materials.
Applicants for all awards may be from any
country. Applications are particularly
encouraged from younger members of the
Society and from those at the beginning of
their careers. Recipients need not have an
academic or institutional appointment and the
Ph.D. is not required.

FINANCIAL DATA:
Amount of support per award: $1,000.

APPLICATION INFO:
Applicants are asked to submit a resume and
a two-page description of their projects,
including a timeline and an indication of
where the results might be published. At
least one recommendation should be sent
separately. Submissions will not be accepted
via e-mail.

For translation submissions, send one copy of
the translation (of the published version, if
relevant), with a letter of reference from
someone acquainted with both languages
assessing the quality of the translation.
Translations should have been completed
within the past five years.

For teaching materials, no letters of
recommendation are needed, but enclose a
cover letter describing the ways in which the
materials might be (or already have been)
used in learning situations.

Duration: One year.

Deadline: December 15. Announcement by
January 15.

PUBLICATIONS:
Announcement.

ADDRESS INQUIRIES TO:
Jane Carlin, President
E-mail: us@morrissociety.org

NATIONAL ENDOWMENT FOR THE ARTS [440]
400 7th Street, S.W.
Washington, DC 20506
(202) 682-5400
(202) 682-5403
Fax: (202) 682-5609
E-mail: webmgr@arts.gov
Web Site: www.arts.gov/grants

FOUNDED: 1965

AREAS OF INTEREST:
National artistic accomplishments of the past,
present and future.

NAME(S) OF PROGRAMS:
● **Art Works**
● **Challenge America**
● **Creative Writing Fellowships**
● **Our Town**
● **Partnership Agreements**
● **Research: Art Works**
● **Translation Projects**

TYPE:
Fellowships; Project/program grants. The
National Endowment for the Arts has three
grant categories: Grants for Organizations,
Grants for Individuals and Partnership
Agreements. Under Grants for Organizations,
the Endowment funds projects only.

Art Works: An organization grant to support
the creation of art that meets the highest
standards of excellence, public engagement
with diverse and excellent art, lifelong
learning in the arts and the strengthening of
communities through the arts.

Challenge America: An organization grant to
support projects that extend the reach of the
arts to underserved populations.

Creative Writing Fellowships: An individual
grant offering fellowships in fiction, poetry
and creative nonfiction which enable
recipients to set aside time for writing,
research, travel and general career
advancement.

Our Town: An organization grant for creative
placemaking projects that contribute to the
livability of communities and place the arts
at their core. The Our Town program offers
support for projects in two areas: Arts
Engagement, Cultural Planning, and Design
Projects; and Projects that Build Knowledge
About Creative Placemaking.

Partnership Agreements: Operates in
conjunction with state arts agencies (SAAs)
and regional arts organizations (RAOs).

Research: Art Works: An organization grant
to support research that investigates the value
and/or impact of the arts, either as individual
components of the U.S. arts ecology or as
they interact with each other and/or with
other domains of American life.

Translation Projects: An individual grant that
enables recipients to translate work from
other languages into English.

YEAR PROGRAM STARTED: 1966

PURPOSE:
To support artists, art forms, art events, art
education, and to conserve highly significant
works of art.

LEGAL BASIS:
The National Foundation on the Arts and
Humanities Act of 1965, Public Law 89-209,
as amended.

ELIGIBILITY:
Contact the Endowment for details.

GEOG. RESTRICTIONS: United States, American
Samoa, Guam, Puerto Rico or the United
States Virgin Islands.

FINANCIAL DATA:
Amount of support per award: Art Works:
Grants generally $10,000 to $100,000.
Challenge America: Grants for $10,000.
Creative Writing Fellowships: $25,000. Our
Town: Grants $25,000 to $200,000. Research:
Art Works: Grants $10,000 to $30,000.
Translation Projects: $12,500 or $25,000.

Total amount of support: Varies.

Matching fund requirements: Art Works and
Challenge America: A minimum cost
share/match equal to the grant amount is
required. Our Town and Research: Art Works
are also matching grants.

APPLICATION INFO:
Contact Endowment or consult its web site.

Deadline: Varies.

ADDRESS INQUIRIES TO:
Nicki Jacobs, Grants Director
Tel: (202) 682-5546

NATIONAL YOUNGARTS FOUNDATION [441]
2100 Biscayne Boulevard
Miami, FL 33137
(305) 377-1140
(800) 970-2787
Fax: (305) 377-1149
E-mail: info@youngarts.org
Web Site: www.youngarts.org

FOUNDED: 1981

AREAS OF INTEREST:
To identify and nurture the most
accomplished young artists in the visual,
literary, design and performing arts and assist
them at critical junctures in their educational
and professional development.

CONSULTING OR VOLUNTEER SERVICES:
Offers the names of registrants and awardees
of its YoungArts® program nationally to
colleges, universities and performing arts
institutions which subscribe to the
Foundation's Scholarship List Service (SLS).

NAME(S) OF PROGRAMS:
- **National YoungArts Week**
- **U.S. Presidential Scholars in the Arts**
- **YoungArts Los Angeles**
- **YoungArts Miami**
- **YoungArts New York**

TYPE:
Awards/prizes; Conferences/seminars;
Internships. Cash grants and scholarship
opportunities to young artists.

YEAR PROGRAM STARTED: 1981

PURPOSE:
To recognize and support aspiring artists in
their formative years and provide career entry
opportunities.

LEGAL BASIS:
Private nonprofit, 501(c)(3), operating
national foundation.

ELIGIBILITY:
YoungArts applicant must be 15 to 18 years
old, or a high school student in grades 10 to
12. Participants must be U.S. citizens or
permanent residents.

NFAA offers a conference for high school
arts educators on preparing students for
college auditions.

20 U.S. Presidential Scholars in the Arts are
selected exclusively from YoungArts
participants by the White House Commission
on Presidential Scholars.

GEOG. RESTRICTIONS: United States.

FINANCIAL DATA:
Up to 170 national finalists attend YoungArts
Week in Miami, all expenses paid.
Amount of support per award: YoungArts
Gold Awards: $10,000 each; YoungArts
Silver Awards: $5,000; YoungArts Award:
Level I, $3,000; Level II, $1,500; Level III,
$1,000; Honorable Mention, $250.
Total amount of support: Approximately
$800,000 annually.

CO-OP FUNDING PROGRAMS: NFAA works in
partnership with other arts organizations to
offer workshops, internships and residencies
to students in advanced stages of their arts
training.

NO. MOST RECENT APPLICANTS: YoungArts:
Approximately 11,000 per year.

NO. AWARDS: Approximately 800 total awards
per year; approximately 450 cash awards per
year.

APPLICATION INFO:
There is a $35 registration fee per category.
Deadline: YoungArts: Early registration May
16, regular registration through October 14.
Audition/portfolio materials due late October.

IRS I.D.: 59-2141837

ADDRESS INQUIRIES TO:
Stacey Glassman Mizener
Vice President of Development
(See address above.)

NEBRASKA ARTS COUNCIL [442]
1004 Farnam Street, Lower Level
Omaha, NE 68102
(402) 595-2122
Fax: (402) 595-2334
E-mail: nac.info@nebraska.gov
Web Site: artscouncil.nebraska.gov

FOUNDED: 1965

AREAS OF INTEREST:
Architecture, visual arts, artists, art
organizations, literature, museums and
libraries, performing arts, aged, children and
youth, community and rural development and
services and education.

CONSULTING OR VOLUNTEER SERVICES:
Technical (staff) services for requesting
organizations who desire assistance in arts
programming efforts. Developmental aspects
of assistance to arts organizations and/or
individuals is predominant.

NAME(S) OF PROGRAMS:
- **Accessibility Grant**
- **Artists-in-Schools/Communities Grants**
- **Arts Learning Projects**
- **Arts Project Grants**
- **Basic Support Grants**
- **Individual Artist Fellowships**
- **Mini Grants**
- **Nebraska Touring Program**
- **School Bus for the Arts Grants**

TYPE:
Fellowships; General operating grants;
Matching gifts; Project/program grants.
Grants to encourage growth and activity in
the arts for the citizens of the state of
Nebraska.

YEAR PROGRAM STARTED: 1965

PURPOSE:
To stimulate and encourage, throughout the
state, the study and presentation of the visual
and performing arts and public interest and
participation therein; to promote the arts,
cultivate resources and support excellence in
artistic endeavors for all Nebraskans.

LEGAL BASIS:
Government agency under state legislation.
Agency also accepts federal funds (from the
National Endowment for the Arts) and
private funds for purposes of its intent.

ELIGIBILITY:
Nonprofit, incorporated status is required of
applying organizations. Applicant
organizations must have federal tax-exempt
status or proof of application for that status
at the time of application. Individuals not
connected with nonprofit organizations are
eligible only for Individual Artist Fellowships
and must be Nebraska residents. The NAC
does not provide funding for capital
expenditures or existing deficits.

GEOG. RESTRICTIONS: Nebraska.

FINANCIAL DATA:
Amount of support per award: Basic Support
Grants: Up to $50,000; All other grants: Up
to $7,500.
Total amount of support: Approximately
$1,400,000.
Matching fund requirements: Must be in
cash.

CO-OP FUNDING PROGRAMS: Support is provided
for organizations desiring programming in
the Mid-America Arts Alliance (six-state
consortium consisting of Arkansas, Kansas,
Missouri, Nebraska, Oklahoma and Texas).

APPLICATION INFO:
Application form is available on the web site.
Duration: One year.
Deadline: March 15 and October 1.

PUBLICATIONS:
Guide to Programs and Services; Artist
Directory.

STAFF:
Jennifer Dreibelbis, Grants Data
Administrator

ADDRESS INQUIRIES TO:
See e-mail address above.

*SPECIAL STIPULATIONS:
Please contact NAC prior to applying for the
first time.

NEVADA ARTS COUNCIL [443]
716 North Carson Street
Suite A
Carson City, NV 89701
(775) 687-6680
Fax: (775) 687-6688
E-mail: infonvartscouncil@nevadaculture.org
Web Site: www.nvartscouncil.org

FOUNDED: 1967

AREAS OF INTEREST:
Visual, literary, performing, design and folk
arts, as well as community development.

CONSULTING OR VOLUNTEER SERVICES:
Provide consulting on arts management,
resources in the arts, grants workshops,
community arts and professional arts needs.

NAME(S) OF PROGRAMS:
- **Artist Services Program**
- **Arts Learning Program**
- **Community Arts Development**
- **Folklife Program**
- **Grants Program**

TYPE:
Awards/prizes; Challenge/matching grants;
Conferences/seminars; Development grants;
Fellowships; General operating grants;
Project/program grants; Residencies;
Technical assistance; Training grants;
Work-study programs. Grants to Nevada
nonprofit groups, individual artists, public
institutions and for arts in education.

YEAR PROGRAM STARTED: 1967

PURPOSE:
To enrich the cultural life of the state through
leadership that preserves, supports,
strengthens and makes accessible excellence
in the arts to all Nevadans.

LEGAL BASIS:
Government agency.

ELIGIBILITY:
Nevada nonprofit organizations with IRS
tax-exempt status and individual artists with

one-year minimum residency may apply for grants. Artists may also apply for artist residencies. Fellowships require residency.

GEOG. RESTRICTIONS: Nevada.

FINANCIAL DATA:
Amount of support per award: Varies.
Total amount of support: Varies.
Matching fund requirements: Varies.

NO. MOST RECENT APPLICANTS: 700.

NO. AWARDS: 346.

APPLICATION INFO:
Applications are available on the web site.
Duration: Six months to two years.
Deadline: Varies.

IRS I.D.: 88-6000022

OFFICERS:
Gail Rappa, Chairperson
Tony Manfredi, Executive Director
Kari Ward, Administrative Services Officer

NEW ENGLAND FOUNDATION FOR THE ARTS   [444]
145 Tremont Street
Seventh Floor
Boston, MA 02111-1254
(617) 951-0010
Fax: (617) 951-0016
E-mail: info@nefa.org
Web Site: www.nefa.org

FOUNDED: 1975

AREAS OF INTEREST:
Performing artists, ensembles, socially engaged art, public art, cultural diplomacy, Native American art, cultural organizations and creative economy research.

NAME(S) OF PROGRAMS:
- **Center Stage**
- **Creative City Boston**
- **Fund for the Arts**
- **National Dance Project**
- **National Theater Project**
- **New England Dance Fund**
- **New England Presenter Travel Fund**
- **New England States Touring Program**
- **New Work New England**
- **Public Art Learning Fund**

TYPE:
Awards/prizes; Development grants; Project/program grants; Travel grants. Production and touring grants; Professional development grants.

PURPOSE:
To facilitate the movement of people, ideas and resources in the arts within New England and beyond; to make vital connections between artists and audiences; to build the strength, knowledge and leadership of the region's creative sector.

LEGAL BASIS:
Public/private partnership.

FINANCIAL DATA:
Amount of support per award: Varies by program.
Total amount of support: Varies.

NO. AWARDS: 450.

APPLICATION INFO:
Contact the Foundation.
Duration: Varies.
Deadline: Varies.

NEW HAMPSHIRE STATE COUNCIL ON THE ARTS   [445]
19 Pillsbury Street
Concord, NH 03301
(603) 271-2789
Fax: (603) 271-3584
TTY/TDD: (800) 735-2964
E-mail: cassandra.mason@dncr.nh.gov
Web Site: www.nh.gov/nharts

FOUNDED: 1965

AREAS OF INTEREST:
The arts in New Hampshire.

CONSULTING OR VOLUNTEER SERVICES:
Artists as Entrepreneurs Workshops, Fall Arts in Education Partnership Conference and Grants Information Services Workshops.

NAME(S) OF PROGRAMS:
- **Apprenticeships**
- **Artist Entrepreneurial Workshops**
- **Artist in Residence**
- **Artist Services**
- **Arts in Education**
- **Arts in Health Project Grants**
- **Cultural Conservation**
- **General Project Grants**
- **Operating Grants**
- **Percent for Art**
- **Public Value Partnerships**
- **Traditional Arts Apprenticeship**
- **Youth Arts Project Grants**

TYPE:
Awards/prizes; Challenge/matching grants; Conferences/seminars; Fellowships; General operating grants; Project/program grants; Residencies; Technical assistance. Grant assistance to New Hampshire organizations and individual artists.

YEAR PROGRAM STARTED: 1965

PURPOSE:
To support and promote excellence, education and community investment in the arts for people in New Hampshire.

LEGAL BASIS:
Agency of the state of New Hampshire.

ELIGIBILITY:
Organizations must be incorporated in New Hampshire. Individual artists must reside in New Hampshire for at least one year.

GEOG. RESTRICTIONS: New Hampshire.

FINANCIAL DATA:
Amount of support per award: $250 to $26,000.
Total amount of support: $593,060 for the year 2019.
Matching fund requirements: Varies.

NO. MOST RECENT APPLICANTS: Varies.

NO. AWARDS: Varies.

APPLICATION INFO:
A completed application form is required for all grants. Submissions must be made online. Support materials are required from all applicants; work sample required from individual artists. IRS tax-exempt 501(c)(3) letter is required from nonprofit organizations.
Duration: One to two years.
Deadline: Varies.

PUBLICATIONS:
E-News; *E-Opps*.

STAFF:
Ginnie Lupi, Director

ADDRESS INQUIRIES TO:
Cassandra Mason
Chief Grants Officer
(See address above.)

*SPECIAL STIPULATIONS:
Funding is restricted to New Hampshire artists, organizations, schools, libraries, branches of government and communities.

NEW JERSEY STATE COUNCIL ON THE ARTS   [446]
P.O. Box 306
Trenton, NJ 08625-0306
(609) 292-6130
E-mail: feedback@sos.nj.gov
Web Site: www.nj.gov/state/njsca/index.html

FOUNDED: 1966

AREAS OF INTEREST:
Dance, music, opera, musical theatre, theatre, visual arts, crafts, media arts, presenters, multi- and interdisciplinary, arts education, folk art, local arts and literary arts.

NAME(S) OF PROGRAMS:
- **Artists-in-Education Residency Grant Program (AIE)**
- **Arts Project Support (APS)**
- **Folk Arts Apprenticeships**
- **General Operating Support (GOS)**
- **General Program Support (GPS)**

TYPE:
Fellowships; General operating grants; Internships; Project/program grants; Residencies; Technical assistance. Apprenticeships; local arts grants. Fellowships and matching grants to provide money to New Jersey artists and organizations. Local arts grants (for local arts) are available to designated county arts agencies only.

Artists-in-Education Residency Grant Program places practicing professional artists in long-term residencies (20 to 100 days) in schools across the state.

Arts Project Support is awarded annually to New Jersey-based, nonprofit organizations and agencies to help support single public arts events.

Folk Arts Apprenticeships are awarded to New Jersey residents to support an apprentice learning a traditional art form from a master in their shared community.

General Operating Support Grants are awarded every three years to New Jersey-based, nonprofit arts organizations to help underwrite the expense of their total operation including their expense of producing and presenting arts events.

General Program Support Grants are awarded every three years to other New Jersey-based, nonprofit organizations, agencies, institutions or units of local government to help underwrite the expense of presenting major, ongoing arts programs.

YEAR PROGRAM STARTED: 1966

PURPOSE:
To improve the quality of life of New Jersey, its people and communities by helping the arts to flourish.

LEGAL BASIS:
State governmental agency.

ELIGIBILITY:
The Council awards grants on a highly competitive basis, employing standardized criteria for eligibility and evaluation published in guidelines and convening panels

of independent experts in the various fields of endeavor for objective feedback and recommendations. A New Jersey resident or a nonprofit organization incorporated in the State of New Jersey committed to professionalism in the arts may apply.

GEOG. RESTRICTIONS: New Jersey.

FINANCIAL DATA:
Amount of support per award: Varies.
Total amount of support: $15,000,000 for fiscal year 2020.
Matching fund requirements: Fellowships are non-matching. Matching grants to organizations must be on a basis of at least 1:1, 3:1 for operating and program support grants.

APPLICATION INFO:
Details are available on the Council web site.

STAFF:
Tammy Herman, Director of Programs and Services

ADDRESS INQUIRIES TO:
Tammy Herman, Director of Programs and Services
(See address above.)

NEW MEXICO ARTS   [447]
Bataan Memorial Building
407 Galisteo Street, Suite 270
Santa Fe, NM 87501
(505) 827-6490
(505) 827-6492
Fax: (505) 827-6043
E-mail: JeniceE.Gharib@state.nm.us
Web Site: www.nmarts.org

FOUNDED: 1966

AREAS OF INTEREST:
Arts.

TYPE:
General operating grants; Project/program grants. Funds are available for arts projects; arts in social service; traditional folk arts; arts learning; colleges, universities and government entities; major cultural organizations; local arts councils and service organizations; economic and entrepreneurial development; arts trails; and community arts development.

PURPOSE:
To promote the arts in New Mexico.

ELIGIBILITY:
Applicants must be a New Mexico organization, government or tribal entity. Organizations must have 501(c)(3) not-for-profit status, although they can use a fiscal agent. Religious organizations can apply for grants. No grants are made to individuals.

GEOG. RESTRICTIONS: New Mexico, with a preference for rural New Mexico.

FINANCIAL DATA:
Amount of support per award: Average: $3,000 to $9,000.
Total amount of support: Average $1,000,000 annually.
Matching fund requirements: 50% match is required; half of the match can be in-kind.

NO. MOST RECENT APPLICANTS: 201.

NO. AWARDS: 201.

APPLICATION INFO:
Application is online and available each September and must include the

organization's 501(c)(3) letter from the IRS. New applicants must submit an advance review application in October.
Duration: One year; applicants must reapply for renewal each year.
Deadline: Advance review in October; final review in December. Contact organization for exact dates.

ADDRESS INQUIRIES TO:
Jenice E. Gharib, Grants Program and Policy Director
(See address or e-mail above.)

*SPECIAL STIPULATIONS:
Consult guidelines for eligible expenses and specific category eligibility requirements.

NEW YORK FOUNDATION FOR THE ARTS   [448]
20 Jay Street, Suite 740
Brooklyn, NY 11201
(212) 366-6900
Fax: (212) 366-1778
E-mail: fellowships@nyfa.org
Web Site: www.nyfa.org

FOUNDED: 1971

AREAS OF INTEREST:
The arts, with a primary focus on New York state.

NAME(S) OF PROGRAMS:
● **Artists' Fellowships**

TYPE:
Awards/prizes; Development grants; Fellowships; Grants-in-aid. Cash awards made to individual or pairs of originating artists living and working in the state of New York for use in career development. Funds are unrestricted.

YEAR PROGRAM STARTED: 1985

PURPOSE:
To provide the time and resources for the creative mind and the artistic spirit to think, work and prosper.

ELIGIBILITY:
Applicant must be 25 years of age or older and cannot be enrolled in a degree-granting program. Applicant must be a resident of New York state for the two years prior to the deadline.

GEOG. RESTRICTIONS: New York state.

FINANCIAL DATA:
Since its inception, the program has provided over $30,000,000 in unrestricted cash grants to artists in 15 disciplines at critical stages in their creative development.
Amount of support per award: $7,000 cash awards.
Total amount of support: $623,000 for the year 2018.

NO. MOST RECENT APPLICANTS: 2,000 to 4,000 each cycle.

NO. AWARDS: 94 for the year 2019.

APPLICATION INFO:
Contact the Foundation.
Deadline: January 22, 11:59 P.M.

STAFF:
Michael L. Royce, Executive Director

NEW YORK STATE COUNCIL ON THE ARTS   [449]
300 Park Avenue South, 10th Floor
New York, NY 10010
(212) 459-8800
Fax: (212) 477-1471
E-mail: public.affairs@arts.ny.gov
Web Site: www.arts.ny.gov

FOUNDED: 1960

AREAS OF INTEREST:
Public support for the arts in New York state.

CONSULTING OR VOLUNTEER SERVICES:
Technical assistance is available for eligible nonprofit arts organizations.

TYPE:
Awards/prizes; Capital grants; Challenge/matching grants; Conferences/seminars; Development grants; General operating grants; Internships; Residencies; Technical assistance. Grants are awarded to eligible New York state nonprofit organizations through 16 discipline-based funding programs: Architecture and Design; Facilities; Arts Education; Dance; Electronic Media and Film; Folk Arts; Individual Artists; Literature; Museum; Music; Presenting; Regional Economic Development; Special Arts Services; State and Local Partnerships; Theater; and Visual Arts. In addition, NYSCA support reaches an additional 1,300 community-based organizations each year in the form of regrants, which are administered by a statewide network of Local Arts Councils through NYSCA's Decentralization program.

YEAR PROGRAM STARTED: 1960

PURPOSE:
To ensure that the role of the arts in New York's communities will continue to grow and play a more significant part in the welfare and education of New York's citizens.

LEGAL BASIS:
State agency.

ELIGIBILITY:
Grants are awarded to nonprofit organizations incorporated in New York state, Indian tribes, and units of local government. Individuals and unincorporated groups may only apply through an eligible nonprofit organization.

GEOG. RESTRICTIONS: New York state.

FINANCIAL DATA:
Amount of support per award: Varies by program.
Matching fund requirements: Varies by program.

NO. AWARDS: Over 2,400 annually.

APPLICATION INFO:
Applications and guidelines are available online. New applicants (except municipalities and Indian tribes) must submit proof of nonprofit status. Returning applicants who have applied in the past three years must certify that their nonprofit status remains valid.
Duration: One calendar year. Organizations may reapply each year.

PUBLICATIONS:
Program guidelines.

STAFF:
Katherine A. Nicholls, Chairperson
Mara Manus, Executive Director
Abigail Young, Director of Operations
Megan White, Deputy Director of Programs

ADDRESS INQUIRIES TO:
Office of Public and Governmental Affairs
(See address above.)

NORTH CAROLINA ARTS COUNCIL   [450]

Department of Natural and
Cultural Resources
109 East Jones Street
Raleigh, NC 27601
(919) 814-6500
Fax: (919) 715-0189
E-mail: ncarts@ncdcr.gov
tanya.mcguire@ncdcr.gov
Web Site: www.ncarts.org

FOUNDED: 1964

AREAS OF INTEREST:
Arts development throughout North Carolina.

CONSULTING OR VOLUNTEER SERVICES:
Offer consulting services to arts
organizations.

NAME(S) OF PROGRAMS:
- **Artist Fellowships**
- **Arts in Education Grants**
- **Grassroots Arts Program**
- **Military and Veteran Healing Arts Grants**
- **Organizational Development**
- **Program Support**
- **Regional Artist Project Grants**
- **SmART Initiative**
- **State Arts Resources**
- **Statewide Service Organizations**

TYPE:
Challenge/matching grants; Development
grants; Fellowships; General operating grants;
Internships; Project/program grants;
Residencies; Technical assistance. Per capita
distribution of funds for arts development,
general operating support, project grants,
local government challenge grants,
arts-in-education grants, new works grants,
discipline-development grants, individual
artist fellowships, fee subsidy for touring
groups, consultant grants, scholarship grants
and workshops.

Artist Fellowships: To support the creative
development of North Carolina artists. In
even years, fellowships are awarded to
writers, songwriters, composers, playwrights
and screenwriters. In odd years, fellowships
are awarded in the areas of visual art, craft,
film/video and choreography.

Arts in Education Grants: For schools and
nonprofit organizations to strengthen the use
of the arts in pre-K-through-12 settings.

Grassroots Arts Program: Distributes funds
for arts programming, primarily through local
arts councils, to all 100 North Carolina
counties using a per capita-based formula.

Military and Veteran Healing Arts Grants:
Grants are awarded to arts organizations that
have a track record of working with military
or veteran audiences.

Organizational Development: Through the
New Realities Program, organizations can
work with a consultant over a period of two
to three years to address long-term issues,
including leadership transition, restructuring,
and repositioning.

Program Support: To help arts organizations
broaden, deepen and diversify participation in
their arts programs.

Regional Artist Project Grants: For regional
consortia of local arts councils, which award
project grants to artists in their regions.

SmART Initiative is a catalyst for arts-driven
economic development projects across the
state.

State Arts Resources: For mature arts
organizations that, over time, have
consistently produced strong arts programs
and demonstrated strong management and
financial accountability.

Statewide Service Organizations: Support is
provided to organizations that provide
programs and services to the arts community
on a statewide or regional basis.

YEAR PROGRAM STARTED: 1967

PURPOSE:
To enrich cultural life in North Carolina by
nurturing and supporting excellence in the
arts and by providing opportunities for every
North Carolinian to experience the arts.

LEGAL BASIS:
Agency of the state of North Carolina.

ELIGIBILITY:
Except for fellowships to individual artists
who are North Carolina residents, the
Council awards grants to North Carolina
agencies and organizations which qualify as
tax-exempt and nonprofit under Section
501(c)(3) of the Internal Revenue Code of
1954.

GEOG. RESTRICTIONS: North Carolina.

FINANCIAL DATA:
Amount of support per award: Varies.
Total amount of support: Varies.
Matching fund requirements: When required,
1:1 cash match, except for fellowships.

APPLICATION INFO:
Application form is available online.
Deadline: Organizational grant applications:
March 1. Individuals: November 1.

STAFF:
Wayne Martin, Executive Director

ADDRESS INQUIRIES TO:
Tanya McGuire, Grants Manager
E-mail: tanya.mcguire@ncdcr.gov
(See address above.)

NORTH DAKOTA COUNCIL ON THE ARTS   [451]

1600 East Century Avenue
Suite 6
Bismarck, ND 58503
(701) 328-7590
Fax: (701) 328-7595
E-mail: comserv@nd.gov
Web Site: www.nd.gov/arts

FOUNDED: 1967

AREAS OF INTEREST:
Arts.

NAME(S) OF PROGRAMS:
- **Arts in Education Collaboration Grant (AIEC)**
- **Arts-in-Education/Artists in Residence**
- **Community Arts Access**
- **Individual Artists Fellowships**
- **Institutional Support**
- **Professional Development**
- **Special Projects**
- **Traditional Arts Apprenticeships**

TYPE:
Conferences/seminars; Exchange programs;
Fellowships; General operating grants;
Project/program grants; Residencies.
Matching grants.

YEAR PROGRAM STARTED: 1967

PURPOSE:
To sustain, advocate and inspire growth for
all North Dakota arts.

LEGAL BASIS:
North Dakota Legislative Assembly.

ELIGIBILITY:
Grants are awarded only to nonprofit
organizations, schools, government
subdivisions and individuals in North Dakota.
Requirements vary according to program.
Organizations which do not have 501(c)(3)
status may be considered for funding on a
case-by-case basis.

GEOG. RESTRICTIONS: North Dakota.

FINANCIAL DATA:
Amount of support per award: Varies by
program.
Total amount of support: $836,753 for fiscal
year 2018.
Matching fund requirements: Varies by grant.

CO-OP FUNDING PROGRAMS: Institutional
Support and Arts-in-Education.

NO. MOST RECENT APPLICANTS: 215 for fiscal
year 2018.

NO. AWARDS: 203 funded for fiscal year 2018.

APPLICATION INFO:
Contact the Council.
Duration: Up to one year.
Deadline: Varies.

PUBLICATIONS:
Grant guidelines; brochures; eNewsletter;
cultural guide.

IRS I.D.: 45-0283965

OFFICER:
David Trottier, Chairperson

ADDRESS INQUIRIES TO:
Kim Konikow, Executive Director
(See address above.)

OHIO ARTS COUNCIL   [452]

30 East Broad Street
33rd Floor
Columbus, OH 43215
(614) 728-4429
Fax: (614) 466-4494
TDD: (800) 750-0750
E-mail: dia.foley@oac.ohio.gov
Web Site: oac.ohio.gov

FOUNDED: 1965

AREAS OF INTEREST:
Arts.

CONSULTING OR VOLUNTEER SERVICES:
Staff assistance related to applications and
program development.

NAME(S) OF PROGRAMS:
- **Artists with Disabilities Access**
- **Arts Access**
- **Arts Learning: Artist Express**
- **Arts Learning: Arts Partnership**
- **Arts Learning: TeachArtsOhio**
- **ArtsNEXT**
- **ArtSTART**
- **Big Yellow School Bus**
- **Building Cultural Diversity**
- **Capacity Building**

- **Individual Artist Grants and Services: Traditional Arts Apprenticeships**
- **Ohio Artists on Tour**
- **Ohio Heritage Fellowship Awards**
- **Sustainability**

TYPE:
Assistantships; Awards/prizes; Conferences/seminars; Fellowships; Formula grants; General operating grants; Internships; Project/program grants; Residencies; Technical assistance. Special projects.

YEAR PROGRAM STARTED: 1965

PURPOSE:
To fund and support quality arts experiences to strengthen Ohio communities culturally, educationally and economically.

LEGAL BASIS:
State agency.

ELIGIBILITY:
All applicants for grants must meet the following legal requirements including intending your project to be nonprofit, having the fact that every tax-exempt organization must have an Employer Identification Number, every applicant having to be an Ohio resident or Ohio-based to receive direct grant support, producing projects of high aesthetic quality and artistic merit.

No person or persons shall, on the grounds of race, color, national origin, handicap, age, sex or religion, be excluded from participation in, be denied benefits of or be otherwise subjected to discrimination under any program, service or benefit advocated, authorized or provided by the state of Ohio.

GEOG. RESTRICTIONS: Ohio.

FINANCIAL DATA:
Amount of support per award: $200 to $400,000.
Total amount of support: $12,000,000 for fiscal year 2018.
Matching fund requirements: Generally, 1:1 cash match.

REPRESENTATIVE AWARDS:
Cleveland Orchestra, Cleveland, OH; Worthington Arts Council, Worthington, OH; Lima Symphony Orchestra, Lima, OH; Actor's Summer Theatre, Columbus, OH; Southern Ohio Museum, Portsmouth, OH.

APPLICATION INFO:
Applicants must use OAC's web-based application system to submit an application.
Duration: July 1 through June 30.
Deadline: Artists with Disabilities Access and Big Yellow School Bus: Applications are accepted year-round; Arts Access and ArtsNEXT: March 1; Arts Learning-Artist Express: Application due in six weeks prior to the date of the visit; Arts Learning-Arts Partnership: March 1; Arts Learning-TeachArtsOhio and Sustainability: February 1; ArtSTART: April 1; Building Cultural Diversity: June 1 and December 1; Capacity Building: June 1; Individual Artist Grants and Services: January 15 for Traditional Arts Apprenticeships and September 1 for Individual Excellence Awards; Ohio Artists on Tour: May 15; Ohio Heritage Fellowship Awards: January 15.

PUBLICATIONS:
Guidelines; *Arts Ohio; Ohio Festivals & Competitions Guide; Focusing the Light: The Arts and Practice of Planning; Appreciative Journey: A Guide to Developing International Cultural Exchange.*

IRS I.D.: 31-1334820

OFFICERS:
Donna S. Collins, Executive Director
Dan Katona, Deputy Director
Dia Foley, Investment Director

ADDRESS INQUIRIES TO:
Dan Katona, Deputy Director
(See address above.)

OKLAHOMA ARTS COUNCIL   [453]
Jim Thorpe Building, Room 640
2101 North Lincoln Boulevard
Oklahoma City, OK 73105
(405) 521-2931
Fax: (405) 521-6418
E-mail: grants@arts.ok.gov
Web Site: www.arts.ok.gov

FOUNDED: 1965

AREAS OF INTEREST:
Arts.

NAME(S) OF PROGRAMS:
- **Capitol Art Travel Subsidies**
- **Major Grant Support**
- **Organizational Support**
- **Small Grant Support**
- **Small Grant Support for Schools**

TYPE:
Project/program grants; Technical assistance. State-appropriated funds and federal funds from the National Endowment for the Arts are disbursed to nonprofit, tax-exempt and nonreligious organizations for arts projects statewide.

YEAR PROGRAM STARTED: 1965

PURPOSE:
To further the arts in the state of Oklahoma.

LEGAL BASIS:
State agency.

ELIGIBILITY:
Nonprofit, tax-exempt and nonreligious Oklahoma organizations are eligible to apply. Funding is also provided for schools, universities, libraries as well as city, county and tribal governments.

GEOG. RESTRICTIONS: Oklahoma.

FINANCIAL DATA:
Amount of support per award: Varies.

APPLICATION INFO:
Contact the Council.
Duration: Projects receiving funding must be completed during the fiscal year.
Deadline: Capitol Art Travel Subsidies: 30 days before travel. Major Grant Support: February 15. Organizational Support: March 1. Small Grant Support and Small Grant Support for Schools: 60 days before program.

PUBLICATIONS:
Program Guidelines; general brochures.

OFFICERS:
Ann Neal, Chairperson
Amber Sharples, Executive Director

ADDRESS INQUIRIES TO:
Thomas Tran, Grants Director
(See address above.)

OREGON ARTS COMMISSION   [454]
775 Summer Street, N.E.
Suite 200
Salem, OR 97301-1280
(503) 986-0082
Fax: (503) 581-5115
E-mail: oregon.artscomm@oregon.gov
Web Site: www.oregonartscommission.org

FOUNDED: 1967

AREAS OF INTEREST:
Arts.

NAME(S) OF PROGRAMS:
- **Access Reimbursement Grants**
- **Arts Build Communities**
- **Arts Learning Grants**
- **Career Opportunity Grants**
- **Individual Artists Fellowship Grants**
- **Operating Support Grants**
- **Oregon Media Arts Fellowship**
- **Small Operating Grants**

TYPE:
Awards/prizes; Conferences/seminars; Fellowships; General operating grants; Project/program grants; Technical assistance; Training grants; Travel grants. Services provided to arts institutions statewide.

YEAR PROGRAM STARTED: 1967

PURPOSE:
To enhance the quality of life for all Oregonians through the arts by stimulating creativity, leadership and economic vitality.

LEGAL BASIS:
Agency of the state of Oregon.

ELIGIBILITY:
Grants are available to nonprofit organizations and professional, nonstudent artists.

GEOG. RESTRICTIONS: Oregon.

FINANCIAL DATA:
Amount of support per award: Varies.
Matching fund requirements: Minimum 1:1.

NO. MOST RECENT APPLICANTS: Varies.

NO. AWARDS: Varies.

APPLICATION INFO:
Detailed information is available on the web site.
Duration: One year.
Deadline: Varies.

IRS I.D.: 93-0563386

PENNSYLVANIA COUNCIL ON THE ARTS   [455]
216 Finance Building
Commonwealth and North Streets
Harrisburg, PA 17120
(717) 787-6883
Fax: (717) 783-2538
E-mail: ra-arts@pa.gov
Web Site: www.arts.pa.gov

FOUNDED: 1966

AREAS OF INTEREST:
Arts.

NAME(S) OF PROGRAMS:
- **Arts Organization Grants**

TYPE:
General operating grants; Residencies. General support grants, specific support grants, and peer-to-peer consultation.

YEAR PROGRAM STARTED: 1966

PURPOSE:
To foster the excellence, diversity and vitality of the arts in Pennsylvania; to broaden the availability and appreciation of those arts throughout the state.

LEGAL BASIS:
State agency.

ELIGIBILITY:
Incorporated nonprofit organizations located in Pennsylvania and serving residents of the state may apply.

GEOG. RESTRICTIONS: Pennsylvania.

FINANCIAL DATA:
Funding comes from state-appropriated funds and federal grants.
Total amount of support: Varies.
Matching fund requirements: Usually a dollar-for-dollar match for organizations.

APPLICATION INFO:
Contact the Council.
Duration: One year.
Deadline: Varies.

PUBLICATIONS:
Guide to Fellowship Programs; Guide to Programs and Services; Guide to the Arts-in-Education Program.

STAFF:
Karl Blischke, Executive Director
Heather Doughty, Deputy Executive Director
Jamie Dunlap, Chief of Creative Catalysts and Lifelong Learning
Amy Gabriele, Chief of Finance and Administration
Matt Serio, Director of Creative Opportunities
Dana Payne, Director of DEI Initiatives, Diverse Cultures and Heritage
Norah Janson, Director of Public Awareness and External Affairs

ADDRESS INQUIRIES TO:
Director of Pertinent Arts Discipline
(See address above.)

PERPETUAL TRUSTEE COMPANY LTD.   [456]
Level 6, 123 Pitt Street
Sydney N.S.W. 2000 Australia
(61) 1800 501 227
Fax: (61) 02 8256 1471
E-mail: philanthropy@perpetual.com.au
Web Site: www.shervingallery.com.au/portiageach

FOUNDED: 1961

AREAS OF INTEREST:
Portrait painting.

NAME(S) OF PROGRAMS:
● **Portia Geach Memorial Award**

TYPE:
Awards/prizes. Cash award for the best portrait painted from life of a man or woman distinguished in Art, Letters or the Sciences, by any female artist resident in Australia.

YEAR PROGRAM STARTED: 1965

PURPOSE:
To recognize the portrait painted from life of the highest artistic merit.

LEGAL BASIS:
Trustees of the Portia Geach Memorial Fund.

ELIGIBILITY:
Entrants must be female Australian residents who are either Australian-born, naturalized, or British-born. Entries must be the original

work of the competitor. Works must have been executed entirely during the commenced year previously. Each entry must be a portrait painted from life of a man or woman distinguished in Art, Letters or the Sciences. Self-portraits are accepted. Works must be two-dimensional and must use the medium of paint.

Sculptures, photographic and video works are not eligible. There is no limit to the number of entries an artist can submit.

GEOG. RESTRICTIONS: Australia.

FINANCIAL DATA:
Amount of support per award: $30,000 (AUD) for the year 2019.

NO. AWARDS: 1.

APPLICATION INFO:
Application information will be available on the web site when the award cycle opens.

ADDRESS INQUIRIES TO:
Philanthropic Services
Portia Geach Memorial Award
(See e-mail address above.)

RAGDALE FOUNDATION   [457]
1260 North Green Bay Road
Lake Forest, IL 60045
(847) 234-1063
E-mail: admissions@ragdale.org
Web Site: www.ragdale.org

FOUNDED: 1976

AREAS OF INTEREST:
Visual arts, poetry, fiction, nonfiction writing, music composition, performance art, play/screenwriting and interdisciplinary arts.

NAME(S) OF PROGRAMS:
● **Residencies at Ragdale Foundation**

TYPE:
Awards/prizes; Fellowships; Internships; Residencies. Low-cost subsidized residencies at Ragdale Foundation, an artist's community, providing a place to work undisturbed on creative projects. Some financial aid and fellowships are available upon acceptance.

YEAR PROGRAM STARTED: 1976

PURPOSE:
To provide a place for artists to work undisturbed on creative projects.

LEGAL BASIS:
Not-for-profit, tax-exempt foundation.

ELIGIBILITY:
Residents are chosen by selection committees composed of professionals in the arts. Writers, composers, visual artists and artists of other disciplines are accepted. Couples and collaborators are not accepted unless each qualifies independently.

FINANCIAL DATA:
Amount of support per award: Residencies with room and board provided. Standard fee is $630 for 18-day residencies and $875 for 25-day residencies.
Total amount of support: Varies.

NO. MOST RECENT APPLICANTS: 600.

NO. AWARDS: Approximately 200.

APPLICATION INFO:
Completed application must be submitted along with references, resume, work samples and project description. Application process is online through the Submittable portal. A

$25 application fee is required. Financial aid application must be completed after acceptance.
Duration: 18 or 25 days.
Deadline: May 15.

PUBLICATIONS:
Application guidelines; two newsletters annually.

IRS I.D.: 36-2937927

OFFICER:
Jeanna Park, President

ADDRESS INQUIRIES TO:
Amy Sinclair
Grants and Admissions Manager
(See address above.)

RHODE ISLAND STATE COUNCIL ON THE ARTS   [458]
One Capitol Hill, 3rd Floor
Providence, RI 02908
(401) 222-3880
(401) 222-3882
Fax: (401) 222-3018
E-mail: todd.trebour@arts.ri.gov
Web Site: www.arts.ri.gov

FOUNDED: 1967

AREAS OF INTEREST:
Arts.

NAME(S) OF PROGRAMS:
● **Artist Initiated Skill Share**
● **Artists Open Studio Tours Grant (AOST)**
● **Arts Access Grant (AAG)**
● **Big Yellow School Bus**
● **Fellowships**
● **Folk Arts Apprenticeships and Fellowships**
● **Investments in Arts and Culture (IAC)**
● **Project Grants for Education (PGE and PGA)**
● **Project Grants for Individuals (PGI)**
● **Project Grants in Healthcare**

TYPE:
Fellowships; General operating grants; Project/program grants. Organizational support includes general operating grants and project/program grants; funding for Rhode Island nonprofit organizations doing arts programming. Individual artist support includes Fellowships, Project Grants for Individuals, and Folk Arts Apprenticeships. Educational Support includes Project Grants in Education.

YEAR PROGRAM STARTED: 1967

PURPOSE:
To support and develop increased and substantial arts opportunities for Rhode Island.

LEGAL BASIS:
Agency of the state of Rhode Island.

ELIGIBILITY:
Varies with each grant category.

GEOG. RESTRICTIONS: Rhode Island.

FINANCIAL DATA:
Amount of support per award: Varies.
Total amount of support: $1,646,882 for fiscal year 2019.
Matching fund requirements: All grants, except for individual artists, require matching funds.

CO-OP FUNDING PROGRAMS: State and local cooperative programs.

APPLICATION INFO:
Contact the specific Program Director.

Duration: Varies with program.

Deadline: April 1 and October 1.

IRS I.D.: 05-6000523

OFFICERS:
Randall Rosenbaum, Executive Director
Maggie Anderson, Program Director, Arts in Education (Education Partnerships)
Elena Calderon-Patino, Program Director, Community Arts and Atrium Gallery
Mollie Flanagan, Program Director, Individual Artists
Todd Trebour, Program Director, Organizations
Elizabeth Keithline, Program Director, Public Art
Donna Fiske, Fiscal and Office Manager

ADDRESS INQUIRIES TO:
Elena Calderon-Patino, Program Director
Community Arts and Atrium Gallery
(See address above.)
Tel: (401) 222-6996

Mollie Flanagan
Program Director, Individual Artists
(See address above.)
Tel: (401) 222-3881

Todd Trebour
Program Director, Organizations
(See address or e-mail above.)
Tel: (401) 222-3882

Maggie Anderson, Program Assistant
Arts in Education
(See address above.)
Tel: (401) 222-1146

SAN FRANCISCO FOUNDATION [459]

One Embarcadero Center, Suite 1400
San Francisco, CA 94111
(415) 733-8500
Fax: (415) 477-2783
E-mail: kfsmith@sff.org
Web Site: sff.org

FOUNDED: 1948

AREAS OF INTEREST:
Fine arts.

NAME(S) OF PROGRAMS:
- **Edwin Anthony and Adelaide Boudreaux Cadogan Scholarships**
- **Jack K. and Gertrude Murphy Fellowships**

TYPE:
Fellowships; Scholarships.

YEAR PROGRAM STARTED: 1986

PURPOSE:
To assist San Francisco Bay Area students in pursuing graduate academic fine arts study at various Bay Area institutions.

LEGAL BASIS:
Community foundation.

ELIGIBILITY:
Applicants must be M.F.A. students currently pursuing a graduate degree in one of the following San Francisco Bay Area colleges and universities: Mills College, San Francisco State University, Stanford University, The California College of the Arts, The San Francisco Art Institute, and UC Berkeley. Students may self-nominate for the award.

Students must have completed at least one semester of graduate school by the time they apply, must be continuously enrolled in the same program and be in good academic standing.

GEOG. RESTRICTIONS: San Francisco Bay Area, California.

FINANCIAL DATA:
Amount of support per award: Cadogan Award: Typically $6,500 in tuition assistance, based on available funding; Murphy Award: Varies based on available funding.

NO. MOST RECENT APPLICANTS: Varies.

NO. AWARDS: Cadogan Scholarship: 17 for the year 2018; Murphy Award: 1.

APPLICATION INFO:
Contact the Foundation.
Deadline: May of each year.

ADDRESS INQUIRIES TO:
E-mail: programs@sff.org

SAN FRANCISCO FOUNDATION [460]

One Embarcadero Center
Suite 1400
San Francisco, CA 94111
(415) 733-8500
Fax: (415) 477-2783
E-mail: kfsmith@sff.org
Web Site: sff.org

FOUNDED: 1948

AREAS OF INTEREST:
Literature, visual arts, film and video, and playwriting

NAME(S) OF PROGRAMS:
- **Art Awards**

TYPE:
Awards/prizes.

PURPOSE:
To foster individual artistic growth within the community.

LEGAL BASIS:
Community foundation.

ELIGIBILITY:
Poets, writers, sculptors, painters, filmmakers, media artists, photographers, printmakers and performing artists are eligible.

GEOG. RESTRICTIONS: Alameda, Contra Costa, Marin, San Francisco and San Mateo counties, California.

FINANCIAL DATA:
Amount of support per award: $2,000.
Total amount of support: Varies.

NO. AWARDS: Varies.

APPLICATION INFO:
Contact the Foundation.
Deadline: Varies.

ADDRESS INQUIRIES TO:
Art Awards Program
E-mail: programs@sff.org

*PLEASE NOTE:
Some art awards that are administered by the Foundation are by nomination only. They are not open application processes.

SILICON VALLEY CREATES [461]

310 South First Street
San Jose, CA 95113
(408) 998-2787 ext. 204
E-mail: alyssae@svcreates.org
Web Site: www.svcreates.org

FOUNDED: 1982

AREAS OF INTEREST:
Arts organizations, individual artists and community arts.

NAME(S) OF PROGRAMS:
- **Artist Laureates**
- **Local Arts Grants**

TYPE:
Awards/prizes; Conferences/seminars; General operating grants; Technical assistance. Laureate awards.

Artist Laureate Awards provide awards to recognize the accomplishments of individual artists.

Local Arts Grants provide general operating support to arts organizations for activities that:
(1) promote artistic excellence while reflecting the dynamic diverse and innovative character of Santa Clara County;
(2) support the professional development of small and mid-sized arts organizations;
(3) recognize and encourage nonprofessional, volunteer involvement as an essential part of the county's cultural environment and;
(4) stimulate local support, particularly at the grassroots level.

LEGAL BASIS:
Private, nonprofit arts council.

GEOG. RESTRICTIONS: Santa Clara County, California.

FINANCIAL DATA:
Amount of support per award: Artist Laureates: $5,000; Local Arts Grants: $4,000 to $10,000, depending on funding level.
Total amount of support: $443,238 for fiscal year 2018.

NO. AWARDS: Artist Laureates: 6; Impact Grants: 19; Operating Grants: 70 for the year 2019.

APPLICATION INFO:
Applications are submitted through the online grant portal.
Deadline: Varies.

PUBLICATIONS:
Annual report.

IRS I.D.: 94-2825213

ADDRESS INQUIRIES TO:
Alyssa Erickson, Program Manager
(See address above.)

SMITHSONIAN INSTITUTION

Office of Fellowships and Internships
470 L'Enfant Plaza, S.W., Suite 7102
MRC 902, P.O. Box 37012
Washington, DC 20013-7012
(202) 633-7070
E-mail: siofi@si.edu
Web Site: www.smithsonianofi.com

TYPE:
Fellowships. Offered to qualified scholars for research to be conducted in residence at the Smithsonian in association with the staff, using collections and research facilities.

See entry 1671 for full listing.

SOUTH CAROLINA ARTS COMMISSION [462]

1026 Sumter Street, Suite 200
Columbia, SC 29201
(803) 734-8696
E-mail: info@arts.sc.gov
Web Site: www.southcarolinaarts.com

FOUNDED: 1967

AREAS OF INTEREST:
Arts education, community arts development
and artist development.

NAME(S) OF PROGRAMS:
- **Arts Education**
- **Community Organizations
  Grants/Programs**
- **Individual Artist Grants/Programs**

TYPE:
Awards/prizes; Fellowships; General
operating grants; Project/program grants;
Seed money grants; Technical assistance;
Training grants; Travel grants.

ELIGIBILITY:
Individuals who apply must be citizens or
residents of the U.S. Grants are awarded to
South Carolina artists, organizations and
units of government.

FINANCIAL DATA:
Amount of support per award: Varies.
Total amount of support: Varies.

APPLICATION INFO:
Consult the Commission web site.
Deadline: Varies.

SOUTH DAKOTA ARTS
COUNCIL   [463]
711 East Wells Avenue
Pierre, SD 57501-3369
(605) 773-3301
(800) 952-3625
Fax: (605) 773-5977
E-mail: sdac@state.sd.us
Web Site: artscouncil.sd.gov

FOUNDED: 1966

AREAS OF INTEREST:
Statewide arts programming in all arts
disciplines.

NAME(S) OF PROGRAMS:
- **Artist Career Development Grants**
- **Artist Collaboration Grants**
- **Artist Fellowships**
- **Artists in Schools & Communities
  (AISC) Grants**
- **Arts Challenge Grants**
- **Importation of Musicians Grants**
- **Project Grants**
- **Statewide Services Grants**
- **Touring Arts**
- **Traditional Arts Apprenticeship Grants**

TYPE:
Challenge/matching grants; Fellowships;
General operating grants; Grants-in-aid;
Project/program grants; Residencies; Seed
money grants; Technical assistance; Travel
grants. Artist grants; arts challenge
grants/general operating support.

YEAR PROGRAM STARTED: 1968

PURPOSE:
To support development of the arts.

LEGAL BASIS:
State agency.

ELIGIBILITY:
Requirements vary with projects. Most grants
are available to South Dakota residents only,
with the exception of Touring Arts.

GEOG. RESTRICTIONS: South Dakota.

FINANCIAL DATA:
Amount of support per award: Generally
$500 to $5,000. Large cultural organizations:
$4,000 to $40,000.

Total amount of support: $1,360,000 for
fiscal year 2020.

Matching fund requirements: Required except
for Artist Collaboration Grants, Artist Grants
and Folk Arts Apprenticeship Grants.

NO. AWARDS: 332 grants and fellowships for
fiscal year 2020.

APPLICATION INFO:
Applications are accepted through an online
e-grant system.
Duration: Generally one fiscal year.
Renewable.
Deadline: March 1 for Organizations and
Artist Grants. September 1 for Touring Arts
and Artist in Schools & Communities.

PUBLICATIONS:
Arts Alive, newsletter; strategic long-range
plan; annual report.

STAFF:
Patrick Baker, Director
Rebecca Cruse, Assistant Director
Paul Mehlhaff, Grants Officer
Kate Vandel, Program Coordinator

ADDRESS INQUIRIES TO:
Patrick Baker, Director
(See address above.)

H. CHASE STONE TRUST   [464]
c/o JPMorgan
370 17th Street, Suite 3200
Denver, CO 80202
(303) 607-7810
Fax: (303) 607-7761
E-mail: julie.golden@jpmorgan.com
Web Site: www.jpmorgan.com/onlinegrants

AREAS OF INTEREST:
Primarily performing, literary and fine arts.

TYPE:
Project/program grants.

PURPOSE:
To support, sustain and develop charitable
organizations operating in the El Paso
County community.

ELIGIBILITY:
Performing, literary and fine arts
organizations serving the entire El Paso
County community are eligible to apply.
Must have 501(c)(3) not-for-profit status. No
grants to individuals.

GEOG. RESTRICTIONS: El Paso County,
Colorado.

FINANCIAL DATA:
Amount of support per award: $2,500 to
$50,000.
Total amount of support: $160,000.

NO. MOST RECENT APPLICANTS: 12.

NO. AWARDS: 10.

APPLICATION INFO:
Application and guidelines are available
online. Organization must provide current
copy of IRS determination letter showing
tax-exempt status under Section 501(c)(3)
and public charity status under Section
509(a).
Duration: One year. No renewals.
Deadline: June 30.

ADDRESS INQUIRIES TO:
Julie Golden, Trust Advisor
(See address above.)

*SPECIAL STIPULATIONS:
JPMorgan will only accept applications
submitted online.

THE FRANK M. TAIT
FOUNDATION
40 North Main Street
Suite 1530
Dayton, OH 45423
(937) 222-2401
E-mail: taitfoundation@gmail.com

TYPE:
Project/program grants. Focus on youth
development, particularly early childhood
development.

See entry 1045 for full listing.

TENNESSEE ARTS
COMMISSION   [465]
401 Dr. Martin Luther King Jr. Boulevard
Nashville, TN 37243-0780
(615) 741-6395
Fax: (615) 741-8559
E-mail: diane.williams@tn.gov
Web Site: tnartscommission.org

FOUNDED: 1967

AREAS OF INTEREST:
All arts disciplines in Tennessee.

CONSULTING OR VOLUNTEER SERVICES:
Consultant, informational and developmental
services are offered to arts groups, individual
artists, museums and arts councils throughout
the state.

NAME(S) OF PROGRAMS:
- **Division of Arts Programs**
- **Division of Communications,
  Information & Technology**

TYPE:
Conferences/seminars; Fellowships; General
operating grants; Project/program grants;
Residencies; Technical assistance; Training
grants. Professional development. Matching
grants. Arts Programs consist of grants to
institutions, individuals, coordinating
agencies and entities of government.
Consultation information and development
assistance to state arts constituency is also
provided.

Grant Programs: Funds may not be used for
capital improvements or for permanent
equipment.

YEAR PROGRAM STARTED: 1967

PURPOSE:
To support and encourage the life and growth
of the arts and craft in the state of Tennessee
and preservation of the state's cultural
heritage.

LEGAL BASIS:
Independent state agency.

ELIGIBILITY:
Grants categories are limited to residents,
artists and organizations of Tennessee. Grants
are made to individuals, nonprofit
organizations and/or entities of government.

GEOG. RESTRICTIONS: Tennessee.

FINANCIAL DATA:
Amount of support per award: $200 to
$100,000.
Matching fund requirements: Most grant
awards require a 1:1 match.

NO. MOST RECENT APPLICANTS: 1,000.

NO. AWARDS: 850.

APPLICATION INFO:
Details are available on the web site.

Duration: One fiscal year, July to June.
Deadline: Varies.

PUBLICATIONS:
Weekly online newsletter.

COMMISSION MEMBERS:
Stephen Bailey, Chairperson
Andrea J. Loughry, Vice Chairperson
Hank Dye, Secretary
Patsy White Camp
Michael Dumont
Mary D. Johnson
Joe D. Kilgore
Jan McNally
Cindy C. Ogle
Dr. Shawn Pitts
Johnnie Wheeler
Jennifer Wolfe

ADDRESS INQUIRIES TO:
Diane Williams, Director of
Grants Management
(See address above.)

TEXAS COMMISSION ON THE ARTS [466]
E.O. Thompson Building
920 Colorado, 5th Floor
Austin, TX 78701
(512) 463-5535
Fax: (512) 475-2699
E-mail: laura@arts.texas.gov
Web Site: www.arts.texas.gov

FOUNDED: 1965

AREAS OF INTEREST:
Operational support and project support to
nonprofit Texas arts organizations for
ongoing programs and/or arts education,
health and human services, economic
development, public safety and criminal
justice, and natural resources and agriculture;
performance support for civic, cultural and
other nonprofit organizations.

CONSULTING OR VOLUNTEER SERVICES:
Seminars, information services, technical
assistance and funding. Services provided to
institutions statewide.

NAME(S) OF PROGRAMS:
● **TCA Grant Programs**

TYPE:
Block grants; Challenge/matching grants;
Conferences/seminars; Exchange programs;
General operating grants; Project/program
grants; Residencies; Technical assistance;
Training grants; Travel grants; Visiting
scholars. Organizational support, project
support and touring support.

YEAR PROGRAM STARTED: 1965

PURPOSE:
To advance the state economically and
culturally by investing in a creative Texas.

LEGAL BASIS:
Texas Government Code, Chapter 444,
Section 021.

ELIGIBILITY:
Any 501(c)(3) organization, educational
institution, or form of government may apply.
Presenters and producers of performing arts
whose programs are designed to stimulate
artistic activity and to heighten awareness of
and broaden public access to the arts in rural
and underserved areas of the state are eligible
to apply.

Award made according to project cost,
program limits, ability to meet funding
criteria and available funds.

GEOG. RESTRICTIONS: Texas.

FINANCIAL DATA:
Total amount of support: $5,000,000 for the
year 2019.
Matching fund requirements: Funds provided
by the state through the grants process must
be matched by the applicant organization.
Matching funds are generally expected to be
in cash.

NO. MOST RECENT APPLICANTS: 1,500.

APPLICATION INFO:
Guidelines available online. All applications
submitted electronically. Contact TCA staff
to obtain user ID and password.
Duration: Up to one year.
Deadline: Varies.

PUBLICATIONS:
Guide to Programs and Services.

STAFF:
Dr. Gary Gibbs, Executive Director

COMMISSION MEMBERS:
Dale W. Brock, Chairperson
S. Shawn Stephens, Vice-Chairperson
Karen Partee, Treasurer
Mila Gibson, Secretary
Marci Roberts, Parliamentarian
Adrian Guerra, At-Large

ADDRESS INQUIRIES TO:
Laura Wiegand
Director of Programs and Technology
(See address above.)

TWO TEN FOOTWEAR FOUNDATION
1466 Main Street
Waltham, MA 02451
(800) 346-3210 ext. 1512
Fax: (781) 736-1555; (781) 736-1554
E-mail: wweatherly@twoten.org
Web Site: twoten.org

TYPE:
Scholarships. Intended for students who are
interested in pursuing a career in footwear
design.

See entry 1605 for full listing.

UNITARIAN UNIVERSALIST ASSOCIATION OF CONGREGATIONS [467]
UU Funding Program
P.O. Box 301149
Jamaica Plain, MA 02130
(617) 971-9600
E-mail: uufunding@gmail.com
Web Site: uua.org/college/scholarships/stanfield

FOUNDED: 1986

AREAS OF INTEREST:
Limited to the fine arts of painting, drawing,
enameling, printmaking, photography and
sculpture.

NAME(S) OF PROGRAMS:
● **Stanfield and D'Orlando Art
Scholarships**

TYPE:
Scholarships. Annual scholarship to be
awarded to an applicant majoring in fine art,
for further study in that major, at an
accredited school.

YEAR PROGRAM STARTED: 1980

PURPOSE:
To aid a Unitarian Universalist student
majoring in fine arts.

LEGAL BASIS:
Religious organization.

ELIGIBILITY:
Applicants must be members in good
standing for at least one year before date of
application or sponsored by a member of a
Unitarian Universalist Congregation and must
be enrolled in an accredited school. Eligible
art fields include drawing, painting, sculpture,
enameling, printmaking and photography.

GEOG. RESTRICTIONS: United States.

FINANCIAL DATA:
Payment is made directly to the recipient.
Amount of support per award: Average
$1,000.
Total amount of support: Varies.

NO. AWARDS: Varies.

APPLICATION INFO:
Applications should include a short essay on
applicant, photos or slides of at least six
works by applicant, two letters of
recommendation, statement of tuition costs
where applicant is enrolled, an application
which has been signed, financial statement
and proof of need.
Duration: One academic year. May reapply.
Deadline: February 15. Notification in May.

*SPECIAL STIPULATIONS:
Affiliation with Unitarian Universalist
Congregation required.

UNITED ARTS COUNCIL OF RALEIGH AND WAKE COUNTY, INC. [468]
410 Glenwood Avenue, Suite 170
Raleigh, NC 27603
(919) 839-1498 ext. 203
Fax: (919) 839-6002
E-mail: cphaneuf@unitedarts.org
Web Site: www.unitedarts.org

FOUNDED: 1990

AREAS OF INTEREST:
Arts, arts education, music education, theatre
arts education, humanities-community
development, and teacher-preparation
education.

NAME(S) OF PROGRAMS:
● **Artists-in-Schools Grants Program**
● **Professional Development Grants for
Artists**
● **Program Support Grants**

TYPE:
Project/program grants; Seed money grants.

YEAR PROGRAM STARTED: 1989

PURPOSE:
To enhance and strengthen arts and arts
education in Wake County, NC.

ELIGIBILITY:
Funds are available to Wake County (NC)
grades K-12 schools, individual artists, arts
organizations and municipalities with specific
arts programming.

GEOG. RESTRICTIONS: Wake County, North
Carolina.

FINANCIAL DATA:
Amount of support per award: $1,000 to
$20,000.
Total amount of support: Varies.
Matching fund requirements: Required for
some programs.

NO. MOST RECENT APPLICANTS: Over 300.

NO. AWARDS: Varies.

APPLICATION INFO:
Application information is available on the web site.
Duration: Varies by grant program annually.
Deadline: Varies by grant program annually.

PUBLICATIONS:
Guidelines.

IRS I.D.: 56-0770175

UNIVERSITY OF MINNESOTA
Room 113, Elmer L. Andersen Library
222 21st Avenue South
Minneapolis, MN 55455
(612) 624-4576
E-mail: asc-clrc@umn.edu
Web Site: www.lib.umn.edu/clrc

TYPE:
Research grants; Travel grants; Visiting scholars. Award to travel to Kerlan Collection, University of Minnesota, plus per diem.

See entry 656 for full listing.

UNIVERSITY OF MINNESOTA   [469]
Room 113, Elmer L. Andersen Library
222 21st Avenue South
Minneapolis, MN 55455
(612) 624-4576
E-mail: asc-clrc@umn.edu
Web Site: www.lib.umn.edu/clrc

AREAS OF INTEREST:
Research and children's literature.

NAME(S) OF PROGRAMS:
● **Marilyn Hollinshead Fellowship**

TYPE:
Travel grants. Award to travel to Kerlan Collection, University of Minnesota, as well as per diem.

PURPOSE:
To fund children's literature research with manuscripts and/or original illustrations.

FINANCIAL DATA:
Award covers travel, food or lodging.
Amount of support per award: Up to $1,500.
Total amount of support: $1,500.

NO. AWARDS: 1 per year.

APPLICATION INFO:
Electronic application acceptable by deadline.
Duration: Grants are awarded annually and are nonrenewable.
Deadline: January 30 of research year.

ADDRESS INQUIRIES TO:
Fellowship Committee
(See address above.)

THE UNIVERSITY OF TEXAS AT AUSTIN   [470]
The Graduate School, Main Building 101
110 Inner Campus Drive, GO400
Austin, TX 78712-1710
(512) 232-3612
E-mail: adameve@austin.utexas.edu
wolfkill@austin.utexas.edu
Web Site: dobiepaisano.utexas.edu

AREAS OF INTEREST:
Competitive writing fellowships.

NAME(S) OF PROGRAMS:
● **The Dobie Paisano Fellowship Program**

TYPE:
Project/program grants. Provides an opportunity for creative or nonfiction writers to live and write for an extended period in an environment that offers isolation and tranquility.

Ralph A. Johnston Memorial Fellowship is aimed at writers who have demonstrated some publishing and critical success.

Jesse H. Jones Writing Fellowship is aimed at, but not limited to, writers who are early in their careers.

Both fellowships provide and require free residence at the ranch.

YEAR PROGRAM STARTED: 1967

PURPOSE:
To stimulate creative writing by making it possible for a person to work without distractions in an environment that offers isolation and tranquility.

ELIGIBILITY:
Criteria for making the awards include quality of work, character of the proposed project, and suitability of the applicant for life at Paisano, the late J. Frank Dobie's ranch near Austin, TX.

At the time of application, the applicant must meet one of the following:
(1) be a native Texan;
(2) have lived in Texas at some time for at least three years or;
(3) have published significant work with a Texas subject.

FINANCIAL DATA:
Amount of support per award: Ralph A. Johnston Memorial Fellowship: Stipend of $6,250 per month; Jesse H. Jones Writing Fellowship: Stipend of $3,000 per month.
Total amount of support: Ralph A. Johnston Memorial Fellowship: $25,000; Jesse H. Jones Writing Fellowship: $18,000.

NO. MOST RECENT APPLICANTS: Ralph A. Johnston Memorial Fellowship: 27; Jesse H. Jones Writing Fellowship: 50.

NO. AWARDS: 1 each annually.

APPLICATION INFO:
Application process begins on November 1. Application fee of $20 for one fellowship or $30 for both fellowships is required. If applying for both fellowships, include the fee with the Johnston Memorial Fellowship application and check the appropriate box at the top of the Johnston application form. Application fees are nonrefundable.

Applicants must submit each application in triplicate and its accompanying materials in separate packets. Make checks or money orders payable to The University of Texas at Austin.

Both application forms can be downloaded and printed from the web site. To request a printed copy of either application, send a self-addressed, stamped envelope (2 ounces postage) to the address above.
Duration: Ralph A. Johnston Memorial Fellowship: Four months. Jesse H. Jones Writing Fellowship: Six months.
Deadline: January 15.

ADDRESS INQUIRIES TO:
Robert T. Wolfkill, Associate Director
(See address above.)

*SPECIAL STIPULATIONS:
Applicant must demonstrate ability to live in a rustic secluded rural location. Fellows must reside at Paisano Ranch.

UTAH DIVISION OF ARTS & MUSEUMS   [471]
617 East South Temple
Salt Lake City, UT 84102
(801) 236-7550
Fax: (801) 236-7556
E-mail: lalder@utah.gov
Web Site: artsandmuseums.utah.gov

FOUNDED: 1899

AREAS OF INTEREST:
Arts and museums funding in Utah.

NAME(S) OF PROGRAMS:
● **Artists Learning**
● **Arts Organization Capacity Building**
● **Arts Project A/B**
● **Folk Arts Scholarships**
● **Local Arts Councils**
● **Museum Operating Support**
● **Museum Project**

TYPE:
Development grants; General operating grants; Matching gifts; Residencies; Scholarships.

PURPOSE:
To provide funding to art organizations and museums in Utah.

LEGAL BASIS:
Government agency.

ELIGIBILITY:
Varies with each grant. Organizations must have IRS 501(c)(3) not-for-profit status or be government entities. No grants to individuals or religious organizations.

GEOG. RESTRICTIONS: Utah.

FINANCIAL DATA:
Amount of support per award: $500 to $50,000.
Total amount of support: $1,500,000.
Matching fund requirements: 1:1 cash match.

NO. MOST RECENT APPLICANTS: 260.

NO. AWARDS: 250.

APPLICATION INFO:
Procedure is done online. Applying organizations must have a Charitable Solicitation Permit.
Duration: One year. Nonrenewable.
Deadline: Varies.

STAFF:
Laurel Cannon Alder, Grants Manager
Racquel Cornali, Grants Coordinator

ADDRESS INQUIRIES TO:
Laurel Cannon Alder
Grants Manager
(See address above.)

VCCA (VIRGINIA CENTER FOR THE CREATIVE ARTS)   [472]
154 San Angelo Drive
Amherst, VA 24521
(434) 946-7236
Fax: (434) 946-7239
E-mail: vcca@vcca.com
Web Site: www.vcca.com

FOUNDED: 1971

TYPE:
Fellowships; Residencies. International exchange programs. Virginia Center for the Creative Arts (VCCA) hosts over 400 visual artists, writers and composers each year. Artists, whether emerging or established, are selected by peer review on the basis of the important or innovative work they are doing in their respective fields. In residence, Fellows are provided with an individual studio, private bedroom and three prepared meals a day so they can focus exclusively on their work. While uninterrupted time is assured and participation in community events or public engagement is voluntary, the dynamic interaction among the 25 Fellows in residence together, as they share work, discuss process, and enjoy each other's company, is an important component of the creative space of VCCA. With a tradition of hospitality and welcome, VCCA schedules a diverse cohort of artists across disciplines.

YEAR PROGRAM STARTED: 1971

PURPOSE:
To provide time and space for national and international writers, visual artists, and composers of talent and promise to bring forth their finest works because the arts are vital, diversity is a strength, and creativity is essential.

LEGAL BASIS:
Nonprofit corporation.

ELIGIBILITY:
Achievement or outstanding promise within a field of art must be demonstrated.

FINANCIAL DATA:
All fellowships are for periods of residency. No cash awards are offered. Some fellowships do offer stipends.
Amount of support per award: Varies.
Total amount of support: Varies.

NO. AWARDS: Over 400.

APPLICATION INFO:
Application must include two references from professionals in the applicant's field, samples of applicant's work and a curriculum vitae. Residencies available for three composers, nine visual artists and 13 writers at any time.
Duration: Two to eight weeks.
Deadline: January 15 for fellowships running from June to September. May 15 for fellowships running from October to January. September 15 for fellowships running from February to May.

PUBLICATIONS:
Application form; annual report; newsletters.

STAFF:
Sheila Gulley Pleasants, Deputy Director

ADDRESS INQUIRIES TO:
Sheila Gulley Pleasants, Deputy Director
(See address above.)

VERMONT ARTS COUNCIL [473]
136 State Street
Montpelier, VT 05633
(802) 828-3292
E-mail: mbell@vermontartscouncil.org
Web Site: www.vermontartscouncil.org

FOUNDED: 1964

AREAS OF INTEREST:
Visual arts including painting, sculpture, drawing, printmaking, architectural and cultural facilities design, crafts, film and photography; performing arts in music, theatre and dance; literature.

NAME(S) OF PROGRAMS:
- **Art in State Buildings Program**
- **Artist Development Grants**
- **Artists in Schools**
- **Arts Impact Grants**
- **Arts Partnership Grants**
- **Creation Grants**
- **Cultural Facilities Grants**
- **Project Grants**

TYPE:
Development grants; Project/program grants; Travel grants. Professional development grants. Cultural facilities improvements. Arts partnerships.

YEAR PROGRAM STARTED: 1966

PURPOSE:
To advance and preserve the arts at the center of Vermont communities.

LEGAL BASIS:
Official state arts agency and a nonprofit membership corporation.

ELIGIBILITY:
Applicants must be nonprofit organizations, agencies of town, county, state government and/or individual artists of demonstrated ability who are residents of Vermont for at least one year.

Funding is not available for:
(1) academic tuition;
(2) activities in which artists are not appropriately compensated;
(3) construction of new facilities, renovation of existing facilities, or other capital improvements (exceptions in cases that comply with Cultural Facilities Grants);
(4) deficits and debts incurred from past activities;
(5) events that present faculty members on the campus of their own institutions;
(6) events which are predominantly religious or sectarian;
(7) events whose sponsors are not in compliance with the requirements of the Americans with Disabilities Act of 1990 and Section 504 of the Rehabilitation Act of 1973;
(8) food and beverages;
(9) for-profit organizations;
(10) fund-raising events;
(11) international travel (airline tickets);
(12) lobbying expenses;
(13) private events to which the public is not invited and;
(14) purchase of permanent equipment (exceptions in cases that comply with Cultural Facilities Grants).

GEOG. RESTRICTIONS: Vermont.

FINANCIAL DATA:
Amount of support per award: Varies according to each program.
Total amount of support: $754,168 in grants and services for the year 2018.
Matching fund requirements: Generally 1:1.

CO-OP FUNDING PROGRAMS: Cultural Facilities Grants with the state of Vermont.

NO. MOST RECENT APPLICANTS: 250.

NO. AWARDS: 135.

APPLICATION INFO:
Interested applicants can view the *Arts Council Grant Guidelines* and application online. Individual artists are required to submit samples of work.

Duration: Typically one to three years.
Deadline: Varies.

IRS I.D.: 03-0218115

ADDRESS INQUIRIES TO:
Meredith Bell
Grants and Information Associate
(See address above.)

VETERANS OF FOREIGN WARS AUXILIARY [474]
National Headquarters
406 West 34th Street, 10th Floor
Kansas City, MO 64111
(816) 561-8655
Fax: (816) 931-4753
E-mail: info@vfwauxiliary.org
Web Site: vfwauxiliary.org

AREAS OF INTEREST:
Creative art for patriotic American youth.

NAME(S) OF PROGRAMS:
- **Young American Creative Patriotic Art Awards**

TYPE:
Awards/prizes.

YEAR PROGRAM STARTED: 1979

PURPOSE:
To promote artistic creativity in patriotic American youth.

LEGAL BASIS:
Nonprofit.

ELIGIBILITY:
Students must be in grades 9 through 12 and must attend school in the same state as the sponsoring VFW Auxiliary. Home-schooled students are eligible; foreign exchange students are not. National winners of the past contests may not compete in future Young American Creative Patriotic Art Contests. Students must be no older than 18 years of age and U.S. citizens or U.S. nationals.

GEOG. RESTRICTIONS: United States.

FINANCIAL DATA:
Amount of support per award: National Scholarships: $10,000 for first place; $5,000 for second place; $2,500 for third place; $1,500 for fourth place; $500 for fifth through eighth place.
Total amount of support: $21,000.

NO. MOST RECENT APPLICANTS: More than 4,600 for the year 2017.

NO. AWARDS: 8 annually.

APPLICATION INFO:
Two-dimensional art must be on paper or canvas. Water color, pencil, pastel, charcoal, tempera, crayon, acrylic, pen-and-ink, or oil may be used.

Art work must not be framed. Canvas entries must be submitted on stretcher frames or canvas board. Other entries must be matted on white. Other color mats must not be used. In matting, heavy paper must be used to reinforce back. Mounted and floating mats may also be used. The art should be no smaller than 8 x 10-inch, but no larger than 18 x 24-inch, not including mat.

Three-dimensional art can be paper, papier-mache, pottery, clay, metal work or fabric. Pieces should be no smaller than 8 x 24-inch in any direction. Art cannot be more than five pounds in weight.

Digital art, jewelry and photography is not accepted.

Applicant must be sure to complete entry form and to attach to back of entry. Submit a typed explanation of patriotism expressed in art (150 words or less).

Deadline: Student: Participants must submit entries to a local VFW Auxiliary Scholarships Chairman by March 31. Department: VFW Auxiliary or District entries must be received by the Department Scholarships Chairman by April 15. National: Department entries in the National Contest must be received at VFW Auxiliary VFW National Headquarters by May 5.

ADDRESS INQUIRIES TO:
Director of Programs and Communications
(See address above.)

*SPECIAL STIPULATIONS:
Only the first place department winner (from each state) is eligible for the national competition.

VIRGIN ISLANDS COUNCIL ON THE ARTS   [475]
5070 Norre Gade, Suite 1
St. Thomas, VI 00802-6762
(340) 774-5984
Fax: (340) 774-6206
E-mail: tasidakelch@yahoo.com
vicastt@hotmail.com
Web Site: www.vicouncilonarts.org

FOUNDED: 1966

AREAS OF INTEREST:
Fine arts, language and literature, music, creative, visual and performing arts and crafts.

NAME(S) OF PROGRAMS:
● **Expanding Opportunities for Participation in the Arts**

TYPE:
Awards/prizes; Exchange programs; General operating grants; Project/program grants; Residencies; Technical assistance; Training grants; Travel grants. Professional development artist or art teacher grants. Grants and technical assistance to individual artists, arts organizations and arts institutions in the Virgin Islands.

YEAR PROGRAM STARTED: 1966

PURPOSE:
To encourage wider participation in the arts by means of individual creative development and the strengthening of cultural organizations.

LEGAL BASIS:
Government agency.

ELIGIBILITY:
Applicants must be residents of the Virgin Islands for at least two years. Grants are made to Virgin Island-based projects or applicants.

GEOG. RESTRICTIONS: Virgin Islands.

FINANCIAL DATA:
Amount of support per award: Up to approximately $10,000. Organizations can receive a maximum of $10,000 and individuals can receive a maximum of $5,000.
Total amount of support: Depends on government, local and federal funding.
Matching fund requirements: The amount varies depending on category of grant. Usually 1:1.

NO. MOST RECENT APPLICANTS: Approximately 185 grant requests.

NO. AWARDS: Approximately 150 grants awarded.

REPRESENTATIVE AWARDS:
$10,000 to Reichhold Center for the Performing Arts.

APPLICATION INFO:
Official application information is available on the Council's web site.
Duration: One year. Renewable on reapplication and reconsideration by the Board of Directors.
Deadline: January 31 and August 31.

STAFF:
Tasida Kelch, Executive Director

ADDRESS INQUIRIES TO:
Jaria Lynch, Special Projects Coordinator
(See address above.)

VIRGINIA COMMISSION FOR THE ARTS   [476]
600 East Main Street, Suite 330
Richmond, VA 23219
(804) 225-3132
Fax: (804) 225-4327
Web Site: www.arts.virginia.gov

FOUNDED: 1968

AREAS OF INTEREST:
Arts activities including but not limited to performances, exhibitions, demonstrations, workshops, readings and other presentations or participatory experiences in the fields of crafts, dance, folk arts, literature, museum work, music, public media, theatre and visual arts, provided by artists or arts organizations located in the state of Virginia.

TYPE:
Fellowships; General operating grants; Project/program grants; Technical assistance. Touring grants; In-school, after-school residency arts programs; Arts programs for adults including aging, military and incarcerated individuals; Training programs for artists; Local government challenge grants; Arts and education grants; Cultural/arts tourism marketing program.

YEAR PROGRAM STARTED: 1968

PURPOSE:
To encourage participation and invest in the arts for all Virginians.

LEGAL BASIS:
State agency.

ELIGIBILITY:
Applicants must be nonprofit, tax-exempt organizations, schools or professional artists, government units.

GEOG. RESTRICTIONS: Virginia.

FINANCIAL DATA:
Amount of support per award: Varies.
Total amount of support: $3,704,210 for fiscal year 2019.
Matching fund requirements: Varies according to program.

NO. MOST RECENT APPLICANTS: Approximately 1,000 for fiscal year 2019.

NO. AWARDS: Approximately 740 for fiscal year 2019.

APPLICATION INFO:
Contact the Commission.
Duration: One year.
Deadline: March 1 and April 1 for most programs. Varies for other programs.

PUBLICATIONS:
Tour directory.

IRS I.D.: 54-0843105

ADDRESS INQUIRIES TO:
Executive Director
(See address above.)

VIRGINIA MUSEUM OF FINE ARTS   [477]
Art and Education Division
200 North Boulevard
Richmond, VA 23220-4007
(804) 204-2685
Fax: (804) 204-2675
E-mail: vmfafellowships@vmfa.museum
Web Site: www.vmfa.museum/fellowships

FOUNDED: 1940

AREAS OF INTEREST:
Education and careers in the visual arts.

NAME(S) OF PROGRAMS:
● **Professional Fellowship Program**
● **Student Fellowship Program**

TYPE:
Awards/prizes; Fellowships. Awards for undergraduate students, graduate students and professionals in the visual arts including painting, sculpture, crafts, photography, filmmaking, video, printmaking, mixed media, new/emerging media, and drawing. Art history is for graduate students only.

YEAR PROGRAM STARTED: 1940

PURPOSE:
To aid Virginians who seek financial aid for additional education or experience in the arts.

LEGAL BASIS:
State agency administering funds from an endowment and private foundations.

ELIGIBILITY:
All Applicants: Persons must be citizens or permanent residents of the U.S. and current legal residents of Virginia. A legal resident has a valid Virginia driver's license and/or pays income taxes in Virginia and/or is a registered Virginia voter. Applicants must be able to provide verification of residency upon request.

Student Applicants: Persons must be current legal residents of Virginia, and must have been legal residents for at least 12 consecutive months prior to the application deadline. Students paying in-state tuition to an accredited Virginia college, university or school of the arts qualify as legal residents of Virginia. Students must be enrolled full-time at an accredited college, university or school of the arts for the grant period of August 2020 to May 2021. Half-year fall semester Fellowship awards will be considered on a case-by-case basis for full-time students in the final year of a degree program who plan to graduate in December 2020.

Professional Applicants: Persons must be current legal residents of Virginia, and must have been legal residents for at least 24 consecutive months prior to the application deadline. Professional applicants must not be degree-seeking students at the time of the application deadline nor during the grant period of August 2020 to May 2021.

GEOG. RESTRICTIONS: Virginia.

FINANCIAL DATA:
Amount of support per award: Professional Fellowships: $8,000; Undergraduate Fellowships: $4,000; Graduate Fellowships: $6,000.

Total amount of support: $167,000 for the year 2019-20.

NO. MOST RECENT APPLICANTS: 753 for the year 2019-20.

NO. AWARDS: 28 for the year 2019-20.

APPLICATION INFO:
Contact the Museum or visit its web site.

Duration: August to May. No renewals.

Deadline: November 1, 2019. Notification in February 2020.

STAFF:
Sara Mazzullo, Fellowship Program Coordinator

ADDRESS INQUIRIES TO:
See e-mail address above.

*PLEASE NOTE:
Awards are made to applicants of highest artistic merit whose education and/or careers will benefit from financial assistance.

KURT WEILL FOUNDATION FOR MUSIC   [478]
7 East 20th Street, 3rd Floor
New York, NY 10003-1106
(212) 505-5240
Fax: (212) 353-9663
E-mail: bsansone@kwf.org
Web Site: www.kwf.org

FOUNDED: 1962

AREAS OF INTEREST:
The study and performance of music by Kurt Weill and Marc Blitzstein.

TYPE:
Grants-in-aid; Project/program grants; Research grants. College/University Performance: Grants to colleges and universities in support of general production expenses for performances of Kurt Weill's and Marc Blitzstein's stage works; grants are available to cover musical expenses in connection with performance of complete Weill and Blitzstein concert works.

Educational Outreach: Grants are awarded to performing and educational organizations which may request funding for educational activities (workshops, symposia, scholarly conferences, lectures in connection with performances, study days, secondary and college-level educational initiatives, etc.) focusing on Kurt Weill, Lotte Lenya and/or Marc Blitzstein, including payment of speakers' honoraria and travel expenses, preparation and printing of supporting materials, etc.

Publication Assistance: Grants assist in expenses related to preparing manuscripts for publication in a recognized scholarly medium, including editing, indexing, design and reproduction fees. Not-for-profit publishing companies are encouraged to apply.

Research and Travel: Grants support research and travel expenses to locations of primary source material for applicants who are researching a topic related to Kurt Weill, Lotte Lenya and/or Marc Blitzstein.

Kurt Weill Dissertation Fellowship: Assists Ph.D. candidates in Weill-research activities.

PURPOSE:
To preserve and perpetuate the legacies of composer Kurt Weill (1900-1950) and actress-singer Lotte Lenya (1898-1981).

ELIGIBILITY:
Broadcasts: Proposals are welcome from producers and not-for-profit broadcasters to support programs that feature Kurt Weill's or Marc Blitzstein's life and/or music. A complete description of the project must be accompanied by a written commitment from the broadcaster.

College/University Performance: Stage Works - All works must be presented in their authorized versions and orchestrations. Performances of *Die sieben Todsonden* are fundable only in Weill's original orchestration and keys. Concert works - Grants are available to cover musical expenses in connection with performance of complete Weill and Blitzstein concert works. Compilation properties consisting solely of Weill's or Blitzstein's songs do not qualify for support.

Educational Outreach: Performing and educational organizations may request funding for educational activities (workshops, symposia, scholarly conferences, lectures in connection with performances, study days, secondary and college-level educational initiatives, etc.) focusing on Weill, Lenya and/or Blitzstein, including payment of speakers' honoraria and travel expenses, preparation and printing of supporting materials, etc.

Professional Performance: Funding may be requested by professional opera companies, theater companies, dance companies and concert groups. All works must be presented in their authorized versions and orchestrations. Applicants must furnish evidence (recordings, reviews) of the artistic merit of the organization's previous performances. Compilation properties consisting solely of Weill's songs do not qualify for support.

Publication Assistance: Funds may be requested to assist in expenses related to preparing manuscripts for publication in a recognized scholarly medium, including editing, indexing, design and reproduction fees. Not-for-profit publishing companies are encouraged to apply. All proposals must have been subject to peer review. Normally conference proceedings are ineligible unless the essays have undergone significant revision and editing as components of a book.

Research and Travel: Applicants must be researching a topic related to Kurt Weill, Lotte Lenya and/or Marc Blitzstein.

Kurt Weill Dissertation Fellowship: Applicants must be writing their dissertation on a topic related to Kurt Weill.

Kurt Weill Mentors: Grants are awarded to aid in preparation of Weill or Blitzstein stage or concert performances, to present workshops or lectures or to participate in scholarly symposia; performing arts organizations and educational institutions may request support to engage performers, conductors, directors and scholars who have been designated "Weill Mentors" by the Kurt Weill Foundation. Such requests may be considered even when the relevant performances would not otherwise be eligible

for support under the Foundation's grant program. Applicants should contact the Foundation for further information.

FINANCIAL DATA:
Amount of support per award: Varies.

Total amount of support: Varies.

NO. MOST RECENT APPLICANTS: 20.

NO. AWARDS: Varies.

APPLICATION INFO:
All applications must include the following:
(1) Application Cover Sheet and Performance Grant Fact Sheet, if applying for a performance grant, available at the Foundation web site;
(2) a detailed description of the project;
(3) information about the applicant, including relevant qualifications and past achievements; performance grant applicants should also include a DVD or audio recording of a past performance and;
(4) a detailed and itemized budget specifying entire project expenses and income, including ticket revenue and income anticipated from other funding sources and date of determination. Applicants must notify the Foundation if other grants are awarded.

In addition, specific items are requested for each category:
Broadcasts: a complete description of the project must be accompanied by a written commitment from the broadcaster;
College/University Performance: applicants must furnish evidence (recordings, reviews) of the artistic merit of the organization's previous performances;
Educational Outreach: applications must include detailed description of the educational activities and vitae for expert participants;
Professional Performance: applicants must furnish evidence (recordings, reviews) of the artistic merit of the organization's previous performances;
Publication Assistance: all proposals must have been subject to peer review; such reviews must be submitted in support of the application, along with a copy of the manuscript;
Research and Travel: grant applicants must submit a detailed outline of the proposed project, a writing sample, and at least one letter of recommendation;
Weill Dissertation Fellowship: applicants must include a copy of the dissertation proposal, at least one writing sample, and two letters of recommendation, one of which must be from the applicant's faculty advisor.

Deadline: November 1 for the following calendar year, academic year or cultural season. Applications for support of major professional productions/festivals/exhibitions, etc., will be evaluated on a case-by-case basis without application or performance deadlines. An additional application deadline of June 1 has been established, limited exclusively to College/University Performance grants for productions taking place in the fall semester of the current academic year.

ADDRESS INQUIRIES TO:
Brady Sansone, Director
(See address above.)

WEST VIRGINIA DEPARTMENT OF ARTS, CULTURE AND HISTORY [479]

The Culture Center
State Capitol Complex
1900 Kanawha Boulevard East
Charleston, WV 25305-0300
(304) 558-0220
Fax: (304) 558-2779
E-mail: lance.e.schrader@wv.gov
Web Site: www.wvculture.org

FOUNDED: 1967

AREAS OF INTEREST:
Artists and arts organizations, including
community development, touring, institutions,
special projects and support for artists,
cultural facilities purchase and rehabilitation.

CONSULTING OR VOLUNTEER SERVICES:
Consultation in a variety of fields is
available.

TYPE:
Capital grants; Challenge/matching grants;
General operating grants; Internships;
Project/program grants; Residencies;
Technical assistance; Training grants; Travel
grants. Long-range planning. Individual
artists grants.

YEAR PROGRAM STARTED: 1967

PURPOSE:
To provide financial and technical assistance
to further the promotion, presentation and
development of the arts throughout the state
of West Virginia.

LEGAL BASIS:
Government agency.

ELIGIBILITY:
Nonprofit 501(c)(3) organizations and public
agencies may apply. Nonprofits must have
been based in West Virginia one year prior to
application. Individual artists must be
residents of West Virginia one year prior to
application.

GEOG. RESTRICTIONS: West Virginia.

FINANCIAL DATA:
Generally, grants cover 50% of project cost.
Amount of support per award: $125 to
$100,000.
Total amount of support: Approximately
$2,521,590 for the year 2017.
Matching fund requirements:
Dollar-for-dollar.

NO. MOST RECENT APPLICANTS: 60.

NO. AWARDS: 50.

APPLICATION INFO:
Copies of application guidelines and
application forms are available upon request
to the Commission or can be found on the
Division web site. Online applications are
preferred.
Duration: One year. Must reapply for
additional funding.
Deadline: Varies.

PUBLICATIONS:
Annual report; application guidelines;
ArtWorks, newsletter.

STAFF:
Randall Reid-Smith, Curator

ADDRESS INQUIRIES TO:
Lance E. Schrader, Arts Director
(See address above.)

WHITAKER FOUNDATION [480]

308 North 21st Street
Suite 400
St. Louis, MO 63103
(314) 241-4352
E-mail: info@thewhitakerfoundation.org
Web Site: www.thewhitakerfoundation.org

FOUNDED: 1975

AREAS OF INTEREST:
The arts, the use of and preservation of
parks.

TYPE:
Project/program grants. Project/program
grants are for urban parks and the arts.

PURPOSE:
To enrich lives through the arts; to encourage
the preservation and use of parks.

LEGAL BASIS:
Private foundation.

ELIGIBILITY:
Organizations must be tax-exempt 501(c)(3).
Project support is preferred. No support for
social events.

The Foundation does not make grants to
individuals.

GEOG. RESTRICTIONS: Metropolitan area of St.
Louis, Missouri.

FINANCIAL DATA:
Amount of support per award: Varies.
Total amount of support: $818,950 for the
year 2019.

NO. AWARDS: Approximately 20 for the year
2019.

APPLICATION INFO:
Application process begins with a Letter of
Inquiry, which must be submitted online.
Applicants, even those previously funded,
must call the Foundation in advance to
discuss their intent to apply.
Duration: Varies.
Deadline: Letters of Inquiry: August 1,
November 1 and February 1; Invited
Proposals: December 1, March 1 and
September 1, respectively.

PUBLICATIONS:
Guidelines.

ADDRESS INQUIRIES TO:
Christy Gray, Executive Director
(See address above.)

WISCONSIN ARTS BOARD [481]

201 West Washington Avenue
2nd Floor
Madison, WI 53703
(608) 266-0190
Fax: (608) 267-0380
E-mail: artsboard@wisconsin.gov
Web Site: artsboard.wisconsin.gov

FOUNDED: 1973

AREAS OF INTEREST:
All arts disciplines in Wisconsin.

CONSULTING OR VOLUNTEER SERVICES:
Workshops and individual consultations.

NAME(S) OF PROGRAMS:
● **Creation and Presentation**
● **Creative Communities**
● **Folk Arts Apprenticeship Program**
● **Wisconsin Regranting Program**

TYPE:
Challenge/matching grants; Internships;
Project/program grants; Technical assistance.

Inquiry services, research and funding.
Services provided to institutions and
individuals statewide in Wisconsin.

Creative Communities Grants include Arts in
Education, Local Arts and Folk Arts.

PURPOSE:
To provide support of arts projects and
activities in the state of Wisconsin.

LEGAL BASIS:
Agency of the state of Wisconsin.

ELIGIBILITY:
Applicants must be organizations located in
Wisconsin, operating for three years and have
501(c)(3) tax-exempt status.

GEOG. RESTRICTIONS: Wisconsin.

FINANCIAL DATA:
Amount of support per award: $1,500 to
$20,000 depending on the program.
Total amount of support: $1,259,810 for the
year 2018.
Matching fund requirements: All grants must
be matched.

NO. AWARDS: Varies.

APPLICATION INFO:
Application form is available online.
Duration: One year.
Deadline: Varies.

STAFF:
George Tzougros, Executive Director

ADDRESS INQUIRIES TO:
Karen Goeschko, Assistant Director
Programs and Services
(See address above.)

WOMEN IN FILM

4221 Wilshire Boulevard
Suite 130
Los Angeles, CA 90010
(323) 935-2211
Fax: (323) 935-2212
E-mail: mverdugo@wif.org
Web Site: womeninfilm.org/film-finishing-fund

TYPE:
Project/program grants. Awards for
completion of films on subjects that meet the
stated guidelines of WIF on an annual basis.

See entry 1003 for full listing.

WOMEN'S STUDIO WORKSHOP (WSW) [482]

722 Binnewater Lane
Kingston, NY 12401
(845) 658-9133
E-mail: info@wsworkshop.org
Web Site: www.wsworkshop.org

FOUNDED: 1974

AREAS OF INTEREST:
Book arts.

NAME(S) OF PROGRAMS:
● **Artists' Book Residency Grants**

TYPE:
Project/program grants; Residencies.

YEAR PROGRAM STARTED: 1979

PURPOSE:
To enable artists to produce a limited edition
artists' book while in residence at the
Women's Studio Workshop.

ELIGIBILITY:
Open to artists working in printmaking or the
book arts.

FINANCIAL DATA:
Amount of support per award: $350 per
week artist stipend, up to $750 materials, up
to $250 travel costs within the continental
U.S., access to all studios, and housing.

NO. MOST RECENT APPLICANTS: Approximately
100.

NO. AWARDS: 2.

APPLICATION INFO:
Application and instructions are available
online.
Duration: Eight to 10 weeks. Nonrenewable.
Deadline: November 15.

ADDRESS INQUIRIES TO:
Erin Zona, Artistic Director
(See address above.)

WOMEN'S STUDIO WORKSHOP (WSW) [483]
722 Binnewater Lane
Kingston, NY 12401
(845) 658-9133
Fax: (845) 658-9031
E-mail: info@wsworkshop.org
Web Site: www.wsworkshop.org

FOUNDED: 1974

AREAS OF INTEREST:
Art-in-education.

NAME(S) OF PROGRAMS:
● **Art-in-Education Artists' Book Residency Grant**

TYPE:
Residencies. With National Endowment for
the Arts (NEA) support, WSW awards two
eight-week residencies to artists in the book
arts. This is a residency grant.

PURPOSE:
To help grantees create new work while they
simultaneously teach young people through
the workshop's studio-based art-in-education
program.

ELIGIBILITY:
Open to artists working in printmaking or the
book arts.

FINANCIAL DATA:
Amount of support per award: $350 per
week stipend, $750 materials budget,
housing, travel costs up to $250 within the
continental U.S. and unlimited studio access.

APPLICATION INFO:
Application and instructions are available
online.
Duration: Eight to 10 weeks.
Deadline: November 15.

ADDRESS INQUIRIES TO:
Erin Zona, Artistic Director
(See address above.)

*PLEASE NOTE:
Normally, residencies are September to
October or January to April. Specific dates
are determined by the academic calendar and
vary annually.

WOMEN'S STUDIO WORKSHOP (WSW) [484]
722 Binnewater Lane
Kingston, NY 12401
(845) 658-9133
E-mail: info@wsworkshop.org
Web Site: www.wsworkshop.
org/residencies/studio-residency-grant

FOUNDED: 1974

AREAS OF INTEREST:
Visual artists.

NAME(S) OF PROGRAMS:
● **Studio Residency Grant**

TYPE:
Residencies.

YEAR PROGRAM STARTED: 1999

PURPOSE:
To provide artists with time and resources to
create a new body of work.

ELIGIBILITY:
Printmakers, papermakers, book artists,
ceramists, photographers or artist
collaborators can apply.

FINANCIAL DATA:
Amount of support per award: $350 per
week artist stipend, up to $500 for materials,
up to $250 for travel within the continental
U.S., plus housing and unlimited studio use.

NO. MOST RECENT APPLICANTS: Approximately
100.

NO. AWARDS: 2.

APPLICATION INFO:
All applications must be submitted through
the web site listed above. Application must
include:
(1) a current resume;
(2) a description of the project (100 to 200
words), including the studio the applicant
would prefer to work in;
(3) 10 images of recent work and;
(4) an image script, including title, medium,
dimension and date of each image.
Duration: Eight to 10 weeks. Nonrenewable.
Deadline: June 30.

ADDRESS INQUIRIES TO:
Erin Zona, Artistic Director
(See address above.)

THE HELENE WURLITZER FOUNDATION OF NEW MEXICO [485]
218 Los Pandos Road
Taos, NM 87571
(575) 758-2413
Fax: (575) 758-2559
E-mail: wurlitzerfoundation@gmail.com
Web Site: wurlitzerfoundation.org

FOUNDED: 1954

AREAS OF INTEREST:
Creative, not interpretive, work in all media
and allied fields.

TYPE:
Residencies. Residence grants for national
and international artists involved in creative
work, including writing, painting, sculpture
and musical composition.

YEAR PROGRAM STARTED: 1954

PURPOSE:
To encourage and stimulate creative work in
all media, including visual arts, literary arts
and musical composition.

LEGAL BASIS:
Tax-exempt under Section 501(c)(3) and
Section 4945(j)(3), (g)(3) and (g)(1).

ELIGIBILITY:
No restrictions are made on the basis of race,
sex, age or religious or ethnic background or
national origin.

FINANCIAL DATA:
No direct monetary grants are made.
Residences are located in Taos, NM and are
furnished with free utilities and rent.
Amount of support per award: Varies.
Total amount of support: Varies.

CO-OP FUNDING PROGRAMS: Robert Chesley
Foundation.

NO. MOST RECENT APPLICANTS: 475.

NO. AWARDS: 13.

APPLICATION INFO:
Application information is available on the
Foundation web site. Form may be completed
online or printed and mailed to the address
above.
Duration: 10 to 12 weeks, depending on the
session.
Deadline: January 18.

IRS I.D.: 85-0128634

OFFICERS AND BOARD OF DIRECTORS:
Peggy Nelson, President
Bill Ebie, Vice President
Michael Knight, Treasurer
Harald Hahn, Secretary
Nic Knight, Executive Director
Joseph Caldwell
Tito Naranjo
Rena Rosequist

ADDRESS INQUIRIES TO:
Nic Knight, Executive Director
(See address above.)

*SPECIAL STIPULATIONS:
Single occupancy only; no pets, no smoking,
no outside employment while in residence.

WYOMING ARTS COUNCIL [486]
2301 Central Avenue
Barrett Building, 2nd Floor
Cheyenne, WY 82002
(307) 214-7819
E-mail: karen.merklin@wyo.gov
Web Site: wyoarts.state.wy.us

FOUNDED: 1967

AREAS OF INTEREST:
Arts within the state of Wyoming.

NAME(S) OF PROGRAMS:
● **Blanchan/Doubleday Fellowships**
● **Community Support Grants**
● **Folk & Traditional Arts Mentoring Project Grants**
● **Pattie Layser Greater Yellowstone Creative Writing & Journalism Fellowship**
● **Literary Arts Fellowships**
● **Performing Arts Fellowships**
● **Professional Development/Career Advancement Grants**
● **Rural Arts Access Grants**
● **Visual Arts Fellowships**

TYPE:
Awards/prizes; Conferences/seminars;
Development grants; Fellowships; General
operating grants; Project/program grants;
Technical assistance. Individual fellowships
are provided in visual, literary and
performing arts to Wyoming residents.

Folk & Traditional Arts Mentoring Project
Grants are designed to support the
transmission of Wyoming's finest folk and
traditional skills through the natural process
of in-person, hands-on instruction from a
master artist to a worthy apprentice.

Pattie Layser Fellowship is a national call open to writers and journalists and seeks to intersect science, education, current events, and conservation to effectively communicate the Greater Yellowstone's natural history and singular importance to society through creative and exceptional writing and subject communication.

YEAR PROGRAM STARTED: 1967

PURPOSE:
To assist artistic programs of outstanding quality that serve the needs of Wyoming citizens, further public interest in the state's cultural heritage and resources and encourage artistic expression, essential for the well-being of the arts.

LEGAL BASIS:
Agency of the state of Wyoming.

ELIGIBILITY:
Grants are provided to 501(c)(3) nonprofit organizations, educational institutions and governmental entities within the state, including arts centers, museums, symphonies, schools, dance workshops, theatre and local arts councils. Individual artists may apply for the Blanche/Doubleday Fellowships, Folk & Traditional Arts Mentoring Project Grants, and Professional Development/Career Advancement Grants.

GEOG. RESTRICTIONS: Wyoming.

FINANCIAL DATA:
Amount of support per award: Varies.

Total amount of support: Varies.

Matching fund requirements: A one-to-one cash match is required on some grants.

NO. MOST RECENT APPLICANTS: More than 200.

NO. AWARDS: Over 200 grants are awarded each year.

APPLICATION INFO:
Apply online for most grant programs.

Duration: One fiscal year (July 1 to the following June 30).

Deadline: Varies.

PUBLICATIONS:
Newsletter.

STAFF:
Michael Lange, Executive Director
Rachel Clifton, Assistant Director
Karen Merklin, Grants Manager
Mary Billiter, Art Education Specialist
Kelsey Girous, Community Development and DEI Specialist
Taylor Craig, Creative Arts Specialist
Josh Chrysler, Folklorist and Health and Wellness Specialist
Brittany Perez, Public Outreach and Events Coordinator

ADDRESS INQUIRIES TO:
Karen Merklin, Grants Manager
(See address above.)

Performing arts

ACADEMY FOUNDATION OF THE ACADEMY OF MOTION PICTURE ARTS AND SCIENCES [487]

1313 North Vine Street
Los Angeles, CA 90028
(310) 247-3010
Fax: (310) 247-3794
E-mail: nicholl@oscars.org
Web Site: www.oscars.org/nicholl

FOUNDED: 1927

AREAS OF INTEREST:
Motion picture arts and sciences.

NAME(S) OF PROGRAMS:
- **The Academy Nicholl Fellowships in Screenwriting**

TYPE:
Awards/prizes; Fellowships. Awards provide a portion of living expenses for one year for promising new writers so that they may concentrate during that period on writing for the screen.

YEAR PROGRAM STARTED: 1985

PURPOSE:
To foster the development of the art of motion picture screenwriting.

LEGAL BASIS:
Nonpublic foundation.

ELIGIBILITY:
Applicants may not have earned more than $25,000 or any other consideration as a screenwriter for theatrical films or television or sold or optioned screen or television rights to any original story, treatment, outline screenplay or teleplay.

FINANCIAL DATA:
Amount of support per award: Up to $35,000 per year.

NO. MOST RECENT APPLICANTS: 7,302 for the year 2019.

NO. AWARDS: Up to 5 fellowships each year.

APPLICATION INFO:
Applicants must submit one copy of an original screenplay in PDF format, no shorter than 70 pages, and no longer than 160 pages in length, written in screenplay format standard to the U.S. motion picture industry. Submissions must have been written originally in English; translations will not be accepted. Submissions must be the original work of the applicant and may not be based, in whole or in part, on any other person's or persons' fictional or nonfictional material, published or unpublished, produced or unproduced. Sequels utilizing characters or storylines from produced motion pictures, television shows or published fiction are not eligible. Nor are adaptations eligible, unless the source material is solely the entrant's original work.

Applicants must also fill out an application form via an online account, completed in its entirety and pay a nonrefundable entry fee. This fee will be applied against judging and administrative costs. Applications and screenplays are accepted online only. Submitted materials will not be returned.

Duration: One year, commencing around the first week of November.

Deadline: Uploaded by 11:59 P.M., May 1. Announcement in late October.

PUBLICATIONS:
Guidelines.

ADDRESS INQUIRIES TO:
Academy Nicholl Fellowships
(See address above.)

*PLEASE NOTE:
Each fellowship is payable quarterly for one year. The first payment will be made at the start of the fellowship year. The second, third, fourth and final payments will be made subject to satisfactory progress of the recipient's work, as judged by the Academy's Nicholl Fellowship Committee. The Academy reserves the right to grant no awards if, in the opinion of the Academy Nicholl Fellowship Committee, no application is of sufficient merit.

*SPECIAL STIPULATIONS:
Academy Nicholl Fellowships may not be held concurrently with other fellowships. During the fellowship year, Academy Nicholl Fellows are expected to complete an original screenplay approximately 90 to 120 pages in length.

AMERICAN DANCE FESTIVAL [488]

Box 90772
Durham, NC 27708-0772
(919) 684-6402
Fax: (919) 684-5459
E-mail: adf@americandancefestival.org
Web Site: www.americandancefestival.org

NAME(S) OF PROGRAMS:
- **Tuition Scholarships**

TYPE:
Scholarships.

PURPOSE:
To offer assistance to promising students.

ELIGIBILITY:
Open to promising students who have a high level of technical ability, creative potential and who have experience in either performing and/or choreography.

GEOG. RESTRICTIONS: Primarily United States.

FINANCIAL DATA:
Amount of support per award: $200 to full tuition.

Total amount of support: Varies.

APPLICATION INFO:
Student must complete the online application and submit the $40 application fee. Each program has different scholarship process requirements. Refer to the scholarship web page located at www.americandancefestival.org/education/school.

Duration: Five-and-a-half weeks.

Deadline: Details are available on the web site.

ADDRESS INQUIRIES TO:
School Staff Administration
(See address above.)

AMERICAN SOCIETY FOR THEATRE RESEARCH (ASTR) [489]

P.O. Box 922
Santa Cruz, CA 95061
(628) 222-4088
Fax: (651) 290-2266
E-mail: info@astr.org
Web Site: www.astr.org

FOUNDED: 1956

AREAS OF INTEREST:

Theatre studies (history, criticism, theory), performance studies, and dance studies.

NAME(S) OF PROGRAMS:

- **The ASTR Collaborative Research Award**
- **ATHE-ASTR Award for Excellence in Digital Scholarship**
- **Biennial Sally Banes Publication Prize**
- **Oscar G. Brockett Essay Prize**
- **Cambridge University Press Prize**
- **Helen Krich Chinoy Dissertation Research Fellowships**
- **Co-sponsored Events Awards**
- **Selma Jeanne Cohen Conference Presentation Award**
- **Distinguished Scholar Award**
- **Grants for Researchers with Heavy Teaching Loads**
- **Barnard Hewitt Award**
- **Errol Hill Award**
- **Gerald Kahan Scholar's Prize**
- **David Keller Travel Grants**
- **Thomas F. Marshall Graduate Student Awards**
- **Brooks McNamara Publishing Subvention**
- **Research Fellowships**
- **Targeted Research Areas Grants**

TYPE:

Awards/prizes; Conferences/seminars; Development grants; Exchange programs; Fellowships; Research grants; Scholarships; Seed money grants; Travel grants; Visiting scholars. The ASTR Collaborative Research Award aims to foster the exchange of research across different academic and community contexts within the U.S. or between U.S. scholars/artists and those abroad. It also aims to foster long-term relationships benefiting faculty who work in different types of institutional environments and to foster the exchange of research in subject areas underrepresented in U.S. theatre scholarship, pedagogy, and performance practice.

ATHE-ASTR Award for Excellence in Digital Scholarship is awarded each year to an individual or team that demonstrates innovation and rigor in the use of electronic/digital media for the purpose of producing or disseminating knowledge about theatre and performance.

Biennial Sally Banes Publication Prize is presented in even-numbered years for the publication (book or essay) that best explores the intersections of theatre and dance/movement in the previous two calendar years.

Oscar G. Brockett Essay Prize is jointly awarded by the Society and the Oscar G. Brockett Center for Theatre History and Criticism at the University of Texas - Austin for the best essay published in English in a refereed scholarly journal or volume published by a scholarly press. The essay can relate to any subject in theatre research, broadly construed.

The Cambridge University Press Prize is given for a Society conference plenary paper written by a first-time plenary presenter.

Helen Krich Chinoy Dissertation Research Fellowships assist Ph.D. candidates with travel to national and international collections to conduct research connected with their dissertations.

Co-sponsored Events Awards assist with events that fulfill ASTR's purpose through collaboration with other organizations and institutions and increase the visibility of the work of both ASTR and the award recipient within a wider professional context.

Selma Jeanne Cohen Conference Presentation Award goes to a scholar to participate in a plenary or working session at the ASTR conference. The presentation must explore the intersections of theatre and dance/movement.

Distinguished Scholar Award is given each year to a scholar whose body of work has made a significant contribution to the field of theatre, dance, opera, and/or performance studies.

Grants for Researchers with Heavy Teaching Loads promote scholarly and practical exchange among theatre researchers by providing opportunities to faculty at institutions with heavy teaching loads and limited support for scholarship.

The Barnard Hewitt Award for Outstanding Research in Theatre History is awarded each year to the best book in "theatre history or cognate disciplines" published during the previous calendar year. The Department of Theatre at the University of Illinois, Urbana-Champaign, provides the monetary prize.

Errol Hill Award is given in recognition of outstanding scholarship in African American theatre, drama, and/or performance studies. The book or article must be published during the previous calendar year.

Gerald Kahan Scholar's Prize is awarded for the best essay written by a junior scholar and published in English in a refereed scholarly journal on any subject in theatre research, broadly construed.

David Keller Travel Grants encourage untenured scholars with terminal degrees to become active members of the Society by helping them to meet the expenses of attending the ASTR annual meeting in November.

Thomas F. Marshall Graduate Student Awards encourage active student membership in the Society by helping to meet the expenses of attending the ASTR annual meeting.

Brooks McNamara Publishing Subvention supports the costs of securing rights to reproduce illustrations for publication, costs of acquiring illustrations, and/or the costs of reproducing illustrations in conjunction with a book under contract for publication. (Electronic publications will also be considered.)

Research Fellowships underwrite some expenses associated with projects in the field of theatre and/or performance studies.

Targeted Research Areas Grants support specific projects in areas currently underrepresented. Such areas include, but are not limited to, pre-1900 research; Asian, African, Latin American, and Middle Eastern theatre, dance and performance. Translations of important theatre documents, including plays, are also considered.

YEAR PROGRAM STARTED: 1976

LEGAL BASIS:

Nonprofit learned society.

ELIGIBILITY:

The ASTR Collaborative Research Award: At least one participant from a host institution must be a current ASTR member.

ATHE-ASTR Award for Excellence in Digital Scholarship: The principal investigator should be a member of either ATHE or ASTR, but co-principal investigators need not all be members for the project to be considered.

Biennial Sally Banes Publication Prize: Any independent, tenured or untenured scholar; eligible books and articles must have been published in the previous two calendar years.

Oscar G. Brockett Essay Prize: Author must have been a member of ASTR for at least three years and be at least seven years beyond the Ph.D. Essays must have been published in the previous calendar year and may not have appeared elsewhere previously.

Cambridge University Press Prize: ASTR conference plenary paper written by a first-time plenary presenter.

Helen Krich Chinoy Dissertation Research Fellowships: Ph.D. candidates who have passed their qualifying exams within the last two years (or will have passed their qualifying exams by June of the current year) and have begun working on their dissertations. The project must be part of the dissertation research.

Co-sponsored Events Awards: Applications may come from individuals, institutions or a combination, to support events of regional, national or international significance in the form of conferences, colloquia, symposia, summits, etc. Events must foster scholarship on theatre and performance.

Selma Jeanne Cohen Conference Presentation Award: Tenured, untenured and contingent faculty, independent scholars and graduate students are eligible to apply.

Distinguished Scholar Award: Nominations are accepted from ASTR members and previous recipients of the award. In addition to contributions made to theatre, dance, opera and/or performance studies, involvement in ASTR is also a criterion of the award.

Grants for Researchers with Heavy Teaching Loads: Any full-time or contingent instructor at the college level, with a terminal degree and a heavy teaching load or the equivalent load based on heavy production and/or service obligations.

Barnard Hewitt Award: Eligible books must have been published in the previous calendar year. They must be written by a scholar or scholars residing in the Americas, or by a scholar or scholars located outside the Americas but writing on an American topic. Plays, edited collections and anthologies are not eligible for this prize.

Errol Hill Award: The book or article must have been published in the previous calendar year. Authors may nominate their own works; nominations from publishers and editors are also accepted.

Gerald Kahan Scholar's Prize: The author must be untenured and within seven years of the Doctorate, or must be enrolled in a doctoral program, at the time the essay is published.

David Keller Travel Grants: Any untenured scholars with terminal degrees, including independent scholars and tenure-track and adjunct faculty.

Thomas F. Marshall Graduate Student Awards: Any student majoring in theatre/performance studies in any academic department at any level of higher education.

Brooks McNamara Publishing Subvention: Any scholar holding a terminal degree and who has been a member of ASTR for at least three years. Applicant must hold a book contract to qualify. Preference is given to junior scholars.

Research Fellowships: Anyone who holds a terminal degree and has been a member of the Society for at least three years is eligible to apply.

Targeted Research Areas Grants: Any independent, tenured or untenured scholar who is currently a member of the Society and holds a terminal degree, or any graduate student who is applying in support of a project that is not directly related to her/his dissertation.

FINANCIAL DATA:
Amount of support per award: Varies.
Total amount of support: Varies.

NO. MOST RECENT APPLICANTS: Varies.

NO. AWARDS: 18.

APPLICATION INFO:
Application information is available on the web site, under "Awards."
Duration: Varies.
Deadline: Varies.

ADDRESS INQUIRIES TO:
Vice President for Awards
(See address above.)

ARTS MIDWEST   [490]
2908 Hennepin Avenue, Suite 200
Minneapolis, MN 55408-1954
(612) 341-0755
E-mail: christy@artsmidwest.org
Web Site: www.artsmidwest.org

FOUNDED: 1985

AREAS OF INTEREST:
Performing arts booking conference and performing arts grants to presenting organizations.

NAME(S) OF PROGRAMS:
• **Arts Midwest Conference**
• **Arts Midwest Touring Fund**

TYPE:
Conferences/seminars. Performing arts grants.

YEAR PROGRAM STARTED: 1985

PURPOSE:
To connect people throughout the Midwest and the world to meaningful arts opportunities, sharing creativity, knowledge, and understanding across boundaries.

LEGAL BASIS:
Nonprofit.

ELIGIBILITY:
Nonprofit performing arts presenters within our nine-state region.

GEOG. RESTRICTIONS: Illinois, Indiana, Iowa, Michigan, Minnesota, North Dakota, Ohio, South Dakota and Wisconsin.

FINANCIAL DATA:
Amount of support per award: Up to 20% of the artist's contracted fee, $500 to $4,000.
Total amount of support: Varies.

NO. MOST RECENT APPLICANTS: 180.

APPLICATION INFO:
Application information is available online. Only one application may be submitted.
Duration: Varies.
Deadline: April.

THE BANFF CENTRE   [491]
107 Tunnel Mountain Drive
Banff AB T1L 1H5 Canada
(403) 762-6180
Fax: (403) 762-6345
E-mail: registrars_office@banffcentre.ca
Web Site: www.banffcentre.ca/programs

FOUNDED: 1933

AREAS OF INTEREST:
Performing arts, literary, visual and new media arts.

TYPE:
Conferences/seminars; Residencies; Scholarships. Practicum.

PURPOSE:
To provide financial assistance to deserving artists for a residency at The Banff Centre.

ELIGIBILITY:
Open to advanced students who have been accepted for a program at The Banff Centre.

FINANCIAL DATA:
Amount of support per award: Varies.
Total amount of support: Varies depending on program.

APPLICATION INFO:
Application information can be accessed online. Applicants must submit a completed application form, accompanied by requested documentation.
Duration: Varies.
Deadline: Varies per program.

ADDRESS INQUIRIES TO:
Office of the Registrar
The Banff Centre
(See e-mail address above.)

CAPEZIO/BALLET MAKERS DANCE FOUNDATION, INC. [492]
One Campus Road
Totowa, NJ 07512
(973) 595-9000
Fax: (973) 595-9120
Web Site: www.capezio.com

FOUNDED: 1952

AREAS OF INTEREST:
National, state and some local dance profession service organizations. Annual Capezio Dance Award in recognition of significant contribution to the art form.

NAME(S) OF PROGRAMS:
• **Capezio Dance Award**
• **Grants Program**

TYPE:
Awards/prizes; Development grants; General operating grants; Project/program grants. Grants to national, state and some local dance service organizations such as dance alliances, dance festivals and other organizations having a major impact on the field.

Capezio Dance Award is given annually by the Trustees to an individual, company or organization that brings respect, stature and distinction to dance in America.

YEAR PROGRAM STARTED: 1952

PURPOSE:
To create a greater awareness and appreciation of dance as an art form and support efforts which service and increase interest in the dance field.

LEGAL BASIS:
Private tax-exempt, corporate foundation.

ELIGIBILITY:
National, state and local organizations that provide essential services to the dance field may apply. Organization must have 501(c)(3) status. No support for individual dancers, companies or schools.

GEOG. RESTRICTIONS: United States.

FINANCIAL DATA:
Amount of support per award: $1,000 to $10,000.
Total amount of support: $50,000 to $100,000.

NO. MOST RECENT APPLICANTS: 200.

NO. AWARDS: 50 to 70.

APPLICATION INFO:
Guidelines are available on the Foundation web site.
Duration: No limitations.
Deadline: April 1.

PUBLICATIONS:
Brochure of guidelines and criteria; listing of grantees and Capezio Award winners.

IRS I.D.: 13-6161198

*PLEASE NOTE:
Does not fund individuals, schools, colleges or universities, films or media or dance companies.

CHOPIN FOUNDATION OF THE U.S.
1440 79th Street Causeway, Suite 117
Miami, FL 33141
(305) 868-0624
Fax: (305) 865-5150
E-mail: info@chopin.org
Web Site: www.chopin.org

TYPE:
Scholarships. Scholarship program supporting young American pianists, 14 to 17 years of age.

See entry 705 for full listing.

MARTHA GRAHAM SCHOOL OF CONTEMPORARY DANCE, INC. [493]
55 Bethune Street, 11th Floor
New York, NY 10014
(212) 229-9200
Fax: (212) 202-7831
E-mail: info@marthagraham.org
jpatten@marthagraham.org
Web Site: marthagraham.edu

FOUNDED: 1926

AREAS OF INTEREST:
Training professional dancers.

NAME(S) OF PROGRAMS:
• **Accelerated Program**
• **Graham 2 Company**
• **Independent Program**
• **Summer Intensive**
• **Teacher Training Program**
• **Teens@Graham Young Artists Program**

- **Two-Year Certificate Program**
- **Winter Intensive**

TYPE:
Conferences/seminars; General operating grants; Internships; Matching gifts; Project/program grants; Research grants; Residencies; Scholarships; Work-study programs. Awards for class tuition.

Scholarship students work at the school.

YEAR PROGRAM STARTED: 1966

PURPOSE:
To provide help to the most promising dance students who are studying at the Martha Graham School.

LEGAL BASIS:
Nonprofit private school.

ELIGIBILITY:
Scholarships are available on a limited merit and need-based system. Scholarships are offered for Graham 2 Company members and understudies in the form of School Assistantships and through faculty-determined Program Director Scholarships. Scholarships require regular attendance.

Proficiency in dancing with special proficiency in the Martha Graham Technique is required. On-site scholarship auditions.

FINANCIAL DATA:
Amount of support per award: Graham 2: $1,500 per semester; Graham 2 Understudy and School Assistantships: $1,000 per semester; Program Director Scholarships: Varies.

Total amount of support: Varies.

NO. MOST RECENT APPLICANTS: 210.

NO. AWARDS: 24.

APPLICATION INFO:
Students are automatically considered as part of their program audition and application submission.

Duration: Normally awarded on a 12-month basis, on the basis of competition.

Deadline: Rolling admissions and international applicants: July 1.

IRS I.D.: 13-1834089

STAFF:
LaRue Allen, Executive Director
Jennifer Patten, Head of School
Tami Alesson, Dean of Students
Janet Eilber, Artistic Director

BOARD OF TRUSTEES:
Kenneth Bloom, Chairman
Inger Witter, President
Lorraine Oler, Secretary
LaRue Allen
Amy Blumenthal
Barbara Cohen
Janet Eilber
Merrie S. Frankel
Inga M. Golay
Sandra Harris
Emil Kang
Jayne Millard
Hooman Yazhari

ADDRESS INQUIRIES TO:
Jennifer Patten, Head of School
(See address above.)

JACOB'S PILLOW, INC. [494]

358 George Carter Road
Becket, MA 01223
(413) 243-9919
Fax: (413) 243-4744
E-mail: info@jacobspillow.org
Web Site: www.jacobspillow.org

FOUNDED: 1932

AREAS OF INTEREST:
Nurturing and sustaining artistic creation, presentation, education and preservation as well as engaging and deepening public appreciation and support for dance.

NAME(S) OF PROGRAMS:
- **The School at Jacob's Pillow**

TYPE:
Assistantships; Awards/prizes; Exchange programs; Fellowships; Residencies; Scholarships; Training grants; Visiting scholars. The School at Jacob's Pillow, one of the most prestigious and sought-after professional advancement training centers in the world, has four intensive programs: Ballet, Cultural Traditions, Contemporary and Musical Theatre Dance, all including awards/prizes/scholarships.

There are creative development residencies available.

PURPOSE:
To provide professional development training to advanced dancers in summer dance programs.

ELIGIBILITY:
Open to U.S. and foreign nationals who are 16 years of age or older and complete application requirements for the program(s) selected.

FINANCIAL DATA:
The School at Jacob's Pillow provides scholarships applicable toward tuition, room and board.

Amount of support per award: Varies.

Total amount of support: Varies.

NO. MOST RECENT APPLICANTS: 3,500.

NO. AWARDS: 100 per year.

APPLICATION INFO:
All dancers wishing to be considered for acceptance in The School's Summer Intensive Programs should follow their program-specific instructions and upload all required materials and videos to complete the online program application. To pre-register for a Master Class or Workshop, a program application must be submitted.

Duration: One to three weeks.

Deadline: March.

ADDRESS INQUIRIES TO:
See e-mail address above.

JACOB'S PILLOW, INC. [495]

358 George Carter Road
Becket, MA 01223
(413) 243-9919
Fax: (413) 243-4714
E-mail: info@jacobspillow.org
internprogram@jacobspillow.org
Web Site: www.jacobspillow.org

AREAS OF INTEREST:
Nurturing and sustaining artistic creation, presentation, education and preservation, as well as engaging and deepening public appreciation and support for dance.

NAME(S) OF PROGRAMS:
- **The Intern Program at Jacob's Pillow**

TYPE:
Internships. The Intern Program at Jacob's Pillow supports training in arts administration and technical theater production.

PURPOSE:
To provide real work projects and responsibilities that build practical experience and develop professional skills.

ELIGIBILITY:
Interested and engaged college students looking for professional advancement opportunities in arts administration may apply.

FINANCIAL DATA:
Amount of support per award: $1,500 stipend.

NO. MOST RECENT APPLICANTS: Approximately 311.

NO. AWARDS: Approximately 100.

APPLICATION INFO:
Online application form requires a cover letter explaining applicant's wish to intern at Jacob's Pillow, their qualifications and interests for the position(s) indicated on the application form, and their goals and expectations for the internship. A resume, two references, support materials, if requested, and a letter of recommendation are also required.

Duration: Up to three months.

Deadline: February.

ADDRESS INQUIRIES TO:
E-mail: internprogram@jacobspillow.org

NATIONAL OPERA ASSOCIATION, INC.

2403 Russell Long Boulevard
Canyon, TX 79016
(806) 651-2843
Fax: (806) 651-2958
E-mail: rhansen@noa.org
rhansen@wtamu.edu
Web Site: www.noa.org

TYPE:
Awards/prizes. Cash prizes awarded to Artist Division winners and Scholarship Division winners. Also scholarships to AIMS, awarded in both divisions. Productions of winning operas in Chamber Opera Competition will be scheduled for annual convention.

See entry 726 for full listing.

NEW DRAMATISTS [496]

424 West 44th Street
New York, NY 10036
(212) 757-6960
Fax: (646) 390-8705
E-mail: newdramatists@newdramatists.org
Web Site: www.newdramatists.org

FOUNDED: 1949

AREAS OF INTEREST:
Service organization for resident member playwrights. Work with resident member writers on new plays, providing them with workshops, readings and staged readings. Involves directors, actors and dramaturges, among other artists, in writer-led development work programming.

TYPE:
Awards/prizes; Internships; Residencies. Resident playwrights are selected by an

admissions panel which consists of current resident playwrights, alumni playwrights, and other theatre professionals. The panel changes completely from year to year.

YEAR PROGRAM STARTED: 1949

PURPOSE:
To provide playwrights with the tools and freedom to make lasting contributions to the theatre.

LEGAL BASIS:
Not-for-profit corporation.

ELIGIBILITY:
Open to U.S. citizens.

GEOG. RESTRICTIONS: United States.

NO. MOST RECENT APPLICANTS: 522 for the year 2018-19.

NO. AWARDS: 5 to 8 residencies per year.

APPLICATION INFO:
Information is available online.
Deadline: Varies.

PUBLICATIONS:
Application guidelines; brochure.

OFFICERS:
David C. Rosenzweig, Chairman
Abbie Van Nostrand, President

NEW MUSIC USA
90 Broad Street, Suite 1902
New York, NY 10004
(212) 645-6949
Fax: (646) 490-0998
E-mail: info@newmusicusa.org
Web Site: www.newmusicusa.org

TYPE:
Awards/prizes; General operating grants; Project/program grants; Residencies. The Impact Fund supports and promotes small, artist-driven ensembles, presenters, and venues in New York City.

Music Alive supports composer-in-residence positions in orchestras of all sizes.

Project Grants offer project-specific funding to individuals and organizations.

See entry 729 for full listing.

PEN AMERICA   [497]
588 Broadway, Suite 303
New York, NY 10012
(212) 334-1660 ext. 4813
Fax: (212) 334-2181
E-mail: awards@pen.org
Web Site: pen.org

FOUNDED: 1922

AREAS OF INTEREST:
American theater.

NAME(S) OF PROGRAMS:
● **PEN/Laura Pels International Foundation for Theater Award - Mid-Career Playwright**

TYPE:
Awards/prizes. Honors a midcareer playwright whose literary achievements are vividly apparent.

PURPOSE:
To honor the accomplishments of American playwrights.

ELIGIBILITY:
Candidates must be playwrights writing in English who have had a professional production of at least two full-length works

mounted in a theater of at least 299 seats and contracted specifically for either limited or open runs. Authors who have written only one-acts or books for musicals, or who have only translated the works of others for English-language audiences, will not be considered.

Candidates must be American citizens.

Candidates may be nominated by writers, playwrights, or members of the theater community. One need not be a PEN member to submit a nomination.

The works of writers produced by regional theaters across the U.S. will be given consideration equal to work produced in major metropolitan centers.

FINANCIAL DATA:
Amount of support per award: $10,000.
Total amount of support: $10,000.

NO. AWARDS: 1 annually.

APPLICATION INFO:
Any playwright, writer or member of the theater community may submit a nomination.
Deadline: August 15 of each year.

ADDRESS INQUIRIES TO:
See e-mail address above.

PEW FELLOWSHIPS AT THE PEW CENTER FOR ARTS & HERITAGE
1608 Walnut Street, 18th Floor
Philadelphia, PA 19103
(267) 350-4920
Fax: (267) 350-4997
E-mail: mfranklin@pewcenterarts.org
Web Site: www.pewcenterarts.org

TYPE:
Fellowships. Opportunities for contemporary artists in the Philadelphia five-county area to concentrate on the development and creation of art. Fellowships to support artists at critical junctures in any stage of their career development. Fellows will be expected to participate annually in at least three meetings with other fellowship recipients.

See entry 520 for full listing.

PRINCESS GRACE FOUNDATION-USA   [498]
150 East 58th Street, 25th Floor
New York, NY 10155
(212) 317-1470
E-mail: grants@pgfusa.org
Web Site: www.pgfusa.org

FOUNDED: 1982

AREAS OF INTEREST:
Theater, dance, choreography, film and playwriting.

NAME(S) OF PROGRAMS:
● **Princess Grace Awards**

TYPE:
Awards/prizes; Fellowships; Scholarships. Dedicated to identifying and assisting emerging artists in theater, dance and film through grants.

YEAR PROGRAM STARTED: 1984

PURPOSE:
To identify and assist emerging artists in the fields of dance, theater and film within the U.S.

LEGAL BASIS:
Not-for-profit, tax-exempt, publicly supported charity.

ELIGIBILITY:
Must be a U.S. citizen or permanent resident.

GEOG. RESTRICTIONS: United States.

FINANCIAL DATA:
Amount of support per award: Theater, Animation, Dance and Film Awards: $7,500 to $30,000 average; Playwrighting Award: $7,500; Choreography Awards: $10,000.
Total amount of support: More than $13,000,000 since inception.

NO. MOST RECENT APPLICANTS: Theater, animation, dance, choreography and film: 250; Playwrighting: 600.

NO. AWARDS: Over 800 since inception.

APPLICATION INFO:
All applicants, except playwrights, must be nominated by a school department chair/dean or company artistic director. The nominating organization must be a registered 501(c)(3). Detailed information is available online.
Duration: September 1 to August 31.
Deadline: Must be postmarked by March 31 for theater and playwriting; April 30 for animation, dance and choreography; June 1 for film.

PUBLICATIONS:
Fact sheet; mission statement; press releases; newsletter.

IRS I.D.: 23-2218331

OFFICERS:
Hon. John F. Lehman, Chairman
Robert O. Marx, Vice Chairman
Brisa Trinchero, Chief Executive Officer

ADDRESS INQUIRIES TO:
Diana Kemppainen, Program Director
(See address above.)

FOREST ROBERTS THEATRE   [499]
Northern Michigan University
1401 Presque Isle Avenue
Marquette, MI 49855-5364
(906) 227-2082
Fax: (906) 227-2567
E-mail: newplays@nmu.edu
wdigneit@nmu.edu
Web Site: www.nmu.edu/forestrobertstheatre

FOUNDED: 1977

AREAS OF INTEREST:
Performing arts and playwriting.

NAME(S) OF PROGRAMS:
● **Mildred and Albert Panowski Playwriting Award**

TYPE:
Awards/prizes.

YEAR PROGRAM STARTED: 1977

PURPOSE:
To encourage and stimulate artistic growth among educational and professional playwrights; to provide students with the creative opportunity to produce an original work on the university stage.

LEGAL BASIS:
Tax-exempt, nonprofit.

FINANCIAL DATA:
The award will include a spring or summer workshop reading of the play and fully mounted production in the subsequent production season, and a trip to Marquette to

act as Artist-in-Residence during the reading of the play and dress rehearsals leading to opening night of the show. Room and board will be provided. Conducting informal seminars and workshops will be a part of this residency. A professional dramaturge will respond to the script and work with the playwright and director.

Amount of support per award: $2,000.

NO. MOST RECENT APPLICANTS: 430.

NO. AWARDS: Generally 1 award in even-numbered years.

REPRESENTATIVE AWARDS:
Mark Rigney for "Bears;" David J. Swanson for "A Paper Tiger in the Rain."

APPLICATION INFO:
The contest has a different theme for each cycle. Applications are to be submitted online.

Duration: One year. Renewal possibilities on a biennial basis.

Deadline: Entries accepted in odd-numbered years only. Entries must be received on or before December 1 to be considered for the current theme. Winner will be announced within six months after the December 1 deadline.

PUBLICATIONS:
Brochure.

ADDRESS INQUIRIES TO:
Playwriting Coordinator
E-mail: wdigneit@nmu.edu

THE SHUBERT FOUNDATION, INC. [500]

234 West 44th Street
New York, NY 10036
(212) 944-3777
Fax: (212) 944-3767
Web Site: www.shubertfoundation.org

FOUNDED: 1945

AREAS OF INTEREST:
Arts-related organizations, dance, education and theatre.

TYPE:
General operating grants.

YEAR PROGRAM STARTED: 1945

PURPOSE:
To sustain and advance the live performing arts, in particular the American theatre and secondarily dance.

LEGAL BASIS:
Private foundation.

ELIGIBILITY:
The Foundation supports not-for-profit theatre and dance companies, as well as some arts-related organizations that assist in the development of the theatre. Applicants must be nonprofit organizations with Internal Revenue Code 501(c)(3) status. Organizations must submit audited financial statements. No grants to individuals.

GEOG. RESTRICTIONS: United States.

FINANCIAL DATA:
All grants cover general operating support only.

Amount of support per award: $10,000 to $325,000.

Total amount of support: $32,000,000 for the year 2019.

NO. AWARDS: 556 for the year 2019.

REPRESENTATIVE AWARDS:
$25,000 to Open Stage of Harrisburg, Harrisburg, PA; $225,000 to La Jolla Playhouse, La Jolla, CA; $250,000 to Manhattan Theatre Club.

APPLICATION INFO:
Grant requests must be submitted on the Foundation's Grant Portal. Organizations that have fully audited financial statements with an annual budget under $150,000 should contact the Foundation before making a formal application. Applications cannot be requested or submitted via e-mail.

Duration: One year. Renewal only with reapplication.

Deadline: December 2 for theatre category; October 15 for dance and other categories. Announcement in May each year.

PUBLICATIONS:
Annual report with application guidelines.

OFFICERS:
Philip J. Smith, Chairman of the Board
Diana Phillips, President
Wyche Fowler, Jr.
Richard J. Poccia
Lee J. Seidler
Stuart Subotnick
Robert E. Wankel

ADDRESS INQUIRIES TO:
Vicki Reiss, Executive Director
(See address above.)

WAGNER COLLEGE [501]

Wagner College Theater
One Campus Road
Staten Island, NY 10301
(718) 390-3223
E-mail: diane.catalano@wagner.edu
Web Site: wagner.edu/theatre/stanley-drama

FOUNDED: 1957

AREAS OF INTEREST:
Playwriting.

NAME(S) OF PROGRAMS:
● **Stanley Drama Award**

TYPE:
Awards/prizes; Project/program grants. Annual award for the best play or musical submitted to the competition.

YEAR PROGRAM STARTED: 1957

PURPOSE:
To call attention to and encourage new playwrights.

LEGAL BASIS:
University.

ELIGIBILITY:
The Award is offered for an original full-length play, musical or one-act play sequence that has not been professionally produced or received trade book publication. Writers of musicals are urged to submit music on tape or CD.

The Stanley Award competition will consider only one submission per playwright. Plays entered previously in the competition may not be resubmitted. Former Stanley Award winners are not eligible to compete.

FINANCIAL DATA:
Amount of support per award: $2,000.

NO. MOST RECENT APPLICANTS: 100.

NO. AWARDS: 3 (1 winner, 2 finalists).

APPLICATION INFO:
Applications may be obtained by sending a self-addressed, stamped envelope to the address above or on the web site. All scripts must be accompanied by a completed application. A reading fee of $30 must accompany the manuscript.

Deadline: October 31. Announcement the following March.

PUBLICATIONS:
Application guidelines.

ADDRESS INQUIRIES TO:
Diane Catalano
Stanley Drama Award
(See address above.)

*SPECIAL STIPULATIONS:
Previous winners are ineligible.

THE LOREN L. ZACHARY SOCIETY FOR THE PERFORMING ARTS

2250 Gloaming Way
Beverly Hills, CA 90210-1717
(310) 276-2731
Fax: (310) 275-8245
E-mail: infoz@zacharysociety.org
Web Site: www.zacharysociety.org

TYPE:
Awards/prizes.

See entry 742 for full listing.

Fine arts

ACADEMY FOUNDATION OF THE ACADEMY OF MOTION PICTURE ARTS AND SCIENCES [502]

1313 North Vine Street
Los Angeles, CA 90028
(310) 247-3000
E-mail: sguthrie@oscars.org
Web Site: www.oscars.org

AREAS OF INTEREST:
Filmmakers.

NAME(S) OF PROGRAMS:
● **Student Academy Awards Competition**

TYPE:
Awards/prizes.

PURPOSE:
To recognize outstanding achievements in student filmmaking; to support and encourage filmmakers with no previous professional experience who are enrolled in accredited colleges and universities.

ELIGIBILITY:
To be eligible, the filmmaker must be a full-time student at an accredited U.S. college, university, film school or art school. The film must have been made in a teacher-student relationship within the curricular structure of that institution. The film must be in one of the following categories: Alternative, Animated, Documentary and Narrative.

FINANCIAL DATA:
Amount of support per award: $5,000 Gold Award, $3,000 Silver Award, and $2,000 Bronze Award.

NO. MOST RECENT APPLICANTS: 1,587.

NO. AWARDS: Approximately 17.

APPLICATION INFO:
Nominees are selected by Academy members.

Deadline: June 1.

ADDRESS INQUIRIES TO:
Shawn Guthrie
Student Academy Awards and Grants Manager
(See address above.)

AMERICAN ORIENTAL SOCIETY [503]

Hatcher Graduate Library
University of Michigan
Ann Arbor, MI 48109-1190
(734) 747-4760
E-mail: jrodgers@umich.edu
Web Site: www.americanorientalsociety.org

FOUNDED: 1842

AREAS OF INTEREST:
Archaeology, fine arts, history, philosophy, language, literature, religion and theology.

NAME(S) OF PROGRAMS:
- **Louise Wallace Hackney Fellowship**

TYPE:
Fellowships. Fellowship for the study of Chinese art with special relation to painting.

YEAR PROGRAM STARTED: 1946

PURPOSE:
To encourage basic research in the languages and literatures of Asia.

LEGAL BASIS:
Nonprofit.

ELIGIBILITY:
Graduate students who have successfully completed at least three years of Chinese language study at a recognized university and have some knowledge or training in art. Students must have completed all requirements for the Ph.D. except research, travel and the written dissertation. Applicants should have the sponsorship of recognized scholars in the fields of Chinese language and culture.

U.S. citizenship is required.

GEOG. RESTRICTIONS: United States.

FINANCIAL DATA:
Amount of support per award: $8,000.
Total amount of support: $8,000 annually.

NO. MOST RECENT APPLICANTS: Approximately 3.

NO. AWARDS: 1 annually.

APPLICATION INFO:
Applicants should submit the following materials in duplicate:
(1) a transcript of their undergraduate and graduate course work;
(2) a statement of personal finances;
(3) a three- or four-page summary of the proposed project to be undertaken during the year of the fellowship award, appended with a financial statement explaining expenses involved in this study and;
(4) no less than three letters of recommendation.

Any scholarly papers or published materials in the area of Chinese painting are welcome along with the other application materials.

Duration: 12 months, July to June. Renewals of appointment are possible but not usually considered.

Deadline: Applications should be submitted no later than March 1. Announcement in May.

PUBLICATIONS:
Application guidelines.

DIRECTORS AND OFFICERS:
Jonathan Rodgers, Secretary and Treasurer
Stephanie W. Jamison, Editor

ADDRESS INQUIRIES TO:
Jonathan Rodgers, Secretary and Treasurer
(See address above.)

BRUCEBO FINE ART SCHOLARSHIP FOUNDATION [504]

Concordia University
1455 De Maisonneuve Boulevard West
Montreal QC H3G 1M8 Canada
(514) 848-2424 ext. 4600
E-mail: fineartsresearch@concordia.ca
Web Site: www.bruceboscholarships.ca
www.concordia.ca/finearts

FOUNDED: 1971

AREAS OF INTEREST:
Promotion of fine arts; Canada-Sweden relationships; artist residencies.

CONSULTING OR VOLUNTEER SERVICES:
Evaluation Committee members provide free services.

NAME(S) OF PROGRAMS:
- **W.B. Bruce European Fine Art Travel Scholarship**
- **Brucebo Fine Art Summer Residency Scholarship**

TYPE:
Development grants; Research grants; Residencies; Scholarships; Travel grants. Grant principally in the fields of fine arts, visual art and design. Grant is either for stay at the Brucebo Studio on the Island of Hanseatic Gotland, Sweden, in the Baltic Sea, for three months during the summer annually, or for undertaking a European Fine Art Travel-Study journey.

YEAR PROGRAM STARTED: 1971

PURPOSE:
To support talented Canadian fine arts graduated students and fine arts practitioners, B.F.A. or M.F.A. persons, in the emerging years of their respective careers.

LEGAL BASIS:
Private.

ELIGIBILITY:
Scholarships are granted through competitions, based on academic merit, to full-time students pursing a Master's or doctorate degree in the Faculty of Fine Arts at Concordia University nearing the completion of their degrees. Degree holders include those with a research-creation studio-based practice, including M.A., M.F.A, M.Des., as well as the M.A./Ph.D. Individualized Program and the Interdisciplinary Ph.D. Program, with a primary supervisor in the Faculty of Fine Arts. Performance-based art practices are not eligible for consideration unless they are undertaken within the context of contemporary visual arts practices and form a minority of the applicant's practice.

Scholarships are open to Canadian citizens and permanent residents only.

GEOG. RESTRICTIONS: Europe, with specific reference to the Nordic countries and Baltic Rim (coastal corridor).

FINANCIAL DATA:
Amount of support per award: Travel Scholarship: $5,000 (CAN); Summer Residency Scholarship: $7,500 (CAN).
Total amount of support: $12,500 (CAN).

NO. MOST RECENT APPLICANTS: Approximately 70.

NO. AWARDS: 1 per award.

APPLICATION INFO:
Application form and guidelines can be found on the Faculty of Arts web site.
Duration: Three months. Nonrenewable.
Deadline: March 9.

PUBLICATIONS:
Research reports.

ADDRESS INQUIRIES TO:
Interim Research Coordinator
Faculty of Studio Arts
Concordia University
(See address and e-mail above.)

*SPECIAL STIPULATIONS:
Canadian citizens and permanent residents only. Recipient submits a report on his or her activities engaged in after return to Canada.

THE CENTER FOR PHOTOGRAPHY AT WOODSTOCK [505]

59 Tinker Street
Woodstock, NY 12498
(845) 679-9957
E-mail: info@cpw.org
Web Site: www.cpw.org

FOUNDED: 1977

AREAS OF INTEREST:
Photography.

NAME(S) OF PROGRAMS:
- **Art Administration Interns**
- **Woodstock A-I-R**

TYPE:
Project/program grants; Residencies; Work-study programs. Woodstock A-I-R is a residency program for artists of color working in the photographic arts.

PURPOSE:
To support artists working in photography and related media and engaging their audiences through opportunities in which creation, discovery and learning are made possible.

LEGAL BASIS:
Not-for-profit arts and educational organization.

FINANCIAL DATA:
Amount of support per award: Varies.

CO-OP FUNDING PROGRAMS: The Center receives funds from the National Endowment for the Arts and the New York State Council on the Arts and has received grants from IBM and the New York Council for the Humanities, The Avery Foundation, Eastman Kodak, Canon, U.S.A. and Andy Warhol Foundation.

NO. AWARDS: Art Administration Interns: Up to 4 seasonally; Woodstock A-I-R: 8.

APPLICATION INFO:
Application information can be found on the web site.

IRS I.D.: 14-1592639

OFFICERS:
Hannah Frieser, Executive Director

ADDRESS INQUIRIES TO:
See e-mail address above.

DALLAS MUSEUM OF ART [506]

1717 North Harwood
Dallas, TX 75201
(214) 922-1334
Fax: (214) 922-1354
E-mail: a2a@dma.org
Web Site: dma.org/about/awards-artists

FOUNDED: 1903

AREAS OF INTEREST:
Contemporary art.

NAME(S) OF PROGRAMS:
● **Clare Hart DeGolyer Memorial Fund**

TYPE:
Awards/prizes.

YEAR PROGRAM STARTED: 1980

PURPOSE:
To support younger, emerging visual artists
who reside in the southwestern part of the
U.S.

LEGAL BASIS:
Nonprofit, tax-exempt arts organization.

ELIGIBILITY:
Applicants must be between 15 and 25 years
of age, have lived in the southwestern part of
the U.S. (Arizona, Colorado, New Mexico,
Oklahoma and Texas) for the past three years
and currently reside there.

Grants are not available for college or art
school tuition.

GEOG. RESTRICTIONS: Arizona, Colorado, New
Mexico, Oklahoma and Texas.

FINANCIAL DATA:
Amount of support per award: Maximum
$1,500.

NO. MOST RECENT APPLICANTS: 25.

NO. AWARDS: 3 to 5.

APPLICATION INFO:
Applications must be submitted via the
online form.
Deadline: January 31. Notification by March
or April.

PUBLICATIONS:
Bimonthly *DMAgenda*; permanent collection
and exhibition catalogues.

ADDRESS INQUIRIES TO:
Awards to Artists
(See address above.)

DALLAS MUSEUM OF ART [507]

1717 North Harwood
Dallas, TX 75201
(214) 922-1334
Fax: (214) 922-1354
E-mail: a2a@dma.org
Web Site: dma.org/about/awards-artists

FOUNDED: 1903

AREAS OF INTEREST:
Contemporary art.

NAME(S) OF PROGRAMS:
● **Arch and Anne Giles Kimbrough Fund**

TYPE:
Awards/prizes. Direct grants to artists.

YEAR PROGRAM STARTED: 1980

PURPOSE:
To support younger, emerging visual artists in
Texas.

LEGAL BASIS:
Nonprofit, tax-exempt arts organization.

ELIGIBILITY:
Applicants must be under 30 years of age,
have lived in Texas for the past three years
and currently reside there.

GEOG. RESTRICTIONS: Texas.

FINANCIAL DATA:
Amount of support per award: Maximum
$3,500.

NO. MOST RECENT APPLICANTS: 35.

NO. AWARDS: 3 to 5.

APPLICATION INFO:
Applications must be submitted via the
online form.
Deadline: January 31. Notification by March
or April.

PUBLICATIONS:
Bimonthly *DMAgenda*; permanent collection
and exhibition catalogues.

ADDRESS INQUIRIES TO:
Awards to Artists
(See address above.)

DALLAS MUSEUM OF ART [508]

1717 North Harwood
Dallas, TX 75201
(214) 922-1334
Fax: (214) 720-0862
E-mail: a2a@dma.org
Web Site: dma.org/about/awards-artists

FOUNDED: 1903

AREAS OF INTEREST:
Art. Collections include contemporary art,
Pre-Columbian, Asian, African, American
and European painting and sculpture,
decorative arts and textiles.

NAME(S) OF PROGRAMS:
● **Otis and Velma Davis Dozier Travel
Grant**

TYPE:
Awards/prizes; Travel grants.

YEAR PROGRAM STARTED: 1990

PURPOSE:
To recognize exceptional talent in
professional artists who wish to expand their
artistic horizons through domestic or foreign
travel.

LEGAL BASIS:
Nonprofit, tax-exempt arts organization.

ELIGIBILITY:
Artists eligible for the grant must be
practicing professionals, be 30 years of age
or older, have lived in Texas for the past
three years and be currently living in Texas.
Financial need will be given consideration
but will not be the determining factor in
making the awards.

GEOG. RESTRICTIONS: Texas.

FINANCIAL DATA:
Amount of support per award: Varies.
Total amount of support: Varies.

NO. MOST RECENT APPLICANTS: 40 annually.

NO. AWARDS: 1 or 2.

APPLICATION INFO:
Applications must be submitted via the
online form.

Deadline: January 31. Notification by March
or April.

PUBLICATIONS:
Bimonthly *DMAgenda*; permanent collection
and exhibition catalogues.

ADDRESS INQUIRIES TO:
Awards to Artists
(See address above.)

FINE ARTS WORK CENTER IN PROVINCETOWN [509]

24 Pearl Street
Provincetown, MA 02657
(508) 487-9960
Fax: (508) 487-8873
E-mail: info@fawc.org
sblood@fawc.org
Web Site: www.fawc.org

FOUNDED: 1968

AREAS OF INTEREST:
Visual arts and creative writing.

NAME(S) OF PROGRAMS:
● **Visual Arts Fellowship**
● **Writing Fellowship**

TYPE:
Fellowships; Residencies.

YEAR PROGRAM STARTED: 1968

PURPOSE:
To offer opportunities to emerging artists and
writers.

LEGAL BASIS:
Nonprofit corporation.

ELIGIBILITY:
Fellowships are offered to selected writers
and visual artists. Applicants must be in the
emerging phase of their careers and must
demonstrate significant talent and
commitment.

Applicants must be individuals (visual artists
and creative writers) who have spent time
working on their own and have created a
considerable body of work which can be
presented in the form of slides or manuscript.

FINANCIAL DATA:
In addition to the stipend, fellows are
provided with an apartment and studio in
Provincetown, MA, and have the support of a
resident staff. Each residency includes private
living and/or working studio in
Provincetown, MA.
Amount of support per award: Stipend of
$1,000 per month and $1,000 at departure.
Total amount of support: $16,000.

NO. MOST RECENT APPLICANTS: 1,400.

NO. AWARDS: 20.

APPLICATION INFO:
Applicants must apply through the online
portal. Application fee is $45.
Duration: Seven months, October 1 to April
30.
Deadline: Writers: December 1. Visual Arts:
February 1. Announcement by May 15.

PUBLICATIONS:
Shankpainter, online literary magazine.

OFFICERS OF THE TRUSTEES:
Ted Chapin, Co-Chairperson
Marty Davis, Co-Chairperson
Margaret Murphy, President
Michael Cunningham, First Vice President
Allison Nichols Ferring, Second Vice
President

ADDRESS INQUIRIES TO:
Susan Blood, Grant Writer
(See address above.)

*SPECIAL STIPULATIONS:
Fellowships are reserved for emerging writers and visual artists.

J. PAUL GETTY TRUST, GETTY FOUNDATION [510]

1200 Getty Center Drive
Suite 800
Los Angeles, CA 90049-1685
(310) 440-7320
Fax: (310) 440-7703
E-mail: gettyfoundation@getty.edu
Web Site: www.getty.edu/foundation

FOUNDED: 1984

AREAS OF INTEREST:
Strengthening art history as a global discipline, promoting the interdisciplinary practice of conservation, increasing access to museums and archival collections, and developing current and future professionals and leaders.

TYPE:
Conferences/seminars; Fellowships; Internships; Project/program grants; Research grants; Training grants.

YEAR PROGRAM STARTED: 1984

PURPOSE:
To advance the understanding and preservation of the visual arts locally and throughout the world.

ELIGIBILITY:
Requirements vary according to grant category. Individuals at the undergraduate and graduate level may be eligible to apply for internships. Eligibility for all other grant categories is limited to nonprofit organizations.

Generally, grants are not made for operating or endowment purposes, for construction or maintenance of buildings or for acquisition of works of art.

FINANCIAL DATA:
Amount of support per award: Varies.
Total amount of support: $9,700,000 for the year 2018.

NO. MOST RECENT APPLICANTS: Approximately 1,300 for fiscal year 2018.

NO. AWARDS: 178 for the year 2018.

REPRESENTATIVE AWARDS:
$135,000 to Max Weber Stiftung-Deutsche Geisteswissenschaftliche Institute im Ausland, Bonn, Germany, for the research seminar "Paris - Capital of Modernity" for Chinese scholars in Paris, France; $89,000 to AAMC Foundation, New York, NY, for "The Networked Curator: a Pilot Program of Digital Training for Museum Curators;" $195,000 to Instituto Lina Bo e P.M. Bardi, Sao Paulo, Brazil, for the preparation of a conservation management plan for Lina Bo Bardi's Casa de Vidro; $240,000 to University of Southern California Annenberg School for Communication and Journalism, Los Angeles, CA, for "Musical Interventions," a series of music events and an accompanying publication in conjunction with Pacific Standard Time: L.A./L.A.; $44,000 to Los Angeles County Arts Commission, Los Angeles, CA, for educational programming related to the 2016 Arts Internship Program.

APPLICATION INFO:
Funding priorities and application information are available on the Foundation web site.
Duration: Varies. Typically one to three years, depending upon the grant category.
Deadline: Varies.

PUBLICATIONS:
Annual report of J. Paul Getty Trust.

IRS I.D.: 95-1790021

OFFICERS:
Deborah Marrow, Director, The Getty Foundation
Joan Weinstein, Deputy Director
Katie Underwood, Assistant Director

ADDRESS INQUIRIES TO:
The Getty Foundation
(See address above.)

ADOLPH AND ESTHER GOTTLIEB FOUNDATION, INC. [511]

380 West Broadway
New York, NY 10012
(212) 226-0581
Fax: (212) 274-1476
E-mail: sross@gottliebfoundation.org
Web Site: www.gottliebfoundation.org

FOUNDED: 1976

AREAS OF INTEREST:
Visual artists.

NAME(S) OF PROGRAMS:
● **Emergency Grant Program**
● **Individual Support Program**

TYPE:
Grants-in-aid. Emergency Grant Program provides cash award to mature creative painters, sculptors and printmakers who are experiencing financial hardship resulting from a current or recent emergency.

Individual Support Program was designed to encourage those artists who have dedicated their lives to developing their art, regardless of their level of commercial success.

YEAR PROGRAM STARTED: 1984

PURPOSE:
To provide interim financial assistance to qualified artists during times of emergencies (such as fire, flood, medical or other unexpected, catastrophic events), or to provide financial assistance as an encouragement to artists who have dedicated their lives to developing their art.

LEGAL BASIS:
Nonprofit corporation.

ELIGIBILITY:
Emergency Grant Program: Applicant must be able to demonstrate a minimum involvement of 10 years in a mature phase of his or her work as a creative painter, sculptor or printmaker and his or her need must result from current or recent emergency beyond the artist's usual circumstances (medical, fire, flood, etc.). This Program does not consider requests for dental work, chronic situations, capital improvements, or projects of any kind; nor can it consider situations resulting from general indebtedness or lack of employment.

Individual Support Program: Applicant will be able to demonstrate work in a mature phase of his or her art for at least 20 years. Eligibility is also determined by applicant's

current financial need. The Foundation does not provide funding for organizations, projects of any type, educational institutions, students, graphic artists, or those working in crafts. The disciplines of photography, film, video or related forms are not eligible unless the work directly involves, or can be interpreted as, painting, printmaking or sculpture.

FINANCIAL DATA:
Amount of support per award: Emergency Grant Program: Maximum $15,000; typical amount is $5,000. Individual Support Program: $25,000.
Total amount of support: $300,000 per program.

NO. AWARDS: Individual Support Grants: 12.

APPLICATION INFO:
Emergency Grant Program: Application forms are available online.

Individual Support Program: Application forms are available online in early September.
Deadline: Emergency Grant Program: Available throughout the year, as budget permits. Individual Support Program: December 15.

PUBLICATIONS:
Information brochure.

BOARD OF DIRECTORS:
Sanford Hirsch, Executive Director
Lynda Benglis
Charlotta Kotik
Robert Mangold
Gordon Marsh
Brooke Rapaport

ADDRESS INQUIRIES TO:
Sheila Ross, Grants Manager
(See address above.)

*SPECIAL STIPULATIONS:
The Emergency Grant Program is to assist individuals in emergency situations only.

THE ELIZABETH GREENSHIELDS FOUNDATION [512]

1814 Sherbrooke Street West
Montreal QC H3H 1E4 Canada
(514) 937-9225
E-mail: info@greenshieldsfoundation.ca
Web Site: www.
elizabethgreenshieldsfoundation.org

FOUNDED: 1955

AREAS OF INTEREST:
Painting, drawing, printmaking and sculpture.

NAME(S) OF PROGRAMS:
● **The Elizabeth Greenshields Foundation Grant**

TYPE:
Grants for artists.

YEAR PROGRAM STARTED: 1955

PURPOSE:
To provide financial assistance, by way of grants, to young artists who are pursuing their studies or are in the early or developmental stage of their career, are working in a representational style of painting, drawing, sculpture or printmaking, and demonstrate the determination and talent to pursue a lifetime career in their art practice.

LEGAL BASIS:
Charitable foundation.

ELIGIBILITY:

Applicants must be pursuing their studies or be in the early or development stage of their career and demonstrate the determination and talent to pursue a lifetime career in their art practice. Only those applicants who work in a representational style of painting, drawing, sculpture or printmaking will be considered. No other artistic activities or disciplines are funded. In particular, illustration, graphic design, photography, animation, video art, film, digital art, crafts, decorative arts, any work that uses a photograph or digital image as the principal medium or that is produced using computer software or graphics, and any work or activity that falls primarily into any of the foregoing categories, are not eligible for a grant. The Foundation does not provide funding for the pursuit of abstract or non-objective art.

Applicants must be at least 18 years of age and no older than 41 years of age.

The Foundation has no geographic, citizenship or residency requirements.

Applicants must be individuals applying on their own behalf. Artistic groups, collectives and organizations are not eligible.

FINANCIAL DATA:

Amount of support per award: First grants are in the amount of $15,000 (CAN) each. Subsequent grants are in the amount of $18,000 (CAN) each (maximum of three grants per artist). The Foundation reserves the right to award grants in other amounts and to disburse funds in whole or in part, as it deems advisable. Grants are made directly to the beneficiaries, not through other organizations.

APPLICATION INFO:

Candidates may only access the application by creating an account and completing an eligibility questionnaire on the Foundation's web site. Applications must be completed and submitted online. Applications submitted in any other manner, including e-mail, mail or otherwise, will not be accepted.

The material and documents required to apply include:
(1) government issued photo identification and proof of citizenship, current address and date of birth;
(2) images of six representative works (no more or less) produced in the last two years. These must be original works produced by the applicant alone;
(3) if the applicant is applying to further his or her art education or training, proof of acceptance or enrollment from the institution where he or she intends to study or train;
(4) a description of the proposed work, project or course of study or training that the applicant intends to undertake with a grant from the Foundation;
(5) a brief artist statement relating to the applicant's previous and current work;
(6) a budget for the proposed work, project, or course of study or training described in the applicant's Artistic Proposal and;
(7) a letter of reference from a teacher or professor, an artist or curator who is familiar with both the applicant and the applicant's work and is able to support his or her application.

All documents and materials (including the letter of reference) must be submitted in English or French.

Duration: Award winners may reapply for another grant one year after a grant was awarded. Applicants who were not awarded a grant may reapply two years from the last decision.

Deadline: The Foundation welcomes applications throughout the year. However, in order to allow for proper response time, it is strongly recommended that applicants file their applications six months prior to the date on which funds are required.

PUBLICATIONS:
Application guidelines.

ADDRESS INQUIRIES TO:
Applications Coordinator
(See address above.)

*PLEASE NOTE:

The Elizabeth Greenshields Foundation grant is one of the most prestigious grants available to emerging figurative artists, as well as one of the most substantial. It is one of the longest standing, with an illustrious history of recipients spanning more than half a century. It is also unique in its scope, in that it is available to students and artists around the world. To date, the Foundation has provided financial assistance to more than 1,900 students and artists in 40 countries.

SAMUEL H. KRESS FOUNDATION [513]

174 East 80th Street
New York, NY 10075
(212) 861-4993
E-mail: lisa.schermerhorn@kressfoundation.org
Web Site: www.kressfoundation.org
www.kressfoundation.fluxx.io (grant portal)

FOUNDED: 1929

AREAS OF INTEREST:
Art history, art conservation and art interpretation in museums.

NAME(S) OF PROGRAMS:
- **Conservation Fellowships**
- **Conservation Grant Program**
- **Digital Art History Grant Program**
- **History of Art Grant Program**
- **History of Art: Institutional Fellowships**
- **Interpretive Fellowships at Art Museums**

TYPE:
Fellowships; Research grants; Travel grants. Grants: Competitive grants only awarded to nonprofit institutions. The grant programs support scholarly projects that promote the appreciation, interpretation, preservation, study and teaching of European art from antiquity to the early 19th century.

Fellowships: Competitive fellowships are awarded to art historians and art conservators in the final stages of their preparation for professional careers, as well as to students of art history and related fields who are interested in art museum education and curating.

YEAR PROGRAM STARTED: 1963

PURPOSE:
To advance the history, conservation and enjoyment of European art, architecture and archaeology from antiquity to the pre-modern era.

LEGAL BASIS:
Private foundation.

ELIGIBILITY:
Contact the Foundation for specific eligibility and application requirements for each grant and fellowship program.

FINANCIAL DATA:
Amount of support per award: Varies.
Total amount of support: Varies.

NO. MOST RECENT APPLICANTS: Approximately 500 in fiscal year 2019.

NO. AWARDS: Approximately 200 to 250 annually.

APPLICATION INFO:
Fellowship and grant applications must be submitted via the online grantmaking portal.

The first step in the application process for all grant programs is the submission of a Letter of Inquiry via the Foundation's online grantmaking portal. Institutions invited to apply for a grant will be notified via e-mail within seven business days of the LOI submission deadline.

Duration: Varies.

Deadline: Fellowships: Conservation Fellowships: January 22. Institutional Fellowships: November 30. Interpretive Fellowships: April 1.

Grant LOIs: March 1, September 1 and December 1 for Conservation Grants and History of Art Grants; March 1 and September 1 for Digital Art History Grants.

PUBLICATIONS:
Annual Report.

IRS I.D.: 13-1624176

STAFF:
Wyman Meere, Program Administrator

OFFICERS AND TRUSTEES:
Carmela Vircillo Franklin, Chairman
Max Marmor, President
Elizabeth Eveillard
William Higgins
Ken Lee
Robert B. Loper
Theodore V. H. Mayer
Nina Scherago
Daniel H. Weiss

ADDRESS INQUIRIES TO:
Lisa W. Schermerhorn, Deputy Director
(See address above.)

*SPECIAL STIPULATIONS:
No applications accepted via fax or e-mail.

LIGHT WORK [514]

316 Waverly Avenue
Syracuse, NY 13210
(315) 443-1300
E-mail: info@lightwork.org
Web Site: www.lightwork.org

FOUNDED: 1972

AREAS OF INTEREST:
Photography.

CONSULTING OR VOLUNTEER SERVICES:
All aspects of visual arts and programs for artists.

NAME(S) OF PROGRAMS:
- **Central New York Light Work Grant**
- **Light Work Artist-in-Residence Program**

TYPE:
Project/program grants; Residencies; Visiting scholars. Artist-in-Residence, exhibitions, publications, sponsored projects, lectures and regrants.

Central New York Light Work Grant supports regional artists near Syracuse, NY.

Light Work Artist-in-Residence Program supports international artists.

YEAR PROGRAM STARTED: 1973

PURPOSE:
To support artists in photography.

LEGAL BASIS:
Not-for-profit organization.

ELIGIBILITY:
Applicants must be working in photography or related visual arts including video, installation and electronic media. Students are ineligible to apply.

GEOG. RESTRICTIONS: Central New York Light Work Grant: Central New York.

FINANCIAL DATA:
Amount of support per award: Central New York Light Work Grant: $3,000; Light Work Artist-in-Residence Program: $5,000 stipend.
Total amount of support: Varies.

CO-OP FUNDING PROGRAMS: Yes.

NO. MOST RECENT APPLICANTS: 900 to 1,000.

NO. AWARDS: 12 to 15.

APPLICATION INFO:
Applicants are encouraged to use the online application process.
Duration: One month.
Deadline: Central New York Light Work Grant: April 1. Light Work Artist-in-Residence Program: July 1.

STAFF:
Shane Lavalette, Director

ADDRESS INQUIRIES TO:
Shane Lavalette, Director
(See address above.)

*PLEASE NOTE:
Housing is provided for residencies.

THE ROBERTO LONGHI FOUNDATION FOR THE STUDY OF THE HISTORY OF ART   [515]

Via Benedetto Fortini, 30
50125 Florence Italy
(39) 055 6580794
Fax: (39) 055 6580794
E-mail: longhi@fondazionelonghi.it
Web Site: www.fondazionelonghi.it

FOUNDED: 1971

AREAS OF INTEREST:
Italian and European art from the 13th to the 18th centuries.

NAME(S) OF PROGRAMS:
● Art History Fellowships in Florence

TYPE:
Fellowships.

PURPOSE:
To promote and further the study of art history by keeping Roberto Longhi's cultural legacy and methods alive.

LEGAL BASIS:
Private foundation.

ELIGIBILITY:
Open to Italian citizens who possess a degree from an Italian university with a thesis in the history of art, and to non-Italian citizens who have graduated in the history of art at an accredited university or an institution of

equal standing. Students who have reached their 32nd birthday before the application deadline are not eligible.

Designed for those who want to seriously dedicate themselves to research in the history of art. Fellowship holders may make use of the study materials available in the Institute. They must frequent the Institute and collaborate on a specific group research project selected by the Scientific Committee. In particular, successful candidates must give the assurance that they can dedicate their full time to the research for which the fellowship is assigned. They must live in Florence for the duration of the fellowship, except for travel required for their research. They may not exceed the periods of vacation fixed by the Institute. They are required to attend seminars, lectures and other activities arranged by the Institute. In addition, Fellows must submit a written report at the end of their stay in Florence, relating the findings of their individual research undertaken at the Longhi Foundation. The nonobservance of the above conditions will be considered sufficient grounds for the cancellation of a fellowship.

FINANCIAL DATA:
Amount of support per award: EUR 5,400 (paid in monthly installments over a period of nine months).

NO. MOST RECENT APPLICANTS: 30 for the year 2018.

NO. AWARDS: 8 for the year 2018-19.

APPLICATION INFO:
Applications should be addressed to the Secretariat of the Foundation at the address above and should contain the candidate's biographical data (place and date of birth, domicile, citizenship), a transcript of the candidate's undergraduate and graduate records, a copy of the degree thesis (if available) and other original works, published or unpublished, a "curriculum studiorum," also indicating the knowledge of foreign languages spoken and written, letters of reference from at least two persons of academic standing who are acquainted with the candidate's work, the subject of the research that the candidate is interested in pursuing within the range of the history of art and two passport photographs.

Recipients of fellowships are asked to communicate within 15 days of notification their acceptance and willingness to comply with the conditions and rules as stated.
Duration: Nine months beginning in October.
Deadline: May 15.

PUBLICATIONS:
Proporzioni, art review.

OFFICERS:
Mina Gregori, Chairman and President

MARYLAND INSTITUTE COLLEGE OF ART   [516]

Office of Graduate Admission
131 North Avenue
Baltimore, MD 21201
(410) 225-2256
Fax: (410) 225-5275
E-mail: graduate@mica.edu
Web Site: www.mica.edu

FOUNDED: 1826

AREAS OF INTEREST:
Fine arts, design and art education.

NAME(S) OF PROGRAMS:
● **Business of Art and Design (MPS)**
● **Filmmaking (MFA)**
● **LeRoy E. Hoffberger School of Painting (MFA)**
● **MA Graphic Design**
● **MA Illustration**
● **MA Social Design**
● **Master of Arts in Teaching**
● **MBA/MA in Design Leadership**
● **MFA Community Arts**
● **MFA Curatorial Practice**
● **MFA Illustration Practice**
● **MFA in Graphic Design**
● **Mt. Royal School of Art (MFA)**
● **MPS in Information Visualization**
● **Photographic and Electronic Media (MFA)**
● **Rinehart School of Sculpture (MFA)**
● **Studio Art (Low-residency MFA)**
● **UX Design (MPS)**

TYPE:
Awards/prizes; Challenge/matching grants; Conferences/seminars; Fellowships; Internships; Research grants; Residencies; Scholarships; Travel grants; Visiting scholars. Teaching internships. Post-Baccalaureate Program awards certificates in fine arts.

YEAR PROGRAM STARTED: 1896

LEGAL BASIS:
Nonprofit institution.

ELIGIBILITY:
Bachelor's degree is required.

FINANCIAL DATA:
Amount of support per award: Varies.
Total amount of support: Varies.

NO. MOST RECENT APPLICANTS: 1,100.

NO. AWARDS: 225.

APPLICATION INFO:
Candidates apply for all programs online through mica.slideroom.com or mica.edu/gradprograms.
Duration: One to two years.
Deadline: January 3. Announcement April 1.

ADDRESS INQUIRIES TO:
Christopher Harring
Associate Vice President of Graduate Admission
E-mail: charring@mica.edu

THE PAUL MELLON CENTRE FOR STUDIES IN BRITISH ART

16 Bedford Square
London WC1B 3JA England
(44) 020 7580 0311
Fax: (44) 020 7636 6730
E-mail: info@paul-mellon-centre.ac.uk
Web Site: www.paul-mellon-centre.ac.uk

TYPE:
Conferences/seminars; Fellowships; Project/program grants; Research grants. Educational Programme Grants for lectures, symposia, seminars or conferences on British art or architectural history.

The Junior Fellowship is to pursue ongoing doctoral research at an American or British university.

The Paul Mellon Centre Rome Fellowship offers fellowships to scholars working on Grand Tour subjects or in the field of Anglo-Italian cultural and artistic relations.

Mid-Career Fellowships are offered for research in the field of British art and architectural history.

The Postdoctoral Fellowship works to transform doctoral research into publishable form such as a book, series of articles, or exhibition catalogues.

Research Support Grants are for expenses in pursuit of research.

The Senior Fellowship supports an established scholar in the field of British art and architectural history to complete a manuscript or book for immediate publication.

Terra-PMC Fellowship is designed to facilitate original, rigorous and exciting scholarship that investigates an aspect of the artistic dialogue between Britain and the U.S. from any period up to 1980.

See entry 383 for full listing.

THE METROPOLITAN MUSEUM OF ART   [517]
1000 Fifth Avenue
New York, NY 10028-0198
(212) 570-3710
E-mail: collegeprograms@metmuseum.org
Web Site: www.metmuseum.org

FOUNDED: 1870

AREAS OF INTEREST:
Internships in art museums.

TYPE:
Internships. Internships for graduate and undergraduate students.

YEAR PROGRAM STARTED: 1972

PURPOSE:
To provide pre-career training and experience for students and graduates in art museums.

ELIGIBILITY:
Many projects require strong preparation in the history of art. Applicants of diverse backgrounds and disciplines are encouraged to apply.

FINANCIAL DATA:
Amount of support per award: Varies by program.
Total amount of support: Varies.

NO. AWARDS: 42.

APPLICATION INFO:
Applications must be completed through the Museum's online portal. No hard copies will be accepted.
Duration: Up to 12 months.
Deadline: Varies.

ADDRESS INQUIRIES TO:
Internship Programs
(See address and e-mail above.)

THE METROPOLITAN MUSEUM OF ART   [518]
1000 Fifth Avenue
New York, NY 10028-0198
(212) 650-2763
E-mail: academic.programs@metmuseum.org
Web Site: www.metmuseum.org

AREAS OF INTEREST:
All fields related to art history and visual culture.

NAME(S) OF PROGRAMS:
● **History of Art and Visual Culture Fellowships**

TYPE:
Fellowships. Fellowship awards to Ph.D. candidates, postdoctoral researchers, and senior scholars studying art history and/or conducting research in a field pertaining to the Met's collections.

YEAR PROGRAM STARTED: 1974

PURPOSE:
To promote research in the fine arts.

ELIGIBILITY:
Applicants should have received the Doctorate, have completed substantial work toward it, or be mature scholars of demonstrated ability.

FINANCIAL DATA:
Amount of support per award: $52,000 stipend for senior fellows for one year, $42,000 for predoctoral fellows, and up to an additional $6,000 for travel and miscellaneous expenses.

APPLICATION INFO:
Applications must be completed through the online portal. No hard copies will be accepted.
Duration: Normally, a fellow will be in residence at The Metropolitan Museum of Art for a maximum of one year. Shorter terms are available for senior fellows.
Deadline: Application and required letters of recommendation must be received by the first Friday in November. Announcement of awards will be made by late March.

STAFF:
Marcie Karp, Senior Managing Educator, Academic and Professional Programs, Education Department

ADDRESS INQUIRIES TO:
See e-mail address above.

MUSEUM OF EARLY SOUTHERN DECORATIVE ARTS (MESDA)   [519]
924 South Main Street
Winston-Salem, NC 27101-5335
(336) 721-7369
Fax: (336) 721-7367
E-mail: mesdaeducation@oldsalem.org
Web Site: mesda.org

FOUNDED: 1965

AREAS OF INTEREST:
Decorative arts of the South before 1860.

NAME(S) OF PROGRAMS:
● **Horton Fellowship**

TYPE:
Fellowships.

YEAR PROGRAM STARTED: 1976

PURPOSE:
To combine the study of history and objects in a museum context.

LEGAL BASIS:
Nonprofit.

ELIGIBILITY:
Graduate student status or present employment in museum-related professions required.

FINANCIAL DATA:
Covers partial tuition for three credit hours.
Amount of support per award: $4,500 maximum.
Total amount of support: $20,000 for the year 2018.

NO. MOST RECENT APPLICANTS: Approximately 20 per year.

NO. AWARDS: Up to 10 per year.

APPLICATION INFO:
Applicant must submit a completed application form and letters of recommendation.
Duration: Four weeks.
Deadline: February 15. Notification March 1.

IRS I.D.: 56-0587289

STAFF:
Daniel Ackermann, Curator of MESDA Collections

ADDRESS INQUIRIES TO:
MESDA Summer Institute
(See address above.)

PEW FELLOWSHIPS AT THE PEW CENTER FOR ARTS & HERITAGE   [520]
1608 Walnut Street, 18th Floor
Philadelphia, PA 19103
(267) 350-4920
Fax: (267) 350-4997
E-mail: mfranklin@pewcenterarts.org
Web Site: www.pewcenterarts.org

FOUNDED: 1991

AREAS OF INTEREST:
Fellowships are awarded for various art forms, including Choreography, Craft Arts, Folk and Traditional Arts, Literature (Fiction, Literary Non-Fiction and Poetry), Media Arts, Music Composition, Painting, Performance Art, Playwriting, Works on Paper and Visual Arts 3-D.

TYPE:
Fellowships. Opportunities for contemporary artists in the Philadelphia five-county area to concentrate on the development and creation of art. Fellowships to support artists at critical junctures in any stage of their career development. Fellows will be expected to participate annually in at least three meetings with other fellowship recipients.

YEAR PROGRAM STARTED: 1991

PURPOSE:
To provide financial support directly to artists so that they will have the opportunity to dedicate themselves wholly to the development of their artwork; to provide such support at a critical juncture in an artist's career, when a concentration on artistic development and exploration is most likely to contribute to personal and professional growth.

ELIGIBILITY:
Artists are nominated and invited to apply for the fellowship. Candidates must be residents of Bucks, Chester, Delaware, Montgomery or Philadelphia counties, PA, for two years or longer. Matriculated students, full or part-time, or immediate family members of a panelist for the year applied or of Pew Fellowships staff are not eligible.

There is no restriction as to citizenship.

GEOG. RESTRICTIONS: Bucks, Chester, Delaware, Montgomery and Philadelphia counties, Pennsylvania.

FINANCIAL DATA:
Fellowship funds are awarded in installments. Funds may be used to support costs such as equipment, materials, assistants, training and travel. The specific use of grant funds will be up to the recipient artist.
Amount of support per award: $75,000.

CO-OP FUNDING PROGRAMS: Program funded by the Pew Charitable Trusts.

NO. MOST RECENT APPLICANTS: Varies.

NO. AWARDS: Up to 12 each year.

APPLICATION INFO:
Application by nomination only.

The application procedure involves a panel review by artists and arts professionals. The first level of review is discipline-based; the second level of review is interdisciplinary; the final selection of candidates is based on the applicant's accomplishments or promise in his or her discipline, and the degree to which the fellowship will address a critical juncture in the artist's career and/or artistic development.
Duration: Up to two years.

STAFF:
Melissa Franklin, Director, Pew Fellowships

ADDRESS INQUIRIES TO:
Melissa Franklin
Director, Pew Fellowships
(See e-mail address above.)

THE POLLOCK-KRASNER FOUNDATION, INC.   [521]
863 Park Avenue
New York, NY 10075
(212) 517-5400
Fax: (212) 288-2836
E-mail: grants@pkf.org
Web Site: www.pkf.org

FOUNDED: 1985

AREAS OF INTEREST:
Visual arts.

TYPE:
Grants-in-aid. Grants to individual visual artists for personal and professional needs.

YEAR PROGRAM STARTED: 1985

PURPOSE:
To aid internationally working artists who have embarked on professional careers.

LEGAL BASIS:
Private foundation.

ELIGIBILITY:
Grants are made to painters, sculptors and artists who work on paper, including printmakers who have taken up art as a professional career. The Foundation will not accept applications from commercial artists, photographers, video artists, filmmakers, craft-makers or any artist whose work primarily falls into these categories. It does not make grants to students nor fund academic study.

The Foundation does not make grants to pay for past debts, legal fees, the purchase of real estate, moves to other cities or to pay for the costs of installations, commissions or projects ordered by others. With very few exceptions, the Foundation will not fund travel expenses.

FINANCIAL DATA:
Amount of support per award: The size of the grant is determined by the individual circumstances of the artist.
Total amount of support: Varies.

APPLICATION INFO:
Artists are required to submit a cover letter, a curriculum vitae, artist statement (optional), an application, and 10 images of current work. Applications are to be submitted online.

Duration: One year.
Deadline: Grants are awarded throughout the year.

PUBLICATIONS:
Biannual report; application guidelines.

STAFF:
Caroline Black, Program Director
Beth Cochems, Grants Manager

ROSWELL ARTIST-IN-RESIDENCE PROGRAM   [522]
409 East College Boulevard
Roswell, NM 88201
(575) 623-5600
E-mail: larrybob@rair.org
Web Site: www.rair.org

FOUNDED: 1967

AREAS OF INTEREST:
Studio-based, fine-art residencies.

TYPE:
Residencies. Roswell Artist-in-Residence Program is for artists who work in drawing, painting, sculpture, photography, printmaking, video and other fine art media.

YEAR PROGRAM STARTED: 1967

PURPOSE:
To provide time for artists to focus on their work, without distractions or interruptions.

FINANCIAL DATA:
Amount of support per award: $800 per month, plus housing, studio and utilities and $100 per dependent.
Matching fund requirements: Artists cover phone service, food, art materials and transportation.

NO. MOST RECENT APPLICANTS: Approximately 270 average.

NO. AWARDS: Approximately 6 each year.

APPLICATION INFO:
Application information is available on the web site.
Duration: One year.
Deadline: Varies from year to year.

IRS I.D.: 33-0999247

STAFF:
Larry Bob Phillips, Director
Nancy Fleming, Programs and Publications and Museum Director

ADDRESS INQUIRIES TO:
Roswell Artist-in-Residence Program
(See e-mail address above.)

SAN DIEGO ART INSTITUTE   [523]
1439 El Prado
House of Charm, Balboa Park
San Diego, CA 92101
(619) 236-0011
E-mail: jasilverman@sandiego-art.org
Web Site: www.sandiego-art.org

FOUNDED: 1941

AREAS OF INTEREST:
Contemporary art.

NAME(S) OF PROGRAMS:
● **Matthew J. Mahoney Artist-in-Residence Program**

TYPE:
Conferences/seminars; Internships. Annual lectures, discussions and workshops.

YEAR PROGRAM STARTED: 2015

PURPOSE:
To advance contemporary art through exhibition, outreach and education.

LEGAL BASIS:
501(c)(3) nonprofit arts organization.

ELIGIBILITY:
Artists and curators working in all media and any stages of their career are welcome to apply for an approximate three-month residency.

FINANCIAL DATA:
Awards include monetary compensation.
Amount of support per award: Varies.
Total amount of support: Varies.

NO. AWARDS: Varies.

APPLICATION INFO:
Open to all media. Open calls for exhibition opportunities.
Duration: Approximately three months.

IRS I.D.: 95-1816068

ADDRESS INQUIRIES TO:
Jacqueline A. Silverman, Executive Director
(See address and e-mail above.)

SCHOOL OF THE MUSEUM OF FINE ARTS AT TUFTS UNIVERSITY, BOSTON   [524]
230 The Fenway
Boston, MA 02115
(617) 627-0047
E-mail: kaitlyn.clark@tufts.edu
Web Site: smfa.tufts.edu

FOUNDED: 1876

AREAS OF INTEREST:
Contemporary visual art.

NAME(S) OF PROGRAMS:
● **Traveling Fellowship Award**

TYPE:
Fellowships. Awarded for travel and study abroad.

YEAR PROGRAM STARTED: 1899

PURPOSE:
To further the professional development of the artist recipients.

LEGAL BASIS:
A part of the Museum of Fine Arts, a nonprofit Massachusetts corporation.

ELIGIBILITY:
Applicants must be alumni of the School of the Museum of Fine Arts.

FINANCIAL DATA:
Amount of support per award: Up to $10,000.
Total amount of support: Approximately $100,000 annually.

NO. MOST RECENT APPLICANTS: 128.

NO. AWARDS: Up to 10.

APPLICATION INFO:
Proposed plan of travel and study, including itinerary, must be submitted with a presentation of art work.
Duration: Varies according to proposal. Normally not more than one year. Nonrenewable.
Deadline: August 13. Announcement in September or October.

ADDRESS INQUIRIES TO:
Kaitlyn Clark, SMFA Exhibitions and
Public Programs
(See address above.)

SKOWHEGAN SCHOOL OF PAINTING AND SCULPTURE [525]

136 West 22nd Street
New York, NY 10011
(212) 529-0505
Fax: (212) 473-1342
E-mail: mail@skowheganart.org
Web Site: www.skowheganart.org

FOUNDED: 1946

AREAS OF INTEREST:
All visual arts.

TYPE:
Scholarships; Travel grants.

YEAR PROGRAM STARTED: 1946

PURPOSE:
To bring together a gifted and diverse group
of individuals who have demonstrated a
commitment to art-making and inquiry to
create the most stimulating environment
possible for a concentrated period of artistic
creation, interaction and growth.

LEGAL BASIS:
Not-for-profit educational institution.

ELIGIBILITY:
Based on need. Candidate must be at least 21
years old.

FINANCIAL DATA:
Scholarships cover room, board and tuition.
Amount of support per award: Varies.

NO. MOST RECENT APPLICANTS: 2,400.

NO. AWARDS: 65.

APPLICATION INFO:
Application information is available online.
Duration: Nine-week summer program,
mid-June to mid-August.

ADDRESS INQUIRIES TO:
Sarah Workneh, Co-Director
(See address above.)

W. EUGENE SMITH MEMORIAL FUND [526]

79 Essex Street
New York, NY 10002
(212) 857-0001
E-mail: info@smithfund.org
Web Site: www.smithfund.org

FOUNDED: 1979

AREAS OF INTEREST:
Photography.

NAME(S) OF PROGRAMS:
● **W. Eugene Smith Grant in Humanistic Photography**

TYPE:
Project/program grants.

PURPOSE:
To support a photographer working on a
project in the humanistic tradition of W.
Eugene Smith, in order to pursue the work.

ELIGIBILITY:
Open to outstanding photographers of any
nationality.

FINANCIAL DATA:
Amount of support per award: $10,000.

Total amount of support: $50,000 for the
year 2020.

NO. MOST RECENT APPLICANTS: Approximately
200 annually.

NO. AWARDS: 5 for the year 2020.

APPLICATION INFO:
Initial application is online only. Applicants
should include a written proposal, biography
and curriculum vitae, and up to 40 images.
Entry fee of $50 is required.
Duration: One year.
Deadline: April 30.

*SPECIAL STIPULATIONS:
Grant recipients agree to give to the W.
Eugene Smith Memorial Fund, Inc., as an
unrestricted gift, 12 digital images and 12
prints of work completed as part of the
project proposed, within 18 months of the
award and shall become part of the Legacy
Collection.

SIR JOHN SOANE MUSEUM FOUNDATION

120 Broadway, 20th Floor
New York, NY 10271
(646) 740-1976
E-mail: fellowships@soanefoundation.org
Web Site: www.soanefoundation.org

TYPE:
Fellowships. Designed to help graduate
students and scholars pursue research projects
related to the work of Sir John Soane's
Museum and its collections.

See entry 387 for full listing.

THE JOHN F. AND ANNA LEE STACEY SCHOLARSHIP FUND [527]

c/o National Cowboy and Western Heritage
Museum
1700 N.E. 63rd Street
Oklahoma City, OK 73111
(405) 478-2250
Fax: (405) 478-4714
E-mail: registrar@nationalcowboymuseum.org
Web Site: nationalcowboymuseum.org

FOUNDED: 1955

AREAS OF INTEREST:
Drawing and painting in the conservative
mode.

TYPE:
Awards/prizes. Cash awards to be used to
further the development of young painters in
the classical conservative tradition.

YEAR PROGRAM STARTED: 1975

PURPOSE:
To foster a high standard in the study of
form, color, drawing, painting, design and
technique, as these are expressed in modes
showing patent affinity with the classical
tradition of western culture.

LEGAL BASIS:
Nonprofit.

ELIGIBILITY:
Open to U.S. citizens between 18 and 35
years of age. Only those who are skilled and
devoted to the painting or drawing of
classical or conservative tradition of western
culture should apply.

GEOG. RESTRICTIONS: United States.

FINANCIAL DATA:
Amount of support per award: $500 to
$5,000.
Total amount of support: Varies.

NO. MOST RECENT APPLICANTS: More than 350.

NO. AWARDS: 3 to 5.

APPLICATION INFO:
Guidelines and application are posted online
by November 1 for the following year. All
applicants will be required to upload images
to the Fund's FTP site. Not more than six
images of their work (clearly labeled with
name, title, dimensions, medium and date of
execution of the work) in the following
categories: painting from life, drawing from
the figure (nude), composition, landscape and
others.

Application forms must accompany all
submissions.
Duration: One year.
Deadline: Entries need to be uploaded by
February 1 of each year.

PUBLICATIONS:
Guidelines.

STAFF:
Melissa Owens, Registrar and Exhibits
Coordinator

ADDRESS INQUIRIES TO:
E-mail:
scholarship@nationalcowboymuseum.org

STUDIO ARTS COLLEGE INTERNATIONAL (SACI) [528]

Palazzo dei Cartelloni
Via Sant' Antonino 11
50123 Florence Italy
(212) 248-7225
Fax: (212) 248-7222
E-mail: admissions@saci-florence.edu
Web Site: www.saci-florence.edu

FOUNDED: 1975

AREAS OF INTEREST:
Studio art, art history, art conservation,
Italian language and culture.

NAME(S) OF PROGRAMS:
● **Fall/Spring/Summer Study Abroad**
● **MA in Art History**
● **MFA in Studio Art**
● **Post Baccalaureate Certificate Program in Conservation**

TYPE:
Awards/prizes; Scholarships.
Fall/Spring/Summer Study Abroad:
Undergraduate and graduate visiting students
may attend for a term or more. SACI offers a
wide variety of both traditional and
cutting-edge studio art and design courses as
well as classes in art history covering
medieval and contemporary art. For
conservation students, there is the unique
opportunity to participate hands-on in the
conservation of historic works in Florence.
Studio Art courses include Fresco Painting,
Serigraphy, Printmaking, Photography, Digital
Multimedia, Video, Jewelry Making, Batik,
Book Making, Sculpture, Ceramics, and
many more.

MFA in Studio Art is a two-year program in
which students work in a creative
environment of rigorous critical and technical
inquiry utilizing the unique artistic and
cultural resources of Florence to prepare for
careers as artists and college instructors.
Students pursue a curriculum integrating
practical and critical skills that encourages

individual innovation, creative collaboration, mentorships and instruction from SACI's outstanding faculty.

Post Baccalaureate Certificate Program in Conservation is a one-year program of intensive graduate study. The study program includes graduate seminars, reviews, field trips, lecture series and exhibitions.

YEAR PROGRAM STARTED: 1975

PURPOSE:
To study Studio Art, Art History or Conservation at a U.S.-accredited institution in Florence, Italy.

ELIGIBILITY:
Selection is based on academic/artistic merit as well as financial need.

FINANCIAL DATA:
Amount of support per award: Varies.

NO. MOST RECENT APPLICANTS: 120.

NO. AWARDS: 100.

APPLICATION INFO:
Application information is available on the web site.
Duration: One semester to full year.
Deadline: Fall: March 15. Spring: October 15. Summer: March 1.

ADDRESS INQUIRIES TO:
Studio Arts College International (SACI)
454 West 19th Street
New York, NY 10011
(See e-mail address above.)

UNIVERSITY OF ILLINOIS AT URBANA-CHAMPAIGN   [529]
College of Fine and Applied Arts
608 East Lorado Taft Drive, Suite 100
Champaign, IL 61820
(217) 333-1661
(217) 333-1660
Fax: (217) 244-8381
E-mail: faa@illinois.edu
Web Site: www.faa.illinois.edu/alumni-friends/kate-neal-kinley-memorial-fellowship

FOUNDED: 1931

AREAS OF INTEREST:
Art, architecture, dance, landscape architecture, music, theatre, and urban and regional planning.

NAME(S) OF PROGRAMS:
● **Kate Neal Kinley Memorial Fellowship**

TYPE:
Fellowships. Awarded for advanced study in the fine arts in the U.S. or abroad, in an approved educational institution, with an approved private teacher or in independent study.

Three major Fellowships will be awarded:
(1) one in any field of music;
(2) one in architectural design and history, art and design, theatre, dance, or instrumental or vocal music and;
(3) one in art, architecture, dance, landscape architecture, theatre, or urban and regional planning.

YEAR PROGRAM STARTED: 1931

PURPOSE:
To help defray expenses of advanced study of the fine and applied arts in America or abroad.

Provides a meaningful opportunity for students to enhance their professional status, aid their pursuit of an advanced degree, or finance a special project within the field.

ELIGIBILITY:
Open to graduates of the College of Fine and Applied Arts of the University of Illinois at Urbana-Champaign and to graduates of similar institutions of equal educational standing whose principal or major studies have been in the fields of art, architecture, dance, landscape architecture, music, theatre, and urban and regional planning.

Although there is no age limitation for applicants, other factors being equal, preference will be given to applicants who have not reached their 25th birthday.

Fellowships will be awarded upon the basis of unusual promise in the fine arts as attested by:
(1) high attainment in the applicant's major field of study as evidenced by academic marks and quality of work submitted or performed;
(2) high attainment in related cultural fields as evidenced by academic marks;
(3) the character, merit and suitability of the program proposed by the applicant and;
(4) excellence of personality, seriousness of purpose and good moral character.

FINANCIAL DATA:
The fellowships are to be used by the recipients toward defraying the expenses of advanced study in America or abroad.
Amount of support per award: Major fellowships: Up to $20,000 in any field of music, up to $20,000 in architectural design and history, art and design, theatre, dance, or instrumental or vocal music, and up to $9,000 in art, architecture, dance, landscape architecture, theatre, or urban and regional planning.

CO-OP FUNDING PROGRAMS: Funded partially by the John Robert Gregg Fund at Community Funds, Inc. and the New York Community Trust.

NO. AWARDS: 3 major fellowships, plus up to 3 additional fellowships of lesser amounts, depending upon committee recommendations.

APPLICATION INFO:
Application form and guidelines are available online.
Duration: Tenable for one academic year.
Deadline: December 1.

ADDRESS INQUIRIES TO:
Kate Neal Kinley
Memorial Fellowship Committee
(See address and telephone number above.)

UNIVERSITY OF SOUTHERN CALIFORNIA ROSKI SCHOOL OF ART AND DESIGN   [530]
Watt Hall 104
850 West 37th Street
Los Angeles, CA 90089-0292
(213) 740-9153
Fax: (213) 740-8938
E-mail: roski@usc.edu
Web Site: roski.usc.edu

FOUNDED: 1883

AREAS OF INTEREST:
Art.

NAME(S) OF PROGRAMS:
● **Macomber Travel Grant**

TYPE:
Travel grants. Selected through a competitive process, the prize will support proposed

projects involving research-based travel, the production of new art work, and a public presentation of the new work.

YEAR PROGRAM STARTED: 1960

PURPOSE:
To educate artists.

LEGAL BASIS:
Private university.

ELIGIBILITY:
Undergraduate applicants must be third-year Roski majors who will begin their senior year in the fall following the award. Graduate applicants must be current first-year Roski M.F.A or M.A. students. Students are allowed to submit team proposals, but the financial award will remain the same and will be shared. The awardee must be in good academic standing at the time of the award and remain in good standing throughout the culminating year. The awardee must be without prior or pending issues of conduct.

FINANCIAL DATA:
Amount of support per award: $7,500.

NO. AWARDS: Maximum 4.

APPLICATION INFO:
Applications must be submitted on SlideRoom. Application must include a proposal, itinerary, and budget of expenses for travel related to the research, development, production, and presentation of an independent art project.
Duration: One year.
Deadline: March 29.

ADDRESS INQUIRIES TO:
Penelope Jones
Assistant Dean of Student Services
(See address above.)

History

AGRICULTURAL HISTORY SOCIETY   [531]
Mount Royal University
Faculty of Arts
4825 Mount Royal Gate, S.W.
Calgary AB T3E 6K6 Canada
(403) 440-8796
E-mail: aghistorysociety@gmail.com
Web Site: www.aghistorysociety.org

AREAS OF INTEREST:
Agricultural and rural history.

NAME(S) OF PROGRAMS:
● **Everett E. Edwards Awards in Agricultural History**
● **Gilbert C. Fite Dissertation Award**
● **Wayne D. Rasmussen Award**
● **Theodore Saloutos Book Award**
● **Henry A. Wallace Award**

TYPE:
Awards/prizes. The Everett E. Edwards Award is presented to the graduate student who submits the best manuscript on any aspect of agricultural history and rural studies during the current calendar year.

The Gilbert C. Fite Dissertation Award will be presented to the author of the best dissertation on any aspect of agricultural history completed during the current calendar year.

The Wayne D. Rasmussen Award is given to the author of the best article on agricultural history published by a journal other than *Agricultural History* during the current calendar year.

The Theodore Saloutos Book Award is presented to the author of a book on any aspect of agricultural history in the U.S. within the current year, broadly interpreted.

The Henry A. Wallace Award is presented to the author of a book on any aspect of agricultural history outside of the U.S. within the current year, broadly interpreted.

PURPOSE:
To promote research and publication in the field of agricultural and rural history.

FINANCIAL DATA:
Amount of support per award: Edwards Award: Honorarium of $200 and publication in *Agricultural History*; Fite Dissertation Award: Honorarium of $300 and a certificate; Rasmussen Award: Honorarium of $200 for the author and certificates for the author and publisher; Saloutos Book Award: $500 to the author.

APPLICATION INFO:
Contact the Society for details.
Deadline: January 15.

AMERICAN ANTIQUARIAN SOCIETY (AAS)
185 Salisbury Street
Worcester, MA 01609-1634
(508) 755-5221
Fax: (508) 754-9069
E-mail: nwolverton@mwa.org
Web Site: www.americanantiquarian.org

TYPE:
Fellowships. Visiting fellowship for historical research by creative and performing artists, writers, filmmakers and journalists.

See entry 313 for full listing.

AMERICAN ANTIQUARIAN SOCIETY (AAS)
185 Salisbury Street
Worcester, MA 01609-1634
(508) 755-5221
Fax: (508) 754-9069
E-mail: nwolverton@mwa.org
Web Site: www.americanantiquarian.org

TYPE:
Conferences/seminars; Fellowships. Fellowships provide support for residence at the Society's library for research on any topic supported by the collections. All awards are for research and writing using the library's resources.

See entry 312 for full listing.

AMERICAN CATHOLIC HISTORICAL ASSOCIATION   [532]
Mount St. Mary's University
16300 Old Emmitsburg Road
Emmitsburg, MD 21727
(301) 447-5799
E-mail: acha@achahistory.org
Web Site: www.achahistory.org

FOUNDED: 1919

AREAS OF INTEREST:
The history of Catholicism from antiquity to the present.

NAME(S) OF PROGRAMS:
● **The Howard R. Marraro Prize**

TYPE:
Awards/prizes. This Prize is given annually to the author of a book that is judged by a committee of experts to be the most distinguished work dealing with Italian history or Italo-American history or relations that has been published in a preceding 12-month period. It is named in memory of Howard A. Marraro (1879-1972), professor, Columbia University and the author of more than a dozen books on Italian literature, history and culture.

YEAR PROGRAM STARTED: 1973

PURPOSE:
To stimulate interest in the history of Catholicism among young scholars.

LEGAL BASIS:
An endowed fund owned by the Association.

ELIGIBILITY:
To be entered in the competition, a work must be of book length, in English, already published and must deal with Italian history or Italian-American history or relations. To be eligible for the prize, an author must be a citizen or resident of the U.S. or Canada. The work must have an imprint of the previous year.

FINANCIAL DATA:
Amount of support per award: $1,500.

NO. AWARDS: 1 per annum.

APPLICATION INFO:
Nominators must complete the online Data Collection Form. One copy of each entry must be sent to each of the three committee members.
Deadline: May 15.

ADDRESS INQUIRIES TO:
Prize Administrator
Tel: (202) 544-2422
E-mail: dschaffer@historians.org

AMERICAN CATHOLIC HISTORICAL ASSOCIATION
Mount St. Mary's University
16300 Old Emmitsburg Road
Emmitsburg, MD 21727
(301) 447-5799
E-mail: acha@achahistory.org
Web Site: www.achahistory.org

TYPE:
Awards/prizes; Challenge/matching grants; Conferences/seminars; Travel grants. A prize awarded annually to the author whose article, dealing with the history of the Catholic Church, is the first of his or her professional career and is judged to be the best of those in that category accepted for publication in any given year by the editors of the *Catholic Historical Review*.

See entry 745 for full listing.

AMERICAN CATHOLIC HISTORICAL ASSOCIATION
Mount St. Mary's University
16300 Old Emmitsburg Road
Emmitsburg, MD 21727
(301) 447-5799
E-mail: acha@achahistory.org
Web Site: www.achahistory.org

TYPE:
Awards/prizes. This Prize is given annually to the author of a book, published during a preceding 12-month period, which is judged by a committee of experts to have made the most original and distinguished contribution to knowledge of the history of the Catholic Church.

See entry 746 for full listing.

AMERICAN CATHOLIC HISTORICAL ASSOCIATION
Mount St. Mary's University
16300 Old Emmitsburg Road
Emmitsburg, MD 21727
(301) 447-5799
E-mail: acha@achahistory.org
Web Site: www.achahistory.org

TYPE:
Awards/prizes; Challenge/matching grants; Conferences/seminars; Research grants; Travel grants. ACHA Graduate Student Summer Research Grant is awarded to an ACHA graduate student member who has completed all requirements for the Doctorate except the dissertation.

John Tracy Ellis Dissertation Award memorializes the scholarship and teaching of Monsignor Ellis (1905-1992).

Presidential Graduate Travel Grant was created in 2010 by the Association from donations from former presidents.

See entry 747 for full listing.

AMERICAN CATHOLIC HISTORICAL ASSOCIATION
Mount St. Mary's University
16300 Old Emmitsburg Road
Emmitsburg, MD 21727
(301) 447-5799
E-mail: acha@achahistory.org
Web Site: www.achahistory.org

TYPE:
Awards/prizes. The Msgr. Harry C. Koenig Award for Catholic Biography (Article Award) is awarded on a competitive basis every two years (in odd-numbered years) to the author who has produced a journal article that focuses on the life of a Catholic personage from any period of Christian history.

The Msgr. Harry C. Koenig Award for Catholic Biography (Book Award) is offered every two years (in even-numbered years) and recognizes an outstanding monograph that focuses on the life of a Catholic personage of any age or time.

See entry 748 for full listing.

THE AMERICAN HISTORICAL ASSOCIATION   [533]
400 A Street, S.E.
Washington, DC 20003
(202) 544-2422
Fax: (202) 544-8307
E-mail: awards@historians.org
Web Site: www.historians.org

FOUNDED: 1884

AREAS OF INTEREST:
Promotion of historical studies, the collection and preservation of historical manuscripts and the dissemination of historical research.

NAME(S) OF PROGRAMS:
- **The Herbert Baxter Adams Prize**
- **The George Louis Beer Prize**
- **The Jerry Bentley Prize**
- **The Albert J. Beveridge Award**
- **The Albert J. Beveridge Grant**
- **The James Henry Breasted Prize**
- **The John H. Dunning Prize in United States History**
- **The John K. Fairbank Prize in East Asian History**
- **The Herbert Feis Award**
- **The Morris D. Forkosch Prize**
- **The Leo Gershoy Award**
- **The Clarence H. Haring Prize**
- **J. Franklin Jameson Award**
- **The Friedrich Katz Prize**
- **The Joan Kelly Memorial Prize in Women's History**
- **Martin A. Klein Prize in African History**
- **Michael Kraus Research Grant**
- **The Waldo G. Leland Prize**
- **Littleton-Griswold Grant**
- **The Littleton-Griswold Prize in American Law and Society**
- **The J. Russell Major Prize**
- **The Helen and Howard R. Marraro Prize in Italian History**
- **The George L. Mosse Prize**
- **The John E. O'Connor Film Award**
- **The James A. Rawley Prize in Atlantic History**
- **John F. Richards Prize in South Asian History**
- **The Dorothy Rosenberg Prize**
- **Bernadotte E. Schmitt Grant**
- **The Wesley-Logan Prize**

TYPE:
Awards/prizes; Fellowships; Research grants. Prizes and awards for distinguished scholarly publications written in English on historical subjects as follows:

Herbert Baxter Adams Prize: Awarded annually for a distinguished book by an American author in the field of European history.

Beer Prize: Awarded annually for the best work on European international history by a U.S. citizen.

Bentley Prize: Awarded annually for the best book in the field of world history.

Beveridge Award: Awarded annually for the best book in English on the history of the U.S., Canada, or Latin America from 1492 to the present.

Beveridge Grant: Given for research pertaining to the Western Hemisphere.

Breasted Prize: Awarded annually for an outstanding book in English in any field of history prior to 1000 A.D.

Dunning Prize: For a book on any subject relating to American history. Awarded biennially in odd years.

Fairbank Prize: Awarded annually for an outstanding book on the history of China proper, Vietnam, Chinese Central Asia, Mongolia, Manchuria, Korea or Japan since the year 1800.

Feis Award: Awarded for distinguished contributions to public history.

Forkosch Prize: Awarded annually in recognition of the best book in English in the field of British, British Imperial or British Commonwealth History.

Gershoy Prize: Awarded annually for an outstanding work published in English on any aspect of the fields of 17th and 18th century western European history.

Haring Prize: For a Latin American who, in the opinion of the committee, has published the most outstanding book on Latin American history during the preceding five years. Awarded every five years.

J. Franklin Jameson Award: Given for outstanding achievement in the editing of historical sources.

Friedrich Katz Prize: Awarded annually for the best book in Latin American and Caribbean history.

Kelly Memorial Prize: Awarded annually for the best work in women's history and/or feminist theory.

Martin A. Klein Prize: Awarded in the study of African history.

Michael Kraus Research Grant: Awarded for the study of colonial American history.

Leland Prize: Offered every five years for the outstanding reference tool in the field of history, i.e., bibliographies, indexes, encyclopedias and other scholarly apparatus.

Littleton-Griswold Grant: Awarded in U.S. legal history and law and society, broadly defined.

Littleton-Griswold Prize: Awarded annually for the best book in any subject on the history of American law and society, broadly defined.

J. Russell Major Prize: Awarded annually for the best work in English on any aspect of French history.

Marraro Prize: Awarded annually for the best work on any epoch of Italian history or Italian-American relations.

George L. Mosse Prize: Awarded annually for an outstanding major work of extraordinary scholarly distinction, creativity, and originality in the intellectual and cultural history of Europe since the Renaissance.

John E. O'Connor Film Award: Awarded annually to recognize outstanding interpretations of history through the medium of film.

James A. Rawley Prize in Atlantic History: Awarded annually in recognition of outstanding historical writing that explores aspects of integration of Atlantic worlds before the 20th century.

John F. Richards Prize in South Asian History: Awarded annually for the most distinguished work of scholarship on South Asian history published in English.

Dorothy Rosenberg Prize: Book prize for the Jewish Diaspora Community.

Bernadette Schmitt Grant: Given for research of Europe, Asia and Africa.

Wesley-Logan Prize: Awarded annually for an outstanding book on African diaspora history.

PURPOSE:
To promote and honor good historical writing and scholarship.

LEGAL BASIS:
Nonprofit association.

ELIGIBILITY:
Applicant must be a member to apply for grants. Preference will be given to Ph.D. candidates and postgraduates.

FINANCIAL DATA:
Amount of support per award: Varies.

NO. AWARDS: 1 in each program on the yearly basis.

PUBLICATIONS:
Annual report; *American Historical Review*; *Perspectives in History*.

OFFICERS:
John McNeill, President
James R. Grossman, Executive Director
Alan Lichtenstein, Editor, *American Historical Review*

ADDRESS INQUIRIES TO:
Gabriella Folsom
Communications and Operations Assistant
(See address above.)

THE AMERICAN HISTORICAL ASSOCIATION [534]
400 A Street, S.E.
Washington, DC 20003
(202) 544-2422
Fax: (202) 544-8307
E-mail: awards@historians.org
Web Site: www.historians.org

FOUNDED: 1884

AREAS OF INTEREST:
Scholarly research.

NAME(S) OF PROGRAMS:
- **The J. Franklin Jameson Fellowship**

TYPE:
Fellowships. Award in American history offered annually by the Library of Congress and the American Historical Association.

YEAR PROGRAM STARTED: 1977

PURPOSE:
To support significant scholarly research in the collections of the Library of Congress by scholars at an early stage in their careers in history.

LEGAL BASIS:
Nonprofit association.

ELIGIBILITY:
At the time of application, applicants must hold the Ph.D. degree or equivalent, must have received this degree within the past seven years and must not have published or had accepted for publication a book-length historical work. The fellowship will not be awarded to complete a doctoral dissertation.

The applicant's project in American history must be one for which the general and special collections of the Library of Congress offer unique research support. Applicants should include a statement substantiating this relationship.

Before the conclusion of the fellowship, the Jameson fellow will summarize the results of his or her research at a professional gathering arranged by the American Historical Association and the Library of Congress. Jameson fellows are not required to complete their project during the tenure of the fellowship, nor need they necessarily have published the results as a discrete work.

The American Historical Association encourages nontenured faculty, public historians, independent scholars and two-year faculty to apply.

FINANCIAL DATA:
Amount of support per award: $5,000 stipend.

NO. MOST RECENT APPLICANTS: 5 to 10 annually.

NO. AWARDS: 1 annually.

APPLICATION INFO:
Letter of application should include a vitae, statement concerning the proposed project and its relationship to Library of Congress holdings, tentative schedule for tenure of the fellowship and three letters of recommendation by persons qualified to judge the project and the applicant's fitness to undertake it.
Duration: Two to three months in full-time residency in Washington, DC.
Deadline: April 1. Award announced in June.

PUBLICATIONS:
Annual report.

OFFICERS:
John McNeill, President
James R. Grossman, Executive Director
Alex Lichtenstein, Editor, *American Historical Review*

ADDRESS INQUIRIES TO:
Gabriella Folsom
Communications and Operations Assistant
(See address above.)

THE AMERICAN HISTORICAL ASSOCIATION   [535]
400 A Street, S.E.
Washington, DC 20003
(202) 544-2422
Fax: (202) 544-8307
E-mail: awards@historians.org
Web Site: www.historians.org

FOUNDED: 1884

AREAS OF INTEREST:
Scholarly research.

NAME(S) OF PROGRAMS:
● **Fellowship in Aerospace History**

TYPE:
Fellowships. The Association annually funds at least one fellow for a period of six to nine months, to undertake a proposed research project related to aerospace history. The Fellowship is supported by the National Aeronautics and Space Administration (NASA).

YEAR PROGRAM STARTED: 1986

PURPOSE:
To provide a fellow with an opportunity to engage in significant and sustained advanced research in all aspects of the history of aerospace from the earliest human interest in flight to the present, including cultural and intellectual history, economic history, history of law and public policy and the history of science, engineering and management.

LEGAL BASIS:
Nonprofit association.

ELIGIBILITY:
Applicant must possess a Doctorate degree in history or in a closely related field or be enrolled as a student, having completed all course work, in a doctoral degree-granting program. Preference is given to applicants in the early stages of their careers.

Stipends may be awarded only to U.S. citizens or permanent residents.

FINANCIAL DATA:
Amount of support per award: $21,250 stipend for a six- to nine-month fellowship, including travel expenses.

NO. AWARDS: 1 per year.

APPLICATION INFO:
Applicants must complete an application form, available online, and offer a specific and detailed research proposal that will be the basis of the fellow's research during the term.
Duration: Six to nine months.
Deadline: April 1.

PUBLICATIONS:
Annual report.

OFFICERS:
John McNeill, President
James R. Grossman, Executive Director
Alex Lichtenstein, Editor, *American Historical Review*

ADDRESS INQUIRIES TO:
Gabriella Folsom
Communications and Operations Assistant
(See address above.)

*SPECIAL STIPULATIONS:
Funds may not be used to support tuition or fees. A fellow may not hold other major fellowships or grants during the fellowship term, except sabbatical and supplemental grants from their own institutions and small grants from other sources for specific research expenses. Sources of anticipated support must be listed in the application form.

AMERICAN INSTITUTE OF THE HISTORY OF PHARMACY
University of Wisconsin School of Pharmacy
Rennebohm Hall
777 Highland Avenue
Madison, WI 53705-2222
(608) 262-5378
E-mail: aihp@aihp.org
Web Site: www.aihp.org

TYPE:
Grants-in-aid; Research grants.

See entry 2331 for full listing.

BERKSHIRE CONFERENCE OF WOMEN HISTORIANS   [536]
Rutgers University, History Department
16 Seminary Place
New Brunswick, NJ 08901
(848) 932-7905
E-mail: secretary@berksconference.org
Web Site: www.berksconference.org

FOUNDED: 1930

AREAS OF INTEREST:
Women's history.

TYPE:
Awards/prizes. One prize awarded annually for the best first book and one for the best article of historical scholarship published by a woman historian in any field of history during the preceding year.

YEAR PROGRAM STARTED: 1972

PURPOSE:
To promote historical scholarship by women.

ELIGIBILITY:
The book or article must have been published in the year preceding the award date.

FINANCIAL DATA:
Amount of support per award: $1,000 for each book prize; $500 for each article prize.
Total amount of support: $1,500.

NO. MOST RECENT APPLICANTS: 150.

NO. AWARDS: 1 award in each category per year.

APPLICATION INFO:
Detailed guidelines are available on the Conference web site.
Deadline: January 15. Notification in June.

ADDRESS INQUIRIES TO:
Dr. Marisa J. Fuentes, Secretary
(See e-mail address above.)

JOHN CARTER BROWN LIBRARY   [537]
Brown University
94 George Street
Providence, RI 02906
(401) 863-2725
Fax: (401) 863-3477
E-mail: jcb-fellowships@brown.edu
Web Site: www.jcbl.org

FOUNDED: 1846

AREAS OF INTEREST:
Historical studies pertaining to the Age of Exploration, Latin American history before 1830, North American history to approximately 1800, European impressions of America, New World travel, exploration and colonization. Also, Indian language, cartography, West Indies and Caribbean studies, maritime, slave trade, and the Jewish Experience in the colonial Americas, North and South.

NAME(S) OF PROGRAMS:
● **The John Carter Brown Library Research Fellowships**

TYPE:
Fellowships. The John Carter Brown Library (JCB), an independently funded institution for advanced research at Brown University, contains one of the world's premier collections of primary materials related to the discovery, exploration, and settlement of the New World to 1825, including books, maps, newspapers and other printed objects.

The Library offers both Short-term and Long-term Fellowships.

YEAR PROGRAM STARTED: 1981

PURPOSE:
To promote scholarly research at the library.

LEGAL BASIS:
Independently funded and administered library and research center.

ELIGIBILITY:
Fellowships and grants are reserved exclusively for scholars whose work is centered on colonial history of the Americas, North and South, including all aspects of European, African, and Native American engagements in global and comparative contexts.

Short-term fellowships are open to individuals who are engaged in pre- and postdoctoral, or independent research, regardless of nationality.

Fellowships funded by the NEH are only available to citizens of the U.S., or to those applicants residing in the U.S. for the three years preceding application. Applicants of all nationalities, however, will be considered for long-term fellowships.

FINANCIAL DATA:
Amount of support per award: Short-term Fellowships: $2,100 per month; Long-term Fellowships: $4,200 per month.

Total amount of support: Varies.

NO. AWARDS: Approximately 40 for the year 2019-20.

APPLICATION INFO:
Applicants must submit:
(1) a narrative description of the proposed project, including an explanation of its historiographical significance, progress to date on the project, identification of specific materials to be consulted at the Library, and plan for work to be completed while in residence;
(2) current curriculum vitae;
(3) a complete application form and;
(4) two letters of recommendation to support their proposed project.

Applicants may submit proposals in English, French, Portuguese or Spanish, although English is generally preferred by the Committee.
Duration: Short-term Fellowships: Two to four months; Long-term Fellowships: Five to 10 months.
Deadline: December 1.

PUBLICATIONS:
Application guidelines.

ADDRESS INQUIRIES TO:
See e-mail address above.

*PLEASE NOTE:
Recipients of all Fellowships must relocate to Providence and be in continuous residence at the John Carter Brown Library for the entire term of the award. Rooms are available for rent at Fiering House, the JCB Fellows' residence, a beautifully restored 1869 house just four blocks from the Library. Those living within commuting distance of the Library (approximately 45 miles distant) are ordinarily not eligible for JCB Fellowships.

CANADIAN INSTITUTE OF UKRAINIAN STUDIES   [538]
University of Alberta
4-30 Pembina Hall
Edmonton AB T6G 2H8 Canada
(780) 492-2972
E-mail: cius@ualberta.ca
Web Site: www.cius.ca

FOUNDED: 1976

AREAS OF INTEREST:
Studies in history, literature, language, education, social sciences, library sciences and women's studies.

NAME(S) OF PROGRAMS:
● **The Helen Darcovich Memorial Doctoral Fellowship**
● **Neporany Doctoral Fellowship**
● **Research Grants**

TYPE:
Fellowships; Research grants; Scholarships. The Helen Darcovich Memorial Doctoral Fellowship is awarded annually to a student writing a dissertation on a Ukrainian or Ukrainian-Canadian topic in education, history, humanities, social sciences, law or library sciences.

The Neporany Doctoral Fellowship, offered by the Canadian Foundation for Ukrainian Studies, is awarded to one ore more doctoral students specializing on Ukraine in political science, economics, and related fields.

Research Grants are awarded in support of projects that have scholarly value, well-defined work plans, and modest budgets.

PURPOSE:
To foster, develop, and support Ukrainian studies in Canada and internationally.

ELIGIBILITY:
The Helen Darcovich Memorial Doctoral Fellowship: Because funding is for dissertation work only, all other degree requirements must be completed by the time the award is taken up. Applications will be judged on a points system based on the dissertation proposal, letters of reference, writing sample, academic grades, and publishing record. Canadian citizens and permanent residents of Canada, who may hold the fellowship at any institution of higher learning, and foreign students enrolled at the University of Alberta, will receive extra points.

Neporany Doctoral Fellowship is offered to doctoral students specializing on Ukraine in political science, economics, and related fields (social sciences and political, economic, and social history). Preference will be given to students completing their dissertations as well as to students at Canadian universities or Canadian citizens and residents.

FINANCIAL DATA:
Amount of support per award: Helen Darcovich Memorial Doctoral Fellowship: $12,500 (CAN); Neporany Doctoral Fellowship: $5,000 to $20,000 (CAN).
Total amount of support: Over $100,000 for the year 2018.

NO. MOST RECENT APPLICANTS: Over 100.

NO. AWARDS: Helen Darcovich Memorial Doctoral Fellowship: 1; Neporany Doctoral Fellowship: 1 or more; Research grants: Over 40.

APPLICATION INFO:
Research grant applicants should read the Research Grant Application Guide prior to filling out the application form.
Duration: Varies.
Deadline: March 1.

ADDRESS INQUIRIES TO:
Serge Cipko, Assistant Director of Research (See address above.)

COLLEGE OF PHYSICIANS OF PHILADELPHIA   [539]
Francis Clark Wood Institute
for the History of Medicine
19 South 22nd Street
Philadelphia, PA 19103-3097
(215) 399-2301
Fax: (215) 569-0356
E-mail: travelgrants@collegeofphysicans.org
Web Site: www.collegeofphysicians.org/library/wood-institute

FOUNDED: 1787

AREAS OF INTEREST:
The history of medicine.

NAME(S) OF PROGRAMS:
● **Wood Institute Travel Grants**

TYPE:
Travel grants; Visiting scholars. This program allows scholars to conduct short-term research in the College's Library and/or Mutter Museum.

YEAR PROGRAM STARTED: 1983

PURPOSE:
To encourage the study and appreciation of medicine in the broader historical and social context in response to current health care issues and public and professional interests.

LEGAL BASIS:
501(c)(3) not-for-profit educational institution.

ELIGIBILITY:
Applicants must reside more than 75 miles from Philadelphia to be eligible. Grants are available to scholars and bona fide researchers.

FINANCIAL DATA:
Amount of support per award: Up to $1,500.
Total amount of support: Up to $1,500.

NO. MOST RECENT APPLICANTS: 15.

NO. AWARDS: Varies.

APPLICATION INFO:
Applicants should submit:
(1) one-page statement of the research project and the applicability of the College's resources;
(2) curriculum vitae (not to exceed three pages in length);
(3) budget estimate of travel and lodging needs and;
(4) one letter of reference (to be sent directly from the source to the College).

Electronic applications are strongly encouraged.
Duration: One to two weeks.
Deadline: Applications are accepted on a rolling basis until annual funding is depleted.

ADDRESS INQUIRIES TO:
Director, Wood Institute for the History of Medicine
Travel Grants
(See address above.)

COLUMBIA UNIVERSITY   [540]
517 Butler Library
535 West 114th Street
New York, NY 10027
(212) 854-2247
Fax: (212) 854-4972
E-mail: annthornton@columbia.edu
Web Site: library.columbia.edu/about/awards/bancroft.html

FOUNDED: 1754

NAME(S) OF PROGRAMS:
● **Bancroft Prizes**

TYPE:
Awards/prizes. Prizes of equal rank to be awarded to the authors of distinguished works in either or both American History, including biography and diplomacy.

YEAR PROGRAM STARTED: 1948

PURPOSE:
To honor the authors of books of distinguished merit and distinction, upon the subject of American history in its broadest sense.

LEGAL BASIS:
University.

ELIGIBILITY:
Awards are made for books first published in the previous calendar year. The competition is open to all persons whether connected with Columbia University or not, and whether citizens of the U.S. or any other country.

The word "American" is interpreted to include all the Americas, North, Central and South; however, the award is confined to works originally written in English or of which there is a published translation in English. Volumes of papers, letters and speeches of famous Americans, unless edited by the author himself, are not eligible. Autobiography comes within the terms of the prize, but books reporting on recent personal experiences of Americans, within a limited area both in time and geography, are not considered eligible.

Previous winners are eligible for an award in a later year.

FINANCIAL DATA:
Amount of support per award: $10,000.
Total amount of support: $20,000 to $30,000 annually.

NO. MOST RECENT APPLICANTS: 230.

NO. AWARDS: 2.

APPLICATION INFO:
Works submitted in competition may be sent to the Bancroft Prize Committee at the address above. It is requested that four copies be furnished, three for jury members and one for the Libraries of Columbia University. A letter should accompany the books so that acknowledgement may be made.
Deadline: Works may be submitted after June 1 and before November 1. Page-proof copy may be submitted after November 1 provided the work will be published after that date and before December 31 of the year preceding the award.

ADDRESS INQUIRIES TO:
Bancroft Prize Committee
(See address above.)

THE COORDINATING COUNCIL FOR WOMEN IN HISTORY, INC.

3118 Chaucer Drive
Charlotte, NC 28210
(773) 960-2092
E-mail: execdir@theccwh.org
Web Site: www.theccwh.org

TYPE:
Awards/prizes. The Catherine Prelinger Award is given to a scholar, with a Ph.D. or A.B.D., whose career has not followed a traditional academic path through secondary and higher education and whose work has contributed to women in the historical profession.

See entry 984 for full listing.

THE COORDINATING COUNCIL FOR WOMEN IN HISTORY, INC. [541]

3118 Chaucer Drive
Charlotte, NC 28210
(773) 960-2092
E-mail: execdir@theccwh.org
Web Site: www.theccwh.org

AREAS OF INTEREST:
Women's history.

NAME(S) OF PROGRAMS:
● **CCWH/Berkshire Conference of Women Historians Graduate Student Fellowship**
● **Nupur Chaudhuri First Article Prize**
● **Carol Gold Best Article Award**
● **Ida B. Wells Graduate Student Fellowship**

TYPE:
Awards/prizes; Fellowships.

PURPOSE:
To support the exploration of the diverse experiences and histories of all women; to educate men and women on the status of women in the historical profession; to promote research and interpretation in areas of women's history.

ELIGIBILITY:
CCWH/Berkshire Conference of Women Historians Graduate Student Fellowship: Applicant must be a graduate student completing a dissertation in a history department.

Nupur Chaudhuri First Article Prize: Applicant must be a CCWH member whose first article is published in a refereed journal.

Carol Gold Best Article Award: Applicant must have received the rank of Associate Professor at the time of publication and must be a current member of the CCWH.

Ida B. Wells Graduate Student Fellowship: Applicant must be an A.B.D. graduate student working on a historical dissertation, not necessarily in a history department. Applicants in interdisciplinary areas such as women's studies or ethnic studies are particularly welcome.

FINANCIAL DATA:
Funds are issued in U.S. dollars only.
Amount of support per award: CCWH/Berkshire Conference, Nupur Chaudhuri Prize and Wells Fellowships: $1,000; Carol Gold Best Article Award: $500.

APPLICATION INFO:
Applications are available on the Council web site.
Deadline: May 15.

ADDRESS INQUIRIES TO:
Elizabeth Everton, Ph.D., Executive Director
(See e-mail address above.)

CUSHWA CENTER FOR THE STUDY OF AMERICAN CATHOLICISM [542]

407 Geddes Hall
University of Notre Dame
Notre Dame, IN 46556
(574) 631-5441
Fax: (574) 631-8471
E-mail: cushwa@nd.edu
Web Site: cushwa.nd.edu

NAME(S) OF PROGRAMS:
● **Hibernian Research Award**

TYPE:
Research grants; Travel grants. The Hibernian Research Award is offered to further the scholarly study of Irish America by scholars of any academic discipline engaged in a research project studying the Irish experience in the U.S.

PURPOSE:
To promote the scholarly study of the Irish in the U.S.

ELIGIBILITY:
Awards are made to scholars in any academic discipline.

FINANCIAL DATA:
Amount of support per award: Maximum $2,000.
Total amount of support: Varies.

NO. AWARDS: 2 to 3.

APPLICATION INFO:
Applicant must submit the following documents via e-mail:
(1) completed application form;
(2) current curriculum vitae, including a representative list of applicant's publications and;
(3) a brief description of the research project (maximum 1,000 words).
Deadline: December 31. Applicants will be notified in March.

STAFF:
Kathleen Sprows Cummings, Director
MaDonna Noak, Administrative Coordinator

ADDRESS INQUIRIES TO:
MaDonna Noak, Administrative Coordinator
(See address above.)

CUSHWA CENTER FOR THE STUDY OF AMERICAN CATHOLICISM [543]

407 Geddes Hall
University of Notre Dame
Notre Dame, IN 46556
(574) 631-5441
Fax: (574) 631-8471
E-mail: cushwa@nd.edu
Web Site: cushwa.nd.edu

FOUNDED: 1980

AREAS OF INTEREST:
Catholicism in the U.S.

NAME(S) OF PROGRAMS:
● **Research Travel Grants**

TYPE:
Travel grants. Research Travel Grants support projects that require substantial use of the collection of the library and/or the archives of the University of Notre Dame and help to defray travel and lodging costs.

YEAR PROGRAM STARTED: 1980

PURPOSE:
To make it possible for scholars to make use of the Notre Dame archives.

LEGAL BASIS:
University.

ELIGIBILITY:
Grants are made to scholars in any academic discipline.

FINANCIAL DATA:
Amount of support per award: Up to $2,000. Assistance at finding affordable accommodations is available.
Total amount of support: Varies.

NO. AWARDS: 8 to 12.

APPLICATION INFO:
Applicant must submit the following documents via e-mail:
(1) completed application form;
(2) current curriculum vitae;
(3) 1,000-word description of the project to be undertaken at the center and;
(4) proposed budget estimating travel, lodging and research expenses.
Duration: Varies.
Deadline: December 31. Applicants will be notified in March.

STAFF:
Kathleen Sprows Cummings, Director
MaDonna Noak, Administrative Coordinator

ADDRESS INQUIRIES TO:
MaDonna Noak, Administrative Coordinator
(See address above.)

CUSHWA CENTER FOR THE STUDY OF AMERICAN CATHOLICISM   [544]

407 Geddes Hall
University of Notre Dame
Notre Dame, IN 46556
(574) 631-5441
Fax: (574) 631-8471
E-mail: cushwa@nd.edu
Web Site: cushwa.nd.edu

FOUNDED: 2012

AREAS OF INTEREST:
Catholicism in the U.S.

NAME(S) OF PROGRAMS:
● **Peter R. D'Agostino Research Travel Grant**

TYPE:
Travel grants. Offered in conjunction with Italian Studies at Notre Dame, the Peter R. D'Agostino Research Travel Grant supports research in Roman archives for a significant publication project on U.S. Catholic history.

YEAR PROGRAM STARTED: 2012

PURPOSE:
To facilitate the study of the American past from an international perspective.

LEGAL BASIS:
University.

FINANCIAL DATA:
Amount of support per award: Maximum $5,000.
Total amount of support: Varies.

NO. AWARDS: 1.

APPLICATION INFO:
Applicant must submit the following documents via e-mail:
(1) completed application form;
(2) current curriculum vitae, including a representative list of applicant's publications;
(3) a brief description of the research project (maximum 1,000 words) and;
(4) a detailed budget including travel, lodging and research expenses, and noting cost-sharing with any other potential sources of funding.
Duration: Varies.
Deadline: December 31. Applicants will be notified by March.

STAFF:
Kathleen Sprows Cummings, Director
MaDonna Noak, Administrative Coordinator

ADDRESS INQUIRIES TO:
MaDonna Noak, Administrative Coordinator
(See address above.)

CUSHWA CENTER FOR THE STUDY OF AMERICAN CATHOLICISM   [545]

407 Geddes Hall
University of Notre Dame
Notre Dame, IN 46556
(574) 631-5441
Fax: (574) 631-8471
E-mail: cushwa@nd.edu
Web Site: cushwa.nd.edu

FOUNDED: 1980

AREAS OF INTEREST:
Catholicism in the U.S.

NAME(S) OF PROGRAMS:
● **Mother Theodore Guerin Research Travel Grant**

TYPE:
Travel grants. The Mother Theodore Guerin Research Travel Grant supports scholars who seek to move Catholic women to the forefront of historical narratives.

PURPOSE:
To make it possible for scholars to make use of the Notre Dame archives.

LEGAL BASIS:
University.

ELIGIBILITY:
Grants are made to scholars in any academic discipline whose projects seek to feature Catholic women more predominantly in stories of the past.

FINANCIAL DATA:
Amount of support per award: Up to $1,500.
Total amount of support: Varies.

NO. AWARDS: 4 to 5.

APPLICATION INFO:
Applicant must submit the following documents via e-mail:
(1) completed application form;
(2) current curriculum vitae;
(3) 1,000-word description of the project, including research plan detailing any research repositories or oral history subjects applicant plans to visit and any advance contact between applicant and relevant archivists or others and;
(4) proposed budget estimating travel, lodging and research expenses.
Duration: Varies.
Deadline: December 31. Applicants will be notified in March.

STAFF:
Kathleen Sprows Cummings, Director
MaDonna Noak, Administrative Coordinator

ADDRESS INQUIRIES TO:
MaDonna Noak, Administrative Coordinator
(See address above.)

SHELBY CULLOM DAVIS CENTER FOR HISTORICAL STUDIES   [546]

Princeton University
129 Dickinson Hall
Princeton, NJ 08544-1017
(609) 258-4997
Fax: (609) 258-5326
E-mail: jhoule@princeton.edu
Web Site: history.princeton.edu

FOUNDED: 1968

AREAS OF INTEREST:
Historical research.

TYPE:
Fellowships.

YEAR PROGRAM STARTED: 1969

LEGAL BASIS:
Center is part of a Charitable Educational Institution.

ELIGIBILITY:
Candidates must have a Ph.D. degree. Fellowships are awarded on the strength of the candidate's research projects, the relationship of those projects to the Center's theme, the candidate's previous scholarly work, and the candidate's ability to contribute to the intellectual life and intellectual exchange of the Center.

Princeton faculty members are not eligible.

Applicants who are non-U.S. nationals or who are members of traditionally underrepresented groups are encouraged to apply.

FINANCIAL DATA:
Fellowship includes salary plus research expenses.
Amount of support per award: Varies.
Total amount of support: Varies.

NO. AWARDS: 8 for the year 2020-21.

APPLICATION INFO:
Applicants must apply online and submit the following:
(1) cover letter;
(2) curriculum vitae;
(3) research proposal, preceded by a one paragraph abstract and;
(4) contact information for three references.
Duration: One semester or one academic year. Nonrenewable.
Deadline: December 1. Notification in early March.

ADDRESS INQUIRIES TO:
Jennifer Goldman, Manager
(See address above.)

THE DIRKSEN CONGRESSIONAL CENTER

2815 Broadway
Pekin, IL 61554
(309) 347-7113
E-mail: fmackaman@dirksencenter.org
Web Site: www.dirksencongressionalcenter.org

TYPE:
Research grants; Seed money grants; Travel grants. Financial awards to individuals conducting research about the U.S. Congress and its leaders.

See entry 1816 for full listing.

FENIMORE ART MUSEUM

5798 State Highway 80
Cooperstown, NY 13326
(607) 547-1416
Fax: (607) 547-1404
E-mail: publications@fenimoreart.org
Web Site: www.fenimoreartmuseum.org

TYPE:
Awards/prizes. Prizes for published catalogues treating collections located or exhibited in New York state.

See entry 410 for full listing.

FENIMORE ART MUSEUM   [547]

5798 State Highway 80
Cooperstown, NY 13326
(607) 547-1416
Fax: (607) 547-1404
E-mail: publications@fenimoreart.org
Web Site: www.fenimoreartmuseum.org

FOUNDED: 1899

AREAS OF INTEREST:
The history of New York state.

NAME(S) OF PROGRAMS:
● **The Dixon Ryan Fox Manuscript Prize of the Fenimore Art Museum**

TYPE:
Awards/prizes. Annual cash prize and publication assistance.

YEAR PROGRAM STARTED: 1973

PURPOSE:
To award the best unpublished, book-length monograph dealing with the history of New York state, as judged by an editorial committee.

LEGAL BASIS:
Private nonprofit association.

ELIGIBILITY:
Manuscripts may deal with any aspect of New York state history. Biographies of individuals whose careers illuminate aspects of the history of the state are also eligible, as are manuscripts dealing with such cultural matters as literature and the arts, provided that in such cases the methodology used is historical. Works of fiction are not eligible.

FINANCIAL DATA:
Amount of support per award: $3,000.
Total amount of support: $3,000.

NO. MOST RECENT APPLICANTS: 5 for the year 2017.

NO. AWARDS: 1 annually.

APPLICATION INFO:
Manuscripts must be typed, double-spaced, with at least one-inch margins. Please send two copies. Clear, readable photocopies or computer printouts are acceptable.
Duration: One-time award. Nonrenewable.
Deadline: March 1. Announcement by July 30 annually.

PUBLICATIONS:
Application guidelines.

OFFICERS AND TRUSTEES:
Jeffrey H. Pressman, M.D., Chairman of the Board
Thomas O. Putnam, Vice Chairman
Douglas E. Evelyn
Kathleen Flanagan
Nellie Gipson
Shelley Graham
Robert S. Hanft
Josef E. Jelinek
Charles B. Kieler
Doris Fischer Malesardi
Erna Morgan McReynolds
Anne G. Older
Ellen Tillapaugh
Richard C. Vanison

ADDRESS INQUIRIES TO:
Ashley Werner
Executive Assistant to the President
E-mail: a.werner@fenimore.org

GERMAN HISTORICAL INSTITUTE   [548]
1607 New Hampshire Avenue, N.W.
Washington, DC 20009-2562
(202) 387-3355
E-mail: fellowships@ghi-dc.org
Web Site: www.ghi-dc.org

FOUNDED: 1987

AREAS OF INTEREST:
German and U.S. history, transatlantic studies and comparative studies in economic, social, cultural and political history.

NAME(S) OF PROGRAMS:
● **Doctoral and Postdoctoral Fellowships**

TYPE:
Fellowships. The Institute awards short-term fellowships to German and American doctoral students as well as postdoctoral scholars/Habilitanden in the fields of German

history, the history of German-American relations, and the role of Germany and the U.S. in international relations.

YEAR PROGRAM STARTED: 1989

PURPOSE:
To support research programme for doctoral students and postdoctoral scholars in the fields of German history, the history of German-American relations, the role of Germany and the U.S. in international relations.

ELIGIBILITY:
Open to German and U.S. doctoral and postdoctoral students.

FINANCIAL DATA:
Amount of support per award: Monthly stipend of EUR 2,000 for doctoral students and EUR 3,400 for postdoctoral scholars.

NO. MOST RECENT APPLICANTS: 100 annually.

NO. AWARDS: 20 to 25 annually.

APPLICATION INFO:
Applications should include cover letter, curriculum vitae, proof of academic degree (or transcripts), project description (3,000 words), research schedule for the fellowship period, and at least one letter of reference. Although applicants may write in either English or German, it is recommended that they use the language in which they are most proficient.
Duration: One to five months, but can be extended one month.
Deadline: April 1 and October 1 annually.

ADDRESS INQUIRIES TO:
Bryan Hart, Program Officer
(See address above.)

HAGLEY MUSEUM AND LIBRARY   [549]
Hagley Library
298 Buck Road
Wilmington, DE 19807
(302) 658-2400 ext. 243
E-mail: clockman@hagley.org
Web Site: www.hagley.org

FOUNDED: 1953

AREAS OF INTEREST:
American business, economic and labor history and the history of technology and science.

NAME(S) OF PROGRAMS:
● **Henry Belin du Pont Dissertation Fellowship in Business, Technology, and Society**
● **Henry Belin du Pont Research Grants**
● **Hagley Exploratory Research Grant**

TYPE:
Fellowships; Research grants; Travel grants; Visiting scholars. Grants to support short-term research in the imprint, manuscript, pictorial and artifact collections of the Hagley Museum and Library.

The Henry Belin du Pont Dissertation Fellowship in Business, Technology, and Society supports research and writing by candidates for doctoral degrees. Projects should demonstrate superior intellectual quality and make substantial use of Hagley's collections.

Henry Belin du Pont Research Grants support research in the collections of the museum and library.

Hagley Exploratory Research Grant supports a one-week visit by scholars who believe that their project will benefit from Hagley research collections, but need the opportunity to explore them on-site to determine if a Henry Belin du Pont research grant application is warranted.

YEAR PROGRAM STARTED: 1962

PURPOSE:
To encourage and support research in the collections.

LEGAL BASIS:
Nonprofit educational institution.

ELIGIBILITY:
Degree candidates and advanced scholars working in Hagley's areas of collecting and research interest are invited to apply. Applications should include research proposals specifying the collections or materials to be studied. Residential award, not a scholarship for college or graduate school.

Hagley Exploratory Research Grant: Priority will be given to junior scholars with innovative projects that seek to expand on existing scholarships.

FINANCIAL DATA:
Amount of support per award: Hagley Exploratory Research Grant: Stipend of $400; Henry Belin du Pont Dissertation Fellowship: Up to $6,500; Henry Belin du Pont Research Grants: $400 per week for recipients residing more than 50 miles from Hagley, and $200 per week for those within 50 miles; International Research: $500 plus travel and on-site housing.
Total amount of support: Approximately $27,100.

NO. MOST RECENT APPLICANTS: 56.

NO. AWARDS: 40.

APPLICATION INFO:
Application forms and guidelines are available online.
Duration: Hagley Exploratory Research Grant: One week; Henry Belin du Pont Dissertation Fellowship: Up to four months; Henry Belin du Pont Research Grants: Up to eight weeks.
Deadline: Hagley Exploratory Research Grant and Henry Belin du Pont Research Grants: March 31, June 30 and October 31; Henry Belin du Pont Dissertation Fellowship in Business, Technology, and Society: November 15.

PUBLICATIONS:
Guides to Collection; application; guidelines.

STAFF:
Jill McKenzie, Executive Director
Roger Horowitz, Center Director
Carol Ressler Lockman, Center Manager

RESEARCH STAFF:
Erik Rau, Director of Library
Max Moeller, Curator, Published Collections
Kevin Martin, Andrew W. Mellon Curator of Audiovisual Collections

ADDRESS INQUIRIES TO:
Carol Ressler Lockman, Center Manager
(See address above.)

THE HISTORIC NEW ORLEANS COLLECTION [550]
410 Chartres Street
New Orleans, LA 70130
(504) 523-4662
Fax: (504) 293-8162
E-mail: wrc@hnoc.org
Web Site: www.hnoc.org

FOUNDED: 1966

AREAS OF INTEREST:
Louisiana history and recognition of published book-length research in the field.

NAME(S) OF PROGRAMS:
● **Kemper and Leila Williams Prize in Louisiana History**

TYPE:
Awards/prizes.

YEAR PROGRAM STARTED: 1974

PURPOSE:
To encourage excellence in the writing and publishing of Louisiana history.

LEGAL BASIS:
Nonprofit foundation.

ELIGIBILITY:
Published books are eligible, but only in the year of their publication or completion.

FINANCIAL DATA:
Amount of support per award: $1,500.
Total amount of support: $1,500.

NO. MOST RECENT APPLICANTS: 22.

NO. AWARDS: 1.

APPLICATION INFO:
Application forms are available on the web site. Four copies of each entry must be submitted.
Deadline: January 15 for works published the previous calendar year. Announcement in March.

PUBLICATIONS:
Application guidelines.

STAFF:
Daniel Hammer, President and Chief Executive Officer

BOARD OF DIRECTORS:
Drew Jardine, Chairperson
John Kallenborn, Vice Chairperson
Hilton S. Bell
Bonnie Boyd
Charles Lapeyre
E. Alexandra Stafford
Lisa H. Wilson

ADDRESS INQUIRIES TO:
Chairperson
Williams Prize Committee
(See address above.)

THE HISTORIC NEW ORLEANS COLLECTION [551]
410 Chartres Street
New Orleans, LA 70130
(504) 598-7183
Fax: (504) 598-7168
E-mail: wrc@hnoc.org
Web Site: www.hnoc.org/research/prizes-and-fellowships

FOUNDED: 1966

AREAS OF INTEREST:
Louisiana history and support of research in the field.

NAME(S) OF PROGRAMS:
● **The Dianne Woest Fellowship in the Arts and Humanities**

TYPE:
Fellowships.

YEAR PROGRAM STARTED: 2005

PURPOSE:
To encourage research using The Historic New Orleans Collection, as well as other research facilities in the greater New Orleans area.

ELIGIBILITY:
Open to doctoral candidates, academic and museum professionals and independent scholars. U.S. citizenship not required, but applicants should be fluent in English.

Fellows will be expected to:
(1) present a public lecture during their term of residence and;
(2) acknowledge The Collection in any published work drawing on fellowship research.

FINANCIAL DATA:
Amount of support per award: Maximum $4,000 stipend.
Total amount of support: Varies.

NO. MOST RECENT APPLICANTS: 32.

NO. AWARDS: 1 to 3.

APPLICATION INFO:
Information may be obtained by e-mailing Jason Wiese, Chief Curator, at jason.wiese@hnoc.org.
Duration: One to three months.
Deadline: November 15. Announcement February 1. Research to begin on or after April 1.

ADDRESS INQUIRIES TO:
Jason Wiese, Chief Curator
(See address above.)

*SPECIAL STIPULATIONS:
Fellows may select their period of residence, but all research must commence and conclude during the specified fiscal year April 1 to March 31.

HISTORY COLORADO STATE HISTORICAL FUND [552]
1200 Broadway
Denver, CO 80203
(303) 866-3493
Fax: (303) 866-2041
E-mail: hc_shs@state.co.us
Web Site: www.historycolorado.org/state-historical-fund

FOUNDED: 1990

AREAS OF INTEREST:
Historic preservation.

TYPE:
Project/program grants. Grants for historic preservation projects.

The State Historical Fund was created by the 1990 constitutional amendment allowing limited gaming in the towns of Cripple Creek, Central City and Black Hawk. The amendment directs that a portion of the gaming tax revenues be used for historic preservation throughout the state.

YEAR PROGRAM STARTED: 1990

PURPOSE:
To promote historic preservation throughout the state of Colorado.

ELIGIBILITY:
Criteria vary for different types of grants. Funds are distributed through a competitive process, and all projects must demonstrate strong public benefit and community support. The Fund assists in a wide variety of preservation projects, including restoration and rehabilitation of historic buildings, architectural assessments, archaeological excavations, designation and interpretation of historic places, preservation planning studies, and education and training programs.

Organizations have to have 501(c)(3) not-for-profit status. Religious organizations may apply, but no grants are given to individuals.

Historic preservation projects in the state of Colorado only.

GEOG. RESTRICTIONS: Colorado.

FINANCIAL DATA:
Amount of support per award: Mini-grants: Up to $35,000. Full grants: Up to approximately $200,000.

APPLICATION INFO:
Contact the History Colorado office and use the application on its web site. Colorado Substitute W9 Form for documentation required.
Duration: Varies; grantees can reapply for new projects.
Deadline: April 1 and October 1.

ADDRESS INQUIRIES TO:
Megan Eflin, Outreach Coordinator
(See address above.)

HISTORY OF SCIENCE SOCIETY [553]
440 Geddes Hall
University of Notre Dame
Notre Dame, IN 46556
(574) 631-1194
E-mail: info@hssonline.org
Web Site: www.hssonline.org

FOUNDED: 1924

AREAS OF INTEREST:
History of science and its cultural influences.

NAME(S) OF PROGRAMS:
● **Derek Price/Rod Webster Prize**

TYPE:
Awards/prizes. Prize for the best scholarly article published in *Isis* during the past three years.

YEAR PROGRAM STARTED: 1979

PURPOSE:
To acknowledge the best scholarly work to appear in *Isis*.

LEGAL BASIS:
Nonprofit 501(c)(3).

ELIGIBILITY:
Applicant must have published an article in *Isis*.

FINANCIAL DATA:
Amount of support per award: $1,000.

NO. AWARDS: 1 per year.

APPLICATION INFO:
All eligible articles are automatically nominated for this prize.
Deadline: April 1.

PUBLICATIONS:
Syllabus samplers, Topical Essays for Teachers, Non-Western Science.

ADDRESS INQUIRIES TO:
Robert J. Malone, Executive Director
(See address above.)

HISTORY OF SCIENCE SOCIETY [554]

440 Geddes Hall
University of Notre Dame
Notre Dame, IN 46556
(574) 631-1194
E-mail: info@hssonline.org
Web Site: www.hssonline.org

FOUNDED: 1924

AREAS OF INTEREST:
History of science, women in science and science service.

NAME(S) OF PROGRAMS:
- **Watson Davis and Helen Miles Davis Prize**
- **Joseph H. Hazen Education Prize**
- **Suzanne J. Levinson Prize**
- **Philip J. Pauly Prize**
- **Pfizer Prize**
- **Ronald Rainger Prize**
- **Nathan Reingold Prize**
- **Margaret W. Rossiter History of Women in Science Prize**

TYPE:
Awards/prizes. The Davis Prize honors books in the history of science directed to a wide public and was established through a long-term pledge from Miles and Audrey Davis.

The Joseph H. Hazen Education Prize recognizes excellence in teaching in the history of science.

The Levinson Prize is awarded in even-numbered years to an outstanding book in the life sciences and natural history.

The Philip J. Pauly Prize is awarded to the best first book on the history of science in the Americas.

The Pfizer Prize honors the best English-language work related to the history of science published in the preceding three years.

The Ronald Rainger Prize is awarded for early career work in the history of earth and environmental sciences.

The Nathan Reingold Prize is given for an original essay in the history of science and its cultural influences.

The Margaret W. Rossiter History of Women in Science Prize honors an outstanding book, or in even-numbered years an article, published in the preceding four years.

YEAR PROGRAM STARTED: 1955

PURPOSE:
To recognize and reward distinguished writing in the field of the history of science.

LEGAL BASIS:
Nonprofit.

ELIGIBILITY:
For the Davis Prize, books should be introductory in assuming no previous knowledge of the subject and be directed to audiences of beginning students and general readers. Books should introduce an entire field, a chronological period, a national tradition or the work of a noteworthy individual. Multi-authored or edited books are eligible, whereas unrevised reprints of previously published works are ineligible.

For the History of Women in Science Prize, books may take a biographical, institutional, theoretical or other approach. Include in the topic, "Women in Science," discussions of women's activities in science, analyses of past scientific practices that deal explicitly with gender and investigations regarding women as viewed by scientists. These may relate to medicine, technology and the social sciences as well as the natural sciences.

The Levinson Prize is open to all books in the life sciences and natural history published in the four years prior to the award year.

For the Philip J. Pauly Prize, the book must have been published within the last three calendar years.

The Pfizer Prize is open to all books published in English. The quality of the work is the overriding criterion.

The Ronald Rainger Prize is open to single, specific works, such as an article, exhibition, or interactive resource, whose primary topic is the history of the earth and environmental sciences broadly construed. Works in languages other than English must be accompanied by an English translation.

The Reingold Prize is open to graduate students at any International college. Essays dealing with medical subjects are not accepted, though papers dealing with the relations between medicine and the natural sciences are welcome. Essay must be no more than 8,000 words in length and thoroughly documented.

FINANCIAL DATA:
Amount of support per award: Davis, Hazen, Levinson and Rossiter History of Women in Science Awards: $1,000; Pfizer Prize: $2,500; Reingold Prize: $500 award, $500 in travel expenses.

APPLICATION INFO:
Contact the Society for details.
Deadline: Reingold Prize: June 1: All others: April 1.

PUBLICATIONS:
Newsletter.

OFFICERS:
Bernard Lightman, President
Jan Golinski, Vice President
Gwen Kay, Treasurer
Luis Campos, Secretary
Alexandria Hui, Editor
Matthew Lavine, Editor

ADDRESS INQUIRIES TO:
Robert J. Malone, Executive Director
(See address above.)

*PLEASE NOTE:
Society does not give grants, scholarships or fellowships.

HOOVER PRESIDENTIAL FOUNDATION

P.O. Box 696
West Branch, IA 52358
(319) 643-5327
Fax: (319) 643-2391
E-mail: info@hooverpf.org
Web Site: www.hooverpresidentialfoundation.org

TYPE:
Research grants; Travel grants. Money is only available for travel to the Hoover Presidential Library in West Branch, IA. The program seeks to encourage scholarly use of the holdings of the Herbert Hoover Presidential Library. It is specifically intended to promote the study of subjects of interest and concern to Herbert Hoover, Lou Henry Hoover, their associates and other public figures as reflected in the Library's 150 manuscript collections.

See entry 1822 for full listing.

IEEE HISTORY CENTER [555]

Stevens Institute of Technology
Samuel C. Williams Library, Third Floor
One Castle Point Terrace
Hoboken, NJ 07030
(732) 562-5468
Fax: (732) 562-6020
E-mail: ieee-history@ieee.org
Web Site: www.ieee.org/history_center

FOUNDED: 1884

AREAS OF INTEREST:
History of technology and sociology of technology.

NAME(S) OF PROGRAMS:
- **IEEE Fellowship in the History of Electrical and Computing Technology**
- **The Elizabeth and Emerson Pugh Young Scholar in Residence at the IEEE History Center**

TYPE:
Fellowships; Internships. Fellowship in the History of Electrical and Computing Technology: Award for one year of full-time doctoral or postdoctoral work in the history of electrical engineering and technology at a college or university of recognized standing:

The Elizabeth and Emerson Pugh Young Scholar in Residence: Two-month internship for graduate research.

YEAR PROGRAM STARTED: 1980

ELIGIBILITY:
Fellowship in the History of Electrical and Computing Technology: Individuals doing graduate or postgraduate work in the history of electrical technology.

The Elizabeth and Emerson Pugh Young Scholar in Residence: Scholars at the beginning of their career studying the history of electrical technology and computing.

FINANCIAL DATA:
Total amount of support: Fellowship in the History of Electrical and Computing Technology: $25,000 annually; The Elizabeth and Emerson Pugh Young Scholar in Residence: $5,000.

NO. MOST RECENT APPLICANTS: 14.

NO. AWARDS: 1 Fellowship and 1 Internship annually.

APPLICATION INFO:
Identification and description of a research project of value is an important part of the application procedure. Further information is available upon request to the Institute.
Duration: Fellowship in the History of Electrical and Computing Technology: One academic year; The Elizabeth and Emerson Pugh Young Scholar in Residence: Two months.
Deadline: Fellowship in the History of Electrical and Computing Technology: February 1; The Elizabeth and Emerson Pugh Young Scholar in Residence: March 1.

PUBLICATIONS:
Newsletter.

ADDRESS INQUIRIES TO:
   Director, IEEE History Center
   (See address above.)

THE INTERCOLLEGIATE STUDIES INSTITUTE

3901 Centerville Road
Wilmington, DE 19807
(302) 652-4600
(302) 524-6148
Fax: (302) 652-1760
E-mail: caguda@isi.org
Web Site: www.isi.org

TYPE:
   Awards/prizes; Fellowships; Scholarships.
   The Weaver Fellowship is granted to students
   who intend to use their advanced degree to
   teach.

See entry 1824 for full listing.

ISTITUTO ITALIANO PER GLI STUDI STORICI   [556]

Via Benedetto Croce, 12
80134 Naples Italy
(39) 081 5517159
(39) 081 5512390
Fax: (39) 081 5514813
E-mail: info@iiss.it
Web Site: www.iiss.it

FOUNDED: 1947

AREAS OF INTEREST:
   Institute for the study of history, philosophy
   and literature.

NAME(S) OF PROGRAMS:
   ● **Federico II Scholarship**
   ● **Istituto italiano per gli studi storici
      Scholarships for Graduate Students
      and Young Postdocs**

TYPE:
   Awards/prizes; Conferences/seminars;
   Research grants; Scholarships. Awards for
   historical, literature and philosophical studies
   at the Istituto Italiano per gli Studi Storici in
   Naples.

   Federico II Scholarship: Funded by the
   Universita di Napoli Federico II for graduates
   from Italian universities with medieval
   studies final dissertation.

YEAR PROGRAM STARTED: 1947

PURPOSE:
   To promote historical, philosophical and
   literature research.

LEGAL BASIS:
   Private institution.

ELIGIBILITY:
   These annual scholarships are offered to
   young graduates and young postdoctorates,
   both Italian and non-Italian, in the disciplines
   of history, philosophy and literature.
   Applicants must have presented their final
   university dissertation before the final
   application date and must be less than 32
   years of age.

   Applications will not be accepted from
   candidates who:
   (1) already received a scholarship from the
   Istituto in past years;
   (2) will receive payment from another type
   of activity;
   (3) will have their Ph.D. course funded by
   other institutions or;
   (4) hold a scholarship from other institutions
   for the same year.

Italian language competence is required.

FINANCIAL DATA:
   The scholarship will be paid to the successful
   candidates in 12 monthly installments starting
   from November of the year of application.
   Amount of support per award: Scholarships:
   EUR 9,700 for Campania Region; EUR
   12,000 for students residing outside of
   Campania; Federico II Scholarship: EUR
   10,300.
   Total amount of support: EUR 260,000.

NO. MOST RECENT APPLICANTS: 200.

NO. AWARDS: 1 Federico II Scholarship; 14
Scholarships for Graduate Students and
Young Postdocs.

APPLICATION INFO:
   Application form must be sent duly filled in
   and signed, together with the following
   documents:
   (1) copy of the identity card or passport;
   (2) curriculum studiorum, including linguistic
   competences (Italian is mandatory);
   (3) degree or Ph.D. certificate showing marks
   for individual exams and/or overall
   evaluation;
   (4) copy of the graduation or Ph.D.
   dissertation and a maximum of five published
   or draft research publications, both in hard
   copy and digital file (in case of e-mail
   submission, only digital version is required);
   (5) research project (maximum five pages)
   including aims, timing, materials, and other
   institutions where the research can be carried
   out and;
   (6) two academic letters of reference.

   Applications which do not completely satisfy
   the above conditions will not be considered.
   Duration: Twelve months (December to May
   for courses and June to November for
   research). The scholarship can be renewed
   for a second year.
   Deadline: Application materials must be
   received no later than the deadline published
   on the IISS web site. (Postal dates will not
   be accepted.)

PUBLICATIONS:
   *Annali dell'Istituto Italiano per gli studi
   storici*; series of monographs; series of
   historical, philosophical and literary texts;
   lectures; essays; inventories.

DIRECTORS:
   Roberto Giordano, Chief Executive Officer
   Prof. Natalino Irti, President

ADMINISTRATIVE OFFICERS:
   Dr. Marta Herling, Secretary-General

ADDRESS INQUIRIES TO:
   Dr. Marta Herling, General Secretary
   (See address above.)

*SPECIAL STIPULATIONS:
   Fellows must carry out their research project
   and attend lessons until the end of the
   academic year.

   From December to May, fellows must reside
   in Naples in order to follow the courses and
   seminars organized by the Institute. In the
   five months that follow, they can carry out
   their research at another institution, either in
   Italy or abroad. They must make a first report
   about their research activities by June 30 and
   a final one by October 31.

   The Institute reserves the right to withdraw
   funding should fellows prove themselves to
   be seriously inadequate.

ITALIAN AMERICAN STUDIES ASSOCIATION   [557]

P.O. Box 487
Millbrae, CA 94030
(408) 738-4564
Fax: (408) 864-5629
E-mail: quinnroseanne@deanza.edu
Web Site: www.italianamericanstudies.net

FOUNDED: 1966

AREAS OF INTEREST:
   Encouragement of Italian-American studies,
   collection, preservation, study and
   popularization of materials that illuminate the
   Italian-American experience in the U.S. and
   Canada.

CONSULTING OR VOLUNTEER SERVICES:
   Sponsors an annual national conference,
   resource depositories and maintains an
   information network.

NAME(S) OF PROGRAMS:
   ● **IASA Memorial Fellowship**

TYPE:
   Fellowships.

YEAR PROGRAM STARTED: 1970

PURPOSE:
   To promote understanding of the Italian
   experience in America.

LEGAL BASIS:
   Nonprofit, tax-exempt organization.

ELIGIBILITY:
   Graduate students in any discipline whose
   work focuses on Italian American culture are
   eligible and encouraged to apply. Student
   must be in good standing in their own home
   institution's graduate program (i.e., fully
   enrolled, degree-seeking, completing work in
   a timely manner, and no academic
   probation). Prior candidates are especially
   encouraged to resubmit previously
   non-funded applications. Qualifications,
   seniority, and quality of application will be
   considered in decision making.

FINANCIAL DATA:
   Amount of support per award: $1,000.
   Total amount of support: $1,000.

NO. AWARDS: 1.

APPLICATION INFO:
   Guidelines are available online.
   Duration: One year.
   Deadline: September.

PUBLICATIONS:
   Annual Proceedings.

OFFICERS:
   Alan J. Gravano, President

ADDRESS INQUIRIES TO:
   Dr. Roseanne Giannini Quinn
   (See address above.)

THE LYNDON BAINES JOHNSON FOUNDATION

2313 Red River Street
Austin, TX 78705-5702
(512) 721-0263
E-mail: grants@lbjfoundation.org
Web Site: www.lbjlibrary.org/page/foundation

TYPE:
   Fellowships; Research grants.

See entry 1826 for full listing.

KENTUCKY HISTORICAL SOCIETY [558]

100 West Broadway
Frankfort, KY 40601
(502) 564-1792
E-mail: khsfellowship@ky.gov
Web Site: history.ky.gov

FOUNDED: 1836

AREAS OF INTEREST:
Historical research, publishing, and public history.

NAME(S) OF PROGRAMS:
- **Scholarly Research Fellowship Program**

TYPE:
Fellowships; Research grants; Travel grants. Scholarly Research Fellowship Program encourages and promotes advanced research on all aspects of Kentucky-related local, regional, national and transnational history.

PURPOSE:
To assist - through these fellowships - researchers with travel and living expenses while using the Kentucky Historical Society research collections.

ELIGIBILITY:
These short-term fellowships are intended to support serious scholarly work. They enable individuals to pursue advanced study and research in the collections of the Kentucky Historical Society. Applications are welcome from independent scholars, as well as from college and university professors, graduate students, and scholars working in other related disciplines.

FINANCIAL DATA:
Amount of support per award: Typically $500 (for one week) to up to $2,000 (for four weeks).

APPLICATION INFO:
Applications are available on the Kentucky Historical Society web site. All applications are peer-reviewed by a panel of leading historians.
Deadline: October 1 and March 1.

ADDRESS INQUIRIES TO:
Stephanie M. Lang, Ph.D.
Coordinator, Research Fellowship Program
(See telephone and e-mail address above.)

LIBRARY COMPANY OF PHILADELPHIA [559]

1314 Locust Street
Philadelphia, PA 19107
(215) 546-3181
Fax: (215) 546-5167
E-mail: jgreen@librarycompany.org
Web Site: www.librarycompany.org

FOUNDED: 1731

AREAS OF INTEREST:
American studies.

NAME(S) OF PROGRAMS:
- **Albert M. Greenfield Foundation Dissertation Fellowships**
- **NEH Postdoctoral Fellowships**
- **Program in African-American History**
- **Program in Early American Economy and Society**
- **Research Fellowships in American History and Culture**

TYPE:
Fellowships. Albert M. Greenfield Foundation Dissertation Fellowship: Supports dissertation research in residence at the Library Company on any subject relevant to its collections.

Program in African-American History: Its Mellon Scholars Fellowship Program offers postdoctoral, dissertation and short-term fellowships to support scholarly work in African-American history from the 17th through the 19th centuries.

Program in Early American Economy and Society: Pre-1860 American economic and business history.

Research Fellowships in American History and Culture: 18th and 19th Century American social and cultural history.

YEAR PROGRAM STARTED: 1988

PURPOSE:
To promote early American historic studies.

ELIGIBILITY:
Both the short-term and long-term Fellowships support postdoctoral and dissertation research. Both also require that the project proposal demonstrate that the Library Company has a primary source central to the research topic. NEH fellows must be U.S. citizens or residents at least three years.

FINANCIAL DATA:
Amount of support per award: Long-term: $20,000 to $50,000; Short-term: $2,000.
Total amount of support: Approximately $170,000 annually.

CO-OP FUNDING PROGRAMS: The short-term fellowships are jointly sponsored with the Historical Society of Pennsylvania.

NO. MOST RECENT APPLICANTS: 200.

NO. AWARDS: Long-term: 11; Short-term: 44.

APPLICATION INFO:
For the short-term fellowships, applicants must complete the required electronic cover sheet and submit one portable document format (PDF) containing a resume and a two- to four-page description of the proposed research. One letter of recommendation should arrive under separate cover in PDF format as well. E-mail materials to fellowships@librarycompany.org.
Duration: Short-term: One month; Long-term: Three to nine months.
Deadline: Program and Research Fellowships: March 1; Long-term Postdoctoral Fellowships: November 1.

ADDRESS INQUIRIES TO:
Jim Green, Fellowship Office
(See address above.)

JAMES MADISON MEMORIAL FELLOWSHIP FOUNDATION [560]

1613 Duke Street
Alexandria, VA 22314
(800) 525-6928
Fax: (703) 838-2180 (VA); (507) 931-8924 (MN)
E-mail: madison@scholarshipamerica.org
Web Site: www.jamesmadison.gov

FOUNDED: 1986

AREAS OF INTEREST:
The roots, principles, framing and development of the U.S. Constitution.

NAME(S) OF PROGRAMS:
- **James Madison Fellowship Program**

TYPE:
Fellowships. The Foundation awards fellowships to college seniors and college graduates without teaching experience (Junior Fellows) and to experienced secondary school teachers in grades seven-12 (Senior Fellows) who will normally enroll respectively in full- and part-time graduate study leading to one of the following Master's degrees: Master's degree in American history or political science, a degree of Master of Arts in Teaching in history or political science, or a related Master's degree in education that permits a concentration in American history, American government or civics.

YEAR PROGRAM STARTED: 1992

PURPOSE:
To support the graduate study of the roots, principles, framing and development of the U.S. Constitution.

LEGAL BASIS:
Foundation.

ELIGIBILITY:
Each fellowship recipient must take at least 12 semester hours or their equivalent in topics directly related to the framing and history of the U.S. Constitution.

A James Madison Fellow must be a U.S. citizen or U.S. national, qualify for study toward one of the qualifying Master's degrees indicated and agree to teach full-time in a secondary school for no less than one year for each full academic year of study under a fellowship.

A Senior Fellow must be a full-time teacher of American history, American government, or civics in grades seven through 12 during the previous year and be under contract or prospective contract to teach full-time as a secondary school teacher of the same subjects for the upcoming academic year.

A Junior Fellow must possess a Bachelor's degree or plan to receive a Bachelor's degree no later than August 31 of the year of application.

GEOG. RESTRICTIONS: United States and its territories.

FINANCIAL DATA:
Amount of support per award: Up to $24,000 for each award.

NO. MOST RECENT APPLICANTS: 250 for the year 2018.

NO. AWARDS: 1 per state per year, as funding permits.

APPLICATION INFO:
Applicant must register online to complete the application process.
Duration: Up to five years for Senior Fellows. Up to two years for Junior Fellows.
Deadline: March 1, annually.

ADDRESS INQUIRIES TO:
James Madison Fellowship Program
One Scholarship Way
St. Peter, MN 56082

*SPECIAL STIPULATIONS:
No funding for Ph.D. programs.

JACOB RADER MARCUS CENTER OF THE AMERICAN JEWISH ARCHIVES

3101 Clifton Avenue
Cincinnati, OH 45220-2408
(513) 221-1875
Fax: (513) 221-7812
E-mail: lfrankel@huc.edu
Web Site: www.americanjewisharchives.org

TYPE:
Fellowships. The Marcus Center's Fellowship Program provides recipients with month-long fellowships for research and writing at The Jacob Rader Marcus Center of the American Jewish Archives. Fellowship stipends will be sufficient to cover transportation and living expenses while in residence.

See entry 757 for full listing.

THE MASSACHUSETTS HISTORICAL SOCIETY   [561]

1154 Boylston Street
Boston, MA 02215
(617) 536-1608
Fax: (617) 859-0074
E-mail: research_programs@masshist.org
Web Site: www.masshist.org

FOUNDED: 1791

AREAS OF INTEREST:
Civil War history, Massachusetts, New England, and U.S. history.

NAME(S) OF PROGRAMS:
- **Suzanne and Caleb Loring Fellowship**

TYPE:
Fellowships. Fellowship funds research on the Civil War, its origins, and consequences, for projects that use the resources at the Massachusetts Historical Society and the Boston Athenaeum. Research must be conducted for at least four weeks at each of the two participating institutions.

YEAR PROGRAM STARTED: 2008

PURPOSE:
To support scholarship on the history of Massachusetts and the nation; to encourage projects that draw on the Civil War resources of the participating organizations.

ELIGIBILITY:
Open to independent scholars, advanced graduate students and holders of a Ph.D. or equivalent. Applicants must be U.S. citizens or already hold the J-1 visa or equivalent documents that will allow them to accept the stipend.

FINANCIAL DATA:
Amount of support per award: $4,000.

NO. AWARDS: 1.

APPLICATION INFO:
Applicants must submit the following materials online:
(1) cover letter;
(2) current curriculum vitae;
(3) project proposal, approximately 1,000 words in length, which includes a description of the project, a statement explaining the historiographical significance of the project, and an indication of the specific Massachusetts Historical Society and Boston Athenaeum collections the applicant wishes to consult and;
(4) for those not holding a Ph.D., a letter of recommendation from a faculty member familiar with the student's work and with the project being proposed.

Duration: Minimum of 20 days at each of the two institutions, for a total of 40 days.
Deadline: Applications must be submitted by 11:59 P.M. on February 15.

ADDRESS INQUIRIES TO:
E-mail: fellowships@masshist.org

THE MASSACHUSETTS HISTORICAL SOCIETY   [562]

1154 Boylston Street
Boston, MA 02215-3695
(617) 536-1608
(617) 646-0588
Fax: (617) 859-0074
E-mail: education@masshist.org
Web Site: www.masshist.org

FOUNDED: 1791

AREAS OF INTEREST:
Massachusetts, New England and U.S. history.

NAME(S) OF PROGRAMS:
- **Kass Teacher Fellowships at MHS**
- **Swensrud Teacher Fellowships at MHS**

TYPE:
Fellowships. Kass and Swensrud Teacher Fellowships are offered to public and/or parochial schoolteachers and library media specialists for on-site research at the Society.

YEAR PROGRAM STARTED: 2001

PURPOSE:
To support four weeks of research at the Society for the creation of a curriculum unit.

ELIGIBILITY:
Applications are welcome from any K-12 teacher or library media specialist who has a serious interest in using the collections at the MHS to prepare primary-source-based curricula, supported by documents and visual aids, in the fields of American history, world history or English/language arts.

The fellowship process is competitive. Awards are made on the strength of:
(1) project design;
(2) the plan for using the Society collections;
(3) the creativity of the proposed classroom activities;
(4) usability in other classrooms and;
(5) recommendations.

Open to U.S. residents only.

GEOG. RESTRICTIONS: United States.

FINANCIAL DATA:
Amount of support per award: Kass Teacher Fellowships: Stipend of $2,000; Swensrud Teacher Fellowships: Stipend of $4,000.

NO. MOST RECENT APPLICANTS: Kass Teacher Fellowships: 15; Swensrud Teacher Fellowships: 35.

NO. AWARDS: Kass Teacher Fellowships: Minimum of 1; Swensrud Teacher Fellowships: Minimum of 3.

APPLICATION INFO:
Application information is available on the web site.
Duration: Four weeks.
Deadline: February.

ADDRESS INQUIRIES TO:
Kate Melchior
Assistant Director of Education
Center for the Teaching of History
Tel: (617) 646-0588
(See address above.)

THE MASSACHUSETTS HISTORICAL SOCIETY   [563]

1154 Boylston Street
Boston, MA 02215
(617) 536-1608
Fax: (617) 859-0074
E-mail: research_programs@masshist.org
Web Site: www.masshist.org

FOUNDED: 1791

AREAS OF INTEREST:
Massachusetts, New England and U.S. history.

NAME(S) OF PROGRAMS:
- **Short-Term Research Fellowship**

TYPE:
Fellowships. Research fellowship to use the Society's collection to complete a major project.

YEAR PROGRAM STARTED: 1983

PURPOSE:
To support scholarship on the history of Massachusetts and the nation.

ELIGIBILITY:
Must be U.S. citizens or foreign nationals holding appropriate U.S. government status. Open to independent scholars, advanced graduate students, and holders of a Ph.D. or equivalent.

FINANCIAL DATA:
Amount of support per award: Stipend of $2,000.

NO. AWARDS: Approximately 20.

APPLICATION INFO:
Applicants must submit the following materials online:
(1) cover letter;
(2) current curriculum vitae;
(3) project proposal, approximately 1,000 words in length, which includes a description of the project, a statement explaining the historiographical significance of the project, and an indication of the specific MHS collections the applicant wishes to consult and;
(4) for applicants not holding a Ph.D., a letter of recommendation from a faculty member familiar with the student's work and with the project being proposed.
Duration: Minimum of 20 days.
Deadline: Applications must be submitted by 11:59 P.M. on March 1.

ADDRESS INQUIRIES TO:
E-mail: fellowships@masshist.org

THE MASSACHUSETTS HISTORICAL SOCIETY   [564]

1154 Boylston Street
Boston, MA 02215
(617) 536-1608
Fax: (617) 859-0074
E-mail: research_programs@masshist.org
Web Site: www.masshist.org

FOUNDED: 1791

AREAS OF INTEREST:
Massachusetts, New England and U.S. history.

NAME(S) OF PROGRAMS:
- **Long-Term Research Fellowship**

TYPE:
Fellowships. Research fellowship to use the Society's collection to complete a major project.

YEAR PROGRAM STARTED: 1983

PURPOSE:
To support scholarship on the history of Massachusetts and the nation.

ELIGIBILITY:
Applicants must be U.S. citizens or foreign nationals who have lived in the U.S. for at least three years prior to the application deadline. Applicants must have completed their professional training. Fellowship is not available to graduate students. Awards committee will pay special attention both to the quality of proposed projects and to their relationship to the Society's collections. Preference will be given to candidates who have not held a long-term grant during the preceding three years.

FINANCIAL DATA:
There is an allowance for professional expenses.
Amount of support per award: $5,000 per month stipend with up to $500 per month housing allowance.

NO. AWARDS: 4 for the year 2020.

APPLICATION INFO:
Applicants must submit the following materials online:
(1) cover letter;
(2) current curriculum vitae;
(3) project proposal, approximately 1,000 words in length, which includes a description of the project, a statement explaining the historiographical significance of the project, and an indication of the specific MHS collections the applicant wishes to consult;
(4) Certification for Participants form and;
(5) two letters of recommendation.
Duration: Four to 12 months of continuous tenure.
Deadline: January 15, 11:59 P.M.

ADDRESS INQUIRIES TO:
E-mail: fellowships@masshist.org

THE MEDIEVAL ACADEMY OF AMERICA [565]
6 Beacon Street
Suite 500
Boston, MA 02108
(617) 491-1622
Fax: (617) 492-3303
E-mail: info@themedievalacademy.org
Web Site: www.medievalacademy.org

FOUNDED: 1925

AREAS OF INTEREST:
Any aspect of medieval studies, 500 to 1500 A.D.

NAME(S) OF PROGRAMS:
- **Birgit Baldwin Fellowship**
- **John Nicholas Brown Prize**
- **Van Courtlandt Elliott Prize**
- **Medieval Academy Dissertation Grants**
- **Schallek Awards**
- **Schallek Fellowship**

TYPE:
Awards/prizes; Fellowships; Research grants. Cash prizes for publications of material on medieval topics.

Birgit Baldwin Fellowship supports a graduate student studying in a North American university researching and writing a significant dissertation for a Ph.D. on any subject in French medieval history. Research must be in archives and libraries of France.

The Brown Prize is awarded annually to a first book or monograph on a medieval topic.

The Elliott Prize is awarded annually for a first published article in the medieval field, judged by the selection committee to be of outstanding quality.

Medieval Academy Dissertation Grants support advanced graduate students who are writing Ph.D. dissertations on medieval topics.

Schallek Awards support graduate students conducting doctoral research in any relevant discipline dealing with late-Medieval Britain (*circa* 1350-1500).

Schallek Fellowship supports Ph.D. dissertation research in any relevant discipline dealing with late-Medieval Britain (*circa* 1350-1500).

YEAR PROGRAM STARTED: 1940

PURPOSE:
To promote publication on medieval topics.

LEGAL BASIS:
Nonprofit corporation.

GEOG. RESTRICTIONS: North America.

FINANCIAL DATA:
Medieval Academy Dissertation Grants and Schallek Awards: These programs help defray research expenses such as the cost of travel to research collections and the cost of photographs, photocopies, microfilms and other research materials. The cost of books or equipment (e.g., computers) is not included.
Amount of support per award: Birgit Baldwin Fellowship: $20,000; Brown Prize: $1,000; Elliott Prize: $500; Medieval Academy Dissertation Grants and Schallek Awards: $2,000; Schallek Fellowship: $30,000.

NO. MOST RECENT APPLICANTS: 30.

NO. AWARDS: Medieval Academy Dissertation Grants: 10. Schallek Awards: 5. Other programs: 1 each annually.

APPLICATION INFO:
All submissions must be made online.
Duration: Fellowships: One year. Baldwin Fellowship is renewable for a second year.
Deadline: Baldwin: November 15. Schallek Fellowships and Brown Prize: October 15. Announcement in April. Medieval Academy Dissertation Grants and Schallek Awards: February 15.

ADDRESS INQUIRIES TO:
Sheryl Mullane-Corvi
Assistant to the Executive Director
(See address above.)

MOUNT VERNON HOTEL MUSEUM & GARDEN [566]
421 East 61st Street
New York, NY 10065
(212) 838-6878
E-mail: t.daly@mvhm.org
Web Site: www.mvhm.org

AREAS OF INTEREST:
American social history, material culture, historic preservation and museum education.

NAME(S) OF PROGRAMS:
- **William Randolph Hearst Foundation Fellowship**

TYPE:
Fellowships. Provides fellowships to graduate or undergraduate students who are interested in American social history, material culture, historic preservation and museum education.

YEAR PROGRAM STARTED: 1984

PURPOSE:
To promote the study of American history.

ELIGIBILITY:
Applicants must currently be enrolled in a college, university or graduate program.

FINANCIAL DATA:
Amount of support per award: $2,750.
Total amount of support: $5,500.

CO-OP FUNDING PROGRAMS: Fellowship is funded by the William Randolph Hearst Foundation.

NO. AWARDS: 2.

APPLICATION INFO:
Students must submit the completed application form, a short essay explaining the applicant's interest in the fellowship, resume and two letters of recommendation e-mailed directly from the individuals writing the recommendations. Applications are available on the web site.
Duration: Nine weeks in June and July.
Deadline: Approximately March.

ADDRESS INQUIRIES TO:
Terri Daly, Director
(See address above.)

NANTUCKET HISTORICAL ASSOCIATION [567]
P.O. Box 1016
Nantucket, MA 02554-1016
(508) 228-1894
E-mail: aholmes@nha.org
Web Site: www.nha.org/research/research-library/verney-fellowship

AREAS OF INTEREST:
History.

NAME(S) OF PROGRAMS:
- **E. Geoffrey and Elizabeth Thayer Verney Fellowship**

TYPE:
Fellowships; Residencies. The Verney Fellowship, which is a residency program to pursue historical research pertaining to Nantucket, MA, encourages research in the collections of the Nantucket Historical Association Research Library. The Association is the principal repository of Nantucket history, with extensive archives, collections of historic properties, and art and artifacts that broadly illustrate Nantucket's past.

YEAR PROGRAM STARTED: 1999

PURPOSE:
To enhance the public's knowledge and understanding of the heritage of Nantucket, MA.

ELIGIBILITY:
Open to graduate students, independent scholars and academics in any field to conduct research in the collections of the Association.

FINANCIAL DATA:
Amount of support per award: $300 per week stipend; housing will be provided. Travel is reimbursed up to $600.
Total amount of support: Up to $1,500.

NO. MOST RECENT APPLICANTS: 6.

NO. AWARDS: 2 for the year 2020.

APPLICATION INFO:
Applicants must e-mail a full description of the proposed project, a curriculum vitae, the names of three references, and an estimate of anticipated time and duration of stay to Catherine A. Taylor, Director of Museum Resources, at the e-mail address listed above.
Duration: Up to three weeks.
Deadline: January 17.

ADDRESS INQUIRIES TO:
Amelia Holmes, Associate Director
Research Library
(See e-mail address above.)

*PLEASE NOTE:
The Verney Fellow resides in the Thomas Macy House, a historic property owned by the Association, for up to a three-week period.

*SPECIAL STIPULATIONS:
NHA Visiting Research Scholars are expected to produce an article suitable for publication in *Historic Nantucket*, the NHA's biannual journal, and to deliver a public lecture on the subject of their research. Projects resulting in the publication of a book, article, conference paper, or other media, are looked upon favorably.

NATIONAL HISTORICAL PUBLICATIONS AND RECORDS COMMISSION [568]

National Archives and Records Administration
700 Pennsylvania Avenue, N.W., Room 114
Washington, DC 20408-0001
(202) 357-5010
Fax: (202) 357-5914
E-mail: nhprc@nara.gov
Web Site: www.archives.gov/nhprc

FOUNDED: 1934

AREAS OF INTEREST:
Archives and historical manuscripts relating to American history.

TYPE:
Project/program grants; Research grants; Technical assistance; Training grants. Grants to support the collection, preservation, digitization, arrangement, description, editing and publishing of documentary source material relating to the history of the U.S., the papers of American leaders and documents treating major subjects and events in American history.

YEAR PROGRAM STARTED: 1964

PURPOSE:
To promote the preservation and use of historical records important for an understanding and appreciation of the history of the U.S.

LEGAL BASIS:
44 U.S.C. 2501-2506.

ELIGIBILITY:
Tribal, state and local government agencies, nonprofit organizations and institutions.

GEOG. RESTRICTIONS: United States and its territories.

FINANCIAL DATA:
Amount of support per award: Average $100,000.
Total amount of support: Up to $6,000,000 (appropriated) for the year 2018.

Matching fund requirements: Generally, 1:1.

NO. MOST RECENT APPLICANTS: 170 for fiscal year 2018.

NO. AWARDS: 66 for fiscal year 2018.

REPRESENTATIVE AWARDS:
$148,000 to the Massachusetts Historical Society to edit *The Papers of John Adams*; $112,693 to Appalachian State University, Boone, NC to process and provide online access to primary research materials within the W.L. Eury Appalachian Collection.

APPLICATION INFO:
All applications must be submitted through Grants.gov.
Duration: Up to three years, depending on the individual project.
Deadline: Varies by program.

PUBLICATIONS:
Newsletter and special reports.

ADDRESS INQUIRIES TO:
See e-mail address above.

NATIONAL SOCIETY DAUGHTERS OF THE AMERICAN REVOLUTION [569]

1776 D Street, N.W.
Washington, DC 20006-5303
(202) 879-3263
E-mail: nsdarscholarships@nsdar.org
Web Site: www.dar.org

FOUNDED: 1895

AREAS OF INTEREST:
American history.

NAME(S) OF PROGRAMS:
● **Dr. Aura-Lee A. and James Hobbs Pittenger American History Scholarship**

TYPE:
Scholarships. The American History Scholarship is awarded to graduating high school students in the upper one-fifth of the class or home schooled who will have a concentrated study of a minimum of 24 credit hours in American History and American Government.

PURPOSE:
To provide ways and means to help students to attain higher education; to perpetuate the memory and spirit of men and women who achieved American independence by acquisition and protection of historical spots and erection of monuments; to carry out injunction of Washington in his farewell address to American people; to maintain institutions of American Freedom; to aid liberty.

LEGAL BASIS:
Incorporated historical society.

ELIGIBILITY:
Scholarships are awarded without regard to race, religion, sex or national origin. All four-year, or more, scholarships must be for consecutive years and are renewable only upon review and approval of annual transcript. Candidates must be U.S. citizens and must attend an accredited college or university in the U.S. No affiliation or relationship to DAR is required for qualification. Awards are judged on the basis of academic excellence, commitment to field of study, as required, and financial need.

GEOG. RESTRICTIONS: United States.

FINANCIAL DATA:
Amount of support per award: $2,000 per year for maximum of $8,000.
Total amount of support: Varies.

NO. AWARDS: Varies.

APPLICATION INFO:
Applicants must use the DAR Scholarship Committee's online submission process found on the DAR public web site. Once applicants have set up their scholarship profile, they will be able to complete the application. If necessary, applicants will be able to provide access to individuals wishing to submit confidential letters of recommendations or school transcripts.
Duration: One academic year. Renewable for up to four years upon annual transcript review and approval.
Deadline: February 15.

PUBLICATIONS:
American Spirit, magazine.

ADDRESS INQUIRIES TO:
National Vice Chairman
E-mail: pittengeramericanhistoryscholarship@nsdar.org

NATIONAL TRUST FOR HISTORIC PRESERVATION [570]

2600 Virginia Avenue, N.W.
Suite 1100
Washington, DC 20037
(202) 588-6277
E-mail: grants@savingplaces.org
Web Site: forum.savingplaces.org/build/funding

FOUNDED: 1949

AREAS OF INTEREST:
To encourage public participation in the preservation of sites, buildings and objects significant in American history and culture.

NAME(S) OF PROGRAMS:
● **National Trust Preservation Funds (NTPF)**

TYPE:
Challenge/matching grants; Project/program grants; Seed money grants; Technical assistance; Training grants. Education program curricula. Project grants to support consultants with professional expertise in areas such as architecture, law, planning, economics, archeology and graphic design. Conferences that address subjects of particular importance to historic preservation also are funded. In addition, grants are made for curriculum development in preservation education directed at select audiences.

YEAR PROGRAM STARTED: 1979

PURPOSE:
To increase the flow of information and ideas in the field of preservation by helping stimulate public discussion, enabling local groups to gain the technical expertise needed for particular projects, introducing students to preservation concepts and crafts and encouraging participation by the private sector in preservation.

LEGAL BASIS:
Nonprofit corporation.

ELIGIBILITY:
Organizational Forum members or Main Street America members of the National Trust are eligible to apply for funding from the National Trust Preservation Funds. Additionally, applicant must be a public agency, 501(c)(3) or other nonprofit organization to be considered. Applicants that

have received previous National Trust financial assistance are eligible provided that all grant requirements are current. No more than three grants will be awarded in any two-year period to a single grantee. Only one grant will be awarded for a particular project phase.

Activities eligible for National Trust Preservation Funds grants include hiring consultants to undertake preservation planning or design projects, obtaining professional advice to strengthen management capabilities, sponsoring preservation conferences, designing and implementing innovative preservation education programs targeted to a specific audience and undertaking other planning activities that will lead to implementation of a specific preservation project.

Grants can be used for professional consultant services, preservation education programs and conferences and rehabilitation feasibility studies. Projects, programs and conferences are not funded retroactively.

Bricks-and-mortar construction projects and the funding of ongoing staff positions are not eligible activities. In addition, historic resource surveys to create inventories or to list resources on local, state or national registers are generally not eligible for funding.

GEOG. RESTRICTIONS: United States and its territories.

FINANCIAL DATA:
Amount of support per award: $2,500 to $5,000.
Total amount of support: $1,800,000 for fiscal year 2017.
Matching fund requirements: Each grantee must match the funds on at least a dollar-for-dollar basis using cash contributions.

NO. AWARDS: 174 grants for fiscal year 2017.

APPLICATION INFO:
Guidelines and application forms may be found on the web site. Applications must be completed and submitted online by the appropriate deadline. Incomplete applications will not be considered.
Duration: Usually a one-time award.
Deadline: Applicants should contact the National Trust Grants Office to obtain information regarding application deadlines.

IRS I.D.: 53-0210807

ADDRESS INQUIRIES TO:
Grants Coordinator
National Trust Preservation Funds
(See address above.)

NEW ENGLAND REGIONAL FELLOWSHIP CONSORTIUM [571]
1154 Boylston Street
Boston, MA 02215
(617) 646-0577
Fax: (617) 859-0074
E-mail: kmorris@masshist.org
Web Site: www.masshist.org

FOUNDED: 1791

AREAS OF INTEREST:
Massachusetts, New England and U.S. history.

TYPE:
Fellowships. Research fellowship to use the resources at a minimum of three different participating institutions.

YEAR PROGRAM STARTED: 1999

PURPOSE:
To encourage projects that draw on the resources of the participating organizations.

ELIGIBILITY:
Open to individuals with a serious need to use the collections and facilities of the participating organizations.

Fellows must work at each of at least three chosen organizations for at least two weeks.

FINANCIAL DATA:
Amount of support per award: Stipend of $5,000 for a minimum of eight weeks of research at participating institutions.

NO. MOST RECENT APPLICANTS: Approximately 100.

NO. AWARDS: Approximately 25.

APPLICATION INFO:
Guidelines and fellowship applications are available on the New England Regional Fellowship Consortium (NERFC) web site. (The Massachusetts Historical Society web site provides a link to it.)
Duration: Minimum of eight weeks.
Deadline: February 1.

ADDRESS INQUIRIES TO:
Katy Morris, Research Coordinator
(See address above.)

NEW JERSEY HISTORIC TRUST [572]
101 South Broad Street
Trenton, NJ 08608-2401
(609) 984-0473
Fax: (609) 984-7590
E-mail: njht@dca.nj.gov
Web Site: www.njht.org

FOUNDED: 1967

AREAS OF INTEREST:
Historic preservation.

NAME(S) OF PROGRAMS:
● **Discover New Jersey History License Plate Fund for Heritage Tourism**
● **Preserve New Jersey Historic Preservation Fund for Planning Grants**

TYPE:
Challenge/matching grants. Planning grants. Discover New Jersey History grant program provides funding for heritage tourism.

Preserve New Jersey Historic Preservation Fund provides funding for the preservation planning of historic properties.

YEAR PROGRAM STARTED: 2013

PURPOSE:
To develop and promote visitor-ready sites as heritage tourism destinations.

LEGAL BASIS:
Public Law 2016-12. New Jersey Administrative Code 5:101-1.1.

ELIGIBILITY:
Applicants must be state, county or municipal governments or nonprofit organizations.

GEOG. RESTRICTIONS: New Jersey.

FINANCIAL DATA:
Amount of support per award: Discover New Jersey History License Plate Fund: Up to $5,000; Preserve New Jersey Historic Preservation Fund: Up to $50,000.
Total amount of support: Varies.
Matching fund requirements: Preserve New Jersey Historic Preservation Fund Planning Grants require a three-to-one match.

NO. MOST RECENT APPLICANTS: 30.

NO. AWARDS: Varies.

REPRESENTATIVE AWARDS:
$3,000 to First Presbyterian Church of Elizabeth for development of Historic Burial Groups Visitor App.

APPLICATION INFO:
Guidelines are available on the Trust web site.
Duration: Varies.
Deadline: Varies.

PUBLICATIONS:
Annual report; program announcement; *Economic Impact of Historic Preservation in New Jersey* (1997), funding resources for history; *Economic and Fiscal Impacts of Heritage Tourism in New Jersey; Keeping the Past Present: The New Jersey Historic Trust, 1967-2013.*

IRS I.D.: 22-3113979

STAFF:
Dorothy Guzzo, Executive Director

ADDRESS INQUIRIES TO:
See e-mail address above.

NEW JERSEY HISTORIC TRUST [573]
101 South Broad Street
Trenton, NJ 08608-2401
(609) 984-0473
Fax: (609) 984-7590
E-mail: njht@dca.nj.gov
Web Site: www.njht.org

FOUNDED: 1967

AREAS OF INTEREST:
Capital preservation of historic properties.

NAME(S) OF PROGRAMS:
● **Emergency Loans**
● **Preserve New Jersey Historic Preservation Fund for Capital Projects**

TYPE:
Capital grants. Loans. Emergency loans may be used for emergency repair or stabilization, planning or research necessary to preserve an endangered property, limited rehabilitation, restoration or improvement, acquisition of a historic property or the purchase of an option to acquire a historic property.

YEAR PROGRAM STARTED: 1990

PURPOSE:
To provide emergency funding for capital preservation projects of historic properties.

LEGAL BASIS:
Government-approved program. Statutory Citation: P.L. 1967, c. 124.

ELIGIBILITY:
Applicants must be nonprofit, tax-exempt organizations or agencies of county or municipal governments. All properties must be listed or eligible for listing in the State and National Registers of Historic Places. For

all requests other than acquisition, applicants must demonstrate control of the property through a deed or a valid lease.

GEOG. RESTRICTIONS: New Jersey.

FINANCIAL DATA:
Awards are short-term low-interest loans.
Amount of support per award: $1,000 to $10,000 for emergency loan; Up to $750,000 for a capital project.
Total amount of support: Varies.
Matching fund requirements: Matching funds for loans are encouraged but not required for emergency loans. Capital projects up to $150,000 require a three-to-one match; capital projects up to $750,000 require a one-to-one match.

NO. MOST RECENT APPLICANTS: 64.

NO. AWARDS: Varies.

REPRESENTATIVE AWARDS:
$10,000 to Newark Museum for stabilization of skylight in historic Polhemus House.

APPLICATION INFO:
A nonrefundable application fee of $25 must be submitted with each application.
Applicants must consult with Trust staff before making application for these funds.
Duration: Varies.
Deadline: Early spring.

PUBLICATIONS:
Program announcement.

IRS I.D.: 21-6000928

STAFF:
Dorothy Guzzo, Executive Director

ADDRESS INQUIRIES TO:
See e-mail address above.

NEW JERSEY HISTORICAL COMMISSION   [574]
New Jersey Department of State
33 West State Street, Fourth Floor
Trenton, NJ 08625-0305
(609) 292-6062
Fax: (609) 633-8168
E-mail: shawn.crisafulli@sos.nj.gov
Web Site: www.history.nj.gov

FOUNDED: 1969

AREAS OF INTEREST:
New Jersey history.

NAME(S) OF PROGRAMS:
● **General Operating Support Grants**

TYPE:
General operating grants. Provide general assistance to historical organizations, museums, historic sites, archives, libraries and similar organizations with collections or programming relating to the history of New Jersey.

YEAR PROGRAM STARTED: 2000

PURPOSE:
To provide operating support for New Jersey history organizations.

LEGAL BASIS:
Agency within the Department of State, State of New Jersey.

ELIGIBILITY:
To be eligible to apply for a General Operating Support Grant, an organization must:
(1) have an annual budget of at least $100,000 in non-state history funds;
(2) document that 25% of its audience (both virtual and actual) comes from beyond a 20-mile radius from its headquarters location;
(3) be a not-for-profit corporation or government (municipal or county) agency, commission or other organization;
(4) be based in New Jersey;
(5) be governed by a board responsible for the programs and policies of the organization;
(6) have a clearly stated mission of service to the promotion, preservation, research, interpretation or public presentation of New Jersey history;
(7) have a two-year track record of providing programs and services to the public that fulfill that mission and;
(8) be in good standing with the New Jersey Historical Commission.

GEOG. RESTRICTIONS: New Jersey.

FINANCIAL DATA:
Amount of support per award: Applicants may apply for grants of up to 33% of the non-state operating income from the last completed fiscal year and current projected year.
Matching fund requirements: Ratio of 3:1 (grantee: Commission).

NO. AWARDS: Approximately 40 for the year 2020.

APPLICATION INFO:
The Commission offers assistance to applicants in the technical aspects of completing the application. Applicants may visit the Commission web site or call Commission staff at the telephone number listed above.
Duration: Three-year funding cycle.

PUBLICATIONS:
Application guidelines.

ADMINISTRATION:
Shawn Crisafulli, Chief Grants Officer

ADDRESS INQUIRIES TO:
Shawn Crisafulli
Chief Grants Officer
P.O. Box 305
Trenton, NJ 08625-0305

*PLEASE NOTE:
The General Operating Support program is a three-year cycle. Applications for fiscal year round 2023 will be accepted in 2022.

*SPECIAL STIPULATIONS:
All funding is based on state appropriations.

NEW JERSEY HISTORICAL COMMISSION   [575]
New Jersey Department of State
33 West State Street, Fourth Floor
Trenton, NJ 08625-0305
(609) 292-6062
Fax: (609) 633-8168
E-mail: shawn.crisafulli@sos.nj.gov
Web Site: www.history.nj.gov

FOUNDED: 1967

AREAS OF INTEREST:
New Jersey history.

NAME(S) OF PROGRAMS:
● **Project Grants**

TYPE:
Project/program grants. Funding for expenses of specific projects relating to New Jersey history. Examples of successful projects include conservation of historical materials (manuscripts, books, costumes, historical visuals), editorial and publication projects, educational initiatives, exhibitions, media (films, radio, videotape, digital media), public programs, and research (including archaeological projects, fellowships, oral history, and national and New Jersey registers of historic places nominations).

YEAR PROGRAM STARTED: 1975

PURPOSE:
To engage diverse audiences in the active exploration, enjoyment, interpretation, understanding and preservation of New Jersey history.

LEGAL BASIS:
Agency within the New Jersey Department of State.

ELIGIBILITY:
Grants are available for both individuals and organizations. There are general standards of eligibility, as well as specific requirements for programs. Organizations must have an annual budget of at least $100,000 in non-state history funds and must document that 25% of its audience (both virtual and actual) comes from beyond a 20-mile radius from its headquarters location.

FINANCIAL DATA:
Amount of support per award: Projects: $1 to $15,000.
Matching fund requirements: Organizations with annual operating budgets of at least $500,000 are expected to show a match equal to 50% of the grant request. The match need not be all in cash; it may include donated services.

NO. AWARDS: Approximately 20 for the year 2020.

APPLICATION INFO:
Applicants must submit a Declaration of Intent online prior to submitting an application.
Deadline: Declaration of Intent and Application: Typically early spring.

PUBLICATIONS:
Application guidelines.

ADMINISTRATION:
Shawn Crisafulli, Chief Grants Officer

ADDRESS INQUIRIES TO:
Shawn Crisafulli
Chief Grants Officer
P.O. Box 305
Trenton, NJ 08625-0305

NEW YORK LANDMARKS CONSERVANCY   [576]
One Whitehall Street, 21st Floor
New York, NY 10004-2127
(212) 995-5260
Fax: (212) 995-5268
E-mail: info@nylandmarks.org
Web Site: www.nylandmarks.org

FOUNDED: 1973

AREAS OF INTEREST:
Historic preservation and restoration of buildings.

NAME(S) OF PROGRAMS:
● **City Ventures Fund**
● **Historic Properties Fund**
● **Sacred Sites Program**
● **Technical Services Program**

TYPE:
Project/program grants.

PURPOSE:
To provide financial and technical services to nonprofit housing corporations, community development organizations, social service agencies, homesteading groups, religious institutions and mutual housing associations.

LEGAL BASIS:
501(c)(3) not-for-profit.

ELIGIBILITY:
Eligible organizations must be IRS 501(c)(3) tax-exempt.

GEOG. RESTRICTIONS: New York.

FINANCIAL DATA:
Amount of support per award: Varies.
Total amount of support: Varies.

APPLICATION INFO:
Prospective applicants should first contact the Conservancy.
Duration: Varies.
Deadline: Varies.

IRS I.D.: 23-7181785

ADDRESS INQUIRIES TO:
Peg Breen, President
(See phone or e-mail address above.)

THE NEWBERRY LIBRARY [577]

Newberry Institute for Research and Education
60 West Walton Street
Chicago, IL 60610
(312) 255-3666
E-mail: research@newberry.org
Web Site: www.newberry.org/fellowships

FOUNDED: 1887

AREAS OF INTEREST:
The humanities of Western Europe, England and the Americas from the late Middle Ages to the early 20th century.

NAME(S) OF PROGRAMS:
- **American Society for Eighteenth-Century Studies (ASECS) Fellowships**

TYPE:
Fellowships. For scholars wishing to use the Newberry's collections to study the period 1660 to 1815.

PURPOSE:
To help provide access to Newberry resources for people who live beyond commuting distance.

LEGAL BASIS:
Private research library.

ELIGIBILITY:
Applicants must have received their Ph.D. or equivalent degree, or be a Ph.D. candidate at dissertation level.

Applicants must be members of the ASECS at the time of award.

Applicants must live outside the Chicago area.

FINANCIAL DATA:
Amount of support per award: $2,500 per month.

NO. MOST RECENT APPLICANTS: 15.

NO. AWARDS: 1 per year.

APPLICATION INFO:
Applications must be submitted through the online webform.
Duration: One month.
Deadline: December 15.

STAFF:
D. Bradford Hunt, Vice President for Research and Academic Programs

ADDRESS INQUIRIES TO:
See e-mail address above.

OMOHUNDRO INSTITUTE OF EARLY AMERICAN HISTORY AND CULTURE [578]

400 Landrum Drive, Ground Floor
Swem Library
Williamsburg, VA 23185
(757) 221-1114
Fax: (757) 221-1047
E-mail: oieahc@wm.edu
Web Site: oieahc.wm.edu/fellowship

FOUNDED: 1943

AREAS OF INTEREST:
Research leading to book publication on any area of early American studies.

NAME(S) OF PROGRAMS:
- **Omohundro Institute-NEH Postdoctoral Fellowship**

TYPE:
Fellowships. The Omohundro Institute of Early American History and Culture, located on the campus of The College of William and Mary, annually offers one postdoctoral fellowship to a promising young scholar in any area of early American studies whose dissertation shows potential for making a significant book-length contribution to scholarship.

Fellows have the opportunity of teaching at the College of William and Mary with a concurrent appointment as visiting assistant professor in the appropriate department.

YEAR PROGRAM STARTED: 1945

LEGAL BASIS:
Independent, nonprofit research institution.

ELIGIBILITY:
Fellows must have successfully defended their dissertation and completed all requirements for the Doctorate by the time they begin the fellowship and may not have previously published a book or have a book under contract. Foreign nationals who have been in continuous residence in the U.S. for the three years immediately preceding the date of application are eligible to apply.

FINANCIAL DATA:
Amount of support per award: $50,400 per year stipend.

CO-OP FUNDING PROGRAMS: The fellowships are supported by the Omohundro Institute and the National Endowment for the Humanities.

NO. AWARDS: 1 annually.

APPLICATION INFO:
Applicants should apply via the Institute web site.
Duration: Two years.
Deadline: November 1 for the term beginning the following July 1.

PUBLICATIONS:
William and Mary Quarterly, scholarly journal; *Uncommon Sense*, newsletter; books.

STAFF:
Karin A. Wulf, Executive Director

ADDRESS INQUIRIES TO:
Karin A. Wulf, Executive Director
(See e-mail address above.)

*SPECIAL STIPULATIONS:
The Institute holds first rights to publishing the resulting book manuscript.

OMOHUNDRO INSTITUTE OF EARLY AMERICAN HISTORY AND CULTURE [579]

400 Landrum Drive, Ground Floor
Swem Library
Williamsburg, VA 23185
(757) 221-1114
Fax: (757) 221-1047
E-mail: oieahc@wm.edu
Web Site: oieahc.wm.edu/fellowship

FOUNDED: 1943

AREAS OF INTEREST:
Promoting the study of early American history and culture.

NAME(S) OF PROGRAMS:
- **Georgian Papers Programme Fellowships**
- **Jamestown Rediscovery-Omohundro Institute (JR-OI) Short-Term Visiting Fellowship**

TYPE:
Fellowships. Georgian Papers Programme Fellowships: With support from the Lapidus Initiative, the Omohundro Institute has entered into an international partnership that will provide opportunities for scholars to do research in the historically rich trove of Georgian materials housed at the Royal Archives in Windsor Castle's Round Tower. The Georgian Papers Programme is a five-year project that by 2020 will create an open online archive and library of approximately 350,000 digitized items from the Georgian monarchs.

Jamestown Rediscovery-Omohundro Institute (JR-OI) Short-Term Visiting Fellowship: Fellows in this program will make use of the College of William and Mary's Swem Library and collections at Historic Jamestowne as well as other resources in the Historic Triangle and Richmond region. This fellowship will also provide the opportunity to experience the Omohundro Institute's editorial expertise and intellectual community of early Americanists.

LEGAL BASIS:
Independent, nonprofit research institution.

ELIGIBILITY:
Georgian Papers Programme Fellowships: Open to scholars - from advanced graduate students to senior scholars; restricted to U.S. or U.K. citizens. Successful applicants will be required to undergo a security clearance before beginning work at Windsor Castle.

JR-OI Short-Term Visiting Fellowship: Open to scholars - from advanced graduate students to senior scholars. Scholars with strong interests in colonial history, historical archaeology, Atlantic history, Native American history, African American studies, early Jamestown, the Chesapeake, and material culture, 1500-1720, are encouraged to apply.

FINANCIAL DATA:
Amount of support per award: Georgian Papers Programme Fellowships: $2,500 stipend with up to $1,500 in additional support for travel. JR-OI Short-Term Visiting Fellowship: Stipend of $2,500.

CO-OP FUNDING PROGRAMS: JR-OI Short-Term Visiting Fellowship: This program is offered in conjunction with the Jamestown Rediscovery Foundation.

NO. AWARDS: Georgian Papers Programme Fellowships: Up to 8 annually. JR-OI Short-Term Visiting Fellowship: Up to 4 annually.

APPLICATION INFO:
Georgian Papers Programme Fellowships: Applicants need to submit a letter of application (including a description of the proposed project and its potential match with the collections), a curriculum vitae and two letters of recommendation. The letter and curriculum vitae should be uploaded via the Institute web site (above). Recommenders should e-mail letters directly to the e-mail address listed above.

JR-OI Short-Term Visiting Fellowship: Applicants need to submit an electronic file with a brief project description (1,000 words maximum) and a curriculum vitae via the Institute web site. In addition, two letters of recommendation should be sent directly to the Institute via the e-mail address above.

Duration: One month.

Deadline: March 1 and November 1.

ADDRESS INQUIRIES TO:
Omohundro Institute of Early American History and Culture
(See e-mail address above.)

OMOHUNDRO INSTITUTE OF EARLY AMERICAN HISTORY AND CULTURE   [580]
400 Landrum Drive, Ground Floor
Swem Library
Williamsburg, VA 23185
(757) 221-1114
Fax: (757) 221-1047
E-mail: oieahc@wm.edu
Web Site: oieahc.wm.edu/fellowship

FOUNDED: 1943

AREAS OF INTEREST:
Graduate student research related to Early American and transatlantic print culture.

NAME(S) OF PROGRAMS:
● **Lapidus-OI Fellowship**

TYPE:
Fellowships. The Lapidus-OI Fellowship is offered annually to support advanced graduate student research related to Early American and transatlantic print culture, including authorship, production, circulation and reception.

LEGAL BASIS:
Independent, nonprofit research institution.

FINANCIAL DATA:
Amount of support per award: $1,000.

CO-OP FUNDING PROGRAMS: Fellowships are made possible through the generous support of Sid Lapidus.

NO. AWARDS: Up to 8 annually.

APPLICATION INFO:
Applicants must submit an electronic file with a 500-word description of their dissertation project, a curriculum vitae, and a one-paragraph research agenda.

Deadline: November 1.

STAFF:
Karin A. Wulf, Executive Director

ADDRESS INQUIRIES TO:
Fellowship Program
(See e-mail address above.)

*SPECIAL STIPULATIONS:
Fellowship recipients must provide a one-page report of their progress no more than 12 months after notification of their award.

PHI ALPHA THETA HISTORY HONOR SOCIETY   [581]
University of South Florida
4202 East Fowler Avenue, SOC107
Tampa, FL 33620-8100
(800) 394-8195
(813) 974-8212
Fax: (813) 974-8215
E-mail: info@phialphatheta.org
Web Site: phialphatheta.org

FOUNDED: 1921

AREAS OF INTEREST:
History.

NAME(S) OF PROGRAMS:
● **Member's Best First Book Award**
● **Member's Best Subsequent Book Award**

TYPE:
Awards/prizes. Awards for the best books published by members of Phi Alpha Theta, one for his or her first book, one for subsequent books (second, third, etc.), published in the field of history.

PURPOSE:
To encourage the publication of distinctive books in history.

LEGAL BASIS:
Nonprofit, 501(c)(3).

ELIGIBILITY:
Books to be judged must be published from August 1 of the previous year to June 30 of the following (award) year to be eligible for that year's award. Awards restricted to society members.

FINANCIAL DATA:
Amount of support per award: $1,000 each.
Total amount of support: $2,000.

NO. MOST RECENT APPLICANTS: 4.

NO. AWARDS: 2 for the year 2020.

APPLICATION INFO:
Six copies of each book and a completed application must be forwarded to the Society's Book Award Committee at the address above.

Deadline: July 1 of the award year.

OFFICERS:
Wendy M. Tunstall, Executive Director

ADDRESS INQUIRIES TO:
Wendy M. Tunstall, Executive Director
(See address above.)

PHI ALPHA THETA HISTORY HONOR SOCIETY   [582]
University of South Florida
4202 East Fowler Avenue, SOC107
Tampa, FL 33620-8100
(800) 394-8195
(813) 974-8212
Fax: (813) 974-8215
E-mail: info@phialphatheta.org
Web Site: phialphatheta.org

FOUNDED: 1921

AREAS OF INTEREST:
History.

NAME(S) OF PROGRAMS:
● **Gordon Morris Bakken Scholarship in Western History**
● **Thomas S. Morgan Memorial Scholarship**
● **William E. Parrish Scholarship**
● **Graydon A. Tunstall Undergraduate Student Scholarship**
● **A.F. Zimmerman Scholarship**

TYPE:
Awards/prizes; Scholarships. The Gordon Morris Bakken Scholarship in Western History is awarded to a graduate student in history researching the Trans-Mississippi West.

The Thomas S. Morgan, William E. Parrish and A.F. Zimmerman Scholarships are given to student members entering graduate school for the first time in the fall for work leading to a Master's degree in history.

The Graydon A. Tunstall Undergraduate Student Scholarship is given to exceptional junior-year students majoring in Modern European History (1815 to present).

PURPOSE:
To promote the study of history at the graduate level.

LEGAL BASIS:
Nonprofit, 501(c)(3).

ELIGIBILITY:
Applicants must be initiated members of the Phi Alpha Theta History Honor Society. Applicant must not be enrolled in an online degree program.

For the Morgan, Parrish and Zimmerman Scholarships, members must be entering graduate school for the first time in the fall of the award year and must be pursuing a Master's degree in History. Students currently enrolled in a graduate program are not eligible to apply.

For the Graydon A. Tunstall Undergraduate Student Scholarship, students must be entering the fall semester of their senior year and majoring in Modern European History (1815 to the present).

FINANCIAL DATA:
Amount of support per award: Bakken Scholarship: $500; Morgan, Parrish and Tunstall Scholarships: $1,000 each; Zimmerman Scholarship: $1,250. In some years, there may be two additional awards of $850 each for Doctoral Scholarships.
Total amount of support: Varies.

NO. MOST RECENT APPLICANTS: 20.

NO. AWARDS: Graduate: 4; Undergraduate: 1.

APPLICATION INFO:
Consult the Society web site.

Duration: One year.

Deadline: Applications must be received on or before March 1.

OFFICERS:
Wendy M. Tunstall; Executive Director

ADDRESS INQUIRIES TO:
Wendy M. Tunstall, Executive Director
(See address above.)

*SPECIAL STIPULATIONS:
Applicants must be members of Phi Alpha Theta.

PHI ALPHA THETA HISTORY HONOR SOCIETY [583]

University of South Florida
4202 East Fowler Avenue, SOC107
Tampa, FL 33620-8100
(800) 394-8195
(813) 974-8212
Fax: (813) 974-8215
E-mail: info@phialphatheta.org
Web Site: phialphatheta.org

FOUNDED: 1921

AREAS OF INTEREST:
History.

NAME(S) OF PROGRAMS:
● **The Nels Andrew Cleven Founder's Paper Prize Awards**
● **Dr. George P. Hammond Paper Prize**
● **Dr. Lynn W. Turner Paper Prize**

TYPE:
Awards/prizes. The George P. Hammond Prize award is for the best paper by a graduate student member of the Society.

The Dr. Lynn W. Turner Prize is awarded for the best paper by an undergraduate student member of the Society.

The four Founder's Paper Prizes are awarded to two graduate and two undergraduate student members of the Society.

PURPOSE:
To promote historical research.

LEGAL BASIS:
501(c)(3).

ELIGIBILITY:
All students must be initiated members.

FINANCIAL DATA:
Amount of support per award: Founder's Awards: $400; Hammond Prize and Turner Award: $500 each.

NO. MOST RECENT APPLICANTS: 20.

NO. AWARDS: 6.

APPLICATION INFO:
Essay should combine original historical research on significant subjects, based on source material and manuscripts if possible, with good English composition and superior style. Papers should not exceed 25 typewritten double-spaced pages in length, excluding bibliography. Entries received that do not comply with these guidelines will be disqualified.

Title page of the paper must include the applicant's name, mailing address, phone number and e-mail address, as well as the college/university, graduate or undergraduate status and year at which he or she joined Phi Alpha Theta.

Entrants must submit five copies of each manuscript and a letter of recommendation from either the Faculty Advisor or History Department Chair indicating the applicant's chapter affiliation and whether the individual is a graduate or an undergraduate student. Send to:
Christopher M. Kennedy, Ph.D.
Office of the Provost
Francis Marion University
P.O. Box 100547
Florence, SC 29502-0547
E-mail: ckennedy@fmarion.edu
Deadline: July 1.

OFFICERS:
Wendy M. Tunstall, Executive Director

ADDRESS INQUIRIES TO:
Wendy M. Tunstall, Executive Director
(See address above.)

PONTIFICAL INSTITUTE OF MEDIAEVAL STUDIES [584]

59 Queen's Park Crescent East
Toronto ON M5S 2C4 Canada
(416) 926-7142
Fax: (416) 926-7292
E-mail: allan.smith@utoronto.ca
Web Site: www.pims.ca

FOUNDED: 1929

AREAS OF INTEREST:
Medieval studies.

NAME(S) OF PROGRAMS:
● **Mellon Postdoctoral Fellowships**

TYPE:
Fellowships.

YEAR PROGRAM STARTED: 1998

PURPOSE:
To develop a candidate's personal research in the context of the Institute's mission.

ELIGIBILITY:
Open to scholars engaged in medieval studies. Level of study is postdoctoral.

FINANCIAL DATA:
Amount of support per award: Approximately $40,000 (CAN).
Total amount of support: Approximately $160,000 (CAN).

NO. MOST RECENT APPLICANTS: 26 for the year 2020.

NO. AWARDS: Up to 4.

APPLICATION INFO:
Application must include official confirmation that the Ph.D. has been examined and that its award has been approved by the appropriate authority.
Duration: One year.
Deadline: February 1.

ADDRESS INQUIRIES TO:
Barbara North, Secretary
E-mail: barbara.north@utoronto.ca

ROCK ISLAND ARSENAL MUSEUM [585]

Rock Island Arsenal Historical Society
R. Maguire Scholarship Committee
One Rock Island Arsenal
Rock Island, IL 61299-5000
(309) 782-5021
Fax: (309) 782-3598
E-mail: contact@arsenalhistoricalsociety.org
rimahoch@aol.com
Web Site: www.arsenalhistoricalsociety.org

AREAS OF INTEREST:
Postgraduate, Master's or Doctorate studies in history and museum study.

NAME(S) OF PROGRAMS:
● **Richard C. Maguire Scholarship**

TYPE:
Scholarships.

PURPOSE:
To provide financial support to a student working for a Master's or Doctorate degree in the fields of history, archaeology or museum study.

ELIGIBILITY:
Applicants must be U.S. citizens. Grants will be awarded on an objective and

nondiscriminatory basis without regard to age, sex, race, religion or affiliation. Level of study is postdoctoral and postgraduate.

GEOG. RESTRICTIONS: United States.

FINANCIAL DATA:
Amount of support per award: $1,000.

APPLICATION INFO:
Application is available on the Museum web site or can be obtained by writing to the Museum. Applicant must enclose a self-addressed, stamped envelope.
Duration: One year.
Deadline: May 2.

ADDRESS INQUIRIES TO:
E-mail: contact@arsenalhistoricalsociety.org

ROCKEFELLER ARCHIVE CENTER [586]

15 Dayton Avenue
Sleepy Hollow, NY 10591
(914) 366-6309
Fax: (914) 366-6017
E-mail: archive@rockarch.org
Web Site: www.rockarch.org

FOUNDED: 1974

AREAS OF INTEREST:
Preservation of and research in the records of The Rockefeller University, the Rockefeller Foundation, the Rockefeller Brothers Fund, the Rockefeller family, the Ford Foundation, the Commonwealth Fund, the Social Science Research Council, the Asian Cultural Council, and other foundations, cultural organizations, research institutions and associated organizations and individuals which include major concentrations in philanthropy, education, history of medicine, science, public health, the arts, agriculture, social sciences, urban affairs and public policy.

CONSULTING OR VOLUNTEER SERVICES:
Reports on holdings and their relevance to research topics and provides assistance to visiting scholars.

NAME(S) OF PROGRAMS:
● **Research Stipend Program at the Rockefeller Archive Center**

TYPE:
Grants-in-aid. Grants-in-Aid to individual scholars to defray costs of travel and accommodation expenses while doing research at the Rockefeller Archive Center in the Center's collections.

YEAR PROGRAM STARTED: 1977

PURPOSE:
To foster, promote and support research by serious scholars in the collections located at the Rockefeller Archive Center, which includes the records of the Rockefeller Family and their far-reaching philanthropic endeavors, such as the Rockefeller University, Rockefeller Foundation, and Rockefeller Brothers Fund.

LEGAL BASIS:
Nonprofit and educational.

ELIGIBILITY:
Grants will be made on a competitive basis to applicants from any discipline, usually graduate students or postdoctoral scholars, who are engaged in research that requires use of the collections at the Center.

FINANCIAL DATA:
Grants are for receipted, approved expenses. Expenses are reimbursed after the completion of the research visit.
Amount of support per award: Up to $5,000.
Total amount of support: $140,000 annually.

NO. MOST RECENT APPLICANTS: 87 for the year 2018.

NO. AWARDS: 52 for the year 2018.

APPLICATION INFO:
Two letters supporting the Grant-in-Aid application are required.
Duration: Applications for second- and third-year support will be considered, but preference is given to new applicants.
Deadline: November 1. Announcement of awards at the beginning of March.

PUBLICATIONS:
Research Reports OnLine from the Rockefeller Archive Center; guides to manuscripts and photograph collections; surveys of holdings on specific subjects.

OFFICERS AND STAFF:
Jack Meyers, President
James A. Smith, Vice President

ADDRESS INQUIRIES TO:
Norine Hochman, Executive Assistant
(See address above.)

FRANKLIN D. ROOSEVELT LIBRARY AND MUSEUM [587]
4079 Albany Post Road
Hyde Park, NY 12538
(845) 486-7770
E-mail: grants.fdr@nara.gov
Web Site: fdrlibrary.org/research-grants

FOUNDED: 1941

AREAS OF INTEREST:
Archives, museum, education and public programs relating to the life and times of Franklin and Eleanor Roosevelt.

NAME(S) OF PROGRAMS:
● **Roosevelt Institute Research Grants**

TYPE:
Grants-in-aid; Research grants. The Roosevelt Institute - the Library's nonprofit partner - supports a program of small grants-in-aid, in support of research on the "Roosevelt years" or clearly related subjects.

PURPOSE:
To foster research and education on the life and times of Franklin and Eleanor Roosevelt.

ELIGIBILITY:
The grants program is particularly designed to encourage younger scholars to expand the knowledge and understanding of the Roosevelt period. The Roosevelt Institute Grants Committee makes its decision on whether or not to provide a grant based on the merits of each research topic and its potential contribution to scholarship.

FINANCIAL DATA:
Funds are awarded for the sole purpose of helping to defray living, travel and related expenses incurred while conducting research at the Roosevelt Library.
Amount of support per award: Up to $2,500.

NO. AWARDS: Determined based on the merit of the applications.

APPLICATION INFO:
Application instructions are found on the Library web site. Applicants are required to submit to the grants administrator an original grant application and one copy detailing the nature and scope of their research project, the names and institutions of three references and a budget outlining the amount needed for travel, lodging and any other research expenses. Each application is evaluated by the Library's archival staff to ascertain that there is material at the Library appropriate for the research topic, approximately how long such research might be expected to take, and per diem.
Duration: Use of the grants is to occur within a year of the grant announcement letter.
Deadline: November 15. Grants are awarded at the beginning of each year.

ADDRESS INQUIRIES TO:
See e-mail address above.

*SPECIAL STIPULATIONS:
Letters are sent to all applicants informing them of the Roosevelt Institute Grants Committee's decision on whether or not to grant funding. Grantees are informed that the use of their grants is to occur within a year of their letter. Grantees will receive their award when they arrive for research at the Library.

SANTA BARBARA MISSION ARCHIVE-LIBRARY [588]
2201 Laguna Street
Santa Barbara, CA 93105
(805) 682-4713 ext. 152
E-mail: research@sbmal.org
Web Site: www.sbmal.org

FOUNDED: 1786

AREAS OF INTEREST:
Preservation, cataloging and public history.

NAME(S) OF PROGRAMS:
● **Geiger Memorial Internship**

TYPE:
Internships; Residencies.

YEAR PROGRAM STARTED: 1978

PURPOSE:
To support an opportunity to gain experience working in an archive.

ELIGIBILITY:
Consideration will be given to graduate and undergraduate students furthering their studies or a career in public history, art history, library and information technology, archive management or museum studies.

FINANCIAL DATA:
Amount of support per award: $2,500 stipend.

NO. AWARDS: 1 annually.

APPLICATION INFO:
Application information is available online.
Duration: Eight weeks during the summer.
Deadline: Summer.

ADDRESS INQUIRIES TO:
Brittany Bratcher, Archivist
(See address and e-mail above.)

SMITHSONIAN NATIONAL AIR AND SPACE MUSEUM
601 Independence Avenue, S.W.
Room 3762, MRC 305
Washington, DC 20560
(202) 633-2214
Fax: (202) 633-1957
E-mail: fay-lukic@si.edu
Web Site: airandspace.si.edu/support/get-involved/internships

TYPE:
Internships. Full-time interns work 40 hours per week from approximately the first week in June until the second week in August.

See entry 2412 for full listing.

SOCIETY FOR FRENCH HISTORICAL STUDIES [589]
Colorado College, Department of History
Palmer Hall, No. 208B
14 East Cache La Poudre Street
Colorado Springs, CO 80903
E-mail: tragan@coloradocollege.edu
Web Site: www.societyforfrenchhistoricalstudies.net

FOUNDED: 1955

AREAS OF INTEREST:
French history.

NAME(S) OF PROGRAMS:
● **The Gilbert Chinard Prize**
● **Natalie Zemon Davis Graduate Student Award**
● **Marjorie M. and Lancelot L. Farrar Memorial Awards**
● **The William Koren, Jr. Prize**
● **The David H. Pinkney Prize**
● **Research Travel Award**

TYPE:
Awards/prizes. The Chinard Prize is for a recent book on historical relations between France and the Americas.

Davis Graduate Student Award is given for the best paper presented by a graduate student at the Society's annual meeting.

Farrar Award is for dissertation research.

The Koren Prize is for a recent journal article written on French history.

The Pinkney Prize is for a recent book written on French history.

Research Travel Award is for recent recipients of Doctorates (awarded jointly with Western Society for French History).

YEAR PROGRAM STARTED: 1955

PURPOSE:
To further the study of French history in the U.S. and Canada.

ELIGIBILITY:
Gilbert Chinard Prize: Historical studies of any area or period are acceptable.

Marjorie M. and Lancelot L. Farrar Awards: Must be a doctoral student in French history at a North American university.

William Koren, Jr. Prize: Must be a North American scholar who published an article on any era of French History in an American, European or Canadian journal.

David Pinkney Prize: Must be a citizen of the U.S. or Canada or an author with a full-time appointment at a U.S. or Canadian college or university. Books on any aspect and period of French history will be considered.

Research Travel Award: Granted to an outstanding American or Canadian scholar who has received the Doctorate in History in the five-year period prior to the award.

FINANCIAL DATA:
Amount of support per award: Chinard and Koren Prize: $1,000; Davis Graduate Student Award: $500; Farrar Awards: $5,000 each; Pinkney Prize: $1,500; Research Travel Award: $2,000.

NO. AWARDS: Chinard Prize, Davis Graduate Student Award, Koren Prize, Pinkney Prize and Research Travel Award: 1; Farrar Awards: 2.

APPLICATION INFO:
Application information is available on the web site.
Deadline: Chinard, Koren and Pinkney Prize: January 1; Davis Graduate Student Award: May 15; Farrar Memorial Awards and Research Travel Award: February 15.

ADDRESS INQUIRIES TO:
Bryant T. Ragan, Executive Director
(See address above.)

THE SOCIETY OF AMERICAN HISTORIANS [590]
Columbia University
Graduate School of Journalism
2950 Broadway
New York, NY 10027
(212) 854-6495
E-mail: amhistsociety@columbia.edu
Web Site: www.sah.columbia.edu

FOUNDED: 1939

AREAS OF INTEREST:
American history and biography.

NAME(S) OF PROGRAMS:
● **Allan Nevins Dissertation Prize**
● **Francis Parkman Prize**
● **SAH Prize for Historical Fiction**

TYPE:
Awards/prizes. Allan Nevins Dissertation Prize: Annual award for the best written doctoral dissertation on an American subject completed in the previous year.

Francis Parkman Prize: Annual award for the best nonfiction book in American history published the previous calendar year that is distinguished for its literary merit.

SAH Prize for Historical Fiction: Biennial award in odd-numbered years for a book of historical fiction on an American subject that makes a significant contribution to historical understanding, portrays authentically the people and events of the historical past, and displays skills in narrative construction and prose style published within the previous two calendar years.

YEAR PROGRAM STARTED: 1960

PURPOSE:
To encourage literary distinction in the writing of history and biography.

LEGAL BASIS:
Nonprofit.

ELIGIBILITY:
Allan Nevins Dissertation Prize: Eligible dissertation must have been defended or the Ph.D. received in the previous calendar year; dissertations must be nominated and submitted by the student's program chair or dissertation sponsor.

FINANCIAL DATA:
Amount of support per award: $2,000 per prize.

NO. AWARDS: Allan Nevins Dissertation and Francis Parkman Prizes: 1 each biennially; SAH Prize for Historical Fiction: 1 biennially in odd-numbered years.

APPLICATION INFO:
Application information and guidelines are available online.
Deadline: Allan Nevins Dissertation Prize: December 31 annually. Francis Parkman Prize: December 1 annually. SAH Prize for Historical Fiction: December 1, 2020.

OFFICERS:
Alice Kessler-Harris, President
Andie Tucher, Executive Secretary

ADDRESS INQUIRIES TO:
See e-mail address above.

THE SONS OF THE REPUBLIC OF TEXAS [591]
SRT Office
1717 Eighth Street, Suite 12
Bay City, TX 77414
(979) 245-6644
Fax: (979) 244-3819
E-mail: aa-srt@son-rep-texas.net
Web Site: www.srttexas.org

FOUNDED: 1893

AREAS OF INTEREST:
Spanish colonial period of Texas history.

NAME(S) OF PROGRAMS:
● **Presidio La Bahia Award**

TYPE:
Awards/prizes. Presidio La Bahia Award is intended to promote suitable preservation of relics, appropriate dissemination of data, and research into Texas heritage, with particular emphasis on the Spanish colonial period.

PURPOSE:
To encourage literary effort and research about historical events and personalities during the days of the Spanish colonial period of Texas history, and to stimulate interest in this period.

ELIGIBILITY:
Open to all persons interested in the Spanish colonial influence on Texas culture.

Research writings have proved in the past to be the most successful type of entry. However, careful consideration will be given to other literary forms, as well as to art, architecture, and archaeological discovery.

FINANCIAL DATA:
Amount of support per award: First place: a minimum of $1,200 for the best published book. At its discretion, the organization may award a second-place book prize. There is a separate category with a prize for the best published paper, article published in a periodical, or project of a nonliterary nature.
Total amount of support: A total of $2,000 is available annually for winning participants in the competition at the discretion of the judges.

NO. AWARDS: 1 for the year 2019.

APPLICATION INFO:
Applicants must submit four copies of published writings to the office. Galley proofs are not acceptable.
Deadline: Entries are accepted from June 1 to September 30.

ADDRESS INQUIRIES TO:
Janet Knox, Administrative Assistant
The Sons of the Republic of Texas
(See address above.)

THE SONS OF THE REPUBLIC OF TEXAS [592]
SRT Office
1717 Eighth Street, Suite 12
Bay City, TX 77414
(979) 245-6644
Fax: (979) 244-3819
E-mail: aa-srt@son-rep-texas.net
Web Site: www.srttexas.org

FOUNDED: 1893

AREAS OF INTEREST:
Republic of Texas (1836-1846).

NAME(S) OF PROGRAMS:
● **Summerfield G. Roberts Award**

TYPE:
Awards/prizes. Cash award to the author of a work of creative writing on the Republic of Texas.

PURPOSE:
To encourage literary effort and research about historical events and personalities during the days of the Republic of Texas (1836-1846), and to stimulate interest in this period.

LEGAL BASIS:
Nonprofit organization.

ELIGIBILITY:
The competition is open to all writers everywhere; they need not reside in Texas nor must the publishers be in Texas. Manuscripts may be either fiction or nonfiction, poems, essays, plays, short stories, novels, or biographies.

FINANCIAL DATA:
Amount of support per award: $2,500.
Total amount of support: $2,500 annually.

NO. AWARDS: 1 annually.

APPLICATION INFO:
Manuscripts must be written or published during the calendar year for which the award is given. The title page must have the contestant's full name, address and phone number. Five copies of each entry must be mailed to the General Office of The Sons of the Republic of Texas at the address above. No copies will be returned.
Duration: One-time award.
Deadline: Postmarked no later than January 15 of the year following the qualifying year of the award.

ADDRESS INQUIRIES TO:
Janet Knox, Administrative Assistant
The Sons of the Republic of Texas
(See address above.)

THE SUMMERLEE FOUNDATION
5556 Caruth Haven Lane
Dallas, TX 75225
(214) 363-9000
Fax: (214) 363-1941
E-mail: info@summerlee.org
Web Site: www.summerlee.org

TYPE:
Project/program grants; Research grants; Technical assistance.

See entry 1264 for full listing.

HARRY S. TRUMAN LIBRARY INSTITUTE

5151 Troost Avenue
Suite 300
Kansas City, MO 64110
(816) 400-1216
Fax: (816) 400-1213
E-mail: lisa.sullivan@trumanlibraryinstitute.org
Web Site: www.trumanlibraryinstitute.org

TYPE:
Awards/prizes; Fellowships; Grants-in-aid; Research grants; Travel grants. The Dissertation Year Fellowships are given to encourage historical scholarship of the public career of Harry S. Truman or the Truman era. Support is given annually to one or two graduate students who have completed the dissertation research and are in the writing stage. Preference will be given to projects based on extensive research at the Truman Library. Successful applicants will be expected to deposit one copy of their completed dissertation, or any publication resulting therefrom, with the Truman Library.

Research Grants are intended to enable graduate students as well as postdoctoral scholars to come to the Library for one to three weeks to use its archival facilities.

The Scholar's Award is given every other year, even-numbered years only, to a scholar engaged in a study of either the public career of Harry S. Truman or some aspect of the history of the Truman administration or of the U.S. during that administration. The scholar's work must be based on extensive research at the Truman Library and must be designed to result in the publication of a book-length manuscript. One copy of such book (and/or any other publication resulting from work done under this award) shall be deposited by the author with the Harry S. Truman Library.

The Harry S. Truman Book Award is given in even years for the best book dealing with some aspect of history of the U.S. between April 12, 1945 and January 20, 1953 or with the public career of Harry S. Truman.

See entry 1838 for full listing.

U.S. ARMY CENTER OF MILITARY HISTORY [593]

Dissertation Fellowship Committee
Collins Hall, Building 35
102 Fourth Avenue, Fort Lesley J. McNair
Washington, DC 20319-5060
(202) 685-2305
Fax: (202) 685-2077
E-mail: usarmy.mcnair.cmh.mbx.dissfellow@mail.mil
Web Site: www.history.army.mil/index.html

FOUNDED: 1942

AREAS OF INTEREST:
History of warfare on land, with special emphasis on the history of the U.S. Army.

NAME(S) OF PROGRAMS:
● **Dissertation Year Fellowships**

TYPE:
Fellowships. The Center offers two Dissertation Fellowships each year and sometimes awards a third fellowship to exceptional dissertations on museum-related topics. The Center will consider dissertations on the history of land warfare; preference is given to topics on the history of the U.S. Army.

YEAR PROGRAM STARTED: 1970

PURPOSE:
To encourage scholarship in military history.

LEGAL BASIS:
Government agency.

ELIGIBILITY:
Applicants must be civilian citizens or nationals of the U.S. that have demonstrated ability and special aptitude for advanced training and study in military history, be enrolled in a recognized graduate school and have successfully completed by September of the year of the award all requirements for the Ph.D. except the dissertation.

FINANCIAL DATA:
Amount of support per award: Stipend of $10,000.
Total amount of support: Up to $30,000.

NO. MOST RECENT APPLICANTS: 11 for the year 2017-18.

NO. AWARDS: Up to 3 annually.

REPRESENTATIVE AWARDS:
"Bickering Brass: Defense Unification, Interservice Rivalry, and the Pacific War;" "The Killing Spirit: American War Criminals and Military Justice, 1942-1945."

APPLICATION INFO:
Applicants must submit by mail the following materials:
(1) completed, typed application form;
(2) proposed research plan and reasons for interest in this topic (not to exceed 10 double-spaced, typed pages);
(3) letter of recommendation from dissertation director confirming dissertation proposal has been accepted by the committee;
(4) two other letters of recommendation;
(5) a writing sample of approximately 25 double-spaced, typed pages (e.g., seminar paper, published scholarly article, excerpt from M.A. thesis or Ph.D. dissertation) and;
(6) transcripts from all undergraduate and graduate schools attended.
Duration: One year.
Deadline: January 15. Announcement April 1.

ADDRESS INQUIRIES TO:
Dr. Jeffrey Seiken
CMH Dissertation Fellowship Committee
(See address above.)

U.S. ARMY MILITARY HISTORY INSTITUTE [594]

U.S. Army Heritage and Education Center
950 Soldiers Drive
Carlisle, PA 17013-5021
(717) 245-3803
E-mail: usarmy.carlisle.awc.mbx.ahec-ves@mail.mil
Web Site: ahec.armywarcollege.edu/ridgway.cfm

FOUNDED: 1967

AREAS OF INTEREST:
Military history with emphasis on the U.S. Army.

NAME(S) OF PROGRAMS:
● **General and Mrs. Matthew B. Ridgway Military History Research Grant**

TYPE:
Research grants; Travel grants. Research and travel fellowships to cover expenses incurred while conducting individual research in USAMHI holdings. These grants may not be used to cover costs for travel to and research at other institutions.

YEAR PROGRAM STARTED: 1977

PURPOSE:
To stimulate utilization of holdings of the Institute in preparation of scholarly, mature publications in military history (theses, dissertations or books).

LEGAL BASIS:
U.S. Department of the Army.

ELIGIBILITY:
Applicants must be actively engaged in the study of military history, to include research as part of a Masters or Doctorate program in military history (or a related field) or research toward a book, monograph, or scholarly article.

FINANCIAL DATA:
Amount of support per award: Up to $2,500.
Total amount of support: Varies.

NO. MOST RECENT APPLICANTS: 18 for the year 2019.

NO. AWARDS: 8 for the year 2019.

APPLICATION INFO:
Electronic submissions only.
Duration: Until December 31 of the following year.
Deadline: Applications are due to the committee by December 31. Final announcement of recipients by March 15.

ADDRESS INQUIRIES TO:
Ridgway Research Grants
(See address above.)

*SPECIAL STIPULATIONS:
Must do research in U.S. Army Military History Institute holdings.

UNITED STATES HOLOCAUST MEMORIAL MUSEUM - JACK, JOSEPH AND MORTON MANDEL CENTER FOR ADVANCED HOLOCAUST STUDIES [595]

100 Raoul Wallenberg Place, S.W.
Washington, DC 20024-2126
(202) 314-7829
Fax: (202) 479-9726
E-mail: vscholars@ushmm.org
Web Site: www.ushmm.org/research/opportunities-for-academics

FOUNDED: 1993

AREAS OF INTEREST:
Holocaust and genocide studies.

NAME(S) OF PROGRAMS:
● **International Academic Programs**

TYPE:
Exchange programs; Fellowships. The Jack, Joseph and Morton Mandel Center for Advanced Holocaust Studies is an integral part of the United States Holocaust Memorial Museum, which serves as America's national institution for Holocaust education and remembrance. The Mandel Center awards fellowships to support significant research and writing about the Holocaust. Awards are granted on a competitive basis. The Mandel Center welcomes proposals from scholars in all relevant academic disciplines, including history, political science, literature, Jewish studies, philosophy, religion, psychology, comparative genocide studies, law and others.

Visiting scholars at the Mandel Center have access to more than 100 million pages of Holocaust-related archival documentation; the Museum's extensive library; oral history, film, photo, art, artifacts and memoir collections; and Holocaust survivor database.

YEAR PROGRAM STARTED: 1994

PURPOSE:
To support scholarship and publication in the field of Holocaust studies; to promote the growth of Holocaust studies at universities; to seek to foster strong relationships between American and international scholars; to organize programs to ensure the ongoing training of future generations of scholars specializing in the Holocaust.

ELIGIBILITY:
Fellowships are awarded to candidates working on their dissertations (ABD), postdoctoral researchers, and senior scholars. Immediate postdoctorals and faculty between appointments will also be considered.

FINANCIAL DATA:
Amount of support per award: Up to $3,700 monthly.
Total amount of support: Varies.

NO. MOST RECENT APPLICANTS: 116.

NO. AWARDS: Approximately 30 to 35.

APPLICATION INFO:
Details are available on the web site listed above.
Duration: Three to eight months. Must be a minimum of three consecutive months.
Deadline: Typically, November of each year.

PUBLICATIONS:
Program announcement.

ADDRESS INQUIRIES TO:
Samantha Hinckley, Program Manager
(See address above.)

THE UNIVERSITY OF DELAWARE-HAGLEY GRADUATE PROGRAM [596]

Department of History, John Munroe Hall
University of Delaware
Newark, DE 19716
(302) 831-8226
Fax: (302) 831-1538
E-mail: dianec@udel.edu
Web Site: www.udel.edu/hagley
www.history.udel.edu

FOUNDED: 1954

AREAS OF INTEREST:
Technology, business, consumption, and work in industrial and post-industrial societies.

TYPE:
Assistantships; Fellowships. The University of Delaware, in association with the Hagley Museum, sponsors a premier graduate resident program for the study of technology, business, consumption, and work in industrial and post-industrial societies leading to a Master of Arts or Ph.D. in History. Students have access to faculty with international reputations in American, European and non-Western history, and benefit from strong interdisciplinary ties to museum studies and material culture programs, as well as the Hagley Museum and Library.

YEAR PROGRAM STARTED: 1954

PURPOSE:
To prepare students planning careers as college teachers and as professionals in museums and historical agencies.

LEGAL BASIS:
Not-for-profit organization classified by IRS as 501(c)(3) organization.

ELIGIBILITY:
All Hagley Scholars are required to complete 30 credits (ten classes). Some of these classes must be selected to fulfill History Department requirements. Hagley Scholars also must take two "Hagley courses" which reflect student and faculty interests. These are offered every semester. Ph.D. students take a written comprehensive examination and write a dissertation. A thesis is optional for M.A. students.

FINANCIAL DATA:
All Hagley Scholars receive a stipend and tuition remission. M.A. students are supported for two years. Ph.D. students receive five years of funding. In exchange, Scholars work as teaching assistants during half the semesters in which they are funded. Hagley Scholars also receive an allowance of $600 a year for travel and research expenses. The Program and the History Department also have additional funds which can be used to support internships and Ph.D. research.

NO. MOST RECENT APPLICANTS: Varies.

NO. AWARDS: Varies.

APPLICATION INFO:
Interested applicants should complete the online application for the UD History Graduate Program. Applicant should clearly indicate on the top of the personal statement that he or she wishes to be considered for the Hagley Program.
Duration: Two years for Master's students; Five years for Ph.D. students.
Deadline: January 15.

ADDRESS INQUIRIES TO:
Diane Clark, Academic Support Coordinator
(See address above.)

*SPECIAL STIPULATIONS:
This is a resident graduate program.

UNIVERSITY OF DELAWARE, DEPARTMENT OF HISTORY [597]

46 West Delaware Avenue
Newark, DE 19716
(302) 831-8226
Fax: (302) 831-1538
E-mail: dianec@udel.edu
Web Site: www.udel.edu
www.history.udel.edu

AREAS OF INTEREST:
Professional training in historical studies.

NAME(S) OF PROGRAMS:
● **E. Lyman Stewart Fellowship**

TYPE:
Fellowships. Residential program in history.

PURPOSE:
To provide a program of graduate study leading to an M.A. or Ph.D. degree for students who plan careers as museum professionals, historical agency administrators or seek careers in college teaching and public history.

ELIGIBILITY:
Open to nationals of any country.

FINANCIAL DATA:
Amount of support per award: M.A. students receive $20,000, plus tuition; Ph.D. students receive $23,000, plus tuition.

Total amount of support: Varies.

NO. AWARDS: Varies.

APPLICATION INFO:
Applications must be submitted online using the University of Delaware application form and include transcripts, Graduate Record Examination scores, TOEFL scores (where applicable), plus three letters of recommendation and a writing sample.
Duration: Two to five years.
Deadline: January 5.

ADDRESS INQUIRIES TO:
Diane Clark, Academic Support Coordinator
(See address above.)

WISCONSIN HISTORICAL SOCIETY PRESS [598]

816 State Street
Madison, WI 53706-1482
(608) 264-6582
E-mail: whspress@wisconsinhistory.org
Web Site: www.wisconsinhistory.org/whspress

FOUNDED: 1846

AREAS OF INTEREST:
Wisconsin history and culture.

NAME(S) OF PROGRAMS:
● **D.C. Everest Fellowship**
● **Amy Louise Hunter Fellowship**
● **Alice E. Smith Fellowship**

TYPE:
Fellowships; Research grants. Fellowships awarded for research and writing for publication in book form by the Society press on Wisconsin history topics.

YEAR PROGRAM STARTED: 2000

PURPOSE:
To promote research and writing on Wisconsin history topics.

LEGAL BASIS:
Agency of the state of Wisconsin.

ELIGIBILITY:
Fellowships are awarded to individuals. Organizations are not eligible to apply.

FINANCIAL DATA:
Amount of support per award: $1,000 to $2,000.

NO. AWARDS: 1 per award.

APPLICATION INFO:
Application must include a cover sheet, resume and completed book proposal.
Duration: One-time award.

PUBLICATIONS:
Program announcement.

YIVO INSTITUTE FOR JEWISH RESEARCH [599]

15 West 16th Street, 3rd Floor
New York, NY 10011-6301
(917) 606-8290
Fax: (212) 292-1892
E-mail: bkaplan@yivo.cjh.org
Web Site: yivo.org

FOUNDED: 1925

AREAS OF INTEREST:
Yiddish, East European and American Jewish history and culture.

NAME(S) OF PROGRAMS:
● **Fellowship in American Jewish Studies**

TYPE:
Fellowships. The Rose and Isidore Drench
Memorial Fellowship and the Dora and
Mayer Tendler Endowed Fellowship in
Jewish Studies are dedicated to doctoral or
postdoctoral research in American Jewish
history, with special consideration given to
scholars working on some aspect of the
Jewish labor movement. This Fellowship is
for research at the YIVO Library and
Archives.

YEAR PROGRAM STARTED: 1990

PURPOSE:
To further research of American Jewish
history, based on resources from the YIVO
Library and Archives.

LEGAL BASIS:
Tax-exempt 501(c)(3) organization.

ELIGIBILITY:
Applicants must be working in American
Jewish history with special consideration
toward the Jewish Labor Movement. The
research must be conducted at YIVO in New
York City.

FINANCIAL DATA:
Amount of support per award: Combined
stipend of $10,000

Total amount of support: $10,000.

NO. AWARDS: 1.

APPLICATION INFO:
Application materials should be sent by
regular mail, fax or e-mail to:
Chairperson, Fellowship Committee
YIVO Institute for Jewish Research.

Applicants should include the following
materials:
(1) curriculum vitae, including all contact
information and detailing education,
publications, other scholarly activity (papers
presented, etc.), teaching and other relevant
work experience, knowledge of relevant
languages, honors, awards and fellowships,
etc.;
(2) research proposal of no more than four
pages, including aims for research during the
period of fellowship; whether the proposed
work is part of a larger project, such as a
dissertation, book, etc.; how the resources of
YIVO will contribute to the work and;
(3) two letters of support, which discuss the
importance of the applicant's work for the
relevant field, as well as the applicant's
ability to carry out the proposed work.

Applicants may apply for only one
fellowship.
Duration: Three months.
Deadline: January 15.

PUBLICATIONS:
Yedies: News from YIVO.

BOARD OF DIRECTORS:
Ruth Levine, Chairman
Irena Pletka, Vice Chairman
Edward Blank
Martin Flumenbaum
Emil Kleinhaus
Dr. Chava Lapin
Leo Melamed
Jacob Morowitz
Eliza New
Ilya Prizel
John Richmond
Harry Wagner

ADDRESS INQUIRIES TO:
Ben Kaplan, Director of Education
Max Weinreich Center for
Advanced Jewish Studies
(See address above.)

*PLEASE NOTE:
Each fellowship requires up to three months'
research stay and at least one public lecture
by the holder.

YIVO INSTITUTE FOR JEWISH RESEARCH   [600]
15 West 16th Street, 3rd Floor
New York, NY 10011-6301
(917) 606-8290
Fax: (212) 292-1892
E-mail: bkaplan@yivo.cjh.org
Web Site: www.yivo.org

FOUNDED: 1925

AREAS OF INTEREST:
Yiddish, East European and American Jewish
history and culture.

NAME(S) OF PROGRAMS:
- **Fellowship in East European Arts, Music, and Theater**
- **Fellowship in East European Jewish Literature**

TYPE:
Fellowships. Fellowship in East European
Arts, Music, and Theater is designed to assist
an undergraduate, graduate or postgraduate
researcher in the fields of Eastern European
Jewish arts, music and theater.

Fellowship in East European Jewish
Literature is designed to assist an
undergraduate, graduate or postgraduate
researcher in Eastern European Jewish
literature.

The stipend is intended to defray expenses
connected with research in YIVO's music, art
and theater collections and library.

YEAR PROGRAM STARTED: 1994

PURPOSE:
To further research in Yiddish Studies, based
on resources from the YIVO Library and
Archives.

LEGAL BASIS:
Tax-exempt 501(c)(3) organization.

FINANCIAL DATA:
Amount of support per award: Fellowship in
East European Arts, Music, and Theater:
Stipend of $7,000; Fellowship in East
European Jewish Literature: Stipend of
$5,000.

NO. AWARDS: 1 per award.

APPLICATION INFO:
Application materials should be sent by
regular mail, fax or e-mail to:
Chairperson, Fellowship Committee
YIVO Institute for Jewish Research.

Applicants should include the following
materials:
(1) curriculum vitae, including all contact
information and detailing education;
publications; other scholarly activity (papers
presented, etc.); teaching and other relevant
work experience; knowledge of relevant
languages; honors, awards and fellowships,
etc.;
(2) research proposal of no more than four
pages, including aims for research during the
period of fellowship; whether the proposed
work is part of a larger project, such as a

dissertation, book, etc.; how the resources of
YIVO will contribute to the work and;
(3) two letters of support, which discuss the
importance of the applicant's work for the
relevant field, as well as the applicant's
ability to carry out the proposed work.

Applicants may apply for one fellowship
only.
Duration: Two to three months.
Deadline: January 15.

PUBLICATIONS:
Yedies: News from YIVO.

BOARD OF DIRECTORS:
Ruth Levine, Chairman
Irena Pletka, Vice Chairman
Edward Blank
Martin Flumenbaum
Emil Kleinhaus
Dr. Chava Lapin
Leo Melamed
Jacob Morowitz
Eliza New
Ilya Prizel
John Richmond
Harry Wagner

ADDRESS INQUIRIES TO:
Ben Kaplan, Director of Education
Max Weinreich Center for
Advanced Jewish Studies
(See address above.)

*PLEASE NOTE:
Each fellowship requires up to three months'
research stay and at least one public lecture
by the holder.

YIVO INSTITUTE FOR JEWISH RESEARCH   [601]
15 West 16th Street, 3rd Floor
New York, NY 10011-6301
(212) 246-6080
Fax: (212) 292-1892
E-mail: eportnoy@yivo.cjh.org
Web Site: www.yivo.org

FOUNDED: 1925

AREAS OF INTEREST:
Eastern European Jewish studies.

NAME(S) OF PROGRAMS:
- **Fellowship in Baltic Jewish Studies**
- **Fellowship in East European Jewish Studies**
- **Fellowship in Polish Jewish Studies**

TYPE:
Fellowships. Fellowship in Baltic Jewish
Studies supports original doctoral or
postdoctoral research in the field of
Lithuanian Jewish history at the YIVO
Library and Archives or travel for Ph.D.
dissertation research in archives and libraries
of the Baltic states.

Fellowship in East European Jewish Studies
supports doctoral or postdoctoral research in
the field of East European Jewish studies.
Research is to be conducted at the YIVO
Library and Archives.

Fellowship in Polish Jewish Studies supports
doctoral or postdoctoral research on
Polish-Jewish history in the modern period,
particularly Jewish-Polish relations, including
the Holocaust period, and Jewish
contributions to Polish literature and culture.
This Fellowship is for research at the YIVO
Library and Archives.

PURPOSE:
To advance Eastern European Jewish studies.

FINANCIAL DATA:
Amount of support per award: Fellowship in Baltic Jewish Studies: $6,000; Fellowship in East European Jewish Studies: $20,000; Fellowship in Polish Jewish Studies: $8,000.

NO. AWARDS: 1 per award.

APPLICATION INFO:
Applications should include a curriculum vitae, a research proposal (four-page maximum), and two letters of support.
Duration: Varies.
Deadline: January 1.

ADDRESS INQUIRIES TO:
Dr. Eddy Portnoy
Max Weinreich Center Academic Advisor and Research Associate
(See address above.)

*PLEASE NOTE:
Fellows are usually expected to spend four to six weeks in residence and are required to give one public lecture.

*SPECIAL STIPULATIONS:
Applicants may apply for one fellowship only.

YIVO INSTITUTE FOR JEWISH RESEARCH   [602]
15 West 16th Street, 3rd Floor
New York, NY 10011-6301
(212) 246-6080
Fax: (212) 292-1892
E-mail: eportnoy@yivo.cjh.org
Web Site: www.yivo.org

FOUNDED: 1925

AREAS OF INTEREST:
Eastern European Jewish studies.

NAME(S) OF PROGRAMS:
● **The Dina Abramowicz Emerging Scholar Fellowship**
● **The Workmen's Circle/Dr. Emanuel Patt Visiting Professorship**

TYPE:
Fellowships; Visiting scholars. The Dina Abramowicz Emerging Scholar Fellowship is intended for postdoctoral research on a topic in Eastern European Jewish studies. The work should lead to a significant scholarly publication and may encompass the revision of a doctoral dissertation. The Fellowship carries a stipend for the holder to conduct research at the YIVO Library and Archives.

The Workmen's Circle/Dr. Emanuel Patt Visiting Professorship in Eastern European Jewish Studies, established by the Van Cortlandt Workmen's Circle Community House, is designed to support postdoctoral research at the YIVO Library and Archives.

PURPOSE:
To advance Eastern European Jewish studies.

FINANCIAL DATA:
Amount of support per award: Abramowicz Fellowships: $5,000; Workmen's Circle: $10,000.

APPLICATION INFO:
Applications should include a cover letter indicating one choice of fellowship, a curriculum vitae, a research proposal (four-page maximum), and two letters of support.
Duration: Varies.
Deadline: January 1.

ADDRESS INQUIRIES TO:
Dr. Eddy Portnoy
Max Weinreich Center Academic Advisor and Research Associate
(See address above.)

*PLEASE NOTE:
Fellows are usually expected to spend four to six weeks in residence and are required to give one public lecture.

*SPECIAL STIPULATIONS:
Applicants may apply for one fellowship only.

Languages

THE AMERICAN CLASSICAL LEAGUE   [603]
860 N.W. Washington Boulevard
Suite A
Hamilton, OH 45013
(513) 529-7741
Fax: (513) 529-7742
E-mail: info@aclclassics.org
Web Site: www.aclclassics.org

FOUNDED: 1919

AREAS OF INTEREST:
Latin and Classical Studies of ancient Rome and Greece.

CONSULTING OR VOLUNTEER SERVICES:
Placement service for teachers of Latin.

NAME(S) OF PROGRAMS:
● **McKinlay Scholarship**

TYPE:
Grants-in-aid; Scholarships.

YEAR PROGRAM STARTED: 1975

PURPOSE:
To assist teachers of Latin and Greek further their educational background.

LEGAL BASIS:
Nonprofit.

ELIGIBILITY:
Applicant must be a member of American Classical League for the preceding three years and current year and teaching Latin or Greek courses.

FINANCIAL DATA:
Amount of support per award: Maximum $2,000 per individual.
Total amount of support: Varies.

NO. MOST RECENT APPLICANTS: 50.

NO. AWARDS: 50.

APPLICATION INFO:
The application form and guidelines are available on the League web site.
Duration: One-time award.
Deadline: January 15 and March 15. Awards announced February 15 and April 15, respectively.

ADDRESS INQUIRIES TO:
Sherwin Little, Executive Director
(See address above.)

AMERICAN INSTITUTE OF INDIAN STUDIES   [604]
1130 East 59th Street
Chicago, IL 60637
(773) 702-8638
E-mail: aiis@uchicago.edu
Web Site: www.indiastudies.org

FOUNDED: 1961

AREAS OF INTEREST:
Indian studies.

NAME(S) OF PROGRAMS:
● **Advanced Language Program in India**

TYPE:
Fellowships. Awards for studies in India in an Indian language.

YEAR PROGRAM STARTED: 1969

PURPOSE:
To provide advanced language training in India.

LEGAL BASIS:
Cooperative, nonprofit organization of 90 American colleges and universities.

ELIGIBILITY:
Open to graduate and junior or senior-level undergraduate students in U.S. colleges and universities who have had a minimum of two years or 240 class hours of classroom instruction in Bengali, Hindi or Tamil and intend to pursue teaching degrees. Applicants for other Indian languages may be considered, but they should contact the AIIS for further information and advice. Applicants must be U.S. citizens.

FINANCIAL DATA:
Grants will be awarded on a competitive basis and will include round-trip airfare to India and a maintenance allowance sufficient to cover living expenses. No funding will be provided for dependents.

APPLICATION INFO:
Application forms are available online. All applications must include a $25 processing fee.
Duration: Nine months.
Deadline: December 31.

EXECUTIVE STAFF:
Elise Auerbach, Administrator

ADDRESS INQUIRIES TO:
Elise Auerbach, Administrator
(See address above.)

AMERICAN RESEARCH INSTITUTE IN TURKEY, INC.
c/o The University of Pennsylvania Museum
3260 South Street
Philadelphia, PA 19104-6324
(215) 898-3474
Fax: (215) 898-0657
E-mail: leinwand@sas.upenn.edu
Web Site: ccat.sas.upenn.edu/ARIT

TYPE:
Fellowships. Bogazici University Summer Language Program: For summer study in Turkey. Also offer travel, stipend and tuition grants. This intensive program offers the equivalent of one full academic year of study in advanced Turkish language at the college level.

See entry 816 for full listing.

THE JAPAN FOUNDATION, NEW YORK
1700 Broadway
15th Floor
New York, NY 10019
(212) 489-0299
Fax: (212) 489-0409
E-mail: info@jfny.org
Web Site: www.jfny.org

TYPE:
Conferences/seminars; Fellowships; Professorships; Project/program grants; Research grants; Travel grants. The Japanese Studies Fellowship Program has three components: Doctoral Fellowship, Long-term Research Fellowship, and Short-term Research Fellowship.

See entry 785 for full listing.

KOBE COLLEGE CORPORATION-JAPAN EDUCATION EXCHANGE
540 West Frontage Road, Suite 3335
Northfield, IL 60093
(847) 386-7661
Fax: (847) 386-7662
E-mail: programs@kccjee.org
Web Site: www.kccjee.org

TYPE:
Awards/prizes. The KCC-JEE High School Essay Contest includes a one-month trip to Japan. It incorporates intensive language study, college credit and a home stay with a Japanese family.

See entry 849 for full listing.

LUSO-AMERICAN EDUCATION FOUNDATION   [605]
7080 Donlon Way
Suite 200
Dublin, CA 94568
(925) 828-3883
Fax: (925) 828-4554
E-mail: education@luso-american.org
Web Site: www.luso-american.org/laef

FOUNDED: 1963

AREAS OF INTEREST:
Perpetuation of the Portuguese language and culture in the U.S.

NAME(S) OF PROGRAMS:
- **Luso-American Education Foundation Scholarships**

TYPE:
Scholarships.

LEGAL BASIS:
Tax-exempt corporation.

ELIGIBILITY:
For the General Youth Scholarship, the applicant must currently be a high school graduating senior, enrolled to begin classes at a community or four-year college/university, and an official U.S. resident. He or she must also meet one of the following requirements: (1) being of Portuguese descent, with a minimum grade point average of 3.5; (2) currently taking Portuguese classes at high school level, with a minimum grade point average of 3.0 or; (3) having attended the Luso-American Education Foundation Cultural Youth Summer Camp for a minimum of two years, with a minimum grade point average of 3.0.

FINANCIAL DATA:
Amount of support per award: Varies in amount, depending on applicant's need and Foundation funds allocated.

NO. AWARDS: 23 for the year 2017.

APPLICATION INFO:
The following materials must be submitted: (1) a complete application by printing (in pen) or typing all information requested; (2) an official transcript of all completed high

school work and SAT/ACT scores (if applicable); these must be issued and certified by a school official, along with a completed Student Counselor Report (found on web site); (3) a letter of recommendation submitted directly from two individuals who can attest to applicant's character and/or financial needs; each letter of recommendation must be submitted with a Letter of Recommendation Cover Sheet (found on web site) and; (4) a recent wallet-size photo of applicant (no photocopies).

Duration: Nonrenewable.

Deadline: Key dates are posted on the Foundation web site.

PUBLICATIONS:
Program announcement.

ADDRESS INQUIRIES TO:
Bernice Pelicas
Administrative Director
(See address or e-mail above.)

LUSO-AMERICAN EDUCATION FOUNDATION   [606]
7080 Donlon Way
Suite 200
Dublin, CA 94568
(925) 828-3883
Fax: (925) 828-4554
E-mail: education@luso-american.org
Web Site: www.luso-american.org/laef

FOUNDED: 1963

AREAS OF INTEREST:
Perpetuation of the Portuguese language and culture in the U.S., Portuguese education and the teaching of Portuguese in California schools and universities.

CONSULTING OR VOLUNTEER SERVICES:
Provides advisory and reference services, assists teachers and school districts in setting up Portuguese language and literature courses, choosing texts, etc., makes referrals to other sources of information, permits on-site use of collection and holds annual Conference on Portuguese-American Education for educators, administrators and community persons. Services are free and available to people across the U.S.

NAME(S) OF PROGRAMS:
- **Educational Grant Program**

TYPE:
Grants-in-aid; Research grants. The Foundation provides a variety of grant programs: research grants, Portuguese language-program grants, study-abroad (in Portugal) grants, and educator (of Portuguese language and/or culture) grants.

YEAR PROGRAM STARTED: 1970

PURPOSE:
To lead initiatives for the advances of the Portuguese culture and language; to support qualified students in accessing higher education; and to foster life-long learning programs.

LEGAL BASIS:
Tax-exempt corporation.

ELIGIBILITY:
Varies with the program.

FINANCIAL DATA:
Amount of support per award: Grants vary in amount, depending on the applicant's need and Foundation funds allocated.

Total amount of support: Varies.

NO. AWARDS: Varies.

APPLICATION INFO:
Form can be downloaded from the Foundation web site.

Deadline: Key days are posted on the Foundation web site.

PUBLICATIONS:
The Luso-American, annual; *Portuguese Presence in California; Literatura de Expressao Portuguesa Nos Estados Unidos;* bibliographies; annual report.

ADDRESS INQUIRIES TO:
Bernice Pelicas
Administrative Director
(See address or e-mail above.)

MODERN LANGUAGE ASSOCIATION OF AMERICA   [607]
85 Broad Street, Suite 500
New York, NY 10004-2434
(646) 576-5000
(646) 576-5141
Fax: (646) 458-0030
E-mail: awards@mla.org
Web Site: www.mla.org

FOUNDED: 1883

AREAS OF INTEREST:
Literary studies, languages and education.

NAME(S) OF PROGRAMS:
- **Morton N. Cohen Award for a Distinguished Edition of Letters**
- **Kenneth W. Mildenberger Prize**
- **Modern Language Association Prize for a Scholarly Edition**
- **Modern Language Association Prize for Independent Scholars**
- **Mina P. Shaughnessy Prize**

TYPE:
Awards/prizes.

PURPOSE:
To recognize outstanding scholarly work.

LEGAL BASIS:
Membership association.

ELIGIBILITY:
Authors are not required to be members of the Association.

The Morton N. Cohen Award is presented biennially in odd-numbered years for important collections of letters published in either of the two preceding years. A multivolume edition is eligible if at least one volume was published during that period. Editors can apply regardless of the fields they and the authors of the letters represent. The winning collection will be one that provides a clear, accurate and readable text, necessary background information, and succinct and eloquent introductory material and annotations. The collection should be in itself a work of literature.

The Kenneth W. Mildenberger Prize is presented biennially in odd-numbered years for an outstanding publication in the field of teaching foreign languages and literatures.

The Modern Language Association Prize for a Scholarly Edition will be given biennially in odd-numbered years to a book published in either of the two preceding years without regard to the field or language either of the editor or of the text presented in the edition. To qualify for the award, an edition should be based on an examination of all available relevant textual sources; the source texts and the edited text's deviations from them should be fully described; the edition should employ editorial principles appropriate to the materials edited, and those principles should be clearly articulated in the volume; the text should be accompanied by appropriate textual and other historical contextual information; the edition should exhibit the highest standards of accuracy in the presentation of its text and apparatus; and the text and apparatus should be presented as accessibly and elegantly as possible.

The Modern Language Association Prize for Independent Scholars is awarded biennially in even-numbered years for a distinguished scholarly book published in the field of English or another modern language or literature. Authors enrolled in a program leading to an academic degree and authors holding a tenured, tenure-accruing or tenure-track position in a postsecondary institution at the time of publication of the book are not eligible. Tenure is understood to include any comparable provision for job security in a postsecondary educational institution.

The Mina P. Shaughnessy Prize is presented biennially in even-numbered years for an outstanding scholarly book in the fields of language, culture, literacy and literature that has a strong application to the teaching of English.

FINANCIAL DATA:
Amount of support per award: Varies.
Total amount of support: Varies.

APPLICATION INFO:
Application form is required for submissions to the Prize for Independent Scholars. To enter book into competition for other prizes, no special form or procedure is needed. Shipments of books should be preceded or accompanied by letters identifying the works.
Duration: One-time award.
Deadline: May 1.

ADDRESS INQUIRIES TO:
Annie M. Reiser, Coordinator of Book Prizes (See address above.)

MODERN LANGUAGE ASSOCIATION OF AMERICA   [608]
85 Broad Street, Suite 500
New York, NY 10004-2434
(646) 576-5000
(646) 576-5141
Fax: (646) 458-0030
E-mail: awards@mla.org
Web Site: www.mla.org

FOUNDED: 1883

AREAS OF INTEREST:
Literary studies, languages and education.

NAME(S) OF PROGRAMS:
- **Matei Calinescu Prize**
- **Katherine Singer Kovacs Prize**
- **Fenia and Yaakov Leviant Memorial Prize in Yiddish Studies**
- **James Russell Lowell Prize**
- **Howard R. Marraro Prize**
- **MLA Prize for a First Book**
- **MLA Prize for an Edited Collection**
- **MLA Prize for Collaborative, Bibliographical or Archival Scholarship**

- **MLA Prize in United States Latina and Latino and Chicana and Chicano Literary and Cultural Studies**
- **Lois Roth Award for a Translation of a Literary Work**
- **Aldo and Jeanne Scaglione Prize for a Translation of a Literary Work**
- **Aldo and Jeanne Scaglione Prize for a Translation of a Scholarly Study of Literature**
- **Aldo and Jeanne Scaglione Prize for Comparative Literary Studies**
- **Aldo and Jeanne Scaglione Prize for French and Francophone Studies**
- **Aldo and Jeanne Scaglione Prize for Italian Studies**
- **Aldo and Jeanne Scaglione Prize for Studies in Slavic Languages and Literatures**
- **Aldo and Jeanne Scaglione Prize for Studies in Germanic Languages and Literatures**
- **Aldo and Jeanne Scaglione Publication Award for a Manuscript in Italian Literary Studies**
- **William Sanders Scarborough Prize**

TYPE:
Awards/prizes. To recognize outstanding scholarly works in the fields of English, French, Italian, Germanic languages and Slavic languages, Yiddish literature and culture, Black American literature and culture, Latino/Latina and Chicana/Chicano literature and culture. Germanic languages include Danish, Dutch, German, Icelandic, Norwegian, Swedish and Yiddish.

The Fenia and Yaakov Leviant Memorial Prize in Yiddish Studies, the Howard R. Marraro Prize, the Aldo and Jeanne Scaglione Prize for a Translation of a Literary Work and the Aldo and Jeanne Scaglione Prize for Studies in Germanic Languages and Literatures are offered biennially in even-numbered years. The MLA Prize in United States Latina and Latino and Chicana and Chicano Literary and Cultural Studies, the Lois Roth Award for a Translation of a Literary Work, the Aldo and Jeanne Scaglione Prize for a Translation of a Scholarly Study of Literature, the Aldo and Jeanne Scaglione Prize for Italian Studies, and the Aldo and Jeanne Scaglione Prize for Studies in Slavic Languages and Literatures are offered biennially in odd-numbered years. All others are awarded annually.

PURPOSE:
To recognize outstanding scholarly work.

LEGAL BASIS:
Membership association.

ELIGIBILITY:
For all awards, works of literary history, literary criticism, philology or literary theory are eligible. Except for translation prizes, books that are primarily translations are ineligible. For French, Germanic, Italian, Lowell, First Book and Marraro Prizes, books must be written by a current member of the Association.

FINANCIAL DATA:
Amount of support per award: Varies.

APPLICATION INFO:
To enter books into competition for prizes, no special form or procedure is needed. Four to six copies of each work are required, depending upon the prize. Shipments of books should be preceded or accompanied by

letters identifying the works and where necessary, confirming the author's membership in the MLA.
Duration: One-time awards.

Deadline: James Russell Lowell Prize and Prize for a First Book: March 1. Matei Calinescu Prize, Lois Roth Award and Scaglione Prize for a Translation of a Literary Work: April 1. Scaglione Publication Award for a Manuscript in Italian Literary Studies: June 1. All other awards: May 1.

ADDRESS INQUIRIES TO:
Annie M. Reiser, Coordinator of Book Prizes (See address above.)

NATIONAL SCIENCE FOUNDATION   [609]
Division of Behavioral and Cognitive Sciences
2415 Eisenhower Avenue, W13
Alexandria, VA 22314
(703) 292-8046
E-mail: jmaling@nsf.gov
Web Site: www.nsf.gov

FOUNDED: 1950

NAME(S) OF PROGRAMS:
- **Linguistics: Dynamic Language Infrastructure-Doctoral Dissertation Research Improvement Grants (DLI-DDRI)**
- **Linguistics Program**
- **Linguistics Program-Doctoral Dissertation Research Improvement Grants (Ling-DDRI)**
- **NSF Dynamic Language Infrastructure-NEH Documenting Endangered Languages (DLI-DEL)**

TYPE:
Research grants. Conferences/workshops. Awards provide support for research into the syntactic, morphological, semantic, phonological and phonetic properties of individual languages and of language in general. Research into the acquisition of language, the psychological processes in the production and perception of language, the social influences on language and dialect variation, and the formal and mathematical properties of language models is also supported.

YEAR PROGRAM STARTED: 1975

PURPOSE:
To support scientific research and education to strengthen research potential in language sciences.

LEGAL BASIS:
National Science Foundation Act of 1950.

ELIGIBILITY:
Applicants may be U.S. colleges and universities on behalf of their staff members, nonprofit, nonacademic research institutions, such as independent museums, observatories, research laboratories and similar organizations, private profit organizations and, under special circumstances, unaffiliated U.S. scientists.

FINANCIAL DATA:
Support may cover research assistantships, staff benefits if a direct cost, permanent equipment, travel, publication costs, computer costs and certain other direct and indirect costs.
Amount of support per award: Averages $350,000 over three-year grant period; DLI-DDRI: Not more than $15,000 in direct costs; Ling-DDRI: Not more than $12,000 in direct costs.

Total amount of support: Approximately $6,250,000 for fiscal year 2019; $3,100,000 for DLI-DEL.

CO-OP FUNDING PROGRAMS: DLI-DEL in partnership with the National Endowment for the Humanities.

NO. MOST RECENT APPLICANTS: Approximately 250 for the year 2019; 80 for DLI-DEL.

APPLICATION INFO:
Proposal should include information about the institution, principal investigator and business administrator, title and description of proposed research, desired effective date of grant, duration of support, facilities, personnel, biographical sketches, current support and pending applications and budget.
Duration: Most grants are for two to three years.
Deadline: Linguistics Program, including DDRIs: Target dates are July 15 for Fall review and January 15 for Spring review. Proposals received too late for one round of review will be reviewed in the following round with a corresponding delay in the availability of funding. DLI-DDRI: September 15 annually. DLI-DEL dissertation proposals may be submitted at any time.

PUBLICATIONS:
NSF Proposal & Award Policies & Procedures Guide (PAPPG).

STAFF:
Joan Maling, Program Director

ADDRESS INQUIRIES TO:
Joan Maling, Program Director
(See address above.)

PEN AMERICA   [610]
588 Broadway, Suite 303
New York, NY 10012
(212) 334-1660 ext. 4813
Fax: (212) 334-2181
E-mail: awards@pen.org
Web Site: pen.org

FOUNDED: 1922

AREAS OF INTEREST:
Translated prose from any language into English.

NAME(S) OF PROGRAMS:
● **PEN Translation Prize**

TYPE:
Awards/prizes. Translation prize awarded for a distinguished translation into English from any language published in the U.S. in 2020.

YEAR PROGRAM STARTED: 1962

PURPOSE:
To promote the art of translation; to pay tribute to the profession.

LEGAL BASIS:
Nonprofit organization affiliated with International PEN.

ELIGIBILITY:
Although all eligible books must have been published in the U.S. in 2021, translators may be of any nationality; U.S. residency or citizenship is not required. There are no restrictions on the subject matter of translated works, although eligible titles should be of a literary character; technical, scientific, or bibliographical translations will not be considered. Translators and authors may not submit their own work. Submissions will only be accepted from publishers and literary agents.

FINANCIAL DATA:
Amount of support per award: $3,000.
Total amount of support: $3,000 annually.

NO. MOST RECENT APPLICANTS: Approximately 200.

NO. AWARDS: 1 each year.

REPRESENTATIVE AWARDS:
Martin Aitken, translator of *Love,* by Hanne Orstavik.

APPLICATION INFO:
Online application form can be found on the Center web site beginning June 1. One copy of a book-length literary translation published during the calendar year under consideration may be submitted by publishers or literary agents. Early submissions are strongly recommended.
Deadline: August 15.

ADDRESS INQUIRIES TO:
See e-mail address above.

THE PHI BETA KAPPA SOCIETY
1606 New Hampshire Avenue, N.W.
Washington, DC 20009
(202) 745-3287
Fax: (202) 986-1601
E-mail: awards@pbk.org
Web Site: www.pbk.org

TYPE:
Fellowships. Fellowship for at least six months of study in France. One award given annually.

See entry 859 for full listing.

SOUTH ATLANTIC MODERN LANGUAGE ASSOCIATION [611]
Georgia State University
Department of English
25 Park Place, N.E., Suite 2425
Atlanta, GA 30303
(404) 413-5816
Fax: (404) 413-5830
E-mail: samla@gsu.edu
Web Site: samla.memberclicks.net

FOUNDED: 1928

AREAS OF INTEREST:
All humanities.

NAME(S) OF PROGRAMS:
● **Graduate Student Creative Writing Award**
● **Graduate Student Essay Prize**
● **Harper Fund Award**
● **SAMLA Studies Award**
● **SAR Prize**
● **Undergraduate Essay Award**

TYPE:
Assistantships; Awards/prizes; Conferences/seminars; Internships; Professorships; Travel grants. SAMLA Studies Award is for the best scholarly book written by a SAMLA member. Presses and individual members may nominate their recent publications in the year prior to the year of the convention.

YEAR PROGRAM STARTED: 1934

PURPOSE:
To encourage and honor distinguished scholarship in the modern languages and literatures.

LEGAL BASIS:
Nonprofit organization.

ELIGIBILITY:
Open to SAMLA members.

FINANCIAL DATA:
Amount of support per award: Graduate Student Creative Writing Award and Graduate Student Essay Prize: $250 per award; Harper Fund Award: Based on annual donations and not to exceed $500; SAMLA Studies Award: $1,000; SAR Prize: $500; Undergraduate Essay Award: $125.
Total amount of support: Varies.

NO. MOST RECENT APPLICANTS: Varies.

NO. AWARDS: Varies.

APPLICATION INFO:
SAMLA Studies Award: Applicants must be SAMLA members who have a scholar nominate their recent publications.
Duration: One-time award. Nonrenewable.
Deadline: February 15.

PUBLICATIONS:
South Atlantic Review, quarterly journal; *SAMLA News,* newsletter.

IRS I.D.: 62-0800246

OFFICERS:
Adrienne Angelo, President
Rudyard Alcocer, First Vice President
Christina McDonald, Second Vice President

EXECUTIVE COMMITTEE:
Leticia Perez Alonso
Martine Boumtje
Ren Denton, M.F.A., Ph.D.
Bryan Giemza
Amy Hodges Hamilton
Jay Lutz

ADDRESS INQUIRIES TO:
Dan Abitz, Associate Director
(See address above.)

U.S. DEPARTMENT OF EDUCATION   [612]
International and Foreign Language Education (IFLE)
Advanced Training and Research Division
400 Maryland Avenue, S.W.
Washington, DC 20202
(202) 453-7854
Fax: (202) 453-5780
E-mail: ifle@ed.gov
Web Site: www.ed.gov/ope/iegps

AREAS OF INTEREST:
Foreign language and area studies.

NAME(S) OF PROGRAMS:
● **Foreign Language and Area Studies Fellowships**

TYPE:
Fellowships. The Foreign Language and Area Studies Fellowships program provides allocations of academic year and summer fellowships to institutions of higher education or consortia of institutions of higher education to assist meritorious undergraduate students and graduate students undergoing training in modern foreign languages and related international or area studies.

YEAR PROGRAM STARTED: 1959

LEGAL BASIS:
Section 602, Title VI of the Higher Education Act of 1965, as amended.

ELIGIBILITY:
FLAS grants are awarded to institutions for a four-year project period. Institutions conduct competitions to select eligible undergraduate and graduate students to receive fellowships.

Funds may be used overseas with prior approval from IFLE.

GEOG. RESTRICTIONS: United States.

FINANCIAL DATA:
Each fellowship includes an institutional payment and a subsistence allowance.

Amount of support per award: The estimated institutional payment for 2019-20 academic year fellowship is $18,000 for a graduate student and $10,000 for an undergraduate student. The estimated institutional payment for summer 2019 fellowship is $5,000 for graduate and undergraduate students.

The estimated subsistence allowance for academic year 2019-20 fellowship is $15,000 for a graduate student and $5,000 for an undergraduate student. The subsistence allowance for summer 2019 fellowship is $2,500 for graduate and undergraduate students.

APPLICATION INFO:
An electronic application form is available at the web site.

Duration: Institutions: Four years.
Individuals: Academic year or summer.

ADDRESS INQUIRIES TO:
Carolyn Collins, Program Officer
(See address above.)

*PLEASE NOTE:
The next competition will take place in 2022.

U.S. DEPARTMENT OF EDUCATION [613]
International and Foreign Language Education
400 Maryland Avenue, S.W.
Room 258-24
Washington, DC 20202
(202) 453-6891
Fax: (202) 453-5780
E-mail: ddra@ed.gov
Web Site: www.ed.
gov/programs/iegpsddrap/index.html

AREAS OF INTEREST:
Foreign languages.

NAME(S) OF PROGRAMS:
● **Fulbright-Hays Doctoral Dissertation Research Abroad**

TYPE:
Fellowships. Fellowships to support doctoral dissertation research abroad in modern foreign languages and related area studies. For the purpose of these programs, area studies is defined as a program of comprehensive study of the aspects of a society or societies, including the study of their geography, history, culture, economy, politics, international relations and languages. The program is designed to develop research knowledge and capability in world areas not widely included in American curricula. Awards will not be available for projects focusing on Western Europe.

YEAR PROGRAM STARTED: 1964

PURPOSE:
To enable graduate students who plan to teach in the U.S. to undertake doctoral dissertation research in the field of modern foreign languages and area studies; to assist with the development of language and area studies specialists.

LEGAL BASIS:
The Mutual Educational and Cultural Exchange Act of 1961, Public Law 87-256, as amended (commonly known as the Fulbright-Hays Act), Section 102(b)(6).

ELIGIBILITY:
A student is eligible to receive a fellowship if he or she:
(1) is a citizen or national of the U.S. or is a permanent resident of the U.S.;
(2) is a graduate student in good standing at an institution of higher education who, when the fellowship begins, is admitted to candidacy in a doctoral program in modern foreign languages and area studies at that institution;
(3) is planning a teaching career in the U.S. upon graduation and;
(4) possesses adequate skills in the language(s) necessary to carry out the dissertation project.

FINANCIAL DATA:
Travel expenses, including excess baggage to and from the residence of the fellow to the host country of research. Maintenance allowance based on the cost of living in country(ies) of research for the fellow and his or her dependent(s). Project allowance for research-related expenses such as books, affiliation fees, local travel and other incidental expenses. Health and accident insurance premiums. $100 administrative fee to applicant institution.

Amount of support per award: $33,461 average for the year 2017.

Total amount of support: $3,011,504 for the year 2017.

NO. MOST RECENT APPLICANTS: 300.

NO. AWARDS: 90 new for the year 2017.

REPRESENTATIVE AWARDS:
$19,303 for "Testing AIDS Treatment Efficacy by a Northern Thai Community;" $28,565 for "Rethinking Community Through Suburban Nepal;" $22,364 for "Culture, Nationalism and Ethnicity in Twentieth Century Lesotho."

APPLICATION INFO:
Official application materials are available from college and university graduate schools concerned with the fellowship program. Prospective applicants must apply electronically through their institutions. The completed materials are then forwarded electronically by the institution to the U.S. Education Department's Application Control Center (ACC) in accordance with instructions published in the *Federal Register*.

Duration: Fellowships provide support for a minimum period of six months and a maximum period of 12 months.

Deadline: March 25.

ADDRESS INQUIRIES TO:
Dr. Pamela Maimer
E-mail: pamela.maimer@ed.gov

U.S. DEPARTMENT OF EDUCATION [614]
Office of Postsecondary Education
International and Foreign Language Education (IFLE)
400 Maryland Avenue, S.W., Suite 258
Mail Stop 258-40
Washington, DC 20202
(202) 453-5690
E-mail: IFLE@ed.gov
Web Site: www2.ed.gov/programs/iegpsnrc

AREAS OF INTEREST:
Foreign language and area studies.

NAME(S) OF PROGRAMS:
● **National Resource Centers (NRC) Program**

TYPE:
Project/program grants; Training grants. The NRC Program provides grants to institutions of higher education and consortia of institutions to establish, strengthen and operate comprehensive and undergraduate centers that will be national resources for:
(1) teaching of any modern foreign language;
(2) instruction in fields needed to provide full understanding of areas, regions or countries in which the modern foreign language is commonly used;
(3) research and training in international studies and the international and foreign language aspects of professional and other fields of study and;
(4) instruction and research on issues in world affairs that concern one or more countries.

This program operates on a four-year grant cycle.

PURPOSE:
To establish, strengthen and operate language and area or international studies centers that will be national resources for teaching any modern foreign language.

LEGAL BASIS:
Authorized under Section 602, Title VI of the Higher Education Act, as amended.

ELIGIBILITY:
Any institution of higher education or a combination of institutions of higher education can apply.

FINANCIAL DATA:
Amount of support per award: $188,000 to $270,000 per year.

Total amount of support: $22,743,107 (appropriated) for the year 2018.

NO. AWARDS: 96 institutional grants.

APPLICATION INFO:
Guidelines are available on the NRC Program web site.

Duration: Four years.

ADDRESS INQUIRIES TO:
Cheryl E. Gibbs, Senior Director
International Foreign Language Education Office
(See address above.)

*PLEASE NOTE:
The NRC Program competes every four years. The next competition will be in fiscal year 2022. This is not a cost-share or matching grant program.

U.S. DEPARTMENT OF EDUCATION [615]
International and Foreign Language Education (IFLE)
Language Resource Centers Program
400 Maryland Avenue, S.W.
Mail Stop 258-40
Washington, DC 20202
(202) 453-7854
E-mail: carolyn.collins@ed.gov
Web Site: www2.ed.
gov/programs/iegpslrc/index.html

AREAS OF INTEREST:
Foreign language education.

NAME(S) OF PROGRAMS:
● **Language Resource Centers Program**

TYPE:
General operating grants. Language Resource Centers Program provides grants for establishing, strengthening and operating centers that serve as resources for improving the nation's capacity for teaching and learning foreign languages through teacher training, research, materials development and dissemination projects.

PURPOSE:
To provide grants to institutions of higher education to establish, strengthen and operate resource centers that serve to improve the nation's capacity to teach and learn foreign languages.

ELIGIBILITY:
Applicant organizations must be institutions of higher education.

FINANCIAL DATA:
Amount of support per award: Average award: $171,673.
Total amount of support: $2,746,768 appropriated for fiscal year 2018.

NO. AWARDS: 16 new awards for fiscal year 2018.

APPLICATION INFO:
Details are available on the Program web site. Applications are submitted through grants.gov.
Duration: Four-year cycle.

ADDRESS INQUIRIES TO:
Carolyn Collins, Program Officer
Language Resource Centers Program
(See address above.)

*PLEASE NOTE:
The next competition will be in fiscal year 2022.

U.S. DEPARTMENT OF EDUCATION
International and Foreign Language Education
400 Maryland Avenue, S.W.
Washington, DC 20202
(202) 453-6304
E-mail: corey.neal@ed.gov
Web Site: www2.ed.gov/programs/iegpsgpa/index.html

TYPE:
Exchange programs; Project/program grants; Seed money grants; Training grants; Travel grants. Also, study grants and grants for foreign language and area study programs of educational development for projects to be undertaken abroad. Grants are awarded to higher education institutions, nonprofit educational organizations, state department of education and consortium of such institutions, departments, organizations and institutions which, in turn, enable professors, college and elementary and secondary school teachers and advanced students to attend seminars abroad and to travel and study in foreign countries in order to strengthen the institution's programs in foreign languages, area studies and world affairs.

See entry 865 for full listing.

U.S. DEPARTMENT OF EDUCATION
International and Foreign Language Education
400 Maryland Avenue, S.W.
Washington, DC 20202
(202) 453-6391
E-mail: tanyelle.richardson@ed.gov
Web Site: www.ed.gov/ope/iegps

TYPE:
Project/program grants; Seed money grants. Grants to plan, develop, and carry out a program to strengthen and improve undergraduate instruction in international studies and foreign languages. Projects primarily focus on curriculum and faculty development. Institutions of higher education and public and private nonprofit agencies and organizations may apply for funds to develop projects which have the potential for making an especially significant contribution to the improvement of undergraduate instruction in international and foreign language studies in the U.S.

See entry 1487 for full listing.

YIVO INSTITUTE FOR JEWISH RESEARCH
15 West 16th Street, 3rd Floor
New York, NY 10011-6301
(917) 606-8290
Fax: (212) 292-1892
E-mail: bkaplan@yivo.cjh.org
Web Site: www.yivo.org

TYPE:
Fellowships. Fellowship in East European Arts, Music, and Theater is designed to assist an undergraduate, graduate or postgraduate researcher in the fields of Eastern European Jewish arts, music and theater.

Fellowship in East European Jewish Literature is designed to assist an undergraduate, graduate or postgraduate researcher in Eastern European Jewish literature.

The stipend is intended to defray expenses connected with research in YIVO's music, art and theater collections and library.

See entry 600 for full listing.

Literature

THE AMERICAN-SCANDINAVIAN FOUNDATION   [616]
58 Park Avenue
New York, NY 10016
(212) 847-9724
Fax: (212) 686-1157
E-mail: grants@amscan.org
Web Site: www.amscan.org/fellowships-grants/translation-competition

FOUNDED: 1910

AREAS OF INTEREST:
Translations of poetry, fiction, drama or literary prose by a Scandinavian author born after 1900.

NAME(S) OF PROGRAMS:
● **American-Scandinavian Foundation Translation Competition**

TYPE:
Awards/prizes. Prize for translation of fiction (50 double-spaced manuscript pages) or poetry (25 double-spaced manuscript pages).

YEAR PROGRAM STARTED: 1980

PURPOSE:
To encourage English translation of contemporary Scandinavian literature.

LEGAL BASIS:
Nonprofit educational institution qualifying under statutes 501(c)(3), 509(a)(1) and 170(c)(2) of the IRS code.

ELIGIBILITY:
Entry must be work by one author, though not necessarily from a single work. It should be conceived as part of a book manuscript. A table of contents for the proposed book should also be included.

FINANCIAL DATA:
Amount of support per award: First prize: $2,500; Second and Third Prize: $2,000 each.
Total amount of support: $6,500.

NO. MOST RECENT APPLICANTS: 15.

NO. AWARDS: 3.

APPLICATION INFO:
Request rules for Translation Prize Competition. Applicants should submit one copy of work in original language and one copy of translation, including title page and table of contents. Name, address and phone number of translator and title and author of the manuscript with the original language specified should be on a separate page. Translator must include written permission from author or author's agent for translation to be entered in competition and published in *Scandinavian Review.* Manuscripts accompanied by self-addressed, stamped envelope will be returned.
Duration: One-time award.
Deadline: June 15. Awards announced by November 1.

PUBLICATIONS:
Competition rules.

OFFICER:
Edward P. Gallagher, President

ADDRESS INQUIRIES TO:
Translation Prize Committee
(See e-mail address above.)

THE ASCAP FOUNDATION   [617]
250 West 57th Street
New York, NY 10107
(212) 621-6588
E-mail: jlapore@ascap.com
Web Site: www.ascap.com

FOUNDED: 1914

AREAS OF INTEREST:
Writing on the subject of music.

NAME(S) OF PROGRAMS:
● **The ASCAP Foundation Deems Taylor/Virgil Thomson Awards**

TYPE:
Awards/prizes. The ASCAP Foundation Deems Taylor/Virgil Thomson Awards program recognizes books and articles on the subject of music selected for their excellence.

YEAR PROGRAM STARTED: 1967

PURPOSE:
To encourage, recognize and reward excellence in a field that is vital to the health and growth of America's musical heritage.

LEGAL BASIS:
Membership association.

ELIGIBILITY:
Any books or articles published anywhere in the U.S. (the 50 states and Puerto Rico) in English during the calendar year preceding the award will be eligible. The subject matter may be biographical or critical, reportorial or historical - almost any form of nonfiction

prose about music and/or its creators - not an instructional textbook, how-to guide, or a work of fiction.

Paperbacks that were originally published in hardcover are not eligible.

GEOG. RESTRICTIONS: United States.

FINANCIAL DATA:
Amount of support per award: Several categories of cash prizes, from $200 to $500.
Total amount of support: Varies.

NO. MOST RECENT APPLICANTS: 150.

NO. AWARDS: 11 for the year 2019.

APPLICATION INFO:
Application may be made online. The following information is required:
(1) title of the book or article;
(2) copyright date of book or date of publication for the article;
(3) name, street address, e-mail address and daytime phone number of all authors of the book or article and;
(4) contact name, address and daytime phone number of the publisher or publication in which the article appeared.

Four copies of each entry are required. Submissions will not be returned. For articles and books, submissions are limited to one entry per author. When submitting one or more articles, be sure that a copy of every article is put into each of four letter-sized file folders. Label each folder with one's full name only. (This is for the competition judges who will review the entries.)

Submissions should be addressed to ASCAP Deems Taylor/Virgil Thomson Awards; American Society of Composers, Authors and Publishers at the address listed above.
Duration: Annual award.
Deadline: May 31.

ADDRESS INQUIRIES TO:
Julie Lapore
The ASCAP Foundation Deems Taylor/Virgil Thomson Awards
(See address above.)

ASIAN AMERICAN WRITERS' WORKSHOP   [618]
112 West 27th Street
Suite 600
New York, NY 10001
E-mail: desk@aaww.org
Web Site: aaww.org

FOUNDED: 1991

AREAS OF INTEREST:
Creative writing.

NAME(S) OF PROGRAMS:
● **The Margins Fellowship**
● **Open City Fellowship**

TYPE:
Fellowships; Grants-in-aid. The Margins Fellowship supports writers of fiction, creative nonfiction, and poetry through a year-long program that includes a grant, mentorship with an established writer, residency time at the Millay Colony for the Arts, publication opportunities, and career guidance.

The Open City Fellowship is awarded to journalists and nonfiction writers who write from and about New York City's Asian and Muslim immigrant neighborhoods, including

Sunset Park, Bay Ridge, Richmond Hill, and Jackson Heights. Fellows receive a grant and publication on *Open City*.

PURPOSE:
To nurture a new generation of Asian diasporic writers.

ELIGIBILITY:
Fellowships are offered to emerging writers of color based in New York City.

The Margins Fellowship: Applicants must be aged 30 or under.

GEOG. RESTRICTIONS: New York, New York.

FINANCIAL DATA:
Amount of support per award: The Margins Fellowship: $5,000; Open City Fellowship: $2,500.

NO. AWARDS: The Margins Fellowship: 4; Open City Fellowship: 2.

APPLICATION INFO:
Details are available online.
Duration: The Margins Fellowship: One year. Open City Fellowship: Six months.

STAFF:
Jafreen Uddin, Executive Director
Jyothi Natarajan, Editorial Director
Yasmin Adele Majeed, Assistant Editor
Kelly Kuwabara, Grantwriting Consultant

BOARD OF DIRECTORS:
Manan Ahmed
Jin Auh
Mariko Gordon
Jennifer Hayashida
Hua Hsu
Anne Ishii
Kirby Kim
Jennifer 8. Lee
Tan Lin
Monica Youn

ADDRESS INQUIRIES TO:
Jafreen Uddin, Executive Director
(See address above.)

THE ASSOCIATION OF WRITERS & WRITING PROGRAMS   [619]
5700 Rivertech Court, Suite 225
Riverdale Park, MD 20737-1250
(240) 696-7700
(240) 696-7683
E-mail: supriya@awpwriter.org
Web Site: www.awpwriter.org

FOUNDED: 1967

AREAS OF INTEREST:
Creative writing; four genres: short fiction, poetry, creative nonfiction and the novel.

CONSULTING OR VOLUNTEER SERVICES:
The office provides information on curricula for courses or programs in creative writing and members of the Board of Directors occasionally visit campuses in order to consult with departments wishing to establish or improve creative writing programs. The office also sponsors the INTRO Journals Project, an annual competition of fiction, nonfiction and poetry by students of creative writing; runs job placement service for members interested in obtaining teaching and writing-oriented positions.

NAME(S) OF PROGRAMS:
● **AWP Award Series in Creative Nonfiction**
● **AWP Award Series in the Novel**

● **Donald Hall Prize in Poetry**
● **Grace Paley Prize in Short Fiction**

TYPE:
Awards/prizes. Annual open competitions for book-length manuscripts: a collection of short stories, a collection of poems, or a work of creative nonfiction of more than 60,000 words. The award in each case is the publication of the winning manuscript by a university press and a cash honorarium from AWP in addition to royalties from the publisher.

YEAR PROGRAM STARTED: 1974

PURPOSE:
To support American writers and creative writing programs in U.S. colleges and universities; to encourage the publication and distribution of good fiction, poetry and other creative writing; to improve the quality of literary education primarily at the college level, as well as at the public school level; to disseminate information useful to writers and students of writing.

LEGAL BASIS:
Nonprofit, tax-exempt corporation.

ELIGIBILITY:
Original works written in English are eligible.

Only book-length manuscripts are eligible (poetry: 48 pages minimum; short story collection and creative nonfiction: 150 to 300 manuscript pages; novel: at least 60,000 words).

The AWP Award Series is open to all authors writing original works in English. No mixed-genre manuscripts can be accepted. Criticism and scholarly monographs are not acceptable for creative nonfiction, which the Award Series defines as factual and literary writing that has the narrative, dramatic, meditative and lyrical elements of novels, plays, poetry, and memoirs.

To avoid conflict of interest and to avoid the appearance of a conflict of interest, former students of a judge (former students who studied with a judge in an academic degree-conferring program or its equivalent) are ineligible to enter the competition in the genre for which their former teacher is serving as judge.

FINANCIAL DATA:
Negotiations regarding book royalties are left to the author and publisher, but AWP has established minimum standards.

Amount of support per award: AWP Prize for Creative Nonfiction and AWP Prize for the Novel: $2,500 each; Donald Hall Prize in Poetry and Grace Paley Prize in Short Fiction: $5,500 each.

NO. MOST RECENT APPLICANTS: Nonfiction: 168; Novel: 283; Poetry: 785; Short Fiction: 276.

NO. AWARDS: 1 winner per genre; 2 finalists per genre.

APPLICATION INFO:
For the Award Series, submissions are only accepted via Submittable (online submissions manager).

Manuscripts must be uploaded between January 1 and February 28. If the author's name appears anywhere except the cover page, the manuscript will be disqualified. Do not attach acknowledgement of previous publications or a biographical note. No manuscripts will be returned. There is a $30 entry/reading fee for nonmembers, $20 for AWP members. Please read guidelines on Association's web site before uploading one's manuscript through Submittable.

Deadline: Manuscripts are accepted only with postmark between January 1 and February 28.

PUBLICATIONS:
Guidelines; *The Writer's Chronicle*, six times per year.

IRS I.D.: 05-0314999

EXECUTIVE DIRECTOR:
Cynthia Sherman

ADDRESS INQUIRIES TO:
Supriya Bhatnagar
Director of Publications
(See address above.)

*PLEASE NOTE:
Reading period from February 1 to September 30 each year.

BREAD LOAF WRITERS' CONFERENCE   [620]
Middlebury College
204 College Street
Middlebury, VT 05753
(802) 443-5286
Fax: (802) 443-2087
E-mail: blwc@middlebury.edu
Web Site: www.middlebury.edu/bread-loaf-conferences/bl_writers

FOUNDED: 1926

AREAS OF INTEREST:
Poetry, fiction and nonfiction.

NAME(S) OF PROGRAMS:
● **Fellowship and Scholarship Program for Writers**

TYPE:
Fellowships; Scholarships. Fellowships and scholarships pay all or part of conference fees.

YEAR PROGRAM STARTED: 1926

PURPOSE:
To encourage writers at the beginning of their careers.

LEGAL BASIS:
Nonprofit.

ELIGIBILITY:
Fellowship candidates must have had one or two original books published. Privately printed books are not considered.

Candidates for tuition scholarships must have had their work published in recognized literary periodicals, but will not have published in book form.

People under 18 are not eligible.

FINANCIAL DATA:
Fellowships pay all conference fees, tuition, room and board. Tuition scholarships pay all conference fees, tuition but not room and board. Working scholarships pay part of tuition and room and board; recipients earn the remainder.

Amount of support per award: Varies.
Total amount of support: Varies.

NO. MOST RECENT APPLICANTS: 2,000.

NO. AWARDS: 60.

APPLICATION INFO:
Information is available online.
Duration: Usually one-time award.

Deadline: February 15. Announcement in May.

DIRECTORS:
Jennifer Grotz, Director
Lauren Francis-Sharma, Assistant Director

ADDRESS INQUIRIES TO:
Jason Lamb, Coordinator
(See address above.)

THE WITTER BYNNER FOUNDATION FOR POETRY, INC.   [621]
P.O. Box 10169
Santa Fe, NM 87504-0169
(505) 699-5178
E-mail: witterb123@gmail.com
Web Site: bynnerfoundation.org

FOUNDED: 1972

AREAS OF INTEREST:
Poetry, with special interest in developing the poetry audience, the process of poetry translation, uses of poetry (including but not limited to dramatic, educational, therapeutic, etc.) and the support of individual poets through existing institutional programs.

TYPE:
Project/program grants.

YEAR PROGRAM STARTED: 1972

PURPOSE:
To develop the poetic art through grant support to nonprofit organizations and individuals represented by such organizations.

LEGAL BASIS:
Exempt, private foundation.

ELIGIBILITY:
Only applications from nonprofit tax-exempt organizations will be accepted. No grants to individuals. Publication projects, endowment funds, capital improvements, continued support and operating expenses are not generally funded.

GEOG. RESTRICTIONS: United States.

FINANCIAL DATA:
Amount of support per award: $1,000 to $10,000.
Total amount of support: $70,000 for the year 2017-18.

NO. MOST RECENT APPLICANTS: 115 letters of intent for the year 2017-18.

NO. AWARDS: 15 grant programs for the year 2017-18.

REPRESENTATIVE AWARDS:
$5,000 to New Mexico School for the Arts; $3,000 to Partners in Education; $5,000 to Reel Fathers; $6,000 to White Pine Press.

APPLICATION INFO:
Upon request, the Foundation's guidelines, an annual report, and a list of the most recent grants will be provided. Applicants must submit a letter of intent prior to application.
Duration: One-year grants only. May be renewed at the discretion of the Board of Directors.
Deadline: February 15 annually. Announcement in May. Letters of intent accepted from August 1 to December 31 annually.

PUBLICATIONS:
Annual report; application guidelines.

IRS I.D.: 23-7169999

BOARD OF DIRECTORS:
Dr. Mark McDaniel, President
Fletcher Catron, Secretary/Treasurer
Kelsey Brown

ADDRESS INQUIRIES TO:
See e-mail address above.

*SPECIAL STIPULATIONS:
The Foundation is interested particularly in using its limited funds as a means to help attract additional monies from other sources to advance the art of poetry. Applications to support the development of seed-money proposals in each of the above areas, therefore, are especially encouraged. While the Foundation has traditionally been supportive of the four areas listed above, it may consider the support of other creative and innovative projects in poetry.

CARNEGIE FUND FOR AUTHORS   [622]
P.O. Box 409
Lenox Hill Station
New York, NY 10021
E-mail: carnegiefundforauthors@gmail.com
Web Site: www.carnegiefundforauthors.org

FOUNDED: 1942

AREAS OF INTEREST:
Literary interests.

TYPE:
Grants-in-aid.

YEAR PROGRAM STARTED: 1942

PURPOSE:
To award grants to authors whose need has come about because of illness or other emergency.

ELIGIBILITY:
Applicants must be authors who have had at least one book of reasonable length published by a mainstream publisher. Applicants cannot use any publication they paid to have published.

Grants are made to individuals who must be U.S. citizens or residents. Applicants must live in the U.S.

Grants are for authors in acute pressing need, not for those with chronic problems.

FINANCIAL DATA:
Amount of support per award: No fixed sum; based on need.

NO. AWARDS: 20 for the year 2018.

APPLICATION INFO:
Applicants must request an application form and submit to the address above with all supporting documentation.
Duration: Lump-sum grant.
Deadline: Grants are voted on and distributed year-round.

IRS I.D.: 13-6084244

*PLEASE NOTE:
Grants are not given for travel, study or to complete projects.

CHILDREN'S LITERATURE ASSOCIATION   [623]
3525 Piedmont Road
Building 5, Suite 300
Atlanta, GA 30305
(630) 571-4520
Fax: (708) 876-5598
E-mail: info@childlitassn.org
Web Site: www.childlitassn.org

FOUNDED: 1973

AREAS OF INTEREST:
All aspects of children's literature scholarship, research and criticism.

NAME(S) OF PROGRAMS:
● **ChLA Diversity Research Grant**

TYPE:
Project/program grants; Research grants. ChLA Diversity Research Grant is a grant to support research related to children's and young adult cultural artifacts (including media, culture and texts) about populations that have been traditionally underrepresented or marginalized culturally and/or historically. Applications for this grant are to be considered annually and will be awarded as warranted.

YEAR PROGRAM STARTED: 2013

PURPOSE:
To promote scholarship and criticism in children's literature.

LEGAL BASIS:
International; tax-exempt 501(c)(3), nonprofit scholarly organization.

ELIGIBILITY:
Applications will be evaluated based upon the quality of the proposal and the potential of the project to enhance or advance Children's Literature studies. Funds may be used for - but are not restricted to - research-related expenses such as travel to special collections, subvention funds, or purchasing materials and supplies. The awards may not be used for obtaining advanced degrees, for researching or writing a thesis or dissertation, for textbook writing or for pedagogical projects. Winners must be members of the Children's Literature Association before they receive any funds. Winners must acknowledge ChLA in any publication or other presentation resulting from the grant.

Members of the ChLA Diversity Committee are not eligible to apply. Recipients of a Diversity Research Grant are not eligible to reapply until the third year from the date of the first award. (In the event the ChLA Board institutes another time interval - whether longer or shorter - the vote of the Board shall supersede the three-year interval rule.)

In a given year, if there are no proposals for the Diversity Research Grant that the Diversity and/or Grants Committee deems of sufficient quality to support ChLA's aims, no grants will be given; conversely, if there are multiple Diversity Research Grant proposals of high quality, it is possible that multiple grants will be made, in which case the award may be less than the proposed budget.

FINANCIAL DATA:
Amount of support per award: $500 to $1,500, depending upon the winning proposal's projected budgetary considerations.

APPLICATION INFO:
Forms and instructions are available on the Association's web site.
Deadline: Only applications that are complete and received as of midnight on February 1 will be considered. Winners will be notified in April, and the awards will be announced at the ChLA annual conference.

IRS I.D.: 38-2005828

ADDRESS INQUIRIES TO:
ChLA Grants Committee
(See address above.)

*SPECIAL STIPULATIONS:
Grant recipients are required to submit a progress report of the project to the chair of the Diversity Committee by April/May of the year following the award and a summary report of the completed project to the chair of the Diversity Committee by April/May of the second year, prior to the presentation of the ideas at the conference.

Each grant will be awarded with the expectation that the undertaking will lead to publication and make a significant contribution to the field of children's literature scholarship or criticism. Within two years of receiving the grant, the recipient will be asked to submit a paper proposal based upon the project for presentation at a ChLA annual conference.

CHILDREN'S LITERATURE ASSOCIATION   [624]
3525 Piedmont Road
Building 5, Suite 300
Atlanta, GA 30305
(630) 571-4520
Fax: (708) 876-5598
E-mail: info@childlitassn.org
Web Site: www.childlitassn.org

FOUNDED: 1973

AREAS OF INTEREST:
All aspects of children's literature scholarship, research and criticism.

NAME(S) OF PROGRAMS:
● **ChLA Beiter Graduate Student Research Grants**
● **ChLA Faculty Research Grants**

TYPE:
Conferences/seminars; Grants-in-aid; Project/program grants; Research grants. ChLA Beiter Graduate Student Research Grants are awarded for proposals of original scholarship with the expectation that the undertaking will lead to publication or a conference presentation and contribute to the field of children's literature criticism.

ChLA Faculty Research Grants are awarded for proposals dealing with criticism or original scholarship with the expectation that the undertaking will lead to publication and make a significant contribution to the field of children's literature in the area of scholarship or criticism. Proposals that deal with critical or original work in the areas of fantasy or science fiction for children or adolescents will be awarded the Margaret P. Esmonde Memorial Scholarship.

YEAR PROGRAM STARTED: 1978

PURPOSE:
To promote scholarship and criticism in children's literature.

LEGAL BASIS:
International; tax-exempt 501(c)(3), nonprofit scholarly organization.

ELIGIBILITY:
ChLA Beiter Research Grants for Graduate Students: Grant funds are not intended as income to assist in the completion of a graduate degree, but as support for research that may be related to the dissertation or Master's thesis. The grant may be used to purchase supplies and materials (e.g., books, videos, equipment), as research support (photocopying, etc.), or to underwrite travel to special collections or libraries. Winners must either be members of the Children's

Literature Association or join the Association before they receive any funds. Students of ChLA Executive Board members or Scholarship Committee members are not eligible to apply.

ChLA Faculty Research Grants: Applications will be evaluated based upon the quality of the proposal and the potential of the project to enhance or advance children's literature studies. Funds may be used for (but are not restricted to) research-related expenses such as travel to special collections or purchasing materials and supplies. The awards may not be used for obtaining advanced degrees, for researching or writing a thesis or dissertation, for textbook writing, or for pedagogical projects. Winners must either be members of the Children's Literature Association or join the Association before they receive any funds. Members of the Executive Board of ChLA and of the Scholarship Committee are not eligible to apply.

FINANCIAL DATA:
ChLA Faculty Research Grants may be used for such expenses as transportation, living expenses or materials and supplies, but not for obtaining advanced degrees.
Amount of support per award: $500 to $1,500.
Total amount of support: Up to $10,000 annually for both grants.

NO. AWARDS: Varies.

APPLICATION INFO:
Forms and instructions are available on the Association's web site.
Duration: Varies. Usually a one-time award to run the length of the project or course of study.
Deadline: February 1. Announcement at the annual conference.

PUBLICATIONS:
Application guidelines.

IRS I.D.: 38-2005828

ADDRESS INQUIRIES TO:
ChLA Grants Committee
(See address above.)

*SPECIAL STIPULATIONS:
Winners should acknowledge ChLA in any publication resulting from the award.

GREAT LAKES COLLEGES ASSOCIATION NEW WRITERS AWARDS   [625]
535 West William Street
Suite 301
Ann Arbor, MI 48103
(734) 661-2350
Fax: (734) 661-2349
E-mail: wegner@glca.org
Web Site: www.glca.org

FOUNDED: 1962

AREAS OF INTEREST:
Education.

NAME(S) OF PROGRAMS:
● **New Writers Awards**

TYPE:
Awards/prizes. Winners invited to tour up to 13 Great Lakes Colleges. Honorarium and expenses included. Awards are made for yearly, first published best book of fiction, best book of poetry and best book of creative

nonfiction. Judges of the awards are faculty members of literature and creative writing at member colleges.

YEAR PROGRAM STARTED: 1970

PURPOSE:
To promote new writers, literature and colleges.

LEGAL BASIS:
Association of independent, liberal arts colleges in Michigan, Indiana, Ohio and Pennsylvania.

ELIGIBILITY:
The book must be the first published volume in fiction, poetry, or creative nonfiction by the author. Only publishers may submit, on behalf of the author, one book in each category, four copies.

Entries submitted must be written in English and published in the U.S. or Canada.

GEOG. RESTRICTIONS: United States and Canada.

FINANCIAL DATA:
The award also covers the costs of a writer's travel when visiting GLCA member colleges.
Amount of support per award: At least $500 per college visited.

NO. MOST RECENT APPLICANTS: 150.

NO. AWARDS: 1 each for creative nonfiction, fiction and poetry.

APPLICATION INFO:
Visit the GLCA web site to download submission packet.
Deadline: June 25.

ADDRESS INQUIRIES TO:
New Writers Awards
(See address above.)

ITALIAN AMERICAN STUDIES ASSOCIATION
P.O. Box 487
Millbrae, CA 94030
(408) 738-4564
Fax: (408) 864-5629
E-mail: quinnroseanne@deanza.edu
Web Site: www.italianamericanstudies.net

TYPE:
Fellowships.

See entry 557 for full listing.

JEWISH BOOK COUNCIL [626]
520 Eighth Avenue, 4th Floor
New York, NY 10018-4393
(212) 201-2920
Fax: (212) 532-4952
E-mail: jbc@jewishbooks.org
Web Site: www.jewishbookcouncil.org

FOUNDED: 1943

AREAS OF INTEREST:
Jewish literature.

NAME(S) OF PROGRAMS:
- **National Jewish Book Award-American Jewish Studies**
- **National Jewish Book Award-Anthologies and Collections**
- **National Jewish Book Award-Autobiography and Memoir**
- **National Jewish Book Award-Biography**
- **National Jewish Book Award-Book Club**
- **National Jewish Book Award-Children's Literature**
- **National Jewish Book Award-Contemporary Jewish Life and Practice**
- **National Jewish Book Award-Debut Fiction**
- **National Jewish Book Award-Education and Jewish Identity**
- **National Jewish Book Award-Fiction**
- **National Jewish Book Award-Food Writing and Cookbooks**
- **National Jewish Book Award-History**
- **National Jewish Book Award-Holocaust**
- **National Jewish Book Award-Modern Jewish Thought and Experience**
- **National Jewish Book Award-Poetry**
- **National Jewish Book Award-Scholarship**
- **National Jewish Book Award-Sephardic Culture**
- **National Jewish Book Award-Visual Arts**
- **National Jewish Book Award-Women's Studies**
- **National Jewish Book Award-Writing Based on Archival Material**
- **National Jewish Book Award-Young Adult Literature**

TYPE:
Awards/prizes. National Jewish Book Awards:
(1) Award to the author of a nonfiction book about the Jewish experience in North America;
(2) Award to the author of a book of essays, biographies, short stories, or other collected works by more than one author;
(3) Award to the author of an autobiography or personal memoir. The subject need not be a Jewish person or family, but must have significant relevance to the Jewish experience.
(4) Award to the author of a biography or family history. The subject need not be a Jewish person or family, but must have significant relevance to the Jewish experience;
(5) Award recognizing the power of books to inspire Jewish community and thought-provoking discussions.
(6) Award to the author of a book on a Jewish theme that is intended for children;
(7) Award to the author of a nonfiction book about current tools and resources of Jewish living within the greater Ashkenazic and Sephardic communities. These include, but are not limited to, cookbooks, holiday how-to books and life-cycle books;
(8) Award to the author of a debut novel or short-story collection with Jewish content;
(9) Award to the author of a nonfiction work that focuses on theory, history and/or practice of Jewish education. Textbooks are not eligible;
(10) Award to the author of a novel or short-story collection with Jewish content;
(11) Award to honor books that illuminate Jewish life, identity, and culture through a culinary lens.
(12) Award to the author of a nonfiction work about the Jewish historical experience. Books focusing primarily on the Holocaust do not belong in this category;
(13) Award to the author of a nonfiction book concerning the Holocaust including autobiographies, memoirs and academic studies;
(14) Award to the author of a nonfiction work addressing Sephardic and/or Ashkenazic Jewish thought and experience;
(15) Award to the author of a book of verse consisting primarily of poems of Jewish concern;
(16) Award to the author of a nonfiction selection that makes an original contribution to Jewish learning. This includes, but is not limited to, works on Bible, Rabbinics and Jewish Law;
(17) Award to the author of a book that explores the traditions and practices unique to Sephardic Jews;
(18) Award to the author of a work of one or more visual artists (painters, weavers, sculptors, photographers, etc.) which includes illustrations and images of Jewish content as a dominant component;
(19) Award to the author of a nonfiction book about women's role in the Jewish experience;
(20) Award to the author of a book of modern historical writing published in English based on archival material including footnotes and bibliography and;
(21) Award to the author of a book on a Jewish theme that is intended for young adults.

YEAR PROGRAM STARTED: 1949

PURPOSE:
To promote greater awareness of works of Jewish literature and scholarship.

LEGAL BASIS:
Not-for-profit organization.

ELIGIBILITY:
Books published during the current calendar year will be eligible, except anthologies of previously published material or collections of writings by various authors or reprints and revised editions, unless otherwise specified. No manuscripts are accepted.

Books must be published in the English language unless otherwise specified. This includes books translated into English from any other language.

FINANCIAL DATA:
Amount of support per award: Varies.
Total amount of support: Varies.

NO. MOST RECENT APPLICANTS: 400.

NO. AWARDS: 18 to 20 each year. Some awards are biennial.

APPLICATION INFO:
Guidelines and submission forms are available online in June.
Duration: One year.
Deadline: Submissions accepted early summer to late September.

PUBLICATIONS:
Application guidelines.

EXECUTIVE DIRECTOR:
Naomi Firestone-Teeter

ADDRESS INQUIRIES TO:
Naomi Firestone-Teeter, Executive Director
or
Evie Saphire-Bernstein, Program Director
(See address above.)

ROBERT F. KENNEDY HUMAN RIGHTS [627]
1300 19th Street, N.W.
Suite 750
Washington, DC 20036
(202) 463-7575
Fax: (202) 463-6606
E-mail: info@rfkhumanrights.org
Web Site: rfkhumanrights.org

FOUNDED: 1968

NAME(S) OF PROGRAMS:
- **RFK Book Award**
- **RFK Journalism Awards**

TYPE:
Awards/prizes. The RFK Book Award recognizes authors whose works of moral insight and imagination uphold a vision of political inclusion, compassion and justice.

The RFK Journalism Awards celebrate excellence in journalism in 13 categories, from investigative journalism to satirical cartoons and documentary film.

YEAR PROGRAM STARTED: 1980

PURPOSE:
To carry forward the mission of Robert F. Kennedy.

LEGAL BASIS:
Tax-exempt public charity.

ELIGIBILITY:
Fiction and nonfiction books published in the U.S. in the previous calendar year are eligible.

FINANCIAL DATA:
Amount of support per award: Book Award: $2,500 Grand Prize; Journalism Awards: $1,000 to individual or news organization and $500 to college and high school winners.
Total amount of support: Varies.

NO. MOST RECENT APPLICANTS: 75.

NO. AWARDS: Varies.

APPLICATION INFO:
Entries may be made by either individual authors or publishers. There is a handling fee of $75 per entry. Books must be submitted in quadruplicate with an entry form clipped inside the front cover of each book.
Duration: One-time award.
Deadline: Varies.

PUBLICATIONS:
Rules for entry.

ADDRESS INQUIRIES TO:
Monica Duran, Development Associate
(See address above.)

KNIGHTS OF COLUMBUS VATICAN FILM LIBRARY AT ST. LOUIS UNIVERSITY [628]
Pius XII Memorial Library
St. Louis University
3650 Lindell Boulevard
St. Louis, MO 63108-3302
(314) 977-3090
Fax: (314) 977-3108
E-mail: vfl@slu.edu
Web Site: lib.slu.edu/special-collections/research/fellowship

AREAS OF INTEREST:
History, philosophy, theology, literature, art, science, paleogeography, codicology, illumination, text editing, and library history.

NAME(S) OF PROGRAMS:
- **Vatican Film Library Mellon Fellowship**

TYPE:
Fellowships; Travel grants. Stipendiary fellowship which includes cost of air travel within the continental U.S.

YEAR PROGRAM STARTED: 1976

PURPOSE:
To conduct research into Medieval and Renaissance manuscripts containing microfilm in the Vatican Film Library.

ELIGIBILITY:
Applicants must be at the postdoctoral level or be a graduate student formally admitted to Ph.D. candidacy and working on their dissertation. U.S. citizens and foreign nationals are eligible.

FINANCIAL DATA:
Fellowship provides the cost of air travel within the continental U.S.
Amount of support per award: $2,250 per month living allowance.
Total amount of support: Varies. Maximum allowance of $4,500 plus air travel.

NO. AWARDS: Varies.

APPLICATION INFO:
Applicants must write a brief project description and notify of the manuscripts to be consulted (for availability), including dates of proposed study, a curriculum vitae, as well as a select bibliography on titles related to project. Proposals should not exceed more than two to three pages. Doctoral applicants must include a letter of recommendation from their advisor.
Duration: Two to eight weeks. Fellows can reapply the following year.
Deadline: March 1 for June to August. June 1 for September to December. October 1 for January to May.

STAFF:
Gregory A. Pass, Ph.D., Assistant Dean for Special Collections and Director, Vatican Film Library

ADDRESS INQUIRIES TO:
See e-mail address above.

STEPHEN LEACOCK ASSOCIATES [629]
P.O. Box 854
Orillia ON L3V 6K8 Canada
E-mail: bettewalkerca@gmail.com
info@leacock.ca
Web Site: www.leacock.ca

FOUNDED: 1946

AREAS OF INTEREST:
Writing of humour by Canadians.

NAME(S) OF PROGRAMS:
- **Stephen Leacock Memorial Medal for Humour**

TYPE:
Awards/prizes. Stephen Leacock Memorial Medal for Humour is presented for a book of humour published in the current calendar year and written by a Canadian. A cash prize accompanies this award.

YEAR PROGRAM STARTED: 1947

PURPOSE:
To promote the writing of Canadian humour.

LEGAL BASIS:
Nonprofit charitable organization.

ELIGIBILITY:
The major emphasis of each entry must be on humor, but literary merit and insightful comment are also important. Books of cartoons and graphic novels are eligible only if they contain a substantial amount of textual material. All entries must carry an ISBN, and have been published in the current year. The language of the entry must be English. In the case of a translation from another language, the translation must have been published in the current year.

The author or authors must be Canadian citizens or landed immigrants and living at the time of publication.

FINANCIAL DATA:
Amount of support per award: Awardee receives a sterling silver medal plus a $15,000 (CAN) cash prize; two runners-up receive $3,000 (CAN) each.
Total amount of support: $21,000 (CAN).

NO. MOST RECENT APPLICANTS: 68.

NO. AWARDS: 1.

APPLICATION INFO:
There is an entry fee of $200 per entry to be sent by check in Canadian funds. Send eight copies of each title plus author biography to Stephen Leacock Associates. Work must be published in previous calendar year. Books are nonreturnable. Entries should be sent to: Mrs. Bette Walker, 149 Peter Street North, Orillia, ON L3V 4Z4 Canada.
Deadline: December 31.

PUBLICATIONS:
Newspacket.

BOARD OF DIRECTORS:
Michael Hill, President
Bette Walker, Vice President and Chairman, Award Committee
John Hughes, Treasurer
Anne Kallin, Secretary

ADDRESS INQUIRIES TO:
Bette Walker, Vice President and Chairman, Award Committee
E-mail: awardschair@leacock.ca
(See address above.)

*SPECIAL STIPULATIONS:
Authors must agree to be present for the Gala dinner.

WILLIAM MORRIS SOCIETY IN THE U.S.
P.O. Box 53263
Washington, DC 20009
E-mail: wmsusmembership@gmail.com
Web Site: www.morrissociety.org

TYPE:
Fellowships; Research grants; Scholarships; Travel grants; Visiting scholars; Research contracts. Supports scholarly, creative, and translation projects about William Morris and his designs, writings and other work.

See entry 439 for full listing.

NATIONAL FEDERATION OF STATE POETRY SOCIETIES, INC. [630]
49 Kitchen Avenue
Harveys Lake, PA 18618
E-mail: paperlesspoets@gmail.com
Web Site: www.nfsps.com

FOUNDED: 1989

AREAS OF INTEREST:
Poetry.

NAME(S) OF PROGRAMS:
- **NFSPS College Undergraduate Poetry (CUP) Competition**

TYPE:
Awards/prizes; Travel grants. The College Undergraduate Poetry Competition consists of two awards: The Edna Meudt Memorial Award and the Florence Kahn Memorial Award.

YEAR PROGRAM STARTED: 1989

PURPOSE:
To encourage the study and writing of poetry.

ELIGIBILITY:
All undergraduate levels of study at an accredited U.S. university or college are eligible (freshman through senior).

GEOG. RESTRICTIONS: United States.

FINANCIAL DATA:
Amount of support per award: Each awardee receives $500 plus 75 copies of published manuscript and an additional $300 stipend for travel to the NFSPS Convention to give a reading.

NO. MOST RECENT APPLICANTS: Up to 25.

NO. AWARDS: 2.

APPLICATION INFO:
Applicant must submit a manuscript of 10 original poems. Consult web site for complete application information. Submissions may be made online via submittable.com.

Deadline: Applications are accepted December 1 to January 31. One anonymous, highly qualified judge will evaluate, judge and select scholarship winners on or before March 12.

ADDRESS INQUIRIES TO:
Steven Concert, Chairperson
College Undergraduate Poetry Competition
(See address above.)

THE NATIONAL POETRY SERIES [631]

57 Mountain Avenue
Princeton, NJ 08540
(609) 430-0999
Fax: (609) 430-9933
E-mail: npspoetry@gmail.com
Web Site: nationalpoetryseries.org

FOUNDED: 1978

AREAS OF INTEREST:
Poetry.

NAME(S) OF PROGRAMS:
● **National Poetry Series Open Competition**

TYPE:
Awards/prizes.

YEAR PROGRAM STARTED: 1978

PURPOSE:
To recognize and promote excellence in contemporary poetry.

LEGAL BASIS:
Nonprofit, private.

ELIGIBILITY:
The National Poetry Series seeks book-length manuscripts of poetry written by American residents or American citizens living abroad. All manuscripts must be previously unpublished, although some or all of the individual poems may have appeared in periodicals. Translations, chapbooks, small groups of poems and books previously self-published are not eligible. Manuscript length is not limited; however, a length of 48 to 64 pages is suggested.

GEOG. RESTRICTIONS: United States.

FINANCIAL DATA:
Arrangements are between author and publisher.

Amount of support per award: $10,000 and book publication.

Total amount of support: $50,000.

NO. MOST RECENT APPLICANTS: 1,850.

NO. AWARDS: 5.

APPLICATION INFO:
Manuscripts are submitted online via the web site. Each manuscript must be accompanied by an entrance fee of $35.

Manuscripts must include two cover pages:
(1) title of manuscript, author's name, address and telephone number (this should be the only page with author's identification) and;
(2) title of manuscript only.

Manuscripts must be paginated and contain a Table of Contents. Do not include acknowledgments, explanatory statements, resumes, autobiographical statements, photographs, illustrations or artwork. These will not be considered.

A list of previous publications or appearances in periodicals should not be included.

Duration: One-time award.

Deadline: February 28 (postmark).

PUBLICATIONS:
Guidelines.

STAFF:
Daniel Halpern, Director
Beth Dial, Coordinator

ADDRESS INQUIRIES TO:
Coordinator, National Poetry Series
(See address above.)

PEN AMERICA [632]

588 Broadway, Suite 303
New York, NY 10012
(212) 334-1660 ext. 4813
Fax: (212) 334-2181
E-mail: awards@pen.org
Web Site: pen.org

NAME(S) OF PROGRAMS:
● **PEN/Hemingway Award for a Debut Novel**

TYPE:
Awards/prizes. Awarded annually for the first published book-length work of fiction by an American writer.

YEAR PROGRAM STARTED: 1976

PURPOSE:
To recognize literary excellence and to honor debut fiction.

LEGAL BASIS:
Nonprofit organization affiliated with International PEN.

ELIGIBILITY:
First published novel by an American citizen or resident, published in the U.S. in 2020. Self-published books are not eligible.

GEOG. RESTRICTIONS: United States.

FINANCIAL DATA:
Amount of support per award: $25,000.
Total amount of support: $25,000.

NO. MOST RECENT APPLICANTS: 150.

NO. AWARDS: 1 winner and 2 honorable mentions.

APPLICATION INFO:
Application process begins on June 1. Submissions are only accepted from publishers or literary agents. Authors may not submit their own book. Full guidelines are available on the web site.

Duration: One-time award.

Deadline: August 15.

ADDRESS INQUIRIES TO:
See e-mail address above.

*SPECIAL STIPULATIONS:
Self-published books, electronic submissions or e-books are not eligible for consideration.

PEN AMERICA [633]

588 Broadway, Suite 303
New York, NY 10012-5258
(212) 334-1660
Fax: (212) 334-2181
E-mail: prisonwriting@pen.org
Web Site: pen.org

FOUNDED: 1922

AREAS OF INTEREST:
Writing of literature and poetry.

NAME(S) OF PROGRAMS:
● **PEN Prison Writing Program**

TYPE:
Awards/prizes.

YEAR PROGRAM STARTED: 1971

PURPOSE:
To help incarcerated writers develop their writing talents and to promote writing as a means of rehabilitation.

LEGAL BASIS:
Tax-exempt, nonprofit organization.

ELIGIBILITY:
U.S. federal, state or county prisoners in the year before the deadline may apply. Only unpublished manuscripts will be considered, except those that have appeared in a prison publication.

GEOG. RESTRICTIONS: United States.

FINANCIAL DATA:
In addition to prize money, all winners are awarded the opportunity to correspond with a writing mentor.

Amount of support per award: First prize: $250, Second prize: $150, Third prize: $100, honorable mention: $25. Prizes are given for each of five categories: Poetry, Fiction, Essay, Memoir and Drama.

NO. MOST RECENT APPLICANTS: 1,500.

NO. AWARDS: Approximately 35 annually.

APPLICATION INFO:
Manuscripts must be typewritten (double-spaced) or clearly printed on standard letter-size paper. Also accept alternative submissions. Authors must not submit more than one entry in each category except in poetry. Name, inmate number and address must appear on each submission.

Duration: One-time award.

Deadline: September 1. Winners announced in Spring.

PUBLICATIONS:
PEN Handbook for Writers in Prison (lists resources available to inmates and journals interested in prison writing).

STAFF:
Robert Pollock, Prison and Justice Writing Program Manager

ADDRESS INQUIRIES TO:
PEN Writing Award for Prisoners
(See address above.)

PEN AMERICA [634]

588 Broadway, Suite 303
New York, NY 10012
(212) 334-1660
Fax: (212) 334-2181
E-mail: writersfund@pen.org
Web Site: pen.org/writers-emergency-fund

FOUNDED: 1922

AREAS OF INTEREST:
Literature, free expression and international literary fellowship.

NAME(S) OF PROGRAMS:
● **Pen America Writers' Emergency Fund**

TYPE:
Grants-in-aid. Emergency fund for professional (published or produced) writers in acute, emergency financial crisis.

YEAR PROGRAM STARTED: 1958

PURPOSE:
To assist professional literary writers in times of short-term financial emergency and also to assist writers and editors with AIDS or HIV; to advance literature, defend free expression and foster international literary fellowship.

LEGAL BASIS:
Nonprofit organization affiliated with International PEN.

ELIGIBILITY:
The fund aims to assist professional (published or produced) writers facing unexpected financial and medical emergencies, and those who are HIV-positive. The fund does not exist for research purposes, for completing projects or to support publications or organizations. Must be a permanent U.S. resident or citizen. Self-published writers are not eligible.

GEOG. RESTRICTIONS: United States.

FINANCIAL DATA:
Amount of support per award: $500 to $1,000.

NO. AWARDS: Varies.

APPLICATION INFO:
Applicants should submit a completed application form, published writing samples, documentation of financial emergency and professional resume. Applications are accepted year-round and are reviewed every three months by the Writers' Fund Committee.

Application can be found at the above web site address.

Deadline: Mid-March, mid-June, mid-September and mid-December.

PUBLICATIONS:
Application; guidelines.

ADDRESS INQUIRIES TO:
See e-mail address above.

*SPECIAL STIPULATIONS:
Repeat grants to any one individual will not be given within a three-year period since last grant.

PEN AMERICA [635]

588 Broadway, Suite 303
New York, NY 10012
(212) 334-1660 ext. 4813
Fax: (212) 334-2181
E-mail: awards@pen.org
Web Site: pen.org

FOUNDED: 1922

AREAS OF INTEREST:
Fiction, literary nonfiction, biography/memoir and poetry.

NAME(S) OF PROGRAMS:
● **PEN Open Book Award**

TYPE:
Awards/prizes. Invites submissions of book-length writings by authors of color, published during the calendar year.

PURPOSE:
To encourage racial and ethnic diversity within the literary and publishing communities.

ELIGIBILITY:
Open to authors of color who have not received wide media coverage. U.S. residency or citizenship is not required. Works of fiction, literary nonfiction, biography/memoir and other works of literary character are strongly preferred. Authors may not submit their own work. Submissions will only be accepted from publishers or literary agents.

FINANCIAL DATA:
Amount of support per award: $5,000.

NO. MOST RECENT APPLICANTS: Approximately 250.

NO. AWARDS: 1.

APPLICATION INFO:
Online application form can be found on the Center web site beginning June 1. Publishers and agents may submit one copy of a book-length writing by an author of color published during the calendar year under consideration, with an official letter of recommendation. Self-published books are not eligible. Early submissions are strongly recommended.

Deadline: August 15 of each year.

ADDRESS INQUIRIES TO:
See e-mail address above.

PEN AMERICA [636]

588 Broadway, Suite 303
New York, NY 10012
(212) 334-1660 ext. 4813
Fax: (212) 334-2181
E-mail: awards@pen.org
Web Site: pen.org

FOUNDED: 1922

AREAS OF INTEREST:
Poetry.

NAME(S) OF PROGRAMS:
● **PEN/Osterweil Award for Poetry**

TYPE:
Awards/prizes. Recognizes the high literary character of the published work to date of a new and emerging American poet of any age and the promise of further literary achievement.

PURPOSE:
To recognize the achievements of new and emerging American poets.

ELIGIBILITY:
Poets nominated for the Award have to be selected by a PEN member.

FINANCIAL DATA:
Amount of support per award: $5,000 awarded in odd-numbered years.

NO. AWARDS: 1.

APPLICATION INFO:
Letters of nomination are accepted from PEN members only.

ADDRESS INQUIRIES TO:
See e-mail address above.

PEN AMERICA [637]

588 Broadway, Suite 303
New York, NY 10012
(212) 334-1660 ext. 4813
Fax: (212) 334-2181
E-mail: awards@pen.org
Web Site: pen.org

FOUNDED: 1922

AREAS OF INTEREST:
Children's/young adult fiction.

NAME(S) OF PROGRAMS:
● **PEN/Phyllis Naylor Grant for Children's and Young Adult Novelists**

TYPE:
Awards/prizes. The Fellowship is offered annually to an author of children's or young adult fiction.

PURPOSE:
To recognize the fact that many writers' work is of high literary caliber but has not yet attracted a broad readership.

ELIGIBILITY:
A candidate is a writer of children's or young adult fiction demonstrating financial need. Candidate must have published at least one novel for children or young adults which have been warmly received by literary critics, but have not generated sufficient income to support the author. The writer's books must be published by a U.S. publisher.

FINANCIAL DATA:
Amount of support per award: $5,000.

NO. MOST RECENT APPLICANTS: 20.

NO. AWARDS: 1.

APPLICATION INFO:
Nomination process begins on April 1. Writers may nominate themselves or a fellow writer. This Fellowship will be judged blindly - the administrators will be aware of the nominee's names, but the judges will not. The application process is entirely online. Hard copy materials will no longer be accepted. The online application will require the following materials:
(1) a letter describing in some detail how they meet the criteria for the Fellowship, including a list of their published novel(s) for children or young adults;
(2) copies of at least three reviews of their novel(s) from professional publications;
(3) a letter of recommendation from an editor or fellow writer;
(4) one copy of the outline of the current novel in progress;
(5) one copy of 50 to 75 pages of the text. Picture books are not eligible. The writers' name should not appear anywhere on the manuscript, in order to ensure anonymity for the judging process and;
(6) on a separate piece of paper, a brief description of the candidate's recent earnings and a statement about why monetary support will make a particular difference in the applicant's writing life at this time. If the candidate is married or living with a domestic partner, please include a brief description of total family income and expense.

Deadline: August 1 each year.

ADDRESS INQUIRIES TO:
See e-mail address above.

PEN AMERICA   [638]

588 Broadway, Suite 303
New York, NY 10012
(212) 334-1660 ext. 4813
Fax: (212) 334-2181
E-mail: awards@pen.org
Web Site: pen.org

FOUNDED: 1922

AREAS OF INTEREST:
Poetry in translation.

NAME(S) OF PROGRAMS:
• **PEN Award for Poetry in Translation**

TYPE:
Awards/prizes. The award recognizes
book-length translations of poetry from any
language into English published during the
current calendar year and is judged by a
single translator of poetry appointed by the
PEN Translation Committee. The award was
made possible originally by a bequest from
the late translator and PEN member Rae
Dalven, and has received current support
from The Kaplen Foundation. It is conferred
every spring in New York.

YEAR PROGRAM STARTED: 1963

PURPOSE:
To recognize book-length translations of
poetry from any language into English
published during the current calendar year.

ELIGIBILITY:
Although all eligible books must have been
published in the U.S., translators may be of
any nationality; U.S. residency or citizenship
is not required.

Self-published books or books with more
than two translators are not eligible.
Translators and authors may not submit their
own work. Submissions will only be accepted
from publishers and literary agents.

FINANCIAL DATA:
Amount of support per award: $3,000.

NO. MOST RECENT APPLICANTS: 50.

NO. AWARDS: 1.

APPLICATION INFO:
Application process opens on June 1. One
copy of book-length translations of poetry
published during the calendar year under
consideration may be submitted by
publishers, agents, or the translators
themselves. Early submissions are strongly
recommended.
Deadline: August 15 each year.

ADDRESS INQUIRIES TO:
See e-mail address above.

PEN AMERICA   [639]

588 Broadway, Suite 303
New York, NY 10012
(212) 334-1660 ext. 4813
Fax: (212) 334-2181
E-mail: awards@pen.org
Web Site: pen.org

FOUNDED: 1922

AREAS OF INTEREST:
Poetry.

NAME(S) OF PROGRAMS:
• **PEN/Voelcker Award for Poetry**

TYPE:
Awards/prizes. The Award, established by a
bequest from Hunce Voelcker, will be
presented to an American poet whose
distinguished and growing body of work to

date represents a notable and accomplished
presence in American literature, for whom
the promise seen in earlier work has been
fulfilled, and who has matured with each
successive volume of poetry.

PURPOSE:
To honor an American poet whose
distinguished and growing body of work to
date represents a notable and accomplished
presence in American literature.

ELIGIBILITY:
Candidates must be American residents and
can be nominated only by professional
members of PEN. It is understood that all
nominations made for the Award supplement
internal nominations made by the panel of
judges. There are no restrictions whatsoever
to the age of the poet or to the style of his or
her work.

FINANCIAL DATA:
Amount of support per award: $5,000
awarded in even-numbered years.

NO. AWARDS: 1.

APPLICATION INFO:
All letters of nomination (one to two pages is
expected) should describe the scope and
literary caliber of the candidate's work, and
summarize the candidate's publications. Most
importantly, nominations should articulate the
degree of accomplishment the nominated
poet has attained, and the esteem in which
the candidate's work is held within the
American literary community. Letters of
nomination must be submitted through PEN's
online nomination portal.
Deadline: Offered in even-numbered years.

ADDRESS INQUIRIES TO:
See e-mail address above.

PEN AMERICA   [640]

588 Broadway, Suite 303
New York, NY 10012
(212) 334-1660 ext. 4813
Fax: (212) 334-2181
E-mail: awards@pen.org
Web Site: pen.org

FOUNDED: 1922

AREAS OF INTEREST:
Debut short story collections.

NAME(S) OF PROGRAMS:
• **PEN/Robert W. Bingham Prize for
Debut Short Story Collection**

TYPE:
Awards/prizes. The PEN/Robert W. Bingham
Prize is awarded annually and honors an
exceptionally talented fiction writer whose
debut work of short stories published in the
prior year represents distinguished literary
achievement and suggests great promise.

YEAR PROGRAM STARTED: 1990

PURPOSE:
To promote the professional careers of
exceptionally talented fiction writers.

LEGAL BASIS:
Nonprofit organization affiliated with
International PEN.

ELIGIBILITY:
Candidate's first (and only first) collection of
short fiction must have been published by a
U.S. trade publisher between January 1 and
December 31 of the prior year. Candidates
must be U.S. residents. American citizenship
is not required. There are no restrictions on

the candidate's age or on the style of his or
her work. Self-published books are not
eligible. Authors may not submit their own
work. Submissions will only be accepted
from publishers and literary agents.

FINANCIAL DATA:
Amount of support per award: $25,000.

NO. MOST RECENT APPLICANTS: 75.

NO. AWARDS: 1.

APPLICATION INFO:
Application process begins June 1.
Submissions will only be accepted from
publishers and literary agents. Submitter is
expected to mail one copy of book to mailing
address provided.
Deadline: August 15 of each year.

ADDRESS INQUIRIES TO:
See e-mail address above.

PEN AMERICA   [641]

588 Broadway, Suite 303
New York, NY 10012
(212) 334-1660 ext. 4813
Fax: (212) 334-2181
E-mail: awards@pen.org
Web Site: pen.org

FOUNDED: 1922

AREAS OF INTEREST:
Promoting the professional development of
talented fiction writers.

NAME(S) OF PROGRAMS:
• **PEN/Robert J. Dau Short Story Prize
for Emerging Writers**

TYPE:
Awards/prizes. The PEN/Robert J. Dau Short
Story Prize for Emerging Writers recognizes
emerging fiction writers for their debut short
story published in a literary magazine or
cultural web site and aims to support the
launch of their careers as fiction writers.

PURPOSE:
To recognize emerging fiction writers for
their debut short story published in a literary
magazine or journal.

LEGAL BASIS:
Nonprofit organization affiliated with
International PEN.

ELIGIBILITY:
Submissions must be from editors of eligible
publications. Authors may not submit their
own work. Stories must have been published
(or forthcoming) in 2020. Participating
publications may be online magazines, print
magazines distributed in the U.S., or cultural
web sites.

Editors from eligible publications may only
submit a short story by a debut writer. The
story must be the writer's first English
publication of any genre that has undergone
an editorial review process and been accepted
and published in a literary journal, book,
media outlet, or other publication that the
author is not academically or professionally
associated with. Editors from eligible
publications may submit up to four eligible
stories (up to 12,000 word) from eligible
authors in a given award year.

The editor and author must agree to the
award's declaration of eligibility and consent,
which outlines serials rights for *Catapult*'s
forthcoming anthology.

FINANCIAL DATA:
Total amount of support: $2,000 and
publication in an anthology.

NO. MOST RECENT APPLICANTS: 150.

NO. AWARDS: 12.

APPLICATION INFO:
Submissions are accepted from June 1 to November 15. Submissions will not be considered unless officially submitted via the online form and received at the PEN America New York office with the corresponding declaration of eligibility and consent.

Deadline: November 15.

ADDRESS INQUIRIES TO:
See e-mail address above.

PEN AMERICA   [642]
588 Broadway, Suite 303
New York, NY 10012
(212) 334-1660 ext. 4813
Fax: (212) 334-2181
E-mail: awards@pen.org
Web Site: pen.org

FOUNDED: 1922

AREAS OF INTEREST:
Promoting the professional development of talented writers.

NAME(S) OF PROGRAMS:
- **PEN/Diamonstein-Spielvogel Award for the Art of the Essay**

TYPE:
Awards/prizes. The PEN/Diamonstein-Spielvogel Award for the Art of the Essay honors a writer whose collection of individual essays, published in the current calendar year, is an expansion of their exceptional body of work focusing on the essay as an art form. This is considered a mid- to late career achievement award.

YEAR PROGRAM STARTED: 1991

PURPOSE:
To recognize a writer whose collection of individual essays expands their exceptional body of work focusing on the essay as an art form.

LEGAL BASIS:
Nonprofit organization affiliated with International Pen.

ELIGIBILITY:
Author must be a permanent U.S. resident or U.S. citizen. Eligible titles must have been published by a U.S. trade publisher during the applicable calendar year. There are no restrictions on the subject matter. Essays may deal with a range of subjects or may explore one specific theme.

The book must be a series of individual essays published by a single author. Anthologies with multiple authors are ineligible.

Individual essays may have been previously published in magazines, journals, or anthologies.

Books submitted for this award may not be submitted to any additional PEN America Literary Award, with the exception of the PEN Open Book Award.

Self published books and single book-length works of nonfiction are not eligible.

FINANCIAL DATA:
Amount of support per award: $10,000.

NO. MOST RECENT APPLICANTS: 100.

NO. AWARDS: 1.

APPLICATION INFO:
Submissions are only accepted from publishers or literary agents. Authors may not submit their own book. Book submissions will not be considered unless officially submitted via the online form and received at the PEN America New York office with the corresponding Declaration of Eligibility.

Duration: One-time award.

Deadline: August 15.

ADDRESS INQUIRIES TO:
See e-mail address above.

PEN AMERICA   [643]
588 Broadway, Suite 303
New York, NY 10012
(212) 334-1660 ext. 4813
Fax: (212) 334-2181
E-mail: awards@pen.org
Web Site: pen.org

FOUNDED: 1922

AREAS OF INTEREST:
Promoting the professional development of talented writers.

NAME(S) OF PROGRAMS:
- **PEN/E.O. Wilson Prize for Literary Science Writing**

TYPE:
Awards/prizes. The PEN/E.O. Wilson Literary Science Award was founded by scientist and author Dr. Edward O. Wilson, activist and actor Harrison Ford, and the E.O. Wilson Biodiversity Foundation. The award celebrates writing that exemplifies literary excellence on the subject of the physical or biological sciences and communicates complex scientific concepts to a lay audience.

YEAR PROGRAM STARTED: 2011

PURPOSE:
To recognize the art of literary science writing.

LEGAL BASIS:
Nonprofit organization affiliated with International PEN.

ELIGIBILITY:
Eligible titles must have been published between January 1 and December 1 of the current award cycle. Authors of the work must be permanent U.S. residents or U.S. citizens.

Books submitted for this award may not be submitted for any additional PEN America Literary Award, with the exception of the PEN Open Book Award.

Anthologies and self-published books are not eligible.

FINANCIAL DATA:
Amount of support per award: $10,000.

NO. MOST RECENT APPLICANTS: 80.

NO. AWARDS: 1.

APPLICATION INFO:
Submissions will only be accepted from publishers and literary agents. Authors may not submit their own book for this award. Book submissions will not be considered unless officially submitted via the online form and received at the PEN America New York office with the corresponding Declaration of Eligibility.

Duration: One-time award.

Deadline: August 15.

ADDRESS INQUIRIES TO:
See e-mail address above.

PEN AMERICA   [644]
588 Broadway, Suite 303
New York, NY 10012
(212) 334-1660 ext. 4813
Fax: (212) 334-2181
E-mail: awards@pen.org
Web Site: pen.org

FOUNDED: 1922

AREAS OF INTEREST:
Promoting the professional development of talented writers.

NAME(S) OF PROGRAMS:
- **PEN/Jacqueline Bograd Weld Award for Biography**

TYPE:
Awards/prizes. The PEN/Jacqueline Bograd Weld Award for Biography is awarded for excellence in the art of biography. This prize goes to the author of a distinguished work published in the U.S. during the previous calendar year. The winning title is considered by the judges to be a work of exceptional literary, narrative, and artistic merit, based on scrupulous research.

PURPOSE:
To recognize a work of exceptional literary, narrative, and artistic merit, based on scrupulous research.

LEGAL BASIS:
Nonprofit organization affiliated with International PEN.

ELIGIBILITY:
A candidate's book of nonfiction must have been published by a trade publisher in the U.S. between January 1 and December 31 of the award year. Candidates need not be U.S. residents.

Books must be works by an author about another person.

Books submitted for this award may not be submitted for any additional PEN America Literary Award, with the exception of the PEN Open Book Award.

Memoirs, autobiographies, and self-published books are not eligible.

FINANCIAL DATA:
Amount of support per award: $5,000.

NO. MOST RECENT APPLICANTS: 120.

NO. AWARDS: 1.

APPLICATION INFO:
Submissions will only be accepted from publishers or literary agents. Authors may not submit their own book for this award. Book submissions will not be considered unless officially submitted via the online form and received at the PEN America New York office with the corresponding Declaration of Eligibility.

Duration: One-time award.

Deadline: August 15.

ADDRESS INQUIRIES TO:
See e-mail address above.

PEN AMERICA   [645]
588 Broadway, Suite 303
New York, NY 10012
(212) 334-1660 ext. 4813
Fax: (212) 334-2181
E-mail: awards@pen.org
Web Site: pen.org

FOUNDED: 1922

AREAS OF INTEREST:
Promoting the professional development of talented nonfiction writers.

NAME(S) OF PROGRAMS:
- **PEN/Jean Stein Grant for Literary Oral History**

TYPE:
Grants-in-aid; Project/program grants. The PEN/Jean Stein Grant for Literary Oral History recognizes a literary work of nonfiction that uses oral history to illuminate an event, individual, place, or movement. The grant is meant to help the author maintain or complete their ongoing project.

This grant is made possible by a substantial contribution from American author and editor Jean Stein, whose groundbreaking work helped popularize literary oral history.

PURPOSE:
To recognize the work of talented nonfiction writers.

LEGAL BASIS:
Nonprofit organization affiliated with International PEN.

ELIGIBILITY:
The submitted project must be the work of a single individual, written in English, and must be an unpublished work-in-progress. The project must be a work of literary nonfiction. Oral history must be a significant component of the project and its research.

Scholarly or academic writing is not eligible.

FINANCIAL DATA:
Amount of support per award: $10,000.

NO. MOST RECENT APPLICANTS: 60.

NO. AWARDS: 1.

APPLICATION INFO:
Application process is entirely online. Hard copy applications will not be accepted. The online submission form requires the following, submitted as one PDF file:
(1) a one- to two-page, single-spaced description of the work, its importance, and why the author chose to undertake this project. One can additionally use this space to discuss relevant permissions, contracts, rights, or other aspects of the project;
(2) a one- to two-page, single-spaced statement explaining why and how oral history was used in the project;
(3) a 300- to 500-word statement explaining how a grant would aid in the completion of the project;
(4) a curriculum vitae for the author of the project, which should include information on any previous publications;
(5) an outline that includes the work completed thus far and the work remaining. The outline should include the names of all participants;
(6) transcripts of the project interviews (six to 10 pages) and;
(7) a writing sample from the project (20 to 40 pages, double-spaced).

Duration: One-time award.

Deadline: June 1.

ADDRESS INQUIRIES TO:
See e-mail address above.

PEN AMERICA [646]

588 Broadway, Suite 303
New York, NY 10012
(212) 334-1660 ext. 4813
Fax: (212) 334-2181
E-mail: awards@pen.org
Web Site: pen.org

FOUNDED: 1922

AREAS OF INTEREST:
Promoting the professional development of talented writers.

NAME(S) OF PROGRAMS:
- **PEN/Heim Translation Fund Grant**

TYPE:
Grants-in-aid. The PEN/Heim Translation Fund was established by an endowed gift from Michael Henry Heim and Pricilla Heim, in response to the dismayingly low number of literary translations currently appearing in English.

YEAR PROGRAM STARTED: 2003

PURPOSE:
To promote the publication and reception of translated international literature in English.

LEGAL BASIS:
Nonprofit organization affiliated with International PEN.

ELIGIBILITY:
Grants support the translation of book-length works of fiction, creative nonfiction, poetry, or drama that have not previously appeared in English in print or have appeared only in an outdated or otherwise flawed translation. Works should be translations-in-progress, as the grant aims to provide support for completion. Preference will be given to translators at the beginning of their career, and to works by underrepresented writers working in underrepresented languages.

There are no restrictions on the nationality or citizenship of the translator, but the works must be translated into English.

The Fund seeks to encourage translators to undertake projects they might not otherwise have had the means to attempt.

Works with multiple translators, literary criticism, and scholarly or technical texts do not quality.

Translators may only submit one project per year.

FINANCIAL DATA:
Amount of support per award: $3,000 to $5,000.

NO. MOST RECENT APPLICANTS: 250.

NO. AWARDS: 10 to 12.

APPLICATION INFO:
Application must be submitted with the following:
(1) a one- to two-page, single-spaced statement outlining the work and describing its importance;
(2) a biography and bibliography of the author, including information on translations of his or her work into other languages and;
(3) curriculum vitae of the translator, no longer than three pages.

If the book is not in the public domain and the project is not yet under contract, include a photocopy of the copyright notice from the book published in its original language and a letter from the copyright holder stating that English-language rights to the book are available. A letter or copy of an e-mail from the copyright holder is sufficient. If the translation is currently under contract with a publisher, submit a copy of the contract.

Translator must also include a 10- to 12-page, single-spaced sample of the translation and the same passage in the original language. If the work has been previously translated, the same passage in the earlier version.

Deadline: June 1.

ADDRESS INQUIRIES TO:
See e-mail address above.

*PLEASE NOTE:
Translators who have previously been awarded grants by the Fund are ineligible to reapply for three years after the year in which they receive a grant. Projects that have been previously submitted and have not received a grant are unlikely to be reconsidered in a subsequent year.

PEN/FAULKNER FOUNDATION [647]

641 S Street, N.W.
3rd Floor
Washington, DC 20001
(202) 898-9063
E-mail: shahenda@penfaulkner.org
Web Site: www.penfaulkner.org

FOUNDED: 1980

AREAS OF INTEREST:
Fiction.

NAME(S) OF PROGRAMS:
- **PEN/Faulkner Award for Fiction**

TYPE:
Awards/prizes. Cash awards for a published winning author and four finalists.

YEAR PROGRAM STARTED: 1981

PURPOSE:
To honor literary excellence.

LEGAL BASIS:
Nonprofit 501(c)(3) organization.

ELIGIBILITY:
Candidates must be living American permanent residents. Books must be published within the calendar year of the award. No self-published books.

GEOG. RESTRICTIONS: United States.

FINANCIAL DATA:
Amount of support per award: $15,000 for the winner. $5,000 to each of four finalists.
Total amount of support: $35,000.

NO. MOST RECENT APPLICANTS: 450.

NO. AWARDS: 5.

APPLICATION INFO:
Candidates should submit four copies of their book. Complete information is available on the Foundation web site.

Deadline: Submissions must be postmarked by October 31. Announcement by mid-March.

IRS I.D.: 52-1431622

OFFICER:
Tracy B. McGillvary, President

EXECUTIVE DIRECTOR:
Gwydion Suilebhan

ADDRESS INQUIRIES TO:
Shahenda Helmy, Program Logistics Director
Awards Department
(See address above.)

*PLEASE NOTE:
This is not a grant program, but a prize for published work.

PERPETUAL TRUSTEE COMPANY LTD. [648]

Level 6, 123 Pitt Street
Sydney N.S.W. 2000 Australia
(61) 1800 501 227
Fax: (61) 02 8256 1471
E-mail: philanthropy@perpetual.com.au
Web Site: www.perpetual.com.au/milesfranklin

FOUNDED: 1954

AREAS OF INTEREST:
The advancement, improvement and betterment of Australian literature.

NAME(S) OF PROGRAMS:
- **Miles Franklin Literary Award**

TYPE:
Awards/prizes. Annual cash award for a published book on Australian life.

YEAR PROGRAM STARTED: 1957

PURPOSE:
To improve the educational style of authors; to help and give incentive to authors and to provide them with additional monetary support to enable them to improve their literary efforts.

LEGAL BASIS:
Trustees of estate of the late Miles Franklin.

ELIGIBILITY:
All works must be in English. No special requirements as regards nationality, age, etc. The book must be published in the year of entry of the award and be of the highest literary merit and must present Australian life in any of its phases. More than one entry may be submitted by each author. Novels or plays written by two or more authors in collaboration are eligible.

Biographies, collections of short stories, children's books and poetry are not eligible. Judges will not consider any text that has only had Internet publication.

FINANCIAL DATA:
Amount of support per award: $60,000 (AUD) for the year 2020.

NO. AWARDS: 1 per year.

APPLICATION INFO:
Application information is available on the web site when the award cycle opens. Publishers are required to submit the novels on the authors' behalf.

PUBLICATIONS:
Application guidelines.

ADDRESS INQUIRIES TO:
Scholarship and Awards
Miles Franklin Literary Award
(See e-mail address above.)

THE PHI BETA KAPPA SOCIETY [649]

1606 New Hampshire Avenue, N.W.
Washington, DC 20009
(202) 745-3287
Fax: (202) 986-1601
E-mail: awards@pbk.org
Web Site: www.pbk.org

FOUNDED: 1776

NAME(S) OF PROGRAMS:
- **The Phi Beta Kappa Book Awards**

TYPE:
Awards/prizes. The Phi Beta Kappa Book Awards consist of three book awards given annually to outstanding scholarly books that have been published in the U.S. in the fields of the humanities, the social sciences, the natural sciences and mathematics.

The Ralph Waldo Emerson Book Award is offered annually for scholarly studies that contribute significantly to interpretations of the intellectual and cultural condition of humanity. This award may recognize work in the fields of history, philosophy and religion; these fields are conceived in sufficiently broad terms to permit the inclusion of appropriate work in related fields such as anthropology and the social sciences. Biographies of public figures may be eligible if their critical emphasis is primarily on the intellectual and cultural condition of humanity.

The Christian Gauss Award is offered for books in the field of literary scholarship or criticism. The prize honors the late Christian Gauss, the distinguished Princeton University scholar, teacher, and dean, who also served as president of the Phi Beta Kappa Society. To be eligible, a literary biography must have a predominantly critical emphasis.

Phi Beta Kappa Book Award in Science is offered for outstanding contributions by scientists to the literature of science. The Award's intent is to encourage literate and scholarly interpretations of the physical and biological sciences and mathematics; monographs and compendiums are not eligible. To be eligible, biographies of scientists must have a substantial critical emphasis on their scientific research.

PURPOSE:
To recognize outstanding printed work in several fields including the social sciences, humanities, natural science and math.

LEGAL BASIS:
National scholarly honorary society.

ELIGIBILITY:
Awards are given for works published in the U.S. during the previous calendar year. Entries must be original publications. Translations and works previously published as a whole are not eligible. Books that contain chapters or sections previously published as articles in periodicals will be considered only if they have very clear, unifying themes and are not random collections. Books that consist entirely of previously published articles are unlikely to qualify.

Entries ordinarily will be the work of a single writer. Exceptions may be made for books written by small teams of scholars working in close collaboration. Books that are collections of chapters by several different authors are not eligible. Entries should not be highly technical in character, nor should they treat subjects of narrowly limited interest. Monographs and reports on research as such are not eligible. In all cases, the subject and style of the entries should be accessible to the general, literate reader.

Authors must be citizens or residents of the U.S. Entries must have been published originally in the U.S. A book may not be entered for more than one of the awards. All entries must be submitted by the publisher. Publishers may submit no more than one entry for each award.

GEOG. RESTRICTIONS: United States.

FINANCIAL DATA:
Amount of support per award: $10,000 to the winning author.
Total amount of support: $30,000 annually.

NO. MOST RECENT APPLICANTS: Varies.

NO. AWARDS: 1 award in each category each year.

APPLICATION INFO:
Inquiries and entries should be addressed to the appropriate award committee at the address above. Entries must be submitted by the publisher.
Duration: No renewal.
Deadline: January 31.

PUBLICATIONS:
Application guidelines.

ADDRESS INQUIRIES TO:
Aurora Sherman, Executive Assistant to the Secretary and Awards Coordinator
(See address above.)

PITT POETRY SERIES [650]

University of Pittsburgh Press
7500 Thomas Boulevard
Pittsburgh, PA 15260
(412) 383-2456
Fax: (412) 383-2466
E-mail: info@upress.pitt.edu
Web Site: upittpress.org

FOUNDED: 1967

AREAS OF INTEREST:
Contemporary American poetry.

NAME(S) OF PROGRAMS:
- **Agnes Lynch Starrett Poetry Prize**

TYPE:
Awards/prizes. Cash prize, plus publication in the Pitt Poetry Series.

YEAR PROGRAM STARTED: 1980

LEGAL BASIS:
University.

ELIGIBILITY:
Starrett Prize awarded annually for a manuscript in English by a writer who has not previously published a full-length book of poetry.

FINANCIAL DATA:
Amount of support per award: $5,000, plus book publication.
Total amount of support: $5,000.

NO. MOST RECENT APPLICANTS: 600 for the year 2019.

NO. AWARDS: 1 each year.

REPRESENTATIVE AWARDS:
Eleanor Boudreau, *Earnest, Earnest?*

APPLICATION INFO:
Send one copy of manuscript on good quality white paper, with no fewer than 48 and no more than 100 typescript pages. Clean, legible photocopies are acceptable. Name, address, phone number, and e-mail address should be on the title page. Also include curriculum vitae. A $25 reading fee per manuscript is required.

Application can also be submitted through www.submittable.com.
Deadline: Between March 1 and April 30 only. Announcement in the fall.

PUBLICATIONS:
Competition rules.

OFFICERS:
Ed Ochester, Editor, Pitt Poetry Series

ADDRESS INQUIRIES TO:
See e-mail address above.

*SPECIAL STIPULATIONS:
Competition for the Starrett Prize is severe.
Casual submissions are not encouraged.
Publisher cannot provide critiques of
manuscripts.

Manuscripts will not be returned.

THE PLAYWRIGHTS' CENTER [651]

2301 Franklin Avenue East
Minneapolis, MN 55406
(612) 332-7481 ext. 1115
Fax: (612) 332-6037
E-mail: info@pwcenter.org
juliab@pwcenter.org
Web Site: pwcenter.org

FOUNDED: 1971

AREAS OF INTEREST:
Playwriting.

CONSULTING OR VOLUNTEER SERVICES:
Advice on career development, jobs and
production for playwrights.

NAME(S) OF PROGRAMS:
- **Affiliated Writer Program**
- **Core Apprentice Program**
- **Core Writer Program**
- **Jerome Fellowships**
- **Many Voices Fellowships**
- **Many Voices Mentorships**
- **McKnight Fellowships in Playwriting**
- **McKnight National Residency and Commission**
- **McKnight Theater Artist Fellowships**
- **New Plays on Campus**

TYPE:
Awards/prizes; Conferences/seminars;
Development grants; Fellowships;
Internships; Project/program grants. Core
Apprentice Program provides student
playwrights with such benefits as a year of
mentorship with a professional playwright
and a full workshop of a new play at the
Playwrights' Center.

Core Writer Program confers additional
membership benefits to committed
professional playwrights.

Jerome Fellowships provide grants to
emerging playwrights, who receive access to
Center's developmental services.

Many Voices Fellowships are awarded to
playwrights of color.

Many Voices Mentorships are awarded to
Minnesota-based beginning writers of color.

McKnight Fellowships in Playwriting provide
grants to midcareer Minnesota-based
playwrights.

McKnight National Residency and
Commission aids in the creation and
development of new works from nationally
recognized playwrights not residing in
Minnesota.

McKnight Theater Artist Fellowships are
awarded to Minnesota theater artists (other
than playwrights).

YEAR PROGRAM STARTED: 1971

PURPOSE:
To assist playwrights.

LEGAL BASIS:
Tax-exempt and nonprofit.

ELIGIBILITY:
Core Writer Program is open to professional
playwrights in the U.S.

Jerome Fellowships are open to emerging
playwrights in the U.S. (citizens or
permanent residents).

Many Voices Fellowships are available to
national and local writers of color.

Many Voices Mentorships are available to
Minnesota-based beginning playwrights.

McKnight Fellowships in Playwriting are
open to Minnesota residents only.

McKnight Theater Artist Fellowships are
open to Minnesota writers only.

McKnight National Residency and
Commission is for playwrights residing
outside of Minnesota.

Additional criteria vary for each program.

GEOG. RESTRICTIONS: Many Voices
Mentorships, McKnight Fellowships in
Playwriting and McKnight Theater Artist
Fellowships: Minnesota.

FINANCIAL DATA:
Amount of support per award: Varies.
Total amount of support: Over $250,000.

NO. MOST RECENT APPLICANTS: 200 for
fellowships. 500 for all programs.

NO. AWARDS: For the year 2018-19: Core
Apprentices: 3; Core Writers: 29; Jerome
Fellowships: 3; Many Voices Fellowships: 2;
Many Voices Mentorship: 1; McKnight
Fellowships in Playwriting: 2; McKnight
National Residency and Commission: 1;
McKnight Theater Artist Fellowships: 3.

APPLICATION INFO:
Application information is available on the
web site.
Duration: Core Writer: Three years; All
other fellowships: One year.
Deadline: Varies.

PUBLICATIONS:
Annual report; newsletter.

IRS I.D.: 41-6170139

STAFF:
Jeremy Cohen, Producing Artistic Director
Hayley Finn, Associate Artistic Director
Julia Brown, Artistic Programs Administrator

ADDRESS INQUIRIES TO:
Julia Brown, Artistic Programs Administrator
(See address above.)

*SPECIAL STIPULATIONS:
Playwright must be in residence in Minnesota
for one year for Jerome Fellowship.
Recipients of McKnight Advancement
Fellowships, McKnight Theater Artist
Fellowships, and Many Voices Fellowships
must maintain residence in Minnesota during
program year.

SOCIETY OF CHILDREN'S BOOK WRITERS AND ILLUSTRATORS [652]

6363 Wilshire Boulevard
Suite 425
Los Angeles, CA 90048
(323) 782-1010
Fax: (323) 782-1892
E-mail: scbwi@scbwi.org
Web Site: www.scbwi.org

FOUNDED: 1968

AREAS OF INTEREST:
Writers, editors and illustrators of children's
books.

NAME(S) OF PROGRAMS:
- **Don Freeman Memorial Grant-in-Aid**
- **Work-In-Progress Grants**

TYPE:
Grants-in-aid; Project/program grants. The
Freeman Memorial Grant-In-Aid has been
established to enable picture-book artists to
further their understanding, training and work
in any aspect of the picture-book genre.

Work-In-Progress Grants have been
established to assist children's book writers
to complete a specific project. Grants are
given in seven categories: Picture Book Text,
Chapter Books/Early Readers, Middle Grade,
Young Adult Fiction, Nonfiction,
Multicultural Fiction or Nonfiction, and
Translation.

YEAR PROGRAM STARTED: 1974

PURPOSE:
To encourage continuing excellence in the
creation of children's literature and to
provide assistance and support to those
working in the children's book field.

LEGAL BASIS:
Corporation.

ELIGIBILITY:
Both grants are available to full and associate
members of the Society of Children's Book
Writers. The SCBW Grant Committee
reserves the right to withhold the grants for
any given year.

FINANCIAL DATA:
Amount of support per award: Freeman
Memorial Grant-In-Aid: $1,000.
Total amount of support: Freeman Memorial
Grant-In-Aid: $2,000.

NO. MOST RECENT APPLICANTS: 285.

NO. AWARDS: Freeman Memorial Grant-In-Aid:
2; Work-In-Progress Grant: 1 in each
category.

APPLICATION INFO:
All applications must be digital and sent as a
single PDF. Full details are available on the
Society's web site.
Duration: One-time grant.
Deadline: March 31. Work-In-Progress Grant
recipients announced in September.

PUBLICATIONS:
Grants brochure.

OFFICERS:
Stephen Mooser, President
Lin Oliver, Executive Director

ADDRESS INQUIRIES TO:
For the Freeman Memorial Grant-In-Aid:
E-mail: sarahbaker@scbwi.org

For the Work-In-Progress Grants:
SCBW Grant Committee
(See address above.)

SYRACUSE UNIVERSITY [653]

English Graduate Office
420 Hall of Languages
Syracuse, NY 13244-1170
(315) 443-2174
Fax: (315) 443-3660
E-mail: tazollo@syr.edu
Web Site: english.syr.edu

FOUNDED: 1861

AREAS OF INTEREST:
American and British literature and culture, creative writing, critical theory, gender studies, cultural studies and film and screen studies.

NAME(S) OF PROGRAMS:
- **Graduate Program in Creative Writing**

TYPE:
Assistantships; Awards/prizes; Fellowships; Scholarships; Travel grants. Fellowships and teaching assistantships in creative writing.

YEAR PROGRAM STARTED: 1963

PURPOSE:
To assist talented writers to pursue graduate degrees at Syracuse University.

ELIGIBILITY:
Applicants must be an outstanding Arts and Sciences seniors with minimum 3.6 grade point average and must be nominated to the Arts and Sciences selection committee by department chairpersons or program directors, or individuals designated by them.

FINANCIAL DATA:
Fellowships and assistantships include remission of tuition costs for graduate study.
Amount of support per award: Annual stipend $15,430 to $17,000. University Fellowships: $25,290.
Total amount of support: Varies.

APPLICATION INFO:
Applications must be submitted online through CollegeNET's ApplyWeb. Additional information required varies by program.
Duration: Three years.
Deadline: December 15.

ADDRESS INQUIRIES TO:
Terri Zollo
Graduate English Office Coordinator
(See e-mail address above.)

TOWSON UNIVERSITY [654]
College of Liberal Arts
8000 York Road
Towson, MD 21252
(410) 704-2128
Fax: (410) 704-6392
E-mail: cla@towson.edu
Web Site: www.towson.edu/cla

FOUNDED: 1866

NAME(S) OF PROGRAMS:
- **Towson University Prize for Literature**

TYPE:
Awards/prizes. Awarded to Maryland writer of a single book or book-length manuscript of fiction, poetry, drama or imaginative nonfiction.

YEAR PROGRAM STARTED: 1980

PURPOSE:
To honor a published work of fiction, poetry or imaginative nonfiction by a Maryland resident.

LEGAL BASIS:
Special endowment.

ELIGIBILITY:
Applicant must be a Maryland resident for at least three years at the time of the award. Prize is awarded on the basis of literary and aesthetic excellence. Book must have been published in the three years prior to the award.

The winning author must be willing to be present at the awards ceremony and to grant to Towson State University the right to quote from the winning work in any publicity related to the prize.

GEOG. RESTRICTIONS: Maryland.

FINANCIAL DATA:
Amount of support per award: Generally $1,000.
Total amount of support: $1,000.

NO. MOST RECENT APPLICANTS: 15.

NO. AWARDS: 1 annually.

APPLICATION INFO:
Any individual, institution, group or publisher may nominate one or more works for the prize. Submit three copies of the work by certified mail, bound if published or typewritten if manuscript. If manuscript, proof of acceptance by a publisher and proposed date of publication must be provided. A completed nomination form must accompany entry.
Duration: One-time award.
Deadline: June 15 each year. Announcement in early Spring.

ADDRESS INQUIRIES TO:
Dean, College of Liberal Arts, LA 2213
Towson University
(See address above.)

THE UNIVERSITY OF IOWA [655]
Iowa Writers' Workshop
102 Dey House
507 North Clinton Street
Iowa City, IA 52242-1000
(319) 335-0416
Fax: (319) 335-0420
E-mail: deb-west@uiowa.edu
Web Site: writersworkshop.uiowa.edu

AREAS OF INTEREST:
Short story collection.

NAME(S) OF PROGRAMS:
- **The Iowa Short Fiction Award**
- **The John Simmons Short Fiction Award**

TYPE:
Awards/prizes. Publication of short story collection/manuscript.

YEAR PROGRAM STARTED: 1969

PURPOSE:
To encourage writing of short stories.

ELIGIBILITY:
Any writer who has not previously published a volume of prose fiction is eligible. Revised manuscripts which have been previously entered may be resubmitted. Writers who have published a volume of poetry are eligible.

The manuscript must be a collection of short stories of at least 150 word-processed, double-spaced pages. Stories previously published in periodicals are eligible.

CO-OP FUNDING PROGRAMS: The awards are provided with cooperation of the Iowa Writers' Workshop and the University of Iowa Press.

NO. MOST RECENT APPLICANTS: 400.

NO. AWARDS: 1 of each annually.

APPLICATION INFO:
No application forms are necessary. Manuscripts should be mailed to: Iowa Short

Fiction Award, Iowa Writers' Workshop, at the address listed above. Do not send the only copy of the manuscript. Xeroxed copies are encouraged. Stamped, self-addressed packaging may be included for return of the manuscript, but is not required.
Deadline: Entries should be postmarked between August 1 and September 30. Announcement of the winners will be made early in the following year.

STAFF:
Lan Samantha Chang, Director

ADDRESS INQUIRIES TO:
Sasha Khmelnik, Program Associate
(See address above.)

UNIVERSITY OF MINNESOTA [656]
Room 113, Elmer L. Andersen Library
222 21st Avenue South
Minneapolis, MN 55455
(612) 624-4576
E-mail: asc-clrc@umn.edu
Web Site: www.lib.umn.edu/clrc

AREAS OF INTEREST:
Children's book artist development.

NAME(S) OF PROGRAMS:
- **The Ezra Jack Keats/Kerlan Memorial Fellowship**

TYPE:
Research grants; Travel grants; Visiting scholars. Award to travel to Kerlan Collection, University of Minnesota, plus per diem.

YEAR PROGRAM STARTED: 1985

PURPOSE:
To fund the artist development of a talented writer and/or illustrator of children's books.

ELIGIBILITY:
Grants are awarded to individuals based on need. Special consideration will be given to those who would find it difficult to finance a visit to the Kerlan Collection. Candidates do not have to be U.S. citizens or residents.

FINANCIAL DATA:
Recipient will receive transportation cost and a per diem allotment.
Amount of support per award: Up to $3,000.
Total amount of support: Up to $3,000.

NO. AWARDS: 1.

APPLICATION INFO:
Electronic application acceptable by deadline.
Duration: Grants are awarded annually and are nonrenewable.
Deadline: January 30 (postmark).

ADDRESS INQUIRIES TO:
Ezra Jack Keats/Kerlan Collection Memorial Fellowship Committee
(See address above.)

THE UNIVERSITY OF SOUTHERN MISSISSIPPI [657]
118 College Drive
Box 5148
Hattiesburg, MS 39406
(601) 266-4349
Fax: (601) 266-6269
E-mail: ellen.ruffin@usm.edu
Web Site: www.degrummond.org/fellowships

FOUNDED: 1966

AREAS OF INTEREST:
American and British children's literature.

NAME(S) OF PROGRAMS:
- **Ezra Jack Keats/Janina Domanska Children's Literature Research Fellowship**

TYPE:
Fellowships; Research grants.

PURPOSE:
To encourage imaginative and productive research in children's literature.

ELIGIBILITY:
Applicants of any discipline who engage in projects which require substantial use of the de Grummond Collection may apply. Awards will be based upon the applicant's scholarly qualifications, the merits of the proposal submitted, and the appropriateness of the proposal to the resources of the de Grummond Collection. Preference will be given to projects which have a good likelihood of being published.

FINANCIAL DATA:
Fellowship monies can be used for travel, lodging, and meals.
Amount of support per award: Up to $1,600.
Total amount of support: Varies.

NO. MOST RECENT APPLICANTS: Average 5 to 7.

NO. AWARDS: 1 for the year 2017.

APPLICATION INFO:
Application information is available on the web site.
Duration: One year. Grants not renewable.
Deadline: October 15.

ADDRESS INQUIRIES TO:
Ellen H. Ruffin, Curator
de Grummond Children's Literature Collection
(See address above.)

UNIVERSITY OF VIRGINIA PRESS [658]
210 Sprigg Lane
Charlottesville, VA 22903
(434) 924-3361
Fax: (434) 982-2655
E-mail: arh2h@virginia.edu
Web Site: www.upress.virginia.edu

FOUNDED: 1963

AREAS OF INTEREST:
18th century studies.

NAME(S) OF PROGRAMS:
- **Walker Cowen Memorial Prize**

TYPE:
Awards/prizes.

YEAR PROGRAM STARTED: 1989

LEGAL BASIS:
University.

ELIGIBILITY:
Submissions should be a work in 18th century studies in history, literature, philosophy or the arts. The work may cover Europe, the Americas, or the Atlantic world. Translation candidates must submit any unpublished, book-length manuscript in English.

FINANCIAL DATA:
Amount of support per award: $5,000 and an advance publishing contract.

NO. MOST RECENT APPLICANTS: Approximately 10.

NO. AWARDS: 1 annually.

APPLICATION INFO:
Applicant must include three copies of their curriculum vitae and a description (one to two typescript pages) of the manuscript's content, scope, and intended readership. For new manuscripts, two identical copies of the manuscript must be submitted simultaneously. For translation candidates, one copy of the work in the original language must be submitted together with copies of any published reviews. If possible, submit an introduction or other sample material from the book translated into English.
Deadline: November 1 (postmark). Award announcement in the following March.

ADDRESS INQUIRIES TO:
Angie Hogan, Associate Editor
(See address above.)

THE WORD WORKS, INC. [659]
P.O. Box 42164
Washington, DC 20015
E-mail: editor@wordworksbooks.org
Web Site: www.wordworksbooks.org

FOUNDED: 1974

AREAS OF INTEREST:
Poetry and literature.

NAME(S) OF PROGRAMS:
- **The Washington Prize**

TYPE:
Awards/prizes.

YEAR PROGRAM STARTED: 1981

PURPOSE:
To encourage and promote contemporary American poetry.

LEGAL BASIS:
Nonprofit corporation.

ELIGIBILITY:
The Washington Prize is awarded for a volume of original poetry in English by a living American or Canadian writer.

GEOG. RESTRICTIONS: Canada and United States.

FINANCIAL DATA:
Amount of support per award: $1,500 plus book publication.

NO. AWARDS: 1 each year.

APPLICATION INFO:
Application must be submitted online. There is an entry fee of $25 (U.S.) drawn on a U.S. bank only, payable to The Word Works.
Deadline: January 15 to March 15. Decision by August.

IRS I.D.: 52-1042022

BOARD OF DIRECTORS:
Karren L. Alenier, Chairperson of the Board
Nancy White, President
J.H. Beall
Nina Budabin-McQuown
Andrea Carter-Brown

ADDRESS INQUIRIES TO:
Andrea Carter-Brown
Washington Prize Series Editor
P.O. Box 42164
Washington, DC 20015

*PLEASE NOTE:
The Washington Prize is for support of poets. It is not an academic scholarship for higher education.

THE WORD WORKS, INC. [660]
P.O. Box 42164
Washington, DC 20015
E-mail: editor@wordworksbooks.org
Web Site: www.wordworksbooks.org

FOUNDED: 1974

AREAS OF INTEREST:
Poetry.

NAME(S) OF PROGRAMS:
- **Tenth Gate Prize**

TYPE:
Awards/prizes. Award is given to a living poet with at least two full-length collections of poetry published by literary presses.

PURPOSE:
To encourage and promote contemporary American poetry.

ELIGIBILITY:
Submitted work must be a volume of original poetry written in English. Applicant must have had at least two full-length collections of poetry published by literary presses.

FINANCIAL DATA:
Amount of support per award: $1,000 plus standard publishing contract.

APPLICATION INFO:
Application must be made online. There is an entry fee of $25 (U.S.). Detailed information can be found on the web site.
Deadline: June 1 to July 15. Decision by October 1.

ADDRESS INQUIRIES TO:
Nancy White, Series Director
Tenth Gate Prize
Adirondack Community College
640 Bay Road
Queensbury, NY 12804

*PLEASE NOTE:
Include a self-addressed, stamped envelope with all regular mail inquiries.

Museums and libraries

ALABAMA LIBRARY ASSOCIATION SCHOLARSHIP FUND, INC. [661]
Alabama Library Association
6030 Monticello Drive
Montgomery, AL 36117
(334) 414-0113
E-mail: allaadmin@allanet.org
Web Site: www.allanet.org

FOUNDED: 1904

AREAS OF INTEREST:
Library science.

NAME(S) OF PROGRAMS:
- **Scholarships in Library Science**

TYPE:
Scholarships. Scholarships for graduate study in library science/library media.

YEAR PROGRAM STARTED: 1945

PURPOSE:
To provide professional training for librarians and prospective librarians.

LEGAL BASIS:
Nonprofit corporation.

ELIGIBILITY:
Residents of Alabama who have been accepted by an accredited institution offering

a graduate course in library science are eligible to apply. Recipients will be selected based on academic achievement, potential service to the library profession and financial need.

GEOG. RESTRICTIONS: Alabama.

FINANCIAL DATA:
Amount of support per award: ALLA Centennial Memorial Scholarship: Minimum $500, with additional funds up to $1,000 based on contributions to the scholarship fund each year; ALLA Memorial Scholarship: Up to $1,000 per award.
Total amount of support: Up to $2,500.

NO. AWARDS: 2.

APPLICATION INFO:
Applicant must submit:
(1) an application form;
(2) a certified final transcript from the institution that awarded applicant's undergraduate degree;
(3) a certified transcript of any graduate work undertaken;
(4) a certified transcript of test scores on the GRE or MAT;
(5) proof of acceptance at an ALA-accredited library school and;
(6) recommendation forms from three references.
Duration: One academic year.
Deadline: June 1.

PUBLICATIONS:
Brochure; application guidelines.

AMERICAN ASSOCIATION OF LAW LIBRARIES [662]
105 West Adams Street
Suite 3300
Chicago, IL 60603
(312) 939-4764
Fax: (312) 431-1097
E-mail: membership@aall.org
Web Site: www.aallnet.org

FOUNDED: 1906

AREAS OF INTEREST:
Librarianship, law librarianship and law.

NAME(S) OF PROGRAMS:
● **Library Degree for Law School Graduates**
● **Library Degree for Non-Law School Graduates**
● **Library School Graduates Attending Law School**
● **Library School Graduates Seeking a Non-Law Degree**

TYPE:
Scholarships. For study of law or librarianship, with support intended for prospective law librarians.

YEAR PROGRAM STARTED: 1966

PURPOSE:
To assist qualified persons who are interested in becoming professional law librarians.

LEGAL BASIS:
Not-for-profit corporation.

ELIGIBILITY:
Preference is given to AALL members, but scholarships are not restricted to members. Evidence of financial need must be submitted.

GEOG. RESTRICTIONS: United States.

FINANCIAL DATA:
Amount of support per award: $1,000 to $3,000. Amounts vary according to available funds and may be limited at the discretion of the Scholarships Committee.
Total amount of support: Varies.

NO. MOST RECENT APPLICANTS: 30.

NO. AWARDS: Varies.

APPLICATION INFO:
Application information is available on the web site.
Duration: Varies by scholarship.
Deadline: April 1.

ADDRESS INQUIRIES TO:
Kylie Weller
Membership Services Manager
(See address above.)

AMERICAN ASSOCIATION OF LAW LIBRARIES [663]
105 West Adams Street
Suite 3300
Chicago, IL 60603
(312) 939-4764
Fax: (312) 431-1097
E-mail: membership@aall.org
Web Site: www.aallnet.org

FOUNDED: 1906

AREAS OF INTEREST:
Librarianship, law librarianship and minorities.

NAME(S) OF PROGRAMS:
● **George A. Strait Minority Stipend Scholarship Endowment**

TYPE:
Scholarships. Stipend for graduate study leading to a degree at an accredited school of library or information science or an accredited law school. Preference will be given to individuals with previous service to, or interest in, law librarianship.

YEAR PROGRAM STARTED: 1966

PURPOSE:
To assist qualified persons who are interested in becoming professional law librarians.

LEGAL BASIS:
Not-for-profit corporation.

ELIGIBILITY:
Application is limited to minority group members defined by current guidelines of the U.S. government. Applicant must be a degree candidate in an ALA-accredited library school or ABA-accredited law school and intend to have a career in law librarianship.

GEOG. RESTRICTIONS: United States.

FINANCIAL DATA:
Amount of support per award: Up to $2,500.
Total amount of support: Varies.

NO. MOST RECENT APPLICANTS: 11.

NO. AWARDS: Varies.

APPLICATION INFO:
Application packet must include:
(1) an official transcript or unofficial copy of transcript from the school where applicant completed most recent degree;
(2) a letter from the Admissions Officer of the library school, stating the program for which the applicant has been accepted and the date the courses begin, or, if applicant has already begun pursuing the degree, a transcript showing they are a degree

candidate in good standing, or, if the applicant is attending law school, a transcript showing they are a degree candidate in good standing;
(3) two letters of recommendation from persons who have knowledge of the applicant's abilities and who can evaluate and comment upon law library employment experience;
(4) a personal statement discussing the applicant's interest in law librarianship, reason for applying for this scholarship, career goals as a law librarian, and statement of financial need and;
(5) a resume.
Duration: One year.
Deadline: April 1.

ADDRESS INQUIRIES TO:
Kylie Weller
Membership Services Manager
(See address above.)

AMERICAN ASSOCIATION OF SCHOOL LIBRARIANS [664]
225 North Michigan Avenue
Suite 1300
Chicago, IL 60601
(800) 545-2433 ext. 4385
Fax: (312) 280-5276
E-mail: aasl@ala.org
Web Site: www.ala.org/aasl

FOUNDED: 1951

AREAS OF INTEREST:
Libraries and librarianship.

NAME(S) OF PROGRAMS:
● **AASL Collaborative School Library Award**
● **AASL Frances Henne Award**
● **AASL Innovative Reading Grant**
● **AASL National School Library of the Year Award**
● **ABC-CLIO Leadership Grant**

TYPE:
Awards/prizes; Development grants; Project/program grants.

PURPOSE:
To honor distinguished service and foster professional growth in the school library profession.

ELIGIBILITY:
Requirements vary by award or grant.

FINANCIAL DATA:
Amount of support per award: $1,250 to $10,000.
Total amount of support: Varies.

NO. MOST RECENT APPLICANTS: 50.

NO. AWARDS: Varies.

APPLICATION INFO:
Application form and information are available from the Association.
Deadline: AASL National School Library of the Year Award: January 1; AASL Collaborative School Library Award, AASL Frances Henne Award, AASL Innovative Reading Grant and ABC-CLIO Leadership Grant: February 1.

EXECUTIVE DIRECTOR:
Sylvia Norton

ADDRESS INQUIRIES TO:
Allison Cline, Deputy Executive Director
(See e-mail address above.)

AMERICAN ASSOCIATION OF SCHOOL LIBRARIANS [665]

225 North Michigan Avenue
Suite 1300
Chicago, IL 60601
(800) 545-2433 ext. 4385
Fax: (312) 280-5276
E-mail: aasl@ala.org
Web Site: www.ala.org/aasl

FOUNDED: 1951

AREAS OF INTEREST:
Libraries.

NAME(S) OF PROGRAMS:
● **Distinguished Service Award**

TYPE:
Awards/prizes. Rosen provides funding for this award.

YEAR PROGRAM STARTED: 1978

PURPOSE:
To honor distinguished service and foster professional growth in the school library field.

ELIGIBILITY:
Nominator and nominee must be members of AASL.

FINANCIAL DATA:
Amount of support per award: $3,000 and a citation.
Total amount of support: $3,000.

NO. AWARDS: 1.

APPLICATION INFO:
Application form and information are available from the Association.
Deadline: February 1.

ADDRESS INQUIRIES TO:
Allison Cline, Deputy Executive Director
(See e-mail address above.)

AMERICAN LIBRARY ASSOCIATION (ALA) [666]

225 North Michigan Avenue
Suite 1300
Chicago, IL 60601
(312) 280-3247
(800) 545-2433 ext. 3247
E-mail: awards@ala.org
Web Site: www.ala.org

FOUNDED: 1876

AREAS OF INTEREST:
Librarianship.

NAME(S) OF PROGRAMS:
● **ALA Awards**

TYPE:
Awards/prizes; Conferences/seminars; Development grants; Fellowships; Research grants; Scholarships; Seed money grants; Travel grants. Cash and noncash awards for achievement/distinguished service, authors/illustrators/publishers, exhibits, funding, intellectual freedom, literacy, professional development, public relations, publications/articles and special services, as well as scholarships, fellowships and research grants sponsored by ALA and its units.

PURPOSE:
To honor distinguished service and foster professional growth.

FINANCIAL DATA:
Amount of support per award: Awards: $250 to $10,000; Research Grants and Fellowships: $500 to $10,000.

Total amount of support: Varies.

NO. AWARDS: Varies.

REPRESENTATIVE AWARDS:
Academic or Research Librarian of the Year Award for outstanding contribution to academic and research librarianship and library development, $3,000 (donated by Baker & Taylor); The H.W. Wilson Library Staff Development Grant to library organization for a program to further its goals and objectives, $3,500 (donated by The H.W. Wilson Company); Frances Henne Research Grant to provide seed money to an individual, institution or group for a project to encourage research on library service to young adults, $500 minimum (donated by Voice of Youth Advocates); David H. Clift Scholarship to worthy U.S. or Canadian citizen to begin an M.L.S. degree in an ALA-accredited program, $3,000 (donated by scholarship endowment interest, individual contributions).

APPLICATION INFO:
Application information is available on the web site.
Duration: Varies.
Deadline: Varies.

ADDRESS INQUIRIES TO:
Cheryl Malden, Program Officer
(See address above.)

ASSOCIATION FOR LIBRARY AND INFORMATION SCIENCE EDUCATION (ALISE) [667]

4 Lan Drive, Suite 310
Westford, MA 01886
(978) 674-6190
Fax: (978) 250-1117
E-mail: office@alise.org
Web Site: www.alise.org

FOUNDED: 1915

AREAS OF INTEREST:
Library and information science education.

NAME(S) OF PROGRAMS:
● **ALISE Research Awards**

TYPE:
Awards/prizes; Research grants. Award for an outstanding research proposal in the field of librarianship and information science.

YEAR PROGRAM STARTED: 1976

PURPOSE:
To provide support for research which will help to promote excellence in education for librarianship and information science.

LEGAL BASIS:
Nonprofit 501(c)(3) corporation.

ELIGIBILITY:
Determined on the basis of the project's appropriateness to the goals of the ALISE, evidence of an established methodology and a viable research design, likelihood of completion in 12 to 18 months and on the qualifications of the researcher, who should be an ALISE member. Evidence that other funds are not available for the project should be presented.

The award cannot be used to support a doctoral dissertation. At least one applicant in a group submitting a proposal must be a personal member of the Association as of the deadline date. Staff training, general operating or overhead expenses, and other indirect costs are not funded.

Recipients of the award must present a progress report at the ALISE Annual Conference, submit written quarterly reports to the Executive Director of ALISE, who will pay the grant in periodic installments as the research progresses, submit the results of the funded study to the Association's *Journal of Education for Library and Information Science* (JELIS) for possible publication prior to submission to other publications, that is, the Journal will have first option on publication, acknowledge the support of ALISE in any publicity or presentation based on the funded study and inform the Executive Director if they receive research funding in addition to that provided by ALISE.

FINANCIAL DATA:
Staff training, general operating or overhead expenses, and other indirect costs are not funded.
Amount of support per award: Up to $5,000.
Total amount of support: $5,000 annually.

NO. AWARDS: 1 or more.

REPRESENTATIVE AWARDS:
Lynn Bowker, University of Ottawa, for "Against the Clock: Developing and Testing a Framework for Speed Training in LIS Education."

APPLICATION INFO:
Proposals should be succinct and precise. No more than 20 double-spaced, typed pages. If necessary, supporting information may be included in an appendix. Proposals must include the following information to be considered in the competition:
(1) abstract of the project in no greater than 200 words;
(2) problem statement and literature review including justification and need for the research;
(3) project objectives;
(4) project description;
(5) research design, methodology and analysis techniques;
(6) detailed budget (including institutional or departmental contributions, if any);
(7) expected benefits and impact from the research and;
(8) vita(e) of project investigator(s).
Duration: One year.
Deadline: March 15.

PUBLICATIONS:
Application guidelines.

IRS I.D.: 51-0193882

STAFF:
Cambria Happ, MPA, CAE, Executive Director

BOARD OF DIRECTORS AND OFFICERS:
Stephen Bajjaly, President
Heather Moulaison Sandy, Secretary/Treasurer
Rong Tang, Director for External Relations
Denice Adkins, Director of Membership
Lilia Pavlovsky, Director for Special Interest Groups

ADDRESS INQUIRIES TO:
ALISE Awards
(See address above.)

*SPECIAL STIPULATIONS:
The Research Grant award cannot be used to support a doctoral dissertation.

ASSOCIATION FOR LIBRARY AND INFORMATION SCIENCE EDUCATION (ALISE) [668]

4 Lan Drive, Suite 310
Westford, MA 01886
(978) 674-6190
Fax: (978) 250-1117
E-mail: office@alise.org
Web Site: www.alise.org

FOUNDED: 1915

AREAS OF INTEREST:
Library and information science education.

NAME(S) OF PROGRAMS:
- **ALISE/ProQuest Methodology Paper Competition**
- **The Eugene Garfield/ALISE Doctoral Dissertation Competition**
- **Bohdan S. Wynar Research Paper Competition**

TYPE:
Awards/prizes. Awards for an outstanding unpublished research paper, methodology paper and for each of two outstanding doctoral dissertations, respectively.

YEAR PROGRAM STARTED: 1977

PURPOSE:
To encourage research in the field of library and information science education and related areas.

LEGAL BASIS:
Nonprofit 501(c)(3) corporation.

ELIGIBILITY:
ALISE/ProQuest Methodology Paper Competition is open to all types of methodology. Papers must be limited to description and discussion of a research method or a technique associated with a particular research method. Papers must explain the particular method/technique, including methodological implications for library and information science. Examples to illustrate its value can come from LIS-related published studies, proposed studies, and works in progress. Papers that stress findings are not eligible.

The Eugene Garfield/ALISE Doctoral Dissertation Competition is open to doctoral students who have recently graduated in any field of study, or who will have completed their dissertations by the deadline. Dissertations must deal with substantive issues related to library and information science, but applicants may be from within or outside LIS programs.

Bohdan S. Wynar Research Paper Competition is open to research papers concerning any aspect of library and information science. This competition is not limited to research regarding LIS education. Any research methodology is acceptable.

FINANCIAL DATA:
Amount of support per award:
ALISE/ProQuest Methodology Paper and The Eugene Garfield/ALISE Doctoral Dissertation Competitions: $500 each.

NO. AWARDS: ALISE/ProQuest Methodology Paper Competition: 1; The Eugene Garfield/ALISE Doctoral Dissertation and Bohdan S. Wynar Research Paper Competitions: Up to 2 each.

APPLICATION INFO:
Application information is available on the web site.
Deadline: March 15.

IRS I.D.: 51-0193882

STAFF:
Cambria Happ, MPA, CAE, Executive Director

BOARD OF DIRECTORS AND OFFICERS:
Stephen Bajjaly, President
Heather Moulaison Sandy, Secretary/Treasurer
Rong Tang, Director for External Relations
Denice Adkins, Director for Membership Services
Lilia Pavlovsky, Director for Special Interest Groups

ADDRESS INQUIRIES TO:
ALISE Awards
(See address above.)

BETA PHI MU [669]

P.O. Box 42139
Philadelphia, PA 19101
(267) 361-5018
E-mail: headquarters@betaphimu.org
Web Site: www.betaphimu.org

FOUNDED: 1948

AREAS OF INTEREST:
Library and information studies.

NAME(S) OF PROGRAMS:
- **Eugene Garfield Doctoral Dissertation Fellowship**
- **Harold Lancour Foreign Research Fellowship**
- **Sarah Rebecca Reed Scholarship**
- **Frank B. Sessa Scholarship for Continuing Professional Education of Beta Phi Mu Members**
- **Blanche E. Woolls Scholarship for School Library Media Service**

TYPE:
Fellowships; Scholarships. Eugene Garfield Doctoral Dissertation Fellowship is funded through the generosity of Eugene Garfield, and provides fellowships for up to six students per year. They are awarded to foster high-quality research in the field and to expedite the movement of new Doctorates into teaching positions.

The Harold Lancour Fellowship is given for foreign study.

The Sarah Rebecca Reed Scholarship is given to a beginning student at the Master's level accepted in an American Library Association-accredited program.

The Frank B. Sessa Scholarship is given for Continuing Education for a Beta Phi Mu member.

The Blanche Woolls Scholarship is given to a beginning student at the Master's level accepted in an American Library Association-Accredited Program majoring in School Media Services.

PURPOSE:
To assist qualified persons who are interested in completing a course of advanced study in library and information studies.

LEGAL BASIS:
Nonprofit organization.

FINANCIAL DATA:
Amount of support per award: Garfield Doctoral Dissertation Fellowship: $3,000; Lancour Fellowship: $1,750; Reed and Woolls Scholarships: $2,250 each; Sessa Scholarship: $150.

Total amount of support: Varies.

NO. AWARDS: Garfield Doctoral Dissertation Fellowship: 6; Lancour Fellowship, Reed Scholarship and Woolls Scholarship: 1 per award; Sessa Scholarship: 10.

APPLICATION INFO:
Forms are available on the Society's web site.
Duration: One-time award. Nonrenewable.
Deadline: March 15.

PUBLICATIONS:
The Pipeline, online newsletter.

STAFF:
Alison M. Lewis, Ph.D., Executive Director

ADDRESS INQUIRIES TO:
Alison M. Lewis, Ph.D., Executive Director
(See address above.)

GLADYS BROOKS FOUNDATION

1055 Franklin Avenue
Suite 208
Garden City, NY 11530-2903
(516) 746-6103
Fax: (516) 877-1758
E-mail: kathy@gladysbrooksfoundation.org
Web Site: www.gladysbrooksfoundation.org

TYPE:
Capital grants; Challenge/matching grants; Demonstration grants; Development grants; Endowments; Matching gifts; Project/program grants; Scholarships. Grants to private, not-for-profit publicly supported libraries, educational institutions, hospitals and clinics in the eastern U.S.

See entry 1084 for full listing.

CALIFORNIA LIBRARY ASSOCIATION [670]

1055 East Colorado Boulevard
Suite 500
Pasadena, CA 91106
(626) 204-4071
E-mail: info@cla-net.org
Web Site: www.cla-net.org

FOUNDED: 1896

AREAS OF INTEREST:
Librarianship.

NAME(S) OF PROGRAMS:
- **Begun Scholarship**
- **CLA Scholarship for Minority Students in Memory of Edna Yelland**

TYPE:
Scholarships. Support for minority library school students. Support for graduate students in reference/information service librarianship.

YEAR PROGRAM STARTED: 1973

PURPOSE:
To help support the educational goals of minority students in the library service field.

LEGAL BASIS:
Nonprofit.

ELIGIBILITY:
Applicant must be accepted by a graduate library school in California, accredited by the American Library Association, be of ethnic origin and show financial need. California residents and U.S. citizens or permanent U.S. residents may apply.

GEOG. RESTRICTIONS: California.

FINANCIAL DATA:
Amount of support per award: Generally $2,500 per Edna Yelland Scholarship; $3,000 for Begun Scholarship.
Total amount of support: $10,500.

NO. MOST RECENT APPLICANTS: 25.

NO. AWARDS: 4.

APPLICATION INFO:
Application information can be found on the Association's web site.
Duration: One-time award.
Deadline: Mid-March.

CAMBRIDGE UNIVERSITY LIBRARY   [671]
West Road
Cambridge CB3 9DR England
(44) 01223 333000
Fax: (44) 01223 333160
E-mail: library@lib.cam.ac.uk
Web Site: www.lib.cam.ac.uk/munby

FOUNDED: 1400

AREAS OF INTEREST:
Bibliographic research.

NAME(S) OF PROGRAMS:
● **The Munby Fellowship in Bibliography**

TYPE:
Fellowships. Graduate fellowships for bibliographical research based on the collections of Cambridge libraries.

YEAR PROGRAM STARTED: 1977

LEGAL BASIS:
University.

ELIGIBILITY:
Open to university graduates in any discipline, with preference given to graduates of postdoctoral or equivalent level, of any nationality or age. Research must be bibliographical.

FINANCIAL DATA:
Amount of support per award: GBP 35,211 for the year 2019-20.

NO. MOST RECENT APPLICANTS: 50.

NO. AWARDS: 1.

APPLICATION INFO:
Applications are accepted through the Cambridge University Job Opportunities link. Applicant must log on to create an online application form. Statement outlining research proposal (maximum two pages), cover letter, and curriculum vitae must be uploaded with the application form.
Duration: 10 months, October 1 to July 31.
Deadline: Advertised in autumn for post to begin October the following year. Election normally made by early January.

PUBLICATIONS:
Application guidelines.

ADDRESS INQUIRIES TO:
Library Syndicate
(See address above.)

CONNECTICUT LIBRARY ASSOCIATION   [672]
234 Court Street
Middletown, CT 06457
(860) 346-2444
Fax: (860) 344-9199
E-mail: cla@ctlibrarians.org
Web Site: www.ctlibraryassociation.org

AREAS OF INTEREST:
Library conferences, workshops and professional level opportunities.

NAME(S) OF PROGRAMS:
● **Proficiency Enhancement Grants (PEG)**

TYPE:
Grants-in-aid. Grants for personnel at all levels of library work.

YEAR PROGRAM STARTED: 1976

PURPOSE:
To support the educational goals of library science students in Connecticut.

LEGAL BASIS:
Nonprofit organization.

ELIGIBILITY:
Grants are made to CLA members only.

GEOG. RESTRICTIONS: Connecticut.

FINANCIAL DATA:
Amount of support per award: Up to $400.
Total amount of support: Up to $2,500 annually.

NO. AWARDS: Up to 4 or 5 grants per year.

APPLICATION INFO:
Application form is available online. Apply to the Chairperson, Program for Educational Grants, at the address above.
Duration: One year. Not renewable.
Deadline: Proposals are reviewed on an ongoing basis.

ADDRESS INQUIRIES TO:
Peter F. Ciparelli, PEG Chairman
Killingly Public Library
25 Westcott Road
Danielson, CT 06239-2928
E-mail: pciparelli@biblio.org
Tel: (860) 779-5383

*PLEASE NOTE:
Only for continuing education, workshops and seminars. Any other applications will be considered at the discretion of the committee.

COOPERSTOWN GRADUATE PROGRAM   [673]
SUNY College at Oneonta
Cooperstown Graduate Program in Museum Studies
5838 State Route 80
Cooperstown, NY 13326-2502
(607) 547-2586
Fax: (607) 547-8926
E-mail: melanie.bruce@oneonta.edu
gretchen.sorin@oneonta.edu
Web Site: www.oneonta.edu/academics/cgp

FOUNDED: 1964

AREAS OF INTEREST:
History museum studies and science museum studies.

TYPE:
Assistantships; Fellowships; Scholarships. Awards for museum studies for Cooperstown Graduate Program students only.

YEAR PROGRAM STARTED: 1964

PURPOSE:
To provide professionally trained individuals for the museum field.

ELIGIBILITY:
Applicants must have a strong academic record, an interest in public service, excellent

writing skills and a demonstrated commitment to the field through museum work in either staff or volunteer capacity.

FINANCIAL DATA:
Amount of support per award: $4,000 to $12,000 per year.
Total amount of support: $175,000.

CO-OP FUNDING PROGRAMS: Co-sponsored with SUNY College at Oneonta.

NO. MOST RECENT APPLICANTS: Approximately 60.

NO. AWARDS: Approximately 50 awards for students.

APPLICATION INFO:
Applications and further information may be obtained from the web site. Applications are to be submitted online.
Duration: Tenable in Cooperstown, NY, for 24 months.
Deadline: May 1 for fellowship application.

PUBLICATIONS:
Viewbook.

ADDRESS INQUIRIES TO:
Melanie Bruce
Outreach and Engagement Coordinator
P.O. Box 4
Cooperstown, NY 13326-0004

THE FOUNDATION FOR ADVANCEMENT IN CONSERVATION (FAIC)   [674]
727 15th Street, N.W.
Suite 500
Washington, DC 20005
(202) 452-9545
Fax: (202) 452-9328
E-mail: cap@culturalheritage.org
Web Site: www.culturalheritage.org/cap

FOUNDED: 1973

AREAS OF INTEREST:
Conservation assessment of museum collections.

CONSULTING OR VOLUNTEER SERVICES:
Professional consulting services.

NAME(S) OF PROGRAMS:
● **Collections Assessment for Preservation (CAP)**

TYPE:
Technical assistance. Provides funds for an independent, professional conservation assessment of a museum's collections and building environment. The assessor's resulting report will identify conservation priorities to assist the museum in developing a long-term plan for collections care and management.

YEAR PROGRAM STARTED: 2017

PURPOSE:
To make collections care and conservation a fundamental priority of museums and historical societies.

LEGAL BASIS:
Private and nonprofit.

ELIGIBILITY:
Institutions including museums, zoos, aquariums, botanical gardens and arboreta are eligible for assistance. CAP will also support the on-site participation of an architectural assessor. Zoos and aquariums that do not have an assessment of the animals' physical conditions and habitats can use the program for a general assessment of those collections.

GEOG. RESTRICTIONS: United States.

FINANCIAL DATA:
Institutions will normally pay travel costs and a portion of assessors fees.

Amount of support per award: $3,500 to $3,900.

Total amount of support: Varies.

CO-OP FUNDING PROGRAMS: Program funded through Institute of Museum and Library Services.

NO. MOST RECENT APPLICANTS: 100.

NO. AWARDS: 76.

APPLICATION INFO:
Notification of the release of CAP application online will be publicized on the FAIC web site by November 1.

Duration: One year.

Deadline: February 1.

PUBLICATIONS:
CAP brochure.

STAFF:
Tiffani Emig, Program Director and Administrative Manager

ADDRESS INQUIRIES TO:
Collections Assessment for Preservation
(See address above.)

GEORGIA LIBRARY ASSOCIATION [675]

P.O. Box 30324
Savannah, GA 31410
(912) 376-9155
E-mail: membership.gla@gmail.com
Web Site: gla.georgialibraries.
org/resources/scholarships

FOUNDED: 1897

AREAS OF INTEREST:
Library professional development.

NAME(S) OF PROGRAMS:
● **Beard Scholarship**
● **Hubbard Scholarship**

TYPE:
Scholarships. Awards for graduate study of library science.

PURPOSE:
To recruit excellent librarians for Georgia.

LEGAL BASIS:
Professional association.

ELIGIBILITY:
Applicants must be accepted for admission to a Master's program at an ALA-accredited library school and must indicate intention to complete the Master's program within three years. Recipient must work in a library in Georgia for at least one year after graduation from ALA-accredited library school. Beard Scholarship is for candidates who demonstrate leadership potential.

GEOG. RESTRICTIONS: Georgia.

FINANCIAL DATA:
Amount of support per award: Beard Scholarship: $1,500; Hubbard Scholarship: $3,000.

Total amount of support: $4,500 annually.

NO. AWARDS: 1 each annually.

APPLICATION INFO:
Applicant must submit to the Chair the following:
(1) one official application form (applicant may be considered for both scholarships via one form and other accompanying

documentation; do not submit duplicate materials);
(2) proof of admission to an American Library Association-accredited Master's program/library school, i.e., a letter from the dean of the school/program certifying acceptance (photocopy is acceptable);
(3) three letters of reference sent directly from the reference to the Committee Chair and;
(4) official transcripts of all academic work sent directly to the Chair from each college or university attended.

Duration: Remainder of MLIS Program.

Deadline: May 15.

ADDRESS INQUIRIES TO:
GLA Scholarship Fund
Georgia Library Association
(See address above.)

*SPECIAL STIPULATIONS:
The scholarship winners must agree to work in Georgia for one year following receipt of the Master's degree or agree to pay back a prorated amount of the award plus interest. Repayment must be made within two years.

HARTFORD PUBLIC LIBRARY [676]

500 Main Street
Hartford, CT 06103-3075
(860) 695-6300
Fax: (860) 722-6900
E-mail: mjarry@hplct.org
Web Site: www.hplct.org

FOUNDED: 1774

AREAS OF INTEREST:
Children's librarianship.

NAME(S) OF PROGRAMS:
● **The Caroline M. Hewins Scholarship**

TYPE:
Scholarships. Awarded to candidates for M.L.S. who will work with children.

YEAR PROGRAM STARTED: 1926

PURPOSE:
To assist in graduate Library Science study, leading to a career in library service with children.

ELIGIBILITY:
Students who plan to specialize in library work with children, who have received or are about to receive a four-year undergraduate degree and who have been admitted to or are attending an ALA-accredited library school are eligible. Preference is given to applicants who plan to pursue a career in public library service.

FINANCIAL DATA:
Amount of support per award: Up to $4,000.

Total amount of support: Up to $4,000 annually.

NO. MOST RECENT APPLICANTS: 25.

NO. AWARDS: 1 annually.

APPLICATION INFO:
The application form can be downloaded from the Library's web site.

Deadline: Completed applications must be submitted by between July 1 and September 1.

ADDRESS INQUIRIES TO:
Marie Jarry, Director of Public Services
(See address above.)

INDIANA LIBRARY FEDERATION [677]

941 East 86th Street
Suite 260
Indianapolis, IN 46240
(317) 257-2040
Fax: (317) 257-1389
E-mail: askus@ilfonline.org
Web Site: www.ilfonline.org

FOUNDED: 1891

AREAS OF INTEREST:
Librarian education and training.

NAME(S) OF PROGRAMS:
● **The Esther Schlundt Fund**
● **The Sue Marsh Weller Fund**

TYPE:
Scholarships. Awards for graduate study of library science at ALA-accredited schools.

PURPOSE:
To aid students in financial need who have strong undergraduate records and who show unusual ability in the library field either public or academic.

LEGAL BASIS:
Professional association.

ELIGIBILITY:
Applicants must be legal residents of Indiana who intend to work in an Indiana library for at least one year after completing library education and must be enrolled in an ALA-accredited graduate program of library science.

GEOG. RESTRICTIONS: Indiana.

FINANCIAL DATA:
Amount of support per award: Up to $1,000.

Total amount of support: Varies.

NO. MOST RECENT APPLICANTS: 8 for the year 2018.

NO. AWARDS: 12 for the year 2018.

APPLICATION INFO:
Application must be made in writing. Further information may be requested from the Federation.

Deadline: June 30.

ADDRESS INQUIRIES TO:
Lucinda Nord, Executive Director
(See address above.)

INSTITUTE OF MUSEUM AND LIBRARY SERVICES [678]

955 L'Enfant Plaza North, S.W.
Suite 4000
Washington, DC 20024
(202) 653-4657
Fax: (202) 653-4600
TTY: (202) 606-8636
E-mail: imlsinfo@imls.gov
Web Site: www.imls.gov

FOUNDED: 1996

AREAS OF INTEREST:
Museums in all disciplines including art, history, science, as well as aquariums and zoological parks, botanical gardens, arboretums, planetariums, nature centers, natural history and children's museums.

NAME(S) OF PROGRAMS:
● **Museum Assessment Program**
● **Museum Grants for African American History and Culture**
● **Museums for America**
● **National Leadership Grants for Museums**

- **National Medal for Museum and Library Service**
- **Native American/Native Hawaiian Museum Services Program**
- **Sparks! Ignition Grants for Museums**

TYPE:
Awards/prizes; Challenge/matching grants; Conferences/seminars; Demonstration grants; Development grants; Fellowships; Formula grants; Internships; Project/program grants; Research grants; Scholarships; Seed money grants; Technical assistance; Training grants; Research contracts. Museum Assessment Program (MAP) grants help strengthen museum operations, plan for the future and meet national standards through self-study and a site visit from a peer reviewer.

Museum Grants for African American History and Culture strengthen African American museums by improving care of collections, developing professional management or providing internships and fellowship opportunities.

Museums for America grants support activities that strengthen museums as active resources for lifelong learning, vital components of livable communities and good stewards of the nation's collections.

National Leadership Grants for Museums support projects that address challenges or needs of the museum field, have broad impact and demonstrate innovation and collaboration.

National Medal for Museum and Library Service is the nation's highest honor for libraries and museums and is awarded by IMLS to outstanding institutions that make exceptional contributions to their communities.

Native American/Native Hawaiian Museum Services Program grants enhance museum services to sustain heritage, culture and knowledge.

Sparks! Ignition Grants for Museums provide an opportunity to expand and test the boundaries of museum services and practices.

YEAR PROGRAM STARTED: 1977

PURPOSE:
To foster leadership, innovation and lifetime learning by supporting museums and libraries.

LEGAL BASIS:
Federal independent agency within the Executive Branch.

ELIGIBILITY:
All types of museums, large and small, are eligible for funding. An eligible museum must be a public or private nonprofit institution that exists on a permanent basis for educational or aesthetic purposes.

Funds cannot be used for construction, renovation of facilities, endowment or acquisition of objects. Contact IMLS for program-specific eligibility.

GEOG. RESTRICTIONS: United States, American Samoa, Guam, the Marshall Islands, Micronesia, Northern Mariana Islands, Palau, Puerto Rico and the Virgin Islands.

FINANCIAL DATA:
Amount of support per award: Varies.
Total amount of support: Varies.

CO-OP FUNDING PROGRAMS: The Museum Assessment Program is funded by the Institute of Museum and Library Services and administered by the American Alliance for Museums.

NO. MOST RECENT APPLICANTS: Varies.

NO. AWARDS: Varies.

APPLICATION INFO:
Grant program guidelines and application instructions are available at IMLS web site.
Deadline: Varies.

PUBLICATIONS:
Annual report.

INSTITUTE OF MUSEUM AND LIBRARY SERVICES   [679]
955 L'Enfant Plaza North, S.W.
Suite 4000
Washington, DC 20024
(202) 653-4657
(202) 653-4700
Fax: (202) 653-4600
E-mail: imlsinfo@imls.gov
Web Site: www.imls.gov

FOUNDED: 1996

AREAS OF INTEREST:
Libraries, including public libraries, school libraries, state libraries, college and university libraries, digital libraries, research libraries and archives that are not an integral part of an institution of higher education and that make publicly available library services and materials, and private or special libraries deemed eligible to participate by the state in which the library is located. Organizations, including graduate schools of library and information science, library consortia and library associations. There are special funding categories for state library administrative agencies, tribal libraries and organizations providing library services to Native Hawaiians.

NAME(S) OF PROGRAMS:
- **Laura Bush 21st Century Librarian Program**
- **Grants to State Library Administrative Agencies**
- **National Leadership Grants for Libraries**
- **Native American Library Services: Basic Grants and Enhancement Grants**
- **Native Hawaiian Library Services Grant**
- **Sparks! Ignition Grants for Libraries**

TYPE:
Project/program grants. Laura Bush 21st Century Librarian Program: Grants support professional development, graduate education and continuing education to help libraries and archives develop human capital capacity.

Grants to State Library Administrative Agencies: This is the largest grant program run by IMLS. It provides funds to State Library Administrative Agencies (SLAAs) using a population-based formula.

National Leadership Grants for Libraries: This program supports projects that address challenges faced by the library and archive fields and that have the potential to advance practice in those fields.

Native American Library Services: Basic Grants and Enhancement Grants: Provide funds for core library operations, technical

assistance, and innovative project grants for libraries serving Native Americans and Alaska Native villages.

A Native Hawaiian Library Services Grant is awarded annually to organizations providing library services to Native Hawaiians.

Sparks! Ignition Grants for Libraries provide an opportunity to expand and test the boundaries of library and archive services and practices.

PURPOSE:
To foster leadership, innovation and lifetime learning by supporting museums and libraries.

LEGAL BASIS:
Federal independent agency within the Executive Branch.

ELIGIBILITY:
Restricted funding categories exist for state library administrative agencies and for library services to Native Americans and Native Hawaiians.

Funds cannot be used for construction, renovation of facilities, endowment or acquisition of objects. Contact IMLS for program-specific eligibility.

GEOG. RESTRICTIONS: United States and territories.

FINANCIAL DATA:
Amount of support per award: Varies.
Total amount of support: Varies.

NO. MOST RECENT APPLICANTS: Varies.

NO. AWARDS: Varies.

APPLICATION INFO:
Application information is available online.
Duration: Varies per award.
Deadline: Varies.

MEDICAL LIBRARY ASSOCIATION   [680]
225 West Wacker Drive
Suite 650
Chicago, IL 60606
(312) 419-9094
E-mail: awards@mail.mlahq.org
Web Site: www.mlanet.org

FOUNDED: 1898

AREAS OF INTEREST:
Health sciences librarianship.

NAME(S) OF PROGRAMS:
- **MLA Doctoral Fellowship**
- **MLA Scholarship**

TYPE:
Fellowships; Scholarships. Awarded for study and doctoral work in health sciences librarianship.

YEAR PROGRAM STARTED: 1986

PURPOSE:
To support and encourage individuals who are qualified to make a contribution to librarianship.

LEGAL BASIS:
Nonprofit.

ELIGIBILITY:
Citizens or permanent residents of the U.S. or Canada are eligible to apply.

For the MLA Doctoral Fellowship, applicants must be members of MLA and graduates of an ALA-accredited library school or have equivalent graduate credentials in related information science disciplines (i.e., computer science, biomedical informatics). They must also have been accepted to candidacy in a Ph.D. program in health sciences librarianship with an emphasis on biomedical and health-related information science. A past recipient of the MLA Doctoral Fellowship is ineligible.

Applicants for the MLA Scholarship must be entering an ALA-accredited graduate library school Master's program or, at the time of the granting of the scholarship (February), have completed no more than one-half of the academic requirements of the graduate program. An applicant who is a past recipient of the MLA Scholarship or the MLA Scholarship for Underrepresented Students is ineligible.

GEOG. RESTRICTIONS: United States and Canada.

FINANCIAL DATA:
Amount of support per award: MLA Doctoral Fellowship: $2,000; MLA Scholarship: Up to $5,000.

NO. AWARDS: MLA Doctoral Fellowship: 1 every two years; MLA Scholarships: 1 each per year.

APPLICATION INFO:
MLA Doctoral Fellowship, applicant must submit the following:
(1) application form and pertinent documentation;
(2) signed statement of terms and conditions;
(3) two letters of reference, submitted by the reference directly to MLA, Professional Development Department;
(4) transcripts of graduate work or proof of enrollment in the graduate program and a list of courses completed and;
(5) name, title, address, phone and e-mail of doctoral advisor.

For the MLA Scholarship, applicant must submit an application form, essay, and all related documents plus a single copy of transcripts, two letters of reference and a copy of applicant's library school catalog or web page, which states the number of credits needed for one's degree.

Application and all supporting documents must be received by the deadline to be valid.
Duration: One year.
Deadline: December 1.

STAFF:
Maria Lopez, Grants, Scholarships and Awards Coordinator

ADDRESS INQUIRIES TO:
Coordinator
Grants, Scholarships and Awards
(See address above.)

MEDICAL LIBRARY ASSOCIATION   [681]
225 West Wacker Drive
Suite 650
Chicago, IL 60606
(312) 419-9094
E-mail: awards@mail.mlahq.org
Web Site: www.mlanet.org

FOUNDED: 1898

AREAS OF INTEREST:
Health sciences librarianship.

NAME(S) OF PROGRAMS:
● **Estelle Brodman Award for the Academic Medical Librarian of the Year**
● **Lois Ann Colaianni Award for Excellence and Achievement in Hospital Librarianship**
● **Louise Darling Medal for Distinguished Achievement in Collection Development in the Health Sciences**
● **Janet Doe Lectureship**
● **Ida and George Eliot Prize**
● **Erich Meyerhoff Prize**
● **Marcia C. Noyes Award**
● **Rittenhouse Award**
● **Frank Bradway Rogers Information Advancement Award**

TYPE:
Awards/prizes; Visiting scholars. Awards to honor service to libraries and librarianship.

The Estelle Brodman Award for the Academic Medical Librarian of the Year recognizes an academic medical librarian at the midcareer level who demonstrates significant achievement or the potential for leadership and continuing excellence.

The Lois Ann Colaianni Award for Excellence and Achievement in Hospital Librarianship is given to an MLA-member who has made significant contributions to the profession in the area of hospital librarianship.

The Louise Darling Medal for Distinguished Achievement in Collection Development in the Health Sciences is given annually for outstanding collection development in the health sciences.

The Janet Doe Lectureship chooses an individual to present the lecture at the MLA's annual meeting. Recipients are chosen for their unique perspective on the history or philosophy of medical librarianship.

The Ida and George Eliot Prize is presented annually for a work published in the preceding calendar year that has been judged most effective in furthering medical librarianship.

The Erich Meyerhoff Prize is awarded annually for the best unpublished essay on the history of medicine and allied health sciences written by a health sciences librarian.

The Marcia C. Noyes Award is the highest professional distinction of the MLA. It recognizes a career that has resulted in lasting and outstanding contributions to medical librarianship.

The Rittenhouse Award recognizes an outstanding unpublished paper written by a library student or intern on health sciences librarianship or medical informatics.

Fellows and Honorary Members are selected for outstanding lifetime contributions to the advancement of the purposes of the MLA and are ordinarily chosen from members at or near the close of an active professional career. Honorary members are nonmembers who have made outstanding contributions to the advancement of the purposes of the Association.

The Frank Bradway Rogers Information Advancement Award is presented annually to recognize the application of technology to the delivery of health sciences information to the science of information, or to the facilitation of the delivery of health sciences information.

PURPOSE:
To honor those who have rendered distinguished service to libraries and medical librarianship.

LEGAL BASIS:
Nonprofit organization.

ELIGIBILITY:
Applicants must be health science librarians. Essays submitted must be on the history of medicine or the allied sciences and must be unpublished.

Membership in MLA is required.

FINANCIAL DATA:
Amount of support per award: Brodman Award, Colaianni Award for Excellence and Achievement in Hospital Librarianship, Rittenhouse Award and Rogers Award: $500 each; Darling Medal: $1,000; Janet Doe Lectureship: $500 and up to $1,700 for travel, lodging and registration; Eliot Prize: $200; Meyerhoff Prize: $500.

CO-OP FUNDING PROGRAMS: The Rittenhouse Award established and sponsored by the Rittenhouse Book Distributors, Philadelphia, PA.

NO. AWARDS: 1 per award each year.

APPLICATION INFO:
Nominations forms and guidelines are available on the web site.
Deadline: November 1.

PUBLICATIONS:
Honors and awards program announcement.

STAFF:
Maria Lopez, Grants, Scholarships and Awards Coordinator

ADDRESS INQUIRIES TO:
Coordinator
Grants, Scholarships and Awards
(See address above.)

MEDICAL LIBRARY ASSOCIATION
225 West Wacker Drive
Suite 650
Chicago, IL 60606
(312) 419-9094
E-mail: awards@mail.mlahq.org
Web Site: www.mlanet.org

TYPE:
Fellowships; Travel grants; Work-study programs. Work-study program for medical librarians from countries other than the U.S. or Canada for a time period of at least two weeks.

See entry 884 for full listing.

MEDICAL LIBRARY ASSOCIATION
225 West Wacker Drive
Suite 650
Chicago, IL 60606
(312) 419-9094
E-mail: awards@mail.mlahq.org
Web Site: www.mlanet.org

TYPE:
Awards/prizes; Scholarships. Awarded for study in health sciences librarianship.

See entry 915 for full listing.

THE METROPOLITAN MUSEUM OF ART [682]

1000 Fifth Avenue
New York, NY 10028-0198
(212) 650-2763
E-mail: academic.programs@metmuseum.org
Web Site: www.metmuseum.org

AREAS OF INTEREST:
Art conservation and research.

NAME(S) OF PROGRAMS:
● **Conservation and Scientific Research Fellowships**

TYPE:
Fellowships. Fellowship awards for recent Master's graduates, Ph.D. candidates, postdoctoral scholars, and senior scientists in the fields of conservation and scientific research.

ELIGIBILITY:
Applicants should have reached an advanced level of experience or training.

FINANCIAL DATA:
Amount of support per award: $52,000 stipend for senior fellows for one year, $42,000 for predoctoral fellows, and up to an additional $6,000 for travel and miscellaneous expenses.

APPLICATION INFO:
Applications must be completed through the Museum's online portal. No hard copies will be accepted.
Duration: Normally, a fellow will be in residence at The Metropolitan Museum of Art for a maximum of one year. Shorter terms are available for senior fellows.
Deadline: Application and required letters of recommendation must be received by the first Friday in December. Announcements of awards will be made by late March.

STAFF:
Marcie Karp, Senior Managing Educator, Academic and Professional Programs, Education Department

ADDRESS INQUIRIES TO:
See e-mail address above.

*SPECIAL STIPULATIONS:
All fellowship recipients will be expected to spend the fellowship in residence in the department with which they are affiliated.

MINNESOTA DEPARTMENT OF EDUCATION [683]

State Library Services
1500 Highway 36 West
Roseville, MN 55113-4266
(651) 582-8791
Fax: (651) 582-8752
E-mail: mde.lst@state.mn.us
Web Site: education.mn.gov/MDE/dse/Lib/sls/

FOUNDED: 1899

AREAS OF INTEREST:
Supporting innovation in library services, cooperation among all types of libraries, public library accessibility, library technology and resource sharing.

CONSULTING OR VOLUNTEER SERVICES:
Assistance provided on a range of library issues.

NAME(S) OF PROGRAMS:
● **Library Accessibility and Improvement Grants**
● **Library Services and Technology Act Competitive Grants**

● **Multi-Type Library Cooperation Aid**
● **Regional Library Telecommunications Aid**
● **Regional Public Libraries Systems Support**

TYPE:
Capital grants; Development grants; Formula grants; General operating grants; Project/program grants; Seed money grants; Technical assistance; Training grants. Matching capital grants for library accessibility and improvement. Competitive grants that address activities and priorities in the Minnesota Five-Year Plan.

YEAR PROGRAM STARTED: 1957

PURPOSE:
To extend and improve library and information services for the people of Minnesota through public libraries and cooperation among all types of libraries.

LEGAL BASIS:
Government agency.

ELIGIBILITY:
Specific requirements vary by program and include local public libraries; Minnesota county and regional public library systems; and multicounty, multitype library systems meeting minimum support requirements. Academic libraries and school library media centers are also eligible to apply. Contact the Department for details.

GEOG. RESTRICTIONS: Minnesota.

FINANCIAL DATA:
Amount of support per award: Varies by grant program.
Total amount of support: Varies by year.
Matching fund requirements: Varies by program.

NO. MOST RECENT APPLICANTS: Varies by grant program.

NO. AWARDS: Varies by grant program.

APPLICATION INFO:
Applications available online.
Duration: Varies by grant program.
Deadline: Varies by grant program.

ADDRESS INQUIRIES TO:
Jennifer R. Nelson, Director and State Librarian
(See address above.)

NATIONAL HOME LIBRARY FOUNDATION [684]

3804 Williams Lane, Lower Level
Chevy Chase, MD 20815
(301) 986-4854
Fax: (301) 986-4855
E-mail: grants@homelibraryfoundation.org
Web Site: homelibraryfoundation.org

FOUNDED: 1932

AREAS OF INTEREST:
Literacy.

TYPE:
Project/program grants. Grants in support of libraries, books and publications.

PURPOSE:
To assist in the distribution of books and other literacy-related resources to libraries and community groups with limited access to sources of specific areas of information; to assist in support, promotion and development of programs with the goal of combating illiteracy and/or encouraging an interest in

reading and the literacy arts among all ages; to encourage development of programs relating primarily to literary or cultural topics that utilize various means of communications.

ELIGIBILITY:
Applicants must be tax-exempt groups with appropriate interests and activities.

GEOG. RESTRICTIONS: United States, with preference to Maryland, Virginia and Washington, DC, areas.

FINANCIAL DATA:
Amount of support per award: $500 to $5,000.
Total amount of support: Approximately $30,000 for the year 2017.

REPRESENTATIVE AWARDS:
$2,500 to Centre Ridge Elementary School, Centreville, VA, for the purchase of books and communications materials; $1,000 to Fairfax Library Foundation, Fairfax, VA, for the purchase of books and communications materials; $2,500 to Reading Partners, Baltimore, MD, for the purchase of books and communications materials.

APPLICATION INFO:
Application takes the form of a proposal stating the nature of the project and its sponsors, along with a budget and financial statement.
Duration: Grants are usually awarded for one year.
Deadline: Applications may be submitted at any time and are reviewed in the spring and fall.

IRS I.D.: 52-6051013

OFFICERS:
Lynda J. Robb, President
Kathleen M. Vance, Vice President
Sue Bell, Treasurer

TRUSTEES:
Sue Bell
Vandna Wendy Bhagat
Ervin S. Duggan
Michael R. Gardner
Lynda J. Robb
Ricardo M. Urbina
Kathleen M. Vance
Ashton J. Wingate

ADDRESS INQUIRIES TO:
Aisha Karimah, Executive Director
(See address above.)

NEW HAMPSHIRE LIBRARY ASSOCIATION [685]

c/o NH State Library
20 Park Street
Concord, NH 03301-6314
(603) 624-6550
E-mail: cpearman@manchesternh.gov
Web Site: nhlibrarians.org

FOUNDED: 1889

AREAS OF INTEREST:
Library and information science education.

NAME(S) OF PROGRAMS:
● **Rosalie Norris Scholarship**
● **F. Mabel Winchell Loan Fund**

TYPE:
Scholarships. The Norris Scholarship is awarded to New Hampshire residents or individuals working in a New Hampshire library for graduate library study. The Winchell Loan Fund provides for interest-free

loans to New Hampshire residents or individuals working in a New Hampshire library to attend graduate library schools.

YEAR PROGRAM STARTED: 1949

PURPOSE:
To promote good library service from all types of libraries to all people of the state.

LEGAL BASIS:
Nonprofit.

ELIGIBILITY:
An applicant must be a member of the New Hampshire Library Association and have been accepted into the appropriate program. Applicant must live in New Hampshire or be employed by a New Hampshire library and must be enrolled in an ALA- accredited program.

GEOG. RESTRICTIONS: New Hampshire.

FINANCIAL DATA:
Amount of support per award: Scholarship grant provides a maximum of $1,000. Loan provides $2,000 (interest-free) to be repaid in four years.
Total amount of support: Varies.

NO. AWARDS: 2 Norris Scholarships for the year 2020.

APPLICATION INFO:
Applications are approved by the New Hampshire Library Association Scholarship Committee. Mail applications to: Carlos Pearman, Scholarship Chairperson, New Hampshire Library Association, c/o Manchester City Library, 405 Pine Street, Manchester, NH 03104.
Duration: One year.
Deadline: April 1 and September 1.

ADDRESS INQUIRIES TO:
Carlos Pearman, Scholarship Chairperson
(See address above.)

NEW JERSEY LIBRARY ASSOCIATION [686]
P.O. Box 1534
Trenton, NJ 08607
(609) 394-8032
Fax: (609) 394-8164
E-mail: njla_office@njla.org
Web Site: www.njla.org

FOUNDED: 1890

AREAS OF INTEREST:
Education, training of members and recruitment into the profession.

NAME(S) OF PROGRAMS:
● **Scholarships**

TYPE:
Scholarships. Offered to residents of New Jersey for study leading to a degree in library science at a graduate library school with an ALA-accredited degree program.

YEAR PROGRAM STARTED: 1926

PURPOSE:
To give financial support for tuition to worthy candidates, of New Jersey residency, desiring to work toward a graduate degree in library service as a profession.

LEGAL BASIS:
Nonprofit status.

ELIGIBILITY:
Applicants for scholarships must:
(1) be residents of New Jersey at the time of application or have worked in any New

Jersey library for at least 12 months on a full-time or part-time basis;
(2) show substantial financial need and;
(3) present worthy scholarship, as shown by official transcript, a written essay describing what the applicant can contribute to librarianship, and two recommendations by people in the field of librarianship if possible.

FINANCIAL DATA:
Scholarships are awarded in the spring for the following school year for full- or part-time study. Funds must be used for tuition only and are sent directly to the college. Any unused monies are refunded to the treasurer of the New Jersey Library Association.
Amount of support per award: Varies depending on funding.

APPLICATION INFO:
Applications and guidelines are available on the Association web site.
Duration: One year.
Deadline: March. Announcement in winter.

ADDRESS INQUIRIES TO:
See e-mail address above.

NEW MEXICO LIBRARY ASSOCIATION [687]
P.O. Box 26074
Albuquerque, NM 87125
(505) 400-7309
Fax: (505) 544-5740
E-mail: contact@nmla.org
Web Site: nmla.org/scholarships-grants

FOUNDED: 1923

AREAS OF INTEREST:
Promoting libraries and librarianship in New Mexico.

NAME(S) OF PROGRAMS:
● **College Scholarship Fund**
● **Continuing Education Grants**
● **Marion Dorroh Memorial Scholarship**

TYPE:
Scholarships. The scholarships support study in an accredited library school program. The continuing grants support attending workshops, conferences and educational activities of practicing New Mexico librarians.

YEAR PROGRAM STARTED: 1953

PURPOSE:
To support and promote libraries and the development of library personnel.

LEGAL BASIS:
Nonprofit corporation.

ELIGIBILITY:
College Scholarship Fund: Application is intended for New Mexico library workers who are pursuing an undergraduate program culminating in a degree in Library Technology or school library certification. It can also be used for graduate study toward a teacher-librarian endorsement.

Marion Dorroh Memorial Scholarship: Applicant must be accepted or currently enrolled in an ALA-accredited college or university as a full- or part-time student for an advanced degree in Library and Information Science.

The Continuing Education Grants support is based upon financial need. The Grants are intended for New Mexico library workers to

promote professional development. They may be used to attend workshops, conferences and related activities.

GEOG. RESTRICTIONS: New Mexico.

FINANCIAL DATA:
Amount of support per award: Continuing Education Grants: Up to $200.
Total amount of support: Varies.

NO. AWARDS: 1 per award.

APPLICATION INFO:
Application forms are available on the Association web site.
Duration: One year.
Deadline: College Scholarship and Marion Dorroh Memorial Scholarship: May 1. Continuing Education Grants: Applications are accepted on a rolling basis.

IRS I.D.: 23-7024820

ADDRESS INQUIRIES TO:
Chairperson
NMLA Education Committee
(See address above.)

NORTH CAROLINA LIBRARY ASSOCIATION [688]
c/o Scholarships Committee
265 East Chester Drive
Suite 133, No. 364
High Point, NC 27262
(919) 839-6252
Fax: (888) 977-3143
E-mail: nclaonline@gmail.com
Web Site: www.nclaonline.org

FOUNDED: 1904

AREAS OF INTEREST:
The promotion of libraries and library service in North Carolina.

NAME(S) OF PROGRAMS:
● **The Appalachian Scholarship**
● **The North Carolina Library Association Memorial Scholarship**
● **The Query-Long Scholarship**

TYPE:
Scholarships. Scholarships and loans to promote the education of qualified librarians.

PURPOSE:
To promote libraries, library and information services, librarianship, intellectual freedom and literacy.

LEGAL BASIS:
Professional association.

ELIGIBILITY:
Applicants must have been a legal resident of North Carolina for two years, have a genuine interest in professional library work, demonstrate need of financial assistance, hold an undergraduate degree and be accepted by a library school. (Persons whose library school applications are pending may apply for the scholarships.)

GEOG. RESTRICTIONS: North Carolina.

FINANCIAL DATA:
Amount of support per award: $1,000 per award.
Total amount of support: Varies.

APPLICATION INFO:
Application forms and instructions can be found on the Association web site.
Duration: One year.
Deadline: May 31. Notification in the summer. Awarded biennially in Conference years.

ADDRESS INQUIRIES TO:
Amy Funberburk
Chairperson for Scholarships
North Carolina Library Association
(See address above.)

ROCK ISLAND ARSENAL MUSEUM

Rock Island Arsenal Historical Society
R. Maguire Scholarship Committee
One Rock Island Arsenal
Rock Island, IL 61299-5000
(309) 782-5021
Fax: (309) 782-3598
E-mail: contact@arsenalhistoricalsociety.org
rimahoch@aol.com
Web Site: www.arsenalhistoricalsociety.org

TYPE:
Scholarships.

See entry 585 for full listing.

STATE LIBRARY AND ARCHIVES OF FLORIDA   [689]

R.A. Gray Building
500 South Bronough Street
Tallahassee, FL 32399-0250
(850) 245-6620
Fax: (850) 245-6643
E-mail: marian.deeney@dos.myflorida.com
Web Site: dos.myflorida.com/library-archives/services-for-libraries/grants/lsta

FOUNDED: 1925

AREAS OF INTEREST:
Public libraries, public elementary school or secondary school libraries, academic libraries, research libraries, private libraries, or library consortium.

CONSULTING OR VOLUNTEER SERVICES:
Provide advice to public and institution libraries and libraries for the blind and handicapped.

NAME(S) OF PROGRAMS:
● **Library Services and Technology Act**

TYPE:
Project/program grants. Project grants congruent with the state long-range plan.

YEAR PROGRAM STARTED: 1997

PURPOSE:
To stimulate excellence and promote access to learning and information resources in all types of libraries for individuals of all ages; to promote library services that provide all users access to information through state, regional, national, and international electronic networks; to provide linkages among and between libraries; to promote targeted library services to people of diverse geographic, cultural, and socioeconomic backgrounds, to individuals with disabilities and to people with limited functional literacy or information skills.

LEGAL BASIS:
Based on U.S. Library Services and Technology Act (P.L. 104-208, as amended) and Florida Statutes 257.12, 257.191 and 257.192.

ELIGIBILITY:
Applicants must be Florida libraries that provide free library service or institution libraries that are operated or substantially supported by the state.

GEOG. RESTRICTIONS: Florida.

FINANCIAL DATA:
Amount of support per award: Varies.
Total amount of support: $8,971,754 for fiscal year 2020-21.
Matching fund requirements: At least one-third of the grant request or award must be met with matching funds.

NO. MOST RECENT APPLICANTS: 40.

APPLICATION INFO:
Application must be submitted online. Applicants should supply project proposal.
Duration: One year. Must reapply for each year.
Deadline: Varies.

PUBLICATIONS:
Grant guidelines.

IRS I.D.: 59-3466865

ADDRESS INQUIRIES TO:
David Beach, Library Program Specialist
Tel: (850) 245-6630
E-mail: david.beach@dos.myflorida.com

TEXAS LIBRARY ASSOCIATION   [690]

3355 Bee Cave Road, Suite 401
Austin, TX 78746-6763
(512) 328-1518
(800) 580-2852
Fax: (512) 328-8852
E-mail: tla@txla.org
Web Site: www.txla.org

FOUNDED: 1902

AREAS OF INTEREST:
Library and information science.

NAME(S) OF PROGRAMS:
● **Walter H. Escue Memorial Scholarship**
● **Vivian Greenfield Education Award**
● **Ray C. Janeway Scholarship**
● **TLA Summer School Scholarship**
● **Van Dusen-Tobin-Kaiser Scholarship**

TYPE:
Scholarships. Awards for graduate study leading to a Master's degree in library science.

YEAR PROGRAM STARTED: 1998

PURPOSE:
To help support the educational goals of students who want to get an advanced degree in library science.

LEGAL BASIS:
Professional association.

ELIGIBILITY:
Applicants must be members of TLA.

Walter Escue Scholars must be Texas residents concentrating studies in technical services, systems administration or library automation, attained at least a "B" average during the last two years of a Baccalaureate degree program and have been accepted as a graduate student to a Texas ALA-accredited library education program.

Vivian Greenfield Award applicants must reside in Texas and write a goals statement outlining a desired educational endeavor revolving around youth services.

Janeway Scholarship applicants must be Texas residents, attained at least a "B" average during the last two years of a Baccalaureate program and have been accepted as a graduate student at a Texas ALA-accredited library education program.

TLA Summer School Scholar must be a Texas resident, attained at least a "B" average during the last two years of a Baccalaureate degree program, and must be registered for MLS degree courses during a summer session at a Texas ALA-accredited library education program. (The scholarship applies only to the summer session.)

Van Dusen-Tobin-Kaiser Scholars must be Texas residents and must be pursuing graduate studies leading to a career as an elementary school or children's librarian, attained at least a "B" average during the last two years of a Baccalaureate degree program, and accepted as a graduate student at a Texas ALA-accredited library education program.

GEOG. RESTRICTIONS: Texas.

FINANCIAL DATA:
Amount of support per award: Escue Scholarship: $1,000; Greenfield Award: $1,500; Janeway Scholarship: $2,000, awarded annually; TLA Summer School Scholarship: $500; Van Dusen-Tobin-Kaiser Scholarship: $1,000, awarded biennially in even-numbered years.
Total amount of support: Varies.

NO. AWARDS: Varies.

APPLICATION INFO:
Application must be submitted online.
Duration: One year.
Deadline: Completed applications must be submitted no later than January 31.

IRS I.D.: 74-6014110

ADDRESS INQUIRIES TO:
Sherra R. Bowers, Director, Operations
(See address above.)

*SPECIAL STIPULATIONS:
Scholarships and grants are to be awarded to Texas residents only and only to applicants attending an institution of higher learning in Texas with an accredited School of Library Science.

UNITED STATES HOLOCAUST MEMORIAL MUSEUM - JACK, JOSEPH AND MORTON MANDEL CENTER FOR ADVANCED HOLOCAUST STUDIES

100 Raoul Wallenberg Place, S.W.
Washington, DC 20024-2126
(202) 314-7829
Fax: (202) 479-9726
E-mail: vscholars@ushmm.org
Web Site: www.ushmm.org/research/opportunities-for-academics

TYPE:
Exchange programs; Fellowships. The Jack, Joseph and Morton Mandel Center for Advanced Holocaust Studies is an integral part of the United States Holocaust Memorial Museum, which serves as America's national institution for Holocaust education and remembrance. The Mandel Center awards fellowships to support significant research and writing about the Holocaust. Awards are granted on a competitive basis. The Mandel Center welcomes proposals from scholars in all relevant academic disciplines, including history, political science, literature, Jewish studies, philosophy, religion, psychology, comparative genocide studies, law and others.

Visiting scholars at the Mandel Center have access to more than 100 million pages of Holocaust-related archival documentation; the

Museum's extensive library; oral history, film, photo, art, artifacts and memoir collections; and Holocaust survivor database.

See entry 595 for full listing.

UNIVERSITY OF ARIZONA SCHOOL OF INFORMATION [691]

University of Arizona
1103 East Second Street, Room 409
Tucson, AZ 85721
(520) 621-3565
Fax: (520) 621-3279
E-mail: si_info@email.arizona.edu
Web Site: ischool.arizona.edu

FOUNDED: 1963

AREAS OF INTEREST:
Information science.

TYPE:
Assistantships; Internships; Scholarships. Graduate assistantships; Research assistantships; Undergraduate internships and scholarships. Awarded to qualified students to attend the School of Information.

YEAR PROGRAM STARTED: 1963

PURPOSE:
To prepare students to tackle the challenges of an information-based society; to enable students to seize opportunities to succeed in emerging industries.

LEGAL BASIS:
Nonprofit, tax-exempt.

ELIGIBILITY:
Any student receiving financial aid must be accepted into the SI degree program. Awards are made to students who meet the criteria set by the School. (This includes students participating in the program online.) The School requires that the student be enrolled for the required number of hours for the semester of award. Assistance is awarded on a semester basis.

A new financial aid form must be completed each semester that a student wishes to be considered for aid. To be considered for financial assistance, an applicant must meet the deadlines posted. Criteria for financial aid are: stellar academic performance, financial status, and other qualifications as defined by specific scholarships.

FINANCIAL DATA:
Amount of support per award: Varies by program.
Total amount of support: Varies.

APPLICATION INFO:
Applicant must complete the Financial Assistance Application section of Library Science Application for Admission.
Duration: One or two semesters.
Deadline: Varies.

ADDRESS INQUIRIES TO:
See e-mail address above.

THE UNIVERSITY OF DELAWARE-HAGLEY GRADUATE PROGRAM

Department of History, John Munroe Hall
University of Delaware
Newark, DE 19716
(302) 831-8226
Fax: (302) 831-1538
E-mail: dianec@udel.edu
Web Site: www.udel.edu/hagley
www.history.udel.edu

TYPE:
Assistantships; Fellowships. The University of Delaware, in association with the Hagley Museum, sponsors a premier graduate resident program for the study of technology, business, consumption, and work in industrial and post-industrial societies leading to a Master of Arts or Ph.D. in History. Students have access to faculty with international reputations in American, European and non-Western history, and benefit from strong interdisciplinary ties to museum studies and material culture programs, as well as the Hagley Museum and Library.

See entry 596 for full listing.

UNIVERSITY OF TORONTO [692]

Faculty of Information
140 St. George Street
Toronto ON M5S 3G6 Canada
(416) 978-3234
Fax: (416) 978-5762
E-mail: inquire.ischool@utoronto.ca
Web Site: www.ischool.utoronto.ca

FOUNDED: 1928

AREAS OF INTEREST:
Education.

NAME(S) OF PROGRAMS:
● **Patricia Fleming Visiting Fellowship in Bibliography and Book History**

TYPE:
Fellowships. Fellowship is awarded biennially in even-numbered years.

YEAR PROGRAM STARTED: 2005

PURPOSE:
To encourage outstanding scholars to conduct research in the field of bibliographical studies or book history.

LEGAL BASIS:
University.

GEOG. RESTRICTIONS: Canada.

FINANCIAL DATA:
Amount of support per award: $2,000 (CAN).

NO. MOST RECENT APPLICANTS: 7.

NO. AWARDS: 1.

APPLICATION INFO:
Applicants should submit a resume, two letters of recommendation, a one- to two-page research proposal describing the project, and the proposed timing of the fellowship.
Duration: One month.
Deadline: March 31.

ADDRESS INQUIRIES TO:
Student Services
(See address above.)

UTAH DIVISION OF ARTS & MUSEUMS

617 East South Temple
Salt Lake City, UT 84102
(801) 236-7550
Fax: (801) 236-7556
E-mail: lalder@utah.gov
Web Site: artsandmuseums.utah.gov

TYPE:
Development grants; General operating grants; Matching gifts; Residencies; Scholarships.

See entry 471 for full listing.

Music

ACCADEMIA MUSICALE CHIGIANA [693]

Via di Città, 89
53100 Siena Italy
(39) 0577 22091
Fax: (39) 0577 288124
E-mail: accademia.chigiana@chigiana.it
Web Site: www.chigiana.it

FOUNDED: 1932

AREAS OF INTEREST:
Music.

NAME(S) OF PROGRAMS:
● **Scholarships for Summer Music Courses**

TYPE:
Awards/prizes; Scholarships. Merit scholarships to those who are registered as active students at the Academy, which offers various summer music master courses in orchestral conducting, composition, voice and various instruments.

In addition, there are other scholarships financed by public institutions or private donors and are awarded at the discretion of the Accademia Chigiana Direction.

YEAR PROGRAM STARTED: 1932

PURPOSE:
To allow young musicians from all over the world to perfect themselves in the principal instruments, studying with many world famous musicians.

ELIGIBILITY:
Applicants can be students of any nationality. Active students must hold an Italian music diploma or an equivalent foreign certificate (exception made for the courses of guitar and singing) and must pass an entrance examination. Age limits are as follows: Conducting, 30 years for the session dedicated to the classical orchestral repertoire; 40 years for the session dedicated to the modern symphonic repertoire; Voice, 32 years (sopranos and tenors), 34 years (mezzo sopranos, baritones and basses); Instruments, 30 years; Chamber Music, average of 30 years. The Italian government also finances scholarships for attendance of summer master classes at the Accademia Chigiana.

Scholarships offered by the Accademia Musicale Chigiana are awarded on the basis of the results of the entrance examination and student merit.

No scholarship will be granted to students already benefiting from financial help from other institutions or to those who do not take the entrance examination on the established date.

FINANCIAL DATA:
Amount of support per award: Scholarships consist of reimbursement of tuition fees (after detraction of the added value tax) plus a daily grant of EUR 35 gross.

Total amount of support: EUR 60,000 (with funds of the Academy) plus EUR 30,000 (by public institutions or private donors).

APPLICATION INFO:
Detailed information and application forms are available from the address above. For details of requirements and application formalities about scholarships awarded by the Italian government, candidates should write directly to the Italian Culture Institute or to the Italian Embassy in their own country.

Deadline: May 15 for the Orchestral Conducting Course; May 31 for Composition Course; June 10 for all other courses.

PUBLICATIONS:
Courses booklet (information and application form).

OFFICERS:
Carlo Rossi, President
Marco Comporti, Vice President
Angelo Armiento, Administrative Director
Nicola Sani, Artistic Director

ADDRESS INQUIRIES TO:
Fondazione Accademia Musicale Chigiana
(See address above.)

AMERICAN ACADEMY OF ARTS AND LETTERS   [694]
633 West 155th Street
New York, NY 10032-7599
(212) 368-5900
Fax: (212) 491-4615
E-mail: academy@artsandletters.org
Web Site: www.artsandletters.org

FOUNDED: 1898

NAME(S) OF PROGRAMS:
• **The Richard Rodgers Awards**

TYPE:
Awards/prizes. Completed musical scripts are accepted by the Academy for this annual competition. The award subsidizes staged readings, studio productions or productions in New York City by a not-for-profit theater group of a musical play by composers and writers who are not already established in this field.

YEAR PROGRAM STARTED: 1978

PURPOSE:
To further the art of the musical theater in the U.S.

LEGAL BASIS:
Nonprofit Internal Revenue Code 501(c)(3).

ELIGIBILITY:
Open only to U.S. citizens or permanent residents of any age. While students may enter the competition, it is primarily intended for work at a professional level.

GEOG. RESTRICTIONS: United States.

FINANCIAL DATA:
Award money is given to the not-for-profit theater for production expenses.
Amount of support per award: Varies.

NO. MOST RECENT APPLICANTS: 133.

NO. AWARDS: 1 to 4.

APPLICATION INFO:
Application form can be downloaded from the Academy web site. The name(s) of the author(s) must be blocked out on each of the items submitted, with the exception of the application form. Write only the title of the work on the script, plot summary and CD. Entries must include the following items:
(1) script with lyrics, preferably with no binders or metal clips. Do not send score, videos or visuals;

(2) half-page synopsis of the action and a list of characters;
(3) CD which must contain at least 45 minutes of music, including a minimum of eight songs, recorded in chronological order. Orchestrations are not necessary; piano and vocals are sufficient. Songs must be in sequence on the CD and each song clearly keyed into the script. Please include a separate track sheet of recorded songs with page numbers indicating where they appear in the script, and specify the total number of minutes recorded. Audio tapes will not be accepted and;
(4) application form signed by all collaborators in a sealed envelope with the title of the work on the outside. Applicants submitting work which has already been produced must give full information concerning these productions, including programs. A work is not eligible if one of the collaborators is deceased.

If the submitted work (or a portion thereof) is an adaptation of material which is not in the public domain, candidates must submit licenses, permissions, or authorizations necessary to permit the work to be produced in conformity with applicable copyright laws. The music must be original.

Materials will be returned if a self-addressed, stamped mailer is enclosed. Addresses must be valid for at least six months. The Academy will take all due care of materials, but it cannot be held responsible for their safe return.

Deadline: November 1. Notification by March.

PUBLICATIONS:
Application guidelines.

STAFF:
Cody Upton, Executive Director
Ashley Fedor, Coordinator, Richard Rodgers Awards

ADDRESS INQUIRIES TO:
The Richard Rodgers Awards
(See address above.)

*SPECIAL STIPULATIONS:
Musical submitted may not be entered again, even if revised.

AMERICAN ACCORDION MUSICOLOGICAL SOCIETY   [695]
322 Haddon Avenue
Westmont, NJ 08108
(856) 854-6628
E-mail: acmeaccordion@gmail.com
Web Site: aamsaccordionfestival.com

FOUNDED: 1968

AREAS OF INTEREST:
Research and symposiums on accordion history in the U.S.

CONSULTING OR VOLUNTEER SERVICES:
Library services, books and music on the accordion, and records, CDs and DVDs for rental.

NAME(S) OF PROGRAMS:
• **Annual Symposium and Festival**

TYPE:
Awards/prizes; Work-study programs. The Annual Symposium and Festival is held on a weekend in March.

YEAR PROGRAM STARTED: 1970

PURPOSE:
To help and stimulate young composers to write for the accordion.

LEGAL BASIS:
Nonprofit professional association.

ELIGIBILITY:
Composer must be acquainted with the various types of accordions.

FINANCIAL DATA:
Amount of support per award: $300.

NO. AWARDS: 1.

APPLICATION INFO:
Applicants should write for entry forms or send an e-mail to the address above.
Deadline: Contact the Society.

ADDRESS INQUIRIES TO:
Joanna Darrow, Director
(See address above.)

THE AMERICAN BANDMASTERS ASSOCIATION   [696]
2602 Pine Valley Drive
Champaign, IL 61822
(217) 721-5156
E-mail: caneva@bsu.edu
Web Site: www.americanbandmasters.org

FOUNDED: 1929

AREAS OF INTEREST:
Concert band and band music.

NAME(S) OF PROGRAMS:
• **Sousa/ABA/Ostwald Award**

TYPE:
Awards/prizes. Prize sponsored by the American Bandmasters Association and Sousa Foundation, involving cash award and performance of the winning band or wind ensemble composition. One award is presented in odd years for grades 1-4; one award is presented in even years for grades 5-6.

YEAR PROGRAM STARTED: 1955

PURPOSE:
To enrich the spectrum of concert band activity.

ELIGIBILITY:
Details are available on the Association web site.

FINANCIAL DATA:
Amount of support per award: $5,000.
Total amount of support: $5,000.

NO. MOST RECENT APPLICANTS: 91.

NO. AWARDS: 1.

APPLICATION INFO:
Send scores (PDFs only) and recordings (mp3 of live performances only) and direct all inquiries to the Chairman of the Contest Committee at the e-mail address above. Additional requirements are provided on the Association web site.
Deadline: August 1. Announcement on October 1.

PUBLICATIONS:
Journal of Band Research.

IRS I.D.: 36-6112860

OFFICERS:
Jay Gephart, President
Kerry Taylor, President-Elect
Michael Colburn, Vice President
Thomas V. Fraschillo, Secretary-Treasurer
Lowell Graham, Chairperson, Nominating Committee

BOARD OF DIRECTORS:
  Linda Moorhouse, Chairman
  Dr. Daniel Bolin
  Bobby R. Francis
  Mark Heidel
  J. Steven Moore
  Michael Nakasone
  Stephen Peterson
  Robert W. Smith

ADDRESS INQUIRIES TO:
  Tom Caneva, Chairperson
  Sousa/ABA/Ostwald Committee
  (See e-mail address above.)

*SPECIAL STIPULATIONS:
  All inquiries and correspondence must be in
  the form of an e-mail.

AMERICAN MATTHAY
ASSOCIATION FOR PIANO   [697]

1924 Fox Road
Tuscaloosa, AL 35406
E-mail: k.t.chance@gmail.com
Web Site: www.matthay.org

FOUNDED: 1925

AREAS OF INTEREST:
  Piano performance and teaching.

NAME(S) OF PROGRAMS:
  ● Clara Wells Fellowships

TYPE:
  Conferences/seminars; Scholarships;
  Work-study programs. Two annual awards,
  one for high school and one for collegiate,
  for travel to and accommodation at the
  Matthay Annual Piano Festival. The award
  includes attendance at the festival, mentoring
  by members, a recital performance,
  performance in a master class, a collection of
  books and CDs.

YEAR PROGRAM STARTED: 1970

PURPOSE:
  To foster the teaching principles of Tobias
  Matthay.

LEGAL BASIS:
  Nonprofit organization.

ELIGIBILITY:
  Candidates must be between 15 to 30 years
  of age, as of the application deadline.

FINANCIAL DATA:
  Amount of support per award: $1,000.
  Total amount of support: $2,000.

NO. MOST RECENT APPLICANTS: 6 to 10 per
  year.

NO. AWARDS: 2.

APPLICATION INFO:
  Applicants must submit an unedited video
  recording (DVD or flash drive) containing
  two works of contrasting period, style and
  tempo. The combined music on the recording
  must comprise a minimum of 10 minutes.
  Application must include a cover letter
  containing:
  (1) applicant's name, age, school grade,
  address, phone and e-mail contacts;
  (2) length of piano study and names of
  teachers;
  (3) experience, including performances,
  awards and scholarships;
  (4) a brief statement as to why applicant
  wants to be a Clara Wells Scholar and;
  (5) name and contact information for
  applicant's current teacher.

  There is a $20 application fee
  (nonrefundable).

Deadline: March 15. Notification no later
than April 1.

PUBLICATIONS:
  The Matthay News.

ADDRESS INQUIRIES TO:
  Dr. Kevin Chance
  Competition Chairperson
  Attn.: Clara Wells
  (See e-mail address above.)

AMERICAN MUSICOLOGICAL
SOCIETY   [698]

20 Cooper Square, 2nd Floor
New York, NY 10003
(212) 992-6340
(877) 679-7648
Fax: (877) 679-7648
E-mail: amsmusicology.org
Web Site: www.amsmusicology.org

FOUNDED: 1934

AREAS OF INTEREST:
  Scholastic work in musicology.

NAME(S) OF PROGRAMS:
  ● AMS Teaching Award
  ● The Philip Brett Award
  ● The H. Robert Cohen/RIPM Award
  ● Early Music Award
  ● The Alfred Einstein Award
  ● Noah Greenberg Award
  ● Thomas Hampson Award
  ● The Roland Jackson Award
  ● The Otto Kinkeldey Award
  ● Lewis Lockwood Award
  ● Music in American Culture Award
  ● Claude V. Palisca Award
  ● Paul A. Pisk Prize
  ● H. Colin Slim Award
  ● Ruth A. Solie Award
  ● Robert M. Stevenson Award
  ● Judy Tsou Critical Race Studies Award

TYPE:
  Awards/prizes. AMS Teaching Award honors
  an exceptional pedagogical resource for
  musicology published during the previous
  two years. By "resource" is meant a
  published article, book (including textbook),
  digital, or online material that best
  exemplifies the highest qualities of
  originality, theory, application, and
  communication for the teaching of
  musicology or music history.

  The Philip Brett Award honors exceptional
  musicological work in the field of gay,
  lesbian, bisexual, transgender/transsexual
  studies completed during the previous two
  calendar years in any country and in any
  language. By "work" is meant a published
  article, book, edition, annotated translation, a
  paper read at a conference, teaching materials
  (course descriptions and syllabi), and other
  scholarly work accepted by the award
  committee that best exemplifies the highest
  qualities of originality, interpretation, theory
  and communication in this field of study.

  The H. Robert Cohen/RIPM Award honors a
  publication related to the goals of RIPM
  (Retrospective Index to Music Periodicals).
  Works include, but are not limited to, books,
  articles, or widely-disseminated databases
  focusing on one or more journals, music
  critics and criticism, reception history, critical
  and cultural histories, and issues of access
  and preservation.

  Early Music Award honors a substantial,
  single-author work of scholarship on music
  before 1550. By "work" is meant a variety of

formats: articles, books, and scholarly
editions with significant editorial
commentaries published during the preceding
three calendar years in any language and in
any country.

The Alfred Einstein Award honors a
musicological article of exceptional merit,
published during the previous year in any
language and in any country, by a scholar in
the early stages of his or her career.

The Noah Greenberg Award is intended as a
grant-in-aid to stimulate active cooperation
between scholars and performers by
recognizing and fostering outstanding
contributions to historical performing
practices. Both scholars and performers may
apply, since the Award may subsidize the
publication costs of articles, monographs, or
editions, as well as public performance,
recordings, or other projects.

The Thomas Hampson Award is dedicated to
fostering editions and scholarship on classic
song in all its contexts as well as new and
innovative technologies for promoting and
understanding classic song via interactive
media and the Internet.

The Roland Jackson Award recognizes an
article in the English language of exceptional
merit in the field of music analysis. Awards
are made in three separate subject categories,
in successive years, on music from circa
1800 to the present, music circa 1600 to
1800, and music before 1600.

The Otto Kinkeldey Award will honor each
year a musicological book of exceptional
merit published during the previous year in
any language and in any country by a scholar
who is past the early stages of his or her
career.

The Lewis Lockwood Award honors each
year a musicological book of exceptional
merit published during the previous year in
any language and in any country by a scholar
in the early stages of his or her career who is
a member of the AMS or a citizen or
permanent resident of Canada or the U.S.

The Music in American Culture Award
honors each year a book of exceptional merit
that both illuminates some important aspect
of the music of the U.S. and places that
music in a rich cultural context. Books
published in the previous year in any
language and in any country are eligible. The
author must be a citizen or permanent
resident of the U.S. or Canada.

The Claude V. Palisca Award honors each
year a scholarly edition or translation in the
field of musicology published during the
previous year in any language and in any
country by a scholar who is a member of the
AMS or a citizen or permanent resident of
Canada or the U.S., deemed by a committee
of scholars to best exemplify the highest
qualities of originality, interpretation, logic
and clarity of thought, and communication.

The Paul A. Pisk Prize is awarded annually
to a graduate music student for a scholarly
paper to be presented at the Annual Meeting
of the Society.

The H. Colin Slim Award honors each year a
musicological article of exceptional merit,
published during the previous year in any
language and in any country by a scholar
who is past the early stages of his or her
career and who is a member of the AMS or a
citizen or permanent resident of Canada or
the U.S.

The Ruth A. Solie Award honors each year a collection of musicological essays of exceptional merit published during the preceding calendar year in any language and in any country and edited by a scholar or scholars who are members of the AMS or citizens or permanent residents of Canada or the U.S.

The Robert M. Stevenson Award recognizes outstanding scholarship in Iberian music. The prize will be awarded annually to a book, monograph, edition, or journal article by a member of the AMS. The publication must be written in English and must have been published during the preceding three calendar years.

Judy Tsou Critical Race Studies Award honors outstanding musicological work in the field of critical race and/or critical ethnic studies. By "work" is meant a published article, book, edition, or other scholarly entity that best exemplifies the highest qualities of originality, interpretation, theory, and communication in this area. Work must have been published during the preceding three calendar years.

Winners of all awards receive a monetary prize, conferred at the Annual Business Meeting and Awards Presentation of the Society by the chair of the committee.

YEAR PROGRAM STARTED: 1967

LEGAL BASIS:
Private.

GEOG. RESTRICTIONS: United States and Canada.

FINANCIAL DATA:
Amount of support per award: Varies.
Total amount of support: Varies.

APPLICATION INFO:
Application information is available on the web site.
Deadline: Noah Greenburg Award and Thomas Hampson Award: August 15. Paul A. Pisk Prize: October 1. Claude V. Palisca Award: January 31. All others; May 1.

IRS I.D.: 23-1577392

ADDRESS INQUIRIES TO:
See e-mail address above.

AMERICAN MUSICOLOGICAL SOCIETY   [699]
20 Cooper Square, 2nd Floor
New York, NY 10003
(212) 992-6340
(877) 679-7648
Fax: (877) 679-7648
E-mail: amsmusicology.org
Web Site: www.amsmusicology.org

FOUNDED: 1934

AREAS OF INTEREST:
Research in the various fields of music as a branch of learning and scholarship.

NAME(S) OF PROGRAMS:
● **Holmes/D'Accone Dissertation Fellowship in Opera Studies**
● **Howard Mayer Brown Fellowship**
● **Alvin H. Johnson AMS 50 Dissertation Fellowships**

TYPE:
Fellowships. The Holmes/D'Accone Fellowship for dissertation research recognizes academic achievement and future

promise in the study of opera. An approved dissertation proposal in the subfield of opera studies is required.

The Howard Mayer Brown Fellowship is intended to increase the presence of minority scholars and teachers in musicology. The fellowship supports one year of graduate work for a member of a historically underrepresented group.

The Alvin H. Johnson AMS Dissertation Fellowships are intended for support of the early stages of research; it is expected that a Fellow's dissertation be completed within the fellowship year. Any submission for a doctoral degree in which the emphasis is on musical scholarship will be considered.

YEAR PROGRAM STARTED: 1989

PURPOSE:
To support the advancement of research in various fields of music.

LEGAL BASIS:
Nonprofit organization.

ELIGIBILITY:
For the AMS Fellowship, applicants must be registered for a Doctorate at a North American university and have completed all formal degree requirements except the dissertation.

The Howard Mayer Brown Fellowship will be awarded to a student who has completed at least one year of graduate work, and who intends to complete a Ph.D. in the field. Applications are encouraged from African-Americans, Native Americans, Latinos, Asian-Americans and, in Canada, visible minorities. There are no restrictions as to age or sex.

FINANCIAL DATA:
Amount of support per award: Varies.
Total amount of support: Varies.

APPLICATION INFO:
Applications must be submitted electronically.
Duration: One year.
Deadline: December 15.

IRS I.D.: 23-1577392

ADDRESS INQUIRIES TO:
See e-mail address above.

ARD INTERNATIONAL MUSIC COMPETITION   [700]
Internationaler Musikwettbewerb der ARD
Bayerischer Rundfunk
Rundfunkplatz 1
D-80335 Munich Germany
(49) 89 5900 42471
Fax: (49) 89 5900 3573
E-mail: ard.musikwettbewerb@br.de
Web Site: www.br.de/ard-musikwettbewerb

FOUNDED: 1952

AREAS OF INTEREST:
International music competition.

TYPE:
Awards/prizes. Cash prizes; Competition for music.

Intended for a selection of young musicians who are interested in following an international career. The standards are, therefore, high and the prizes are awarded only for outstanding performances. Program categories differ each year. For 2020: flute, trombone, piano and string quartet.

YEAR PROGRAM STARTED: 1952

PURPOSE:
To create gifted musicians and international soloists.

ELIGIBILITY:
Open to musicians of all nations born between 1991 and 2003 in the categories flute, trombone and piano. String Quartet: Total age maximum 120; single members neither younger than 17 nor older than 35.

FINANCIAL DATA:
Amount of support per award: Soloists: First prize, EUR 10,000; Second prize, EUR 7,500; Third prize, EUR 5,000. Wind Quintet: First prize, EUR 25,000; Second prize, EUR 20,000; Third prize, EUR 15,000. Piano Duo: First prize, EUR 12,000; Second prize, EUR 9,000; Third prize, EUR 6,000. String Quartet: First prize, EUR 24,000; Second prize, EUR 18,000; Third prize, EUR 12,000. Piano Trio: First Prize, EUR 18,000; Second prize, EUR 13,500; Third prize, EUR 9,000.
Total amount of support: EUR 121,500 for the year 2020.

CO-OP FUNDING PROGRAMS: Theodor - Rogler - Foundation, Alice - Rosner - Foundation, Siemens Arts Program and others.

NO. MOST RECENT APPLICANTS: Approximately 400 each year.

NO. AWARDS: 12.

APPLICATION INFO:
A valid statement of type and duration of study should accompany the entry form. Students must have permission from their current teacher to participate. A list of the applicant's complete repertoire is required. Upon arrival in Munich, each competitor should present a birth certificate or a valid passport at the Competition Office.

Preselections with videos are obligatory for all categories.
Deadline: March 31.

PUBLICATIONS:
Annual prospectus with application guidelines and programs.

OFFICERS:
Oswald Beaujean, Artistic Director
Meret Forster, Artistic Director
Elisabeth Kozik, Managing Director
Anja Krainz, Project Management

ADDRESS INQUIRIES TO:
Competition Office
(See address above.)

THE ASCAP FOUNDATION
250 West 57th Street
New York, NY 10107
(212) 621-6588
E-mail: jlapore@ascap.com
Web Site: www.ascap.com

TYPE:
Awards/prizes. The ASCAP Foundation Deems Taylor/Virgil Thomson Awards program recognizes books and articles on the subject of music selected for their excellence.
See entry 617 for full listing.

THE ASCAP FOUNDATION   [701]
250 West 57th Street
New York, NY 10107
(212) 621-6588
E-mail: concertmusic@ascap.com
Web Site: www.ascapfoundation.org

FOUNDED: 1975

AREAS OF INTEREST:
Music, music composition and music education.

NAME(S) OF PROGRAMS:
- **The ASCAP Foundation Morton Gould Young Composer Awards**

TYPE:
Awards/prizes.

YEAR PROGRAM STARTED: 1978

PURPOSE:
To encourage talented young American composers.

LEGAL BASIS:
Publicly supported foundation, 501(c)(3) organization.

ELIGIBILITY:
Individuals must have not reached their 30th birthday as of January 1 of the year of application and must be U.S. citizens, permanent residents or enrolled students with student visas.

Previous recipients are eligible to reapply for the award.

GEOG. RESTRICTIONS: United States.

FINANCIAL DATA:
Amount of support per award: $500 to $3,500, at discretion of judges.
Total amount of support: $25,000.

NO. MOST RECENT APPLICANTS: Approximately 700.

NO. AWARDS: 15 or more.

APPLICATION INFO:
A completed application form must be submitted along with one reproduction of an original manuscript or score, a listing of music studies and compositions to date, and biographical information.
Deadline: February 1.

PUBLICATIONS:
Annual report; contributions policy; application guidelines.

BOARD OF DIRECTORS:
Paul Williams, President
Irwin Z. Robinson, Vice President
Dean Kay, Treasurer
Ginny Mancini, Secretary
Marilyn Bergman
Charles Bernstein
Bruce Broughton
Tita Cahn
Desmond Child
Dan Foliart
Arthur Hamilton
James M. Kendrick
Robert Kimball
Michelle Lewis
Johnny Mandel
James McBride
Roger McNulty
Marcus Miller
Jason Mraz
Michael Price
Geoffrey Sargeant
Stephen Schwartz
Alex Shapiro
Valerie Simpson
Doug Wood

ADMINISTRATION:
Colleen McDonough, Executive Director
Julie Lapore, Associate Director

ADDRESS INQUIRIES TO:
Cia Toscanini
Vice President, Concert Music
(See address above.)

BRANDON UNIVERSITY [702]

School of Music
270 18th Street
Brandon MB R7A 6A9 Canada
(204) 727-7388
Fax: (204) 728-6839
E-mail: music@brandonu.ca
Web Site: www.brandonu.ca/music

AREAS OF INTEREST:
Music education, performance and literature (piano, collaborative piano, strings, composition, clarinet, trumpet, conducting and jazz).

TYPE:
Assistantships; Scholarships.

YEAR PROGRAM STARTED: 1980

PURPOSE:
To afford graduate students the opportunity to gain professional experience while studying and to provide monetary assistance.

ELIGIBILITY:
Open to candidates with a Bachelor's degree in music or music education with a minimum grade point average of 3.0 during the final year.

FINANCIAL DATA:
Amount of support per award: Up to $5,000 per year.
Total amount of support: $20,000 per year.

NO. MOST RECENT APPLICANTS: 15.

NO. AWARDS: 9.

APPLICATION INFO:
Applications available both online and from the Graduate Music Office.
Duration: Two years.
Deadline: May 1.

ADDRESS INQUIRIES TO:
Kerry DuWors, Chairperson
Graduate Music Department
(See address above.)

CHAMBER MUSIC AMERICA [703]

12 West 32nd Street, 7th Floor
New York, NY 10001
(212) 242-2022 ext. 102
E-mail: sdadian@chamber-music.org
Web Site: www.chamber-music.org

FOUNDED: 1977

AREAS OF INTEREST:
The promotion of public interest in and appreciation of chamber music and the promotion of cooperation among and advancement of professional American chamber music ensembles and presenters.

CONSULTING OR VOLUNTEER SERVICES:
Technical assistance provided in such areas as fund-raising, marketing and residency design and implementation.

NAME(S) OF PROGRAMS:
- **Residency Partnership Program**

TYPE:
Project/program grants. Direct grants for ensembles and concert presenters.

YEAR PROGRAM STARTED: 1978

PURPOSE:
To stimulate the establishment of chamber music residencies.

LEGAL BASIS:
Nonprofit arts service organization.

ELIGIBILITY:
Candidates must be an ensemble member or a presenter in good standing of CMA and have experience in workshops or other residency-related activities.

GEOG. RESTRICTIONS: United States and its territories.

FINANCIAL DATA:
Amount of support per award: Up to $6,000.
Total amount of support: Varies.
Matching fund requirements: CMA funds up to 75% of the requested amount.

NO. MOST RECENT APPLICANTS: 45.

NO. AWARDS: 8.

APPLICATION INFO:
Telephone consultations and workshops held by teleconference with CMA staff are available for organizations with questions about the application process.
Duration: Must take place within one month's time.
Deadline: October 18.

PUBLICATIONS:
Chamber Music, magazine; newsletter; application guidelines.

ADDRESS INQUIRIES TO:
Susan Dadian, Program Director
CMA Classical/Contemporary
(See address above.)

*SPECIAL STIPULATIONS:
Residencies must take place within the U.S. or its territories.

CHAMBER MUSIC AMERICA [704]

12 West 32nd Street, 7th Floor
New York, NY 10001
(212) 242-2022 ext. 102
E-mail: sdadian@chamber-music.org
Web Site: www.chamber-music.org

FOUNDED: 1977

AREAS OF INTEREST:
The promotion of public interest in and appreciation of chamber music and the promotion of cooperation among and advancement of professional American chamber music ensembles and presenters.

NAME(S) OF PROGRAMS:
- **Chamber Music America Classical Commissioning Program**

TYPE:
Project/program grants. Classical Commissioning provides support to U.S. member ensembles and presenters for commissions of new chamber works by American composers. Grants are made for commissioning fees, copying costs and ensemble rehearsal honoraria.

YEAR PROGRAM STARTED: 1983

PURPOSE:
To stimulate the composition of new works for chamber ensembles.

LEGAL BASIS:
Nonprofit arts service organization.

ELIGIBILITY:
Ensembles and presenters must be organizational members of Chamber Music America. Compositions must be written for small ensembles (two to 10 musicians)

performing one to a part, and may represent a diverse musical spectrum, including contemporary art music, world music, and works that include electronics.

GEOG. RESTRICTIONS: United States and its territories.

FINANCIAL DATA:
Amount of support per award: Up to $20,000 for composer fee, copying allotment of $1,000 and subsidy of $1,000 per musician.
Total amount of support: Varies.

NO. MOST RECENT APPLICANTS: 166.

NO. AWARDS: 13.

APPLICATION INFO:
Guidelines may be obtained in January from the web site listed above.
Duration: Applicants may reapply after one cycle.
Deadline: April 3.

PUBLICATIONS:
Guidelines and applications.

ADDRESS INQUIRIES TO:
Susan Dadian, Program Director
CMA Classical/Contemporary
(See address above.)

CHOPIN FOUNDATION OF THE U.S. [705]

1440 79th Street Causeway, Suite 117
Miami, FL 33141
(305) 868-0624
Fax: (305) 865-5150
E-mail: info@chopin.org
Web Site: www.chopin.org

FOUNDED: 1977

AREAS OF INTEREST:
Chopin and the promotion of classical music in the community by the support of young American pianists.

NAME(S) OF PROGRAMS:
● **Scholarship Program for Young Pianists**

TYPE:
Scholarships. Scholarship program supporting young American pianists, 14 to 17 years of age.

YEAR PROGRAM STARTED: 1997

PURPOSE:
To support talented young American musicians in their struggle for career recognition; to make classical music available to the community.

ELIGIBILITY:
Open to qualified American pianists (citizens or legal residents) not younger than 14 and not older than 17 years of age on the application deadline, whose field of study is music and whose major is piano. If applicant is older than 17 years of age, he or she may only be accepted if currently in this scholarship program.

GEOG. RESTRICTIONS: United States.

FINANCIAL DATA:
Amount of support per award: $1,000.
Total amount of support: $18,000 for the year 2018-19.

NO. AWARDS: 18 for the year 2018-19.

APPLICATION INFO:
Scholarship applications must be submitted online. The following documents are required and must be uploaded with the application:

(1) statement of career goals;
(2) two recommendations from piano teachers or professional piano performers;
(3) an unedited video recording of Chopin's works as required for Years One to Four. Video must be recorded in one session, but must be saved and uploaded as separate files. Uploaded file must be labeled with the name of the piece and the edition used;
(4) proof of current school enrollment or statement of being homeschooled;
(5) copy of birth certificate or proof of U.S. naturalization/legal residency and;
(6) non-refundable $25 application fee.

Incomplete applications will not be considered.
Duration: One year. Renewable up to four years as long as the recipient continues to study piano, maintains satisfactory progress, and each year submits an audiocassette, CD or DVD recording of unedited performances of Chopin's works for evaluation as per renewal information.
Deadline: May 15.

IRS I.D.: 59-1778404

ADDRESS INQUIRIES TO:
Barbara Muze, Executive Director
(See address above.)

*SPECIAL STIPULATIONS:
Registration fee of $25 must be included with application.

CIVIC ORCHESTRA OF CHICAGO [706]

220 South Michigan Avenue
Chicago, IL 60604
(312) 294-3400
Fax: (312) 294-3329
E-mail: civic@cso.org
Web Site: cso.org/civic

FOUNDED: 1919

AREAS OF INTEREST:
Training young musicians for professional work in the orchestral field at the highest level with an emphasis on artistic excellence, community engagement and advocacy.

NAME(S) OF PROGRAMS:
● **Civic Orchestra Lesson Scholarship Stipends**

TYPE:
Fellowships; Scholarships. Stipends to help defray cost of private study with Chicago Symphony members and additional music training-related costs. Scholarship funds may be used for full-time two-year graduate-level study at a local academic institution.

YEAR PROGRAM STARTED: 1919

PURPOSE:
To promote the development of aesthetic sensitivity and playing technique through personal instruction with skilled pedagogues.

LEGAL BASIS:
The Civic Orchestra is a training orchestra under the auspices of the Chicago Symphony Orchestra, which is incorporated as a nonprofit, tax-exempt organization.

ELIGIBILITY:
Scholarships are available to all Civic Orchestra members.

FINANCIAL DATA:
Amount of support per award: $8,500 average for 30-week season.
Total amount of support: Varies.

NO. MOST RECENT APPLICANTS: 565.

NO. AWARDS: 90 each season.

APPLICATION INFO:
Application forms can be filled out when auditioning for the Civic Orchestra. Membership application forms are available from the Civic Orchestra office. Auditions are held in February and March.
Duration: 30 weeks, September to June. Renewal possible for up to two years.
Deadline: Mid-January.

OFFICERS:
Helen Zell, Chairperson
Jeff Alexander, President, Chicago Symphony Orchestra

ADDRESS INQUIRIES TO:
Jonathan McCormick
Director of Education
(See address above.)

CLEVELAND INSTITUTE OF MUSIC [707]

11021 East Boulevard
Cleveland, OH 44106
(216) 791-5000
Fax: (216) 791-3168
E-mail: dale.hedding@cim.edu
Web Site: www.cim.edu

FOUNDED: 1920

NAME(S) OF PROGRAMS:
● **Cleveland Institute of Music Scholarships**

TYPE:
Scholarships.

PURPOSE:
To provide talented students with a professional, world-class education in the art of music.

ELIGIBILITY:
CIM Scholarship is a merit-based, need-informed award. CIM faculty recommendations of the applicant audition are the primary component for this award. In addition to grades, test scores, outside letters of recommendation and expectation of student potential are considered.

FINANCIAL DATA:
Amount of support per award: Varies.

NO. MOST RECENT APPLICANTS: Varies.

APPLICATION INFO:
Students must apply online.
Deadline: Application timelines are posted online.

ADDRESS INQUIRIES TO:
Jerrod Price
Admissions and Enrollment Management
(See address above.)

COLUMBIA UNIVERSITY

709 Pulitzer Hall
2950 Broadway
New York, NY 10027
(212) 854-3841
E-mail: pulitzer@pulitzer.org
Web Site: www.pulitzer.org

TYPE:
Awards/prizes; Fellowships. Awards in journalism, books and music.

Pulitzer Prizes in Journalism are awarded based on material appearing in a text-based U.S. newspaper or news site that publishes at

least once a week during the year. Awards given for:
(1) meritorious public service by a newspaper through the use of its journalistic resources which may include editorials, cartoons, photographs, graphics and online material;
(2) local, state or national reporting of breaking news;
(3) investigative reporting by an individual or team, presented as a single article or series;
(4) explanatory journalism that illuminates a significant or complex subject, demonstrating mastery of the subject, lucid writing and clear presentation;
(5) reporting on significant issues of local concern;
(6) reporting on national affairs;
(7) reporting on international affairs, including United Nations correspondence;
(8) feature writing giving prime consideration to high literary quality and originality;
(9) commentary;
(10) criticism;
(11) editorial writing;
(12) cartoon or portfolio of cartoons;
(13) breaking news photography in black and white or color, which may consist of a photograph or photographs, a sequence or an album;
(14) feature photography in black and white or color with the same stipulations as above and;
(15) audio journalism that serves the public interest.

Prizes in Letters are restricted to works first published in the U.S. during the year in book form and available for purchase by the general public. Awards given for:
(1) fiction by an American author, preferably dealing with American life;
(2) a play by an American author, preferably original in its source and dealing with American life, produced in the U.S. January 1 to December 31;
(3) appropriately documented book on the history of the U.S.;
(4) appropriately documented biography or autobiography by an American author;
(5) volume of original verse by an American author and;
(6) appropriately documented book of nonfiction by an American author that is not eligible for consideration in any other category.

A prize in music is given for distinguished musical composition by an American that has had its first performance in the U.S. during the year.

Four fellowships enable outstanding graduates to travel, report and study abroad. One fellowship is given to an outstanding graduate who wishes to specialize in drama, music, literary, film or television criticism.

See entry 1757 for full listing.

CONTEMPORARY MUSIC FESTIVAL   [708]
School of Music
Indiana State University
Terre Haute, IN 47809
(812) 237-2743
Fax: (812) 237-3009
E-mail: kurt.fowler@indstate.edu
Web Site: www.indstate.edu/cas/cmf

FOUNDED: 1966

AREAS OF INTEREST:
Contemporary orchestra music.

NAME(S) OF PROGRAMS:
- **Competition for Orchestral Compositions**

TYPE:
Awards/prizes; Conferences/seminars. Performance of new music by the Indianapolis Chamber Orchestra. Winning composers will take part in seminars that are part of the festival and will receive an honorarium to cover expenses.

YEAR PROGRAM STARTED: 1966

PURPOSE:
Performance of new orchestral music.

ELIGIBILITY:
Contestants must be citizens or legal residents of the U.S. Winners of the competition within the last five years are not eligible.

FINANCIAL DATA:
Amount of support per award: First place: $1,000.

NO. MOST RECENT APPLICANTS: 50.

NO. AWARDS: 1.

APPLICATION INFO:
Guidelines are available on the web site.
Deadline: June 1.

ADDRESS INQUIRIES TO:
Indianapolis Chamber Orchestra
4603 Clarendon Road, Suite 36
Indianapolis, IN 46208
Tel: (317) 940-9607

AARON COPLAND FUND FOR MUSIC, INC.   [709]
254 West 31st Street, 15th Floor
New York, NY 10001
(212) 461-6956
Fax: (212) 810-4567
E-mail: info@coplandfund.org
onlinegrants@coplandfund.org
Web Site: www.coplandfund.org

FOUNDED: 1992

AREAS OF INTEREST:
Music.

NAME(S) OF PROGRAMS:
- **Performance Program**
- **Recording Program**
- **Supplemental Program**

TYPE:
General operating grants; Project/program grants. Performance Program: Provides support to performing organizations whose artistic excellence encourages and improves public knowledge and appreciation of serious contemporary American music. Organizations whose principal function is to support a specific performing ensemble should apply to this program.

Recording Program: Documents and provides wider exposure for the music of contemporary American composers, develops audiences for contemporary American music through record distribution and other retail markets, and supports the release and dissemination of recordings of previously unreleased contemporary American music and the reissuance of recordings that are no longer available.

Supplemental Program: Provides support to nonprofit organizations that have a history of substantial commitment to contemporary American music but whose needs are not addressed by the Fund's programs of support

for performing organizations and recording projects, such as presenters and music service organizations.

YEAR PROGRAM STARTED: 1992

PURPOSE:
To encourage and improve public knowledge and appreciation of contemporary American music.

LEGAL BASIS:
Foundation.

ELIGIBILITY:
For the Performance Program, applicants must be nonprofit professional performing ensembles with a history of substantial commitment to contemporary American music and with plans to continue that commitment. Ensembles must have been in existence for at least two years at the time of application. Festivals are only eligible to apply for their professional core ensembles. Individuals, student ensembles, presenters without a core ensemble are not eligible. Grants will not be made for the purpose of commissions to composers.

For the Recording Program, applicants must be nonprofit performance ensembles, presenting institutions or nonprofit or commercial recording companies. Any applicant who, as of the deadline date, has one or more Recording Program grants that have been paid but that have not been released within two years after receiving funds will not be eligible to apply for a Recording Program grant. Grants will not be made for the purpose of commissions to composers.

Supplemental Program: Applications may be submitted by nonprofit organizations that have a history of substantial commitment to contemporary American music but whose needs are not addressed by the Fund's programs of support for performing organizations and recording projects. Organizations must have been in existence for at least two years at the time of application.

FINANCIAL DATA:
Amount of support per award: $1,000 to $20,000 for Performance Program and Supplemental Program; Up to $20,000 for the Recording Program.
Total amount of support: Varies.

NO. MOST RECENT APPLICANTS: Approximately 550.

NO. AWARDS: Varies.

APPLICATION INFO:
Fund guidelines and application procedures are available to prospective applicants on the Fund's web site.
Duration: Varies depending on needs and nature of the request.

ADDRESS INQUIRIES TO:
Grants Manager
E-mail: grantsmanager@coplandfund.org
(See address above.)

THE CURTIS INSTITUTE OF MUSIC   [710]
1726 Locust Street
Philadelphia, PA 19103
(215) 717-3117
E-mail: admissions@curtis.edu
Web Site: www.curtis.edu

FOUNDED: 1924

AREAS OF INTEREST:
Musical performance.

NAME(S) OF PROGRAMS:
- **Bachelor of Music Degree Program**
- **Diploma Program**
- **Master of Music in Opera**

TYPE:
Scholarships. The training of young performing musicians, admitted by competitive audition for a tuition-free musical education.

YEAR PROGRAM STARTED: 1924

PURPOSE:
To train exceptionally gifted young musicians for careers as performing artists on the highest professional level.

LEGAL BASIS:
The school is operated under a Charter granted by the Commonwealth of Pennsylvania and is also included in the list of "Colleges and Universities in Pennsylvania approved by the State Council of Education for the Granting of Degrees."
The U.S. Government has duly approved the Curtis Institute of Music as an institution of learning for the attendance of nonimmigrant students, under the Immigration and Nationality Act.

ELIGIBILITY:
All are eligible for the competitive audition, regardless of race, origin or geographic distribution.

For Bachelor of Music Degree Program and Diploma Program, eligibility requirements consist of a competitive audition, high school diploma or GED, SAT Scores, English achievement scores and TOEFL for foreign students.

For Master of Music Degree Programs, eligibility requirements consist of a competitive audition and previous Bachelor's degree.

FINANCIAL DATA:
All students are on a scholarship basis exclusively and pay no tuition fees.
Amount of support per award: Varies depending upon award program.
Total amount of support: Varies.

APPLICATION INFO:
The application, required supporting documents, and $150 application fee must be submitted online.
Duration: One-time award.
Deadline: December 16.

PUBLICATIONS:
The Curtis Institute of Music Catalogue (includes application form).

IRS I.D.: 23-1585611

ADDRESS INQUIRIES TO:
Christopher Hodges, Director of Admissions
(See address above.)

EASTMAN SCHOOL OF MUSIC OF THE UNIVERSITY OF ROCHESTER   [711]
26 Gibbs Street
Rochester, NY 14604
(585) 274-1560
Fax: (585) 274-1088
E-mail: gdean@esm.rochester.edu
Web Site: www.esm.rochester.edu

AREAS OF INTEREST:
Music.

NAME(S) OF PROGRAMS:
- **Eastman School of Music Graduate Awards**

TYPE:
Assistantships; Awards/prizes; Fellowships; Internships; Scholarships; Visiting scholars.

PURPOSE:
To support the School's academic programs.

ELIGIBILITY:
Open to nationals of all countries. Candidates should have the qualifications necessary for admission to the Eastman School of Music. Non-U.S. citizens are usually offered service scholarships in ensemble work at graduate level.

FINANCIAL DATA:
Amount of support per award: Up to $21,000 in stipend and $41,520 in tuition scholarship per year.
Total amount of support: Approximately $9,000,000 annually.

NO. AWARDS: 350.

APPLICATION INFO:
Applicants must complete an application form. In addition, awards require an interview in Rochester or at one of the regional auditions.
Duration: One academic year. Renewable.
Deadline: December 1.

ADDRESS INQUIRIES TO:
Admissions Office
Eastman School of Music
(See address above.)

AVERY FISHER ARTIST PROGRAM   [712]
c/o Veronique Firkusny
155 West 68th Street, Suite 1130
New York, NY 10023
(917) 363-4380
E-mail: averyfisherartistprogram@firkusny.org
Web Site: www.averyfisherartistprogram.org

FOUNDED: 1974

AREAS OF INTEREST:
Music, specifically classical instrumentalists.

NAME(S) OF PROGRAMS:
- **The Avery Fisher Career Grants**
- **The Avery Fisher Prize**

TYPE:
Awards/prizes; Grants-in-aid. Awards for excellence and help in launching major careers.

YEAR PROGRAM STARTED: 1974

PURPOSE:
To recognize outstanding classical instrumentalists and chamber ensembles.

LEGAL BASIS:
Not-for-profit, tax-exempt.

ELIGIBILITY:
Instrumentalists who are U.S. citizens or permanent residents may be nominated.

FINANCIAL DATA:
Amount of support per award: Avery Fisher Career Grants: $25,000 each; Avery Fisher Prize: $100,000.
Total amount of support: Varies.

NO. AWARDS: Up to 5 Career Grants per year. Avery Fisher Prize is considered every year, but awarded at the discretion of the Executive Committee.

APPLICATION INFO:
Individual artists may not apply directly. Nominations are made by the Recommendation Board, which comprises nationally known instrumentalists, conductors, chamber ensembles, music educators and presenters. Final selections are made by the Executive Committee. The Program is administered by the Lincoln Center for the Performing Arts, Inc.
Deadline: Varies.

EXECUTIVE COMMITTEE:
Emanuel Ax
Deborah Borda
Marylou Falcone
David Finckel
Henry Fogel
Anthony Fogg
Pamela Frank
Jeremy Geffen
Ara Guzelimian
Wu Han
Yo-Yo Ma
Jane S. Moss
Chad Smith
Matias Tarnopolsky
Henry Timms

ADDRESS INQUIRIES TO:
Veronique Firkusny, Executive Director
(See address above.)

FONDATION DES ETATS-UNIS   [713]
15, boulevard Jourdan
75014 Paris France
(33) 1 53 80 68 80
Fax: (33) 1 53 80 68 99
E-mail: culture@feusa.org
Web Site: www.feusa.org/harriet-hale-woolley-scholarship

FOUNDED: 1929

AREAS OF INTEREST:
Grants for musicians, artists, and psychiatry residents.

CONSULTING OR VOLUNTEER SERVICES:
Office of Cultural Affairs.

NAME(S) OF PROGRAMS:
- **Harriet Hale Woolley Scholarship**

TYPE:
Awards/prizes; Development grants; Scholarships. Bequeathed to the Fondation des Etats-Unis, Cite Internationale Universitaire de Paris in the early 1930s, the Harriet Hale Woolley Scholarship is awarded annually to a select number of exceptional American artists and musicians who plan to pursue their studies in Paris.

A scholarship is also available to French, Swiss and American medical postgraduates specializing in psychiatry with an internship in a Parisian hospital.

The scholarship is not intended for research in art history or musicology, nor for dance or theater.

YEAR PROGRAM STARTED: 1933

PURPOSE:
To promote artistic and cultural exchange between the U.S. and France.

LEGAL BASIS:
Fondation Reconnue d'Utilite Publique (FRUP).

ELIGIBILITY:
Requirements include:
(1) American citizenship;

(2) between 21 and 29 years of age;
(3) graduation with high academic standing from an American college, university, or professional school of recognized standing;
(4) evidence of accomplishment in the candidate's field of expertise;
(5) proposal of a unique and detailed artistic project related to one's field of study that requires a one-year residency in Paris and;
(6) good moral character, personality and adaptability, plus good physical health and emotional stability.

Scholarship recipient must reside at the Fondation des Etats-Unis for the academic year.

FINANCIAL DATA:
The Scholarship is designed to assist with living expenses while in Paris.
Amount of support per award: Stipend of EUR 10,000 (may vary subject to fund earnings), payable in four installments during the academic year (October 1 to June 30).

NO. MOST RECENT APPLICANTS: 15 to 20.

NO. AWARDS: Artists and musicians: Up to 5; Postgraduates in Psychiatry: 1.

APPLICATION INFO:
Application should be made by e-mail. Instructions are available online.
Duration: One academic year.
Deadline: All application dossiers and their supporting materials must be received no later than January 31, for the current academic year.

STAFF:
Dr. Anne Cremieux, Director
Dr. Sophie Vasset, Director
Noëmi Haire-Sievers, Culture and International Relations Manager

ADDRESS INQUIRIES TO:
Harriet Hale Woolley Scholarship
(See address above.)

*SPECIAL STIPULATIONS:
As this project should include enrollment in a recognized institution, it is strongly suggested that the candidate establish a significant contact with a teacher or institution prior to arriving in France and to show evidence of this contact in his or her application dossier.

FROMM MUSIC FOUNDATION AT HARVARD [714]
Department of Music
3 Oxford Street
Harvard University
Cambridge, MA 02138
(617) 495-2791
Fax: (617) 496-8081
E-mail: musicdpt@fas.harvard.edu
Web Site: frommfoundation.fas.harvard.edu

FOUNDED: 1972

AREAS OF INTEREST:
Commissioning and performance of contemporary music.

TYPE:
Commission and grant-in-aid.

YEAR PROGRAM STARTED: 1952

PURPOSE:
To bring contemporary music closer to the public by providing support to composers and performers.

LEGAL BASIS:
Private foundation.

ELIGIBILITY:
Composers must be citizens or residents of the U.S. For these purposes, "residents" shall be deemed to include only lawful permanent residents, temporary residents, asylees, refugees and nonimmigrants who have lawfully been admitted to the U.S. for a term of one year or more.

FINANCIAL DATA:
Amount of support per award: $12,000.

NO. MOST RECENT APPLICANTS: 250.

NO. AWARDS: 12 annually.

APPLICATION INFO:
Applicants must contact the Foundation for an application.
Deadline: June 1 for consideration in following fall. Commissions will be awarded in December.

PUBLICATIONS:
Application guidelines.

STAFF:
Enrique Marquez, Administrator

DIRECTORS:
Ingrid Monson, Chairperson
George Lewis
Chen Yi

ADDRESS INQUIRIES TO:
Enrique Marquez, Administrator
(See address above.)

*SPECIAL STIPULATIONS:
For those who have previously received a Fromm Commission, there is a 15-year waiting period before you can apply again. The Fromm Commission cannot be applied to projects that have been awarded other commissions.

THE GRAMMY MUSEUM [715]
888 South Figueroa Street
Los Angeles, CA 90017
(310) 581-1260
E-mail: grants@grammy.com
Web Site: www.grammymuseum.
org/programs/grants-program

FOUNDED: 1989

AREAS OF INTEREST:
Music research, archiving and preserving and the medical and occupational well-being of music professionals.

TYPE:
Challenge/matching grants; Project/program grants; Research grants. The GRAMMY Museum Grant Program funds the following areas:
(1) Scientific Research Projects - Grants to organizations and individuals to support efforts that advance the research and/or broad reaching implementations of original scientific research projects related to the impact of music on the human condition, such as the links between music study and early childhood development, the effects of music therapy and the medical and occupational well-being of music professionals.
(2) Archiving and Preservation Projects - Grants to organizations and individuals to support efforts that advance the archiving and preservation of the music and recorded sound heritage of the Americas. The Archiving and Preservation area has two funding categories:
(a) Preservation Implementation and (b) Planning, Assessment and/or Consultation.

YEAR PROGRAM STARTED: 1989

PURPOSE:
To cultivate the understanding, appreciation and advancement of the contribution of recorded music to American culture.

ELIGIBILITY:
Priority is given to music projects of national significance that achieve a broad reach and whose final results are accessible to the general public.

The GRAMMY Museum, Inc., will not fund:
(1) chapters, trustees, officers or staff;
(2) organizations that discriminate on the basis of race, sex, religion, national origin, disability or age;
(3) recording projects, demo tapes or live performances designed to promote the career of an individual or group;
(4) faculty and staff salaries unrelated to the project;
(5) performance events;
(6) purchase or repairs of music instruments or equipment;
(7) competitions and related expenses;
(8) work toward academic degrees;
(9) regular ongoing business activities of corporate clients;
(10) organizations or individuals for more than three consecutive years;
(11) organizations not based in the U.S. or;
(12) documentaries, endowments and web sites.

FINANCIAL DATA:
Amount of support per award: Up to $20,000.
Total amount of support: Varies.

NO. AWARDS: 14 for the year 2018.

APPLICATION INFO:
Letters of inquiry are only accepted online. Guidelines are available on the Foundation web site. Applicants must use current grant application only and should also include:
(1) evidence of organization's nonprofit status and copy of IRS tax determination letter;
(2) general description, history and accomplishments of the organization;
(3) current resume for individual applicants and organization's key personnel;
(4) two letters of support for the project and;
(5) an itemized budget.

Late or incomplete applications will not be reviewed.
Duration: Six to 24 months.
Deadline: October 15. Invitation to submit full proposal sent in November. Notification following spring.

ADDRESS INQUIRIES TO:
Derek Spencer, Senior Coordinator
Grants and Education
(See address above.)

*SPECIAL STIPULATIONS:
Projects must be completed and a final report submitted within 12 to 24 months of project start date. A full set of the completed project is due to The GRAMMY Museum within 90 days of the project completion date. Grantees must formally credit The GRAMMY Museum in all published materials and announcements.

GUITAR FOUNDATION OF AMERICA [716]
P.O. Box 2900
Palos Verdes Peninsula, CA 90274
(877) 570-1651
E-mail: info@guitarfoundation.org
Web Site: www.guitarfoundation.org

FOUNDED: 1973

AREAS OF INTEREST:
Classical guitar.

NAME(S) OF PROGRAMS:
- **International Concert Artists Competition**
- **International Youth Competition**
- **Regional Events**

TYPE:
Awards/prizes; Conferences/seminars. International Youth Competition awarded in two divisions: Division I for ages 15 to 18 years old and Division II for ages 14 years old and under.

PURPOSE:
To support the serious study of the guitar in its historic and performance aspects; to promote the guitar as an ensemble instrument; to encourage composition and arrangements of ensemble music involving the guitar; to preserve and make available literature on the guitar.

LEGAL BASIS:
501(c)(3).

ELIGIBILITY:
Open to competitors worldwide.

FINANCIAL DATA:
Amount of support per award: Varies.
Total amount of support: Varies.

NO. AWARDS: 3 grand prize winners annually.

IRS I.D.: 51-0147668

ADDRESS INQUIRIES TO:
E-mail: ekhamas@guitarfoundation.org

THE KOSCIUSZKO FOUNDATION, INC.   [717]
15 East 65th Street
New York, NY 10065
(212) 734-2130 ext. 414
E-mail: chopin@thekf.org
Web Site: www.kfchopin.org

FOUNDED: 1925

AREAS OF INTEREST:
Polish culture in the U.S., friendship and understanding between the U.S. and Poland through educational and cultural programs.

NAME(S) OF PROGRAMS:
- **Chopin Piano Competition**

TYPE:
Awards/prizes; Scholarships.

YEAR PROGRAM STARTED: 1949

PURPOSE:
To encourage gifted young pianists to further their studies and perform the works of Chopin, Szymanowski and other Polish composers.

LEGAL BASIS:
501(c)(3) not-for-profit organization.

ELIGIBILITY:
The competition is open to pianists of all nationalities representing a professional level of performance, born between January 1, 1989 and December 31, 2001. It is expected that applicants will have demonstrated exceptional talent and artistic achievement. Contestants may apply to compete in the preliminaries in New York. Each contestant should have a program of at least 60 minutes and is expected to perform complete works from memory.

GEOG. RESTRICTIONS: United States.

FINANCIAL DATA:
Amount of support per award: $10,000 first prize; $5,000 second prize; $3,000 third prize.
Total amount of support: $20,000.

APPLICATION INFO:
Official application materials are available upon request to the Foundation. Send business-size, self-addressed, stamped envelope. These materials are also available on the web site.
Deadline: January 1.

PUBLICATIONS:
KF newsletter; annual report.

IRS I.D.: 13-1628179

STAFF:
Marek Skulimowski, President and Executive Director

ADDRESS INQUIRIES TO:
Chopin Piano Competition
(See address above.)

THE LEEDS INTERNATIONAL PIANO COMPETITION   [718]
The Piano Competition Office
The University of Leeds
169B Woodhouse Lane
Leeds LS2 9JT England
(44) 0113 244 6586
Fax: (44) 0113 234 6106
E-mail: info@leedspiano.com
Web Site: www.leedspiano.com

FOUNDED: 1961

AREAS OF INTEREST:
Piano.

TYPE:
Awards/prizes. Prizes in piano awarded every third year.

YEAR PROGRAM STARTED: 1963

PURPOSE:
To provide a competition for professional pianists.

LEGAL BASIS:
Charity.

ELIGIBILITY:
The Competition is open to professional pianists of all nationalities born between October 1, 1988 and April 1, 1998.

FINANCIAL DATA:
Amount of support per award: GBP 1,000 to GBP 25,000.
Total amount of support: Prize money in excess of GBP 70,000.

APPLICATION INFO:
Application may be made online. Competitors must complete the form in English and upload both an audio recording of a performance from the audition repertoire and a set of documents as specified online.
Deadline: October 31.

ADDRESS INQUIRIES TO:
Linda Wellings, Operations Director
(See e-mail address above.)

THE LESCHETIZKY ASSOCIATION, INC.   [719]
880 West 181st Street
Apartment 3H
New York, NY 10033
(212) 781-5377
E-mail: tleschetizky@gmail.com
alison.thomas@verizon.net
Web Site: www.leschetizky.org
www.concertocompetitionTL.org

FOUNDED: 1942

AREAS OF INTEREST:
Piano playing and instruction.

CONSULTING OR VOLUNTEER SERVICES:
Performance opportunities and workshops.

NAME(S) OF PROGRAMS:
- **Concerto Competition "Theodor Leschetizky" for Gifted Young Pianists**

TYPE:
Awards/prizes. First prize winner plays full concerto with orchestra in New York City.

PURPOSE:
To perpetuate Theodor Leschetizky's principles of pianism and teaching by offering programs and performing opportunities for pianists, piano teachers and students.

LEGAL BASIS:
Tax-exempt organization under the IRS code 501(c)(3).

ELIGIBILITY:
Open to pianists aged 17 and younger, internationally.

FINANCIAL DATA:
Amount of support per award: $300 to $1,000.
Total amount of support: $10,000.

NO. MOST RECENT APPLICANTS: Varies.

NO. AWARDS: First and second prize; other awards at the discretion of judges.

APPLICATION INFO:
Information is available online. Entry materials may be mailed to Alison Thomas at the address below.

PUBLICATIONS:
Annual bulletin.

OFFICERS:
Zelma Bodzin, President
Dr. Alison Thomas, Competition Chairman

ADDRESS INQUIRIES TO:
Dr. Alison Thomas, Competition Chairman
(See address above.)

LONG-THIBAUD-CRESPIN COMPETITION   [720]
32, avenue Matignon
75008 Paris France
(33) 1 42 66 66 80
Fax: (33) 1 42 66 06 43
E-mail: contact@long-thibaud-crespin.org
Web Site: www.long-thibaud-crespin.org

FOUNDED: 1943

AREAS OF INTEREST:
Music.

TYPE:
Awards/prizes. International competition for piano, violin and voice. The competition varies yearly: The Crespin Singing Competition (2020); The Thibaud Violin Competition (2021); The Long Piano Competition (2022).

ELIGIBILITY:
Candidate maximum age of 30 years on January 1 of the year of the contest.

FINANCIAL DATA:
Amount of support per award: First Grand Prize: EUR 25,000. There are other prizes also in each competition.

NO. MOST RECENT APPLICANTS: 57.

NO. AWARDS: Varies with the competition.

APPLICATION INFO:
Information about the various competitions can be found on the web site.
Duration: One week.
Deadline: Varies.

PUBLICATIONS:
Brochures.

OFFICERS:
Bernard Volker, President

ADDRESS INQUIRIES TO:
Delegate General
Long-Thibaud-Crespin Competition
(See address above.)

E. NAKAMICHI FOUNDATION   [721]
10736 Jefferson Boulevard
P.M.B. 523
Culver City, CA 90230
(714) 771-9677
E-mail: enakamichi.foundation@gmail.com
Web Site: www.enfoundation.com

FOUNDED: 1985

AREAS OF INTEREST:
Music.

TYPE:
Project/program grants. Performance of music by classical and romantic period composers.

YEAR PROGRAM STARTED: 1986

PURPOSE:
To support appreciation of music by classical and romantic period composers.

LEGAL BASIS:
Private foundation.

ELIGIBILITY:
Eligible organizations must be 501(c)(3) tax-exempt. Individuals and religious organizations are ineligible.

GEOG. RESTRICTIONS: Japan and United States.

FINANCIAL DATA:
Amount of support per award: $3,000 to $10,000.
Total amount of support: Generally $100,000 to $200,000 per year.

NO. MOST RECENT APPLICANTS: 60.

NO. AWARDS: 25.

APPLICATION INFO:
Contact the Foundation for application procedures.
Duration: Single/multiple performances.
Deadline: March 15 and October 15.

IRS I.D.: 95-3870341

ADDRESS INQUIRIES TO:
Gayle Yamazaki, President
(See address above.)

*PLEASE NOTE:
The Foundation is only accepting grant applications from those organizations that were successfully awarded a grant in the years 2000 through 2007.

NATIONAL ASSOCIATION OF COMPOSERS, USA (NACUSA)   [722]
P.O. Box 49256
Barrington Station
Los Angeles, CA 90049
(541) 418-1182
E-mail: gregsteinke@mail.music-usa.org
Web Site: nacusa.us

FOUNDED: 1932

AREAS OF INTEREST:
The performance, publication, broadcasting and archiving of new American concert hall music.

NAME(S) OF PROGRAMS:
• **Young Composers' Competition**

TYPE:
Awards/prizes; Conferences/seminars. Cash awards and guaranteed performances.

YEAR PROGRAM STARTED: 1978

PURPOSE:
To recognize and encourage young talent.

LEGAL BASIS:
501(c)(3) nonprofit organization.

ELIGIBILITY:
Open to all NACUSA members who are American citizens or residents, who have reached their 18th birthday, but have not yet reached their 32nd birthday by the submission deadline. Compositions submitted should not exceed 10 to 12 minutes. Compositions should not be published nor have won other competitions. Two works may be submitted.

Instrumentation varies from year to year; check NACUSA web site for current instrumentation and other details.

GEOG. RESTRICTIONS: United States.

FINANCIAL DATA:
Amount of support per award: First prize: $500 and a guaranteed performance at a NACUSA concert; Second prize: $400; Third prize: $300 and possible performances at a NACUSA concert.

CO-OP FUNDING PROGRAMS: Contest is supported, in part, by grants from ASCAP and BMI.

NO. MOST RECENT APPLICANTS: 30.

NO. AWARDS: 15 annually.

APPLICATION INFO:
Complete information and electronic application submission is available on the Association web site.
Deadline: December 15.

PUBLICATIONS:
Composer/USA, newsletter.

IRS I.D.: 51-0166704

ADDRESS INQUIRIES TO:
Dr. Greg A. Steinke, President
(See e-mail address above.)

NATIONAL FEDERATION OF MUSIC CLUBS   [723]
1646 West Smith Valley Road
Greenwood, IN 46142
(317) 882-4003
Fax: (317) 882-4019
E-mail: info@nfmc-music.org
Web Site: www.nfmc-music.org

FOUNDED: 1898

AREAS OF INTEREST:
Vocal and instrumental music, dance and composition.

NAME(S) OF PROGRAMS:
• **NFMC Competitions and Awards**

TYPE:
Awards/prizes. Competitions. Awards for students and adults who show proficiency in the fields of voice, instrumental performance, dance, composition, etc. The Federation provides a wide range of awards.

PURPOSE:
To support performance and promotion of American music.

LEGAL BASIS:
Nonprofit.

ELIGIBILITY:
Competitions cover a wide range of age groups from age 10 through adult. In general, applicants must be native-born or naturalized American citizens and must be members or become members of the National Federation of Music Clubs either by individual or group affiliation before applications are accepted.

GEOG. RESTRICTIONS: United States.

FINANCIAL DATA:
Amount of support per award: $25 to $20,000.
Total amount of support: Over $750,000 at the local, state and national level.

APPLICATION INFO:
Award requirements and application forms are available on the NFMC web site or contact the Chair of the specific award. All award applications must be submitted online by uploading them to the NFMC web site.
Duration: One-time award.

PUBLICATIONS:
Competitions and awards chart; *Junior Keynotes Magazine; Music Club Magazine.*

OFFICERS:
Michael Edwards, President
Barbara Hildebrand, Treasurer
Jeanne Hryniewicki, Recording Secretary

STAFF:
Jennifer Griffin, Executive Director

ADDRESS INQUIRIES TO:
Jennifer Griffin, Executive Director
(See address above.)

NATIONAL FEDERATION OF MUSIC CLUBS   [724]
1646 West Smith Valley Road
Greenwood, IN 46142
(317) 882-4003
Fax: (317) 882-4019
E-mail: info@nfmc-music.org
Web Site: www.nfmc-music.org

FOUNDED: 1898

AREAS OF INTEREST:
Vocal and instrumental music and composition.

NAME(S) OF PROGRAMS:
• **Award Program for Summer Music Festivals and Music Centers**

TYPE:
Awards/prizes. Prizes for the performance and promotion of American music at summer music festivals.

PURPOSE:
To support performance and promotion of
American music.

LEGAL BASIS:
Nonprofit.

ELIGIBILITY:
Program open to summer music festivals,
centers and camps in the U.S. and its
territories. In general, applicants must be
native-born or naturalized American citizens
and must be members or become members of
the National Federation of Music Clubs
either by individual or group affiliation
before applications are accepted.

GEOG. RESTRICTIONS: United States.

FINANCIAL DATA:
Amount of support per award: Average $200
to $3,000.

NO. AWARDS: Over 38.

OFFICERS:
Michael Edwards, President
Barbara Hildebrand, Treasurer
Jeanne Hryniewicki, Recording Secretary

STAFF:
Jennifer Griffin, Executive Director

ADDRESS INQUIRIES TO:
Jennifer Griffin, Executive Director
(See address above.)

NATIONAL FEDERATION OF MUSIC CLUBS   [725]

1646 West Smith Valley Road
Greenwood, IN 46142
(317) 882-4003
Fax: (317) 882-4019
E-mail: info@nfmc-music.org
Web Site: www.nfmc-music.org

FOUNDED: 1898

AREAS OF INTEREST:
Dedicated to finding and fostering young
musical talent.

NAME(S) OF PROGRAMS:
● **Dorothy Dann Bullock Music Therapy
Award**

TYPE:
Grants-in-aid. Financial assistance.

PURPOSE:
To support performance and promotion of
American music.

LEGAL BASIS:
Nonprofit.

ELIGIBILITY:
Offered to Music Therapy Majors (college
sophomores, juniors or seniors) in accredited
schools offering Music Therapy degrees
approved by American Music Therapy
Association. Applicants must be native-born
or naturalized American citizens and must be
members or become members of NFMC
either by individual or group affiliation
before applications are accepted.

GEOG. RESTRICTIONS: United States.

FINANCIAL DATA:
Amount of support per award: $1,500.
Total amount of support: $1,500 annually.

NO. AWARDS: 1 annually.

APPLICATION INFO:
Application information is available on the
web site.
Deadline: March 1.

OFFICERS:
Michael Edwards, President
Barbara Hildebrand, Treasurer
Jeanne Hryniewicki, Recording Secretary

STAFF:
Jennifer Griffin, Executive Director

ADDRESS INQUIRIES TO:
Bullock Music Therapy Award
(See address above.)

NATIONAL OPERA ASSOCIATION, INC.   [726]

2403 Russell Long Boulevard
Canyon, TX 79016
(806) 651-2843
Fax: (806) 651-2958
E-mail: rhansen@noa.org
rhansen@wtamu.edu
Web Site: www.noa.org

FOUNDED: 1955

AREAS OF INTEREST:
Opera production, opera composition,
promotion of operatic talent and opera
education.

CONSULTING OR VOLUNTEER SERVICES:
Distinguished members available for
consultation and workshops.

NAME(S) OF PROGRAMS:
● **Carolyn Bailey and Dominick Argento
Vocal Competition**
● **Biennial Dissertation Competition**
● **Chamber Opera Competition**
● **Collegiate Opera Scenes Competition**
● **Opera Production Competition**
● **Scholarly Paper Competition**

TYPE:
Awards/prizes. Cash prizes awarded to Artist
Division winners and Scholarship Division
winners. Also scholarships to AIMS, awarded
in both divisions. Productions of winning
operas in Chamber Opera Competition will
be scheduled for annual convention.

YEAR PROGRAM STARTED: 1977

PURPOSE:
To assist young opera singers in furthering
their training for an operatic career and to
honor the best of the new chamber operas
and the outstanding opera productions by
universities and colleges.

LEGAL BASIS:
Nonprofit organization.

ELIGIBILITY:
All applicants must submit an entrance fee
depending on category and membership
status.

FINANCIAL DATA:
Amount of support per award: $500 to
$2,000 for singing competitors.
Total amount of support: Approximately
$10,000.

NO. MOST RECENT APPLICANTS: 180 for vocal
competition, 80 for opera production
competition and 45 for chamber opera
competition.

NO. AWARDS: Approximately 10.

APPLICATION INFO:
Application information is available on the
web site.
Duration: Varies.
Deadline: Varies by contest.

PUBLICATIONS:
Opera Journal; NOA Newsletter.

ADDRESS INQUIRIES TO:
Robert Hansen, Executive Director
(See address above.)

NATIONAL ORCHESTRAL INSTITUTE   [727]

3800 Clarice Smith Performing Arts Center
University of Maryland School of Music
College Park, MD 20742
(301) 405-2317
Fax: (301) 405-5977
E-mail: noi@umd.edu
Web Site: theclarice.umd.edu/noi

FOUNDED: 1988

AREAS OF INTEREST:
Orchestral music.

TYPE:
Residencies; Scholarships; Training grants;
Visiting scholars. Advanced orchestral
training program offering talented musicians
on the threshold of their professional careers
a four-week opportunity to study and perform
under internationally renowned conductors
and principal musicians from leading
American orchestras.

YEAR PROGRAM STARTED: 1988

PURPOSE:
To prepare musicians for professional
orchestral careers.

LEGAL BASIS:
University.

ELIGIBILITY:
Applicants must be between the ages of 18
and 28 with appropriate orchestral music
skill.

FINANCIAL DATA:
Support includes tuition at the Institute.
Amount of support per award: Over $4,000.
Total amount of support: Varies.

NO. AWARDS: Approximately 750.

APPLICATION INFO:
Applicants should submit an application,
resume and one letter of recommendation.
They should also audition at one of the
audition centers in cities across the U.S.
between January and March.
Duration: June 1 to June 30.
Deadline: Varies by audition location.

PUBLICATIONS:
Program announcement.

ADDRESS INQUIRIES TO:
Richard Scerbo, Director
(See address above.)

THE WALTER W. NAUMBURG FOUNDATION, INC.   [728]

120 Claremont Avenue
New York, NY 10027
(917) 493-4040
E-mail: naumburgfoundation@gmail.com
Web Site: www.naumburg.org

FOUNDED: 1925

AREAS OF INTEREST:
Sponsorship of international competitions for
various musical instruments and voice.

TYPE:
Awards/prizes.

ELIGIBILITY:
This competition is open to musicians of all
nationalities. Requirements differ by
category.

FINANCIAL DATA:
Amount of support per award: $25,000 first prize, $15,000 second prize and $10,000 third prize.

APPLICATION INFO:
Application forms may be obtained online.
Duration: One-time award.

ADDRESS INQUIRIES TO:
Debra Kinzler, Associate Director
(See address above.)

*PLEASE NOTE:
The solo competition disciplines rotate from year to year.

NEW MUSIC USA   [729]
90 Broad Street, Suite 1902
New York, NY 10004
(212) 645-6949
Fax: (646) 490-0998
E-mail: info@newmusicusa.org
Web Site: www.newmusicusa.org

FOUNDED: 2011

AREAS OF INTEREST:
Living composers and contemporary music of all kinds.

NAME(S) OF PROGRAMS:
● **Impact Fund**
● **Music Alive**
● **Project Grants**

TYPE:
Awards/prizes; General operating grants; Project/program grants; Residencies. The Impact Fund supports and promotes small, artist-driven ensembles, presenters, and venues in New York City.

Music Alive supports composer-in-residence positions in orchestras of all sizes.

Project Grants offer project-specific funding to individuals and organizations.

PURPOSE:
To increase opportunities for composers by fostering the creation, performances, dissemination, and appreciation of their music; to fund the creation of new work; to support direct contact between composers and audiences; to create education programs that deepen the understanding of composers and their work; to establish innovative private- and public-sector partnerships that create new opportunities.

LEGAL BASIS:
Nonprofit corporation.

GEOG. RESTRICTIONS: United States.

FINANCIAL DATA:
Amount of support per award: Impact Fund: $3,000 to $10,000; Project Grants: $250 to $15,000.

Total amount of support: Approximately $1,000,000 annually.

APPLICATION INFO:
Guidelines are available online.
Duration: Varies.
Deadline: Varies.

IRS I.D.: 13-0432981

BOARD OF DIRECTORS:
Frederick Peters, Chairperson
Amy Iwano, Vice Chairperson
Joseph M. Walker, Treasurer
Matias Tarnopolsky, Secretary

ADDRESS INQUIRIES TO:
Scott Winship
Director of Grantmaking Programs
(See address above.)

ORCHESTRE SYMPHONIQUE DE MONTREAL (OSM)   [730]
1600, rue Saint-Urbain
Montreal QC H2X 0S1 Canada
(514) 840-7400 ext. 7415
Fax: (514) 842-0728
E-mail: concours@osm.ca
Web Site: www.osm.ca/en/competition

FOUNDED: 1937

AREAS OF INTEREST:
Music.

NAME(S) OF PROGRAMS:
● **OSM Competition**

TYPE:
Awards/prizes; Scholarships. Grand prize includes money prize, a performance with the Orchestre symphonique de Montreal, concert opportunities with various organizations throughout Canada, scholarships at leading North American summer academies and a professional recording by ICI Musique.

YEAR PROGRAM STARTED: 1940

PURPOSE:
To encourage young Canadian musicians.

LEGAL BASIS:
Symphony orchestra.

ELIGIBILITY:
Open to Canadian citizens or landed immigrants in the following categories: Piano and Strings, up to 25 years of age; Woodwinds and Brass, 16 to 25 years of age (except tuba, 16 to 30 years of age); Percussion, 16 to 30 years of age; Voice, 22 to 30 years of age.

Each year is for a different category.

FINANCIAL DATA:
Amount of support per award: One grand prize: $15,000 (CAN); two first prizes: $10,000 (CAN). Three second prizes: $5,000 (CAN). Three third prizes: $2,500 (CAN). Three prizes for the best interpretation of a Canadian work: $2,500 (CAN).

Total amount of support: More than $100,000 (CAN) in prizes, scholarships and concert opportunities.

NO. MOST RECENT APPLICANTS: 85 to 95.

NO. AWARDS: Approximately 15 annually.

APPLICATION INFO:
Include application form, registration fee, proof of age and of Canadian citizenship and curriculum vitae. Applicants must contact OSM Competition to acquire full details of application process.
Deadline: May 10.

ADDRESS INQUIRIES TO:
OSM Competition
(See address above.)

*PLEASE NOTE:
Musical program approved by the jury members of the competition.

PERCUSSIVE ARTS SOCIETY   [731]
110 West Washington Street
Suite A
Indianapolis, IN 46204
(317) 974-4488
Fax: (317) 974-4499
E-mail: percarts@pas.org
Web Site: www.pas.org

FOUNDED: 1961

AREAS OF INTEREST:
Percussive arts, including music education, performance and literature related to percussion instruments.

CONSULTING OR VOLUNTEER SERVICES:
The Society has consulting committees on acoustics, education curricula, literature, etc.

NAME(S) OF PROGRAMS:
● **Terry Gibbs Vibraphone Scholarship**
● **John E. Grimes Timpani Scholarship**
● **Freddie Gruber Scholarship**
● **Internship Program**
● **PASIC International Scholarship**
● **PASIC Scholarships**
● **PAS/Armand Zildjian Percussion Scholarship**
● **PAS/Remo, Inc. Fred Hoey Memorial Scholarship**
● **Percussion Composition Contest**
● **Zildjian Family Opportunity Fund**

TYPE:
Awards/prizes; Internships; Project/program grants; Scholarships.

YEAR PROGRAM STARTED: 1961

PURPOSE:
To promote percussion education, research, performance and appreciation.

LEGAL BASIS:
Not-for-profit corporation.

ELIGIBILITY:
Applicants must be members of the Society.

Internships are open to enrolled music business major students in an accredited university program.

FINANCIAL DATA:
Amount of support per award: Varies.
Total amount of support: Approximately $60,000 in grants and scholarships annually.

APPLICATION INFO:
Application may be submitted online. Consult Society web site.
Duration: Education scholarships and grants: One year.
Deadline: Varies.

PUBLICATIONS:
Percussive Notes, magazine; *Rhythm! Scene,* digital magazine.

IRS I.D.: 73-1385751

STAFF:
Joshua Simonds, Executive Director

ADDRESS INQUIRIES TO:
Amber Fox, Program Manager
(See address above.)

THE PITTSBURGH NEW MUSIC ENSEMBLE, INC.   [732]
Wellington Square, Suite 102
1225 South Main Street
Greensburg, PA 15601
(512) 785-6255
E-mail: kevin@pnme.org
Web Site: www.pnme.org

FOUNDED: 1975

AREAS OF INTEREST:
New music.

NAME(S) OF PROGRAMS:
- **Harvey Gaul Music Composition Contest**

TYPE:
Awards/prizes.

YEAR PROGRAM STARTED: 1975

PURPOSE:
To promote new music and support composers.

LEGAL BASIS:
Nonprofit corporation.

ELIGIBILITY:
Contestants must be U.S. citizens.

FINANCIAL DATA:
Amount of support per award: $6,000 commission.

NO. AWARDS: 1.

APPLICATION INFO:
An entry form is required. An entry fee of $20 must accompany each composition. Contestants should send a score and CD of a representative instrumental work, along with a current biography and contact information. No MIDI realizations.

PUBLICATIONS:
Application guidelines.

IRS I.D.: 25-1364030

OFFICERS:
Samantha Bennett, Executive Director
Catherine Noe'Rourke, Executive Director
Kevin Noe, Artistic Director

ADDRESS INQUIRIES TO:
Kevin Noe, Artistic Director
(See address above.)

*PLEASE NOTE:
Contest is on an as needed basis, not every year.
The Ensemble does not award scholarships.

PRESSER FOUNDATION   [733]
1501 Cherry Street
Philadelphia, PA 19102
(267) 519-5350
E-mail: trodgers@presserfoundation.org
Web Site: www.presserfoundation.org

FOUNDED: 1939

AREAS OF INTEREST:
Music education and music philanthropy.

NAME(S) OF PROGRAMS:
- **Advancement of Music**
- **Assistance to Worthy Music Teachers**
- **Capital Support**
- **The Presser Foundation Graduate Music Award**
- **The Presser Foundation Undergraduate Scholar Award**
- **Special Projects**

TYPE:
Awards/prizes; General operating grants; Project/program grants.

YEAR PROGRAM STARTED: 1939

PURPOSE:
To provide financial awards to promising undergraduate and graduate students at qualified higher education institutions; to provide grants for the construction and renovation of suitable buildings for musical instruction and performance; to administer emergency aid to worthy music teachers in distress; to provide support to innovative projects and collaborations between music organizations; to provide operating support to worthy music organizations in the Greater Philadelphia area.

LEGAL BASIS:
Private foundation.

GEOG. RESTRICTIONS: United States.

FINANCIAL DATA:
Total amount of support: Advancement of Music: $2,500 to $60,000; Capital Support: $25,000 to $500,000; The Presser Foundation Graduate Music Award: $10,000; The Presser Foundation Undergraduate Scholar Award: Approximately $4,000; Special Projects: $5,000 to $100,000.

APPLICATION INFO:
Applicant must apply through the online grant management system.
Duration: Varies.
Deadline: Advancement of Music: November 15. Capital Support: February 1. The Presser Foundation Undergraduate Scholar Award: September 1. Special Projects: October 15.

ADDRESS INQUIRIES TO:
Teresa Araco Rodgers, Executive Director
(See e-mail address above.)

THE QUEEN ELISABETH INTERNATIONAL MUSIC COMPETITION OF BELGIUM   [734]
20, rue aux Laines
B-1000 Brussels Belgium
(32) 2 213 40 50
E-mail: info@queenelisabethcompetition.be
Web Site: queenelisabethcompetition.be
concoursreineelisabeth.de/en

FOUNDED: 1951

AREAS OF INTEREST:
Voice, violin, piano and cello.

TYPE:
Awards/prizes.

PURPOSE:
To support young artists and thus help to establish their reputations with both professionals and the public through an international competition for music interpretation.

LEGAL BASIS:
Nonprofit organization.

ELIGIBILITY:
Programs alternate each year. The competition is dedicated to the cello in 2021, the voice in 2022, and the violin in 2023.

The competition is open to musicians of all nationalities. The minimum age for applicants is 18. Maximum age is 30 for pianists, violinists, and cellists, and 32 for singers. Instrumental competitors play both assigned works and pieces of their own selection. The competition is divided into selection rounds and final round.

FINANCIAL DATA:
Amount of support per award: Varies.

NO. MOST RECENT APPLICANTS: 331 pianists for the year 2020.

NO. AWARDS: 24 for the year 2020.

APPLICATION INFO:
Applications for registration should be downloaded online and accompanied by the following:
(1) a copy of birth certificate;
(2) proof of nationality;
(3) one photograph in the form of a TIFF file (minimum 300 dpi) for the programme;
(4) curriculum vitae;
(5) documentation providing proof of his or her skill (for example, higher diplomas, repertoire list with works performed in public, prizes and diplomas received from other competitions, press reviews, etc.) and;
(6) a video recording (image and sound) with appropriate music programme.
Deadline: Early December of the year preceding the competition.

PUBLICATIONS:
Competition announcement and rules; brochures.

OFFICERS:
Baron Jan Huyghebaert, Chairman
Nicolas Dernoncourt, Secretary General

ADDRESS INQUIRIES TO:
The Secretariat of the Competition
(See address above.)

SAN FRANCISCO CONSERVATORY OF MUSIC   [735]
50 Oak Street
San Francisco, CA 94102
(415) 503-6214
Fax: (415) 503-6299
E-mail: dhoward@sfcm.edu
Web Site: www.sfcm.edu

FOUNDED: 1917

AREAS OF INTEREST:
Music.

NAME(S) OF PROGRAMS:
- **Performance Scholarships in Music for Students in Bachelor and Master of Music Programs**

TYPE:
Assistantships; Scholarships; Work-study programs. Awards for the study of music at the Conservatory.

YEAR PROGRAM STARTED: 1917

PURPOSE:
To enable talented, needy students to attend the Conservatory.

LEGAL BASIS:
Conservatory of Music.

ELIGIBILITY:
U.S. and foreign citizens may apply. Candidates must have had considerable experience in musical performance and must attend the Conservatory on a full-time basis.

FINANCIAL DATA:
Scholarships are to be applied toward tuition at the Conservatory.
Amount of support per award: $1,000 and up.
Total amount of support: $11,016,000 for the academic year 2018-19.

NO. MOST RECENT APPLICANTS: 950.

NO. AWARDS: 456 for the academic year 2018-19.

APPLICATION INFO:
Applicants must submit the San Francisco Conservatory of Music Application and either the Free Application for Federal Student Aid or International Student Certification of

Finances. CSS/Financial Aid Profile is required for all international students and domestic students under the age of 26.

Duration: Tenable for one year and may be renewed.

Deadline: February 15.

OFFICER:
Doris Howard, Director of Financial Aid

ADDRESS INQUIRIES TO:
Financial Aid
E-mail: finaid@sfcm.edu
(See address above.)

SAN FRANCISCO OPERA CENTER [736]

War Memorial Opera House
301 Van Ness Avenue
San Francisco, CA 94102-4509
(415) 565-3244
Fax: (415) 551-6305
E-mail: sfoperacenter@sfopera.com
Web Site: sfopera.com/about-us/opera-center/

FOUNDED: 1954

AREAS OF INTEREST:
Young professional singers, pianists/accompanists and stage directors interested in a sequence of opera performance and career development opportunities.

CONSULTING OR VOLUNTEER SERVICES:
Board of Directors of Merola Opera Program and a full staff of conductors, coaches, stage directors and instructors in singing, acting, movement, stage combat, auditioning, career development and other activities.

NAME(S) OF PROGRAMS:
● **Adler Fellowships**
● **Merola Opera Program**

TYPE:
Fellowships; Internships; Technical assistance. Auditions by application are held in the fall of each year for the following summer's Merola Opera Program in various cities throughout the U.S. Participants will also be considered for Adler Fellowships (singers/pianists).

YEAR PROGRAM STARTED: 1977

PURPOSE:
To provide professional opera training and performance opportunities for talented young opera professionals.

LEGAL BASIS:
Nonprofit.

ELIGIBILITY:
Open to all singers, pianists/accompanists and stage directors. All voice types are eligible, between the ages of 20 and 34.

To participate in the Adler Fellowships, applicants must complete one month of the Merola Summer Program.

FINANCIAL DATA:
Merola Opera Program participants receive shared housing accommodations, weekly allowance and round-trip airfare from place of residence to San Francisco. Adler Fellowships are for a salaried 12-month contract.

Total amount of support: Varies.

APPLICATION INFO:
Auditions are held nationally. Details are available on the web site.

Duration: Adler Fellowships: 12-month contract. Merola Opera Program: June to August.

Deadline: Refer to the National Auditions page on the Center's web site.

PUBLICATIONS:
Application guidelines.

OFFICERS:
Sheri Greenawald, Director

ADDRESS INQUIRIES TO:
Chris Bragg, Administrative Director
(See e-mail address above.)

SIGMA ALPHA IOTA PHILANTHROPIES, INC. [737]

One Tunnel Road
Asheville, NC 28805-1229
(828) 251-0606
Fax: (828) 251-0644
E-mail: nh@sai-national.org
Web Site: www.sai-national.org

FOUNDED: 1903

AREAS OF INTEREST:
Music, new compositions.

CONSULTING OR VOLUNTEER SERVICES:
Local volunteers in music.

NAME(S) OF PROGRAMS:
● **Inter-American Music Awards**

TYPE:
Awards/prizes. Music composition contest.

YEAR PROGRAM STARTED: 1948

PURPOSE:
To give to the fraternity, and to the public, compositions of high musical merit; to bring distinction to winning composers; to offer royalties and other benefits coincident with publication of winning music.

LEGAL BASIS:
Nonprofit corporation.

ELIGIBILITY:
Requirements change each triennium; however, applicants must be residents of North, Central or South America.

GEOG. RESTRICTIONS: North, Central and South America.

FINANCIAL DATA:
Amount of support per award: $2,500 prize, plus winning composition published by a major music publisher.

NO. MOST RECENT APPLICANTS: 45.

NO. AWARDS: 1.

APPLICATION INFO:
Application information is available on the web site.

Duration: One-time award.

Deadline: September 1, 2023.

PUBLICATIONS:
Brochure.

STAFF:
Ruth Sieber Johnson, SAI Executive Director

ADDRESS INQUIRIES TO:
Ruth Sieber Johnson
SAI Executive Director
(See address above.)

SYMPHONY OF THE MOUNTAINS [738]

Kingsport Renaissance Center, Suite 311
1200 East Center Street
Kingsport, TN 37660
(423) 392-8423
Fax: (423) 392-8428
E-mail: info@symphonyofthemountains.org
Web Site: www.symphonyofthemountains.org

FOUNDED: 1946

AREAS OF INTEREST:
Symphonic concerts and educational and social activities.

NAME(S) OF PROGRAMS:
● **Elizabeth Harper Vaughn Concerto Competition**

TYPE:
Awards/prizes. Cash prize and appearance with the Symphony of the Mountains Orchestra.

YEAR PROGRAM STARTED: 1969

PURPOSE:
To recognize excellence in music performance, with the potential for career advancement.

LEGAL BASIS:
Not-for-profit corporation.

ELIGIBILITY:
Open to musicians 25 years of age and under, with recommendation of private instructor.

FINANCIAL DATA:
Amount of support per award: $750.
Total amount of support: $750.

NO. MOST RECENT APPLICANTS: 10.

NO. AWARDS: 1 in odd-numbered years.

APPLICATION INFO:
Requires recommendation of private instructor and CD or DVD of performance (full concerto or other appropriate musical arrangement with orchestral accompaniment).

Duration: One-time award.

Deadline: September 1.

PUBLICATIONS:
Posters, postcards, programs for subscription concerts.

IRS I.D.: 62-0534228

STAFF:
Cornelia Laemmli Orth, Music Director/Chief Operating Officer

ADDRESS INQUIRIES TO:
Cornelia Laemmli Orth
Music Director/Chief Operating Officer
(See address above.)

THE RICHARD TUCKER MUSIC FOUNDATION, INC. [739]

1790 Broadway
Suite 715
New York, NY 10019-1412
(212) 757-2218
Fax: (212) 757-2347
E-mail: info@richardtucker.org
Web Site: www.richardtucker.org

FOUNDED: 1975

AREAS OF INTEREST:
Financial aid to American opera singers and opera companies with development programs for American singers.

NAME(S) OF PROGRAMS:
● **Richard Tucker Award**

- **Richard Tucker Career Grants**
- **Sara Tucker Study Grants**

TYPE:
Awards/prizes.

YEAR PROGRAM STARTED: 1978

PURPOSE:
To help further the careers of young American singers.

LEGAL BASIS:
Tax-exempt, not-for-profit organization.

ELIGIBILITY:
Nominees must already be performing in opera. Open to males and females in all vocal categories. Singers cannot apply; they must be recommended by a professional in the field. Applicants must also be U.S.-born.

GEOG. RESTRICTIONS: United States.

FINANCIAL DATA:
Amount of support per award: Richard Tucker Award: $50,000. Richard Tucker Career Grants: Unrestricted grant of $10,000. Sara Tucker Study Grants: Unrestricted grant of $5,000.
Total amount of support: Approximately $105,000.

NO. MOST RECENT APPLICANTS: 100 to 120.

NO. AWARDS: Richard Tucker Award: 1. Richard Tucker Career Grants and Sara Tucker Study Grants: 3 to 5 each.

APPLICATION INFO:
Information on the nominating process for the awards is available on the web site or by telephoning the Foundation. Application is via a confidential anonymous nomination process.
Duration: Varies, but most of the awards are one-time awards.
Deadline: Recommendations are due December 31.

IRS I.D.: 23-7431029

BOARD OF DIRECTORS:
Jeffrey Manocherian, Chairman
Barry Tucker, President
Sherrill Milnes, Vice President

ADDRESS INQUIRIES TO:
Peter H. Carwell, Executive Director
(See address above.)

THE VIOLIN SOCIETY OF AMERICA   [740]

14070 Proton Road
Suite 100
Dallas, TX 75244
(972) 233-9107 ext. 205
Fax: (972) 490-4219
E-mail: info@vsaweb.org
Web Site: www.vsaweb.org

FOUNDED: 1973

AREAS OF INTEREST:
Making and restoring stringed instruments and their bows, the history of stringed instruments and performers, technique, performance practice, repertory and the acoustics of bowed stringed instruments. The Society also sponsors conventions that include lectures, demonstrations, symposia and concerts, biennial international competitions for new stringed instruments and their bows, a Music Fair and a periodical covering all aspects of bowed string instruments.

NAME(S) OF PROGRAMS:
- **Kaplan-Goodkind Memorial Scholarship Fund**
- **Kun Scholarship Fund**
- **Aram and Rose Nigogosian Fund**

TYPE:
Scholarships. Tuition grants to students of violin-making and bow-making enrolled in a full-time violin-making school.

YEAR PROGRAM STARTED: 1982

PURPOSE:
To bring together people from various fields to exchange ideas and skills and to help people learn about the making of bows and stringed instruments.

LEGAL BASIS:
Tax-exempt educational organization.

ELIGIBILITY:
Students must be U.S. citizens, have satisfactorily completed at least one full year of study in the program, have shown serious effort, talent and future promise, and have financial need.

GEOG. RESTRICTIONS: United States.

FINANCIAL DATA:
Amount of support per award: $1,000 average.
Total amount of support: Varies.

NO. MOST RECENT APPLICANTS: 15.

NO. AWARDS: 8 to 12 annually.

APPLICATION INFO:
Apply through the program director of an approved program.
Duration: One-time tuition grant.
Deadline: Grants made on a continuing basis.

PUBLICATIONS:
The Journal, newsletter.

IRS I.D.: 23-7354645

OFFICERS:
Marilyn Wallin, President
Zachary Moen, President-Elect/Secretary
Nicholas Lampo, First Vice President
Julian Cossman Cooke, Second Vice President
Richard Dodson, Treasurer

ADDRESS INQUIRIES TO:
Elizabeth Kirkendoll, General Manager
(See address above.)

YOUNG CONCERT ARTISTS, INC.   [741]

1776 Broadway
Suite 1500
New York, NY 10019
(212) 307-6655
Fax: (212) 581-8894
E-mail: yca@yca.org
Web Site: www.yca.org

FOUNDED: 1961

AREAS OF INTEREST:
Young composers, young solo classical musicians (instruments and voice) and string quartets.

NAME(S) OF PROGRAMS:
- **Young Concert Artists International Auditions**

TYPE:
Awards/prizes. Artist management. YCA sponsors the Young Concert Artists Series in New York City at Carnegie's Zankel Hall, Lincoln Center's Alice Tully Hall, Kaufman Music Center's Merkin Hall, and in Washington, DC at the Kennedy Center; books concert engagements in the U.S. and abroad; offers career guidance and development; and provides all promotion and publicity materials, at no cost to the artists. YCA membership generally continues until the artists are signed by commercial management. The organization's work is made possible by contributions from corporations, foundations, individuals and government agencies.

YEAR PROGRAM STARTED: 1961

PURPOSE:
To discover and launch the careers of exceptional young musicians.

LEGAL BASIS:
Nonprofit, tax-exempt.

ELIGIBILITY:
Instrumentalists and singers must perform required repertoire and have letters of recommendation.

NO. MOST RECENT APPLICANTS: 275.

NO. AWARDS: Varies. Winners are selected only against a standard of excellence; any number can win who are selected by the jury.

APPLICATION INFO:
Auditions dates, application form and requirements are available online.
Duration: Each winner signs a multiyear renewable contract with Young Concert Artists, which may be extended by mutual consent.
Deadline: Contact the organization.

PUBLICATIONS:
Brochure.

IRS I.D.: 13-1951681

OFFICER:
Daniel Kellogg, President

ADDRESS INQUIRIES TO:
Daniel Kellogg, President

Auditions:
Mr. Erol Gurol
(See address above.)

THE LOREN L. ZACHARY SOCIETY FOR THE PERFORMING ARTS   [742]

2250 Gloaming Way
Beverly Hills, CA 90210-1717
(310) 276-2731
Fax: (310) 275-8245
E-mail: infoz@zacharysociety.org
Web Site: www.zacharysociety.org

FOUNDED: 1972

AREAS OF INTEREST:
Performing arts, operatic vocal and chamber ensemble.

NAME(S) OF PROGRAMS:
- **Annual Loren L. Zachary National Vocal Competition for Young Opera Singers**

TYPE:
Awards/prizes.

YEAR PROGRAM STARTED: 1973

PURPOSE:
To assist in the development of the careers of young opera singers through financial support and performance opportunities.

LEGAL BASIS:
Educational, tax-exempt, nonprofit corporation.

ELIGIBILITY:
Open to singers between the ages of 21 and 35, who have completed proper operatic training and are prepared to pursue professional stage careers. Awards are available only through participation in the annual vocal competition in New York and Los Angeles. All singers with completed applications are guaranteed an audition.

GEOG. RESTRICTIONS: United States and Canada.

FINANCIAL DATA:
Amount of support per award: Top six awards for the year 2019: $18,000, $12,000, $8,000, $5,000, $3,500, and $2,500. Remaining four grants $2,000 each.

Total amount of support: $56,650 for the year 2019.

NO. MOST RECENT APPLICANTS: 150.

NO. AWARDS: 10 for the year 2019.

APPLICATION INFO:
Application and rules are available at the web site, or submit a letter requesting audition information and applications in October. Singers must be present in Los Angeles or New York for all phases of the Competition. Recordings are not acceptable. No fax or e-mail requests.

For more information, contact the Competition Director at the phone number above.

Duration: February to May.

Deadline: January (for New York Auditions) and February (for Los Angeles Auditions); exact date varies each year.

PUBLICATIONS:
Application; guidelines.

IRS I.D.: 95-2800160

OFFICERS:
Nedra Zachary, President and Founder
Peter Hubner, Vice President
Allan J. Stephan, Vice President
Michele Patazkis, Secretary
Joseph Givens, Treasurer

ADVISORY BOARD:
John DeMain
Stephen De Maio
Michael Fabiano
Dr. George Fritthum
Peter Guth
Michael Hampe
Ioan Holender
Marilyn Horne
David Hulme
Marjan Kiepura
Mrs. George London
Peter Mark
Thea Musgrave
Arlene Shrut
Barbara Ann Testa

ADDRESS INQUIRIES TO:
Nedra Zachary, Director of Competition
(See address above.)

Religion and theology

AMERICAN ACADEMY OF RELIGION [743]
825 Houston Mill Road, N.E.
Suite 300
Atlanta, GA 30329
(404) 727-3049
Fax: (404) 727-7959
E-mail: info@aarweb.org
Web Site: www.aarweb.org

FOUNDED: 1909

AREAS OF INTEREST:
Religion and theology.

NAME(S) OF PROGRAMS:
- **Collaborative Research Grants**
- **Individual Research Grants**
- **International Dissertation Research Grant**

TYPE:
Research grants. Collaborative Research Grants and Individual Research Grants provide support for important aspects of research such as travel to archives and libraries, research assistance, field work and released time. However, funds are not provided for dissertation research.

International Dissertation Research Grants support AAR student members whose dissertation research requires them to travel outside of the country in which their school or university is located. Grants are intended to help candidates complete their doctoral degrees by offsetting costs of travel, lodging, and other dissertation research-related expenses.

YEAR PROGRAM STARTED: 1989

PURPOSE:
To promote research and scholarship in the field of religion; to foster excellence in teaching in the field of religion; to support and encourage members' professional development; to develop programming and participation in AAR regional groups; to advance publication and scholarly communication in the field of religion; to contribute to the public understanding of religion; to welcome the various voices in the field of religion and to support and encourage diversity within the AAR; to help to advance and secure the future of the academic study of religion.

LEGAL BASIS:
501(c)(3).

ELIGIBILITY:
Applicants must be current AAR members who have been in good standing for the previous three years and have not received an AAR Research Award in the previous five years.

FINANCIAL DATA:
Amount of support per award: Collaborative and Individual Research Grants: $500 to $5,000; International Dissertation Research Grant: $5,000.

APPLICATION INFO:
Individual or Collaborative grant applicants should submit through the Academy's electronic system:
(1) cover page that includes the following:
(a) name, (b) institutional affiliation, (c) title of the project and, (d) grant type - Individual or Collaborative;
(2) abstract of 50 words or fewer describing the project;

(3) project budget;
(4) two-page focused description of the research project that details its aims and significance and explains how the award would be used. Collaborative project descriptions should include brief descriptions of the scholarly role of each collaborator and a plan to have the research published and;
(5) curriculum vitae of no more than two pages.

International Dissertation Research Grant applicants must submit the following materials through the online form:
(1) letter of application (no longer than three pages) that describes their research project and how support for on-site research is critical for the completion of their dissertation;
(2) current curriculum vitae;
(3) proposed budget and project timeline and;
(4) letter of support from their dissertation supervisor.

Duration: Individual or Collaborative Grant: Research projects may be undertaken any time within that academic year and up to the end of the following calendar year. International Dissertation Research Grant: Funds must be expended by the end of the calendar year awarded.

Deadline: Collaborative Grant and Individual Research Grant: August 1; International Dissertation Grant: December 1.

IRS I.D.: 25-6063005

STAFF:
Elizabeth Hardcastle, Service Coordinator

ADDRESS INQUIRIES TO:
Elizabeth Hardcastle, Service Coordinator
(See address above.)

AMERICAN ACADEMY OF RELIGION [744]
825 Houston Mill Road, N.E.
Suite 300
Atlanta, GA 30329
(404) 727-3049
Fax: (404) 727-7959
E-mail: info@aarweb.org
Web Site: www.aarweb.org

FOUNDED: 1909

AREAS OF INTEREST:
To support projects within the regions that promise to benefit the scholarly and professional life of AAR members and the work of the regions.

NAME(S) OF PROGRAMS:
- **Regional Development Grants**

TYPE:
Development grants. Workshops, special programs, training events and other innovative regional projects may be funded through this source.

PURPOSE:
To promote research and scholarship in the field of religion; to foster excellence in teaching in the field of religion; to support and encourage members' professional development; to develop programming and participation in AAR regional groups; to advance publication and scholarly communication in the field of religion; to contribute to the public understanding of religion; to welcome into our conversation the various voices in the field of religion and to support and encourage diversity within the AAR; to help to advance and secure the future of the academic study of religion.

LEGAL BASIS:
501(c)(3).

ELIGIBILITY:
Applicant must be a current member of AAR and maintain their membership throughout the grant period.

GEOG. RESTRICTIONS: United States.

FINANCIAL DATA:
Amount of support per award: Maximum $4,000.

NO. MOST RECENT APPLICANTS: 15.

NO. AWARDS: 4.

APPLICATION INFO:
Grant applications must be submitted electronically through the Online Submissions System. Proposals should include the following:
(1) complete contact information for all parties involved in developing the grant proposal;
(2) a narrative description of the project detailing how the project promises to benefit the scholarly and professional life of AAR members and the work of the region;
(3) a statement on how this project or activities may be adapted to other regional groups or a brief explanation of why this project is region-specific;
(4) a clear timeline for the completion of the grant. Please note that projects are to be completed within one year of award announcement, unless other arrangements have been made with the AAR Executive Office and;
(5) a detailed budget, including office expenses, travel expenses, honoraria, stipend, and other expenses. Institutional overhead costs may not be included in this budget.
Duration: One year.
Deadline: June 1.

IRS I.D.: 20-5478525

ADDRESS INQUIRIES TO:
Regional Coordinator

AMERICAN CATHOLIC HISTORICAL ASSOCIATION   [745]
Mount St. Mary's University
16300 Old Emmitsburg Road
Emmitsburg, MD 21727
(301) 447-5799
E-mail: acha@achahistory.org
Web Site: www.achahistory.org

FOUNDED: 1919

AREAS OF INTEREST:
The history of Catholicism from antiquity to the present.

NAME(S) OF PROGRAMS:
● **The Peter Guilday Prize**

TYPE:
Awards/prizes; Challenge/matching grants; Conferences/seminars; Travel grants. A prize awarded annually to the author whose article, dealing with the history of the Catholic Church, is the first of his or her professional career and is judged to be the best of those in that category accepted for publication in any given year by the editors of the *Catholic Historical Review*.

YEAR PROGRAM STARTED: 1972

PURPOSE:
To stimulate interest in the history of Catholicism among young scholars.

LEGAL BASIS:
Learned society.

ELIGIBILITY:
The article must deal with some aspect of the history of the Catholic Church broadly considered. Anyone who has already published an historical book or an article in a learned journal will not be eligible for competition. Articles based on doctoral dissertations will be welcome, provided they are self-contained studies. Manuscripts must not exceed 30 typewritten pages (footnotes included). The author must be a citizen or permanent resident of the U.S. or Canada.

GEOG. RESTRICTIONS: United States and Canada.

FINANCIAL DATA:
Amount of support per award: $250.
Total amount of support: $250 per annum.

NO. MOST RECENT APPLICANTS: 3.

NO. AWARDS: 1 per annum.

APPLICATION INFO:
Inquiries and manuscripts should be sent to the address above.
Deadline: September 1.

ADDRESS INQUIRIES TO:
Charles Strauss
Executive Secretary-Treasurer
(See e-mail address above.)

AMERICAN CATHOLIC HISTORICAL ASSOCIATION   [746]
Mount St. Mary's University
16300 Old Emmitsburg Road
Emmitsburg, MD 21727
(301) 447-5799
E-mail: acha@achahistory.org
Web Site: www.achahistory.org

FOUNDED: 1919

AREAS OF INTEREST:
The history of Catholicism from antiquity to the present.

NAME(S) OF PROGRAMS:
● **The John Gilmary Shea Prize**

TYPE:
Awards/prizes. This Prize is given annually to the author of a book, published during a preceding 12-month period, which is judged by a committee of experts to have made the most original and distinguished contribution to knowledge of the history of the Catholic Church.

YEAR PROGRAM STARTED: 1945

PURPOSE:
To stimulate interest in the history of Catholicism among young scholars.

LEGAL BASIS:
Learned society.

ELIGIBILITY:
Any author who is a citizen or permanent resident of the U.S. or Canada is eligible to apply. The work submitted must have been published within the previous calendar year.

GEOG. RESTRICTIONS: United States and Canada.

FINANCIAL DATA:
Amount of support per award: $1,500.
Total amount of support: $1,500 per annum.

NO. AWARDS: 1 per annum.

APPLICATION INFO:
No formal application is required. Publishers or authors may enter by sending three copies of the work to be considered. Write or e-mail to the above address for further details.
Deadline: June 15.

ADDRESS INQUIRIES TO:
Charles Strauss
Executive Secretary-Treasurer
See e-mail address above.)

AMERICAN CATHOLIC HISTORICAL ASSOCIATION   [747]
Mount St. Mary's University
16300 Old Emmitsburg Road
Emmitsburg, MD 21727
(301) 447-5799
E-mail: acha@achahistory.org
Web Site: www.achahistory.org

FOUNDED: 1919

AREAS OF INTEREST:
The history of Catholicism from antiquity to the present.

NAME(S) OF PROGRAMS:
● **ACHA Graduate Student Summer Research Grant**
● **John Tracy Ellis Dissertation Award**
● **Presidential Graduate Travel Grant**

TYPE:
Awards/prizes; Challenge/matching grants; Conferences/seminars; Research grants; Travel grants. ACHA Graduate Student Summer Research Grant is awarded to an ACHA graduate student member who has completed all requirements for the Doctorate except the dissertation.

John Tracy Ellis Dissertation Award memorializes the scholarship and teaching of Monsignor Ellis (1905-1992).

Presidential Graduate Travel Grant was created in 2010 by the Association from donations from former presidents.

PURPOSE:
To stimulate interest in the history of Catholicism among young scholars.

LEGAL BASIS:
Learned society.

ELIGIBILITY:
ACHA Graduate Student Summer Research Grant: Awarded to an ACHA graduate student member who has completed all requirements for the Doctorate except the dissertation and is attending an accredited institution of higher learning.

John Tracy Ellis Dissertation Award: Applicants must be citizens or authorized residents of the U.S. or Canada, and must be enrolled in a doctoral program at a recognized institution of higher education.

Presidential Graduate Travel Grant: Given on a competitive basis to two graduate students who are current members of the Association and who have papers accepted at either the Annual or Spring meetings.

FINANCIAL DATA:
Amount of support per award: ACHA Graduate Student Summer Research Grant $2,500 per award; John Tracy Ellis Dissertation Award: A purse of $1,500; Presidential Graduate Travel Grant: $500 per award.

NO. AWARDS: ACHA Graduate Student Summer Research Grant: 4; Presidential Graduate Travel Grant: 2 for the Annual Meeting and 2 for the Spring Meeting.

APPLICATION INFO:
Presidential Graduate Travel Grant: Applicants should provide a letter formally applying for the grant and detailing the content of his or her paper, a mini-curriculum vitae (one page), and a letter of recommendation from a faculty member (preferably the dissertation director).

Deadline: ACHA Graduate Student Summer Research Grant: April 30; John Tracy Ellis Dissertation Award: September 30; Presidential Graduate Travel Grant: Applications should be submitted two months prior to either the Annual or Spring meeting.

ADDRESS INQUIRIES TO:
Charles Strauss
Executive Secretary-Treasurer
(See e-mail address above.)

AMERICAN CATHOLIC HISTORICAL ASSOCIATION [748]
Mount St. Mary's University
16300 Old Emmitsburg Road
Emmitsburg, MD 21727
(301) 447-5799
E-mail: acha@achahistory.org
Web Site: www.achahistory.org

FOUNDED: 1919

AREAS OF INTEREST:
The history of Catholicism from antiquity to the present.

NAME(S) OF PROGRAMS:
● **The Msgr. Harry C. Koenig Award for Catholic Biography (Article Award)**
● **The Msgr. Harry C. Koenig Award for Catholic Biography (Book Award)**

TYPE:
Awards/prizes. The Msgr. Harry C. Koenig Award for Catholic Biography (Article Award) is awarded on a competitive basis every two years (in odd-numbered years) to the author who has produced a journal article that focuses on the life of a Catholic personage from any period of Christian history.

The Msgr. Harry C. Koenig Award for Catholic Biography (Book Award) is offered every two years (in even-numbered years) and recognizes an outstanding monograph that focuses on the life of a Catholic personage of any age or time.

ELIGIBILITY:
The Msgr. Harry C. Koenig Award for Catholic Biography (Article Award): Submission can either be published originally in English or translated into English and must be of a substantial length. Graduate students (Master's or doctoral level) from accredited institutions of higher learning, independent scholars or faculty members are eligible to compete. Single and multi-authored works will be considered. Book articles and edited volume articles do not qualify. Preference will be given to a submission that has appeared in a scholarly journal.

The Msgr. Harry C. Koenig Award for Catholic Biography (Book Award): Entries must have first been published in English.

FINANCIAL DATA:
Amount of support per award: Article Award: $500; Book Award: $1,500.

NO. AWARDS: 1 per award.

APPLICATION INFO:
Application information is available on the web site.
Deadline: Article Award: April 30. Book Award: June 1.

ADDRESS INQUIRIES TO:
Charles Strauss
Executive Secretary-Treasurer
(See e-mail address above.)

THE CHATLOS FOUNDATION, INC. [749]
P.O. Box 915048
Longwood, FL 32791-5048
(407) 862-5077
E-mail: info@chatlos.org
Web Site: www.chatlos.org

FOUNDED: 1953

AREAS OF INTEREST:
Bible colleges, seminaries, religion, liberal arts colleges, medical and social concerns.

TYPE:
General operating grants; Project/program grants; Scholarships; Technical assistance; Training grants. Scholarships are not provided directly to individuals but rather to colleges and seminaries which in turn provide monies to the students of their choice.

YEAR PROGRAM STARTED: 1953

LEGAL BASIS:
Private foundation.

ELIGIBILITY:
The Foundation only funds nonprofit organizations which are tax-exempt for U.S. federal income tax purposes around the globe. Less emphasis on grant requests for bricks and mortar, endowments, conference and administrative expenses and multiyear grants. No grants for medical research, individual church congregations, primary/secondary schools, organizations in existence for less than two years, arts organizations or individuals. Contributions cannot be made to organizations which discriminate on the basis of race, color, sex, creed, age or national origin.

FINANCIAL DATA:
Amount of support per award: Bible colleges: $5,000 to $20,000; Religious causes and medical concerns: $5,000 to $15,000; Liberal arts colleges: $2,500 to $7,500; Social concerns: $2,000 to $5,000.

Initially, the Foundation tends to fund requests for amounts around $10,000.
Total amount of support: Approximately $2,000,000 for the year 2017.

NO. MOST RECENT APPLICANTS: 558 for the year 2017.

NO. AWARDS: 111 grants for the year 2017.

APPLICATION INFO:
Application may be submitted by mail or online. Details are available on the Foundation web site.
Duration: Varies, although multiyear grants are rarely considered.
Deadline: Applications are accepted throughout the year.

PUBLICATIONS:
Application guideline brochure.

IRS I.D.: 13-6161425

ADDRESS INQUIRIES TO:
Grants Administrator
(See address above.)

EPISCOPAL CHURCH FOUNDATION [750]
475 Riverside Drive, Suite 750
New York, NY 10115
(212) 870-2852
(800) 697-2858
Fax: (212) 297-0142
E-mail: ecf@episcopalfoundation.org
Web Site: www.episcopalfoundation.org

FOUNDED: 1949

AREAS OF INTEREST:
Innovative programs in leadership development, education and philanthropy for the clergy and laity of the Episcopal Church.

CONSULTING OR VOLUNTEER SERVICES:
Capital campaigns, planned giving and endowment management services.

NAME(S) OF PROGRAMS:
● **ECF Fellowship Partners Program**

TYPE:
Fellowships. Religious studies. Fellowship Partners Program consists of two tracks: Academic Fellowships and Ministry Fellowships.

YEAR PROGRAM STARTED: 1964

PURPOSE:
To support doctoral study for Episcopalians planning teaching careers in theological education in the Episcopal Church in the U.S.

ELIGIBILITY:
Applications from both lay and ordained Episcopalians are welcome.

Academic Fellowship applicants on the academic track must be engaged in or embarking on a course of study at the graduate level, except for first professional degrees (e.g., M.Div., J.D., M.D.). Acceptable courses of study include doctoral- and Master's-level programs, as well as clinical study or training at the postundergraduate level.

Ministry Fellowship applicants will be asked to demonstrate how their ministry has the potential to transform community at the grassroots level, and special consideration will be given to programs in locations with limited resources or among underserved communities.

GEOG. RESTRICTIONS: United States.

FINANCIAL DATA:
Amount of support per award: Up to $15,000 per year.
Total amount of support: Approximately $100,000 annually.

NO. AWARDS: 4 for the year 2019.

APPLICATION INFO:
Application information is available on the web site.

Duration: One year. Fellowship is renewable for two more years.

Deadline: Mid-March. Notification by late May.

PUBLICATIONS:
ECF Vital Practices.

ADDRESS INQUIRIES TO:
Kjerstin Besser
Associate Program Director
(See address above.)

GENERAL BOARD OF HIGHER EDUCATION AND MINISTRY, THE UNITED METHODIST CHURCH   [751]

1001 19th Avenue South
Nashville, TN 37212
(615) 340-7338
Fax: (615) 340-7529
E-mail: mbigord@gbhem.org
Web Site: www.gbhem.org

AREAS OF INTEREST:
Religion.

NAME(S) OF PROGRAMS:
● **Georgia Harkness Scholarships**

TYPE:
Awards/prizes; Scholarships. Awards to encourage women over age 35 to prepare for ordained ministry as an Elder in the United Methodist Church as a second career. The scholarship is to be used for study toward the basic seminary degree in an accredited school of theology.

YEAR PROGRAM STARTED: 1975

PURPOSE:
To support and encourage women for ordained ministry as an Elder in the United Methodist Church.

LEGAL BASIS:
Nonprofit organization.

ELIGIBILITY:
Applicant must be a member of the United Methodist Church for a minimum of three years and be a certified candidate for Elder in the year they are applying. Women over age 35 who have received a Bachelor of Arts or equivalent degree, have been accepted in an accredited school of theology, and have affirmed a specific interest in preparation for ordination as an Elder in the United Methodist Church are eligible. A 3.0 grade point average is required.

FINANCIAL DATA:
Amount of support per award: $5,000.

NO. AWARDS: Varies.

APPLICATION INFO:
Applicants can access the application at the Board web site.

Duration: One year.

Deadline: Early March.

ADDRESS INQUIRIES TO:
Marcie Bigord, Assistant Director
Office of Loans and Scholarships
(See address above.)

*PLEASE NOTE:
Full-time enrollment required.

GENERAL COMMISSION ON ARCHIVES AND HISTORY OF THE UNITED METHODIST CHURCH   [752]

36 Madison Avenue
Madison, NJ 07940
(973) 408-3189
Fax: (973) 408-3909
E-mail: atday@gcah.org
Web Site: www.gcah.org

FOUNDED: 1968

AREAS OF INTEREST:
History of the United Methodist Church and antecedent bodies.

NAME(S) OF PROGRAMS:
● **John Harrison Ness Memorial Award**

TYPE:
Awards/prizes. Awards to the students of accredited seminaries whose professor submits the best papers on various aspects of United Methodist denominational history. In general, comprehensive subjects on the history of some phase of the denomination will be preferred, but papers on local church or annual conference subjects will be accepted if approved by the professor advising the project.

YEAR PROGRAM STARTED: 1979

PURPOSE:
To stimulate interest in history of the United Methodist Church.

LEGAL BASIS:
Private church-related organization.

ELIGIBILITY:
The paper must have been appraised by the professor of church history under whom the student has been studying and who will submit the paper. The paper must be properly annotated and be a minimum length of 3,000 words. It is desired that the project be undertaken only after the student has had a course in United Methodist history or at least during the enrollment in such.

FINANCIAL DATA:
Amount of support per award: First prize: $500; Second prize: $300.

Total amount of support: $800 annually.

NO. AWARDS: 2.

APPLICATION INFO:
Details are available online.

Duration: Annual. A recipient may resubmit if he or she is still in seminary.

Deadline: February 1. Announcement approximately three months later.

OFFICERS:
Rev. Alfred T. Day, III, General Secretary

ADDRESS INQUIRIES TO:
Rev. Alfred T. Day III, General Secretary
(See address above.)

THE STEWART HUSTON CHARITABLE TRUST   [753]

50 South 1st Avenue
Coatesville, PA 19320
(610) 384-2666
Fax: (610) 384-3396
E-mail: admin@stewarthuston.org
Web Site: www.stewarthuston.org

FOUNDED: 1989

AREAS OF INTEREST:
Historic preservation, health and human services, civic and Protestant Christian organizations.

CONSULTING OR VOLUNTEER SERVICES:
General nonprofit organizational issues. Finance and fund-raising.

TYPE:
Capital grants; Challenge/matching grants; General operating grants; Matching gifts; Project/program grants.

YEAR PROGRAM STARTED: 1989

PURPOSE:
To provide funds, technical assistance and collaboration on behalf of nonprofit organizations engaged exclusively in religious, charitable or educational work; to extend opportunities to deserving needy persons.

LEGAL BASIS:
Private foundation.

ELIGIBILITY:
Applicants must be tax-exempt and address a particular community need. Grants are not awarded for scholarship support to individuals, endowment purposes, purchase of tickets or advertising for benefit purposes, coverage of continuing operating deficits, and document publication costs. Support is not provided to intermediate or pass-through organizations (other than United Way), groups such as fraternal organizations, political campaigns, veterans, labor or local civic groups, volunteer fire companies, and groups engaged in influencing legislation.

According to Stewart Huston's Indenture of Trust, 60% of distributions go to Trinitarian/Evangelical organizations as defined by the Chester County Orphans Court: "The grant applicant must be organized and operated exclusively to further religious and charitable activities carried on by Protestant churches, other than Unitarian churches, and affiliated or related organizations; grant proceeds must be used exclusively for one or both of the following two activities: dissemination of the Christian Gospel by preaching and conducting religious services, offering a Christian education, etc.; and promotion of Christian principles through charity."

The remaining 40% is to be distributed for secular purposes within a 100-mile radius from Coatesville, PA.

GEOG. RESTRICTIONS: Chester County, Pennsylvania and Savannah, Georgia areas.

FINANCIAL DATA:
Amount of support per award: Maximum grant: $20,000; Average $5,000 to $10,000.

Total amount of support: $650,000 in grants for the year ended December 31, 2018.

NO. MOST RECENT APPLICANTS: 130.

NO. AWARDS: 44.

REPRESENTATIVE AWARDS:
$10,000 to The Living Vine; $5,000 to Chester County Food Bank; $20,000 to Christ Church Episcopal; $15,000 to Bridge of Hope; $10,000 to Habitat for Humanity.

APPLICATION INFO:
Applications must be submitted online. Applicants are encouraged to call and discuss their project with the staff. The application form should be submitted with a grant proposal and include the following attachments:
(1) IRS tax-exemption letter;
(2) Pennsylvania charitable organizations registration certificate (any organization with gross revenue over $25,000, regardless of

location). Churches exempt;

(3) by-laws;

(4) last independent financial audit;

(5) list of the organization's major public and private funding sources;

(6) list of the Board of Directors with their community/professional affiliations;

(7) agency's current operating budget;

(8) most recent Form 990 filed with the IRS;

(9) latest annual report;

(10) list of the public and private sources being solicited to fund the project;

(11) detailed project budget;

(12) statement that there has been no change in purpose, character or method of operation since the agency's IRS tax ruling was issued and;

(13) a few examples of media reviews about the organization's program.

Duration: No multiyear commitments.

Deadline: April 1 for civic and health organizations; April 1 and October 1 for Protestant Christian organizations.

PUBLICATIONS:
Program announcement; guidelines; annual report.

IRS I.D.: 23-2612599

TRUSTEES:
Charles L. Huston, III
Elinor Lashley
Shelton Sanford

ADDRESS INQUIRIES TO:
Scott G. Huston, Executive Director
(See address above.)

IMMANUEL BIBLE FOUNDATION   [754]

1301 South Fell Avenue
Normal, IL 61761
(309) 452-6710
Fax: (309) 862-4121
E-mail: execdiribf@gmail.com
Web Site: ibfoundation.org

FOUNDED: 1944

AREAS OF INTEREST:
Local charities and youth-serving organizations.

TYPE:
General operating grants. Special needs grants.

YEAR PROGRAM STARTED: 1949

PURPOSE:
To promote the gospel and serve as a resource for the Christian community.

LEGAL BASIS:
Tax-exempt private foundation.

ELIGIBILITY:
Tax-exempt organizations, entirely local to the Foundation's immediate area, may apply. Out-of-state applications are not accepted. No grants to individuals.

GEOG. RESTRICTIONS: McLean County, Illinois.

FINANCIAL DATA:
Amount of support per award: $500.
Total amount of support: Up to $7,500.

APPLICATION INFO:
Applications are currently available by mail. Contact the Executive Director.

Duration: Varies by need.

Deadline: Applications accepted January 1 to May 1. Announcement by September 1.

IRS I.D.: 37-0688539

ADDRESS INQUIRIES TO:
Annette Klinzing, Executive Director
(See address above.)

KOCH FOUNDATION, INC.   [755]

4421 N.W. 39th Avenue
Building 1, Suite 1
Gainesville, FL 32606
(352) 373-7491
Fax: (352) 337-1548
E-mail: staff@thekochfoundation.org
Web Site: www.thekochfoundation.org

FOUNDED: 1979

AREAS OF INTEREST:
Roman Catholic evangelization.

TYPE:
Fellowships; Grants-in-aid; Project/program grants; Training grants. Grants are made for direct evangelization programs, preparation of evangelists, resource-poor Catholic schools that are the principal means of evangelization in the community.

YEAR PROGRAM STARTED: 1979

PURPOSE:
To provide financial support for evangelization efforts to Catholic organizations throughout the world that propagate the Roman Catholic faith.

LEGAL BASIS:
Not-for-profit corporation.

ELIGIBILITY:
U.S. Catholic organizations must be 501(c)(3) and appear in the *Official Catholic Directory*. Non-U.S. Catholic organizations must have a fiscal agent in the U.S. who is willing to disburse grant funds for them, should a grant be awarded.

FINANCIAL DATA:
Amount of support per award: Varies depending on needs and nature of the request; typical grant $15,000.
Total amount of support: $4,717,100 in total support for fiscal year 2018-19.

NO. MOST RECENT APPLICANTS: 455 for fiscal year 2016-17.

NO. AWARDS: 342 approved grants for fiscal year 2018-19.

APPLICATION INFO:
Application forms are available January 1 to May 1. Briefly describe the project when writing for a grant application. All requests must be in English to assure appropriate attention. Faxed requests are not accepted. Completed applications must be returned within 90 days. Applications must include a budget, a statement of the desired impact on evangelization and, if international, the country and diocese where the program will take place and the U.S. fiscal agent who will be responsible for distributing the funds. Applications for a continuing project must be accompanied by a six-month progress report or yearly evaluation.

Duration: Varies.

Deadline: May 1. Announcement in mid-March.

PUBLICATIONS:
Application guidelines.

IRS I.D.: 59-1885997

BOARD OF DIRECTORS:
William A. Bomberger, President
Inge L. Vraney, Vice President
Carolyn L. Bomberger, Treasurer

Rachel A. Bomberger, Secretary
Lawrence E. Vraney, Jr., Assistant Treasurer
Michelle H. Bomberger, Assistant Secretary
Matthew A. Bomberger
Charlotte L. Spacinsky
Jeffrey Vraney
Lori Vraney
Maura J. Vraney

ADDRESS INQUIRIES TO:
Executive Director
(See address above.)

LUTHERAN FOUNDATION OF ST. LOUIS   [756]

8860 Ladue Road
Suite 200
St. Louis, MO 63124
(314) 231-2244 ext. 111
Fax: (314) 727-7688
E-mail: info@lutheranfoundation.org
Web Site: www.lutheranfoundation.org

FOUNDED: 1984

AREAS OF INTEREST:
Christian voluntarism, congregation social service outreach, Lutheran education, services to ex-offenders and their families, foreign-born populations, and older adults maintaining independence.

TYPE:
Project/program grants.

YEAR PROGRAM STARTED: 1984

PURPOSE:
To provide grant awards in the areas of Christian voluntarism, congregation social service outreach ministry, Lutheran education, prevention and early intervention in children's mental health, and services to prisoners, ex-offenders and their families.

LEGAL BASIS:
Religious foundation.

ELIGIBILITY:
Applicant must be a 501(c)(3), serve the St. Louis metropolitan area, address one or more of the funding focus areas, and complement the Foundation's core values.

The Foundation does not make grants to individuals.

GEOG. RESTRICTIONS: Metropolitan St. Louis, Missouri area.

FINANCIAL DATA:
Amount of support per award: Varies.
Total amount of support: Varies.
Matching fund requirements: Varies depending on the grant.

NO. AWARDS: Average 125 per year.

APPLICATION INFO:
Application information is available on the Foundation's web site.

Duration: Varies.

Deadline: June 1 and December 1. Announcement in August and February, respectively.

IRS I.D.: 43-1379359

BOARD OF DIRECTORS:
Robert A. Boyle, Chairperson
Jonathan D. Schultz, Vice Chairperson
Linda L. Moen, Secretary
Rev. Robert K. Bernhardt
William A. Brinkmeyer
Jeffrey P. Cloeter
Emily A. Elam
Rev. Micah A. Glenn

Charles F. Heisner
Shirley A. Jackson
Cyril D. Loum
Michael S. Murphy
Bruce H. Pompe
Sharon Rohrbach
Aaron L. Schmeerbauch
Ann L. Vazquez

ADDRESS INQUIRIES TO:
Grants Manager
(See address above.)

JACOB RADER MARCUS CENTER OF THE AMERICAN JEWISH ARCHIVES [757]

3101 Clifton Avenue
Cincinnati, OH 45220-2408
(513) 221-1875
Fax: (513) 221-7812
E-mail: lfrankel@huc.edu
Web Site: www.americanjewisharchives.org

FOUNDED: 1947

AREAS OF INTEREST:
American and western hemisphere Jewish history.

NAME(S) OF PROGRAMS:
● The American Jewish Archives Fellowship Program

TYPE:
Fellowships. The Marcus Center's Fellowship Program provides recipients with month-long fellowships for research and writing at The Jacob Rader Marcus Center of the American Jewish Archives. Fellowship stipends will be sufficient to cover transportation and living expenses while in residence.

YEAR PROGRAM STARTED: 1977

PURPOSE:
To collect, preserve and publish the history of the American Jewish experience.

LEGAL BASIS:
A division of the Hebrew Union College, Jewish Institute of Religion; tax-exempt.

ELIGIBILITY:
Applicants must be conducting serious research in some area relating to the history of North American Jewry. Typically, fellowships will be awarded to postdoctoral candidates, Ph.D. candidates who are completing dissertations, and senior or independent scholars.

FINANCIAL DATA:
Grant amount is based upon the individual's research. Fellowship stipends will help offset transportation and living expenses while in residence in Cincinnati.
Amount of support per award: Varies.
Total amount of support: Varies.

APPLICATION INFO:
In addition to a Fellowship application, Fellowship applicants must provide a research proposal (no more than five typewritten, double-spaced pages), and two recommendations, preferably from academic colleagues (for graduate and doctoral students, one of these recommendations must be from the candidate's dissertation advisor). Research must be done for one month on campus through the archives.

Application should not be made to individually named fellowship funds of the Center. Applicants will be considered for all available Center fellowships.

Prior to completion of the Fellowship applications, the Center strongly recommends that applicants familiarize themselves with its collection. The American Jewish Archives web site contains a list of holdings and a number of finding aids for applicant to peruse. An archivist can be contacted directly for information at the number above (ext. 403).
Duration: Up to one month.
Deadline: February 19.

PUBLICATIONS:
Program description.

STAFF:
Dr. Gary P. Zola, Executive Director
Lisa B. Frankel, Director of Educational Outreach and Administration
Dr. Dana Herman, Director, Fellowship Program

ADDRESS INQUIRIES TO:
Dr. Dana Herman
Director, Fellowship Program
E-mail: dherman@huc.edu

VERNE CATT MCDOWELL CORPORATION [758]

432 Ferry Street, S.W.
Albany, OR 97321
(541) 619-3270

FOUNDED: 1963

AREAS OF INTEREST:
Graduate theological education.

NAME(S) OF PROGRAMS:
● Verne Catt McDowell Scholarship

TYPE:
Scholarships. Financial assistance for men and women attending an approved seminary to become ordained in the Christian Church (Disciples of Christ) denomination and work actively in that church.

YEAR PROGRAM STARTED: 1966

PURPOSE:
To train men and women to become pastors in the Christian Church (Disciples of Christ) Denomination.

LEGAL BASIS:
Private nonprofit corporation.

ELIGIBILITY:
A graduate from an accredited college and/or university who plans to enter an approved seminary of the Christian Church (Disciples of Christ) is eligible to apply. Study must take place in the U.S. Candidates must plan to be ordained in the Christian Church (Disciples of Christ) Denomination and work actively in that church.

Preference given to students from Oregon.

FINANCIAL DATA:
Amount of support per award: Varies.
Total amount of support: Varies.

NO. AWARDS: 3 to 5 per year.

APPLICATION INFO:
Write for application and include eligibility and where information regarding program was found.
Duration: Varies with each student; continues support until completion of seminary, as long as eligibility criteria are met.
Deadline: May 1. Awards are usually announced after annual meeting in June.

IRS I.D.: 93-6022991

OFFICERS:
Sara Staton, President
Nadine M. Wood, Business Manager

ADDRESS INQUIRIES TO:
Nadine M. Wood, Business Manager
(See address above.)

MEMORIAL FOUNDATION FOR JEWISH CULTURE [759]

50 Broadway, 34th Floor
New York, NY 10004
(212) 425-6606
Fax: (212) 425-6602
E-mail: office@mfjc.org
Web Site: www.mfjc.org

FOUNDED: 1964

AREAS OF INTEREST:
Support for Jewish cultural and educational programs all over the world, in cooperation with universities and established scholarly organizations.

NAME(S) OF PROGRAMS:
● **International Doctoral Scholarship for Studies Specializing in Jewish Fields**
● **International Fellowship in Jewish Studies and Jewish Culture**

TYPE:
Fellowships; Scholarships.

PURPOSE:
To help assure a creative Jewish future throughout the world by encouraging Jewish scholarship, Jewish education and Jewish cultural creativity.

LEGAL BASIS:
IRS Section 501(c)(3) charity; not a private foundation.

ELIGIBILITY:
Individual requirements vary according to the scholarship or fellowship.

FINANCIAL DATA:
Amount of support per award: Up to $10,000 per year.

APPLICATION INFO:
Guidelines and application forms for scholarships and fellowships are available on written request to the Foundation at the address above.
Duration: One academic year.
Deadline: October 31 for doctoral scholarships and fellowships.

OFFICERS:
Marlene Bethlehem, President
Jeni S. Friedman, Executive Vice President

ADDRESS INQUIRIES TO:
Jeni S. Friedman
Executive Vice President
(See address above.)

PONTIFICAL INSTITUTE OF MEDIAEVAL STUDIES

59 Queen's Park Crescent East
Toronto ON M5S 2C4 Canada
(416) 926-7142
Fax: (416) 926-7292
E-mail: allan.smith@utoronto.ca
Web Site: www.pims.ca

TYPE:
Fellowships.

See entry 584 for full listing.

PRESBYTERIAN CHURCH (U.S.A.)   [760]
100 Witherspoon Street
Louisville, KY 40202-1396
(502) 569-5224
(800) 728-7228 ext. 5224
Fax: (502) 569-8766
E-mail: finaid@pcusa.org
Web Site: www.pcusa.org/financialaid

NAME(S) OF PROGRAMS:
• **Presbyterian Study Grants**

TYPE:
Grants-in-aid; Scholarships.

PURPOSE:
To assist graduate students who are
communicant members of the Presbyterian
Church (U.S.A.) in their preparation for
professional church occupations.

ELIGIBILITY:
Applicants must demonstrate financial need,
be enrolled on a full-time basis, be in good
academic standing, be studying in a
Presbyterian Church (U.S.A.) seminary, and
must be studying in one of the two categories
listed below:
(1) students preparing for ordination must be
full-time M.Div. and must be enrolled as an
inquirer with or received as a candidate by a
Presbyterian Church (U.S.A.) presbytery for
a church occupation or;
(2) students preparing for occupations as a
Christian educator must be full-time
M.A.C.E. students.

GEOG. RESTRICTIONS: United States.

FINANCIAL DATA:
Grants are meant to be supplemental to other
assistance a student has sought and is
receiving from presbytery, seminary, home
church, etc. Grants are not available for
summer study, intern year or studying
abroad.
Amount of support per award: Up to $7,000
for the academic year, depending upon
demonstrated need and availability of funds.
Total amount of support: Varies.

APPLICATION INFO:
Detailed information and forms are available
on the web site.
Duration: One academic year. Renewals
possible (annually).
Deadline: May 15 for Part 1.

*SPECIAL STIPULATIONS:
No grants are available for doctoral study.

RASKOB FOUNDATION FOR CATHOLIC ACTIVITIES   [761]
P.O. Box 4019
Wilmington, DE 19807
(302) 655-4440
Fax: (302) 655-3223
E-mail: info@rfca.org
Web Site: www.rfca.org

FOUNDED: 1945

AREAS OF INTEREST:
Catholic activities.

TYPE:
Project/program grants.

YEAR PROGRAM STARTED: 1945

PURPOSE:
To engage in such exclusively religious,
charitable, literary and educational activities

as will aid the Roman Catholic Church and
institutions and organizations identified with
it.

LEGAL BASIS:
Nonprofit foundation.

ELIGIBILITY:
Applicants must be Catholic organizations
with nonprofit status.

FINANCIAL DATA:
Since inception, the Foundation has awarded
nearly $200,000,000, both domestically and
internationally, for a wide variety of causes.
Amount of support per award: $5,000 to
$60,000.
Total amount of support: $6,706,778 for the
year 2019.

NO. MOST RECENT APPLICANTS: 739 for the
year 2019.

NO. AWARDS: 223 for the year 2019.

APPLICATION INFO:
Process and requirements for Domestic and
International Programs are available on the
Foundation's web site. The International
Program is comprised of two phases. The
abstract phase is open to
organizations/projects meeting the outlined
requirements. After abstracts are reviewed,
the Foundation will notify each organization
whether or not they are invited to the
application phase.
Duration: Varies.
Deadline: Domestic applications:
Applications are accepted from January 1
through the last business day in January for
Board decision at the Foundation's May
meeting and from June 1 through the last
business day in June for Board decision at
the Foundation's November meeting.
International applications: Abstracts may be
submitted from May 1 through the last
business day of May. Decisions regarding
abstracts will be sent in mid-September.

PUBLICATIONS:
Application guidelines.

IRS I.D.: 51-0070060

STAFF:
Theresa G. Robinson, Executive Vice
President

ADDRESS INQUIRIES TO:
Janine Harlam, Grants Administrator
(See address above.)

SUBCOMMITTEE ON CATHOLIC HOME MISSIONS   [762]
United States Conference of Catholic Bishops
3211 4th Street, N.E.
Washington, DC 20017-1194
(202) 541-5400
Fax: (202) 541-3473
E-mail: homemissions@usccb.org
Web Site: www.usccb.org

FOUNDED: 1924

AREAS OF INTEREST:
Catholic missions and diocesan programs in
America, including evangelization, catechesis,
parish life, Hispanic ministry, youth outreach,
prison ministry, and personnel training.

TYPE:
General operating grants; Project/program
grants; Seed money grants; Training grants.
Annual grants to fund home mission and
diocesan activities, such as evangelization

through proclamation of the Word, pastoral
services, personnel training and the formation
of faith communities in the U.S. and its
territories. Home mission activities may be
centered at the national, regional, diocesan or
local level and may address the country as a
whole, a particular group of people or a
particular place.

YEAR PROGRAM STARTED: 1924

ELIGIBILITY:
Eligible applicants may come from diocesan
bishops of home mission dioceses for
activities that serve to establish or strengthen
the church in their dioceses. No funds are
available for endowments or loans.

GEOG. RESTRICTIONS: United States and its
Caribbean and Pacific territories.

FINANCIAL DATA:
Amount of support per award: Varies
depending on needs and nature of the
request.
Total amount of support: $9,400,000 for the
year 2018.

NO. MOST RECENT APPLICANTS: 84.

NO. AWARDS: 83.

APPLICATION INFO:
Application materials are available January of
each year. Contact office for other
requirements.
Duration: Grants are renewable.
Deadline: April 1. Announcement in October.
Disbursements are made semiannually,
January to December.

PUBLICATIONS:
Annual report; guidelines; *Neighbors*,
quarterly newsletter.

OFFICERS:
Bishop Shawn McKnight, Chairman
Kevin Day, Director

ADDRESS INQUIRIES TO:
Kevin Day, Director
(See telephone and e-mail address above.)

*PLEASE NOTE:
Currently considering grants from dioceses
only.

UNITED JEWISH APPEAL-FEDERATION OF JEWISH PHILANTHROPIES OF NEW YORK   [763]
130 East 59th Street
New York, NY 10022
(212) 980-1000
(212) 836-1321
Fax: (212) 836-1353
E-mail: feinsteinl@ujafedny.org
Web Site: www.ujafedny.org

FOUNDED: 1917

AREAS OF INTEREST:
Human services, Jewish identity and
education, rescue and resettlement of Jewish
communities in distress.

CONSULTING OR VOLUNTEER SERVICES:
Offers numerous opportunities to volunteer.
Please call Resource Line: (212) 836-1447.

TYPE:
Awards/prizes; Block grants; Capital grants;
Challenge/matching grants;
Conferences/seminars; Demonstration grants;
Development grants; Fellowships; General
operating grants; Internships; Matching gifts;
Project/program grants; Research grants;
Scholarships; Technical assistance; Travel
grants; Research contracts.

YEAR PROGRAM STARTED: 1917

PURPOSE:
To care for people in need; to inspire a passion for Jewish life and learning; to strengthen Jewish communities in New York, in Israel, and around the world.

LEGAL BASIS:
501(c)(3).

ELIGIBILITY:
No grants to individuals. Applicants must be 501(c)(3) organizations.

GEOG. RESTRICTIONS: New York including the five boroughs, Nassau, Suffolk and Westchester counties.

FINANCIAL DATA:
Amount of support per award: Varies depending upon needs and nature of the request.

Total amount of support: $141,600,000 for fiscal year 2019.

APPLICATION INFO:
Application form required. Organizations must include documentation of IRS nonprofit status with their application.

Duration: One year. Renewal possible.

Deadline: January for most programs.

PUBLICATIONS:
Annual Report to the Community.

IRS I.D.: 51-0172429

ADDRESS INQUIRIES TO:
E-mail: grants@ujafedny.org

UNITED METHODIST COMMUNICATIONS
810 12th Avenue South
Nashville, TN 37203-4704
(615) 742-5400
Fax: (615) 742-5423
E-mail: scholarship@umcom.org
Web Site: www.umcom.org

TYPE:
Fellowships. Assists one United Methodist student in postgraduate study at an accredited U.S. college or university who intends to pursue a career in religious journalism.

See entry 1789 for full listing.

THE WABASH CENTER FOR TEACHING AND LEARNING IN THEOLOGY AND RELIGION [764]
301 West Wabash Avenue
Crawfordsville, IN 47933
(765) 361-6047
Fax: (765) 361-6051
E-mail: wabashcenter@wabash.edu
Web Site: www.wabashcenter.wabash.edu

FOUNDED: 1995

AREAS OF INTEREST:
Teaching religion and theology, higher education pedagogy in theology and religion.

NAME(S) OF PROGRAMS:
* **Educational Environments**
* **Faculty Practices and Vocation**

TYPE:
Conferences/seminars; Fellowships; Project/program grants; Research grants.

YEAR PROGRAM STARTED: 1995

PURPOSE:
To strengthen and enhance the teaching of religion and theology in North American theological schools and religion departments in colleges and universities.

ELIGIBILITY:
Full-time faculty members in religion departments of colleges and universities in North America and in theological schools accredited by the Association of Theological Schools are eligible to apply for these grants.

GEOG. RESTRICTIONS: United States and Canada.

FINANCIAL DATA:
Amount of support per award: Up to $30,000.

NO. MOST RECENT APPLICANTS: Approximately 100.

NO. AWARDS: 80.

APPLICATION INFO:
Grant proposals should consist of an application form, project proposal (including budget) and letter of support. Specific format for grant proposals is explained in detail on the Center's web site.

Deadline: February 15.

PUBLICATIONS:
Teaching Theology and Religion, published quarterly by Wiley-Blackwell Publishers.

ADDRESS INQUIRIES TO:
Paul O. Myhre, Associate Director
(See address above.)

INTERNATIONAL AFFAIRS AND AREA STUDIES

International affairs and area studies

AMERICAN INSTITUTE OF PAKISTAN STUDIES [765]

University of Wisconsin-Madison
B488 Medical Sciences Center
1300 University Avenue
Madison, WI 53706
(608) 265-1471
Fax: (608) 265-3302
E-mail: aips@pakistanstudies-aips.org
Web Site: www.pakistanstudies-aips.org

FOUNDED: 1973

AREAS OF INTEREST:
All fields of humanities and social sciences if engaged in research on Pakistan and relations between Pakistan and other countries.

NAME(S) OF PROGRAMS:
- **AIPS Post Doctoral Fellowship**
- **AIPS Pre-Doctoral Fellowship**
- **Community College Faculty Exchange**
- **Lecture Series**
- **Workshop Series**

TYPE:
Awards/prizes; Conferences/seminars; Fellowships; Travel grants; Visiting scholars. Awarded in several categories including predoctoral research, postdoctoral study, library service and professional development.

YEAR PROGRAM STARTED: 1973

PURPOSE:
To promote research on Pakistan.

ELIGIBILITY:
Applicants must be scholars and advanced graduate students who are American citizens and are engaged in research on Pakistan in ancient, medieval and modern times, in all fields of the humanities and social sciences. Research topics comparing aspects of Pakistan with other Muslim countries are especially encouraged.

Graduate student applicants must have fulfilled all residence, language and preliminary examination requirements for the Doctorate and have an approved dissertation topic.

FINANCIAL DATA:
The award will provide a maintenance allowance for the scholar and dependents, plus travel and other benefits.
Amount of support per award: Varies.
Total amount of support: Approximately $100,000.

NO. MOST RECENT APPLICANTS: 15.

NO. AWARDS: Varies.

APPLICATION INFO:
Predoctoral applications should include a proposal (five pages), curriculum vitae, a transcript, a letter from the dissertation advisor and contact information for two references. Postdoctoral applications should include a proposal (five pages), curriculum vitae, and contact information for two referees.
Duration: Two to nine months.
Deadline: Varies.

STAFF:
Laura Hammond, U.S. Director

ADDRESS INQUIRIES TO:
Laura Hammond, U.S. Director
(See address above.)

THE KATHRYN AMES FOUNDATION [766]

c/o Pierson & Pierson
305 West Chesapeake Avenue, Suite 308
Towson, MD 21204
(410) 821-3006
Fax: (410) 821-3007
E-mail: info@kathrynames.org
Web Site: www.kathrynames.org

FOUNDED: 1993

AREAS OF INTEREST:
Israel, education, health care, poverty relief and pluralism.

TYPE:
General operating grants; Project/program grants.

YEAR PROGRAM STARTED: 1993

PURPOSE:
To benefit organizations located in Israel which are working for charitable and benevolent purposes.

LEGAL BASIS:
Private foundation.

ELIGIBILITY:
Eligible organizations must be nonprofit and located in Israel.

GEOG. RESTRICTIONS: Israel.

FINANCIAL DATA:
Amount of support per award: $7,500 to $40,000; Average: $11,389.
Total amount of support: $432,801 for the year 2019.

NO. MOST RECENT APPLICANTS: Letters of Inquiry: 214; Full Applications: 60 for the year 2019.

NO. AWARDS: 38 for the year 2019.

APPLICATION INFO:
Application form is available online.
Duration: Typically one year.

PUBLICATIONS:
Application guidelines.

ADDRESS INQUIRIES TO:
Lu Pierson, Grants Administrator
(See address above.)

ARCHAEOLOGICAL INSTITUTE OF AMERICA [767]

44 Beacon Street
Boston, MA 02108
(857) 305-9360
Fax: (857) 233-4270
E-mail: fellowships@archaeological.org
Web Site: www.archaeological.org

FOUNDED: 1879

AREAS OF INTEREST:
Archaeological research and publication.

NAME(S) OF PROGRAMS:
- **The Archaeology of Portugal Fellowship**

TYPE:
Fellowships. The Fellowship supports projects pertaining to the archaeology of Portugal. These include, but are not limited to, research projects, colloquia, symposia, publication, research-related travel, or travel to academic meetings for the purpose of presenting papers on the archaeology of Portugal.

PURPOSE:
To promote archaeological studies pertaining to Portugal.

ELIGIBILITY:
Portuguese, American and other international scholars are invited to apply. Applicants must have been AIA members in good standing for at least two consecutive years (one year for graduate students).

FINANCIAL DATA:
Amount of support per award: Award may vary based on the merit of the proposal. Typically $4,000.
Total amount of support: Typically $2,000 to $8,000.

NO. MOST RECENT APPLICANTS: 8.

NO. AWARDS: 1 for the year 2020.

APPLICATION INFO:
Application information is available on the web site.
Duration: One year; work to be conducted between July 1 of the award year and the following June 30.
Deadline: November 1. Announcement by February 1.

ADDRESS INQUIRIES TO:
Laurel Nilsen Sparks
Lecture and Fellowship Coordinator
(See address above.)

ASHBURN INSTITUTE INC. [768]

198 Okatie Village Drive
Suite 103, PMB 301
Bluffton, SC 29909
(703) 728-6482
Fax: (843) 705-7643
E-mail: info@ashburninstitute.org
Web Site: www.ashburninstitute.org

FOUNDED: 1940

AREAS OF INTEREST:
International relations, political science, Middle Eastern studies, and international security.

NAME(S) OF PROGRAMS:
- **Frank Educational Fund**

TYPE:
Research grants; Scholarships. The Institute carries out its own scholarship program for graduate students through an annual endowment received in perpetuity. Half of the funds must be awarded to U.S. citizens. The best papers which meet the goals of the conference, as outlined in the "Call for Papers," will reimburse the graduate authors by covering their conference travel and lodging expenses. Locations for the conference may be anywhere in the world. The top papers are selected for publication with due credit to the authors.

Funding is provided by the gracious endowment left by Mayme and Herb Frank for the purpose of promoting international integration and harmonization.

YEAR PROGRAM STARTED: 1991

PURPOSE:
To support the study of federalism and international integration at the graduate and postgraduate level.

ELIGIBILITY:
Open to graduate students of good academic standing working on a thesis or dissertation relating to international integration and federalism or doing coursework that places major weight on international integration and

federalism. International (foreign institutions) graduate students are eligible, as well as U.S. students.

FINANCIAL DATA:
Amount of support per award: $1,000 to $2,000.

Total amount of support: $20,000 annually.

APPLICATION INFO:
Application information can be found on the Institute's web site. Please submit abstract paper for consideration at the International Conference.

Deadline: Determined by future conference dates.

ADDRESS INQUIRIES TO:
Frank Fund Manager
(See address above.)

AUSTRO-AMERICAN ASSOCIATION OF BOSTON [769]

34 Cutting Cross Way
Wayland, MA 01778
(978) 579-2191
E-mail: scholarship@austria-boston.org
Web Site: www.austria-boston.org

FOUNDED: 1944

AREAS OF INTEREST:
All aspects of Austrian society, especially culture; music; and Austrian-American relations.

TYPE:
Research grants; Scholarships. Scholarship award provides support for a project relating to Austrian music, history, literature, science, art, architecture, contemporary life or other aspects of the Austrian contribution to culture.

YEAR PROGRAM STARTED: 1976

PURPOSE:
To further interest in Austrian culture.

LEGAL BASIS:
Organized and established as of July 6, 1970 by the Secretary of the Commonwealth.

ELIGIBILITY:
The project must be related to Austria.

Undergraduate or graduate students at New England colleges or universities are eligible. They must be willing to present the results of their project at an event of the Austro-American Association.

GEOG. RESTRICTIONS: New England.

FINANCIAL DATA:
The scholarship award does not support tuition or other expenses related to a course of study.

Amount of support per award: $3,000.

Total amount of support: $3,000.

NO. MOST RECENT APPLICANTS: 6.

NO. AWARDS: 1 per year (when funds are available).

APPLICATION INFO:
Applications should include a curriculum vitae, a detailed description of the proposed project and two letters of recommendation from faculty members well acquainted with the applicant's background and potential. Applicants will be invited to present the results of their project at a meeting of the Association. A personal interview will be required.

Duration: One year.

Deadline: March 23.

OFFICERS:
Traude Schieber-Acker, President
Marta Stasa, Vice President
Hana Sittler, Treasurer
Judy Zohn, Secretary

ADDRESS INQUIRIES TO:
Traude Schieber-Acker, President and Chairperson, Scholarship Panel
Austro-American Association of Boston, Inc.
(See address and e-mail above.)

*PLEASE NOTE:
E-mail correspondence and electronic submission are requested.

CENTER FOR INTERNATIONAL SECURITY AND COOPERATION (CISAC)   [770]

Freeman Spogli Institute for International Studies
Stanford University
Encina Hall, C222, 616 Serra Street
Stanford, CA 94305-6165
(650) 736-4566
Fax: (650) 723-0089
E-mail: cisacfellowship@stanford.edu
Web Site: cisac.fsi.stanford.edu

FOUNDED: 1970

AREAS OF INTEREST:
CISAC fellows may focus on any of the following topics: nuclear weapons policy and nonproliferation; nuclear energy; digital security; biosecurity and global health; insurgency; terrorism; civil conflict; national security strategies; and global governance.

NAME(S) OF PROGRAMS:
● Cybersecurity and International Security Fellowship
● Human-Centered Artificial Intelligence (HAI)
● The MacArthur Foundation Nuclear Security Fellowship
● Natural Sciences or Engineering International Security Fellowship
● Social Sciences or Humanities International Security Fellowship
● Stanford International Observatory Research Fellowship
● The Stanton Nuclear Security Fellowship

TYPE:
Fellowships.

PURPOSE:
To produce policy-relevant research on international security topics; to teach and train the next generation of security specialists; to influence policymaking in international security; to develop a more informed public discussion.

LEGAL BASIS:
University.

ELIGIBILITY:
Must be in Ph.D. program, have a Ph.D. or equivalent, or extraordinary professional experience.

FINANCIAL DATA:
Amount of support per award: Varies.
Total amount of support: Varies.

NO. MOST RECENT APPLICANTS: Over 220.

NO. AWARDS: 10 to 20.

APPLICATION INFO:
Application information is available on the CISAC web site.

Duration: Nine to 11 months.
Deadline: January.

ADDRESS INQUIRIES TO:
CISAC Fellowship Program
(See address above.)

CENTER FOR U.S. - MEXICAN STUDIES, UNIVERSITY OF CALIFORNIA, SAN DIEGO   [771]

School of Global Policy and Strategy
9500 Gilman Drive, No. 0519
La Jolla, CA 92093-0519
(858) 822-1696
Fax: (858) 534-6447
E-mail: usmex@ucsd.edu
Web Site: usmex.ucsd.edu

FOUNDED: 1979

AREAS OF INTEREST:
The study of U.S. and Mexico relations and the study of Mexico within the social sciences and history.

NAME(S) OF PROGRAMS:
● USMEX Visiting Fellows Program

TYPE:
Fellowships.

YEAR PROGRAM STARTED: 1980

PURPOSE:
To support the write-up of a Ph.D. dissertation or the write-up of a postdoctoral research project.

ELIGIBILITY:
Open to Mexican citizens, advanced graduate students, junior faculty and advanced faculty members from any campus of the University of California system, as well as other institutions.

GEOG. RESTRICTIONS: United States and Mexico.

FINANCIAL DATA:
Amount of support per award: Stipends average $10,000 to $22,500 for the academic year.

Total amount of support: $150,000.

NO. MOST RECENT APPLICANTS: 70.

NO. AWARDS: 8.

APPLICATION INFO:
Applicants must submit a one-page letter of intent describing the work to be completed during residence. Letters are to be submitted by e-mail to Greg Mallinger, Fellows Coordinator, gmallinger@ucsd.edu.

Duration: Four to nine months. Former Visiting Fellows are eligible to apply again after five years.

Deadline: November.

ADDRESS INQUIRIES TO:
Greg Mallinger, Fellows Coordinator
(See address above.)

THE CHRISTENSEN FUND

487 Bryant Street
Second Floor
San Francisco, CA 94107
(415) 644-1600
Fax: (415) 644-1601
E-mail: info@christensenfund.org
Web Site: www.christensenfund.org

TYPE:
General operating grants; Project/program grants; Research grants.

See entry 59 for full listing.

COUNCIL FOR EUROPEAN STUDIES AT COLUMBIA UNIVERSITY [772]

475 Riverside Drive
Office 308i
New York, NY 10115
(646) 745-8550
E-mail: awards@ces-europe.org
Web Site: councilforeuropeanstudies.org

FOUNDED: 1970

AREAS OF INTEREST:
The study of Europe.

NAME(S) OF PROGRAMS:
- **Book Award**
- **CES Small Event Grants**
- **Conference Travel Grants**
- **First Article Prize in Humanities and Social Sciences**
- **Mellon-CES Dissertation Completion Fellowship in European Studies**
- **SAE-CES Pre-Dissertation Research Fellowships**

TYPE:
Awards/prizes; Conferences/seminars; Fellowships; Internships; Scholarships; Travel grants. The CES Book Award honors talented emerging scholars with an award for the best first book on any subject in European studies. The award is given every two years.

CES Conference Travel Grants support transcontinental travel for junior faculty and graduate students already scheduled to present at the Council's International Conference of Europeanists.

CES Small Event Grants support workshops, lectures, symposia and other small events that share research on Europe with a wider community.

First Article Prize awards one prize to a scholar working in the humanities and one to a scholar working in the social sciences. These prizes will honor the writers of the best first articles on European studies published within a two-year period.

Mellon-CES Dissertation Completion Fellowships are intended to facilitate the timely completion of the doctoral degree by late-stage graduate students focused on topics in European studies.

SAE-CES Pre-Dissertation Research Fellowships are intended to fund student's first major research project in Europe.

YEAR PROGRAM STARTED: 1971

ELIGIBILITY:
Book Award: Must be scholar's first book on any subject in European studies. Books may be nominated by the author, a CES member, or by a publisher.

Pre-Dissertation Research Fellowships are limited to graduate students currently enrolled in a doctoral program at a university that is a member of the Council for European Studies Academic Consortium. Member universities and additional eligibility requirements can be found online.

First Article Prize nominees meet the following criteria:
(1) be the first article published by the nominee in the field of European studies in a peer-reviewed journal;
(2) be published between October 1, 2018 and September 30, 2020;
(3) be the work of one author only or be an article on which the nominee is the first author and;

(4) be authored by a member of the Council for European Studies or a faculty/student of an institution that is a member. Nominations may be submitted by the publisher, editor, author, or admiring colleagues.

To be eligible for the Mellon-CES Dissertation Completion Fellowship, the applicant must be ABD, be enrolled at a higher education institution in the U.S., and can have no more than one full year of dissertation work remaining at the start of the fellowship year as certified by his or her dissertation advisor. The applicant must also have exhausted the dissertation completion funding normally provided by his or her academic department or university, and he or she must be working on a topic within or substantially overlapping European studies. To be eligible to receive the fellowship, applicants must also be enrolled in an institution that is a member of the CES Academic Consortium. However, students whose universities are not currently members of the CES consortium may apply, but they are encouraged to apply early in the application season so that every effort may be made to enroll the institution in the CES member consortium and, thus, establish the student's eligibility by the application deadline.

FINANCIAL DATA:
Book Award recipient receives a certificate, $1,000 and all-expenses-paid trip to International Conference and award ceremony. Fellowship recipients receive a stipend, travel support for attending and presenting at the CES International Conference of Europeanists, and the opportunity to publish in *Perspectives on Europe*.
Amount of support per award: Book Award: $1,000; CES Small Event Grants: $300 to $1,500; Conference Travel Grant: equivalent of $725, $500 cash grant and waiver of registration fee; First Article Prize: $500; Mellon-CES Dissertation Completion Fellowship: $27,500 stipend to be paid in six bimonthly installments; Pre-Dissertation Research Fellowship: $5,000 stipend.
Total amount of support: Varies.

APPLICATION INFO:
Applications and guidelines are available online.
Deadline: Book Award: Mid-October; CES Small Event Grants: December 1 for spring and July 15 for fall; Conference Travel Grant: January 9; First Article Prize: October 1; Mellon-CES Dissertation Completion Fellowship and Pre-Dissertation Research Fellowship: January.

COUNCIL ON FOREIGN RELATIONS [773]

58 East 68th Street
New York, NY 10065
(212) 434-9740
Fax: (212) 434-9870
E-mail: fellowships@cfr.org
Web Site: www.cfr.org/fellowships

FOUNDED: 1921

AREAS OF INTEREST:
International relations, international affairs, Japan, U.S.-Japan relations, U.S.-Japan politics, Japanese studies, Japanese-American relations, foreign policy, policymaking, and public service.

NAME(S) OF PROGRAMS:
- **International Affairs Fellowship in Japan (IAF-J)**

TYPE:
Fellowships. The International Affairs Fellowship in Japan (IAF-J), sponsored by Hitachi, Ltd., provides a selected group of midcareer U.S. citizens the opportunity to expand their professional horizons by spending a period of research or other professional activity in Japan. Fellows are drawn from academia, business, government, media, NGOs and think tanks. In cooperation with the Council on Foreign Relations (CFR), the program's sponsor, Hitachi, Ltd., assists fellows in finding suitable host organizations in Japan.

YEAR PROGRAM STARTED: 1997

PURPOSE:
To strengthen mutual understanding and cooperation between the rising generations of leaders in the U.S. and Japan.

ELIGIBILITY:
The IAF-J is only open to U.S. citizens between the ages of 27 and 45. The program is intended primarily for those without substantial prior experience in Japan, although the selection committee has made exceptions when it considered that the fellowship would allow an individual to add a significant new dimension to his or her career. Knowledge of the Japanese language is not a requirement.

FINANCIAL DATA:
The program awards a stipend in yen, which covers travel and living expenses in Japan. Fellows are considered independent contractors rather than employees of CFR, and are not eligible for employment benefits, including health insurance.

CO-OP FUNDING PROGRAMS: Hitachi, Ltd.

NO. AWARDS: Approximately 3 to 5 per year.

APPLICATION INFO:
Interested candidates who meet the program's eligibility requirements can apply online via the CFR web site between June 1 and October 1 on an annual basis. Candidates who are selected as IAF-J finalists will be notified between December and January, with finalist interviews scheduled in Washington, DC, and New York, NY, between January and February. Official selections and announcement of IAF-J awards will be made between February and March.
Duration: Three to 12 months.
Deadline: October 31.

ADDRESS INQUIRIES TO:
See telephone or e-mail address above.

COUNCIL ON FOREIGN RELATIONS

58 East 68th Street
New York, NY 10065
(212) 434-9740
Fax: (212) 434-9870
E-mail: fellowships@cfr.org
Web Site: www.cfr.org/fellowships

TYPE:
Fellowships. The Edward R. Murrow Press Fellow spends nine months full-time in residence at the Council on Foreign Relations' (CFR) headquarters in New York. The program enables the fellow to engage in sustained analysis and writing, expand his or her intellectual and professional horizons,

and extensively participate in CFR's active program of meetings and events. The Fellow will be part of the David Rockefeller Studies Program, CFR's think tank, alongside the program's full-time, adjunct and visiting fellows, whose expertise extends across the broad range of significant foreign policy issues facing the U.S. and the international community.

See entry 1759 for full listing.

COUNCIL ON FOREIGN RELATIONS [774]

58 East 68th Street
New York, NY 10065
(212) 434-9740
Fax: (212) 434-9800
E-mail: fellowships@cfr.org
Web Site: www.cfr.org/fellowships

FOUNDED: 1921

AREAS OF INTEREST:
International affairs, international relations, policymaking, U.S. foreign policy, foreign affairs, public service, government, and academia.

NAME(S) OF PROGRAMS:
● **International Affairs Fellowship (IAF)**

TYPE:
Fellowships. The International Affairs Fellowship (IAF) Program aims to strengthen career development by helping outstanding individuals acquire and apply foreign policy skills beyond the scope of their professional and scholarly achievements. The distinctive character of the IAF Program lies in the contrasting professional experiences fellows obtain through their 12-month appointment. Selected fellows from academia and the private sector spend fellowship tenures in public service and policy-oriented settings, while government officials spend their tenures in a scholarly atmosphere free from operational pressure.

YEAR PROGRAM STARTED: 1967

PURPOSE:
To assist midcareer scholars and professionals in advancing their analytic capabilities and broadening their foreign policy experience.

ELIGIBILITY:
The IAF Program is only open to U.S. citizens and permanent residents between the ages of 27 and 35 who are eligible to work in the U.S. CFR does not sponsor for visas. While a Ph.D. is not a requirement, selected fellows generally hold an advanced degree and possess a strong record of work experience as well as a firm grounding in the field of foreign policy. The program does not fund pre- or postdoctoral research, work toward a degree, or the completion of projects for which substantial progress has been made prior to the Fellowship period.

FINANCIAL DATA:
Fellows are considered independent contractors rather than employees of CFR, and are not eligible for employment benefits, including health insurance.
Amount of support per award: Stipend of $105,000.

NO. AWARDS: 8 to 10 annually.

APPLICATION INFO:
Interested candidates who meet the program's eligibility requirements can apply online via the Council web site between June 1 and October 31 on an annual basis.

Duration: 12 months, preferably beginning in September. Though deferment is not an option, requests to do so, for up to one year only, will be considered on a case-by-case basis and under special circumstances.
Deadline: October 31. Notification between December and January. Announcement between February and March.

ADDRESS INQUIRIES TO:
See telephone or e-mail address above.

COUNCIL ON FOREIGN RELATIONS [775]

58 East 68th Street
New York, NY 10065
(212) 434-9740
Fax: (212) 434-9870
E-mail: fellowships@cfr.org
Web Site: www.cfr.org/fellowships

FOUNDED: 1921

AREAS OF INTEREST:
Nuclear security, nuclear weapons, nuclear proliferation, nuclear terrorism, nuclear energy, nuclear force posture, nuclear arms, international relations, international affairs, foreign affairs, government, and public policy.

NAME(S) OF PROGRAMS:
● **Stanton Nuclear Security Fellowship Program (SNSF)**

TYPE:
Fellowships. The Stanton Nuclear Security Fellowship (SNSF) Program, made possible by a grant from the Stanton Foundation, offers younger scholars studying nuclear security issues the opportunity to spend a period of 12 months at the Council on Foreign Relations' (CFR) offices in New York or Washington, DC, conducting policy-relevant research. The Fellowships will be awarded on the basis of academic and professional accomplishments and promise, and on the merits of the specific research projects proposed.

YEAR PROGRAM STARTED: 2009

PURPOSE:
To stimulate the development of the next generation of thought leaders in nuclear security. The fellows could work on a wide range of issues, including nuclear terrorism, nuclear proliferation, nuclear weapons, nuclear force posture, and nuclear energy.

ELIGIBILITY:
Qualified candidates must be junior (non-tenured) faculty, postdoctoral fellows, or predoctoral candidates from any discipline who are working on a nuclear security-related issue. The program is only open to U.S. citizens and permanent residents who are eligible to work in the U.S. CFR does not sponsor for visas.

FINANCIAL DATA:
Payment will be made in 12 equal monthly installments. Fellows are considered independent contractors rather than employees of CFR, and are not eligible for employment benefits, including health insurance.
Amount of support per award: A stipend of $110,000 for junior (non-tenured) faculty and $80,000 for postdoctoral fellows.

CO-OP FUNDING PROGRAMS: The SNSF Program is made possible by a generous grant from the Stanton Foundation.

NO. AWARDS: 1 to 2 annually.

APPLICATION INFO:
Interested candidates who meet the program's eligibility requirements must submit an application form, a cover letter, a curriculum vitae, and a proposal outlining the work proposed to conduct (as specified on the CFR web site). Each applicant should arrange to have two letters of recommendation sent assessing the policy relevance of the applicant's proposed project as well as the applicant's qualifications for carrying it out.

All application materials must be sent to the e-mail address above.
Duration: 12 months, preferably beginning in September.
Deadline: December 15.

ADDRESS INQUIRIES TO:
See telephone or e-mail address above.

CULTURAL VISTAS [776]

233 Broadway, Suite 2120
New York, NY 10279
(212) 497-3510
E-mail: alfa@culturalvistas.org
Web Site: www.culturalvistas.org/alfa
www.alfafellowship.org

FOUNDED: 2004

AREAS OF INTEREST:
Culture, business, law, politics, public policy, government, journalism, mass communications, finance and economics.

NAME(S) OF PROGRAMS:
● **Alfa Fellowship Program**

TYPE:
Exchange programs; Fellowships; Internships. A high-level professional development exchange program placing qualified American, British and German citizens in work assignments at leading organizations in Russia in the fields of business, economics, journalism, law and public policy. The program includes language training, seminar programs, and extended professional work experience. Fellows receive a stipend, travel, housing and insurance.

YEAR PROGRAM STARTED: 2004

PURPOSE:
To foster a new generation of future American, British and German leaders with in-depth practical experience in the modern business and public policy environment of the Russian Federation.

ELIGIBILITY:
Open to U.S., U.K. and German citizens with a Bachelor's degree, work experience and professional interest or background in above fields. Russian language proficiency preferred, but not required.

Applicants must:
(1) have U.S., U.K. or German citizenship;
(2) be 25 to 35 years of age at time of application;
(3) have a Bachelor's degree in business, economics, journalism, law or public policy and;
(4) have at least two years relevant work experience in their field of expertise.

GEOG. RESTRICTIONS: United States, United Kingdom, Germany and Russia.

FINANCIAL DATA:
Monthly stipend, free accommodations in Russia, all in-country program-related travel,

round-trip flight to Moscow, and limited international health, accident and liability insurance during the program in Russia.

NO. MOST RECENT APPLICANTS: Approximately 120.

NO. AWARDS: 18.

APPLICATION INFO:
Candidates must submit application online with all supporting materials by the deadline.
Duration: 11 months, June to April.
Deadline: November 15.

ADDRESS INQUIRIES TO:
Melissa Graves, Program Director
Alfa Fellowship Program
(See address above.)

J.W. DAFOE FOUNDATION   [777]
Department of Political Studies
University of Manitoba
c/o 529 Fletcher Argue Building
Winnipeg MB R3T 5V5 Canada
(204) 474-8546
Fax: (204) 474-7645
E-mail: andrea.rounce@umanitoba.ca
Web Site: www.dafoefoundation.ca

AREAS OF INTEREST:
International relations, economics, history and political science.

NAME(S) OF PROGRAMS:
- **Dafoe Book Prize**
- **John W. Dafoe Graduate Fellowship**

TYPE:
Awards/prizes; Conferences/seminars; Fellowships; Project/program grants; Research grants. Dafoe Book Prize is awarded to the best book on Canada, Canadians, and/or Canada's place in the world published in the previous calendar year.

Graduate Fellowships for study in international relations, economics, history or political studies.

PURPOSE:
To encourage graduate study in international relations; to further international understanding.

LEGAL BASIS:
University association.

ELIGIBILITY:
Dafoe Book Prize: Distinguished writing by Canadians, or authors resident in Canada, that contributes to the understanding of Canada, Canadians, and/or Canada's place in the world are eligible. Co- or multiple-authored books are eligible, but not edited books consisting of chapters from many different authors.

Dafoe Graduate Fellowship will be offered to a graduate student who:
(1) is enrolled full-time in the Faculty of Graduate Studies entering the first or second year of a Master's program in any of the following departments: the Department of Economics, History, Political Studies, the Arthur V. Mauro Centre for Peace and Justice, or the Faculty of Law at the University of Manitoba;
(2) has achieved a minimum grade point average of 3.5 (or equivalent) in the previous 60 credit hours of study and;
(3) is pursuing a thesis stream program related to the field of international relations and/or international comparative studies.

GEOG. RESTRICTIONS: Canada.

FINANCIAL DATA:
Amount of support per award: $10,000 (CAN).
Total amount of support: $20,000 (CAN) annually.

NO. AWARDS: 1 per award.

APPLICATION INFO:
Dafoe Book Prize: Publishers and individuals are encouraged to submit their entries (in four copies), with the appropriate submission fee. Late entries for books published in later November and December will be accepted into the new year.

Dafoe Graduate Fellowship: Applicants are required to submit a cover letter, detailed research proposal, three letters of reference, and official transcripts to the Awards Office at the Faculty of Graduate Studies at the University of Manitoba.
Duration: Fellowships are for one year and are nonrenewable.
Deadline: Dafoe Book Prize: December 13. Dafoe Graduate Fellowship: April 1.

TRUSTEES:
Catherine Auld, Chairperson

*SPECIAL STIPULATIONS:
A submission fee of $50 per entry is required for the J.W. Dafoe Book Prize.

THE EAST-WEST CENTER   [778]
1601 East West Road
Honolulu, HI 96848-1601
(808) 944-7735
Fax: (808) 944-7730 (Award Services Office)
E-mail: scholarships@eastwestcenter.org
Web Site: www.eastwestcenter.
org/studentprograms

FOUNDED: 1960

AREAS OF INTEREST:
Economics; environmental change, vulnerability and governance; population and health; politics, governance and security, at a local, national and/or regional level in the Asia Pacific region.

NAME(S) OF PROGRAMS:
- **East-West Center Graduate Degree Fellowship**

TYPE:
Fellowships.

YEAR PROGRAM STARTED: 1960

PURPOSE:
To strengthen relations and understanding among the peoples and nations of Asia, the Pacific and the U.S.; to serve as a vigorous hub for cooperative research, education and dialogue on critical issues of common concern to the Asia Pacific region and the U.S.

LEGAL BASIS:
Public, nonprofit educational corporation established in Hawaii in 1960 by the U.S. Congress.

ELIGIBILITY:
Candidates must have obtained a four-year Bachelor's degree or its equivalent, must be a citizen or permanent resident of the U.S. or a country in Asia or the Pacific, and must come to the Center on the exchange visitor (J-1) visa.

Priority in the student selection process is given to applicants with a commitment to the Asia Pacific region seeking degrees in fields of study related to research themes at the East-West Center.

GEOG. RESTRICTIONS: Hawaii.

FINANCIAL DATA:
Award may include housing, stipend, tuition, health insurance, when relevant, and book allowance as approved. Costs may be shared by collaborating institutions.
Amount of support per award: Varies.
Total amount of support: Varies.
Matching fund requirements: Cost-sharing on any Center award is actively sought.

CO-OP FUNDING PROGRAMS: Funding for the Center comes from the U.S. government, with additional support provided by private agencies, individuals, foundations, corporations, and the governments of the region.

NO. MOST RECENT APPLICANTS: 150.

NO. AWARDS: Varies based on funding.

APPLICATION INFO:
Applications are available online.
Duration: Initially 12 months with possible renewal up to two years for Master's Degree or doctoral studies, contingent upon funding, performance and academic progress.
Deadline: December 1 for forwarding to the Award Services Office.

ADDRESS INQUIRIES TO:
Award Services Office
(See address above.)

*SPECIAL STIPULATIONS:
Study must be at the University of Hawaii at Manoa.

THE EAST-WEST CENTER   [779]
1601 East-West Road
Honolulu, HI 96848-1601
(808) 944-7646
Fax: (808) 944-7070 (Attn: APLP)
E-mail: aplp@eastwestcenter.org
Web Site: www.eastwestcenter.org/aplp

FOUNDED: 1960

AREAS OF INTEREST:
Issues related to the Asia Pacific region.

NAME(S) OF PROGRAMS:
- **Asia Pacific Leadership Program**

TYPE:
Fellowships. Links advanced and interdisciplinary analysis of emergent regional issues with experiential leadership learning.

YEAR PROGRAM STARTED: 2001

PURPOSE:
To create a network of action focused on building a peaceful, prosperous and just Asia Pacific community.

LEGAL BASIS:
Public, nonprofit educational corporation.

ELIGIBILITY:
Candidates must have at least a three-year Bachelor's degree or its equivalent from an accredited U.S. college or university or from a recognized institution of higher learning abroad, at least five years of work experience, a demonstrated commitment to promoting peace and prosperity in the Asia Pacific region, and a deep interest in experiential leadership development training.

Priority in the student selection process is given to candidates with professional work experience:

(1) international experience and aptitude, including overseas residence, language skills, intercultural and diversity exposure;
(2) leadership track record in professional, public and/or personal realms;
(3) volunteer and community service experience;
(4) Asia Pacific engagement and evidence of interest in the region, as well as commitment to its future prosperity; this might include classes taken at university, time spent in the region, languages spoken, membership and fellowships, specific projects, field studies and areas of research interest and;
(5) experience working collaboratively in small teams or in large groups.

GEOG. RESTRICTIONS: Hawaii.

FINANCIAL DATA:
Award includes program fees, living expenses, field study costs, and other academic expenses.
Amount of support per award: Varies.
Total amount of support: Varies.

NO. AWARDS: 25 to 30 each year.

APPLICATION INFO:
Application form is available online.
Duration: Early August to early December.
Deadline: Priority Deadline: December 1. Final Deadline: March 1.

PUBLICATIONS:
Annual report.

ADDRESS INQUIRIES TO:
Asia Pacific Leadership Program
(See address above.)

THE EISENHOWER INSTITUTE AT GETTYSBURG COLLEGE [780]

818 Connecticut Avenue, N.W.
Suite 400
Washington, DC 20006
(202) 628-4444
Fax: (202) 628-4445
E-mail: ei@gettysburg.edu
Web Site: www.eisenhowerinstitute.org

FOUNDED: 1983

AREAS OF INTEREST:
World affairs.

NAME(S) OF PROGRAMS:
● **Eisenhower Institute Scholarship Programs**

TYPE:
Conferences/seminars; Endowments; Fellowships; Internships; Scholarships.

PURPOSE:
To promote sound and forward-looking policies that lay the intellectual and civic groundwork for the next generation of opinion-leaders, policy-shapers and public servants.

ELIGIBILITY:
Open to American high school, undergraduate, and graduate students.

FINANCIAL DATA:
Amount of support per award: Scholarships and fellowships: $4,000 to $10,000.

APPLICATION INFO:
Application procedures are available online.

IRS I.D.: 52-1306218

ADDRESS INQUIRIES TO:
Erika Butts, Administrative Assistant
(See address above.)

GRADUATE INSTITUTE OF INTERNATIONAL AND DEVELOPMENT STUDIES [781]

Chemin Eugene-Rigot 2A
P.O. Box 1672
CH - 1211 Geneva 1 Switzerland
(41) 22 908 57 00
Fax: (41) 22 908 57 10
E-mail: info@graduateinstitute.ch
Web Site: graduateinstitute.ch

FOUNDED: 1927

AREAS OF INTEREST:
Development, anthropology and sociology of development, and international relations.

NAME(S) OF PROGRAMS:
● **Financial Aid for Study at The Graduate Institute of International and Development Studies**

TYPE:
Assistantships; Awards/prizes; Exchange programs; Fellowships; Residencies; Scholarships; Visiting scholars. Financial aid in advanced study in international relations including intensive research and study towards the Master's degree and the Ph.D. Tenable at the Institute.

PURPOSE:
To support the scientific study of contemporary international relations and development studies and the pursuit of advanced studies based on personal work and research.

LEGAL BASIS:
Foundation.

ELIGIBILITY:
Each year, financial assistance is awarded by the Institute in the form of scholarships covering the minimum needs of students. They are allocated on the basis of applicants' academic performance and financial needs.

Scholarships also awarded for young lecturers from the global south.

FINANCIAL DATA:
Scholars are exempted from Institute fees, but not from the obligatory fees of the University of Geneva which confers the Doctorate.
Amount of support per award: Full scholarship: CHF 18,000 per academic year.

NO. AWARDS: 250 scholarships annually.

APPLICATION INFO:
Online application form is available from mid-September.
Duration: One academic year. Renewable.
Deadline: January 15.

PUBLICATIONS:
Annual report.

ADDRESS INQUIRIES TO:
E-mail: executive@graduateinstitute.ch

INSTITUTE OF CURRENT WORLD AFFAIRS [782]

1779 Massachusetts Avenue, N.W.
Suite 605
Washington, DC 20036
(202) 364-4068
E-mail: icwa@icwa.org
Web Site: www.icwa.org

FOUNDED: 1925

AREAS OF INTEREST:
Current world affairs.

TYPE:
Fellowships. Fellowships are not scholarships, and are not awarded to support work toward academic degrees or for collaborative research projects, or to write books.

YEAR PROGRAM STARTED: 1925

PURPOSE:
To provide talented and promising individuals with an opportunity to develop a deep understanding of an issue, country or region outside the U.S. and to share that understanding with a wider public.

ELIGIBILITY:
Fellowships are for self-designed independent study only. Applicants must have a good command of written and spoken English and be women and men under 36 years of age who demonstrate initiative, integrity, outstanding character, good communications skills, seriousness of purpose and enthusiasm for their chosen fields.

FINANCIAL DATA:
The Institute provides sufficient, though not unlimited, financial support for its fellows and their immediate families, allowing them to live in good health and reasonable comfort in order to fulfill the purposes of the fellowship.
Amount of support per award: Varies.
Total amount of support: Varies.

NO. AWARDS: 2.

APPLICATION INFO:
Applicants should write an initial letter of interest to the Executive Director explaining the personal background and professional experience that would qualify them for the fellowship they have in mind. They should describe the activities they would like to carry out during two years overseas and enclose a resume or curriculum vitae. Select candidates will be invited to submit a more detailed application.

Initial letter should be by e-mail, although regular mail will be accepted. Further information may be obtained from the Institute's web site.
Duration: Minimum period of two years.
Deadline: June 15 for December appointment.

ADDRESS INQUIRIES TO:
E-mail: apply@icwa.org

INSTITUTE OF INTERNATIONAL EDUCATION [783]

1400 K Street, N.W.
Suite 700
Washington, DC 20005
(202) 686-8665
Fax: (202) 686-4029
E-mail: sir@iie.org
Web Site: www.cies.org/sir

FOUNDED: 1947

AREAS OF INTEREST:
Humanities or social sciences, or any field that will benefit from an international perspective.

NAME(S) OF PROGRAMS:
● **Fulbright Scholar-in-Residence Program**

TYPE:
Awards/prizes; Exchange programs; Visiting scholars. Grants support a visiting lecturer from outside the U.S. to teach regular courses or develop new ones, team teach or participate in special seminars or serve as a resource to faculty and students and, through outreach, to the community at large.

PURPOSE:
To initiate or develop international programs at colleges and universities by using a foreign scholar-in-residence to internationalize the curriculum, set up global studies or area-specific programs or otherwise expand contacts of students and faculty with other cultures and to strengthen or enrich existing international or area studies programs.

LEGAL BASIS:
Public Law 87-256, as amended, The Mutual Educational and Cultural Exchange Act of 1961.

ELIGIBILITY:
U.S. colleges and universities, including community colleges, are invited to submit proposals to obtain a foreign scholar-in-residence. Preference is given to proposals in the humanities or social sciences, although other fields focusing on international issues will be considered.

GEOG. RESTRICTIONS: United States.

FINANCIAL DATA:
Monthly stipend as well as round-trip international travel, excess baggage allowance, accident and sickness insurance, and allowances for books, professional development and dependents.
Amount of support per award:
Approximately $2,710 to $3,145 per month, depending on the cost of living in the city where the scholar will reside.
Total amount of support: Over $1,000,000 for the year 2017.
Matching fund requirements: Some cost sharing by the host institution is encouraged, either supplementary funding or in-kind support, such as housing.

CO-OP FUNDING PROGRAMS: U.S. Department of State.

NO. AWARDS: 30 to 35.

APPLICATION INFO:
Guidelines are available in March. Application must be submitted online.
Duration: One semester to one academic year.
Deadline: November 1.

PUBLICATIONS:
Directory of Visiting Scholars; descriptive brochure; annual report.

ADDRESS INQUIRIES TO:
Kailey Atwater, Program Manager
(See address above.)

THE INTERNATIONAL FOUNDATION [784]
55 Lane Road
Suite 300
Fairfield, NJ 07004
E-mail: info@intlfoundation.org
Web Site: intlfoundation.org

FOUNDED: 1948

AREAS OF INTEREST:
Agriculture, health, education, social development, the environment and community development.

TYPE:
Development grants; Project/program grants; Seed money grants; Technical assistance; Training grants.

YEAR PROGRAM STARTED: 1948

PURPOSE:
To help people of the developing world in their endeavors to solve some of their problems, to attain a better standard of living, and to obtain a reasonable degree of self-sufficiency.

LEGAL BASIS:
Private foundation.

ELIGIBILITY:
The Foundation funds only projects of U.S.-based, IRS-certified philanthropies.

GEOG. RESTRICTIONS: United States.

FINANCIAL DATA:
Amount of support per award: Up to $25,000.

NO. AWARDS: Approximately 100.

APPLICATION INFO:
Applications are to be submitted on the Foundation's web site. Proposals must include a statement from IRS of not-for-profit status, a brief overview of the proposal, amount of funds requested from The Foundation, a brief background of organization applying, a statement of the problem addressed by project, objectives of the project, plan of operation/method of achieving objectives, beneficiaries of the project, methods of project evaluation and report, project budget, sources of other funding applied for or received and date.

All appropriate communications will be answered.
Duration: One year. Must reapply.
Deadline: Grant applications are accepted on a rolling basis. They are reviewed quarterly by the Grants Committee.

PUBLICATIONS:
Brochure, includes application guidelines.

IRS I.D.: 13-1962255

BOARD OF DIRECTORS AND OFFICERS:
Letitia K. Butler, Chairperson
Douglas P. Walker, Vice Chairperson
John D'A. Tyree, Treasurer
Hilda Arellano
Gary Dicovitsky
Kathy Gaiser
William M. McCormack, M.D.

ADDRESS INQUIRIES TO:
Hilda Arellano
Grants Committee Chairperson
(See address above.)

THE JAPAN FOUNDATION, NEW YORK [785]
1700 Broadway
15th Floor
New York, NY 10019
(212) 489-0299
Fax: (212) 489-0409
E-mail: info@jfny.org
Web Site: www.jfny.org

FOUNDED: 1972

AREAS OF INTEREST:
Arts and cultural exchange, Japanese studies, intellectual exchange and grassroots exchange and education.

NAME(S) OF PROGRAMS:
- **Abe Fellowship for Journalists Program**
- **Abe Fellowship Program**
- **CGP Grant Program - Discretionary Grants**
- **CGP Grant Program - Education Grants**
- **CGP Grant Program - Grassroots Program**
- **CGP Grant Program - Intellectual Exchange**
- **Exhibition Abroad Support Program**
- **Institutional Project Support Grant Program for Japanese Studies**
- **Institutional Project Support Small Grant Program for Japanese Studies**
- **Japanese Studies Fellowship Program**
- **JFNY Grant for Japanese Studies**
- **JFNY Grant Program - Arts and Culture**
- **Performing Arts Japan Program**
- **Support Program for Translation and Publication on Japan**
- **U.S. and European Museum Infrastructure Support Program**
- **U.S.-Southeast Asia-Japan Collaboration and Exchange Initiative**

TYPE:
Conferences/seminars; Fellowships; Professorships; Project/program grants; Research grants; Travel grants. The Japanese Studies Fellowship Program has three components: Doctoral Fellowship, Long-term Research Fellowship, and Short-term Research Fellowship.

PURPOSE:
To promote international cultural exchange and mutual understanding between Japan and other countries by providing assistance for Arts and Cultural Exchange, Japanese Studies, Intellectual Exchange, and Grassroots Exchange and Education programs in the U.S.

LEGAL BASIS:
Independent administrative institution.

ELIGIBILITY:
Varies according to program.

FINANCIAL DATA:
For Fellowships, the Foundation will provide a round-trip, economy-class airfare to and from Japan. The stipend is determined in accordance with the grantee's professional status.
Amount of support per award: Varies according to program.
Matching fund requirements: Varies according to program.

APPLICATION INFO:
Program announcements and application forms are available on the web site. Arts and Culture grant applications from Alaska, Arizona, California, Colorado, Hawaii, Idaho, Montana, Nevada, New Mexico, Oregon, Utah, Washington and Wyoming should be sent to the Japan Foundation, Los Angeles Office, 5700 Wilshire Boulevard, Suite 100, Los Angeles, CA 90036; Tel: (323) 761-7510; Fax: (323) 761-7517; E-mail: jflainfo@jflalc.org. Arts and Culture Grant applications from all other states should be sent directly to the Japan Foundation New York Office. Grant applications for all other programs should be sent to the New York office to the section in charge of the grant program.
Duration: Varies according to program.
Deadline: Varies according to program.

PUBLICATIONS:
Annual report.

IRS I.D.: 13-2974222

STAFF:
Osamu Honda, Director General
Kenji Matsumoto, Deputy Director General
Koji Nozaki, Program Director, Arts and
Cultural Exchange
Takeshi Yoshida, Program Director,
Grassroots Exchange and Education
Moto Ono, Program Director, Intellectual
Exchange
Kanako Mabuchi, Program Director, Japanese
Studies and Japanese-Language Course

ADDRESS INQUIRIES TO:
See e-mail address above.

JAPAN-U.S. FRIENDSHIP COMMISSION   [786]
1201 15th Street, N.W.
Suite 330
Washington, DC 20005
(202) 653-9800
Fax: (202) 653-9802
E-mail: jusfc@jusfc.gov
Web Site: www.jusfc.gov

FOUNDED: 1976

AREAS OF INTEREST:
Cultural and educational activities between
Japan and the U.S., including language and
area studies, economic relations, media and
public education.

TYPE:
Project/program grants. Programs of
institutional support. Grants for projects of
research, training and exchange with Japan.

YEAR PROGRAM STARTED: 1977

PURPOSE:
To enhance reciprocal people-to-people
understanding and friendship between the
U.S. and Japan.

LEGAL BASIS:
Independent agency of the U.S. government.

ELIGIBILITY:
Grants are offered to cultural and educational
institutions in the U.S. and Japan.

GEOG. RESTRICTIONS: United States and Japan.

FINANCIAL DATA:
U.S. government trust fund of $40,000,000.
Amount of support per award: Varies.
Total amount of support: Varies.

CO-OP FUNDING PROGRAMS: NEA.

NO. MOST RECENT APPLICANTS: Varies by
program.

NO. AWARDS: Approximately 30 annually.

APPLICATION INFO:
Application forms are available on the web
site.
Duration: One year.
Deadline: July 1. Notification in October.

PUBLICATIONS:
Biennial report; program
information/guidelines; application form.

OFFICERS:
Dr. Sheila Smith, Chairman
Dr. Edward Lincoln
Dr. Patricia Maclachlan
Dr. Deanna Marcum
Dr. Samuel C. Morse
Dr. Leonard J. Schoppa, Jr.

David Sneider
Dr. William M. Tsutsui

ADDRESS INQUIRIES TO:
Paige Cottingham-Streater, Executive
Director
(See address above.)

*SPECIAL STIPULATIONS:
Institution grants only.

THE JAPANESE AMERICAN CITIZENS LEAGUE (JACL)   [787]
Washington, DC Office
1629 K Street, N.W., Suite 400
Washington, DC 20006
(202) 223-1240
Fax: (202) 296-8082
E-mail: dinoue@jacl.org
Web Site: www.jacl.org

FOUNDED: 1929

AREAS OF INTEREST:
Cultural exchange.

NAME(S) OF PROGRAMS:
● **JACL Kakehashi Program**

TYPE:
Travel grants. The Kakehashi Program is a
new international program, part of JACL's
leadership development. It is for college
students and consists of five webinars and a
nine-day trip to Japan.

PURPOSE:
To strengthen cultural ties between Japan and
the U.S.

ELIGIBILITY:
This Program is for college students in good
standing between the ages of 18 and 25.
Students are selected for their community
service, leadership experience and academic
accomplishments. Eligible students must be
either of Japanese ancestry or Asian ancestry,
and must be a U.S. citizen. Students who
have previously participated in a program
sponsored by the government of Japan are
ineligible.

NO. AWARDS: 185 students are to be selected for
the Program.

APPLICATION INFO:
Contact JACL.

ADDRESS INQUIRIES TO:
David Inoue, Executive Director
E-mail: japanprogram@jacl.org
(See address above.)

A.J. MUSTE MEMORIAL INSTITUTE
168 Canal Street, 6th Floor
New York, NY 10013
(212) 533-4335
E-mail: info@ajmuste.org
Web Site: www.ajmuste.org

TYPE:
Grants-in-aid. The Institute's regular grant
fund annually funds international, national
and local projects in the U.S. and around the
world. It gives priority to those with small
budgets and little chance of funding from
more traditional sources. It also offers fiscal
sponsorship. The Institute does not provide
academic scholarships.

See entry 1367 for full listing.

THE NATIONAL COUNCIL FOR EURASIAN AND EAST EUROPEAN RESEARCH   [788]
1828 L Street, N.W.
Suite 1200
Washington, DC 20036
(202) 572-9095
Fax: (866) 937-9872
E-mail: info@nceeer.org
Web Site: www.nceeer.org

FOUNDED: 1978

AREAS OF INTEREST:
The program is limited to research designed
to contribute to knowledge of current
developments and analysis of their
significance in Eastern Europe and the
successor states of the former Soviet Union.

TYPE:
Research grants; Research contracts.
Institutional grants and research contracts and
policy research scholarships and related
activities, such as meetings and conferences,
research-specific training, contact among
scholars and specialists in government and
private enterprise, development of databanks
and other reference aids and dissemination of
research data, methodology and findings,
both in scholarly forms and through public
media.

YEAR PROGRAM STARTED: 1978

PURPOSE:
To encourage and sustain high-quality
research on Eastern Europe, the former
Soviet Union and its successor states, in the
social sciences (including geography,
demography and environmental studies) and
history.

LEGAL BASIS:
Incorporated, nonprofit, autonomous
academic body.

ELIGIBILITY:
Limited to scholars at the postdoctoral level
for academic participants and to an
equivalent degree of maturity and
professional employment for those from other
fields. Applicant must be a U.S. citizen.
Applications must be submitted to the
Council by U.S. nonprofit institutions in the
form of grant or contract proposals.

GEOG. RESTRICTIONS: United States.

FINANCIAL DATA:
Amount of support per award: Varies;
normally not more than $70,000 for any
individual project.
Matching fund requirements: Cost sharing at
a minimum of 20% from non-federal funds is
mandatory.

APPLICATION INFO:
Application guidelines, compliance with
which is required, should be obtained from
the Council, at the address above. Required
documentation includes:
(1) identification form;
(2) one-page summary;
(3) detailed description of project;
(4) curriculum vitae and bibliographies for
principal personnel;
(5) description of proposed written or other
products and dissemination methods;
(6) budget and;
(7) letters of recommendation.
Duration: Varies.
Deadline: December 31.

PUBLICATIONS:
Guidelines.

ADDRESS INQUIRIES TO:
President
(See address above.)

NUCLEAR AGE PEACE FOUNDATION [789]

PMB 121
1187 Coast Village Road, Suite 1
Santa Barbara, CA 93108
(805) 965-3443
Fax: (805) 568-0466
E-mail: wagingpeace@napf.org
Web Site: www.wagingpeace.org

FOUNDED: 1982

AREAS OF INTEREST:
Achieving a nuclear weapon-free world, international law, international relations, liberty, justice, human dignity, human rights, nonviolence, responsible use of technology, peace education, and youth empowerment.

NAME(S) OF PROGRAMS:
● **Barbara Mandigo Kelly Peace Poetry Awards**

TYPE:
Awards/prizes; Internships. An annual series of awards to encourage poets to explore and illuminate positive visions of peace and the human spirit.

PURPOSE:
To play an important role in making the 21st century a time of peace and justice, and a time in which the rights of all individuals to peace, security and a healthy environment will be realized.

FINANCIAL DATA:
Amount of support per award: Adults: $1,000; Youth (13-18): $200; Youth (12 and under): $200.
Total amount of support: $1,400.

APPLICATION INFO:
Application information and guidelines are available at www.peacecontests.org.
Deadline: April 30.

ORGANIZATION OF AMERICAN STATES [790]

1889 F Street, N.W.
Seventh Floor
Washington, DC 20006
(202) 370-9771
Fax: (202) 458-3967
E-mail: scholarships@oas.org
Web Site: www.oas.org/scholarships

FOUNDED: 1890

AREAS OF INTEREST:
To promote the economic, social, scientific and cultural development of the Member States in order to achieve a stronger bond and better understanding among the peoples of the Americas through the advanced training of its citizens in the priority areas requested by the countries.

NAME(S) OF PROGRAMS:
● **Academic Studies**
● **Professional Development**

TYPE:
Fellowships; Scholarships; Technical assistance. Awarded for graduate academic studies and/or research, and last two years of undergraduate studies for students in the English-speaking Caribbean, for training in areas contributing to the economic, social, technical and cultural development of OAS member countries.

YEAR PROGRAM STARTED: 1958

PURPOSE:
Program of Scholarships and Training: to assist the member states with their domestic efforts in pursuit of integral development goals by supporting human resource development in the priority areas established by the member countries.

ELIGIBILITY:
Candidates must be citizens or permanent residents of an OAS member country, with a university degree in the case of academic studies, or who have demonstrated ability to pursue advanced training in the field chosen for professional development courses. Scholarships are for graduate or undergraduate studies, research, or professional training in any field, with the exception of the medical sciences and related areas and introductory language studies. Candidates must know the language of the study country. Studies must be undertaken at an institution in a member country of the OAS, with the exception of the country of which the candidate is a citizen or permanent resident.

Graduate scholarships are offered for study towards a Master's or Doctorate degree. They may also be used for research, if required by a specific academic program. Scholarships are awarded for an initial period of one academic year and may be extended subsequently for up to one additional year. Under the Self-Placed in an OAS Non-Consortium University, candidates apply directly for admission to the universities or educational institutions of their choice, and present their application for an OAS scholarship. Only one candidate per country will be awarded with this type of scholarship. In the Self-Placed in an OAS Consortium University, candidates apply directly to up to three programs in different universities, part of the OAS Consortium University, located in three different countries. Applying to this type of scholarship increases the applicant's chances of being offered an OAS scholarship. Undergraduate scholarships are available only to citizens of the English-speaking Caribbean member countries for the last two years of study for an undergraduate degree.

No fellowships will be awarded retroactively, and no benefits will be provided to the family of the fellowship holder.

FINANCIAL DATA:
Fellowship may include, depending upon the circumstances of each fellow, a round-trip ticket, tuition fees, study materials, health insurance, and partial subsistence allowance (which varies from country to country).

Amount of support per award: Academic Studies: Minimum U.S. $10,000 for one year, maximum not to exceed U.S. $20,000 for up to two years; Professional Development: Varies.

Matching fund requirements: Students are responsible for covering a portion of their subsistence costs.

APPLICATION INFO:
Application materials are available at the web site. Except for applicants in the U.S., applications must be presented to the National Liaison Offices (ONEs) of the applicant's country of origin or permanent residence. The ONE is the official channel identified by each government for submission of applications for OAS scholarships. U.S. citizens can send applications directly to the Organization's mailing address.
Duration: Fellowships are tenable for not less than one year nor more than two years.
Deadline: For presentation of applications to the National Liaison Office (ONE): Differs from country to country and should therefore be confirmed with the National Liaison Office (ONE) in the applicant's country of origin or permanent residence.

ADDRESS INQUIRIES TO:
Department of Human Development, Education and Employment
(See address above.)

*SPECIAL STIPULATIONS:
For countries other than the U.S., the fellowship form must be presented to the General Secretariat of the OAS in Washington, DC, through the official channels established by each government.

HERBERT SCOVILLE, JR., PEACE FELLOWSHIP [791]

820 First Street, N.E.
Suite LL-180
Washington, DC 20002
(202) 446-1565
E-mail: info@scoville.org
Web Site: scoville.org

FOUNDED: 1987

AREAS OF INTEREST:
Climate and security, emerging technology threats, nuclear nonproliferation and weapons of mass destruction, and peace building and conflict resolution.

TYPE:
Fellowships.

YEAR PROGRAM STARTED: 1987

PURPOSE:
To provide an opportunity for college graduates to gain practical knowledge and experience by contributing to the efforts of nonprofit, public-interest organizations working on peace and security issues.

LEGAL BASIS:
Nonprofit program.

ELIGIBILITY:
Prospective Fellows are expected to demonstrate excellent academic accomplishments and a strong interest in issues of peace and security. Graduate study, a college major, course work, or substantial independent reading that reflects the substantive focus of the Fellowship is also a plus. Prior experience with public-interest activism or advocacy is highly desirable. It is preferred, but not required, that such activities be focused on peace and security issues.

Candidates are required to have completed a Baccalaureate degree by the time the Fellowship commences. Preference is given to U.S. citizens, although a Fellowship to a foreign national residing in the U.S. is awarded periodically based on availability of funding. The Scoville Fellowship is not intended for students or scholars interested in pursuing independent research in Washington, DC.

Preference will be given to individuals who have not had substantial prior public-interest or government experience in the Washington, DC area.

FINANCIAL DATA:
Amount of support per award: $3,300 per month, plus travel expenses to the Washington, DC area to begin fellowship, health insurance, and up to $1,000 in professional development.
Total amount of support: Varies.

NO. MOST RECENT APPLICANTS: 300 to 350.

NO. AWARDS: 6 to 8 per year.

APPLICATION INFO:
Information is available on the web site. All application materials must be submitted by e-mail to apply@scoville.org.
Duration: Six to nine months.
Deadline: Spring Fellowship: October 2; Fall Fellowship: January 4.

PUBLICATIONS:
Application guidelines; organization description.

ADDRESS INQUIRIES TO:
Paul Revsine, Executive Director
(See address above.)

SOCIAL SCIENCE RESEARCH COUNCIL [792]

One Pierrepont Plaza
15th Floor
Brooklyn, NY 11201
(212) 377-2700 ext. 3672
E-mail: japan@ssrc.org
Web Site: www.ssrc.org/fellowships/jsps-fellowship

FOUNDED: 1923

AREAS OF INTEREST:
Social sciences and humanities.

NAME(S) OF PROGRAMS:
● **SSRC/JSPS Long-Term Fellowship**
● **SSRC/JSPS Short-Term Fellowship**

TYPE:
Fellowships; Research grants. The Japan Society for the Promotion of Science (JSPS) Postdoctoral Fellowship for Foreign Researchers provides promising and highly qualified recent Ph.Ds. and ABDs with funding to conduct research in Japan. JSPS guidelines target the applicant who wishes to conduct cooperative research under the leadership of a host researcher, thereby advancing the Fellow's own research and at the same time stimulating Japanese academic circles through close collaboration with young Japanese researchers.

YEAR PROGRAM STARTED: 1967

PURPOSE:
To stimulate Japanese academic circles through close collaboration with young foreign researchers.

LEGAL BASIS:
Not-for-profit organization.

ELIGIBILITY:
Applicants must be U.S. citizens or permanent residents at the time of application

and not be of Japanese descent. Citizens of other countries are eligible for short-term fellowships if they have completed a Master's or Ph.D. course at an institution of higher education in the U.S. and, upon completing the course, have for at least three continuous years conducted high-level research at a university in the U.S. Japanese nationals are not eligible for a fellowship regardless of current residency status. Applicants currently in Japan are not eligible for short-term fellowships.

Applicants for long-term fellowships must submit a copy of a Ph.D. diploma from a university outside Japan dated no more than six years prior to April 1, 2020.

Applicants for short-term fellowships must submit a copy of a Ph.D. diploma from a university outside Japan dated no more than six years prior to April 1, 2020 or a letter from their institution stating that the applicant is a Ph.D. candidate within two years of receiving a Ph.D.

Scholars who have previously received funding from JSPS for the Short-Term Fellowship are eligible to apply for the JSPS Long-Term Fellowship.

FINANCIAL DATA:
Grants are to be used for maintenance, travel and research expenses.
Amount of support per award: Varies based on length of research term and doctoral status.
Total amount of support: Varies.

NO. MOST RECENT APPLICANTS: Long-Term and Short-Term Fellowships: 21.

NO. AWARDS: Long-Term Fellowships: 4; Short-Term Fellowships: 5.

APPLICATION INFO:
Application information is available on the web site.
Duration: Long-Term Fellowships: 12 to 24 months; Short-Term Fellowships: One to 12 months.
Deadline: December 1.

PUBLICATIONS:
Annual report; *Items*, newsletter; *Fellowships and Grants for Training and Research*, brochure.

STAFF:
Nicole Levit, Japan Associate Director
Bree Brinson, Program Assistant

ADDRESS INQUIRIES TO:
Bree Brinson, Program Assistant
Japan Program
Social Science Research Council
(See address above.)

SOCIAL SCIENCE RESEARCH COUNCIL [793]

300 Cadman Plaza West
15th Floor
Brooklyn, NY 11201
(212) 377-2700 ext. 3644
Fax: (212) 377-2727
E-mail: idrf@ssrc.org
Web Site: www.ssrc.org/programs/idrf

FOUNDED: 1923

AREAS OF INTEREST:
Fellowships in the humanities and humanistic social sciences.

NAME(S) OF PROGRAMS:
● **International Dissertation Research Fellowship Program (IDRF)**

TYPE:
Fellowships. Support to graduate students in the humanities and humanistic social sciences who are enrolled in doctoral programs in the U.S. and conducting dissertation research outside of the U.S.

YEAR PROGRAM STARTED: 1997

PURPOSE:
To support the advancement of social science and humanistic research.

LEGAL BASIS:
Not-for-profit corporation.

ELIGIBILITY:
Applicants must be enrolled in a full-time doctoral program at a U.S. university. U.S. citizenship is not required. Research must be conducted outside of the U.S. and on a non-U.S. topic.

FINANCIAL DATA:
Amount of support per award: Average $23,000.

NO. MOST RECENT APPLICANTS: More than 1,000.

NO. AWARDS: 70.

APPLICATION INFO:
Application information is available on the web site usually the first week in August.
Duration: Nine to 12 months.
Deadline: Typically the first week in November.

ADDRESS INQUIRIES TO:
See e-mail address above.

SOCIAL SCIENCE RESEARCH COUNCIL [794]

One Pierrepont Plaza
15th Floor
Brooklyn, NY 11201
(212) 377-2700 ext. 3672
E-mail: abe@ssrc.org
Web Site: www.ssrc.org/fellowships/abe-fellowship

FOUNDED: 1923

AREAS OF INTEREST:
International multidisciplinary research on topics of pressing global concern.

NAME(S) OF PROGRAMS:
● **Abe Fellowship Program**

TYPE:
Fellowships; Research grants. The program encourages international multidisciplinary research on topics of pressing global concern and fosters the development of a new generation of researchers interested in policy-relevant topics of long-range importance and willing to become key members of a bilateral and global research network built around such topics.

The Abe Fellowship Program administers an annual fellowship competition that provides scholars and nonacademic research professionals in the social sciences and related disciplines with support for research projects addressing one or more of three themes: (1) Threats to Personal, Societal and International Security; (2) Growth and Sustainable Development; (3) Social, Scientific and Cultural Trends and Transformations and; (4) Governance, Empowerment and Participation.

YEAR PROGRAM STARTED: 1991

PURPOSE:
To encourage international multidisciplinary research on topics of pressing global concern.

ELIGIBILITY:
Competition is open to citizens of the U.S. and Japan as well as to nationals of other countries who can demonstrate strong and serious long-term affiliations with research communities in Japan or the U.S. Applicants must hold the Ph.D. or the terminal degree in their field, or have attained an equivalent level of professional experience. Applications from researchers in professions other than academia are encouraged. Previous language training is not a prerequisite for this Fellowship. However, if the research project requires language ability, the applicant should provide evidence of adequate proficiency to complete the project. Projects proposing to address key policy issues or seeking to develop a concrete policy proposal must reflect nonpartisan positions.

GEOG. RESTRICTIONS: Japan and United States.

FINANCIAL DATA:
Awards may be used for maintenance, travel and research expenses.
Amount of support per award: Varies.
Total amount of support: Varies.

NO. MOST RECENT APPLICANTS: 71 for the year 2019.

NO. AWARDS: 10.

APPLICATION INFO:
Applications are available by early summer and must be submitted online at applications.ssrc.org.
Duration: Three to 12 months of full-time support over a 24-month period. Fellowship tenure must begin between April 1 and December 31 of a given year.
Deadline: Typically late fall.

STAFF:
Nicole Levit, Associate Director
Bree Brinson, Program Assistant

ADDRESS INQUIRIES TO:
Abe Fellowship Program
Social Science Research Council
(See address above.)

SOCIETY FOR FRENCH HISTORICAL STUDIES
Colorado College, Department of History
Palmer Hall, No. 208B
14 East Cache La Poudre Street
Colorado Springs, CO 80903
E-mail: tragan@coloradocollege.edu
Web Site: www.societyforfrenchhistoricalstudies.net

TYPE:
Awards/prizes. The Chinard Prize is for a recent book on historical relations between France and the Americas.

Davis Graduate Student Award is given for the best paper presented by a graduate student at the Society's annual meeting.

Farrar Award is for dissertation research.

The Koren Prize is for a recent journal article written on French history.

The Pinkney Prize is for a recent book written on French history.

Research Travel Award is for recent recipients of Doctorates (awarded jointly with Western Society for French History).

See entry 589 for full listing.

SWEDISH WOMEN'S EDUCATIONAL ASSOCIATION INC. [795]
P.O. Box 4128
Fort Lauderdale, FL 33338-4128
E-mail: litstip@swea.org
Web Site: swea.org

AREAS OF INTEREST:
Sweden's culture, history and language.

NAME(S) OF PROGRAMS:
● **SWEA Scholarship in Literature, Language and Area Studies**

TYPE:
Scholarships. Funds may be used to study in Sweden. Previous trips to Sweden, or lack thereof, are of no consideration. Willingness to travel to Sweden for dissertation work is a plus, but not a requirement.

PURPOSE:
To promote and preserve the Swedish language, cultures and traditions.

ELIGIBILITY:
The applicant must:
(1) be a well-merited doctoral candidate, studying at a non-Swedish university and reside permanently outside of Sweden;
(2) have filed a dissertation topic and;
(3) have a good knowledge of the Swedish language (written and spoken).

FINANCIAL DATA:
Amount of support per award: $10,000.
Total amount of support: $10,000.

NO. AWARDS: 1.

APPLICATION INFO:
The applicant must submit an application, curriculum vitae, a detailed description of the dissertation project, a statement explaining how the scholarship money will be used, a presentation of himself or herself in Swedish, and three letters of recommendation. Applications are available online.
Duration: One year. Recipients may reapply.
Deadline: January 15.

ADDRESS INQUIRIES TO:
SWEA International Committee for Literary Scholarship
(See e-mail address above.)

*SPECIAL STIPULATIONS:
There is no discrimination on the basis of gender, race, color, age, religion or nationality.

TINKER FOUNDATION INC. [796]
55 East 59th Street
New York, NY 10022
(212) 421-6858
Fax: (212) 223-3326
E-mail: tinker@tinker.org
Web Site: www.tinker.org

FOUNDED: 1959

AREAS OF INTEREST:
Institutional grants for projects addressing democratic governance, sustainable resource management, and education, with a geographic focus on the Spanish- and Portuguese-speaking countries of Latin America.

NAME(S) OF PROGRAMS:
● **Institutional Grants**
● **Tinker Field Research Grants**
● **Tinker Visiting Professor**

TYPE:
Travel grants; Visiting scholars. Travel grants (issued to universities) are to be used to support brief periods of individual research in Latin America by graduate students.

YEAR PROGRAM STARTED: 1979

PURPOSE:
To enable emerging scholars to work in the Spanish- and Portuguese-speaking countries of Latin America, enabling them to acquire a comprehensive knowledge of language, cultures and terrain, and to gather research data and develop contacts with scholars and institutions in their respective fields.

LEGAL BASIS:
Private foundation.

ELIGIBILITY:
Open to all recognized Centers or Institutes of Latin American Studies with graduate doctoral programs at accredited U.S. universities. Field Research Grants, awarded to individuals by the appropriate university institutes/centers, are to reflect the Foundation's broad areas of interest.

The Foundation's selection criteria include the quality of the overall graduate program in Latin American studies, the immediate benefits to the Latin American studies program that will result from the availability of Field Research Grants at the university and the level of general university support for Latin American studies as demonstrated by past commitments and future projects.

Institutional Grants: Open to any 501(c)(3) (or equivalent foreign) organization doing work in and on the Spanish- and Portuguese-speaking countries of Latin America.

GEOG. RESTRICTIONS: Latin America, excluding Puerto Rico.

FINANCIAL DATA:
Amount of support per award: Field Research Grants: $10,000 and $15,000; Institutional Grants: Up to $150,000.
Total amount of support: $3,500,000 annually.
Matching fund requirements: Field Research Grant Awards require the university to match the award on a 1:1 ratio.

NO. MOST RECENT APPLICANTS: Field Research Grants: 11; Institutional Grants: Approximately 500.

NO. AWARDS: Field Research Grants: Up to 6 new annually; Institutional Grants: Varies.

APPLICATION INFO:
Application instructions and forms can be accessed via the web site.
Duration: Maximum of three years.
Deadline: Field Research Grants: October 1. Institutional Grants: January or February and July or August.

STAFF:
Margaret J. Cushing, Associate Director
Susan Vega, Director of Administration and Finance
Avi Richman, Education Program Officer
Angelina Pienczykowski, Grants Manager

DIRECTORS AND OFFICERS:
Alan Stoga, Chairman
Caroline B. Kronley, President
Kathleen Waldron, Treasurer
Luis Rubio, Secretary
Sally Grooms Cowal
Shannon K. O'Neil

Arturo C. Porzecanski
Susan L. Segal
Bradford K. Smith

ADDRESS INQUIRIES TO:
Angelina Pienczykowski, Grants Manager
(See address above.)

U.S. DEPARTMENT OF EDUCATION

International and Foreign Language Education
(IFLE)
Advanced Training and Research Division
400 Maryland Avenue, S.W.
Washington, DC 20202
(202) 453-7854
Fax: (202) 453-5780
E-mail: ifle@ed.gov
Web Site: www.ed.gov/ope/iegps

TYPE:
Fellowships. The Foreign Language and Area
Studies Fellowships program provides
allocations of academic year and summer
fellowships to institutions of higher education
or consortia of institutions of higher
education to assist meritorious undergraduate
students and graduate students undergoing
training in modern foreign languages and
related international or area studies.

See entry 612 for full listing.

U.S. DEPARTMENT OF EDUCATION

International and Foreign Language Education
400 Maryland Avenue, S.W.
Room 258-24
Washington, DC 20202
(202) 453-6891
Fax: (202) 453-5780
E-mail: ddra@ed.gov
Web Site: www.ed.
gov/programs/iegpsddrap/index.html

TYPE:
Fellowships. Fellowships to support doctoral
dissertation research abroad in modern
foreign languages and related area studies.
For the purpose of these programs, area
studies is defined as a program of
comprehensive study of the aspects of a
society or societies, including the study of
their geography, history, culture, economy,
politics, international relations and languages.
The program is designed to develop research
knowledge and capability in world areas not
widely included in American curricula.
Awards will not be available for projects
focusing on Western Europe.

See entry 613 for full listing.

U.S. DEPARTMENT OF EDUCATION

Office of Postsecondary Education
International and Foreign Language Education
(IFLE)
400 Maryland Avenue, S.W., Suite 258
Mail Stop 258-40
Washington, DC 20202
(202) 453-5690
E-mail: IFLE@ed.gov
Web Site: www2.ed.gov/programs/iegpsnrc

TYPE:
Project/program grants; Training grants. The
NRC Program provides grants to institutions
of higher education and consortia of
institutions to establish, strengthen and

operate comprehensive and undergraduate
centers that will be national resources for:
(1) teaching of any modern foreign language;
(2) instruction in fields needed to provide full
understanding of areas, regions or countries
in which the modern foreign language is
commonly used;
(3) research and training in international
studies and the international and foreign
language aspects of professional and other
fields of study and;
(4) instruction and research on issues in
world affairs that concern one or more
countries.

This program operates on a four-year grant
cycle.

See entry 614 for full listing.

U.S. DEPARTMENT OF EDUCATION   [797]

International and Foreign Language Education
(IFLE)
400 Maryland Avenue, S.W., Suite 258
Mail Stop 258-40
Washington, DC 20202
(202) 453-5690
E-mail: cheryl.gibbs@ed.gov
Web Site: www2.ed.gov/programs/iegpsaorc

AREAS OF INTEREST:
Area studies.

NAME(S) OF PROGRAMS:
● **American Overseas Research Centers (AORC) Program**

TYPE:
Project/program grants; Research grants;
Training grants. The AORC Program
provides grants to consortia of U.S.
institutions of higher education to establish or
operate an AORC that promotes postgraduate
research, exchanges and area studies.

LEGAL BASIS:
Authorized under Section 609 of the Higher
Education Act of 1965, as amended.

ELIGIBILITY:
Any American overseas research center can
qualify that meets the following conditions:
(1) be a consortium of U.S. institutions of
higher education that receives more than 50%
of its funding from public or private U.S.
sources;
(2) have a permanent presence in the country
in which the center is located and;
(3) be an organization described in Section
501(c)(3) of the Internal Revenue Code of
1993, which is exempt from taxation under
Section 501(a) of the Code.

FINANCIAL DATA:
AORC grants may be used to pay all or a
portion of the cost of establishing or
operating a center or program including:
(1) the cost of operation and maintenance of
overseas facilities;
(2) the cost of organizing and managing
conferences;
(3) the cost of teaching and research
materials;
(4) the cost of acquisition, maintenance and
preservation of library collections;
(5) the cost of bringing visiting scholars and
faculty to the center to teach or to conduct
research;
(6) the cost of faculty and staff stipends and
salaries;
(7) the cost of faculty, staff and student travel
and;

(8) the cost of publication and dissemination
of materials for the scholarly and general
public.
Amount of support per award: Average
annual grant: $65,000.

APPLICATION INFO:
Duration: Up to 48 months.

ADDRESS INQUIRIES TO:
Cheryl E. Gibbs, Senior Director
International Foreign Language Education
Office
(See address above.)

*PLEASE NOTE:
The AORC Program competes every four
years. New competition is anticipated in the
spring of 2020.

U.S. INSTITUTE OF PEACE   [798]

Jennings Randolph Fellowship
Programs for International Peace
2301 Constitution Avenue, N.W.
Washington, DC 20037-2900
(202) 429-7812
Fax: (202) 429-6063
E-mail: jrprogram@usip.org
Web Site: www.usip.org

FOUNDED: 1984

AREAS OF INTEREST:
Topics and disciplines related to international
peace, conflict and conflict management.

NAME(S) OF PROGRAMS:
● **Jennings Randolph Senior Fellowship Programs for International Peace**
● **USIP Peace Scholar Dissertation Fellowship**

TYPE:
Fellowships; Residencies. Residential
program for senior fellows, but not for Peace
Scholars. The U.S. Institute of Peace is an
independent, nonpartisan institution created
by Congress to strengthen the nation's
capacity to promote the peaceful resolution
of international conflict.

Under the Jennings Randolph Senior
Fellowship Programs for International Peace,
Senior Fellowships and Peace Scholar
Dissertation Fellowships are awarded on a
competitive basis.

Senior Fellowships are awarded annually to
scholars and practitioners from a variety of
professions, including college and university
faculty, journalists, diplomats, writers,
educators, military officers, international
negotiators and lawyers, and staff of civil
society organizations. Fellows are supported
for varying periods of time to conduct
research on themes defined by USIP centers
in their Calls for Applications, which will be
published on USIP's web site, consult with
staff and contribute to the ongoing work of
the Institute.

Peace Scholar program supports doctoral
dissertations that explore the sources and
nature of international conflict, and strategies
to prevent or end conflict and to sustain
peace. Peace Scholars work at their
university or appropriate field research sites.
Successful applicants must demonstrate that
their work is relevant for policy and/or
practice in the field of conflict analysis,
prevention and management, and postconflict
peacebuilding.

YEAR PROGRAM STARTED: 1986

PURPOSE:
To enable outstanding scholars, practitioners and doctoral students to focus their efforts on critical problems of international peace and conflict.

Fellows undertake research and education projects that will increase knowledge and spread awareness among the public and policymakers and the public about topics concerning the sources and nature of international conflict and the full range of ways to end or prevent conflict and to sustain peace.

LEGAL BASIS:
Independent, nonpartisan and educational institution created by the U.S. Congress.

ELIGIBILITY:
Senior Fellowships: The competition is open to citizens of all nations. Fellowship topics will vary.

Peace Scholar Dissertation Fellowships: Citizens of all countries are eligible, but must be enrolled in an accredited college or university registered in the U.S. Applicants must have completed all requirements for the degree except the dissertation by the commencement of the award (September 1). Priority will be given to projects that contribute knowledge relevant to the formulation of policy or to understanding of best practices on international peace and conflict issues.

FINANCIAL DATA:
Senior Fellows receive a stipend that will vary according to the particular call for applications.
Amount of support per award: Senior Fellows can receive up to $100,000 each for a 10-month period. Peace Scholar Dissertation Fellows receive a $20,000 flat stipend, which may be used to support writing or field research.
Total amount of support: Varies each year.

NO. MOST RECENT APPLICANTS: 50 for Jennings Randolph Senior Fellowships; 115 for Peace Scholar Awards.

NO. AWARDS: Jennings Randolph Senior Fellowships: Up to 3; Peace Scholar Awards: 6 to 12 per year.

APPLICATION INFO:
For application forms for either the Senior Fellowships or the Peace Scholar Dissertation Fellowships, please visit the Institute's web site or contact the Jennings Randolph Fellowship Programs at the address above. Please note that the applications for both competitions are online only.
Duration: Senior Fellowships: Varies; Peace Scholar Dissertation Fellowships: One academic year (nine months).
Deadline: Jennings Randolph Senior Fellowships: Varies. There may be up to four competitions per year. Peace Scholar Fellows: November.

PUBLICATIONS:
Program Description with guidelines; application form; brochure.

STAFF:
Kathleen Kuehnast, Director
Jeremy Moore, Senior Program Officer
Tina Hegadorn, Senior Program Specialist
Jordon Lee, Senior Program Assistant

ADDRESS INQUIRIES TO:
Jennings Randolph Fellowship Programs for International Peace
(See address above.)

*PLEASE NOTE:
Research on conflict within the U.S. may not be supported under the terms of the Institute's mandate.

*SPECIAL STIPULATIONS:
No phone calls please.

U.S. INSTITUTE OF PEACE [799]

2301 Constitution Avenue, N.W.
Washington, DC 20037
(202) 457-1700
E-mail: jrprogram@usip.org
Web Site: www.usip.org/grants-fellowships

FOUNDED: 1984

AREAS OF INTEREST:
International peace and conflict management and related fields. Topic areas of interest include, but are not restricted to, international conflict resolution, diplomacy, negotiation theory, functionalism and "track two" diplomacy, methods of third-party dispute settlement, international law, international organizations and collective security, deterrence and balance of power, arms control, psychological theories about international conflict, the role of nonviolence and nonviolent sanctions, moral and ethical thought about conflict and conflict resolution and theories about relationships among political institutions, human rights and conflict.

NAME(S) OF PROGRAMS:
- **U.S. Institute of Peace Grants & Fellows Program**

TYPE:
Conferences/seminars; Project/program grants; Research grants; Research contracts. Support for research, education and training and the dissemination of information on international peace and conflict resolution.

YEAR PROGRAM STARTED: 1986

PURPOSE:
To carry out basic and applied research on the causes of war and other international conflicts; to develop curricula and texts for high school through postgraduate study and to conduct teacher-training institutes, workshops and seminars; to conduct training, symposia and continuing education programs for practitioners, policymakers, policy implementers and the public; to undertake public information efforts; to increase the store of information on international peace and conflict resolution.

LEGAL BASIS:
Independent, nonpartisan federal institution created and funded by the U.S. Congress.

ELIGIBILITY:
Grant applicants must be nonprofit organizations, official public institutions and, both U.S. and foreign nationals, including the following: institutions of postsecondary, community and secondary education, public and private education, training or research institutions and libraries and public departments and agencies (including state and territorial departments of education and commerce).

Individuals requesting support for degree work are not eligible.

For additional questions regarding eligibility, please contact the appropriate program center at USIP listed online.

FINANCIAL DATA:
Amount of support per award: The amount of any grant is based on the proposed budget and on negotiations with successful applicants.

NO. MOST RECENT APPLICANTS: 200.

NO. AWARDS: 16.

APPLICATION INFO:
Application information is available on the web site.
Duration: One to two years.
Deadline: Varies by program. Specific dates are posted online.

PUBLICATIONS:
Program announcement.

STAFF:
Kathleen Kuehnast, Director
Jeremy Moore, Senior Program Officer
Tina Hegadorn, Senior Program Specialist
Jordon Lee, Senior Program Assistant

ADDRESS INQUIRIES TO:
The Grant Program
United States Institute of Peace
(See address above.)

*SPECIAL STIPULATIONS:
The Institute does not support funding for degree work.

U.S. INSTITUTE OF PEACE [800]

2301 Constitution Avenue, N.W.
Washington, DC 20037
(202) 457-1700
Fax: (202) 429-6063
E-mail: publiceducation@usip.org
Web Site: www.usip.org/public-education/students/AFSAEssayContest

FOUNDED: 1984

AREAS OF INTEREST:
International affairs, peace, conflict resolution, history, writing and research.

NAME(S) OF PROGRAMS:
- **AFSA National High School Essay Contest**

TYPE:
Awards/prizes; Scholarships. The American Foreign Service Association's National High School Essay Contest engages high school students in learning and writing about issues of peace and conflict. It encourages an appreciation for diplomacy's role in building partnerships that can advance peacebuilding and protect national security.

YEAR PROGRAM STARTED: 1987

PURPOSE:
To have students research and write about issues dealing with international conflict resolution and peacemaking.

LEGAL BASIS:
Independent, nonpartisan institution created by the U.S. Congress.

ELIGIBILITY:
Students whose parents are not in the Foreign Service are eligible to participate if they are in grades nine to 12 in any of the 50 states, the District of Columbia, the U.S. territories, or if they are U.S. citizens attending high school overseas. Students may be attending a public, private or parochial school. Entries from home students are also accepted.

Previous first-place winners and immediate relatives of directors or staff of the American Foreign Service Association and Semester at Sea are not eligible to participate.

FINANCIAL DATA:
First-place winner receives an all-expense-paid, two-day trip to Washington, DC to meet members of the Senior State Department Leadership and tour the U.S. Institute of Peace, as well as a full-tuition-paid voyage with Semester at Sea upon his or her enrollment at an accredited university.

Runner-up receives a full scholarship to participate in the International Diplomacy Program of the National Student Leadership Conference, held annually in Washington, DC.

Amount of support per award: First-place winner: $2,500. Runner-up: $1,250.

CO-OP FUNDING PROGRAMS: The National High School Essay Contest is conducted in conjunction with the U.S. Institute of Peace, Semester at Sea, and the National Student Leadership Conference.

NO. MOST RECENT APPLICANTS: 450.

APPLICATION INFO:
Up-to-date information and details can be found on the American Foreign Service Association's web site (www.afsa.org/essay-contest).
Duration: One-time award. This is an annual contest.
Deadline: March 15.

ADDRESS INQUIRIES TO:
Theo Horn
Awards Manager
American Foreign Service Association
2101 E Street, N.W.
Washington, DC 20037
E-mail: horn@afsa.org

UNITED STATES-JAPAN FOUNDATION   [801]
145 East 32nd Street
12th Floor
New York, NY 10016
(212) 481-8753
(212) 481-8757
Fax: (212) 481-8762
E-mail: programs@us-jf.org
Web Site: www.us-jf.org

FOUNDED: 1980

AREAS OF INTEREST:
Precollege education and policy studies, communication and public opinion.

NAME(S) OF PROGRAMS:
● **Grants**
● **Elgin Heinz Outstanding Teacher Award**
● **U.S.-Japan Leadership Program**

TYPE:
Awards/prizes; General operating grants; Project/program grants; Research grants; Travel grants. In the area of Precollege Education, the Foundation supports the improvement and enhancement of instruction of Japan in the U.S. and on the U.S. in Japan in secondary and elementary schools through programs which foster the creative use of the Internet in education, teacher training, professional development, intensive study tours, and curriculum design. The Foundation also supports the improvement of Japanese language instruction.

In the area of Policy Studies, the Foundation supports joint policy research and has established several nongovernmental channels for ongoing discussions between small groups of prominent experts. Policy projects have been active in such fields as trade and international finance, the environment, multilateral crisis management, and Northeast Asian security.

The Foundation will consider communication/public opinion projects that not only raise awareness about Japan in the U.S. and of the U.S. in Japan, but also deal with concrete issues that affect the bilateral relationship. Using creative approaches, these programs should reach broad audiences to stimulate balanced, in-depth and quality media coverage of issues that are central to U.S.-Japan relations.

Projects that link civil society organizations in the two countries are also supported.

YEAR PROGRAM STARTED: 1980

PURPOSE:
To promote stronger ties between Americans and Japanese through education, communication, policy studies and similar activities that foster greater mutual knowledge and understanding regarding each other and issues of common concern.

LEGAL BASIS:
Not-for-profit private foundation.

ELIGIBILITY:
Certain types of programs fall outside the Foundation's current interests. These include undergraduate education, cultural performances or exhibitions, sports exchanges, publication subsidies, scientific research and research conferences. As a rule, grants cannot be made to individuals applying on their own behalf for independent study, research, travel or participation in meetings; grants also cannot be made to for-profit organizations.

Because the Foundation is interested primarily in supporting program activities, it does not award grants as contributions to capital campaigns, endowment funds or deficit operations. In addition, it does not award grants for the construction or maintenance of buildings or other physical premises or for the purchase of equipment.

The Foundation does not administer programs which it supports. Foundation grants may not be used to influence legislation or election to public office.

GEOG. RESTRICTIONS: United States or Japan.

FINANCIAL DATA:
Amount of support per award: Varies.
Total amount of support: Approximately $2,000,000 annually.

NO. MOST RECENT APPLICANTS: 150 to 200.

NO. AWARDS: Approximately 45.

REPRESENTATIVE AWARDS:
Education: $30,000 to Concordia Language Villages, Moorhead, MN, to support a Japanese language scholarship program for middle and high school students in a 12-state region that aims to improve Japanese language study throughout the Midwest; Community/Public Opinion: $73,441 to University of Nebraska Medical Center, Department of Emergency Medicine, Omaha, NE, to support a knowledge exchange between the U.S. and Japan concerning screening, assessment, and treatment of abuse victims; Policy Studies: $39,000 to Dartmouth College, Hanover, NH, to support a project to assess the Japanese citizen's perception of Self-Defense Forces.

APPLICATION INFO:
Applicants should submit a preproposal letter of inquiry, including a brief description of the proposed project and its objectives, any necessary background information on the project and applicant, and a brief budget estimate. If there is interest, the applicant will be invited to prepare a full proposal.
Duration: 12 months. Annual renewal possible.

ADDRESS INQUIRIES TO:
Director of Foundation Grants
(See address above.)

WORLD LEARNING INC.   [802]
1015 15th Street, N.W.
7th Floor
Washington, DC 20005
(202) 408-5420
E-mail: fulbrightspecialist@worldlearning.org
Web Site: fulbrightspecialist.worldlearning.org

FOUNDED: 1947

AREAS OF INTEREST:
Scholarly exchange.

NAME(S) OF PROGRAMS:
● **Fulbright Specialist Program**

TYPE:
Exchange programs; Project/program grants. The Fulbright Specialist Program is designed to provide short-term project opportunities for U.S. faculty and professionals. Grant recipients have a chance to participate in a variety of new and exciting activities: collaborate with counterparts in other countries on curriculum and faculty development, assist in institutional planning, deliver a series of lectures or provide other expertise, etc.

YEAR PROGRAM STARTED: 2001

PURPOSE:
To promote mutual understanding and scholarship.

LEGAL BASIS:
Private, nonprofit organization that receives funding from the U.S. State Department.

ELIGIBILITY:
The Fulbright Specialist Program is open to qualified U.S. scholars and professionals in various fields. Applicants will be considered without regard to race, color, religion, sex, age, national origin and/or physical impairment.

Applicants must meet all of the following minimum eligibility requirements:
(1) U.S. citizen at the time of application; permanent resident status is not sufficient;
(2) for academics, a Ph.D. or equivalent professional/terminal degree at the time of application plus a minimum of five years of postdoctoral teaching or professional experience in the field in which person is applying;
(3) for professionals and artists outside academe, recognized professional standing and substantial professional accomplishments plus a minimum of five years of professional experience in the field in which person is applying;
(4) disclosure of prior conviction, current indictment or arrest for commission of a felony or misdemeanor (excluding minor traffic violations); prior conviction or current indictment may result in disqualification and;
(5) U.S. residency required at the time of selection for a grant.

In matching candidates with grant opportunities, preference will be given to candidates with the most relevant professional experience.

FINANCIAL DATA:
Grants awarded will include travel and per diem plus a $200 per day honorarium. Per diem costs, which are in-country costs for lodging, meals and in-country transportation, will be covered by the host institution.
Amount of support per award: Varies.

NO. MOST RECENT APPLICANTS: 600.

NO. AWARDS: Approximately 350 to 450 per year.

APPLICATION INFO:
Qualified U.S. scholars and professionals apply throughout the calendar year for candidacy on the Fulbright Specialists Roster. Peer review is conducted six times each year. CIES builds lists of qualified Specialist candidates for each eligible discipline and facilitates matching Specialist candidates with project requests. There is a two-tier application process for U.S. scholars.

Non-U.S. postsecondary degree-granting academic institutions and other eligible institutions with education-focused programming submit Specialist project requests through the appropriate Fulbright agency in their country. Once approved by the Fulbright Commission or U.S. Embassy, the Specialist project request is forwarded to the U.S. Department of State for final approval.
Duration: Two to six weeks.

ADDRESS INQUIRIES TO:
See e-mail address above.

International studies and research abroad

AFS INTERCULTURAL PROGRAMS/USA [803]
120 Wall Street, 4th Floor
New York, NY 10005
(800) 237-4636
(646) 751-2011
Fax: (212) 299-9090
E-mail: studyabroad@afsusa.org
Web Site: www.afsusa.org

FOUNDED: 1947

AREAS OF INTEREST:
International exchange of high school students who live with host families and attend local schools. Participants go to and from 60 countries.

CONSULTING OR VOLUNTEER SERVICES:
More than 100,000 volunteers around the world.

NAME(S) OF PROGRAMS:
- **AFS Faces of America Diversity Scholarship Program**
- **AFS Global Prep**
- **AFS Semester Program**
- **AFS Summer Program**
- **AFS Year Program**
- **AFSNext**
- **Congress-Bundestag Youth Exchange (CBX)**
- **Kennedy-Lugar Youth Exchange and Study Abroad (YES Abroad)**
- **National Securities Languages Initiative for Youth (NSLI-Y)**

TYPE:
Exchange programs; Scholarships. U.S. students abroad. Scholarships are for AFS-run programs only.

YEAR PROGRAM STARTED: 1947

PURPOSE:
To provide cross-cultural learning experiences for young people in another environment.

LEGAL BASIS:
Incorporated under the Not-for-Profit Corporation Laws of the state of New York. Exempt from New York state, New York City and federal taxes.

ELIGIBILITY:
Age, health, academic background, motivation and personality are considered.

FINANCIAL DATA:
Amount of support per award: Varies depending on merit and need.
Total amount of support: Approximately $3,000,000.

NO. AWARDS: Nearly 50% of all participants receive financial aid. AFS deals with 4,400 students each year.

APPLICATION INFO:
Candidate must submit health record, school record, applicant essay, screening group recommendation, interview forms and parental essay.
Duration: Two to six weeks to one year. Nonrenewable.
Deadline: Dependent on program.

PUBLICATIONS:
Annual report; application forms; AFS program catalog; *Partnerships*, newsletter.

IRS I.D.: 39-1711417

ADDRESS INQUIRIES TO:
See e-mail address above.

ALBRIGHT INSTITUTE OF ARCHAEOLOGICAL RESEARCH (AIAR) [804]
P.O. Box 40151
Philadelphia, PA 19106
(215) 238-1290
Fax: (215) 238-1540
E-mail: scohen@aiar.org
Web Site: www.aiar.org

FOUNDED: 1900

AREAS OF INTEREST:
Fellowships are open to those in Near Eastern studies from prehistory through the early Islamic period, including the fields of anthropology, archaeology, art history, Bible, epigraphy, historical geography, history, language, literature, philology and religion, and related disciplines.

NAME(S) OF PROGRAMS:
- **Fellowships at the Albright Institute of Archaeological Research in Jerusalem**

TYPE:
Fellowships; Professorships; Scholarships; Travel grants; Visiting scholars. Fellowships are for study at the Albright Institute in Jerusalem, Israel.

The ACLS Recent Doctoral Recipients Fellowship is available to awardees and alternates of the Mellon/ACLS Dissertation Completion Fellowships the prior year.

The George A. Barton Fellowship is awarded for one month and is open to all doctoral students or recent Ph.D. recipients.

The Marcia and Oded Borowski Research Fellowship provides a one-month fellowship to doctoral and postdoctoral candidates of all nationalities.

The Council of American Overseas Research Centers (CAORC) Multi-Country Research Fellowships are open to U.S. doctoral candidates and scholars who have already earned their Ph.D. in fields in the humanities, social sciences, or allied natural sciences and wish to conduct research of regional or transregional significance. Fellowships require scholars to conduct research in more than one country, at least one of which hosts a participating American overseas research center. (Apply at www.caorc.org/programs/index.html.)

Educational and Cultural Affairs Fellowships (ECA): (1) Junior Research Fellowships consist of two fellowships of up to nine months each; these fellowships are open to doctoral students and recent Ph.D. recipients who are U.S. citizens and; (2) Associate Fellowships consist of 13 administrative fee awards for senior and junior fellows (one or two semesters).

Ernest S. Frerichs Annual Professorship is for nine months and is open to doctoral and postdoctoral scholars of all nationalities. Recipient is expected to assist the Albright's Director in planning and implementing the Ernest S. Frerichs Program for Albright Fellows, which requires a working knowledge of living and traveling in Israel.

The Seymour Gitin Distinguished Professorship is open to internationally recognized senior scholars of all nationalities who have made significant contributions to their field of study.

Glassman Holland Research Fellowship is for three months and is open to all European postdoctoral researchers who are permanently resident in Europe.

Carol and Eric Meyers Doctoral Dissertation Fellowship provides one month of study for doctoral students whose research involves the study of archaeology and society in the biblical or early postbiblical periods. Topics dealing with society at the household level are encouraged.

National Endowment for the Humanities (NEH) Fellowships are awarded for four to nine months. Open to postdoctoral scholars who are U.S. citizens or alien residents in the U.S. for at least three years.

The Lydie T. Shufro Summer Research Fellowship is for one month during the summer and open to scholars at all levels and nationalities.

YEAR PROGRAM STARTED: 1940

PURPOSE:
To help scholars undertake high-quality research and field projects in the Near East; to encourage interdisciplinary study and communication among scholars.

LEGAL BASIS:
Nonprofit, archaeological research corporation.

ELIGIBILITY:
Fellowships are open to those in Near Eastern studies from prehistoric through the early Islamic period, including the fields of archaeology, anthropology, art history, Bible, epigraphy, gender studies, historical geography, history, language, literature, philology and religion and related disciplines. The research period should be continuous, without frequent trips outside the country. Residence at the Albright is required. The option to accommodate dependents is subject to space available at the Albright.

FINANCIAL DATA:
Amount of support per award: Varies.
Total amount of support: $330,000 in fellowships and awards.

CO-OP FUNDING PROGRAMS: With various organizations and foundations, such as the NEH.

NO. AWARDS: Up to 32 in fellowships and awards from the Institute; 32 Associate Fellows receive funding from other sources.

APPLICATION INFO:
All eligible persons are encouraged to apply for as many awards as they wish, but each awardee can hold only one AIAR award at a time. Persons who have received an award in one year can reapply for the same or other awards the following year, but new applicants will be given priority.
Duration: Up to one year.
Deadline: January 15 and October 15.

PUBLICATIONS:
Applications.

STAFF:
Dr. Matthew J. Adams, Director

ADDRESS INQUIRIES TO:
Dr. Susan Cohen, Chair
Albright Fellowship Committee
(See e-mail address above.)

THE AMERICAN ACADEMY IN BERLIN [805]

Am Sandwerder 17-19
D-14109 Berlin Germany
(49) 30 804 83 106
Fax: (49) 30 804 83 111
E-mail: cs@americanacademy.de
Web Site: www.americanacademy.de

FOUNDED: 1994

AREAS OF INTEREST:
History, political science, literature, economics, German studies, art history, musicology, anthropology, law, writing, journalism, religious studies and sociology.

NAME(S) OF PROGRAMS:
● **Berlin Prize Fellowship**

TYPE:
Fellowships. Academic semester fellowship in Berlin with residence at the Hans Arnhold Center.

YEAR PROGRAM STARTED: 1998

PURPOSE:
To further scholarly professional development; to foster greater understanding between the people of the U.S. and the people of Germany.

LEGAL BASIS:
Private, independent, nonprofit center.

ELIGIBILITY:
Must be either a U.S. citizen or permanent resident, and have completed their Doctorate or equivalent professional degree. Open to scholars, artists, and professionals who wish to engage in independent study in Berlin for an academic semester or, in rare cases, for an entire academic year. Candidates need not work on German topics, but their project descriptions should explain how a residency in Berlin will contribute to further professional development. Writers must have published at least one book at time of application.

FINANCIAL DATA:
Amount of support per award: Stipend of $5,000 per month, round-trip airfare, and an apartment and partial board at the Hans Arnhold Center.

NO. MOST RECENT APPLICANTS: 300 to 400.

NO. AWARDS: Approximately 20.

APPLICATION INFO:
General Application is available online from late May to the end of September.
Duration: One academic semester.
Deadline: September.

STAFF:
Carol Scherer, Manager of Fellows Selection

ADDRESS INQUIRIES TO:
Carol Scherer
Manager of Fellows Selection
(See address above.)

AMERICAN ACADEMY IN ROME

7 East 60th Street
New York, NY 10022-1001
(212) 751-7200
Fax: (212) 751-7220
E-mail: info@aarome.org
Web Site: www.aarome.org

TYPE:
Awards/prizes; Fellowships; Residencies. Fellowships for independent work in architecture, landscape architecture, design, musical composition, visual arts, historic preservation/conservation, literature, ancient studies, medieval studies, renaissance and early modern studies, and modern Italian studies. Supported projects must be conducted at American Academy in Rome facilities.

See entry 311 for full listing.

AMERICAN ACADEMY IN ROME

7 East 60th Street
New York, NY 10022
(212) 751-7200
Fax: (212) 751-7220
E-mail: info@aarome.org
Web Site: www.aarome.org

TYPE:
Awards/prizes; Fellowships; Residencies. Provides a residential year at the American Academy in Rome for an American landscape architect for advanced study, travel and association with other fellows in the arts and humanities.

See entry 1983 for full listing.

AMERICAN CENTER OF ORIENTAL RESEARCH [806]

209 Commerce Street
Alexandria, VA 22314
(703) 789-9231
E-mail: usa.office@acorjordan.org
Web Site: www.acorjordan.org

FOUNDED: 1968

AREAS OF INTEREST:
The study of humanistic disciplines, such as art and architecture, literature, philology, prehistory and topography, relating in particular to the Middle East from prehistoric times to the modern era. Projects involving Islamic studies are especially encouraged.

The American Center of Oriental Research in Amman, Jordan serves as a center of operations for scholars of all nationalities wishing to conduct research in Jordan.

NAME(S) OF PROGRAMS:
● **ACOR-CAORC Fellowship**
● **ACOR-CAORC Postgraduate Fellowships**
● **Pierre and Patricia Bikai Fellowship**
● **Bert and Sally de Vries Fellowship**
● **Jennifer C. Groot Fellowships in the Archaeology of Jordan**
● **Harrell Family Fellowship**
● **MacDonald/Sampson Fellowship**
● **National Endowment for the Humanities (NEH) Fellowship**
● **Kenneth W. Russell Fellowship**
● **James A. Sauer Fellowship**

TYPE:
Fellowships; Research grants; Visiting scholars. ACOR-CAORC Fellowships are for M.A. and doctoral students. Fields of study include all areas of the humanities and the natural and social sciences. Topics should contribute to scholarship in Near Eastern studies; U.S. citizenship required.

ACOR-CAORC Postgraduate Fellowships are for postdoctoral scholars and scholars with a terminal degree in their field, pursuing research or publication projects in the natural and social sciences, humanities, and associated disciplines relating to the Near East; U.S. citizenship required.

Pierre and Patricia Bikai Fellowship is for a residency at ACOR in Amman and is open to enrolled graduate students of any nationality, except Jordanian citizens, participating in an archaeological project or conducting archaeological work in Jordan.

Bert and Sally de Vries Fellowship supports a student for participation on an archaeological project or research in Jordan. Senior project staff members whose expenses are being borne largely by the project are ineligible. Open to enrolled undergraduate or graduate students of any nationality except Jordanian citizens.

The Jennifer C. Groot Fellowships support beginners in archaeological fieldwork who have been accepted as team members on archaeological projects with ASOR/CAP affiliation in Jordan. Open to undergraduate or graduate students of U.S. or Canadian citizenship.

Harrell Family Fellowship supports a graduate student for participation on an archaeological project or research in Jordan. Senior project staff members whose expenses are being borne largely by the project are ineligible. Open to enrolled graduate students of any nationality except Jordanian citizens.

MacDonald/Sampson Fellowship is for a residency at ACOR for research in the fields of Ancient Near Eastern languages and history, archaeology, Bible studies, or comparative religion, or a travel grant to assist with participation in an archaeological field project in Jordan. Open to enrolled undergraduate or graduate students of Canadian citizenship or landed immigrant status.

The National Endowment for the Humanities (NEH) Fellowship is for scholars who have a Ph.D. or have completed their professional training. Fields of research include modern and classical languages, linguistics, literature, history, jurisprudence, philosophy, archaeology, comparative religion, ethics, and the history, criticism and theory of the arts. Social and political scientists are encouraged to apply. Applicants must be U.S. citizens or foreign nationals living in the U.S. three years immediately preceding the application deadline.

James A. Sauer Fellowship is open to enrolled graduate students of U.S. or Canadian citizenship participating on an archaeological project or research in Jordan.

YEAR PROGRAM STARTED: 1968

PURPOSE:
To help scholars undertake high-quality research and field projects in the Middle East; to encourage interdisciplinary study and communication among scholars.

LEGAL BASIS:
Nonprofit, archaeological research corporation.

ELIGIBILITY:
Most fellowships are restricted to U.S. or Canadian citizens.

CAORC, NEH, MacDonald/Sampson and Bikai Fellows will reside at the ACOR facility in Amman while conducting their research. Recipients are expected to participate actively in the formal and informal activities of the Center.

FINANCIAL DATA:
Amount of support per award:
ACOR-CAORC Fellowships: $23,800 maximum; ACOR-CAORC Postgraduate Fellowships: $32,400 maximum; Pierre and Patricia Bikai Fellowship: $600 monthly stipend plus room and board at ACOR; Bert and Sally de Vries Fellowship and Groot Fellowships: $1,500; Harrell Family Fellowship: $2,000; MacDonald/Sampson Fellowship: $400 stipend, plus room and board at ACOR, or travel grant of $2,000 to help with any project-related expenses; National Endowment for the Humanities

(NEH) Fellowship: $50,000 maximum; Kenneth W. Russell Fellowship: $1,800; James A. Sauer Fellowship: $1,250.
Total amount of support: Varies.

CO-OP FUNDING PROGRAMS: With various organizations and foundations, such as the NEH.

NO. MOST RECENT APPLICANTS: 81 for all programs.

NO. AWARDS: ACOR-CAORC Fellowships and ACOR-CAORC Postgraduate Fellowships: 2 or more each; Bikai Fellowship: 1 to 2; Bert and Sally de Vries, Harrell Family, MacDonald/Sampson, NEH and Sauer Fellowships: 1 each; Groot Fellowships: Up to 4.

APPLICATION INFO:
Prospective applicants are encouraged to consult with the ACOR Administrative Director about application procedures, the competitiveness of their applications, or any other questions they might have about the awards program.

Online application portal can be found at orcfellowships.fluidreview.com.

All eligible persons are encouraged to apply for as many awards as they wish, but each awardee can hold only one ACOR award at a time. Persons who have received an award in one year can reapply for the same or other awards the following year, but new applicants will be given priority.
Duration: ACOR-CAORC Fellowships/Postgraduate Fellowships: Two to six months; Bikai Fellowship: One to two months; National Endowment for the Humanities (NEH) Fellowship: Four to 10 months; Sauer Fellowship: One month.
Deadline: February 1.

PUBLICATIONS:
Program announcements.

IRS I.D.: 23-7084091

ADDRESS INQUIRIES TO:
ACOR Fellowship Committee
(See address above.)

AMERICAN FRIENDS OF THE ALEXANDER VON HUMBOLDT FOUNDATION [807]
1401 K Street
Suite 1005
Washington, DC 20005
(202) 783-1907
E-mail: info@americanfriendsofavh.org
Web Site: www.americanfriendsofavh.org

FOUNDED: 1953

AREAS OF INTEREST:
Intercultural exchange.

NAME(S) OF PROGRAMS:
● **German Chancellor Fellowship**

TYPE:
Exchange programs; Fellowships; Project/program grants. Fellowship for one-year stay in Germany for professional development, study or research. Applicants design individual projects specific to Germany and decide at which institutions to pursue them.

YEAR PROGRAM STARTED: 1990

PURPOSE:
To strengthen ties between Germany and the U.S. through fellowship recipient's profession or studies.

ELIGIBILITY:
Intended for career-oriented individuals from any profession or field of study who show outstanding potential for U.S. leadership. Selected fellows represent the private, public, not-for-profit, cultural and academic sectors. Applicant must be from (and current national of) the U.S., Russia, China or Brazil.

FINANCIAL DATA:
Stipend covers housing and living expenses. In addition, the Fellowship also covers travel expenses to and from Germany and the costs of a German language course, introductory seminar, study tour, and final meeting in Bonn.
Amount of support per award: Monthly stipend of EUR 2,150 to EUR 2,750, based on qualifications.
Total amount of support: Varies.

NO. MOST RECENT APPLICANTS: 37 (from U.S.).

NO. AWARDS: 10 annually (from U.S.).

APPLICATION INFO:
Applications must be submitted to the Foundation's Bonn, Germany office.
Duration: One year.
Deadline: September 15. Fellowship period begins the following year on September 1.

STAFF:
Brian Craft, Alumni Relations and Annual Fund Program Coordinator
Alexis Brouwer-Ancher, Communications and Events Program Coordinator

ADDRESS INQUIRIES TO:
Program Coordinator
(See address above.)

*SPECIAL STIPULATIONS:
Prior to submitting an application, applicants are expected to have established contact with a mentor in Germany who agrees to provide professional and/or scholarly assistance throughout the program year.

AMERICAN FRIENDS OF THE ALEXANDER VON HUMBOLDT FOUNDATION [808]
1401 K Street
Suite 1005
Washington, DC 20005
(202) 783-1907
E-mail: info@americanfriendsofavh.org
Web Site: www.americanfriendsofavh.org

FOUNDED: 1953

AREAS OF INTEREST:
Postgraduate research in Germany.

NAME(S) OF PROGRAMS:
● **Humboldt Research Fellowship for Experienced Researchers**

TYPE:
Fellowships; Project/program grants; Research grants. This program allows a researcher to carry out a long-term research project (six to 18 months) at a research institution in Germany which the applicant has selected in cooperation with an academic host.

PURPOSE:
To support highly qualified scholars and scientists of all nationalities and disciplines so that they may carry out a long-term research project.

ELIGIBILITY:
Open to scientists and scholars from outside Germany, with above-average qualifications,

who:
(1) have completed their Doctorate less than 12 years ago;
(2) already have his or her own research profile and;
(3) are working at least at the level of Assistant Professor or Junior Research Group Leader or have a record of several years of independent academic work.

Fellowships are awarded on the basis of academic achievement, the quality and feasibility of the proposed research and the candidate's publications.

FINANCIAL DATA:
In addition to a monthly stipend, special allowances are available for accompanying family members, travel expenses, and German language instruction.
Amount of support per award: EUR 3,150 monthly stipend.
Total amount of support: Varies.

NO. MOST RECENT APPLICANTS: Approximately 1,800.

NO. AWARDS: Approximately 600.

APPLICATION INFO:
Application documents can be downloaded from www.humboldt-foundation.de.
Duration: Six to 18 months. Fellowships may be divided into a maximum of three visits of at least three months each.
Deadline: Applications may be submitted at any time to the Humboldt Foundation in Bonn, Germany. The review process takes four to seven months, and the selection committee meets three times a year to review applications.

STAFF:
Brian Craft, Alumni Relations and Annual Fund Program Coordinator
Alexis Brouwer-Ancher, Communications and Events Program Coordinator

ADDRESS INQUIRIES TO:
Program Coordination
(See address above.) or

Alexander von Humboldt Stiftung
Jean-Paul-Strasse 12
D-53173 Bonn
Germany
Tel: 49 (0228) 833-0
Fax: 49 (0228) 833-199
E-mail: info@avh.de

*SPECIAL STIPULATIONS:
Applicant must have received Ph.D. within 12 years.

AMERICAN INSTITUTE FOR SRI LANKAN STUDIES (AISLS)   [809]

155 Pine Street
Belmont, MA 02478
E-mail: rogersjohnd@aol.com
Web Site: www.aisls.org

FOUNDED: 1996

AREAS OF INTEREST:
The promotion of scholarly excellence in Sri Lankan studies.

NAME(S) OF PROGRAMS:
● **AISLS Fellowship Program**

TYPE:
Fellowships. Program supports research in Sri Lanka by U.S. citizens who already hold a Ph.D. or the equivalent at the time they begin their fellowship tenure.

PURPOSE:
To foster excellence in American research and teaching on Sri Lanka; to promote the exchange of scholars and scholarly information between the U.S. and Sri Lanka.

ELIGIBILITY:
Applicants must hold U.S. citizenship and a Ph.D. or equivalent academic degree, or show that they will hold such a degree before taking up the fellowship. Scholars at all ranks are eligible. Applicants must plan to spend at least two months in Sri Lanka and complete the fellowship within the time frame listed under eligibility guidelines. Projects in all fields in the social sciences and humanities are eligible.

FINANCIAL DATA:
Fellowship includes reimbursement up to $2,000 for round-trip airfare between the U.S. and Colombo via U.S. carriers, and a limited budget for research expenses, to be negotiated.
Amount of support per award: Stipend of $3,700 per month.

APPLICATION INFO:
The completed application should contain the following items:
(1) AISLS Fellowship Application Cover Sheet;
(2) curriculum vitae, not to exceed three pages;
(3) description of the proposed study, not to exceed three single-spaced pages. This is the most important part of the application. It should cover the questions to be addressed by the project, the approach to be taken, work done to date, work to be accomplished during the fellowship period, the applicant's competence to carry out the project, how the project addresses the criteria of the competition, and a statement of other support received or being sought for the project and;
(4) one-page bibliography, including a selected list of publications by other scholars or primary sources that have been or will be used in the project.
Duration: Two to six months.
Deadline: December 1.

ADDRESS INQUIRIES TO:
John Rogers, U.S. Director
(See address above.)

AMERICAN INSTITUTE FOR SRI LANKAN STUDIES (AISLS)   [810]

155 Pine Street
Belmont, MA 02478
E-mail: rogersjohnd@aol.com
Web Site: www.aisls.org

FOUNDED: 1996

AREAS OF INTEREST:
The promotion of scholarly excellence in Sri Lankan studies.

NAME(S) OF PROGRAMS:
● **AISLS Dissertation Planning Grant**

TYPE:
Research grants. Grant to assist graduate students intending to do dissertation research in Sri Lanka.

YEAR PROGRAM STARTED: 2006

PURPOSE:
To enable graduate students to make a pre-dissertation visit to Sri Lanka to investigate the feasibility of their topic, to

sharpen their research design, or to make other practical arrangements for future research.

ELIGIBILITY:
Applicants must be enrolled in a Ph.D. program (or equivalent) in a U.S. university. There are no citizenship requirements. Applicants should have completed most of their graduate coursework by the time they take up their grant. The grant is especially intended for students who are in the process of completing their dissertation proposals and preparing applications for funds to support their dissertation research, but other purposes may be proposed. Applicants should plan to spend at least six weeks in Sri Lanka.

GEOG. RESTRICTIONS: United States.

FINANCIAL DATA:
Grant includes reimbursement up to $2,000 for round-trip airfare between U.S. and Colombo, reimbursement for any visa fees paid to the Sri Lankan government, and a per diem for six to eight weeks.
Amount of support per award: Per diem of $560 per week.

APPLICATION INFO:
The completed application should contain the following items:
(1) AISLS Dissertation Planning Grant Application Cover Sheet;
(2) curriculum vitae, not to exceed two pages, which should include the name and e-mail address of the applicant's dissertation supervisor;
(3) copy of the applicant's graduate transcript. An unofficial copy is acceptable;
(4) project narrative, not to exceed two single-spaced pages. This is the most important part of the application and should contain a summary of the proposed dissertation project, or, if the purpose of the planning grant is to define a dissertation project, a summary of the more general questions the applicant hopes to address in his or her dissertation, a description of what the applicant intends to do during the grant period, and the applicant's competence to carry out his or her proposed project, including language training;
(5) one-page project bibliography, including a selected list of publications by other scholars or primary sources that have been or will be used in the project and;
(6) a confidential letter of recommendation from the applicant's dissertation supervisor. This letter should cover the applicant's academic record and be specific about the applicant's progress to date within the graduate program concerned. This letter should be sent directly to John Rogers at the address listed above.
Duration: Six to eight weeks.
Deadline: December 1. Early submission is encouraged.

ADDRESS INQUIRIES TO:
John Rogers, U.S. Director
(See address above.)

AMERICAN INSTITUTE OF BANGLADESH STUDIES   [811]

B488 Medical Sciences Center
1300 University Avenue
Madison, WI 53706
(608) 265-1471
Fax: (608) 265-3302
E-mail: aibs@southasia.wisc.edu
Web Site: www.aibs.net

FOUNDED: 1989

AREAS OF INTEREST:
Bangladesh culture and society.

NAME(S) OF PROGRAMS:
- **Junior Fellowship**
- **Pre-Dissertation Fellowships**
- **Seminar and Conference Support**
- **Senior Fellowship**
- **Undergraduate Research Initiative**
- **Workshops in U.S. and Bangladesh**

TYPE:
Awards/prizes; Conferences/seminars; Fellowships; Research grants; Travel grants. Junior Fellowship is for those who are in the ABD phase of their Ph.D. program. Applicants must be prepared to commence field research at the start of the fellowship period.

Pre-Dissertation Fellowships are short-term grants offered to graduate students pursuing studies of Bangladesh or another country outside the U.S. The grant provides a stay of between two and four months in Bangladesh that may be used for language study, resource assessment, or network building to aid the completion of a competitive dissertation proposal.

The Senior Fellowship is for those who have a Ph.D. They may already have research experience in Bangladesh or may be interested in developing a research area on Bangladesh.

YEAR PROGRAM STARTED: 1989

PURPOSE:
To improve the scholarly understanding of Bangladesh culture and society in the U.S. and to promote educational exchange between the U.S. and Bangladesh.

ELIGIBILITY:
Applicants must be U.S. citizens or permanent residents and have their Ph.D.

Pre-Dissertation Fellowship: At the time of application, students must have completed at least one year of graduate study in a recognized Ph.D.-granting institution.

FINANCIAL DATA:
Amount of support per award: Junior Fellowship: $920 monthly allowance; Senior Fellowship: $1,150 plus research and dependents' allowances per month in non-convertible Bangladesh Taka. Round-trip air transportation will be provided via the most direct route and using the Bangladesh carrier whenever possible.
Total amount of support: Varies.

APPLICATION INFO:
Application forms and complete details are available online.
Duration: Junior Fellowship: Six to 10 months; Pre-Dissertation Fellowship: Two to four months; Senior Fellowship: Four to 12 months.
Deadline: Varies depending upon program.

ADDRESS INQUIRIES TO:
See e-mail address above.

AMERICAN INSTITUTE OF INDIAN STUDIES

1130 East 59th Street
Chicago, IL 60637
(773) 702-8638
E-mail: aiis@uchicago.edu
Web Site: www.indiastudies.org

TYPE:
Fellowships. Awards for studies in India in an Indian language.
See entry 604 for full listing.

AMERICAN INSTITUTE OF INDIAN STUDIES [812]

1130 East 59th Street
Chicago, IL 60637
(773) 702-8638
E-mail: aiis@uchicago.edu
Web Site: www.indiastudies.org

FOUNDED: 1961

AREAS OF INTEREST:
Indian studies.

NAME(S) OF PROGRAMS:
- **AIIS Fellowships**

TYPE:
Fellowships; Research grants. Senior (postdoctoral) Research Fellowships are awarded to academic specialists in Indian studies who possess the Ph.D. or equivalent. While in India, each Senior Research Fellow will be formally affiliated with an Indian university.

Fellowships for Senior Scholarly Development are awarded to established scholars who have not previously specialized in Indian studies and to established professionals who have not previously worked or studied in India. Proposals in this category should have a substantial research or project component and the anticipated results should be clearly defined. While in India, each Fellow will be formally affiliated with an Indian university.

Junior (dissertation) Fellowships are awarded to graduate students from all academic disciplines whose dissertation research requires study in India. Junior Fellows will have formal affiliation with Indian universities and Indian research supervisors.

Senior Performing Arts Fellowships are awarded to accomplished practitioners of the performing arts of India who demonstrate that studying in India will enhance their skills, develop their capabilities to teach or perform in the U.S., enhance American involvement with India's artistic traditions and strengthen their links with peers in India.

YEAR PROGRAM STARTED: 1962

PURPOSE:
To support the advancement of knowledge and understanding of India, its people and culture, primarily through research conducted in India by American scholars.

LEGAL BASIS:
Cooperative, nonprofit organization of 90 American colleges and universities.

ELIGIBILITY:
U.S. citizens are eligible for AIIS grants, as are foreign nationals enrolled or teaching full-time at American colleges or universities. U.S. and Indian government employees are ineligible for AIIS grants. Eligible applicants who are unaffiliated or who are from nonmember institutions are encouraged to apply.

FINANCIAL DATA:
Fellowships include a maintenance allowance and international travel. Fellowships for four months or less have significant travel restrictions. Fellowships for six months or more may include limited dependent

coverage if funds are available. Award funds are generally made available in foreign currency only.

NO. AWARDS: Determined by the amount of support received by AIIS.

APPLICATION INFO:
Application forms are available online. All applications must include a $25 processing fee.
Duration: Up to nine months for Senior Research Fellowships, Fellowships for Senior Scholarly Development and Senior Performing Arts Fellowships; Up to 11 months for Junior Fellowships.
Deadline: July 1. Awards are announced in early October. Awards begin in June of the following year.

EXECUTIVE STAFF:
Elise Auerbach, Administrator

ADDRESS INQUIRIES TO:
Elise Auerbach, Administrator
(See address above.)

THE AMERICAN JEWISH JOINT DISTRIBUTION COMMITTEE [813]

220 East 42nd Street
New York, NY 10017
(212) 687-6200
E-mail: jdcentwine@jdc.org
miriam.bader@jdc.org
Web Site: www.jdcentwine.org/lead/ralph-i-goldman-fellowship

AREAS OF INTEREST:
International Jewish communal service.

NAME(S) OF PROGRAMS:
- **The Ralph I. Goldman Fellowship**

TYPE:
Fellowships. Premier leadership opportunity awarded to one person annually for young thinkers and doers - writers, artists, policy shapers, business innovators and community builders.

YEAR PROGRAM STARTED: 1987

PURPOSE:
To provide young Jewish leaders with an insider's perspective on JDC's global programs, while also giving them the opportunity to participate in the life of international Jewish communities.

ELIGIBILITY:
Candidates should have the following credentials:
(1) Bachelor's degree or equivalent and proven academic excellence;
(2) professional achievement in the candidate's chosen career;
(3) demonstrated exceptional leadership and communication skills;
(4) strong interest in international Jewish affairs and public service;
(5) knowledge of foreign language(s) is a plus, but not a requirement and;
(6) formal and/or informal Jewish education.

FINANCIAL DATA:
Amount of support per award:
Approximately $50,000 stipend plus international travel expenses.

NO. AWARDS: 1 annually.

APPLICATION INFO:
Candidates should send an e-mail to the address above. Application includes a short personal essay, two letters of recommendation, and a 90-second video.

Duration: One year, beginning in January.

AMERICAN RESEARCH CENTER IN EGYPT, INC.   [814]

909 North Washington Street
Suite 320
Alexandria, VA 22314
(703) 721-3479
E-mail: info@arce.org
fellows@arce.org
Web Site: www.arce.org

FOUNDED: 1948

AREAS OF INTEREST:
Research on Egypt and in Egypt on all phases of Egyptian civilization and culture from earliest times to the present.

NAME(S) OF PROGRAMS:
● **Fellowships for Research in Egypt**

TYPE:
Fellowships; Research grants; Travel grants. Fellowships awarded to doctoral students in the all-but-dissertation (ABD) stage as well as to postdoctoral scholars. Topics for research fellowship encompass the humanities, social sciences and art and archaeology and cover periods from ancient times to the present. A limited number of predissertation travel grants are awarded in the same categories as fellowships.

YEAR PROGRAM STARTED: 1974

PURPOSE:
To obtain a fresh and more profound knowledge of Egypt and the Near East through scholarly research; to train American specialists in Near Eastern Studies in academic disciplines which require familiarity with Egypt; to disseminate knowledge of Egypt and thus understanding of the whole Near East and promote American-Egyptian cultural relations.

LEGAL BASIS:
Nonprofit organization.

ELIGIBILITY:
Criteria for selections rest on the Committee's judgment of the applicant's intellectual capacity and maturity, fitness for field work in Egypt, the significance and relevance of the proposed topic and its potential contribution to scholarly research in Egypt. No special consideration is given to applicants from member institutions and candidates need not be members of the ARCE. Awards are open to all qualified candidates without regard to sex, race and religion. All applicants, pre- and postdoctoral, must be U.S. citizens due to funding guidelines. Under certain circumstances, funding is available through the NEH for non-U.S. postdoctoral scholars living in the U.S. for more than three consecutive years to receive funding. Therefore, it is advisable to contact fellows@arce.org for further clarification.

GEOG. RESTRICTIONS: Egypt.

FINANCIAL DATA:
Monthly per diem plus round-trip airfare between the U.S. and Cairo. Fellows may receive stipends only for the period of time during which they are present in Egypt. A small dependent allowance for accompanying family members is available.

Amount of support per award: $2,200 to $3,650 monthly per diem; NEH all-inclusive award: $4,200 per month.

Total amount of support: Varies.

CO-OP FUNDING PROGRAMS: NEH and CAORC/ECA.

NO. MOST RECENT APPLICANTS: 15 for the year 2017-18.

NO. AWARDS: 7.

APPLICATION INFO:
Electronic submission is preferred. Original letters of recommendation and transcripts, if applicable, may also be scanned and sent electronically.

All applicants must submit three letters of recommendation. Predoctoral applicants must submit a fourth recommendation attesting to their capacity in ancient or modern languages as related to their proposed research.

Duration: CAORC/ECA: Three to 12 months; NEH all-inclusive award: Four to 10 months.

Deadline: Mid-January.

PUBLICATIONS:
Annual report; application guidelines; journal; bulletin; e-newsletter.

IRS I.D.: 04-2319500

GOVERNING BOARD:
Betsy Bryan, President
David Anderson, Vice President
Richard Larson, Treasurer

ADDRESS INQUIRIES TO:
Djodi Deutsch
Academic Programs Manager
E-mail: fellows@arce.org

AMERICAN RESEARCH INSTITUTE IN TURKEY, INC.   [815]

c/o The University of Pennsylvania Museum
3260 South Street
Philadelphia, PA 19104-6324
(215) 898-3474
Fax: (215) 898-0657
E-mail: leinwand@sas.upenn.edu
Web Site: ccat.sas.upenn.edu/ARIT

FOUNDED: 1964

AREAS OF INTEREST:
Research and study in Turkey, including all fields of the humanities and social sciences.

NAME(S) OF PROGRAMS:
● **ARIT Fellowship Program**

TYPE:
Fellowships. ARIT offers a number of fellowships for research in Turkey in humanities and social sciences. Grants for tenures of up to one academic year will be considered; some preference is given to projects of shorter duration. ARIT operates hostel, research and study facilities for researchers in Turkey at its branch centers in Istanbul and Ankara.

YEAR PROGRAM STARTED: 1964

PURPOSE:
To support research in humanities and social sciences in Turkey.

LEGAL BASIS:
Funded in part by grants from U.S. Department of State, Bureau of Educational and Cultural Affairs.

ELIGIBILITY:
Scholars and advanced graduate students engaged in research on ancient, medieval or modern times in Turkey, in any field of the humanities and social sciences, are eligible. Student applicants must have fulfilled all

preliminary requirements for the Doctorate except the dissertation by June of the program year, and before beginning any ARIT-sponsored research. Non-U.S. applicants who currently reside in the U.S. or Canada are expected to maintain an affiliation with an educational institution in the U.S. or Canada. For questions of eligibility and procedures, please check with the ARIT office in Philadelphia.

FINANCIAL DATA:
Awards cover international travel to and from Turkey and provide a stipend based on Turkish living standards and the fellow's academic status.

Amount of support per award: Generally $2,500 to $15,500.

Total amount of support: Varies.

CO-OP FUNDING PROGRAMS: The Fellowship program is supported in part by a grant from the U.S. Department of State, Bureau of Educational and Cultural Affairs.

NO. MOST RECENT APPLICANTS: 75 for the year 2017-18.

NO. AWARDS: 4 for the year 2018.

APPLICATION INFO:
Turkish law requires foreign scholars to obtain formal permission for any research to be carried out at institutions in Turkey. ARIT fellowship applicants are responsible for obtaining the appropriate research permissions and visas. In general, researchers should seek permission to carry out research directly from the director(s) of the institution(s) where they intend to work; this includes researchers who wish to work in libraries housed in Turkish museums. For archival and library research with tenures of less than three months, some foreign scholars may enter Turkey on a tourist visa and apply for the research permit and visa from within Turkey, or scholars may choose to procure a research visa from the Turkish embassy in advance of their arrival. Scholars wishing to carry out research in Turkey for terms longer than three months should apply for the research permit and in addition secure a research visa prior to entering Turkey. Non-U.S. researchers should consult the Turkish Consulate for specific procedures.

Researchers who wish to work with collections housed in the Turkish archaeological museums, however, should make their applications through the Ministry of Culture and Tourism, General Directorate for Cultural Heritage and Museums. In addition, if the material they wish to work with is part of an excavation, researchers must submit a letter with their application signed by the excavation director giving permission to carry out the research. The research permit application regulations and format for researchers are posted on the ARIT web site. ARIT reserves the right to withhold payment of fellowship stipends if appropriate research permission is not obtained.

Please include three letters of reference with one's application. Graduate student applicants must provide a copy of their graduate transcript.

Duration: Up to one academic year.

Deadline: November 1.

OFFICERS:
A. Kevin Reinhart, President

Nick Cahill, Vice President
Maria de Jong Ellis, Treasurer

ADDRESS INQUIRIES TO:
Nancy W. Leinwand
(See telephone and e-mail above.)

AMERICAN RESEARCH INSTITUTE IN TURKEY, INC. [816]

c/o The University of Pennsylvania Museum
3260 South Street
Philadelphia, PA 19104-6324
(215) 898-3474
Fax: (215) 898-0657
E-mail: leinwand@sas.upenn.edu
Web Site: ccat.sas.upenn.edu/ARIT

FOUNDED: 1964

AREAS OF INTEREST:
Turkey.

NAME(S) OF PROGRAMS:
● **Bogazici University Summer Language Program for Intensive Advanced Turkish Language Study**

TYPE:
Fellowships. Bogazici University Summer Language Program: For summer study in Turkey. Also offer travel, stipend and tuition grants. This intensive program offers the equivalent of one full academic year of study in advanced Turkish language at the college level.

YEAR PROGRAM STARTED: 1981

PURPOSE:
To support the study of advanced Turkish language.

LEGAL BASIS:
Consortium of universities. Funding from the U.S. Department of Education.

ELIGIBILITY:
Full-time students and scholars affiliated at academic institutions are eligible to apply. To be a fellowship applicant, one must:
(1) be a citizen, national or permanent resident of the U.S.;
(2) be enrolled in an undergraduate- or graduate-level academic program, or be faculty;
(3) have a minimum B average in one's studies, if still a student and;
(4) perform at the high-intermediate level on a proficiency-based admissions examination.

FINANCIAL DATA:
Fellowships cover round-trip airfare to Istanbul, application and tuition fees, and a maintenance stipend.

CO-OP FUNDING PROGRAMS: Funded by U.S. Department of Education, Office of Post-Secondary Education.

NO. MOST RECENT APPLICANTS: Approximately 40.

NO. AWARDS: Approximately 15 for the year 2019.

APPLICATION INFO:
Application information is available on the web site.

Duration: Approximately eight weeks (late June through early August).

Deadline: February 1.

OFFICERS:
C. Brian Rose, President
Ahmet Karamustafa, Vice President
Brian Peasnall, Treasurer
John Curry, Secretary

ADDRESS INQUIRIES TO:
Dr. Sylvia Onder
Eastern Mediterranean Languages
Department of Arabic and Islamic Studies
Georgetown University
210 North Poulton Hall
1437 37th Street, N.W.
Washington, DC 20007
E-mail: aritfellowship@georgetown.edu or

Nancy Leinwand
American Research Institute in Turkey
(See address and e-mail above.)

AMERICAN RESEARCH INSTITUTE IN TURKEY, INC. [817]

c/o The University of Pennsylvania Museum
3260 South Street
Philadelphia, PA 19104-6324
(215) 898-3474
Fax: (215) 898-0657
E-mail: leinwand@sas.upenn.edu
Web Site: ccat.sas.upenn.edu/ARIT

FOUNDED: 1964

AREAS OF INTEREST:
Turkey covering all periods of history in the general range of the humanities and including humanistically oriented aspects of the social sciences, prehistory, history, art, archaeology, literature and linguistics, as well as interdisciplinary aspects of cultural history.

NAME(S) OF PROGRAMS:
● **NEH Fellowships for Research in Turkey**

TYPE:
Fellowships. These advanced fellowships are made possible by support from the National Endowment for the Humanities. The fields of study cover all periods of history in the general range of the humanities and include humanistically oriented aspects of the social sciences, prehistory, history, art, archaeology, literature and linguistics, as well as interdisciplinary aspects of cultural history.

ARIT maintains two research institutes in Turkey. ARIT in Istanbul has a research library concentrated on Byzantine and Ottoman Turkey. The ARIT Ankara center focuses on art, archaeology, and ancient history in its library, and serves Turkish and American archaeologists through its programs. Both institutes have residential facilities for fellows and provide general assistance as well as introductions to colleagues, institutions and authorities in Turkey.

YEAR PROGRAM STARTED: 1991

PURPOSE:
To support long-term postdoctoral research in Turkey in the humanities.

LEGAL BASIS:
Consortium of universities. Funding from the National Endowment for the Humanities.

ELIGIBILITY:
Scholars who have completed their formal academic training by the application deadline and plan to carry out research in Turkey may apply. Applicants may be U.S. citizens or three-year residents of the U.S. Please consult ARIT headquarters on questions of eligibility. Advanced scholars may also apply for ARIT Fellowships in the Humanities and Social Sciences.

FINANCIAL DATA:
Amount of support per award: Stipend of $4,200 per month, awarded on the basis of individual proposals.

NO. MOST RECENT APPLICANTS: 12.

NO. AWARDS: 1 to 3 advanced fellowships for the 2019-20 academic year.

APPLICATION INFO:
Turkish law requires foreign scholars to obtain formal permission to carry out research at institutions in Turkey. ARIT fellowship applicants are responsible for obtaining the appropriate research permissions and visas. In general, researchers should seek permission to carry out research from the director(s) of the institution(s) where they intend to work; this includes researchers who wish to work in libraries housed in Turkish museums. For archival and library research with tenure of less than three months, some foreign scholars may enter Turkey on a tourist visa and apply for the research permit and visa from within Turkey; or they may choose to procure a research visa via the Turkish Embassy in advance of their arrival. Scholars wishing to carry out research in Turkey for terms longer than three months should apply for the research permit and in addition secure a research visa prior to entering Turkey. Non-U.S. researchers should consult the Turkish Consulate for specific procedures.

Researchers who wish to work with collections housed in the Turkish archaeological museums, however, should make their applications through the Ministry of Culture and Tourism, General Directorate for Cultural Heritage and Museums. In addition, if the material they wish to work with is part of an excavation, researchers must submit a letter with their application signed by the excavation director giving permission to carry out the research. The research permit application regulations and format for researchers are posted on the ARIT web site (ccat.sas.upenn.edu/ARIT/Research Permit.htm). ARIT reserves the right to withhold payment of fellowship stipends if appropriate research permission is not obtained.

Duration: Four to 12 continuous months.

Deadline: November 1 for the following academic year. Applicants will be notified by the end of January of that following year.

PUBLICATIONS:
Program announcement.

OFFICERS:
C. Brian Rose, President
Ahmet Karamustafa, Vice President
Brian Peasnall, Treasurer
John Curry, Secretary

ADDRESS INQUIRIES TO:
Nancy W. Leinwand
(See telephone number above.)

THE AMERICAN-SCANDINAVIAN FOUNDATION [818]

58 Park Avenue
New York, NY 10016
(212) 779-3587
(615) 881-1532
Fax: (212) 686-1157
E-mail: grants@amscan.org
Web Site: www.amscan.org

FOUNDED: 1910

AREAS OF INTEREST:
Advanced study in Scandinavia.

NAME(S) OF PROGRAMS:
- **ASF Awards for Study in Scandinavia**

TYPE:
Fellowships; Research grants. Short-term project grants and long-term fellowships for advanced study in a field which may be pursued with particular merit in one of the Scandinavian countries (Denmark, Finland, Iceland, Norway or Sweden).

Fellowships are intended to support an academic year-long stay. Priority is given to candidates at the graduate level for dissertation-related study or research.

Grants are considered especially suitable for postgraduate scholars, professionals and candidates in the arts to carry out research or study visits of one to three months' duration.

YEAR PROGRAM STARTED: 1911

PURPOSE:
To advance cultural and intellectual understanding between the U.S. and Scandinavia, primarily through exchange programs, cultural programs and publications.

LEGAL BASIS:
Nonprofit educational institution qualifying under statutes 501(c)(3), 509(a)(1) and 170(c)(2) of the IRS code.

ELIGIBILITY:
Applicants must have a well-defined research or study project that makes a stay in Scandinavia essential. Applicants must be U.S. citizens or permanent residents who will have completed their undergraduate education by the start of their project in Scandinavia. Team projects are eligible, but each member must apply as an individual, submitting a separate, fully documented application. First priority will be given to applicants who have not previously received an ASF award. Only in exceptional cases will a third award be considered. The ASF considers it desirable that all candidates have at least some ability in the language of the host country, even if it is not essential for the execution of the research plan. For projects that require a command of one or more Scandinavian (or other) languages, candidates should defer application until they have the necessary proficiency. Evidence of a confirmed invitation or affiliation is an important factor in award consideration.

ASF does not fund the following:
(1) travel for attendance at professional meetings, conferences, seminars or conventions;
(2) performances or exhibitions;
(3) publication costs;
(4) equipment purchases, including personal computers, software and cell phones;
(5) research assistants;
(6) institutional overhead costs;
(7) tuition fees from U.S. home institution;
(8) foregone salary;
(9) supplementation of substantial sabbatical support;
(10) support for dependents;
(11) personal obligations, including repayment of loans and mortgages;
(12) acquisition of language skills;
(13) study in programs especially designed for English-speaking students, or at English-language institutions;
(14) beginning studies in any subject or;
(15) retroactive program support.

Projects must be undertaken in Denmark, Finland, Iceland, Norway or Sweden.

GEOG. RESTRICTIONS: Scandinavia.

FINANCIAL DATA:
The awards support project-related costs, including maintenance, transatlantic round-trip travel, in-country travel, tuition and fees (where applicable) and materials expenditures (e.g., books, photocopying, art supplies).

Amount of support per award: Grants normally up to $5,000, especially suited for short visits of one to three months and fellowships of up to $23,000, intended for a full academic year of study or research.

Total amount of support: Over $400,000 for the 2018-19 competition.

NO. MOST RECENT APPLICANTS: 84.

NO. AWARDS: Varies each year according to total funds available. Awards were made to 26 Americans in the 2018-19 competition.

APPLICATION INFO:
Only applications on current official ASF forms will be considered. Such applications are available online. Incomplete applications cannot be processed. Unsuccessful applications will be discarded.

Applicants for Awards for Study in Scandinavia are urged to arrange their academic or professional affiliations as far in advance as possible. Applicants must secure these placements or affiliations on their own; the ASF cannot assist in establishing contacts. The ASF requires confirmation of invitation or affiliation from the institution or individuals detailed in the proposal. Since July and August are traditionally holiday months in Scandinavia, many people may not be available for consultation. Applicants are cautioned to plan their projects accordingly. Applicants are expected to devote full-time to their proposed study or research, and must justify the length of time needed to complete their project. Awards are based on the application submitted; subsequent changes in the proposal are discouraged and may not be considered.

Duration: Grants: One to three months. Fellowships: One academic year.

Deadline: November 1 for receipt of fully documented applications. Awards announced by the following April 15.

PUBLICATIONS:
Annual report; fellowship and grant application guidelines; *Scandinavian Review*; *Scan*, newsletter; *Study in Scandinavia*, guide.

ADMINISTRATION:
Edward P. Gallagher, President
Lynn Carter, Secretary to the Board
Carl Fritscher, Fellowships and Grants Officer

ADDRESS INQUIRIES TO:
Fellowships and Grants
(See address above.)

*SPECIAL STIPULATIONS:
ASF awards may require supplementation from other sources, but they should not duplicate the benefits of additional awards (and vice versa). Candidates must notify the ASF if they have received other award offers. The ASF will not provide funds if, in its judgment, a proposal can be carried out without its assistance.

AMERICAN SCHOOL OF CLASSICAL STUDIES AT ATHENS   [819]

6-8 Charlton Street
Princeton, NJ 08540-5232
(609) 683-0800
Fax: (609) 924-0578
E-mail: application@ascsa.org
Web Site: www.ascsa.edu.gr

FOUNDED: 1881

AREAS OF INTEREST:
Classical studies.

NAME(S) OF PROGRAMS:
- **National Endowment for the Humanities Fellowships**

TYPE:
Fellowships. Fellowships for postdoctoral scholars and professionals in the humanities.

LEGAL BASIS:
Graduate research and teaching center.

ELIGIBILITY:
Postdoctoral scholars and professionals in relevant fields including architecture and art history who are U.S. citizens or foreign nationals who have lived in the U.S. for the three years immediately preceding the application deadline may apply. Applicants must already hold their Ph.D. or have completed all requirements, except for the actual conferral of the degree, by the application deadline.

FINANCIAL DATA:
School fees are waived and the award provides lunches at Loring Hall five days per week. The NEH fellow will pay for travel costs, housing, residence permit, and other living expenses from the stipend.

Amount of support per award: Stipend of $4,200 per month.

Total amount of support: $75,600 annually.

NO. MOST RECENT APPLICANTS: 31.

NO. AWARDS: 2 to 4.

APPLICATION INFO:
Correspondence about fellowships and admission to membership in the school should be directed to the address above. Applicants must submit an online application form, a short abstract of the project, a statement of the project (up to five pages), curriculum vitae, and the names of three recommenders who will write letters of reference.

Applicants should indicate their preference for the length and dates of tenure of the award to coincide with the American School's academic year: September to June for a nine-month fellowship, January to June for a five-month fellowship, or September to December for a four-month fellowship.

Duration: Four, five or nine months.

Deadline: October 31.

STAFF:
Jenifer Neils, Director

ADDRESS INQUIRIES TO:
See e-mail address above.

AMERICAN SCHOOL OF CLASSICAL STUDIES AT ATHENS [820]

6-8 Charlton Street
Princeton, NJ 08540-5232
(609) 683-0800
Fax: (609) 924-0578
E-mail: application@ascsa.org
Web Site: www.ascsa.edu.gr

FOUNDED: 1881

AREAS OF INTEREST:
Late Antique through Modern Greek Studies, including but not limited to the Byzantine, Frankish, Post-Byzantine, and Ottoman periods.

NAME(S) OF PROGRAMS:
- **M. Alison Frantz Fellowship in Post-Classical Studies at the Gennadius Library**

TYPE:
Fellowships. The M. Alison Frantz Fellowship is part of the Student Associate Program, which is open to advanced graduate students in the same fields as the Regular Academic Program (classical studies and ancient Mediterranean studies and related fields such as history of art, anthropology, prehistory, studies in postclassical Greece, etc.), who plan to pursue independent research projects and who do not wish to commit to the full Regular Academic Program.

YEAR PROGRAM STARTED: 1963

PURPOSE:
To provide financial assistance to advanced graduate students who plan to pursue independent research projects but do not wish to commit to the American School's full Regular Academic Program.

LEGAL BASIS:
Graduate educational institution (non-degree granting).

ELIGIBILITY:
Ph.D. candidates and recent Ph.Ds. (up to five years) from a U.S. or Canadian institution may apply. Candidates should demonstrate their need to work in the Gennadius Library.

FINANCIAL DATA:
Amount of support per award: Stipend of $11,500, plus room, board and waiver of School fees.

NO. AWARDS: 1.

APPLICATION INFO:
Application must be made online on the ASCSA web site. Applicants must submit the Fellowship Application Form, a curriculum vitae, a description of the proposed project (up to 750 words), and three letters of reference online. Students must submit transcripts.
Duration: One academic year (September to June).
Deadline: January 15.

STAFF:
Jenifer Neils, Director

ADDRESS INQUIRIES TO:
Chair, Committee on Libraries and Archives
(See address above.)

*SPECIAL STIPULATIONS:
Fellows are expected to be in residence at the School for the full academic year. A final report is due at the end of the award period,

and the ASCSA expects that copies of all publications that result from research conducted as a Fellow of the ASCSA be contributed to the Gennadius Library.

AMERICAN SCHOOL OF CLASSICAL STUDIES AT ATHENS [821]

6-8 Charlton Street
Princeton, NJ 08540-5232
(609) 683-0800
Fax: (609) 924-0578
E-mail: application@ascsa.org
Web Site: www.ascsa.edu.gr

FOUNDED: 1881

AREAS OF INTEREST:
Classical studies, history of art, history of architecture, pottery, Mycenaean archaeology, Athenian architecture and archaeology.

NAME(S) OF PROGRAMS:
- **Advanced Fellowships**

TYPE:
Fellowships. Several Fellowships awarded by the School for the full academic year: the Gorham Phillips Stevens Fellowship in the history of architecture; the Ione Mylonas Shear Fellowship in Mycenaean archaeology or Athenian architecture and/or archaeology; the Homer A. and Dorothy B. Thompson Fellowship in the study of pottery. Additionally, three Fellowships are unrestricted as to field: the Edward Capps, the Doreen Canaday Spitzer, and the Eugene Vanderpool Fellowships.

PURPOSE:
To support work on a specific project by students who wish to study at the School for a year.

ELIGIBILITY:
Students who have completed the Regular Program or one year as a Student Associate Member at the ASCSA and plan to return to the School to pursue independent research, usually for the Ph.D. dissertation, may apply. Given only if candidates meet a standard acceptable to the Director and the Committee.

School programs are generally open to qualified students and scholars at colleges or universities in the U.S. or Canada; restrictions may apply for specific fellowships and programs. The American School of Classical Studies at Athens does not discriminate on the basis of race, age, sex, sexual orientation, color, religion, ethnic origin, or disability when considering admission to any form of membership.

GEOG. RESTRICTIONS: United States and Canada.

FINANCIAL DATA:
Amount of support per award: Stipend of $11,500, plus room, board and waiver of School fees.

NO. MOST RECENT APPLICANTS: 9.

NO. AWARDS: 7.

APPLICATION INFO:
Submit application form, curriculum vitae, transcripts, letters of recommendation and a detailed statement of the project to be pursued in Greece. Application must be made online on the ASCSA web site.
Duration: One year.
Deadline: February 15.

STAFF:
Jenifer Neils, Director

ADDRESS INQUIRIES TO:
See e-mail address above.

*SPECIAL STIPULATIONS:
Membership application to the ASCSA must be made online on the web site at the same time one applies to any outside funding organization for work at the School.

AMERICAN SCHOOL OF CLASSICAL STUDIES AT ATHENS [822]

6-8 Charlton Street
Princeton, NJ 08540-5232
(609) 683-0800
Fax: (609) 924-0578
E-mail: application@ascsa.org
Web Site: www.ascsa.edu.gr

FOUNDED: 1881

AREAS OF INTEREST:
Ancient Greek law.

NAME(S) OF PROGRAMS:
- **The Harry Bikakis Fellowship**

TYPE:
Fellowships. Research fellowship awarded periodically, but not more frequently than once a year.

PURPOSE:
To promote research.

ELIGIBILITY:
North American or Greek graduate students researching ancient Greek law, or Greek graduate students working on a School excavation.

School programs are generally open to qualified students and scholars at colleges or universities in the U.S. or Canada; restrictions may apply for specific fellowships and programs. The American School of Classical Studies at Athens does not discriminate on the basis of race, age, sex, sexual orientation, color, religion, ethnic origin, or disability when considering admission to any form of membership.

FINANCIAL DATA:
Amount of support per award: $1,875. School fees are waived.

NO. MOST RECENT APPLICANTS: 1.

NO. AWARDS: 1.

APPLICATION INFO:
Submit Associate Member application, including an outline of the proposed project, and two letters of reference online on the ASCSA web site.
Deadline: January 15.

STAFF:
Jenifer Neils, Director

ADDRESS INQUIRIES TO:
See e-mail address above.

*SPECIAL STIPULATIONS:
Membership application to the ASCSA must be made online on the web site at the same time one applies to any outside funding organization for work at the School.

AMERICAN SCHOOL OF CLASSICAL STUDIES AT ATHENS   [823]

6-8 Charlton Street
Princeton, NJ 08540-5232
(609) 683-0800
Fax: (609) 924-0578
E-mail: application@ascsa.org
Web Site: www.ascsa.edu.gr

FOUNDED: 1881

AREAS OF INTEREST:
Gennadeion collections.

NAME(S) OF PROGRAMS:
- **Cotsen Traveling Fellowship for Research in Greece**

TYPE:
Fellowships. Short-term grant.

PURPOSE:
To assist students and scholars in the pursuit of research topics requiring the use of Gennadeion collections.

ELIGIBILITY:
Senior scholars and graduate students for projects and research at the Gennadius Library. Requires residency in Athens of at least one month during the academic year from September 1 to June 1. The recipient is expected to take part in the activities of the Library and of the School in addition to pursuing research.

School programs are generally open to qualified students and scholars at colleges or universities in the U.S. or Canada; restrictions may apply for specific fellowships and programs. The American School of Classical Studies at Athens does not discriminate on the basis of race, age, sex, sexual orientation, color, religion, ethnic origin, or disability when considering admission to any form of membership.

FINANCIAL DATA:
Fellowship does not include costs for School trips, housing or board.
Amount of support per award: Stipend of $2,000. School fees are waived for a maximum of two months.

NO. MOST RECENT APPLICANTS: 10.

NO. AWARDS: 1.

APPLICATION INFO:
Application must be made online and should include the following:
(1) curriculum vitae;
(2) letter (up to 750 words) describing the project, proposed dates, budget, and explanation of the relation of the Gennadius Library's collection to the research project and;
(3) two letters of recommendation.
Duration: Minimum one month.
Deadline: January 15.

STAFF:
Dr. Maria Georgopoulou, Director, Gennadius Library

ADDRESS INQUIRIES TO:
Director, Gennadius Library
(See address above.)

*SPECIAL STIPULATIONS:
Membership application to the ASCSA must be made online on the web site at the same time one applies to any outside funding organization for work at the School.

AMERICAN SCHOOL OF CLASSICAL STUDIES AT ATHENS   [824]

6-8 Charlton Street
Princeton, NJ 08540-5232
(609) 683-0800
Fax: (609) 924-0578
E-mail: ascsa@ascsa.org (for information)
application@ascsa.org (to apply)
Web Site: www.ascsa.edu.gr

FOUNDED: 1881

AREAS OF INTEREST:
Skeletal, faunal, geoarchaeological, environmental studies and archaeological science.

NAME(S) OF PROGRAMS:
- **Wiener Laboratory Post-Doctoral Fellowship**
- **Wiener Laboratory Pre-Doctoral Fellowship**
- **Wiener Laboratory Programmatic Post-Doctoral Fellowship**
- **Wiener Laboratory Research Associateships**

TYPE:
Fellowships; Research grants. The Malcolm H. Wiener Laboratory for Archaeological Science at ASCSA provides funding for scholars pursuing interdisciplinary research on archaeological questions pertaining to the ancient Greek world and adjacent areas. Three different types of funding are offered: Post-Doctoral (three-year term), Pre-Doctoral (two-year term), and Programmatic Post-Doctoral (three-year term). The School also offers shorter-duration, more focused Research Associate positions.

PURPOSE:
To promote laboratory research pertinent to the American School of Classical Studies at Athens.

ELIGIBILITY:
Applicants are welcome from any college or university worldwide. The American School of Classical Studies at Athens does not discriminate on the basis of race, age, sex, sexual orientation, color, religion, ethnic origin, or disability when considering admission to any form of membership or application for employment.

Post-Doctoral Fellowship: Eligibility limited to individuals who have received their Ph.D. within the last seven years.

Pre-Doctoral Fellowship: Eligibility limited to individuals actively enrolled in a graduate program who have passed all qualifying exams and have an approved Ph.D. proposal.

Programmatic Post-Doctoral Research Fellowship: Eligibility limited to individuals who received their Ph.Ds. and are applying to work on material related to an ASCSA archaeological project.

Research Associateships: Eligibility limited to individuals actively enrolled in a graduate program and individuals with a higher-level degree in a relevant discipline.

FINANCIAL DATA:
Amount of support per award: Post-Doctoral and Programmatic Post-Doctoral Fellowship: Stipend of $35,000 per year; Pre-Doctoral Fellowship: Stipend up to $20,000 per year; Research Associateships: Stipend variable up to $7,000.

NO. AWARDS: Varies.

APPLICATION INFO:
Applicants should consult the web site for updated information about the application process. Application must be made online on the ASCSA web site.
Duration: Post-Doctoral and Programmatic Post-Doctoral Fellowship: Three-year term. Pre-Doctoral Fellowship: Two-year term. Research Associateships: Up to nine months.
Deadline: January 15. Announcement by March 15.

ADDRESS INQUIRIES TO:
Dr. Panagiotis Karkanas
Director, Wiener Laboratory
E-mail: TKarkanas@ascsa.edu.gr

*SPECIAL STIPULATIONS:
Membership application to the ASCSA must be made online on the web site at the same time one applies to any outside funding organization for work at the School.

AMERICAN SCHOOL OF CLASSICAL STUDIES AT ATHENS   [825]

6-8 Charlton Street
Princeton, NJ 08540-5232
(609) 683-0800
Fax: (609) 924-0578
E-mail: application@ascsa.org
Web Site: www.ascsa.edu.gr

FOUNDED: 1881

AREAS OF INTEREST:
Research at the ASCSA excavations at Ancient Corinth in Greece.

NAME(S) OF PROGRAMS:
- **Henry S. Robinson Corinth Research Fellowship**

TYPE:
Fellowships. Fellowship for research on a doctoral dissertation or primary publication, specifically on Corinth. Program is offered every other year. Robinson Fellowship for 2020-21 to be announced in the fall of 2019.

PURPOSE:
To revive field work at Corinth.

ELIGIBILITY:
Open to established scholars or Ph.D. candidates, for research on a doctoral dissertation or primary publication specifically on Corinth, requiring the use of the resources, archaeological site and collections at the ASCSA excavations at Ancient Corinth in Greece. Open to all nationalities.

FINANCIAL DATA:
The Fellowship does not allow travel costs (to and from country of origin or within Greece). Funding is for research activities at Corinth, to be used to cover living expenses, including room, board, fees and other costs associated with the study, such as photography and drawings. Availability of rooms and work space is limited during the excavation season from April to June.
Amount of support per award: Stipend up to $4,000 for one or more individuals. School fees are waived.

NO. MOST RECENT APPLICANTS: 8.

NO. AWARDS: 1 or more.

APPLICATION INFO:
Submit Associate Membership application online, including curriculum vitae and proposal statement, which should have the

following items:
(1) project outline;
(2) explanation of goals;
(3) statement of the significance of the project;
(4) work completed to date;
(5) schedule for completion;
(6) dates for project;
(7) budget and;
(8) two letters of support, including one from dissertation advisor if applicant is a Ph.D. candidate.

Duration: Up to three months within the 12-month period July 1 to June 30. Nonrenewable.

Deadline: January 15. Announcement mid-March.

*SPECIAL STIPULATIONS:
The Robinson Fellowship may not be held concurrently with another School fellowship. Preference is given to candidates who have not previously held the Robinson Fellowship or received substantial ASCSA funding for the same project.

AMERICAN SCHOOL OF CLASSICAL STUDIES AT ATHENS   [826]
6-8 Charlton Street
Princeton, NJ 08540-5232
(609) 683-0800
Fax: (609) 924-0578
E-mail: application@ascsa.org
Web Site: www.ascsa.edu.gr

FOUNDED: 1881

AREAS OF INTEREST:
Archaeology.

NAME(S) OF PROGRAMS:
● **Jacob Hirsch Fellowship**

TYPE:
Fellowships.

PURPOSE:
To provide an opportunity for students who are Ph.D. candidates writing their dissertations in archaeology or recent Ph.Ds. completing a project, such as a revision of a dissertation for publication, who require a lengthy residence in Greece.

LEGAL BASIS:
Graduate educational institution (non-degree granting).

ELIGIBILITY:
Students who hold U.S. or Israeli citizenship, and who are Ph.D. candidates writing their dissertations in archaeology or recent Ph.Ds. completing a project may apply.

FINANCIAL DATA:
Stipend plus room, board, and waiver of School fees.
Amount of support per award: Stipend of $11,500.

NO. AWARDS: 1.

APPLICATION INFO:
Applicant must submit "Associate Membership with Fellowship" application online. The application should include a curriculum vitae, a detailed description of the project to be pursued in Greece (250-word abstract and a statement up to three pages, single-spaced), and three letters of recommendation. Student applicants are required to submit legible PDF scans of academic transcripts as part of the online application.

Duration: One academic year (September to June).
Deadline: January 15.

STAFF:
Jenifer Neils, Director

ADDRESS INQUIRIES TO:
Chair, Committee on Admissions and Fellowships
(See address above.)

*SPECIAL STIPULATIONS:
A final report is due at the end of the award period, and the ASCSA expects that copies of all publications that result from research conducted as a Fellow of the ASCSA be contributed to the relevant library of the School.

AMERICAN SCHOOL OF CLASSICAL STUDIES AT ATHENS   [827]
6-8 Charlton Street
Princeton, NJ 08540-5232
(609) 683-0800
Fax: (609) 924-0578
E-mail: application@ascsa.org
Web Site: www.ascsa.edu.gr

FOUNDED: 1881

AREAS OF INTEREST:
Archaeology, classical studies, history, classical literature, art history, and Bronze Age archaeology.

NAME(S) OF PROGRAMS:
● **Regular Member Program Fellowships**

TYPE:
Fellowships. The Heinrich Schliemann and the John Williams White Fellowships in Archaeology are awarded based on the student's performance on the archaeology examination.

The Thomas Day Seymour Fellowship in History and Literature is awarded based on the student's combined performance on the history and literature examination.

Nine fellowships are unrestricted to field. These are the Virginia Grace, the Michael Jameson, the Philip Lockhart, the Lucy Shoe Meritt, the Fowler Merle-Smith, the Martin Ostwald, and the James Rignall Wheeler Fellowships. The Bert Hodge Hill Fellowship is unrestricted, but with a preference for a student in art history. The Emily Townsend Vermeule Fellowship is unrestricted, but with a preference for Bronze Age archaeology.

PURPOSE:
To provide members with full funding and lodging to pursue research.

LEGAL BASIS:
Graduate educational institution (non-degree granting).

ELIGIBILITY:
Students at colleges or universities in the U.S. or Canada may apply. Student must first be accepted into the Regular Member Program.

GEOG. RESTRICTIONS: United States and Canada.

FINANCIAL DATA:
Stipend plus room, board, and waiver of School fees.
Amount of support per award: Stipend of $11,500.

NO. AWARDS: Up to 12.

APPLICATION INFO:
Students will automatically be considered for these fellowships upon the submission of their application and completion of the ASCSA Entrance Exams.
Duration: One academic year (September to June 1).
Deadline: January 15.

AMERICAN SCHOOLS OF ORIENTAL RESEARCH (ASOR)   [828]
209 Commerce Street
Alexandria, VA 22314
(703) 789-9229
E-mail: info@asor.org
Web Site: www.asor.org

FOUNDED: 1900

AREAS OF INTEREST:
The study of humanistic disciplines, such as anthropology, archaeology, Biblical studies, epigraphy, history, history of art and architecture, literature, philology, prehistory and topography, relating in particular to the Middle East from prehistoric times to the modern era.

NAME(S) OF PROGRAMS:
● **William G. Dever Fellowship for Biblical Scholars**
● **Foundation for Biblical Archaeology Scholarships**
● **Harris Grants**
● **Heritage Fellowships**
● **P.E. MacAllister Fellowships**
● **Member Supported Fellowships**
● **Mesopotamian Fellowship**
● **Eric and Carol Meyers Fellowships**
● **Shirlee Meyers/G. Ernest Wright Fellowships**
● **Platt Fellowships**
● **Harva L. Sheeler Excavation Fellowships**
● **Strange/Midkiff Families Fellowships**
● **Student Travel Grants**
● **Study of Collections Fellowships**

TYPE:
Conferences/seminars; Fellowships; Scholarships; Travel grants.

YEAR PROGRAM STARTED: 1940

PURPOSE:
To encourage scholars to undertake study and research about the ancient Near East.

LEGAL BASIS:
Nonprofit, archaeological research corporation.

ELIGIBILITY:
The Fellowship is open to qualified students and scholars from any country. Applicants must be or become individual professional members of ASOR, or must be affiliated with an institution that is a member of ASOR.

FINANCIAL DATA:
Amount of support per award: Dever Fellowship: $7,000; Foundation for Biblical Archaeology Scholarships: $700; Harris Grants: $5,000; Heritage, MacAllister, Member-Supported, Meyers, Meyers/Wright, Platt, Sheeler, Strange/Midkiff and Study of Collections Fellowships: $2,000 each; Mesopotamian Fellowship: $9,000; Student Travel Grants: $250.

Total amount of support: Approximately $63,000.

NO. MOST RECENT APPLICANTS: Varies.

NO. AWARDS: Varies.

APPLICATION INFO:

All eligible persons are encouraged to apply for as many fellowships and professorships as they wish, but a person can hold only one award at a time. Persons who have received an award in one year can reapply for the same or other awards the following year, but new applicants will have priority.

Deadline: Dever, Heritage, MacAllister, Member Supported, Meyers, Meyers/Wright, Platt, Sheeler and Strange/Midkiff Fellowships: February. Foundation for Biblical Archaeology Scholarships and Student Travel Grants: Mid-August. Harris Grants: January. Mesopotamian Fellowships: November 1.

STAFF:

Andrew G. Vaughn, Ph.D., Executive Director

ADDRESS INQUIRIES TO:

Office Coordinator
(See address above.)

*SPECIAL STIPULATIONS:

Applicants must be or become members of ASOR or attend an ASOR-affiliated institution.

THE AMERICAN SWEDISH INSTITUTE   [829]

2600 Park Avenue South
Minneapolis, MN 55407
(612) 871-4907
Fax: (612) 871-8682
E-mail: info@asimn.org
Web Site: asimn.org

FOUNDED: 1929

AREAS OF INTEREST:
Swedish culture.

NAME(S) OF PROGRAMS:
● **Lilly Lorénzen Scholarship**

TYPE:
Scholarships; Travel grants.

YEAR PROGRAM STARTED: 1980

PURPOSE:
To foster and preserve Swedish culture in America.

ELIGIBILITY:
Must be a Minnesota resident with demonstrated achievement in their field of study who plans to study in Sweden, has a working knowledge of the Swedish language and will contribute to American-Swedish exchange.

FINANCIAL DATA:
Amount of support per award: $1,000.
Total amount of support: $1,000.

NO. MOST RECENT APPLICANTS: 10.

NO. AWARDS: 1.

APPLICATION INFO:
Updated information and application are available on the ASI web site.
Duration: One-time award.
Deadline: May 1.

ADDRESS INQUIRIES TO:
Britta Walstron, ASI Programs Manager
E-mail: brittaw@asimn.org

BELGIAN AMERICAN EDUCATIONAL FOUNDATION, INC.   [830]

195 Church Street
New Haven, CT 06510
(203) 785-4055
E-mail: emile.boulpaep@yale.edu
Web Site: www.baef.us
www.baef.be

FOUNDED: 1920

AREAS OF INTEREST:
Educational exchange between the U.S. and Belgium.

NAME(S) OF PROGRAMS:
● **B.A.E.F. Fellowships for Study in Belgium**

TYPE:
Fellowships. Predoctoral and postdoctoral fellowships for advanced study in most fields of knowledge with supported work to be undertaken at a Belgian university or an institution of higher learning. Fellowships for Belgian students are also available.

YEAR PROGRAM STARTED: 1920

PURPOSE:
To allow American candidates to pursue independent study and research in Belgium on projects for which Belgium provides special advantages.

LEGAL BASIS:
Public foundation.

ELIGIBILITY:
The applicant must be a citizen or permanent resident of the U.S. and either have a Bachelor's degree, Master's degree or equivalent degree, or be working towards a Ph.D. or equivalent degree while holding the B.A.E.F. Fellowship. Preference is given to applicants under the age of 30. Knowledge of Dutch, French or German is optional.

FINANCIAL DATA:
Fellowships carry a fixed stipend for living expenses, travel and tuition, if any. Health insurance coverage is also provided.
Amount of support per award: $28,000 for Master's or Ph.D. student; $32,000 for Postdoctoral Fellows for 12 months.

NO. MOST RECENT APPLICANTS: 55 U.S. applicants per academic year.

NO. AWARDS: Up to 10 awards to American students per academic year.

APPLICATION INFO:
Applicant shall furnish a completed application form with all its appropriate attachments. Application blanks are available on www.baef.us. Completed applications must be submitted electronically with attachments in PDF format to the e-mail address above.
Duration: 12 months preferred; no less than six months.
Deadline: October 31, for the following academic year. Fellowship starting as early as July 1 of that following year.

DIRECTORS:
Dr. Emile L. Boulpaep, President and Chairman
Marcel Crochet, Vice President
Olivier Trouveroy, Treasurer
L. Gilles Sion, Secretary
Maryan Ainsworth
Luc Coene
Jacques de Groote
Diego du Monceau

Susan Friberg
Margaret Hoover
Daniel Janssen
Filip Moerman
William S. Moody
Dirk Wauters
Jacques Willems

ADDRESS INQUIRIES TO:
Dr. Emile L. Boulpaep, President
(See address above.)

BRUCEBO FINE ART SCHOLARSHIP FOUNDATION

Concordia University
1455 De Maisonneuve Boulevard West
Montreal QC H3G 1M8 Canada
(514) 848-2424 ext. 4600
E-mail: fineartsresearch@concordia.ca
Web Site: www.bruceboscholarships.ca
www.concordia.ca/finearts

TYPE:
Development grants; Research grants; Residencies; Scholarships; Travel grants. Grant principally in the fields of fine arts, visual art and design. Grant is either for stay at the Brucebo Studio on the Island of Hanseatic Gotland, Sweden, in the Baltic Sea, for three months during the summer annually, or for undertaking a European Fine Art Travel-Study journey.

See entry 504 for full listing.

CANADIAN BUREAU FOR INTERNATIONAL EDUCATION (CBIE)   [831]

220 Laurier Avenue West, Suite 1550
Ottawa ON K1P 5Z9 Canada
(613) 237-4820
Fax: (613) 237-1073
E-mail: scholarships-bourses@cbie.ca
Web Site: www.educanada.ca/scholarships-bourses

FOUNDED: 1981

AREAS OF INTEREST:
All disciplines at the Master's or doctoral levels.

NAME(S) OF PROGRAMS:
● **Foreign Government Awards Program**

TYPE:
Scholarships. The Government of the Republic of Korea, through the National Institute for International Education Development (NIIED), offers scholarships for study or research at the Master's or Ph.D. level in Korean studies, humanities, social sciences, natural sciences, engineering, and other fields of study.

PURPOSE:
To provide opportunities for Canadians to pursue studies or research at institutions of higher education abroad.

ELIGIBILITY:
Applicants must:
(1) be Canadian citizens. Neither the applicant nor their parents can hold Korean citizenship;
(2) be under 40 years of age as of the beginning of the scholarship period;
(3) hold or be expecting to hold an undergraduate or Master's degree by August 31 preceding the start of the scholarship;
(4) not have completed an undergraduate, Master's, or doctoral degree program in South Korea;

(5) have a minimum A- average from the previously attended institution;
(6) select the university and subject of study from the list of eligible universities and programs designated by NIIED and;
(7) be in good health, both mentally and physically, to complete the program of study successfully.

Priority may be given to candidates who have certified scores on their proficiency in Korean or who apply for studies in natural sciences and engineering.

FINANCIAL DATA:
Funding includes airfare, tuition and monthly living allowances. These scholarships are subject to the availability of funding.

NO. AWARDS: 6 for the academic year 2020-21.

APPLICATION INFO:
Further information and application forms are available on the web site above.
Duration: Up to two years at the Master's level, plus up to 12 months for language training (if necessary); Up to three years at the doctoral level, plus up to 12 months for language training (if necessary).
Deadline: March.

ADDRESS INQUIRIES TO:
Program Coordinator
International Scholarship Programs
(See address above.)

*SPECIAL STIPULATIONS:
Candidates may not hold other awards concurrently.

CANADIAN BUREAU FOR INTERNATIONAL EDUCATION (CBIE) [832]

220 Laurier Avenue West, Suite 1550
Ottawa ON K1P 5Z9 Canada
(613) 237-4820
Fax: (613) 237-1073
E-mail: scholarships-bourses@cbie.ca
Web Site: www.educanada.ca/scholarships-bourses

AREAS OF INTEREST:
Higher education.

NAME(S) OF PROGRAMS:
● **Commonwealth Scholarship Plan**

TYPE:
Scholarships. Under the Commonwealth Scholarship and Fellowship Plan, scholarships are available for Canadians to pursue studies or research at the Ph.D. level that lead to a degree at a university in New Zealand.

PURPOSE:
To provide opportunities for candidates to pursue studies and/or research at higher education institutions in the Commonwealth.

ELIGIBILITY:
Applicants must be Canadian citizens and have completed an undergraduate degree with a minimum A- average or equivalent. Applicants are responsible to seek their own admission to the universities or educational institutions of their choice and ensure the necessary admission requirements are met. In addition, applicants whose native language is not English may be required to complete the academic International English Language Testing System (IELTS).

In business, management and related fields, the applicant may be required to complete the Graduate Management Admission Test (GMAT).

In economics and related fields, applicant should note that some universities require the Graduate Record Examination (GRE).

FINANCIAL DATA:
Funding includes airfare, tuition, medical and travel insurance, and an annual grant. These scholarships are subject to the availability of funding.
Amount of support per award: Varies by institution.

NO. AWARDS: Varies.

APPLICATION INFO:
Further information and application forms are available on the web site above.
Duration: Up to three years.
Deadline: July.

ADDRESS INQUIRIES TO:
Program Coordinator
International Scholarship Programs
(See address above.)

CANADIAN BUREAU FOR INTERNATIONAL EDUCATION (CBIE) [833]

220 Laurier Avenue West, Suite 1550
Ottawa ON K1P 5Z9 Canada
(613) 237-4820
Fax: (613) 237-1073
E-mail: scholarships-bourses@cbie.ca
Web Site: www.educanada.ca/scholarships-bourses

FOUNDED: 1981

AREAS OF INTEREST:
All disciplines at the Master's, doctoral or postdoctoral levels.

NAME(S) OF PROGRAMS:
● **Canada-China Scholars' Exchange Program**

TYPE:
Exchange programs; Scholarships. Global Affairs Canada and the Chinese Ministry of Education offer short-term scholarships to Canadians wishing to study abroad in China. Scholarships are awarded for studies, research, language studies or a combination of studies and language studies at participating Chinese institutions.

PURPOSE:
To provide opportunities for Canadians to pursue studies or research at institutions of higher education abroad.

ELIGIBILITY:
Applicants must:
(1) be Canadian citizens residing in Canada;
(2) be a full-time professor or research staff at a recognized postsecondary education or research institution in Canada, a student enrolled in either a college, undergraduate or graduate program at a recognized postsecondary education institution in Canada, or a midcareer professional from a Canadian government, media or cultural organization, or national education association, who has a graduate (Master's or doctoral) degree and has managerial, policy development or decision making responsibilities for at least three years with the organization;
(3) have achieved the required level of written and spoken Chinese by the host institution in China (if applicable);
(4) undertake studies in an approved subject area in a Chinese institution;
(5) not be seeking a degree in China and;

(6) be under 45 years of age for "General Scholar" category or under 50 years of age for "Senior Scholar" category.

FINANCIAL DATA:
Funding includes tuition, accommodation, and comprehensive medical insurance.
Amount of support per award: Varies by level of study.

APPLICATION INFO:
Applicant must complete the following two-step process:
(1) Applicants must first complete and submit the online application form of the Department of Foreign Affairs, Trade and Development (DFATD) available on the CBIE web site and provide the supporting documents as requested and;
(2) Applicants must complete and submit the CSC online application from the China Scholarship Council web site, as well as an application package submitted by mail.
Duration: Four to 12 months for students; Eight weeks to 12 months for midcareer professionals and faculty members.
Deadline: January 23.

ADDRESS INQUIRIES TO:
Program Coordinator
International Scholarship Programs
(See address above.)

CANADIAN INSTITUTE FOR ADVANCED LEGAL STUDIES

P.O. Box 43538, Leaside Post Office
1601 Bayview Avenue
Toronto ON M4G 4G8 Canada
(416) 429-3292
Fax: (416) 429-9805
E-mail: info@canadian-institute.com
Web Site: www.canadian-institute.com

TYPE:
Scholarships.

See entry 1799 for full listing.

CANADIAN INSTITUTE IN GREECE/L'INSTITUT CANADIEN EN GRECE

Brock University, Department of Classics
1812 Sir Isaac Brock Way
St. Catharines ON L2S 3A1 Canada
(905) 688-5550 ext. 3798
Fax: (905) 984-4859
E-mail: rsmith@brocku.ca
Web Site: www.cig-icg.gr

TYPE:
Fellowships; Internships; Travel grants. Intended to support the graduate work of a person who needs to study in Greece.

See entry 323 for full listing.

WINSTON CHURCHILL FOUNDATION OF THE UNITED STATES [834]

600 Madison Avenue, Suite 1601
New York, NY 10022-1737
(212) 752-3200
Fax: (212) 246-8330
E-mail: info@churchillscholarship.org
Web Site: www.churchillscholarship.org

FOUNDED: 1959

AREAS OF INTEREST:
Science, math and engineering.

NAME(S) OF PROGRAMS:
- **Churchill Scholarship**

TYPE:
Scholarships. Scholarship for one year of graduate work at University of Cambridge. Churchill Scholarship may also include a Special Research Grant.

YEAR PROGRAM STARTED: 1963

PURPOSE:
To encourage Anglo-American cooperation and American scientific and technological talent.

LEGAL BASIS:
Public charity.

ELIGIBILITY:
Candidate must be a citizen of the U.S., have a Bachelor's degree from an accredited U.S. college or university and be enrolled at one of 123 participating American institutions.

FINANCIAL DATA:
Amount of support per award: Churchill Scholarship: Tuition, plus GBP 14,500 living allowance, $1,500 travel allowance and reimbursement of visa application fees. Total individual package is approximately $60,000; Churchill Scholars may also receive a Special Research Grant of up to $2,000.
Total amount of support: Approximately $900,000 for the year 2018.

NO. MOST RECENT APPLICANTS: 105.

NO. AWARDS: 16 scholarships for the year 2018.

APPLICATION INFO:
Application forms are available from Foundation representatives at participating institutions. Information also available on Foundation's web site.
Duration: One year.
Deadline: October 31.

OFFICERS:
John L. Loeb, Jr., Chairman
Patrick A. Gerschel, President
Michael Morse, Executive Director
David D. Burrows, Treasurer
James A. Fitzpatrick, Jr., Secretary

ADDRESS INQUIRIES TO:
Michael Morse, Executive Director
(See address above.)

CORPUS CHRISTI COLLEGE   [835]
Trumpington Street
Cambridge CB2 1RH England
(44) 01223 338038
Fax: (44) 01223 765589
E-mail: graduate-tutor@corpus.cam.ac.uk
Web Site: www.corpus.cam.ac.uk

FOUNDED: 1352

AREAS OF INTEREST:
All subjects of postgraduate research at the University of Cambridge.

NAME(S) OF PROGRAMS:
- **Postgraduate Research at the University of Cambridge**

TYPE:
Scholarships.

PURPOSE:
To enable the candidate to pursue, as a member of the college, research in any subject leading to a research degree of Cambridge University.

LEGAL BASIS:
University College.

ELIGIBILITY:
Applicants must have a first degree from a recognized university and name Corpus Christi College as their college of first preference on GAF. Candidates must become registered as University of Cambridge graduate students.

FINANCIAL DATA:
Amount of support per award: Varies.
Matching fund requirements: It is a requirement that individuals who are eligible apply to other funding bodies, e.g. Cambridge Trusts.

APPLICATION INFO:
Applications are submitted through the Applicant Portal located at www.graduatestudy.cam.ac.uk. Paper application can be requested by e-mailing graduateadmissions@admin.cam.ac.uk for those unable to apply online.
Duration: Up to three years.

ADDRESS INQUIRIES TO:
Tutor for Advanced Students
(See e-mail address above.)

COUNCIL OF AMERICAN OVERSEAS RESEARCH CENTERS (CAORC)   [836]
P.O. Box 37012
MRC 178
Washington, DC 20013-7012
(202) 633-1599
E-mail: fellowships@caorc.org
Web Site: www.caorc.org

FOUNDED: 1981

AREAS OF INTEREST:
Promoting the work of American overseas research centers.

NAME(S) OF PROGRAMS:
- **Multi-Country Research Fellowship Program**

TYPE:
Fellowships; Research grants. Requires scholars to conduct research in two or more countries outside the U.S., at least one of which hosts a participating American overseas research center.

YEAR PROGRAM STARTED: 1993

PURPOSE:
To advance higher learning and scholarly research by providing a forum for communication and cooperation among American overseas advanced research centers; to provide general and continuing publicity about the importance and contributions of the centers; to exchange operational and administrative information among the centers; to exchange scholarly and research information among the centers; to encourage joint research projects.

LEGAL BASIS:
501(c)(3) organization.

ELIGIBILITY:
Program is open to U.S. doctoral candidates and scholars who have already earned their Ph.D. in fields in the humanities, social sciences, or allied natural sciences and wish to conduct research of regional or trans-regional significance. Must be U.S. citizen or permanent resident.

U.S. State Department travel restrictions apply. U.S. citizens may not travel to Afghanistan, Iraq, Yemen or Pakistan (senior scholars allowed only).

FINANCIAL DATA:
Amount of support per award: Up to $11,000.

NO. AWARDS: 9.

APPLICATION INFO:
A complete application consists of:
(1) application form;
(2) project description (1,500 words or less) describing the nature of the proposal and competence to carry out the required research;
(3) project bibliography/literature review (one page maximum);
(4) two signed letters of recommendation;
(5) curriculum vitae (three pages maximum) and;
(6) graduate transcripts (Ph.D. candidates only).

Applicants are urged to review the Application Instructions before submitting the application.
Duration: Ph.D./Postdoctoral: Minimum of 90 days.
Deadline: Late January.

ADDRESS INQUIRIES TO:
Program Manager
(See address above.)

*SPECIAL STIPULATIONS:
Fellows must complete their research within a specific time.

COUNCIL ON FOREIGN RELATIONS
58 East 68th Street
New York, NY 10065
(212) 434-9740
Fax: (212) 434-9870
E-mail: fellowships@cfr.org
Web Site: www.cfr.org/fellowships

TYPE:
Fellowships. The International Affairs Fellowship in Japan (IAF-J), sponsored by Hitachi, Ltd., provides a selected group of midcareer U.S. citizens the opportunity to expand their professional horizons by spending a period of research or other professional activity in Japan. Fellows are drawn from academia, business, government, media, NGOs and think tanks. In cooperation with the Council on Foreign Relations (CFR), the program's sponsor, Hitachi, Ltd., assists fellows in finding suitable host organizations in Japan.

See entry 773 for full listing.

CULTURAL VISTAS   [837]
233 Broadway, Suite 2120
New York, NY 10279
(212) 497-3555
E-mail: ragnello@culturalvistas.org
Web Site: culturalvistas.org

FOUNDED: 1968

AREAS OF INTEREST:
All areas of culture, business, technical, and engineering.

NAME(S) OF PROGRAMS:
- **Congress-Bundestag Youth Exchange for Young Professionals**

TYPE:
Exchange programs; Fellowships; Internships; Scholarships; Work-study programs.
Language learning. Scholarship program with

a strong focus on cultural exchange.
One-year scholarship for work/study program
to Germany including German language
training, academic semester in Germany and
internship component.

YEAR PROGRAM STARTED: 1983

PURPOSE:
To give participants understanding for
everyday life, education and professional
training in Germany.

ELIGIBILITY:
Requirements include:
(1) U.S. citizenship;
(2) 18 and one-half to 24 years of age at start
of program;
(3) at least high school diploma or equivalent
and;
(4) clear career goals, a solid academic
background, and relevant work experience or
internships in field strongly preferred.

German language proficiency preferred, but
not required.

FINANCIAL DATA:
Funding provided for international airfare,
language training and study costs, living
expenses during study phases, all seminars,
and sickness and accident insurance while
abroad.

CO-OP FUNDING PROGRAMS: Funded in U.S. by
the Bureau of Educational and Cultural
Affairs of the Department of State and
through the Administration of the Bundestag
in Germany.

NO. MOST RECENT APPLICANTS: 650.

NO. AWARDS: 75.

APPLICATION INFO:
Electronic submission only.
Duration: One year (July to July).
Deadline: December 1 for the following
program year.

ADDRESS INQUIRIES TO:
Congress-Bundestag Youth Exchange
for Young Professionals
(See address above.)

*SPECIAL STIPULATIONS:
Must be U.S. citizens, 18 and one-half to 24
years of age at the start of the program.
Previous recipients of Congress-Bundestag
scholarships are not eligible for this program.

CYPRUS AMERICAN
ARCHAEOLOGICAL RESEARCH
INSTITUTE   [838]
209 Commerce Street
Alexandria, VA 22314
(703) 789-9231
E-mail: usa.office@caari.org.cy
Web Site: www.caari.org

FOUNDED: 1900

AREAS OF INTEREST:
The study of humanistic disciplines, such as
anthropology, archaeology, Biblical studies,
epigraphy, history, history of art and
architecture, literature, philology, prehistory
and topography, relating in particular to the
Middle East from prehistoric times to the
modern era.

Cyprus American Archaeological Research
Institute is the only residential archaeological
institute on the island of Cyprus and serves
as a center for the dissemination of
information about the archaeology of Cyprus.

NAME(S) OF PROGRAMS:
● **The Anita Cecil O'Donovan Fellowship**
● **The Danielle Parks Memorial
  Fellowship**
● **The Helena Wylde Swiny and Stuart
  Swiny Fellowship**

TYPE:
Fellowships; Research grants; Residencies;
Travel grants. There are a large variety of
fellowships available through the Near
Eastern Fellowship Program for the
American Schools of Oriental Research and
affiliated overseas research centers. Besides
The Cyprus American Archaeological
Research Institute in Nicosia, Cyprus
(CAARI), there are also The American
Center of Oriental Research in Amman,
Jordan (ACOR) and the W.F. Albright
Institute of Archaeological Research in
Jerusalem, Israel (AIAR). Contact the
American Schools of Oriental Research for
full details.

The Anita Cecil O'Donovan Fellowship is an
award to a graduate student of any
nationality, enrolled in a graduate program in
any nation, to pursue research on a project
relevant to the archaeology and/or culture of
Cyprus.

The Danielle Parks Memorial Fellowship is
for a graduate student of any nationality who
needs to work in Cyprus to further his or her
research on a subject of relevance to Cypriot
archaeology and culture.

The Helena Wylde Swiny and Stuart Swiny
Fellowship is a grant to a graduate student of
any nationality in a U.S. or Canadian
university or college to pursue a research
project relevant to an ongoing field project in
Cyprus or that requires work on Cyprus
itself.

YEAR PROGRAM STARTED: 1940

PURPOSE:
To help scholars undertake high-quality
research and field projects in the Middle
East; to encourage interdisciplinary study and
communication among scholars.

LEGAL BASIS:
Nonprofit, archaeological research
corporation.

ELIGIBILITY:
All ASOR awards are open to qualified
students and scholars from any country.
Applicants must be affiliated with an
institution that is a member of the ASOR
corporation or must be an individual
professional member. Prime consideration is
given to applicants whose projects are
affiliated with ASOR.

ASOR does not conduct the competition nor
take part in the selection process for the
Fulbright Fellowships, but encourages
qualified scholars to apply for these awards.

FINANCIAL DATA:
The Anita Cecil O'Donovan Fellowship and
The Helena Wylde Swiny and Stuart Swiny
Fellowship will be used to fund research time
in residence at CAARI and to help defray
costs of travel.

The Danielle Parks Memorial Fellowship
covers travel to and living expenses in
Cyprus.
Amount of support per award: $2,000 each.
Total amount of support: $6,000.

NO. MOST RECENT APPLICANTS: 13 for the year
2020.

NO. AWARDS: 1 each.

APPLICATION INFO:
Application form is available on the Institute
web site. All eligible persons are encouraged
to apply for as many fellowships and
professorships as they wish, but a person can
hold only one award at a time. Persons who
have received an award in one year can
reapply for the same or other awards the
following year, but new applicants will have
priority.
Duration: One-time awards.
Deadline: December.

ADDRESS INQUIRIES TO:
See e-mail address above.

*SPECIAL STIPULATIONS:
For the O'Donovan, Parks and Swiny
Fellowships, residence at CAARI is
mandatory.

For the Danielle Parks Memorial Fellowship,
the fellow is expected during his or her stay
to give a presentation at CAARI on a subject
related to his or her research. The fellow will
periodically keep the Director of CAARI
apprised of his or her research activities and
will acknowledge CAARI and the Danielle
Parks Memorial Fellowship in any
publication that emerges from the research
carried during the Fellowship.

CYPRUS AMERICAN
ARCHAEOLOGICAL RESEARCH
INSTITUTE   [839]
209 Commerce Street
Alexandria, VA 22314
(703) 789-9231
E-mail: usa.office@caari.org.cy
Web Site: www.caari.org

FOUNDED: 1900

AREAS OF INTEREST:
The study of humanistic disciplines, such as
anthropology, archaeology, Biblical studies,
epigraphy, history, history of art and
architecture, literature, philology, prehistory
and topography, relating in particular to the
Middle East from prehistoric times to the
modern era.

Cyprus American Archaeological Research
Institute is the only residential archaeological
institute on the island of Cyprus and serves
as a center for the dissemination of
information about the archaeology of Cyprus.

NAME(S) OF PROGRAMS:
● **CAARI/CAORC Research Fellowships**
● **Edgar J. Peltenburg Postdoctoral
  Research Fellowship in Cypriot
  Prehistory**

TYPE:
Fellowships; Research grants; Travel grants.
CAARI/CAORC Research Fellowships are
designed for scholars who already have their
Ph.Ds., whose research engages the
archaeology, history, culture, or geography of
Cyprus, and who would derive significant
benefits from a month's research time on the
island.

The Edgar J. Peltenburg Postdoctoral
Research Fellowship honors the late
Professor Edgar Peltenburg and provides a
stipend to conduct research on Cypriot
prehistory (from the first visitors to the
transition to the Iron Age).

PURPOSE:
To help scholars undertake high-quality research and field projects in the Middle East; to encourage interdisciplinary study and communication among scholars.

LEGAL BASIS:
Nonprofit, archaeological research corporation.

ELIGIBILITY:
CAARI/CAORC Research Fellowship: Scholars who already have their Ph.D., whose research engages the archaeology, history, culture, or geography of Cyprus, may apply. Applicants must be U.S. citizens. Particular consideration is given to applicants whose projects enable them to include Cyprus in their teaching.

Edgar J. Peltenburg Postdoctoral Research Fellowship: Applicants of all nationalities are encouraged to apply provided they have been awarded a Ph.D. by the start of the fellowship. Although the fellowship is open to scholars of all ages, priority will be given to early career candidates who have received their Ph.D. within five years of the start of the fellowship.

FINANCIAL DATA:
Amount of support per award:
CAARI/CAORC Research Fellowship: $5,500 (up to $1,500 for transportation and up to $4,000 for research expenses on the island); Peltenburg Fellowship: $14,000 stipend and up to $1,500 travel expenses for those traveling to Cyprus from abroad.

NO. AWARDS: CAARI/CAORC Research Fellowship: 2.

APPLICATION INFO:
Application form is available on the Institute web site. All eligible persons are encouraged to apply for as many fellowships as they wish, but a person can hold only one award at a time. Persons who have received an award in one year can reapply for the same or other awards the following year, but new applicants will have priority.

Duration: CAARI/CAORC Research Fellowship: Minimum one month. Peltenburg Fellowship: Nine months. Renewable in exceptional cases for an additional nine months.

Deadline: January.

ADDRESS INQUIRIES TO:
See e-mail address above.

*SPECIAL STIPULATIONS:
A minimum of 30 days residence at CAARI is required for the CAARI/CAORC Research Fellowship.

Peltenburg Fellow will normally be expected to reside at CAARI for the duration of the fellowship. In addition, he or she is expected to play an active role in the CAARI community and contribute to the academic environment with research-related and/or outreach events.

THE LADY DAVIS FELLOWSHIP TRUST   [840]
The Sprinzak Building, Room 103
The Edmond Safra Campus, Hebrew University
Jerusalem 91904 Israel
(972) 2-651-2306 (voice mail)
(972) 2-658-4723
Fax: (972) 2-566-3848
E-mail: ld.fellows@mail.huji.ac.il
Web Site: ldft.huji.ac.il

FOUNDED: 1973

NAME(S) OF PROGRAMS:
● **Postdoctoral Researchers Fellowship**
● **Visiting Professorships Fellowship**

TYPE:
Fellowships.

YEAR PROGRAM STARTED: 1973

LEGAL BASIS:
University association.

ELIGIBILITY:
Postdoctoral Researchers: If applying for academic year 2020-21, must have received Doctorate no earlier than October 1, 2015.

Visiting Professorships: Must be a full or associate professor and have an academic sponsor.

FINANCIAL DATA:
The Trust pays round-trip airfare from the fellow's country of origin to Israel and half the medical insurance if purchased and paid for in Israel.
Amount of support per award: Postdoctoral Researchers: $1,485 (per month) for candidates who have held their Doctorates for less than two years before they take up the fellowship. Postdoctoral candidates who have their Doctorates for more than two years will receive $1,641 (per month) plus rental allowance; Visiting Professorships: $2,711 (per month).

APPLICATION INFO:
Prospective candidates must establish contact with the relevant department at the Hebrew University, and ensure that there is a faculty member willing to sponsor the application.
Duration: Postdoctoral Researchers: Nine to 12 months. May request an extension of one year only. Visiting Professorships: Two to four months.
Deadline: Postdoctoral Researchers: December 31. Visiting Professorships: November 30.

*SPECIAL STIPULATIONS:
Fellowships may not be deferred from one year to the next.

Fellows who have won another concurrent fellowship must disclose this to the Trust, whereupon the amount of the award will be reviewed.

A Fellow is expected to take up the Fellowship within the period of the academic year for which he has applied (in other words, between October 1 and September 30 in the following year). Attempts are made to be as elastic as possible should a Fellow expect to arrive before or after October 1.

EMBASSY OF FRANCE IN THE U.S., SCAC   [841]
4101 Reservoir Road, N.W.
Washington, DC 20007
(202) 944-6000
Fax: (202) 944-6268
E-mail: hss.coordinator@chateaubriand-fellowship.org
Web Site: frenchhighereducation.org

FOUNDED: 1980

AREAS OF INTEREST:
Higher education, study abroad, research, France, and French language.

NAME(S) OF PROGRAMS:
● **Chateaubriand Humanities & Social Sciences (HSS) Fellowship Program**
● **France on Campus Award**
● **Teaching Assistant Program in France**
● **Transatlantic Mobility Program**

TYPE:
Assistantships; Exchange programs; Fellowships; Grants-in-aid; Project/program grants; Research grants; Training grants; Travel grants. Chateaubriand Fellowship Program: Offered by the embassy of France in the U.S., each year this program allows doctoral students enrolled in American universities to conduct research in France for up to nine months.

Teaching Assistant Program in France: The French Ministry of Education and the Cultural Services Department of the French Embassy in Washington, DC offer over 1,100 teaching assistantships each year for American citizens and permanent residents of the U.S. to teach English in French schools. Assistants may work in primary schools or secondary schools.

YEAR PROGRAM STARTED: 1980

PURPOSE:
To promote the exchange of ideas between France and the U.S.

LEGAL BASIS:
Embassy.

ELIGIBILITY:
Details are available online.

FINANCIAL DATA:
Amount of support per award: Chateaubriand Fellowship Program: EUR 1,500 monthly, a round-trip ticket to France and health insurance; France on Campus Award: $500 to $2,000 per project; Teaching Assistant Program in France: EUR 785 per month; Transatlantic Mobility Program: Up to $15,000 per U.S. higher education institution.

NO. AWARDS: Chateaubriand Fellowship Program: 10 to 15; France on Campus Award: 3 to 10; Teaching Assistant Program in France: Over 1,100; Transatlantic Mobility Program: 6 to 8.

APPLICATION INFO:
Details are available online.
Duration: Chateaubriand Fellowship Program: Four or eight months; Teaching Assistant Program in France: Seven months.
Deadline: Details are available online.

ADDRESS INQUIRIES TO:
Chateaubriand Fellowship Program
E-mail:
hss.coordinator@chateaubriand-fellowship.org
France on Campus Award
E-mail: franceoncampus@frenchculture.org
Teaching Assistant Program in France:
E-mail:
teaching-assistant-program@frenchculture.org
Transatlantic Mobility Program
E-mail:
transatlanticmobilityprogram@ambafrance-us.org

THE GARDEN CLUB OF AMERICA
14 East 60th Street, Third Floor
New York, NY 10022
(212) 753-8287
Fax: (212) 753-0134
E-mail: scholarshipapplications@gcamerica.org
Web Site: www.gcamerica.org/scholarships

TYPE:
Exchange programs; Fellowships. A graduate academic year in the U.S. for a British

student and a work-study program for an American at universities and botanical gardens in the U.K. in fields related to horticulture, botany and landscape design.

See entry 1993 for full listing.

THE GARDEN CLUB OF AMERICA

14 East 60th Street, Third Floor
New York, NY 10022
(212) 753-8287
Fax: (212) 753-0134
E-mail: scholarshipapplications@gcamerica.org
Web Site: www.gcamerica.org/scholarships

TYPE:
Research grants. Financial assistance to college seniors and graduate students to study habitat-related issues that will benfit threatened or endangered bird species and lend useful information for land management decisions.

See entry 1994 for full listing.

GERMAN ACADEMIC EXCHANGE SERVICE   [842]

871 United Nations Plaza, 14th Floor
New York, NY 10017
(212) 758-3223
Fax: (212) 755-5780
E-mail: daadny@daad.org
Web Site: www.daad.org

FOUNDED: 1925

AREAS OF INTEREST:
International exchanges in education, research in higher education, and academic teaching staff; scholarships to German and foreign students.

CONSULTING OR VOLUNTEER SERVICES:
DAAD serves on a consultancy service in the field of international academic mobility.

NAME(S) OF PROGRAMS:
- **DAAD Emigre Memorial German Internship Program (EMGIP-Bundestag)**
- **DAAD German Studies Research Grant**
- **DAAD Research Grant**
- **DAAD Research Internships in Science and Engineering (RISE)**
- **DAAD Research Stays for University Academics and Scientists**
- **DAAD RISE Professional**
- **DAAD Study Scholarship**
- **DAAD University Summer Course Grant**
- **DAAD Visiting Professorship**

TYPE:
Awards/prizes; Conferences/seminars; Exchange programs; Fellowships; Internships; Professorships; Project/program grants; Research grants; Scholarships; Visiting scholars. The German Academic Exchange Service is the New York office of the Deutscher Akademischer Austausch Dienst (DAAD), a German organization with its head office in Bonn. DAAD offers a wide range of opportunities to students, scholars and higher education institutions of the U.S. and Canada, from undergraduate students to faculty, for study and research in Germany.

PURPOSE:
To provide information on study and research opportunities in higher education at home and abroad; to promote international higher

education and research through scholarships; to recruit and place German academic teaching staff from all disciplines at foreign institutions of higher education; to maintain a network of former scholarship holders abroad.

LEGAL BASIS:
Registered association under private law.

ELIGIBILITY:
DAAD grants are available to faculty and students in the U.S. and Canada to participate in a wide variety of academic activities. Funding is restricted to travel to Germany, including German higher education institutions, research institutions and archives in Germany.

GEOG. RESTRICTIONS: United States and Canada.

FINANCIAL DATA:
Amount of support per award: Varies.
Total amount of support: Varies.

APPLICATION INFO:
Application information is available on the web site.
Duration: Varies.
Deadline: Varies.

PUBLICATIONS:
Grants for Study and Research in Germany.

ADDRESS INQUIRIES TO:
See contact form on DAAD web site.

GERMAN HISTORICAL INSTITUTE

1607 New Hampshire Avenue, N.W.
Washington, DC 20009-2562
(202) 387-3355
E-mail: fellowships@ghi-dc.org
Web Site: www.ghi-dc.org

TYPE:
Fellowships. The Institute awards short-term fellowships to German and American doctoral students as well as postdoctoral scholars/Habilitanden in the fields of German history, the history of German-American relations, and the role of Germany and the U.S. in international relations.

See entry 548 for full listing.

GRADUATE WOMEN INTERNATIONAL (GWI)

Chemin du Grand-Montfleury, 48
CH-1290 Versoix Geneva Switzerland
(41) 22 731 23 80
Fax: (41) 22 738 04 40
E-mail: gwi@graduatewomen.org
Web Site: www.graduatewomen.org

TYPE:
Awards/prizes; Fellowships; Internships; Research grants; Training grants. Graduate Women International fellowships and grants are awarded triennially to encourage and enable women graduates to undertake original research or obtain further training in the humanities, social sciences and natural sciences.

See entry 988 for full listing.

THE HAGUE ACADEMY OF INTERNATIONAL LAW

Peace Palace
Carnegieplein 2
2517 KJ The Hague The Netherlands
(31) 70 3024242
E-mail: registration@hagueacademy.nl
Web Site: www.hagueacademy.nl

TYPE:
Project/program grants. Study programs. Residential scholarships for doctoral candidates from developing countries whose thesis, in private international law or public international law, is in the process of completion, who reside in their home country and who do not have access to scientific sources.

See entry 1804 for full listing.

THE HAGUE ACADEMY OF INTERNATIONAL LAW

Peace Palace
Carnegieplein 2
2517 KJ The Hague The Netherlands
(31) 70 3024242
E-mail: registration@hagueacademy.nl
Web Site: www.hagueacademy.nl

TYPE:
Project/program grants; Scholarships. Study programs. A limited number of scholarships are given to cover tuition and living expenses while studying at the three-week summer session of the Hague Academy of International Law. Because of the limited number, granting of scholarships is based solely on academic merit.

See entry 1805 for full listing.

THE HAGUE ACADEMY OF INTERNATIONAL LAW

Peace Palace
Carnegieplein 2
2517 KJ The Hague The Netherlands
(31) 70 3024242
E-mail: centre@hagueacademy.nl
Web Site: www.hagueacademy.nl

TYPE:
Project/program grants.

See entry 1802 for full listing.

THE HAGUE ACADEMY OF INTERNATIONAL LAW

Peace Palace
Carnegieplein 2
2517 KJ The Hague The Netherlands
(31) 70 3024242
E-mail: registration@hagueacademy.nl
Web Site: www.hagueacademy.nl

TYPE:
Project/program grants. External Programme is held each year, in turn in Africa, Asia and Latin America, upon the invitation of host governments or international organizations. It is designed for approximately 20 participants from the countries in the region (who are resident in their own country), whose traveling expenses are usually financed by the Academy and whose accommodation is financed by the government of the host state or organization. In addition, 20 participants come from the host state itself.

See entry 1803 for full listing.

HEINRICH HERTZ-STIFTUNG [843]

Ministerium fuer Kultur und Wissenschaft
des Landes Nordrhein-Westfalen
Heinrich Hertz-Stiftung
Voelklinger Strasse 49
D-40221 Duesseldorf Germany
(49) 211 896-4266
Fax: (49) 211 896-4407
E-mail: martina.schoeler@heinrich-hertz-stiftung.nrw.de
Web Site: www.heinrich-hertz-stiftung.de

FOUNDED: 1961

AREAS OF INTEREST:
International exchange of scientists.

TYPE:
Exchange programs; Scholarships.
Scholarships to promote the sciences through
the exchange of university teachers and
young scientists (without special restrictions).

YEAR PROGRAM STARTED: 1962

PURPOSE:
To promote sciences.

LEGAL BASIS:
Public foundation.

ELIGIBILITY:
University teachers and young scientists are
eligible. Non-German citizens should have a
working knowledge of German and German
citizens a working knowledge of the
language of the host country.

GEOG. RESTRICTIONS: Land
Nordrhine-Westphalia.

FINANCIAL DATA:
Amount of support per award: Award values
are dependent upon individual needs.
Total amount of support: Varies.

NO. MOST RECENT APPLICANTS: 14.

NO. AWARDS: 12 for the year 2019.

APPLICATION INFO:
Applications should be submitted only by
third persons. A curriculum vitae,
examination record, two references and a full
description of the planned project with a
timetable are to be included. Further
information may be obtained on request.
Duration: Dependent upon individual needs.
Two years maximum.

PUBLICATIONS:
Hinweise auf die Antragstellung; *Die
Heinrich Hertz-Stiftung*, booklet; Heinrich
Hertz-Stiftung, folder.

STAFF:
Susanne Schneider-Salomon, Chief Executive
Officer
Martina Schoeler, Head of Office

ADDRESS INQUIRIES TO:
Ministerium fuer Kultur und Wissenschaft
des Landes Nordrhein-Westfalen
Heinrich Hertz-Stiftung
(See address above.)

INSTITUTE FOR THE INTERNATIONAL EDUCATION OF STUDENTS (IES)

33 West Monroe Street
Suite 2300
Chicago, IL 60603-5405
(312) 944-1750
(800) 995-2300
Fax: (312) 944-1448
E-mail: info@IESabroad.org
Web Site: www.IESabroad.org

TYPE:
Awards/prizes; Scholarships. Boren and
Gilman Scholarship Support Grants: This
program offers recipients of these prestigious
scholarships the opportunity to apply for
additional financial support.

Disability Grants: This program's purpose is
to enhance study abroad opportunities for
students with disabilities. It offers grants to
students whose disabilities may add
significant costs to their study abroad
experience.

Diversity Scholarships: This program offers
one way to encourage and support students
from a range of institutions and
underrepresented populations.
Underrepresented students include students
from underrepresented racial and ethnic
groups, first-generation-to-college students,
students from low-income families and
students with a history of overcoming
adversity.

Donor Funded Scholarships: These
scholarship opportunities have been created
through the generosity of various donors who
support the important mission of IES Abroad.

Need Based Aid: This program is available
to students with demonstrated financial need.
Priority is given to Pell Grant recipients.

Partner University Scholarships: These
scholarships are funded by IES Abroad
partner universities in countries where IES
has programs.

Public University Grants: This program offers
an automatic $2,000 credit toward a semester
or academic year program.

See entry 1534 for full listing.

INSTITUTE OF INTERNATIONAL EDUCATION [844]

Fulbright U.S. Student Program
809 United Nations Plaza
New York, NY 10017-3580
(800) 272-6994
E-mail: fbstudent@iie.org
Web Site: www.us.fulbrightonline.org

FOUNDED: 1919

AREAS OF INTEREST:
International educational and cultural
exchange for graduate-level students and
early career professionals.

NAME(S) OF PROGRAMS:
● **Fulbright U.S. Student Program**

TYPE:
Exchange programs; Scholarships. Grants for
graduate study, research or English Teaching
Assistantships abroad.

YEAR PROGRAM STARTED: 1946

PURPOSE:
To give U.S. students the opportunity to live,
study, teach or do research in a foreign
country for one academic year and to
increase mutual understanding between the
people of the U.S. and other countries
through the exchange of persons, knowledge
and skills.

LEGAL BASIS:
Nonprofit, as described under Internal
Revenue Code 501(c)(3).

ELIGIBILITY:
The program is open to all disciplines and
fields of study, except medical degree study.
Candidates must possess U.S. citizenship, a
Bachelor's degree by the beginning date of
the grant, language proficiency sufficient to
carry out the project overseas and good
health. Preference in selecting candidates is
for those who have had the majority of high
school and undergraduate college education
at educational institutions in the U.S and
little experience living, studying or working
in the country of application. Candidates may
not hold a doctoral degree at the time of
application.

FINANCIAL DATA:
Fulbright Grants provide round-trip
transportation, orientation program, books,
maintenance for one academic year and
health benefits package. Some country
programs may provide tuition and language
study courses. The maintenance allowance is
based on living costs in the host country and
is sufficient to meet normal expenses of a
single person at the graduate-study level.
Dependents allowances vary by country.
Amount of support per award: Varies by
country.

CO-OP FUNDING PROGRAMS: Funds from other
scholarships, fellowships or grants in dollars
or foreign currency received concurrently
with a Fulbright Grant will be deducted if
they duplicate the Fulbright benefits. No
deduction is made if other grants are for
assistance in meeting family expenses of
grantees or other expenses not covered by the
grant.

NO. MOST RECENT APPLICANTS: 10,400.

NO. AWARDS: Approximately 2,500.

APPLICATION INFO:
Enrolled students should contact the
Fulbright Program Adviser on their campus.
Candidates who are not enrolled in an
educational institution should contact IIE,
U.S. Student Programs Division, at the
address above.
Duration: One academic year.
Deadline: Enrolled students should submit
their applications to their campus Fulbright
Program Advisers by the dates set by them.
At-large candidates must submit their
applications to the IIE office in October.

ADDRESS INQUIRIES TO:
Daniel Kramer, Director of
Fulbright U.S. Student Program
(See address above.)

INTERNATIONAL DEVELOPMENT RESEARCH CENTRE (IDRC)

150 Kent Street
Ottawa ON K1P 0B2 Canada
(613) 696-2098
E-mail: awards@idrc.ca
Web Site: www.idrc.ca
www.crdi.ca

TYPE:
Internships. Program provides training in
research management and grant
administration under the guidance of Centre
program staff. Approximately 50% of the
time spent on own research project.

See entry 1194 for full listing.

INTERNATIONAL DEVELOPMENT RESEARCH CENTRE (IDRC)

150 Kent Street
Ottawa ON K1P 0B2 Canada
(613) 696-2098
E-mail: awards@idrc.ca
Web Site: www.idrc.ca
www.crdi.ca

TYPE:
Fellowships. Fellowship is awarded for research on the relationship between forest resources and the social, economic, cultural and environmental welfare of people in developing countries.

See entry 1192 for full listing.

INTERNATIONAL RESEARCH & EXCHANGES BOARD (IREX) [845]

1275 K Street, N.W.
Suite 600
Washington, DC 20005
(202) 628-8188
Fax: (202) 628-8189
E-mail: irex@irex.org
Web Site: www.irex.org

FOUNDED: 1968

AREAS OF INTEREST:
Academic research exchanges and professional training programs in Europe, Eurasia, the Middle East and North Africa, and Asia.

NAME(S) OF PROGRAMS:
- **International Leaders in Education Program (ILEP)**
- **Regional Assistance Program (RAP)**
- **Teaching Excellence and Achievement Program (TEA)**

TYPE:
Conferences/seminars; Exchange programs; Fellowships; Project/program grants; Research grants; Training grants; Travel grants; Visiting scholars. ILEP: Grants to secondary teachers from around the globe to the U.S. to further develop expertise in their subject areas, enhance their teaching skills, and increase their knowledge about the U.S.

Regional Assistance Program (RAP) works with civil society organizations to advance political, social and economic reform across the Middle East and North Africa.

TEA: Grants to secondary-school teachers from Eurasia and South Asia with unique opportunities to develop expertise in their subject areas, enhance their teaching skills, and increase their knowledge about the U.S.

YEAR PROGRAM STARTED: 1968

PURPOSE:
To promote advanced field research and professional training programs between the U.S. and the countries of Europe, Eurasia, Asia and the Middle East and North Africa.

LEGAL BASIS:
Nonprofit organization.

GEOG. RESTRICTIONS: United States, Europe, Eurasia, the Middle East, Asia and North Africa.

FINANCIAL DATA:
Amount of support per award: Varies per program.

APPLICATION INFO:
Application information is available upon request.

PUBLICATIONS:
Policy papers, application materials.

ADDRESS INQUIRIES TO:
Program Coordinator
(See address above.)

ISTITUTO ITALIANO PER GLI STUDI STORICI

Via Benedetto Croce, 12
80134 Naples Italy
(39) 081 5517159
(39) 081 5512390
Fax: (39) 081 5514813
E-mail: info@iiss.it
Web Site: www.iiss.it

TYPE:
Awards/prizes; Conferences/seminars; Research grants; Scholarships. Awards for historical, literature and philosophical studies at the Istituto Italiano per gli Studi Storici in Naples.

Federico II Scholarship: Funded by the Universita di Napoli Federico II for graduates from Italian universities with medieval studies final dissertation.

See entry 556 for full listing.

JAPAN INFORMATION CENTER [846]

Consulate General of Japan
299 Park Avenue, 18th Floor
New York, NY 10171
(212) 418-4463
E-mail: scholarship@ny.mofa.go.jp
Web Site: www.ny.us.emb-japan.go.jp

FOUNDED: 1955

AREAS OF INTEREST:
Japanese language and cultural studies.

NAME(S) OF PROGRAMS:
- **Japanese Government (Monbukagakusho) Scholarships for Japanese Studies**

TYPE:
Scholarships. Undergraduate scholarships awarded to foreign students who wish to pursue Japanese language and cultural studies in Japan. The program offers students an intensive course of Japanese language and introduction to Japanese studies in various aspects.

YEAR PROGRAM STARTED: 1955

PURPOSE:
To provide funding for non-Japanese students who want to pursue a course of Japanese and cultural studies in Japan.

LEGAL BASIS:
Japanese government agency.

ELIGIBILITY:
Applicants must:
(1) be nationals of the country to which the scholarships are offered;
(2) be at least 18 years and less than 29 years of age as of April 1 of the year of application;
(3) be regular students who follow an undergraduate course at a university in their own country or a third country and who are mainly first- to third-year Bachelor's students or above in that course;
(4) be specializing in a field concerning Japanese language or Japanese culture at their university;

(5) have good knowledge of the Japanese language and;
(6) be in good health.

Applicants must have a background in Japanese studies to qualify. A written Japanese examination will be given to selected applicants before being considered by the government offices in Japan.

FINANCIAL DATA:
Amount of support per award: Varies.
Total amount of support: Varies.

NO. AWARDS: Varies.

APPLICATION INFO:
Applicants should contact the appropriate Japanese consulate. Consulates General are located in Anchorage, Atlanta, Boston, Chicago, Denver, Detroit, Hagatna (Guam), Honolulu, Houston, Los Angeles, Miami, Nashville, New York City, Portland, Saipan, San Francisco, Seattle, and Washington, DC.
Duration: One academic year.
Deadline: Varies.

PUBLICATIONS:
Application guidelines.

ADDRESS INQUIRIES TO:
Local Japanese Consulate General

*PLEASE NOTE:
Placement of grantees to universities will be decided by Monbukagakusho after consultation with the universities concerned.

JAPAN INFORMATION CENTER [847]

Consulate General of Japan
299 Park Avenue, 18th Floor
New York, NY 10171
(212) 418-4463
Fax: (212) 371-1294
E-mail: scholarship@ny.mofa.go.jp
Web Site: www.ny.us.emb-japan.go.jp

FOUNDED: 1955

AREAS OF INTEREST:
Humanities and social sciences: literature, history, aesthetics, law, politics, economics, commerce, pedagogy, psychology, sociology, music, fine arts, natural sciences, pure science, engineering, agriculture, fisheries, pharmacology, medicine, dentistry and home economics.

NAME(S) OF PROGRAMS:
- **Japanese Government (Monbukagakusho) Scholarships for Research Students**

TYPE:
Scholarships. Graduate scholarships awarded to foreign students who wish to study at Japanese universities as nondegree research students.

PURPOSE:
To help students wishing to pursue Japan-related studies.

LEGAL BASIS:
Japanese government agency.

ELIGIBILITY:
Applicants must:
(1) be nationals of the country to which the scholarships are offered;
(2) be under 36 years of age as of April 1 of the year of the award;
(3) be university or college Bachelor or Master's degree graduates;
(4) be willing to study the Japanese language

and to receive instruction in that language and;

(5) be in good health.

The study area must be in the same field as the applicant has studied (or is now studying) or a related one.

FINANCIAL DATA:
Amount of support per award: Varies.
Total amount of support: Varies.

NO. AWARDS: Varies.

APPLICATION INFO:
Applicants should contact the appropriate Japanese consulate. Consulates General are located in Anchorage, Atlanta, Boston, Chicago, Denver, Detroit, Hagatna (Guam), Honolulu, Houston, Los Angeles, Miami, Nashville, New York City, Portland, Saipan, San Francisco, Seattle, and Washington, DC.
Duration: 18 months to two years, including a six-month language course.
Deadline: Varies.

PUBLICATIONS:
Application guidelines.

ADDRESS INQUIRIES TO:
Local Japanese Consulate General

*PLEASE NOTE:
Field of study must be one of those available at the Japanese universities and practical training given by factories or companies is excluded.

HERBERT D. KATZ CENTER FOR ADVANCED JUDAIC STUDIES   [848]
420 Walnut Street
Philadelphia, PA 19106
(215) 746-1290
E-mail: carrielo@upenn.edu
Web Site: katz.sas.upenn.edu

AREAS OF INTEREST:
Advanced research in Judaic and related studies.

NAME(S) OF PROGRAMS:
● **Judaic and Related Studies Postdoctoral Fellowships**

TYPE:
Fellowships.

PURPOSE:
To support education in Judaic and related studies.

ELIGIBILITY:
Postdoctoral scholars in the humanities, social sciences and the arts at all levels may apply. All scholars whose work fits within the proposed research topics are eligible to apply. National and international scholars who meet the application terms may apply. International scholars are appointed under a J-1 visa only. No exceptions can be made. Applicants should consult the international programs office at their current university to confirm eligibility before applying for this fellowship.

Fellowships may be granted for one semester or the full academic year. Scholars are required to spend the term of the fellowship in residence in Philadelphia at the Katz Center.

FINANCIAL DATA:
Amount of support per award: Up to $60,000.

NO. AWARDS: 20.

APPLICATION INFO:
Application information is available on the web site.
Duration: Up to one year. Fellowships are not renewable.
Deadline: Mid-September.

ADDRESS INQUIRIES TO:
Carrie Love
Fellowship Program Administrator
(See address above.)

KOBE COLLEGE CORPORATION-JAPAN EDUCATION EXCHANGE   [849]
540 West Frontage Road, Suite 3335
Northfield, IL 60093
(847) 386-7661
Fax: (847) 386-7662
E-mail: programs@kccjee.org
Web Site: www.kccjee.org

AREAS OF INTEREST:
Japanese culture and language.

NAME(S) OF PROGRAMS:
● **The KCC-JEE High School Essay Contest**

TYPE:
Awards/prizes. The KCC-JEE High School Essay Contest includes a one-month trip to Japan. It incorporates intensive language study, college credit and a home stay with a Japanese family.

YEAR PROGRAM STARTED: 1995

PURPOSE:
To provide American high school students the opportunity to experience Japanese culture firsthand, enhancing their Japanese language skills and deepening their appreciation of Japanese culture and values by living in Japan for one month.

ELIGIBILITY:
Applicant must meet the following requirements:
(1) be an American citizen or permanent resident alien, 16 years of age by June 1 of the year contest is held;
(2) must have had at least one year of accredited Japanese language study;
(3) attend a public or private high school in the U.S. and;
(4) be available to study during the four weeks established for this program.

GEOG. RESTRICTIONS: United States.

FINANCIAL DATA:
Prize includes round-trip airfare, tuition, and room and board in a Japanese home.
Amount of support per award: Approximately $4,000.

APPLICATION INFO:
Application and complete information can be found online.
Duration: One summer month (typically July). Nonrenewable.
Deadline: February.

THE KOSCIUSZKO FOUNDATION, INC.   [850]
15 East 65th Street
New York, NY 10065
(212) 734-2130 ext. 412
E-mail: addy@thekf.org
Web Site: www.thekf.org/kf/programs/study

FOUNDED: 1925

AREAS OF INTEREST:
Strengthening of cultural and educational bonds between the U.S. and Poland through an exchange program to Poland for the purpose of Polish language, culture and history studies.

NAME(S) OF PROGRAMS:
● **Summer Study Abroad Programs**

TYPE:
Exchange programs; Scholarships. Summer programs. The Summer Study Abroad Programs offer a variety of courses from July through August at the Jagiellonian University in Krakow and at the John Paul II Catholic University of Lublin, Poland. Polish language, culture, history, art and many other subjects are available. The Foundation sponsors this program mainly for paying students; however, the Tomaszkiewicz-Florio and Frances E. Wyszynski Scholarships are available for the program at the Jagiellonian University in Krakow.

YEAR PROGRAM STARTED: 1970

PURPOSE:
To enable American students to pursue a short-term course of Polish language, culture, history and art studies abroad.

LEGAL BASIS:
501(c)(3) not-for-profit organization.

ELIGIBILITY:
The Summer Study Abroad Programs are open to U.S. undergraduate and graduate students as well as graduating high school students who will be 18 years of age by the first day of the program.

Students of Polish descent can apply for funding to attend the Foundation's three-week program at the Jagiellonian University via the Foundation's Tomaszkiewicz-Florio Scholarship.

GEOG. RESTRICTIONS: United States.

FINANCIAL DATA:
Program fee includes tuition, course materials, cultural events and sightseeing trips, a language placement test, language classes, afternoon classes, shared dormitory room, two meals a day and assistance from Polish university students. The scholarships which are available cover program fees for three-week programs at the Jagiellonian University in Krakow.
Amount of support per award: Varies.
Total amount of support: $31,860 awarded towards Summer Studies in Krakow for the year 2019.

NO. AWARDS: 18 for the year 2019.

APPLICATION INFO:
Required forms are available on the Summer Study Abroad Programs web page. There is a nonrefundable fee of $35.
Duration: Two- to eight-week programs are available.
Deadline: Mid-April for scholarship applicants. Mid-May for students who wish to pay their own way.

PUBLICATIONS:
KF Newsletter; annual report.

IRS I.D.: 13-1628179

STAFF:
Marek Skulimowski, President and Executive Director

ADDRESS INQUIRIES TO:
Addy Tymczyszyn, Coordinator
Summer Study Abroad Programs
(See e-mail address above.)

*PLEASE NOTE:
Students submit scholarship applications to
the Foundation's chapters. Pay-to-go
applicants must submit application materials
to Kosciuszko Foundation's headquarters in
New York City.

*SPECIAL STIPULATIONS:
Students who receive scholarships are
required to submit a report upon completion
of the program. The report is forwarded to
the donors of the scholarship.

THE KOSCIUSZKO
FOUNDATION, INC.   [851]
15 East 65th Street
New York, NY 10065
(212) 734-2130 ext. 413
E-mail: exchangetopoland@thekf.org
Web Site: www.thekf.
org/kf/scholarships/exchange-poland/year-abroad

FOUNDED: 1925

AREAS OF INTEREST:
Strengthening of cultural and educational
bonds between the U.S. and Poland through
an exchange program to Poland for the
purpose of Polish language, culture and
history studies.

NAME(S) OF PROGRAMS:
● **The Kosciuszko Foundation Year**
  Abroad Program

TYPE:
Exchange programs; Scholarships. The Year
Abroad Program at the Center for Polish
Language and Culture in the World,
Jagiellonian University (Krakow) offers
American students the opportunity to study
Polish language, history, literature and culture
for one academic year or one semester. This
program allows students to spend their
undergraduate junior or senior year in
Poland. Undergraduate credit may be
transferred. Students at the Master's level
may also apply.

PURPOSE:
To enable American students to pursue an
undergraduate course of Polish language,
literature, history and culture at the Center
for Polish Language and Culture, Jagiellonian
University, Krakow.

LEGAL BASIS:
501(c)(3) not-for-profit organization.

ELIGIBILITY:
U.S. citizens enrolled at a U.S. college or
university who will be entering their junior
or senior year can apply. Graduate students,
with the exception of those at the dissertation
level, can also apply. Minimum grade point
average of 3.0 is required.

GEOG. RESTRICTIONS: United States.

FINANCIAL DATA:
Scholarship offers a tuition waiver, housing
and a monthly stipend of 1,600 Polish zloty
per month from the Polish government
towards living expenses. Recipients also
receive $900 per semester from the
Foundation for living expenses.
Transportation to and from Poland and other
personal expenses are not included.

Amount of support per award: $900 per
semester plus additional funding from the
Polish National Agency for Academic
Exchange in the amount of 1,600 Polish
zloty per month of study.
Total amount of support: Varies.

NO. MOST RECENT APPLICANTS: 18.

NO. AWARDS: 7.

APPLICATION INFO:
Details are available on the Foundation web
site.
Duration: One semester (October to February
or February to June) or one academic year
(October to June).
Deadline: February 20. Notification in May.
Funding is for the following academic year.

PUBLICATIONS:
Guidelines; *KF Newsletter*; annual report.

IRS I.D.: 13-1628179

STAFF:
Marek Skulimowski, President and Executive
Director
Gosia Szymanska, Exchange Program Officer

ADDRESS INQUIRIES TO:
Gosia Szymanska, Exchange Program Officer
(See e-mail address above.)

THE KOSCIUSZKO
FOUNDATION, INC.   [852]
15 East 65th Street
New York, NY 10065
(212) 734-2130 ext. 413
E-mail: exchangetopoland@thekf.org
Web Site: www.thekf.
org/kf/scholarships/exchange-poland/research

FOUNDED: 1925

AREAS OF INTEREST:
Strengthening of cultural and educational
bonds between the U.S. and Poland through
an exchange program for graduate-level
students and scholars who wish to conduct
research programs in Poland.

NAME(S) OF PROGRAMS:
● **The Kosciuszko Foundation Graduate**
  Studies and Research in Poland

TYPE:
Exchange programs; Research grants;
Scholarships. This program enables American
students and scholars to pursue a course of
graduate or postgraduate study and research
in Poland. It is also open to university faculty
who wish to spend a sabbatical conducting
research in Poland.

Research may be conducted during the Polish
academic year, October through June only.

PURPOSE:
To assist Americans in continuing their
graduate and postgraduate studies and
research at institutions of higher learning in
Poland.

LEGAL BASIS:
501(c)(3) not-for-profit organization.

ELIGIBILITY:
U.S. citizens with strong Polish language
skills who wish to conduct research in
Poland may apply. Funding is granted for
research at institutions of higher learning in
Poland which fall under the jurisdiction of
the Polish National Agency for Academic
Exchange.

GEOG. RESTRICTIONS: United States.

FINANCIAL DATA:
Scholarship does not cover tuition costs.
Participants receive a stipend from the Polish
government towards housing and living
expenses. No provisions are made for
dependents. Transportation to and from
Poland is at the expense of the participant.
Personal expenses are not included.
Amount of support per award: $300 per
month of approved study/research, plus 1,600
zloty per month from the Polish National
Agency for Academic Exchange.
Total amount of support: Varies.

NO. MOST RECENT APPLICANTS: Approximately
10.

NO. AWARDS: 5.

APPLICATION INFO:
Details are available on the Foundation web
site.
Duration: Maximum of nine months.
Research may be conducted from October to
June.
Deadline: February 20. Notification in May
for funding in the following academic year.

PUBLICATIONS:
KF Newsletter; annual report.

IRS I.D.: 13-1628179

STAFF:
Marek Skulimowski, President and Executive
Director

ADDRESS INQUIRIES TO:
Gosia Szymanska, Exchange Program Officer
(See e-mail address above.)

THE KOSCIUSZKO
FOUNDATION, INC.   [853]
15 East 65th Street
New York, NY 10065
(212) 734-2130 ext. 407
E-mail: dorwat@thekf.org
Web Site: www.thekf.
org/kf/programs/teaching_english_in_poland

FOUNDED: 1925

AREAS OF INTEREST:
Educational and cultural exchange program
in Poland.

NAME(S) OF PROGRAMS:
● **Teaching English in Poland**

TYPE:
Summer educational and cultural exchange
program for American teachers and teaching
assistants in Poland.

YEAR PROGRAM STARTED: 1991

PURPOSE:
To provide Polish students with English
language experiences within an American
cultural context; to familiarize Polish students
with various aspects of American life and
culture; to introduce American teachers and
teaching assistants to Polish culture, history,
traditions and people of Poland so that their
knowledge and impressions will be shared.

LEGAL BASIS:
501(c)(3) not-for-profit organization.

ELIGIBILITY:
Experienced teachers/administrators certified
in the U.S., educators with private/parochial
school or other verifiable teaching
experience, college/university faculty, and
those engaged in student services (school
nurse, social worker, guidance counselor,
school psychologist, etc.) are eligible for

participation. Group flight arrangements will be made by the Foundation. Participants are encouraged to travel to Poland with the group.

GEOG. RESTRICTIONS: United States.

FINANCIAL DATA:
Registration fee of $300 for teachers and $250 for teaching assistants and peer tutors. Medical insurance, required by The Kosciuszko Foundation, is covered. This is a volunteer opportunity. Applicant pays for airfare. Room and board during the teaching program as well as sightseeing in Poland after the program's end are covered by Polish hosts.

Amount of support per award: Varies.

Matching fund requirements: In-kind donations such as art and sport equipment towards the program are accepted.

CO-OP FUNDING PROGRAMS: Delta Kappa Gamma support in the amount of $14,000.

NO. MOST RECENT APPLICANTS: 120.

NO. AWARDS: 31.

APPLICATION INFO:
Applications must be completed on the Foundation's web site.

Duration: Two and one-half to four weeks.

Deadline: January 31.

PUBLICATIONS:
KF Newsletter; Annual Report.

IRS I.D.: 13-1628179

STAFF:
Mary Kay Pieski, Ph.D.

ADDRESS INQUIRIES TO:
Teaching English in Poland Program
(See address above.)

THE ROBERTO LONGHI FOUNDATION FOR THE STUDY OF THE HISTORY OF ART

Via Benedetto Fortini, 30
50125 Florence Italy
(39) 055 6580794
Fax: (39) 055 6580794
E-mail: longhi@fondazionelonghi.it
Web Site: www.fondazionelonghi.it

TYPE:
Fellowships.

See entry 515 for full listing.

MARSHALL AID COMMEMORATION COMMISSION   [854]

ACU
Woburn House
20-24 Tavistock Square
London WC1H 9HF England
(44) 207 380 6704
(44) 207 380 6703
E-mail: apps@marshallscholarship.org
Web Site: www.marshallscholarship.org

FOUNDED: 1953

NAME(S) OF PROGRAMS:
● **Marshall Scholarships**

TYPE:
Scholarships. Tenable at any university in the U.K. in any subject leading to the award of a British university degree, which recipients are required to take.

Marshall Scholarships finance young Americans of high ability to study for a degree in the U.K. in a system of higher education recognized for its excellence. These grants have been established to express British gratitude for the European Recovery Program (the Marshall Plan) instituted by General of the Army George C. Marshall.

YEAR PROGRAM STARTED: 1954

PURPOSE:
To enable intellectually distinguished young Americans to study in the U.K.; to contribute to the advancement of knowledge in science, technology, the humanities and social sciences and the creative arts at Britain's centers of academic excellence.

LEGAL BASIS:
Programme established by British Parliamentary Act.

ELIGIBILITY:
Scholarships are offered to U.S. citizens for study in the U.K. Graduates of a degree-granting college or university who have graduated from their undergraduate college or university no more than three years before the year the award will be taken up are eligible (e.g., for awards tenable from October 2021, candidates must have graduated after April 2018). Candidates must be American citizens at the time of application and must have obtained a grade point average of not less than 3.7 (or A-).

FINANCIAL DATA:
Scholarships include a personal allowance, tuition fees, grants for books, travel, thesis and fares to and from Britain.

Amount of support per award: Currently GBP 1,110 per month (GBP 1,362 for those registered within the London Metropolitan Police district).

Total amount of support: GBP 2,550,000 for the year ended March 31, 2019.

NO. MOST RECENT APPLICANTS: Approximately 1,000.

NO. AWARDS: Up to 50 awards annually.

APPLICATION INFO:
Application should be made to a British Consulate-General (in Atlanta, Boston, Chicago, Houston, Los Angeles, New York and San Francisco) or to the British Embassy in Washington, DC.

Duration: One to two years. May be extended for a third year.

Deadline: Early October of the year preceding the award.

OFFICERS:
Caroline Harrison, Executive Secretary
Mary C. Denyer, Assistant Secretary

COMMISSION MEMBERS:
Christopher Fisher, Chairperson
Alan Bookbinder
Prof. Judith Buchanan
Adrian Greer
Suzanne McCarthy
Dr. Alice Prochaska
Prof. Adam Smith
Dr. Leslie Vinjamuri
Xenia Wickett
Lord Wood of Anfield

THE MATSUMAE INTERNATIONAL FOUNDATION   [855]

4-14-46, Kamiogi, Suginami-ku
Tokyo 167-0043 Japan
(81) 3-3301-7600
Fax: (81) 3-3301-7601
E-mail: contact@mif-japan.org
Web Site: www.mif-japan.org

FOUNDED: 1979

AREAS OF INTEREST:
Natural sciences, engineering and medicine are given first priority.

NAME(S) OF PROGRAMS:
● **Fellowship Program**

TYPE:
Fellowships; Research grants.

YEAR PROGRAM STARTED: 1980

PURPOSE:
To provide opportunity to foreign scientists to conduct research at Japanese institutions.

LEGAL BASIS:
Private foundation.

ELIGIBILITY:
Citizenship is unrestricted. Those of non-Japanese nationality who meet all of the following eligibility requirements are invited to submit the required application documents:
(1) Applicants must hold a Ph.D. degree, or be recognized by the Foundation as possessing equivalent academic qualifications;
(2) Applicants must be 49 years of age or under at the time of application;
(3) Applicants must have sufficient conversational ability in English or Japanese to prevent insurmountable difficulties during their research activities in Japan;
(4) Applicants should not have been in Japan in the past and/or in the present and;
(5) Applicants should have firm positions and professions in their home countries and should return to their countries upon completion of their fellowship stay by the Foundation.

FINANCIAL DATA:
Awards include stipend for research and stay, lump sum on arrival, round-trip travel and insurance.

Amount of support per award: Monthly allowance of JPY 220,000; lump sum on arrival of 120,000 JPY.

NO. MOST RECENT APPLICANTS: 852 researchers from 119 countries for the year 2019.

NO. AWARDS: Approximately 20 per year.

APPLICATION INFO:
Application form required. Applicants should obtain the current issue of the Fellowship Announcement from the Foundation. To obtain the announcement, write to the Foundation with name and address by postal mail, or by e-mail. The announcement can also be downloaded from the web page of the Foundation; the Application Form must be printed out in PDF format or MS Word file.

Application must be submitted from the applicant's home country. Under no circumstances will an application be accepted from a person already in Japan. The Foundation does not accept applications by fax or e-mail.

All documents must be typewritten in English. The following documents (A4 in size) must be included and submitted on one

occasion by the applicant:
(1) a photograph (taken within the last three months) along with the fully completed application form (signed and dated);
(2) a description of the research project by the applicant;
(3) complete list of publications;
(4) reprint of what the applicant considers to be his or her most important publication;
(5) a personal history (curriculum vitae);
(6) a letter of recommendation from the applicant's employer and/or supervisor testifying to academic ability and achievements and confirming the availability of study leave covering the grant period;
(7) a certified copy of the applicant's academic certificates (Ph.D., Master's, Bachelor's) issued by the university concerned (in English, or document with English translation attached) and;
(8) an invitation letter with signature from the host scientist confirming the period of stay, the research project, the availability of research facilities/materials and the arrangement of lodging accommodation under the Foundation Fellowship Program.

Submitted applications which do not contain all of the required documents will automatically be rejected.

The Foundation will not be responsible for costs incurred in submitting an application and reserves the right to request additional documents if necessary. All documents received become the property of the Foundation and will not be returned. The Foundation will not respond to individual inquiry concerning the status/arrival of application documents.

Duration: Three to six months; extension/reduction of the granted period is not allowed.

Deadline: Applications must be received by the Foundation by June 30 for the following year's fellowship.

PUBLICATIONS:
Program announcement.

ADDRESS INQUIRIES TO:
Fellowship Program
(See address above.)

*PLEASE NOTE:
To promote deeper understanding of Japan, the Foundation organizes a Study Tour during the invitation period in Japan.

Each year, the Foundation issues a "Research Report" containing summaries of research activities or results which are kindly submitted by the Fellows.

In order to keep in touch with Fellows after their return home, the Foundation issues a "Newsletter" and "Fellowship Directory" annually.

MICHIGAN STATE UNIVERSITY [856]
Office for Education Abroad
427 North Shaw Lane, Room 109
East Lansing, MI 48824
(517) 353-8920
Fax: (517) 432-2082
E-mail: abroad@msu.edu
Web Site: educationabroad.msu.edu

NAME(S) OF PROGRAMS:
● **MSU Education Abroad Scholarships**

TYPE:
Scholarships. Academic study abroad scholarships for college-level credit. The program includes over 275 overseas study programs in more than 60 countries in a wide variety of academic fields.

PURPOSE:
To assist Michigan State University students who will benefit from study abroad.

LEGAL BASIS:
University.

ELIGIBILITY:
Applicants must be MSU students. Participation in study abroad program is:
(1) based on financial need. Applicant must have FAFSA application on file with MSU office of financial aid and have a minimum 2.0 grade point average and;
(2) based on academic performance. Applicant must have a minimum 3.5 grade point average and submit an essay explaining how study abroad would enhance the student's education.

FINANCIAL DATA:
Amount of support per award: $250 to $1,750 available per student.
Total amount of support: Approximately $400,000 annually.

NO. MOST RECENT APPLICANTS: Approximately 1,200.

NO. AWARDS: Approximately 400 per year.

APPLICATION INFO:
Application information is available on the web site.
Duration: Varies.
Deadline: October 1 and March 1.

STAFF:
Lynn Aguado, Study Abroad Program Coordinator

ADDRESS INQUIRIES TO:
Jennifer Somerville, Budget and Financial Manager
E-mail: somervi5@msu.edu

NATIONAL SECURITY EDUCATION PROGRAM [857]
Boren Scholarships
Institute of International Education
1400 K Street, N.W., 7th Floor
Washington, DC 20005-2403
(800) 618-6737
E-mail: boren@iie.org
Web Site: www.borenawards.org

FOUNDED: 1991

AREAS OF INTEREST:
Languages and cultures of world regions that are critical to U.S. interests and underrepresented in study abroad, including Africa, Asia, Central and Eastern Europe, Eurasia, Latin America, and the Middle East.

NAME(S) OF PROGRAMS:
● **Boren Scholarships**

TYPE:
Scholarships. Boren Scholarships provide funding for U.S. undergraduate students to study less commonly taught languages in world regions that are critical to U.S. interests and underrepresented in study abroad.

PURPOSE:
To provide American undergraduates with the resources and encouragement they need to acquire language skills and cultural experiences in areas of the world critical to national security, broadly defined. In exchange for funding, recipients commit to working in the federal government for a minimum of one year after graduation.

ELIGIBILITY:
Must be a U.S. citizen at the time of application. Open to high school graduates, or those who have earned a GED, and are matriculated as a freshman, sophomore, junior, or senior in a U.S. postsecondary institution, including universities, colleges, and community colleges. Applicant must plan to study abroad in Africa, Asia, Central and Eastern Europe, Eurasia, or the Middle East. The countries of Western Europe, Canada, Australia, and New Zealand are excluded. The study abroad program must meet home institution standards and end prior to graduation.

FINANCIAL DATA:
Amount of support per award: Summer: Up to $8,000; Semester: Up to $10,000; Full academic year: Up to $20,000.

NO. MOST RECENT APPLICANTS: 851.

NO. AWARDS: 244.

APPLICATION INFO:
Complete details and application information can be found on the Boren Awards web site.
Duration: Summer (minimum eight weeks), fall or spring semester, and full academic year.
Deadline: February 5.

ADDRESS INQUIRIES TO:
See e-mail address or phone number above.

*SPECIAL STIPULATIONS:
In exchange for funding, recipients agree to the National Security Education Program (NSEP) Service Requirement. The NSEP Service Requirement stipulates that an award recipient work for a minimum of one year in the federal government in a position with national security responsibilities. The Departments of Defense, Homeland Security, State, or any element of the Intelligence Community are priority agencies.

NATIONAL SECURITY EDUCATION PROGRAM [858]
Boren Fellowships
Institute of International Education
1400 K Street, N.W., 7th Floor
Washington, DC 20005-2403
(800) 618-6737
E-mail: boren@iie.org
Web Site: www.borenawards.org

FOUNDED: 1991

AREAS OF INTEREST:
Boren Fellowships support study and research in areas of the world that are critical to U.S. interests, including Africa, Asia, Central and Eastern Europe, Eurasia, Latin America, and the Middle East.

NAME(S) OF PROGRAMS:
● **Boren Fellowships**

TYPE:
Fellowships. Fellowships for U.S. graduate students to provide support for overseas study or a combination of overseas and domestic study.

PURPOSE:
To encourage U.S. graduate students to add an important international and language component to their graduate education through specialization in area study, language study, or increased language proficiency; to support study and research in areas of the

world that are critical to U.S. interests, including Africa, Asia, Central and Eastern Europe, Eurasia, Latin America, and the Middle East.

ELIGIBILITY:
Must be a U.S. citizen at the time of application. Applicants must be matriculated in or applying to a graduate degree program at an accredited U.S. college or university located within the U.S. Boren Fellows must remain matriculated in their graduate programs for the duration of the fellowship. Applicant must plan an overseas program that meets home institution standards in Africa, Asia, Central and Eastern Europe, Eurasia, Latin America, and the Middle East. The countries of Western Europe, Canada, Australia, and New Zealand are excluded.

FINANCIAL DATA:
Amount of support per award: Up to $24,000 for overseas study; Up to $30,000 for a combination of domestic and overseas study.

NO. MOST RECENT APPLICANTS: 273.

NO. AWARDS: 106.

APPLICATION INFO:
Complete details and application information can be found on the Boren Awards web site.
Duration: Minimum 12 weeks for overseas study. Preference will be given to programs of six to 12 months.
Deadline: January 29.

ADDRESS INQUIRIES TO:
See e-mail address or phone number above.

*SPECIAL STIPULATIONS:
In exchange for funding, recipients agree to the National Security Education Program (NSEP) Service Requirement. The NSEP Service Requirement stipulates that an award recipient work for a minimum of one year in the federal government in a position with national security responsibilities. The Departments of Defense, Homeland Security, State, or any element of the Intelligence Community are priority agencies.

THE PHI BETA KAPPA
SOCIETY   [859]
1606 New Hampshire Avenue, N.W.
Washington, DC 20009
(202) 745-3287
Fax: (202) 986-1601
E-mail: awards@pbk.org
Web Site: www.pbk.org

AREAS OF INTEREST:
French language, literature and culture.

NAME(S) OF PROGRAMS:
● **The Walter J. Jensen Fellowship for French Language, Literature and Culture**

TYPE:
Fellowships. Fellowship for at least six months of study in France. One award given annually.

YEAR PROGRAM STARTED: 2001

PURPOSE:
To help educators and researchers improve education in standard French language, literature and culture, and in the study of standard French in the U.S.

ELIGIBILITY:
Candidates must be U.S. citizens under 40 years of age who can demonstrate their career does or will involve active use of the

French language. They must have earned a Baccalaureate degree from an accredited four-year institution, and have a 3.0 minimum grade point average in French language and literature as a major. They must demonstrate superior competence in French, according to the standards established by the American Association of Teachers of French. Preference may be given to members of Phi Beta Kappa and educators at the secondary school level or above.

GEOG. RESTRICTIONS: United States.

FINANCIAL DATA:
Includes single round-trip, economy-class ticket for travel to France.
Amount of support per award: $16,400 for the year 2018.

NO. MOST RECENT APPLICANTS: Varies.

NO. AWARDS: Minimum 1 annually.

APPLICATION INFO:
The application booklet contains:
(1) the Application for the Walter J. Jensen Fellowship;
(2) two Transcript Request forms and;
(3) the Letter of Recommendation Form.

Applicant must submit three complete sets of documents. The Letter of Recommendation and Transcript Request forms may be duplicated. Please indicate the Fellowship name on all correspondence.

Applicant should send the application, official transcripts, and confidential letters of recommendation (in sealed envelopes) to the Walter J. Jensen Fellowship Committee in care of the Phi Beta Kappa Society.
Duration: At least six months.
Deadline: January 15.

ADDRESS INQUIRIES TO:
Aurora Sherman, Executive Assistant to the Secretary and Awards Coordinator
(See address above.)

THE ROTARY FOUNDATION OF
ROTARY INTERNATIONAL   [860]
One Rotary Center
1560 Sherman Avenue
Evanston, IL 60201-3698
(866) 976-8279
(847) 866-3000
E-mail: rotarypeacecenters@rotary.org
Web Site: www.rotary.org/en/peace-fellowships

FOUNDED: 2002

AREAS OF INTEREST:
Higher education.

NAME(S) OF PROGRAMS:
● **Rotary Peace Fellowships**

TYPE:
Fellowships. The Rotary Peace Centers offer individuals committed to peace and cooperation the opportunity to pursue a one- to two-year Master's-level degree or a three-month professional certificate in international studies, peace studies and conflict resolution at one of the six Rotary Peace Centers. The university partners are: Duke University and the University of North Carolina at Chapel Hill (North Carolina, U.S.A.); International Christian University (Tokyo, Japan); University of Bradford (West Yorkshire, England); University of Queensland (Brisbane, Queensland, Australia); Uppsala University (Uppsala, Sweden); and Chulalongkorn University (Bangkok, Thailand).

YEAR PROGRAM STARTED: 2002

PURPOSE:
To further peace and international understanding.

LEGAL BASIS:
Incorporated not-for-profit foundation.

ELIGIBILITY:
For the Master's Degree Program, applicants must have:
(1) a minimum of three years of related full-time work or volunteer experience and a Bachelor's degree;
(2) proficiency in English; proficiency in a second language is strongly recommended;
(3) a strong commitment to international understanding and peace as demonstrated through professional and academic achievements and personal or community service and;
(4) excellent leadership skills.

For the Professional Development Certificate Program, applicants must have:
(1) a minimum of five years of relevant full-time work or volunteer experience and a strong academic background;
(2) proficiency in English; proficiency in a second language is strongly recommended;
(3) a strong commitment to international understanding and peace demonstrated through professional and academic achievements and personal and community service activities and;
(4) excellent leadership skills.

Rotary Peace Fellowship may not be used for doctoral study. The following people are not eligible for the Master's Degree Program:
(1) active Rotarians;
(2) employees of a Rotary club, Rotary International, or other Rotary entity;
(3) spouses, lineal descendants (children or grandchildren by blood or legal adoption), spouses of lineal descendants or ancestors (parents or grandparents by blood) of any living person in the categories above and;
(4) former Rotarians and their relatives as described above.

FINANCIAL DATA:
Fellowship will include funding for tuition and required fees, room and board, transportation, contingency expenses and other funding, including paid internship experience.
Amount of support per award: Master's Program: Average $75,000; Professional Development Certificate: Average $12,000.
Total amount of support: Varies.

NO. MOST RECENT APPLICANTS: 325.

NO. AWARDS: Approximately 100 each year.

APPLICATION INFO:
Applicants are required to submit their application and all supplementary materials to a Rotary district. Rotary clubs can help to connect applicants with a Rotary district. It is strongly recommended that applicants connect to a club near their legal or permanent place of residence, full-time study, or employment to assist with the application process. Applications must be submitted to the applicant's chosen Rotary district by May 31, and it is recommended that the applicants contact a club and/or district when they begin the application process.

Application checklist and essay requirements are available on the Rotary web site.
Duration: Master's Program: 15 to 24 months. Professional Development Certificate: Three months.

Deadline: May 31.

PUBLICATIONS:
Application; brochure.

ADDRESS INQUIRIES TO:
Local Rotary Club or Contact Center
(See e-mail address above.)

ST. ANDREW'S SOCIETY OF THE STATE OF NEW YORK [861]

150 East 55th Street, 3rd Floor
New York, NY 10022
(212) 223-4248
Fax: (212) 233-0748
E-mail: office@standrewsny.org
Web Site: standrewsny.org

FOUNDED: 1756

AREAS OF INTEREST:
Charitable support of needy persons of
Scottish descent and scholarship program.

NAME(S) OF PROGRAMS:
● **Scholarship Program for Graduate
Study in Scotland**

TYPE:
Scholarships. Scholarships for American
students of Scottish descent for one year of
graduate study in any Scottish university.

YEAR PROGRAM STARTED: 1956

PURPOSE:
To promote cultural interchange and goodwill
between Scotland and the U.S.

LEGAL BASIS:
Tax-exempt charitable organization.

ELIGIBILITY:
An applicant must be in senior year of
undergraduate study, exhibit financial need,
possess an outstanding scholastic and activity
record, provide evidence of Scottish descent,
and reside within a 250-mile radius of New
York state.

GEOG. RESTRICTIONS: New Jersey, New York,
Pennsylvania and the New England states.

FINANCIAL DATA:
Award is to be used initially against tuition,
then board, room, transportation and other
expenses.
Amount of support per award: $35,000.
Total amount of support: Varies each year.

NO. MOST RECENT APPLICANTS: 100.

NO. AWARDS: 2 per year (for U.S. applicants).

APPLICATION INFO:
The applicant must contact the Fellowships
Office at their current academic institution.
Each college or university is invited to send
only one candidate forward to the St.
Andrew's Society Selection Committee.
Referral must be by the president of the
institution the applicant is attending.
Duration: One year. Nonrenewable.
Deadline: December 15. Announcement in
early March.

PUBLICATIONS:
Quarterly newsletter.

IRS I.D.: 13-5602329

OFFICERS:
Donald S. Whamond, Jr., President
David M. Murphy, First Vice President
Richard Porter, Second Vice President
John A.D. Needham, Treasurer
Thomas Burt, Secretary

ADDRESS INQUIRIES TO:
Samuel S. Abernethy, Scholarship Chairman
(See address above.)

*SPECIAL STIPULATIONS:
Candidates must be from northeastern U.S.
and of Scottish descent, and must be U.S.
citizens.

SCUOLA NORMALE SUPERIORE [862]

Piazza dei Cavalieri, 7
Palazzo D'Ancona
56124 Pisa Italy
(39) 050 509237
(39) 050 509111
Fax: (39) 050 563513
E-mail: mario.landucci@sns.it
phd@sns.it
Web Site: www.sns.it

FOUNDED: 1813

AREAS OF INTEREST:
Classical philology, linguistics and history,
modern philology and linguistics, history, art
history, philosophy, mathematics and physics
and their applications in chemistry and
biology.

NAME(S) OF PROGRAMS:
● **Graduate School Scholarships for
Study in Italy**

TYPE:
Scholarships. Scholarships for study at the
Scuola Normale Superiore, Pisa, Italy, for
postgraduate study in the disciplinary areas
of the humanities and of mathematics,
physics and natural sciences listed above.

PURPOSE:
To promote research and study in Italy.

LEGAL BASIS:
State-owned university.

ELIGIBILITY:
Citizens of all countries who have an M.A.
degree and know Italian may apply. Students
over 30 at the time of application cannot be
admitted to the graduate courses. Applicants
may not be receiving other forms of
assistance.

FINANCIAL DATA:
Amount of support per award:
Perfezionamento (Ph.D.): Study grant of
EUR 17,000 per year.

NO. AWARDS: 76 for the year 2020-21.

APPLICATION INFO:
Information is available online. The new
announcement appears around May to June
each year.
Duration: Up to three years; fellowship may
be extended for an additional year for
justified academic and/or scientific reasons if
possible within the budget.
Deadline: February 27 for spring session;
August 27 for autumn session.

ADDRESS INQUIRIES TO:
Student Secretariat
Dott. Mario Landucci
(See address above.)

SHASTRI INDO-CANADIAN INSTITUTE (SICI) [863]

Room 1418, Education Tower
2500 University Drive, N.W.
Calgary AB T2N 1N4 Canada
(403) 220-3220
E-mail: maldeen@ucalgary.ca
Web Site: www.shastriinstitute.org

AREAS OF INTEREST:
Knowledge creation and mobilization, faculty
and student mobility, building institutional
partnerships and understanding between India
and Canada.

TYPE:
Fellowships; Internships; Travel grants.
Collaborative research grants; Publication
grants.

YEAR PROGRAM STARTED: 1968

PURPOSE:
To promote understanding between Canada
and India, mainly through facilitating
academic activities.

ELIGIBILITY:
Applicants must be Canadian citizens or
permanent residents.

FINANCIAL DATA:
Amount of support per award: Varies.
Total amount of support: Varies.

CO-OP FUNDING PROGRAMS: Department of
Education, Ministry of Human Resources,
Government of India.

NO. MOST RECENT APPLICANTS: 30 to 70 per
grant.

NO. AWARDS: Varies.

APPLICATION INFO:
Application information is available on the
web site.
Duration: Three months to two years.
Deadline: Varies.

ADDRESS INQUIRIES TO:
See e-mail address above.

SOMMERHOCHSCHULE-UNIVERSITY OF VIENNA [864]

Alser Strasse 4/Hof 1/Tuer 1.16
1090 Vienna Austria
(43) 1-4277-24131
E-mail: sommerhochschule@univie.ac.at
Web Site: shs.univie.ac.at

FOUNDED: 1949

AREAS OF INTEREST:
European Studies (with focus on the legal,
economic, political and cultural aspects)
taught in English; German Language Courses
(A1, A2, B1, B2).

NAME(S) OF PROGRAMS:
● **International Summer Program
(Summer Campus Strobl/St.
Wolfgang/Austria)**

TYPE:
Scholarships. The European Studies courses
focus on the political, economic and legal,
but also historical and cultural, aspects of
Europe and the EU. The German language
courses are offered at four different levels of
proficiency (beginners to advanced).

YEAR PROGRAM STARTED: 1949

PURPOSE:
To contribute to an increased understanding
of the EU and its possible future shape and
to create an environment which encourages
intercultural and social exchange and favors
mutual understanding among participants.

LEGAL BASIS:
A subcompany of the University of Vienna;
nonprofit status; state supported.

ELIGIBILITY:
Applicants have to be at least 18 years old and must have completed at least two years of studies at college or university level in their countries of residence or have an educational background equivalent to one year at a European university before the beginning of the program.

FINANCIAL DATA:
A limited number of partial scholarships are available for the European Studies section of the program. The scholarships are awarded on the basis of academic excellence and financial need.
Amount of support per award: EUR 400 to 2,800.

NO. MOST RECENT APPLICANTS: 80 to 100.

NO. AWARDS: Varies based on the size of the scholarships.

APPLICATION INFO:
Applicants must submit the following documents:
(1) completed application form;
(2) transcript of grades;
(3) a letter of recommendation (academic or professional);
(4) official proof of proficiency in English;
(5) statement of purpose (one page maximum) and;
(6) two passport-size photos taken within the past year.

All documents have to be submitted either in original or as a certified copy and have to be translated into English or German.

Application material must be sent to the office of the Sommerhochschule (faxed or e-mailed applications cannot be accepted).
Duration: Four weeks, middle of July to middle of August.
Deadline: February 28 for scholarship applications; April 30 for regular applications.

PUBLICATIONS:
Annual brochures and leaflets for the International Summer Program of the Sommerhochschule.

STAFF:
Dr. Franz-Stefan Meissel, Director
Verena Bauer, Program Coordinator
Nina Gruber, Program Coordinator

ADDRESS INQUIRIES TO:
Nina Gruber, Program Coordinator
(See address above.)

U.S. DEPARTMENT OF EDUCATION   [865]
International and Foreign Language Education
400 Maryland Avenue, S.W.
Washington, DC 20202
(202) 453-6304
E-mail: corey.neal@ed.gov
Web Site: www2.ed.
gov/programs/iegpsgpa/index.html

FOUNDED: 1967

AREAS OF INTEREST:
Foreign languages and area studies.

NAME(S) OF PROGRAMS:
● **Fulbright-Hays Group Projects Abroad Program**

TYPE:
Exchange programs; Project/program grants; Seed money grants; Training grants; Travel grants. Also, study grants and grants for foreign language and area study programs of educational development for projects to be undertaken abroad. Grants are awarded to higher education institutions, nonprofit educational organizations, state department of education and consortium of such institutions, departments, organizations and institutions which, in turn, enable professors, college and elementary and secondary school teachers and advanced students to attend seminars abroad and to travel and study in foreign countries in order to strengthen the institution's programs in foreign languages, area studies and world affairs.

YEAR PROGRAM STARTED: 1967

PURPOSE:
To contribute to the development and improvement of the study of foreign languages and area studies in the U.S. by providing opportunities for faculty, teachers, upperclassmen and/or graduate students to travel to foreign countries in group projects for research, training and curriculum development.

LEGAL BASIS:
The Mutual Educational and Cultural Exchange Act of 1961, Public Law 87-256 (Fulbright Hays Act), Section 102(b)(6).

ELIGIBILITY:
Under the program, grants are awarded to institutions of higher education, state departments of education, private nonprofit educational organizations and consortiums of such institutions, departments and organizations to conduct overseas group projects in research, training and curriculum development, by groups of individuals engaged in a common endeavor.

A participant must be a citizen, national or permanent resident of the U.S. and either a faculty member in modern foreign languages or area studies, an experienced educator responsible for planning, conducting or supervising programs in modern foreign languages or area studies at the elementary, secondary or postsecondary levels, a graduate student or upperclassman who plans a teaching career in modern foreign languages or area studies.

The grant does not provide funds for project-related expenses within the U.S. Funds may be used only for a maintenance stipend based on 50% of the amount established in the U.S. Department of State publication, *Maximum Travel Per Diem Allowances for Foreign Areas*, round-trip international travel, a local travel allowance for necessary project-related transportation within the country of study, exclusive of the purchase of transportation equipment, the purchase of project-related artifacts, books and other teaching materials in the country of study, rent for instructional facilities in the country of study, and clerical and professional services performed by resident instructional personnel in the country of study.

FINANCIAL DATA:
Amount of support per award: Varies.
Total amount of support: $2,507,907 for the year 2018.

APPLICATION INFO:
Application information is available on the web site.
Duration: Four weeks to one year. No renewals.
Deadline: March.

ADDRESS INQUIRIES TO:
Corey Neal, Program Officer
(See e-mail address above.)

*PLEASE NOTE:
Annual competition contingent upon receiving a Congressional Appropriation.

UNIVERSITY OF BRISTOL   [866]
Senate House
Tyndall Avenue
Bristol BS8 1TH England
(44) 0117 928 9000
(44) 0117 331 7972
Fax: (44) 0117 331 7873
E-mail: student-funding@bristol.ac.uk
Web Site: www.bris.ac.uk

FOUNDED: 1909

AREAS OF INTEREST:
Faculties of arts, engineering, biomedical sciences, health sciences, science, social sciences and law.

NAME(S) OF PROGRAMS:
● **Postgraduate Research Scholarships**

TYPE:
Scholarships. Postgraduate research scholarships for study toward the Ph.D. degree in one of the Schools of the University of Bristol.

YEAR PROGRAM STARTED: 1989

PURPOSE:
To attract excellent research students.

LEGAL BASIS:
University.

ELIGIBILITY:
Scholarships are available for the U.K., Europe and overseas students.

APPLICATION INFO:
Information is available from the Student Funding Office at the University of Bristol or online.
Duration: Up to four years, subject to satisfactory academic progress and according to the particular discipline and training programme.
Deadline: Varies.

PUBLICATIONS:
Annual report; research prospectus.

ADDRESS INQUIRIES TO:
Student Funding Office
(See address above.)

UNIVERSITY OF ILLINOIS AT URBANA-CHAMPAIGN
College of Fine and Applied Arts
608 East Lorado Taft Drive, Suite 100
Champaign, IL 61820
(217) 333-1661
(217) 333-1660
Fax: (217) 244-8381
E-mail: faa@illinois.edu
Web Site: www.faa.illinois.edu/alumni-friends/kate-neal-kinley-memorial-fellowship

TYPE:
Fellowships. Awarded for advanced study in the fine arts in the U.S. or abroad, in an approved educational institution, with an approved private teacher or in independent study.

Three major Fellowships will be awarded:
(1) one in any field of music;
(2) one in architectural design and history, art and design, theatre, dance, or instrumental or

vocal music and;
(3) one in art, architecture, dance, landscape architecture, theatre, or urban and regional planning.

See entry 529 for full listing.

THE UNIVERSITY OF MANCHESTER   [867]
Manchester Doctoral College
Oxford Road
Manchester M13 9PL England
(44) 0161 275 8792
E-mail: mdc@manchester.ac.uk
Web Site: www.manchester.ac.
uk/study/postgraduate-research/funding

FOUNDED: 1824

AREAS OF INTEREST:
Arts, economic, social and legal studies, education, science, engineering, medicine and biological sciences.

NAME(S) OF PROGRAMS:
● **British Marshall Scholarships**
● **Fulbright - University of Manchester Award**
● **North American Foundation Awards**
● **President's Doctoral Scholar Award**

TYPE:
Assistantships; Awards/prizes; Block grants; Conferences/seminars; Endowments; Exchange programs; Fellowships; Research grants; Scholarships; Training grants; Travel grants; Visiting scholars. Research studentships for postgraduate-taught and research programmes in the fields above.

North American Foundation Awards are for postgraduate study at the University of Manchester (NAFUM).

The University of Manchester is also a recognized institution for the purpose of U.S. federal loans and Canadian student loans.

FINANCIAL DATA:
Studentships include payment of fees at U.K. level and/or maintenance allowance.
Amount of support per award: Varies.

ADDRESS INQUIRIES TO:
Student Services Centre
E-mail: ssc@manchester.ac.uk

UNIVERSITY OF OSLO INTERNATIONAL SUMMER SCHOOL   [868]
Oslo International Summer School
c/o St. Olaf College
1520 St. Olaf Avenue
Northfield, MN 55057-1098
(507) 786-3269
(800) 639-0058
E-mail: iss@stolaf.edu
Web Site: www.uio.no/summerschool

FOUNDED: 1947

AREAS OF INTEREST:
The International Summer School offers undergraduate and graduate courses in the following areas:
General course offerings - Norwegian language, Norwegian art history, Norwegian architecture and design, Norwegian literature, history, political science, culture and society, international relations and gender equality in Nordic countries;
Graduate courses - peace research, international development, gender equality,

international community health, energy and sustainable development, human rights, and a changing Arctic.

TYPE:
Scholarships.

YEAR PROGRAM STARTED: 1947

PURPOSE:
To offer academic instruction to a gathering of many nationalities in the hope of a modest but concrete increase in understanding and goodwill among nations.

LEGAL BASIS:
Part of the University of Oslo.

ELIGIBILITY:
Scholarships awarded only to students accepted into the Oslo International Summer School program. Scholarship applicants must meet the entrance requirements of the International Summer School and must present evidence of attending or having attended a recognized university and have a good academic record. One year or more of college or university is required. In addition, seriousness of academic purpose and personal qualities likely to make the applicant a good representative of his or her country.

FINANCIAL DATA:
Amount of support per award: Varies.
Total amount of support: Varies.

NO. MOST RECENT APPLICANTS: Approximately 30.

NO. AWARDS: Varies.

APPLICATION INFO:
A financial aid application form and the application for admission to the International Summer School and the supporting letters of recommendation are used by the Financial Aid Committee to choose financial aid recipients.
Duration: Six weeks during the summer, from late June to early August. No renewal possibilities.
Deadline: February 1. Results are announced the first week in April.

PUBLICATIONS:
ISS catalog.

ADMINISTRATION:
Nita Kapoor, Director, International Summer School Norwegian Office
Torild Homstad, Administrator, North American Admissions Office

ADDRESS INQUIRIES TO:
Non-North American students should request information from:
International Summer School
Postbox 1082
NO-0317 Oslo, Norway
Tel: (011) 47 2285-6385

All other applicants can use the North American address above.

THE UNIVERSITY OF SYDNEY   [869]
Scholarships Office
Level 4, Jane Foss Russell Building G02
The University of Sydney N.S.W. 2006
Australia
61 (02) 8627 1444
E-mail: scholarships.officer@sydney.edu.au
Web Site: www.sydney.edu.au/scholarships

FOUNDED: 1850

NAME(S) OF PROGRAMS:
● **Research Training Program (RTP)**

TYPE:
Scholarships. Awarded for research leading to a higher degree. Tenable at the University of Sydney.

LEGAL BASIS:
University.

ELIGIBILITY:
The scholarships are awarded on academic merit and research ability to qualified candidates. Open to qualified foreign graduates from any country eligible to commence a higher degree by research. Australian and New Zealand citizens or permanent residents are not eligible.

FINANCIAL DATA:
Amount of support per award: $35,000 AUD for the year 2020.

NO. AWARDS: Varies.

APPLICATION INFO:
Application information is available on the web site.
Duration: Two years for a Master's research degree and three years for a Ph.D. Extension of up to six months possible for Ph.D. candidate subject to satisfactory progress.

UNIVERSITY OF VIRGINIA [870]
New Cabell Hall
1605 Jefferson Park Avenue
Charlottesville, VA 22904
(434) 243-0807
Fax: (434) 243-2140
E-mail: gradstudies@virginia.edu
Web Site: www.virginia.edu

FOUNDED: 1872

AREAS OF INTEREST:
International law and politics, international economics, international institutions and international development.

NAME(S) OF PROGRAMS:
● **Albert Gallatin Research Fellowship**

TYPE:
Exchange programs; Fellowships.

YEAR PROGRAM STARTED: 1976

PURPOSE:
To support advanced doctoral study in international affairs.

LEGAL BASIS:
University.

ELIGIBILITY:
Ph.D. students in international affairs at the dissertation stage of their work. U.S. citizens and permanent residents enrolled in a U.S. doctoral institution. Intended for students who plan to study at the Graduate Institute of International Studies, Geneva, Switzerland.

GEOG. RESTRICTIONS: United States.

FINANCIAL DATA:
Total amount of support: Varies.

NO. MOST RECENT APPLICANTS: 7.

NO. AWARDS: 1 or more annually.

APPLICATION INFO:
Student nominations should be routed through the home department or program. Departments should submit all nominations at once. Departments must provide a cover letter that includes a priority ranking of applications/nominations.

Nominations should include:
(1) a cover letter;
(2) a two-page, single-spaced description of the study to be undertaken (written by the

nominee);
(3) two letters of reference from faculty or others familiar with the project;
(4) a University of Virginia transcript (unofficial transcript is satisfactory);
(5) a statement of all other awards, including amounts for which the nominee has applied during the same time period and for the same research proposal;
(6) a curriculum vitae and;
(7) a detailed budget outlining specific research related travel and expenditures.

Duration: One academic year. Shorter term grants are also available.

Deadline: Nominations: March 14.
Announcement: March 30.

PUBLICATIONS:
Application guidelines.

ADDRESS INQUIRIES TO:
Office of Graduate and Postdoctoral Affairs
(See e-mail address above.)

*SPECIAL STIPULATIONS:
Applicant must be engaged in the dissertation phase of Ph.D. work in international affairs.

VILLA I TATTI: THE HARVARD UNIVERSITY CENTER FOR ITALIAN RENAISSANCE STUDIES   [871]
Via di Vincigliata, 26
50135 Florence Italy
E-mail: fellowships@itatti.harvard.edu
Web Site: itatti.harvard.edu/fellowships

FOUNDED: 1961

AREAS OF INTEREST:
All aspects of the Italian Renaissance: fine arts, literature, music, science, philosophy, religion and political, intellectual, economic and social history.

CONSULTING OR VOLUNTEER SERVICES:
Library, photographic collection and archive.

NAME(S) OF PROGRAMS:
- **Berenson Fellowship**
- **Fellowship in the Digital Humanities**
- **I Tatti Fellowship**
- **Craig Hugh Smyth Fellowships**
- **David and Julie Tobey Fellowship**
- **Wallace Fellowship**

TYPE:
Fellowships. Berenson Fellowship supports postdoctoral research of scholars who explore "Italy in the World." Projects should address the transnational dialogues between Italy and other cultures during the Renaissance, broadly understood historically to include the period from the 14th to the 17th century.

Fellowship in the Digital Humanities supports research of scholars in the humanities or social sciences, librarians, archivists, and data science professionals whose research interests or practice cut across traditional disciplinary boundaries and actively employ technology in their work.

I Tatti Fellowship supports postdoctoral research in any aspect of the Italian Renaissance.

Craig Hugh Smyth Fellowship is designed for curators and conservators pursuing advanced research in any aspect of the Italian Renaissance.

David and Julie Tobey Fellowship supports postdoctoral research on drawings, prints, and illustrated manuscripts from the Italian

Renaissance, and especially the role that these works played in the creative process, the history of taste and collecting, and questions of connoisseurship.

Wallace Fellowship supports postdoctoral research on the historiography and impact of the Italian Renaissance in the modern era, namely the 19th to 21st centuries.

YEAR PROGRAM STARTED: 1961

PURPOSE:
To promote advanced interdisciplinary study in Renaissance fields.

LEGAL BASIS:
Part of Harvard University.

ELIGIBILITY:
Criteria for each fellowship varies. Applicants should refer to the Center's web site for requirements.

FINANCIAL DATA:
Stipends will be given in accord with the individual needs of the approved applicants and the availability of funds.

Amount of support per award: Berenson, Fellowship in the Digital Humanities, Smyth, Tobey and Wallace Fellowships: $4,200 per month, plus a one-time supplement (maximum $1,500) towards relocation expenses. An additional $1,000 per month will be offered to help offset rental costs, if applicable; I Tatti Fellowship: $60,000, plus relocation supplement and housing or housing supplement.

CO-OP FUNDING PROGRAMS: Deborah Loeb Brice Fellowship, Committee to Rescue Italian Art, Francesco E. de Dombrowski Bequest, Florence Gould Foundation, Hanna Kiel Fellowship, Melville J. Kahn Fellowship Fund, Samuel H. Kress Foundation, Robert Lehman Fellowship, Jean Francois Malle Fellowship Fund, Andrew W. Mellon Foundation, Ahmanson Foundation, Lila Wallace - Reader's Digest Endowment Fund.

NO. AWARDS: Berenson, Fellowship in the Digital Humanities and Wallace Fellowship: Up to 4; I Tatti Fellowship: 15; Smyth Fellowship: 2; Tobey Fellowship: 1.

APPLICATION INFO:
Application forms are available online. Applications by fax are not accepted.
Duration: I Tatti Fellowship: One year from July 1 to June 30. All others: Four to six months.
Deadline: Varies.

IRS I.D.: 04-2103580

ADDRESS INQUIRIES TO:
Alina Payne, Director
(See address above.)

VILLA I TATTI: THE HARVARD UNIVERSITY CENTER FOR ITALIAN RENAISSANCE STUDIES   [872]
Via di Vincigliata, 26
50135 Florence Italy
E-mail: fellowships@itatti.harvard.edu
Web Site: itatti.harvard.edu/fellowships

FOUNDED: 1961

AREAS OF INTEREST:
History, with preference given to advanced research projects that address the history of science and knowledge related to early modern Italy, including transnational connections between Italy and other cultures.

CONSULTING OR VOLUNTEER SERVICES:
Library, photographic collection and archive.

NAME(S) OF PROGRAMS:
- **Warburg/I Tatti Joint Fellowship**

TYPE:
Fellowships. Villa I Tatti - The Harvard University Center for Italian Renaissance Studies in Florence, Italy, and the Warburg Institute School of Advanced Study at the University of London offer a joint, residential fellowship. Fellows will spend the fall term (September to December) in London and the spring term (January to June) in Florence. The fellowship is designed for early and midcareer scholars in the field of history, with preference given to advanced research projects that address the history of science and knowledge related to early modern Italy, including transnational connections between Italy and other cultures. Scholars can also apply to work on the transmission and circulation of ideas, objects, and people during the Renaissance, into and beyond the Italian peninsula, or on the historiography of the Italian Renaissance, including the rebirth of interest in the Renaissance in later periods.

PURPOSE:
To promote advanced interdisciplinary study in Renaissance fields.

LEGAL BASIS:
Part of Harvard University.

ELIGIBILITY:
Applicants must have their Ph.D. in hand by the time they apply. Applicants must be conversant in English and have at least a reading knowledge of Italian, with a solid background in Italian Renaissance Studies. Each successful candidate must be approved by both the Warburg Institute and Villa I Tatti.

Priority will be given to applicants with no previous association with either I Tatti or the Warburg Institute.

Applications will not be accepted from candidates proposing to revise their doctoral dissertation for publication.

FINANCIAL DATA:
Amount of support per award: Spring Term at Villa I Tatti: Stipend of $4,000 per month, plus up to $1,500 for relocation expenses. An additional $1,000 per month will be offered to offset rental costs, if applicable; Autumn Term at Warburg Institute: Stipend of GBP 1,500 per month.

NO. AWARDS: 1.

APPLICATION INFO:
Applications must be written in English and must be submitted electronically. Scholars can apply to only one type of fellowship at I Tatti per academic year.

Applicants must have two scholars who know their work well submit recommendations online by the deadline. These recommendations must be written in English.

Duration: 10 months.

Deadline: November 15.

IRS I.D.: 04-2103580

ADDRESS INQUIRIES TO:
Alina Payne, Director
(See address above.)

VILLA I TATTI: THE HARVARD UNIVERSITY CENTER FOR ITALIAN RENAISSANCE STUDIES [873]

Via di Vincigliata, 26
50135 Florence Italy
E-mail: fellowships@itatti.harvard.edu
Web Site: itatti.harvard.edu/fellowships
byzantinestudies.boun.edu.tr

FOUNDED: 1961

AREAS OF INTEREST:
Interaction between Italy and the Byzantine Empire (ca. 1300 to ca. 1700).

CONSULTING OR VOLUNTEER SERVICES:
Library, photographic collection and archive.

NAME(S) OF PROGRAMS:
- **Villa I Tatti-Bogazici University Joint Fellowship**

TYPE:
Fellowships. Villa I Tatti: The Harvard University Center for Italian Renaissance Studies and the Byzantine Studies Research Center of Bogazici University offer a joint, residential fellowship to support research on the interaction between Italy and the Byzantine Empire (ca. 1300 to ca. 1700). This collaboration aims to foster the development of research on Late Byzantine-Italian relations by supporting early-career scholars whose work explores Byzantium's cross-cultural contacts in the late medieval and early modern Mediterranean world through the study of art, architecture, archaeology, history, literature, material culture, music, philosophy, religion, or science.

PURPOSE:
To foster the development of research on Late Byzantine-Italian relations.

LEGAL BASIS:
Part of Harvard University.

ELIGIBILITY:
Candidates must have received their Ph.D. on or after 2010. Candidates must be conversant in English and have at least a reading knowledge of Italian. They must have a solid background in Italian Renaissance and/or Byzantine studies.

Priority will be given to applicants with no previous association with Villa I Tatti or the Byzantine Studies Research Center.

FINANCIAL DATA:
Amount of support per award: Stipend for the autumn semester in Istanbul is $1,800 per month, plus a one-time supplement (maximum $1,500) towards airfare to and from Istanbul; stipend for the spring semester in Italy is $4,200 per month plus a one-time supplement (maximum $1,500) towards relocation expenses. An additional $1,000 per month will be offered to offset rental costs, if applicable.

NO. AWARDS: 1.

APPLICATION INFO:
Applications must be written in English and must be submitted electronically. Scholars can apply to only one type of fellowship at I Tatti per academic year.

Duration: Fall term (September to December) in Istanbul and spring term (January to June) in Florence.

Deadline: November 15.

IRS I.D.: 04-2103580

ADDRESS INQUIRIES TO:
Alina Payne, Director
(See address above.)

VILLA I TATTI: THE HARVARD UNIVERSITY CENTER FOR ITALIAN RENAISSANCE STUDIES [874]

Via di Vincigliata, 26
50135 Florence Italy
E-mail: fellowships@itatti.harvard.edu
Web Site: itatti.harvard.edu/fellowships

FOUNDED: 1961

AREAS OF INTEREST:
Art history, with preference given to advanced research projects that address the relationship between Spain and Italy, including transnational connections and dialogues with Latin America, during the Renaissance.

CONSULTING OR VOLUNTEER SERVICES:
Library, photographic collection and archive.

NAME(S) OF PROGRAMS:
- **I Tatti/Museo Nacional del Prado Joint Fellowship**

TYPE:
Fellowships. Joint fellowship designed to support early and midcareer scholars in the field of art history.

PURPOSE:
To promote advanced interdisciplinary study in Renaissance fields.

LEGAL BASIS:
Part of Harvard University.

ELIGIBILITY:
Applicants must have their Ph.D. certificate by the time they apply. They must be conversant in English and Spanish and have at least a reading knowledge of Italian, with a solid background in Italian and/or Spanish and Latin American studies.

Priority will be given to applicants with no previous association with either I Tatti or the Museo del Prado.

FINANCIAL DATA:
Amount of support per award: Stipend for autumn semester in Madrid is EUR 3,000 per month; stipend for the spring semester in Florence is $4,000 per month, plus a one-time supplement (maximum $1,500) towards relocation expenses. An additional $1,000 per month will be offered to offset rental costs, if applicable.

CO-OP FUNDING PROGRAMS: Centro de Estudios de Europa Hispanica.

NO. AWARDS: 1.

APPLICATION INFO:
Applications must be written in English and must be submitted electronically. Scholars can apply to only one type of fellowship at I Tatti per academic year.

Duration: Fall semester (September to December) in Madrid and spring semester (January to June) in Florence.

Deadline: November 15.

IRS I.D.: 04-2103580

ADDRESS INQUIRIES TO:
Alina Payne, Director
(See address above.)

THOMAS J. WATSON FELLOWSHIP PROGRAM

233 Broadway
Suite 2709
New York, NY 10279
(212) 245-8859
E-mail: tjw@tjwf.org
Web Site: watson.foundation

TYPE:
Fellowships. The Foundation provides Fellows an opportunity for a focused and disciplined "Wanderjahr" of their own devising or design-time in which to explore with thoroughness a particular interest, test their aspirations and abilities, view their lives and American society in greater perspective and concomitantly, to develop a more informed sense of international concern. The Fellowship experience is intended to provide Fellows an opportunity to immerse themselves in cultures other than their own for an entire year. The candidate's proposed project should involve investigation into an area of demonstrated concern and personal interest.

See entry 1491 for full listing.

WEIZMANN INSTITUTE OF SCIENCE [875]

Feinberg Graduate School
David Lopatie Hall of Graduate Studies
P.O. Box 26
234 Herzl Street
Rehovot 7610001 Israel
(972) 8-934-2924
Fax: (972) 8-934-4114
E-mail: FGS@weizmann.ac.il
Web Site: www.weizmann.ac.il/feinberg

FOUNDED: 1934

AREAS OF INTEREST:
Life sciences, chemistry, physics, mathematics, computer science and science teaching.

NAME(S) OF PROGRAMS:
- **Postdoctoral Fellowships Program at the Weizmann Institute of Science**

TYPE:
Fellowships. The Feinberg Graduate School of the Weizmann Institute of Science offers a limited number of postdoctoral fellowships in all areas of research in which the Weizmann Institute is engaged. The fellowships are offered in various fields of biology, chemistry, physics, biochemistry-biophysics, mathematics, computer science and science teaching.

YEAR PROGRAM STARTED: 1976

PURPOSE:
To train postgraduate research students to senior positions in academia, scientific research, medical research, industry, education, and government systems.

LEGAL BASIS:
Research institute.

ELIGIBILITY:
Postdoctoral fellowship applicants must have received a Ph.D. or equivalent degree within seven years of the start of the fellowship program. Candidates may be citizens of any country.

FINANCIAL DATA:
The annual stipend is adjusted periodically in accordance with living costs. Also offered is a small relocation allowance and a one-way, economy-class airfare (round-trip airfare in case the fellowship is extended to two years).

Amount of support per award:
Approximately $31,000 per year.

APPLICATION INFO:
Application forms and additional information may be obtained from the Feinberg Graduate School, Weizmann Institute of Science and from the web site.

Duration: 12 months. Possible renewal for a second and third year.

Deadline: Applications may be submitted year-round.

OFFICERS:
Prof. Gilad Perez, President
Prof. Michael Fainzilber, Chairperson, Postdoctoral Fellowship Program

ADDRESS INQUIRIES TO:
Feinberg Graduate School
(See address above.)

YOUTH FOR UNDERSTANDING USA   [876]

6856 Eastern Avenue, N.W.
Suite 310
Washington, DC 20012
(202) 774-5200 ext. 5203
(800) 833-6243
Fax: (202) 588-7571
E-mail: admissions@yfu.org
mckendree@yfu.org
Web Site: www.yfuusa.org

FOUNDED: 1957

AREAS OF INTEREST:
The exchange of U.S. and international high school students in more than 60 countries.

CONSULTING OR VOLUNTEER SERVICES:
Intercultural education and training and research.

NAME(S) OF PROGRAMS:
● **Americans Overseas Summer, Semester and Year Programs**
● **Congress-Bundestag Youth Exchange Program**
● **Corporate Scholarship Program**
● **International Semester and Year Programs**
● **Japan-U.S. Senate Youth Exchange Program**

TYPE:
Exchange programs; Grants-in-aid; Scholarships; Travel grants. Students on summer semester and year programs live with volunteer host families overseas. Students on semester and academic year programs also attend school. International students live and study at U.S. high schools or community colleges. Competitive, full and partial scholarships for Corporate, Japan-U.S. Senate Programs and Japan-America Friendship Scholars Program.

YEAR PROGRAM STARTED: 2001

PURPOSE:
To advance intercultural understanding, mutual respect and social responsibility through educational exchanges for youth, families and communities.

LEGAL BASIS:
Tax-exempt, 501(c)(3) international educational organization.

ELIGIBILITY:
Applicants must be U.S. or international high school students between the ages of 15 and 18. Full scholarships for special programs are awarded through merit competition. Partial scholarships (10 to 25%) are awarded on the basis of need.

FINANCIAL DATA:
Amount of support per award: From $500 to full support.

CO-OP FUNDING PROGRAMS: Funding sources for scholarships include a multitude of governments, corporations, foundations and individuals.

NO. AWARDS: Approximately 250.

APPLICATION INFO:
Applicants for programs involving full scholarships must complete special application materials. For corporate programs, applicants must meet special eligibility requirements. Applicants for partial scholarships must complete financial aid forms.

Duration: Scholarships awarded for the program period.

Deadline: Scholarships: December 1. Programs: March 1. Announcement between February and April.

IRS I.D.: 02-0557010

OFFICERS:
Scott J. Messing, President and Chief Executive Officer
Martin Nichols, Treasurer
Dianne Bradley, Secretary

BOARD OF TRUSTEES:
Ambassador Laurence Wohlers, Chairman
Andrew Towne, Vice Chairman
Eric Biga
Dianne Bradley
Jyarland Daniels
William Dant
Gloria Garcia
Susan Harcourt
Kristan McMahon
Seena Mortazavi
Martin Nichols
Mamiko Reeves
Donna Schnaars
Bastian Von Beschwitz
Daryl Weinert

ADDRESS INQUIRIES TO:
Jennifer McKendree, Marketing Manager
(See address and toll-free telephone number above.)

Programs for foreign scholars

AMERICA-ISRAEL CULTURAL FOUNDATION   [877]

322 Eighth Avenue
Suite 1702
New York, NY 10001
(212) 557-1600
Fax: (212) 557-1611
E-mail: admin@aicf.org
Web Site: www.aicf.org

FOUNDED: 1939

AREAS OF INTEREST:
Music, dance, theater, visual arts, film and television.

NAME(S) OF PROGRAMS:
● **Scholarship Program for Israelis**

TYPE:
Awards/prizes; Endowments; Fellowships; Project/program grants; Scholarships. For study in the arts of music, painting and sculpture, dance and drama, film and television, to be pursued either in Israel or in other countries.

YEAR PROGRAM STARTED: 1952

PURPOSE:
To further Israeli talent in the fields of music, visual arts, dance and drama, film and television.

ELIGIBILITY:
Only Israeli nationals that live and study in Israel are eligible to apply for domestic scholarships. Israeli nationals studying abroad are able to apply for scholarships to any international location of study.

FINANCIAL DATA:
Amount of support per award: $600 to $10,000.

Total amount of support: $1,300,000 per year.

NO. MOST RECENT APPLICANTS: Approximately 2,500.

NO. AWARDS: Approximately 600.

APPLICATION INFO:
Application materials are available upon request to America-Israel Cultural Foundation, 20 Dr. George Wise Street, Broshim Center, Tel Aviv 6997712, Israel.

Duration: Grants are awarded for one to two years of study. Teachers of the arts may also apply for up to six-month fellowships.

Deadline: Varies.

IRS I.D.: 13-1664048

ADDRESS INQUIRIES TO:
Scholarships: Iris Reff Ronen
Executive Director
20 Dr. George Wise Street
Broshim Center
Tel Aviv 6997712, Israel

AMERICAN ASSOCIATION OF FAMILY AND CONSUMER SCIENCES (AAFCS)   [878]

400 North Columbus Street
Suite 202
Alexandria, VA 22314-2752
(703) 706-4600
(800) 424-8080
Fax: (703) 706-4663
E-mail: awards@aafcs.org
Web Site: www.aafcs.org/resources/recognition

FOUNDED: 1909

AREAS OF INTEREST:
Family and consumer sciences.

NAME(S) OF PROGRAMS:
● **National Fellowship**

TYPE:
Fellowships. AAFCS awards fellowships to individuals who have exhibited the potential to make contributions to the family and consumer sciences profession.

PURPOSE:
To support graduate study in the field of family and consumer sciences.

LEGAL BASIS:
501(c)(3) nonprofit charity.

FINANCIAL DATA:
Amount of support per award: $5,000 fellowship, plus up to $1,000 of support.

Total amount of support: Varies.

NO. MOST RECENT APPLICANTS: 15.

NO. AWARDS: 1 to 5.

APPLICATION INFO:
Application information is available on the web site.
Duration: One academic year.
Deadline: Varies.

PUBLICATIONS:
Brochure.

ADDRESS INQUIRIES TO:
See e-mail address above.

AMERICAN ASSOCIATION OF UNIVERSITY WOMEN [879]
1310 L Street, N.W.
Suite 1000
Washington, DC 20005
(202) 785-7700
E-mail: aauw@applyists.com
Web Site: www.aauw.org

FOUNDED: 1888

AREAS OF INTEREST:
Advancement of educational and professional opportunities for women in the U.S. and around the globe.

NAME(S) OF PROGRAMS:
- **AAUW International Fellowships**

TYPE:
Fellowships. Awarded to women pursuing full-time graduate or postdoctoral study in the U.S. who are not U.S. citizens or permanent residents.

YEAR PROGRAM STARTED: 1917

PURPOSE:
To provide advanced study and training for non-American women (i.e., women who are not U.S. citizens or permanent residents) of outstanding academic ability who may be expected to give effective leadership in their homelands.

ELIGIBILITY:
International Fellowships are awarded for full-time study or research in the U.S. to women who are not U.S. citizens or permanent residents. Both graduate and postgraduate studies at accredited U.S. institutions are supported. Applicants must have earned the equivalent of a U.S. Bachelor's degree by November 15, 2019, and must have applied to their proposed institutions of study by the time of the application. Up to five International Master's/First Professional Degree Fellowships are renewable for a second year.

Recipients are selected for academic achievement and demonstrated commitment to women and girls. Recipients return to their home countries to become leaders in business, government, academia, community activism, the arts and sciences.

FINANCIAL DATA:
Amount of support per award: $18,000 to $30,000.

APPLICATION INFO:
Applicant must create an account through the "apply now" link to the vendor site located on the funding opportunity page.
Deadline: November 15.

ADDRESS INQUIRIES TO:
See e-mail address above.

AMERICAN INSTITUTE OF BANGLADESH STUDIES [880]
B488 Medical Sciences Center
1300 University Avenue
Madison, WI 53706
(608) 265-1471
Fax: (608) 265-3302
E-mail: aibs@southasia.wisc.edu
Web Site: www.aibs.net

FOUNDED: 1989

AREAS OF INTEREST:
Bangladesh culture and society.

NAME(S) OF PROGRAMS:
- **AIBS Fellowship**

TYPE:
Fellowships. Fellowships for Bangladeshi scholars interested in conducting research in the U.S. that involves all academic disciplines.

PURPOSE:
To improve the scholarly understanding of Bangladesh culture and society in the U.S.; to promote educational exchange between the U.S. and Bangladesh.

ELIGIBILITY:
Applicants must:
(1) be Bangladesh citizens;
(2) be affiliated with an AIBS partner institution in Bangladesh and;
(3) coordinate with a sponsor at an AIBS member institution to oversee their proposed research.

Scholars must have a letter of reference or sponsorship from a professor at the sponsoring institution in the U.S.

FINANCIAL DATA:
Fellowships include stipend, plus up to $2,500 for economy round-trip air transportation and visa expenses, $1,500 per month for housing, $250 per month for supplies, health insurance, and an institutional bench fee of $750 to the sponsoring U.S. institution.

Amount of support per award: Stipend of $1,500 per month.

NO. AWARDS: 5.

APPLICATION INFO:
Applications must be submitted via the online application package. Be sure to select the AIBS Fellowship (Bangladesh Applicant Only) link. Application will include:
(1) narrative proposal (maximum 10 pages);
(2) curriculum vitae (maximum two pages);
(3) three letters of reference and;
(4) letter of sponsorship from U.S. host institution. Send letter to aibs@southasia.wisc.edu and contact.aibs.dhk@gmail.com.

Duration: Any period of two months between January 10 and June 30.

Deadline: December.

ADDRESS INQUIRIES TO:
See e-mail address above.

*SPECIAL STIPULATIONS:
Scholars awarded a fellowship will be required to give lectures at AIBS member institutions or at institutions within the surrounding region.

THE AMERICAN SOCIETY OF MECHANICAL ENGINEERS AUXILIARY, INC.
2 Park Avenue, MS-RB
New York, NY 10016-5990
(212) 591-7650
E-mail: bigleyr@asme.org
Web Site: go.asme.org/scholarships

TYPE:
Scholarships. Lucy and Charles W.E. Clarke Scholarship is for high school seniors participating on a FIRST team.

Baldwin, Cartwright, Chenoweth, Farny, Kezios and Scharp Scholarships are for undergraduate students in mechanical engineering.

Parsons and Rothermel Scholarships are for graduate students with a degree in mechanical engineering, to be used to pursue a Master's or Ph.D. degree in mechanical engineering.

Rice-Cullimore Scholarship is for foreign students at the graduate level.

Student Loan Fund is for juniors, seniors or graduate students enrolled as degree candidates in good standing.

See entry 2427 for full listing.

BELGIAN AMERICAN EDUCATIONAL FOUNDATION, INC.
195 Church Street
New Haven, CT 06510
(203) 785-4055
E-mail: emile.boulpaep@yale.edu
Web Site: www.baef.us
www.baef.be

TYPE:
Fellowships. Predoctoral and postdoctoral fellowships for advanced study in most fields of knowledge with supported work to be undertaken at a Belgian university or an institution of higher learning. Fellowships for Belgian students are also available.

See entry 830 for full listing.

INTERNATIONAL ROAD FEDERATION [881]
500 Montgomery Street, Suite 525
Alexandria, VA 22314
(703) 535-1001
Fax: (703) 535-1007
E-mail: psankey@irf.global
info@irf.global
Web Site: www.irf.global

FOUNDED: 1948

AREAS OF INTEREST:
Highway engineering, management and policy.

NAME(S) OF PROGRAMS:
- **IRF Fellowship Program**

TYPE:
Fellowships; Scholarships. Annual awards for graduate study in highway and traffic engineering for graduate engineers and policymakers.

YEAR PROGRAM STARTED: 1949

PURPOSE:
To train personnel in the field of highways and highway transport.

LEGAL BASIS:
Private foundation.

ELIGIBILITY:
Open to non-U.S. graduate students.
Qualified civil engineers must return to home
country following completion of program.

FINANCIAL DATA:
Amount of support per award: $2,500 to
$15,000 to defray partially one year of
graduate study.
Total amount of support: Approximately
$90,000 annually.
Matching fund requirements: Home country
donors must make up differential.

NO. MOST RECENT APPLICANTS: 45 for the year
2016.

NO. AWARDS: 4.

APPLICATION INFO:
Applications must be submitted directly to
the IRF web site during the open enrollment
period.
Duration: One year.
Deadline: October 13.

PUBLICATIONS:
Annual Report; *Directory of Students.*

IRS I.D.: 52-0793883

STAFF:
C. Patrick Sankey, President and Chief
Executive Officer

ADDRESS INQUIRIES TO:
C. Patrick Sankey, President
(See address above.)

THE KENNEDY MEMORIAL TRUST   [882]

3 Birdcage Walk
Westminster
London SW1H 9JJ England
(44) 020 7222 1151
Fax: (44) 020 7222 7189
E-mail: emily@kennedytrust.org.uk
Web Site: www.kennedytrust.org.uk

FOUNDED: 1966

NAME(S) OF PROGRAMS:
● **Kennedy Scholarships**

TYPE:
Scholarships. Awarded for postgraduate work
for one year at Harvard University or the
Massachusetts Institute of Technology (MIT).
Field of study is unrestricted.

YEAR PROGRAM STARTED: 1966

PURPOSE:
To award graduate scholarships as part of the
British memorial to President Kennedy.

LEGAL BASIS:
Private.

ELIGIBILITY:
Those applying for the Kennedy Scholarships
must be all of the following:
(1) British citizens at the time of application;
(2) ordinarily resident in the U.K.;
(3) wholly or mainly educated in the U.K.
and;
(4) graduates of a British university.

Awards will not be made to postdoctoral
candidates wishing to pursue further research
in their own field. Applications cannot be
accepted from those already in the U.S.
Marriage is not a bar to the award of a
Kennedy Scholarship, but there is no extra
funding for a spouse.

FINANCIAL DATA:
Full tuition and health insurance fees, plus a
stipend for living costs and a grant for
vacation travel within the U.S.
Amount of support per award: Means-tested
stipend of up to $27,250.

NO. MOST RECENT APPLICANTS: 160.

NO. AWARDS: 10 for the year 2020-21.

APPLICATION INFO:
Applications for awards are available on The
Trust web site starting in mid- to late August.
In the same application season, candidates
should make a separate and independent
application to the programme(s) of their
choice at Harvard and/or MIT.

Applications must be submitted online. In
addition to completing an online form,
applicants will be asked to submit an essay
(not to exceed 1,000 words) giving an
account of their academic pursuits and
intellectual interests, their general activities,
their reasons for their choice of course and
institution, and their current plans for the
future.
Duration: One year.
Deadline: Late October.

OFFICERS AND TRUSTEES:
Prof. Sir Mark Walport, FRS, Chairman
Dr. Emily Charnock, Director
Matt Clifford
Dr. Peter Englander
Stephanie Flanders
Prof. Fiona Macpherson
Prof. Anthony Saich
Mary Ann Sieghart
Moira Wallace
Prof. Martin Weale
Prof. Andrew Whittle

ADDRESS INQUIRIES TO:
Dr. Emily Charnock, Director
(See address above.)

LASPAU, INC.   [883]

25 Mount Auburn Street
Suite 203
Cambridge, MA 02138-6095
(617) 495-5255
Fax: (617) 495-8990
E-mail: laspau-webmaster@calists.harvard.edu
Web Site: www.laspau.harvard.edu

FOUNDED: 1965

AREAS OF INTEREST:
Designing and administering academic and
professional exchange programs in Latin
America, the Caribbean, Canada and the U.S.

CONSULTING OR VOLUNTEER SERVICES:
Specialized educational consulting services
are offered by Laspau.

TYPE:
Exchange programs; Fellowships;
Project/program grants; Scholarships;
Technical assistance; Training grants; Travel
grants. Laspau administers school programs,
institutional development programs through
executive training, and graduate admission
tests. Laspau is involved in these exchange
areas: professional/business,
students/educators and training.

YEAR PROGRAM STARTED: 1966

PURPOSE:
To strengthen human capital in Latin
America and the Caribbean through
educational and professional development
opportunities.

LEGAL BASIS:
Nonprofit organization.

ELIGIBILITY:
In most cases, individuals wishing to apply
for a scholarship must be nominated through
the program sponsor by a participating Latin
American, Caribbean or other institution.
(Similarly, all scholarship and loan recipients
agree to return promptly to their home
institutions.)

Laspau gives special priority to regional,
socio-economic and ethnic diversity in order
to broaden opportunities for underserved
populations. Independent applications are
accepted only for certain programs; details
are available at the Programs section on the
web site.

GEOG. RESTRICTIONS: Latin America and the
Caribbean.

FINANCIAL DATA:
Laspau provides grantees and their sponsors
with comprehensive financial services,
disbursement of scholarship grants and
regular reports to sponsoring agencies.
Amount of support per award: Varies.
Total amount of support: Approximately
$13,000,000.

APPLICATION INFO:
Application procedures vary by program.
Check the Programs section on the web site
for details.

PUBLICATIONS:
eNewsletter, annual report; newsletter;
brochures; grantee guides.

MEDICAL LIBRARY ASSOCIATION   [884]

225 West Wacker Drive
Suite 650
Chicago, IL 60606
(312) 419-9094
E-mail: awards@mail.mlahq.org
Web Site: www.mlanet.org

FOUNDED: 1898

AREAS OF INTEREST:
Health sciences librarianship.

NAME(S) OF PROGRAMS:
● **Cunningham Memorial International
Fellowship**

TYPE:
Fellowships; Travel grants; Work-study
programs. Work-study program for medical
librarians from countries other than the U.S.
or Canada for a time period of at least two
weeks.

YEAR PROGRAM STARTED: 1972

PURPOSE:
To assist in the education and training of
medical librarians from countries outside the
continental U.S. and Canada in areas where
improved medical library service is essential
to the health and welfare of the people
through the education of physicians and
scientists.

LEGAL BASIS:
Nonprofit.

ELIGIBILITY:
Candidate must be working in a medical
library or be preparing to work in one in
their country and must have an undergraduate
and a Master's-level library degree. (The
latter requirement may be waived.) Candidate
must have a statement from a responsible
official of the institution where they are
working or plans to work that they will be

guaranteed a position in a medical library when they return to their country; they must also pass the TOEFL exam to demonstrate competence in English and he or she must present three letters of recommendation and a health certificate. Past recipients of the Fellowship are ineligible.

FINANCIAL DATA:

The Fellowship pays a stipend toward living, travel and tuition expenses in the U.S. and Canada. These funds are for the fellow only. No support is provided for spouses or dependents. Payment for travel to and from the U.S. or Canada is the responsibility of the fellow.

Amount of support per award: Up to $4,000.

Matching fund requirements: Candidate may need additional resources during the period of this fellowship.

NO. AWARDS: 1 per year.

APPLICATION INFO:

Applicant must submit the following:
(1) three letters of reference, in English, from responsible persons who are familiar with the applicant's qualifications;
(2) a signed statement, in English, from a responsible official of the institution where he or she is working or plans to work, guaranteeing a position in a health sciences library upon his or her return;
(3) a certificate of good physical health, written in English, from a licensed physician;
(4) a video with a typed transcript and;
(5) an essay.

Duration: At least two to three weeks.

Deadline: December 1. Announcement in March.

STAFF:

Maria Lopez, Grants, Scholarships and Awards Coordinator

ADDRESS INQUIRIES TO:

Coordinator
Grants, Scholarships and Awards
(See address above.)

ORGANIZATION OF AMERICAN STATES

1889 F Street, N.W.
Seventh Floor
Washington, DC 20006
(202) 370-9771
Fax: (202) 458-3967
E-mail: scholarships@oas.org
Web Site: www.oas.org/scholarships

TYPE:

Fellowships; Scholarships; Technical assistance. Awarded for graduate academic studies and/or research, and last two years of undergraduate studies for students in the English-speaking Caribbean, for training in areas contributing to the economic, social, technical and cultural development of OAS member countries.

See entry 790 for full listing.

ORGANIZATION OF AMERICAN STATES [885]

Department of Human Development, Education and Employment
1889 F Street, N.W., Seventh Floor
Washington, DC 20006
(202) 370-9760
Fax: (202) 458-3167
E-mail: rowefund@oas.org
Web Site: www.oas.org/en/rowefund

FOUNDED: 1948

AREAS OF INTEREST:

Any field of study.

NAME(S) OF PROGRAMS:

● **The Leo S. Rowe Pan American Fund**

TYPE:

Assistantships; Awards/prizes; Scholarships; Visiting scholars. Loan program. The Leo S. Rowe Pan American Fund awards interest-free student loans to citizens from Latin America and the Caribbean countries, to help them finance their higher studies or research in accredited universities across the U.S. The Rowe Fund Program is available to foreign students and foreign scholars in U.S. universities.

YEAR PROGRAM STARTED: 1948

PURPOSE:

To provide a loan program to qualified citizens from Latin America and the Caribbean countries to help them finance their higher education or research at accredited institutions in the U.S. by awarding interest-free loans.

ELIGIBILITY:

Rowe Fund loans are granted to individuals currently studying or wishing to pursue graduate, postgraduate or the last two years of undergraduate studies. Additionally, professionals or university faculty who are currently pursuing, or wish to pursue, advanced training, research or technical certificates at accredited institutions in the U.S. are also eligible. This includes semester-abroad programs and professional development courses, with the exception of English-as-a-Second-Language courses. Most fields of study are accepted.

Applicants must be citizens of the following countries: Antigua and Barbuda, Argentina, Barbados, Belize, Bolivia, Brazil, Chile, Colombia, Costa Rica, Dominica (Commonwealth of), Dominican Republic, Ecuador, El Salvador, Grenada, Guatemala, Guyana, Haiti, Honduras, Jamaica, Mexico, Nicaragua, Panama, Paraguay, Peru, Saint Kitts and Nevis, Saint Lucia, Saint Vincent and the Grenadines, Suriname, The Bahamas (Commonwealth of), Trinidad and Tobago, Uruguay or Venezuela (Bolivarian Republic of).

Candidates must:
(1) be nationals of a Latin American or Caribbean member state of the OAS (U.S. and Canadian citizens are not eligible);
(2) have an international student visa (F or J) allowing them to study full-time in the U.S.;
(3) be accepted as a full-time student in an accredited institution of higher learning in the U.S.;
(4) have adequate academic records (grade point average greater than or equal to 3.0);
(5) be able to demonstrate other sources of financing (such as savings, employment, fellowship, funds supplied by the university or relatives, etc.) to cover the greater portion of their academic expenses;
(6) ensure that loans are underwritten by a guarantor (citizen or permanent resident of the U.S.) and;
(7) promise that upon completion of his or her studies, he or she will repay the loan in full and return to his or her country; (if OPT is granted, the return date can be extended up to a year upon completion of studies).

FINANCIAL DATA:

Loans can be used to cover a portion of the tuition and other university fees, essential

books and supplies, room and board and/or emergencies not covered by their principal source of funding. No application or processing fees. Funding is sent directly to the student after approval.

Amount of support per award: Up to U.S. $7,500 per academic semester. Loan recipients may apply for additional loans for subsequent academic semesters, providing the total amount of loans granted does not exceed U.S. $15,000 over the course of the studies for which the loan is granted.

Total amount of support: $15,000 (U.S.) per Rowe Fund recipient.

Matching fund requirements: The prospective applicant must demonstrate other sources of financing (such as savings, employment, a fellowship, funds supplied by the university or relatives, etc.), to cover the greater part of their academic expenses and must present a guarantor.

NO. AWARDS: Averaging 100.

APPLICATION INFO:

Instructions are available on the Rowe Fund web site.

Duration: Two years maximum.

Deadline: A person may apply for a Rowe Fund loan at any time during the course of their studies in the U.S.

STAFF:

Lina M. Sevillano, Program Coordinator

ADDRESS INQUIRIES TO:

Leo S. Rowe Pan American Fund
(See address above.)

*SPECIAL STIPULATIONS:

Repayment is deferred while the loan recipient is in school. Loan repayment is scheduled in 50 equal monthly payments starting three months after completion of studies.

These loans are made with the understanding that, upon completing those studies, loan recipients commit to repay the loan in full and return to their home countries within a year to apply their knowledge and training as well as continue fostering friendship and communication among the peoples of the Americas.

P.E.O. SISTERHOOD [886]

P.E.O. Executive Office
3700 Grand Avenue
Des Moines, IA 50312
(515) 255-3153
Fax: (515) 255-3820
E-mail: ips@peodsm.org
Web Site: www.peointernational.org

FOUNDED: 1869

NAME(S) OF PROGRAMS:

● **P.E.O. International Peace Scholarship**

TYPE:

Scholarships. Awards for selected women from countries other than the U.S. and Canada to pursue graduate study in the U.S. or Canada. Support is available for advanced study in any field except for research. No new applications at the dissertation level.

YEAR PROGRAM STARTED: 1949

PURPOSE:

To promote world peace and understanding through scholarship aid to selected women from other countries to further their education in the U.S. and Canada.

LEGAL BASIS:
Nonprofit organization.

ELIGIBILITY:
Prerequisites for applicants:
(1) Applicant must be qualified for admission to full-time graduate study, working toward a graduate degree in the accredited college or university she will attend in the U.S. or Canada;
(2) A copy of the applicant's confirmation of admission must be submitted with the application. This notice must specify the graduate degree program. No consideration will be given to applicants lacking evidence of admission and;
(3) Prerequisites 1 and 2 do not apply to the applicant who enrolls at Cottey College (Nevada, MO), which is owned and operated by the P.E.O. Sisterhood. The applicant shall present evidence of admission to Cottey.

In order to qualify for her first scholarship, an applicant must have a full year of coursework remaining and be enrolled and on campus for the entire school year. Doctoral students who have completed coursework and are working on dissertations only are not eligible as first-time applicants. Doctoral students in medicine or dentistry will be considered only in the final two years of coursework, internship or residency.

Upon completion of the degree program or Optional Practical Training, the applicant must promise to return to her home country or to a location outside the U.S. or Canada within 60 days, depending on visa status.

A student holding citizenship or permanent residency in the U.S. or Canada is ineligible. Scholarships are not given for online courses, research, internships or for practical training if not combined with coursework. Scholarships are not awarded for travel or repayment of past debt.

FINANCIAL DATA:
Scholarships to students studying in Canadian universities will be paid in Canadian dollars.
Amount of support per award: $12,500 maximum per year, based upon need.

NO. MOST RECENT APPLICANTS: Approximately 450.

NO. AWARDS: Approximately 180.

APPLICATION INFO:
In order to be considered for an IPS Scholarship, a student must submit an eligibility form electronically through the P.E.O. International web site. Paper forms sent to the P.E.O. International office will not be accepted. The online eligibility form can be submitted from September 15 to December 15.
Duration: Initial support is for a period not to exceed one year (two semesters fall-spring), with one renewal possible. Not to exceed a total of two years.
Deadline: To establish eligibility: December 15. Final date to submit completed application materials from applicants already enrolled in the graduate program and school for which their scholarship is intended: March 1. Final date to submit completed application materials from applicants not yet enrolled in the graduate program or school for which the scholarship is intended: April 1. Last date to submit completed application materials for applicants who will be attending Cottey College: April 1. Notification of scholarships: May. Final date for student acceptance of scholarships: June 1.

No eligibility information will be accepted before September 15 or after December 15.

PUBLICATIONS:
Information sheet.

ADDRESS INQUIRIES TO:
Project Supervisor
(See address above.)

*SPECIAL STIPULATIONS:
Applicant must have round-trip or return travel expense guaranteed at the time of application.

THE UNIVERSITY OF SYDNEY   [887]
Scholarships Office
Level 4, Jane Foss Russell Building G02
The University of Sydney N.S.W. 2006
Australia
61 (02) 8627 1444
E-mail: scholarships.officer@sydney.edu.au
Web Site: www.sydney.edu.au/scholarships

FOUNDED: 1850

NAME(S) OF PROGRAMS:
● **Walter Mersh Strong Scholarship**

TYPE:
Scholarships. Awarded for studies at postgraduate level. Tenable at the University of Sydney. The scholarship is available for a Master by coursework program in agriculture, education and social work, or public health.

PURPOSE:
To provide opportunities for graduate students from Papua New Guinea to attend the University of Sydney to undertake a Master by coursework program in agriculture, education and social work, or public health.

LEGAL BASIS:
University.

ELIGIBILITY:
Only citizens from Papua New Guinea may apply. Applicants must have completed the equivalent of an Australian Bachelor degree qualification with outstanding results based on the Australian grading system.

Students who have already commenced postgraduate studies or students transferring with credit exemptions and/or advanced standing are not eligible.

GEOG. RESTRICTIONS: Papua New Guinea.

FINANCIAL DATA:
Amount of support per award: Tuition fees and living allowance of $35,000 AUD per annum for the year 2020.

NO. AWARDS: 1.

APPLICATION INFO:
Application information is available on the web site.
Deadline: As advertised, when funds are available.

Technical assistance and cooperative research

NATIONAL INSTITUTES OF HEALTH   [888]
Division of International Relations
Fogarty International Center
Building 31, Room B2C11
31 Center Drive, MSC 2220
Bethesda, MD 20892-2220
(301) 496-4784
Fax: (301) 480-3414
E-mail: tina.chung@nih.gov
Web Site: www.fic.nih.
gov/programs/pages/japan-fellowships.aspx

AREAS OF INTEREST:
Biomedical and behavioral sciences.

NAME(S) OF PROGRAMS:
● **Japan Society for the Promotion of Science Postdoctoral Research Fellowships (Extramural)**

TYPE:
Fellowships. A limited number of postdoctoral research fellowships are provided by the Japan Science and Technology Agency (JSTA) to U.S. scientists to conduct research in Japan. Types of activity supported include collaboration in basic or clinical research and familiarization with or utilization of special techniques and equipment not otherwise available to the applicant.

YEAR PROGRAM STARTED: 1987

PURPOSE:
To provide a research experience in the biomedical, clinical and behavioral sciences in Japanese laboratories.

LEGAL BASIS:
Government agency.

ELIGIBILITY:
Applicants for the program must be U.S. citizens or permanent U.S. residents, hold a Doctorate in one of the clinical, behavioral or biomedical sciences and make prior arrangements with the appropriate Japanese host researcher as to the research plan.

The program does not provide support for activities that have as their principal purpose brief observational visits, attendance at scientific meetings or independent study.

NO. AWARDS: Up to 10 short-term, 2 long-term.

APPLICATION INFO:
Application information is available on the web site.
Duration: Short-term: One to 12 months; Long-term: 12 to 24 months.
Deadline: Short-term: March 31 and October 1. Long-term: March 31.

ADDRESS INQUIRIES TO:
Tina Chung, M.P.H., Program Officer
(See address above.)

NORTH ATLANTIC TREATY ORGANIZATION   [889]
Emerging Security Challenges Division (ESCD)
NATO HQ, Boulevard Leopold III
B-1110 Brussels Belgium
Fax: (32) 2 707 4232
E-mail: sps.info@hq.nato.int
Web Site: www.nato.int/science

FOUNDED: 1958

AREAS OF INTEREST:
Scientific cooperation between NATO Allies and partner countries.

NAME(S) OF PROGRAMS:
● **Science for Peace and Security (SPS) Programme**

TYPE:
Multiyear projects; workshops and training.

Offers grants to scientists in NATO and Partner countries to collaborate on priority research topics, which include NATO priorities and additional Partner country priorities.

In addition to activities funded by the NATO international budget, the Science for Peace and Security Programme also engages in activities funded directly by one or more nations. These consist of pilot studies, short-term projects and topical workshops which are aligned with NATO's Strategic Objectives and are in areas of priority to NATO or Partner countries. Any NATO or Partner country can initiate a new proposal. The initiating nation seeks the participation of other NATO and Partner nations and this participation is always voluntary. Support Grant Programme is open to experts from both NATO countries and those Partner countries eligible for support.

YEAR PROGRAM STARTED: 1960

PURPOSE:
To stimulate collaboration between laboratories in different countries and thus enhance the effectiveness of research.

GEOG. RESTRICTIONS: NATO countries: Albania, Belgium, Bulgaria, Canada, Croatia, Czech Republic, Denmark, Estonia, France, Germany, Greece, Hungary, Iceland, Italy, Latvia, Lithuania, Luxembourg, Montenegro, Netherlands, Norway, Poland, Portugal, Romania, Slovak Republic, Slovenia, Spain, Turkey, United Kingdom and United States.

FINANCIAL DATA:
Covering project-related costs, organizational costs, travel and living expenses.

Amount of support per award: Typical three-year projects are EUR 150,000 to EUR 300,000.

APPLICATION INFO:
Applications should be presented on the official application forms that can be downloaded from the Science for Peace and Security web site. Applications should be submitted via e-mail to sps.applications@hq.nato.int.

Duration: Depends on the mechanism. Up to three years for the multiyear projects.

Deadline: February 1, June 1 and October 1. Applications may be submitted at any time. Applications received later than this deadline date will be considered during the next evaluation cycle.

PUBLICATIONS:
NATO Science Series.

ADDRESS INQUIRIES TO:
See e-mail address above.

U.S.-ISRAEL BINATIONAL SCIENCE FOUNDATION (BSF)   [890]
P.O. Box 45086 (Hamarpeh Street, No. 8)
Har Hotzvim
Jerusalem 91450 Israel
(972) 2-582-8239
Fax: (972) 2-582-8306
E-mail: bsf@bsf.org.il
Web Site: www.bsf.org.il

FOUNDED: 1972

AREAS OF INTEREST:
Science.

TYPE:
Research grants. Promotes cooperation between the countries in research concerned with science and technology for peaceful purposes through grants to cooperative research projects. Grants are for bilateral, cooperative research between U.S. and Israeli scientists for research conducted in either country.

YEAR PROGRAM STARTED: 1974

PURPOSE:
To strengthen U.S.-Israel science cooperation.

LEGAL BASIS:
Established by government-to-government agreement.

ELIGIBILITY:
Any scientist on the staff of a U.S. or Israel nonprofit research institution may apply by submitting a cooperative research proposal.

Eligible research areas are health sciences, life sciences, physics, chemistry, mathematical sciences, atmospheric and earth sciences, oceanography and limnology, materials research, environmental research, energy research, biomedical engineering, economics, sociology, social and developmental psychology, and computer sciences.

Submission of grant applications is on a split-program basis; namely, eligibility is limited, in alternate years, to either health and life sciences or to exact, natural and social sciences.

FINANCIAL DATA:
Awards are made to cover the direct cost of executing the approved research, i.e., salaries for research assistants, supplies, travel, etc. Salaries of principal investigators are not included.

Amount of support per award: Regular Grant: Up to $230,000 for four years; Start-up Grant: Up to $75,000 over two years.

Total amount of support: Approximately $17,000,000.

APPLICATION INFO:
Proposals are unsolicited and should be submitted jointly by the collaborating scientists via the prospective grantee institution where the research will be performed. Proposals should be submitted via the BSF web site.

Duration: Up to four years.

Deadline: The completed application form must reach the BSF by November 15 for a grant to be awarded in the following year. Awards are made annually and are announced in July.

OFFICERS:
Dr. Yair Rotstein, Executive Director
Dr. Rachel Haring, Assistant Executive Director

ADDRESS INQUIRIES TO:
Dr. Yair Rotstein, Executive Director
(See address above.)

SPECIAL POPULATIONS

Special Populations

THE ABLE TRUST [891]

3320 Thomasville Road
Suite 200
Tallahassee, FL 32308
(850) 224-4493
Fax: (850) 224-4496
E-mail: info@abletrust.org
Web Site: www.abletrust.org

FOUNDED: 1991

AREAS OF INTEREST:
Disabilities and handicapped persons.

NAME(S) OF PROGRAMS:
- **Board Directed Initiative Grants**
- **General Support for Employment Placement Programs**
- **Strategic Employment Placement Initiatives**

TYPE:
Project/program grants. Board Directed Initiative Grants: This program is defined through an announcement by the Board of Directors for proposals that address a specific issue. The release of an Initiative Request is at the discretion of the Board and may occur at any time during a fiscal year. Funding parameters in this category will be described in the published Initiative Request and will correspond to the described objective of the Board Directed Initiative.

General Support for Employment Placement Programs: This program is for general support of employment programs for a grant year. Requests should result in employment placement for participating individuals with disabilities and could encompass equipment and/or staffing needs of an applicant organization to expand an existing program in a new way or create a new program. Awards for this category will occur twice a year at the Fall and Summer Board Meetings.

Strategic Employment Placement Initiatives: This is the primary grant program of The Foundation, and such proposals address the employment placement of Floridians with disabilities. Consideration for these large grants will occur at the Third Quarter Board Meeting of The Foundation.

YEAR PROGRAM STARTED: 1990

PURPOSE:
To be a key leader in providing Floridians with disabilities opportunities for successful employment.

LEGAL BASIS:
501(c)(3) public-private partnership foundation.

ELIGIBILITY:
Proposals will be accepted from Florida-based nonprofit organizations with 501(c)(3) status serving disabled Florida citizens. Each organization may have only one active grant in any one-year time period.

GEOG. RESTRICTIONS: Florida.

FINANCIAL DATA:
Amount of support per award: Average award is $50,000 for organizations. General Support for Employment Placement Programs: Up to $65,000. Strategic Employment Placement Initiatives: Up to $250,000.
Total amount of support: $2,072,119 for fiscal year 2018.

NO. MOST RECENT APPLICANTS: 90.

NO. AWARDS: 78.

APPLICATION INFO:
Application guidelines are available on the Able Trust web site.
Duration: Board Directed Initiative Grants and General Support for Employment Placement Programs: One year. Strategic Employment Placement Initiatives: Three years.
Deadline: General Support for Employment Placement Programs: April 5 and July 5. Strategic Employment Placement Initiatives: December 6.

IRS I.D.: 59-3052307

STAFF:
Tony Carvajal, President and Chief Executive Officer

ADDRESS INQUIRIES TO:
Tony Carvajal
President and Chief Executive Officer
(See address above.)

THE ACTUARIAL FOUNDATION

475 North Martingale Road
Suite 600
Schaumburg, IL 60173-2226
(847) 706-3535
E-mail: Scholarships@ActFnd.org
Web Site: www.actuarialfoundation.org

TYPE:
Scholarships. This scholarship promotes diversity in the profession through an annual scholarship program for Black/African American, Hispanic, Native North American and Pacific Islander students. The scholarship award recognizes and encourages academic achievements by awarding scholarships to full-time undergraduate students pursuing a degree that may lead to a career in the actuarial profession.

See entry 1907 for full listing.

ALZHEIMER'S DRUG DISCOVERY FOUNDATION

57 West 57th Street
Suite 904
New York, NY 10019
(212) 901-8000
Fax: (212) 901-8010
E-mail: info@alzdiscovery.org
grants@alzdiscovery.org
Web Site: www.alzdiscovery.org

TYPE:
Awards/prizes; Conferences/seminars; Research grants.

See entry 2022 for full listing.

THE AMERICAN ACADEMY OF ESTHETIC DENTISTRY

225 West Wacker Drive
Suite 650
Chicago, IL 60606
(312) 981-6770
Fax: (312) 265-2908
E-mail: info@estheticacademy.org
Web Site: www.estheticacademy.org

TYPE:
Research grants.

See entry 2132 for full listing.

AMERICAN ASSOCIATION OF LAW LIBRARIES

105 West Adams Street
Suite 3300
Chicago, IL 60603
(312) 939-4764
Fax: (312) 431-1097
E-mail: membership@aall.org
Web Site: www.aallnet.org

TYPE:
Scholarships. Stipend for graduate study leading to a degree at an accredited school of library or information science or an accredited law school. Preference will be given to individuals with previous service to, or interest in, law librarianship.

See entry 663 for full listing.

AMERICAN BAR FOUNDATION [892]

750 North Lake Shore Drive
Fourth Floor
Chicago, IL 60611
(312) 988-6500
Fax: (312) 988-6579
E-mail: fellowships@abfn.org
Web Site: www.americanbarfoundation.org

FOUNDED: 1952

AREAS OF INTEREST:
Law and social science.

NAME(S) OF PROGRAMS:
- **Summer Undergraduate Research Fellowships**

TYPE:
Internships. Fellows spend the summer gaining hands-on research experience, touring legal institutions and law schools, and meeting with legal practitioners and scholars.

YEAR PROGRAM STARTED: 1988

PURPOSE:
To promote access to legal education and the academy for historically underrepresented individuals by immersing highly talented diverse students in a rigorous empirical and interdisciplinary research environment, while introducing multiple career paths to the legal profession and the academy.

LEGAL BASIS:
Private foundation.

ELIGIBILITY:
Must be a U.S. citizen or permanent resident. The program is open, but not limited to, persons who are African-American, Hispanic/Latino, Native American, or Puerto Rican. Applicants must be sophomores or juniors in college with a grade point average of at least 3.0 on a scale of 4.0 and must be moving toward an academic major in one of the social science or humanities disciplines.

GEOG. RESTRICTIONS: United States.

FINANCIAL DATA:
Amount of support per award: $3,600.

NO. MOST RECENT APPLICANTS: 160.

NO. AWARDS: 4 each year.

APPLICATION INFO:
Application form is available online.
Duration: Eight weeks during the summer.
Deadline: January.

PUBLICATIONS:
Annual report, application guidelines and forms.

ADDRESS INQUIRIES TO:
   Marcilena Shaeffer, Program Coordinator
   (See address above.)

AMERICAN COUNCIL FOR POLISH CULTURE (ACPC)
4628 Columbia Road
Annandale, VA 22003
(301) 717-0662
E-mail: thomaspayne52@verizon.net
Web Site: www.polishcultureacpc.org

TYPE:
   Scholarships.

See entry 1496 for full listing.

AMERICAN COUNCIL OF THE BLIND
1703 North Beauregard Street
Suite 420
Alexandria, VA 22311
(202) 467-5081
(800) 424-8666
Fax: (703) 465-5085
E-mail: info@acb.org
Web Site: www.acb.org

TYPE:
   Assistantships; Awards/prizes; Internships;
   Scholarships. Scholarships for outstanding
   blind students enrolled in academic,
   vocational, technical or professional training
   programs beyond the high school level.

See entry 1497 for full listing.

THE AMERICAN GEOSCIENCES INSTITUTE (AGI)
4220 King Street
Alexandria, VA 22302-1502
(703) 379-2480
Fax: (703) 379-7563
E-mail: wallacescholarship@agiweb.org
Web Site: www.americangeosciences.
org/workforce/harriet-evelyn-wallace-scholarship

TYPE:
   Scholarships. Open to all women pursuing a
   Master's or Doctorate degree in geosciences
   at an accredited institution of higher
   education in a recognized geoscience
   program.

See entry 1893 for full listing.

THE AMERICAN HELLENIC EDUCATIONAL PROGRESSIVE ASSOCIATION   [893]
1909 Q Street, N.W.
Suite 500
Washington, DC 20009
(202) 232-6300
Fax: (202) 232-2140
E-mail: ahepa@ahepa.org
Web Site: www.ahepa.org

FOUNDED: 1922

AREAS OF INTEREST:
   Culture, history, and issues relating to Greece
   and Cyprus.

TYPE:
   Scholarships.

PURPOSE:
   To promote, encourage, induce and advance
   education at the college, university and
   graduate school level.

ELIGIBILITY:
   Applicants must be of Hellenic heritage,
   although their ancestry does not have to be
   100% Greek. The applicant must be a
   member in good standing of AHEPA or
   affiliated organizations, demonstrate financial
   need and have no criminal record.

FINANCIAL DATA:
   Amount of support per award: Up to $2,000.
   Total amount of support: $100,000 for the
   year 2020.

NO. AWARDS: Varies.

APPLICATION INFO:
   Scholarship application is posted online.
   Duration: One year. Renewal possible.
   Deadline: March 31.

ADDRESS INQUIRIES TO:
   Basil Mossaidis, Executive Director
   (See address above.)

THE AMERICAN INSTITUTE OF ARCHITECTS
1735 New York Avenue, N.W.
Washington, DC 20006-5292
(202) 626-7529
Fax: (202) 626-7399
E-mail: scholarships@aia.org
Web Site: www.aia.org

TYPE:
   Scholarships. Awards to provide an
   opportunity for financially disadvantaged
   and/or minority groups to pursue a
   professional degree in architecture.

See entry 375 for full listing.

AMERICAN INSTITUTE OF CHEMICAL ENGINEERS (AICHE)
120 Wall Street, Floor 23
New York, NY 10005-4020
(800) 242-4363
Fax: (646) 495-1503
E-mail: awards@aiche.org
Web Site: www.aiche.org

TYPE:
   Scholarships.

See entry 2416 for full listing.

AMERICAN PLANNING ASSOCIATION   [894]
205 North Michigan Avenue
Suite 1200
Chicago, IL 60601
(312) 786-6345
E-mail: foundation@planning.org
Web Site: www.planning.
org/foundation/scholarships

FOUNDED: 1909

AREAS OF INTEREST:
   Urban and regional planning and the
   promotion of the art and science of planning.

NAME(S) OF PROGRAMS:
   ● **APA Foundation Scholarship**

TYPE:
   Scholarships.

YEAR PROGRAM STARTED: 1970

PURPOSE:
   To celebrate planning by providing partial
   funding for all women and minority (African
   American, Hispanic American or Native
   American) students.

LEGAL BASIS:
   Private, nonprofit educational association.

ELIGIBILITY:
   Applicants must be citizens of the U.S. and
   enrolled or accepted for enrollment in a
   planning program accredited by the Planning
   Accreditation Board (PAB). Applicants must
   document the need for financial assistance.

GEOG. RESTRICTIONS: United States.

FINANCIAL DATA:
   Scholarship provides partial funding for
   tuition and one-year student membership in
   the American Planning Association.
   Amount of support per award: $4,000 to
   $5,000 paid directly to the student's school.
   Total amount of support: Varies.

NO. MOST RECENT APPLICANTS: 86.

NO. AWARDS: 4 annually.

APPLICATION INFO:
   Contact the Association.
   Duration: One academic year.
   Deadline: June.

PUBLICATIONS:
   Program announcement.

ADDRESS INQUIRIES TO:
   See e-mail address above.

AMERICAN POLITICAL SCIENCE ASSOCIATION
1527 New Hampshire Avenue, N.W.
Washington, DC 20036
(202) 483-2512
Fax: (202) 483-2657
E-mail: kmealy@apsanet.org
Web Site: www.apsanet.org/mfp

TYPE:
   Fellowships; Grants-in-aid; Scholarships.
   Awards to aid prospective African American,
   Asian Pacific, Latino/Latina and Native
   American political science students beginning
   the doctoral study of political science.

See entry 1812 for full listing.

AMERICAN PSYCHOLOGICAL ASSOCIATION
Minority Fellowship Program/APA
750 First Street, N.E.
Washington, DC 20002-4242
(202) 336-6127
Fax: (202) 336-6012
E-mail: mfp@apa.org
Web Site: www.apa.org/pi/mfp

TYPE:
   Fellowships. Fellowship is geared to those
   pursuing careers as practitioners specializing
   in the delivery of behavioral health services
   to ethnic minority populations. Students
   specializing in clinical, school and counseling
   psychology are encouraged to apply.

See entry 2357 for full listing.

AMERICAN PSYCHOLOGICAL ASSOCIATION
Minority Fellowship Program/APA
750 First Street, N.E.
Washington, DC 20002-4242
(202) 336-6127
Fax: (202) 336-6012
E-mail: mfp@apa.org
Web Site: www.apa.org/pi/mfp

TYPE:
Fellowships.

See entry 2355 for full listing.

AMERICAN SOCIETY FOR MICROBIOLOGY

Education Department
1752 N Street, N.W.
Washington, DC 20036
(202) 942-9282
Fax: (202) 942-9329
E-mail: fellowships@asmusa.org
Web Site: www.asm.org

TYPE:
Fellowships. Research Capstone Fellowship provides funding for professional development and career networking to underrepresented minority students.

Undergraduate Research Fellowships provide undergraduate, community college and post-Baccalaureate students the opportunity to perform summer research with an ASM faculty member, in addition to receiving professional development training at the Microbe Academy for Professional Development (MAPD).

See entry 1961 for full listing.

AMERICAN SOCIETY FOR MICROBIOLOGY

Education Board
1752 N Street, N.W.
Washington, DC 20036
E-mail: education@asmusa.org
Web Site: www.asm.org

TYPE:
Travel grants. Career Development Grants for Postdoctoral Women are given to support the career development of the candidate by providing funds to travel to a meeting, visit another laboratory, take a course in a geographically distant place, or for other travel to advance the candidate's career. The fields covered by the award are any of those represented by Divisions of the American Society for Microbiology.

See entry 1962 for full listing.

AMERICAN SOCIOLOGICAL ASSOCIATION   [895]

1430 K Street, N.W.
Suite 600
Washington, DC 20005
(202) 383-9005 ext. 842
TDD: (202) 638-0981
E-mail: diversity@asanet.org
Web Site: www.asanet.org

FOUNDED: 1905

AREAS OF INTEREST:
All areas of sociology.

NAME(S) OF PROGRAMS:
● **Minority Fellowship Program**

TYPE:
Fellowships. Predoctoral training fellowships for minority-group members studying sociology.

YEAR PROGRAM STARTED: 1974

PURPOSE:
To provide predoctoral students with financial support, academic and research training, and mentoring, in coordination with university graduate programs, in order to increase the talent pool of minority sociologists in the U.S.

LEGAL BASIS:
Nonprofit professional association.

ELIGIBILITY:
Applicants must be citizens, noncitizen nationals of the U.S. or have been lawfully admitted to the U.S. for permanent residence, DACA eligible, and have in their possession an Alien Registration Card, and they must be enrolled in (and have completed one full academic year) in a program that grants the Ph.D. in sociology.

In addition, applicants must be members of an underrepresented racial and ethnic group, including African Americans, Latinos (e.g., Mexican, Cuban, Puerto Rican), American Indians or Alaskan Natives and Asians (e.g., Chinese, Japanese, Korean, Southeast Asian) or Pacific Islanders (e.g., Hawaiian, Guamanian, Samoan, Filipino).

GEOG. RESTRICTIONS: United States.

FINANCIAL DATA:
Award includes stipend and some tuition assistance.
Amount of support per award: $18,000.
Total amount of support: Varies.

NO. MOST RECENT APPLICANTS: 100.

NO. AWARDS: Up to 5 annually.

APPLICATION INFO:
Applicants must submit completed application forms, transcripts, letters of recommendation and two essays. Selection is based upon evidence of scholarship, writing ability, research potential, financial need and racial and ethnic minority identification.
Duration: Fellowships are tenable for one calendar year.
Deadline: January 31. Announcement by April 30.

STAFF:
Maliyah Grant, Program Coordinator

ADDRESS INQUIRIES TO:
Maliyah Grant, Program Coordinator
(See address above.)

ARMENIAN GENERAL BENEVOLENT UNION

55 East 59th Street, 7th Floor
New York, NY 10022-1112
(212) 319-6383
Fax: (212) 319-6507
E-mail: scholarship@agbu.org
Web Site: www.agbu-scholarship.org

TYPE:
Fellowships; Scholarships.

See entry 1504 for full listing.

ARMENIAN RELIEF SOCIETY OF EASTERN U.S.A., INC.   [896]

80 Bigelow Avenue
Suite 200
Watertown, MA 02472
(617) 926-3801
Fax: (617) 924-7238
E-mail: arseastus@gmail.com
Web Site: www.arseastusa.org

FOUNDED: 1910

NAME(S) OF PROGRAMS:
● **A.R.S. Lazarian Graduate Scholarship**
● **A.R.S. Undergraduate Scholarship**

TYPE:
Awards/prizes; Scholarships. Scholarships to assist students of Armenian ancestry in their higher education studies.

PURPOSE:
To aid Armenian students residing in the U.S.

LEGAL BASIS:
Nonprofit organization.

ELIGIBILITY:
Undergraduate students must meet the following requirements:
(1) must be of Armenian descent;
(2) must be an undergraduate student who has completed at least one college semester at an accredited four-year college or university in the U.S. or must be enrolled in a two-year college and transferring to a four-year college or university as a full-time student in the fall.

Applicants for the Lazarian Scholarship must be of Armenian descent, have graduated from an accredited four-year college or university in the U.S., and be in need of financial assistance. Applicants must be pursuing their studies at the graduate level (Master's or Doctorate degree) in the field of law, history, political science, international relations, journalism, government, economics, business administration, medicine public service, or a similar field.

Scholarships are awarded on the basis of financial need, academic merit and involvement in the Armenian community.

FINANCIAL DATA:
Amount of support per award: Varies, according to donations.

NO. MOST RECENT APPLICANTS: Undergraduate: 25; Graduate: 20.

APPLICATION INFO:
Application form must be downloaded from the web site and mailed to the address listed above.

Undergraduate Scholarship applicant must submit the following with the completed application:
(1) first two pages of their parent's most recent income tax returns;
(2) first two pages of their most recent income tax returns;
(3) sealed official transcript;
(4) two letters of recommendation and;
(5) tuition costs (submit one copy of the school's cost for the academic year).

Lazarian Graduate Scholarship applicant must submit the following with a completed application:
(1) official transcript of undergraduate, as well as graduate, college grades. No faxes or copies will be accepted;
(2) tuition costs (submit one copy of the school's costs for the current academic year);
(3) applicant's most recent income tax return (form 1040). If an income tax return has not been filed, a copy of FAFSA, SAR, or the parents' income tax return must be submitted;
(4) three letters of recommendation and;
(5) proof of enrollment in a graduate program or proof of acceptance into a graduate program.
Duration: One year. No automatic renewal. An individual who receives an award may apply for a scholarship during the following year. Applicants may receive a total of two awards.

Deadline: April 1.

STAFF:
Vart Chiloyan, Executive Secretary

ADDRESS INQUIRIES TO:
Scholarship Committee
(See address above.)

ASTRAEA LESBIAN FOUNDATION FOR JUSTICE   [897]

116 East 16th Street, 7th Floor
New York, NY 10003
(212) 529-8021
Fax: (212) 982-3321
E-mail: info@astraeafoundation.org
Web Site: www.astraeafoundation.org

FOUNDED: 1977

AREAS OF INTEREST:
Racial, economic and gender justice for
lesbian, gay, bisexual, transgender, and
intersex (LGBTI) peoples in the global south
and east.

NAME(S) OF PROGRAMS:
● **International Fund**

TYPE:
General operating grants; Grants-in-aid;
Project/program grants.

PURPOSE:
To provide critically needed financial support
to lesbian-led, LGBTI and progressive
organizations striving to eliminate oppression
based on race, age, sex, religion, sexual
orientation, gender identity, economic
exploitation, physical and mental ability,
anti-semitism, and other such factors.

ELIGIBILITY:
Must be charitable nongovernmental
organizations and meet the criteria used in
determining 501(c)(3) status in the U.S.
Those eligible to apply are:
(1) groups led by and/or for LGBTI
communities;
(2) groups doing work towards social change
on issues affecting LGBTI people;
(3) nongovernmental, not-for-profit groups
with organizational budgets of $500,000
(U.S.) or less and;
(4) groups active for at least one year at the
time of proposal.

Organizations applying must not have a
budget of over $500,000 (U.S.).

GEOG. RESTRICTIONS: Africa, Asia and the
Pacific, Eastern Europe/Commonwealth of
Independent States, Latin America and the
Caribbean, and the Middle East.

FINANCIAL DATA:
Amount of support per award: $7,000 to
$20,000; Average grant: $10,000.
Total amount of support: Varies.

APPLICATION INFO:
Organizations must submit letter of interest.
Full applications are by invitation only.
Duration: One year. Must reapply.
Deadline: Letter of interest: December 15.

ADDRESS INQUIRIES TO:
Namita Chad
Associate Director, Programs or
Miabi Chatterji
Senior Grants Manager
(See address above.)

ASTRAEA LESBIAN FOUNDATION FOR JUSTICE   [898]

116 East 16th Street, 7th Floor
New York, NY 10003
(212) 529-8021
Fax: (212) 982-3321
E-mail: info@astraeafoundation.org
Web Site: www.astraeafoundation.org

FOUNDED: 1977

AREAS OF INTEREST:
Social change organizations and projects
(including film, video, media and cultural
projects) that directly address the depth and
complexity of critical issues in LGBTQ
communities.

NAME(S) OF PROGRAMS:
● **U.S. General Fund**

TYPE:
General operating grants; Grants-in-aid;
Project/program grants. Grants are provided
to LGBTQ people of color-led organizations
fighting for racial and economic justice.

PURPOSE:
To provide critically needed financial support
to lesbian-led, LGBTQ and progressive
organizations striving to eliminate oppression
based on race, age, sex, religion, sexual
orientation, gender identity, economic
exploitation, physical and mental ability,
anti-semitism, and other such factors.

ELIGIBILITY:
501(c)(3) organizations. No grants to
individuals.

GEOG. RESTRICTIONS: United States and its
territories.

FINANCIAL DATA:
Amount of support per award: $7,000 to
$30,000; Average grant: $10,000
Total amount of support: Varies.

APPLICATION INFO:
Unsolicited proposals are not accepted.
Duration: One year. Must reapply.

ADDRESS INQUIRIES TO:
Namita Chad
Associate Director, Programs or
Miabi Chatterji
Senior Grants Manager
(See address above.)

ASTRAEA LESBIAN FOUNDATION FOR JUSTICE   [899]

116 East 16th Street, 7th Floor
New York, NY 10003
(212) 529-8021
Fax: (212) 982-3321
E-mail: info@astraeafoundation.org
Web Site: www.astraeafoundation.org

FOUNDED: 1977

AREAS OF INTEREST:
Impactful art by LGBTQI people and
organizations.

NAME(S) OF PROGRAMS:
● **Global Arts Fund**

TYPE:
Awards/prizes.

YEAR PROGRAM STARTED: 2013

PURPOSE:
To recognize the work of LGBTQI artists
and organizations by providing support to
those who show artistic merit and whose art
and perspective reflect a commitment to
Astraea's mission and efforts to promote
LGBTQI visibility and social justice in
marginalized LGBTQI communities in the
face of exploitations wrought by
globalization, imperialism, and
neocolonialism.

ELIGIBILITY:
LGBTQI people and organizations with
limited access to resources are eligible. The
Fund will consider submissions, requested
through a nomination process, in many
artistic expressions: video, film, poetry,
fictional prose, photography, painting,
performance, dance, theater, music and other
interdisciplinary expressions.

GEOG. RESTRICTIONS: United States, the Global
East and the Global South.

FINANCIAL DATA:
Amount of support per award: $5,000 to
$30,000.

NO. AWARDS: 4 to 10.

APPLICATION INFO:
The Fund only considers submissions
through a nomination process, nominators
having been grantees.
Deadline: Varies.

ADDRESS INQUIRIES TO:
Namita Chad
Associate Director, Programs or
Miabi Chatterji
Senior Grants Manager
(See address above.)

*PLEASE NOTE:
Nominations are not currently accepted for
the Global Arts Fund.

ALEXANDER GRAHAM BELL ASSOCIATION FOR THE DEAF AND HARD OF HEARING   [900]

3417 Volta Place, N.W.
Washington, DC 20007
(202) 337-5220
Fax: (202) 337-8314
E-mail: scholarships@agbell.org
Web Site: www.agbell.org

FOUNDED: 1890

AREAS OF INTEREST:
All areas of study.

NAME(S) OF PROGRAMS:
● **Alexander Graham Bell College
Scholarship Awards**

TYPE:
Scholarships.

YEAR PROGRAM STARTED: 1967

PURPOSE:
To assist students with pre-lingual, bilateral
hearing loss, who use listening and spoken
language, to attend mainstream colleges.

ELIGIBILITY:
Based on age of diagnosis, degree of hearing
loss and grade point average.

FINANCIAL DATA:
Amount of support per award: $1,500 to
$2,500.
Total amount of support: Varies.

NO. MOST RECENT APPLICANTS: Approximately
100.

NO. AWARDS: Approximately 20.

APPLICATION INFO:
Applicants should download the application (preferred) or request via e-mail. Photocopies are not accepted.

Duration: One year. Nonrenewable.

Deadline: Varies. Details posted online in December.

IRS I.D.: 53-0196644

ADDRESS INQUIRIES TO:
College Scholarships
(See address and e-mail above.)

BEN & JERRY'S FOUNDATION [901]

30 Community Drive
South Burlington, VT 05403-6828
(802) 846-1500
E-mail: info@benandjerrysfoundation.org
Web Site: www.benandjerrysfoundation.org

FOUNDED: 1985

AREAS OF INTEREST:
Economic, environmental, social justice and grassroots organizing.

TYPE:
General operating grants; Project/program grants. Grants to nonprofit organizations which facilitate progressive social change by addressing the underlying conditions of societal and/or environmental problems using organizing as a strategy to create change.

YEAR PROGRAM STARTED: 1986

PURPOSE:
To support and encourage organizations that facilitate progressive social change by addressing the underlying conditions of societal and environmental problems.

LEGAL BASIS:
Private foundation.

ELIGIBILITY:
The Foundation generally funds organizations with budgets less than $500,000. Applicant must be a nonprofit 501(c)(3) organization or have a sponsoring agent that has this status. No grants to support basic services. Applicants need to demonstrate that their projects will lead to societal, institutional or environmental change, help ameliorate an unjust or destructive situation by empowering constituents and address the root causes of social and/or environmental problems.

No funding for discretionary or emergency requests, colleges or universities, individuals or scholarships, research projects, religious projects, state agencies, international or foreign programs or direct-service programs.

GEOG. RESTRICTIONS: United States and its territories.

FINANCIAL DATA:
Amount of support per award: $1,000 to $20,000.

Total amount of support: $2,000,000.

REPRESENTATIVE AWARDS:
$10,000 to Ohio Valley Environmental Coalition to continue funding to support their work organizing broad-based opposition to mountaintop removal/valley fill coal mining practices as well as unsafe coal waste ponds; $10,000 to Little Village Environmental Justice Organization to continue funding for the People United for Dignity, Democracy and Justice project.

APPLICATION INFO:
Contact the Foundation.

Duration: One year. Must reapply.

Deadline: Pre-Applications: On or about April 15 and October 15.

PUBLICATIONS:
Annual report; application guidelines; grant recipients list.

IRS I.D.: 03-0300865

STAFF:
Lisa Pendolino, Managing Director
Rebecca Golden, Director of Programs

*PLEASE NOTE:
The Foundation does not accept mailed letters of interest. Please apply online.

JACOB AND HILDA BLAUSTEIN FOUNDATION [902]

One South Street
Suite 2900
Baltimore, MD 21202
(410) 347-7201
E-mail: info@blaufund.org
Web Site: www.blaufund.org

FOUNDED: 1957

AREAS OF INTEREST:
Jewish life and Israel, education, human rights, health and mental health, and the arts.

TYPE:
General operating grants; Matching gifts; Project/program grants.

ELIGIBILITY:
Grants are made to organizations that have tax-exempt status under Section 501(c)(3) of the Internal Revenue Code. No grants are made to individuals.

GEOG. RESTRICTIONS: United States (primarily Baltimore, Maryland) and Israel.

FINANCIAL DATA:
Amount of support per award: Varies.

Total amount of support: $7,900,000 for the year 2018.

APPLICATION INFO:
Application information is available on the Foundation's web site.

Duration: Typically one to two years.

ADDRESS INQUIRIES TO:
Betsy F. Ringel
Executive Director
(See address above.)

CALIFORNIA LIBRARY ASSOCIATION

1055 East Colorado Boulevard
Suite 500
Pasadena, CA 91106
(626) 204-4071
E-mail: info@cla-net.org
Web Site: www.cla-net.org

TYPE:
Scholarships. Support for minority library school students. Support for graduate students in reference/information service librarianship.

See entry 670 for full listing.

CARING FOR MILITARY FAMILIES: THE ELIZABETH DOLE FOUNDATION [903]

600 New Hampshire Avenue, N.W.
10th Floor
Washington, DC 20037
(202) 249-7171
E-mail: molly@elizabethdolefoundation.org
Web Site: www.elizabethdolefoundation.org

FOUNDED: 2012

AREAS OF INTEREST:
Military and veteran caregivers.

NAME(S) OF PROGRAMS:
● **Hidden Heroes Fund**

TYPE:
Project/program grants; Research grants. The Elizabeth Dole Foundation provides grants to qualified nonprofits as part of the Hidden Heroes Fund. This fund is dedicated to supporting innovative programs that make a direct impact on the lives of America's military and veteran caregivers.

YEAR PROGRAM STARTED: 2016

PURPOSE:
To spur targeted support for military caregivers, providing funding to leading nonprofit organizations with an exemplary track record.

ELIGIBILITY:
Organizations must be 501(c)(3) registered, and projects must directly impact the lives of military and veteran caregivers, the spouses, parents, and other loved-ones caring for our nation's wounded warriors at home. Projects must fall under one or more of the Foundation's five pillars of impact: families and communities, education and training, employment and workplace support, financial and/or legal support, and health and well-being.

Use of the Foundation's RAND study data or other relevant research in designing and implementing the project is highly encouraged.

FINANCIAL DATA:
The Foundation has awarded $1,000,000 in grants since inception.

Amount of support per award: Varies depending on the project.

NO. MOST RECENT APPLICANTS: 175.

NO. AWARDS: 16.

APPLICATION INFO:
Information may be obtained by contacting the Foundation at the e-mail address above.

Duration: Funding until completion of the specific project. Project duration is negotiated during the application process. Grant not renewable; however, organizations are allowed to apply more than once.

Deadline: Applications are accepted on a year-round basis.

ADDRESS INQUIRIES TO:
Pavel Sullivan, Vice President of Operations
(See address above.)

*SPECIAL STIPULATIONS:
The program or project must support military caregivers directly. Programs supporting veterans, with incidental or tangential support for their caregivers, will not be considered.

THE CENTER FOR LGBTQ STUDIES [904]

The Graduate Center/CUNY
365 Fifth Avenue, Room 7115
New York, NY 10016
(212) 817-1955
E-mail: clagsfellowships@gmail.com
Web Site: clags.org

FOUNDED: 1991

AREAS OF INTEREST:
Scholarly research on the lesbian, gay, bisexual, transgender, and queer experience.

NAME(S) OF PROGRAMS:
- **The Duberman-Zal Fellowship**

TYPE:
Awards/prizes; Fellowships. An endowed fellowship named for CLAGS founder and first executive director, Martin Duberman, and partner, Eli Zal.

PURPOSE:
To promote the study of historical, cultural, and political issues of vital concern to lesbian, gay, bisexual, and transgendered individuals.

ELIGIBILITY:
Graduate students, independent scholars, or adjunct from any country doing scholarly research on the lesbian/gay/bisexual/transgender/queer (LGBTQ) experience may apply. University affiliation is not necessary.

FINANCIAL DATA:
Amount of support per award: $2,500.

NO. AWARDS: 1.

APPLICATION INFO:
Applications must include the following:
(1) a cover letter with contact information (address, phone number, and e-mail), project title, names of recommenders, and the fellowship being applied for;
(2) a research proposal of seven to 10 pages (double-spaced) including references;
(3) a brief statement of how the funds will be used;
(4) a curriculum vitae and;
(5) two letters of recommendation.

All submissions must be sent electronically to the e-mail listed above.

Letters of recommendation should be electronically directly from recommenders to the e-mail listed above.
Deadline: Mid-November. Final decisions are made in Spring.

PUBLICATIONS:
Annual report.

ADDRESS INQUIRIES TO:
Jasmina Sinanovic, Director of Development and Finance
(See address above.)

*SPECIAL STIPULATIONS:
Fellowship recipient may be asked to participate in CLAG's programming the following academic year to present their research project.

CINTAS FOUNDATION

8724 Sunset Drive
P.M.B. 528
Miami, FL 33173
E-mail: info@cintasfoundation.org
Web Site: www.cintasfoundation.org

TYPE:
Awards/prizes; Fellowships. Awarded to persons of Cuban citizenship or lineage residing outside Cuba for achievement of a creative nature in architecture, painting, sculpture, printmaking, music composition and literature.

See entry 401 for full listing.

THE CONSORTIUM FOR GRADUATE STUDY IN MANAGEMENT

229 Chesterfield Business Parkway
Chesterfield, MO 63005
(636) 681-5553
Fax: (636) 681-5499
E-mail: recruiting@cgsm.org
Web Site: www.cgsm.org

TYPE:
Fellowships. Competitive Advantage is a career and graduate school readiness program for underrepresented minority college students.

Graduate fellowships for minority students interested in management careers in business.

See entry 1724 for full listing.

COUNCIL ON SOCIAL WORK EDUCATION [905]

1701 Duke Street, Suite 200
Alexandria, VA 22314-3457
(703) 683-8080
Fax: (703) 683-8099
E-mail: dnguyen@cswe.org
Web Site: www.cswe.org

FOUNDED: 1952

AREAS OF INTEREST:
Improvement of social services and mental health.

NAME(S) OF PROGRAMS:
- **The Mental Health and Substance Abuse Fellowship Program**

TYPE:
Fellowships. Awards for doctoral-level studies in social work, specializing in mental health and substance abuse-related education, research, policy and practice.

YEAR PROGRAM STARTED: 1974

PURPOSE:
To reduce health disparities and improve health care outcomes of racially and ethnically diverse populations by increasing the number of culturally competent behavioral health professionals available to underserved populations in the public and private nonprofit sectors.

LEGAL BASIS:
Nonprofit organization.

ELIGIBILITY:
Applicants must be American citizens, noncitizen nationals, or have permanent residence status. International students, Deferred Action for Childhood Arrivals students, and work visa holders are not eligible to apply. The fellowship targets, but is not limited to, minority ethnic and racial groups.

Applicant must have a Master's degree in social work from a CSWE-accredited program and be starting full-time study leading to a doctoral degree in social work, or be currently enrolled as a full-time student in a doctoral social work program.

Applicant's career goals should center on leadership in practice, research, teaching, or policy promulgation with underrepresented and underserved persons facing mental health and/or substance abuse challenges.

FINANCIAL DATA:
Fellowship awards include a monthly stipend for one year to help meet living and doctoral study expenses.
Amount of support per award: Varies.
Total amount of support: Varies.

CO-OP FUNDING PROGRAMS: Funded by the Center for Mental Health Services, Center for Substance Abuse Prevention, and the Center for Substance Abuse Treatment in the Substance Abuse and Mental Health Services Administration (SAMHSA).

NO. AWARDS: Up to 25.

APPLICATION INFO:
Complete information is available at the Council web site.
Duration: Three years maximum. Renewable each year subject to availability of funds and progress in program.
Deadline: February 28.

ADDRESS INQUIRIES TO:
E-mail: mfp@cswe.org
(See telephone number above.)

DARTMOUTH COLLEGE [906]

Office of Graduate Studies
Eastman/Marshall
37 Dewey Field Road, Suite 6062, Room 437
Hanover, NH 03755-3526
(603) 646-2106
Fax: (603) 646-8762
E-mail: jane.b.seibel@dartmouth.edu
Web Site: graduate.dartmouth.edu

FOUNDED: 1769

AREAS OF INTEREST:
Fellowships for underrepresented minority scholars (including African-American and Native American scholars) and other graduate scholars with a demonstrated commitment and ability to advance educational diversity.

NAME(S) OF PROGRAMS:
- **Eastman/Marshall Dissertation Fellowships**

TYPE:
Exchange programs; Fellowships.

YEAR PROGRAM STARTED: 1991

PURPOSE:
To increase the number of underrepresented minority faculty in American higher education by supporting African-American, Native American and other scholars with a demonstrated commitment to the advancement of educational diversity.

LEGAL BASIS:
University.

ELIGIBILITY:
Applicants will be chosen on the basis of academic achievement and promise, membership in a racial or ethnic group that is currently underrepresented among faculty in the applicant's academic field, demonstrated commitment to increasing opportunities for underrepresented minorities and increasing cross-racial understanding, and potential for serving as an advocate and mentor for minority undergraduate and graduate students.

GEOG. RESTRICTIONS: United States and Canada.

FINANCIAL DATA:
Fellowship provides stipend, office space, library privileges and research assistance.
Amount of support per award: $36,000 stipend and $2,500 research assistance.
Total amount of support: $77,000 annually.

NO. AWARDS: 2.

APPLICATION INFO:
Application form required. Contact the Office of Graduate Studies. Supporting documentation includes abstract of dissertation prospectus, statement of academic career plan, curriculum vitae, transcripts and three letters of reference.
Duration: Two years.
Deadline: February 18. Announcement April 1.

PUBLICATIONS:
Program announcement.

ADDRESS INQUIRIES TO:
Jane Seibel, Assistant Dean
(See address above.)

*SPECIAL STIPULATIONS:
Fellows are expected to complete the dissertation during the tenure of the Fellowship and may have the opportunity to participate in teaching, either as a primary instructor or as part of a team.

DAUGHTERS OF PENELOPE FOUNDATION, INC. [907]
1909 Q Street, N.W., Suite 500
Washington, DC 20009
(202) 234-9741
Fax: (202) 483-6983
E-mail: president@dopfoundationinc.com
dophq@ahepa.org
Web Site: www.dopfoundationinc.com
www.daughtersofpenelope.org

FOUNDED: 1983

AREAS OF INTEREST:
Philanthropic, educational and cultural activities pertaining to Greek culture.

NAME(S) OF PROGRAMS:
● **Daughters of Penelope National Scholarship Awards**

TYPE:
Scholarships. Academic and Financial Need.

YEAR PROGRAM STARTED: 1984

PURPOSE:
To promote the social, ethical and intellectual interests of members; to perpetuate the study of American ideals and to encourage Hellenic study; to cultivate citizenship and patriotism.

ELIGIBILITY:
Applicant must be a woman and have a current member of their immediate family or legal guardian (court-appointed) in the Daughters of Penelope or the Order of Ahepa, in good standing for a minimum of two years, or be a member in good standing for two years in the Daughters of Penelope or the Maids of Athena.

FINANCIAL DATA:
Amount of support per award: $500 to $2,500 depending on scholarship.
Total amount of support: Varies.

NO. MOST RECENT APPLICANTS: Varies.

NO. AWARDS: 8 for the year 2018.

APPLICATION INFO:
Application is available on the Foundation web site.

Duration: One year.
Deadline: May 1.

ADDRESS INQUIRIES TO:
E-mail:
dopfoundationscholarship@gmail.com

EDUCATIONAL TESTING SERVICE
660 Rosedale Road
Princeton, NJ 08541
E-mail: internfellowships@ets.org
Web Site: www.ets.org/research/internship-fellowship

TYPE:
Internships. Interns in this eight-week program participate in research under the guidance of ETS mentors in one of the areas of interest listed above at ETS office located in Princeton, N.J. Interns also participate in seminars and workshops on a variety of topics.

See entry 1402 for full listing.

FEDERAL HIGHWAY ADMINISTRATION
Center of Transportation Workforce Development
1200 New Jersey Avenue, S.E.
Washington, DC 20590
(703) 235-0538
E-mail: transportationedu@dot.gov
Web Site: www.fhwa.dot.gov/ugp

TYPE:
Fellowships; Internships; Research grants. Dwight David Eisenhower Transportation Fellowship Program's objectives are to attract the nation's brightest minds to the field of transportation, to enhance the careers of transportation professionals by encouraging them to seek advanced degrees, and to retain top talent in the transportation industry of the U.S. This Program encompasses all areas of transportation. The Program has seven award categories:
(1) Eisenhower Graduate (GRAD) Fellowships enable students to pursue Master's degrees or Doctorates in transportation-related fields at the university of their choice;
(2) Eisenhower Grants for Research (GRF) Fellowships acquaint undergraduate and graduate students with transportation research, development and technology-transfer activities at the U.S. Department of Transportation facilities;
(3) Eisenhower Historically Black Colleges and Universities (HBCU) Fellowships provide HBCU students with additional opportunities to enter careers in transportation. The Fellowships also serve as a feeder for other Eisenhower fellowships;
(4) Eisenhower Hispanic Serving Institutions (HSI) Fellowships provide HSI students with additional opportunities to enter careers in transportation. The Fellowships also serve as a feeder for other Eisenhower fellowships;
(5) Eisenhower Tribal College and Universities Fellowships (TCU) provides students with additional opportunities to enter careers in transportation. The Fellowships also serve as a feeder for other Eisenhower fellowships;
(6) Eisenhower Intern Fellowships (EIF) provides students with opportunities to perform a wide range of transportation-related activities at public and private-sector transportation organizations and;
(7) Eisenhower Community College Fellowships provide students at community colleges with opportunities to enter careers in transportation. The Fellowships also serve as a feeder for other Eisenhower fellowships.

See entry 2395 for full listing.

FEEA SCHOLARSHIP PROGRAM
1641 Prince Street
Alexandria, VA 22314
(202) 554-0007
Fax: (202) 559-1298
E-mail: fedshelpingfeds@feea.org
Web Site: feea.org

TYPE:
Scholarships. Merit-based scholarship competition program open exclusively to federal employees, their spouses and their children.

See entry 1521 for full listing.

FOUNDATION FOR SCIENCE AND DISABILITY [908]
503 N.W. 89th Street
Gainesville, FL 32607
(352) 374-5774
E-mail: rmankin1@ufl.edu
Web Site: stemd.org

FOUNDED: 1978

AREAS OF INTEREST:
Science, mathematics, medicine, engineering and computer science.

TYPE:
Grants-in-aid; Research grants.

YEAR PROGRAM STARTED: 1978

PURPOSE:
To assist disabled students who are interested in obtaining a graduate degree in one of the above fields.

LEGAL BASIS:
Affiliate of American Association for Advancement of Science.

ELIGIBILITY:
Open to college seniors and graduate students who have some physical or sensory disability and who have been accepted to graduate or professional school. Selection is based on sincerity of purpose and scholarship and/or research ability.

FINANCIAL DATA:
Funds may be used for an assistive device or instrument, or as financial support to work with a professor on an individual research project, or for some other special need.
Amount of support per award: $1,000.

NO. MOST RECENT APPLICANTS: 5.

NO. AWARDS: At least 1.

APPLICATION INFO:
Application forms may be obtained by writing or e-mailing Dr. Richard Mankin, as listed above, or can be downloaded from the Foundation web site.

Applicants should submit a copy of college transcript, two letters of recommendation, 250-word summary of educational goals including what the funds will be used for, if awarded, and a copy of a U.S. birth or naturalization certificate.

Deadline: December 1.

ADDRESS INQUIRIES TO:
Dr. Richard Mankin, Chairperson
Science Student Grant Committee
(See address above.)

THE FOUNDATION OF THE AMERICAN COLLEGE OF HEALTHCARE EXECUTIVES
300 South Riverside Plaza
Suite 1900
Chicago, IL 60606-6698
(312) 424-9400
Fax: (312) 424-9405
E-mail: contact@ache.org
Web Site: www.ache.org/scholarships

TYPE:
Scholarships. Offered annually, the Albert W.
Dent and the Foster G. McGaw Graduate
Student Scholarships are designated for
students enrolled in their final year of
classroom work in a health care management
graduate program.

Albert W. Dent Graduate Student Scholarship
is only available to minority students.

See entry 1307 for full listing.

4A'S   [909]
1065 Avenue of the Americas, 16th Floor
New York, NY 10018
(212) 682-2500
Fax: (212) 682-8391
E-mail: maip@aaaa.org
Web Site: foundation.aaaa.org

FOUNDED: 1917

AREAS OF INTEREST:
Advertising, media, marketing, data/analytics
and design.

NAME(S) OF PROGRAMS:
● **Multicultural Advertising Intern Program (MAIP)**

TYPE:
Fellowships; Scholarships.

YEAR PROGRAM STARTED: 1973

PURPOSE:
To assist multicultural students in attaining
skills and knowledge necessary for careers in
advertising and to assist advertising agencies
in recruiting multicultural persons for the
professional level.

LEGAL BASIS:
Nonprofit organization.

ELIGIBILITY:
Open to any Black, Native Hawaiian or
Pacific Islander, American Indian or Alaska
Native, Asian, Hispanic, multiracial or
multiethnic student. Students must be
currently enrolled in an undergraduate or
graduate program at any accredited,
degree-granting college or university, or a
student attending a participating 4A's
portfolio school and have completed at least
their junior year by the time of the
internship. Applicants must have a grade
point average minimum of 3.0 on a scale of
4.0 and must be citizens or permanent
residents of the U.S. Applicants must be able
to show their passion to launch an
advertising career through their essays.

Students have the opportunity to work in one
of the basic career areas of advertising
including account management, media buying
and planning, art direction, community

management, copywriting, design,
production, project management, public
relations and strategy.

GEOG. RESTRICTIONS: United States.

FINANCIAL DATA:

Amount of support per award: $12 per hour.
Total amount of support: Varies.

NO. MOST RECENT APPLICANTS: 342.

NO. AWARDS: 100 to 200.

APPLICATION INFO:
Candidates must submit an application,
resume, letters of recommendation, school
transcripts and supporting materials (such as
artwork). $25 application fee required.
Semi-finalists are interviewed before final
selections are made.
Duration: 22 weeks (12-week online Spring
Training and a 10-week internship).
Deadline: Mid- to end of October.

ADDRESS INQUIRIES TO:
Reema Elghossain, Vice President
Talent, Engagement and Inclusion
(See e-mail address above.)

GSBA SCHOLARSHIP FUND   [910]
400 East Pine Street, Suite 322
Seattle, WA 98122
(206) 363-9188
Fax: (206) 568-3123
E-mail: scholarship@thegsba.org
Web Site: www.thegsba.org

FOUNDED: 1991

AREAS OF INTEREST:
Leadership and service in the LGBTQ
community.

TYPE:
Awards/prizes; Scholarships. Scholarships are
intended for college, creative study,
vocational training and postsecondary
education.

YEAR PROGRAM STARTED: 1991

PURPOSE:
To expand economic opportunities for the
Lesbian, Gay, Bisexual and Transgender
community and those who support equality
for all.

LEGAL BASIS:
501(c)(3) nonprofit.

ELIGIBILITY:
Applicants must demonstrate proven
leadership skills, strong academic
achievement and a commitment to making a
positive difference in the world. Applicant
must be a current Washington state resident
pursuing a postsecondary degree in the U.S.

GEOG. RESTRICTIONS: Washington state.

FINANCIAL DATA:
The Fund has awarded over $4,000,000 since
its founding.
Amount of support per award: Up to
$13,000.
Total amount of support: $500,000 for the
year 2019.

NO. MOST RECENT APPLICANTS: 800 for the
year 2019.

NO. AWARDS: 50 for the year 2019.

APPLICATION INFO:
Applicants must submit the online application
form, letters of recommendation and
transcripts.
Duration: One year. Renewable up to four
years.
Deadline: January 10.

PUBLICATIONS:
Guide/Directory, business listing and
resources; *Perspective*, monthly newsletter.

IRS I.D.: 94-3138514

STAFF:
Louise Chernin, President and Chief
Executive Officer
Ilona Lohrey, Vice President of Membership
and Programs
Rachel Chernin, Vice President of Operations
and Finance
Matt Landers, Director of Public Policy and
Government Affairs
Mark Rosen, Deputy Director
Amy Burdick, Senior Business Relationship
Manager
Jeff Boyer, Senior Development Officer
Christine Arrington, Development Manager
and Capitol Hill Specialist
Levi Coffin, Grant Manager and Business
Training Specialist
Toraya Miller, Membership and Program
Manager
Joey Chapman, Membership Development
Manager
Carlos Chavez, Program Events Manager
Taylor Briggs, Scholarship Program Manager
Cade Schmidt, Marketing Specialist

BOARD OF DIRECTORS:
Stephanie Dallas, Chairman
Jay Petterson, Vice Chairman
Carolyn Hojaboom, Treasurer
Brandon Chun, Secretary
Carrie Carson, Scholarship Chairperson
David Blandford
Leda Chahim
Danny Cords
Linda DiLello-Morton
Roz Edison
Rigo Garcia Ortega
Gladys Gillis
Eve Gourley
Jenny Harding
Andrew Held
James Hing
Katie Mooney
Mike Novasio
Alex Oh
Dustin O'Quinn
Lisa Sterritt
Masoud Torabi
Barb Wilson
Beto Yarce

MYRTLE E. AND WILLIAM G. HESS CHARITABLE TRUST [911]
c/o JPMorgan
28660 Northwestern Highway
Southfield, MI 48034
(248) 738-6169
Fax: (800) 919-3085
E-mail: kimberly.l.thomas@jpmorgan.com
Web Site: www.jpmorgan.com/onlinegrants

FOUNDED: 1985

AREAS OF INTEREST:
Catholic charitable organizations located in
Oakland County, MI; Catholic charitable,
educational and scientific objectives.

TYPE:
   Capital grants; Development grants;
   Endowments; General operating grants;
   Project/program grants.

YEAR PROGRAM STARTED: 1985

PURPOSE:
   To provide funds in perpetuity for charitable
   purposes.

LEGAL BASIS:
   Private foundation.

ELIGIBILITY:
   Limited to Catholic organizations with
   charitable, educational and scientific
   objectives. Particular preference being given
   to such objectives within the confines of
   Waterford and White Lake Townships.

GEOG. RESTRICTIONS: Waterford and White
   Lake townships in Oakland County,
   Michigan.

FINANCIAL DATA:
   Amount of support per award: $2,500 to
   $25,000.
   Total amount of support: Varies.

NO. MOST RECENT APPLICANTS: 28.

NO. AWARDS: 26.

APPLICATION INFO:
   Only online applications are accepted.
   Duration: One year. Renewals possible.
   Deadline: April 30.

ADDRESS INQUIRIES TO:
   Kimberly Thomas, Trust Officer
   (See address above.)

IMMUNE DEFICIENCY
FOUNDATION   [912]
110 West Road
Suite 300
Towson, MD 21204
(800) 296-4433
Fax: (410) 321-9165
E-mail: dantilla@primaryimmune.org
Web Site: www.primaryimmune.org

FOUNDED: 1980

AREAS OF INTEREST:
   Immunodeficiency diseases.

NAME(S) OF PROGRAMS:
   ● **The Varun Bhaskaran (WAS)**
     Scholarship Program of IDF

TYPE:
   Scholarships.

YEAR PROGRAM STARTED: 2013

ELIGIBILITY:
   Scholarship for undergraduate or graduate
   students living with Wiskott-Aldrich
   Syndrome.

GEOG. RESTRICTIONS: United States.

FINANCIAL DATA:
   Amount of support per award: Varies.
   Total amount of support: Varies.

APPLICATION INFO:
   Contact the Foundation for application
   procedures.
   Duration: Renewable yearly based on
   financial need and academic participation.
   Deadline: Usually February 1 to April 1.

ADDRESS INQUIRIES TO:
   Dan Antilla, Program Manager
   (See address above.)

INSTITUTE OF INDUSTRIAL
AND SYSTEMS ENGINEERS
(IISE)
3577 Parkway Lane
Building 5, Suite 200
Norcross, GA 30092
(770) 449-0461
Fax: (770) 441-3295
E-mail: bcameron@iise.org
Web Site: www.iise.org

TYPE:
   Fellowships; Scholarships. The Institute
   supports the advancement of engineering
   education and research through scholarships
   and fellowships to recognize and support
   these types of endeavors.

See entry 2434 for full listing.

THE JAPANESE AMERICAN
CITIZENS LEAGUE (JACL)
Washington, DC Office
1629 K Street, N.W., Suite 400
Washington, DC 20006
(202) 223-1240
Fax: (202) 296-8082
E-mail: dinoue@jacl.org
Web Site: www.jacl.org

TYPE:
   Travel grants. The Kakehashi Program is a
   new international program, part of JACL's
   leadership development. It is for college
   students and consists of five webinars and a
   nine-day trip to Japan.

See entry 787 for full listing.

JEWISH COMMUNITY
FOUNDATION OF LOS
ANGELES
6505 Wilshire Boulevard
Suite 1200
Los Angeles, CA 90048
(323) 761-8700
Fax: (323) 761-8720
E-mail: info@jewishfoundationla.org
Web Site: www.jewishfoundationla.org

TYPE:
   Awards/prizes; Capital grants;
   Project/program grants; Seed money grants.
   Capital Grants: Construction and renovation
   projects for facilities that predominantly
   serve members of the Los Angeles Jewish
   community.

   Cutting Edge Grants: New programs with the
   potential for transformative impact that
   address critical needs in the Los Angeles
   Jewish community.

   General Community Grants: Programs by
   organizations outside of the Jewish
   community which address high-priority
   concerns in the Los Angeles community.

   Israel Grants: Programs that have an impact
   on economic development and pluralistic
   Jewish identity in Israel.

   Next Stage Grants: Capacity building support
   for select former Cutting Edge Grant
   recipients to get to the next stage of their
   success.

See entry 1195 for full listing.

JEWISH FEDERATION OF
METROPOLITAN CHICAGO
ACADEMIC SCHOLARSHIP
PROGRAM
JVS Career and Employment/JCFS Chicago
216 West Jackson Boulevard, Suite 700
Chicago, IL 60606-6921
(312) 673-3444
Fax: (312) 553-5544
E-mail: jvsscholarship@jcfs.org
Web Site: www.jcfs.org/jvsscholarships

TYPE:
   Awards/prizes; Scholarships. Awards to
   individuals for the academic year.

See entry 1540 for full listing.

THE LUCIUS N. LITTAUER
FOUNDATION, INC.   [913]
220 Fifth Avenue, 19th Floor
New York, NY 10001-7708
(646) 237-5158
E-mail: adivack@littauerfoundation.org
Web Site: littauerfoundation.org

FOUNDED: 1929

AREAS OF INTEREST:
   Access to opportunity for low-income and
   marginalized populations in New York and
   Israel, support for Jewish communal life in
   New York, and Judaica librairies and
   archives.

TYPE:
   General operating grants; Project/program
   grants; Seed money grants; Training grants;
   Loan forgiveness programs.

YEAR PROGRAM STARTED: 1929

PURPOSE:
   To support education, health care and social
   welfare in the Jewish world and beyond.

LEGAL BASIS:
   Independent foundation.

ELIGIBILITY:
   Funds are awarded to nonprofit 501(c)(3)
   institutions. No grants to individuals.

GEOG. RESTRICTIONS: New York, New York and
   Israel.

FINANCIAL DATA:
   Amount of support per award: Varies.
   Total amount of support: $3,029,350 for the
   year 2019.

NO. AWARDS: 95 for the year 2019.

APPLICATION INFO:
   All grant requests must be made online
   through the Foundation web site. Application
   includes a full description of project, budget
   request, timetable for completion, institution
   which will administer grant and contact
   person.
   Duration: Varies. Renewal possible.
   Deadline: Applications are accepted on a
   rolling basis.

PUBLICATIONS:
   Guidelines.

IRS I.D.: 13-1688027

ADDRESS INQUIRIES TO:
Alan Divack, Program Director
(See address above.)

LUSO-AMERICAN EDUCATION FOUNDATION

7080 Donlon Way
Suite 200
Dublin, CA 94568
(925) 828-3883
Fax: (925) 828-4554
E-mail: education@luso-american.org
Web Site: www.luso-american.org/laef

TYPE:
Scholarships.

See entry 605 for full listing.

MARINE BIOLOGICAL LABORATORY

7 MBL Street
Woods Hole, MA 02543
(508) 289-7173
Fax: (508) 289-7934
E-mail: researchprograms@mbl.edu
Web Site: www.mbl.edu

TYPE:
Research grants.

See entry 1969 for full listing.

MAURICE J. MASSERINI TRUST   [914]

c/o Wells Fargo Private Bank
4365 Executive Drive, 18th Floor
San Diego, CA 92121
(858) 622-6958
Fax: (858) 622-6848
E-mail: grantadministration@wellsfargo.com
Web Site: www.wellsfargo.com/private-foundations/masserini-trust

AREAS OF INTEREST:
Underprivileged children, the elderly,
religious, human services, health,
environment/animals, education, and arts and
culture.

TYPE:
Project/program grants.

ELIGIBILITY:
Eligible organizations must be IRS 501(c)(3)
tax-exempt and be located in San Diego
County, CA. Start-up organizations or
salaries are generally not supported.

GEOG. RESTRICTIONS: San Diego County,
California.

FINANCIAL DATA:
Amount of support per award: Generally
$5,000 to $15,000.
Total amount of support: Varies.

NO. AWARDS: 20 per year.

APPLICATION INFO:
Applications are submitted through an online
application process.
Duration: One year. Renewable by
reapplication.
Deadline: June 30.

ADDRESS INQUIRIES TO:
Wells Fargo Philanthropic Services
(See e-mail address above.)

MEDICAL LIBRARY ASSOCIATION   [915]

225 West Wacker Drive
Suite 650
Chicago, IL 60606
(312) 419-9094
E-mail: awards@mail.mlahq.org
Web Site: www.mlanet.org

FOUNDED: 1898

AREAS OF INTEREST:
Health sciences librarianship.

NAME(S) OF PROGRAMS:
● **MLA Scholarship for
Underrepresented Students**

TYPE:
Awards/prizes; Scholarships. Awarded for
study in health sciences librarianship.

YEAR PROGRAM STARTED: 1964

PURPOSE:
To contribute to the support of
underrepresented individuals who are
qualified to make a contribution to health
sciences librarianship.

LEGAL BASIS:
Nonprofit.

ELIGIBILITY:
Applicant must be:
(1) a member of an underrepresented group;
(2) entering a Master's program at an
ALA-accredited graduate library school or
must have completed no more than half of
their graduate program academic
requirements at the time the award is made
and;
(3) a citizen of or have permanent residence
status in the U.S. or Canada.

A past recipient of the MLA Scholarship or
the MLA Scholarship for Underrepresented
Students is ineligible. Membership in MLA
is not required.

FINANCIAL DATA:
Amount of support per award: Up to $5,000.

NO. AWARDS: 1 per year.

APPLICATION INFO:
Applicant must submit the following:
(1) a completed online application;
(2) two letters of reference from persons not
related to the applicant who are
knowledgeable about the applicant's
character, education and abilities;
(3) official transcript from each college or
university attended, sent directly from the
respective institution that grants either
Baccalaureate degree or library study degree
and;
(4) copy of catalog or web page of
applicant's library school, which states the
number of credits needed for applicant's
degree.
Duration: One year.
Deadline: December 1.

STAFF:
Maria Lopez, Grants, Scholarships and
Awards Coordinator

ADDRESS INQUIRIES TO:
Coordinator
Grants, Scholarships and Awards
(See address above.)

MICHIGAN STATE UNIVERSITY, THE GRADUATE SCHOOL   [916]

Chittenden Hall
466 West Circle Drive
East Lansing, MI 48824
(517) 353-3220
Fax: (517) 353-3355
E-mail: gradschool@grd.msu.edu
Web Site: grad.msu.edu

FOUNDED: 1855

AREAS OF INTEREST:
Higher education.

NAME(S) OF PROGRAMS:
● **Academic Achievement Graduate
Assistantships**
● **Education Opportunity Fellowship**
● **University Distinguished Fellowships**
● **University Enrichment Fellowships**

TYPE:
Assistantships; Fellowships.

YEAR PROGRAM STARTED: 1970

PURPOSE:
To increase participation by all U.S. students
in graduate programs leading to advanced
degrees in fields that do not yet reflect the
inclusive diversity of the U.S. population; to
enhance their retention and degree
completion.

LEGAL BASIS:
University.

ELIGIBILITY:
Candidates are considered for the Academic
Achievement Graduate Assistantship if
nominated by the academic unit of the
graduate program. Candidates for the
Education Opportunity Fellowship may apply
directly upon admission into a graduate
program.

Candidate must be admitted to or enrolled in
a graduate/professional degree-granting
program at Michigan State University. Some
programs require a student to demonstrate
financial need. To be considered for financial
support under the Graduate Education
Opportunity Programs, all recipients must be
able to prove U.S. citizenship or permanent
residency. Funding based on financial need.

University Distinguished Fellowship and
University Enrichment Fellowship are
merit-based recruitment fellowships. Students
must be nominated by a department/college.

GEOG. RESTRICTIONS: United States.

FINANCIAL DATA:
Amount of support per award: Academic
Achievement Graduate Assistantship
(AAGA): Level I, half-time, $13,032 to
$23,361, plus nine credits (Fall/Spring),
including health care; Education Opportunity
Fellowship (EOF): $1,500 per semester, plus
$100 to $200 per dependent for each
semester; University Distinguished
Fellowships (UDF) and University
Enrichment Fellowships (UEF): $29,000, plus
six to 10 credits (Fall/Spring) or three to five
credits (Summer), including health care.
Total amount of support: Approximately
$270,000.

APPLICATION INFO:
Contact the Graduate School.
Duration: Five to 11 semesters.
Deadline: April 15.

ADDRESS INQUIRIES TO:
Thomas Jeitschko
Dean of the Graduate School
(See address above.)

*SPECIAL STIPULATIONS:
Students must be enrolled in a graduate/professional program at Michigan State University.

MITSUBISHI ELECTRIC AMERICA FOUNDATION

1300 Wilson Boulevard
Suite 210
Arlington, VA 22209
(703) 276-8240
E-mail: mea.foundation@meus.mea.com
Web Site: www.meaf.org

TYPE:
Demonstration grants; Internships; Matching gifts; Project/program grants; Seed money grants; Technical assistance; Training grants. Grants are offered to make a better world for all by helping young people with disabilities to maximize their potential and participation in society.

See entry 1457 for full listing.

THE NATIONAL ACADEMIES OF SCIENCES, ENGINEERING, AND MEDICINE [917]

Fellowships Office
Ford Foundation Fellowship Programs
500 Fifth Street, N.W.
Washington, DC 20001
(202) 334-2872
E-mail: FordApplications@nas.edu
Web Site: www.nationalacademies.org/ford

FOUNDED: 1979

AREAS OF INTEREST:
Behavioral and social sciences, humanities, engineering, mathematics, physical sciences, biological sciences, education and interdisciplinary programs comprised of two or more eligible disciplines supported by the fellowship program.

NAME(S) OF PROGRAMS:
● **Ford Foundation Fellowship Programs**

TYPE:
Fellowships. Awards for study in research-based doctoral programs leading to the Ph.D. or Sc.D. degrees, as well as postdoctoral studies.

YEAR PROGRAM STARTED: 1986

PURPOSE:
To increase the diversity of the nation's college and university faculties by increasing their ethnic and racial diversity, to maximize the educational benefits of diversity, and to increase the number of professors who can and will use diversity as a resource for enriching the education of all students.

LEGAL BASIS:
Private foundation.

ELIGIBILITY:
Applicants to these Ford Foundation Fellowships must be U.S. citizens, U.S. permanent residents, or U.S. nationals, individuals granted deferred action status under Deferred Action for Childhood Arrivals Program, political asylees, or refugees by the application deadline.

Predoctoral Fellowships are intended for students who plan to work toward the Ph.D. or Sc.D. degree in selected academic disciplines that lead to careers in teaching and research at the college or university level, and who have at least three years remaining in their program. They may be college seniors, or individuals who have completed undergraduate study, or who have completed some graduate study, or who have already enrolled in a Ph.D. or Sc.D. program.

Dissertation Fellowships are intended for Ph.D. or Sc.D. degree candidates who, by the application deadline, have completed all departmental and institutional requirements for the Ph.D. or Sc.D., except for the writing and defense of the dissertation. Fellowship support is intended for the final year of dissertation writing.

Predoctoral and Dissertation Fellowships: Persons holding a doctoral degree earned at any time and in any field are not eligible to apply. Applicants must be Ph.D. or Sc.D. degree candidates studying one of the fields in the behavioral and social sciences, humanities, social sciences, life sciences, chemistry, earth sciences, physics and astronomy, engineering, mathematics, computer science, education, or interdisciplinary programs composed of two or more eligible disciplines supported by the fellowship program. They must aspire to a teaching and research career. Awards are not made for practice-oriented programs in business administration and management, health sciences, public health, home economics, library science, speech pathology and audiology, personnel and guidance, social work, fine arts and performing arts and education.

Postdoctoral Fellowships are intended for fellows to engage in a year of postdoctoral research and scholarship in an environment free from the interference of their normal professional duties. Applicants are required to have earned a Ph.D. or Sc.D. degree from a U.S. educational institution within a specified time period. Only those individuals already engaged in a teaching and research career or those planning such a career are eligible to apply in this program. Previous Ford Foundation postdoctoral fellows may not reapply. Awards will be made in research-based areas of the behavioral and social sciences, humanities, life sciences, chemistry, earth sciences, physics and astronomy, engineering, mathematics, computer science, education, or for interdisciplinary programs composed of two or more eligible disciplines supported by the fellowship program.

FINANCIAL DATA:
Amount of support per award: Dissertation Fellowships: $25,000 for one year and invitation to attend one Conference of Ford Fellows; Predoctoral Fellowships: Annual $24,000 stipend, invitation to attend at least one Conference of Ford Fellows; Postdoctoral Fellowships: $45,000 stipend and invitation to attend one Conference of Ford Fellows.

CO-OP FUNDING PROGRAMS: Program funded by the Ford Foundation.

NO. MOST RECENT APPLICANTS: Approximately 3,000 reviewed applicants.

NO. AWARDS: 70 Predoctoral Fellowships, 36 Dissertation Fellowships, and 20 Postdoctoral Fellowships.

APPLICATION INFO:
Applications are to be submitted online.
Duration: Predoctoral Fellowships: Three years; Dissertation and Postdoctoral Fellowships: Nine or 12 months.

Deadline: Predoctoral Fellowships: December 17, 5 P.M.; Dissertation and Postdoctoral Fellowships: December 10, 5 P.M.

PUBLICATIONS:
Program announcement.

ADDRESS INQUIRIES TO:
See e-mail address above.

NATIONAL ACTION COUNCIL FOR MINORITIES IN ENGINEERING, INC. (NACME)

One North Broadway
Suite 601
New York, NY 10601
(914) 539-4010
Fax: (914) 539-4032
E-mail: scholarships@nacme.org
Web Site: www.nacme.org

TYPE:
Block grants; Scholarships. The NACME Bridge Scholarship program is designed to support students who have received and accepted freshman admission to an undergraduate engineering or computer science program at a NACME Partner Institution and have been invited to attend a residential academic program the summer prior to freshman matriculation. The scholarship covers the published cost of participation of the Bridge program.

The NACME Collegiate Scholarship provides support for qualified underrepresented students, Black/African American, Native/American Indian, and Laninx/Hispanic American, who have directly applied to an engineering or computer science undergraduate program at a NACME Partner Institution.

See entry 2436 for full listing.

NATIONAL ACTION COUNCIL FOR MINORITIES IN ENGINEERING, INC. (NACME)

One North Broadway
Suite 601
New York, NY 10601
(914) 539-4010
Fax: (914) 539-4032
E-mail: scholarships@nacme.org
Web Site: www.nacme.org

TYPE:
Fellowships; Scholarships. Americas Styrenics Scholarship provides financial support that will promote high academic achievement, leadership qualities and commitment to excellence at Louisiana State University.

Autodesk NACME Scholarship is designed to provide financial support and work experience that will promote high academic achievement among underrepresented students enrolled in an undergraduate computer science or computer engineering program. The award is accompanied by a summer internship.

Bechtel Undergraduate Scholarship Award is a financial support program that encourages and recognizes high academic achievement of students interested in pursuing a corporate career in a construction-related engineering discipline. The award is accompanied by an internship and mentoring opportunities.

Bechtel Undergraduate Women in Engineering Scholarship is geared towards female students who are rising juniors or seniors.

Chevron Scholarship Program awards current matriculating students in engineering, specifically mechanical, chemical, electrical, civil and petroleum as well as computer science (and qualifying information technology programs), who have the potential to excel as scholars, leaders and potential contributors to Chevron Corporation. Assessment will be based on academic merit and leadership potential.

Sidney and Katherine Friend Scholarship is a joint endowment established between NACME and New York University, Tandon School of Engineering.

William Randolph Hearst Endowment Scholarship is supported by the William Randolph Hearst Foundation.

Phillip D. Reed Undergraduate Endowment Fellowship is made possible through an endowment from the Phillip D. Reed Foundation.

See entry 2437 for full listing.

NATIONAL ASSOCIATION OF HISPANIC JOURNALISTS   [918]

1050 Connecticut Avenue, N.W.
5th Floor
Washington, DC 20036
(202) 853-7760
(202) 909-6880
E-mail: nahj@nahj.org
lafrank@nahj.org
Web Site: nahj.org

FOUNDED: 1984

AREAS OF INTEREST:
English or Spanish language print, photo, broadcast or online journalism.

NAME(S) OF PROGRAMS:
- **Jonathan Camuy Scholarship**
- **NAHJ Cecilia Alvear Scholarship**
- **NAHJ Facebook Journalism Project Scholarship**
- **NAHJ General Scholarships (Ruben Salazar Fund)**
- **NAHJ Maria Elena Salinas Scholarship**
- **NAHJ/NBC News Summer Fellows Program**

TYPE:
Awards/prizes; Conferences/seminars; Fellowships; General operating grants; Internships; Matching gifts; Project/program grants; Research grants; Scholarships; Seed money grants; Training grants; Travel grants.

YEAR PROGRAM STARTED: 1986

PURPOSE:
To encourage the study and practice of journalism and mass communications by Hispanics.

ELIGIBILITY:
Open to high school seniors, college undergraduates and first-year graduate students pursuing careers in print, photo, broadcast or online journalism.

GEOG. RESTRICTIONS: United States and Puerto Rico.

FINANCIAL DATA:
Amount of support per award: Jonathan Camuy Scholarship: $1,500; NAHJ Cecilia Alvear Scholarship and NAHJ Maria Elena

Salinas Scholarship: $2,500; NAHJ Facebook Journalism Scholarship: $10,000; NAHJ General Scholarships: $2,000.

NO. MOST RECENT APPLICANTS: Approximately 230.

NO. AWARDS: 50 scholarships.

APPLICATION INFO:
Scholarship applications are available online in January of each year.
Duration: One year.
Deadline: March.

IRS I.D.: 95-3927141

ADDRESS INQUIRIES TO:
Scholarships Department
(See address above.)

NATIONAL FEDERATION OF THE BLIND   [919]

NFB Scholarship Program
200 East Wells Street at Jernigan Place
Baltimore, MD 21230
(410) 659-9314 ext. 2415
E-mail: scholarships@nfb.org
Web Site: www.nfb.org/scholarships

FOUNDED: 1940

AREAS OF INTEREST:
Improving the quality of life for blind persons by creating opportunity and combating discrimination.

CONSULTING OR VOLUNTEER SERVICES:
Major programs in scholarships, promoting employment for the blind, civil rights litigation, helping parents of blind children, public education, etc.

NAME(S) OF PROGRAMS:
- **National Federation of the Blind Scholarship Program**

TYPE:
Scholarships. Awarded on the basis of academic excellence, service to the community and leadership. Provides a one-time grant plus a continuing program of mentors and seminars for blind college students.

PURPOSE:
To create opportunities for blind persons residing in and attending college or university in the U.S. or Puerto Rico.

LEGAL BASIS:
Nonprofit, tax-deductible, nationwide membership organization of the blind.

ELIGIBILITY:
Applicants residing in the U.S. or Puerto Rico must be legally blind and pursuing or planning to pursue a full-time postsecondary course of study in the upcoming fall semester in the U.S or Puerto Rico. One scholarship, however, may be given to a person working full-time while attending school part-time. In addition, some scholarships have been further restricted by the donor. Recipients of Federation scholarships need not be members of the National Federation of the Blind. International students are not eligible unless they reside in the U.S. or Puerto Rico.

GEOG. RESTRICTIONS: United States and Puerto Rico.

FINANCIAL DATA:
Scholarship includes financial assistance to attend the NFB Annual Convention and other gifts.
Amount of support per award: $3,000 to $12,000; other gifts vary in value.

Total amount of support: Over $120,000 annually.

NO. MOST RECENT APPLICANTS: 470.

NO. AWARDS: 30 (1 $12,000 scholarship, 1 $10,000 scholarship, 2 $8,000 scholarships, 4 $5,000 scholarships and 22 $3,000 scholarships).

APPLICATION INFO:
Application information is available on the web site. Those interested in applying should read the rules of eligibility, the timeline, the Submission Checklist and the Scholarship FAQ, then fill in the online Scholarship Application Form. Supply the required documents and complete one telephone interview with the NFB representative.
Duration: One year. Renewals possible upon reapplication.
Deadline: Scholarship applications are accepted from November 1 of the previous year to March 31 of the year in which the scholarship is to be awarded. All documentation and the interview request must be received by the deadline. Notification by June 1.

ADDRESS INQUIRIES TO:
Scholarship Committee
(See address above.)

*SPECIAL STIPULATIONS:
Applicants must be legally blind in both eyes. Winners are assisted to attend the NFB Annual Convention in July. Attendance is required and a part of the prize awarded to each winner.

THE NATIONAL GEM CONSORTIUM   [920]

1430 Duke Street
Alexandria, VA 22314
(703) 562-3646
Fax: (202) 207-2518
E-mail: info@gemfellowship.org
Web Site: www.gemfellowship.org

FOUNDED: 1976

AREAS OF INTEREST:
Engineering at the Master's and Doctorate levels and science at the Doctorate level.

CONSULTING OR VOLUNTEER SERVICES:
Mentor/protege training, graduate study preparedness training, success training, programs and publications designed to promote graduate education in engineering and science.

NAME(S) OF PROGRAMS:
- **The GEM M.S. Engineering Fellowship**
- **The GEM Ph.D. Engineering Fellowship**
- **The GEM Ph.D. Science Fellowship**
- **GRAD Lab**
- **Graduate and Faculty Development Program**

TYPE:
Fellowships; Internships. All-expense fellowship for graduate study (tuition and stipend) and paid summer work experience in a scientific or engineering environment.

YEAR PROGRAM STARTED: 1976

PURPOSE:
To increase the number of minorities with graduate degrees in engineering and science.

LEGAL BASIS:
Incorporated in the State of Virginia; 501(c)(3) tax-exempt.

ELIGIBILITY:

Must be a U.S. citizen or permanent resident and an American Indian, Black American, Mexican American or Hispanic American.

FINANCIAL DATA:

Amount of support per award: M.S. Fellowship: Tuition and fees, plus a $16,000 stipend over entire M.S. program. Master's-level students also are assigned to a paid internship. Ph.D. Fellowships: $16,000 stipend applied in one academic year. Additional stipend support from GEM University.

Total amount of support: Varies.

NO. MOST RECENT APPLICANTS: 1,700.

NO. AWARDS: 200 for the year 2018.

APPLICATION INFO:

Three recommendations, GRE scores, and unofficial transcript of all college work.

Duration: Average three semesters or four quarters for Master's; five years renewable for Doctorate.

Deadline: November 15. Announcement May 31.

PUBLICATIONS:

Annual report; application brochure.

OFFICERS:

Michael Greene, President

ADDRESS INQUIRIES TO:

Fellowship Administration Team (See address above.)

NATIONAL INSTITUTE OF GENERAL MEDICAL SCIENCES

National Institutes of Health
45 Center Drive, MSC 6200
Bethesda, MD 20892-6200
(301) 496-7301
Fax: (301) 402-0224
E-mail: info@nigms.nih.gov
Web Site: www.nigms.nih.gov

TYPE:

Fellowships; Research grants; Training grants; Research contracts. Capacity building. The National Institute of General Medical Sciences (NIGMS) supports basic research that increases understanding of biological processes and lays the foundation for advances in disease diagnosis, treatment and prevention. NIGMS-funded scientists investigate how living systems work at a range of levels, from molecules and cells to tissues, whole organisms and populations. The Institute also supports research in certain clinical areas, primarily those that affect multiple organ systems. To assure the vitality and continued productivity of research enterprise, NIGMS provides leadership in training the next generation of scientists, in enhancing the diversity of scientific workforce, and in developing research capacities throughout the country.

See entry 2086 for full listing.

NATIONAL INSTITUTE OF GENERAL MEDICAL SCIENCES

Center for Research Capacity Building
45 Center Drive, Room 2AS-43
Bethesda, MD 20892
(301) 594-3900
Fax: (301) 480-2753
E-mail: irina.krasnova@nih.gov
Web Site: www.nigms.nih.gov

TYPE:

Development grants; Research grants. Grants to assist eligible institutions to strengthen the institutions' biomedical research capabilities and provide opportunities to students to engage in biomedical or behavioral research and other activities in preparation for Ph.D. training in these areas.

See entry 2087 for full listing.

NATIONAL INSTITUTE ON MINORITY HEALTH AND HEALTH DISPARITIES [921]

6707 Democracy Boulevard, Suite 800
MSC 5465
Bethesda, MD 20892-5465
(301) 402-1366
Fax: (301) 480-4049
Web Site: www.nimhd.nih.gov

AREAS OF INTEREST:

Minority opportunities in biomedical and behavioral science.

NAME(S) OF PROGRAMS:

- **Minority Health and Health Disparities Research Training Program (MHRT)**

TYPE:

Research grants; Training grants. The NIMHD Minority Health Research Training Program (MHRT) funds U.S. institutions to offer short-term research training opportunities in international and domestic settings to undergraduate and graduate students, postdoctoral and medical students from health disparity backgrounds. Institutions with MHRT funding provide training and international and domestic exposure to students to conduct research at foreign and domestic sites in the biomedical, clinical, social, or behavioral sciences. Although the training time of the 10- to 12-week (or longer) training period varies by institution, it often takes place during the summer or for one semester during the academic year.

YEAR PROGRAM STARTED: 1993

PURPOSE:

To provide research training opportunities for minority undergraduate students, minority medical students and postdoctorates in biomedical and behavioral research; to support faculty members to serve as mentors to students abroad and at home.

ELIGIBILITY:

Minority participants must be from underrepresented minority groups including African Americans, Asian Americans, Native Americans, Hispanic Americans, Alaskan Natives, Native Hawaiians and Pacific Islanders.

Applicants must be undergraduate or graduate students pursuing a doctoral degree in the biomedical or behavioral sciences, a medical degree, or a postdoctorate pursuing a degree in the biomedical or behavioral sciences.

GEOG. RESTRICTIONS: United States and its territories.

FINANCIAL DATA:

Amount of support per award: Up to $250,000 in direct costs annually.

Total amount of support: Approximately $5,000,000 in grants annually.

NO. AWARDS: Up to 12.

APPLICATION INFO:

NIMHD does not work directly with students interested in the MHRT Program. Students who are interested in MHRT must apply through the MHRT Program at a specific college or university (see roster of programs on the web site).

Duration: Up to five years.

Deadline: Varies.

PUBLICATIONS:

Program announcement; guidelines.

ADDRESS INQUIRIES TO:

Richard Berzon, Ph.D.
Health Scientist Administrator
(See address above.)

THE NATIONAL ITALIAN AMERICAN FOUNDATION

1860 19th Street, N.W.
Washington, DC 20009-5501
(202) 939-3114
Fax: (202) 387-0800
E-mail: scholarships@niaf.org
Web Site: www.niaf.org/scholarships

TYPE:

Scholarships. The National Italian American Foundation (NIAF) will award scholarships and grants to outstanding students for use during the following academic year. The awards will be made on the basis of academic merit and divided between two groups of students.

See entry 1556 for full listing.

NATIONAL MEDICAL FELLOWSHIPS, INC.

12 East 46th Street
Suite 5E
New York, NY 10017
(212) 483-8880
Fax: (212) 483-8897
E-mail: scholarships@nmfonline.org
Web Site: www.nmfonline.org

TYPE:

Awards/prizes; Project/program grants; Scholarships. Service learning. NMF supports underrepresented minority medical students and health professions students enrolled in U.S. accredited programs as they matriculate. Awards are available to students M1 to M4/5. In addition to financial support, NMF provides opportunities for aspiring doctors to take their learning into the community.

See entry 2096 for full listing.

NATIONAL TAXIDERMISTS ASSOCIATION [922]

1615 Montana Street
Missoula, MT 59801
(406) 721-1214
Web Site: www.nationaltaxidermists.com

AREAS OF INTEREST:

Taxidermy and education.

NAME(S) OF PROGRAMS:

- **Charlie Fleming Scholarship**

TYPE:

Scholarships.

PURPOSE:

To promote higher education and taxidermy education.

ELIGIBILITY:

Students must be a member, spouse or dependent of the NTA for three consecutive years.

FINANCIAL DATA:
Amount of support per award: $1,500.

NO. AWARDS: 2 per year.

APPLICATION INFO:
Contact the Organization for application procedures.

Applicant must submit an essay incorporating the MTA mission statement, their personal desires and ambitions and the educator the applicant wishes to study under.
Duration: One year.
Deadline: May 15.

NEW JERSEY OFFICE OF THE SECRETARY OF HIGHER EDUCATION (OSHE)
One John Fitch Plaza
P.O. Box 542
Trenton, NJ 08625-0542
(609) 341-3808
Fax: (609) 292-7225
E-mail: hasani.carter@oshe.nj.gov
Web Site: www.state.nj.
us/highereducation/EOF/EOF_Description.shtml

TYPE:
Grants-in-aid. Student support. The Educational Opportunity Fund (EOF) is administered through the Office of the Secretary of Higher Education (OSHE). Created by law in 1968, EOF is one of the state's most comprehensive student support programs that provides access to higher education for those who come from low income and educationally disadvantaged backgrounds. EOF is not an entitlement grant program.

See entry 1567 for full listing.

NEWMEXICOWOMEN.ORG [923]
1807 2nd Street, Suite 76
Santa Fe, NM 87505
(505) 750-1732
E-mail: sarah@newmexicowomen.org
Web Site: newmexicowomen.org

FOUNDED: 2012

AREAS OF INTEREST:
Gender justice and healing.

TYPE:
General operating grants.

PURPOSE:
To advance opportunities for women and girls statewide so they can lead self-sufficient, healthy and empowered lives.

ELIGIBILITY:
Tax-exempt, nonprofit organizations may apply.

GEOG. RESTRICTIONS: New Mexico.

FINANCIAL DATA:
Amount of support per award: $1,000 to $20,000.
Total amount of support: $120,000 for the year 2018.

NO. AWARDS: 25 for the year 2018.

APPLICATION INFO:
Instructions are available online.
Duration: One year.
Deadline: July 26.

ADDRESS INQUIRIES TO:
Sarah Ghiorse, Executive Director
(See address above.)

ORDER SONS OF ITALY IN AMERICA, GRAND LODGE OF FLORIDA
2021 Pine Needle Trail
Kissimmee, FL 34746
(321) 286-6787
E-mail: gertd830@gmail.com
Web Site: osiaflorida.org

TYPE:
Awards/prizes; Grants-in-aid; Scholarships. Scholarships are provided to high school students entering college.

Financial aid is given in support of charitable programs, such as Alzheimer's disease, Cooley's anemia, autism, and cancer.

See entry 1579 for full listing.

PEN AMERICA
588 Broadway, Suite 303
New York, NY 10012
(212) 334-1660 ext. 4813
Fax: (212) 334-2181
E-mail: awards@pen.org
Web Site: pen.org

TYPE:
Awards/prizes. Invites submissions of book-length writings by authors of color, published during the calendar year.

See entry 635 for full listing.

PRIDE FOUNDATION [924]
2014 East Madison Street
Suite 300
Seattle, WA 98122
(206) 323-3318
Fax: (206) 323-1017
E-mail: grants@pridefoundation.org
Web Site: www.pridefoundation.org

FOUNDED: 1985

AREAS OF INTEREST:
Arts and recreation; education outreach and advocacy; HIV/AIDS; lesbian health; youth and family; and other health and community services.

TYPE:
Endowments; General operating grants; Project/program grants; Scholarships; Seed money grants. Short-term grants.

YEAR PROGRAM STARTED: 1987

PURPOSE:
To inspire giving; to expand opportunities and advance full equality for LGBTQ people across the Northwest.

ELIGIBILITY:
Organizations applying for grant funds must have 501(c)(3) nonprofit tax status, or be affiliated with an organization that has 501(c)(3) status that will assume responsibility for administering all funds received and expended.

Organizations and/or projects must encompass LGBTQ issues and/or populations.

GEOG. RESTRICTIONS: Alaska, Idaho, Montana, Oregon and Washington.

FINANCIAL DATA:
Amount of support per award: $2,500 to $10,000.
Total amount of support: $550,000.

NO. MOST RECENT APPLICANTS: Approximately 130 annually.

NO. AWARDS: Approximately 30 annually.

APPLICATION INFO:
Detailed instructions are available on the Foundation web site.
Duration: One year.
Deadline: Varies.

PUBLICATIONS:
e-Newsletter, bimonthly.

IRS I.D.: 91-1325007

ADDRESS INQUIRIES TO:
Jeremiah Allen, Director of Programs
(See address above.)

PROSPANICA [925]
2711 LBJ Freeway
Suite 800
Dallas, TX 75234
(877) 467-4622
E-mail: info@prospanica.org
Web Site: www.prospanica.org

AREAS OF INTEREST:
Business administration.

NAME(S) OF PROGRAMS:
● **Prospanica Scholarship Program**

TYPE:
Awards/prizes; Conferences/seminars; Scholarships.

YEAR PROGRAM STARTED: 1989

PURPOSE:
To empower Hispanic business professionals to achieve their full educational, economic and social potential.

LEGAL BASIS:
501(c)(3) organization.

ELIGIBILITY:
Applicant must:
(1) be a U.S. citizen or legal permanent resident;
(2) be of Hispanic/Latino heritage;
(3) have a minimum grade point average of 3.0 on a 4.0 scale (or equivalent) or have a minimum 2.75 grade point average on a 4.0 scale (or equivalent) in combination with two years of full-time work experience;
(4) have a Prospanica membership (member ID required);
(5) for the Graduate Awards, be enrolled in a Master's degree program in the business school at a college or university in the U.S. or Puerto Rico accredited by AACSB and;
(6) for the Undergraduate Awards, be a sophomore or higher pursuing a Bachelor's degree within the business school at a college or university in the U.S. or Puerto Rico accredited by AACSB.

GEOG. RESTRICTIONS: United States and Puerto Rico.

FINANCIAL DATA:
Amount of support per award: $2,000 to $5,000.

APPLICATION INFO:
Applications are submitted on the Prospanica web site. Round 1 requires no outside documentation. For Round 2, the following information will be needed for the application process:
(1) personal statement (maximum 300 words or 3,000 characters);
(2) Prospanica essay;
(3) college academic information, including complete transcripts of grades from all colleges attended;

(4) list of work, Prospanica participation, and community service experience and;
(5) financial information from the family's most recently submitted tax return.

Applicants should review their application before submission. All application pages with required fields must be completed in the format described in order to submit the application. It is recommended the applicant print a hard copy for their records. Once the application is submitted, no further revisions can be made.

To complete the application process, the following documents must be uploaded or mailed to Prospanica before the deadline:
(1) complete undergraduate and graduate school transcripts of grades from all colleges attended. Online transcripts must display student name, school name, grades and credit hours for each course and term in which each course was taken and;
(2) two recommendation forms from professors, advisors or employers.

It is the applicant's responsibility to gather and submit all required information. An e-mail confirmation will be generated when the application is successfully submitted. Late submissions and incomplete applications will not be considered. Applicant should contact Prospanica to check on the completeness of their application.

Duration: One academic year.

Deadline: Round 1: April 20. Round 2: June 11, by invitation only.

RIGHTEOUS PERSONS FOUNDATION [926]

400 South Beverly Drive, Suite 420
Beverly Hills, CA 90212
(310) 314-8393
E-mail: grants@righteouspersons.org
Web Site: www.righteouspersons.org

FOUNDED: 1994

AREAS OF INTEREST:
Primarily Jewish organizations.

TYPE:
General operating grants; Matching gifts; Project/program grants; Seed money grants; Technical assistance.

PURPOSE:
To strengthen Jewish life in America.

LEGAL BASIS:
Nonprofit.

ELIGIBILITY:
Applicants must be tax-exempt organizations. Priority is given to national organizations and projects which create meaningful experiences for Jewish youth, promote Jewish learning, provide leadership training grounded in Jewish tradition, employ the arts and media to explore the relevance of modern Jewish identity, promote tolerance and understanding between Jews and non-Jews, and encourage Jews to participate in the work of social justice.

The Foundation does not make grants to individuals. Also, the Foundation does not support university faculty chairs, individual synagogues or day schools, research, the publication of books or magazines, or organizations or projects based outside of the U.S. In addition, the Foundation generally does not support endowments, capital campaigns, building funds, or social service projects.

GEOG. RESTRICTIONS: United States.

FINANCIAL DATA:
Amount of support per award: Varies.
Total amount of support: Varies.

APPLICATION INFO:
Applicants should submit a two- to three-page letter of inquiry including:
(1) a description of the proposed project including the issues the project will address and the target population(s);
(2) a brief description of the organization's mission, activities and history;
(3) the total amount of the organization's operating budget;
(4) the total amount requested from the Foundation;
(5) the name, mailing address and telephone number of a contact person;
(6) a detailed project budget;
(7) a list of the organization's board of directors;
(8) documentation of the organization's 501(c)(3) status;
(9) the total amount requested from the Foundation and;
(10) a list of the organization/project's primary sources of support over the last two years including names of foundations and amounts provided each year.

If there is a fiscal sponsor for the project, include a current copy of the sponsor's tax-exempt letter from the IRS as well as a letter of support from the sponsor acknowledging their responsibilities. Do not send full proposals or video or audio tapes unless otherwise requested. Faxed applications will not be considered.

Duration: Varies.

PUBLICATIONS:
Program announcement; guidelines.

STAFF:
Rachel Levin, Executive Director
Shayna Rose Triebwasser, Senior Program Officer

BOARD OF DIRECTORS:
Steven Spielberg, Chairman
Gerald Breslauer, President
Tammy Anderson

ADDRESS INQUIRIES TO:
Shayna Rose Triebwasser, Program Officer
(See address above.)

JACKIE ROBINSON FOUNDATION (JRF) [927]

75 Varick Street, 2nd Floor
New York, NY 10013-1917
(212) 290-8600
Fax: (212) 290-8081
E-mail: general@jackierobinson.org
Web Site: www.jackierobinson.org

FOUNDED: 1973

AREAS OF INTEREST:
Providing college education and a comprehensive set of support services for academically gifted, highly motivated students of color with financial need.

NAME(S) OF PROGRAMS:
- **Extra Innings Fellowship Program (EIF)**
- **Mentoring and Leadership Program**
- **Rachel Robinson International Fellowship Program (RRIF)**

TYPE:
Conferences/seminars; Fellowships; Scholarships. The Foundation Scholarship

Program (Mentoring and Leadership Program) is designed to address the financial needs of college students and provide comprehensive mentoring services through its 42 Strategies for Success Curriculum.

The Fellowship programs are follow-up programs to the JRF Scholars program (Mentoring and Leadership Program).

The Extra Innings Fellowship Program helps highly motivated JRF Scholars to fund the cost of advanced professional or graduate training.

The Rachel Robinson International Fellowship Program promotes and supports international service and study opportunities for JRF Scholars.

PURPOSE:
To award four-year college scholarships to academically gifted students of color with financial need, enabling them to attend the college of their choice.

ELIGIBILITY:
Applicants must complete the JRF Scholars Program (Mentoring and Leadership Program) to be eligible for the Fellowship Programs. Foundation Scholar applicants must meet all of the following criteria:
(1) have U.S. citizenship;
(2) be a minority student;
(3) be a high school senior enrolling in college in the coming fall;
(4) have a SAT score (combined math and critical reading sections) of 1,000 or above, an ACT of 21 or above;
(5) have leadership potential and;
(6) be in financial need.

FINANCIAL DATA:
JRF Scholars program includes financial sponsorship to attend JRF's annual, four-day "Mentoring and Leadership Conference" in New York City as well as other regional events throughout the year.

Amount of support per award: Scholarships: Up to $7,000 per year; maximum $28,000 over four years.

NO. MOST RECENT APPLICANTS: Scholarships: Approximately 5,000 per year.

NO. AWARDS: Scholarships: 60 per year.

APPLICATION INFO:
Application information is available at the Foundation web site. Scholarship application is available for online review on October 15, and goes live on November 1.

Duration: Four years.

Deadline: The application is due February 1. Applicants are notified of status April 30; final selection of Scholars is announced on June 15.

ADDRESS INQUIRIES TO:
Mentoring and Leadership Program
Jackie Robinson Foundation
(See address above.)

RRF FOUNDATION FOR AGING [928]

8765 West Higgins Road
Suite 430
Chicago, IL 60631-4170
(773) 714-8080
Fax: (773) 714-8089
E-mail: info@rrf.org
Web Site: www.rrf.org

FOUNDED: 1950

AREAS OF INTEREST:
Aging.

NAME(S) OF PROGRAMS:
- **Organizational Capacity Building**
- **Responsive Grants**

TYPE:
Project/program grants; Research grants; Technical assistance; Training grants. Grants program support projects that have a significant focus on older adults, ages 65 and older, in the following areas:
Advocacy - Achieve enduring social change around issues that affect older Americans;
Direct Service - Improve availability and quality of community-based and residential long-term services and supports;
Professional Education and Training - Increase the competency of professionals and paraprofessionals who serve older adults and;
Research - Seek causes and solutions to significant problems for older adults.

Organizational Capacity Building - Designed to strengthen the effectiveness of Illinois nonprofit groups serving older people Priority is given to proposals addressing caregiving, economic security in later life, housing, and social and intergenerational connectedness.

YEAR PROGRAM STARTED: 1979

PURPOSE:
To improve the quality of life for the nation's older population.

LEGAL BASIS:
Private foundation.

ELIGIBILITY:
To be eligible for support, organizations, congregations and institutions must qualify under the regulations of the IRS.

GEOG. RESTRICTIONS: Direct-service grants limited to Florida, Illinois, Iowa, Kentucky, Michigan, Missouri and Wisconsin; OCB Grants are limited to the Chicago, Illinois area.

FINANCIAL DATA:
Assets of $136,091,407 for the year 2018.
Amount of support per award: $46,400 average for the year 2019.
Total amount of support: $6,403,453 for the year 2019.

NO. MOST RECENT APPLICANTS: 245 for the year 2019.

NO. AWARDS: 138 for the year 2019.

APPLICATION INFO:
The Foundation has an online application process. Visit the Foundation web site to find information about submitting a proposal.
Deadline: Responsive Grants: February 1, May 1 and August 1, with award announcement three to four months after submission date.

TRUSTEES AND OFFICERS:
Ruth Ann Watkins, Chairman of the Board
Irene Frye, President
Downey R. Varey, Treasurer
Michael J. Starshak, Secretary
John Bouman
Kathleen Kolodgy
Thomas D. Kuczmarski
Adrienne D. Mims, M.D.
Anthony J. Perry, M.D.
Thomas R. Prohaska, Ph.D.

ADDRESS INQUIRIES TO:
See e-mail address above.

SANTA FE COMMUNITY FOUNDATION [929]

501 Halona Street
Santa Fe, NM 87505
(505) 988-9715
Fax: (505) 988-1829
E-mail: foundation@santafecf.org
Web Site: www.santafecf.org

FOUNDED: 1981

AREAS OF INTEREST:
Animal welfare, cultural vibrancy, educational success and career pathways, economic opportunity, health, lesbian, gay, bisexual and transgender community, Native Americans, sustainable agriculture and stewardship of resources, and well-being.

NAME(S) OF PROGRAMS:
- **Community Leadership Fund**
- **Dollars 4 Schools**
- **Envision Fund**
- **Local Impact Investing Initiative**
- **MoGro**
- **Native American Advised Fund**
- **NM Health Equity Partnership**
- **Santa Fe Baby Fund**

TYPE:
General operating grants; Project/program grants.

YEAR PROGRAM STARTED: 1981

PURPOSE:
To promote charitable community outreaches.

LEGAL BASIS:
Community foundation.

ELIGIBILITY:
The Foundation awards grants to nonprofit organizations only. The Foundation does not award grants for religious or political purposes, capital outlay, endowment or to individuals.

GEOG. RESTRICTIONS: Santa Fe and northern New Mexico.

FINANCIAL DATA:
Amount of support per award: $5,000 to $15,000.
Total amount of support: $10,000,000 (including donor-advised funds) for the year 2018.

CO-OP FUNDING PROGRAMS: Hispanics in Philanthropy, Opportunity Santa Fe, Law Enforcement Assisted Diversion, and Early Childhood Funders Network.

NO. MOST RECENT APPLICANTS: Approximately 200 for the year 2018.

NO. AWARDS: 55 for the year 2018.

APPLICATION INFO:
Applicants must submit proof of IRS 501(c)(3) status.
Duration: One year.
Deadline: Spring and Fall.

PUBLICATIONS:
Giving Together, catalogue.

IRS I.D.: 85-0303044

OFFICER:
William Smith, President and Chief Executive Officer

ADDRESS INQUIRIES TO:
Christa Coggins
Vice President for Community Philanthropy
(See address above.)

SONS OF ITALY FOUNDATION [930]

219 E Street, N.E.
Washington, DC 20002
(202) 547-2900
Fax: (202) 546-8168
E-mail: scholarships@osia.org
Web Site: www.osia.org

FOUNDED: 1959

AREAS OF INTEREST:
Cultural preservation and advancement for Italian Americans; education.

NAME(S) OF PROGRAMS:
- **National Leadership Grant Competition**

TYPE:
Awards/prizes; Scholarships. The Foundation provides Italian language scholarships, study-abroad scholarships and merit-based higher education scholarships.

YEAR PROGRAM STARTED: 1959

PURPOSE:
To help educate Italian Americans and improve their lives.

LEGAL BASIS:
Public, tax-exempt organization as defined by Section 501(c)(3) and Section 509(a)(1) of the Internal Revenue Code.

ELIGIBILITY:
Applicants must be U.S. citizens of Italian descent (at least one Italian or Italian-American grandparent) enrolled in a four-year undergraduate program or a graduate program at an accredited academic institution for the fall term.

FINANCIAL DATA:
Amount of support per award: Scholarships: $4,000 to $25,000.
Total amount of support: Varies.

NO. MOST RECENT APPLICANTS: 1,000.

NO. AWARDS: 10 to 12.

APPLICATION INFO:
Contact the Foundation.
Duration: One year.
Deadline: February 28.

PUBLICATIONS:
Annual report; *Grant Priorities, Guidelines and Procedures,* booklet.

ADDRESS INQUIRIES TO:
Michelle Ment, Chairperson
Scholarship, Education and Culture Committee
(See address above.)

U.S. DEPARTMENT OF EDUCATION

Office of English Language Acquisition
LBJ Education Building, MS-6510
400 Maryland Avenue, S.W.
Washington, DC 20202-6510
(202) 401-1433 (NPD Program)
(202) 453-6054 (NAM Program)
Web Site: www.ed.gov/offices/oela

TYPE:
Formula grants. National Professional Development Program provides grants for eligible entities to implement professional development activities intended to improve instruction for English Learners (ELs) and assists education personnel working with ELs to meet high professional standards. Professional development activities may include both pre-service and in-service activities.

Native American and Alaska Native Children in School Program awards grants to eligible entities to develop and enhance capacity to provide effective instruction and support to Native American students who are identified as English Learners (ELs). The goal of this program is to support the teaching, learning and studying of Native American languages while also increasing the English language proficiency of students served to achieve the same challenging state academic content and achievement standards for all students.

See entry 1446 for full listing.

UCLA INSTITUTE OF AMERICAN CULTURES (IAC) [931]
2329 Murphy Hall, Box 957244
Los Angeles, CA 90095-7244
(310) 825-6815
Fax: (310) 825-3994
E-mail: iaccoordinator@conet.ucla.edu
Web Site: www.iac.ucla.edu

FOUNDED: 1969

AREAS OF INTEREST:
Advancing knowledge, strengthening and integrating interdisciplinary research and enriching instruction on African Americans, American Indians, Asian Americans and Chicanos.

NAME(S) OF PROGRAMS:
- **Institute of American Cultures Visiting Research Scholar Fellowship Program in Ethnic Studies**

TYPE:
Fellowships. Deals with arts and humanities, education and teacher training, fine arts, applied arts, law, social sciences, and sciences. The IAC, in cooperation with UCLA's four Ethnic Studies Research Centers (American Indian Studies Center, Asian American Studies Center, Bunche Center for African American Studies, and Chicano Studies Research Center), offers awards to visiting scholars to support research on African Americans, American Indians, Asian Americans and Chicanas/os.

PURPOSE:
To enable Ph.D. scholars wishing to work in association with the American Indian Studies Center, the Bunche Center for African American Studies, the Asian American Studies Center, and the Chicano Studies Research Center, in order to conduct research and publish books or manuscripts.

ELIGIBILITY:
Open to U.S. citizens or permanent residents of the U.S. who hold a Ph.D. from an accredited college or university (or, in the case of the arts, a terminal degree) in the appropriate field at the time of appointment. UCLA faculty, staff and currently enrolled students are not eligible to apply.

FINANCIAL DATA:
Amount of support per award: Up to $35,000 stipend and up to $4,000 in research support. Amount contingent upon rank, experience and date of completion of terminal degree.

NO. AWARDS: Up to 4.

APPLICATION INFO:
Applicants are encouraged to contact the Studies Research Center of interest prior to applying. Application process begins in November.
Duration: Up to three quarters (nine months).

Deadline: Dates are posted on the IAC web site.

ADDRESS INQUIRIES TO:
IAC Coordinator
(See address above.)

UNITED METHODIST COMMUNICATIONS [932]
810 12th Avenue South
Nashville, TN 37203-4744
(615) 742-5400
Fax: (615) 742-5777
E-mail: scholarship@umcom.org
Web Site: www.umcom.org

FOUNDED: 1948

AREAS OF INTEREST:
Religious communications.

NAME(S) OF PROGRAMS:
- **The Leonard M. Perryman Communications Scholarship for Ethnic Minority Students**

TYPE:
Fellowships; Scholarships. Award for junior or senior undergraduate study in religion journalism or mass communications. The term *communications* is meant to cover various media as audio-visual, electronic and print journalism.

PURPOSE:
To enable the recipient to continue his or her studies in communication; to promote a level of excellence in communication on the undergraduate level by an ethnic minority student.

ELIGIBILITY:
Applicants must be United Methodist ethnic minority undergraduate students, junior or senior, who have an intention to pursue a career in religion journalism or mass communications and are enrolled in an accredited U.S. college or university.

FINANCIAL DATA:
Amount of support per award: $2,500.
Total amount of support: $2,500 per academic year.

NO. AWARDS: 1.

APPLICATION INFO:
Applicant must submit:
(1) an application form (completed and submitted electronically or printed and mailed);
(2) official transcripts from the current institution of higher education and any others attended. Transcripts should be mailed by the school directly to the address listed in the application packet;
(3) three letters of recommendation, one from the local church pastor or a denominational official, one from the chairperson of the department in which the applicant is majoring as an undergraduate student, and one from an employer or supervisor in a position to evaluate the applicant's communications skills;
(4) an essay (no more than 500 words) about the applicant's commitment to the Christian faith and interest in communications, and how the applicant sees the two intersecting in their life presently and in the future;
(5) three examples of journalistic work (audiovisual, electronic, print). If requested in writing, these materials will be returned after the committee has completed its selection and;

(6) a recent photograph, preferably head and shoulders, suitable for publicity use if awarded the scholarship.
Duration: One academic year.
Deadline: March 15 (postmarked).

PUBLICATIONS:
Application guidelines.

ADDRESS INQUIRIES TO:
Relationship Team
(See address above.)

*SPECIAL STIPULATIONS:
Candidates must be in their junior or senior year to qualify.

UNIVERSITY OF CALIFORNIA [933]
President's Postdoctoral Fellowship Program
402 Sproul Hall
Berkeley, CA 94720-1508
(510) 643-8235
E-mail: ppfpinfo@berkeley.edu
Web Site: ppfp.ucop.edu/info

FOUNDED: 1869

AREAS OF INTEREST:
Education and research.

NAME(S) OF PROGRAMS:
- **University of California President's Postdoctoral Fellowship Program**

TYPE:
Fellowships. Awarded for research conducted under faculty sponsorship on any one of the University of California's 10 campuses.

YEAR PROGRAM STARTED: 1984

PURPOSE:
To encourage outstanding women and minority Ph.D. recipients to pursue academic careers at the University of California; to offer research fellowships to all qualified candidates who are committed to university careers in research, teaching and service that will enhance the diversity of the academic community at the University of California.

LEGAL BASIS:
University.

ELIGIBILITY:
Applicants must be U.S. citizens or permanent residents and must hold or receive a Ph.D. from an accredited university. Applicants should expect to have earned their Ph.D. degree by June 30 of the year for which they are applying.

The program will prefer candidates who have research interests focusing on underserved populations and understanding issues of racial or gender inequalities.

The program also prefers candidates with a record of leadership or significant experience teaching and mentoring students from groups that have been historically underrepresented in higher education.

FINANCIAL DATA:
The award includes salary, health, vision and dental benefits, and up to $5,000 for research-related and program travel expenses.
Amount of support per award:
Approximately $50,760 per fellow, depending upon the field and level of experience, plus benefits for self and dependents.

NO. AWARDS: 42 new for the year 2020-21.

APPLICATION INFO:
Application consists of curriculum vitae, research proposal, dissertation abstract, personal statement, writing sample, mentor support letter and thesis advisor letter.

Duration: Initially one academic year beginning July 1. Renewal for a second year will be granted upon demonstration of academic productivity and participation in program events.

Deadline: November 1. Announcement of awardees in the spring.

STAFF:
Mark A. Lawson, Ph.D., Director
Kimberly M. Adkinson, Assistant Director

ADDRESS INQUIRIES TO:
Kimberly M. Adkinson, Assistant Director
President's Postdoctoral Fellowship Program
(See address above.)

UNIVERSITY OF CALIFORNIA, LOS ANGELES   [934]

Asian American Studies Center
3230 Campbell Hall
Los Angeles, CA 90095-1546
(310) 825-2974
Fax: (310) 206-9844
E-mail: melanyd@ucla.edu
Web Site: www.aasc.ucla.edu/scholarships

FOUNDED: 1969

AREAS OF INTEREST:
Asian American studies, policy, social science, public health, law, education, and humanities research on Asian Americans and Pacific Islanders.

NAME(S) OF PROGRAMS:
● **Ethnic Studies Fellowships**

TYPE:
Awards/prizes; Conferences/seminars; Fellowships; Research grants; Scholarships; Visiting scholars; Work-study programs. Support for visiting scholars and researchers.

YEAR PROGRAM STARTED: 1969

PURPOSE:
To provide funding for studies in the field of Asian American arts, humanities, social sciences and applied research.

LEGAL BASIS:
University.

ELIGIBILITY:
Applicants must have the Ph.D. in place at the time Fellowship is awarded. UCLA faculty members are not eligible for support.

FINANCIAL DATA:
Visiting Scholars may use the funds to supplement sabbatical support, though the total available will not exceed the maximum stipend levels, and when combined with sabbatical funds may not exceed the candidate's current institutional salary.

Visiting Scholars will be paid through their home institutions and will be expected to continue their health benefits through that source. Awardees may receive up to $4,000 in research support (through reimbursements of research expenses).

Amount of support per award: Maximum stipend of $35,000, contingent upon rank, experience and date of completion of terminal degree.

Total amount of support: Varies.

NO. MOST RECENT APPLICANTS: 10.

NO. AWARDS: 1.

APPLICATION INFO:
Contact the University.

Duration: Nine months.

Deadline: Approximately January 10, 2021.

STAFF:
Melany De La Cruz-Viesca, Associate Director/IAC Coordinator

ADDRESS INQUIRIES TO:
Melany De La Cruz-Viesca
Associate Director/IAC Coordinator
Asian American Studies Center
(See address above.)

UNIVERSITY OF SOUTHERN CALIFORNIA

USC Graduate School
3601 Trousdale Parkway, STU 301
Los Angeles, CA 90089-0894
(213) 740-9033
Fax: (213) 740-9048
E-mail: gradfllw@usc.edu
Web Site: graduateschool.usc.edu

TYPE:
Fellowships. Merit fellowships. Fellowships will be combined with matching funds from individual schools to provide four or more years of funding toward the Ph.D.

See entry 1628 for full listing.

VIRGINIA POLYTECHNIC INSTITUTE AND STATE UNIVERSITY   [935]

MAOP Office
280 Stanger Street
Blacksburg, VA 24061
(540) 231-5023
Fax: (540) 231-2618
E-mail: maop@vt.edu
Web Site: www.maop.vt.edu

AREAS OF INTEREST:
Graduate programs particularly in science, math and technology.

NAME(S) OF PROGRAMS:
● **Multicultural Academic Opportunity Graduate Student Scholars Program**

TYPE:
Assistantships; Fellowships; Internships; Scholarships. The program assists with graduate school financing in exchange for assistance to MAOP administration. Graduate students assist with programming implementation such as mentoring to undergraduate students.

YEAR PROGRAM STARTED: 1973

PURPOSE:
To improve professional and educational opportunities for minority students in architecture, planning, public and international affairs, and landscape architecture.

ELIGIBILITY:
Candidate must maintain a 3.0 cumulative grade point average, attend and participate in monthly Graduate Scholar workshops, and remain engaged with the MAOP program.

FINANCIAL DATA:
Amount of support per award: $6,000 to $16,000 per academic year.

NO. AWARDS: 12.

APPLICATION INFO:
Complete application includes a 500-word essay, two letters of recommendation and departmental commitment of funding.

Duration: One year. Renewable.

Deadline: April 1.

ADDRESS INQUIRIES TO:
Monica Hunter, Interim Director
MAOP Office
(See address above.)

WIDENER MEMORIAL FOUNDATION IN AID OF HANDICAPPED CHILDREN [936]

4060 Butler Pike
Suite 225
Plymouth Meeting, PA 19462
(610) 825-8900
Fax: (610) 825-8904
E-mail: jhagerty@erdixon.com

FOUNDED: 1912

AREAS OF INTEREST:
Orthopedically handicapped children.

TYPE:
Capital grants.

PURPOSE:
To benefit orthopedically handicapped children.

LEGAL BASIS:
Special interest foundation.

ELIGIBILITY:
Applicants must be 501(c)(3) organizations that are not classified as private foundations. Organizations must benefit orthopedically handicapped children in some way.

GEOG. RESTRICTIONS: Greater Delaware Valley area (including the city of Philadelphia, Pennsylvania), and Bucks, Burlington, Camden, Chester, Delaware, Gloucester, Montgomery and Philadelphia counties.

FINANCIAL DATA:
Amount of support per award: Varies.

Total amount of support: Approximately $900,000 to $1,000,000 annually.

NO. MOST RECENT APPLICANTS: 26.

NO. AWARDS: 17.

APPLICATION INFO:
Applicant should include a letter describing the purpose for which grant would be used, persons who would benefit from the activity for which the grant is requested, specifically orthopedically handicapped children, and statements showing that the organization is exempt under 501(c)(3) of the Internal Revenue Code and also not classified as a private foundation.

Duration: Typically one year. Must reapply.

Deadline: May 15 and October 15. Board meets in May or June and November to approve grant requests.

IRS I.D.: 23-6267223

OFFICERS:
Edith D. Miller, President
Heike Sullivan, Esq., Vice President and Trustee
Edith R. Dixon, Treasurer and Trustee
George W. Dixon, Secretary
Bruce L. Castor, Esq., Trustee
Mark S. DePillis, Esq., Trustee
Linda Grobman, Ed.D., Trustee
John Keleher, Trustee
Robert Mack, Ed.D., Trustee

ADDRESS INQUIRIES TO:
Edith D. Miller, President
P.O. Box 178
Lafayette Hill, PA 19444-0178

WITH FOUNDATION [937]

2225 East Bayshore Road, Suite 200
Palo Alto, CA 94303
(650) 320-1715
Fax: (650) 320-1716
E-mail: info@withfoundation.org
Web Site: withfoundation.org

FOUNDED: 2002

AREAS OF INTEREST:
Health care access and health care research benefiting adults with developmental disabilities.

TYPE:
Challenge/matching grants; Conferences/seminars; General operating grants; Project/program grants; Research grants; Technical assistance.

YEAR PROGRAM STARTED: 2002

PURPOSE:
To provide financial support to organizations that promote the establishment of comprehensive health care for adults with developmental disabilities.

ELIGIBILITY:
Organizations must be nonprofit 501(c)(3). Only grant proposals consistent with the Foundation's mission statement will be eligible for funding. No grants are made to individuals.

GEOG. RESTRICTIONS: United States.

FINANCIAL DATA:
Amount of support per award: $30,000 to $50,000.
Total amount of support: Approximately $750,000 annually.
Matching fund requirements: By invitation only.

NO. MOST RECENT APPLICANTS: 50.

NO. AWARDS: 16 for the year 2018.

APPLICATION INFO:
Letter of interest must be completed online during open grant cycles.
Duration: Typically one year.

ADDRESS INQUIRIES TO:
E-mail: grants@withfoundation.org

African-American

CONGRESSIONAL BLACK CAUCUS FOUNDATION, INC. [938]

1720 Massachusetts Avenue, N.W.
Washington, DC 20036
(202) 263-2800
Fax: (202) 263-0846
E-mail: scholarships@cbcfinc.org
Web Site: www.cbcfinc.org

FOUNDED: 1976

AREAS OF INTEREST:
Promoting educational and leadership opportunities for African Americans.

NAME(S) OF PROGRAMS:
• **CBC Spouses Education Scholarship**

TYPE:
Scholarships. The CBC Spouses Education Scholarship is a national program that awards scholarships to academically talented and highly motivated students who intend to pursue full-time undergraduate, graduate or doctoral degrees.

PURPOSE:
To provide support to students, particularly African-Americans, who exhibit leadership skills, are involved in their community, and are pursuing higher education.

LEGAL BASIS:
Nonpartisan, nonprofit foundation.

ELIGIBILITY:
Undergraduate or graduate students residing or attending school in district of CBC member may apply.

FINANCIAL DATA:
Amount of support per award: Varies.
Total amount of support: Varies.

NO. AWARDS: Varies.

APPLICATION INFO:
The Foundation utilizes an online application process.
Duration: One year. Must reapply.
Deadline: End of May.

PUBLICATIONS:
Policy review; annual report.

IRS I.D.: 52-1160561

ADDRESS INQUIRIES TO:
Leadership Institute for Public Service (See address or e-mail above.)

CONGRESSIONAL BLACK CAUCUS FOUNDATION, INC. [939]

1720 Massachusetts Avenue, N.W.
Washington, DC 20036
(202) 263-2800
Fax: (202) 263-0846
E-mail: scholarships@cbcfinc.org
Web Site: www.cbcfinc.org

FOUNDED: 1976

NAME(S) OF PROGRAMS:
• **CBC Spouses Performing Arts Scholarship**
• **CBC Spouses Visual Arts Scholarship**

TYPE:
Scholarships. CBC Spouses Performing Arts Scholarship, developed in honor of the late Curtis Mayfield, is intended to ensure that students pursuing a career in the performing arts receive the financial assistance to achieve their goals.

CBC Spouses Visual Arts Scholarship was established for students who are pursuing a career in the visual arts.

PURPOSE:
To encourage education in the performing and visual arts among minority students.

ELIGIBILITY:
Applicant must:
(1) be a U.S. citizen or permanent U.S. resident;
(2) be preparing to pursue an undergraduate degree full-time, or be a current full-time student in good academic standing at a U.S. accredited college or university;
(3) have a minimum 2.5 grade point average and;
(4) exhibit leadership ability and participate in community service activities.

The scholarships do not have a residency requirement.

GEOG. RESTRICTIONS: United States.

FINANCIAL DATA:
Amount of support per award: $3,000.
Total amount of support: Up to $60,000.

NO. AWARDS: Up to 10 scholarships annually.

APPLICATION INFO:
The Foundation utilizes an online application process.
Duration: One year. Must reapply.
Deadline: Late April to early May.

ADDRESS INQUIRIES TO:
Leadership Institute for Public Service (See address or e-mail above.)

CONGRESSIONAL BLACK CAUCUS FOUNDATION, INC. [940]

1720 Massachusetts Avenue, N.W.
Washington, DC 20036
(202) 263-2800
Fax: (202) 263-0846
E-mail: info@cbcfinc.org
internships@cbcfinc.org
Web Site: www.cbcfinc.org

AREAS OF INTEREST:
Promoting educational and leadership opportunities for African Americans.

NAME(S) OF PROGRAMS:
• **The CBCF Congressional Fellows Program**
• **The CBCF Congressional Internship Program**

TYPE:
Fellowships; Internships. The CBCF Congressional Fellows Program helps participants gain invaluable experience as they assist in the development of legislation and public policy initiatives while working as congressional staff for a year. This program targets early career policy professionals who have completed a professional and/or graduate degree and have demonstrated commitment to improving the lives and services for individuals living in underserved communities. Fellows work on Capitol Hill in the office of a Congressional Black Caucus member.

The CBCF Congressional Internship Program provides undergraduate students with an in-depth orientation to Capitol Hill and the legislative process through actual work experience in the offices of Congressional Black Caucus Members. In this way interns prepare to become decision makers in the policymaking process.

PURPOSE:
To increase the number of African Americans on congressional committees and subcommittees by providing students the opportunity to participate in all aspects of the legislative process.

LEGAL BASIS:
Nonpartisan, nonprofit foundation.

ELIGIBILITY:
Fellows Program applicants must have completed graduate coursework. Internship Program applicants must be college undergraduates.

FINANCIAL DATA:
Fellows are responsible for their own travel arrangements, expenses and housing accommodations. CBCF provides health and dental insurance coverage during term of fellowship. Interns receive a stipend and housing at a local university.

Amount of support per award: Fellows Program: $40,000 annual stipend; Internship Program: $3,000 stipend.

Total amount of support: Varies.

NO. AWARDS: 6 to 9 fellowships per year.

APPLICATION INFO:
Submit a completed application with detailed resume, certificate of academic standing and/or faculty certification, a writing sample of up to 10 pages, three letters of recommendation, one of which must be from the dean, department chairperson, faculty or advisor and an official transcript from each school attended.

Duration: Fellowships: 20 months; Internships: Nine weeks during the Summer, 16 weeks during the Spring and Fall.

Deadline: Spring: November; Summer: March; Fall: July.

IRS I.D.: 52-1160561

ADDRESS INQUIRIES TO:
Leadership Institute for Public Service (See address above.)

FREDERICK DOUGLASS INSTITUTE FOR AFRICAN AND AFRICAN-AMERICAN STUDIES

311 Morey Hall
University of Rochester
P.O. Box 270440
Rochester, NY 14627-0440
(585) 276-5744
Fax: (585) 256-2594
E-mail: FDI@rochester.edu
Web Site: www.sas.rochester.edu/aas

TYPE:
Awards/prizes; Conferences/seminars; Fellowships.

See entry 1401 for full listing.

FLORIDA DEPARTMENT OF EDUCATION   [941]

Office of Student Financial Assistance
325 West Gaines Street, Suite 1314
Tallahassee, FL 32399-0400
(888) 827-2004
Fax: (850) 487-1809
E-mail: osfa@fldoe.org
Web Site: www.floridastudentfinancialaidsg.org

NAME(S) OF PROGRAMS:
● **Rosewood Family Scholarship Program**

TYPE:
Scholarships. Financial assistance for descendants of the Rosewood family affected by the incidents of January 1923, to attend a state university, public community college or public postsecondary vocational-technical school.

PURPOSE:
To encourage and assist minority students to continue on to higher education.

LEGAL BASIS:
Governmental agency.

ELIGIBILITY:
To receive funding, the applying student must meet the following initial eligibility requirements:
(1) not owe a repayment or be in default under any state or federal grant, loan or scholarship program unless satisfactory arrangements to repay have been made;
(2) not have previously received a Baccalaureate degree;

(3) enroll full-time at an eligible participating postsecondary institution in a program of study leading to an undergraduate degree, a certificate or a diploma and;
(4) must provide copies of documents of ancestry by April 1; mail copies to Florida Department of Education, Office of Student Financial Assistance, State Scholarship and Grant Programs.

FINANCIAL DATA:
Amount of support per award: Varies; may not exceed $6,100.

NO. MOST RECENT APPLICANTS: 172 for the year 2017-18.

NO. AWARDS: 28 for the year 2017-18.

APPLICATION INFO:
Detailed program information can be found on the web site.

Duration: Renewable for 100% of student's programs.

Deadline: April 1 for submitting a fully completed, error-free Florida Financial Aid Application. Florida residents must complete and submit the Free Application for Federal Student Aid (FAFSA) online in time to be processed error-free by the U.S. Department of Education on or before May 15. Florida nonresidents must complete and submit the FAFSA in time to receive the Student Aid Report (SAR) from the processor and postmark a copy of the SAR to OSFA by May 15.

ADDRESS INQUIRIES TO:
State Scholarship and Grant Programs (See address above.)

THE JACK AND JILL OF AMERICA FOUNDATION   [942]

1930 17th Street, N.W.
Washington, DC 20009-6207
(202) 232-5290
Fax: (202) 232-1747
E-mail: administration@jackandjillfoundation.org
Web Site: www.jackandjillfoundation.org

FOUNDED: 1968

AREAS OF INTEREST:
African American families, education, and health and wellness.

CONSULTING OR VOLUNTEER SERVICES:
Volunteer services.

NAME(S) OF PROGRAMS:
● **Education**
● **Health and Wellness**
● **Our Village**
● **Reading Corner Literacy Grant**
● **Teen Community Service Award**

TYPE:
Project/program grants; Scholarships. Volunteer opportunities.

YEAR PROGRAM STARTED: 1968

PURPOSE:
To influence the ongoing positive development of children.

LEGAL BASIS:
Public charity.

ELIGIBILITY:
Grants are made to 501(c)(3), 501(c)(4) and IRS charitable organizations.

GEOG. RESTRICTIONS: United States.

FINANCIAL DATA:
Amount of support per award: $3,000 to $10,000.

Total amount of support: Varies.

NO. MOST RECENT APPLICANTS: 500.

NO. AWARDS: Varies.

APPLICATION INFO:
Applicant should carefully read the Information for Grant Applicants on the Foundation web site before submitting an application on the designated form. Furthermore, answers on the application coversheet must be given in the space provided; no additional sheets can be attached. Type the application (using at least 10-point type). Applications may not be faxed. All signatures should be signed in blue ink. A complete application consists of an application coversheet along with the following materials:
(1) proposal;
(2) copy of IRS 501(c)(3) letter or documentation of 501(c)(4) status, whichever is applicable;
(3) most recent audited income statement or 990 tax return, if 501(c)(3) organization, or most recent year-end statement of income and expenses, if 501(c)(4) organization and;
(4) brief resume or bio of the organization's Project Director and other relevant supporting material.

Duration: One year.

Deadline: April 21.

PUBLICATIONS:
Newsletter; annual report; application guidelines.

IRS I.D.: 51-0224656

STAFF:
Pier A.H. Blake, Executive Director

ADDRESS INQUIRIES TO:
Pier A.H. Blake, Executive Director (See address above.)

THE NAACP LEGAL DEFENSE AND EDUCATIONAL FUND, INC.   [943]

40 Rector Street
5th Floor
New York, NY 10006
(212) 965-2244
Fax: (212) 226-7592
E-mail: scholarships@naacpldf.org
eanderson@naacpldf.org
Web Site: www.naacpldf.org/scholarships

FOUNDED: 1964

AREAS OF INTEREST:
Financial assistance for African-American undergraduates and for law students with a demonstrable interest in civil rights.

NAME(S) OF PROGRAMS:
● **LDF Herbert Lehman Education Fund Scholarship Program**
● **LDF Earl Warren Legal Training Program**

TYPE:
Awards/prizes; Grants-in-aid; Internships; Scholarships. LDF Herbert Lehman Education Fund Scholarship Program: Scholarships for African-American high school seniors, high school graduates and college freshmen to attend four-year accredited colleges and universities.

LDF Earl Warren Legal Training Program: Scholarships for law students to attend three-year accredited law schools.

YEAR PROGRAM STARTED: 1964

PURPOSE:
To encourage students to continue the work of the Legal Defense Fund; to encourage young people to be involved in public service; to increase the presence of African-American students in colleges, universities and law schools in the U.S.

LEGAL BASIS:
501(c)(3) corporation.

ELIGIBILITY:
Applicants must be U.S. citizens. Candidates must have outstanding potential evidenced by their recommendations, high school academic records, test scores and essays. They must understand their educational goals and academic abilities. Candidates should have a clear commitment to working in the public service as exemplified by their community and school involvements. Candidates should have exceptional leadership potential with an ability to work well in diverse settings.

Law students already enrolled in law school are not eligible to apply for the LDF Earl Warren Legal Training Program.

Applicants are encouraged to visit the Fund's web site.

GEOG. RESTRICTIONS: United States.

FINANCIAL DATA:
Amount of support per award: LDF Herbert Lehman Education Fund Scholarship Program: $2,000 per year; LDF Earl Warren Legal Training Program: $10,000 per year.

NO. MOST RECENT APPLICANTS: Over 2,000.

NO. AWARDS: Herbert Lehman Scholarship: 25; Earl Warren Program: 5 annually.

APPLICATION INFO:
Applications will be available for online submission by November 30 of each year. Applicants who do not meet the basic criteria for eligibility or do not satisfy program requirements for the completion of applications will not be considered.

Duration: Herbert Lehman Scholarship: Up to four years depending upon availability of funds. Renewable during undergraduate career, if student remains in good standing with their college or university. Earl Warren Program: Three years provided scholar remains in good academic standing and meets scholarship criteria.

Deadline: April 1 for the Lehman Scholarship and May 1 for the Warren Legal Training Program. Notification normally takes place at the end of July, prior to the fall semester of the student's first academic year.

STAFF:
Eve Anderson, Program Assistant

ADDRESS INQUIRIES TO:
Eve Anderson, Program Assistant
(See address above.)

NATIONAL ASSOCIATION FOR EQUAL OPPORTUNITY IN HIGHER EDUCATION (NAFEO) [944]
110 Maryland Avenue, N.E.
Suite 509
Washington, DC 20002
(202) 552-3300
Fax: (202) 552-3330
E-mail: nafeocareers@nafeo.org
Web Site: www.nafeonation.org

FOUNDED: 1969

AREAS OF INTEREST:
Equal opportunity in higher education.

NAME(S) OF PROGRAMS:
- **NAFEO Internship Program**

TYPE:
Internships. NAFEO Internship Program offers full-time paid internships in the summer, spring and fall.

YEAR PROGRAM STARTED: 1997

PURPOSE:
To provide lifelong learning experiences that enhance personal and professional development.

ELIGIBILITY:
Preference will be given to students enrolled in undergraduate or graduate programs at historically or predominantly black colleges and universities. A grade point average of 3.0 or above on a 4.0 scale is required. (Some internships require U.S. citizenship.)

FINANCIAL DATA:
Stipends are paid according to a student's classification at the time of application. Round-trip travel: Students selected for summer internships only who reside outside of the Washington, DC, metropolitan area will receive a travel allowance. A housing stipend will be provided. Local travel: Interns receive an allowance to subsidize daily travel to and from their work assignments.

Amount of support per award: Undergraduate students, $11 per hour; graduate students, $13 to $15 per hour.

NO. AWARDS: Approximately 20.

APPLICATION INFO:
Applicant must submit:
(1) complete application;
(2) current resume;
(3) unofficial transcript - by request only;
(4) official transcript - by request only and;
(5) two completed faculty recommendation forms - by request only.

In conjunction with NAFEO member institutions, NAFEO staff reviews applications to ensure that applicants are eligible and that the applications are complete. NAFEO staff then refers applications to employing agencies based on the academic disciplines they are seeking. Employing agencies review the applications, conduct interviews if necessary, and make all final selections.

Selected students will be notified by NAFEO staff and provided with an official internship offer.

Duration: Summer: 10 weeks; Fall and spring: 15 weeks.

Deadline: Varies.

ADDRESS INQUIRIES TO:
Internship Coordinator
(See address above.)

THE NATIONAL ASSOCIATION OF BLACK SOCIAL WORKERS [945]
2305 Martin Luther King Jr. Avenue, S.E.
Washington, DC 20020
(202) 678-4570
Fax: (202) 678-4572
E-mail: officedirector@nabsw.org
Web Site: www.nabsw.org

FOUNDED: 1968

AREAS OF INTEREST:
Social work and community advocacy.

NAME(S) OF PROGRAMS:
- **Emma and Meloid Algood Tuition Scholarship (Undergraduate)**
- **Dr. Joyce Beckett Scholarship**
- **Selena Danette Brown Book Scholarship**
- **Stella Browne Book Scholarship**
- **Thaddeus P. Matthis Book Scholarship**
- **Dr. Theresa L. Roberts Book Scholarship**
- **Cenie Jomo Williams Tuition Scholarship**

TYPE:
Scholarships.

YEAR PROGRAM STARTED: 1968

PURPOSE:
To promote the welfare, survival and liberation of communities of African ancestry.

LEGAL BASIS:
Nonprofit membership association.

ELIGIBILITY:
Student must:
(1) be an active paid member of NABSW;
(2) have a 2.5 grade point average on a 4.0 scale;
(3) express research interest in African Americans or those of African ancestry and;
(4) be enrolled for full-time study at an accredited U.S. social work program for the semester that the award will be granted.

GEOG. RESTRICTIONS: United States.

FINANCIAL DATA:
Amount of support per award: $250 to $2,500.
Total amount of support: Varies.

NO. AWARDS: Varies.

APPLICATION INFO:
Scholarship applications can be obtained from the National Office.
Duration: One-time award. May reapply for the Emma and Meloid Algood Tuition Scholarship.
Deadline: February 15.

PUBLICATIONS:
Quarterly newsletters.

IRS I.D.: 13-2779773

ADDRESS INQUIRIES TO:
Melanie Bryant, National Office Director
(See address above.)

NATIONAL BLACK MBA ASSOCIATION [946]
400 West Peachtree Street, N.W.
Suite 203
Atlanta, GA 30308
(404) 260-5444
E-mail: scholarship@nbmbaa.org
Web Site: nbmbaa.org

AREAS OF INTEREST:
The economic and intellectual wealth of the black community.

NAME(S) OF PROGRAMS:
- **NBMBAA Undergraduate Scholarship Program**

TYPE:
Scholarships.

PURPOSE:
To help create economic and intellectual wealth for the Black community; to identify

and increase the pool of Black talent for business, public, private and nonprofit sectors.

ELIGIBILITY:
Applicant must:
(1) be a student in their first, second, third or fourth year enrolled full-time at an accredited college or university at the time of award (September);
(2) be a financially active member of the National Black MBA Association;
(3) be a U.S. or Canadian citizen;
(4) submit an essay on provided topic;
(5) submit a current resume;
(6) have a grade point average of 3.0 or above;
(7) demonstrate academic excellence;
(8) demonstrate exceptional leadership potential;
(9) be actively involved in their local communities through service to others and;
(10) be recommended by faculty advisor.

GEOG. RESTRICTIONS: United States and Canada.

FINANCIAL DATA:
Amount of support per award: Up to $5,000 for the 2017-18 academic year.

APPLICATION INFO:
Applicant is strongly advised to contact the Association at the e-mail address above for up-to-date details.

The following application materials must be submitted:
(1) application (must be completed online);
(2) a 500-word essay completed on the selected topic (submitted online only);
(3) a current resume no more than two pages long;
(4) a copy uploaded of applicant's most recent official transcript(s) and;
(5) a professional headshot (photograph) in jpeg format (image should be at least 1024 x 768).

ADDRESS INQUIRIES TO:
See e-mail address above.

*SPECIAL STIPULATIONS:
Scholarship recipients are required to agree to participate in limited public relations activities.

NATIONAL BLACK NURSES ASSOCIATION, INC.
8630 Fenton Street
Suite 910
Silver Spring, MD 20910
(301) 589-3200
Fax: (301) 589-3223
E-mail: info@nbna.org
Web Site: www.nbna.org

TYPE:
Scholarships.

See entry 2281 for full listing.

NATIONAL SOCIETY OF BLACK ENGINEERS
205 Daingerfield Road
Alexandria, VA 22314
(703) 549-2207
Fax: (703) 683-5312
E-mail: scholarships@nsbe.org
Web Site: apply.nsbe.org

TYPE:
Awards/prizes; Scholarships. The Society offers a variety of NSBE and

corporate-sponsored scholarship and award opportunities to its precollege, collegiate undergraduate and graduate student members as well as technical professional members.

See entry 1561 for full listing.

NEED   [947]
The Law and Finance Building
429 Fourth Avenue, 20th Floor
Pittsburgh, PA 15219
(412) 566-2760
Fax: (412) 471-6643
E-mail: needpgh@gmail.com
Web Site: www.needld.org

FOUNDED: 1963

AREAS OF INTEREST:
Higher education, college access services.

CONSULTING OR VOLUNTEER SERVICES:
Counseling for postsecondary education; assistance to students and parents needing help with the completion of financial aid forms; mentoring services.

NAME(S) OF PROGRAMS:
● **Access to College and Career Education (ACE) Program**
● **African American Male Mentoring Initiative (AAMMI)**
● **Future NEED Scholars**
● **The NEED HBCU (Historically Black Colleges and Universities) Educational Tour**
● **Science, Technology, Engineering, Art and Math (STEAM) Female Mentoring Program**
● **Unmet NEED Grants and Scholarships**

TYPE:
Internships; Matching gifts; Scholarships. Supplemental grants for postsecondary education at colleges and business, trade and technical schools.

YEAR PROGRAM STARTED: 1963

PURPOSE:
To provide career and college access services which empower youth from the Pittsburgh region to aspire to, learn about, prepare for, and complete higher education.

LEGAL BASIS:
Incorporated nonprofit, tax-exempt.

ELIGIBILITY:
Applicant must meet the following requirements:
(1) be a high school student planning to enroll, or a student already enrolled, full-time in a college or university;
(2) be a resident of a county in the Pittsburgh area for one year prior to entering a school or college;
(3) have a minimum cumulative grade point average of 2.0;
(4) be a U.S. citizen;
(5) demonstrate unmet financial need of at least $1,000 after the financial aid award package has been determined and;
(6) have an Expected Family Contribution (EFC) less than $5,000.

GEOG. RESTRICTIONS: Allegheny, Armstrong, Beaver, Butler, Fayette, Greene, Lawrence, Washington and Westmoreland counties, Pennsylvania.

FINANCIAL DATA:
Amount of support per award: $1,000 to $3,500.

Total amount of support: Varies.

APPLICATION INFO:
Applicant must submit:
(1) NEED application;
(2) high school, college or school transcript (whichever is most recent) and;
(3) photo.
Duration: Academic year. May reapply in subsequent years.
Deadline: May 31.

PUBLICATIONS:
Annual report.

OFFICERS:
TiAnda Blount, Chairperson of the Board

ADDRESS INQUIRIES TO:
Student Services Department
(See address above.)

THE SCHOMBURG CENTER FOR RESEARCH IN BLACK CULTURE
515 Malcolm X Boulevard
New York, NY 10037-1801
(212) 491-2228
E-mail: sir@nypl.org
Web Site: www.nypl.org/about/locations/schomburg/fellowships

TYPE:
Fellowships. Awarded to scholars and professionals whose research in African diasporic studies can benefit from extended access to the Center's collections. Seminars, colloquia, forums, symposia and conferences complement the residency program.

See entry 362 for full listing.

UNITED NEGRO COLLEGE FUND (UNCF)   [948]
1805 Seventh Street, N.W.
Washington, DC 20001
(800) 331-2244
(202) 810-0258
E-mail: scholarships@uncf.org
Web Site: www.uncf.org

FOUNDED: 1944

TYPE:
Fellowships; Internships; Scholarships; Technical assistance. The Fund, since its founding, has raised money for 37 private, historically Black colleges and universities.

Faculty fellowship programs make it possible for hundreds of instructors to earn doctoral degrees.

Mentoring and internship opportunities are provided for hundreds of UNCF students.

Scholarships are offered to a pool of more than 60,000 talented students attending UNCF colleges and universities. The Fund oversees more than 450 scholarship programs in the following general categories:
(1) geographically based scholarships;
(2) scholarships based on academic major;
(3) scholarships based on merit and need and;
(4) financial aid for graduate study.

PURPOSE:
To provide low-cost quality education in an environment that enables students to excel.

FINANCIAL DATA:
Amount of support per award: Scholarships: $500 to $10,000.

Total amount of support: Varies.

APPLICATION INFO:
Contact the Fund for detailed information.

OFFICERS:
Michael L. Lomax, Ph.D, President and Chief Executive Officer

ADDRESS INQUIRIES TO:
James Lander, Senior Director of Program Management
(See address above.)

Native American

AMERICAN INDIAN COLLEGE FUND [949]

8333 Greenwood Boulevard
Denver, CO 80221
(303) 426-8900
Fax: (303) 426-1200
E-mail: scholarships@collegefund.org
Web Site: collegefund.org

FOUNDED: 1989

AREAS OF INTEREST:
Scholarship funding for Native American and Alaska Native students.

NAME(S) OF PROGRAMS:
- **Full Circle Scholarship Program**
- **TCU Scholarship Program**

TYPE:
Scholarships.

YEAR PROGRAM STARTED: 1989

PURPOSE:
To educate the mind and spirit of Native American communities by providing undergraduate and graduate Native student scholarships and programmatic support for the nation's 34 accredited tribal colleges and universities to provide access to an affordable, quality higher education while preserving Native cultures and languages; to make scholarships available to undergraduate and graduate Native students at any accredited public or private (nonprofit) college.

ELIGIBILITY:
Minimum requirements for all American Indian College Fund Full Circle Scholarships include:
(1) U.S. citizenship;
(2) enrollment full-time in an accredited tribal, public or private (nonprofit) college or university;
(3) ability to trace Indian ancestry; registered as a member of a federal- or state-recognized tribe, or a descendant of at least one grandparent or parent who is an enrolled tribal member; Alaska Natives may use Native Corporation membership;
(4) minimum grade point average of 2.0 mandatory (many Full Circle Scholarships funded by Fund's partners are more competitive) and;
(5) submission of a completed online application.

Eligible organizations must be 501(c)(3) not-for-profit. No grants are made to religious organizations.

GEOG. RESTRICTIONS: United States.

FINANCIAL DATA:
Amount of support per award: Scholarships: Average $1,200 per year.

APPLICATION INFO:
Guidelines and application form are available on the web site.

Deadline: Full Circle Scholarship: Applications accepted January 1 to May 31 each year. TCU Scholarship: Varies by college.

ADDRESS INQUIRIES TO:
See e-mail address above.

AMERICAN INDIAN GRADUATE CENTER [950]

3701 San Mateo Boulevard, N.E.
Suite 200
Albuquerque, NM 87110
(505) 881-4584
Fax: (505) 884-0427
E-mail: fellowships@aigcs.org
Web Site: www.aigcs.org

FOUNDED: 1969

AREAS OF INTEREST:
Graduate and undergraduate-level education in any field.

NAME(S) OF PROGRAMS:
- **Fellowships for American Indians or Alaskan Natives**

TYPE:
Fellowships; Grants-in-aid; Scholarships. Grants on an academic year basis. Summer funding available to continuing students only; these are students who are currently in the fellowship program.

YEAR PROGRAM STARTED: 1969

PURPOSE:
To help open doors to graduate education and help tribes obtain the educated professionals they need to become more self-sufficient and exercise their rights to self-determination.

LEGAL BASIS:
IRS status 501(c)(3), tax-exempt, incorporated in New Mexico.

ELIGIBILITY:
An applicant must be an enrolled member of a U.S. federally recognized American Indian tribe or Alaska Native group, or possess one-fourth degree Indian blood from a federally recognized tribe. Applicant must be pursuing a Master's, Doctorate or professional degree as a full-time graduate student at an accredited graduate school in the U.S. and must be in financial need. They must submit an essay as described in the application packet. Applicants must apply for federal financial and campus-based aid at the financial aid office of the university they plan to attend.

GEOG. RESTRICTIONS: United States.

FINANCIAL DATA:
Awards are based on each applicant's unmet financial need as verified by the applicant's college financial aid office. Fellowships are supplementary grants and are only a percentage of a student's total unmet financial need.

Amount of support per award: Varies.

Total amount of support: Varies.

Matching fund requirements: Universities are encouraged to provide assistance.

CO-OP FUNDING PROGRAMS: The organization works with other scholarship agencies to assure that there will be no overfunding of students.

NO. MOST RECENT APPLICANTS: Over 3,000 for the year 2017.

NO. AWARDS: Over 900 for the year 2017.

APPLICATION INFO:
Application must be submitted online.
Duration: One academic year at a time. Students may reapply each year.
Deadline: Varies depending on scholarship.

PUBLICATIONS:
Annual report; newsletter; brochure.

IRS I.D.: 85-0222386

STAFF:
Josh Lucio, Program Associate
Lakota Coriz, Program Assistant

ADDRESS INQUIRIES TO:
See e-mail address above.

AMERICAN INDIAN SCIENCE AND ENGINEERING SOCIETY (AISES) [951]

6899 Winchester Circle
Suite 102A
Boulder, CO 80301
(720) 552-6123
Fax: (720) 526-6940
E-mail: info@aises.org
Web Site: www.aises.org

FOUNDED: 1977

AREAS OF INTEREST:
American Indian education in the science and engineering fields.

TYPE:
Academic and travel scholarships. AISES scholarships are intended to partially defray tuition and other educational expenses, thereby increasing access to higher education and improving college retention rates for AISES members.

AISES scholarships are made possible by corporations, government agencies, foundations, and individuals who wish to support the advancement of American Indians/Alaskan Natives. Scholarships are distributed in two disbursements and awarded for one academic year, unless otherwise specified. Recipients cannot receive more than one scholarship in any of the programs.

Scholarships are also awarded to members of AISES who are American Indian/Alaskan Native college students who meet the eligibility requirements for each scholarship.

YEAR PROGRAM STARTED: 1983

PURPOSE:
To significantly increase the number of American Indian/Alaskan Native scientists and engineers, and develop knowledgeable leaders within native communities; to foster the building of community by bridging science and technology with traditional native values.

LEGAL BASIS:
Private, nonprofit corporation.

ELIGIBILITY:
Each scholarship has its own eligibility requirements regarding grade point average, majors and academic status. Minimum requirements include:
(1) Applicant must be an AISES member at the time of application and;
(2) Applicant must be an enrolled member or a descendant of an enrolled member of a federal or state recognized American Indian Tribe or Alaska Native Village, or Native Hawaiian or descendant from a Native Hawaiian, or Pacific Islander or descendant from a Pacific Islander, or Indigenous person of Canada. Enrollment documents and/or a copy of birth certificate(s) showing

descendancy from an enrolled citizen, Indigenous group of Canada, Native Hawaiian, or Pacific Islander are acceptable. Applicant may also, instead, provide a copy of their Certificate of Degree of Indian Blood or Certificate of Degree of Alaska Native Blood (CDIB) card.

GEOG. RESTRICTIONS: United States and Canada.

FINANCIAL DATA:
Amount of support per award: Varies.
Total amount of support: Varies.

NO. MOST RECENT APPLICANTS: 1,719.

NO. AWARDS: 178.

APPLICATION INFO:
Student must complete a General Applicant Profile through the Online Scholarship Application Information System (OASIS) provided by Indigenous Education, Inc., which is located at cobellscholar.academicworks.com.
Duration: One academic year.
Deadline: March 15.

PUBLICATIONS:
AISES Scholarship Program brochure.

IRS I.D.: 73-1023474

ADDRESS INQUIRIES TO:
Dr. Johnny Poolaw, Associate Director of Student Success Services
(See address above.)

AMERICAN PHILOSOPHICAL SOCIETY [952]

104 South Fifth Street
Philadelphia, PA 19106-3387
(215) 440-3429
E-mail: lmusumeci@amphilsoc.org
Web Site: www.amphilsoc.org/grants/phillips-fund-native-american-research

FOUNDED: 1743

AREAS OF INTEREST:
Scholarly research.

NAME(S) OF PROGRAMS:
● **Phillips Fund for Native American Research**

TYPE:
Grants-in-aid; Research grants. Postgraduate grants for research in Native American linguistics, ethnohistory and the history of studies of Native Americans in the continental U.S. and Canada. The Committee prefers supporting the work of younger scholars/graduate students for research on Master's or doctoral dissertations. Grants are for travel costs, tapes, films and consultants' fees.

YEAR PROGRAM STARTED: 1940

LEGAL BASIS:
Nonprofit learned society.

ELIGIBILITY:
Open to graduate students and postdoctoral candidates.

The grants described above are for research in Native American linguistics and ethnohistory, as well as in the history of studies of Native Americans. There are no ethnic restrictions on applicants. Work must be on groups located in the continental U.S. and Canada.

The Committee sometimes approves more than two awards to the same person within a five-year period. Grants are not made for

projects in archaeology, ethnography, psycholinguistics, or for the preparation of pedagogical materials, general maintenance or purchase of permanent equipment (tape recorders, books, etc.).

FINANCIAL DATA:
The grants are intended for such extra costs as travel, tapes, films, consultants' fees, etc., but not for the purchase of permanent equipment (tape recorders, computers, etc.)
Amount of support per award: Awards average $3,000; grants do not exceed $3,500.
Total amount of support: $49,900 for the year 2020.

NO. MOST RECENT APPLICANTS: 32.

NO. AWARDS: 17 for the year 2020.

APPLICATION INFO:
Application must be submitted electronically through the Society's online portal. Up to two additional pages may be submitted for the project statement.

Two letters of support are required.

The application and both letters of reference must be received by the deadline.
Duration: One year.
Deadline: March 1. Notification by May.

ADDRESS INQUIRIES TO:
Linda Musumeci
Director of Grants and Fellowships
(See address above.)

ASSOCIATION ON AMERICAN INDIAN AFFAIRS [953]

966 Hungerford Drive, Suite 30-A
Rockville, MD 20850
(240) 314-7155
E-mail: general.aaia@indian-affairs.org
Web Site: www.indian-affairs.org/scholarships.html

FOUNDED: 1922

AREAS OF INTEREST:
Sovereignty, culture preservation, youth education and capacity building of Indian country.

NAME(S) OF PROGRAMS:
● **Association on American Indian Affairs Scholarship Program**

TYPE:
Scholarships. Undergraduate and graduate scholarships for citizens of federally recognized Tribes and unrecognized Tribes.

PURPOSE:
To promote the welfare of American Indians and Alaska Natives by supporting efforts to sustain and perpetuate their cultures and languages; to protect their sovereignty, constitutional, legal and human rights and natural resources; to improve their health, education and economic and community development.

LEGAL BASIS:
Charitable nonprofit foundation.

ELIGIBILITY:
The applicant must meet the following basic requirements:
(1) be enrolled in one's tribe;
(2) be attending an accredited school full-time both fall and spring semesters;
(3) be seeking a Master's degree in any curriculum, Ph.D., law degree or medical degree and;
(4) have a minimum 2.5 grade point average.

GEOG. RESTRICTIONS: Continental United States and Alaska.

FINANCIAL DATA:
Amount of support per award: Varies.

NO. MOST RECENT APPLICANTS: 370.

NO. AWARDS: 27.

APPLICATION INFO:
Application period opens at the end of May. Information is available online.
Duration: Life of the student's academic career, as long as the student maintains a 2.5 grade point average and full-time status.
Deadline: Mid-June.

BNSF RAILWAY FOUNDATION [954]

2500 Lou Menk Drive
Building AOB-2
Fort Worth, TX 76131-2830
(817) 867-6458
E-mail: bnsffoundation@bnsf.com
Web Site: www.bnsffoundation.org

NAME(S) OF PROGRAMS:
● **Native American Scholarship Program**

TYPE:
Scholarships. Awarded annually to outstanding Native American high school seniors from funds provided by the Foundation, for up to four years or until undergraduate degree requirements are completed, whichever occurs first. Scholarship winners may attend any accredited college (two-year leading to a four-year degree) or university in the U.S.

LEGAL BASIS:
Corporate foundation.

ELIGIBILITY:
High school seniors having one-fourth or more Indian blood are eligible. Applicants need not be related to Burlington Northern Santa Fe personnel to qualify. Two scholarships are provided exclusively for members of the Navajo Tribe and the other three are available to any Native American high school students residing in Arizona, California, Colorado, Kansas, Minnesota, Montana, New Mexico, North Dakota, Oklahoma, Oregon, South Dakota, or Washington.

Winners are selected on the basis of strong academic performance in high school, with award preference being given to the study of any of the sciences such as medicine, engineering, natural and physical sciences, as well as business, education and health administration.

GEOG. RESTRICTIONS: Arizona, California, Colorado, Kansas, Minnesota, Montana, New Mexico, North Dakota, Oklahoma, Oregon, South Dakota and Washington.

FINANCIAL DATA:
Amount of support per award: $1,000 to $2,500 annually for up to four years or until undergraduate degree requirements are completed, whichever occurs first (but not to exceed five years). Financial need determines the amount awarded.

NO. AWARDS: 5.

APPLICATION INFO:
The scholarship is administered by the American Indian Science and Engineering Society (AISES) and all winners are selected by the organization. Applications may be obtained by writing American Indian Science

and Engineering Society, P.O. Box 9828, Albuquerque, NM 87119-9828. All correspondence and questions should be directed to AISES.

Duration: Up to four years or until undergraduate degree requirements are completed, whichever occurs first, but not to exceed five years.

ADDRESS INQUIRIES TO:
American Indian Science and Engineering Society
(See address above.)

BUREAU OF INDIAN AFFAIRS [955]

Office of Indian Services
Division of Workforce Development
1849 C Street, N.W., Room 4520
Washington, DC 20240
(202) 513-7625
E-mail: Terrence.Parks@bia.gov
Web Site: www.indianaffairs.gov

FOUNDED: 1824

AREAS OF INTEREST:
Vocational training, job placement, education, childcare and related services.

NAME(S) OF PROGRAMS:
● **Indian Employment Assistance**
● **Public Law 102-477**

TYPE:
Project/program grants; Training grants. Vocational training and job placement, advisory services and counseling, education, childcare and youth development programs.

YEAR PROGRAM STARTED: 1956

PURPOSE:
To provide individual grants for adult vocational training and job placement services for Indians.

LEGAL BASIS:
Public Law 67-85, The Snyder Act of November 2, 1921; Public Law 84-959, Indian Adult Vocational Training Act of August 3, 1956; Public Law 102-477.

ELIGIBILITY:
Applicant must be a member of a federally recognized tribe, band or group of Indians, whose residence is on or near an Indian reservation under the jurisdiction of BIA.

GEOG. RESTRICTIONS: United States.

FINANCIAL DATA:
Total amount of support: Over $100,000,000 annually.

CO-OP FUNDING PROGRAMS: Indian Education, Training and Employment.

NO. MOST RECENT APPLICANTS: 6,500.

NO. AWARDS: 455 for the year 2017.

APPLICATION INFO:
Applicants should make application to the nearest Agency or Tribal Employment Assistance. Contact tribal office nearest to place of residence.
Duration: One year. Renewal possible if continuing training.

STAFF:
Terrence Parks, Division Chief

ADDRESS INQUIRIES TO:
Terrence Parks, Division Chief
(See address above.)

BUREAU OF INDIAN AFFAIRS [956]

Office of Indian Energy and Economic Development
Division of Energy and Mineral Development
13922 Denver West Parkway, Suite 200
Lakewood, CO 80401
(303) 969-5270
Fax: (303) 969-5273
E-mail: IEEDgrants@bia.gov
Web Site: www.bia.gov/as-ia/ieed

AREAS OF INTEREST:
Energy development; renewable energy; development capacity; oil, gas and coal development.

NAME(S) OF PROGRAMS:
● **Tribal Energy Development Capacity (TEDC) Grant**

TYPE:
Project/program grants.

PURPOSE:
To help tribes in assessing, developing or obtaining the managerial, organizational and technical capacity needed to develop energy resources on Indian land and to properly account for resulting energy production and revenues, as provided for in Title V, Section 503, of the Energy Policy Act.

LEGAL BASIS:
Public Law 67-85, The Snyder Act of November 2, 1921; The Energy Policy Act of 2005 (25 U.S.C. 3501 et seq.)

ELIGIBILITY:
Federally recognized Indian tribes and tribal energy resource development organizations.

GEOG. RESTRICTIONS: United States.

FINANCIAL DATA:
Amount of support per award: Up to $300,000 appropriated annually.
Total amount of support: Over $1,500,000.

NO. AWARDS: Up to 35.

APPLICATION INFO:
Applicants should refer to the solicitation notice on www.grants.gov.
Duration: 12 months; renewal possible.

STAFF:
Stephen Manydeeds, Division Chief
Winter Jojola-Talburt, Deputy Division Chief
Amy Wilson, TEDC Program Manager

ADDRESS INQUIRIES TO:
Amy Wilson, TEDC Program Manager
(See address above.)

BUREAU OF INDIAN AFFAIRS [957]

Office of Indian Energy and Economic Development
Division of Energy and Mineral Development
13922 Denver West Parkway, Suite 200
Lakewood, CO 80401
(303) 969-5270
Fax: (303) 969-5273
E-mail: IEEDgrants@bia.gov
Web Site: www.bia.gov/as-ia/ieed

AREAS OF INTEREST:
Energy development; mineral development; feasibility study; renewable energy; oil, gas and coal development.

NAME(S) OF PROGRAMS:
● **Energy and Mineral Development Program (EMDP) Grant**

TYPE:
Project/program grants.

PURPOSE:
To promote energy and mineral development projects that explore for energy and mineral resources, inventory or assess known resources, or perform feasibility or market studies that tend to promote the use and development of known energy and mineral resources.

LEGAL BASIS:
Public Law 67-85, The Snyder Act of November 2, 1921; The Energy Policy Act of 2005 (25 U.S.C. 3501 et seq.)

ELIGIBILITY:
Federally recognized Indian tribes and tribal energy resource development organizations.

GEOG. RESTRICTIONS: Indian land within the United States.

FINANCIAL DATA:
Amount of support per award: Up to $600,000 appropriated annually.
Total amount of support: Over $5,000,000; total funds are contingent on annual appropriations.

NO. AWARDS: Approximately 15.

APPLICATION INFO:
Applicants should refer to the solicitation notice on www.grants.gov.
Duration: 12 months; renewal possible.
Deadline: May.

STAFF:
Stephen Manydeeds, Division Chief
Winter Jojola-Talburt, Deputy Division Chief
Amy Wilson, Program Manager

ADDRESS INQUIRIES TO:
Amy Wilson, Program Manager
(See address above.)

BUREAU OF INDIAN AFFAIRS [958]

Office of Indian Energy and Economics Development (IEED)
U.S. Department of the Interior, Room 4138 MIB
1849 C Street, N.W.
Washington, DC 20240
(202) 595-4766
E-mail: IEEDgrants@bia.gov
jamesr.west@bia.gov
Web Site: www.indianaffairs.gov/as-ia/ieed/content

AREAS OF INTEREST:
Economic development, feasibility study.

NAME(S) OF PROGRAMS:
● **Native American Business Development Institute (NABDI)**

TYPE:
Project/program grants.

PURPOSE:
To study the viability of an economic development project or business or the practicality of a technology an eligible recipient may choose to pursue.

LEGAL BASIS:
Public Law 67-85, The Snyder Act of November 2, 1921.

ELIGIBILITY:
Federally recognized Indian tribes.

GEOG. RESTRICTIONS: United States.

FINANCIAL DATA:
Amount of support per award:
Approximately $35,000 to $50,000.

Total amount of support: Varies. Total funds are contingent on annual appropriations.

NO. MOST RECENT APPLICANTS: 50 to 80.

NO. AWARDS: 12 to 22.

APPLICATION INFO:
Applicants should refer to the solicitation notice on www.grants.gov.

Duration: 12 months. Renewal possible.

Deadline: Varies.

STAFF:
James R. West, IEED Grant Manager

BUREAU OF INDIAN EDUCATION   [959]

12220 Sunrise Valley Drive
Reston, VA 20191
(703) 390-6697
E-mail: katherine.campbell@bie.edu
Web Site: www.bie.edu

FOUNDED: 1824

AREAS OF INTEREST:
Elementary and secondary education tribal colleges.

NAME(S) OF PROGRAMS:
● **Higher Education Grant Program for American Indians and Alaska Natives**

TYPE:
Fellowships; Scholarships.

YEAR PROGRAM STARTED: 1949

PURPOSE:
To provide financial aid to eligible Indian students enabling them to attend accredited institutions of higher education.

LEGAL BASIS:
Snyder Act.

ELIGIBILITY:
Applicant must be a member of a tribe eligible for services from the Bureau, enrolled or accepted for enrollment in an accredited college and have financial need as determined by the institution's financial aid office.

FINANCIAL DATA:
The grants are intended to supplement the financial aid package prepared by the educational institution's financial aid officer. The grant meets the unmet need portion of the package.

Amount of support per award: Varies.

Total amount of support: Varies.

Matching fund requirements: Meets the unmet need portion of the institution's financial aid package.

CO-OP FUNDING PROGRAMS: Other donor's funding programs are a part of the financial aid package.

NO. MOST RECENT APPLICANTS: 20,000.

NO. AWARDS: 15,000.

APPLICATION INFO:
Candidates should request an application from a home agency or tribal Higher Education Grant Program (HEGP). Contact the BIA/Tribal census office to obtain a Certificate of Degree of Indian Blood (CDIB) and tribal enrollment and submit with the application. Write to the admissions office of the chosen school for an application. Request a financial aid packet from the school's Financial Aid Officer, who will prepare a financial aid package based on the applicant's

need. Then submit all these forms to the appropriate offices well in advance of the deadline.

Duration: One academic year. Must renew annually.

Deadline: Varies.

ADDRESS INQUIRIES TO:
Home agency or tribally administered Higher Education Grant Program

CATCHING THE DREAM   [960]

8200 Mountain Road, N.E.
Suite 103
Albuquerque, NM 87110
(505) 262-2351
Fax: (505) 262-0534
E-mail: NScholarsh@aol.com
Web Site: www.catchingthedream.org

FOUNDED: 1986

AREAS OF INTEREST:
Scholarships for Native college students and improvement of Indian schools and postsecondary education for Native American students in the fields of math, engineering, science, business, education and computers.

CONSULTING OR VOLUNTEER SERVICES:
The Fund assists Native American students who need help in locating other sources of funding and provides fund-raising, management training, conferences, and seminars.

NAME(S) OF PROGRAMS:
● **Math and Science Teaching (MAST)**
● **MESBEC (Math, Engineering, Science, Business, Education and Computers) Program**
● **Native American Leadership in Education (NALE) Program**
● **Reading Award Program (RAP)**
● **Tribal Business Management (TBM) Program**

TYPE:
Conferences/seminars; Development grants; Grants-in-aid; Scholarships; Technical assistance. CTD also works to improve Indian schools through a program of grants and technical assistance. This work has led to the development of 40 Exemplary Programs in Indian education since 1988. The annual Exemplary Institute is a meeting of these Exemplary Programs, where they teach other people how to develop similar programs.

MAST program makes grants of $5,000 to Indian high schools to improve their math and science teaching.

MESBEC Program consists of competitive scholarships for high-potential Native Americans studying in math, engineering, science, business, education and computers.

NALE Program consists of competitive scholarships for high-potential paraprofessional Native Americans who plan to complete their degrees and obtain credentials as teachers, counselors or administrators.

RAP makes grants to Indian schools to improve the reading ability of their students.

Tribal Business Management (TBM) Program consists of competitive scholarships for Native students in all fields of business.

YEAR PROGRAM STARTED: 1986

PURPOSE:
To help tribes prepare young people to work in the fields which are critical for economic, social, business and political development in Indian Country.

LEGAL BASIS:
Nonprofit organization.

ELIGIBILITY:
Applicants must be at least one-quarter blood member of a federally recognized, state recognized or terminated Indian tribe. They must have high potential for the field of study and work for which they are preparing. They must attend an accredited U.S. college or university. They must have clear goals in mind and have done some work toward accomplishing these goals. The goals must be related to the betterment of Indian people or the betterment of an Indian tribe or community. Progress toward accomplishing a goal may be demonstrated by study, by work, by volunteer work or by other means.

Students with no clear goals are discouraged from applying. Normally, successful applicants will plan to earn a four-year degree or a graduate degree. In a few cases, associate degrees are approved. Applicants must apply for all other sources of funding for which they are eligible, including private scholarship sources, corporate traineeships, federal funds, loans, jobs, grants and so forth.

Students can contact CTD up to three years in advance.

GEOG. RESTRICTIONS: United States.

FINANCIAL DATA:
Amount of support per award: $500 to $5,000.

Total amount of support: Approximately $168,000 for the year 2016-17.

NO. AWARDS: MAST: 6; RAP: 12; All other programs: 169 for the year 2015-16.

APPLICATION INFO:
Contact Catching the Dream.

Duration: Until completion of degree.

Deadline: March 15 for summer school. September 15 for winter quarter and spring semester. April 30 for fall semester.

PUBLICATIONS:
The National Indian Grant Directory; Reading for College; Racism in Indian Country; The Secret of No Face; Basic Fund Raising; How to Write Winning Proposals; Literacy in Indian Country.

IRS I.D.: 85-0360858

BOARD OF DIRECTORS:
James Lujan, President
Dr. Lester Sandoval, Vice President
John Tohtsoni, Jr., Treasurer
Jodie Palmer, Secretary
Dr. Dean Chavers
Ms. Lynn Okon Scholnick

CHEROKEE NATION   [961]

P.O. Box 948
Tahlequah, OK 74465
(918) 453-5000
(918) 453-5465
Fax: (918) 458-6286
E-mail: collegeresources@cherokee.org
Web Site: www.cherokee.org

FOUNDED: 1904

AREAS OF INTEREST:
Planning and development (individual and tribal), health, education and welfare.

CONSULTING OR VOLUNTEER SERVICES:
Tribal government administration consultants and volunteers in all interest areas available to eligible tribal members.

NAME(S) OF PROGRAMS:
● **College Resource Center**

TYPE:
Project/program grants; Scholarships; Technical assistance. Financial and other support through all programs to eligible tribal members.

YEAR PROGRAM STARTED: 1964

PURPOSE:
To serve its tribes and members in the areas indicated.

LEGAL BASIS:
Federally recognized Indian tribe.

ELIGIBILITY:
Tribal membership is required.

GEOG. RESTRICTIONS: Primarily northeast Oklahoma.

FINANCIAL DATA:
Amount of support per award: Varies.
Total amount of support: Varies.

APPLICATION INFO:
Guidelines and application form are available on the web site.
Duration: Varies.
Deadline: Varies.

ADDRESS INQUIRIES TO:
College Resource Center
(See e-mail address above.)

FIRST NATIONS DEVELOPMENT INSTITUTE [962]

2432 Main Street, Second Floor
Longmont, CO 80501
(303) 774-7836
Fax: (303) 774-7841
E-mail: info@firstnations.org
Web Site: www.firstnations.org

FOUNDED: 1980

AREAS OF INTEREST:
Nourishing Native foods and health, investing in Native youth, achieving Native financial empowerment, strengthening tribal and community institutions, and advancing household and community asset building strategies.

CONSULTING OR VOLUNTEER SERVICES:
Yes.

TYPE:
Program development grants. First Nations works to improve economic conditions for Native Americans through technical assistance and training, advocacy and policy, and direct financial grants in the five key areas of interest.

YEAR PROGRAM STARTED: 1993

PURPOSE:
To strengthen American Indian economies to support healthy Native communities.

LEGAL BASIS:
Nonprofit organization.

ELIGIBILITY:
Eligible organizations include:
(1) fiscally sponsored Native community organizations;
(2) Native controlled nonprofit organizations;

(3) Native 7871 organizations and;
(4) Federal and state recognized tribal government and tribal government programs.

Grants are not made to individuals for for-profit businesses, programs serving exclusively urban Native communities, programs serving Natives but not controlled by a majority of Natives, for-profit Native consulting firms, for-profit Native businesses except those associated with a nonprofit Native enterprise, or religious organizations (except for traditional Native American spiritual programs).

GEOG. RESTRICTIONS: United States and its territories.

FINANCIAL DATA:
Amount of support per award: Varies.
Total amount of support: Varies.

NO. AWARDS: 148 grants for the year 2019.

APPLICATION INFO:
Application must be made online. Complete information is available on the web site.
Duration: Typically one year.
Deadline: Varies.

PUBLICATIONS:
List of publications; annual report.

IRS I.D.: 54-1254491

ADDRESS INQUIRIES TO:
Kendall Tallmadge, Senior Program Officer
(See address above.)

NATIONAL SOCIETY DAUGHTERS OF THE AMERICAN REVOLUTION

1776 D Street, N.W.
Washington, DC 20006-5303
(202) 879-3263
E-mail: nsdarscholarships@nsdar.org
Web Site: www.dar.org

TYPE:
Scholarships. Intended to help Native American college/university and technical school students at the undergraduate or graduate level.

See entry 1558 for full listing.

NATIONAL SOCIETY DAUGHTERS OF THE AMERICAN REVOLUTION

1776 D Street, N.W.
Washington, DC 20006-5303
(202) 879-3263
E-mail: nsdarscholarships@nsdar.org
Web Site: www.dar.org

TYPE:
Scholarships. Intended to help Native American students enrolled full-time at a two- or four-year college or university.

See entry 1559 for full listing.

NATIVE AMERICAN COMMUNITY BOARD (NACB) [963]

P.O. Box 572
Lake Andes, SD 57356-0572
(605) 487-7072
Fax: (605) 487-7964
E-mail: charon@charles-mix.com
Web Site: www.nativeshop.org

FOUNDED: 1986

AREAS OF INTEREST:
Civil rights, women's rights, reproductive justice, and a healthy environment.

NAME(S) OF PROGRAMS:
● **College Intern Program**

TYPE:
Internships.

PURPOSE:
To address pertinent issues of health, education, land and water rights, and economic development of Native American people.

ELIGIBILITY:
College juniors, seniors or graduate students interested in Native American rights and health issues. Priority will be given to those wishing to stay long-term (six months or longer).

FINANCIAL DATA:
Amount of support per award: $250 biweekly.
Total amount of support: Varies.

NO. AWARDS: 8.

APPLICATION INFO:
Contact the NACB for application procedures.
Duration: Three months to one year, with three months being the preferred minimum stay.
Deadline: Contact the NACB for openings.

ADDRESS INQUIRIES TO:
Charon Asetoyer, Executive Director
(See e-mail address above.)

THE NEWBERRY LIBRARY [964]

Newberry Institute for Research and Education
60 West Walton Street
Chicago, IL 60610
(312) 255-3666
E-mail: research@newberry.org
Web Site: www.newberry.org/fellowships

AREAS OF INTEREST:
Native American women, humanities and social sciences.

NAME(S) OF PROGRAMS:
● **Frances C. Allen Fellowships**

TYPE:
Fellowships; Visiting scholars. Allen fellows are expected to spend a significant part of their tenure in residence at the Newberry D'Arcy McNickle Center for American Indian and Indigenous Studies.

PURPOSE:
To encourage study by Native American women of the humanities and social sciences.

LEGAL BASIS:
Private research library.

ELIGIBILITY:
Applicants must be women of American Indian heritage. While candidates for this award may be working on any graduate or pre-professional field related to the Newberry's collection, the particular goal of the Fellowship is to encourage American Indian women in their studies of the humanities and social sciences.

FINANCIAL DATA:
Amount of support per award: $2,500 per month stipend.

NO. MOST RECENT APPLICANTS: 5.

NO. AWARDS: 1 to 2.

APPLICATION INFO:
Applications must be submitted through the online webform.

Duration: One to two months.

Deadline: December 15.

STAFF:
D. Bradford Hunt, Vice President for Research and Academic Programs

ADDRESS INQUIRIES TO:
See e-mail address above.

*SPECIAL STIPULATIONS:
Allen Fellows are expected to spend a significant part of their tenure in residence at the D'Arcy McNickle Center for American Indian and Indigenous Studies.

RUNNING STRONG FOR AMERICAN INDIAN YOUTH   [965]
8301 Richmond Highway
Alexandria, VA 22309
(703) 317-9881
Fax: (703) 659-6231
E-mail: info@indianyouth.org
Web Site: www.indianyouth.org

FOUNDED: 1986

AREAS OF INTEREST:
Native Americans.

TYPE:
Capital grants; Challenge/matching grants; General operating grants; Project/program grants; Seed money grants.

YEAR PROGRAM STARTED: 1986

PURPOSE:
To help American Indian people meet their immediate survival needs - food, water and shelter - while implementing and supporting programs designed to create opportunities for self-sufficiency and self-esteem, particularly for tribal youth.

ELIGIBILITY:
No grants are made to individuals or fund-raising events. Grants made only to programs that support Native Americans.

GEOG. RESTRICTIONS: United States.

FINANCIAL DATA:
Amount of support per award: Up to $5,000 for new applicants.

Total amount of support: Varies.

NO. AWARDS: Varies.

APPLICATION INFO:
E-mail or call for grant guidelines.

Duration: Up to five years. Must reapply each year.

PUBLICATIONS:
Annual report; application guidelines.

IRS I.D.: 54-1594578

ADDRESS INQUIRIES TO:
Lauren Haas Finkelstein
Executive Director
(See address above.)

U.S. DEPARTMENT OF EDUCATION   [966]
Office of Indian Education
400 Maryland Avenue, S.W.
LBJ Building, 3W101
Washington, DC 20202-6335
(202) 260-3774
Fax: (202) 205-0606
E-mail: indian.education@ed.gov
Web Site: www2.ed.gov/programs/indianformula/index.html

NAME(S) OF PROGRAMS:
• **Indian Education-Formula Grants to Local Education Agencies (LEAs)**

TYPE:
Formula grants. Grants to provide financial assistance to LEAs and tribal schools to address the unique cultural, language and educationally related academic needs of American Indian and Alaska Native students, including preschool children.

LEGAL BASIS:
Public Law 92-318, Title IV, Part A, as amended (25 U.S.C. 2601-2606, 2651).

ELIGIBILITY:
Local educational agencies which have at least 10 Indian children or in which Indians constitute at least 25% of the total enrollment may apply. However, these enrollment requirements do not apply to an LEA in Alaska, California or Oklahoma that serves Indian children or an LEA on, or in proximity to, an Indian reservation. An Indian tribe or an organization controlled or sanctioned by an Indian tribal government and that operates a school for children of that tribe is eligible if that school provides its students an educational program that meets the standards established by the Bureau of Indian Affairs (BIA) or is operated by that tribe or organization under a contract with the BIA.

FINANCIAL DATA:
Amount of support per award: Varies.

Total amount of support: Varies.

NO. AWARDS: Varies.

APPLICATION INFO:
Application instructions and forms are available upon request.

Duration: One year, July 1 to June 30.

Deadline: Varies.

ADDRESS INQUIRIES TO:
Indian Education Programs
(See address above.)

U.S. DEPARTMENT OF HEALTH AND HUMAN SERVICES   [967]
Mary E. Switzer Memorial Building, Room 4126
330 C Street, S.W.
Washington, DC 20416
(877) 922-9262 (Help Desk)
Fax: (202) 690-8145
E-mail: anacomments@acf.hhs.gov
Web Site: www.acf.hhs.gov/ana

FOUNDED: 1974

AREAS OF INTEREST:
General community programming, training and technical assistance and research, demonstration and evaluation.

NAME(S) OF PROGRAMS:
• **Environmental Regulatory Enhancement**

• Native Languages
• **Social and Economic Development Strategies (SEDS) for Native Americans**

TYPE:
Demonstration grants; Development grants; Project/program grants; Research grants; Seed money grants; Technical assistance; Training grants. Financial Assistance grants may be used for such purposes as, but not limited to, Governance Projects, development of codes and ordinances and status clarification activities; Economic Development Projects, to promote business starts for Native-owned businesses and improve Native American housing management; and Social Development Projects, to assume local control of planning and delivering social services in Native American communities, developing local models related to comprehensive planning and delivery of social services and developing or coordinating activities with state-funded projects in decreasing the incidence of child abuse, neglect and fetal alcohol syndrome.

YEAR PROGRAM STARTED: 1973

PURPOSE:
To support projects that improve social and economic conditions of Native Americans within their communities and increase the effectiveness of Indian Tribes and Native American organizations in meeting their economic and social goals.

LEGAL BASIS:
Native American Programs Act of 1974, as amended, Public Law 93-644; Older Americans Act Amendments of 1987, Title V, Public Law 100-175; Indian Reorganization Act Amendments, Section 215, Public Law 100-581; Older Americans Act Amendments of 1992, Title VIII, Public Law 102-375; 42 U.S.C. 2991 et. seq.

ELIGIBILITY:
Governing bodies of Indian tribes, Alaskan Native villages and regional associations established by the Alaska Native Claims Settlement Act, Indian and Alaska Native Organizations in urban or rural nonreservation areas, public and nonprofit agencies serving Native Hawaiians and other Native American Pacific Islanders which include the Native peoples from Guam, American Samoa, Palau or the Commonwealth of the Northern Mariana Islands. The populations served may be located on those islands or in the U.S.

GEOG. RESTRICTIONS: United States.

FINANCIAL DATA:
Amount of support per award: Approximately $125,000 average.

Total amount of support: Approximately $38,500,000 annually.

Matching fund requirements: A matching share of 20% is required unless waived in accordance with criteria which is published in 45 CFR, Part 1336.50. This program has maintenance of effort requirements.

NO. AWARDS: 64 for the year 2018.

APPLICATION INFO:
In order to apply for a grant, an organization must complete the grants.gov registration process.

Duration: One year with possibility of multiyear funding.

Deadline: Varies.

STAFF:
Jeannie Hovland, Commissioner

ADDRESS INQUIRIES TO:
Administration for Native Americans
(See address above.)

THE MORRIS K. UDALL AND STEWART L. UDALL FOUNDATION [968]

130 South Scott Avenue
Tucson, AZ 85701
(520) 901-8564
Fax: (520) 901-8570
E-mail: curley@udall.gov
Web Site: www.udall.gov

FOUNDED: 1992

AREAS OF INTEREST:
Educating young Americans in our nation's heritage, environmental studies, Native American affairs and public policy conflict resolution.

NAME(S) OF PROGRAMS:
• **Congressional Internships**

TYPE:
Internships. Congressional Internships: Native American college, graduate and law students work in congressional offices and federal agencies to gain a firsthand understanding of the federal government. The Foundation arranges meetings with elected officials, staff at Native American advocacy and public interest organizations, and Native American professionals in Washington, DC. They also take field trips and meet with congressional members, agency heads and cabinet secretaries.

YEAR PROGRAM STARTED: 1996

PURPOSE:
To educate a new generation of Americans to preserve and protect their national heritage through studies in the environment, Native American health and tribal policy and effective public policy conflict resolution.

LEGAL BASIS:
The Foundation is an executive branch agency. The President of the U.S. appoints its board of trustees with the advice and consent of the U.S. Senate.

ELIGIBILITY:
Interns will be selected by an independent committee. Applicants must demonstrate a commitment to learning about the federal government. They must be self-motivated and interested in taking advantage of the rich and diverse resources available to them in Washington, DC. Additionally, candidates for the internship program must:
(1) be an enrolled member of a recognized tribe or state-recognized tribe;
(2) be a college junior, senior, graduate student, law student or graduating from a tribal college;
(3) have a minimum 3.0 grade point average or a "B" average and;
(4) have an interest in tribal government and policy.

FINANCIAL DATA:
Interns are provided with airfare to and from Washington, DC, lodging convenient to Capitol Hill, and a daily allowance sufficient for meals, transportation and incidentals.
Amount of support per award: $1,200 educational stipend to be paid at the conclusion of the internship.

NO. MOST RECENT APPLICANTS: 50.

NO. AWARDS: 12.

APPLICATION INFO:
Application information is available on the web site.
Duration: 10 weeks.
Deadline: January 31 (postmark).

STAFF:
Jason Curley, Program Manager

ADDRESS INQUIRIES TO:
Jason Curley, Program Manager
(See address above.)

UNITED SOUTH AND EASTERN TRIBES, INC. [969]

711 Stewarts Ferry Pike
Suite 100
Nashville, TN 37214
(615) 872-7900
Fax: (615) 872-7417
E-mail: kfairbend@usetinc.org
Web Site: www.usetinc.org

FOUNDED: 1969

AREAS OF INTEREST:
Indian tribes.

TYPE:
Scholarships.

PURPOSE:
To enhance the development of Indian Tribes; to improve the capabilities of Tribal governments; to assist the member Tribes and their governments in dealing effectively with public policy issues and in serving the broad needs of Indian people.

ELIGIBILITY:
Supplemental monies are awarded to USET area Indian students who are enrolled members of one of the 30 USET member Tribal Nations.

Must be an Indian student that meets the following criteria:
(1) satisfactory scholastic standing and;
(2) current enrollment or acceptance in a postsecondary educational institution.

FINANCIAL DATA:
Amount of support per award: Selected undergraduate applicants receive an equal amount in any award period in increments of no less than $750. In addition, selected graduate applicants receive an equal amount in any award period in increments of no less than $1,000.
Total amount of support: Varies.

NO. MOST RECENT APPLICANTS: 36.

NO. AWARDS: 22.

APPLICATION INFO:
Contact the Organization for application procedures. Information is also available online.
Duration: Annual supplemental scholarship. Must reapply for additional term.
Deadline: January 15.

ADDRESS INQUIRIES TO:
USET Scholarship Fund
Attn: Karen Fairbend
(See address above.)

UNIVERSITY OF CALIFORNIA, LOS ANGELES [970]

American Indian Studies Center
UCLA - 3220 Campbell Hall, Box 951548
Los Angeles, CA 90095-1548
(310) 825-7315
Fax: (310) 206-7060
E-mail: aisc@ucla.edu
Web Site: www.aisc.ucla.edu

FOUNDED: 1970

AREAS OF INTEREST:
American Indian studies and related topics in policy, education, economics, culture and community.

NAME(S) OF PROGRAMS:
• **Institute of American Cultures Grant**

TYPE:
Fellowships; Research grants; Visiting scholars.

YEAR PROGRAM STARTED: 1969

PURPOSE:
To conduct research in Native American Studies.

LEGAL BASIS:
University research organization; nonprofit organization.

ELIGIBILITY:
Applicants must be citizens or permanent residents of the U.S. and hold a Ph.D. from an accredited college or university (or, in the case of the arts, an appropriate terminal degree) in a relevant field at the time of appointment. UCLA faculty, staff and currently enrolled students are not eligible to apply.

FINANCIAL DATA:
Visiting Researchers may use funds to supplement sabbatical support for a total that does not exceed the candidate's current institutional salary. Visiting Researchers will be paid through their home institutions and will be expected to continue their health benefits through that source as well. Awardees may receive up to $4,000 in research support (through reimbursement of research expenses).
Amount of support per award: Maximum stipend $35,000.
Total amount of support: Varies.

APPLICATION INFO:
Application information is available on the web site.
Duration: Nine to 12 months. Nonrenewable.
Deadline: Varies.

PUBLICATIONS:
American Indian Culture and Research Journal; brochures; books.

IRS I.D.: 95-6006143

STAFF:
Shannon Speed, Director
Pam Grieman, Assistant Director

ADDRESS INQUIRIES TO:
AISC Coordinator
(See address above.)

WASHINGTON STUDENT ACHIEVEMENT COUNCIL   [971]

American Indian Endowed Scholarship
917 Lakeridge Way
Olympia, WA 98502
(360) 753-7843
Fax: (360) 704-6243
E-mail: aies@wsac.wa.gov
Web Site: readysetgrad.wa.
gov/college/american-indian-endowed-
scholarship

AREAS OF INTEREST:
Student financial aid.

NAME(S) OF PROGRAMS:
● **American Indian Endowed Scholarship Program**

TYPE:
Scholarships.

YEAR PROGRAM STARTED: 1993

PURPOSE:
To create an educational opportunity for students with close social and cultural ties to the American Indian community to pursue undergraduate and graduate studies who might not be able otherwise to attend and graduate from higher education institutions in Washington state.

LEGAL BASIS:
Government agency.

ELIGIBILITY:
Applicants must be students of an in-state institution with close social and cultural ties to the American Indian community in the state. Must be a resident of the state of Washington and in financial need. Applicant must have applied for financial aid via FAFSA. Applicant must intend to return service to the state Native American community. Academic merit is also a consideration.

FINANCIAL DATA:
Amount of support per award: $500 to $2,000.
Total amount of support: Varies.

APPLICATION INFO:
Application includes statement of commitment to return service to Washington American Indian communities, statement of close social and cultural ties, three letters of recommendation, completed application and release of information form and transcripts.
Duration: One year. Must reapply for renewal for a maximum of four additional years.
Deadline: February 1. Announcement will be made by late Spring.

ADDRESS INQUIRIES TO:
Ann Voyles, Program Associate
American Indian Endowed Scholarship
P.O. Box 43430
Olympia, WA 98504-3430
E-mail: aies@wsac.wa.gov

Spanish-speaking

CONGRESSIONAL HISPANIC CAUCUS INSTITUTE   [972]

1128 16th Street, N.W.
Washington, DC 20036
(202) 543-1771
Fax: (202) 546-2143
E-mail: programs@chci.org
Web Site: www.chci.org

FOUNDED: 1978

AREAS OF INTEREST:
Leadership training in the legislative process for promising Latino undergraduates.

NAME(S) OF PROGRAMS:
● **CHCI Congressional Internship**

TYPE:
Internships. Internships provide college students with a paid work placement in a congressional office or federal agency for a period of 12 weeks (Spring and Fall Programs) or 10 weeks (Summer Program), as well as extensive professional development and leadership trainings.

PURPOSE:
To expose young Latinos to the legislative process and to strengthen their professional leadership skills, ultimately promoting the presence of Latinos on Capitol Hill and in federal agencies.

ELIGIBILITY:
Students must currently be enrolled full-time and working towards their undergraduate degree.

Student must display:
(1) high academic achievement (preference of 3.0 grade point average or higher);
(2) evidence of leadership skills and potential for leadership growth;
(3) demonstrated commitment to public service-oriented activities and;
(4) superior analytical skills, outstanding oral and written communication skills.

Applicants must be U.S. citizens, lawful permanent residents, asylees, or individuals who are lawfully authorized to work full-time without restriction for any U.S. employer and who, at the time of application, possess lawful evidence of employment authorization.

GEOG. RESTRICTIONS: United States.

FINANCIAL DATA:
Internship includes stipend, domestic round-trip transportation to Washington, DC, housing (all expenses covered) and academic credit if eligible.
Amount of support per award: Spring and Fall Programs: $3,750 stipend; Summer Program: $3,125.

NO. AWARDS: 70 per year.

APPLICATION INFO:
A complete application consists of a one-page PDF resume, curriculum vitae, most recent unofficial transcript, and two letters of recommendation.
Duration: Spring and Fall Programs: 12 weeks; Summer Program: 10 weeks. Internships are not renewable.
Deadline: Spring Program: October 21. Fall Program: February 21. Summer Program: December 1.

CONGRESSIONAL HISPANIC CAUCUS INSTITUTE   [973]

1128 16th Street, N.W.
Washington, DC 20036
(202) 543-1771
(202) 548-8796
Fax: (202) 546-8799
E-mail: programs@chci.org
Web Site: chci.org

FOUNDED: 1978

AREAS OF INTEREST:
Higher education, secondary education, health, housing, law, and public policy.

NAME(S) OF PROGRAMS:
● CHCI Graduate Fellowship Program
● CHCI Public Policy Fellowship

TYPE:
Fellowships. Graduate Fellowship Program offers exceptional Latinos who have earned a graduate degree or higher related to a chosen policy issue area within three years of program start date unparalleled exposure to hands-on experience in public policy.

Public Policy Fellowship offers talented Latinos who have earned a Bachelor's degree within two years of the program start date the opportunity to gain hands-on experience at the national level in public policy.

PURPOSE:
To help increase opportunities for Hispanics to participate in and contribute to the American policymaking process.

ELIGIBILITY:
Applicants must:
(1) demonstrate high academic achievement (preference of 3.0 grade point average or higher);
(2) show evidence of leadership skills and potential for leadership growth;
(3) demonstrate commitment to public service-oriented activities and;
(4) possess superior analytical skills, outstanding oral and written communication skills.

Graduate Fellowship Program applicants must have completed a Master's degree or postgraduate degree prior to the program start date.

Public Policy Fellowship applicants must have earned a Bachelor's degree within two years of the program start date.

Applicants must be U.S. citizens, lawful permanent residents, asylees, or individuals who are lawfully authorized to work full-time without restriction for any U.S. employer and who, at the time of application, possess lawful evidence of employment authorization.

GEOG. RESTRICTIONS: United States.

FINANCIAL DATA:
Amount of support per award: CHCI Graduate Fellowship Program: Stipend of $29,700; CHCI Public Policy Fellowship: Stipend of $26,100.

APPLICATION INFO:
A complete application consists of a one-page PDF resume, curriculum vitae, most recent unofficial transcript, and a letter of recommendation.
Duration: Nine months: Late August to late May.
Deadline: January 30.

FLORIDA DEPARTMENT OF EDUCATION   [974]

Office of Student Financial Assistance
325 West Gaines Street, Suite 1314
Tallahassee, FL 32399-0400
(888) 827-2004
Fax: (850) 487-1809
E-mail: osfa@fldoe.org
Web Site: www.floridastudentfinancialaidsg.org

NAME(S) OF PROGRAMS:
● **Jose Marti Scholarship Challenge Grant Fund**

TYPE:
Challenge/matching grants; Grants-in-aid. Jose Marti Scholarship Challenge Grant Fund is a need-based merit scholarship that provides financial assistance to eligible students of Hispanic origin who will attend Florida public or eligible private institutions.

YEAR PROGRAM STARTED: 1986

PURPOSE:
To provide financial assistance to Hispanic-American high school seniors and graduate students in Florida.

LEGAL BASIS:
Florida Department of Education.

ELIGIBILITY:
Applicants for undergraduate study must apply during their senior year of high school. Graduate students may apply; however, priority for the scholarship is given to graduating high school seniors.

For the applying student, initial eligibility requirements to receive funding are as follows:
(1) be a Florida resident and a U.S. citizen or eligible noncitizen; a student's residency and citizenship status are determined by the postsecondary institution; consult the financial aid office or admissions office of the institution the student plans to attend for questions;
(2) not owe a repayment or be in default under any state or federal grant, loan or scholarship program unless satisfactory arrangements to repay have been made;
(3) be of Spanish culture, born in or having a natural parent who was born in either Mexico, or a Hispanic country of the Caribbean, Central or South America, regardless of race;
(4) have earned, by the end of the seventh semester, a minimum unweighted cumulative grade point average of 3.0 on a 4.0 scale in high school for an undergraduate scholarship, or a 3.0 institutional cumulative grade point average for undergraduate college work if applying for a graduate-level scholarship;
(5) enroll as a degree-seeking student at an eligible postsecondary institution and enroll each academic term for a minimum of 12 credit hours for undergraduate study or nine credit hours for graduate study and;
(6) demonstrate a minimum $2,000 in financial need by timely completing and submitting the FAFSA.

GEOG. RESTRICTIONS: Florida.

FINANCIAL DATA:
Amount of support per award: Typically $2,000.
Total amount of support: $124,000 for the year 2018-19.

NO. MOST RECENT APPLICANTS: 17,955 for the year 2018-19.

NO. AWARDS: 65 for the year 2018-19.

APPLICATION INFO:
Detailed program information can be found on the web site.
Duration: One academic year.
Deadline: For undergraduate study, submit a fully completed error-free Florida Financial Aid Application during the student's last year in high school by April 1. For graduate study, submit a fully completed error-free Florida Financial Aid Application by April 1 prior to the year of graduate study.

ADDRESS INQUIRIES TO:
State Scholarship and Grant Programs
(See address above.)

THE HISPANIC NATIONAL BAR FOUNDATION
1900 K Street, N.W.
Suite 100
Washington, DC 20006
(786) 340-9991
E-mail: info@hnbf.org
Web Site: www.hnbf.org

TYPE:
Conferences/seminars; Training grants. Nine-day program held by the Foundation in Washington, DC which provides Latino high school students with the opportunity to learn more about the legal profession. The Summer Law Institute offers students the chance to come to the nation's capital and learn more about the college application process, meet influential Latino leaders, and tour national monuments and various government agencies.

See entry 1807 for full listing.

HISPANIC SCHOLARSHIP FUND [975]
1411 West 190th Street
Suite 700
Gardena, CA 90248
(877) 473-4636
(310) 975-3700
Fax: (310) 349-3328
E-mail: info@hsf.net
scholar1@hsf.net
Web Site: www.hsf.net

FOUNDED: 1975

AREAS OF INTEREST:
College scholarships for Hispanic American students.

NAME(S) OF PROGRAMS:
● **General College Scholarship Program**

TYPE:
Scholarships. Awarded to Hispanic community college, undergraduate and graduate students.

YEAR PROGRAM STARTED: 1975

PURPOSE:
To strengthen America by generating support for the educational advancement of Hispanics by increasing the rate of Hispanics earning a college degree.

LEGAL BASIS:
Nonprofit 501(c)(3) organization.

ELIGIBILITY:
Applicant must:
(1) be of Hispanic heritage;
(2) be a U.S. citizen or legal permanent resident;
(3) have a minimum 3.0 cumulative grade point average (on a 4.0 scale) and;
(4) apply for federal financial aid using FAFSA.

FINANCIAL DATA:
Amount of support per award: $500 to $5,000.
Total amount of support: Approximately $500,000,000.

NO. MOST RECENT APPLICANTS: 50,000.

NO. AWARDS: 1,000.

APPLICATION INFO:
Electronic application only; forms available at the web site.
Duration: Students may reapply until they obtain a degree, providing they satisfy full-time enrollment.
Deadline: February 15.

PUBLICATIONS:
Annual report; newsletter.

IRS I.D.: 52-1051044

BOARD OF DIRECTORS:
Gene Camarena, Chairperson
Elizabeth Oliver-Farrow, Vice Chairperson
Anthony Salcido, Treasurer
Fidel A. Vargas, President and Chief Executive Officer
Daniel J. Acosta
Michael J. Bender
Walter Dolhare
Nely Galan
Phillip Hyun
James McNamara
Angel Luis Morales
Ida Nieto
Bea Perez
Adam Rodriguez
Gina Rodriguez
Maria Elena Salinas
Peggy Turner
Cesar Vargas

UCLA CHICANO STUDIES RESEARCH CENTER [976]
193 Haines Hall
Box 951544
Los Angeles, CA 90095
(310) 825-2363
Fax: (310) 206-1784
E-mail: csrcinfo@chicano.ucla.edu
Web Site: www.chicano.ucla.edu
www.iac.ucla.edu

FOUNDED: 1969

AREAS OF INTEREST:
Chicano Studies and relevant fields.

NAME(S) OF PROGRAMS:
● **Institute of American Cultures Visiting Research Scholar Program in Ethnic Studies**

TYPE:
Fellowships; Visiting scholars.

YEAR PROGRAM STARTED: 1976

PURPOSE:
To foster learning and scholarship pertaining to the Chicano-Latino community.

LEGAL BASIS:
University program.

ELIGIBILITY:
Applicant must be a U.S. citizen or permanent resident. At the time of appointment, applicant must hold a Ph.D. from an accredited college or university, or in the case of the arts, an appropriate terminal degree.

UCLA faculty, staff and currently enrolled students are not eligible to apply.

FINANCIAL DATA:
Amount of support per award: Up to $35,000 to home institution and up to $4,000 research grant.
Total amount of support: Up to $39,000.

NO. AWARDS: 1.

APPLICATION INFO:
Application information available upon request.
Duration: Up to nine months.
Deadline: January. Notification in March.

OFFICERS:
Chon A. Noriega, Director

ADDRESS INQUIRIES TO:
Grants and Fellowships Coordinator
(See address above.)

Women

THE ISABEL ALLENDE FOUNDATION [977]
116 Caledonia Street
Sausalito, CA 94965
(415) 289-0992
E-mail: lori@isabelallende.com
Web Site: www.isabelallendefoundation.org

FOUNDED: 1996

AREAS OF INTEREST:
Reproductive rights, economic independence and freedom from violence for women and girls.

NAME(S) OF PROGRAMS:
- **Esperanza Grants**

TYPE:
Project/program grants. Promotes and preserves the fundamental rights of women and children to be empowered and protected.

PURPOSE:
To invest in the power of women and girls to secure reproductive rights, economic independence and freedom from violence.

ELIGIBILITY:
Nonprofit 501(c)(3) grassroots organizations and equivalent international organizations that benefit the San Francisco Bay area and/or Chile are eligible to apply. No grants to individuals.

The Foundation does not fund capital campaigns, individual trips or tours, conferences or events, and projects that benefit political, religious, and/or military organizations.

Unsolicited requests are not accepted.

GEOG. RESTRICTIONS: San Francisco Bay area, California and Chile.

FINANCIAL DATA:
Amount of support per award: Varies.
Total amount of support: Varies.

APPLICATION INFO:
New organization proposals are not being accepted at this time. Current grantees may apply for renewal and will receive instructions from the Foundation on how to apply.
Duration: One year. Must submit report for renewal.
Deadline: Varies.

ADDRESS INQUIRIES TO:
Lori Barra, Executive Director
(See address above.)

AMERICAN ASSOCIATION OF UNIVERSITY WOMEN [978]
1310 L Street, N.W.
Suite 1000
Washington, DC 20005
(202) 785-7700
E-mail: aauw@applyists.com
Web Site: www.aauw.org

FOUNDED: 1888

AREAS OF INTEREST:
Advancement of educational and professional opportunities for women in the U.S.

NAME(S) OF PROGRAMS:
- **AAUW Selected Professions Fellowships**

TYPE:
Fellowships. Awarded to women who are U.S. citizens or permanent residents who are pursuing full-time study in a Master's or professional degree program in which women are underrepresented, including STEM, law, business and medicine.

YEAR PROGRAM STARTED: 1970

PURPOSE:
To encourage women's participation in fields where they have been traditionally underrepresented.

ELIGIBILITY:
The Association awards Selected Professions Fellowships to women who are citizens or permanent residents of the U.S. who have achieved high standards of academic excellence and show promise of distinction in their respective fields. Applicants must be full-time students at an accredited U.S. institution during the fellowship year, and should be pursuing a course of study in the U.S. over the full academic year. Priority is given to women who do not already hold a Master's or first professional degree.

Selected Professions Fellowships are awarded for the following Master's programs:
(1) Architecture;
(2) Computer/information sciences;
(3) Engineering and;
(4) Mathematics/statistics.

Fellowships in the following degree programs are restricted to women of color, who have been underrepresented in these fields:
(1) Master's in business administration - applicants may apply for second year of study only;
(2) Law - applicants may apply for third year of study only and;
(3) Doctorate in medicine - applicants may apply for third or fourth year of study only.

GEOG. RESTRICTIONS: United States.

FINANCIAL DATA:
Amount of support per award: $5,000 to $18,000.

APPLICATION INFO:
Applicant must create an account through the "apply now" link to the vendor site located on the funding opportunity page.
Deadline: December 1.

AMERICAN ASSOCIATION OF UNIVERSITY WOMEN [979]
1310 L Street, N.W.
Suite 1000
Washington, DC 20005
(202) 785-7700
E-mail: aauw@applyists.com
Web Site: www.aauw.org

FOUNDED: 1888

AREAS OF INTEREST:
Advancement of educational and professional opportunities for women in the U.S. and around the globe.

NAME(S) OF PROGRAMS:
- **American Fellowships**

TYPE:
Fellowships; Visiting scholars. Awarded to women who are U.S. citizens or permanent residents pursuing full-time study to complete dissertations, conducting postdoctoral research full-time, or preparing research for publication for eight consecutive weeks.

YEAR PROGRAM STARTED: 1888

PURPOSE:
To support women scholars who are completing dissertations, planning research leave from accredited institutions or preparing research for publication.

ELIGIBILITY:
Applicants must be citizens or permanent residents of the U.S. There are no restrictions as to place of study or age. Fellowship is open to women who will have completed all requirements for the Doctorate, except the writing of the dissertation, by November 15 preceding the fellowship year, July 1 to June 30, or who hold the Ph.D. at the time of application. Applicants are evaluated by academic professionals on the scholarly excellence of their proposals, quality and originality of project design, and experience teaching or mentoring female students. In addition, applicants will be asked to outline their commitment to helping women and girls through community service, service in their profession and/or service in their field of research.

GEOG. RESTRICTIONS: United States.

FINANCIAL DATA:
Amount of support per award: $6,000 to $30,000.

APPLICATION INFO:
Applicant must create an account through the "apply now" link to the vendor site located on the funding opportunity page.
Deadline: November 1.

AMERICAN ASSOCIATION OF UNIVERSITY WOMEN
1310 L Street, N.W.
Suite 1000
Washington, DC 20005
(202) 785-7700
E-mail: aauw@applyists.com
Web Site: www.aauw.org

TYPE:
Fellowships. Awarded to women pursuing full-time graduate or postdoctoral study in the U.S. who are not U.S. citizens or permanent residents.

See entry 879 for full listing.

AMERICAN ASSOCIATION OF UNIVERSITY WOMEN [980]
1310 L Street, N.W.
Suite 1000
Washington, DC 20005
(202) 785-7700
E-mail: aauw@applyists.com
Web Site: www.aauw.org

FOUNDED: 1888

AREAS OF INTEREST:
Nontraditional fields.

NAME(S) OF PROGRAMS:
- **AAUW Career Development Grants**

TYPE:
Grants-in-aid. Awarded to women who are U.S. citizens or permanent residents pursuing a certificate or degree to advance their

careers, change careers or re-enter the workforce and whose Bachelor's degree was received at least five years before the award period.

YEAR PROGRAM STARTED: 1972

PURPOSE:
To assist women who are continuing their self-development through higher education.

ELIGIBILITY:
Career Development Grants provide funding to women who hold a Bachelor's degree and are preparing to advance or change careers or re-enter the workforce. Primary consideration is given to women of color and women pursuing their first advanced degree or credentials in nontraditional fields.

Applicants must be U.S. citizens or permanent residents whose last degree was received before June 30, 2015. Funds are available for tuition, fees, books, supplies, local transportation and dependent care.

Grants provide support for course work beyond a Bachelor's degree, including a Master's degree, second Bachelor's degree, certification program or specialized training in technical or professional fields. Course work must be taken at an accredited two- or four-year college or university in the U.S. or at a technical school that is fully licensed or accredited by the U.S. Department of Education. Funds are not available for Doctorate-level work.

GEOG. RESTRICTIONS: United States.

FINANCIAL DATA:
Amount of support per award: $2,000 to $12,000.

APPLICATION INFO:
Applicant must create an account through the "apply now" link to the vendor site located on the funding opportunity page.
Deadline: November 15.

AMERICAN NUCLEAR SOCIETY (ANS)
555 North Kensington Avenue
LaGrange Park, IL 60526
(708) 352-6611
Fax: (708) 352-0499
E-mail: scholarships@ans.org
Web Site: www.ans.org

TYPE:
Scholarships. Delayed Education for Women Scholarship is designed for women in a nuclear-related field whose formal studies have been delayed or interrupted for at least one year.

Landis Scholarships are administered by the ANS NEED Committee, and are awarded to undergraduate and graduate students who have greater-than-average financial need.
See entry 2419 for full listing.

BERKSHIRE CONFERENCE OF WOMEN HISTORIANS
Rutgers University, History Department
16 Seminary Place
New Brunswick, NJ 08901
(848) 932-7905
E-mail: secretary@berksconference.org
Web Site: www.berksconference.org

TYPE:
Awards/prizes. One prize awarded annually for the best first book and one for the best

article of historical scholarship published by a woman historian in any field of history during the preceding year.
See entry 536 for full listing.

BOSTON WOMEN'S FUND   [981]
2 Oliver Street
Suite 800
Boston, MA 02109
(617) 725-0035
Fax: (617) 725-0277
E-mail: info@bostonwomensfund.org
Web Site: bostonwomensfund.org

FOUNDED: 1984

AREAS OF INTEREST:
Women organized for racial, economic and social justice.

TYPE:
Grants-in-aid; Project/program grants; Seed money grants.

PURPOSE:
To pool funds from individuals; to channel money to support women's and girls' organizations for economic and social justice.

LEGAL BASIS:
Public foundation.

ELIGIBILITY:
Applicants or their fiscal agents must be 501(c)(3) organizations. Also funded are direct-service projects which have an organizing component. Groups just getting started are encouraged to apply, particularly those women who are most vulnerable and have the least access to other resources including women of color, low-income women, disabled women, lesbians, girls, older women, transgender people, immigrant and refugee women. Applicants with organizational budgets of less than $350,000 per year are preferred. No grants to individuals.

GEOG. RESTRICTIONS: Preference given to the Boston metropolitan area, and to selected outlying areas such as Brockton, Lawrence, Lowell and Worcester, Massachusetts.

FINANCIAL DATA:
Amount of support per award: Up to $15,000.

NO. MOST RECENT APPLICANTS: Varies.

NO. AWARDS: Varies.

APPLICATION INFO:
Send an e-mail to request the application.
Duration: Typically one year.

PUBLICATIONS:
Application guidelines; donor contribution information in annual report.

ADDRESS INQUIRIES TO:
E-mail: programs@bostonwomensfund.org

BROOKHAVEN WOMEN IN SCIENCE   [982]
P.O. Box 183
Upton, NY 11973
(631) 344-7153
E-mail: bwisawards@bnl.gov
Web Site: www.bnl.gov/bwis/scholarships.php

FOUNDED: 1979

AREAS OF INTEREST:
Advancement of women in the natural sciences, engineering or mathematics fields.

NAME(S) OF PROGRAMS:
• **Renate W. Chasman Scholarship for Women**

TYPE:
Awards/prizes; Scholarships. These scholarships are offered to encourage women to pursue careers in the sciences technology, engineering or mathematics.

YEAR PROGRAM STARTED: 1986

PURPOSE:
To encourage women to resume their formal education in a technical field.

LEGAL BASIS:
Tax-exempt, incorporated under the Educational Laws of New York state.

ELIGIBILITY:
Applicants must be:
(1) women;
(2) graduate students at an accredited educational institution;
(3) performing research at Brookhaven National Laboratory in the STEM disciplines (science, technology, engineering or mathematics) and;
(4) receiving their degree not prior to May of the competition year.

FINANCIAL DATA:
Amount of support per award: $2,500.

NO. AWARDS: 1 per year.

APPLICATION INFO:
Requests for application via mail must include a self-addressed, stamped envelope.
Duration: One-time award.
Deadline: January 30. Announcement in spring.

ADDRESS INQUIRIES TO:
Chasman Scholarship Fund
Brookhaven Women in Science
(See address or e-mail above.)

CANADIAN FEDERATION OF UNIVERSITY WOMEN   [983]
331 Cooper Street, Suite 502
Ottawa ON K2P 0G5 Canada
(613) 234-8252
(888) 220-9606
Fax: (613) 234-8221
E-mail: fellowships@cfuw.org
Web Site: www.cfuw.org
www.cfuwcharitabletrust.ca

FOUNDED: 1919

AREAS OF INTEREST:
Graduate education for women.

NAME(S) OF PROGRAMS:
• **Ruth Binnie Fellowship**
• **Canadian Home Economics Association (CHEA) Fellowship**
• **CFUW Aboriginal Women's Award (AWA)**
• **CFUW Bourse Georgette Lemoyne**
• **CFUW Dr. Alice E. Wilson Awards**
• **CFUW Dr. Margaret McWilliams Pre-Doctoral Fellowship**
• **CFUW Elizabeth and Rachel Massey Award**
• **CFUW Linda Souter Humanities Award**
• **CFUW Memorial Fellowship**
• **CFUW 1989 Ecole Polytechnique Commemorative Awards**

TYPE:
Awards/prizes; Fellowships. The Ruth Binnie Fellowship is for Master's studies with a

focus on one or more aspects of the field of home economics. The candidate may be studying abroad.

Canadian Home Economics Association Fellowship candidate must be studying one or more aspects in the field of home economics at the Master's or doctoral level in Canada.

CFUW Aboriginal Women's Award candidate must be a Canadian Aboriginal woman studying in Canada, who holds an undergraduate university degree or equivalent and has applied to be a full-time student in any year of an eligible program at a recognized or accredited Canadian post-secondary degree-granting institution. Eligible programs include: programs leading to a first degree in law, i.e., Bachelor of Laws (LLB) or Juris Doctor (JD); programs leading to first degrees in medicine, i.e., Medical Doctor (M.D.) or Doctor of Optometry (O.D.); programs leading to qualifying for a license to practice as a Nurse Practitioner in the province or territory of the graduate's choice; and programs leading to a Master's degree in fields dealing with important Canadian aboriginal issues at the time the AWA is given as defined by most recent Canadian report by the United Nations Special Rapporteur on the rights of indigenous peoples.

CFUW Bourse Georgette Lemoyne Fellowship is for graduate study at a Canadian university. The candidate must be studying in French.

CFUW Dr. Alice E. Wilson Award is for graduate studies in any field, with special consideration given to mature students returning to study after at least three years.

CFUW Dr. Margaret McWilliams Pre-Doctoral Fellowship candidate must have completed at least one full calendar year as a full-time student in doctoral-level studies and be a full-time student in Canada or abroad at the time of application.

CFUW Elizabeth and Rachel Massey Award is for postgraduate studies in the visual arts such as painting, sculpture or in music in Canada or abroad.

CFUW Linda Souter Humanities Award is for Master's or doctoral students. Generally, study in the humanities is theoretical and does not involve empirical methodology. Humanities could include English language and literature, history, languages study, classics, philosophy, film studies, communication studies and culture studies.

CFUW Memorial Fellowship candidate must be enrolled in a Master's degree program in science, mathematics, or engineering in Canada or abroad.

CFUW 1989 Ecole Polytechnique Commemorative Award is for graduate studies in any field. The candidate must justify the relevance of her work to women.

YEAR PROGRAM STARTED: 1921

PURPOSE:
To support the education of women at the postgraduate level in Canada and abroad.

LEGAL BASIS:
Foundation of a nonprofit organization.

ELIGIBILITY:
Candidates must hold at least a Bachelor's degree or equivalent from a recognized

university, have been accepted into the proposed program and place of study, and be a Canadian citizen or permanent resident.

GEOG. RESTRICTIONS: Canada.

FINANCIAL DATA:
Amount of support per award: $5,000 to $25,000 (CAN).
Total amount of support: Approximately $100,000 for the year 2018.

NO. MOST RECENT APPLICANTS: 363 for the year 2019.

NO. AWARDS: 10 different categories, with 14 awards.

APPLICATION INFO:
Application form and guidelines are posted in August on the Federation's web site.
Duration: One year. Grants not renewable, except the CFUW Aboriginal Women's Award.
Deadline: January 14. Announcement April 15.

PUBLICATIONS:
The Communicator; CFUW Charitable Trust Annual Report; CFUW Fellowships and Awards, e-newsletter; *CFUW External Annual Report; CFUW News & Updates; CFUW Week in Review.*

ADDRESS INQUIRIES TO:
Betty Dunlop
Fellowships Program Manager
(See address above.)

THE COORDINATING COUNCIL FOR WOMEN IN HISTORY, INC. [984]

3118 Chaucer Drive
Charlotte, NC 28210
(773) 960-2092
E-mail: execdir@theccwh.org
Web Site: www.theccwh.org

FOUNDED: 1969

AREAS OF INTEREST:
Women's history, gender and sexuality, and activism for women.

NAME(S) OF PROGRAMS:
● **Catherine Prelinger Award**

TYPE:
Awards/prizes. The Catherine Prelinger Award is given to a scholar, with a Ph.D. or A.B.D., whose career has not followed a traditional academic path through secondary and higher education and whose work has contributed to women in the historical profession.

YEAR PROGRAM STARTED: 1998

PURPOSE:
To explore the diverse experiences and histories of all women; to honor scholars that have not followed a traditional academic path of uninterrupted and completed secondary, undergraduate, and graduate degrees leading into a tenured faculty position and whose work has contributed to women in the historical profession; to promote research and interpretation in areas of women's history; to recognize or to enhance the ability of the recipient to contribute significantly to women in history, whether in the profession in the present or in the study of women in the past.

ELIGIBILITY:
The applicant:
(1) must be a member in good standing of the Coordinating Council for Women in

History;
(2) must hold either A.B.D. status or the Ph.D. at the time of application;
(3) shall be actively engaged in scholarship that is historical in nature, although the degree may be in related fields;
(4) shall have already contributed or shown potential for contributing significantly to women in history, whether in the profession in the present or in the study of women in the past and;
(5) has not followed a traditional academic path of uninterrupted and completed secondary, undergraduate and graduate degrees leading to a tenure-track faculty position.

FINANCIAL DATA:
Funds issued in U.S. dollars only.
Amount of support per award: $20,000.

NO. MOST RECENT APPLICANTS: 30 to 50.

NO. AWARDS: 1.

APPLICATION INFO:
Contact the organization.
Deadline: May 15.

ADDRESS INQUIRIES TO:
Elizabeth Everton, Ph.D., Executive Director (See e-mail address above.)

*SPECIAL STIPULATIONS:
All recipients will be required to submit a final paper to CCWH on how the award was expended and summarizing the scholarly work completed.

THE COORDINATING COUNCIL FOR WOMEN IN HISTORY, INC.

3118 Chaucer Drive
Charlotte, NC 28210
(773) 960-2092
E-mail: execdir@theccwh.org
Web Site: www.theccwh.org

TYPE:
Awards/prizes; Fellowships.

See entry 541 for full listing.

DAUGHTERS OF PENELOPE FOUNDATION, INC. [985]

1909 Q Street, N.W., Suite 500
Washington, DC 20009
(202) 234-9741
Fax: (202) 483-6983
E-mail: dophq@ahepa.org
Web Site: www.dopfoundationinc.com

FOUNDED: 1983

AREAS OF INTEREST:
Education, health and philanthropy.

NAME(S) OF PROGRAMS:
● **Paula J. Alexander Memorial Scholarship (Undergraduate)**
● **Helen J. Beldecos, Past Grand President, Scholarship (Undergraduate)**
● **The Big Five Graduate Scholarship**
● **Daughters of Penelope Past Grand Presidents Memorial Scholarship (Undergraduate)**
● **Daughters of Penelope Past Grand Presidents Undergraduate Scholarship**
● **Daughters of Penelope - St. Basil's Academy**
● **Eos #1 Mother Lodge Chapter Scholarship (Undergraduate)**
● **Joanne V. Hologgitas, Ph.D., Past Grand President, Scholarship (Undergraduate)**
● **Hopewell Agave Chapter #224 Scholarship (Undergraduate)**

- **Mary Kandaras Memorial Scholarship** (Undergraduate)
- **Kottis Family Scholarship** (Undergraduate)
- **Clara R. Payne Memorial Scholarship**
- **Dorothy Lillian Quincey Memorial Graduate Scholarship**
- **Alexandra Apostolides Sonenfeld Memorial Undergraduate Scholarship**
- **Sonja B. Stefanadis Graduate Student Scholarship**
- **Barbara Edith Quincey Thorndyke Memorial Undergraduate Scholarship**
- **Mary M. Verges, Past Grand President, Scholarship (Undergraduate)**
- **The Sotiri Zervoulias & Lea Soupata Scholarship (St. Basil's Academy)**

TYPE:
Scholarships.

YEAR PROGRAM STARTED: 1983

PURPOSE:
To support education for women of Greek descent.

LEGAL BASIS:
The Foundation is a recognized 501(c)(3) organization; tax-exempt.

ELIGIBILITY:
Scholarships are based on financial need or academic merit (or both). Contact the organization for full details.

GEOG. RESTRICTIONS: Canada, Greece and United States.

FINANCIAL DATA:
Amount of support per award: $500 to $2,500.

Total amount of support: Varies.

NO. AWARDS: 15 for the year 2018.

APPLICATION INFO:
Information and guidelines are available online.

Deadline: May 1.

PUBLICATIONS:
President's Bulletin, monthly publication.

IRS I.D.: 52-1346043

ADDRESS INQUIRIES TO:
Elena Saviolakis
Executive Director
(See address above.)

*SPECIAL STIPULATIONS:
Scholarship may not be deferred to be used at a later date. These awards are not renewable and must be used strictly for tuition and/or books. Application must be typewritten. All requirements must be met and all questions answered or applicant will be disqualified.

DAUGHTERS OF THE CINCINNATI

271 Madison Avenue
Suite 1408
New York, NY 10016
(212) 991-9945
E-mail: scholarships@daughters1894.org
Web Site: www.daughters1894.org

TYPE:
Scholarships. Undergraduate scholarships.

See entry 1517 for full listing.

DREXEL UNIVERSITY COLLEGE OF MEDICINE [986]

The Legacy Center:
Archives and Special Collections
2900 West Queen Lane
Philadelphia, PA 19129
(215) 991-8340
E-mail: com_archives@drexel.edu
Web Site: archives.drexelmed.edu

FOUNDED: 1977

AREAS OF INTEREST:
Medicine as it relates to women in professional practice.

NAME(S) OF PROGRAMS:
- **M. Louise Gloeckner, M.D., Summer Research Fellowship**

TYPE:
Fellowships. For four to six weeks of research at The Legacy Center. Collections house the business and academic records of the Woman's Medical College of Pennsylvania, the Medical College of Pennsylvania, and Drexel University College of Medicine, the personal papers of women physicians, records of national and international women's medical organizations, schools, associations, hospitals and a historic photograph collection.

YEAR PROGRAM STARTED: 1985

PURPOSE:
To encourage the use of the institution's archival collections in the study of women in medicine, and history generally.

LEGAL BASIS:
University.

ELIGIBILITY:
Applicants must be either undergraduate or graduate students, medical students, faculty members or independent researchers. Preference is given to researchers with well-defined projects to be completed in one summer.

FINANCIAL DATA:
Total amount of support: $4,000.

NO. AWARDS: 1 annually.

APPLICATION INFO:
Guidelines and application form are available on the web site.
Duration: Four to six weeks depending on project.
Deadline: March 1.

PUBLICATIONS:
Program announcement.

STAFF:
Joanne Murray, Historian and Director

ADDRESS INQUIRIES TO:
Joanne Murray, Historian and Director
(See address above.)

THE EDUCATIONAL FOUNDATION FOR WOMEN IN ACCOUNTING

136 South Keowee Street
Dayton, OH 45402-2241
(937) 424-3391
Fax: (937) 222-5794
E-mail: info@efwa.org
Web Site: www.efwa.org

TYPE:
Scholarships. Laurels Fund provides a one-year academic scholarship for women pursuing a Ph.D. in accounting.

Women in Need Scholarship is available to women in their third, fourth or fifth year of academic pursuit who need the financial support to complete their degrees. It is renewable annually upon satisfactory completion of course requirements.

Women in Transition Scholarship is intended for women returning to school as freshmen to earn a Bachelor's degree in accounting. It is renewable annually upon satisfactory completion of course requirements.

See entry 1727 for full listing.

GENERAL BOARD OF HIGHER EDUCATION AND MINISTRY, THE UNITED METHODIST CHURCH

1001 19th Avenue South
Nashville, TN 37212
(615) 340-7338
Fax: (615) 340-7529
E-mail: mbigord@gbhem.org
Web Site: www.gbhem.org

TYPE:
Awards/prizes; Scholarships. Awards to encourage women over age 35 to prepare for ordained ministry as an Elder in the United Methodist Church as a second career. The scholarship is to be used for study toward the basic seminary degree in an accredited school of theology.

See entry 751 for full listing.

GLOBAL FUND FOR WOMEN [987]

800 Market Street, 7th Floor
San Francisco, CA 94102
(415) 248-4800
Fax: (415) 248-4801
E-mail: grantsinfo@globalfundforwomen.org
Web Site: www.globalfundforwomen.org

FOUNDED: 1987

AREAS OF INTEREST:
Female human rights, women's access to communications, economic autonomy of women, and girls' education.

TYPE:
Conferences/seminars; General operating grants; Seed money grants; Technical assistance; Training grants. The Global Fund for Women is a grantmaking foundation that brings together a worldwide network of women and men to strengthen women's rights around the world. Initiatives include promoting women's economic independence, girls' education, women's rights within religious and cultural tradition, and women's health and safety. The Fund also provides assistance to groups overseas that wish to establish philanthropic organizations designed to benefit women.

YEAR PROGRAM STARTED: 1987

PURPOSE:
To promote a world of equality and social justice; to provide the financial means to enable women to attain this vision.

LEGAL BASIS:
Nonprofit corporation, 501(c)(3) tax-exempt.

ELIGIBILITY:
The Global Fund does not make grants to individuals, groups based and working primarily or solely in the U.S., groups whose main or only purpose is to generate income

for its members or the community or groups headed and managed by men and without women in important management functions.

The Global Fund considers support to groups which demonstrate a clear commitment to women's equality and female human rights, are governed and directed primarily by women, have defined plans to strengthen the work of the group over time and may be unlikely to obtain funding from other sources.

FINANCIAL DATA:
Amount of support per award: $5,000 to $30,000.

Total amount of support: $7,794,845 for fiscal year 2017-18.

NO. MOST RECENT APPLICANTS: Approximately 2,500 annually.

NO. AWARDS: Approximately 500 annually.

APPLICATION INFO:
Applicants may request and respond to grant request guidelines or send a letter describing the group and including contact information, organizational information and grant request information.
Duration: Varies depending on needs and nature of the request.

PUBLICATIONS:
Annual report; brochure; *Raising Our Voices*, newsletter.

IRS I.D.: 77-0155782

STAFF:
Musimbi Kanyoro, President and Chief Executive Officer
Leila Hessini, Vice President Programs

GRADUATE WOMEN IN SCIENCE
P.O. Box 7
Mullica Hill, NJ 08062
E-mail: fellowships@gwis.org
Web Site: www.gwis.org

TYPE:
Fellowships.

See entry 1653 for full listing.

GRADUATE WOMEN INTERNATIONAL (GWI)   [988]
Chemin du Grand-Montfleury, 48
CH-1290 Versoix Geneva Switzerland
(41) 22 731 23 80
Fax: (41) 22 738 04 40
E-mail: gwi@graduatewomen.org
Web Site: www.graduatewomen.org

FOUNDED: 1919

AREAS OF INTEREST:
Secondary, tertiary, continuing and nontraditional education for girls and women, human rights, status of women.

CONSULTING OR VOLUNTEER SERVICES:
At the international level, Graduate Women International has working relationships with a number of nongovernmental organizations, consultative status with ECOSOC, ILO and UNESCO, as well as periodic cooperation with other United Nations bodies. At the national level, affiliates in 58 countries work to accomplish Graduate Women International's goals and to address issues of global concern, both through project work and interaction with their governments and other interested groups.

NAME(S) OF PROGRAMS:
- **BFWG Marjorie Shaw Fellowship**
- **FfWG Crosby Hall Fellowship**
- **NZFGW Daphne Purves Grant**
- **Caroline Spurgeon Centenary Fellowship**

TYPE:
Awards/prizes; Fellowships; Internships; Research grants; Training grants. Graduate Women International fellowships and grants are awarded triennially to encourage and enable women graduates to undertake original research or obtain further training in the humanities, social sciences and natural sciences.

YEAR PROGRAM STARTED: 1919

PURPOSE:
To promote understanding and friendship among the university women of the world, irrespective of their race, nationality, religion or political opinions; to encourage international cooperation; to further the development of education; to represent university women in international organizations; to encourage the full application of members' skills to the problems which arise at all levels of public life, whether local, national, regional or worldwide; to encourage their participation in the solving of these problems.

LEGAL BASIS:
International nongovernmental organization, based in Geneva, Switzerland.

ELIGIBILITY:
Open to women graduates:
(1) who are members of Graduate Women International enrolled in a Ph.D. programme of which they have completed the first year and;
(2) who are nonmembers and independent members of less than the nominated period of membership; these may apply subject to payment of an administrative fee.

Applications are welcomed from the humanities, social sciences and natural sciences. Membership in a national association is also an eligibility factor.

FINANCIAL DATA:
Candidates must provide evidence of adequate budgetary provision to meet the costs of their studies over and above the amount requested for the GWI award.
Amount of support per award: Fellowships: CHF 2,000 to 12,000; Grants: CHF 3,000 to 6,000.

NO. AWARDS: 5 to 15 fellowships and grants are offered in each competition.

APPLICATION INFO:
All applications must be submitted electronically. Application forms are available on the web site. Members of one of GWI's national affiliates must submit applications when completed with required supporting documentation to their NFA. Independent members and nonmembers must submit their completed applications directly to the GWI Office in Geneva with any administrative fee that is required.
Duration: Fellowships are intended to cover eight to 12 months of work. Grants are awarded for a minimum of two months of work. The awards are not renewable.
Deadline: June 30.

ADDRESS INQUIRIES TO:
See e-mail address above.

*SPECIAL STIPULATIONS:
Women graduates only.

KENTUCKY FOUNDATION FOR WOMEN   [989]
1215 Heyburn Building
332 West Broadway
Louisville, KY 40202-2184
(502) 562-0045
E-mail: team@kfw.org
Web Site: www.kfw.org

FOUNDED: 1985

AREAS OF INTEREST:
Arts, social change and feminism.

NAME(S) OF PROGRAMS:
- **Art Meets Activism**
- **Artist Enrichment**
- **Hopscotch House Artist Retreat Center**

TYPE:
Awards/prizes; Project/program grants; Residencies.

YEAR PROGRAM STARTED: 1985

PURPOSE:
To promote positive social change through feminist expression in the arts.

ELIGIBILITY:
Individuals must be residents of Kentucky.

GEOG. RESTRICTIONS: Kentucky.

FINANCIAL DATA:
Amount of support per award: $1,000 to $7,500.

Total amount of support: $200,000 annually.

NO. MOST RECENT APPLICANTS: Varies.

NO. AWARDS: Varies.

APPLICATION INFO:
Guidelines and application form are available on the Foundation web site.
Duration: One year.
Deadline: Art Meets Activism: First Friday of March; Artist Enrichment: First Friday of September.

STAFF:
Sharon LaRue, Executive Director
Jenrose Fitzgerald, Grant Program Manager
Janae Hall, Hopscotch House Retreat Manager

ADDRESS INQUIRIES TO:
Sharon LaRue, Executive Director
(See address above.)

THE LALOR FOUNDATION, INC.
c/o GMA Foundations
2 Liberty Square, Suite 500
Boston, MA 02109
(617) 426-7080
(617) 391-3088
Fax: (617) 426-7087
E-mail: fellowshipmanager@gmafoundations.com
Web Site: lalorfound.org

TYPE:
Project/program grants.

See entry 2291 for full listing.

THE LEEWAY FOUNDATION [990]

1315 Walnut Street
Suite 832
Philadelphia, PA 19107
(215) 545-4078
Fax: (215) 545-4021
E-mail: info@leeway.org
Web Site: www.leeway.org

FOUNDED: 1993

AREAS OF INTEREST:
Women and trans artists creating art for social change.

NAME(S) OF PROGRAMS:
- **Art and Change Grant**
- **Leeway Transformation Award**

TYPE:
Awards/prizes; Project/program grants. Art and Change Grants provide project-based grants to fund art for social change projects.

Leeway Transformation Award is an unrestricted award (not project-based) for women and trans people demonstrating a commitment of five years or more to art for social change work.

YEAR PROGRAM STARTED: 1998

PURPOSE:
To support women and trans artists who create art for social change.

ELIGIBILITY:
Women and trans artists living in the Delaware Valley region may apply. The Transformation Award is open to women and trans people working in any art form who create art and social change and have done so for the past five years or more, demonstrating a commitment to art for social change work.

GEOG. RESTRICTIONS: Camden County, New Jersey; Bucks, Chester, Delaware, Montgomery and Philadelphia counties, Pennsylvania.

FINANCIAL DATA:
Amount of support per award: Art and Change Grant: $2,500; Leeway Transformation Award: $15,000.
Total amount of support: Varies.

NO. MOST RECENT APPLICANTS: Varies.

NO. AWARDS: Varies.

APPLICATION INFO:
Contact the Foundation for application or download a copy of the current application and guideline procedures from the web site.
Duration: Varies based on project need.
Deadline: Art and Change Grant: March 1 and August 1; Leeway Transformation Award: May 15.

STAFF:
Denise Brown, Executive Director

ADDRESS INQUIRIES TO:
Melissa Hamilton
Interim Program Director
(See address above.)

MICHIGAN WOMEN FORWARD [991]

1155 Brewery Park Boulevard
Suite 350
Detroit, MI 48207
(313) 962-1920
Fax: (313) 962-1926
E-mail: support@miwf.org
Web Site: www.miwf.org

FOUNDED: 1986

AREAS OF INTEREST:
Needs of women and girls.

NAME(S) OF PROGRAMS:
- **Young Women for Change**

TYPE:
General operating grants; Project/program grants; Seed money grants. Specific focus changes yearly and is determined by each of seven chapters.

YEAR PROGRAM STARTED: 1986

PURPOSE:
To develop young women through the process of philanthropy and grantmaking into successful, fiscally responsible and socially responsive women.

LEGAL BASIS:
Nonprofit 501(c)(3) organization.

ELIGIBILITY:
Eligible organizations must be IRS 501(c)(3) tax-exempt.

GEOG. RESTRICTIONS: Michigan.

FINANCIAL DATA:
Amount of support per award: $500 to $5,000.
Total amount of support: Varies.

APPLICATION INFO:
Guidelines and application form are available on the web site.
Duration: One year.

PUBLICATIONS:
Trillium, newsletter.

IRS I.D.: 38-2689979

ADDRESS INQUIRIES TO:
See e-mail address above.

MONEY FOR WOMEN/BARBARA DEMING MEMORIAL FUND, INC. [992]

P.O. Box 717
Bearsville, NY 12409
E-mail: demingfund@gmail.com
Web Site: demingfund.org

FOUNDED: 1975

AREAS OF INTEREST:
Visual art, fiction, nonfiction and poetry.

NAME(S) OF PROGRAMS:
- **Individual Artist Support Grants**

TYPE:
Awards/prizes. Small grants awarded annually to individual feminists in the arts.

YEAR PROGRAM STARTED: 1975

PURPOSE:
To support feminists in the arts.

LEGAL BASIS:
Private foundation.

ELIGIBILITY:
Open to individual feminist women in the arts, in visual art, fiction (prose), nonfiction (prose) and poetry whose work addresses women's concerns and/or speaks for peace and justice from a feminist perspective. Applicants must be citizens with primary residence in the U.S. or Canada. No educational or study scholarships.

GEOG. RESTRICTIONS: United States and Canada.

FINANCIAL DATA:
Amount of support per award: $500 to $1,500.
Total amount of support: Varies.

NO. MOST RECENT APPLICANTS: 550.

NO. AWARDS: 21 for the year 2019.

REPRESENTATIVE AWARDS:
Amber Caron (fiction), Logan, UT, *The Handler*; Patricia Maciesz (mixed genre), Oakland, CA, *Bill the Patriarchy*; Carol Larson (art), Petaluma, CA, *Defining Moments: Stiched Perspectives on Becoming a Woman*.

APPLICATION INFO:
Visit the Fund web site to complete electronic application. Completed applications require an application/processing fee of $25.
Deadline: January 1 to January 31, 2021 for nonfiction and poetry. January 1 to January 31, 2022 for fiction, visual art and mixed genre. Announcement by May.

PUBLICATIONS:
Newsletter.

IRS I.D.: 51-0176956

BOARD OF DIRECTORS:
Elvia R. Arriola
Maureen Brady
Gabrielle Calvocoressi
Daisy Hernandez
Martha Hughes
Alice Templeton
Crystal Williams

ADDRESS INQUIRIES TO:
See e-mail address above.

MS. FOUNDATION FOR WOMEN [993]

12 Metro Tech Center
26th Floor
Brooklyn, NY 11201
(212) 742-2300
Fax: (212) 742-1653
E-mail: info@ms.foundation.org
Web Site: forwomen.org

FOUNDED: 1972

AREAS OF INTEREST:
Economic justice, women's health, and safety.

NAME(S) OF PROGRAMS:
- **Economic Justice**
- **Women's Health**
- **Women's Safety**

TYPE:
Project/program grants; Technical assistance. General support. Capacity building.

YEAR PROGRAM STARTED: 1976

PURPOSE:
To support the efforts of women and girls to govern their own lives and influence the world around them; to champion an equitable society by effecting change in public consciousness, law, philanthropy and social policy through its leadership, expertise and financial support.

LEGAL BASIS:
Public foundation.

ELIGIBILITY:
Funding is by invitation only. Within its funding priorities, the Foundation gives priority to:
(1) efforts that engage women and girls in crafting activist solutions to the particular

challenges they face in their communities based on gender, race, ethnicity, class, age, disability, sexual orientation and culture and; (2) national-, regional- or state-level public policy advocacy informed by local organizing work and undertaken by organizations with strong linkages to a grassroots constituency.

Special consideration is given to the organizations that:
(1) are pro-women's empowerment, proactively antiracist and working to dismantle heterosexism, class oppression and discrimination based on disability;
(2) address the particular challenges faced by low-income women and girls;
(3) clearly articulate and respond to issues of gender as related to class and race/ethnicity;
(4) are multi-issue and involved in a form of cross-constituency organizing and coalition work;
(5) encourage intergenerational work that empowers younger as well as older women;
(6) include in leadership positions those who are affected most directly by the issues addressed and;
(7) have limited access to other funding sources.

The Foundation does not fund direct-service projects, stand-alone cultural or media projects, publications, individuals, scholarships, religious institutions, conferences, university-based research or government agencies.

GEOG. RESTRICTIONS: United States.

FINANCIAL DATA:
Amount of support per award: Varies.
Total amount of support: Varies.

NO. AWARDS: Over 100.

APPLICATION INFO:
Applications are accepted by invitation only through targeted Requests for Proposals. From time to time, however, the Foundation will launch open calls for proposals, which will be posted on the Foundation web site.
Duration: Generally one-time grants. Some renewal funding.
Deadline: Varies per program.

PUBLICATIONS:
Annual report; application guidelines; most recent grants list.

BOARD OF DIRECTORS:
Jocelyn Frye, Chairperson
Alicia Lara, Vice Chairperson
Jenna Bussman-Wise, Treasurer
Gail Wasserman, Secretary
Angela Glover Blackwell
Wade Davis
Susan Dickler
Lauren Embrey
Cathy Hartnett
Suzanne Lerner
Yin Ling Leung
Danielle Moodie-Mills
Jenna Scalan
Rinku Sen
Tom Watson
Catherine Yelverton

NATIONAL FEDERATION OF REPUBLICAN WOMEN [994]
124 North Alfred Street
Alexandria, VA 22314
(703) 548-9688
E-mail: scholarships@nfrw.org
Web Site: www.nfrw.org

FOUNDED: 1938

AREAS OF INTEREST:
The political process.

NAME(S) OF PROGRAMS:
- **Dorothy Kabis Internship**
- **National Pathfinder's Scholarship**
- **Betty Rendel Scholarship**

TYPE:
Internships; Scholarships. Dorothy Kabis Internship includes a six- to eight-week internship in Washington, DC, housing, travel and stipend.

National Pathfinder's Scholarships are given to the best nominated candidates.

Betty Rendel Scholarships are given to undergraduate women who are majoring in political science, government or economics.

PURPOSE:
To involve more women in the political process and provide educational opportunities.

ELIGIBILITY:
National Pathfinder's Scholarship is open to young women seeking undergraduate or postgraduate degrees, college sophomores, juniors, seniors and students enrolled in a Master's program. Recent high school graduates and first-year college women are not eligible.

Betty Rendel Scholarship applicants must be undergraduate women who are majoring in political science, government or economics. Open only to women who have successfully completed two years of college work.

GEOG. RESTRICTIONS: United States.

FINANCIAL DATA:
Dorothy Kabis Internship includes a small stipend, housing and airfare.
Amount of support per award: National Pathfinder's Scholarship: $2,500; Betty Rendel Scholarship: $1,000.

NO. AWARDS: 3 per scholarship and 2 internships.

APPLICATION INFO:
All grant information, including a printable version of the application, can be found online.
Duration: One-time award.
Deadline: June 1 for the National Pathfinder's Scholarship and Betty Rendel Scholarship. December 1 for Dorothy Kabis Internship.

ADDRESS INQUIRIES TO:
Scholarship Coordinator
(See address above.)

*SPECIAL STIPULATIONS:
Applicants must be U.S. citizens and may only apply to one program in a given year. Winners may not reapply.

NATIVE AMERICAN COMMUNITY BOARD (NACB)
P.O. Box 572
Lake Andes, SD 57356-0572
(605) 487-7072
Fax: (605) 487-7964
E-mail: charon@charles-mix.com
Web Site: www.nativeshop.org

TYPE:
Internships.

See entry 963 for full listing.

THE NEWBERRY LIBRARY
Newberry Institute for Research and Education
60 West Walton Street
Chicago, IL 60610
(312) 255-3666
E-mail: research@newberry.org
Web Site: www.newberry.org/fellowships

TYPE:
Fellowships; Visiting scholars. Allen fellows are expected to spend a significant part of their tenure in residence at the Newberry D'Arcy McNickle Center for American Indian and Indigenous Studies.

See entry 964 for full listing.

P.E.O. SISTERHOOD
P.E.O. Executive Office
3700 Grand Avenue
Des Moines, IA 50312
(515) 255-3153
Fax: (515) 255-3820
E-mail: ips@peodsm.org
Web Site: www.peointernational.org

TYPE:
Scholarships. Awards for selected women from countries other than the U.S. and Canada to pursue graduate study in the U.S. or Canada. Support is available for advanced study in any field except for research. No new applications at the dissertation level.

See entry 886 for full listing.

THE PHI BETA KAPPA SOCIETY [995]
1606 New Hampshire Avenue, N.W.
Washington, DC 20009
(202) 745-3287
Fax: (202) 986-1601
E-mail: awards@pbk.org
Web Site: www.pbk.org

FOUNDED: 1776

AREAS OF INTEREST:
French language, literature and culture; Greek language, literature and history.

NAME(S) OF PROGRAMS:
- **Mary Isabel Sibley Fellowship**

TYPE:
Fellowships. Grant to women scholars made in alternate years for advanced research dealing with Greek language, literature, history or archaeology (odd-numbered years) or with French language or literature (even-numbered years).

YEAR PROGRAM STARTED: 1934

PURPOSE:
To assist women scholars conducting original research.

LEGAL BASIS:
National scholarly honorary society.

ELIGIBILITY:
Unmarried women between 25 and 35 years of age (inclusive) are eligible to apply. They must hold the Doctorate or have fulfilled all requirements for the Doctorate except the dissertation. Applicants must have demonstrated ability to carry on original research and must plan to devote full-time work to research during the fellowship year. Eligibility is not restricted to members of the Society or to U.S. citizens.

FINANCIAL DATA:
The Fellowship carries a $20,000 stipend with one-half of the amount payable after July following announcement of the Fellowship and the balance after another six months have elapsed.
Amount of support per award: $20,000.
Total amount of support: $20,000.

NO. MOST RECENT APPLICANTS: Varies.

NO. AWARDS: 1 each year.

APPLICATION INFO:
Official application materials are available upon request to the Awards Coordinator or on the web site. Fellowships are awarded alternately in the fields of Greek language, literature, history or archaeology (odd-numbered years) and French language or literature (even-numbered years). Send brief description of intended research project when requesting an application.
Duration: The Fellowship is tenable for one year.
Deadline: January 15.

ADDRESS INQUIRIES TO:
Mary Isabel Sibley Fellowship Committee (See address above.)

ROCHESTER AREA COMMUNITY FOUNDATION [996]
500 East Avenue
Rochester, NY 14607-1912
(585) 271-4100
Fax: (585) 271-4292
E-mail: racf@racf.org
Web Site: www.racf.org

FOUNDED: 1972

AREAS OF INTEREST:
Women in poverty, organizational capacity building, aging, arts, the environment, civic engagement, youth and families, historical preservation, health, racial equity, concentrated poverty, academic and achievement gap.

TYPE:
Project/program grants; Scholarships.

PURPOSE:
To support community responsibility and leadership, healthy options for young people and their families, early childhood development and quality of life.

LEGAL BASIS:
Tax-exempt public charity.

GEOG. RESTRICTIONS: Genesee, Livingston, Monroe, Ontario, Orleans, Seneca, Wayne and Yates counties, New York.

FINANCIAL DATA:
Amount of support per award: Varies.
Total amount of support: Approximately $22,000,000 for the year 2017.

IRS I.D.: 23-7250641

ADDRESS INQUIRIES TO:
Jennifer Leonard
President and Executive Director (See address above.)

SKILLBUILDERS FUND [997]
4707 College Boulevard, Suite 201
Leawood, KS 66211
(913) 608-7545
E-mail: info@skillbuildersfund.org
Web Site: www.skillbuildersfund.org

FOUNDED: 1983

AREAS OF INTEREST:
Programs benefiting low-income women and girls.

TYPE:
Matching gifts; Project/program grants; Scholarships. Programs that help women and girls with economic self-sufficiency. Matching gifts are for directors only. Scholarships are only given to organizations, not to individuals.

YEAR PROGRAM STARTED: 1984

PURPOSE:
To enhance the capabilities of women and girls of all ages in the Kansas City metropolitan area and to realize their full potential.

LEGAL BASIS:
Private foundation.

ELIGIBILITY:
Organizations must be IRS 501(c)(3) not-for-profit. Funding primarily is directed to 501(c)(3) organizations that specifically benefit women and girls. Individuals, businesses and other for-profit organizations do not qualify.

GEOG. RESTRICTIONS: Kansas City metropolitan area, including Cass, Clay, Jackson, Johnson, Leavenworth, Platte, Ray and Wyandotte counties.

FINANCIAL DATA:
Amount of support per award: $15,000 to $25,000.
Total amount of support: Varies.

NO. AWARDS: 3 to 9 annually.

APPLICATION INFO:
Application information is available on the web site. Applicants must include a copy of their IRS tax determination letter with the application.
Duration: One year.
Deadline: Varies from year to year.

PUBLICATIONS:
Information brochure with application procedures.

IRS I.D.: 48-0984713

ADDRESS INQUIRIES TO:
Jennifer Sullivan, Grants Administrator and Executive Assistant
(See address above.)

SOCIETY OF DAUGHTERS OF THE U.S. ARMY
11804 Grey Birch Place
Reston, VA 20191-4223

TYPE:
Scholarships.

See entry 1592 for full listing.

SOCIETY OF WOMEN ENGINEERS [998]
130 East Randolph Street
Suite 3500
Chicago, IL 60601
(312) 596-5223
(877) 793-4636
Fax: (312) 312-9550
E-mail: scholarships@swe.org
Web Site: societyofwomenengineers.swe.org/scholarships

FOUNDED: 1950

AREAS OF INTEREST:
Engineering.

NAME(S) OF PROGRAMS:
● **Society of Women Engineers Scholarship Program**

TYPE:
Awards/prizes; Conferences/seminars; Scholarships. Support for undergraduate and graduate engineering studies including women who have been out of the engineering job market and out of school for a minimum of two years and who will return to school for an engineering program.

PURPOSE:
To encourage women to achieve their utmost in careers as professional engineers and as the leaders of tomorrow and to attain high levels of education.

LEGAL BASIS:
Nonprofit educational organization under IRS 501(c)(3) classification.

ELIGIBILITY:
Scholarships are open only to students identifying as female studying an accredited engineering program in a school, college, or university. Candidate is evaluated on the basis of scholastic standing in high school and/or activity.

Some scholarships require applicant to be a U.S. citizen.

Additional criteria can be found on the Society web site.

FINANCIAL DATA:
Scholarship payments are made directly to academic institutions on the recipient's behalf.
Amount of support per award: $1,000 to $17,000.
Total amount of support: Over $810,000 for the year 2019.

NO. AWARDS: 260 new and renewed for the year 2019.

APPLICATION INFO:
Completed application form and letters of reference are required.
Duration: One year. Possible renewal.
Deadline: May 1 for freshmen. February 15 for sophomore, junior, senior and graduate. Announcement in late spring and summer, respectively, for use during the following academic year.

PUBLICATIONS:
Applications; *SWE* magazine.

IRS I.D.: 13-1947735

ADDRESS INQUIRIES TO:
See e-mail address above.

TEXAS WOMEN'S FOUNDATION [999]
Campbell Centre II
8150 North Central Expressway, Suite 110
Dallas, TX 75206
(214) 965-9977
Fax: (214) 526-3633
E-mail: ldelagarza@txwf.org
Web Site: www.txwf.org

FOUNDED: 1985

AREAS OF INTEREST:
Leadership and education, economic security, health and safety, and women's issues.

TYPE:
General operating grants; Project/program grants.

YEAR PROGRAM STARTED: 1985

PURPOSE:
To invest in women and girls; to empower women's philanthropy to build a better world.

LEGAL BASIS:
Community organization.

ELIGIBILITY:
Applicants must be 501(c)(3) organizations with 50% of the recipients residing in Dallas, Denton or Collin counties, TX. The applying program must serve at least 75% women and/or girls, inclusive of sexual orientation, gender identity and gender expression.

GEOG. RESTRICTIONS: Collin, Dallas and Denton counties, Texas.

FINANCIAL DATA:
Amount of support per award: Up to $30,000.
Total amount of support: Approximately $4,400,000 per year.

APPLICATION INFO:
The guidelines and application form are available online.
Duration: One year.
Deadline: Varies according to program area.

IRS I.D.: 75-2048261

STAFF:
Roslyn Dawson Thompson, President and Chief Executive Officer
Ashley Harris, Vice President of Development
Dawn Hooper, Vice President, Operations and Finance
Lisa De La Garza, Vice President of Programs
Mary Valadez, Associate Vice President of Grants

ADDRESS INQUIRIES TO:
Shonda Barnett
Manager, Grants and Research
E-mail: sbarnett@txwf.org

WASHINGTON UNIVERSITY

The Graduate School
One Brookings Drive
Campus Box 1186
St. Louis, MO 63130
(314) 935-6848
Fax: (314) 935-4887
E-mail: shmiller@wustl.edu
Web Site: graduateschool.wustl.edu/olin-fellowship

TYPE:
Fellowships. The Olin Fellowships are open to candidates for any of the following graduate and professional schools at Washington University: architecture, art, arts and sciences, business, engineering, law, medicine, and social work.

See entry 1634 for full listing.

WELLESLEY COLLEGE   [1000]

Career Education
Green Hall 439, 106 Central Street
Wellesley, MA 02481-8203
(781) 283-2347
Fax: (781) 283-3674
E-mail: fellowships@wellesley.edu
Web Site: www.wellesley.
edu/careereducation/fellowships-and-scholarships

AREAS OF INTEREST:
Graduate education.

NAME(S) OF PROGRAMS:
- **Anne Louise Barrett Fellowship**
- **Margaret Freeman Bowers Fellowship**
- **The Eugene L. Cox Fellowship**
- **Professor Elizabeth F. Fisher Fellowship**
- **Ruth Ingersoll Goldmark Fellowship**
- **Horton-Hallowell Fellowship**
- **Peggy Howard Fellowship in Economics**
- **Edna V. Moffett Fellowship**
- **Alice Freeman Palmer Fellowship**
- **Kathryn Conway Preyer Fellowship**
- **Vida Dutton Scudder Fellowship**
- **Harriet A. Shaw Fellowship**
- **Mary Elvira Stevens Traveling Fellowship**
- **Maria Opasnov Tyler '52 Scholarship**
- **Sarah Perry Wood Medical Fellowship**
- **Fanny Bullock Workman Fellowship**

TYPE:
Fellowships; Research grants. The Anne Louise Barrett Fellowship is given preferably in music and primarily for study or research in musical theory, composition, or in the history of music, abroad or in the U.S.

The Margaret Freeman Bowers Fellowship is given for graduate/professional study in fields leading to a career of service to others. Fields include social work, law, public health, policy and administration, and development studies. Business, medicine, and science also qualify, as long as they are dedicated to addressing social challenges in the U.S. and around the world.

The Eugene L. Cox Fellowship is for graduate study in medieval or renaissance history and culture abroad or in the U.S.

The Professor Elizabeth F. Fisher Fellowship is given for research or further study in geology or geography, including urban, environmental or ecological studies.

The Ruth Ingersoll Goldmark Fellowship is awarded for graduate study in English literature, English composition or in the classics.

The Horton-Hallowell Fellowship is awarded for graduate study in any field, preferably in the last two years of candidacy for the Ph.D. degree, or its equivalent, or for private research of equivalent standard.

The Peggy Howard Fellowship in Economics is given to provide financial aid for Wellesley students or alumnae continuing their study of economics. Administered by the economics faculty who may name one or two recipients depending on the income available.

The Edna V. Moffett Fellowship is given to a young alumna, preferably for a first year of graduate study in history.

The Alice Freeman Palmer Fellowship is awarded for study or research abroad or in the U.S.

The Kathryn Conway Preyer Fellowship is for advanced study in history.

The Vida Dutton Scudder Fellowship is given for study in the field of social science, political science or literature.

The Harriet A. Shaw Fellowship is given for study or research in music and the allied arts, in the U.S. or abroad.

Mary Elvira Stevens Traveling Fellowship is awarded for travel or study outside the U.S.

The Maria Opasnov Tyler '52 Scholarship is for graduate study in Russian studies.

The Sarah Perry Wood Medical Fellowship is awarded for the study of medicine at an accredited medical school approved by the American Medical Association.

The Fanny Bullock Workman Fellowship is given for graduate study in any field.

ELIGIBILITY:
Requirements are available on the College web site.

FINANCIAL DATA:
Amount of support per award: Varies.
Total amount of support: Varies.

APPLICATION INFO:
Details are posted online.
Deadline: Peggy Howard Fellowship: Early April. Mary Elvira Stevens Fellowship: Early December. All other awards: Early January.

PUBLICATIONS:
Program announcement.

*PLEASE NOTE:
Eligibility requirements change frequently. Wellesley College prefers applicants use the web site as the main source of information.

*SPECIAL STIPULATIONS:
These fellowships are for study at institutions other than Wellesley College. Applicants must be graduating seniors or alumnae of Wellesley College for all fellowships.

WELLESLEY COLLEGE   [1001]

Career Education
Green Hall 439, 106 Central Street
Wellesley, MA 02481-8203
(781) 283-2347
Fax: (781) 283-3674
E-mail: fellowships@wellesley.edu
Web Site: www.wellesley.
edu/careereducation/fellowships-and-scholarships

AREAS OF INTEREST:
Graduate study for women.

NAME(S) OF PROGRAMS:
- **Mary McEwen Schimke Scholarship**
- **M.A. Cartland Shackford Medical Fellowship**

TYPE:
Fellowships; Scholarships. Awards are made to female applicants who plan for full-time graduate study for the coming year.

The Mary McEwen Schimke Scholarship is a supplemental award given to afford relief from household and child care expenses while pursuing graduate study.

The M.A. Cartland Shackford Medical Fellowship is given for study of medicine with a view to general practice, not psychiatry.

ELIGIBILITY:
Requirements are posted on the College web site.

FINANCIAL DATA:
Amount of support per award: Varies.
Total amount of support: Varies.

APPLICATION INFO:
Application information is available on the web site.
Duration: One year.
Deadline: Mid-January.

PUBLICATIONS:
Announcement.

*PLEASE NOTE:
Eligibility requirements change from year to year. Wellesley College prefers applicants use the web site as their main source of information.

WOMEN IN DEFENSE [1002]

WID HORIZONS
2101 Wilson Boulevard, Suite 700
Arlington, VA 22201
(703) 247-2570
Fax: (703) 522-1885
E-mail: wid@ndia.org
Web Site: www.womenindefense.net

AREAS OF INTEREST:
Increasing women's participation in national security fields.

NAME(S) OF PROGRAMS:
- **Horizons Foundation Scholarship Program**

TYPE:
Scholarships. The Horizons Foundation Scholarship Program is supported by accredited colleges and universities. Awards are made on an annual basis. The Foundation selects all scholarship recipients based on criteria it sets. Scholarships are awarded to applicants who require financial assistance, demonstrate strong academic credentials and a commitment to a career in national security.

YEAR PROGRAM STARTED: 1988

PURPOSE:
To encourage women to pursue careers related to the national security interests of the U.S.; to provide development opportunities to women who are already working in national security fields.

ELIGIBILITY:
Scholarship Program applicants should be pursuing studies in engineering, computer science, security studies, military history, government relations, cyber security, physics, mathematics, business, law, international relations, political science, operations research or economics. Other disciplines will be considered if the applicant can successfully demonstrate relevance to a career in the areas of national security or defense.

Scholarship Program applicants also must meet the following criteria (no exceptions will be considered):
(1) be a female currently enrolled at an accredited university or college, either full-time or part-time;
(2) undergraduate and graduate students are eligible; undergraduates must have attained at least junior-level status (60 credits);
(3) demonstrate interest in pursuing a career related to national security/national defense;
(4) demonstrate financial need;
(5) have a minimum grade point average of 3.25 and;
(6) be a citizen of the U.S.

Recipients of past awards may apply for future financial assistance.

FINANCIAL DATA:
Amount of support per award: Varies.
Total amount of support: Varies.

NO. MOST RECENT APPLICANTS: 99.

NO. AWARDS: Varies.

APPLICATION INFO:
Applications must be completed in full and include only the following requested items:
(1) one essay in three segments (no more than 500 words);
(2) official academic transcripts;
(3) two recommendation letters and;
(4) proof of U.S. citizenship.

Do not include copies of awards, certificates or photographs. Only students meeting eligibility requirements will be considered.
Deadline: March 15.

ADDRESS INQUIRIES TO:
Tameka Brown, Associate Director
E-mail: tbrown@ndia.org

*PLEASE NOTE:
Interested applicants should monitor WID's web site for detailed instructions and application deadlines.

WOMEN IN FILM [1003]

4221 Wilshire Boulevard
Suite 130
Los Angeles, CA 90010
(323) 935-2211
Fax: (323) 935-2212
E-mail: mverdugo@wif.org
Web Site: womeninfilm.org/film-finishing-fund

FOUNDED: 1985

AREAS OF INTEREST:
Filmmaking.

NAME(S) OF PROGRAMS:
- **Women in Film Finishing Fund**

TYPE:
Project/program grants. Awards for completion of films on subjects that meet the stated guidelines of WIF on an annual basis.

YEAR PROGRAM STARTED: 1985

PURPOSE:
To increase employment and promote equal opportunities for women; to encourage individual creative projects by women; to enhance media images of women; to further the professional development of women; to influence prevailing attitudes and practices regarding and on behalf of women.

LEGAL BASIS:
Nonprofit organization.

ELIGIBILITY:
Filmmaker must have completed 90% of principal photography and have a rough cut at the time of application. Membership in Women In Film is not required. Writer and Director must identify as female or the Writer or Director must identify as female and the Protagonist must be female.

Applications are encouraged from around the world.

Student projects and web series are not eligible for funding.

FINANCIAL DATA:
Amount of support per award: Up to $25,000 in cash and/or in-kind services.
Total amount of support: Varies.

NO. MOST RECENT APPLICANTS: 390 for the year 2018.

NO. AWARDS: 8 for the year 2018.

APPLICATION INFO:
Detailed guidelines and application form may be obtained from the Foundation's web site.
Duration: Varies.

Deadline: July 7.

ADDRESS INQUIRIES TO:
Melissa Verdugo, Manager of Programs
(See e-mail address above.)

*SPECIAL STIPULATIONS:
Projects must be in post-production by the deadline. Filmmakers must submit a rough cut of their films to be considered.

WOMEN'S CONGRESSIONAL POLICY INSTITUTE (WCPI) [1004]

409 12th Street, S.W.
Suite 702
Washington, DC 20024
(202) 554-2323
Fax: (202) 554-2346
E-mail: cindy@wcpinst.org
Web Site: www.womenspolicy.org

FOUNDED: 1995

AREAS OF INTEREST:
Women's public policy issues.

NAME(S) OF PROGRAMS:
- **Congressional Fellowships on Women and Public Policy**

TYPE:
Fellowships.

YEAR PROGRAM STARTED: 1980

PURPOSE:
To encourage more effective participation by women in the formulation of policy options that recognize the needs of all people; to promote activities that encourage the translation of research into policy; to raise awareness that national and international issues concerning women are interdependent; to increase understanding that those issues often defined as women's issues are, in fact, human issues of equal importance to both women and men.

LEGAL BASIS:
501(c)(3) nonprofit organization.

ELIGIBILITY:
Applicants must be currently enrolled in, or have graduated within the last 18 months from, a graduate or professional degree program in the U.S. Preliminary selection is based on academic performance, writing skills, experience with community groups and interest in the analysis of gender differences as they affect federal laws and legislating. Candidates from all academic disciplines are considered. Final selection follows an interview by WCPI.

FINANCIAL DATA:
Amount of support per award: Monthly stipends of $3,400, plus $1,000 health care allowance.
Total amount of support: $25,000 per awardee for academic year 2016.

NO. MOST RECENT APPLICANTS: Approximately 100.

NO. AWARDS: Approximately 5.

APPLICATION INFO:
Applications are available in early March. Applicants must submit all academic transcripts, three letters of recommendation, completed application form and an essay.
Duration: January to August. No renewals.
Deadline: June 1. Regional interviews of semi-finalists are held in June and awards made by July 31.

IRS I.D.: 52-1914894

STAFF:
  Cindy Hall, President
  Cheryl Williams, Vice President

ADDRESS INQUIRIES TO:
  Cindy Hall, President
  (See address above.)

*SPECIAL STIPULATIONS:
  Foreign students at international universities
  are not eligible. Must come to Washington to
  work full-time in a congressional office from
  January until July/August.

WOMEN'S FOUNDATION OF MINNESOTA   [1005]

105 Fifth Avenue South
Suite 300
Minneapolis, MN 55401-6050
(612) 337-5010
Fax: (612) 337-0404
E-mail: contactus@wfmn.org
Web Site: www.wfmn.org

FOUNDED: 1983

AREAS OF INTEREST:
  Women and girls in Minnesota.

NAME(S) OF PROGRAMS:
  - **girlsBEST Fund**
  - **Innovation Fund**
  - **MN Girls Are Not For Sale Fund**
  - **Ripley Memorial Foundation**
  - **Young Women's Initiative**

TYPE:
  Development grants; General operating
  grants; Project/program grants; Technical
  assistance. Start-up grants. The girlsBEST
  program has four program tracks: Academic;
  Entrepreneurial; Employment Development
  and High-Paying/High-Skill Careers; Public
  Education and Advocacy.

YEAR PROGRAM STARTED: 1986

PURPOSE:
  To fund "social change" through our
  grantmaking; to make grants to programs that
  result in shifts in individual, cultural and
  community attitudes and behaviors, and shifts
  in institutions and policies that serve as
  barriers to gender equality.

LEGAL BASIS:
  Public foundation.

ELIGIBILITY:
  Must primarily benefit women and girls and
  be not-for-profit or informal not-for-profit.
  Foundation does not fund direct service
  programs.

GEOG. RESTRICTIONS: Minnesota.

FINANCIAL DATA:
  Amount of support per award: $5,000 to
  $100,000.
  Total amount of support: Over $2,200,000
  total funding in all programs.

NO. MOST RECENT APPLICANTS: 500.

APPLICATION INFO:
  Detailed instructions and guidelines are
  available from the Foundation.
  Duration: One to three years.
  Deadline: Varies.

PUBLICATIONS:
  Annual report; equality report; brochure;
  grant guidelines; research/issue reports.

IRS I.D.: 41-1635761

BOARD OF TRUSTEES:
  Susan Segal, Chairperson

Nevada Littlewolf, Vice Chairperson
Gail Polley-Nordhaus, Treasurer
Chanda Smith-Baker, Secretary
Jennifer Alstad
Julia Classen
Joanne Green
Katharine L. Kelly
Rebecca Klevan
George Martin
Elena Brito Sifferlin
Roderic Southall
Valerie Spencer
Pheng Thao
Sandy Vargas

ADDRESS INQUIRIES TO:
  Jasmine Sanchez, Program Officer and
  Grants Manager
  (See address above.)

*SPECIAL STIPULATIONS:
  Funds only in Minnesota.

WOMEN'S SPORTS FOUNDATION   [1006]

Eisenhower Park
1899 Hempstead Turnpike, Suite 400
East Meadow, NY 11554
(516) 542-4700
(800) 227-3988
Fax: (516) 542-0095
E-mail: info@womenssportsfoundation.org
Web Site: www.womenssportsfoundation.org

FOUNDED: 1974

AREAS OF INTEREST:
  The Foundation - the leading authority on the
  participation of women and girls in sports -
  advocates for equality, educates the public,
  conducts research and offers grants to
  promote sports and physical activity for girls
  and women.

NAME(S) OF PROGRAMS:
  - **Travel & Training Fund**

TYPE:
  Training grants; Travel grants.

YEAR PROGRAM STARTED: 1984

PURPOSE:
  To advance the lives of girls and women
  through sports and physical activity; to
  provide direct financial assistance to aspiring
  female athletes with successful competitive
  records who have potential to achieve even
  higher performance levels and rankings.

LEGAL BASIS:
  501(c)(3) nonprofit organization.

ELIGIBILITY:
  Individual applicants and all members of a
  team must be female U.S. citizens or legal
  residents and be eligible to compete for a
  U.S. national team. Applicants must have
  amateur status.

GEOG. RESTRICTIONS: United States.

FINANCIAL DATA:
  Amount of support per award: $2,500 to
  $10,000.
  Total amount of support: Minimum $100,000
  annually.

NO. AWARDS: Varies.

APPLICATION INFO:
  Contact the Foundation for guidelines.
  Duration: One year.
  Deadline: Online applications must be
  submitted by 5 P.M. May 10. Grants will be
  disbursed during the second quarter of the
  year.

PUBLICATIONS:
  Annual report; research reports; educational
  guides; educational curriculum.

IRS I.D.: 23-7380557

OFFICERS:
  Dr. Deborah Antonine, Chief Executive
  Officer
  Grete Eliassen, President

ADDRESS INQUIRIES TO:
  Elizabeth Flores, Program Officer
  (See address above.)

*SPECIAL STIPULATIONS:
  Applicants must demonstrate
  accomplishments and potential to be
  considered. No travel grants outside the U.S.
  An individual or team may be awarded only
  one grant per calendar year and a maximum
  of three grants in a lifetime.

ZONTA INTERNATIONAL FOUNDATION

1200 Harger Road, Suite 330
Oak Brook, IL 60523
(630) 928-1400
Fax: (630) 928-1559
E-mail: programs@zonta.org
Web Site: www.zonta.org

TYPE:
  Fellowships. Awarded annually to women for
  graduate study in aerospace-related sciences
  or aerospace-related engineering at any
  university or college offering accredited
  graduate courses and degrees.

See entry 1875 for full listing.

ZONTA INTERNATIONAL FOUNDATION

1200 Harger Road, Suite 330
Oak Brook, IL 60523
(630) 928-1400
Fax: (630) 928-1559
E-mail: programs@zonta.org
Web Site: www.zonta.org

TYPE:
  Awards/prizes; Scholarships. For women of
  any nationality pursuing degrees in business
  who demonstrate outstanding potential in the
  field of business.

See entry 1747 for full listing.

ZONTA INTERNATIONAL FOUNDATION   [1007]

1200 Harger Road, Suite 330
Oak Brook, IL 60523
(630) 928-1400
Fax: (630) 928-1559
E-mail: programs@zonta.org
Web Site: www.zonta.org

FOUNDED: 1919

AREAS OF INTEREST:
  Encouraging women's involvement in public
  affairs.

NAME(S) OF PROGRAMS:
  - **Young Women in Public Affairs
    Awards**

TYPE:
  Awards/prizes.

YEAR PROGRAM STARTED: 1990

PURPOSE:
  To encourage young women's involvement
  and interest in public affairs.

LEGAL BASIS:
Incorporated in the state of Illinois as a nonprofit organization.

ELIGIBILITY:
Women of ages 16 to 19 on April 1 of each year, living in a Zonta district/region, or a citizen of a Zonta country, who demonstrate evidence of the following, are eligible to apply:
(1) active commitment to volunteerism;
(2) experience in local government, student government or workplace leadership (paid or unpaid);
(3) volunteer leadership achievements;
(4) knowledge of Zonta International and its programs and;
(5) advocating for Zonta International's mission of advancing the status of women worldwide.

Applicants from geographic areas within a Zonta district/region where no clubs are located will be considered and also eligible to apply for the district/region award.

FINANCIAL DATA:
Amount of support per award: District award recipients receive $1,500 (U.S.) from the Zonta International Foundation YWPA Fund. Districts may choose to add to this award amount. Also, 10 international award recipients are selected from district recipients and receive an additional $4,000 (U.S.)
Total amount of support: Varies.

NO. MOST RECENT APPLICANTS: 32.

NO. AWARDS: 32.

APPLICATION INFO:
The YWPA Awards program operates at the club, district and international levels of Zonta International and is managed by Zonta members. To apply, contact the Zonta Club within the applicant's district/region for deadlines and an address to mail application. (Such contact information is available on the web site.) Alternatively, one can e-mail one's name and contact information to the Young Women in Public Affairs Committee Chairman at ywpachairman@zonta.org.

Deadline: Must contact Zonta Club directly for deadline.

ADDRESS INQUIRIES TO:
Programs Coordinator
(See e-mail address above.)

URBAN AND REGIONAL AFFAIRS

Children and youth

THE JOHN W. ALDEN TRUST [1008]

c/o Emma M. Greene, Senior V.P.
Philanthropic Client Dir., U.S. Trust
Bank of America Private Wealth Management
225 Franklin Street, MA1-225-04-02
Boston, MA 02110
(617) 951-1108
E-mail: susan.t.monahan@gmail.com
Web Site: www.cybergrants.com/alden

AREAS OF INTEREST:
Education and therapy for children who are blind, retarded, disabled, mentally or physically ill; medical and scientific research for the prevention and/or cure of the conditions.

TYPE:
Capital grants; Challenge/matching grants; Conferences/seminars; Demonstration grants; Development grants; Matching gifts; Project/program grants; Research grants; Seed money grants; Technical assistance; Training grants.

LEGAL BASIS:
Private foundation.

ELIGIBILITY:
Organizations must be IRS 501(c)(3) tax-exempt and serve residents of eastern Massachusetts.

FINANCIAL DATA:
Amount of support per award: Generally up to $20,000.
Total amount of support: $552,500 for fiscal year 2019.
Matching fund requirements: Determined on a case-by-case basis.

NO. AWARDS: 38 grants for the year 2019.

REPRESENTATIVE AWARDS:
$10,000 to Silver Lining Mentoring; $10,000 to Triangle; $20,000 to House of Possibilities.

APPLICATION INFO:
All applications must be submitted online.
Duration: Varies.
Deadline: Approximately January 5, April 5, July 5 and October 5.

PUBLICATIONS:
Guidelines.

TRUSTEES:
Emma Green
Susan T. Monahan, Grants Coordinator

ADDRESS INQUIRIES TO:
Susan T. Monahan
Grants Coordinator and Trustee
(See e-mail address above.)

THE ISABEL ALLENDE FOUNDATION

116 Caledonia Street
Sausalito, CA 94965
(415) 289-0992
E-mail: lori@isabelallende.com
Web Site: www.isabelallendefoundation.org

TYPE:
Project/program grants. Promotes and preserves the fundamental rights of women and children to be empowered and protected.

See entry 977 for full listing.

AMERICAN ACADEMY OF CHILD AND ADOLESCENT PSYCHIATRY

3615 Wisconsin Avenue, N.W.
Washington, DC 20016-3007
(202) 966-7300 ext. 117
Fax: (202) 966-5894
E-mail: aarcher@aacap.org
Web Site: www.aacap.org

TYPE:
Conferences/seminars; Fellowships; Research grants; Travel grants. Educational Outreach Program provides travel support for residents and CAP fellows to travel to the Annual Meeting and network with child and adolescent psychiatrists.

Joshi International Scholar Awards recognize midcareer international physicians who primarily work with children and adolescents providing mental health services outside the U.S.

Junior Investigator Award is offered for one child and adolescent psychiatry junior faculty to pursue innovative research. The research may be basic or clinical in nature but must be relevant to the understanding, treatment and prevention of child and adolescent mental health disorders. The award also includes the cost of attending AACAP's Annual Meeting for five days.

Life Members Mentorship Grant for Medical Students provides travel support for medical student recipients to receive a formal overview of child and adolescent psychiatry, establish mentor relationships with child and adolescent psychiatrists, and experience AACAP's Annual Meeting.

Pilot Awards are offered to members with a career interest in child and adolescent mental health research.

Ülgür International Scholar Award recognizes a child and adolescent psychiatrist or a physician in the international community who has made significant contributions to the enhancement of mental health services for children and adolescents.

See entry 2350 for full listing.

AMERICAN ACADEMY OF CHILD AND ADOLESCENT PSYCHIATRY

3615 Wisconsin Avenue, N.W.
Washington, DC 20016-3007
(202) 966-7300 ext. 117
Fax: (202) 966-5894
E-mail: aarcher@aacap.org
Web Site: www.aacap.org

TYPE:
Project/program grants; Research grants; Travel grants. The Marilyn B. Benoit, M.D., Child Maltreatment Mentorship Award facilitates the completion of a project in which the applicant collaborates with a mentor specializing in the areas of child welfare, foster care, and/or children maltreatment prevention/intervention.

The Psychodynamic Faculty Training and Mentorship Initiative provides a reimbursable travel stipend to cover travel support for attending the required program events during AACAP's Annual Meeting.

See entry 2351 for full listing.

AMERICAN ACADEMY OF CHILD AND ADOLESCENT PSYCHIATRY

3615 Wisconsin Avenue, N.W.
Washington, DC 20016-3007
(202) 966-7300 ext. 117
Fax: (202) 966-5894
E-mail: aarcher@aacap.org
Web Site: www.aacap.org

TYPE:
Awards/prizes; Conferences/seminars; Fellowships; Research grants; Travel grants. Jeanne Spurlock Minority Medical Student Research Fellowship in Substance Abuse and Addiction provides support for research training in substance abuse and addiction under a mentor with experience in the type of research that is being proposed, and whose work includes children and adolescents participants.

Summer Medical Student Fellowship provides clinical or research training under a child and adolescent psychiatrist mentor.

See entry 2349 for full listing.

ANDRUS FAMILY FUND

200 Madison Avenue, 25th Floor
New York, NY 10016
(212) 687-6975
E-mail: jkaizer@affund.org
info@affund.org
Web Site: affund.org

TYPE:
Project/program grants.

See entry 1065 for full listing.

BAINUM FAMILY FOUNDATION [1009]

7735 Old Georgetown Road, Suite 1000
Bethesda, MD 20814
(240) 450-0000
Fax: (240) 450-4115
E-mail: vgentilcore@bainumfdn.org
Web Site: www.bainumfdn.org

FOUNDED: 1968

AREAS OF INTEREST:
Underserved children and youth; early childhood (birth to three years of age).

YEAR PROGRAM STARTED: 1968

PURPOSE:
To support educational programs assisting underserved children/youth.

LEGAL BASIS:
Private foundation.

ELIGIBILITY:
Eligible organizations must be IRS 501(c)(3) tax-exempt.

GEOG. RESTRICTIONS: Baltimore, Maryland and Washington, DC metropolitan areas.

FINANCIAL DATA:
Amount of support per award: $58,000.
Total amount of support: $20,000,000.

NO. MOST RECENT APPLICANTS: 343.

NO. AWARDS: 343.

APPLICATION INFO:
Applications are accepted by invitation only.

ADDRESS INQUIRIES TO:
Shantelice White
Senior Grants Manager
(See address above.)

BASEBALL TOMORROW FUND [1010]

245 Park Avenue
New York, NY 10167
(212) 931-7991
E-mail: btf@mlb.com
Web Site: www.baseballtomorrowfund.com

FOUNDED: 1999

AREAS OF INTEREST:
Youth baseball and softball.

TYPE:
Capital grants; Challenge/matching grants; Project/program grants. These grants are offered to promote and enhance the growth of youth baseball and softball in the U.S., Canada and throughout the world.

YEAR PROGRAM STARTED: 2000

PURPOSE:
To promote and enhance the growth of baseball in the U.S., Canada and throughout the world by funding programs, fields and equipment purchases, designed to encourage and maintain youth participation in the game.

ELIGIBILITY:
Grants are made to support participation growth and incremental programs and/or for facilities for youth baseball and softball. Organizations must be nonprofit or tax-exempt.

FINANCIAL DATA:
Amount of support per award: $40,000 average grant.
Total amount of support: $2,000,000 annually.
Matching fund requirements: 50% match required.

NO. MOST RECENT APPLICANTS: 200.

NO. AWARDS: Over 1,000 since inception.

APPLICATION INFO:
An online application is available on the web site. Letters of inquiry and requests for support are not accepted by mail or e-mail.
Deadline: January 1, April 1, July 1 and October 1.

ADDRESS INQUIRIES TO:
See e-mail address above.

THE BOY SCOUTS OF AMERICA, NATIONAL EAGLE SCOUT ASSOCIATION [1011]

1325 West Walnut Hill Lane
P.O. Box 152079
Irving, TX 75015-2079
(972) 580-2000
E-mail: nesa@scouting.org
Web Site: www.nesa.org

AREAS OF INTEREST:
Scouting and youth.

NAME(S) OF PROGRAMS:
- **Bailey Scholarship**
- **Hall/McElwain Merit Scholarships**
- **Robert and Rebeca Palmer Scholarship**

TYPE:
Scholarships.

PURPOSE:
To serve Eagle Scouts and through them, the entire movement of Scouting.

ELIGIBILITY:
Must be graduating high school senior or an undergraduate college student no later than completion of their junior year. Applicant

must have demonstrated leadership ability in scouting and a strong record of participation in activities outside of scouting.

Applicant must be a member of the National Eagle Scout Association and must supply Scout history and participation. Award is not based on financial need or grades.

FINANCIAL DATA:
Scholarships are for tuition, room, board and books.
Amount of support per award: $2,500 to $5,000.
Total amount of support: Varies.

NO. AWARDS: Varies, depending on funds available.

APPLICATION INFO:
Application process begins August 1. Information is available on the Association web site. Application must be submitted online.
Duration: One-time award.
Deadline: October 31.

ADDRESS INQUIRIES TO:
Jeff Laughlin, Manager
(See address above.)

*PLEASE NOTE:
This scholarship is not available to students attending any of the U.S. military academies.

*SPECIAL STIPULATIONS:
Applicant must fill out new application each year.

THE BOY SCOUTS OF AMERICA, NATIONAL EAGLE SCOUT ASSOCIATION [1012]

1325 West Walnut Hill Lane
P.O. Box 152079
Irving, TX 75015-2079
(972) 580-2000
E-mail: nesa@scouting.org
Web Site: www.nesa.org

AREAS OF INTEREST:
Scouting and youth.

NAME(S) OF PROGRAMS:
- **Mabel and Lawrence S. Cooke Scholarship**
- **National Eagle Scout Scholarship Fund**
- **STEM Scholarship**

TYPE:
Scholarships.

PURPOSE:
To serve Eagle Scouts and through them, the entire movement of Scouting.

ELIGIBILITY:
For the Mabel and Lawrence S. Cooke Scholarship, applicant must register and maintain status as a full-time student at a college/university. The scholarship is not available to students attending any of the U.S. military academies, because the U.S. government pays expenses that are covered by NESA scholarships at these academies.

National Eagle Scout Scholarship Fund applicants must register and maintain status as a full-time student at a college/university. Applicant must be a member of the National Eagle Scout Association.

FINANCIAL DATA:
Funds are for tuition, room, board, and books.
Amount of support per award: Mabel and Lawrence S. Cooke Scholarship: One scholarship of up to $48,000 (up to $12,000

per year for four years) and four $25,000 scholarships ($6,250 per year for four years) are given annually; National Eagle Scout Scholarship Fund: Varies each year, depending on the funds available; STEM Scholarship: Up to $50,000 for four years ($12,500 per year).
Total amount of support: Varies.

NO. AWARDS: Varies.

APPLICATION INFO:
Application information is available on the web site. Application must be submitted online.
Duration: Up to four years.
Deadline: Applications open August 1; submit no later than October 31.

ADDRESS INQUIRIES TO:
Jeff Laughlin, Manager
(See address above.)

THE LOUIS CALDER FOUNDATION [1013]

999 18th Street
Suite 2350S
Denver, CO 80202
(720) 943-9865
E-mail: proposals@calderfdn.org
Web Site: www.louiscalderfoundation.org

FOUNDED: 1951

AREAS OF INTEREST:
Education.

TYPE:
Capital grants; Project/program grants. Curriculum development.

YEAR PROGRAM STARTED: 1951

PURPOSE:
To promote scholastic development of children and youth by improving elementary and secondary education through its support of charter and parochial schools.

LEGAL BASIS:
Private foundation.

ELIGIBILITY:
Nonprofit 501(c)(3) organizations.

Grants are not made to individuals, private foundations, governmental organizations or publicly operated educational institutions. The Foundation generally does not provide support to annual funds or special events.

GEOG. RESTRICTIONS: Continental United States.

FINANCIAL DATA:
Amount of support per award: Average $100,000.
Total amount of support: Approximately $6,500,000 annually.

NO. AWARDS: Over 50.

REPRESENTATIVE AWARDS:
$100,000 to Great Hearts Academies for Headmaster College and Residency Program; $100,000 to Quill for development of online literacy tool; $50,000 to Stellar Collegiate Charter School for grade-level growth of new elementary school.

APPLICATION INFO:
The Foundation does not accept unsolicited proposals. Organizations unfamiliar to the Foundation, or those that are not current grantees, are encouraged to submit a letter of inquiry via the web site. If the organization's programming falls within the parameters of

the current grantmaking strategy and is selected for further review, a full proposal will be requested.

Duration: Varies.

PUBLICATIONS:
Annual report.

IRS I.D.: 13-6015562

TRUSTEES:
M. Alexander Calder
Peter D. Calder
Frank E. Shanley

ADDRESS INQUIRIES TO:
Holly Nuechterlein, Program Director
(See e-mail address above.)

CAMPBELL FOUNDATION, INC.   [1014]

705 York Road
Towson, MD 21204
(410) 828-1961
Fax: (410) 821-8814
E-mail: lsperato@stoycpa.com

AREAS OF INTEREST:
Social services, education, arts and cultural programs.

TYPE:
Capital grants; General operating grants; Project/program grants.

PURPOSE:
To provide support for cultural, educational and social services and institutions.

LEGAL BASIS:
Nonprofit foundation.

ELIGIBILITY:
Organization must have 501(c)(3) status.

GEOG. RESTRICTIONS: Maryland, primarily Baltimore.

FINANCIAL DATA:
Amount of support per award: $2,500 to $5,000 general operating grant; $15,000 to $20,000 capital grant.
Total amount of support: Average $190,000 per year.

NO. AWARDS: Average 80 per year.

APPLICATION INFO:
Organizations must submit a written proposal, up to two pages in length, including program specifications. Proof of 501(c)(3) status required.
Duration: One year. Renewal by reapplication.
Deadline: November 15.

ADDRESS INQUIRIES TO:
Virginia T. Campbell, President
(See address above.)

THE CARSON SCHOLARS FUND, INC.

305 West Chesapeake Avenue
Suite 310
Towson, MD 21204
(410) 828-1005
Fax: (410) 828-1007
E-mail: lrichards@carsonscholars.org
Web Site: carsonscholars.org

TYPE:
Scholarships. The Carson Scholars Fund awards college scholarships to students in grades 4-11 who excel academically and are dedicated to serving their communities.

See entry 1511 for full listing.

THOMAS AND AGNES CARVEL FOUNDATION   [1015]

35 East Grassy Sprain Road
Yonkers, NY 10710
(914) 793-7300
Fax: (914) 793-7381
E-mail: tacarvelfoundation@gmail.com

AREAS OF INTEREST:
Children, youth, health and religion.

TYPE:
General operating grants; Grants-in-aid; Matching gifts; Project/program grants; Research grants.

ELIGIBILITY:
Applicants must be 501(c)(3) tax-exempt organizations. Grants may be given to religious organizations that meet geographic requirements. No grants to individuals.

GEOG. RESTRICTIONS: Connecticut, New Jersey and New York.

FINANCIAL DATA:
Amount of support per award: Varies, depending on needs and nature of the request.

APPLICATION INFO:
No application form required. Applicants must provide IRS tax-exempt documentation.
Duration: One year. Renewable.

ADDRESS INQUIRIES TO:
Peter A. Smith, President
(See address above.)

THE CENTER AT SIERRA HEALTH FOUNDATION

1321 Garden Highway
Suite 210
Sacramento, CA 95833
(916) 993-7701
E-mail: impact@shfcenter.org
Web Site: www.shfcenter.org

TYPE:
Matching gifts; Project/program grants.

See entry 1351 for full listing.

CHILDREN'S BUREAU   [1016]

Administration on Children, Youth and Families
330 C Street, S.W.
Washington, DC 20201
(202) 205-8172
E-mail: jan.shafer@acf.hhs.gov
Web Site: www.acf.hhs.gov/cb

FOUNDED: 1974

AREAS OF INTEREST:
Prevention, identification, assessment and treatment of child abuse and neglect, sexual abuse, incidence of abuse and neglect.

NAME(S) OF PROGRAMS:
● **Child Abuse Prevention and Treatment Act (CAPTA) State Grants**

TYPE:
Demonstration grants; Project/program grants; Research grants; Technical assistance; Training grants.

YEAR PROGRAM STARTED: 1974

PURPOSE:
To assist state, local and voluntary agencies and organizations to strengthen their capacities to prevent child abuse and neglect, identify and assess abused and neglected children and provide necessary ameliorative services to them and their families.

LEGAL BASIS:
Public Law 102-295, 45 CFR Subtitle B, part 1340.

ELIGIBILITY:
Grants for demonstration programs or projects and research projects may be made to states, public agencies, community-based organizations, or public or private organizations.

FINANCIAL DATA:
$25,310,000 budgeted for fiscal year 2019.
Amount of support per award: Average $400,000.

APPLICATION INFO:
Standard grant application forms provided by the agency must be used. Complete instructions and necessary forms are issued with each announcement or solicitation.
Duration: Normally 36 to 60 months.
Deadline: Varies.

ADDRESS INQUIRIES TO:
Jan Shafer, Director
Division of Program Innovation
(See address above.)

*SPECIAL STIPULATIONS:
Financial and program progress reports are required semiannually; a final report and an expenditure report are required no later than 90 days after the completion of the project. Audits conducted. Records must be maintained for three years.

ADOLPH COORS FOUNDATION   [1017]

215 St. Paul Street, Suite 300
Denver, CO 80206
(303) 388-1636
Fax: (303) 388-1684
E-mail: info@acoorsfdn.org
Web Site: coorsfoundation.org

FOUNDED: 1976

AREAS OF INTEREST:
Primarily youth, job training, and self-sufficiency.

TYPE:
Capital grants; General operating grants; Project/program grants.

PURPOSE:
To build a stronger, healthier society.

ELIGIBILITY:
Organizations must be classified as 501(c)(3) and operate within the U.S. The Foundation does not consider grants to organizations that in policy or practice discriminate on the basis of race, creed or gender. No grants to religious organizations or individuals.

GEOG. RESTRICTIONS: Colorado.

FINANCIAL DATA:
Amount of support per award: Varies.
Total amount of support: $8,809,370 for the year 2019.

NO. AWARDS: 120 for the year 2019.

APPLICATION INFO:
Applications may only be submitted online.
Duration: One year.
Deadline: March 1, July 1 and November 1.

ADDRESS INQUIRIES TO:
Carrie Tynan, Executive Director
(See address above.)

THE CRAIL-JOHNSON FOUNDATION [1018]

461 West 6th Street
Suite 300
San Pedro, CA 90731
(310) 519-7413
Fax: (310) 519-7221
Web Site: www.crail-johnson.org

FOUNDED: 1987

AREAS OF INTEREST:
Underserved children, youth and families in the areas of health, education and human services.

TYPE:
General operating grants; Project/program grants.

YEAR PROGRAM STARTED: 1987

PURPOSE:
To promote the well-being of children in need through effective application of human and financial resources.

LEGAL BASIS:
Private foundation.

ELIGIBILITY:
Applicants must be tax-exempt 501(c)(3) organizations. No grants to individuals.

GEOG. RESTRICTIONS: Los Angeles, California.

FINANCIAL DATA:
Amount of support per award: $5,000 to $30,000.

APPLICATION INFO:
Consult applications procedure page of web site.
Duration: Typically one year.
Deadline: Varies.

PUBLICATIONS:
Guidelines.

OFFICERS:
Craig C. Johnson, Chairman
Alan C. Johnson, President
Byung Kim, Chief Financial Officer

MICHAEL AND SUSAN DELL FOUNDATION [1019]

P.O. Box 163867
Austin, TX 78716
Fax: (512) 600-5501
E-mail: info@msdf.org
Web Site: www.dell.org

AREAS OF INTEREST:
Education, family economic stability, and childhood health.

TYPE:
Project/program grants. Grants to support and initiate programs that directly serve the needs of children living in urban poverty.

PURPOSE:
To improve outcomes for children, living in urban poverty around the world, in a measurable way.

ELIGIBILITY:
Eligible organizations must be 501(c)(3) or have a fiscal sponsor which is 501(c)(3).

GEOG. RESTRICTIONS: United States, India and South Africa.

FINANCIAL DATA:
Foundation will not fund more than 25% of a project's budget or more than 10% of an organization's total annual operating expenses.
Amount of support per award: Varies.

Total amount of support: Varies.

APPLICATION INFO:
All grant requests should be submitted via online form.
Duration: Varies.

THE CLEVELAND H. DODGE FOUNDATION, INC. [1020]

420 Lexington Avenue, Suite 2331
New York, NY 10170
(212) 972-2800
Fax: (212) 972-1049
E-mail: emommsen@chdodgefoundation.org
Web Site: www.chdodgefoundation.org

FOUNDED: 1917

AREAS OF INTEREST:
Educational institutions and welfare agencies serving the educational needs and character development of young people, as well as early childhood literacy (grades Nursery through K).

TYPE:
Project/program grants.

YEAR PROGRAM STARTED: 1917

PURPOSE:
To help better mankind by providing funds for education and social welfare organizations.

LEGAL BASIS:
Private foundation.

ELIGIBILITY:
Grants are made to nonprofit, 501(c)(3) organizations in the Foundation's areas of interest. No grants are made to individuals.

GEOG. RESTRICTIONS: United States.

FINANCIAL DATA:
Amount of support per award: $5,000 to $500,000; average grant: $25,000.
Total amount of support: $2,300,000 for the year 2018.

NO. MOST RECENT APPLICANTS: Approximately 150.

NO. AWARDS: 48.

APPLICATION INFO:
Applicants must provide:
(1) a letter describing the organization and grant request, including budget;
(2) annual report and;
(3) proof of 501(c)(3) status.
Duration: Typically one year. Multi-year commitments are rare.
Deadline: January 15, April 15 and September 15.

IRS I.D.: 13-6015087

ADDRESS INQUIRIES TO:
Emily Mommsen, Executive Director
(See address above.)

DUPONT PIONEER [1021]

7100 N.W. 62nd Avenue
Johnston, IA 50131
(515) 535-7719
(800) 247-6803 ext. 57719
Fax: (515) 535-4842
E-mail: community.investment@pioneer.com
Web Site: www.pioneer.com

AREAS OF INTEREST:
Education, food security and community betterment.

NAME(S) OF PROGRAMS:
- **Community Betterment**
- **Food Security**
- **PreK-12 Education**

TYPE:
General operating grants; Matching gifts; Project/program grants. Community outreach programs. Matching gifts are for educational institutions.

PURPOSE:
To help improve the quality of life in the communities in which customers and employees live and work.

LEGAL BASIS:
Corporation giving program.

ELIGIBILITY:
Must be an IRS tax-exempt 501(c)(3) organization. No grants to individuals or religious organizations that promote a particular doctrine.

FINANCIAL DATA:
Amount of support per award: Up to $5,000.
Total amount of support: Varies.

NO. AWARDS: Approximately 1,000 per year.

APPLICATION INFO:
Applications are by invitation only.
Duration: One year.

EAST TENNESSEE FOUNDATION [1022]

520 West Summit Hill Drive
Suite 1101
Knoxville, TN 37902
(865) 524-1223
(877) 524-1223
Fax: (865) 637-6039
E-mail: etf@etf.org
Web Site: www.easttennesseefoundation.org

FOUNDED: 1986

AREAS OF INTEREST:
Arts and culture, youth-at-risk, community development, affordable housing construction, and scholarships.

CONSULTING OR VOLUNTEER SERVICES:
A variety of technical assistance to applicants and grantees.

TYPE:
Project/program grants; Scholarships; Seed money grants; Technical assistance. The Foundation is comprised of 400 philanthropic funds and nine supporting organizations.

PURPOSE:
To make the region a better place today and for future generations.

LEGAL BASIS:
Community foundation; 501(c)(3) organization.

ELIGIBILITY:
Grants are awarded to 501(c)(3) public charities, units of government, or educational institutions. The Foundation does not make grants or loans to individuals.

GEOG. RESTRICTIONS: Counties in East Tennessee.

FINANCIAL DATA:
Amount of support per award: Funding support generally $500 to $10,000 per year for competitive grants and scholarships; $15,000 to $140,000 in Affordable Housing Trust Fund (AHTF) grants.
Total amount of support: Varies.

APPLICATION INFO:
Applications are accepted online.

Duration: Varies.

Deadline: Varies.

PUBLICATIONS:
Connections, Funding Focus, quarterly newsletter; annual reports; documents; brochures.

IRS I.D.: 62-0807696

STAFF:
Michael McClamroch, President and Chief Executive Officer
Carolyn Schwenn, Executive Vice President and Secretary
Tamara Boyer, Vice President for Advancement
Jan Elston, Vice President for Competitive Grant Program
Deanene Catani, Director of Communications

ADDRESS INQUIRIES TO:
Michael McClamroch
President and Chief Executive Officer
(See address above.)

*PLEASE NOTE:
Organizations located outside of the Foundation's service area are not eligible for funding.

THE EISNER FOUNDATION [1023]

9401 Wilshire Boulevard
Suite 735
Beverly Hills, CA 90212
(310) 228-6808
E-mail: info@eisnerfoundation.org
Web Site: eisnerfoundation.org

FOUNDED: 1996

AREAS OF INTEREST:
Intergenerational programs.

TYPE:
Capital grants; General operating grants; Project/program grants. The Eisner Foundation supports organizations offering intergenerational solutions to society's greatest challenges through its grant-making programs.
Capacity-Building Grants support training or planning.
Capital Project Grants support buying, constructing or renovating facilities.
General Operating Grants offer unrestricted support.
Opportunity Grants aim to help smaller organizations grow and gain credibility, and encourage organizations to be innovative and entrepreneurial in developing new intergenerational solutions.
Project Support Grants offer funding for specific projects or initiatives.

PURPOSE:
To identify, advocate for, and invest in high-quality and innovative programs that unite multiple generations for the betterment of our communities.

LEGAL BASIS:
501(c)(3) organization.

ELIGIBILITY:
Tax-exempt 501(c)(3) organizations based in Los Angeles County or doing work that benefits populations in Los Angeles County are eligible to apply. Grants are available for general operating expenses, project support, capacity-building, and capital projects.

Opportunity Grants are offered to smaller organizations or larger organizations launching new intergenerational initiatives.

GEOG. RESTRICTIONS: Los Angeles County, California.

FINANCIAL DATA:
Amount of support per award: Typically $100,000 to $300,000; Opportunity Grants: Up to $25,000.
Total amount of support: Approximately $7,500,000 per year.

REPRESENTATIVE AWARDS:
$125,000 to CASA of Los Angeles to recruit volunteer court advocates for children in the child welfare system; $50,000 to Heart of Los Angeles to increase access to services for seniors and create volunteer opportunities that will facilitate intergenerational connections with HOLA youth; $150,000 (over two years) to Turnaround Arts to bring high-quality arts education resources to Los Angeles County's lowest performing elementary and middle schools.

APPLICATION INFO:
Before submitting a Letter of Inquiry, organization must answer brief questions online to determine eligibility.
Duration: One year or multiyear. Opportunity Grants are available for one-year terms and are renewable for small organizations. Large organizations with successful initiatives may apply for additional grant funds after one year, but cannot renew an Opportunity Grant.
Deadline: Letters of Intent are accepted year-round. Full grant proposals are presented to the Board for quarterly review with the exception of Opportunity Grant proposals, which are presented in June and December.

IRS I.D.: 95-4607191

STAFF:
Trent Stamp, Chief Executive Officer
Cathy Choi, Director of Programs
Chelsea Mason, Director of Communications
Madison Miller, Foundation Administrator

ADDRESS INQUIRIES TO:
Trent Stamp, Chief Executive Officer
(See address above.)

FOSTER CARE TO SUCCESS

23811 Chagrin Boulevard
Suite 210
Cleveland, OH 44122
(571) 203-0270
E-mail: scholarships@fc2success.org
Web Site: www.fc2success.org

TYPE:
Scholarships.

See entry 1405 for full listing.

H.B. FULLER COMPANY FOUNDATION [1024]

1200 Willow Lake Boulevard
St. Paul, MN 55110
(651) 236-5900
E-mail: hbfullerfoundation@hbfuller.com
Web Site: www.hbfuller.com/community

FOUNDED: 1974

AREAS OF INTEREST:
STEM education for youth (science, technology, engineering and math) and youth leadership development.

NAME(S) OF PROGRAMS:
- **Leadership Development for Youth**
- **STEM Education**

TYPE:
Project/program grants. Leadership Development for Youth supports organizations and programs that help young people become successful, productive adults.
STEM Education supports youth education initiatives in the areas of science, technology, engineering and math (STEM).

PURPOSE:
To support charitable activities of the company.

ELIGIBILITY:
Must be an eligible, tax-exempt 501(c)(3) organization. Projects must be aligned with the Company's focus areas and must aim to benefit people where employees live and work.

GEOG. RESTRICTIONS: Greater Atlanta, Georgia; Aurora, Illinois; South Bend, Indiana; Paducah, Kentucky; Peabody, Massachusetts; Grand Rapids and Michigan Center, Michigan; Twin Cities metropolitan area, Minnesota; Rexdale, Ontario; Simpsonville, South Carolina; and Vancouver, Washington.

FINANCIAL DATA:
Amount of support per award: Varies. Individual grants typically are from $5,000 to $10,000.
Total amount of support: Varies.

APPLICATION INFO:
Online application process.
Duration: Typically one year.
Deadline: Minnesota STEM/Youth Leadership grants: Proposals accepted March 1 to 31 and August 1 to 31. All other North American grants: April 1 to July 31.

ADDRESS INQUIRIES TO:
H.B. Fuller Community Affairs
(See e-mail address above.)

THE GERBER FOUNDATION [1025]

4747 West 48th Street
Suite 153
Fremont, MI 49412
(231) 924-3175
Fax: (231) 924-7906
E-mail: tgf@gerberfoundation.org
Web Site: www.gerberfoundation.org

FOUNDED: 1952

AREAS OF INTEREST:
Enhancing the quality of life of infants and young children in nutrition, care and development.

TYPE:
Matching gifts; Research grants. Grants to ensure the continuity of scientific and educational research in infant nutrition and child health. Matching gifts to 501(c)(3) educational, health and human services institutions within the U.S.

YEAR PROGRAM STARTED: 1952

PURPOSE:
To enhance the quality of life of infants and young children.

LEGAL BASIS:
Private foundation.

ELIGIBILITY:
Must be 501(c)(3).

GEOG. RESTRICTIONS: United States.

FINANCIAL DATA:

Amount of support per award: Matching Gifts: $75 to $2,250; Research Grants: $20,000 to $350,000.

Total amount of support: $3,479,766 for the year 2017.

Matching fund requirements: Must be a Gerber Products Company retiree and have retired before July 1, 2002.

NO. MOST RECENT APPLICANTS: 350 for the year 2017.

NO. AWARDS: 107 for the year 2017.

APPLICATION INFO:

Research grant applicants should submit a two- to three-page letter of inquiry initially. Applications for all programs are submitted through the gerberfoundation.smartsimple.com web site.

Duration: One-time award with annual review.

Deadline: Letters of inquiry due May 15 and November 15.

PUBLICATIONS:

Guidelines; application.

IRS I.D.: 38-6068090

OFFICERS:

Barbara J. Ivens, President
Fernando Flores-New, Vice President
Stan VanderRoest, Treasurer
Tracy Baker, Secretary

ADDRESS INQUIRIES TO:

Catherine Obits, Program Manager
(See address above.)

THE WILLIAM T. GRANT FOUNDATION [1026]

One Grand Central Place, 43rd Floor
60 East 42nd Street
New York, NY 10165
(212) 752-0071
Fax: (212) 752-1398
E-mail: info@wtgrantfdn.org
Web Site: wtgrantfoundation.org

FOUNDED: 1936

AREAS OF INTEREST:

Supporting research to improve the lives of young people in the U.S.

NAME(S) OF PROGRAMS:

- **William T. Grant Scholars Program**
- **Institutional Challenge Grant**
- **Research Grants Program**
- **Youth Service Improvement Grants Program**

TYPE:

Project/program grants; Research grants. William T. Grant Scholars Program supports promising early career researchers from diverse disciplines. The award is intended to facilitate the professional development of early career scholars who have demonstrated success in conducting high-quality research and are seeking to further develop their skills and research program.

The Institutional Challenge Grant encourages university-based research institutes, schools and centers to build sustained research-practice partnerships with public agencies or nonprofit organizations to reduce inequality in youth outcomes.

The Youth Service Improvement Grants Program supports activities conducted by community-based organizations in the five boroughs of New York City to improve the quality of services for young people ages 8 to 25.

YEAR PROGRAM STARTED: 1936

PURPOSE:

To help create a society that values young people and enables them to reach their full potential. In pursuit of this goal, the Foundation invests in research and in people and projects that use evidence-based approaches.

LEGAL BASIS:

Private foundation.

ELIGIBILITY:

Organization must have 501(c)(3) status. No grants to individuals.

GEOG. RESTRICTIONS: United States.

FINANCIAL DATA:

Amount of support per award: William T. Grant Scholars Program: Up to $350,000; Institutional Challenge Grant: $650,000; Research Grants: $100,000 to $600,000; Youth Service Improvement Grants Program: $25,000.

Total amount of support: Varies.

NO. AWARDS: William T. Grant Scholars Program: 4 to 6 annually; Institutional Challenge Grant: 1 annually; Youth Service Improvement Grants Program: Varies.

APPLICATION INFO:

Application, requirements and procedures are available online.

Duration: William T. Grant Scholars Program: Five years; Institutional Challenge Grant: Three years; Investigator Initiated Grants: Two to three years.

Deadline: Varies.

PUBLICATIONS:

Annual report; guidelines; *William T. Grant Scholars*, brochure.

TRUSTEES:

Russell P. Pennoyer, Chairperson
Andres A. Alonso
Margaret R. Burchinal
Prudence L. Carter
Greg Duncan
Scott Evans
Adam Gamoran
Kenji Hakuta
Mary Patillo
Judson Reis
Estelle B. Richman
Mark Soler
Noah Walley

STAFF:

Adam Gamoran, President
Vivian Tseng, Senior Vice President, Programs
Rosanna Aybar, Vice President, Finance and Administration
Kimberly DuMont, Senior Program Officer
Tricia Denton, Director, Grantmaking Operations
Sharon Brewster, Grants Coordinator, Discretionary Grants
Nancy Rivera-Torres, Grants Coordinator, Major Grants
Irene Williams, Grants Coordinator, William T. Grant Scholars

HASBRO CHILDREN'S FUND [1027]

One Hasbro Place
Providence, RI 02903
(401) 727-5084
Fax: (401) 721-7275
Web Site: corporate.hasbro.com

FOUNDED: 2006

AREAS OF INTEREST:

The welfare and development of children.

NAME(S) OF PROGRAMS:

- **Community Grants**

TYPE:

Product donations; Project/program grants. Grants made by the Hasbro Children's Fund focus on three core principles:
(1) Programs which provide hope to children who need it most;
(2) Play for children who otherwise would not be able to experience that joy and;
(3) Empowerment of youth through service.

YEAR PROGRAM STARTED: 1985

PURPOSE:

To assist children in triumphing over critical life obstacles as well as bringing the joy of play into their lives.

ELIGIBILITY:

U.S.-based 501(c)(3) organizations who deliver programs to children in Los Angeles, CA; Boulder, CO; Miami, FL; Renton, WA; and Rhode Island.

FINANCIAL DATA:

Amount of support per award: Varies.

Total amount of support: Varies.

APPLICATION INFO:

All interested organizations are asked to apply through the Fund's online application system.

CHARLES HAYDEN FOUNDATION [1028]

140 Broadway, 51st Floor
New York, NY 10005
(212) 785-3677
Fax: (212) 785-3689
E-mail: fdn@chf.org
Web Site: www.charleshaydenfoundation.org

FOUNDED: 1937

AREAS OF INTEREST:

Education and youth agencies.

TYPE:

Project/program grants. Grant priorities focus on institutions and programs primarily serving youth at risk of not reaching their full potential, especially youth in low-income communities. Support is provided for youth development programs, charter schools, independent and parochial schools, and informal educational enrichment programs.

YEAR PROGRAM STARTED: 1937

PURPOSE:

To promote the mental, moral and physical development of children and youth three to 18 years of age in the New York and Boston metropolitan areas.

LEGAL BASIS:

Private foundation.

ELIGIBILITY:

Grants are restricted to institutions and organizations in the New York and Boston metropolitan areas, as defined by the Foundation. The Foundation focuses on those grants primarily serving youth, three to 18 years of age, that are most at-risk of not reaching their full potential, especially youth in low-income communities. Grants are available for capital and program support. Program grants must have clear goals to be met within the specified time frame. Program support goes mainly for new and expanded programs. No grants are awarded to individuals.

GEOG. RESTRICTIONS: New York and Boston, Massachusetts metropolitan areas.

FINANCIAL DATA:
Amount of support per award: Varies.
Total amount of support: $13,869,028 for the year 2019.

APPLICATION INFO:
Applicants should submit a request online through the Foundation web site.

Interviews, if required or requested, are not arranged until the written grant application has been submitted and the preliminary review is completed.
Duration: Most grants are for one year. Grant renewals are sometimes considered.

IRS I.D.: 13-5562237

OFFICERS:
Dean H. Steeger, Chairman of the Board
Kenneth D. Merin, President and Chief Executive Officer
Kristen J. McCormack, Treasurer
Robert Andrews, Secretary
Sonni Holland, Assistant Secretary
Carol Van Atten, Assistant Secretary

BOARD OF TRUSTEES:
Robert Andrews
Jose Claxton
Robert Howitt
Kristen J. McCormack
Kenneth D. Merin
Dean H. Steeger

ADDRESS INQUIRIES TO:
Kenneth D. Merin
President and Chief Executive Officer
(See address above.)

*SPECIAL STIPULATIONS:
Institutions receiving capital support must wait two years before seeking additional assistance.

THE JACK AND JILL OF AMERICA FOUNDATION
1930 17th Street, N.W.
Washington, DC 20009-6207
(202) 232-5290
Fax: (202) 232-1747
E-mail: administration@jackandjillfoundation.org
Web Site: www.jackandjillfoundation.org

TYPE:
Project/program grants; Scholarships.
Volunteer opportunities.

See entry 942 for full listing.

KANSAS HEALTH FOUNDATION
309 East Douglas
Wichita, KS 67202
(316) 262-7676
(800) 373-7681
Fax: (316) 262-2044
E-mail: info@khf.org
Web Site: kansashealth.org

TYPE:
Project/program grants.

See entry 1321 for full listing.

THE KLINGENSTEIN THIRD GENERATION FOUNDATION
80 8th Avenue
Suite 1400
New York, NY 10011
(332) 219-0601
E-mail: info@klingenstein.org
Web Site: www.ktgf.org

TYPE:
Fellowships; Research grants. The Foundation funds research and other programs related to childhood and adolescent ADHD and depression. All funding is directed towards three research fellowship programs (funding postdoctoral research in ADHD, depression and access to care) and the medical student training program. The Foundation does not accept general applications for project or research funding.

See entry 2371 for full listing.

THE AGNES M. LINDSAY TRUST [1029]
15 Constitution Drive
Suite 1A, Office
Bedford, NH 03110
(603) 669-1366
(603) 488-1213
E-mail: admin@lindsaytrust.org
Web Site: www.lindsaytrust.org

FOUNDED: 1939

AREAS OF INTEREST:
Broad charitable giving and special community needs, including handicapped, elderly, children's homes, youth organizations, homeless shelters and food banks.

NAME(S) OF PROGRAMS:
- **Camp Scholarships**
- **Dental Health**
- **Education**
- **Health and Welfare**

TYPE:
Capital grants. Awards grants for capital campaigns, capital items and renovation needs. Also, supports a number of health and welfare organizations, health projects, dental projects, special needs including blind, deaf and learning-disabled, elderly, children's hospitals, children's homes, youth organizations, youth and family services and summer camperships (summer enrichment programs).

YEAR PROGRAM STARTED: 1939

PURPOSE:
To support the education of poor and deserving students from rural communities; to relieve suffering through child welfare.

ELIGIBILITY:
Eligible organizations must be IRS 501(c)(3) tax-exempt and be located in the New England states of Maine, Massachusetts, New Hampshire and Vermont. The Trust does not fund in Connecticut or Rhode Island.

The Trust does not make grants to individuals.

The Trust rarely, if ever, approves grants for general operating funds, nor does it fund grant requests from public entities, municipalities, sectarian organizations, or individuals.

GEOG. RESTRICTIONS: Maine, Massachusetts, New Hampshire and Vermont.

FINANCIAL DATA:
$25,000,000 in assets for the year ended 2018.
Amount of support per award: $1,000 to $5,000.
Total amount of support: $953,520 in total grants for the year 2018.

NO. MOST RECENT APPLICANTS: 582 for the year 2018.

NO. AWARDS: Approximately 294 for the year 2018.

APPLICATION INFO:
Guidelines are available online. Application must be downloaded and e-mailed to either address listed above.
Duration: One year.
Deadline: Trustees meet monthly. It generally takes two months from time of submission of application to receipt of letter of decision.

IRS I.D.: 02-6004971

TRUSTEES:
Michael S. DeLucia
Ernest E. Dion
Alan G. Lampert

ADDRESS INQUIRIES TO:
Susan Bouchard, Administrative Director
(See address above.)

*PLEASE NOTE:
It is highly recommended that applicants review the information available online prior to submission of a grant proposal.

*SPECIAL STIPULATIONS:
If your organization is awarded a grant, the Trust requests that your organization wait one year before applying for future funding.

LOS ANGELES RAMS FOUNDATION [1030]
29899 Agoura Road
Agoura Hills, CA 91301
(818) 540-2016
Web Site: www.therams.com/community

FOUNDED: 1997

AREAS OF INTEREST:
Youth health, fitness and character education.

TYPE:
General operating grants; Project/program grants.

YEAR PROGRAM STARTED: 1997

PURPOSE:
To support programs designed to engage youth in activities that promote health, fitness and character development.

ELIGIBILITY:
Grants are made to organizations that have tax-exempt status under Section 501(c)(3) of the Internal Revenue Code. No unsolicited grants are accepted.

FINANCIAL DATA:
Since 1997, the Foundation has donated more than $10,000,000 in cash, grants, merchandise and tickets to area charities.
Amount of support per award: Varies based on program or project scope.

Total amount of support: Up to $250,000 annually.

NO. AWARDS: 30 to 50.

APPLICATION INFO:
Proposals are accepted by invitation only; however, letters and collateral material from potential grant recipients are welcome.

ADDRESS INQUIRIES TO:
Director of Community Outreach
(See address above.)

THE DR. JOHN T. MACDONALD FOUNDATION, INC.   [1031]

1550 Madruga Avenue, Suite 215
Coral Gables, FL 33146
(305) 667-6017
Fax: (305) 667-9135
E-mail: info@jtmacdonaldfdn.org
Web Site: www.jtmacdonaldfdn.org

FOUNDED: 1992

AREAS OF INTEREST:
Health education, prevention and early detection of disease, children, economically disadvantaged, and medical rehabilitation.

TYPE:
Project/program grants.

YEAR PROGRAM STARTED: 1992

PURPOSE:
To provide funding for programs and projects designed to improve, preserve or restore the health and health care of people in Miami-Dade County, FL.

LEGAL BASIS:
Private.

ELIGIBILITY:
Tax-exempt organizations that are registered to solicit funds under Florida law. The Foundation funds projects for medical and health-related programs. The Foundation does not fund national projects, multiyear funding requests, for-profit organizations, political candidates or campaigns, religious projects, support for individuals, or other grantmaking foundations.

GEOG. RESTRICTIONS: Miami-Dade County, Florida.

FINANCIAL DATA:
Amount of support per award: $5,000 to $50,000.
Total amount of support: $1,500,000 for the year 2019.

NO. AWARDS: 19, plus 4 scholarships and awards; 2 major multimillion-dollar awards.

APPLICATION INFO:
Letter of Inquiry must be filed electronically. Application information and instructions are available on the Foundation web site.
Deadline: Letters of inquiry are accepted February 1 to April 15.

PUBLICATIONS:
Program announcement; guidelines; application packet (online).

IRS I.D.: 59-0818918

ADDRESS INQUIRIES TO:
John Edward Smith
Managing Director
(See address above.)

MAURICE J. MASSERINI TRUST

c/o Wells Fargo Private Bank
4365 Executive Drive, 18th Floor
San Diego, CA 92121
(858) 622-6958
Fax: (858) 622-6848
E-mail: grantadministration@wellsfargo.com
Web Site: www.wellsfargo.com/private-foundations/masserini-trust

TYPE:
Project/program grants.

See entry 914 for full listing.

R.J. MCELROY TRUST   [1032]

425 Cedar Street, Suite 312
Waterloo, IA 50701-1351
(319) 287-9102
Fax: (319) 287-9105
E-mail: megan@mcelroytrust.org
Web Site: www.mcelroytrust.org

FOUNDED: 1965

AREAS OF INTEREST:
Education, children and youth.

TYPE:
Capital grants; Challenge/matching grants; General operating grants; Internships; Project/program grants; Scholarships; Seed money grants; Technical assistance.

PURPOSE:
To invest in nonprofit and public organizations that inspire and transform youth.

LEGAL BASIS:
Private.

ELIGIBILITY:
The Trust only supports programs, projects or endeavors that help young people. Applicant must be nonprofit or tax-exempt.

The Trust does not make grants to religious organizations for religious programming or to schools or school districts for one-to-one technology/computers for students.

GEOG. RESTRICTIONS: Allamakee, Black Hawk, Bremer, Buchanan, Butler, Chickasaw, Clayton, Delaware, Fayette, Grundy, Tama and Winneshiek counties, Iowa.

FINANCIAL DATA:
Amount of support per award: Varies per project.
Total amount of support: Approximately $1,900,000 for the year 2019.
Matching fund requirements: The Trust seldom funds 100% of a project.

NO. AWARDS: Approximately 60 per year.

APPLICATION INFO:
Applications are available online.
Duration: One year. Renewal possible.
Deadline: Applications accepted on a rolling basis.

IRS I.D.: 42-6173496

TRUSTEES:
Dr. Raleigh D. Buckmaster
Kathy Flynn
Sally Hollis
Robert Smith, Jr.
James B. Waterbury
Mike Young
Rick Young

STAFF:
Megan McKenzie, Executive Director
Shanlee McNally, Program Officer

ADDRESS INQUIRIES TO:
Megan McKenzie, Executive Director
(See address above.)

*PLEASE NOTE:
Contact the Executive Director before applying.

THE MCJ AMELIOR FOUNDATION   [1033]

310 South Street
Morristown, NJ 07960
(973) 540-1946

AREAS OF INTEREST:
Youths at risk, children, community empowerment and mentoring.

TYPE:
Challenge/matching grants; General operating grants; Project/program grants; Seed money grants.

LEGAL BASIS:
Private foundation.

ELIGIBILITY:
Applicants must be 501(c)(3) organizations.

GEOG. RESTRICTIONS: Newark, New Jersey.

FINANCIAL DATA:
Amount of support per award: Varies.
Total amount of support: Varies.

APPLICATION INFO:
The Foundation does not accept unsolicited proposals.
Duration: Varies.

STAFF:
Suzanne Spero, Executive Director
Christine C. Gilfillan, President

ADDRESS INQUIRIES TO:
Suzanne Spero, Executive Director
(See address above.)

MEBANE CHARITABLE FOUNDATION, INC.   [1034]

232 South Main Street
Mocksville, NC 27028
(336) 936-0041
Fax: (336) 936-0038
E-mail: lcolbourne@mebanefoundation.com
Web Site: www.mebanefoundation.com

FOUNDED: 1992

AREAS OF INTEREST:
Children's education.

NAME(S) OF PROGRAMS:
● **The Early Childhood Development Program**
● **Literacy Interventions PreK-3rd Grades**
● **The Teacher Training and Professional Development Program**

TYPE:
Project/program grants.

PURPOSE:
To teach children first to read then to further their education at all levels of learning, thereby attempting to break the cycle of poverty.

ELIGIBILITY:
Organizations qualified for exemption under Section 501(c)(3) of the IRS Code and not private foundations as defined by Section 509(a).

GEOG. RESTRICTIONS: Mainly North Carolina, Southeast.

FINANCIAL DATA:
Amount of support per award: $250 to $298,499.

Total amount of support: $2,027,150 for the year 2019.

NO. MOST RECENT APPLICANTS: Over 100 for the year 2019.

NO. AWARDS: 54.

APPLICATION INFO:
Organization must first complete a phone interview with the President to determine if their proposal is within the objectives and interest of the Foundation.

Duration: Varies.

Deadline: Application must be postmarked by July 1 for fall meeting of the board of directors, or by January 1 for spring meeting.

ADDRESS INQUIRIES TO:
Larry Colbourne, President
(See address above.)

NATIONAL FOOTBALL LEAGUE FOUNDATION

345 Park Avenue
New York, NY 10154
(212) 450-2000
E-mail: alexia.gallagher@nfl.com
Web Site: www.nflfoundation.org

TYPE:
Awards/prizes; Challenge/matching grants; General operating grants; Project/program grants; Research grants; Seed money grants; Training grants.

See entry 1220 for full listing.

NATIONAL FOSTER PARENT ASSOCIATION [1035]

1102 Prairie Ridge Trail
Pflugerville, TX 78660
(512) 686-1948
(800) 557-5238
Fax: (888) 925-5634
E-mail: info@nfpaonline.org
Web Site: www.nfpaonline.org

FOUNDED: 1972

AREAS OF INTEREST:
Foster parents and children in foster care.

NAME(S) OF PROGRAMS:
- **NFPA Youth Scholarship**
- **Walk Me Home Program**

TYPE:
Conferences/seminars; Scholarships. Scholarships for youth living in foster families whose foster parents are members of NFPA.

Walk Me Home Program is a walk program to raise awareness of foster care and the need for more foster families, as well as to raise funds for recruitment and other activities.

YEAR PROGRAM STARTED: 1972

PURPOSE:
To support foster youth and children of foster parents that wish to further their education beyond high school, including college or university studies, vocational and job training, and correspondence courses, including the GED.

LEGAL BASIS:
Nonprofit, volunteer organization established in 1972, with tax-exempt status under Section 501(c)(3) of the Internal Revenue Code.

ELIGIBILITY:
Must be a foster youth or an adoptive or birth child of foster parent members who is a college- or university-bound senior or is 17 years of age (either in school or out) in pursuit of vocational/job training/correspondence GED/other educational advancement.

GEOG. RESTRICTIONS: United States and territories.

FINANCIAL DATA:
Amount of support per award: $500.
Total amount of support: $2,500.

NO. MOST RECENT APPLICANTS: 23.

NO. AWARDS: 5 scholarships; 3 to foster children, 1 to an adoptive child, and 1 to a biological child of foster parents.

APPLICATION INFO:
Application is available from the Association at the address above. A minimum of two letters of recommendation and a typewritten statement of 300 to 500 words on "Why I want to further my education and why I should be considered for a National Foster Parent Association Scholarship" is also required.

Duration: Possible renewal.

Deadline: Applications must be postmarked on or before March 15.

IRS I.D.: 06-0894870

ADDRESS INQUIRIES TO:
Irene Clements, Executive Director
(See address above.)

NATIONAL JEWISH COMMITTEE ON SCOUTING

1325 West Walnut Hill Lane
Irving, TX 75038
(972) 580-2425
Fax: (972) 580-2535
E-mail: anthony.berger@scouting.org
Web Site: www.jewishscouting.org

TYPE:
Scholarships.

See entry 1557 for full listing.

ORLANDO MAGIC YOUTH FOUNDATION [1036]

8701 Maitland Summit Boulevard
Orlando, FL 32810
(407) 916-2400
Fax: (407) 916-2985
E-mail: omyf@orlandomagic.com
Web Site: www.omyf.org

FOUNDED: 1988

AREAS OF INTEREST:
Children and families at risk in central Florida in the areas of child and youth education, health and wellness with a specific focus on childhood obesity prevention, and homelessness.

TYPE:
Development grants; General operating grants; Project/program grants.

PURPOSE:
To nourish the minds and bodies of children who need it most in central Florida.

ELIGIBILITY:
Organizations must be classified as 501(c)(3) or 170(c)(3) by the IRS and have a constituency open to all segments of the community with a focus on low income. The Fund does not typically provide funding for private schools, legal aid societies, political, lobbying or advocacy groups, or capital requests for building and/or major improvements, except those for equipment/supplies that are critical to the delivery of a program or service.

GEOG. RESTRICTIONS: Orange, Osceola and Seminole counties, Florida.

FINANCIAL DATA:
Amount of support per award: $10,000 to $100,000.

Total amount of support: $1,000,000 annually.

NO. MOST RECENT APPLICANTS: 75.

NO. AWARDS: 15.

APPLICATION INFO:
Applicants are invited to submit Letter of Inquiry.

Duration: One year. May reapply.

Deadline: Letter of Inquiry: Late April.

LUCILE PACKARD FOUNDATION FOR CHILDREN'S HEALTH [1037]

400 Hamilton Avenue, Suite 340
Palo Alto, CA 94301
(650) 736-0675
(650) 497-8365
Fax: (650) 498-2619
E-mail: grants@lpfch.org
Web Site: www.lpfch-cshcn.org

FOUNDED: 1997

AREAS OF INTEREST:
Children's health.

TYPE:
Project/program grants.

YEAR PROGRAM STARTED: 2000

PURPOSE:
To promote the health and well-being of children through statewide and local partnerships; to improve the system of health care for children, especially those with chronic or complex health problems.

ELIGIBILITY:
Organizations must be 501(c)(3) nonprofit.

GEOG. RESTRICTIONS: California.

FINANCIAL DATA:
Amount of support per award: Varies.

NO. MOST RECENT APPLICANTS: 20.

NO. AWARDS: Varies.

APPLICATION INFO:
The Foundation generally invites specific applications for proposals. However, unsolicited proposals for projects that contribute to achieving the program's goals are welcome. Proposals initiated by applicants should be presented to the Foundation as a letter of inquiry. It is strongly recommended that applicants carefully review the program goals, priorities and restrictions before submitting a letter of inquiry.

Duration: Typically six months to two years.

ADDRESS INQUIRIES TO:
Jenny Ly, Grants Manager
(See address above.)

PARENTS WITHOUT PARTNERS

6798 Cheddar Valley Drive
Brighton, MI 48116
(810) 333-5920
(800) 637-7974
E-mail: pwpintoffice@gmail.com
Web Site: www.parentswithoutpartners.org

TYPE:
Scholarships.

See entry 1438 for full listing.

THE PINKERTON FOUNDATION   [1038]

610 Fifth Avenue
Suite 316
New York, NY 10020
(212) 332-3385
E-mail: grantsmanager@pinkertonfdn.org
Web Site: www.thepinkertonfoundation.org

FOUNDED: 1966

AREAS OF INTEREST:
After-school and summer learning, career
readiness, education, youth and family
justice.

TYPE:
General operating grants; Internships;
Project/program grants. Support for programs
that develop individual competencies, instill
values and increase opportunities to
participate in society.

Support for community-based programs with
preference given to projects for children,
youth and families that intervene before a
pattern of failure has been established.

YEAR PROGRAM STARTED: 1968

PURPOSE:
To improve the lives of young people in poor
neighborhoods throughout New York City.

LEGAL BASIS:
Not-for-profit corporation organized in the
state of Delaware in 1966.

ELIGIBILITY:
Grant applicants must be nonprofit public
charitable organizations which are tax-exempt
under Section 501(c)(3) of the Internal
Revenue Code. The Foundation does not
make grants to individuals or give loans or
emergency assistance, nor does it support
medical research or the direct provision of
health care or religious education. It
generally does not make grants to support
conferences, publications, media or to
building renovations or other capital projects,
unless they are integrally related to the
Foundation's program objectives or are an
outgrowth of one of its grantee's programs.

GEOG. RESTRICTIONS: New York, New York.

FINANCIAL DATA:
Amount of support per award: $25,000 to
$480,000; average $75,000.
Total amount of support: Approximately
$30,518,200.

NO. AWARDS: Approximately 250 annually.

APPLICATION INFO:
Applications must be submitted through the
Foundation's Grant Portal.
Duration: Usually up to three years.
Deadline: Letters of inquiry are accepted at
any time. Decisions are made immediately
following board meetings in May and
December.

OFFICERS:
Daniel L. Mosley, Chairman

Richard M. Smith, President
James Piereson, Treasurer
Marnie S. Pillsbury, Secretary

STAFF:
Laurie Dien, Vice President, Programs
Julie Peterson, Senior Program Officer
Jennifer Negron, Program Officer

ADDRESS INQUIRIES TO:
Yvonne Schonborg, Grants Manager
(See e-mail address above.)

PRITCHETT TRUST   [1039]

BMO Harris Bank
790 North Water Street, Floor 11
Milwaukee, WI 53202
(414) 287-7250
Fax: (414) 287-8580
E-mail: trust.custody@bmo.com

AREAS OF INTEREST:
Children, families and youth.

TYPE:
Project/program grants; Seed money grants.

YEAR PROGRAM STARTED: 1995

PURPOSE:
To improve the quality of life in Crawford
County and southeast Kansas by supporting
initiatives that serve these populations.

LEGAL BASIS:
Private trust.

ELIGIBILITY:
Applicants for grants must be located or
operating in southeastern Kansas and a
strong, if not exclusive, preference is given to
applicants located or operating in Crawford
County. The applicant must qualify as a
charitable organization described in Section
501(c)(3) of the Internal Revenue Code or as
a political subdivision of the State of Kansas
including municipalities, school districts and
Pittsburg State University.

GEOG. RESTRICTIONS: Southeast Kansas, with
an emphasis on Crawford County.

FINANCIAL DATA:
Amount of support per award: Varies.
Total amount of support: $400,000 to
$500,000.

NO. MOST RECENT APPLICANTS: 72.

NO. AWARDS: 43.

APPLICATION INFO:
Requests should be submitted in the form of
a one-page synopsis, together with a package
containing the full proposal.
Duration: One year. Renewal possible.
Deadline: June 1.

ADDRESS INQUIRIES TO:
BMO Trust and Custody Services
(See address above.)

RONALD MCDONALD HOUSE CHARITIES   [1040]

110 North Carpenter Street
Chicago, IL 60607
(630) 623-7048
E-mail: info@rmhc.org
Web Site: www.rmhc.org

FOUNDED: 1984

AREAS OF INTEREST:
Primarily, the health and well-being of
children.

NAME(S) OF PROGRAMS:
- **Africa and South Asia: Child and
  Maternal Health**
- **U.S. Grants: Children's Oral Health
  Care**

TYPE:
Challenge/matching grants; Grants-in-aid;
Project/program grants; Training grants.

YEAR PROGRAM STARTED: 1984

PURPOSE:
To directly improve the health and well-being
of children.

LEGAL BASIS:
Nonprofit, 501(c)(3) tax-exempt organization.

ELIGIBILITY:
Not-for-profit tax-exempt organizations,
based in the U.S. but operating either
domestically or internationally. Projects must
be sustainable and measurable. Proposed
projects must directly benefit children. No
grants to individuals, political campaigns,
secular religious activities, for salaries, travel
or ongoing expenses, or capital expenses.
Projects must include a "Train-the-Trainer"
component in the methodology.

Grant requests from organizations more
regional in nature will be referred to the
closest local chapter.

FINANCIAL DATA:
Amount of support per award: $100,000 and
up.
Total amount of support: Approximately
$4,000,000.

NO. MOST RECENT APPLICANTS: 150.

NO. AWARDS: 11.

REPRESENTATIVE AWARDS:
$169,043 over two years to Curamericas,
Liberia; $179,800 to Lwala Community
Alliance, Kenya; $627,637 to Resurge, Nepal
and India; $50,000 to Wyman Center, U.S.

APPLICATION INFO:
Application information is available on the
web site.
Duration: One-year to multiyear funding.

PUBLICATIONS:
Application form; annual report; application
guidelines.

BOARD OF TRUSTEES:
Steven Ramirez, Chairman of the Board
Sheila Musolino, President and Chief
Executive Officer

*SPECIAL STIPULATIONS:
Applications only accepted online.

HENRY AND RUTH BLAUSTEIN ROSENBERG FOUNDATION

One South Street, Suite 2900
Baltimore, MD 21202
(410) 347-7201
Fax: (410) 347-7210
E-mail: info@blaufund.org
Web Site: www.blaufund.org

TYPE:
Capital grants; General operating grants;
Project/program grants. Programs of benefit
to the underserved community in the
Baltimore, MD area.

See entry 1242 for full listing.

THE SAIGH FOUNDATION [1041]

231 South Bemiston Avenue
Suite 735
St. Louis, MO 63105
(314) 862-3055
Fax: (314) 862-9288
E-mail: saigh@thesaighfoundation.org
Web Site: thesaighfoundation.org

FOUNDED: 2000

AREAS OF INTEREST:
Children and youth in the field of education and health care in the St. Louis metropolitan area.

TYPE:
Development grants; Endowments; General operating grants; Internships; Project/program grants; Research grants; Scholarships; Technical assistance; Training grants.

PURPOSE:
To enhance the quality of life in St. Louis metropolitan region through support for charitable projects and initiatives which primarily benefit children and youth through education and health care.

LEGAL BASIS:
501(c)(3).

ELIGIBILITY:
St. Louis area nonprofit organizations benefiting children and youth in the areas of education and health care may apply.

GEOG. RESTRICTIONS: St. Louis, Missouri metropolitan area.

FINANCIAL DATA:
Amount of support per award: Varies.
Total amount of support: Varies.

NO. MOST RECENT APPLICANTS: Approximately 225.

APPLICATION INFO:
Applications are to be submitted using the Missouri Common Grant Application, which can be found on the Foundation's web site.
Deadline: January 15, April 15, July 15 and October 15.

STAFF:
Elke Buckland, Executive Director
Julie Hantman, Assistant Director

ADDRESS INQUIRIES TO:
Elke Buckland, Executive Director
(See address above.)

THE SCHUMANN FUND FOR NEW JERSEY [1042]

21 Van Vleck Street
Montclair, NJ 07042
(973) 509-9883
E-mail: astrickland@schumannfund.org
Web Site: fdnweb.org/schumann

FOUNDED: 1988

AREAS OF INTEREST:
Children and youth, education, racial and economic equity, and public policy (statewide) as well as social services in Essex County, NJ.

TYPE:
Demonstration grants; General operating grants; Project/program grants. Priorities include early childhood development, supporting efforts to heighten the chances of academic and social success for young children, especially the urban poor. Other focus areas include public policy and local activities directed at solving community problems, with particular concern for families with young children and education.

YEAR PROGRAM STARTED: 1988

LEGAL BASIS:
Tax-exempt, private foundation.

ELIGIBILITY:
Organizations seeking grants must be designated 501(c)(3) by the IRS. No applications for capital campaigns, annual giving, endowment, direct support of individuals and local programs in counties other than Essex. Projects in the arts, health care and housing development normally fall outside the Schumann Fund priority areas.

GEOG. RESTRICTIONS: New Jersey, with special emphasis on Essex County.

FINANCIAL DATA:
Amount of support per award: $15,000 to $50,000.
Total amount of support: Approximately $500,000.

APPLICATION INFO:
There is no standard application form to be used in presenting a request to the Schumann Fund. The Fund, however, encourages the use of the New York/New Jersey Common Application Form. A written proposal should be submitted which includes a detailed description of the purpose for which assistance is desired and the plan for accomplishment. The proposal should be accompanied by a copy of the organization's latest financial statement, an expense budget which identifies all sources of income, the project's time frame and future funding plans, a list of the organization's Board of Directors, IRS documents confirming the organization's status as a 501(c)(3) tax-exempt organization and not a private foundation, and the most recent audit.
Duration: Usually one year. Multiyear grants possible.
Deadline: January 15, April 15, July 15 and October 15.

PUBLICATIONS:
Annual report.

IRS I.D.: 52-1556076

TRUSTEES:
Anthony Cicatello
Leonard S. Coleman, Jr.
Christopher J. Daggett
Martha Day
Roger Pratt

EXECUTIVE DIRECTOR:
Annette Strickland

ADDRESS INQUIRIES TO:
Annette Strickland, Executive Director
(See address above.)

*PLEASE NOTE:
Grants are restricted to projects in New Jersey.

THE SEYBERT FOUNDATION [1043]

P.O. Box 52758
Philadelphia, PA 19115
(215) 821-8144
E-mail: admin@seybertfoundation.org
Web Site: www.seybertfoundation.org

FOUNDED: 1914

AREAS OF INTEREST:
Operating support for nonprofit organizations serving disadvantaged children and youth who are residents of the city of Philadelphia. The Institution is limited under the terms of the will setting up the fund to disadvantaged boys and girls of the city of Philadelphia only.

TYPE:
General operating grants.

LEGAL BASIS:
501(c)(3) charitable foundation.

ELIGIBILITY:
Grants are limited to nonprofit organizations serving disadvantaged young people through the high school ages who are residents of the city of Philadelphia. Grants are made to qualifying tax-exempt organizations under Sections 501(c)(3) and 509(a) of the Internal Revenue Code. Priority is given to organizations with operating budgets of less than $1,500,000.

GEOG. RESTRICTIONS: Philadelphia, Pennsylvania.

FINANCIAL DATA:
Amount of support per award: $10,000 per year.

NO. MOST RECENT APPLICANTS: 109 for the year 2018.

NO. AWARDS: 28 for the year 2018.

REPRESENTATIVE AWARDS:
Big Picture Alliance; Mighty Writers; Philadelphia Youth Basketball.

APPLICATION INFO:
Guidelines are available on the Foundation web site.
Duration: Two years.
Deadline: June 15. No more than one request will be considered per calendar year except under special circumstances.

PUBLICATIONS:
Application guidelines.

IRS I.D.: 23-6260105

OFFICERS AND BOARD OF DIRECTORS:
Marissa Meyers, Acting President
Matthew A. Grande, Treasurer
Cat Lavigne, Secretary
Noor Bowman
Landon Jones, Esq.
Miguel Morel
Cicely Peterson-Mangum, Esq.
Rich Sedmak
Deepa Vasudevan

ADDRESS INQUIRIES TO:
Theresa Jackson, Manager
(See address above.)

*PLEASE NOTE:
Grants must benefit poor boys and girls of the city of Philadelphia.

SIERRA HEALTH FOUNDATION

1321 Garden Highway
Sacramento, CA 95833
(916) 922-4755
Fax: (916) 922-4024
E-mail: info@sierrahealth.org
Web Site: www.sierrahealth.org

TYPE:
Project/program grants. Sponsorship. Specific to funding opportunities - solicited.

See entry 1377 for full listing.

SILICON VALLEY COMMUNITY FOUNDATION

2440 West El Camino Real
Suite 300
Mountain View, CA 94040-1498
(650) 450-5400
Fax: (650) 450-5401
E-mail: info@siliconvalleycf.org
Web Site: www.siliconvalleycf.org

TYPE:
General operating grants; Project/program grants; Scholarships; Seed money grants. Nonprofit organizations that provide services or programs related to the specific five grantmaking strategies in San Mateo and Santa Clara counties may be eligible to apply for funding from the Foundation's endowment. Scholarships for college-bound students are also open to application.

See entry 1257 for full listing.

STUART FOUNDATION [1044]

500 Washington Street
Eighth Floor
San Francisco, CA 94111
(415) 393-1551
Fax: (415) 568-9815
E-mail: info@stuartfoundation.org
Web Site: www.stuartfoundation.org

FOUNDED: 1985

NAME(S) OF PROGRAMS:
- **Education**

TYPE:
Development grants; General operating grants; Project/program grants; Research grants; Technical assistance; Training grants. Systematic change and collaborative service delivery.

YEAR PROGRAM STARTED: 1985

PURPOSE:
To provide a coordinated set of programs, activities, research, and policy analysis that improve opportunities for children and youth in California and Washington to become self-reliant, responsible and contributing members of their communities.

LEGAL BASIS:
Private foundation.

ELIGIBILITY:
No grants to individuals.

GEOG. RESTRICTIONS: California and Washington.

FINANCIAL DATA:
Amount of support per award: Average grant of $100,000.

Total amount of support: Approximately $16,000,000 annually.

APPLICATION INFO:
The Foundation does not accept unsolicited requests for funding.
Duration: Grants are approved for one year at a time, although projects can be funded for several years.

IRS I.D.: 20-0882784

BOARD MEMBERS:
Dwight L. Stuart, Jr., Chairman

ADDRESS INQUIRIES TO:
Jade Nelson, Grants and Operations Manager
(See address above.)

*PLEASE NOTE:
The Foundation does not accept unsolicited requests for funding.

SUBARU OF AMERICA FOUNDATION, INC.

One Subaru Drive
Camden, NJ 08103
(856) 488-5099
Fax: (856) 254-1367
E-mail: foundation@subaru.com
Web Site: www.subaru.com/about-subaru/subaru-foundation

TYPE:
General operating grants; Project/program grants. Employee matching gift program.

See entry 1441 for full listing.

THE FRANK M. TAIT FOUNDATION [1045]

40 North Main Street
Suite 1530
Dayton, OH 45423
(937) 222-2401
E-mail: taitfoundation@gmail.com

FOUNDED: 1955

AREAS OF INTEREST:
Early childhood development, youth development and cultural activities for underserved youth.

TYPE:
Project/program grants. Focus on youth development, particularly early childhood development.

YEAR PROGRAM STARTED: 1956

PURPOSE:
To provide programs that develop youth (particularly early childhood development programs); to provide cultural enrichment experiences for underserved youth.

LEGAL BASIS:
Ohio corporation, not for profit.

ELIGIBILITY:
Organizations must be exempt under 501(c)(3). No private foundations.

The Foundation does not fund:
(1) medical research or equipment;
(2) operating budgets or annual fund drives;
(3) emergency requests for crash programs;
(4) endowment funds;
(5) religious programs or activities or;
(6) lobbying or propaganda activities.

GEOG. RESTRICTIONS: Montgomery County, Ohio.

FINANCIAL DATA:
Amount of support per award: Typically $5,000 to $50,000.

Total amount of support: $345,675 for the year 2017.

APPLICATION INFO:
Must contact the Executive Director at the phone number or e-mail address above to discuss the prospective grant proposal and to obtain approval for its subsequent submission.
Duration: Usually one year. Reapply for renewal.
Deadline: Requests are reviewed quarterly. Contact the Executive Director at the phone number above to confirm deadlines.

PUBLICATIONS:
Guidelines.

IRS I.D.: 31-6037499

ADDRESS INQUIRIES TO:
Jenni Roer, Executive Director
(See address above.)

TURRELL FUND [1046]

21 Van Vleck Street
Montclair, NJ 07042-2358
(973) 783-9358
E-mail: turrell@turrellfund.org
Web Site: www.turrellfund.org

FOUNDED: 1935

AREAS OF INTEREST:
Agencies rendering direct services to at-risk children in the state of Vermont, and, primarily, in the New Jersey counties of Essex, Hudson, Passaic and Union; policy initiatives for the very young child. While there are exceptions, the Fund's emphasis is on programs serving children, from birth to five years of age, and advocacy programs which support children in the same age range.

TYPE:
General operating grants; Project/program grants.

YEAR PROGRAM STARTED: 1935

PURPOSE:
To financially and strategically support organizations which directly provide or foster the creation and delivery of high-quality, developmental and educational services to at-risk children, especially the youngest and their families in Vermont and designated areas of New Jersey.

LEGAL BASIS:
Tax-exempt private foundation.

ELIGIBILITY:
Tax-exempt 501(c)(3) organizations in New Jersey and Vermont only may apply. In New Jersey, emphasis is on northern urban areas centered in Essex, Hudson, Passaic and Union counties only. No grants are awarded for lobbying, endowments or research. No grants to individuals and most hospital work and health delivery services. Only organizations providing direct services and advocacy for children and youth are eligible.

GEOG. RESTRICTIONS: Essex, Hudson, Passaic and Union counties, New Jersey and Vermont.

FINANCIAL DATA:
Amount of support per award: $1,000 to $350,000; $16,000 average grant.

Total amount of support: Approximately $4,600,000.

NO. MOST RECENT APPLICANTS: Approximately 400 per year.

NO. AWARDS: Approximately 250 per year.

APPLICATION INFO:
Applications are accepted online only. Scanned into the proposal should be the following:
(1) a brief letter describing the project;
(2) a copy of the IRS letter granting tax exemption;
(3) operating and project budgets and;
(4) either a 990 form or audited statement from most recent year available.

The proposal should include:
(1) background information about the organization;
(2) identification of board members;
(3) staff qualifications;

(4) a financial report;
(5) current budget and;
(6) project costs.

Duration: One year.

Deadline: August 1 and February 1. Announcement in early June and early December.

PUBLICATIONS:
Annual report.

IRS I.D.: 22-1551936

OFFICERS:
S. Lawrence Prendergast, Chairman of the Board
Richard A. Rubio, Treasurer
Curtland E. Fields, Secretary
Kim Keiser, Assistant Secretary

TRUSTEES:
Robert E. Angelica
Elizabeth W. Christie
Curtland E. Fields
Rev. William S. Gannon
William H. Hammond, Jr.
Matthew E. Melmed
Dr. Julia A. Miller
Rev. Dr. John P. Mitchell
John Morning
S. Lawrence Prendergast
Mark Sustic

ADDRESS INQUIRIES TO:
Curtland E. Fields
President and Chief Executive Officer
(See address above.)

U.S. DEPARTMENT OF HEALTH AND HUMAN SERVICES   [1047]

Administration for Children and Families
300 C Street, S.W., 4th Floor
Washington, DC 20024
(866) 763-6481
(202) 205-8573
Fax: (202) 205-9721
E-mail: headstart@eclkc.info
Web Site: www.acf.hhs.gov/ohs

NAME(S) OF PROGRAMS:
● Head Start

TYPE:
Project/program grants. Grants for comprehensive programs focused primarily upon children from low-income families who have not reached the age of compulsory school attendance. Supported projects should involve:
(1) comprehensive health (including medical and dental examinations), nutritional, social, psychological, educational and mental health services;
(2) appropriate activities to encourage and provide opportunities for participation of parents and effective use of provided services and;
(3) other pertinent training, technical assistance, evaluation and follow-through activities.

YEAR PROGRAM STARTED: 1965

PURPOSE:
To promote school readiness for children in low-income families by offering educational, nutritional, health, social and other services.

LEGAL BASIS:
Omnibus Budget and Reconciliation Act of 1981 (Public Law 97-35).

ELIGIBILITY:
Public or private nonprofit organizations, including community-based and faith-based organizations, or for-profit agencies within a community that wish to compete for funds, are eligible to apply.

FINANCIAL DATA:
Federal funds may not exceed 80% except in certain limited situations where grantees may be relieved of all or part of the nonfederal share.

Amount of support per award: Varies.

Total amount of support: $9,838,693,013 (federal appropriation) for fiscal year 2018.

Matching fund requirements: Grantees are required to provide 20% of the total cost of the project.

APPLICATION INFO:
Applications from organizations which are not current grantees are accepted only in response to announcements in the *Federal Register.* Applicants for a Head Start grant should contact the Health and Human Services regional office in their area. Parents wishing to enroll their children should consult the local Head Start Program in their Community.

U.S. DEPARTMENT OF HEALTH AND HUMAN SERVICES   [1048]

Administration for Children and Families
Family and Youth Services Bureau
330 C Street, S.W.
Washington, DC 20201
(202) 205-8102
Fax: (202) 260-9333
E-mail: requests@ncfy.com
Web Site: www.acf.hhs.gov/fysb

FOUNDED: 1974

AREAS OF INTEREST:
Crisis and referral services for runaway and homeless youth.

NAME(S) OF PROGRAMS:
● Runaway and Homeless Youth (RHY) Programs

TYPE:
Development grants; General operating grants; Project/program grants; Technical assistance. Title III of the Juvenile Justice and Delinquency Prevention Act of 1974, et seq., to authorize the Runaway and Homeless Youth Program.

Basic Center, Street Outreach, and Transitional Living are components of this Program.

Through Basic Center, the Bureau provides financial assistance to establish or strengthen community-based programs that address the immediate needs of runaway and homeless youth and their families. These programs are designed to provide youth with emergency shelter, food, clothing, counseling and referrals for health care.

Through Street Outreach, the Bureau awards grants to private, nonprofit agencies to conduct outreach designed to build relationships between grantee staff and street youth. These efforts are intended to help young people leave the streets.

Through Transitional Living, the Bureau targets LGBTQ projects that provide longer-term residential services to homeless youth, 16 to 21 years of age, for up to 18 months. Services are intended to help homeless youth make a successful transition to self-sufficient living. Transitional Living also supports youth maternity group home.

YEAR PROGRAM STARTED: 1974

PURPOSE:
To establish or strengthen locally controlled community programs that address the immediate needs of runaway and homeless youth and their families. Services must be provided outside of the law enforcement, juvenile justice system, child welfare or mental health. The program is designed to alleviate problems of RHY youth, reunite youth with their families, and encourage the resolution of intrafamily problems through counseling and other services, strengthen family relationships and encourage stable living conditions for youth and help youth decide upon constructive courses of action.

ELIGIBILITY:
Grants are available to states, localities, nonprofit private agencies, coordinated networks and Indian Tribes.

GEOG. RESTRICTIONS: United States and its territories.

FINANCIAL DATA:
Amount of support per award: Basic Center: $50,000 to $200,000; Street Outreach: $90,000 to $150,000; Transitional Living: $100,000 to $250,000.

Total amount of support: Over $28,000,000 for the year 2019.

NO. MOST RECENT APPLICANTS: Varies.

NO. AWARDS: Basic Center: 89; Street Outreach: 52; Transitional Living: 18.

APPLICATION INFO:
Guidelines available on the web site.

Duration: Three years for Basic Center and Street Outreach. Five years for Transitional Living.

Deadline: July.

ADDRESS INQUIRIES TO:
National Clearinghouse on Families and Youth
8120 Woodmont Avenue, Suite 850
Bethesda, MD 20814

U.S. DEPARTMENT OF HEALTH AND HUMAN SERVICES   [1049]

Administration for Children and Families
Children's Bureau
330 C Street, S.W.
Washington, DC 20201
(202) 205-8618
Fax: (202) 205-9721
Web Site: www.acf.hhs.gov/cb

AREAS OF INTEREST:
Adoption, child abuse and neglect, child welfare services, foster care, guardianship and tribes.

NAME(S) OF PROGRAMS:
● Child Welfare Waiver Demonstration Projects
● Discretionary Grant Programs
● State & Tribal Grant Programs

TYPE:
Formula grants; Project/program grants. The Child Welfare Waiver Demonstration authority provides states with an opportunity to use federal funds more flexibly in order to test innovative approaches to child welfare service delivery and financing. The states can design and demonstrate a wide range of approaches to reforming child welfare and improving outcomes in the areas of safety, permanency, and well-being.

Discretionary Grants are awarded for research and program development through a competitive peer-review process, to State, Tribal and local agencies, faith-based and community-based organizations, and other nonprofit and for-profit groups.

State & Tribal Grant Programs provide matching funds to States and Tribes to help them operate every aspect of their child welfare systems - from prevention of child abuse and neglect to adoption and the information systems necessary to support these programs.

PURPOSE:
To fund projects, programs and research that serve children, families or the community to states, territories and tribes.

ELIGIBILITY:
Discretionary Grants: States, local governments, tribes, public agencies or private agencies or organizations with expertise in providing technical assistance related to family preservation, family support, time-limited family reunification and adoption promotion and support.

State & Tribal Grant Programs: States, territories and certain Indian Tribes are eligible.

FINANCIAL DATA:
Amount of support per award: Varies.
Total amount of support: Varies.

APPLICATION INFO:
ACF requires electronic submission of applications. Information on applying electronically is available at Grants.gov. Applicants who do not have an Internet connection or sufficient capacity to upload large files to the Internet may contact ACF for an exception that will allow these applicants to submit an application in paper format.

Duration: Discretionary Grants are generally for a 12-, 24- or 36-month period; some may be renewed for up to five years.

Deadline: Contact the headquarters or regional office, as appropriate, for application deadlines.

ADDRESS INQUIRIES TO:
Catherine Heath, Program Specialist
(See address above.)

U.S. DEPARTMENT OF JUSTICE

Office of Juvenile Justice and
Delinquency Prevention
810 Seventh Street, N.W., 7th Floor
Washington, DC 20531
(202) 307-5911
Fax: (202) 353-9093
E-mail: lynnell.clarke@usdoj.gov
Web Site: www.ojjdp.gov

TYPE:
Block grants; Challenge/matching grants; Demonstration grants; Formula grants; Internships; Project/program grants; Research grants; Technical assistance; Training grants. Grants to increase the capacity of state and local governments to conduct effective juvenile justice and delinquency prevention programs as developed in the state comprehensive action plan.

See entry 1292 for full listing.

USDA FOOD AND NUTRITION SERVICE   [1050]

Child Nutrition Service
3101 Park Center Drive, Room 628
Alexandria, VA 22302
(703) 305-2054
Fax: (703) 305-2879
Web Site: www.fns.usda.gov

FOUNDED: 1969

AREAS OF INTEREST:
Child nutrition.

NAME(S) OF PROGRAMS:
- **The Child and Adult Care Food Program**
- **The Fresh Fruit and Vegetable Program**
- **The National School Lunch Program**
- **The School Breakfast Program**
- **The Special Milk Program**
- **The Summer Food Service Program**

TYPE:
Formula grants; Grants-in-aid; Project/program grants. Reimbursement for the support of food service in schools, child and adult care institutions to improve nutrition.

The Child and Adult Care Food Program helps child care facilities and institutions serve nutritious meals and snacks to preschool and school-age children. To participate, facilities and institutions must be licensed or approved to provide child care services. They must also meet certain other eligibility requirements. The program operates in nonresidential day care centers, settlement houses, outside-school-hours care centers, family day care homes, institutions providing day care for handicapped children and others. Participating facilities and institutions get cash assistance, USDA-donated foods and technical guidance. In child care centers, the amount of cash assistance varies according to the family size and income of children served. In day care homes, the amount of cash assistance is based on a food service payment rate. Similar benefits are also now available to adult day care centers which serve functionally impaired adults or persons 60 years of age or older.

The Fresh Fruit and Vegetable Program introduces school children to a variety of produce that they otherwise might not have the opportunity to sample. The goal is to improve children's overall diet and create healthier eating habits to impact their present and future health.

The National School Lunch Program makes well-planned nutritious meals available to school children. Any public or nonprofit private schools of high school grade or under and licensed public or nonprofit private residential child care institutions are eligible to participate in the National School Lunch and School Breakfast Programs. Schools that participate are required to provide free and reduced-price meals to children unable to pay the full price. Eligibility is based on application information submitted by a parent or guardian. The household income limit for free lunches is set at or below 130% of the federal poverty level and for reduced price lunches household income must be above 130% or at or below 185% of the federal poverty level. Children from households not eligible for free or reduced-price meals must pay the school's full price charge for lunch.

Cash and donated commodities are provided to participating schools and institutions according to the number of meals served.

The School Breakfast Program makes nutritious breakfasts available to school children under the same eligibility guidelines and general requirements as the National School Lunch Program.

The Special Milk Program makes it possible for all children attending a participating school or institution to purchase milk at a reduced price or receive it free, if they are eligible. Reimbursement is provided for each half-pint of milk served under the program. Schools and institutions that participate in other federal child nutrition programs authorized under the National School Lunch Act or the Child Nutrition Act of 1966 may not participate in the Special Milk Program, except for split-session kindergarten programs conducted in schools in which the children do not have access to the other meal program.

The Summer Food Service Program helps communities serve meals to needy children when school is not in session. The program is sponsored by public or private nonprofit school food authorities or local, municipal, county or state governments. Public or private nonprofit residential camps, other private nonprofit organizations, colleges and universities which participate in the National Youth Sports Program also may be sponsors. The program operates in areas in which at least 50% of the children meet the income criteria for free and reduced-price school meals. USDA reimburses sponsors for operating costs of food services up to a specified maximum rate for each meal served. In addition, sponsors receive some reimbursement for planning, operating and supervising expenses.

YEAR PROGRAM STARTED: 1946

PURPOSE:
To help safeguard the health and well-being of the nation's children and to encourage the domestic consumption of nutritious agricultural commodities and other foods.

LEGAL BASIS:
The National School Lunch Act as amended and the Child Nutrition Act of 1966, as amended.

ELIGIBILITY:
Family size and number of children based on income poverty levels.

GEOG. RESTRICTIONS: United States and its territories.

FINANCIAL DATA:
Amount of support per award: Varies.
Total amount of support: Varies.
Matching fund requirements: Varies.

APPLICATION INFO:
Official application materials are available upon request to state educational agencies or other state-designated agency. In states where education agencies do not administer the programs for nonprofit private schools, contact the appropriate Food and Nutrition Service Regional Office of the Department of Agriculture for more information.

Deadline: Applications are accepted throughout the year.

VETERANS OF FOREIGN WARS AUXILIARY
National Headquarters
406 West 34th Street, 10th Floor
Kansas City, MO 64111
(816) 561-8655
Fax: (816) 931-4753
E-mail: info@vfwauxiliary.org
Web Site: vfwauxiliary.org

TYPE:
Awards/prizes.

See entry 474 for full listing.

JOSEPH B. WHITEHEAD FOUNDATION [1051]
191 Peachtree Street, Suite 3540
Atlanta, GA 30303
(404) 522-6755
Fax: (404) 522-7026
E-mail: fdns@woodruff.org
Web Site: jbwhitehead.org

FOUNDED: 1937

AREAS OF INTEREST:
Human services, public education, children and youth services, and early childhood education.

TYPE:
Capital grants; General operating grants; Project/program grants.

LEGAL BASIS:
Private foundation.

ELIGIBILITY:
Organization must:
(1) be a 501(c)(3) charity;
(2) be located or operating in metropolitan Atlanta, as defined by the United Way of Greater Atlanta to include Butts, Cherokee, Clayton, Cobb, Coweta, DeKalb, Douglas, Fayette, Fulton, Gwinnett, Henry, Paulding, and Rockdale counties and;
(3) align with the Foundation's program interests in early childhood education, K-12 education, children and youth, human services, or health.

GEOG. RESTRICTIONS: Metropolitan Atlanta, Georgia.

FINANCIAL DATA:
Amount of support per award: $40,000 to $15,000,000 for the year 2019.
Total amount of support: $62,868,379 for the year 2019.

NO. MOST RECENT APPLICANTS: 57 for the year 2019.

NO. AWARDS: 42 for the year 2019.

APPLICATION INFO:
Applicants are encouraged to review the eligibility requirements, grantmaking guidelines and program interests and submit an informal inquiry to the Foundation's e-mail address to determine grant eligibility before submitting a formal request. Formal proposals should be submitted through the online grant portal and should include the following information:
(1) a description of the organization, its purposes, programs, staffing and governing board;
(2) organization's latest financial statements, including the most recent report;
(3) a description of the proposed project and full justification for its funding;
(4) an itemized project budget, including other sources of support in hand anticipated and;

(5) evidence from the IRS of the organization's tax-exempt status and the applying organization itself is not a private foundation.
Duration: One year.
Deadline: February 1 and August 15.

TRUSTEES:
E. Jenner Wood, III, Chairman
Lawrence L. Gellerstedt, III, Vice Chairman

OFFICERS:
P. Russell Hardin, President
Erik S. Johnson, Secretary and Treasurer

ADDRESS INQUIRIES TO:
P. Russell Hardin, President
(See address above.)

WIDENER MEMORIAL FOUNDATION IN AID OF HANDICAPPED CHILDREN
4060 Butler Pike
Suite 225
Plymouth Meeting, PA 19462
(610) 825-8900
Fax: (610) 825-8904
E-mail: jhagerty@erdixon.com

TYPE:
Capital grants.

See entry 936 for full listing.

Community development and services

ABEL FOUNDATION [1052]
1815 Y Street
Lincoln, NE 68508
(402) 434-1212
Fax: (402) 434-1799
Web Site: www.abelfoundation.org

AREAS OF INTEREST:
Health and human services, higher education and community development programs.

TYPE:
Capital grants; Matching gifts; Project/program grants.

PURPOSE:
To improve the quality of life, particularly in communities where the company has facilities.

ELIGIBILITY:
Grants are made to organizations that have tax-exempt status under Section 501(c)(3) of the Internal Revenue Code. No grants are made to individuals.

GEOG. RESTRICTIONS: Nebraska, particularly Lincoln.

FINANCIAL DATA:
Amount of support per award: Varies.
Total amount of support: $820,400 for the year 2018.

APPLICATION INFO:
Applicants are requested to use the Lincoln/Lancaster County Grant Maker Common Application Form.
Duration: One year. Renewal possible.
Deadline: March 31, July 15 and October 31. Foundation meets in May, September and December, respectively, to review funding requests.

ADDRESS INQUIRIES TO:
J. Ross McCown, Vice President
(See address above.)

AKRON COMMUNITY FOUNDATION [1053]
345 West Cedar Street
Akron, OH 44307-2407
(330) 376-8522
Fax: (330) 376-0202
E-mail: jgarofalo@akroncf.org
Web Site: www.akroncf.org

FOUNDED: 1955

AREAS OF INTEREST:
Arts and culture, civic affairs, health and human services, and education.

TYPE:
Capital grants; General operating grants; Project/program grants; Scholarships; Seed money grants.

YEAR PROGRAM STARTED: 1955

PURPOSE:
To embrace and enhance the work of charitable people who make a permanent commitment to the good of the community.

LEGAL BASIS:
Community foundation.

ELIGIBILITY:
Organizations must be tax-exempt.

GEOG. RESTRICTIONS: Summit County, Ohio.

FINANCIAL DATA:
Assets of $220,710,000 for the year ended December 31, 2019.
Amount of support per award: Average $14,000 to $18,000.
Total amount of support: $10,444,435 for the year 2019.

CO-OP FUNDING PROGRAMS: City of Akron Neighborhood Partnership.

NO. AWARDS: 1,516 for the year 2019.

APPLICATION INFO:
Applicants must contact the Foundation before submitting an application.
Duration: One year.
Deadline: Arts and Culture: April 1; Civic Affairs: July 1; Health and Human Services: October 1; Education: December 15.

PUBLICATIONS:
Guidelines.

IRS I.D.: 34-1087615

ADDRESS INQUIRIES TO:
John F. Garofalo
Vice President of Community Investment
(See address above.)

ALBION COMMUNITY FOUNDATION [1054]
P.O. Box 156
Albion, MI 49224-0156
(517) 629-3349
Fax: (517) 629-8027
E-mail: foundation@albionfoundation.org
Web Site: www.albionfoundation.org

FOUNDED: 1969

AREAS OF INTEREST:
Promoting philanthropy addressing community needs through grantmaking, and providing leadership on key community issues.

TYPE:
Capital grants; Challenge/matching grants;
Development grants; Project/program grants.

PURPOSE:
To provide a favorable ratio between the
amount of money requested and the number
of people served, show innovation and
creativity in addressing a community need
that demonstrates careful planning that
provides for successful completion of the
project.

LEGAL BASIS:
501(c)(3).

ELIGIBILITY:
Any nonprofit charity, as defined by Sections
501(c)(3) and 509(a) of the Internal Revenue
Code, located within the greater Albion area
or directly serving residents of the greater
Albion area is eligible to apply for funding.
Faith institutions, public entities, and schools
directly serving the great Albion area
community are also eligible for specific
projects subject to restrictions.

GEOG. RESTRICTIONS: Greater Albion, Michigan
area.

FINANCIAL DATA:
Amount of support per award: $150 to
$10,000, depending on the fund.
Total amount of support: Approximately
$80,000 to $100,000 each year.

APPLICATION INFO:
Details and application forms are available
online. One complete, hard copy of the
application and attachments, with original
signatures, can be sent to the Foundation at
the address above. Alternatively, electronic
applications are accepted through the
Foundation's web site.
Deadline: January 10, March 10, May 10 and
September 10.

ALBUQUERQUE COMMUNITY FOUNDATION   [1055]

624 Tijeras, N.W.
Albuquerque, NM 87102
(505) 883-6240
Fax: (505) 883-3629
E-mail: joanna@abqcf.org
Web Site: www.albuquerquefoundation.org

FOUNDED: 1981

AREAS OF INTEREST:
Arts and culture, education, environmental
and historic preservation, economic and
workforce development, health and human
services.

TYPE:
Challenge/matching grants; General operating
grants; Project/program grants; Scholarships;
Seed money grants; Technical assistance.

YEAR PROGRAM STARTED: 1983

PURPOSE:
To improve the quality of life in the greater
Albuquerque area by providing support for
projects and organizations that serve the
community.

LEGAL BASIS:
Community foundation.

ELIGIBILITY:
Grants are made to nonprofit organizations.
Foundation grants are generally not made to
individuals, for political or religious
purposes, to retire indebtedness, for the
payment of interest or taxes, annual

campaigns, endowments, emergency funding,
to influence legislation or elections, to private
foundations and other grantmaking
organizations, or to organizations that
discriminate on the basis of race, creed or
sex.

GEOG. RESTRICTIONS: Albuquerque, New
Mexico.

FINANCIAL DATA:
Amount of support per award: Varies.
Total amount of support: Varies.

APPLICATION INFO:
Current guidelines and criteria are available
on the web site.
Duration: One year.

PUBLICATIONS:
Report to the Community.

IRS I.D.: 85-0295444

STAFF:
Randy Royster, President and Chief
Executive Officer
Joanna Colangelo, Vice President of
Community Impact
Kelli Cooper, Vice President of Philanthropic
Services
Nick Williams, Finance Director

BOARD OF TRUSTEES:
William P. Lang, Chairperson
Steve Maestas, Chairperson-elect
Beverly R. Bendicksen, Treasurer
Debbie Johnson, Secretary
Patrick Apodaca
Carl M. Alongi
Arellana Cordero
Kathleen D. Davis
Paul DiPaola
Anna Doss
William E. Ebel
Glenn Fellows
Debbie Harmes
Rebecca Harrington
Pam Hurd-Knief
Albert T. Jorgensen
Steven W. Keene
Kenneth C. Leach
Marcus Mims, C.P.A.
Linda H. Parker
Jerrald J. Roehl
Anne Sapon
Charlotte Schoenmann
George Stanfield
Walter E. Stern
Jose Viramontes

ADDRESS INQUIRIES TO:
Joanna Colangelo, Vice President of
Community Impact
(See address above.)

ALGER REGIONAL COMMUNITY FOUNDATION   [1056]

P.O. Box 39
Munising, MI 49862
(906) 387-3900
E-mail: algercf@yahoo.com
Web Site: www.algercf.com

FOUNDED: 1992

AREAS OF INTEREST:
Cultural arts, community service, education,
the environment and conservation, health and
human services, and youth.

TYPE:
Endowments; Project/program grants;
Scholarships.

YEAR PROGRAM STARTED: 1995

PURPOSE:
To provide support to organizations that
enhance the quality of life in Alger County.

ELIGIBILITY:
Grants are made to organizations that have
tax-exempt status under Section 501(c)(3) of
the Internal Revenue Code. Nonsectarian
religious programs may apply. Organizations
must serve or be located in Alger County,
MI. No grants are made to individuals.

GEOG. RESTRICTIONS: Alger County, Michigan.

FINANCIAL DATA:
Amount of support per award: Varies.

APPLICATION INFO:
Foundation staff members are available to
talk with potential applicants who are
interested in learning about opportunities and
needs in the community.

ALLEGAN COUNTY COMMUNITY FOUNDATION   [1057]

112 Locust Street
Allegan, MI 49010
(269) 673-8344
E-mail: theresa.accf@gmail.com
Web Site: www.alleganfoundation.org

FOUNDED: 1965

AREAS OF INTEREST:
Education, health and human services,
culture, community development,
environmental issues and art.

TYPE:
General operating grants; Project/program
grants; Scholarships; Technical assistance.
Grants fall into the following categories:
youth and general.

PURPOSE:
To positively impact the Allegan County
community through the establishment of
permanently endowed funds.

LEGAL BASIS:
Community foundation.

ELIGIBILITY:
Applications accepted from charitable
organizations serving Allegan County, MI
residents. No funding for individuals except
for scholarships.

GEOG. RESTRICTIONS: Allegan County,
Michigan.

FINANCIAL DATA:
Amount of support per award: $500 to
$20,000.

APPLICATION INFO:
Applications must include a copy of the IRS
501(c)(3) tax determination letter.
Duration: One year.
Deadline: TAG: First Friday in September;
Legacy: December.

IRS I.D.: 38-6189947

ADDRESS INQUIRIES TO:
Theresa Bray, Executive Director
(See address above.)

*SPECIAL STIPULATIONS:
Potential applicants must meet with the
Executive Director before receiving the grant
application(s). .

ALTMAN FOUNDATION [1058]

8 West 40th Street
19th Floor
New York, NY 10018-2263
(212) 682-0970
Fax: (212) 682-1648
E-mail: info@altman.org
Web Site: www.altmanfoundation.org

FOUNDED: 1913

AREAS OF INTEREST:
Strengthening communities, health,
education, independent and non-public
schools, arts and culture.

TYPE:
Project/program grants.

YEAR PROGRAM STARTED: 1913

PURPOSE:
To support programs and organizations
within the five boroughs of New York City
working in the Foundation's four program
areas.

LEGAL BASIS:
Private foundation.

ELIGIBILITY:
Must have a current IRS 501(c)(3)
tax-exemption letter. No grants to individuals.
No grants for bricks and mortar or capital
equipment.

GEOG. RESTRICTIONS: Five boroughs of New
York City.

FINANCIAL DATA:
Amount of support per award: Varies.
Total amount of support: Varies.

NO. MOST RECENT APPLICANTS: Approximately
300.

APPLICATION INFO:
Applicants should review material on the
Foundation's web site regarding funding
approach, guidelines, limitations and
procedures.
Duration: One year. Renewal possible.

PUBLICATIONS:
Annual report.

IRS I.D.: 13-1623879

STAFF:
Deborah T. Velazquez, President
Megan McAllister, Senior Program Officer
Rachael N. Pine, J.D., Senior Program
Officer

ADDRESS INQUIRIES TO:
Deborah T. Velasquez, President
(See address above.)

AMARILLO AREA FOUNDATION [1059]

801 South Fillmore
Suite 700
Amarillo, TX 79101
(806) 376-4521
Fax: (806) 373-3656
E-mail: kathie@aaf-hf.org
Web Site: www.amarilloareafoundation.org

FOUNDED: 1957

AREAS OF INTEREST:
Community, arts and culture, education,
health and human services, teen pregnancy
prevention, youth-oriented programs and
elderly services.

TYPE:
Project/program grants; Scholarships.
Discretionary grants.

PURPOSE:
To exercise leadership on charitable issues,
advance the cause of philanthropy throughout
the region and promote efficient and effective
delivery of services from nonprofit
organizations.

LEGAL BASIS:
501(c)(3).

ELIGIBILITY:
No grants to individuals. Scholarships go to
educational institutions.

GEOG. RESTRICTIONS: 26 northernmost counties
in the Texas panhandle.

FINANCIAL DATA:
Amount of support per award: $20,000 to
$250,000.
Total amount of support: Varies.

APPLICATION INFO:
Contact Grants Coordinator for counseling
prior to submitting application. Application is
available online for download as a Word
document.
Duration: Typically one year.

ADDRESS INQUIRIES TO:
Kathie Grant, Grant Administrator
(See address above.)

AMERICAN PLANNING ASSOCIATION

205 North Michigan Avenue
Suite 1200
Chicago, IL 60601
(312) 786-6345
E-mail: foundation@planning.org
Web Site: www.planning.
org/foundation/scholarships

TYPE:
Scholarships.

See entry 894 for full listing.

AMERICAN PLANNING ASSOCIATION [1060]

205 North Michigan Avenue
Suite 1200
Chicago, IL 60601
(312) 786-6705
E-mail: foundation@planning.org
Web Site: www.planning.
org/foundation/scholarships

FOUNDED: 1909

AREAS OF INTEREST:
Urban and regional planning and promotion
of the art and science of planning.

NAME(S) OF PROGRAMS:
● **Charles Abrams Scholarship Program**

TYPE:
Scholarships. For a student enrolled in a
graduate planning program, leading to a
Master's degree, who attends one of the
following schools:
(1) Columbia University, Division of Urban
Planning;
(2) Harvard University, Urban Planning
Program, Harvard Graduate School of
Design;
(3) Massachusetts Institute of Technology,
Department of Urban Studies and Planning;
(4) New School University, Urban Policy
Analysis and Management Program, Robert
J. Milano Graduate School of Management
and Urban Policy or;
(5) University of Pennsylvania, Department
of City and Regional Planning.

PURPOSE:
To aid students who will pursue careers as
practicing planners.

LEGAL BASIS:
Private, nonprofit educational association.

ELIGIBILITY:
An applicant must be a U.S. citizen and have
been accepted into the graduate planning
program of one of the five eligible schools.
Incoming students are eligible. An applicant
must be in need of financial assistance, as
determined by a review of the applicant's
financial needs. A nomination by the
department chair is required.

FINANCIAL DATA:
Student also receives one-year membership in
the American Planning Association.
Amount of support per award: $2,000 paid
directly to the student's school to defray
tuition costs.
Total amount of support: $2,000 each year.

NO. MOST RECENT APPLICANTS: 5.

NO. AWARDS: 1 each year.

APPLICATION INFO:
An eligible applicant should apply through
one of the five designated schools on forms
supplied to the participating university by
APA. Applicant needs to be nominated by
Department Chair.
Duration: One academic year.
Deadline: June.

ADDRESS INQUIRIES TO:
See e-mail address above.

AMPCO-PITTSBURGH CHARITABLE FOUNDATION [1061]

726 Bell Avenue, Suite 301
Carnegie, PA 15106
(412) 456-4418
Fax: (412) 456-4436
E-mail: rhoover@ampcopgh.com

AREAS OF INTEREST:
Universities and community funds.

TYPE:
Cash contributions.

PURPOSE:
To provide support for community funds and
higher education.

ELIGIBILITY:
Organizations classified as 501(c)(3) by the
IRS can apply. No grants to individuals.

GEOG. RESTRICTIONS: United States.

FINANCIAL DATA:
Amount of support per award: $250 to
$1,000.
Total amount of support: $400,000 per year.

APPLICATION INFO:
Request should be in letter format.
Deadline: October 31.

ADDRESS INQUIRIES TO:
Rose Hoover
Chairman of Board and Trustee
(See address above.)

THE ANDERSEN CORPORATE FOUNDATION [1062]

White Pine Building
342 Fifth Avenue North, Suite 200
Bayport, MN 55003
(651) 275-4450
Fax: (651) 439-9480
E-mail: andersencorpfdn@srinc.biz
Web Site: www.andersencorporation.com/sustainability/community

FOUNDED: 1941

AREAS OF INTEREST:
Education and youth development, health and safety, human services, and affordable housing.

TYPE:
Capital grants; General operating grants; Project/program grants.

YEAR PROGRAM STARTED: 1941

PURPOSE:
To better people's lives and strengthen communities, focusing primarily where Andersen employees live and work.

LEGAL BASIS:
Private foundation.

ELIGIBILITY:
Qualified tax-exempt organizations. Primary focus on Washington County, MN and portions of western Wisconsin.

GEOG. RESTRICTIONS: Washington County, Minnesota; Dunn, Polk and St. Croix counties, Wisconsin. Limited support to organizations serving Ramsey County, Minnesota.

FINANCIAL DATA:
$50,000,000 in assets as of December 31, 2019.
Amount of support per award: $1,500 to $100,000.
Total amount of support: $2,100,000 for the year 2018-19.

NO. AWARDS: 138 for the year 2018-19.

APPLICATION INFO:
Applications are accepted by invitation only. New organizations must complete the Inquiry Form available on the web site and submit to the e-mail address listed above.
Duration: One year. Renewal by reapplication.
Deadline: November 15, February 15 and June 15.

PUBLICATIONS:
Application guidelines.

IRS I.D.: 41-6020912

OFFICERS AND BOARD OF DIRECTORS:
Karen Richard, President
Eliza Chlebeck, Vice President
Chris Galvin, Treasurer
Phil Donaldson
Jeanne Junker
Jay Lund

ADDRESS INQUIRIES TO:
Chloette Haley, Program Officer
(See address above.)

*PLEASE NOTE:
Foundation prefers that the proposal be sent to the address above.

FRED C. AND KATHERINE B. ANDERSEN FOUNDATION [1063]

P.O. Box 80
Bayport, MN 55003
(651) 264-7355
Fax: (651) 264-7245
E-mail: marygillstrom@sbcglobal.net

FOUNDED: 1959

AREAS OF INTEREST:
Education, youth, elderly and health programs.

TYPE:
Capital grants; Challenge/matching grants; General operating grants; Project/program grants. The Foundation supports four-year accredited colleges and universities that do not accept state or federal funding.

YEAR PROGRAM STARTED: 1959

PURPOSE:
To support organizations of higher learning that are four-year institutions that do not accept state or federal funding.

LEGAL BASIS:
Private foundation.

ELIGIBILITY:
Grants are made to organizations that have tax-exempt status under Section 501(c)(3) of the Internal Revenue Code. No grants are made to individuals. No grants for endowment.

GEOG. RESTRICTIONS: Washington County, Minnesota; Pierce, Polk and St. Croix counties, Wisconsin.

FINANCIAL DATA:
Total market value of $800,000 for the year 2019.
Amount of support per award: Varies by need.
Total amount of support: $35,967,000 for the year 2019.

APPLICATION INFO:
Organizations should submit a letter of intent to the Foundation.
Duration: One year. Must reapply for future grants.
Deadline: March 15, June 15 and September 15.

IRS I.D.: 41-6020920

ADDRESS INQUIRIES TO:
Mary Gillstrom, Vice President/Secretary
(See address above.)

HUGH J. ANDERSEN FOUNDATION [1064]

342 Fifth Avenue North, Suite 200
Bayport, MN 55003-4502
(651) 275-4489
Fax: (651) 439-9480
E-mail: hjafdn@srinc.biz
Web Site: www.srinc.biz/foundations/hugh-j-andersen-foundation

FOUNDED: 1962

AREAS OF INTEREST:
Humanities, arts/culture, elementary and secondary education, health care, human services, women and homelessness.

TYPE:
Capital grants; General operating grants; Project/program grants. Supports focused efforts that foster inclusivity, promotes equality, and lends to increased human independence, self-sufficiency and dignity.

PURPOSE:
To improve the quality of life in the St. Croix Valley.

LEGAL BASIS:
Private organization.

ELIGIBILITY:
Eligible organizations must be IRS 501(c)(3) tax-exempt.

GEOG. RESTRICTIONS: Primarily Washington County, Minnesota and Pierce, Polk, and St. Croix counties in Wisconsin, with secondary focus in St. Paul, Minnesota.

FINANCIAL DATA:
Amount of support per award: $500 to $75,000.
Total amount of support: $4,404,000 for fiscal year ended February 28, 2019.

NO. AWARDS: 244.

APPLICATION INFO:
The Foundation requires a full proposal when applying for a grant. A full proposal consists of:
(1) Request Cover Form;
(2) Proposal Checklist and;
(3) all documentation as indicated on the Checklist.

Although the Foundation prefers the use of the Hugh J. Andersen Foundation Request Cover Form and Checklist for a complete proposal, the Minnesota Common Grant Application Form will be accepted provided the Foundation's Request Cover Form and Proposal Checklist are also included.
Duration: One year. Renewal by reapplication.
Deadline: March 15, June 15, August 15 and November 15.

PUBLICATIONS:
Annual report; application guidelines.

IRS I.D.: 41-6020914

ADDRESS INQUIRIES TO:
Brad Kruse, Philanthropy Director
(See address above.)

ANDRUS FAMILY FUND [1065]

200 Madison Avenue, 25th Floor
New York, NY 10016
(212) 687-6975
E-mail: jkaizer@affund.org
info@affund.org
Web Site: affund.org

FOUNDED: 2000

AREAS OF INTEREST:
Juvenile justice and foster care.

NAME(S) OF PROGRAMS:
● **Foster Care Program**
● **Juvenile Justice Program**

TYPE:
Project/program grants.

YEAR PROGRAM STARTED: 2000

PURPOSE:
To contribute to the body of knowledge and experience about what is necessary to create and sustain effective social change.

LEGAL BASIS:
501(c)(3).

ELIGIBILITY:
Groups must be tax-exempt under Section 501(c)(3) of the IRS. Organizations can also submit Letters of Inquiry through a sponsoring organization if the sponsor has a 501(c)(3) status.

The Andrus Family Fund does not fund individuals, capital campaigns or building construction, purchasing of equipment, or conference scholarships.

GEOG. RESTRICTIONS: United States.

FINANCIAL DATA:
Amount of support per award: $50,000 to $200,000.

Total amount of support: $3,500,000 to $4,000,000.

APPLICATION INFO:
Applicants are encouraged to review the guidelines on the Foundation web site thoroughly before submitting a grant application.

Deadline: Grants are awarded by the trustees, who meet in September.

ADDRESS INQUIRIES TO:
Manuela Arciniegas, Director
(See address above.)

ANN ARBOR AREA COMMUNITY FOUNDATION [1066]

301 North Main Street
Suite 300
Ann Arbor, MI 48104-1133
(734) 663-0401
(734) 436-7587
Fax: (734) 663-3514
E-mail: info@aaacf.org
kvideto@aaacf.org
Web Site: www.aaacf.org

FOUNDED: 1963

AREAS OF INTEREST:
Environment, arts, health and human services, youth and seniors.

NAME(S) OF PROGRAMS:
- **The African American Endowment Fund**
- **The Anna Botsford Bach Fund**
- **Community Grantmaking**
- **Coordinated Funding**
- **Cultural Economic Development**
- **Youth Council**
- **The Ypsilanti Area Community Fund**

TYPE:
Demonstration grants; Development grants; General operating grants; Project/program grants; Scholarships; Seed money grants; Technical assistance.

YEAR PROGRAM STARTED: 1963

PURPOSE:
To improve the quality of life in the Foundation's region.

ELIGIBILITY:
AAACF welcomes grant applications from 501(c)(3) nonprofit organizations whose programs and services benefit the people of Washtenaw County, MI.

GEOG. RESTRICTIONS: Washtenaw County, Michigan.

FINANCIAL DATA:
Amount of support per award: Varies.
Total amount of support: Varies.

APPLICATION INFO:
A guideline on how to apply and application form are available on the Foundation web site.
Duration: One year.
Deadline: Varies.

OFFICER:
Neel Hajra, President and Chief Executive Officer

ADDRESS INQUIRIES TO:
Jillian Rosen, Vice President for Community Investment
E-mail: jrosen@aaacf.org

THE ANNENBERG FOUNDATION

2000 Avenue of the Stars
Suite 1000 S
Los Angeles, CA 90067
(310) 209-4560
Fax: (310) 209-1631
E-mail: info@annenberg.org
requests@annenberg.org
Web Site: www.annenberg.org

TYPE:
General operating grants; Grants-in-aid; Project/program grants; Technical assistance.

See entry 16 for full listing.

ARIZONA COMMUNITY FOUNDATION [1067]

2201 East Camelback Road
Suite 405-B
Phoenix, AZ 85016
(602) 381-1400
(800) 222-8221
Fax: (602) 381-1575
E-mail: info@azfoundation.org
Web Site: www.azfoundation.org

FOUNDED: 1978

AREAS OF INTEREST:
Children's mental health and prevention programs, economic development, arts and culture, youth agencies and health agencies.

NAME(S) OF PROGRAMS:
- **Communities for All Ages**

TYPE:
Project/program grants.

YEAR PROGRAM STARTED: 1978

PURPOSE:
To benefit the quality of life in the Phoenix, AZ community and the surrounding area.

LEGAL BASIS:
Community foundation.

ELIGIBILITY:
Tax-exempt, nonprofit organizations. No grants are made to individuals.

GEOG. RESTRICTIONS: Arizona.

FINANCIAL DATA:
Amount of support per award: $10,000 average.

APPLICATION INFO:
Application information is available on the web site.
Duration: Typically, one year.

PUBLICATIONS:
Annual report.

OFFICERS:
Stephen O. Evans, Chairman
Robbin M. Coulon, Esq., Vice Chairman
Rufus Glasper, Treasurer
Leezie Kim, Esq., Secretary

ADDRESS INQUIRIES TO:
Lora Golke
Senior Director, Philanthropic Services
(See address above.)

ARKANSAS COMMUNITY FOUNDATION [1068]

5 Allied Drive
Suite 51110
Little Rock, AR 72202
(501) 372-1116
Fax: (501) 372-1166
E-mail: arcf@arcf.org
Web Site: www.arcf.org

FOUNDED: 1976

AREAS OF INTEREST:
Grants are made in all fields.

TYPE:
Project/program grants; Scholarships.

PURPOSE:
To promote smart giving to improve communities.

LEGAL BASIS:
Community foundation.

ELIGIBILITY:
Applicants must be nonprofit organizations with projects to benefit Arkansans. Few unrestricted grants are made. Only Arkansas organizations need apply.

Most funds are restricted or designated for specific organizations. Very few unrestricted grants are made.

GEOG. RESTRICTIONS: Arkansas.

FINANCIAL DATA:
Total amount of support: $40,966,916 for the year 2019.

APPLICATION INFO:
Application information is available on the web site.
Duration: One year.

PUBLICATIONS:
Annual report; newsletter.

IRS I.D.: 52-1055743

BOARD OF DIRECTORS:
Philip Tappan, Chairperson
Heather Larkin, President and Chief Executive Officer
Ramsay Ball
Kandice Bell
Alison Bradford-White
Tracy Cude
Jackson Farrow
Don Greenland
Dennis Hunt
Eric Hutchinson
Heather Loftis
Creshelle Nash, M.D.
Steve Nipper
Paige Partridge-Hix
Andy Peeler
Robert Thompson
Robert Zunick

ADDRESS INQUIRIES TO:
Grants Coordinator
(See address above.)

THE AUSTIN COMMUNITY FOUNDATION [1069]

4315 Guadalupe Street
Suite 300
Austin, TX 78751
(512) 472-4483
Fax: (512) 472-4486
E-mail: info@austincf.org
Web Site: www.austincf.org

FOUNDED: 1977

AREAS OF INTEREST:
Arts and culture, community engagement, education, recreation and animal-related services, environment and public space, human services/basic needs, and health and wellness.

NAME(S) OF PROGRAMS:
- **Community Grant Program**

TYPE:
Project/program grants; Scholarships.

YEAR PROGRAM STARTED: 1977

PURPOSE:
To promote philanthropy in central Texas; to improve the quality of life now and in the future.

ELIGIBILITY:
Organizations must be 501(c)(3) or 170(b)(1)(a)(vi) and located in the central Texas area, including Bastrop, Burnet, Caldwell, Hays, Travis and Williamson counties. Funds are not given to individuals.

GEOG. RESTRICTIONS: Central Texas.

FINANCIAL DATA:
Amount of support per award: Varies; average competitive grant is $25,000.
Total amount of support: $2,300,000.

NO. MOST RECENT APPLICANTS: 240.

NO. AWARDS: 95.

APPLICATION INFO:
Applications is available on the Foundation web site.
Duration: One year. Must reapply.
Deadline: Proposals are reviewed on an ongoing basis; four- to six-month process.

IRS I.D.: 74-1934031

ADDRESS INQUIRIES TO:
Meagan A. Longley
Vice President Community Impact
(See address above.)

AUTRY FOUNDATION   [1070]
4383 Colfax Avenue
Studio City, CA 91604
(818) 752-7770
Fax: (818) 752-7779
E-mail: mhansen@autry.com

AREAS OF INTEREST:
Culture, education, children's and seniors' groups, hunger and health.

TYPE:
Project/program grants.

PURPOSE:
To offer assistance to communities in southern California.

LEGAL BASIS:
Private foundation.

ELIGIBILITY:
Eligible organizations must be IRS 501(c)(3) tax-exempt.

GEOG. RESTRICTIONS: Southern California.

FINANCIAL DATA:
Amount of support per award: Varies.
Total amount of support: Varies.

APPLICATION INFO:
Applicants should submit a letter and include a copy of the IRS tax determination letter.
Duration: Depends on project. Renewable.

ADDRESS INQUIRIES TO:
Maxine Hansen, Director
(See address above.)

BADGER METER FOUNDATION, INC.   [1071]
4545 West Brown Deer Road
Milwaukee, WI 53223-2479
(414) 371-5742

AREAS OF INTEREST:
Social services, education, conservation and community funds.

TYPE:
Capital grants.

PURPOSE:
To support education and community service organizations, health associations, the handicapped, the arts and conservation.

ELIGIBILITY:
Organizations classified as 501(c)(3) by the IRS can apply. No grants to individuals and religious organizations.

GEOG. RESTRICTIONS: Southeastern Milwaukee area, Wisconsin.

FINANCIAL DATA:
Amount of support per award: Varies.
Total amount of support: Varies.

NO. AWARDS: 30 for the year 2018.

APPLICATION INFO:
Request must be submitted on organization's letterhead paper.
Duration: One year. Grants are renewable.

ADDRESS INQUIRIES TO:
John Biever, Treasurer and Secretary
(See address above.)

BALTIMORE COMMUNITY FOUNDATION
2 East Read Street, 9th Floor
Baltimore, MD 21202
(410) 332-4171
Fax: (410) 837-4701
E-mail: info@bcf.org
Web Site: www.bcf.org

TYPE:
Scholarships. Neighborhood grants. Education grants.

See entry 29 for full listing.

BARAGA COUNTY COMMUNITY FOUNDATION   [1072]
100 Hemlock Street
Baraga, MI 49908
(906) 353-7898
E-mail: baragacf@up.net
Web Site: www.baragacountyfoundation.org

FOUNDED: 1994

AREAS OF INTEREST:
Arts and culture, community development, education, senior well-being, and youth development.

TYPE:
Capital grants; Challenge/matching grants; Endowments; Project/program grants; Scholarships; Seed money grants; Technical assistance. Community convening.

YEAR PROGRAM STARTED: 1994

PURPOSE:
To enhance the quality of life for the citizens of the community.

LEGAL BASIS:
501(c)(3).

ELIGIBILITY:
Grants are made to organizations that have tax-exempt status under Section 501(c)(3) of the Internal Revenue Code.

GEOG. RESTRICTIONS: Baraga County, Michigan.

FINANCIAL DATA:
Amount of support per award: Varies depending upon the needs and nature of the request; $1,500 common.
Total amount of support: Approximately $38,000.

NO. AWARDS: Varies.

APPLICATION INFO:
Application information is available upon request.
Duration: One year. Renewal possible.
Deadline: Varies.

IRS I.D.: 38-3198122

ADDRESS INQUIRIES TO:
Gordette Cote Leutz, Executive Director
(See address above.)

BARNES GROUP FOUNDATION   [1073]
123 Main Street
Bristol, CT 06010
(860) 583-7070
E-mail: info@bginc.com
Web Site: www.bginc.com

FOUNDED: 1945

AREAS OF INTEREST:
Cultural arts, education, and health and welfare.

TYPE:
General operating grants; Scholarships. Employee scholarship program.

PURPOSE:
To support higher education, cultural arts, and health and welfare.

ELIGIBILITY:
Organizations classified as 501(c)(3) by the IRS can apply. Individuals and religious organizations are ineligible.

GEOG. RESTRICTIONS: United States, with emphasis on Connecticut and New England.

FINANCIAL DATA:
Amount of support per award: Varies.
Total amount of support: Varies.

APPLICATION INFO:
Applicants must write to the Foundation for an application form.
Duration: One year. Grants are renewable.

ADDRESS INQUIRIES TO:
Tom Barnes, Secretary
(See address above.)

BARR FOUNDATION   [1074]
2 Atlantic Avenue, Lewis Wharf
Fourth Floor
Boston, MA 02110
(617) 854-3500
Fax: (617) 854-3501
E-mail: info@barrfoundation.org
Web Site: www.barrfoundation.org

FOUNDED: 1987

AREAS OF INTEREST:
Education, the environment, arts and cultural activities with a focus on Boston, MA.

TYPE:
Capital grants; Challenge/matching grants; Conferences/seminars; Development grants; Endowments; Fellowships; General operating grants; Matching gifts; Project/program grants; Technical assistance. The work of the Foundation focuses on three critical areas with a focus on Boston, MA:
(1) closing education opportunity gaps;
(2) mitigating climate change and;
(3) enhancing cultural vitality.

PURPOSE:
To enhance the quality of life for all of Boston's citizens.

ELIGIBILITY:
Barr does not make grants to individuals or for scholarships. It is also rare to fund capital projects, event sponsorships, program-related investments, or organizations not classified as public charities and tax-exempt under Section 501(c)(3) of the Internal Revenue Code.

GEOG. RESTRICTIONS: Regional Boston, Massachusetts and New England areas.

FINANCIAL DATA:
Amount of support per award: Varies.
Total amount of support: $85,000,000 budgeted for the year 2018.

APPLICATION INFO:
Generally, by invitation only. From time to time, Barr issues open requests for proposals, to provide broad access to funding opportunities, and to ensure the Foundation remains open to new ideas and new partnerships. Organizations are encouraged to subscribe to the Foundation's newsletter to stay informed about future RFP opportunities.
Deadline: Quarterly, in conjunction with quarterly meeting.

PUBLICATIONS:
Newsletter.

IRS I.D.: 04-6579815

ADDRESS INQUIRIES TO:
Kerri Ann Hurley
Director of Grants Management
(See address above.)

BAYER FUND [1075]
800 North Lindbergh Boulevard
St. Louis, MO 63167
(314) 694-4391
Fax: (314) 694-7658
E-mail: monsanto.fund@monsanto.com
Web Site: www.monsantofund.org

FOUNDED: 1964

AREAS OF INTEREST:
Community development, education, and food and nutrition.

TYPE:
Project/program grants.

PURPOSE:
To strengthen communities where Bayer customers and employees live and work; to address families in underresourced areas, with an emphasis on children.

ELIGIBILITY:
Applicants must be nonprofit 501(c)(3) or units of government 170(c)(1). Proposed projects must fit within one of the focus areas. Must be an experienced, established and reputable organization (not a start-up organization), financially sound with a diverse funding base, and be audited annually.

Grants are not given to religious organizations.

FINANCIAL DATA:
Amount of support per award: $2,500 to $250,000.
Total amount of support: Varies.

APPLICATION INFO:
Application information is available online.
Duration: One to two years.
Deadline: Varies.

NORWIN S. AND ELIZABETH N. BEAN FOUNDATION [1076]
40 Stark Street
Manchester, NH 03101
(603) 493-7257
E-mail: kcook@beanfoundation.org
Web Site: www.beanfoundation.org

FOUNDED: 1967

AREAS OF INTEREST:
Arts and humanities, education, environment, health, social and community services and development of the voluntary sector.

TYPE:
Capital grants; Challenge/matching grants. Grants to tax-exempt charitable organizations operating in Amherst or Manchester, NH, for broad charitable purposes. Generally, at least two-thirds of available funds are awarded as grants for programs undertaken by nonprofit organizations and public agencies. The remaining one-third is allocated for capital needs, including acquisition of equipment, renovation or construction of facilities and additions to endowment.

General operating support grants are not made to ongoing programs, nor are grants made to eliminate previously incurred deficits. Short-term operating support may be provided to new organizations or for new program initiatives of established organizations. Generally, grants are provided for expenditure over a period of one year.

YEAR PROGRAM STARTED: 1967

PURPOSE:
To promote the general welfare.

LEGAL BASIS:
Private foundation.

ELIGIBILITY:
Applications are accepted from nonprofit 501(c)(3) organizations, municipal and public agencies serving the communities of Amherst or Manchester, NH. Priority consideration is given to organizations operating primarily in those two communities. However, the Foundation will consider applications from statewide or regional organizations which provide a substantial and documented level of service to Manchester and Amherst. The Foundation does not make grants to individuals or provide scholarship aid.

GEOG. RESTRICTIONS: Amherst or Manchester, New Hampshire.

FINANCIAL DATA:
Amount of support per award: $1,000 to $50,000.
Total amount of support: $591,715 for fiscal year 2017.

NO. MOST RECENT APPLICANTS: 60.

NO. AWARDS: 40 for the year 2017.

REPRESENTATIVE AWARDS:
$5,000 to Currier Museum of Art to support the Earn and Learn Teen Volunteer Program;

$15,000 to New Hampshire Community Loan Fund to strengthen the business practices of child care centers in Manchester; $19,088 to UpReach Therapeutic Equine Center to provide psycho-educational equine curriculum to children exposed to trauma and/or violence and their parents; $5,000 to Operation Warm to provide new winter coats to Manchester children in need; $5,000 to Rimmon Heights Neighborhood to support beautification of a section of Piscataquog River Park.

APPLICATION INFO:
Applications must be submitted electronically. Applications should include a completed cover letter sheet and proposal with appropriate enclosures explaining the purpose of the project, describing how the project will be accomplished, and indicating the amount of grant support sought.
Duration: Grants are usually awarded for a one-year period only. The Foundation does not consider multiyear grants except in very rare circumstances.
Deadline: April 1, September 1 and December 1 for decisions made in February, June and November, respectively.

PUBLICATIONS:
Guidelines.

STAFF:
Kathleen D. Cook, Grant Manager

BOARD OF TRUSTEES:
Anna Thomas, Chairperson
David Chen
Michael Delaney
John F. Dinkel, Jr.
Thomas J. Donovan
Maria Mongan
Leslee Stewart

ADDRESS INQUIRIES TO:
Kathleen D. Cook, Grant Manager
(See address above.)

BENTON FOUNDATION
727 Chicago Avenue
Evanston, IL 60202
(847) 328-3040
E-mail: info@benton.org
Web Site: www.benton.org

TYPE:
Technical assistance. Program is funded for preserving, protecting and strengthening the public benefits in America's media environment.

See entry 1750 for full listing.

BERKS COUNTY COMMUNITY FOUNDATION [1077]
237 Court Street
Reading, PA 19601
(610) 685-2223
E-mail: info@bccf.org
Web Site: www.bccf.org

FOUNDED: 1994

AREAS OF INTEREST:
Community, health, energy, smart growth and public policy.

TYPE:
Project/program grants; Scholarships.

PURPOSE:
To promote philanthropy and improve the quality of life in Berks County; to encourage and nurture performing artists at critical points in their careers.

LEGAL BASIS:
501(c)(3).

ELIGIBILITY:
Tax-exempt or nonprofit organizations, individuals, associations and public or private agencies are eligible to apply. Grant must be used for charitable purposes only.

GEOG. RESTRICTIONS: Berks County, Pennsylvania.

FINANCIAL DATA:
$77,800,000 in assets.
Amount of support per award: Varies, depending on fund.
Total amount of support: Varies.

APPLICATION INFO:
Applications are submitted through the Foundation's Grant Application System.
Duration: Varies.

PUBLICATIONS:
Annual report.

ADDRESS INQUIRIES TO:
See e-mail address above.

WILLIAM BLAIR AND COMPANY FOUNDATION   [1078]
150 North Riverside Plaza
Chicago, IL 60606
(312) 364-8037
E-mail: lcoy@williamblair.com
Web Site: www.williamblair.com

AREAS OF INTEREST:
Cultural programs, education, health and human services, social services, youth and entrepreneurship.

TYPE:
Matching gifts; Project/program grants.

ELIGIBILITY:
Organizations must be classified as 501(c)(3) by the IRS. No grants to individuals. Limited to employees of William Blair. Not open to the public.

FINANCIAL DATA:
Amount of support per award: Varies.
Total amount of support: Varies.
Matching fund requirements: Employee donations are matched 1:1 up to $1,500 per calendar year.

NO. MOST RECENT APPLICANTS: Varies.

NO. AWARDS: Over 500.

APPLICATION INFO:
Contact the Foundation.
Duration: One year.

ADDRESS INQUIRIES TO:
Laura Coy, Director of Philanthropy Strategy
(See address above.)

*PLEASE NOTE:
All Foundation grants are employee inspired.

BLOWITZ-RIDGEWAY FOUNDATION   [1079]
1701 East Woodfield Road
Suite 201
Schaumburg, IL 60173-5127
(847) 330-1020
E-mail: serena@blowitzridgeway.org
Web Site: blowitzridgeway.org

FOUNDED: 1984

AREAS OF INTEREST:
Health care and housing.

TYPE:
General operating grants; Project/program grants.

YEAR PROGRAM STARTED: 1984

PURPOSE:
To improve the health of the uninsured, underinsured and low-income metropolitan Chicago residents and the community through increased access to community-based preventive and primary health services, such as medical, dental, vision, mental health, and case management; to support housing programs and services that provide access to prevention, intervention, follow-up, supportive services, and employment training for individuals and families who are homeless or at-risk of being homeless.

LEGAL BASIS:
Private independent foundation.

ELIGIBILITY:
Organizations classified as 501(c)(3) by the IRS can apply. Preference will be given to organizations in Illinois and to programs or services which benefit youth, seniors or individuals lacking sufficient resources to care for themselves. No grants to individuals, religious or political organizations, government agencies, organizations that subsist mainly on third-party funding nor for the production or writing of audio-visual materials.

GEOG. RESTRICTIONS: City of Chicago and the six collar counties of Cook, DuPage, Kane, Lake, McHenry, and Will, Illinois.

FINANCIAL DATA:
Assets of $38,000,000 for the year ended September 30, 2019.
Amount of support per award: Generally, $10,000 to $15,000; some larger grants.
Total amount of support: Approximately $1,030,000 for fiscal year 2019.

NO. MOST RECENT APPLICANTS: 170 for the year 2019.

NO. AWARDS: 89 for the year 2019.

APPLICATION INFO:
The Blowitz-Ridgeway Foundation no longer accepts paper applications or applications submitted by mail. Applications are only accepted through the online grant program. If declined, applicants must reapply the following year.
Duration: One year. Grants are renewable.

PUBLICATIONS:
Annual report; application guidelines.

IRS I.D.: 36-2488355

ADDRESS INQUIRIES TO:
Serena Moy, Executive Director
(See address above.)

BLUE MOUNTAIN COMMUNITY FOUNDATION   [1080]
P.O. Box 603
Walla Walla, WA 99362-0015
(509) 529-4371
Fax: (509) 529-5284
E-mail: bmcf@bluemountainfoundation.org
Web Site: www.bluemountainfoundation.org

FOUNDED: 1984

AREAS OF INTEREST:
Social and community services, education, health, and the arts and humanities.

TYPE:
Endowments; Project/program grants; Scholarships. The Foundation administers and awards scholarships to local area students to enable them to attend college, graduate school or trade school.

PURPOSE:
To seek, steward and share charitable gifts in the Blue Mountain area.

ELIGIBILITY:
The Foundation awards grants to nonprofit, tax-exempt organizations in the Foundation's service area which includes the counties of Columbia, Garfield and Walla Walla in the state of Washington and the communities in Umatilla County, OR. It strives to make awards to agencies and programs that meet community needs and bring the most benefit to people in the Blue Mountain area.

GEOG. RESTRICTIONS: Columbia, Garfield and Walla Walla counties in Washington, and Umatilla County in Oregon.

FINANCIAL DATA:
Amount of support per award: Varies.
Total amount of support: Approximately $2,000,000 annually.

APPLICATION INFO:
Grant guidelines and application forms can be obtained through the Foundation's web site. Application must be submitted electronically.
Duration: Typically one year.
Deadline: Grants: July 1; Scholarships: March 2.

THE BNY MELLON FOUNDATION OF SOUTHWESTERN PENNSYLVANIA   [1081]
P.O. Box 185
Pittsburgh, PA 15230-0185
(412) 234-0620
Fax: (412) 236-1662
E-mail: ryan.ricarte@bnymellon.com
Web Site: www.bnymellon.com

FOUNDED: 1974

AREAS OF INTEREST:
Humanitarian and social impact through pro bono volunteerism and donations.

TYPE:
Project/program grants; Technical assistance.

YEAR PROGRAM STARTED: 1974

PURPOSE:
To identify and support initiatives that improve the social and economic conditions of residents where the company does business and where employees live and work. Through powering potential, the company's strategic philanthropic investments.

LEGAL BASIS:
Corporate foundation, part of BNY Mellon's Charitable Giving Program.

ELIGIBILITY:
Organizations requesting support must have 501(c)(3) tax-exempt charitable status and must be public charities as defined under Section 509(a)(1) of the Internal Revenue Code.

No support is available for loans or direct grants to individuals, religious programs of churches or other sectarian organizations and political parties, campaigns or candidates. As a general rule, support is not available for fraternal organizations, such as police or fire associations, scholarships, fellowships and travel grants, conference or seminar attendance, specialized health campaigns, endowment campaigns, individual United Way agencies which already benefit from the Corporation's gift to the United Way appeal, national organizations, projects or programs or those which operate outside the U.S. and multiyear commitments.

GEOG. RESTRICTIONS: Southwestern Pennsylvania.

FINANCIAL DATA:
Amount of support per award: Varies.
Total amount of support: Approximately $4,000,000 for the year 2017.

NO. MOST RECENT APPLICANTS: Approximately 500.

NO. AWARDS: Approximately 125.

APPLICATION INFO:
Contact the Foundation.
Duration: One year.
Deadline: Requests are considered upon receipt.

PUBLICATIONS:
Annual report which contains contributions policy and application guidelines.

STAFF:
Kenya T. Boswell, President
Ryan Ricarte, Administrator

ADDRESS INQUIRIES TO:
Ryan Ricarte, Administrator
(See address above.)

THE BOSTON FOUNDATION [1082]

75 Arlington Street, Third Floor
Boston, MA 02116-3936
(617) 338-1700
Fax: (617) 338-1604
E-mail: grantsinfo@tbf.org
Web Site: www.tbf.org

FOUNDED: 1915

AREAS OF INTEREST:
Health, welfare, educational, cultural, planning and housing needs of the Boston metropolitan area community.

TYPE:
General operating grants; Project/program grants; Technical assistance. Capacity building. Grants for new or experimental programs of both new and established institutions.

LEGAL BASIS:
Community foundation established in 1915 in Massachusetts by agreement and declaration of trust. Incorporated in 1917.

ELIGIBILITY:
Grants are made to organizations or for programs in the Boston standard metropolitan statistical area only. Organizations must be 501(c)(3) public charity or have federal tax-exempt status or a fiscal nonprofit agent. No grants are made to individuals. Grants are not made for scholarship, travel, medical or scientific research, religious purposes, publications or films or for national/international organizations.

GEOG. RESTRICTIONS: Greater Boston, Massachusetts.

FINANCIAL DATA:
Amount of support per award: Averages approximately $10,000 to $150,000.
Total amount of support: Approximately $16,000,000 annually.
Matching fund requirements: Varies.

NO. MOST RECENT APPLICANTS: Approximately 550.

NO. AWARDS: Approximately 220.

APPLICATION INFO:
Information may be obtained from the Foundation web site.
Duration: Up to five years.

PUBLICATIONS:
Annual report; application guidelines; quarterly newsletters.

OFFICERS:
Sandra M. Edgerley, Chairperson
Linda Mason, Vice Chairperson
Paul S. Grogan, President and Chief Executive Officer
Alfred F. Van Ranst, Jr., Treasurer and Chief Financial Officer
Stephen Chan, Secretary
George C. Wilson, Assistant Treasurer
John Ho, Assistant Secretary

BOARD MEMBERS:
Zamawa Arenas
Andrew Arnott
Vanessa Calderon-Rosado, Ph.D.
Elyse Cherry
Brian Conway
Pam Y. Eddinger, Ph.D.
Sandra M. Edgerley
Michael R. Eisenson
Paul C. Gannon
Paul S. Grogan
Rev. Dr. Gregory G. Groover, Sr.
Paul W. Lee
Linda Mason
Dr. Myechia Minter-Jordan
J. Keith Motley, Ph.D.
Peter Nessen
Ron O'Hanley
Dwight Poler
T.J. Rose
Scott E. Squillace, Esq.
C.A. Webb

ADDRESS INQUIRIES TO:
Grants Manager or Program Officer
(See address above.)

OTTO BREMER TRUST [1083]

30 East 7th Street
Suite 2900
St. Paul, MN 55101
(651) 227-8036
(888) 291-1123
Fax: (651) 312-3665
E-mail: twilliams@ottobremer.org
Web Site: ottobremer.org

AREAS OF INTEREST:
Community economic, civic, and social betterment.

TYPE:
Capital grants; Challenge/matching grants; General operating grants; Project/program grants.

PURPOSE:
To assist people in achieving full economic, civic and social participation in and for the betterment of their communities.

ELIGIBILITY:
Grants are restricted to private nonprofit or public tax-exempt organizations for purposes defined under Section 501(c)(3) of the Internal Revenue Code. Grants are only made to organizations whose beneficiaries are residents of Minnesota, North Dakota or Wisconsin. Grants are not made to individuals.

GEOG. RESTRICTIONS: Minnesota, North Dakota and western Wisconsin.

FINANCIAL DATA:
Amount of support per award: $1,000 to $500,000; average $35,000.
Total amount of support: Approximately $50,000,000 for the year 2018.

NO. AWARDS: Approximately 850 per year.

APPLICATION INFO:
Applicants must complete the eligibility questions through the link on the Trust web site. Those encouraged to continue the application process will be directed to the landing page.
Duration: One year. Must reapply.
Deadline: Varies.

GLADYS BROOKS FOUNDATION [1084]

1055 Franklin Avenue
Suite 208
Garden City, NY 11530-2903
(516) 746-6103
Fax: (516) 877-1758
E-mail: kathy@gladysbrooksfoundation.org
Web Site: www.gladysbrooksfoundation.org

FOUNDED: 1981

AREAS OF INTEREST:
Libraries, education, hospitals and clinics.

TYPE:
Capital grants; Challenge/matching grants; Demonstration grants; Development grants; Endowments; Matching gifts; Project/program grants; Scholarships. Grants to private, not-for-profit publicly supported libraries, educational institutions, hospitals and clinics in the eastern U.S.

YEAR PROGRAM STARTED: 1981

PURPOSE:
To provide for the intellectual, moral and physical welfare of the people of this country by establishing and supporting nonprofit libraries, educational institutions, hospitals and clinics.

ELIGIBILITY:
Applicants must be publicly supported, not-for-profit tax-exempt organizations. Generally speaking, grant applications will only be considered where outside funding, including governmental, is not available. The project will be largely funded by the grant unless the grant request covers a discrete component of a larger project. The funds will be used for capital projects including equipment or endowments. Applications for direct salary support will not be accepted.

Grant applications will be considered for major expenditures generally between $50,000 and $100,000 and greater or lesser amounts in certain circumstances.

GEOG. RESTRICTIONS: Connecticut, Florida, Illinois, Indiana, Louisiana, Maine, Maryland, Massachusetts, New Jersey, New York, Pennsylvania, Rhode Island and Tennessee.

FINANCIAL DATA:
  Amount of support per award: $50,000 to
  $100,000.

APPLICATION INFO:
  The initial step in seeking a grant is
  completion of the Request Form and
  submitting it electronically to the Foundation.
  In doing so, the applicant will automatically
  be provided with all the information required
  for the Grant Proposal Letter. This step will
  also initiate the two-week period by the end
  of which the Grant Proposal Letter must be
  submitted.
  Duration: One year.
  Deadline: May 31.

PUBLICATIONS:
  Annual report.

GOVERNING BOARD:
  James J. Daly, Chairman
  Michael P. Connors
  Thomas Q. Morris, M.D.

*PLEASE NOTE:
  All grant awards are made on the condition
  that the entirety of the funds advanced shall
  be utilized in direct furtherance of the project
  and that no portion thereof shall be
  appropriated by the grantee as an
  administrative or processing fee, for
  overseeing the project or for its general
  overhead.

BRUNSWICK FOUNDATION, INC.   [1085]

26125 North Riverwoods Boulevard
Suite 500
Mettawa, IL 60045
(847) 735-4344
Fax: (847) 735-4765
E-mail: lisa.debartolo@brunswick.com
Web Site: www.brunswick.com

FOUNDED: 1957

AREAS OF INTEREST:
  Organizations that support the company's
  products.

NAME(S) OF PROGRAMS:
  • **Brunswick Employee Sons and
    Daughters Scholarship**
  • **Dollars for Doers Volunteer Program**

TYPE:
  General operating grants. Scholarships to
  employee's children.

PURPOSE:
  To support causes and/or projects that are
  related to fitness activities.

LEGAL BASIS:
  Private foundation.

ELIGIBILITY:
  Organizations in areas of company operation
  classified as 501(c)(3) by the IRS will be
  considered. Scholarship applicants must be
  children of current employees at the
  company.

FINANCIAL DATA:
  Amount of support per award: Dollars for
  Doers: $75 to $1,000.
  Total amount of support: Approximately
  $250,000.

NO. MOST RECENT APPLICANTS: 250.

NO. AWARDS: Varies.

APPLICATION INFO:
  Applications are sent out by invitation only.
  Duration: One year.

Deadline: End of February.

IRS I.D.: 36-6033576

STAFF:
  Lisa DeBartolo, Coordinator

DIRECTORS:
  Judith Zelisko, President
  Brenna Preisser, Vice President
  William L. Metzger, Treasurer
  Marsha Vaughn, Secretary

ADDRESS INQUIRIES TO:
  Lisa DeBartolo, Coordinator
  (See address above.)

THE BUHL FOUNDATION   [1086]

650 Smithfield Street
Suite 2300
Pittsburgh, PA 15222
(412) 566-2711
Fax: (412) 566-2714
E-mail: buhl@buhlfoundation.org
Web Site: www.buhlfoundation.org
www.onenorthsidepgh.org

FOUNDED: 1927

AREAS OF INTEREST:
  Education, youth development, human
  services and economic and community
  development, particularly with regard to the
  Northside of Pittsburgh.

CONSULTING OR VOLUNTEER SERVICES:
  Wide variety of community initiatives to
  improve quality of life in the greater
  Pittsburgh area in general, and the Northside
  of Pittsburgh in particular.

TYPE:
  Demonstration grants; Development grants;
  Grants-in-aid; Project/program grants; Seed
  money grants; Training grants. Capacity
  building. Grants-in-aid, primarily to
  institutions in the Pittsburgh metropolitan
  area, Allegheny County and western
  Pennsylvania for developmental and
  innovative projects in education, children and
  youth, and community services. More
  recently, a place-based granting focus on the
  Northside of Pittsburgh.

YEAR PROGRAM STARTED: 1928

PURPOSE:
  To support efforts that contribute to the
  vibrancy and well-being of the Northside and
  the Pittsburgh region, create learning
  environments so that young people will thrive
  and be prepared for adulthood, encourage
  innovation and entrepreneurial solutions to
  improve quality of life, and make a definitive
  difference in addressing persistent community
  challenges or unmet needs of at-risk
  neighborhoods.

LEGAL BASIS:
  Independent private foundation established by
  will probated on June 20, 1927.

ELIGIBILITY:
  Tax-exempt, nonprofit institutions with
  appropriate interests in southwestern
  Pennsylvania are eligible to apply. Emphasis
  is on grants to institutions in the Pittsburgh
  metropolitan area, with a particular focus on
  the Northside of Pittsburgh. Programs and
  projects which combine different professional
  interests and relate agencies in cooperative
  endeavors are often recognized as worthy of
  a grant. Grants are not made to individuals.

GEOG. RESTRICTIONS: Southwestern
  Pennsylvania, including Pittsburgh and
  Allegheny counties, with a focus on the
  Northside of Pittsburgh.

FINANCIAL DATA:
  Total amount of support: $2,706,653 for the
  year ended June 30, 2018.

NO. MOST RECENT APPLICANTS: 110.

NO. AWARDS: 69.

REPRESENTATIVE AWARDS:
  $175,000 to New Sun Rising to support the
  administration of the 2018 One Northside
  Neighbor-to-Neighbor Mini-Grant program;
  $180,000 to Auberle to provide a workforce
  solution for Northside residents by launching
  the Northside Employment Institute;
  $105,875 to United Way of Southwestern
  Pennsylvania to support a stipend-based
  program to encourage community
  participation in One Northside education
  efforts; $75,000 to Foundation of HOPE to
  implement a diversion program on the
  Northside for low- to medium-risk,
  nonviolent offenders intended to decrease the
  participant's likelihood of re-offending.

APPLICATION INFO:
  Applicants must write a letter of inquiry to
  the President at the address above, followed,
  if requested, by a formal proposal. Interviews
  and other follow-up procedures are then
  initiated by staff. Applications must contain a
  statement of objectives and the proposed
  means of attaining these, a description of the
  program and budget as well as information
  regarding the applicant agency, its
  organization and structure, its tax status and
  its capacity to implement the project.
  Duration: Usually one year. Some grants
  cover two or three years.

PUBLICATIONS:
  Annual report; application procedures.

IRS I.D.: 25-0378910

OFFICERS:
  Diana A. Bucco, President

TRUSTEES:
  Peter F. Mathieson, Chairperson
  Saleem H. Ghubril, Vice Chairperson
  Kim Tillotson Fleming, Secretary and
  Treasurer
  Quintin B. Bullock
  Carolyn Duronio
  Anne Lewis
  Lara E. Washington

ADDRESS INQUIRIES TO:
  Diana A. Bucco, President
  (See address above.)

PATRICK AND AIMEE BUTLER FAMILY FOUNDATION   [1087]

2356 University Avenue West
Suite 420
St. Paul, MN 55114
(651) 222-2565
E-mail: roberth@butlerfamilyfoundation.org
Web Site: butlerfamilyfoundation.org

FOUNDED: 1951

AREAS OF INTEREST:
  Arts and culture, environment, and human
  services.

TYPE:
  General operating grants; Project/program
  grants.

YEAR PROGRAM STARTED: 1951

PURPOSE:
To foster safety, opportunity, and growth for individuals and families by supporting effective, nonprofit organizations in the arts, environment and human services.

LEGAL BASIS:
Private foundation.

ELIGIBILITY:
Eligible organizations must be IRS 501(c)(3) tax-exempt. The Foundation does not fund criminal justice, economic development or education, employment or vocational programs, films or videos, health, hospitals or medical research, loans or grants to individuals, secondary or elementary education, theater or dance, or projects outside the U.S.

GEOG. RESTRICTIONS: Twin Cities Metropolitan area, Minnesota.

FINANCIAL DATA:
Amount of support per award: Average $30,000.

Total amount of support: $5,279,525 for the year 2017.

NO. MOST RECENT APPLICANTS: 140 for the year 2017.

NO. AWARDS: 117 for the year 2017.

APPLICATION INFO:
Must apply online through web site link.
Duration: Two years.
Deadline: April 1.

PUBLICATIONS:
Guidelines.

TRUSTEES:
Peter K. Butler, Chairperson
Paul S. Butler, Vice Chairperson
John K. Butler, Treasurer
Catherine C. Butler, Secretary
Brigid M. Butler
Patricia M. Butler
Patrick Butler, Jr.
Suzanne A. LeFevour
Bridget E. McElroy
Bridget A. O'Brien
Temple Peterson

STAFF:
Robert Hybben, Director of Program Operations
JoAnne Peters, Manager of Community Grants

ADDRESS INQUIRIES TO:
Robert Hybben
Director of Program Operations
(See address above.)

CALIFORNIA COMMUNITY FOUNDATION [1088]

221 South Figueroa Street, Suite 400
Los Angeles, CA 90012
(213) 413-4130
Fax: (213) 383-2046
E-mail: info@calfund.org
Web Site: www.calfund.org

FOUNDED: 1915

AREAS OF INTEREST:
Education, health, housing and homelessness, and immigration.

NAME(S) OF PROGRAMS:
- **Education**
- **Health**
- **Housing**
- **Immigration**

TYPE:
Fellowships; General operating grants; Project/program grants; Scholarships. Policy analysis and advocacy.

YEAR PROGRAM STARTED: 1915

PURPOSE:
To lead positive systemic change that strengthens Los Angeles communities.

LEGAL BASIS:
Community foundation, designated a public charity by the IRS.

ELIGIBILITY:
The Foundation will consider applications that are consistent with current program priorities and goals. Eligible organizations are:
(1) nonprofit agencies with evidence of tax-exempt status under Section 501(c)(3) of the Internal Revenue Code and not classified as a private foundation;
(2) located within and primarily serving residents of Los Angeles County, with the exception of regional, statewide or national public policy efforts that may benefit a substantial portion of the local population and;
(3) operated and organized so that they do not discriminate in the hiring of staff or the provision of services on the basis of race, religion, gender, sexual orientation, age, national origin or disability.

GEOG. RESTRICTIONS: Los Angeles County, California.

FINANCIAL DATA:
Amount of support per award: Nonprofit Organization Grants: Generally $75,000 to $100,000; Scholarships: Generally $250 to $15,000; Fellowship for Visual Artists Awards: $15,000 to $20,000.
Total amount of support: $242,000,000 for the year 2018.

CO-OP FUNDING PROGRAMS: Building a Lifetime of Options and Opportunities for Men - BLOOM; Early Childhood Alliance; Home L.A. Fund; L.A. Justice Fund.

NO. AWARDS: 632.

APPLICATION INFO:
Information about how to apply can be found on the web site.
Duration: Generally two years.
Deadline: Varies.

PUBLICATIONS:
Annual report; application form; application guidelines; philanthropic white papers; fund brochures.

IRS I.D.: 95-3510055

STAFF:
Antonia Hernandez, President and Chief Executive Officer
Steven J. Cobb, Chief Financial Officer
John E. Kobara, Chief Operating Officer
Teresa Mosqueda, Vice President, Development and Donor Relations
Efrain Escobeda, Vice President, Education and Immigration
Ann Sewill, Vice President, Health and Housing

BOARD OF DIRECTORS:
Patrick T. Dowling, M.D., Chairperson
James E. Berliner
Peter Berliner
Louise Henry Bryson
Alejandra Campoverdi
William C. Choi
Elyssa Elbaz

Xavier A. Gutierrez
Meloni M. Hallock
Antonia Hernandez
Eva Ho
Melvin D. Lindsey
Robert Lovelace
Hon. Gloria Molina
David Wheeler Newman
Thomas A. Saenz
Miguel A. Santana
Therese Tucker
Fidel A. Vargas
Karim Webb
Daniel G. Weiss

CALLAWAY FOUNDATION, INC. [1089]

209 Broome Street
LaGrange, GA 30240
(706) 884-7348
Fax: (706) 884-0201
E-mail: tpenn@callawayfoundation.org
Web Site: www.callawayfoundation.org

FOUNDED: 1943

AREAS OF INTEREST:
Charitable, religious and educational interests.

TYPE:
Capital grants; Challenge/matching grants; Matching gifts. Matching grants focus on construction.

YEAR PROGRAM STARTED: 1943

PURPOSE:
To improve the quality of life in the city of LaGrange and Troup County, Georgia.

LEGAL BASIS:
Private foundation.

ELIGIBILITY:
Eligible organizations must be IRS 501(c)(3). Each application is considered on its merits.

GEOG. RESTRICTIONS: City of LaGrange and Troup County, Georgia.

FINANCIAL DATA:
Amount of support per award: Varies.
Total amount of support: Varies.

NO. MOST RECENT APPLICANTS: 100.

NO. AWARDS: Varies.

REPRESENTATIVE AWARDS:
$3,000,000 to LaGrange College; $450,000 to Downtown LaGrange Development Authority; $155,000 to Lafayette Society for Performing Arts.

APPLICATION INFO:
Applicants may submit a written proposal and must include a copy of the IRS tax determination letter. Application can be found on Foundation's web site.
Duration: Varies.
Deadline: March 31, June 30, September 30 and December 31.

PUBLICATIONS:
Annual report.

IRS I.D.: 58-0566147

ADDRESS INQUIRIES TO:
Paul S. (Tripp) Penn, III, President
(See address above.)

CAPITAL REGION COMMUNITY FOUNDATION [1090]

330 Marshall Street
Suite 300
Lansing, MI 48912
(517) 272-2870
Fax: (517) 272-2871
E-mail: chales@ourcommunity.org
Web Site: www.ourcommunity.org

FOUNDED: 1987

AREAS OF INTEREST:
Arts, education, environment, health care, human services, humanities and youth.

TYPE:
Capital grants; Challenge/matching grants; Development grants; General operating grants; Project/program grants; Scholarships. Impact grants. Capacity building grants.

YEAR PROGRAM STARTED: 1989

PURPOSE:
To build a permanent endowment; to meet charitable needs in the tri-county area.

LEGAL BASIS:
Community foundation.

ELIGIBILITY:
Eligible organizations must be IRS 501(c)(3) tax-exempt and be located in the tri-county area.

GEOG. RESTRICTIONS: Clinton, Eaton and Ingham counties, Michigan.

FINANCIAL DATA:
Amount of support per award: Varies.
Total amount of support: Varies.

APPLICATION INFO:
Application information is available on the web site.
Duration: One year. No renewals.

PUBLICATIONS:
Annual report; grant guidelines.

IRS I.D.: 38-2776652

ADDRESS INQUIRIES TO:
Cindy Hales
Director of Community Investment
(See address above.)

*PLEASE NOTE:
No grants are made to individuals. Do not apply for college scholarships.

THE CARPENTER FOUNDATION [1091]

824 East Main Street
Suite 102
Medford, OR 97504
(541) 772-5851
(541) 772-5732
Fax: (541) 773-3970
E-mail: pwilliams@carpenter-foundation.org
Web Site: www.carpenter-foundation.org

FOUNDED: 1958

AREAS OF INTEREST:
Arts, education, human services and public interest issues.

TYPE:
Capital grants; Challenge/matching grants; Demonstration grants; Development grants; General operating grants; Matching gifts; Project/program grants; Scholarships; Technical assistance; Training grants.

YEAR PROGRAM STARTED: 1958

PURPOSE:
To add opportunity, choice, inclusiveness, enrichment and a climate for change for those living in the Rogue Valley.

LEGAL BASIS:
Private family foundation.

ELIGIBILITY:
Grant applications will be accepted from tax-exempt agencies only. No grants are made to individuals. Only one grant per year to any agency is usually considered. The Foundation makes grants within Jackson and Josephine counties, with the exception of a few statewide public interest issues directly affecting persons living in these counties. The Foundation rarely makes multiyear grants, grants for historical applications, hospital construction or equipment, group or individual trips, or activities for religious purposes.

GEOG. RESTRICTIONS: Jackson and Josephine counties, Oregon.

FINANCIAL DATA:
Total assets of $19,104,231 for fiscal year ended June 30, 2018.
Amount of support per award: Varies.
Total amount of support: $774,527 in grants for fiscal year ended June 30, 2018.

CO-OP FUNDING PROGRAMS: The Foundation works in partnership with other agencies, organizations and public entities.

NO. MOST RECENT APPLICANTS: Approximately 150.

NO. AWARDS: 90.

APPLICATION INFO:
Cover letter (no more than one page) from the applicant organization summarizing the scope of the project, the amount of the request, and the name, address, telephone number and e-mail address of the person to contact regarding the request is required.

Proposal information (no more than four pages) including:
(1) description of proposal or project, and the community needs or strengths that it addresses;
(2) review of the applicant agency, its purpose and services to the community, its staffing and use of volunteers;
(3) the project budget, showing specifically how the grant funds will be used, as well as other possible funding sources for this project;
(4) description of how the project will be funded in the future (if applicable);
(5) the planning process, staffing and timeline for the project;
(6) result expected and proposed evaluation method and;
(7) any recent independent board fund-raising efforts.

Required attachments (do not staple or clip):
(1) detailed budget for the agency's current year and the year for which the project is proposed (if different);
(2) income statement and balance sheet from the most recently completed fiscal year (or audit, if available); no 990s please;
(3) list of board of directors, occupations and addresses;
(4) approval of the application by the agency's board of directors and;
(5) copy of the IRS exemption letter under Section 501(c)(3).
Duration: One year.

Deadline: Applications are reviewed on a quarterly basis.

BOARD OF TRUSTEES:
Emily C. Mostue, President
Karen C. Allan, Vice President/Secretary
William Moffat, Treasurer
Mary Curtis Gramley
Linda Hugle
Lee Murdoch
Sue Naumes
Paul Nicholson
Dan Thorndike

ADDRESS INQUIRIES TO:
Polly Williams, Program Officer
Tel: (541) 772-5732
(See e-mail address above.)

CATERPILLAR FOUNDATION [1092]

100 N.E. Adams Street
Peoria, IL 61629-1480
(309) 675-1000
Web Site: www.caterpillar.com/en/company/caterpillar-foundation.html
www.togetherstronger.com

FOUNDED: 1952

AREAS OF INTEREST:
Poverty alleviation via programs with measurable outcomes in the areas of basic human needs, education and environment.

TYPE:
General operating grants; Project/program grants.

PURPOSE:
To support local and community activities where the company has a major manufacturing presence, as well as national and international organizations; to alleviate poverty and place people on the path to prosperity.

ELIGIBILITY:
Organizations in areas of company manufacturing operations and classified as 501(c)(3) by the IRS can apply. No grants to individuals and religious organizations.

FINANCIAL DATA:
Amount of support per award: Varies.

APPLICATION INFO:
Applicant must complete eligibility questionnaire. Grant application process is by invitation only.
Duration: One year. Grants are renewable.

CATHOLIC CAMPAIGN FOR HUMAN DEVELOPMENT [1093]

3211 4th Street, N.E.
Washington, DC 20017
(202) 541-3210
Fax: (202) 541-3329
E-mail: cchdgrants@usccb.org
Web Site: www.usccb.org/cchd

FOUNDED: 1970

AREAS OF INTEREST:
Humanitarianism.

NAME(S) OF PROGRAMS:
• **Community Development Grant**
• **Economic Development Grant**

TYPE:
Project/program grants.

YEAR PROGRAM STARTED: 1970

PURPOSE:
To address the root causes of poverty by nurturing solidarity between the poor and non-poor and facilitating the participation of people living in poverty.

LEGAL BASIS:
Roman Catholic Church-sponsored funding agency.

ELIGIBILITY:
To qualify for CCHD funds, applicant organizations must not promote, in any way, activities that work against Catholic values. CCHD's grants to local anti-poverty efforts are screened, awarded and monitored in close partnership with local Catholic dioceses. CCHD grants to groups in a local community require the explicit approval of the Bishop of that diocese.

GEOG. RESTRICTIONS: United States and territories.

FINANCIAL DATA:
Amount of support per award: $25,000 to $75,000.
Total amount of support: Varies.

NO. AWARDS: Approximately 180 for the year 2018.

APPLICATION INFO:
Contact CCHD for guidelines.
Duration: Community Development Grant: Six years; Economic Development Grant: Three years.
Deadline: Proposals accepted September 1 to November 1.

ADDRESS INQUIRIES TO:
Grants Administrator
(See address above.)

CENTRAL INDIANA COMMUNITY FOUNDATION [1094]

615 North Alabama Street
Indianapolis, IN 46204
(317) 634-2423 ext. 112
Fax: (317) 684-0943
E-mail: info@cicf.org
Web Site: www.cicf.org

FOUNDED: 1997

AREAS OF INTEREST:
Arts, culture, civic affairs, education, environment, parks, and health and human services.

TYPE:
General operating grants; Project/program grants; Scholarships.

PURPOSE:
To strengthen Marion and Hamilton counties by attracting charitable endowments; to maximize benefits to donors; to make effective grants; to provide leadership to address community needs by developing productive citizens, building strong neighborhoods, embracing inclusiveness, and promoting community amenities.

LEGAL BASIS:
Community foundation.

ELIGIBILITY:
Grants are made to nonprofit charitable organizations exempt from federal taxation under Section 501(c)(3) of the Internal Revenue Code. Priority is given to programs and projects which expect to have a positive effect on Marion and Hamilton counties.

GEOG. RESTRICTIONS: Mostly Marion and Hamilton counties, Indiana.

FINANCIAL DATA:
Amount of support per award: $250 to $100,000.
Total amount of support: Varies.

APPLICATION INFO:
Application information is available on the web site.
Duration: Typically one year.
Deadline: Varies.

PUBLICATIONS:
Annual report; newsletter.

IRS I.D.: 35-1793630

ADDRESS INQUIRIES TO:
Haley Logan
Community Investment Coordinator
E-mail: haleyl@cicf.org

CENTRAL NEW YORK COMMUNITY FOUNDATION [1095]

431 East Fayette Street
Suite 100
Syracuse, NY 13202-3314
(315) 422-9538
Fax: (315) 471-6031
E-mail: info@cnycf.org
Web Site: cnycf.org

FOUNDED: 1927

AREAS OF INTEREST:
Literacy, poverty, lead poisoning, capacity building, leadership development, and strengthening nonprofit capacity.

TYPE:
Capital grants; Project/program grants. Capital, programmatic, and organizational development grants that support new ideas and scale up projects with proven impact.

PURPOSE:
To support programs that strengthen nonprofits and prepare leaders for the future; to build, sustain, and share community knowledge; to promote collaboration to address community issues.

LEGAL BASIS:
Community foundation.

ELIGIBILITY:
Applicants must be tax-exempt, 501(c)(3) not-for-profit organizations in Madison and Onondaga counties which will fund innovative programs that address unmet community needs.

The Foundation encourages proposals that:
(1) suggest practical solutions to community problems;
(2) promote cooperation among not-for-profits without duplicating existing services;
(3) generate community support, both professional and volunteer;
(4) strengthen the organization's effectiveness or stability;
(5) demonstrate the organization's ability to secure realistic funding and;
(6) address prevention as well as remediation.

The Foundation does not make grants for annual operating budgets, endowments, sectarian purposes, loans or assistance to individuals, medical or academic research except when directed by donor, or activities that occurred before the Community Foundation's decision date.

GEOG. RESTRICTIONS: Madison and Onondaga counties, New York.

FINANCIAL DATA:
Amount of support per award: Varies.
Total amount of support: Over $12,000,000 for the year ended March 31, 2019.

NO. AWARDS: 3,157 grants to 1,240 nonprofits for the year ended March 31, 2019.

APPLICATION INFO:
Standard application forms are available. Foundation staff is available to answer questions or discuss with any prospective applicant the appropriateness of a request.
Duration: Varies.
Deadline: March and October.

PUBLICATIONS:
Annual report.

OFFICERS:
Peter A. Dunn, President and Chief Executive Officer
Kim Sadowski, Senior Vice President and Chief Financial Officer
Katrina M. Crocker, Vice President, Communications
Frank M. Ridzi, Vice President, Community Investment

ADDRESS INQUIRIES TO:
Peter Dunn, Chief Executive Officer
(See address above.)

THE CH FOUNDATION

6102 82nd Street
Suite 8A
Lubbock, TX 79424
(806) 792-0448
Fax: (806) 792-7824
E-mail: hhocker@chfoundation.com
Web Site: www.chfoundationlubbock.com

TYPE:
Capital grants; Project/program grants.
See entry 1935 for full listing.

HARRY CHAPIN FOUNDATION [1096]

16 Gerard Street
Huntington, NY 11743
(631) 423-7558
Fax: (631) 423-7598
E-mail: harrychapinfound@aol.com
Web Site: harrychapinfoundation.org

FOUNDED: 1981

AREAS OF INTEREST:
Community education, arts-in-education, agriculture and environment.

TYPE:
Challenge/matching grants; Project/program grants.

YEAR PROGRAM STARTED: 1981

PURPOSE:
To address the problems of the disadvantaged and promote educational programs that lead to a greater understanding of human suffering.

ELIGIBILITY:
Only programs operating in the U.S. will be funded. Applicants must be 501(c)(3) nonprofit. Organizations with annual budgets less than $500,000 are favored. Complete description of focus areas is available on the Foundation web site.

No grants to individuals.

GEOG. RESTRICTIONS: United States.

FINANCIAL DATA:
Amount of support per award: Up to
$10,000.

NO. AWARDS: Approximately 20 to 25 annually.

APPLICATION INFO:
Application should be made in a brief written
proposal to Ms. Leslie Ramme, Executive
Director, at the HCF Office. HCF also
accepts the New York/New Jersey Area
Common Grant Application Form.

Duration: One year. Must reapply.

Deadline: Applications are accepted on an
ongoing basis.

EXECUTIVE DIRECTOR:
Leslie Ramme

ADDRESS INQUIRIES TO:
Leslie Ramme, Executive Director
(See address above.)

CHARLESTON AREA CHARITABLE FOUNDATION [1097]

c/o Gilbert, Metzger & Madigan
P.O. Box 677
Charleston, IL 61920
(217) 345-2128
Fax: (217) 345-2315

AREAS OF INTEREST:
Community and education.

TYPE:
Grants-in-aid; Project/program grants.

PURPOSE:
To enhance and support the quality of life in
Charleston, IL area.

ELIGIBILITY:
Grants are made to organizations that have
tax-exempt status under Section 501(c)(3) of
the Internal Revenue Code. No grants are
made to individuals.

GEOG. RESTRICTIONS: Charleston, Illinois and
surrounding area.

FINANCIAL DATA:
Amount of support per award: Grants vary in
amount, depending upon the needs and
nature of the request.

Total amount of support: Varies.

APPLICATION INFO:
Applicants must submit a brief letter
outlining the purpose of the grant.

Duration: One-time grants.

Deadline: Quarterly; two weeks prior to
Board meetings to be held in February, May,
August and November.

ADDRESS INQUIRIES TO:
Michael Metzger, President
(See address above.)

THE CHAUTAUQUA REGION COMMUNITY FOUNDATION [1098]

418 Spring Street
Jamestown, NY 14701
(716) 661-3390
Fax: (716) 488-0387
E-mail: tirgang@crcfonline.org
Web Site: www.crcfonline.org

FOUNDED: 1978

AREAS OF INTEREST:
Arts and leisure, economic development,
education, health care, and workforce
development.

NAME(S) OF PROGRAMS:
● Axel W. Carlson Award
● John D. Hamilton Community Service Award

TYPE:
Awards/prizes; Capital grants;
Challenge/matching grants; Endowments;
General operating grants; Matching gifts;
Project/program grants; Scholarships; Seed
money grants; Technical assistance; Training
grants. Axel W. Carlson Award has been a
tribute to the unsung heroes of our
community. These individuals have made
significant contributions through their efforts
while neither receiving nor expecting reward
or recognition.

The John D. Hamilton Community Service
Award recognizes an individual's dedication,
leadership and support in furthering
community spirit and enhancing the quality
of life in the Chautauqua Community.

YEAR PROGRAM STARTED: 1978

PURPOSE:
To enrich the quality of life in the
Chautauqua region.

LEGAL BASIS:
501(c)(3).

ELIGIBILITY:
Grants are available to 501(c)(3) nonprofit
organizations. Scholarships are provided to
students for higher education.

GEOG. RESTRICTIONS: Chautauqua region, New
York.

FINANCIAL DATA:
Amount of support per award: Varies.

Total amount of support: Over $3,200,000 in
grants and scholarships for the year 2018.

Matching fund requirements: Varies
depending on the request.

NO. MOST RECENT APPLICANTS: 1,000.

NO. AWARDS: 850.

APPLICATION INFO:
Carlson and Hamilton Awards: Nominations
are to be submitted by letter or e-mail, with
the full name, address and detailed
explanation of that person's contributions and
accomplishments, along with an explanation
of why the nominee is deserving of the
award. If the nominator is uncertain if they
should submit the nomination or has
additional questions, please contact the office
via telephone for clarification.

Online grant application can be completed by
visiting ChautauquaGrants.org.

Duration: One calendar year.

Deadline: Carlson Award: March 1;
Hamilton Award: April 1. Grant deadlines
vary.

PUBLICATIONS:
Annual report; newsletters; scholarship
booklet.

IRS I.D.: 16-1116837

STAFF:
Tory L. Irgang, Executive Director
Sarah M. Shelters, Communications Officer
Jacob S. Schrantz, Fiscal Officer
Lisa W. Lynde, Program Officer
Michelle Frederickson, Program Associate

ADDRESS INQUIRIES TO:
Tory L. Irgang, Executive Director
(See address above.)

CHESTER COUNTY COMMUNITY FOUNDATION [1099]

28 West Market Street
West Chester, PA 19382
(610) 696-8211
Fax: (610) 696-8213
E-mail: grants@chescocf.org
Web Site: www.chescocf.org

FOUNDED: 1994

AREAS OF INTEREST:
Quality of life in the Chester County,
Pennsylvania area.

TYPE:
Capital grants; Challenge/matching grants;
General operating grants; Grants-in-aid;
Project/program grants; Scholarships.

YEAR PROGRAM STARTED: 1994

PURPOSE:
To improve the quality of life in communities
within Chester County, PA.

LEGAL BASIS:
501(c)(3) public charity.

GEOG. RESTRICTIONS: Primarily Chester County,
Pennsylvania.

FINANCIAL DATA:
Approximately $60,000,000 in assets.

Amount of support per award: $1,000 to
$15,000.

Total amount of support: $2,400,000 for
fiscal year 2018.

NO. MOST RECENT APPLICANTS: 160 for the
year 2018.

NO. AWARDS: Approximately 700 for the year
2018.

APPLICATION INFO:
Information may be obtained from the
Foundation web site.

Duration: One year. Renewal by
reapplication.

Deadline: Proposals are accepted year-round.

ADDRESS INQUIRIES TO:
Beth Harper Briglia, Executive Vice
President of
Philanthropy Services
(See address above.)

THE CHICAGO COMMUNITY TRUST [1100]

225 North Michigan Avenue
Suite 2200
Chicago, IL 60601
(312) 616-8000
Fax: (312) 616-7955
E-mail: grants@cct.org
Web Site: www.cct.org

FOUNDED: 1915

AREAS OF INTEREST:
The well-being of the residents of Cook
County, IL in the fields of health, basic
human needs, community development,
education, cultural arts, sustainability and the
environment.

TYPE:
General operating grants; Project/program
grants; Technical assistance. Grants to
tax-exempt institutions and organizations for
charitable purposes. Special initiatives are
developed periodically.

YEAR PROGRAM STARTED: 1915

PURPOSE:
To provide for the broad charitable needs of the community in a manner which will assure response to the most pressing problems of the day.

LEGAL BASIS:
Community foundation.

ELIGIBILITY:
Applicants must be tax-exempt, 501(c)(3) organizations. Funded projects must benefit the residents of Cook County, IL. Some grants are made for the region.

GEOG. RESTRICTIONS: Cook County, Illinois.

FINANCIAL DATA:
Amount of support per award: Varies.
Total amount of support: Approximately $240,000,000 for the year 2018.

NO. MOST RECENT APPLICANTS: 700 to 800.

APPLICATION INFO:
Applicants must register through the online grant system. Paper letters of inquiry will not be accepted.
Duration: One year.

PUBLICATIONS:
Guidelines; annual report.

STAFF:
Helene D. Gayle, President and Chief Executive Officer

ADDRESS INQUIRIES TO:
See e-mail address above.

ROBERT STERLING CLARK FOUNDATION [1101]
135 East 64th Street
New York, NY 10065
(212) 288-8900
Fax: (212) 288-1033
E-mail: rscf@rsclark.org
Web Site: www.rsclark.org

FOUNDED: 1952

AREAS OF INTEREST:
Leadership and leadership development.

TYPE:
Project/program grants.

PURPOSE:
To support, encourage and invest in people and the nonprofit organizations that develop them in communities across New York City.

LEGAL BASIS:
501(c)(3).

ELIGIBILITY:
Applicants must be nonprofit organizations.

PUBLICATIONS:
Annual report; guidelines.

BOARD OF DIRECTORS:
James Allen Smith, Chairman
Julie Muraco, Treasurer
Paul Dolan
John Hoyt Stookey

OFFICER:
Philip Li, President

ADDRESS INQUIRIES TO:
Philip Li, President
(See address above.)

THE CLEVELAND FOUNDATION [1102]
1422 Euclid Avenue
Suite 1300
Cleveland, OH 44115-2001
(216) 861-3810
Fax: (216) 861-1729
E-mail: grantsmgmt@clevefdn.org
Web Site: www.clevelandfoundation.org

FOUNDED: 1914

AREAS OF INTEREST:
Economic development, public education reform, neighborhood and housing, human services and youth development strengthening the quality of life in early childhood, strengthening the arts and cultural community and greater university circle.

TYPE:
Project/program grants; Scholarships.

YEAR PROGRAM STARTED: 1914

PURPOSE:
To enhance the quality of life for all citizens of greater Cleveland, now and for generations to come, by building endowment, addressing needs through grantmaking and providing leadership on key community issues.

LEGAL BASIS:
Community foundation.

ELIGIBILITY:
Grantmaking is restricted to programs and services in the Greater Cleveland community, Cuyahoga, Geauga and Lake counties. Requests are considered from tax-exempt agencies in the following areas: civic affairs, economic development, education, health, social services, arts and culture, and environment. Careful consideration is given to such criteria as benefit the entire community and applicant's ability to successfully carry out the proposed activity. Applicant must be a nonprofit organization.

Giving is limited to the Greater Cleveland area unless specified by the donor. No grants to individuals or religious institutions for religious purposes. No support for community services such as fire and police protection, fund-raising campaigns, memberships and travel. No support for publications or audiovisual materials unless they are an integral part of a key program. Capital support for buildings, major equipment, land or renovation is only provided when there is strong evidence that the project has high priority for the community.

GEOG. RESTRICTIONS: Greater Cleveland, Cuyahoga, Geauga and Lake counties, Ohio.

FINANCIAL DATA:
Amount of support per award: $200 to $4,000,000; average $50,000.
Total amount of support: $101,000,000 for the year 2017.
Matching fund requirements: Depending upon proposal, grants may be authorized contingent upon receipt of matching funds from agency's own or other sources.

CO-OP FUNDING PROGRAMS: Neighborhood Connections Program.

NO. AWARDS: 4,768 grants authorized for the year 2017.

APPLICATION INFO:
The Foundation requires organizations to submit inquiries and applications electronically. Guidelines can be found on the web site.

Duration: Usually one year.

PUBLICATIONS:
Annual report; *Giving Voice*, quarterly; Grantee e-newsletter.

IRS I.D.: 34-0714588

COASTAL COMMUNITY FOUNDATION OF SOUTH CAROLINA [1103]
635 Rutledge Avenue
Suite 201
Charleston, SC 29403
(843) 723-3635
Fax: (843) 577-3671
E-mail: info@coastalcommunityfoundation.org
Web Site: www.coastalcommunityfoundation.org

FOUNDED: 1974

AREAS OF INTEREST:
Community development, health, education, human needs, environment and arts.

NAME(S) OF PROGRAMS:
- **Specialized Grants**
- **Regional Grants**

TYPE:
Challenge/matching grants; Endowments; Project/program grants; Scholarships; Technical assistance; Training grants.

YEAR PROGRAM STARTED: 1974

PURPOSE:
To help create vibrant communities by uniting people and investing resources.

ELIGIBILITY:
Generally, applicants must be charitable 501(c)(3) organizations in Beaufort, Berkeley, Charleston, Colleton, Dorchester, Georgetown, Hampton, Horry and Jasper counties, South Carolina.

GEOG. RESTRICTIONS: Coastal South Carolina.

FINANCIAL DATA:
Amount of support per award: Generally $20,000 maximum.
Total amount of support: Varies.

NO. MOST RECENT APPLICANTS: Approximately 550 for the year 2018.

NO. AWARDS: Approximately 330 for the year 2018.

APPLICATION INFO:
Application and instructions are available online.
Duration: Grantees typically have 12 months from receipt to expend their awards.
Deadline: Mid-January and early June.

IRS I.D.: 23-7390313

THE COLUMBUS FOUNDATION [1104]
1234 East Broad Street
Columbus, OH 43205
(614) 251-4000
Fax: (614) 251-4009
E-mail: contactus@columbusfoundation.org
Web Site: www.columbusfoundation.org

FOUNDED: 1943

AREAS OF INTEREST:
Advancing philanthropy, arts and humanities, urban affairs, conservation, education, health and social services.

NAME(S) OF PROGRAMS:
- **Fund for Capital Improvements**

- Fund for Financial Innovation
- Fund for Innovative Operations
- Fund for Targeted Needs

TYPE:
Capital grants; Development grants; Fellowships; General operating grants; Project/program grants; Scholarships. The Foundation awards competitive grants from the unrestricted and field-of-interest funds created by donors.

The Fund for Capital Improvements supports projects designed to improve the delivery, quality, and efficiency of nonprofit programs and services that serve vulnerable populations.

The Fund for Financial Innovation will support nonprofit leaders and their organizations to adapt to the new economic reality.

The Fund for Innovative Operations addresses significant needs of local organizations through grants supporting continuous improvement, capacity-building, and arts and cultural efforts.

The Fund for Targeted Needs addresses basic needs, disadvantaged children, developmental disabilities (traditional grants program), as well as more narrow and specific grant programs.

YEAR PROGRAM STARTED: 1943

PURPOSE:
To assist donors and others in strengthening and improving the community for the benefit of all its residents.

LEGAL BASIS:
Community foundation, exempt under Section 501(c)(3) of the Internal Revenue Code.

ELIGIBILITY:
Organizations in the central Ohio region having recognition under Section 501(c)(3) of the Internal Revenue Code. No grants are made to individuals.

GEOG. RESTRICTIONS: Primarily Franklin County and surrounding area.

FINANCIAL DATA:
Amount of support per award: $250 to $1,250,000.
Total amount of support: Varies.

NO. MOST RECENT APPLICANTS: 403.

NO. AWARDS: 292.

REPRESENTATIVE AWARDS:
Capacity Building and Leadership Grants: $6,000 to Jeanne B. McCoy Community Center for the Arts Corporation to support the fund-raising planning component of the business plan; Innovative Operations-Continuous Improvement: $273,500 to Ohio Association of Second Harvest Foodbanks to support overall operations; Basic Needs: $95,000 to Community Shelter Board to support general operating expenses to address homelessness.

APPLICATION INFO:
Those seeking grants may submit a Letter of Intent or a Full Proposal to the Foundation by accessing its online grant application system through its web site.
Duration: Typically one year.
Deadline: Varies.

PUBLICATIONS:
Annual yearbook; application guidelines.

IRS I.D.: 31-6044264

STAFF:
Douglas F. Kridler, President and Chief Executive Officer
Scott G. Heitkamp, Vice President and Chief Financial Officer
Dan A. Sharpe, Vice President, Community Research and Grants Management

ADDRESS INQUIRIES TO:
Melissa McCool
Grants Management Coordinator
(See address above.)

COLUMBUS JEWISH FOUNDATION   [1105]

Robins Center for Philanthropy
1175 College Avenue
Columbus, OH 43209
(614) 338-2365
Fax: (614) 338-2361
E-mail: susan@jewishcolumbus.org
Web Site: www.jewishcolumbus.org

FOUNDED: 1955

AREAS OF INTEREST:
Jewish education, Jewish leadership development and the preservation of the integrity of the Jewish family.

TYPE:
Challenge/matching grants; Demonstration grants; Seed money grants.

YEAR PROGRAM STARTED: 1955

PURPOSE:
To develop sustainable financial resources to fulfill the Foundation's mission to ensure continuity of Jewish life and to meet changing needs locally, in Israel, and in our worldwide community.

LEGAL BASIS:
Public charity.

ELIGIBILITY:
Applicants must be 501(c)(3) organizations. Money will be designated for pilot projects or as seed money only. Particular emphasis on central Ohio Jewish organizations.

No grants to individuals. No operating support.

FINANCIAL DATA:
Amount of support per award: Varies depending on needs and nature of the request.
Total amount of support: $473,300 for fiscal year ended June 30, 2019.

CO-OP FUNDING PROGRAMS: The Foundation prefers to set up networks for funding with other organizations.

NO. MOST RECENT APPLICANTS: 22.

NO. AWARDS: 14 anticipated for the year 2019.

REPRESENTATIVE AWARDS:
Columbus Torah Academy Experiential Learning Initiative; Columbus Jewish Day School Math and English Arts Coaching; Columbus Jewish Cemetery Association for cemetery repairs and geo-tagging.

APPLICATION INFO:
Formal request forms are available from the Foundation.
Duration: Generally one year.
Deadline: September 15 and February 15.

PUBLICATIONS:
Annual report; guidelines.

IRS I.D.: 31-1384772

OFFICERS:
Jim Bowman, President
Harlan W. Robins, Vice President
William Byers, Treasurer
Michael Schlonsky, Secretary

ADDRESS INQUIRIES TO:
Susan Tanur, Director of Grants
(See address and e-mail above.)

COMMON COUNSEL FOUNDATION   [1106]

1624 Franklin Street
Suite 1022
Oakland, CA 94612
(510) 834-2995
Fax: (510) 834-2998
E-mail: info@commoncounsel.org
Web Site: www.commoncounsel.org

FOUNDED: 1988

AREAS OF INTEREST:
Economic, environmental and social justice.

TYPE:
General operating grants; Training grants; Travel grants.

PURPOSE:
To offer strategic philanthropic advisory services to donors and family foundations while serving the community at large.

ELIGIBILITY:
501(c)(3) nonprofit organizations. Religious organizations must be working in interfaith coalitions. Grants are not made to individuals. Also, must involve low- and moderate-income members in grassroots community organizing to bring about long-term policy change. Organizational budget must be $400,000 or less except for the small Grassroots Exchange Fund (travel grants), which considers requests from organizations with budgets up to $1,000,000 (higher priority is given to those with budgets less than $750,000).

FINANCIAL DATA:
Amount of support per award: Travel and training grants: $500 to $1,000 with an average of approximately $800; General operating grants: $5,000 to $15,000.

CO-OP FUNDING PROGRAMS: Abelard Foundation West; Acorn Foundation; Victor and Lorraine Honig Fund; Grassroots Exchange Fund; Native Voices Rising; Social and Economic Justice Fund; Still We Rise Fund.

NO. MOST RECENT APPLICANTS: 280.

APPLICATION INFO:
Applicant should submit a letter of inquiry. Full proposals for most of the Funds are by invitation only.
Deadline: January 15 and June 15 (or February through November for Grassroots Exchange Fund).

COMMUNITY FOUNDATION FOR A GREATER RICHMOND   [1107]

3409 Moore Street
Richmond, VA 23230
(804) 330-7400
Fax: (804) 330-5992
E-mail: sblackwell@cfrichmond.org
info@cfrichmond.org
Web Site: www.cfrichmond.org

FOUNDED: 1968

AREAS OF INTEREST:
Children, families, communities, health care, education and arts.

NAME(S) OF PROGRAMS:
- **The Jenkins Foundation: Improving the Health of Greater Richmond**
- **R.E.B. Awards for Teaching Excellence**
- **Sheltering Arms Fund**

TYPE:
Project/program grants; Scholarships. Competitive grants.

YEAR PROGRAM STARTED: 1968

PURPOSE:
To improve life for generations of children; to improve public education; to support innovative health care projects.

LEGAL BASIS:
Charitable trust.

ELIGIBILITY:
Proposals are accepted from charitable 501(c)(3) organizations serving residents of Greater Richmond and/or the Tri-Cities.

GEOG. RESTRICTIONS: Richmond and central Virginia.

FINANCIAL DATA:
Amount of support per award: Jenkins Fund: Up to $75,000; R.E.B. Awards: $4,000 to $12,000; Sheltering Arms: $5,000 to $20,000.
Total amount of support: Varies.

APPLICATION INFO:
Guidelines and application forms are available on the web site.
Duration: Typically one year.
Deadline: Varies per program.

PUBLICATIONS:
Annual report.

OFFICERS:
Pamela J. Royal, M.D., Chairperson
Austin Brockenbrough, IV, Vice Chairperson
Sherry Armstrong, President and Chief Executive Officer
Philip M. Goodpasture, Treasurer
Kristen Hager, Secretary

ADDRESS INQUIRIES TO:
Jenkins Foundation and Sheltering Arms:
Eric Clay, Senior Program Officer
Health Initiatives

R.E.B. Awards:
Stacey Keeley, Director of Philanthropic Services
(See address above.)

COMMUNITY FOUNDATION FOR GREATER ATLANTA, INC. [1108]

191 Peachtree Street, N.E.
Suite 1000
Atlanta, GA 30303
(404) 688-5525
Fax: (404) 688-3060
E-mail: rrodriguez@cfgreateratlanta.org
Web Site: www.cfgreateratlanta.org

FOUNDED: 1951

AREAS OF INTEREST:
Operational grants to nonprofits serving a 23-county region in Georgia.

NAME(S) OF PROGRAMS:
- **A Place to Perform**
- **An Extra Wish**
- **Atlanta AIDS Fund**
- **Civic Engagement Fund**

- **Metropolitan Atlanta Arts Fund**
- **Neighborhood Fund**
- **Newton Fund**
- **Nonprofit Toolbox**
- **Strategic Restructuring Fund**

TYPE:
General operating grants; Project/program grants; Scholarships; Technical assistance; Training grants. Project/program grants support organizations implementing creative and impactful programs and policies that increase the equity of opportunity.

YEAR PROGRAM STARTED: 1951

PURPOSE:
To provide quality services to donors and innovative leadership on community issues.

LEGAL BASIS:
501(c)(3) community foundation.

ELIGIBILITY:
Applicant organizations must have 501(c)(3) status. Project must be within the metropolitan Atlanta area. Request for funding may not exceed 10% of organization's operational budget. For general operation grants, organization must have an operating budget of $100,000.

Grant funds cannot be used for regranting, fund-raising or capital campaigns. No grants to individuals.

GEOG. RESTRICTIONS: 23 counties in the metropolitan Atlanta area.

FINANCIAL DATA:
Amount of support per award: Maximum $75,000.

NO. MOST RECENT APPLICANTS: 290 for discretionary monies.

APPLICATION INFO:
Grant application guidelines are available online.
Duration: No grants are awarded on a continuing basis. Generally, grants are one or two years.
Deadline: Arts Fund and Common Good: May; Grants: February and October.

PUBLICATIONS:
Annual report; policy and application guidelines.

IRS I.D.: 58-1344646

STAFF:
Alicia Philipp, President
Diana Champ Davis, Chief Financial Officer and Vice President, Capacity
Lita Ugarte Pardi, Vice President, Community
Elyse Hammett, Vice President, Marketing and Communications

BOARD MEMBERS:
Susan Grant, Chairperson
Frank Bell
Rabbi Peter S. Berg
Millard Choate
Bert Clark
Richard W. Courts, IV
Patrice Greer
Doug Hooker
Julia A. Houston
Wonya Lucas
Jeffrey S. Muir
Barbara Bing Pliner
Bryan Rand
John C. Reid
Dave Stockert
Ramon Tome
Dr. Gregory J. Vaughn

Benjamin T. White, Legal Counsel
Jerry Wilkinson
Studie Young

ADDRESS INQUIRIES TO:
Ryan Rodriguez, Grants Manager
(See address above.)

COMMUNITY FOUNDATION FOR GREATER BUFFALO [1109]

726 Exchange Street
Suite 525
Buffalo, NY 14210
(716) 852-2857
Fax: (716) 852-2861
E-mail: mail@cfgb.org
Web Site: cfgb.org

FOUNDED: 1919

TYPE:
Grants-in-aid; Scholarships. Grants to organizations in the eight counties of western New York state.

YEAR PROGRAM STARTED: 1919

PURPOSE:
To connect people, ideas and resources to improve lives in western New York state. The four community goals of the Foundation are:
(1) Improve educational achievement for students living in low-income households;
(2) Increase racial/ethnic equity;
(3) Protect and restore significant environmental resources and promote equitable access and;
(4) Strengthen the region as a center for architecture, arts and culture.

LEGAL BASIS:
Community trust; 501(c)(3) tax determination; public charity under Section 170(b)(1)(a)(vi).

ELIGIBILITY:
Programs and agencies must benefit residents of the eight counties of western New York state.

GEOG. RESTRICTIONS: Eight counties of western New York state.

FINANCIAL DATA:
Amount of support per award: $5,522 to $45,000 for the year 2018.
Total amount of support: $529,622.

NO. MOST RECENT APPLICANTS: 114 for the year 2018.

NO. AWARDS: 23.

APPLICATION INFO:
Application information is available on the web site.
Deadline: Letters of Intent accepted from January 1 to February 1. Selected Letters of Intent invited to submit a full proposal by May 3. Applicants notified by mid-July.

STAFF:
Clotilde Perez-Bode Dedecker, President/Chief Executive Officer
Brendan Harrington, Chief Financial Officer/Chief Administrative Officer
Cindy Odom, Chief Community Impact Officer
Betsy Constantine, Executive Vice President, Giving Strategies
Jean McKeown, Vice President, Community Impact
Myra Lawrence, Vice President, Finance
Colleen Becht, Controller
Kate Masiello, Senior Director, Client Relations
Mary Bradach, Senior Director, Gift Planning

Felicia Beard, Senior Director, Racial Equity
Initiatives
Leah Angel Daniel, Director, Communities of
Giving Legacy Initiative
Bridget Niland, Director, Youth Sports
Initiatives
Ba Zin Lin, Senior Program Officer
Darren Penoyer, Senior Program Officer
Sira Faye, Program Officer
Allie Urbanski, Program Officer
Alexandra Warner, Program Officer
Aubrey Hammond, Scholarship Officer
Linda Gallagher, Accounting Manager
Alicia Dziak, Communications Content
Manager
Mark Vanderwerken, Operations Manager
Mary Sheehan, Senior Accountant
Nora Kennon, Giving Strategies Associate
Laura Schwamborn, Giving Strategies
Associate

BOARD OF DIRECTORS:
Tamara O. Alsace, Ph.D.
Jennifer Chalmers Balbach
Melissa Baumgart
James Biltekoff
Gary Crosby
Bonnie R. Durand, Ph.D.
Ross J. Eckert
Steve Finch
Lawrence C. Franco
Dottie Gallagher
Allen (Pete) Grum
Alice Jacobs, J.D.
Cheryl A. Jankowski
William Joyce
Alex Montante
Gary L. Mucci
Hal D. Payne
Hon. Rose H. Sconiers
John F. Somers
Francisco M. Vasquez, Ph.D.
John N. Walsh, III

ADDRESS INQUIRIES TO:
Darren Penoyer, Senior Program Officer
(See address above.)

THE COMMUNITY FOUNDATION FOR GREATER NEW HAVEN [1110]

70 Audubon Street
New Haven, CT 06510-9755
(203) 777-2386
Fax: (203) 787-6584
E-mail: contactus@cfgnh.org
Web Site: www.cfgnh.org

FOUNDED: 1928

AREAS OF INTEREST:
Health, education, community development,
regional and economic development, arts and
culture, youth, environment, and food and
shelter.

TYPE:
Capital grants; General operating grants;
Matching gifts; Project/program grants;
Scholarships. Capacity building grants.
Support for youth and welfare agencies,
social services, hospitals and health agencies,
educational institutions, community funds
and the humanities, including music and art,
to organizations serving the residents of
greater New Haven.

PURPOSE:
To create positive and sustainable change in
greater New Haven, CT.

LEGAL BASIS:
Community foundation established in
Connecticut by Resolution and Declaration of
Trust.

ELIGIBILITY:
The Foundation welcomes grant requests
from greater New Haven area organizations
that are defined as tax-exempt under Section
501(c)(3) or any applicable statute of the
Internal Revenue Code. While grants are
occasionally made to governmental agencies,
local nonprofits receive priority.

GEOG. RESTRICTIONS: Greater New Haven,
Connecticut: Ansonia, Bethany, Branford,
Cheshire, Derby, East Haven, Guilford,
Hamden, Madison, Milford, New Haven,
North Branford, North Haven, Orange,
Oxford, Seymour, Shelton, Wallingford, West
Haven, Woodbridge.

FINANCIAL DATA:
Amount of support per award: Varies.
Total amount of support: Over $20,000,000
each year.

NO. MOST RECENT APPLICANTS: Varies.

NO. AWARDS: Varies.

REPRESENTATIVE AWARDS:
$50,000 to Bridges Healthcare, Inc., to
provide general operating support for a
comprehensive range of prevention, mental
health and addiction recovery programs for
adults, children and families; $120,000 to
New Haven Reads to provide general
operating support for the promotion of
literacy through tutoring, family engagement,
college preparation and a free book bank;
$30,000 to JUNTA for Progressive Action to
support leadership transition activities
including a national Executive Search, a staff
retreat and board development.

APPLICATION INFO:
Application information is available on the
Foundation's web site.
Duration: One year with multiyears
considered annually.
Deadline: Varies from year to year.

PUBLICATIONS:
Annual report; grant guidelines; newsletters.

IRS I.D.: 06-6032106

STAFF:
William W. Ginsberg, President and Chief
Executive Officer
Christina M. Ciociola, Senior Vice President
for Grantmaking and Strategy
A.F. Drew Alden, Senior Vice President for
Investments, Chief Financial Officer and
Chief Compliance Officer

ADDRESS INQUIRIES TO:
Denise Canning, Director of
Grant Operations
(See address above.)

COMMUNITY FOUNDATION FOR MONTEREY COUNTY [1111]

2354 Garden Road
Monterey, CA 93940
(831) 375-9712
Fax: (831) 375-4731
E-mail: info@cfmco.org
Web Site: www.cfmco.org/grants

FOUNDED: 1945

AREAS OF INTEREST:
Animal welfare, arts and culture, community
development, education, environment, health,
human services, historic preservation and
youth development.

NAME(S) OF PROGRAMS:
- **Community Impact Grants Program**
- **Neighborhood Grants Program**
- **Opportunity Grants**
- **Organizational Development Grants**

TYPE:
Capital grants; General operating grants;
Project/program grants; Scholarships;
Technical assistance.

PURPOSE:
To inspire philanthropy and be a catalyst for
strengthening communities throughout
Monterey County.

LEGAL BASIS:
Community foundation.

ELIGIBILITY:
Community-based, nonprofit organizations
whose programs benefit the residents of
Monterey County, CA.

The Foundation does not make Community
Impact Grants to support individuals, for
normal operating costs usually covered by
operating income, for endowment funds, to
support sectarian religious programs, for
annual campaigns, dinners, or special events,
to pay off past debts or existing obligations,
for scholarships, fellowships or travel grants,
or for technical or specialized research.

GEOG. RESTRICTIONS: Monterey County,
California.

FINANCIAL DATA:
Amount of support per award: Varies
depending on type of grant.
Total amount of support: Varies.

APPLICATION INFO:
Detailed guidelines and application form can
be obtained at the Foundation web site.
Duration: One year. Reapplication annually.
Deadline: Varies.

IRS I.D.: 94-1615897

ADDRESS INQUIRIES TO:
Director of Grantmaking or
Grants and Programs Coordinator
E-mail: grants@cfmco.org

THE COMMUNITY FOUNDATION FOR NORTHEAST FLORIDA [1112]

245 Riverside Avenue
Suite 310
Jacksonville, FL 32202
(904) 356-4483
Fax: (904) 356-7910
E-mail: kshaw@jaxcf.org
Web Site: www.jaxcf.org

AREAS OF INTEREST:
Early childhood, seniors, and the arts.

TYPE:
Project/program grants.

PURPOSE:
To stimulate philanthropy to build a better
community.

ELIGIBILITY:
Eligible organizations must be IRS 501(c)(3)
tax-exempt.

GEOG. RESTRICTIONS: Baker, Clay, Duval, Nassau and St. Johns counties in northern Florida.

FINANCIAL DATA:
Amount of support per award: Varies.
Total amount of support: Varies.

APPLICATION INFO:
Application information is available on the web site.
Duration: Up to 24 months.
Deadline: Varies.

PUBLICATIONS:
Newsletter; annual report.

STAFF:
John Zell, Vice President, Development
Kathleen Shaw, Vice President, Programs

ADDRESS INQUIRIES TO:
Kathleen Shaw
Vice President, Programs
(See address above.)

COMMUNITY FOUNDATION FOR NORTHEAST GEORGIA [1113]

6500 Sugarloaf Parkway, Suite 220
Duluth, GA 30097
(770) 813-3380
Fax: (770) 813-3375
E-mail: rredner@cfneg.org
Web Site: www.cfneg.org

FOUNDED: 1985

AREAS OF INTEREST:
The quality of life in northeast Georgia.

TYPE:
Grants-in-aid.

PURPOSE:
To improve the quality of life throughout northeast Georgia.

ELIGIBILITY:
Grants can be made to tax-exempt private agencies that the IRS classifies as 501(c)(3) organizations, public charities and government agencies. The Foundation will consider organizations that serve people in the areas of education, health and human services, community service and the arts.

GEOG. RESTRICTIONS: Northeast Georgia.

FINANCIAL DATA:
Approximately $80,000,000 has been granted since inception.
Amount of support per award: Varies.
Total amount of support: Varies.

NO. AWARDS: Varies.

APPLICATION INFO:
The grant request must be completed according to the standard Grant Proposal Guidelines issued by the Foundation. Application can be downloaded from the web site.
Duration: Typically one year.
Deadline: March.

ADDRESS INQUIRIES TO:
Margaret Bugbee, Chief Financial Officer
(See address above.)

COMMUNITY FOUNDATION FOR NORTHEAST MICHIGAN [1114]

100 North Ripley
Suite F
Alpena, MI 49707
(989) 354-6881
Fax: (989) 356-3319
E-mail: pheraghty@cfnem.org
Web Site: www.cfnem.org

FOUNDED: 1974

AREAS OF INTEREST:
Education, health, youth services, arts, community needs and issues important to women.

TYPE:
Conferences/seminars; Development grants; Endowments; Project/program grants; Scholarships; Seed money grants; Training grants. Tobacco-related programs/projects. Women's Giving Circle for issues important to women. Youth-related programs/projects.

YEAR PROGRAM STARTED: 1974

PURPOSE:
To provide resources for community projects.

LEGAL BASIS:
Community foundation.

ELIGIBILITY:
Eligible organizations must be IRS 501(c)(3) tax-exempt, government schools or churches, providing the project is nonsectarian. No grants to individuals.

GEOG. RESTRICTIONS: Alcona, Alpena, Montmorency and Presque Isle counties, Michigan.

FINANCIAL DATA:
Amount of support per award: Community Impact Grant: Up to $5,000; Women's Giving Circle and Youth-related programs/projects: Up to $2,500.
Total amount of support: Over $250,000 in grants for fiscal year 2018-19.

CO-OP FUNDING PROGRAMS: Collaboration between organizations is encouraged.

NO. MOST RECENT APPLICANTS: Approximately 225.

NO. AWARDS: Varies.

REPRESENTATIVE AWARDS:
High School Orchard Project; Eighth Grade University Visits; Elementary School and High School Robotics; Safety and Mobility for Seniors; Fiftieth Anniversary Capital Campaign.

APPLICATION INFO:
Applications may be obtained online.
Duration: One year, with the possibility of a six-month extension.
Deadline: Varies.

PUBLICATIONS:
Annual report; biannual newsletter; brochures; application guidelines.

IRS I.D.: 23-7384822

EXECUTIVE DIRECTOR:
Patrick Heraghty

ADDRESS INQUIRIES TO:
For Grants:
Kara LeMonds, Program Officer

For Women's Giving Circle:
Julie Wiesen, Program Director
(See address above.)

COMMUNITY FOUNDATION FOR PALM BEACH AND MARTIN COUNTIES [1115]

700 South Dixie Highway
Suite 200
West Palm Beach, FL 33401-5854
(561) 659-6800
Fax: (561) 832-6542
E-mail: info@cfpbmc.org
Web Site: www.yourcommunityfoundation.org

FOUNDED: 1972

AREAS OF INTEREST:
Community revitalization, positive youth development, education attainment, arts and culture, hunger and capacity building, and environment.

TYPE:
Challenge/matching grants; Conferences/seminars; Development grants; Project/program grants; Scholarships; Technical assistance; Training grants.

PURPOSE:
To develop a shared vision of building a sense of community.

ELIGIBILITY:
501(c)(3) organizations are eligible to apply for grants.

GEOG. RESTRICTIONS: Martin and Palm Beach counties, Florida.

FINANCIAL DATA:
Amount of support per award: Varies.
Total amount of support: $9,200,000 for the year ended June 30, 2018.
Matching fund requirements: Varies.

NO. MOST RECENT APPLICANTS: Approximately 600 grant applicants and 450 scholarship applicants for the year ended June 30, 2017.

NO. AWARDS: 618 grants and scholarships for the year ended June 30, 2017.

APPLICATION INFO:
Applicants must complete a proposal summary and budget form. Check online for application and submission information.
Duration: Scholarships: Up to four years. Grants: Varies.
Deadline: Scholarships: February 1. Grants: Varies.

PUBLICATIONS:
Annual report; newsletter.

IRS I.D.: 23-7181875

OFFICERS:
Bradley Hurlburt, President and Chief Executive Officer
Steve Erjavec, Chief Financial Officer

ADDRESS INQUIRIES TO:
Daryl Houston
Senior Community Impact Officer
(See address above.)

THE COMMUNITY FOUNDATION FOR THE GREATER CAPITAL REGION [1116]

2 Tower Place
Albany, NY 12203
(518) 446-9638
Fax: (518) 446-9708
E-mail: info@cfgcr.org
Web Site: www.cfgcr.org

FOUNDED: 1968

AREAS OF INTEREST:
Health, science, education, youth and environment.

NAME(S) OF PROGRAMS:
- **Capacity-Building Grant Initiative**
- **Regular Competitive Grants**

TYPE:
Capital grants; Challenge/matching grants; General operating grants; Matching gifts; Project/program grants; Research grants; Scholarships; Technical assistance. Small, flexible grants to support some of the costs associated with organizational capacity-building.

The Foundation creates networks of opportunity - opportunities to bring together interested donors and community service providers to address a particular problem or need in the local community served. It serves the Capital Region of New York state by funding creative, visionary and sensitive projects - often seed money for innovative programs - that address the evolving needs of the community. The Foundation also serves as a vehicle for individuals, families, corporations, private foundations and nonprofit organizations to use in carrying out their long-term philanthropic plans.

Homelessness: Grants are designed to eliminate homelessness in the Capital Region.

Disabilities: The purpose of these grants is to serve the needs of the mentally and/or physically disabled, including the hearing- and sight-impaired.

Health: Program and capital grants are available for health care organizations working to improve the health of residents of the four-county region around Albany, NY.

Science: This program makes grants to support and promote discovery and development in medicine, science and technology in the Capital District.

PURPOSE:
To support capacity-building efforts of organizations including projects that are designed to generate new thinking about ways to improve an organization's ability to serve the community, more effectively carry out its mission, and plan for the future.

LEGAL BASIS:
Classified by the Internal Revenue Code as a public charity.

ELIGIBILITY:
Grants are made to applicants that qualify under Section 501(c)(3) of the Internal Revenue Code as a nonprofit organization, or operate under the fiscal sponsorship of an organization that does, and serve residents and be located within the ten-county Greater Capital Region. No grants are made to individuals. Nonsectarian religious programs may apply.

The Foundation's competitive grants support organizations that do not discriminate in their employment practices, volunteer opportunities, or delivery of programs or services on the basis of race, color, religion, gender, national origin, ancestry, age, medical condition, disability, veteran status, marital status, sexual orientation, or any other characteristic protected by law.

GEOG. RESTRICTIONS: Albany, Columbia, Fulton, Greene, Montgomery, Rensselaer, Saratoga, Schenectady, Schoharie, or Washington counties, New York.

FINANCIAL DATA:
Assets of over $83,000,000.

Amount of support per award: $1,000 to $30,000.

Total amount of support: $6,400,000 in grants and scholarships for the year 2019.

NO. AWARDS: Over 1,374 grants and scholarships for the year 2019.

APPLICATION INFO:
An application form is required and may be obtained online. Prospective applicants may discuss their plans with the Foundation's program staff prior to submitting an application.
Duration: Varies.
Deadline: Varies.

PUBLICATIONS:
Grantmaking Guidelines.

ADDRESS INQUIRIES TO:
See e-mail address above.

COMMUNITY FOUNDATION OF ABILENE [1117]
850 North First
Abilene, TX 79601
(325) 676-3883
Fax: (325) 676-4206
E-mail: mparrish@cfabilene.org
Web Site: www.cfabilene.org

FOUNDED: 1986

AREAS OF INTEREST:
Human services, arts and culture, education, health, community development and civic affairs.

TYPE:
Capital grants; Challenge/matching grants; Project/program grants; Technical assistance.

PURPOSE:
To increase the quality of life in Abilene, TX; to increase the awareness of philanthropy in the area.

ELIGIBILITY:
Eligible organizations must be IRS 501(c)(3) tax-exempt and be located in the immediate Abilene, TX area.

GEOG. RESTRICTIONS: Abilene, Texas.

FINANCIAL DATA:
Amount of support per award: $1,000 to $25,000.

Total amount of support: Approximately $5,400,000.

NO. MOST RECENT APPLICANTS: 75.

NO. AWARDS: 50.

APPLICATION INFO:
Applicants must submit required documentation online.
Duration: One year.
Deadline: Spring and fall.

ADDRESS INQUIRIES TO:
Michelle Parrish, Grants Director
(See address above.)

COMMUNITY FOUNDATION OF COLLIER COUNTY [1118]
1110 Pine Ridge Road, Suite 200
Naples, FL 34108
(239) 649-5000
Fax: (239) 649-5337
E-mail: ekeesler@cfcollier.org
Web Site: www.cfcollier.org

FOUNDED: 1985

AREAS OF INTEREST:
Health, human services, basic needs, education, civic affairs, environment, arts and humanities, women and girls, economic development and animal welfare.

TYPE:
Development grants; Matching gifts; Project/program grants; Scholarships. Capacity-building grants. Community Grant Programs in the area of professional development.

YEAR PROGRAM STARTED: 1985

PURPOSE:
To improve the quality of life in Collier County by connecting donors to community needs; to provide leadership on critical community issues.

LEGAL BASIS:
Public foundation.

ELIGIBILITY:
Eligible organizations must be IRS 501(c)(3) tax-exempt.

GEOG. RESTRICTIONS: Primarily Collier County, Florida.

FINANCIAL DATA:
Amount of support per award: Varies.
Total amount of support: Varies.

APPLICATION INFO:
Guidelines are available on the Foundation web site. Applications must be submitted through the online grant portal.
Duration: Varies.
Deadline: Varies.

PUBLICATIONS:
Guidelines; annual report; newsletter; *Vital Signs*, report; *Donor Advised Fund Handbook*; issue papers.

STAFF:
Eileen Connolly-Keesler, President and Chief Executive Officer
Lisette Holmes, Chief Financial Officer
Laura Simmelink, Senior Director of Programs

ADDRESS INQUIRIES TO:
Eileen Connolly-Keesler
President and Chief Executive Officer
(See address above.)

COMMUNITY FOUNDATION OF EASTERN CONNECTICUT [1119]
68 Federal Street
New London, CT 06320
(860) 442-3572
Fax: (860) 442-0584
E-mail: jennob@cfect.org
Web Site: www.cfect.org

FOUNDED: 1982

AREAS OF INTEREST:
Arts and culture, civic affairs, community needs and development, education, empowering youth, promoting basic needs and rights, preserving the environment, and advancing animal welfare.

NAME(S) OF PROGRAMS:
- **Animal Welfare Grants**
- **Community Foundation Scholarships**
- **Environmental Grants**
- **Northeast Area Women and Girls Fund**
- **Norwich Area Women and Girls Fund**
- **Norwich Youth Grants**
- **Southeast Area Women and Girls Fund**

- **Southeastern General Grants**
- **Windham Area Women and Girls Fund**

TYPE:
General operating grants; Project/program grants; Scholarships.

YEAR PROGRAM STARTED: 1982

PURPOSE:
To connect the generosity of private donors with the changing needs of the residents of eastern Connecticut by promoting local philanthropy and funding local projects.

ELIGIBILITY:
Federally recognized 501(c)(3) organizations and most charitable, educational and civic institutions that serve the towns listed below.

GEOG. RESTRICTIONS: Towns of Ashford, Bozrah, Brooklyn, Canterbury, Chaplin, Colchester, Columbia, Coventry, Eastford, East Lyme, Franklin, Griswold, Groton, Hampton, Killingly, Lebanon, Ledyard, Lisbon, Lyme, Mansfield, Montville, New London, North Stonington, Norwich, Old Lyme, Plainfield, Pomfret, Preston, Putnam, Salem, Scotland, Sprague, Stafford, Sterling, Stonington, Thompson, Union, Voluntown, Waterford, Willington, Windham, and Woodstock, Connecticut.

FINANCIAL DATA:
Amount of support per award: Grants: $1,000 to $50,000; Scholarships: $500 to $12,000.
Total amount of support: Varies.

NO. MOST RECENT APPLICANTS: Grants: 200; Scholarships: Over 500.

NO. AWARDS: Approximately 150 grants and 300 scholarships.

APPLICATION INFO:
Information is available on the Foundation web site or contact the Foundation for specific details on the various grant programs.
Duration: Typically one to four years.
Deadline: Varies by program.

ADDRESS INQUIRIES TO:
Jennifer O'Brien, Program Director
(See address above.)

THE COMMUNITY FOUNDATION OF FREDERICK COUNTY, MD, INC. [1120]

312 East Church Street
Frederick, MD 21701
(301) 695-7660
Fax: (301) 695-7775
E-mail: info@frederickcountygives.org
Web Site: www.frederickcountygives.org

FOUNDED: 1986

AREAS OF INTEREST:
Community development.

TYPE:
Project/program grants; Scholarships.

YEAR PROGRAM STARTED: 1986

PURPOSE:
To make charitable dreams come true by working with donors to establish funds that award grants and scholarships.

ELIGIBILITY:
Requirements can be found on the Foundation web site.

GEOG. RESTRICTIONS: Frederick County, Maryland.

FINANCIAL DATA:
Amount of support per award: Varies depending on need.
Total amount of support: Grants: Over $5,000,000 for fiscal year ended June 30, 2019; Scholarships: Over $1,000,000 annually.

NO. AWARDS: Over 280 grants to nonprofits for the year ended June 30, 2019; 430 scholarships to 314 individuals for the academic year 2019-20.

APPLICATION INFO:
Information may be found on the Foundation web site.
Duration: Grants: Varies. Scholarships: One academic year.
Deadline: Varies.

PUBLICATIONS:
Annual report; newsletters; grant applications.

IRS I.D.: 52-1488711

ADDRESS INQUIRIES TO:
See e-mail address above.

THE COMMUNITY FOUNDATION OF GREATER CHATTANOOGA, INC. [1121]

1400 Williams Street
Chattanooga, TN 37408
(423) 265-0586 ext. 11
Fax: (423) 265-0587
E-mail: rsuttles@cfgc.org
Web Site: cfgc.org

FOUNDED: 1963

AREAS OF INTEREST:
Nonprofit organizations.

TYPE:
Scholarships.

YEAR PROGRAM STARTED: 1963

PURPOSE:
To encourage giving and inspire action to improve lives in the Chattanooga area.

LEGAL BASIS:
501(c)(3).

ELIGIBILITY:
Each scholarship fund has specific eligibility criteria. Most funds require the applicant:
(1) be a graduating high school senior from a Hamilton County, TN high school;
(2) demonstrate financial need;
(3) applied to or have been accepted to attend a regionally accredited two- or four-year, technical, nonproprietary or community college or university and;
(4) have at least a cumulative grade point average of 2.5 or higher.

GEOG. RESTRICTIONS: Hamilton County, Tennessee.

FINANCIAL DATA:
Amount of support per award: Varies.

APPLICATION INFO:
Students must complete an eligibility quiz before being provided access to the scholarship application.
Duration: Varies.
Deadline: Varies.

IRS I.D.: 62-6045999

STAFF:
Meaghan Jones, President
Marisa Ogles, Vice President, Donor Services and Engagement
Rebecca Suttles, Director of Scholarships

BOARD OF DIRECTORS:
Julie Stowe, Chairperson
John Clark, Vice Chairperson
Dallas Joseph, Vice Chairperson
Elizabeth Williams, Vice Chairperson
Barry Large, Treasurer
Ansley Moses, Corporate Secretary
Ben Brown
Rondell Crier
Stacy Johnson
Cheryl Key
Travis Lytle
Gladys Pineda
Chantelle Roberson
Ray Ryan
Greg Willett

ADDRESS INQUIRIES TO:
Rebecca Suttles
Director of Scholarships
(See address above.)

THE COMMUNITY FOUNDATION OF GREATER CHATTANOOGA, INC. [1122]

1400 Williams Street
Chattanooga, TN 37408
(423) 265-0586 ext. 15
Fax: (423) 265-0587
E-mail: rposey@cfgc.org
Web Site: cfgc.org

FOUNDED: 1963

AREAS OF INTEREST:
Improving the quality of life in the Chattanooga, TN area.

TYPE:
Project/program grants.

PURPOSE:
To inspire giving and encourage action to improve lives in the Chattanooga area.

LEGAL BASIS:
501(c)(3).

ELIGIBILITY:
Organizations have to be 501(c)(3) public charities located in Hamilton County, TN and/or primarily serving Hamilton County.

GEOG. RESTRICTIONS: Hamilton County, Tennessee.

FINANCIAL DATA:
Amount of support per award: Varies.
Total amount of support: Approximately $900,000.

APPLICATION INFO:
Application information is available on the Foundation web site.
Duration: Generally one year.
Deadline: Contact Foundation for exact date.

ADDRESS INQUIRIES TO:
Robin Posey
Director of Community Impact
(See address above.)

COMMUNITY FOUNDATION OF GREATER GREENSBORO [1123]

330 South Greene Street
Suite 100
Greensboro, NC 27401
(336) 379-9100
Fax: (336) 378-0725
E-mail: info@cfgg.org
Web Site: cfgg.org

FOUNDED: 1983

AREAS OF INTEREST:
Capacity-building for nonprofits serving the Greater Greensboro, NC area.

NAME(S) OF PROGRAMS:
- **College and University Scholarships**
- **Community Grants Program**
- **Pre-College Scholarships**

TYPE:
Challenge/matching grants; Conferences/seminars; Demonstration grants; Development grants; Endowments; General operating grants; Project/program grants; Scholarships. Recognition Awards.

ELIGIBILITY:
Grant applicant must be a 501(c)(3) nonprofit organization located in or serving the greater Greensboro area. No grants to individuals.

GEOG. RESTRICTIONS: Greater Greensboro, North Carolina area.

FINANCIAL DATA:
Amount of support per award: Average grant: $3,000 to $5,000. Scholarships: Varies.
Total amount of support: Varies.

APPLICATION INFO:
Applications and guidelines are available online.
Duration: Varies.
Deadline: Varies.

IRS I.D.: 56-1380249

ADDRESS INQUIRIES TO:
H. Walker Sanders, President
(See address above.)

COMMUNITY FOUNDATION OF GREATER ROCHESTER   [1124]
P.O. Box 80431
Rochester, MI 48308-0431
(248) 608-2804
Fax: (248) 608-2826
E-mail: director@cfound.org
Web Site: www.cfound.org

FOUNDED: 1983

AREAS OF INTEREST:
Arts, conservation of natural resources, community needs and development, culture, education, environment, health, historic preservation and human services.

TYPE:
Endowments; Project/program grants; Scholarships; Travel grants. Community grants.

PURPOSE:
To enhance the quality of life for the citizens of Greater Rochester area by serving as a community endowment builder, grantmaker and leader.

ELIGIBILITY:
Grants are made to organizations that have tax-exempt status under Section 501(c)(3) of the Internal Revenue Code. Nonsectarian religious programs may apply.

GEOG. RESTRICTIONS: Primarily Greater Rochester, Michigan and surrounding area.

FINANCIAL DATA:
Amount of support per award: Varies.
Total amount of support: Varies.

APPLICATION INFO:
Contact the Foundation for application procedures.
Duration: Varies.
Deadline: Varies.

ADDRESS INQUIRIES TO:
Johanna Allen, Executive Director
(See address above.)

THE COMMUNITY FOUNDATION OF HERKIMER & ONEIDA COUNTIES, INC.   [1125]
2608 Genesee Street
Utica, NY 13502
(315) 735-8212
Fax: (315) 735-9363
E-mail: info@foundationhoc.org
Web Site: foundationhoc.org

FOUNDED: 1952

AREAS OF INTEREST:
Economic development, education, health and wellness, arts and culture.

TYPE:
Capital grants; Challenge/matching grants; Project/program grants; Scholarships; Seed money grants; Technical assistance; Training grants.

PURPOSE:
To improve the quality of life of the residents of Herkimer and Oneida counties in New York.

LEGAL BASIS:
Community foundation.

ELIGIBILITY:
Applications are entertained from organizations that are tax-exempt under Section 501(c)(3) of the Internal Revenue Code. Grants may be made for program or capital expenses. Operating funds will receive consideration on a short-term or emergency basis, with the understanding that applicants must submit a clear, realistic plan to secure alternative funding at the end of a specific time.

The Community Foundation does not make grants for religious purposes, nor does it provide financial assistance or scholarships directly to individuals, support for nonemergency expenses already incurred or ongoing operating support.

GEOG. RESTRICTIONS: Herkimer and Oneida counties, New York.

FINANCIAL DATA:
Amount of support per award: Average $34,000.
Total amount of support: $8,087,000.

NO. MOST RECENT APPLICANTS: 475.

NO. AWARDS: 891 grants and scholarships.

APPLICATION INFO:
Details are available on the Foundation web site.
Duration: One year; multi-year grants available occasionally on case-by-case basis.
Deadline: Grant requests are accepted on an ongoing basis.

PUBLICATIONS:
Annual report; newsletters.

IRS I.D.: 15-6016932

ADDRESS INQUIRIES TO:
Jan Squadrito
Senior Community Investment Manager
(See address above.)

COMMUNITY FOUNDATION OF JACKSON HOLE   [1126]
245 East Simpson Avenue
Jackson, WY 83001
(307) 739-1026
Fax: (307) 734-2841
E-mail: info@cfjacksonhole.org
Web Site: www.cfjacksonhole.org

FOUNDED: 1989

AREAS OF INTEREST:
Art, civic involvement, education, environment, health and human services, and recreation.

TYPE:
Development grants; General operating grants; Grants-in-aid; Project/program grants; Research grants.

PURPOSE:
To improve lives through philanthropic leadership.

LEGAL BASIS:
501(c)(3).

ELIGIBILITY:
Must be a 501(c)(3) corporation.

GEOG. RESTRICTIONS: Teton County, Wyoming.

FINANCIAL DATA:
Amount of support per award: Varies.
Total amount of support: Approximately $23,000,000 for the year 2018.

APPLICATION INFO:
Application information is available on the web site.
Deadline: Varies.

IRS I.D.: 83-0308856

ADDRESS INQUIRIES TO:
Laurie Andrews, President
(See address above.)

THE COMMUNITY FOUNDATION OF LORAIN COUNTY   [1127]
9080 Leavitt Road
Elyria, OH 44035
(440) 984-7390
Fax: (440) 984-7399
E-mail: foundation@peoplewhocare.org
Web Site: www.peoplewhocare.org

FOUNDED: 1980

AREAS OF INTEREST:
Arts and culture, civic affairs, education, health, and social services.

TYPE:
General operating grants; Project/program grants. Grants are given to improve the quality of life in Lorain County.

YEAR PROGRAM STARTED: 1980

PURPOSE:
To connect people who care with causes that matter.

ELIGIBILITY:
Organization or sponsor must be 501(c)(3). Funding must serve the people of Lorain County.

GEOG. RESTRICTIONS: Lorain County, Ohio.

FINANCIAL DATA:
Amount of support per award: Varies.
Total amount of support: Varies.

APPLICATION INFO:
Application is available on the web site.

Deadline: Dates are posted online.

ADDRESS INQUIRIES TO:
Linda Styer, Senior Program Officer
E-mail: grants@peoplewhocare.org

COMMUNITY FOUNDATION OF NORTH CENTRAL WISCONSIN [1128]

500 First Street
Suite 2600
Wausau, WI 54403
(715) 845-9555
E-mail: info@cfoncw.org
Web Site: www.cfoncw.org

FOUNDED: 1987

AREAS OF INTEREST:
Arts, education, health and human services, and resource preservation.

TYPE:
Capital grants; Development grants; Project/program grants; Scholarships; Seed money grants; Technical assistance.

YEAR PROGRAM STARTED: 1987

PURPOSE:
To enhance the quality of north central Wisconsin.

ELIGIBILITY:
Consideration is given primarily to those organizations that are tax-exempt under Section 501(c)(3) of the Internal Revenue Code.

GEOG. RESTRICTIONS: Greater Wausau area, Marathon County, Wisconsin.

FINANCIAL DATA:
Amount of support per award: $1,000 to $50,000.
Total amount of support: Varies.

CO-OP FUNDING PROGRAMS: Community Arts Grants are funded through the Wisconsin Arts Board; B.A. and Esther Greenheck Foundation and Community Foundation.

NO. MOST RECENT APPLICANTS: Average 100 per year.

NO. AWARDS: Average 50 to 60 per year.

REPRESENTATIVE AWARDS:
Medical College of Wisconsin; Boys & Girls Club; United Way.

APPLICATION INFO:
Application information is available on the web site.
Duration: One year.
Deadline: Applications are due the first business day of March, June, September and December.

STAFF:
Jean Tehan, President/Chief Executive Officer
Sue Nelson, Program Officer
Pam Eckmann, Director of Finance

ADDRESS INQUIRIES TO:
Sue Nelson, Program Officer
(See address above.)

COMMUNITY FOUNDATION OF SAINT JOSEPH COUNTY [1129]

P.O. Box 837
South Bend, IN 46624
(574) 232-0041
Fax: (574) 233-1906
E-mail: info@cfsjc.org
Web Site: www.cfsjc.org

AREAS OF INTEREST:
Arts and culture; community development and urban affairs; health and human services; parks, recreation, and environment; youth and education.

NAME(S) OF PROGRAMS:
- **African American Community Fund**
- **ArtsEverywhere Fund**
- **Leighton Award for Nonprofit Excellence**
- **Senior Living Initiative**
- **Special Project Challenge Grant**

TYPE:
Capital grants; Challenge/matching grants; Project/program grants; Scholarships. Donor-advised grants.

PURPOSE:
To promote organizations whose programs benefit the residents of St. Joseph County; to assist existing agencies to better respond to the needs of the community.

ELIGIBILITY:
Grants are made to organizations that have tax-exempt status under Section 501(c)(3) of the Internal Revenue Code. No grants are made to individuals. Nonsectarian religious programs may apply. Funded projects should benefit a significant constituency within the community and the organization must exhibit the ability to raise the required matching funds, if applicable.

GEOG. RESTRICTIONS: Saint Joseph County, Indiana.

FINANCIAL DATA:
Amount of support per award: Varies per award.
Matching fund requirements: Some programs require matching funds.

APPLICATION INFO:
Application information is available on the web site.
Duration: Varies.
Deadline: Special Project Challenge Grant: March 1 and October 1; Senior Living Initiative and ArtsEverywhere Fund: May 1 and November 1; Leighton Award for Nonprofit Excellence: August 1 of odd-numbered years.

STAFF:
Rose Meissner, President

ADDRESS INQUIRIES TO:
Emily Slatt, Program Officer
(See address above.)

THE COMMUNITY FOUNDATION OF SHELBY COUNTY [1130]

Courtview Center, Suite 202
100 South Main Avenue
Sidney, OH 45365-2771
(937) 497-7800
Fax: (937) 497-7799
E-mail: info@commfoun.com
Web Site: www.commfoun.com

FOUNDED: 1952

AREAS OF INTEREST:
Arts and culture, family and community, education, environment, and health.

TYPE:
Capital grants; Project/program grants; Scholarships; Seed money grants.

PURPOSE:
To improve the quality of life and to cultivate, administer and distribute legacy gifts for the benefit of its local community.

ELIGIBILITY:
Organizations must have 501(c)(3) status.

GEOG. RESTRICTIONS: Shelby County, Ohio.

FINANCIAL DATA:
Amount of support per award: Discretionary grants: $500 to $5,000.
Total amount of support: $88,000 in discretionary grants for the year 2020; $2,700,000 in total grantmaking for fiscal year 2018.

NO. MOST RECENT APPLICANTS: Varies.

NO. AWARDS: Varies.

APPLICATION INFO:
Applicants must call the Executive Director of the Foundation to discuss the grant request idea and whether the project appears to fit within the Foundation's guidelines. Preliminary Grant Proposals and Full Proposals will not be accepted if they have not been requested by the Executive Director.

Applications for most of the scholarships are available online.
Deadline: Grants: Approximately February 1 and August 1. Scholarships: Varies.

ADDRESS INQUIRIES TO:
Marian Spicer, Executive Director
(See address above.)

THE COMMUNITY FOUNDATION OF SOUTH ALABAMA [1131]

212 St. Joseph Street
Mobile, AL 36602
(251) 438-5591
Fax: (251) 438-5592
E-mail: jberson@communityfoundationsa.org
Web Site: communityfoundationsa.org

FOUNDED: 1976

AREAS OF INTEREST:
Arts and culture, economic opportunity, civic engagement, and health and wellness.

TYPE:
Project/program grants; Scholarships. Capacity-building grants. Special initiative grants.

PURPOSE:
To assemble and direct philanthropic assets to make Southwestern Alabama a better place.

LEGAL BASIS:
Alabama not-for-profit corporation/community foundation.

ELIGIBILITY:
Eligible organizations must be IRS 501(c)(3) tax-exempt and located in southwest Alabama.

GEOG. RESTRICTIONS: Southwestern Alabama (Baldwin, Choctaw, Clarke, Conecah, Escambia, Mobile, Monroe and Washington counties).

FINANCIAL DATA:
Amount of support per award: Varies.
Total amount of support: Varies.

APPLICATION INFO:
Guidelines and application form are available online.

Duration: Typically one year. Renewal by reapplication. Some multiyear grants may be awarded.

Deadline: Varies.

PUBLICATIONS:
Annual report; newsletter; application guidelines; *Charitable Gift Annuity*; *Real Estate Gifts*.

IRS I.D.: 63-0695166

STAFF:
Rebecca Byrne, President and Chief Executive Officer
Jena Berson, Director of Communications and Programs
Carolyn Marston, Director of Operations

ADDRESS INQUIRIES TO:
Jena Berson, Director of Communications and Programs
(See address and telephone number above.)

COMMUNITY FOUNDATION OF THE EASTERN SHORE   [1132]

1324 Belmont Avenue, Suite 401
Salisbury, MD 21804
(410) 742-9911
Fax: (410) 742-6638
E-mail: hmahler@cfes.org
Web Site: www.cfes.org

FOUNDED: 1984

AREAS OF INTEREST:
Arts, civic affairs, community needs, conservation, culture, education, health and historic preservation.

NAME(S) OF PROGRAMS:
* **Community Needs Grants**
* **Education Grants Program**
* **Richard A. Henson Award of Excellence**
* **Mini Grants**
* **Frank H. Morris Humanitarian Award**
* **Nonprofit Support Program**
* **Women's Fund Grants**
* **Workforce Development Grants**

TYPE:
Awards/prizes; Challenge/matching grants; Demonstration grants; Project/program grants; Scholarships; Seed money grants; Technical assistance; Training grants.

YEAR PROGRAM STARTED: 1984

PURPOSE:
To improve the quality of life in the area by acting as a funding source for present and future generations.

ELIGIBILITY:
Grants are made to organizations that have tax-exempt status under Section 501(c)(3) of the Internal Revenue Code and not classified as a private foundation that is located or serves the residents of the counties. No grants are made to individuals. Nonsectarian religious programs may apply. Agencies must be operated and organized so that they do not discriminate in the hiring of staff on the basis of race, religion, gender, sexual orientation, age, national origin or disability.

GEOG. RESTRICTIONS: Somerset, Wicomico and Worcester counties, Maryland.

FINANCIAL DATA:
Amount of support per award: Community Needs, Education Grants and Women's Fund Grants: Maximum $5,000; Henson and Morris Awards: Approximately $1,000; Mini Grants: Maximum $1,500.

Total amount of support: Over $5,000,000 in grants and scholarships annually.

APPLICATION INFO:
Varies by program. All request for funding must be submitted through the Foundation's e-grant portal.

Duration: One year.

Deadline: Community Needs: February 1 and August 1; Education Grants Program: August; Henson and Morris Awards: September 1; Mini Grants: 15th of each month; Women's Fund: March 30; Workforce Development: October 1.

STAFF:
Heather Mahler, Program Director

ADDRESS INQUIRIES TO:
Heather Mahler, Program Director
(See address above.)

COMMUNITY FOUNDATION OF THE FOX RIVER VALLEY   [1133]

111 West Downer Place
Suite 312
Aurora, IL 60506
(630) 896-7800
Fax: (630) 896-7811
E-mail: info@cffrv.org
Web Site: www.cffrv.org

AREAS OF INTEREST:
Education, health care, social services, the arts, and other charitable fields.

TYPE:
Capital grants; Scholarships.

PURPOSE:
To support worthwhile projects in the served communities.

ELIGIBILITY:
Grants are made to organizations that have tax-exempt status under Section 501(c)(3) of the Internal Revenue Code. No grants are made to individuals.

GEOG. RESTRICTIONS: Aurora, southern Kane County, and Kendall County, Illinois.

FINANCIAL DATA:
Amount of support per award: Varies.
Total amount of support: Varies.

NO. MOST RECENT APPLICANTS: Scholarships: Approximately 700 for the year 2019.

NO. AWARDS: Scholarships: Approximately 380 for the year 2019.

APPLICATION INFO:
Applications may be obtained from the Foundation web site.

Duration: Varies.

Deadline: Letter of Intent: March 31 and September 30. Grant proposals: May 1 and November 1. Scholarships: January.

ADDRESS INQUIRIES TO:
Julie Christman, President and Chief Executive Officer
(See address above.)

COMMUNITY FOUNDATION OF THE OZARKS   [1134]

425 East Trafficway
Springfield, MO 65806
(417) 864-6199
Fax: (417) 864-8344
E-mail: bdierks@cfozarks.org
Web Site: cfozarks.org

AREAS OF INTEREST:
Health and social services; arts, culture and environment; education and community development.

TYPE:
Challenge/matching grants; Demonstration grants; Development grants; Endowments; Project/program grants; Scholarships. Initiative grants. Technical/Capacity-building grants.

PURPOSE:
To build a community endowment; to provide leadership; to prompt collaboration on community issues; to improve the quality of life for citizens in Greene County, MO and the surrounding region.

LEGAL BASIS:
Community foundation.

ELIGIBILITY:
Eligible organizations must be IRS 501(c)(3) tax-exempt and located in Greene County, MO or counties represented by the Foundation's affiliate organizations which are located throughout the central and southern half of Missouri.

GEOG. RESTRICTIONS: Central and southern Missouri.

FINANCIAL DATA:
Amount of support per award: Grants: $1,500 to $25,000; Initiative Awards: $100,000 to $1,000,000.

Total amount of support: Discretionary Grants and Scholarships Programs: $2,000,000.

APPLICATION INFO:
Complete application information is available online.

Duration: Typically one year.

Deadline: Varies.

ADDRESS INQUIRIES TO:
Bridget Dierks, Vice President of Programs
(See address above.)

COMMUNITY FOUNDATION OF THE TEXAS HILL COUNTRY   [1135]

420 Water Street
Suite 108
Kerrville, TX 78028
(830) 896-8811
E-mail: austin@communityfoundation.net
Web Site: www.communityfoundation.net

FOUNDED: 1982

AREAS OF INTEREST:
Art and heritage, religion, basic human needs and youth development.

TYPE:
Challenge/matching grants; Development grants; Grants-in-aid; Matching gifts; Project/program grants; Scholarships; Technical assistance.

PURPOSE:
To improve the quality of life in the Texas Hill Country of Texas.

LEGAL BASIS:
Corporation.

ELIGIBILITY:
Organization must be located in or provide services to Bandera, Blanco, Edwards, Gillespie, Kendall, Kerr, Kimble, Mason, Real or Uvalde County, TX. Organization must be IRS 501(c)(3) tax-exempt. Grants are not awarded to individuals.

FINANCIAL DATA:
More than $23,000,000 in assets for the year ended December 31, 2018.

Amount of support per award: Varies.

Total amount of support: Varies.

NO. AWARDS: Varies.

APPLICATION INFO:
Application information is available on the Foundation web site.

IRS I.D.: 74-2225369

STAFF:
Austin Dickson, Executive Director
Amy Rector, Business Manager
Ingrid Cunyus, Grants and Scholarships Manager
Jayne Zirkel, Marketing and Events Manager

ADDRESS INQUIRIES TO:
Austin Dickson, Executive Director
(See address above.)

COMMUNITY FOUNDATION OF WEST TEXAS [1136]

6102 82nd Street, Suite 8B
Lubbock, TX 79424
(806) 762-8061
E-mail: tami@
communityfoundationofwesttexas.org
Web Site: www.cfwtx.org

FOUNDED: 1981

AREAS OF INTEREST:
Charitable organizations and community development.

NAME(S) OF PROGRAMS:
● **Mini Grant for Teachers Program**

TYPE:
Project/program grants; Scholarships; Technical assistance. Responsiveness to changing or emerging community needs approach for solving community problems in South Plains area.

YEAR PROGRAM STARTED: 1981

PURPOSE:
To improve the quality of life in the South Plains area of Texas.

ELIGIBILITY:
Organizations must be 501(c)(3) not-for-profit.

GEOG. RESTRICTIONS: Lubbock and the surrounding 14 counties of Texas.

FINANCIAL DATA:
Amount of support per award: Grant awards: Up to $5,000; Mini Grant for Teachers Program: Up to $1,000.

Total amount of support: Varies.

CO-OP FUNDING PROGRAMS: Affiliate Endowment Challenges, Community Endowment Challenge, Mini Grant for Teachers.

APPLICATION INFO:
Application information is available on the web site.

Duration: One year. Must reapply.

Deadline: Mini Grant for Teachers: June 15. All others: Varies.

ADDRESS INQUIRIES TO:
See e-mail address above.

COMMUNITY FOUNDATION OF WESTERN MASSACHUSETTS (CFWM) [1137]

333 Bridge Street
Springfield, MA 01103
(413) 732-2858
Fax: (413) 733-8565
E-mail: wmass@communityfoundation.org
Web Site: communityfoundation.org

FOUNDED: 1991

AREAS OF INTEREST:
Human services, economic development, education, arts and culture, health, housing and environment.

TYPE:
Capital grants; Project/program grants; Scholarships. Capacity building. Equipment.

YEAR PROGRAM STARTED: 1991

PURPOSE:
To enrich the quality of life of the people of our region.

ELIGIBILITY:
Grants are restricted to worthy public charities serving residents of Franklin, Hampden and Hampshire counties in Massachusetts.

GEOG. RESTRICTIONS: Franklin, Hampden and Hampshire counties, Massachusetts.

FINANCIAL DATA:
Amount of support per award: Varies.

Total amount of support: Approximately $2,000,000 awarded annually through competitive grant opportunities.

CO-OP FUNDING PROGRAMS: Informal linkages as well as funds established by family foundations within the community foundation.

NO. MOST RECENT APPLICANTS: 129 for the year 2018.

NO. AWARDS: 106 for the year 2018.

APPLICATION INFO:
Contact the Foundation for application procedures.

Duration: One year. Nonrenewable.

Deadline: Varies.

PUBLICATIONS:
Annual report; newsletter; brochures for donors and applicants.

STAFF:
Katie Allan Zobel, President and Chief Executive Officer
James Ayres, Vice President for Programs and Strategy

ADDRESS INQUIRIES TO:
James Ayres
Vice President for Programs and Strategy
(See address above.)

COMMUNITY FOUNDATIONS OF THE HUDSON VALLEY [1138]

80 Washington Street, Suite 201
Poughkeepsie, NY 12601
(845) 452-3077
Fax: (845) 452-3083
E-mail: grant@communityfoundationshv.org
Web Site: www.communityfoundationshv.org

FOUNDED: 1969

AREAS OF INTEREST:
Health, education and social services.

NAME(S) OF PROGRAMS:
● **Community Response Grants**

● **Farm Fresh Food Initiatives**
● **Fund for Excellence in Education Grants**

TYPE:
Project/program grants; Scholarships; Training grants. Equipment to improve office operations.

PURPOSE:
To improve the quality of life in Dutchess, Putnam and Ulster counties, New York.

ELIGIBILITY:
Eligible organizations must be IRS 501(c)(3) tax-exempt or have a fiscal sponsor.

GEOG. RESTRICTIONS: Primarily Dutchess, Putnam and Ulster counties, New York.

FINANCIAL DATA:
Amount of support per award: Varies.

Total amount of support: Approximately $27,000,000 for the year 2019.

APPLICATION INFO:
Application information is available on the web site. Applications are submitted through the online application system.

PUBLICATIONS:
Annual report; newsletters.

IRS I.D.: 23-7026859

ADDRESS INQUIRIES TO:
See e-mail address above.

*SPECIAL STIPULATIONS:
Review web site, if possible, for grant information. Applicants may contact the organization for details of its grants.

COMMUNITYGIVING [1139]

101 7th Avenue South, No. 100
St. Cloud, MN 56301
(320) 253-4380
(877) 253-4380
Fax: (320) 240-9215
E-mail: kgrochow@communitygiving.org
Web Site: www.communitygiving.org

FOUNDED: 1985

AREAS OF INTEREST:
Philanthropy to support arts and culture, education, environment, youth and families, and human services.

TYPE:
Challenge/matching grants; Conferences/seminars; General operating grants; Project/program grants; Scholarships; Seed money grants; Technical assistance.

PURPOSE:
To attract and administer funds to improve the quality of life for citizens of central Minnesota.

LEGAL BASIS:
Community foundation.

ELIGIBILITY:
Eligible organizations must be IRS 501(c)(3) tax-exempt and located within Benton, Sherburne and Stearns counties, Minnesota. Funding to religious organizations of a nonsectarian nature, which benefits the entire community. No grants to individuals.

GEOG. RESTRICTIONS: Benton, Sherburne and Stearns counties, Minnesota.

FINANCIAL DATA:
$149,000,000 in assets as of June 30, 2019.

Amount of support per award: Average: $5,096.

Total amount of support: $13,746,040 in grants paid as of June 30, 2019.

NO. AWARDS: 2,697.

APPLICATION INFO:
Online application and required documents
are available online. Applicant must include a
copy of the IRS 501(c)(3) tax determination
letter.
Duration: One year.
Deadline: Varies.

PUBLICATIONS:
Annual report; application guidelines.

IRS I.D.: 36-3412544

ADDRESS INQUIRIES TO:
Kathy Grochow
Director of Community Programs
(See address above.)

CONNECTICUT COMMUNITY FOUNDATION [1140]
43 Field Street
Waterbury, CT 06702
(203) 753-1315
Fax: (203) 756-3054
E-mail: info@conncf.org
Web Site: www.conncf.org

FOUNDED: 1923

AREAS OF INTEREST:
Arts and culture, cradle to career (youth
development/education), economic vitality,
environment, grassroots engagement, healthy
communities, older adults, technology and
women's issues.

CONSULTING OR VOLUNTEER SERVICES:
Nonprofit advisor services available.

NAME(S) OF PROGRAMS:
- **Capacity Building Grants**
- **Nonprofit Assistance Initiative**
- **Program Grants**
- **Scholarships**
- **Training Programs**

TYPE:
Capital grants; Challenge/matching grants;
Project/program grants; Scholarships; Seed
money grants; Technical assistance.
Sponsorships. Organizational development.

YEAR PROGRAM STARTED: 1923

PURPOSE:
To serve the people of the Greater Waterbury
and Litchfield Hills to improve the quality of
life.

LEGAL BASIS:
Community foundation.

ELIGIBILITY:
Applicant must:
(1) be a not-for-profit organization
recognized under Section 501(c)(3) of the
Internal Revenue Code, or a municipal entity
seeking a grant for public purposes;
(2) have a board, representative of the
community, of which a majority is neither
employees nor relatives of employees;
(3) be located within and/or providing
services to residents of the Foundation's
21-town service area: Beacon Falls,
Bethlehem, Bridgewater, Cheshire, Goshen,
Litchfield, Middlebury, Morris, Naugatuck,
New Milford, Oxford, Prospect, Roxbury,
Southbury, Thomaston, Warren, Washington,
Waterbury, Watertown, Wolcott or Woodbury
and;
(4) have a Nonprofit Registration to Solicit
Funds (or exemption, if appropriate) from the
Connecticut Department of Consumer
Protection. Registration must be renewed
annually.

Grant requests for political or religious
purposes or for capital expenditures on
buildings not owned by a nonprofit are not
accepted. Religious organizations or
municipalities are not eligible to apply for
grants for buildings or expenses related to
buildings. However, they may apply for
equipment that is specifically part of an
eligible programmatic request.

GEOG. RESTRICTIONS: Greater Waterbury and
Litchfield Hills, Connecticut.

FINANCIAL DATA:
Amount of support per award: Varies.
Total amount of support: Approximately
$4,000,000 in grants and scholarships.

NO. AWARDS: Over 900 grants and scholarships.

APPLICATION INFO:
Guidelines and application form may be
obtained online.
Duration: One year. Multiyear funding
should be applied for at the outset and is
subject to review.
Deadline: Varies.

PUBLICATIONS:
Annual report.

IRS I.D.: 06-6038074

ADDRESS INQUIRIES TO:
Josh Carey, Director of Grants Management
(See address above.)

COOK FAMILY FOUNDATION [1141]
120 West Exchange Street
Suite 202
Owosso, MI 48867
(989) 725-1621
Fax: (989) 936-5910
E-mail: tom@cookfamilyfoundation.org
Web Site: www.cookfamilyfoundation.org

FOUNDED: 1978

AREAS OF INTEREST:
Community organizations, education and
youth, environment, and University of
Michigan.

TYPE:
Capital grants; Challenge/matching grants;
Demonstration grants; Development grants;
Matching gifts; Project/program grants;
Scholarships; Seed money grants; Technical
assistance. Educational support.

YEAR PROGRAM STARTED: 1978

PURPOSE:
To strengthen and invest in the future of
community institutions in Shiawassee
County; to support the University of
Michigan.

LEGAL BASIS:
Family (private) foundation.

ELIGIBILITY:
Eligible organizations must be IRS 501(c)(3)
tax-exempt. The Foundation does not give
grants for religious purposes and upholds
federal law which prohibits the expenditure
of funds for political campaigns or direct
lobbying activities. With the exception of
scholarships, the Foundation does not give
grants to individuals.

GEOG. RESTRICTIONS: Shiawassee County,
Michigan.

FINANCIAL DATA:
Amount of support per award: Typically
$5,000 to $50,000.

Total amount of support: $1,114,248 in
grants for the year 2019.
Matching fund requirements: Varies based on
grant; average 20% cash/in-kind.

APPLICATION INFO:
Applicants should submit a short letter of
inquiry.
Deadline: First consideration will be given to
grant applications submitted by April 1.
Applications should be made no later than
November 1.

STAFF:
Yvette Collard, Associate Director

ADDRESS INQUIRIES TO:
Thomas Cook, Executive Director
P.O. Box 278
Owosso, MI 48867

*PLEASE NOTE:
The Foundation establishes a total annual
grant budget in January for that year and
addresses applications on a first-come,
first-served basis within that budget.

COOPERATIVE DEVELOPMENT FOUNDATION [1142]
1775 I Street, N.W.
Eighth Floor
Washington, DC 20006
(202) 442-2302
E-mail: kboyette@ncba.coop
Web Site: www.cdf.coop
www.heroes.coop

FOUNDED: 1944

AREAS OF INTEREST:
Community, economic and social
development through cooperative enterprise.

TYPE:
Grants-in-aid. The Foundation makes grants
and loans for cooperative development
through its various funds.

PURPOSE:
To promote self-help and mutual aid in
community, economic and social
development through cooperative enterprise.

LEGAL BASIS:
501(c)(3) organization.

ELIGIBILITY:
The Foundation does not award grants for
purely personal needs. It works only in the
cooperative sector.

GEOG. RESTRICTIONS: Primarily the United
States.

FINANCIAL DATA:
Amount of support per award: Varies.
Total amount of support: Varies.

NO. MOST RECENT APPLICANTS: Approximately
70.

NO. AWARDS: 45.

APPLICATION INFO:
Contact the Foundation after reviewing the
various fund descriptions to determine if the
proposed project fits within the Foundation's
funding priorities. The Foundation supports
cooperative development only.

PUBLICATIONS:
Annual report.

STAFF:
Leslie Mead, Executive Director
Kirstie Boyette, Fund-raising and Fund
Manager

ADDRESS INQUIRIES TO:
See e-mail address above.

The Foundation supports cooperative
development only.

ADOLPH COORS FOUNDATION
215 St. Paul Street, Suite 300
Denver, CO 80206
(303) 388-1636
Fax: (303) 388-1684
E-mail: info@acoorsfdn.org
Web Site: coorsfoundation.org

TYPE:
Capital grants; General operating grants;
Project/program grants.

See entry 1017 for full listing.

CORPORATION FOR NATIONAL AND COMMUNITY SERVICE [1143]
250 E Street, S.W.
Washington, DC 20525
(202) 606-5000
(800) 942-2677
E-mail: VISTA@americorps.gov
Web Site: www.nationalservice.
gov/programs/americorps/americorps-
programs/americorps-vista

FOUNDED: 1965

AREAS OF INTEREST:
Anti-poverty or poverty-related activities.

NAME(S) OF PROGRAMS:
● **AmeriCorps VISTA**

TYPE:
Project/program grants. Provides full-time,
full-year volunteers at the request of
community groups to work on clearly defined
tasks that lead to mobilization of the
community's resources. The volunteers live
among the people they serve at subsistence
levels of support.

YEAR PROGRAM STARTED: 1965

PURPOSE:
To supplement efforts to eliminate poverty
and poverty-related problems.

LEGAL BASIS:
Domestic Volunteer Service Act of 1973, as
amended (P.L. 93-113).

ELIGIBILITY:
Sponsors applying for AmeriCorps VISTA
must be nonprofit organizations. They may
be public or private and include state and
local governments.

GEOG. RESTRICTIONS: United States and its
territories.

FINANCIAL DATA:
Organizations receive AmeriCorps VISTA
member slots. Those VISTA members
receive a basic monthly substance allowance.
An end-of-service stipend or the Segal
AmeriCorps Educational Award is paid upon
completion of service.
Amount of support per award:
Approximately $22,000 per VISTA slot.
Total amount of support: Varies.

NO. MOST RECENT APPLICANTS: Organizations:
Approximately 1,000; Individuals:
Approximately 5,500.

NO. AWARDS: Organizations: Approximately
900.

APPLICATION INFO:
Application information is available online.

Duration: One to five years.
Deadline: Applications accepted on an
ongoing basis.

ADDRESS INQUIRIES TO:
E-mail: VISTA@cns.gov

THE DALLAS FOUNDATION [1144]
3963 Maple Avenue
Suite 390
Dallas, TX 75219
(214) 741-9898
Fax: (214) 741-9848
E-mail: info@dallasfoundation.org
Web Site: www.dallasfoundation.org

FOUNDED: 1929

AREAS OF INTEREST:
Arts, education, health and human services,
social services, and public/civic benefit.

TYPE:
Capital grants; Project/program grants;
Scholarships.

YEAR PROGRAM STARTED: 1929

PURPOSE:
To improve the quality of life for residents of
the city and county of Dallas.

LEGAL BASIS:
Community foundation.

ELIGIBILITY:
Applicant organizations must be tax-exempt
nonprofit focused on needs within Dallas
County. Grants from the field of interest
funds require a match between the purpose of
the grant and the purpose of the available
funds. Grants from the unrestricted funds
may be given to any type of need within
Dallas County.

Funds are not available from discretionary
funds for individuals, endowments, research,
debt retirement, annual campaigns,
underwriting of fund-raising events, or for
organizations that have received support
within the preceding three to five years.

GEOG. RESTRICTIONS: City and county of
Dallas, Texas.

FINANCIAL DATA:
Amount of support per award: Varies.
Total amount of support: Varies.

NO. MOST RECENT APPLICANTS: 400.

NO. AWARDS: 50.

APPLICATION INFO:
The application form is available on the
Foundation web site, or by request.
Unrestricted funds must have a letter of
inquiry submitted by August 1.
Duration: Varies.
Deadline: Field of Interest funds: January 31
with announcement in June. Unrestricted
funds: August 1 with announcement in
December.

PUBLICATIONS:
Annual report; application guidelines.

ADDRESS INQUIRIES TO:
Brittani Trusty, Program Officer
(See address above.)

DANIELS FUND
101 Monroe Street
Denver, CO 80206-4467
(303) 393-7220
E-mail: info@danielsfund.org
grantsinfo@danielsfund.org
Web Site: www.danielsfund.org

TYPE:
Capital grants; General operating grants;
Project/program grants; Scholarships. Daniels
Fund Ethics Initiative delivers principle-based
ethics education and reinforces the value of
ethical business and personal conduct. The
Ethics Initiative consists of a Collegiate
Program, High School Program, Middle
School Program, Community College
Program, Elementary School Program, Law
Enforcement Program, Business Program,
and an online Case Bank. Each of the Ethics
Initiative's components utilizes a specific
approach to reach its target audience.
Funding is provided through the Daniels
Fund Grants Program.

Daniels Fund Grants Program supports highly
effective nonprofit organizations in Colorado,
New Mexico, Utah and Wyoming.

Daniels Fund Scholarship Program consists
of the Daniels Scholarship Program and the
Boundless Opportunity Scholarship Program.
The Daniels Scholarship Program provides a
comprehensive, four-year annually-renewable
college scholarship for highly motivated
students to earn a Bachelor's degree that
helps them build a successful career and
rewarding life. Daniels Scholars are honest,
respectful, self-reliant, and compassionate.
They are proud Americans who value our
free enterprise system and are prepared to
give the world their very best shot. The
scholarship applies toward the expense of
attaining a Bachelor's degree at any
nonprofit, accredited college or university in
the U.S. The Boundless Opportunity
Scholarship Program provides college
scholarships for non-traditional students of all
ages, awarded by select colleges and
universities using funds provided by the
Daniels Fund.

See entry 86 for full listing.

IRENE E. AND GEORGE A. DAVIS FOUNDATION [1145]
One Monarch Place
Suite 1300
Springfield, MA 01144-1300
(413) 734-8336
Fax: (413) 734-7845
E-mail: info@davisfdn.org
Web Site: www.davisfdn.org

FOUNDED: 1970

AREAS OF INTEREST:
Community, social services and early
education.

TYPE:
Capital grants; General operating grants.

PURPOSE:
To make strategically significant investments
in organizations and projects that promise
demonstrable long-range benefits improving
the quality of life of citizens residing in
Hampden County, MA.

LEGAL BASIS:
Private foundation.

ELIGIBILITY:
Grants are made to organizations that have
tax-exempt status under Section 501(c)(3) of
the Internal Revenue Code. Catholic
organizations may apply. No grants are made
to individuals.

GEOG. RESTRICTIONS: Hampden County, Massachusetts.

FINANCIAL DATA:
Amount of support per award: Varies.
Total amount of support: Varies.

NO. MOST RECENT APPLICANTS: 200.

NO. AWARDS: 125.

APPLICATION INFO:
Guidelines and application form are available on the Foundation web site. An initial Letter of Inquiry is required to determine the interest and appropriateness of a full proposal.
Duration: Typically one year.
Deadline: Proposals are accepted throughout the year.

ADDRESS INQUIRIES TO:
See telephone number above.

DEARBORN COMMUNITY FOUNDATION, INC. [1146]
322 Walnut Street
Lawrenceburg, IN 47025
(812) 539-4115
E-mail: fmccarter@dearborncf.org
Web Site: www.dearborncf.org

FOUNDED: 1997

AREAS OF INTEREST:
Art, culture and humanities, community and public benefit, education, environment and animal protection, human services, public safety, and youth programs.

TYPE:
Capital grants; Challenge/matching grants; Development grants; General operating grants; Project/program grants; Scholarships; Seed money grants; Technical assistance; Training grants.

YEAR PROGRAM STARTED: 1997

PURPOSE:
To connect people who care with causes that improve the quality of life in the community by advancing cultural, educational and social opportunities, while preserving the community's heritage and helping donors create a permanent legacy in Dearborn County, IN.

ELIGIBILITY:
Grants are made to organizations that are tax-exempt under Section 501(c)(3) of the Internal Revenue Code and recognized by the state of Indiana as current and active not-for-profit organizations. No grants are made to individuals outside of scholarships and/or educational grants. Nonsectarian religious programs may apply.

GEOG. RESTRICTIONS: Dearborn County, Indiana.

FINANCIAL DATA:
Amount of support per award: Varies.
Total amount of support: $1,700,000 for the year 2017.

APPLICATION INFO:
Applications are submitted online.
Duration: One year.
Deadline: Varies.

STAFF:
Fred McCarter, Executive Director

ADDRESS INQUIRIES TO:
Fred McCarter, Executive Director
(See address above.)

DELAWARE COUNTY FOUNDATION [1147]
737 Enterprise Drive
Suite A
Lewis Center, OH 43035
(614) 764-2332
Fax: (614) 764-2333
E-mail: foundation@delawarecf.org
Web Site: www.delawarecf.org

FOUNDED: 1995

AREAS OF INTEREST:
Arts, civic affairs, community needs, culture, education, environment, health and human services.

NAME(S) OF PROGRAMS:
● **Designated Funds**
● **Donor Advised Funds**
● **Field of Interest Funds**
● **Organizational Endowment Funds**
● **Scholarship Funds**
● **Special Project Funds**
● **Unrestricted Funds**

TYPE:
Scholarships.

PURPOSE:
To enhance the quality of life for Delaware County residents.

ELIGIBILITY:
Grants are made to organizations that have tax-exempt status under Section 501(c)(3) of the Internal Revenue Code that serve Delaware County. No grants are made to individuals, religious programs, political groups or for deficit reduction.

GEOG. RESTRICTIONS: Delaware County, Ohio.

FINANCIAL DATA:
Amount of support per award: $500 to $6,000.
Total amount of support: $1,137,603 in grants and scholarships for the year 2019.

NO. AWARDS: 372 grants and 171 scholarships for the year 2019.

APPLICATION INFO:
Information may be obtained from the Foundation web site.
Duration: Typically one year.
Deadline: Scholarships: March 1 and June. Grants: July 10.

STAFF:
Chris Baker, President and Chief Executive Officer

ADDRESS INQUIRIES TO:
See e-mail address above.

ROGER L. AND AGNES C. DELL CHARITABLE TRUST [1148]
101 East Fifth Street, EP-MN-S14
Suite 1400
St. Paul, MN 55101
(855) 452-4015
Fax: (651) 466-8742
E-mail: charitableservicesgroupmpls@usbank.com

AREAS OF INTEREST:
Arts and culture, education and youth in the Fergus Falls, MN region.

TYPE:
Capital grants; General operating grants; Project/program grants.

PURPOSE:
To improve the quality of life in Fergus Falls, MN and the surrounding area.

ELIGIBILITY:
Eligible organizations must be IRS 501(c)(3) tax-exempt.

GEOG. RESTRICTIONS: Fergus Falls, Minnesota and the surrounding area.

FINANCIAL DATA:
Amount of support per award: Varies.
Total amount of support: Varies.

APPLICATION INFO:
Application should be submitted in writing outlining the nature of the request.
Deadline: Varies.

ADDRESS INQUIRIES TO:
Matt McGovern
Pemberton Sorlie Rufer Kershner PLLP
110 North Mill Street
P.O. Box 866
Fergus Falls, MN 56538-0866

*SPECIAL STIPULATIONS:
Unsolicited proposals not accepted.

DEPAUW UNIVERSITY KEY CLUB INTERNATIONAL BONNER SCHOLARSHIP [1149]
204 East Seminary Street
Greencastle, IN 46135
(765) 658-4187
(800) 447-2495
Fax: (765) 658-4137
E-mail: jenniecoy@depauw.edu
Web Site: www.keyclub.org

AREAS OF INTEREST:
Leadership and community service.

NAME(S) OF PROGRAMS:
● **Bonner Scholarship**

TYPE:
Scholarships.

PURPOSE:
To encourage youth to become actively involved in the community around them.

ELIGIBILITY:
Applicant must be a college-bound graduating high school senior with a grade point average of B or higher and have been an active Key Club member for two years, not serving as International Board member or governor.

Selection is based on academic achievement, commitment to community service, and leadership.

Women, ethnic minorities, and high-need students are encouraged to apply.

GEOG. RESTRICTIONS: United States.

FINANCIAL DATA:
Amount of support per award: $2,500.

CO-OP FUNDING PROGRAMS: Corella and Bertram F. Bonner Foundation.

NO. MOST RECENT APPLICANTS: 125.

NO. AWARDS: 9.

APPLICATION INFO:
No special application is required. Applicants involved in Key Club will be identified via their admissions application.
Duration: Four years.
Deadline: March 1 for early consideration; however, applications will be received until all selections are made.

ADDRESS INQUIRIES TO:
DePauw University Office of Admission
Bonner Scholarship Program
Greencastle, IN 46135-1778

*SPECIAL STIPULATIONS:
Bonner scholars are expected to maintain
good academic standing at DePauw (2.5
grade point average or better), participate in
educational and enrichment activities,
successfully complete the Bonner Program
First-Year Student Seminar, as well as
participate in community-service programs
for an average of eight hours per week
during the school year, and complete two
summer internships consisting of 280 hours
each.

DICKINSON AREA COMMUNITY FOUNDATION [1150]

333 South Stephenson Avenue
Suite 204
Iron Mountain, MI 49801
(906) 774-3131
Fax: (906) 774-7640
E-mail: tjuul@dickinsonareacf.org
dacfofficemgr@dickinsonareacf.org
Web Site: www.
dickinsonareacommunityfoundation.org

FOUNDED: 1995

AREAS OF INTEREST:
Arts, community needs and development,
culture, education, environment, health and
human services.

TYPE:
Grants-in-aid; Scholarships.

PURPOSE:
To encourage philanthropic investment in
Dickinson County and surrounding
Wisconsin communities.

LEGAL BASIS:
501(c)(3) tax-exempt organization.

ELIGIBILITY:
Grants are made to organizations that have
tax-exempt status under Section 501(c)(3) of
the Internal Revenue Code. No grants are
made to individuals. Nonsectarian religious
programs may apply.

GEOG. RESTRICTIONS: Dickinson County,
Michigan and surrounding Wisconsin and
Michigan communities.

FINANCIAL DATA:
Amount of support per award: Varies by fund
or scholarship.
Total amount of support: Varies.

APPLICATION INFO:
When grants are available, application
information is available on the web site.

Scholarship applicants can apply at their
local schools.
Duration: One year.
Deadline: Scholarships: March 15. Grants:
October 15.

PUBLICATIONS:
Brochures.

ADDRESS INQUIRIES TO:
Tamara Juul, Executive Director
(See address above.)

THE DIXON FOUNDATION [1151]

One Chase Corporate Center
Suite 400
Birmingham, AL 35244-7001
(205) 313-6501
E-mail: joy.levio@dixon-group.com

FOUNDED: 1986

AREAS OF INTEREST:
Local community.

TYPE:
General operating grants.

PURPOSE:
To support social services in northern
Alabama and northern Georgia.

ELIGIBILITY:
Eligible organizations must be IRS 501(c)(3)
tax-exempt. No funding to individuals.

GEOG. RESTRICTIONS: Central Alabama and
northern Georgia.

FINANCIAL DATA:
Amount of support per award: Varies.
Total amount of support: Up to $10,000.

APPLICATION INFO:
Applicants should send in a brief summary,
budget, and copy of IRS 501(c)(3) tax
determination letter.
Duration: One year. Grants renewable by
reapplication.
Deadline: September 30.

ADDRESS INQUIRIES TO:
Joy Levio, Vice President and
Treasurer
(See address above.)

THE JEAN AND LOUIS DREYFUS FOUNDATION, INC. [1152]

64 West 48th Street
Suite 1408
New York, NY 10036
(212) 599-1931
Fax: (646) 992-8091
E-mail: jk@jldreyfus.org
Web Site: www.jldreyfus.org

FOUNDED: 1979

AREAS OF INTEREST:
Aging and disadvantaged, arts-in-education,
education and literacy, and social services.

TYPE:
Challenge/matching grants; General operating
grants; Project/program grants. Funding to
direct-service organizations and those
projects which will produce systemic change.

PURPOSE:
To enhance the quality of life of New
Yorkers, particularly the aging and
disadvantaged.

ELIGIBILITY:
Nonprofit 501(c)(3) direct-service
organizations focusing on enhancing the
quality of life of New Yorkers.

GEOG. RESTRICTIONS: New York City (five
boroughs), New York.

FINANCIAL DATA:
Total amount of support: $771,300 in grants
for the year 2018.

APPLICATION INFO:
Initially, a one- to two-page letter of inquiry
describing the grantee organization and
outlining the project in question. Letters
should be sent by mail to the attention of
Ms. Edmee de M. Firth, Executive Director.

Letters of inquiry from organizations not
previously funded are not being accepted at
this time.
Duration: One year. Must reapply.
Deadline: Letter of Inquiry: January 15 and
July 15.

ADDRESS INQUIRIES TO:
Edmee de M. Firth, Executive Director
(See address above.)

*PLEASE NOTE:
Letters of inquiry from organizations not
previously funded are not being accepted at
this time.

DULUTH SUPERIOR AREA COMMUNITY FOUNDATION [1153]

222 East Superior Street
Suite 302
Duluth, MN 55802
(218) 726-0232
Fax: (218) 726-0257
E-mail: grantsinfo@dsacommunityfoundation.
com
Web Site: www.dsacommunityfoundation.org

FOUNDED: 1982

AREAS OF INTEREST:
Arts, community and economic development,
education, environment and human services.

TYPE:
Challenge/matching grants; Development
grants; Project/program grants; Scholarships;
Seed money grants.

YEAR PROGRAM STARTED: 1983

PURPOSE:
To improve the quality of life in Duluth,
Superior and surrounding counties.

LEGAL BASIS:
Community foundation.

ELIGIBILITY:
Eligible organizations must be IRS 501(c)(3)
tax-exempt.

GEOG. RESTRICTIONS: Aitkin, Carlton, Cook,
Itasca, Koochiching, Lake and St. Louis
counties, Minnesota; Ashland, Bayfield and
Douglas counties, Wisconsin.

FINANCIAL DATA:
Amount of support per award: Varies.
Total amount of support: Varies.

APPLICATION INFO:
Information regarding the inquiry process is
available online.
Duration: Grants: Usually one year.
Nonrenewable. Scholarships: One year. Most
are renewable.
Deadline: Varies according to program.

PUBLICATIONS:
Elements, newsletter; annual report.

ADDRESS INQUIRIES TO:
See e-mail address above.

THE JOHN G. DUNCAN TRUST [1154]

c/o Wells Fargo Wealth Management
100 North Main Street, 6th Floor
MAC D4001-065
Winston-Salem, NC 27101
(888) 235-4351
Fax: (877) 746-5889
E-mail: grantadministration@wellsfargo.com
Web Site: www.wellsfargo.com/private-
foundations/duncan-charitable-trust

FOUNDED: 1955

AREAS OF INTEREST:
Animals, environment, culture and humanities, human services, health, education, religion, arts and public/society benefit.

TYPE:
Project/program grants.

YEAR PROGRAM STARTED: 1956

PURPOSE:
To support charitable, benevolent, educational and religious purposes within the state of Colorado.

LEGAL BASIS:
Private foundation.

ELIGIBILITY:
501(c)(3) tax-exempt organizations in Colorado may apply. Grants are not made for individuals, general operating expenses, endowments, organizations outside of Colorado, or other grantmaking organizations.

Organizations receiving a grant are not eligible to apply for a grant in the following calendar year.

GEOG. RESTRICTIONS: Colorado.

FINANCIAL DATA:
Amount of support per award: Typically $5,000 to $10,000.
Total amount of support: Approximately $300,000 per year.

APPLICATION INFO:
Applications must be submitted online during the application periods for specific program areas in order to be reviewed at the grant meetings held after each application deadline date.
Duration: No grants are made on a continuing basis.
Deadline: Arts, Culture, Humanities and Education: March. Environment, Animals and Human Services: June 30. Health, Public/Society Benefit and Religion: September 30.

ADDRESS INQUIRIES TO:
See e-mail address above.

*SPECIAL STIPULATIONS:
Periodic progress reports and final reports may be required for funded projects.

THE EAST BAY COMMUNITY FOUNDATION   [1155]
De Domenico Building
200 Frank H. Ogawa Plaza
Oakland, CA 94612
(510) 836-3223
Fax: (510) 836-7418
E-mail: grantmaking@eastbaycf.org
Web Site: www.ebcf.org

FOUNDED: 1928

AREAS OF INTEREST:
Early childhood success, arts and environment, economic empowerment, and policy advocacy and civic engagement.

TYPE:
Project/program grants. Building leadership capacity grants.

YEAR PROGRAM STARTED: 1928

PURPOSE:
To transform the lives of people in the East Bay with pressing needs.

LEGAL BASIS:
Public foundation.

ELIGIBILITY:
Eligible organizations must be IRS 501(c)(3) tax-exempt.

GEOG. RESTRICTIONS: Alameda and Contra Costa counties, California.

FINANCIAL DATA:
Amount of support per award: Varies.
Total amount of support: Over $57,000,000 in grants and over $157,000 in scholarships for the year 2018.

APPLICATION INFO:
Guidelines and application are available online.
Duration: Varies.

PUBLICATIONS:
Guidelines.

EAST TEXAS COMMUNITIES FOUNDATION   [1156]
315 North Broadway Avenue
Suite 210
Tyler, TX 75702-5712
(903) 533-0208
Fax: (903) 533-0258
E-mail: mlsmith@etcf.org
Web Site: etcf.org

FOUNDED: 1989

AREAS OF INTEREST:
Community development.

TYPE:
Grants-in-aid; Scholarships. The Foundation administers scholarship funds for donors, nonprofit organizations, civic clubs, service groups and businesses.

PURPOSE:
To promote charitable giving which enhances the quality of life for the people of east Texas.

ELIGIBILITY:
Grants are made to 501(c)(3) organizations. Scholarship applicants must be citizens or permanent residents of the U.S.

GEOG. RESTRICTIONS: East Texas.

FINANCIAL DATA:
Amount of support per award: Varies.
Total amount of support: Varies.

APPLICATION INFO:
Application information is available on the web site. Scholarship applications must be submitted electronically.
Duration: Varies.
Deadline: Varies.

ADDRESS INQUIRIES TO:
Mary Lynn Smith, Program Officer
(See address above.)

EAU CLAIRE COMMUNITY FOUNDATION   [1157]
306 South Barstow Street, Suite 104
Eau Claire, WI 54701
(715) 552-3801
Fax: (715) 552-3802
E-mail: info@eccfwi.org
Web Site: www.eccommunityfoundation.org

FOUNDED: 1997

AREAS OF INTEREST:
Serving the charitable needs of the Eau Claire, WI area.

TYPE:
Project/program grants.

YEAR PROGRAM STARTED: 1997

PURPOSE:
To strengthen our community by offering donors opportunities to establish charitable legacies, by making grants, and by serving as a catalyst to address community needs.

LEGAL BASIS:
Nonprofit community foundation.

ELIGIBILITY:
Eligible organizations must have 501(c)(3) status. Grants are available to religious organizations when recipients of services are not required to profess membership or belief in the religious organization.

GEOG. RESTRICTIONS: Eau Claire County, Wisconsin.

FINANCIAL DATA:
Amount of support per award: Varies.
Total amount of support: $2,500,000 (unaudited) for the year 2019.

CO-OP FUNDING PROGRAMS: Women's Giving Circle.

NO. MOST RECENT APPLICANTS: 60 for the year 2019.

NO. AWARDS: 43 full or partial grant awards for the year 2019.

APPLICATION INFO:
Application must be submitted online.
Duration: One year.
Deadline: February 1.

PUBLICATIONS:
Annual report; newsletters.

IRS I.D.: 39-1891064

STAFF:
Sue Bornick, Executive Director

ADDRESS INQUIRIES TO:
Sue Bornick, Executive Director
(See address above.)

ECOLAB FOUNDATION   [1158]
One Ecolab Place
St. Paul, MN 55102
(651) 250-2923
E-mail: ecolabfoundation@ecolab.com
Web Site: www.ecolab.com/about/corporate-responsibility/community-involvement

FOUNDED: 1986

AREAS OF INTEREST:
Arts and culture, youth and education, environment and conservation, and civic and community development.

CONSULTING OR VOLUNTEER SERVICES:
501(c)(3) organizations.

TYPE:
General operating grants; Project/program grants. Employee matching gifts.

YEAR PROGRAM STARTED: 1986

PURPOSE:
To enrich the quality of life in communities where Ecolab operates.

LEGAL BASIS:
Corporate foundation.

ELIGIBILITY:
Eligible organizations must be IRS 501(c)(3) tax-exempt.

Employee matching gifts to accredited schools only.

GEOG. RESTRICTIONS: City of Industry,
California; Jacksonville, FL; McDonough,
Georgia; Elk Grove Village, Joliet and
Naperville, Illinois; Huntington, Indiana;
Garyville, Louisiana; St. Paul, Minnesota;
Columbus, Mississippi; Greensboro, North
Carolina; Ellwood City, Pennsylvania;
Corsicana, Fort Worth, Garland and Sugar
Land, Texas; Martinsburg, West Virginia; and
Beloit, Wisconsin.

FINANCIAL DATA:
Amount of support per award: $5,000 to
$60,000.

Total amount of support: $9,000,000 total
giving for the year 2019.

Matching fund requirements: Must be a
full-time Ecolab employee.

NO. MOST RECENT APPLICANTS: 300.

NO. AWARDS: 200.

APPLICATION INFO:
Application form is available online.
Duration: One year.
Deadline: Varies per geographic region.

ADDRESS INQUIRIES TO:
Lisa Maloney-Vinz
Community Relations Director
(See address above.)

*PLEASE NOTE:
Requests for matching gifts must be made
through the Ecolab Giving Site (employees
only).

EL PASO COMMUNITY
FOUNDATION   [1159]
333 North Oregon Street
2nd Floor
El Paso, TX 79901
(915) 533-4020
Fax: (915) 532-0716
E-mail: info@epcf.org
Web Site: www.epcf.org

FOUNDED: 1977

AREAS OF INTEREST:
Arts and humanities, education, economic
development, health and disabilities,
environment and animals, and human
services.

TYPE:
General operating grants; Scholarships. A
charitable fund established at the Foundation
by individuals, corporations or organizations.

PURPOSE:
To improve the quality of life in the El Paso
region, TX.

LEGAL BASIS:
Permanent endowment.

ELIGIBILITY:
Grant request will be considered only from
501(c)(3) agencies located within or offering
services to the community which includes far
west Texas, southern New Mexico and
northern Chihuahua, Mexico. Grants are not
made to individuals or religious
organizations.

GEOG. RESTRICTIONS: Far west Texas, southern
New Mexico and northern Chihuahua,
Mexico.

FINANCIAL DATA:
Amount of support per award: $5,000 to
$40,000.

Total amount of support: $19,018,078 in
grants and projects for the year 2019.

APPLICATION INFO:
The Foundation utilizes an online application
process.
Duration: One year.
Deadline: Grants: February 1 and August 1.

ADDRESS INQUIRIES TO:
Bonita Johnson, Grants Manager
(See address above.)

FRED L. EMERSON
FOUNDATION, INC.   [1160]
5654 South Street Road
Auburn, NY 13021
(315) 253-9621
E-mail: info@emersonfoundation.com
Web Site: www.emersonfoundation.com

FOUNDED: 1932

AREAS OF INTEREST:
Education (primarily private higher
education), hospital and health programs,
community agencies, cultural institutions,
youth and community service programs, and
social welfare agencies.

TYPE:
Capital grants; Challenge/matching grants;
Endowments; Project/program grants;
Research grants.

PURPOSE:
To improve the quality of life in Auburn,
Cayuga County and upstate New York.

ELIGIBILITY:
Organizations must be tax-exempt. No grants
are made to individuals or for-profit
organizations. No sponsorship of fund-raising
events or political activities. Proposals
seeking support solely for recurring operating
expenses of an organization are strongly
discouraged.

GEOG. RESTRICTIONS: Focus on upstate New
York with a concentration in the community
of Auburn, Cayuga County and the
surrounding region.

FINANCIAL DATA:
Amount of support per award: Varies.
Total amount of support: $3,337,165 for the
year 2018.

NO. AWARDS: 133 for the year 2018.

APPLICATION INFO:
All proposals submitted for consideration
must be completed through the Foundation's
Online Application portal or using the
printable Grant Proposal Submission Form.
Duration: Varies.
Deadline: Colleges and universities: March 1
and September 1. All other proposals are
accepted on an ongoing basis.

PUBLICATIONS:
Guidelines.

ADDRESS INQUIRIES TO:
Daniel J. Fessenden
Executive Director
(See address above.)

ENTERPRISE COMMUNITY
PARTNERS
334 Boylston Street, Suite 400
Boston, MA 02116
(781) 235-2006
E-mail: rosefellowship@enterprisecommunity.
org
Web Site: www.enterprisecommunity.org/rose

TYPE:
Fellowships. The Rose Fellowship partners
community-engaged architects and artists
with local community development
organizations. Architectural fellows are
designers with an accredited degree in
architecture and a passion for applying their
skills in a community development context.
Artists are defined as socially-engaged
creative practitioners, teaching artists, and
culture bearers working in all disciplines.

See entry 379 for full listing.

ESSEX COUNTY COMMUNITY
FOUNDATION   [1161]
175 Andover Street
Suite 101
Danvers, MA 01923
(978) 777-8876 ext. 133
Fax: (978) 777-9454
E-mail: c.lavoieschuster@eccf.org
Web Site: www.eccf.org

FOUNDED: 1999

AREAS OF INTEREST:
Arts and culture, education, environment,
health, social and community services and
youth services.

CONSULTING OR VOLUNTEER SERVICES:
Nonprofit organizations in Essex County,
MA.

NAME(S) OF PROGRAMS:
● **Emergency Fund**
● **First Jobs Fund**
● **Fund for Excellence in Essex County**
● **Greater Lawrence Community Fund**
● **Greater Lawrence Disaster Relief
   Fund-Relief and Recovery**
● **Greater Lawrence Summer Fund**
● **Impact Essex County Fund**
● **Institute for Trustees**
● **Merrimack Valley Municipal Business
   Development and Recovery Fund**
● **North Shore Community Health
   Network**
● **Dee & King Webster Memorial Fund
   for Greater Lawrence**
● **The Women's Fund of Essex County**

TYPE:
Capital grants; Conferences/seminars;
Endowments; General operating grants;
Project/program grants; Scholarships;
Technical assistance. Capacity-building
grants. Various grantmaking funds. Mostly
project/program grants. Agencies can
establish endowment funds.

The Foundation has 222 grant funds and 30
scholarship programs.

YEAR PROGRAM STARTED: 1999

PURPOSE:
To promote philanthropy in Essex County by
managing charitable funds for donors; to
provide grants and services to nonprofit
organizations; to engage in community
leadership activities.

LEGAL BASIS:
Public 501(c)(3) charity.

ELIGIBILITY:
Organizations offering programs and services
in Essex County (MA) communities,
recognized as tax-exempt under Section
501(c)(3) of the Internal Revenue Code and,
in some cases, to agencies of local or state
government. Organizations with a qualified
fiscal sponsor are also considered.

GEOG. RESTRICTIONS: Primarily Essex County, Massachusetts.

FINANCIAL DATA:
Approximately $91,000,000 in assets under management.
Amount of support per award: $2,000 to $20,000 for competitive grants;
donor-advised funds may award larger grants.
Total amount of support: $7,800,000 for fiscal year 2019.

NO. AWARDS: 1,288 grants and scholarships for fiscal year 2019.

REPRESENTATIVE AWARDS:
$15,000 (over three years) to Raw Art Works to support after-school and out-of-school arts programs for underserved girls and women; $7,500 to Essex County Greenbelt Association to determine meaningful collectible data sets for strategic decision making.

APPLICATION INFO:
Competitive grant applications are accepted online. Scholarship applicants should inquire at their local school.
Duration: Up to three years, depending on fund.
Deadline: Varies.

PUBLICATIONS:
Annual report; newsletter; brochure.

IRS I.D.: 04-3407816

STAFF:
Beth Francis, President and Chief Executive Officer

ADDRESS INQUIRIES TO:
Carol Lavoie Schuster, Vice President for Grants and Services
(See address above.)

SAMUEL S. FELS FUND   [1162]
1528 Walnut Street
Suite 1002
Philadelphia, PA 19102
(215) 731-9455
E-mail: info@samfels.org
Web Site: www.samfels.org

FOUNDED: 1935

AREAS OF INTEREST:
Refugees and immigrants, youth in the foster care system, arts and community, and social, racial and economic justice.

NAME(S) OF PROGRAMS:
● **Arts and Culture**
● **Focused Populations**
● **Social, Racial and Economic Justice**

TYPE:
General operating grants; Project/program grants. In the area of Arts and Culture, the Fund invests in arts and cultural organizations whose primary mission is to preserve, strengthen and/or share social or cultural identities and traditions and those that amplify marginalized voices and perspectives in pursuit of social change.

In the area of Focused Populations, the Fund supports developing services and policies that improve integration, opportunity and advancement for refugees and immigrants or improve safety, stability and opportunity for youth in and exiting the child welfare system.

In the area of Social, Racial and Economic Justice, the Fund supports new ideas and proven approaches, including legal and other

direct services for marginalized communities (excluding those that fall under one of the previous focus areas), that address social inequities, protect civil liberties and human rights, and advance diversity and inclusion within and among nonprofits.

YEAR PROGRAM STARTED: 1936

PURPOSE:
To improve conditions and opportunities for marginalized communities within the city of Philadelphia; to support services, advocacy and activities that move us towards a more socially, racially and economically just society with opportunities for all.

LEGAL BASIS:
Private foundation.

ELIGIBILITY:
Applicants must be agencies located in the city of Philadelphia. Excluded from the Fund's program of grants are contributions to national organizations, capital campaigns, scholarships, fellowships and grants-in-aid for travel, research and publication, or grants to individual day care or afterschool programs. No grants are made to individuals.

GEOG. RESTRICTIONS: Philadelphia, Pennsylvania.

FINANCIAL DATA:
Amount of support per award: $20,000 to $35,000.
Total amount of support: $1,500,000 to $1,800,000.

NO. AWARDS: Varies.

APPLICATION INFO:
Guidelines are available on the web site.
Duration: Primarily one year.

PUBLICATIONS:
Annual report; guidelines for applicants.

TRUSTEES:
Pari Hashemi, Chairperson
Ida K. Chen, Vice Chairperson
Tamer Makary, Treasurer
Dannyelle Austin
Will Gonzalez
John L. Jackson, Jr.
Fariha Khan

STAFF:
Sarah Martinez-Helfman, President
Tim Murray, Proposal and Budget Officer
Shanell Ransom, Grants Operations Manager

ADDRESS INQUIRIES TO:
Sarah Martinez-Helfman, President
(See telephone number above.)

FIRST HORIZON
FOUNDATION   [1163]
P.O. Box 84
Memphis, TN 38101-0084
(901) 523-4444
(901) 523-4112
E-mail: foundation@firsthorizon.com
Web Site: firsthorizonfoundation.com

FOUNDED: 1864

AREAS OF INTEREST:
Arts and culture, education and leadership, environment, financial literacy, health and human services.

TYPE:
Capital grants; Challenge/matching grants; Development grants; General operating grants; Matching gifts.

YEAR PROGRAM STARTED: 1993

PURPOSE:
To generate economic development in core market; to preserve and enhance what is special about core market and its communities; to leverage additional resources for the community.

LEGAL BASIS:
Corporate contributions program.

ELIGIBILITY:
Grants are made to 501(c)(3) tax-exempt organizations whose activities meet the objectives outlined above. First Horizon National Corp. does not use corporate contributions to support individuals, K-12 schools, charities sponsored solely by a single civic organization, charities which redistribute funds to other charitable organizations, except in the case of recognized united fund-type organizations, agencies supported by United Way or united arts funds, religious, social, athletic or fraternal organizations, political organizations or those having the primary purpose of influencing legislation or promoting a particular ideological point of view, trips and tours, operating budget deficits, multiyear commitments of four years or more and/or endowments.

Grants are limited to communities where First Horizon National Corp. has a presence.

FINANCIAL DATA:
Amount of support per award: Varies.
Total amount of support: Over $11,000,000 for the year 2019.

NO. AWARDS: Grants to more than 600 organizations in 2019.

APPLICATION INFO:
Funding requests must be formally submitted through the Foundation's online grant system.
Duration: Typically one year. Funding is not automatically renewed. Recipients desiring continued support should submit a request for review in the fall.
Deadline: Varies.

PUBLICATIONS:
Program guidelines and application procedures.

STAFF:
Lockie Dearman Wade, Community Investment Manager

ADDRESS INQUIRIES TO:
Lockie Dearman Wade
Community Investment Manager
(See address above.)

*PLEASE NOTE:
Impact reports are required following receipt of grants.

*SPECIAL STIPULATIONS:
Grants are limited to communities served by First Horizon National Corp.

THE FLINN FOUNDATION
1802 North Central Avenue
Phoenix, AZ 85004
(602) 744-6800
E-mail: info@flinn.org
Web Site: flinn.org

TYPE:
Demonstration grants; Fellowships; Project/program grants; Scholarships; Seed money grants. The arts and culture grants program assists Arizona's large arts and

culture organizations in generating capital through creative programming and fiscal planning.

The Foundation's biosciences grant projects aim to strengthen Arizona's biosciences infrastructure and thereby improve the state's capacity to compete nationally and internationally in the biosciences economy.

The Arizona Center for Civic Leadership seeks to strengthen civic leadership in Arizona.

The Flinn Scholars Program annually awards top Arizona high school graduates full scholarship support.

See entry 115 for full listing.

THE FOUNDATION FOR ENHANCING COMMUNITIES [1164]

200 North Third Street, 8th Floor
Harrisburg, PA 17101
(717) 236-5040
Fax: (717) 231-4463
E-mail: info@tfec.org
Web Site: www.tfec.org

FOUNDED: 1920

AREAS OF INTEREST:
Education, human services, arts and culture, children and youth, environment and community development.

CONSULTING OR VOLUNTEER SERVICES:
Offers consulting services.

NAME(S) OF PROGRAMS:
● **The Fund for Women and Girls**

TYPE:
Challenge/matching grants; Conferences/seminars; Endowments; Internships; Matching gifts; Project/program grants; Scholarships; Seed money grants; Technical assistance. Management services.

YEAR PROGRAM STARTED: 1920

PURPOSE:
To inspire giving by partnering with donors to achieve their charitable goals; to strengthen our local communities by investing in them now and for future generations.

LEGAL BASIS:
Community foundation.

ELIGIBILITY:
Eligible organizations must have 501(c)(3) status. No grants are made to individuals or religious organizations for religious purposes.

GEOG. RESTRICTIONS: Dillsburg area, Cumberland, Dauphin, Franklin, Lebanon and Perry counties, Pennsylvania.

FINANCIAL DATA:
Assets of $108,600,000 for the year ended December 31, 2019.
Amount of support per award: $4,011 average.
Total amount of support: Approximately $758,263 annually.

NO. MOST RECENT APPLICANTS: 288.

NO. AWARDS: 189.

APPLICATION INFO:
Applicants should:
(1) review the grantmaking guidelines for each regional foundation;
(2) contact the Program Officer to determine eligibility to apply and discuss the proposal

and;
(3) submit a grant application according to the guidelines provided on the Foundation's web site.
Duration: One year. Nonrenewable.

PUBLICATIONS:
Annual report.

IRS I.D.: 01-0564355

STAFF:
Janice Black, President and Chief Executive Officer
Kirk Demyan, Vice President and Chief Financial Officer
Jennifer Doyle, Vice President of Philanthropy and Community Investment
Allison Brubaker, Marketing and Communications Officer
Debbie Garrison, Philanthropic Officer
Heather LaManna, Philanthropic Officer
Jennifer Strechay, Program Officer for Community Investment
Jim Martin, Senior Financial Services Associate
Andrea R. Iguina-Perez, Community Investment Associate
Billie Jo Lake, Financial Services Associate
Raeann Buskey, Marketing and Communications Associate
Thomas Bradley, III, Scholarship Associate
Faith Elmes, Scholarship Coordinator
Leslie Fick, Early Education Specialist
Jeane Predmore, Early Education Specialist

ADDRESS INQUIRIES TO:
Director of Development and Community Investment
(See address above.)

*SPECIAL STIPULATIONS:
All discretionary grants must be awarded in the five-county region of Cumberland, Dauphin, Franklin, Lebanon and Perry counties or the Dillsburg area.

FOUNDATION FOR THE CAROLINAS [1165]

220 North Tryon Street
Charlotte, NC 28202
(704) 973-4500
(704) 973-4556
(800) 973-7244
Fax: (704) 973-7244
E-mail: bcollier@fftc.org
Web Site: www.fftc.org

FOUNDED: 1958

AREAS OF INTEREST:
Education, human services, health and medical research, arts, environment and historical preservation, youth, senior programs and social capital.

TYPE:
Demonstration grants; General operating grants; Project/program grants; Scholarships; Seed money grants.

YEAR PROGRAM STARTED: 1958

PURPOSE:
To advance philanthropy by serving donors, increasing charitable giving and improving communities in its area of service.

LEGAL BASIS:
Community foundation.

ELIGIBILITY:
Grants will be made only to organizations recognized by the IRS as 501(c)(3) in the greater Charlotte area.

The Foundation generally does not fund capital campaigns and buildings, computers, vehicles and similar equipment, publication of books and production of videos, conferences and travel, grants to individuals or endowment funds.

GEOG. RESTRICTIONS: Greater Charlotte, 13-county region in North and South Carolina.

FINANCIAL DATA:
Amount of support per award: $2,500 to $100,000.
Total amount of support: Varies.

APPLICATION INFO:
Contact the Foundation.
Duration: One year.
Deadline: Varies.

BOARD OF DIRECTORS:
Jewell D. Hoover, Chairperson
Kendall Alley
Gwin C. Barr
Cathy Bessant
Chantay Bouler
Marian Steele Clark
Jesse Cureton
Al de Molina
Lynn Good
Barnes Hauptfuhrer
Kelly King
Todd Mansfield
Arrington Mixon
Janice Patrick
Chris Poplin
Kevin Roche
Lynne Scott Safrit
Ruth Shaw
Fred Whitfield

ADDRESS INQUIRIES TO:
Brian Collier, Executive Vice President
(See address above.)

FOUNDATION FOR THE MID SOUTH [1166]

134 East Amite Street
Jackson, MS 39201
(601) 355-8167
Fax: (601) 355-6499
E-mail: iallen@fndmidsouth.org
Web Site: www.fndmidsouth.org

FOUNDED: 1989

AREAS OF INTEREST:
Improving the quality of life for residents in the states of Arkansas, Louisiana and Mississippi, with a primary focus on education, community development, health and wellness, and wealth building.

NAME(S) OF PROGRAMS:
● **Community Development**
● **Education**
● **Health & Wellness**
● **Wealth Building**

TYPE:
Conferences/seminars; General operating grants; Internships; Project/program grants; Training grants.

PURPOSE:
To nurture families and children; to improve schools; to build the economy for all people in the region.

ELIGIBILITY:
Applicants must be tax-exempt organizations under Section 501(c)(3) of the Internal Revenue Code.

GEOG. RESTRICTIONS: Arkansas, Louisiana and Mississippi.

FINANCIAL DATA:
Amount of support per award: Varies.
Total amount of support: Varies.

APPLICATION INFO:
The Foundation has an internal process for identifying and selecting grantees. Unsolicited grant proposals, inquiries or letters of intent are not accepted.
Duration: One to three years.
Deadline: 12 weeks prior to award periods in February, May and November.

FOUNDATION FOR THE TRI-STATE COMMUNITY, INC. [1167]

855 Central Avenue
Suite 300
Ashland, KY 41101
(606) 324-3888
Fax: (606) 324-5961
E-mail: mwwiseman@tristatefoundation.org
Web Site: www.tristatefoundation.org

FOUNDED: 1972

AREAS OF INTEREST:
Arts and cultural programs, education, science and charity.

NAME(S) OF PROGRAMS:
● **21st Century Endowment Fund**

TYPE:
Challenge/matching grants; Project/program grants; Scholarships; Seed money grants; Technical assistance.

YEAR PROGRAM STARTED: 1980

PURPOSE:
To improve the quality of life in the tri-state area by encouraging, raising, administering and distributing gifts for charitable, cultural, educational and scientific purposes.

LEGAL BASIS:
Community foundation.

ELIGIBILITY:
Priority will be given to organizations which are 501(c)(3) and other organizations that meet the Foundation's special charitable grant guidelines. The Foundation does not fund sectarian activities or individuals.

GEOG. RESTRICTIONS: Boyd and Greenup counties, Kentucky; Lawrence County, Ohio; Cabell and Wayne counties, West Virginia.

FINANCIAL DATA:
Amount of support per award: $500 to $5,000.
Total amount of support: Approximately $15,000 per quarter.

NO. AWARDS: 16 for the year 2018.

APPLICATION INFO:
Contact Foundation for grant application and to discuss proposed project.
Duration: One-time award. Applicants may reapply after a one-year period.
Deadline: January 10, April 10, July 10 and October 10.

PUBLICATIONS:
Annual report; *How We've Grown*; grant guidelines; 35th anniversary report.

IRS I.D.: 61-0729266

STAFF:
Mary Witten Wiseman, President
Kathryn Davis Lamp, Vice President

ADDRESS INQUIRIES TO:
Mary Witten Wiseman, President
(See address above.)

THE FRIST FOUNDATION [1168]

3100 West End Avenue, Suite 1200
Nashville, TN 37203-1348
(615) 292-3868
Fax: (615) 292-5843
E-mail: askfrist@fristfoundation.org
Web Site: www.fristfoundation.org

FOUNDED: 1982

AREAS OF INTEREST:
Health, human services, education, technology, civic affairs and the arts.

CONSULTING OR VOLUNTEER SERVICES:
Management consulting.

NAME(S) OF PROGRAMS:
● **The Frist Foundation Awards of Achievement**
● **The Frist Foundation Technology Grants Program**

TYPE:
Capital grants; General operating grants; Technical assistance. The Foundation makes direct grants to tax-exempt organizations in the greater Nashville area in the fields of health, human services, education, civic affairs and the arts, with a special emphasis on vulnerable populations.

In addition to conducting a grantmaking program responsive to external requests, the Frist Foundation actively seeks out and initiates programs addressing particular needs. Among these programs are the Center for Nonprofit Management, a community-wide effort to provide specialized management training and consulting to nonprofit community organizations.

Operating grants are given to organizations that offer management assistance, training, volunteers, goods or services to large numbers of Nashville agencies.

YEAR PROGRAM STARTED: 1983

PURPOSE:
To invest its resources in selected not-for-profit organizations in the greater Nashville area in ways that strengthen their ability to provide services; to enhance unique community assets in Nashville; to develop new sources of revenue through social enterprise.

LEGAL BASIS:
509(a) private foundation.

ELIGIBILITY:
Grantees must be tax-exempt under Section 501(c)(3) of the Internal Revenue Code and not private foundations as described in Section 509(a). The Foundation ordinarily does not make grants or provide support to:
(1) international, regional or local organizations outside the Nashville area;
(2) projects, programs or organizations that serve a limited audience or a relatively small number of people;
(3) hospitals, biomedical or clinical research, or disease-specific organizations seeking support for national projects and programs;
(4) organizations during their first three years of operation;
(5) endowments;
(6) social events, fund-raising activities or telethons;
(7) individuals or their projects;
(8) political activities;

(9) religious organizations for religious purposes;
(10) private foundations;
(11) advertising sponsorships or;
(12) schools below the college level, except for projects intended to serve the broader community.

Special emphasis is placed on organizations that provide services to vulnerable populations.

GEOG. RESTRICTIONS: Nashville, Tennessee area.

FINANCIAL DATA:
Amount of support per award: $500 to $100,000. Average $3,500.
Total amount of support: $17,177,505 for the year 2018.

NO. MOST RECENT APPLICANTS: Approximately 200 for the year 2019.

NO. AWARDS: 179 for the year 2018.

APPLICATION INFO:
If an organization wishes to apply for support, it should make contact by phone, by letter of inquiry, or by completing an application through the web site. If applying by mail, the letter should describe in no more than two pages:
(1) the organization and its record of accomplishment;
(2) the objectives of the program to be funded and whom it would benefit;
(3) the amount sought from the Foundation in relation to the total need;
(4) exactly how Foundation funds would be used and;
(5) the proposed method to evaluate the program's success.

The initial inquiry should also include an annual report, if available, and a copy of the IRS letter confirming that the organization is tax-exempt under Section 501(c)(3) of the Internal Revenue Code and not a private foundation as described in Section 509(a).
Duration: Up to three years. Renewals are not automatic. Applications from organizations supported in the past will be considered new requests.

IRS I.D.: 62-1134070

STAFF:
Peter F. Bird, Jr., President and Chief Executive Officer
Colette R. Easter, Treasurer
Corinne C. Bergeron, Program Officer

DIRECTORS:
William R. Frist, Chairman
Peter F. Bird, Jr.
Chuck Elcan
Lauren Elcan
Patricia Frist Elcan
Jennifer Frist
Julie D. Frist
Thomas F. Frist, III

ADDRESS INQUIRIES TO:
Peter F. Bird, Jr.
President and Chief Executive Officer
(See address above.)

THE GIFFORD FOUNDATION [1169]

100 Clinton Square
126 North Salina Street, 3rd Floor
Syracuse, NY 13202
(315) 474-2489
Fax: (315) 475-4983
E-mail: sheena@giffordfoundation.org
Web Site: www.giffordfoundation.org

FOUNDED: 1954

AREAS OF INTEREST:
Youth development, education and job readiness, and capacity building.

TYPE:
Challenge/matching grants; Conferences/seminars; Demonstration grants; Development grants; General operating grants; Project/program grants; Research grants; Seed money grants; Training grants.

YEAR PROGRAM STARTED: 1954

PURPOSE:
To provide funds for general charitable purposes.

LEGAL BASIS:
Private.

ELIGIBILITY:
Only tax-exempt organizations may apply. Organizations must show evidence of problems to be solved and how proposed solution will benefit constituency and the community. No grants to individuals.

FINANCIAL DATA:
Amount of support per award: Varies.
Total amount of support: Varies.

APPLICATION INFO:
The Foundation only invites community grant proposals after reviewing a letter of inquiry.
Duration: One year.

PUBLICATIONS:
Application guidelines; statement of policies; mission statement.

STAFF:
Sheena Soloman, Executive Director
Lindsay McClung, Director of Community Grantmaking
Megan Wagner-Flynn, Program Officer and Grants Manager

ADDRESS INQUIRIES TO:
Lindsay McClung
Director of Community Grantmaking
(See address above.)

LISA AND DOUGLAS GOLDMAN FUND [1170]

One Montgomery Street, Suite 3440
San Francisco, CA 94104
(415) 771-1717
E-mail: grantsmanager@ldgfund.org
Web Site: www.ldgfund.org

FOUNDED: 1992

AREAS OF INTEREST:
Jewish affairs, environment, democracy and civil liberties, health and recreation, literacy and education, and reproductive health and rights.

TYPE:
Capital grants; Project/program grants.

YEAR PROGRAM STARTED: 1992

PURPOSE:
To improve the quality of life, primarily in San Francisco.

LEGAL BASIS:
Private foundation.

ELIGIBILITY:
Eligible organizations must be IRS 501(c)(3) tax-exempt.

GEOG. RESTRICTIONS: Primarily San Francisco area, California.

FINANCIAL DATA:
Amount of support per award: $10,000 to $150,000.
Total amount of support: Generally $10,000,000.

APPLICATION INFO:
Online application process. Applicants must include a copy of the IRS tax determination letter. Letter of inquiry must be submitted before proposal.
Duration: Varies.

PUBLICATIONS:
Annual report; application guidelines.

GOLDSEKER FOUNDATION [1171]

1040 Park Avenue
Suite 310
Baltimore, MD 21201
(410) 837-5100
E-mail: terri@goldsekerfoundation.org
Web Site: www.goldsekerfoundation.org

FOUNDED: 1973

AREAS OF INTEREST:
Community development and the nonprofit sector.

TYPE:
Challenge/matching grants; General operating grants; Matching gifts; Project/program grants; Technical assistance. Project grants and ongoing operating support.

The Foundation maintains a two-track grantmaking program that designates two priority areas, but retains the ability to initiate and respond to new ideas and opportunities within established program areas, namely community affairs, education, and human services. In each of the priority grant areas - community development and the nonprofit sector - the Foundation is a directly engaged and active partner. Grants include a mix of Foundation initiatives and projects submitted independently by potential grantees.

YEAR PROGRAM STARTED: 1976

PURPOSE:
To support programs which directly benefit the people of the Baltimore metropolitan area.

LEGAL BASIS:
Private, nonprofit.

ELIGIBILITY:
Qualified nonprofit, charitable and educational organizations as defined under federal and state laws as permissible grantees of private foundations. Support is limited to institutions in the Baltimore metropolitan area with special emphasis on disadvantaged persons, giving priority to programs intended to assist children and families and to strengthen neighborhoods.

No support for endowment, capital, deficits, annual giving, publications, religious purposes, arts and culture, specific diseases or disabilities or projects typically supported with public funds.

GEOG. RESTRICTIONS: Metropolitan Baltimore, Maryland.

FINANCIAL DATA:
No distribution in any calendar year to any single institution is to exceed five percent of the Foundation's net income for that year.
Amount of support per award: Varies.

Total amount of support: Approximately $4,000,000 for the year 2018.
Matching fund requirements: Varies with specific request.

NO. AWARDS: 62 for the year 2018.

REPRESENTATIVE AWARDS:
$30,000 to Community Law Center; $50,000 to Baltimore Arts Realty Corporation; $60,000 to The Loading Dock; $75,000 to Venture for America.

APPLICATION INFO:
Applicants must submit a brief letter describing their program. It should include: (1) evidence of 501(c)(3) and 509(a) tax-exempt status; (2) background information about the applicant; (3) objectives of the proposed project; (4) methods for accomplishing objectives and; (5) projected program budget and amount sought from the Foundation.

The Foundation welcomes telephone inquiries about funding throughout the year.
Duration: Typically one year. Occasional multiyear grants.
Deadline: Requests will be considered at one of four quarterly meetings of the Board of Directors.

PUBLICATIONS:
Annual report; program guidelines.

IRS I.D.: 52-0983502

OFFICERS:
Sheldon Goldseker, Chairman
Deby Goldseker, Vice Chairman
Matthew D. Gallagher, President and Chief Executive Officer
Sharna Goldseker, Treasurer
Ana Goldseker, Secretary

STAFF:
Laurie Latuda Kinkel, Program Officer

BOARD OF DIRECTORS:
Ana Goldseker
Deby Goldseker
Sharna Goldseker
Sheldon Goldseker
Shelley Goldseker
Susan B. Katzenberg
Howard M. Weiss

ADDRESS INQUIRIES TO:
Program Officer
(See address above.)

*SPECIAL STIPULATIONS:
Grantmaking is limited to the metropolitan area of Baltimore, MD.

THE GRACO FOUNDATION [1172]

P.O. Box 1441
Minneapolis, MN 55440-1441
(612) 623-6153
E-mail: gracofoundation@graco.com
Web Site: www.graco.com/foundation

FOUNDED: 1956

AREAS OF INTEREST:
Education, especially STEM; workforce development; youth development.

CONSULTING OR VOLUNTEER SERVICES:
Through established community programs.

NAME(S) OF PROGRAMS:
● **Financial Grants of Support**

TYPE:
Capital grants; Development grants; Scholarships.

YEAR PROGRAM STARTED: 1956

PURPOSE:
To help organizations grow their ability to serve community needs through grants focused on capital projects, specific programs and technology needs.

LEGAL BASIS:
Established under the Minnesota Nonprofit Corporation Act as a nonprofit corporation under the provisions of Chapter 317, Minnesota Statutes 1953 and Acts amendatory thereof.

ELIGIBILITY:
Priority is placed on organizations that have a proven track record of enabling people to become self-sufficient and more productive.

FINANCIAL DATA:
Amount of support per award: Varies.
Total amount of support: $1,173,146 in grants for the year 2018.

APPLICATION INFO:
New grant applications by invitation only.

PUBLICATIONS:
Annual report/guidelines available on web site.

IRS I.D.: 41-6023537

BOARD OF DIRECTORS:
Patrick J. McHale, President
Karen P. Gallivan, Vice President
Janel French, Treasurer
Charlotte Boyd, Secretary

ADDRESS INQUIRIES TO:
Charlotte Boyd, Foundation Manager
(See address above.)

*PLEASE NOTE:
Unsolicited requests are not accepted.

GRAND HAVEN AREA COMMUNITY FOUNDATION   [1173]
One South Harbor Drive
Grand Haven, MI 49417
(616) 842-6378
Fax: (616) 842-9518
E-mail: info@ghacf.org
Web Site: www.ghacf.org

FOUNDED: 1971

AREAS OF INTEREST:
Arts and culture, diversity and inclusion, economic and community betterment, education, environment, and health and human services.

TYPE:
Project/program grants; Scholarships; Seed money grants. Pool of funds contributed by donors for the benefit of the Northwest Ottawa County area.

YEAR PROGRAM STARTED: 1971

PURPOSE:
To enrich and enhance the quality of life in the Northwest Ottawa County area; to link donors' interests with the needs of the community.

LEGAL BASIS:
Community foundation.

ELIGIBILITY:
Grant applicants must be charitable organizations recognized under Section 501(c)(3) of the Internal Revenue Code. Grants are also awarded to units of

government, educational institutions and churches that are providing services which benefit the Tri-Cities community.

GEOG. RESTRICTIONS: Northwest Ottawa County, Michigan.

FINANCIAL DATA:
Amount of support per award: Varies depending on needs and nature of the request.
Total amount of support: $5,241,536 in competitive and donor-advised grants for the year 2017.

NO. MOST RECENT APPLICANTS: 1,190.

NO. AWARDS: 1,100.

REPRESENTATIVE AWARDS:
$100,000 to No More Sidelines for the Building Belongings Campaign to renovate the athletic facilities at the Folkert Community Hub; $75,000 (over three years) to Grand Rapids Community Foundation to support organizations and programs designed to combat youth homelessness; $24,832 to Pathways of Arbor Circle for Ottawa Substance Abuse Prevention NW Quadrant Rebuilding.

APPLICATION INFO:
Applicant must submit Letter of Inquiry form online. Upon staff review and determination of project alignment with Foundation's priorities, applicant will be prompted to submit a full application.
Duration: Varies.
Deadline: Letter of Inquiry: November 21, February 20 and August 21.

PUBLICATIONS:
Annual report; application.

STAFF:
Hadley Streng, President
Patty McDonald, Director of Finance and Administration
Holly Cole, Director of Grants and Program

BOARD OF TRUSTEES:
Randy Hansen, Chairperson
Chad Bush, Vice Chairperson
Tammy Bailey, Treasurer
Nelson Jacobson, Secretary
Cindy Anderson
Sandy Huber
Mark Kleist
Anil Mandala
Mark Pereira
Barb VanHeest
Pat VerDuin

ADDRESS INQUIRIES TO:
Holly Cole, Director of Grants and Program
(See address above.)

THE GREATER CEDAR RAPIDS COMMUNITY FOUNDATION   [1174]
324 Third Street, S.E.
Cedar Rapids, IA 52401
(319) 366-2862
Fax: (319) 366-2912
E-mail: grants@gcrcf.org
Web Site: www.gcrcf.org

FOUNDED: 1948

AREAS OF INTEREST:
Arts and culture, community development, education, environment, health and human services.

NAME(S) OF PROGRAMS:
● **Endowment Challenge Fund**
● **Linn County Fund**
● **Nonprofit Network**
● **Organizational Development Fund**
● **President's Fund**
● **Program Fund**

TYPE:
Challenge/matching grants; General operating grants; Project/program grants; Scholarships; Seed money grants; Technical assistance.

YEAR PROGRAM STARTED: 1989

PURPOSE:
To enrich the quality of life in Linn County, IA.

LEGAL BASIS:
Community foundation.

ELIGIBILITY:
Eligible organizations must be IRS 501(c)(3) tax-exempt, public agencies/units of government or have a fiscal sponsor.

GEOG. RESTRICTIONS: Cedar Rapids and surrounding Linn County, Iowa.

FINANCIAL DATA:
Amount of support per award: $250 to $60,000 depending on fund.
Total amount of support: $11,000,000 for the year 2019.

CO-OP FUNDING PROGRAMS: A variety of donor advisors operate competitive funds.

NO. MOST RECENT APPLICANTS: Varies.

NO. AWARDS: 1,761 for the year 2019.

APPLICATION INFO:
Applications must be made online.
Duration: One to three years for most funds. Renewal by reapplication.
Deadline: Approximately February 15, June 15 and September 20.

PUBLICATIONS:
Annual report; "Community" newsletter; guidelines.

ADDRESS INQUIRIES TO:
See e-mail address above.

*SPECIAL STIPULATIONS:
The Foundation makes competitive grant awards only within Linn County, IA and its immediate vicinity.

GREATER CINCINNATI FOUNDATION   [1175]
720 East Pete Rose Way
Suite 120
Cincinnati, OH 45202
(513) 241-2880
Fax: (513) 768-6133
E-mail: werisetogether@gcfdn.org
Web Site: www.gcfdn.org

FOUNDED: 1963

AREAS OF INTEREST:
Racial equity and justice, affordable housing production, preservation and protection, women's economic mobility, arts, education, environment, community organizing and advocacy, and safety net services.

NAME(S) OF PROGRAMS:
● **All-In Cincinnati Racial Equity Coalition**
● **Community-Wide Affordable Housing Strategy**
● **COVID-19 Response**
● **Racial Equity Matters**
● **Women's Fund of Greater Cincinnati Foundation**

TYPE:
Capital grants; Development grants; Project/program grants. Funds for capacity building, programmatic support, and transformative projects addressing systemic issues.

PURPOSE:
To lead the charge toward a more vibrant Greater Cincinnati for everyone, now and for generations to come.

LEGAL BASIS:
Tax-exempt under Section 501(c)(3) of IRS code.

ELIGIBILITY:
Recipient must be a local agency in the Greater Cincinnati area and must be tax-exempt under Section 501(c)(3) of the IRS code.

GEOG. RESTRICTIONS: Greater Cincinnati, Ohio, northern Kentucky and southeast Indiana.

FINANCIAL DATA:
Amount of support per award: $1,000 to $100,000.

Total amount of support: Over $80,000,000 for the year 2019.

CO-OP FUNDING PROGRAMS: Over 800 for the year 2019.

NO. MOST RECENT APPLICANTS: Over 600 for the year 2019.

REPRESENTATIVE AWARDS:
Dan Beard Council, Boy Scouts of America; Children's Protective Service, Cincinnati Association for the Blind.

APPLICATION INFO:
Application information is available on the web site.

Unsolicited proposals are not accepted under the Community Grants program.

Duration: One to three years.

Deadline: Varies.

IRS I.D.: 31-0669700

STAFF:
Ellen Katz, President and Chief Executive Officer
Will Woodward, Chief Financial Officer
Philip Lanham, Vice President for Giving Strategy
Ronald C. Christian, Esq., Legal Counsel

GOVERNING BOARD:
Delores Hargrove-Young, Chairperson
George H. Vincent, Esq., Vice Chairperson
Calvin Buford
Robin F. Chatman, M.D.
Thomas Croft
John Domaschko
Steven Jemison
Mike Keating
Uma R. Kotagal, M.D.
Timothy J. Maloney
Ernest F. McAdams, Jr., Esq.
David Osborn, C.F.A.
Maribeth Rahe
Dianne M. Rosenberg
Ryan Rybolt
Ann Schwister
Ellen van der Horst
Sally Westheimer

ADDRESS INQUIRIES TO:
Inquiries must be submitted through www.gcfdn.org/submitinquiry

GREATER GREEN BAY COMMUNITY FOUNDATION [1176]

320 North Broadway
Suite 260
Green Bay, WI 54303
(920) 432-0800
Fax: (920) 432-5577
E-mail: amberpaluch@ggbcf.org
Web Site: www.ggbcf.org

FOUNDED: 1991

AREAS OF INTEREST:
Promoting a better future for the entire community of northeastern Wisconsin.

TYPE:
General operating grants; Project/program grants; Scholarships. Capacity-building grants; Donor-advised funds.

YEAR PROGRAM STARTED: 1991

PURPOSE:
To inspire and encourage charitable giving in northeast Wisconsin by connecting caring people with solutions that strengthen our community.

ELIGIBILITY:
Eligible organizations must have 501(c)(3) not-for-profit status. Schools and governmental entities may also apply. No grants are made to individuals.

GEOG. RESTRICTIONS: Brown, Door, Kewaunee and Oconto counties, Wisconsin.

FINANCIAL DATA:
Amount of support per award: Varies.
Total amount of support: $9,000,000 annually.

NO. AWARDS: 2,000 annually.

APPLICATION INFO:
All applicants should share their ideas with the Foundation prior to the submission of a formal application.

Duration: Varies by grant program.
Deadline: Varies by grant program.

IRS I.D.: 39-1699966

ADDRESS INQUIRIES TO:
Vice President of Community Engagement (See address above.)

THE GREATER KANAWHA VALLEY FOUNDATION [1177]

Huntington Square, Suite 1600
900 Lee Street East
Charleston, WV 25301
(304) 346-3620
Fax: (304) 346-3640
E-mail: shyre@tgkvf.org
Web Site: www.tgkvf.org

FOUNDED: 1962

AREAS OF INTEREST:
Education, health, community economic development, basic needs, and arts and culture.

TYPE:
Project/program grants; Scholarships.

YEAR PROGRAM STARTED: 1964

PURPOSE:
To serve the greater Kanawha Valley and surrounding areas.

LEGAL BASIS:
501(c)(3).

ELIGIBILITY:
Grant applicant must be a 501(c)(3) nonprofit organization as determined by the IRS, a faith-based organization, or a government entity located in or directly benefiting residents of the Greater Kanawha Valley.

GEOG. RESTRICTIONS: Boone, Clay, Fayette, Kanawha, Lincoln and Putnam, West Virginia.

FINANCIAL DATA:
Amount of support per award: Varies.
Total amount of support: $7,304,646 in donor-advised and donor-designated grants and $3,287,372 in discretionary grants for the year ended December 31, 2019; $740,612 in scholarships for the academic year 2019-20.
Matching fund requirements: Must have a match, in-kind or cash, not a specific percent.

NO. MOST RECENT APPLICANTS: Varies.

NO. AWARDS: 440 donor-advised and donor-designated grants for the year 2019; 368 scholarships for the academic year 2019-20.

APPLICATION INFO:
Applications are accepted online only.
Duration: Varies.
Deadline: Grants: Varies. Scholarships: January 15.

PUBLICATIONS:
Annual report.

IRS I.D.: 55-6024430

STAFF:
Stephanie Hyre, Senior Program Officer, Education and Arts
Derek Vance, Program Officer, Basic Needs and Special Initiatives
Todd Dorcas, Program Officer, Community Economic Development
Megan Simpson, Program Officer, Health
Susan Hoover, Scholarship Program Officer

ADDRESS INQUIRIES TO:
For Basic Needs and Special Initiative Grants:
Derek Vance, Program Officer
E-mail: dvance@tgkvf.org

For Community Economic Development Grants:
Todd Dorcas, Program Officer
E-mail: tdorcas@tgkvf.org
(See address above.)

For Education and Arts Grants:
Stephanie Hyre, Senior Program Officer
E-mail: shyre@tgkvf.org

For Health Program Grants:
Megan Simpson, Program Officer
E-mail: msimpson@tgkvf.org
(See address above.)

For scholarships:
Susan Hoover, Scholarship Program Officer
E-mail: shoover@tgkvf.org
(See address above.)

THE GREATER KANSAS CITY COMMUNITY FOUNDATION AND AFFILIATED TRUSTS [1178]

1055 Broadway Boulevard, Suite 130
Kansas City, MO 64105
(816) 842-0944
(866) 719-7886
(816) 627-3417
Fax: (816) 842-8079
E-mail: info@growyourgiving.org
Web Site: www.growyourgiving.org

FOUNDED: 1978

AREAS OF INTEREST:
Public education and life sciences.

CONSULTING OR VOLUNTEER SERVICES:
Grantmaking services.

TYPE:
Project/program grants; Scholarships. Grants in the areas of public education and life sciences and scholarships are given to make a positive support of the nonprofit sector and to promote philanthropy for the benefit of the community.

PURPOSE:
To improve the quality of life in greater Kansas City by increasing charitable giving, connecting donors to community needs they care about, and providing leadership on critical community issues.

LEGAL BASIS:
Public foundation.

ELIGIBILITY:
The Community Foundation does not ordinarily fund endowment campaigns, debt reduction, annual appeals and membership contributions, operating expenses and fund-raising projects of religious organizations, capital fund drives, including brick and mortar, land acquisition, equipment purchases, renovation or purchase of buildings, construction or the improvement of public spaces or financial assistance for individuals.

GEOG. RESTRICTIONS: Greater Kansas City, Missouri.

FINANCIAL DATA:
Amount of support per award: Varies.
Total amount of support: $464,000,000 for the year 2019.

NO. MOST RECENT APPLICANTS: 1,734 grant applicants for the year 2019.

NO. AWARDS: 841 grants for the year 2019.

APPLICATION INFO:
Unsolicited applications will not be accepted.
Duration: Typically one year.
Deadline: Varies.

IRS I.D.: 43-1152398

OFFICERS:
Deborah L. Wilkerson, President and Chief Executive Officer
Brenda Chumley, Senior Vice President of Foundation Relations and Operations
Katie Gray, Senior Vice President of Finance and Foundation Services

ADDRESS INQUIRIES TO:
See e-mail address above.

*PLEASE NOTE:
Unsolicited requests will not be accepted.

THE GREATER LANSING FOUNDATION [1179]
120 North Washington Square
Suite 650
Lansing, MI 48933
(517) 334-5232
Fax: (517) 334-5445
E-mail: info@crcfoundation.org

FOUNDED: 1947

AREAS OF INTEREST:
Arts, education, general charitable giving, handicapped and health.

NAME(S) OF PROGRAMS:
- **The Greater Lansing Foundation General Fund**

TYPE:
Capital grants; Development grants; Project/program grants; Scholarships; Seed money grants; Training grants; Work-study programs. General support for seed money and capital funds.

YEAR PROGRAM STARTED: 1947

PURPOSE:
To promote the well-being of the inhabitants of Clinton, Eaton and Ingham counties by distributing income to local charitable, public or educational institutions.

LEGAL BASIS:
Private foundation.

ELIGIBILITY:
Applicants must have a 501(c)(3) IRS exemption and be a public charity.

GEOG. RESTRICTIONS: Clinton, Eaton and Engham counties, Michigan.

FINANCIAL DATA:
Amount of support per award: Up to $10,000.
Total amount of support: Approximately $50,000 annually.

APPLICATION INFO:
Grant application requests should be made to:
Capital Region Community Foundation
c/o The Greater Lansing Foundation Fund
330 Marshall Street, Suite 300
Lansing, MI 48912
E-mail: info@crcfoundation.org
Tel: (517) 272-2870.
Duration: One year.
Deadline: April 1.

IRS I.D.: 38-6057513

ADDRESS INQUIRIES TO:
Margo Chicosky, Secretary
(See e-mail address above.)

GREATER MILWAUKEE FOUNDATION [1180]
101 West Pleasant Street
Suite 210
Milwaukee, WI 53212
(414) 272-5805
Fax: (414) 272-6235
E-mail: info@greatermilwaukeefoundation.org
Web Site: www.greatermilwaukeefoundation.org

FOUNDED: 1915

AREAS OF INTEREST:
Unrestricted grantmaking in the areas of strengthening neighborhoods, strengthening education, increasing economic opportunities, and promoting equity and inclusion.

TYPE:
Awards/prizes; Capital grants; Challenge/matching grants; Demonstration grants; Development grants; Matching gifts; Professorships; Project/program grants; Research grants; Scholarships; Seed money grants; Technical assistance; Training grants. The Foundation's unrestricted grantmaking does not support general operations.

The Foundation operates as a community trust, a public nonprofit organization established to administer charitable funds for the benefit of the people of the community. It is composed of more than 1,200 funds, each created by donors to serve the charitable causes of their choice. Donors can make grants locally, nationally or around the world.

The component funds are of several types, depending upon the wishes of the donor expressed at the time the originating gift or bequest was made:
(1) Unrestricted funds are those in which the Foundation's Board is given full discretion in determining how income can best be disbursed each year for charitable purposes;
(2) Field of interest funds are administered with a particular charitable purpose in mind, such as support of the arts, child welfare or education;
(3) Designated funds have been established to favor specific charitable agencies and institutions; the income earned by this type of fund is paid annually to a particular agency or agencies named by the donor; grants are usually intended to provide general sustaining support for current agency operations and;
(4) Donor-advised funds are those established by gifts from individuals, foundations or corporations in which the original contributors make suggestions to the Foundation Board about grant distributions.

YEAR PROGRAM STARTED: 1915

PURPOSE:
To inspire philanthropy, serve donors, and strengthen communities now and for future generations.

LEGAL BASIS:
Public nonprofit organization exempt from federal taxation under Section 501(c)(3) of the Internal Revenue Code.

ELIGIBILITY:
The Greater Milwaukee Foundation Board welcomes grant applications from agencies serving the people of the greater Milwaukee community. Details regarding grantmaking criteria are available online.

The Foundation is committed to promoting equity and inclusion with a focus on racial equity in its community. This commitment applies to its grantmaking. Nonprofit board diversity is the first of many things it considers. Eligible nonprofits must have board membership that is at least 10% people of color (African Americans, Asian Americans, Hispanic/Latino Americans and all other persons not categorized as white by the U.S. Census).

GEOG. RESTRICTIONS: Greater Milwaukee, Wisconsin, including Milwaukee, Ozaukee, Washington and Waukesha counties.

FINANCIAL DATA:
The funds vary in size from $25,000 to $27,000,000.
Amount of support per award: $18,191 average for the year 2018.
Total amount of support: $62,400,000 for the year 2019.

CO-OP FUNDING PROGRAMS: Nonprofit Management Fund; Milwaukee Teen Pregnancy Prevention Initiative Collaborative Fund; Milwaukee Succeeds Funders Collaborative.

NO. AWARDS: 4,478 grants for the year 2019.

APPLICATION INFO:
Applicant organization should update or add its information to the Foundation's online Grants Portal. Details for grant seekers are available online.
Duration: Generally, one year.

Deadline: Funding decisions are made quarterly.

PUBLICATIONS:
Newsletter; magazine; annual report.

IRS I.D.: 39-6036407

STAFF:
Kenneth Robertson, Vice President and Chief Financial Officer
Kathryn Dunn, Vice President, Community Investment
Kristen Mekemson, Vice President, Development and Philanthropic Services
Michael D. Hoffman, Vice President, Human Resources and Organizational Learning
Laura Porfilio Glawe, Vice President, Marketing and Communications
Danae Davis, Executive Director, Milwaukee Succeeds

BOARD OF DIRECTORS:
Jacqueline Herd-Barber, Chairperson
Paul J. Jones, Vice Chairperson
Wendy Reed Bosworth
Pedro Colon
David J. Drury
Susan Ela
Thomas W. Florsheim, Jr.
Cecelia Gore
Dale Kent
David J. Kundert
Gregory S. Marcus
Darryl D. Morin
Cory L. Nettles
Greg Oberland
Marie L. O'Brien
Mary Ellen Stanek
Derek L. Tyus
Gregory M. Wesley

OFFICER:
Ellen M. Gilligan, President and Chief Executive Officer

ADDRESS INQUIRIES TO:
Laura Porfilio Glawe
Vice President, Marketing and Communications
(See address above.)

THE GREATER NEW ORLEANS FOUNDATION [1181]

919 St. Charles Avenue
New Orleans, LA 70130
(504) 598-4663
Fax: (504) 598-4676
E-mail: richard@gnof.org
Web Site: www.gnof.org

AREAS OF INTEREST:
Housing, environment, health, workforce development, arts and culture, and children and youth.

TYPE:
Project/program grants; Scholarships. The Foundation provides start-up funds for promising new organizations or programs. It also funds demonstration grants to new or established organizations with innovative program models and offers transition grants to nonprofit organizations moving into a new state of organizational development.

PURPOSE:
To create a resilient, sustainable, vibrant community for all in the greater New Orleans region.

ELIGIBILITY:
The Foundation makes grants to nonprofit, tax-exempt organizations that serve the greater New Orleans area.

GEOG. RESTRICTIONS: Southeastern Louisiana and greater New Orleans region.

FINANCIAL DATA:
Amount of support per award: Varies.
Total amount of support: Varies.

APPLICATION INFO:
Guidelines are available online.
Duration: Typically one year. Renewal by reapplication.
Deadline: Varies.

PUBLICATIONS:
Guidelines.

*SPECIAL STIPULATIONS:
Upon completion of the funded project, or within one year, grant recipients must provide an end-of-grant report based on their proposed program evaluation.

THE GRUNDY FOUNDATION [1182]

680 Radcliffe Street
Bristol, PA 19007
(215) 788-5460
Fax: (215) 788-0915
E-mail: ejw@grundyfoundation.com
Web Site: www.grundyfoundation.com

FOUNDED: 1961

AREAS OF INTEREST:
Arts and culture, education and human services.

TYPE:
Capital grants. Capital grants for 501(c)(3) organizations throughout Bucks County, PA, primarily Lower Bucks County. Operating/programmatic support only for preselected organizations primarily in Bristol, PA and other parts of Lower Bucks County.

YEAR PROGRAM STARTED: 1961

PURPOSE:
To promote the well-being of the Commonwealth of Pennsylvania, with a particular emphasis in Bucks County.

LEGAL BASIS:
501(c)(3) private foundation.

ELIGIBILITY:
Applicants must be nonprofit organizations that have public charity status. No grants to individuals or for fellowships or loans.

GEOG. RESTRICTIONS: Primarily Lower Bucks County, Pennsylvania.

FINANCIAL DATA:
Amount of support per award: Excluding two impact grants each year, average grant $4,292.
Total amount of support: Varies.
Matching fund requirements: Stipulated with specific programs.

NO. AWARDS: 10 for the year 2017.

APPLICATION INFO:
Applicants should use the Philanthropy Network of Greater Philadelphia Common Grant Form found at www.philanthropynetwork.org.
Duration: No grants are awarded on a continuing basis.

PUBLICATIONS:
Application guidelines.

ADDRESS INQUIRIES TO:
Eugene J. Williams, Executive Director
(See address above.)

GULF COAST COMMUNITY FOUNDATION [1183]

601 Tamiami Trail South
Venice, FL 34285
(941) 486-4600
Fax: (941) 486-4699
E-mail: info@gulfcoastcf.org
Web Site: www.gulfcoastcf.org

FOUNDED: 1995

AREAS OF INTEREST:
Arts and culture, civic affairs, the environment, education, health and human services, and economic development.

TYPE:
Project/program grants.

YEAR PROGRAM STARTED: 1995

PURPOSE:
To improve the quality of life in communities the Foundation serves.

LEGAL BASIS:
Community foundation.

ELIGIBILITY:
Nonprofit organizations, 501(c)(3) tax-exempt, are eligible to apply.

GEOG. RESTRICTIONS: Charlotte, DeSoto, Lee, Manatee and Sarasota counties, Florida.

FINANCIAL DATA:
Amount of support per award: Varies.
Total amount of support: Varies.
Matching fund requirements: Varies.

REPRESENTATIVE AWARDS:
Charlotte County Homeless Coalition to provide first-year operating support for Safe House Shelter; Legal Aid of Manasota to provide free legal representation for southern Sarasota County homeowners facing foreclosure on their homes; United Way of Sarasota County to fund site coordinators who will facilitate the new Volunteer Income Tax Assistance Program.

APPLICATION INFO:
Application information is available on the web site.
Duration: Varies.
Deadline: Varies.

PUBLICATIONS:
Annual report; application guidelines.

ADDRESS INQUIRIES TO:
See e-mail address above.

HALL FAMILY FOUNDATION

P.O. Box 419580
Mail Drop 323
Kansas City, MO 64141-6580
(816) 274-8516
Fax: (816) 274-8547
E-mail: hff@hallmark.com
Web Site: www.hallfamilyfoundation.org

TYPE:
Capital grants; Project/program grants; Training grants.

See entry 137 for full listing.

HAMILTON COMMUNITY FOUNDATION [1184]

120 King Street West, Suite 700
Hamilton ON L8P 4V2 Canada
(905) 523-5600
Fax: (905) 523-0741
E-mail: grants@hamiltoncommunityfoundation.
ca
Web Site: www.hamiltoncommunityfoundation.
ca

FOUNDED: 1954

AREAS OF INTEREST:
Community development and services for
Hamilton, ON.

TYPE:
Project/program grants.

YEAR PROGRAM STARTED: 1954

PURPOSE:
To foster the growth of community
philanthropy; to build and prudently manage
community endowments; to provide
exceptional services to donors; to address
needs through strategic grantmaking and
organizational support; to provide leadership
on key community issues.

LEGAL BASIS:
Community foundation.

ELIGIBILITY:
Grants only to registered Canadian charities
and others qualified as described in Section
110 of the Income Tax Act. On occasion,
not-for-profit organizations without charitable
status may be sponsored by a registered
charity.

GEOG. RESTRICTIONS: Community of Hamilton,
Ontario, Canada.

FINANCIAL DATA:
Amount of support per award: Varies.
Total amount of support: $11,400,000 in
grants and community leadership for the year
2018-19.

NO. AWARDS: 850 grants to 307 organizations
for the year 2018-19.

APPLICATION INFO:
Application information is available on the
web site.
Duration: Varies by fund.

STAFF:
Terry Cooke, President and Chief Executive
Officer

ADDRESS INQUIRIES TO:
Matt Goodman, Vice President
Grants and Community Initiatives
(See address above.)

THE HAMPTON ROADS COMMUNITY FOUNDATION [1185]

101 West Main Street
Suite 4500
Norfolk, VA 23510
(757) 622-7951
Fax: (757) 622-1751
E-mail: grants@hamptonroadscf.org
Web Site: www.hamptonroadscf.org

FOUNDED: 1950

AREAS OF INTEREST:
Community development, education and
social welfare.

TYPE:
Capital grants; Development grants;
Project/program grants; Research grants;

Scholarships. Planning grants. Grants for
Vibrant Places (facilities and capital
campaigns), environmental stewardship,
educational success, cultural vitality, health
and wellness, economic stability, and special
interest.

YEAR PROGRAM STARTED: 1950

PURPOSE:
To provide opportunity for all through
leadership, philanthropy and civic
engagement.

LEGAL BASIS:
Nonprofit corporation.

ELIGIBILITY:
501(c)(3) nonprofit organizations that provide
benefits to the residents.

GEOG. RESTRICTIONS: Southeastern Virginia.

FINANCIAL DATA:
Amount of support per award: $500 to
$650,000.
Total amount of support: Approximately
$19,000,000 for the year 2020.

NO. MOST RECENT APPLICANTS: Approximately
125.

NO. AWARDS: Approximately 80.

APPLICATION INFO:
Application information is available on the
web site.
Duration: Grants: One year to multiyear;
Scholarships: One to four years.
Deadline: Varies depending upon program.

PUBLICATIONS:
Annual report; application guidelines;
quarterly newsletter.

IRS I.D.: 54-2035996

STAFF:
Deborah M. DiCroce, President and Chief
Executive Officer
Robin Foreman, Vice President for
Administration
Leigh Evans Davis, Vice President for Donor
Engagement
Linda Rice, Vice President for Grantmaking
Vivian Oden, Vice President for Special
Projects
Gina Kelly, Grants Manager

ADDRESS INQUIRIES TO:
See e-mail address above.

HAWAII COMMUNITY FOUNDATION [1186]

827 Fort Street Mall
Honolulu, HI 96813
(808) 537-6333
(888) 731-3863 (Hawaii)
Fax: (808) 521-6286
E-mail: give@hawaiicommunityfoundation.org
Web Site: www.hawaiicommunityfoundation.org

FOUNDED: 1916

AREAS OF INTEREST:
Culture and art, natural resources
conservation, education, health and medical
research, human services, disability,
mentoring and media, scholarships, neighbor
island assistance, persons in need and the
FLEX Program.

TYPE:
Development grants; Project/program grants;
Scholarships; Seed money grants; Technical
assistance; Training grants; Travel grants.

PURPOSE:
To build community among the people of
Hawaii.

LEGAL BASIS:
Community foundation.

ELIGIBILITY:
Grantseeker must be a tax-exempt
organization, either a unit of government or
one classified by the IRS as a 501(c)(3)
charity which is not a private foundation. The
organization must serve Hawaii's people and
environment and have leadership which
represents the community served. It must
make a request that is time-limited or has
other source of future funding.

The Foundation supports innovative and
creative programs that fit within specific
areas. It also provides scholarships for
college studies.

GEOG. RESTRICTIONS: Hawaii.

FINANCIAL DATA:
Foundation has more than $284,000,000 in
charitable assets.
Amount of support per award: Varies.
Total amount of support: Varies.

APPLICATION INFO:
Applicant must consult the Foundation web
site for instructions, as there are various
forms for each program.
Duration: Varies.
Deadline: Varies by program.

PUBLICATIONS:
Annual report.

THE HEALTH FOUNDATION OF GREATER INDIANAPOLIS, INC.

429 East Vermont Street, Suite 300
Indianapolis, IN 46202-3698
(317) 630-1805
Fax: (317) 630-1806
E-mail: rmcconnell@thfgi.org
Web Site: www.thfgi.org

TYPE:
Project/program grants.

See entry 1355 for full listing.

THE HEALTHCARE FOUNDATION FOR ORANGE COUNTY

1505 East 17th Street
Suite 113
Santa Ana, CA 92705
(714) 245-1650
Fax: (714) 245-1653
E-mail: info@hfoc.org
Web Site: www.hfoc.org

TYPE:
Demonstration grants; Development grants;
General operating grants; Project/program
grants; Technical assistance; Training grants.

See entry 1315 for full listing.

HILLSDALE COUNTY COMMUNITY FOUNDATION [1187]

2 South Howell
Hillsdale, MI 49242-1634
(517) 439-5101
Fax: (517) 439-5109
E-mail: s.bisher@abouthccf.org
Web Site: www.abouthccf.org

FOUNDED: 1991

AREAS OF INTEREST:
Arts, education, community needs, scholarships and philanthropy.

TYPE:
Project/program grants; Scholarships.

YEAR PROGRAM STARTED: 1991

PURPOSE:
To improve the quality of life in Hillsdale County.

LEGAL BASIS:
Community foundation.

ELIGIBILITY:
For grants, organizations must be in and benefit Hillsdale County and be IRS 501(c)(3) tax-exempt. For scholarships, students must be graduates of Hillsdale County High School, residents of Hillsdale County and citizens of the U.S.

GEOG. RESTRICTIONS: Hillsdale County, Michigan.

FINANCIAL DATA:
Amount of support per award: $300 to $25,000.
Total amount of support: Varies.

NO. MOST RECENT APPLICANTS: 15 to 20.

NO. AWARDS: 10.

APPLICATION INFO:
Applications are available at the address above and must include all required documentation, completed application according to requirements, and a copy of the IRS 501(c)(3) tax determination letter.
Duration: One year.
Deadline: Foundation Grants: May 1 and November 1.

ADDRESS INQUIRIES TO:
Sharon Bisher, President and Chief Executive Officer
(See address above.)

THE HOME DEPOT FOUNDATION [1188]
2455 Paces Ferry Road, C-17
Atlanta, GA 30339
Fax: (770) 384-3908
E-mail: hd_foundation@homedepot.com
Web Site: corporate.homedepot.com/community

FOUNDED: 1978

AREAS OF INTEREST:
Affordable housing, sustainable community development and community affairs.

CONSULTING OR VOLUNTEER SERVICES:
Team Depot volunteer program.

NAME(S) OF PROGRAMS:
● **Community Impact Grants Program**
● **Disaster Relief Program**
● **National Partner Grants Program**
● **Team Depot**
● **Veteran Housing Grants Program**

TYPE:
Challenge/matching grants; Development grants; Product donations; Project/program grants. Environmental research grants.

YEAR PROGRAM STARTED: 2002

PURPOSE:
To improve the homes and lives of U.S. military veterans and their families; to respond to communities in disaster.

LEGAL BASIS:
Corporate giving program.

ELIGIBILITY:
Most grants are made in communities where The Home Depot operates stores. No grants to individuals, religious, fraternal, political, labor, athletic, social or veterans groups, fund-raising benefits, dinners, exhibits, conferences and sports events, charities sponsored solely by a single civic organization, courtesy or journal advertising campaigns, multiyear commitments, or organizations that are not 501(c)(3) or Revenue Canada-designated charities.

GEOG. RESTRICTIONS: United States, Canada and Mexico.

FINANCIAL DATA:
Amount of support per award: Community Impact Grants: Up to $5,000; Veteran Housing Grants Program: $100,000 to $500,000.
Matching fund requirements: Employees making contributions to recognized nonprofits may apply for matching gifts up to $500 through The Home Depot Matching Gift Program.

APPLICATION INFO:
Contact the Foundation for application guidelines.
Duration: Varies.
Deadline: Varies according to program.

PUBLICATIONS:
Brochure; *Social Responsibility Report.*

ADDRESS INQUIRIES TO:
See e-mail address above.

HOUSING EDUCATION AND RESEARCH ASSOCIATION (HERA) [1189]
581 Stargazer Way
Florence, MT 59833
(406) 580-4836
E-mail: heraballen@gmail.com
Web Site: www.housingeducators.org

AREAS OF INTEREST:
Housing education.

NAME(S) OF PROGRAMS:
● **Tessie Agan Award Competition**

TYPE:
Awards/prizes.

ELIGIBILITY:
Open to graduate and undergraduate students.

FINANCIAL DATA:
Amount of support per award: Graduate Award: $750 presented at the HERA Annual Meeting; Undergraduate Award: $250.

APPLICATION INFO:
Information and specific guidelines pertaining to all grants can be found online.
Duration: One-time award.

ADDRESS INQUIRIES TO:
Barbara Allen, Executive Director
(See address above.)

*SPECIAL STIPULATIONS:
Award is contingent upon attending the meeting and presenting the paper. Conference registration fees are waived.

HUDSON-WEBBER FOUNDATION [1190]
333 West Fort Street
Suite 1310
Detroit, MI 48226-3134
(313) 963-7777
Fax: (313) 963-2818
Web Site: hudson-webber.org

FOUNDED: 1943

AREAS OF INTEREST:
The primary concern of the Foundation is the vitality of the metropolitan Detroit community. The Foundation's Trustees have defined four specific program missions in which they will concentrate their efforts and resources: Community and Economic Development, Safe and Just Communities, Built Environment, and Arts and Culture.

TYPE:
Project/program grants.

YEAR PROGRAM STARTED: 1943

PURPOSE:
To improve the quality of life of the metropolitan Detroit community.

LEGAL BASIS:
Private foundation.

ELIGIBILITY:
The Foundation assigns highest priority of support to programs in the city of Detroit. Programs outside of Detroit generally are not supported.

The Foundation does not make grants for endowments, fund-raising social events, conferences or exhibits. With the exception of the Foundation's program for Hudsonians, the Foundation does not make grants to individuals.

GEOG. RESTRICTIONS: Southeastern Michigan, specifically the city of Detroit.

FINANCIAL DATA:
Amount of support per award: $5,000 to $1,000,000.
Total amount of support: $7,321,475 for the year 2018.

NO. AWARDS: 63.

APPLICATION INFO:
Information may be obtained from the Foundation's web site.
Duration: One year.

BOARD OF TRUSTEES:
Jennifer Hudson Parke, Chairperson
Melanca D. Clark, President and Chief Executive Officer
David E. Meador, Treasurer
Amanda Van Dusen, Secretary
Toby Barlow
Matthew P. Cullen
Stephen R. D'Arcy
Stephen Henderson
Gilbert Hudson
Joseph L. Hudson, IV
Barbara McQuade
Joseph R. Parke
Robert G. Riney
Matthew Simoncini
Reginald M. Turner
Jean Hudson Witmer

ADDRESS INQUIRIES TO:
Stephanie Armes, Grants Manager
(See address above.)

HUMBOLDT AREA FOUNDATION [1191]

363 Indianola Road
Bayside, CA 95524
(707) 442-2993
Fax: (707) 442-3811
E-mail: sarad@hafoundation.org
Web Site: www.hafoundation.org

FOUNDED: 1972

AREAS OF INTEREST:
Children, youth and families; community, economy and the environment; health and well-being; arts and humanities; native cultures.

NAME(S) OF PROGRAMS:
- **Community Grants**
- **Consulting Grant**
- **Field of Interest Grant Program**
- **Grassroots Grant Program**
- **Native Cultures Fund**
- **Rapid Response Grants**
- **School Enrichment Grant Program**
- **Summer Youth Program**

TYPE:
Awards/prizes; Capital grants; Challenge/matching grants; General operating grants; Project/program grants; Scholarships; Seed money grants; Technical assistance.

YEAR PROGRAM STARTED: 1972

PURPOSE:
To improve the quality of life on the north coast of California.

ELIGIBILITY:
Eligible organizations must be IRS 501(c)(3) tax-exempt. Applications will be evaluated using the following criteria: need, planning and management, leadership and collaboration.

The Foundation will not fund projects outside of its service area, projects without sound planning and development, deferred maintenance, annual operating costs, travel, scholarships and fellowships, or projects which violate the nonprofit public laws.

GEOG. RESTRICTIONS: Curry, Del Norte, Humboldt and Trinity counties, California.

FINANCIAL DATA:
Amount of support per award: Varies.
Total amount of support: Varies.

APPLICATION INFO:
Information, guidelines and applications are available online.
Duration: Varies.
Deadline: Varies.

PUBLICATIONS:
Guidelines.

IRS I.D.: 23-7310660

ADDRESS INQUIRIES TO:
Sara Dronkers
Director of Grantmaking
(See address above.)

INTERNATIONAL DEVELOPMENT RESEARCH CENTRE (IDRC) [1192]

150 Kent Street
Ottawa ON K1P 0B2 Canada
(613) 696-2098
E-mail: awards@idrc.ca
Web Site: www.idrc.ca
www.crdi.ca

FOUNDED: 1970

AREAS OF INTEREST:
Research for international development.

NAME(S) OF PROGRAMS:
- **IDRC John G. Bene Research Fellowship in Developing Countries**

TYPE:
Fellowships. Fellowship is awarded for research on the relationship between forest resources and the social, economic, cultural and environmental welfare of people in developing countries.

PURPOSE:
To support field research in all developing countries.

ELIGIBILITY:
Applicant must meet the following criteria:
(1) hold Canadian citizenship or permanent residency status;
(2) be registered at a Canadian university at the Master's or doctoral level;
(3) have an academic background that combines forestry or agroforestry with social sciences. Applicants from interdisciplinary programs (e.g., environmental studies) may also be eligible;
(4) have approval of the research proposal by applicant's supervisor;
(5) proposed field research must take place in a developing country;
(6) applicant must be affiliated with an institution or organization in the region in which the research will take place and provide proof and;
(7) applicant must have completed course work and passed comprehensive examinations before taking up the award.

FINANCIAL DATA:
Amount of support per award: Up to $15,000 (CAN).

NO. AWARDS: 1.

APPLICATION INFO:
Application forms are available on the funding page of the IDRC web site.
Duration: 10 weeks to 12 months.
Deadline: June or July. Exact date is posted online in April.

ADDRESS INQUIRIES TO:
IDRC Centre Awards
(See e-mail address above.)

INTERNATIONAL DEVELOPMENT RESEARCH CENTRE (IDRC) [1193]

150 Kent Street
Ottawa ON K1P 0B2 Canada
(613) 696-2098
E-mail: awards@idrc.ca
Web Site: www.idrc.ca
www.crdi.ca

FOUNDED: 1970

NAME(S) OF PROGRAMS:
- **IDRC Doctoral Research Awards (IDRA)**

TYPE:
Awards/prizes. These awards are offered once a year and are intended for field research in one or more developing countries. Candidates must conduct their research in areas corresponding to IDRC's research priorities.

PURPOSE:
To support the field research of Canadian graduate students and developing country nationals enrolled in a Canadian university for doctoral research on a topic of relevance to sustainable and equitable development.

ELIGIBILITY:
Applicants must meet the following conditions for eligibility:
(1) hold Canadian citizenship (or permanent residency status), or hold citizenship of a developing country;
(2) be enrolled at a Canadian university at the doctoral level;
(3) research proposal is for a doctoral thesis and has been approved by the thesis supervisor;
(4) proposed field research must take place in one or more developing countries and be conducted for a doctoral dissertation;
(5) provide evidence of affiliation with an institution or organization in the developing-country region(s) in which the research will take place and;
(6) have completed course work and passed comprehensive examinations before taking up the award.

FINANCIAL DATA:
Total amount of support: Up to $20,000 (CAN).

NO. AWARDS: Approximately 20 per year.

APPLICATION INFO:
Applications are to be submitted online from the IDRC funding page. E-mail applications are not accepted.
Duration: 10 weeks to 12 months.
Deadline: May.

ADDRESS INQUIRIES TO:
IDRC Centre Awards
(See e-mail address above.)

INTERNATIONAL DEVELOPMENT RESEARCH CENTRE (IDRC) [1194]

150 Kent Street
Ottawa ON K1P 0B2 Canada
(613) 696-2098
E-mail: awards@idrc.ca
Web Site: www.idrc.ca
www.crdi.ca

FOUNDED: 1970

AREAS OF INTEREST:
Research for international development.

NAME(S) OF PROGRAMS:
- **IDRC Research Awards**

TYPE:
Internships. Program provides training in research management and grant administration under the guidance of Centre program staff. Approximately 50% of the time spent on own research project.

PURPOSE:
To provide exposure to research for international development through a program of training in research management and grant administration.

ELIGIBILITY:
Canadian citizens, permanent residents of Canada, and citizens of developing countries are eligible. Applicant must be registered in a Master's or Ph.D. program or have completed a Master's or Ph.D. degree in a recognized university.

Additional requirements are available on the IDRC funding page.

FINANCIAL DATA:
Amount of support per award: $41,310 to $47,822.

NO. AWARDS: Approximately 10 per year.

APPLICATION INFO:
Applications must be submitted online from the IDRC funding page.

Duration: One year.

Deadline: Posted on the IDRC web site in June.

ADDRESS INQUIRIES TO:
IDRC Centre Awards
(See e-mail address above.)

JEWISH COMMUNITY FOUNDATION OF LOS ANGELES [1195]

6505 Wilshire Boulevard
Suite 1200
Los Angeles, CA 90048
(323) 761-8700
Fax: (323) 761-8720
E-mail: info@jewishfoundationla.org
Web Site: www.jewishfoundationla.org

FOUNDED: 1954

AREAS OF INTEREST:
Jewish life, community and health services, education, social services, arts and culture, and civic life.

CONSULTING OR VOLUNTEER SERVICES:
Center for Designed Philanthropy - consultation with family foundations and individual funders regarding the effectiveness of their grantmaking.

NAME(S) OF PROGRAMS:
- **Capital Grants**
- **Cutting Edge Grants**
- **General Community Grants**
- **Israel Grants**
- **Next Stage Grants**

TYPE:
Awards/prizes; Capital grants; Project/program grants; Seed money grants. Capital Grants: Construction and renovation projects for facilities that predominantly serve members of the Los Angeles Jewish community.

Cutting Edge Grants: New programs with the potential for transformative impact that address critical needs in the Los Angeles Jewish community.

General Community Grants: Programs by organizations outside of the Jewish community which address high-priority concerns in the Los Angeles community.

Israel Grants: Programs that have an impact on economic development and pluralistic Jewish identity in Israel.

Next Stage Grants: Capacity building support for select former Cutting Edge Grant recipients to get to the next stage of their success.

YEAR PROGRAM STARTED: 1976

PURPOSE:
To provide endowment resources to enable the community to initiate model programs, assist agencies to address the diverse and demanding challenges to face emergencies and the needs of the Jewish community and the Los Angeles community at large.

LEGAL BASIS:
Jewish community foundation.

ELIGIBILITY:
Grants are made to nonprofit 501(c)(3) organizations.

GEOG. RESTRICTIONS: Primarily Los Angeles and Israel.

FINANCIAL DATA:
The Foundation currently manages assets of approximately 1.1 billion.

Amount of support per award: Capital Grants: Up to $200,000 over a two-year period; Cutting Edge Grants: Up to $300,000; General Community Grants: $10,000 to $25,000; Israel Grants: $100,000 to $250,000; Next Stage Grants: Up to $250,000 over a three-year period.

Total amount of support: The Foundation and its donors distribute approximately $81,000,000 in grants.

REPRESENTATIVE AWARDS:
$70,000 to Chrysalis for Direct Hire Program; $250,000 to the Jewish Federation of Greater Los Angeles for the Campaign for Civil Discourse; $250,000 to Project Miracle for the Miracle Masters Program.

APPLICATION INFO:
Application information is available on the web site. General Community Grants and Israel Grants are by invitation only.

Duration: Most grants one to three years. No renewals. Cutting Edge Grants: Three to five years.

Deadline: Varies.

PUBLICATIONS:
Annual report.

IRS I.D.: 95-6111928

OFFICERS:
William R. Feiler, Chairperson
Marvin I. Schotland, President and Chief Executive Officer
Anthony Chanin, Vice President
Abby Feinman, Vice President
Marcia Weiner Mankoff, Vice President
Harold Masor, Vice President
Evan Schlessinger, Vice President
Mark Schwartz, Vice President
Eugene Stein, Vice President
Adlai Wertman, Vice President
Scott Richland, Treasurer
Selwyn Gerber, Secretary

EXECUTIVE STAFF:
Marvin I. Schotland, President and Chief Executive Officer
Daniel M. Rothblatt, Executive Vice President, Philanthropic Services
David Carroll, Senior Vice President, Finance and Administration/Chief Financial Officer
Lori Klein, Vice President, Center for Designed Philanthropy
Lewis Groner, Vice President, Marketing and Communications
Natella Royzman, Director, Charitable Gift Planning
Ellen Rosen, General Counsel

THE KANTZLER FOUNDATION [1196]

Pere Marquette Depot
1000 Adams Street, Suite 200
Bay City, MI 48708
(989) 893-4438
Fax: (989) 893-4448
E-mail: kathy@kantzler.org
Web Site: www.kantzler.org

FOUNDED: 1974

AREAS OF INTEREST:
Education, science, arts, culture, human services, conservation, beautification and recreation projects in the Bay County area.

TYPE:
Capital grants; Development grants; Project/program grants.

YEAR PROGRAM STARTED: 1974

PURPOSE:
To provide financial support for charitable projects and programs that directly benefit the residents of Bay County, MI.

LEGAL BASIS:
Michigan nonprofit corporation.

ELIGIBILITY:
Organizations must be IRS 501(c)(3) tax-exempt. Priority is given to projects that will have a multiplier effect upon the community. The grants must be used to finance the cost of special projects and capital improvements and not to defray current operating expenses. The Foundation will not provide the entire support for a project and will expect that others will share the costs.

GEOG. RESTRICTIONS: Bay County area, Michigan.

FINANCIAL DATA:
Assets of approximately $6,000,000.

Amount of support per award: $1,000 to $250,000.

Total amount of support: Varies.

APPLICATION INFO:
Organizations wishing to submit a grant request must first call the Foundation to register their intent to submit the request. At that time they will be provided helpful information and assistance. If the request meets preliminary qualification criteria, the applicant will be assigned a login and password to the online application form. Applications must be completed and filed online, but supporting documents, endorsement letters, financial documents and public filings may be submitted in hard copy form.

Duration: Usually one year.

Deadline: Mid-March, early June, early September and late November.

PUBLICATIONS:
Brochure.

ADDRESS INQUIRIES TO:
Administrator for the Board of Trustees
(See address above.)

EDWARD BANGS KELLEY & ELZA KELLEY FOUNDATION, INC. [1197]

20 North Main Street
South Yarmouth, MA 02664
(508) 775-3117
Fax: (508) 760-3640
E-mail: contact@kelleyfoundation.org
Web Site: www.kelleyfoundation.org

FOUNDED: 1954

AREAS OF INTEREST:
Health, psychology, sociology, education, culture, and environment.

TYPE:
Capital grants; Challenge/matching grants; Development grants; Matching gifts; Project/program grants.

YEAR PROGRAM STARTED: 1954

PURPOSE:
To promote the health and welfare of the residents of Barnstable County.

LEGAL BASIS:
Private foundation.

ELIGIBILITY:
Applicants must be U.S. citizens, residents of Barnstable County, or organizations who serve Barnstable County. Grants must benefit health and welfare of Barnstable County (MA) residents.

GEOG. RESTRICTIONS: Barnstable County, Massachusetts.

FINANCIAL DATA:
Amount of support per award: Varies.
Total amount of support: Approximately $250,000.

CO-OP FUNDING PROGRAMS: Cape Cod Grantmakers Collaborative, other foundations.

APPLICATION INFO:
Grant applicants should contact Robert Talerman, President of the Foundation, for information and application forms. Additional information is available on the web site.
Duration: One year.

IRS I.D.: 04-6039660

ADDRESS INQUIRIES TO:
See e-mail address above.

THE KETTERING FUND   [1198]
40 North Main Street
Suite 1480
Dayton, OH 45423
(937) 228-1021
E-mail: info@ketteringfamilyphilanthropies.org
Web Site: www.cfketteringfamilies.com

FOUNDED: 1958

AREAS OF INTEREST:
The environment, medical research, teaching, the arts, human services, and higher education.

TYPE:
Capital grants; Challenge/matching grants; Development grants; Endowments; Matching gifts; Project/program grants; Research grants.

YEAR PROGRAM STARTED: 1958

PURPOSE:
To support scientific, medical, social and educational studies and research conducted by nonprofit, charitable organizations that are located in Ohio.

LEGAL BASIS:
Private foundation.

ELIGIBILITY:
Applicants must be tax-exempt 501(c)(3) nonprofit organizations. The Fund does not support individuals, partisan political causes or candidates, public elementary or secondary schools, scholarships or travel.

GEOG. RESTRICTIONS: Ohio.

FINANCIAL DATA:
Amount of support per award: Varies.
Total amount of support: $3,088,500 in grants paid for the year 2018.

NO. AWARDS: 10 to 15.

REPRESENTATIVE AWARDS:
$40,000 to Ohio Arts Council; $20,000 to Ohio Foundation of Independent Colleges.

APPLICATION INFO:
The Kettering Fund requires a letter of inquiry, to be submitted online, as a preliminary step before an application is requested. Check online for availability of funding.
Duration: Varies with project.
Deadline: Letter of inquiry: Generally late January and July.

PUBLICATIONS:
Application guidelines.

ADDRESS INQUIRIES TO:
Kathy Reed, Administrative Director
(See address above.)

KEWEENAW COMMUNITY FOUNDATION   [1199]
236 Quincy Street
Hancock, MI 49930
(906) 482-9673
Fax: (906) 482-9679
E-mail: mail@k-c-f.org
Web Site: www.keweenawgives.org

FOUNDED: 1994

AREAS OF INTEREST:
Environment, health, arts, recreation, and youth.

TYPE:
Awards/prizes; Challenge/matching grants; Development grants; Endowments; Project/program grants; Scholarships.

YEAR PROGRAM STARTED: 1994

PURPOSE:
To inspire giving that invests in our community's quality of life.

ELIGIBILITY:
Grants are made to organizations that have tax-exempt status under Section 501(c)(3) of the Internal Revenue Code. No grants are made to individuals. Religious programs may apply. Grants can also be given to governmental units or eligible educational institutions.

GEOG. RESTRICTIONS: Houghton and Keweenaw counties, Michigan.

FINANCIAL DATA:
Amount of support per award: Grants vary in amount, depending upon the needs and nature of the request.
Total amount of support: Varies.

APPLICATION INFO:
Information is available on the web site.
Duration: One year. Renewal possible.

IRS I.D.: 38-3223079

STAFF:
Erin Minne, Executive Director
Lisa Broemer, Finance and Fund Development
Andrew Ranville, Communications Coordinator

ADDRESS INQUIRIES TO:
Lisa Broemer, Finance and Fund Development
(See address above.)

KITSAP COMMUNITY FOUNDATION   [1200]
9657 Levin Road, N.W.
Suite 220
Silverdale, WA 98383
(360) 698-3622
E-mail: kcf@kitsapfoundation.org
Web Site: www.kitsapfoundation.org

FOUNDED: 1993

NAME(S) OF PROGRAMS:
● **Annual Competitive Grant Program**

TYPE:
General operating grants; Project/program grants; Scholarships.

YEAR PROGRAM STARTED: 1999

PURPOSE:
To improve the quality of life in the community.

LEGAL BASIS:
501(c)(3).

ELIGIBILITY:
Grant support mostly for nonprofit organizations serving Kitsap County, WA and surrounding areas.

GEOG. RESTRICTIONS: Kitsap County, Washington and its surrounding areas.

FINANCIAL DATA:
$11,000,000 in assets as of September 30, 2019.
Amount of support per award: $500 to $5,000.
Total amount of support: $80,000 in grants for the year 2019.

NO. MOST RECENT APPLICANTS: 62.

NO. AWARDS: 25.

APPLICATION INFO:
Applications are to be submitted online at commongrantapplication.com.
Duration: One year.
Deadline: September 28.

PUBLICATIONS:
Newsletter; annual report.

IRS I.D.: 94-3205217

STAFF:
Shaine Schramling, Funds and Grants Officer

ADDRESS INQUIRIES TO:
Shaine Schramling
Funds and Grants Officer
(See address above.)

THE KROGER COMPANY FOUNDATION   [1201]
1014 Vine Street
Cincinnati, OH 45202-1100
(513) 762-4000
Fax: (513) 762-1100
E-mail: krogerfoundation@kroger.com
Web Site: www.thekrogerco.com/community

FOUNDED: 1987

AREAS OF INTEREST:
Hunger relief.

TYPE:
General operating grants.

YEAR PROGRAM STARTED: 1987

PURPOSE:
To feed the hungry and assist local grassroots organizations.

LEGAL BASIS:
Corporate giving program.

ELIGIBILITY:
Only proposals from 501(c)(3) organizations located in communities where the Kroger Company has operations are considered.

FINANCIAL DATA:
Amount of support per award: Typically $10,000.

APPLICATION INFO:
Grant request must be submitted at www.communitygifts.com. All requests must include a 501(c)(3) tax determination letter from the IRS.

PUBLICATIONS:
Program announcement; application guidelines.

ADDRESS INQUIRIES TO:
Foundation Administrator
(See address above.)

*SPECIAL STIPULATIONS:
Funding limited to organizations serving communities where Kroger operates.

LAWRENCE COUNTY COMMUNITY FOUNDATION   [1202]

1324 K Street, Suite 150
Bedford, IN 47421
(812) 279-2215
Fax: (812) 279-1984
E-mail: lccf@cfpartner.org
Web Site: www.cfpartner.org

AREAS OF INTEREST:
Community improvement.

TYPE:
Endowments; Project/program grants; Scholarships. Collaborative projects. Classroom grants.

PURPOSE:
To be proactive in creating and growing an enduring source of charitable assets that will help to identify and respond to the emerging and changing needs of the community.

ELIGIBILITY:
Organizations and agencies who may or may not be tax-exempt according to Section 501(c)(3) of the Internal Revenue Code or for-profit entities interested in funding a charitable, not-for profit program are eligible. Population served by the program must be within Lawrence County, IN.

GEOG. RESTRICTIONS: Lawrence County, Indiana.

FINANCIAL DATA:
Amount of support per award: Varies.
Total amount of support: Varies.

APPLICATION INFO:
Application form can be requested from the Foundation or downloaded from the web site. Applicants must submit the following documents with the application form:
(1) concise summary of the proposed project, two or three paragraphs in length, stating the community need to be addressed by the project and why the organization is qualified to address the need, the target population and estimated number to be served, the organization's experience with similar projects, and a description of how the project will fit into and further the organization's overall mission;
(2) description of the activities or steps that will be taken to carry out the project, including project timeline;
(3) summary of funding details, including how the funds will be used, as well as other funding sources. Attach a detailed budget sheet showing projected income and expenses for the project;
(4) an explanation of how the success of this project will be evaluated. If the organization plans to continue the project, explain how will it be sustained after grant funding is

expended and;
(5) list of names and amounts from sources contributing 10% or more of the organization's budget in the past two years. Also list affiliations with religious groups.

Application must be signed by the organization President or another nonpaid board officer. Staple or clip each grant application copy.
Duration: Funding for a multiyear project will usually be considered on an annual basis and not extend beyond three years.

ADDRESS INQUIRIES TO:
Hope Flores, Chief Executive Officer
(See address above.)

THE JOHN J. LEIDY FOUNDATION   [1203]

305 West Chesapeake Avenue
Suite 308
Towson, MD 21204
(410) 821-3006
Fax: (410) 821-3007
E-mail: info@leidyfoundation.org
Web Site: www.leidyfoundation.org

FOUNDED: 1957

AREAS OF INTEREST:
Education, health care, arts/culture, food services, human services, children and youth.

TYPE:
General operating grants; Project/program grants.

PURPOSE:
To improve the quality of life in the Baltimore area.

LEGAL BASIS:
Private foundation.

ELIGIBILITY:
Organizations must be IRS 501(c)(3) tax-exempt and be located in Maryland. The Foundation does not fund individuals.

GEOG. RESTRICTIONS: Baltimore metropolitan area.

FINANCIAL DATA:
Amount of support per award: $350 to $20,000.
Total amount of support: $728,154 for the year 2018.

NO. MOST RECENT APPLICANTS: 125.

NO. AWARDS: 75 for the year 2018.

APPLICATION INFO:
Applications must include the proposed budget and a copy of the IRS tax-exempt letter. Application submission via e-mail is preferred.
Duration: Typically one year.

PUBLICATIONS:
Application guidelines.

OFFICER:
Robert L. Pierson, President

ADDRESS INQUIRIES TO:
Lu Pierson, Grants Administrator
(See address above.)

LOCAL INITIATIVES SUPPORT CORPORATION   [1204]

28 Liberty Street
34th Floor
New York, NY 10005
(212) 455-9800
Fax: (212) 682-5929
E-mail: info@lisc.org
Web Site: www.lisc.org

FOUNDED: 1980

AREAS OF INTEREST:
Urban and rural community revitalization.

TYPE:
Project/program grants; Technical assistance. Equity. Organizational support.

YEAR PROGRAM STARTED: 1980

PURPOSE:
To support community development; to equip struggling communities with the capital, strategy and know-how to become places where people can thrive; to build sustainable communities, which are good places to work, do business and raise children.

ELIGIBILITY:
Nonprofit 501(c)(3) IRS status.

GEOG. RESTRICTIONS: United States.

FINANCIAL DATA:
Amount of support per award: Varies.
Total amount of support: Varies.
Matching fund requirements: A strict matching requirement, dollar-for-dollar of new money from local private sources.

APPLICATION INFO:
Contact LISC local offices or the Corporation.
Duration: Varies.

IRS I.D.: 13-3030229

BOARD OF DIRECTORS:
Robert E. Rubin, Chairman
Maurice Jones, President and Chief Executive Officer

LONG ISLAND COMMUNITY FOUNDATION   [1205]

900 Walt Whitman Road
Suite 205
Melville, NY 11747
(631) 991-8800 ext. 233
Fax: (631) 991-8801
E-mail: jdemaio@licf.org
Web Site: www.licf.org

FOUNDED: 1978

AREAS OF INTEREST:
Arts, education, community development, environment, health, mental health, hunger, technical assistance, youth development and progressive social change.

NAME(S) OF PROGRAMS:
● **Henry Phillip Kraft Memorial Fund-Environmental Grants**
● **LIUU Fund-Progressive Social Change Grants**

TYPE:
Project/program grants.

YEAR PROGRAM STARTED: 1978

PURPOSE:
To provide leadership in identifying current and future community needs, and building a permanent endowment to address these needs.

LEGAL BASIS:
501(c)(3) or fiscal agent.

ELIGIBILITY:
Programs and projects benefiting Long Island, NY. Nonprofit organizations headquartered outside of Nassau and Suffolk Counties may apply if the project benefits Nassau and Suffolk counties.

GEOG. RESTRICTIONS: Nassau and Suffolk counties, New York.

FINANCIAL DATA:
Amount of support per award: $10,000 to $25,000.

NO. AWARDS: Over 50 annually.

APPLICATION INFO:
The Foundation has three grant cycles throughout the year. Detailed instructions are provided on the Foundation's web site. Applicants should review the instructions carefully before submitting an application.
Duration: One year.

STAFF:
Marie Smith, Director of Donor Relations
Sol Marie Alfonso-Jones, Senior Program Officer
Jeannie DeMaio, Grants Administrator

EXECUTIVE DIRECTOR:
David Okorn

ADDRESS INQUIRIES TO:
Jeannie DeMaio, Grants Administrator
(See address above.)

M & M AREA COMMUNITY FOUNDATION   [1206]

1110 10th Avenue, Suite L-1
Menominee, MI 49858
(906) 864-3599
E-mail: info@mmacf.org
Web Site: www.mmacf.org

FOUNDED: 1994

AREAS OF INTEREST:
Arts, charity, civic affairs, community development, culture, education, health, historic preservation and human services.

TYPE:
Project/program grants; Scholarships.

YEAR PROGRAM STARTED: 1997

PURPOSE:
To inspire people to provide lasting legacies which enrich our communities.

ELIGIBILITY:
Grants are made to organizations that have tax-exempt status under Section 501(c)(3) of the Internal Revenue Code. No grants are made to individuals.

GEOG. RESTRICTIONS: Menominee County, Michigan and Marinette County, Wisconsin.

FINANCIAL DATA:
Amount of support per award: Varies.
Total amount of support: $250,000 in grants and scholarships annually.

NO. AWARDS: 20 scholarships in fiscal year 2020.

APPLICATION INFO:
Applications must be submitted online.
Duration: Varies.
Deadline: Varies.

ADDRESS INQUIRIES TO:
Paula Gruszynski
Executive Director
(See e-mail address above.)

MADISON COMMUNITY FOUNDATION   [1207]

111 North Fairchild Street
Suite 260
Madison, WI 53703
(608) 232-1763
Fax: (608) 232-1772
E-mail: tlinfield@madisongives.org
grants@madisongives.org
Web Site: www.madisongives.org

FOUNDED: 1942

AREAS OF INTEREST:
Arts and culture, community development, environment, capacity building, and learning.

TYPE:
Capital grants; Project/program grants. Endowment challenge grants. Program grants support new programs or expansion of existing programs. Capital grants support the construction, acquisition and renovation of facilities and the purchase of equipment. Investments in technology are given to significantly enhance the organization's ability to operate or to improve services. Endowment grants are 1:2 or 1:3 challenge grants to grow agency endowment funds.

PURPOSE:
To enhance the quality of life for residents in Dane County.

LEGAL BASIS:
Community foundation.

ELIGIBILITY:
Organizations must be nonprofit IRS 501(c)(3) tax-exempt, serve the people of Dane County, employ a staff, elect a governing board, and conduct business without discrimination on the basis of race, religion, gender, sexual preference, age, marital status, disability or national origin.

Generally grants are not made for operating expenses, individuals, endowments, debt retirement, lobbying, annual campaigns, scholarships, religious organizations for religious purposes, conferences, fund-raising, celebrations or substance abuse treatment.

GEOG. RESTRICTIONS: Dane County, Wisconsin.

FINANCIAL DATA:
Approximately 25% of grant applications are funded at some level. The Foundation is rarely the sole funder of projects; other sources will be sought to accomplish project goals.
Amount of support per award: Program average: $35,000; Capital average: $55,000.
Total amount of support: Approximately $2,000,000 in unrestricted and field-of-interest grants.

NO. MOST RECENT APPLICANTS: 80.

NO. AWARDS: 23.

REPRESENTATIVE AWARDS:
Neighborhood Center STEM Project; Madison Public Library Capital Campaign; Madison Parks Foundation; Boys and Girls Club; Madison Opera.

APPLICATION INFO:
Guidelines and applications are available from the Foundation. Full proposals must be submitted in both paper and electronic form. Proposals by fax are not accepted. An online letter of inquiry (LOI) is required.
Duration: One to two years.
Deadline: Letter of Inquiry: August 1. Those asked to submit a full proposal: October 1.

PUBLICATIONS:
Grantmaking Guidelines.

ADDRESS INQUIRIES TO:
Tom Linfield
Vice President, Community Impact
(See address above.)

MARIETTA COMMUNITY FOUNDATION   [1208]

100 Putnam Street
Marietta, OH 45750
(740) 373-3286
E-mail: heather@mcfohio.org
Web Site: www.mcfohio.org

FOUNDED: 1974

AREAS OF INTEREST:
Civic affairs, the elderly, community needs and education.

TYPE:
Challenge/matching grants; Conferences/seminars; Development grants; Endowments; Grants-in-aid; Matching gifts; Scholarships; Seed money grants; Technical assistance; Training grants.

YEAR PROGRAM STARTED: 1974

PURPOSE:
To support philanthropy and the efforts of citizens to improve natural, human and civic resources.

LEGAL BASIS:
Community foundation.

ELIGIBILITY:
Must be a 501(c)(3) organization in or serving Washington County, OH.

GEOG. RESTRICTIONS: Greater Washington County, Ohio, and surrounding area.

FINANCIAL DATA:
Amount of support per award: $200 to $20,000.
Total amount of support: $150,000 unrestricted for the year 2016.

NO. MOST RECENT APPLICANTS: 60.

NO. AWARDS: 35.

APPLICATION INFO:
Organizations may either send a one-page letter of inquiry or submit a formal application form.
Duration: Varies.
Deadline: Proposals are accepted at any time during the year. To be considered in a particular quarter, the in-hand deadlines are February 15 and September 15. Applicants should allow 45 to 75 days for processing and response.

PUBLICATIONS:
Annual report; grant guidelines; memorial brochure.

FREDA MAYTAG-GRACE CRAWFORD TRUST

c/o JPMorgan Private Foundation Services
P.O. Box 227237, TX1-2963
Dallas, TX 75222-7237
(214) 965-2901
Fax: (800) 888-7695
E-mail: jpmorgan.pcs.grants@jpmchase.com
Web Site: www.jpmorgan.com/onlinegrants

TYPE:
Project/program grants.

See entry 1324 for full listing.

LUTHER T. MCCAULEY CHARITABLE TRUST [1209]

c/o JPMorgan
370 17th Street, Suite 3200
Denver, CO 80202
(303) 607-7810
Fax: (303) 607-7761
E-mail: julie.golden@jpmorgan.com
Web Site: www.jpmorgan.com/onlinegrants

AREAS OF INTEREST:
Economically deprived, the socially disadvantaged, mentally and physically handicapped citizens, with preference made toward the youth of the community for their educational, social, recreational and medical needs.

TYPE:
Project/program grants.

ELIGIBILITY:
Qualifying charities, agencies and institutions which direct their attention to the economically deprived, the socially disadvantaged and the mentally and physically handicapped citizens of El Paso County, CO. No grants to individuals.

Organization must provide copy of current IRS determination letter showing tax-exempt status under Section 501(c)(3) and public charity status under Section 509(a).

GEOG. RESTRICTIONS: El Paso County, Colorado.

FINANCIAL DATA:
Total amount of support: Average: $7,500.

APPLICATION INFO:
Applications must be submitted online. No physical applications will be accepted.
Duration: One year. No renewals.
Deadline: November 1. Decision by end of first quarter of the following year.

ADDRESS INQUIRIES TO:
Julie Golden, Trust Advisor
(See address above.)

RICHARD KING MELLON FOUNDATION [1210]

BNY/Mellon Center
500 Grant Street, Suite 4106
Pittsburgh, PA 15219-2502
(412) 392-2800
Fax: (412) 392-2837
E-mail: lreed@rkmf.org
Web Site: www.rkmf.org

FOUNDED: 1947

AREAS OF INTEREST:
Conservation; regional economic development; education; human services and nonprofit capacity building.

TYPE:
Capital grants; Challenge/matching grants; Grants-in-aid; Project/program grants. Grant program for improving the quality of life in southwestern Pennsylvania.

PURPOSE:
To promote conservation, economic development, education, human services and programs in the public interest.

ELIGIBILITY:
Must be 501(c)(3) nonprofit organizations. Priority is given to projects and programs that have clearly defined outcomes and an evaluation component. Funding is almost exclusively committed to southwestern Pennsylvania. Preference is given for support

of established organizations with specific objectives, and for partnering with other donors rather than solely underwriting the entire cost of projects.

GEOG. RESTRICTIONS: Southwestern Pennsylvania.

FINANCIAL DATA:
Amount of support per award: Varies.
Total amount of support: $127,591,006 in grants paid for the year 2018.

NO. AWARDS: 180 for the year 2018.

APPLICATION INFO:
Applications must be submitted online.
Duration: Varies.
Deadline: Applications accepted on a rolling basis.

ADDRESS INQUIRIES TO:
Lisa Reed, Information and Grants Manager
(See address above.)

EUGENE AND AGNES E. MEYER FOUNDATION [1211]

1250 Connecticut Avenue, N.W.
Suite 800
Washington, DC 20036
(202) 483-8294
E-mail: jward@meyerfdn.org
Web Site: www.meyerfoundation.org

FOUNDED: 1944

AREAS OF INTEREST:
Housing, employment, education, asset building, and capacity-building.

TYPE:
General operating grants; Project/program grants. Capacity-building grants. Grants for a wide variety of projects in the above areas of interest in the Washington, DC metropolitan area.

YEAR PROGRAM STARTED: 1944

PURPOSE:
To pursue and invest in solutions that build on equitable greater Washington, DC community in which economically vulnerable people thrive.

LEGAL BASIS:
Private foundation.

ELIGIBILITY:
The Foundation distributes its funds to and through tax-exempt nonprofit organizations. It does not make grants for projects that are primarily sectarian in character. Grants are seldom made for projects outside the geographical boundaries of Greater Washington and are never made to individuals. The Foundation does not support endowment drives, scientific or medical research, scholarship programs, seasonal programs, special or annual events or conferences.

GEOG. RESTRICTIONS: Montgomery and Prince George's counties, Maryland; Arlington, Fairfax and Prince William counties and the cities of Alexandria, Falls Church, Manassas and Manassas Park, Virginia; Washington, DC.

FINANCIAL DATA:
Amount of support per award: Most grants $10,000 to $50,000.
Total amount of support: $8,100,000 in grants authorized for the year 2018.

CO-OP FUNDING PROGRAMS: Occasional joint funding.

NO. MOST RECENT APPLICANTS: Approximately 425.

NO. AWARDS: Approximately 220 grants annually.

APPLICATION INFO:
Applications must be submitted online via link on the Foundation's web site.
Duration: Generally one-year support from date of award.

PUBLICATIONS:
E-newsletter.

IRS I.D.: 53-0241716

STAFF:
Nicky Goren, President and Chief Executive Officer
Karen FitzGerald, Vice President, Community Partnerships and Learning
Janice Thomas, Vice President, Finance and Operations
Jane Ward, Grants Director
Nadine Duplessy Kearns, Program Director, DC
Julian A. Haynes, Program Director, Maryland
Sonia Quinonez, Program Director, Northern Virginia
Melody Fitzgerald, Executive Office and Governance Manager
Andrew Brown, Grants Manager
Jenny Burke, Operations Manager
Edward Erskine, Finance and Operations Associate
Kari Den Otter, Partnerships Associate
Alexis Martinez, Partnerships Coordinator

OFFICERS AND BOARD OF DIRECTORS:
Charlene M. Dukes, Chairperson
Bo Menkiti, Vice Chairperson
Nicky Goren, President and Chief Executive Officer
Tram Nguyen, Treasurer
Tori O'Neil-McElrath, Secretary
Winell Belfonte
William Dunbar
David Harrington
Lidia Soto-Harmon
Karen Wawrzaszek
Ryan Young

ADDRESS INQUIRIES TO:
Nicky Goren, President and Chief Executive Officer
(See address above.)

MICHIGAN GATEWAY COMMUNITY FOUNDATION [1212]

111 Days Avenue
Buchanan, MI 49107-1609
(269) 695-3521
Fax: (269) 695-4250
E-mail: info@mgcf.org
Web Site: mgcf.org

FOUNDED: 1978

AREAS OF INTEREST:
Health, culture, education and community development.

TYPE:
Challenge/matching grants; Development grants; Project/program grants; Scholarships; Seed money grants.

YEAR PROGRAM STARTED: 1978

PURPOSE:
To address the changing needs of the community in Cass and South Berrien counties; to foster a community of philanthropy, for good, forever.

LEGAL BASIS:
501(c)(3) nonprofit foundation.

ELIGIBILITY:
Eligible organizations must be IRS 501(c)(3) tax-exempt.

GEOG. RESTRICTIONS: Cass and South Berrien counties, Michigan.

FINANCIAL DATA:
Amount of support per award: Varies.
Total amount of support: Varies.

APPLICATION INFO:
Applicants may use the Common Grant Application Form of the Council of Michigan Foundations. Applications must include a copy of the IRS tax determination letter. Applications for grants and scholarships are available on the web site.

Applicants for grants are strongly encouraged to contact the Foundation for an appointment before completing an application.
Duration: One year. Most grants not renewable.
Deadline: Grants from unrestricted grant sources: February 1 and August 1.

PUBLICATIONS:
Annual report; scholarship programs.

IRS I.D.: 38-2180730

ADDRESS INQUIRIES TO:
Robert N. Habicht
President and Chief Executive Officer
(See address above.)

THE MINNEAPOLIS FOUNDATION   [1213]
800 IDS Center
80 South Eighth Street
Minneapolis, MN 55402
(612) 672-3878
Fax: (612) 672-3846
E-mail: e-mail@mplsfoundation.org
Web Site: www.minneapolisfoundation.org

FOUNDED: 1915

AREAS OF INTEREST:
Civic engagement, economic vitality, education.

CONSULTING OR VOLUNTEER SERVICES:
Philanthropic services for other foundations.

TYPE:
General operating grants; Project/program grants.

PURPOSE:
To invest the Foundation's unrestricted resources towards specific results in order to achieve social, economic and racial equity for Minneapolis residents.

LEGAL BASIS:
Community foundation incorporated in Minnesota.

ELIGIBILITY:
Organizations must advance social, economic, and/or racial equity to be eligible for funding. The Foundation grants to 501(c)(3) organizations, some 501(c)(4) nonprofits, governmental or tribal organizations, and groups organized for nonprofit purposes (informal, emerging or collaborative groups).

The Foundation does not fund individuals, organizations/activities outside of Minnesota, conference registration fees, memberships, direct religious activities, political organizations or candidates' fund-raising efforts, conferences, events or sponsorships, financial deficits, replacement of public sector funds, emergency/safety net services, regranting/loans, production of housing units, or purchase or repair of vehicles.

GEOG. RESTRICTIONS: Primarily Minneapolis, Minnesota.

FINANCIAL DATA:
Amount of support per award: Competitive grants: $57,000 average.
Total amount of support: $4,076,000 in competitive grants for the year 2019.

NO. AWARDS: 80 to 90 competitive grants per year.

REPRESENTATIVE AWARDS:
$35,000 to African Development Center of Minnesota to produce affordable housing opportunities and support a more competitive workforce; $40,000 to State Voices to increase voter participation in communities of color; $50,000 to EMPOWER to recruit, prepare, train and mobilize a cohort of underserved and underrepresented low-income and communities of color across Minneapolis to advocate for high-quality educational options for all children.

APPLICATION INFO:
Application information and updates on the Foundation grantmaking cycle are available on the web site.
Duration: One year. Must reapply for additional funding. No multiyear grants.

IRS I.D.: 41-6029402

OFFICERS:
R.T. Rybak, President and Chief Executive Officer

ADDRESS INQUIRIES TO:
Community Grantmaking
(See address above.)

MIZUHO USA FOUNDATION, INC.   [1214]
Mizuho Americas
1251 Avenue of the Americas, 31st Floor
New York, NY 10020-1104
(212) 282-4192
E-mail: mizuho.usa.foundation@mizuhogroup.com
Web Site: www.mizuhoamericas.com/foundation

FOUNDED: 2003

AREAS OF INTEREST:
Community development, with a focus on affordable housing, economic development and workforce development.

NAME(S) OF PROGRAMS:
- **Fostering Economic Self-Sufficiency**
- **Mizuho Community Involvement Grants Program**
- **Mizuho Matching Gifts Program**
- **Promoting Economic Development**
- **Strengthening Affordable Housing**

TYPE:
Demonstration grants; Matching gifts; Project/program grants; Seed money grants. The Foundation awards grants to not-for-profit charitable organizations for community development programs that help sustain and revitalize economically distressed urban communities, and assist individuals who live in these neighborhoods.

Fostering Economic Self-Sufficiency funds programs that strengthen the workforce development field through the provision of technical assistance and/or training to not-for-profit organizations.

Mizuho Community Involvement Grants Program makes small grants available to the not-for-profit charitable organizations with which Mizuho Corporate Bank volunteer activities take place.

Mizuho Matching Gifts Program is for qualifying contributions made by eligible Mizuho Financial Group U.S. employees to qualifying not-for-profit charitable organizations in the areas of education, arts and culture, health and community affairs.

Promoting Economic Development supports programs that promote economic and commercial revitalization of communities by fostering small business development, entrepreneurship, job creation and job retention.

Strengthening Affordable Housing provides funding for programs that facilitate access to affordable housing for low- and moderate-income individuals and families.

YEAR PROGRAM STARTED: 2003

PURPOSE:
To provide grants to not-for-profit charitable organizations to support community development programs that contribute to the strength and vitality of urban neighborhoods; to serve as a catalyst for innovative programs in the U.S. that strengthen urban communities.

LEGAL BASIS:
Corporate foundation.

ELIGIBILITY:
Organizations applying to the Foundation must:
(1) be recognized as tax-exempt under Section 501(c)(3) of the Internal Revenue Code and classified as a public charity under Section 509(a)(1) or (2) of the Internal Revenue Code and not a supporting organization under Section 509(a)(3);
(2) present a proposal that satisfies the Foundation's guidelines;
(3) not discriminate against a person or group on the basis of age, race, national origin, ethnicity, gender, disability, sexual orientation, political affiliation or religious belief and;
(4) be in full compliance with U.S. anti-terrorism laws and regulations, including the USA Patriot Act and Executive Order 13224, pertaining to U.S.-based, not-for-profit charitable organizations conducting activities outside of the U.S.

The Foundation does not fund:
(1) general operating support;
(2) individuals;
(3) religious, sectarian, fraternal, veteran, athletic or labor groups;
(4) organizations or programs outside the U.S.;
(5) political organizations, political candidates or political activity;
(6) organizations whose primary purpose is to influence legislation;
(7) fund-raising activities such as charitable dinners or sporting events;
(8) advertising and;
(9) endowment or capital campaigns.

GEOG. RESTRICTIONS: New York City, New York.

FINANCIAL DATA:
Foundation's endowment is approximately $14,000,000 as of July 31, 2019.

Amount of support per award: $10,000 to $100,000; average $50,000.

Total amount of support: $606,500, including approximately $515,000 in program grants, for the year 2019.

Matching fund requirements: Mizuho Matching Gifts Program: 1:1 match for qualifying contributions. Requests for matching gifts must come from eligible employees of the Mizuho Financial Group in the U.S.

CO-OP FUNDING PROGRAMS: Neighborhood Opportunities Fund (New York City, NY) and New York City Workforce Development Fund.

NO. AWARDS: 34 grants for the year 2019.

REPRESENTATIVE AWARDS:
$25,000 to Association for Neighborhood and Housing Development to support community organizations by providing trainings that advance their skills, knowledge, and abilities to tackle complex community development issues; $50,000 to The Door to expand a program to help more young people who are at greatest risk of not succeeding in college gain admission and make a successful transition to college; $30,000 to Local Initiatives Support Coalition to support the expansion of a program that helps affordable housing developers in New York City integrate green, health measures and energy efficiency retrofits in their buildings to reduce building costs and improve the health of residents.

APPLICATION INFO:
Qualifying organizations must submit a short concept paper of up to three pages for preliminary review. The concept paper should include:
(1) a brief description of the organization including its legal name, history, mission/goals, activities and web address;
(2) copy of the IRS determination letter indicating 501(c)(3) tax-exempt status and 509(1) public charity classification and;
(3) a description of the program for which funding is sought, including statement of need, goals and objectives of the program, expected outcomes and evaluation methods, projected time frame, population(s)/geographies served, grant amount requested, and a preliminary program budget, with projected expenses and revenues, including funding commitments received to date for the program as well as pending requests (may be provided in attachment form).

The Foundation staff will review all initial submissions and invite organizations on a selective basis to submit more detailed proposals. Each applicant will be notified of the Foundation's interest within eight weeks of the annual deadline. Selected proposals are presented to the Foundation's Board of Directors, which makes funding decisions each fall.

Duration: Usually one year; some multiyear grants may be awarded.

Deadline: July 1 or first business day in July, to be considered for funding in the same year.

PUBLICATIONS:
Brochure; application guidelines.

IRS I.D.: 13-3550008

OFFICERS:
John H. Higgs, Chairman
Hiroyuki Kasama, President

Paul Dankers, Treasurer
Koichi Zaiki, Secretary
Lesley H. Palmer, Executive Director
Albert Scarola, Assistant Treasurer
Leah Markham, Program Officer

BOARD OF DIRECTORS:
Nancy Bercovici
John H. Higgs
Hiroyuki Kasama
Teiji Teramoto
Koichi Zaiki

ADDRESS INQUIRIES TO:
Lesley H. Palmer, Executive Director
(See address above.)

MONTANA COMMUNITY FOUNDATION [1215]

33 South Last Chance Gulch
Suite 2A
Helena, MT 59601
(406) 443-8313
Fax: (406) 442-0482
E-mail: info@mtcf.org
Web Site: www.mtcf.org

FOUNDED: 1988

AREAS OF INTEREST:
General charitable purposes.

NAME(S) OF PROGRAMS:
● **Social Justice Montana**
● **Women's Foundation of Montana**

TYPE:
Grants-in-aid; Scholarships. The Foundation provides $2,000,000 annually in grants and scholarships, with almost all of that money designated. It also has a large number of donor-advised and scholarship funds. The only competitive granting programs are the following:
(1) Social Justice Montana: The mission of this Fund is to promote tolerance and combat bigotry and discrimination, with a focus on youth, ages elementary through high school and;
(2) Women's Foundation of Montana: Its mission is to promote economic self-sufficiency and a brighter future for women and girls.

PURPOSE:
To cultivate a culture of giving so Montana communities can flourish.

LEGAL BASIS:
501(c)(3) organization.

ELIGIBILITY:
Applicants must be 501(c)(3) tax-exempt organizations or an exempt government unit.

GEOG. RESTRICTIONS: Montana.

FINANCIAL DATA:
Assets of approximately $100,500,000 as of June 30, 2018.

Amount of support per award: Social Justice Montana: Up to $5,000. Women's Foundation of Montana: Up to $10,000. Scholarships: Generally $500 to $5,000.

Total amount of support: $6,400,000 in grants and scholarships distributed in fiscal year 2018.

APPLICATION INFO:
Application information is posted online. Only one application per organization will be accepted.

Duration: Varies.

Deadline: Scholarships: March 18.

ADDRESS INQUIRIES TO:
Jessica Stewart-Kuntz
Operations and Grants Manager
(See address above.)

THE MORTON-KELLY CHARITABLE TRUST [1216]

c/o Jensen Baird Gardner & Henry
10 Free Street
Portland, ME 04112
(207) 775-7271
Fax: (207) 775-7935
E-mail: mquinlan@jbgh.com
Web Site: www.morton-kelly.org

FOUNDED: 1988

AREAS OF INTEREST:
Educational programs, cultural projects, historic preservation projects and environmental initiatives.

TYPE:
Capital grants; Challenge/matching grants; Development grants; Project/program grants; Seed money grants. One-time cash award.

YEAR PROGRAM STARTED: 1988

PURPOSE:
To support organizations in the arts, education, environment and history.

LEGAL BASIS:
Private foundation.

ELIGIBILITY:
Organizations must be IRS 501(c)(3) tax-exempt and be located in Maine.

GEOG. RESTRICTIONS: Maine.

FINANCIAL DATA:
Amount of support per award: Varies.
Total amount of support: $913,000 for the year 2019.

NO. MOST RECENT APPLICANTS: 158 for the year 2019.

NO. AWARDS: 92 for the year 2019.

REPRESENTATIVE AWARDS:
$5,000 to 317 Main Community Music Center; $5,000 to Kennebec Estuary Land Trust; $4,000 to Friends of L.C. Bates Museum; $15,000 to Maine Humanities Council; $5,000 to Penobscot Theatre Council.

APPLICATION INFO:
Applicants may submit a written proposal and must include a copy of the IRS tax determination letter.

Duration: One year.

Deadline: October 1.

IRS I.D.: 01-0442078

ADDRESS INQUIRIES TO:
Michael J. Quinlan, Secretary
(See address above.)

*PLEASE NOTE:
Applications not accepted before July 1 each year.

CHARLES STEWART MOTT FOUNDATION [1217]

Mott Foundation Building
503 South Saginaw Street, Suite 1200
Flint, MI 48502-1851
(810) 238-5651
Fax: (810) 766-1753
E-mail: info@mott.org
Web Site: www.mott.org

FOUNDED: 1926

AREAS OF INTEREST:
Civil society, environment, education and Flint, MI area, besides exploratory interests.

TYPE:
Challenge/matching grants; Demonstration grants; General operating grants; Project/program grants; Seed money grants; Technical assistance; Training grants. Grants for improvement of the quality of living in the community through pilot ventures in a number of human service areas. Emphasis is on improving opportunity for the individual, partnership with the community, effectiveness of community systems and leadership.

PURPOSE:
To support efforts that promote a just, equitable and sustainable society.

LEGAL BASIS:
Private foundation.

ELIGIBILITY:
Applicants must be organizations and institutions with appropriate interests. No grants to individuals. Tax-exempt status is required.

FINANCIAL DATA:
Amount of support per award: $15,000 to $250,000.
Total amount of support: $132,000,000 for the year 2018.

NO. AWARDS: 358 for the year 2018.

APPLICATION INFO:
Letter of Inquiry form must be completed on the Foundation web site.
Duration: One year; occasionally multiyear.

PUBLICATIONS:
Annual report.

TRUSTEES:
Ridgway H. White, Chairman and Chief Executive Officer
Frederick S. Kirkpatrick, Vice Chairman
A. Marshall Acuff, Jr.
Lizabeth Ardisana
Tiffany W. Lovett
Webb F. Martin
Olivia P. Maynard
John Morning
Maryanne Mott
Charlie Nelms
Douglas X. Patiño
Jeremy Piper
William H. Piper
George E. Ross
Marise M.M. Stewart
Helen Taylor

ADDRESS INQUIRIES TO:
Office of Proposal Entry
(See address above.)

MUSKINGUM COUNTY COMMUNITY FOUNDATION [1218]

534 Putnam Avenue
Zanesville, OH 43701
(740) 453-5192
Fax: (740) 453-5734
E-mail: giving@mccf.org (grants)
scholarshipcentral@mccf.org (scholarships)
Web Site: www.mccf.org

FOUNDED: 1985

AREAS OF INTEREST:
Improving the quality of life in Muskingum County, OH.

CONSULTING OR VOLUNTEER SERVICES:
Assistance to college-bound students, grantseekers and grantmakers in the Muskingum County, OH area.

NAME(S) OF PROGRAMS:
● **Scholarship Central**

TYPE:
Awards/prizes; Challenge/matching grants; Conferences/seminars; Development grants; Endowments; Project/program grants; Scholarships; Seed money grants; Technical assistance; Visiting scholars. Scholarships for Muskingum County, OH residents and others designated in fund agreements.

YEAR PROGRAM STARTED: 1985

PURPOSE:
To improve the quality of life and to serve the charitable needs of the community by attracting and administering charitable funds.

LEGAL BASIS:
Ohio nonprofit corporation classified by the IRS as a 501(c)(3) entity.

ELIGIBILITY:
Organization with primary or sole impact on Muskingum County, OH.

GEOG. RESTRICTIONS: Muskingum and contiguous counties, Ohio.

FINANCIAL DATA:
Amount of support per award: Varies.
Total amount of support: Approximately $1,000,000 annually.

NO. AWARDS: Grants and scholarships: Over 100 yearly.

APPLICATION INFO:
Varies per grant or scholarship.
Duration: Grants and scholarships: Varies.
Deadline: Varies.

ADDRESS INQUIRIES TO:
Brian Wagner, Chief Executive Officer
(See address above.)

NATIONAL BLACK MBA ASSOCIATION [1219]

400 West Peachtree Street, N.W.
Suite 203
Atlanta, GA 30308
(404) 260-5444
E-mail: scholarship@nbmbaa.org
Web Site: nbmbaa.org

AREAS OF INTEREST:
The economic and intellectual wealth of the black community.

NAME(S) OF PROGRAMS:
● **NBMBAA Graduate Scholarship Program**

TYPE:
Scholarships.

PURPOSE:
To help create economic and intellectual wealth for the black community; to identify and increase the pool of Black talent for business, public, private and nonprofit sectors.

ELIGIBILITY:
Applicant must:
(1) be a financially active member of the National Black MBA Association;
(2) be a U.S. or Canadian citizen;
(3) be a student entering their first year (Fall 2018), or continuing in a full or part-time Master's program at an accredited college or university at the time of award (September

2019);
(4) have a 3.0 or above grade point average;
(5) demonstrate academic excellence;
(6) demonstrate exceptional leadership potential;
(7) be actively involved in their local communities through service to others and;
(8) be recommended by a faculty member or individual familiar with applicant's academic achievements or supervisor in a business workplace.

GEOG. RESTRICTIONS: United States and Canada.

FINANCIAL DATA:
The Association has awarded over $5,000,000 in scholarships to deserving youth and minority students (undergraduate, graduate and doctoral).
Amount of support per award: Up to $10,000.
Total amount of support: Over $500,000.

NO. MOST RECENT APPLICANTS: 550.

NO. AWARDS: Minimum of 25.

APPLICATION INFO:
Application materials include:
(1) application (must be completed online);
(2) essay (500 words on the selected topic, submitted online only);
(3) current resume no more than two pages long;
(4) copy of most recent official transcript(s) uploaded and;
(5) headshot in jpeg format (image should be at least 1024 x 768).
Deadline: June 6.

ADDRESS INQUIRIES TO:
See e-mail address above.

NATIONAL BLACK MBA ASSOCIATION

400 West Peachtree Street, N.W.
Suite 203
Atlanta, GA 30308
(404) 260-5444
E-mail: scholarship@nbmbaa.org
Web Site: nbmbaa.org

TYPE:
Scholarships.

See entry 946 for full listing.

NATIONAL FOOTBALL LEAGUE FOUNDATION [1220]

345 Park Avenue
New York, NY 10154
(212) 450-2000
E-mail: alexia.gallagher@nfl.com
Web Site: www.nflfoundation.org

FOUNDED: 1973

AREAS OF INTEREST:
Health and safety, youth football, and community.

NAME(S) OF PROGRAMS:
● **Field Grants**
● **Player Foundation Grants**
● **Pro Bowl Grants**
● **Youth Football Grants**

TYPE:
Awards/prizes; Challenge/matching grants; General operating grants; Project/program grants; Research grants; Seed money grants; Training grants.

YEAR PROGRAM STARTED: 1973

PURPOSE:
To support youth-oriented programs that promote education, physical fitness and the value of a healthy lifestyle.

LEGAL BASIS:
Private foundation.

ELIGIBILITY:
Grants will be awarded to organizations that focus on youth-centered educational and recreational programming on a national scale.

GEOG. RESTRICTIONS: United States.

FINANCIAL DATA:
Amount of support per award: Varies.
Total amount of support: Varies.

NO. MOST RECENT APPLICANTS: Approximately 1,200.

NO. AWARDS: Varies.

APPLICATION INFO:
Application information is available on the web site.
Deadline: Varies.

IRS I.D.: 23-7315236

ADDRESS INQUIRIES TO:
Alexia Gallagher, Executive Director
(See address above.)

NATIONAL TRUST FOR HISTORIC PRESERVATION
2600 Virginia Avenue, N.W.
Suite 1100
Washington, DC 20037
(202) 588-6277
E-mail: grants@savingplaces.org
Web Site: forum.savingplaces.org/build/funding

TYPE:
Challenge/matching grants; Project/program grants; Seed money grants; Technical assistance; Training grants. Education program curricula. Project grants to support consultants with professional expertise in areas such as architecture, law, planning, economics, archeology and graphic design. Conferences that address subjects of particular importance to historic preservation also are funded. In addition, grants are made for curriculum development in preservation education directed at select audiences.

See entry 570 for full listing.

NBCC FOUNDATION, INC.
3 Terrace Way
Greensboro, NC 27403
(336) 232-0376
Fax: (336) 232-0010
E-mail: foundation@nbcc.org
Web Site: www.nbccf.org

TYPE:
Fellowships; Scholarships. Academic scholarships for individuals pursuing a graduate-level degree in professional counseling.

See entry 1563 for full listing.

NEW MEXICO FOUNDATION [1221]
8 Calle Medico
Santa Fe, NM 87505
(505) 820-6860
E-mail: edavila@newmexicofoundation.org
info@newmexicofoundation.org
Web Site: www.newmexicofoundation.org

FOUNDED: 1983

AREAS OF INTEREST:
New Mexico's communities and their people.

NAME(S) OF PROGRAMS:
● **Education and Leadership**
● **Emergency Grants**

TYPE:
Endowments; Grants-in-aid; Scholarships. New Mexico Community Foundation provides grants that help nonprofit organizations, community groups and charities statewide expand their efforts, increase their impact and advance their unique mission and vision to achieve success today and tomorrow. Although the Foundation does not have a regular open or revolving grant cycle, programmatic grant opportunities are available from time to time. It has the following program areas of focus:

Education and Leadership: Included in this program area are College Scholarships, which have originated through donor-advised funds and which assist high school graduates to pursue their academic goals; Fiscal Sponsorship Program, which enables new organizations to raise money for programs and provides guidance and oversight as needed to expand capacity and develop best practices; and Native American Preparatory Scholars Fund, an initiative and endowment fund of the Foundation that supports increasing the number of New Mexico Native American students who shall aspire to, be prepared for, and graduate from colleges and universities.

Emergency Grants provide help for individuals and families facing crisis situations.

LEGAL BASIS:
501(c)(3) organization.

GEOG. RESTRICTIONS: New Mexico.

FINANCIAL DATA:
Amount of support per award: Varies.

ADDRESS INQUIRIES TO:
Erika Davila, Scholarships and Grants Manager
(See address above.)

THE NORCLIFFE FOUNDATION
600 University Street
Suite 2003
Seattle, WA 98101
(206) 682-4820
E-mail: info@norcliffefoundation.org
Web Site: www.norcliffefoundation.org

TYPE:
Capital grants; General operating grants; Project/program grants.

See entry 223 for full listing.

NORTHEAST AGRICULTURAL EDUCATION FOUNDATION
220 South Warren Street
9th Floor
Syracuse, NY 13202
(315) 671-0588
Fax: (315) 671-0589
E-mail: info@northeastagriculture.org
Web Site: www.northeastagriculture.org

TYPE:
Project/program grants.

See entry 1949 for full listing.

NORTHERN TRUST CORPORATION [1222]
50 South LaSalle Street, L7
Chicago, IL 60603
(312) 630-6000
Fax: (312) 630-1809
E-mail: communityaffairs@northerntrust.com
Web Site: www.northerntrust.com

FOUNDED: 1889

AREAS OF INTEREST:
Education, social welfare, and culture and the arts.

NAME(S) OF PROGRAMS:
● **The Northern Trust Company Charitable Trust**
● **The Northern Trust Matching Gift Program**
● **Volunteer Grants Program**

TYPE:
Capital grants; Endowments; General operating grants; Matching gifts; Project/program grants; Technical assistance; Training grants. Grants within the Bank's areas of interest, including matching gifts to hospitals, educational institutions, cultural institutions and social welfare organizations.

YEAR PROGRAM STARTED: 1966

PURPOSE:
To reach out to people in the Chicago area who are in need or face obstacles that impede their full participation in society.

LEGAL BASIS:
Northern Trust Company is a multi-bank holding company.

ELIGIBILITY:
Applicant must be a not-for-profit organization, tax-exempt under IRS requirements and located in the U.S., Chicago metropolitan area.

Normally, contributions will not be made to support individuals, fraternal groups, individual churches or sectarian organizations, political activity, research, tickets or advertising for fund-raising benefits and agencies receiving more than 5% of their funding from the United Way.

GEOG. RESTRICTIONS: Chicago, Illinois.

FINANCIAL DATA:
Amount of support per award: Typical grant is $10,000 to $15,000.

Total amount of support: $4,499,271 in grants for the year 2017.

Matching fund requirements: Will match 100% of any gifts at least $25 to a maximum of $2,000 per person per year.

APPLICATION INFO:
New applicants must submit an online letter of inquiry eight weeks before application deadline. If proposal is approved, then applicant must submit:
(1) a completed application form;
(2) a copy of organization's IRS 501(c)(3) notification letter;
(3) a copy of organization's operating budget and specific project budget, if applicable;
(4) financial information for previous two years;
(5) a list of Chicago-area corporate and foundation contributors and amounts given in the last and the current year;
(6) a list of board members, with affiliations and;
(7) a list of organization's management staff and their qualifications.

Prior successful applicants are not required to submit the letter of inquiry.

Duration: Grants are annual. Multiyear pledges for capital or endowments. Requests for renewals are considered annually.

Deadline: Varies.

PUBLICATIONS:
Annual report.

IRS I.D.: 36-6147253

STAFF:
Deborah Liverett, Senior Vice President
Alexis Sutton, Vice President
Chastity Davis, Officer
Edrea Jones, Coordinator
Dawn McGovern, Coordinator

ADDRESS INQUIRIES TO:
See e-mail address above.

THE NORTHWEST MINNESOTA FOUNDATION [1223]

201 Third Street, N.W.
Bemidji, MN 56601
(218) 759-2057
Fax: (218) 759-2328
E-mail: info@nwmf.org
Web Site: www.nwmf.org

FOUNDED: 1986

AREAS OF INTEREST:
Community planning, civic engagement, business development, housing, child care, health equity, and philanthropy.

TYPE:
Challenge/matching grants; Demonstration grants; Project/program grants; Research grants; Scholarships; Seed money grants; Technical assistance.

YEAR PROGRAM STARTED: 1986

PURPOSE:
To invest resources, facilitate collaboration, and promote philanthropy to make the region a better place to live and work.

ELIGIBILITY:
Applicants must be a public agency or private nonprofit organization with a 501(c)(3) federal tax-exempt status. If an organization does not meet these criteria, it may work with an affiliated tax-exempt organization that may be the applicant and fiscal agent for the project. The affiliate must be a parent organization, provide similar services and/or define in writing its participation in project implementation. No grants are made to individuals.

GEOG. RESTRICTIONS: Beltrami, Clearwater, Hubbard, Kittson, Lake of the Woods, Mahnomen, Marshall, Norman, Pennington, Polk, Red Lake and Roseau counties, Minnesota.

FINANCIAL DATA:
Amount of support per award: Varies depending on the grant type.
Total amount of support: Varies.
Matching fund requirements: 50% typically required.

NO. MOST RECENT APPLICANTS: 40.

NO. AWARDS: 30.

APPLICATION INFO:
A preproposal must be submitted on the NMF preproposal application form. Applicants are encouraged to contact NMF staff to discuss projects prior to submission. Once a project has been determined to be

eligible, a full application is invited and NMF staff will explain the process for submitting additional information.

Duration: Up to two years; multiyear depending upon grant.

Deadline: Preproposals may be submitted at any time.

ADDRESS INQUIRIES TO:
Nate Dorr
Senior Program Officer-Grants
(See address above.)

THE NORTHWESTERN MUTUAL FOUNDATION [1224]

720 East Wisconsin Avenue
Milwaukee, WI 53202
(414) 665-2200
(877) 877-2129
Fax: (414) 665-7519
E-mail: foundationonline@northwesternmutual.com
Web Site: foundation.northwesternmutual.com

FOUNDED: 1992

AREAS OF INTEREST:
Education, childhood cancer, building neighborhood capacity and volunteerism.

CONSULTING OR VOLUNTEER SERVICES:
MutualFriends is the name of the corporate employee volunteer program.

TYPE:
Project, program and capacity-building support, matching gifts, scholarships, disaster relief, United Way and UPAF support.

PURPOSE:
To improve the lives of children and families in need.

ELIGIBILITY:
Organization must have tax-exempt classification under Section 501(c)(3) of the Internal Revenue Code. No grants to organizations that advocate, support or practice activities inconsistent with Northwestern Mutual's nondiscrimination policies.

GEOG. RESTRICTIONS: Milwaukee, Wisconsin. United States for National Childhood Cancer Program.

FINANCIAL DATA:
Amount of support per award: Varies.

APPLICATION INFO:
Guidelines and deadlines are communicated annually on the Foundation web site. Foundation accepts online applications only through its web site.

Duration: One year. Must reapply.

OFFICER:
Eric Christophersen, President

ADDRESS INQUIRIES TO:
See e-mail address above.

OKLAHOMA CITY COMMUNITY FOUNDATION, INC. [1225]

P.O. Box 1146
Oklahoma City, OK 73101-1146
(405) 235-5603
Fax: (405) 235-5612
E-mail: info@occf.org
Web Site: occf.org

FOUNDED: 1969

AREAS OF INTEREST:
Beautification, education, the arts, social services and civic organizations.

TYPE:
Project/program grants; Scholarships. Support for philanthropic agencies designated by donors. Discretionary grants by the Foundation's trustees are relatively modest.

PURPOSE:
To serve the charitable purposes of its donors and the charitable needs of the Oklahoma City area through the development and administration of endowment and other charitable funds with the goal of preserving capital and enhancing value.

LEGAL BASIS:
Public foundation.

ELIGIBILITY:
Applicants can be any IRS 501(c)(3) organization.

GEOG. RESTRICTIONS: Oklahoma City, Oklahoma and surrounding area.

FINANCIAL DATA:
Assets of $1,175,030,000 for the year ended June 30, 2019.
Amount of support per award: Varies.
Total amount of support: $37,521,000 in grant distributions for fiscal year ended June 30, 2019.

APPLICATION INFO:
Application information is available on the web site.

Duration: Varies.

IRS I.D.: 23-7024262

ADDRESS INQUIRIES TO:
Nancy Anthony, President
(See address above.)

OMAHA COMMUNITY FOUNDATION

3555 Farnam Street
Suite 222
Omaha, NE 68131
(402) 342-3458
Fax: (402) 342-3582
E-mail: info@omahafoundation.org
Web Site: www.omahafoundation.org

TYPE:
Capital grants; General operating grants; Project/program grants; Technical assistance. Donors can contribute through the Omaha Community Foundation to any nonprofit agency. The OCF also has 10 discretionary grant programs.

See entry 229 for full listing.

OPEN SOCIETY INSTITUTE - BALTIMORE [1226]

201 North Charles Street
Suite 1300
Baltimore, MD 21201
(410) 234-1091
Fax: (410) 234-2816
E-mail: osi.baltimore@opensocietyfoundations.org
Web Site: www.osibaltimore.org

AREAS OF INTEREST:
Drug addiction.

NAME(S) OF PROGRAMS:
• **Addiction and Health Equity Program**

TYPE:
Project/program grants. The Drug Addiction Treatment Program seeks to ensure universal access to treatment services for all in need regardless of income or insurance status.

YEAR PROGRAM STARTED: 1998

PURPOSE:
To focus on critical national urban issues as they are expressed locally.

LEGAL BASIS:
Foundation.

ELIGIBILITY:
Grants are made to organizations that have tax-exempt status under Section 501(c)(3) of the Internal Revenue Code. No grants are made to individuals. Nonsectarian religious programs may apply.

GEOG. RESTRICTIONS: Baltimore City, Maryland.

FINANCIAL DATA:
Amount of support per award: Varies.
Total amount of support: Varies.

APPLICATION INFO:
Applicants should submit a letter of inquiry of two to three pages which includes:
(1) a description of the program to be funded;
(2) the qualifications of the organization to carry out the program;
(3) the ways in which the program reflects the priorities of The Drug Addiction Treatment Program;
(4) the amount requested and;
(5) a copy of the IRS letter stating the organization's tax-exempt status.
Duration: Varies.
Deadline: Grant applications are accepted on an ongoing basis.

ADDRESS INQUIRIES TO:
Scott Nolen, Program Director
Drug Addiction Treatment
(See address above.)

THE ORDEAN FOUNDATION [1227]
501 Ordean Building
424 West Superior Street
Duluth, MN 55802
(218) 726-4785
E-mail: dness@ordean.org
Web Site: www.ordean.org

FOUNDED: 1933

AREAS OF INTEREST:
Social services, education and health, services to low-income, mentally and physically handicapped, elderly, mentally ill, chemically dependent, prevention of delinquency, and scholarships for certain health-related majors at Duluth colleges.

TYPE:
Challenge/matching grants; Demonstration grants; General operating grants; Project/program grants; Scholarships.

YEAR PROGRAM STARTED: 1933

LEGAL BASIS:
Private foundation.

ELIGIBILITY:
Applicants must be nonprofit, tax-exempt IRS 501(c)(3) organizations located or providing services in Greater City of Duluth, MN.

GEOG. RESTRICTIONS: Greater City of Duluth, Minnesota.

FINANCIAL DATA:
Amount of support per award: $5,000 to $170,000.
Total amount of support: $1,400,000 for the year 2020.

NO. AWARDS: Approximately 45.

REPRESENTATIVE AWARDS:
$125,000 to Lake Superior Community Health Center; $100,000 to Mentor North to match caring adults with at-risk youths.

APPLICATION INFO:
Guidelines are available from the Foundation office at the address above.
Duration: Varies.
Deadline: January 15, February 15, May 15, August 15, October 15 and November 15 for the February, March, June, September, November and December meetings, respectively.

STAFF:
Don Ness, Executive Director
Joe Everett, Program Director

BOARD OF DIRECTORS:
Jim Vizanko, President
Chuck Walt, Vice President
Traci Morris, Treasurer
Jon Nelson, Secretary
Marsha Hystead
Maria Isley
Stacy Johnston
Marcus Jones
John Strange
Tony Yung

ADDRESS INQUIRIES TO:
Joe Everett, Program Director
(See address above.)

THE OREGON COMMUNITY FOUNDATION [1228]
1221 S.W. Yamhill Street, Suite 100
Portland, OR 97205-2108
(503) 227-6846
E-mail: info@oregoncf.org
Web Site: www.oregoncf.org

FOUNDED: 1973

AREAS OF INTEREST:
Health and well-being, education, arts and culture, economic vitality, and community livability, environment and engagement.

NAME(S) OF PROGRAMS:
● **Community Grants Program**

TYPE:
Capital grants; Challenge/matching grants; Matching gifts; Project/program grants; Scholarships.

YEAR PROGRAM STARTED: 1974

PURPOSE:
To strengthen the social fabric of our communities by awarding grants that build civic leadership and engagement and address evolving, community-identified needs.

LEGAL BASIS:
Community foundation.

ELIGIBILITY:
Applicants for programs must be nonprofit, tax-exempt organizations in Oregon.

Applicants must have received a community grant only once during the previous 12 months and must have completed evaluation reports for all prior grants. The Foundation gives preference to projects that demonstrate strong local support and promise tangible benefits or means of solving community problems or concerns.

GEOG. RESTRICTIONS: Oregon.

FINANCIAL DATA:
Amount of support per award: $5,000 to $50,000. Average grant $20,000.
Total amount of support: $110,000,000 in grants, including $10,000,000 in scholarships and $7,000,000 for the Community Grants Program.

NO. MOST RECENT APPLICANTS: 600 to 700 proposals per year.

NO. AWARDS: Community Grants: Approximately 350 annually.

APPLICATION INFO:
Application information is available on the web site. Application must be submitted via the online system.
Duration: Small grants: One year; Large grants: One to three years.
Deadline: Community Grants Program: January 15 and July 15.

IRS I.D.: 23-7315673

ADDRESS INQUIRIES TO:
Program Officer
(See address above.)

*SPECIAL STIPULATIONS:
Generally funds only in Oregon.

OUTER BANKS COMMUNITY FOUNDATION [1229]
13 Skyline Road
Southern Shores, NC 27949
(252) 261-8839
Fax: (252) 261-0371
E-mail: info@obcf.org
Web Site: www.obcf.org

FOUNDED: 1982

AREAS OF INTEREST:
Outer Banks, from Corolla to Ocracoke Island.

TYPE:
Project/program grants; Scholarships. 55 different scholarship funds available to local students. Grants available for local nonprofit programs and projects.

YEAR PROGRAM STARTED: 1982

PURPOSE:
To help meet local needs in the Outer Banks of North Carolina, from Corolla to Ocracoke Island.

LEGAL BASIS:
501(c)(3).

GEOG. RESTRICTIONS: Corolla area of Currituck County, Dare County and Ocracoke Island in Hyde County, North Carolina.

FINANCIAL DATA:
Amount of support per award: Varies.
Total amount of support: Varies.

APPLICATION INFO:
Application information is available on the web site.
Deadline: Varies.

IRS I.D.: 58-1516313

ADDRESS INQUIRIES TO:
Lorelei Costa, Executive Director
(See address above.)

PERMIAN BASIN AREA FOUNDATION [1230]

3312 Andrews Highway
Midland, TX 79703
(432) 617-3213
Fax: (432) 617-0151
E-mail: mharris@pbaf.org
Web Site: www.pbaf.org

FOUNDED: 1989

AREAS OF INTEREST:
Community development.

TYPE:
Grants-in-aid; Scholarships.

PURPOSE:
To enrich the quality of life for the
communities of the Permian Basin area of
Texas.

LEGAL BASIS:
501(c)(3) organization.

GEOG. RESTRICTIONS: Communities of the
Permian Basin region of Texas.

FINANCIAL DATA:
The Foundation has awarded nearly
$100,000,000 in grants and scholarships since
inception.

Amount of support per award: Grants:
Average $15,000; Scholarships: $1,000 to
$2,500.

APPLICATION INFO:
Organizations wishing to apply for a grant
must fully complete and submit one copy of
the Pre-Application Summary (SF-1).
Organizations that have received funding
during a previous grant cycle must also
complete and submit the Grant Award
Follow-up Form (SF-FW). Do not include a
cover letter with the application.

A full application will be complete when one
copy of the appropriate Standard Forms and
additional documents indicated on the
Standard Form Checklist are completed and
submitted to the Foundation by the full
application due date. (The list of required
forms differs depending on the purpose of
the grant request.) Upon receiving a full
application, the Foundation will conduct a
full application review which may include an
applicant interview, a site visit, and/or a
request for additional information.

All scholarship applications must contain the
following:
(1) transcript with fall semester grades;
(2) college transcript if student is enrolled in
concurrent college courses and;
(3) at least one letter of recommendation, but
not more than three.

Some applications require an essay. Check
the individual scholarship criteria to
determine if an essay is required and the
designated topic.

Duration: Grants: Typically one year. Can
reapply every two years.

Deadline: Grant proposals: April 1 for Spring
and October 1 for Fall.

ADDRESS INQUIRIES TO:
Grants Administrator
(See address above.)

PETOSKEY-HARBOR SPRINGS AREA COMMUNITY FOUNDATION [1231]

616 Petoskey Street, Suite 203
Petoskey, MI 49770
(231) 348-5820
Fax: (231) 348-5883
E-mail: info@phsacf.org
Web Site: www.phsacf.org

FOUNDED: 1992

AREAS OF INTEREST:
Arts, education, environment, health, human
service and community development.

TYPE:
Grants-in-aid; Scholarships. Grants are given
for scholarships or for charitable needs.

YEAR PROGRAM STARTED: 1992

PURPOSE:
To build an endowment to serve community
needs.

LEGAL BASIS:
Community foundation.

ELIGIBILITY:
Grants must be for charitable purposes, but
not for individuals.

GEOG. RESTRICTIONS: Emmet County,
Michigan.

FINANCIAL DATA:
Over $40,000,000 in assets.
Amount of support per award: $500 to
$15,000.
Total amount of support: Varies.

APPLICATION INFO:
Applications are available at the address
above and must include a copy of the IRS
tax determination letter. Call before you
apply.
Duration: One year.
Deadline: March 1 and October 1.

PUBLICATIONS:
Annual report; application guidelines.

ADDRESS INQUIRIES TO:
Director of Community Philanthropy
(See address above.)

THE PHILADELPHIA FOUNDATION [1232]

1835 Market Street
Suite 2410
Philadelphia, PA 19103-2968
(215) 563-6417
Fax: (215) 563-6882
E-mail: info@philafound.org
Web Site: www.philafound.org

FOUNDED: 1918

AREAS OF INTEREST:
Arts, culture, humanities, education,
environment, health, human services and
public/community development.

NAME(S) OF PROGRAMS:
● **Advocacy Program**
● **Advocacy Unrestricted**
● **Direct Service**
● **Impact Grant**
● **Leadership Grant**

TYPE:
General operating grants; Project/program
grants; Scholarships. The Philadelphia
Foundation's grantmaking strategies are
sensitive to the needs of diverse population

groups in the community and reflect a
commitment to stabilizing the infrastructure
of nonprofit organizations.

YEAR PROGRAM STARTED: 1918

PURPOSE:
To serve as a vehicle and resource for
philanthropy in the greater Philadelphia area,
PA; to develop, manage and allocate
community resources in partnership with
donors and grantees to build on community
assets, to respond to the needs of the entire
community, and to promote empowerment,
leadership, and civic participation among
underserved groups; to practice and
encourage diversity, equity, and inclusiveness
as fundamental values of community life.

LEGAL BASIS:
Community foundation established in
Pennsylvania by bank resolution.

ELIGIBILITY:
Organization must be IRS 501(c)(3), located
in five-county area of southeastern
Pennsylvania.

GEOG. RESTRICTIONS: Greater Philadelphia area,
Pennsylvania.

FINANCIAL DATA:
Amount of support per award: $3,000 to
$50,000 (but not more than 10% of an
organization's budget).
Total amount of support: $25,000,000
annually.

CO-OP FUNDING PROGRAMS: The Nonprofit
Repositioning Fund.

NO. AWARDS: 1,000 annually.

APPLICATION INFO:
Applicants must take the Eligibility Wizard
quiz as the initial step.
Duration: Usually one year.
Deadline: Varies.

PUBLICATIONS:
Newsletters; annual report.

OFFICERS:
Pedro A. Ramos, Esq., President and Chief
Executive Officer
Orlando C. Esposito, Chief Financial Officer

ADDRESS INQUIRIES TO:
Grantmaking Services Department
E-mail: grantmakingservices@philafound.org
(See address above.)

THE PITTSBURGH FOUNDATION [1233]

5 PPG Place
Suite 250
Pittsburgh, PA 15222
(412) 391-5122
Fax: (412) 391-7259
E-mail: contactus@pghfdn.org
Web Site: www.pittsburghfoundation.org

FOUNDED: 1945

AREAS OF INTEREST:
Education, family life, economic
development, health care and the arts.

TYPE:
Capital grants; General operating grants;
Project/program grants; Research grants;
Scholarships. The Foundation promotes and
champions the betterment of the greater
Pittsburgh community and the quality of life
for all its citizens by helping a wide variety
of donors fulfill significant community needs
and providing a vehicle to make giving easy,

personally satisfying and effective. The Foundation awards grants through restricted and unrestricted funds. Purposes for which unrestricted grants are awarded include: organizational capacity building; systemic change; improved service delivery; planning and program development; capital and equipment (in limited and special circumstances) through one targeted fund; operating (in very limited and defined circumstances); research (in special circumstances).

Scholarships and medical research grants are awarded from specific funds established for this purpose.

PURPOSE:
To achieve educational excellence and equity; to support families; to foster economic development; to eliminate disparities in health outcomes; to advance the arts.

LEGAL BASIS:
Community foundation established in Pennsylvania by bank resolution and declaration of trust.

ELIGIBILITY:
Grant applicants must be tax-exempt, public charitable organizations and institutions located in Pittsburgh and southwestern Pennsylvania. Generally, grants are nonrecurring and are not granted for operating budgets and not made to individuals.

GEOG. RESTRICTIONS: Pittsburgh and southwestern Pennsylvania.

FINANCIAL DATA:
Amount of support per award: Varies.
Total amount of support: Approximately $15,000,000 in unrestricted funds; $20,000,000 in donor-directed funds.

NO. MOST RECENT APPLICANTS: Approximately 2,380.

NO. AWARDS: 2,255.

APPLICATION INFO:
Application form is available online and must be submitted electronically.
Duration: Up to three years.

PUBLICATIONS:
Annual report; newsletter; donor information; application guidelines; scholarship brochure.

IRS I.D.: 25-0965466

STAFF:
Lisa Schroeder, President and Chief Executive Officer
Jonathan Brelsford, Senior Vice President of Finance and Investments

BOARD OF DIRECTORS:
Edith L. Shapira, M.D., Chairperson
John C. Harmon, Esq., Vice Chairperson
John R. McGinley, Jr., Vice Chairperson
Kim Tillotson Fleming, Treasurer
Walter H. Smith, Jr., Ph.D., Secretary
Edward J. Donnelly, III, M.D.
Patrick Dowd, Ph.D.
Laura Ellsworth
Lee B. Foster, II
William Generett, Jr.
Rev. Glenn Grayson
Laura Shapira Karet
Brian R. Lenart
Anne Lewis
Terry Miller, M.S.W.
Kamal Nigam
William Strickland

ADDRESS INQUIRIES TO:
Lisa Schroeder
President and Chief Executive Officer
(See address above.)

PRINCETON AREA COMMUNITY FOUNDATION [1234]

15 Princess Road
Lawrenceville, NJ 08648
(609) 219-1800
Fax: (609) 219-1850
E-mail: info@pacf.org
Web Site: pacf.org

FOUNDED: 1991

AREAS OF INTEREST:
Arts and culture, housing, social services, civil rights and public policy, religion, health, education, and children, youth and families.

TYPE:
General operating grants; Project/program grants; Scholarships.

PURPOSE:
To connect people who care with causes that matter across central New Jersey.

LEGAL BASIS:
A public benefit (nonprofit) organization.

ELIGIBILITY:
Eligible organizations must have 501(c)(3) status.

FINANCIAL DATA:
Since its founding, the Foundation has granted nearly $126,000,000 to its community area of service.
Amount of support per award: Varies.
Total amount of support: Over $20,000,000 in grants and $330,000 in scholarships for the year 2018.

NO. AWARDS: 2,080 grants for the year 2017.

APPLICATION INFO:
Application information is available on the web site.
Duration: One year. Renewable.

STAFF:
Jeffrey M. Vega, President and Chief Executive Officer
Laura J. Longman, MBA, Chief Financial Officer
Marcia Schakelford, Chief Philanthropy Officer

ADDRESS INQUIRIES TO:
Grants and Programs
Princeton Area Community Foundation
(See address above.)

PROLITERACY WORLDWIDE [1235]

101 Wyoming Street
Syracuse, NY 13204
(315) 422-9121
Fax: (315) 422-6369
E-mail: nbf@proliteracy.org
Web Site: www.proliteracy.org

FOUNDED: 1955

AREAS OF INTEREST:
Literacy, adult basic education, English as a second language, and family literacy.

NAME(S) OF PROGRAMS:
● **National Book Fund (NBF)**

TYPE:
Project/program grants; Technical assistance.

YEAR PROGRAM STARTED: 1995

PURPOSE:
To provide grants for books and other materials local programs can use to expand their current volunteer literacy programs; to develop, promote and expand literacy programs in the U.S.

LEGAL BASIS:
Nonprofit organization.

ELIGIBILITY:
Adult literacy and adult basic education programs only.

GEOG. RESTRICTIONS: United States.

FINANCIAL DATA:
Amount of support per award: Typically $500 to $2,000.
Total amount of support: Varies.
Matching fund requirements: Up to 20% match required for non-ProLiterary members.

NO. MOST RECENT APPLICANTS: More than 100 annually.

NO. AWARDS: 92 for the year 2019-20.

APPLICATION INFO:
Application information is available online. Applications may be submitted beginning February 1.
Duration: One year. NBF grantee eligible again in three years or two full funding cycles.
Deadline: March 15.

PUBLICATIONS:
Guidelines.

IRS I.D.: 16-1214734

ADDRESS INQUIRIES TO:
Alicia Suskin
National Book Fund Program Director
(See e-mail address above.)

RANCHO SANTA FE FOUNDATION [1236]

162 South Rancho Santa Fe Road
Suite B-30
Encinitas, CA 92024
(858) 756-6557
Fax: (858) 756-6561
E-mail: christy@rsffoundation.org
Web Site: www.rsffoundation.org

FOUNDED: 1981

AREAS OF INTEREST:
Military, workforce development for at-risk youth, human trafficking prevention, and capacity building support for regional nonprofits.

NAME(S) OF PROGRAMS:
● **The Patriots Connection**
● **Rancho Santa Fe Women's Fund**

TYPE:
Challenge/matching grants; Development grants; Endowments; General operating grants; Project/program grants; Scholarships.

YEAR PROGRAM STARTED: 1981

PURPOSE:
To connect donors with regional and global needs through visionary community leadership, personalized service and effective grantmaking.

LEGAL BASIS:
Community foundation.

ELIGIBILITY:
Organizations must have tax-exempt status under Section 501(c)(3) of the Internal Revenue Code. Additional requirements are listed on the Foundation web site.

FINANCIAL DATA:
Amount of support per award: $5,000 to $100,000.

Total amount of support: Varies.

NO. MOST RECENT APPLICANTS: 60 to 75.

NO. AWARDS: Varies.

APPLICATION INFO:
The Foundation accepts applications by invitation only. The Foundation does not accept unsolicited grant requests, except for the Rancho Santa Fe Women's Fund. Women's Fund application process opens August 1.

Duration: Typically one year.

Deadline: Patriots Connection: Mid-April. Awarded in June; Women's Fund: August 1. Awarded in May.

PUBLICATIONS:
Annual report.

IRS I.D.: 95-3709639

STAFF:
Christina P. Wilson, President and Chief Executive Officer
Karen Sprigle, Chief Operations Officer
Debbie Anderson, Programs Director
Dan Beals, Finance Director
Megan Fletcher, Communications Manager
Korri Ball, Administrative Coordinator, Women's Fund

ADDRESS INQUIRIES TO:
Christina P. Wilson, President and Chief Executive Officer
(See address above.)

RBC FOUNDATION - U.S.A. [1237]
RBC Plaza
60 South Sixth Street
Minneapolis, MN 55402-4422
(612) 371-2936
Fax: (612) 371-7933
E-mail: fndapplications@rbc.com
Web Site: www.rbcwealthmanagement.com

AREAS OF INTEREST:
Arts and culture, youth, health and human services.

NAME(S) OF PROGRAMS:
● **RBC Emerging Artists Project**
● **RBC Youth Mental Well-being Project**

TYPE:
Project/program grants. In the area of arts and culture, the Emerging Artists Program supports initiatives that help artists in their early years of development and that bridge the gap between their academic experiences to professional careers in the arts.

In the area of health and human services, grants are exclusively directed to the RBC Youth Mental Well-being Project focusing on programs that are helping youth and families access the right care at the right time. To foster economic independence and promote self-sufficiency, the Foundation also focuses on organizations providing emergency food, shelter and basic needs, and adult literacy and employment training programs.

In the area of youth, grants are focused on programs that prepare students for future success.

PURPOSE:
To improve the quality of life in communities where the company has facilities.

LEGAL BASIS:
Corporate foundation.

ELIGIBILITY:
Organizations must have their 501(c)(3) registered nonprofit status for a minimum of three years, a minimum annual operating budget of $100,000 and an established relationship with an RBC Wealth Management employee, preferably board involvement.

The Foundation does not support capital and endowment campaigns, multiyear commitments, or start-up organizations.

FINANCIAL DATA:
Total amount of support: $2,600,000 for the year 2019.

APPLICATION INFO:
Guidelines and application forms are available on the web site.

Duration: One year.

Deadline: Varies.

ADDRESS INQUIRIES TO:
Julie Allen
E-mail: julie.allen@rbc.com

THE REINBERGER FOUNDATION [1238]
30000 Chagrin Boulevard, Suite 300
Cleveland, OH 44124
(216) 292-2790
E-mail: info@reinbergerfoundation.org
Web Site: www.reinbergerfoundation.org

FOUNDED: 1968

AREAS OF INTEREST:
Arts, education and human service.

NAME(S) OF PROGRAMS:
● **Arts, Culture and Humanities**
● **Education**
● **Human Service**

TYPE:
Capital grants; Challenge/matching grants; General operating grants; Matching gifts; Project/program grants.

PURPOSE:
To help individuals move toward self-sufficiency; to provide opportunity for enrichment in the community.

LEGAL BASIS:
Private foundation.

ELIGIBILITY:
Eligible organizations must be IRS 501(c)(3) tax-exempt. Priority will be given to those organizations who received Reinberger Foundation support in the past five years.

GEOG. RESTRICTIONS: Northeast Ohio or greater Columbus area.

FINANCIAL DATA:
Since its beginning, the Foundation has provided more than $120,000,000 in funding support to the community.

Amount of support per award: $2,500 to $150,000 for the year 2019.

Total amount of support: $3,028,309 for the year 2019.

NO. MOST RECENT APPLICANTS: 218 for the year 2019.

NO. AWARDS: 128 for the year 2019.

APPLICATION INFO:
Online application is available on the web site.

Duration: Up to five years.

Deadline: March 15 for Education, July 14 for Human Service and November 15 for Art.

ADDRESS INQUIRIES TO:
Karen L. Hooser, President
(See address above.)

LUTHER I. REPLOGLE FOUNDATION [1239]
1720 N Street, N.W.
Washington, DC 20036-2907
(202) 213-1657
Fax: (202) 580-6579
E-mail: gwenn@lirf.org
Web Site: reploglefoundation.org

FOUNDED: 1966

AREAS OF INTEREST:
At-risk youth, children and families, with particular attention to improving educational opportunities for inner-city children.

TYPE:
General operating grants; Project/program grants. The Foundation supports programs that:
(1) address the needs of youth and children living in, or at risk of, long-term poverty, especially children of inner-city residents. Of particular interest are programs for teen pregnancy prevention, counseling, broad-spectrum social services, and other programs that help young people improve their own lives and;
(2) improve educational opportunities for inner-city children, including enrichment programs in the arts and sciences, alternative schools, after-school tutoring and mentoring, and scholarship programs.

PURPOSE:
To address the needs of youth and children living in, or at risk of, long-term poverty; to improve educational opportunities for inner-city children; to support programs for affordable and supportive housing that reach groups of people frequently left out of traditional shelter programs.

ELIGIBILITY:
Organizations must be not-for-profit 501(c)(3) with revenues less than $6,000,000.

GEOG. RESTRICTIONS: Washington, DC; Chicago, Illinois; Minneapolis/St. Paul, Minnesota.

FINANCIAL DATA:
Amount of support per award: Usually $5,000 to $10,000.

Total amount of support: Approximately $450,000 for the year 2018.

NO. MOST RECENT APPLICANTS: Over 50.

NO. AWARDS: 2 new and 22 renewals.

APPLICATION INFO:
Application is available on the Foundation web site.

Duration: Renewable if grantee sends report.

Deadline: August 15 for new requests. September 15 for renewals.

IRS I.D.: 36-6141697

ADDRESS INQUIRIES TO:
Gwenn H.S. Gebhard, Executive Director
(See address above.)

ROCHESTER AREA FOUNDATION [1240]

12 Elton Hills Drive, N.W.
Rochester, MN 55901
(507) 282-0203
Fax: (507) 616-7608
E-mail: raf-info@rochesterarea.org
Web Site: www.rochesterarea.org

FOUNDED: 1944

AREAS OF INTEREST:
General grants to benefit residents of the Greater Rochester area.

TYPE:
Capital grants; Challenge/matching grants; Project/program grants; Scholarships; Seed money grants.

YEAR PROGRAM STARTED: 1944

PURPOSE:
To use its resources to improve the quality of life, promote greater equality of opportunities and to support development of effective methods to assist those in need in the Greater Rochester area.

LEGAL BASIS:
Community foundation.

ELIGIBILITY:
Applicants must be 501(c)(3) organizations or units of government agencies or government-created public agencies located in or serving the Greater Rochester area. Grants are not given to individuals.

GEOG. RESTRICTIONS: Greater Rochester, Minnesota.

FINANCIAL DATA:
Amount of support per award: Varies.
Total amount of support: $3,335,000 for the year 2018.

NO. AWARDS: 728 for the year 2018.

APPLICATION INFO:
Pre-approved and approved application forms are required. Applicant organizations must include an IRS letter of tax determination.
Duration: One-time grants.
Deadline: January 1 and August 1.

PUBLICATIONS:
Annual report with consolidated financials.

ROSE COMMUNITY FOUNDATION [1241]

600 South Cherry Street
Suite 1200
Denver, CO 80246-1712
(303) 398-7400
Fax: (303) 398-7430
E-mail: grantsmanager@rcfdenver.org
krojas@rcfdenver.org
Web Site: www.rcfdenver.org

FOUNDED: 1995

AREAS OF INTEREST:
Child and family development, education, the elderly, health of the community, Jewish life, human service, transportation (aging only), early childhood education, family self-sufficiency, health preventive, low-income health access and health policy leadership.

TYPE:
Capital grants; Challenge/matching grants; General operating grants; Project/program grants; Seed money grants; Technical assistance. Capacity-building grants.

YEAR PROGRAM STARTED: 1995

PURPOSE:
To enhance the quality of life of the greater Denver community through leadership, resources, traditions and values.

ELIGIBILITY:
Applicants must be charitable, nonprofit organizations classified as 501(c)(3) by the IRS or be a tax-supported institution, such as a school or government agency. New or emerging organizations are permitted to apply through a sponsoring tax-exempt organization. Applicants (including university departments) may have only one proposal pending at any given time.

The Foundation will not support grants to individuals or endowments, including academic chairs, grants to one organization to be passed to another, annual appeals or membership drives, fund-raising events, or political candidates.

GEOG. RESTRICTIONS: Denver metropolitan area, specifically Adams, Arapahoe, Boulder, Broomfield, Denver, Douglas and Jefferson counties, Colorado.

FINANCIAL DATA:
Amount of support per award: Varies depending on needs and nature of the request.
Total amount of support: Approximately $14,700,000 for the year 2018.
Matching fund requirements: Varies by nature of award.

NO. AWARDS: Approximately 600.

APPLICATION INFO:
It is recommended to speak with a Program Officer prior to submitting an application to discuss the program, project or organization.
Duration: Varies.

IRS I.D.: 84-0920862

ADDRESS INQUIRIES TO:
Kelli Rojas, Grants Manager
(See address above.)

HENRY AND RUTH BLAUSTEIN ROSENBERG FOUNDATION [1242]

One South Street, Suite 2900
Baltimore, MD 21202
(410) 347-7201
Fax: (410) 347-7210
E-mail: info@blaufund.org
Web Site: www.blaufund.org

AREAS OF INTEREST:
Arts and culture, youth development, adult self-sufficiency, and health.

TYPE:
Capital grants; General operating grants; Project/program grants. Programs of benefit to the underserved community in the Baltimore, MD area.

PURPOSE:
To promote arts and culture, youth development, and adult self-sufficiency within the underserved community.

ELIGIBILITY:
501(c)(3) nonprofit organizations. No grants to individuals.

GEOG. RESTRICTIONS: Baltimore, Maryland.

FINANCIAL DATA:
Amount of support per award: $5,000 to $25,000.
Total amount of support: Approximately $1,400,000.

APPLICATION INFO:
Send two- to three-page letter of intent or application. IRS tax status determination letter is required. Faxed and e-mailed letters of intent are not accepted.
Duration: One to two years. Prior grantee organizations may be renewable.

ADDRESS INQUIRIES TO:
Betsy F. Ringel, Executive Director
(See address above.)

ROSS FOUNDATION [1243]

202 South Fifth Street
Arkadelphia, AR 71923
(870) 246-9881
Fax: (870) 246-9674
E-mail: info@rossfoundation.us
Web Site: www.rossfoundation.us

FOUNDED: 1966

AREAS OF INTEREST:
Education, culture, conservation and community activities.

TYPE:
Conferences/seminars; Matching gifts; Project/program grants; Research grants.

YEAR PROGRAM STARTED: 1966

LEGAL BASIS:
Private foundation.

ELIGIBILITY:
Applicants must be IRS 501(c)(3) organizations located in Clark County or Arkadelphia, AR. No grants to individuals.

GEOG. RESTRICTIONS: Clark County or Arkadelphia, Arkansas.

FINANCIAL DATA:
Amount of support per award: Generally $500 to $25,000.
Total amount of support: $679,000 for the year 2018.
Matching fund requirements: Varies.

CO-OP FUNDING PROGRAMS: Arkadelphia Promise Foundation.

NO. MOST RECENT APPLICANTS: Approximately 30 for the year 2018.

NO. AWARDS: 22 for the year 2018.

APPLICATION INFO:
Application form is available online.
Duration: Typically one year.
Deadline: Proposals are reviewed March, July and October.

ADDRESS INQUIRIES TO:
Mary Elizabeth Eldridge
Director of Programs or
Amanda Fenocchi, Assistant Grants Officer
(See address above.)

THE RUSSELL FAMILY FOUNDATION [1244]

3025 Harborview Drive
Gig Harbor, WA 98335
(253) 858-5050
Fax: (253) 851-0460
E-mail: info@trff.org
Web Site: www.trff.org

FOUNDED: 1999

AREAS OF INTEREST:
Elimination of poverty, healthy educational and extracurricular activities for youth, and social justice.

NAME(S) OF PROGRAMS:
- **Jane's Fellowship Program**

TYPE:
Fellowships. Fellowship program for individuals who plan to work in the Foundation's areas of interest.

YEAR PROGRAM STARTED: 2004

PURPOSE:
To support grassroots leaders in Pierce County and Tacoma, WA.

ELIGIBILITY:
Must be a grassroots leader who has demonstrated exceptional creativity, courage and commitment in serving diverse needs in Tacoma and countywide.

GEOG. RESTRICTIONS: Pierce County and Tacoma, Washington.

FINANCIAL DATA:
Amount of support per award: Varies.
Total amount of support: Varies.

NO. AWARDS: Up to 13.

APPLICATION INFO:
Application information is available on the web site.
Duration: 15 months.
Deadline: Varies.

ADDRESS INQUIRIES TO:
E-mail: jfp.app@trff.org

SAGINAW COMMUNITY FOUNDATION   [1245]
One Tuscola Street, Suite 100
Saginaw, MI 48607
(989) 755-0545
Fax: (989) 755-6524
E-mail: brian@saginawfoundation.org
Web Site: www.saginawfoundation.org

FOUNDED: 1984

AREAS OF INTEREST:
Arts, community development, culture, education, health, youth and human services.

CONSULTING OR VOLUNTEER SERVICES:
Seminars, group presentations and one-on-one consultation.

TYPE:
Grants-in-aid; Project/program grants; Scholarships.

YEAR PROGRAM STARTED: 1984

PURPOSE:
To fulfill donor wishes and enable community initiatives to come to life, now and forever; to provide strategic leadership in the community; to practice impactful grantmaking in the areas of youth development, early education, and community improvement; to provide stewardship of the Foundation's resources, human and financial.

ELIGIBILITY:
Grants are made to organizations that have tax-exempt status under Section 501(c)(3) of the Internal Revenue Code, local units of government and religious institutions to support projects or programs benefiting the citizens and communities of Saginaw County. Except for scholarships, no grants are made to individuals. Nonsectarian religious programs may apply.

GEOG. RESTRICTIONS: Saginaw County, Michigan.

FINANCIAL DATA:
Amount of support per award: Grants vary in amount, depending upon the needs and nature of the request.
Total amount of support: $3,770,651 for the year 2018.
Matching fund requirements: Varies by program.

NO. MOST RECENT APPLICANTS: 6,800.

NO. AWARDS: 627.

APPLICATION INFO:
Application information is available on the web site.

ADDRESS INQUIRIES TO:
Program Officer
(See address above.)

ST. CROIX VALLEY FOUNDATION   [1246]
516 Second Street, Suite 214
Hudson, WI 54016
(715) 386-9490
Fax: (715) 386-1250
E-mail: info@scvfoundation.org
Web Site: www.scvfoundation.org

FOUNDED: 1995

AREAS OF INTEREST:
Arts, civic affairs, community needs and development, environment, health and human services, and education.

NAME(S) OF PROGRAMS:
- **Health and Wellness Grant**
- **Music Education Grant**
- **Valley Arts Initiative Grant**

TYPE:
Project/program grants; Scholarships. Environmental and humane grants.

YEAR PROGRAM STARTED: 1995

PURPOSE:
To advance the quality of life in the St. Croix Valley of Wisconsin and Minnesota.

LEGAL BASIS:
501(c)(3).

ELIGIBILITY:
Grants are made to organizations that have tax-exempt status under Section 501(c)(3) of the Internal Revenue Code or serving the St. Croix Valley of Wisconsin and Minnesota. Nonsectarian religious programs may apply.

GEOG. RESTRICTIONS: Burnett, Pierce, Polk and St. Croix counties in St. Croix Valley, Wisconsin; Chicago and Washington counties in Minnesota.

FINANCIAL DATA:
Amount of support per award: Maximum $5,000; $2,450 average.
Total amount of support: Approximately $100,000 per year.

NO. MOST RECENT APPLICANTS: 82.

NO. AWARDS: 46.

APPLICATION INFO:
For full guidelines, refer to the Foundation web site.
Duration: Varies depending on the field of interest.
Deadline: Music Education Grant: October 4. Health and Wellness Grant: March 6. Valley Arts Initiative Grant: December 13.

IRS I.D.: 41-1817315

ADDRESS INQUIRIES TO:
Angela Pilgrim
Grants and Programs Officer
E-mail: apilgrim@scvfoundation.org

SAINT-GOBAIN CORPORATION FOUNDATION   [1247]
20 Moores Road
Malvern, PA 19355
(610) 893-5484
Fax: (855) 639-6629
E-mail: SGNorthAmericaInfo@saint-gobain.com
Web Site: www.saint-gobain-northamerica.com

FOUNDED: 2001

AREAS OF INTEREST:
Education, energy conservation, environmental concerns, STEM (science, technology, engineering and math), local communities, housing and community development.

NAME(S) OF PROGRAMS:
- **Direct Grants Program**

TYPE:
Project/program grants.

PURPOSE:
To play a vital role in the economic, social and educational development of the community.

LEGAL BASIS:
Corporation foundation.

ELIGIBILITY:
Eligible organizations must be IRS 501(c)(3) tax-exempt and be located in areas where Saint-Gobain Corporation has manufacturing locations.

GEOG. RESTRICTIONS: Massachusetts and Pennsylvania.

FINANCIAL DATA:
Amount of support per award: Varies.
Total amount of support: Varies.

APPLICATION INFO:
Applicants must complete the online Direct Grants Application Form. All completed applications must include the following in order to be considered:
(1) full details of the proposed program;
(2) a brief overview of the organization and a description of its history, mission, goals and key achievements;
(3) IRS letter confirming tax-exempt status as 501(c)(3);
(4) proof of accreditation and IRS Tax Identification Number for education institutions;
(5) current listing of organization's officers and board of directors, including their affiliations;
(6) current board-approved organizational budget and the budget for the proposed project;
(7) major sources of funding and;
(8) a copy of the most recent audited financial statement.
Duration: Typically one year.
Deadline: Applications must be submitted by end of February for April Board Meeting and by end of July for September Board Meeting.

ADDRESS INQUIRIES TO:
Patty Tarantino, Communications Coordinator
E-mail: patricia.a.tarantino@saint-gobain.com

SAN ANGELO AREA FOUNDATION [1248]

221 South Irving Street
San Angelo, TX 76903
(325) 947-7071
Fax: (325) 947-7322
E-mail: infosaaf@saafound.org
Web Site: www.saafound.org

FOUNDED: 2002

AREAS OF INTEREST:
Community development.

TYPE:
Grants-in-aid; Scholarships. To build a legacy of philanthropy by attracting and prudently managing endowed gifts in order to match donor interests with community needs of the area.

PURPOSE:
To improve the quality of life in the San Angelo, TX area.

LEGAL BASIS:
Community foundation.

ELIGIBILITY:
Must be a 501(c)(3) nonprofit organization. Grant funds must be used within and for the benefit of residents and communities of the 17 counties of the San Angelo area.

GEOG. RESTRICTIONS: San Angelo area, Texas.

FINANCIAL DATA:
Amount of support per award: Varies.
Total amount of support: Varies.

APPLICATION INFO:
Application and proposal forms are available online.
Duration: Grants: Typically one year. Scholarships: One to eight semesters.
Deadline: Grants: February 1 for spring cycle and September 1 for fall cycle. Scholarships: March 1.

ADDRESS INQUIRIES TO:
Matt Lewis, President and Chief Executive Officer
(See address above.)

SAN ANTONIO AREA FOUNDATION [1249]

303 Pearl Parkway
Suite 114
San Antonio, TX 78215
(210) 225-2243
Fax: (210) 225-1980
E-mail: info@saafdn.org
Web Site: www.saafdn.org

FOUNDED: 1964

AREAS OF INTEREST:
Animal services, arts and culture, biomedical research, community and human services, high school completion, strengthening nonprofits, children and youth, seniors, and medicine and health care.

NAME(S) OF PROGRAMS:
● **Annual Responsive Grants**
● **San Antonio Area African-American Community Fund**
● **Special and Urgent Needs**
● **Women and Girls Development Fund**

TYPE:
Capital grants; General operating grants; Project/program grants; Research grants; Scholarships; Technical assistance.

YEAR PROGRAM STARTED: 1964

PURPOSE:
To help donors achieve their charitable goals for the greater benefit of the community.

LEGAL BASIS:
Community foundation.

ELIGIBILITY:
Eligible organizations must be IRS 501(c)(3) tax-exempt and located in Bexar County or surrounding counties. Endowments and debt reduction will not be funded. The Foundation does not provide grants to individuals.

GEOG. RESTRICTIONS: Bexar County and surrounding counties, Texas.

FINANCIAL DATA:
Amount of support per award: Varies.
Total amount of support: $52,000,000 in grants and scholarships for the year 2017.

APPLICATION INFO:
Application and guidelines are available on the web site.
Duration: One year. Must reapply for additional funding.
Deadline: Varies.

PUBLICATIONS:
Newsletter; annual report.

IRS I.D.: 74-6065414

ADDRESS INQUIRIES TO:
Community, Engagement and Impact Team
(See e-mail address above.)

*SPECIAL STIPULATIONS:
The Foundation does not fund statewide; only in Bexar County and surrounding counties.

THE SAN DIEGO FOUNDATION [1250]

2508 Historic Decatur Road
Suite 200
San Diego, CA 92106-6138
(619) 235-2300
Fax: (619) 239-1710
E-mail: info@sdfoundation.org
Web Site: www.sdfoundation.org

FOUNDED: 1975

AREAS OF INTEREST:
Civil society, economic/employment development, education, health and human services, environment, arts and culture, capacity building, science and technology.

TYPE:
Awards/prizes; Capital grants; Challenge/matching grants; Demonstration grants; Development grants; Fellowships; General operating grants; Matching gifts; Project/program grants; Research grants; Scholarships; Seed money grants; Technical assistance; Training grants.

YEAR PROGRAM STARTED: 1975

PURPOSE:
To improve the quality of life for all San Diegans through effective responsible philanthropy.

LEGAL BASIS:
Community foundation.

ELIGIBILITY:
Applicant organizations must be IRS 501(c)(3).

GEOG. RESTRICTIONS: San Diego County, California.

FINANCIAL DATA:
Amount of support per award: Varies.
Total amount of support: Over $40,000,000 annually.
Matching fund requirements: On a case-by-case basis.

NO. AWARDS: 2,800.

APPLICATION INFO:
Requests for proposals in the area of Community Partnerships must include a project budget, organization budget, and letter of qualification. Unsolicited proposals are not accepted for Donor-Advised Funds.
Duration: Generally, one year.
Deadline: Varies.

PUBLICATIONS:
Annual report; newsletters.

IRS I.D.: 95-2942582

*SPECIAL STIPULATIONS:
Most grants made only in San Diego region.

SAN FRANCISCO FOUNDATION [1251]

One Embarcadero Center
Suite 1400
San Francisco, CA 94111
(415) 733-8500
Fax: (415) 477-2783
E-mail: info@sff.org
Web Site: sff.org

FOUNDED: 1948

AREAS OF INTEREST:
Societal and civic issues, health and environment, and arts and humanities.

NAME(S) OF PROGRAMS:
● **Community Leadership Awards**

TYPE:
Awards/prizes.

YEAR PROGRAM STARTED: 1963

PURPOSE:
To recognize individuals and organizations whose leadership has made a significant impact in the Bay Area.

LEGAL BASIS:
Community foundation.

ELIGIBILITY:
Organizations must be 501(c)(3).

GEOG. RESTRICTIONS: Alameda, Contra Costa, Marin, San Francisco and San Mateo counties, California.

FINANCIAL DATA:
Amount of support per award: Individual leaders: $10,000; Organizations: $20,000.
Total amount of support: Varies.

NO. MOST RECENT APPLICANTS: 275.

NO. AWARDS: Varies.

APPLICATION INFO:
Details are available online at the web site.
Deadline: Varies.

ADDRESS INQUIRIES TO:
Community Leadership Award Program
E-mail: ebrown@sff.org

SANTA BARBARA FOUNDATION [1252]

1111 Chapala Street, Suite 200
Santa Barbara, CA 93101
(805) 963-1873
Fax: (805) 966-2345
E-mail: info@sbfoundation.org
Web Site: www.sbfoundation.org

FOUNDED: 1928

AREAS OF INTEREST:
Arts and culture expression, living and dying with dignity, lifelong learning, safety, education, civic engagement, sustainable protection of environment/historic places, and the local food system.

NAME(S) OF PROGRAMS:
- **Community Disaster Relief Fund**
- **Children, Early Care and Education Grants**
- **Get Together Grant Program**
- **Small Impact Building Grants**

TYPE:
Capital grants; Challenge/matching grants; Development grants; General operating grants; Project/program grants.

YEAR PROGRAM STARTED: 1928

PURPOSE:
To enrich the lives of the people of Santa Barbara County, CA.

LEGAL BASIS:
Community foundation incorporated in California.

ELIGIBILITY:
501(c)(3) organizations only. Funds must be used to benefit the people of Santa Barbara County, CA.

GEOG. RESTRICTIONS: Santa Barbara County, California.

FINANCIAL DATA:
Amount of support per award: Community Grants: Up to $50,000; Children, Early Care and Education Grants: $5,000 to $20,000; Small Capacity Building Grants: Up to $5,000.
Total amount of support: Approximately $3,700,000 in discretionary grants for the year ended December 31, 2018.
Matching fund requirements: Varies.

APPLICATION INFO:
Application information is available on the web site.
Duration: One year. No guarantee for continuation.
Deadline: Community Grants: First Monday of each month, February to November.

PUBLICATIONS:
Annual report; application guidelines; quarterly newsletter.

IRS I.D.: 95-1866094

STAFF:
Ron Gallo, President and Chief Executive Officer
Pedro Paz, Director of Grantmaking

ADDRESS INQUIRIES TO:
Grants Associate
(See address above.)

CHARLES AND LYNN SCHUSTERMAN FAMILY FOUNDATION   [1253]
110 West Seventh Street, Suite 2000
Tulsa, OK 74119
(212) 548-9810
Fax: (918) 392-9724
E-mail: information@schusterman.org
Web Site: www.schusterman.org

FOUNDED: 1987

AREAS OF INTEREST:
Child advocacy, Jewish life, education, and community service.

TYPE:
Capital grants; General operating grants; Project/program grants.

PURPOSE:
To fund projects of interest to the Foundation including, but not limited to, those working with education, community life and Jewish affairs.

LEGAL BASIS:
Family foundation.

ELIGIBILITY:
Tax-exempt U.S. and international organizations that enhance Jewish life and nonsectarian Oklahoma-based organizations focused on child advocacy, education and youth leadership through service are eligible.

FINANCIAL DATA:
Amount of support per award: Varies.
Total amount of support: Varies.

NO. AWARDS: 117.

APPLICATION INFO:
Grants are by invitation only.
Duration: One year; seldom more than three years. Must reapply for renewal based on performance.
Deadline: Applications are received on a rolling basis.

ADDRESS INQUIRIES TO:
See e-mail address above.

SCRANTON AREA FOUNDATION   [1254]
615 Jefferson Avenue, Suite 102
Scranton, PA 18510
(570) 347-6203
E-mail: safinfo@safdn.org
Web Site: www.safdn.org

FOUNDED: 1954

AREAS OF INTEREST:
The people and community of the city of Scranton and Lackawanna County, PA.

TYPE:
Challenge/matching grants; Demonstration grants; Grants-in-aid; Project/program grants; Scholarships; Seed money grants; Training grants.

PURPOSE:
To strengthen the local community; to enrich the lives of the people of Scranton and Lackawanna County, PA.

ELIGIBILITY:
Grants to 501(c)(3) nonprofits serving Lackawanna County, PA.

GEOG. RESTRICTIONS: The city of Scranton and Lackawanna County, Pennsylvania.

FINANCIAL DATA:
Amount of support per award: Varies.
Total amount of support: Varies.

APPLICATION INFO:
Applicant must submit a letter of intent through the Foundation web site.
Duration: Varies.

ADDRESS INQUIRIES TO:
Cathy Fitzpatrick, Grants Manager
E-mail: cathyf@safdn.org

THE SELF FAMILY FOUNDATION   [1255]
120 Main Street
Greenwood, SC 29646
(864) 941-4011
(864) 953-2441
E-mail: mamienic@selffoundation.org
Web Site: www.selffoundation.org

FOUNDED: 1942

AREAS OF INTEREST:
Community wellness, education, with emphasis on early childhood development and youth, and health with emphasis on prevention.

TYPE:
Challenge/matching grants; Project/program grants. Project grants in areas of the Foundation's interest.

YEAR PROGRAM STARTED: 1942

PURPOSE:
To help people to help themselves in South Carolina.

LEGAL BASIS:
Tax-exempt, private foundation.

ELIGIBILITY:
Applicants must be tax-exempt organizations in South Carolina only. No grants are awarded directly to individuals.

GEOG. RESTRICTIONS: South Carolina, with preference to Greenwood.

FINANCIAL DATA:
Amount of support per award: $1,000 to $500,000. Typical grant: $25,000.
Total amount of support: $1,100,000 for the year 2019.
Matching fund requirements: Stipulated with specific programs.

NO. AWARDS: 40 for the year 2019.

REPRESENTATIVE AWARDS:
$300,000 to Humane Society of Greenwood County for the spay and neuter clinic; $25,000 to Healthy Learners for the Healthy Learners Greenwood program; $10,000 to Greenwood Performing Arts for the Inter-generational Outreach Program.

APPLICATION INFO:
Application form is available on the Foundation web site.
Duration: No grants on a continuing basis.
Deadline: March 1, September 1 and November 1. Announcements in April, October and December.

IRS I.D.: 57-0400594

OFFICERS:
J.C. Self, III, Chairman
Sally E. Self, M.D., Vice Chairman
Mamie Nicholson, President
W.M. Self, Jr., Treasurer
Cade Jackson, Secretary

TRUSTEES:
Virginia Self Goldsmith
Cade Jackson
Matt Logan, M.D.
Lucas McMillan, Ph.D.
Laurie Self Pulver, M.D.
Furman C. Self
J.C. Self, III
Sally E. Self, M.D.
W.M. Self
W.M. Self, Jr.
Mary Andrews Self Whittington

ADDRESS INQUIRIES TO:
Mamie Nicholson, President
(See address above.)

SHASTA REGIONAL COMMUNITY FOUNDATION [1256]

1335 Arboretum Drive, Suite B
Redding, CA 96003
(530) 244-1219
E-mail: amanda@shastarcf.org
Web Site: www.shastarcf.org

FOUNDED: 2000

AREAS OF INTEREST:
Arts and culture, community development, education, health and human services.

NAME(S) OF PROGRAMS:
● **The McConnell Fund**
● **Redding Rancheria Community Fund**

TYPE:
Project/program grants.

PURPOSE:
To enhance the quality of life of Shasta and Siskiyou communities through philanthropy, education and information.

ELIGIBILITY:
To be eligible for funding, the applicant must be a nonprofit 501(c)(3) organization or public agency and provide specific and direct benefits to residents of Shasta and/or Siskiyou counties, primarily, or to Modoc, Tehama or Trinity counties.

GEOG. RESTRICTIONS: Primarily Shasta and Siskiyou counties, California. Limited funding to Modoc, Tehama and Trinity counties, California.

FINANCIAL DATA:
Net investment assets of $32,200,000 in 2019.
Amount of support per award: Varies.
Total amount of support: $4,300,000 in grants and $272,300 in scholarships awarded in 2019.

NO. AWARDS: Grants: Varies; Scholarships: More than 200 annually.

APPLICATION INFO:
Consult the Foundation web site.
Duration: Varies.
Deadline: Varies.

ADDRESS INQUIRIES TO:
Grants:
Amanda Hutchings
Director of Community Impact
(See e-mail address above.)

Scholarships:
Miriam Leal, Program Associate
(See phone number above.)

SILICON VALLEY COMMUNITY FOUNDATION [1257]

2440 West El Camino Real
Suite 300
Mountain View, CA 94040-1498
(650) 450-5400
Fax: (650) 450-5401
E-mail: info@siliconvalleycf.org
Web Site: www.siliconvalleycf.org

FOUNDED: 2007

AREAS OF INTEREST:
This community foundation utilizes five grantmaking strategies: economic security; education (closing the middle school achievement gap in mathematics); immigrant integration; regional planning (land use and transportation planning); and a community opportunity fund currently focused on safety-net services of food and shelter.

TYPE:
General operating grants; Project/program grants; Scholarships; Seed money grants. Nonprofit organizations that provide services or programs related to the specific five grantmaking strategies in San Mateo and Santa Clara counties may be eligible to apply for funding from the Foundation's endowment. Scholarships for college-bound students are also open to application.

YEAR PROGRAM STARTED: 2008

PURPOSE:
To advance philanthropic solutions to challenging problems, engaging donors to make our region and world a better place for all.

LEGAL BASIS:
Community foundation.

ELIGIBILITY:
To be eligible for a grant, an organization should have current evidence of tax-exempt status under Section 501(c)(3) from the IRS, be a public entity or have a fiscal sponsor with tax-exempt status.

In general, the Foundation does not make grants from its endowment for or to:
(1) activities not directly benefiting the residents of San Mateo and Santa Clara counties;
(2) organizations that are discriminatory;
(3) individuals (contact the Foundation for exceptions to this rule);
(4) costs already incurred;
(5) fraternal organizations, unless sponsoring a specific program open to the entire community;
(6) religious purposes; however, organizations with religious affiliations will be considered for grants if their programs seek to address the needs of the wider community without regard to religious beliefs;
(7) fund-raising events such as walk-a-thons, tournaments and fashion shows and general fund-raising solicitations;
(8) organizations and programs designed to elect candidates to public office or;
(9) out-of-area travel.

GEOG. RESTRICTIONS: San Mateo and Santa Clara counties, California.

FINANCIAL DATA:
Amount of support per award: $10,000 to $250,000, with average grant size less than $100,000. Grant size varies according to the type of project, needs of the organization, and the Foundation's annual giving budget and program concentration.
Total amount of support: Dependent on the Foundation's annual giving budget.

NO. MOST RECENT APPLICANTS: 360.

APPLICATION INFO:
The first step for any potential applicant is to learn the specific components of the grantmaking strategies. If the potential applicant's organization does work or plans to do work related to one of the grantmaking strategies and a Request for Proposal (RFP) regarding that strategy is open for application, then a representative should attend a grant information session. This will give the potential applicant an opportunity to learn more about the grantmaking strategy, the RFP process and talk with a program officer.

The second step would be to submit a proposal with all the required information outlined in the RFP application checklist.

The Foundation encourages submission of proposals via e-mail and accepts proposals postmarked and submitted electronically by the respective deadline date.
Duration: Grants are usually for one year, and should not be considered a source of ongoing support.
Deadline: Contact the Foundation for the appropriate grantmaking strategy application.

PUBLICATIONS:
Annual report; RFP guidelines; research papers; *One Magazine.*

IRS I.D.: 20-5205488

BOARD OF DIRECTORS:
Daniel Lewin, Chairperson
Marie Oh Huber, Vice Chairperson
Nicole Taylor, President and Chief Executive Officer
Alan Zafran, Secretary/Treasurer
George Brown
Rebecca Guerra
Greta S. Hansen
Larry Kramer
Julie Miraglia Kwon
Wade W. Loo
David P. Lopez, Ed.D.
Judy Minor
Kate Mitchell
Daniel Perez
Luz Urrutia
Thurman V. White, Jr.

*SPECIAL STIPULATIONS:
Funding limited to San Mateo and Santa Clara counties only.

SOUTHWEST FLORIDA COMMUNITY FOUNDATION [1258]

2031 Jackson Street
Suite 100
Fort Myers, FL 33901
(239) 274-5900
Fax: (239) 274-5930
E-mail: info@floridacommunity.com
bkelly@floridacommunity.com
Web Site: www.floridacommunity.com

FOUNDED: 1976

AREAS OF INTEREST:
Community design, arts communities and culture, economy and jobs, education, health safety, animals, environment, equity empowerment, climate change, resources for change, philanthropy and community trust.

TYPE:
Demonstration grants; Project/program grants; Scholarships.

PURPOSE:
To connect donors and their philanthropic aspirations with evolving community needs.

LEGAL BASIS:
501(c)(3).

ELIGIBILITY:
Grants are made to organizations that have tax-exempt status under Section 501(c)(3) of the Internal Revenue Code. No grants are made to individuals. Nonsectarian religious programs may apply. Must serve the needs of the communities listed below.

GEOG. RESTRICTIONS: Charlotte, Collier, Glades, Hendry and Lee counties, Florida.

FINANCIAL DATA:
Amount of support per award: $5,000 to $25,000; Initiative Grant Awards: Up to $50,000.

Total amount of support: $5,200,000 in grants and $901,729 in scholarships for fiscal year 2018.

NO. MOST RECENT APPLICANTS: Varies.

NO. AWARDS: Grants: 20; Scholarships: 135.

APPLICATION INFO:
Contact the Foundation for application procedures.
Duration: One year.
Deadline: Varies per program.

PUBLICATIONS:
Annual report; quarterly newsletter.

IRS I.D.: 59-6580974

ADMINISTRATORS:
Sarah Owen, President and Chief Executive Officer

ADDRESS INQUIRIES TO:
Barbara Kelly, Impact Coordinator
(See address above.)

STARK COMMUNITY FOUNDATION   [1259]
400 Market Avenue North
Suite 200
Canton, OH 44702-2107
(330) 454-3426
Fax: (330) 454-5855
E-mail: info@starkcf.org
Web Site: www.starkcf.org

FOUNDED: 1963

AREAS OF INTEREST:
Advancement of the health, social welfare, education, culture or civic improvement of the community.

TYPE:
Capital grants; Challenge/matching grants; Demonstration grants; Development grants; General operating grants; Matching gifts; Project/program grants; Research grants; Scholarships; Seed money grants; Technical assistance; Training grants; Loan forgiveness programs.

YEAR PROGRAM STARTED: 1965

PURPOSE:
To improve the quality of life for residents of Stark County, OH.

LEGAL BASIS:
Community foundation.

ELIGIBILITY:
Organizations with 501(c)(3) status serving Stark County, OH, are eligible. The Foundation will not support operating expenses of well-established organizations, deficit programs, or capital expenditures, endowment funds, religious organizations or religious purposes, annual appeal or membership contributions, conferences or recognition events.

GEOG. RESTRICTIONS: Stark County, Ohio.

FINANCIAL DATA:
Total assets $252,824,162 as of January 31, 2018.
Amount of support per award: $1,000 to $225,000.
Total amount of support: Approximately $11,992,673 for the year 2018.
Matching fund requirements: No general requirements.

NO. MOST RECENT APPLICANTS: Approximately 200.

NO. AWARDS: 130 Discretionary Field of Interest and 60 Pro-Active Initiatives.

APPLICATION INFO:
Application information is available on the web site.
Duration: One year.
Deadline: Varies.

PUBLICATIONS:
Annual report; guidelines and policies; *Community and Commitment*, newsletter.

STAFF:
Mark Samolczyk, President

ADDRESS INQUIRIES TO:
Mark Samolczyk, President
(See address above.)

THE STEELE-REESE FOUNDATION   [1260]
32 Washington Square West
New York, NY 10011
(917) 331-2741
Fax: (212) 286-8513
E-mail: charles@steele-reese.org
Web Site: www.steele-reese.org

FOUNDED: 1955

AREAS OF INTEREST:
Education, health, social welfare, the humanities and the environment.

TYPE:
General operating grants; Project/program grants. Funding is only provided for rural projects of interest to the Foundation. The projects must serve people in the geographic area served by the Foundation.

In Appalachian Kentucky, grants are awarded for elementary and secondary school education purposes only.

YEAR PROGRAM STARTED: 1955

LEGAL BASIS:
Private foundation.

ELIGIBILITY:
Funding is provided to nonprofit organizations servicing communities in Appalachian Kentucky and the western states of Idaho and Montana.

All organizations seeking funds must demonstrate additional local community support for their programming.

GEOG. RESTRICTIONS: Appalachian Kentucky, Idaho and Montana.

FINANCIAL DATA:
Amount of support per award: Typically $5,000 to $50,000. Larger grants are typically for multiyear support.
Matching fund requirements: Some grants require that an organization raise a specific matching amount.

NO. MOST RECENT APPLICANTS: 200 to 250.

NO. AWARDS: Approximately 60.

APPLICATION INFO:
The Foundation welcomes proposals that are accurately aimed. The Foundation's policies and guidelines in detail are available for review online. All applicants must submit proposal materials electronically through the Foundation's web site.
Duration: Grants payable over one to three years. Absolutely no renewals.
Deadline: Appalachian Kentucky: March 1 for consideration during the current fiscal year. Idaho and Montana: Approximately January 9.

PUBLICATIONS:
Annual report.

ADDRESS INQUIRIES TO:
For general inquiries about Foundation policies:
William T. Buice, Trustee
The Steele-Reese Foundation
(See address above.) or

Charles U. Buice, Trustee
The Steele-Reese Foundation
123 Fort Greene Place, No. 4
Brooklyn, NY 11217
(See e-mail address above.)

For Kentucky:
Judy Owens, Appalachian Director
2613 Clubside Court
Lexington, KY 40513
Tel & Fax: (859) 313-5225
E-mail: jkowensjd@aol.com

For Idaho or Montana:
Linda Tracy, Western Program Director
P.O. Box 8311
Missoula, MT 59807-8311
Tel: (406) 207-7984
Fax: (207) 470-3872
E-mail: linda@steele-reese.org

THE ABBOT AND DOROTHY H. STEVENS FOUNDATION   [1261]
P.O. Box 111
North Andover, MA 01845
(978) 688-7211
E-mail: grantprocess@stevensfoundation.com

AREAS OF INTEREST:
Education, community welfare, arts and youth programs.

TYPE:
Capital grants; General operating grants; Project/program grants.

PURPOSE:
To improve the quality of life in greater Lawrence and Merrimack Valley.

ELIGIBILITY:
Eligible organizations must be IRS 501(c)(3) tax-exempt.

GEOG. RESTRICTIONS: Greater Lawrence and Merrimack Valley, Massachusetts.

FINANCIAL DATA:
Amount of support per award: $8,000 average.
Total amount of support: Varies.

APPLICATION INFO:
Applicants must include a copy of their IRS 501(c)(3) tax determination letter.
Duration: One year.
Deadline: Trustees meet monthly with the exception of July and August.

PUBLICATIONS:
Guidelines.

ADDRESS INQUIRIES TO:
Joshua Miner, Executive Director
(See address above.)

THE NATHANIEL AND ELIZABETH P. STEVENS FOUNDATION   [1262]
P.O. Box 111
North Andover, MA 01845
(978) 688-7211
E-mail: grantprocess@stevensfoundation.com

AREAS OF INTEREST:
Education, community welfare, arts and youth programs.

TYPE:
Capital grants; General operating grants; Project/program grants.

PURPOSE:
To improve the quality of life in the greater Lawrence and Merrimack Valley.

ELIGIBILITY:
Eligible organizations must be IRS 501(c)(3) tax-exempt.

GEOG. RESTRICTIONS: Greater Lawrence and Merrimack Valley, Massachusetts.

FINANCIAL DATA:
Amount of support per award: $8,000 average.
Total amount of support: Varies.

APPLICATION INFO:
Applications must include a copy of the IRS 501(c)(3) tax determination letter.
Duration: One year.
Deadline: Trustees meet monthly with the exception of July and August.

PUBLICATIONS:
Guidelines.

ADDRESS INQUIRIES TO:
Joshua Miner, Executive Director
(See address above.)

H. CHASE STONE TRUST

c/o JPMorgan
370 17th Street, Suite 3200
Denver, CO 80202
(303) 607-7810
Fax: (303) 607-7761
E-mail: julie.golden@jpmorgan.com
Web Site: www.jpmorgan.com/onlinegrants

TYPE:
Project/program grants.

See entry 464 for full listing.

SUDBURY FOUNDATION   [1263]

326 Concord Road
Sudbury, MA 01776
(978) 443-0849
Fax: (978) 579-9536
E-mail: contact@sudburyfoundation.org
Web Site: www.sudburyfoundation.org

FOUNDED: 1952

AREAS OF INTEREST:
Scholarships, environment, food initiatives and charitable grants for communities in the Sudbury area; children, youth and families.

NAME(S) OF PROGRAMS:
- **The Atkinson Scholarship Program**
- **Children, Youth and Families Program**
- **Farm and Local Food Program**
- **The Sudbury Program**

TYPE:
Project/program grants; Scholarships. Capacity-building grants.

YEAR PROGRAM STARTED: 1952

PURPOSE:
To improve the quality of life in Sudbury and the surrounding communities.

ELIGIBILITY:
Eligible organizations must be IRS 501(c)(3) tax-exempt. The Foundation funds projects in Sudbury and the 10 communities surrounding

Sudbury that address the issues of Youth Development and Opportunity, Community Building, and Preservation of Community Character and Assets.

The Atkinson Scholarship Program provides college financial aid to students connected to Sudbury, MA.

Farm and Local Food program focuses on food and local farm initiatives in Massachusetts.

GEOG. RESTRICTIONS: Sudbury, Massachusetts and surrounding areas.

FINANCIAL DATA:
Scholarships are administered to the schools earmarked for specific students.
Amount of support per award: Scholarships: Up to $5,000 annually; Grants: $5,000 to $50,000.
Total amount of support: Varies.

NO. AWARDS: Scholarships: 15 new awards per year; Grants to nonprofits: 35 per year.

APPLICATION INFO:
Details are available on the Foundation web site.
Duration: Typically one year.
Deadline: Varies.

ADDRESS INQUIRIES TO:
Marilyn Martino, Executive Director
(See address above.)

*SPECIAL STIPULATIONS:
Scholarship program open to local high school seniors only for undergraduate education.

THE SUMMERLEE FOUNDATION   [1264]

5556 Caruth Haven Lane
Dallas, TX 75225
(214) 363-9000
Fax: (214) 363-1941
E-mail: info@summerlee.org
Web Site: www.summerlee.org

FOUNDED: 1988

AREAS OF INTEREST:
Animal protection and Texas history.

NAME(S) OF PROGRAMS:
- **Animal Protection Program**
- **Texas History**

TYPE:
Project/program grants; Research grants; Technical assistance.

YEAR PROGRAM STARTED: 1988

PURPOSE:
To promote animal protection and the prevention of cruelty to animals; to research and document all facets of Texas history.

LEGAL BASIS:
Charitable foundation.

ELIGIBILITY:
No grants are made for religious purposes or to individuals. Must be 501(c)(3).

FINANCIAL DATA:
Amount of support per award: $5,000 to $10,000.

NO. MOST RECENT APPLICANTS: Approximately 200.

NO. AWARDS: 84.

APPLICATION INFO:
Guidelines are available on the Foundation web site.

Duration: Generally one year; occasionally multiyear.
Deadline: Varies.

IRS I.D.: 75-2252355

OFFICERS:
John W. Crain, Chairman
Mary Volcansek, Ph.D., Vice Chairman
Gary N. Smith, President
Jim Bruseth, Ph.D., Treasurer
Hon. David D. Jackson, Assistant Secretary

BOARD OF DIRECTORS:
Melanie K. Anderson
Jim Bruseth, Ph.D.
Joan Casey
John W. Crain
Hon. Nikki DeShazo
Ron Tyler, Ph.D.
Mary Volcansek, Ph.D.

ADDRESS INQUIRIES TO:
Melanie K. Anderson
Program Director-Animal Protection or
Gary N. Smith
Program Director-Texas History
(See address above.)

THE SUMMIT FOUNDATION   [1265]

103 South Harris Street
Breckenridge, CO 80424
(970) 453-5970
E-mail: tsfadmin@summitfoundation.org
Web Site: www.summitfoundation.org

FOUNDED: 1984

AREAS OF INTEREST:
Art and culture, health and human service, education, environment and sports.

TYPE:
Capital grants; Challenge/matching grants; Endowments; General operating grants; Project/program grants; Scholarships; Technical assistance. The Foundation supports scholarship programs at Summit High School and neighboring community high schools. Scholarships are available to graduating seniors each year.

YEAR PROGRAM STARTED: 1984

PURPOSE:
To improve the quality of life for residents and guests of Summit County and neighboring communities.

LEGAL BASIS:
Community foundation.

ELIGIBILITY:
Grants are made to organizations that have tax-exempt status under Section 501(c)(3) of the Internal Revenue Code. No grants are made to individuals.

GEOG. RESTRICTIONS: Summit County and neighboring communities of Alma, Fairplay, Kremmling and Leadville, Colorado.

FINANCIAL DATA:
Amount of support per award: Varies.
Total amount of support: Approximately $2,700,000 for the year 2017.

NO. AWARDS: Over 100.

APPLICATION INFO:
Applications are accepted through the online grant portal.
Deadline: Typically April and October.

IRS I.D.: 74-2341399

ADDRESS INQUIRIES TO:
Executive Director
(See address above.)

SYNTHOMER/OMNOVA SOLUTIONS FOUNDATION [1266]

25435 Harvard Road
Beachwood, OH 44122-6201
(216) 682-7067
Fax: (216) 453-0113
E-mail: theresa.carter@omnova.com
Web Site: www.omnova.com

FOUNDED: 1999

AREAS OF INTEREST:
Support of educational, cultural and 501(c)(3) organizations in areas where Synthomer/OMNOVA Solutions has large concentrations of employment.

TYPE:
Capital grants; Development grants; Endowments; General operating grants; Matching gifts; Product donations; Project/program grants; Scholarships.

YEAR PROGRAM STARTED: 1999

PURPOSE:
To support education and other charitable organizations in the communities where Synthomer/OMNOVA Solutions has facilities.

LEGAL BASIS:
Nonprofit corporation, private foundation.

ELIGIBILITY:
501(c)(3) tax-exempt organizations are eligible.

GEOG. RESTRICTIONS: Georgia, Massachusetts, North Carolina, Ohio, Pennsylvania and South Carolina.

FINANCIAL DATA:
Amount of support per award: $100 to $50,000. Average $5,000.
Total amount of support: $1,195,689 for the year 2019.

NO. AWARDS: Approximately 271 for the year 2019.

REPRESENTATIVE AWARDS:
American Red Cross; Akron Community Service Center and Urban League; Akron Symphony Orchestra; United Way; Great Akron and Greater Cleveland Food Banks.

APPLICATION INFO:
Application is available on the Foundation web site.
Duration: One year. Renewable.
Deadline: October 30.

PUBLICATIONS:
Application guidelines; annual report.

IRS I.D.: 34-1909350

TRUSTEES:
Paul DeSantis, Chairman
Christopher Weber, Treasurer
Erin Hagen
Jackie Laurich
Marshall Moore

STAFF:
Kim Huff, Community Relations Representative

ADDRESS INQUIRIES TO:
Theresa Carter, President
(See address above.)

THOMAS THOMPSON TRUST   [1267]

c/o Rackemann, Sawyer & Brewster
160 Federal Street, 15th Floor
Boston, MA 02110-1700
(617) 951-1108
Fax: (617) 542-7437
E-mail: smonahan@rackemann.com
Web Site: www.thomasthompsontrust.org

AREAS OF INTEREST:
Education, health/mental health, social services and cultural.

TYPE:
Capital grants; Challenge/matching grants; Conferences/seminars; Demonstration grants; Development grants; Endowments; Professorships; Project/program grants; Seed money grants; Technical assistance; Training grants; Research contracts. Support for special programs, capital support, new construction, renovation and equipment.

PURPOSE:
To promote health, education, or general social and civic betterment.

LEGAL BASIS:
Private foundation.

ELIGIBILITY:
Eligible organizations must be in operation for three consecutive years prior to submitting an application.

GEOG. RESTRICTIONS: Dutchess County, New York, particularly in Rhinebeck; and Windham County, Vermont, particularly in Brattleboro.

FINANCIAL DATA:
Amount of support per award: $5,000 to $25,000.
Total amount of support: $670,000 for fiscal year 2018.
Matching fund requirements: Determined on case-by-case basis.

NO. MOST RECENT APPLICANTS: 55.

NO. AWARDS: 42 for fiscal year 2018.

REPRESENTATIVE AWARDS:
Brattleboro Boys and Girls Club; Windham Housing Trust; Groundworks Collaborative; Culture Connect.

APPLICATION INFO:
Applications must be submitted online.
Duration: Varies.
Deadline: Generally January 5, April 1, July 1 and October 1.

PUBLICATIONS:
Application guidelines.

TRUSTEES:
Susan T. Monahan
Maura E. Murphy, Esq.
Michael F. O'Connell, Esq.

ADDRESS INQUIRIES TO:
Susan T. Monahan
Grants Coordinator and Trustee
(See address or e-mail above.)

TIDES FOUNDATION   [1268]

P.O. Box 29198
San Francisco, CA 94129-0198
(415) 561-6400
Fax: (415) 561-6401
E-mail: info@tides.org
Web Site: www.tides.org

FOUNDED: 1976

AREAS OF INTEREST:
Civic participation, economic development, economic and racial justice, environment, environmental justice, LGBTIQ communities, HIV/AIDS, native communities, progressive media, arts and culture, violence prevention, women's empowerment and reproductive health, and youth organizing and development.

NAME(S) OF PROGRAMS:
- **Colin Higgins Youth Courage Awards**
- **Antonio Pizzigati Prize for Software in the Public Interest**
- **Mario Savio Young Activist Award**

TYPE:
General operating grants; Project/program grants.

YEAR PROGRAM STARTED: 1976

PURPOSE:
To partner with donors to increase and organize resources for social change.

LEGAL BASIS:
Public foundation.

FINANCIAL DATA:
Amount of support per award: Varies.
Total amount of support: $235,556,871 in grants (U.S. and international) in 2017.

NO. AWARDS: 3,600 total grants in 2017.

APPLICATION INFO:
The Fund does not accept unsolicited grant requests.

IRS I.D.: 51-0198509

ADDRESS INQUIRIES TO:
Adam Michaelsson, Grants Specialist
(See address above.)

TOLEDO COMMUNITY FOUNDATION   [1269]

300 Madison Avenue, Suite 1300
Toledo, OH 43604
(419) 241-5049
E-mail: toledocf@toledocf.org
Web Site: www.toledocf.org

FOUNDED: 1973

AREAS OF INTEREST:
Education, social services, physical and mental health, neighborhood and urban affairs, natural resources and the arts.

TYPE:
Challenge/matching grants; Project/program grants; Seed money grants. The Foundation has a particular interest in providing seed money for new programs designed to meet emerging community needs or to expand existing successful programs. Emphasis is placed on programs that will:
(a) create safe, positive living environments;
(b) enable families to develop the skills/resources needed to support and nurture each member and;
(c) foster the development of responsible young people who are capable of achieving their fullest potential.

PURPOSE:
To enrich the quality of life for individuals and families in the greater Toledo, OH service area.

ELIGIBILITY:
Grants are awarded only to nonprofit, charitable organizations that are IRS 501(c)(3) tax-exempt. The Foundation usually will not make grants from its unrestricted funds to support general operating budgets

(or budget deficits) of established organizations, annual campaigns, capital campaigns, purchase of equipment such as computer hardware/software or motor vehicles, production of films, videos, television programs, etc., or for sectarian activities of religious organizations.

GEOG. RESTRICTIONS: Northwest Ohio and southeast Michigan, with particular emphasis on the greater Toledo, Ohio area.

FINANCIAL DATA:
Amount of support per award: Varies.

APPLICATION INFO:
Online grant application must be completed. No hard copies accepted.
Duration: Generally one year.
Deadline: January 15 and September 15.

PUBLICATIONS:
Guidelines.

ADDRESS INQUIRIES TO:
Patrick Johnston, Senior Program Officer
(See address above.)

THE TRULL FOUNDATION [1270]

404 Fourth Street
Palacios, TX 77465
(361) 972-5241
Fax: (361) 972-1109
E-mail: info@trullfoundation.org
Web Site: www.trullfoundation.org

FOUNDED: 1967

AREAS OF INTEREST:
Children, substance abuse problems, Texas coastal environment, and The Palacios County area.

CONSULTING OR VOLUNTEER SERVICES:
Assists local projects and organizations in Texas, with a priority to rural Texas.

TYPE:
Challenge/matching grants; Development grants; General operating grants; Project/program grants; Scholarships.

YEAR PROGRAM STARTED: 1948

PURPOSE:
To support charitable and educational programs.

LEGAL BASIS:
Private (family) foundation.

ELIGIBILITY:
Applicants must have federal tax-exemption letter from IRS.

GEOG. RESTRICTIONS: Primarily in rural Texas.

FINANCIAL DATA:
Amount of support per award: $2,000 to $5,000 average.
Total amount of support: Approximately $1,000,000 for the year 2018.

NO. AWARDS: 113 for the year 2018.

REPRESENTATIVE AWARDS:
$5,000 to Camp Fire North Texas, Wichita Falls, TX; $10,000 to Palacios Volunteer Fire Department, Palacios, TX; $8,000 to Katy Prairie Conservancy, Houston, TX; $15,000 to Palmer Drug Abuse Program of Corpus Christi, Inc., Corpus Christi, TX.

APPLICATION INFO:
Each applicant should submit the following:
(1) cover letter (two-page maximum);
(2) proposal fact sheet (two-page maximum);
(3) current agency budget (one to three pages), including sources of income;

(4) one-page project budget, if different from operating budget;
(5) documentation of IRS status 501(c)(3). If there is any matter which might affect the IRS status to cause the revocation of the exemption, include information about this matter and;
(6) selected additional material or information (limit five pages) (optional).

Proposals sent by fax or e-mail are not accepted.

The Foundation may request additional information if there is an interest in the proposal.
Duration: Usually no more than one year per project.
Deadline: Announcement within three months after receipt of proposal.

PUBLICATIONS:
Biennial report; application guidelines; proposal fact sheet.

IRS I.D.: 23-7423943

TRUSTEES:
R. Scott Trull, Chairman
Cara P. Herlin, Vice Chairman
Kristan B. Olfers, Secretary/Treasurer
Sarah H. Olfers, Trustee
Marsha Baumann, Advisory Trustee
Cathy Wakefield, Advisory Trustee
Bill Wigmore, Advisory Trustee

ADDRESS INQUIRIES TO:
Nellie Lee, Executive Director
(See address above.)

U.S. BANCORP FOUNDATION [1271]

BC-MN-H21B
800 Nicollet Mall
Minneapolis, MN 55402
(612) 303-4000
E-mail: usbankgrants@usbank.com
Web Site: www.usbank.com/community/index.aspx

FOUNDED: 1979

AREAS OF INTEREST:
Workforce education and economic prosperity, neighborhood stability and revitalization, and artistic and cultural enrichment and learning through play.

NAME(S) OF PROGRAMS:
● **Community Possible**

TYPE:
Capital grants; Development grants; General operating grants; Matching gifts; Project/program grants.

PURPOSE:
To improve the quality of life in communities where U.S. Bancorp employees live and work.

LEGAL BASIS:
Corporate foundation.

ELIGIBILITY:
Organizations must be IRS 501(c)(3) tax-exempt and must be located in communities where United States Bank operates.

The Foundation charitable contributions program will not provide funding for:
(1) organizations not tax-exempt under Internal Revenue Code Section 501(c)(3);
(2) fraternal organizations, merchant associations, chamber memberships or programs, or 501(c)(4) or (6) organizations;

(3) fund-raising events or sponsorships, "pass through" organizations or private foundations;
(4) organizations outside U.S. Bancorp communities;
(5) programs operated by religious organizations for religious purposes;
(6) political organizations or organizations designed primarily to lobby;
(7) individuals;
(8) travel and related expenses;
(9) endowment campaigns;
(10) deficit reduction;
(11) organizations receiving primary funding from the United Way or;
(12) organizations whose practices are not in keeping with the Company's equal opportunity policy.

GEOG. RESTRICTIONS: Communities where United States Bank has operations.

FINANCIAL DATA:
Amount of support per award: Varies.
Total amount of support: Varies.

APPLICATION INFO:
Application and guidelines are available online.
Duration: One year.
Deadline: Varies.

PUBLICATIONS:
Guidelines; Corporate Citizenship Report.

IRS I.D.: 41-1359579

U.S. DEPARTMENT OF HEALTH AND HUMAN SERVICES [1272]

Office of Innovation
330 C Street, S.W.
Washington, DC 20201
(202) 401-4634
Web Site: www.acl.gov

AREAS OF INTEREST:
Developmental disabilities.

NAME(S) OF PROGRAMS:
● **Projects of National Significance for Persons with Developmental Disabilities**

TYPE:
Demonstration grants; Technical assistance; Training grants. Model demonstration grants. Support for persons with developmental disabilities.

YEAR PROGRAM STARTED: 1975

PURPOSE:
To support policy development and awards funding that enhance the independence, productivity, inclusion and integration of people with developmental disabilities and their families.

LEGAL BASIS:
Government agency.

ELIGIBILITY:
Applicants must be nonprofit organizations, state agencies, or consortia.

GEOG. RESTRICTIONS: United States and its territories.

FINANCIAL DATA:
Amount of support per award: Varies.
Total amount of support: $9,000,750 for the year 2016.
Matching fund requirements: 25% local match.

NO. AWARDS: Approximately 29 for the year 2016.

APPLICATION INFO:
Application information is available on the web site.
Duration: 12 to 60 months.
Deadline: Varies.

OFFICERS:
Julie Hocker, Commissioner, Administration on Disabilities

ADDRESS INQUIRIES TO:
Allison Cruz, Director
(See address above.)

U.S. DEPARTMENT OF HOUSING AND URBAN DEVELOPMENT   [1273]
Entitlement Communities Division
451 7th Street, S.W., Room 7282
Washington, DC 20410
(202) 708-3587 (Office of Block Grant Assistance)
(202) 708-1577 (Entitlement Division)
(202) 708-1322 (State/Small Cities Division)
Fax: (202) 401-2044
E-mail: gloria.l.coates@hud.gov
Web Site: www.hudexchange.info

FOUNDED: 1974

AREAS OF INTEREST:
Community development.

NAME(S) OF PROGRAMS:
● **Community Development Block Grant Program: Entitlement Communities Program**

TYPE:
Block grants; Project/program grants. Acquisition, construction of certain public works, facilities and improvements, clearance, housing rehabilitation, relocation and demolition, public services (limited), activities relating to conservation and renewable energy resources, neighborhood revitalization and economic development projects, including assistance to micro enterprises.

YEAR PROGRAM STARTED: 1975

PURPOSE:
To develop viable urban communities, including decent housing and a suitable living environment and expand economic opportunities, principally for persons of low and moderate income.

LEGAL BASIS:
Units of general local government under Title I of the Housing and Community Development Act of 1974 (PL 93-383).

ELIGIBILITY:
The following units of general local government and states are all entitled to receive block grants from the CDBG Entitlement Communities Program and State and Small Cities Program. Grant amounts are determined by a statutory formula:
(1) principal cities of Metropolitan Statistical Areas (MSAs);
(2) other metropolitan cities with a population of at least 50,000 and;
(3) qualified urban counties, as defined in the Act, with populations of at least 200,000 (excluding the population of entitled cities).

Under the HUD Administered Small Cities Program, HUD directly awards grants to non-entitled units of general local government within the state of Hawaii by formula. The total value of grants awarded through this Program is determined by statutory formula.

FINANCIAL DATA:
Amount of support per award: Varies from city to city.
Total amount of support: Approximately $3 billion for fiscal year 2019.

APPLICATION INFO:
For the CDBG Entitlement Communities Program, a grantee must develop and submit to HUD its consolidated plan, which is a jurisdiction's comprehensive planning document and application for funding under the Community Planning and Development formula grant programs: CDBG, HOME, Emergency Shelter Grants (ESG) and Housing Opportunities for Persons with AIDS (HOPWA). In its consolidated plan, the jurisdiction must identify its goals for these community planning and development programs, as well as for housing programs. These goals will serve as the criteria against which HUD will evaluate a jurisdiction's plan and its performance under the plan. In addition, the consolidated plan must include required certifications, including that not less than 70% of the CDBG funds expended over a one-, two- or three-year period specified by the grantee, will be used for activities that benefit low- and moderate-income persons. A consolidated plan submission will be approved by HUD unless the plan (or a portion of it) is inconsistent with the purposes of the National Affordable Housing Act or it is substantially incomplete.

Under the HUD Administered Small Cities Program, to receive a grant, the counties of Hawaii, Maui and Kauai in Hawaii must prepare and submit a consolidated plan to HUD.

ADDRESS INQUIRIES TO:
Office of Block Grant Assistance
(See address above.)

*SPECIAL STIPULATIONS:
Block grants made to states and local governments, not individuals.

THE UNITY FOUNDATION OF LAPORTE COUNTY   [1274]
422 Franklin Street
Suite C
Michigan City, IN 46360
(219) 879-0327
Fax: (219) 210-3881
E-mail: unity@uflc.net
Web Site: www.uflc.net

FOUNDED: 1992

AREAS OF INTEREST:
Community development in LaPorte County, IN.

CONSULTING OR VOLUNTEER SERVICES:
Technical assistance to nonprofits and donors.

NAME(S) OF PROGRAMS:
● **Community Fund**

TYPE:
Challenge/matching grants; Grants-in-aid; Project/program grants; Scholarships; Technical assistance. Community Fund makes grants to education, the arts, health and human services, and the environment to the whole community. Grants are based on what the community needs at a given time.

YEAR PROGRAM STARTED: 1992

PURPOSE:
To improve the quality of life in LaPorte County, IN.

LEGAL BASIS:
Indiana corporation 501(c)(3).

ELIGIBILITY:
Nonprofits serving people of LaPorte County, IN.

GEOG. RESTRICTIONS: LaPorte County, Indiana.

FINANCIAL DATA:
Amount of support per award: Community grants: Up to $3,000.
Total amount of support: More than $700,000 in community grants and more than $130,000 in scholarships each year.

NO. MOST RECENT APPLICANTS: Grants: 89.

NO. AWARDS: 81.

APPLICATION INFO:
Applications should follow the format outlined in the online directions. The following information is required:
(1) narrative describing the program or specific need to be addressed, its significance to the community and its particular benefit to those living in the LaPorte County area, and the names and qualifications of those persons who will carry it out;
(2) complete budget for the project, including funding plan, amount of the request, and names of other funding sources the organization has applied to for assistance and;
(3) description of applicant organization(s) including the name, address, telephone and fax number of the contact person, a list of the officers and board members, a copy of the IRS letter designating the organization as 501(c)(3) federal tax-exempt, latest annual financial report, and any descriptive brochures or promotional literature.
Deadline: Grants: April 1; Scholarships: January 1.

PUBLICATIONS:
Report to Community.

STAFF:
Maggi Spartz, President

ADDRESS INQUIRIES TO:
Maggi Spartz, President
(See address above.)

VAN LOEBENSELS/REMBEROCK FOUNDATION   [1275]
131 Steuart Street
Suite 301
San Francisco, CA 94105
(415) 512-0500
Fax: (415) 371-0227
E-mail: nwiltsek@vlsrr.org
Web Site: www.vlsrr.org

FOUNDED: 1964

AREAS OF INTEREST:
Legal services.

TYPE:
General operating grants; Project/program grants; Seed money grants.

YEAR PROGRAM STARTED: 1964

PURPOSE:
To support projects that will test potentially useful innovations in the areas of public interest law.

LEGAL BASIS:
Private independent foundation.

ELIGIBILITY:
Grants are restricted to northern California. Grants are not ordinarily made for projects requiring medical, scientific or other technical knowledge for evaluation, operating budgets of well-established organizations, capital expenditures, to national organizations unless for a specific local project, to individuals or for scholarships.

GEOG. RESTRICTIONS: Northern California.

FINANCIAL DATA:
Amount of support per award: Average grant: $15,000.

Total amount of support: $1,757,000 for the year 2017.

NO. AWARDS: 74 for the year 2017.

REPRESENTATIVE AWARDS:
$35,000 to East Bay Community Law Center.

APPLICATION INFO:
Application information is available on the web site.

Duration: Most grants are awarded on a single-year basis, but may be renewed if warranted.

Deadline: Proposals are considered every two to three months. Deadlines are four times a year, dates of which are posted on the Foundation web site. Announcement several days after Board meetings.

BOARD OF DIRECTORS:
Toni Rembe, President
Brian Wong, Treasurer
Julie Divola, Secretary
Irma Herrera
Thomas C. Layton

EXECUTIVE DIRECTOR:
Nancy Wiltsek

ADDRESS INQUIRIES TO:
Nancy Wiltsek, Executive Director
(See address above.)

VENTURA COUNTY COMMUNITY FOUNDATION [1276]

4001 Mission Oaks Boulevard
Suite A
Camarillo, CA 93012
(805) 330-6672
Fax: (805) 484-2700
E-mail: pwiggins@vccf.org
Web Site: www.vccf.org

FOUNDED: 1987

AREAS OF INTEREST:
Community needs and development, culture, education, health, human services, women's issues and Latino issues.

TYPE:
Project/program grants; Scholarships.

YEAR PROGRAM STARTED: 1987

PURPOSE:
To promote and enable philanthropy to improve our community, for good, forever.

ELIGIBILITY:
Must qualify under the Internal Revenue Code Section 501(c)(3) as a nonprofit organization, or operate under the fiscal sponsorship of an organization that does, and serve residents of Ventura County, CA.

GEOG. RESTRICTIONS: Ventura County, California.

FINANCIAL DATA:
Amount of support per award: Varies.

Total amount of support: Varies.

NO. AWARDS: 802.

APPLICATION INFO:
Applications accepted only in response to an open request for proposals.

Duration: Varies per program.

ADDRESS INQUIRIES TO:
Appropriate program officer, as outlined in the Request for Proposals.

VICTORIA FOUNDATION, INC. [1277]

31 Mulberry Street, Fifth Floor
Newark, NJ 07102
(973) 792-9200
Fax: (973) 792-1300
E-mail: info@victoriafoundation.org
Web Site: www.victoriafoundation.org

FOUNDED: 1924

AREAS OF INTEREST:
Education, neighborhood revitalization, youth and families in Newark, NJ, as well as statewide environmental issues.

TYPE:
Capital grants; Challenge/matching grants; General operating grants; Project/program grants. The focus in Education includes after-school programs, educational enrichment, teacher training and curriculum development.

Neighborhood Revitalization includes community development, employment training, housing programs and community organizing.

The focus in Youth and Families includes youth development programs and efforts to strengthen families.

The concentration in Environment includes open space preservation in New Jersey, particularly in the Highlands and Pinelands.

YEAR PROGRAM STARTED: 1924

PURPOSE:
To promote education, urban environment, neighborhood development and urban revitalization, and youth and families in the city of Newark; to preserve and conserve resources including land and water in the state of New Jersey and within the city of Newark.

LEGAL BASIS:
Independent foundation.

ELIGIBILITY:
Organizations must be nonprofit per Internal Revenue Code 501(c)(3) and must address the Foundation's interests. No grants are made to individuals or for programs dealing with specific diseases, afflictions or geriatric needs. Proposals from arts organizations will be considered only if they directly bear on education.

General programs are focused within Newark, NJ. Environmental programs encompass the areas of New Jersey Highlands, Pine Barrens, Kittatinny Ridge and Valley Regions of New Jersey.

GEOG. RESTRICTIONS: Newark, New Jersey.

FINANCIAL DATA:
Amount of support per award: Varies.

Total amount of support: $11,880,500 in total grants paid for the year 2016.

NO. MOST RECENT APPLICANTS: Approximately 300.

NO. AWARDS: 204 for the year ended December 31, 2016.

REPRESENTATIVE AWARDS:
$75,000 to New Jersey Symphony Orchestra to support the Newark Early Strings Program, which provides Suzuki violin instruction to over 500 elementary school children; $130,000 to Ironbound Community Corporation towards general operating support.

APPLICATION INFO:
Application information is available on the web site. Applicants must apply through the online portal. No mail-in applications will be accepted.

Duration: One year. Renewal based upon careful trustee and staff review of subsequent proposal submissions.

Deadline: Current grantees: Mid-January and mid-July; New applicants: Early January and mid- to late June; School applications: February 1; Summer camp: First week of September. Announcements in late June and December; Environment land acquisitions accepted on a rolling basis.

PUBLICATIONS:
Annual report.

IRS I.D.: 22-1554541

OFFICERS:
Frank Alvarez, President
Margaret H. Parker, Vice President
Gary M. Wingens, Treasurer
Irene Cooper-Basch, Executive Officer and Secretary

TRUSTEES:
Frank Alvarez
Henry Amoroso
Ana Baptista
Michael Catania
Sally Chubb
Robert Holmes
Robert L. Johnson, M.D.
Franklin E. Parker, IV
John F. Parker
Margaret H. Parker
Denise Rodgers
Sara Chubb Sauvayre
Bei Saville
Grizel Ubarry
Gary M. Wingens
A. Zachery Yamba

ADDRESS INQUIRIES TO:
Irene Cooper-Basch, Executive Officer
(See address above.)

THE WACO FOUNDATION [1278]

1227 North Valley Mills Drive
Suite 235
Waco, TX 76710
(254) 754-3404
(254) 752-9457 (MAC Program)
Fax: (254) 753-2887
E-mail: mac@wacofoundation.org
Web Site: www.wacofoundation.org

FOUNDED: 1958

AREAS OF INTEREST:
Residents of McLennan County, TX.

NAME(S) OF PROGRAMS:
• **MAC College Money Program**

TYPE:
Scholarships. Intended to promote postsecondary educational opportunities in

the community, and thereby promote greater employment opportunities for those of working age.

YEAR PROGRAM STARTED: 1995

PURPOSE:
To make a positive difference in the lives and future of the people who live in Waco and McLennan County through grantmaking, promotion of community philanthropy, and support of the not-for-profit sector.

ELIGIBILITY:
Must have graduated from McLennan County high schools and have family income of less than $50,000.

GEOG. RESTRICTIONS: McLennan County, Texas.

FINANCIAL DATA:
Amount of support per award: Varies.
Total amount of support: $500,000 in contributions annually.

APPLICATION INFO:
High school seniors must submit completed application form and FAFSA.
Duration: Two years. Renewable for two years.
Deadline: May 1 of student's senior year of high school.

ADDRESS INQUIRIES TO:
Rolando Rodriguez, MAC and Scholarship Coordinator
(See address above.)

DENNIS & PHYLLIS WASHINGTON FOUNDATION [1279]

P.O. Box 16630
Missoula, MT 59808
(406) 523-1300
Fax: (800) 381-2942
E-mail: info@dpwfoundation.org
Web Site: www.dpwfoundation.org

FOUNDED: 1987

AREAS OF INTEREST:
Direct service, youth-focused programs in arts and culture, community service, health and human services, and education.

TYPE:
Project/program grants; Scholarships.

YEAR PROGRAM STARTED: 1987

PURPOSE:
To invest in people to improve the quality of their lives.

LEGAL BASIS:
Private foundation.

ELIGIBILITY:
Eligible organizations must be IRS 501(c)(3) tax-exempt. Low administrative costs required. Indirect or overhead costs not directly related to implementation of a grant are not allowed.

GEOG. RESTRICTIONS: Montana and communities where Washington has services.

FINANCIAL DATA:
Amount of support per award: Varies.
Total amount of support: Varies.

APPLICATION INFO:
Grant applicants must complete the online application process which includes reading grant guidelines and completion of a short eligibility review. If qualified, the organization will be invited to submit a full application online.

Scholarship applicants can review application guidelines on the Foundation's web site.
Duration: One to three years.
Deadline: Applications are accepted on a rolling basis.

ADDRESS INQUIRIES TO:
See e-mail address above.

WASHINGTON FORREST FOUNDATION [1280]

2407 Columbia Pike, Suite 200
Arlington, VA 22204
(703) 920-3688
Fax: (703) 920-0130
E-mail: allison@washingtonforrest.org
Web Site: washingtonforrest.org

FOUNDED: 1968

AREAS OF INTEREST:
Human services, education and community development organizations or programs serving South Arlington, VA.

TYPE:
Capital grants; General operating grants; Project/program grants; Seed money grants. Pilot project grants.

PURPOSE:
To improve and enhance the quality of life in South Arlington, VA.

LEGAL BASIS:
Public foundation.

ELIGIBILITY:
Eligible organizations must be IRS 501(c)(3) tax-exempt and be located in northern Virginia.

Capital grants to existing grantees only.

Pilot project grants and seed money grants are usually awarded to existing organizations for unique programs.

GEOG. RESTRICTIONS: South Arlington, Virginia.

FINANCIAL DATA:
Amount of support per award: $5,000 to $30,000.
Total amount of support: $750,000.

NO. MOST RECENT APPLICANTS: 59.

NO. AWARDS: 59.

APPLICATION INFO:
Applicants should first call the Foundation to discuss the proposal. Applications must include a copy of the IRS tax determination letter.
Duration: One year. Renewal by reapplication.
Deadline: One month prior to board meetings held in September, December and March. Dates will be posted online.

ADDRESS INQUIRIES TO:
Allison A. Erdle, Executive Director
(See address above.)

*SPECIAL STIPULATIONS:
Organization must be located in or have a program operating in South Arlington, VA.

WEGE FOUNDATION [1281]

99 Monroe Avenue, N.W.
Suite 902
Grand Rapids, MI 49503
(616) 957-0480
Fax: (616) 957-0616
E-mail: kfurtado@wegefoundation.org
Web Site: www.wegefoundation.org

FOUNDED: 1968

AREAS OF INTEREST:
Education, environment, health care, human services and the arts in west Michigan.

TYPE:
Capital grants; Endowments; General operating grants; Project/program grants.

YEAR PROGRAM STARTED: 1968

PURPOSE:
To assist programs and projects in the areas of education, environment, health care, arts and culture, and human services.

ELIGIBILITY:
Grants are made to tax-exempt, nonprofit organizations which meet the Foundation's current program priorities and are located in the west Michigan area.

GEOG. RESTRICTIONS: Grand Rapids, Kent County and west Michigan.

FINANCIAL DATA:
Amount of support per award: $500 to $40,000.
Total amount of support: Approximately $20,000,000 annually.

NO. MOST RECENT APPLICANTS: 316 for the year 2019.

NO. AWARDS: 269 for the year 2019.

APPLICATION INFO:
Applications must be submitted through the Foundation's web site.
Duration: One year. Renewal possible.
Deadline: Proposals are accepted twice per year for Spring and Fall grant review.

BOARD OF DIRECTORS AND TRUSTEES:
Jonathan Wege, Chairman
Mark Van Putten, President and Chief Executive Officer
Dale Reitberg, Secretary
Christopher Carter
Mary Goodwillie Nelson
Johanna Osman
Caitlin Wege
Christopher Wege
Diana Wege
Laura Wege

THE HARRY AND JEANETTE WEINBERG FOUNDATION, INC. [1282]

7 Park Center Court
Owings Mills, MD 21117
(410) 654-8500
Fax: (410) 654-3943
Web Site: www.hjweinbergfoundation.org

FOUNDED: 1959

AREAS OF INTEREST:
Housing, health, jobs, education, and community services.

TYPE:
Capital grants; Challenge/matching grants; General operating grants; Matching gifts; Project/program grants.

ELIGIBILITY:
Grants are made to nonprofit 501(c)(3) organizations that provide direct services to low-income and vulnerable individuals and families, primarily in the U.S. and Israel. Grants are focused on meeting basic needs and enhancing an individual's ability to meet those needs with emphasis on older adults,

the Jewish community and the hometown communities of Maryland, northeastern Pennsylvania and Hawaii.

Religious organizations are eligible to apply.

The Foundation does not give grants to individuals.

FINANCIAL DATA:
Amount of support per award: Varies.
Total amount of support: Varies.

APPLICATION INFO:
Applicants must first determine eligibility by completing the online questionnaire.
Deadline: Grant requests are accepted throughout the year.

THOMAS H. WHITE FOUNDATION [1283]

1422 Euclid Avenue, Suite 966
Cleveland, OH 44115-1952
(216) 696-7273
Fax: (216) 621-8198
E-mail: sclancy@fmscleveland.com
Web Site: thomaswhitefoundation.org

FOUNDED: 1913

AREAS OF INTEREST:
Early childhood education, middle school to high school education, high school to higher education, and human services.

TYPE:
Project/program grants. The Foundation will focus its grantmaking in two major areas: Education and Human Services. Specifically, the Foundation is interested in supporting programs that address four critical areas: (1) Workforce readiness: programs that emphasize science and technology education, adequate employment preparation, support systems and the relationship to earning potential; (2) School retention: programs that emphasize the critical transition issues that occur during early teenage years and affect family relationships and school attendance; (3) Early childhood enrichment: programs which enhance the learning environment; provide support, training and ancillary services to parents; and/or enhance the recruitment and training of day care providers and; (4) Programs that support education in science, technology, engineering and math.

Organizations and programs that contribute generally to the quality of life in Greater Cleveland may also be considered at the Foundation's discretion.

YEAR PROGRAM STARTED: 1913

PURPOSE:
To improve educational resources and support charitable purposes in the city of Cleveland, OH.

LEGAL BASIS:
Private foundation.

ELIGIBILITY:
Grants awarded to tax-exempt, nonprofit charitable and educational institutions located within Cuyahoga County, OH, if such organizations, and their services and facilities, primarily serve residents of the city of Cleveland.

Applicants are discouraged from submitting requests for endowment, general operating support, research, symposia or seminars. No grants are awarded to individuals. The

Foundation does not respond to general solicitations or annual fund-raising campaigns.

GEOG. RESTRICTIONS: Cuyahoga County, Ohio; primarily the city of Cleveland.

FINANCIAL DATA:
Amount of support per award: $1,000 to $100,000.
Total amount of support: Approximately $1,000,000 annually.
Matching fund requirements: Stipulated with individual programs.

APPLICATION INFO:
Application forms and guidelines are available on the Foundation web site.
Deadline: December 1, April 1 and August 1, for meetings held in March, June and September, respectively.

ADDRESS INQUIRIES TO:
Sherri Clancy, Consultant
(See address above.)

*SPECIAL STIPULATIONS:
Local giving only.

WICHITA COMMUNITY FOUNDATION [1284]

301 North Main Street
Suite 100
Wichita, KS 67202
(316) 264-4880
Fax: (316) 264-7592
E-mail: wcf@wichitacf.org
Web Site: www.wichitacf.org

FOUNDED: 1986

AREAS OF INTEREST:
Arts, conservation, education, environmental health, humanities and social services.

TYPE:
Project/program grants; Scholarships; Seed money grants.

PURPOSE:
To provide a permanent resource for building community philanthropy.

LEGAL BASIS:
Community foundation.

ELIGIBILITY:
Grants are made to organizations that have tax-exempt status under Section 501(c)(3) of the Internal Revenue Code. No grants are made to individuals.

GEOG. RESTRICTIONS: Sedgwick County, Kansas.

FINANCIAL DATA:
Amount of support per award: $10,000 to $100,000.
Total amount of support: Approximately $5,500,000 for the year 2019.

APPLICATION INFO:
Grant application information is available on the web site. High school students may apply for scholarships online.
Duration: Typically one year.
Deadline: Grant applications are accepted throughout the year; deadlines vary. Scholarship applications: March 15.

ADDRESS INQUIRIES TO:
James Woods
Director of Donor Services
(See address above.)

THE WINSTON-SALEM FOUNDATION [1285]

751 West Fourth Street
Suite 200
Winston-Salem, NC 27101-2702
(336) 725-2382
Fax: (336) 727-0581
E-mail: info@wsfoundation.org
Web Site: www.wsfoundation.org

FOUNDED: 1919

AREAS OF INTEREST:
Human services, education, arts, culture, health, environment, animal welfare, community and economic development, public interest, and recreation.

NAME(S) OF PROGRAMS:
- **Black Philanthropy Initiative Grants**
- **Community Grants**
- **Elkin/Tri-County Grants**
- **Student Aid Scholarships**
- **Teacher Grants**
- **Women's Fund of Winston-Salem Grants**
- **Youth Grantmakers in Action**

TYPE:
Development grants; Endowments; Project/program grants; Scholarships; Seed money grants; Training grants. Capacity-building grants; Capital campaign grants. Discretionary grants given to organizations providing benefit to citizens within the greater Forsyth County, NC area, subject to limitations on program areas expressed by the donor of the source fund. Student scholarships primarily for Forsyth County residents.

YEAR PROGRAM STARTED: 1919

PURPOSE:
To help agencies initiate, innovate and experiment, as well as to provide other types of support as appropriate.

LEGAL BASIS:
Community foundation.

ELIGIBILITY:
Applicants must be charitable organizations and publicly supported charities. No grants are made to individuals.

GEOG. RESTRICTIONS: Forsyth County, North Carolina and contiguous counties.

FINANCIAL DATA:
Amount of support per award: $300 to $100,000.
Total amount of support: $1,900,000 in grants for the year 2018.

NO. MOST RECENT APPLICANTS: Approximately 150.

NO. AWARDS: Approximately 95.

APPLICATION INFO:
Community Grant information is available on the web site.
Duration: Generally, grants are for one year.

PUBLICATIONS:
Annual report; guidelines for donors and grantseekers; newsletters.

IRS I.D.: 56-6037615

STAFF:
Scott F. Wierman, President
Lisa Purcell, Executive Vice President

ADDRESS INQUIRIES TO:
Madelyn McCaully, Grants Manager
(See address above.)

WOODS CHARITABLE FUND, INC. [1286]

1248 O Street, Suite 1130
Lincoln, NE 68508
(402) 436-5971
E-mail: twoods@woodscharitable.org
Web Site: www.woodscharitable.org

FOUNDED: 1941

AREAS OF INTEREST:
Children, youth and families, education, community development and housing, arts and humanities.

TYPE:
Challenge/matching grants; Demonstration grants; General operating grants; Project/program grants; Seed money grants; Technical assistance. Grants to support organizations and projects located in and directly serving the residents of Lincoln, NE.

YEAR PROGRAM STARTED: 1941

PURPOSE:
To strengthen the community by improving opportunities and life outcomes for all people in Lincoln, NE.

LEGAL BASIS:
Private foundation.

ELIGIBILITY:
Grants are made only to tax-exempt organizations described in Section 501(c)(3) of the IRS Code and which have a written ruling from the IRS that they also qualify under 509(a)(1), (2) or (3) of the Code (publicly supported organizations and their affiliates).

Geographically, grants are limited to organizations in Lincoln. Occasionally, the Fund reviews proposals from outside the city if the proposed activities have statewide impact and a significant Lincoln component. While the Fund makes grants in very diverse fields, fund-raising benefits or program advertising, individual needs, endowments, scholarships or fellowships are not eligible for grant review.

GEOG. RESTRICTIONS: Lincoln, Nebraska.

FINANCIAL DATA:
Amount of support per award: Average payment: $28,710 for the year 2019.
Total amount of support: $1,529,200 in grants paid for the year 2019.

NO. MOST RECENT APPLICANTS: Approximately 180.

NO. AWARDS: 53.

REPRESENTATIVE AWARDS:
$55,000 to Released and Restored, Inc. toward reducing recidivism rates in Nebraska by preparing individuals for release from incarceration by providing inmates with tools and support systems needed for learning how to live moral, ethical, productive and legal lives upon return to their communities; $75,000 to City of Lincoln Policy Department toward human trafficking prevention and deterrence efforts; $40,000 to Lincoln Lancaster County Habitat for Humanity, Inc., to enhance programs educating and assisting low-income homeowners on repair, maintenance and rehabilitation of their properties in order to foster homeownership success.

APPLICATION INFO:
Guidelines are available on the Fund web site. Before submitting a full proposal, applicants should contact the Fund with a two-page summary request and budget or a phone call. If the request appears suitable, a full proposal will be requested.
Deadline: April 15 to 30 for November Board Meeting. October 15 to 31 for May Board Meeting. Proposals that arrive well before the deadline have a better chance for careful review.

IRS I.D.: 47-6032847

STAFF:
Tom Woods, President and Secretary
Nicole Juranek, Community Investment Director
Kathy Steinauer Smith, Community Investment Director
Joan Stolle, Operations Manager

DIRECTORS:
Nelle Woods Jamison, Chairperson
Candice Howell, Vice Chairperson
Hank Woods, Treasurer
Michael J. Tavlin, Assistant Treasurer
Pablo Cervantes
Jay Conrad
Michelle Suarez
Ed Wimes

ADDRESS INQUIRIES TO:
Tom Woods, President
(See address above.)

WOODS FUND CHICAGO [1287]

35 East Wacker Drive
Suite 1760
Chicago, IL 60601
(312) 782-2698
Fax: (312) 782-4155
E-mail: dclark@woodsfund.org
Web Site: www.woodsfund.org

FOUNDED: 1941

AREAS OF INTEREST:
Racial equity, economic justice, public policy advocacy, and integration of community organizing.

TYPE:
General operating grants; Project/program grants.

PURPOSE:
To advance racial equity and economic justice.

LEGAL BASIS:
Nonprofit.

ELIGIBILITY:
The Woods Fund will support organizations that:
(1) have an explicit racial equity and economic justice focus. The organization's commitment to racial equity and economic justice should be present in their mission, vision, and/or values;
(2) prioritize and engage people most impacted by structural racism and economic injustice to lead the process of defining problems and developing solutions;
(3) have the majority of people of color in their leadership, including senior staff and board membership and;
(4) lead with community organizing and/or public policy advocacy as the strategies for change.

GEOG. RESTRICTIONS: Metropolitan Chicago, Illinois.

FINANCIAL DATA:
Amount of support per award: Funding amounts depend on the size, capacity and demonstrated efficacy of the organization. Typically grants are $15,000 to $55,000. New applicants generally receive $15,000 to $25,000 annually for the initial year(s) of funding.
Total amount of support: Typically $2,300,000 in grants annually.

APPLICATION INFO:
Instructions are available at the Fund web site.
Duration: One to two years.

*PLEASE NOTE:
Contact program officer prior to applying for grant.

WYOMING ARTS COUNCIL

2301 Central Avenue
Barrett Building, 2nd Floor
Cheyenne, WY 82002
(307) 214-7819
E-mail: karen.merklin@wyo.gov
Web Site: wyoarts.state.wy.us

TYPE:
Awards/prizes; Conferences/seminars; Development grants; Fellowships; General operating grants; Project/program grants; Technical assistance. Individual fellowships are provided in visual, literary and performing arts to Wyoming residents.

Folk & Traditional Arts Mentoring Project Grants are designed to support the transmission of Wyoming's finest folk and traditional skills through the natural process of in-person, hands-on instruction from a master artist to a worthy apprentice.

Pattie Layser Fellowship is a national call open to writers and journalists and seeks to intersect science, education, current events, and conservation to effectively communicate the Greater Yellowstone's natural history and singular importance to society through creative and exceptional writing and subject communication.

See entry 486 for full listing.

Crime prevention

INTERNATIONAL CENTRE FOR COMPARATIVE CRIMINOLOGY [1288]

University of Montreal
C.P. 6128, Succursale Centre-Ville
Montreal QC H3C 3J7 Canada
(514) 343-7065
Fax: (514) 343-2269
E-mail: cicc@umontreal.ca
Web Site: www.cicc-iccc.org

FOUNDED: 1969

AREAS OF INTEREST:
Sociology of crime and deviance, comparative studies on criminal justice, police, courts, prisons, victims, national and international research, terrorism and counterterrorism.

CONSULTING OR VOLUNTEER SERVICES:
In all the fields of criminal justice.

NAME(S) OF PROGRAMS:
● **Research Fieldwork**

TYPE:
Conferences/seminars; Exchange programs; Fellowships. The Centre brings visiting professors and specialists to confer on

projects and cooperate on research investigation and invites graduate and postgraduate students to do fieldwork at the Centre.

YEAR PROGRAM STARTED: 1969

PURPOSE:
To provide funding to encourage continued study in the field of crime and criminal justice.

LEGAL BASIS:
University.

ELIGIBILITY:
Applicant must:
(1) hold a Ph.D. degree before starting the postdoctoral research and for no more than three years prior to the proposed starting date of the fellowship;
(2) be supervised by a regular researcher from the CICC. The researcher must formally agree to supervise the candidate in the postdoctoral research and will guarantee the feasibility of the project;
(3) have completed university studies in a field relevant or related to criminology: anthropology, forensics, law, history, psychiatry, psycho-education, psychology, political science, sociology, applied social sciences statistics, and social work are the principal related fields and;
(4) master French or English. Applicant must be able to write scientific papers, either in French or English.

Priority will be given to candidates who are co-supervised.

FINANCIAL DATA:
Amount of support per award: Postdoctoral Fellowships: $33,485 (CAN) for the year 2019.

NO. MOST RECENT APPLICANTS: 6.

NO. AWARDS: Postdoctoral Fellowships: 1 or 2 per year.

APPLICATION INFO:
Detailed instructions are available on the Centre's web site.
Duration: One year, January to December.
Deadline: July 15.

PUBLICATIONS:
Annual report; Revue *Criminologie.*

OFFICERS:
M. Remi Boivin, Director

ADDRESS INQUIRIES TO:
See e-mail address above.

NATIONAL INSTITUTE OF JUSTICE, U.S. DEPARTMENT OF JUSTICE [1289]
810 Seventh Street, N.W.
Washington, DC 20531
(202) 307-2942
Web Site: www.nij.gov

FOUNDED: 1968

AREAS OF INTEREST:
Criminal justice research and evaluation, program development, dissemination of research-based criminal justice, and fellowships.

NAME(S) OF PROGRAMS:
● **Research Grants**

TYPE:
Research grants. Grants and contracts related to topics in criminal justice and social science, physical science, and forensic science, including those for evaluative research; research and development grants and contracts in science and technology for criminal justice applications.

The focus of NIJ research is on generating information that is useful to state and local public officials in developing policies related to crime reduction.

YEAR PROGRAM STARTED: 1968

PURPOSE:
To increase knowledge of the causes, prevention, and control of crime, the effectiveness and efficiency of the criminal justice system, and the responsiveness of the nation's law enforcement and justice administration systems; to disseminate this knowledge to the federal, state, and local policymakers.

LEGAL BASIS:
Omnibus Crime Control and Safe Streets Act of 1968; Homeland Security Act of 2002.

ELIGIBILITY:
NIJ awards grants to or enters into cooperative agreements with educational institutions, nonprofit organizations, public agencies, individuals, and profit-making organizations that are willing to waive their fees. Special eligibility criteria are indicated in NIJ's solicitations for proposals.

GEOG. RESTRICTIONS: United States.

FINANCIAL DATA:
All NIJ awards must be used to supplement existing funds, not to replace those already appropriated for the same purpose.
Amount of support per award: $10,000 to $500,000.
Total amount of support: Approximately $250,000,000 annually.
Matching fund requirements: Units of state and local governments are encouraged to contribute matching funds and other applicants are encouraged to seek matching contributions from government agencies or private organizations.

NO. AWARDS: Approximately 400.

APPLICATION INFO:
Guidelines, applications, and information about specific solicitations for proposals are available on the web site.
Duration: Normally two years maximum. Renewal possible.
Deadline: Varies.

ADDRESS INQUIRIES TO:
National Criminal Justice Reference Service
P.O. Box 6000
Rockville, MD 20849-6000
Tel: (800) 851-3420

U.S. DEPARTMENT OF JUSTICE [1290]
Bureau of Justice Statistics
810 7th Street, N.W.
Washington, DC 20531
(202) 307-0765
E-mail: askbjs@usdoj.gov
Web Site: www.bjs.gov

FOUNDED: 1969

AREAS OF INTEREST:
Statistics on crime, victims of crime, criminal offenders and operations of justice systems at all levels of government throughout the U.S.

NAME(S) OF PROGRAMS:
● **State Justice Statistics for Statistical Analysis Centers**

TYPE:
Development grants; Research grants. Cooperative agreements for the development of statistical methods and techniques and the aggregation and analysis of statistical information on crime and criminal justice in the states.

YEAR PROGRAM STARTED: 1972

PURPOSE:
To develop and enhance the capabilities of the states in gathering, analyzing and using statistical information pertaining to crime and the criminal justice system and to obtain selected types of data for multistate aggregation.

LEGAL BASIS:
Government agency formed under the Justice System Improvement Act of 1979.

ELIGIBILITY:
Applicants must be state agencies whose activities include statistical analysis at the state level.

FINANCIAL DATA:
Amount of support per award: $75,000 to $210,000.
Total amount of support: Varies.

NO. MOST RECENT APPLICANTS: Approximately 39 for the year 2018.

APPLICATION INFO:
Applicants must register in the OJP Grants Management System prior to submitting an application.
Duration: 12 to 36 months.
Deadline: March 29.

ADDRESS INQUIRIES TO:
Devon Adams, Chief, Criminal Justice Data Improvement Program
(See address above.)

U.S. DEPARTMENT OF JUSTICE [1291]
Office of Juvenile Justice and Delinquency Prevention
810 Seventh Street, N.W., 7th Floor
Washington, DC 20531
(202) 307-5911
Fax: (202) 353-9093
E-mail: lynnell.clarke@usdoj.gov
Web Site: www.ojjdp.gov

FOUNDED: 1975

AREAS OF INTEREST:
Delinquency prevention research, juvenile gangs, serious violent juvenile offenders and juvenile justice statistics.

NAME(S) OF PROGRAMS:
● **Juvenile Justice and Delinquency Prevention Program**

TYPE:
Conferences/seminars; Development grants; Fellowships; Internships; Project/program grants; Research grants; Residencies; Visiting scholars; Research contracts. Grants to conduct research, evaluation and development on juvenile justice and delinquency prevention activities, including the development of new or improved approaches, techniques, systems and program models to conduct behavioral research on the causes of juvenile crime, means of, intervention and prevention, and to evaluate juvenile programs and procedures.

YEAR PROGRAM STARTED: 1975

PURPOSE:
To encourage, coordinate and conduct research and evaluation of juvenile justice and delinquency prevention activities; to provide a clearinghouse and information center for collecting, publishing and distributing information on juvenile delinquency; to conduct a national training program; to establish standards for the administration on juvenile justice. Current emphasis is work in the area of serious and violent juvenile crime, drug involvement by youth and missing children.

LEGAL BASIS:
Juvenile Justice Reform Act of 2018, Public Law 115-385, as amended.

ELIGIBILITY:
Public or private agencies, organizations, including institutions of higher learning, or individuals.

GEOG. RESTRICTIONS: United States and its territories.

FINANCIAL DATA:
Amount of support per award: Varies.
Total amount of support: Varies.

NO. MOST RECENT APPLICANTS: 100.

NO. AWARDS: 80.

REPRESENTATIVE AWARDS:
Law Enforcement Agencies Policies Regarding Missing Children; School Crime and Discipline Research and Discipline; Causes and Correlates of Delinquency.

APPLICATION INFO:
Contact the U.S. Department of Justice.
Duration: Generally one to three years.
Deadline: Varies.

PUBLICATIONS:
Annual report; annual program plan; various project reports.

ADDRESS INQUIRIES TO:
Juvenile Justice Clearinghouse
National Criminal Justice
Reference Service
P.O. Box 6000
Rockville, MD 20849-6000
Tel: (800) 851-3420
Fax: (301) 240-5830

U.S. DEPARTMENT OF JUSTICE [1292]

Office of Juvenile Justice and
Delinquency Prevention
810 Seventh Street, N.W., 7th Floor
Washington, DC 20531
(202) 307-5911
Fax: (202) 353-9093
E-mail: lynnell.clarke@usdoj.gov
Web Site: www.ojjdp.gov

AREAS OF INTEREST:
Juvenile justice, delinquency prevention and child protection.

NAME(S) OF PROGRAMS:
● **Juvenile Justice and Delinquency Prevention Allocation to States**

TYPE:
Block grants; Challenge/matching grants; Demonstration grants; Formula grants; Internships; Project/program grants; Research grants; Technical assistance; Training grants. Grants to increase the capacity of state and local governments to conduct effective juvenile justice and delinquency prevention programs as developed in the state comprehensive action plan.

YEAR PROGRAM STARTED: 1974

LEGAL BASIS:
Juvenile Justice Reform Act of 2018, Public Law 115-385, as amended.

ELIGIBILITY:
To receive an award, states must, each year, satisfy 28 state plan requirements. If a state does not meet these requirements, it is not eligible to receive its Formula Grants program allocation for that year.

GEOG. RESTRICTIONS: United States and its territories.

FINANCIAL DATA:
Amount of support per award: Varies.
Total amount of support: Varies.
Matching fund requirements: Formula is based upon population of people under age 18. No match is required except for construction programs, where the match is 50%. Seven and one half percent administrative funds are matched 100%.

NO. MOST RECENT APPLICANTS: 60.

NO. AWARDS: 60.

APPLICATION INFO:
Contact the U.S. Department of Justice.
Duration: One to three years from the fiscal year of awards.
Deadline: Varies.

ADDRESS INQUIRIES TO:
Juvenile Justice Clearinghouse
National Criminal Justice
Reference Service
P.O. Box 6000
Rockville, MD 20849-6000
Tel: (800) 851-3420
Fax: (301) 240-5830

Public health

AAA FOUNDATION FOR TRAFFIC SAFETY [1293]

607 14th Street, N.W.
Suite 201
Washington, DC 20005
(202) 639-3401
E-mail: info@aaafoundation.org
Web Site: www.aaafoundation.org

FOUNDED: 1947

AREAS OF INTEREST:
Traffic safety.

TYPE:
Demonstration grants; Project/program grants; Research grants; Research contracts.

YEAR PROGRAM STARTED: 1947

PURPOSE:
To save lives and reduce injuries by preventing traffic crashes; to reduce injuries when crashes do occur.

LEGAL BASIS:
Publicly supported not-for-profit 501(c)(3).

ELIGIBILITY:
Foundation grants to organizations only.

The Foundation does not fund research to develop new devices, grants for community action initiatives or other purely local traffic safety programs, or projects outside the field of traffic safety.

GEOG. RESTRICTIONS: Primarily United States and Canada.

FINANCIAL DATA:
Amount of support per award: $5,000 to $1,000,000.
Total amount of support: Approximately $5,000,000.
Matching fund requirements: Encourage co-funding, but not required.

NO. MOST RECENT APPLICANTS: 125.

NO. AWARDS: 12.

APPLICATION INFO:
Contact the Foundation for application procedures.
Duration: Six months to five years.
Deadline: May 15.

PUBLICATIONS:
Annual report.

IRS I.D.: 52-0794368

ADDRESS INQUIRIES TO:
Joanne But, Program Coordinator
(See address above.)

AGENCY FOR HEALTHCARE RESEARCH AND QUALITY (AHRQ) [1294]

Office of Management Services
Division of Grants Management
5600 Fishers Lane, 7th Floor
Rockville, MD 20857
(301) 427-1104 (specify funding area)
(301) 427-1450
E-mail: gmi@ahrq.hhs.gov
Web Site: www.ahrq.gov

FOUNDED: 1968

AREAS OF INTEREST:
AHRQ is the primary source of federal support for research on problems related to the quality and delivery of health services.

NAME(S) OF PROGRAMS:
● **AHRQ Research Grants**

TYPE:
Conferences/seminars; Development grants; Fellowships; Project/program grants; Research grants; Training grants. Dissertation support highlighting primary care, market forces, cost containment, managed care, the cost of treating AIDS, the improvement of treatment for persons with HIV, rural health care, infant mortality, medical liability, malpractice reform, health care of the aged and disabled and policy studies.

YEAR PROGRAM STARTED: 1969

PURPOSE:
To support research to improve the quality, effectiveness, accessibility and cost effectiveness of health care.

LEGAL BASIS:
AHCPR Research Grants: Section 304, 5, 7, 8, of the Public Health Service Act.

ELIGIBILITY:
Any academic institution, agency of a state or local government, nonprofit organization or individual is eligible to submit grant proposals under this program. For-profit entities are not eligible.

FINANCIAL DATA:

Amount of support per award: Varies according to the project type and nature of the individual research proposal.

Total amount of support: Varies.

APPLICATION INFO:

Contact the Agency.

Duration: One to five years.

Deadline: Varies.

STAFF:

Kishena Wadhwani, Director, Division of Scientific Review

ADDRESS INQUIRIES TO:

Office of Management Services
Division of Grants Management
(See address above.)

THE AMERICAN FOUNDATION FOR SUICIDE PREVENTION

199 Water Street
11th Floor
New York, NY 10038
(212) 363-3500 ext. 2015
Fax: (212) 363-6237
E-mail: grantsmanager@afsp.org
Web Site: afsp.org/research-grant-information

TYPE:

Research grants.

See entry 1382 for full listing.

THE AMERICAN FOUNDATION FOR SUICIDE PREVENTION

199 Water Street
11th Floor
New York, NY 10038
(212) 363-3500 ext. 2015
Fax: (212) 363-6237
E-mail: grantsmanager@afsp.org
Web Site: afsp.org/research-grant-information

TYPE:

Fellowships; Research grants; Training grants.

See entry 1383 for full listing.

THE AMERICAN FOUNDATION FOR SUICIDE PREVENTION

199 Water Street
11th Floor
New York, NY 10038
(212) 363-3500 ext. 2015
Fax: (212) 363-6237
E-mail: grantsmanager@afsp.org
Web Site: afsp.org/research-grant-information

TYPE:

Research grants.

See entry 1384 for full listing.

THE AMERICAN FOUNDATION FOR SUICIDE PREVENTION

199 Water Street
11th Floor
New York, NY 10038
(212) 363-3500 ext. 2015
Fax: (212) 363-6237
E-mail: grantsmanager@afsp.org
Web Site: afsp.org/research-grant-information

TYPE:

Research grants. Standard Research Grants are awarded to individual investigators. An additional annual stipend is available for

mentors on Young Investigator Awards in which the investigator is at the level of Assistant Professor or lower.

See entry 1385 for full listing.

AMERICAN MEDICAL WOMEN'S ASSOCIATION, INC.

1100 East Woodfield Road
Suite 350
Schaumburg, IL 60173
(847) 517-2801
Fax: (847) 517-7229
E-mail: associatedirector@amwa-doc.org
Web Site: www.amwa-doc.org

TYPE:

Awards/prizes; Conferences/seminars; General operating grants; Project/program grants; Training grants; Travel grants. Support for clinics serving the poor in medically underserved areas, scholarships and loans to qualifying women medical students, and continuing medical education for physicians in areas related to women's health.

See entry 2029 for full listing.

AMERICAN PSYCHOLOGICAL ASSOCIATION

Government Relations Office
Public Interest Directorate
750 First Street, N.E.
Washington, DC 20002-4242
(202) 336-5931
Fax: (202) 336-6063
E-mail: gtwose@apa.org
Web Site: www.apa.org/about/gr/fellows/index.aspx

TYPE:

Fellowships. Program provides trained scientists and practitioners an opportunity for enhanced understanding of and involvement in the federal policymaking process by serving as congressional staff in Washington, DC.

See entry 2356 for full listing.

ARCHSTONE FOUNDATION   [1295]

301 East Ocean Boulevard
Suite 1850
Long Beach, CA 90802
(562) 590-8655
Fax: (562) 495-0317
E-mail: archstone@archstone.org
Web Site: www.archstone.org

FOUNDED: 1985

AREAS OF INTEREST:

Aging in community, depression in late life, and family caregiving.

TYPE:

Challenge/matching grants; Conferences/seminars; Demonstration grants; Development grants; Project/program grants; Technical assistance; Training grants.

YEAR PROGRAM STARTED: 1985

PURPOSE:

To contribute toward the preparation of society in meeting the needs of an aging population.

ELIGIBILITY:

501(c)(3) organizations. Individuals may not apply. No funding available for capital expenditures, fund-raisers or research.

GEOG. RESTRICTIONS: Southern California.

FINANCIAL DATA:

Limited indirect costs to 10%.

Amount of support per award: Varies.

Total amount of support: $1,778,903 in grants payable for the year ended June 30, 2018.

NO. AWARDS: 51 during fiscal years 2018 and 2019.

APPLICATION INFO:

Application forms and reporting guidelines are available on the Foundation's web site.

Duration: One year. May be renewed for up to three years.

IRS I.D.: 33-0133359

BOARD OF DIRECTORS:

Diana M. Bonta, Chairperson
Cynthia D. Banks
Hon. Lynn Daucher
Christopher A. Langston, Ph.D.
Amye L. Leong, MBA
Theresa J. Marino
Hon. Renee B. Simon, M.S., M.L.S.
Rocky Suares, C.F.P.
Peter C. Szutu, M.P.H.
Heather M. Young, Ph.D., R.N.

ADDRESS INQUIRIES TO:

Tanisha Davis, Grants Manager
(See address above.)

MAX BELL FOUNDATION   [1296]

105 12 Avenue, S.E.
Suite 970
Calgary AB T2G 1A1 Canada
(403) 215-7310
E-mail: amccarry@maxbell.org
Web Site: www.maxbell.org

FOUNDED: 1972

AREAS OF INTEREST:

Health and wellness, education and the environment.

TYPE:

Challenge/matching grants; Development grants; Internships; Project/program grants.

YEAR PROGRAM STARTED: 1972

PURPOSE:

To develop innovative ideas that impact public policies and practices.

LEGAL BASIS:

Private foundation.

ELIGIBILITY:

Organizations must have a registered Canadian charitable number issued by Revenue Canada. Grants are not made for conferences and workshops, scholarships, individuals, sabbaticals, equipment purchases, capital campaigns, fund-raising drives or annual charitable appeals.

GEOG. RESTRICTIONS: Canada.

FINANCIAL DATA:

Amount of support per award: Varies.

Total amount of support: Approximately $1,800,000 (CAN).

Matching fund requirements: Varies.

APPLICATION INFO:

All applications must be submitted online.

Duration: Development grants: Typically four months. Project/program grants: One to three years. Nonrenewable.

STAFF:

Allan Northcott, President

Arlene McCarry, Administrator
Margaret Herriman, Program Officer
Dr. David Elton, Special Advisor

BOARD OF DIRECTORS:
Brenda Eaton, Chairman
Ken Marra, Vice Chairman
Dr. Paul Boothe
Provost Christopher Manfredi
Margaret-Jean Mannix
Donna Miller
Doug Moen

ADDRESS INQUIRIES TO:
Margaret Herriman, Program Officer
(See address above.)

BRIGHAM AND WOMEN'S HOSPITAL [1297]

75 Francis Street
Boston, MA 02115
(617) 732-5500
Fax: (617) 582-6112
E-mail: bwhdeland@partners.org
Web Site: www.brighamandwomens.org

AREAS OF INTEREST:
Health care.

NAME(S) OF PROGRAMS:
● **Deland Fellowship Program in Health Care and Society**

TYPE:
Fellowships.

YEAR PROGRAM STARTED: 1988

PURPOSE:
To train outstanding future leaders in health care.

ELIGIBILITY:
It is anticipated that candidates will come from a variety of careers and educational backgrounds including business, law, economics, public policy, medicine and nursing. Candidates are required to have an advanced degree from a U.S. accredited institution.

NO. AWARDS: 2 annually.

APPLICATION INFO:
Brigham and Women's Hospital is using the National Council on Administrative Fellowship's centralized application system. Candidates can apply at nafcas.liaisoncas.com. If there is a reason that the potential candidate cannot apply through NAFCAS, please contact the program director for consideration of a direct application.
Duration: One year.
Deadline: First Monday in October. Notification in November.

ADDRESS INQUIRIES TO:
Director, Deland Fellowship Program
(See e-mail address above.)

BRIGHT FOCUS FOUNDATION [1298]

22512 Gateway Center Drive
Clarksburg, MD 20871
(301) 948-3244
(800) 437-2423
Fax: (301) 948-4403
E-mail: researchgrants@brightfocus.org
Web Site: www.brightfocus.org

FOUNDED: 1997

AREAS OF INTEREST:
Macular degeneration.

NAME(S) OF PROGRAMS:
● **Macular Degeneration Research Program**

TYPE:
Research grants.

YEAR PROGRAM STARTED: 1998

PURPOSE:
To fund research on and educate the public about macular degeneration.

LEGAL BASIS:
501(c)(3) nonprofit charitable organization.

ELIGIBILITY:
Grants are awarded on the basis of the proposal's scientific merit and its relevance to understanding the diseases studied. No funds for large equipment, institutional overhead cost, construction or building expenses.

The Foundation is particularly interested in receiving letters from new investigators and from established investigators seeking to explore new directions in macular degeneration research.

FINANCIAL DATA:
Amount of support per award: Innovative Research Grant: Up to $600,000; New Investigator Grant: Up to $450,000; Postdoctoral Fellowship: Up to $200,000.
Total amount of support: Varies.

NO. AWARDS: 20 for the year 2019.

APPLICATION INFO:
Must send initial letter of intent. Subsequent proposal by invitation.
Duration: Innovative Research Grant and New Investigator Grant: Up to three years; Postdoctoral Fellowship: Up to two years.
Deadline: Letter of Intent: July 29.

PUBLICATIONS:
Annual report; newsletters; clinical brochures.

ADDRESS INQUIRIES TO:
See e-mail address above.

THE CALIFORNIA ENDOWMENT [1299]

1000 North Alameda Street
Los Angeles, CA 90012
(213) 928-8645
(800) 449-4149
Fax: (213) 928-8871
E-mail: destrada@calendow.org
Web Site: www.calendow.org

FOUNDED: 1996

AREAS OF INTEREST:
Health care access, disparities in health, public health, multicultural health, health and well-being, cultural competency and work force diversity.

NAME(S) OF PROGRAMS:
● **Building Healthy Communities Initiative**

TYPE:
Challenge/matching grants; General operating grants; Matching gifts; Project/program grants.

YEAR PROGRAM STARTED: 1998

PURPOSE:
To improve access to affordable, quality health care for underserved individuals and communities; to promote fundamental improvements in the health status of the people of California; to improve the health of Californians through community-based

programs, collaborations and partnerships that strengthen leadership, stimulate policy development and contribute to systems change.

ELIGIBILITY:
Grants are awarded to tax-exempt organizations only. No grants to individuals.

GEOG. RESTRICTIONS: California.

FINANCIAL DATA:
Amount of support per award: Varies.

APPLICATION INFO:
Applications by invitation only.

IRS I.D.: 95-4523232

CALIFORNIA HEALTHCARE FOUNDATION [1300]

1438 Webster Street
Suite 400
Oakland, CA 94612
(510) 238-1040
Fax: (510) 238-1388
E-mail: info@chcf.org
Web Site: www.chcf.org

FOUNDED: 1996

AREAS OF INTEREST:
Advancing meaningful, measurable improvements in the way the health care delivery system provides care to the people of California.

NAME(S) OF PROGRAMS:
● **Health Innovation Fund**
● **HighValue Care**
● **Improving Access**
● **Informing Decision-Makers**

TYPE:
Project/program grants.

PURPOSE:
To commission research and analysis; to publish and disseminate information; to convene stakeholders and fund development of programs and models aimed at improving the health care delivery and financing systems.

GEOG. RESTRICTIONS: California.

FINANCIAL DATA:
Amount of support per award: Varies.
Total amount of support: Varies.

APPLICATION INFO:
Letters of inquiry are preferred for unsolicited projects with description, timeline and estimated budget.
Duration: Varies.

ADDRESS INQUIRIES TO:
Lisa Kang
Director, Grants Administration
(See address above.)

THE CALIFORNIA WELLNESS FOUNDATION [1301]

City National Plaza, Suite 1100
515 South Flower Street
Los Angeles, CA 90071
(818) 702-1900
Fax: (818) 702-1999
E-mail: grants@calwellness.org
info@calwellness.org
Web Site: www.calwellness.org

FOUNDED: 1991

AREAS OF INTEREST:
Access and quality health care, healthy and safe neighborhoods, and education and employment.

NAME(S) OF PROGRAMS:
- **Advancing Wellness Grants Program**

TYPE:
Conferences/seminars; Demonstration grants; General operating grants; Project/program grants; Seed money grants.

YEAR PROGRAM STARTED: 1992

PURPOSE:
To improve the health of the people of California by making grants for health promotion, wellness education and disease prevention.

LEGAL BASIS:
Private foundation.

ELIGIBILITY:
Applicants must be nonprofit organizations that are exempt under Section 501(c)(3) of the IRS and are defined as "not a private foundation" under Section 509(a)(1). The Foundation also funds government agencies.

The Foundation does not fund Section 509(a)(3) Type III non-functionally integrated supporting organizations and does not provide international funding or fund organizations located outside of the U.S. Grants are not made for annual fund drives, building campaigns, major equipment, biomedical research or to activities that exclusively benefit members of sectarian or religious organizations.

GEOG. RESTRICTIONS: California.

FINANCIAL DATA:
Amount of support per award: Varies depending on needs and nature of the request.

Total amount of support: Approximately $36,800,000 for the year 2017.

NO. AWARDS: 694 for the year 2018.

APPLICATION INFO:
Applicant must submit a Letter of Interest through Cal Wellness' Grants Portal. If asked to submit a full proposal, guidance will be provided about how to submit the proposal.

Duration: Varies.

PUBLICATIONS:
Annual report; brochure; quarterly newsletter.

IRS I.D.: 95-4292101

STAFF:
Margaret W. Minnich, Chief Financial Officer
Arun Baheti, Vice President of Operations
Fatima Angeles, Vice President of Programs
Amber Lopez Gamble, Acting Director of Grants Management
Crystal D. Crawford, Program Director
Alex M. Johnson, Program Director
Jeffrey S. Kim, Program Director
Earl Lui, Program Director

BOARD OF DIRECTORS:
Joseph M. Lumarda, MBA, Chairperson
Dr. Pamela J. Simms-Mackey, Treasurer
M. Isabel Becerra, Secretary
Xochitl Castaneda
Elizabeth Hallman, R.N.
Terence Mulligan
Debra Nakatomi
Arnold X.C. Perkins
Angelica Salas
Ernest J. Wilson, III
Geri Yang-Johnson

EXECUTIVE STAFF:
Judy Belk, President and Chief Executive Officer

ADDRESS INQUIRIES TO:
Amber Lopez Gamble
Acting Director of Grants Management
(See address above.)

CENTER FOR SCIENCE IN THE PUBLIC INTEREST
1220 L Street, N.W.
Suite 300
Washington, DC 20005
(202) 332-9110
Fax: (202) 265-4954
E-mail: hr@cspinet.org
Web Site: www.cspinet.org

TYPE:
Internships. These unpaid internships allow interns to work on specific projects under the direction of a Project Director or the Executive Director.

See entry 2455 for full listing.

CHICAGO BOARD OF TRADE FOUNDATION　　　　[1302]
141 West Jackson Boulevard
Suite 1404
Chicago, IL 60604
(312) 789-8225
Fax: (312) 604-6118
E-mail: cbotfoundation@hctech.com
Web Site: www.cbotfoundation.org

AREAS OF INTEREST:
Youth, education, seniors, wildlife, social and human services.

TYPE:
General operating grants; Project/program grants.

PURPOSE:
To assist children in need, seniors, people with disabilities, social and human services within the Chicago community.

ELIGIBILITY:
Organizations classified as 501(c)(3) by the IRS can apply. Individuals and religious organizations are ineligible. Must be nondiscriminatory in its practices and may not give funds to ancillary organizations.

GEOG. RESTRICTIONS: Greater Chicago, Illinois metropolitan area.

FINANCIAL DATA:
Amount of support per award: $1,000 to $20,000.

NO. MOST RECENT APPLICANTS: 50 for the year 2018.

NO. AWARDS: 30 for the year 2018.

APPLICATION INFO:
Applicant must submit a copy of proposal, 501(c)(3), (4) or (10) documentation, and a recent financial statement.

Duration: One year. Grants are renewable.

ADDRESS INQUIRIES TO:
Dawn Andersen
(See address above.)

THE COLORADO TRUST　　[1303]
1600 Sherman Street
Denver, CO 80203-1604
(303) 837-1200
Fax: (303) 839-9034
E-mail: gwyn@coloradotrust.org
Web Site: www.coloradotrust.org

FOUNDED: 1985

AREAS OF INTEREST:
Policies and information related to advancing health equity, as well as projects that address health equity in partnership with communities throughout Colorado.

NAME(S) OF PROGRAMS:
- **Community Partnerships**
- **Health Data and Information**
- **Health Equity Investments**
- **Health Equity Learning Series**
- **Health Policy and Advocacy**

TYPE:
General operating grants; Project/program grants; Research grants; Technical assistance.

YEAR PROGRAM STARTED: 1985

PURPOSE:
To advance the health and well-being of the people of Colorado.

LEGAL BASIS:
Private foundation.

ELIGIBILITY:
The following types of organizations are eligible to apply for Colorado Trust funding opportunities:
(1) nonprofit organizations that are exempt under Section 501(c)(3) of the Internal Revenue Code and are classified as "not a private foundation" under Section 509(a);
(2) independent, sponsored projects of a nonprofit 501(c)(3) organization acting as a fiscal sponsor and;
(3) government and public agencies.

GEOG. RESTRICTIONS: Colorado.

FINANCIAL DATA:
Amount of support per award: Varies.
Total amount of support: $18,400,000 in charitable expenditures for fiscal year 2018.

APPLICATION INFO:
Applications are accepted following the release of Requests for Proposals issued by The Colorado Trust. Application requirements are detailed specifically in Requests for Proposals.
Duration: Varies.

PUBLICATIONS:
Annual report; health equity stories; evaluation reports; program reports; *Advance*, newsletter.

IRS I.D.: 84-0994055

BOARD OF TRUSTEES:
Ned Calonge, M.D., President and Chief Executive Officer
Brenda J. Allen, Ph.D.
Wendy Dominguez
John P. Hopkins
Warren Johnson, M.D.
Donald Mares
Tim Schultz
Colleen Schwarz, MBA
Alan Synn, M.D.
Betty Velasquez
Rev. Louise Westfall

ADDRESS INQUIRIES TO:
Gwyn Barley, Vice President of Community Partnerships and Grants
(See address and e-mail above.)

THE CULLEN TRUST FOR HEALTH CARE　　[1304]
2727 Allen Parkway, Suite 1000
Houston, TX 77019
(713) 651-8837
E-mail: gina@cullenfdn.org
Web Site: www.cullentrust.org

FOUNDED: 1978

AREAS OF INTEREST:
Health care.

TYPE:
Capital grants; Development grants; Endowments; General operating grants; Project/program grants. Clinical-based research grants.

YEAR PROGRAM STARTED: 1978

PURPOSE:
To provide financial assistance and to benefit institutions providing health care.

LEGAL BASIS:
Charitable trust.

ELIGIBILITY:
Applicants must be tax-exempt 501(c)(3).

GEOG. RESTRICTIONS: Primarily Houston, Texas area.

FINANCIAL DATA:
Amount of support per award: Average $50,000.
Total amount of support: Varies.

APPLICATION INFO:
Applications are only accepted through the Trust web site.
Duration: One to three years.
Deadline: February 15 and September 1.

ADDRESS INQUIRIES TO:
Gina McEvily, Grant Administrator
(See address above.)

RAY EDWARDS MEMORIAL TRUST   [1305]

800 Nicollet Mall
Suite 800
Minneapolis, MN 55402
(855) 452-4015
E-mail: charitableservicesgroupmpls@usbank. com

FOUNDED: 1961

AREAS OF INTEREST:
Hospital-based health care delivery and direct health care services to indigent.

TYPE:
Capital grants; General operating grants; Project/program grants.

YEAR PROGRAM STARTED: 1961

PURPOSE:
To provide hospital-based health care services for those who are in greatest financial need and are enduring or experiencing serious illnesses.

LEGAL BASIS:
Private foundation.

ELIGIBILITY:
Eligible organizations must be IRS 501(c)(3) tax-exempt.

GEOG. RESTRICTIONS: Greater St. Paul, Minnesota and the metropolitan area to the east.

FINANCIAL DATA:
Amount of support per award: $1,000 to $150,000.
Total amount of support: Up to $845,000 annually.

NO. MOST RECENT APPLICANTS: Approximately 100.

NO. AWARDS: Average 35 annually.

APPLICATION INFO:
Applications must include four copies of the following:

(1) one-page cover letter signed by Chief Executive Officer or Board Chair;
(2) Minnesota Common Grant Application (cover page only);
(3) audited financial statement from most recent fiscal year;
(4) IRS tax-exempt determination letter;
(5) Board of Directors listing and;
(6) report describing use and impact of any recent grants from the Trust.

The Foundation does not accept letters of inquiry. No electronic media will be accepted.
Duration: Typically one year. Capital projects: Multiyear.
Deadline: May 1.

PUBLICATIONS:
Application guidelines.

ADDRESS INQUIRIES TO:
See e-mail address above.

*SPECIAL STIPULATIONS:
No inquiry letters. Submit proposals only.

THE FOUNDATION FOR SPIRITUALITY AND MEDICINE   [1306]

c/o Daniel Ford, M.D.
5 Bafford Court
Glen Arm, MD 21057
(410) 614-0986
E-mail: dford@jhmi.edu
Web Site: www.foundationspiritmed.com

FOUNDED: 1981

AREAS OF INTEREST:
Health, health education and spirituality.

TYPE:
Challenge/matching grants; Conferences/seminars; Demonstration grants; Development grants; General operating grants; Project/program grants; Research grants; Seed money grants; Training grants.

YEAR PROGRAM STARTED: 1995

PURPOSE:
To promote the integration of spirituality into health care.

ELIGIBILITY:
Grants are given to any nonprofit organization whose mission is the training of professionals in the healing arts, the delivery of health care, or the provision of spiritual services. Preference may be given to applicants who demonstrate matching funds by their organization or from other sources.

GEOG. RESTRICTIONS: Primarily Maryland.

FINANCIAL DATA:
Amount of support per award: Maximum $25,000 per year.
Total amount of support: Approximately $100,000 per year.
Matching fund requirements: Matching funds are preferred.

NO. AWARDS: Varies.

APPLICATION INFO:
Applications must be no more than 10 pages in length (double-spaced) and should include the following:

(1) description and history of the project;
(2) description of organization and personnel;
(3) rationale for proposed project;
(4) goals and objectives of the project;
(5) short-term and long-term benefits expected from the project;

(6) plans for a continuation of the project;
(7) timetable and;
(8) budget.

Grantees must meet Foundation requirements for regular financial and project reporting, and submit an annual and final written report. An oral presentation to the board of directors of the Foundation may be requested as part of the application process and/or as part of the report.

Applicants are requested to submit applications electronically to smdcdaneker@comcast.net. In addition, applicants are required to mail at least two paper copies of the application to the Foundation's address.
Duration: Up to two years.
Deadline: January 15 and July 15.
Announcements April 1 and October 1.

PUBLICATIONS:
Brochure.

IRS I.D.: 52-1238713

ADDRESS INQUIRIES TO:
David C. Daneker, Chairman
(See address above.)

THE FOUNDATION OF THE AMERICAN COLLEGE OF HEALTHCARE EXECUTIVES   [1307]

300 South Riverside Plaza
Suite 1900
Chicago, IL 60606-6698
(312) 424-9400
Fax: (312) 424-9405
E-mail: contact@ache.org
Web Site: www.ache.org/scholarships

FOUNDED: 1933

AREAS OF INTEREST:
Health care management.

NAME(S) OF PROGRAMS:
● **Albert W. Dent Graduate Student Scholarship**
● **Foster G. McGaw Graduate Student Scholarship**

TYPE:
Scholarships. Offered annually, the Albert W. Dent and the Foster G. McGaw Graduate Student Scholarships are designated for students enrolled in their final year of classroom work in a health care management graduate program.

Albert W. Dent Graduate Student Scholarship is only available to minority students.

YEAR PROGRAM STARTED: 1969

PURPOSE:
To provide financial aid, increase the enrollment in health care management graduate programs and to encourage students to obtain positions in the middle and upper levels of health care management.

ELIGIBILITY:
An applicant must:
(1) be a full-time student entering the final year of classroom work in a health care management graduate program;
(2) be able to demonstrate financial need;
(3) be a U.S. or Canadian citizen;
(4) have not been a previous recipient of the scholarship and;
(5) be a minority if applying for the Albert W. Dent Graduate Student Scholarship.

GEOG. RESTRICTIONS: United States and
Canada.

FINANCIAL DATA:
Amount of support per award: $5,000.
Total amount of support: Varies.

CO-OP FUNDING PROGRAMS: The initial gift for
the McGaw Student Scholarship was from
the Foster G. McGaw Charitable Fund.
Additional gifts were made by Mr. McGaw
from his personal funds before his death in
1986.

NO. MOST RECENT APPLICANTS: 200 to 250.

NO. AWARDS: Up to 15 scholarships awarded
per year.

APPLICATION INFO:
Application is submitted online via the
Foundation web site.
Duration: One year.
Deadline: March 31.

ADDRESS INQUIRIES TO:
Scholarship Committee
Division of Member Services
(See address above.)

THE DAVID GEFFEN FOUNDATION [1308]

12011 San Vicente Boulevard
Suite 606
Los Angeles, CA 90049
(310) 581-5955
E-mail: ddishman@geffenco.com

FOUNDED: 1986

AREAS OF INTEREST:
AIDS/HIV, civil liberties, health and health
care, the arts and issues of concern to the
Jewish community.

TYPE:
General operating grants; Project/program
grants.

PURPOSE:
To support the arts, health care, issues of
concern to the Jewish community, HIV/AIDS
and civil liberties.

LEGAL BASIS:
Private foundation.

ELIGIBILITY:
Applicants must be 501(c)(3) organizations.
No grants for documentaries, audio-visual
programming or publications. No grants to
individuals.

GEOG. RESTRICTIONS: Primarily New York City
and Los Angeles, California.

FINANCIAL DATA:
Amount of support per award: Varies
depending on needs and nature of the
request.
Total amount of support: $41,175,591 for the
year 2019.

APPLICATION INFO:
No application form. Proposals should
include summary and description of the
project or program, background information
of the organization, description of key staff,
list of Board of Directors, IRS letter
confirming tax-exempt status and financial
information including annual operating and
project budgets. Applicants should not send
videotapes or additional materials unless
otherwise requested.
Duration: One-time grant and multiyear
support. Renewal possible.

Deadline: Applications accepted throughout
the year. Each request may take up to three
months to evaluate.

PUBLICATIONS:
Application guidelines.

IRS I.D.: 95-4085811

STAFF:
J. Dallas Dishman, Ph.D., Executive Director

ADDRESS INQUIRIES TO:
J. Dallas Dishman, Ph.D., Executive Director
(See address above.)

HCR MANORCARE FOUNDATION [1309]

333 North Summit Street
Toledo, OH 43604
(419) 252-5989
Fax: (419) 252-5521
E-mail: gives@hcr-manorcare.com
Web Site: www.hcr-manorcare.com

FOUNDED: 1997

AREAS OF INTEREST:
Community service and outreach,
hospice-related programs, research and public
education for diseases and disorders that
affect the elderly, those requiring post-acute
services and those requiring hospice or
end-of-life care.

TYPE:
Challenge/matching grants; Project/program
grants.

YEAR PROGRAM STARTED: 1997

PURPOSE:
To support organizations involved in research
and public education about diseases and
disorders affecting the elderly, and
organizations which provide community
service and outreach to such individuals; to
provide support to programs addressing
end-of-life care; to provide support for
hospice.

LEGAL BASIS:
Corporate foundation.

ELIGIBILITY:
Preference is given to organizations in states
where HCR ManorCare Corporation has
strategic operations. Organizations must be
IRS 501(c)(3) tax-exempt and have one other
source of support.

HCR ManorCare will not fund advertising or
fund-raising events, individuals, for-profit
organizations, building or capital campaigns,
endowments, organizations with primary
service areas in non-HCR ManorCare states,
multiyear commitments, research projects
with overhead fees in excess of 10% or
organizations that have applied for funding
within the last 12 months.

GEOG. RESTRICTIONS: United States.

FINANCIAL DATA:
Amount of support per award: Varies.
Total amount of support: Varies.

NO. MOST RECENT APPLICANTS: 300.

NO. AWARDS: 150.

APPLICATION INFO:
The Foundation does not accept unsolicited
applications. Grants are only given through
HCR ManorCare Corporation locations.
Duration: One year.

IRS I.D.: 52-2031975

ADDRESS INQUIRIES TO:
Bill White, Executive Director
(See address above.)

HEALTH EFFECTS INSTITUTE (HEI) [1310]

75 Federal Street
Suite 1400
Boston, MA 02110-1817
(617) 488-2338
Fax: (617) 488-2335
E-mail: jrutledge@healtheffects.org
Web Site: www.healtheffects.org

FOUNDED: 1980

AREAS OF INTEREST:
Health effects of air pollution.

NAME(S) OF PROGRAMS:
● **Health Effects of Air Pollution**
● **Walter A. Rosenblith New Investigator
Award**

TYPE:
Research contracts.

YEAR PROGRAM STARTED: 1980

PURPOSE:
To provide high-quality, impartial, and
relevant science on the health effects of air
pollution.

LEGAL BASIS:
Public/Private partnership.

ELIGIBILITY:
Requirements vary according to program.

FINANCIAL DATA:
Amount of support per award: Health Effects
of Air Pollution: $500,000 to $800,000;
Rosenblith New Investigator Award: Up to
$500,000 over three years.
Total amount of support: Varies.

APPLICATION INFO:
Application information is available online.
Duration: Up to three years.
Deadline: Varies.

ADDRESS INQUIRIES TO:
For Health Effects:
Lissa McBurney
Tel: (617) 488-2345

For Walter A. Rosenblith New Investigator
Award:
Dr. Eleanne van Vliet
Tel: (617) 488-2322
(See address above.)

THE HEALTH FOUNDATION OF GREATER INDIANAPOLIS, INC. [1311]

429 East Vermont Street, Suite 300
Indianapolis, IN 46202-3698
(317) 630-1805
Fax: (317) 630-1806
E-mail: rmcconnell@thfgi.org
Web Site: www.thfgi.org

FOUNDED: 1985

AREAS OF INTEREST:
Childhood obesity, school-based health and
HIV/AIDS.

NAME(S) OF PROGRAMS:
● **Indiana AIDS Fund**

TYPE:
Grants-in-aid.

YEAR PROGRAM STARTED: 2019

PURPOSE:
To serve the community's most vulnerable citizens by funding health-related projects and organizations not easily supported by other means.

ELIGIBILITY:
Any Indiana-based nonprofit 501(c)(3) group, organization or agency that provides HIV/AIDS-related programs or services to local constituencies may apply for funding.

GEOG. RESTRICTIONS: Indiana.

FINANCIAL DATA:
Amount of support per award: Varies.
Total amount of support: Varies.

NO. MOST RECENT APPLICANTS: 33.

NO. AWARDS: 31.

APPLICATION INFO:
The Foundation does not accept unsolicited proposals.
Duration: 12 months.
Deadline: Varies.

ADDRESS INQUIRIES TO:
Jason Grisell, MBA
President and Chief Executive Officer
(See address above.)

HEALTH FOUNDATION OF SOUTH FLORIDA   [1312]
One Biscayne Tower
2 South Biscayne Boulevard, Suite 1710
Miami, FL 33131
(305) 374-7200
Fax: (305) 374-7003
E-mail: fkuchkarian@hfsf.org
Web Site: www.hfsf.org

FOUNDED: 1993

AREAS OF INTEREST:
Access to care, health coverage, healthy safety-net, social determinants of health, social needs, health and housing, systems change, policy and advocacy, and anchor institutions.

TYPE:
Challenge/matching grants; General operating grants; Project/program grants; Technical assistance; Training grants.

PURPOSE:
To invest in and be a catalyst for collaborations, policy, and systems change that improves the health of South Florida communities, with a focus on vulnerable, low- to moderate income populations.

ELIGIBILITY:
Eligible organizations must be IRS 501(c)(3) tax-exempt and be located in south Florida.

GEOG. RESTRICTIONS: South Florida counties of Broward, Miami-Dade and Monroe.

FINANCIAL DATA:
Amount of support per award: Typically $10,000 to $300,000.
Total amount of support: $4,500,000.

NO. AWARDS: 52.

APPLICATION INFO:
Concept proposals must be submitted electronically through the Foundation's web site. Applicants are encouraged to reach out to the Foundation program staff before applying.
Duration: Multiyear.
Deadline: Proposals are accepted year-round.

ADDRESS INQUIRIES TO:
Fernanda Kuchkarian
Director, Programs
(See address above.)

THE HEALTH TRUST   [1313]
3180 Newberry Drive
Suite 200
San Jose, CA 95118
(408) 513-8700
Fax: (408) 448-4055
E-mail: grants@healthtrust.org
Web Site: www.healthtrust.org

FOUNDED: 1996

AREAS OF INTEREST:
Public health.

NAME(S) OF PROGRAMS:
● **Community Grants**

TYPE:
Project/program grants.

YEAR PROGRAM STARTED: 1996

PURPOSE:
To support events and projects that build health equity in Silicon Valley.

LEGAL BASIS:
Nonprofit, public charity, qualifying as IRS 501(c)(3) organization.

ELIGIBILITY:
The organization must be tax-exempt and nonprofit. Health services must be provided within Santa Clara County and the following three zip codes of San Benito County: 95045, 95023 and 95024.

GEOG. RESTRICTIONS: Santa Clara and northern San Benito counties, California.

FINANCIAL DATA:
Amount of support per award: $250 to $2,500.
Total amount of support: Varies.

NO. MOST RECENT APPLICANTS: Approximately 38.

APPLICATION INFO:
Guidelines are available on the Trust web site. Event Grant application must be submitted online.
Duration: One year.
Deadline: Applications are accepted on a rolling basis.

STAFF:
Maria Garcia, Program Officer

ADDRESS INQUIRIES TO:
Grants Administrator
(See address above.)

THE HEALTH TRUST   [1314]
3180 Newberry Drive
Suite 200
San Jose, CA 95118
(408) 513-8700
Fax: (408) 448-4055
E-mail: grants@healthtrust.org
Web Site: www.healthtrust.org

FOUNDED: 1996

AREAS OF INTEREST:
Public health.

NAME(S) OF PROGRAMS:
● **Health Partnership Grants**

TYPE:
Project/program grants.

PURPOSE:
To make grants to programs and projects that advance specific priorities under three focus areas: Improving Health Through Food, Making Chronic Conditions More Preventable and Manageable, and Prioritizing Health Through Housing.

LEGAL BASIS:
Nonprofit, public charity.

ELIGIBILITY:
Organization must be tax-exempt and nonprofit. Health services must be provided within Santa Clara County and the following three zip codes of San Benito County: 95045, 95023 and 95024.

GEOG. RESTRICTIONS: Santa Clara and northern San Benito counties, California.

FINANCIAL DATA:
Amount of support per award: Varies.
Total amount of support: Varies.

APPLICATION INFO:
Applications must be submitted online.
Duration: Varies.
Deadline: Varies.

ADDRESS INQUIRIES TO:
Grants Administrator
(See address above.)

THE HEALTHCARE FOUNDATION FOR ORANGE COUNTY   [1315]
1505 East 17th Street
Suite 113
Santa Ana, CA 92705
(714) 245-1650
Fax: (714) 245-1653
E-mail: info@hfoc.org
Web Site: www.hfoc.org

FOUNDED: 1996

AREAS OF INTEREST:
Health care and community health.

CONSULTING OR VOLUNTEER SERVICES:
Some training and technical assistance.

NAME(S) OF PROGRAMS:
● **Partnership for a Healthy Orange County**

TYPE:
Demonstration grants; Development grants; General operating grants; Project/program grants; Technical assistance; Training grants.

YEAR PROGRAM STARTED: 1999

PURPOSE:
To promote health and support health care for the benefit of the people of Orange County, CA; to improve the health of the neediest and most underserved residents of the county.

LEGAL BASIS:
Private 501(c)(3) foundation.

ELIGIBILITY:
Grants are made to nonprofit organizations that are exempt from taxation under Section 501(c)(3) of the Internal Revenue Code and that are defined as "not a private foundation" under Section 509(a). Government agencies may also be funded.

Grants are not generally awarded for annual fund drives, building campaigns, major equipment or biomedical research. Activities that exclusively benefit the members of a religious or fraternal organization are not funded.

GEOG. RESTRICTIONS: Primarily Anaheim, Orange, Santa Ana and Tustin, California.

FINANCIAL DATA:
Amount of support per award: Varies.
Total amount of support: $660,000 for the year 2019.

CO-OP FUNDING PROGRAMS: Health Funders Partnership.

NO. MOST RECENT APPLICANTS: 29 for the year 2018.

NO. AWARDS: 15 for the year 2018.

APPLICATION INFO:
Requests for proposals may be obtained from the Foundation.
Duration: One year; multiyear funding at the Board's discretion.
Deadline: September 6.

IRS I.D.: 33-0644620

ADDRESS INQUIRIES TO:
Foundation Coordinator
(See address above.)

HUGOTON FOUNDATION   [1316]
900 Park Avenue, Suite 17E
New York, NY 10075
(212) 734-5447
Fax: (212) 734-5447

AREAS OF INTEREST:
Patient care and health.

TYPE:
Project/program grants.

PURPOSE:
To improve patient care.

LEGAL BASIS:
Nonprofit organization.

ELIGIBILITY:
Eligible organizations must be IRS 501(c)(3) tax-exempt and be located in Miami, FL or the borough of Manhattan, NY.

GEOG. RESTRICTIONS: Miami, Florida and borough of Manhattan, New York.

FINANCIAL DATA:
Amount of support per award: $1,000 to $250,000.

APPLICATION INFO:
Application should be made by letter and include a copy of the IRS tax determination letter.
Duration: One year. Nonrenewable.

ADDRESS INQUIRIES TO:
Joan K. Stout, President
(See address above.)

IRVINE HEALTH FOUNDATION   [1317]
18301 Von Karman Avenue
Suite 440
Irvine, CA 92612-0120
(949) 253-2959
E-mail: info@ihf.org
Web Site: www.ihf.org

FOUNDED: 1986

AREAS OF INTEREST:
Technology-enabled healthy living, with a focus on the veteran and senior populations of Orange County, CA.

YEAR PROGRAM STARTED: 1987

PURPOSE:
To intensify focus on approaches that improve individual healthy behaviors, especially those using technologies that provide broader access to effective health practices; to highlight systems that bolster the well-being of Orange County's seniors and veterans.

LEGAL BASIS:
Independent, nonprofit foundation.

ELIGIBILITY:
Applicants must be qualified tax-exempt charitable organizations recognized as such by the IRS. To receive favorable consideration, a project or program must be economically viable, provide effective management and serve a legitimate purpose which avoids duplicating work performed by other organizations.

The Foundation is accelerating its efforts to form new partnerships with technology companies, academic and philanthropy organizations, investors, innovators, and the development of nontraditional approaches.

GEOG. RESTRICTIONS: Orange County, California.

FINANCIAL DATA:
Amount of support per award: Varies.
Total amount of support: Varies.
Matching fund requirements: Varies.

APPLICATION INFO:
Focus grants by invitation only.
Duration: Varies.

IRS I.D.: 33-0141599

STAFF:
Edward B. Kacic, CAIA, President
Ellen A. Young, Vice President

BOARD OF DIRECTORS:
Timothy L. Strader, Chairman
Jeffrey E. Flocken, Vice Chairman
Thomas C. Cesario, M.D., Secretary/Treasurer
Douglas M. Mancino, Esq., Director
Carol Mentor McDermott, Director
Margarita Pereyda, M.D., Director

*SPECIAL STIPULATIONS:
Funding requests are by invitation only. Unsolicited inquiries are not accepted.

THE JENKINS FOUNDATION   [1318]
3409 Moore Street
Richmond, VA 23230
(804) 330-7400
Fax: (804) 330-5992
E-mail: info@cfrichmond.org
Web Site: www.jenkinsfoundation-va.org

FOUNDED: 1995

AREAS OF INTEREST:
Access to primary care, access to mental health care, and the prevention and treatment of substance use disorders in the greater Richmond, VA area.

TYPE:
General operating grants; Project/program grants.

YEAR PROGRAM STARTED: 1996

PURPOSE:
To expand access to community-based health care programs and improved health care in the greater Richmond area.

LEGAL BASIS:
Supporting organization of The Community Foundation Serving Richmond and Central Virginia.

ELIGIBILITY:
Eligible organizations must be IRS 501(c)(3) tax-exempt and serve the greater Richmond, VA area.

GEOG. RESTRICTIONS: Richmond and the counties of Chesterfield, Goochland, Hanover, Henrico and Powhatan, Virginia.

FINANCIAL DATA:
Amount of support per award: Up to $75,000.
Total amount of support: $2,129,153 for the year 2019.

NO. AWARDS: 40.

APPLICATION INFO:
Application forms are available online.
Duration: Annually. May reapply.

PUBLICATIONS:
Guidelines; annual report (online).

ADDRESS INQUIRIES TO:
Arnette Cousins
Tel: (804) 409-5594
E-mail: acousins@cfrichmond.org

THE JEWISH HEALTHCARE FOUNDATION OF PITTSBURGH   [1319]
Centre City Tower, Suite 2400
650 Smithfield Street
Pittsburgh, PA 15222
(412) 594-2550
Fax: (412) 232-6240
E-mail: info@jhf.org
Web Site: www.jhf.org

FOUNDED: 1990

AREAS OF INTEREST:
Aging and long-term care, Jewish community, professional education and workforce, public health, and quality and safety.

CONSULTING OR VOLUNTEER SERVICES:
Research, planning, convening and technical assistance.

TYPE:
Challenge/matching grants; Demonstration grants; Fellowships; Project/program grants; Research grants; Seed money grants; Technical assistance; Training grants.

YEAR PROGRAM STARTED: 1991

PURPOSE:
To improve health outcomes for elderly, poor and disabled residents in and beyond the Pittsburgh region; to improve health care quality, cost and efficiency.

LEGAL BASIS:
Public charity.

ELIGIBILITY:
Applicants must be 501(c)(3) organizations. No grants to programs without a health care component, general operations, endowments, capital campaigns, retirement of debt, scholarships, fellowships, travel or individual research grants.

GEOG. RESTRICTIONS: Pittsburgh region, Pennsylvania.

FINANCIAL DATA:
Amount of support per award: Average $50,000.

Total amount of support: Over $2,500,000 for the year 2017.

NO. AWARDS: 27 for the year 2017.

REPRESENTATIVE AWARDS:
United Way of Allegheny County; WESA; Jewish Federation of Greater Pittsburgh.

APPLICATION INFO:
Send letter of intent (not to exceed six pages), including program objectives, timetable, long-term plans, board of directors list, budget, documentation of 501(c)(3) status and most recent financial statements.

The Foundation also accepts the common grant application designed by Grantmakers of Western Pennsylvania.

Duration: Varies.

Deadline: Applications accepted on a continual basis.

PUBLICATIONS:
Annual report; *Roots*, reports; *Branches*, periodical.

IRS I.D.: 25-1624347

STAFF:
Karen Wolk Feinstein, Ph.D., President and Chief Executive Officer
Nancy D. Zionts, MBA, Chief Operating Officer and Chief Program Officer

ADDRESS INQUIRIES TO:
Nancy D. Zionts, Chief Operating Officer and Chief Program Officer
(See address above.)

THE JOHNS HOPKINS CENTER FOR ALTERNATIVES TO ANIMAL TESTING   [1320]

Johns Hopkins University
615 North Wolfe Street, Room W7032
Baltimore, MD 21205
(410) 614-4990
Fax: (410) 614-2871
E-mail: caat@jhu.edu
Web Site: altweb.jhsph.edu

FOUNDED: 1981

AREAS OF INTEREST:
Health and safety.

TYPE:
Development grants; Research grants.

YEAR PROGRAM STARTED: 1982

PURPOSE:
To develop innovative non-whole animal methods to evaluate fully commercial and/or therapeutic products to ensure the health and safety of the public. CAAT accomplishes this goal by funding research which will lead to the refinement, replacement or reduction of animals in toxicity testing and by disseminating scientifically correct information about these methods and their applications.

LEGAL BASIS:
University research program.

ELIGIBILITY:
Grants are made to institutions which have an established mechanism for handling private funding. Grant proposals should provide the fundamental knowledge base to develop alternative methods to whole animals for the safety evaluation of commercial products. CAAT encourages the development of in vitro approaches to toxicity evaluation including, but not limited to, methods using human cells/cell lines and studies in the areas

of skin hypersensitivity/toxicity, phototoxicity, target organ toxicity (e.g., neurotoxicity) and structure-activity relationships.

FINANCIAL DATA:
Amount of support per award: $40,000 maximum per year, including 15% overhead or actual costs, whichever is less.

APPLICATION INFO:
Applicants must submit and receive approval of prepoposal by deadline date using CAAT prepoposal form.

Duration: Up to two years.

Deadline: May 16 for prepoposal abstracts.

PUBLICATIONS:
CAAT Newsletter; technical reports; *Alternatives in Toxicology*, book series.

IRS I.D.: 52-0595110

ADDRESS INQUIRIES TO:
Michele Downes, Grants Coordinator
(See address above.)

KANSAS HEALTH FOUNDATION   [1321]

309 East Douglas
Wichita, KS 67202
(316) 262-7676
(800) 373-7681
Fax: (316) 262-2044
E-mail: info@khf.org
Web Site: kansashealth.org

FOUNDED: 1985

AREAS OF INTEREST:
Health equity and civic health.

NAME(S) OF PROGRAMS:
• **Impact Capacity Grant**

TYPE:
Project/program grants.

YEAR PROGRAM STARTED: 2017

PURPOSE:
To improve the health of all Kansans.

ELIGIBILITY:
Applicants must be tax-exempt under Section 501(c)(3), a government entity, or a church (with certain exclusions), located within the state, and not a previous recipient of a grant within the calendar year.

GEOG. RESTRICTIONS: Kansas.

FINANCIAL DATA:
Amount of support per award: Up to $25,000 per organization.

Total amount of support: Up to $2,000,000 annually in two cycles per year.

NO. AWARDS: Varies.

APPLICATION INFO:
Applications are to be submitted using the Online Impact Capacity Grant Application Form.

Letters of Inquiry are accepted from organizations that believe they have a project fitting the Foundation's funding priorities.

Duration: One year.

Deadline: Varies.

PUBLICATIONS:
Grant announcement press release.

IRS I.D.: 48-0873431

ADDRESS INQUIRIES TO:
Chan Brown, Program Officer
(See address above.)

LA84 FOUNDATION   [1322]

2141 West Adams Boulevard
Los Angeles, CA 90018
(323) 730-4600
Fax: (323) 730-9637
E-mail: info@la84.org
Web Site: la84.org

FOUNDED: 1984

AREAS OF INTEREST:
Youth sports.

TYPE:
Capital grants; Project/program grants. Field of play activities.

PURPOSE:
To promote and enhance youth sports opportunities in southern California.

LEGAL BASIS:
Private nonprofit foundation.

ELIGIBILITY:
Grants are made only to organizations with nonrestrictive membership operating open to all, regardless of race, creed, sex, sexual orientation, religious affiliation, or nationality. No grants to individuals. Grants are discouraged for endowments, travel outside of southern California, general operating expenses, land purchases, or debt recovery and liability. Grants are need-based.

GEOG. RESTRICTIONS: Imperial, Los Angeles, Orange, Riverside, San Bernardino, San Diego, Santa Barbara and Ventura counties, California.

FINANCIAL DATA:
Amount of support per award: Small grants: Generally $10,000 or less. Other grants: Average $25,000 to $50,000.

Total amount of support: Approximately $4,000,000 per year.

NO. AWARDS: Approximately 80 per year.

REPRESENTATIVE AWARDS:
$36,400 to Aceing Autism Inc. for personnel, equipment and facility fees for a tennis program serving autistic youth; $25,000 to Catholic Charities of Los Angeles, Inc. for program personnel and referees for a middle school soccer program; $80,000 to Play Rugby, Inc. for personnel, administrative expenses and equipment for a rugby program.

APPLICATION INFO:
Application guidelines will be posted on the Foundation web site in October or later.

Duration: One year.

Deadline: Applications are accepted year-round.

PUBLICATIONS:
Biannual report.

IRS I.D.: 95-3792725

OFFICERS:
Renata Simril, President and Chief Executive Officer
Marcia Suzuki, Vice President, Finance and Operations
Anne-Marie Jones, Vice President, Grants and Programs
Jeremy Rosenberg, Vice President, Marketing and Communications

STAFF:
Oscar Delgado, Director, Partnerships and Development

ADDRESS INQUIRIES TO:
Anne-Marie Jones
Vice President, Grants and Programs
E-mail: grants@la84.org

LIVINGSTON MEMORIAL FOUNDATION [1323]

c/o Musick, Peeler and Garrett
2801 Townsgate Road, Suite 200
Westlake Village, CA 91361-5842
(805) 418-3115
Fax: (805) 418-3101
E-mail: l.mcavoy@mpglaw.com
Web Site: www.livingstonmemorialfoundation.org

FOUNDED: 1974

AREAS OF INTEREST:
Medical and health care in Ventura County, CA.

NAME(S) OF PROGRAMS:
- **Operational Program Grants**
- **Special Project Grants**

TYPE:
Capital grants; General operating grants; Project/program grants; Travel grants. Capital grants are for medical and health care services.

Operational grants support well-established programs that continue to provide positive results.

Special project grants support those agencies and institutions that can demonstrate the need for assistance in funding a special project or with the cost of medical equipment that promises significant positive results.

YEAR PROGRAM STARTED: 1976

PURPOSE:
To promote medical and health-related services of benefit to the underserved and uninsured people of Ventura County, CA.

LEGAL BASIS:
Private Foundation under the Internal Revenue Code.

ELIGIBILITY:
Grant applications are assessed according to criteria that include giving preferential treatment to programs or projects that offer measurable medical benefits, are patient-specific or involve hands-on care.

Grants are not usually made to individuals, for projects or programs normally financed from government sources, conferences, seminars, workshops, exhibits, travel, or publishing activities.

GEOG. RESTRICTIONS: Ventura County, California.

FINANCIAL DATA:
Amount of support per award: $1,000 to $204,500.
Total amount of support: $414,000 for the year 2019-20.

NO. MOST RECENT APPLICANTS: 22 for the year 2019-20.

NO. AWARDS: 18.

APPLICATION INFO:
Organizations should first submit a brief introductory letter, not to exceed three pages. The letter should include a concise statement of the need for the funds, the amount requested, pertinent factual information, and state the desired type of grant. Current verification of tax-exempt status should also

be included. After review, eligible organizations may be invited to submit a formal grant application.

Duration: One year.

Deadline: Formal applications are received in late November. Awards are announced in April of each year.

IRS I.D.: 23-7364623

DIRECTORS AND OFFICERS:
Laura K. McAvoy, Esq., President and Chairman
Richard M. Loft, M.D., Vice President and Vice Chairman
Thomas P. Pecht, Vice President, Vice Chairman and Assistant Secretary
Kathleen F. Deutschman, Secretary and Assistant Chief Financial Officer
Marcia L. Donlon, Assistant Secretary
John R. Walters, M.D., Chief Financial Officer

ADDRESS INQUIRIES TO:
Laura K. McAvoy, Esq.
President and Chairman
(See address above.)

THE DR. JOHN T. MACDONALD FOUNDATION, INC.

1550 Madruga Avenue, Suite 215
Coral Gables, FL 33146
(305) 667-6017
Fax: (305) 667-9135
E-mail: info@jtmacdonaldfdn.org
Web Site: www.jtmacdonaldfdn.org

TYPE:
Project/program grants.

See entry 1031 for full listing.

FREDA MAYTAG-GRACE CRAWFORD TRUST [1324]

c/o JPMorgan Private Foundation Services
P.O. Box 227237, TX1-2963
Dallas, TX 75222-7237
(214) 965-2901
Fax: (800) 888-7695
E-mail: jpmorgan.pcs.grants@jpmchase.com
Web Site: www.jpmorgan.com/onlinegrants

AREAS OF INTEREST:
Tuberculosis and other respiratory diseases; preservation of a clean and healthy environment.

TYPE:
Project/program grants.

PURPOSE:
To provide medical and nursing care for individuals in the Colorado Springs community who are afflicted with tuberculosis or other respiratory diseases.

ELIGIBILITY:
Grants to 501(c)(3) nonprofit organizations. No grants to individuals.

GEOG. RESTRICTIONS: Colorado Springs, Colorado.

FINANCIAL DATA:
Amount of support per award: Varies.

APPLICATION INFO:
Application and guidelines are available online.

Duration: Varies.

Deadline: March 20, June 20, September 20 and December 20.

ADDRESS INQUIRIES TO:
Stephany Lewis, Trust Officer
E-mail: stephany.n.lewis@jpmorgan.com

MT. SINAI HEALTH CARE FOUNDATION [1325]

11000 Euclid Avenue
Cleveland, OH 44106-1714
(216) 421-5500
E-mail: mitchell.balk@case.edu
Web Site: www.mtsinaifoundation.org

FOUNDED: 1996

AREAS OF INTEREST:
Urban health, Jewish community, health policy, academic medicine and bioscience.

TYPE:
Challenge/matching grants; Demonstration grants; Development grants; Project/program grants; Seed money grants.

YEAR PROGRAM STARTED: 1997

PURPOSE:
To improve the health of the citizens in the greater Cleveland, OH area.

LEGAL BASIS:
Public charity.

ELIGIBILITY:
Eligible organizations must be IRS 501(c)(3) tax-exempt.

GEOG. RESTRICTIONS: Greater Cleveland, Ohio.

FINANCIAL DATA:
Amount of support per award: Varies.
Total amount of support: $7,300,000 for the year 2019.

APPLICATION INFO:
Application information may be obtained by contacting the Foundation or visiting the web site listed above.

Duration: Varies.

Deadline: January 1, April 1, July 1 and October 1.

PUBLICATIONS:
Guidelines; annual report; *Legacy*, newsletter.

IRS I.D.: 34-1777878

ADDRESS INQUIRIES TO:
Mitchell Balk, President
(See address above.)

NATIONAL HEALTH SERVICE CORPS (NHSC) [1326]

U.S. Department of Health and Human Services
Health Resources and Services Administration
5600 Fishers Lane
Rockville, MD 20857
(800) 221-9393
Web Site: bhw.hrsa.gov
nhsc.hrsa.gov

AREAS OF INTEREST:
Competitive scholarships for students enrolled in schools of osteopathic and allopathic medicine, family nurse practitioner, nurse midwifery and physician assistant training programs and dental school.

NAME(S) OF PROGRAMS:
- **National Health Service Corps Scholarship Program**

TYPE:
Scholarships. The scholarship award includes the payment of a monthly stipend, an amount for other reasonable educational expenses, tuition and required fees. Recipients owe one year of professional clinical service in a

health professional shortage area (HPSA) for each year of support, with a two-year service minimum.

YEAR PROGRAM STARTED: 1973

PURPOSE:
To provide the National Health Service Corps with an adequate supply of trained health professionals to serve in health professional shortage areas.

ELIGIBILITY:
All applicants must be citizens or nationals of the U.S. at the time they apply, enrolled or accepted for enrollment in an accredited health professions education program.

GEOG. RESTRICTIONS: United States and its territories.

FINANCIAL DATA:
Scholarship recipients receive a monthly stipend, one annual payment for other reasonable educational expenses, and payment to the school, on their behalf, of tuition and required fees. The stipend is taxable only for certain scholarships.
Amount of support per award: Based on costs for every student in the program.
Total amount of support: Varies.

NO. MOST RECENT APPLICANTS: 2,068 for the year 2017.

NO. AWARDS: 181 for the year 2017.

APPLICATION INFO:
Complete information is available on the web site.
Duration: The scholarship award is only for one school year, with a two-year full-time or four-year half-time minimum service obligation.
Deadline: Varies.

PUBLICATIONS:
Applicant information bulletin.

ADDRESS INQUIRIES TO:
See telephone or e-mail address above.

*SPECIAL STIPULATIONS:
Recipients must serve where needed in a designated Health Professional Shortage Area (HPSA).

NATIONAL INSTITUTE ON AGING [1327]
Division of Extramural Activities
7201 Wisconsin Avenue
Bethesda, MD 20892-9205
(301) 496-9322
E-mail: kenneth.santora@nih.gov
Web Site: www.nia.nih.gov

FOUNDED: 1975

AREAS OF INTEREST:
Biology of aging research, geriatrics and gerontology research, neuroscience research on aging, behavioral and social research on aging. Particular focus in Alzheimer's disease and related dementias.

NAME(S) OF PROGRAMS:
• Aging Research

TYPE:
Conferences/seminars; Fellowships; Grants-in-aid; Project/program grants; Research grants; Technical assistance; Training grants; Research contracts. Career development grants; Loan repayment programs.

PURPOSE:
To support biomedical, clinical, social, neuroscience, neuropsychology and behavioral research and research training directed toward greater understanding of the aging process and the needs and problems of older people. The primary goal is to improve the health and well-being of older people through the development of new knowledge.

LEGAL BASIS:
Government agency.

ELIGIBILITY:
Grants and contracts are available to universities, colleges, medical, dental and nursing schools, schools of public health, laboratories, hospitals, state and local health departments and other public or private profit or nonprofit institutions.

NRSA awards are provided for individual postdoctoral and institutional pre-and postdoctoral research training in health and health-related areas which are periodically specified by the National Institutes of Health. Individuals with a professional or scientific degree are eligible. Applicants must be citizens of the U.S. or be admitted for permanent residency.

GEOG. RESTRICTIONS: United States.

FINANCIAL DATA:
Amount of support per award: Average: $491,619 for research project grants.
Total amount of support: Varies.

NO. MOST RECENT APPLICANTS: 4,983 for fiscal year 2019.

NO. AWARDS: 1,001.

APPLICATION INFO:
Contact the Institute.
Duration: One year to multiyear.
Deadline: Varies.

OFFICERS:
Kenneth Santora, Ph.D., Director

ADDRESS INQUIRIES TO:
Division of Extramural Activities
(See address above.)

NATIONAL INSTITUTE ON ALCOHOL ABUSE AND ALCOHOLISM [1328]
Office of Extramural Activities
6700B Rockledge Drive, Room 1458
Bethesda, MD 20817
(301) 443-9737
Fax: (301) 443-6077
E-mail: bautista@mail.nih.gov
Web Site: www.niaaa.nih.gov

FOUNDED: 1971

NAME(S) OF PROGRAMS:
• **Career Enhancement Award for Stem Cell Research (K18)**
• **Independent Scientist Awards (K02)**
• **Mentored Patient-Oriented Research Career Development Award (K23)**
• **Mentored Quantitative Research Career Development Award (K25)**
• **Midcareer Investigator Award in Patient-Oriented Research (K24)**
• **NIH Pathway to Independence Award (K99/R00)**
• **Scientist Development Awards for Mentored Clinical (K08)**
• **Scientist Development Awards for Mentored Research (K01)**

TYPE:
Research grants. Support for full-time research on a long-term (five years) basis for research scientists.

Career Enhancement Award for Stem Cell Research (K18) is to encourage investigators to obtain the training they need to appropriately use stem cells in their research.

Independent Scientist Awards (K02) support advanced research experience.

NIH Pathway to Independence (PI) Award (K99/R00) will provide up to five years of support consisting of two phases. The PI award is limited to postdoctoral trainees.

Scientist Development Awards for Mentored Research (K01) and Scientist Development Awards for Mentored Clinical (K08) support individuals with one to four years of postdoctoral training or experience, but no extensive research experience.

PURPOSE:
To provide salary support to talented investigators so that they can engage in full-time research on a long-term basis and develop their full research potential.

LEGAL BASIS:
PHS Act, Section 301 as amended (42 U.S.C. 241).

ELIGIBILITY:
Applicants can either be public or nonprofit private organizations and institutions located in the U.S. or its territories and possessions or U.S. citizens or permanent residents. Citizenship is mandatory for renewal beyond the initial five-year award.

FINANCIAL DATA:
Amount of support per award: Varies.
Total amount of support: Varies.

APPLICATION INFO:
Application kits are available at most institutional offices of sponsored research and may be obtained from the Grants Information Office.
Duration: Generally five years. Renewal possible.
Deadline: Standard due dates vary with specific grant. Consult web site.

PUBLICATIONS:
NIAAA additional information to the NIH Career Development Program Announcements (K Awards).

ADDRESS INQUIRIES TO:
Dr. Raye Litten, Director
Division of Treatment
and Recovery Research
Tel: (301) 443-0636 or

Dr. Michael Hilton, Deputy Director
Division of Epidemiology
and Prevention Research
Tel: (301) 402-9402 or

Dr. Kathy Jung
Division of Metabolism
and Health Effects
Tel: (301) 443-8744 or

Dr. Antonio Noronha
Division of Neuroscience and Behavior
Tel: (301) 443-4223
(See address above.)

NATIONAL INSTITUTE ON ALCOHOL ABUSE AND ALCOHOLISM [1329]

National Institutes of Health
6700 Rockledge Drive, Room 1324
Bethesda, MD 20892
(301) 443-4225
Fax: (301) 594-0673
E-mail: mryan1@mail.nih.gov
Web Site: www.niaaa.nih.gov

FOUNDED: 1971

AREAS OF INTEREST:
Pharmaceuticals, diagnostic instruments, and the prevention and treatment of alcoholism and alcohol abuse.

NAME(S) OF PROGRAMS:
● **Small Business Innovation Research Program**

TYPE:
Research grants; Research contracts. Separate grant applications are awarded for Phase I and Phase II of the program. Phase I is designed to establish the feasibility of the technological innovation and determine the quality of performance. The objective of Phase II is to further demonstrate the efficacy of the product for commercial exploitation. Only funded applicants from Phase I are eligible to apply for Phase II.

YEAR PROGRAM STARTED: 1983

PURPOSE:
To stimulate technological innovation in the alcohol field, increase private-sector commercialization of innovations derived from federal research and development and foster and encourage participation by minority and disadvantaged firms in technological innovation.

LEGAL BASIS:
The Small Business Innovation Development Act, P.L. 97-219.

ELIGIBILITY:
Each organization must qualify as a small business in accordance with the stipulations set forth in the Omnibus Solicitation of the PHS Small Business Innovation Research Program. In general, the organization must be independently owned and operated, must be located in the U.S. and at least 51% of the ownership must be by U.S. citizens or lawfully admitted permanent resident aliens. The primary employment of the principal investigator must be with the firm at the time of award and during the conduct of the proposed project. The performance site must be in the U.S.

GEOG. RESTRICTIONS: United States.

FINANCIAL DATA:
Amount of support per award: May not exceed $150,000 for both direct and indirect costs for Phase I. May not exceed $1,000,000 for two years in total costs for Phase II. If costs exceed these amounts, contact the program officer named in the solicitation or the SBIR coordinator.

APPLICATION INFO:
The electronic submission process is multi-step. Details on applying can be found at sbir.nih.gov.
Duration: Varies for Phase I. Two years for Phase II.
Deadline: Contracts: Early November; Grants: April 5, September 5 and January 5.

PUBLICATIONS:
Omnibus solicitation for SBIR grant applications.

ADDRESS INQUIRIES TO:
Megan Ryan, SBIR Coordinator
(See address above.)

NATIONAL INSTITUTES OF HEALTH

Division of International Relations
Fogarty International Center
Building 31, Room B2C11
31 Center Drive, MSC 2220
Bethesda, MD 20892-2220
(301) 496-4784
Fax: (301) 480-3414
E-mail: tina.chung@nih.gov
Web Site: www.fic.nih.
gov/programs/pages/japan-fellowships.aspx

TYPE:
Fellowships. A limited number of postdoctoral research fellowships are provided by the Japan Science and Technology Agency (JSTA) to U.S. scientists to conduct research in Japan. Types of activity supported include collaboration in basic or clinical research and familiarization with or utilization of special techniques and equipment not otherwise available to the applicant.

See entry 888 for full listing.

LUCILE PACKARD FOUNDATION FOR CHILDREN'S HEALTH

400 Hamilton Avenue, Suite 340
Palo Alto, CA 94301
(650) 736-0675
(650) 497-8365
Fax: (650) 498-2619
E-mail: grants@lpfch.org
Web Site: www.lpfch-cshcn.org

TYPE:
Project/program grants.

See entry 1037 for full listing.

THE PATRON SAINTS FOUNDATION [1330]

260 South Los Robles Avenue, No. 201
Pasadena, CA 91101
(626) 564-0444
Fax: (626) 564-0444
E-mail: patronsaintsfdn@sbcglobal.net
Web Site: patronsaintsfoundation.org

FOUNDED: 1986

AREAS OF INTEREST:
Health care.

TYPE:
Project/program grants. Limited operating support will be awarded at the discretion of the Board of Directors.

YEAR PROGRAM STARTED: 1986

PURPOSE:
To improve the health of individuals residing in the West San Gabriel Valley through health care programs that are consistent with the moral and religious teachings of the Roman Catholic Church.

LEGAL BASIS:
Private foundation.

ELIGIBILITY:
Organizations must be IRS 501(c)(3) tax-exempt.

GEOG. RESTRICTIONS: West San Gabriel Valley, California.

FINANCIAL DATA:
Amount of support per award: $5,000 to $15,000.
Total amount of support: $427,500 for fiscal year ended June 30, 2019.

NO. MOST RECENT APPLICANTS: 35.

NO. AWARDS: 28 for fiscal year ended June 30, 2019.

APPLICATION INFO:
Two copies of the application (not to exceed three pages, no less than 11-point type, one stapled and one paper-clipped) must be mailed to the Foundation, along with other required documents including financial statements, copy of the organization's 501(c)(3) determination letter and IRS Form 990.
Duration: One year. Renewal by reapplication.
Deadline: First Friday in March and first Friday in October.

PUBLICATIONS:
Grant guidelines; grant application form; brochure.

IRS I.D.: 95-3484257

EXECUTIVE DIRECTOR:
Kathleen T. Shannon

ADDRESS INQUIRIES TO:
Kathleen T. Shannon, Executive Director
(See address above.)

THE DOROTHY RIDER POOL HEALTH CARE TRUST [1331]

645 West Hamilton Street
Suite 202
Allentown, PA 18101
(610) 770-9346
E-mail: info@pooltrust.org
Web Site: www.pooltrust.org

FOUNDED: 1975

AREAS OF INTEREST:
Community health, health services research, leadership development and medical education, recruitment and retention of outstanding health care providers, access to care, health studies, and clinical innovation.

TYPE:
Challenge/matching grants; Development grants; Project/program grants. Grants addressing at least one of the key components of the Trust's Philanthropic Agenda: improved health status of the citizens of the region, recruitment and retention of outstanding health care providers, clinical innovation, access to care, medical education, community health and health service research.

PURPOSE:
To serve as a resource that enables Lehigh Valley Hospital to be a superior regional hospital and improve the health of the citizens of the region it serves.

ELIGIBILITY:
The Trust considers proposals from nonprofit organizations and institutions within the Trust's interest areas.

GEOG. RESTRICTIONS: Allentown, Pennsylvania and surrounding area.

FINANCIAL DATA:
Amount of support per award: Varies.

Total amount of support: $840,447 for the year 2018.

APPLICATION INFO:
Funding requests should be initiated with a letter of intent from the applicant. The letter should be two to four pages summarizing the need, objective, strategy, evaluation, budget and duration.

Electronic application process is available on the web site.
Duration: Varies.

PUBLICATIONS:
Annual report.

IRS I.D.: 23-6627932

TRUSTEES:
Denise M. Gargan
John P. Jones, III
Peter M. Leibold, Esq.
Mary D. Naylor, Ph.D., FAAN
James O. Woolliscroft, M.D.

STAFF:
Edward F. Meehan, M.P.H., Executive Director
Ronald C. Dendas, M.S., Program Officer
Bridget I. Rassler, Manager, Finance and Administration
Regina M. Gabriel, Program Secretary

ADDRESS INQUIRIES TO:
Edward F. Meehan, M.P.H., Executive Director
(See address above.)

QUANTUM FOUNDATION   [1332]
2701 North Australian Avenue, Suite 200
West Palm Beach, FL 33407
(561) 832-7497
Fax: (561) 832-5794
E-mail: randy@quantumfnd.org
Web Site: www.quantumfnd.org

FOUNDED: 1995

AREAS OF INTEREST:
Health access, health education, health workforce, and basic needs to support health.

TYPE:
Capital grants; Challenge/matching grants; Demonstration grants; Matching gifts; Project/program grants; Seed money grants.

YEAR PROGRAM STARTED: 1997

PURPOSE:
To inspire and fund bold initiatives that improve the health of our communities through quality health.

LEGAL BASIS:
Private foundation.

ELIGIBILITY:
Eligible organizations must be IRS 501(c)(3) tax-exempt and defined as a public charity under Section 509(a)(1), (2) or (3), an accredited school or university, or a unit of government or public agency, typically tax-exempt under Section 107(c)(1) or Section 511(a)(2)(B), providing services in Palm Beach County.

GEOG. RESTRICTIONS: Palm Beach County, Florida.

FINANCIAL DATA:
Amount of support per award: Varies.
Total amount of support: Approximately $6,000,000 annually.

APPLICATION INFO:
Submit a Letter of Inquiry at the Foundation's web site.

Duration: One to three years.
Deadline: Varies.

STAFF:
Randy Scheid, Vice President of Programs
Shannon Hawkins, Senior Program Officer

ADDRESS INQUIRIES TO:
Randy Scheid, Vice President of Programs
(See e-mail address above.)

RESEARCH MANITOBA   [1333]
A201 Chown Building
753 McDermot Avenue
Winnipeg MB R3E 0T6 Canada
(204) 775-1096
E-mail: info@researchmb.ca
Web Site: researchmanitoba.ca

FOUNDED: 1980

AREAS OF INTEREST:
Basic research in health, natural and social sciences, engineering and the humanities in the province of Manitoba.

TYPE:
Awards/prizes; Research grants; Scholarships. New investigator operating grants; Innovative proof of concept grants.

YEAR PROGRAM STARTED: 1981

PURPOSE:
To promote, support and coordinate the funding of research in health, natural and social sciences, engineering and humanities in Manitoba.

LEGAL BASIS:
Established by an Act of the Provincial Legislature and provincially funded.

ELIGIBILITY:
Grants are awarded to individuals in the Province of Manitoba.

GEOG. RESTRICTIONS: Manitoba, Canada.

FINANCIAL DATA:
Amount of support per award: Varies.
Total amount of support: $12,000,000 budgeted annually.

CO-OP FUNDING PROGRAMS: Canadian Foundation for Innovation.

NO. AWARDS: 104 for the year 2018-19.

APPLICATION INFO:
Applications must be made on the appropriate Research Manitoba forms online.
Duration: Varies.
Deadline: Specific deadlines for each program are posted on the Research Manitoba web site.

PUBLICATIONS:
Annual report; awards guide; GMS user guide.

STAFF:
Christina Weise, Chief Executive Officer
Nicole Barry, Director of Finance and Administration
Kristen Hooper, Communications Officer
Necole Sommersell, Manager, Evaluation and Impact
Jennifer Cleary, Manager, Programs
Freyja Arnason, Manager, RITHiM
Judi Bahl, Manager, Strategic Partnerships

BOARD MEMBERS:
Tracey Maconachie, Chairperson
Dr. Digvir Jayas, Vice-Chairperson
Dr. Rashid Ahmed
Doreen Bilodeau
Dr. Hani El-Gabalawy

Luis Escobar
Earl Gardiner
Chris Johnson
Andrea Legary

ADDRESS INQUIRIES TO:
See e-mail address above.

JOSEPHINE G. RUSSELL
TRUST   [1334]
9 Bartlet Street, Suite 343
Andover, MA 01810
E-mail: russelltrust@yahoo.com

FOUNDED: 1933

AREAS OF INTEREST:
Education, health care, poverty and social services.

TYPE:
General operating grants; Project/program grants; Scholarships.

PURPOSE:
To provide care, healing and nursing of the sick and injured; to provide relief and aid to the poor; to provide training and education of the young; to assist in any other manner of social service in the City of Lawrence.

LEGAL BASIS:
Private charitable trust.

ELIGIBILITY:
Eligible organizations must be IRS 501(c)(3) tax-exempt and serve the Lawrence area. No grants to individuals. No grants are made for endowments, equipment, capital campaigns, construction or renovations of buildings and facilities. No matching gifts.

Organizations intending to submit applications for funds must be able to demonstrate that, if funds are awarded by the Trust, the program will confer a direct benefit to Lawrence residents who are sick, injured or poor; or for education or in any other manner of social services upon the people of the city of Lawrence, MA.

GEOG. RESTRICTIONS: Lawrence, Massachusetts.

FINANCIAL DATA:
Total amount of support: $440,000 for the year 2019.

NO. MOST RECENT APPLICANTS: 55.

NO. AWARDS: 46.

APPLICATION INFO:
Updated guidelines may be requested from the e-mail address above. Applicants may submit a written proposal and must include a copy of the IRS tax determination letter, budget and list of trustees in the organization.

Once application is completed, individual copies must be sent to all designated trustees.
Duration: One year. Renewal possible.
Deadline: January 31.

PUBLICATIONS:
Guidelines.

STAFF:
Marsha E. Rich, Managing Trustee

ADDRESS INQUIRIES TO:
See e-mail address above.

*PLEASE NOTE:
Guidelines require submissions of grant proposals to all trustees.

*SPECIAL STIPULATIONS:
Funded organizations are required to submit expenditure letter by December 31 of funding year.

EUNICE KENNEDY SHRIVER NATIONAL INSTITUTE OF CHILD HEALTH AND HUMAN DEVELOPMENT [1335]

Division of Extramural Research (DER)
6710B Rockledge Drive
Room 2314, MSC 7002
Bethesda, MD 20817
(800) 370-2943
(301) 945-7573
Fax: (866) 760-5947
E-mail: NICHDInformationResourceCenter@
mail.nih.gov
Web Site: www.nichd.nih.
gov/about/org/der/branches

FOUNDED: 1963

AREAS OF INTEREST:
All health sciences pertaining to mothers and children.

NAME(S) OF PROGRAMS:
- **Child Development and Behavior Branch (CDBB)**
- **Contraception Research Branch (CRB)**
- **Developmental Biology and Structural Variation Branch (DBSVB)**
- **Fertility and Infertility (FI) Branch**
- **Gynecologic Health and Disease Branch (GHDB)**
- **Intellectual and Developmental Disabilities Branch (IDDB)**
- **Maternal and Pediatric Infectious Disease Branch (MPIDB)**
- **Obstetric and Pediatric Pharmacology and Therapeutics Branch (OPPTB)**
- **Pediatric Growth and Nutrition Branch (PGNB)**
- **Pediatric Trauma and Critical Illness Branch (PTCIB)**
- **Population Dynamics Branch (PDB)**
- **Pregnancy and Perinatology Branch (PPB)**

TYPE:
Conferences/seminars; Development grants; Fellowships; General operating grants; Project/program grants; Training grants; Research contracts. Project grants and research contracts to expand the health and well-being of individuals from the moment of conception and extending through the later teenage years.

PURPOSE:
To discover new knowledge through research.

LEGAL BASIS:
Public Health Service Act, Sections 301(c), 444 and 472.

ELIGIBILITY:
Universities, colleges, medical, dental and nursing schools, schools of public health, laboratories, hospitals, state and local health departments, other public or private nonprofit institutions and commercial organizations are eligible. Individuals may apply for grants for academic and research training. They must have a professional or scientific degree and be citizens or permanent residents of the U.S.

FINANCIAL DATA:
Amount of support per award: Varies.

APPLICATION INFO:
Contact the Institute.

Duration: One year to multiyear funding.

ADDRESS INQUIRIES TO:
See e-mail address above.

SICKKIDS FOUNDATION [1336]

525 University Avenue, Suite 835
Toronto ON M5G 2L3 Canada
(416) 813-8104
(800) 661-1083 ext. 2354
E-mail: national.grants@sickkidsfoundation.com
Web Site: www.sickkidsfoundation.com/about-us/grants

FOUNDED: 1973

AREAS OF INTEREST:
Health and well-being of children.

NAME(S) OF PROGRAMS:
- **Community Conference Grants Program**
- **New Investigator Research Grants**

TYPE:
Awards/prizes; Conferences/seminars; Project/program grants; Research grants. Community Conference Grants program brings together families with researchers and clinicians for medical presentations and family-oriented discussions. It helps ensure knowledge exchange with families so that they are able to access the most up-to-date information about their children's health.

New Investigator Research Grants program focus is to ensure that there continues to be well-trained researchers across the country working to address the most pressing childhood diseases and conditions.

YEAR PROGRAM STARTED: 1974

PURPOSE:
To promote quality programs in child health, research and public health education in the field.

LEGAL BASIS:
Public foundation with charitable registration.

ELIGIBILITY:
Community Conference Grants: Eligible events must have a focus on information sharing between health professionals, community organizations and families. Academic conferences are not eligible for funding. Eligible events must:
(1) address issues that are relevant to child health in Canada;
(2) support the parent-child-professional partnership by having a focus on information sharing between families, health professionals, and community organizations;
(3) include knowledgeable and credible presenters;
(4) take place in Canada and;
(5) be sponsored by a registered Canadian charitable organization.

Preference will be given to events which are organized by smaller, community-based organizations, have interactive/knowledge exchange sessions with families, involve parents as panel/speakers, and have the potential to make an impact on practice or policy.

New Investigator Grants: Principal investigator must be eligible to apply for independent research grants and be formally affiliated with an eligible institution, where that institution is willing to financially administer the grant. The Principal Investigator will usually hold a doctoral degree (Ph.D.) or equivalent degree and have had formal research training. If there are two applicants, both must be eligible as a New Investigator. Eligible applicants are required to include a mentorship plan and to work with a clearly-identified mentor(s).

GEOG. RESTRICTIONS: Canada.

FINANCIAL DATA:
Amount of support per award: Community Conference Grants: Maximum $5,000; New Investigator Grants: Up to $100,000 per year.
Total amount of support: Varies.

NO. AWARDS: Community Conference Grants: Up to 12; New Investigator Research Grants: Up to 6.

APPLICATION INFO:
Application guidelines are available online. All applications are submitted through the Online Application Portal.

Duration: New Investigator Grants: Maximum of three years with annual review of progress. No renewals.

Deadline: Community Conference Grants: January 31, May 31 and September 30. New Investigator Research Grant: Mid-April.

SISTERS OF ST. JOSEPH HEALTHCARE FOUNDATION [1337]

440 South Batavia
Orange, CA 92868-3998
(714) 633-8121 ext. 7109
E-mail: rfox@csjorange.org
Web Site: www.csjorange.org

FOUNDED: 1992

AREAS OF INTEREST:
Health care and health access, mental health, violence prevention, and homelessness.

TYPE:
General operating grants; Project/program grants. The Foundation sponsors or supports long-term efforts which are closely identified with the Sisters of St. Joseph of Orange and their mission of bringing unity and healing where divisiveness and oppression exist.

PURPOSE:
To fund programs which directly serve the needs of the underserved, especially families and children at risk; to support programs and organizations that work to prevent violence and homelessness.

LEGAL BASIS:
Public foundation.

ELIGIBILITY:
Applicants must be nonprofit organizations operating in Humbolt County, southern California and San Francisco Bay area which have programs that directly serve the needs of the underserved, especially families and children at risk, as well as programs of education and advocacy which are directed at improving health and access to health care. Religious organizations also receive support. Capital projects will not be considered.

The Foundation desires to fund programs and organizations that:
(1) provide direct health-related services;
(2) support and transform the individual, social, economic, institutional, and cultural aspects of communities;
(3) provide change within larger societal systems to benefit low-income and at-risk populations and;
(4) develop the leadership and capacity for self-determination of those served by the Foundation's funding.

GEOG. RESTRICTIONS: Southern California, Humbolt County and San Francisco Bay area.

FINANCIAL DATA:
Total amount of support: $1,917,000 for the year 2019.

NO. MOST RECENT APPLICANTS: 200 for the year 2019.

NO. AWARDS: 80 for the year 2019.

APPLICATION INFO:
Contact the Foundation.

Duration: One year.

Deadline: Contact Foundation for exact dates.

ADDRESS INQUIRIES TO:
Sister Regina Fox, S.S.N.D.
Executive Director
(See address above.)

GERTRUDE E. SKELLY CHARITABLE FOUNDATION

4600 North Ocean Boulevard
Suite 206
Boynton Beach, FL 33435
(561) 276-1008
Fax: (561) 272-2793
E-mail: ejoh@hhk.com

TYPE:
Challenge/matching grants;
Conferences/seminars; Project/program grants; Research grants; Scholarships;
Training grants. Emergency grants for continued education.

See entry 1484 for full listing.

THE CHRISTOPHER D. SMITHERS FOUNDATION, INC. [1338]

P.O. Box 67
Mill Neck, NY 11765
(516) 676-0067
E-mail: info@smithersfoundation.org
Web Site: smithersfoundation.org

FOUNDED: 1952

AREAS OF INTEREST:
Education and prevention of alcoholism.

TYPE:
Conferences/seminars; Project/program grants; Research grants; Technical assistance; Training grants.

YEAR PROGRAM STARTED: 1952

PURPOSE:
To prevent alcoholism through education.

APPLICATION INFO:
Grant proposal must include:
(1) brief description of the program and grant amount requested (budget);
(2) copy of 501(c)(3) nonprofit status and;
(3) copy of most recent annual report.

PUBLICATIONS:
Annual report.

OFFICERS:
Adele C. Smithers, Chairman
Nikki Smithers, President
Samuel B. Bacharach, Ph.D., Vice President
Stacia Murphy, Treasurer
Brinkley Smithers, Secretary

DIRECTORS:
Nicholas A. Pace, M.D.
M. Elizabeth Brothers, Honorary Director

ARTEMAS W. STEARNS TRUST [1339]

9 Bartlet Street, Suite 343
Andover, MA 01810
E-mail: stearnstrust@yahoo.com

FOUNDED: 1896

AREAS OF INTEREST:
The aged and poor, health care in the Lawrence area, social services and education.

TYPE:
General operating grants; Project/program grants; Scholarships. Elder and infirm support.

YEAR PROGRAM STARTED: 1896

PURPOSE:
To pay income to such nonprofit and charitable homes, nursing homes, convalescent homes, retirement homes, sanitaria, homes for the aged, hospitals, agencies and such other similar institutions, organizations and agencies as may provide for or care, in whole or in part, for the indigent aged people of both sexes; to provide relief of the deserving poor of the City of Lawrence, without distinction of nationality or religious belief.

LEGAL BASIS:
Private charitable trust.

ELIGIBILITY:
Eligible organizations must be IRS 501(c)(3) tax-exempt. No grants to individuals. No grants are made for endowments, equipment, capital campaigns, construction or renovations of buildings and facilities.

Organizations intending to submit applications for funds must be able to demonstrate that, if funds are awarded by the Trust, the program will confer a direct benefit upon the indigent aged people or to the deserving poor of the city of Lawrence, MA exclusively.

GEOG. RESTRICTIONS: Lawrence, Massachusetts.

FINANCIAL DATA:
Amount of support per award: Varies.

Total amount of support: $189,000 for the year 2019.

NO. MOST RECENT APPLICANTS: 45.

NO. AWARDS: 40.

APPLICATION INFO:
Updated guidelines may be requested from the e-mail address above. Applicants may submit a written proposal and must include a copy of the IRS tax determination letter, budget and list of trustees in the organization.

Once application is completed, individual copies must be sent to all designated trustees.

Duration: One year. Renewal possible.

Deadline: January 31.

PUBLICATIONS:
Application guidelines.

STAFF:
Marsha E. Rich, Managing Trustee

ADDRESS INQUIRIES TO:
See e-mail address above.

*PLEASE NOTE:
Guidelines require submissions of grant proposals to all trustees.

*SPECIAL STIPULATIONS:
Funded organizations are required to submit expenditure letter by December 31 of funding year.

U.S. DEPARTMENT OF HEALTH AND HUMAN SERVICES [1340]

Health Resources and Services Administration
Bureau of Primary Health Care
Parklawn Building, 5600 Fishers Lane
Room 1874
Rockville, MD 20857
(301) 594-4300
(301) 594-4110
Web Site: bphc.hrsa.gov

FOUNDED: 1976

AREAS OF INTEREST:
Assisting communities located in medically underserved areas to develop needed primary health care services.

CONSULTING OR VOLUNTEER SERVICES:
Information and technical assistance is available from U.S. Public Health Service Regional Office staff.

NAME(S) OF PROGRAMS:
● **The Health Center Program**

TYPE:
Project/program grants. Grants may be made for planning and development of a community health center and for operations.

YEAR PROGRAM STARTED: 1975

PURPOSE:
To provide primary health care in ambulatory care settings located in severely medically underserved areas and to develop a network of services involving as many other health programs and facilities operating in the area as possible; to arrange for other federal programs not operating in the area to establish services within the federally funded primary care center whenever possible.

LEGAL BASIS:
Government agency.

ELIGIBILITY:
Grants may be made to public or private not-for-profit entities. Area to be served must be medically underserved. Priority will be given to areas of highest need.

GEOG. RESTRICTIONS: United States.

FINANCIAL DATA:
Amount of support per award:
Approximately $650,000.

Matching fund requirements: The applicant must assume part of the project costs determined on a case-by-case basis.

CO-OP FUNDING PROGRAMS: Funding along with other federal programs, such as Migrant Health Centers, National Health Service Corps, MCH, or Mental Health Alcohol and Drug Abuse is encouraged, as well as cooperation with state and local programs.

APPLICATION INFO:
Information available from HRSA Grant Application Center, 901 Russell Avenue, Suite 450, Gaithersburg, MD 20879, or call (877) 477-2123.

Duration: Project periods may be up to three years, with annual budget periods.

PUBLICATIONS:
Application guidelines.

STAFF:
Jim Macrae, Associate Administrator to Bureau of Primary Health Care Director

U.S. DEPARTMENT OF HEALTH AND HUMAN SERVICES   [1341]

Centers for Medicare and Medicaid Services
7500 Security Boulevard
Baltimore, MD 21244-1850
(410) 786-3000
(877) 267-2323
Fax: (410) 786-1008
E-mail: medicaid.gov@cms.hhs.gov
Web Site: www.medicaid.gov

FOUNDED: 1967

NAME(S) OF PROGRAMS:
- **Medicaid**

TYPE:
Formula grants. Financial assistance to states
for in- and outpatient hospital services, other
laboratory services, home health care, family
planning, physicians' services and early
diagnosis and treatment for persons who are
medically needy.

LEGAL BASIS:
Title XIX, Social Security Act as amended;
Public Law 89-97; Public Law 90-248;
Public Law 91-56; 42 U.S.C. 1396, et seq.
Public Law 92-223; Public Law 92-603.

ELIGIBILITY:
State and local welfare agencies operating
under an approved Medicaid plan are eligible
for support.

GEOG. RESTRICTIONS: United States.

FINANCIAL DATA:
Amount of support per award: Varies.
Total amount of support: Varies.

APPLICATION INFO:
Application forms are available from the
address above or from regional or local
offices of the Medical Services
Administration to whom applications should
be submitted.
Duration: Quarterly.
Deadline: States must submit quarterly
estimates of funds no later than May 15,
August 15, November 15 and February 15 in
order to receive quarterly grant awards.

UNITED HOSPITAL FUND OF NEW YORK   [1342]

1411 Broadway, 12th Floor
New York, NY 10018
(212) 494-0761
Fax: (212) 494-0801
E-mail: hholmes@uhfnyc.org
Web Site: uhfnyc.org

FOUNDED: 1879

AREAS OF INTEREST:
Expanding health insurance coverage,
improving quality of care, and redesigning
health care services.

NAME(S) OF PROGRAMS:
- **Health Care Improvement Grant Program**

TYPE:
Project/program grants; Seed money grants.

YEAR PROGRAM STARTED: 1938

PURPOSE:
To provide support to innovative projects by
nonprofit hospitals and health care and other
organizations to improve the quality of health
care for all New Yorkers.

LEGAL BASIS:
Public charity.

ELIGIBILITY:
Nonprofit 501(c)(3) tax-exempt organizations
in or to the benefit of New York City are
eligible for support. No grants to individuals,
capital or endowment campaigns or general
operating grants.

GEOG. RESTRICTIONS: Primarily New York, New
York, including the five boroughs.

FINANCIAL DATA:
Amount of support per award: Typically
$50,000 to $125,000.
Total amount of support: Approximately
$1,000,000 annually.
Matching fund requirements: Varies.

NO. MOST RECENT APPLICANTS: 60.

REPRESENTATIVE AWARDS:
$75,833 to BronxCare Health System;
$79,948 to Mount Sinai Hospital; $72,691 to
St. John's Episcopal Hospital.

APPLICATION INFO:
The Foundation is not accepting Letters of
Intent or unsolicited proposals at this time.
Duration: One to two years. Nonrenewable.

PUBLICATIONS:
Annual report; application guidelines.

OFFICERS:
John C. Simons, Chairman
Anthony Shih, M.D., M.P.H., President
Sheila M. Abrams, Senior Vice President and
Treasurer
Sally J. Rogers, Senior Vice President
Chad Shearer, Senior Vice President
Jo Ivey Boufford, M.D., Vice Chairman
Amanda A. Williams, Corporate Secretary

BOARD OF DIRECTORS:
Jo Ivey Boufford, M.D.
Dale C. Christensen, Jr.
J. Barclay Collins, II
Margaret Crotty
Samuel J. Daniel, M.D.
Christophe Durand
Robert S. Galvin, M.D.
Jennifer L. Howse, Ph.D.
Eugene Keilin
Cary A. Kravet
Josh N. Kuriloff
Meera Mani, M.D., Ph.D.
Howard P. Milstein
Susana R. Morales, M.D.
Robert C. Osborne, Jr.
Seun Salami
Anthony Shih, M.D., M.P.H.
Anthony Shorris
John C. Simons
Eileen M. Sullivan-Marx, Ph.D.
Mary Beth C. Tully
Barbara A. Yastine

ADDRESS INQUIRIES TO:
Hollis Holmes, Grants Manager
(See address above.)

US COMMUNITY PARTNERSHIPS   [1343]

GSK
5 Moore Drive
Research Triangle Park, NC 27709
E-mail: us.communitypartnerships@gsk.com
Web Site: us.gsk.com

AREAS OF INTEREST:
Nutrition and physical activity for children
and youth, STEM education, and disaster
preparedness and response.

TYPE:
Project/program grants.

PURPOSE:
To foster increased understanding of
scientific, clinical and health care issues; to
contribute to improving patient care.

LEGAL BASIS:
Corporate foundation.

ELIGIBILITY:
Applicants must be nonprofit organizations
with proposals consistent with guidelines and
interest areas. No grants for capital projects,
operating expenses, conferences, symposia,
publications, fund-raising events, lobbying to
influence legislation, religious organizations,
sporting events, universities, free-standing
research centers, scholar aid, expeditions or
individuals.

GEOG. RESTRICTIONS: United States.

FINANCIAL DATA:
Amount of support per award: Varies
depending on needs and nature of the
request.

APPLICATION INFO:
Applicants must first register on the U.S.
Community Partnerships Charitable Grant
Request System. Once registration is
approved (approximately 10 days),
organization may be required to submit
additional information including:
(1) copy of 501(c)(3) or 501(c)(1), if a public
school, IRS letter of determination;
(2) member list for the Board of Directors;
(3) program literature;
(4) program evaluation (if an ongoing
program for three or more years);
(5) most recent audited financials and;
(6) additional information as required per
Impact Awards or Impact Grants programs.
Duration: Typically one year.
Deadline: Applications accepted throughout
the year.

THE WHITEHORSE FOUNDATION   [1344]

Westlake Tower
1601 Fifth Avenue, Suite 1900
Seattle, WA 98101
(206) 515-2131
(206) 622-2294
Fax: (206) 622-7673
E-mail: c.erickson@seattlefoundation.org
Web Site: www.seattlefoundation.org

FOUNDED: 1990

AREAS OF INTEREST:
Preventative human services to improve the
lives of children, youth and families.

TYPE:
Project/program grants.

YEAR PROGRAM STARTED: 1990

PURPOSE:
To fund comprehensive preventive social
service programs in Snohomish County, WA.

LEGAL BASIS:
Community foundation.

ELIGIBILITY:
Applicant organizations must be IRS
501(c)(3) tax-exempt. No grants to
individuals.

GEOG. RESTRICTIONS: Snohomish County,
Washington.

FINANCIAL DATA:
Amount of support per award: Varies.

NO. MOST RECENT APPLICANTS: 30.

NO. AWARDS: 15.

APPLICATION INFO:
Applications guidelines are available on the web site. Letter of Inquiry must be submitted to grantmaking@seattlefoundation.org.
Duration: Up to several years.

STAFF:
Ceil Erickson, Program Director

ADDRESS INQUIRIES TO:
Ceil Erickson, Program Director
(See address above.)

MR. AND MRS. P.A. WOODWARD'S FOUNDATION   [1345]
1055 West Hastings Street, Suite 300
Vancouver BC V6E 2E9 Canada
(604) 682-8116
E-mail: pawoodwardfoundation@gmail.com
Web Site: www.woodwardfoundation.ca

FOUNDED: 1951

AREAS OF INTEREST:
Health care.

TYPE:
The Foundation supports those projects which affect the people of the Province of British Columbia where there is clear indication of the health benefit anticipated. The Foundation is charged with aiding in the purchase of the latest medical equipment of proven performance that provides direct benefit to the patient. A preference was expressed to fund items with direct patient benefit, as contrasted to research done in the laboratory with uncertain or delayed benefits and programs that create awareness.

PURPOSE:
To assist in projects which could contribute to better health care.

LEGAL BASIS:
Charitable foundation.

ELIGIBILITY:
Organizations applying for funding must be domiciled within the Province of British Columbia. All individuals and organizations applying must be in possession of a Charitable Gift Registration Number as issued by the Department of National Revenue of Canada.

The Foundation will consider applications in the following general areas:
(1) health care equipment of proven effectiveness and;
(2) special projects which will benefit the health of British Columbians.

The Foundation will not support routine operational budgets, fundamental research not directly related to patient care, conferences or annual meetings, endowments or capital building costs.

GEOG. RESTRICTIONS: British Columbia, Canada.

FINANCIAL DATA:
Amount of support per award: Grants vary in amount, depending upon the needs and nature of the request.

NO. AWARDS: Varies.

APPLICATION INFO:
Applications will be received by invitation only. Organizations must e-mail a Letter of Intent indicating what they would like to apply for. Organizations may then be invited to submit a full application.

Deadline: Beginning of February for March Board meeting; beginning of May for June Board meeting; Middle of September for October Board meeting. Actual dates are posted on the Foundation web site.

OFFICERS:
Christopher C. Woodward, President
Jill Leversage, Treasurer
Paul Langley, Secretary
Jim Allworth

MEMBERS AND DIRECTORS:
Jim Allworth
Paul Langley
Jill Leversage
Gregory J.D. McKinstry
Hon. Madam Justice Mary V. Newbury
David Ostrow
Christopher C. Woodward

ADDRESS INQUIRIES TO:
Executive Director
(See address above.)

Social welfare

THE ABELARD FOUNDATION-EAST   [1346]
P.O. Box 148
Lincoln, MA 01773
E-mail: eastabel@aol.com
Web Site: fdnweb.org/abelardeast

AREAS OF INTEREST:
Progressive social change, community organizing, civil and human rights.

TYPE:
General operating grants; Project/program grants.

PURPOSE:
To support local progressive social change activities that expand and protect civil liberties and civil and human rights, and promote and strengthen community involvement in, and control over, the decisions that affect their lives.

ELIGIBILITY:
Applicants must represent or be associated with a nonprofit, 501(c)(3) tax-exempt organization. Priority is given to projects that are in their first years of development and have budgets less than $300,000.

GEOG. RESTRICTIONS: Eastern United States, east of the Mississippi River.

FINANCIAL DATA:
Amount of support per award: Average $10,000.
Total amount of support: Approximately $140,000 annually.

NO. AWARDS: Approximately 15 new and renewals.

APPLICATION INFO:
Applicants should submit one copy of a proposal (no more than seven to 10 pages) which includes:
(1) background of the organization;
(2) description of the work for which funds are being sought;
(3) explanation of need and;
(4) impact the project will have.

Proposals prepared in a "common application" format will also be accepted.

Applying organizations must include IRS 501(c)(3) determination letter.

Duration: One year. Up to two renewals possible.
Deadline: Applications mailed by March 15 will be reviewed for the spring meeting. Applications mailed by September 15 will be reviewed for the fall meeting.

ADDRESS INQUIRIES TO:
Susan Collins, Trustee
The Abelard Foundation-East
(See address above.)

EMMA J. ADAMS MEMORIAL FUND, INC.   [1347]
328 Eldert Lane
Brooklyn, NY 11208
(347) 789-6717
Fax: (347) 789-6717

FOUNDED: 1933

AREAS OF INTEREST:
Geriatric institutions, welfare, elderly, and needy, mostly through organizations.

TYPE:
Grants-in-aid. Financial support and organized aid to geriatric, needy and/or elderly institutional agencies and occasionally to referred respectable, aged indigent persons in financial difficulty through no fault of their own, in the greater New York City area.

YEAR PROGRAM STARTED: 1936

PURPOSE:
To aid elderly, needy and indigent people and geriatric institutions.

LEGAL BASIS:
Nonprofit corporation.

ELIGIBILITY:
Most grants are awarded to operating geriatric institutions.

No scholarships, program grants, administrative expenses, and no brick-and-mortar grants.

GEOG. RESTRICTIONS: Greater New York area.

FINANCIAL DATA:
Amount of support per award: Varies.
Total amount of support: Average $40,000 per year.

NO. MOST RECENT APPLICANTS: Over 150.

NO. AWARDS: 15 to 20.

APPLICATION INFO:
Application forms available upon request. The letter must indicate the referral source. No telephone requests honored.
Duration: Varies.
Deadline: September 1.

IRS I.D.: 13-6116503

DIRECTORS:
Jill Harvey
Betsy Rowe
Sally Saran
Elizabeth H.J. Scott
Carolyn Swayze

ADDRESS INQUIRIES TO:
Sally Saran, President
(See address above.)

JUDD S. ALEXANDER FOUNDATION   [1348]
500 First Street, Suite 10
Wausau, WI 54403
(715) 845-4556
Fax: (715) 843-9018
E-mail: office@alexanderprop.org
Web Site: juddsalexanderfoundation.org

FOUNDED: 1978

AREAS OF INTEREST:
Education, recreation, human services, children's services and economic development.

TYPE:
Capital grants; Challenge/matching grants; Project/program grants; Seed money grants. Support is provided for capital building and emergency funds.

YEAR PROGRAM STARTED: 1978

PURPOSE:
To support quality of life and economic development in Marathon County, WI.

LEGAL BASIS:
Private foundation.

ELIGIBILITY:
Organizations classified as 501(c)(3) by the IRS can apply. The Foundation does not make grants to individuals or private businesses.

GEOG. RESTRICTIONS: Marathon County, Wisconsin.

FINANCIAL DATA:
Amount of support per award: Varies.
Total amount of support: Varies.

APPLICATION INFO:
Five copies, unbound, of the proposal should be submitted. Proposal material should not be placed in protective covers or other presentation formats. Videos and other supplementary materials are not encouraged and will not be returned to applicants. A fully reviewable proposal will include:
(1) a cover page with the exact name and location of the proposed grant recipient, along with the name, title, address and phone number of an individual at the organization;
(2) a project overview, which includes a description of the organization's main activities and whether it is a public, private or not-for-profit entity, a description of the project or activity for which funding is requested, and specific outcomes and goals and;
(3) a project budget which includes revenue and expense pages and a budget narrative.

The following items must also be attached:
(1) the organization's current annual operating budget, including revenues and expenses;
(2) a list of the organization's governing body and its officers, showing business, professional and/or community affiliations, along with officers' financial contributions to the organization;
(3) letters of support and letters from other agencies indicating their intent to collaborate (as appropriate);
(4) other documents to supplement the above information, provided it is not duplicative of other material or information contained in the narratives or budget presentation;
(5) the most recent audited financial statements and;
(6) the most recent IRS determination letter.

The Foundation does not accept proposals by fax or e-mail.
Duration: Typically one year. Must reapply.

ADDRESS INQUIRIES TO:
Gary W. Freels, President
(See address above.)

THE ALLSTATE FOUNDATION [1349]
3075 Sanders Road
Northbrook, IL 60062
E-mail: foundation@allstate.com
Web Site: www.allstatefoundation.org

FOUNDED: 1952

AREAS OF INTEREST:
Domestic violence, youth empowerment, nonprofit leadership and volunteerism.

TYPE:
Matching gifts; Project/program grants. Program support in the Foundation's areas of focus; matching gifts for higher education only.

YEAR PROGRAM STARTED: 1952

PURPOSE:
To assist deserving organizations serving the fields of domestic violence and youth empowerment.

LEGAL BASIS:
Corporate foundation.

ELIGIBILITY:
If invited to apply, an organization must be exempt under Section 501(c)(3) of the IRS code, or be a municipal, state or federal government entity.

GEOG. RESTRICTIONS: United States.

FINANCIAL DATA:
Amount of support per award: National programs: $100,000; Local/regional grants: $5,000 to $20,000.
Total amount of support: Approximately $25,000,000 in grants for the year 2018.
Matching fund requirements: For colleges and universities.

APPLICATION INFO:
Unsolicited grant applications will not be accepted.
Duration: One year. Renewal based on program outcome and results.

PUBLICATIONS:
Guidelines.

IRS I.D.: 36-6116535

ADDRESS INQUIRIES TO:
See e-mail address above.

THE CALIFORNIA ENDOWMENT
1000 North Alameda Street
Los Angeles, CA 90012
(213) 928-8645
(800) 449-4149
Fax: (213) 928-8871
E-mail: destrada@calendow.org
Web Site: www.calendow.org

TYPE:
Challenge/matching grants; General operating grants; Matching gifts; Project/program grants.

See entry 1299 for full listing.

CAMPBELL FOUNDATION, INC.
705 York Road
Towson, MD 21204
(410) 828-1961
Fax: (410) 821-8814
E-mail: lsperato@stoycpa.com

TYPE:
Capital grants; General operating grants; Project/program grants.

See entry 1014 for full listing.

CATHOLIC CHARITIES USA [1350]
2050 Ballenger Avenue, Suite 400
Alexandria, VA 22314
(703) 549-1390
Fax: (703) 549-1656
E-mail: info@catholiccharitiesusa.org
Web Site: catholiccharitiesusa.org

AREAS OF INTEREST:
The aged, community services, homeless, emergency relief and family services.

TYPE:
Assistantships; Project/program grants.

PURPOSE:
To provide service to those in need and to advocate justice in societal structures.

LEGAL BASIS:
Nonprofit organization.

ELIGIBILITY:
Grants are only offered to the 1,700 Catholic Charities member agencies. Any organization which is not affiliated with Catholic Charities is ineligible for support.

GEOG. RESTRICTIONS: United States.

FINANCIAL DATA:
Amount of support per award: Varies depending on project and need of the geographic area being served.
Total amount of support: Varies.

APPLICATION INFO:
Organizations should contact their local or diocesan chapters of Catholic Charities for application information and materials.
Duration: Up to five years.

THE CENTER AT SIERRA HEALTH FOUNDATION [1351]
1321 Garden Highway
Suite 210
Sacramento, CA 95833
(916) 993-7701
E-mail: impact@shfcenter.org
Web Site: www.shfcenter.org

AREAS OF INTEREST:
Improving health outcomes and reducing health disparities.

NAME(S) OF PROGRAMS:
- **Building Healthy Communities**
- **California Funders for Boys and Men of Color**
- **Leadership Development for Racial Equity**
- **My Brother's Keeper Sacramento Collaborative**
- **Positive Youth Justice Initiative**
- **San Joaquin Valley Health Fund**

TYPE:
Matching gifts; Project/program grants.

PURPOSE:
To eradicate health inequities across the state; to bring people, ideas and infrastructure together to create positive change.

LEGAL BASIS:
501(c)(3) nonprofit.

ELIGIBILITY:
Applicant must be a public entity or designated 501(c)(3) organization by the IRS

with 509(a)(1) or 509(a)(2) status. No grants to individuals, endowments or activities which exclusively benefit members of private or religious organizations.

GEOG. RESTRICTIONS: California, with a focus on underserved San Joaquin Valley.

FINANCIAL DATA:
Amount of support per award: Varies.

OFFICERS:
Chet Hewitt, President and Chief Executive Officer
Gil Alvarado, Senior Vice President of Finance and Administration
Kaying Hang, Vice President of Programs and Partnerships

BOARD OF DIRECTORS:
Debra McKenzie, Chairman
Jose Hermocillo, Vice Chairman
David W. Gordon
Chet Hewitt
Nancy P. Lee
Robert Petersen, C.P.A.
Dr. Claire Pomeroy
Carol Whiteside

ADDRESS INQUIRIES TO:
See e-mail address above.

THE COMMONWEALTH FUND   [1352]
One East 75th Street
New York, NY 10021
(212) 606-3800
Fax: (212) 606-3500
E-mail: grants@cmwf.org
Web Site: www.commonwealthfund.org

FOUNDED: 1918

AREAS OF INTEREST:
Supporting independent research on health care issues, and making grants to improve health care practice and policy.

NAME(S) OF PROGRAMS:
- **Advancing Medicare**
- **Controlling Health Care Costs**
- **Federal and State Health Policy**
- **Health Care Coverage and Access**
- **Health Care Delivery System Reform**
- **International Health Policy and Practice Innovations**
- **Tracking Health System Performance**

TYPE:
Fellowships; Project/program grants; Research grants; Scholarships; Research contracts.

YEAR PROGRAM STARTED: 1918

PURPOSE:
To promote a high-performing health care system that achieves better access, improved quality, and greater efficiency, particularly for society's most vulnerable, including low-income people, the uninsured, minority Americans, young children and elderly adults.

The Fund carries out this mandate by supporting independent research on health care issues and making grants to improve health care practice and policy. An international program in health policy is designed to stimulate innovative policies and practices in the U.S. and other industrialized countries.

LEGAL BASIS:
Private foundation.

ELIGIBILITY:
The Fund makes grants only to tax-exempt organizations and public agencies. No grants to individuals.

FINANCIAL DATA:
Amount of support per award: Varies.

Total amount of support: $19,600,000 in grants for fiscal year 2017-18.

NO. MOST RECENT APPLICANTS: 850.

NO. AWARDS: 170.

REPRESENTATIVE AWARDS:
$20,000 to Grantmakers in Aging, Inc., for engaging philanthropy in complex care; $345,900 to Issues Research, Inc., for case studies and tools to support the spread of promising practices in health care delivery and cost control; $121,771 to Bipartisan Policy Center, Inc., for development of policy options for addressing barriers to care improvement for patients with complex care needs.

APPLICATION INFO:
The Fund requests letters of inquiry to initiate the grant application process. Applicants are encouraged to submit letters of inquiry using the online form. While the Fund will continue to accept letters of inquiry via regular mail and fax, such submissions will take longer to process than those received online. Letters of inquiry are acknowledged when received. Applicants are typically advised of the results of an initial staff review within two months. Program staff will contact applicants if more detailed information is required.

Duration: Typically one year, although some multiyear funding available.

Deadline: Applications may be submitted at any time.

IRS I.D.: 13-1635260

STAFF:
David Blumenthal, M.D., President
Kathleen Regan, Executive Vice President and Chief Operating Officer
Donald Moulds, Executive Vice President for Programs
Eric C. Schneider, M.D., Senior Vice President for Policy and Research
Barry A. Scholl, Senior Vice President for Communications and Publishing
Andrea Landes, Vice President of Grants Management

BOARD OF DIRECTORS:
Benjamin K. Chu, M.D., Chairman
Maureen Bisognano
David Blumenthal, M.D.
Mitchell J. Blutt, M.D.
Sheila P. Burke, R.N.
Michael V. Drake, M.D.
Margaret A. Hamburg, M.D.
Kathryn D. Haslanger
Vivian S. Lee, M.D.
Lois Quam
Mark D. Smith, M.D.
Simon Stevens
Laura Walker, MBA
William Y. Yun

ADDRESS INQUIRIES TO:
Andrea Landes
Vice President of Grants Management
(See address above.)

COMMUNITY FOUNDATION OF THE VERDUGOS   [1353]
111 East Broadway, Suite 200
Glendale, CA 91205
(818) 241-8040
Fax: (818) 241-8045
E-mail: info@cfverdugos.org
Web Site: www.cfverdugos.org

FOUNDED: 1956

AREAS OF INTEREST:
Arts and culture, children, education, health, homeless services, human services, senior services and environment.

TYPE:
Capital grants; Development grants; Project/program grants; Scholarships.

YEAR PROGRAM STARTED: 1956

PURPOSE:
To meet current and changing needs in the community; to provide grants that create impact on the community.

LEGAL BASIS:
Community foundation.

ELIGIBILITY:
Eligible organizations must be schools or IRS 501(c)(3) tax-exempt.

GEOG. RESTRICTIONS: Burbank, Glendale, La Canada/Flintridge, La Crescenta, Montrose and Verdugo City, California.

FINANCIAL DATA:
Amount of support per award: Grants: $5,000 minimum; average grant $8,000 to $12,000; Scholarships: Varies.

Total amount of support: Approximately $400,000 to $500,000 annually.

CO-OP FUNDING PROGRAMS: Through restricted, donor-advised funds within the Foundation.

APPLICATION INFO:
Guidelines and application form are available on the Foundation web site.

Duration: One year. Agency can reapply one year after the grant ends.

Deadline: June 1.

PUBLICATIONS:
Annual report; quarterly newsletters.

IRS I.D.: 95-6068137

ADDRESS INQUIRIES TO:
Chief Executive Officer
(See address above.)

CORPORATION FOR NATIONAL AND COMMUNITY SERVICE   [1354]
250 E Street, S.W.
Washington, DC 20024
(202) 606-5000
(800) 942-2677
Fax: (202) 606-3475
TTY: (800) 833-3722
E-mail: info@cns.gov
Web Site: www.nationalservice.gov/programs/senior-corps

FOUNDED: 1971

AREAS OF INTEREST:
Volunteer service.

NAME(S) OF PROGRAMS:
- **Foster Grandparent Program**
- **Retired and Senior Volunteer Program (RSVP)**
- **Senior Companion Program**

TYPE:
Demonstration grants; General operating grants; Grants-in-aid; Project/program grants; Technical assistance. Grants to provide meaningful opportunities for low-income persons age 55 years and over, specifically providing person-to-person service to children with special needs as Foster Grandparents and providing services to adults with special needs as Senior Companions. The Retired and Senior Volunteer Program helps people 55 and older put their skills and life experience to work in their communities.

PURPOSE:
To provide volunteer service opportunities for older Americans.

LEGAL BASIS:
Federal agency.

ELIGIBILITY:
State and local public agencies, private nonprofit organizations, and tribal entities may apply.

GEOG. RESTRICTIONS: United States and territories.

FINANCIAL DATA:
Amount of support per award: Foster Grandparent Program: $328,000 average. Retired Senior Volunteer Program: $77,000 average. Senior Companion Program: $204,000 average.

Matching fund requirements: 10% for Foster Grandparent Program and Senior Companion Program. For Retired Senior Volunteer Program, 10-20-30%.

CO-OP FUNDING PROGRAMS: Local public and private nonprofit agencies receive grants to sponsor and operate FGP, RSVP and SCP.

APPLICATION INFO:
Contact the Corporation.
Duration: Three years with opportunity to amend annually.
Deadline: Varies.

PUBLICATIONS:
Grant application; guidelines.

IRS I.D.: 53-0260397

CARL M. FREEMAN FOUNDATION
31556 Winterberry Parkway
Selbyville, DE 19975
(302) 483-7639
Fax: (302) 483-7639
E-mail: grantsmanager@freemanfoundation.org
Web Site: www.carlfreemanfoundation.org

TYPE:
Capital grants; Challenge/matching grants; General operating grants.

See entry 413 for full listing.

THE HEALTH FOUNDATION OF GREATER INDIANAPOLIS, INC. [1355]
429 East Vermont Street, Suite 300
Indianapolis, IN 46202-3698
(317) 630-1805
Fax: (317) 630-1806
E-mail: rmcconnell@thfgi.org
Web Site: www.thfgi.org

FOUNDED: 1985

AREAS OF INTEREST:
Childhood obesity, school-based health and HIV/AIDS.

TYPE:
Project/program grants.

PURPOSE:
To serve the community's most vulnerable citizens by funding health-related projects and organizations not easily supported by other means.

ELIGIBILITY:
Applicant must be a 501(c)(3) group, organization or agency that provides health-related programs or services within Indiana. Must also function without discrimination or segregation based on race, gender, age, religion, national origin, sexual orientation, disability, military or marital status in hiring, termination, assignment and promotion of staff, selection of board members or provisions of services. No grants are made to individuals. Nonsectarian religious programs may apply.

GEOG. RESTRICTIONS: Indiana.

FINANCIAL DATA:
Amount of support per award: Varies.
Total amount of support: Varies.

NO. MOST RECENT APPLICANTS: 38.

NO. AWARDS: 37.

APPLICATION INFO:
The Foundation does not accept unsolicited proposals. The Board of Directors identify relevant health issues and direct the staff to connect organizations to one another.
Duration: One year.
Deadline: Varies.

IRS I.D.: 35-6203550

ADDRESS INQUIRIES TO:
Jason Grisell, MBA
President and Chief Executive Officer
(See address above.)

VICTOR AND LORRAINE HONIG FUND [1356]
1624 Franklin Street
Suite 1022
Oakland, CA 94612
(510) 834-2995
Fax: (510) 834-2998
E-mail: info@commoncounsel.org
Web Site: www.commoncounsel.org

AREAS OF INTEREST:
Social change, community development, environment, public policy and empowerment.

TYPE:
General operating grants; Project/program grants.

PURPOSE:
To support community organizations that are working to advance equality, opportunity, justice and civil rights for low-income communities and communities of color in the San Francisco Bay area and beyond; to support organizations that connect local social justice efforts with national and international movements for peace and justice.

LEGAL BASIS:
Family foundation.

ELIGIBILITY:
Grants made only to IRS 501(c)(3) tax-exempt organizations. No grants are made to social service programs offering ongoing or direct delivery of services, medical, educational or cultural institutions,

emergency funding, scholarship funds or other aids to individuals, organizations which have sophisticated fund-raising capabilities, capital expenditure, construction or renovation programs or programs undertaken at government initiative. Priority is given to grassroots community organizations in low-income areas.

GEOG. RESTRICTIONS: California.

FINANCIAL DATA:
Amount of support per award: $1,000 to $25,000.
Total amount of support: Varies.

NO. MOST RECENT APPLICANTS: 50 to 100.

NO. AWARDS: Varies.

APPLICATION INFO:
Letters of Inquiry and Proposals are by invitation only.
Duration: Most grants are for one year.

ADDRESS INQUIRIES TO:
Grants Administrator
(See address above.)

A.V. HUNTER TRUST, INC. [1357]
650 South Cherry Street
Suite 535
Glendale, CO 80246
(303) 399-5450
Fax: (303) 399-5499
E-mail: barbarahowie@avhuntertrust.org
Web Site: avhuntertrust.org

FOUNDED: 1924

AREAS OF INTEREST:
Disabled, seniors, youth, indigent, and individuals with medical needs.

NAME(S) OF PROGRAMS:
• **Direct Operating Grants**
• **Funds for One**

TYPE:
General operating grants. Grants to qualifying nonprofit organizations offering direct services to assist those in need.

Funds for One assists qualified individuals with the purchase of eyeglasses, hearing aids, durable medical equipment, and limited dental procedures through applications from a Case Manager.

YEAR PROGRAM STARTED: 1924

PURPOSE:
To give aid, comfort, support or assistance to children or aged persons or indigent adults.

LEGAL BASIS:
Private foundation.

ELIGIBILITY:
Applicants must be organizations classified as 501(c)(3) by the IRS. The Trust will consider only one request from an organization during any 12-month period. Institutions or organizations supported by tax-derived monies, including those which have lost governmental funding, will not be considered. The Trustees will not consider grants or loans to individuals, developmental or start-up funds, research, publications, films or other media projects, capital campaigns or acquisitions, including construction and renovations, education or scholarship aid, grants to cover deficits or retirement of debt, purchase of memberships or blocks of tickets, endowments, recruiting and training of staff or gathering and disseminating information.

GEOG. RESTRICTIONS: Colorado.

FINANCIAL DATA:
Amount of support per award: $5,000 to $30,000. Average: $15,000.

Total amount of support: $2,530,960 for the year 2018.

NO. AWARDS: 224 grants to organizations and 279 grants to individuals for the year 2018.

REPRESENTATIVE AWARDS:
$10,000 to Boys & Girls Clubs of Fremont County; $10,000 to Greeley Transitional Housing; $10,000 to Senior Resource Services.

APPLICATION INFO:
Letters of Inquiry and grant applications must be submitted online.

STAFF:
Barbara L. Howie, Executive Director
Charlotte A. Gillespie, Senior Program Officer
Kary L. Cramer, Program Officer, Funds for One
Ryan O. Campbell, Program Officer, Grants

BOARD OF TRUSTEES:
Bruce K. Alexander, President
Allan B. Adams, Vice President
Mary K. Anstine, Treasurer
W. Robert Alexander
Jeremy O. May

ADDRESS INQUIRIES TO:
Barbara L. Howie, Executive Director
(See address above.)

THE STEWART HUSTON CHARITABLE TRUST

50 South 1st Avenue
Coatesville, PA 19320
(610) 384-2666
Fax: (610) 384-3396
E-mail: admin@stewarthuston.org
Web Site: www.stewarthuston.org

TYPE:
Capital grants; Challenge/matching grants; General operating grants; Matching gifts; Project/program grants.

See entry 753 for full listing.

THE HYAMS FOUNDATION, INC.   [1358]

50 Federal Street, 9th Floor
Boston, MA 02110
(617) 426-5600
Fax: (866) 497-2260
E-mail: info@hyamsfoundation.org
Web Site: www.hyamsfoundation.org

FOUNDED: 1921

AREAS OF INTEREST:
Community issues, racial justice, equitable housing, fair wages and benefits, and school-to-prison.

TYPE:
General operating grants; Project/program grants; Technical assistance. General operating.

PURPOSE:
To reduce racial and ethnic disparaties in Boston and Chelsea, MA.

LEGAL BASIS:
Nonprofit foundation.

ELIGIBILITY:
Applicants must be Massachusetts charitable corporations, tax-exempt under Section

501(c)(3) and designated as not a private foundation under Section 509(a). No grants will be made to one organization for the programs of another organization which has not itself received both such determinations. The Foundation ordinarily will consider only one application from an organization in any given 12-month period. However, a single application may include a request for more than one program or purpose.

Grants are not given to individuals, educational institutions for standard educational or capital programs, any municipal, state or federal agency, hospital capital campaigns, endowments and religious organizations for sectarian religious purposes.

Grants are rarely made for curriculum development, conferences, film production, scholarships or to national or international organizations.

GEOG. RESTRICTIONS: Boston and Chelsea, Massachusetts.

FINANCIAL DATA:
Total amount of support: $4,974,500 in grants in 2016.

NO. AWARDS: Funding provided to 76 local nonprofit organizations in 2016.

APPLICATION INFO:
Application form required. Organizations which are unsure about whether they meet the Foundation's funding priorities and criteria are encouraged to submit a one-page letter of interest to the Foundation. This letter should describe the reason for seeking support and the geographic area(s) and population(s) to be served.

Application form is available online.
Duration: Typically one year. Multiyear grants also given.
Deadline: March 1, September 1 and December 1.

TRUSTEES:
Penn S. Loh, Chairperson
Willma H. Davis, Treasurer
Omar Simmons, Assistant Treasurer
Iris Gomez, Clerk
Julie Goodridge
Lucas H. Guerra
Rahsaan D. Hall
Karen L. Mapp
Martella Wilson-Taylor

STAFF:
Jocelyn Sargent, Executive Director
Mark Paley, Director of Administration and Finance
R. Shani Pankam, Grants Manager
Sergio Marin Luna, Program Officer
David Moy, Senior Program Officer, Civic Engagement
Maria Mulkeen, Program Officer, Affordable Housing
Nahir Torres, Program Officer, Teen Development

ADDRESS INQUIRIES TO:
R. Shani Pankam, Grants Manager
(See address above.)

ITTLESON FOUNDATION, INC.   [1359]

15 East 67th Street
New York, NY 10065
(212) 794-2008
Fax: (212) 794-0351
Web Site: www.ittlesonfoundation.org

FOUNDED: 1932

AREAS OF INTEREST:
Mental health, environment and AIDS.

TYPE:
Demonstration grants; Project/program grants; Seed money grants. Seed money for the start-up of innovative programs in the fields of mental health, AIDS, and the environment.

In the area of AIDS, the Foundation supports cutting-edge prevention efforts. It is also particularly interested in new model, pilot, and demonstration efforts which address the needs of underserved at-risk populations, respond to the challenges facing community-based AIDS service organizations, provide meaningful school-based sex education, make treatment information accessible, available, and easily understandable to those in need of it, and address the psycho-social needs of those infected and affected by AIDS, especially adolescents.

In the area of environment, the Foundation supports innovative pilot, model and demonstration projects that will help move individuals, communities and organizations from environmental awareness to environmental activism. The Foundation seeks to support the present generation of environmental activists, educate and engage the next generation, strengthen the infrastructure of the environmental movement with a particular focus on efforts at the grassroots and statewide levels, and activate new constituencies.

In the area of mental health, the Foundation continues to support efforts to address the needs of underserved populations. It also seeks pilot, model and demonstration projects which fight the stigma associated with mental illness, utilize new knowledge and current technological advances to improve programs and services for people with mental illness, bring the full benefits of this new knowledge and technology to those who presently do not have access to them, and advance preventative mental health efforts, especially those targeted to youth and adolescents.

PURPOSE:
To launch and disseminate innovative projects in the areas of mental health, AIDS and the environment.

ELIGIBILITY:
Grants are available to nonprofit organizations within the U.S. Preference is given to pilot projects, test and demonstration projects and applied research which ideally should inform public policy, if successful. The Foundation also supports dissemination projects.

The Foundation does not usually support capital building projects, endowments, grants to individuals, scholarships or internships (except as part of a program), or continuing support to existing programs. Moreover, the Foundation does not support programs of direct service to individuals with only a local focus or constituency. The Foundation does not make international grants.

GEOG. RESTRICTIONS: United States.

FINANCIAL DATA:
Amount of support per award: Average $45,000 to $90,000.

Total amount of support: $375,000 for the year 2019.

APPLICATION INFO:
There are no application forms. Applicants should write a brief letter to the Executive Director describing the basic organization and the work for which funds are being sought, along with a budget and evidence of tax-exempt status. If the activity falls within the current scope of the Foundation's interests, the applicant will be asked to supply additional information as required. Applicant should consult web site for current year's focus.

Duration: Generally one year. Multiyear when appropriate. No renewals.

Deadline: Letters of Intent must be received by September 1.

OFFICERS AND DIRECTORS:
H. Anthony Ittleson, Chairman and President
Andrew Auchincloss, Vice Chairman and Director
Pamela Syrmis, Vice President and Director
H. Davison, Treasurer
Anthony C. Wood, Secretary and Executive Director
H. Philip Ittleson, Director
Stephanie Ittleson, Director
Christina Ittleson Smith, Director
Victor Talbot, M.D., Director

ADDRESS INQUIRIES TO:
Anthony C. Wood, Executive Director
(See address above.)

JACKSONVILLE JAGUARS FOUNDATION
One TIAA Bank Field Drive
Jacksonville, FL 32202
(904) 633-5437
Fax: (904) 633-5683
Web Site: www.jaguars.com/community

TYPE:
General operating grants; Project/program grants. Limited capital grants that target economically and socially "at-risk" youths in northeast Florida.

See entry 153 for full listing.

THE CARL W. AND CARRIE MAE JOSLYN CHARITABLE TRUST [1360]
c/o JPMorgan Private Foundation Services
2200 Ross Avenue, Floor 5
Dallas, TX 75201
Fax: (800) 883-7695
E-mail: grant.reports@jpmorgan.com
Web Site: www.jpmorgan.com/onlinegrants

FOUNDED: 1975

AREAS OF INTEREST:
Children, elderly and handicapped persons of El Paso County, CO.

TYPE:
Project/program grants. Small project grants and general operating support.

YEAR PROGRAM STARTED: 1975

LEGAL BASIS:
Tax-exempt charitable trust.

ELIGIBILITY:
Organizations serving children, the elderly and handicapped persons in El Paso County, CO, are eligible to apply.

GEOG. RESTRICTIONS: El Paso County, Colorado.

FINANCIAL DATA:
Amount of support per award: Varies.

Total amount of support: Varies.

NO. MOST RECENT APPLICANTS: 75.

NO. AWARDS: 30.

APPLICATION INFO:
Application must be made online; paper applications will not be accepted.

Duration: One year. Nonrenewable.

Deadline: October 15.

ADDRESS INQUIRIES TO:
Stephany Lewis, Executive Director
JPMorgan
(See address above.)

LIBERTY HILL FOUNDATION [1361]
6420 Wilshire Boulevard
Suite 700
Los Angeles, CA 90048
(323) 556-7200
Fax: (323) 556-7240
E-mail: info@libertyhill.org
Web Site: www.libertyhill.org

FOUNDED: 1976

AREAS OF INTEREST:
Economic justice, environmental justice, LGBTQ justice, and racial justice.

NAME(S) OF PROGRAMS:
- **Brothers, Sons, Selves**
- **Fund for Change**
- **Wally Marks Leadership Institute for Change**

TYPE:
General operating grants; Project/program grants; Seed money grants; Technical assistance. The Brothers, Sons, Selves program is a coalition of community-based organizations from across Los Angeles County that are organizing and working with African-American, Latino and Asian-Pacific Islander youth in low-income communities to address inequities through grassroots policy campaigns and leadership development.

Fund for Change supports high-impact social change through cultivating effective community leaders, seeding emerging organizations, and developing a base of grassroots activists within the areas of economic and racial justice, environmental justice and LGBTQ justice.

The Wally Marks Leadership Institute for Change invests in community leaders at the front lines of change with intensive on-the-job training for community organizers.

YEAR PROGRAM STARTED: 1976

PURPOSE:
To advance social change through a strategic combination of grants, leadership training and campaigns.

LEGAL BASIS:
Public foundation.

ELIGIBILITY:
Fund for Change: The Foundation considers applications from nonprofit 501(c)(3) organizations, or those organizations having a fiscal sponsorship agreement with a nonprofit organization which complies with Liberty Hill's policy on fiscal sponsorship, in Los Angeles County, CA, that actively work toward a more just distribution of resources and power, develop grassroots activism and leadership, are building their organizational infrastructure and promote a society free from discrimination.

The Foundation does not fund capital campaigns for land or buildings, individual efforts, films or video projects, profit-making ventures, direct union organizing, electioneering for candidates in public office, one-time events or conferences that are not linked to social change organizing strategies, or projects that only serve communities outside Los Angeles County.

GEOG. RESTRICTIONS: Primarily Los Angeles County, California.

FINANCIAL DATA:
Amount of support per award: Fund for Change: $10,000 to $50,000.

Total amount of support: $729,000 for the year 2017.

CO-OP FUNDING PROGRAMS: Donor-advised program.

NO. MOST RECENT APPLICANTS: 72.

NO. AWARDS: 35.

APPLICATION INFO:
Letter of Inquiry for Fund for Change must be submitted electronically. Submissions by fax will not be accepted.

Unsolicited proposals will not be accepted.

Duration: One to two years.

Deadline: Letter of Inquiry: Varies.

PUBLICATIONS:
Guidelines; newsletter.

IRS I.D.: 51-0181191

STAFF:
Shane Goldsmith, President and Chief Executive Officer
Joanna Kabat, Director of Grantmaking

ADDRESS INQUIRIES TO:
Joanna Kabat
Director of Grantmaking
E-mail: jkabat@libertyhill.org

*PLEASE NOTE:
Applicants must submit a Letter of Inquiry. Unsolicited proposals will not be accepted.

THE AGNES M. LINDSAY TRUST
15 Constitution Drive
Suite 1A, Office
Bedford, NH 03110
(603) 669-1366
(603) 488-1213
E-mail: admin@lindsaytrust.org
Web Site: www.lindsaytrust.org

TYPE:
Capital grants. Awards grants for capital campaigns, capital items and renovation needs. Also, supports a number of health and welfare organizations, health projects, dental projects, special needs including blind, deaf and learning-disabled, elderly, children's hospitals, children's homes, youth organizations, youth and family services and summer camperships (summer enrichment programs).

See entry 1029 for full listing.

LUTHERAN FOUNDATION OF ST. LOUIS
8860 Ladue Road
Suite 200
St. Louis, MO 63124
(314) 231-2244 ext. 111
Fax: (314) 727-7688
E-mail: info@lutheranfoundation.org
Web Site: www.lutheranfoundation.org

TYPE:
Project/program grants.

See entry 756 for full listing.

M & M AREA COMMUNITY FOUNDATION

1110 10th Avenue, Suite L-1
Menominee, MI 49858
(906) 864-3599
E-mail: info@mmacf.org
Web Site: www.mmacf.org

TYPE:
Project/program grants; Scholarships.

See entry 1206 for full listing.

MAINE INITIATIVES   [1362]

56 North Street, Suite 100
Portland, ME 04101
(207) 607-4070
E-mail: info@maineinitiatives.org
Web Site: www.maineinitiatives.org

FOUNDED: 1993

AREAS OF INTEREST:
Supporting social change in Maine.

NAME(S) OF PROGRAMS:
• **Grants for Change**

TYPE:
General operating grants; Seed money grants;
Technical assistance. Grants provide funding
to Maine groups advancing social, economic,
and environmental justice at the grassroots
level.

YEAR PROGRAM STARTED: 1994

PURPOSE:
To cultivate social, economic and
environmental justice through grants and
other support to grassroots organizations in
Maine communities.

ELIGIBILITY:
Organization must be tax-exempt. Religious
organizations are eligible but not for religious
purposes.

GEOG. RESTRICTIONS: Maine.

FINANCIAL DATA:
Amount of support per award: Up to $25,000
over three years.
Total amount of support: Varies.

NO. AWARDS: Up to 10.

APPLICATION INFO:
Copies of IRS 501(c)(3) designation letters
are requested. Contact the organization for
application.
Duration: Up to three years.
Deadline: July 15.

PUBLICATIONS:
Newsletter; annual report.

IRS I.D.: 01-0484310

STAFF:
Phil Walsh, Executive Director

ADDRESS INQUIRIES TO:
See e-mail address above.

MAZON: A JEWISH RESPONSE TO HUNGER   [1363]

10850 Wilshire Boulevard
Suite 400
Los Angeles, CA 90024
(310) 442-0020
Fax: (310) 442-0030
E-mail: mazonmail@mazon.org
amiller@mazon.org
Web Site: www.mazon.org

FOUNDED: 1986

AREAS OF INTEREST:
Anti-hunger advocacy pertaining to local,
state and federal nutrition safety-net services.

NAME(S) OF PROGRAMS:
• **Quick Reaction Fund (QRF)**

TYPE:
Demonstration grants; General operating
grants; Internships; Project/program grants.
Capacity building grants. Quick Reaction
Fund, launched in September of 2017,
recognizes the need for anti-hunger
movement leaders to respond quickly to
pressing issues that will disproportionally
impact the lives of food insecure people.
QRF addresses this need by providing
one-time grants to leaders to help leverage
immediate, innovative and time-sensitive
advocacy opportunities in response to
unforeseen legislation, political development,
public attacks, or public messaging
opportunities.

YEAR PROGRAM STARTED: 1986

PURPOSE:
To prevent and alleviate hunger among
people of all faiths and backgrounds.

GEOG. RESTRICTIONS: United States and Israel.

FINANCIAL DATA:
Amount of support per award: QRF: $500 to
$15,000; All others: Varies.
Total amount of support: Varies.

NO. MOST RECENT APPLICANTS: 171.

NO. AWARDS: 153.

APPLICATION INFO:
All MAZON applications are by invitation
only.
Duration: One year.

PUBLICATIONS:
Program announcement; guidelines.

ADDRESS INQUIRIES TO:
Alexis Miller, Program Officer
E-mail: amiller@mazon.org

THE MCKNIGHT FOUNDATION   [1364]

710 South Second Street
Suite 400
Minneapolis, MN 55401
(612) 333-4220
Fax: (612) 332-3833
E-mail: info@mcknight.org
Web Site: www.mcknight.org

FOUNDED: 1953

AREAS OF INTEREST:
Regional economic and community
development, Minnesota's arts and artists,
education equity, Midwest climate and
energy, Mississippi River water quality,
neuroscience research, and international crop
research.

NAME(S) OF PROGRAMS:
• **Arts**

• **Education**
• **International**
• **Midwest Climate and Energy**
• **Neuroscience**

TYPE:
General operating grants; Project/program
grants.

YEAR PROGRAM STARTED: 1953

PURPOSE:
To advance climate solutions in the Midwest;
to support the arts, international crop
research, and neuroscience.

LEGAL BASIS:
Family foundation.

ELIGIBILITY:
Applicants must be classified as tax-exempt,
nonprofit organizations by the IRS.

GEOG. RESTRICTIONS: Minnesota, with emphasis
on the Minneapolis-St. Paul area, Mississippi
River Corridor, and select international areas
of work.

FINANCIAL DATA:
Total amount of support: Approximately
$200,000 for the year 2018.

NO. AWARDS: 315 for the year 2019.

APPLICATION INFO:
Applications are available online.
Deadline: Varies. Specific dates are posted
on the Foundation web site.

PUBLICATIONS:
Annual report, including grants list;
grantmaking guidelines for all programs.

OFFICERS:
Pamela Wheelock, President
Nichol Higdon, Vice President of Finance
and Compliance

BOARD:
Dana Anderson
Anne Binger
Erika Binger
Meghan Binger Brown
Phyllis Goff
Debby Landesman
Perry Moriearty
Luther Ragin, Jr.
Roger Sit
Noa Staryk
Ted Staryk
Kathy Tunheim

ADDRESS INQUIRIES TO:
Stephanie Duffy, Director of
Grants and Information Management
(See address above.)

MARIETTA MCNEILL MORGAN AND SAMUEL TATE MORGAN, JR. TRUST   [1365]

Bank of America Private Bank
1800 K Street, N.W., Mail Code
DC1-842-05-01
Washington, DC 20006
(202) 442-7460
E-mail: dc.grantmaking@ustrust.com
Web Site: www.bankofamerica.
com/grantmaking

FOUNDED: 1962

AREAS OF INTEREST:
Arts, culture and humanities, education, and
human services.

TYPE:
Capital grants.

LEGAL BASIS:
Private foundation.

ELIGIBILITY:
Nonprofit organizations in the
Commonwealth of Virginia who are classified
by IRS as tax-exempt and are not private
foundations. Grants for capital only. No
grants to individuals, for endowment funds or
operating funds.

GEOG. RESTRICTIONS: Virginia.

FINANCIAL DATA:
Amount of support per award: $5,000 to
$75,000 dispersed in a single payment;
average $40,000.
Total amount of support: Varies.

CO-OP FUNDING PROGRAMS: Other funding
sources encouraged.

NO. MOST RECENT APPLICANTS: 58.

NO. AWARDS: 29.

APPLICATION INFO:
Applications are submitted online.
Duration: One year.
Deadline: April 1. Notification by June 30.

ADDRESS INQUIRIES TO:
Lee Parker, Senior Vice President
(See address above.)

MRG FOUNDATION [1366]
P.O. Box 12489
Portland, OR 97212
(503) 289-1517
Fax: (503) 232-1731
E-mail: grants@mrgf.org
Web Site: www.mrgfoundation.org

FOUNDED: 1976

AREAS OF INTEREST:
Community-based groups working for
progressive social, racial, economic and
environmental justice change.

NAME(S) OF PROGRAMS:
● **Capacity Building Grants**
● **Critical Response Grants**
● **General Fund Grants**
● **Travel Grants**

TYPE:
General operating grants; Internships; Seed
money grants; Travel grants. Funds special
project grants and general support.

Critical Response Grants provide
community-based groups with the additional
capacity needed to organize a progressive
response to an unexpected crisis or
opportunity for organizing.

Travel Grants help MRG grantees make
national and regional connections and
develop the leadership and skills needed for
effective organizational development and
organizing.

YEAR PROGRAM STARTED: 1976

PURPOSE:
To empower those impacted by injustice; to
promote social change.

LEGAL BASIS:
Nonprofit, tax-exempt 501(c)(3) public
foundation.

ELIGIBILITY:
Organizations must do tax-exempt activities
in the state of Oregon and fit criteria of
social change work listed in fields of interest.
No grants to individuals. The Foundation
does not fund food co-ops, health centers,
schools or social services.

Grant applicants for the Critical Response
Grant and the Travel Grant must have an
organizational budget under $500,000 to be
eligible.

GEOG. RESTRICTIONS: Oregon.

FINANCIAL DATA:
Amount of support per award: Critical
Response Grants: Up to $2,000; General
Fund: $2,000 to $20,000; Travel Grants: Up
to $1,000.
Total amount of support: $470,000.

NO. MOST RECENT APPLICANTS: 100.

NO. AWARDS: 34.

REPRESENTATIVE AWARDS:
Center for Intercultural Organizing;
Community Alliance of Tenants;
Salem/Keizer Coalition for Equality.

APPLICATION INFO:
Application forms and information are
available upon request.
Duration: Six to 12 months.
Deadline: Critical Response Grants and
Travel Grants have no application deadline,
but are subject to exhaustion of annual
funding monies. General Fund: September
and March.

PUBLICATIONS:
Applying for a Grant from MRG.

OFFICERS:
Lizzie Martinez, Chairperson

*PLEASE NOTE:
Formerly known as the McKenzie River
Gathering Foundation.

A.J. MUSTE MEMORIAL INSTITUTE [1367]
168 Canal Street, 6th Floor
New York, NY 10013
(212) 533-4335
E-mail: info@ajmuste.org
Web Site: www.ajmuste.org

FOUNDED: 1974

AREAS OF INTEREST:
Peace and disarmament, social and economic
justice, racial and gender equality, human
rights, and the labor movement.

TYPE:
Grants-in-aid. The Institute's regular grant
fund annually funds international, national
and local projects in the U.S. and around the
world. It gives priority to those with small
budgets and little chance of funding from
more traditional sources. It also offers fiscal
sponsorship. The Institute does not provide
academic scholarships.

YEAR PROGRAM STARTED: 1974

PURPOSE:
To promote peace and disarmament, social
and economic justice, racial and sexual
equality, and the labor movement.

ELIGIBILITY:
The Institute funds projects which seek to
advance nonviolent grassroots education and
action for social and economic justice. The
Institute does not make grants for general
support of ongoing operations. It does not
generally accept proposals from organizations
with annual budgets over $500,000 or for
projects with budgets over $50,000. It will
also not accept a new request from a
previously funded group for two years after a

grant. Grants are not made to individuals and
generally not to religious organizations or
development projects.

FINANCIAL DATA:
Amount of support per award: Average grant:
$5,000; reviewed in quarterly cycles.
Total amount of support: Varies.

NO. AWARDS: Varies.

APPLICATION INFO:
Complete information is available on the
Institute web site.
Duration: Varies.
Deadline: Varies according to program.

ADDRESS INQUIRIES TO:
Heidi Boghosian, Executive Director
(See address above.)

NATIONAL COUNCIL ON FAMILY RELATIONS [1368]
661 Lasalle Street
Suite 200
St. Paul, MN 55114
(763) 781-9331
Fax: (763) 781-9348
E-mail: info@ncfr.org
Web Site: www.ncfr.org

FOUNDED: 1938

AREAS OF INTEREST:
Family science, family research, family
practice, family education, sociology,
psychology, social work, human
development, child development, and certified
family life education.

NAME(S) OF PROGRAMS:
● **Felix Berardo Mentoring Award**
● **Czaplewski Fellowship Award**
● **Ruth Jewson Award**
● **NCFR Student Award**
● **Cindy Winter Award**

TYPE:
Awards/prizes. Awards given for
contributions to the area of family science.
All of the awards require NCFR membership.

YEAR PROGRAM STARTED: 1938

PURPOSE:
To share in the development and
dissemination of knowledge about families
and family relationships; to establish
professional standards; to work to promote
family well-being.

LEGAL BASIS:
501(c)(3) education and research association.

ELIGIBILITY:
Criteria are posted on the Council web site.

FINANCIAL DATA:
Amount of support per award: $250 to $500.
Total amount of support: Varies.

NO. MOST RECENT APPLICANTS: 150.

NO. AWARDS: 45 to 50.

APPLICATION INFO:
Application information is available on the
web site.
Duration: One year.
Deadline: Berardo Award, Jewson Award,
NCFR Student Award and Winter Award:
May 1.

PUBLICATIONS:
*Journal of Marriage and the Family; Family
Relations; Journal of Family Theory and
Review.*

OFFICERS:
Anisa Zvonkovic, President

ADDRESS INQUIRIES TO:
E-mail: membership@ncfr.org

*PLEASE NOTE:
Czaplewski Fellowship Award will be
awarded only when there is a request for
support, but not more often than once very
other year.

JESSIE SMITH NOYES
FOUNDATION
122 East 42nd Street
Suite 2501
New York, NY 10168
(212) 684-6577
Fax: (212) 689-6549
E-mail: noyes@noyes.org
Web Site: noyes.org

TYPE:
General operating grants; Project/program
grants.

See entry 2006 for full listing.

OPEN SOCIETY INSTITUTE -
BALTIMORE   [1369]
201 North Charles Street
Suite 1300
Baltimore, MD 21201
(410) 234-1091
Fax: (410) 234-2816
E-mail: osi.baltimore@opensocietyfoundations.
org
Web Site: www.osibaltimore.org

AREAS OF INTEREST:
Criminal justice reform.

NAME(S) OF PROGRAMS:
• **Criminal and Juvenile Justice Program**

TYPE:
Project/program grants. The Criminal and
Juvenile Justice Program seeks to reduce the
use of incarceration and its social and
economic costs without compromising public
safety, and promote justice systems that are
fair, are used as a last resort, and offer
second chances. The Program supports
advocacy, public education, research,
grassroots organizing, litigation and
demonstration projects that focus on
reforming racial and social inequities at
critical stages of the criminal and juvenile
justice systems - from arrest to re-entry into
the community.

YEAR PROGRAM STARTED: 1998

PURPOSE:
To reduce Maryland's overuse of
incarceration and its social and economic
costs without compromising public safety.

LEGAL BASIS:
Foundation.

ELIGIBILITY:
Grants are made to organizations that have
tax-exempt status under Section 501(c)(3) of
the Internal Revenue Code. No grants are
made to individuals.

GEOG. RESTRICTIONS: Baltimore City, Maryland.

FINANCIAL DATA:
Amount of support per award: Varies.
Total amount of support: Varies.

APPLICATION INFO:
Applicants should submit a letter of inquiry
of two to three pages which includes:

(1) a description of the program to be
funded;
(2) the qualifications of the organization to
carry out the program;
(3) the ways in which the program reflects
the priorities of the Criminal and Juvenile
Justice Program;
(4) the amount of the budget and the funds
requested and;
(5) a copy of the IRS letter stating the
organization's tax-exempt status.
Duration: Varies.
Deadline: Grant applications are accepted on
an ongoing basis.

ADDRESS INQUIRIES TO:
Tara Huffman, Program Director
Criminal and Juvenile Justice Program
(See address above.)

PASADENA COMMUNITY
FOUNDATION   [1370]
301 East Colorado Boulevard
Suite 810
Pasadena, CA 91101
(626) 796-2097
Fax: (626) 583-4738
E-mail: jdevoll@pasadenacf.org
Web Site: pasadenacf.org

FOUNDED: 1954

AREAS OF INTEREST:
Charitable organizations (Pasadena area
only), children, youth and family, community
development, environment education, arts and
the humanities, health and people with
special needs.

TYPE:
Capital grants; Project/program grants. Grants
for non-recurring capital needs, such as
equipment, building repairs and vehicles.

YEAR PROGRAM STARTED: 1954

PURPOSE:
To support charitable organizations in the
Pasadena area.

LEGAL BASIS:
Nonprofit public benefit corporation.

ELIGIBILITY:
Applicants must be 501(c)(3) organizations.
No personal grants to individuals, churches
or schools. No grants out of the Pasadena
area.

GEOG. RESTRICTIONS: Greater Pasadena area,
California.

FINANCIAL DATA:
Amount of support per award: Capital grants:
Up to $25,000; Project/program grants: Up to
$30,000.
Total amount of support: $5,334,738 in
grants awarded for the year 2018.

REPRESENTATIVE AWARDS:
$15,632 to Kidspace Children's Museum;
$12,361 to Peace Over Violence; $30,000 to
Pasadena Educational Foundation.

APPLICATION INFO:
Guidelines are available on the Foundation
web site.
Duration: One year.
Deadline: Project/program grants: Early
February or late March. Capital grants: Early
August.

PUBLICATIONS:
Application guidelines; formal application
form; newsletter.

IRS I.D.: 20-0253310

ADDRESS INQUIRIES TO:
Mike deHilster, Program Officer
E-mail: mdehilster@pasadenacf.org

JAY AND ROSE PHILLIPS
FAMILY FOUNDATION OF
MINNESOTA   [1371]
615 First Avenue, N.E.
Suite 400
Minneapolis, MN 55413
(612) 623-1654
Fax: (612) 623-1653
E-mail: info@phillipsfamilymn.org
Web Site: phillipsfamilymn.org

FOUNDED: 1944

AREAS OF INTEREST:
Education, small business development and
entrepreneurship.

TYPE:
Project/program grants. Grants to improve
organizational effectiveness.

YEAR PROGRAM STARTED: 1944

PURPOSE:
To provide support for organizations and
projects that address unmet human and social
needs.

LEGAL BASIS:
Private foundation.

ELIGIBILITY:
Grants are made to organizations that have
tax-exempt status under Section 501(c)(3) of
the Internal Revenue Code. No grants are
made to individuals.

The Foundation's preference is to support
projects that represent new thinking about
community needs and innovative efforts.

GEOG. RESTRICTIONS: North Minneapolis,
Minnesota.

FINANCIAL DATA:
Amount of support per award: Typically,
$15,000 to $50,000.
Total amount of support: Varies.

NO. AWARDS: Varies.

APPLICATION INFO:
Application by invitation only.
Duration: Typically one year.

PUBLICATIONS:
Annual report; application guidelines.

IRS I.D.: 27-4196509

ADDRESS INQUIRIES TO:
Tracy Lamparty
Grants and Operations Manager
(See address above.)

*SPECIAL STIPULATIONS:
Unsolicited requests are not accepted.

PLOUGH FOUNDATION   [1372]
62 North Main, Suite 201
Memphis, TN 38103
(901) 521-2779
Fax: (901) 529-4063
E-mail: mail@plough.org
Web Site: www.plough.org

FOUNDED: 1960

AREAS OF INTEREST:
Families in crisis, public education and
youth, crime, health and economic
development.

TYPE:
Capital grants; Challenge/matching grants; Seed money grants.

YEAR PROGRAM STARTED: 1960

PURPOSE:
To make payments or distributions to charitable organizations or for charitable purposes which will benefit the greatest number of people in the City of Memphis and/or Shelby County, TN.

LEGAL BASIS:
Private, independent foundation.

ELIGIBILITY:
No grants for assistance to address a crisis management situation caused by poor initial planning, individuals and projects outside the Memphis/Shelby County (TN) area. No grants for funding for private schools K-12, public charter schools, funding for annual fund-raising, or to individuals.

GEOG. RESTRICTIONS: Shelby County, Tennessee.

FINANCIAL DATA:
Amount of support per award: Varies.
Total amount of support: Varies.

REPRESENTATIVE AWARDS:
University of Memphis; Memphis Child Advocacy Center; Memphis College of Art; Memphis Shelby Crime Commission.

APPLICATION INFO:
Applications are accepted by invitation only.
Duration: One to three years.
Deadline: Dates are posted on the Foundation web site.

PUBLICATIONS:
Brochure.

IRS I.D.: 23-7175983

BOARD OF TRUSTEES:
Diane Rudner, Chairperson
Patricia R. Burnham
Eugene J. Callahan
D.D. Eisenberg
Johnny B. Moore, Jr.
Peter Pettit
Steven Wishnia

ADDRESS INQUIRIES TO:
Bob Wallace, Chief Operating Officer and Chief Financial Officer
(See address above.)

PRITCHETT TRUST

BMO Harris Bank
790 North Water Street, Floor 11
Milwaukee, WI 53202
(414) 287-7250
Fax: (414) 287-8580
E-mail: trust.custody@bmo.com

TYPE:
Project/program grants; Seed money grants.

See entry 1039 for full listing.

KATE B. REYNOLDS CHARITABLE TRUST [1373]

128 Reynolda Village
Winston-Salem, NC 27106-5123
(336) 397-5500
Fax: (336) 723-7765
E-mail: laura@kbr.org
Web Site: kbr.org

FOUNDED: 1947

AREAS OF INTEREST:
Human services and health care for the financially disadvantaged.

NAME(S) OF PROGRAMS:
● **Forsyth County Program Area**
● **Health Improvement in North Carolina**

TYPE:
Capital grants; Challenge/matching grants; Conferences/seminars; Demonstration grants; Fellowships; Project/program grants; Seed money grants; Technical assistance; Training grants; Research contracts. Capacity building. Through the Forsyth County Program Area, the Trust responds to basic life needs and invests in solutions that improve the quality of life for financially needy residents of Forsyth County. This Division seeks impact through two program areas: Increasing Self Reliance and Providing Basic Needs.

Through the Health Improvement in North Carolina, the Trust responds to health and wellness needs and invests in solutions that improve the quality of health for financially needy residents of North Carolina. This Division seeks impact through two program areas: Supporting Prevention and Providing Treatment.

YEAR PROGRAM STARTED: 1947

PURPOSE:
To improve the quality of life and quality of health for the financially needy of North Carolina; to accelerate positive movement on critical community issues and to effect enduring systemic change.

LEGAL BASIS:
Private foundation.

ELIGIBILITY:
Organizations eligible for grants are those that have qualified for exemption under Section 501(c)(3) and are not private foundations or a Type III supporting organization. Grants are not made to individuals or for medical research. Advance consultations are required prior to accepting an application.

GEOG. RESTRICTIONS: North Carolina.

FINANCIAL DATA:
Amount of support per award: Average $20,000 to $200,000.

APPLICATION INFO:
The Trust requires prospective applicants to call for an advance consultation prior to submitting an application. Applications are only accepted electronically.
Duration: Generally one to three years.
Deadline: Second Tuesday in February and August.

PUBLICATIONS:
Newsletter.

IRS I.D.: 56-6036515

STAFF:
Laura Gerald, President
Stephanie Cooper-Lewter, Executive Vice President, Programs and Administration
Joel T. Beeson, Director of Administration
Nora Ferrell, Director of Communications
Alan G. Welch, Information Systems Manager

ADDRESS INQUIRIES TO:
Laura Gerald, President
(See address above.)

SAILORS' SNUG HARBOR OF BOSTON [1374]

c/o GMA Foundations
Two Liberty Square, Suite 500
Boston, MA 02109
(617) 391-3097
Fax: (617) 426-7087
E-mail: phall@gmafoundations.com
Web Site: www.sailorssnugharbor.org

FOUNDED: 1852

AREAS OF INTEREST:
Elderly and fishing families.

TYPE:
General operating grants; Project/program grants.

PURPOSE:
To address the social service needs of fishermen, their families, and low-income elders residing in coastal communities of Massachusetts.

LEGAL BASIS:
Private foundation.

ELIGIBILITY:
Grants are made to organizations that have tax-exempt status under Section 501(c)(3) of the Internal Revenue Code. No grants are made to individuals. Nonsectarian religious programs may apply.

GEOG. RESTRICTIONS: Massachusetts.

FINANCIAL DATA:
Amount of support per award: Typical one-year grant: $10,000; Multiyear grants: Up to $50,000 per year.
Total amount of support: $407,400 for the year 2019.

NO. AWARDS: 17 for the year 2019.

APPLICATION INFO:
Applications must be submitted online.
Duration: One or three years. One-year grant is renewable by reapplication.
Deadline: August 15.

ADDRESS INQUIRIES TO:
Phil Hall, Foundation Administrator
(See address above.)

GEORGE J. AND EFFIE L. SEAY MEMORIAL TRUST [1375]

Bank of America
1111 East Main Street, 12th Floor
Richmond, VA 23219
(202) 442-7460
E-mail: dc.grantmaking@ustrust.com
Web Site: www.bankofamerica.com/philanthropic/foundation.go

FOUNDED: 1959

AREAS OF INTEREST:
Arts, culture, humanities, education, and human services.

TYPE:
Project/program grants. Grants for specific needs.

PURPOSE:
To enhance the quality of life in the Commonwealth of Virginia.

LEGAL BASIS:
Private foundation.

ELIGIBILITY:
Nonprofit organizations only in the Commonwealth of Virginia. No grants to individuals or to endowment funds.

GEOG. RESTRICTIONS: Virginia.

FINANCIAL DATA:
Amount of support per award: $10,000 to $50,000.
Total amount of support: Varies.
Matching fund requirements: Stipulated for specific grants.

CO-OP FUNDING PROGRAMS: Other funding sources are encouraged.

APPLICATION INFO:
Guidelines are available online. Application must be submitted through the "Apply Now" link.
Duration: One year.
Deadline: April 1. Decision by June 30.

PUBLICATIONS:
Application guidelines.

ADDRESS INQUIRIES TO:
See e-mail address above.

*SPECIAL STIPULATIONS:
Grants made only to organizations in Virginia.

SHARE OUR STRENGTH   [1376]

1030 15th Street, N.W.
Suite 1100 W
Washington, DC 20005
(800) 969-4767
E-mail: info@strength.org
Web Site: www.nokidhungry.org

FOUNDED: 1984

AREAS OF INTEREST:
Domestic childhood hunger, hunger prevention and alleviation limited to summer meals, after-school meals, school breakfast and nutrition education.

NAME(S) OF PROGRAMS:
● No Kid Hungry

TYPE:
Project/program grants. Grants are focused on increasing participation in the federal nutrition programs, including summer meals, after-school meals, school breakfast, and on nutrition education.

YEAR PROGRAM STARTED: 1984

PURPOSE:
To end childhood hunger in the United States.

LEGAL BASIS:
Nonprofit organization.

ELIGIBILITY:
Applicants must be 501(c)(3) organizations, schools/school districts, churches/faith-based organizations or other organizations/agencies eligible to receive grants.

GEOG. RESTRICTIONS: United States.

FINANCIAL DATA:
Amount of support per award: Varies.
Total amount of support: $10,924,850 in grants payable for fiscal year 2018.

NO. AWARDS: 1,110 grants approved in fiscal year 2018.

APPLICATION INFO:
Applications will be accepted by invitation only.
Duration: One year. Renewal possible.
Deadline: Varies.

PUBLICATIONS:
Annual report.

SIERRA HEALTH FOUNDATION   [1377]

1321 Garden Highway
Sacramento, CA 95833
(916) 922-4755
Fax: (916) 922-4024
E-mail: info@sierrahealth.org
Web Site: www.sierrahealth.org

FOUNDED: 1984

AREAS OF INTEREST:
Improving health outcomes and reducing health disparities.

NAME(S) OF PROGRAMS:
● **Conference and Education Center**
● **Health Leadership Program**
● **Healthy Sacramento Coalition**
● **Nonprofit Event Sponsorships**
● **Responsive Grants Program**

TYPE:
Project/program grants. Sponsorship. Specific to funding opportunities - solicited.

YEAR PROGRAM STARTED: 1984

PURPOSE:
To invest in and serve as a catalyst for ideas, partnerships and programs that improve health and quality of life in northern California through convening, educating and strategic grantmaking.

LEGAL BASIS:
Private foundation.

ELIGIBILITY:
Applicant must be a public entity or designated 501(c)(3) organization by the IRS with 509(a)(1) or 509(a)(2) status. No grants to individuals, endowments or activities which exclusively benefit members of private or religious organizations.

GEOG. RESTRICTIONS: Northern California counties.

FINANCIAL DATA:
Amount of support per award: Varies by program.
Total amount of support: Varies.

PUBLICATIONS:
Healthy Youth Healthy Regions; *Renewing Juvenile Justice.*

IRS I.D.: 68-0050036

OFFICERS:
Chet P. Hewitt, President and Chief Executive Officer
Gil Alvarado, Senior Vice President of Finance and Administration and Chief Financial Officer
Kaying Hang, Vice President of Programs and Partnerships

BOARD OF DIRECTORS:
David W. Gordon
Jose Hermocillo
Chet P. Hewitt
Nancy P. Lee
Debra McKenzie
Robert Petersen, C.P.A.
Dr. Claire Pomeroy
Carol Whiteside

ADDRESS INQUIRIES TO:
See e-mail address above.

SOCIAL JUSTICE FUND NORTHWEST   [1378]

1904 Third Avenue, Suite 806
Seattle, WA 98101
(206) 624-4081 ext. 107
Fax: (206) 382-2640
E-mail: info@socialjusticefund.org
Web Site: socialjusticefund.org

FOUNDED: 1978

AREAS OF INTEREST:
Funding community-based groups to promote social justice activities and organizations attempting to establish a society that is politically and economically democratic, equitable and environmentally sound.

CONSULTING OR VOLUNTEER SERVICES:
Facilitates regional networking and general foundation information.

TYPE:
General operating grants; Project/program grants; Seed money grants; Training grants. Rapid response grants.

YEAR PROGRAM STARTED: 1978

PURPOSE:
To be a resource for organizations working for social justice in the states of Idaho, Montana, Oregon, Washington and/or Wyoming attempting to establish a society that is politically and economically democratic, equitable and environmentally just.

LEGAL BASIS:
Nonprofit, 501(c)(3), public foundation.

ELIGIBILITY:
Applicant must address fundamental issues facing Northwest/Northern Rockies or any organizations that work in and have a direct impact on the people of Idaho, Montana, Oregon, Washington and/or Wyoming. Considered are organizations that are led by the people most impacted.

GEOG. RESTRICTIONS: Idaho, Montana, Oregon, Washington and Wyoming.

FINANCIAL DATA:
Amount of support per award: Average grant: $15,000.
Total amount of support: Over $1,000,000 for the year 2018.

APPLICATION INFO:
Application information is available on the web site.
Duration: Two years.
Deadline: Varies.

PUBLICATIONS:
Guidelines; monthly e-mail newsletter; annual report.

IRS I.D.: 91-1036971

BOARD OF DIRECTORS:
Yen Baynes
Maya Berkowitz
Emily Bookstein
Rob Cato
Rebecca Chan
Gita Mehrotra
Aaron Oravillo
Kim Powe
Uma Rao
Carolanne Sanders
Ranfis Giannettino Villatoro

ADDRESS INQUIRIES TO:
Magan Do, Grantmaking Director
(See address above.)

THE STODDARD CHARITABLE TRUST [1379]

370 Main Street. 12th Floor
Worcester, MA 01608
(508) 459-8000

FOUNDED: 1939

AREAS OF INTEREST:
Culture, education and social services.

TYPE:
Capital grants. Grants to support activities in the Trustees' areas of interest.

YEAR PROGRAM STARTED: 1939

PURPOSE:
To provide funding to worthy causes in the Worcester, MA area and to help that community during times of need.

LEGAL BASIS:
Private, charitable foundation.

ELIGIBILITY:
Nonprofit organizations.

GEOG. RESTRICTIONS: Worcester, Massachusetts.

FINANCIAL DATA:
Amount of support per award: Varies.
Total amount of support: Approximately $4,822,000 for the year 2016.

APPLICATION INFO:
Applications should be made by letter (four copies) summarizing the request, together with background information. Include a copy of the IRS tax determination letter.
Duration: One year.
Deadline: Two weeks prior to one of five or six annual distribution meetings.

OFFICERS AND TRUSTEES:
Warner S. Fletcher, Chairman
Judith S. King, Treasurer
Valerie S. Loring, Secretary
Allen W. Fletcher

ADDRESS INQUIRIES TO:
Warner S. Fletcher, Chairman
(See address above.)

THE SUMMIT FOUNDATION

103 South Harris Street
Breckenridge, CO 80424
(970) 453-5970
E-mail: tsfadmin@summitfoundation.org
Web Site: www.summitfoundation.org

TYPE:
Capital grants; Challenge/matching grants; Endowments; General operating grants; Project/program grants; Scholarships; Technical assistance. The Foundation supports scholarship programs at Summit High School and neighboring community high schools. Scholarships are available to graduating seniors each year.

See entry 1265 for full listing.

SUNNEN FOUNDATION [1380]

7910 Manchester Avenue
St. Louis, MO 63143
(314) 781-2100

FOUNDED: 1953

AREAS OF INTEREST:
Grants for specific goal-oriented activities to protect reproductive and First Amendment rights and for youth and family services.

TYPE:
Capital grants; Challenge/matching grants; Development grants; Matching gifts; Project/program grants.

YEAR PROGRAM STARTED: 1953

LEGAL BASIS:
Private foundation.

ELIGIBILITY:
Limited to those organizations having tax-exempt status. No scholarship, research or travel grants are made to or for specific individuals.

GEOG. RESTRICTIONS: St. Louis, Missouri.

FINANCIAL DATA:
Assets of $16,771,971 (unaudited) as of December 31, 2017.
Amount of support per award: $1,000 to $430,700 for the year 2017.
Total amount of support: $724,700 for the year 2017.

NO. MOST RECENT APPLICANTS: Approximately 30.

NO. AWARDS: 15 for the year 2017.

REPRESENTATIVE AWARDS:
$155,000 to Planned Parenthood of St. Louis.

APPLICATION INFO:
The Sunnen Foundation has no formal application form. Proposal should include:
(1) summary page that describes the project and amount of funds requested;
(2) organizational background that includes mission, history, types of programs offered and constituencies served;
(3) project description that justifies the need, outlines specific goals, objectives and activities planned to meet the goals and objectives, a project timeline and specific methods of evaluation;
(4) project budget that notes anticipated expenses, including details of how the Sunnen Foundation funds will be used and anticipated income, including information about other grantmakers approached for funding;
(5) organizational budget that notes the current year budget and proposed budget for project year(s) showing income and expenses, the organization's most recent audited financial statement and public and private sources of funds and;
(6) supporting documents that should include a list of current board members, annual report and evidence of 501(c)(3) status.

Five copies of the proposal should be submitted.
Duration: Varies.
Deadline: Applications are accepted on a rolling basis. Board meets June and December to review.

PUBLICATIONS:
Guidelines.

IRS I.D.: 43-6029156

OFFICERS:
Kurt J. Kallaus, President and Director
Matthew S. Kreider, Vice President and Director
Susan S. Brasel, Treasurer and Director
Ruth Cardinale, Secretary and Director
Helen S. Sly, Director

ADDRESS INQUIRIES TO:
Kurt J. Kallaus, President
(See address above.)

TIDES FOUNDATION

P.O. Box 29198
San Francisco, CA 94129-0198
(415) 561-6400
Fax: (415) 561-6401
E-mail: info@tides.org
Web Site: www.tides.org

TYPE:
General operating grants; Project/program grants.

See entry 1268 for full listing.

UNITED JEWISH APPEAL-FEDERATION OF JEWISH PHILANTHROPIES OF NEW YORK

130 East 59th Street
New York, NY 10022
(212) 980-1000
(212) 836-1321
Fax: (212) 836-1353
E-mail: feinsteinl@ujafedny.org
Web Site: www.ujafedny.org

TYPE:
Awards/prizes; Block grants; Capital grants; Challenge/matching grants; Conferences/seminars; Demonstration grants; Development grants; Fellowships; General operating grants; Internships; Matching gifts; Project/program grants; Research grants; Scholarships; Technical assistance; Travel grants; Research contracts.

See entry 763 for full listing.

UNITED METHODIST HEALTH MINISTRY FUND [1381]

100 East First Avenue
Hutchinson, KS 67501
(620) 662-8586
Fax: (620) 662-8597
E-mail: healthfund@healthfund.org
Web Site: healthfund.org

FOUNDED: 1986

AREAS OF INTEREST:
Health care.

NAME(S) OF PROGRAMS:
- **Access to Health Care-System Change and Advocacy**
- **Early Childhood Development**
- **Healthy Congregations Program**

TYPE:
Challenge/matching grants; Conferences/seminars; Demonstration grants; General operating grants; Project/program grants; Seed money grants; Technical assistance; Training grants.

YEAR PROGRAM STARTED: 1986

PURPOSE:
To advance health, healing and wholeness for persons within and beyond the bounds of the former Kansas West Conference of the United Methodist Church.

LEGAL BASIS:
Church foundation.

ELIGIBILITY:
Projects and partners are chosen based on their potential to impact the health of Kansans.

GEOG. RESTRICTIONS: Kansas.

FINANCIAL DATA:
Amount of support per award:
Approximately $20,000 average grant.

Total amount of support: $2,000,000 to $3,500,000.

NO. MOST RECENT APPLICANTS: Approximately 130.

NO. AWARDS: Approximately 100.

REPRESENTATIVE AWARDS:
$250,000 to Enroll America to support expanded outreach efforts-Affordable Care Act enrollment; $150,400 to Prairie View, Inc., Newton, KS, for a Tri-County Mental Health Project to improve and increase mental health services.

APPLICATION INFO:
Grant proposals are accepted by invitation only.
Duration: Varies.

Deadline: January, March, July and October. Contact Fund for exact dates.

PUBLICATIONS:
Annual report; special publications.

IRS I.D.: 48-1019578

STAFF:
David Jordan, President
Katie Schoenhoff, Director of Programs
Dashinika Poindexter, Program Coordinator

ADDRESS INQUIRIES TO:
Katie Schoenhoff, Director of Programs
(See address above.)

*SPECIAL STIPULATIONS:
Preference for United Methodist Churches and agencies in Kansas.

WICHITA COMMUNITY FOUNDATION

301 North Main Street
Suite 100
Wichita, KS 67202
(316) 264-4880
Fax: (316) 264-7592
E-mail: wcf@wichitacf.org
Web Site: www.wichitacf.org

TYPE:
Project/program grants; Scholarships; Seed money grants.

See entry 1284 for full listing.

EDUCATION

Educational projects and research (general)

THE AMERICAN FOUNDATION FOR SUICIDE PREVENTION [1382]

199 Water Street
11th Floor
New York, NY 10038
(212) 363-3500 ext. 2015
Fax: (212) 363-6237
E-mail: grantsmanager@afsp.org
Web Site: afsp.org/research-grant-information

FOUNDED: 1987

AREAS OF INTEREST:
Suicide prevention.

NAME(S) OF PROGRAMS:
- **Pilot Innovation Grant**

TYPE:
Research grants.

PURPOSE:
To provide seed funding for new projects that have the potential to lead to larger investigations.

ELIGIBILITY:
Grants are awarded to investigators at any level affiliated with not-for-profit institutions or organizations. Grant applications are not accepted from for-profit organizations, or from federal or state government agencies. Applications from the Veterans Administration are eligible.

FINANCIAL DATA:
Amount of support per award: Up to $30,000.

NO. MOST RECENT APPLICANTS: 30.

NO. AWARDS: Varies.

APPLICATION INFO:
Applications must be submitted online at the Foundation web site.
Duration: One or two years.
Deadline: Mid-November.

ADDRESS INQUIRIES TO:
Carl Niedzielski, Research Grants Manager
(See address above.)

THE AMERICAN FOUNDATION FOR SUICIDE PREVENTION [1383]

199 Water Street
11th Floor
New York, NY 10038
(212) 363-3500 ext. 2015
Fax: (212) 363-6237
E-mail: grantsmanager@afsp.org
Web Site: afsp.org/research-grant-information

FOUNDED: 1987

AREAS OF INTEREST:
Suicide prevention.

NAME(S) OF PROGRAMS:
- **Postdoctoral Research Fellowships**

TYPE:
Fellowships; Research grants; Training grants.

YEAR PROGRAM STARTED: 1987

PURPOSE:
To enable young investigators to quality for independent careers in suicide research.

ELIGIBILITY:
Postdoctoral Research Fellowships are awarded for full-time training projects by investigators who have received an M.D. or Ph.D. degree within the preceding six years and have not had more than three years of fellowship support.

FINANCIAL DATA:
Amount of support per award: Up to $120,000 (stipend $50,000 per year and $10,000 per year institutional allowance).

NO. MOST RECENT APPLICANTS: 15.

NO. AWARDS: Varies.

APPLICATION INFO:
Applications must be submitted online at the Foundation web site.
Duration: Two years.
Deadline: Mid-November.

ADDRESS INQUIRIES TO:
Carl Niedzielski, Research Grants Manager
(See address above.)

THE AMERICAN FOUNDATION FOR SUICIDE PREVENTION [1384]

199 Water Street
11th Floor
New York, NY 10038
(212) 363-3500 ext. 2015
Fax: (212) 363-6237
E-mail: grantsmanager@afsp.org
Web Site: afsp.org/research-grant-information

FOUNDED: 1987

AREAS OF INTEREST:
Suicide prevention.

NAME(S) OF PROGRAMS:
- **Distinguished Investigator Award**

TYPE:
Research grants.

YEAR PROGRAM STARTED: 1987

PURPOSE:
To advance knowledge of suicide and the ability to prevent it; to fund new directions and initiatives in suicidology.

ELIGIBILITY:
Applicant must be an associate professor or higher with a proven history of research and publication in the area of suicide.

FINANCIAL DATA:
Amount of support per award: $125,000 ($62,500 per year).

NO. MOST RECENT APPLICANTS: 10.

NO. AWARDS: Varies.

APPLICATION INFO:
Applications must be submitted online at the Foundation web site.
Duration: Up to two years.
Deadline: Mid-November.

ADDRESS INQUIRIES TO:
Carl Niedzielski, Research Grants Manager
(See address above.)

THE AMERICAN FOUNDATION FOR SUICIDE PREVENTION [1385]

199 Water Street
11th Floor
New York, NY 10038
(212) 363-3500 ext. 2015
Fax: (212) 363-6237
E-mail: grantsmanager@afsp.org
Web Site: afsp.org/research-grant-information

FOUNDED: 1987

AREAS OF INTEREST:
Suicide prevention.

NAME(S) OF PROGRAMS:
- **Standard Research Grants**
- **Young Investigator Grants**

TYPE:
Research grants. Standard Research Grants are awarded to individual investigators. An additional annual stipend is available for mentors on Young Investigator Awards in which the investigator is at the level of Assistant Professor or lower.

YEAR PROGRAM STARTED: 1987

PURPOSE:
To advance the knowledge of suicide and the ability to prevent it; to promote the study of clinical, biological and psychosocial aspects of suicide.

ELIGIBILITY:
Grants are awarded to not-for-profit organizations.

FINANCIAL DATA:
Amount of support per award: Up to $100,000 for a Standard Research Grant or $90,000 over two years with a mentor on Young Investigator Grant.

NO. MOST RECENT APPLICANTS: Standard Research Grants: 80; Young Investigator Grants: 30.

NO. AWARDS: Varies.

APPLICATION INFO:
Applications must be submitted online at the Foundation web site.
Duration: Two years.
Deadline: Mid-November.

ADDRESS INQUIRIES TO:
Carl Niedzielski, Research Grants Manager
(See address above.)

AMERICAN HONDA FOUNDATION [1386]

1919 Torrance Boulevard
Torrance, CA 90501
(310) 781-4090
E-mail: ahf@ahm.honda.com
Web Site: www.honda.com/community

FOUNDED: 1984

AREAS OF INTEREST:
Youth education in the areas of science, technology, engineering, mathematics, environment, job training and literacy.

TYPE:
Challenge/matching grants; General operating grants; Project/program grants.

YEAR PROGRAM STARTED: 1984

PURPOSE:
To fund programs which strive to educate communities in the process of problem solving and planning; to educate minority youth in the areas of science and math.

LEGAL BASIS:
501(c)(3) corporate foundation.

ELIGIBILITY:
Applicants must be 501(c)(3) organizations, national in scope, impact and outreach and focused on youth and scientific education. To be considered for possible funding, programs related to youth and scientific education should be dedicated to improving the human

condition of all mankind, soundly managed and administered by enthusiastic and dedicated individuals who approach their jobs in a youthful way, look to the future or foresightful programs, innovative and creative programs that propose untried methods which ultimately may result in providing solutions to the complex cultural, educational, scientific and social concerns currently facing American society, broad in scope, intent, impact and outreach, possess a high potential for success with a relatively low incidence of duplication of effort, operate from a position of financial soundness, in urgent need of funding from a priority basis (not necessarily financial need), i.e., the relative importance of the program or project to the public and represent a minimal risk in terms of venture capital investment.

Grants are not given to individuals or for scholarships, politics, fund-raising activities, religious activities, arts and culture, medical or educational research, sponsorships for nonprofit, or disaster relief.

No in-kind contributions from the Foundation. No donations of Honda products.

GEOG. RESTRICTIONS: United States.

FINANCIAL DATA:
Amount of support per award: $20,000 to $75,000 per year; $30,000 to $50,000 average.
Total amount of support: $1,800,000 for fiscal year 2017.

APPLICATION INFO:
Proposals must be submitted online. No paper or faxed applications will be accepted.
Duration: One year.
Deadline: February 1 and August 1 for organizations that have never received funding from the Foundation. May 1 for organizations that have received at least one year of funding support in the last 10 years.

ADDRESS INQUIRIES TO:
See e-mail address above.

*SPECIAL STIPULATIONS:
One proposal per year, per grant seeker.

AMERICAN INSTITUTE OF CERTIFIED PUBLIC ACCOUNTANTS (AICPA)   [1387]

220 Leigh Farm Road
Durham, NC 27707
(919) 402-4473
E-mail: scholarships@aicpa.org
Web Site: thiswaytocpa.com/education/aicpa-legacy-scholarships

AREAS OF INTEREST:
Accounting.

NAME(S) OF PROGRAMS:
● **AICPA Scholarship for Minority Accounting Students**

TYPE:
Scholarships.

YEAR PROGRAM STARTED: 1969

PURPOSE:
To provide financial assistance to minority students who show significant potential to become C.P.As.

ELIGIBILITY:
An applicant must meet the following requirements:
(1) be an underrepresented minority in the accounting profession (e.g., Black or African

American, Hispanic or Latino, Native American or Asian American);
(2) enrolled as a full-time undergraduate (12 semester-hours or equivalent) or a full-time graduate-level student (nine semester-hours or equivalent) for the 2019-20 academic year; an exception may be granted if the student plans to participate in an internship;
(3) pursuing an undergraduate- or graduate-level degree in an "accounting-related" major ("accounting-related" shall be as determined by Sponsor in Sponsor's sole discretion);
(4) planning to pursue the C.P.A. licensure but not presently be a C.P.A.;
(5) completed at least 30 semester-hours (or equivalent) of college coursework, including at least six semester-hours (or equivalent) in accounting, by end of spring 2019;
(6) applied to or been accepted into a public or private, 501(c) four-year college or university located in the U.S. or its territories; the business program must be accredited by the AACSB and/or ACBSP;
(7) maintained an overall and major grade point average of at least 3.0 (on a 4.0 scale);
(8) be an AICPA student affiliate member (or have submitted a new member application); those interested can apply on the web site at no cost;
(9) be a U.S. citizen or permanent resident (green card holder) and;
(10) have some financial need (i.e., not receiving a full or partial scholarship(s) and/or grant(s) that cover and/or exceed one's educational expenses).

AICPA staff and their family members are not eligible to receive this scholarship.

GEOG. RESTRICTIONS: United States and its territories.

FINANCIAL DATA:
Amount of support per award: $3,000 to $5,000.
Total amount of support: Approximately $450,000 for the academic year 2018-19.

NO. AWARDS: Up to 90 per academic year.

APPLICATION INFO:
Information is available online.
Duration: One year. Renewable.
Deadline: March 1.

ADDRESS INQUIRIES TO:
AICPA Scholarship for Minority Accounting Students Program
(See e-mail address above.)

*SPECIAL STIPULATIONS:
Students selected to receive an AICPA scholarship must participate in the AICPA Legacy Scholars program, which includes performing at least eight hours of community service per semester to advocate for the C.P.A. profession. Through their community service efforts, AICPA Legacy Scholars enhance their leadership and communication skills by building relationships with both aspiring and seasoned C.P.As.

THE AMERICAN SOCIETY FOR NONDESTRUCTIVE TESTING, INC.   [1388]

1711 Arlingate Lane
Columbus, OH 43228
(614) 274-6003
(800) 222-2768 ext. 233 (U.S. and Canada)
Fax: (614) 274-6899
E-mail: james@asnt.org
Web Site: www.asnt.org

FOUNDED: 1997

AREAS OF INTEREST:
Promotion of nondestructive testing.

NAME(S) OF PROGRAMS:
● **ASNT Faculty Grant Award**

TYPE:
Development grants. The Society sponsors an annual award that will provide grants to foster the development of nondestructive testing and evaluation courses (NDT & NDE) as an integral part of its engineering curricula.

PURPOSE:
To provide incentive to faculty members of engineering or science programs at U.S. universities or colleges to revise their existing NDT courses or to develop new courses to teach NDT by providing financial resources in the form of a grant.

LEGAL BASIS:
501(c)(3) corporation.

ELIGIBILITY:
Faculty members from engineering or science programs at U.S. universities and colleges are encouraged to apply.

FINANCIAL DATA:
Amount of support per award: $10,000.
Total amount of support: Varies.

NO. AWARDS: Up to 2.

APPLICATION INFO:
Guidelines and application are available online.
Duration: One year.
Deadline: December 1. Funding will begin the following July.

ADDRESS INQUIRIES TO:
Jessica Ames, ASNT Program Coordinator (See address above.)

THE KATHRYN AMES FOUNDATION

c/o Pierson & Pierson
305 West Chesapeake Avenue, Suite 308
Towson, MD 21204
(410) 821-3006
Fax: (410) 821-3007
E-mail: info@kathrynames.org
Web Site: www.kathrynames.org

TYPE:
General operating grants; Project/program grants.

See entry 766 for full listing.

ARCHAEOLOGICAL INSTITUTE OF AMERICA

44 Beacon Street
Boston, MA 02108
(857) 305-9360
Fax: (857) 233-4270
E-mail: fellowships@archaeological.org
Web Site: www.archaeological.org

TYPE:
Fellowships. The Fellowship supports projects pertaining to the archaeology of Portugal. These include, but are not limited to, research projects, colloquia, symposia, publication, research-related travel, or travel to academic meetings for the purpose of presenting papers on the archaeology of Portugal.

See entry 767 for full listing.

ARIZONA STATE UNIVERSITY [1389]

P.O. Box 870901
Tempe, AZ 85287-0901
(480) 965-9139
E-mail: lsp@asu.edu
Web Site: eoss.asu.edu/lsp

AREAS OF INTEREST:
Leadership.

NAME(S) OF PROGRAMS:
● **ASU Leadership Scholarship Program**

TYPE:
Scholarships.

YEAR PROGRAM STARTED: 1977

PURPOSE:
To recognize outstanding high school graduating seniors who have achieved excellence in leadership.

ELIGIBILITY:
Applicant must be nominated by their high school counselor. Only one applicant per high school will be considered. Additionally, applicant must:
(1) have an unweighted grade point average of 3.25;
(2) have a history of community service or volunteering and involvement with clubs and organizations and;
(3) have a completed ASU application for undergraduate admission on file.

FINANCIAL DATA:
Amount of support per award: In-state: $10,000 per year; Out-of-state: $13,000 per year.

NO. AWARDS: 25 per year.

APPLICATION INFO:
Guidelines are available on the University web site.
Duration: Eight consecutive semesters.
Deadline: Early January.

ADDRESS INQUIRIES TO:
Lara Klinkner, Assistant Director
(See e-mail address above.)

ASSOCIATION OF INTERNATIONAL CERTIFIED PROFESSIONAL ACCOUNTANTS (THE ASSOCIATION)

220 Leigh Farm Road
Durham, NC 27707
(919) 402-4682
E-mail: scholarships@aicpa.org
academics@aicpa.org
Web Site: www.aicpa.org

TYPE:
Fellowships. Awarded annually to full-time minority accounting scholars who demonstrate significant potential to become accounting educators.

See entry 1506 for full listing.

BAT CONSERVATION INTERNATIONAL [1390]

500 North Capital of Texas Highway
Building One
Austin, TX 78746
(512) 327-9721
E-mail: grants@batcon.org
Web Site: www.batcon.org

FOUNDED: 1982

AREAS OF INTEREST:
Mammals, ecology, conservation and biology; specifically bats.

NAME(S) OF PROGRAMS:
● **BCI Student Research Scholarships**

TYPE:
Research grants; Scholarships. Support graduate students in research.

YEAR PROGRAM STARTED: 1990

PURPOSE:
To conserve bats and their habitat worldwide; to support research that specifically provides for bat conservation progress.

ELIGIBILITY:
Must be currently enrolled in a degree-granting program.

FINANCIAL DATA:
Amount of support per award: Varies.
Total amount of support: Varies.
Matching fund requirements: Varies.

NO. MOST RECENT APPLICANTS: 70 to 90.

NO. AWARDS: Varies.

APPLICATION INFO:
Open Requests for Proposals are posted online. Requests for student proposals will be offered mid- to late October.
Duration: One year.
Deadline: Varies.

IRS I.D.: 74-2553144

ADDRESS INQUIRIES TO:
Rebecca Patterson
Conservation Programs Coordinator
(See address above.)

BATON ROUGE AREA FOUNDATION

100 North Street
Suite 900
Baton Rouge, LA 70802
(225) 387-6126
E-mail: rschutte@braf.org
Web Site: www.braf.org

TYPE:
Capital grants; Challenge/matching grants; Conferences/seminars; Demonstration grants; Development grants; Matching gifts; Project/program grants; Scholarships; Seed money grants; Technical assistance; Training grants; Visiting scholars.

See entry 399 for full listing.

BAYER USA FOUNDATION

100 Bayer Road
Pittsburgh, PA 15205
(412) 777-2000
(800) 422-9374
Fax: (412) 778-4413
E-mail: bayerusafoundation@bayer.com
Web Site: www.bayer.us

TYPE:
General operating grants; Project/program grants.

See entry 1646 for full listing.

BETHESDA LUTHERAN COMMUNITIES [1391]

600 Hoffmann Drive
Watertown, WI 53094
(920) 261-3050
Fax: (920) 261-8441
E-mail: jenna.wegner@bethesdalc.org
Web Site: bethesdalc.org

AREAS OF INTEREST:
Developmental disabilities.

NAME(S) OF PROGRAMS:
● **Intellectual and Developmental Disabilities Scholastic Achievement Scholarships**

TYPE:
Scholarships.

PURPOSE:
To encourage Lutheran youth to develop God-pleasing attitudes and actions toward people with individual differences, and to consider careers in the field of intellectual and developmental disabilities services.

ELIGIBILITY:
Must be an active, communicant member of a Lutheran congregation, be classified as a freshman, sophomore or junior at an accredited four-year college or university, have a minimum 3.0 grade point average on a 4.0 scale, and have a career objective in the field of intellectual and developmental disabilities services.

GEOG. RESTRICTIONS: United States.

FINANCIAL DATA:
Amount of support per award: $3,000.
Total amount of support: Varies.

NO. MOST RECENT APPLICANTS: 30.

NO. AWARDS: Up to 10.

APPLICATION INFO:
Application requirements include:
(1) a completed application form;
(2) documentation of 100 hours of service to people with intellectual and/or developmental disabilities, volunteer or paid. Service must be completed within the past two years;
(3) a 250- to 300-word essay on how the intended academic course of study will support their career in the field of intellectual and/or developmental disabilities;
(4) four letters of recommendation (pastor, professor/teacher and two unrelated others);
(5) an official college/university transcript(s) and;
(6) a photograph showing applicant in service of someone with developmental disabilities (not required, but helpful).

Applicant may include any other material that will assist the committee to better know them.
Deadline: May 15. Announcement end of July.

ADDRESS INQUIRIES TO:
Jenna Wegner
Executive Administrative Assistant
(See address above.)

BIBLIOGRAPHICAL SOCIETY OF AMERICA [1392]

P.O. Box 1537
Lenox Hill Station
New York, NY 10021
(212) 452-2710
E-mail: bsa@bibsocamer.org
Web Site: www.bibsocamer.org

FOUNDED: 1904

AREAS OF INTEREST:
Study of books and manuscripts and other textual artifacts in traditional and emerging formats.

NAME(S) OF PROGRAMS:
● **BSA Fellowship Program**

TYPE:
Fellowships. Stipend in support of travel, living and research expenses.

YEAR PROGRAM STARTED: 1983

PURPOSE:
To support bibliographical inquiry as well as research in the history of the book trades and in publishing history.

ELIGIBILITY:
Open to Doctorates, postdoctorates and postgraduates. Applicants of any nationality can apply. Eligible topics may concentrate on books and documents in any field, but should focus on the book or manuscript (the physical object) as historical evidence. Such topics may include establishing a text or studying the history of book production, publication, distribution, collecting, or reading. Enumerative listings do not fall within the scope of this program.

FINANCIAL DATA:
Amount of support per award: Varies.
Total amount of support: Varies.

APPLICATION INFO:
Instructions on how to apply and application form are available on the Society's web site.
Deadline: November 1.

ADDRESS INQUIRIES TO:
Hope Mayo, Chair of the
Fellowship Committee
E-mail: bsafellowships@bibsocamer.org

BROWARD EDUCATION FOUNDATION   [1393]
600 S.E. Third Avenue, First Floor
Fort Lauderdale, FL 33301
(754) 321-2030
Fax: (754) 321-2706
E-mail: befinfo@browardschools.com
Web Site: browardeducationfoundation.org

FOUNDED: 1983

AREAS OF INTEREST:
Education.

NAME(S) OF PROGRAMS:
● **Broward Education Foundation School Supply Center**
● **Innovative Teacher Grants**
● **Student Scholarships**

TYPE:
Grants-in-aid; Scholarships.

YEAR PROGRAM STARTED: 1983

PURPOSE:
To provide resources for Broward County Public Schools students and teachers that increase achievement success in education.

LEGAL BASIS:
501(c)(3) education foundation.

GEOG. RESTRICTIONS: Broward County, Florida.

FINANCIAL DATA:
Amount of support per award: Varies.
Total amount of support: Approximately $2,885,000 for fiscal year 2017-18.

NO. MOST RECENT APPLICANTS: 1,300.

APPLICATION INFO:
Contact the Foundation for program-specific information.
Duration: Varies.
Deadline: Varies.

PUBLICATIONS:
Financial report.

ADDRESS INQUIRIES TO:
Coco Burns, Program Director
(See address above.)

THE BROWN FOUNDATION, INC.   [1394]
P.O. Box 130646
Houston, TX 77219-0646
(713) 523-6867
Fax: (713) 523-2917
E-mail: bfi@brownfoundation.org
Web Site: www.brownfoundation.org

FOUNDED: 1951

AREAS OF INTEREST:
Education, arts and humanities, civic/public affairs, medicine and science, and human services.

TYPE:
Assistantships; Capital grants; Challenge/matching grants; Fellowships; General operating grants; Matching gifts; Professorships; Project/program grants; Seed money grants.

YEAR PROGRAM STARTED: 1951

PURPOSE:
To distribute funds for public charitable purposes, principally for the support, encouragement and assistance to education, the arts and community service.

LEGAL BASIS:
Private foundation.

ELIGIBILITY:
Funding given to 501(c)(3) nonprofit institutions only. No grants to individuals.

GEOG. RESTRICTIONS: Primarily Texas.

FINANCIAL DATA:
Amount of support per award: Varies.
Total amount of support: $64,036,648 for fiscal year ended June 30, 2018.

APPLICATION INFO:
Grant proposals must include the purpose of the organization requesting funds, tax-exempt determination letter, audited financial statement, summary of proposed project, budget and letter of approval from a chief administrator. Applications will not be processed until all required information is included.
Duration: Typically one year.

PUBLICATIONS:
Application guidelines.

OFFICERS AND TRUSTEES:
William N. Mathis, Chairman
Isabel Lummis, President
Holbrook F. Dorn, Treasurer
Louisa Sarofim, Secretary
Andrew B. Abendshein, Assistant Treasurer
A. Maconda Abinader
Elisa S. Pye

ADDRESS INQUIRIES TO:
Ann Ziker, Executive Director
(See address above.)

FRITZ B. BURNS FOUNDATION   [1395]
21800 Oxnard Street
Suite 490
Woodland Hills, CA 91367
(818) 313-8818
Fax: (818) 313-8821

FOUNDED: 1955

AREAS OF INTEREST:
Education.

TYPE:
Capital grants; Scholarships. Grants are educational in nature. The emphasis is on buildings, equipment, endowments (not for operational expenses), scholarships, faculty fellowships, hospitals and hospital equipment and medical research.

YEAR PROGRAM STARTED: 1955

LEGAL BASIS:
Private foundation.

ELIGIBILITY:
Eligible organizations must have IRS 501(c)(3) not-for-profit status. Grants are not made to individuals or to religious organizations.

GEOG. RESTRICTIONS: California and Nevada.

FINANCIAL DATA:
Amount of support per award: $500 to $100,000.
Total amount of support: Varies.

APPLICATION INFO:
Applicant organizations must provide IRS 501(c)(3) documentation. Financial statements and a list of the organization's board of directors must be included with the application.
Duration: One year.
Deadline: September 30.

OFFICER:
Rex Rawlinson, President

ADDRESS INQUIRIES TO:
Rex Rawlinson, President
(See address above.)

THE CEMALA FOUNDATION   [1396]
330 South Greene Street, Suite 101
Greensboro, NC 27401
(336) 274-3541
Fax: (336) 272-8153
E-mail: cemala@cemala.org
Web Site: www.cemala.org

FOUNDED: 1986

AREAS OF INTEREST:
Early childhood development, workforce development, and transformational spaces and opportunities.

TYPE:
Capital grants; Challenge/matching grants; Development grants; Grants-in-aid; Project/program grants; Seed money grants; Technical assistance.

PURPOSE:
To better the quality of life for the citizens of Greensboro, NC.

LEGAL BASIS:
Private foundation.

ELIGIBILITY:
Eligible organizations must be IRS 501(c)(3) tax-exempt.

GEOG. RESTRICTIONS: Primarily Greensboro, North Carolina.

FINANCIAL DATA:
Amount of support per award: Varies.
Total amount of support: Varies.

APPLICATION INFO:
The Cemala Foundation is no longer accepting unsolicited grant proposals. It is making strategic investments in projects

compatible with the Foundation's vision. Consult its web site for additional information.

Duration: Typically one year. Renewal possible.

Deadline: March 1 and September 1.

STAFF:
Susan Schwartz, Executive Director
Melissa Burroughs, Assistant Treasurer

ADDRESS INQUIRIES TO:
Susan Schwartz, Executive Director
(See address above.)

THE COCA-COLA FOUNDATION, INC.   [1397]

P.O. Box 1734
Atlanta, GA 30301
(404) 676-2121
E-mail: cocacolacommunityrequest@coca-cola.com
Web Site: www.coca-colacompany.com/our-company/the-coca-cola-foundation

FOUNDED: 1984

AREAS OF INTEREST:
Water stewardship, healthy and active lifestyles, community recycling, and education.

TYPE:
Project/program grants.

PURPOSE:
To help develop and maintain vibrant, sustainable and local communities; to support initiatives and programs that respond in a meaningful way to community needs and priorities.

LEGAL BASIS:
Corporate foundation.

ELIGIBILITY:
Grants are made only to nonprofit 501(c)(3) or equivalent organizations. No grants to individuals, religious organizations or endeavors, or political, legislative, lobbying or fraternal organizations.

FINANCIAL DATA:
Amount of support per award: Varies.
Total amount of support: Varies.

APPLICATION INFO:
Detailed instructions and application form are available online.

Duration: Typically one year.

Deadline: Requests accepted and reviewed on a year-round basis.

PUBLICATIONS:
Annual report.

THE COMMUNITY FOUNDATION FOR THE GREATER CAPITAL REGION   [1398]

2 Tower Place
Albany, NY 12203
(518) 446-9638
Fax: (518) 446-9708
E-mail: info@cfgcr.org
Web Site: www.cfgcr.org

AREAS OF INTEREST:
Education.

TYPE:
Scholarships.

YEAR PROGRAM STARTED: 1968

PURPOSE:
To assist outstanding students who plan to pursue postsecondary education in college and vocational programs.

LEGAL BASIS:
Community foundation.

ELIGIBILITY:
Eligible students must be high school seniors enrolling in a full-time undergraduate course of study at an accredited college, university, or vocational-technical school.

GEOG. RESTRICTIONS: Varies according to scholarship opportunity.

FINANCIAL DATA:
Amount of support per award: Varies.
Total amount of support: Varies.

NO. AWARDS: Varies.

APPLICATION INFO:
Applications are posted online as they become available.

Duration: One year.

Deadline: Generally March to May.

ADDRESS INQUIRIES TO:
See e-mail address above.

COMMUNITY FOUNDATION OF THE LOWCOUNTRY, INC.   [1399]

4 Northridge Drive, Suite A
Hilton Head Island, SC 29926
(843) 681-9100
Fax: (843) 681-9101
E-mail: ksmith@cf-lowcountry.org
Web Site: www.cf-lowcountry.org

FOUNDED: 1994

TYPE:
Community impact grants. Community investment grants. Opportunity grants. Organization development grants.

PURPOSE:
To maintain and enhance the educational, social, culture, health, civic and environmental resources of the community.

LEGAL BASIS:
501(c)(3) and SC Secretary of State annual registration.

ELIGIBILITY:
501(c)(3) organizations.

GEOG. RESTRICTIONS: Hilton Head area, South Carolina.

FINANCIAL DATA:
Amount of support per award: Community Impact Grants and Community Investment Grants: $10,000 or more; Organizational Development Grants: Up to $5,000.
Total amount of support: Approximately $5,000,000 for fiscal year 2018.

APPLICATION INFO:
Applicants must attend a grants information session and register on the Giving Marketplace. In order to determine project eligibility, applicants are then required to meet with the Vice President for Grantmaking. Those eligible are invited to apply.

Duration: One year.

Deadline: January 15, May 15 and September 15.

ADDRESS INQUIRIES TO:
Kevin Smith, Grants
(See e-mail address above.)

COUNCIL ON TECHNOLOGY AND ENGINEERING TEACHER EDUCATION (CTETE)   [1400]

Rhode Island College
Department of Educational Studies
600 Mount Pleasant Avenue
Providence, RI 02809-1991
(401) 456-8793
E-mail: cmclaughlin@ric.edu
Web Site: ctete.org

FOUNDED: 1950

AREAS OF INTEREST:
Technology and engineering teacher education.

CONSULTING OR VOLUNTEER SERVICES:
NCATE state guideline preparation found on web site.

NAME(S) OF PROGRAMS:
• **Outstanding Research Award**

TYPE:
Challenge/matching grants; Conferences/seminars; Project/program grants; Research grants; Research contracts. Field study support and curriculum development.

YEAR PROGRAM STARTED: 1996

PURPOSE:
To discover philosophical rationales, theoretical models, principles and/or practices that potentially increase the effectiveness and efficiency of pre-service or in-service engineering and technology teacher education.

LEGAL BASIS:
Special-interest foundation.

ELIGIBILITY:
Applicants must be members of the Council on Technology and Engineering Teacher Education.

FINANCIAL DATA:
Amount of support per award: $500.

APPLICATION INFO:
Candidates may nominate themselves or be nominated by someone else. The application process consists of an initial screening by the CTETE Research and Scholarship Committee based on a brief abstract, followed by a peer review of papers submitted by selected finalists.

Duration: Typically one year.

Deadline: December 31.

ADDRESS INQUIRIES TO:
Charles McLaughlin, Past President
(See address above.)

THE DANA FOUNDATION

505 Fifth Avenue, Sixth Floor
New York, NY 10017
(212) 223-4040
Fax: (212) 317-8721
E-mail: danainfo@dana.org
Web Site: www.dana.org

TYPE:
Awards/prizes; Research grants. The Foundation focuses on brain research. Grants in these areas are made principally through competitive Clinical Hypotheses Programs in immuno-imaging, neuroimaging and brain-cardiovascular system interactions. These competitive grants programs support pilot testing of experimental and innovative ideas that in immunology and neuroscience research have the potential of advancing

clinical applications. The Foundation also supports an invitational program in which leading scientists are invited to compete for research grants designed to improve immune system responses to biological agents.

The Foundation has supported advances in education throughout its history. Its current interest is focused primarily on professional development programs that foster improved teaching of the performing arts in public schools. Programs emphasize innovative training projects that are exported from, or imported to, New York City, Washington, DC, Los Angeles and their surrounding areas.

See entry 2053 for full listing.

FREDERICK DOUGLASS INSTITUTE FOR AFRICAN AND AFRICAN-AMERICAN STUDIES   [1401]

311 Morey Hall
University of Rochester
P.O. Box 270440
Rochester, NY 14627-0440
(585) 276-5744
Fax: (585) 256-2594
E-mail: FDI@rochester.edu
Web Site: www.sas.rochester.edu/aas

FOUNDED: 1986

AREAS OF INTEREST:
African and African-American studies and graduate education through advanced research at the University of Rochester.

NAME(S) OF PROGRAMS:
● **FDI Postdoctoral Fellowship**

TYPE:
Awards/prizes; Conferences/seminars; Fellowships.

PURPOSE:
To promote the development of African and African-American studies and graduate education through advanced research at the University of Rochester; specifically, to support the completion of a project.

ELIGIBILITY:
Open to scholars who hold a Ph.D. degree in a field related to African and African-American studies.

FINANCIAL DATA:
Amount of support per award: Annual stipend of $40,000 and a $3,000 fund for research-related activities.

NO. MOST RECENT APPLICANTS: Approximately 30 to 40.

NO. AWARDS: 2 annually.

APPLICATION INFO:
Applicants must submit the following information online via www.rochester.edu/fort/fdi_postdoc:
(1) a completed FDI fellowship application form;
(2) a curriculum vitae;
(3) a three- to five-page description of the project (plus a short bibliography);
(4) a sample of published or unpublished writing on a topic related to the proposal and;
(5) three letters of recommendation that comment upon the value and feasibility of the work proposed, to be sent by the referees.
Duration: September 1 to May 31.
Deadline: December 31.

ADDRESS INQUIRIES TO:
Ghislaine Radegonde-Eison
Program Manager
(See e-mail address above.)

EDUCATIONAL TESTING SERVICE   [1402]

660 Rosedale Road
Princeton, NJ 08541
E-mail: internfellowships@ets.org
Web Site: www.ets.org/research/internship-fellowship

FOUNDED: 1947

AREAS OF INTEREST:
Psychometrics, validity, natural language processing and computational linguistics, cognitive psychology, learning sciences, linguistics, second language learning, teaching English as a second language, speech recognition and processing, teaching and classroom research, and statistics.

NAME(S) OF PROGRAMS:
● **Summer Internship Program for Graduate Students**

TYPE:
Internships. Interns in this eight-week program participate in research under the guidance of ETS mentors in one of the areas of interest listed above at ETS office located in Princeton, N.J. Interns also participate in seminars and workshops on a variety of topics.

YEAR PROGRAM STARTED: 1963

PURPOSE:
To provide research opportunities to individuals enrolled in a doctoral program in the fields described above.

LEGAL BASIS:
Not-for-profit organization.

ELIGIBILITY:
Graduate students who are currently enrolled in a full-time doctoral program in one of the areas listed above and who have completed a minimum of two years of coursework toward their Ph.D. or Ed.D. prior to the program start date are eligible to apply.

GEOG. RESTRICTIONS: Princeton, New Jersey.

FINANCIAL DATA:
Amount of support per award: $6,000 salary and transportation allowance for relocating to and from the Princeton area; housing will be provided for interns commuting more than 50 miles.

NO. MOST RECENT APPLICANTS: Average of 200.

NO. AWARDS: Approximately 10 to 15.

APPLICATION INFO:
The application process opens in November. Applicants must complete the electronic application form.
Duration: Eight weeks in June and July.
Deadline: February 1. Applicants will be notified by April 1.

PUBLICATIONS:
Program announcement.

STAFF:
Georgiana Weingart, Program Coordinator

ADDRESS INQUIRIES TO:
See e-mail address above.

FEDERATION OF AMERICAN CONSUMERS AND TRAVELERS   [1403]

318 Hillsboro Avenue
P.O. Box 104
Edwardsville, IL 62025
(618) 656-0454
(800) 872-3228
Fax: (618) 656-5369
E-mail: vrolens@usafact.org
Web Site: www.usafact.org

FOUNDED: 1984

AREAS OF INTEREST:
Education.

NAME(S) OF PROGRAMS:
● **Classroom and Community Grants**
● **Educational Grant Program**

TYPE:
Project/program grants; Scholarships. Education Grant Program provides scholarships to members and their immediate families, with the hope of increasing accessibility to advanced education.

PURPOSE:
To help provide supplies or to otherwise support a classroom project for which funds may not be readily available somewhere else; to improve the teacher's ability to teach and the students' opportunity to learn.

ELIGIBILITY:
Classroom Grants: Any dues-paying member of FACT may nominate any teacher to apply for a grant. Only one nomination per year per member.

Educational Grant: All applicants must be FACT members, their children or grandchildren.

GEOG. RESTRICTIONS: United States.

FINANCIAL DATA:
Amount of support per award: Classroom and Community Grants: $100 to $2,500; Educational Grant: Varies.
Total amount of support: Varies.

APPLICATION INFO:
Contact the Federation for guidelines.
Duration: Annual awards.
Deadline: Classroom and Community Grants: January, April, July and October; Educational Grant: Awarded quarterly.

ADDRESS INQUIRIES TO:
Vicki Rolens, Managing Director
(See address above.)

FLORIDA EDUCATION FUND   [1404]

201 East Kennedy Boulevard
Suite 1525
Tampa, FL 33602
(813) 272-2772 ext. 203
Fax: (813) 272-2784
E-mail: cjackson@fefonline.org
mdf@fefonline.org
Web Site: www.fefonline.org

FOUNDED: 1984

AREAS OF INTEREST:
Arts and sciences, mathematics, business, engineering, health sciences, nursing, higher education, visual and performing arts.

NAME(S) OF PROGRAMS:
● **McKnight Doctoral Fellowship**

TYPE:
Fellowships.

YEAR PROGRAM STARTED: 1984

PURPOSE:
To address the underrepresentation of African American and Hispanic faculty at colleges and universities in the state of Florida by increasing the pool of citizens qualified with Ph.D. degrees to teach at the college and university levels, thus expanding employment opportunities in the industry.

LEGAL BASIS:
Corporation.

ELIGIBILITY:
Applicants must be African American or Hispanic, U.S. citizens, and hold a minimum of a Bachelor's degree from a regionally accredited college or university. The Fellowship will be awarded only to persons who intend to seek the Ph.D. degree in one of the disciplines as described on the Fund's web site.

GEOG. RESTRICTIONS: United States.

FINANCIAL DATA:
Fellowships include a $12,000 stipend, plus up to $5,000 for tuition and fees. Any tuition and fees over $5,000 are waived.
Amount of support per award: Up to $17,000 per year.

NO. MOST RECENT APPLICANTS: 500.

NO. AWARDS: Up to 50 per academic year.

APPLICATION INFO:
Online application is available at the web site.
Duration: Three years, with fourth and fifth years supported by the institution if necessary.
Deadline: January 15.

PUBLICATIONS:
Annual report.

ADDRESS INQUIRIES TO:
Charles Jackson, Program Manager
(See address above.)

FOSTER CARE TO SUCCESS [1405]

23811 Chagrin Boulevard
Suite 210
Cleveland, OH 44122
(571) 203-0270
E-mail: scholarships@fc2success.org
Web Site: www.fc2success.org

FOUNDED: 1981

AREAS OF INTEREST:
Foster children.

NAME(S) OF PROGRAMS:
● **FCS Scholarship Fund**

TYPE:
Scholarships.

YEAR PROGRAM STARTED: 1986

PURPOSE:
To recognize outstanding scholarship and community service by a college student who has no family supporting their goals and efforts.

LEGAL BASIS:
501(c)(3), nonprofit organization.

ELIGIBILITY:
Applicants must:
(1) have been in public or private foster care for the 12 consecutive months leading up to and including their 18th birthday, or have been adopted or placed into legal guardianship from foster care after their 16th birthday, or they must have been orphaned for at least one year at the time of their 18th birthday;
(2) have been accepted into or expect to be accepted into an accredited, Pell-eligible college or other postsecondary school;
(3) be under the age of 25 on March 31 of the year in which they apply if they have not previously received scholarship funding from FC2S and;
(4) have been in foster care or orphaned while living in the U.S.

U.S. citizenship is not required.

GEOG. RESTRICTIONS: United States.

FINANCIAL DATA:
Funds may be used for tuition and books.
Amount of support per award: $2,500 to $5,000.
Total amount of support: Varies.

NO. MOST RECENT APPLICANTS: 2,200.

NO. AWARDS: 75 new; 300 repeat recipients.

APPLICATION INFO:
Information may be obtained from the address above or online from January 1 to March 31.
Duration: One academic year. Renewable up to five years if student remains eligible.
Deadline: March 31 for online application and postmark no later than April 15 for submission of additional materials required of applicant.

IRS I.D.: 52-1238437

EXECUTIVE DIRECTOR:
Eileen McCaffrey

ADDRESS INQUIRIES TO:
Dana Brown, Director of Scholarships and Grants
(See address above.)

FOUNDATION FOR TECHNOLOGY AND ENGINEERING EDUCATION [1406]

1914 Association Drive
Suite 201
Reston, VA 20191-1539
(703) 860-2100
Fax: (703) 860-0353
E-mail: iteea@iteea.org
Web Site: www.iteea.org

FOUNDED: 1939

AREAS OF INTEREST:
Technology education.

NAME(S) OF PROGRAMS:
● **Maley/FTEE Scholarship Technology and Engineering Teacher Professional Development**

TYPE:
Scholarships.

PURPOSE:
To support teachers in their preparation to increase the positive outcomes of technology and engineering education.

ELIGIBILITY:
Applicant must be a technology and engineering teacher at any grade level who is beginning or continuing graduate study. Criteria includes evidence of teaching success, plans for action research, recommendations, plans for professional development, and the applicant's needs.
Applicant must be a member of the International Technology and Engineering Educators Association.

FINANCIAL DATA:
Amount of support per award: $500.

NO. AWARDS: 1.

APPLICATION INFO:
Applicant must send an application package, which is to include the following required items:
(1) letter of application explaining plans for graduate study, plans for action research, the applicant's need and the school's name, address, telephone, grade level, and home address;
(2) resume (not to exceed four pages) describing current position, professional activities and achievements;
(3) official college transcript(s);
(4) documentation of acceptance into graduate school and;
(5) three letters of recommendation from among the following: undergraduate faculty, graduate faculty and school administration.
Duration: One year.
Deadline: December 1.

ADDRESS INQUIRIES TO:
Maley/FTEE Scholarship
Foundation for Technology and Engineering Education
(See address above.)

*SPECIAL STIPULATIONS:
Applicant must be a member of the ITEEA.

THE GAMBLE FOUNDATION [1407]

1660 Bush Street, Suite 300
San Francisco, CA 94109
(415) 561-6540 ext. 250
E-mail: jcallahan@pfs-llc.net
Web Site: www.gamblefoundation.org

FOUNDED: 1968

AREAS OF INTEREST:
Environment and agriculture.

TYPE:
Project/program grants.

YEAR PROGRAM STARTED: 1968

PURPOSE:
To promote the holistic management of preserved lands through grants to organizations focused mainly in the San Francisco Bay, CA area.

LEGAL BASIS:
Private foundation.

ELIGIBILITY:
Grants are made to organizations that have tax-exempt status under Section 501(c)(3) of the Internal Revenue Code. No grants are made to individuals.

GEOG. RESTRICTIONS: San Francisco, Marin and Napa counties, California.

FINANCIAL DATA:
Amount of support per award: $1,500 to $40,000.
Total amount of support: Varies.

APPLICATION INFO:
Proposals are accepted by invitation only.
Duration: One to four years.

ADDRESS INQUIRIES TO:
Grants Manager
(See address above.)

HAMILTON FAMILY CHARITABLE TRUST [1408]

200 Eagle Road
Suite 308
Wayne, PA 19087
(610) 293-2225
Fax: (610) 293-0967
E-mail: nwingo@218enterprises.com
Web Site: www.hfctrust.org

FOUNDED: 1992

AREAS OF INTEREST:
Education, youth and literacy-based education programs for underserved children and youth.

TYPE:
Challenge/matching grants; Project/program grants.

YEAR PROGRAM STARTED: 1996

PURPOSE:
To promote quality programs of education for economically underserved youth.

LEGAL BASIS:
Private foundation.

ELIGIBILITY:
Grants are made to organizations that have tax-exempt status under Section 501(c)(3) of the Internal Revenue Code. No grants are made to individuals.

GEOG. RESTRICTIONS: Philadelphia, Pennsylvania and surrounding counties.

FINANCIAL DATA:
Amount of support per award: $5,000 to $100,000.

APPLICATION INFO:
Application form and guidelines are available on the Trust web site.
Duration: One calendar year.
Deadline: November 1, February 1, May 1 and August 1.

STAFF:
Nancy Wingo, Executive Director

ADDRESS INQUIRIES TO:
Nancy Wingo, Executive Director
(See address above.)

HANNAFORD CHARITABLE FOUNDATION [1409]

145 Pleasant Hill Road
Scarborough, ME 04074
E-mail: hannafordcharitablefoundation@hannaford.com
Web Site: www.hannaford.com

AREAS OF INTEREST:
Education, health through healthy communities and food security.

TYPE:
Capital grants; Project/program grants. Employee scholarships.

YEAR PROGRAM STARTED: 1994

PURPOSE:
To provide financial support to nonprofit organizations dedicated to improving the communities where Hannaford operates.

LEGAL BASIS:
Private foundation.

ELIGIBILITY:
Preference for funding is given to organizations or programs that involve Hannaford associates, are located in Hannaford's marketing area, and have the potential to provide ongoing services to Foundation customers.

The Foundation does not offer support to individuals, tax-supported institutions or scholarship (employee) programs outside of their marketing area.

GEOG. RESTRICTIONS: Maine, Massachusetts, New Hampshire, New York and Vermont.

FINANCIAL DATA:
Amount of support per award: Varies.
Total amount of support: Varies.

NO. AWARDS: Varies.

APPLICATION INFO:
Instructions and requirements are available on the Foundation web site.
Duration: Typically one year.
Deadline: Grants submissions are reviewed quarterly.

HARBUS FOUNDATION [1410]

Harvard Business School
Soldiers Field
Boston, MA 02163
(617) 495-6528
Fax: (617) 495-8619
E-mail: foundation@harbus.org
Web Site: www.harbus.org/foundation

FOUNDED: 1997

AREAS OF INTEREST:
Education, journalism and literacy.

TYPE:
Project/program grants. The Foundation, which was formed by the student-run Harbus News Corporation at Harvard Business School, seeks to give back to the community by supporting programs of educational development in the communities where students live and learn.

PURPOSE:
To support small, community-based organizations, individuals, or local schools with limited resources to establish and sustain new and innovative programs in the areas of literacy, journalism, and/or education.

ELIGIBILITY:
Proposals will be accepted from individuals and tax-exempt organizations as defined by Section 501(c)(3) of the Internal Revenue Code for purposes to be carried out within the greater Boston area.

The Foundation does not fund scholarships and fellowships, religious organizations for religious purposes, city or state governments, capital campaigns, for-profit organizations or purely personal needs.

GEOG. RESTRICTIONS: Greater Boston, Massachusetts area with priority given to the communities of Allston and Brighton.

FINANCIAL DATA:
Amount of support per award: $20,000.
Total amount of support: $60,000 for the year 2018.

NO. AWARDS: 3 for the year 2018.

APPLICATION INFO:
Application for funding is by invitation only. However, if one's organization aligns with the Foundation mission, send e-mail with a brief description of this organization and desired use of the Foundation resources.
Duration: One year. Renewal possible by reapplication for a maximum of three years.
Deadline: December 1.

PUBLICATIONS:
Brochure.

THE PHIL HARDIN FOUNDATION [1411]

2750 North Park Drive
Meridian, MS 39305
(601) 483-4282
Fax: (601) 483-5665
E-mail: info@philhardin.org
Web Site: www.philhardin.org

FOUNDED: 1964

AREAS OF INTEREST:
Education with special (but not exclusive) emphasis on preK-12th grade.

TYPE:
Challenge/matching grants; Conferences/seminars; Endowments; Internships; Matching gifts; Project/program grants. Foundation's current primary focus is improving student achievement for preK-12th grade.

YEAR PROGRAM STARTED: 1964

PURPOSE:
To improve teaching and learning for Mississippians from grades preK-12.

LEGAL BASIS:
Tax-exempt, private foundation.

ELIGIBILITY:
Tax-exempt organizations in and out of Mississippi for projects to improve the education of Mississippians. No individual grants.

GEOG. RESTRICTIONS: Mississippi.

FINANCIAL DATA:
Amount of support per award: $2,000 to $500,000.
Total amount of support: $2,500,000 per year for all programs.
Matching fund requirements: Stipulated with specific program.

NO. MOST RECENT APPLICANTS: 68.

NO. AWARDS: 25 to 30.

APPLICATION INFO:
Proposals are to be based on current research and best practices. If not available, then prior approval to submit proposal must be obtained. Applications must be submitted online and include the following:
(1) IRS tax-exempt determination letter;
(2) list of board members, affiliations and contact information;
(3) most recent audited financial statement, including 990;
(4) copy of operating budget and;
(5) list of past and present funders.

The Foundation does not accept videotapes, faxed or e-mailed proposals.
Duration: One-time, one-year or multiyear grants. Some renewals possible.

OFFICERS:
Robert Ward, President and Chairperson
R.B. Deen, Jr., Senior Vice President
Marty Davidson, Vice President for Investments and Treasurer
Ronnie L. Walton, Secretary and General Counsel

DIRECTORS:
Kacey Bailey
Jim McGinnis
Michael Van Veckhoven

ADDRESS INQUIRIES TO:
Administrative Assistant
(See address above.)

HEALTH RESOURCES AND SERVICES ADMINISTRATION [1412]
5600 Fishers Lane, Room 15-N78
Rockville, MD 20857
(301) 443-2909
Fax: (301) 451-5629
E-mail: SDSProgram@hrsa.gov
Web Site: bhw.hrsa.gov

AREAS OF INTEREST:
Health professions and nursing education.

NAME(S) OF PROGRAMS:
- **Scholarships for Disadvantaged Students**

TYPE:
Scholarships. Funds made available to eligible schools for the purpose of providing scholarships to full-time financially needy students from disadvantaged backgrounds. Students must apply at the financial aid office of school where enrolled or admitted for enrollment.

YEAR PROGRAM STARTED: 1991

PURPOSE:
To improve and expand health care services for underserved people.

LEGAL BASIS:
Government agency.

ELIGIBILITY:
Student must be a citizen or permanent resident of the U.S. enrolled in a health profession or nursing program and be from a disadvantaged background.

GEOG. RESTRICTIONS: United States.

FINANCIAL DATA:
Amount of support per award: Up to $40,000 per student.
Total amount of support: Varies.

NO. AWARDS: Approximately 79.

APPLICATION INFO:
Contact student financial aid office at the school attended for application procedure.
Duration: Four years. Must reapply for additional funding after four years.
Deadline: March.

WILLIAM G. AND MYRTLE E. HESS CHARITABLE TRUST [1413]
c/o JPMorgan
28660 Northwestern Highway
Southfield, MI 48034
(248) 738-6169
Fax: (800) 919-3085
E-mail: kimberly.l.thomas@jpmorgan.com
Web Site: www.jpmorgan.com/onlinegrants

FOUNDED: 1969

AREAS OF INTEREST:
Science, education and charity.

TYPE:
General operating grants; Grants-in-aid; Project/program grants.

YEAR PROGRAM STARTED: 1969

PURPOSE:
To benefit organizations in Michigan.

ELIGIBILITY:
Eligible organizations must be nonprofit, 501(c)(3) tax-exempt. Grants are not given to individuals or for religious or political purposes.

GEOG. RESTRICTIONS: Michigan.

FINANCIAL DATA:
Amount of support per award: $1,000 to $10,000.
Total amount of support: Varies.

APPLICATION INFO:
Applications are to be submitted online.
Duration: Typically one year.
Deadline: August 15. Decisions on grant requests made annually in September.

ADDRESS INQUIRIES TO:
Kimberly Thomas, Trust Officer
(See address above.)

*PLEASE NOTE:
Applications received late will be held until the following year.

HUTCHINSON COMMUNITY FOUNDATION
One North Main Street
Suite 501
Hutchinson, KS 67501
(620) 663-5293
Fax: (620) 663-9277
E-mail: info@hutchcf.org
Web Site: hutchcf.org

TYPE:
Project/program grants; Seed money grants.

See entry 420 for full listing.

INTERNATIONAL ASSOCIATION OF ICE CREAM DISTRIBUTORS AND VENDORS (IAICDV) [1414]
3601 East Joppa Road
Baltimore, MD 21234
(410) 931-8100
Fax: (410) 931-8111
E-mail: info@iaicdv.org
Web Site: www.iaicdv.org

FOUNDED: 1969

AREAS OF INTEREST:
The ice cream vending and distributing industries.

NAME(S) OF PROGRAMS:
- **IAICDV Annual Scholarship**

TYPE:
Scholarships.

YEAR PROGRAM STARTED: 1990

PURPOSE:
To award deserving applicants who are determined to further their profession, and our industry, through advanced education.

ELIGIBILITY:
The following criteria apply:
(1) Applicant must be an owner of a member company, employee of a member company or a dependent (natural or adopted) of a member company; the member company must be in good standing with the IAICDV;
(2) Applicant must be or have been working in the ice cream industry during the award year and;
(3) Applicant must use the scholarship for their postsecondary education, including university, college or trade school.

FINANCIAL DATA:
Amount of support per award: $10,000.
Total amount of support: $10,000.

NO. MOST RECENT APPLICANTS: 15.

NO. AWARDS: 1.

APPLICATION INFO:
Contact the Association for detailed guidelines.
Duration: One-time award.
Deadline: August 1.

ADDRESS INQUIRIES TO:
IAICDV Scholarship Program
(See address above.)

INTERNATIONAL LITERACY ASSOCIATION (ILA) [1415]
P.O. Box 8139
Newark, DE 19714-8139
(800) 336-7323 (U.S. and Canada)
(302) 731-1600 (all other countries)
E-mail: ilaawards@reading.org
Web Site: www.literacyworldwide.org

FOUNDED: 1956

AREAS OF INTEREST:
Reading and literacy through professional development, advocacy, partnership, research, and global literacy development.

NAME(S) OF PROGRAMS:
- **Jeanne S. Chall Research Fellowship**
- **Elva Knight Research Grant**
- **Constance McCullough International Research Grant**
- **Helen M. Robinson Grant**
- **Nila Banton Smith Teacher as Researcher Grant**
- **Steven A. Stahl Research Grant**

TYPE:
Awards/prizes; Fellowships; Grants-in-aid; Research grants. Jeanne S. Chall Research Fellowship encourages and supports reading research by promising scholars. Its special emphasis is to support research efforts in the areas of beginning reading, readability, reading difficulty, stages of reading development, the relation of vocabulary to reading, and diagnosing and teaching adults with limited reading ability.

Elva Knight Research Grant is awarded annually to support reading or literacy.

Constance McCullough International Research Grant is awarded annually to assist a member of the International Literacy Association in the investigation of reading-related problems and to encourage international professional development activities that are carried out in countries outside the U.S. or Canada.

Helen M. Robinson Grant is given annually to assist doctoral students at the early stages of their dissertation research in the areas of reading and literacy.

Nila Banton Smith Teacher as Researcher Grant supports classroom teachers who undertake action research inquiries about literacy and instruction.

Steven A. Stahl Research Grant encourages and supports promising graduate students in their research. The grant will be awarded annually to a recipient with at least three years of teaching experience who is conducting classroom research (including action research) focused on improving reading instruction and children's reading achievement.

PURPOSE:
To promote reading by continuously
advancing the quality of literacy instruction
and research worldwide.

FINANCIAL DATA:
Amount of support per award: Jeanne S.
Chall, Elva Knight and Nila Banton Smith:
$5,000; Constance McCullough: $2,000;
Helen M. Robinson: $1,200; Steven A. Stahl:
$1,000.
Total amount of support: Varies.

NO. AWARDS: 1 each annually. Research grants
vary.

APPLICATION INFO:
Application guidelines are available online.
Deadline: March 15.

PUBLICATIONS:
Application guidelines.

ADDRESS INQUIRIES TO:
Dawn Roberts, Human Resources Associate
E-mail: mroberts@reading.org
(See address above.)

INTERNATIONAL LITERACY ASSOCIATION (ILA)   [1416]

P.O. Box 8139
Newark, DE 19714-8139
(800) 336-7323 (U.S. and Canada)
(302) 731-1600 (all other countries)
E-mail: ilaawards@reading.org
Web Site: www.literacyworldwide.org

FOUNDED: 1956

AREAS OF INTEREST:
Reading and literacy through professional
development, advocacy, partnership, research,
and global literacy development.

NAME(S) OF PROGRAMS:
● **ILA Erwin Zolt Digital Literacy Game
   Changer Award**
● **ILA Jerry Johns Outstanding Teacher
   Educator in Reading Award**

TYPE:
Awards/prizes; Research grants; Travel
grants. ILA Erwin Zolt Digital Literacy
Game Changer Award is presented annually
to honor literacy game changers in online
collaboration, who are making an outstanding
and innovative contribution to the use of
technology in literacy education.

ILA Jerry Johns Outstanding Teacher
Educator in Reading Award honors an
outstanding college or university teacher of
reading methods or reading-related courses.
Nominees must be Association members,
affiliated with a college or a university, and
engaged in teacher preparation in reading at
the undergraduate and/or graduate levels.

PURPOSE:
To promote literacy worldwide.

FINANCIAL DATA:
Amount of support per award: Jerry Johns:
$1,000.

APPLICATION INFO:
Forms and guidelines can be obtained at the
Association web site.
Deadline: March 15.

ADDRESS INQUIRIES TO:
Dawn Roberts, Human Resources Associate
E-mail: mroberts@reading.org
(See address above.)

JELLISON BENEVOLENT SOCIETY   [1417]

P.O. Box 145
Junction City, KS 66441-0145
(785) 762-5566
E-mail: s_williams1948@yahoo.com

FOUNDED: 1947

AREAS OF INTEREST:
Higher education.

TYPE:
Scholarships.

PURPOSE:
To aid area students in pursuit of higher
education.

LEGAL BASIS:
Private foundation.

ELIGIBILITY:
Must be a high school senior or older,
preferably a resident of Geary County, KS.

GEOG. RESTRICTIONS: Typically Geary County,
Kansas.

FINANCIAL DATA:
Amount of support per award: $500 to
$1,500 per semester.
Total amount of support: Varies.

NO. MOST RECENT APPLICANTS: 75.

NO. AWARDS: 71.

APPLICATION INFO:
Contact the Society for guidelines.
Duration: One year. Renewable by supplying
copy of grades above 2.0.
Deadline: June 20 and November 20.

IRS I.D.: 48-6106092

STAFF:
Dale Ann Clore, President
Susan E. Williams, Secretary

ADDRESS INQUIRIES TO:
Susan E. Williams, Secretary
(See address above.)

JPRO NETWORK (JEWISH PROFESSIONAL RESOURCE ORGANIZATION)   [1418]

25 Broadway, Suite 1700
New York, NY 10004
(212) 284-6945
E-mail: info@jpro.org
Web Site: www.jpro.org

FOUNDED: 1899

AREAS OF INTEREST:
Jewish communal services.

NAME(S) OF PROGRAMS:
● **Norman Edell Scholarship**
● **Graduate Student Network**
● **Local Groups Network**
● **Mandelkorn Distinguished Service
   Award**
● **Professional Development Programs**
● **Young Professional Award**

TYPE:
Awards/prizes; Conferences/seminars;
Internships. Support of local groups of
Jewish professionals.

YEAR PROGRAM STARTED: 1899

PURPOSE:
To enrich Jewish education in the communal
service field; to connect and enhance
professionals working on behalf of the
Jewish community.

LEGAL BASIS:
Nonprofit corporation.

GEOG. RESTRICTIONS: United States and
Canada.

FINANCIAL DATA:
Amount of support per award: Varies.

NO. AWARDS: 2.

APPLICATION INFO:
Contact JPRO Network through its web site
for application procedures.

PUBLICATIONS:
Journal of Jewish Communal Service;
monthly newsletter.

STAFF:
Ilana Aisen, Executive Director
Erica Goldman, Director of Program and
Operations

ADDRESS INQUIRIES TO:
Erica Goldman, Director of
Program and Operations
(See e-mail address above.)

WILLIAM R. KENAN, JR. CHARITABLE TRUST   [1419]

360 Kenan Center Drive, Floor 5
Chapel Hill, NC 27599
(919) 391-7222
Fax: (919) 962-3331
E-mail: dzinn@kenancharitabletrust.org
Web Site: www.kenancharitabletrust.org

FOUNDED: 1965

AREAS OF INTEREST:
Education.

TYPE:
Project/program grants.

PURPOSE:
To support educational programs of interest
to the Trust.

LEGAL BASIS:
Private foundation.

ELIGIBILITY:
The Foundation does not accept unsolicited
proposals.

GEOG. RESTRICTIONS: United States, primarily
within Florida, Kentucky, New York and
North Carolina.

FINANCIAL DATA:
Amount of support per award: Varies.
Total amount of support: Varies.

APPLICATION INFO:
Trustee's statement of guidelines, areas of
interest and required procedures are available
on request.
Duration: Varies.

ADDRESS INQUIRIES TO:
Douglas Zinn, Executive Director
(See address above.)

*PLEASE NOTE:
The Trust does not accept unsolicited
proposals.

CHARLES G. KOCH CHARITABLE FOUNDATION   [1420]

1320 North Courthouse Road
Suite 500
Arlington, VA 22201
(703) 875-1770
Fax: (703) 875-1766
E-mail: grants@charleskochfoundation.org
Web Site: www.charleskochfoundation.org

FOUNDED: 1980

AREAS OF INTEREST:
Higher education, research, and professional education programs.

TYPE:
Fellowships; Project/program grants; Research grants; Seed money grants; Travel grants. Dissertation grants.

YEAR PROGRAM STARTED: 1980

PURPOSE:
To advance an understanding of how economic freedom improves the well-being of people around the world.

LEGAL BASIS:
Private foundation.

ELIGIBILITY:
The Foundation primarily makes grants to Section 501(c)(3) public charities. The Foundation does not support for-profit corporations or individuals. Grant proposals for capital construction, debt reduction, or general fund-raising drives or events are discouraged. The Foundation does not make grants intended to support lobbying activities or candidates for political office, and rarely funds endowments.

Proposals will be considered for dissertations across a variety of disciplines that examine foundational, system-level and applied research questions.

The Foundation invites recent Ph.D.s and doctoral candidates with an expected graduation date of spring 2021 to apply for postdoctoral fellowships.

GEOG. RESTRICTIONS: United States.

FINANCIAL DATA:
Amount of support per award: Dissertation grants: Up to $5,000; All others: Varies depending on program.

APPLICATION INFO:
Organizations seeking grants must submit a proposal online. If the proposal meets the initial requirements, it is reviewed to assess whether it fits within the Foundation's priorities. Prospective grantees may be contacted for further information.
Duration: Varies depending on needs and nature of the request.
Deadline: Proposals are evaluated on a rolling basis.

STAFF:
Brian Hooks, President
Vonda Holliman, Secretary and Treasurer
Ryan Stowers, Executive Director
Matthew Brown, Policy Research Director
Teri Akpovi, Senior Programs Recruiter
Hussein Hussein, Program Officer
Elizabeth Brannen, Human Resource Coordinator

ADDRESS INQUIRIES TO:
Teri Akpovi, Senior Programs Recruiter
(See address above.)

THE JEAN AND E. FLOYD KVAMME FOUNDATION   [1421]
P.O. Box 2494
Saratoga, CA 95070
(408) 395-2829
Fax: (408) 354-0804

AREAS OF INTEREST:
Arts, charitable and cultural, education, health, medical research and Christian religious organizations.

TYPE:
Capital grants; Development grants; General operating grants; Project/program grants. Medical grants are given primarily in the areas of Alzheimers, leukemia, arthritis, and spondylitis; however, grants for research in other areas are considered.

PURPOSE:
To support organizations and institutes that promote arts, cultural, education, health, medical, scientific and social advancement of the international communities.

LEGAL BASIS:
Corporate contributions.

ELIGIBILITY:
Grants are made to organizations that have tax-exempt status under Section 501(c)(3) of the Internal Revenue Code and international Christian organizations. No grants are made to individuals.

GEOG. RESTRICTIONS: Artistic and educational grants: Northern California.

FINANCIAL DATA:
Amount of support per award: Varies.
Total amount of support: Varies.

APPLICATION INFO:
Applicants must submit a brief (one-page) letter of intent with a brief description of the project, dollar amount and verification of 501(c)(3) status.
Duration: One year.

TRUSTEE:
Jean Kvamme

ADDRESS INQUIRIES TO:
Jean Kvamme, Trustee
(See address above.)

LEARNING FOR LIFE   [1422]
1325 West Walnut Hill Lane
Irving, TX 75038
(972) 580-2433
Fax: (214) 256-4078
E-mail: exploring@lflmail.org
Web Site: www.learningforlife.org
www.exploring.org

AREAS OF INTEREST:
Career opportunities, life skills, service learning, character education and leadership experience.

NAME(S) OF PROGRAMS:
● **Exploring Program**

TYPE:
Awards/prizes; Scholarships. Exploring provides exciting activities and one-on-one mentorship for youth looking to discover their future.

PURPOSE:
To provide young men and women, ages 10 to 20, with an opportunity to learn about a wide variety of career fields and network with professionals already working in those fields; to offer hands-on experience, valuable networking contacts and interaction with other youth who share the same interests and aspirations.

ELIGIBILITY:
Open to young men and women 10 to 20 years old. Must be a participant in the Learning for Life Exploring Program to receive scholarship.

FINANCIAL DATA:
Amount of support per award: Varies per award.

Total amount of support: Varies.

APPLICATION INFO:
Guidelines are available on the web site.
Duration: One year. Must reapply.
Deadline: Varies per program.

ADDRESS INQUIRIES TO:
Tim Anderson, Senior Director of Exploring, Team Lead
(See address above.)

MARSHALL COMMUNITY FOUNDATION   [1423]
614 Homer Road
Marshall, MI 49068
(269) 781-2273
Fax: (269) 781-9747
E-mail: info@marshallcf.org
Web Site: www.marshallcf.org

FOUNDED: 1970

AREAS OF INTEREST:
Arts and education, culture, environment, health and well-being, human services, youth and seniors, and community/economic development.

TYPE:
Project/program grants; Scholarships.

YEAR PROGRAM STARTED: 1985

PURPOSE:
To support projects that promote the educational, recreational, environmental and cultural development of the Marshall area and Calhoun County.

LEGAL BASIS:
Community foundation.

ELIGIBILITY:
Grants are made to organizations that have tax-exempt status under Section 501(c)(3) and 509(a)(1) or (2) of the Internal Revenue Code. Nonsectarian religious programs meeting a general community need may apply. No grants are made to individuals.

GEOG. RESTRICTIONS: Calhoun County, Michigan.

FINANCIAL DATA:
Amount of support per award: Varies.
Total amount of support: Varies.

APPLICATION INFO:
Application information is available online.
Duration: One year.
Deadline: January 1, April 1, July 1 and October 1.

ADDRESS INQUIRIES TO:
Shannon Tiernan, Executive Director
(See address above.)

THE MUSTARD SEED FOUNDATION   [1424]
7115 Leesburg Pike, Suite 304
Falls Church, VA 22043
(703) 524-5620
Fax: (703) 533-7340
E-mail: ljackson@msfdn.org
Web Site: msfdn.org

FOUNDED: 1983

AREAS OF INTEREST:
Education and religion.

NAME(S) OF PROGRAMS:
● **Harvey Fellows Program**

TYPE:
Fellowships.

YEAR PROGRAM STARTED: 1992

PURPOSE:
To encourage students who are committed to Jesus Christ to pursue vocations that are culturally influential and to pursue vocational credentials in the most prestigious graduate programs; to validate exceptional abilities in academics and leadership as gifts from God worthy of cultivation and development.

LEGAL BASIS:
Nonprofit.

ELIGIBILITY:
The Harvey Fellows must be Christian graduate students and attend a graduate school program that is considered to be one of the top five in a given subject area or specialty in the world.

FINANCIAL DATA:
Amount of support per award: $16,000 per year.
Total amount of support: Varies.

NO. AWARDS: Varies.

APPLICATION INFO:
The application process has two stages. First, the application must be completed and submitted through the online application system. No paper applications are accepted. The online application does not need to be completed all at once. Secondly, specific required materials must be submitted via mail (e.g., official transcripts, letters of recommendation, test scores). All required materials must be collected by the applicant, bundled, and sent directly to the Foundation. A complete list of the required documents can be found on the Foundation's web site.
Duration: One year. Optional renewal up to two additional years.
Deadline: November 1.

ADDRESS INQUIRIES TO:
See e-mail address above.

THE NAACP LEGAL DEFENSE AND EDUCATIONAL FUND, INC.
40 Rector Street
5th Floor
New York, NY 10006
(212) 965-2244
Fax: (212) 226-7592
E-mail: scholarships@naacpldf.org
eanderson@naacpldf.org
Web Site: www.naacpldf.org/scholarships

TYPE:
Awards/prizes; Grants-in-aid; Internships; Scholarships. LDF Herbert Lehman Education Fund Scholarship Program: Scholarships for African-American high school seniors, high school graduates and college freshmen to attend four-year accredited colleges and universities.

LDF Earl Warren Legal Training Program: Scholarships for law students to attend three-year accredited law schools.

See entry 943 for full listing.

THE NATIONAL ACADEMY OF EDUCATION   [1425]
500 Fifth Street, N.W.
Washington, DC 20001
(202) 334-2341
Fax: (202) 334-2350
E-mail: info@naeducation.org
Web Site: www.naeducation.org

FOUNDED: 1965

AREAS OF INTEREST:
All aspects of educational research.

NAME(S) OF PROGRAMS:
- **National Academy of Education/Spencer Dissertation Fellowship**
- **National Academy of Education/Spencer Postdoctoral Fellowship**

TYPE:
Fellowships. The Dissertation Fellowship seeks to encourage a new generation of scholars from a wide range of disciplines and professional fields to undertake research relevant to the improvement of education. These fellowships support individuals whose dissertations show potential for bringing fresh and constructive perspectives to the history, theory or practice of formal or informal education anywhere in the world. The program develops the careers of its recipients through professional development activities involving the National Academy of Education.

The Postdoctoral Fellowship is nonresidential and funds proposals that make significant scholarly contributions to the field of education. The program develops the careers of its recipients through professional development activities involving National Academy of Education members.

PURPOSE:
To support early career scholars working in critical areas of education research.

LEGAL BASIS:
Private operating foundation.

ELIGIBILITY:
Dissertation Fellowship: Open to students at U.S. institutions. Non-U.S. citizens enrolled at a graduate school in the U.S. are eligible to apply. The basic selection criteria are the importance of the research question to education, the quality of the research approach and feasibility of the work plan, and the applicant's future potential as a researcher and interest in educational research.

Postdoctoral Fellowship: Primary criterion for selection is promise as an educational research scholar, with special emphasis on potential to make a significant contribution to our understanding of education. Applicant must have received Ph.D., Ed.D. or equivalent degree in the past five years.

FINANCIAL DATA:
Dissertation Fellowship: The Fellowship funding is to support the writing of the dissertation only. The Fellowship funding must not be spent on data collection.

Postdoctoral Fellowship: Terms of the award do not permit institutional overhead. If the scholar transfers institutions, the grant transfers with him or her. The money may be spent toward any salary, supplies, etc., that aid the grantee in pursuing research described in the Fellowship application.

Amount of support per award: Dissertation Fellowship: $27,500 for one year. Postdoctoral Fellowship: $70,000 over one year, 18 months or two years.

NO. MOST RECENT APPLICANTS: Dissertation Fellowship: Approximately 400 annually. Postdoctoral Fellowship: Approximately 200 annually.

NO. AWARDS: Dissertation Fellowship: 35. Postdoctoral Fellowship: 30.

APPLICATION INFO:
Application material is available in June.
Duration: Dissertation Fellowship: One or two years. Postdoctoral Fellowship: Up to two years.
Deadline: Dissertation Fellowship: October 3. Postdoctoral Fellowship: November 7.

ADDRESS INQUIRIES TO:
See e-mail address above.

NATIONAL CENTER FOR LEARNING DISABILITIES   [1426]
One Thomas Circle
Suite 700
Washington, DC 20005
(646) 616-1211
Fax: (212) 545-9665
E-mail: afscholarship@ncld.org
info@ncld.org
Web Site: www.ncld.org/scholarships-and-awards

FOUNDED: 2001

AREAS OF INTEREST:
Education and learning disabilities.

NAME(S) OF PROGRAMS:
- **Anne Ford Scholarship**
- **Allegra Ford Thomas Scholarship**

TYPE:
Scholarships. Anne Ford Scholarship is a four-year scholarship granted to a graduating high school senior with a documented learning disability and/or ADHD who will be enrolled in a full-time Bachelor's degree program.

Allegra Ford Thomas Scholarship is a one-time scholarship awarded to a graduating high school senior with a documented learning disability and/or ADHD who will be enrolled in a two-year community college, a vocational or technical training program, or a specialized program for students with LD.

YEAR PROGRAM STARTED: 2001

PURPOSE:
To support a high school senior of high merit with a documented learning disability and/or ADHD, who is pursuing an undergraduate degree.

LEGAL BASIS:
Nonprofit organization.

ELIGIBILITY:
Anne Ford Scholarship applicant must:
(1) be a graduating high school senior who will be attending a four-year Bachelor's degree program;
(2) have an overall grade point average of 3.0 or higher on a four-point scale (or equivalent);
(3) provide most current documentation of an identified learning disability and/or ADHD and;
(4) be a U.S. citizen.

Allegra Ford Thomas Scholarship applicant must:
(1) be a graduating high school senior who will be attending a two-year community college, a vocational/technical training program, or specialized program for students with LD;
(2) demonstrate financial need;
(3) provide most current documentation of an identified learning disability and/or ADHD and;
(4) be a U.S. citizen.

GEOG. RESTRICTIONS: United States.

FINANCIAL DATA:
Amount of support per award: Anne Ford Scholarship: $10,000 ($2,500 per year over four years). Allegra Ford Thomas Scholarship: $2,500.

NO. AWARDS: 1 of each award per year.

APPLICATION INFO:
Application information is available on the web site.
Duration: Anne Ford Scholarship: Four years. Allegra Ford Thomas Scholarship: One-time scholarship.
Deadline: Varies. Check web site for specific dates.

ADDRESS INQUIRIES TO:
NCLD Team
E-mail: info@ncld.org

*SPECIAL STIPULATIONS:
The scholars will be required to submit annual reports detailing their progress in school and describing their insights about their personal growth.

NATIONAL COALITION OF BLACK MEETING PLANNERS (NCBMP)   [1427]
1800 Diagonal Road
Suite 600
Alexandria, VA 22314
(571) 366-1779
E-mail: info@ncbmp.org
Web Site: www.ncbmp.com

FOUNDED: 1983

AREAS OF INTEREST:
Professional meeting planning and hospitality management.

TYPE:
Conferences/seminars; Scholarships.

YEAR PROGRAM STARTED: 1983

PURPOSE:
To be the preeminent organization in educating the African American meeting planner in all aspects of the meeting planning profession; to improve the meetings, conferences, exhibitions, and convocations that African Americans manage.

ELIGIBILITY:
Students seeking careers in meeting planning and enrolled in a hospitality management program.

GEOG. RESTRICTIONS: United States.

FINANCIAL DATA:
Amount of support per award: $1,000 to $2,500.
Total amount of support: $3,000 annually.

NO. AWARDS: 3.

APPLICATION INFO:
Contact the Coalition for application procedures.
Duration: One-time award.
Deadline: November.

ADDRESS INQUIRIES TO:
Marlinda Henry, Executive Director
(See address above.)

NATIONAL COUNCIL FOR THE SOCIAL STUDIES
8555 16th Street, Suite 500
Silver Spring, MD 20910
(301) 588-1800 ext. 110
(800) 296-7840
Fax: (301) 588-2049
E-mail: awards@ncss.org
Web Site: www.socialstudies.org

TYPE:
Awards/prizes; Grants-in-aid. The Septima Clark Book Awards were first presented in 2019 and are intended to recognize the most distinguished books and encourage the writing, publishing and dissemination of outstanding social studies books for young readers that treat topics related to women's issues sensitively and accurately.

Exemplary Research in Social Studies Award acknowledges and encourages scholarly inquiry into significant issues and possibilities for social studies education. Research must be published and have a social education focus.

Jean Dresden Grambs Distinguished Career in Social Studies Award recognizes professionals who have made extensive contributions to knowledge concerning significant areas of social studies education through meritorious research.

Larry Metcalf Exemplary Dissertation Award recognizes outstanding research completed in pursuit of the doctoral degree and encourages scholarly inquiry into significant issues and possibilities for social studies education. Research must be published and have a social education focus.

The annual NCSS Outstanding Teacher of the Year Awards recognize exceptional classroom social studies teachers for grades K-6, 5-8 and 7-12 who teach social studies regularly and systematically in elementary school settings, and at least half-time in middle or junior high and high school settings.

Carter G. Woodson Book Award encourages the writing, publishing and dissemination of outstanding social studies books for young readers that treat topics related to ethnic minorities and relations sensitively and accurately.

See entry 1688 for full listing.

NATIONAL COUNCIL FOR THE SOCIAL STUDIES
8555 16th Street, Suite 500
Silver Spring, MD 20910
(301) 588-1800 ext. 110
(800) 296-7840
Fax: (301) 588-2049
E-mail: awards@ncss.org
Web Site: www.socialstudies.org

TYPE:
Awards/prizes. Annual award for projects representing excellence and innovation in social studies education and having the potential of serving as a model for other teachers.

See entry 1689 for full listing.

NATIONAL COUNCIL FOR THE SOCIAL STUDIES
8555 16th Street, Suite 500
Silver Spring, MD 20910
(301) 588-1800 ext. 110
(800) 296-7840
Fax: (301) 588-2049
E-mail: awards@ncss.org
Web Site: www.socialstudies.org

TYPE:
Awards/prizes. Award to promote school geography education programs that encourage the integration of geography into the social studies curriculum/classroom and enhance the geographic literacy of students at the classroom, district or statewide level.

See entry 1690 for full listing.

NATIONAL COUNCIL FOR THE SOCIAL STUDIES
8555 16th Street, Suite 500
Silver Spring, MD 20910
(301) 588-1800 ext. 110
(800) 296-7840
Fax: (301) 588-2049
E-mail: awards@ncss.org
Web Site: www.socialstudies.org

TYPE:
Awards/prizes. Award for Global Understanding recognizes a social studies educator (or a team of educators) who has made notable contributions in helping social studies students increase their understanding of the world.

See entry 1691 for full listing.

NATIONAL COUNCIL OF TEACHERS OF ENGLISH RESEARCH FOUNDATION [1428]
340 North Neil Street
Suite 104
Champaign, IL 61820
(217) 328-3870
(877) 369-6283
E-mail: researchfoundation@ncte.org
Web Site: www.ncte.org/research-foundation

FOUNDED: 1911

AREAS OF INTEREST:
Teaching and learning of language, literacy and culture.

TYPE:
Project/program grants; Research grants. Support for projects related to the teaching and learning of language, literacy and culture.

YEAR PROGRAM STARTED: 1960

PURPOSE:
To encourage research, experimentation and investigation in the teaching of English.

LEGAL BASIS:
Separate entity within nonprofit, tax-exempt organization.

ELIGIBILITY:
Applicants must be members of NCTE. Funds are not available for commercial teaching materials, dissertation support, tuition expenses, indirect overhead or benefit costs, previously incurred expenses related to the project, researcher salaries, or refreshments.

GEOG. RESTRICTIONS: United States.

NO. MOST RECENT APPLICANTS: 15.

NO. AWARDS: 2.

REPRESENTATIVE AWARDS:
Hui Jiang, Special Education Itinerant Teacher, Marie Pense Center, NJ for "Bringing Funds of Knowledge to School: Culturally Responsive Approaches that Connect Home Culture with School Practice for Preschool-Aged Children in Chinese Immigrant Families;" Toby Emert, Associate Professor and Chair, Department of Education, Agnes Scott College for "ESL Learners and High-Tech Storytelling: Promoting Academic Confidence;" Jennifer Escobar, English Instructor, Moreno Valley College for "Examining the Effects of a Critical Reading Selection Framework and Process in the Community College Classroom."

APPLICATION INFO:
Applicant must submit an application cover sheet, grant proposal and one-page resume.
Duration: Generally one year. Applicants may reapply to Trustees for extension.
Deadline: Research Grant: March 15 in odd-numbered years. Notification by June 1. Teacher Research Grant: October 1 in odd-numbered years. Notification by December 3.

PUBLICATIONS:
Application guidelines.

IRS I.D.: 37-0715886

ADDRESS INQUIRIES TO:
See e-mail address above.

*PLEASE NOTE:
Research grants are awarded in alternating years. Next grant cycle is 2021.

NATIONAL FOSTER PARENT ASSOCIATION

1102 Prairie Ridge Trail
Pflugerville, TX 78660
(512) 686-1948
(800) 557-5238
Fax: (888) 925-5634
E-mail: info@nfpaonline.org
Web Site: www.nfpaonline.org

TYPE:
Conferences/seminars; Scholarships. Scholarships for youth living in foster families whose foster parents are members of NFPA.

Walk Me Home Program is a walk program to raise awareness of foster care and the need for more foster families, as well as to raise funds for recruitment and other activities.

See entry 1035 for full listing.

NATIONAL INSTITUTE ON DRUG ABUSE   [1429]

6001 Executive Boulevard, Room 4246
MSC 9550
Bethesda, MD 20892-9550
(301) 443-1124
E-mail: tracy.waldeck@nih.gov
Web Site: www.drugabuse.gov/funding/research-training

AREAS OF INTEREST:
Drug abuse and addiction.

TYPE:
Awards/prizes. The Institute supports a variety of training and career development grant awards for all career stages.

PURPOSE:
To support research training and/or career development at predoctoral, postdoctoral (including postresident or research-track resident), and junior faculty levels.

ELIGIBILITY:
Specific eligibility criteria vary based on the award.

FINANCIAL DATA:
Amount of support per award: Varies.

ADDRESS INQUIRIES TO:
Tracy Waldeck, Ph.D., Director
(See address above.)

NATIONAL MOLE DAY FOUNDATION

3896 Leaman Court
Freeland, MI 48623
(989) 964-8020
E-mail: moleday@hotmail.com
Web Site: www.moleday.org

TYPE:
Grants-in-aid. The George Hague Memorial Travel Award is given to financially support a young chemistry instructor (with two to five years of chemistry experience) in attending a biennial ChemEd conference.

The National Mole of the Year Award (MOTY) is given to a member of the National Mole Day Foundation who has contributed the most to furthering the cause of Mole Day and chemistry education.

See entry 1886 for full listing.

NATIONAL OCEANIC AND ATMOSPHERIC ADMINISTRATION   [1430]

200 Harry S. Truman Parkway
Suite 460
Annapolis, MD 21401
(410) 267-5660
Fax: (410) 267-5666
E-mail: kevin.schabow@noaa.gov
Web Site: chesapeakebay.noaa.gov

FOUNDED: 1985

AREAS OF INTEREST:
Fisheries habitat, ecosystem services, and ecosystem-based fisheries research in Chesapeake Bay.

NAME(S) OF PROGRAMS:
● **Chesapeake Bay Fisheries Research Program**

TYPE:
Project/program grants; Research grants. Research cooperative agreements.

YEAR PROGRAM STARTED: 1985

PURPOSE:
To support stock assessment, multispecies and ecosystem-based fisheries research in Chesapeake Bay.

LEGAL BASIS:
Government agency.

ELIGIBILITY:
Individuals who are U.S. citizens or residents and organizations, including religious, classified as 501(c)(3) by the IRS can apply.

GEOG. RESTRICTIONS: United States, with a focus on Chesapeake Bay/mid-Atlantic.

FINANCIAL DATA:
Amount of support per award: Up to $250,000.

Total amount of support: Up to $500,000.

NO. MOST RECENT APPLICANTS: 10.

NO. AWARDS: 2 to 4.

APPLICATION INFO:
Application information is available on the web site. RFPs released between October and February.
Duration: Multiyear.
Deadline: Varies each year.

PUBLICATIONS:
Application guidelines; annual report.

ADDRESS INQUIRIES TO:
Kevin Schabow, Grants Manager
National Marine Fisheries Service
(See address above.)

NATIONAL SCIENCE FOUNDATION

Directorate for Education and Human Resources
Division of Research on Learning in Formal and Informal Settings
2415 Eisenhower Avenue
Alexandria, VA 22314
(703) 292-8620
Fax: (703) 292-9044; (703) 292-9046
E-mail: acarroll@nsf.gov
Web Site: www.nsf.gov

TYPE:
Conferences/seminars; Demonstration grants; Development grants; Project/program grants; Research grants; Training grants. Advanced Informal STEM Learning (AISL) program invests in projects that develop and implement informal learning experiences designed to increase interest, engagement and understanding of science, technology, engineering and mathematics (STEM) by individuals of all ages and backgrounds, as well as projects that advance knowledge and practice of informal science education.

With an emphasis on two-year colleges, the Advanced Technological Education (ATE) program focuses on the education of technicians for the high-technology fields that drive the nation's economy.

Discovery Research PreK-12 (DR K12) funds research, development and evaluation activities through knowledge generation and application to improve PreK-12 learning and teaching.

Innovative Technology Experiences for Students and Teachers (ITEST) is designed to increase the opportunities for students and teachers to learn about, experience, and use information technologies within the context of science, technology, engineering and mathematics (STEM), including Information Technology (IT) courses. It is in direct response to the concern about shortages of information technology workers in the U.S.

Research and Evaluation on Education in Science and Engineering (REESE) supports basic and applied research and evaluation that enhances science, technology, engineering and mathematics (STEM) learning and teaching.

See entry 1458 for full listing.

NATIVE AMERICAN COMMUNITY BOARD (NACB) [1431]

P.O. Box 572
Lake Andes, SD 57356-0572
(605) 487-7097
(605) 487-7072
Fax: (605) 487-7964
E-mail: charon@charles-mix.com
Web Site: www.nativeshop.org

AREAS OF INTEREST:
Native American women.

NAME(S) OF PROGRAMS:
- **NACB Internship Program**

TYPE:
Internships. Internships at the Native
American Women's Health Education
Resource Center and the Women's Lodge.

PURPOSE:
To support young women interested in
learning about indigenous issues and willing
to serve indigenous communities.

LEGAL BASIS:
Nonprofit tax-exempt 501(c)(3) organization.

ELIGIBILITY:
Internships are open to college and graduate
students or recent graduates looking for some
work experience. Applicants need to be
interested in Native American rights and
health issues and have a desire to actively
promote civil rights, women's rights and a
healthy environment. Priority will be given to
those wishing to stay six months or longer.

FINANCIAL DATA:
Internship includes free room at the shelter
and partial board from the Resource Center's
food pantry.
Amount of support per award: $250
biweekly.
Total amount of support: Varies.

APPLICATION INFO:
A resume with references is required, and the
Board needs to know the time frame in
which the intern expects to serve. Applicant
should mail personal resume to the Internship
Coordinator; Native American Women's
Health Education Resource Center; at the
mailing address above, send it to the fax
number above or e-mail it to the address
above.
Duration: Three months to one year.
Deadline: Internship positions are available
all year-round.

ADDRESS INQUIRIES TO:
Charon Asetoyer, Executive Director
(See e-mail address above.) or

The Native American Women's
Health Education Resource Center
(See phone numbers above.)

*PLEASE NOTE:
Each intern will be assigned to the Resource
Center and to the Domestic Violence Shelter,
which is located nearby. After arrival and an
orientation period, assignments will be given
out based on the individual's experience,
strengths, interests and, if necessary,
academic requirements.

THE NEA FOUNDATION [1432]

1201 16th Street, N.W., Suite 416
Washington, DC 20036
(202) 822-7840
Fax: (202) 822-7779
E-mail: neafoundation@nea.org
Web Site: www.neafoundation.org

AREAS OF INTEREST:
Public education.

TYPE:
Awards/prizes. Recognizes and awards the
excellence demonstrated by educators
nationwide.

PURPOSE:
To advance student achievement, through the
unique strength of the Foundation's
partnership with educators, by investing in
public education that will prepare each of
America's children to learn and thrive in a
rapidly changing world.

GEOG. RESTRICTIONS: United States.

FINANCIAL DATA:
Amount of support per award: State level:
$650 gift to teacher's school and travel to
Annual Salute to Excellence in Education
Gala. Five finalists from the state level:
$10,000 courtesy of the Horace Mann
Educators Corporation. National awardee:
$25,000 total from NEA Member Benefits
Company.

APPLICATION INFO:
Applicants must complete proposals through
the Foundation's online grant system.
Deadline: May 1.

THE NEA FOUNDATION [1433]

1201 16th Street, N.W., Suite 416
Washington, DC 20036-3207
(202) 822-7840
Fax: (202) 822-7779
E-mail: neafoundation@nea.org
Web Site: www.neafoundation.org

FOUNDED: 1969

AREAS OF INTEREST:
Education.

NAME(S) OF PROGRAMS:
- **NEA Foundation Learning and
  Leadership Grants**
- **NEA Foundation Student Achievement
  Grants**

YEAR PROGRAM STARTED: 1999

PURPOSE:
To improve the academic achievement of
students in U.S. public schools and public
higher education institutions in any subject
area(s); to support public school teachers,
public education support professionals, and/or
faculty and staff in public institutions of
higher education.

ELIGIBILITY:
Applicants must be practicing U.S. public
school teachers in grades PreK-12, public
school education support professionals, or
faculty or staff at public higher education
institutions.

Applicants must be members of the National
Education Association. The NEA Foundation
encourages grant applications from education
support professionals.

Learning and Leadership Grant: All
professional development must improve
practice, curriculum, and student
achievement. Decisions regarding the content
of the professional growth activities must be
based upon an assessment of student work
undertaken with colleagues, and must be
integrated into the institutional planning
process. Funds may not be used to pursue
degrees, pay direct costs, grant administration
fees, or salaries, or support travel costs or
conference fees for more than one person.

Student Achievement Grant: The proposed
work should engage students in critical
thinking and problem solving that deepens
their knowledge of standards-based subject
matter. The work should also improve
students' habits of inquiry, self-directed
learning, and critical reflection. Proposals for
work resulting in low-income and minority
student success with honors, advanced
placement, or other challenging curricula are
particularly encouraged. Funds may be used
for resource materials, supplies, equipment,
transportation, software, or
scholars-in-residence. Although some funds
may be used to support the professional
development necessary to implement the
project, the majority of grant funds must be
spent on materials or educational experiences
for students.

GEOG. RESTRICTIONS: United States.

FINANCIAL DATA:
Amount of support per award: Learning and
Leadership Grants: $2,000 (individuals) and
$5,000 (groups engaged in collegial study);
Student Achievement Grants: $2,000 and
$5,000.

NO. MOST RECENT APPLICANTS: 950.

NO. AWARDS: 170.

APPLICATION INFO:
All proposals must be submitted through the
Foundation's online grant system.
Duration: Annual. Nonrenewable.
Deadline: February 1, June 1 and October
15.

ADDRESS INQUIRIES TO:
Jesse Graytock, Grants Manager
(See address above.)

NELLIE MAE EDUCATION FOUNDATION [1434]

1250 Hancock Street, Suite 701N
Quincy, MA 02169
(781) 348-4200
E-mail: info@nmefoundation.org
Web Site: www.nmefoundation.org

FOUNDED: 1998

AREAS OF INTEREST:
Systems change and racial equity in public
education.

TYPE:
Matching gifts; Research grants.

YEAR PROGRAM STARTED: 1998

PURPOSE:
To promote accessibility, quality and
effectiveness of education, especially for
underserved populations in the six New
England states.

LEGAL BASIS:
Public charity.

ELIGIBILITY:
Organizations must be 501(c)(3) or public
schools. No grants are made to individuals.

GEOG. RESTRICTIONS: Connecticut, Maine,
Massachusetts, New Hampshire, Rhode
Island and Vermont.

FINANCIAL DATA:
Amount of support per award: Varies.
Total amount of support: Varies.

APPLICATION INFO:
Open grant opportunities are posted online.

Duration: Varies.

Deadline: Varies.

ADDRESS INQUIRIES TO:
Ellen Wang, Senior Program Officer
E-mail: ewang@nmefoundation.org

NICSA   [1435]
1420 New York Avenue, N.W.
5th Floor
Washington, DC 20005
(508) 485-1500
Fax: (508) 485-1560
E-mail: info@nicsa.org
Web Site: www.nicsa.org

FOUNDED: 1962

AREAS OF INTEREST:
Education.

NAME(S) OF PROGRAMS:
● **The NICSA/William T. Blackwell Scholarship Fund**

TYPE:
Scholarships.

PURPOSE:
To provide leadership and innovation in educational programming and information exchange within the operations sector of the mutual fund industry worldwide; to recognize outstanding students of the NICSA Family with financial support for postsecondary education.

ELIGIBILITY:
Applicants must be dependent children of full-time employees of NICSA member companies and be enrolled in or planning to pursue a full-time course of study leading to a Bachelor's degree from an accredited four-year college or university.

Must maintain a 3.0 grade point average for renewal.

FINANCIAL DATA:
Amount of support per award: Up to $5,000 per year.

Total amount of support: Maximum of $40,000 annually.

APPLICATION INFO:
Application information is available online.

Duration: Up to four years.

Deadline: May 10.

NORTH CAROLINA GLAXOSMITHKLINE FOUNDATION   [1436]
5 Moore Drive
P.O. Box 13398
Research Triangle Park, NC 27709
(919) 483-2140
Fax: (919) 315-3015
E-mail: info@ncgskfoundation.org
Web Site: www.ncgskfoundation.org

FOUNDED: 1986

AREAS OF INTEREST:
Science, health and education at all educational and professional levels.

NAME(S) OF PROGRAMS:
● **Child Health Recognition Awards**
● **Ribbon of Hope**
● **Traditional Grants**
● **Women in Science Scholars Program**

TYPE:
Project/program grants; Seed money grants. Support for activities which help meet the educational and health needs of today's society and future generations.

Child Health Recognition Awards program honors local health departments, public health staff, and individuals for innovative, collaborative programs that improve the lives of North Carolina's children.

Ribbon of Hope provides one-time grants to nonprofits for projects furthering health, science and education in their communities.

The Traditional Grants program provides for larger grants that may be multiyear in nature, to support programs advancing health, science and education throughout the state of North Carolina.

Women in Science Scholars Program offers an educational opportunity to young women by coupling college scholarships with a mentoring program.

YEAR PROGRAM STARTED: 1986

PURPOSE:
To provide programs that emphasize the understanding and applications of science, health and education at all academic and professional levels.

LEGAL BASIS:
Foundation.

ELIGIBILITY:
Ribbon of Hope: North Carolina community-based nonprofit, charitable organizations and institutions exempt under Section 501(c)(3) of the Internal Revenue Code are eligible to apply. Individuals may not apply. Nonprofits with proposals pertaining to science, health and education as well as collaborative partnerships between several community-based organizations are encouraged to apply.

Traditional Grants: Grant applicants must be nonprofit, charitable organizations and institutions exempt under Section 501(c)(3) of the Internal Revenue Code. No grants are made to individuals, for construction or restoration projects, or for international programs. The primary focus of the Foundation is to provide seed funds for new and worthwhile educational programs. This policy does not preclude the consideration and possible funding of ongoing projects.

GEOG. RESTRICTIONS: North Carolina.

FINANCIAL DATA:
Amount of support per award: Ribbon of Hope: $25,000; Traditional Grants: $25,000 and up.

Total amount of support: Approximately $3,000,000 paid out annually.

REPRESENTATIVE AWARDS:
Ribbon of Hope: Airlie Gardens Foundation, New Hanover County, to support the "Educator in the Gardens" program; Cradle of Forestry in America Interpretive Association, Transylvania County, to support programming that provides learning experiences on forest ecology, accessing public lands safely, and improving overall health through guided hikes, field trips, and natural science education classes; Anson County Partnership for Children, Anson County, to launch the Motheread program, providing parents with lessons to gain literacy skills and ways to also effectively teach their children literacy skills.

Traditional Grants: $1,577,718 (over five years) to The University of North Carolina-Asheville to support the Chemistry and Biology Fellows and Scholars undergraduate research; $1,100,000 (over four years) to The Hill Center to build statewide effectiveness, diversity, and scale their initiatives to provide educational support to struggling students; $125,000 to Bladen County Community College to develop a writing center for students.

APPLICATION INFO:
Applications are submitted through the Foundation web site.

Duration: Ribbon of Hope: One-time grant; Traditional Grants: Up to five years.

Deadline: Child Health Recognition Awards: May 31. Ribbon of Hope: April 1 and October 1. Traditional Grants: January 1, April 1, July 1 and October 1.

PUBLICATIONS:
Annual report; application; brochure.

IRS I.D.: 58-1698610

STAFF:
Marilyn E. Foote-Hudson, Executive Director

BOARD OF DIRECTORS:
Robert A. Ingram, Chairman
Margaret B. Dardess, President
Thomas R. Haber, Treasurer
Paul A. Holcombe, Jr., Secretary

ADDRESS INQUIRIES TO:
See e-mail address above.

OAK GROVE SCHOOL FOUNDATION   [1437]
P.O. Box 150
South China, ME 04358
(207) 445-3333
E-mail: austinlaw@fairpoint.net
Web Site: www.ogsfoundation.org

FOUNDED: 1989

AREAS OF INTEREST:
Education, secondary school curriculum augmenting, limited secondary school scholarships, and some not-for-profits.

NAME(S) OF PROGRAMS:
● **Grants Program**
● **Tuition Assistance**

TYPE:
Demonstration grants; General operating grants; Grants-in-aid; Project/program grants; Scholarships. Scholarships are for Quaker high schools.

YEAR PROGRAM STARTED: 1991

PURPOSE:
To foster secondary education innovation in proximate geographic area; to provide tuition assistance.

LEGAL BASIS:
Private foundation.

ELIGIBILITY:
Secondary schools and 501(c)(3) organizations in Central Maine. For tuition assistance, candidates may be either currently enrolled or accepted for enrollment in a Quaker secondary school and must be a resident of Maine or children or grandchildren of Oak Grove School or Oak Grove-Coburn School alumni/ae. In addition, children and grandchildren of former Oak Grove or Oak Grove-Coburn faculty and staff are eligible applicants.

GEOG. RESTRICTIONS: Central Maine.

FINANCIAL DATA:
Amount of support per award: Grants: $3,000 to $5,000; Scholarships: Varies.
Total amount of support: Approximately $130,000 annually.

NO. MOST RECENT APPLICANTS: Approximately 150.

NO. AWARDS: Approximately 100 yearly.

APPLICATION INFO:
Application forms are available from the Foundation web site.
Duration: Grants: One year. Renewal possible upon review for up to two more years.
Deadline: Large grants: April 1. Small grants: Early October.

IRS I.D.: 01-0211537

ADDRESS INQUIRIES TO:
Joann Austin, Counselor and Attorney at Law
Austin Law
(See address above.)

PARENTS WITHOUT PARTNERS [1438]
6798 Cheddar Valley Drive
Brighton, MI 48116
(810) 333-5920
(800) 637-7974
E-mail: pwpintoffice@gmail.com
Web Site: www.parentswithoutpartners.org

FOUNDED: 1957

AREAS OF INTEREST:
Education of children of single parents belonging to the organization.

NAME(S) OF PROGRAMS:
● **Parents Without Partners International Scholarship**

TYPE:
Scholarships.

PURPOSE:
To provide single parents and their children with an opportunity for enhancing personal growth, self-confidence, and sensitivity towards others by offering an environment for support, friendship and the exchange of parenting techniques.

LEGAL BASIS:
Nonprofit.

ELIGIBILITY:
Applicants must be dependent children, up to 25 years of age, of active PWP members. Applicants must be members of a current senior class of any high school and planning to enter and have applied to a school of higher education for the following year, or be an undergraduate student planning to continue higher education for the following year. Applications will be accepted for trade and vocational schools, as well as colleges and universities.

GEOG. RESTRICTIONS: United States and Canada.

FINANCIAL DATA:
Amount of support per award: Varies.
Total amount of support: Varies.

APPLICATION INFO:
Forms are available on the PWP web site.
Duration: One year. Nonrenewable. Must reapply.
Deadline: April 15.

ADDRESS INQUIRIES TO:
Mary Anne Britton, International Vice President
Family and Educational Programming
E-mail: maryannebritton@provide net

THE MABEL LOUISE RILEY FOUNDATION [1439]
2 Liberty Square
Suite 500
Boston, MA 02109
(617) 399-1850
Fax: (617) 399-1851
E-mail: info@rileyfoundation.com
Web Site: www.rileyfoundation.com

FOUNDED: 1972

AREAS OF INTEREST:
Emphasis on priority needs in social services, human services and education, especially for youth, community development including cultural, housing and urban environmental programs.

TYPE:
Capital grants; Challenge/matching grants; Development grants; Project/program grants; Seed money grants; Training grants.

LEGAL BASIS:
Private foundation.

ELIGIBILITY:
Requests are considered only from corporations organized under the laws of Massachusetts for purposes to be carried out within Massachusetts and those who have a 501(c)(3) IRS determination.

GEOG. RESTRICTIONS: Greater Boston area, with a primary focus on the city of Boston, Massachusetts.

FINANCIAL DATA:
Amount of support per award: $50,000 to $100,000.
Total amount of support: $3,222,500 for the year 2018.

NO. AWARDS: 52.

APPLICATION INFO:
Applicants are required to submit a brief summary (LOI) of their proposal, not more than two pages, without a cover letter before submitting a formal grant request. This summary should briefly describe the purposes and objectives of the proposal, a brief history of the applicant and the amount requested from the Foundation. In addition to the two-page summary, a copy of the IRS 501(c)(3) Determination Letter and a program budget relative to the request should be included.

The Foundation will notify the applicant if the submission of a formal grant request is invited. Formal grant proposal must be made using the Common Proposal Form of the Associated Grant Makers.
Duration: One year. Renewals possible. Two-year waiting period is requested before applying again for those who have been awarded a grant.
Deadline: Meetings are held in March, June, September and December with deadlines for receipt of full grant proposals set 60 days prior to each meeting.

PUBLICATIONS:
Guidelines.

IRS I.D.: 04-6278857

TRUSTEES:
Grace Fey

Robert W. Holmes, Jr.
Joannie Jaxtimer

ADDRESS INQUIRIES TO:
Nancy A. Saunders, Administrator
(See address above.)

ROSS FOUNDATION
202 South Fifth Street
Arkadelphia, AR 71923
(870) 246-9881
Fax: (870) 246-9674
E-mail: info@rossfoundation.us
Web Site: www.rossfoundation.us

TYPE:
Conferences/seminars; Matching gifts; Project/program grants; Research grants.
See entry 1243 for full listing.

GEORGE J. AND EFFIE L. SEAY MEMORIAL TRUST
Bank of America
1111 East Main Street, 12th Floor
Richmond, VA 23219
(202) 442-7460
E-mail: dc.grantmaking@ustrust.com
Web Site: www.bankofamerica.com/philanthropic/foundation.go

TYPE:
Project/program grants. Grants for specific needs.
See entry 1375 for full listing.

SMITHSONIAN ENVIRONMENTAL RESEARCH CENTER (SERC)
647 Contees Wharf Road
Edgewater, MD 21037
(443) 482-2217
Fax: (443) 482-2380
E-mail: gustafsond@si.edu
Web Site: serc.si.edu

TYPE:
Fellowships; Internships. The Internship Program enables undergraduates, recent graduates and graduate students to work on specific projects under the direction of the Center's professional staff and is tailored to provide the maximum educational benefit to each participant. Graduate students and undergraduates may conduct independent projects with the approval of the staff member with whom they plan to study.

Subject matter of the projects includes terrestrial and estuarine environmental research within the disciplines of mathematics, chemistry, microbiology, botany, zoology, and environmental education.

Fellowships are offered annually at the postdoctoral, predoctoral and graduate levels.

Internships are offered three times per year at the undergraduate levels, recent graduate, or beginning Master's student.
See entry 2010 for full listing.

SPENCER FOUNDATION [1440]
625 North Michigan Avenue
Suite 1600
Chicago, IL 60611
(312) 337-7000
Fax: (312) 337-0282
E-mail: abrinkman@spencer.org
Web Site: www.spencer.org

FOUNDED: 1962

AREAS OF INTEREST:
Research on education as approached from scholars in the social sciences and humanities.

NAME(S) OF PROGRAMS:
- **Conference Grants**
- **Large Research Grants**
- **Research-Practice Partnershp Grants**
- **Small Research Grants**
- **Lyle Spencer Research Awards**

TYPE:
Research grants. Conference grants. Grants for research to expand knowledge and understanding of the problems and processes of education.

YEAR PROGRAM STARTED: 1970

PURPOSE:
To support research that gives promise of yielding new knowledge leading to the improvement of education, broadly defined.

LEGAL BASIS:
Independent foundation.

ELIGIBILITY:
The Foundation is interested in a wide variety of disciplinary and interdisciplinary approaches to the study of education. The principal investigator ordinarily must have an earned Doctorate in an academic discipline or in the field of education and must have an affiliation with a nonprofit organization such as a college or university, a research facility, or a cultural institution.

FINANCIAL DATA:
Amount of support per award: Varies.

Total amount of support: Approximately $24,000,000 annually.

NO. MOST RECENT APPLICANTS: Approximately 2,000.

NO. AWARDS: 150.

APPLICATION INFO:
Application procedures differ by program. Researchers seeking support should view the Foundation's web site for general program information.

Duration: Varies.

Deadline: Varies.

PUBLICATIONS:
Annual report.

OFFICERS:
Na'ilah Suad Nasir, President

BOARD OF DIRECTORS:
Pamela Grossman, Chairperson
Richard Murnane, Vice Chairperson
Carl Cohen
Na'ilah Suad Nasir
Erick Odmark
Eduardo Padron
Stephen Raudenbush
Cybele Raver
Rob Reich
Cecilia Rios-Aguilar
Mark Vander Ploeg
Mike Williams

ADDRESS INQUIRIES TO:
Annie Brinkman, Grants Manager
(See address above.)

SUBARU OF AMERICA FOUNDATION, INC.   [1441]

One Subaru Drive
Camden, NJ 08103
(856) 488-5099
Fax: (856) 254-1367
E-mail: foundation@subaru.com
Web Site: www.subaru.com/about-subaru/subaru-foundation

FOUNDED: 1984

AREAS OF INTEREST:
Career exploration for at-risk middle and high school students and job training for unemployed and underemployed young adults, ages 16 to 26.

TYPE:
General operating grants; Project/program grants. Employee matching gift program.

YEAR PROGRAM STARTED: 1984

PURPOSE:
To help un- and low-employed young people become self-sufficient through job training, mentoring and work experience leading to obtaining and retaining employment.

LEGAL BASIS:
Corporate foundation.

ELIGIBILITY:
Only organizations that are tax exempt under section 501(c)(3) of the Internal Revenue Code may apply. The Foundation will consider partnerships with established organizations with proven records of success in training and gainful employment strategies that achieve the following:
(1) work with underserved communities and youth ages 16 to 26;
(2) help develop the soft and hard skills necessary to connect to employment pathways;
(3) provide STEAM-based training leading to employment opportunities;
(4) provide a support network for mentoring, coaching and counseling as it relates to building employment skills and eliminating barriers to success;
(5) assist in obtaining industry-appropriate certifications that may aid in getting employment;
(6) create and nurture partnerships for internships and job placement and;
(7) track employment of participants for at least one year past graduation.

GEOG. RESTRICTIONS: Only proposals serving the geographic locations listed will be considered:
Corporate Headquarters: southern New Jersey (mainly Camden and Burlington counties);
Eastern Region: Washington, District of Columbia; Orlando, Florida; Atlanta, Georgia; Frederick, Howard, Montgomery and Prince Georges counties in Maryland; Florence, New Jersey; Philadelphia, Pennsylvania and Fairfax, Loudon and Prince William counties in Virginia;
Central Region: Chicago, Illinois; Minneapolis, Minnesota; Columbus, Ohio; and Dallas, Texas;
Western Region: Phoenix, Arizona; Los Angeles, San Diego and San Francisco, California; Denver, Colorado; Portland, Oregon; and Seattle, Washington.

FINANCIAL DATA:
Amount of support per award: Varies.

Matching fund requirements: Contributions for the matching gift program must be made by Subaru of America employees at a $25 minimum or $2,000 maximum per employee per fiscal year.

APPLICATION INFO:
Application form is available online as a Word document. Grant application and all required supporting documentation must be submitted at the same time as one package and should be mailed to the address above to arrive by the deadline (not postmarked by the deadline). Grant applications with missing information or documentation will not be considered.

Deadline: March 30 and October 12.

IRS I.D.: 22-2531774

STAFF:
Sandra E. Capell, Philanthropy and Corporate Responsibility Manager

ADDRESS INQUIRIES TO:
Sandra E. Capell
Philanthropy and Corporate Responsibility Manager
(See address above.)

TAILHOOK EDUCATIONAL FOUNDATION   [1442]

9696 Business Park Avenue
San Diego, CA 92131-1643
(858) 689-9223
Fax: (858) 578-8839
E-mail: rlw@tailhook.net
Web Site: tailhook.net/tef-home

FOUNDED: 1992

AREAS OF INTEREST:
Education.

NAME(S) OF PROGRAMS:
- **Tailhook Educational Foundation Scholarship Award**

TYPE:
Scholarships. The Foundation awards merit-based scholarships.

YEAR PROGRAM STARTED: 1992

PURPOSE:
To support dependents of the Naval Aviation community with their educational needs.

LEGAL BASIS:
501(c)(3).

ELIGIBILITY:
To be eligible for consideration, an individual must be a high school graduate and the natural, step, or adopted son, daughter, or grandchild of a current or former (U.S. Navy, U.S. Marine Corps or U.S. Coast Guard) Naval Aviator, Naval Flight Officer, or Naval Aircrewman. Also eligible are individuals or children/grandchildren of individuals who are serving or have served on board a U.S. Navy Aircraft Carrier in ship's company or the Air Wing. Eligible applicants must be accepted for undergraduate enrollment at an accredited college.

GEOG. RESTRICTIONS: United States.

FINANCIAL DATA:
Amount of support per award: $2,500 to $15,000.

Total amount of support: $311,000.

NO. MOST RECENT APPLICANTS: Approximately 700 for the year 2018.

NO. AWARDS: 107 for the year 2018.

APPLICATION INFO:
Application information is available on the web site.
Duration: One year. Must reapply.
Deadline: March 1.

IRS I.D.: 33-0487778

TRIANGLE COMMUNITY FOUNDATION   [1443]

800 Park Offices Drive, Suite 201
Research Triangle Park, NC 27709
(919) 474-8370
Fax: (919) 941-9208
E-mail: jessica@trianglecf.org
Web Site: www.trianglecf.org

AREAS OF INTEREST:
Projects of excellence.

TYPE:
Grants-in-aid; Scholarships. General grantmaking.

YEAR PROGRAM STARTED: 1984

PURPOSE:
To expand philanthropy.

ELIGIBILITY:
Organizations, including religious, classified as 501(c)(3) by the IRS can apply. No grants to individuals.

GEOG. RESTRICTIONS: Chatham, Durham, Orange and Wake counties, North Carolina.

FINANCIAL DATA:
Amount of support per award: Minimum $250.
Total amount of support: Varies.

APPLICATION INFO:
Application available online.
Duration: Grants are not renewable.

PUBLICATIONS:
Annual report.

ADDRESS INQUIRIES TO:
Jessica Aylor
Vice President Community Engagement
(See address above.)

U.S. DEPARTMENT OF EDUCATION   [1444]

550 12th Street, S.W.
Washington, DC 20024
(202) 245-7274
Fax: (202) 245-6752
E-mail: ies@ed.gov
ellie.pelaez@ed.gov
Web Site: ies.ed.gov

FOUNDED: 1972

AREAS OF INTEREST:
Basic and applied research, evaluations and analyses in education practice and policy.

NAME(S) OF PROGRAMS:
● **Education Research**

TYPE:
Project/program grants; Research grants. Grants competitions.

The Institute supports research on a diverse set of student outcomes including: school readiness for prekindergarten; academic outcomes in kindergarten through Grade 12 that include learning, achievement, and higher order thinking in the core academic content areas of reading, writing, mathematics, and science measured by specific assessments (e.g.,

researcher-developed assessments, standardized tests, grades, end of course exams, exit exams) as well as course completion, grade retention, high school graduation and dropout rates; social skills, dispositions, and behaviors that support academic outcomes for students from prekindergarten through high school; access to, retention in, and completion of postsecondary education; and reading, writing, and mathematics skills for adult learners (i.e., students at least 16 years old and outside of the K-12 system). The Institute supports research from prekindergarten through Grade 12 for the typically developing student. For postsecondary and adult learners the Institute supports research on typically developing students and students with disabilities. The Institute supports research on students with disabilities from birth through high school through a different grant program run by the Institute's National Center for Special Education Research.

LEGAL BASIS:
Public Law 92-318, as amended.

ELIGIBILITY:
Applicants must be colleges, universities, state departments of education, local education agencies, other public or private profit and nonprofit agencies, organizations, groups and individuals. Support is restricted to basic and applied research, planning studies, evaluations, investigations, experiments and developmental activities directly related to research in the field of education.

Most funds provide continuing support for long-term research and development programs. The remaining funds are used for new projects, announced as Grants Competitions in specific areas of interest.

FINANCIAL DATA:
Amount of support per award: Varies.
Total amount of support: Varies.

APPLICATION INFO:
Application information is available on the web site.
Duration: Varies.
Deadline: Specific date changes each year, but application deadlines generally fall between June and September.

ADDRESS INQUIRIES TO:
Ellie Pelaez
Management and Program Analyst
(See above address.)

U.S. DEPARTMENT OF EDUCATION   [1445]

Office of Career, Technical and Adult Education
550 12th Street, S.W., 11th Floor
Washington, DC 20202-7100
(202) 245-7700
Fax: (202) 245-7838
E-mail: octae@ed.gov
Web Site: www2.ed.gov/about/offices/list/ovae

FOUNDED: 1965

AREAS OF INTEREST:
Adult basic education, basic literacy skills, English as a second language and adult secondary education.

CONSULTING OR VOLUNTEER SERVICES:
Technical assistance is provided to state educational agencies.

TYPE:
Grants-in-aid. The program provides grants to states to fund local programs of adult education and literacy services, including workplace literacy services, family literacy services, English language learning and integrated English literacy/civics education programs. Basic grants to all states including the District of Columbia as well as the Virgin Islands, American Samoa, Guam, Northern Mariana Islands and Palau.

YEAR PROGRAM STARTED: 1965

PURPOSE:
To provide educational opportunities for educationally disadvantaged adults.

LEGAL BASIS:
The Adult Education and Family Literacy Act (AEFLA), enacted as Title II of the Workforce Investment Act (WIA) of 1998, is the principal source of federal support for adult basic and literacy education programs for adults who lack basic skills, a high school diploma, or proficiency in English.

ELIGIBILITY:
Individuals and local providers cannot receive grant money directly from the Office of Vocational and Adult Education (OVAE).

Adult education and literacy programs are funded through federal grants to the states. The amount each state receives is based on a formula established by Congress. States, in turn, distribute funds to local eligible entities to provide adult education and literacy services.

The Division provides assistance to states to improve program quality and capacity.

GEOG. RESTRICTIONS: United States and its territories.

FINANCIAL DATA:
AEFLA funds are distributed by formula to states using census data on the number of adults (ages 16 and older) in each state who lack a high school diploma and who are not enrolled in school. States must match 25% of the federal contribution with state or local funds, but many states contribute considerably more.

Amount of support per award: Varies.

Total amount of support: Approximately $1.9 billion annually.

Matching fund requirements: 25% of grant award.

NO. MOST RECENT APPLICANTS: 57.

NO. AWARDS: 57.

APPLICATION INFO:
Applicants interested in participating in the State-Administered Program should contact the appropriate state educational agency for information.

Duration: One year and continuing based on appropriations.

ADDRESS INQUIRIES TO:
Office of Career, Technical and Adult Education
Adult Education and Literacy Division
400 Maryland Avenue, S.W.
Washington, DC 20202-7100

U.S. DEPARTMENT OF EDUCATION [1446]

Office of English Language Acquisition
LBJ Education Building, MS-6510
400 Maryland Avenue, S.W.
Washington, DC 20202-6510
(202) 401-1433 (NPD Program)
(202) 453-6054 (NAM Program)
Web Site: www.ed.gov/offices/oela

AREAS OF INTEREST:
English language acquisition, language enhancement and academic achievement for Limited English Proficient (LEP) children.

NAME(S) OF PROGRAMS:
- **National Professional Development Program**
- **Native American and Alaska Native Children in School Program**

TYPE:
Formula grants. National Professional Development Program provides grants for eligible entities to implement professional development activities intended to improve instruction for English Learners (ELs) and assists education personnel working with ELs to meet high professional standards. Professional development activities may include both pre-service and in-service activities.

Native American and Alaska Native Children in School Program awards grants to eligible entities to develop and enhance capacity to provide effective instruction and support to Native American students who are identified as English Learners (ELs). The goal of this program is to support the teaching, learning and studying of Native American languages while also increasing the English language proficiency of students served to achieve the same challenging state academic content and achievement standards for all students.

YEAR PROGRAM STARTED: 1968

LEGAL BASIS:
Elementary and Secondary Education Act of 1965, as amended by No Child Left Behind Act of 2001.

ELIGIBILITY:
National Professional Development Program: Institutions of higher education in consortia with local education agencies or state education agencies may apply.

Native American and Alaska Native Children in School Program: Entities that operate the following kinds of elementary, secondary and postsecondary schools primarily for Native American children (including Alaska Native children) are eligible applicants under this program:
(1) Indian tribes;
(2) tribally sanctioned educational authorities;
(3) Native Hawaiian or Native American Pacific Islander native language educational organizations;
(4) elementary schools or secondary schools that are operated or funded by the Bureau of Indian Education (BIE), or a consortium of such schools;
(5) elementary schools or secondary schools operated under a contract with or grant from the BIE in consortium with another such school or a tribal or community organization and;
(6) elementary schools or secondary schools operated by the BIE and an institution of higher education (IHE), in consortium with elementary schools or secondary schools operated under a contract with or a grant from the BIE or a tribal or community organization.

GEOG. RESTRICTIONS: United States and its Commonwealths and territories.

FINANCIAL DATA:
Total amount of support: National Professional Development Program: $45,691,345 appropriated for fiscal year 2018; Native American and Alaska Native Children in School Program: $5,000,000.

STAFF:
Supreet Anand, Deputy Director

ADDRESS INQUIRIES TO:
National Professional Development Program:
Francisco Javier Lopez
Tel: (202) 401-1433

Native American and Alaska Native Children in School Program:
Celeste McLaughlin
Tel: (202) 453-6054

U.S. DEPARTMENT OF STATE, FULBRIGHT TEACHER EXCHANGES [1447]

1275 K Street, N.W.
Suite 600
Washington, DC 20005
(202) 628-8188
Fax: (202) 628-8189
E-mail: jbferguson@irex.org
Web Site: www.fulbrightteacherexchanges.org

FOUNDED: 1946

AREAS OF INTEREST:
K-12 education; all teaching disciplines including, but not limited to, mathematics, science, English, English as a Second Language (ESL), foreign language and history.

NAME(S) OF PROGRAMS:
- **Fulbright Teacher Exchanges**

TYPE:
Exchange programs; Travel grants. Fulbright Teacher Exchanges encompass the following programs:
Fulbright Distinguished Awards in Teaching Research Program, Fulbright Distinguished Awards in Teaching Short-Term Program and Fulbright Teachers for Global Classrooms Program are for U.S. educators;
Fulbright Leaders for Global Schools Program is for U.S. administrators and;
Fulbright Teaching Excellence & Achievement Program and Fulbright Distinguished Awards in Teaching for International Teachers Program are for international educators.

YEAR PROGRAM STARTED: 1946

PURPOSE:
To increase mutual understanding between the people of the U.S. and the people of other countries through the funding of K-12 educator exchanges.

LEGAL BASIS:
Mutual Educational and Cultural Exchange Act (Fulbright Hays Act) of 1961.

ELIGIBILITY:
Applicants must meet the following general requirements:
(1) be a U.S. citizen or hold citizenship and be a resident in one of the participating countries;
(2) be fluent in English;
(3) hold a Master's degree or higher (for U.S. educators; international applicant requirements vary);
(4) be employed full-time at an accredited school in the U.S., its territories, or in one of the participating countries;
(5) spend at least 50% of their time teaching or working directly with students and;
(6) have taught for at least five years.

FINANCIAL DATA:
In most cases, the U.S. educator secures a leave of absence with or without pay from his or her home institution (as does the foreign teacher). Exchange grants include a summer orientation program and round-trip transportation for grantee only.
Amount of support per award: Varies.
Total amount of support: Varies.

NO. MOST RECENT APPLICANTS: 1,000 across all programs.

NO. AWARDS: 400 annually.

APPLICATION INFO:
All applications must be submitted through the online application system.
Duration: U.S. Educators: Two weeks to six months; International Educators: Six weeks to four months.
Deadline: Varies. E-mail contact.fulbrightteachers@irex.org for information.

ADDRESS INQUIRIES TO:
See e-mail address above.

*PLEASE NOTE:
All programs are tentative and are subject to the availability of funds.

UNIVERSITY OF MANITOBA [1448]

Faculty of Graduate Studies
500 University Centre
Winnipeg MB R3T 2N2 Canada
(204) 474-6703
Fax: (204) 474-7553
E-mail: sara.sealey@umanitoba.ca
Web Site: umanitoba.ca/graduate_studies

AREAS OF INTEREST:
Teaching and cutting-edge research.

NAME(S) OF PROGRAMS:
- **University of Manitoba Graduate Fellowships**

TYPE:
Fellowships. Any discipline taught at graduate level at the university.

PURPOSE:
To reward academic excellence.

ELIGIBILITY:
At the time of application, students do not need to have been accepted by the department or faculty, but at the time of taking up the award must be regular full-time graduate students who have been admitted to and registered in advanced degree programmes, e.g., Master's or Ph.D., but not pre-Master's in any field of study or faculty of the University of Manitoba. Students beyond the second year in the Master's programme or beyond the fourth year in the Ph.D. programme are not eligible to apply for or hold a University of Manitoba Fellowship.

FINANCIAL DATA:
Amount of support per award: $18,000 for Ph.D.; $14,000 for Master's.

APPLICATION INFO:
Applicant must request information from the department to which he or she is applying at the University of Manitoba.

Duration: One year.

ADDRESS INQUIRIES TO:
Sara Sealey, Awards Officer
(See address above.)

DENNIS & PHYLLIS WASHINGTON FOUNDATION

P.O. Box 16630
Missoula, MT 59808
(406) 523-1300
Fax: (800) 381-2942
E-mail: info@dpwfoundation.org
Web Site: www.dpwfoundation.org

TYPE:
Project/program grants; Scholarships.

See entry 1279 for full listing.

FRED B. AND RUTH B. ZIGLER FOUNDATION   [1449]

P.O. Box 986
Jennings, LA 70546-0986
(337) 824-2413
Fax: (337) 824-2414
E-mail: ziglerfoundation@gmail.com

FOUNDED: 1956

AREAS OF INTEREST:
Education.

TYPE:
Project/program grants; Scholarships.

PURPOSE:
To benefit Jefferson-Davis Parish area.

LEGAL BASIS:
Private foundation.

ELIGIBILITY:
Grants are made to organizations that have tax-exempt status under Section 501(c)(3) of the Internal Revenue Code. No grants are made to individuals.

GEOG. RESTRICTIONS: Jefferson-Davis Parish area, Louisiana.

FINANCIAL DATA:
Amount of support per award: Varies.
Total amount of support: $100,000 to $400,000.

NO. AWARDS: Approximately 30 each year.

APPLICATION INFO:
Applicants must submit a brief letter outlining the purpose of the grant.
Duration: Up to four years.
Deadline: 30 days prior to the Board meeting. The Board meets every other month starting in January.

ADDRESS INQUIRIES TO:
Julie G. Berry, President
(See address above.)

Elementary and secondary education

ALTMAN FOUNDATION

8 West 40th Street
19th Floor
New York, NY 10018-2263
(212) 682-0970
Fax: (212) 682-1648
E-mail: info@altman.org
Web Site: www.altmanfoundation.org

TYPE:
Project/program grants.

See entry 1058 for full listing.

THE BELK FOUNDATION   [1450]

6832 Morrison Boulevard
Suite 100
Charlotte, NC 28211
(704) 544-5444
E-mail: britt@belkfoundation.org
Web Site: www.belkfoundation.org

FOUNDED: 1928

AREAS OF INTEREST:
Education.

TYPE:
General operating grants; Project/program grants; Research grants; Training grants. Core achievement in grades K-3; Teacher and Leader development.

PURPOSE:
To invest in schools and organizations that work aggressively to ensure all students graduate from high school and continue on an intentional path toward college, career and life.

ELIGIBILITY:
Charitable organizations, with 501(c)(3) status, located in Charlotte, NC and select state-level initiatives in North Carolina.

No grants made to individuals, private elementary or secondary schools, international programs and/or organizations, and organizations for the primary purpose of fund-raising.

GEOG. RESTRICTIONS: North Carolina.

FINANCIAL DATA:
Amount of support per award: $5,000 to $500,000.
Total amount of support: Varies.

APPLICATION INFO:
Applications are accepted by invitation only. Applicant must complete online Eligibility Quiz. If prompted, applicant will submit Letter of Inquiry.
Deadline: April 1 and October 1.

STAFF:
Johanna Anderson, Executive Director
C.T. Anderson, Program Associate
Britt Benavidez, Program Assistant

*PLEASE NOTE:
The Foundation dedicates its resources to two areas:
(1) Teaching and Leading and;
(2) K-3 Achievement.

*SPECIAL STIPULATIONS:
Currently the Foundation is only accepting Letters of Inquiry from organizations serving the community of Charlotte, NC and select state-level initiatives in North Carolina.

THE LOUIS CALDER FOUNDATION

999 18th Street
Suite 2350S
Denver, CO 80202
(720) 943-9865
E-mail: proposals@calderfdn.org
Web Site: www.louiscalderfoundation.org

TYPE:
Capital grants; Project/program grants. Curriculum development.

See entry 1013 for full listing.

SAMUEL N. AND MARY CASTLE FOUNDATION   [1451]

733 Bishop Street, Suite 1275
Honolulu, HI 96813
(808) 522-1101
Fax: (808) 522-1103
E-mail: snandmarycastle@hawaii.rr.com
Web Site: fdnweb.org/castle/

FOUNDED: 1894

AREAS OF INTEREST:
Early education and care, cultural arts, human services for children, teacher training, and some maternal/child health support.

CONSULTING OR VOLUNTEER SERVICES:
Castle colleagues training for directors of early childhood centers.

TYPE:
Scholarships; Technical assistance; Training grants.

YEAR PROGRAM STARTED: 1894

PURPOSE:
To support training for early childhood education professionals; to support early education, preschools, scholarships, and select higher education programs in teacher training; to support early education.

LEGAL BASIS:
Private family foundation.

GEOG. RESTRICTIONS: Hawaii.

FINANCIAL DATA:
Amount of support per award: Typically $10,000 to $100,000.
Total amount of support: $2,100,000 for the year 2018.
Matching fund requirements: Varies.

NO. MOST RECENT APPLICANTS: 125.

NO. AWARDS: Approximately 50.

REPRESENTATIVE AWARDS:
$50,000 to Catholic Charities for families with children; $100,000 (over two years) to Chaminade University for student scholarships; $125,000 to University of Hawaii for scholarships.

APPLICATION INFO:
The applicant organization should review the Foundation's priorities and policies to determine whether it is eligible to be considered for funding and whether the type of activity proposed is in one of the Foundation's funding areas. Applicants are required to contact the Foundation's Executive Director by letter, e-mail, phone or personal visit before making fund application.

Proposals may be hand delivered or mailed and should include the following:
(1) proposal (one copy);
(2) one copy of each of the additional materials as defined on the Foundation's web

site (e.g., IRS determination letter, audited financial statements);
(3) one- to two-page executive summary (two copies);
(4) budget (two copies) and;
(5) Board of Directors list (two copies).

Organizations which have submitted their charters, bylaws and 501(c)(3) may submit complete applications by e-mail attachment.

Applicant organizations should not bind their proposals or submit videos or other items which have not been requested by the Foundation.
Duration: One year. Renewal possible up to three years.
Deadline: January 15, May 15, and September 5.

OFFICERS:
Dr. Robert Peters, President
Dr. Kittredge A. Baldwin, Vice President
Alfred L. Castle, Treasurer and Executive Director
Cynthia Quisenberry, Secretary

ADDRESS INQUIRIES TO:
Alfred L. Castle, Executive Director
(See address above.)

*SPECIAL STIPULATIONS:
All applicants must be prescreened before applying.

HUGH AND HAZEL DARLING FOUNDATION

520 South Grand Avenue, Suite 395
Los Angeles, CA 90071
(213) 683-5200
Fax: (213) 627-7795
E-mail: rstack@darlingfoundation.org

TYPE:
Block grants; Capital grants; Challenge/matching grants; Matching gifts; Scholarships; Training grants.

See entry 1470 for full listing.

FIRSTENERGY FOUNDATION   [1452]

76 South Main Street
Akron, OH 44308
(330) 384-5022
Fax: (330) 245-5566
E-mail: fe_comm_involve@firstenergycorp.com
Web Site: www.firstenergycorp.com/community

AREAS OF INTEREST:
Science, technology, engineering and mathematics education.

NAME(S) OF PROGRAMS:
• **STEM Grants Program**

TYPE:
Project/program grants. Project/program grants in the classroom setting.

YEAR PROGRAM STARTED: 1985

PURPOSE:
To support classroom projects and teacher professional development initiatives focusing on STEM (science, technology, engineering and mathematics).

ELIGIBILITY:
Educators (grades preK-12) and youth group leaders in the service areas of FirstEnergy and communities where FirstEnergy has facilities are encouraged to apply. Any creative project dealing with science, technology, engineering and mathematics is

eligible. Projects that involve students directly, incorporate matching funds, community resources, interdisciplinary or team-teaching and involve various age groups are highly favored. Teacher training projects are highly favored. Completed projects or those previously funded are not eligible.

GEOG. RESTRICTIONS: Maryland, New Jersey, Ohio, Pennsylvania and West Virginia.

FINANCIAL DATA:
Grants may be used to compensate experts who come to work with the students, but not to pay teachers or staff.
Amount of support per award: Up to $1,000.
Total amount of support: $97,000 for the year 2019.

NO. AWARDS: 116 for the year 2019.

APPLICATION INFO:
Application can be downloaded and completed electronically.
Duration: One school year.
Deadline: Usually third week in September.

PUBLICATIONS:
Bright Ideas for Educators.

ADDRESS INQUIRIES TO:
Community Involvement Department
(See address above.)

*SPECIAL STIPULATIONS:
Grants are only available to schools or groups in the FirstEnergy service area or in communities where it has facilities.

CHARLES HAYDEN FOUNDATION

140 Broadway, 51st Floor
New York, NY 10005
(212) 785-3677
Fax: (212) 785-3689
E-mail: fdn@chf.org
Web Site: www.charleshaydenfoundation.org

TYPE:
Project/program grants. Grant priorities focus on institutions and programs primarily serving youth at risk of not reaching their full potential, especially youth in low-income communities. Support is provided for youth development programs, charter schools, independent and parochial schools, and informal educational enrichment programs.

See entry 1028 for full listing.

INVESTED   [1453]

606 Oakesdale Avenue, S.W.
Suite C-202
Renton, WA 98057
(206) 352-1199 ext. 1
E-mail: jwalters@invested.org
Web Site: www.invested.org

FOUNDED: 1963

AREAS OF INTEREST:
Secondary schools and immediate support for disadvantaged students.

NAME(S) OF PROGRAMS:
• **InvestED School Partnership/Funding Program**

TYPE:
Grants-in-aid; Matching gifts. Support for partner schools only.

YEAR PROGRAM STARTED: 1963

PURPOSE:
To support middle and senior high school aid program providing for grants to both accredited public and private schools (grades 6-12) within the state of Washington to enable these schools to assist individual students who have needs their families cannot afford.

LEGAL BASIS:
Public charity.

ELIGIBILITY:
Grants are restricted to a program aiding students in Washington state.

School must submit year-end report May 1 to June 30 to be eligible for grant the following year.

GEOG. RESTRICTIONS: Washington state.

FINANCIAL DATA:
Amount of support per award: $350 to over $3,000 in initial funding; up to $500 matching grant per school, per school year.
Total amount of support: $510,000 initial funding and $175,000 in matching grants.

NO. MOST RECENT APPLICANTS: 660 schools.

NO. AWARDS: 660 schools.

APPLICATION INFO:
Contact the Organization for guidelines.
Duration: One year. Renewable.
Deadline: June 30.

IRS I.D.: 23-7189670

STAFF:
Joyce Walters, Executive Director
Elizabeth Benedict, Development Director
Judy Simpson, Communications Manager
Christopher Coleman, Development Associate
Samantha Cox, Program Coordinator

DIRECTORS:
Tom Horton, Chairperson
Mack Miller, First Vice President
Sam Howard, Second Vice President
Sourabh Mathur, Treasurer
Sandy Bennett-Scott, Secretary
Steven D. Brown
Trevor Carlson
Mia Coffman
Trish Millines Dziko
Thomas Gilbert, Ph.D.
Brian Kistler
Andy Knapp
Marcie Maxwell
Joe Osborne
Dr. Damien Pattenaude
Jeff Richards
Kerry Swanson
Dave Wilson

ADDRESS INQUIRIES TO:
Executive Director
(See address above.)

MARTHA HOLDEN JENNINGS FOUNDATION   [1454]

The Halle Building
1228 Euclid Avenue, Suite 240
Cleveland, OH 44115-1811
(216) 589-5700
Web Site: www.mhjf.org

FOUNDED: 1959

AREAS OF INTEREST:
Ohio elementary and secondary education.

NAME(S) OF PROGRAMS:
• **Grants-to-Educators Program**
• **Open Grants**

TYPE:
Project/program grants. Project/program grants are for education only. Support to aide the improvement of elementary and secondary public school education in Ohio.

YEAR PROGRAM STARTED: 1959

PURPOSE:
To foster the development of individual capabilities of young people to the maximum extent through improving the quality of teaching in secular primary and secondary schools; to provide a means for greater accomplishment on the part of Ohio's teachers by encouraging creativity in teaching and bringing greater recognition to the teaching profession.

LEGAL BASIS:
Nonprofit foundation.

ELIGIBILITY:
For Grants-to-Educators, applicants must be teachers or public school administrators and are intended for classroom, schoolwide or districtwide projects. For other grants, applicants must be tax-exempt with 501(c)(3) status from the IRS.

Open Grants are available to any public school district, nonreligious private school working with public schools, or tax-exempt organization that assists elementary and secondary schools in Ohio. No grants for capital improvements or graduate study, and generally no grants for equipment or travel.

GEOG. RESTRICTIONS: Ohio.

FINANCIAL DATA:
Amount of support per award:
Grants-to-Educators: Up to $3,000; Open Grants: Varies depending on needs and nature of the request. Average: $15,000.
Total amount of support: $3,318,433 for the year 2019.

NO. MOST RECENT APPLICANTS: 279.

NO. AWARDS: 235 for the year 2019.

REPRESENTATIVE AWARDS:
$10,000 to Invent Now, Inc., North Canton, OH, for Camp Invention Program; $10,000 to Idea Stream, Cleveland, OH, for News Depth Program; $8,000 to Mount Vernon City Schools for STEM Robotics Program; $9,500 to Northwest Local Schools for LETRS Training.

APPLICATION INFO:
There are two funding categories within the Grants-to-Educators and Open Grants programs: Excellent Teaching and Deep Learning. Applicants need to understand the rationale behind these grant categories before completing a proposal. Applicants must indicate the category or categories for which they are seeking funds within each program.

All grant requests must be submitted online at the Foundation web site.
Duration: One year. Proposal may be resubmitted for a second or third year.
Deadline: Proposals must be submitted by the 15th of the month preceding the month in which they are to be considered.

Grants-to-Educators: The Distribution Committee meets ten months a year (not in July or December).

Open Grants: The Board of Directors does not meet in February, July, October or December. Decisions on grant applications are generally communicated within two months of submission.

PUBLICATIONS:
Guidelines; *Pro-Excellentia.*

STAFF:
Dr. Daniel J. Keenan, Executive Director

KLINGENSTEIN CENTER FOR INDEPENDENT SCHOOL LEADERSHIP [1455]
Teachers College, Columbia University
525 West 120th Street, Box 125
New York, NY 10027-6696
(212) 678-3156
Fax: (212) 678-3156
E-mail: klingenstein@tc.columbia.edu
Web Site: klingensteincenter.org

FOUNDED: 1977

AREAS OF INTEREST:
Leadership development for independent and international education.

NAME(S) OF PROGRAMS:
- **Klingenstein Heads of Schools Program**
- **Klingenstein Summer Institute for Early Career Teachers**
- **Master's Degree in Private School Leadership**

TYPE:
Scholarships. The Klingenstein Heads of Schools Program gathers heads of independent and international schools from throughout the nation and the world for two weeks of intensive study among professional peers.

The Klingenstein Summer Institute gathers teachers in the beginning years of their careers for an exploration of teaching styles, educational philosophies and issues, and personal development.

The Master's Degree in Private School Leadership, with a focus in independent and international school leadership, gathers independent school teachers and administrators for a rigorous degree program. The Two Summers Master's Program is the two-summer version of the full-year degree program. Either program can be paired with an MBA from either Columbia Business School or INSEAD in France or Singapore to earn an M.A./MBA dual degree. The majority of students get generous tuition scholarships.

YEAR PROGRAM STARTED: 1978

PURPOSE:
To draw attention to outstanding leadership.

LEGAL BASIS:
Private foundation.

ELIGIBILITY:
Teachers and administrators working in an independent or international school with a nondiscriminatory admissions policy are eligible to apply. All programs are open to international applicants.

FINANCIAL DATA:
All programs offer tuition funding. The Heads of Schools Program and the Summer Institute for Early Career Teachers are fully-funded fellowships. Students in Master's programs are eligible for financial aid and scholarships.
Amount of support per award: Varies.
Total amount of support: Varies.

APPLICATION INFO:
Applicant must submit application, transcripts, autobiographical information and recommendations from sponsoring school. Master's program applicants must submit GMAT or GRE scores.
Duration: Varies.
Deadline: Klingenstein Heads of Schools Program: May 1; Summer Institute and Full-Year Master's Degree: January 15; Two Summers Master's Program: November 1 of even-numbered years.

PUBLICATIONS:
Klingbrief.

ADDRESS INQUIRIES TO:
Assistant Director
(See address above.)

MCCARTHEY DRESSMAN EDUCATION FOUNDATION [1456]
610 East South Temple Street
Suite 110
Salt Lake City, UT 84102
(801) 578-1260
Fax: (801) 578-1261
E-mail: info@mccartheydressman.org
Web Site: mccartheydressman.org

AREAS OF INTEREST:
Student learning and educational quality.

NAME(S) OF PROGRAMS:
- **Academic Enrichment Grants**
- **Student Teaching Scholarship**
- **Teacher Development Grants**

TYPE:
Development grants; Project/program grants; Scholarships. Academic Enrichment Grants aim to maximize innovation and results in classrooms and education departments.

Student Teaching Scholarships offer financial and mentoring support to educators who will be student teaching in their final year of a qualified teacher education program. Foundation mentors offer one-on-one guidance and attention to nurture the next generation of teachers. Scholarship recipients acquire and strengthen exemplary teaching practices that promote learning by their own students.

Teacher Development Grants aim to increase the effectiveness of individual educators and small teams of teachers. These grants provide opportunities for teachers to integrate fresh strategies that encourage critical inquiry and to observe their effects on students. Teachers have the opportunity to reflect and write about their projects, as well as to share their results with other teachers.

PURPOSE:
To serve as a catalyst in maximizing the skills and creativity of educators at the K-12 levels; to cultivate pioneering approaches to teaching that result in dynamic student learning.

ELIGIBILITY:
Applications for Academic Enrichment Grants are considered from educators who are employed by schools or nonprofit organizations, have the background and experience to complete the project successfully, have direct and regular contact with students in grades preK-12, work with students from low-income households, and are willing to work in collaboration with the Foundation. A project may have one to many participants involved in its planning and implementation. However, the Foundation does require that each application by

submitted in the name of one individual even if there are two or more participants involved in a single project.

Student Teaching Scholarship applicants must be full-time students in good standing and in the final year of the teacher education program at New Mexico State University, the University of California Santa Cruz, the University of Texas at Austin or the Stephen F. Austin State University. They must specialize in elementary or secondary education and have the background and experience to complete the project successfully. Applicant must be willing to work with a trustee of the Foundation during the student teaching experience.

Applications for Teacher Development Grants are considered from educators who are licensed K-12 teachers employed in public or private schools, have the background and experience to complete the project successfully, and are willing to work in collaboration with the Foundation. A project may have one to many participants involved in its planning and implementation. However, the Foundation does require that each application be submitted in the name of one individual even if there are two or more participants involved in a single project.

FINANCIAL DATA:
Amount of support per award: Academic Enrichment Grants and Teacher Development Grants: Up to $10,000 per year; Student Teaching Scholarship: $6,000.

NO. MOST RECENT APPLICANTS: Maximum 350 (175 Academic Enrichment, 50 Student Teaching and 125 Teacher Development).

NO. AWARDS: Academic Enrichment Grants: 5; Student Teaching Scholarship: 4; Teacher Development Grants: 4 for the year 2019-20.

APPLICATION INFO:
Applications are submitted online. Letters of recommendation are required.

Duration: Academic Enrichment Grants and Teacher Development Grants: Up to three years, provided eligibility requirements continue to be met. Student Teaching Scholarship: One year.

Deadline: April 15. Awards announced July 15.

TRUSTEES:
Judy A. Abbott
Michael Borish
Mark Dressman
Carmen Gonzales
Sarah McCarthey
Carolyn Schubach
Patrick Scott
Kip Tellez
Phil Wilder
Jo Worthy

MEBANE CHARITABLE FOUNDATION, INC.
232 South Main Street
Mocksville, NC 27028
(336) 936-0041
Fax: (336) 936-0038
E-mail: lcolbourne@mebanefoundation.com
Web Site: www.mebanefoundation.com

TYPE:
Project/program grants.

See entry 1034 for full listing.

MITSUBISHI ELECTRIC AMERICA FOUNDATION [1457]
1300 Wilson Boulevard
Suite 210
Arlington, VA 22209
(703) 276-8240
E-mail: mea.foundation@meus.mea.com
Web Site: www.meaf.org

FOUNDED: 1991

AREAS OF INTEREST:
People with disabilities, including education, employment, independence and community inclusion.

TYPE:
Demonstration grants; Internships; Matching gifts; Project/program grants; Seed money grants; Technical assistance; Training grants. Grants are offered to make a better world for all by helping young people with disabilities to maximize their potential and participation in society.

YEAR PROGRAM STARTED: 1991

PURPOSE:
To help young people with disabilities maximize their potential and participation in society.

LEGAL BASIS:
Foundation.

ELIGIBILITY:
Applicants must meet criteria as stated in Foundation guidelines. Priority given to applicants in communities where MEUS facilities are located.

GEOG. RESTRICTIONS: United States.

FINANCIAL DATA:
Amount of support per award: Typically $10,000 to $75,000 per year.

Total amount of support: $985,221,000 for the year 2018.

Matching fund requirements: Mitsubishi Electric employee must submit a request to match for qualified organizations.

NO. MOST RECENT APPLICANTS: 100.

NO. AWARDS: 6 to 12 annually.

REPRESENTATIVE AWARDS:
$187,500 to support the Autistic Self-Advocacy Network Autism Campus Inclusion Program; $150,000 to the University of Pittsburgh to support the Advancing Inclusive Manufacturing (AIM) Program; $150,000 to the U.S. Business Leadership Network to support the Career Link Mentoring Program.

APPLICATION INFO:
Submit a two-page concept paper (click on the "How to Apply" tab on the Foundation web site) including a budget summary and description of the need and objectives for the funds requested. Instructions for full proposals will be sent after initial screening. Concept papers are reviewed throughout the year.

Applicants are requested not to telephone the Foundation during the application process.

Duration: One to three years. Renewal possible on a case-by-case basis.

Deadline: October 15 to be considered for following year funding.

BOARD OF DIRECTORS:
Mike Corbo
Mike DeLano
Chris Gerdes
Brian Heery

Keijiro Hora
Mitsuharu Kiwada
Mark Kuntz
Perry Pappous
Scott Summerville
Dr. Richard C. Waters

ADDRESS INQUIRIES TO:
Kevin R. Webb, Senior Director
(See address above.)

NATIONAL ENDOWMENT FOR THE HUMANITIES
The Constitution Center
400 7th Street, S.W.
Washington, DC 20506
(202) 606-8424
Fax: (202) 606-8240
E-mail: communications@neh.gov
Web Site: www.neh.gov

TYPE:
Conferences/seminars. Grants support summer seminars and national institutes in the humanities for college and school teachers. These faculty development activities are conducted at colleges and universities across the country. Lists of pending seminars and institutes are available from the program.

See entry 347 for full listing.

NATIONAL SCIENCE FOUNDATION [1458]
Directorate for Education and Human Resources
Division of Research on Learning in Formal and Informal Settings
2415 Eisenhower Avenue
Alexandria, VA 22314
(703) 292-8620
Fax: (703) 292-9044; (703) 292-9046
E-mail: acarroll@nsf.gov
Web Site: www.nsf.gov

FOUNDED: 1950

AREAS OF INTEREST:
Science, mathematics, technology education content; pedagogy; applied research; development of resources and tools for instruction, assessment, evaluation and informal science.

NAME(S) OF PROGRAMS:
- **Advanced Informal STEM Learning (AISL)**
- **Advanced Technological Education (ATE)**
- **Discovery Research PreK-12 (DR K12)**
- **Innovative Technology Experiences for Students and Teachers (ITEST)**

TYPE:
Conferences/seminars; Demonstration grants; Development grants; Project/program grants; Research grants; Training grants. Advanced Informal STEM Learning (AISL) program invests in projects that develop and implement informal learning experiences designed to increase interest, engagement and understanding of science, technology, engineering and mathematics (STEM) by individuals of all ages and backgrounds, as well as projects that advance knowledge and practice of informal science education.

With an emphasis on two-year colleges, the Advanced Technological Education (ATE) program focuses on the education of technicians for the high-technology fields that drive the nation's economy.

Discovery Research PreK-12 (DR K12) funds research, development and evaluation activities through knowledge generation and application to improve PreK-12 learning and teaching.

Innovative Technology Experiences for Students and Teachers (ITEST) is designed to increase the opportunities for students and teachers to learn about, experience, and use information technologies within the context of science, technology, engineering and mathematics (STEM), including Information Technology (IT) courses. It is in direct response to the concern about shortages of information technology workers in the U.S.

Research and Evaluation on Education in Science and Engineering (REESE) supports basic and applied research and evaluation that enhances science, technology, engineering and mathematics (STEM) learning and teaching.

PURPOSE:
To promote quality programs of education in mathematics, science and technology for all the nation's youth, and informal learning opportunities in these fields for youth and adults.

LEGAL BASIS:
The National Science Foundation Act of 1950, Public Law 81-507, as amended.

GEOG. RESTRICTIONS: United States.

FINANCIAL DATA:
Amount of support per award: Grants vary in amount, depending upon the needs and nature of the request and availability of funds.

Total amount of support: $180,000,000.

APPLICATION INFO:
Application information is available on the Foundation's web site.

Duration: One to five years.

Deadline: Varies.

THE RADIANT PEACE FOUNDATION INTERNATIONAL, INC. [1459]

P.O. Box 40822
St. Petersburg, FL 33743-0822
(727) 343-8212
E-mail: radiantpeaceintl@gmail.com
Web Site: www.radiantpeace.org

FOUNDED: 1990

NAME(S) OF PROGRAMS:
● **Radiant Peace Education Awards**

TYPE:
Awards/prizes. Recognizes and awards children, teachers and schools for Radiant Peace essays, art, projects, and videos.

YEAR PROGRAM STARTED: 1990

PURPOSE:
To inspire, promote and encourage Radiant Peace worldwide.

LEGAL BASIS:
A 501(c)(3) nonprofit educational organization.

ELIGIBILITY:
All students grades one-12 including home schools and youth groups.

FINANCIAL DATA:
Amount of support per award: $25 to $500.
Total amount of support: Varies by year.

NO. AWARDS: 109.

APPLICATION INFO:
Invitations and guidelines posted online.

Deadline: December and April.

ADDRESS INQUIRIES TO:
Office Manager
(See address above.)

SONY CORPORATION OF AMERICA [1460]

25 Madison Avenue, 27th Floor
New York, NY 10010-8601
(212) 833-6851
E-mail: erin.amaty@sony.com
Web Site: www.sony.com

FOUNDED: 1972

AREAS OF INTEREST:
Arts, culture and technology, with primary focus in education; environmental issues; civic affairs; disaster relief.

TYPE:
General operating grants; Matching gifts; Product donations; Project/program grants.

YEAR PROGRAM STARTED: 1972

PURPOSE:
To meet the needs of the communities where Sony has a presence; to support national organizations which extend into Sony presence areas.

ELIGIBILITY:
No grants to individuals, political or religious organizations, labor unions, endowments, capital campaigns, lobbying groups, testimonial dinners, for-profit publications seeking advertisements and foreign or non-U.S. organizations.

GEOG. RESTRICTIONS: United States.

FINANCIAL DATA:
Amount of support per award: Varies.

Total amount of support: Varies.

Matching fund requirements: Sony matches contributions made by full-time employees to educational institutions, hospitals and health care organizations, cultural organizations, and environmental organizations.

APPLICATION INFO:
Send brief letter describing organization, amount requested, objectives of organization, recent audited financial statement and proof of tax-exempt status. Phone calls not accepted, only written requests.

Duration: One year. Must reapply for continued support.

Deadline: Requests accepted throughout the year. Notification within three months.

PUBLICATIONS:
Contribution guidelines.

OFFICERS:
Karen E. Kelso, Senior Director, Corporate Social Responsibility

ADDRESS INQUIRIES TO:
Erin Amaty, Senior Coordinator
Corporate Social Responsibility
(See address above.)

STATE LIBRARY AND ARCHIVES OF FLORIDA

R.A. Gray Building
500 South Bronough Street
Tallahassee, FL 32399-0250
(850) 245-6620
Fax: (850) 245-6643
E-mail: marian.deeney@dos.myflorida.com
Web Site: dos.myflorida.com/library-archives/services-for-libraries/grants/lsta

TYPE:
Project/program grants. Project grants congruent with the state long-range plan.

See entry 689 for full listing.

W. CLEMENT & JESSIE V. STONE FOUNDATION [1461]

70 East Lake Street, Suite 1020
Chicago, IL 60601
(800) 288-4859
E-mail: info@wcstonefnd.org
Web Site: www.wcstonefnd.org

FOUNDED: 1958

AREAS OF INTEREST:
Education, early childhood and youth development.

TYPE:
General operating grants; Project/program grants; Technical assistance.

YEAR PROGRAM STARTED: 1958

PURPOSE:
To make the world a better place by supporting programs in education, early childhood and youth development.

ELIGIBILITY:
Grants are made to organizations that have tax-exempt status under Section 501(c)(3) of the Internal Revenue Code. Nonsectarian religious programs may apply. No grants are made to individuals.

GEOG. RESTRICTIONS: San Francisco Bay area, California; Chicago, Illinois; Boston, Massachusetts; New York City, New York; and Philadelphia, Pennsylvania.

FINANCIAL DATA:
Amount of support per award: $10,000 to $100,000, depending upon the program.
Total amount of support: Approximately $5,500,000 for the year 2019.

NO. AWARDS: 100.

APPLICATION INFO:
The Foundation does not accept unsolicited proposals. Organizations may call if they feel there is a strong match between their work and the Foundation's grantmaking priorities.

Duration: One year. Renewal possible.

Deadline: Late April to early May and late October.

IRS I.D.: 36-2498125

OFFICERS AND DIRECTORS:
Norman C. Stone, Chairman
Sandra Stone, President
Steven M. Stone, Treasurer
Michael A. Stone, Secretary
Sara Slaughter, Executive Director
Amy Stone
Barbara Stone
David Stone
Debbie Stone
Jeffrey Stone
Jennifer Stone
Norah Stone

Sara Stone
Chad Tingley

ADDRESS INQUIRIES TO:
Sara Slaughter, Executive Director
(See address above.)

TOSHIBA AMERICA FOUNDATION [1462]

1251 Avenue of the Americas, 41st Floor
New York, NY 10020
(212) 596-0620
E-mail: tai-foundation@toshiba.com
Web Site: www.toshiba.com/tai

FOUNDED: 1990

AREAS OF INTEREST:
Mathematics and science education for
grades K-12.

TYPE:
Project/program grants.

YEAR PROGRAM STARTED: 1990

PURPOSE:
To improve science and math education at
the pre-college level (grades K-12 only).

LEGAL BASIS:
Corporate foundation.

ELIGIBILITY:
Grants are made to private or public schools.
Preference is given to programs or projects
that take place in science or math
classrooms. The Foundation does not fund
grants for general operating costs,
endowments, scholarships, conferences,
summer programs, purchase of equipment
(product or donations), sponsorships, or
individuals.

GEOG. RESTRICTIONS: United States.

FINANCIAL DATA:
Amount of support per award: $1,000 to
$20,000.
Total amount of support: Approximately
$500,000.

NO. AWARDS: 150 annually.

APPLICATION INFO:
Applications are available on the
Foundation's web site.
Duration: One year.
Deadline: Grades K-5: October 1. Grades
6-12: May 1 and November 1 for requests
more than $5,000.

IRS I.D.: 13-3596612

ADDRESS INQUIRIES TO:
Program Officer
(See address above.)

U.S. DEPARTMENT OF EDUCATION

Office of Indian Education
400 Maryland Avenue, S.W.
LBJ Building, 3W101
Washington, DC 20202-6335
(202) 260-3774
Fax: (202) 205-0606
E-mail: indian.education@ed.gov
Web Site: www2.ed.
gov/programs/indianformula/index.html

TYPE:
Formula grants. Grants to provide financial
assistance to LEAs and tribal schools to
address the unique cultural, language and

educationally related academic needs of
American Indian and Alaska Native students,
including preschool children.

See entry 966 for full listing.

U.S. DEPARTMENT OF EDUCATION

Office of Post Secondary Education
Federal TRIO Programs
400 Maryland Avenue, S.W.
Washington, DC 20202
(202) 453-6273
(202) 453-6914
Fax: (202) 502-7857
E-mail: OPE_TRIO@ed.gov
Web Site: www.ed.gov/ope/trio

TYPE:
Project/program grants. There are three types
of grants under the Upward Bound program:
Regular Upward Bound Grants, Veterans
Upward Bound Grants, and Upward Bound
Math and Science Grants.

The Regular Upward Bound projects are
designed to generate in participants the skills
and motivation necessary for success in
education beyond secondary school. The
Veterans Upward Bound projects are
designed to assist veterans in preparing for a
program of postsecondary education. The
Upward Bound Math and Science projects
are designed to prepare high school students
for postsecondary education programs that
lead to careers in the fields of math and
science.

See entry 1486 for full listing.

YOUTH FOR UNDERSTANDING USA

6856 Eastern Avenue, N.W.
Suite 310
Washington, DC 20012
(202) 774-5200 ext. 5203
(800) 833-6243
Fax: (202) 588-7571
E-mail: admissions@yfu.org
mckendree@yfu.org
Web Site: www.yfuusa.org

TYPE:
Exchange programs; Grants-in-aid;
Scholarships; Travel grants. Students on
summer semester and year programs live
with volunteer host families overseas.
Students on semester and academic year
programs also attend school. International
students live and study at U.S. high schools
or community colleges. Competitive, full and
partial scholarships for Corporate, Japan-U.S.
Senate Programs and Japan-America
Friendship Scholars Program.

See entry 876 for full listing.

Higher education projects and research

ABEL FOUNDATION

1815 Y Street
Lincoln, NE 68508
(402) 434-1212
Fax: (402) 434-1799
Web Site: www.abelfoundation.org

TYPE:
Capital grants; Matching gifts;
Project/program grants.

See entry 1052 for full listing.

AMERICAN FLORAL ENDOWMENT

1001 North Fairfax Street
Suite 201
Alexandria, VA 22314
(703) 838-5211
Fax: (703) 838-5212
E-mail: afe@endowment.org
Web Site: endowment.org

TYPE:
Internships; Project/program grants; Research
grants; Scholarships. The Endowment funds
research and educational development in
floriculture and environmental horticulture
designed to produce solutions to industry
needs and promote the growth and
improvement of the floral industry for the
benefit of the grower, wholesale, retail, allied
segments and the general public.

The Endowment supports educational
programs focused on attracting young people
to the industry, and educational endeavors to
identify and solve industry needs and/or
challenges. The programs are divided into
two major areas:
(1) paid floriculture internships/scholarships
for full-time college students and;
(2) general educational grants to national
programs.

See entry 1932 for full listing.

AMERICAN FOUNDATION FOR PHARMACEUTICAL EDUCATION (AFPE) [1463]

6076 Franconia Road, Suite C
Alexandria, VA 22310-1758
(703) 875-3095
Fax: (703) 875-3098
E-mail: hardimon@afpepharm.org
Web Site: afpepharm.org

FOUNDED: 1942

AREAS OF INTEREST:
Education.

NAME(S) OF PROGRAMS:
● **AFPE Predoctoral Fellowships in the
Pharmaceutical Sciences**

TYPE:
Fellowships.

YEAR PROGRAM STARTED: 1942

PURPOSE:
To encourage an outstanding pharmacy
school graduate to pursue an advanced
degree in the pharmaceutical sciences; to
identify and support students who have the
potential to become leaders in the
pharmaceutical profession.

ELIGIBILITY:
Eligible applicants must meet the following
criteria:
(1) be a U.S. citizen or permanent resident;
(2) be a full-time student enrolled in a
graduate Ph.D. program in pharmaceutical
science administered by or officially affiliated
with a U.S. college of pharmacy accredited
by ACPE;
(3) have at least three semesters of study
completed in the current Ph.D. program;
(4) have no more that three and a half years

remaining to obtain the Ph.D. degree and; (5) may be a joint Pharm.D./Ph.D. student who has completed the equivalent of three full semesters of graduate credit toward the Ph.D. and will be awarded the Ph.D. degree within three additional years.

GEOG. RESTRICTIONS: United States.

FINANCIAL DATA:
The Fellowship stipend may be used for a purpose decided by the awardee and college that will enable the student to make progress in their pursuit of the Ph.D., such as student stipend, laboratory supplies, books, materials, travel, etc. None of the funds shall be used for indirect costs by the institution.
Amount of support per award: $10,000 stipend.
Total amount of support: Varies.

NO. MOST RECENT APPLICANTS: 150.

NO. AWARDS: 42.

APPLICATION INFO:
Application and guidelines are available online.
Duration: One year, September to August. Renewable.

AMERICAN FOUNDATION FOR PHARMACEUTICAL EDUCATION (AFPE)
6076 Franconia Road, Suite C
Alexandria, VA 22310-1758
(703) 875-3095
Fax: (703) 875-3098
E-mail: hardimon@afpepharm.org
Web Site: afpepharm.org

TYPE:
Fellowships.
See entry 2330 for full listing.

AMERICAN FRIENDS OF THE ALEXANDER VON HUMBOLDT FOUNDATION   [1464]
1401 K Street
Suite 1005
Washington, DC 20005
(202) 783-1907
E-mail: info@americanfriendsofavh.org
Web Site: www.americanfriendsofavh.org

FOUNDED: 1953

AREAS OF INTEREST:
Postgraduate research in Germany.

NAME(S) OF PROGRAMS:
● **Humboldt Research Fellowship for Postdoctoral Researchers**

TYPE:
Fellowships; Project/program grants; Research grants; Scholarships. This program supports highly qualified scholars and scientists of all nationalities and disciplines so that they may carry out long-term research projects that the applicant has selected in cooperation with an academic host the applicant has selected at a research institution in Germany.

PURPOSE:
To support highly qualified scholars and scientists of all nationalities and disciplines so that they may carry out long-term research projects in Germany.

ELIGIBILITY:
Open to scientists and scholars who completed a doctoral degree within four years prior to the application submission date.

Fellowships are awarded on the basis of academic achievement, the quality and feasibility of the proposed research and the candidate's publications.

FINANCIAL DATA:
In addition to a monthly stipend, special allowances are available for accompanying family members, travel expenses and German language instruction.
Amount of support per award: EUR 2,650 monthly.
Total amount of support: Varies.

NO. MOST RECENT APPLICANTS: Approximately 1,800.

NO. AWARDS: Approximately 600 total fellowships for postdoctoral researchers and experienced researchers each year.

APPLICATION INFO:
Application information is available on the web site.
Duration: Six to 24 months in Germany.
Deadline: Continuous. The review process takes several months, and the selection committee meets three times a year to review applications.

STAFF:
Brian Craft, Alumni Relations and Annual Fund Program Coordinator
Alexis Brouwer-Ancher, Communications and Events Program Coordinator

ADDRESS INQUIRIES TO:
Program Coordination
(See address above.) or

Alexander von Humboldt Stiftung
Jean-Paul-Strasse 12
D-53173 Bonn
Germany
Tel: 49 (0228) 833-0
Fax: 49 (0228) 833-199
E-mail: info@avh.de

*SPECIAL STIPULATIONS:
Applicant must have received Ph.D. within four years.

AMERICAN LIBRARY ASSOCIATION (ALA)   [1465]
225 North Michigan Avenue
Suite 1300
Chicago, IL 60601
(312) 280-4279
(800) 545-2433 ext. 4279
Fax: (312) 280-4279
E-mail: scholarships@ala.org
Web Site: www.ala.org/educationcareers/scholarships

FOUNDED: 1969

AREAS OF INTEREST:
Library science.

NAME(S) OF PROGRAMS:
● **ALA Spectrum Scholarship**
● **ALA/Century Scholarship**
● **ALSC/Bound-to-Stay-Bound Books Scholarship**
● **ALSC/Frederic G. Melcher Scholarship**
● **David H. Clift Scholarship**
● **Tom and Roberta Drewes Scholarship**
● **Mary V. Gaver Scholarship**
● **Miriam L. Hornback Scholarship**

● **Christopher J. Hoy/ERT Scholarship**
● **Tony B. Leisner Scholarship**
● **LITA/Christian Larew Memorial Scholarship**
● **Peter Lyman Memorial/SAGE Scholarships**
● **W. David Rozkuszka Scholarship**

TYPE:
Scholarships. All scholarships are for librarians entering a Master's degree program.

ALA/Century Scholarship is for an individual with a disability entering a Master's degree or Ph.D. program.

ALSC and Gaver Scholarships are for a youth services librarian.

Clift, Hoy/ERT and Rozkuszka are general scholarships.

Drewes, Hornback and Leisner Scholarships are for paid library support staff currently working in a library.

SAGE Scholarship is for a new media services librarian.

PURPOSE:
To support library staff education.

ELIGIBILITY:
Applicants must be U.S. or Canadian citizens, or permanent residents thereof.

Applicants must demonstrate academic excellence, leadership qualities and evidence of commitment to a career in librarianship.

Applicants may not have completed more than 12 semester hours or the equivalent towards a Master's degree in library science prior to June 1.

GEOG. RESTRICTIONS: United States and Canada.

FINANCIAL DATA:
Amount of support per award: Varies.
Total amount of support: Over $300,000 annually.

APPLICATION INFO:
Applications and reference forms are submitted online. Applicants are required to submit their undergraduate transcripts.
Deadline: March 1.

STAFF:
Kimberly Redd, Program Manager

ADDRESS INQUIRIES TO:
Kimberly Redd, Program Manager
(See address above.)

THE AMERICAN-SCANDINAVIAN FOUNDATION   [1466]
58 Park Avenue
New York, NY 10016
(212) 779-3587
(615) 881-1532
Fax: (212) 686-1157
E-mail: grants@amscan.org
Web Site: www.amscan.org

FOUNDED: 1910

AREAS OF INTEREST:
Cross-cultural exchange at an academic level.

NAME(S) OF PROGRAMS:
● **Visiting Lectureships**

TYPE:
Exchange programs. The Foundation invites U.S. colleges and universities to apply for

funding to host a visiting lecturer from Norway or Sweden. Lectureships should be in the area of contemporary studies with an emphasis in one of the following areas: (1) public policy; (2) conflict resolution; (3) environmental studies; (4) multiculturalism and; (5) health care.

PURPOSE:
To promote international understanding through educational and cultural exchange between the U.S. and Scandinavia.

ELIGIBILITY:
The competition is open to all American colleges and universities. The award is appropriate for any department or interdisciplinary program with an interest in incorporating a Scandinavian focus into its course offerings. The lecturer must be a Norwegian or Swedish citizen and a scholar or expert in a field appropriate to the host department or program.

FINANCIAL DATA:
Amount of support per award: $20,000 teaching/research stipend plus a $5,000 travel stipend for lecture appearances outside home institution.

NO. MOST RECENT APPLICANTS: 1.

NO. AWARDS: 1.

APPLICATION INFO:
Application and instructions are available on the Foundation web site.
Duration: One semester.
Deadline: February 15. Announcement April 15.

*SPECIAL STIPULATIONS:
The selected lecturer is expected to teach one course (undergraduate or graduate-level) and perform modest public activities (lectures, etc.) for which he or she will receive $20,000.

ARCHAEOLOGICAL INSTITUTE OF AMERICA   [1467]
44 Beacon Street
Boston, MA 02108
(857) 305-9360
Fax: (857) 233-4270
E-mail: fellowships@archaeology.org
Web Site: www.archaeological.org

FOUNDED: 1879

AREAS OF INTEREST:
Archaeological research and publication.

NAME(S) OF PROGRAMS:
● **Helen M. Woodruff Fellowship of the AIA and the American Academy in Rome**

TYPE:
Fellowships. A predoctoral or postdoctoral fellowship for study of archaeology and classical studies established by the Institute at the American Academy in Rome. Award supports a Rome Prize.

PURPOSE:
To promote the study of archaeology and classical studies.

ELIGIBILITY:
Applicant must be a citizen or permanent resident of the U.S.

GEOG. RESTRICTIONS: United States.

FINANCIAL DATA:
Amount of support per award: $10,000.
Total amount of support: $10,000.

NO. AWARDS: 1 in odd-numbered years.

APPLICATION INFO:
Applications must be sent to the American Academy in Rome; 7 East 60th Street; New York, NY 10022.
Duration: One year.
Deadline: November 1 of even-numbered years.

ADDRESS INQUIRIES TO:
Fellowship Coordinator
Tel: (212) 571-7200

ARCHITECTURAL LEAGUE OF NEW YORK
594 Broadway, Suite 607
New York, NY 10012
(212) 753-1722
Fax: (212) 486-9173
E-mail: info@archleague.org
Web Site: archleague.org

TYPE:
Travel grants. The Deborah J. Norden Fund, established in 1995 in memory of architect and arts administrator Deborah Norden, awards travel/study grants to students and recent graduates in the field of architecture, architectural history, and urban studies.

See entry 377 for full listing.

ARCTIC INSTITUTE OF NORTH AMERICA   [1468]
The University of Calgary
2500 University Drive, N.W., ES 1040
Calgary AB T2N 1N4 Canada
(403) 220-7515
Fax: (403) 282-4609
E-mail: arctic@ucalgary.ca
Web Site: www.arctic.ucalgary.ca

FOUNDED: 1945

AREAS OF INTEREST:
Arctic natural and social sciences.

NAME(S) OF PROGRAMS:
● **AINA Grants-in-Aid**

TYPE:
Grants-in-aid; Scholarships.

YEAR PROGRAM STARTED: 1945

PURPOSE:
To provide funding to young investigators, especially graduate students, to augment their research.

ELIGIBILITY:
Proposed projects can include field, library or office-intensive investigations. Although there is no limitation on the area of investigation, the Institute encourages applications focused on the natural sciences and social sciences, including anthropology and economics, in the North.

FINANCIAL DATA:
Funding can be used for travel, supplies, equipment and services, but not for salary or wages.
Amount of support per award: $1,000.
Total amount of support: Varies each year, depending on number of applications received.

NO. MOST RECENT APPLICANTS: 80.

NO. AWARDS: Varies.

APPLICATION INFO:
Applications may be submitted online.
Duration: One year.

Deadline: February 1.

PUBLICATIONS:
Arctic Journal.

ADDRESS INQUIRIES TO:
Arctic Institute of North America
(See e-mail address above.)

BARNES GROUP FOUNDATION
123 Main Street
Bristol, CT 06010
(860) 583-7070
E-mail: info@bginc.com
Web Site: www.bginc.com

TYPE:
General operating grants; Scholarships. Employee scholarship program.

See entry 1073 for full listing.

ROY J. CARVER CHARITABLE TRUST   [1469]
202 Iowa Avenue
Muscatine, IA 52761-3733
(563) 263-4010
Fax: (563) 263-1547
E-mail: info@carvertrust.org
Web Site: www.carvertrust.org

FOUNDED: 1982

AREAS OF INTEREST:
Biomedical and scientific research; elementary, secondary and higher education; youth recreation.

TYPE:
Capital grants; Challenge/matching grants; Professorships; Project/program grants; Research grants; Scholarships.

YEAR PROGRAM STARTED: 1982

PURPOSE:
To support medical and scientific research, scholarships, general education and programs addressing the needs of youth.

LEGAL BASIS:
Trust.

ELIGIBILITY:
Eligible organizations must be IRS 501(c)(3) tax-exempt.

GEOG. RESTRICTIONS: Iowa and portions of western Illinois.

FINANCIAL DATA:
Amount of support per award: Varies.
Total amount of support: Varies.

NO. AWARDS: Approximately 68.

APPLICATION INFO:
Detailed information is available online.
Duration: Varies.
Deadline: February 15, May 15, August 15 and November 15.

ADDRESS INQUIRIES TO:
Troy K. Ross, Ph.D.
Executive Administrator
(See address above.)

CENTER FOR CALIFORNIA STUDIES, CAPITAL FELLOWS PROGRAMS
California State University, Sacramento
6000 J Street, MS 6081
Sacramento, CA 95819-6081
(916) 278-6906
Fax: (916) 278-5199
E-mail: calstudies@csus.edu
Web Site: www.csus.edu/center/center-california-studies

TYPE:
Fellowships. Sponsored by the Center for California Studies at California State University, Sacramento. Full-time fellowships for 64 fellows across four programs, 10 to 11 months, and graduate units earned from California State University, Sacramento.

See entry 1814 for full listing.

CORNELL UNIVERSITY
Society for the Humanities
A.D. White House
121 Presidents Drive
Ithaca, NY 14853-1101
(607) 255-9274
(607) 255-4086
Fax: (607) 255-1422
E-mail: humctr@cornell.edu
Web Site: societyhumanities.as.cornell.edu/fellowships

TYPE:
Fellowships. Postdoctoral teaching-research fellowships in the humanities, each awarded for a two-year period. While in residence at Cornell, postdoctoral fellows hold department affiliation and have limited teaching duties and the opportunity for scholarly work.

See entry 332 for full listing.

HUGH AND HAZEL DARLING FOUNDATION [1470]
520 South Grand Avenue, Suite 395
Los Angeles, CA 90071
(213) 683-5200
Fax: (213) 627-7795
E-mail: rstack@darlingfoundation.org

FOUNDED: 1987

AREAS OF INTEREST:
Education.

TYPE:
Block grants; Capital grants; Challenge/matching grants; Matching gifts; Scholarships; Training grants.

YEAR PROGRAM STARTED: 1987

PURPOSE:
To support education in California, with principle emphasis on legal education.

LEGAL BASIS:
Private foundation.

ELIGIBILITY:
Grants are made only to tax-exempt 501(c)(3) organizations. No grants are made to individuals.

GEOG. RESTRICTIONS: California.

FINANCIAL DATA:
Amount of support per award: Varies.
Total amount of support: $1,925,000 for the year 2019.

NO. MOST RECENT APPLICANTS: 100.

NO. AWARDS: 41 for the year 2019.

APPLICATION INFO:
Send letter and literature.
Deadline: Applications accepted throughout the year.

IRS I.D.: 95-6874901

OFFICERS:
Richard L. Stack, Trustee

ADDRESS INQUIRIES TO:
Richard L. Stack, Trustee
(See address above.)

DELOITTE FOUNDATION [1471]
695 East Main Street
Stamford, CT 06901
(203) 761-3413
Fax: (877) 366-1742
E-mail: plevine@deloitte.com
Web Site: www.deloitte.com/us/df

FOUNDED: 1928

AREAS OF INTEREST:
Higher education, specializing in accounting and business.

TYPE:
Conferences/seminars; Fellowships; Matching gifts; Professorships; Research grants.

YEAR PROGRAM STARTED: 1956

PURPOSE:
To support education through a variety of initiatives that help develop the talent of the future and their influencers and promote excellence in teaching, research and curriculum innovation.

LEGAL BASIS:
Foundation.

ELIGIBILITY:
Doctoral Fellowship Program applicants must be doctoral candidates pursuing a Ph.D. in accounting at U.S. colleges and universities.

GEOG. RESTRICTIONS: United States.

FINANCIAL DATA:
Amount of support per award: Doctoral Fellowship Program: $25,000.
Total amount of support: Fellowship: $250,000 each year.

NO. MOST RECENT APPLICANTS: Approximately 50.

NO. AWARDS: Doctoral Fellowship Program: Up to 10.

APPLICATION INFO:
Application required only for Doctoral Fellowship Program and can be obtained through head of university accounting program. Send letter for other grant requests.
Duration: Doctoral Fellowship Program: Up to two years.
Deadline: Doctoral Fellowships: October 15. Announcement in late January or early February. No deadline for Research Grants.

PUBLICATIONS:
Information brochure.

BOARD OF DIRECTORS:
Mike Fucci, Chairman
Antoinette Leatherberry, President
Sam Silvers, Secretary and Treasurer

ADDRESS INQUIRIES TO:
Peg Levine, Specialist
(See address above.)

HALBERT CENTRE FOR CANADIAN STUDIES [1472]
Hebrew University of Jerusalem
Mount Scopus
Jerusalem 9190501 Israel
(972) 2-588-1344
Fax: (972) 2-582-6267
E-mail: mscanada@mail.huji.ac.il
Web Site: canadianstudies.huji.ac.il

FOUNDED: 1944

AREAS OF INTEREST:
Canadian studies.

NAME(S) OF PROGRAMS:
● **Halbert Centre for Canadian Studies Visiting Professors Program**

TYPE:
Professorships; Visiting scholars.

YEAR PROGRAM STARTED: 1945

PURPOSE:
To build bridges and strengthen ties between Canadian and Israeli scholars.

LEGAL BASIS:
Nonprofit.

ELIGIBILITY:
Applicants should hold university teaching positions in the social sciences, humanities or law. Applicants will be expected to combine broad teaching and research experience in their field with an ability to emphasize Canadian content. An expression of interest in participating in cooperative work to emphasize the development of joint Israel-Canada research will be of advantage to the applicant.

GEOG. RESTRICTIONS: Canada.

FINANCIAL DATA:
Remuneration includes up to $3,000 (CAN) for cost of airfare to Israel and housing.
Total amount of support: Varies.

NO. AWARDS: 5 for the academic year 2017-18.

APPLICATION INFO:
Application must be submitted by the chair of the hosting department at the Hebrew University. The hosting department is requested to submit a plan reflecting the nature and scope of the visit, as well as the applicant's curriculum vitae and a short bio.

Curriculum vitae should not exceed two pages in length, and should only include the candidate's experience in the last five years.
Duration: One to four weeks.
Deadline: February 20. Decision by end of March.

PUBLICATIONS:
Program announcement.

ADDRESS INQUIRIES TO:
See e-mail address above.

THE HALLETT CHARITABLE TRUSTS [1473]
P.O. Box 14729
Minneapolis, MN 55414
(612) 346-7777
E-mail: info@halletttrusts.org
Web Site: www.halletttrusts.org

AREAS OF INTEREST:
Higher education, social services, children's services, health, economic and cultural services.

TYPE:
Project/program grants.

PURPOSE:
To directly impact the population of the community in a manner that will measurably enrich its educational, health, economic and cultural opportunities.

ELIGIBILITY:
Grants are made to organizations that have tax-exempt status under Section 501(c)(3) of the Internal Revenue Code. No grants are made to individuals.

GEOG. RESTRICTIONS: Cuyuna Lakes area, Minnesota.

FINANCIAL DATA:
    Amount of support per award: Varies.
    Total amount of support: $500,000 to
    $600,000.

NO. AWARDS: 30 for the year 2019.

APPLICATION INFO:
    Application information is available on the
    web site.
    Duration: Typically one year. Trustees may
    make multiyear commitments for grants.
    Deadline: October 31.

ADDRESS INQUIRIES TO:
    Sally Godfrey, Executive Director
    (See address above.)

HALLIBURTON FOUNDATION, INC.   [1474]
Plaza 1, 3320 T
3000 North Sam Houston Parkway East
Houston, TX 77032
(281) 871-3558
E-mail: brinda.maxwell@halliburton.com
Web Site: www.halliburton.com

FOUNDED: 1965

AREAS OF INTEREST:
    Higher education and elementary/secondary
    education.

TYPE:
    Matching gifts; Project/program grants.

LEGAL BASIS:
    Corporate giving program.

ELIGIBILITY:
    Direct grant process is by invitation.
    Applicants are accredited junior colleges,
    colleges and universities or accredited
    elementary/secondary schools.

    No grants are awarded for building programs,
    financial assistance to students or support of
    student activities and organizations.

GEOG. RESTRICTIONS: United States.

FINANCIAL DATA:
    Amount of support per award: Varies.
    Total amount of support: Varies.
    Matching fund requirements: Contributions of
    directors, officers and employees of the
    Halliburton companies to accredited junior
    colleges, colleges/universities and
    elementary/secondary schools are matched
    2.25:1 under certain conditions.

NO. AWARDS: Over 500.

APPLICATION INFO:
    Requests for support should be mailed to the
    address listed above. Lengthy proposals are
    not required.
    Duration: One year.

PUBLICATIONS:
    Guidelines.

ADDRESS INQUIRIES TO:
    Brinda Maxwell, Administrator
    (See address above.)

THE HOROWITZ FOUNDATION FOR SOCIAL POLICY
P.O. Box 7
Rocky Hill, NJ 08553-0007
(732) 445-2280
E-mail: info@horowitz-foundation.org
Web Site: www.horowitz-foundation.org

TYPE:
    Research grants. Grants to doctoral
    candidates at the dissertation level with
    emphasis on social policy-related studies.
    See entry 1684 for full listing.

THE GEORGE A. AND ELIZA GARDNER HOWARD FOUNDATION   [1475]
University Hall, Room 406
Brown University
One Prospect Street
Providence, RI 02912
(401) 863-2429
Fax: (401) 863-1339
E-mail: howard_foundation@brown.edu
Web Site: www.brown.edu/howard-foundation

FOUNDED: 1952

TYPE:
    Fellowships. The Foundation awards a
    limited number of fellowships each year for
    independent projects in fields selected on a
    rotational basis.

YEAR PROGRAM STARTED: 1952

PURPOSE:
    To aid the professional development of
    promising individuals at the crucial early-mid
    stages of their careers.

LEGAL BASIS:
    Private foundation.

ELIGIBILITY:
    Nominees should normally have the rank of
    assistant or associate professor or their
    nonacademic equivalents. Support is intended
    to augment paid sabbatical leaves, making it
    financially possible for grantees to have time
    off in which to pursue their projects, free of
    any other professional responsibilities.
    Accepted nominees should therefore be
    eligible for sabbaticals or other leave with
    guaranteed additional support.

    The project undertaken by a Howard Fellow
    should also be comprehensible to persons
    outside the immediate field of specialization.
    Candidates, regardless of their country of
    citizenship, must be professionally based in
    the U.S. either by affiliation with an
    institution or by residence.

GEOG. RESTRICTIONS: United States.

FINANCIAL DATA:
    Amount of support per award: $35,000 for
    the year 2020-21.
    Total amount of support: Approximately
    $280,000.

NO. MOST RECENT APPLICANTS: 100.

NO. AWARDS: Approximately 9 per year.

APPLICATION INFO:
    Application process opens on July 1.
    Instructions are available on the web site.
    Duration: One academic year, July 1 to June
    30.
    Deadline: November 1.

IRS I.D.: 05-0275563

ADMINISTRATION:
    Joseph Meisel, Administrative Director
    Edward Goll, Administrative Coordinator

ADDRESS INQUIRIES TO:
    Edward Goll
    Administrative Coordinator
    George A. and Eliza
    Gardner Howard Foundation

P.O. Box 1857
Brown University
Providence, RI 02912

INSTITUTE OF INTERNATIONAL EDUCATION/COUNCIL FOR INTERNATIONAL EXCHANGE OF SCHOLARS   [1476]
1400 K Street, N.W.
Suite 700
Washington, DC 20005-2403
(202) 686-4000
Fax: (202) 686-4029
E-mail: iea@iie.org
Web Site: www.cies.org/iea

FOUNDED: 1947

AREAS OF INTEREST:
    Scholarly exchange.

NAME(S) OF PROGRAMS:
    ● **Fulbright International Education
      Administrators Program**

TYPE:
    Conferences/seminars; Exchange programs;
    Project/program grants; Research grants;
    Travel grants. Through its short-term
    seminars, the Fulbright International
    Education Administrators Program can help
    U.S. higher education administrators establish
    lasting connections within the social, cultural
    and education systems of other countries.
    Selected administrators have the opportunity
    to gain in-depth knowledge about the host
    country's higher education system as well as
    to establish networks of U.S. and
    international colleagues. Grantees return
    home with enhanced ability to serve
    international students and encourage
    prospective study-abroad students.

YEAR PROGRAM STARTED: 1947

PURPOSE:
    To promote mutual understanding between
    people of the U.S. and people of other
    nations.

LEGAL BASIS:
    Public Law 87-256, as amended, The Mutual
    Educational and Cultural Exchange Act of
    1961.

ELIGIBILITY:
    Applicants must be U.S. citizens.

    U.S.-France and U.S.-India IEA Programs are
    open to experienced international education
    administrators and senior administrators
    responsible for enhancing the international
    dimensions of their institutions.

    U.S.-Germany IEA Program is open to
    experienced administrators in international
    exchanges, foreign admissions, study-abroad,
    international education, career services,
    alumni affairs and development/fund-raising.

    U.S.-Japan IEA Program is open to
    experienced international education
    administrators and senior administrators
    responsible for enhancing the international
    dimensions of their institutions. Preference is
    given to applicants who have not had
    significant professional visits to Japan in the
    last five years and who indicate an
    institutional interest in increasing the number
    of Japanese students on their campus.

    U.S.-Korea IEA Program is open to
    experienced international education
    administrators and senior administrators
    responsible for enhancing the international

dimensions of their institutions. Preference is given to applicants who have an existing population of Korean students on campus.

Applicants to any of these IEA programs are not required to hold a Ph.D.

GEOG. RESTRICTIONS: United States.

FINANCIAL DATA:
Grants generally include round-trip airfare, travel within the host country, lodging, and a lump sum supplement for incidentals.
Amount of support per award: Varies.

NO. MOST RECENT APPLICANTS: Approximately 70.

NO. AWARDS: U.S.-France IEA: Up to 12; U.S.-Germany IEA: Up to 15; U.S.-India IEA and U.S.-Japan IEA: Up to 10; U.S.-Korea IEA: Up to 8; U.S.-Russia IEA: 5; U.S.-Taiwan IEA: Up to 12.

APPLICATION INFO:
Guidelines are available on the CIES web site. Applications must be submitted online.
Duration: U.S.-India IEA: Two weeks in March; U.S.-Japan and U.S.-Korea IEA: Two weeks in June; U.S.-France and U.S. Germany IEA: Two weeks in October. U.S.-Russia IEA and U.S.-Taiwan IEA: Two weeks in April.
Deadline: U.S.-Japan IEA and U.S.-Korea IEA: November 1; U.S.-France IEA and U.S.-Germany IEA: February 3; U.S.-India IEA: August 1; U.S.-Russia IEA: October 15; U.S.-Taiwan IEA: September 16.

PUBLICATIONS:
Descriptive brochure; annual awards catalog; annual report.

ADDRESS INQUIRIES TO:
Fulbright International Education Administrators Program
(See e-mail and address above.)

THE FLETCHER JONES FOUNDATION [1477]
1055 East Colorado Boulevard
5th Floor
Pasadena, CA 91106
(626) 204-4012
Fax: (626) 535-9508
E-mail: mary@fletcherjonesfdn.org
Web Site: www.fletcherjonesfdn.org

FOUNDED: 1969

AREAS OF INTEREST:
Primarily, support to private independent colleges and universities in California.

TYPE:
Capital grants; Endowments; Fellowships; Grants-in-aid; Internships; Professorships; Project/program grants; Scholarships. Equipment grants. Academic programs.

YEAR PROGRAM STARTED: 1969

PURPOSE:
To assist private higher education in California.

LEGAL BASIS:
Private foundation.

ELIGIBILITY:
Grants are made to nonprofit, 501(c)(3) organizations. 90% of grants are for private colleges and universities in California. Grants are not made to carry on propaganda, to influence legislation or elections, to promote voter registration, to political candidates, to

political campaigns, or to organizations engaged in such activities. Grants are not made to individuals.

The Foundation generally does not favor requests for projects which should be financed by government agencies, nor does it normally make grants to operating funds, elementary or secondary schools, deficit financing, or contingencies.

GEOG. RESTRICTIONS: California.

FINANCIAL DATA:
Amount of support per award: Varies.

NO. AWARDS: Varies.

REPRESENTATIVE AWARDS:
$1,000,000 to Pomona College; $300,000 to Biola University.

APPLICATION INFO:
The Foundation primarily supports private, nonprofit, degree-granting colleges and universities in California. An institution which believes it meets these criteria may contact the Executive Director for discussion. A link to the online application must be provided by the Executive Director after preliminary consultation.
Deadline: Applications are accepted throughout the year and reviewed quarterly.

IRS I.D.: 23-7030155

STAFF:
Mary Spellman, Executive Director and Treasurer

OFFICERS AND TRUSTEES:
Peter K. Barker, President
John D. Pettker, Vice President and Secretary
Samuel P. Bell, Vice President
Patrick C. Haden, Vice President
Parker S. Kennedy, Vice President
Daniel E. Lungren, Vice President
Donald E. Nickelson, Vice President
Hon. Rockwell Schnabel, Vice President
Stewart R. Smith, Vice President

ADDRESS INQUIRIES TO:
Mary Spellman
Executive Director and Treasurer
(See address above.)

LUMINA FOUNDATION [1478]
30 South Meridian Street, Suite 700
Indianapolis, IN 46204-3503
(317) 951-5300
(800) 834-5756
Fax: (317) 951-5063
E-mail: gm@luminafoundation.org
Web Site: www.luminafoundation.org

FOUNDED: 2000

AREAS OF INTEREST:
Promoting educational improvements and access. Focus beginning in 2013: Mobilizing to reach Goal 2025 and designing and building a 21st-century higher education system.

TYPE:
Project/program grants; Research contracts. The Foundation has worked with and made grants to many colleges, universities, peer foundations, associations and other organizations that work to improve student access and outcomes across the nation.

PURPOSE:
To help people achieve their potential by expanding access to and success in education beyond high school. Specific goal: To

increase the proportion of Americans with high-quality college degrees, certificates and credentials to 60% by 2025.

ELIGIBILITY:
Organizations that are classified as tax-exempt under Section 501(c)(3) of the Internal Revenue Code and as public charities under Section 509(a)(1), (2) or (3) or to public organizations that are designated under Section 170(c) of the Code, not individuals. Grants will not be made to supporting organizations controlled by disqualified persons to Lumina or Type III supporting organizations that are not functionally integrated Type III supporting organizations (as defined in the Internal Revenue Code).

GEOG. RESTRICTIONS: United States and its territories.

FINANCIAL DATA:
Amount of support per award: Average grant amount: $200,000.
Total amount of support: More than $55,000,000 for the year 2018.

APPLICATION INFO:
All unsolicited inquiries should be submitted as formal Letters of Inquiry (LOI) so that Foundation staff may carefully review the request. Preference is submission online. Complete information can be found on the web site. Full proposals are by invitation.
Duration: One to three years. Grant is not renewable.

ADDRESS INQUIRIES TO:
Grants Management
P.O. Box 1806
Indianapolis, IN 46206-1806

MONROE-BROWN FOUNDATION [1479]
P.O. Box 51716
Kalamazoo, MI 49005
(269) 324-5586
E-mail: lmauzy@monroebrown.org
Web Site: www.monroebrown.org

FOUNDED: 1984

AREAS OF INTEREST:
Higher education and economic development.

TYPE:
Internships; Scholarships.

PURPOSE:
To advance the public well-being through higher education and economic development.

LEGAL BASIS:
Private foundation.

ELIGIBILITY:
Organizations must qualify as a nonprofit under Section 501(c)(3) of the Internal Revenue Code.

GEOG. RESTRICTIONS: Kalamazoo, Michigan.

FINANCIAL DATA:
Amount of support per award: Varies.
Total amount of support: Varies.

APPLICATION INFO:
Application information is available on the web site.
Duration: Varies.

ADDRESS INQUIRIES TO:
A.J. Todd, President
(See address above.)

NATIONAL ASSOCIATION OF SCHOLARS   [1480]

420 Madison Avenue
7th Floor
New York, NY 10017
(917) 551-6770
E-mail: contact@nas.org
Web Site: www.nas.org

NAME(S) OF PROGRAMS:
- **The Peter Shaw Memorial Award**

TYPE:
Awards/prizes. The Peter Shaw Memorial Award recognizes exemplary writing on issues pertaining to higher education and American intellectual culture.

PURPOSE:
To enrich the substance and strengthen the integrity of scholarship and teaching.

ELIGIBILITY:
Candidates must be chosen by the Association.

FINANCIAL DATA:
Award includes a plaque and travel expenses to attend the Association's National Conference and present a speech.
Amount of support per award: $1,000.

*PLEASE NOTE:
Awards are not given on an annual basis, but only when the Association holds a National Conference.

NATIONAL WILDLIFE FEDERATION

11100 Wildlife Center Drive
Reston, VA 20190-5362
(703) 438-6265
Fax: (703) 438-6468
E-mail: fellows@nwf.org
ecoleaders@nwf.org
Web Site: www.nwf.org
www.nwfecoleaders.org

TYPE:
Fellowships.

See entry 2004 for full listing.

THE SAMUEL ROBERTS NOBLE FOUNDATION   [1481]

2510 Sam Noble Parkway
Ardmore, OK 73401
(580) 224-6213
Fax: (580) 224-6212
E-mail: granting@noblefoundation.org
Web Site: www.noblefoundation.org

FOUNDED: 1945

AREAS OF INTEREST:
Higher education (primarily in Oklahoma), capital funding for higher education, health research, health delivery systems, and social services and community.

TYPE:
Capital grants; Challenge/matching grants; General operating grants; Project/program grants.

YEAR PROGRAM STARTED: 1946

PURPOSE:
To advance agricultural science and practice by conducting field and laboratory research, and by providing consultations to farmers, ranchers, and land managers in the Southern Great Plains; to foster sustainable agricultural practices; to support worthy charities through a program of grants with the aim of building stronger communities.

LEGAL BASIS:
Private foundation.

ELIGIBILITY:
Organizations must be classified as 501(c)(3) by the IRS and are primarily located in Oklahoma. No loans or grants are made to individuals.

GEOG. RESTRICTIONS: Oklahoma.

FINANCIAL DATA:
Amount of support per award: Varies.
Total amount of support: Varies.

NO. AWARDS: 32 grants approved for the year 2017.

APPLICATION INFO:
Letters of Inquiry must be submitted through the online grants management system.
Deadline: Letters of inquiry will be accepted online January 1 through June 1.

IRS I.D.: 73-0606209

STAFF:
Alexis Carter-Black, Director of Philanthropy
Stacy Newman, Program Officer

ADDRESS INQUIRIES TO:
Stacy Newman, Program Officer
(See address above.)

NORTH CAROLINA ASSOCIATION OF EDUCATORS   [1482]

NCAE Center for Instructional Advocacy
700 South Salisbury Street
Raleigh, NC 27601
(919) 832-3000
(800) 662-7924
Fax: (919) 829-1626
E-mail: awards@ncae.org
Web Site: www.ncae.org

FOUNDED: 1970

AREAS OF INTEREST:
Teaching.

NAME(S) OF PROGRAMS:
- **Mary Morrow/Edna Richards Scholarship Fund**

TYPE:
Scholarships. To be used for college expenses in senior year.

YEAR PROGRAM STARTED: 1994

PURPOSE:
To aid worthy students who plan to teach in North Carolina after graduation.

LEGAL BASIS:
Nonprofit organization.

ELIGIBILITY:
The applicant must be in their junior year in a North Carolina college or university, planning to teach and willing to teach in the public schools of North Carolina for at least two years following graduation. Selection is based on character, personality, scholastic achievement, evidence of promise as a teacher and financial need.

GEOG. RESTRICTIONS: North Carolina.

FINANCIAL DATA:
Amount of support per award: $1,000 per year.
Total amount of support: Varies.

NO. MOST RECENT APPLICANTS: Varies.

NO. AWARDS: Varies.

APPLICATION INFO:
Application forms are mailed in Fall to the heads of the department of education in colleges in North Carolina, both state-supported and private. The department head is requested to give the application forms to two juniors of his or her selection.
Duration: One year.
Deadline: January 30 (postmark).

ADDRESS INQUIRIES TO:
NCAE Center for Instructional Advocacy
(See address above.)

RADCLIFFE INSTITUTE FOR ADVANCED STUDY, HARVARD UNIVERSITY   [1483]

Radcliffe Institute Fellowship Program
Byerly Hall
8 Garden Street
Cambridge, MA 02138
E-mail: fellowships@radcliffe.harvard.edu
Web Site: www.radcliffe.harvard.edu

FOUNDED: 1960

NAME(S) OF PROGRAMS:
- **Radcliffe Institute Fellowship Program**

TYPE:
Fellowships. The Radcliffe Institute for Advanced Study is a scholarly community where individuals pursue advanced work across a wide range of academic disciplines, professions or creative arts. Within this broad purpose, and in recognition of Radcliffe's historic contributions to the education of women and to the study of issues related to women, the Radcliffe Institute sustains a continuing commitment to the study of women, gender and society, although applicants' projects need not focus on gender.

Radcliffe Institute Fellowships are designed to support scholars, scientists, artists and writers of exceptional promise and demonstrated accomplishment who wish to pursue independent work in academic and professional fields, and in the creative arts.

YEAR PROGRAM STARTED: 1999

PURPOSE:
To offer support to The Radcliffe Institute for Advanced Study Fellowship programs for a scholarly community where individuals pursue advanced work across a wide range of academic disciplines, professions and creative arts.

LEGAL BASIS:
Department of Harvard University, nonprofit.

ELIGIBILITY:
For all programs, residence in the Boston area and participation in the Institute community are required during the fellowship appointment.

FINANCIAL DATA:
Some support for relocation expenses provided when relevant. If so directed, Radcliffe will pay stipend to home institution if the institution is U.S.-based.
Amount of support per award: Stipends up to $78,000 for one year, plus $5,000 to cover project expenses.

NO. MOST RECENT APPLICANTS: Over 1,350 for the year 2019.

NO. AWARDS: Up to 50 fellowships.

APPLICATION INFO:
Applications are available online in late
Spring.

Duration: September 1 to May 31.

Deadline: Humanities and Social Sciences
and Creative Arts: Mid-September. Science,
Engineering and Mathematics: Early October.

STAFF:
Alison Ney, Administrator of Fellowships

ADDRESS INQUIRIES TO:
See e-mail address above.

*SPECIAL STIPULATIONS:
Fellows are expected to present their
work-in-progress and to attend other fellows'
events.

THE NELL J. REDFIELD FOUNDATION

P.O. Box 61
Reno, NV 89504
(775) 323-1373
Fax: (775) 323-4476
E-mail: gsmith@redfieldfoundation.org

TYPE:
Capital grants; Challenge/matching grants;
Development grants; Matching gifts;
Project/program grants. Grants for higher
education. Medical and social welfare for
disadvantaged children and seniors.

See entry 250 for full listing.

GERTRUDE E. SKELLY CHARITABLE FOUNDATION [1484]

4600 North Ocean Boulevard
Suite 206
Boynton Beach, FL 33435
(561) 276-1008
Fax: (561) 272-2793
E-mail: ejoh@hhk.com

FOUNDED: 1991

AREAS OF INTEREST:
Nursing education and medical care for
indigents.

TYPE:
Challenge/matching grants;
Conferences/seminars; Project/program
grants; Research grants; Scholarships;
Training grants. Emergency grants for
continued education.

YEAR PROGRAM STARTED: 1991

PURPOSE:
To provide scholarships for individuals to
obtain educational opportunities and/or
medical care.

LEGAL BASIS:
Private foundation.

ELIGIBILITY:
Eligible applicants are colleges and
universities, and other IRS 501(c)(3)
tax-exempt organizations. No grants are given
to agencies which do not provide direct
services or scholarships.

GEOG. RESTRICTIONS: United States.

FINANCIAL DATA:
Amount of support per award: Maximum
$50,000.

Total amount of support: $750,000 for the
year 2020.

Matching fund requirements: Tailored to
specific projects.

NO. MOST RECENT APPLICANTS: 100.

NO. AWARDS: 100.

APPLICATION INFO:
Write to the address above for application
guidelines.

Duration: One year.

Deadline: June 30. Award announcement the
following January or second quarter of the
following year.

TRUSTEES:
Erik Edward Joh

ADDRESS INQUIRIES TO:
Erik Edward Joh, Trustee
(See address above.)

TARAKNATH DAS FOUNDATION [1485]

South Asia Institute
Columbia University
606 West 122nd Street, Room 213
New York, NY 10027
E-mail: lg17@columbia.edu
Web Site: www.sai.columbia.edu/taraknath-das-foundation

FOUNDED: 1930

AREAS OF INTEREST:
Indian national graduate students studying
any field in a U.S. university.

TYPE:
Grants-in-aid.

YEAR PROGRAM STARTED: 1935

PURPOSE:
To promote friendly relations and cultural
cooperation between the U.S. and India.

LEGAL BASIS:
Special interest foundation.

ELIGIBILITY:
Applicants are not limited by discipline or
subject area. Applicants must be Indian
nationals (holding Indian passports) and must
have completed at least one year of graduate
study in the U.S.

FINANCIAL DATA:
Amount of support per award: $3,000 to
$8,000.

Total amount of support: Approximately
$25,000.

NO. MOST RECENT APPLICANTS: 20.

NO. AWARDS: About 4 annually.

APPLICATION INFO:
Applicants must submit all application
materials together. Only complete
applications will be judged for the awards.
Complete applications include:
(1) completed application form;
(2) transcript from most recent academic
institution;
(3) three sealed letters of recommendation,
including one from the applicant's academic
advisor;
(4) academic plans of applicant and;
(5) photocopy of applicant's passport.

Duration: One year.

Deadline: October 1.

ADDRESS INQUIRIES TO:
Leonard Gordon, Director
(See address above.)

U.S. DEPARTMENT OF EDUCATION [1486]

Office of Post Secondary Education
Federal TRIO Programs
400 Maryland Avenue, S.W.
Washington, DC 20202
(202) 453-6273
(202) 453-6914
Fax: (202) 502-7857
E-mail: OPE_TRIO@ed.gov
Web Site: www.ed.gov/ope/trio

AREAS OF INTEREST:
Education for low-income youth.

NAME(S) OF PROGRAMS:
● **Upward Bound**

TYPE:
Project/program grants. There are three types
of grants under the Upward Bound program:
Regular Upward Bound Grants, Veterans
Upward Bound Grants, and Upward Bound
Math and Science Grants.

The Regular Upward Bound projects are
designed to generate in participants the skills
and motivation necessary for success in
education beyond secondary school. The
Veterans Upward Bound projects are
designed to assist veterans in preparing for a
program of postsecondary education. The
Upward Bound Math and Science projects
are designed to prepare high school students
for postsecondary education programs that
lead to careers in the fields of math and
science.

YEAR PROGRAM STARTED: 1966

PURPOSE:
To generate participation skills and the
motivation necessary for success in education
beyond school.

LEGAL BASIS:
Title IV of the Higher Education Act of
1965, as amended.

ELIGIBILITY:
Institutions of higher education, public and
private agencies and organizations including
community-based organizations with
experience serving disadvantaged youth,
combinations of such institutions, agencies
and organizations, and, as appropriate to the
purposes of the program, secondary schools
may apply. Students must have completed the
eighth grade, be between the ages of 13 and
19, and have a need for academic support in
order to pursue a program of postsecondary
education. All students must be either from
low-income families or be potential
first-generation college students. The program
requires that two-thirds of the participants in
a project must be both low-income and
potential first-generation students. The
remaining one-third must be either
low-income, first-generation college students,
or students who have a high risk for
academic failure.

GEOG. RESTRICTIONS: United States.

FINANCIAL DATA:
Amount of support per award: Average
$367,727 for fiscal year 2018.

Total amount of support: $355,592,015
allocated for fiscal year 2018.

NO. MOST RECENT APPLICANTS: 70,914.

NO. AWARDS: 967.

APPLICATION INFO:
Applications are submitted through
grants.gov.

Duration: Five-year grant award cycles.

ADDRESS INQUIRIES TO:
Kenneth Waters, Program Specialist
(See address above.)

U.S. DEPARTMENT OF EDUCATION   [1487]

International and Foreign Language Education
400 Maryland Avenue, S.W.
Washington, DC 20202
(202) 453-6391
E-mail: tanyelle.richardson@ed.gov
Web Site: www.ed.gov/ope/iegps

NAME(S) OF PROGRAMS:
● **Undergraduate International Studies and Foreign Language Program**

TYPE:
Project/program grants; Seed money grants.
Grants to plan, develop, and carry out a
program to strengthen and improve
undergraduate instruction in international
studies and foreign languages. Projects
primarily focus on curriculum and faculty
development. Institutions of higher education
and public and private nonprofit agencies and
organizations may apply for funds to develop
projects which have the potential for making
an especially significant contribution to the
improvement of undergraduate instruction in
international and foreign language studies in
the U.S.

YEAR PROGRAM STARTED: 1972

PURPOSE:
To assist institutions to internationalize the
curriculum. Applicants may propose to
initiate a global studies program or a
program focusing on a single world area and
its languages; to develop a program which
focuses on issues or topics, such as
environmental studies or international
business; to combine the teaching of
international studies with professional or
preprofessional training; to integrate
undergraduate studies with Master's degree
programs; to combine international studies
with teacher training programs.

LEGAL BASIS:
Title VI, section 604A, Higher Education
Act, as amended in 1986.

ELIGIBILITY:
Proposals are invited from institutions of
higher education, including universities and
two- to four-year colleges, and consortia of
such institutions. The proposed program
should include plans to initiate new or
revised courses in international studies or
area studies, and to improve or expand
instruction in foreign languages. The program
should be comparative or interdisciplinary in
nature and strengthen linkages among
disciplines and professional fields.

GEOG. RESTRICTIONS: United States.

FINANCIAL DATA:
Amount of support per award: Single
Institutions: Average $89,000 per year;
Organizations, Associations and Institutional
Consortia: Average $140,000 per year.
Total amount of support: $2,800,000 for
fiscal year 2020.
Matching fund requirements: Dollar-for-dollar
primarily within in-kind contributions.

NO. MOST RECENT APPLICANTS: 92.

NO. AWARDS: Approximately 30 new awards for
fiscal year 2020.

APPLICATION INFO:
Applications are required to be submitted
electronically using the grants.gov system.
Duration: Single Institutions: Up to two
years; Organizations, Associations and
Institutional Consortia: Up to three years.
Deadline: Summer.

STAFF:
Tanyelle Richardson, Senior Program Officer

ADDRESS INQUIRIES TO:
Tanyelle Richardson, Senior Program Officer
(See e-mail address above.)

*PLEASE NOTE:
Competition held every two years contingent
upon receiving a Congressional
Appropriation.

U.S. DEPARTMENT OF EDUCATION

400 Maryland Avenue, S.W.
Washington, DC 20024
(202) 453-7521
E-mail: timothy.duvall@ed.gov
Web Site: www2.ed.
gov/programs/iegpscibe/index.html

TYPE:
Project/program grants. The program
provides grants to eligible institutions of
higher education or combinations of these
institutions for planning, establishing and
operating Centers for International Business
Education.

See entry 1744 for full listing.

U.S. DEPARTMENT OF EDUCATION

International and Foreign Language Education
(IFLE)
Language Resource Centers Program
400 Maryland Avenue, S.W.
Mail Stop 258-40
Washington, DC 20202
(202) 453-7854
E-mail: carolyn.collins@ed.gov
Web Site: www2.ed.
gov/programs/iegpslrc/index.html

TYPE:
General operating grants. Language Resource
Centers Program provides grants for
establishing, strengthening and operating
centers that serve as resources for improving
the nation's capacity for teaching and
learning foreign languages through teacher
training, research, materials development and
dissemination projects.

See entry 615 for full listing.

UCLA INSTITUTE OF AMERICAN CULTURES (IAC)

2329 Murphy Hall, Box 957244
Los Angeles, CA 90095-7244
(310) 825-6815
Fax: (310) 825-3994
E-mail: iaccoordinator@conet.ucla.edu
Web Site: www.iac.ucla.edu

TYPE:
Fellowships. Deals with arts and humanities,
education and teacher training, fine arts,
applied arts, law, social sciences, and
sciences. The IAC, in cooperation with
UCLA's four Ethnic Studies Research
Centers (American Indian Studies Center,
Asian American Studies Center, Bunche

Center for African American Studies, and
Chicano Studies Research Center), offers
awards to visiting scholars to support
research on African Americans, American
Indians, Asian Americans and Chicanas/os.

See entry 931 for full listing.

THE UNIVERSITY OF CALGARY   [1488]

Faculty of Graduate Studies
Earth Sciences Building, Room 1010
2500 University Drive, N.W.
Calgary AB T2N 1N4 Canada
(403) 220-4938
Fax: (403) 289-7635
E-mail: gsaward@ucalgary.ca
Web Site: grad.ucalgary.ca/awards

AREAS OF INTEREST:
Management.

NAME(S) OF PROGRAMS:
● **Robert A. Willson Doctoral Management Scholarship**

TYPE:
Awards/prizes; Scholarships.

PURPOSE:
To produce a noteworthy leader in
management teaching and research who has a
broad appreciation of management's role in
society, both nationally and internationally.

ELIGIBILITY:
Open to candidates who, at the time of
tenure, are registered in a full-time program
leading to a doctoral degree in Management
at the University of Calgary, Haskayne
School of Business. While academic
excellence is essential, candidates should also
present evidence of leadership in their
academic or professional background.
Students with international experience and
orientation will be particularly considered.

FINANCIAL DATA:
Amount of support per award: $10,000.
Total amount of support: $10,000.

CO-OP FUNDING PROGRAMS: The donor of this
scholarship program is the Haskayne School
of Business.

NO. AWARDS: 1 per annum.

APPLICATION INFO:
No application is required. The Haskayne
School of Business will recommend a
recipient on the basis of academic and
professional leadership. The Graduate
Coordinator will submit recommendations to
the Graduate Scholarship Office. The
recommendation is subject to final approval
of the Graduate Scholarship Committee.
Duration: One year.
Deadline: May 15.

PUBLICATIONS:
Academic calendar.

ADDRESS INQUIRIES TO:
Graduate Scholarship Office
(See address above.)

UNIVERSITY OF CALIFORNIA

President's Postdoctoral Fellowship Program
402 Sproul Hall
Berkeley, CA 94720-1508
(510) 643-8235
E-mail: ppfpinfo@berkeley.edu
Web Site: ppfp.ucop.edu/info

TYPE:
Fellowships. Awarded for research conducted under faculty sponsorship on any one of the University of California's 10 campuses.

See entry 933 for full listing.

THE UNIVERSITY OF TEXAS AT AUSTIN [1489]

LBJ School of Public Affairs
P.O. Box Y
Austin, TX 78713-8925
(512) 471-4292
Fax: (512) 471-8455
E-mail: lbjadmit@austin.utexas.edu
Web Site: lbj.utexas.edu

AREAS OF INTEREST:
Public policy.

NAME(S) OF PROGRAMS:
● **Lyndon B. Johnson School of Public Affairs**

TYPE:
Assistantships; Fellowships. Merit fellowships are available to assist graduate students with financial support for education at the Master's and doctoral level.

ELIGIBILITY:
Applicants must be graduate students enrolled in Lyndon B. Johnson School of Public Affairs.

FINANCIAL DATA:
Amount of support per award: $4,000 to $60,000.

NO. AWARDS: Varies.

APPLICATION INFO:
Contact the University for application procedures.
Duration: One to two years. Grants not renewable.
Deadline: Varies.

ADDRESS INQUIRIES TO:
Office of Student Affairs and Admissions
(See address above.)

THE WABASH CENTER FOR TEACHING AND LEARNING IN THEOLOGY AND RELIGION

301 West Wabash Avenue
Crawfordsville, IN 47933
(765) 361-6047
Fax: (765) 361-6051
E-mail: wabashcenter@wabash.edu
Web Site: www.wabashcenter.wabash.edu

TYPE:
Conferences/seminars; Fellowships; Project/program grants; Research grants.

See entry 764 for full listing.

JEANNETTE K. WATSON FELLOWSHIP [1490]

233 Broadway
Suite 2709
New York, NY 10279
(212) 245-8859
E-mail: jkw@watson.foundation
Web Site: watson.foundation

TYPE:
Fellowships. The program offers 15 students each year, from 12 New York City colleges, the opportunity for paid internships for three consecutive summers. The internships offer closely supervised, challenging work from which the student can learn. The expectation is that three summers in different sectors (nonprofit organizations, public service and for-profit firms) in New York City and overseas will make fellows more compelling candidates for national fellowships, graduate admissions and good jobs.

YEAR PROGRAM STARTED: 2000

PURPOSE:
To develop talent, leadership and motivation for service.

ELIGIBILITY:
Applicant must:
(1) be enrolled at one of the invited colleges (Baruch College, Brooklyn College, City College, College of Staten Island, Hunter College, John Jay College, Lehman College, Long Island University-Brooklyn Campus, Marymount Manhattan College, Pace University-Manhattan Campus, Queens College, and St. John's University);
(2) be a second-semester freshman or a sophomore;
(3) not be older than 25 on March 1 of application year;
(4) be enrolled in a liberal arts program;
(5) be a U.S. citizen or a "green card" holder and;
(6) be willing to participate in three successive summer internships and their collateral summer and term-time seminars.

FINANCIAL DATA:
Amount of support per award: $5,500 for the first summer; $6,500 for the second summer, and $7,000 for the third summer, plus $2,000 discovery fund.
Total amount of support: $255,000 annually.

APPLICATION INFO:
Application information is available on the web site.
Duration: Three consecutive summer internships of 10 weeks plus year-round activities.
Deadline: February.

STAFF:
Chris Kasabach, Foundation Executive Director

THOMAS J. WATSON FELLOWSHIP PROGRAM [1491]

233 Broadway
Suite 2709
New York, NY 10279
(212) 245-8859
E-mail: tjw@tjwf.org
Web Site: watson.foundation

FOUNDED: 1968

AREAS OF INTEREST:
Independent study outside of the U.S. for graduating college seniors.

TYPE:
Fellowships. The Foundation provides Fellows an opportunity for a focused and disciplined "Wanderjahr" of their own devising or design-time in which to explore with thoroughness a particular interest, test their aspirations and abilities, view their lives and American society in greater perspective and concomitantly, to develop a more informed sense of international concern. The Fellowship experience is intended to provide Fellows an opportunity to immerse themselves in cultures other than their own for an entire year. The candidate's proposed project should involve investigation into an area of demonstrated concern and personal interest.

YEAR PROGRAM STARTED: 1968

PURPOSE:
To give exceptional college graduates the freedom to engage in a year of independent study, purposeful exploration and travel outside of the U.S. in order to enhance their capacity for resourcefulness, imagination, openness and leadership, and to foster their humane and effective participation in the world community.

LEGAL BASIS:
Private foundation.

ELIGIBILITY:
The Foundation welcomes applicants from a diverse range of backgrounds and academic disciplines. Only graduating seniors at one of 40 partner colleges are eligible for nomination by their institution.

GEOG. RESTRICTIONS: United States.

FINANCIAL DATA:
Amount of support per award: $30,000.
Total amount of support: Varies.

NO. MOST RECENT APPLICANTS: 220.

NO. AWARDS: 40 each year.

APPLICATION INFO:
Students must first be nominated by their college or university, and then compete on a national level. Application form required.
Duration: One year.
Deadline: Nominations and nominees' completed applications should arrive by first Tuesday in November. Announcement made in mid-March.

PUBLICATIONS:
Guidelines.

IRS I.D.: 13-6038151

STAFF:
Sneha Subramanian, Program Manager

*SPECIAL STIPULATIONS:
All Fellows are required to maintain contact with the fellowship office during their year abroad. In addition to quarterly progress reports, they must submit a final evaluation of the Fellowship year together with a financial accounting of the expenditure of Fellowship funds. The Fellowship is taxable and must be reported by recipients as income. Taxes are not withheld by the Foundation.

TODD WEHR FOUNDATION [1492]

9212 Wilson Boulevard
Wauwatosa, WI 53226
(414) 258-6481

FOUNDED: 1954

AREAS OF INTEREST:
Education and inner-city Milwaukee capital projects for the benefit of children.

TYPE:
Capital grants.

ELIGIBILITY:
Organizations must have 501(c)(3) tax-exempt status. No grants to individuals.

GEOG. RESTRICTIONS: Wisconsin, with emphasis on Milwaukee.

FINANCIAL DATA:
Amount of support per award: $5,000 to $500,000.

NO. AWARDS: 1 to 10.

APPLICATION INFO:
Send brief letter of inquiry along with full proposal.

Duration: One to 10 years.

Deadline: Applications accepted throughout the year.

ADDRESS INQUIRIES TO:
Allan E. Iding, Chairman of the Board (See address above.)

Scholar aid programs (all disciplines)

ALABAMA COMMISSION ON HIGHER EDUCATION   [1493]
100 North Union Street
Montgomery, AL 36104-3702
(334) 242-2273
Fax: (334) 242-2269
E-mail: cheryl.newton@ache.edu
Web Site: ache.edu

FOUNDED: 1977

AREAS OF INTEREST:
Continuing higher education.

NAME(S) OF PROGRAMS:
● **Senior Adult Scholarship Program**

TYPE:
Grants-in-aid; Scholarships. A free tuition program for senior citizens who meet the admission requirements.

ELIGIBILITY:
Alabama residents who are 60 years of age or older and who attend public two-year postsecondary educational institutions in Alabama are eligible to apply.

GEOG. RESTRICTIONS: Alabama.

APPLICATION INFO:
Applications can be obtained by contacting the financial aid office at any public two-year postsecondary educational institution in Alabama.

ADDRESS INQUIRIES TO:
Cheryl B. Newton, Grants Coordinator (See address above.)

ALABAMA COMMISSION ON HIGHER EDUCATION   [1494]
100 North Union Street
Montgomery, AL 36104-3702
(334) 242-2273
Fax: (334) 242-2269
E-mail: cheryl.newton@ache.edu
Web Site: ache.edu

FOUNDED: 1977

AREAS OF INTEREST:
Higher education.

NAME(S) OF PROGRAMS:
● **Alabama National Guard Educational Assistance Program**

TYPE:
Awards/prizes. An award to be used for tuition, educational fees and books/supplies for Alabama National Guard members to attend a public or private postsecondary educational institution in Alabama.

YEAR PROGRAM STARTED: 1984

ELIGIBILITY:
Students who are active members in good standing with a federally recognized unit of the Alabama National Guard are eligible to apply. Participants may receive federal veterans benefits, but must show a cost-less-aid amount of at least $100. Awards are based on need.

GEOG. RESTRICTIONS: Alabama.

FINANCIAL DATA:
Amount of support per award: Awards are limited to $1,000 per term and no more than $2,000 per year.

APPLICATION INFO:
Application forms are available from Alabama National Guard Units. Funds are limited, so students who are Guard members are encouraged to apply early. Forms must be signed by a representative of the Alabama Military Department and the financial aid officer at the college or university the student plans to attend. All applicants must have the Free Application for Federal Student Aid (FAFSA) on file.

ADDRESS INQUIRIES TO:
Cheryl B. Newton, Grants Coordinator (See address above.)

ALABAMA COMMISSION ON HIGHER EDUCATION   [1495]
100 North Union Street
Montgomery, AL 36104-3702
(334) 242-2273
Fax: (334) 242-2269
E-mail: cheryl.newton@ache.edu
Web Site: ache.edu

FOUNDED: 1977

AREAS OF INTEREST:
Higher education.

NAME(S) OF PROGRAMS:
● **Alabama Student Assistance Program**
● **Alabama Student Grant Program**

TYPE:
Awards/prizes; Grants-in-aid; Scholarships. The Alabama Student Assistance Program is a need-based, state grant. Awards are limited to undergraduate work.

The Alabama Student Grant Program is an award of grant assistance at an eligible independent Alabama college or university. Award is not based on need. Maximum amount available only when sufficient funds are available.

ELIGIBILITY:
Applicants for the Alabama Student Assistance Program must be undergraduate students who are Alabama residents attending eligible Alabama institutions. 55 Alabama institutions participate in the program.

Applicants for the Alabama Student Grant Program must be undergraduate students either half-time or full-time who are Alabama residents attending Amridge University, Birmingham-Southern College, Concordia College, Faulkner University, Huntington College, Judson College, Miles College, Oakwood College, Samford University, Spring Hill College, Stillman College, U.S. Sports Academy or the University of Mobile.

GEOG. RESTRICTIONS: Alabama.

FINANCIAL DATA:
Amount of support per award: Student Assistance Program: $300 to $5,000; Student Grant Program: Up to $1,200.

Total amount of support: ASAP: $2,805,633; ASGP: $4,088,870 for the year 2017-18.

NO. AWARDS: ASAP: 4,216; ASGP: 5,619 for the year 2017-18.

APPLICATION INFO:
Application forms are available at the institution that the applicant is planning on attending.

ADDRESS INQUIRIES TO:
Cheryl B. Newton, Grants Coordinator (See address above.)

AMERICAN ASSOCIATION OF UNIVERSITY WOMEN
1310 L Street, N.W.
Suite 1000
Washington, DC 20005
(202) 785-7700
E-mail: aauw@applyists.com
Web Site: www.aauw.org

TYPE:
Fellowships. Awarded to women who are U.S. citizens or permanent residents who are pursuing full-time study in a Master's or professional degree program in which women are underrepresented, including STEM, law, business and medicine.

See entry 978 for full listing.

AMERICAN COUNCIL FOR POLISH CULTURE (ACPC) [1496]
4628 Columbia Road
Annandale, VA 22003
(301) 717-0662
E-mail: thomaspayne52@verizon.net
Web Site: www.polishcultureacpc.org

NAME(S) OF PROGRAMS:
● **ACPC Scholarship, Summer Studies in Poland**
● **Polish Studies Scholarship**
● **Pulaski Scholarships for Advanced Studies**
● **Wladyslaw Zachariasiewicz Memorial Journalism Scholarship**

TYPE:
Scholarships.

ELIGIBILITY:
ACPC Scholarship, Summer Studies in Poland: American of Polish descent entering junior or senior year at accredited college or university. Must have an ACPC affiliation.

Polish Studies Scholarship: Intended for students pursuing some Polish studies (major may be in other fields) at universities in the U.S. who have completed at least two years of college or university work. Scholarships awarded for the fall term.

Pulaski Scholarships for Advanced Studies: Applicant must be of Polish heritage and have completed at least two years in advanced studies at a U.S. university.

Wladyslaw Zachariasiewicz Memorial Journalism Scholarship: Applicant must be a U.S. citizen, or one currently applying for U.S. citizenship, admitted for a fully accredited university in the U.S. or Poland. Special consideration will be given to students of Polish-American heritage and those of non-Polish heritage who have a clear and thorough understanding of Polish culture and values. Awards are based solely on professional and academic merit with an appreciation for issues that affect Polish-Americans.

FINANCIAL DATA:
Amount of support per award: ACPC Scholarship, Summer Studies in Poland: $2,000 toward transportation and tuition; Polish Studies Scholarship: $3,000; Pulaski Scholarships for Advanced Studies: $5,000; Zachariasiewicz Scholarship: $5,000 toward tuition and school-related expenses other than room and board.

APPLICATION INFO:
Instructions and application form, if required, are available online.
Deadline: ACPC Scholarship, Summer Studies in Poland: April 1. Polish Studies Scholarship: May 3. Pulaski Scholarships for Advanced Studies: March 15. Zachariasiewicz Scholarship: March 31.

ADMINISTRATION:
Raymond Glembocki, President

ADDRESS INQUIRIES TO:
ACPC Scholarship, Summer Studies in Poland:
Robert Synakowski
E-mail: syracusepolishhome@yahoo.com

Polish Studies Scholarship:
Deborah M. Majka
E-mail: dziecko2@comcast.net

Pulaski Scholarships for Advanced Studies:
Dr. Steven Medvec
E-mail: samedvec@comcast.net

Wladyslaw Zachariasiewicz Memorial Scholarship Committee:
Mark G. Dillon, Chairperson
E-mail: mglendillon@aol.com

AMERICAN COUNCIL OF THE BLIND [1497]
1703 North Beauregard Street
Suite 420
Alexandria, VA 22311
(202) 467-5081
(800) 424-8666
Fax: (703) 465-5085
E-mail: info@acb.org
Web Site: www.acb.org

FOUNDED: 1961

AREAS OF INTEREST:
Independence, security, equality of opportunity and quality of life for all blind and visually impaired.

NAME(S) OF PROGRAMS:
● **American Council of the Blind Scholarships**

TYPE:
Assistantships; Awards/prizes; Internships; Scholarships. Scholarships for outstanding blind students enrolled in academic, vocational, technical or professional training programs beyond the high school level.

YEAR PROGRAM STARTED: 1982

PURPOSE:
To assist blind postsecondary students with educational expenses.

LEGAL BASIS:
Nonprofit membership organization.

ELIGIBILITY:
Applicants must be legally blind persons admitted or under consideration for admission to postsecondary training programs for the next school year, who are U.S. citizens or resident aliens and who have submitted a completed application and the required supporting materials.

GEOG. RESTRICTIONS: United States.

FINANCIAL DATA:
Amount of support per award: Minimum $1,000.
Total amount of support: $66,500 for the year 2018.

NO. AWARDS: 18 for the year 2018.

APPLICATION INFO:
Applicant must provide two letters of recommendation, certificate of legal blindness and a letter of acceptance from a postsecondary school.
Duration: One academic year. Nonrenewable, but recipient may reapply.
Deadline: Postmarked by February 15. Announcement June 1.

PUBLICATIONS:
Annual report; *Braille Forum*; *Student Advocate*.

IRS I.D.: 58-0914436

OFFICERS:
Kim Charlson, President
Dan Spoone, First Vice President
John McCann, Second Vice President

ADDRESS INQUIRIES TO:
Scholarship Coordinator
6300 Shingle Creek Parkway
Suite 195
Brooklyn Center, MN 55430

AMERICAN FRIENDS OF THE ALEXANDER VON HUMBOLDT FOUNDATION [1498]
1401 K Street
Suite 1005
Washington, DC 20005
(202) 783-1907
E-mail: info@americanfriendsofavh.org
Web Site: www.americanfriendsofavh.org

FOUNDED: 1953

AREAS OF INTEREST:
Scholarly research and academic cooperation through provision of awards and fellowships. All countries and all disciplines.

NAME(S) OF PROGRAMS:
● **Humboldt Research Award Programme**

TYPE:
Awards/prizes; Fellowships; Project/program grants; Research grants; Scholarships. Research awards for outstanding achievements in the fields of humanities and social sciences, natural sciences, medicine and engineering sciences providing for visits to German research institutes.

YEAR PROGRAM STARTED: 1972

PURPOSE:
To strengthen scientific cooperation between foreign and German researchers.

LEGAL BASIS:
Government agency run according to private law.

ELIGIBILITY:
Open to internationally renowned scientists and scholars having full professor or equivalent standing.

FINANCIAL DATA:
Amount of support per award: Up to EUR 60,000, plus travel expenses for awardee and accompanying family members.
Total amount of support: Varies.

NO. MOST RECENT APPLICANTS: Approximately 285.

NO. AWARDS: 100.

APPLICATION INFO:
Awards are made by nomination and by eminent German scholars only. No self-nomination is allowed.
Duration: Visits to German institutes from six to 12 months. No renewal of the award is possible, but recipient may be invited to Germany again.
Deadline: Nominations may be submitted at any time.

STAFF:
Brian Craft, Alumni Relations and Annual Fund Program Coordinator
Alexis Brouwer-Ancher, Communications and Events Program Coordinator

ADDRESS INQUIRIES TO:
See e-mail address above.

AMERICAN INDIAN COLLEGE FUND
8333 Greenwood Boulevard
Denver, CO 80221
(303) 426-8900
Fax: (303) 426-1200
E-mail: scholarships@collegefund.org
Web Site: collegefund.org

TYPE:
Scholarships.

See entry 949 for full listing.

AMERICAN INDIAN GRADUATE CENTER
3701 San Mateo Boulevard, N.E.
Suite 200
Albuquerque, NM 87110
(505) 881-4584
Fax: (505) 884-0427
E-mail: fellowships@aigcs.org
Web Site: www.aigcs.org

TYPE:
Fellowships; Grants-in-aid; Scholarships. Grants on an academic year basis. Summer funding available to continuing students only; these are students who are currently in the fellowship program.

See entry 950 for full listing.

AMERICAN INDIAN SCIENCE AND ENGINEERING SOCIETY (AISES)
6899 Winchester Circle
Suite 102A
Boulder, CO 80301
(720) 552-6123
Fax: (720) 526-6940
E-mail: info@aises.org
Web Site: www.aises.org

TYPE:
Academic and travel scholarships. AISES scholarships are intended to partially defray tuition and other educational expenses, thereby increasing access to higher education and improving college retention rates for AISES members.

AISES scholarships are made possible by corporations, government agencies, foundations, and individuals who wish to support the advancement of American Indians/Alaskan Natives. Scholarships are distributed in two disbursements and awarded for one academic year, unless otherwise specified. Recipients cannot receive more than one scholarship in any of the programs.

Scholarships are also awarded to members of AISES who are American Indian/Alaskan Native college students who meet the eligibility requirements for each scholarship.

See entry 951 for full listing.

AMERICAN INSTITUTE OF CERTIFIED PUBLIC ACCOUNTANTS (AICPA)

220 Leigh Farm Road
Durham, NC 27707
(919) 402-4473
E-mail: scholarships@aicpa.org
Web Site: thiswaytocpa.com/education/aicpa-legacy-scholarships

TYPE:
Scholarships.

See entry 1387 for full listing.

AMERICAN LEGION AUXILIARY - DEPARTMENT OF WISCONSIN   [1499]

P.O. Box 140
Portage, WI 53901-0140
(608) 745-0124
Fax: (608) 745-1947
E-mail: deptsec@amlegionauxwi.org
Web Site: www.amlegionauxwi.org

FOUNDED: 1921

AREAS OF INTEREST:
Scholar aid programs for children of Veterans.

NAME(S) OF PROGRAMS:
● **American Legion Auxiliary Badger Girls State Scholarships**
● **American Legion Auxiliary National Scholarships**
● **Child Welfare Scholarship**
● **Health Careers Scholarships**
● **Eileen Knox Memorial Scholarship**
● **H.S. and Angeline Lewis Scholarships**
● **Merit and Memorial Scholarships**
● **State President's Scholarships**
● **Della Van Deuren Scholarships**

TYPE:
Scholarships.

PURPOSE:
To enable students to secure Baccalaureate degrees.

ELIGIBILITY:
Applicant must be a daughter, son, stepdaughter, stepson, wife or widow of a veteran. Granddaughters, grandsons, great-granddaughters, great-grandsons, step-granddaughters, step-grandsons, step-great-granddaughters, step-great-grandsons of a Wisconsin American Legion Auxiliary member may also apply. If the applicant is a member of a Wisconsin American Legion Auxiliary Unit, a Wisconsin American Legion Post or a Wisconsin Sons of The American Legion Squadron, they do not need to reside in Wisconsin. Applicant must:
(1) be in need of financial help to continue their education;
(2) have at least a 3.5 grade point average on a 4.0 grade base and;
(3) be a resident of Wisconsin, except as noted above.

Applicant may apply for more than one scholarship, but can only receive one scholarship from the American Legion Auxiliary-Department of Wisconsin, awarded on a one-time only basis, nonrenewable. School selected to attend must be an accredited school, but need not be located in Wisconsin. Judges reserve the right to determine the type of scholarship awarded and their decision is final.

GEOG. RESTRICTIONS: Wisconsin.

FINANCIAL DATA:
Amount of support per award: Varies depending on available funds.
Total amount of support: $25,000 for the year 2019.

NO. MOST RECENT APPLICANTS: Approximately 150.

NO. AWARDS: 26 for the year 2019.

APPLICATION INFO:
Applicants must use only the application form designated for the year that they are applying for. For the Lewis, State President's, Merit and Memorial, Child Welfare, Health Careers and Registered Nurse Scholarships, one application form may be used regardless of how many programs an applicant may be eligible for.
Duration: One year.
Deadline: March 15.

ADDRESS INQUIRIES TO:
Bonnie Dorniak
Executive Secretary/Treasurer
(See address above.)

AMERICAN MEDICAL ASSOCIATION FOUNDATION   [1500]

330 North Wabash Avenue
Suite 39300
Chicago, IL 60611-5885
(312) 464-4200
Fax: (312) 464-4142
E-mail: amafoundation@ama-assn.org
Web Site: www.amafoundation.org

FOUNDED: 1950

AREAS OF INTEREST:
Public health and medical education.

NAME(S) OF PROGRAMS:
● **Excellence in Medicine**
● **Joan F. Giambalvo Memorial Scholarship**
● **Physicians of Tomorrow Scholarship**

TYPE:
Awards/prizes; Project/program grants; Scholarships. Excellence in Medicine Awards are given to recognize physicians and medical students who are improving the health of their communities and the lives of those who are most in need.

The Joan F. Giambalvo Memorial Scholarship is presented in conjunction with the AMA's Women Physicians Congress to provide a research grant to help researchers advance the progress of women in the medical profession and identify and address the needs of women physicians and medical students.

The Physicians of Tomorrow Scholarships are awarded to rising fourth-year medical students based on financial need and academic excellence.

PURPOSE:
To bring together physicians and communities to improve our nation's health.

LEGAL BASIS:
Public foundation.

ELIGIBILITY:
Scholarships are based on academic excellence and financial need. Student must be nominated through the medical school dean's office designate and currently enrolled in an accredited U.S. allopathic or osteopathic medical school. Student must be a permanent resident or citizen of the U.S.

GEOG. RESTRICTIONS: United States.

FINANCIAL DATA:
Amount of support per award: Joan F. Giambalvo Scholarship: Up to $10,000; Physicians of Tomorrow Scholarship: $10,000.

APPLICATION INFO:
Information is available on the Foundation web site.
Duration: Scholarships: One year.
Deadline: Varies.

PUBLICATIONS:
Brochure; program announcement; e-newsletter; quarterly newsletter.

ADDRESS INQUIRIES TO:
Emily Demko, Program Associate
(See address above.)

AMERICAN OSTEOPATHIC FOUNDATION

142 East Ontario Street, Suite 1450
Chicago, IL 60611-2864
(312) 202-8235
Fax: (312) 202-8216
E-mail: info@aof.org
Web Site: www.aof.org

TYPE:
Awards/prizes; Scholarships. Research, community service and international outreach grants.

See entry 2317 for full listing.

THE AMERICAN SOCIETY FOR NONDESTRUCTIVE TESTING, INC.   [1501]

1711 Arlingate Lane
Columbus, OH 43228
(614) 274-6003
(800) 222-2768
Fax: (614) 274-6899
E-mail: james@asnt.org
Web Site: www.asnt.org

FOUNDED: 1941

AREAS OF INTEREST:
Nondestructive testing and engineering.

NAME(S) OF PROGRAMS:
● **Engineering Undergraduate Award**
● **Robert B. Oliver Scholarship**

TYPE:
Scholarships.

YEAR PROGRAM STARTED: 1998

PURPOSE:
To provide incentive to students in the field of nondestructive testing.

LEGAL BASIS:
501(c)(3) corporation.

ELIGIBILITY:
Engineering Undergraduate Award:
Undergraduate students enrolled in colleges
and universities in the U.S. with recognized
engineering department programs are eligible
for the scholarship. Students must have an
anticipated graduation date that is later than
the date the funds are distributed.

Oliver Scholarship: Students must be enrolled
in an Associate degree or certificate program
which includes studies in NDT.

FINANCIAL DATA:
Amount of support per award: Engineering
Undergraduate Award: $3,000; Oliver
Scholarship: $2,500.

Total amount of support: Engineering
Undergraduate Award: $9,000; Oliver
Scholarship: $7,500.

NO. AWARDS: Up to 3 per year per award.

APPLICATION INFO:
Information and application are available
online.

Duration: One year.

Deadline: Engineering Undergraduate Award:
December 15. Oliver Scholarship: February
15.

ADDRESS INQUIRIES TO:
Jessica Ames
ASNT Program Coordinator
(See address above.)

AMERICAN SOCIETY OF HEMATOLOGY

2021 L Street, N.W.
Suite 900
Washington, DC 20036
(202) 776-0544
E-mail: awards@hematology.org
Web Site: www.hematology.org

TYPE:
Awards/prizes; Fellowships; Research grants;
Scholarships.

See entry 2033 for full listing.

AMVETS   [1502]

4647 Forbes Boulevard
Lanham, MD 20706-4380
(301) 683-4027
Fax: (301) 683-3027
E-mail: klathroum@amvets.org
Web Site: www.amvets.org

FOUNDED: 1944

NAME(S) OF PROGRAMS:
- **AMVETS National Scholarship Program: Entering College Freshman Scholarship**
- **AMVETS National Scholarship Program: JROTC Scholarship**

TYPE:
Scholarships. National scholarship program
for high school seniors who are children or
grandchildren of veterans.

PURPOSE:
To make the goal of postsecondary education
more attainable for the children and
grandchildren of veterans by assisting
deserving students who might not otherwise
have the financial means to achieve their
educational goals.

ELIGIBILITY:
Applicant must:
(1) be a graduating high school senior
entering at the college freshman level in the
upcoming fall or be an active JROTC cadet
and currently a high school senior;
(2) have a minimum grade point average of
3.0 (or documented evidence of extenuating
circumstances that caused a lower grade
point average);
(3) be the child or grandchild of a U.S.
veteran, active duty, National Guard, or
Reservist;
(4) be a U.S. citizen;
(5) demonstrate academic promise and
financial need and;
(6) agree to authorize AMVETS to publicize
their scholarship award, if they are selected.

GEOG. RESTRICTIONS: United States.

FINANCIAL DATA:
Amount of support per award: Entering
College Freshman Scholarship: $4,000
($1,000 per year of a four-year program);
JROTC Scholarship: $1,000.

NO. AWARDS: Entering College Freshman
Scholarship: 6; JROTC Scholarship: 1.

APPLICATION INFO:
Applications must be completed online.

Duration: One to four years. Nonrenewable.

Deadline: April 30.

ADDRESS INQUIRIES TO:
Karla Lathroum
(See e-mail address above.)

ARCHAEOLOGICAL INSTITUTE OF AMERICA   [1503]

44 Beacon Street
Boston, MA 02108
(857) 305-9360
Fax: (857) 233-4270
E-mail: fellowships@archaeological.org
Web Site: www.archaeological.org

FOUNDED: 1879

AREAS OF INTEREST:
Archaeological research and publication.

NAME(S) OF PROGRAMS:
- **The AIA Publication Subvention Program**
- **Samuel H. Kress Grants for Research and Publication in Classical Art and Architecture**

TYPE:
Grants-in-aid. The AIA Publication
Subvention Program offers subventions from
the AIA's Bothmer Publication Fund in
support of new book-length publications in
the field of Greek, Roman, and Etruscan
archaeology and art history.

Samuel H. Kress Grants for Research and
Publication in Classical Art and Architecture
funds publication preparation or research
leading to publication undertaken by
professional members of the AIA.

PURPOSE:
To support the scholarly publication of
archaeological works.

ELIGIBILITY:
Applicants must have been AIA members in
good standing for at least two consecutive
years (one year for graduate students) before
the application deadline.

FINANCIAL DATA:
Amount of support per award: AIA
Publication Subvention Program: Average
$5,000. Samuel H. Kress Grants: $3,000.

Total amount of support: Varies.

NO. MOST RECENT APPLICANTS: AIA
Publication Subvention Program: 3; Samuel
H. Kress Grants: 3.

NO. AWARDS: AIA Publication Subvention
Program: 4; Samuel H. Kress Grants: 2.

APPLICATION INFO:
Applications must be completed online. Full
details are available on the Institute web site.

Duration: Typically one year.

Deadline: March 1 and November 1.

ADDRESS INQUIRIES TO:
Laurel Nilsen Sparks
Lecture and Fellowship Coordinator
(See address above.)

ARMENIAN GENERAL BENEVOLENT UNION   [1504]

55 East 59th Street, 7th Floor
New York, NY 10022-1112
(212) 319-6383
Fax: (212) 319-6507
E-mail: scholarship@agbu.org
Web Site: www.agbu-scholarship.org

AREAS OF INTEREST:
Education.

NAME(S) OF PROGRAMS:
- **Heritage Scholar Grant**
- **International Scholarship**
- **Performing Arts Scholarship**
- **Religious Studies Scholarship**
- **U.S. Graduate Scholarship**

TYPE:
Fellowships; Scholarships.

PURPOSE:
To provide financial assistance to students of
Armenian descent.

ELIGIBILITY:
Students must be of Armenian descent
enrolled in college or university.

FINANCIAL DATA:
Amount of support per award: Heritage
Scholar Grant: Up to $2,000; International
Scholarship: Up to $3,000; Performing Arts
Scholarship: $1,000 to $5,000; Religious
Studies Scholarship: Up to $5,000; U.S.
Graduate Scholarship: $5,000 average.

Total amount of support: Approximately
$1,000,000 annually.

NO. MOST RECENT APPLICANTS: Over 1,000.

NO. AWARDS: Over 500.

APPLICATION INFO:
Applicants must check their eligibility before
gaining access to the application.

Deadline: Heritage Scholar Grant: April 15;
International Scholarship: June 1; Performing
Arts and Religious Studies Scholarships: May
31; U.S. Graduate Scholarship: April 30.

ADDRESS INQUIRIES TO:
Scholarship Program
(See address above.)

ASIAN AMERICAN JOURNALISTS ASSOCIATION   [1505]

5 Third Street
Suite 1108
San Francisco, CA 94103
(415) 346-2051 ext. 107
Fax: (415) 346-6343
E-mail: danielg@aaja.org
Web Site: www.aaja.org

FOUNDED: 1981

AREAS OF INTEREST:
Journalism.

NAME(S) OF PROGRAMS:
● **Stanford Chen Internship Grant**
● **Lloyd LaCuesta Internship Grant**
● **William Woo Print & Online News Internship Grant**

TYPE:
Grants-in-aid; Scholarships.

YEAR PROGRAM STARTED: 1981

PURPOSE:
To encourage Asian-American students to pursue journalism careers.

ELIGIBILITY:
Must be a full-time college student pursuing journalism as a major.

Detailed information regarding each program is posted on the Association web site.

GEOG. RESTRICTIONS: United States.

FINANCIAL DATA:
Amount of support per award: Stanford Chen Internship Grant and William Woo Internship Grant: $2,000; Lloyd LaCuesta Internship Grant: $1,000.
Total amount of support: Varies.

NO. MOST RECENT APPLICANTS: 50.

NO. AWARDS: 7.

APPLICATION INFO:
Application information is available on the web site.
Duration: One-time award. No renewals.
Deadline: April.

IRS I.D.: 95-3755203

STAFF:
Daniel Garcia, Program Associate

ADDRESS INQUIRIES TO:
Daniel Garcia, Program Associate
(See address above.)

ASSOCIATION OF INTERNATIONAL CERTIFIED PROFESSIONAL ACCOUNTANTS (THE ASSOCIATION)   [1506]

220 Leigh Farm Road
Durham, NC 27707
(919) 402-4682
E-mail: scholarships@aicpa.org
academics@aicpa.org
Web Site: www.aicpa.org

AREAS OF INTEREST:
Accounting/doctoral program.

NAME(S) OF PROGRAMS:
● **AICPA Fellowship for Minority Doctoral Students**

TYPE:
Fellowships. Awarded annually to full-time minority accounting scholars who demonstrate significant potential to become accounting educators.

PURPOSE:
To ensure that C.P.As. of diverse backgrounds are visible in college and university classrooms; to increase the number of minority C.P.As. who serve as role models and mentors to young people in the academic environment.

ELIGIBILITY:
To be considered, applicants must meet the following requirements:
(1) have applied to a doctoral program and awaiting word on acceptance, or have been accepted into a doctoral program or already matriculated in a doctoral program and pursuing appropriate coursework;
(2) have earned a Master's degree and/or completed a minimum of three years of full-time experience in the practice of accounting;
(3) be a minority student of Black or African American, Hispanic or Latino, Native American, Native Hawaiian or Pacific Islander ethnicity;
(4) attend school on a full-time basis and plan to remain enrolled full-time until attaining one's doctoral degree;
(5) agree not to work full-time in a paid position or accept responsibility for teaching more than one course per semester as a teaching assistant, or dedicate more than one quarter of the time as a research assistant;
(6) be a C.P.A. or plan to pursue the C.P.A. credential and;
(7) be a U.S. citizen or permanent resident (green card holder).

GEOG. RESTRICTIONS: United States and its territories.

FINANCIAL DATA:
Amount of support per award: $12,000.
Total amount of support: $300,000 for the academic year 2019-20.

NO. AWARDS: 25 for the academic year 2019-20.

APPLICATION INFO:
Instructions are available online, or send an e-mail to the Association.
Duration: One year. Renewable up to five years.
Deadline: May 30.

ADDRESS INQUIRIES TO:
AICPA Minority Doctoral Fellowship Program
E-mail: academics@aicpa.org
(See address above.)

ASSOCIATION ON AMERICAN INDIAN AFFAIRS

966 Hungerford Drive, Suite 30-A
Rockville, MD 20850
(240) 314-7155
E-mail: general.aaia@indian-affairs.org
Web Site: www.indian-affairs.org/scholarships.html

TYPE:
Scholarships. Undergraduate and graduate scholarships for citizens of federally recognized Tribes and unrecognized Tribes.

See entry 953 for full listing.

ALEXANDER GRAHAM BELL ASSOCIATION FOR THE DEAF AND HARD OF HEARING

3417 Volta Place, N.W.
Washington, DC 20007
(202) 337-5220
Fax: (202) 337-8314
E-mail: scholarships@agbell.org
Web Site: www.agbell.org

TYPE:
Scholarships.

See entry 900 for full listing.

BINC FOUNDATION

3135 South State Street
Suite 203
Ann Arbor, MI 48108
(866) 733-9064
Fax: (734) 477-2806
E-mail: info@bincfoundation.org
Web Site: www.bincfoundation.org

TYPE:
Challenge/matching grants; Grants-in-aid; Scholarships.

See entry 39 for full listing.

BNSF RAILWAY FOUNDATION

2500 Lou Menk Drive
Building AOB-2
Fort Worth, TX 76131-2830
(817) 867-6458
E-mail: bnsffoundation@bnsf.com
Web Site: www.bnsffoundation.org

TYPE:
Scholarships. Awarded annually to outstanding Native American high school seniors from funds provided by the Foundation, for up to four years or until undergraduate degree requirements are completed, whichever occurs first. Scholarship winners may attend any accredited college (two-year leading to a four-year degree) or university in the U.S.

See entry 954 for full listing.

THE LYNDE AND HARRY BRADLEY FOUNDATION, INC.   [1507]

1400 North Water Street
Suite 300
Milwaukee, WI 53202
(414) 291-9915
Fax: (414) 291-9991
Web Site: www.bradleyfdn.org

FOUNDED: 1942

AREAS OF INTEREST:
Humanities, social sciences and law.

NAME(S) OF PROGRAMS:
● **Bradley Fellowship Program**

TYPE:
Fellowships. To strengthen America's "intellectual infrastructure" at a higher-education level, providing useful assistance to young scholars during a critical phase in their education.

YEAR PROGRAM STARTED: 1986

PURPOSE:
To encourage projects that focus on cultivating a renewed, healthier, and more vigorous sense of citizenship among the American people, and among peoples of other nations, as well.

ELIGIBILITY:
Selected candidates must be intelligent doctoral and postdoctoral fellows within the discretion of participating professors or nominators. The principal consideration is excellence and merit. Candidates must also be U.S. citizens or residents.

GEOG. RESTRICTIONS: United States.

FINANCIAL DATA:
Amount of support per award: Up to $25,000 per academic year.

APPLICATION INFO:
Recipients must be nominated by participating professors or nominators.
Duration: One year.

ADDRESS INQUIRIES TO:
Senior Program Director
(See address above.)

BROADCAST EDUCATION ASSOCIATION
One M Street, S.E.
Washington, DC 20003
(202) 602-0587
Fax: (202) 609-9940
E-mail: help@beaweb.org
Web Site: www.beaweb.org

TYPE:
Scholarships. BEA is the professional development association for professors, industry professionals and students involved in teaching and research related to radio, television and other electronic media. BEA administers scholarships annually, to honor broadcasters and the entire electronic media profession.

John Bayliss and Abe Voron Awards: Study toward a career in radio.

BEA Founders, Richard Eaton, Peter B. Orlik and Vincent T. Wasilewski Awards: Study in any electronic media area. (Wasilewski Award is for graduate students only.)

Library of American Broadcasting Foundation Award is for graduate students focusing on broadcast history.

For the BEA Founders Award, preference is given to students enrolled in a BEA Two-Year/Small College Member Institution or graduates of these programs now enrolled in a BEA Four-Year Institution.

All other scholarships are awarded to juniors, seniors and graduate students at BEA Member institutions.

See entry 1751 for full listing.

BROADCAST EDUCATION ASSOCIATION
One M Street, S.E.
Washington, DC 20003
(202) 602-0587
Fax: (202) 609-9940
E-mail: help@beaweb.org
Web Site: www.beaweb.org

TYPE:
Scholarships. PILOT Media Technology and Innovation Scholarships are awarded to college sophomores, juniors, seniors entering graduate school and graduate students for pursuit of studies related to media technology and innovation.

See entry 1752 for full listing.

BUREAU OF INDIAN EDUCATION
12220 Sunrise Valley Drive
Reston, VA 20191
(703) 390-6697
E-mail: katherine.campbell@bie.edu
Web Site: www.bie.edu

TYPE:
Fellowships; Scholarships.
See entry 959 for full listing.

CALIFORNIA STUDENT AID COMMISSION   [1508]
P.O. Box 419026
Rancho Cordova, CA 95741-9026
(888) 224-7268
Fax: (916) 464-8002
E-mail: studentsupport@csac.ca.gov
Web Site: www.csac.ca.gov

FOUNDED: 1955

NAME(S) OF PROGRAMS:
● **Cal Grants A, B and C**

TYPE:
Assistantships; Grants-in-aid. Grant A will help pay for tuition and fees at public and private colleges, and some private career colleges. Grant B provides low-income students with a living allowance and assistance with tuition and fees. Most five-year students receive an allowance for books and living expenses. Grant C helps pay for tuition and training costs at occupational or career technical schools.

YEAR PROGRAM STARTED: 1956

PURPOSE:
To assist with tuition and books for students attending college in California.

LEGAL BASIS:
California Education Code.

ELIGIBILITY:
Student must be a U.S. citizen or eligible noncitizen and a California resident for at least one year.

GEOG. RESTRICTIONS: California.

FINANCIAL DATA:
Amount of support per award: Grants A and B: Varies by type of college; Grant C: Up to $2,462 for tuition and fees and $1,094 for books, tools and equipment.

NO. MOST RECENT APPLICANTS: 350,000.

NO. AWARDS: 75,000.

APPLICATION INFO:
Students should submit the Free Application for Federal Student Aid (FAFSA) or the California Dream Act Application and a verified Cal Grant grade point average. The FAFSA is available online.
Duration: Up to four years.
Deadline: March 2. California Community College students: March 2 and September 2.

PUBLICATIONS:
Fund Your Future; Financial Aid for Students, booklet.

CALIFORNIA STUDENT AID COMMISSION   [1509]
P.O. Box 419029
Rancho Cordova, CA 95741-9029
(888) 224-7268
Fax: (916) 464-8002
E-mail: specialized@csac.ca.gov
Web Site: www.csac.ca.gov

FOUNDED: 1955

AREAS OF INTEREST:
Dependents of law enforcement personnel.

NAME(S) OF PROGRAMS:
● **Law Enforcement Personnel Dependents' Grant Program (LEPD)**

TYPE:
Grants-in-aid. The program provides need-based educational grants to dependents and spouses of California peace officers (Highway Patrol, marshals, sheriffs, police officers), Department of Corrections and California Youth Authority employees and permanent/full-time firefighters, employed by public entities who have been killed in the performance of duty or totally disabled as a result of an accident or injury caused by external violence or physical force incurred in the performance of duty.

Grant awards are for attendance at WASC-accredited colleges in California.

YEAR PROGRAM STARTED: 1969

LEGAL BASIS:
California Labor Code, Section 4709. State agency.

ELIGIBILITY:
Dependents and spouses of California peace officers, Department of Corrections and California Youth Authority employees and permanent/full-time firefighters employed by public entities killed or totally disabled in the performance of duty.

GEOG. RESTRICTIONS: California.

FINANCIAL DATA:
Amount of support per award: $100 to $12,192.
Total amount of support: Varies.

APPLICATION INFO:
Eligible students must file the following documents with the Specialized Programs Branch:
(1) a Law Enforcement Personnel Dependent's Grant application;
(2) a copy of the Student Aid Report (SAR), which is generated after filing a FAFSA;
(3) birth certificate (not required for spouse);
(4) the death certificate of the parent or spouse and the coroner's report (if appropriate), police report, and any other documentation that shows evidence that the death or total disability was caused by external violence or physical force incurred in the line of duty (for peace and law enforcement officers), by the direct action of an inmate (for officers and employees of the Department of Corrections and Rehabilitation), or in the performance of duty (for firefighters);
(5) findings of the Workers' Compensation Appeals Board or other evidence that the fatality or 100% disabling accident or injury was compensable under Division 4.0 and 4.5 (commencing with Section 6100) of the Labor Code and;
(6) proof of enrollment at a California postsecondary institution as described above for the applicable academic year.
Duration: Up to four years.

PUBLICATIONS:
Financial Aid for Students, booklet.

STAFF:
Marlene L. Garcia, Executive Director

ADDRESS INQUIRIES TO:
　See e-mail address above.

CANADIAN FRIENDS OF THE HEBREW UNIVERSITY　　[1510]
4950 Yonge Street
Suite 1202
Toronto ON M2N 6K1 Canada
(416) 485-8000
(888) 432-7398
E-mail: inquiry@cfhu.org
Web Site: www.cfhu.org

FOUNDED: 1944

AREAS OF INTEREST:
　Law, dentistry, social sciences, economics, humanities, the sciences, medicine and computer science.

TYPE:
　Awards/prizes; Scholarships. The Canadian Friends of the Hebrew University sponsors Canadian college or university students who participate in programs at the Hebrew University of Jerusalem.

YEAR PROGRAM STARTED: 1944

PURPOSE:
　To give the financial support necessary for Canadian students to study at Hebrew University in Jerusalem, Israel; to raise funds in support of the Hebrew University research programs.

LEGAL BASIS:
　Nonprofit.

ELIGIBILITY:
　Applicants must be Canadian citizens or landed immigrants. Awards are given based on need. Some scholarships are designated for Israeli students.

GEOG. RESTRICTIONS: Canada.

FINANCIAL DATA:
　Amount of support per award: $1,000 to $3,000.
　Total amount of support: Varies.

NO. AWARDS: Varies.

APPLICATION INFO:
　Contact Chris Carabott at ccarabott@cfhu.org.
　Duration: At least one year.
　Deadline: May 1.

STAFF:
　Rami Kleinmann, Chief Executive Officer and President

ADDRESS INQUIRIES TO:
　Kris Hreczynski, Officer Manager
　(See address above.)

THE CARSON SCHOLARS FUND, INC.　　[1511]
305 West Chesapeake Avenue
Suite 310
Towson, MD 21204
(410) 828-1005
Fax: (410) 828-1007
E-mail: lrichards@carsonscholars.org
Web Site: carsonscholars.org

FOUNDED: 1994

AREAS OF INTEREST:
　Education.

NAME(S) OF PROGRAMS:
● **Carson Scholarships**

TYPE:
　Scholarships. The Carson Scholars Fund awards college scholarships to students in grades 4-11 who excel academically and are dedicated to serving their communities.

YEAR PROGRAM STARTED: 1994

PURPOSE:
　To operate on the principle that if children could be taught early to excel, they would stay motivated and have a higher chance of educational success later in life.

ELIGIBILITY:
　Students must be nominated by the principal at his or her school. Only one student from each school is able to apply. Carson Scholars must have a grade point average of 3.75 and display humanitarian qualities through community service. Scholarships are awarded solely on the basis of academic achievements and humanitarian qualities, without regard to financial need or ethnicity. Carson Scholars must be U.S. citizens or residents.

GEOG. RESTRICTIONS: United States.

FINANCIAL DATA:
　Scholarship winners receive the honor of being named "Carson Scholars" and are awarded an Olympic-sized medal and a trophy for their school. Winners receive a recognition package and an invitation to attend an awards banquet.
　Amount of support per award: $1,000.

NO. AWARDS: 501 for the year 2018.

APPLICATION INFO:
　Students must be nominated by the principal of his or her school to compete. Only one student from each school is able to apply. Complete information is on the web site.
　Duration: One-time award.
　Deadline: Nominations open in October and close the beginning of January. Notification is made in March.

ADDRESS INQUIRIES TO:
　Lacey Richards, Scholarship Director
　(See e-mail address above.)

CATCHING THE DREAM
8200 Mountain Road, N.E.
Suite 103
Albuquerque, NM 87110
(505) 262-2351
Fax: (505) 262-0534
E-mail: NScholarsh@aol.com
Web Site: www.catchingthedream.org

TYPE:
　Conferences/seminars; Development grants; Grants-in-aid; Scholarships; Technical assistance. CTD also works to improve Indian schools through a program of grants and technical assistance. This work has led to the development of 40 Exemplary Programs in Indian education since 1988. The annual Exemplary Institute is a meeting of these Exemplary Programs, where they teach other people how to develop similar programs.

　MAST program makes grants of $5,000 to Indian high schools to improve their math and science teaching.

　MESBEC Program consists of competitive scholarships for high-potential Native Americans studying in math, engineering, science, business, education and computers.

　NALE Program consists of competitive scholarships for high-potential paraprofessional Native Americans who plan

to complete their degrees and obtain credentials as teachers, counselors or administrators.

　RAP makes grants to Indian schools to improve the reading ability of their students.

　Tribal Business Management (TBM) Program consists of competitive scholarships for Native students in all fields of business.

See entry 960 for full listing.

CHATHAM UNIVERSITY　　[1512]
Woodland Road
Berry Hall
Pittsburgh, PA 15232
(412) 365-1825
Fax: (412) 365-1609
E-mail: admission@chatham.edu
undergraduate@chatham.edu
Web Site: www.chatham.edu/admission/financial-aid/undergraduate/scholarships

FOUNDED: 1869

AREAS OF INTEREST:
　Providing scholarship opportunities to students who have shown academic promise during their high school career and who are enrolled at Chatham University.

NAME(S) OF PROGRAMS:
● **The Chatham University Merit Scholarship Programs**

TYPE:
　Awards/prizes; Endowments; Formula grants; General operating grants; Grants-in-aid; Internships; Scholarships. The Chatham University Merit Scholarship Programs include the Presidential, Trustee, Dean, and Founder, as well as Chatham Grants. Additional scholarship opportunities include the S-STEM Scholarship, the Heffer Family Scholarship, the Girl Scout Gold Scholarship, the Minna Kaufmann Ruud Music Scholarship, the Eden Hall Scholarship for Sustainability, the AFS/YFU/Rotary International Scholarship, the Visual Arts Scholarship, the Interior Architecture Scholarship, the Girl Scout Leadership Award, the Legacy Award, the Family Heritage Award, the Phi Theta Kappa Scholarship, and the Rachel Carson Book Award.

YEAR PROGRAM STARTED: 1978

PURPOSE:
　To attract outstanding students to Chatham University and to provide recognition of their academic performance.

ELIGIBILITY:
　Chatham University Merit Scholars are chosen based on their performance in high school, grades, and SAT or ACT scores.

　Grants are based strictly on need; many of the scholars are from families for whom the choice of a college such as Chatham would not be possible without this support.

FINANCIAL DATA:
　Amount of support per award: Presidential Scholarship pays full tuition. Other Scholarships are from $3,000 per year to $16,000 per year.
　Total amount of support: Varies.

NO. MOST RECENT APPLICANTS: Approximately 1,000 annually.

APPLICATION INFO:
All applicants must complete an application for admission to Chatham University which includes SAT or ACT scores, high school transcript, and application.

First-year students who choose not to submit the SAT/ACT will be required to submit a graded writing sample and resume or list of activities as well as complete an interview. Applicants will also have the option to submit a portfolio or special project/activity.

Duration: Four years of the undergraduate career, provided the high academic criteria expected of such scholars is maintained. Renewable annually based on grade point average of 3.0 or higher for Presidential Scholarship and 2.0 or higher for the other scholarships, and full-time enrollment.

Deadline: February 1.

STAFF:
Amy Becher, Vice President for Enrollment Management
Dr. Jennifer Burns, Assistant Vice President of Financial Aid

ADDRESS INQUIRIES TO:
Office of Enrollment Management
(See address above.)

CHINESE AMERICAN MEDICAL SOCIETY
11 East Broadway, Unit 4-C
New York, NY 10038
(212) 334-4760
Fax: (646) 304-6373
E-mail: jlove@camsociety.org
Web Site: www.camsociety.org

TYPE:
Fellowships; Scholarships.

See entry 2052 for full listing.

THE CLARK FOUNDATION [1513]
5229 State Highway 28
Cooperstown, NY 13326
(607) 547-9927
Fax: (607) 547-8598
Web Site: www.clarkscholarship.org

FOUNDED: 1931

NAME(S) OF PROGRAMS:
● **Clark Foundation Scholarship Program**

TYPE:
Scholarships. Undergraduate college scholarships.

YEAR PROGRAM STARTED: 1961

PURPOSE:
To assist Cooperstown area students in their pursuit of higher education.

LEGAL BASIS:
Nonprofit foundation.

ELIGIBILITY:
Individual undergraduate college scholarships are awarded to graduates of Central School, Cooperstown, NY and 12 surrounding rural central school districts.

GEOG. RESTRICTIONS: Cooperstown and the 12 surrounding New York rural central school districts of Cherry Valley-Springfield, Edmeston, Gilbertsville, Laurens, Milford, Morris, Mount Markham, Mount Upton, Richfield Springs, Schenevus, Worcester and Owen D. Young.

FINANCIAL DATA:
Amount of support per award:
Approximately $3,800.

Total amount of support: $3,800,000.

NO. MOST RECENT APPLICANTS: 331.

NO. AWARDS: 193.

APPLICATION INFO:
Students are recommended by their respective schools.

Duration: One year. Possible renewal each year for duration of undergraduate education.

Deadline: First week in February.

OFFICERS:
Jane Forbes Clark, President
Kevin S. Moore, Treasurer
Douglas Bauer, Executive Director and Secretary

ADDRESS INQUIRIES TO:
Gary Kuch, Director
Clark Foundation Scholarship Office
P.O. Box 427
Cooperstown, NY 13326

COCA-COLA SCHOLARS FOUNDATION [1514]
P.O. Box 442
Atlanta, GA 30301-0442
(800) 306-2653
Fax: (404) 733-5439
E-mail: scholars@coca-cola.com
Web Site: www.coca-colascholars.org

FOUNDED: 1986

AREAS OF INTEREST:
Enhancing educational opportunities in the U.S.

NAME(S) OF PROGRAMS:
● **Coca-Cola Scholars Program**

TYPE:
Scholarships. Awards based on leadership, academics and community service.

YEAR PROGRAM STARTED: 1989

PURPOSE:
To enhance educational opportunities in the U.S. through scholarship awards and enrichment programs for young people who demonstrate, through academic excellence and leadership in their communities, their capacity for and commitment to making a difference in the world.

ELIGIBILITY:
Current high school (or home-schooled) seniors attending school in the U.S. (or select DoD schools). Applicant must not graduate prior to deadline.

GEOG. RESTRICTIONS: United States.

FINANCIAL DATA:
Program has awarded over $69,000,000 in scholarships since inception.
Amount of support per award: $20,000.
Total amount of support: Over $3,000,000 annually.

NO. MOST RECENT APPLICANTS: 50,000 to 100,000 annually.

NO. AWARDS: 150 annually.

APPLICATION INFO:
Application must be submitted online.
Duration: Four to 10 years.
Deadline: October 31.

ADDRESS INQUIRIES TO:
See e-mail address above.

CONCORDIA UNIVERSITY [1515]
1455 de Maisonneuve Boulevard West
Graduate Awards Office, Room S-GM 930.01
Montreal QC H3G 1M8 Canada
(514) 848-2424 ext. 3385
Fax: (514) 848-2812
E-mail: graduate-awards@concordia.ca
Web Site: www.concordia.ca/sgs.html

FOUNDED: 1974

AREAS OF INTEREST:
All disciplines.

NAME(S) OF PROGRAMS:
● **Concordia University Graduate Fellowships**

TYPE:
Assistantships; Awards/prizes; Conferences/seminars; Endowments; Fellowships; Scholarships. Postgraduate full-time fellowships.

PURPOSE:
To recruit highly qualified graduate students to doctoral programs.

ELIGIBILITY:
Candidates must be planning to pursue full-time doctoral studies at Concordia University. Academic merit is the prime consideration in the granting of the award.

All new admissions will be considered for awards.

GEOG. RESTRICTIONS: Canada.

FINANCIAL DATA:
Amount of support per award: $14,000 (CAN) per year.

NO. MOST RECENT APPLICANTS: Over 1,000.

NO. AWARDS: 100 or more.

APPLICATION INFO:
Guidelines are available on the University's web site.
Duration: One to four years.

COOK FAMILY FOUNDATION
120 West Exchange Street
Suite 202
Owosso, MI 48867
(989) 725-1621
Fax: (989) 936-5910
E-mail: tom@cookfamilyfoundation.org
Web Site: www.cookfamilyfoundation.org

TYPE:
Capital grants; Challenge/matching grants; Demonstration grants; Development grants; Matching gifts; Project/program grants; Scholarships; Seed money grants; Technical assistance. Educational support.

See entry 1141 for full listing.

JACK KENT COOKE FOUNDATION [1516]
44325 Woodridge Parkway
Lansdowne, VA 20176-5297
(703) 723-8000
(800) 941-3300
E-mail: scholarships@jkcf.org
Web Site: www.jkcf.org

FOUNDED: 2000

AREAS OF INTEREST:
Education.

NAME(S) OF PROGRAMS:
● **College Scholarship Program**

- **Undergraduate Transfer Scholarship**
- **Young Scholars Program**

TYPE:
Fellowships; Scholarships. College Scholarship Program is available to high-performing high school seniors with financial need who seek to attend and graduate from the nation's best four-year colleges and universities.

Undergraduate Transfer Scholarship honors excellence by supporting outstanding community college students with financial need to transfer to and complete their Bachelor's degrees at the nation's top four-year colleges and universities.

Young Scholars Program seeks high-achieving seventh-grade students with financial need, and cultivates their talents and abilities throughout high school by providing the personalized advising and financial support needed to secure challenging academic opportunities.

PURPOSE:
To help students of exceptional promise reach their full potential through education.

GEOG. RESTRICTIONS: United States.

FINANCIAL DATA:
Amount of support per award: College Scholarship Program and Undergraduate Transfer Scholarship: Up to $40,000 per year. Young Scholars Program: Varies.

NO. MOST RECENT APPLICANTS: College Scholarship Program: 5,520; Undergraduate Transfer Scholarship: 1,494; Young Scholars Program: 2,302 for the year 2019.

NO. AWARDS: College Scholarship Program: Approximately 60; Undergraduate Transfer Scholarship: Approximately 60; Young Scholars: Approximately 50.

APPLICATION INFO:
An application form needs to be completed. Application information is available on the web site.

Duration: College Scholarship Program: Up to four years. Undergraduate Transfer Scholarship: Two to three years.

Deadline: College Scholarship Program and Undergraduate Transfer Scholarship: Opens August, closes late November. Young Scholars Program: Opens January, closes April.

ADDRESS INQUIRIES TO:
See e-mail address above.

DARTMOUTH COLLEGE

Office of Graduate Studies
Eastman/Marshall
37 Dewey Field Road, Suite 6062, Room 437
Hanover, NH 03755-3526
(603) 646-2106
Fax: (603) 646-8762
E-mail: jane.b.seibel@dartmouth.edu
Web Site: graduate.dartmouth.edu

TYPE:
Exchange programs; Fellowships.

See entry 906 for full listing.

DAUGHTERS OF PENELOPE FOUNDATION, INC.

1909 Q Street, N.W., Suite 500
Washington, DC 20009
(202) 234-9741
Fax: (202) 483-6983
E-mail: dophq@ahepa.org
Web Site: www.dopfoundationinc.com

TYPE:
Scholarships.

See entry 985 for full listing.

DAUGHTERS OF THE CINCINNATI   [1517]

271 Madison Avenue
Suite 1408
New York, NY 10016
(212) 991-9945
E-mail: scholarships@daughters1894.org
Web Site: www.daughters1894.org

FOUNDED: 1894

NAME(S) OF PROGRAMS:
- **Daughters of the Cincinnati Scholarship Program**

TYPE:
Scholarships. Undergraduate scholarships.

YEAR PROGRAM STARTED: 1906

PURPOSE:
To assist high school seniors entering college with financial aid (annually for the four years).

LEGAL BASIS:
Nonprofit, tax-exempt organization.

ELIGIBILITY:
Applicant must be a senior in high school who is the daughter of a career officer commissioned in the regular Army, Navy, Air Force, Coast Guard or Marine Corps (active, retired or deceased). The daughters of officers in the Reserves, National Guard and State Militia are not eligible to apply for this scholarship.

FINANCIAL DATA:
Aid for tuition and room and board.
Amount of support per award: Average $4,000 to $5,000 annually.
Total amount of support: Varies.

NO. MOST RECENT APPLICANTS: Approximately 100.

NO. AWARDS: Approximately 3 to 4 annually.

APPLICATION INFO:
The application is accessible from the web site after supplying the parent's branch of service and rank.
Duration: Four years, or as long as the student attends college up to that length of time. Reviewed annually.
Deadline: Postmarked by March 15. Announcement in mid-May.

PUBLICATIONS:
Information sheet.

ADDRESS INQUIRIES TO:
Scholarship Administrator
(See address above.)

DAVIDSON INSTITUTE   [1518]

9665 Gateway Drive, Suite B
Reno, NV 89521
(775) 852-3483
E-mail: tmoessner@davidsongifted.org
davidsonfellows@davidsongifted.org
Web Site: www.davidsongifted.org/Fellows-Scholarship

FOUNDED: 1999

AREAS OF INTEREST:
Encouraging the development of academically gifted students.

NAME(S) OF PROGRAMS:
- **Davidson Fellows**

TYPE:
Awards/prizes; Scholarships.

YEAR PROGRAM STARTED: 2001

PURPOSE:
To award students working at the college graduate level on projects that have the potential to benefit society.

ELIGIBILITY:
Students must be 18 or younger as of October 1 of the year of application, must be U.S. citizens or permanent residents residing in the U.S. and must have completed a significant piece of work.

FINANCIAL DATA:
Amount of support per award: Scholarships of $10,000, $25,000 or $50,000 to be used at an accredited college or university.
Total amount of support: $480,000 for the year 2019.

NO. MOST RECENT APPLICANTS: 400.

NO. AWARDS: 20.

APPLICATION INFO:
Application categories are Science, Technology, Engineering, Mathematics, Literature, Music, Philosophy and Outside the Box. The application is completely online. Students must submit a project, two essays and a video; they must also have two nominators.
Duration: The scholarship is available for 10 years and is not renewable.
Deadline: The second Wednesday in February.

ADDRESS INQUIRIES TO:
Tacie Moessner, Director
Davidson Fellows Scholarship Program
(See e-mail address above.)

MICHAEL AND SUSAN DELL FOUNDATION   [1519]

P.O. Box 163867
Austin, TX 78716-3867
(877) 600-5587
(800) 294-2039 (apply)
Fax: (512) 600-5501
E-mail: info@msdf.org
Web Site: www.dell.org
www.dellscholars.org

NAME(S) OF PROGRAMS:
- **Dell Scholars Program**

TYPE:
Scholarships. Need-based scholarship that recognizes academic potential in lower-income and underserved students. Applicants must demonstrate a drive to succeed while overcoming personal obstacles.

YEAR PROGRAM STARTED: 2004

PURPOSE:
To assist students who have worked hard to prepare themselves for higher education yet may have lower grade point averages and test scores because of adverse personal situations or surroundings.

ELIGIBILITY:
Applicants must:
(1) be high school seniors who have

participated in a Michael and Susan Dell Foundation-approved college readiness program;
(2) be a U.S. citizen or legal permanent resident;
(3) have financial need confirmed through eligibility for a Federal Pell Grant;
(4) have a minimum 2.4 grade point average on a 4.0 scale and;
(5) be planning to enroll full-time in a Bachelor's degree program at an accredited higher education institution in the fall directly after high school graduation.

Scholarship may be used at any accredited two- or four-year institution in the U.S. where credits can be earned towards a Baccalaureate degree, including community and junior colleges. Technical colleges and vocational programs are not eligible.

GEOG. RESTRICTIONS: United States.

FINANCIAL DATA:
Award may be applied to any cost of acquiring an education. Also provide other means of support, such as mentoring.
Amount of support per award: $20,000 over a maximum of six years.
Total amount of support: Varies.

NO. AWARDS: 500 annually.

APPLICATION INFO:
Application, which becomes available in October, must be completed online. No paper applications will be accepted.
Duration: Up to six years.
Deadline: December 1.

ADDRESS INQUIRIES TO:
E-mail: apply@dellscholars.org

THE EBELL OF LOS ANGELES   [1520]
743 South Lucerne Boulevard
Los Angeles, CA 90005-3707
(323) 931-1277 ext. 184
Fax: (323) 937-0272
E-mail: Scholarship@ebelloflosangeles.com
Web Site: www.ebellla.org

FOUNDED: 1894

AREAS OF INTEREST:
Higher education.

NAME(S) OF PROGRAMS:
● **Ebell/Flint Scholarship**

TYPE:
Scholarships.

YEAR PROGRAM STARTED: 1919

PURPOSE:
To support scholarships for qualified college students.

LEGAL BASIS:
Private foundation.

ELIGIBILITY:
To be eligible for an Ebell scholarship, applicant must:
(1) be a U.S. citizen;
(2) be a permanent resident of Los Angeles County;
(3) be at least a full-time freshman attending an accredited Los Angeles County college or university;
(4) achieve at least a 3.25 cumulative grade point average;
(5) demonstrate community commitment and;
(6) be available for an in-person interview with the Ebell Scholarship Committee on the Ebell campus.

GEOG. RESTRICTIONS: Los Angeles County, California.

FINANCIAL DATA:
Amount of support per award: Four-year colleges: $5,000 per year (12 months) paid semiannually in September and February; Two-year colleges: $3,000 per year.
Total amount of support: Over $200,000 annually.

NO. AWARDS: 53.

APPLICATION INFO:
Guidelines and application form are available on the web site.
Duration: Three years or when the student attains Bachelor's degree, whichever comes first.
Deadline: April 2.

IRS I.D.: 23-7049580

ADDRESS INQUIRIES TO:
See e-mail address above.

THE EISENHOWER FOUNDATION
200 S.E. 4th Street
Abilene, KS 67410
(785) 263-6771
Fax: (785) 263-6715
E-mail: info@eisenhowerfoundation.net
Web Site: www.EisenhowerFoundation.net

TYPE:
Travel grants. Travel grants are awarded to individual researchers on a competitive basis to cover a portion of expenses while in Abilene, KS, using the presidential library.

See entry 1818 for full listing.

FEEA SCHOLARSHIP PROGRAM   [1521]
1641 Prince Street
Alexandria, VA 22314
(202) 554-0007
Fax: (202) 559-1298
E-mail: fedshelpingfeds@feea.org
Web Site: feea.org

AREAS OF INTEREST:
Education.

TYPE:
Scholarships. Merit-based scholarship competition program open exclusively to federal employees, their spouses and their children.

PURPOSE:
To financially aid hard-working federal employees, their spouses and their children in their college education.

ELIGIBILITY:
Children, step-children and legal dependents of full- or part-time permanent federal civilian or postal workers employed with the federal government for more than three years, as well as their spouses may apply. Dependents may first apply as high school seniors. Dependents must be full-time students enrolled in or planning to enroll in an accredited postsecondary school in a course of study that leads to a two-year, four-year or graduate degree. 3.0 grade point average on a 4.0 scale is required.

GEOG. RESTRICTIONS: United States.

FINANCIAL DATA:
Amount of support per award: $1,000 to $5,000.

NO. MOST RECENT APPLICANTS: 2,700.

NO. AWARDS: 217.

APPLICATION INFO:
Scholarship catalog and application instructions are available on the FEEA web site. Required material includes:
(1) complete high school or college transcripts;
(2) one written recommendation or letter of reference;
(3) a short essay (topic changes annually);
(4) a list of community service, extracurricular activities and awards and;
(5) a copy of the employee sponsor's most recent SF-50.

Specific instructions and any additional requirements are listed on each year's application.
Duration: One year. May reapply each year if still eligible.
Deadline: End of March. Exact date will be posted online.

*PLEASE NOTE:
Top student applicants have the opportunity to win one of two additional awards.

THE JAMES MARSTON FITCH CHARITABLE FOUNDATION
c/o The Neighborhood Preservation Center
232 East 11th Street
New York, NY 10003
(212) 252-6809
Fax: (212) 471-9987
E-mail: cpena@fitchfoundation.org
Web Site: fitchfoundation.org

TYPE:
Research grants. Richard L. Blinder Award was created to promote studies that explore the architecture of cultural buildings which integrate historic preservation and new construction - past, present and future; presented biennially.

Mid-Career Fellowship: This grant is the primary mission and the signature grant of this Foundation. The grants are intended to support projects of innovative original research or creative design that advance the practice of historic preservation in the U.S.

See entry 380 for full listing.

FLORIDA DEPARTMENT OF EDUCATION
Office of Student Financial Assistance
325 West Gaines Street, Suite 1314
Tallahassee, FL 32399-0400
(888) 827-2004
Fax: (850) 487-1809
E-mail: osfa@fldoe.org
Web Site: www.floridastudentfinancialaidsg.org

TYPE:
Scholarships. Financial assistance for descendants of the Rosewood family affected by the incidents of January 1923, to attend a state university, public community college or public postsecondary vocational-technical school.

See entry 941 for full listing.

FLORIDA DEPARTMENT OF EDUCATION [1522]

Office of Student Financial Assistance
325 West Gaines Street, Suite 1314
Tallahassee, FL 32399-0400
(888) 827-2004
Fax: (850) 487-1809
E-mail: osfa@fldoe.org
Web Site: www.floridastudentfinancialaidsg.org

AREAS OF INTEREST:
Financial aid for Florida undergraduate students.

NAME(S) OF PROGRAMS:
- **Access to Better Learning and Education Grant Program (ABLE)**
- **Mary McLeod Bethune Scholarship Program (MMB)**
- **Effective Access to Student Education (EASE)**
- **First Generation Matching Grant Program (FGMG)**
- **Florida Farmworker Student Scholarship Program**
- **Florida Student Assistance Grant Program (FSAG)**
- **Florida Work Experience Program (FWEP)**
- **Scholarships for Children and Spouses of Deceased or Disabled Veterans (CSDDV)**

TYPE:
Challenge/matching grants; Grants-in-aid; Scholarships. The Access to Better Learning and Education (ABLE) Grant Program provides tuition assistance to Florida undergraduate students enrolled in degree programs at eligible private Florida colleges or universities. ABLE is a decentralized program, and each participating institution determines application procedures, deadlines and student eligibility.

The Mary McLeod Bethune Scholarships (MMB) are awarded to undergraduate students who meet scholastic requirements attending Bethune-Cookman University, Edward Waters College, Florida A&M University, or Florida Memorial University.

The Effective Access to Student Education (EASE) grants are provided to full-time Florida undergraduates attending an eligible private, nonprofit Florida college or university.

The First Generation Matching Grant Program (FGMG) provides need-based grants to degree-seeking, resident, undergraduate students who demonstrate financial need, are enrolled in participating postsecondary institutions, and whose parents have not earned Baccalaureate or higher degrees.

The Florida Farmworker Student Scholarship Program requires one parent to be a farmer.

The Florida Student Assistance Grant Program (FSAG) is a need-based grant program available to degree-seeking and certificate-seeking, resident, undergraduate students who demonstrate substantial financial need and are enrolled in participating postsecondary institutions.

The Florida Work Experience Program (FWEP) provides eligible Florida students the opportunity to secure work experiences that will complement and reinforce the students' educational and career goals.

Scholarships for Children and Spouses of Deceased or Disabled Veterans (CSDDV) provides scholarships for dependent children and unremarried spouses of Florida veterans who died as a result of service-connected injuries, diseases, or disabilities sustained while on active duty or have been certified by the Florida Department of Veterans' Affairs as having service-connected 100% total and permanent disabilities.

PURPOSE:
To provide financial assistance to Florida students continuing their education.

LEGAL BASIS:
State agency.

GEOG. RESTRICTIONS: Florida.

FINANCIAL DATA:
Amount of support per award: Varies per program.
Total amount of support: Varies.

NO. AWARDS: Access to Better Learning and Education Grant Program: 2,298 disbursed; Mary McLeod Bethune Scholarship Program: 136 disbursed; Effective Access to Student Education: 45,839 disbursed; First Generations Matching Grant Program: 11,911 disbursed; Florida Student Assistance Grant Program: 183,225 disbursed; Florida Work Experience Program: 790 disbursed; Scholarships for Children and Spouses of Deceased or Disabled Veterans: 1,684 disbursed.

APPLICATION INFO:
Applicant must submit a completed, error-free Florida Financial Aid Application (FFAA) or Free Application for Federal Student Aid (FAFSA) as designated online.
Duration: Varies.
Deadline: CSDDV: April 1. All others: Determined by institution.

ADDRESS INQUIRIES TO:
See telephone and e-mail address above.

FLORIDA DEPARTMENT OF EDUCATION

Office of Student Financial Assistance
325 West Gaines Street, Suite 1314
Tallahassee, FL 32399-0400
(888) 827-2004
Fax: (850) 487-1809
E-mail: osfa@fldoe.org
Web Site: www.floridastudentfinancialaidsg.org

TYPE:
Challenge/matching grants; Grants-in-aid. Jose Marti Scholarship Challenge Grant Fund is a need-based merit scholarship that provides financial assistance to eligible students of Hispanic origin who will attend Florida public or eligible private institutions.

See entry 974 for full listing.

FLORIDA DEPARTMENT OF EDUCATION [1523]

Office of Student Financial Assistance
325 West Gaines Street, Suite 1314
Tallahassee, FL 32399-0400
(888) 827-2004
Fax: (850) 487-1809
E-mail: osfa@fldoe.org
Web Site: www.floridastudentfinancialaidsg.org

NAME(S) OF PROGRAMS:
- **Florida Bright Futures Scholarship Program**

TYPE:
Scholarships. The Florida Bright Futures Scholarship Program is the umbrella program for three state-funded scholarships based on academic achievement in high school: Florida Academic Scholars (FAS) Award, Florida Medallion Scholars (FMS) Award, Florida Gold Seal Vocational Scholars (GSV) Award, and Florida Gold Seal Cape Award.

YEAR PROGRAM STARTED: 1997

PURPOSE:
To reward Florida's high school graduates who merit recognition of high academic achievement.

LEGAL BASIS:
State agency.

ELIGIBILITY:
Initial eligibility requirements to receive funding are as follows:
(1) be a Florida resident and a U.S. citizen or eligible noncitizen; student's residency and citizenship status are determined by the postsecondary institution; consult the financial aid office or admissions office of the institution one plans to attend;
(2) meet specific coursework, volunteer service hours, and minimum grade point average and test score requirements and;
(3) not be found guilty of, or pled nolo contendere to, a felony charge, unless the student has been granted clemency by the Governor and Cabinet sitting as the Executive Office of Clemency.

GEOG. RESTRICTIONS: Florida.

FINANCIAL DATA:
Amount of support per award: Varies.
Total amount of support: Varies.

NO. MOST RECENT APPLICANTS: 191,622 for the year 2017-18.

NO. AWARDS: 126,218 eligible with 103,385 disbursed for the year 2018-19.

APPLICATION INFO:
Detailed program information can be found on the web site.
Duration: One year; renewable up to five years from high school graduation or a first Baccalaureate degree, whichever comes first.
Deadline: Florida Financial Aid Application must be submitted no later than August 31 after high school graduation.

ADDRESS INQUIRIES TO:
State Scholarship and Grant Programs (See address above.)

FOUNDATION FOR TECHNOLOGY AND ENGINEERING EDUCATION [1524]

1914 Association Drive
Suite 201
Reston, VA 20191-1539
(703) 860-2100
Fax: (703) 860-0353
E-mail: iteea@iteea.org
Web Site: www.iteea.org

FOUNDED: 1939

AREAS OF INTEREST:
Technology education.

NAME(S) OF PROGRAMS:
- **FTEE Undergraduate Scholarship**

TYPE:
Scholarships. The scholarship is for an undergraduate student majoring in technology and engineering education teacher preparation.

PURPOSE:
To support teacher preparation in technology and engineering education.

ELIGIBILITY:
Applicant must be a member of the International Technology and Engineering Educators Association and be a current, full-time undergraduate majoring in technology and engineering education teacher preparation. Applicant must not be a senior by application deadline.

FINANCIAL DATA:
Amount of support per award: $500.

NO. MOST RECENT APPLICANTS: 2.

NO. AWARDS: 1.

APPLICATION INFO:
Applicants must submit the application package, which is to include the following required items:
(1) letter of transmittal that includes a statement about personal interest in teaching technology and engineering and applicant's address with day and evening telephone numbers;
(2) resume or vitae which indicate career goals, current professional and college activities and achievements (maximum three pages);
(3) photocopy of college transcript (required 2.5 grade point average on 4.0 scale) and;
(4) three faculty letters of recommendation from among his or her professors and/or advisor.

Application may be submitted electronically to the e-mail address listed above.
Duration: One year.
Deadline: December 1.

ADDRESS INQUIRIES TO:
FTEE Undergraduate Scholarship Foundation for Technology and Engineering Education
(See address above.)

*SPECIAL STIPULATIONS:
Applicant must be a member of the ITEEA.

FOUNDATION FOR TECHNOLOGY AND ENGINEERING EDUCATION   [1525]
1914 Association Drive
Suite 201
Reston, VA 20191-1539
(703) 860-2100
Fax: (703) 860-0353
E-mail: iteea@iteea.org
Web Site: www.iteea.org

FOUNDED: 1939

AREAS OF INTEREST:
Technology education.

NAME(S) OF PROGRAMS:
● **Litherland/FTEE Scholarship Undergraduate Major in Technology and Engineering Education**

TYPE:
Scholarships.

PURPOSE:
To assist an undergraduate student majoring in technology education and engineering teacher preparation.

ELIGIBILITY:
Applicant must be member of the International Technology and Engineering Educators Association and a current,

full-time undergraduate majoring in technology education and engineering teacher preparation. The student must not be a senior by application deadline. The award is based upon interest in teaching, academic ability, need and faculty recommendations.

FINANCIAL DATA:
Amount of support per award: $500.

NO. MOST RECENT APPLICANTS: 2.

NO. AWARDS: 1.

APPLICATION INFO:
Applicants must submit an application package, which is to include the following required items:
(1) a letter of transmittal that includes a statement about his or her personal interest in teaching technology and engineering and applicant's address with day and evening telephone numbers;
(2) resume or vitae identifying career goals, current professional activities and achievements;
(3) photocopy of college transcript and;
(4) three faculty letters of recommendation from among his or her professors and/or advisor.
Duration: One year.
Deadline: December 1.

ADDRESS INQUIRIES TO:
Litherland/FTEE Scholarship Foundation for Technology and Engineering Education
(See address above.)

*SPECIAL STIPULATIONS:
Applicant must be a member of the ITEEA.

FREEDOM ALLIANCE   [1526]
22570 Markey Court, Suite 240
Dulles, VA 20166
(703) 444-7940
(800) 475-6620
Fax: (703) 444-9893
E-mail: wanda.cruz@freedomalliance.org
Web Site: www.fascholarship.com

FOUNDED: 1990

AREAS OF INTEREST:
Scholarship aid to the children of American military personnel who have been killed or injured in military service.

NAME(S) OF PROGRAMS:
● **Freedom Alliance Scholarship Fund**

TYPE:
Scholarships. Freedom Alliance Scholarship Fund provides college scholarships to the sons and daughters of America's military heroes - those who sacrifice life or limb in defense of America's freedom.

YEAR PROGRAM STARTED: 1990

PURPOSE:
To honor the bravery and dedication exhibited by Americans in the U.S. armed forces who have sacrificed life and limb by providing educational scholarships to their children.

LEGAL BASIS:
501(c)(3) educational and charitable foundation.

ELIGIBILITY:
Students must be a dependent child of a service member who was killed or was permanently disabled (100% rating) in the line of duty, or who is currently certified as POW or MIA. The applicant must also be a

senior in high school, a high school graduate, or enrolled in an institution of higher learning, including colleges, universities or vocational schools.

FINANCIAL DATA:
Amount of support per award: Varies.
Total amount of support: $2,100,000.

NO. MOST RECENT APPLICANTS: 695 for the year 2019.

NO. AWARDS: 499 for the year 2019.

APPLICATION INFO:
Eligible students seeking a Freedom Alliance scholarship must first complete an application form. Applications will not be considered by the scholarship committee unless all required materials listed below accompany the application package:
(1) certificate of death/disability or proof of POW/MIA status as defined in the instructions;
(2) proof of dependency as defined in the instructions;
(3) 500-word essay as explained in the instructions;
(4) official transcripts from high school and all post-high school educational institutions;
(5) photo of applicant and;
(6) photo of parent.

DD Form 214 is also required in the case of a student whose parent is permanently disabled, in addition to the VA rating letter demonstrating permanent disability in the application packet.
Duration: Scholarships are awarded annually and are renewable for a total of four scholarships.
Deadline: Applications are accepted on a rolling basis.

STAFF:
Thomas Kilgannon, President
Calvin Coolidge, Executive Director

BOARD OF DIRECTORS AND OFFICERS:
Gerald Lindholm, Chairman
Rita Scott, Secretary/Treasurer
Lt Gen Jerry Boykin, USA (Ret.)
Ed Daily
Bob Garthwait

FOUNDERS:
Lt Col Oliver L. North, USMC (Ret.),
Honorary Chairman
Lt Gen Edward J. Bronars, USMC

ADDRESS INQUIRIES TO:
Wanda Cruz, Program Assistant
(See address above.)

*PLEASE NOTE:
No graduate scholarships are provided.

GOLDEN KEY INTERNATIONAL HONOUR SOCIETY, INC.   [1527]
1040 Crown Pointe Parkway
Suite 900
Atlanta, GA 30338
(678) 689-2200
(800) 377-2401
Fax: (678) 689-2297
E-mail: awards@goldenkey.org
Web Site: goldenkey.org

AREAS OF INTEREST:
Nonprofit academic honors organization that recognizes the top 15% of juniors and seniors in all undergraduate fields.

NAME(S) OF PROGRAMS:
● **Advisor Professional Development Grant**

- **Chartering Officer Scholarship**
- **GEICO Life Scholarship**
- **The Golden Key Graduate Scholarship Award**
- **Golden Key Research Grants**
- **Professor Jeff Johnson Study Abroad Scholarship**
- **Joan Nelson Study Abroad Scholarship**
- **Undergraduate Achievement Scholarship**

TYPE:
Awards/prizes; Scholarships; Travel grants. Advisor Professional Development Grant allows current Golden Key chapter advisors the ability to attend professional development conferences or pursue research within their academic disciplines.

Chartering Officer Scholarship recognizes members who have chartered or re-chartered their local chapter in the previous academic year.

GEICO Life Scholarship: Recognizes outstanding members who achieve academic excellence while balancing additional commitments such as family and/or career.

The Golden Key Graduate Scholar Award: Golden Key's premier scholarship program. Supports members' post-Baccalaureate study at accredited universities anywhere in the world.

Golden Key Research Grants: Allow members to conduct thesis research and/or present their research at professional conferences or student research symposia.

Professor Jeff Johnson and Joan Nelson Study Abroad Scholarships assist members who are going to participate in a study abroad program.

Undergraduate Achievement Scholarship recognizes members for their excellence throughout their undergraduate careers.

PURPOSE:
To enable members to realize their potential.

ELIGIBILITY:
Open to Golden Key members.

FINANCIAL DATA:
Amount of support per award: $1,000 to $10,000.

Total amount of support: $500,000 for the year 2016.

APPLICATION INFO:
Golden Key's scholarships and awards require a formal application. Each scholarship has a unique submission deadline and application process. Details about each of the scholarship programs can be found under the Scholarships and Awards Listing on the web site. All scholarship submissions must be written in English.

Deadline: Varies.

ADDRESS INQUIRIES TO:
Chris Yarbrough
Director, Programs and Operations
(See address above.)

*SPECIAL STIPULATIONS:
Only Golden Key members may apply for these scholarships and awards.

THE GREATER KANAWHA VALLEY FOUNDATION
Huntington Square, Suite 1600
900 Lee Street East
Charleston, WV 25301
(304) 346-3620
Fax: (304) 346-3640
E-mail: shyre@tgkvf.org
Web Site: www.tgkvf.org

TYPE:
Project/program grants; Scholarships.

See entry 1177 for full listing.

THE HIGHER EDUCATION STUDENT ASSISTANCE AUTHORITY   [1528]
P.O. Box 540
Trenton, NJ 08625-0540
(609) 588-3300
E-mail: clientservices@hesaa.org
Web Site: www.hesaa.org

FOUNDED: 1959

AREAS OF INTEREST:
State financial assistance for college students.

NAME(S) OF PROGRAMS:
- **Law Enforcement Officer Memorial Scholarship**
- **New Jersey Governor's Industry Vocations Scholarship for Women and Minorities (NJ-GIVS)**
- **New Jersey Student Tuition Assistance Reward Scholarship (NJ STARS)**
- **New Jersey Student Tuition Assistance Reward Scholarship II (NJ STARS II)**
- **New Jersey World Trade Center Scholarship**
- **NJBEST Scholarship**
- **Survivor Tuition Benefits Program**

TYPE:
Scholarships. Law Enforcement Officer Memorial Scholarship provides financial aid for eligible children of law enforcement officers killed in the line of duty.

New Jersey Governor's Industry Vocations Scholarship for Women and Minorities pays for an eligible certificate or degree-granting program in a construction-related field at one of New Jersey's eligible institutions.

New Jersey Student Tuition Assistance Reward Scholarship provides access to higher education for the state's highest achieving students.

New Jersey Student Tuition Assistance Reward Scholarship II enables successful NJ STARS scholars to transfer to a New Jersey four-year college or university and earn a Bachelor's degree.

New Jersey World Trade Center Scholarship benefits dependent children and surviving spouses of New Jersey residents who were killed in or who died of the terrorist attacks against the U.S. on September 11, 2001.

NJBEST Scholarship is a one-time scholarship to beneficiaries in the NJBEST 529 college savings plan, who are enrolled at least half-time in his or her first year, first semester of postsecondary education at a New Jersey institution.

Survivor Tuition Benefits Program benefits dependent children and surviving spouses of New Jersey firefighters, emergency service workers or law enforcement officers who were killed in the line of duty.

PURPOSE:
To provide financial assistance to college students demonstrating academic proficiency, and/or need.

ELIGIBILITY:
Student must be a U.S. citizen or eligible noncitizen and registered with the Selective Service. For some programs, New Jersey residency and a current-year FAFSA are required. Application deadlines, years of eligibility and payment limits apply to all programs. Contact HESAA for details.

GEOG. RESTRICTIONS: New Jersey.

FINANCIAL DATA:
Amount of support per award: New Jersey Governor's Industry Vocations Scholarship for Women and Minorities: Up to $2,000 per year or up to the cost of tuition, less any federal, state or institutional aid. NJBEST Scholarship: Varies depending upon the number of years open and level of contributions. Survivor Tuition Benefits Program: Covers the cost of tuition at any New Jersey public college or university. Students enrolled at an independent New Jersey college or university may receive up to the highest tuition charges at a New Jersey public institution.

APPLICATION INFO:
Application information as well as applications are available on the HESAA web site. Some programs require a FAFSA to be filed before applying.

Deadline: All programs have deadline dates for fall and spring terms. Contact HESAA for application deadline dates.

STAFF:
Kathryn Safran, Director, Grants and Scholarships

THE HIGHER EDUCATION STUDENT ASSISTANCE AUTHORITY   [1529]
P.O. Box 540
Trenton, NJ 08625-0540
(609) 588-3300
E-mail: clientservices@hesaa.org
Web Site: www.hesaa.org

FOUNDED: 1959

AREAS OF INTEREST:
State financial assistance for college students.

NAME(S) OF PROGRAMS:
- **Tuition Aid Grant (TAG)**

TYPE:
Grants-in-aid. The Higher Education Student Assistance Authority (HESAA) is a New Jersey authority that provides students and families with the financial and informational resources for students to pursue their education beyond high school. With roots dating back to 1959, HESAA's singular focus has always been to benefit the students it serves. HESAA provides state supplemental loans, grants and scholarships. HESAA also administers the state's college savings plan.

YEAR PROGRAM STARTED: 1969

PURPOSE:
To provide financial assistance to needy students attending approved New Jersey institutions. This is calculated by estimating what a family can contribute from income and assets plus a contribution from the student's earnings and savings. The amount

and type of aid will depend upon program eligibility, available funds and the degree of need.

LEGAL BASIS:
New Jersey Higher Education Tuition Aid Act.

ELIGIBILITY:
Applicants must be New Jersey residents for at least 12 consecutive months prior to receiving an award, and will be enrolled in an approved New Jersey institution. Student must be a U.S. citizen or eligible noncitizen and be registered with the Selective Service, if applicable. Grants are renewable annually based upon satisfactory academic progress and continued financial need. Students who have received a Baccalaureate degree are not eligible.

GEOG. RESTRICTIONS: New Jersey.

FINANCIAL DATA:
Amount of support per award: Award amounts are based on the student's New Jersey Eligibility Index, tuition charged and appropriated funds.

NO. AWARDS: Based upon appropriations.

APPLICATION INFO:
Applicants must file the Free Application for Federal Student Aid (FAFSA), including the additional New Jersey questions.
Duration: Renewable for four years of undergraduate study providing eligibility continues and an application is filed.
Deadline: February 15 for fall and spring terms. September 15 for spring term only. Renewals April 15 for fall and spring terms.

PUBLICATIONS:
State and Federal Financial Aid Programs for New Jersey Students, brochure.

HISPANIC SCHOLARSHIP FUND
1411 West 190th Street
Suite 700
Gardena, CA 90248
(877) 473-4636
(310) 975-3700
Fax: (310) 349-3328
E-mail: info@hsf.net
scholar1@hsf.net
Web Site: www.hsf.net

TYPE:
Scholarships. Awarded to Hispanic community college, undergraduate and graduate students.
See entry 975 for full listing.

THE HONOR SOCIETY OF PHI KAPPA PHI [1530]
7576 Goodwood Boulevard
Baton Rouge, LA 70806
(225) 388-4917 ext. 235
(800) 804-9880 ext. 235
Fax: (225) 388-4900
E-mail: kpartin@phikappaphi.org
Web Site: www.phikappaphi.org

FOUNDED: 1897

AREAS OF INTEREST:
Scholastic excellence in all academic fields.

NAME(S) OF PROGRAMS:
● **The Phi Kappa Phi Fellowship**

TYPE:
Fellowships. Support for the first year of graduate or professional school.

YEAR PROGRAM STARTED: 1932

PURPOSE:
To stimulate members of Phi Kappa Phi to go to graduate or professional school.

LEGAL BASIS:
Honor Society incorporated in Michigan, May 20, 1972. Authorized to operate in Louisiana, September 1978. Tax-exempt under IRS 501(c)(3). Companion organization, the Phi Kappa Phi Foundation, incorporated in California, December 17, 1969, as a Public Benefit Foundation, tax-exempt under IRS 501(c)(3).

ELIGIBILITY:
Applicant must be a member of Phi Kappa Phi, maintain high scholastic standing and be recommended by a chapter of Phi Kappa Phi.

FINANCIAL DATA:
Amount of support per award: $8,500 to $35,000.
Total amount of support: $615,000 for the year 2018.

CO-OP FUNDING PROGRAMS: Awards made through Phi Kappa Phi Foundation, a companion organization to the Society.

NO. AWARDS: 58 (50 valued at $8,500, 6 valued at $20,000 and 2 valued at $35,000) for the year 2018.

APPLICATION INFO:
Completed application packet must be returned to the local chapter on or before the deadline.
Duration: One academic year. Nonrenewable.

IRS I.D.: 95-1856406

STAFF:
Kelli Partin, Awards Manager

ADDRESS INQUIRIES TO:
Kelli Partin, Awards Manager
(See address above.)

HORTICULTURAL RESEARCH INSTITUTE, INC. [1531]
2130 Stella Court
Columbus, OH 43215
(614) 487-1117
Fax: (614) 487-1216
E-mail: jenniferg@americanhort.org
Web Site: www.hriresearch.org

AREAS OF INTEREST:
Nursery, landscape research and horticulture.

NAME(S) OF PROGRAMS:
● **Carville M. Akehurst Memorial Scholarship**
● **Timothy Bigelow and Palmer W. Bigelow, Jr. Scholarship**
● **Bryan A. Champion Memorial Scholarship**
● **Muggets Scholarship**
● **Spring Meadow Nursery Scholarship**
● **Usrey Family Scholarship**
● **Susie and Bruce Usrey Education Scholarship**

TYPE:
Scholarships.

YEAR PROGRAM STARTED: 1988

PURPOSE:
To aid students seeking a career in the horticulture industry.

LEGAL BASIS:
Nonprofit organization.

ELIGIBILITY:
Varies.

GEOG. RESTRICTIONS: Varies.

FINANCIAL DATA:
Amount of support per award: $500 to $5,000.
Total amount of support: Varies.

NO. AWARDS: 9 for the academic year 2019-20.

APPLICATION INFO:
Applications are available online.
Deadline: September 8.

IRS I.D.: 52-1052547

ADDRESS INQUIRIES TO:
See e-mail address above.

ILLINOIS RESTAURANT ASSOCIATION EDUCATIONAL FOUNDATION [1532]
33 West Monroe, Suite 250
Chicago, IL 60603
(312) 787-4000
E-mail: kkramer@illinoisrestaurants.org
Web Site: www.illinoisrestaurants.org

FOUNDED: 1973

AREAS OF INTEREST:
Foodservice/restaurant/hospitality.

NAME(S) OF PROGRAMS:
● **IRA Educational Foundation Scholarship Program**

TYPE:
Product donations; Scholarships.

YEAR PROGRAM STARTED: 1973

PURPOSE:
To build the Illinois hospitality workforce through the ProStart® curriculum, career exploration, workforce development and scholarships for high school students.

LEGAL BASIS:
Not-for-profit organization.

ELIGIBILITY:
Applicants must be permanent residents of the state of Illinois who are applying to or enrolled in an accredited culinary school, college or university and who are enrolled full-time or substantial part-time, taking a minimum of nine credit hours each term, majoring in a culinary restaurant management or foodservice-related program.

GEOG. RESTRICTIONS: Illinois.

FINANCIAL DATA:
Scholarships provide assistance toward tuition and materials.
Amount of support per award: Varies.

NO. MOST RECENT APPLICANTS: 84.

NO. AWARDS: 84.

APPLICATION INFO:
Application forms are available on the web site.
Duration: One academic year. Renewal is not automatic.
Deadline: April 29.

IRS I.D.: 36-3271510

ADDRESS INQUIRIES TO:
ProStart® Manager
Tel: 312-380-4117
Fax: 312-787-4792
(See address above.)

INDIANA COMMISSION FOR HIGHER EDUCATION, DIVISION OF STUDENT FINANCIAL AID   [1533]

101 West Ohio Street
Suite 300
Indianapolis, IN 46204-4206
(317) 464-4400
(888) 528-4719
Fax: (317) 232-3260
E-mail: awards@che.in.gov
Web Site: www.in.gov/che/4498.htm

FOUNDED: 1965

AREAS OF INTEREST:
    Student financial aid.

NAME(S) OF PROGRAMS:
  • **William A. Crawford Minority Teacher Scholarship**
  • **Mitch Daniels Early Graduation Scholarship**
  • **EARN Indiana (State Work Study)**
  • **National Guard Supplemental Grant**
  • **Next Generation Hoosier Educators Scholarship**
  • **The Frank O'Bannon Grant**
  • **Earlene S. Rodgers Student Teaching Stipend for Minorities**
  • **Student Teaching Stipend for High-Needs Fields**
  • **21st Century Scholars Program**

TYPE:
    Grants-in-aid; Project/program grants; Scholarships; Work-study programs. Monetary grants awarded annually toward the cost of tuition.

    The Crawford Minority Teacher Scholarship was created to address the critical shortage of Black and Hispanic teachers in Indiana.

    The Next Generation Hoosier Educators Scholarship provides high-achieving high school and college students interested in pursuing a career in education the opportunity to earn a renewable scholarship. In exchange, students agree to teach for five years at an eligible Indiana school or repay the corresponding, prorated amount of the scholarship.

    The Rodgers Student Teaching Stipend for Minorities is for minority students (defined as Black and Hispanic) who plan to teach.

    Student Teaching Stipend for High-Needs Fields is for students who plan to teach in "high-need" fields, which means a teaching specialty that affects the economic vitality of Indiana and in which there is a shortage of candidates.

    21st Century Scholars Program was created as Indiana's way of raising the educational aspirations of low- and moderate-income families.

YEAR PROGRAM STARTED: 1971

PURPOSE:
    To provide financial assistance to students attending colleges within the state of Indiana.

LEGAL BASIS:
    Indiana Scholarship Act, I.C. 20-12-21. I.C. 20-12-21.1.

ELIGIBILITY:
    An applicant must be an Indiana resident, a U.S. citizen or eligible noncitizen and must attend an eligible institution located within the state of Indiana as a full-time undergraduate student (12 to 15 hours per term).

GEOG. RESTRICTIONS: Indiana.

FINANCIAL DATA:
    Amount of support per award: Varies.
    Total amount of support: Varies.
    Matching fund requirements: Only in EARN Indiana.

NO. AWARDS: Varies.

APPLICATION INFO:
    Free Application for Federal Student Aid (FAFSA) must be received by deadline for The Frank O'Bannon Grant.

    21st Century Scholars Program: Must sign and submit pledge affirmation before March 10. File for state and federal financial aid by completing the FAFSA on time. Apply for admission and institutional financial aid at the Indiana college attending by the deadline for each college. Enroll as a full-time college student and maintain Indiana residency.

    Duration: Four years. Reapplication required annually.

    Deadline: Mitch Daniels Early Graduation and Minority Teacher Scholarships: September 4. EARN Indiana, The Frank O'Bannon Grant and 21st Century Scholars Program: March 10. Student Teaching Stipend: October 4 for fall term and January 31 for spring term.

PUBLICATIONS:
    Application guidelines.

ADDRESS INQUIRIES TO:
    Indiana Commission for Higher Education (See address above.)

INSTITUTE FOR THE INTERNATIONAL EDUCATION OF STUDENTS (IES)   [1534]

33 West Monroe Street
Suite 2300
Chicago, IL 60603-5405
(312) 944-1750
(800) 995-2300
Fax: (312) 944-1448
E-mail: info@IESabroad.org
Web Site: www.IESabroad.org

FOUNDED: 1950

AREAS OF INTEREST:
    International education (JYA).

NAME(S) OF PROGRAMS:
  • **Boren and Gilman Scholarship Support Grants**
  • **Disability Grants**
  • **Diversity Scholarships**
  • **Donor Funded Scholarships**
  • **Need Based Aid**
  • **Partner University Scholarships**
  • **Public University Grants**

TYPE:
    Awards/prizes; Scholarships. Boren and Gilman Scholarship Support Grants: This program offers recipients of these prestigious scholarships the opportunity to apply for additional financial support.

    Disability Grants: This program's purpose is to enhance study abroad opportunities for students with disabilities. It offers grants to students whose disabilities may add significant costs to their study abroad experience.

    Diversity Scholarships: This program offers one way to encourage and support students from a range of institutions and underrepresented populations. Underrepresented students include students from underrepresented racial and ethnic

groups, first-generation-to-college students, students from low-income families and students with a history of overcoming adversity.

    Donor Funded Scholarships: These scholarship opportunities have been created through the generosity of various donors who support the important mission of IES Abroad.

    Need Based Aid: This program is available to students with demonstrated financial need. Priority is given to Pell Grant recipients.

    Partner University Scholarships: These scholarships are funded by IES Abroad partner universities in countries where IES has programs.

    Public University Grants: This program offers an automatic $2,000 credit toward a semester or academic year program.

YEAR PROGRAM STARTED: 1950

PURPOSE:
    To provide study opportunities abroad for qualified undergraduate students from U.S. colleges and universities.

LEGAL BASIS:
    Not-for-profit educational organization organized under the laws of Illinois.

ELIGIBILITY:
    All aid categories require applicants to be accepted to and attend an IES Abroad standard program. (Customized programs are not eligible for IES Abroad aid.)

    Some aid categories require that applicants attend a college or university that is part of the IES Abroad Consortium and that transfers at least 75% of institutional aid for study abroad expenses.

FINANCIAL DATA:
    Amount of support per award: Boren and Gilman Scholarship Support Grants: $500 for summer program; $1,000 for fall or spring program. Disability Grants: $500. Diversity Scholarships: Up to $5,000 depending on category. Donor Funded Scholarships: Award amounts vary by category. Need Based Aid: Up to $5,000 (fall or spring programs); up to $1,000 (summer programs). Public University Grants: $2,000.

    Total amount of support: For the 2017-18 academic year: $55,000 in Boren and Gilman Scholarship Support Grants; $2,000 in Disability Grants; $85,000 in Diversity Scholarships; $318,650 in Donor Funded Scholarships; $908,800 in Need Based Aid; $43,573 in Partner University Scholarships; $3,422,000 in Public University Grants; $271,269 in other miscellaneous aid.

NO. MOST RECENT APPLICANTS: Approximately 3,000.

NO. AWARDS: Boren and Gilman Scholarship Support Grants: 63; Disability Grants: 4; Diversity Scholarships: 37; Donor Funded Scholarships: 171; Need Based Aid: 617; Partner University Scholarships: 11; Public University Grants: 1,711; Miscellaneous Aid: 148.

APPLICATION INFO:
    Applications may be submitted online.

    Duration: Academic year, one semester, or summer (need-based only). Nonrenewable.

    Deadline: May 1 for fall semester and academic year; November 1 for spring semester; April 1 for summer.

PUBLICATIONS:
Annual report; IES Abroad Alumni Exchange Newsletter; IES Abroad catalogs; IES MAP©.

IRS I.D.: 36-2251912

GOVERNING BOARD:
Ezio Vergani, Chairperson
Robert Browne
Mary Cahillane
Susan Carty
James Crawford
Debora de Hoyos
Dr. Mary Dwyer
Marie Fioramonti
Dr. Pamela Brooks Gann
Phyllis Haberman
Rhonda Jordan
Robert McNeill
Mary O'Brien Pearlman
Dr. Marla Salmon
Alan Schwartz
Clayton Spencer
Sheila A. Stamps
Peter E. Sundman
Dr. Lara Tiedens
Monica Vachher

ADDRESS INQUIRIES TO:
Joseph Sevigny, Associate Vice President of Enrollment Management
(See address above.)

INTERNATIONAL ASSOCIATION OF FIRE CHIEFS FOUNDATION, INC. [1535]

4795 Meadow Wood Lane
Suite 100
Chantilly, VA 20151
(703) 273-0911
Fax: (703) 273-9363
E-mail: foundation@iafc.org
Web Site: www.iafcf.org

FOUNDED: 1974

AREAS OF INTEREST:
Fire prevention and research.

NAME(S) OF PROGRAMS:
- **International Association of Fire Chiefs Foundation Scholarship Program**

TYPE:
Scholarships. Scholarships for advanced study in fire science, fire department administration and operation, public administration or any fire-related program.

YEAR PROGRAM STARTED: 1974

PURPOSE:
To aid in better fire service administration and to support training in this area.

ELIGIBILITY:
Under the regulations, any member of the fire service who is an active member of U.S. or Canadian Fire Service in a state, county, provincial, municipal, community, industrial or federal fire department, and who has demonstrated proficiency as a member, is eligible to apply for a scholarship to a recognized institution of higher education of his or her choice. Applicants must have the approval of their department chiefs. Dependents are not eligible.

GEOG. RESTRICTIONS: United States.

FINANCIAL DATA:
Amount of support per award: Generally $250 to $2,000, providing a maximum of this dollar amount toward tuition costs.

Total amount of support: Approximately $45,000 per year.

NO. MOST RECENT APPLICANTS: 57.

NO. AWARDS: Approximately 46.

APPLICATION INFO:
Application information is available on the web site.
Duration: One year.
Deadline: April 30.

PUBLICATIONS:
Application guidelines.

ADDRESS INQUIRIES TO:
Terry Monroe
Association Manager for Foundation
(See address above.)

INTERNATIONAL DEVELOPMENT RESEARCH CENTRE (IDRC)

150 Kent Street
Ottawa ON K1P 0B2 Canada
(613) 696-2098
E-mail: awards@idrc.ca
Web Site: www.idrc.ca
www.crdi.ca

TYPE:
Awards/prizes. These awards are offered once a year and are intended for field research in one or more developing countries. Candidates must conduct their research in areas corresponding to IDRC's research priorities.

See entry 1193 for full listing.

IODE [1536]

40 Orchard View Boulevard, Suite 219
Toronto ON M4R 1B9 Canada
(416) 487-4416
Fax: (416) 487-4417
E-mail: iodecanada@bellnet.ca
Web Site: www.iode.ca

FOUNDED: 1900

AREAS OF INTEREST:
Education, social service and citizenship.

NAME(S) OF PROGRAMS:
- **War Memorial Scholarships**

TYPE:
Scholarships. Postgraduate scholarships tenable in any university in Canada and the Commonwealth.

YEAR PROGRAM STARTED: 1920

PURPOSE:
To provide scholarships for educational purposes as a memorial to Canadian men and women who gave their lives in defense of freedom during World Wars I and II.

LEGAL BASIS:
Charitable organization.

ELIGIBILITY:
Candidates must be Canadian citizens. At the time of application, candidates must hold a first degree from a Canadian university and be enrolled in at least the second year of a doctoral program.

GEOG. RESTRICTIONS: Canada and the Commonwealth.

FINANCIAL DATA:
Amount of support per award: $15,000 (CAN) for study in Canada and for study overseas within the Commonwealth for the 2020-21 academic year.

NO. AWARDS: 3 for the 2020-21 academic year.

APPLICATION INFO:
A candidate must apply to the War Memorial Convener in the province in which the first degree was obtained. The names of Conveners change from year to year, but appear in the scholarship folder. Application must be submitted online.
Duration: One year.
Deadline: Applications must reach the Convener of the province from which the first degree was obtained by November 1.

OFFICERS:
Hazel MacLeod, National War Memorial Officer

TRUSTEES:
Carol McCall, National President

ADDRESS INQUIRIES TO:
E-mail: iodewarmemorial@gmail.com

THE JAPAN FOUNDATION, LOS ANGELES [1537]

5700 Wilshire Boulevard
Suite 100
Los Angeles, CA 90036
(323) 761-7510
Fax: (323) 761-7517
E-mail: culture@jflalc.org
Web Site: www.jflalc.org

FOUNDED: 1983

AREAS OF INTEREST:
Japanese arts, culture and language education.

NAME(S) OF PROGRAMS:
- **Arts & Culture Grants**
- **J-LEAP**
- **Japanese Language Grants**

TYPE:
Conferences/seminars; Exchange programs; Fellowships; Grants-in-aid; Product donations; Project/program grants; Research grants; Training grants; Visiting scholars.

PURPOSE:
To support grants that promote Japanese arts, culture, language and education.

ELIGIBILITY:
Candidates must be citizens or permanent residents of the U.S.

GEOG. RESTRICTIONS: United States.

FINANCIAL DATA:
Amount of support per award: Varies.
Total amount of support: Varies.

APPLICATION INFO:
Guidelines are available online.
Duration: Arts & Culture Grants and Japanese Language Grants: One year; J-LEAP: Two years.
Deadline: Varies.

THE JAPANESE AMERICAN CITIZENS LEAGUE (JACL) [1538]

JACL National Office
1629 K Street, Suite 400
Washington, DC 20006
(202) 223-1240
E-mail: sfjacl@yahoo.com
policy@jacl.org
Web Site: www.jacl.org

FOUNDED: 1929

AREAS OF INTEREST:
Education, cultural preservation, and civil rights.

NAME(S) OF PROGRAMS:
- **JACL National Scholarship and Awards Program**

TYPE:
Scholarships. JACL offers more than 30 scholarships and student aid awards (financial aid).

Scholarship categories: Entering Freshman (High School Senior), Undergraduate, Graduate, Law, Creative and Performing Arts, and Financial Aid.

YEAR PROGRAM STARTED: 1946

PURPOSE:
To recognize education as a key to greater opportunities for its members.

ELIGIBILITY:
Applicant must be an active National JACL member at either an individual or student/youth level. Applicants must be planning to attend full-time an institution of higher learning within the U.S. at the undergraduate or graduate school level. Applicants may apply under only one scholarship category. Entering freshman applicants must be high school seniors. Creative and performing arts applicants cannot be professional artists.

JACL membership is open to everyone of any ethnic background.

FINANCIAL DATA:
Amount of support per award: $1,000 to $5,000.
Total amount of support: Over $70,000 in scholarships.

APPLICATION INFO:
Information brochure and applications are posted on the JACL web site annually in November.

Freshman applications must be postmarked and mailed to the local JACL chapter to which the applicant belongs. All other applications must be postmarked and mailed to the address on the application form.
Duration: One year. Limited to a total of two awards.
Deadline: Freshman Application: March 1; All others: First week of April.

ADDRESS INQUIRIES TO:
Patty Wada, Regional Director
E-mail: pwada@jacl.org

JEWISH FAMILY AND CHILDREN'S SERVICES   [1539]
2150 Post Street
San Francisco, CA 94115
(415) 449-1226
Fax: (844) 492-3928
TDD: (415) 567-1044
E-mail: michellel@jfcs.org
Web Site: www.jfcs.org

FOUNDED: 1850

AREAS OF INTEREST:
Jewish individuals and their families, college tuition and expenses, vocational training and loans for business and professional endeavors.

NAME(S) OF PROGRAMS:
- **Educational Loans and Grants Program**

TYPE:
Grants-in-aid. Need-based loans and grants.

PURPOSE:
To provide educational loans and grants to Jewish graduate and undergraduate students.

LEGAL BASIS:
Nonprofit.

ELIGIBILITY:
Applicants must be students of Jewish descent who have demonstrated academic achievement (generally demonstrated by a 3.0 grade point average on a 4.0 scale), financial need, broad-based extracurricular activities and in-depth community involvement and acceptance to an accredited college, university or vocational school.

GEOG. RESTRICTIONS: Marin, San Francisco, San Mateo, Santa Clara, or Sonoma counties, California.

FINANCIAL DATA:
Amount of support per award: Need-based grants: $500 to $2,500; Loans: $1,000 to $6,000.
Total amount of support: Up to $6,000 per student, per year.

NO. MOST RECENT APPLICANTS: 65.

NO. AWARDS: Varies per year.

APPLICATION INFO:
Application information is available on the web site beginning the first week of May. Contact the organization's Director of Financial Aid Center for more information.
Duration: One academic year.
Deadline: First week of July. However, applications will be accepted until funding is exhausted.

PUBLICATIONS:
Program announcement.

ADDRESS INQUIRIES TO:
Michelle Lamphere
Director, JFCS Financial Aid Center
(See address above.)

JEWISH FEDERATION OF METROPOLITAN CHICAGO ACADEMIC SCHOLARSHIP PROGRAM   [1540]
JVS Career and Employment/JCFS Chicago
216 West Jackson Boulevard, Suite 700
Chicago, IL 60606-6921
(312) 673-3444
Fax: (312) 553-5544
E-mail: jvsscholarship@jcfs.org
Web Site: www.jcfs.org/jvsscholarships

FOUNDED: 1959

AREAS OF INTEREST:
Higher education for Jewish students in full-time academic programs in the helping professions, legally domiciled in the metropolitan Chicago (IL) area.

TYPE:
Awards/prizes; Scholarships. Awards to individuals for the academic year.

YEAR PROGRAM STARTED: 1959

PURPOSE:
To provide financial support to Jewish men and women for their full-time academic programs.

LEGAL BASIS:
Tax-exempt private foundation.

ELIGIBILITY:
Scholarships are awarded on the basis of financial need. Applicants must be full-time

students of Jewish background, legally domiciled in the metropolitan Chicago area. Applicants must have demonstrated career promise. Assistance is available for the fields listed below, including but not limited to:
(1) the helping professions such as medicine, dentistry, social work, education, psychology, the rabbinate and noncorporate areas of law;
(2) mathematics, engineering and other sciences and;
(3) communications within the College of Media at the University of Illinois at Urbana-Champaign.

Additional requirements:
(1) undergraduates entering or who have entered the junior year in career-specific programs which require no postgraduate education for professional-level employment in one of the professional areas mentioned above or;
(2) students entering or who have entered a graduate or professional school in a helping profession described above or;
(3) students in a vocational training program with a specific educational goal in the helping professions.

Newcomers who are refugees or asylees are encouraged to apply. Citizenship is not a prerequisite.

FINANCIAL DATA:
Amount of support per award: Up to $8,000.
Total amount of support: Approximately $500,000 per year.

CO-OP FUNDING PROGRAMS: Program is administered by JVS Career and Employment/JCFS Chicago.

NO. MOST RECENT APPLICANTS: Approximately 130 for the year 2018.

NO. AWARDS: Approximately 90.

APPLICATION INFO:
Application submission must include application form, budget worksheet, personal and financial data, IRS Form 1040, proof of (Cook County) legal domicility, two reference letters, autobiography and official academic transcript. Applicants must be available for a personal interview at JVS Career and Employment/JCFS Chicago offices located throughout the Chicago metropolitan area prior to April 20.

Applications are available in the fall and can be downloaded from the JVS Career and Employment/JCFS Chicago web site. (Click on "Scholarship Services.").
Duration: One academic year. Recipients may reapply for renewal.
Deadline: February 1 for submission of applications.

OFFICERS:
Sally Yarberry, Scholarship Coordinator

ADDRESS INQUIRIES TO:
Scholarship Coordinator
(See address and phone number above.)

*SPECIAL STIPULATIONS:
All applicants must be available for a personal interview at the JVS Career and Employment/JCFS Chicago offices located throughout the Chicago metropolitan area.

KANSAS BOARD OF REGENTS [1541]

1000 S.W. Jackson, Suite 520
Topeka, KS 66612-1368
(785) 430-4240
Fax: (785) 430-4233
E-mail: dlindeman@ksbor.org
Web Site: www.kansasregents.org

FOUNDED: 1925

AREAS OF INTEREST:
Higher education.

NAME(S) OF PROGRAMS:
- **Kansas Comprehensive Grant**

TYPE:
Grants-in-aid. Grant-in-aid is available to students with demonstrated financial need attending the four-year public and independent colleges and universities in Kansas.

YEAR PROGRAM STARTED: 1999

PURPOSE:
To provide access and choice for needy students attending either public or independent four-year colleges and universities in the state.

ELIGIBILITY:
Students must be U.S. citizens or residents and Kansas resident undergraduates, attending either a four-year public or independent college/university, and have demonstrated financial need as determined by the Free Application for Federal Student Aid (FAFSA) need analysis.

GEOG. RESTRICTIONS: Kansas.

FINANCIAL DATA:
Amount of support per award: Eligible students attending four-year public colleges and universities may be awarded up to $1,500 annually. Eligible students attending four-year independent colleges and universities may be awarded up to $3,500 annually.
Total amount of support: $15,758,338 for the 2017-18 academic year.

NO. MOST RECENT APPLICANTS: 25,826.

NO. AWARDS: 9,200.

APPLICATION INFO:
No application other than the FAFSA.
Duration: Annual award. Students need to file their FAFSA annually.
Deadline: Priority deadline is April 1 annually.

ADDRESS INQUIRIES TO:
Diane Lindeman
Director of Student Financial Assistance
(See address above.)

KENTUCKY HIGHER EDUCATION ASSISTANCE AUTHORITY (KHEAA) [1542]

P.O. Box 798
Frankfort, KY 40602-0798
(800) 928-8926
Fax: (502) 696-7373
E-mail: studentaid@kheaa.com
Web Site: www.kheaa.com

FOUNDED: 1966

AREAS OF INTEREST:
Postsecondary student financial assistance.

NAME(S) OF PROGRAMS:
- **College Access Program (CAP)**
- **Kentucky Educational Excellence Scholarship (KEES)**
- **Kentucky Tuition Grant (KTG)**

TYPE:
Grants-in-aid; Scholarships. Need-based or incentive-based student aid; College Access Program helps Kentucky's financially needy undergraduate students attend eligible public and private Kentucky colleges, universities, proprietary schools and technical colleges.

Kentucky Educational Excellence Scholarship awards scholarships to Kentucky high school students based on grade point average and ACT/SAT scores to encourage them to attend a college or university in Kentucky. Low-income students may earn additional awards based on Advanced Placement (AP) or International Baccalaureate (IB) exam scores.

Kentucky Tuition Grant provides a tuition equalization grant to help Kentucky residents attend eligible Kentucky private colleges.

PURPOSE:
To provide financial aid to students.

ELIGIBILITY:
Applicant must be a U.S. citizen or resident.

College Access Program: Student must reside in Kentucky, demonstrate financial need, attend an eligible college or university, have no past due financial obligations to KHEAA or any Title IV program, and be enrolled at least half-time in a program of study at least two years in length.

Kentucky Educational Excellence Scholarship: Student must earn at least a 2.5 grade point average in any year of high school in Kentucky while meeting Kentucky Educational Excellence Scholarship curriculum requirements. Student must reside in Kentucky and attend and graduate from a certified Kentucky high school. Student must have an ACT composite score of 15 or higher for ACT bonus. Convicted felons will be disqualified.

Kentucky Tuition Grant: Student must reside in Kentucky, demonstrate financial need, attend an eligible college or university, have no past due financial obligations to KHEAA or any Title IV program, and be enrolled full-time in an Associate or Bachelor's degree program.

FINANCIAL DATA:
Amount of support per award: College Access Program: Up to $2,000 per academic year at two-year schools, up to $2,200 per academic year at four-year schools; Kentucky Educational Excellence Scholarship: Varies by student; Kentucky Tuition Grant: Up to $3,000 per academic year.

NO. AWARDS: CAP: 55,100; KEES: 70,900; CTG: 12,800.

APPLICATION INFO:
College Access Program and Kentucky Tuition Grant : Applicant must complete the Free Application for Federal Student Aid (FAFSA) (available at www.fafsa.ed.gov).
Duration: College Access Program and Kentucky Tuition Grant: Awarded on an annual basis. Nonrenewable. Kentucky Educational Excellence Scholarship: Funds awarded based on high school academic performance. Renewal requirements must be met annually once the student is in college.
Deadline: College Access Program and Kentucky Tuition Grant: End of FAFSA processing year, which is the end of the academic year.

ADDRESS INQUIRIES TO:
Customer Care
Kentucky Higher Education
Assistance Authority
(See address or phone number above.)

KENTUCKY HIGHER EDUCATION ASSISTANCE AUTHORITY (KHEAA) [1543]

P.O. Box 798
Frankfort, KY 40602-0798
(800) 928-8926
Fax: (502) 696-7373
E-mail: studentaid@kheaa.com
Web Site: www.kheaa.com

FOUNDED: 1966

AREAS OF INTEREST:
Postsecondary student financial assistance.

NAME(S) OF PROGRAMS:
- **Kentucky National Guard Tuition Award Program**

TYPE:
Need-based student aid; Military service grant. Kentucky National Guard Tuition Award Program provides tuition assistance for active members of the Kentucky National Guard to attend a Kentucky college or university.

PURPOSE:
To provide financial aid to students.

ELIGIBILITY:
Applicants must be U.S. citizens or residents. Student must be an active member of the Kentucky National Guard, maintain all minimum eligibility standards, be eligible for all positive personnel actions, and have completed basic training or its equivalent.

FINANCIAL DATA:
Amount of support per award: Up to in-state tuition for full- or part-time study at a Kentucky public university.

NO. AWARDS: 1,100.

APPLICATION INFO:
Application available online (https://ky.ngb.army.mil/tuitionstudent) or contact the Boone National Guard at (502) 607-1039.

ADDRESS INQUIRIES TO:
Student Aid
Kentucky Higher Education
Assistance Authority
(See address or phone number above.)

KNIGHTS OF COLUMBUS [1544]

One Columbus Plaza
New Haven, CT 06510
(203) 752-4332
Fax: (203) 752-4103
E-mail: scholarships@kofc.org
Web Site: www.kofc.org/scholarships

AREAS OF INTEREST:
Educational support.

NAME(S) OF PROGRAMS:
- **Bishop Charles P. Greco Graduate Fellowships**
- **John W. McDevitt (Fourth Degree) Scholarships**
- **Pro Deo and Pro Patria Scholarships**

TYPE:
Fellowships; Project/program grants; Scholarships. Scholarships and fellowships are awarded to members of The Knights of

Columbus in good standing, a son or daughter of such a member or deceased member, or to a member of the Columbian Squires.

The Bishop Greco Graduate Fellowships are for full-time graduate study leading to a Master's degree in a program for classroom teachers of persons with intellectual disabilities.

The John W. McDevitt (Fourth Degree) Scholarships are awarded to students entering the freshman class of undergraduate study at a Catholic college or university in the U.S.

For the Pro Deo and Pro Patria Scholarships, students must be entering the freshman class in a college program leading to a Bachelor's degree. Scholarships are available at The Catholic University of America in Washington, DC and to students entering other Catholic colleges in the U.S.

PURPOSE:
To provide support for community activities, education; to provide financial assistance to children of members in good standing.

ELIGIBILITY:
For Bishop Greco Graduate Fellowships, applicants must be enrolled in a graduate study program leading to a Master's degree in a program designed for the preparation of classroom teachers of persons with intellectual disabilities. Membership requirements as listed for the scholarship above also apply for this award.

For McDevitt (Fourth Degree) Scholarships, applicants must be members in good standing of the Knights of Columbus or the wife, widow, son or daughter of such a member or deceased member.

For Pro Deo and Pro Patria Scholarships, applicants must be students entering in the freshman class in a Catholic college program leading to a Bachelor's degree. An applicant must be a member in good standing of the Knights of Columbus or the son or daughter of such a member, a deceased member or a member in good standing of the Columbian Squires.

GEOG. RESTRICTIONS: United States.

FINANCIAL DATA:
Amount of support per award: Bishop Greco Graduate Fellowships: $2,000 maximum per year; McDevitt (Fourth Degree) Scholarships: $1,500; Pro Deo and Pro Patria Scholarships: $1,500 per year.

Total amount of support: $711,519 in scholarships for the academic year 2017-18.

NO. AWARDS: 450 for the academic year 2017-18.

APPLICATION INFO:
Application order form required. Candidates are required to submit supporting documents to substantiate eligibility.

To be considered on a financial basis, applicant must include SAR report (within the FAFSA).

Duration: Pro Deo and Pro Patria Scholarships: Up to four years. Greco Graduate Fellowship: Up to two years.

Deadline: March 1 for U.S. students. May 1 for Canadian students.

ADDRESS INQUIRIES TO:
Department of Scholarships
(See address above.)

*SPECIAL STIPULATIONS:
Candidates for Educational Trust Fund scholarships will be required to submit supporting documents to substantiate the claim.

THE KOSCIUSZKO FOUNDATION, INC. [1545]
15 East 65th Street
New York, NY 10065
(212) 734-2130 ext. 412
E-mail: addy@thekf.org
Web Site: www.thekf.org/kf/scholarships/tuition/
FOUNDED: 1925

AREAS OF INTEREST:
Scholarships and grant support for Americans of Polish descent and to Americans whose majors focus on Polish language, history and culture; funding for graduate-level studies in the U.S.

NAME(S) OF PROGRAMS:
● **The Kosciuszko Foundation Tuition Scholarship**

TYPE:
Scholarships. Offers funding to American citizens of Polish descent and to Polish citizens who have permanent residency status in the U.S. Scholarships are for Master's and Ph.D. students for full-time studies only. Undergraduate seniors may apply for a scholarship towards their first year of Master's-level studies. Americans (non-Polish descent) are eligible for graduate-level studies when majoring in Polish language, history or culture.

All majors are supported. However, the Kosciuszko Foundation has special funding allocated in the following areas: law and engineering studies at DePaul University and nonpublic colleges and universities in Illinois, Indiana, Iowa, Kansas, Michigan, Minnesota, Missouri, Nebraska, North Dakota, Ohio, South Dakota, Wisconsin and Bayonne, NJ residents; residents of Connecticut, particularly Fairfield and New Haven counties; Amsterdam, NY, Chicopee, MA and New Hampshire and; for violin and piano.

Contact Foundation for additional funding opportunities.

YEAR PROGRAM STARTED: 1950

PURPOSE:
To promote higher education of Americans of Polish descent and Polish studies.

LEGAL BASIS:
501(c)(3) not-for-profit organization which is engaged in educational and cultural relations between the U.S. and Poland.

ELIGIBILITY:
Applicants must:
(1) be U.S. citizens of Polish descent or;
(2) be Polish citizens who have legal permanent residency status in the U.S. or;
(3) be Americans of non-Polish descent who are pursuing Polish majors and;
(4) have a minimum grade point average of 3.0.

Scholarships are awarded on the basis of academic excellence and evidence of identification with the Polish-American community. Financial need is taken into consideration. Scholarships are for full-time graduate study in the U.S. and certain programs in Poland.

Within the parameters of the scholarship program are special opportunities for studies in journalism, nursing, teaching, business, piano performance, law, arts, social sciences and education.

GEOG. RESTRICTIONS: United States and Poland.

FINANCIAL DATA:
Funding for tuition and educational expenses such as books and fees associated with attendance at colleges and universities.
Amount of support per award: $1,000 to $7,000.
Total amount of support: $267,435 for the academic year 2019.

NO. AWARDS: 91.

APPLICATION INFO:
Detailed instructions are available on the Foundation web site. Completed applications must be accompanied by a nonrefundable $35 application fee.
Duration: One academic year. Possible renewal for a second year upon reapplication.
Deadline: Mid-January. Notification in May. Funding for the following academic year.

PUBLICATIONS:
Guidelines; *KF Newsletter*; grants brochure; annual report.

IRS I.D.: 13-1628179

STAFF:
Marek Skulimowski, President and Executive Director

ADDRESS INQUIRIES TO:
Addy Tymczyszyn, Coordinator
(See e-mail address above.)

*SPECIAL STIPULATIONS:
Scholarship checks are issued upon proof of full-time status.

THE KOSCIUSZKO FOUNDATION, INC. [1546]
15 East 65th Street
New York, NY 10065
(212) 734-2130 ext. 412
E-mail: addy@thekf.org
Web Site: www.thekf.org/kf/programs/study/wsips

AREAS OF INTEREST:
Strengthening of cultural and educational bonds between the U.S. and Poland through an exchange program to Poland for the purpose of Polish language and culture studies.

NAME(S) OF PROGRAMS:
● **Wisconsin Study in Poland (WSIP)**

TYPE:
Scholarships. The Wisconsin Study in Poland program offers a four- or six-week Polish language and culture scholarship at the Jagiellonian University in Krakow during the summer session.

PURPOSE:
To enable Wisconsin residents of Polish descent the opportunity to pursue a short-term course of Polish language and culture studies abroad.

LEGAL BASIS:
501(c)(3) not-for-profit organization.

ELIGIBILITY:
Applicant must meet all requirements for the Summer Study Abroad Program. Applicant must be a Wisconsin resident of Polish descent. Consideration may also be given to nonresident Wisconsin students of Polish descent if they are attending Wisconsin

college or university. Candidate must have a cumulative grade point average of 3.0 or higher.

Previous knowledge of the Polish language is not required.

FINANCIAL DATA:
Scholarship covers the cost of program fees, including tuition, course materials and textbooks, a shared room, two meals per day, and complementary programs such as sightseeing. Scholarship recipients will be responsible for their own transportation, health care coverage and all other costs.
Total amount of support: $4,840 for the year 2019.

NO. AWARDS: 2 scholarships per year.

APPLICATION INFO:
Details are available on the Foundation web site. A $35 nonrefundable scholarship application fee is required.
Duration: Four- or six-week program, to begin in July.
Deadline: Mid-April. E-mail notification in May.

PUBLICATIONS:
KF Newsletter; annual report.

IRS I.D.: 13-1628179

STAFF:
Marek Skulimowski, President and Executive Director

ADDRESS INQUIRIES TO:
Addy Tymczyszyn, Coordinator
Wisconsin Study in Poland
(See e-mail address above.)

*PLEASE NOTE:
Students who receive scholarship funding will be required to submit a $95 nonrefundable registration fee, as well as additional application materials.

LORAN SCHOLARS FOUNDATION   [1547]
460 Richmond Street West, Suite 502
Toronto ON M5V 1Y1 Canada
(416) 646-2120
Fax: (416) 646-0846
E-mail: info@loranscholar.ca
Web Site: www.loranscholar.ca
www.boursierloran.ca

FOUNDED: 1988

AREAS OF INTEREST:
Higher education.

NAME(S) OF PROGRAMS:
● **Loran Awards**

TYPE:
Scholarships. Grants for graduating high school students about to enter a university in Canada. These awards include an annual stipend and matching tuition waiver, access to $10,000 in funding for summer internships, one-on-one mentorship, and annual retreats and scholar gatherings.

PURPOSE:
To identify and support talented students who demonstrate character, promise of leadership and a strong commitment to service in the community; to fund these citizens to study on Canadian campuses, to the benefit of their future and ours.

ELIGIBILITY:
Applicant must:
(1) be in the graduating year of uninterrupted

full-time studies in high school or CEGEP. Exceptions may be considered for those who have undertaken a gap year for academic pursuits or community service-based activities;
(2) present a minimum cumulative average of 85% and;
(3) hold Canadian citizenship or permanent resident status.

GEOG. RESTRICTIONS: Canada.

FINANCIAL DATA:
Amount of support per award: Valued at $100,000 for four years.
Total amount of support: $3,700,000 (CAN).

NO. AWARDS: 130 to 140 annually.

APPLICATION INFO:
Applications are available early September and can be completed online. Students should speak to their guidance counselor about their school's nomination process.
Duration: Up to four years.
Deadline: Mid-October.

ADDRESS INQUIRIES TO:
See e-mail address above.

*PLEASE NOTE:
Loran Award Finalist and Provincial Awards are tenable at any public university in Canada. Loran Awards are tenable at participating Canadian consortium universities only.

LOUISIANA DIVISION OF THE ARTS, DEPARTMENT OF CULTURE, RECREATION AND TOURISM
1051 North Third Street, Room 420
Baton Rouge, LA 70802
(225) 342-8200
Fax: (225) 342-8173
E-mail: arts@crt.la.gov
Web Site: www.crt.state.la.us/cultural-development/arts

TYPE:
General operating grants; Technical assistance. Grants in a variety of programs are offered to arts organizations across the state.

General operating support grants are offered in three levels of operating support to nonprofit arts organizations.

See entry 429 for full listing.

MARINE CORPS SCHOLARSHIP FOUNDATION, INC.   [1548]
909 North Washington Street
Suite 400
Alexandria, VA 22314
(703) 549-0060
Fax: (703) 549-9474
E-mail: scholarship@mcsf.org
Web Site: www.mcsf.org

FOUNDED: 1962

AREAS OF INTEREST:
Scholarships to eligible children of Marines and children of qualifying Navy Corpsmen, chaplains, and religious program specialists.

TYPE:
Scholarships. Scholarships are for accredited undergraduate (post-high school) college or career technical education (CTE).

YEAR PROGRAM STARTED: 1962

PURPOSE:
To provide need-based scholarships to the children of Marines and qualifying Navy Corpsmen who attend college or career training; to honor Marines by educating their children.

LEGAL BASIS:
Nonprofit, tax-exempt corporation.

ELIGIBILITY:
Applicant must be the child of an active duty or reserve U.S. Marine, or a veteran U.S. Marine who has received an honorable discharge or who was killed while serving in the U.S. Marine Corps. Children of U.S. Navy Corpsmen, chaplains, or religious specialists attached to a Marine unit may also qualify. Applicant must be planning to attend, or already attending, an accredited college or vocational/technical institution, have a grade point average of at least 2.0, and pursuing their first degree or technical certificate. Graduate study is not eligible. An income requirement must be met. Special funding is available for children of those who were wounded or killed in combat.

FINANCIAL DATA:
The Scholarship Foundation has provided over 40,000 scholarships valued at over $135,000,000 since 1962.
Amount of support per award: $1,500 to $10,000 per year.
Total amount of support: $8,200,000 for the 2019-20 academic year.

NO. MOST RECENT APPLICANTS: Over 2,900 for the 2019-20 academic year.

NO. AWARDS: Over 2,300 for the 2019-20 academic year.

APPLICATION INFO:
Application available online beginning January 1.
Duration: One year. Renewable for up to three years. Recipients must reapply.
Deadline: March 1.

PUBLICATIONS:
Annual report; guidelines; yearbook; trifold; newsletter.

IRS I.D.: 22-1905062

STAFF:
Steven D. Peterson, Chief Operating Officer
Jeanna Adams, Director, Scholarship Programs

ADDRESS INQUIRIES TO:
Director of Scholarship Programs
(See address above.)

*SPECIAL STIPULATIONS:
Cannot violate civil or campus law.

THURGOOD MARSHALL COLLEGE FUND (TMCF)   [1549]
901 F Street, N.W.
Suite 700
Washington, DC 20004
(202) 507-4861
Fax: (202) 652-2934
E-mail: scholarships@tmcf.org
Web Site: tmcf.org

FOUNDED: 1987

AREAS OF INTEREST:
Business, teaching, communications and public relations.

NAME(S) OF PROGRAMS:
● **TMCF Scholarships**

TYPE:

Scholarships. Scholarship for full-time students pursuing a degree at one of the 47 TMCF "member schools."

ELIGIBILITY:

Students must:

(1) have a minimum cumulative grade point average of 3.0 on a 4.0 scale;
(2) apply for financial aid using the Free Application for Federal Student Aid;
(3) attend one of the 47 TMCF member-schools (unless otherwise stated on the application);
(4) be a U.S. citizen or legal permanent resident with a valid permanent resident card or passport stamped;
(5) demonstrate leadership qualities and service experience and;
(6) be recommended by a faculty or staff member of one's current school.

Awards are merit-based.

GEOG. RESTRICTIONS: United States.

FINANCIAL DATA:

TMCF scholarships are restricted for payment of tuition, on-campus room and board, and books and fees.

Amount of support per award: Average $3,100 per semester.

Total amount of support: Varies.

NO. AWARDS: Nearly 500 scholarships per year.

APPLICATION INFO:

Apply online only.

Duration: Usually one academic year.

Deadline: Varies.

MARYLAND HIGHER EDUCATION COMMISSION   [1550]

Office of Student Financial Assistance (OSFA)
6 North Liberty Street
Baltimore, MD 21201
(410) 767-3301
(410) 767-3300
(800) 974-0203 (toll-free)
Fax: (410) 332-0250; (410) 332-0252
TTY: (800) 735-2258
E-mail: osfamail.mhec@maryland.gov
Web Site: mhec.maryland.gov

FOUNDED: 1961

NAME(S) OF PROGRAMS:

● **Maryland State Scholarships**

TYPE:

Grants-in-aid; Scholarships; Loan forgiveness programs. Career and occupational programs. The Howard P. Rawlings Program of Educational Excellence Awards is the state's largest need-based program. It has two components: the Educational Assistance Grant and the Guaranteed Access Grant. The Educational Assistance Grant is targeted to low- to moderate-income families and is based on financial need (40% of calculated financial need for four-year institutions, 60% for community colleges). The Guaranteed Access Grant is for very low-income high school students and requires a 2.5 high school grade point average (100% of student need up to a maximum of $19,100).

The Part-Time Grant supports part-time, degree-seeking, undergraduate students.

The Graduate and Professional School Scholarship provides support to full-time and part-time graduate and professional students in nursing, pharmacy, dentistry, law, medicine, veterinary science, and social work.

Senatorial Scholarships: Each member of the state senate may award scholarships each year.

Delegate Scholarships: Each member of the House of Delegates may award scholarships to students attending approved Maryland postsecondary institutions.

Maryland also offers a number of career/occupational and unique population financial assistance programs.

LEGAL BASIS:

Government agency.

ELIGIBILITY:

Candidate must be a resident of the state and generally enrolled or intending to enroll in a college or university in Maryland.

GEOG. RESTRICTIONS: Maryland.

FINANCIAL DATA:

Amount of support per award: Educational Assistance Grant: $400 to $3,000; Guaranteed Access Grant: Up to $19,100; Part-Time Grant: $200 to $2,000; Graduate and Professional School Scholarship: $1,000 to $5,000; Senatorial Scholarships: $400 to $11,800 annually per member of the state senate; Delegate Scholarships: Minimum $200.

Total amount of support: $1,110,000 for all aid programs (including loan repayment programs) for the 2017-18 award year. Educational Assistance Grant: $54,500,000; Guaranteed Access Grant: $21,520,592; Part-Time Grant: $5,087,780; Graduate and Professional School Scholarship: $1,168,030; Senatorial Scholarships: $6,913,562; Delegate Scholarships: $6,148,599.

NO. MOST RECENT APPLICANTS: One-time FAFSA applications: 121,243.

NO. AWARDS: 51,687, including all state grant and loan repayment programs.

APPLICATION INFO:

Use the Free Application for Federal Student Aid (FAFSA) or special program application.

Duration: Up to four years. Renewable.

Deadline: March 1 for state-administered, need-based aid program; other deadlines vary throughout the year.

PUBLICATIONS:

A Quick Guide to Cash for College and How to Get it; Student Guide to Higher Education and Financial Aid In Maryland; 6 Steps to Choosing the Right School.

ADDRESS INQUIRIES TO:

See e-mail address above.

MASSACHUSETTS MEDICAL SOCIETY (MMS)   [1551]

860 Winter Street
Waltham Woods Corporate Center
Waltham, MA 02451-1411
(781) 893-4610
(800) 322-2303
Fax: (781) 893-8009
E-mail: info@massmed.org
Web Site: www.massmed.org

FOUNDED: 1781

NAME(S) OF PROGRAMS:

● **Massachusetts Medical Society International Health Studies Grant Program**
● **Massachusetts Medical Society (MMS) Annual Scholars Program**
● **MMS Medical Information Technology Awards**
● **MMS Student Section Community Service Grants**

TYPE:

Awards/prizes; Grants-in-aid; Research grants; Scholarships. Massachusetts Medical Society International Health Studies Grant Program: Grants to defray the costs of study abroad.

Massachusetts Medical Society (MMS) Annual Scholars Program: Awarded to four students from each of the four Massachusetts medical schools.

MMS Medical Information Technology Awards: Given annually to one medical student and one resident physician.

MMS Student Section Community Service Grants: Funding for each of two service projects per medical school chapter of the Section, per calendar year.

PURPOSE:

To advance medical knowledge; to develop and maintain the highest professional and ethical standards of medical practice and health care; to promote medical institutions formed on liberal principles for the health, benefit, and welfare of the citizens of the Commonwealth.

ELIGIBILITY:

Massachusetts Medical Society International Health Studies Grant Program: MMS medical student or resident; preference given to applicants planning a career serving underprivileged populations. Massachusetts Medical Society (MMS) Annual Scholars Program: MMS member; fourth-year medical students expected to graduate each year and enrolled in a Massachusetts medical school. MMS Medical Information Technology Awards: MMS member; medical students or residents enrolled in one of the four Massachusetts Medical Schools or a Massachusetts hospital or training program. MMS Student Section Community Service Grants: Current medical student members of the MMS whose projects meet objectives in community and social service, public health activism and education or volunteer mentorship activities.

FINANCIAL DATA:

Amount of support per award: Massachusetts Medical Society International Health Studies Grant Program: Up to $2,000. Massachusetts Medical Society (MMS) Annual Scholars Program: $10,000. MMS Medical Information Technology Awards: $5,000 annually. MMS Student Section Community Service Grants: Up to $250.

NO. AWARDS: Massachusetts Medical Society International Health Studies Grant Program: 5 to 7. Massachusetts Medical Society (MMS) Annual Scholars Program: 16. MMS Medical Information Technology Awards: 1 medical student and 1 resident physician. MMS Student Section Community Service Grants: 2 service projects per medical school chapter of the Section, per calendar year.

APPLICATION INFO:

Application information is available on the web site.

Deadline: Massachusetts Medical Society International Health Studies Grant Program: Mid-November. Massachusetts Medical Society (MMS) Annual Scholars Program: Mid-January. MMS Medical Information

Technology Awards: Mid-November. MMS Student Section Community Service Grants: Accepted on a rolling deadline basis.

PUBLICATIONS:
Application guidelines.

ADDRESS INQUIRIES TO:
MMS International Health Studies Grant Program:
Jennifer Day, MMS and Alliance Charitable Foundation Director
Tel: (781) 434-7044
E-mail: jday@mms.org

MMS Annual Scholars Program:
Applicant's Office of Student Affairs or Lisa Smith, Membership Services Specialist
MMS Membership Communications and Marketing
Tel: (781) 434-7759
E-mail: lsmith@mms.org

MMS Medical Information Technology Awards
Leon Q. Barzin, MMS Technical Program Portfolio Director
Tel: (800) 322-2303 ext. 7048
E-mail: lbarzin@mms.org

MMS Student Section Community Service Grants:
Colleen Hennessey
Manager, Member Relations
Tel: (781) 434-7315
E-mail: chennessey@mms.org

MASSACHUSETTS OFFICE OF STUDENT FINANCIAL ASSISTANCE [1552]
75 Pleasant Street
Malden, MA 02148
(617) 391-6070
Fax: (617) 391-6085
E-mail: cmccurdy@dhe.mass.edu
Web Site: www.mass.edu/osfa

FOUNDED: 1980

AREAS OF INTEREST:
Financial assistance to Massachusetts students.

NAME(S) OF PROGRAMS:
● **Massachusetts Cash Grant**
● **Massachusetts Gilbert Matching Student Grant Program**
● **MASSGrants**

TYPE:
Grants-in-aid. Massachusetts Cash Grant is intended to assist needy students in meeting institutionally held charges such as mandatory fees and non-state-supported tuition. Designed as an offset of the Tuition Waiver Program, these grants provide financial support to those individuals who would otherwise be denied the opportunity for higher education.

Massachusetts Gilbert Matching Student Grant Program is based on financial need and awarded to Massachusetts residents enrolled in nonprofit private colleges.

MASSGrants are state grants in all undergraduate fields, based solely on financial need, renewable for up to four years of undergraduate study. State grants must be used at accredited institutions in Massachusetts and reciprocal states.

PURPOSE:
To assist those who are unable to meet the costs of postsecondary education.

ELIGIBILITY:
For Massachusetts Cash Grant, applicant must be a permanent legal resident of Massachusetts for one year prior to the academic year for which the grant is awarded, be a U.S. citizen or eligible noncitizen, and be in compliance with applicable laws. For Massachusetts Gilbert Matching Student Grant Program, applicants must be permanent Massachusetts residents for at least one year, attending full-time in Massachusetts. MASSGrant applicants may attend school in Massachusetts, Pennsylvania, Vermont or Washington, DC.

GEOG. RESTRICTIONS: Primarily Massachusetts.

FINANCIAL DATA:
Amount of support per award: Massachusetts Cash Grant and MASSGrant: Varies; Massachusetts Gilbert Matching Student Grant Program: $200 to $2,500 per academic year.
Total amount of support: Varies.

APPLICATION INFO:
Applicants must file the Free Application for Federal Student Aid (FAFSA) after October 1.
Deadline: Massachusetts Cash Grant and Massachusetts Gilbert Matching Student Grant Program is determined by college. MASSGrant: FAFSA must be completed by May 1 each year.

Students must meet the FAFSA priority date for Massachusetts Cash Grant, Massachusetts Gilbert Matching Student Grant Program and other state financial aid programs that are awarded directly by the college.

PUBLICATIONS:
Guidelines.

ADDRESS INQUIRIES TO:
Clantha McCurdy
Senior Deputy Commissioner
(See address above.)

MICHIGAN STATE UNIVERSITY, THE GRADUATE SCHOOL
Chittenden Hall
466 West Circle Drive
East Lansing, MI 48824
(517) 353-3220
Fax: (517) 353-3355
E-mail: gradschool@grd.msu.edu
Web Site: grad.msu.edu

TYPE:
Assistantships; Fellowships.

See entry 916 for full listing.

MISSOURI DEPARTMENT OF HIGHER EDUCATION AND WORKFORCE DEVELOPMENT [1553]
P.O. Box 1469
Jefferson City, MO 65102-1469
(573) 751-2361
(800) 473-6757 (option 4)
Fax: (573) 751-6635
E-mail: info@dhewd.mo.gov
Web Site: dhewd.mo.gov

FOUNDED: 1986

NAME(S) OF PROGRAMS:
● **Missouri Higher Education Academic Scholarship Program ("Bright Flight")**

TYPE:
Scholarships. Provides undergraduate student financial aid to qualified Missouri students who wish to attend qualified Missouri institutions of higher education, both public and private.

PURPOSE:
To enable qualified full-time students to attend a participating postsecondary institution (public and private).

LEGAL BASIS:
RSMO Supp. 173.250. Government agency.

ELIGIBILITY:
Applicant must be a resident of Missouri and a U.S. citizen or permanent resident and enrolled in an eligible Missouri institution, be a high school senior who plans to enroll as a first-time, full-time student and have a composite score on the American College Testing Program (ACT) or the Scholastic Aptitude Test (SAT) in the top five percent of all Missouri students taking the tests.

Student must take the ACT or SAT assessment and receive the required test score on or before the June test date of their senior year. GED and home-schooled students may also qualify. The Missouri Department of Higher Education will obtain the ACT or SAT assessment records, whichever the student has taken, and will notify students, high schools and postsecondary institutions of scholarship awards. Scholarships may not be used for theology for divinity studies.

GEOG. RESTRICTIONS: Missouri.

FINANCIAL DATA:
Amount of support per award: Statutory maximum award for an academic year is $3,000 for the top three percent and $1,000 for the fourth/fifth percentile.
Total amount of support: $21,254,230 for the 2019-20 academic year.

NO. AWARDS: 7,470 for the 2019-20 academic year.

APPLICATION INFO:
Eligible students will receive approval letters for qualifying scores.
Duration: One academic year. Renewable annually until students have obtained a Baccalaureate degree or completed a total of 10 semesters.
Deadline: Student applicant has to achieve the qualified score by the June test date.

ADDRESS INQUIRIES TO:
Information Center
(See address above.)

MISSOURI DEPARTMENT OF HIGHER EDUCATION AND WORKFORCE DEVELOPMENT [1554]
P.O. Box 1469
Jefferson City, MO 65102-1469
(573) 751-2361
(800) 473-6757 (option 4)
Fax: (573) 751-6635
E-mail: info@dhewd.mo.gov
Web Site: dhewd.mo.gov

FOUNDED: 1986

NAME(S) OF PROGRAMS:
● **Access Missouri Financial Assistance Program**

TYPE:
Grants-in-aid. Undergraduate student financial aid to qualified Missouri students

who wish to attend qualified Missouri institutions of higher education, both public and private.

YEAR PROGRAM STARTED: 2007

PURPOSE:
To enable full-time students to attend a participating postsecondary institution (public and private).

LEGAL BASIS:
Section 173.1101-173.1107, RSMo. Government agency.

ELIGIBILITY:
Initially, applicants must meet the following requirements:
(1) have a FAFSA on file by April 1;
(2) have any FAFSA corrections made by July 31 (if one is eligible, school choices may be added until September 30 by contacting the MDHE);
(3) be a U.S. citizen or permanent resident and a Missouri resident;
(4) be an undergraduate student enrolled full-time at a participating Missouri school (students with documented disabilities who are enrolled in at least six credit hours may be considered to be enrolled full-time);
(5) have an Expected Family Contribution (EFC) of $12,000 or less;
(6) not be pursuing a degree or certificate in theology or divinity and;
(7) not have received the first Bachelor's degree, completed the required hours for a Bachelor's degree, or completed 150 semester credit hours.

Renewal students must continue to meet the eligibility requirements for initial students and additionally:
(1) continue to meet the eligibility requirements for initial students;
(2) maintain a minimum cumulative grade point average of 2.5 and otherwise maintain satisfactory academic progress as defined by the applicant's school (if this is the first academic year in which one has received an Access Missouri payment, this requirement does not apply) and;
(3) not have received an Access Missouri award for a maximum of five semesters at a two-year school or 10 semesters at any combination of two-year or four-year schools, whichever occurs first.
If Charles Gallagher or Missouri College Guarantee awardee in past semesters, those semesters are counted in the 10-semester limit, along with any semester in which the applicant has received an Access Missouri award.

GEOG. RESTRICTIONS: Missouri.

FINANCIAL DATA:
Amount of support per award: Award amounts are based on the type of school one is attending when award is received. If applicant transfers to a different school, his or her award amount may change based on the type of school to which he or she transfers. Public two-year: $300 to $940. Public four-year and State Technical College of Missouri: $1,500 to $2,050. Private: $1,500 to $2,050. (Note: Maximum award amounts may be less than these figures; it depends on the amount of funding that is available for the program.)
Total amount of support: $67,909,710 for the 2019-20 academic year.

NO. AWARDS: 44,208 for the 2019-20 academic year.

APPLICATION INFO:
Contact the Department or consult the web site.
Duration: One academic year. Renewable.
Deadline: FAFSA on file by April 1. Priority deadline: February 1. Final deadline: April 1.

ADDRESS INQUIRIES TO:
Information Center
(See address above.)

NATIONAL FEDERATION OF THE BLIND

NFB Scholarship Program
200 East Wells Street at Jernigan Place
Baltimore, MD 21230
(410) 659-9314 ext. 2415
E-mail: scholarships@nfb.org
Web Site: www.nfb.org/scholarships

TYPE:
Scholarships. Awarded on the basis of academic excellence, service to the community and leadership. Provides a one-time grant plus a continuing program of mentors and seminars for blind college students.

See entry 919 for full listing.

NATIONAL INSTITUTE FOR LABOR RELATIONS RESEARCH   [1555]

5211 Port Royal Road
Suite 510
Springfield, VA 22151
(703) 321-9606
(703) 770-2247
Fax: (703) 321-0676
E-mail: clj@nrtw.org
Web Site: www.nilrr.org

FOUNDED: 1975

AREAS OF INTEREST:
Organization of public opposition to compulsory unionism in the education community.

NAME(S) OF PROGRAMS:
● **Applegate/Jackson Parks Future Teacher Scholarship**

TYPE:
Scholarships. Scholarship awarded annually to the education student who exemplifies dedication to principle and high professional standards.

YEAR PROGRAM STARTED: 1989

PURPOSE:
To promote awareness of compulsory unionism.

LEGAL BASIS:
Nonprofit 501(c)(3) organization.

ELIGIBILITY:
Applicants are limited to undergraduates and graduate students majoring in education in institutions of higher learning throughout the U.S. Foreign students may apply, as long as they are attending an institution of higher learning in the U.S. Applicants who will be considered must demonstrate potential for successful completion of educational requirements in a college or university Department of Education program and the potential of successful application for a teaching license and demonstrate, by means of a written essay, an understanding of the individual freedom issue as it applies to the problem of compulsory unionism in the education community.

GEOG. RESTRICTIONS: United States.

FINANCIAL DATA:
Amount of support per award: $1,000 per scholarship.
Total amount of support: $1,000.

NO. MOST RECENT APPLICANTS: Approximately 212.

NO. AWARDS: 1.

APPLICATION INFO:
Applications may be submitted electronically. A total application will consist of a completed application form and a typewritten essay of approximately 500 words clearly demonstrating an interest in and a knowledge of the Right to Work principle as it applies to educators. All applicants will be requested to submit an official copy of his or her most recent transcript of grades.
Duration: One year. Nonrenewable.
Deadline: Applications must be postmarked on or by December 31.

ADDRESS INQUIRIES TO:
Cathy Jones, Scholarship Administrator
(See address above.)

*SPECIAL STIPULATIONS:
Applicant must be an education major attending college or have been admitted to an institution of higher learning in the U.S.

THE NATIONAL ITALIAN AMERICAN FOUNDATION [1556]

1860 19th Street, N.W.
Washington, DC 20009-5501
(202) 939-3114
Fax: (202) 387-0800
E-mail: scholarships@niaf.org
Web Site: www.niaf.org/scholarships

NAME(S) OF PROGRAMS:
● **NIAF Scholarship Program**

TYPE:
Scholarships. The National Italian American Foundation (NIAF) will award scholarships and grants to outstanding students for use during the following academic year. The awards will be made on the basis of academic merit and divided between two groups of students.

PURPOSE:
To assist Italian American students or those interested in Italian studies.

ELIGIBILITY:
To be eligible for a NIAF scholarship, a student must meet the following criteria:
(1) be a member of NIAF or have a parent, grandparent or guardian with an active NIAF membership;
(2) be enrolled in a U.S. accredited institution of higher education for the fall semester;
(3) have a grade point average of at least 3.5 out of 4.0 (or the equivalent). Some scholarships require a lower grade point average requirement for eligibility. Students that are part of a pass-fail system are also eligible to apply;
(4) be a U.S. citizen or permanent resident alien and;
(5) must have at least one ancestor who has immigrated from Italy.

GEOG. RESTRICTIONS: United States.

FINANCIAL DATA:
Each scholarship award can only cover tuition and university-provided room and board. Scholarship monies not used during the academic year are not transferable to the following academic year.
Amount of support per award: $2,500 to $12,000.
Total amount of support: Varies.

NO. MOST RECENT APPLICANTS: Over 4,000.

NO. AWARDS: 60 to 70.

APPLICATION INFO:
In order to be complete, an application must include the following:
(1) completed online application form;
(2) recent transcripts (either official or unofficial);
(3) recent resume outlining academic achievement, awards received, extracurricular involvement and work experience and;
(4) one letter of recommendation.

Students applying for need-based scholarships will be required to upload their FAFSA Student Aid Report (SAR).
Duration: One academic year.
Deadline: March 1.

PUBLICATIONS:
Scholarship brochure.

ADDRESS INQUIRIES TO:
See e-mail address above.

NATIONAL JEWISH COMMITTEE ON SCOUTING [1557]
1325 West Walnut Hill Lane
Irving, TX 75038
(972) 580-2425
Fax: (972) 580-2535
E-mail: anthony.berger@scouting.org
Web Site: www.jewishscouting.org

NAME(S) OF PROGRAMS:
● **Rick Arkans Eagle Scout Scholarship**
● **Chester M. Vernon Memorial Eagle Scout Scholarship**
● **Frank L. Weil Memorial Eagle Scout Scholarship**

TYPE:
Scholarships.

PURPOSE:
To promote Boy Scouting among Jewish youth; to help Jewish institutions and local council Jewish committees to provide Scouting opportunities for Jewish youth; to promote Jewish values in Scouting.

ELIGIBILITY:
Applicants must:
(1) be a registered, active member of a Boy Scout troop, Varsity Scout team, or Venturing crew;
(2) have received the Eagle Scout Award;
(3) be an active member of a synagogue and must have received the Ner Tamid or Etz Chaim religious emblem;
(4) have demonstrated practical citizenship in his synagogue, school, Scouting unit, and community and;
(5) be enrolled in an accredited high school and in his final year at the time of selection, except Scouts whose Eagle Scout boards of review are held the same year of their high school graduation may apply in that calendar year. They may receive a scholarship one time only.

Applicants for Rick Arkans and Chester M. Vernon Memorial Eagle Scout Scholarships must also demonstrate financial need.

GEOG. RESTRICTIONS: United States.

FINANCIAL DATA:
Amount of support per award: Rick Arkans Eagle Scout Scholarship: $1,000; Chester M. Vernon Memorial Eagle Scout Scholarship: $1,000 per year; Frank L. Weil Memorial Eagle Scout Scholarship: $1,000 first place award and two $500 second place awards.

NO. AWARDS: 6.

APPLICATION INFO:
Applicants for the Arkans and Vernon Scholarships must submit a copy of the Free Application for Federal Student Assistance (FAFSA).

All sections of the scholarship application should be completed with as much information as possible. However, except for the required letter of recommendation (and FAFSA), no additional pages may be attached.
Duration: One year. Chester M. Vernon Memorial Eagle Scout Scholarship: Up to four years.
Deadline: Application submitted no later than January 31. Announcements by June 1.

ADDRESS INQUIRIES TO:
Anthony Berger, Staff Advisor
(See address above.)

NATIONAL SOCIETY DAUGHTERS OF THE AMERICAN REVOLUTION [1558]
1776 D Street, N.W.
Washington, DC 20006-5303
(202) 879-3263
E-mail: nsdarscholarships@nsdar.org
Web Site: www.dar.org

FOUNDED: 1890

AREAS OF INTEREST:
Furthering the education of Native Americans.

NAME(S) OF PROGRAMS:
● **American Indian Scholarship**

TYPE:
Scholarships. Intended to help Native American college/university and technical school students at the undergraduate or graduate level.

PURPOSE:
To provide scholarship assistance to Native American students of any age or tribe, in any state, striving to get an education.

ELIGIBILITY:
Applicants must:
(1) be Native Americans (proof required by letter or proof papers) in financial need;
(2) be U.S. citizens/residents and;
(3) have a grade point average of 3.25 or higher.

Graduate students are eligible; however, undergraduate students are given preference.

GEOG. RESTRICTIONS: United States.

FINANCIAL DATA:
Amount of support per award: $4,000.
Total amount of support: Varies.

NO. AWARDS: Up to 5.

APPLICATION INFO:
Applicants must use the DAR Scholarship Committee's online submission process found

on the DAR public web site. Once applicants have set up their scholarship profile, they will be able to complete the application. If necessary, applicants will be able to provide access to individuals wishing to submit confidential letters of recommendations or school transcripts.
Duration: One-time award.
Deadline: February 15.

ADDRESS INQUIRIES TO:
National Vice Chairman
E-mail: americanindianschol@nsdar.org

NATIONAL SOCIETY DAUGHTERS OF THE AMERICAN REVOLUTION [1559]
1776 D Street, N.W.
Washington, DC 20006-5303
(202) 879-3263
E-mail: nsdarscholarships@nsdar.org
Web Site: www.dar.org

FOUNDED: 1890

AREAS OF INTEREST:
Furthering the education of Native Americans.

NAME(S) OF PROGRAMS:
● **Frances Crawford Marvin American Indian Scholarship**

TYPE:
Scholarships. Intended to help Native American students enrolled full-time at a two- or four-year college or university.

PURPOSE:
To provide scholarship assistance to Native American students.

ELIGIBILITY:
Applicants must:
(1) be enrolled full-time at a two- or four-year college or university;
(2) be Native Americans (proof required by letter or proof papers);
(3) be U.S. citizens/residents;
(4) demonstrate financial need and academic achievement and;
(5) have a grade point average of 3.25 or higher.

A recipient may reapply and be considered along with members of the applicant pool.

GEOG. RESTRICTIONS: United States.

FINANCIAL DATA:
Amount of support per award: Varies.

NO. AWARDS: 1.

APPLICATION INFO:
Applicants must use the DAR Scholarship Committee's online submission process found on the DAR public web site. Once applicants have set up their scholarship profile, they will be able to complete the application. If necessary, applicants will be able to provide access to individuals wishing to submit confidential letters of recommendations or school transcripts.
Duration: One year. Renewable.
Deadline: February 15.

ADDRESS INQUIRIES TO:
National Vice Chairman
E-mail: fcmarvinamericanindianscholarship@nsdar.org

NATIONAL SOCIETY OF ACCOUNTANTS SCHOLARSHIP FOUNDATION   [1560]

1330 Braddock Place
Suite 540
Alexandria, VA 22314
(703) 549-6400
(800) 966-6679
Fax: (703) 549-2984
E-mail: members@nsacct.org
Web Site: www.nsacct.org

FOUNDED: 1969

AREAS OF INTEREST:
Accounting.

NAME(S) OF PROGRAMS:
● **NSA Scholarships**
● **The Stanley H. Stearman Award**

TYPE:
Scholarships.

PURPOSE:
To provide financial encouragement to students who select accounting as a career.

LEGAL BASIS:
501(c)(3) charitable organization.

ELIGIBILITY:
Must be an undergraduate accounting major who is a U.S. or Canadian citizen that attends a U.S.-accredited school and maintains a "B" or better overall grade point average.

For the Stearman Award, applicant must be the spouse, son, daughter, grandchild, niece, nephew, daughter-in-law or son-in-law of an active or retired NSA living or deceased member. The member must have held membership for at least one year prior to the annual distribution of applications in October.

GEOG. RESTRICTIONS: United States.

FINANCIAL DATA:
Amount of support per award: $500 to $2,200.
Total amount of support: $31,200 for the year 2018.

NO. AWARDS: 25 for the year 2018.

APPLICATION INFO:
Guidelines are available on the Foundation web site.
Duration: One year. Nonrenewable, except for the Stearman Award which cannot exceed three years.
Deadline: March 31 (postmark).

NATIONAL SOCIETY OF BLACK ENGINEERS   [1561]

205 Daingerfield Road
Alexandria, VA 22314
(703) 549-2207
Fax: (703) 683-5312
E-mail: scholarships@nsbe.org
Web Site: apply.nsbe.org

FOUNDED: 1975

AREAS OF INTEREST:
All areas of engineering.

TYPE:
Awards/prizes; Scholarships. The Society offers a variety of NSBE and corporate-sponsored scholarship and award opportunities to its precollege, collegiate undergraduate and graduate student members as well as technical professional members.

PURPOSE:
To increase the number of culturally responsible Black engineers who excel academically, succeed professionally and positively impact the community.

ELIGIBILITY:
For scholarships, applicant must be an active, paid NSBE member.

FINANCIAL DATA:
Amount of support per award: $500 to $10,000.
Total amount of support: Approximately $400,000 given annually in scholarships.

NO. MOST RECENT APPLICANTS: 2,661.

NO. AWARDS: Approximately 250 scholarships annually.

APPLICATION INFO:
Application information is available on the web site. Application must be submitted online.
Duration: One year. Nonrenewable.
Deadline: Spring cycle: Applications open in April with a deadline of June 30. Fall cycle: Applications open in September with a deadline of January 3.

*SPECIAL STIPULATIONS:
Each scholarship recipient cannot be awarded more than two scholarships in a given program year. Members that apply for more than one scholarship that has an internship requirement must rank acceptance of scholarship for awarding, if selected as a recipient. (A member cannot accept both internships for a given time period; thus he or she must decide prior to selection which scholarship/internship they would want to accept in priority order.)

NATSO FOUNDATION   [1562]

Bill and Carolyn Moon Scholarships
1330 Braddock Place, Suite 501
Alexandria, VA 22314
(703) 549-2100
Fax: (703) 684-4525
E-mail: billmoonscholarship@natsofoundation.org
Web Site: www.natso.com/natsofoundation/billmoonscholarship

FOUNDED: 1989

AREAS OF INTEREST:
Research, scholarships and public outreach.

NAME(S) OF PROGRAMS:
● **Bill and Carolyn Moon Scholarships**

TYPE:
Scholarships. These scholarships provide much needed and deserved assistance to industry students planning for their postsecondary education.

PURPOSE:
To aid travel plaza employees and their dependents with educational expenses.

ELIGIBILITY:
Must be a truck stop/travel plaza employee or the legal dependent of a truck stop/travel plaza employee.

FINANCIAL DATA:
Amount of support per award: $5,000.
Total amount of support: Varies.

NO. AWARDS: 5.

APPLICATION INFO:
Applications are submitted online.
Duration: One semester.

Deadline: Mid-May.

ADDRESS INQUIRIES TO:
See e-mail address above.

NBCC FOUNDATION, INC. [1563]

3 Terrace Way
Greensboro, NC 27403
(336) 232-0376
Fax: (336) 232-0010
E-mail: foundation@nbcc.org
Web Site: www.nbccf.org

FOUNDED: 2005

AREAS OF INTEREST:
Philanthropy, mental health care, professional counseling, credentialing, scholarships and grant funding.

NAME(S) OF PROGRAMS:
● **ACS Training Award**
● **BCC Training Award**
● **CCE Professional Development Award**
● **Doctoral Minority Fellowship**
● **GCDF Scholarship**
● **Master's Youth Addictions Minority Fellowship**
● **Master's Youth Minority Fellowship**
● **NBCC Foundation Military Scholarship**
● **NBCC Foundation Rural Scholarship**

TYPE:
Fellowships; Scholarships. Academic scholarships for individuals pursuing a graduate-level degree in professional counseling.

YEAR PROGRAM STARTED: 2009

PURPOSE:
To increase the availability of counselors in underserved areas, with the current priority areas of minority, rural and military communities. Military Scholarship: To increase the number of counselors available to serve active duty service members and veterans. Minority Fellowship: To increase counseling resources available to underserved minority populations. Rural Scholarship: To increase access to needed counseling services in remote areas.

ELIGIBILITY:
For the ACS Training Award, the applicant must:
(1) currently hold the NCC certification maintained with no ethical holds or missed payments for a minimum of one year;
(2) have extensive clinical experience in providing mental health or substance abuse counseling services and;
(3) commit to applying for the ACS credential within one year of the award.

For the BCC Training Award, the applicant must:
(1) not be currently or previously certified as a BCC;
(2) commit to applying for the BCC and;
(3) demonstrate exceptional coaching potential through one or more of the following: having access to the population in need of coaching or working in a setting conducive to coaching; having a background in leadership; and holding or pursuing a degree from a relevant program.

For the CCE Professional Development Award, applicant must:
(1) currently hold a CCE credential maintained in good standing for a minimum of one year and;
(2) promote their CCE credential or contribute to the related field through one or more of the following: providing

credential-related training for others; bringing programs that promote the credential to their campus or organization; delivering a presentation at a relevant conference; conducting relevant research; writing for a relevant publication; holding leadership positions in relevant groups or associations; and mentoring another who is pursuing the credential.

For the Doctoral Minority Fellowship, the applicant must:
(1) be a U.S. citizen or have permanent resident status;
(2) not receive any other federal funds (except for federal loans) or work for a federal agency;
(3) must currently hold the National Certified Counselor (NCC) certification and be in good standing or document all of the following: a full state license as a professional counselor; a passing score on the National Counselor Examination for Licensure and Certification (NCE) or the National Clinical Mental Health Counseling Examination (NCMHCE); and a commitment to obtain the NCC certification within three months if awarded a fellowship;
(4) be enrolled full-time and be in good standing in a CACREP-accredited, doctoral-level counseling program;
(5) have demonstrated knowledge and experience with racially and ethnically diverse populations and;
(6) commit to provide mental health and substance abuse services to underserved minority populations in the private nonprofit and public sectors through direct practice or the training of direct practitioners.
African Americans, Alaska Natives, American Indians, Asian Americans, Hispanics/Latinos, Native Hawaiians and Pacific Islanders are especially encouraged to apply.

For the GCDF Scholarship, the applicant must:
(1) (if a U.S. applicant) hold an active GCDF credential in good standing and be enrolled in a Master's-level program accredited by the Council for Accreditation of Counseling & Related Educational Programs (CACREP);
(2) (if an international applicant) either hold an active GCDF credential in good standing and be enrolled in an advanced education program in counseling or be a student currently enrolled in both a GCDF training program and a post-Bachelor's counseling program, as appropriate to their country and;
(3) commit to providing career counseling services for two years.

For the Master's Youth Addictions Minority Fellowship, the applicant must:
(1) be a U.S. citizen or have permanent resident status;
(2) not receive any other federal funds (except for federal student loans) or work for a federal agency;
(3) be entering their last year of study in the upcoming fall academic year;
(4) be enrolled full-time in either an accredited addictions counseling Master's program or a CACREP-accredited Master's program with a concentration in addictions counseling;
(5) demonstrate knowledge of and experience with racially and ethnically diverse populations;
(6) commit to applying for the National Certified Counselor (NCC) certification prior to graduation and to completing the application process and;
(7) commit to providing addictions

counseling services to underserved minority transition-age youth (16 to 25) populations for two years.
African Americans, Alaska Natives, American Indians, Asian Americans, Hispanics/Latinos, Native Hawaiians and Pacific Islanders are especially encouraged to apply.

For the Master's Youth Minority Fellowship, the applicant must:
(1) be a U.S. citizen or have permanent resident status;
(2) not receive any other federal funds (except for federal student loans) or work for a federal agency;
(3) be enrolled full-time in a CACREP-accredited counseling Master's program;
(4) must demonstrate knowledge of and experience with racially and ethnically diverse populations;
(5) must commit to applying for the National Certified Counselor (NCC) certification prior to graduation and to completing the application process and;
(6) must commit to providing mental health services to underserved minority transition-age youth (16 to 25) populations for two years.
African Americans, Alaska Natives, American Indians, Asian Americans, Hispanics/Latinos, Native Hawaiians and Pacific Islanders are especially encouraged to apply.

For the Military Scholarship, the applicant must:
(1) be enrolled full-time in a CACREP-accredited counseling Master's program;
(2) be former or current active duty U.S. military service members or spouses of a military service member whose service was within the past five years; veterans must have served in the military within the past five years and have received an honorable discharge;
(3) commit to applying for the National Certified Counselor (NCC) certification prior to graduation and to completing the application process and;
(4) commit to providing mental health services to service members and/or veterans for at least two years.

For the Rural Scholarship, the applicant must:
(1) be enrolled full-time in a CACREP-accredited counseling Master's program;
(2) reside in a rural area as defined by the Health Resources and Services Administration (HRSA);
(3) commit to applying for the National Certified Counselor (NCC) certification prior to graduation and to completing the application process and;
(4) commit to providing mental health services in a rural area for at least two years.

FINANCIAL DATA:
Awards go directly to recipients for any expenses associated with educational pursuit.

Amount of support per award: ACS Training Award: $500. BCC Training Award: Up to $3,000. CCE Professional Development Award: $500. Doctoral Minority Fellowship: Up to $20,000. GCDF Scholarship: $5,000. Master's Youth Addictions Minority Fellowship: Up to $11,000. Master's Youth

Minority Fellowship: Up to $8,000. Military and Rural Scholarships: $5,000 (subject to change upon annual review).

APPLICATION INFO:
Application information is available on the web site.
Duration: One-time scholarship award. Not renewable.
Deadline: Varies from year to year.

ADDRESS INQUIRIES TO:
Program Coordinator
(See address above.)

NEBRASKA'S COORDINATING COMMISSION FOR POSTSECONDARY EDUCATION [1564]
140 North 8th Street, Suite 300
Lincoln, NE 68508
(402) 471-2847
E-mail: ritchie.morrow@nebraska.gov
Web Site: www.ccpe.nebraska.gov

FOUNDED: 1991

AREAS OF INTEREST:
Higher education in Nebraska.

NAME(S) OF PROGRAMS:
● **Nebraska Opportunity Grant**

TYPE:
Scholarships. Nebraska Opportunity Grant is a need-based aid program to assist Nebraska students working on an undergraduate degree.

YEAR PROGRAM STARTED: 2003

PURPOSE:
To assist with costs of attending a Nebraska college or university.

ELIGIBILITY:
Applicant must be a Nebraska resident who has not earned a Bachelor's, Master's or professional degree. He or she must complete Free Application for Federal Student Aid (FAFSA) and have an Expected Family Contribution (EFC) equal to or less than the yearly maximum.

GEOG. RESTRICTIONS: Nebraska.

FINANCIAL DATA:
Amount of support per award: Varies.
Total amount of support: $17,978,264 for the year 2018-19.

NO. AWARDS: 12,753 for the year 2018-19.

APPLICATION INFO:
Must complete the FAFSA. Institutions may have additional application requirements.
Duration: Up to one academic year. Renewable.
Deadline: Applications are accepted on a rolling basis.

ADDRESS INQUIRIES TO:
J. Ritchie Morrow, M.S.Ed.
Financial Aid Officer
Nebraska's Coordinating Commission for Postsecondary Education
P.O. Box 95005
Lincoln, NE 68509-5005
(See telephone number above.)

NEED
The Law and Finance Building
429 Fourth Avenue, 20th Floor
Pittsburgh, PA 15219
(412) 566-2760
Fax: (412) 471-6643
E-mail: needpgh@gmail.com
Web Site: www.needld.org

TYPE:
Internships; Matching gifts; Scholarships. Supplemental grants for postsecondary education at colleges and business, trade and technical schools.

See entry 947 for full listing.

NEW JERSEY DEPARTMENT OF MILITARY AND VETERANS AFFAIRS [1565]

DVS-VBB
P.O. Box 340
Trenton, NJ 08625-0340
(609) 530-6854
Fax: (609) 530-6970
E-mail: patty.richter@dmava.nj.gov
Web Site: www.nj.gov/military

FOUNDED: 1959

AREAS OF INTEREST:
State financial assistance for postsecondary students.

NAME(S) OF PROGRAMS:
● **Veterans Tuition Credit Program (VTCP)**

TYPE:
Grants-in-aid. Tuition assistance grant for attendance at any eligible undergraduate, graduate or vocational institution in the U.S.

YEAR PROGRAM STARTED: 1977

PURPOSE:
To provide tuition assistance to U.S. veterans of the Armed Forces of the U.S. who served on active duty between December 31, 1960 and May 7, 1975 who were, or are, eligible for federal veterans' educational assistance (G.I. Bill).

LEGAL BASIS:
Entitlement.

ELIGIBILITY:
Applicant must be a veteran of the armed forces of the U.S. who is or was eligible for veterans educational assistance pursuant to federal law and served on active duty in the armed forces of the U.S. between December 31, 1960 and May 7, 1975. Applicant must have been a legal New Jersey resident at the time of induction into the armed forces, or at the time of discharge from active duty or for at least one year prior to the time of application, excluding the time spent in active duty. If a veteran was not a New Jersey resident at time of induction or separation, veteran must provide documentation reflecting residency – copy of NJ Income Tax Return, letter from postmaster, home mortgage or apartment lease. Applicant must be currently enrolled in an approved state approving agency course of study at any eligible academic, professional or vocational institution in the U.S.

GEOG. RESTRICTIONS: New Jersey.

FINANCIAL DATA:
Amount of support per award: Eligible veterans may receive a maximum award of $400 a year for full-time attendance or $200 a year for half-time attendance as provided by regulations and available appropriations.

NO. MOST RECENT APPLICANTS: 17.

NO. AWARDS: Based upon appropriations.

APPLICATION INFO:
Applications are available at campus Veterans Affairs offices or by calling the New Jersey Department of Military and Veterans

Information Number, Tel: (888) 865-8387, available from any location in New Jersey, Monday through Friday, 8:30 A.M. to 4:30 P.M.

Duration: Eligible veterans may receive up to four academic years of payment.

Deadline: October 1 for fall and spring terms. March 1 for spring term only.

OFFICERS:
Tom DeShields, Director, Fiscal Operations

ADDRESS INQUIRIES TO:
Patricia Richter, Bureau Chief, VBB
(See address above.)

NEW JERSEY DEPARTMENT OF MILITARY AND VETERANS AFFAIRS [1566]

DVS-VBB
P.O. Box 340
Trenton, NJ 08625-0340
(609) 530-6854
Fax: (609) 530-6970
E-mail: patty.richter@dmava.nj.gov
Web Site: www.nj.gov/military

FOUNDED: 1959

AREAS OF INTEREST:
State financial assistance for college students, 16 to 21 years of age.

NAME(S) OF PROGRAMS:
● **Prisoner of War/Missing in Action (POW/MIA) Program**

TYPE:
Grants-in-aid; Scholarships.

YEAR PROGRAM STARTED: 1978

LEGAL BASIS:
Entitlement.

ELIGIBILITY:
Applicants must be dependent children (any child born before, during or after the period of time its parent was a POW/MIA) of military service personnel who were officially declared "Prisoner of War" or "Person Missing in Action" after January 1, 1960. The POW or MIA must have been a resident of New Jersey at the time he or she entered the Armed Forces of the U.S. or whose official residence is New Jersey.

GEOG. RESTRICTIONS: New Jersey.

FINANCIAL DATA:
Amount of support per award: Full tuition costs will be paid on behalf of the eligible dependent to any New Jersey public or independent college or university upon certification of full-time enrollment.

APPLICATION INFO:
Applications are available by contacting the New Jersey Department of Military and Veterans Affairs, Veterans Service Office, located in Mercer County.

Deadline: October 1 for fall and spring term benefits. March 1 for spring term benefits only.

OFFICERS:
Tom DeShields, Director, Fiscal Operations

ADDRESS INQUIRIES TO:
Patricia Richter, Bureau Chief, VBB
(See address above.)

NEW JERSEY OFFICE OF THE SECRETARY OF HIGHER EDUCATION (OSHE) [1567]

One John Fitch Plaza
P.O. Box 542
Trenton, NJ 08625-0542
(609) 341-3808
Fax: (609) 292-7225
E-mail: hasani.carter@oshe.nj.gov
Web Site: www.state.nj.us/highereducation/EOF/EOF_Description.shtml

FOUNDED: 1968

AREAS OF INTEREST:
State financial and student support assistance for low-income college students.

NAME(S) OF PROGRAMS:
● **The New Jersey Educational Opportunity Fund (EOF) Program**

TYPE:
Grants-in-aid. Student support. The Educational Opportunity Fund (EOF) is administered through the Office of the Secretary of Higher Education (OSHE). Created by law in 1968, EOF is one of the state's most comprehensive student support programs that provides access to higher education for those who come from low income and educationally disadvantaged backgrounds. EOF is not an entitlement grant program.

YEAR PROGRAM STARTED: 1968

PURPOSE:
To ensure meaningful access to higher education for those who come from backgrounds of economic and educational disadvantage.

LEGAL BASIS:
New Jersey Educational Opportunity Act of 1968.

ELIGIBILITY:
Applicants must meet both the EOF statewide and institutional requirements. Applicants must be New Jersey residents for at least 12 consecutive months prior to receiving an award. Applicants must be full-time, matriculated students in an approved New Jersey college or university in an approved program of study. Household income cannot exceed established guidelines. The amount of the grant varies based on financial need, cost of attendance and available funding.

GEOG. RESTRICTIONS: New Jersey.

FINANCIAL DATA:
Amount of support per award: Dependent upon annual appropriations, financial need, cost of attendance, and enrollment status.

Public four-year institution: $775 a semester for a resident student; $650 a semester for a commuter student. County/community college: $600 a semester. Independent college/university: $1,325 a semester.

Total amount of support: $31,679,000.

NO. AWARDS: 13,247 undergraduates, unduplicated.

APPLICATION INFO:
Space is limited and admission into EOF is conducted at the campus level. Applicants should contact the participating institution for more information regarding their respective EOF admission process. Participating institutions are listed at www.nj.gov/highereducation/EOF/EOF_programs.shtml.

Duration: Financial assistance is renewable for four years of undergraduate study providing student is making satisfactory academic progress, demonstrates unmet need, and an application is filed by the deadline.

Deadline: September 15 for fall term and February 15 for spring term.

PUBLICATIONS:
State and Federal Financial Aid Programs for New Jersey Students, brochure.

ADDRESS INQUIRIES TO:
Dr. Hasani Carter
EOF Executive Director
Office of the Secretary
of Higher Education
(See address above.)

NEW YORK STATE EDUCATION DEPARTMENT [1568]
Office of Higher Education
Education Building, Room 971 EBA
Albany, NY 12234
(518) 474-3719
Fax: (518) 474-7468
E-mail: scholar@nysed.gov
Web Site: www.highered.nysed.
gov/kiap/scholarships

NAME(S) OF PROGRAMS:
● **Regents Physician Loan Forgiveness Award Program**
● **Scholarships for Academic Excellence**

TYPE:
Scholarships. Regents Physician Loan Forgiveness Award Program: Designed to increase the number of physicians practicing in areas of New York state designated by the Regents as having a shortage of physicians. Emphasis is placed on primary care.

Scholarships for Academic Excellence: For use only at colleges and universities within New York state. Students are nominated by their high schools for this award.

PURPOSE:
To encourage specially talented youth to continue their education.

GEOG. RESTRICTIONS: New York state.

FINANCIAL DATA:
Amount of support per award: Regents Physician Loan Forgiveness Award Program: Up to $10,000 per year for two years, then reapply for up to two more years at same amount; Scholarships for Academic Excellence: $500 to $1,500.
Total amount of support: Varies.

NO. AWARDS: Regents Physician Loan Forgiveness Award Program: Minimum of 80; Scholarships for Academic Excellence; 2,000 $1,500 scholarships, 6,000 $500 scholarships.

APPLICATION INFO:
Regents Physician Loan Forgiveness Award Program: Consult the Department web site. Scholarships for Academic Excellence: Available through the student's high school.
Duration: Regents Physician Loan Forgiveness Award Program: Two years, after which the physician must reapply; physician then may be able to get two more years of funding. Scholarships for Academic Excellence: Four years.
Deadline: Regents Physician Loan Forgiveness Award Program: Posted online. Scholarships for Academic Excellence: February 15.

ADDRESS INQUIRIES TO:
See telephone or e-mail address above.

NEW YORK STATE HIGHER EDUCATION SERVICES CORPORATION [1569]
99 Washington Avenue
Albany, NY 12255
(888) 697-4372
(518) 473-1574
Fax: (518) 474-3749
E-mail: barbara.hochberg@hesc.ny.gov
Web Site: www.hesc.ny.gov

FOUNDED: 1975

AREAS OF INTEREST:
Postsecondary student financial aid.

NAME(S) OF PROGRAMS:
● **Military Service Recognition Scholarship (MSRS)**
● **NYS Memorial Scholarships**

TYPE:
Grants-in-aid; Scholarships. Military Service Recognition Scholarship (MSRS) provides financial aid to children, spouses and financial dependents of members of the armed forces of the U.S. or of a state-organized militia who, at any time on or after August 2, 1990, while a New York state resident, died or became severely and permanently disabled while engaged in hostilities or training for hostilities. It is for study in New York state.

NYS Memorial Scholarships (NYS Memorial Scholarships for Families of Deceased Firefighters, Volunteer Firefighters, Police Officers, Peace Officers, and Emergency Medical Service Workers) provides financial aid to children, spouses and financial dependents of deceased members of these branches of public service who have died as the result of injuries sustained in the line of duty in service to the state of New York. It is for study in New York state.

The Corporation administers more than 25 grant, scholarship, award and other programs providing college financial aid for New York state residents.

YEAR PROGRAM STARTED: 2004

PURPOSE:
To provide special financial assistance for postsecondary study for children in certain categories.

LEGAL BASIS:
Article 13 of the Education Law. New York state agency.

ELIGIBILITY:
Students must:
(1) study at an approved postsecondary institution in New York state;
(2) have graduated from high school in the U.S., earned a GED, or passed a federally approved "Ability to Benefit" test as defined by the Commissioner of the State Education Department;
(3) be enrolled as a full-time student taking 12 or more credits per semester;
(4) be matriculated in an approved program of study and be in good academic standing and;
(5) not be in default on a student loan guaranteed by HESC or any repayment of state awards.

GEOG. RESTRICTIONS: New York state.

FINANCIAL DATA:
Amount of support per award: Varies.

Total amount of support: Varies.

APPLICATION INFO:
Applicants must complete and submit either the Military Service Recognition Scholarship Web Supplement or the NYS Memorial Scholarship Web Supplement. Be sure to print the Web Supplement confirmation, sign the supplement, and submit it along with the required documentation according to the instructions. FAFSA must be completed after eligibility is established and applicant has been assigned an account number.
Duration: Four years of full-time undergraduate study or five years of undergraduate study if the student is enrolled in an approved five-year program.
Deadline: June 30.

ADDRESS INQUIRIES TO:
E-mail: scholarships@hesc.ny.gov

NEW YORK STATE HIGHER EDUCATION SERVICES CORPORATION [1570]
99 Washington Avenue
Albany, NY 12255
(888) 697-4372
(518) 473-1574
Fax: (518) 474-3749
Web Site: www.hesc.ny.gov

FOUNDED: 1975

AREAS OF INTEREST:
Postsecondary student financial aid.

NAME(S) OF PROGRAMS:
● **NYS Aid for Part-Time Study (APTS)**

TYPE:
Grants-in-aid. College-based program providing grant assistance for eligible part-time students enrolled in approved undergraduate studies.

YEAR PROGRAM STARTED: 1984

PURPOSE:
To help pay tuition for eligible students enrolled in approved certificate or degree programs.

LEGAL BASIS:
State agency.

ELIGIBILITY:
To be considered for an award, a student must enroll part-time in a degree or an approved certificate program at a degree-granting institution, meet specific income limits, be a New York state resident, be either a U.S. citizen or eligible noncitizen, have a tuition charge of at least $100 per year, and not have used up Tuition Assistance Program (TAP) eligibility.

For this program, part-time study means being enrolled for at least three, but less than 12, semester-hours per semester, or four, but less than eight, credit hours per trimester. A participating college selects recipients from among eligible students.

GEOG. RESTRICTIONS: New York state.

FINANCIAL DATA:
Award amount is based on the student's need and the amount of money available at the institution.
Amount of support per award: Up to $2,000 per year.

APPLICATION INFO:
Awards are made through each college offering the program. Students should contact the college financial aid office to find out how to apply at their school.

Duration: Renewable up to four years.

Deadline: Varies.

ADDRESS INQUIRIES TO:
E-mail: scholarships@hesc.ny.gov

NEW YORK STATE HIGHER EDUCATION SERVICES CORPORATION   [1571]

99 Washington Avenue
Albany, NY 12255
(888) 697-4372
(518) 473-1574
Fax: (518) 474-3749
E-mail: barbara.hochberg@hesc.ny.gov
Web Site: www.hesc.ny.gov

FOUNDED: 1975

AREAS OF INTEREST:
Postsecondary student financial aid.

NAME(S) OF PROGRAMS:
● **New York State Tuition Assistance Program (TAP)**

TYPE:
Grants-in-aid. New York's largest grant program, the Tuition Assistance Program helps eligible New York residents attending in-state postsecondary institutions pay for tuition. TAP grants are based on the applicant's and his or her family's New York state net taxable income.

YEAR PROGRAM STARTED: 1976

PURPOSE:
To partially defray tuition charges to students.

LEGAL BASIS:
Article 13 of the Education Law.

ELIGIBILITY:
Legal New York state residents who are U.S. citizens or eligible noncitizens, who are full-time students at an approved postsecondary institution in New York state, and who meet income eligibility limitations are eligible to apply.

GEOG. RESTRICTIONS: New York state.

FINANCIAL DATA:
Grant varies according to New York net taxable income of the applicant and the family. Student must attend an institution charging at least $200 annual tuition.

Amount of support per award: Up to $5,165.

Total amount of support: Varies.

NO. AWARDS: Unlimited.

APPLICATION INFO:
Student must complete the annual FAFSA online application; from there he or she can proceed via online link to the HESC TAP application, which must also be completed. The TAP application is also available by accessing the HESC web site (above).

Duration: Up to four or five years of undergraduate study if the student is enrolled in an approved five-year program.

Deadline: June 30 of the current school year.

ADDRESS INQUIRIES TO:
Student Information
(See address above.)

THE CHARLOTTE W. NEWCOMBE FOUNDATION   [1572]

35 Park Place
Princeton, NJ 08542-6918
(609) 924-7022
Fax: (609) 252-1773
E-mail: info@newcombefoundation.org
Web Site: www.newcombefoundation.org

FOUNDED: 1979

AREAS OF INTEREST:
College scholarship funds to colleges and universities.

NAME(S) OF PROGRAMS:
● **Newcombe Fellowships**
● **Newcombe Scholarships for Mature Students**
● **Newcombe Scholarships for Students with Disabilities**
● **Special Scholarship Endowment Grants**

TYPE:
Challenge/matching grants; Endowments; Fellowships; Internships; Scholarships. Endowment challenges build up current Newcombe Scholarship Endowments at colleges in a Newcombe program.

Newcombe Fellowships are designed to encourage original and significant study of ethical and religious values in all areas of human endeavor. The selection process and all administration for this continuing fellowship program are handled by the Woodrow Wilson National Fellowship Foundation of Princeton, NJ. All doctoral requirements except the dissertation must be completed by November of the year preceding the Fellowship award. Student must be attending a graduate school in the U.S.

Newcombe Scholarships for Mature Students are for students age 25 and older who have completed half the credits required for their Bachelor's degrees. These scholarships are available at selected colleges which offer support services for mature students. Preference in this program is given to four-year colleges with excellent support services for mature students. It is Foundation policy not to provide grants in this program to professional schools, including theological seminaries and those training health care professionals; 31 colleges are in this program.

Newcombe Scholarships for Students with Disabilities are intended to recognize the extraordinary expenses these students incur because of their disabilities and to supplement other sources of aid. The Newcombe Foundation offers special disability expense scholarships, internship scholarships and partial tuition scholarships through the counseling offices of colleges which provide excellent support services for disabled students. Preference in this program is given to four-year colleges which render exceptional service to large numbers of disabled students. 11 colleges are in the Newcombe Program.

Special Scholarship Endowment Grants are awarded to selected institutions to benefit students from a specified economically disadvantaged population that the institution serves.

The Foundation makes no awards to individual students. All grants are made to colleges, universities and other institutions of higher education.

YEAR PROGRAM STARTED: 1981

PURPOSE:
To provide selected colleges and universities with scholarship funds for specifically targeted groups of students.

LEGAL BASIS:
Private.

ELIGIBILITY:
No grants to individuals. Scholarship aid only. No funds for program development staffing or support. The Foundation provides grants to colleges, universities and foundations to create scholarships for designated undergraduate and graduate students. No aid is available for postdoctoral fellowships.

GEOG. RESTRICTIONS: Scholarships for Disabled Students and Mature Students are generally limited to the mid-Atlantic states.

FINANCIAL DATA:
Amount of support per award: Varies.

Total amount of support: $2,300,000 for the year 2018-19.

Matching fund requirements: Varies.

NO. AWARDS: Varies.

APPLICATION INFO:
For Newcombe Fellowships, contact Woodrow Wilson National Fellowship Foundation, P.O. Box 5281, Princeton, NJ 08543-5281 for application materials. Tel: (609) 452-7007. Web site: www.woodrow.org.

For Newcombe Scholarships for Mature Students and Students with Disabilities, colleges within geographic area should contact the Foundation for applications. Individuals should contact their college of choice for availability of these scholarships.

Duration: Varies.

Deadline: Inquiries are accepted on an ongoing basis. Proposals by invitation.

PUBLICATIONS:
Annual report.

IRS I.D.: 23-2120614

STAFF:
Dr. Gianna Durso-Finley, Executive Director
Lindsey G. Bohra, Associate Executive Director

BOARD OF TRUSTEES:
Robert M. Adams
Dale Robinson Anglin
Elizabeth T. Frank
Louise U. Johnson
J. Barton Luedeke

ADDRESS INQUIRIES TO:
Dr. Gianna Durso-Finley, Executive Director
(See address above.)

*PLEASE NOTE:
No grants to individuals.

*SPECIAL STIPULATIONS:
Grants are made to colleges and universities exclusively for student scholarships. Two programs (Mature Students and Students with Disabilities) are generally limited to mid-Atlantic states.

NORTH CAROLINA STATE EDUCATION ASSISTANCE AUTHORITY/COLLEGE FOUNDATION OF NORTH CAROLINA [1573]

P.O. Box 14103
Research Triangle Park, NC 27709
(919) 549-8614
(866) 866-2362
E-mail: programinformation@cfnc.org
Web Site: www.cfnc.org

AREAS OF INTEREST:
Financial aid for North Carolina students.

TYPE:
Grants-in-aid; Scholarships.

PURPOSE:
To provide access to higher education and information for the citizens of North Carolina.

ELIGIBILITY:
Varies with program. All applicants must be North Carolina residents and intend to use funds for tuition purposes only.

GEOG. RESTRICTIONS: North Carolina.

FINANCIAL DATA:
Amount of support per award: Varies.
Total amount of support: Varies.

APPLICATION INFO:
Applications may be obtained online or by telephone request.
Duration: Varies.
Deadline: Varies.

ADDRESS INQUIRIES TO:
NCSEAA Grants Training and Outreach
(See address above.)

NORTHERN CHAUTAUQUA COMMUNITY FOUNDATION [1574]

212 Lake Shore Drive West
Dunkirk, NY 14048
(716) 366-4892
Fax: (716) 366-3905
E-mail: info@nccfoundation.org
Web Site: www.nccfoundation.org

FOUNDED: 1986

AREAS OF INTEREST:
Youth development and economic development.

TYPE:
Challenge/matching grants; Project/program grants; Scholarships. Youth Development and Economic Development grants.

YEAR PROGRAM STARTED: 1986

PURPOSE:
To enhance the northern Chautauqua community.

LEGAL BASIS:
Community foundation.

ELIGIBILITY:
Applicants must be registered 501(c)(3) organizations that serve the northern Chautauqua County community.

GEOG. RESTRICTIONS: Northern Chautauqua County, New York.

FINANCIAL DATA:
Amount of support per award: $25 to $10,000.
Total amount of support: $1,168,662 in grants and scholarships for the year 2017.

APPLICATION INFO:
Call the Foundation for information or visit its web site.
Deadline: Community Grants: March 1 and September 1.

PUBLICATIONS:
Annual report; Spring and Fall newsletters.

IRS I.D.: 16-1271663

STAFF:
Diane E. Hannum, Executive Director
Eileen Ardillo, Program Coordinator
Ida Lord, Community Relations and Development Coordinator
Victoria Howell, Administrative Scholarship Coordinator

ADDRESS INQUIRIES TO:
For Grants:
Eileen Ardillo, Program Coordinator

For Scholarships:
Victoria Howell
Administrative Scholarship Coordinator
(See address above.)

*SPECIAL STIPULATIONS:
Scholarships to northern Chautauqua County residents only.

THE NRA [1575]

11250 Waples Mill Road
Fairfax, VA 22030
(703) 267-1087
(800) 554-9498
Fax: (703) 267-1083
E-mail: jebrayscholarship@nrahq.org
Web Site: nra.org

NAME(S) OF PROGRAMS:
● **Jeanne E. Bray Memorial Scholarship**

TYPE:
Scholarships. For children of peace officers.

YEAR PROGRAM STARTED: 1988

PURPOSE:
To assist children of peace officers, who are current NRA members, in furthering their education.

ELIGIBILITY:
Must be an adult or junior member of the NRA and the son or daughter of a currently serving, full-time/deceased, full-time/retired, full-time, or disabled and retired commissioned peace officer who is also a current NRA member or was at the time of death. Eligible students can be senior high school students through senior college students. Applicants must have a satisfactory academic record and be enrolled full-time. Must be U.S. citizens or residents.

GEOG. RESTRICTIONS: United States.

FINANCIAL DATA:
Amount of support per award: Up to $12,000 or four years, whichever comes first.

NO. AWARDS: Varies.

APPLICATION INFO:
Applicant will need to contact Chandra Bolland to receive the personal reference forms.
Duration: Up to four semesters.
Deadline: November 15.

ADDRESS INQUIRIES TO:
Chandra Bolland
Jeanne E. Bray Memorial Scholarship Committee
(See address and e-mail above.)

OHIO DEPARTMENT OF HIGHER EDUCATION [1576]

Office of Financial Aid
25 South Front Street
Columbus, OH 43215
(614) 466-6000
Fax: (614) 752-5903
E-mail: hotline@highered.ohio.gov
Web Site: www.ohiohighered.org/ohio-war-orphans

NAME(S) OF PROGRAMS:
● **Ohio War Orphans Scholarship**

TYPE:
Scholarships. Full-time undergraduate scholarships.

YEAR PROGRAM STARTED: 1954

PURPOSE:
To provide tuition assistance to the children of deceased or severely disabled Ohio veterans who served in the armed forces during a period of declared war or conflict.

LEGAL BASIS:
State agency.

ELIGIBILITY:
Applicant must be 16 to 25 years of age and a child of disabled or deceased Ohio war veteran or child of Vietnam conflict MIA or POW. Veteran parent must have at least a 60% combined disability rating. Applicant must also be enrolled as a full-time student in an eligible institution of higher education.

GEOG. RESTRICTIONS: Ohio.

FINANCIAL DATA:
Students attending Ohio nonprofit and profitmaking institutions of higher education will receive amounts no greater than the average amount paid for students attending public institutions; tuition coverage at public institutions varies each year.
Amount of support per award: Varies.
Total amount of support: $8,372,500 for the year 2018-19.

NO. AWARDS: 1,275 for the year 2018-19.

APPLICATION INFO:
Student must submit a completed application form.
Duration: Scholarships are automatically renewable for up to five years of undergraduate education.
Deadline: May 15. Announcements in early August.

STAFF:
Ramah Church, Program Manager

ADDRESS INQUIRIES TO:
Ramah Church, Program Manager
(See address above.)

*SPECIAL STIPULATIONS:
This program is not for graduate students.

OHIO DEPARTMENT OF HIGHER EDUCATION [1577]

Office of Financial Aid
25 South Front Street
Columbus, OH 43215
(614) 466-6000
Fax: (614) 752-5903
E-mail: ocog_admin@highered.ohio.gov
Web Site: www.ohiohighered.org/ocog

FOUNDED: 1963

NAME(S) OF PROGRAMS:
- **Ohio College Opportunity Grant Program (OCOG)**

TYPE:
General operating grants. Grants for college-bound students or current undergraduate students.

YEAR PROGRAM STARTED: 2006

PURPOSE:
To assist in achieving the goals of access and choice for low-income and middle-income students.

LEGAL BASIS:
State agency.

ELIGIBILITY:
Applicant must be an Ohio resident, demonstrate financial need, and be seeking an Associate's degree, a Bachelor's degree, or nursing diploma at an eligible institution.

GEOG. RESTRICTIONS: Ohio and Pennsylvania.

FINANCIAL DATA:
Amount of support per award: Varies.
Total amount of support: $102,023,190 for the year 2018.

NO. AWARDS: 69,454 for the year 2018.

APPLICATION INFO:
Student must submit a Free Application for Federal Student Aid (FAFSA).
Duration: One academic year. Renewable for a maximum of 10 semesters of full-time study.
Deadline: October 1.

ADDRESS INQUIRIES TO:
Tamika Braswell, Director
(See address above.)

*SPECIAL STIPULATIONS:
This program is not for graduate students.

OHIO NATIONAL GUARD SCHOLARSHIP PROGRAM [1578]

The Adjutant General's Department
2825 West Dublin Granville Road
Columbus, OH 43235-2789
(614) 336-7143
(888) 400-6484
Fax: (614) 336-7195
E-mail: ng.oh.oharng.mbx.ong-scholarship@mail.mil
lonny.r.kirby.nfg@mail.mil
Web Site: www.ong.ohio.gov/information/education/scholarship_index.html

FOUNDED: 1977

AREAS OF INTEREST:
Associate or undergraduate general education.

TYPE:
Scholarships. Grants for undergraduate students attending three credit hours or more.

YEAR PROGRAM STARTED: 1978

PURPOSE:
To encourage enlistment in Ohio National Guard.

LEGAL BASIS:
Ohio Revised Code. Nonprofit.

ELIGIBILITY:
Applicants must possess a high school diploma or a GED certificate and enlist, re-enlist or extend their current enlistment in the Ohio National Guard for a minimum of three years and up to six years.

GEOG. RESTRICTIONS: Ohio.

FINANCIAL DATA:
Instructional and general fees paid 100% for student attending public institution. For private institutions, the amount paid is equivalent to the average cost of public schools.
Amount of support per award: Varies.
Total amount of support: $21,000,000 annually.

NO. MOST RECENT APPLICANTS: 3,500.

APPLICATION INFO:
An applicant must apply each term so that the application is received in the Scholarship Program Office no later than the established deadlines, which are no later than the close of business (4:30 P.M.).
Duration: Scholarships are renewable for up to four years of undergraduate education. A three- to five-year enlistment will qualify applicants for an A.A. degree. A six-year enlistment will qualify applicants for a B.A. degree.
Deadline: July 1 for fall; November 1 for winter/quarter, semester, trimester/spring semester; February 1 for spring quarter; April 1 for summer.

PUBLICATIONS:
Regulation AGOR 621-1(Army); *35-1*(Air).

STAFF:
Lonny Kirby, Program Coordinator

ADDRESS INQUIRIES TO:
Lonny Kirby, Program Coordinator
(See address above.)

*SPECIAL STIPULATIONS:
Applicant must enlist in Ohio National Guard for not less than three years. Must enroll minimum three credit hours in degree-granting program.

ORDER SONS OF ITALY IN AMERICA, GRAND LODGE OF FLORIDA [1579]

2021 Pine Needle Trail
Kissimmee, FL 34746
(321) 286-6787
E-mail: gertd830@gmail.com
Web Site: osiaflorida.org

FOUNDED: 1953

AREAS OF INTEREST:
Culture, charity and education.

TYPE:
Awards/prizes; Grants-in-aid; Scholarships. Scholarships are provided to high school students entering college.

Financial aid is given in support of charitable programs, such as Alzheimer's disease, Cooley's anemia, autism, and cancer.

YEAR PROGRAM STARTED: 1988

PURPOSE:
To share and help those in need; to support high school students entering college; to support charitable programs.

ELIGIBILITY:
Scholarship program: Applying student must be a U.S. citizen or resident who resides in the state of Florida, be of Italian heritage, and achieve high scholastic grades.

Applying organizations must have 501(c)(3) not-for-profit status. No grants are made to religious organizations.

GEOG. RESTRICTIONS: Florida.

FINANCIAL DATA:
Amount of support per award: Scholarship program: $2,000 per student.
Total amount of support: $10,000.

NO. AWARDS: Scholarship program: Varies with funding; 5 scholarships in 2018.

APPLICATION INFO:
Scholarship application form can be obtained on the web site or at applying student's local high school. Completed application materials must be submitted to the State Scholarship Chairperson.
Duration: One-time awards. Grants are not renewable.
Deadline: March 31.

ADDRESS INQUIRIES TO:
Gertrude Dorries, State Scholarship Chairperson
(See e-mail address above.)

PARAPSYCHOLOGY FOUNDATION, INC.

P.O. Box 1562
New York, NY 10021-0043
(212) 628-1550
Fax: (212) 628-1559
E-mail: office@parapsychology.org
Web Site: parapsychology.org

TYPE:
Scholarships. Assists students attending an accredited college or university in pursuing the academic study of the science of parapsychology.

See entry 2376 for full listing.

PENNSYLVANIA HIGHER EDUCATION ASSISTANCE AGENCY [1580]

1200 North Seventh Street
Harrisburg, PA 17102-1398
(717) 720-2800
(800) 692-7392 (Pennsylvania only)
Fax: (717) 720-3786
E-mail: granthelp@pheaa.org
Web Site: www.pheaa.org

FOUNDED: 1964

NAME(S) OF PROGRAMS:
- **Pennsylvania State Grant Program**

TYPE:
Grants-in-aid. The Pennsylvania State Grant Program allows eligible Pennsylvania residents to obtain financial assistance for undergraduate study at any PHEAA-approved institution of higher education. The Free Application for Federal Student Aid (FAFSA) serves as the program's application.

YEAR PROGRAM STARTED: 1964

PURPOSE:
To assist needy students in obtaining higher education.

LEGAL BASIS:
Government agency.

ELIGIBILITY:
The student applying for Pennsylvania State Grants must:
(1) meet criteria for financial need;
(2) be enrolled on at least a half-time basis in a PHEAA-approved undergraduate program of study and not already have a four-year (or more) undergraduate degree;
(3) be a high school graduate or the recipient

of a GED;

(4) demonstrate academic progress (for continued aid) and;

(5) be a Pennsylvania resident (domiciliary).

Summer school students may also qualify for State Grant funds.

GEOG. RESTRICTIONS: Pennsylvania.

FINANCIAL DATA:
Amount of support per award: Varies annually.

NO. AWARDS: Approximately 130,000.

APPLICATION INFO:
Submit the Free Application for Federal Student Aid (FAFSA) and Pennsylvania State Grant Form. Most renewal students do not have to complete the State Grant Form.

Duration: One academic year. Renewal contingent upon continued eligibility and financial need.

Deadline: Varies.

EXECUTIVE OFFICERS:
James H. Steeley, President and Chief Executive Officer
Elizabeth McCloud, Vice President of State Grants and Special Programs

ADDRESS INQUIRIES TO:
Elizabeth McCloud, Vice President of State Grants and Special Programs
(See address above.)

THE PHI BETA KAPPA SOCIETY [1581]

1606 New Hampshire Avenue, N.W.
Washington, DC 20009
(202) 745-3287
Fax: (202) 986-1601
E-mail: awards@pbk.org
Web Site: www.pbk.org

AREAS OF INTEREST:
Philosophy.

NAME(S) OF PROGRAMS:
● **The Romanell-Phi Beta Kappa Professorship in Philosophy**

TYPE:
Fellowships. Professorship awarded to scholars in the field of philosophy, without restriction to any one school of philosophical thought.

YEAR PROGRAM STARTED: 1983

PURPOSE:
To recognize not only distinguished achievement, but also the recipient's contribution or potential contribution to public understanding of philosophy.

ELIGIBILITY:
Scholar need not be a member of Phi Beta Kappa, but must be on the faculty of an institution sheltering a chapter of Phi Beta Kappa and must be nominated by that chapter.

GEOG. RESTRICTIONS: United States.

FINANCIAL DATA:
In addition to the stipend, the award includes a lecture series and publishing deal with Oxford University Press.

Amount of support per award: $7,500 stipend for the awardee and $1,000 for his or her chapter.

NO. AWARDS: 1 annually.

APPLICATION INFO:
Recipient must be nominated by the chapter of Phi Beta Kappa at the institution in which they are on faculty.

Duration: One year. Nonrenewable.

Deadline: June 30.

ADDRESS INQUIRIES TO:
Aurora Sherman, Executive Assistant to the Secretary and Awards Coordinator
(See address above.)

*SPECIAL STIPULATIONS:
Recipient will be expected to give a series of three special lectures during the year of the Professorship. Such lectures are to be given at the sheltering institution and to be open to the general public as well as to the academic community.

PI GAMMA MU, INTERNATIONAL HONOR SOCIETY IN SOCIAL SCIENCE [1582]

1001 Millington, Suite B
Winfield, KS 67156
(620) 221-3128
E-mail: executivedirector@pigammamu.org
Web Site: www.pigammamu.org

FOUNDED: 1924

AREAS OF INTEREST:
Economics, history, political science, sociology, anthropology, international relations, social work, psychology, social philosophy, history of education and criminal justice, law and human/cultural geography.

NAME(S) OF PROGRAMS:
● **Pi Gamma Mu Scholarships**

TYPE:
Scholarships. Awarded for graduate study.

YEAR PROGRAM STARTED: 1951

PURPOSE:
To promote scholarship in the Society's areas of interest.

LEGAL BASIS:
Nonprofit.

ELIGIBILITY:
Applicant must be a member of Pi Gamma Mu.

FINANCIAL DATA:
Amount of support per award: $1,000 or $2,000.

Total amount of support: Up to $13,000 annually.

NO. MOST RECENT APPLICANTS: Approximately 47.

NO. AWARDS: Up to 10.

APPLICATION INFO:
Resume, personal statement, transcript and three letters of recommendation required.

Duration: One year.

Deadline: February 15. Announcement: Spring. Distribution: Fall.

PUBLICATIONS:
Application guidelines.

OFFICERS:
Dr. C. Laurence Heck, President
Dr. Susan Kinsella, First Vice President
Dr. Clara Small, Second Vice President
Dr. Mari Plikuhn, Secretary and Treasurer
Dr. Charles Hartwig, Chancellor
Katherine Im, Chancellor

Allison G.S. Knox, Chancellor
Dr. Brad Tennant, Chancellor

ADDRESS INQUIRIES TO:
Executive Director

MINNIE STEVENS PIPER FOUNDATION [1583]

1250 N.E. Loop 410, Suite 810
San Antonio, TX 78209-1539
(210) 525-8494
Fax: (210) 341-6627
E-mail: mspf@mspf.org
Web Site: www.mspf.org

FOUNDED: 1950

NAME(S) OF PROGRAMS:
● **Piper Professor Program**
● **Piper Scholar Program**
● **Student Loan Program**

TYPE:
Awards/prizes; Scholarships. Piper Professor Program: Annual awards to professors for superior teaching at the college level.

Piper Scholars: Four-year scholarships awarded to academically promising and superior high school seniors in amounts that assist them in attending the college or university of their choice within the state of Texas.

Student Loan Program: Loans to worthy and needy students at the junior, senior, undergraduate or graduate college level.

PURPOSE:
To support charitable, scientific, or educational undertakings by providing for, or contributing toward, the education of financially limited but worthy students; to assist young men and women residents of Texas, attending or wishing to attend colleges and universities in the state of Texas, to complete their education and obtain degrees; to contribute to community chests; to support any other nonprofit organization or activity dedicated to promoting the general welfare within the state of Texas.

LEGAL BASIS:
Private foundation with Letter Ruling under Section 4945 of the Tax Reform Act of 1969.

ELIGIBILITY:
Piper Professor Program: Candidates must be U.S. citizens and nominated through college/university President's office.

Piper Scholar Program: Participation is by invitation only to high schools in certain geographic areas. Student must be nominated by their high school counselor.

Student Loan Program: Must be full-time status. Restricted to Texas residents attending a college or university within the state of Texas.

GEOG. RESTRICTIONS: Texas.

FINANCIAL DATA:
Amount of support per award: Piper Professor Program: $5,000.

NO. AWARDS: Piper Professor Program: 10; Piper Scholar Program: 25.

APPLICATION INFO:
Student Loan application can be downloaded from the Foundation web site.

Duration: Piper Scholar Program: Four years.

ADDRESS INQUIRIES TO:
Joyce M. Ellis, Executive Director
(See address above.)

*SPECIAL STIPULATIONS:
Piper Professor and Piper Scholars Programs
are by invitation only.

THE PLANNING AND VISUAL EDUCATION PARTNERSHIP   [1584]
4651 Sheridan Street, Suite 470
Hollywood, FL 33021
(954) 241-4800
(954) 241-4834
Fax: (954) 893-8375
E-mail: info@paveglobal.org
Web Site: paveglobal.org

FOUNDED: 1992

AREAS OF INTEREST:
Retail design planning, industrial design and
visual merchandising.

TYPE:
Awards/prizes; Capital grants;
Conferences/seminars; Product donations;
Project/program grants; Scholarships. Student
educational support. Mentorships.

PURPOSE:
To encourage students to study in the field of
retail design, interior design, and planning
and visual merchandising.

FINANCIAL DATA:
Amount of support per award: PAVE Global
Shop Design Project: $15,000; Student Aid
Program: $25,000; Student Design
Competition: $8,000 for first place, $5,500
for second place, $3,000 for third place and
$1,000 for honorable mention.
Total amount of support: $115,000 for the
year 2018-19.

NO. AWARDS: 13.

ADDRESS INQUIRIES TO:
Dash Nagel, Managing Director
(See address above.)

PRESBYTERIAN CHURCH (U.S.A.)   [1585]
100 Witherspoon Street
Louisville, KY 40202-1396
(888) 728-7228 ext. 5224
Fax: (502) 569-8766
E-mail: finaid@pcusa.org
Web Site: www.pcusa.org/financialaid

AREAS OF INTEREST:
Majors in health services/sciences, religious
studies, sacred music, social services and
social sciences.

NAME(S) OF PROGRAMS:
● Student Opportunity Scholarship

TYPE:
Scholarships. Need-based.

YEAR PROGRAM STARTED: 1956

PURPOSE:
To assist undergraduate sophomores, juniors
and seniors already in college, with
preference to racial ethnic students.

ELIGIBILITY:
Scholarship preference to African Americans,
Asian Americans, Middle Eastern Americans
and Hispanic Americans. Applicants must:
(1) demonstrate financial need;
(2) be a member of the Presbyterian Church
(U.S.A.);
(3) be a sophomore, junior or senior already
in college;

(4) have a 2.5 grade point average or greater
and;
(5) be seeking a Bachelor's degree.

GEOG. RESTRICTIONS: United States.

FINANCIAL DATA:
Amount of support per award: Up to $4,000
per academic year.
Total amount of support: Approximately
$160,000 annually.

NO. MOST RECENT APPLICANTS: 120.

NO. AWARDS: 80.

APPLICATION INFO:
Applications can be downloaded from the
web site, beginning April 1.
Duration: Renewable up to three years
depending on need and maintenance of a 2.5
grade point average.
Deadline: May 15 for "getting started" part;
June 15 for financial information.

PUBLICATIONS:
Financial Aid Programs.

ADDRESS INQUIRIES TO:
Financial Aid for Service
(See address above.)

PRESBYTERIAN CHURCH (U.S.A.)   [1586]
100 Witherspoon Street
Louisville, KY 40202-1396
(888) 728-7228 ext. 5224
Fax: (502) 569-8766
E-mail: finaid@pcusa.org
Web Site: www.pcusa.org/financialaid

NAME(S) OF PROGRAMS:
● Samuel Robinson Award

TYPE:
Awards/prizes. Essay contest, awarded to
junior or senior undergraduate students
enrolled full-time in one of the
colleges/universities related to the
Presbyterian Church (U.S.A.).

YEAR PROGRAM STARTED: 1940

PURPOSE:
To instill an interest in the work of the
Presbyterian Church throughout the U.S.

LEGAL BASIS:
Nonprofit.

ELIGIBILITY:
Must be a member of the Presbyterian
Church (U.S.A.) and a junior or senior
attending a Presbyterian-related college or
university.

GEOG. RESTRICTIONS: United States.

FINANCIAL DATA:
Amount of support per award: $1,500 to
$7,500.
Total amount of support: Varies.

NO. MOST RECENT APPLICANTS: 2.

NO. AWARDS: Up to 10.

APPLICATION INFO:
Applications by request. Contact the
Presbyterian Church (U.S.A.) or refer to web
site.
Duration: One-time award.
Deadline: Proposals are reviewed on a
rolling basis. Applications will be reviewed
quarterly.

ADDRESS INQUIRIES TO:
Financial Aid for Service
(See address above.)

*SPECIAL STIPULATIONS:
Open to Presbyterian students attending a
Presbyterian-related school.

THE PRESS CLUB OF ST. LOUIS CHARITABLE FUND - ST. LOUIS PRESS CLUB   [1587]
c/o The Press Club of St. Louis
P.O. Box 410522
Creve Couer, MO 63141
(314) 449-8029
Fax: (314) 317-0031
E-mail: info@stlpressclub.org
Web Site: stlpressclub.org

FOUNDED: 1956

AREAS OF INTEREST:
Journalism.

NAME(S) OF PROGRAMS:
● Joe Bonwich Media Scholarship
● Donald R. Burris Journalism
  Scholarship
● Joan Foster Dames Women's
  Journalism Scholarship
● Fourth Estate Scholarships
● Karl Heinz and Doris Finzel
  Photojournalism Scholarship
● High School Journalism Scholarship
● Journalism Foundation Scholarships
● David S. Lipman Scholarship
● Sarah Bryan Miller Scholarship
● Press Club and St. Louis Post-Dispatch
  Ronald Wade Journalism Scholarship
● Press Club Internship Scholarships
● Press Club Journalism Scholarship
● Press Club Media Summer Internship
  Scholarships
● Press Club Neiman Marcus Media
  Scholarship

TYPE:
Capital grants; Fellowships; Internships;
Project/program grants; Scholarships.

YEAR PROGRAM STARTED: 1970

PURPOSE:
To award scholarships to those entering
sophomore, junior and senior years of college
or graduate school preparing for
journalism/communications careers at
recognized schools, majoring in journalism,
broadcasting, English or related fields; to
award fellowships for journalists to do
investigative stories for publication.

LEGAL BASIS:
Incorporated as nonprofit organization in
state of Missouri.

ELIGIBILITY:
Applicants for scholarships must be currently
enrolled as full-time students who are
intending to pursue a career in journalism,
media communications or a related field;
graduate students must carry at least six
hours. Press Club Fellowship Program:
Journalists with an investigative project
concerning the St. Louis region.

GEOG. RESTRICTIONS: St. Louis, Missouri and
counties of Franklin, Jefferson, Lincoln, St.
Charles, St. Louis and Warren, and Illinois
counties of Bond, Clinton, Jersey, Madison,
Monroe and St. Clair.

FINANCIAL DATA:
Amount of support per award:
Fellowship/Grants Program: Up to $10,000.
Scholarships: $1,000 to $4,000.

CO-OP FUNDING PROGRAMS: Grants from
member organizations.

NO. AWARDS: Grants: 1; Scholarships:
Approximately 15.

APPLICATION INFO:
Consult the Press Club web site.
Deadline: Scholarships: April 15.

PUBLICATIONS:
Courier, newsletter.

IRS I.D.: 43-1489003

STAFF:
Glenda Partlow, Executive Director
Laura Schnarr, Development and Social
Media Coordinator

ADDRESS INQUIRIES TO:
Glenda Partlow
Executive Director, Press Club
(See address above.)

RONALD REAGAN PRESIDENTIAL FOUNDATION AND INSTITUTE [1588]

40 Presidential Drive
Simi Valley, CA 93065
(571) 213-7970
E-mail: ekorsvall@reaganfoundation.org
Web Site: www.reaganfoundation.
org/scholarships

FOUNDED: 1987

NAME(S) OF PROGRAMS:
● **GE-Reagan Foundation Scholarship
Program**

TYPE:
Scholarships. The GE-Reagan Foundation
Scholarship Program rewards college-bound
students who demonstrate exemplary
leadership, drive, integrity and citizenship
with financial assistance to pursue higher
education.

PURPOSE:
To honor the legacy and character of
America's 40th president.

ELIGIBILITY:
Open to current high school seniors.

GEOG. RESTRICTIONS: United States.

FINANCIAL DATA:
Amount of support per award: $10,000 for
each scholarship.

NO. AWARDS: Varies.

APPLICATION INFO:
Application information is available on the
web site.
Duration: One academic year. Renewable for
up to three additional years.
Deadline: Application is available in the fall
and is due the first week of January. The
scholarship will then be awarded for the next
full academic year. Contact the Foundation
for exact details.

ADDRESS INQUIRIES TO:
E-mail: ge-reagan@scholarshipamerica.org
Tel: (844) 402-0354

SID RICHARDSON MEMORIAL FUND [1589]

309 Main Street
Fort Worth, TX 76102
(817) 336-0494
Fax: (817) 339-7245
E-mail: mkuykendall@sidrichardson.org
Web Site: www.sidrichardsonmemorialfund.org

FOUNDED: 1965

AREAS OF INTEREST:
Academic and vocational scholarships.

TYPE:
Scholarships. Scholarships are for both
academic and vocational studies.

YEAR PROGRAM STARTED: 1965

LEGAL BASIS:
Tax-exempt.

ELIGIBILITY:
Limited funds are available to assist in
defraying the cost of college education or of
vocational training. These scholarships are
awarded on a competitive basis according to
academic achievement and/or financial need.

Those eligible to apply for a Sid Richardson
Memorial Fund scholarship are direct
descendants (children or grandchildren) of
persons who qualified for Early Retirement,
Normal Retirement, Disability Retirement, or
Death Benefits from The Bass Retirement
Plan (formerly The Retirement Plan For
Employees of Bass Enterprises Production
Co.), Retirement Plan for Employees of
Barbnet/San Jose Cattle Co., Retirement Plan
for Employees of City Center Development
Co., City Club Retirement Plan, Retirement
Plan for Employees of Richardson Aviation,
G.P., Retirement Plan for Employees of Sid
W. Richardson Foundation, or Retirement
Plan for Employees of Sundance Square.
Those eligible also include direct descendants
(children or grandchildren) of persons
presently employed with a minimum of three
years' full-time service (as of March 31) with
any of the following employers: Barbnet
Investment Co., BBT Capital Management,
LLC, BEPCO, L.P., City Club of Fort Worth,
Richardson Aviation, San Jose Cattle Co.,
SHSM Partners, L.P., Sid Richardson Carbon
Co. (SRCE, L.P.), Sid W. Richardson
Foundation, and Sundance Square
Management, L.P.

FINANCIAL DATA:
Amount of support per award: $1,000 to
$10,000 per student per academic year.
Total amount of support: Approximately
$510,000.

NO. MOST RECENT APPLICANTS: Varies.

NO. AWARDS: 81 for the year 2018.

APPLICATION INFO:
Application request may be submitted via the
Fund's web site. Follow "How to Apply" tab.
You may also direct a written request for an
application to Mary Kuykendall, Sid
Richardson Memorial Fund, at the address,
e-mail or fax number listed above. Include
the student name, address, e-mail and phone
number, as well as the qualifying employee's
name, last 4-digits of Social Security
Number, qualifying company name and dates
of employment, as well as relationship to the
student.
Duration: Considered for renewal annually if
a 2.0 grade point average is maintained for
each semester.
Deadline: Completed applications must be
postmarked no later than March 31 annually
for the following academic year.
Announcement of awards by May 31.

IRS I.D.: 75-1220266

OFFICERS:
Pete Geren, Executive Director
Shanda Ranelle, Treasurer
Mary Kuykendall, Secretary

BOARD OF DIRECTORS:
Thomas White, Chairman

William Jones, Vice President
Heidi McDonald, Vice President
Mitchell Roper, Vice President

ADDRESS INQUIRIES TO:
Mary Kuykendall, Scholarship Coordinator
(See address above.)

JACKIE ROBINSON FOUNDATION (JRF)

75 Varick Street, 2nd Floor
New York, NY 10013-1917
(212) 290-8600
Fax: (212) 290-8081
E-mail: general@jackierobinson.org
Web Site: www.jackierobinson.org

TYPE:
Conferences/seminars; Fellowships;
Scholarships. The Foundation Scholarship
Program (Mentoring and Leadership
Program) is designed to address the financial
needs of college students and provide
comprehensive mentoring services through its
42 Strategies for Success Curriculum.

The Fellowship programs are follow-up
programs to the JRF Scholars program
(Mentoring and Leadership Program).

The Extra Innings Fellowship Program helps
highly motivated JRF Scholars to fund the
cost of advanced professional or graduate
training.

The Rachel Robinson International
Fellowship Program promotes and supports
international service and study opportunities
for JRF Scholars.

See entry 927 for full listing.

THE ROTARY CLUB OF BRYN MAWR [1590]

P.O. Box 84
Bryn Mawr, PA 19010
(484) 254-6377
E-mail: rbcuff@verizon.net
Web Site: www.brynmawrrotary.org

FOUNDED: 1969

AREAS OF INTEREST:
To serve others and satisfy Rotary principles.

NAME(S) OF PROGRAMS:
● **Harry H. Cabell Scholarship Program**

TYPE:
Awards/prizes; Scholarships.

YEAR PROGRAM STARTED: 1985

PURPOSE:
To recognize and reward college students
who meet trust requirements.

LEGAL BASIS:
Not-for-profit society.

ELIGIBILITY:
Financial need, high academic standards and
leadership qualities, service to others and
achievement qualities are important factors in
the decision process. Applicants must be in
an area college or university.

GEOG. RESTRICTIONS: Metropolitan Philadelphia
and surrounding counties.

FINANCIAL DATA:
Amount of support per award: $2,500 for the
year 2017.
Total amount of support: Varies.

NO. AWARDS: 2 for the year 2017.

APPLICATION INFO:
Application form must include recommendation from faculty, statement of good standing from dean, transcript of grades and 300-word essay.

Duration: One year. No renewals.

Deadline: Early March. Announcement approximately April 30.

ADDRESS INQUIRIES TO:
Richard Cuff, Scholarship Committee
Harry H. Cabell Scholarship Awards
(See address above.)

SHASTRI INDO-CANADIAN INSTITUTE (SICI)
Room 1418, Education Tower
2500 University Drive, N.W.
Calgary AB T2N 1N4 Canada
(403) 220-3220
E-mail: maldeen@ucalgary.ca
Web Site: www.shastriinstitute.org

TYPE:
Fellowships; Internships; Travel grants. Collaborative research grants; Publication grants.

See entry 863 for full listing.

HORACE SMITH FUND   [1591]
16 Union Avenue
Suite 2K
Westfield, MA 01085
(413) 739-4222
Fax: (413) 739-1108
E-mail: info@horacesmithfund.org
Web Site: www.horacesmithfund.org

FOUNDED: 1899

AREAS OF INTEREST:
Education, scholarships and fellowships.

TYPE:
Fellowships; Scholarships.

YEAR PROGRAM STARTED: 1899

PURPOSE:
To help students obtain scholarships and fellowships.

ELIGIBILITY:
For scholarships, students must have graduated from a high school in Hampden County. For fellowships, students must be legal residents of Hampden County.

GEOG. RESTRICTIONS: Hampden County, Massachusetts.

FINANCIAL DATA:
Amount of support per award: Scholarships: $3,000 per year for four years; Fellowships: $5,000 per year for up to three years.
Total amount of support: Varies.

NO. MOST RECENT APPLICANTS: Approximately 300 for the year 2019.

NO. AWARDS: Fellowships: 3; Scholarships: 20.

APPLICATION INFO:
Applications are available in September.

Duration: One year. Scholarships renewable up to four years; Fellowships up to three years.

Deadline: March 15.

PUBLICATIONS:
Annual report; contributions policy; application guidelines.

ADDRESS INQUIRIES TO:
Josephine Sarnelli, Executive Director
(See address above.)

*SPECIAL STIPULATIONS:
Hampden County, MA residents only.

SOCIETY OF DAUGHTERS OF THE U.S. ARMY   [1592]
11804 Grey Birch Place
Reston, VA 20191-4223

FOUNDED: 1928

NAME(S) OF PROGRAMS:
● **Society of Daughters of the United States Army Scholarships**

TYPE:
Scholarships.

PURPOSE:
To help daughters or granddaughters (including adopted or step) of career warrant and commissioned Army officers (Warrant Officers through General) who are on active duty, retired after at least 20 years of active service, were medically retired, or died while on active duty or after eligible retirement.

LEGAL BASIS:
Nonprofit corporation.

ELIGIBILITY:
For the Roberts, Wagner, Prickett, Simpson and DUSA Scholarships, applicants must be a daughter or granddaughter (including step or adopted) of a career warrant (WO 1-5) or commissioned (Second & First LT, CPT, MAJ, LTC, COL and BG, MG, LT or full General) officer of the U.S. Army who either:
(1) is currently on active duty;
(2) retired after at least 20 years of active service;
(3) was medically retired before 20 years of active service;
(4) died while on active duty or;
(5) died after retiring with 20 or more years of active service.

U.S. Army must have been the officer's primary occupation. These scholarships are for undergraduate study only and cover academic expenses only. Minimum grade point average is 3.0.

FINANCIAL DATA:
Amount of support per award: $1,000 per year.

NO. MOST RECENT APPLICANTS: 50.

NO. AWARDS: 11.

APPLICATION INFO:
Mail one request with the officer's name, rank, component (active, reserve, retired), inclusive dates of active duty, and the relationship to the applicant, along with a stamped, self-addressed envelope, to the Scholarship Chairman. Do not send any documentation. Requests for applications must be postmarked between November 1 and March 1 for awards in the next academic year. Office is closed between March 2 and October 31. Application is not available when office is closed. Application will not be sent without qualifying information.

Do not send by registered/certified or commercial mail; delivery will be delayed. All application submissions become the property of DUSA.

Duration: One year. The scholarships may be renewed annually for four years, provided a student maintains eligibility.

Deadline: March 1.

STAFF:
Mary P. Maroney, Chairman, Memorial and Scholarship Funds

ADDRESS INQUIRIES TO:
Mary P. Maroney, Scholarship Chairman
Daughters of the United States Army
(See address above.)

SOCIETY OF PHYSICS STUDENTS   [1593]
One Physics Ellipse
College Park, MD 20740-3843
(301) 209-3007
Fax: (301) 209-0839
E-mail: sps@aip.org
Web Site: www.spsnational.org

FOUNDED: 1968

AREAS OF INTEREST:
Physics.

NAME(S) OF PROGRAMS:
● **Society of Physics Students Leadership Scholarship**

TYPE:
Scholarships.

YEAR PROGRAM STARTED: 1985

PURPOSE:
To encourage the study of physics and the pursuit of high scholarship.

LEGAL BASIS:
Not-for-profit, 501(c)(3).

ELIGIBILITY:
Applicants must be a junior according to their institution's definition and plan to be enrolled as an undergraduate for at least one more semester. Only Society of Physics Students members are eligible. Scholarship is awarded on the basis of academic performance and leadership in the Society of Physics Students.

GEOG. RESTRICTIONS: United States.

FINANCIAL DATA:
Amount of support per award: $2,000 to $5,000.

NO. MOST RECENT APPLICANTS: 23.

NO. AWARDS: 17.

APPLICATION INFO:
Completed application form, official transcript of grades, and two letters of recommendation required. Applications are accepted through the online application system only.

Duration: One year. No renewals.

Deadline: March 15.

STAFF:
Mikayla Cleaver, Program Coordinator

ADDRESS INQUIRIES TO:
Mikayla Cleaver, Program Coordinator
(See address above.)

*SPECIAL STIPULATIONS:
Applicant must be an active member of the Society of Physics Students.

THE PAUL & DAISY SOROS FELLOWSHIPS FOR NEW AMERICANS   [1594]
11 West 42nd Street, 3rd Floor
New York, NY 10036
(212) 405-8234
E-mail: pdsoros@pdsoros.org
Web Site: www.pdsoros.org

FOUNDED: 1997

AREAS OF INTEREST:
Financial aid for New Americans.

TYPE:
Fellowships.

PURPOSE:
To provide opportunities for continuing generations of able and accomplished New Americans to achieve leadership in their chosen fields.

ELIGIBILITY:
A New American is defined as an individual who:
(1) is a resident alien (i.e., holds a Green Card);
(2) currently is a DACA (Deferred Action for Childhood Arrivals) recipient and their status is active, is awaiting renewal, or had DACA status, but because the program was rescinded, they no longer have DACA status;
(3) has been naturalized as a U.S. citizen or;
(4) is the child of parents born abroad as non-U.S. citizens.

The applicant must either have a Bachelor's degree or be in his or her final year of undergraduate study.

Upper age limit is 30 years by deadline.

GEOG. RESTRICTIONS: United States.

FINANCIAL DATA:
Amount of support per award: Fellow receives maintenance grant of $25,000 and a tuition grant of one-half tuition cost of U.S. graduate program attended, up to a maximum of $20,000 per annum.

NO. MOST RECENT APPLICANTS: Over 2,200 annually.

NO. AWARDS: 30 per year.

APPLICATION INFO:
Applications must be submitted via the online application system.
Duration: Up to two years.
Deadline: October 29.

ADDRESS INQUIRIES TO:
Yulian Ramos, Deputy Director
(See e-mail address above.)

*SPECIAL STIPULATIONS:
Must be 30 years old or younger by deadline in order to be eligible.

SOUTH CAROLINA HIGHER EDUCATION TUITION GRANTS COMMISSION   [1595]
111 Executive Center Drive
Suite 242
Columbia, SC 29210
(803) 896-1120
E-mail: info@sctuitiongrants.org
Web Site: www.sctuitiongrants.org

FOUNDED: 1970

AREAS OF INTEREST:
Undergraduate student financial aid to eligible South Carolina residents attending in-state, independent colleges on a full-time basis.

CONSULTING OR VOLUNTEER SERVICES:
Assistance to South Carolina high schools and colleges with questions and problems pertaining to student financial aid.

NAME(S) OF PROGRAMS:
● **South Carolina Tuition Grants Program**

TYPE:
Grants-in-aid.

YEAR PROGRAM STARTED: 1970

PURPOSE:
To increase the level of college attendance in South Carolina and to better utilize the existing educational resources of the state; to give students a choice of attending the college that best meets their academic needs.

LEGAL BASIS:
Established by state statute.

ELIGIBILITY:
Applicant must be a South Carolina resident, demonstrate good moral character, be accepted by or enrolled full-time in an eligible South Carolina private college and have financial need. Incoming freshmen must rank in the upper three-quarters of their class or score 900 or higher on the re-centered SAT, score 19 or higher on the ACT, or graduate with a minimum 2.7 grade point average on the SC Uniform Grading Scale. Renewal applicants must complete at least 24 semester-hours per year.

GEOG. RESTRICTIONS: South Carolina.

FINANCIAL DATA:
Awards cannot exceed tuition and fees at the institution, the need of the student and the average per-pupil expenditure by the state at a public college.
Amount of support per award: $100 to $3,600 per year. Average grant $3,100 for the year 2019-20.
Total amount of support: Approximately $44,100,000 total state appropriations for the 2019-20.

NO. MOST RECENT APPLICANTS: 34,531 for the year 2019-20.

NO. AWARDS: 12,850 for the year 2019-20.

APPLICATION INFO:
Application available online.
Duration: One year. Renewable if need continues for up to eight semesters. Must reapply each year.
Deadline: June 30.

PUBLICATIONS:
Annual report; general brochure.

GRANTS COMMITTEE:
Krista Newkirk, Chairperson
Dr. Evans Whitaker, Vice Chairperson
Dr. Roslyn Clark Artis, Secretary
Dr. W. Franklin Evans
Dr. Robert Gustafson
Dr. Darrell Parker
Steve Petit
Dr. Dwaun Warmack

ADDRESS INQUIRIES TO:
Zachary Christian, Deputy Director
(See address above.)

STATE COUNCIL OF HIGHER EDUCATION FOR VIRGINIA   [1596]
James Monroe Building, 10th Floor
101 North 14th Street
Richmond, VA 23219
(804) 225-2600
Fax: (804) 225-2604
E-mail: communications@schev.edu
Web Site: www.schev.edu

FOUNDED: 1956

AREAS OF INTEREST:
Statewide coordination of higher education.

NAME(S) OF PROGRAMS:
● **Virginia Tuition Assistance Grant Program (VTAG)**

TYPE:
Grants-in-aid.

YEAR PROGRAM STARTED: 1972

PURPOSE:
To assist Virginia residents who attend accredited private, nonprofit colleges and universities in Virginia for health profession education.

LEGAL BASIS:
State agency. Program mandated by state law.

ELIGIBILITY:
Recipients must be domiciliary residents of Virginia who are enrolled full-time at an approved private college or university within the state. Not available at Virginia public institutions, for-profit institutions or non-Virginia institutions. Awards are not based on financial need. Students may not be enrolled in a program of religious training or theological education.

GEOG. RESTRICTIONS: Virginia.

FINANCIAL DATA:
Funding is specified biennially by the Appropriations Act.
Amount of support per award: Up to $3,400 for Undergraduate and $1,700 for Graduate for the academic year 2019-20, depending on amount of appropriation and number of recipients.
Total amount of support: $65,812,665 for the academic year 2018-19.

NO. AWARDS: Approximately 23,000 for the academic year 2018-19.

APPLICATION INFO:
Application is available from participating private colleges or universities in Virginia.
Duration: Nine months (academic year). Renewals are reviewed by the institutions.
Deadline: July 31. December 1 for late applications.

ADDRESS INQUIRIES TO:
Applicants should contact the financial aid officer at the participating private Virginia college or university they plan to attend.

STATE OF IDAHO BOARD OF EDUCATION   [1597]
650 West State Street, No. 307
Boise, ID 83720-0037
(208) 332-1595
Fax: (208) 334-2632
E-mail: scholarshiphelp@osbe.idaho.gov
Web Site: www.boardofed.idaho.gov/scholarship/idaho-opportunity-scholarship

FOUNDED: 1891

AREAS OF INTEREST:
Idaho education.

NAME(S) OF PROGRAMS:
● **Idaho Opportunity Scholarship**

TYPE:
Scholarships. Scholarships are available for high school and college students.

YEAR PROGRAM STARTED: 2009

PURPOSE:
To provide scholarships for Idaho citizens who have graduated from an Idaho high school or earned their GED in Idaho.

LEGAL BASIS:
Idaho Code Title 33, Chapter 43 (33-4303).

ELIGIBILITY:
The following scholarship application
requirements apply:
(1) Idaho residency;
(2) graduation from an Idaho high school;
(3) grade point average of 3.0;
(4) demonstration of need by completion of
Free Application for Federal Student Aid
(FAFSA) and;
(5) U.S. citizenship or residency.

GEOG. RESTRICTIONS: Idaho.

FINANCIAL DATA:
Scholarship award cannot exceed cost of
attendance.
Amount of support per award: $3,500.
Total amount of support: $20,777,300 for the
year 2019.

NO. MOST RECENT APPLICANTS: 5,261.

NO. AWARDS: 6,438 new and renewals for the
year 2019.

APPLICATION INFO:
An application form needs to be completed.
Apply online at the web site address above
from December 1 to March 1 of the
following year.
Duration: Four years. Scholarship is
renewable.
Deadline: March 1.

STAFF:
Joy Miller, Scholarships Program Manager

ADDRESS INQUIRIES TO:
Scholarships Program Manager
(See address above.)

STATE OF IDAHO BOARD OF EDUCATION   [1598]
P.O. Box 983
Boise, ID 83701
(208) 342-0777
(208) 334-2270
E-mail: scholarshiphelp@osbe.idaho.gov
Web Site: www.idahogovernorscup.org
www.boardofed.idaho.gov/scholarship/idaho-
governors-cup-scholarship

FOUNDED: 1891

AREAS OF INTEREST:
Idaho education.

NAME(S) OF PROGRAMS:
● **Idaho Governor's Cup Scholarship**

TYPE:
Scholarships. Scholarships are available for
high school seniors and home school students
throughout Idaho.

YEAR PROGRAM STARTED: 1974

PURPOSE:
To provide scholarships for Idaho citizens
who have graduated from an Idaho high
school or earned their GED in Idaho.

LEGAL BASIS:
Idaho Code Title 33, Chapter 43 (33-4303).

ELIGIBILITY:
To qualify for the scholarship, a student must
meet all of the following criteria:
(1) be a resident of Idaho;
(2) be a graduating senior of an Idaho high
school or home school;
(3) enroll as a full-time student in an
academic or technical program at an Idaho
college or university, taking the ACT or SAT
if enrolling in an academic program;
(4) have a cumulative grade point average of

2.8 or above and;
(5) attend the first semester of college
following graduation.

High consideration for selection will be
based on a demonstrated commitment to
public service. Documentation of volunteer
work, leadership, and public service is
required.

GEOG. RESTRICTIONS: Idaho.

FINANCIAL DATA:
Amount of support per award: $3,000.

NO. AWARDS: Approximately 25.

APPLICATION INFO:
Application requires:
(1) completion of the online application;
(2) two letters of recommendation from
individuals who are unrelated to the
applicant, yet know of their interests,
achievements and commitment to public
service;
(3) an essay of no more than 500 words
sharing a little information about the
applicant. Make sure to include academic
interests and what the applicant hopes to
accomplish individually and for others in the
future and;
(4) completed online forms detailing a
commitment to public service including, but
not limited to, school, community and church
volunteer service projects, and participation
in other service organizations and volunteer
work.
Duration: One year. Renewable up to four
years for academic programs and up to three
years for career technical programs.
Deadline: February 15 for academic
programs; March 15 for career technical
programs.

STAFF:
Carlie Foster, Executive Director
Emily Hunter, Assistant Director
Mikayla Mitzel, Scholarship Manager

BOARD OF DIRECTORS AND OFFICERS:
Doug Sayer, President
Mike Reynoldson, Vice President
Cordell Chigbrow, Treasurer
Jeremy Pisca, Secretary
Mike Brassey
Ken Dey
Scott Madison
Jason Kreizenbeck
Jayson Ronk
Pat Sullivan
Anna Torma
Tim Vedder

ADDRESS INQUIRIES TO:
High school counselor or
scholarship program manager
(See e-mail address above.)

STATE OF MICHIGAN DEPARTMENT OF TREASURY   [1599]
P.O. Box 30462
Lansing, MI 48909-7962
(888) 447-2687
Fax: (517) 241-5835
E-mail: mistudentaid@michigan.gov
Web Site: www.michigan.gov/mistudentaid

AREAS OF INTEREST:
Promoting and aiding student higher
education in the state of Michigan.

NAME(S) OF PROGRAMS:
● **Children of Veterans Tuition Grant
(CVTG)**

● **Dual Enrollment**
● **Fostering Futures Scholarship**
● **Michigan Competitive Scholarship
(MCS)**
● **Michigan Gear Up**

TYPE:
Grants-in-aid; Scholarships.

ELIGIBILITY:
All state of Michigan programs require:
(1) high school diploma, certificate of
completion, or GED;
(2) Michigan residency of at least one year
prior to enrollment;
(3) U.S. citizenship, permanent residency or
approved refugee status;
(4) at least half-time enrollment at an
approved Michigan college or university;
(5) student not being in default on a federal
student loan and;
(6) the student meeting Satisfactory
Academic Progress (SAP) standards as set by
the institution.

Children of Veterans Tuition Grant: Student
must be the natural or adopted child of a
Michigan veteran who is totally and
permanently disabled, deceased or missing in
action. Student must be at least 16 and less
than 21 years old and must maintain a
cumulative grade point average of 2.25 for
renewal.

Dual Enrollment: Students attending a private
high school are determined eligible by the
Michigan Department of Education (MDE).

Fostering Futures Scholarship: Student must
have been in foster care after the 13th
birthday. There is no upper age limit and
student can receive funding at any age.
Student must be attending a Michigan public
or private four-year college/university or a
community college. Funding can be used
along with the Education Training Voucher.

Michigan Competitive Scholarship: Student
must have an SAT score of 1200 and a
qualifying ACT score of at least 23
(composite) or 90 (scaled score) and cannot
be attending an institution whose primary
purpose is to prepare students for ordination
or appointment as a member of the clergy of
a church, denomination or religious sect.
Student must maintain a minimum
cumulative 2.0 grade point average.

Michigan Gear Up: Only nominated
participants will be eligible for a scholarship.

FINANCIAL DATA:
Fostering Futures provides eligible foster
youth with scholarship funds for tuition, fees,
room/board, books and supplies/equipment
required for enrollment. Michigan
Competitive Scholarship program is both
merit- and need-based. Limited to tuition and
mandatory fees.
Amount of support per award: Children of
Veterans Tuition Grant: Up to $2,800 per
academic year (award limited to tuition and
mandatory fees); Fostering Futures
Scholarship: Up to $3,000; Michigan
Competitive Scholarship: Up to $1,000 per
academic year; Michigan Gear Up:
Maximum $1,000.

APPLICATION INFO:
Fostering Futures Scholarship: Application
must be submitted with copies of student
financial aid award letter, most recent
transcripts, and documentation supporting
any off-campus expenses requested.

Duration: Children of Veterans Tuition Grant and Michigan Gear Up: Up to four academic years. Michigan Competitive Scholarship: Limited to 10 semesters or 15 terms.

Deadline: Varies.

ADDRESS INQUIRIES TO:
State of Michigan
Student Scholarships and Grants
(See address and e-mail above.)

STATE OF MICHIGAN DEPARTMENT OF TREASURY [1600]

P.O. Box 30462
Lansing, MI 48909-7962
(888) 447-2687
Fax: (517) 241-5835
E-mail: mistudentaid@michigan.gov
Web Site: www.michigan.gov/mistudentaid

NAME(S) OF PROGRAMS:
- **Michigan Tuition Grant (MTG)**
- **Police Officer's and Fire Fighter's Survivor Tuition Grant (STG)**
- **Tuition Incentive Program (TIP)**

TYPE:
Grants-in-aid.

ELIGIBILITY:
Michigan Tuition Grant: Program is need-based. Student must be enrolled at an approved independent, degree-granting Michigan institution. However, student cannot be enrolled in a course of study leading to a degree in theology, divinity or religious education.

Police Officer's and Fire Fighter's Survivor Tuition Grant: For children and surviving spouses of Michigan police officers and firefighters killed in the line of duty. Must provide satisfactory proof. Child must be less than 21 at the time of the police officer's or firefighter's death and must apply before age 21. Award recipient must enroll at least half-time in a program leading to a certificate or degree at an approved Michigan community college or public university. Applicant must, excluding death benefits, be below 400% of the federal poverty level (must demonstrate financial need).

Tuition Incentive Program: Student must have received Medicaid coverage, as determined by The Michigan Department of Human Services (DHS), for 24 months within any 36 consecutive months between the ages of 9 and high school graduation. Awardee must begin using program within four years from high school graduation. Eligibility ends after six years from the date of high school graduation.

FINANCIAL DATA:
Police Officer's and Fire Fighter's Survivor Tuition Grant: Award limited to tuition only. Tuition Incentive Program: Award limited to tuition and mandatory fees; eligible mandatory fees cannot exceed $250 per semester or term.

Amount of support per award: Michigan Tuition Grant: Up to $2,400 per academic year. Award limited to tuition and mandatory fees.

APPLICATION INFO:
Details are available online.

Duration: Michigan Tuition Grant: Limited to 10 semesters or 15 terms. Police Officer's and Fire Fighter's Survivor Tuition Grant: Limited to 9 semesters or 14 terms (124

semester- or 180 term-credits). Tuition Incentive Program: Pays up to 24 semester- or 36 term-credits per academic year; cannot exceed 80 semester- or 120 term-credits.

Deadline: Michigan Tuition Grant: March 1. Tuition Incentive Program: August 31.

ADDRESS INQUIRIES TO:
State of Michigan
Student Scholarships and Grants
(See address and e-mail above.)

SUDBURY FOUNDATION

326 Concord Road
Sudbury, MA 01776
(978) 443-0849
Fax: (978) 579-9536
E-mail: contact@sudburyfoundation.org
Web Site: www.sudburyfoundation.org

TYPE:
Project/program grants; Scholarships. Capacity-building grants.

See entry 1263 for full listing.

SYRACUSE UNIVERSITY [1601]

Graduate School
304 Lyman Hall
Syracuse, NY 13244-1200
(315) 443-1701
E-mail: gradawd@syr.edu
Web Site: www.syr.edu

AREAS OF INTEREST:
Student work/study programs.

NAME(S) OF PROGRAMS:
- **Syracuse University Graduate Assistantships**

TYPE:
Assistantships. Syracuse University Graduate Assistantships are of a teaching or research nature.

FINANCIAL DATA:
Amount of support per award: $15,378 minimum stipend plus up to 24 credit hours of tuition scholarship for the year 2017-18. Majority of stipends are greater than the minimum.

APPLICATION INFO:
Applicants must apply through departments.
Duration: One year. Renewable, depending upon student's performance and departmental need.
Deadline: Varies by program and is dependent upon admission deadline.

ADDRESS INQUIRIES TO:
Academic department of interest.

SYRACUSE UNIVERSITY [1602]

Graduate School
304 Lyman Hall
Syracuse, NY 13244-1200
(315) 443-1701
E-mail: gradawd@syr.edu
Web Site: www.syr.edu

AREAS OF INTEREST:
Graduate university education.

NAME(S) OF PROGRAMS:
- **African American Graduate Fellowship**
- **Hursky Fellowship**
- **STEM Doctoral Fellowships**
- **Syracuse University Fellowship**

TYPE:
Fellowships.

PURPOSE:
To provide a full support package during a student's term of study.

ELIGIBILITY:
African American Graduate Fellowships: Awarded annually to new and continuing students across disciplines whose work supports that of the African American Studies Program.

Hursky Fellowship: Open to graduate students with a Ukrainian background whose area of study is the Ukraine or includes topics related to the Ukraine.

STEM Doctoral Fellowships: Science, technology, engineering and math disciplines. Open to members of an underrepresented group who are U.S. citizens or permanent residents.

Syracuse University Fellowships: Open to nationals of any country.

FINANCIAL DATA:
Fellowships include up to 30 credits of tuition.
Amount of support per award: $15,425 for Master's stipend plus full tuition; $25,290 for Ph.D. stipend for full tuition.

NO. AWARDS: African American Graduate Fellowship: 6 new per year; Hursky Fellowship: 1 new per year; STEM Doctoral Fellowships: Up to 5 new per year; Syracuse University Fellowship: Number of awards determined by each academic college, varies yearly.

APPLICATION INFO:
Applicants must apply through admission application.
Duration: Varies by fellowship type, one to five years.
Deadline: January 1, unless earlier date determined by specific department.

ADDRESS INQUIRIES TO:
See e-mail address above.

TENNESSEE STUDENT ASSISTANCE CORPORATION [1603]

404 James Robertson Parkway
Parkway Towers, Suite 1510
Nashville, TN 37243-0820
(615) 741-1346
(800) 342-1663
Fax: (615) 741-6101
E-mail: tsac.aidinfo@tn.gov
Web Site: www.tn.gov/collegepays

FOUNDED: 1974

NAME(S) OF PROGRAMS:
- **Dependent Children Scholarship Program**
- **Graduate Nursing Loan-Forgiveness Program**
- **Ned McWherter Scholars Program**
- **Minority Teaching Fellows Program**
- **Tennessee Education Lottery Scholarship Program**
- **Tennessee Math & Science Teachers Loan Forgiveness Program**
- **Tennessee Promise**
- **Tennessee Reconnect**
- **Tennessee Student Assistance Award**
- **Tennessee Teaching Scholars Program**

TYPE:
Grants-in-aid; Scholarships; Loan forgiveness programs. Need-based grants for undergraduate Tennessee residents enrolled in an eligible Tennessee institution.

Dependent Children Scholarship Program provides aid for Tennessee residents who are dependent children of a Tennessee law enforcement officer, fireman or an emergency medical service technician who has been killed or totally and permanently disabled while performing duties within the scope of such employment.

Graduate Nursing Loan-Forgiveness Program is designed to encourage Tennessee residents who are nurses to become teachers and administrators in Tennessee nursing education programs. Participants in this program incur an obligation to enter a faculty or administrative position in a nursing education program, in Tennessee, immediately upon completion of the education program.

The Ned McWherter Scholars Program is intended to encourage academically superior Tennessee high school graduates to attend college in Tennessee.

Minority Teaching Fellows Program is intended to encourage talented minority Tennesseans to enter the teaching field in Tennessee.

Tennessee Education Lottery Scholarship Program is for those who have been a Tennessee resident for one year by September 1 of the year of application date.

Tennessee Math & Science Teachers Loan Forgiveness Program provides financial assistance to Tennessee public school teachers seeking an advanced degree in a math or a science, or a certification to teach a math or a science. Loan forgiveness requires employment in a Tennessee public school system two years for each year of the loan funding received.

Tennesee Promise is both a scholarship and mentoring program focused on increasing the number of students that attend college in the state. It provides students a last-dollar scholarship, meaning the scholarship will cover tuition and fees not covered by the Pell grant, the HOPE scholarship, or state student assistance funds. Students may use the scholarship at any of the state's 13 community colleges, 27 colleges of applied technology, or other eligible institutions offering an Associate's degree program.

Tennessee Reconnect is Governor Bill Haslam's initiative to help more of the state's adults enter higher education to gain new skills, advance in the workplace, and fulfill lifelong dreams of completing a degree or credential.

Tennessee Student Assistance Award provides nonrepayable financial assistance to financially needy undergraduate students who are residents of Tennessee.

Tennessee Teaching Scholars Program is intended to encourage exemplary students to enter the teaching field in Tennessee.

YEAR PROGRAM STARTED: 1976

PURPOSE:
To provide grants based on financial need for Tennessee residents.

LEGAL BASIS:
State agency.

ELIGIBILITY:
Applicants for the Ned McWherter Scholars Program must be high school seniors with a 3.5 grade point average, a GED score of 570 and 29 ACT or 1280 SAT, and planning to attend an eligible Tennessee institution.

Applicants for the Minority Teaching Fellows Program are preferably high school seniors with a 2.75 grade point average and 18 ACT or be at the top 25% of their graduating class. Undergraduate applicants must have a 2.5 college grade point average.

Applicants for the Tennessee Education Lottery Scholarship Program must:
(1) be entering freshmen who are Tennessee residents for one year prior to application;
(2) enroll in a Tennessee public college/university or enroll in a Tennessee private college/university that is accredited by the Southern Association of Colleges and Schools and;
(3) be enrolled full-time (part-time prorated), leading to a certificate in the Tennessee Technology Centers or degree in approved colleges and universities. Satisfactory academic progress required.

Applicants for the Tennessee Teaching Scholars Program must be college juniors or seniors or post-Baccalaureate students admitted to teacher education programs in Tennessee colleges or universities and U.S. citizens.

GEOG. RESTRICTIONS: Tennessee.

FINANCIAL DATA:
Amount of support per award: Varies.
Matching fund requirements: For Ned McWherter Scholars Program, the institution must match $3,000.

NO. MOST RECENT APPLICANTS: Ned McWherter Scholars: 900; Minority Teaching Fellows: 150; Tennessee Teaching Scholars: 400.

NO. AWARDS: Ned McWherter Scholars: 50; Minority Teaching Fellows: 29; Tennessee Education Lottery Scholarship Program: 40,000; Tennessee Teaching Scholars: 160.

APPLICATION INFO:
Detailed information is available online.
Duration: Renewable each academic year.
Deadline: Ned McWherter Scholars: February 15; Minority Teaching Fellows: April 15; Tennessee Education Lottery Scholarship Program: September 1 for fall term, February 1 for spring and summer terms; Tennessee Teaching Scholars: April 15.

ADDRESS INQUIRIES TO:
See telephone numbers above.

*SPECIAL STIPULATIONS:
Loan Forgiveness Programs, Tennessee Teaching Scholars and Minority Teaching Fellows: Recipients agree to teach one year for each year of funding in a public Tennessee grades K-12 school or appropriate learning institution or repayment will be required.

TWO TEN FOOTWEAR FOUNDATION   [1604]
Scholarship Department
1466 Main Street
Waltham, MA 02451
(800) 346-3210
Fax: (781) 736-1555; (781) 736-1554
E-mail: wweatherly@twoten.org
Web Site: twoten.org

FOUNDED: 1939

AREAS OF INTEREST:
Footwear industry.

NAME(S) OF PROGRAMS:
● **Two Ten Footwear Foundation College Scholarship Program**

TYPE:
Scholarships. Offered to students affiliated with the footwear, leather or allied industries.

YEAR PROGRAM STARTED: 1969

PURPOSE:
To provide financial assistance to people in the footwear, leather and allied industries.

LEGAL BASIS:
Private foundation.

ELIGIBILITY:
Scholarship applicant must be affiliated with the footwear, leather or allied industries:
(1) either the student must be employed in the above industries, or have a parent (natural, step or adopted) who must be employed in these industries for a minimum of two years prior to January 1 (student must be considered a dependent);
(2) student must display financial need for college costs as calculated by the federal method of need analysis and the Two Ten Selection Committee;
(3) student must be a U.S. citizen or eligible noncitizen and;
(4) student must enroll at an accredited college, university, nursing or vocational/technical school, earning a two- or four-year undergraduate degree.

FINANCIAL DATA:
Amount of support per award: Generally, up to $3,000; Members of National Shoe Travelers and retailers of the National Shoe and Shoe Retailers Association: Up to $5,000.
Total amount of support: Approximately $870,000 for the year 2018.

NO. AWARDS: 350 for the year 2018.

APPLICATION INFO:
Contact the Foundation.
Duration: Up to four years.
Deadline: April 1.

ADDRESS INQUIRIES TO:
Walker Weatherly
(See e-mail address above.)

*SPECIAL STIPULATIONS:
Eligible companies must do at least 50% of their business in footwear, or applicant or parent must work in a specific footwear division.

TWO TEN FOOTWEAR FOUNDATION   [1605]
1466 Main Street
Waltham, MA 02451
(800) 346-3210 ext. 1512
Fax: (781) 736-1555; (781) 736-1554
E-mail: wweatherly@twoten.org
Web Site: twoten.org

AREAS OF INTEREST:
Footwear design.

NAME(S) OF PROGRAMS:
● **Two Ten Footwear Foundation Design Scholarship Program**

TYPE:
Scholarships. Intended for students who are interested in pursuing a career in footwear design.

YEAR PROGRAM STARTED: 2003

PURPOSE:
To provide financial aid to those studying footwear design.

ELIGIBILITY:
Applicant must:
(1) demonstrate an interest and commitment to a career in footwear design;
(2) be a U.S. citizen or eligible noncitizen;
(3) display financial need as calculated by the federal method of need analysis and the Design Scholarship Selection Committee (applicant can estimate Expected Family Contribution at www.finaid.com) and;
(4) attend or plan to attend an approved postsecondary institution.

GEOG. RESTRICTIONS: United States.

FINANCIAL DATA:
Amount of support per award: Up to $3,000.
Total amount of support: Varies.

NO. AWARDS: Varies.

APPLICATION INFO:
Applicants for consideration must submit a portfolio. Interested candidates must contact the director of scholarship for further information.
Duration: Up to four years.
Deadline: April 5.

ADDRESS INQUIRIES TO:
Walker Weatherly
(See e-mail address above.)

U.S. DEPARTMENT OF EDUCATION [1606]
Federal Student Aid Programs
830 First Street, N.E.
Washington, DC 20202
(800) 433-3243
TTY: (800)-730-8913
E-mail: studentaid@ed.gov
Web Site: studentaid.ed.gov

AREAS OF INTEREST:
Student financial aid.

NAME(S) OF PROGRAMS:
● **Pell Grant**

TYPE:
Grants-in-aid. Student aid grants for higher education. Available almost exclusively to undergraduates. Grant does not have to be repaid.

YEAR PROGRAM STARTED: 1973

PURPOSE:
To help undergraduates pay for education after high school.

LEGAL BASIS:
Title IV, Higher Education Act of 1965, as amended.

ELIGIBILITY:
In general, the aid recipient must:
(1) show financial need;
(2) enroll as a regular student in an eligible degree or certificate program;
(3) be a U.S. citizen or eligible noncitizen and;
(4) meet the school's satisfactory academic progress standards in his or her course of study.

The student also must register with the Selective Service, if required.

FINANCIAL DATA:
Amount of support per award: Depends on student's financial need, the cost of attendance (COA) at the student's school, status as full-time or part-time student and how long the student will be enrolled in the academic year in question. The financial aid office at student's college or career school will determine how much financial aid he or she is eligible to receive.

APPLICATION INFO:
Applicants should contact the financial aid office at each school they are considering attending to determine which forms must be submitted. Students can request a copy of the *Student Guide* at the toll-free phone number.
Duration: One year. Renewable. Student can receive Federal Pell Grant for no more than 12 semesters or the equivalent (roughly six years).

PUBLICATIONS:
Funding Education Beyond High School: The Guide to Federal Student Aid.

ADDRESS INQUIRIES TO:
Federal Student Aid Programs
P.O. Box 84
Washington, DC 20044

*PLEASE NOTE:
Applicant may receive only one Pell Grant in an award year, and may not receive Pell Grant funds from more than one school at a time.

U.S. DEPARTMENT OF EDUCATION [1607]
Federal Student Aid Programs
830 First Street, N.E.
Washington, DC 20202
(800) 433-3243
TTY: (800) 730-8913
E-mail: studentaid@ed.gov
Web Site: studentaid.ed.gov

AREAS OF INTEREST:
Student financial aid.

NAME(S) OF PROGRAMS:
● **Federal Work-Study**

TYPE:
Work-study programs. Federal Work-Study program provides part-time jobs for undergraduate and graduate students with financial need. This allows them to earn money to help pay education expenses. Jobs can be on- or off-campus and are available to full-time or part-time students. Students are paid at least federal minimum wage. The money earned does not have to be repaid. The program is administered by schools participating in the Federal Work-Study Program. Interested students should check with their school's financial aid office to determine if their school does participate.

PURPOSE:
To enable students to earn a part of educational expenses.

LEGAL BASIS:
Government agency.

ELIGIBILITY:
In general, the aid recipient must:
(1) show financial need;
(2) be a U.S. citizen or eligible noncitizen with a valid Social Security number (SSN);
(3) be working toward a degree or certificate in an eligible program;
(4) demonstrate one is qualified to obtain a postsecondary education;
(5) register (if not already done so) with the Selective Service, if one is a male between the ages of 18 and 25 and;
(6) maintain satisfactory academic progress once in school.

FINANCIAL DATA:
Federal Work-Study wages will be at least the current federal minimum wage, but may be higher, depending on the type of work and the skills required. The total Federal Work-Study award depends on when a student applies, one's level of need, and the funding level of one's school.
Amount of support per award: Varies.
Total amount of support: Varies.

APPLICATION INFO:
The interested student should consult with his or her school's financial aid office.
Duration: One year. Renewable.

PUBLICATIONS:
Funding Your Education: The Guide to Federal Student Aid.

ADDRESS INQUIRIES TO:
Federal Student Aid Programs
P.O. Box 84
Washington, DC 20044

U.S. DEPARTMENT OF EDUCATION [1608]
Federal Student Aid Programs
830 First Street, N.E.
Washington, DC 20202
(800) 433-3243
TTY: (800) 730-8913 (for hearing-impaired)
E-mail: studentaid@ed.gov
Web Site: studentaid.ed.gov

AREAS OF INTEREST:
Student financial aid.

NAME(S) OF PROGRAMS:
● **Federal Supplemental Educational Opportunity Grant (FSEOG)**

TYPE:
Grants-in-aid. Federal Supplemental Educational Opportunity Grant (FSEOG) is a grant for undergraduate students with exceptional financial need. This grant does not need to be repaid. The program is administered directly by the financial aid office at each participating school and is therefore called "campus-based" aid. Not all schools participate.

PURPOSE:
To help undergraduates with exceptional financial need.

ELIGIBILITY:
FSEOG is awarded to undergraduate students who have exceptional financial need and who have not earned a Bachelor's or graduate degree. Federal Pell Grant recipients receive priority.

FINANCIAL DATA:
Amount of support per award: $100 to $4,000 a year, depending on student's financial need, when student applied, the amount of other aid student has received, and the availability of funds at student's school.

APPLICATION INFO:
Student should check with his or her school's financial aid office to ascertain if the school offers the FSEOG.
Deadline: Each school sets its own deadlines for campus-based funds.

*PLEASE NOTE:
Each participating school receives a certain amount of FSEOG funds each year from the U.S. Department of Education's office of Federal Student Aid. Once the full amount of the school's FSEOG funds has been awarded to students, no more FSEOG awards can be made for that year.

U.S. DEPARTMENT OF EDUCATION [1609]

Federal Student Aid Programs
830 First Street, N.E.
Washington, DC 20202
(800) 433-3243
TTY: (800) 730-8913 (for hearing-impaired)
E-mail: studentaid@ed.gov
Web Site: studentaid.ed.gov

AREAS OF INTEREST:
Student financial aid.

NAME(S) OF PROGRAMS:
- Teacher Education Assistance for College and Higher Education (TEACH) Grant

TYPE:
Grants-in-aid. Grant does not have to be repaid unless recipient fails to carry out the service obligation.

PURPOSE:
To help undergraduate, post-Baccalaureate and graduate students with financial need.

ELIGIBILITY:
The TEACH Grant is intended for undergraduate, post-Baccalaureate and graduate students who plan to become elementary or secondary teachers. Recipient must sign Agreement to Serve saying he or she will teach full-time in a high-need field for four complete years (within eight years of completing the academic program) at an elementary school, secondary school or educational service agency serving children from low-income families. Grant recipient must attend a participating college and meet certain academic achievement requirements. Failure to complete the teaching service commitment will result in the grant being converted to a Direct Unsubsidized Loan that must be repaid.

FINANCIAL DATA:
Amount of support per award: Up to $4,000 per year.

APPLICATION INFO:
Those interested in applying must contact the financial aid office at the school where they will be enrolled to find out whether the school participates in the TEACH Grant Program and to learn about the programs of study at the school that are TEACH-grant eligible.

THE MORRIS K. UDALL AND STEWART L. UDALL FOUNDATION [1610]

130 South Scott Avenue
Tucson, AZ 85701
(520) 901-8564
Fax: (520) 901-8570
E-mail: curley@udall.gov
Web Site: www.udall.gov

FOUNDED: 1992

AREAS OF INTEREST:
Environment, including policy, engineering, science, education, urban planning and renewal, business, justice and economics; Native American health care and tribal public policy, including policy, engineering, science, education and business.

NAME(S) OF PROGRAMS:
- Udall Scholarship

TYPE:
Scholarships. The Udall Foundation seeks future leaders across a wide spectrum of environmental fields, including policy, engineering, science, education, urban planning and renewal, business, justice and economics.

The Udall Foundation also seeks future Native American and Alaska Native leaders in Native American health care and tribal public policy. Tribal policy includes fields related to tribal sovereignty, tribal governance, tribal law, Native American education, Native American justice, natural resource management, cultural preservation and revitalization, Native American economic development and other areas affecting Native American communities. Native American health care includes health care administration, social work, medicine and research into health conditions affecting Native American communities.

YEAR PROGRAM STARTED: 1996

PURPOSE:
To educate a new generation of Americans to preserve and protect their national heritage through studies in the environment, Native American health and tribal policy, and effective public policy conflict resolution.

LEGAL BASIS:
The Foundation is an executive branch agency. The President of the U.S. appoints its board of trustees with the advice and consent of the U.S. Senate.

ELIGIBILITY:
Citizens, nationals or permanent residents of the U.S. are eligible to apply. The scholarship awards are made on the basis of merit to two groups of students:
(1) those who are college sophomores or juniors in the current academic year, have outstanding potential and who study the environment and related fields and;
(2) Native American and Alaska Native students who are college sophomores or juniors in the current academic year, have outstanding potential and are in fields related to health care or tribal public policy.

FINANCIAL DATA:
Amount of support per award: Up to $7,000.
Total amount of support: Varies.

NO. AWARDS: Approximately 55 for the year 2020.

APPLICATION INFO:
Application information is available on the web site.
Duration: One year.
Deadline: Approximately early March each year.

STAFF:
Jason Curley, Program Manager

ADDRESS INQUIRIES TO:
Jason Curley, Program Manager
(See address above.)

*SPECIAL STIPULATIONS:
Students must have support from a faculty or staff member at their college.

UNICO NATIONAL, INC. [1611]

271 U.S. Highway 46 West
Suite F-103
Fairfield, NJ 07004
(973) 808-0035
Fax: (973) 808-0043
E-mail: uniconational@unico.org
Web Site: www.unico.org

FOUNDED: 1922

NAME(S) OF PROGRAMS:
- Maria and Paolo Alessio Southern Italy Scholarship
- Sargeant John Basilone Memorial Graduate Scholarship
- Cottone Postgraduate Scholarship (Medical Only)
- William C. Davini Scholarship
- DiMattio Celli Undergraduate Study Abroad Program
- Major Don S. Gentile Scholarship
- Ella Grasso Literary Scholarship
- Inserra Scholarships
- Guglielmo Marconi Engineering Scholarship
- Theodore Mazza Scholarship
- Alphonse A. Miele Scholarship
- Robert J. Tarte Scholarship for Italian Studies
- Bernard and Carolyn Torraco Nursing Scholarships
- Louise Torraco Memorial Scholarship for Science
- Ralph J. Torraco Fine Arts Scholarship
- Ralph J. Torraco Scholarship
- Ralph J. Torraco Scholarship for Special Education
- Ralph J. Torraco Scholarship for Therapy Sciences

TYPE:
Scholarships. Postgraduate scholarships and undergraduate scholarships.

PURPOSE:
To give financial aid to students of outstanding merit so they may complete their education.

ELIGIBILITY:
Candidates must reside in the home state of an active UNICO Chapter, unless otherwise indicated. Candidates must meet the eligibility requirements stated on each of the respective applications. Online degree programs are not eligible for UNICO scholarships.

Scholarship candidates must, in general, be of Italian heritage, i.e., must have one parent or grandparent of Italian heritage. The Tarte and Torraco Scholarships are open to all ethnicities. The extent to which a candidate has contributed to the life and welfare of school and/or community will be taken into account in the assessment of merit. UNICO member's children are eligible. Each chapter of UNICO National may submit applications for each of the UNICO Foundation scholarships.

A candidate for the undergraduate scholarships must be a citizen of the U.S. and have Italian heritage. An applicant must be a graduating senior at a public or private secondary school.

Applicants to the Alessio Scholarship must be currently attending, full-time students at an accredited campus based college or university program in the U.S. pursuing a degree. Applicant must be of Southern Italian descent, specifically including the regions of Abruzzo, Basilicata, Calabria, Campania, Latium, Molise, Puglia, Sardinia, and Sicilia.

The Basilone Scholarship requires that the applicant be a senior in college or a graduate beginning postgraduate studies.

The Cottone Scholarship requires that a candidate be a college senior or graduate who is beginning postgraduate studies in the field of medicine or is currently enrolled in an accredited medical school in the U.S.

A candidate for either postgraduate program (Basilone or Cottone Scholarship) must be a U.S. citizen of Italian heritage.

A candidate for the Inserra Scholarship must be a full-time student enrolled in an accredited college or university in the U.S. pursuing a degree. Candidate must be a citizen of Italian heritage.

A candidate for the Guglielmo Marconi Engineering Scholarship must be a sophomore, junior or senior student enrolled full-time, in an accredited college/university program in the U.S. majoring in engineering. Applicant must be a U.S. citizen of Italian heritage.

Robert J. Tarte Scholarship is given to a student enrolled full-time in an accredited college or university program in the U.S. pursuing Italian studies.

A candidate for the Bernard and Carolyn Torraco Memorial Nursing Scholarship must currently be enrolled in an accredited nursing degree program in the U.S., completing core nursing courses, at one of the following: An Associate Degree School of Nursing; A Collegiate School of Nursing; A Diploma School of Nursing. Proof of enrollment must be provided. The candidate must have a minimum grade point average of 3.0 or B to qualify. Preference will be given to applicants demonstrating financial need.

A candidate for the Louise Torraco Memorial Scholarship for Science must be enrolled full-time in an accredited college/university program in the U.S. pursuing study in the physical sciences or life sciences. Nominee must hold U.S. citizenship.

Ralph J. Torraco Fine Arts Scholarship is given to students enrolled full-time in an accredited college/university program in the U.S. pursuing a degree in the fine arts. Nominee must hold U.S. citizenship.

Ralph J. Torraco Scholarship requires students to be enrolled full-time in an accredited college/university program in the U.S. pursuing a degree. Nominees must hold U.S. citizenship.

Ralph J. Torraco Scholarship for Special Education requires students to be currently attending, full-time, an accredited campus based college/university program in the U.S. pursuing a degree in the field of special education. A candidate must hold U.S. citizenship.

Ralph J. Torraco Scholarship for Therapy Sciences requires students to be currently attending, full-time, an accredited campus based college/university program in the U.S. pursuing a degree in the field of therapy sciences. A candidate must hold U.S. citizenship.

FINANCIAL DATA:
Amount of support per award: Alessio, Inserra, Torraco Nursing, Louise Toracco Memorial and all Ralph J. Torraco Scholarships: $2,500; Basilone, Davini, Gentile, Mazza and Miele Scholarships: $1,500 per year; Cottone Postgraduate Scholarship: $5,000; DiMattio Celli Program and Guglielmo Marconi Engineering Scholarship: $1,250; Grasso and Tarte Scholarships: $1,000.
Total amount of support: Varies.

NO. AWARDS: Alessio, Cottone, Davini, Gentile, Marconi, Mazza, Miele and Tarte Scholarships: 1; Basilone, DiMattio, Grasso,

Inserra, Louise Torraco and all Ralph J. Torraco Scholarships: 2; Bernard and Carolyn Torraco Scholarship: Up to 10.

APPLICATION INFO:
Applications are to be submitted online. Students will find complete information and submission instructions under the Scholarship tab on the UNICO National web site. Paper applications cannot be accepted.
Duration: Basilone Scholarship: Maximum of two years; Cottone Postgraduate Scholarship: One-time only; Undergraduate scholarships: Maximum of four years.
Deadline: DiMattio Celli Undergraduate Study Abroad Program: March 1. All others: April 15.

ADDRESS INQUIRIES TO:
UNICO National Scholarship Director (See address above.)

UNITED NEGRO COLLEGE FUND (UNCF)
1805 Seventh Street, N.W.
Washington, DC 20001
(800) 331-2244
(202) 810-0258
E-mail: scholarships@uncf.org
Web Site: www.uncf.org

TYPE:
Fellowships; Internships; Scholarships; Technical assistance. The Fund, since its founding, has raised money for 37 private, historically Black colleges and universities.

Faculty fellowship programs make it possible for hundreds of instructors to earn doctoral degrees.

Mentoring and internship opportunities are provided for hundreds of UNCF students.

Scholarships are offered to a pool of more than 60,000 talented students attending UNCF colleges and universities. The Fund oversees more than 450 scholarship programs in the following general categories:
(1) geographically based scholarships;
(2) scholarships based on academic major;
(3) scholarships based on merit and need and;
(4) financial aid for graduate study.

See entry 948 for full listing.

THE UNIVERSITY OF BRITISH COLUMBIA   [1612]
Faculty of Graduate and Postdoctoral Studies
170-6371 Crescent Road
Vancouver BC V6T 1Z2 Canada
(604) 822-2848
Fax: (604) 822-5802
E-mail: graduate.awards@ubc.ca
Web Site: www.grad.ubc.ca/scholarships-awards-funding

AREAS OF INTEREST:
All areas of advanced study.

NAME(S) OF PROGRAMS:
● **Affiliated Fellowships**

TYPE:
Fellowships. For postgraduate studies leading to a Master's or Doctorate degree at the University of British Columbia.

PURPOSE:
To allow outstanding students to devote full-time to research and study leading to a Master's or Doctorate degree.

LEGAL BASIS:
University.

ELIGIBILITY:
Citizens of any country may apply. Applicants must have outstanding academic records.

FINANCIAL DATA:
Amount of support per award: Master's: $175 to $16,000 (CAN); Doctoral: $175 to $30,000 (CAN) per annum. Most approximately $16,000 (CAN).
Total amount of support: Approximately $600,000 (CAN) per annum.

NO. MOST RECENT APPLICANTS: Approximately 800.

NO. AWARDS: Approximately 50 per year.

APPLICATION INFO:
Fellowships are awarded on the basis of applications submitted to graduate programs.
Duration: One or two years.
Deadline: Early December for Master's Program and mid-September for Doctoral Program.

ADDRESS INQUIRIES TO:
See e-mail address above.

THE UNIVERSITY OF BRITISH COLUMBIA   [1613]
Faculty of Graduate and Postdoctoral Studies
170-6371 Crescent Road
Vancouver BC V6T 1Z2 Canada
(604) 822-2848
Fax: (604) 822-5802
E-mail: graduate.awards@ubc.ca
Web Site: www.grad.ubc.ca/scholarships-awards-funding

AREAS OF INTEREST:
Doctoral study in all disciplines.

NAME(S) OF PROGRAMS:
● **Four Year Doctoral Fellowships**

TYPE:
Fellowships.

YEAR PROGRAM STARTED: 2009

PURPOSE:
To attract and retain outstanding doctoral students by offering stable, base-level funding for four years of their Ph.D. studies and research.

ELIGIBILITY:
Open to doctoral students in any discipline. Citizens of any country may apply.

FINANCIAL DATA:
Amount of support per award: Ensures student receives financial support of at least $18,200 (CAN) per year plus tuition.
Total amount of support: Approximately $14,000,000.

NO. AWARDS: 200 new fellowships offered by graduate programs each year.

APPLICATION INFO:
Applicant must first contact graduate program of interest. Fellowships are awarded on basis of nomination made by graduate program.
Duration: Four years.
Deadline: Most funding decisions made in January to March.

ADDRESS INQUIRIES TO:
See e-mail address above.

THE UNIVERSITY OF BRITISH COLUMBIA [1614]

Faculty of Graduate and Postdoctoral Studies
170-6371 Crescent Road
Vancouver BC V6T 1Z2 Canada
(604) 822-2848
Fax: (604) 822-5802
E-mail: graduate.awards@ubc.ca
Web Site: www.grad.ubc.ca/scholarships-awards-funding

AREAS OF INTEREST:
Research-based Master's and doctoral studies.

NAME(S) OF PROGRAMS:
● **Graduate Support Initiative**

TYPE:
Scholarships.

YEAR PROGRAM STARTED: 2008

PURPOSE:
To provide funding for graduate students through entrance scholarships, multiyear funding packages, tuition awards, and scholarship top-ups.

LEGAL BASIS:
University.

ELIGIBILITY:
Citizens of any country may apply.

FINANCIAL DATA:
Amount of support per award: Set by graduate programs.
Total amount of support: Approximately $6,500,000 annually.

APPLICATION INFO:
Student should submit research proposal and academic record to the graduate department of interest.
Duration: Up to four years.
Deadline: Inquiry to graduate program of interest accepted throughout the year. Most funding decisions are made January to March.

ADDRESS INQUIRIES TO:
See e-mail address above.

THE UNIVERSITY OF CALGARY [1615]

Faculty of Graduate Studies
Earth Sciences Building, Room 1010
2500 University Drive, N.W.
Calgary AB T2N 1N4 Canada
(403) 220-4938
Fax: (403) 289-7635
E-mail: gsaward@ucalgary.ca
Web Site: grad.ucalgary.ca/awards

FOUNDED: 1966

AREAS OF INTEREST:
Petroleum industry.

NAME(S) OF PROGRAMS:
● **The Archibald Waynne Dingman Memorial Graduate Scholarship**

TYPE:
Awards/prizes; Scholarships. Graduate scholarship for study in all areas relevant to the petroleum industry. Tenable at The University of Calgary. Award endowed through a bequest of the late Corinne Patteson.

ELIGIBILITY:
Open to qualified graduates of any recognized university who are registered in or admissible to a program leading to a Master's or doctoral degree at The University of Calgary.

FINANCIAL DATA:
Amount of support per award: $3,500 (CAN).
Total amount of support: $3,500 (CAN).

NO. AWARDS: 1.

APPLICATION INFO:
Students should consult the Graduate Award Competition Guidelines and Application available online.
Duration: One year.
Deadline: February 1 to candidate's Graduate Program Office, unless program has an earlier deadline.

ADDRESS INQUIRIES TO:
Graduate Scholarship Office
(See address above.)

THE UNIVERSITY OF CALGARY [1616]

Faculty of Graduate Studies
Earth Sciences Building, Room 1010
2500 University Drive, N.W.
Calgary AB T2N 1N4 Canada
(403) 220-4938
Fax: (403) 289-7635
E-mail: gsaward@ucalgary.ca
Web Site: grad.ucalgary.ca/awards

FOUNDED: 1966

AREAS OF INTEREST:
Medical sciences.

NAME(S) OF PROGRAMS:
● **William H. Davies Medical Research Scholarships**

TYPE:
Awards/prizes; Scholarships. Awards for study in the medical sciences. Tenable at The University of Calgary. Award endowed through a bequest of the late William H. Davies.

ELIGIBILITY:
Open to qualified graduates of any recognized university who will be registered full-time in the Cumming School of Medicine at The University of Calgary. Successful candidates must contact their research program within the Faculty of Medicine; others cannot be considered. Awards are made solely on the basis of academic excellence.

FINANCIAL DATA:
Amount of support per award: $3,000 to $11,000 (CAN), depending upon the candidate's qualifications, experience and graduate program.

NO. AWARDS: Varies.

APPLICATION INFO:
Information is available from the Faculty of Graduate Studies. Candidates should apply to the Associate Dean, Graduate Science Education, Faculty of Medicine. Recommendations from the Faculty of Medicine will be submitted for approval to the Graduate Scholarship Committee.
Duration: One year.
Deadline: November 15.

ADDRESS INQUIRIES TO:
Graduate Scholarship Office
(See address above.)

THE UNIVERSITY OF CALGARY [1617]

Faculty of Graduate Studies
Earth Sciences Building, Room 1010
2500 University Drive, N.W.
Calgary AB T2N 1N4 Canada
(403) 220-4938
Fax: (403) 289-7635
E-mail: gsaward@ucalgary.ca
Web Site: grad.ucalgary.ca/awards

FOUNDED: 1966

AREAS OF INTEREST:
All fields of study, except art.

NAME(S) OF PROGRAMS:
● **Izaak Walton Killam Doctoral Scholarships**

TYPE:
Awards/prizes; Scholarships.

YEAR PROGRAM STARTED: 1967

PURPOSE:
To encourage advanced study, to increase the scientific and scholastic attainment of Canadians and to promote sympathetic understanding between Canadians and the peoples of other countries. Those receiving scholarships would likely contribute to the advancement of learning or win distinction in their profession.

ELIGIBILITY:
Scholarships are normally awarded to students who will be in their first, second, or third year of Ph.D. studies during the tenure of the award. Fourth year students may be considered under exceptional circumstances. The recipients must be registered full-time in a doctoral program at the University of Calgary. Applicants must have completed at least one year of graduate study before taking up an award.

GEOG. RESTRICTIONS: Canada.

FINANCIAL DATA:
$3,000 of this award (a Killam Research Scholarship) is reserved to cover costs associated with special equipment, conferences and/or travel in direct connection with the Ph.D. research.
Amount of support per award: $36,000 (CAN).
Total amount of support: Varies.

NO. AWARDS: Varies.

APPLICATION INFO:
Students should consult the Graduate Award Competition Guidelines and Application. In order to receive the Killam Research Scholarship portion of the award, the student must submit a letter outlining the proposed use of funds. This statement must be signed by the supervisor approving the use. No receipts are required.
Duration: Two years.
Deadline: February 1 to candidate's Graduate Program Office, unless the program has an earlier deadline.

ADDRESS INQUIRIES TO:
Graduate Scholarship Office
(See address above.)

THE UNIVERSITY OF CALGARY [1618]

Faculty of Graduate Studies
Earth Sciences Building, Room 1010
2500 University Drive, N.W.
Calgary AB T2N 1N4 Canada
(403) 220-4938
Fax: (403) 289-7635
E-mail: gsaward@ucalgary.ca
Web Site: grad.ucalgary.ca/awards

FOUNDED: 1966

AREAS OF INTEREST:
Cellular, molecular, microbial and biochemical biology.

NAME(S) OF PROGRAMS:
- **Bettina Bahlsen Memorial Graduate Scholarship**

TYPE:
Awards/prizes; Scholarships. Award for study in the fields of cellular, molecular, microbial or biochemical biology. Tenable at The University of Calgary, Department of Biological Sciences.

PURPOSE:
To assist graduate students from outside Canada who require financial assistance for their first year of study.

ELIGIBILITY:
Open to full-time graduate students entering or enrolled in a doctoral program in the Department of Biological Sciences. Selection will be based on academic excellence. Preference will be accorded to an international student and, if possible, to a student entering the first year of graduate studies.

FINANCIAL DATA:
Amount of support per award: $22,500 (CAN).
Total amount of support: $22,500 (CAN).

NO. AWARDS: 1.

APPLICATION INFO:
Students should consult the Department of Biological Sciences. A recommendation will be forwarded to the Graduate Scholarship Office. The recommendation is subject to final approval of the Graduate Scholarship Committee.

Duration: One year.
Deadline: February 1.

ADDRESS INQUIRIES TO:
Graduate Scholarship Office
(See address above.)

THE UNIVERSITY OF CALGARY [1619]

Faculty of Graduate Studies
Earth Sciences Building, Room 1010
2500 University Drive, N.W.
Calgary AB T2N 1N4 Canada
(403) 220-4938
Fax: (403) 289-7635
E-mail: gsaward@ucalgary.ca
Web Site: grad.ucalgary.ca/awards

FOUNDED: 1966

AREAS OF INTEREST:
Business and management.

NAME(S) OF PROGRAMS:
- **John Labatt Limited Scholarship**
- **ScotiaMcLeod Scholarship**

TYPE:
Awards/prizes; Scholarships. Awards for study in the fields of business, management

and related areas. Tenable at the University of Calgary. Awards are endowed through gifts from John Labatt Limited and ScotiaMcLeod Inc. Matching grants provided from the Province of Alberta's Advanced Education Endowment Fund.

ELIGIBILITY:
Open to students registered full-time in the MBA program at the Haskayne School of Business. Awardees must be engaged in full-time study during the tenure of the award.

FINANCIAL DATA:
Amount of support per award: Labatt Scholarship: $3,600 (CAN); ScotiaMcLeod Scholarship: $4,000 (CAN).
Total amount of support: $7,600 (CAN).

NO. AWARDS: 1 per award.

APPLICATION INFO:
Student should consult with the Haskayne School of Business. A recommendation will be forwarded to the Graduate Scholarship Office. The recommendation is subject to final approval of the Graduate Scholarship Committee.

Duration: One year.
Deadline: May 15.

ADDRESS INQUIRIES TO:
Graduate Scholarship Office
(See address above.)

THE UNIVERSITY OF CALGARY [1620]

Faculty of Graduate Studies
Earth Sciences Building, Room 1010
2500 University Drive, N.W.
Calgary AB T2N 1N4 Canada
(403) 220-4938
Fax: (403) 289-7635
E-mail: gsaward@ucalgary.ca
Web Site: grad.ucalgary.ca/awards

FOUNDED: 1966

NAME(S) OF PROGRAMS:
- **The University of Calgary Silver Anniversary Graduate Fellowships**

TYPE:
Awards/prizes; Fellowships. Graduate fellowships in all fields of study tenable in The Faculty of Graduate Studies at The University of Calgary. Award endowed by an anonymous donor and matched by the Province of Alberta.

ELIGIBILITY:
Open to students who are registered full-time in a doctoral program at The University of Calgary. Candidates must be residents of Canada. Awards are granted on the basis of academic standing and demonstrated potential for advanced study and research.

FINANCIAL DATA:
Amount of support per award: $16,000 to $20,000.
Total amount of support: Varies.

NO. AWARDS: Varies depending on funds.

APPLICATION INFO:
Students should consult the Graduate Award Competition guidelines, which are posted on the web site.

Duration: Two years.
Deadline: February 1, unless specific program has an earlier deadline.

ADDRESS INQUIRIES TO:
Graduate Scholarship Office
(See address above.)

THE UNIVERSITY OF CALGARY [1621]

Faculty of Graduate Studies
Earth Sciences Building, Room 1010
2500 University Drive, N.W.
Calgary AB T2N 1N4 Canada
(403) 220-4938
Fax: (403) 289-7635
E-mail: gsaward@ucalgary.ca
Web Site: grad.ucalgary.ca/awards

FOUNDED: 1966

AREAS OF INTEREST:
Creative writing in English, English literature, and related literary fields.

NAME(S) OF PROGRAMS:
- **The A.T.J. Cairns Memorial Scholarship**

TYPE:
Awards/prizes; Scholarships. Graduate scholarship tenable at The University of Calgary. Award endowed through the estate of the late A.T.J. Cairns, with a matching grant provided by the Province of Alberta's Advanced Education Endowment Fund.

ELIGIBILITY:
Candidates must be registered in or admissible to a Master's or doctoral degree program in the Department of English.

FINANCIAL DATA:
Amount of support per award: $1,000 to $5,000.
Total amount of support: Varies.

NO. AWARDS: Determined annually.

APPLICATION INFO:
Students interested in the award should apply to the Department of English in the first instance. Recommendations from the Department will be considered by the University Graduate Scholarship Committee.

Duration: One year.
Deadline: April 30.

ADDRESS INQUIRIES TO:
Graduate Scholarship Office
(See address above.)

THE UNIVERSITY OF CALGARY [1622]

Faculty of Graduate Studies
Earth Sciences Building, Room 1010
2500 University Drive, N.W.
Calgary AB T2N 1N4 Canada
(403) 220-4938
Fax: (403) 289-7635
E-mail: gsaward@ucalgary.ca
Web Site: grad.ucalgary.ca/awards

FOUNDED: 1966

NAME(S) OF PROGRAMS:
- **Graduate Faculty Council Scholarship**

TYPE:
Awards/prizes; Scholarships. Graduate scholarship in all fields of study tenable at The University of Calgary. Award endowed by The University of Calgary Graduate Faculty Council.

ELIGIBILITY:
Open to students registered full-time in a doctoral program.

FINANCIAL DATA:
Amount of support per award: $10,000 per annum.

Total amount of support: Varies depending on funds available.

NO. AWARDS: Varies.

APPLICATION INFO:
Students should consult the Graduate Award Competition Guidelines and Application available online.

Duration: One year.

Deadline: February 1, unless specific program has an earlier deadline.

ADDRESS INQUIRIES TO:
Graduate Scholarship Office
(See address above.)

THE UNIVERSITY OF CALGARY [1623]

Faculty of Graduate Studies
Earth Sciences Building, Room 1010
2500 University Drive, N.W.
Calgary AB T2N 1N4 Canada
(403) 220-4938
Fax: (403) 289-7635
E-mail: gsaward@ucalgary.ca
Web Site: grad.ucalgary.ca/awards

FOUNDED: 1966

AREAS OF INTEREST:
Humanities.

NAME(S) OF PROGRAMS:
- **Peter C. Craigie Memorial Scholarship**

TYPE:
Awards/prizes; Scholarships. Graduate scholarship tenable at The University of Calgary. Award endowed by friends, family and colleagues of Peter Craigie, who was Vice President (Academic) at the University; matching grant provided from the Province of Alberta's Advanced Education Endowment Fund.

ELIGIBILITY:
Open to students registered full-time who have completed one term of study in a Master's program in one of the following departments: Classics and Religion; English; French, Italian and Spanish; Linguistics, Languages and Cultures; and Philosophy. The recipient must have an outstanding scholastic record and have been or be involved in activities contributing in the general welfare of the university community.

FINANCIAL DATA:
Amount of support per award: $6,000.

Total amount of support: $6,000.

NO. AWARDS: 1.

APPLICATION INFO:
Applicants must complete a statement of eligibility (approximately 400 words) describing their activities contributing to the general welfare of the University of Calgary community. Students should consult the Graduate Awards Competition Guidelines and complete the Graduate Award Scholarship Application through the Student Center.

Duration: One year.

Deadline: February 1, unless the program has an earlier deadline.

ADDRESS INQUIRIES TO:
Graduate Scholarship Office
(See address above.)

THE UNIVERSITY OF CALGARY [1624]

Faculty of Graduate Studies
Earth Sciences Building, Room 1010
2500 University Drive, N.W.
Calgary AB T2N 1N4 Canada
(403) 220-4938
Fax: (403) 289-7635
E-mail: gsaward@ucalgary.ca
Web Site: grad.ucalgary.ca/awards

FOUNDED: 1966

AREAS OF INTEREST:
Economics, geoscience, engineering and management.

NAME(S) OF PROGRAMS:
- **Canadian Natural Resources Limited Graduate Scholarship**

TYPE:
Awards/prizes; Scholarships. Graduate scholarship tenable at the University of Calgary. This Scholarship recognizes the importance training and education play in helping students take advantage of the career and economic prospects available in the oil and gas industry.

PURPOSE:
To recognize the importance training and education play in helping students take advantage of the career and economic prospects available in the oil and gas industry.

ELIGIBILITY:
Open to students who are registered full-time in a thesis-based program in the Faculty of Graduate Studies at the University of Calgary.

FINANCIAL DATA:
Amount of support per award: $10,400.

Total amount of support: $10,400.

CO-OP FUNDING PROGRAMS: Endowed by Canadian Natural Resources Ltd (formerly Sceptre Resources Limited); matching grant provided from the Province of Alberta's Advanced Education Endowment Fund.

NO. AWARDS: 1.

APPLICATION INFO:
Students should consult the Graduate Award Competition Guidelines. Application information is available at the web site address.

Duration: One year.

Deadline: February 1 to the candidate's graduate program office, unless the program has an earlier deadline.

ADDRESS INQUIRIES TO:
Graduate Scholarship Office
(See address above.)

THE UNIVERSITY OF CALGARY [1625]

Faculty of Graduate Studies
Earth Sciences Building, Room 1010
2500 University Drive, N.W.
Calgary AB T2N 1N4 Canada
(403) 220-4938
Fax: (403) 289-7635
E-mail: gsaward@ucalgary.ca
Web Site: grad.ucalgary.ca/awards

AREAS OF INTEREST:
Natural resources, energy and environmental law.

NAME(S) OF PROGRAMS:
- **Faculty of Law Graduate Scholarship**

TYPE:
Awards/prizes; Scholarships.

ELIGIBILITY:
Open to students registered full-time in a graduate program in the Faculty of Law. If, in the opinion of the University of Calgary Graduate Scholarship Selection Committee, no suitable applications are received, no awards will be made.

FINANCIAL DATA:
Amount of support per award: $12,500.

Total amount of support: $12,500.

CO-OP FUNDING PROGRAMS: Endowed through contributions made to the Focus on Natural Resources Law Campaign; matching grant provided from the Province of Alberta.

NO. AWARDS: 1.

APPLICATION INFO:
Application forms are available from the Director, Graduate Programme, Faculty of Law. Awards will be recommended by a committee of the Faculty of Law based upon academic excellence. The Graduate Coordinator, Law, will submit recommendations to the Graduate Scholarship Office. The recommendation is subject to final approval of the Graduate Scholarship Committee.

Duration: One year. Nonrenewable.

Deadline: December 15.

PUBLICATIONS:
Academic calendar.

ADDRESS INQUIRIES TO:
Graduate Scholarship Office
(See address above.)

UNIVERSITY OF KANSAS CHILD LANGUAGE DOCTORAL PROGRAM [1626]

1000 Sunnyside Avenue
Room 3031, Dole Center
Lawrence, KS 66045-7555
(785) 864-4570
Fax: (785) 864-4571
E-mail: childlang@ku.edu
Web Site: clp.ku.edu

AREAS OF INTEREST:
Early childhood education and language research.

NAME(S) OF PROGRAMS:
- **Child Language Doctoral Program**

TYPE:
Conferences/seminars; Research grants; Scholarships.

PURPOSE:
To train individuals on language impairment across the life span.

ELIGIBILITY:
Applicants must have U.S. citizenship or permanent residency status, admission to the Child Language Doctoral Program or Intercampus Program in Speech-Language-Hearing or a related program, submission of a significant research plan of high quality, demonstrated high academic achievements and potential, and research interests congruent with those of one or more of the training program faculty members.

FINANCIAL DATA:
Amount of support per award: $21,180 per year predoctoral award.

Total amount of support: Varies.

APPLICATION INFO:
Applicants must submit:
(1) a curriculum vitae;
(2) a list of all courses taken in relevant areas such as language impairment of children, linguistics, psychology, special education, and speech and hearing sciences;
(3) a research plan describing the applicant's plans for research on language impairments of children;
(4) two official transcripts;
(5) names and phone numbers of three references who can evaluate the applicant's research potential;
(6) scores from the Graduate Record Examinations and;
(7) letter of intent stating willingness to participate in continuous research practicum.
Duration: One year.
Deadline: Beginning of February.

STAFF:
Dr. Mabel L. Rice, Director
Linda Mann, Program Assistant

ADDRESS INQUIRIES TO:
Dr. Mabel L. Rice, Director
(See address above.)

UNIVERSITY OF SOUTHERN CALIFORNIA [1627]
3720 South Flower Street, Third Floor
CUB 303
Los Angeles, CA 90089-0701
(213) 740-8336
Fax: (213) 740-6070
E-mail: jeri.muniz@usc.edu
Web Site: research.usc.edu

AREAS OF INTEREST:
Art history.

TYPE:
Fellowships; Grants-in-aid.

PURPOSE:
To support graduate education in art history at USC.

ELIGIBILITY:
Admission to Ph.D. program in art history.

GEOG. RESTRICTIONS: California.

FINANCIAL DATA:
Amount of support per award: Varies.

APPLICATION INFO:
Applicants must submit the Graduate School Application and the Supplemental Application form along with Graduate Record Exam (GRE) scores and letters of recommendation.
Duration: One year. Renewal possible based on academic progress.
Deadline: December 1.

ADDRESS INQUIRIES TO:
Contracts and Grants
(See address above.)

UNIVERSITY OF SOUTHERN CALIFORNIA [1628]
USC Graduate School
3601 Trousdale Parkway, STU 301
Los Angeles, CA 90089-0894
(213) 740-9033
Fax: (213) 740-9048
E-mail: gradfllw@usc.edu
Web Site: graduateschool.usc.edu

NAME(S) OF PROGRAMS:
- **Annenberg Graduate Fellowship Program**

- **Global Ph.D. Fellowship**
- **Provost's Ph.D. Fellowship Program**
- **Rose Hills Ph.D. Fellowship**

TYPE:
Fellowships. Merit fellowships. Fellowships will be combined with matching funds from individual schools to provide four or more years of funding toward the Ph.D.

YEAR PROGRAM STARTED: 1982

PURPOSE:
To allow outstanding students to devote full-time to research and study at USC leading to a career in university teaching and research.

LEGAL BASIS:
University.

ELIGIBILITY:
Excellent incoming Ph.D. applicants who show outstanding promise for academic careers in research and training.

FINANCIAL DATA:
Amount of support per award: $30,000 plus tuition and mandatory fees.

APPLICATION INFO:
Nomination by department only.
Duration: Two years, awarded annually with at least two years subsequent departmental/school support, based upon continued superior performance.
Deadline: Varies.

PUBLICATIONS:
Program announcements.

ADDRESS INQUIRIES TO:
Kate Tegmeyer, Assistant Director
(See address above.)

UNIVERSITY OF SOUTHERN CALIFORNIA [1629]
USC Undergraduate Programs
3601 Trousdale Parkway, STU 300
Los Angeles, CA 90089-0896
(213) 740-1741
Fax: (213) 740-9757
E-mail: ugp@usc.edu
Web Site: undergrad.usc.edu/experience/research/rose-hills

AREAS OF INTEREST:
Science and engineering.

NAME(S) OF PROGRAMS:
- **Rose Hills Summer Research Fellowships**

TYPE:
Fellowships. Summer fellowship for undergraduate students at USC supporting full-time research in science or engineering.

PURPOSE:
The Rose Hills Foundation, which supports nonprofit organizations for the benefit of the people of southern California, has generously provided funding for a limited number of students who would like to obtain science and engineering fellowships.

ELIGIBILITY:
Applicant must be enrolled at USC during the fall as a junior or senior in a program leading to an undergraduate degree in the life or natural sciences or engineering. USC cumulative grade point average of 3.0 or better is required. (Preference will be given to students whose USC cumulative grade point average is 3.5 or better.) U.S. citizenship is required, with residency in southern California. (A resident of southern

California is defined as a student whose permanent address is south of the Tehachapi Mountains.)

GEOG. RESTRICTIONS: Southern California.

FINANCIAL DATA:
Amount of support per award: Stipend of $5,000.
Total amount of support: $250,000.

NO. MOST RECENT APPLICANTS: 42.

NO. AWARDS: Average of 42 annually.

APPLICATION INFO:
Students must submit an online application and faculty recommendation form to be considered for funding.
Duration: Eight weeks, mid-May through mid-August.
Deadline: Fourth Friday of March. Announcement before mid-April.

ADDRESS INQUIRIES TO:
Dr. David Glasgow, Assistant Vice Provost
Office of Undergraduate Programs
Tel: (213) 740-6146
E-mail: dglasgow@usc.edu

VERMONT STUDENT ASSISTANCE CORPORATION [1630]
10 East Allen Street
Winooski, VT 05404-2601
(800) 642-3177 (continental U.S.)
(802) 655-9602 (Burlington area)
Fax: (802) 654-3765
TDD: (800) 281-3341
E-mail: info@vsac.org
Web Site: www.vsac.org

FOUNDED: 1965

AREAS OF INTEREST:
Students in need.

NAME(S) OF PROGRAMS:
- **Vermont Incentive Grants and Scholarships**
- **Vermont Outreach Programs**

TYPE:
Conferences/seminars; Grants-in-aid; Scholarships. Grants and loans for students enrolled in approved postsecondary institutions.

YEAR PROGRAM STARTED: 1965

PURPOSE:
To ensure that all Vermonters have the necessary financial and informational resources to pursue their educational goals beyond high school.

LEGAL BASIS:
Nonprofit, public corporation.

ELIGIBILITY:
For Incentive Grant, applicant must be a Vermont resident, enrolled full-time at an approved postsecondary institution, and must meet need test.

For Part-Time Grant, applicant must be a Vermont resident, taking fewer than 12 credit hours, have not received a Bachelor's degree, and must meet need test.

For Non-Degree Grant, applicant must be a Vermont resident, not matriculated, and must meet need test.

GEOG. RESTRICTIONS: Vermont.

FINANCIAL DATA:
Amount of support per award: Incentive Grant: $1,000 to $12,200 for the academic

year 2018-19; Non-Degree Grant: Varies; Part-Time Grant: $500 to $9,150 for the academic year 2018-19.

Total amount of support: $19,704,330 for fiscal year 2018.

NO. MOST RECENT APPLICANTS: 21,449 for fiscal year 2017.

NO. AWARDS: 12,476 need-based grants for the year 2018.

APPLICATION INFO:
FAFSA and Vermont Grant application required for Incentive and Part-Time Grant.

Duration: One academic year. Renewal possible under annual reapplication for up to 10 semesters.

Deadline: Applications accepted on a rolling basis for all grants.

ADDRESS INQUIRIES TO:
VSAC Research Department
(See address above.)

VERTICAL FLIGHT FOUNDATION

2701 Prosperity Avenue, Suite 210
Fairfax, VA 22031
(703) 684-6777
Fax: (703) 739-9279
E-mail: bchen@vtol.org
Web Site: www.vtol.org/vff

TYPE:
Awards/prizes; Scholarships. Annual scholarships to undergraduate senior, Master's or Ph.D. students interested in pursuing careers in some technical aspect of helicopter or vertical flight engineering.

See entry 2413 for full listing.

WASHINGTON STUDENT ACHIEVEMENT COUNCIL [1631]

917 Lakeridge Way, S.W.
Olympia, WA 98502
(360) 753-7848
Fax: (855) 480-8718
E-mail: sws@wsac.wa.gov
Web Site: readysetgrad.wa.gov

FOUNDED: 1969

NAME(S) OF PROGRAMS:
● **Washington State Need Grant Program**
● **Washington State Work-Study Program**

TYPE:
Work-study programs. Subsidized employment opportunities.

YEAR PROGRAM STARTED: 1974

PURPOSE:
To provide financial assistance to needy students attending eligible postsecondary institutions in the state of Washington by stimulating and promoting their employment and to provide such needy students, wherever possible, with employment related to their academic pursuits.

LEGAL BASIS:
State agency.

ELIGIBILITY:
Applicants must demonstrate financial need, be enrolled or accepted for enrollment as at least half-time undergraduate, graduate or professional students and be capable, in the opinion of the institution, of maintaining good standing in a course of study while employed under the program.

GEOG. RESTRICTIONS: Washington state.

FINANCIAL DATA:
Amount of support per award: Varies.

Total amount of support: Approximately $7,800,000 for the 2018-19 academic year.

APPLICATION INFO:
There is no separate application for this program. Students are awarded automatically by their school on the basis of their financial need as evidenced from their Free Application for Federal Student Aid (FAFSA) results or Washington Application for State Financial Aid (WASFA).

Duration: Renewable.

STAFF:
Jeffrey Powell, Program Administrator
Debbie Jackson, Program Manager

ADDRESS INQUIRIES TO:
Financial Aid Office at the college or Washington Student Achievement Council
(See address above.)

WASHINGTON STUDENT ACHIEVEMENT COUNCIL [1632]

917 Lakeridge Way, S.W.
Olympia, WA 98504-3430
(888) 535-0747 (option 5)
E-mail: health@wsac.wa.gov
Web Site: www.wsac.wa.gov/health-professionals

AREAS OF INTEREST:
Primary and integrated health care.

NAME(S) OF PROGRAMS:
● **Health Professional Loan Repayment**

TYPE:
Loan repayment program.

YEAR PROGRAM STARTED: 1991

PURPOSE:
To encourage health professionals to work in rural or underserved urban areas of the state of Washington by providing loan repayment.

LEGAL BASIS:
Government agency.

ELIGIBILITY:
Competitive application process for rural and underrepresented primary care needs.

GEOG. RESTRICTIONS: Washington state.

FINANCIAL DATA:
Amount of support per award: $70,000 with a two-year service commitment and $75,000 with a three-year service commitment.

APPLICATION INFO:
Instructions are available on the Council web site.

PUBLICATIONS:
Application form; brochure.

STAFF:
Claudia Shanley, Assistant Director of Health Workforce Programs
Jaclyn Cook, Program Manager

ADDRESS INQUIRIES TO:
Jaclyn Cook, Program Manager
(See address above.)

*SPECIAL STIPULATIONS:
Must commit to employment in Washington state.

WASHINGTON UNIVERSITY [1633]

The Graduate School
One Brookings Drive, Campus Box 1187
St. Louis, MO 63130-4899
(314) 935-7359
Fax: (314) 935-4887
E-mail: cgfp@wustl.edu
Web Site: pages.wustl.edu/cgfp

FOUNDED: 1853

AREAS OF INTEREST:
Anthropology, architecture, art history, archaeology, biology, biomedical sciences, business administration, chemistry, Chinese/Japanese and comparative literature, creative writing, earth and planetary sciences, economics, education, engineering, English, fine arts, German, history, material science and engineering, mathematics, movement science, music, philosophy, physics, political science, psychology, romance languages, statistics, social work, and visual arts.

NAME(S) OF PROGRAMS:
● **The Chancellor's Graduate Fellowship Program at Washington University in St. Louis**

TYPE:
Fellowships; Research grants; Scholarships; Travel grants.

YEAR PROGRAM STARTED: 1991

PURPOSE:
To facilitate training for students interested in becoming college or university professors, and who can contribute to diversity on the Washington University campus.

LEGAL BASIS:
University.

ELIGIBILITY:
Open to students who are admissible into any of Washington University's Ph.D. programs in Arts and Sciences, Business, Engineering or Social Work. Also eligible are students admissible to other Washington University programs providing final disciplinary training for prospective college professors (e.g., M.F.A. in Creative Writing, M.F.A. in Art). Students must be able to contribute to the diversity on the Washington University campus.

Applicants must be in the process of receiving, or will receive, an undergraduate degree from a four-year institution in the U.S. International students may apply, as long as they meet all admissions criteria.

FINANCIAL DATA:
Amount of support per award: Doctoral candidates are provided stipends and allowances of $34,560 per twelve-month year for five years, plus full tuition scholarships, with a total value in excess of $120,000. This combines a fellowship stipend of $33,060 and a $1,500 educational allowance.

CO-OP FUNDING PROGRAMS: Fellows will meet as a community on a regular basis to discuss trends and activities within their various disciplines. Scholars will lead discussions on a multitude of topics and the fellows will participate in an annual conference.

NO. MOST RECENT APPLICANTS: 400.

NO. AWARDS: Varies.

APPLICATION INFO:
Application information is available on the web site.

Duration: Five years for doctoral candidates, contingent upon satisfactory academic progress. Two years for graduate students in

MFA (in Writing, Visual Art and Dance) and M.Arch. (Master of Architecture) programs. Three years for J.D. in Law.

Deadline: Chancellor's Program: January 25.

PUBLICATIONS:
Program announcement.

ADDRESS INQUIRIES TO:
See e-mail address above.

WASHINGTON UNIVERSITY [1634]

The Graduate School
One Brookings Drive
Campus Box 1186
St. Louis, MO 63130
(314) 935-6848
Fax: (314) 935-4887
E-mail: shmiller@wustl.edu
Web Site: graduateschool.wustl.edu/olin-fellowship

FOUNDED: 1974

AREAS OF INTEREST:
Anthropology, architecture, art history, archaeology, audiology, biology, biomedical sciences, business administration, chemistry, Chinese, classics, comparative literature, creative writing, dance, earth and planetary sciences, economics, education, engineering, English, German, history, Japanese, law, materials science, mathematics, medicine, movement science, music, occupational therapy, philosophy, physics, physical therapy, political science, psychology, public health, romance languages, social work, statistics, and visual arts.

NAME(S) OF PROGRAMS:
● Mr. and Mrs. Spencer T. Olin Fellowships for Women

TYPE:
Fellowships. The Olin Fellowships are open to candidates for any of the following graduate and professional schools at Washington University: architecture, art, arts and sciences, business, engineering, law, medicine, and social work.

YEAR PROGRAM STARTED: 1974

PURPOSE:
To encourage women of exceptional promise to prepare for careers in higher education and the professions; to continue and extend the historically important contributions of Monticello College to the education of women; to extend the influence of Washington University by assisting in the advanced education of outstanding young women who are likely to make significant contributions to higher education and the professions.

LEGAL BASIS:
Joint program of a private foundation (The Monticello College Foundation) and of Washington University in St. Louis.

ELIGIBILITY:
Any female graduate of a Baccalaureate institution in the U.S. who plans to prepare for a career in higher education or the professions by full-time advanced study at Washington University is eligible to apply. Applicants are considered without regard to age, handicap, religious creed, race, sexual orientation or national origin and only with regard to the excellence of their qualifications. Applicants must meet the admission requirements of the graduate or professional school of Washington University.

Preference will be given to those who wish to study for the highest earned degree in their chosen field.

FINANCIAL DATA:
The Olin Fellowships are tenable only at Washington University. They carry awards which compare favorably in each discipline with the most attractive financial aid offers available in that discipline at Washington University.

NO. AWARDS: Varies.

APPLICATION INFO:
Application and instructions are available at https://gradapply.wustl.edu/apply/fellowship.

Duration: Given satisfactory academic achievement, awards are renewable for a period of four years or until the completion of the program of academic degree study, whichever is first.

Deadline: Applications, with all supporting documents, must be submitted online no later than January 25 preceding the academic year for which application has been made.

ADDRESS INQUIRIES TO:
E-mail: olinfellowship@wustl.edu

WELLESLEY COLLEGE

Career Education
Green Hall 439, 106 Central Street
Wellesley, MA 02481-8203
(781) 283-2347
Fax: (781) 283-3674
E-mail: fellowships@wellesley.edu
Web Site: www.wellesley.edu/careereducation/fellowships-and-scholarships

TYPE:
Fellowships; Research grants. The Anne Louise Barrett Fellowship is given preferably in music and primarily for study or research in musical theory, composition, or in the history of music, abroad or in the U.S.

The Margaret Freeman Bowers Fellowship is given for graduate/professional study in fields leading to a career of service to others. Fields include social work, law, public health, policy and administration, and development studies. Business, medicine, and science also qualify, as long as they are dedicated to addressing social challenges in the U.S. and around the world.

The Eugene L. Cox Fellowship is for graduate study in medieval or renaissance history and culture abroad or in the U.S.

The Professor Elizabeth F. Fisher Fellowship is given for research or further study in geology or geography, including urban, environmental or ecological studies.

The Ruth Ingersoll Goldmark Fellowship is awarded for graduate study in English literature, English composition or in the classics.

The Horton-Hallowell Fellowship is awarded for graduate study in any field, preferably in the last two years of candidacy for the Ph.D. degree, or its equivalent, or for private research of equivalent standard.

The Peggy Howard Fellowship in Economics is given to provide financial aid for Wellesley students or alumnae continuing their study of economics. Administered by the economics faculty who may name one or two recipients depending on the income available.

The Edna V. Moffett Fellowship is given to a young alumna, preferably for a first year of graduate study in history.

The Alice Freeman Palmer Fellowship is awarded for study or research abroad or in the U.S.

The Kathryn Conway Preyer Fellowship is for advanced study in history.

The Vida Dutton Scudder Fellowship is given for study in the field of social science, political science or literature.

The Harriet A. Shaw Fellowship is given for study or research in music and the allied arts, in the U.S. or abroad.

Mary Elvira Stevens Traveling Fellowship is awarded for travel or study outside the U.S.

The Maria Opasnov Tyler '52 Scholarship is for graduate study in Russian studies.

The Sarah Perry Wood Medical Fellowship is awarded for the study of medicine at an accredited medical school approved by the American Medical Association.

The Fanny Bullock Workman Fellowship is given for graduate study in any field.

See entry 1000 for full listing.

WELLESLEY COLLEGE

Career Education
Green Hall 439, 106 Central Street
Wellesley, MA 02481-8203
(781) 283-2347
Fax: (781) 283-3674
E-mail: fellowships@wellesley.edu
Web Site: www.wellesley.edu/careereducation/fellowships-and-scholarships

TYPE:
Fellowships; Scholarships. Awards are made to female applicants who plan for full-time graduate study for the coming year.

The Mary McEwen Schimke Scholarship is a supplemental award given to afford relief from household and child care expenses while pursuing graduate study.

The M.A. Cartland Shackford Medical Fellowship is given for study of medicine with a view to general practice, not psychiatry.

See entry 1001 for full listing.

WEST VIRGINIA HIGHER EDUCATION POLICY COMMISSION [1635]

1018 Kanawha Boulevard East, Suite 700
Charleston, WV 25301
(304) 558-4016
Fax: (855) 292-1415
E-mail: brian.weingart@wvhepc.edu
Web Site: www.wvhepc.edu

FOUNDED: 1969

AREAS OF INTEREST:
Education.

NAME(S) OF PROGRAMS:
● West Virginia Higher Education Grant Program

TYPE:
Grants-in-aid. Monetary grants awarded to undergraduate students attending approved institutions of higher education.

YEAR PROGRAM STARTED: 1968

PURPOSE:
  To guarantee that the most able and needy students are given the opportunity to continue their program of self-improvement at the postsecondary level by assisting in the removal of financial barriers through monetary awards.

LEGAL BASIS:
  West Virginia Higher Education Grant Program is a government program administered under the authority of West Virginia Code 18-C-5-1.

ELIGIBILITY:
  An applicant must be a citizen of the U.S., have been a resident of West Virginia for at least one year immediately preceding the date of application for a grant or renewal of a grant, require financial assistance to pursue a college education, possess academic promise or be making satisfactory progress and enroll as a full-time undergraduate in an approved educational institution.

  Grants are restricted to approved educational institutions located in West Virginia and Pennsylvania.

GEOG. RESTRICTIONS: West Virginia and Pennsylvania.

FINANCIAL DATA:
  Amount of support per award: Up to $2,800.
  Total amount of support: $37,657,860 total funding for student awards for academic year 2018-19 in state-appropriated funds, special fee revenues allocated by the governing Board.

NO. AWARDS: Approximately 16,334 for academic year 2018-19.

APPLICATION INFO:
  Applicants must submit the Free Application for Federal Student Aid (FAFSA).
  Duration: Total of eight semesters or 12 quarters. The eight semesters do not have to be consecutive. Receipt of a grant in a given year does not guarantee its continuance in a subsequent year even though eligibility may be maintained. Students must reapply each year.

Deadline: April 15 for priority consideration.

IRS I.D.: 55-0517092

STAFF:
  Matt Turner, Vice Chancellor for Administration
  Brian Weingart, Senior Director of Financial Aid

ADDRESS INQUIRIES TO:
  Brian Weingart
  Senior Director of Financial Aid
  (See address above.)

THE WOODROW WILSON NATIONAL FELLOWSHIP FOUNDATION   [1636]
5 Vaughn Drive
Suite 300
Princeton, NJ 08540
(609) 452-7007 ext. 310
E-mail: newcombe@woodrow.org
Web Site: www.woodrow.org

FOUNDED: 1945

AREAS OF INTEREST:
  Higher education.

NAME(S) OF PROGRAMS:
  • **Charlotte W. Newcombe Doctoral Dissertation Fellowships**

TYPE:
  Awards/prizes; Fellowships; Scholarships. Awards to support and encourage original and significant study of ethical and/or religious values in the humanities and social sciences.

YEAR PROGRAM STARTED: 1981

PURPOSE:
  To encourage study of ethical or religious values.

LEGAL BASIS:
  Publicly supported charity.

ELIGIBILITY:
  Doctoral candidates enrolled in a U.S. university, located in the U.S., working on topics of religious or ethical values in the Humanities or Social Sciences may apply.

FINANCIAL DATA:
  Amount of support per award: $25,000 for 12 months of dissertation writing.

CO-OP FUNDING PROGRAMS: Program made available by funds from the Charlotte W. Newcombe Foundation.

NO. MOST RECENT APPLICANTS: 520.

NO. AWARDS: Minimum of 20.

APPLICATION INFO:
  Applications are accepted beginning September 1 and must be submitted electronically.
  Duration: Tenure of the award is for the academic year following the announcement of the winners.
  Deadline: November 15.

ADDRESS INQUIRIES TO:
  See e-mail address above.

*SPECIAL STIPULATIONS:
  Fellowship is for humanities and social sciences. Applicants in highly quantitative fields should not apply.

WOMEN IN DEFENSE
WID HORIZONS
2101 Wilson Boulevard, Suite 700
Arlington, VA 22201
(703) 247-2570
Fax: (703) 522-1885
E-mail: wid@ndia.org
Web Site: www.womenindefense.net

TYPE:
  Scholarships. The Horizons Foundation Scholarship Program is supported by accredited colleges and universities. Awards are made on an annual basis. The Foundation selects all scholarship recipients based on criteria it sets. Scholarships are awarded to applicants who require financial assistance, demonstrate strong academic credentials and a commitment to a career in national security.

See entry 1002 for full listing.

SCIENCES (multiple disciplines)

Sciences (multiple disciplines)

THE ACADEMY OF NATURAL SCIENCES OF PHILADELPHIA [1637]

1900 Benjamin Franklin Parkway
Philadelphia, PA 19103-1101
(215) 299-1065
Fax: (215) 299-1079
E-mail: kepics@ansp.org
Web Site: ansp.org/research/fellowships-endowments/gallagher

FOUNDED: 1812

AREAS OF INTEREST:
Research, exhibition and education in natural sciences.

NAME(S) OF PROGRAMS:
- **John J. and Anna H. Gallagher Fellowship**

TYPE:
Fellowships; Project/program grants; Research grants; Residencies; Training grants; Visiting scholars. The Gallagher Fellowship provides support for original postdoctoral or sabbatical research on the systematics of microscopic invertebrates, with priority for the study of rotifers.

YEAR PROGRAM STARTED: 1990

LEGAL BASIS:
Private, nonprofit natural science museum.

ELIGIBILITY:
Candidates must have a Ph.D. in zoology or in ecology, evolution and biodiversity from a major university. Applicants must provide a research proposal involving microscopic freshwater invertebrate animals, including development of expertise in one or more taxonomic groups and the names of three references who are acknowledged scholars in the field. Preference will be given to candidates specializing in Rotifera.

Work must take place primarily at the Academy of Natural Sciences of Philadelphia and/or in the field and should emphasize utilization of the Academy's collections of literature and specimens. Projects should be scaled for completion during the one-year duration of the fellowship.

FINANCIAL DATA:
Fellowship includes salary, benefits, travel expenses, field and laboratory supplies.
Total amount of support: $30,000 to $50,000.

NO. MOST RECENT APPLICANTS: 9.

NO. AWARDS: 1.

APPLICATION INFO:
Research proposal should include:
(1) curriculum vitae;
(2) statement of research interests;
(3) a three- to five-page description of the project (including salary request, research project costs and a timeline) and;
(4) names and contact information of three references.
Duration: Up to 12 months.
Deadline: Proposals are accepted on a rolling basis.

ADDRESS INQUIRIES TO:
Kristen Kepics, Department Administrator
(See e-mail address above.)

ALABAMA ACADEMY OF SCIENCE, INC. [1638]

2108 Fox Valley Circle
Birmingham, AL 35216
(205) 936-0823
E-mail: krannich@uab.edu
Web Site: www.alabamaacademyofscience.org

FOUNDED: 1924

AREAS OF INTEREST:
Chemistry, biology, archaeology, earth science, forestry, geography, conservation, physics, industry, economics, mathematics, computer science, anthropology, engineering, psychology, behavioral and social sciences, physical sciences, health sciences and ecology.

CONSULTING OR VOLUNTEER SERVICES:
Visiting Scientist Speaker Program for elementary schools, high schools and colleges.

NAME(S) OF PROGRAMS:
- **Gorgas Scholarship**
- **Mason Science Teaching Fellowships**
- **Student Research Grants**
- **Student Travel Awards**

TYPE:
Assistantships; Awards/prizes; Conferences/seminars; Fellowships; Project/program grants; Research grants; Scholarships; Travel grants; Visiting scholars. Grants to college and university students for small research projects and for travel to scientific meetings to present papers.

Fellowships are for teaching science for Alabama teachers.

The Gorgas Scholarships are awarded to high school senior students who were Alabama Science Scholar Search entrants for any Alabama college or university.

YEAR PROGRAM STARTED: 1924

PURPOSE:
To stimulate student science study and research; to promote the development of interested scientific matter in the state; to render public service in scientific matters.

LEGAL BASIS:
Tax-exempt membership organization.

ELIGIBILITY:
Open to individuals committed to the purpose of the Academy.

GEOG. RESTRICTIONS: Alabama.

FINANCIAL DATA:
Amount of support per award: MST Fellowship: $1,000 for teacher and $50 to $100 per award for student research; Student Research Grants: $250; Student Travel Awards: $50; $10,000 in scholarships to high school seniors.
Total amount of support: Up to $13,000 annually.

CO-OP FUNDING PROGRAMS: Gorgas Scholarship Program is supported by the Alabama Power Foundation, Inc. All other programs are funded by membership dues, meeting registrations, exhibits, contributions and university memberships.

NO. MOST RECENT APPLICANTS: 100.

NO. AWARDS: Gorgas Scholarship: 12; MST Fellowship: 1 teacher award and 40 for student research competition; Student Research Grants: 4; Student Travel Awards: 30.

APPLICATION INFO:
Contact the Academy.

Duration: One year.
Deadline: Approximately February 1. Award announcement at annual meeting in March.

PUBLICATIONS:
Journal of the Alabama Academy of Sciences.

IRS I.D.: 63-6050246

ADDRESS INQUIRIES TO:
Larry K. Krannich, Ph.D.
Executive Director
(See address above.)

ALTERNATIVES RESEARCH AND DEVELOPMENT FOUNDATION [1639]

801 Old York Road, Suite 316
Jenkintown, PA 19046
(215) 887-8076
E-mail: grants@ardf-online.org
Web Site: www.ardf-online.org

FOUNDED: 1993

AREAS OF INTEREST:
Development, validation and adoption of non-animal methods in biomedical research, product testing and education.

NAME(S) OF PROGRAMS:
- **Alternatives Research Grant Program**
- **William and Eleanor Cave Award**

TYPE:
Awards/prizes; Research grants.

YEAR PROGRAM STARTED: 1993

PURPOSE:
To fund and promote the development, validation and adoption of non-animal methods in biomedical research, product testing and education.

ELIGIBILITY:
Nonsectarian religious programs may apply. Preference is given to universities and research institutions in the U.S. No grants are made to individuals.

FINANCIAL DATA:
Amount of support per award: Up to $40,000.
Total amount of support: Varies.

APPLICATION INFO:
Primary grant application should be no more than 15 pages, including the Alternatives Research Grant Program Application Form. ADRF encourages electronic submission via dropbox.com. If submitting by mail, send five copies of the primary grant application and supplemental material.

Primary grant application is composed of:
(1) abstract (not to exceed 200 words) that describes the proposed research project and includes an explanation of how the work will

contribute to reducing or replacing current uses of laboratory animals in biomedical research, product safety testings, or educational demonstrations;
(2) proposal that presents a clear research plan and includes sections on materials and methods, expected results, and a list of relevant references;
(3) description of how the proposed research will lead to a significant reduction or replacement of laboratory animals;
(4) detailed budget and justification for equipment and supplies;
(5) description of additional sources of funding for the project currently available or applied for. Also supply information about previous grant support in this project area during the past two years and;
(6) curriculum vitae for the principal investigator.

Supplemental material includes previous publications which directly support the current grant application and curriculum vitae (one page each) for up to three personnel involved other than the principal investigator.

Duration: One year.

Deadline: May 1.

ADDRESS INQUIRIES TO:
Sue Leary, President
(See address above.)

AMERICAN ASSOCIATION FOR THE ADVANCEMENT OF SCIENCE

1200 New York Avenue, N.W.
Washington, DC 20005
(202) 326-6744
E-mail: mmfellowship@aaas.org
Web Site: www.aaas.org/programs/mass-media-fellowship

TYPE:
Fellowships. Fellowships to support undergraduates, graduate students, and postdoctorates in the fields of social, natural and physical sciences, mathematics, and engineering during the summer as reporters in mass media organizations nationwide. Fellows will have the opportunity to observe and participate in the process by which events and ideas become news, improve their communication skills by learning to describe complex technical subjects in a manner understandable to the lay public, and increase their understanding of editorial decision making and the way in which information is effectively disseminated.

Each fellow will work for a specific media organization. Some will work for newspapers or magazines on news and feature writing assignments. Others may be involved in television or radio production.

See entry 1748 for full listing.

AMERICAN INSTITUTE OF CHEMICAL ENGINEERS (AICHE)   [1640]

120 Wall Street, Floor 23
New York, NY 10005-4020
(203) 702-7660
(646) 495-1348
Fax: (203) 775-5177
E-mail: awards@aiche.org
Web Site: www.aiche.org

AREAS OF INTEREST:
Chemical engineering.

NAME(S) OF PROGRAMS:
- **Food, Pharmaceutical and Bioengineering Division Award in Chemical Engineering**

TYPE:
Awards/prizes.

YEAR PROGRAM STARTED: 1970

PURPOSE:
To recognize an individual's outstanding chemical engineering contribution in the food, pharmaceutical and/or bioengineering industry.

LEGAL BASIS:
Professional association.

ELIGIBILITY:
Contribution may have been made in industry, government, or academic areas, or with other organizations.

FINANCIAL DATA:
Amount of support per award: $2,000 and a plaque.
Total amount of support: $2,000.

NO. AWARDS: 1 annually.

APPLICATION INFO:
Nomination form is available on the AIChE web site.
Deadline: April 15.

ADDRESS INQUIRIES TO:
Dr. Wilfred Chen, Gore Professor of Chemical Engineering
224 Colburn Laboratory
Department of Chemical and Biomedical Engineering
University of Delaware
Newark, DE 19716
E-mail: wilfred@udel.edu

THE AMERICAN MUSEUM OF NATURAL HISTORY   [1641]

Richard Gilder Graduate School
Central Park West at 79th Street
New York, NY 10024-5192
(212) 769-5017
Fax: (212) 769-5257
E-mail: fellowships-rggs@amnh.org
assistantdirector-rggs@amnh.org
Web Site: www.amnh.org/our-research/richard-gilder-graduate-school

FOUNDED: 1869

AREAS OF INTEREST:
Anthropology, paleontology and zoology.

NAME(S) OF PROGRAMS:
- **Collection Study Grants**
- **Lerner-Gray Grants for Marine Research**
- **Theodore Roosevelt Memorial Grants**

TYPE:
Grants-in-aid; Research grants. Collection Study Grants enable predoctoral and recent postdoctoral investigators to study any of the scientific collections at the American Museum in the departments of anthropology, earth and planetary sciences, entomology, herpetology, ichthyology, invertebrates, mammalogy, ornithology, and vertebrate paleontology.

The Lerner-Gray Grants for Marine Research provide support to highly qualified persons starting careers in marine zoology.

The Theodore Roosevelt Memorial Grants support research on North American fauna in wildlife conservation or related fields of North American fauna.

YEAR PROGRAM STARTED: 1976

PURPOSE:
To provide modest short-term awards to advanced graduate students and postdoctoral researchers who are commencing their careers in the fields of zoology, paleontology and anthropology.

ELIGIBILITY:
Applicants should be advanced graduate students and postdoctoral researchers who are beginning their careers in the interest areas listed above. Research projects need not be carried out at the American Museum.

FINANCIAL DATA:
Amount of support per award: $500 to $3,500.
Total amount of support: Varies.

NO. AWARDS: Collection Study Grants: 23; Lerner-Gray Grants: 28; Theodore Roosevelt Grants: 34 for the year 2019.

APPLICATION INFO:
Application information is available on the web site.
Duration: Collection Study Grants: Projects of four days or longer are encouraged; Lerner-Gray and Theodore Roosevelt Grants: One year.
Deadline: Collection Study Grants: May 1; Lerner-Gray Grants: March 14; Theodore Roosevelt Memorial Grants: February 15.

ADDRESS INQUIRIES TO:
Maria Rios, Assistant Director
Fellowships and Student Affairs
(See address above.)

THE AMERICAN MUSEUM OF NATURAL HISTORY   [1642]

Richard Gilder Graduate School
Central Park West at 79th Street
New York, NY 10024-5192
(212) 769-5017
Fax: (212) 769-5257
E-mail: fellowships-rggs@amnh.org
assistantdirector-rggs@amnh.org
Web Site: www.amnh.org/our-research/richard-gilder-graduate-school

FOUNDED: 1869

AREAS OF INTEREST:
Vertebrate and invertebrate zoology, paleozoology, anthropology, earth and planetary sciences.

NAME(S) OF PROGRAMS:
- **Postdoctoral Research Fellowship Program**

TYPE:
Fellowships.

YEAR PROGRAM STARTED: 1960

PURPOSE:
To advance the training of recent postdoctoral investigators and established scientists.

LEGAL BASIS:
Nonprofit.

ELIGIBILITY:
Provides training to postdoctoral investigators and established scientists to carry out a specific project, which must fit into the Museum's areas of interest. Postdoctoral Fellows are expected to be in residence at the Museum.

FINANCIAL DATA:
Salary, health insurance and research expenses, as per budget, are provided.
Amount of support per award: Varies.
Total amount of support: Varies.

NO. MOST RECENT APPLICANTS: 50.

NO. AWARDS: 5.

APPLICATION INFO:
Applications require a project description with bibliography, budget, curriculum vitae including a list of publications, and letters of recommendation.
Duration: Up to two years.
Deadline: November 15.

PUBLICATIONS:
Grants and Fellowships of the American Museum of Natural History, booklet.

ADDRESS INQUIRIES TO:
Maria Rios, Assistant Director
Fellowships and Student Affairs
(See address above.)

AMERICAN TINNITUS ASSOCIATION (ATA)   [1643]
8300 Boone Boulevard
Suite 500
Vienna, VA 22182
(800) 634-8978
E-mail: tinnitus@ata.org
Web Site: www.ata.org

FOUNDED: 1971

AREAS OF INTEREST:
Tinnitus.

NAME(S) OF PROGRAMS:
● **ATA Student Research Grant Program**
● **ATA Tinnitus Research Grant Program**

TYPE:
Research grants; Seed money grants.
Financially supports scientific studies about tinnitus.

YEAR PROGRAM STARTED: 1980

PURPOSE:
To identify the mechanisms of tinnitus or to improve tinnitus treatments.

LEGAL BASIS:
501(c)(3) nonprofit association.

ELIGIBILITY:
Tinnitus Research Grant: Postdoctorate.
Student Grant: Doctorate or medical student.
ATA will consider the subject of research, quality of its design, potential for significant advances in basic knowledge or clinical application, available facilities and personnel at the institution and qualifications of investigators. Facility must be nonprofit.

GEOG. RESTRICTIONS: United States.

FINANCIAL DATA:
Amount of support per award: Tinnitus Research Grant: Up to $150,000 ($50,000 per year); Student Grant: $10,000.

APPLICATION INFO:
In addition to the application form, applicants must submit a concisely written research proposal containing detailed descriptions of the following elements:
(1) introduction, statement of the problem and specific aims of the research;
(2) background and significance of the issue;
(3) relevant preliminary or pilot studies;
(4) the facility that will house the study and/or administer the funds;
(5) discussion of relevant literature and,

where appropriate, standardized tinnitus measures;
(6) outline of intended study procedures including study design, sampling and measurement data to be used, and description of analysis and evaluation plan and;
(7) outcomes expected from the study and the study's use.
Duration: Tinnitus Research Grant: Up to three years. Student Grant: One year.
Deadline: November 1.

STAFF:
Torryn Brazell, Chief Executive Officer

ADDRESS INQUIRIES TO:
Torryn Brazell, Chief Executive Officer
(See address above.)

ARGONNE NATIONAL LABORATORY   [1644]
Human Resources Service
9700 South Cass Avenue
Argonne, IL 60439-4845
(630) 252-4114
Fax: (630) 252-3193
E-mail: lisareed@anl.gov
undergrad@anl.gov
Web Site: www.dep.anl.gov

FOUNDED: 1968

AREAS OF INTEREST:
Basic physical and life sciences, mathematics, computer science, engineering, applied research relating to coal, conservation, environmental impact and technology, fission and fusion energy.

NAME(S) OF PROGRAMS:
● **Science Undergraduate Laboratory Internships**

TYPE:
Internships.

PURPOSE:
To encourage the further study of science.

LEGAL BASIS:
Research center of the U.S. Department of Energy.

ELIGIBILITY:
Applicants must be U.S. citizens or legal permanent residents who are full-time students at accredited U.S. colleges or universities. Applicants must have completed at least one year as a matriculated undergraduate student at the time of applying, with an undergraduate cumulative minimum grade point average of 3.0 on a 4.0 scale. Applicants must be 18 years of age or older at the time the internship begins.

GEOG. RESTRICTIONS: United States.

FINANCIAL DATA:
Amount of support per award: $600 per week stipend.
Total amount of support: Varies.

NO. MOST RECENT APPLICANTS: 100.

APPLICATION INFO:
Applications must be submitted at the Department of Energy web site.
Duration: 10 weeks during the summer; 15 weeks during fall or spring.
Deadline: Summer: January 10. Fall: Approximately May 30. Spring: October 30.

ADDRESS INQUIRIES TO:
Lisa Reed, Program Coordinator
(See address above.)

ARGONNE NATIONAL LABORATORY   [1645]
Human Resources Service
9700 South Cass Avenue
Argonne, IL 60439-4845
(630) 252-4114
Fax: (630) 252-3193
E-mail: lisareed@anl.gov
graduate@anl.gov
Web Site: www.dep.anl.gov

FOUNDED: 1946

AREAS OF INTEREST:
Basic physical and life sciences, mathematics, computer science and engineering, applied research relating to coal, conservation, environmental science and energy technologies and fission and fusion energy.

NAME(S) OF PROGRAMS:
● **Graduate Research Program**

TYPE:
Fellowships. Graduate Research Program provides Master's and Ph.D. level candidates an opportunity to conduct work within an Argonne research group or on a specific project for the purpose of supporting the student's thesis work. The university sets the academic standards and awards the degree. In practice, the participation of the faculty member varies from full partnership in the research to general supervision of the student's thesis work. The Argonne staff member keeps the faculty member at the university informed on the student's progress.

YEAR PROGRAM STARTED: 1968

PURPOSE:
To encourage the advanced study of science.

LEGAL BASIS:
Research center of the U.S. Department of Energy.

ELIGIBILITY:
Appointments are available to qualified U.S. and non-U.S. university graduate students who wish to carry out their thesis research at Argonne National Laboratory under the co-sponsorship of an Argonne staff member and a faculty member at the student's home institution.

Applicant must be currently enrolled full-time at an accredited institution and be 18 years of age or older at the time the appointment begins.

GEOG. RESTRICTIONS: United States.

FINANCIAL DATA:
Appointees receive an hourly wage, which is determined by the hiring division and the Educational Programs Office. Travel reimbursement is determined by the hiring division in accordance with laboratory policy. All travel arrangements must be made by the hiring division in order to receive any reimbursement.
Total amount of support: Varies.

NO. AWARDS: Approximately 15.

APPLICATION INFO:
Applications must be submitted electronically.
Duration: Three months to one year. Possibility of renewal.

ADDRESS INQUIRIES TO:
Lisa Reed, Program Coordinator
(See address above.)

BAYER USA FOUNDATION [1646]

100 Bayer Road
Pittsburgh, PA 15205
(412) 777-2000
(800) 422-9374
Fax: (412) 778-4413
E-mail: bayerusafoundation@bayer.com
Web Site: www.bayer.us

FOUNDED: 1953

AREAS OF INTEREST:
Education and workforce development,
environment and sustainability, health and
social services.

TYPE:
General operating grants; Project/program
grants.

PURPOSE:
To take an active role in business
communities; to enhance the quality of life
for Bayer employees and neighbors.

LEGAL BASIS:
Corporate giving program.

ELIGIBILITY:
Proposed projects must impact at least one of
Bayer Corporation's business locations. No
grants to organizations without IRS 501(c)(3)
status, United Way-affiliated agencies for
general operating support, charitable dinners
and events, individuals, political
organizations, endowment funds, deficit
reduction, religious organizations, student
trips or exchange programs, community
advertising, athletic sponsorships or
telephone solicitations.

GEOG. RESTRICTIONS: Berkeley and northern
California; Shawnee, Kansas; Kansas City,
Missouri; northern New Jersey;
Raleigh-Durham, North Carolina; Pittsburgh,
Pennsylvania. STEM proposals with national
focus will be entertained.

FINANCIAL DATA:
Amount of support per award: Varies
depending on needs and nature of the
request.

APPLICATION INFO:
Applications must be submitted online.
Applicants will receive confirmation when an
application is received. Grant applications
will be reviewed on a regular basis, and grant
seekers with approved proposals will be
contacted. If applicant does not hear from the
Foundation, his or her proposal does not
meet the strategic interests of the company.
Deadline: Varies by location.

ADDRESS INQUIRIES TO:
See e-mail address above.

BROOKHAVEN WOMEN IN SCIENCE

P.O. Box 183
Upton, NY 11973
(631) 344-7153
E-mail: bwisawards@bnl.gov
Web Site: www.bnl.gov/bwis/scholarships.php

TYPE:
Awards/prizes; Scholarships. These
scholarships are offered to encourage women
to pursue careers in the sciences technology,
engineering or mathematics.

See entry 982 for full listing.

CARNEGIE INSTITUTION FOR SCIENCE [1647]

1530 P Street, N.W.
Washington, DC 20005
(202) 939-1120
E-mail: tmcdowell@carnegiescience.edu
Web Site: www.carnegiescience.edu

FOUNDED: 1902

AREAS OF INTEREST:
Astronomy, physics, chemistry, earth
sciences, materials science, plant biology,
developmental biology and global ecology.

NAME(S) OF PROGRAMS:
● **Predoctoral and Postdoctoral
   Fellowships at the Carnegie Institution**

TYPE:
Fellowships; Internships; Technical
assistance; Visiting scholars; Research
contracts. Predoctoral and Postdoctoral
fellowships for research training in the fields
of astronomy, geophysics, physics and related
sciences, plant biology, genetics and
developmental biology in residence at one of
the Carnegie Institution's six operating
centers.

PURPOSE:
To encourage in the broadest and most liberal
manner investigation, research and discovery
and the application of knowledge to the
improvement of mankind.

LEGAL BASIS:
Exempt under Section 501(c)(3) of the
Internal Revenue Code.

ELIGIBILITY:
Qualified scientists who have obtained the
doctoral degree or are in the process are
eligible. Candidates are evaluated on the
basis of academic record, recommendations
of professors and associates and the
complementing nature of their research to
work in progress at the Carnegie department.
Women and minorities are encouraged to
apply.

FINANCIAL DATA:
Amount of support per award: Varies by
department.

APPLICATION INFO:
Fellowship applications are submitted online
to the Directors of the Departments of
Carnegie Institution.
Duration: Fellowships are usually awarded
for one year with the possibility of renewal
for another year.
Deadline: Varies.

PUBLICATIONS:
Newsletter.

OFFICERS:
Eric D. Isaacs, President
Timothy Doyle, Chief Operating Officer

DIRECTORS:
Yixian Zheng, Director, Department of
Embryology
Richard Carlson, Director, Department of
Terrestrial Magnetism
Michael Walter, Director, Geophysical
Laboratory
John Mulchaey, Director, Observatories of
the Carnegie Institution
Joe Berry, Acting Director, Department of
Global Ecology
Zhi-yong Wang, Acting Director, Department
of Plant Biology

ADDRESS INQUIRIES TO:
Call first to determine to whom inquiry
should be directed.

Dr. Yixian Zheng
Director, Department of Embryology
3520 San Martin Drive
Baltimore, MD 21218 or

Dr. Richard Carlson
Director, Department of Terrestrial
Magnetism
5241 Broad Branch Road, N.W.
Washington, DC 20015 or

Dr. Michael Walter
Director, Geophysical Laboratory
5251 Broad Branch Road, N.W.
Washington, DC 20015 or

Dr. John Mulchaey
Director, Observatories of the Carnegie
Institution
813 Santa Barbara Street
Pasadena, CA 91101 or

Dr. Joe Berry
Acting Director, Department of Global
Ecology
260 Panama Street
Stanford, CA 94305
Tel: (650) 646-3830 or

Dr. Zhi-yong Wang
Acting Director, Department of Plant Biology
260 Panama Street
Stanford, CA 94305

*SPECIAL STIPULATIONS:
Fellowships are tenable only at one of the
Institution's facilities. No extracurricular
grants.

EARTHWATCH INSTITUTE [1648]

1380 Soldier's Field Road
Suite 2700
Boston, MA 02135
(800) 776-0188
Fax: (978) 450-1200
E-mail: research@earthwatch.org
Web Site: earthwatch.org/research-funding

FOUNDED: 1971

AREAS OF INTEREST:
Earthwatch supports rigorous research that
responds to global challenges - from climate
change to human-wildlife coexistence to
environmental sustainability - while engaging
with local communities.

NAME(S) OF PROGRAMS:
● **Earthwatch Funding for Field
   Research**

TYPE:
Research grants. Financial support for field
research projects. Earthwatch's overarching
goal is to support projects that produce
rigorous, relevant, and impactful science,
address global change, and actively involve
citizen-scientist participants. Through
Earthwatch's citizen science model, research
teams are provided with funding and
volunteers needed to support data collection
in marine, terrestrial, freshwater, and urban
ecosystems. Volunteers take action to help
scientists accomplish their research goals and
contribute to tangible outcomes that advance
conservation.

YEAR PROGRAM STARTED: 1971

PURPOSE:
To engage people worldwide in scientific
field research and education to promote
understanding and action necessary for a
sustainable environment.

LEGAL BASIS:
Incorporated as a nonprofit, tax-exempt organization, 501(c)(3) of the IRS Code.

ELIGIBILITY:
All Principal Investigators must have a Ph.D. and an affiliation with a university, government agency or science-focused NGP. Earthwatch strongly encourages graduate student participation on projects and is particularly interested in helping support early-career scientists and scientists local to the research nation.

Proposals are evaluated on the basis of scientific merit, appropriateness of citizen-scientist activities, expected project outcomes and impacts, safety, and logistics.

GEOG. RESTRICTIONS: Due to safety concerns, Earthwatch is not able to support any research projects in certain regions of the world. More information is provided during the application process.

FINANCIAL DATA:
Amount of support per award: Field grants vary based on project needs. Typical field grants are $20,000 to $80,000 per year per project.

APPLICATION INFO:
Application information is available on the web site.
Duration: Three years, subject to passing an annual performance review. Funding is renewable, upon submitting a research renewal proposal.
Deadline: Projects are developed 18 months in advance of fielding.

PUBLICATIONS:
Earthwatch, magazine; *Project Briefings*; proposal guidelines; grants list.

STAFF:
Dr. Cristina Eisenberg, Chief Scientist

ADDRESS INQUIRIES TO:
Research Department
(See address above.)

EARTHWATCH INSTITUTE [1649]
1380 Soldiers Field Road
2nd Floor
Boston, MA 02135
(800) 776-0188
E-mail: fellowshipawards@earthwatch.org
Web Site: www.earthwatch.org/education

FOUNDED: 1971

AREAS OF INTEREST:
Promoting a sustainable environment.

NAME(S) OF PROGRAMS:
- **Earthwatch Educator Program**
- **Earthwatch Teach Earth USA Program**

TYPE:
Fellowships. Teachers in grades K-12 apply for seven- to 14-day Earthwatch expedition fellowships that take place during the summer. Earthwatch selects teachers from all subject areas across the U.S. to assist scientists on expeditions by collecting data on climate change and sustainable resource management. Funding for these fellowships comes from a variety of donors, e.g., individuals, corporations, family foundations, community organizations and nonprofits. On their return from the field, these teachers must develop a lesson or action plan that ties their experience back to their classroom or community.

YEAR PROGRAM STARTED: 1971

PURPOSE:
To inspire young people to become environmental ambassadors by engaging educators and empowering them to be role models regarding environmental issues and science research; to accomplish this, the Teach Earth USA Fellowship program focuses on engaging teachers from all subject areas and grade levels to assist scientists with research on climate change and sustainable resource management.

LEGAL BASIS:
Incorporated as a nonprofit, tax-exempt organization, 501(c)(3) of the IRS Code.

ELIGIBILITY:
All U.S. teachers that currently teach grades K-12. These teachers must be passionate about teaching, looking to learn more about environmental issues, are interested in how scientific research is conducted, excited to collaborate with a team of teachers, and committed to engaging students and the community outside the classroom. Earthwatch searches for evidence of passionate teaching that stretches beyond the basics of the classroom and engages professionals who may not identify as science experts but are willing to learn and do more.

GEOG. RESTRICTIONS: United States.

FINANCIAL DATA:
Fellowship covers the full cost of the assigned expedition including meals and accommodations and on-site transportation. The fellowship also includes a travel award to offset out-of-pocket travel expenses to and from the expedition. Partially-funded fellowships are also offered.
Amount of support per award: $6,500.
Total amount of support: $377,006.

NO. MOST RECENT APPLICANTS: Approximately 450.

NO. AWARDS: 30.

APPLICATION INFO:
Applicants may contact Earthwatch at the e-mail address listed above.
Duration: Seven- to 14-day expedition.
Deadline: Applications are typically sent out during the fall. Deadline is mid-January to mid-February.

PUBLICATIONS:
Earthwatch, magazine; Project Briefings; proposal guidelines; grants list.

THE ELECTROCHEMICAL SOCIETY [1650]
65 South Main Street, Building D
Pennington, NJ 08534-2839
(609) 737-1902 ext. 124
Fax: (609) 737-2743
E-mail: awards@electrochem.org
Web Site: www.electrochem.org/awards

FOUNDED: 1902

AREAS OF INTEREST:
Advancement of the theory and practice of electrochemical and solid-state science and technology, and allied subjects.

NAME(S) OF PROGRAMS:
- **Edward Goodrich Acheson Award**
- **Allen J. Bard Award**
- **Vittorio de Nora Award**
- **Henry B. Linford Award for Distinguished Teaching**
- **Gordon E. Moore Medal for Outstanding Achievement in Solid State Science and Technology**
- **Olin Palladium Award**
- **Charles W. Tobias Young Investigator Award**
- **Carl Wagner Memorial Award**

TYPE:
Awards/prizes. Edward Goodrich Acheson Award is for distinguished contributions to the advancement of any of the objects, purposes or activities of The Electrochemical Society.

Allen J. Bard Award recognizes distinguished contributions to electrochemical science.

Vittorio de Nora Award is for contributions to the field of electrochemical engineering and technology.

Henry B. Linford Award for Distinguished Teaching recognizes excellence in teaching in subject areas of interest to the Society.

Gordon E. Moore Medal for Outstanding Achievement in Solid State Science and Technology is for distinguished contributions to the field of solid state science.

Olin Palladium Award is for distinguished contributions to the field of electrochemical or corrosion science.

Charles W. Tobias Young Investigator Award recognizes outstanding scientific and/or engineering work in fundamental or applied electrochemistry or solid-state science and technology by a young scientist or engineer.

Carl Wagner Memorial Award recognizes a midcareer achievement and excellence in research areas of interest of the Society, and significant contributions in the teaching or guidance of students or colleagues in education, industry or government.

PURPOSE:
To advance the theory and practice of electrochemical and solid-state science and technology, and allied subjects.

ELIGIBILITY:
Varies by award.

FINANCIAL DATA:
Amount of support per award: Edward Goodrich Acheson Award: Gold medal, wall plaque, and prize of $10,000. Allen J. Bard Award: Wall plaque with glass carbon medal, prize of $7,500, ECS Life Membership, and a complimentary meeting registration to accept the Award. Vittorio de Nora Award: Gold medal, wall plaque and prize of $7,500. Henry B. Linford Award for Distinguished Teaching: Silver medal, wall plaque and prize of $2,500. Olin Palladium Award: Palladium medal, wall plaque and prize of $7,500. Gordon E. Moore Medal for Outstanding Achievement in Solid State Science and Technology: Silver medal, wall plaque and prize of $7,500. Charles W. Tobias Young Investigator Award: Framed scroll, prize of $5,000, ECS Life Membership and travel assistance to the meeting of the award presentation (up to $1,000). Carl Wagner Memorial Award: ECS Life Membership, certificate, sterling silver medal, travel assistance to the meeting of award presentation (up to $1,000).

NO. MOST RECENT APPLICANTS: 5 to 10.

NO. AWARDS: Only 1 winner per award given in any of the award cycles.

APPLICATION INFO:
Application information is available on the web site.

Deadline: Varies by award.

ADDRESS INQUIRIES TO:
E-mail: awards@electrochem.org

THE ELECTROCHEMICAL SOCIETY [1651]

65 South Main Street, Building D
Pennington, NJ 08534-2839
(609) 737-1902
(609) 737-1902 ext. 111
Fax: (609) 737-2743
E-mail: awards@electrochem.org
jessica.wisniewski@electrochem.org
Web Site: www.electrochem.org

FOUNDED: 1902

AREAS OF INTEREST:
Advancement of the theory and practice of electrochemistry, electrometallurgy, solid-state science, electrothermics and allied subjects.

NAME(S) OF PROGRAMS:
● **ECS Summer Fellowships**

TYPE:
Awards/prizes; Conferences/seminars; Development grants; Fellowships; Grants-in-aid; Project/program grants; Research grants; Training grants; Travel grants. Summer Fellowships assist students in pursuit of work in a field of interest to the The Electrochemical Society.

YEAR PROGRAM STARTED: 1928

PURPOSE:
To stimulate and encourage participation and education in the fields of electrochemical science and technology as well as other interests to the Society.

LEGAL BASIS:
Scientific, educational, nonprofit, tax-exempt organization.

ELIGIBILITY:
For Fellowships, the applicant must be a graduate student (between B.S. and Ph.D.) in a college or university who will continue studies following the summer months the award is given.

No limitations on sex, race, nationality or religion.

FINANCIAL DATA:
Amount of support per award: Varies upon approval from the Board of Directors; usually $5,000 each.

Total amount of support: Varies.

NO. MOST RECENT APPLICANTS: 49.

NO. AWARDS: Up to 4 Summer Fellowships annually.

APPLICATION INFO:
Submit a brief statement of educational objectives, work accomplished on thesis, work planned, transcript of undergraduate and graduate work, two letters of recommendation and a letter of agreement not to hold other appointments or fellowships simultaneously.

Duration: June to September.

Deadline: Fellowships: January 15. Notification for Fellowships will be made on or before March 15.

PUBLICATIONS:
Interface Magazine.

STAFF:
Jessica Wisniewski, Human Resources and Operations Manager

ADDRESS INQUIRIES TO:
The Electrochemical Society
Awards/ECS
(See address above.)

FATS AND PROTEINS RESEARCH FOUNDATION, INC. [1652]

500 Montgomery Street
Suite 310
Alexandria, VA 22314
(703) 683-2633
E-mail: dmeeker@nara.org
Web Site: www.fprf.org

FOUNDED: 1962

AREAS OF INTEREST:
Use of rendered product in animal nutrition and other applications; feed safety, biosecurity, and efficiency of processes.

TYPE:
Research grants; Research contracts.

YEAR PROGRAM STARTED: 1962

PURPOSE:
To promote scientific and technological research into new and expanded uses for fats and proteins from animal by-products and processing technology; to encourage cooperative studies.

LEGAL BASIS:
Nonprofit foundation, 501(c)(6).

ELIGIBILITY:
Colleges, universities and research institutes with appropriate interests and capabilities are eligible to apply.

FINANCIAL DATA:
Amount of support per award: Average $35,000.

Total amount of support: $300,000 to $400,000 annually.

CO-OP FUNDING PROGRAMS: Encouraged.

NO. MOST RECENT APPLICANTS: 14 for the year 2019.

NO. AWARDS: 10 for the year 2020.

APPLICATION INFO:
Request proposal format from the above address or visit the web site. Prospective applicants should submit a brief outline of the proposed project (including background information, objectives, scope and mode of approach) along with a statement of the required budget and a brief biographical sketch of personnel to be involved in the research.

Duration: Varies.

Deadline: March 15 and September 15 for review of applications.

PUBLICATIONS:
Annual report; contributions policy; application guidelines.

IRS I.D.: 39-2497869

ADDRESS INQUIRIES TO:
Dr. David L. Meeker, Research Director
(See e-mail address above.)

FLORIDA EDUCATION FUND

201 East Kennedy Boulevard
Suite 1525
Tampa, FL 33602
(813) 272-2772 ext. 203
Fax: (813) 272-2784
E-mail: cjackson@fefonline.org
mdf@fefonline.org
Web Site: www.fefonline.org

TYPE:
Fellowships.

See entry 1404 for full listing.

FOUNDATION FOR SCIENCE AND DISABILITY

503 N.W. 89th Street
Gainesville, FL 32607
(352) 374-5774
E-mail: rmankin1@ufl.edu
Web Site: stemd.org

TYPE:
Grants-in-aid; Research grants.

See entry 908 for full listing.

GRADUATE WOMEN IN SCIENCE [1653]

P.O. Box 7
Mullica Hill, NJ 08062
E-mail: fellowships@gwis.org
Web Site: www.gwis.org

FOUNDED: 1922

AREAS OF INTEREST:
Science and research.

CONSULTING OR VOLUNTEER SERVICES:
A great deal of volunteering is provided by 22 chapters of the organization (e.g., science fair judges, girl scout support in science, etc.).

NAME(S) OF PROGRAMS:
● **GWIS Fellowships Program**

TYPE:
Fellowships.

YEAR PROGRAM STARTED: 1941

PURPOSE:
To increase knowledge in the natural sciences; to encourage research careers in the sciences by women.

ELIGIBILITY:
Applicants must be women scientists who have already completed a Bachelor's degree and are conducting research in the natural sciences. Applicants are encouraged to become SDE/GWIS members at the time of application.

FINANCIAL DATA:
Amount of support per award: Up to $10,000.

Total amount of support: Varies.

NO. MOST RECENT APPLICANTS: 230 for the year 2017.

NO. AWARDS: 5 for the year 2018-19.

APPLICATION INFO:
Information about the application process is available online.

Duration: One year. No renewals.

Deadline: January 11.

PUBLICATIONS:
GWIS Bulletin; GWIS e-news, monthly electronic newsletter.

IRS I.D.: 24-0825560

ADDRESS INQUIRIES TO:
Dr. Vicky Cattani
GWIS Fellowships Committee Chair
(See address above.)

HARVARD TRAVELLERS CLUB, PERMANENT FUND   [1654]

170 Hubbard Street
Lenox, MA 01240
E-mail: jackdeary@harvardtravellersclub.org
Web Site: www.travellersfund.org

FOUNDED: 1937

AREAS OF INTEREST:
Various scientific fields.

TYPE:
Project/program grants; Research grants.
Small grants for research projects.

YEAR PROGRAM STARTED: 1937

PURPOSE:
To foster research and/or exploration which
involves travel.

LEGAL BASIS:
501(c)(3) nonprofit organization.

ELIGIBILITY:
Applicants must have ability to make a
competent contribution in the field of
research. The Fund does not pay travel
expenses unless it is intimately involved with
the research and/or exploration. Preference is
given to applicants working on advanced
degrees.

FINANCIAL DATA:
Amount of support per award: Up to $5,000.
Total amount of support: Maximum $10,000
annually.

NO. MOST RECENT APPLICANTS: 15.

NO. AWARDS: 2.

APPLICATION INFO:
Applicants should submit a curriculum vitae
and proposal of travel/studies.
Duration: Usually one-time grant.
Deadline: Late February. Decision in April.

IRS I.D.: 04-6115589

AWARDS COMMITTEE:
Nils Bonde-Henricksen
Peter Creighton
Jack Deary

ADDRESS INQUIRIES TO:
Jack Deary, Trustee
(See address above.)

*SPECIAL STIPULATIONS:
No scholarships for study at educational
institutions.

THE HERB SOCIETY OF AMERICA, INC.

9019 Kirtland Chardon Road
Kirtland, OH 44094
(440) 256-0514
Fax: (440) 256-0541
E-mail: director@herbsociety.org
Web Site: www.herbsociety.org

TYPE:
Research grants.

See entry 1945 for full listing.

HISTORY OF SCIENCE SOCIETY

440 Geddes Hall
University of Notre Dame
Notre Dame, IN 46556
(574) 631-1194
E-mail: info@hssonline.org
Web Site: www.hssonline.org

TYPE:
Awards/prizes. The Davis Prize honors books
in the history of science directed to a wide
public and was established through a
long-term pledge from Miles and Audrey
Davis.

The Joseph H. Hazen Education Prize
recognizes excellence in teaching in the
history of science.

The Levinson Prize is awarded in
even-numbered years to an outstanding book
in the life sciences and natural history.

The Philip J. Pauly Prize is awarded to the
best first book on the history of science in
the Americas.

The Pfizer Prize honors the best
English-language work related to the history
of science published in the preceding three
years.

The Ronald Rainger Prize is awarded for
early career work in the history of earth and
environmental sciences.

The Nathan Reingold Prize is given for an
original essay in the history of science and
its cultural influences.

The Margaret W. Rossiter History of Women
in Science Prize honors an outstanding book,
or in even-numbered years an article,
published in the preceding four years.

See entry 554 for full listing.

HISTORY OF SCIENCE SOCIETY

440 Geddes Hall
University of Notre Dame
Notre Dame, IN 46556
(574) 631-1194
E-mail: info@hssonline.org
Web Site: www.hssonline.org

TYPE:
Awards/prizes. Prize for the best scholarly
article published in *Isis* during the past three
years.

See entry 553 for full listing.

ILLINOIS STATE ACADEMY OF SCIENCE   [1655]

c/o Research and Collections Center
1011 East Ash Street
Springfield, IL 62703
(217) 782-6436
E-mail: rmyers@museum.state.il.us
Web Site: ilacadofsci.com

FOUNDED: 1907

AREAS OF INTEREST:
Promotion of science in the state of Illinois.

NAME(S) OF PROGRAMS:
● **Scientific Research Grants/Proposal Writing Contest**

TYPE:
Awards/prizes; Grants-in-aid; Project/program
grants; Research grants; Seed money grants.
Cash grants and certificates to Illinois high

school, junior college or college students for
writing a scientific proposal and conducting
the proposed research.

YEAR PROGRAM STARTED: 1981

PURPOSE:
To promote science in the state of Illinois.

LEGAL BASIS:
Nonprofit organization.

ELIGIBILITY:
All public or private high school, junior
college or college students in the state of
Illinois who are sponsored by a signing
instructor are eligible. ISAS membership is
required. Proposals do not have to be
original. They can be a spin-off of a lab
experiment from class or something the
student is interested in as a hobby.

GEOG. RESTRICTIONS: Illinois.

FINANCIAL DATA:
Amount of support per award: High School
students: Up to $200,000; Undergraduate
students: Up to $500; Graduate students: Up
to $1,000.
Total amount of support: Varies each year.

NO. AWARDS: Varies.

APPLICATION INFO:
Students must submit application
electronically through the Academy's web
site.
Duration: One-time award.
Deadline: Application deadline is posted on
the Academy's web site.

PUBLICATIONS:
*Transactions of the Illinois State Academy of
Science.*

IRS I.D.: 37-6043007

ADDRESS INQUIRIES TO:
Travis Wilcoxen
E-mail: t.wilcoxen@millikin.edu or
Robyn L. Myers, Executive Secretary
(See address above.)

INSTITUTE OF FOOD TECHNOLOGISTS FOUNDATION

525 West Van Buren Street
Suite 1000
Chicago, IL 60607
(312) 782-8424
Fax: (312) 416-7919
E-mail: feedingtomorrow@ift.org
Web Site: www.ift.org/scholarships

TYPE:
Scholarships. Freshman Scholarships and
Undergraduate Scholarships encourage
undergraduate enrollment in food science and
technology. Graduate Scholarships support
advanced study in the field of food science
and technology.

See entry 2398 for full listing.

INTERNATIONAL FOUNDATION FOR ETHICAL RESEARCH, INC. (IFER)   [1656]

53 West Jackson Boulevard, Suite 1552
Chicago, IL 60604
(312) 427-6065
Fax: (312) 427-6524
E-mail: ifer@navs.org
Web Site: www.ifer.org

FOUNDED: 1985

AREAS OF INTEREST:
Scientifically valid alternatives to the use of animals in research, product testing, and education.

NAME(S) OF PROGRAMS:
- **Graduate Fellowship Program for Alternatives to the Use of Animals in Science**

TYPE:
Fellowships; Research grants. Graduate Fellowships in Humane Science support research in, but not limited to, tissue, cell and organ cultures, clinical studies using animals or humans, epidemiological studies, enhanced use of extensive tissue repositories and patient databases, public education, and computer modeling to replace the use of animals used in science.

YEAR PROGRAM STARTED: 1985

PURPOSE:
To provide financial incentives to graduate students in science that encourage them at the earliest stages of their career to integrate innovation and discovery with ethics and respect for animals.

LEGAL BASIS:
Nonprofit.

ELIGIBILITY:
Application is open to students enrolled in Master's and Ph.D. programs in the sciences and human or veterinary medicine. Projects in other fields that show promise to increase public awareness or promote changes in the legal system or public policy regarding the use of animals in research, testing and education are also eligible.

Fellowships are awarded to those candidates whose program of study shows the greatest potential to replace the use of animals in science.

FINANCIAL DATA:
Amount of support per award: Up to $12,500 stipend, plus up to $2,500 for supplies per year.

APPLICATION INFO:
Information and preproposal guidelines are available from the Foundation.
Duration: The fellowships are renewable for up to three years.
Deadline: Preproposal: Usually spring. Exact date will be posted online.

PUBLICATIONS:
Newsletter.

IRS I.D.: 22-2628153

THE LALOR FOUNDATION, INC. [1657]

c/o GMA Foundations
2 Liberty Square, Suite 500
Boston, MA 02109
(617) 426-7080
(617) 391-3088
Fax: (617) 426-7087
E-mail: fellowshipmanager@gmafoundations.com
Web Site: lalorfound.org

FOUNDED: 1935

AREAS OF INTEREST:
Basic postdoctoral research in mammalian reproductive physiology and biochemistry bearing on sterilization and/or prevention or termination of pregnancy.

NAME(S) OF PROGRAMS:
- **The Lalor Foundation Postdoctoral Fellowship Program**

TYPE:
Fellowships. Fellowships to institutions for basic postdoctoral research in mammalian reproductive biology as related to the regulation of fertility.

YEAR PROGRAM STARTED: 1937

PURPOSE:
To promote intensive research in mammalian reproductive biology.

LEGAL BASIS:
Tax-exempt philanthropic foundation.

ELIGIBILITY:
Domestic institutions must be exempt from federal income taxes under Section 501(c)(3) of the Internal Revenue Code. Domestic and foreign institutions must qualify under Section 509(a)(1), (2) or (3). Individuals who are nominated by the applicant institution may be citizens of any country and should have training and experience at least equal to the Ph.D. or M.D. level. Potential fellows may not have held the doctoral degree more than two years.

The applicant institution may make its nomination of a fellow from among its own personnel or elsewhere, but, qualifications being equal, candidates from other than the proposing institution itself may carry modest preference. The application must name the institution's nominee for fellowship and include his or her performance record.

FINANCIAL DATA:
Grants for coverage of fellowship stipend and institutional expenses.
Amount of support per award: $50,000 per year.
Total amount of support: $500,000 for fiscal year 2018.

NO. AWARDS: 10 for fiscal year 2018.

APPLICATION INFO:
Application and appendices are to be submitted online.
Duration: One year. Renewable under some circumstances.
Deadline: January 15. Notification by April 15.

IRS I.D.: 51-6000153

OFFICERS:
Cynthia B. Patterson, President
Christopher Burdick, Vice President
Lalor Burdick, Secretary and Treasurer

BOARD OF TRUSTEES:
Christopher Burdick
Lalor Burdick
Carol Chandler, Esq.
Marnie Cochran
Cynthia B. Patterson
Sally H. Zeckhauser

ADDRESS INQUIRIES TO:
Fellowship Manager
(See address above.)

LOS ALAMOS NATIONAL LABORATORY [1658]

P.O. Box 1663
MS-P290
Los Alamos, NM 87545
(505) 665-6406
E-mail: hrstaffing-postdocs@lanl.gov
Web Site: www.lanl.gov/science/postdocs

FOUNDED: 1943

AREAS OF INTEREST:
Biosciences, chemistry, computing, Earth and space science, engineering, materials science, mathematics and physics.

NAME(S) OF PROGRAMS:
- **Richard P. Feynman Postdoctoral Fellowship in Theory and Computing**
- **J. Robert Oppenheimer Postdoctoral Fellowship**
- **Frederick Reines Postdoctoral Fellowship in Experimental Sciences**

TYPE:
Fellowships. The Distinguished Postdoctoral Fellowships provide the opportunity for the recipients to collaborate with LANL scientists and engineers on staff-initiated research. Candidates for these awards must display extraordinary ability in scientific research and show clear and definite promise of becoming outstanding leaders in the research they pursue.

YEAR PROGRAM STARTED: 1960

ELIGIBILITY:
Candidates must have a doctoral degree within the last five years or will have completed all Ph.D. requirements by commencement of their appointment. The Feynman and Reines Fellowships require the ability to obtain a DOE "Q" clearance, which normally requires U.S. citizenship.

Every candidate must be sponsored by a technical staff member before being reviewed by the Postdoctoral Committee.

FINANCIAL DATA:
A generous and comprehensive salary and benefits package is provided, including incoming relocation.
Amount of support per award: Feynman, Oppenheimer and Reines Postdoctoral Fellowships provide a starting salary of $109,000.

NO. AWARDS: Up to 2 in each fellowship category.

APPLICATION INFO:
Details are available online.
Duration: Appointments are for three years.
Deadline: January.

ADDRESS INQUIRIES TO:
See e-mail address above.

MICHIGAN SOCIETY OF FELLOWS

University of Michigan
0540 Rackham Building
915 East Washington Street
Ann Arbor, MI 48109-1070
(734) 763-1259
E-mail: society.of.fellows@umich.edu
Web Site: www.societyoffellows.umich.edu

TYPE:
Fellowships. Fellows are appointed as Assistant Professors in appropriate departments and as Postdoctoral Scholars in the Michigan Society of Fellows. They are expected to be in residence in Ann Arbor during the academic years of the fellowship, to teach for the equivalent of one academic year, to participate in the informal intellectual life of the Society, and to devote time to their independent research or artistic projects.

See entry 343 for full listing.

MICRON TECHNOLOGY FOUNDATION, INC.

P.O. Box 6
Boise, ID 83707-0006
(208) 363-3675
Fax: (208) 368-4435
E-mail: mtf@micron.com
Web Site: www.micron.com/foundation

TYPE:
Matching gifts; Professorships;
Project/program grants; Research grants.

See entry 1913 for full listing.

MICROSCOPY SOCIETY OF AMERICA   [1659]

11130 Sunrise Valley Drive
Suite 350
Reston, VA 20191
(703) 234-4115
E-mail: associationmanagement@microscopy.org
Web Site: www.microscopy.org/awards

FOUNDED: 1942

AREAS OF INTEREST:
Microscopy.

NAME(S) OF PROGRAMS:
● **Undergraduate Research Scholarship Program**

TYPE:
Scholarships.

PURPOSE:
To foster educational and research potential in full-time undergraduate students intent on pursuing microscopy as a career or major research tool.

LEGAL BASIS:
Nonprofit society.

ELIGIBILITY:
The applicant must be a full-time undergraduate student and must have achieved junior or senior standing by the time the work is initiated. Research must be completed prior to graduation. Scholarship funds must be expended within one year of award date.

Applicants may receive only one scholarship and may perform research at an institution other than the one in which the applicant is enrolled. Successful applicants must agree to furnish MSA with an abstract for publication in the Society Journal, *Microscopy & Microanalysis*, describing the results and status of their project within two months after the conclusion of the award period, to acknowledge the award in all resulting publications, and to provide reprints of any other resulting publications to the Society.

FINANCIAL DATA:
Amount of support per award: Up to $3,000.
Total amount of support: Varies.

NO. MOST RECENT APPLICANTS: 20.

NO. AWARDS: Average 5.

APPLICATION INFO:
Required application form should include:
(1) a research proposal not to exceed three pages in length, including a brief introduction, a short methods section and description and itemized goals of the study;
(2) a budget indicating how the awarded funds will be expended;
(3) two letters of reference from scientists or university faculty familiar with the applicant's capabilities;

(4) a letter from the laboratory supervisor where the proposed research will be performed, confirming that the applicant and research project are acceptable;
(5) a curriculum vitae detailing previous education and/or training in microscopy and a brief statement of career goals and;
(6) a letter of recommendation from an MSA member.

An original and four copies of a completed application form and attachments are required, unless all materials are being submitted electronically to the e-mail address above.

Duration: One year. No renewals.
Deadline: December 1. Award announcement January 15.

PUBLICATIONS:
Program announcement.

ADDRESS INQUIRIES TO:
Ashley Carey, Managing Director
(See address above.)

MICROSCOPY SOCIETY OF AMERICA   [1660]

11130 Sunrise Valley Drive
Suite 350
Reston, VA 20191
(703) 234-4115
E-mail: associationmanagement@microscopy.org
Web Site: www.microscopy.org/awards

FOUNDED: 1942

AREAS OF INTEREST:
All phases of microscopy.

NAME(S) OF PROGRAMS:
● **Microscopy & Microanalysis (M & M) Student Award**

TYPE:
Travel grants. Awards are given to outstanding students selected on the basis of the quality and originality of their research abstracts submitted for the Annual MSA Scientific Program. The award consists of free registration for the meeting, a copy of *Proceedings*, and an invitation to the Sunday social event.

PURPOSE:
To promote student interest in microscopy and exchange of information.

LEGAL BASIS:
Nonprofit.

ELIGIBILITY:
Applicants must be bona fide students at a recognized college or university at the time of the meeting. Awards are based on the quality of the paper submitted for presentation at the meeting and the applicant must be the submitted paper's first author. Successful applicants must present their papers personally at the meeting in order to receive the award. They are expected to attend and participate in the entire meeting. Candidates should be juniors or seniors at the time the work is initiated. Former winners are ineligible.

FINANCIAL DATA:
Awardees will be reimbursed up to $1,000 for travel (round-trip, lowest-fare, continental U.S.) and complimentary full-meeting registration to the Microscopy & Microanalysis meeting, and invitation to the Presidential Reception.

Amount of support per award: Varies.

Total amount of support: $30,000.

NO. AWARDS: Varies.

APPLICATION INFO:
Applications consist of a completed Advanced Reservation Form, payment for student registration, a supporting letter from a member of MSA, preferably a research advisor, attesting to the applicant's status, and a scientific paper for presentation accompanied by a completed Data Form.
Deadline: February 15.

PUBLICATIONS:
The MSA Proceedings.

ADDRESS INQUIRIES TO:
See e-mail address above.

NATIONAL CENTER FOR ATMOSPHERIC RESEARCH   [1661]

1850 Table Mesa Drive
Boulder, CO 80305
(303) 497-1607
Fax: (303) 497-1646
E-mail: sbriggs@ucar.edu
Web Site: www.asp.ucar.edu

FOUNDED: 1960

AREAS OF INTEREST:
Research in atmospheric sciences, including such topics as atmospheric dynamics (on all scales) and models, climate science, cloud physics, atmospheric chemistry and radiation, turbulence, upper-atmosphere physics, solar and solar-terrestrial physics (including ionospheric studies and aeronomy), oceanography and atmospheric technology. Also included are studies of the interaction of the atmosphere with the oceans, the cryosphere, the Earth's surface and human society and application of biology, ecology, geology, economics and political science skills to atmospheric issues.

NAME(S) OF PROGRAMS:
● **Postdoctoral Fellowships at NCAR**

TYPE:
Fellowships. The fellowships cover a year's appointment, with a likely extension to two years, at NCAR to take advantage of its educational programs and/or research facilities in the broad field of atmospheric sciences.

YEAR PROGRAM STARTED: 1964

PURPOSE:
To provide an opportunity for talented scientists who have recently received their Ph.Ds. to continue to pursue their research interests and to develop expertise in new areas; to enrich the research talent in the atmospheric sciences by offering an opportunity for highly qualified Ph.D. physicists, chemists, applied mathematicians, engineers and specialists from other disciplines such as biology, geology, science education, economics and geography, as well as atmospheric science, to apply their training to research in the atmospheric sciences.

LEGAL BASIS:
Research institution operated by the nonprofit University Corporation for Atmospheric Research (UCAR) under sponsorship of the National Science Foundation (NSF).

ELIGIBILITY:
Interested scientists who have received their Ph.D., Sc.D. or equivalent are eligible.

NCAR encourages applications from women and minorities. There are no restrictions for foreign applicants.

Primary criteria in selection of postdoctoral appointees are the applicant's scientific capability and potential, originality and independence, and the ability to take advantage of the research opportunities at NCAR.

Appointments are tenable only in residence in Boulder, CO.

FINANCIAL DATA:
All appointees are eligible for life and health insurance in addition to excellent retirement benefits. Travel expenses to NCAR will be reimbursed for the fellow and his or her family. A small allowance for moving and storage is provided.
Amount of support per award: Basic stipend of $66,880 for the first year and $68,540 for the second year, plus a minimum of $3,500 for annual scientific travel support.

NO. MOST RECENT APPLICANTS: 100.

NO. AWARDS: Approximately 10 per year.

APPLICATION INFO:
Contact the Center.
Duration: Two years.
Deadline: January, to be considered for fellowship awards to begin the following summer or fall. Selections announced in March.

PUBLICATIONS:
Program announcement.

ADDRESS INQUIRIES TO:
Scott Briggs, Coordinator
Advanced Study Program
(See address above.)

*SPECIAL STIPULATIONS:
Appointments are tenable only in residence at the National Center for Atmospheric Research.

NATIONAL INVENTORS HALL OF FAME   [1662]
3701 Highland Park, N.W.
North Canton, OH 44720-4535
(800) 968-4332 (option 5)
E-mail: collegiate@invent.org
Web Site: www.invent.org/collegiate-inventors

AREAS OF INTEREST:
Creative invention: science, engineering, mathematics, technology and related fields.

NAME(S) OF PROGRAMS:
● **Collegiate Inventors Competition**

TYPE:
Awards/prizes. National competition in the U.S. that recognizes and rewards innovations, discoveries, and research by college and university students and their faculty advisors.

YEAR PROGRAM STARTED: 1990

PURPOSE:
To promote exploration in invention, science, engineering, technology, and other creative endeavors and provide a window on the future technologies from which society will benefit in the future.

ELIGIBILITY:
Open to students who are enrolled (or have been enrolled) full-time in any U.S. college or university at least part of the 12-month period prior to the date the entry is

submitted. In the case of a team (maximum of four students), at least one member must meet the full-time eligibility criteria.

Entry must be the original idea and work product of the student/advisor team, and must not have been:
(1) made available to the public as a commercial product or process or;
(2) patented or published more than one year prior to the date of competition submission.

Entries must be written in English.

GEOG. RESTRICTIONS: United States.

FINANCIAL DATA:
Finalists will win an all-expense-paid trip in the fall to present their work to a panel of expert judges, including National Inventors Hall of Fame inductees.
Amount of support per award: Up to $15,000.
Total amount of support: Up to $100,000.

NO. MOST RECENT APPLICANTS: 300.

NO. AWARDS: 5.

APPLICATION INFO:
All entries must be submitted on the official application form, which is available online.
Deadline: Mid-June.

ADDRESS INQUIRIES TO:
Collegiate Inventors Competition
(See e-mail address above.)

NATIONAL OCEANIC AND ATMOSPHERIC ADMINISTRATION   [1663]
NOAA/Sea Grant, R/SG
1315 East-West Highway, Room 11735
Silver Spring, MD 20910
(301) 734-1066
Fax: (301) 713-0799
E-mail: sgweb@noaa.gov
Web Site: www.seagrant.noaa.gov

FOUNDED: 1966

AREAS OF INTEREST:
Marine resource development.

NAME(S) OF PROGRAMS:
● **National Sea Grant College Program**

TYPE:
Research grants. Grants for research, education and outreach in oceanography, fisheries science and environmental studies; marine commerce and engineering and marine biotechnology; economic, legal and sociological considerations related to the management and development of natural resources in the marine environment; and development, conservation and economic utilization of resources in the marine environment.

The grant provides training and advisory service activities in order to increase the understanding, development and wise use of ocean, coastal and Great Lakes resources. The Secretary of Commerce, through NOAA, awards grants on a competitive basis for these purposes.

The program is carried out through a network of 33 Sea Grant programs, located in coastal and Great Lakes states, involving hundreds of universities nationwide.

YEAR PROGRAM STARTED: 1966

PURPOSE:
To promote wise utilization of marine and coastal resources.

LEGAL BASIS:
The National Sea Grant College and Program Act of 1966, Public Law 89-688, as amended. (33 U.S.C. 1121, et seq.)

ELIGIBILITY:
Universities and colleges, junior colleges, technical schools, institutes, laboratories and other public or private agencies with appropriate interests are eligible to apply.

FINANCIAL DATA:
Amount of support per award: Varies.
Total amount of support: Approximately $72,000,000 in grant funds per year.

APPLICATION INFO:
Detailed information is available on the web site.
Duration: Generally one to three years.
Deadline: Varies.

ADDRESS INQUIRIES TO:
Jonathan Pennock, Director
(See address above.)

NATIONAL RESEARCH COUNCIL OF CANADA   [1664]
1200 Montreal Road, Building M-58
Room E-109
Ottawa ON K1A 0R6 Canada
(613) 949-4655
E-mail: info@nrc-cnrc.gc.ca
racoordinator.hrb@nrc-cnrc.gc.ca
Web Site: www.nrc-cnrc.gc.ca

FOUNDED: 1916

AREAS OF INTEREST:
Science and engineering.

NAME(S) OF PROGRAMS:
● **National Research Council Research Associate Program**

TYPE:
Associateships. Research Associate Program provides promising scientists and engineers with the opportunity to work in a challenging research environment during the early stages of their career. Applicants will be selected competitively and must demonstrate the ability to perform original, high-quality research in their chosen field.

Research Associates will be offered appointments to the staff of the National Research Council on a term basis and will be offered salaries and benefits currently available to Research Officers.

YEAR PROGRAM STARTED: 1975

PURPOSE:
To undertake, assist or promote scientific and engineering research to further Canada's economic and social development and to give promising scientists and engineers an opportunity to work on challenging research problems.

LEGAL BASIS:
Federal government agency.

ELIGIBILITY:
Applicant must possess a Ph.D. in natural science or engineering or a Master's degree in an engineering field earned within the last five years, or expect to obtain the degree within six months. Applicant must have a demonstrated ability to perform original high-quality research in their chosen field.

Although preference will be given to Canadian citizens and permanent residents, Associateships are open to nationals of all countries. The offer of an Associateship does not ensure foreign nationals permanent residency in Canada. Non-Canadian candidates should apply for non-immigrant status (i.e., temporary status) and an employment visa.

FINANCIAL DATA:
Salaries commensurate with experience are taxable and subject to other deductions.
Amount of support per award: Current annual Ph.D. recruiting rate is $68,997.
Total amount of support: Varies.

APPLICATION INFO:
Applicants must apply online. All applicants must submit university transcripts, two letters of recommendation and resume. Application is valid for one year.
Duration: Two years. Renewal to a maximum of five years.

ADDRESS INQUIRIES TO:
Research Associates Program Coordinator
(See address above.)

NATIONAL SCIENCE FOUNDATION [1665]
Directorate for Education and Human Resources
Division of Graduate Education
2415 Eisenhower Avenue
Alexandria, VA 22314
(703) 292-8630
(866) 673-4737
Fax: (703) 292-9048
E-mail: info@nsfgrfp.org
Web Site: www.nsf.gov/grfp (official program information)
www.nsfgrfp.org (application assistance)

FOUNDED: 1950

AREAS OF INTEREST:
Science, technology, engineering and math.

NAME(S) OF PROGRAMS:
● **NSF Graduate Research Fellowship Program**

TYPE:
Fellowships. Awarded for graduate study leading to research-based Master's and doctoral degrees in science and engineering. The GRFP provides three years of support for the graduate education of individuals who have demonstrated their potential for significant achievements in science and engineering. The ranks of NSF Fellows include individuals who have made transformative breakthrough discoveries in science and engineering, become leaders in their chosen careers and been honored as Nobel laureates.

YEAR PROGRAM STARTED: 1952

PURPOSE:
To help ensure the vitality and diversity of the scientific and engineering workforce in the U.S.

LEGAL BASIS:
Government agency.

ELIGIBILITY:
Applicant must meet all of the following eligibility criteria by the application deadline:
(1) be a U.S. citizen, national or permanent resident;
(2) intend to enroll or be enrolled full-time in a research-based graduate degree program in an eligible field of study in STEM or STEM education;
(3) have never previously accepted a GRFP award, or if previously offered a GRFP award, have declined by the deadline;

(4) have never earned a doctoral or terminal degree in any field;
(5) have never earned a Master's or professional degree in any field, unless returning to graduate study after an interruption of two or more consecutive years immediately preceding the deadline, and are not enrolled in a graduate degree program at the application deadline and;
(6) not be a current NSF employee.

GEOG. RESTRICTIONS: United States.

FINANCIAL DATA:
Amount of support per award: $138,000 per award; $46,000 annually (includes $34,000 stipend to the Fellow and $12,000 cost of education allowance to the institution).

NO. MOST RECENT APPLICANTS: 12,000 for the year 2018.

NO. AWARDS: Approximately 1,600.

APPLICATION INFO:
Application must be completed online.

The following material is required from all applicants:
(1) personal, relevant background and future goals statement;
(2) graduate research plan statement;
(3) three reference letters and;
(4) academic transcripts.
Duration: The fellowship period is five years, during which NSF provides three years of support. Normal tenure is 12 months for each fellowship year. Availability of the second and third years of a support is contingent upon certification by the fellowship institution that progress is being made and availability of appropriated funds.
Deadline: October.

ADDRESS INQUIRIES TO:
Graduate Research Fellowship Program
(See address above.)

*PLEASE NOTE:
Program eligibility requirements subject to change each year.

NATIONAL SCIENCE FOUNDATION [1666]
2415 Eisenhower Avenue
Alexandria, VA 22314
(703) 292-7283
Fax: (703) 292-9068
E-mail: fkronz@nsf.gov
Web Site: www.nsf.gov

FOUNDED: 1950

AREAS OF INTEREST:
Research that uses historical, philosophical, or social scientific methods to investigate the intellectual, material, or social facets of STEM (Science, Technology, Engineering and Mathematics), including medical science. It encompasses a broad spectrum of topics including interdisciplinary studies of ethics, equity, governance, and policy issues closely related to STEM disciplines.

NAME(S) OF PROGRAMS:
● **Science, Technology and Society**

TYPE:
Conferences/seminars; Fellowships; Project/program grants; Research grants; Training grants. Grants support research and educational projects, national meetings, dissemination efforts, cross-disciplinary study, dissertation research, small group training activities, dissertation improvement grants for graduate students, and postdoctoral

fellowships. The proposals that are considered for support use methods from a variety of disciplines including anthropology, communications, history, philosophy, political science, and sociology to investigate STEM theory and practice with regards to their history, socio-cultural formation, philosophical underpinnings, and impacts on quality of life, culture, and society.

YEAR PROGRAM STARTED: 1976

PURPOSE:
To provide educational opportunities for graduate students.

LEGAL BASIS:
Government agency.

ELIGIBILITY:
Individuals, universities, colleges and nonprofit organizations.

FINANCIAL DATA:
Amount of support per award: Generally, $12,000 to $500,000.
Total amount of support: Approximately $6,200,000.

CO-OP FUNDING PROGRAMS: National Institutes of Health; Department of Energy.

NO. AWARDS: 80.

APPLICATION INFO:
Proposers should consult the Science, Technology and Society (STS) Announcement 15-506 and appropriate NSF brochures such as Grant Proposal Guide, available from the address above.
Duration: One to five years.
Deadline: February 2 and August 3.

ADDRESS INQUIRIES TO:
Frederick Kronz, Program Director
(See address above.)

NATIONAL SCIENCE FOUNDATION [1667]
Directorate of Geosciences, Office of Polar Programs
2415 Eisenhower Avenue
Alexandria, VA 22314
(703) 292-8014
Fax: (703) 292-9081
E-mail: dfriscic@nsf.gov
Web Site: www.nsf.gov

FOUNDED: 1950

AREAS OF INTEREST:
Antarctic natural sciences.

NAME(S) OF PROGRAMS:
● **U.S. Antarctic Research Program**

TYPE:
Fellowships; Project/program grants; Research grants. Grants for research projects in all fields of science pertinent to the Antarctic, including both field work in the Antarctic and study in the U.S. of already gathered data and specimens. Support is provided for research projects in astronomy, astrophysics, the behavioral sciences, biology, cartography, geology, glaciology, meteorology, oceanography, solid earth geophysics, upper atmospheric physics and magnetospheric physics. Logistics and support in Antarctica are arranged by the Foundation.

YEAR PROGRAM STARTED: 1959

PURPOSE:
To fund, coordinate and arrange for support of research in all fields of science pertinent to Antarctica.

LEGAL BASIS:
Federal agency under the National Science Foundation Act of 1950, Public Law 81-507, as amended. Also White House memo 6646 dated February 5, 1982.

ELIGIBILITY:
U.S. universities and colleges are the primary participants in the program. Other eligible participants include nonacademic research institutions, profit or nonprofit, and unaffiliated scientists or scientists employed by other federal agencies.

GEOG. RESTRICTIONS: United States.

FINANCIAL DATA:
Amount of support per award: Varies with need.

Total amount of support: $55,000,000.

Matching fund requirements: Grantee institutions are generally required to share in project costs by a contribution to any cost element in the project, direct or indirect.

NO. AWARDS: Approximately 50.

APPLICATION INFO:
Applications are submitted in the form of a proposal with a detailed research plan and budget. Information concerning proposal preparation is available in the PAPPG, NSF 17-1, *Grant Proposal Guide, Antarctic Research Program Announcement.* Information regarding guidelines for the Division of Polar Programs can be found on the web site under the tab "Geosciences."

Deadline: Proposals are accepted on a rolling basis.

ADDRESS INQUIRIES TO:
David Friscic, Tech Information Specialist (See address above.)

NATIONAL SCIENCE FOUNDATION   [1668]
Directorate of Geosciences, Office of Polar Programs
2415 Eisenhower Avenue
Alexandria, VA 22314
(703) 292-8014
Fax: (703) 292-9081
E-mail: dfriscic@nsf.gov
Web Site: www.nsf.gov

FOUNDED: 1950

AREAS OF INTEREST:
Arctic natural sciences, social sciences, Arctic system science, and Arctic observing network.

NAME(S) OF PROGRAMS:
● **Arctic Research Program**

TYPE:
Conferences/seminars; Research grants; Research contracts. Grants and contracts to support scientific research projects relating to the Arctic as well as the subsequent analysis of data. Research may be concerned with problems of marine research, including the polar pack ice; terrestrial biology, including analysis of the ecosystem; meteorology; solar-terrestrial physics; glaciology, including permafrost; geology and geophysics; social sciences; and data and information.

YEAR PROGRAM STARTED: 1971

PURPOSE:
To increase man's knowledge of the Arctic environment and its dynamic parameters; to increase cooperation in research with other agencies and nations having Arctic interests.

LEGAL BASIS:
The National Science Foundation Act of 1950, Public Law 81-507, as amended; Arctic Research and Policy Act of 1984.

ELIGIBILITY:
Proposals may be submitted by U.S. colleges and universities and by academically related nonprofit research organizations. Industry and other organizations are also eligible for support.

GEOG. RESTRICTIONS: United States.

FINANCIAL DATA:
Amount of support per award: Varies.

Total amount of support: $40,000,000 annually.

Matching fund requirements: Cost sharing is not required.

NO. AWARDS: 75 per year, pending availability of funds.

APPLICATION INFO:
Application information may be requested from the Foundation. Information regarding guidelines for the Division of Polar Programs can be found on the web site under the tab "Geosciences."

Because of far-reaching scientific, logistic and international implications of Arctic research projects, it is essential that scientists specify all field needs when submitting proposals. Special procedures and a longer lead time apply to research proposed for Greenland. Proposers should also consult the Foundation's *Proposal and Award Procedures Guide* (PAPPG) (NSF 17-1).

Deadline: Proposals are accepted on a rolling basis.

ADDRESS INQUIRIES TO:
David Friscic, Tech Information Specialist (See address above.)

THE ROYAL SOCIETY OF CANADA   [1669]
Walter House
282 Somerset Street West
Ottawa ON K2P 0J6 Canada
(613) 991-6990 ext. 106
Fax: (613) 991-6996
E-mail: nominations@rsc-src.ca
Web Site: www.rsc-src.ca

FOUNDED: 1883

AREAS OF INTEREST:
Arts and humanities, social sciences and science.

NAME(S) OF PROGRAMS:
● **Yvan Allaire Medal**
● **The Bancroft Award**
● **The Pierre Chauveau Medal**
● **The Sir John William Dawson Medal**
● **The Flavelle Medal**
● **Ursula Franklin Award in Gender Studies**
● **The Jason A. Hannah Medal**
● **The Innis-Gérin Medal**
● **The McLaughlin Medal**
● **Willet G. Miller Medal**
● **The Lorne Pierce Medal**
● **The Miroslaw Romanowski Medal**
● **The Rutherford Memorial Medals**
● **The John L. Synge Award**
● **The Henry Marshall Tory Medal**
● **The J.B. Tyrrell Historical Medal**

TYPE:
Awards/prizes. The Yvan Allaire Medal is awarded in recognition of outstanding research in governance of public and private organizations.

The Bancroft Award is given for publication, instruction and research in the earth sciences that have conspicuously contributed to public understanding and appreciation of the subject.

The Pierre Chauveau Medal is awarded for a distinguished contribution to knowledge in the humanities.

The Sir John William Dawson Medal is awarded for important contributions of knowledge in multiple domains.

The Flavelle Medal is awarded for an outstanding contribution to biological science during the preceding 10 years or for significant additions to a previous outstanding contribution to biological science.

The Ursula Franklin Award in Gender Studies is intended to recognize significant contributions by a Canadian scholar in the humanities and social sciences to furthering our understanding of issues concerning gender.

The Jason A. Hannah Medal is awarded for an important publication in the history of medicine.

The Innis-Gérin Medal is presented for a distinguished and sustained contribution to the literature of the social sciences.

The McLaughlin Medal is awarded for important research of sustained excellence in any branch of the medical sciences.

The Willet G. Miller Medal is given for outstanding research in any branch of earth sciences.

The Lorne Pierce Medal is awarded for an achievement of special significance and conspicuous merit in imaginative or critical literature written in either English or French (critical literature dealing with Canadian subjects has priority over critical literature of equal merit that does not deal with Canadian subjects).

The Miroslaw Romanowski Medal is awarded for significant contributions to the resolution of scientific aspects of environmental problems or for important improvements to the quality of an ecosystem in all aspects - terrestrial, atmospheric and aqueous - brought about by scientific means.

The Rutherford Memorial Medals are awarded for outstanding research in any branch of physics and chemistry.

The John L. Synge Award is given to acknowledge outstanding research in any of the branches of the mathematical sciences.

The Henry Marshall Tory Medal is given for outstanding research in any branch of astronomy, chemistry, mathematics, physics or an allied science.

The J.B. Tyrrell Historical Medal is awarded for outstanding work in the history of Canada.

YEAR PROGRAM STARTED: 1955

PURPOSE:
To annually recognize Canadian citizens for contributions to Canadian academic excellence in various branches.

LEGAL BASIS:
Nonprofit.

ELIGIBILITY:
Awarded to Canadian citizens or those who have had status for at least three years as Canadian Permanent Residents.

GEOG. RESTRICTIONS: Canada.

FINANCIAL DATA:
Amount of support per award: Varies with every medal.

APPLICATION INFO:
Open call for nominations takes place January 15 to March 1.
Duration: The Bancroft Award, The Chauveau Medal, The Sir John William Dawson Medal, The Flavelle Medal, Ursula Franklin Award in Gender Studies, The Jason A. Hannah Medal, The Innis-Gérin Medal, Willet G. Miller Medal, The Lorne Pierce Medal, The Henry Marshall Tory Medal and The J.B. Tyrrell Historical Medal: Every two years. Allaire, McLaughlin, Romanowski and Rutherford Memorial Medals: Every year. The John L. Synge Award: Varies.
Deadline: March 1.

ADDRESS INQUIRIES TO:
Christopher Dragan, Membership and Engagement Coordinator
(See address above.)

SIGMA XI: THE SCIENTIFIC RESEARCH HONOR SOCIETY   [1670]
3200 East NC Highway 54
Suite 300
Research Triangle Park, NC 27709
(919) 549-4691 ext. 206
Fax: (919) 549-0090
E-mail: giar@sigmaxi.org
Web Site: www.sigmaxi.org

FOUNDED: 1886

AREAS OF INTEREST:
The sciences, physical sciences, engineering, social, behavioral and life sciences.

NAME(S) OF PROGRAMS:
- **Grants in Aid of Research**

TYPE:
Grants-in-aid; Project/program grants; Research grants. Grants in Aid support research projects in any field of scientific investigation. Assistance is available for such research-related activities as travel to research location or supplies.

YEAR PROGRAM STARTED: 1922

PURPOSE:
To encourage scientific research.

LEGAL BASIS:
Nonprofit organization.

ELIGIBILITY:
Graduate and undergraduate students with proposals for specific research projects are eligible to apply. Student faculty advisor (first recommender) should be a full, active member of Sigma Xi to compete for Sigma Xi funds. NAS funds in the program are unrestricted and cover the physical, life and medical sciences (excluding the social sciences).

Grants do not cover overhead costs. No grants for publication/presentation costs, travel to meetings or stipends. Will fund travel to a research site.

FINANCIAL DATA:
Amount of support per award: Up to $1,000 for most areas of the sciences and engineering; Up to $5,000 for astronomy; Up to $2,500 for eye/vision research.
Total amount of support: Approximately $200,000.

CO-OP FUNDING PROGRAMS: National Academy of Sciences.

NO. MOST RECENT APPLICANTS: 1,600.

NO. AWARDS: 200.

APPLICATION INFO:
Contact the Society for details.
Duration: Applicants may apply for a second grant after submitting a report on the outcome of the project supported by a first grant.
Deadline: Applications and supporting letters must be received by March 15 or October 1. Awards are announced within 12 weeks.

PUBLICATIONS:
Annual report; application guidelines.

ADDRESS INQUIRIES TO:
Dr. Janelle Simmons, Manager of Programs
E-mail: jsimmons@sigmaxi.org

SMITHSONIAN INSTITUTION   [1671]
Office of Fellowships and Internships
470 L'Enfant Plaza, S.W., Suite 7102
MRC 902, P.O. Box 37012
Washington, DC 20013-7012
(202) 633-7070
E-mail: siofi@si.edu
Web Site: www.smithsonianofi.com

FOUNDED: 1846

AREAS OF INTEREST:
Animal behavior, ecology and environmental science, including an emphasis on the tropics; anthropology, including archaeology; astrophysics and astronomy; earth sciences and paleobiology; evolutionary and systematic biology; history of science and technology; history of art, especially American, contemporary, African and Asian art; 20th-century American crafts and decorative arts; social and cultural history of the U.S.; and folklore.

NAME(S) OF PROGRAMS:
- **Smithsonian Graduate Student Fellowships**
- **Smithsonian Postdoctoral Fellowships**
- **Smithsonian Predoctoral Fellowships**
- **Smithsonian Senior Fellowships**

TYPE:
Fellowships. Offered to qualified scholars for research to be conducted in residence at the Smithsonian in association with the staff, using collections and research facilities.

YEAR PROGRAM STARTED: 1964

PURPOSE:
To provide students and scholars in the sciences, arts and humanities with an opportunity for research utilizing the unique collections and facilities of the Smithsonian, while working with the institution's research staff.

LEGAL BASIS:
Act of Congress approved August 10, 1846; 20 U.S.C. 41 et seq.

ELIGIBILITY:
Smithsonian Fellowships are open to both U.S. citizens and foreign nationals. Fluency in English is required.

For the graduate fellowships, students must be formally enrolled and engaged in a graduate program of study at a degree-granting institution, have completed at least one semester and have not yet been advanced to candidacy if in a Ph.D. program.

For the predoctoral fellowships, students must be enrolled in a university as candidates for the Ph.D. or equivalent. At the time of appointment, the university must approve the undertaking of dissertation research at the Smithsonian and indicate that requirements for the Doctorate, other than the dissertation, have been met.

For the postdoctoral fellowships, applicants must have received the Ph.D., or equivalent, within seven years of the program deadline and must have completed the degree or certificate at the time the fellowship commences.

For the senior fellowships, applicants must have received the Ph.D., or equivalent, seven or more years before the program deadline.

Research must be conducted while in residence at the Smithsonian.

The Smithsonian Institution does not offer financial assistance for degree-granting programs at academic institutions. All forms of financial assistance are to support research in residence at the Smithsonian and its facilities.

FINANCIAL DATA:
Amount of support per award: Varies.

APPLICATION INFO:
Official application materials are available upon request. Specify the fellowship corresponding to your academic level.
Duration: Varies.
Deadline: Varies.

PUBLICATIONS:
Smithsonian Opportunities for Research and Study.

OFFICER:
Eric Woodard, Director

ADDRESS INQUIRIES TO:
Office of Fellowships and Internships
(See address above.)

SOCIETY FOR SCIENCE AND THE PUBLIC   [1672]
1719 N Street, N.W.
Washington, DC 20036
(202) 785-2255
E-mail: sts@societyforscience.org
Web Site: www.societyforscience.org

FOUNDED: 1921

AREAS OF INTEREST:
Sciences, mathematics, engineering and medicine.

NAME(S) OF PROGRAMS:
- **Regeneron Science Talent Search**

TYPE:
Awards/prizes. Competition for high school seniors excelling in science, math and engineering.

YEAR PROGRAM STARTED: 1942

PURPOSE:
To discover at the high school senior year level, those who have the potential to become the scientists, mathematicians and engineers of the future; to make the public aware of the impact that a quality science, mathematics or engineering education has on our future and the future of our nation.

LEGAL BASIS:
Nonprofit educational institution.

ELIGIBILITY:
Student must be in the last year of secondary school in the U.S., Puerto Rico, Guam, Virgin Islands, American Samoa, Wake and Midway Islands, the Marianas, DOD Schools or American schools abroad or for citizens studying abroad.

FINANCIAL DATA:
Amount of support per award: National Semifinalists receive $2,000 and their schools receive $2,000. Top 10 awarded $40,000 to $250,000. Remainder of top 40 receive $25,000.

Total amount of support: Varies.

NO. AWARDS: 300 National Semifinalists; 40 Finalists.

APPLICATION INFO:
There are four components of the application: (1) Applicants enter responses to the basic information and essay questions directly into the text boxes on the web pages of the application;
(2) Documents such as the research report, IRB summary, and IACUC approvals, where applicable, will be uploaded to the application as Word documents or PDF's;
(3) Each student must request at least one Project Recommendation, one High School Report, and one Educator Recommendation. Each applicant has the option of requesting a second recommendation of each type and;
(4) Applicants may mail their transcripts to the Society in hard copy form or ask their High School Report provider to upload a scanned copy to their High School Report. In either case, the timely receipt of the transcript is the responsibility of the student.
Deadline: November.

PUBLICATIONS:
Science News, magazine.

ADDRESS INQUIRIES TO:
Allie Stifel, Program Director
(See address above.)

THE SOCIETY FOR THE SCIENTIFIC STUDY OF SEXUALITY   [1673]
881 Third Street, Suite B-5
Whitehall, PA 18052
(610) 443-3100
E-mail: thesociety@sexscience.org
Web Site: sexscience.org

FOUNDED: 1957

AREAS OF INTEREST:
Sex research, sex therapy and sex education.

NAME(S) OF PROGRAMS:
- **Grants-in-Aid Project**
- **Student Research Grants**

TYPE:
Grants-in-aid; Research grants. Grants-in-Aid Project supports scientific sexuality research in areas not likely to receive support from other sources.

Student Research Grant supports an SSSS student member who is doing human sexuality research.

YEAR PROGRAM STARTED: 1985

PURPOSE:
To assist with the development of quality research projects in the area of sex research.

LEGAL BASIS:
Tax-exempt, private, not-for-profit corporation.

ELIGIBILITY:
Grants-in-Aid Project is open to all professionals conducting research related to human sexuality.

Student Research Grants are open to students who are enrolled in a degree-granting program and student members of SSSS.

FINANCIAL DATA:
Amount of support per award: Grants-in-Aid: $1,000; Student Research Grants: $2,000.

NO. MOST RECENT APPLICANTS: 25.

NO. AWARDS: Varies.

APPLICATION INFO:
Applications and additional information can be found online.
Deadline: Grants-in-Aid Project: Proposals may be submitted at any time during the year. Student Research Grants: September 1.

PUBLICATIONS:
Application guidelines.

IRS I.D.: 13-2642753

SYSTEMS PLUS, INC.
One Research Court
Suite 360
Rockville, MD 20850
(301) 948-4232
E-mail: afsffp.pmo@sysplus.com
Web Site: afsffp.sysplus.com

TYPE:
Fellowships. Research fellowship.

See entry 2448 for full listing.

TOURETTE ASSOCIATION OF AMERICA, INC.
42-40 Bell Boulevard
Suite 205
Bayside, NY 11361-2820
(718) 224-2999
Fax: (718) 279-9596
E-mail: support@tourette.org
Web Site: www.tourette.org

TYPE:
Fellowships; General operating grants; Research grants; Seed money grants; Technical assistance. Research grants available for Ph.D. and M.D. researchers in the following categories:
(1) proposals in basic neuroscience specifically relevant to Tourette Syndrome and;
(2) clinical studies related to the etiology, pathophysiology and treatment of Tourette Syndrome.

Fellowships provide one-year postdoctoral training.

See entry 2274 for full listing.

U.S. ARMY RESEARCH OFFICE   [1674]
800 Park Office Drive
Research Triangle Park, NC 27703
(919) 549-0641
Fax: (919) 549-4310
Web Site: www.arl.army.mil

FOUNDED: 1951

AREAS OF INTEREST:
Biosciences, chemistry, electronics, engineering, environmental sciences, materials sciences, mathematical and computer sciences and physics.

TYPE:
Conferences/seminars; Research grants; Research contracts. Grants and contracts for scientific research in such areas of interest to the U.S. Army as chemistry, engineering, biology, mathematics, metallurgy and materials, physics, electronics and environmental sciences. Support is also provided for symposia on particular aspects of scientific investigation, the results of which further Department of the Army objectives.

YEAR PROGRAM STARTED: 1951

PURPOSE:
To increase knowledge of natural phenomena and environment in an attempt to solve problems in the physical, engineering, environmental and life sciences.

LEGAL BASIS:
Government agency.

ELIGIBILITY:
Organizations with appropriate interests are eligible to apply.

FINANCIAL DATA:
Amount of support per award: Grants and contracts vary in amount, depending upon the needs and nature of the request; $136,000 yearly average.

Total amount of support: $500,000,000 to $550,000,000 including both grants and contracts.

NO. MOST RECENT APPLICANTS: Approximately 550.

NO. AWARDS: Approximately 350.

APPLICATION INFO:
Research awards are selected from proposals submitted in response to an open-ended Broad Agency Announcement (BAA). Contractors interested in submitting proposals should go to the ARL web site and download the ARO BAA.
Duration: One to three years. Continuations possible if work has not been completed.
Deadline: Varies.

ADDRESS INQUIRIES TO:
RDECOM Acquisitions Center
(See address above.)

U.S. DEPARTMENT OF ENERGY
3610 Collins Ferry Road
P.O. Box 880
Morgantown, WV 26507-0880
(304) 285-4764
Fax: (304) 285-4403
Web Site: www.netl.doe.gov

TYPE:
Assistantships; Project/program grants; Research grants. Topics change annually. In general, the program areas could include high performance materials, sensors and controls, simulation-based engineering, and water management research and development.

See entry 2450 for full listing.

U.S. DEPARTMENT OF THE NAVY [1675]

Office of Naval Research, One Liberty Center
875 North Randolph Street, Suite 1425
Arlington, VA 22203-1995
(703) 696-5031
Fax: (703) 696-5940
E-mail: onrpublicaffairs@navy.mil
Web Site: www.onr.navy.mil

FOUNDED: 1946

AREAS OF INTEREST:
Advanced materials, ocean sciences, mathematics, information sciences, physics, electronics, chemistry, mechanics, cognitive and neural sciences.

NAME(S) OF PROGRAMS:
- **University Research Initiative**
- **Young Investigator Program**

TYPE:
Research grants; Research contracts. ONR sponsors long-range scientific research, applied research and advanced technology development which offer potential for advancement and improvement of naval operations. Programs include physics, electronic and solid state sciences, mathematics, operations research, statistics and probability, information science, fluid dynamics, physiology, biochemistry, biophysics, microbiology, naval biology, cognitive and neural sciences research, personnel and training research, Arctic research, coastal sciences, earth and environmental physics, atmospheric sciences, metallurgy and ceramics research, chemistry, energy research, structural mechanics, physical and chemical oceanography, marine geology and geophysics, ocean biology, ocean acoustics and ocean engineering.

YEAR PROGRAM STARTED: 1946

PURPOSE:
To support research in various scientific fields including ocean science and physics.

LEGAL BASIS:
Public Law 588, as amended and Public Law 85-934, as amended.

ELIGIBILITY:
Nonprofit institutions of higher education and organizations whose primary purpose is the conduct of scientific research may apply for contracts or grants. Nonprofit and profit-making institutions, organizations or industrial establishments, as well as qualified individuals, are eligible for contract support.

FINANCIAL DATA:
Amount of support per award: Varies, depending upon the needs and nature of the request.
Total amount of support: Varies.

NO. MOST RECENT APPLICANTS: Approximately 4,000 inquiries.

NO. AWARDS: Approximately 2,500 annually.

APPLICATION INFO:
Before submitting a proposal, interested individuals are encouraged to assess the relevance of their research interests to Navy research priorities by consulting the ONR web page and talking to the relevant ONR Program Manager. Applications are submitted in the form of a proposal which should include:
(1) general statement requesting consideration of the proposal;
(2) brief review of the scientific background of the proposed research;
(3) technical description of the project, including statement of objectives and scientific methods to be employed;
(4) description of available facilities;
(5) background of principal investigator(s) and associates;
(6) bibliography of pertinent publications;
(7) proposed duration of project and annual itemized budget;
(8) other research projects currently undertaken by the principal investigator;
(9) other agencies to whom the proposal is being submitted for possible financial support and;
(10) cost breakdown by year.

WEIZMANN INSTITUTE OF SCIENCE

Feinberg Graduate School
David Lopatie Hall of Graduate Studies
P.O. Box 26
234 Herzl Street
Rehovot 7610001 Israel
(972) 8-934-2924
Fax: (972) 8-934-4114
E-mail: FGS@weizmann.ac.il
Web Site: www.weizmann.ac.il/feinberg

TYPE:
Fellowships. The Feinberg Graduate School of the Weizmann Institute of Science offers a limited number of postdoctoral fellowships in all areas of research in which the Weizmann Institute is engaged. The fellowships are offered in various fields of biology, chemistry, physics, biochemistry-biophysics, mathematics, computer science and science teaching.

See entry 875 for full listing.

THE HELEN HAY WHITNEY FOUNDATION [1676]

20 Squadron Boulevard
Suite 630
New City, NY 10956-5247
(845) 639-6799
Fax: (845) 639-6798
E-mail: office@hhwf.org
Web Site: hhwf.org

FOUNDED: 1947

AREAS OF INTEREST:
Biomedical sciences.

NAME(S) OF PROGRAMS:
- **Early Postdoctoral Research Fellowship Program in Biomedical Sciences**

TYPE:
Fellowships. Postdoctoral research fellowships.

YEAR PROGRAM STARTED: 1957

PURPOSE:
To provide beginning postdoctoral research training to young M.Ds. and Ph.Ds. to further their careers in research in biomedical sciences.

LEGAL BASIS:
Independent foundation.

ELIGIBILITY:
Candidates living in North America or foreign nationals that pursue their fellowship in the U.S., who hold the M.D., Ph.D. or equivalent degree, who are seeking beginning postdoctoral training in basic biomedical research and have no more than one year postdoctoral experience by June 15 are eligible. U.S. citizenship is not a requirement, but fellowships to resident noncitizens are awarded only for training in the U.S. Citizens may train abroad.

Applications from established scientists or advanced fellows will not be considered. Applicants who have already had one year's postdoctoral laboratory training at the time of deadline will not be considered for a Whitney Fellowship.

FINANCIAL DATA:
Amount of support per award: Fellowships provide stipends as follows: $54,000 for the first year, $57,000 for the second year and $60,000 for the third year, plus a $1,500 research allowance to the department for each year of tenure, travel to fellowship location and annual meeting of all fellows. Additionally, there is a dependent child allowance of $1,500 per each dependent child.

NO. MOST RECENT APPLICANTS: 500.

APPLICATION INFO:
Online application is available at the Foundation web site.
Duration: Three years. Contingent upon satisfactory performance.
Deadline: Applications accepted April 15 to June 15. Fellowships begin the following April 1 through September 1.

PUBLICATIONS:
Annual report.

WOODS HOLE OCEANOGRAPHIC INSTITUTION [1677]

Academic Programs Office, Clark 223, MS No. 31
360 Woods Hole Road
Woods Hole, MA 02543-1541
(508) 289-3379
E-mail: education@whoi.edu
Web Site: www.whoi.edu/main/summer-student-fellowship

FOUNDED: 1930

AREAS OF INTEREST:
Research in biological oceanography, marine chemistry and geochemistry, marine geology and geophysics, applied ocean physics and engineering, physical oceanography and marine policy.

NAME(S) OF PROGRAMS:
- **Summer Student Fellowship Program in Oceanography**

TYPE:
Fellowships. Awards for independent research in oceanography/ocean engineering and marine policy projects pursued under the guidance of a member of the research staff of the Woods Hole Oceanographic Institution. Fellowship is for a 10- to 12-week summer study at Woods Hole Oceanographic Institution.

YEAR PROGRAM STARTED: 1954

PURPOSE:
To give a small group of qualified undergraduate science and engineering students experience that will enable them to determine whether they wish to devote lifetime careers to studying the oceans.

LEGAL BASIS:
Charter under the Commonwealth of Massachusetts.

ELIGIBILITY:
Summer Student Fellowships are awarded to undergraduate students who will have

completed their junior year at colleges or universities by the start of the fellowship period. Students who will graduate before the fellowship begins are not eligible to apply. Preference is given to students studying in any of the fields of science or engineering including but not limited to the fields of biology, chemistry, engineering, geology, geophysics, mathematics, meteorology, physics, oceanography, and marine policy. Students must have at least a tentative interest in the ocean sciences, oceanographic engineering, mathematics, or marine policy.

Persons from underrepresented groups are encouraged to apply. WHOI actively recruits underrepresented minorities in ocean science as defined by the National Science Foundation (African-, Hispanic- and Native-Americans, and Pacific Islanders).

Fellows are selected based on the applicant's previous academic and scientific achievements and promise as future ocean scientists or ocean engineers. Important consideration is given to matching each fellow with an appropriate advisor on WHOI's Scientific or Senior Technical Staff.

FINANCIAL DATA:
Award includes weekly stipend, travel allowance of $700 and institutional housing.
Amount of support per award: Stipend of $632 per week.
Total amount of support: Varies.

NO. AWARDS: 25 to 30.

APPLICATION INFO:
Applications must be submitted online. A complete application should include an application form, transcripts of college and university records, at least three personal references, a concise statement of the applicant's research plans and interests, future education and career plans, and reasons for applying to the Institution.

Duration: 10 to 12 weeks.

Deadline: February 15. Notification by March 15.

STAFF:
Margaret K. Tivey, Vice President for Academic Programs and Dean

ADDRESS INQUIRIES TO:
See e-mail address above.

*SPECIAL STIPULATIONS:
Fellows are required to present a mid-summer progress report. At the end of the summer, each fellow is required to prepare a written report describing their research.

SOCIAL SCIENCES

Social sciences (general)

AGENCY FOR HEALTHCARE RESEARCH AND QUALITY (AHRQ)
Office of Management Services
Division of Grants Management
5600 Fishers Lane, 7th Floor
Rockville, MD 20857
(301) 427-1104 (specify funding area)
(301) 427-1450
E-mail: gmi@ahrq.hhs.gov
Web Site: www.ahrq.gov

TYPE:
Conferences/seminars; Development grants;
Fellowships; Project/program grants;
Research grants; Training grants. Dissertation
support highlighting primary care, market
forces, cost containment, managed care, the
cost of treating AIDS, the improvement of
treatment for persons with HIV, rural health
care, infant mortality, medical liability,
malpractice reform, health care of the aged
and disabled and policy studies.

See entry 1294 for full listing.

AMERICAN BAR FOUNDATION
750 North Lake Shore Drive
Fourth Floor
Chicago, IL 60611
(312) 988-6500
Fax: (312) 988-6579
E-mail: fellowships@abfn.org
Web Site: www.americanbarfoundation.org

TYPE:
Internships. Fellows spend the summer
gaining hands-on research experience, touring
legal institutions and law schools, and
meeting with legal practitioners and scholars.

See entry 892 for full listing.

AMERICAN BAR FOUNDATION
750 North Lake Shore Drive
Fourth Floor
Chicago, IL 60611-4403
(312) 988-6500
Fax: (312) 988-6579
E-mail: fellowships@abfn.org
Web Site: www.americanbarfoundation.org

TYPE:
Fellowships. The American Bar Foundation
(ABF), in partnership with AccessLex
Institute (ALI), is committed to developing
the next generation of scholars interested in
empirical and interdisciplinary research on
legal and higher education. This is a
residential fellowship at the ABF.

See entry 1797 for full listing.

BRETT FAMILY FOUNDATION [1678]
1123 Spruce Street
Boulder, CO 80302
(303) 442-1200
Fax: (303) 442-1221
E-mail: info@brettfoundation.org
Web Site: www.brettfoundation.org

FOUNDED: 2000

AREAS OF INTEREST:
Social justice, equal rights and access to
opportunity for individuals and families.

NAME(S) OF PROGRAMS:
- **Nonprofit Media Grant Program**
- **Social Justice Grant Program**

TYPE:
General operating grants.

PURPOSE:
To promote caring communities by investing
in organizations throughout Colorado
working for social justice and nonprofit
media.

GEOG. RESTRICTIONS: Colorado.

FINANCIAL DATA:
Amount of support per award: $2,500 to
$10,000.
Total amount of support: Approximately
$500,000 annually.

REPRESENTATIVE AWARDS:
$7,500 to Colorado Civic Engagement
Roundtable; $3,500 to Family Learning
Center; $10,000 to Colorado Public Radio.

APPLICATION INFO:
By invitation only.
Duration: One year. Must reapply.
Deadline: Varies.

ADDRESS INQUIRIES TO:
Senior Advisor
(See address above.)

CANADIAN FEDERATION FOR THE HUMANITIES AND SOCIAL SCIENCES [1679]
141 Laurier Avenue West
Suite 200
Ottawa ON K1P 5J3 Canada
(613) 238-6112 ext. 319
Fax: (613) 238-6114
E-mail: aspp-paes@ideas-idees.ca
Web Site: www.ideas-idees.ca

FOUNDED: 1941

AREAS OF INTEREST:
Social sciences and humanities.

NAME(S) OF PROGRAMS:
- **Awards to Scholarly Publications Program**

TYPE:
Grants-in-aid. Grants to support the
publication of scholarly books in the social
sciences and humanities.

YEAR PROGRAM STARTED: 1941

PURPOSE:
To assist the publication of books of
advanced scholarship in the humanities and
social sciences that make an important
contribution to knowledge.

LEGAL BASIS:
NGO, nonprofit.

ELIGIBILITY:
Scholarly works in English or French of at
least 40,000 words in length authored by
Canadian citizens or permanent residents of
Canada. The following works are not
eligible: unrevised theses, conference
proceedings, scholarly journals or articles,
textbooks, technical reports, concordances,
memoires and autobiographies. Approved
works must be published in Canada by
ASPP-approved publishers.

GEOG. RESTRICTIONS: Canada.

FINANCIAL DATA:
Grants are paid following publication directly
to the publisher.

Amount of support per award: Publication
Grant: $8,000. Translation Grant: $12,000.

NO. MOST RECENT APPLICANTS: 226.

NO. AWARDS: 180 Publication Grants and 5
Translation Grants per year.

APPLICATION INFO:
Publishers usually apply on the behalf of
authors, though authors may also apply
directly. Visit the program web site to
download the most up-to-date guidelines and
application forms.

PUBLICATIONS:
Application guidelines; application forms.

ADDRESS INQUIRIES TO:
Program Officer, ASPP
(See address above.)

*SPECIAL STIPULATIONS:
Non-Canadians may be eligible for ASPP
support if their work is on a Canadian
subject and is based on Canadian sources.

CANADIAN INSTITUTE OF UKRAINIAN STUDIES
University of Alberta
4-30 Pembina Hall
Edmonton AB T6G 2H8 Canada
(780) 492-2972
E-mail: cius@ualberta.ca
Web Site: www.cius.ca

TYPE:
Fellowships; Research grants; Scholarships.
The Helen Darcovich Memorial Doctoral
Fellowship is awarded annually to a student
writing a dissertation on a Ukrainian or
Ukrainian-Canadian topic in education,
history, humanities, social sciences, law or
library sciences.

The Neporany Doctoral Fellowship, offered
by the Canadian Foundation for Ukrainian
Studies, is awarded to one ore more doctoral
students specializing on Ukraine in political
science, economics, and related fields.

Research Grants are awarded in support of
projects that have scholarly value,
well-defined work plans, and modest budgets.

See entry 538 for full listing.

COUNCIL FOR EUROPEAN STUDIES AT COLUMBIA UNIVERSITY
475 Riverside Drive
Office 308i
New York, NY 10115
(646) 745-8550
E-mail: awards@ces-europe.org
Web Site: councilforeuropeanstudies.org

TYPE:
Awards/prizes; Conferences/seminars;
Fellowships; Internships; Scholarships; Travel
grants. The CES Book Award honors talented
emerging scholars with an award for the best
first book on any subject in European studies.
The award is given every two years.

CES Conference Travel Grants support
transcontinental travel for junior faculty and
graduate students already scheduled to
present at the Council's International
Conference of Europeanists.

CES Small Event Grants support workshops,
lectures, symposia and other small events that
share research on Europe with a wider
community.

First Article Prize awards one prize to a scholar working in the humanities and one to a scholar working in the social sciences. These prizes will honor the writers of the best first articles on European studies published within a two-year period.

Mellon-CES Dissertation Completion Fellowships are intended to facilitate the timely completion of the doctoral degree by late-stage graduate students focused on topics in European studies.

SAE-CES Pre-Dissertation Research Fellowships are intended to fund student's first major research project in Europe.

See entry 772 for full listing.

CROSSROADS FUND   [1680]

3411 West Diversey Avenue, Suite 20
Chicago, IL 60647-1245
(773) 227-7676
Fax: (773) 227-7790
E-mail: info@crossroadsfund.org
Web Site: www.crossroadsfund.org

FOUNDED: 1981

AREAS OF INTEREST:
Social change.

TYPE:
General operating grants; Project/program grants; Seed money grants; Technical assistance.

PURPOSE:
To support grassroots organizations working to alleviate underlying causes of social ills.

LEGAL BASIS:
Public foundation.

ELIGIBILITY:
Projects must be run by community organizations or nonprofits. No individuals. The Foundation only funds groups with annual expenses under $300,000.

GEOG. RESTRICTIONS: Chicago, Illinois metropolitan area and northwestern Indiana.

FINANCIAL DATA:
Amount of support per award: Up to $10,000.
Total amount of support: $820,000 for the year 2019.

APPLICATION INFO:
Application information is available on the web site.
Duration: One year.

PUBLICATIONS:
Application guidelines; newsletter; brochure; annual report.

ADDRESS INQUIRIES TO:
Jane Kimondo, Executive Director
(See address above.)

THE HARRY FRANK GUGGENHEIM FOUNDATION   [1681]

42 West 54th Street
16th Floor
New York, NY 10019
(646) 428-0971
Fax: (646) 428-0981
E-mail: info@hfg.org
Web Site: www.hfg.org

FOUNDED: 1929

AREAS OF INTEREST:
Scholarly research on violence and aggression.

NAME(S) OF PROGRAMS:
● **The Harry Frank Guggenheim Foundation Dissertation Fellowship**

TYPE:
Fellowships. Awarded to individuals who will complete the writing of the dissertation within the award year. Support is for projects which seek to advance and coordinate creative breakthroughs in the social and biological sciences relating to the study of violence and aggression.

YEAR PROGRAM STARTED: 1990

PURPOSE:
To further understanding of human social problems related to violence and aggression.

LEGAL BASIS:
Private foundation.

ELIGIBILITY:
Fellowships are for students in the final year of their doctoral programs. They are designed to support the write-up stage of the dissertation. They are available to citizens of any country in the world.

Recipients of the Dissertation Fellowship must submit a copy of the dissertation, approved and accepted by their institution, within six months after the end of the award year. Any papers, books, articles, or other publications based on the research should also be sent to the Foundation.

FINANCIAL DATA:
Amount of support per award: $20,000.
Total amount of support: $200,000 each year.

NO. MOST RECENT APPLICANTS: Average 225.

NO. AWARDS: 10 or more.

APPLICATION INFO:
Guidelines and application forms are available on the web site.
Duration: Dissertation Fellowships are one-time awards and are not renewable.
Deadline: February 1.

PUBLICATIONS:
Guidelines and Report.

OFFICERS:
Daniel Wilhelm, President
Deirdre Hamill, Director, Finance and Administration
Joel Wallman, Director of Research
Nyeleti Honwana, Program Officer

ADDRESS INQUIRIES TO:
Dissertation Fellowship
(See address above.)

THE HARRY FRANK GUGGENHEIM FOUNDATION   [1682]

42 West 54th Street
16th Floor
New York, NY 10019
(646) 428-0971
Fax: (646) 428-0981
E-mail: info@hfg.org
Web Site: www.hfg.org

FOUNDED: 1929

AREAS OF INTEREST:
Research on violence and aggression.

NAME(S) OF PROGRAMS:
● **The Harry Frank Guggenheim Foundation Research Grant**

TYPE:
Research grants. Support for projects which seek to advance and coordinate creative breakthroughs in the social and biological sciences relating to the study of violence and aggression.

YEAR PROGRAM STARTED: 1972

PURPOSE:
To further understanding of human social problems related to violence and aggression.

LEGAL BASIS:
Private, operating foundation.

ELIGIBILITY:
The Foundation awards research grants to individuals (or a few principal investigators at most) for individual projects and does not award grants to institutions for institutional programs.

Applicants for a research grant may be citizens of any country. While almost all recipients of a Foundation research grant possess a Ph.D., M.D., or equivalent degree, there are no formal degree requirements for the grant. The grant, however, may not be used to support research undertaken as part of the requirements for a graduate degree. Applicants need not be affiliated with an institution of higher learning, although most are college or university professors.

FINANCIAL DATA:
Amount of support per award: Usually $15,000 to $40,000 per year.
Total amount of support: Grants and Fellowships: $400,000 to $500,000.

NO. MOST RECENT APPLICANTS: 175.

NO. AWARDS: Approximately 10.

APPLICATION INFO:
Guidelines and application form are available at the Foundation web site.
Duration: Usually one to two years. Renewal is possible if requested in original application, but not guaranteed.
Deadline: August 1.

PUBLICATIONS:
Guidelines; Annual Report.

OFFICERS:
Daniel Wilhelm, President
Deirdre Hamill, Director, Finance and Administration
Joel Wallman, Director of Research
Nyeleti Honwana, Program Officer

ADDRESS INQUIRIES TO:
Research Grants
(See address above.)

THE JOHN RANDOLPH HAYNES AND DORA HAYNES FOUNDATION   [1683]

888 West Sixth Street, Suite 1150
Los Angeles, CA 90017-2737
(213) 623-9151
Fax: (213) 623-3951
E-mail: info@haynesfoundation.org
Web Site: www.haynesfoundation.org

FOUNDED: 1926

AREAS OF INTEREST:
Public policy for Los Angeles.

TYPE:
Fellowships; Research grants.

YEAR PROGRAM STARTED: 1926

PURPOSE:
To strengthen research in the social sciences into public policy issues of the Los Angeles region.

LEGAL BASIS:
Independent private foundation.

ELIGIBILITY:
501(c)(3) organizations only.

No grants are made to individuals.

GEOG. RESTRICTIONS: California, specifically Los Angeles, Orange, Riverside, San Bernardino, and Ventura counties.

FINANCIAL DATA:
Amount of support per award: $5,000 to $250,000.

Total amount of support: Up to $3,000,000.

NO. AWARDS: 25 grants and 15 fellowships for fiscal year 2018-19.

REPRESENTATIVE AWARDS:
$229,000 to California Institute of Technology; $200,000 to University of California, Riverside; $182,000 to University of California, Los Angeles.

APPLICATION INFO:
Application information is available on the web site.
Duration: One to two years.
Deadline: Varies.

PUBLICATIONS:
Annual report.

IRS I.D.: 95-1644020

BOARD OF TRUSTEES:
Dr. Jane G. Pisano, President
Robert Eckert
Gil Garcetti
Philip M. Hawley
Enrique Hernandez, Jr.
Robin Kramer
Dr. Daniel A. Mazmanian
Gilbert T. Ray
Roberto Suro

ADDRESS INQUIRIES TO:
See e-mail address above.

THE HOROWITZ FOUNDATION FOR SOCIAL POLICY   [1684]
P.O. Box 7
Rocky Hill, NJ 08553-0007
(732) 445-2280
E-mail: info@horowitz-foundation.org
Web Site: www.horowitz-foundation.org

FOUNDED: 1997

AREAS OF INTEREST:
Social sciences, including anthropology, area studies, economics, political science, psychology, sociology, urban studies, as well as newer areas such as evaluation research.

TYPE:
Research grants. Grants to doctoral candidates at the dissertation level with emphasis on social policy-related studies.

YEAR PROGRAM STARTED: 1997

PURPOSE:
To support the advancement of research and understanding in the major fields of the social sciences.

ELIGIBILITY:
Awards are only open to aspiring Ph.Ds. at the dissertation level whose project has received approval from their appropriate

department head/university. Applicants are not required to be U.S. citizens or U.S. residents.

Preference will be given to projects that deal with contemporary issues in the social sciences and issues of policy relevance.

Awards are not allocated so as to insure a representative base of disciplines, but are approved solely on merit.

FINANCIAL DATA:
Amount of support per award: $7,500 plus additional special grants; Additional $5,000 for best overall project.

CO-OP FUNDING PROGRAMS: Determined on a case-by-case basis.

NO. MOST RECENT APPLICANTS: 855 for the year 2019.

NO. AWARDS: Approximately 25 annually.

APPLICATION INFO:
Application guidelines and eligibility criteria can be found at the Foundation web site. Applications must be submitted through the online system. All materials must be submitted, in English, prior to the closing date.
Duration: One year. Nonrenewable.
Deadline: December 1.

IRS I.D.: 31-1612153

BOARD OF TRUSTEES:
Ayse Akincigil
David J. Armor
Hans Martin Boehmer
Jonathan D. Breul
Mary E. Curtis Horowitz
Richard Edwards
Pearl Eliadis
Michal Grinstein-Weiss
Melissa Jonson-Reid
Mary McKay
Nandini Ramanujam
Ray C. Rist
William Rodgers
Jos Vaessen

ADDRESS INQUIRIES TO:
Mary E. Curtis Horowitz
Chairman and Trustee
(See address above.)

INSTITUTE FOR ADVANCED STUDY   [1685]
One Einstein Drive
Princeton, NJ 08540
(609) 734-8250
Fax: (609) 951-4457
E-mail: donne@ias.edu
Web Site: www.sss.ias.edu

FOUNDED: 1930

AREAS OF INTEREST:
Economics, political science, sociology, education, anthropology and history.

NAME(S) OF PROGRAMS:
● **School of Social Science Fellowships**

TYPE:
Fellowships. Postdoctoral research fellowships at the School of Social Science.

YEAR PROGRAM STARTED: 1970

PURPOSE:
To support fundamental research and scholarship in the social sciences and humanities.

LEGAL BASIS:
Private, nonprofit research center.

ELIGIBILITY:
Scholars of any nationality who have obtained their highest degree and whose work is relevant to any aspect of the social sciences are urged to apply.

FINANCIAL DATA:
Amount of support per award:
Approximately $35,000 to $70,000.

Total amount of support: Varies.

Matching fund requirements: Institute strongly encourages applicants to apply for outside funds as well.

NO. MOST RECENT APPLICANTS: 509.

NO. AWARDS: 55.

APPLICATION INFO:
Applications must be submitted online.
Duration: One academic year.
Deadline: November 1.

PUBLICATIONS:
Annual report.

STAFF:
Donne Petito, Administrative Officer

ADDRESS INQUIRIES TO:
School of Social Science
(See address above.)

*SPECIAL STIPULATIONS:
This is a residential (on-site) fellowship.

INSTITUTE FOR QUANTITATIVE SOCIAL SCIENCE, HARVARD UNIVERSITY   [1686]
Henry A. Murray Research Archive
CGIS Knafel Building, Room 318
Cambridge, MA 02138
(617) 496-6528
E-mail: support@dataverse.org
Web Site: www.murray.harvard.edu

FOUNDED: 1976

AREAS OF INTEREST:
Social sciences, psychology and human development, and education.

NAME(S) OF PROGRAMS:
● **Jeanne Humphrey Block Dissertation Award**

TYPE:
Awards/prizes. The Block Dissertation Award is offered by the Henry A. Murray Research Archive.

YEAR PROGRAM STARTED: 1990

PURPOSE:
To support research that best embodies Henry A. Murray's commitment to the in-depth study of individuals in context, over time and from a variety of perspectives.

LEGAL BASIS:
University or research association.

ELIGIBILITY:
Applicant must be a Harvard Ph.D. candidate (third year or above) in the social sciences.

FINANCIAL DATA:
Amount of support per award: $2,500.
Total amount of support: $2,500.

NO. AWARDS: 1.

APPLICATION INFO:
Detailed information and application guidelines are available upon request to the Institute or can be found on its web site.
Duration: One year.
Deadline: March 13.

PUBLICATIONS:
  Program announcement.

IRS I.D.: 04-2103589

ADDRESS INQUIRIES TO:
  E-mail: funding@iq.harvard.edu

*SPECIAL STIPULATIONS:
  Dissertation must utilize data archived in the
  Harvard Dataverse.

KAPPA OMICRON NU HONOR SOCIETY
P.O. Box 798
Okemos, MI 48805-0798
(727) 940-2658 ext. 2003
E-mail: info@kon.org
Web Site: www.kon.org

TYPE:
  Fellowships; Project/program grants;
  Research grants; Scholarships. Awarded to
  members for graduate or postgraduate study
  and research in human sciences or one of its
  specializations at colleges or universities with
  strong research programs and supporting
  disciplines for the chosen major or topic.

See entry 2458 for full listing.

MADDIE'S FUND   [1687]
6150 Stoneridge Mall Road
Suite 125
Pleasanton, CA 94588
(925) 310-5450
E-mail: grants@maddiesfund.org
Web Site: www.maddiesfund.org

AREAS OF INTEREST:
  Animal welfare.

TYPE:
  Project/program grants; Training grants.

PURPOSE:
  To revolutionize the status and well-being of
  companion animals.

ELIGIBILITY:
  To be considered for a grant, an organization
  must meet the following criteria:
  (1) be a U.S.-based 501(c)(3) or government
  animal welfare organization focused on dogs
  and/or cats;
  (2) publicly share annual animal statistics on
  their web site;
  (3) publicly share lifesaving percentage and
  the formula for how it was calculated on
  their web site;
  (4) be an active participant in Shelter
  Animals Count and;
  (5) be an active participant in the Million Cat
  Challenge.

GEOG. RESTRICTIONS: United States.

FINANCIAL DATA:
  Amount of support per award: Varies by
  program.
  Total amount of support: $11,950,000 for the
  year 2019.

NO. AWARDS: 712 for the year 2019.

APPLICATION INFO:
  Applications will be made available when
  each individual grant opportunity is
  announced. Potential applicants can sign up
  for the Maddie Network to receive an e-mail
  when new grant opportunities or application
  periods are open.
  Duration: Varies by program.
  Deadline: Varies by program.

ADDRESS INQUIRIES TO:
  Kelly Clardy, Senior Grants Specialist
  (See address above.)

THE NATIONAL ASSOCIATION OF BLACK SOCIAL WORKERS
2305 Martin Luther King Jr. Avenue, S.E.
Washington, DC 20020
(202) 678-4570
Fax: (202) 678-4572
E-mail: officedirector@nabsw.org
Web Site: www.nabsw.org

TYPE:
  Scholarships.

See entry 945 for full listing.

NATIONAL COUNCIL FOR THE SOCIAL STUDIES   [1688]
8555 16th Street, Suite 500
Silver Spring, MD 20910
(301) 588-1800 ext. 110
(800) 296-7840
Fax: (301) 588-2049
E-mail: awards@ncss.org
Web Site: www.socialstudies.org

FOUNDED: 1921

AREAS OF INTEREST:
  Social studies education.

NAME(S) OF PROGRAMS:
  ● **Septima Clark Book Awards**
  ● **Exemplary Research in Social Studies**
  ● **Jean Dresden Grambs Distinguished Career in Social Studies**
  ● **The Larry Metcalf Exemplary Dissertation Award**
  ● **Outstanding Social Studies Teacher of the Year Awards (Elementary, Middle and Secondary Levels)**
  ● **Carter G. Woodson Book Awards**

TYPE:
  Awards/prizes; Grants-in-aid. The Septima
  Clark Book Awards were first presented in
  2019 and are intended to recognize the most
  distinguished books and encourage the
  writing, publishing and dissemination of
  outstanding social studies books for young
  readers that treat topics related to women's
  issues sensitively and accurately.

  Exemplary Research in Social Studies Award
  acknowledges and encourages scholarly
  inquiry into significant issues and
  possibilities for social studies education.
  Research must be published and have a
  social education focus.

  Jean Dresden Grambs Distinguished Career
  in Social Studies Award recognizes
  professionals who have made extensive
  contributions to knowledge concerning
  significant areas of social studies education
  through meritorious research.

  Larry Metcalf Exemplary Dissertation Award
  recognizes outstanding research completed in
  pursuit of the doctoral degree and encourages
  scholarly inquiry into significant issues and
  possibilities for social studies education.
  Research must be published and have a
  social education focus.

  The annual NCSS Outstanding Teacher of the
  Year Awards recognize exceptional classroom
  social studies teachers for grades K-6, 5-8
  and 7-12 who teach social studies regularly
  and systematically in elementary school
  settings, and at least half-time in middle or
  junior high and high school settings.

Carter G. Woodson Book Award encourages
the writing, publishing and dissemination of
outstanding social studies books for young
readers that treat topics related to ethnic
minorities and relations sensitively and
accurately.

PURPOSE:
  To provide leadership, service and support
  for all social studies educators.

ELIGIBILITY:
  NCSS membership is required, except for the
  Septima Clark and Carter G. Woodson Book
  Awards.

GEOG. RESTRICTIONS: United States.

FINANCIAL DATA:
  Amount of support per award: Grants-in-Aid:
  Up to $3,000; Outstanding Social Studies
  Teacher of the Year Awards: $2,500 and up
  to $500 in transportation/lodging
  reimbursement to attend the annual
  conference.
  Total amount of support: Varies.

NO. MOST RECENT APPLICANTS: Varies.

NO. AWARDS: Exemplary Research in Social
  Studies, Jean Dresden Grambs Award and
  Larry Metcalf Award: 1 per award annually;
  Outstanding Social Studies Teacher Award: 1
  annually per category; Septima Clark Award
  and Carter G. Woodson Award: 3 annually.

APPLICATION INFO:
  Applications must be submitted through the
  online system.
  Deadline: Dates are posted online.

ADDRESS INQUIRIES TO:
  See e-mail address above.

NATIONAL COUNCIL FOR THE SOCIAL STUDIES   [1689]
8555 16th Street, Suite 500
Silver Spring, MD 20910
(301) 588-1800 ext. 110
(800) 296-7840
Fax: (301) 588-2049
E-mail: awards@ncss.org
Web Site: www.socialstudies.org

FOUNDED: 1921

AREAS OF INTEREST:
  Social studies education.

NAME(S) OF PROGRAMS:
  ● **Christa McAuliffe Reach for the Stars Award**

TYPE:
  Awards/prizes. Annual award for projects
  representing excellence and innovation in
  social studies education and having the
  potential of serving as a model for other
  teachers.

YEAR PROGRAM STARTED: 1986

PURPOSE:
  To help a social studies educator make his or
  her dream of innovative social studies a
  reality; to assist classroom teachers in
  developing and implementing imaginative,
  innovative, and illustrative social studies
  teaching strategies; to assist classroom
  teachers in supporting student implementation
  of innovative social studies, citizenship
  projects, field experiences, and community
  connections.

ELIGIBILITY:
  NCSS membership is required. Applicant
  must be a full-time social studies teacher or
  social studies teacher educator currently
  engaged with K-12 students.

GEOG. RESTRICTIONS: United States.

FINANCIAL DATA:
Amount of support per award: $2,500, commemorative gift, presentation session at annual conference, and publicity.

NO. MOST RECENT APPLICANTS: 4.

NO. AWARDS: 1 annually.

APPLICATION INFO:
Applications must be submitted through the online system. No mail-in copies will be allowed.
Deadline: Dates are posted online.

ADDRESS INQUIRIES TO:
See e-mail address above.

NATIONAL COUNCIL FOR THE SOCIAL STUDIES   [1690]
8555 16th Street, Suite 500
Silver Spring, MD 20910
(301) 588-1800 ext. 110
(800) 296-7840
Fax: (301) 588-2049
E-mail: awards@ncss.org
Web Site: www.socialstudies.org

FOUNDED: 1921

AREAS OF INTEREST:
Social studies education.

NAME(S) OF PROGRAMS:
● **Grant for the Enhancement of Geographic Literacy in Honor of James F. Marren**

TYPE:
Awards/prizes. Award to promote school geography education programs that encourage the integration of geography into the social studies curriculum/classroom and enhance the geographic literacy of students at the classroom, district or statewide level.

PURPOSE:
To promote geography education in the schools; to enhance the geographic literacy of students at the classroom, district, or statewide level; to encourage integration of geography into the social studies curriculum/classroom.

ELIGIBILITY:
Programs, not individuals, individual lessons or units, which will enhance the geographic literacy of students at the classroom, district, or statewide levels. Recipients may be individuals or groups in school districts, public institutions, or universities.

GEOG. RESTRICTIONS: United States.

FINANCIAL DATA:
Amount of support per award: $2,500, commemorative gift, presentation session at annual conference, and publicity.

NO. MOST RECENT APPLICANTS: 6.

NO. AWARDS: 1.

APPLICATION INFO:
Instructions and application form are available on the NCSS web site.
Deadline: Dates are posted online.

ADDRESS INQUIRIES TO:
See e-mail address above.

NATIONAL COUNCIL FOR THE SOCIAL STUDIES   [1691]
8555 16th Street, Suite 500
Silver Spring, MD 20910
(301) 588-1800 ext. 110
(800) 296-7840
Fax: (301) 588-2049
E-mail: awards@ncss.org
Web Site: www.socialstudies.org

FOUNDED: 1921

AREAS OF INTEREST:
Social studies education.

NAME(S) OF PROGRAMS:
● **Award for Global Understanding in Honor of James M. Becker**

TYPE:
Awards/prizes. Award for Global Understanding recognizes a social studies educator (or a team of educators) who has made notable contributions in helping social studies students increase their understanding of the world.

PURPOSE:
To recognize a social studies educator (or a team of educators) who has made notable contributions in helping social studies students increase their understanding of the world.

ELIGIBILITY:
NCSS membership is required. Anyone may nominate. Nominees must be social studies educators who are affecting the global understanding of preK-12 students.

FINANCIAL DATA:
Amount of support per award: $2,000 cash award, up to $700 in transportation/lodging reimbursement, a complimentary NCSS conference registration, publicity for a session to present at the NCSS annual conference, and a commemorative gift.

NO. MOST RECENT APPLICANTS: 8.

NO. AWARDS: 1 annually.

APPLICATION INFO:
Instructions and application form are available on the NCSS web site.
Deadline: Dates are posted online.

ADDRESS INQUIRIES TO:
See e-mail address above.

NATIONAL COUNCIL ON FAMILY RELATIONS
661 Lasalle Street
Suite 200
St. Paul, MN 55114
(763) 781-9331
Fax: (763) 781-9348
E-mail: info@ncfr.org
Web Site: www.ncfr.org

TYPE:
Awards/prizes. Awards given for contributions to the area of family science. All of the awards require NCFR membership.
See entry 1368 for full listing.

NATIONAL INSTITUTE OF MENTAL HEALTH   [1692]
Division of Translational Research (DTR)
6001 Executive Boulevard, Room 7111, MSC 9632
Bethesda, MD 20892-9632
(301) 443-9232
E-mail: ftuma@nih.gov
Web Site: www.nimh.nih.gov/about/organization/dtr

AREAS OF INTEREST:
Psychopathology related to trauma, including research on neurobiological, behavioral, cognitive, and other risk and protective factors for psychopathology after traumatic events and the development of interventions for post-traumatic psychopathology.

NAME(S) OF PROGRAMS:
● **Traumatic Stress Research Program**

TYPE:
Fellowships; Project/program grants; Research grants; Technical assistance; Training grants.

YEAR PROGRAM STARTED: 1969

PURPOSE:
To plan, support and administer programs of research, research training and resource development aimed at understanding the pathophysiology of mental illness and hastening the translation of behavioral science and neuroscience advances into innovations in clinical care.

LEGAL BASIS:
Section 301 of the Public Health Service Act, as amended; Public Law 78-410, 42 U.S.C. 241.

ELIGIBILITY:
Applicants can be any public or nonprofit institution such as a university, college, hospital or a community agency, unit of state or local government, an authorized unit of the federal government or a for-profit institution and/or entity.

FINANCIAL DATA:
Amount of support per award: Funding amounts vary by grant type.

APPLICATION INFO:
Forms and instructions are available online.
Duration: Average three to five years.
Deadline: Varies.

ADDRESS INQUIRIES TO:
See e-mail address above.

NATIONAL SCIENCE FOUNDATION
2415 Eisenhower Avenue
Alexandria, VA 22314
(703) 292-7283
Fax: (703) 292-9068
E-mail: fkronz@nsf.gov
Web Site: www.nsf.gov

TYPE:
Conferences/seminars; Fellowships; Project/program grants; Research grants; Training grants. Grants support research and educational projects, national meetings, dissemination efforts, cross-disciplinary study, dissertation research, small group training activities, dissertation improvement grants for graduate students, and postdoctoral fellowships. The proposals that are considered for support use methods from a variety of disciplines including anthropology, communications, history, philosophy, political science, and sociology to investigate STEM theory and practice with regards to their history, socio-cultural formation, philosophical underpinnings, and impacts on quality of life, culture, and society.

See entry 1666 for full listing.

NATIONAL SOCIETY DAUGHTERS OF THE AMERICAN REVOLUTION [1693]

1776 D Street, N.W.
Washington, DC 20006-5303
(202) 879-3263
E-mail: nsdarscholarships@dar.org
Web Site: www.dar.org

FOUNDED: 1895

AREAS OF INTEREST:
Political science, history, government and economics.

NAME(S) OF PROGRAMS:
● **Enid Hall Griswold Memorial Scholarship**

TYPE:
Scholarships. Undergraduate scholarships awarded to a deserving junior or senior accepted or enrolled in an accredited college or university in the U.S. who is majoring in either political science, history, government or economics.

YEAR PROGRAM STARTED: 1982

PURPOSE:
To provide ways and means to aid students to attain higher education.

LEGAL BASIS:
Incorporated historical society.

ELIGIBILITY:
Scholarships are awarded without regard to race, religion, sex or national origin. Candidates must be U.S. citizens and must attend an accredited college or university in the U.S. No affiliation or relationship to DAR is required for qualification. Awards are judged on the basis of academic excellence, commitment to field of study, as required, and financial need.

Candidate must major in political science, history, government or economics.

GEOG. RESTRICTIONS: United States.

FINANCIAL DATA:
Amount of support per award: $5,000.
Total amount of support: $10,000.

NO. AWARDS: 2.

APPLICATION INFO:
Applicants must use the DAR Scholarship Committee's online submission process found on the DAR public web site. Once applicants have set up their scholarship profile, they will be able to complete the application. If necessary, applicants will be able to provide access to individuals wishing to submit confidential letters of recommendations or school transcripts.
Duration: One academic year. Nonrenewable.
Deadline: February 15.

PUBLICATIONS:
American Spirit, magazine.

ADDRESS INQUIRIES TO:
National Vice Chairman
E-mail:
enidhallmemorialscholarship@nsdar.org

THE PHI BETA KAPPA SOCIETY [1694]

1606 New Hampshire Avenue, N.W.
Washington, DC 20009
(202) 265-3808
Fax: (202) 986-1601
E-mail: awards@pbk.org
Web Site: www.pbk.org

AREAS OF INTEREST:
Philosophy.

NAME(S) OF PROGRAMS:
● **The Dr. Martin R. Lebowitz and Eve Lewellis Lebowitz Prize for Philosophical Achievement and Contribution**

TYPE:
Awards/prizes. In conjunction with the American Philosophical Association, the award is presented to a pair of philosophers who hold contrasting views of an important philosophical question that is of current interest both to the field and to an educated public audience. The Lebowitz symposium program ordinarily consists of two annual lectures to be delivered sequentially at a divisional meeting selected by the honorees, or lacking their agreement, by the Phi Beta Kappa Society.

PURPOSE:
To promote the discipline of philosophy.

ELIGIBILITY:
The committee is encouraged to consider candidates who address important philosophical issues using diverse methodologies and perspectives and who, in so doing, are able to communicate important philosophical ideas to specialist and non-specialist audiences.

FINANCIAL DATA:
Amount of support per award:
Approximately $25,000 per person.

Total amount of support: Approximately $50,000 annually.

NO. AWARDS: 1 annually for 1 pair.

APPLICATION INFO:
American Philosophical Association members are eligible to nominate or self-nominate. A complete nomination will consist of the following, and can be uploaded into the form:
(1) two 300-word abstracts, one for each speaker, which details the proposed topic and the approach that will be taken in the symposium;
(2) a complete curriculum vitae for both proposed speakers and;
(3) two letters of recommendation. Ideally, the reference will have knowledge of both proposed speakers. Letters should address the stature of the candidates and the relevance of the selected topic.
Deadline: December 1.

ADDRESS INQUIRIES TO:
Eva Caldera, Associate Secretary
Tel: (202) 745-3244
E-mail: ecaldera@pbk.org

PI GAMMA MU, INTERNATIONAL HONOR SOCIETY IN SOCIAL SCIENCE

1001 Millington, Suite B
Winfield, KS 67156
(620) 221-3128
E-mail: executivedirector@pigammamu.org
Web Site: www.pigammamu.org

TYPE:
Scholarships. Awarded for graduate study.

See entry 1582 for full listing.

SMITH RICHARDSON FOUNDATION, INC. [1695]

60 Jesup Road
Westport, CT 06880
(203) 222-6222
Fax: (203) 222-6282
E-mail: jhollings@srf.org
Web Site: www.srf.org

FOUNDED: 1935

AREAS OF INTEREST:
Improvement of public policy in the fields of social welfare, economic and regulatory schemes and education issues; improvement of American foreign policy, particularly as it relates to national security.

NAME(S) OF PROGRAMS:
● **Domestic Public Policy Program**
● **International Security and Foreign Policy Program**

TYPE:
Conferences/seminars; Project/program grants; Research grants. The Domestic Policy Program primarily supports research on ways to improve public policy in the fields of social welfare, economic and regulatory schemes and education issues. The program has a particular interest in research that examines the effectiveness of institutions which serve children and families at-risk.

The Foreign Policy Program supports projects in national security and defense policy, in military history and strategy, in the political, military and economic affairs of Eastern Europe and the states of the former Soviet Union, economic and security developments in the Asia Pacific, and also in international economic issues of vital interest to American policymakers. The program aims to define the nature of the post-cold war security environment.

YEAR PROGRAM STARTED: 1935

PURPOSE:
To support and promote a vigorous and free society.

LEGAL BASIS:
Private foundation.

ELIGIBILITY:
Organizations sponsoring projects appropriate to the Foundation's interests are eligible. The Foundation originates many of the grant commitments which are made, and the vast majority of unsolicited requests for funding must be rejected. Because of fund limitations, no grants are available for deficit funding of previously established operations, projects relating to building construction (i.e., "brick and mortar"), programs related to the arts, historic restoration projects, or research in the physical sciences. No grants are made directly to individuals or to advocacy organizations. The Foundation does not provide support for the operating costs of direct-service programs or charities. The Foundation rarely provides general support for any organization or funding for conferences and documentaries.

The Foundation awards grants for policy research with national implications. Some small grants are available to support innovative service and educational programs in Connecticut and North Carolina which assist children and families at-risk. Nearly all such local grants are solicited by the staff and the Board of the Foundation. Service programs in states other than Connecticut and North Carolina are ineligible for funding.

GEOG. RESTRICTIONS: Connecticut and North Carolina.

FINANCIAL DATA:
Amount of support per award: Varies.

APPLICATION INFO:
The Foundation has a two-stage application process. Initial inquiries should be submitted by mail to the address above in the form of a concept paper. If the project is determined to be a good candidate for a grant, applicants will be asked to prepare a full-length proposal.
Duration: Varies.
Deadline: Grants are reviewed on an ongoing basis.

PUBLICATIONS:
Annual report.

IRS I.D.: 56-0611550

STAFF:
Allan Song, Senior Program Officer
Mark Steinmeyer, Senior Program Officer
Olga Ramous, Grants Coordinator
Kathy Lavery, Records Coordinator

OFFICERS AND TRUSTEES:
Peter L. Richardson, Chairman of the Board
W. Winburne King, III, Vice-Chairman of the Board, General Counsel and Chief Investment Officer
Marin J. Strmecki, Ph.D., Senior Vice President, Director of Programs
Ross F. Hemphill, Vice President and Chief Financial Officer
Arvid R. Nelson, Ph.D., Secretary
Karla W. Frank, Assistant Secretary
Michael Blair
John Richardson
Lunsford Richardson, Jr.
Nico Richardson
Tyler B. Richardson
E. William Stetson, III

ADDRESS INQUIRIES TO:
Domestic Policy or Foreign Policy Program
(See address above.)

THE ROYAL TOWN PLANNING INSTITUTE [1696]
41 Botolph Lane
London EC3R 8DL England
(020) 7929-9494
Fax: (020) 7929-9490
E-mail: marketing@rtpi.org.uk
Web Site: www.rtpi.org.uk

FOUNDED: 1914

AREAS OF INTEREST:
Urban and regional planning, land use, transport and housing, industrial strategy on planning, rural planning, conservation and recreational planning.

NAME(S) OF PROGRAMS:
● **George Pepler International Award**

TYPE:
Travel grants. This biennial award is made to individuals in their first 10 years of post-qualification experience, who wish to visit Britain or, as residents of Britain, desire to visit another country for a short period to study the theory and practice of town and country planning or some particular aspect of planning.

YEAR PROGRAM STARTED: 1973

PURPOSE:
To provide an international travelling award for young people of any nationality who wish to visit another country in order to study town planning or a related subject.

LEGAL BASIS:
Charitable trust.

ELIGIBILITY:
Young people of any nationality under the age of 30 are eligible to apply. Professional qualifications are not necessary. Each applicant is required to complete a prescribed application form and submit to a panel of advisers a statement showing the nature of the study and suggested itinerary.

FINANCIAL DATA:
Amount of support per award: GBP 3,000 paid in two equal installments.

NO. MOST RECENT APPLICANTS: 15.

NO. AWARDS: 1 biennially.

APPLICATION INFO:
Contact the Institute through its e-mail address for an entry form and details. Application and information can be found online.
Duration: Three to four weeks.
Deadline: September 30.

ADDRESS INQUIRIES TO:
Rebecca Hildreth, Head of Marketing and Communications
(See address above.)

RUSSELL SAGE FOUNDATION [1697]
112 East 64th Street
New York, NY 10065
(212) 750-6000
Fax: (212) 371-4761
E-mail: info@rsage.org
Web Site: www.russellsage.org

FOUNDED: 1907

AREAS OF INTEREST:
Behavioral economics; future of work; race, ethnicity, and immigration; and social inequality. Special initiatives on integrating biology and social science knowledge, computational social science, immigrant and immigrant integration, and non-standard employment.

TYPE:
Research grants; Visiting scholars.
Presidential grants.

YEAR PROGRAM STARTED: 1907

PURPOSE:
To improve social and living conditions in the U.S. by conducting and supporting social science research relevant to public policy issues.

LEGAL BASIS:
Private operating foundation.

ELIGIBILITY:
The Foundation supports focused, empirical research projects under the direction of a principal investigator. Under the terms of the contract, the research must be coordinated through a fiscal agency (university, college or 501(c)(3) organization under the Internal Revenue Code).

The Foundation's awards are restricted to support for basic social science research within its announced programs. These currently include research on the future of work, immigration and the social psychology of social contact.

The Foundation conducts a Visiting Scholar program under which persons working in the areas of current interest to the Foundation join the staff for one year to consult and continue their own research and writing.

GEOG. RESTRICTIONS: United States.

FINANCIAL DATA:
Amount of support per award: Presidential grants: Up to $50,000; Research grants: Up to $175,000.
Total amount of support: Approximately $4,800,000 for the year 2019.

NO. MOST RECENT APPLICANTS: 874.

NO. AWARDS: 89.

APPLICATION INFO:
Applications for awards should be preceded by a letter of inquiry to the Foundation. Guidelines and other details are available on the web site.
Duration: One to three years.
Deadline: Eight weeks prior to Board meetings to be held March, June and November.

PUBLICATIONS:
Biennial report; scholarly books.

IRS I.D.: 13-1635303

OFFICERS:
Sheldon Danziger, President
Claire Gabriel, Secretary

ADDRESS INQUIRIES TO:
E-mail: programs@rsage.org

SOCIAL SCIENCES AND HUMANITIES RESEARCH COUNCIL OF CANADA [1698]
350 Albert Street
Ottawa ON K1P 6G4 Canada
(613) 943-7777
Fax: (613) 943-1329
E-mail: fellowships@sshrc-crsh.gc.ca
Web Site: www.sshrc-crsh.gc.ca

FOUNDED: 1977

AREAS OF INTEREST:
The development and support of research, research training, and scholarly activities in the social sciences and humanities.

NAME(S) OF PROGRAMS:
● **Doctoral Awards**

TYPE:
Awards/prizes; Fellowships; Scholarships. Through its Doctoral Awards program, SSHRC offers two types of funding for doctoral students:
(1) SSHRC Doctoral Fellowships and;
(2) Joseph-Armand Bombardier (JAB) Canada Graduate Scholarships (CGS) program - Doctoral Scholarships.

YEAR PROGRAM STARTED: 1977

PURPOSE:
To develop research skills and assist in the training of highly qualified personnel by supporting students who demonstrate a high standard of scholarly achievement in undergraduate and graduate studies in the social sciences and humanities.

LEGAL BASIS:
Government agency.

ELIGIBILITY:
Applicants must be Canadian citizens or permanent residents of Canada. SSHRC Doctoral Fellowships are tenable at any recognized university in Canada, or abroad,

in which case the award holder has to have at least one previous degree from a Canadian university.

Joseph-Armand Bombardier Canada Graduate Scholarships-Doctoral Scholarships are tenable only at Canadian universities.

FINANCIAL DATA:
Amount of support per award: SSHRC Doctoral Fellowships: $20,000 (CAN) per year; Joseph-Armand Bombardier Canada Graduate Scholarships-Doctoral Scholarships: $35,000 (CAN) per year.

NO. AWARDS: SSHRC Doctoral Fellowships: 508; Joseph-Armand Bombardier Canada Graduate Scholarships-Doctoral Scholarships: 430 for the year 2019-20.

APPLICATION INFO:
On university campuses, information may be obtained from the Faculty of Graduate Studies, the Office of Research Administration, the Registrar, or the Student Awards Office. Inquiries may also be addressed directly to the Research Training Portfolio of the Council, at the address above. Detailed program and application information is available online.

Duration: SSHRC Doctoral Fellowships: One to four years; Joseph-Armand Bombardier Canada Graduate Scholarships-Doctoral Scholarships: Three years. Nonrenewable.

Deadline: For applicants registered at a Canadian university, in the fall on the date set by the university; for other applicants, usually in October.

ADDRESS INQUIRIES TO:
Research Training Portfolio
(See address above.)

SOCIAL SCIENCES AND HUMANITIES RESEARCH COUNCIL OF CANADA [1699]
350 Albert Street
Ottawa ON K1P 6G4 Canada
(613) 943-7777
Fax: (613) 943-1329
E-mail: fellowships@sshrc-crsh.gc.ca
Web Site: www.sshrc-crsh.gc.ca

FOUNDED: 1977

AREAS OF INTEREST:
The development and support of research, research training, and scholarly activities in the social sciences and humanities.

NAME(S) OF PROGRAMS:
• **SSHRC Postdoctoral Fellowships**

TYPE:
Fellowships. For Canadian citizens or permanent residents of Canada, to support postdoctoral research in the humanities and social sciences.

YEAR PROGRAM STARTED: 1977

PURPOSE:
To support promising new scholars in the social sciences and humanities and to assist them in establishing a research base at an important time in their research careers.

LEGAL BASIS:
Government agency.

ELIGIBILITY:
Competition is open to persons who have been awarded an earned Doctorate within the two years preceding competition closing date (or up to five years if the applicant's career was interrupted or delayed for the purpose of

maternity, childrearing, illness or health-related family responsibilities). Applicants must demonstrate that all doctoral requirements will be completed before the proposed starting date of tenure. Awards are for postdoctoral study or research within a university or research institution.

Applicants must be Canadian citizens or permanent residents of Canada at the time of application.

FINANCIAL DATA:
Amount of support per award: $45,000 (CAN) per year for up to two years.

NO. MOST RECENT APPLICANTS: 855 for the year 2018-19.

NO. AWARDS: 151 for the year 2018-19.

APPLICATION INFO:
Before submitting an application, applicants must ensure that they meet the requirements specified under Eligibility on the Council web site. Applicants must complete and submit only one application form, together with the curriculum vitae and required attachments. Instructions for filling out the application form and curriculum vitae are available within the form used by applicants to create their online submission.

Duration: Period of tenure is 12 to 24 months. Nonrenewable.

Deadline: Usually in mid-September. Announcement in February.

ADDRESS INQUIRIES TO:
Research Training Portfolio
(See address or e-mail above.)

SOCIAL SCIENCES AND HUMANITIES RESEARCH COUNCIL OF CANADA [1700]
350 Albert Street
Ottawa ON K1P 6G4 Canada
(613) 943-7777
Fax: (613) 943-1329
E-mail: fellowships@sshrc-crsh.gc.ca
Web Site: www.sshrc-crsh.gc.ca

FOUNDED: 1977

AREAS OF INTEREST:
The development and support of research, research training, and scholarly activities in the social sciences and humanities.

NAME(S) OF PROGRAMS:
• **Joseph-Armand Bombardier Canada Graduate Scholarships Program - Master's Scholarships**
• **Master's Awards**

TYPE:
Awards/prizes; Fellowships; Scholarships.

YEAR PROGRAM STARTED: 2003

PURPOSE:
To develop research skills and assist in the training of highly qualified personnel by supporting students who demonstrate a high standard of scholarly achievement in undergraduate and graduate studies in the social sciences and humanities.

LEGAL BASIS:
Government agency.

ELIGIBILITY:
Applicants must be Canadian citizens or permanent residents of Canada. Joseph-Armand Bombardier Canada Graduate Scholarships-Master's Scholarships are tenable only at Canadian universities.

FINANCIAL DATA:
Amount of support per award:
Joseph-Armand Bombardier Canada Graduate Scholarships - Master's Scholarships: $17,500 (CAN).

NO. AWARDS: 1,262 Joseph-Armand Bombardier Canada Graduate Scholarships - Master's Scholarships for the year 2019-20.

APPLICATION INFO:
Information may be obtained from the Faculty of Graduate Studies or sent directly to the Research Training Portfolio at the e-mail address listed above. Detailed program and application information is available online. Applications must be submitted online using the Research Portal.

Duration: One year. Nonrenewable.

Deadline: December 1.

ADDRESS INQUIRIES TO:
Research Training Portfolio
(See address above.)

SOCIAL SCIENCES AND HUMANITIES RESEARCH COUNCIL OF CANADA [1701]
350 Albert Street
Ottawa ON K1P 6G4 Canada
(613) 943-7777
Fax: (613) 943-1329
E-mail: vanier@cihr-irsc.gc.ca
Web Site: www.vanier.gc.ca

FOUNDED: 2008

AREAS OF INTEREST:
The development and support of research, research training, and scholarly activities in the social sciences and humanities.

NAME(S) OF PROGRAMS:
• **Vanier Canada Graduate Scholarships (CGS)**

TYPE:
Awards/prizes; Fellowships; Scholarships. For doctoral students in the humanities and social sciences. Administered by the Canadian Institutes of Health Research, the Natural Sciences and Engineering Research Council and the Social Sciences Research Council.

YEAR PROGRAM STARTED: 2008

PURPOSE:
To attract and retain world-class doctoral students by supporting students who demonstrate both leadership skills and a high standard of scholarly achievement in graduate studies in social sciences and humanities, natural sciences and engineering, and health.

LEGAL BASIS:
Government agency.

ELIGIBILITY:
Applicants can be citizens or permanent residents of Canada, as well as international students. For full eligibility criteria, visit www.vanier.gc.ca/en/eligibility-admissibilite.html.

GEOG. RESTRICTIONS: Canada.

FINANCIAL DATA:
Amount of support per award: $50,000 (CAN) per year.

NO. MOST RECENT APPLICANTS: 183 for the year 2017-18.

NO. AWARDS: Up to 55 annually.

APPLICATION INFO:
Candidates must be nominated by a Canadian institution with a quota at which they want to study. On university campuses, information

may be obtained from the Dean or Faculty of Graduate Studies, the Office of Research Administration, the Registrar, or the Student Awards Office. Inquiries may also be addressed directly to the Vanier Banting Secretariat at the e-mail address above.

Duration: Three years. Nonrenewable.

Deadline: Nomination deadline is set by the university. The Vanier Banting Secretariat's deadline for nominations submitted by the universities is usually early November.

ADDRESS INQUIRIES TO:
See e-mail address above.

SOCIAL SCIENCES AND HUMANITIES RESEARCH COUNCIL OF CANADA   [1702]

350 Albert Street
Ottawa ON K1P 6G4 Canada
(613) 943-7777
Fax: (613) 943-1329
E-mail: fellowships@sshrc-crsh.gc.ca
Web Site: www.sshrc-crsh.gc.ca

FOUNDED: 2010

AREAS OF INTEREST:
The development and support of research, research training, and scholarly activities in the social sciences and humanities.

NAME(S) OF PROGRAMS:
● **Banting Postdoctoral Fellowships**

TYPE:
Fellowships. For Canadian citizens, permanent residents of Canada and foreign citizens to support postdoctoral research in the humanities and social sciences.

YEAR PROGRAM STARTED: 2010

PURPOSE:
To support promising new scholars in the social sciences and humanities and to assist them in establishing a research base at an important time in their research careers.

LEGAL BASIS:
Government agency.

ELIGIBILITY:
Competition is open to persons who have been awarded an earned Doctorate within the three years preceding competition. Applicants can be citizens or permanent residents of Canada, as well as international students.

Without exception, the Banting Postdoctoral Fellowships:
(1) are tenable only at the institution which supported the original application for the program;
(2) must be taken up no earlier than April 1 and no later than October 1 of the year following the application deadline and;
(3) are for two years from the date of up-take.

FINANCIAL DATA:
Amount of support per award: $70,000 (CAN) per year for two years.

NO. MOST RECENT APPLICANTS: 178 for the year 2017-18.

NO. AWARDS: 23.

APPLICATION INFO:
On university campuses, information may be obtained from the Dean or Faculty of Graduate Studies, the Office of Research Administration, the Registrar, or the Student Awards Office.

For more information, visit www.banting.fellowships-bourses.gc.ca.

Duration: Period of tenure is 24 months. Nonrenewable.

Deadline: Usually mid-September.

ADDRESS INQUIRIES TO:
Research Training Portfolio
(See address above.)

THE SOCIETY FOR THE PSYCHOLOGICAL STUDY OF SOCIAL ISSUES (SPSSI)   [1703]

700 Seventh Street, S.E.
Washington, DC 20003
(202) 675-6956
E-mail: awards@spssi.org
Web Site: www.spssi.org

FOUNDED: 1936

AREAS OF INTEREST:
Social psychology research.

NAME(S) OF PROGRAMS:
● **Gordon Allport Intergroup Relations Prize**

TYPE:
Awards/prizes. The Gordon Allport Intergroup Relations Prize honors the memory of the late Dr. Gordon W. Allport, a founder and past president of SPSSI.

LEGAL BASIS:
Independently incorporated society.

ELIGIBILITY:
Entries must be papers published during the calendar year preceding the year of submission. Submissions are limited to articles, chapters or other works published in their primary form (e.g., appearing in print for print journals or books or online for online-only journals or other volumes) with a formal publication date of the prior year. An individual or group may only submit one paper to SPSSI awards (including the Allport, Klineberg and Dissertation Awards) per award year (January 1 to December 31). All entries must be submitted in English.

The award is given to "the best paper or article of the year on intergroup relations." Originality of the contribution, whether theoretical or empirical, will be given special weight. The research area of intergroup relations includes such dimensions as age, gender, and socioeconomic status, as well as ethnicity.

FINANCIAL DATA:
Amount of support per award: $1,000.

CO-OP FUNDING PROGRAMS: The Award is sponsored by The Gordon W. Allport Memorial Fund of Harvard University and SPSSI.

NO. AWARDS: 1 for the year 2018.

APPLICATION INFO:
Online submissions are the preferred method. Limit the number and size of files uploaded when applying online.

For hard-copy submissions, send five copies to SPSSI.

Duration: Annual award.

Deadline: June 15. Notification by October 15.

ADDRESS INQUIRIES TO:
See e-mail address above.

THE SOCIETY FOR THE PSYCHOLOGICAL STUDY OF SOCIAL ISSUES (SPSSI)   [1704]

700 Seventh Street, S.E.
Washington, DC 20003
(202) 675-6956
E-mail: awards@spssi.org
Web Site: www.spssi.org

FOUNDED: 1936

AREAS OF INTEREST:
Social psychology research.

NAME(S) OF PROGRAMS:
● **Innovative Teaching Award**

TYPE:
Awards/prizes. SPSSI confers an annual award for innovative teaching in areas related to the psychological study of social issues. This award recognizes effective courses, assignments or classroom activities addressing social issues.

LEGAL BASIS:
Independently incorporated society.

ELIGIBILITY:
Nominees should be SPSSI members who have developed innovative pedagogical products that aid in teaching the psychological study of social issues. Nominees may teach at graduate degree-granting institutions, Bachelor's-degree universities and colleges, two-year and community colleges, or as contingent or adjunct faculty.

FINANCIAL DATA:
Recipients will be recognized in the Teaching and Learning column in the SPSSI *Forward* newsletter. Honorable Mention awardees will receive one year of free SPSSI membership.

Amount of support per award: $1,000 and a plaque.

NO. MOST RECENT APPLICANTS: 4.

NO. AWARDS: 1.

APPLICATION INFO:
Application instructions are available on the web site.

Deadline: March 1.

ADDRESS INQUIRIES TO:
See e-mail address above.

THE SOCIETY FOR THE PSYCHOLOGICAL STUDY OF SOCIAL ISSUES (SPSSI)   [1705]

700 Seventh Street, S.E.
Washington, DC 20003
(202) 675-6956
E-mail: awards@spssi.org
Web Site: www.spssi.org

FOUNDED: 1936

AREAS OF INTEREST:
Social issues and psychology.

NAME(S) OF PROGRAMS:
● **Awards for Outstanding Teaching and Mentoring**

TYPE:
Awards/prizes. SPSSI confers one or two annual awards for outstanding teaching and mentoring in areas related to the psychological study of social issues. The award recognizes teaching excellence in a variety of contexts.

PURPOSE:
To recognize outstanding teaching in areas related to the psychological study of social issues.

LEGAL BASIS:
Independently incorporated society.

ELIGIBILITY:
Nominees should be SPSSI members who have made substantial contributions to students in the psychological study of social issues. To be eligible, individuals must have been teaching and/or mentoring students for at least five years full-time since the doctoral degree. Nominees may teach at graduate degree-granting institutions, Bachelor's degree universities and colleges, or two-year and community colleges. Self-nominations are encouraged.

FINANCIAL DATA:
Amount of support per award: $1,000 plus a plaque.

NO. MOST RECENT APPLICANTS: 6.

NO. AWARDS: 1 or 2.

APPLICATION INFO:
Application information is available on the web site.
Deadline: March.

PUBLICATIONS:
Application guidelines.

ADDRESS INQUIRIES TO:
See e-mail address above.

THE SOCIETY FOR THE PSYCHOLOGICAL STUDY OF SOCIAL ISSUES (SPSSI)   [1706]
700 Seventh Street, S.E.
Washington, DC 20003
(202) 675-6956
E-mail: awards@spssi.org
Web Site: www.spssi.org

FOUNDED: 1936

AREAS OF INTEREST:
Social psychology research.

NAME(S) OF PROGRAMS:
- **SPSSI Action Teaching Grants**

TYPE:
Grants-in-aid.

PURPOSE:
To develop, enhance, or measure the impact of an innovative action teaching classroom activity, student assignment, field experience, or web-based resource.

LEGAL BASIS:
Independently incorporated society.

ELIGIBILITY:
Open to regular dues-paying members of SPSSI, including graduate students. Proposed projects will be judged on originality, feasibility, potential teaching effectiveness, and potential impact with respect to one or more social issues.

FINANCIAL DATA:
Amount of support per award: $100 to $1,500.

NO. AWARDS: Maximum 3 annually.

APPLICATION INFO:
Online submissions are the preferred method. Application should include:
(1) SPSSI Action Teaching Grant Application Form;
(2) curriculum vitae or resume;
(3) an abstract of 75 to 100 words summarizing the grant proposal and;
(4) a description of the project, including a statement of what students will learn from the action teaching resource or activity

developed with grant funding, how the action teaching resource or activity will contribute to society or others beyond the class, how student learning will be assessed and its broader impact, why grant funding is needed to develop the action teaching resource or activity, and a budget describing each item and rationale.
Deadline: April 15. Decision by May 15.

ADDRESS INQUIRIES TO:
See e-mail address above.

THE SOCIETY FOR THE PSYCHOLOGICAL STUDY OF SOCIAL ISSUES (SPSSI)   [1707]
700 Seventh Street, S.E.
Washington, DC 20003
(202) 675-6956
E-mail: awards@spssi.org
Web Site: www.spssi.org

FOUNDED: 1936

AREAS OF INTEREST:
Social psychology research.

NAME(S) OF PROGRAMS:
- **SPSSI James Marshall Fellowship in Public Policy**

TYPE:
Fellowships. Fellowship provides support for a postdoctoral level fellow to work full-time for one year in the U.S. Congress in Washington, DC. The fellow should expect to use psychological research to inform the public policymaking process while working full-time in a congressional office.

PURPOSE:
To train early career scientists to contribute to the effective use of scientific knowledge about social issues in the formation of public policy at the federal level; to educate the scientific community about how research can contribute to the development of public policy; to establish a more effective liaison between social scientists and various policymaking mechanisms.

LEGAL BASIS:
Independently incorporated society.

ELIGIBILITY:
Fellowship is open to postdoctoral scientists from any discipline relevant to the psychological study of social issues. Candidates must hold a Ph.D. or Psy.D. before the start of the fellowship and be a member of SPSSI. Candidates must demonstrate interest or involvement in the application of social science to social issues and policies, have a sound scientific background, and demonstrate sensitivity toward policy issues. Candidates must be able to communicate effectively, both orally and in writing. Individual initiative and an ability to work cooperatively with others having diverse viewpoints are critical. Knowledge of policy processes at the national level, along with placement goals, is desirable, but not essential.

FINANCIAL DATA:
Fellowship includes health benefits and paid attendance at the annual SPSSI Conference in June of the fellowship year.
Amount of support per award: Stipend of $60,000.

CO-OP FUNDING PROGRAMS: Supported, in part, by an endowment provided by the James Marshall Fund.

NO. MOST RECENT APPLICANTS: 16.

NO. AWARDS: 1.

APPLICATION INFO:
Applications for the 2020-21 fellowship year are available beginning December 1, 2019. The following documents will be required:
(1) a personal statement (1,000-word limit) describing the applicant's interest and experience in policy activities or social issues, their interest in the fellowship program, how the fellowship fits into their career goals, and what the desired objectives are;
(2) a writing sample (500-word limit) summarizing how the applicant's research fits within its field of study;
(3) curriculum vitae and;
(4) three letters of reference. Letters should address the applicant's abilities, experience and motivation as related to the fellowship program.
Duration: One year, September to August.
Deadline: February 1.

ADDRESS INQUIRIES TO:
Sarah Mancoll, Policy Director
(See address above.)

THE SOCIETY FOR THE PSYCHOLOGICAL STUDY OF SOCIAL ISSUES (SPSSI)   [1708]
700 Seventh Street, S.E.
Washington, DC 20003
(202) 675-6956
E-mail: awards@spssi.org
Web Site: www.spssi.org

FOUNDED: 1936

AREAS OF INTEREST:
Social psychology research.

NAME(S) OF PROGRAMS:
- **Small-Scale Events Advancing SPSSI (SEAS) Grants**

TYPE:
Conferences/seminars; Development grants. Grants for support of small-scale events hosted at a member's institution or other local venue related to the psychological study of social issues. These events may include, but are not limited to, departmental or institutional speakers or speaker series, research symposia, brown-bag events or series, or mini-conferences. Initiatives that enhance SPSSI membership and pre-conferences or small meetings attached to larger conferences where the theme and content of the meeting is related to the psychological study of social issues are also supported.

PURPOSE:
To promote awareness of the Society; to identify potential new members.

LEGAL BASIS:
Independently incorporated society.

ELIGIBILITY:
Current regular dues-paying members of SPSSI may apply. If not a current member of SPSSI, a membership application may be submitted along with the grant application. Graduate student members may apply, with faculty mentor or advisor serving as a co-applicant.

Proposals will be evaluated on the event's potential to attract new SPSSI members, promote SPSSI's basic interests and goals, and to facilitate research links, networks and capacity. Proposals for events drawing attendees from two or more institutions, departments or disciplines are highly encouraged.

FINANCIAL DATA:
Funds may be used to publicize the event, pay speakers' honoraria, reimburse speakers' travel expenses, print collateral materials, or other expenses related to the specific project. Funds may not be used for paying SPSSI membership dues, honoraria for organizers, or costs not directly related to the project or event.

Amount of support per award: Up to $1,000.

NO. AWARDS: 1 for the year 2019.

APPLICATION INFO:
Application should include:
(1) a cover letter;
(2) a brief proposal (up to 1000 words) outlining the purpose of the event and its anticipated outcomes and;
(3) a detailed budget (one page or less) outlining the use of funds, and including additional sources of funding that will be sought to support the event.

Online submissions are the preferred method.

Duration: One year.

Deadline: September 30. Proposals for events that are highly timely and event-specific may be submitted at any time during the year and will be reviewed within one month of receipt on an ad hoc basis.

ADDRESS INQUIRIES TO:
See e-mail address above.

THE SOCIETY FOR THE PSYCHOLOGICAL STUDY OF SOCIAL ISSUES (SPSSI) [1709]
700 Seventh Street, S.E.
Washington, DC 20003
(202) 675-6956
E-mail: awards@spssi.org
Web Site: www.spssi.org

FOUNDED: 1936

AREAS OF INTEREST:
Social psychology research.

NAME(S) OF PROGRAMS:
● **Local- and State-Level Policy Work Grants**

TYPE:
Research grants.

YEAR PROGRAM STARTED: 2015

PURPOSE:
To influence policy at the local and state levels through applied research; to increase the availability of policy opportunities for SPSSI members who are interested in applied research; to encourage younger scholars to become more involved in SPSSI.

LEGAL BASIS:
Independently incorporated society.

ELIGIBILITY:
To be eligible, a group must meet the following criteria:
(1) at least one member of the group must be a current SPSSI member;
(2) the group must consist of a minimum of three social scientists who live in the same state or similar regionally-based jurisdiction outside of the U.S.;
(3) the group members must be working on the same issue, broadly defined and;
(4) the group must compellingly demonstrate

that the members are interested in the policy applications of psychological science and other social science research.

Preference will be given to groups that demonstrate either existing policy expertise or the willingness to learn more about policy work at the local or state level.

FINANCIAL DATA:
Amount of support per award: Up to $2,000 per award.

Total amount of support: Up to $6,000.

NO. MOST RECENT APPLICANTS: 4.

NO. AWARDS: Up to 3.

APPLICATION INFO:
To apply for funding, the group should submit a short proposal (no more than 3,000 words) that:
(1) addresses the criteria delineated above;
(2) explains the outcomes or deliverables;
(3) provides a budget for the year;
(4) specifies agreement to submit a presentation of the work for the annual SPSSI Conference and;
(5) specifies agreement to deliver a summary of the work completed at the end of the grant period. Such a document may take the form of a five- to 10-page summary of the work completed, a policy paper, a research report, or another suitable report.

Duration: One year.

Deadline: June 1 for spring award cycle; November 1 for fall award cycle.

ADDRESS INQUIRIES TO:
Sarah Mancoll, Policy Director
E-mail: smancoll@spssi.org

THE SOCIETY FOR THE PSYCHOLOGICAL STUDY OF SOCIAL ISSUES (SPSSI) [1710]
700 Seventh Street, S.E.
Washington, DC 20003
(202) 675-6956
E-mail: awards@spssi.org
Web Site: www.spssi.org

FOUNDED: 1936

AREAS OF INTEREST:
Social psychology research.

NAME(S) OF PROGRAMS:
● **Dalmas A. Taylor Memorial Summer Minority Policy Fellowship**

TYPE:
Fellowships. This fellowship is to honor the memory of Dalmas A. Taylor, who passed away during his term as President of SPSSI. It provides an opportunity for a graduate student of color to work on public policy issues in Washington, DC.

PURPOSE:
To provide an opportunity for a graduate student of color to work on public policy issues in Washington, DC.

LEGAL BASIS:
Independently incorporated society.

ELIGIBILITY:
Applicants must be currently enrolled and in good standing in an accredited graduate program in psychology or a related field. They must be members of an ethnic minority group (African American, Alaskan Native, American Indian, Asian American, Hispanic and Pacific Islander) or have demonstrated a commitment to a career with a focus on

ethnic minority issues. Applicants should not have completed their graduate program by the time they begin the fellowship.

FINANCIAL DATA:
Fellowship includes travel expenses and up to $1,500 for living expenses to relocate to Washington, DC.

Amount of support per award: Stipend of $3,000.

CO-OP FUNDING PROGRAMS: This fellowship is administered in conjunction with APA and the APA Minority Fellowship Program.

NO. MOST RECENT APPLICANTS: 10.

NO. AWARDS: 1.

APPLICATION INFO:
Application should include:
(1) a cover page stating name, institution, address, telephone number, fax number (if applicable) and e-mail address;
(2) a statement (no more than 1,000 words) which details the reason for interest in this fellowship, previous and current research experiences, indication of interest in ethnic minority psychological issues and statement of how this fellowship would contribute to the applicant's career goals;
(3) two letters of recommendation, which can be uploaded with application materials or sent directly to the e-mail address listed above and;
(4) current curriculum vitae.

A link to the application will be available online beginning January 1. Online submission is the preferred method.

Duration: Typically eight to 12 weeks.

Deadline: March 1. Announcement will be made on or about April 15.

ADDRESS INQUIRIES TO:
See e-mail address above.

THE SOCIETY FOR THE PSYCHOLOGICAL STUDY OF SOCIAL ISSUES (SPSSI) [1711]
700 Seventh Street, S.E.
Washington, DC 20003
(202) 675-6956
E-mail: awards@spssi.org
Web Site: www.spssi.org

FOUNDED: 1936

AREAS OF INTEREST:
Social psychology research.

NAME(S) OF PROGRAMS:
● **SPSSI Grants-in-Aid**

TYPE:
Grants-in-aid.

YEAR PROGRAM STARTED: 1956

PURPOSE:
To support scientific research in social problem areas related to the basic interests and goals of SPSSI and particularly those that are not likely to receive support from traditional sources.

LEGAL BASIS:
Independently incorporated society.

ELIGIBILITY:
The applicant must be a member of SPSSI. Applicants may submit only one application per deadline. If an applicant has applied to the Clara Mayo Grant in the same award year (July 1 to June 30), he or she is not eligible to apply for Grants-in-Aid. Individuals may submit a joint application.

The SPSSI Committee on Grants-in-Aid especially encourages proposals involving: (1) unique and timely research opportunities; (2) underrepresented institutions, graduate students and junior scholars; (3) volunteer research teams and; (4) actual, not pilot, projects.

SPSSI's Grants-in-Aid program will include grants earmarked especially in support of research related to SPSSI's current policy priorities: interpersonal violence, marriage equality, and immigration reform. Proposals within these priorities will receive special consideration, though submissions are not limited to these areas of focus.

FINANCIAL DATA:
Funds are normally not provided for travel to conventions, travel or living expenses while conducting research, stipends of principal investigators, costs associated with manuscript preparation, or the indirect costs of institutions.

Amount of support per award: Usually, up to $2,000 for postdoctoral work and up to $1,000 for predoctoral work.

Total amount of support: Varies.

Matching fund requirements: Applicant is required to submit evidence of a request to match amount offered.

NO. AWARDS: 47 for the year 2018.

APPLICATION INFO:
Application information is available on the web site.

Duration: One year.

Deadline: Spring round May 15, with announcement by July 20. Fall round October 15, with announcement by December 15.

PUBLICATIONS:
Application guidelines.

ADDRESS INQUIRIES TO:
See e-mail address above.

THE SOCIETY FOR THE PSYCHOLOGICAL STUDY OF SOCIAL ISSUES (SPSSI)   [1712]
700 Seventh Street, S.E.
Washington, DC 20003
(202) 675-6956
E-mail: awards@spssi.org
Web Site: www.spssi.org

FOUNDED: 1936

AREAS OF INTEREST:
Intergroup relations, social issues and psychology.

NAME(S) OF PROGRAMS:
● **The Applied Social Issues Internship Program**

TYPE:
Internships.

PURPOSE:
To encourage research that is conducted in cooperation with a community or government organization, public interest group or other not-for-profit entity that will benefit directly from the project.

LEGAL BASIS:
Independently incorporated society.

ELIGIBILITY:
College seniors, graduate students and first-year postdoctorates in psychology,

applied social science, and related disciplines are eligible. Applicant must be an SPSSI member.

FINANCIAL DATA:
Amount of support per award: $300 to $2,500 to cover research costs, community organizing and, in unusual cases, a stipend for the intern.

CO-OP FUNDING PROGRAMS: Cost sharing by sponsoring department or organization is desirable. .

NO. MOST RECENT APPLICANTS: 10.

NO. AWARDS: 6.

APPLICATION INFO:
Application information may be obtained from the web site.

Duration: One year.

Deadline: March 15. Announcement by May 15.

ADDRESS INQUIRIES TO:
See e-mail address above.

THE SOCIETY FOR THE PSYCHOLOGICAL STUDY OF SOCIAL ISSUES (SPSSI)   [1713]
700 Seventh Street, S.E.
Washington, DC 20003
(202) 675-6956
E-mail: awards@spssi.org
Web Site: www.spssi.org

FOUNDED: 1936

AREAS OF INTEREST:
Intergroup relations, social issues and psychology.

NAME(S) OF PROGRAMS:
● **Clara Mayo Grants**

TYPE:
Research grants. Supports Master's theses and predissertation research on sexism, racism or prejudice, with preference given to students enrolled in a terminal Master's program.

PURPOSE:
To support Master's theses or predissertation research on aspects of sexism, racism or prejudice, with preference given to students enrolled in a terminal Master's program. Studies of the application of theory or the design of interventions or treatments to address these problems are welcome.

LEGAL BASIS:
Independently incorporated society.

ELIGIBILITY:
Individuals who are SPSSI members and who have matriculated in graduate programs in psychology, applied social science and related disciplines are eligible to apply. Self-nominations are encouraged. A student who is applying for the Grants-In-Aid program may not apply for the Clara Mayo award in the same award year. Applicants may submit only one Mayo application per calendar year.

Studies of the application of theory or the design of interventions or treatments to address these problems are welcome. Proposals that include a college or university agreement to match the amount requested will be favored, but proposals without matching funds will also be considered.

FINANCIAL DATA:
Amount of support per award: $1,000 maximum.

Total amount of support: Varies.

NO. MOST RECENT APPLICANTS: Approximately 28 per cycle.

NO. AWARDS: Up to 6 each cycle.

APPLICATION INFO:
Application information is available on the web site.

Duration: One to two years.

Deadline: Spring round May, with announcement by July. Fall round October, with announcement by December.

ADDRESS INQUIRIES TO:
See e-mail address above.

THE SOCIETY FOR THE PSYCHOLOGICAL STUDY OF SOCIAL ISSUES (SPSSI)   [1714]
700 Seventh Street, S.E.
Washington, DC 20003
(202) 675-6956
E-mail: awards@spssi.org
Web Site: www.spssi.org

FOUNDED: 1936

AREAS OF INTEREST:
Intergroup relations, social issues and psychology.

NAME(S) OF PROGRAMS:
● **The SAGES Program**

TYPE:
Research grants. Program to encourage retired members to apply their knowledge to helping solve social problems or to assist policymakers to solve social problems. Proposals are invited that use social science research findings to address social problems through direct action projects, consulting with not-for-profit groups, or through preparing reviews of existing social science literature that could be used by policymakers.

LEGAL BASIS:
Independently incorporated society.

ELIGIBILITY:
Applicants must be retired SPSSI members. Members nearing retirement may be considered. Proposals will be evaluated in terms of how well they build on existing social science research and theory, the feasibility of the project, and the importance of the project.

FINANCIAL DATA:
Funding can be submitted for direct costs related to the project. This can be spent over a two-year period. Money can be used for hiring staff (including clerical assistance), computing fees, travel, telephone, or other justifiable expenses. Funding cannot be used as a stipend for the applicant.

Amount of support per award: $2,000 to $3,000; rarely, up to $10,000.

NO. AWARDS: 2 for the year 2019.

APPLICATION INFO:
Online submissions are the preferred method. Please limit the number and size of files uploaded when applying online.

Proposals should include a brief review of the relevant literature underlying the project (no more than five pages), a timetable, a detailed budget, and the curriculum vitae of the applicant. The applicant's employment status must be clearly specified, along with a statement of SPSSI membership. Projects that involve collaboration with some organization should include a letter from the sponsoring organization.

Duration: Up to two years.

Deadline: April 15. Announcement by June 15.

ADDRESS INQUIRIES TO:
See e-mail address above.

THE SOCIETY FOR THE PSYCHOLOGICAL STUDY OF SOCIAL ISSUES (SPSSI) [1715]

700 Seventh Street, S.E.
Washington, DC 20003
(202) 675-6956
E-mail: awards@spssi.org
Web Site: www.spssi.org

FOUNDED: 1936

AREAS OF INTEREST:
Intergroup relations, social issues and psychology.

NAME(S) OF PROGRAMS:
- **The Louise Kidder Early Career Award**

TYPE:
Awards/prizes. This award is named in honor of Louise Kidder for her early career accomplishments and contributions to SPSSI.

PURPOSE:
To recognize social issues researchers who have made substantial contributions to the field early in their careers.

LEGAL BASIS:
Independently incorporated society.

ELIGIBILITY:
Nominees should be investigators who have made substantial contributions to social issues research within 10 years of receiving a graduate degree and who have demonstrated the potential to continue such contributions. Nominees need not be current Society members. Applicants must be scholars who are within 10 years of obtaining their doctoral degree.

FINANCIAL DATA:
Amount of support per award: $500 and plaque.

NO. MOST RECENT APPLICANTS: 17.

NO. AWARDS: 1.

APPLICATION INFO:
Online submissions are the preferred method.
Deadline: June 1. Decisions announced by August 1.

ADDRESS INQUIRIES TO:
See e-mail address above.

THE SOCIETY FOR THE PSYCHOLOGICAL STUDY OF SOCIAL ISSUES (SPSSI) [1716]

700 Seventh Street, S.E.
Washington, DC 20003
(202) 675-6956
E-mail: awards@spssi.org
Web Site: www.spssi.org

FOUNDED: 1936

AREAS OF INTEREST:
Intergroup relations, social issues and psychology.

NAME(S) OF PROGRAMS:
- **The Social Issues Dissertation Award**

TYPE:
Awards/prizes. The Social Issues Dissertation Award is given for the best psychological dissertation concerned with social issues. It is judged upon scientific excellence and potential application to social problems.

PURPOSE:
To award dissertations that best demonstrate scientific excellence and potential application to social problems.

LEGAL BASIS:
Independently incorporated society.

ELIGIBILITY:
Any doctoral dissertation in psychology (or in a social science with psychological subject matter) accepted between March 1 of the previous year and up to the deadline of the current year is eligible. Applicants must have successfully defended their dissertation prior to the current year's award deadline. An individual or group may only submit one paper to one SPSSI award (including the Allport, Klineberg and Dissertation Awards) per award year. Applicants may not submit to the Dissertation Prize more than one time.

FINANCIAL DATA:
Amount of support per award: First prize: $1,000; Second prize: $500.

NO. MOST RECENT APPLICANTS: 47.

NO. AWARDS: 2.

APPLICATION INFO:
Online applications are the preferred method. Limit the number and size of files uploaded when applying online. For hard-copy submissions, mail the complete application to SPSSI, at the address above; Attn: Social Issues Dissertation.

The application should include a 500-word summary of the dissertation. The summary should include title, rationale, methods, and results of dissertation, as well as its implications for social problems. Please also include a cover sheet that states the title of one's dissertation, applicant's name, postal and e-mail addresses, phone number and university granting the degree.

Deadline: May 1. Announcement of finalist status by July 13.

PUBLICATIONS:
Application guidelines.

ADDRESS INQUIRIES TO:
See e-mail address above.

STIFTELSEN RIKSBANKENS JUBILEUMSFOND

Regeringsgatan 67
111 56 Stockholm Sweden
(46) 08-50 62 64 00
E-mail: rj@rj.se
Web Site: www.rj.se

TYPE:
Conferences/seminars; Research grants.

See entry 364 for full listing.

U.S. ARMY RESEARCH INSTITUTE FOR BEHAVIORAL AND SOCIAL SCIENCES [1717]

Building 1464
6000 6th Street
Fort Belvoir, VA 22060-5586
(703) 545-2410

FOUNDED: 1940

AREAS OF INTEREST:
Leadership, interactive training and simulation, individual performance and information comprehension, and social structures affecting army performance.

TYPE:
Fellowships; Research grants; Visiting scholars.

PURPOSE:
To contribute to the cumulative knowledge base in behavioral science, with an eye to building new technologies capable of improving the effectiveness of Army personnel and their units.

LEGAL BASIS:
Government agency.

ELIGIBILITY:
Both single-investigator and collaborative research efforts will be considered, and multidisciplinary approaches to a central problem are encouraged. Collaborative efforts may involve researchers at a single institution or in cooperating institutions and joint university/industry partnerships are welcomed. Interest is welcomed from the widest range of institutions, including historically Black colleges and universities and minority institutions.

No consideration will be given to applied research or investigations whose primary focus is on physiological or chemical mechanisms or psychopathology. Another consideration determining support for the research is the judgment that findings have the potential for feeding into development of new behavioral technologies capable of improving the effectiveness of Army personnel and their units.

FINANCIAL DATA:
Amount of support per award: Grant amounts vary according to funds available and Army requirements. Generally $100,000 to $800,000. Average $200,000 per year.

Total amount of support: $5,600,000 for the year 2019.

APPLICATION INFO:
Interested individuals should seek ARI's Broad Agency Announcement, issued annually between January and June. Preliminary concept papers (three to five pages) as well as formal proposals may be submitted. Concept papers should describe the problem to be addressed, justify the effort's theoretical significance and uniqueness, briefly describe the approach to the problem and state potential benefits to the Army. An estimated budget and project duration should be included, along with brief vitae of the principal investigators.

Concept papers will be reviewed within ARI for their relevance to Army priorities, theoretical significance and technical merit. Offers of highly rated concept papers will be invited to submit formal proposals.

Duration: Maximum five years. Average three years.

Deadline: Varies.

PUBLICATIONS:
Program announcement.

ADDRESS INQUIRIES TO:
Chief of Foundational Science Research Unit (See address above.)

U.S. DEPARTMENT OF JUSTICE

Office of Juvenile Justice and
Delinquency Prevention
810 Seventh Street, N.W., 7th Floor
Washington, DC 20531
(202) 307-5911
Fax: (202) 353-9093
E-mail: lynnell.clarke@usdoj.gov
Web Site: www.ojjdp.gov

TYPE:
   Conferences/seminars; Development grants;
   Fellowships; Internships; Project/program
   grants; Research grants; Residencies; Visiting
   scholars; Research contracts. Grants to
   conduct research, evaluation and development
   on juvenile justice and delinquency
   prevention activities, including the
   development of new or improved approaches,
   techniques, systems and program models to
   conduct behavioral research on the causes of
   juvenile crime, means of, intervention and
   prevention, and to evaluate juvenile programs
   and procedures.

   See entry 1291 for full listing.

UKRAINIAN RESEARCH INSTITUTE AT HARVARD UNIVERSITY

34 Kirkland Street
Cambridge, MA 02138
(617) 495-4053
Fax: (617) 495-8097
E-mail: huri@fas.harvard.edu
Web Site: www.huri.harvard.edu

TYPE:
   Fellowships. The Jacyk Distinguished
   Fellowship is designed to bring senior
   scholars to Harvard University for focused
   research in Ukrainian history, literature,
   philology, culture, and other related areas of
   study in the humanities and social sciences
   fields. This fellowship is awarded biennially.

   See entry 366 for full listing.

UKRAINIAN RESEARCH INSTITUTE AT HARVARD UNIVERSITY

34 Kirkland Street
Cambridge, MA 02138
(617) 495-4053
Fax: (617) 495-8097
E-mail: huri@fas.harvard.edu
Web Site: www.huri.harvard.edu

TYPE:
   Fellowships.

   See entry 367 for full listing.

WOODROW WILSON INTERNATIONAL CENTER FOR SCHOLARS

One Woodrow Wilson Plaza
1300 Pennsylvania Avenue, N.W.
Washington, DC 20004-3027
(202) 691-4170
Fax: (202) 691-4001
E-mail: fellowships@wilsoncenter.org
Web Site: www.wilsoncenter.org

TYPE:
   Fellowships; Research grants; Residencies;
   Scholarships; Visiting scholars. The Center
   seeks to commemorate, through its residential
   fellowship program of advanced research,
   both the scholarly depth and the public

concerns of Woodrow Wilson. The Center
welcomes outstanding project proposals in
the social sciences and humanities on global
issues - topics that intersect with questions of
public policy or provide the historical
framework to illume policy issues of
contemporary importance. The Center
especially welcomes projects likely to foster
communication between the world of ideas
and the world of public affairs.

Projects should have relevance to the world
of public policy. Fellows should be prepared
to interact with policymakers in Washington
and with the Center's staff working on
similar areas.

Fellowships are tenable in residence only at
the Woodrow Wilson International Center for
Scholars. The Center will not provide support
for research to be carried out elsewhere.
Fellows devote their full time to research and
writing.

See entry 369 for full listing.

CARTER G. WOODSON INSTITUTE FOR AFRICAN-AMERICAN AND AFRICAN STUDIES

University of Virginia
McCormick Road, 108 Minor Hall
Charlottesville, VA 22903
(434) 924-3109
Fax: (434) 924-8820
E-mail: woodson@virginia.edu
Web Site: woodson.virginia.edu

TYPE:
   Fellowships. The Woodson Institute offers
   residential fellowships to predoctoral and
   postdoctoral scholars. These fellowships are
   designed to facilitate the completion of works
   in progress by providing scholars with
   unencumbered leave.

   Afro-American and African Studies is
   considered to cover Africa, Africans and
   peoples of African descent in North, Central
   and South America and the Caribbean, past
   and present.

   See entry 372 for full listing.

Business and economics

THE ACTUARIAL FOUNDATION

475 North Martingale Road
Suite 600
Schaumburg, IL 60173-2226
(847) 706-3535
E-mail: Scholarships@ActFnd.org
Web Site: www.actuarialfoundation.org

TYPE:
   Scholarships.

   See entry 1908 for full listing.

THE ACTUARIAL FOUNDATION

475 North Martingale Road
Suite 600
Schaumburg, IL 60173-2226
(847) 706-3535
E-mail: Scholarships@ActFnd.org
Web Site: www.actuarialfoundation.org

TYPE:
   Scholarships. Originally named the John
   Culver Wooddy Scholarship, the Curtis E.

Huntington Memorial Scholarship is awarded
annually to undergraduate seniors enrolled as
full-time students at an accredited U.S.
educational institution.

See entry 1909 for full listing.

AMERICAN INSTITUTE OF CERTIFIED PUBLIC ACCOUNTANTS (AICPA)   [1718]

220 Leigh Farm Road
Durham, NC 27707
(919) 402-4473
Fax: (919) 402-4473
E-mail: scholarships@aicpa.org
Web Site: thiswaytocpa.
com/education/scholarship-search

FOUNDED: 1887

AREAS OF INTEREST:
   Accounting.

NAME(S) OF PROGRAMS:
   ● **AICPA Foundation Scholarship for
      Future CPAs**

TYPE:
   Scholarships.

YEAR PROGRAM STARTED: 2019

PURPOSE:
   To provide financial assistance to outstanding
   students to encourage their pursuit of
   accounting as a major and their ultimate
   entry into the profession; to support
   undergraduate or graduate students interested
   in pursuing the CPA license after graduation.

ELIGIBILITY:
   Applicant must be a U.S. citizen or
   permanent resident and an AICPA Student
   Affiliate member. Applicant must be enrolled
   as a full-time undergraduate (12 semester
   hours or equivalent) or full-time graduate
   level student (nine semester hours or
   equivalent) pursuing an undergraduate or
   graduate-level degree in accounting or an
   accounting-related major at a public or
   private, not-for-profit four-year college or
   university in the U.S. or its territories.
   Student must have completed at least 30
   semester hours (or equivalent) of college
   coursework, including at least six semester
   hours (or equivalent) in accounting. Student
   must maintain an overall grade point average
   of at least 3.0 on a 4.0 scale.

   Applicant must be planning to pursue the
   CPA licensure, but not presently be a CPA.

GEOG. RESTRICTIONS: United States and its
territories.

FINANCIAL DATA:
   Amount of support per award: $5,000.

NO. AWARDS: 25.

APPLICATION INFO:
   Application must be submitted online.

   Duration: One academic year. Nonrenewable.

   Deadline: March 1.

ADDRESS INQUIRIES TO:
   AICPA Scholarship Manager
   (See address above.)

AMERICAN INSTITUTE OF CERTIFIED PUBLIC ACCOUNTANTS (AICPA) [1719]

220 Leigh Farm Road
Durham, NC 27707
(919) 402-4473
E-mail: scholarships@aicpa.org
Web Site: thiswaytocpa.com/education/aicpa-legacy-scholarships

AREAS OF INTEREST:
Accounting and accounting-related fields.

NAME(S) OF PROGRAMS:
● **AWSCPA Scholarship Award**

TYPE:
Scholarships. AWSCPA Scholarship Award provides financial assistance to outstanding female students majoring in accounting or an accounting-related field.

YEAR PROGRAM STARTED: 2019

PURPOSE:
To support the success of women in the accounting profession.

ELIGIBILITY:
Applicant must:
(1) be a woman pursuing an undergraduate or graduate-level degree in an accounting or accounting-related major;
(2) be planning to pursue the C.P.A. licensure, but not presently be a C.P.A.;
(3) attend a public or private, not-for-profit 501(c) four-year college or university in the U.S. or its territories for the full academic year;
(4) be enrolled in a business and/or accounting program that is accredited by the AACSB and/or ACBSP for the full academic year;
(5) have completed at least 30 semester hours (or equivalent) of college coursework, including at least six semester hours (or equivalent) in accounting by spring of the award year;
(6) maintain an overall grade point average of a least 3.0 on a 4.0 scale;
(7) be an AICPA Student Affiliate member, or have submitted a new member application;
(8) be a U.S. citizen or permanent resident;
(9) exhibit some financial need and;
(10) plan to participate in the AICPA Legacy Scholars program for the full academic year.

FINANCIAL DATA:
Amount of support per award: $5,000.
Total amount of support: Up to $20,000 annually.

NO. AWARDS: Varies.

APPLICATION INFO:
Guidelines are available on the web site.
Duration: One academic year. Nonrenewable.
Deadline: March 1.

ADDRESS INQUIRIES TO:
See e-mail address above.

AMERICAN INSTITUTE OF CERTIFIED PUBLIC ACCOUNTANTS (AICPA) [1720]

220 Leigh Farm Road
Durham, NC 27707
(919) 402-4473
E-mail: scholarships@aicpa.org
Web Site: thiswaytocpa.com/education/aicpa-legacy-scholarships

AREAS OF INTEREST:
Accounting.

NAME(S) OF PROGRAMS:
● **AICPA/Robert Half Student Scholarships**

TYPE:
Scholarships. Awarded to accounting majors to encourage them to become a C.P.A.

PURPOSE:
To provide financial assistance to students who are currently majoring in accounting, finance or information systems; to encourage students to consider careers in accounting and business.

ELIGIBILITY:
An applicant must meet the following requirements:
(1) pursuing an undergraduate- or graduate-level degree in an "accounting-related" major ("accounting-related" shall be as determined by Sponsors in Sponsors' sole discretion);
(2) planning to pursue the C.P.A. licensure but not presently be a C.P.A.;
(3) applied to or been accepted into a public or private, 501(c) four-year college or university located in the U.S. or its territories; the business program must be accredited by the AACSB and/or ACBSP;
(4) completed at least 30 semester-hours (or equivalent) of college coursework, including at least six semester-hours (or equivalent) in accounting, by end of spring 2020;
(5) maintained an overall and major grade point average of at least 3.0 (on a 4.0 scale);
(6) enrolled as a full-time undergraduate (12 semester-hours or equivalent) or a full-time graduate-level student (nine semester-hours or equivalent) for the 2020-21 academic year; an exception may be made if one plans to participate in an internship program;
(7) be an AICPA student affiliate member (or have submitted a new member application); those interested can apply on the web site at no cost;
(8) be a U.S. citizen or permanent resident (green card holder) and;
(9) have some financial need (i.e., not receiving a full or partial scholarship(s) and/or grant(s) that cover and/or exceed one's educational expenses).

AICPA and RHI/Accountemps staff and their family members are not eligible to receive this scholarship.

GEOG. RESTRICTIONS: United States and its territories.

FINANCIAL DATA:
Amount of support per award: $10,000.
Total amount of support: Up to $40,000 annually.

NO. AWARDS: Varies.

APPLICATION INFO:
Guidelines are available on the web site.
Duration: One year. Nonrenewable.
Deadline: March 1.

ADDRESS INQUIRIES TO:
See e-mail address above.

*SPECIAL STIPULATIONS:
Students selected to receive an AICPA scholarship must participate in the AICPA Legacy Scholars program, which includes performing at least eight hours of community service per semester to advocate for the C.P.A. profession. Through their community service efforts, AICPA Legacy Scholars enhance their leadership and communication skills by building relationships with both aspiring and seasoned C.P.As.

AMERICAN INSTITUTE OF CERTIFIED PUBLIC ACCOUNTANTS (AICPA) [1721]

220 Leigh Farm Road
Durham, NC 27707
(919) 402-4473
E-mail: scholarships@aicpa.org
Web Site: thiswaytocpa.com/education/aicpa-legacy-scholarships

AREAS OF INTEREST:
Accounting and accounting-related fields.

NAME(S) OF PROGRAMS:
● **AICPA Foundation Two-Year Transfer Scholarship**

TYPE:
Scholarships. AICPA Foundation Two-Year Transfer Scholarship provides financial assistance to students who have earned an Associate's degree in business, accounting, finance or economics with a declared intent to major in accounting at a four-year college or university.

PURPOSE:
To provide financial assistance to students who are currently majoring in accounting, finance or information systems; to encourage students to consider careers in accounting and business.

ELIGIBILITY:
An eligible applicant must be/have:
(1) earned an Associate's degree in business, accounting, finance or economics with a declared intent to major in accounting or an "accounting-related field" at a four-year college or university ("accounting-related" shall be as determined by Sponsors in Sponsors' sole discretion);
(2) planning to pursue the C.P.A. licensure but not presently be a C.P.A.;
(3) proof of acceptance into a public or private, not-for-profit 501(c) four-year college or university located in the U.S. states or territories for the full upcoming academic year; the business program must be accredited by the AACSB and/or ACBSP; (exception may be granted, but not guaranteed, at the discretion of Sponsor; inquire at the e-mail address above if one is unsure of one's eligibility);
(4) maintained an overall and major grade point average of at least 3.0 (on a 4.0 scale);
(5) enrolled as a full-time undergraduate (12 semester hours or equivalent); an exception may be made if one plans to participate in an internship program;
(6) an AICPA student affiliate member (or have submitted a new member application); one can apply online at no cost at the web site above;
(7) a U.S. citizen or permanent resident (green card holder) and;
(8) some financial need (i.e., not receiving a full or partial scholarship(s) and/or grant(s) that cover and/or exceed one's educational expenses).

AICPA staff and their family members are not eligible to receive this scholarship.

FINANCIAL DATA:
Scholarship aid may be used only for the payment of expenses that directly relate to obtaining an accounting education (e.g., tuition, fees, room and board and/or books and materials only). Scholarship payments are sent directly to the student's financial aid office on behalf of the student.

Amount of support per award: $5,000.

Total amount of support: Up to $125,000 annually.

NO. AWARDS: Varies.

APPLICATION INFO:
Guidelines are available on the web site.
Duration: One academic year. Nonrenewable.
Deadline: March 1.

ADDRESS INQUIRIES TO:
See e-mail address above.

*SPECIAL STIPULATIONS:
Students selected to receive an AICPA scholarship must participate in the AICPA Legacy Scholars program, which includes performing at least eight hours of community service per semester to advocate for the C.P.A. profession. Through their community service efforts, AICPA Legacy Scholars enhance their leadership and communication skills by building relationships with both aspiring and seasoned C.P.As.

AMERICAN INSTITUTE OF CERTIFIED PUBLIC ACCOUNTANTS (AICPA)　　[1722]

220 Leigh Farm Road
Durham, NC 27707
(919) 402-4473
E-mail: scholarships@aicpa.org
Web Site: thiswaytocpa.com/education/aicpa-legacy-scholarships

AREAS OF INTEREST:
Accounting.

NAME(S) OF PROGRAMS:
● **John L. Carey Scholarship**

TYPE:
Scholarships.

YEAR PROGRAM STARTED: 2013

PURPOSE:
To provide financial assistance to liberal arts or other nonbusiness-related degree holders pursuing graduate studies in accounting and the C.P.A. designation; to encourage students with little or no previous accounting education to consider professional accounting careers.

ELIGIBILITY:
An applicant must meet the following requirements:
(1) have obtained a liberal arts or other nonbusiness undergraduate degree from a regionally accredited institution in the U.S. prior to enrolling in a graduate accounting program;
(2) have not earned more than 12 credits in accounting or business during his or her undergraduate program;
(3) planning to pursue the C.P.A. licensure but not presently be a C.P.A.;
(4) planning to pursue a graduate-level degree in an "accounting-related" major ("accounting-related" shall be as determined by Sponsor in Sponsor's sole discretion); this program will enable a student to sit for the C.P.A. exam;
(5) applied to or been accepted into a public or private, 501(c) four-year college or university located in the U.S. or its territories; the business program must be accredited by the AACSB and/or ACBSP;
(6) not actively participating in a graduate accounting program;
(7) enrolled as a full-time graduate-level student (nine semester-hours or equivalent) for the 2020-21 academic year; an exception may be granted if one plans to participate in

an internship program;
(8) be an AICPA student affiliate member (or have submitted a new member application) by the beginning of the 2020-21 academic year; those interested can apply on the web site at no cost;
(9) be a U.S. citizen or permanent resident (green card holder) and;
(10) have some financial need (i.e., not already be receiving a full or partial scholarship(s) that covers or exceeds one's educational expenses).
Note: AICPA staff and their family members are not eligible to receive this scholarship.

GEOG. RESTRICTIONS: United States and its territories.

FINANCIAL DATA:
Amount of support per award: $5,000.
Total amount of support: Up to $25,000 annually.

NO. AWARDS: Varies.

APPLICATION INFO:
Guidelines are available on the web site.
Duration: One year. Nonrenewable.
Deadline: March 1.

ADDRESS INQUIRIES TO:
See e-mail address above.

*SPECIAL STIPULATIONS:
Students selected to receive an AICPA scholarship must participate in the AICPA Legacy Scholars program, which includes performing at least eight hours of community service per semester to advocate for the C.P.A. profession. Through their community service efforts, AICPA Legacy Scholars enhance their leadership and communication skills by building relationships with both aspiring and seasoned C.P.As.

APPRAISAL INSTITUTE OF PROFESSIONAL RESOURCES　　[1723]

200 West Madison Street
Suite 1500
Chicago, IL 60606
(312) 335-4226
Fax: (312) 335-4134
E-mail: aierf@appraisalinstitute.org
Web Site: www.aiedtrust.org

NAME(S) OF PROGRAMS:
● **Appraisal Institute Education and Relief Foundation Scholarship**

TYPE:
Scholarships. Graduate and undergraduate scholarships to help worthy and qualified students finance the cost of college work leading to a degree in the fields of real estate appraisal, land economics, real estate and allied fields.

PURPOSE:
To help finance the educational endeavors of individuals concentrating their studies in real estate appraisal, land economics, real estate or allied fields.

ELIGIBILITY:
Applicants must be citizens of the U.S., attending a full-time college, U.S. university or community college, and have the expressed intention of majoring in real estate evaluation and related subjects. Related subjects may include land economics, economics, economic geography, and others similarly related. Levels of education for the scholarship must be sophomore, junior, senior and graduate year of college.

Preference will be given to those applicants whose previous training and whose future course of study indicate that they intend to follow a field of endeavor which comes within the scope of the objectives of the Appraisal Institute. Applicants must also demonstrate qualities of leadership and scholarly attainments.

GEOG. RESTRICTIONS: United States.

FINANCIAL DATA:
Amount of support per award: Graduate: $2,000; Undergraduate: $1,000.

NO. AWARDS: Approximately 20 per year.

APPLICATION INFO:
Scholarship applications are available on the web site.
Duration: One academic year.
Deadline: April 15 for the following academic year.

OFFICERS:
Jim Amorin, Chief Executive Officer

BOARD OF TRUSTEES:
Shelly Tanaka, Chairperson
Miles Hamrick, Sr., Vice Chairperson

ADDRESS INQUIRIES TO:
Scott Brody
Supervisor of Professional Resources
(See address above.)

THE CONSORTIUM FOR GRADUATE STUDY IN MANAGEMENT　　[1724]

229 Chesterfield Business Parkway
Chesterfield, MO 63005
(636) 681-5553
Fax: (636) 681-5499
E-mail: recruiting@cgsm.org
Web Site: www.cgsm.org

FOUNDED: 1966

NAME(S) OF PROGRAMS:
● **Competitive Advantage**
● **Fellowships for Under-Represented Minorities in Management**

TYPE:
Fellowships. Competitive Advantage is a career and graduate school readiness program for underrepresented minority college students.

Graduate fellowships for minority students interested in management careers in business.

YEAR PROGRAM STARTED: 1967

PURPOSE:
To hasten the entry of minorities into management positions in business.

LEGAL BASIS:
Not-for-profit, IRS 501(c)(3) status.

ELIGIBILITY:
U.S. citizenship and permanent residence in the U.S. is required. Applicant must present evidence of their commitment to the Consortium's mission of promoting the inclusion of African Americans, Hispanic Americans and Native Americans in American Business. The undergraduate degree need not be in business or economics.

Fellowships are awarded only by Consortium institutions, including University of California-Berkeley, Carnegie-Mellon University, Dartmouth College, Emory University, Indiana University (Bloomington), New York University, Rice University,

University of Michigan (Ann Arbor),
University of North Carolina (Chapel Hill),
University of Rochester, University of
Southern California, University of Texas
(Austin), University of Virginia, University of
Wisconsin (Madison) and Washington
University (St. Louis).

There are no fellowships awarded for
part-time study.

FINANCIAL DATA:
The fellowship includes full tuition and
required fees.
Total amount of support: $40,000,000 for the
year 2020.

NO. MOST RECENT APPLICANTS: 1,250.

NO. AWARDS: 425.

APPLICATION INFO:
Guidelines and application form are available
on the web site.
Duration: Fellowships are awarded for a
maximum of four semesters of full-time
study.
Deadline: November 15 and January 5.

IRS I.D.: 43-0962198

STAFF:
Peter Aranda, Chief Executive Officer
Glenn Wilen, Vice President of Finance and
Administration

DECA INC. [1725]

1908 Association Drive
Reston, VA 20191
(703) 860-5000
Fax: (703) 860-4013
E-mail: cindy@deca.org
Web Site: www.deca.org

FOUNDED: 1946

AREAS OF INTEREST:
Marketing education, management and
entrepreneurship.

TYPE:
Scholarships.

YEAR PROGRAM STARTED: 1962

PURPOSE:
To prepare emerging leaders and
entrepreneurs in marketing, finance,
hospitality and management in high schools
and colleges around the globe.

LEGAL BASIS:
Nonprofit association.

ELIGIBILITY:
Applicant must be a current member of
DECA.

GEOG. RESTRICTIONS: United States.

FINANCIAL DATA:
Amount of support per award: Varies.
Total amount of support: Over $200,000 in
scholarships provided at the International
Career Development Conference (ICDC)
each year.

NO. MOST RECENT APPLICANTS: 5,000.

NO. AWARDS: 100.

APPLICATION INFO:
Information is available at the web site.
Duration: One year. Renewals are
considered. Must reapply.
Deadline: January.

ADDRESS INQUIRIES TO:
Cindy Allen
Director of Sponsorships
(See e-mail address above.)

ECONOMIC HISTORY ASSOCIATION [1726]

Department of Economics
University of Wisconsin-La Crosse
1725 State Street
La Crosse, WI 54601
(608) 785-6863
E-mail: mhaupert@uwlax.edu
Web Site: www.eh.net/eha

FOUNDED: 1940

AREAS OF INTEREST:
Economic history.

NAME(S) OF PROGRAMS:
● **Arthur H. Cole Grants-in-Aid**

TYPE:
Grants-in-aid. Grants for advanced research
in any aspect of economic history.

YEAR PROGRAM STARTED: 1972

PURPOSE:
To support individual research in the field of
economic history.

LEGAL BASIS:
Nonprofit.

ELIGIBILITY:
Applicants must have completed their Ph.D.
and must be members of the Economic
History Association. Preference is given to
recent Ph.D. recipients.

FINANCIAL DATA:
Amount of support per award: Up to $5,000.
Total amount of support: $15,000 to $20,000.

NO. MOST RECENT APPLICANTS: 18.

NO. AWARDS: 6.

APPLICATION INFO:
Application information is available on the
Association web site.
Duration: One year.
Deadline: Early March.

PUBLICATIONS:
The Journal of Economic History.

IRS I.D.: 13-6128711

THE EDUCATIONAL FOUNDATION FOR WOMEN IN ACCOUNTING [1727]

136 South Keowee Street
Dayton, OH 45402-2241
(937) 424-3391
Fax: (937) 222-5794
E-mail: info@efwa.org
Web Site: www.efwa.org

FOUNDED: 1966

AREAS OF INTEREST:
Women in the accounting field.

NAME(S) OF PROGRAMS:
● **Laurels Fund**
● **Michelle L. McDonald Scholarship**
● **Moss Adams LLP Scholarship**
● **Seattle ASWA Chapter Scholarship**
● **Women in Need Scholarship**
● **Women in Transition Scholarship**

TYPE:
Scholarships. Laurels Fund provides a
one-year academic scholarship for women
pursuing a Ph.D. in accounting.

Women in Need Scholarship is available to
women in their third, fourth or fifth year of
academic pursuit who need the financial
support to complete their degrees. It is
renewable annually upon satisfactory
completion of course requirements.

Women in Transition Scholarship is intended
for women returning to school as freshmen to
earn a Bachelor's degree in accounting. It is
renewable annually upon satisfactory
completion of course requirements.

YEAR PROGRAM STARTED: 1966

PURPOSE:
To support the advancement of women in the
accounting profession through the funding of
education, research, career literature,
publications and other projects; to encourage
and enable women to enter the accounting
profession and empower them to achieve
equal opportunities and equal rewards.

LEGAL BASIS:
501(c)(3) organization.

ELIGIBILITY:
Women who are pursuing accounting degrees
at the undergraduate, graduate and
postgraduate levels.

GEOG. RESTRICTIONS: United States.

FINANCIAL DATA:
Amount of support per award: Varies.
Total amount of support: Varies.

NO. AWARDS: Vary annually.

APPLICATION INFO:
Applications are available on the web site.
Duration: Laurels Fund, Michelle L.
McDonald, Moss Adams LLP and Seattle
ASWA Chapter Scholarships: One year;
Women in Need Scholarship: Two years;
Women in Transition Scholarship: Four
years.
Deadline: Laurels Fund: May 15. All others:
April 30.

IRS I.D.: 36-6149364

ADDRESS INQUIRIES TO:
Foundation Administrator
(See address above.)

ERNST & YOUNG FOUNDATION [1728]

5 Times Square
New York, NY 10036
(212) 773-3000
E-mail: ellen.glazerman@ey.com

FOUNDED: 1937

AREAS OF INTEREST:
Higher education, with specific interests in
accounting, business, computer science,
engineering and information systems.

TYPE:
Fellowships; Matching gifts; Scholarships.

YEAR PROGRAM STARTED: 1937

PURPOSE:
To support higher education.

LEGAL BASIS:
Public charity.

ELIGIBILITY:
No grants to individuals. No cold requests.

GEOG. RESTRICTIONS: United States and its
territories.

FINANCIAL DATA:
Amount of support per award: Varies.
Total amount of support: Varies.

Matching fund requirements: Ernst & Young Foundation will only match contributions to not-for-profit accredited colleges, junior colleges, community colleges, universities, graduate schools or professional schools.

APPLICATION INFO:
The Foundation does not accept unsolicited requests for funding.

Duration: Varies.

Deadline: Grant requests are reviewed continuously.

ADDRESS INQUIRIES TO:
Ellen J. Glazerman, Executive Director
(See address and e-mail above.)

FEDERATION OF AMERICAN CONSUMERS AND TRAVELERS [1729]

318 Hillsboro Avenue
P.O. Box 104
Edwardsville, IL 62025
(618) 656-0454
(800) 872-3228
Fax: (618) 656-5369
E-mail: vrolens@usafact.org
Web Site: www.usafact.org

NAME(S) OF PROGRAMS:
● **Community and Business Project Grants**

TYPE:
Project/program grants; Seed money grants.

PURPOSE:
To support civic club, church, and community projects that are nominated by members.

ELIGIBILITY:
Projects are nominated by members.

GEOG. RESTRICTIONS: United States.

FINANCIAL DATA:
Amount of support per award: $100 to $2,500, based on funding availability and the needs of the specific proposal.

Total amount of support: Varies.

APPLICATION INFO:
Contact the Federation for guidelines.

Duration: One-time award.

Deadline: Quarterly.

ADDRESS INQUIRIES TO:
Vicki Rolens, Managing Director
(See address above.)

*SPECIAL STIPULATIONS:
Applicant must be a FACT member or have been nominated by a FACT member.

4A'S

1065 Avenue of the Americas, 16th Floor
New York, NY 10018
(212) 682-2500
Fax: (212) 682-8391
E-mail: maip@aaaa.org
Web Site: foundation.aaaa.org

TYPE:
Fellowships; Scholarships.

See entry 909 for full listing.

HAGLEY MUSEUM AND LIBRARY

Hagley Library
298 Buck Road
Wilmington, DE 19807
(302) 658-2400 ext. 243
E-mail: clockman@hagley.org
Web Site: www.hagley.org

TYPE:
Fellowships; Research grants; Travel grants; Visiting scholars. Grants to support short-term research in the imprint, manuscript, pictorial and artifact collections of the Hagley Museum and Library.

The Henry Belin du Pont Dissertation Fellowship in Business, Technology, and Society supports research and writing by candidates for doctoral degrees. Projects should demonstrate superior intellectual quality and make substantial use of Hagley's collections.

Henry Belin du Pont Research Grants support research in the collections of the museum and library.

Hagley Exploratory Research Grant supports a one-week visit by scholars who believe that their project will benefit from Hagley research collections, but need the opportunity to explore them on-site to determine if a Henry Belin du Pont research grant application is warranted.

See entry 549 for full listing.

THE S.S. HUEBNER FOUNDATION FOR INSURANCE EDUCATION [1730]

Department of Risk Management and Insurance
Georgia State University
P.O. Box 4036
Atlanta, GA 30302-4036
(404) 413-7466
E-mail: sshore@gsu.edu
Web Site: www.huebnerfoundation.org

FOUNDED: 1940

AREAS OF INTEREST:
Insurance and risk management.

TYPE:
The Foundation's program goals are:
(1) to support the Ph.D. program at Georgia State University that is training the next generation of scholars who will conduct academic research on insurance economics specifically and the efficient allocation of risk in the economy more generally;
(2) to sponsor a periodic summer symposium or occasional lecture series facilitated by leading scholars designed to build collaborative research relationships among young researchers at Georgia State University and elsewhere who are interested in risk-related topics and;
(3) to provide assistance for professionals who seek to develop the research skills necessary to address contemporary insurance and risk problems in such areas as regulation, policy or industry practice.

YEAR PROGRAM STARTED: 1940

PURPOSE:
To advance university-level risk management and insurance scholarship and learning.

APPLICATION INFO:
Contact the Foundation for guidelines.

IRS I.D.: 23-6297325

ADDRESS INQUIRIES TO:
Stephen H. Shore, Ph.D.
Executive Director
(See address above.)

INSTITUTE FOR SUPPLY MANAGEMENT [1731]

309 West Elliot Road, Suite 113
Tempe, AZ 85284-1556
(480) 752-6276
Fax: (480) 752-7890
E-mail: membersvcs@ instituteforsupplymanagement.org
Web Site: www.instituteforsupplymanagement.org

AREAS OF INTEREST:
Supply management, supply chain management and procurement.

NAME(S) OF PROGRAMS:
● **R. Gene Richter Scholarship Program**

TYPE:
Scholarships.

YEAR PROGRAM STARTED: 2008

PURPOSE:
To identify the future leaders of supply management and fast-track those individuals into the profession through a program of tuition assistance, executive mentoring, junior mentoring and networking.

ELIGIBILITY:
Eligible students are:
(1) enrolled full-time in an accredited supply chain management curriculum;
(2) entering their senior year during the 2019-20 academic year;
(3) graduating either in December 2019 or Spring 2020;
(4) a citizen of the U.S. or Canada, or possess a valid green card;
(5) available to attend the Institute for Supply Management Annual International Conference and;
(6) willing to sign a contract pledging that the monetary award will be used for educational expenses.

Scholarship recipients will be chosen based on attained high academic achievement, demonstrated strong leadership ability, demonstrated high ethical standards, and a strong commitment to pursuing a career in the field of supply chain management.

FINANCIAL DATA:
Amount of support per award: $10,000 ($5,000 for December graduates).

CO-OP FUNDING PROGRAMS: R. Gene Richter Scholarship Fund and the R. Gene and Nancy D. Richter Foundation.

NO. AWARDS: 6 for the year 2018-19.

APPLICATION INFO:
Application is available online.

Duration: One academic year.

Deadline: December 31.

THE CALVIN K. KAZANJIAN ECONOMICS FOUNDATION, INC. [1732]

P.O. Box 300
Dallas, PA 18612-0330
(570) 690-4629
E-mail: director@kazanjian.org
Web Site: www.kazanjian.org

FOUNDED: 1947

AREAS OF INTEREST:
Promoting the understanding of economics and addressing the issue of economic illiteracy.

TYPE:
Challenge/matching grants; Demonstration grants. Grants for economic education.

PURPOSE:
To aid in bringing greater happiness and prosperity to all through a better understanding of economics.

ELIGIBILITY:
The Foundation will only give serious consideration to those projects which directly advance its immediate purposes and meet its guidelines. It will only support nonprofit 501(c)(3) organizations and will not support overhead or indirect costs.

GEOG. RESTRICTIONS: United States.

FINANCIAL DATA:
Amount of support per award:
Approximately $25,000 average grant.
Total amount of support: Approximately $400,000.

APPLICATION INFO:
Guidelines and criteria are found on the web site. Applicants must include:
(1) copy of an IRS nonprofit determination letter;
(2) latest audited financial statement;
(3) list of board of directors;
(4) annual budget and;
(5) project budget.
Duration: Varies.
Deadline: September 15 for November/December review. February 15 for May/June review.

IRS I.D.: 06-0665174

ADDRESS INQUIRIES TO:
Dr. Michael MacDowell, Managing Director
(See address above.)

*PLEASE NOTE:
The Foundation does not give scholarships.

KPMG FOUNDATION [1733]

3 Chestnut Ridge Road
Montvale, NJ 07645-0435
(201) 307-7932
Fax: (201) 624-7763
E-mail: tperino@kpmg.com
Web Site: www.kpmgfoundation.org
www.phdproject.org

FOUNDED: 1968

AREAS OF INTEREST:
Academic research, education and professional development in the area of business.

TYPE:
Conferences/seminars; Matching gifts; Professorships; Project/program grants. Special grants, made on the recommendations of the Firm's college relations partners, are for specific projects that create new educational opportunities.

YEAR PROGRAM STARTED: 1968

PURPOSE:
To recognize outstanding achievement in accounting education and research; to recognize academic excellence and community achievement; to help minority students obtain careers in business and industry; to promote research that will benefit the profession now and in the future.

LEGAL BASIS:
501(c)(3) public charity.

ELIGIBILITY:
The Foundation restricts grants to educational purposes related to its firm's functional areas, including accounting, auditing and tax.

GEOG. RESTRICTIONS: United States.

FINANCIAL DATA:
Matching fund requirements: The Matching Gift Program only matches employee/partner gifts to colleges and universities from which the donors are alumni or where KPMG recruits. Minimum $50 for employees and maximum $7,500 per institution per fiscal year.

PUBLICATIONS:
Annual report.

IRS I.D.: 13-6262199

BOARD OF TRUSTEES:
Robert F. Arning, Chairperson
Blane Ruschak, President
Darren H. Burton
David DiCristofaro
Gabriel De La Rosa
Maureen Evers-Willox
Ben Garfunkel
Tandra C. Jackson
Christine M. Kachinsky
Heidi Murdy-Michael
James Powell
Bradley N. Sprong
Sandra B. Torchia

ADDRESS INQUIRIES TO:
Tara Perino, Senior Director
(See address above.)

LIBRA FUTURE FUND [1734]

3 Canal Plaza, Suite 500
Portland, ME 04101
(207) 879-6280
Fax: (207) 879-6281
E-mail: erik@librafoundation.org
Web Site: www.librafoundation.org/libra-future-fund

FOUNDED: 2005

AREAS OF INTEREST:
Economic development and job opportunities in Maine.

NAME(S) OF PROGRAMS:
● **Libra Future Fund Young Adult Grant Program**

TYPE:
Project/program grants. To promote economic development and create job opportunities in Maine.

YEAR PROGRAM STARTED: 2005

PURPOSE:
To capitalize upon the energy and creativity that Maine's young people embody; to combat youth out-migration by supporting initiatives that increase the number of Maine-based professional opportunities.

ELIGIBILITY:
Applicants must be 18 to 29 years of age, reside in Maine at least eight months per year, or be originally from Maine, but attending school out of state.

GEOG. RESTRICTIONS: Maine.

FINANCIAL DATA:
Amount of support per award: $3,000 to $5,000.
Total amount of support: Approximately $38,360 for the year 2018.

APPLICATION INFO:
Complete instructions can be found on the Fund's web site.
Duration: One-time grant.
Deadline: January 23, April 23, July 23, and October 23.

ADDRESS INQUIRIES TO:
Erik Hayward, President
(See address above.)

THE GERALD LOEB AWARDS

UCLA Anderson School of Management
110 Westwood Plaza
Gold Hall, Suite B307
Los Angeles, CA 90095-1481
(310) 825-4478
Fax: (310) 825-4479
E-mail: loeb@anderson.ucla.edu
Web Site: www.anderson.ucla.edu/gerald-loeb-awards

TYPE:
Awards/prizes. Awards to recognize business and financial journalists for important contributions to the understanding of business, finance and the economy.

See entry 1769 for full listing.

LOGISTICS & TRANSPORTATION ASSOCIATION OF NORTH AMERICA (LTNA) [1735]

P.O. Box 426
Union, WA 98592
E-mail: executive.director@ltna.org
Web Site: www.ltna.org

AREAS OF INTEREST:
Transportation logistics, supply-chain management, traffic management and transportation safety.

NAME(S) OF PROGRAMS:
● **Hooper Memorial Scholarship**
● **Denny Lydic Scholarship**
● **Alice Glaisyer Warfield Scholarship**
● **Charlotte Woods Memorial Scholarship**

TYPE:
Scholarships. Charlotte Woods Memorial Scholarship is awarded to a student who is an LTNA member or a dependent of a member.

PURPOSE:
To encourage advanced vocational, undergraduate and graduate study in the field of transportation and traffic management.

ELIGIBILITY:
LTNA awards scholarships to graduating high school seniors and college undergraduate students accepted to or currently enrolled at accredited institutions of higher learning in degree programs in the fields of transportation logistics, supply-chain management, traffic management, and transportation safety.

In addition to the acceptance, enrollment and field of study requirements described above, the basis for awarding LTNA scholarships includes a calculated review and assessment of each applicant's academic record, character, potential and professional interest as revealed through the applicant's application and specified supporting documents.

GEOG. RESTRICTIONS: United States and Canada.

APPLICATION INFO:
In addition to a completed application form, supporting documents include:
(1) certified transcript directly from applicant's college/university;
(2) two or three letters of recommendation and;
(3) a 250-word essay explaining why the applicant has chosen transportation logistics or an allied field as a career path, and outlining the objectives. Essay should be composed separately in Microsoft Word file only. Application form is available at the web site.

All application documents must be mailed to the Executive Director at the address above.

Deadline: No later than July 25.

ADDRESS INQUIRIES TO:
Katie Dejonge, Executive Director
(See address above.)

MARKETING EDGE [1736]

500 Seventh Avenue, 8th Floor
New York, NY 10018
(212) 790-1510
E-mail: admin@marketingedge.org
Web Site: www.marketingedge.org

FOUNDED: 1966

NAME(S) OF PROGRAMS:
- **Collegiate ECHO Marketing Challenge**
- **Collegiate Summit**
- **Robert Kestnbaum Research Program**
- **Marketing EDGE Scholarship Program**
- **Professor's Institute**
- **Shankar-Spiegel Award for the Best Dissertation Proposal in Direct/Interactive Marketing**
- **Student Career Forums**

TYPE:
Awards/prizes; Conferences/seminars; Internships; Research grants; Scholarships; Research contracts. Collegiate ECHO Marketing Challenge provides students worldwide with experiential learning, crafting an integrated marketing plan.

Collegiate Summit is an annual conference focused on digital and data-focused marketing for undergraduate students.

Robert Kestnbaum Research Program is intended to generate leading-edge academic research to impact the future of direct/interactive marketing.

Marketing EDGE Scholarship Program provides education funding support to undergraduate and graduate students nationwide.

Professor's Institute is an invitation-only conference held in conjunction with SMU's Brierly Institute for Customer Engagement, to bring marketing academics and practitioners together to engage in thought-provoking conversations that have the potential to influence marketing curricula and current marketing practice.

Shankar-Spiegel Award for the Best Dissertation Proposal in Direct/Interactive Marketing recognizes doctoral candidates with the best dissertation proposal in direct/interactive marketing. Doctoral students from accredited doctoral programs are eligible to receive this award.

Student Career Forums provides opportunity for college students to meet and network with marketing professionals.

YEAR PROGRAM STARTED: 1966

PURPOSE:
To educate, develop, grow and employ college students in the marketing field.

LEGAL BASIS:
Nonprofit, tax-exempt organization.

ELIGIBILITY:
Varies by program.

GEOG. RESTRICTIONS: United States.

FINANCIAL DATA:
Amount of support per award: $5,000 to $50,000.

CO-OP FUNDING PROGRAMS: Corporate Leadership Program.

APPLICATION INFO:
Form and guidelines are available online.

PUBLICATIONS:
Annual report; conference materials; *Journal of Interactive Marketing*®.

IRS I.D.: 13-6222757

STAFF:
Terri L. Bartlett, Chief Executive Officer and President
Marie Adolphe, Senior Vice President, Program Development

ADDRESS INQUIRIES TO:
Administration Assistant
(See address above.)

THE BURTON D. MORGAN FOUNDATION [1737]

22 Aurora Street
Hudson, OH 44236
(330) 655-1660
Fax: (330) 655-1673
E-mail: grantsmanager@bdmorganfdn.org
Web Site: www.bdmorganfdn.org

FOUNDED: 1967

AREAS OF INTEREST:
Entrepreneurship education, economic development and free enterprise system.

TYPE:
Challenge/matching grants; Conferences/seminars; Endowments; General operating grants; Project/program grants.

YEAR PROGRAM STARTED: 1967

PURPOSE:
To champion the entrepreneurial spirit.

LEGAL BASIS:
Private foundation.

ELIGIBILITY:
Grants are made to organizations classified as public charities and tax-exempt under Section 501(c)(3) of the IRS Code. For-profit companies and startups are not eligible to apply for funding directly from the Foundation. The Foundation does not make grants to individuals.

Projects with national impact are occasionally considered.

GEOG. RESTRICTIONS: Primarily Northeast Ohio.

FINANCIAL DATA:
Amount of support per award: Varies.
Total amount of support: Varies.
Matching fund requirements: Varies.

CO-OP FUNDING PROGRAMS: Forward Cities; Fund for Our Economic Future; JumpStart Higher Education Collaboration Council; Scalerator NEO.

REPRESENTATIVE AWARDS:
$10,000 to First Congregational Church of Hudson; $3,000 to Music from the Western Reserve; $14,000 to Portage County Literary Coalition.

APPLICATION INFO:
Details on how to apply for grants can be found on the Foundation web site.

Duration: One year.

Deadline: Requests greater than $20,000: May 1 for September consideration, September 1 for January or February consideration, and February 1 for June consideration. Requests under $20,000 are considered on a rolling basis.

PUBLICATIONS:
Pipeline, e-newsletter; annual report.

IRS I.D.: 34-6598971

OFFICER:
Deborah D. Hoover, President and Chief Executive Officer

ADDRESS INQUIRIES TO:
Grants Manager
(See address above.)

THE NASDAQ EDUCATIONAL FOUNDATION, INC. [1738]

805 King Farm Boulevard
Rockville, MD 20850
(301) 978-8738
(800) 842-0356
Fax: (301) 978-8472
E-mail: foundation@nasdaq.com
Web Site: www.business.nasdaq.com

FOUNDED: 1994

AREAS OF INTEREST:
Financial markets literacy.

TYPE:
Development grants; Fellowships; Project/program grants; Research grants; Seed money grants. The Foundation offers grants in the following areas:
(1) academic study or research;
(2) Ph.D. dissertation fellowships;
(3) curriculum development and;
(4) educational projects or programs.

PURPOSE:
To promote learning about capital formation, financial markets and entrepreneurship through innovative educational programs.

ELIGIBILITY:
The Foundation will accept proposals from educational institutions and organizations designated as tax-exempt according to Section 501(c)(3) of the Internal Revenue Code.

In limited cases, proposals from highly and specifically qualified individuals, only for the purpose of conducting independent academic study or research on financial markets, are accepted.

FINANCIAL DATA:
Amount of support per award: Varies.
Total amount of support: Varies.

APPLICATION INFO:
Applicants must submit a letter of inquiry and be invited to submit a proposal.

Duration: One year, unless otherwise specified.

Deadline: Varies.

ADDRESS INQUIRIES TO:
Joan C. Conley, Senior Vice President
and Corporate Secretary or
Angela Henson, Project Coordinator
(See address above.)

NATIONAL ENDOWMENT FOR FINANCIAL EDUCATION (NEFE)   [1739]

1331 17th Street, Suite 1200
Denver, CO 80202
(303) 741-6333
Fax: (303) 220-0838
E-mail: nefegrantrequest@nefe.org
Web Site: www.nefe.org

FOUNDED: 1997

AREAS OF INTEREST:
Financial education for the American public.

NAME(S) OF PROGRAMS:
● **NEFE Research Funding Program**

TYPE:
Fellowships; Research grants. NEFE
Research Funding Program recruits qualified
individuals from diverse backgrounds who
share a common interest in working on
projects within NEFE's broad scope of
activities and in gaining nonprofit operations
and management experience. The program
also awards grants for research projects that
will expand the body of knowledge in the
field of financial literacy.

YEAR PROGRAM STARTED: 1998

PURPOSE:
To fund innovative research that can make a
profound contribution to the field of financial
literacy.

ELIGIBILITY:
To be considered for a fellowship
opportunity, candidates must be:
(1) in good standing with their academic
institution and;
(2) a currently registered graduate
degree-seeking student.

Grants are awarded to organizations that have
been designated tax-exempt status according
to Internal Revenue Code Section 501(c)(3)
or its equivalent for colleges and universities.
Grants are not awarded to:
(1) individuals;
(2) organizations that have not been
designated tax-exempt under Section
501(c)(3) or its equivalent;
(3) organizations that discriminate on the
basis of age, color, disability, marital status,
nationality, race, religion, sex, sexual
orientation, or veteran status;
(4) organizations and/or project principals
and team members who fail to meet NEFE's
Strategy Statement and Procedures
requirements concerning the U.S.A. Patriot
Act and related regulations;
(5) foreign organizations;
(6) international programs or projects or;
(7) organizations whose projects include
re-grant of NEFE funding.

Project outcomes should be in the field of
financial literacy and directly relevant to the
public's well-being.

GEOG. RESTRICTIONS: United States.

FINANCIAL DATA:
Amount of support per award: Fellowships:
$3,000 per semester; Grants: Generally
$100,000 up.
Total amount of support: Varies.

NO. MOST RECENT APPLICANTS: 25.

NO. AWARDS: 3.

APPLICATION INFO:
Fellowship Program does not accept
unsolicited applications. Applicants to the
Grant Program must first submit a Letter of
Inquiry. Those projects appearing to have
strong potential will move to a proposal
phase; applicants for those selected projects
will be given further instruction at that time.
Duration: Varies.
Deadline: First Tuesday in December for
spring funding and first Tuesday in June for
fall funding.

PUBLICATIONS:
NEFE Digest.

IRS I.D.: 84-0632115

ADDRESS INQUIRIES TO:
Grants Manager
(See address above.)

THE NATIONAL RESTAURANT ASSOCIATION EDUCATIONAL FOUNDATION   [1740]

2055 L Street, N.W.
Washington, DC 20036
(202) 973-3672
E-mail: scholars@nraef.org
Web Site: www.chooserestaurants.
org/scholarships

FOUNDED: 1987

AREAS OF INTEREST:
Foodservice education and training.

NAME(S) OF PROGRAMS:
● **Professional Development for
Educators Scholarship**

TYPE:
Training grants; Travel grants.

PURPOSE:
To support foodservice educators earning
their Certified Secondary Educators
Foodservice certification; to provide financial
support to attend an NRA Summer Institute
or participate in a "hands-on" industry work
experience.

ELIGIBILITY:
Must be an educator of a restaurant and/or
foodservice-related program in a secondary
school and submit a signed letter of
recommendation on school letterhead that
also verifies employment by an immediate
supervisor or program director. Applicants
must be U.S. citizens/residents.

GEOG. RESTRICTIONS: United States.

FINANCIAL DATA:
Amount of support per award: $1,700.
Total amount of support: Varies.

NO. MOST RECENT APPLICANTS: 150.

NO. AWARDS: Varies.

APPLICATION INFO:
Application information is available online.
Duration: Varies.
Deadline: January 31.

THE NATIONAL RESTAURANT ASSOCIATION EDUCATIONAL FOUNDATION

2055 L Street, N.W.
Washington, DC 20036
(202) 973-3672
E-mail: scholars@nraef.org
Web Site: www.chooserestaurants.
org/scholarships

TYPE:
Scholarships. Provides scholarships for
students who are pursuing an education and
career in the foodservice industry.

See entry 2461 for full listing.

PHI CHI THETA EDUCATIONAL FOUNDATION   [1741]

1508 East Beltline Road, Suite 104
Carrollton, TX 75006
(972) 245-7202
E-mail: foundationinfo@phichitheta.org
Web Site: www.phichitheta.org/foundation

FOUNDED: 1999

AREAS OF INTEREST:
Business and economics.

NAME(S) OF PROGRAMS:
● **Educational and Scholastic
Advancement Programs**

TYPE:
Scholarships. Grants.

YEAR PROGRAM STARTED: 2000

PURPOSE:
To provide scholarships and grants to
members of the Phi Chi Theta Fraternity.

LEGAL BASIS:
Public charity, 501(c)(3) organization.

ELIGIBILITY:
Open to students who are members of Phi
Chi Theta in approved courses in colleges
and universities in the U.S. leading to
Bachelor's, Master's or doctoral degrees in
the fields of business administration and/or
economics. Applicants must have completed
at least one semester of college-level study.
Selection is based on scholastic achievement,
motivation, leadership potential and financial
need.

GEOG. RESTRICTIONS: United States.

FINANCIAL DATA:
Amount of support per award: $500 to
$1,000.
Total amount of support: Varies.

NO. MOST RECENT APPLICANTS: Over 20.

NO. AWARDS: Varies.

APPLICATION INFO:
Applicants must submit an official transcript
and two letters of recommendation.
Duration: One year. Nonrenewable.
Deadline: May 1.

PUBLICATIONS:
Application guidelines.

IRS I.D.: 31-1672618

OFFICERS:
Melissa Bolin, President
Mary Ellen Lewis, Treasurer

PROSPANICA
2711 LBJ Freeway
Suite 800
Dallas, TX 75234
(877) 467-4622
E-mail: info@prospanica.org
Web Site: www.prospanica.org

TYPE:
Awards/prizes; Conferences/seminars;
Scholarships.

See entry 925 for full listing.

CHARLES SCHWAB FOUNDATION [1742]
211 Main Street, SF211 MN-16-205
San Francisco, CA 94105-1905
E-mail: charlesschwabfoundation@schwab.com
Web Site: www.aboutschwab.com/citizenship
www.schwabmoneywise.com

FOUNDED: 1993

AREAS OF INTEREST:
Financial literacy and cultural and social
needs.

NAME(S) OF PROGRAMS:
● **Schwab Moneywise™**

TYPE:
General operating grants; Matching gifts;
Project/program grants. The Charles Schwab
Foundation awards strategic financial support
through direct grants to selected nonprofit
organizations that respond to local cultural
and social needs or support Schwab's
commitment to financial literacy. These
grants provide employees with a voice and
role in supporting the community groups they
care about most.

YEAR PROGRAM STARTED: 1993

PURPOSE:
To give back to communities by supporting
employee-selected causes and fostering
financial literacy through funding,
involvement and expertise.

LEGAL BASIS:
Corporate foundation.

ELIGIBILITY:
The Foundation provides direct grants to
select nonprofit organizations that support
Schwab's commitment to financial literacy
and respond to local cultural and social
needs.

Applicants must meet at least one of the
following selection criteria:
(1) be recommended by a Schwab employee
who is an active volunteer in the
organization;
(2) be performing community work that
corresponds to the Foundation's initiatives or;
(3) promote financial capability.

Greater consideration will be given to those
organizations that already have Schwab
employee volunteer involvement. The more
employees involved, the greater the
opportunity to be considered for a direct
grant.

To qualify for a direct grant, an organization
must:
(1) be based in the U.S. or one of its
territories;
(2) be recognized as a tax-exempt public
charity under Section 501(c)(3) of the U.S.
Internal Revenue Code (per Section 170)
and;
(3) (if an educational institution) be

accredited by a regional accrediting
association or by a recognized independent
accrediting group.

GEOG. RESTRICTIONS: United States.

FINANCIAL DATA:
Total amount of support: More than
$8,500,000 given annually to directly support
nonprofit organizations; $4,100,000 given in
employee gifts and matching donations in
2018.

NO. AWARDS: 2,467 nonprofit organizations
received financial support in 2018.

APPLICATION INFO:
The Foundation is currently accepting grant
requests by invitation only.
Deadline: Proposals are reviewed on a
quarterly basis.

PUBLICATIONS:
Program brochure with application
guidelines.

IRS I.D.: 94-1737782

ADDRESS INQUIRIES TO:
Direct Grant Program
(See address above.)

SIMON FRASER UNIVERSITY [1743]
Maggie Benston Student Services Centre 1100
8888 University Drive
Burnaby BC V5A 1S6 Canada
(778) 782-3042
Fax: (778) 782-3080
E-mail: gradstdy@sfu.ca
Web Site: www.sfu.ca/dean-gradstudies.html

NAME(S) OF PROGRAMS:
● **SFU Graduate Fellowships**

TYPE:
Fellowships.

PURPOSE:
To offer financial support to the University's
students enrolled in a Master's or Ph.D.
program.

ELIGIBILITY:
Open to current or entering Master's or Ph.D.
program students with a grade point average
of 3.5 or above.

FINANCIAL DATA:
Amount of support per award: $3,250 to
$6,500 (CAN).

APPLICATION INFO:
Eligible students apply through their
department of enrollment by completing an
application through the Graduate Award
Application and Adjudication System.
Duration: One term or more. Must reapply.
Deadline: Varies.

ADDRESS INQUIRIES TO:
Specific Department of Enrollment
Simon Fraser University
(Request specific department's address.)

SOCIETY OF ACTUARIES (SOA)
475 North Martingale Road
Suite 600
Schaumburg, IL 60173-2226
(847) 706-3509
Fax: (847) 273-8605
E-mail: ttatsumi@soa.org
Web Site: www.soa.org/doctoral-stipend

TYPE:
Awards/prizes; Scholarships. Society of
Actuaries' James C. Hickman Scholar

Doctoral Stipend Program is designed to
provide stipends to doctoral students who
will, through their studies, address research
and education needs of the profession,
including both the theoretical and practical
aspects.

See entry 1914 for full listing.

SOCIETY OF ACTUARIES (SOA)
475 North Martingale Road
Suite 600
Schaumburg, IL 60173-2226
(847) 706-3509
Fax: (847) 273-8605
E-mail: ttatsumi@soa.org
Web Site: www.soa.org/education/resources/edu-
institution-grant/default.aspx

TYPE:
Awards/prizes; Development grants; General
operating grants; Project/program grants;
Research grants; Scholarships; Travel grants.
Grants to educational institutions.

See entry 1915 for full listing.

U.S. DEPARTMENT OF EDUCATION [1744]
400 Maryland Avenue, S.W.
Washington, DC 20024
(202) 453-7521
E-mail: timothy.duvall@ed.gov
Web Site: www2.ed.
gov/programs/iegpscibe/index.html

AREAS OF INTEREST:
International business education.

CONSULTING OR VOLUNTEER SERVICES:
Offers technical assistance.

NAME(S) OF PROGRAMS:
● **Centers for International Business
Education Program**

TYPE:
Project/program grants. The program
provides grants to eligible institutions of
higher education or combinations of these
institutions for planning, establishing and
operating Centers for International Business
Education.

YEAR PROGRAM STARTED: 1989

PURPOSE:
To provide funding to U.S. institutions of
higher education for curriculum development,
research, and training on issues of
importance to U.S. trade and competitiveness.

LEGAL BASIS:
Government agency.

ELIGIBILITY:
An applicant must be a U.S. institution of
higher education or a combination of such
institutions that establishes a Center Advisory
Council prior to the date that federal
assistance is received. The Center Advisory
Council shall conduct extensive planning
prior to the establishment of the Center for
International Business Education concerning
the scope of the Center's activities and the
design of its programs. Programs and
activities to be conducted by Centers for
International Business Education must meet
the programmatic requirements listed above.

FINANCIAL DATA:
Grant funds may be used to pay the federal
share of costs of faculty and staff travel in
foreign areas, regions or countries, teaching
and research materials, curriculum planning
and development, bringing visiting scholars

and faculty to the center to teach or to conduct research, training and improvement of the staff for the purpose of and subject to such conditions as the Secretary finds necessary for carrying out the objectives of this program and other costs consistent with planning, establishing or operating a center.

Amount of support per award: $305,000 average award for fiscal year 2018.

Total amount of support: $4,571,400 for fiscal year 2018.

NO. MOST RECENT APPLICANTS: 26.

NO. AWARDS: Approximately 15.

APPLICATION INFO:
The Department of Education provides an application package upon request to the Office of Postsecondary Education. Applications become available in May.

Duration: Four years.

Deadline: June. Competition held every four years.

PUBLICATIONS:
Application guidelines; abstracts of grantees.

ADDRESS INQUIRIES TO:
Tim Duvall, Ph.D.
(See address above.)

THE UNIVERSITY OF CALGARY

Faculty of Graduate Studies
Earth Sciences Building, Room 1010
2500 University Drive, N.W.
Calgary AB T2N 1N4 Canada
(403) 220-4938
Fax: (403) 289-7635
E-mail: gsaward@ucalgary.ca
Web Site: grad.ucalgary.ca/awards

TYPE:
Awards/prizes; Scholarships. Awards for study in the fields of business, management and related areas. Tenable at the University of Calgary. Awards are endowed through gifts from John Labatt Limited and ScotiaMcLeod Inc. Matching grants provided from the Province of Alberta's Advanced Education Endowment Fund.

See entry 1619 for full listing.

UNIVERSITY OF NEBRASKA AT OMAHA   [1745]

Mammel Hall, Room 300
6708 Pine Street
Omaha, NE 68182-0048
(402) 554-2341
E-mail: mba@unomaha.edu
Web Site: cba.unomaha.edu/mba

AREAS OF INTEREST:
UNO MBA Program and MS Economics.

NAME(S) OF PROGRAMS:
● **UNO Graduate Assistantships**

TYPE:
Assistantships. Graduate, MBA scholarships in all subjects.

ELIGIBILITY:
Graduate assistantships are available for qualified students who are enrolled in a graduate degree program in the College of Business Administration.

FINANCIAL DATA:
Amount of support per award: Waiver of tuition costs for a minimum of six semester-hours of graduate credit per semester up to a maximum of 12.

NO. MOST RECENT APPLICANTS: Varies.

NO. AWARDS: Varies.

APPLICATION INFO:
Applicants should complete the Graduate Assistantship application that is available on the web site. Application must be submitted to the e-mail address above, along with a resume and letters of recommendation.

Deadline: Varies.

THE DEAN WITTER FOUNDATION   [1746]

57 Post Street, Suite 510
San Francisco, CA 94104
(415) 981-2966
Fax: (415) 981-5218
E-mail: admin@deanwitterfoundation.org
Web Site: www.deanwitterfoundation.org

FOUNDED: 1952

AREAS OF INTEREST:
Research and higher education in finance, wildlife research and conservation projects, and K-12 education.

TYPE:
Challenge/matching grants; Fellowships; General operating grants; Internships; Matching gifts; Professorships; Project/program grants; Research grants; Scholarships; Seed money grants.

YEAR PROGRAM STARTED: 1952

PURPOSE:
To help fund research and higher education in areas of special interest to the Foundation, as well as K-12 education.

LEGAL BASIS:
Private foundation.

ELIGIBILITY:
Grants are made to tax-exempt 501(c)(3) institutions. No grants are made to individuals.

GEOG. RESTRICTIONS: Northern California.

FINANCIAL DATA:
Amount of support per award: $10,000 to $25,000.

Total amount of support: Approximately $3,500,000.

NO. AWARDS: 10.

APPLICATION INFO:
The Foundation does not accept unsolicited proposals.

Duration: One year. Renewal possible.

OFFICERS AND TRUSTEES:
Dean Witter, III, Chairman
Malcolm G. Witter, President
Allison Frey, Secretary
Brooke Witter, Trustee

ADDRESS INQUIRIES TO:
Kenneth J. Blum, Administrative Director
(See address above.)

*PLEASE NOTE:
The Foundation does not accept unsolicited proposals.

ZONTA INTERNATIONAL FOUNDATION   [1747]

1200 Harger Road, Suite 330
Oak Brook, IL 60523
(630) 928-1400
Fax: (630) 928-1559
E-mail: programs@zonta.org
Web Site: www.zonta.org

FOUNDED: 1919

AREAS OF INTEREST:
Financial support for women of any nationality pursuing degrees in business leading to a business management career.

NAME(S) OF PROGRAMS:
● **Jane M. Klausman Women in Business Scholarships**

TYPE:
Awards/prizes; Scholarships. For women of any nationality pursuing degrees in business who demonstrate outstanding potential in the field of business.

YEAR PROGRAM STARTED: 1998

PURPOSE:
To provide financial support for women of any nationality pursuing degrees in business leading to a business management career.

LEGAL BASIS:
Incorporated in the state of Illinois as a nonprofit organization.

ELIGIBILITY:
Applicant must meet the following minimum requirements:
(1) be undertaking a business and/or business-related program at an accredited university, college or institute;
(2) be enrolled in at least the second year of an undergraduate program through the final year of a Master's program at the time the application is submitted (applicants must still be attending school to receive this award in November);
(3) have achieved an outstanding academic record during her academic studies, including business-related subjects;
(4) have demonstrated initiative, ambition and commitment to pursuing a career in business and;
(5) be living or studying in a Zonta region/district.

FINANCIAL DATA:
The scholarship award may be used for tuition, books or living expenses at any university, college or institution offering accredited business courses and degrees.

Amount of support per award: Up to $2,000 at the District Level and 6 international scholarships for $8,000.

Total amount of support: Varies.

NO. MOST RECENT APPLICANTS: Varies.

NO. AWARDS: Up to 32.

APPLICATION INFO:
Applications must be completed in English. English translations must accompany all non-English documents. The Jane M. Klausman Women in Business Scholarship program operates at the club, district and international levels of Zonta International. To apply, contact the Zonta Club within the applicant's district/region for deadlines and an address to mail application. (Such contact information is also available on the web site.) Alternatively, one can e-mail one's name and contact information to Zonta International Headquarters at the address above. Applicants must be nominated by a local Zonta Club first.

Deadline: Must contact Zonta Club for deadlines.

ADDRESS INQUIRIES TO:
Programs Coordinator
(See e-mail address above.)

Communications

AMERICAN ASSOCIATION FOR THE ADVANCEMENT OF SCIENCE   [1748]

1200 New York Avenue, N.W.
Washington, DC 20005
(202) 326-6744
E-mail: mmfellowship@aaas.org
Web Site: www.aaas.org/programs/mass-media-fellowship

FOUNDED: 1848

AREAS OF INTEREST:
Science-related issues in the media and public understanding and appreciation of science technology.

NAME(S) OF PROGRAMS:
● **Mass Media Science and Engineering Fellows Program**

TYPE:
Fellowships. Fellowships to support undergraduates, graduate students, and postdoctorates in the fields of social, natural and physical sciences, mathematics, and engineering during the summer as reporters in mass media organizations nationwide. Fellows will have the opportunity to observe and participate in the process by which events and ideas become news, improve their communication skills by learning to describe complex technical subjects in a manner understandable to the lay public, and increase their understanding of editorial decision making and the way in which information is effectively disseminated.

Each fellow will work for a specific media organization. Some will work for newspapers or magazines on news and feature writing assignments. Others may be involved in television or radio production.

YEAR PROGRAM STARTED: 1974

PURPOSE:
To strengthen the relationship between science and technology and the media and to enhance coverage of science-related issues in the media in order to improve public understanding and appreciation of science and technology.

LEGAL BASIS:
Nonprofit association.

ELIGIBILITY:
Applicants must be currently enrolled as a science student (undergraduate or graduate), be a postdoctoral researcher, or be within one year of completion of any of the above. Applicants must be eligible to work in the U.S.

FINANCIAL DATA:
Fellowships include a stipend, travel costs to and from the media site, and travel and expenses to attend pre- and post-fellowship gatherings in Washington, DC.
Amount of support per award: $7,000.

NO. MOST RECENT APPLICANTS: Approximately 150.

NO. AWARDS: Approximately 25.

APPLICATION INFO:
In addition to the completed application form, candidates must submit a current resume, two writing samples, brief answers to application prompts, and at least two letters of recommendation. Applicants should be available for a telephone interview in March and be able to accept assignments anywhere in the U.S.

Duration: 10 weeks in the summer.
Deadline: January 1. Announcement in April.

STAFF:
Kristin Lewis, Project Director

ADDRESS INQUIRIES TO:
Kristin Lewis, Project Director
Mass Media Science and Engineering Fellows Program
(See address above.)

AMERICAN ASSOCIATION FOR THE ADVANCEMENT OF SCIENCE   [1749]

1200 New York Avenue, N.W.
Washington, DC 20005
(202) 326-6431
E-mail: sja@aaas.org
Web Site: sjawards.aaas.org

FOUNDED: 1848

AREAS OF INTEREST:
Science and engineering.

NAME(S) OF PROGRAMS:
● **AAAS Kavli Science Journalism Awards**

TYPE:
Awards/prizes. Global awards for stories of life, physical and social sciences, engineering and mathematics, published in newspapers, general magazines, aired on radio or podcasts, on video, and online. Entries should be intended for general, nontechnical audiences. There is also an award recognizing excellence in science news reporting for children. Since 2015, the contest has been open to journalists worldwide in all categories.

YEAR PROGRAM STARTED: 1945

PURPOSE:
To encourage newspaper, magazine, audio, video and online science writing.

LEGAL BASIS:
Nonprofit scientific organization.

ELIGIBILITY:
Qualified individuals may apply with appropriate single stories or series published in newspapers or general circulation magazines, or aired on podcasts, radio or video, and online. Awards may not be presented to the same entrant in any two consecutive years, and individuals who have already won three of the annual awards are no longer eligible to apply.

FINANCIAL DATA:
Amount of support per award: Gold Award: $5,000; Silver Award: $3,500.
Total amount of support: $68,000.

CO-OP FUNDING PROGRAMS: Sponsored by The Kavli Foundation.

NO. MOST RECENT APPLICANTS: 1,100.

NO. AWARDS: 16 for the 2020 contest year. Two each for eight categories, including large newspaper, small newspaper, magazine, video in-depth reporting, video spot news/feature reporting, audio, online and children's science news.

APPLICATION INFO:
Online application information and FAQ can be found at the web site.
Deadline: August 1.

OFFICERS:
Dr. Sudip Parikh, Chief Executive Officer

ADDRESS INQUIRIES TO:
Earl Lane, Executive Director
AAAS Kavli Science Journalism Awards
(See address above.)

AMERICAN POLITICAL SCIENCE ASSOCIATION

1527 New Hampshire Avenue, N.W.
Washington, DC 20036
(202) 483-2512
Fax: (202) 483-2657
E-mail: cfp@apsanet.org
Web Site: www.apsanet.org/cfp

TYPE:
Fellowships. Awards to political science professors and journalists in early-career to midcareer status; the award provides an opportunity for support as a full-time aide to a member of the House or Senate or as a staff member for a Congressional committee.

See entry 1811 for full listing.

BENTON FOUNDATION   [1750]

727 Chicago Avenue
Evanston, IL 60202
(847) 328-3040
E-mail: info@benton.org
Web Site: www.benton.org

FOUNDED: 1948

AREAS OF INTEREST:
The use of media and information technology in solving social problems and strengthening communities.

NAME(S) OF PROGRAMS:
● **Media Policy and Public Service Media**

TYPE:
Technical assistance. Program is funded for preserving, protecting and strengthening the public benefits in America's media environment.

PURPOSE:
To articulate a public-interest vision for the digital age and to demonstrate the value of communications for solving social problems; to leverage media and technology in innovative ways as a means to strengthen communities.

LEGAL BASIS:
501(c)(3) private foundation.

FINANCIAL DATA:
Amount of support per award: $500 to $5,000.

APPLICATION INFO:
By invitation only. The Foundation does not accept unsolicited grant applications.
Deadline: Varies.

ADDRESS INQUIRIES TO:
Adrianne Benton Furniss, Executive Director
(See address above.)

BROADCAST EDUCATION ASSOCIATION   [1751]

One M Street, S.E.
Washington, DC 20003
(202) 602-0587
Fax: (202) 609-9940
E-mail: help@beaweb.org
Web Site: www.beaweb.org

FOUNDED: 1923

AREAS OF INTEREST:
Electronic media.

NAME(S) OF PROGRAMS:
- **John Bayliss Scholarship Award**
- **BEA Founders Award**
- **Richard Eaton Foundation Award**
- **Library of American Broadcasting Foundation Award**
- **Peter B. Orlik Award**
- **Abe Voron Award**
- **Vincent T. Wasilewski Award**

TYPE:
Scholarships. BEA is the professional development association for professors, industry professionals and students involved in teaching and research related to radio, television and other electronic media. BEA administers scholarships annually, to honor broadcasters and the entire electronic media profession.

John Bayliss and Abe Voron Awards: Study toward a career in radio.

BEA Founders, Richard Eaton, Peter B. Orlik and Vincent T. Wasilewski Awards: Study in any electronic media area. (Wasilewski Award is for graduate students only.)

Library of American Broadcasting Foundation Award is for graduate students focusing on broadcast history.

For the BEA Founders Award, preference is given to students enrolled in a BEA Two-Year/Small College Member Institution or graduates of these programs now enrolled in a BEA Four-Year Institution.

All other scholarships are awarded to juniors, seniors and graduate students at BEA Member institutions.

YEAR PROGRAM STARTED: 1962

PURPOSE:
To secure mutual advantages that flow from a continuing relationship between broadcasters and institutions of higher learning which offer a high standard of training and guidance for those who plan to enter the electronic media.

LEGAL BASIS:
Private association.

ELIGIBILITY:
Scholarships will be awarded for full-time degree work for the full academic year. One-semester grants are not made. Scholarships must be used exclusively for tuition, student fees, university bookstore course purchases, dormitory and related items eligible to be charged to a student's official campus account. Current scholarship holders are not eligible to reapply in the year following their award. All scholarships must be applied to study at a campus where at least one department is a BEA institutional member. Applicant can visit the Association web site (click on "Scholarship") or phone (at the number above) to verify that one's campus is a member.

The applicant should be able to show substantial evidence of superior academic performance and potential to be an outstanding electronic media professional. There should be compelling evidence that the applicant possesses high integrity and a well-articulated sense of personal and professional responsibility.

FINANCIAL DATA:
Amount of support per award: John Bayliss and Richard Eaton Foundation Awards: $2,500 each; BEA Founders Award: $1,500 each; Library of American Broadcasting Foundation, Orlik and Voron Awards: $3,000 each; Wasilewski Award: $4,000.

Total amount of support: $53,000 for the year 2021-22.

NO. MOST RECENT APPLICANTS: 50 to 100.

NO. AWARDS: Bayliss, Eaton, Library of American Broadcasting Foundation, Orlik and Wasilewski Awards: 1 each; BEA Founders Award: 2; Voron Award: 3.

APPLICATION INFO:
Application forms are available online. Application must be typed to be considered. Each copy of the application must be collated and securely stapled. The forms ask for personal and academic data and transcripts, media and other experience, a written statement of goals, and supportive statements from two references, at least one of which must be an electronic media faculty member.

Submit four completed copies of the application. Each copy should include, in order:
(1) typed application form;
(2) transcript(s) from all collegiate institutions;
(3) two letters of recommendation and;
(4) thesis or dissertation proposal abstract (if applying for the LAB Scholarship).
Do not send disk, tapes, resumes, photos, etc. These will not be considered by the committee. No faxed or e-mailed material will be accepted.

Completed applications should be sent to:
Dr. Peter B. Orlik
BEA Scholarship Committee Chair
613 Kane Street
Mount Pleasant, MI 48858
E-mail: orlik1pb@cmich.edu

Duration: One full-time academic year.

Deadline: Application forms and materials must be received by Dr. Orlik by the close of business on October 15.

PUBLICATIONS:
Journal of Broadcasting & Electronic Media; *Journal of Education Media*; *Journal of Radio Studies*.

ADDRESS INQUIRIES TO:
Dr. Peter B. Orlik, Scholarships
613 Kane Street
Mount Pleasant, MI 48858
E-mail: orlik1pb@cmich.edu
(See address above.)

*PLEASE NOTE:
Due to the large volume of scholarship-related business, phone calls cannot be returned.

*SPECIAL STIPULATIONS:
All scholarships must be applied to study at a campus where at least one department is a BEA institutional member. Applications listing ineligible schools will be disqualified.

BROADCAST EDUCATION ASSOCIATION [1752]
One M Street, S.E.
Washington, DC 20003
(202) 602-0587
Fax: (202) 609-9940
E-mail: help@beaweb.org
Web Site: www.beaweb.org

FOUNDED: 1923

AREAS OF INTEREST:
Electronic media.

NAME(S) OF PROGRAMS:
- **PILOT Media Technology and Innovation Scholarships**

TYPE:
Scholarships. PILOT Media Technology and Innovation Scholarships are awarded to college sophomores, juniors, seniors entering graduate school and graduate students for pursuit of studies related to media technology and innovation.

PURPOSE:
To secure mutual advantages that flow from a continuing relationship between broadcasters and institutions of higher learning which offer a high standard of training and guidance for those who plan to enter the electronic media.

LEGAL BASIS:
Private association.

ELIGIBILITY:
Applicant must be a current college sophomore, junior, senior entering graduate school or continuing graduate student pursuing studies related to media technology and innovation. Eligible academic areas include broadcast television or radio engineering/technology, sports media production or other broadcast content creation, web/online media, mobile media, media-related information technology, audience measurement and media technology research.

FINANCIAL DATA:
Amount of support per award: $5,000.

Total amount of support: Up to $25,000 for the year 2020-21.

NO. AWARDS: Up to 5.

APPLICATION INFO:
Application form requires the following information:
(1) personal contact information;
(2) academic history;
(3) supportive statements from two references;
(4) a 250-word statement of career goals;
(5) listing of relevant accomplishments and experience and;
(6) college transcripts.

Duration: One full-time academic year.

Deadline: October 14.

PUBLICATIONS:
Journal of Broadcasting & Electronic Media; *Journal of Education Media*; *Journal of Radio Studies*.

ADDRESS INQUIRIES TO:
Traci Bailey
Manager, Business Operations
(See address above.)

*PLEASE NOTE:
Due to the large volume of scholarship-related business, phone calls cannot be returned.

COLUMBIA JOURNALISM SCHOOL [1753]
2950 Broadway
New York, NY 10027
(212) 854-6468
Fax: (212) 854-3148
E-mail: cm3443@columbia.edu
Web Site: journalism.columbia.edu/oakes

FOUNDED: 1960

AREAS OF INTEREST:
Environmental journalism.

NAME(S) OF PROGRAMS:
● **John B. Oakes Award**

TYPE:
Awards/prizes. Awarded for distinguished excellence in environmental journalism.

YEAR PROGRAM STARTED: 1993

ELIGIBILITY:
To be considered for this Award, submitted articles must have been written between January 1 and December 31 of previous year. The article must have been published in a U.S.-based publication. An online publication is acceptable.

GEOG. RESTRICTIONS: United States.

FINANCIAL DATA:
Amount of support per award: $5,000 and a certificate.

NO. AWARDS: 1 award yearly.

APPLICATION INFO:
Nomination instructions are available online. Entry fee of $50 required for each nomination (non-refundable).
Duration: Recipients of the Oakes Award can win it a second time.
Deadline: January 31.

ADDRESS INQUIRIES TO:
Caroline Wernecke
Assistant Director, Professional Prizes
(See address above.)

COLUMBIA JOURNALISM SCHOOL [1754]

2950 Broadway
New York, NY 10027-7004
(212) 854-6468
E-mail: cm3443@columbia.edu
Web Site: journalism.columbia.edu/berger

FOUNDED: 1960

NAME(S) OF PROGRAMS:
● **Mike Berger Award**

TYPE:
Awards/prizes. A newspaper competition, covering the previous calendar year, open to reporters nationwide.

YEAR PROGRAM STARTED: 1960

PURPOSE:
To honor distinguished newspaper reporting in the tradition of the late Meyer Berger of the New York Times.

LEGAL BASIS:
University.

ELIGIBILITY:
All newspaper reporters across the country are eligible whether they report for dailies, weeklies, monthlies, newspaper magazines, radio broadcast, digital reporting or online publications. Members of the ethnic press should submit copies of original stories with an English translation.

FINANCIAL DATA:
Winners receive a cash award along with a certificate and hotel and travel expenses to New York.
Amount of support per award: $1,500.

NO. AWARDS: 1 annually.

APPLICATION INFO:
Nominations are solicited from the editors of all daily newspapers across the country, as well as ethnic, weekly and online publications. Judges request that a nominating exhibit include two copies of a

letter from the editor, a brief biographical resume of the reporter, and two copies of not more than five clippings.
Deadline: Early March. Notification in the spring. Presented at Columbia University in May.

ADDRESS INQUIRIES TO:
Caroline Wernecke
Assistant Director, Professional Prizes
(See address above.)

COLUMBIA JOURNALISM SCHOOL [1755]

2950 Broadway
New York, NY 10027
(212) 854-5047
Fax: (212) 854-3148
E-mail: lm3105@columbia.edu
Web Site: journalism.columbia.edu/cabot

AREAS OF INTEREST:
Journalism and inter-American relations.

NAME(S) OF PROGRAMS:
● **Maria Moors Cabot Prizes**

TYPE:
Awards/prizes. The prize program recognizes distinguished journalistic contributions to inter-American understanding. Prizes are awarded annually by the Trustees of Columbia University on recommendations made by the Dean of the Graduate School of Journalism and the Cabot Board.

YEAR PROGRAM STARTED: 1938

PURPOSE:
To recognize sustained and distinguished contributions of journalists to the advancement of understanding among the peoples of the Western Hemisphere.

LEGAL BASIS:
University.

ELIGIBILITY:
Although awards have been made to publishers or others in managerial positions, the board is particularly interested in working journalists throughout the Americas whose writings or broadcasts have contributed to mutual understanding and freedom of the press over a period of time.

GEOG. RESTRICTIONS: Western Hemisphere.

FINANCIAL DATA:
Amount of support per award: $5,000 and a Cabot medal, plus round-trip transportation to Columbia University for the award ceremonies.

NO. AWARDS: 5 for the year 2019.

APPLICATION INFO:
The Committee appreciates the submission of at least five, but no more than 10, newspaper or magazine articles, television or radio programs or Internet stories that are representative of the nominee's work. Complete nomination instructions are available online.
Deadline: March 16.

ADDRESS INQUIRIES TO:
Lauren Meregildo-Santos
Program Coordinator
(See address above.)

COLUMBIA UNIVERSITY [1756]

Graduate School of Journalism
2950 Broadway, Mail Code 3850
New York, NY 10027
(212) 854-2711
E-mail: ann.grimes@columbia.edu
Web Site: www.journalism.columbia.edu/kb

FOUNDED: 1975

AREAS OF INTEREST:
Economics and business journalism for midcareer journalists.

NAME(S) OF PROGRAMS:
● **Knight-Bagehot Fellowship in Economics and Business Journalism**

TYPE:
Awards/prizes; Fellowships. Awarded to midcareer professional journalists to study business and economics at Columbia University.

YEAR PROGRAM STARTED: 1975

PURPOSE:
To improve the quality of business and economics journalism.

LEGAL BASIS:
University-affiliated fellowship program.

ELIGIBILITY:
Applicants must have at least four years' experience in journalism.

FINANCIAL DATA:
The Fellowship includes free tuition plus a stipend to cover living expenses.
Amount of support per award: Up to $60,000.

NO. AWARDS: Up to 10.

APPLICATION INFO:
Application information is available online.
Duration: One academic year.
Deadline: February 15.

PUBLICATIONS:
Annual report.

ADDRESS INQUIRIES TO:
Ann Grimes, Director
Knight-Bagehot Fellowship
(See address above.)

COLUMBIA UNIVERSITY [1757]

709 Pulitzer Hall
2950 Broadway
New York, NY 10027
(212) 854-3841
E-mail: pulitzer@pulitzer.org
Web Site: www.pulitzer.org

FOUNDED: 1917

AREAS OF INTEREST:
Excellence in journalism, books, drama and music.

NAME(S) OF PROGRAMS:
● **Pulitzer Fellowships**
● **Pulitzer Prizes**

TYPE:
Awards/prizes; Fellowships. Awards in journalism, books and music.

Pulitzer Prizes in Journalism are awarded based on material appearing in a text-based U.S. newspaper or news site that publishes at least once a week during the year. Awards given for:
(1) meritorious public service by a newspaper through the use of its journalistic resources which may include editorials, cartoons, photographs, graphics and online material;

(2) local, state or national reporting of breaking news;

(3) investigative reporting by an individual or team, presented as a single article or series;

(4) explanatory journalism that illuminates a significant or complex subject, demonstrating mastery of the subject, lucid writing and clear presentation;

(5) reporting on significant issues of local concern;

(6) reporting on national affairs;

(7) reporting on international affairs, including United Nations correspondence;

(8) feature writing giving prime consideration to high literary quality and originality;

(9) commentary;

(10) criticism;

(11) editorial writing;

(12) cartoon or portfolio of cartoons;

(13) breaking news photography in black and white or color, which may consist of a photograph or photographs, a sequence or an album;

(14) feature photography in black and white or color with the same stipulations as above and;

(15) audio journalism that serves the public interest.

Prizes in Letters are restricted to works first published in the U.S. during the year in book form and available for purchase by the general public. Awards given for:

(1) fiction by an American author, preferably dealing with American life;

(2) a play by an American author, preferably original in its source and dealing with American life, produced in the U.S. January 1 to December 31;

(3) appropriately documented book on the history of the U.S.;

(4) appropriately documented biography or autobiography by an American author;

(5) volume of original verse by an American author and;

(6) appropriately documented book of nonfiction by an American author that is not eligible for consideration in any other category.

A prize in music is given for distinguished musical composition by an American that has had its first performance in the U.S. during the year.

Four fellowships enable outstanding graduates to travel, report and study abroad. One fellowship is given to an outstanding graduate who wishes to specialize in drama, music, literary, film or television criticism.

YEAR PROGRAM STARTED: 1917

PURPOSE:
To recognize excellence in journalism, letters, drama and music.

LEGAL BASIS:
University.

ELIGIBILITY:
Competition for prizes is limited to work done during the calendar year ending December 31.

FINANCIAL DATA:
Amount of support per award: $7,500 for fellowships; $15,000 for prizes.

NO. AWARDS: Fellowships: 5; Prizes in Letters, Drama and Music: 7; Prizes in Journalism: 15.

APPLICATION INFO:
Application form and $75 handling fee required with entries.

Duration: One-time awards. Previous winners are eligible for consideration each year for any award.

Deadline: Prizes in Books: June 15 and October 1; Prizes in Drama and Prize in Music: December 31; Prizes in Journalism: Fourth Friday of January.

PUBLICATIONS:
Award announcement; brochure.

BOARD:
Elizabeth Alexander
Nancy Barnes
Robert Blau
Lee C. Bollinger
Katherine Boo
Neil Brown
Dana Canedy
Nicole Carroll
Steve Coll
Gail Collins
John Daniszewski
Stephen Engelberg
Aminda Marques Gonzales
Steven Hahn
Carlos Lozada
Emily Ramshaw
David Remnick
Tommy Shelby

ADDRESS INQUIRIES TO:
The Pulitzer Prize Board
(See address above.)

COUNCIL FOR THE ADVANCEMENT OF SCIENCE WRITING, INC. [1758]

P.O. Box 17337
Seattle, WA 98127
(206) 880-0177
E-mail: sylviakantor@casw.org
Web Site: www.casw.org

FOUNDED: 1959

AREAS OF INTEREST:
Writing about science, medicine, health, technology, energy, the environment, etc., for the general public via the mass media (distinct from technical writing or technical journalism).

NAME(S) OF PROGRAMS:
- **Evert Clark/Seth Payne Award for Young Science Journalists**
- **The Victor Cohn Prize for Excellence in Medical Science Reporting**
- **Rennie Taylor/Alton Blakeslee Fellowships for Graduate Study in Science Writing**

TYPE:
Awards/prizes; Fellowships. Evert Clark/Seth Payne Award recognizes outstanding reporting and writing in any field of science.

The Victor Cohn Prize salutes general excellence in medical science writing for the mass media. The prize, to be given annually, seeks to honor a writer for a body of work published or broadcast within the last five years which, for reasons of uncommon clarity, accuracy, breadth of coverage, enterprise, originality, insight and narrative power, has made a profound and lasting contribution to public awareness and understanding of critical advances in medical science and their impact on human health and well-being.

Rennie Taylor/Alton Blakeslee Fellowships support graduate students in science journalism and experienced reporters who wish to study science writing at the graduate level.

PURPOSE:
To increase public understanding of science by upgrading the quality and quantity of science and medical writing and by improving relationships between scientists and the press.

LEGAL BASIS:
Nonprofit 501(c)(3).

ELIGIBILITY:
Evert Clark/Seth Payne Award is limited to non-technical, print and online journalism. Articles published in newspapers (including college newspapers), magazines, newsletters and web sites are eligible. Both freelancers and staff writers are eligible. Books, as well as articles in technical journals and trade association publications, are not eligible. Entries will be judged on the basis of accuracy, clarity, insightfulness, fairness, resourcefulness, and timeliness. Applicants must be age 30 or younger.

The Victor Cohn Prize: Editors, colleagues, scientists and others familiar with the candidate's body of work may proffer nominations. Individuals may nominate themselves.

Rennie Taylor/Alton Blakeslee Fellowships: Journalists with two years of experience who wish to specialize in science writing will receive priority selection. Such applicants should be employed by daily newspapers, wire services, news magazines, radio stations, or television stations or networks. Students must have undergraduate degrees in science or journalism and prove to the satisfaction of a selection committee that they have the motivation and ability to pursue a career in science writing. Fellows may attend school full- or part-time.

Fellowships are not available to those who are pursuing or plan to pursue careers in public relations or public information work.

GEOG. RESTRICTIONS: United States.

FINANCIAL DATA:
Amount of support per award: Evert Clark/Seth Payne Award: $1,000 and expenses to attend ScienceWriters Conference; The Victor Cohn Prize: $3,000 and a framed certificate; Rennie Taylor/Alton Blakeslee Fellowships: $5,000.

NO. MOST RECENT APPLICANTS: Evert Clark/Seth Payne Award: 59; Rennie Taylor/Alton Blakeslee Fellowships: 27 for the year 2019.

NO. AWARDS: Evert Clark/Seth Payne Award and The Victor Cohn Prize: 1; Rennie Taylor/Alton Blakeslee Fellowships: 4 full fellowships and 2 half fellowships.

APPLICATION INFO:
Applicants must apply on the Council web site.

Duration: One academic year. Nonrenewable.

Deadline: Evert Clark/Seth Payne Award and The Victor Cohn Prize: June 30. Rennie Taylor/Alton Blakeslee Fellowships: March.

PUBLICATIONS:
Guide to Careers in Science Writing.

IRS I.D.: 13-1953314

OFFICERS AND DIRECTORS:
Alan Boyle, President

Robin Lloyd, Vice President
Richard Harris, Treasurer
Betsy Mason, Secretary
Rosalind Reid, Executive Director
Christie Aschwanden
Deborah Blum
William Kearney
Maggie Koerth
Celeste LeCompte
Thomas Lin
Tariq Malik
Charles Petit
Debbie Ponchner
Cristine Russell
Ashley·Smart
Kenneth P. Trevett
Dan Vergano

ADDRESS INQUIRIES TO:
Rosalind Reid, Executive Director
(See address above.)

*SPECIAL STIPULATIONS:
U.S. citizens only.

COUNCIL ON FOREIGN RELATIONS [1759]

58 East 68th Street
New York, NY 10065
(212) 434-9740
Fax: (212) 434-9870
E-mail: fellowships@cfr.org
Web Site: www.cfr.org/fellowships

FOUNDED: 1921

AREAS OF INTEREST:
International relations, international news, foreign policy, journalism, international journalism, war reporting, foreign affairs, international affairs, and international media.

NAME(S) OF PROGRAMS:
● **Edward R. Murrow Press Fellowship**

TYPE:
Fellowships. The Edward R. Murrow Press Fellow spends nine months full-time in residence at the Council on Foreign Relations' (CFR) headquarters in New York. The program enables the fellow to engage in sustained analysis and writing, expand his or her intellectual and professional horizons, and extensively participate in CFR's active program of meetings and events. The Fellow will be part of the David Rockefeller Studies Program, CFR's think tank, alongside the program's full-time, adjunct and visiting fellows, whose expertise extends across the broad range of significant foreign policy issues facing the U.S. and the international community.

YEAR PROGRAM STARTED: 1949

PURPOSE:
To promote the quality of responsible and discerning journalism that exemplified the work of Edward R. Murrow.

ELIGIBILITY:
The program is only open to applicants who have distinguished credentials in the field of journalism and who have covered international news as a working journalist for print, broadcast or online media widely available in the U.S. Applicants are limited to those individuals who are authorized to work in the U.S. and who will continue to be authorized for the duration of the Fellowship. CFR does not sponsor for visas.

FINANCIAL DATA:
The Fellow is considered an independent contractor rather than an employee of CFR, and is not eligible for employment benefits, including health insurance.
Amount of support per award: A stipend of $75,000, as well as a modest travel grant.

CO-OP FUNDING PROGRAMS: CBS Foundation and Ford Foundation.

NO. AWARDS: 1 per year.

APPLICATION INFO:
Interested candidates who meet the program's eligibility requirements can apply online between January 1 and March 1 on an annual basis.
Duration: Nine months, beginning in September.
Deadline: March 1. Official selections and announcement will be made in April.

ADDRESS INQUIRIES TO:
See telephone or e-mail address above.

THE DOW JONES NEWS FUND [1760]

4300 Route One North
Monmouth Junction, NJ 08852
(609) 452-2820
Fax: (609) 520-5804
E-mail: djnf@dowjones.com
Web Site: dowjonesnewsfund.org

FOUNDED: 1958

AREAS OF INTEREST:
Journalism.

NAME(S) OF PROGRAMS:
● **Multimedia Training Academies**
● **Summer High School Journalism Workshops**
● **Summer Journalism Intern Programs**

TYPE:
Internships. Multimedia Training Academies for professors at historically Black colleges and universities and Hispanic-serving institutions.

Paid Summer Journalism Intern Programs for college juniors, seniors and graduate students.

PURPOSE:
To encourage students to consider careers in copy-editing.

LEGAL BASIS:
Nonprofit foundation.

ELIGIBILITY:
Internships: Applicants must be juniors, seniors or graduate students at any college who have a sincere interest in professional copy-editing news work. Working on a school publication is not a stated requirement, but highly recommended. Applicants must also be U.S. citizens or have a working Visa permitting them to work in the U.S.

GEOG. RESTRICTIONS: United States.

FINANCIAL DATA:
Interns will receive regular wages (minimum $400 per week) from the newspapers for which they work. After the summer of work, a $1,000 scholarship check is awarded to the intern's college, but only if that intern returns to school following the internship.
Amount of support per award: Program grants: $3,000 to $25,000; Scholarships: $1,000.
Total amount of support: Approximately $350,000.

NO. MOST RECENT APPLICANTS: 900.

NO. AWARDS: Multimedia Training Academies: 25 college faculty; Scholarships: Up to 85; Workshops: 150 participants.

APPLICATION INFO:
Internships: Applications available online September 1 to November 1.
Duration: Internships: 11 to 13 weeks. Workshops and training programs: Five to 10 days. All programs occur during the summer.
Deadline: November 1.

OFFICERS:
Richard J. Levine, President
Paul Schmidt, Treasurer
Diana Mitsu Klos, Secretary

STAFF:
Linda Shockley, Managing Director
Denise Jester, Finance and Administration Manager
Heather Taylor, Digital Media and Programs Manager

DIRECTORS:
LaSharah S. Bunting
Thomas E. Engleman
Gail Griffin
Richard S. Holden
Garry D. Howard
Neal Lipschutz
Mark Musgrave
Laurence G. O'Donnell
Dr. Reginald Owens
Karen Miller Pensiero
Dr. Russell G. Todd

ADDRESS INQUIRIES TO:
Internship Coordinator
Editing Intern Programs
(See address above.)

FUND FOR INVESTIGATIVE JOURNALISM [1761]

1110 Vermont Avenue, N.W.
Suite 500
Washington, DC 20005
(202) 378-0953
E-mail: fundfij@gmail.com
Web Site: www.fij.org

FOUNDED: 1969

AREAS OF INTEREST:
Promoting the work of investigative journalism.

TYPE:
Project/program grants. The Fund gives grants to investigative reporters working outside the protection and backing of major news organizations.

PURPOSE:
To provide funding for reporters engaged in investigative journalism.

ELIGIBILITY:
Projects on domestic issues are eligible. To be considered, foreign-based story proposals must come from U.S.-based reporters or have a strong U.S. angle involving American citizens, government or business. All stories must be published in English and have a media outlet in the U.S.

FINANCIAL DATA:
Amount of support per award: Up to $10,000.
Total amount of support: Varies.

APPLICATION INFO:
Applications are to be submitted online. Applicant must write a proposal letter outlining the story, what he or she expects to

prove, how this will be done, and the type of sources for the proof. For projects, include the anticipated completion date.

The letter must be supported by a resume, a detailed budget to justify the size of the grant, no more than two writing samples or one sample chapter in the case of a book applicant, and a letter of commitment from an editor or publisher or an executive of a broadcast news operation or online news outlet stating that the project will be published or broadcast if completed according to the proposal.

A letter of commitment is required for all applicants and is a nonnegotiable requirement. In the case of individuals seeking grants for books, a signed copy of a contract with a publisher is required and should be substituted for the commitment letter.

Deadline: Varies.

ADDRESS INQUIRIES TO:
Eric Ferrero, Executive Director
(See address above.)

WILLIAM RANDOLPH HEARST FOUNDATION [1762]

90 New Montgomery Street, Suite 1212
San Francisco, CA 94105
(415) 908-4565
(800) 841-7048 ext. 4565
Fax: (415) 243-0760
E-mail: jwatten@hearstfdn.org
Web Site: www.hearstawards.org

FOUNDED: 1948

AREAS OF INTEREST:
Writing, photojournalism, broadcast journalism and multimedia.

NAME(S) OF PROGRAMS:
• **Hearst Journalism Awards Program**

TYPE:
Awards/prizes; Scholarships. Awards to the top 10 winners of 14 monthly competitions: five writing, two photojournalism, one radio news coverage, two television news coverage and four multimedia. Entrants must be journalism majors attending one of the 105 accredited schools of journalism. The schools receive a matching grant.

YEAR PROGRAM STARTED: 1960

PURPOSE:
To provide support, encouragement and assistance to education in journalism at the undergraduate college level.

LEGAL BASIS:
Nonprofit foundation.

ELIGIBILITY:
Participation in the program is open only to journalism majors who are undergraduates at the colleges and universities that are members of the Association of Schools of Journalism and Mass Communication.

GEOG. RESTRICTIONS: United States.

FINANCIAL DATA:
Amount of support per award: $3,000 to $10,000, depending upon placement of winners.
Total amount of support: Over $700,000 for the year 2019-20.

NO. MOST RECENT APPLICANTS: 1,400.

NO. AWARDS: 150 scholarships and grants.

APPLICATION INFO:
Full application information may be obtained through individual departments of journalism at participating schools. A list of accredited schools is available at Hearst Foundation's San Francisco address.
Duration: Varies.
Deadline: Monthly during academic year.

STAFF:
Dino Dinovitz, Executive Director
Jan C. Watten, Program Director
Yasi Haerizadeh, Deputy Program Director

BOARD OF DIRECTORS:
William R. Hearst, III, President
James Asher
Annissa Balson
David Barrett
Frank A. Bennack, Jr.
John G. Conomikes
Lisa Hagerman
George R. Hearst, Jr.
Gilbert C. Maurer
Mark Miller
Virginia Randt
Mitchell Scherzer
Steven Swartz

ADDRESS INQUIRIES TO:
Jan C. Watten, Program Director
(See address above.)

THE SIDNEY HILLMAN FOUNDATION, INC. [1763]

330 West 42nd Street
Suite 900
New York, NY 10036
(646) 448-6413
E-mail: alex@hillmanfoundation.org
Web Site: www.hillmanfoundation.org

FOUNDED: 1950

AREAS OF INTEREST:
Civil liberties, civil rights, labor movement, social welfare, housing, economic security and international understanding.

NAME(S) OF PROGRAMS:
• **Hillman Prizes for Journalism**
• **Sidney Awards**

TYPE:
Awards/prizes. Monetary awards for outstanding contributions in the fields of daily or periodical journalism, nonfiction, radio and television, blogs and commentary.

YEAR PROGRAM STARTED: 1950

PURPOSE:
To recognize outstanding contributions to the field of journalism dealing with themes relating to the ideals which Sidney Hillman held throughout his life, including the protection of individual civil liberties, improved race relations, a strengthened labor movement, the advancement of social welfare, housing and economic security, greater world understanding and related problems.

LEGAL BASIS:
Private foundation.

ELIGIBILITY:
Only work published in English in the previous calendar year and distributed in the U.S. and Canada is eligible for consideration. Radio and television contributions must have been produced under professional auspices in the previous calendar year.

GEOG. RESTRICTIONS: United States and Canada.

FINANCIAL DATA:
Amount of support per award: Hillman Prize: $5,000; Sidney Award: $500.

NO. MOST RECENT APPLICANTS: 600.

NO. AWARDS: Hillman Prizes: 7; Sidney Awards: 12.

APPLICATION INFO:
Nominations may be submitted by the author, editor or publication. The entry must be accompanied by a brief cover letter.
Deadline: Hillman Prizes: January 30. Sidney Awards: Last day of each month.

STAFF:
Alexandra Lescaze, Executive Director
Lindsay Beyerstein, Lead Writer

ADDRESS INQUIRIES TO:
Alexandra Lescaze, Executive Director
(See address above.)

INTER AMERICAN PRESS ASSOCIATION (IAPA) [1764]

3511 N.W. 91st Avenue
Miami, FL 33172
(305) 634-2465
Fax: (305) 860-4264
E-mail: info@sipiapa.org
Web Site: www.sipiapa.org

FOUNDED: 1942

AREAS OF INTEREST:
Press freedom.

NAME(S) OF PROGRAMS:
• **IAPA Scholarship Fund**

TYPE:
Exchange programs; Fellowships; Scholarships. Scholarships for American and Canadian working journalists, journalism graduates or journalism students to study in Latin America and for journalists who are citizens or residents of countries outside the U.S. or Canada to study in the U.S. or Canada.

YEAR PROGRAM STARTED: 1954

PURPOSE:
To support the exchange of journalists and journalism students between countries of the Western Hemisphere.

LEGAL BASIS:
Nonprofit association, tax-exempt under Internal Revenue Code 501(c)(3).

ELIGIBILITY:
Journalists or journalism school seniors or graduates between 21 and 35 years of age with a good command of the language they are to use. Students must have completed their degree before beginning the scholarship year.

Language ability for U.S. and Canadian candidates must be confirmed by a recognized authority in Spanish or Portuguese. Latin American candidates must take a TOEFL (Test of English as a Foreign Language).

FINANCIAL DATA:
Amount of support per award: U.S. and Canadian scholars will receive $20,000 for the duration of their stay abroad. Latin American and Caribbean scholars will receive $20,000 and a one-time round-trip airfare for the year.

NO. MOST RECENT APPLICANTS: 95.

NO. AWARDS: 4.

APPLICATION INFO:
Application is available on the web site or by writing to the Association.

Duration: One academic year.

Deadline: January 31.

STAFF:
Ricardo Trotti, Executive Director
Ed McCullough, Coordinator of Scholarship Fund

ADDRESS INQUIRIES TO:
Ed McCullough
Coordinator of Scholarship Fund
(See address above.)

INTERNATIONAL DOCUMENTARY ASSOCIATION
3600 Wilshire Boulevard
Suite 1810
Los Angeles, CA 90010
(213) 232-1660
Fax: (213) 232-1669
E-mail: grants@documentary.org
Web Site: www.documentary.org

TYPE:
Awards/prizes; Internships. IDA Documentary Awards celebrate the best nonfiction films and programs of the year. Prize awarded in seven categories: feature, short, episodic series, curated series, short film series, limited series, and the David L. Wolper Student Documentary Award.

IDA/David L. Wolper Student Documentary Achievement Award recognizes exceptional achievement in nonfiction film and video production at the university level and brings greater public and industry awareness to the work of students in the documentary field.

The Pare Lorentz Award is awarded for films that reflect the spirit and tradition of Pare Lorentz's work. The film should demonstrate one or more of Lorentz's central concerns (the appropriate use of the natural environment, justice for all, and the illumination of pressing social problems) presented as a compelling story by skillful filmmaking.

Pare Lorentz Documentary Fund supports full-length documentary films that reflect the spirit and nature of Pare Lorentz's work, exhibiting objective research, artful storytelling, strong visual style, high production values, artistic writing and outstanding music composition, as well as skillful direction, camerawork and editing.

Los Angeles County Arts Commission Internships are offered to undergraduate students who currently reside or are enrolled in a college or university located in Los Angeles County, CA. Those interested should consult the Association web site for up-to-date details.

See entry 424 for full listing.

INVESTIGATIVE REPORTERS AND EDITORS [1765]
141 Neff Annex
Missouri School of Journalism
Columbia, MO 65211
(573) 882-6668
Fax: (573) 882-5431
E-mail: rescntr@ire.org
Web Site: www.ire.org

FOUNDED: 1975

AREAS OF INTEREST:
Journalism across all media.

NAME(S) OF PROGRAMS:
● **Investigative Reporters and Editors Contest**

TYPE:
Awards/prizes; Fellowships. Investigative Reporters and Editors Contest is an annual investigative reporting contest. The Tom Renner Award (one of the 17 categories of this Contest) is given to the best investigative reporting in print, broadcast or book form, covering crime and its impact on society.

IRE also offers fellowships to minority journalism students and professionals to attend IRE national or regional conferences. There are also fellowships available for small newspaper staffers and for journalism students.

PURPOSE:
To promote high-quality, in-depth journalism.

LEGAL BASIS:
University.

ELIGIBILITY:
Individual journalists and news organizations may submit entries for the Renner Award. No more than 10 stories can be entered. Entries that disregard the rules will be disqualified. Qualifications for IRE minority fellowships include financial need, references and answers to essay questions.

FINANCIAL DATA:
Amount of support per award: Renner Award: $500; Student Award: $250.
Total amount of support: Varies.

NO. MOST RECENT APPLICANTS: 550.

NO. AWARDS: 17.

APPLICATION INFO:
All entry materials are entered online through the IRE Award contest platform. There is no limit on the number of entries allowed from individual journalists.
Deadline: Mid-January. Deadline for fellowships depends on conference dates.

PUBLICATIONS:
Program announcement; entry form.

IRS I.D.: 51-0166741

ADDRESS INQUIRIES TO:
Lauren Grandestaff, Contest Coordinator
(See address above.)

JOURNAL OF THE AMERICAN MEDICAL ASSOCIATION [1766]
330 North Wabash Avenue
Suite 39300
Chicago, IL 60611
(312) 464-4186
Fax: (312) 464-5824
E-mail: robert.golub@jamanetwork.org
Web Site: jamanetwork.org

FOUNDED: 1847

AREAS OF INTEREST:
Public health, physician and health care personnel education and medical publications.

NAME(S) OF PROGRAMS:
● **Morris Fishbein Fellowship in Medical Editing**

TYPE:
Fellowships. Award granted to physicians exclusively as a one-year, full-time editorial fellowship with *The Journal of the American Medical Association.* The successful candidate will work with the editorial and production staff in all facets of editing and publishing a major weekly medical journal. At the completion of the program, it is expected that the candidate will be proficient in all aspects of manuscript selection, peer review, issue makeup, copy editing and styling, issue planning and managing, in addition to the many other elements of medical journal publication.

YEAR PROGRAM STARTED: 1978

PURPOSE:
To provide physicians with an opportunity to learn the editorial functions of a major medical journal.

LEGAL BASIS:
Not-for-profit organization serving members in the medical profession.

ELIGIBILITY:
Applicants must be physicians. Candidates also must have proven writing ability at the time of application because they will be required during the course of the year to prepare articles for publication. Although the fellow will work under the supervision of a physician-editor, ability to work independently is a must. Ability to use a resource library is a strong plus.

Fellow must live in Chicago during the 12-month full-time fellowship (July to June).

FINANCIAL DATA:
Amount of support per award: $70,000.
Total amount of support: $70,000 annually.

NO. MOST RECENT APPLICANTS: 12.

NO. AWARDS: 1 annually.

APPLICATION INFO:
Application forms may be obtained from the address or e-mail listed above.
Duration: One year.
Deadline: Early January.

ADDRESS INQUIRIES TO:
Robert M. Golub, M.D., Deputy Editor
(See e-mail and address above.)

KAPPA TAU ALPHA [1767]
76 Gannett Hall
School of Journalism
University of Missouri
Columbia, MO 65211-1200
(573) 882-7685
E-mail: umcjourkta@missouri.edu
Web Site: www.kappataualpha.org

FOUNDED: 1910

AREAS OF INTEREST:
Journalism research and mass communication.

NAME(S) OF PROGRAMS:
● **Frank Luther Mott KTA Research/Book Award**

TYPE:
Awards/prizes. Annual award for a published book concerned with journalism and mass communications research.

YEAR PROGRAM STARTED: 1944

PURPOSE:
To recognize the top book published in the field of journalism and mass communications research; to promote interest in Kappa Tau Alpha among students and faculty.

LEGAL BASIS:
National society honoring scholarship in journalism and mass communication.

ELIGIBILITY:
Qualified individuals may apply for the award with an appropriate book published during the year.

FINANCIAL DATA:
Amount of support per award: $1,000 and a plaque.

NO. MOST RECENT APPLICANTS: 15 to 20 annually.

NO. AWARDS: 1 annually.

APPLICATION INFO:
Interested applicants should submit six copies of the published work to be considered.
Deadline: December 9.

OFFICERS:
Holly Hall, President
Edward Carter, Vice President
Beverly Horvit, Executive Director

JUDGES:
Edward Carter
Holly Hall
Beverly Horvit

ADDRESS INQUIRIES TO:
Beverly Horvit, Executive Director
(See address above.)

LIVINGSTON AWARDS [1768]

Wallace House, University of Michigan
620 Oxford Road
Ann Arbor, MI 48104
(734) 998-7575
Fax: (734) 998-7979
E-mail: livawards@umich.edu
Web Site: wallacehouse.umich.edu/livingston-awards

FOUNDED: 1981

AREAS OF INTEREST:
Broadcast, print and online journalism.

NAME(S) OF PROGRAMS:
● **Livingston Awards for Young Journalists**

TYPE:
Awards/prizes; Challenge/matching grants; Endowments.

YEAR PROGRAM STARTED: 1981

PURPOSE:
To recognize the best young journalists; to support the work of young journalists; to create modern role models for the next generation of news consumers; to advance excellence in journalism.

LEGAL BASIS:
Foundation.

ELIGIBILITY:
Entries must be directly related to current events or include new information about old events. Features and commentary are eligible. There are no awards for still photography.

Journalists who are 34 years old or younger as of December 31 and whose work appears in print, broadcast or online media may apply.

Submissions must consist of materials prepared in the ordinary course of the journalist's professional production. One entry per individual. Individuals may apply on their own, or be entered by their organization. Multiple bylines are eligible, but all must meet age criteria. Materials prepared by journalists specifically for submission to the Livingston Awards will not qualify and may not be considered. Student media are not eligible.

All entries will be judged on the basis of either a single piece, or in the case of series, a maximum of three related pieces.

FINANCIAL DATA:
Amount of support per award: $10,000.
Total amount of support: $30,000.

NO. AWARDS: 3.

APPLICATION INFO:
Detailed information is available online.
Deadline: February 1. Announcement in June.

PUBLICATIONS:
Program brochure.

STAFF:
Melissa Riley, Program Manager

ADDRESS INQUIRIES TO:
See e-mail address above.

THE GERALD LOEB AWARDS [1769]

UCLA Anderson School of Management
110 Westwood Plaza
Gold Hall, Suite B307
Los Angeles, CA 90095-1481
(310) 825-4478
Fax: (310) 825-4479
E-mail: loeb@anderson.ucla.edu
Web Site: www.anderson.ucla.edu/gerald-loeb-awards

FOUNDED: 1957

AREAS OF INTEREST:
Business, economic and financial news writing and journalism.

TYPE:
Awards/prizes. Awards to recognize business and financial journalists for important contributions to the understanding of business, finance and the economy.

YEAR PROGRAM STARTED: 1957

PURPOSE:
To recognize journalists who make significant contributions to the understanding of business and finance.

LEGAL BASIS:
University.

ELIGIBILITY:
Entries submitted must have been published or broadcast for the first time during the previous calendar year in the U.S.

FINANCIAL DATA:
Amount of support per award: $2,000; $500 Honorable Mention.

APPLICATION INFO:
Guidelines are available on the web site. Application must be submitted online.
Deadline: February 15.

PUBLICATIONS:
Entry brochure.

ADDRESS INQUIRIES TO:
Jonathan Daillak, Deputy Director of Administration and Development
(See address above.)

MASSACHUSETTS INSTITUTE OF TECHNOLOGY [1770]

77 Massachusetts Avenue
E19-623
Cambridge, MA 02139
(617) 452-3513
E-mail: knight-info@mit.edu
Web Site: ksj.mit.edu

AREAS OF INTEREST:
Science journalism.

NAME(S) OF PROGRAMS:
● **Knight Science Journalism Fellowship**

TYPE:
Fellowships. Access to courses, laboratories and researchers for 10 months.

YEAR PROGRAM STARTED: 1983

PURPOSE:
To recognize excellence in explaining science, medicine, technology and the environment to the public; to provide a deeper familiarity with the processes of research and development to widen the fellows' acquaintance with leading engineers, scientists and medical researchers experienced in explaining complex issues.

LEGAL BASIS:
University.

ELIGIBILITY:
Applicants must be full-time journalists, whether they are on staff or freelance. They must have at least three years of full-time experience covering science, technology, medicine or environment. Candidates may be reporters, writers, editors, producers, illustrators, filmmakers or photojournalists. They may work for newspapers, magazines, television, radio, the Web or other media. Journalists from all countries are eligible to apply.

FINANCIAL DATA:
Fellowship includes stipend. During their residence, fellows receive MIT affiliate and extended health plan for individuals, spouses and families.
Amount of support per award: $70,000 plus $2,500 housing stipend.

CO-OP FUNDING PROGRAMS: Sponsored by the John S. and James L. Knight Foundation.

NO. AWARDS: 10 annually.

APPLICATION INFO:
Online submission only.
Duration: Nine months, August to May.
Deadline: January 15. Interviews will begin in March with public announcement in April.

ADDRESS INQUIRIES TO:
Bettina Urcuioli
Program Administrator
Tel: (617) 452-3513
E-mail: bma@mit.edu

NATIONAL ASSOCIATION OF FARM BROADCASTING FOUNDATION [1771]

1100 Platte Falls Road
Platte City, MO 64079
(816) 431-4032
Fax: (816) 431-4087
E-mail: susan@nafb.com
Web Site: www.nafbfoundation.com

AREAS OF INTEREST:
Agricultural journalism and communications.

NAME(S) OF PROGRAMS:
● **Glenn Kummerow Memorial Scholarship**
● **The George Logan Scholarship**
● **Orion Samuelson Scholarship**

TYPE:
Scholarships. Since 1977, the NAFB Foundation has provided financial support

and educational opportunities in the form of college scholarships to assist students in pursuit of careers in agricultural communications. Currently the NAFB Foundation offers three annual college scholarships. These scholarships are recognized at the National NAFB Convention.

YEAR PROGRAM STARTED: 1975

PURPOSE:
To provide financial support and educational opportunities for students in pursuit of careers in agricultural communications.

ELIGIBILITY:
Must be at least junior-year college students, enrolled in an agricultural journalism/agricultural communications curriculum, or plan to transfer to a university which offers a designated professional program of study in agricultural radio-television broadcasting. Selection is by application and is based on agricultural communications aptitude and leadership achievements, academic record and career plans.

FINANCIAL DATA:
Winners receive an expense-paid trip to attend the convention as part of the award.
Amount of support per award: $5,000 each scholarship.
Total amount of support: $15,000.

NO. AWARDS: 1 per award.

APPLICATION INFO:
Applications are available in April on the Foundation web site.
Duration: One school year.
Deadline: June 11.

ADDRESS INQUIRIES TO:
NAFB Member Services Manager
(See address above.)

NATIONAL ASSOCIATION OF HISPANIC JOURNALISTS

1050 Connecticut Avenue, N.W.
5th Floor
Washington, DC 20036
(202) 853-7760
(202) 909-6880
E-mail: nahj@nahj.org
lafrank@nahj.org
Web Site: nahj.org

TYPE:
Awards/prizes; Conferences/seminars; Fellowships; General operating grants; Internships; Matching gifts; Project/program grants; Research grants; Scholarships; Seed money grants; Training grants; Travel grants.

See entry 918 for full listing.

NATIONAL ASSOCIATION OF SCIENCE WRITERS, INC.   [1772]

P.O. Box 7905
Berkeley, CA 94707
(510) 647-9500
E-mail: director@nasw.org
Web Site: www.nasw.org

FOUNDED: 1934

AREAS OF INTEREST:
Dissemination of scientific and medical information to a general lay audience and professional development for science writers.

NAME(S) OF PROGRAMS:
● **Science in Society Awards**

TYPE:
Conferences/seminars; Fellowships; Project/program grants; Seed money grants; Training grants; Travel grants. Separate monetary prizes and awards for writers in five categories:
(1) books;
(2) commentary or opinion;
(3) science reporting (short, medium or long);
(4) science reporting for a local or regional market and;
(5) science reporting series.

YEAR PROGRAM STARTED: 1972

PURPOSE:
To recognize investigative or interpretive reporting about the sciences and their impact on society.

LEGAL BASIS:
Professional membership organization.

ELIGIBILITY:
Any writer (or team) is eligible to submit not more than one entry in each category. Material may be single article or broadcast or a series. Books with a copyright date of 2019 are eligible. Works must be written or spoken, in English, intended for the layperson and published or broadcast in North America between January 1, 2019 and December 31, 2019.

GEOG. RESTRICTIONS: North America.

FINANCIAL DATA:
Amount of support per award: $2,000 and Certificates of Recognition in each category.
Total amount of support: $14,000.

NO. MOST RECENT APPLICANTS: 360.

NO. AWARDS: 7 annually.

APPLICATION INFO:
Details are available online.
Deadline: February 1.

ADDRESS INQUIRIES TO:
Tinsley Davis, Executive Director
(See address above.)

NATIONAL ASSOCIATION OF SCIENCE WRITERS, INC.   [1773]

P.O. Box 7905
Berkeley, CA 94707
(510) 647-9500
E-mail: director@nasw.org
Web Site: www.nasw.org

FOUNDED: 1934

AREAS OF INTEREST:
Dissemination of scientific and medical information to a general audience and professional development for science writers.

NAME(S) OF PROGRAMS:
● **NASW Idea Grants**

TYPE:
Project/program grants. Grants to support projects or programs designed to help science writers in their professional lives and/or benefit the field of science writing.

YEAR PROGRAM STARTED: 2010

PURPOSE:
To award the creativity and initiative of science writers; to create projects and programs that benefit the field and the writers in it.

LEGAL BASIS:
Professional membership organization.

ELIGIBILITY:
Individuals or groups are eligible to apply. Proposals can serve non-members, as well as members. Creative thinking is encouraged.

GEOG. RESTRICTIONS: North America.

FINANCIAL DATA:
Amount of support per award: $1,000 to $50,000.
Total amount of support: Varies.

APPLICATION INFO:
Details are available online.
Deadline: Varies.

ADDRESS INQUIRIES TO:
Tinsley Davis, Executive Director
(See address above.)

NATIONAL ASSOCIATION OF SCIENCE WRITERS, INC.   [1774]

P.O. Box 7905
Berkeley, CA 94707
(510) 647-9500
E-mail: director@nasw.org
Web Site: www.nasw.org

FOUNDED: 1934

AREAS OF INTEREST:
Dissemination of scientific and medical information to a general lay audience and professional development for science writers.

NAME(S) OF PROGRAMS:
● **Excellence in Institutional Writing Awards**

TYPE:
Awards/prizes. Monetary prizes and awards for writers in two categories:
(1) Short form and;
(2) Long form.

YEAR PROGRAM STARTED: 2018

PURPOSE:
To recognize high-caliber, publicly accessible science writing produced on behalf of an institution or other non-media organization.

LEGAL BASIS:
Professional membership organization.

ELIGIBILITY:
Material must be published or broadcast in the January to December preceding the deadline.

FINANCIAL DATA:
Amount of support per award: $2,000 and Certificates of Recognition in each category.
Total amount of support: $4,000.

NO. MOST RECENT APPLICANTS: Over 200.

NO. AWARDS: 2 annually.

APPLICATION INFO:
Details are available online December 1.
Deadline: February 1.

ADDRESS INQUIRIES TO:
Tinsley Davis, Executive Director
(See address above.)

NATIONAL ENDOWMENT FOR THE HUMANITIES   [1775]

The Constitution Center
400 7th Street, S.W.
Washington, DC 20506
(202) 606-8269
Fax: (202) 606-8557
E-mail: publicpgms@neh.gov
Web Site: www.neh.gov

FOUNDED: 1965

AREAS OF INTEREST:
Scholarship, research, education and public programs in the humanities. In the act that established the Endowment, the term humanities includes, but is not limited to, the study of history, philosophy, languages, linguistics, literature, archaeology, jurisprudence, the history, theory and criticism of the arts, ethics, comparative religion and those aspects of the social sciences that employ historical or philosophical approaches.

NAME(S) OF PROGRAMS:
- **Public Humanities Projects**

TYPE:
Project/program grants. Public Humanities Projects grants support projects that bring the ideas and insights of the humanities to life for general audiences. Projects must engage humanities scholarship to illuminate significant themes in disciplines such as history, literature, ethics and art, or to address challenging issues in contemporary life. NEH encourages projects that involve members of the public in collaboration with humanities scholars or that invite contributions from the community in the development and delivery of humanities programming. The grant program supports a variety of forms of audience engagement: Community Conversations: This format supports one- to three-year-long series of community-wide public discussions in which diverse residents creatively address community challenges, guided by the perspectives of the humanities; Exhibitions: This format supports permanent exhibitions that will be on view for at least three years, or traveling exhibitions that will be available to public audiences in at least two venues in the U.S. (including the originating location) and; Historic Places: This format supports the interpretation of historic sites, houses, neighborhoods and regions, which might include living history presentations, guided tours, exhibitions and public programs.

YEAR PROGRAM STARTED: 1969

PURPOSE:
To create an understanding and appreciation of the humanities among the general public.

LEGAL BASIS:
The National Foundation on the Arts and Humanities Act of 1965, Public Law 89-209, as amended.

ELIGIBILITY:
Any U.S. nonprofit organization with IRS tax-exempt status is eligible, as are state and local governmental agencies and federally recognized Indian tribal governments.

GEOG. RESTRICTIONS: United States.

FINANCIAL DATA:
Amount of support per award: Planning: Mostly up to $40,000, with a maximum of $75,000 for complex projects that will reach large national audiences. Implementation: Typically up to $400,000 ($460,000 for projects requesting a Position in Public Humanities); up to $1,000,000 for Chairman's Special Awards.
Total amount of support: Varies.

NO. MOST RECENT APPLICANTS: Average 99.

NO. AWARDS: Average 16.

APPLICATION INFO:
All applications must be submitted via Grants.gov. Applications should follow the parameters set out in one of the three formats listed above. Details are provided on the NEH web site.
Duration: Varies.
Deadline: August. NEH strongly recommends that applicant complete or verify one's Grants.gov registration at least six weeks before the application deadline, as it takes time to process one's registration.

PUBLICATIONS:
Annual report; *Grant Programs*; *Humanities Magazine*.

IRS I.D.: 52-1098584

ADDRESS INQUIRIES TO:
Division of Public Programs
(See telephone or e-mail address above.)

NATIONAL INSTITUTE FOR LABOR RELATIONS RESEARCH   [1776]
5211 Port Royal Road
Suite 510
Springfield, VA 22151
(703) 321-9606
(703) 770-2247
Fax: (703) 321-0676
E-mail: CLJ@nrtw.org
Web Site: www.nilrr.org

FOUNDED: 1985

AREAS OF INTEREST:
Research and analysis exposing the economic and social inequities of compulsory unionism.

NAME(S) OF PROGRAMS:
- **The William B. Ruggles Journalist Scholarship**

TYPE:
Scholarships. Unrestricted scholarship awarded annually to the student who exemplifies the dedication to principle and high journalistic standards of the late William B. Ruggles, the well-known and respected Texas journalist who contributed significantly to the Right to Work movement.

YEAR PROGRAM STARTED: 1974

PURPOSE:
To honor the late William B. Ruggles, former editorial page editor of *The Dallas Morning News.*

LEGAL BASIS:
Nonpartisan coalition of citizens.

ELIGIBILITY:
Applicants are limited to graduate or undergraduate students majoring in journalism or other related majors (communications, multimedia, film, etc.) in institutions of higher learning throughout the U.S. Foreign students are eligible, as long as they are attending an institution of higher learning in the U.S. Graduating high school seniors may apply, if accepted to a journalism or communications school. To be considered, applicants must demonstrate the potential for a successful completion of educational requirements in an accredited journalism program and an understanding of voluntarism and of the problems of compulsory unionism.

GEOG. RESTRICTIONS: United States.

FINANCIAL DATA:
Amount of support per award: $2,000.
Total amount of support: $2,000 each year.

NO. MOST RECENT APPLICANTS: 50.

NO. AWARDS: 1 annually.

APPLICATION INFO:
A total application will consist of a completed formal application form, available from the address above, an official grade transcript from essay finalists and a typewritten essay of approximately 500 words clearly demonstrating an interest in and a knowledge of the Right to Work principle. Application may be submitted electronically or by mail. Online applications are encouraged.
Deadline: Postmark by December 31.

ADDRESS INQUIRIES TO:
Cathy Jones, Scholarship Administrator
(See address above.)

NATIONAL PRESS FOUNDATION   [1777]
1211 Connecticut Avenue, N.W.
Suite 310
Washington, DC 20036
(202) 663-7280
E-mail: jenny@nationalpress.org
Web Site: nationalpress.org

AREAS OF INTEREST:
Journalism.

NAME(S) OF PROGRAMS:
- **Clifford K. and James T. Berryman Award for Editorial Cartoons**
- **Benjamin C. Bradlee Editor of the Year Award**
- **Chairman's Citation**
- **Everett McKinley Dirksen Award for Distinguished Reporting of Congress**
- **The Feddie Reporting Award**
- **Hinrich Foundation Award for Distinguished Reporting on Trade**
- **Innovative Storytelling Award**
- **W.M. Kiplinger Distinguished Contributions to Journalism Award**
- **Carolyn C. Mattingly Award for Mental Health Reporting**
- **Sol Taishoff Award for Excellence in Broadcast Journalism**
- **Technology in Journalism Award**

TYPE:
Awards/prizes; Fellowships. International programs. Each year, the National Press Foundation recognizes the best in American Journalism across 11 award categories.

Benjamin C. Bradlee Editor of the Year Award recognizes significant achievements that enhance the quality of journalism in the U.S.

Chairman's Citation, selected at the sole discretion of the NPF chairman, confers recognition on individuals whose accomplishments fall outside the traditional categories of excellence.

Everett McKinley Dirksen Award for Distinguished Reporting of Congress is intended to recognize U.S.-based journalists whose work shows thoughtful appraisal and insight into the workings of the U.S. Congress and represents the highest standards of journalism.

The Feddie Reporting Award recognizes outstanding reporting about the impact of federal laws and regulations on local communities.

The Hinrich Foundation Award recognizes exemplary journalism that illuminates and advances the public's understanding of international business and trade.

The Innovative Storytelling Award recognizes digital journalism of the highest quality that re-invents the way stories are told to present a compelling audience experience.

W.M. Kiplinger Distinguished Contributions to Journalism Award honors persons who have, through their vision and leadership, strengthened American journalism and furthered the efforts to establish the highest qualify of American journalism.
Carolyn C. Mattingly Award for Mental Health Reporting recognized exemplary journalism that illuminates and advances the understanding of mental health issues and treatments for the illness.

Sol Taishoff Award for Excellence in Broadcast Journalism is awarded to a U.S.-based broadcaster for a body of quality work in video or audio journalism that represents the highest standards of journalism. This award may recognize an individual's accomplishment in field reporting, producing, writing or work at the anchor desk.

Technology in Journalism Award recognizes individuals or organizations that develop, adapt or creatively apply specific tools or technologies in the gathering and reporting of impactful journalism of the highest quality.

PURPOSE:
To help journalists better understand the issues about which they write and broadcast.

ELIGIBILITY:
Clifford K. and James T. Berryman Award for Editorial Cartoons is open to U.S.-based editorial cartoonists for work that exhibits power to influence public opinion, plus good drawing and striking effect.

Benjamin C. Bradlee Editor of the Year Award is open to any U.S.-based editor at any level of a news organization. It recognizes imagination, professional skill, ethics and an ability to motivate staff.

The Feddie Reporting Award is open to any U.S.-based journalist whose work represents the highest standards of journalism.

The Hinrich Award is open to any professional journalist whose work exemplifies the highest standards of journalism and is published by a reputable news organization. This includes print, broadcast and digital journalists.

Innovative Storytelling Award is open to any U.S. journalist or U.S. news organization. Judges will take into consideration the originality of the nominated presentation, and how re-imagined delivery vehicles enhanced the audience's understanding of the underlying journalism.

Technology in Journalism Award is open to anyone at a U.S. news organization. A vendor or technology partner may apply if submitted jointly with a news organization. Judges will take into consideration the originality of the nominated tool or technology, its criticality to shaping the story, and how it is used within larger journalistic efforts.

FINANCIAL DATA:
Amount of support per award: Berryman and Kiplinger Awards: $2,500; Bradlee, Dirksen, Feddie, Innnovative Storytelling, Taishoff and Technology in Journalism Awards: $5,000; Chairman's Citation: $1,000; Hinrich Award and Mattingly Award: $10,000.
Total amount of support: $55,000 in cash prizes.

NO. AWARDS: 1 per award category.

APPLICATION INFO:
Application information is available on the Foundation's web site.

STAFF:
Sonni Efron, President
Jenny Ash-Maher, Director of Operations

NEW YORK STATE SENATE
Legislative Office Building, Suite 1426
Albany, NY 12247
(518) 455-2611
Fax: (518) 426-6827
E-mail: students@nysenate.gov
Web Site: www.nysenate.gov/student-programs

TYPE:
Fellowships. These fellowships are intended for the graduate/postgraduate/midcareer level. Stipends are for bipartisan opportunities to train in government while on-site in Albany, NY. Fellows spend almost a year immersed in the work of the Senate, learning techniques associated with policymaking and legislative process. Placement is usually to the office of an elected Senate member. The Senate Legislative Fellows Program, Biggane Fellowship, Roth Journalism Fellowship and Wiebe Public Service Fellowship constitute the Senate Graduate/Post-Graduate/Mid-Career Fellowships.

See entry 1830 for full listing.

THE NEWSGUILD-CWA (TNG-CWA) [1778]
501 Third Street, N.W.
Washington, DC 20001-2797
(202) 434-7177
Fax: (202) 434-1472
E-mail: communications@newsguild.org
Web Site: www.newsguild.org/heywood-broun-award

FOUNDED: 1933

AREAS OF INTEREST:
Representing journalists and other media workers in the traditional and digital news industry in the U.S., Canada and Puerto Rico. Areas of interest include all matters involving the news media; freedom of the press and other First Amendment issues; and workers' rights.

NAME(S) OF PROGRAMS:
• **Heywood Broun Award**

TYPE:
Awards/prizes. The Heywood Broun Award is given in name and tradition of the famed early 20th-century New York City columnist and NewsGuild founder whose journalism righted wrongs, fought injustice and championed the underdog. The total award package consists of a Top award and two lesser Substantial Distinction awards.

YEAR PROGRAM STARTED: 1941

PURPOSE:
To encourage and recognize individual journalistic achievement in this spirit by members of the working press, particularly if it helps right a wrong or correct an injustice, or shows an "abiding concern for the underdog and the underprivileged."

LEGAL BASIS:
Labor union.

ELIGIBILITY:
All journalists working for professional mass media in the U.S., Canada and Puerto Rico are eligible, whether or not they are Guild members. Entries can be from newspapers, web sites, nonprofit news organizations, magazines, television and radio - any type of professional news broadcast or publication, print or digital.

Entries on behalf of an entire staff of a publication or employer are not eligible. While team entries are eligible, and have been Broun winners, judges are instructed to give more weight to entries by individuals or pairs of journalists.

Entries written or reported by managers are not eligible.

GEOG. RESTRICTIONS: United States, Puerto Rico and Canada.

FINANCIAL DATA:
Amount of support per award: Top award: $5,000 and engraved plaque. Substantial Distinction awards: $1,000 and framed citation.
Total amount of support: $7,000.

NO. MOST RECENT APPLICANTS: 80.

NO. AWARDS: 1 Top award and 2 Substantial Distinction awards annually.

APPLICATION INFO:
Consult the web site address above for details.
Deadline: Last Friday in January.

OFFICERS:
Bernard J. Lunzer, President
Marian Needham, Executive Vice President

ADDRESS INQUIRIES TO:
Broun Award Committee
(See address above.)

THE NEWSGUILD-CWA (TNG-CWA) [1779]
501 Third Street, N.W.
Washington, DC 20001-2797
(202) 434-7177
Fax: (202) 434-1472
E-mail: communications@newsguild.org
Web Site: www.newsguild.org/david-s-barr-award-student-journalism

FOUNDED: 1933

AREAS OF INTEREST:
Representing journalists and other media workers in the traditional and digital news industry in the U.S., Canada and Puerto Rico. Areas of interest include all matters involving the news media; freedom of the press and other First Amendment issues; and workers' rights.

NAME(S) OF PROGRAMS:
• **David S. Barr Award**

TYPE:
Awards/prizes; Scholarships.

YEAR PROGRAM STARTED: 1999

PURPOSE:
To inspire a new generation of journalists by recognizing work that contributes to the pursuit of justice and fairness; to promote

issues of importance to working people; to serve as a lasting memorial and tribute to David S. Barr.

ELIGIBILITY:
The contest is open to:
(1) high school students, including those enrolled in vocational, technical or special education programs and;
(2) part-time or full-time college students, including those in community colleges and in graduate programs.

Students who have worked or are working as professional journalists - excluding internships - are not eligible to enter.

FINANCIAL DATA:
Amount of support per award: $1,000 for high school winner; $1,500 for college winner.

NO. MOST RECENT APPLICANTS: 180.

NO. AWARDS: High School and College: 1 each.

APPLICATION INFO:
Application form is available at the Guild web site. Entry must be mailed to TNG-CWA, along with four copies and the application form. Applicant must refer to the web site for complete details.
Duration: One-time award.
Deadline: Last Friday of January (postmark).

ADDRESS INQUIRIES TO:
Dominique Edmondson, Secretary to Collective Bargaining Department
David S. Barr Award
(See address above.)

NIEMAN FOUNDATION FOR JOURNALISM AT HARVARD   [1780]
Walter Lippmann House
One Francis Avenue
Cambridge, MA 02138
(617) 496-8511
Fax: (617) 495-8976
E-mail: samantha_henry@harvard.edu
Web Site: nieman.harvard.edu

FOUNDED: 1938

AREAS OF INTEREST:
Journalism and investigative reporting.

NAME(S) OF PROGRAMS:
- **Worth Bingham Prize for Investigative Journalism**

TYPE:
Awards/prizes. Honors investigative reporting of stories of national significance where the public interest is being ill-served. These stories may involve state, local or national government, lobbyists or the press itself wherever there exists an "atmosphere of easy tolerance" that journalist Worth Bingham himself once described in his reporting on the nation's capital. The investigative reporting may cover actual violations of the law, rule or code; lax or ineffective administration or enforcement; or activities which create conflicts of interest, entail excessive secrecy or otherwise raise questions of propriety.

YEAR PROGRAM STARTED: 1967

PURPOSE:
To honor exceptional investigative reporting of stories of national significance where the public interest is being ill-served.

ELIGIBILITY:
All submissions must have been published in a U.S. newspaper or magazine or on the newspaper or magazine's web site during the calendar year. Web-based news organizations that follow a strict code of journalistic ethics and publish original reporting on a regular basis may also submit entries. No broadcast-only entries are allowed.

Entries may include a single story, a related series of stories, or up to three unrelated stories. Columns and editorials are eligible. Individuals are encouraged to submit their own entries. In the case of a series, at least half the individual stories must have been published during the contest year.

Winners in any one year will be eligible for future awards without restriction.

GEOG. RESTRICTIONS: United States.

FINANCIAL DATA:
Amount of support per award: $20,000 annually.

NO. AWARDS: 1.

APPLICATION INFO:
Application must be made online. All entries must be accompanied by a $50 entry fee, payable online.
Deadline: January.

ADDRESS INQUIRIES TO:
Samantha Henry
Assistant Director for Programming and Special Projects
(See address above.)

NIEMAN FOUNDATION FOR JOURNALISM AT HARVARD   [1781]
Walter Lippmann House
One Francis Avenue
Cambridge, MA 02138
(617) 495-2238
E-mail: nieman_applications@harvard.edu
Web Site: www.nieman.harvard.edu

FOUNDED: 1938

AREAS OF INTEREST:
Journalism.

NAME(S) OF PROGRAMS:
- **Nieman Fellowships in Journalism**

TYPE:
Fellowships. Provides journalists with the opportunity to spend a year of study at Harvard University. Awards are for U.S. and international journalists.

The Foundation also offers short-term Knight Visiting Nieman Fellowships to journalists and other professionals working on projects to advance journalism. Contact the Foundation for further details.

YEAR PROGRAM STARTED: 1938

PURPOSE:
To provide an opportunity for journalists to deepen their knowledge in a field of specialty, broaden their knowledge in several areas, or prepare for a new journalistic assignment.

LEGAL BASIS:
A foundation of Harvard University.

ELIGIBILITY:
Print, broadcast and online reporters, editors, photographers, producers, editorial writers, columnists, filmmakers and cartoonists with

at least five years of full-time, professional experience in the news media are invited to apply.

During the two years prior to applying, an applicant should not have participated in a fellowship or taken a leave of absence from work that lasted for four months or longer. There are no age limits or academic prerequisites, and a college degree is not required.

All prospective fellows must speak, read and write English fluently.

FINANCIAL DATA:
Nieman Fellows receive a stipend plus housing, child care and health insurance allowance, if applicable.
Amount of support per award: $70,000 stipend.

NO. AWARDS: Approximately 24 annually (around 12 to journalists from the U.S. and around 12 to journalists from other countries).

APPLICATION INFO:
Contact the Foundation.
Duration: Nine months.
Deadline: U.S. applications due January 31 for the academic year beginning in August. International applications are due December 1 for the academic year beginning the following August.

PUBLICATIONS:
Nieman Reports.

STAFF:
Nicole Arias, Fellowship Administrator

ADDRESS INQUIRIES TO:
Nicole Arias, Fellowship Administrator
(See address above.)

NIEMAN FOUNDATION FOR JOURNALISM AT HARVARD   [1782]
Walter Lippmann House
One Francis Avenue
Cambridge, MA 02138
(617) 496-6333
Fax: (617) 495-8976
E-mail: christine_kaye@harvard.edu
Web Site: www.nieman.harvard.edu

FOUNDED: 1938

AREAS OF INTEREST:
Journalism.

NAME(S) OF PROGRAMS:
- **Taylor Family Award for Fairness in Journalism**

TYPE:
Awards/prizes. Established through gifts for an endowment by members of the Taylor family, which published *The Boston Globe* from 1872 to 1999.

YEAR PROGRAM STARTED: 2001

PURPOSE:
To encourage fairness in news coverage by America's journalists and news organizations.

ELIGIBILITY:
Nominations are for a single article, editorial, commentary, photograph, or a series of stories, photographs, editorials, commentaries, or a body of work by an individual journalist. The work must have been published in a U.S. newspaper or magazine or on the newspaper or magazine's web site during the previous calendar year.

GEOG. RESTRICTIONS: United States.

FINANCIAL DATA:
  Amount of support per award: $10,000, plus two $1,000 finalist awards.
  Total amount of support: $12,000.

APPLICATION INFO:
  All entries must be submitted online using the Foundation's online application form.
  Deadline: Date will be posted on the Foundation web site.

ADDRESS INQUIRIES TO:
  Christine Kaye, Event Manager
  (See address above.)

THE ALICIA PATTERSON FOUNDATION   [1783]

1100 Vermont Avenue, N.W.
Suite 900
Washington, DC 20005
(202) 393-5995
Fax: (301) 951-8512
E-mail: info@aliciapatterson.org
Web Site: www.aliciapatterson.org

FOUNDED: 1961

AREAS OF INTEREST:
  Journalism.

NAME(S) OF PROGRAMS:
  • **Fellowship Program for Journalists**

TYPE:
  Fellowships. Awarded to working print journalists for six months or one year of travel and inquiry. On leave from their normal writing, editing or photographing duties, Fellows examine their chosen subjects (areas or problems of significant interest, foreign or domestic) and write quarterly articles for the *APF Reporter*. These articles may be reprinted.

YEAR PROGRAM STARTED: 1965

PURPOSE:
  To foster, promote, sustain and improve the best traditions of American journalism; to provide a few talented and promising American journalists with the opportunity to pursue independent projects.

LEGAL BASIS:
  Section 501(c)(3) of the IRS Code and Not For Profits Corporation Law: New York State.

ELIGIBILITY:
  The program is open to U.S. citizens who are full-time print journalists or to non-U.S. citizens who work full-time for U.S. print publication, either in America or abroad.

FINANCIAL DATA:
  Amount of support per award: $20,000 stipend for six months or $40,000 stipend for the year.
  Total amount of support: Varies.

NO. MOST RECENT APPLICANTS: Varies.

NO. AWARDS: 7 to 10 per year.

APPLICATION INFO:
  Application forms are available in June. Information may be requested from the address above throughout the year.
  Duration: Fellowships support a one-year or six-month leave of absence. The fellowship typically begins within the first three months of the calendar year.
  Deadline: October 1 (postmark).

PUBLICATIONS:
  APF Reporter, quarterly online magazine.

IRS I.D.: 13-6092124

ADDRESS INQUIRIES TO:
  Margaret Engel, Executive Director
  (See address above.)

THE PRESS CLUB OF ST. LOUIS CHARITABLE FUND - ST. LOUIS PRESS CLUB

c/o The Press Club of St. Louis
P.O. Box 410522
Creve Couer, MO 63141
(314) 449-8029
Fax: (314) 317-0031
E-mail: info@stlpressclub.org
Web Site: stlpressclub.org

TYPE:
  Capital grants; Fellowships; Internships; Project/program grants; Scholarships.

See entry 1587 for full listing.

PULLIAM JOURNALISM FELLOWSHIP   [1784]

Indiana Star
130 South Meridian Street
Indianapolis, IN 46225
(317) 213-9830
E-mail: russell.pulliam@indystar.com
Web Site: www.indystar.com/pjf

FOUNDED: 1974

AREAS OF INTEREST:
  Journalism awards.

TYPE:
  Fellowships. Newswriting internship program at *The Indianapolis Star* and *The Arizona Republic*, which are owned by Gannett Co.

YEAR PROGRAM STARTED: 1974

PURPOSE:
  To offer on-the-job experience, plus seminars and writing criticism, to college students seriously pursuing a newspaper journalism career.

LEGAL BASIS:
  Corporate-sponsored.

ELIGIBILITY:
  Applicants are generally college journalism majors or liberal arts majors with part-time newspaper experience, outstanding character references, proven writing ability and a solid academic record.

GEOG. RESTRICTIONS: United States.

FINANCIAL DATA:
  Amount of support per award: $6,500 ($650 per week for 10-week program).

NO. MOST RECENT APPLICANTS: 200.

NO. AWARDS: 25.

APPLICATION INFO:
  Brochures are available from the address above. View the instructions and download the application at the web site.
  Duration: 10 weeks, June to August. No renewals.
  Deadline: November 1 (postmark).

PUBLICATIONS:
  Brochure.

ADDRESS INQUIRIES TO:
  Russ Pulliam, Director
  (See address above.)

QUILL AND SCROLL FOUNDATION   [1785]

School of Journalism and Mass Communication
The University of Iowa
100 Adler Journalism Building, Room W111
Iowa City, IA 52242-2004
(319) 335-3457
(319) 335-3321
E-mail: quill-scroll@uiowa.edu
Web Site: www.quillandscroll.org

FOUNDED: 1926

AREAS OF INTEREST:
  Journalism, high school media, media law and ethics, and scholastic journalism education.

CONSULTING OR VOLUNTEER SERVICES:
  Coordinate judging of K-12 writing, journalism and media contests.

TYPE:
  Scholarships; Training grants.

YEAR PROGRAM STARTED: 1964

PURPOSE:
  To improve the quality of secondary school journalism.

LEGAL BASIS:
  Nonprofit special-interest foundation.

ELIGIBILITY:
  Qualified scholars or educational departments with appropriate interests are eligible to apply.

GEOG. RESTRICTIONS: Primarily United States.

FINANCIAL DATA:
  Amount of support per award: $500 to $1,500.
  Total amount of support: $2,500 for the year 2020.

NO. MOST RECENT APPLICANTS: More than 100.

NO. AWARDS: 4 for the year 2020.

APPLICATION INFO:
  Applications are available online.
  Duration: One-time award.
  Deadline: Students: May 10; Teachers: April 15.

PUBLICATIONS:
  Application guidelines.

IRS I.D.: 42-0795095

TRUSTEES:
  Richard P. Johns, Chairperson
  Yuxing Zheng, Vice Chairperson
  William Casey
  Erica Hernandez
  John Humenik
  Patrick Johnson
  Jack Kennedy
  Anthony Whitten
  Jessica Young

OFFICER:
  Jeff Browne, Executive Director

ADDRESS INQUIRIES TO:
  Jeff Browne, Executive Director
  (See address above.)

RADIO TELEVISION DIGITAL NEWS ASSOCIATION FOUNDATION   [1786]

The National Press Building
529 14th Street, N.W., Suite 1240
Washington, DC 20045
(202) 662-7254
E-mail: katem@rtdna.org
Web Site: www.rtdna.org

FOUNDED: 1946

AREAS OF INTEREST:
Electronic journalism.

NAME(S) OF PROGRAMS:
- **N.S. Biestock Fellowship**
- **Ed Bradley Scholarship**
- **Michele Clark Fellowship**
- **George Foreman Tribute to Lyndon B. Johnson**
- **Jacque I. Minnotte Fellowship**
- **Vada and Barney Oldfield Fellowship for National Security Reporting**
- **Lou and Carole Prato Sports Reporting Scholarship**
- **The President's Scholarships**
- **Mike Reynolds Journalism Scholarship**
- **Carole Simpson Scholarship**
- **Lee Thornton Scholarship**
- **Pete Wilson Scholarship**

TYPE:
Fellowships; Scholarships. Scholarship awards for one year of undergraduate and/or graduate study in broadcast journalism.

YEAR PROGRAM STARTED: 1967

PURPOSE:
To aid in advanced learning of electronic journalism.

LEGAL BASIS:
Incorporated.

ELIGIBILITY:
For scholarships, applicants must be officially enrolled in college and have at least one full academic year remaining, must be a fully enrolled college sophomore or higher, may apply for only one scholarship, and may be enrolled in any major so long as their career intent is television or radio news. Fellowships are available to young professionals with fewer than 10 years in the field. U.S. citizens and international applicants are eligible.

International applicants must have a U.S. Taxpayer ID Number (TIN).

FINANCIAL DATA:
Amount of support per award: Scholarships: $1,000 to $10,000; Fellowships: $1,000 and $2,500.

NO. MOST RECENT APPLICANTS: 250.

NO. AWARDS: Undergraduate: 9; Fellowships: 4.

APPLICATION INFO:
Application must be submitted online.
Duration: Scholarships: One year.
Deadline: Varies.

PUBLICATIONS:
Annual report.

IRS I.D.: 38-1860090

ADDRESS INQUIRIES TO:
Kate McGarrity, Program and Award Manager
(See address above.)

REPORTERS COMMITTEE FOR FREEDOM OF THE PRESS [1787]

1156 15th Street, N.W.
Suite 1020
Washington, DC 20005
(202) 795-9306
Fax: (202) 795-9310
E-mail: kpoole@rcfp.org
Web Site: www.rcfp.org

FOUNDED: 1970

AREAS OF INTEREST:
First Amendment interests of the news media.

NAME(S) OF PROGRAMS:
- **The Reporters Committee Legal Fellowships**

TYPE:
Fellowships. Legal fellows monitor significant developments in First Amendment media law, assist with legal defense requests from reporters, prepare legal memoranda, amicus briefs and other special projects. The Fellowship focuses on media law.

YEAR PROGRAM STARTED: 1987

PURPOSE:
To protect the right to gather and distribute news; to keep government accountable by ensuring access to public records, meetings and courtrooms; to preserve the principles of free speech and unfettered press, as guaranteed by the First Amendment of the U.S. Constitution.

ELIGIBILITY:
Candidates must have received a law degree by August of the year the Fellowship begins. Strong legal research and writing skills are required, and a background in news reporting is very strongly preferred.

FINANCIAL DATA:
Fellowship includes fully paid health benefits.
Amount of support per award: Minimum of $65,000.

NO. AWARDS: 6 to 8 annually.

APPLICATION INFO:
Contact the Committee by e-mail.
Duration: One year, September to August.
Deadline: November 3.

ADDRESS INQUIRIES TO:
E-mail: fellowship@rcfp.org

KURT SCHORK MEMORIAL FUND [1788]

4441 MacArthur Boulevard, N.W.
Washington, DC 20007
(202) 333-2545
E-mail: enquiries@ksmfund.org
Web Site: www.ksmfund.org

FOUNDED: 2001

AREAS OF INTEREST:
International journalism.

NAME(S) OF PROGRAMS:
- **Kurt Schork Awards in International Journalism**

TYPE:
Awards/prizes. Awards for print reporters whose stories shed new light on controversial issues. Three prizes are awarded each year, one to a local reporter in a developing country or nation in transition, one to a freelance journalist covering international news, and one to recognize the unsung work of news fixers.

The awards are underwritten by the Kurt Schork Memorial Fund and Reuters, and administered by the Columbia University Graduate School of Journalism.

YEAR PROGRAM STARTED: 2002

PURPOSE:
To honor Kurt Schork, an American freelance journalist, killed in a military ambush while on assignment for Reuters on May 24, 2000 in Sierra Leone.

ELIGIBILITY:
Local Reporter: Print journalists employed by a local news outlet and residing in a developing country or nation in transition (non-OECD or EU countries), whose work has been published in a local publication, are eligible.

Freelance Journalist: All freelance print journalists and those contracted by news organizations are eligible.

Eligible Media: Entries are welcomed from all types of print-based media including newspapers and magazines and established online publications.

FINANCIAL DATA:
Amount of support per award: $5,000.

NO. AWARDS: 3.

APPLICATION INFO:
Complete information may be found on the Fund web site.
Deadline: May 31.

ADDRESS INQUIRIES TO:
See e-mail address above.

UNITED METHODIST COMMUNICATIONS [1789]

810 12th Avenue South
Nashville, TN 37203-4704
(615) 742-5400
Fax: (615) 742-5423
E-mail: scholarship@umcom.org
Web Site: www.umcom.org

FOUNDED: 1948

AREAS OF INTEREST:
Religion communications.

NAME(S) OF PROGRAMS:
- **The Stoody-West Fellowship**

TYPE:
Fellowships. Assists one United Methodist student in postgraduate study at an accredited U.S. college or university who intends to pursue a career in religious journalism.

YEAR PROGRAM STARTED: 1964

PURPOSE:
To enable the recipient to continue graduate studies in religion journalism; to promote a level of excellence in communication at the graduate level.

LEGAL BASIS:
Nonprofit.

ELIGIBILITY:
Applicant must be a United Methodist student who intends to pursue a career in religion journalism and is enrolled in graduate study at an accredited U.S. college or university (includes electronic and broadcast media as well as print). Employees of United Methodist Communications and members of the General Commission on Communication are not eligible for the Fellowship.

FINANCIAL DATA:
Amount of support per award: $6,000.
Total amount of support: $6,000.

NO. AWARDS: 1 annually.

APPLICATION INFO:
Application forms are available online.

Applicant must submit:
(1) completed application form;
(2) official transcripts of schools attended, including evidence of enrollment as a graduate student in the journalism or communications department of a duly

accredited college or university in the U.S.;
(3) three letters of recommendation;
(4) an essay of not more than 500 words
about their commitment to the Christian
Faith, interest in religion communication, and
how they see the two intersecting in their
life, presently and in the future;
(5) three writing samples and;
(6) recent personal photograph.

If materials must be mailed, use the
following address:
Stoody-West Fellowship Committee
United Methodist Communications
P.O. Box 320
Nashville, TN 37202-0320.

If submitting by FedEx or UPS, send to:
Stoody-West Fellowship Committee, United
Methodist Communications, at the street
address above.

Duration: One academic year.

Deadline: March 15 (postmark).

PUBLICATIONS:
Application guidelines.

ADDRESS INQUIRIES TO:
Relationship Team
(See address above.)

*PLEASE NOTE:
Religious journalism is interpreted to include
news writing for secular press, church press
and for church institutions. Appropriate news
and journalism forms will be considered,
including electronic and broadcast media, as
well as print.

UNITED METHODIST COMMUNICATIONS

810 12th Avenue South
Nashville, TN 37203-4744
(615) 742-5400
Fax: (615) 742-5777
E-mail: scholarship@umcom.org
Web Site: www.umcom.org

TYPE:
Fellowships; Scholarships. Award for junior
or senior undergraduate study in religion
journalism or mass communications. The
term *communications* is meant to cover
various media as audio-visual, electronic and
print journalism.

See entry 932 for full listing.

UNIVERSITY FILM AND VIDEO ASSOCIATION   [1790]

Bentley University
Department of English and Media Studies
AAC 087
Waltham, MA 02452
(781) 891-2862
E-mail: chayward@bentley.edu
Web Site: www.ufva.org

AREAS OF INTEREST:
Film, video and multimedia production.

NAME(S) OF PROGRAMS:
 ● **Carole Fielding Student Grants**

TYPE:
Block grants; Capital grants; Development
grants; General operating grants;
Project/program grants; Research grants;
Seed money grants. Annual support for
student projects in film, video and
multimedia productions or research activities
in historical, critical, theoretical or
experimental studies in film or video.

YEAR PROGRAM STARTED: 1993

PURPOSE:
To support and promote student film and
video makers.

LEGAL BASIS:
UFVA membership funded.

ELIGIBILITY:
An applicant must be a graduate or
undergraduate student at the time the
application is made, be sponsored by a
faculty member who is an active member of
the University Film and Video Association
and agree to present, or have presented by
his or her representative, a report on the
project or production at the next annual
meeting of the Association.

The judges reserve the right not to make an
award if quality or quantity of submissions
so justify.

FINANCIAL DATA:
Amount of support per award: Varies.
Total amount of support: $2,500 per year.

NO. MOST RECENT APPLICANTS: 75.

NO. AWARDS: Varies.

APPLICATION INFO:
Applicants should submit materials online.
The proposal must include a one-page
description of the production or project
which includes a statement of purpose, an
indication of the resources available to
complete the work and a summary of the
proposed film, video production or study. If a
narrative film is proposed, submit a copy of
the script. A documentary proposal should
include a short treatment. An experimental or
animated film proposal should include a
treatment (or script) and/or story boards.
Also include a one-page budget, indicating
what portion of the total project will be
supported by this grant and a statement by a
faculty member who is an active member of
the University Film and Video Association
assessing the feasibility of the project or
production and indicating his or her
willingness to serve as faculty supervisor or
consultant.

Deadline: December 15. Announcements by
March 31.

OFFICERS:
Laura Vazquez, President
Joseph Brown, Executive Vice President
Konstantia Kontaxis, Editorial Vice President

ADDRESS INQUIRIES TO:
Prof. Casey Hayward, UFVA Grants Office
(See e-mail address above.)

THE UNIVERSITY OF CALGARY   [1791]

Faculty of Graduate Studies
Earth Sciences Building, Room 1010
2500 University Drive, N.W.
Calgary AB T2N 1N4 Canada
(403) 220-4938
Fax: (403) 289-7635
E-mail: gsaward@ucalgary.ca
Web Site: grad.ucalgary.ca/awards

FOUNDED: 1966

AREAS OF INTEREST:
Communication and media studies.

NAME(S) OF PROGRAMS:
 ● **Cogeco Inc. Graduate Scholarship**

TYPE:
Awards/prizes; Scholarships.

LEGAL BASIS:
University scholarship program.

ELIGIBILITY:
Applicants must be students admissible to or
registered in a Master's program (either
thesis-based or course-based) in the
Communication and Media Studies Program
at the University of Calgary. Awards will be
made on the basis of academic excellence.

FINANCIAL DATA:
Amount of support per award: $9,000.
Total amount of support: $9,000.

CO-OP FUNDING PROGRAMS: Scholarship is
financed by Cogeco Inc.

NO. AWARDS: 1 each year.

APPLICATION INFO:
Candidates should apply to the
Communication and Media Studies Program
in the first instance. Recommendations will
be submitted to the University of Calgary
Graduate Scholarship Office for approval.
The recommendation is subject to final
approval of the Graduate Scholarship
Committee.

Duration: One year.

Deadline: February 1.

ADDRESS INQUIRIES TO:
Graduate Scholarship Office
(See address above.)

UNIVERSITY OF MICHIGAN   [1792]

Knight-Wallace Fellows
Wallace House
620 Oxford Road
Ann Arbor, MI 48104-2635
(734) 998-7666
Fax: (734) 998-7979
E-mail: kwfellows@umich.edu
Web Site: www.wallacehouse.umich.edu/knight-
wallace

AREAS OF INTEREST:
Journalism, arts, sciences and professions.

NAME(S) OF PROGRAMS:
 ● **Knight-Wallace Fellowships for Journalists**

TYPE:
Fellowships.

YEAR PROGRAM STARTED: 1973

PURPOSE:
To offer a full academic year to midcareer
journalists at the University of Michigan.

LEGAL BASIS:
A part of the Provost's office at the
University of Michigan.

ELIGIBILITY:
Status of eligibility extends to all full-time
print, broadcast, online, photo and film
journalists with five years' experience whose
work appears regularly in U.S.-controlled
news organizations. Freelancers are included.
Work may be related or unrelated to
professional objectives.

FINANCIAL DATA:
Fellowship also includes tuition and fees,
plus travel expenses for our international
news tours.

Amount of support per award: $75,000
stipend.

NO. AWARDS: 20.

APPLICATION INFO:
Application form, a leave of absence (if possible) for the period of the Fellowship, and a support letter from direct supervisor is required. Two statements, an intellectual autobiography, and a proposed program of study must be included. Do not submit more than five examples of applicant's work.

Duration: Eight-month academic year, September to April.

Deadline: February 1 for U.S. applicants. International applicants deadline may vary. Announcement in May.

PUBLICATIONS:
Wall House Journal.

ADDRESS INQUIRIES TO:
Birgit Rieck, Associate Director
(See address above.)

Labor

IMAGINE AMERICA FOUNDATION [1793]
14200 Park Meadow Drive
Suite 117 S
Chantilly, VA 20151
(571) 267-3015
Fax: (866) 734-5812
E-mail: studentservices@imagine-america.org
Web Site: www.imagine-america.org

FOUNDED: 1982

AREAS OF INTEREST:
Private career education, trade schools, and vocational schools.

NAME(S) OF PROGRAMS:
● **Imagine America Adult Excellence Award**
● **Imagine America Adult Skills Education Program (ASEP)**
● **Imagine America High School Scholarship Program**
● **Imagine America LDRSHIP Award**
● **Imagine America Military Award Program (MAP)**
● **Imagine America Promise Scholarship Program**

TYPE:
Awards/prizes; Scholarships; Research contracts. Sponsorships. For the Imagine America High School Scholarship Program, three scholarships are given to each high school listed on the Foundation web site above.

YEAR PROGRAM STARTED: 1982

PURPOSE:
To provide research, scholarship and training for America's career colleges.

LEGAL BASIS:
501(c)(3) nonprofit organization.

ELIGIBILITY:
Applicants for the Adult Skills Education Program must be 19 years of age or older.

Applicants for the Military Award Program must be honorably discharged, active duty, reservist or retired military.

Scholarship applicants must be graduating high school seniors.

GEOG. RESTRICTIONS: United States and Puerto Rico.

FINANCIAL DATA:
Amount of support per award: Adult Skills Education Program, High School Scholarship Program and Military Award Program: $1,000; All others: Varies.

Total amount of support: $18,000,000 annually.

NO. AWARDS: 18,000.

PUBLICATIONS:
Career College Central, magazine.

ADDRESS INQUIRIES TO:
Lee Doubleday
Director of Operations
(See address above.)

U.S. DEPARTMENT OF HEALTH AND HUMAN SERVICES/ADMINISTRATION FOR CHILDREN AND FAMILIES/OFFICE OF FAMILY ASSISTANCE [1794]
Mary E. Switzer Building
330 C Street, S.W.
Washington, DC 20201
(877) 696-6775
Fax: (202) 205-5887
E-mail: rachel.johnson@acf.hhs.gov
info.ofa@acf.hhs.gov
Web Site: www.acf.hhs.gov/ofa

FOUNDED: 1996

AREAS OF INTEREST:
Education, employment and support services, and financial assistance.

NAME(S) OF PROGRAMS:
● **State Family Assistance Grants**
● **Temporary Assistance for Needy Families (TANF)**

TYPE:
Block grants; Internships; Technical assistance. Block grants to states, the District of Columbia, territories, and federally recognized Indian tribes and Alaska Native Organizations for education, employment, training and supportive services to help eligible families move to work and self-sufficiency.

YEAR PROGRAM STARTED: 1996

PURPOSE:
To help needy families achieve self-sufficiency.

LEGAL BASIS:
Social Security Act, Title IV-A and Title IV-F, as amended (42 USC 602-603, 681-687 and 1302) and Public Law 100-485.

ELIGIBILITY:
Grants are awarded to states, the District of Columbia, territories, and federally recognized Indian tribes and Alaska Native Organizations based on a complete TANF plan. Statute precludes any grantees other than those stated above.

FINANCIAL DATA:
Amount of support per award: Calculated share of federal block grant.

Total amount of support: $16.5 billion.

NO. AWARDS: 54 states, the District of Columbia and U.S. territories.

PUBLICATIONS:
TANF Annual Report to Congress; policy announcements; program instructions; information memoranda.

ADDRESS INQUIRIES TO:
Rachel Johnson, Program Analyst
(See address above.)

U.S. DEPARTMENT OF LABOR [1795]
Office of Apprenticeship
Room N-5311
200 Constitution Avenue, N.W.
Washington, DC 20210
(202) 693-2796
E-mail: apprenticeship@dol.gov
Web Site: www.dol.gov/apprenticeship

FOUNDED: 1937

AREAS OF INTEREST:
Apprenticeship, skill and technical training.

CONSULTING OR VOLUNTEER SERVICES:
Provides technical assistance at no cost.

NAME(S) OF PROGRAMS:
● **National Apprenticeship System**

TYPE:
Technical assistance. Management and labor, along with government and the education system, work together at the national, state and local levels to formulate and promote effective apprenticeship programs. The program must be an organized, written plan embodying training and supervision of one or more apprentices in an apprenticeable occupation, as defined in 29 CFR 29.4 and subscribed to by a sponsor who has undertaken to carry out the apprenticeship program.

YEAR PROGRAM STARTED: 1937

PURPOSE:
To formulate, promote and publish labor standards necessary to safeguard the welfare of apprentices, encourage the inclusion of such standards in apprenticeship contracts, bring together employers and labor to create apprenticeship programs, cooperate with state agencies in formulating and promoting apprenticeship standards, and cooperate with the U.S. Department of Education on vocational education and related instruction in apprenticeship.

LEGAL BASIS:
National Apprenticeship Act of 1937 (P.L. 308-75); Title 29, CFR Part 30; Title 29, CFR Part 29.

ELIGIBILITY:
To be eligible as a sponsor, apprenticeship programs must meet the basic standards and established criteria set forth by the Secretary of Labor and may be registered upon request of the program sponsor. Registration of programs and apprentices in states having apprenticeship agencies recognized by the U.S. Department of Labor is performed by the state apprenticeship agencies. Programs in states not having recognized apprenticeship agencies will be registered by the Bureau of Apprenticeship and Training.

To be eligible as a beneficiary, applicants for apprenticeship must be at least 16 years of age. They must have the ability and aptitude to master the occupations and sufficient education to complete satisfactorily the required hours of related theoretical instruction.

GEOG. RESTRICTIONS: United States.

FINANCIAL DATA:
The Department of Labor does not finance apprenticeships. Program sponsors bear the expenses of the program.

NO. MOST RECENT APPLICANTS: 100,000.

APPLICATION INFO:
Notices for accepting applications are published locally by apprenticeship program sponsors. Information may be obtained from local One Stop Centers or may be requested by contacting regional, state or area offices of the Office of Apprenticeship, U.S. Department of Labor, or the ETA Grants Office.

PUBLICATIONS:
Apprenticeship Past and Present; *National Apprenticeship Program*.

ADDRESS INQUIRIES TO:
Grants Department
Division of Grants and Contracts
(See address above.)

W.E. UPJOHN INSTITUTE FOR EMPLOYMENT RESEARCH   [1796]

300 South Westnedge Avenue
Kalamazoo, MI 49007-4686
(269) 343-5541
Fax: (269) 343-3308
E-mail: communications@upjohn.org
Web Site: www.upjohn.org

FOUNDED: 1945

AREAS OF INTEREST:
Policy-relevant research on employment and unemployment at the international, national, state and local levels. The Institute is also receptive to international studies for the purpose of drawing lessons for U.S. policy. Topics of interest include job creation, job stabilization, matching of jobs and people, alleviation of unemployment hazards, the political science of manpower programs and the quality of work life.

CONSULTING OR VOLUNTEER SERVICES:
Both consulting and volunteer services are available, though the latter are limited.

NAME(S) OF PROGRAMS:
• **Early Career Research Awards**

TYPE:
Conferences/seminars; Research grants; Visiting scholars; Research contracts. Early Career Research Awards are intended to provide resources to junior faculty (untenured and within six years of earning the Ph.D.) to carry out policy-related research on labor market issues. The Institute supports and encourages research on all issues related to labor markets and public workforce policy.

YEAR PROGRAM STARTED: 1976

PURPOSE:
To conduct research into the causes and effects of unemployment and measures for the alleviation of unemployment at the national, state and local levels.

LEGAL BASIS:
Public nonprofit organization.

ELIGIBILITY:
Award proposals will be evaluated according to the following criteria:
(1) contribution to important labor market policy issues and to the professional literature;
(2) technical merit and;
(3) professional qualifications.

FINANCIAL DATA:
The Institute does not pay indirect costs but will entertain any legitimate research expense as part of the budget. Acceptable items

include costs for professional, technical, and support personnel, data acquisition, materials and supplies, computer services, and travel. The Institute does not fund dissertation research although it does have a Dissertation Award program. Grant payments are made to the individual upon award.
Amount of support per award: Up to $5,000.

NO. MOST RECENT APPLICANTS: 48.

NO. AWARDS: 17.

APPLICATION INFO:
Applicants should submit a proposal of up to 1,200 words (approximately four double-spaced pages) describing the proposed research and its relevance to labor market policy. The proposal should include an abstract and a brief budget. Applications must also include a current curriculum vitae.

Applications submitted via regular mail are to be addressed to: Institute Grant Committee, W.E. Upjohn Institute for Employment Research, at the address above. Submissions by e-mail are accepted at the Institute's e-mail address.

Duration: Ordinarily one year, which includes research and writing of paper to be submitted to a scholarly journal.

Deadline: Applications: Late January. Announcement: Early March.

PUBLICATIONS:
Program announcement; proposal guidelines.

IRS I.D.: 38-1360419

TRUSTEES:
Donald R. Parfet, Chairman
Marilyn Schlack, Vice Chairman
B. Joseph White, Secretary-Treasurer
John M. Dunn
Sydney Parfet
Frank J. Sardone
Amanda Van Dusen
Dr. Eileen Wilson-Oyelaran

ADDRESS INQUIRIES TO:
Richard Wyrwa, Manager of Publications and Marketing
(See address above.)

*PLEASE NOTE:
Awards are essentially performance-based contracts. Applications and all work submitted under Early Career Research Awards become the property of the Institute. It is Institute policy to require submission of the research paper to its working paper series. Unaccepted proposals and rejected research papers will be returned upon request, without restrictions on further use by others. It is also Institute policy to encourage publication of the sponsored research in scholarly journals following submission of the research paper to the Institute. Submission of any material waives all rights to make any claim because of any use thereof by the W.E. Upjohn Unemployment Trustee Corporation, its agents and employees.

*SPECIAL STIPULATIONS:
Award recipients are expected to write a research paper based on the funded work for submission to the Institute's working paper series, submit the paper to a peer-reviewed journal, and prepare a synopsis of the research for possible publication in the Institute's newsletter, *Employment Research*.

Law

AMERICAN ASSOCIATION OF LAW LIBRARIES

105 West Adams Street
Suite 3300
Chicago, IL 60603
(312) 939-4764
Fax: (312) 431-1097
E-mail: membership@aall.org
Web Site: www.aallnet.org

TYPE:
Scholarships. For study of law or librarianship, with support intended for prospective law librarians.

See entry 662 for full listing.

AMERICAN BAR FOUNDATION   [1797]

750 North Lake Shore Drive
Fourth Floor
Chicago, IL 60611-4403
(312) 988-6500
Fax: (312) 988-6579
E-mail: fellowships@abfn.org
Web Site: www.americanbarfoundation.org

FOUNDED: 1952

AREAS OF INTEREST:
Law, legal institutions, and legal processes and their impact on society.

NAME(S) OF PROGRAMS:
• **ABF/ALI Doctoral Fellowship Program in Legal & Higher Education**

TYPE:
Fellowships. The American Bar Foundation (ABF), in partnership with AccessLex Institute (ALI), is committed to developing the next generation of scholars interested in empirical and interdisciplinary research on legal and higher education. This is a residential fellowship at the ABF.

YEAR PROGRAM STARTED: 2017

PURPOSE:
To assist emerging scholars who are studying issues of access, affordability or value in legal or higher education; to assemble and coordinate a professional network of scholars who will produce innovative, objective, empirical and interdisciplinary research in the field.

LEGAL BASIS:
Private foundation.

ELIGIBILITY:
Applications are invited from outstanding students who are candidates for Ph.D. degrees, across a broad range of disciplines. Doctoral research must address significant issues in the field and show promise of a major contribution to social scientific understanding of legal or higher education. Students from underrepresented minority groups are especially encouraged to apply. There are no citizenship requirements for this fellowship. Non-U.S. nationals are welcome to apply; however, the ABF is unable to sponsor an H-1B visa.

FINANCIAL DATA:
Fellows will receive a stipend for up to 24 months. Fellows may also request up to $3,500 per year to reimburse for expenses associated with research, travel to meet with advisors, or travel to conferences at which

papers are presented. Doctoral Fellows may request reimbursement of reasonable relocation expenses up to $2,500.

Amount of support per award: Varies.

NO. AWARDS: Varies.

APPLICATION INFO:
Application form is available online.
Duration: One year.
Deadline: Current deadlines are posted on the Foundation web site.

ADDRESS INQUIRIES TO:
Marcilena Shaeffer, Program Coordinator
(See address above.)

*PLEASE NOTE:
Fellowships are held in residence at the ABF. Appointments to fellowships are full-time. Fellows are expected to participate fully in the academic life of the ABF so that they may develop close collegial ties with ABF faculty and other scholars in residence.

AMERICAN COLLEGE OF LEGAL MEDICINE

1061 East Main Street
Suite 300
East Dundee, IL 60118
(847) 752-5355
E-mail: info@aclm.org
Web Site: www.aclm.org

TYPE:
Awards/prizes. The Hirsh Award is awarded to a law, dentistry, podiatry, nursing, pharmacy, health science, health care administration, or public health student.

See entry 2024 for full listing.

THE CANADIAN BAR ASSOCIATION [1798]

66 Slater Street
Suite 1200
Ottawa ON K1P 5H1 Canada
(613) 237-2925
(800) 267-8860
Fax: (613) 237-0185
E-mail: info@cba.org
Web Site: www.cba.org

FOUNDED: 1914

AREAS OF INTEREST:
Law and the administration of justice, promoting access to justice and promotion of equality in the professional justice system.

NAME(S) OF PROGRAMS:
- **Viscount Bennett Fellowship**

TYPE:
Awards/prizes; Fellowships. Award is offered annually to one student for postgraduate studies in law.

YEAR PROGRAM STARTED: 1946

PURPOSE:
To encourage a high standard of legal education, training and ethics.

ELIGIBILITY:
Canadian citizens who have graduated from an approved law school in Canada or who, at the time of application, are pursuing final-year studies as undergraduate students at such approved law school. All applicants must be CBA members in good standing. Candidates must have completed and filed an application for graduate studies with the

institution of higher learning of their choice before submitting the fellowship application to the CBA.

GEOG. RESTRICTIONS: Canada.

FINANCIAL DATA:
Amount of support per award: $25,000 (CAN) paid in two equal installments.
Total amount of support: $25,000 (CAN).

NO. MOST RECENT APPLICANTS: 27.

NO. AWARDS: 1.

APPLICATION INFO:
Each applicant must submit a Viscount Bennett Application Form with relevant attachments. Applications must be accompanied by:
(1) a birth or citizenship certificate;
(2) a certified copy of all law school transcripts;
(3) a one-page synopsis highlighting pertinent information from university transcripts;
(4) a synopsis of extracurricular activities during postsecondary studies;
(5) a statement of the course of study to be pursued and;
(6) two letters of reference.

Completed application forms must be submitted to the address above:
Viscount Bennett Fellowship
c/o Senior Director of Communications and Marketing.
Duration: One year. Nonrenewable.
Deadline: November 15 (postmark).

ADDRESS INQUIRIES TO:
Senior Director of Communications and Marketing
(See address above.)

*SPECIAL STIPULATIONS:
As a condition of the Fellowship, recipient(s) of the Viscount Bennett Fellowship must submit a written report at midterm and at the end of the year of graduate study, and must submit a copy of their final thesis at year end.

CANADIAN INSTITUTE FOR ADVANCED LEGAL STUDIES [1799]

P.O. Box 43538, Leaside Post Office
1601 Bayview Avenue
Toronto ON M4G 4G8 Canada
(416) 429-3292
Fax: (416) 429-9805
E-mail: info@canadian-institute.com
Web Site: www.canadian-institute.com

FOUNDED: 1979

AREAS OF INTEREST:
Law.

NAME(S) OF PROGRAMS:
- **French Language Scholarship**
- **The Right Honourable Paul Martin, Sr. Scholarship**

TYPE:
Scholarships.

YEAR PROGRAM STARTED: 1983

PURPOSE:
French Language Scholarship: To study for the equivalent of a Master's or doctoral degree from a Canadian university at a European university where instruction is given in French.

The Right Honourable Paul Martin, Sr. Scholarship: To study for an L.L.M. at the University of Cambridge.

ELIGIBILITY:
French Language Scholarship: The Institute annually awards a scholarship for graduate studies in law toward a second-cycle or third-cycle diploma (the equivalent of a Master's or doctoral degree from a Canadian university) at a European university where instruction is given in French, to a person who has (in the four years before the candidate will commence the proposed studies) been awarded a Bachelor's degree in law from a Canadian university. An applicant must be accepted into a French-language European university for graduate studies in law in order to receive this Scholarship, although such acceptance need not be confirmed at the time of the application for the Scholarship or at the time that the Institute provides the candidate with notice that he or she has been selected to receive the Scholarship.

The Right Honourable Paul Martin, Sr. Scholarship: The Institute annually awards two full scholarships for graduate studies in law at the University of Cambridge (Cambridge, England) to candidates who have been awarded a law degree from a three- or four-year program at a faculty of law in a Canadian university in the four years before the candidate will commence his or her studies at the University of Cambridge (supported by The Right Honourable Paul Martin Sr. Scholarship). An applicant must be accepted into the University of Cambridge and a College of the University of Cambridge for graduate studies in law in order to receive this Scholarship, although such acceptance need not be confirmed at the time of the application for the Scholarship nor at the time that the Institute provides the candidate with notice that he or she has been selected to receive the Scholarship.

FINANCIAL DATA:
French Language Scholarship: Scholarship includes full tuition and includes an allowance to cover a portion of living expenses and reasonable travel expenses to and from the European university, subject to any other awards received by the successful candidate.

The Right Honourable Paul Martin, Sr. Scholarship: Scholarships include full tuition at the University of Cambridge, a monthly living allowance and return airfare, subject to any other awards received by the successful candidate.

Total amount of support: French Language Scholarship: Up to $20,000 (CAN); The Right Honourable Paul Martin, Sr. Scholarship: Approximately $35,000 (CAN).

NO. MOST RECENT APPLICANTS: French Language Scholarship: 2. The Right Honourable Paul Martin, Sr. Scholarship: 20.

NO. AWARDS: French Language Scholarship: 1. The Right Honourable Paul Martin, Sr. Scholarship: 2.

APPLICATION INFO:
French Language Scholarship: Applications must include:
(1) curriculum vitae;
(2) a personal statement indicating why the applicant wishes to undertake graduate studies in law and why the applicant is suited to undertake such studies;
(3) a copy of transcripts for undergraduate and graduate studies, for studies in law or for a Bar Admission Course, as applicable;
(4) a maximum of three letters of reference

and;

(5) a statement of tuition fees and anticipated living and travel expenses.

The Right Honourable Paul Martin, Sr. Scholarship: Applications must include:
(1) curriculum vitae;
(2) a personal statement indicating why the applicant wishes to undertake graduate studies in law at the University of Cambridge and why the applicant is suited to undertake such studies;
(3) a copy of transcripts for undergraduate and graduate studies, for studies in law and for a Bar Admissions Course, as applicable, and;
(4) a maximum of three letters of reference.

Applications may be submitted by mail or e-mail.

Duration: One year.

Deadline: December 31. Notification by April 15.

ADDRESS INQUIRIES TO:
See e-mail address above.

ENVIRONMENTAL LAW INSTITUTE   [1800]

1730 M Street, N.W.
Suite 700
Washington, DC 20036
(202) 939-3800
Fax: (202) 939-3868
E-mail: law@eli.org
Web Site: www.eli.org

FOUNDED: 1969

AREAS OF INTEREST:
Environmental law, management and policy, including economic and scientific aspects and protection of natural areas.

CONSULTING OR VOLUNTEER SERVICES:
Variety of services including tuition scholarships to continuing legal education programs, consulting services and technical assistance.

TYPE:
Scholarships. Scholarships to annual Environmental Law Course.

YEAR PROGRAM STARTED: 1970

PURPOSE:
To provide access to education on environmental law and policy; to improve the level of practice and raise the quality of debate on key legal/policy questions.

LEGAL BASIS:
Nonprofit corporation, 501(c)(3).

ELIGIBILITY:
Open to public interest lawyers, attorneys doing substantial pro bono work, and state and local government attorneys involved in environmental law.

FINANCIAL DATA:
Amount of support per award: Approximately $800 to $900 per scholarship applicant approved.
Total amount of support: Approximately $25,000 annually.

CO-OP FUNDING PROGRAMS: Environmental Law Conference with ALI-CLE.

NO. MOST RECENT APPLICANTS: Approximately 25.

NO. AWARDS: Approximately 25.

APPLICATION INFO:
Send letter of application stating need and expected benefit.

PUBLICATIONS:
Annual report; *Environmental Law Reporter*; *The Environmental Forum*; *National Wetlands Newsletter*.

IRS I.D.: 52-0901863

OFFICERS:
Scott Fulton, President

ADDRESS INQUIRIES TO:
See e-mail address above.

FOOD AND DRUG LAW INSTITUTE (FDLI)   [1801]

1155 15th Street, N.W., Suite 910
Washington, DC 20005-2706
(202) 371-1420
(800) 956-6293
Fax: (202) 371-0649
E-mail: info@fdli.org
Web Site: www.fdli.
org/resources/career/austern-writing-competition

FOUNDED: 1949

AREAS OF INTEREST:
Food and drug law issues.

NAME(S) OF PROGRAMS:
● **H. Thomas Austern Writing Competition**

TYPE:
Awards/prizes. The subject matter of the competition is an in-depth analysis of a current issue relevant to the food and drug field, including a relevant case law, legislative history and other authorities, particularly where the U.S. Food and Drug Administration is involved.

YEAR PROGRAM STARTED: 1978

PURPOSE:
To encourage law students interested in the areas of law affecting FDA regulated industries, foods, drugs, medical devices, dietary supplements, cosmetics, veterinary, cannabis or tobacco and nicotine products, and biologics; to provide a marketplace for discussing food and drug law issues.

LEGAL BASIS:
Nonprofit educational association.

ELIGIBILITY:
The level of study is postgraduate. Entrants must currently be enrolled in a J.D. program at any of the U.S. ABA-accredited law schools.

GEOG. RESTRICTIONS: United States.

FINANCIAL DATA:
Amount of support per award: $750 first prize; $500 second prize; $250 third prize.
Total amount of support: $1,500.

NO. AWARDS: 3 annually.

APPLICATION INFO:
Applicants must submit all materials electronically. Instructions can be found on the web site.
Duration: One year.
Deadline: Mid-June.

PUBLICATIONS:
Food and Drug Law Journal.

ADDRESS INQUIRIES TO:
Ren White
E-mail: ren.white@fdli.org

THE HAGUE ACADEMY OF INTERNATIONAL LAW   [1802]

Peace Palace
Carnegieplein 2
2517 KJ The Hague The Netherlands
(31) 70 3024242
E-mail: centre@hagueacademy.nl
Web Site: www.hagueacademy.nl

FOUNDED: 1914

AREAS OF INTEREST:
Public and private international law.

NAME(S) OF PROGRAMS:
● **Centre for Studies and Research in International Law and International Relations**

TYPE:
Project/program grants.

YEAR PROGRAM STARTED: 1957

PURPOSE:
To bring together young international lawyers of a high standard from all over the world, to undertake original research on a common general theme which is determined each year by the Academy.

ELIGIBILITY:
The program is open to academics or lawyers of a high standard. Applications are open only to those persons who hold advanced university degrees (a Doctorate or the Academy's diploma) or to those who provide evidence of their actual involvement, for at least three years, in international legal matters. Candidates must have real practical experience and an ability to undertake research.

FINANCIAL DATA:
Registration is free of charge and all participants receive a partial reimbursement of travel expenses.

NO. AWARDS: 20 to 24.

APPLICATION INFO:
Candidates should upload the following documents to the online registration form:
(1) a copy of their valid passport or identification;
(2) an identity photograph;
(3) a copy of their highest degree certificate or an official document from their university certifying that the applicant is preparing to obtain a degree;
(4) a curriculum vitae with, if applicable, a list of publications;
(5) a short letter stating the reasons for the application (one to two pages) and;
(6) a recommendation letter from a professor of international law.
Duration: Three weeks.
Deadline: September 1.

PUBLICATIONS:
Books of the Centre for Studies and Research - Hague Academy of International Law.

OFFICERS:
Prof. Yves Daudet, President
Jean-Marc Thouvenin, Secretary-General of the Academy

ADDRESS INQUIRIES TO:
Registration Office
(See address above.)

*PLEASE NOTE:
The research work undertaken at the Centre may be included in a collective work published by the Academy.

*SPECIAL STIPULATIONS:
In principle, no person may participate more than once in the Centre's activities. Each

participant must write an article on a subject arising out of the general theme of the year, which will be determined by the Director of Research. This report must be sent to the relevant Director of Research, by mid-November at the latest.

THE HAGUE ACADEMY OF INTERNATIONAL LAW   [1803]

Peace Palace
Carnegieplein 2
2517 KJ The Hague The Netherlands
(31) 70 3024242
E-mail: registration@hagueacademy.nl
Web Site: www.hagueacademy.nl

FOUNDED: 1914

AREAS OF INTEREST:
Public and private international law.

NAME(S) OF PROGRAMS:
● **External Programme**

TYPE:
Project/program grants. External Programme is held each year, in turn in Africa, Asia and Latin America, upon the invitation of host governments or international organizations. It is designed for approximately 20 participants from the countries in the region (who are resident in their own country), whose traveling expenses are usually financed by the Academy and whose accommodation is financed by the government of the host state or organization. In addition, 20 participants come from the host state itself.

YEAR PROGRAM STARTED: 1969

ELIGIBILITY:
This programme is aimed at persons having studied international law (young university teachers and young civil servants from the ministry of foreign affairs or other ministries), selected by the Secretary-General in the name of the Curatorium on exclusively scientific criteria. Candidates should come from countries in the region of the host country. A list of the eligible nationalities is published every year.

FINANCIAL DATA:
Regional participants receive a daily allowance according to the length of the stay and the reimbursement of their travel expenses. The accommodation is provided by the host country.

NO. MOST RECENT APPLICANTS: 50.

NO. AWARDS: 20.

APPLICATION INFO:
Candidates should apply online with the following:
(1) a curriculum vitae with, if applicable, a list of publications;
(2) a copy of candidate's highest degree certificate or an official document from candidate's university certifying candidate is preparing to obtain a degree. If the original document is not in English or French, please add a translation;
(3) a short letter giving reasons for the application (one to two pages);
(4) a recommendation letter from a professor of international law sent separately;
(5) a copy of candidate's valid passport or ID and;
(6) an identity photograph.
Duration: Eight days.
Deadline: July 31.

OFFICERS:
Prof. Yves Daudet, President
Jean-Marc Thouvenin, Secretary-General of the Academy

ADDRESS INQUIRIES TO:
Registration Office
(See address above.)

*SPECIAL STIPULATIONS:
One is not allowed to participate more than once in the External Programme. Candidates should reside in their home country when applying.

THE HAGUE ACADEMY OF INTERNATIONAL LAW   [1804]

Peace Palace
Carnegieplein 2
2517 KJ The Hague The Netherlands
(31) 70 3024242
E-mail: registration@hagueacademy.nl
Web Site: www.hagueacademy.nl

FOUNDED: 1914

AREAS OF INTEREST:
Private and public international law.

NAME(S) OF PROGRAMS:
● **Doctoral Scholarships in International Law**

TYPE:
Project/program grants. Study programs. Residential scholarships for doctoral candidates from developing countries whose thesis, in private international law or public international law, is in the process of completion, who reside in their home country and who do not have access to scientific sources.

YEAR PROGRAM STARTED: 1923

PURPOSE:
To facilitate the completion of the theses through the use of the Academy, and especially the resources of the Library of the Peace Palace.

LEGAL BASIS:
Non-governmental organization.

ELIGIBILITY:
The candidates' doctoral thesis should be in the process of completion. Applicant should be a national of a non-member state of the OECD, who is a resident in their own country.

FINANCIAL DATA:
Help in the form of a contribution towards travelling expenses may be granted to participants, taking into account the distance of their country of normal residence.
Amount of support per award: EUR 2,250 plus half of the traveling expenses, up to a maximum of EUR 910.

NO. MOST RECENT APPLICANTS: 30.

NO. AWARDS: 4.

APPLICATION INFO:
Application online only. Applications should be accompanied by a recommendation from the professor under whose direction the thesis is being written which mentions the title of the thesis. It should also contain a curriculum vitae, a copy of the highest degree certificate (translated in French or English) and a short letter giving reasons for application.
Duration: Eight weeks, July to September.
Deadline: January 31.

PUBLICATIONS:
Programme de la Session; Collected Courses, series of published lectures.

ADDRESS INQUIRIES TO:
Registration Office
(See address above.)

*SPECIAL STIPULATIONS:
The Academy will verify that recipients of scholarships are effectively resident in The Hague without interruption and that they use the Peace Palace Library on a regular basis.

No person may receive more than one scholarship.

THE HAGUE ACADEMY OF INTERNATIONAL LAW   [1805]

Peace Palace
Carnegieplein 2
2517 KJ The Hague The Netherlands
(31) 70 3024242
E-mail: registration@hagueacademy.nl
Web Site: www.hagueacademy.nl

FOUNDED: 1914

AREAS OF INTEREST:
Private and public international law.

NAME(S) OF PROGRAMS:
● **Hague Academy of International Law Summer Courses**

TYPE:
Project/program grants; Scholarships. Study programs. A limited number of scholarships are given to cover tuition and living expenses while studying at the three-week summer session of the Hague Academy of International Law. Because of the limited number, granting of scholarships is based solely on academic merit.

YEAR PROGRAM STARTED: 1923

PURPOSE:
To support personal and effective participation of members in scientific work related to international law and international affairs.

ELIGIBILITY:
Candidates must have completed at least four consecutive years of university studies, which must have included lectures on International Law, or must hold a three-year law degree on the date of the opening of the courses. All candidates must master one of the two working languages of the Academy - English or French.

FINANCIAL DATA:
Amount of support per award: EUR 2,000 (including registration fees of EUR 1,100) covering accommodation expenses incurred during the three weeks of one of the teaching periods. Travelling expenses will be partially reimbursed either by the relevant donor or by the Academy.

NO. MOST RECENT APPLICANTS: 680.

NO. AWARDS: 100.

APPLICATION INFO:
Application for scholarship should be made through the online registration form. The application must contain an identity photograph, a curriculum vitae, a copy of the highest degree certificate (translated in English or French), a short letter giving reason for the application and a recommendation from a professor of international law, sent separately.
Duration: Three weeks in public international law; three weeks in private international law.

Deadline: Complete files of scholarship candidates should be in the possession of the Secretariat before January 31.

PUBLICATIONS:
Collected Courses, series of published lectures.

OFFICERS:
Prof. Yves Daudet, President
Jean-Marc Thouvenin, Secretary-General of the Academy

ADDRESS INQUIRIES TO:
Registration Office
(See address above.)

*SPECIAL STIPULATIONS:
No person may receive more than one scholarship for the Summer Courses. Recipients of scholarships are required to attend the Academy's courses throughout the session.

THE HISPANIC BAR ASSOCIATION OF D.C. FOUNDATION   [1806]

1341 G Street, N.W.
Suite 500
Washington, DC 20005
(202) 466-8585
Fax: (202) 463-4803
E-mail: foundation@hbadc.org
Web Site: www.hbadc.org

FOUNDED: 1995

AREAS OF INTEREST:
Law and public interest.

NAME(S) OF PROGRAMS:
● **The HBA-DC Foundation Fellowship**

TYPE:
Fellowships.

PURPOSE:
To provide students with valuable work experience and exposure to an area of public interest law.

ELIGIBILITY:
First- and second-year law students attending accredited law schools in the District of Columbia metropolitan area are eligible to apply, once having obtained a job offer from a sponsoring organization.

GEOG. RESTRICTIONS: District of Columbia and the metropolitan area.

FINANCIAL DATA:
Amount of support per award: Minimum $5,000.
Total amount of support: Varies.

NO. AWARDS: 1 or more.

APPLICATION INFO:
Application information is available on the web site. Completed application must be submitted by e-mail to fellowships@hbadc.org.
Duration: Annual.
Deadline: Dates are posted on the Foundation web site.

ADDRESS INQUIRIES TO:
See e-mail address above.

THE HISPANIC NATIONAL BAR FOUNDATION   [1807]

1900 K Street, N.W.
Suite 100
Washington, DC 20006
(786) 340-9991
E-mail: info@hnbf.org
Web Site: www.hnbf.org

FOUNDED: 1985

AREAS OF INTEREST:
Promoting the legal education of persons of Hispanic heritage throughout the U.S. and Puerto Rico.

NAME(S) OF PROGRAMS:
● **Future Latino Leaders Summer Law Institute**

TYPE:
Conferences/seminars; Training grants. Nine-day program held by the Foundation in Washington, DC which provides Latino high school students with the opportunity to learn more about the legal profession. The Summer Law Institute offers students the chance to come to the nation's capital and learn more about the college application process, meet influential Latino leaders, and tour national monuments and various government agencies.

YEAR PROGRAM STARTED: 2005

PURPOSE:
To provide tools and resources necessary to ensure full and equal opportunity for Hispanics to become leaders in the global community, thereby ensuring a brighter future for all.

LEGAL BASIS:
Section 501(c)(3) organization dedicated to charitable and educational purposes.

ELIGIBILITY:
Applicants must meet the following criteria:
(1) be a high school student entering the sophomore, junior or senior year, or be a recent graduate;
(2) have an interest in learning about law school and becoming a lawyer;
(3) be a U.S. citizen, legal permanent resident or be a legal U.S. visitor with a valid visa and passport and;
(4) have a demonstrated interest in helping one's community and building one's leadership skills.

FINANCIAL DATA:
There is no cost to participate in the Summer Law Institute. However, accepted students must pay a $50 application fee, unless a waiver of this fee is requested and granted. Students are also responsible for arranging transportation to Washington, DC. The cost of transportation should not deter one from applying. Upon acceptance to the program, the Foundation is committed to working with the attendee and his or her family in order to ensure that person's ability to attend.
Amount of support per award: Valued at over $3,000 per person.

NO. MOST RECENT APPLICANTS: 100.

NO. AWARDS: 32.

APPLICATION INFO:
Application process begins mid-February. Application can be completed online or sent by mail and must include:
(1) Applicant Information Form;
(2) signed Rules and Regulations Form;
(3) two essays;
(4) two letters of recommendation (from teachers, counselors or employers);
(5) resume (may include community service, leadership positions or civic activities);
(6) certified copy of academic record from high school and;
(7) $50 application fee or fee waiver approval.
Duration: Nine days.

ADDRESS INQUIRIES TO:
See e-mail address above.

JOHN M. LLOYD FOUNDATION   [1808]

11777 San Vicente Boulevard
Suite 745
Los Angeles, CA 90049
(310) 622-1050
E-mail: truejustice@johnmlloyd.org
Web Site: johnmlloyd.org

FOUNDED: 1991

AREAS OF INTEREST:
Criminal justice reform primarily in Los Angeles County, CA.

TYPE:
General operating grants; Project/program grants.

YEAR PROGRAM STARTED: 1992

PURPOSE:
To promote one just criminal justice system in Los Angeles County, CA, a system centered on strong communities and practical resources, not prisons; to help Los Angeles County become a leader in a movement toward true justice nationwide.

LEGAL BASIS:
Private, family foundation.

ELIGIBILITY:
The Foundation does not accept unsolicited requests for funding at this time.

GEOG. RESTRICTIONS: Primarily Los Angeles County, California.

FINANCIAL DATA:
Amount of support per award: Varies; most grants are about $30,000.
Total amount of support: $310,500 for the year 2018.

NO. AWARDS: 13 for the year 2018.

REPRESENTATIVE AWARDS:
Dignity and Power Now; Youth Justice Coalition; Healing Dialogue and Action.

APPLICATION INFO:
Unsolicited formal proposals will not be considered.
Duration: One year and multiyear grants.

IRS I.D.: 36-3766003

BOARD OF DIRECTORS:
Mark-Anthony Clayton-Johnson
Eliot Estrin
Jesse Estrin
Mary Lloyd Estrin
Robert L. Estrin
Griff Foxley
Zoe Lloyd Foxley
Trish Devine Karlin
Linda Dorn Klein
Heidi Mage Lloyd
Pricilla Ocen
Gabrielle Zhuang

ADDRESS INQUIRIES TO:
Melanie Havelin, Executive Director
(See e-mail address above.)

*SPECIAL STIPULATIONS:
Unsolicited formal proposals will not be considered.

MCGILL UNIVERSITY [1809]

Chancellor Day Hall
3644 Peel Street
Montreal QC H3A 1W9 Canada
(514) 398-6616
E-mail: staffappointments.law@mcgill.ca
Web Site: www.mcgill.ca/law

AREAS OF INTEREST:
Law, especially pertaining to the Canadian legal system and legal community. Particular interest in projects relating to Indigenous law.

NAME(S) OF PROGRAMS:
● **Maxwell Boulton Q.C. Fellowship**

TYPE:
Fellowships.

YEAR PROGRAM STARTED: 1983

PURPOSE:
To provide younger scholars with an opportunity to pursue a major research project or to complete the research requirement for a higher degree.

ELIGIBILITY:
Open to candidates who have completed residency requirements for a doctoral degree in law.

FINANCIAL DATA:
Amount of support per award: $45,000 (CAN) per year.

NO. MOST RECENT APPLICANTS: 2.

NO. AWARDS: 1.

APPLICATION INFO:
Information is available on the web site.
Duration: One year.
Deadline: February 1.

ADDRESS INQUIRIES TO:
See e-mail address above.

REPORTERS COMMITTEE FOR FREEDOM OF THE PRESS

1156 15th Street, N.W.
Suite 1020
Washington, DC 20005
(202) 795-9306
Fax: (202) 795-9310
E-mail: kpoole@rcfp.org
Web Site: www.rcfp.org

TYPE:
Fellowships. Legal fellows monitor significant developments in First Amendment media law, assist with legal defense requests from reporters, prepare legal memoranda, amicus briefs and other special projects. The Fellowship focuses on media law.

See entry 1787 for full listing.

RHODE ISLAND STATE GOVERNMENT INTERNSHIP PROGRAM

State House, Room 8AA
Providence, RI 02903
(401) 222-6782
Fax: (401) 222-4447
E-mail: intern@rilegislature.gov
blanzi@rilegislature.gov
Web Site: www.rilegislature.gov/internship

TYPE:
Internships. Funding through General Assembly is also available. Internship opportunities for graduate and undergraduate students in the state government operation. Students are involved in executive, legislative and judicial assignments. The internship is viewed as an extension of the classroom and is seen as complementing and building upon the educational opportunities available on campuses.

This program has established a Summer Internship section, open to Rhode Island residents only, that begins in late June and concludes in August.

See entry 1834 for full listing.

THE UNIVERSITY OF CALGARY [1810]

Faculty of Graduate Studies
Earth Sciences Building, Room 1010
2500 University Drive, N.W.
Calgary AB T2N 1N4 Canada
(403) 220-4938
Fax: (403) 289-7635
E-mail: gsaward@ucalgary.ca
Web Site: grad.ucalgary.ca/awards

FOUNDED: 1966

AREAS OF INTEREST:
Law.

NAME(S) OF PROGRAMS:
● **The Honourable N.D. McDermid Graduate Scholarship in Law**

TYPE:
Awards/prizes; Scholarships. Graduate scholarships in law tenable at The University of Calgary. Awards endowed by the McDermid Law Fund in memory of the late Honourable Neil Douglas McDermid, Q.C., who was a prominent member of the legal profession of Alberta and the Calgary community for many years.

PURPOSE:
To financially assist students who want to study law at the university.

LEGAL BASIS:
University.

ELIGIBILITY:
Graduate students entering or enrolled on a full-time basis in the graduate program in the Faculty of Law at The University of Calgary. If, in the opinion of the Faculty of Graduate Studies Scholarships Selection Committee, no suitable applications are received, no awards will be made.

GEOG. RESTRICTIONS: Canada.

FINANCIAL DATA:
Amount of support per award: $14,000 (award may be divided further to $7,000).
Total amount of support: $28,000.

NO. AWARDS: 2 to 4.

APPLICATION INFO:
Application forms are available from the Dean's Office, Faculty of Law. Applications will be reviewed by a Committee of the Faculty of Law based upon academic excellence. The Graduate Coordinator, Law will submit recommendations to the Graduate Scholarship Office. The recommendation is subject to final approval of the Graduate Scholarship Committee.
Duration: One year. Nonrenewable.
Deadline: December 15.

ADDRESS INQUIRIES TO:
Graduate Scholarship Office
(See address above.)

THE UNIVERSITY OF CALGARY

Faculty of Graduate Studies
Earth Sciences Building, Room 1010
2500 University Drive, N.W.
Calgary AB T2N 1N4 Canada
(403) 220-4938
Fax: (403) 289-7635
E-mail: gsaward@ucalgary.ca
Web Site: grad.ucalgary.ca/awards

TYPE:
Awards/prizes; Scholarships.

See entry 1625 for full listing.

Political science

AMERICAN POLITICAL SCIENCE ASSOCIATION [1811]

1527 New Hampshire Avenue, N.W.
Washington, DC 20036
(202) 483-2512
Fax: (202) 483-2657
E-mail: cfp@apsanet.org
Web Site: www.apsanet.org/cfp

FOUNDED: 1903

AREAS OF INTEREST:
Political science.

NAME(S) OF PROGRAMS:
● **Congressional Fellowship Program**

TYPE:
Fellowships. Awards to political science professors and journalists in early-career to midcareer status; the award provides an opportunity for support as a full-time aide to a member of the House or Senate or as a staff member for a Congressional committee.

YEAR PROGRAM STARTED: 1953

PURPOSE:
To equip outstanding young political scientists and journalists with a better understanding of the national legislative process.

LEGAL BASIS:
Nonprofit association.

ELIGIBILITY:
Open to U.S. political scientists and journalists. Political scientists must have completed their Ph.D. within the last 15 years or will have defended a dissertation by the start of the fellowship year. Applicant journalists must have a Bachelor's degree and between two and 10 years of full-time professional experience in newspaper, magazine, radio or television work. Special fellowships are available for Ph.D.-level scholars of any discipline or journalists with demonstrated professional interest in telecommunications.

FINANCIAL DATA:
Amount of support per award: $52,500 stipend plus travel.

NO. MOST RECENT APPLICANTS: Varies.

NO. AWARDS: Varies.

APPLICATION INFO:
Official application materials are available on the web site.
Duration: 10 months, November to August.
Deadline: Early December

ADDRESS INQUIRIES TO:
See e-mail address above.

AMERICAN POLITICAL SCIENCE ASSOCIATION [1812]

1527 New Hampshire Avenue, N.W.
Washington, DC 20036
(202) 483-2512
Fax: (202) 483-2657
E-mail: kmealy@apsanet.org
Web Site: www.apsanet.org/mfp

FOUNDED: 1903

AREAS OF INTEREST:
Political science.

NAME(S) OF PROGRAMS:
● **APSA Minority Fellows Program**

TYPE:
Fellowships; Grants-in-aid; Scholarships.
Awards to aid prospective African American,
Asian Pacific, Latino/Latina and Native
American political science students beginning
the doctoral study of political science.

YEAR PROGRAM STARTED: 1969

PURPOSE:
To increase the number of minority scholars
in the discipline; to assist minority students
in completing their Doctorates by
concentrating not only on the recruitment of
minorities, but also on the retention of these
groups within the profession.

LEGAL BASIS:
Nonprofit association.

ELIGIBILITY:
Applicants must:
(1) be minority students applying to enter a
doctoral program in political science for the
first time;
(2) be members of one of the following
racial/ethnic minority groups: African
Americans, Asian Pacific Americans,
Latinos/Latinas, and Native Americans
(federal and state recognized tribes);
(3) demonstrate an interest in teaching and
potential for research in political science and;
(4) be a U.S. citizen, U.S. national,
permanent resident or an individual granted
Deferred Action for Childhood Arrivals
(DACA) program status at time of
application.

FINANCIAL DATA:
Amount of support per award: $4,000,
disbursed in two $2,000 payments, one at the
end of their first graduate year and one at the
end of their second, provided that they
remain in good academic standing.

NO. MOST RECENT APPLICANTS: 20.

NO. AWARDS: 16 for the year 2019-20.

APPLICATION INFO:
Forms can be downloaded from the web site.
Duration: One year.
Deadline: Varies.

ADDRESS INQUIRIES TO:
Kimberly Mealy
Senior Director, Diversity and Inclusion
(See address above.)

AMERICAN POLITICAL SCIENCE ASSOCIATION [1813]

1527 New Hampshire Avenue, N.W.
Washington, DC 20036
(202) 483-2512
Fax: (202) 483-2657
E-mail: centennial@apsnet.org
Web Site: www.apsanet.org/smallresearchgrant

AREAS OF INTEREST:
Political science.

NAME(S) OF PROGRAMS:
● **Small Research Grant Program**

TYPE:
Project/program grants; Research grants;
Seed money grants; Technical assistance;
Travel grants. The Association Small
Research Grant Program supports research in
all fields of political science.

PURPOSE:
To support the research of political scientists
who are not employed at Ph.D.-granting
departments in the field, or who are in
non-tenure track or contingent positions
ineligible for departmental funding.

ELIGIBILITY:
Applicants must be Association members at
the time of application and when the funds
are dispersed. The principal investigator and
any coauthor must be one of the following:
(1) a Ph.D. faculty member at a college or
university that does not award a Ph.D. in
political science, public administration, public
policy, international relations, government or
politics and whose primary appointment is in
one of these departments or;
(2) a Ph.D. faculty member at a college or
university that awards the Ph.D. in political
science who is on a non-tenure or contingent
track, and ineligible for departmental funding
or;
(3) a political scientist not affiliated with an
academic institution who is unemployed or
working in a research organization such as a
think tank.

This grant does not provide support for
dissertation research or writing. Graduate
students are not eligible to apply. Applicants
do not have to be U.S. citizens or residents.

FINANCIAL DATA:
Funds may be used for travel to archives,
travel to conduct interviews, administration
and coding of instruments, research
assistance, and purchase of data-sets. Travel
to professional meetings, secretarial costs
except for preparation of the final
manuscripts for publication, and salary
support for the principal investigator are
excluded from funding. Overhead or indirect
costs are not allowable expenses.
Amount of support per award: Up to $2,500.

APPLICATION INFO:
Complete proposal and application
procedures as well as sample proposals can
be found on the web site. Application must
be submitted through the link on the Small
Research Grant Program web page.
Duration: One year. Nonrenewable.
Deadline: Submission date will be posted
online.

*SPECIAL STIPULATIONS:
Funds must be expended between the time
they are received (usually in May) and the
end of the following fiscal year (June 30).

ASHBURN INSTITUTE INC.

198 Okatie Village Drive
Suite 103, PMB 301
Bluffton, SC 29909
(703) 728-6482
Fax: (843) 705-7643
E-mail: info@ashburninstitute.org
Web Site: www.ashburninstitute.org

TYPE:
Research grants; Scholarships. The Institute
carries out its own scholarship program for
graduate students through an annual

endowment received in perpetuity. Half of
the funds must be awarded to U.S. citizens.
The best papers which meet the goals of the
conference, as outlined in the "Call for
Papers," will reimburse the graduate authors
by covering their conference travel and
lodging expenses. Locations for the
conference may be anywhere in the world.
The top papers are selected for publication
with due credit to the authors.

Funding is provided by the gracious
endowment left by Mayme and Herb Frank
for the purpose of promoting international
integration and harmonization.

See entry 768 for full listing.

CENTER FOR CALIFORNIA STUDIES, CAPITAL FELLOWS PROGRAMS [1814]

California State University, Sacramento
6000 J Street, MS 6081
Sacramento, CA 95819-6081
(916) 278-6906
Fax: (916) 278-5199
E-mail: calstudies@csus.edu
Web Site: www.csus.edu/center/center-california-studies

FOUNDED: 1982

AREAS OF INTEREST:
California state government and public
service.

NAME(S) OF PROGRAMS:
● **Executive Fellowship Program**
● **Judicial Fellowship Program**
● **Senate Fellowship Program**
● **Jesse M. Unruh Assembly Fellowship Program**

TYPE:
Fellowships. Sponsored by the Center for
California Studies at California State
University, Sacramento. Full-time fellowships
for 64 fellows across four programs, 10 to 11
months, and graduate units earned from
California State University, Sacramento.

PURPOSE:
To provide insight into the legislative
process, including exposing people with
diverse life experience and backgrounds to
the legislative process; to provide research
and other professional staff assistance to the
Assembly or Senate; to provide an
experiential learning opportunity in California
state government within the Executive
branch, whereby Fellows gain valuable
insight and experience in the realm of public
policy and politics; to enable fellows to
conduct research, advocate on behalf of the
judiciary, develop and implement programs,
seek grants, and engage in education
outreach, strategic, planning, and policy
analysis.

LEGAL BASIS:
University/government program funded by
State Budget-General Budget Fund.

ELIGIBILITY:
Must be 20 years of age by September 1 of
fellowship year and have a minimum
four-year Bachelor's degree with graduation
by September 1 of fellowship year. Graduate,
postgraduate and midcareer applicants are
welcome.

FINANCIAL DATA:
In addition to the stipend, full medical, vision
and dental benefits are provided.

Amount of support per award: $2,794 monthly stipend (taxable income).

NO. MOST RECENT APPLICANTS: 1,300.

NO. AWARDS: 64.

APPLICATION INFO:
Applications will only be accepted online. Applicants must submit all transcripts, three letters of recommendation (minimum), and required writing prompts.

Duration: 10 to 11 months.

Deadline: February. Interviews in southern California and Sacramento in April/May. Fellowship announcement in May.

ADDRESS INQUIRIES TO:
Leonor Ehling, Executive Director
(See address above.)

*SPECIAL STIPULATIONS:
International fellows must have a valid work visa.

CITY OF NEW YORK [1815]

Department of Citywide Administrative Services
One Centre Street, Room 2425
New York, NY 10007
(212) 386-0058
E-mail: urbanfellows@dcas.nyc.gov
Web Site: www.nyc.gov/fellowships

FOUNDED: 1969

AREAS OF INTEREST:
City government and New York City government.

NAME(S) OF PROGRAMS:
● **New York City Urban Fellows Program**

TYPE:
Fellowships. Stipend for full-time work in New York City government agencies. Fellows work closely with city officials on long- and short-term projects and attend weekly seminars to get an academic perspective on the workings and problems of local government. Assignments range over fields such as urban planning, housing, health and social sciences, economic and financial administration, youth service, intergovernmental relations, criminal justice, cultural affairs and innumerable others. Positions are at relatively high levels as assistants to administrators and staff within the various city agencies.

YEAR PROGRAM STARTED: 1969

PURPOSE:
To attract qualified college graduates to participate in a management training program in New York City government.

LEGAL BASIS:
City Government agency.

ELIGIBILITY:
As of September of the program year, applicants must be recent college graduates (no more than two full years out of college). Fellows participate on a full-time basis. Applicants must be able to demonstrate their eligibility to work in the U.S. after graduation and for the entire fellowship period.

FINANCIAL DATA:
A choice of paid health insurance plans is provided.

Amount of support per award: $31,563 for the year 2019-20.

NO. MOST RECENT APPLICANTS: Approximately 300.

NO. AWARDS: 25 annually.

APPLICATION INFO:
Application information is available on the web site.

Duration: Nine months, September to May.

Deadline: Second Friday in January.

PUBLICATIONS:
Application guidelines.

ADDRESS INQUIRIES TO:
New York City Urban Fellows Program
(See address above.)

CONGRESSIONAL BLACK CAUCUS FOUNDATION, INC.

1720 Massachusetts Avenue, N.W.
Washington, DC 20036
(202) 263-2800
Fax: (202) 263-0846
E-mail: scholarships@cbcfinc.org
Web Site: www.cbcfinc.org

TYPE:
Scholarships. The CBC Spouses Education Scholarship is a national program that awards scholarships to academically talented and highly motivated students who intend to pursue full-time undergraduate, graduate or doctoral degrees.

See entry 938 for full listing.

CONGRESSIONAL BLACK CAUCUS FOUNDATION, INC.

1720 Massachusetts Avenue, N.W.
Washington, DC 20036
(202) 263-2800
Fax: (202) 263-0846
E-mail: info@cbcfinc.org
internships@cbcfinc.org
Web Site: www.cbcfinc.org

TYPE:
Fellowships; Internships. The CBCF Congressional Fellows Program helps participants gain invaluable experience as they assist in the development of legislation and public policy initiatives while working as congressional staff for a year. This program targets early career policy professionals who have completed a professional and/or graduate degree and have demonstrated commitment to improving the lives and services for individuals living in underserved communities. Fellows work on Capitol Hill in the office of a Congressional Black Caucus member.

The CBCF Congressional Internship Program provides undergraduate students with an in-depth orientation to Capitol Hill and the legislative process through actual work experience in the offices of Congressional Black Caucus Members. In this way interns prepare to become decision makers in the policymaking process.

See entry 940 for full listing.

CONGRESSIONAL HISPANIC CAUCUS INSTITUTE

1128 16th Street, N.W.
Washington, DC 20036
(202) 543-1771
Fax: (202) 546-2143
E-mail: programs@chci.org
Web Site: www.chci.org

TYPE:
Internships. Internships provide college students with a paid work placement in a congressional office or federal agency for a period of 12 weeks (Spring and Fall Programs) or 10 weeks (Summer Program), as well as extensive professional development and leadership trainings.

See entry 972 for full listing.

CONGRESSIONAL HISPANIC CAUCUS INSTITUTE

1128 16th Street, N.W.
Washington, DC 20036
(202) 543-1771
(202) 548-8796
Fax: (202) 546-8799
E-mail: programs@chci.org
Web Site: chci.org

TYPE:
Fellowships. Graduate Fellowship Program offers exceptional Latinos who have earned a graduate degree or higher related to a chosen policy issue area within three years of program start date unparalleled exposure to hands-on experience in public policy.

Public Policy Fellowship offers talented Latinos who have earned a Bachelor's degree within two years of the program start date the opportunity to gain hands-on experience at the national level in public policy.

See entry 973 for full listing.

THE DIRKSEN CONGRESSIONAL CENTER [1816]

2815 Broadway
Pekin, IL 61554
(309) 347-7113
E-mail: fmackaman@dirksencenter.org
Web Site: www.dirksencongressionalcenter.org

FOUNDED: 1963

AREAS OF INTEREST:
U.S. Congress and its leaders.

NAME(S) OF PROGRAMS:
● **Congressional Research Grants**

TYPE:
Research grants; Seed money grants; Travel grants. Financial awards to individuals conducting research about the U.S. Congress and its leaders.

YEAR PROGRAM STARTED: 1978

PURPOSE:
To foster study of Congress in order to enhance public understanding and appreciation of the legislative branch of the federal government.

LEGAL BASIS:
Independent, nonpartisan, not-for-profit research and educational organization.

ELIGIBILITY:
Open to anyone with a serious interest in studying Congress. The Center seeks applications specifically from political scientists, historians, biographers, scholars of public administration or American studies or journalists. Graduate students may also apply.

The program does not fund undergraduates or pre-Ph.D. study. Organizations are not eligible. No institutional overhead or indirect costs will be covered.

FINANCIAL DATA:
Amount of support per award: Up to $3,500.

Total amount of support: $50,000 for the year 2019.

NO. MOST RECENT APPLICANTS: 45,

NO. AWARDS: Approximately 15 per year.

APPLICATION INFO:
Details on application are available on the web site.

Duration: Usually one year.

Deadline: Applications are accepted on a rolling basis. Announcements made quarterly.

IRS I.D.: 36-6132816

BOARD OF DIRECTORS:
Greg S. Cassidy
Denny Kief
Scott Kriegsman
Janet M. Lange
Carol Merna
Shaun Newell
Kimberly Remmert
Timothy J. Schwartz
Brad Stotler
Kay Sutton
Leslie K. Weyhrich
Tiffany White
James Wolf

ADDRESS INQUIRIES TO:
Frank H. Mackaman
(See address above.)

*SPECIAL STIPULATIONS:
This program does not fund tuition.

DONNER CANADIAN FOUNDATION   [1817]
8 Prince Arthur Avenue, 3rd Floor
Toronto ON M5R 1A9 Canada
(416) 920-6400
Fax: (416) 920-5577
E-mail: mclean@donner.ca
Web Site: www.donnerfoundation.org

FOUNDED: 1950

AREAS OF INTEREST:
Public policy research and education, environment and wildlife preservation, international development and human rights, and social services.

TYPE:
Project/program grants.

PURPOSE:
To determine how government handles public assets in delivering public services.

LEGAL BASIS:
Private foundation.

ELIGIBILITY:
The Foundation only makes grants to charitable organizations under the Income Tax Act of Canada. Grants are usually made for specific projects. The Foundation does not make grants for ongoing expenses, the acquisition of capital (equipment, buildings, land, etc.), endowments, fund-raising drives or to cover budget deficits. The Foundation does not accept unsolicited proposals.

GEOG. RESTRICTIONS: Canada.

FINANCIAL DATA:
Amount of support per award: Varies.
Total amount of support: Approximately $3,800,000 for the year 2019.

NO. AWARDS: More than 70 for the year 2019.

APPLICATION INFO:
The Foundation does not regularly respond to letters of inquiry or unsolicited requests for funding. Charitable organizations may send the Foundation's Executive Director a two- to three-page description of their goals and programs and if there is a potential match between this work and the interests of the Foundation, staff will contact the charity for more information.

Duration: One year.

EXECUTIVE DIRECTOR:
Helen McLean

ADDRESS INQUIRIES TO:
Helen McLean, Executive Director
(See address above.)

*PLEASE NOTE:
The Foundation only provides support to organizations recognized as charitable by the Canada Revenue Agency.

THE EISENHOWER FOUNDATION   [1818]
200 S.E. 4th Street
Abilene, KS 67410
(785) 263-6771
Fax: (785) 263-6715
E-mail: info@eisenhowerfoundation.net
Web Site: www.EisenhowerFoundation.net

AREAS OF INTEREST:
Scholarly research in the fields of history, government, economics, communications and international affairs.

NAME(S) OF PROGRAMS:
● **Travel Grants**

TYPE:
Travel grants. Travel grants are awarded to individual researchers on a competitive basis to cover a portion of expenses while in Abilene, KS, using the presidential library.

PURPOSE:
To assist scholars' research of primary sources in such fields as history, government, economics, communications and international affairs so they may provide informed leadership in American national life.

ELIGIBILITY:
Applicants must be graduate-level students.

FINANCIAL DATA:
Grants are not retroactive and travel must occur within one year of award.
Amount of support per award: Up to $1,000, dependent on application and review board recommendations.
Total amount of support: Varies.

NO. MOST RECENT APPLICANTS: 18.

NO. AWARDS: 17.

APPLICATION INFO:
Applications may be accessed online.
Deadline: Varies.

ADDRESS INQUIRIES TO:
Eisenhower Foundation
P.O. Box 295
Abilene, KS 67410
(See e-mail address above.)

*SPECIAL STIPULATIONS:
If grantee's research results in a thesis, dissertation, book or article, a copy of the final product must be submitted to the Eisenhower Library for its holdings.

GERALD R. FORD PRESIDENTIAL LIBRARY   [1819]
1000 Beal Avenue
Ann Arbor, MI 48109
(734) 205-0555
Fax: (734) 205-0571
E-mail: ford.library@nara.gov
Web Site: www.fordlibrarymuseum.gov

AREAS OF INTEREST:
Domestic issues, foreign policy and politics of the 1970s.

NAME(S) OF PROGRAMS:
● **Research Travel Grant Program**

TYPE:
Research grants; Travel grants. Research Travel Grants are awarded biannually to scholars to help defray the expenses of travel to conduct archival research in the collections of the Ford Library. Library collections focus on federal policies, foreign relations, and politics in the 1970s.

PURPOSE:
To promote research in the holdings of the Ford Library.

ELIGIBILITY:
Overseas applicants are welcome to apply, but they are responsible for costs of travel from their home country to North America.

FINANCIAL DATA:
Amount of support per award: Maximum $2,200.
Total amount of support: Typically, $45,000 annually.

NO. MOST RECENT APPLICANTS: 40.

NO. AWARDS: Varies.

APPLICATION INFO:
Before applying, contact the Library for information about holdings related to your project. Applicants should submit the application form, a curriculum vitae, and a two- or three-page project proposal to the Library. The proposal should provide both a description of the project and the ways in which Ford Library resources can advance the research. Three professional references must submit supporting letters of recommendation.

Materials can be submitted electronically or sent by e-mail to:
travelgrant@38foundation.org.
Duration: Research to be conducted within one year notice of award.
Deadline: March 15 and September 15 (postmark).

ADDRESS INQUIRIES TO:
Kristy Lecceadone, Grants Manager
303 Pearl Street, N.W.
Grand Rapids, MI 49504
Tel: (616) 254-0396
E-mail: travelgrant@38foundation.org

*SPECIAL STIPULATIONS:
The Gerald R. Ford Foundation expects acknowledgment of its support in resulting publication(s) and a donated copy of same to the Gerald R. Ford Presidential Library.

GERALD R. FORD PRESIDENTIAL LIBRARY   [1820]
1000 Beal Avenue
Ann Arbor, MI 48109
(734) 205-0558
Fax: (734) 205-0571
E-mail: ford.library@nara.gov
Web Site: www.fordlibrarymuseum.gov

FOUNDED: 1981

AREAS OF INTEREST:
The U.S. political process, broadly defined, since circa 1970. Of special interest is the role and analysis of public opinion in that process.

NAME(S) OF PROGRAMS:
- **Gerald R. Ford Scholar Award (Dissertation Award) in Honor of Robert M. Teeter**

TYPE:
Awards/prizes; Research grants. Annual award to a doctoral student doing dissertation research and writing on an aspect of the U.S. political process during the latter part of the 20th century. Robert Teeter spent over 30 years as a leader in public opinion analysis and campaign strategy, including the 1976 campaign of President Gerald R. Ford. The majority of written materials from Teeter's career are part of the Gerald R. Ford Presidential Library collections. The Robert M. Teeter Papers document public opinion analysis and political campaign strategy from 1972 to 2004. They also include NBC News and *Wall Street Journal* National Public Opinion Surveys from 1989 to 2004.

PURPOSE:
To promote research regarding the U.S. political process during the latter part of the 20th century.

ELIGIBILITY:
Applicants must have completed all requirements for the Ph.D. program (coursework and examinations) by the application deadline, except for the dissertation.

FINANCIAL DATA:
The Library will present the award when the recipient arrives at the Library to conduct research. The recipient determines use of the award money, including, but not limited to, travel, paper and audiovisual reproductions and administrative costs, and other research and writing expenses.
Amount of support per award: $5,000.

CO-OP FUNDING PROGRAMS: The Award has been made possible by the generous support of the Teeter family and friends, and the United Parcel Service.

NO. AWARDS: 1.

APPLICATION INFO:
Application can be downloaded from the web site listed above. Applicants must submit each of the following:
(1) an abstract describing the dissertation (no longer than 150 words);
(2) a five-page proposal;
(3) three letters of recommendation from individuals who can attest to the applicant's qualifications for the Award (one must be from their academic director that includes a statement approving the dissertation topic);
(4) unofficial transcripts from all graduate schools attended and;
(5) a curriculum vitae.
Deadline: March 31 postmark. Awards are made each spring. Applications may be submitted at any time, but those received after the deadline will automatically be entered for the following year's award.

STAFF:
Lauren White, Grant Coordinator

ADDRESS INQUIRIES TO:
Gerald R. Ford Scholar Award in Honor of Robert M. Teeter
(See address above.)

THE FUND FOR AMERICAN STUDIES [1821]

1706 New Hampshire Avenue, N.W.
Washington, DC 20009
(202) 986-0384
Fax: (202) 986-0390
E-mail: dmccarthy@tfas.org
Web Site: www.tfas.org/programs/robert-novak-journalism-fellowship

FOUNDED: 1990

AREAS OF INTEREST:
Advancement of constitutional principles, a democratic society and a vibrant free enterprise system.

NAME(S) OF PROGRAMS:
- **Robert Novak Journalism Fellowship Program**

TYPE:
Fellowships. One-year writing project on a topic of applicant's choosing, focusing on journalism supportive of American culture and a free society.

YEAR PROGRAM STARTED: 1994

PURPOSE:
To award grants to working print and online journalists who share the Foundation's mission.

ELIGIBILITY:
Applicants must be U.S. citizens and working journalists with less than 10 years of professional experience in print and online journalism and who share the mission to advance constitutional principles, a democratic society and a vibrant free enterprise system.

FINANCIAL DATA:
Amount of support per award: Fellows: $30,000, plus up to $5,000 reimbursement for qualified project expenses; Full Fellows: $50,000 to $60,000, plus expense allowances between $10,000 and $15,000.
Total amount of support: Varies.

NO. AWARDS: Varies, depending upon funding available and the number of qualified applicants.

APPLICATION INFO:
Application materials must be submitted electronically.
Duration: One year.
Deadline: April 6.

IRS I.D.: 13-6223604

ADDRESS INQUIRIES TO:
Daniel McCarthy, Program Director
(See e-mail address above.)

HOOVER PRESIDENTIAL FOUNDATION [1822]

P.O. Box 696
West Branch, IA 52358
(319) 643-5327
Fax: (319) 643-2391
E-mail: info@hooverpf.org
Web Site: www.hooverpresidentialfoundation.org

FOUNDED: 1954

NAME(S) OF PROGRAMS:
- **Herbert Hoover Presidential Travel Grant Program**

TYPE:
Research grants; Travel grants. Money is only available for travel to the Hoover Presidential Library in West Branch, IA. The program seeks to encourage scholarly use of the holdings of the Herbert Hoover Presidential Library. It is specifically intended to promote the study of subjects of interest and concern to Herbert Hoover, Lou Henry Hoover, their associates and other public figures as reflected in the Library's 150 manuscript collections.

YEAR PROGRAM STARTED: 1978

PURPOSE:
To encourage historical research on Herbert Hoover and his connections.

LEGAL BASIS:
Tax-exempt, privately supported educational foundation.

ELIGIBILITY:
Current graduate students, postdoctoral scholars and independent researchers are eligible to apply. Applicant should contact archival staff to determine if Library holdings are pertinent to the applicant's research.

FINANCIAL DATA:
Amount of support per award: Up to $2,000. The Foundation will consider larger requests for extended graduate and postgraduate research at the Library.
Total amount of support: Varies.

NO. MOST RECENT APPLICANTS: 11.

NO. AWARDS: 9.

APPLICATION INFO:
Application materials are available on the web site or upon request from the Foundation. Applicants must consult with the archival staff concerning their topic prior to submitting a request for funding.
Duration: No grants made on a continuing basis. Reapplications for consecutive support periods are accepted. No more than two grants are allowed within a five-year period.
Deadline: March 1. Announcement April 30.

PUBLICATIONS:
Historical Materials in the Herbert Hoover Presidential Library.

ADDRESS INQUIRIES TO:
Delene W. McConnaha
Academic Programs Manager
(See address above.)

INSTITUTE FOR HUMANE STUDIES (IHS) [1823]

3434 Washington Boulevard, MS 1C5
Arlington, VA 22201
(703) 993-4880
Fax: (703) 993-4890
E-mail: funding@theihs.org
Web Site: www.theihs.org

FOUNDED: 1961

AREAS OF INTEREST:
Individual liberty.

NAME(S) OF PROGRAMS:
- **Humane Studies Fellowships**

TYPE:
Fellowships; Research grants. Humane Studies Fellowships cover the fields of the social sciences and humanities.

PURPOSE:
To assist graduate students worldwide with a special interest in individual liberty.

ELIGIBILITY:
Graduate students in a Ph.D. program at a college or university may apply. Applicant

must have a research interest that contributes to liberty-advancing scholarship. Past attendance at an IHS program or event required.

FINANCIAL DATA:
Amount of support per award: Up to $15,000 per year.

Total amount of support: Varies.

APPLICATION INFO:
Application information is available on the web site.

Duration: One academic year. Renewable.

Deadline: March 31.

ADDRESS INQUIRIES TO:
See e-mail address above.

THE INTERCOLLEGIATE STUDIES INSTITUTE   [1824]
3901 Centerville Road
Wilmington, DE 19807
(302) 652-4600
(302) 524-6148
Fax: (302) 652-1760
E-mail: caguda@isi.org
Web Site: www.isi.org

FOUNDED: 1953

AREAS OF INTEREST:
Education.

NAME(S) OF PROGRAMS:
● **Richard M. Weaver Fellowship**

TYPE:
Awards/prizes; Fellowships; Scholarships. The Weaver Fellowship is granted to students who intend to use their advanced degree to teach.

PURPOSE:
To convey to successive generations of college students a better understanding of the values and institutions that sustain a free society.

LEGAL BASIS:
A nonprofit, nonpartisan, tax-exempt educational organization.

ELIGIBILITY:
Applicant must be a member of the Intercollegiate Studies Institute. Applicant must also engage in graduate studies for the purpose of teaching at the college level. Those attending preprofessional schools (such as law, business, medicine and divinity) are ineligible. Applicants must be U.S. citizens who will be enrolled in a full-time graduate program for the upcoming academic year. Applicants may apply for more than one fellowship in any given academic cycle.

FINANCIAL DATA:
Amount of support per award: Five at $15,000 each, three at $10,000 each, and seven at $5,000 each.

Total amount of support: Varies.

NO. AWARDS: 15.

APPLICATION INFO:
Application information is available on the web site.

Deadline: January 23.

ADDRESS INQUIRIES TO:
Academic Program Officer
Program and Fellowships
(See address above.)

THE JAPANESE AMERICAN CITIZENS LEAGUE (JACL) [1825]
Washington, DC Office
1629 K Street, N.W., Suite 400
Washington, DC 20006
(202) 223-1240
E-mail: dinoue@jacl.org
Web Site: www.jacl.org

FOUNDED: 1929

AREAS OF INTEREST:
Public service leadership development.

NAME(S) OF PROGRAMS:
● **Mike M. Masaoka Fellowship Fund Congressional Program**

TYPE:
Fellowships. Congressional fellowship established to help understand the importance of public service at the national level. The Masaoka fellow serves in the Washington, DC office of a member of Congress in either the U.S. House of Representatives or the U.S. Senate.

YEAR PROGRAM STARTED: 1988

PURPOSE:
To develop leaders for public service.

ELIGIBILITY:
Candidates must be U.S. citizens who are graduating college seniors or students in graduate or professional programs. Preference will be given to those who have demonstrated commitment to Asian American and Pacific Islander (AAPI) issues, particularly those affecting the Japanese American community. Membership in the JACL is required. Communication skills, especially in writing, are important.

GEOG. RESTRICTIONS: United States.

FINANCIAL DATA:
Fellowship includes round-trip airfare from fellow's home to Washington, DC.

Amount of support per award: $2,500 monthly stipend.

Total amount of support: Up to $30,000 per fellow.

NO. AWARDS: Up to 4 annually.

APPLICATION INFO:
Completed application materials may be sent via e-mail to dinoue@jacl.org.

Duration: Six to eight months.

Deadline: 11:59 P.M., July 31.

ADDRESS INQUIRIES TO:
David Inoue, Executive Director
E-mail: policy@jacl.org
(See address above.)

THE LYNDON BAINES JOHNSON FOUNDATION   [1826]
2313 Red River Street
Austin, TX 78705-5702
(512) 721-0263
E-mail: grants@lbjfoundation.org
Web Site: www.lbjlibrary.org/page/foundation

FOUNDED: 1969

AREAS OF INTEREST:
Support for the LBJ Presidential Library and the LBJ School of Public Affairs at The University of Texas.

NAME(S) OF PROGRAMS:
● **Middleton Fellowship in Presidential Studies**
● **Moody Research Grants**

TYPE:
Fellowships; Research grants.

YEAR PROGRAM STARTED: 1972

PURPOSE:
To defray living, travel and related expenses incurred while conducting research at the LBJ Library during the period for which the grant is awarded.

LEGAL BASIS:
Nonprofit organization.

ELIGIBILITY:
In accepting a grant, an applicant must agree to the following conditions:
(1) that the product of the research which is made possible through these funds will not be used for any political purpose;
(2) that the funds are for the purpose of helping to defray expenses incurred while conducting research at the Johnson Library;
(3) that the grant must be used in the grant period in which it is awarded and;
(4) that the LBJ Foundation will be promptly provided with a copy of any publication, paper, article or book resulting from research made possible by this grant.

FINANCIAL DATA:
Amount of support per award: Middleton Fellowship: $5,000; Moody Research Grants: $600 to $3,000.

Total amount of support: Middleton Fellowship: $10,000 to $12,000; Moody Research Grants: Approximately $50,000 per grant period.

NO. MOST RECENT APPLICANTS: 7 Middleton Fellowships and 30 Moody Research Grants for Spring.

NO. AWARDS: Middleton Fellowship: 2; Moody Research Grants: 13.

APPLICATION INFO:
Application forms must be accompanied by a written proposal. Candidates should state clearly and precisely how the holdings of the LBJ Library will contribute to the completion of the project.

Middleton Fellowship applicants are also required to submit three letters of recommendation.

Duration: Eight months for spring grant period. Six months for fall grant period.

Deadline: September 15 for January to August grant period. March 15 for June to December grant period.

IRS I.D.: 74-1774063

STAFF:
Amy Barbee, Executive Director
Samantha Stone, Deputy Director

ADDRESS INQUIRIES TO:
Samantha Stone, Deputy Director
(See telephone or e-mail address above.)

NATIONAL ENDOWMENT FOR DEMOCRACY   [1827]
1025 F Street, N.W.
Suite 800
Washington, DC 20004
(202) 378-9700
Fax: (202) 378-9407
E-mail: info@ned.org
Web Site: www.ned.org/grantseekers

FOUNDED: 1983

AREAS OF INTEREST:
Democracy throughout the world.

NAME(S) OF PROGRAMS:
- **National Endowment for Democracy Grants**

TYPE:
Project/program grants.

PURPOSE:
To strengthen democratic institutions throughout the world.

ELIGIBILITY:
Nongovernmental organizations, which include civic organizations, associations, independent media, and other similar organizations, may apply. Individuals, governmental bodies, or state-supported institutions are also eligible.

FINANCIAL DATA:
Amount of support per award: Average $50,000 to $60,000.
Total amount of support: Varies.

NO. MOST RECENT APPLICANTS: Over 8,000.

NO. AWARDS: Approximately 1,600.

APPLICATION INFO:
Application information is available on the web site.
Duration: One year. Renewable.
Deadline: 10 to 12 weeks prior to board meetings held in January, March, June and September.

NATIONAL FEDERATION OF REPUBLICAN WOMEN

124 North Alfred Street
Alexandria, VA 22314
(703) 548-9688
E-mail: scholarships@nfrw.org
Web Site: www.nfrw.org

TYPE:
Internships; Scholarships. Dorothy Kabis Internship includes a six- to eight-week internship in Washington, DC, housing, travel and stipend.

National Pathfinder's Scholarships are given to the best nominated candidates.

Betty Rendel Scholarships are given to undergraduate women who are majoring in political science, government or economics.

See entry 994 for full listing.

NEW YORK STATE ASSEMBLY INTERN COMMITTEE [1828]

Legislative Office Building, Room 104A
Albany, NY 12248
(518) 455-4704
Fax: (518) 455-4705
E-mail: intern@nyassembly.gov
Web Site: www.nyassembly.gov/internship

FOUNDED: 1971

AREAS OF INTEREST:
Government.

NAME(S) OF PROGRAMS:
- **Assembly Session Internships**

TYPE:
Internships. Program provides firsthand knowledge of the legislative process and functions. The interns are assigned research and administrative responsibilities in an Assembly office. They receive a practical educational experience and attend weekly classes. The Assembly benefits from the new ideas and fresh perspectives of the interns. All intern placements are in Albany, NY.

YEAR PROGRAM STARTED: 1971

PURPOSE:
To encourage talented students from all fields to learn about and get involved in state government.

LEGAL BASIS:
Government legislature.

ELIGIBILITY:
Applicants must be matriculated in a U.S. college or university degree program as juniors or seniors. Applications are welcome from students in any academic field. Colleges generally award a full semester of credit for participation. International students should have academic requirements in the U.S. to be eligible.

FINANCIAL DATA:
Session interns receive a stipend and semester of college credit.
Amount of support per award: $6,200 session term.

NO. MOST RECENT APPLICANTS: Over 200.

NO. AWARDS: 150.

APPLICATION INFO:
Applications are available from an Intern Program liaison officer on college campuses. Applications and all supporting documents must be submitted to the Intern Committee in a complete package.

The following documents must be included with the application:
(1) personal statement;
(2) official transcripts of all college courses completed and in progress;
(3) two letters of recommendation;
(4) a letter from an appropriate college official endorsing the student's participation and indicating the amount of credit to be granted by the college and;
(5) a concise writing sample.
Duration: January to mid-May.
Deadline: November 1.

STAFF:
Kathleen McCarty, Director, Assembly Intern Committee

ADDRESS INQUIRIES TO:
Kathleen McCarty, Director
Assembly Intern Committee
(See address above.)

NEW YORK STATE ASSEMBLY INTERN COMMITTEE [1829]

Legislative Office Building, Room 104A
Albany, NY 12248
(518) 455-4704
Fax: (518) 455-4705
E-mail: intern@nyassembly.gov
Web Site: www.nyassembly.gov/internship

FOUNDED: 1971

AREAS OF INTEREST:
Government.

NAME(S) OF PROGRAMS:
- **Graduate Scholar Internship**

TYPE:
Internships. Assignments designed to provide up to 10 graduate students with full-time work placements as Assembly researchers and policy analysts with all the responsibilities and expectations of such positions. The work placements are with Assembly leaders. The interns will have the opportunity to develop a better understanding

of the legislative process while contributing new ideas and fresh perspectives to the legislative decision making process.

YEAR PROGRAM STARTED: 1976

PURPOSE:
To bring the expertise and thinking of the state's best graduate students into the legislative process.

LEGAL BASIS:
Government.

ELIGIBILITY:
All students matriculated in or who have recently completed a graduate degree program may apply. Students with expertise in a variety of public policy issues are being sought. Issues include public finance, education, environmental conservation, etc. Students must work full-time in the Assembly. International students should have academic requirements in the U.S. to be eligible. Credit can often be arranged by the school.

GEOG. RESTRICTIONS: New York state.

FINANCIAL DATA:
Amount of support per award: $15,000 stipend per year.

NO. MOST RECENT APPLICANTS: 50.

NO. AWARDS: Up to 10 each year.

APPLICATION INFO:
Applications are available from graduate schools, directly from the Assembly Intern Committee, or on the web site. Applications must include two letters of recommendation, a letter from graduate program dean or director, official transcripts, a writing sample and a personal statement.
Duration: Six months (January to June). Nonrenewable.
Deadline: September 13 (postmark).

STAFF:
Kathleen McCarty, Director

ADDRESS INQUIRIES TO:
Kathleen McCarty, Director
(See address above.)

NEW YORK STATE SENATE [1830]

Legislative Office Building, Suite 1426
Albany, NY 12247
(518) 455-2611
Fax: (518) 426-6827
E-mail: students@nysenate.gov
Web Site: www.nysenate.gov/student-programs

FOUNDED: 1965

AREAS OF INTEREST:
New York state government and education which includes improved public access to and understanding of government, resulting in enhanced citizenship, career staffing, government administration and leadership.

NAME(S) OF PROGRAMS:
- **James L. Biggane Fellowship in Finance**
- **New York State Senate Legislative Fellows Program**
- **Richard J. Roth Journalism Fellowship**
- **Richard A. Wiebe Public Service Fellowship**

TYPE:
Fellowships. These fellowships are intended for the graduate/postgraduate/midcareer level. Stipends are for bipartisan opportunities to train in government while on-site in Albany, NY. Fellows spend almost a year immersed

in the work of the Senate, learning techniques associated with policymaking and legislative process. Placement is usually to the office of an elected Senate member. The Senate Legislative Fellows Program, Biggane Fellowship, Roth Journalism Fellowship and Wiebe Public Service Fellowship constitute the Senate Graduate/Post-Graduate/Mid-Career Fellowships.

YEAR PROGRAM STARTED: 1965

PURPOSE:
To provide an opportunity for career experience and learning for graduate assistants, career recruitment among superior fellows, and citizenship training in general.

LEGAL BASIS:
Legislative authority.

ELIGIBILITY:
Graduate/Postgraduate/Mid-Career Fellowships: In most cases, Fellows must have completed graduate-level work at an accredited university during the immediately previous spring and fall semesters. Fellowships are open to all majors. Training in the history/politics/government of New York state is not required.

The Biggane Fellow may be a person in midcareer. Biggane applicants need not be currently enrolled in graduate-level study, but must have obtained a previous graduate-level degree. Legislative Fellows will be talented and skilled graduate/postgraduate students from a variety of academic disciplines.

The Roth Fellow may be a student with experience and/or intentions in the fields of communications, journalism and/or public relations.

The Wiebe Fellow will be a student with legal training and a variety of other backgrounds.

Students are not required to presently reside in New York state or attend school in New York state.

FINANCIAL DATA:
The stipend is distributed in biweekly installments prorated from the first day to the last day of enrollment. Some benefit options are available (health, dental, vision, life insurance, and the retirement program). Fellows are not Senate employees; they do not earn vacation or personal leave.

All Senate Fellowships are on-site in Albany, NY. Fellowships are not financial aid for academic work, on-campus or classroom study. Housing in Albany is the responsibility of the Fellow.

Amount of support per award:
Grant-in-Study stipend of $40,000 for the fellowship year September 2021 to June 2022.

NO. MOST RECENT APPLICANTS: 30.

NO. AWARDS: Approximately 16 fellowships each year. Legislative Fellows Program: Up to 13; Biggane, Roth and Wiebe Fellowships: 1 each.

APPLICATION INFO:
Applications must include the following:
(1) course work-in-progress list signed by campus official (if not on transcript);
(2) calling of Office of Student Programs to indicate one's intent to apply;
(3) policy proposal;
(4) rebuttal of policy proposal;
(5) statement of purpose;

(6) writing sample essay;
(7) resume or curriculum vitae;
(8) all official transcripts (graduate and undergraduate) and;
(9) three letters of reference from persons familiar with the applicant's character, academic and/or professional abilities (at least two from faculty members).

Duration: Approximately one year, September through late June. No renewals.

Deadline: Last Friday in April.

PUBLICATIONS:
Program announcement.

ADDRESS INQUIRIES TO:
Director, Office of Student Programs
(See address above.)

NEW YORK STATE
SENATE   [1831]
Legislative Office Building, Suite 1426
Albany, NY 12247
(518) 455-2611
Fax: (518) 426-6827
E-mail: students@nysenate.gov
Web Site: www.nysenate.gov/student-programs

FOUNDED: 1978

AREAS OF INTEREST:
State government internships for undergraduates.

NAME(S) OF PROGRAMS:
● **Undergraduate Session Assistants Program**

TYPE:
Internships. Annual undergraduate internship running early January to late April.

YEAR PROGRAM STARTED: 1978

PURPOSE:
To provide on-site experience at the New York State Senate, Albany, NY.

ELIGIBILITY:
Applicant must be a full-time student in an accredited, undergraduate degree program on a campus in New York state. The program is intended and designed for college juniors and seniors; exceptional sophomores may occasionally be selected. Freshmen are ineligible.

The Senate welcomes majors in all accredited disciplines. Training in the history/politics/government of New York is neither a prerequisite of nor an advantage to selection. Skill and ability, initiative, eagerness to learn, discretion and mature flexibility are essential for success.

Each student should demonstrate a 3.0 grade point average or better and meet the campus/departmental standard for off-campus study; full-time enrollment in the immediately previous spring (not summer) and current fall semester/previous two trimesters. Each standard is to be certified by the Campus Liaison Officer (CLO), student's academic advisor, chairman, dean, or other duly authorized campus official.

Placements are ordinarily to the offices of individual senators. Students may observe, participate in, and/or acquire experience with state government procedures. Combined participation in the program and legislative placement is for a minimum of 35 hours per week. Longer hours are possible and should be expected.

Each applicant must be able to earn campus-awarded credit for participation in the program to be eligible. On-campus faculty is responsible for academic advisement, evaluation, grading and granting of credit for their student participant(s) enrolled in this Senate program.

GEOG. RESTRICTIONS: New York state.

FINANCIAL DATA:
Arrangement of housing in Albany is the responsibility of the individual enrollee.
Amount of support per award: A stipend of $6,600 to offset costs of moving to and living in Albany.

NO. MOST RECENT APPLICANTS: Approximately 40 to 45.

NO. AWARDS: Approximately 30.

APPLICATION INFO:
Enrollment is on-site at the New York State Senate in Albany, NY. Applications are available on campus, from the Student Programs Office, or at the web site.

If there is no CLO on campus, contact Nicholas J. Parrella, Director of Student Programs, at the address listed above.

Duration: Approximately four months.

Deadline: The last Friday in October. Expect an earlier on-campus deadline if one's school has a Campus Liaison Officer (CLO). Announcement of selections is approximately mid-November.

STAFF:
Nicholas J. Parrella, Director of Student Programs

ADDRESS INQUIRIES TO:
Nicholas J. Parrella
Director of Student Programs
(See address above.)

PIPER FUND   [1832]
15 Research Drive
Suite B
Amherst, MA 01002
(413) 256-0349
E-mail: grantsmanager@proteusfund.org
Web Site: www.proteusfund.org

AREAS OF INTEREST:
Campaign finance reform in the American political system.

TYPE:
General operating grants; Project/program grants.

PURPOSE:
To help meet the needs of the growing movement for campaign finance reform in America.

GEOG. RESTRICTIONS: United States.

FINANCIAL DATA:
Amount of support per award: Typically $10,000 to $50,000.

Total amount of support: Approximately $38,000,000 since inception. Over $3,000,000 for the year 2018.

NO. AWARDS: 75 for the year 2019.

APPLICATION INFO:
Applications are accepted by invitation only.
Duration: One year.

ADDRESS INQUIRIES TO:
Kyrstin Thorson Rogers, Grants Manager
(See address above.)

*SPECIAL STIPULATIONS:
Grants are by invitation only.

PRESIDENT'S COMMISSION ON WHITE HOUSE FELLOWSHIPS [1833]

712 Jackson Place, N.W.
Washington, DC 20503
(202) 395-4522
Fax: (202) 395-6179
E-mail: whitehousefellows@who.eop.gov
Web Site: www.whitehouse.gov/get-involved/fellows

FOUNDED: 1964

AREAS OF INTEREST:
Leadership and public service for young professionals.

NAME(S) OF PROGRAMS:
• **White House Fellowships**

TYPE:
Fellowships. The White House Fellows program is America's most prestigious program for leadership and public service. White House Fellowships offer exceptional young men and women firsthand experience working at the highest levels of the federal government.

White House Fellows typically spend a year working as full-time, paid special assistants to senior White House staff, the Vice President, cabinet secretaries and other top-ranking government officials. Fellows also participate in an education program consisting of roundtable discussions with renowned leaders from the private and public sectors, and trips to study U.S. policy in action both domestically and internationally. Fellowships are awarded on a strictly nonpartisan basis.

PURPOSE:
To give those who participate in the program firsthand, high-level experience with the workings of the federal government and to increase their sense of participation in national affairs.

ELIGIBILITY:
The following criteria apply:
(1) applicants must be U.S. citizens;
(2) employees of the federal government are not eligible unless they are career military personnel;
(3) applicants must have completed their undergraduate education by the time they begin the application process and;
(4) there are no formal age restrictions; however, the fellowship program was created to give selected Americans the experience of government service early in their careers.

The Commission awards fellowships on a strict nonpartisan basis and encourages balance and diversity in all aspects of the program.

GEOG. RESTRICTIONS: United States.

FINANCIAL DATA:
Fellows are eligible to purchase health insurance through the Federal Employee Health Benefit Plans.

NO. MOST RECENT APPLICANTS: Up to 1,000.

NO. AWARDS: 11 to 19 fellowships per year.

APPLICATION INFO:
Application must be submitted online and is available beginning in the Fall.
Duration: Typically one year.
Deadline: Mid-January.

RHODE ISLAND STATE GOVERNMENT INTERNSHIP PROGRAM [1834]

State House, Room 8AA
Providence, RI 02903
(401) 222-6782
Fax: (401) 222-4447
E-mail: intern@rilegislature.gov
blanzi@rilegislature.gov
Web Site: www.rilegislature.gov/internship

FOUNDED: 1969

AREAS OF INTEREST:
Communications, business and government.

NAME(S) OF PROGRAMS:
• **Rhode Island State Government Internship Program**

TYPE:
Internships. Funding through General Assembly is also available. Internship opportunities for graduate and undergraduate students in the state government operation. Students are involved in executive, legislative and judicial assignments. The internship is viewed as an extension of the classroom and is seen as complementing and building upon the educational opportunities available on campuses.

This program has established a Summer Internship section, open to Rhode Island residents only, that begins in late June and concludes in August.

YEAR PROGRAM STARTED: 1969

PURPOSE:
To provide a link between the public and state government; to open a channel for the potential recruitment of personnel for state government internship; to supplement college and university course offerings in state and local government; to enable students to develop a knowledge of the structure and procedure of state government.

LEGAL BASIS:
Chapter 47, General Laws, state of Rhode Island.

ELIGIBILITY:
Spring semester interns are chosen by members of the faculties of 11 participating Rhode Island colleges and universities. Students must have junior or senior status. Summer applicants can be out-of-state students who are Rhode Island residents.

FINANCIAL DATA:
Academic credit, up to a maximum of six credits, is available. For the Summer Internship, a student is required to work eight to 10 hours per week and receives a monthly stipend.
Amount of support per award: Summer: $20 per day for a minimum of four hours of work.

APPLICATION INFO:
Interns are selected by the academic committee and referred to Intern Staff.
Duration: 12 weeks in the spring (one school semester) and eight weeks (July and August) for Summer Internship.
Deadline: August 9 for fall program, December 20 for spring program, and April 24 for summer program.

ADDRESS INQUIRIES TO:
Beatrice Lanzi, Executive Director
(See address above.)

FRANKLIN D. ROOSEVELT LIBRARY AND MUSEUM

4079 Albany Post Road
Hyde Park, NY 12538
(845) 486-7770
E-mail: grants.fdr@nara.gov
Web Site: fdrlibrary.org/research-grants

TYPE:
Grants-in-aid; Research grants. The Roosevelt Institute - the Library's nonprofit partner - supports a program of small grants-in-aid, in support of research on the "Roosevelt years" or clearly related subjects.

See entry 587 for full listing.

SARAH SCAIFE FOUNDATION, INC. [1835]

One Oxford Centre, Suite 3900
301 Grant Street
Pittsburgh, PA 15219-6402
(412) 392-2900
Web Site: www.scaife.com

FOUNDED: 1941

AREAS OF INTEREST:
Domestic and international public policy issues.

TYPE:
Challenge/matching grants; Fellowships; General operating grants; Project/program grants; Seed money grants.

YEAR PROGRAM STARTED: 1941

PURPOSE:
To direct money to programs that address major domestic and international issues.

LEGAL BASIS:
Private foundation.

ELIGIBILITY:
The Foundation does not make grants to individuals for any purpose, to nationally organized fund-raising groups, or to organizations that are not publicly supported nonprofit charitable organizations.

FINANCIAL DATA:
Amount of support per award: Average $25,000 to $250,000.

REPRESENTATIVE AWARDS:
$40,000 to American Civil Rights Institute; $250,000 to Foundation for Individual Rights in Education, Inc.; $60,000 to New England Legal Foundation.

APPLICATION INFO:
Grant proposals to the Foundation must contain a cover letter signed by the organization's president or authorized representative and have the approval of the board of directors. The letter should include a concise description of the purpose of the requesting organization and of the specific project or program for which funds are requested (if applicable) along with the following:
(1) program or project budget (if applicable);
(2) timetable (if applicable);
(3) organization's annual budget;
(4) most recent audited financial statements;
(5) current Form 990;
(6) annual report;
(7) list of officers and directors with their affiliations;
(8) list of key supporters and;
(9) IRS determination letter evidencing 501(c)(3) tax-exempt status.
Duration: One year.

Deadline: Board meets quarterly in February, May, September and November. Notification within two to four weeks.

PUBLICATIONS:
Annual report.

OFFICERS:
Michael W. Gleba, Chairman, Chief Executive Officer and Treasurer
Yvonne Marie Bly, Secretary and Assistant Treasurer

ADDRESS INQUIRIES TO:
Michael W. Gleba
Chairman and Chief Executive Officer
(See address above.)

THE SOCIETY FOR THE PSYCHOLOGICAL STUDY OF SOCIAL ISSUES (SPSSI) [1836]
700 Seventh Street, S.E.
Washington, DC 20003
(202) 675-6956
E-mail: awards@spssi.org
Web Site: www.spssi.org

FOUNDED: 1936

AREAS OF INTEREST:
Public policy, social issues, psychology and international relations.

NAME(S) OF PROGRAMS:
● **Otto Klineberg Intercultural and International Relations Award**

TYPE:
Awards/prizes. The Klineberg Award is given for the best paper or article of the year on intercultural or international relations.

PURPOSE:
To award the best paper or article of the year on intercultural or international relations.

LEGAL BASIS:
Independently incorporated society.

ELIGIBILITY:
Entries can be either unpublished manuscripts, in press papers, book chapters, or journal articles published no more than 18 months prior to the submission deadline. Entries cannot be returned. The competition is open to nonmembers and members of SPSSI. Graduate students are especially urged to submit papers. Submissions from across the social sciences are encouraged, however the paper must clearly demonstrate its relevance for psychological theory and research in the domain of intercultural and international relations.

FINANCIAL DATA:
Amount of support per award: $1,000.

NO. MOST RECENT APPLICANTS: 24.

NO. AWARDS: 1.

APPLICATION INFO:
Online submissions are the preferred method. Please limit the number and size of files uploaded when applying online. For hard-copy submissions, send five (5) copies to the address listed above, "Attn: Klineberg Award."

Deadline: March 1.

PUBLICATIONS:
Program announcement; application guidelines.

ADDRESS INQUIRIES TO:
See e-mail address above.

HATTON W. SUMNERS FOUNDATION [1837]
325 North St. Paul Street
Suite 3920
Dallas, TX 75201
(214) 220-2128
Fax: (214) 953-0737
E-mail: info@hattonsumners.org
Web Site: www.hattonsumners.org

FOUNDED: 1949

AREAS OF INTEREST:
Self-government, political science and democracy.

TYPE:
Challenge/matching grants; Conferences/seminars; Endowments; Fellowships; Internships; Project/program grants; Scholarships. Scholarship programs at selected universities and grants to support other educational activities for both students and adults, which are designed to create an appreciation and understanding for the U.S. executive, legislative and judicial processes.

YEAR PROGRAM STARTED: 1949

PURPOSE:
To encourage the study, teaching and research into the science and art of self-government so that the American people may understand the fundamental principles of democracy and be guided thereby in shaping governmental policies.

LEGAL BASIS:
Private charitable foundation.

GEOG. RESTRICTIONS: Arkansas, Kansas, Louisiana, Missouri, Nebraska, New Mexico, Oklahoma and Texas.

FINANCIAL DATA:
Amount of support per award: Varies.

Total amount of support: $2,337,000 for the year 2017.

NO. AWARDS: Varies.

REPRESENTATIVE AWARDS:
$20,000 to Bill of Rights Institute, Arlington, VA, for Constitutional Seminars and curriculum support for teachers in New Mexico; $150,000 to Institute for Policy Innovation, Irving, TX, for lecture series on public policy issues; $15,000 to The Arc of Collin, Dallas and Rockwall Counties, Dallas, TX, for funding of The Leadership Institute.

APPLICATION INFO:
Grant applications must be in writing, but do not need to be formal. The Foundation does not accept applications via fax or e-mail.

Duration: One year. Occasional multiyear funding.

Deadline: August 1. Decision in October.

PUBLICATIONS:
Annual report.

STAFF:
Hugh C. Akin, Executive Director

ADDRESS INQUIRIES TO:
Hugh C. Akin, Executive Director
(See address above.)

HARRY S. TRUMAN LIBRARY INSTITUTE [1838]
5151 Troost Avenue
Suite 300
Kansas City, MO 64110
(816) 400-1216
Fax: (816) 400-1213
E-mail: lisa.sullivan@trumanlibraryinstitute.org
Web Site: www.trumanlibraryinstitute.org

FOUNDED: 1957

AREAS OF INTEREST:
Harry S. Truman and the Truman administration.

NAME(S) OF PROGRAMS:
● **Dissertation Year Fellowships**
● **Research Grant**
● **Scholar's Award**
● **Harry S. Truman Book Award**

TYPE:
Awards/prizes; Fellowships; Grants-in-aid; Research grants; Travel grants. The Dissertation Year Fellowships are given to encourage historical scholarship of the public career of Harry S. Truman or the Truman era. Support is given annually to one or two graduate students who have completed the dissertation research and are in the writing stage. Preference will be given to projects based on extensive research at the Truman Library. Successful applicants will be expected to deposit one copy of their completed dissertation, or any publication resulting therefrom, with the Truman Library.

Research Grants are intended to enable graduate students as well as postdoctoral scholars to come to the Library for one to three weeks to use its archival facilities.

The Scholar's Award is given every other year, even-numbered years only, to a scholar engaged in a study of either the public career of Harry S. Truman or some aspect of the history of the Truman administration or of the U.S. during that administration. The scholar's work must be based on extensive research at the Truman Library and must be designed to result in the publication of a book-length manuscript. One copy of such book (and/or any other publication resulting from work done under this award) shall be deposited by the author with the Harry S. Truman Library.

The Harry S. Truman Book Award is given in even years for the best book dealing with some aspect of history of the U.S. between April 12, 1945 and January 20, 1953 or with the public career of Harry S. Truman.

YEAR PROGRAM STARTED: 1959

PURPOSE:
To encourage study of the history of the Truman administration and the public career of Harry S. Truman; to promote the use of the Truman Library as a national center for historical scholarship.

ELIGIBILITY:
Undergraduate students, doctoral candidates and postdoctoral scholars with appropriate interests are eligible for support. Applicants must be competent researchers with viable topics for which pertinent materials are available at the Truman Library.

FINANCIAL DATA:
Amount of support per award: Dissertation Year Fellowships: $16,000 payable in two installments; Research Grants: Up to $2,500; Scholar's Award: $30,000; Truman Book Award: $2,500.

NO. AWARDS: Dissertation Year Fellowships: Up to 2.

REPRESENTATIVE AWARDS:
Harry S. Truman Book Award: Kevin Peraino, "A Force So Swift: Mao, Truman, and the Birth of Modern China, 1949."

APPLICATION INFO:
Applicants for the Scholar's Award should submit an application and proposal for preliminary screening. If selected, applicants must submit further information including a list of Truman files already utilized or planned to be utilized, a projected timeline for completion, and projected income for the academic year in which the award will be announced. Applicants for Research Grants may receive no more than two grants in this category in any one five-year period.

For the Harry S. Truman Book Award, six copies of each book entered must be submitted to the Book Award Administrator.

Duration: Research Grants: One to three weeks.

Deadline: Dissertation Year Fellowships: February 1. Announcement first week of April. Research Grants: April 1 and October 1. Results announced six weeks later. Scholar's Award: December 15 of odd-numbered years. Announcement no later than March 31. Harry S. Truman Book Award: Books must be received by January 20 in even-numbered years.

PUBLICATIONS:
Program announcement; *Whistle Stop*, newsletter.

OFFICERS:
Clyde F. Wendel, Chairman of the Board
James B. Nutter, Vice Chairperson
Adam P. Sachs, Vice Chairperson
Jeannine Strandjord, Vice Chairperson
John A. MacDonald, Treasurer
Lisa Hardwick, Secretary

BOARD OF DIRECTORS:
Clifton Truman Daniel, Honorary Chairperson
Merilyn K. Berenbom
Paul M. Black
Maureen McMeel Carroll
Robert P. Dunn
Josh Earnest
Susie S. Evans
Greg Gunderson, Ph.D.
Mary Ann Heiss, Ph.D.
Harvey L. Kaplan
Charlotte L. Kemper
Kay Martin
Bridget McCandless, M.D.
Leigh Nottberg
Patrick J. Ottensmeyer
Karen Pack
Jason C. Parker, Ph.D.
James D. Rine
Marny Sherman
Meyer J. Sosland
Timothy W. Triplett
David Von Drehle
Hon. Eileen Weir
Thomas R. Willard

ADDRESS INQUIRIES TO:
Grants Administrator
(See address above.)

THE HARRY S. TRUMAN SCHOLARSHIP FOUNDATION [1839]

712 Jackson Place, N.W.
Washington, DC 20006-4901
(202) 395-4831
Fax: (202) 395-6995
E-mail: office@truman.gov
Web Site: www.truman.gov

FOUNDED: 1975

AREAS OF INTEREST:
Local, state and national government service.

NAME(S) OF PROGRAMS:
● **Harry S. Truman Scholarship Program**

TYPE:
Awards/prizes. Awards for undergraduate students who demonstrate outstanding leadership potential, plan to pursue careers in government or elsewhere in public service and wish to attend graduate school to help prepare for their careers. At least one Truman Scholar is selected each year from each state, the District of Columbia, Puerto Rico and, considered as a single entity, Guam, the Virgin Islands, American Samoa and the Commonwealth of the Northern Mariana Islands. Scholars may attend graduate schools in the U.S. or in foreign countries.

YEAR PROGRAM STARTED: 1975

PURPOSE:
To develop increased opportunities for young Americans to prepare for and pursue careers in public service, whether it be at the local, county, state or national level, through an educational scholarship program. The Foundation defines public service as employment in government at any level, including uniformed services, public-interest organizations, non-governmental research and/or educational organizations and public-service oriented nonprofit organizations such as those whose primary purposes are to help needy or disadvantaged persons or to protect the environment.

LEGAL BASIS:
Authorized by Congress in 1975; the sole Federal memorial to President Harry S. Truman.

ELIGIBILITY:
To be considered for nomination as a Truman Scholar, a student must be:
(1) a full-time student as a junior at a four-year institution pursuing a Bachelor's degree;
(2) enrolled in a four-year accredited institution of higher education;
(3) committed to a career in government or in public service as defined above;
(4) in the upper quarter of his or her class and;
(5) a U.S. citizen or, in the case of nominees from American Samoa or the Commonwealth of the Northern Mariana Islands, a U.S. national.

FINANCIAL DATA:
The award may only be used for tuition, fees, books, room and board and other specifically approved expenses in graduate school.
Amount of support per award: Up to $30,000.

NO. MOST RECENT APPLICANTS: 756.

NO. AWARDS: 62 for the year 2019.

APPLICATION INFO:
All candidates for scholarships are nominated by their institutions of higher education. The Foundation neither solicits nor accepts direct candidate applications. Each participating institution must appoint a faculty representative to serve as liaison between the institution and the Foundation. The Foundation's nomination and supporting information forms are available from faculty representatives.

Duration: Up to four years.

Deadline: February 4.

THE MORRIS K. UDALL AND STEWART L. UDALL FOUNDATION

130 South Scott Avenue
Tucson, AZ 85701
(520) 901-8564
Fax: (520) 901-8570
E-mail: curley@udall.gov
Web Site: www.udall.gov

TYPE:
Internships. Congressional Internships: Native American college, graduate and law students work in congressional offices and federal agencies to gain a firsthand understanding of the federal government. The Foundation arranges meetings with elected officials, staff at Native American advocacy and public interest organizations, and Native American professionals in Washington, DC. They also take field trips and meet with congressional members, agency heads and cabinet secretaries.

See entry 968 for full listing.

WOMEN'S CONGRESSIONAL POLICY INSTITUTE (WCPI)

409 12th Street, S.W.
Suite 702
Washington, DC 20024
(202) 554-2323
Fax: (202) 554-2346
E-mail: cindy@wcpinst.org
Web Site: www.womenspolicy.org

TYPE:
Fellowships.

See entry 1004 for full listing.

Sociology and anthropology

AMERICAN SOCIOLOGICAL ASSOCIATION

1430 K Street, N.W.
Suite 600
Washington, DC 20005
(202) 383-9005 ext. 842
TDD: (202) 638-0981
E-mail: diversity@asanet.org
Web Site: www.asanet.org

TYPE:
Fellowships. Predoctoral training fellowships for minority-group members studying sociology.

See entry 895 for full listing.

L.S.B. LEAKEY FOUNDATION   [1840]

1003B O'Reilly Avenue
San Francisco, CA 94129-1359
(415) 561-4646
Fax: (415) 561-4647
E-mail: grants@leakeyfoundation.org
Web Site: leakeyfoundation.org

FOUNDED: 1968

AREAS OF INTEREST:
Human evolution, including research into the environments, archaeology and human paleontology of the Miocene, Pliocene and Pleistocene, into the behavior, morphology, molecular anthropology and ecology of the great apes and other primate species when it contributes to the development or testing of models of human evolution and into the ecology and adaptations of living hunter-gatherer peoples.

NAME(S) OF PROGRAMS:
- **Leakey Foundation Grants**

TYPE:
Research grants. The General Research Grants priority is normally given to the exploratory phase of promising new projects that most closely meet the stated purpose of the Foundation.

YEAR PROGRAM STARTED: 1968

PURPOSE:
To conduct research related to human origins.

LEGAL BASIS:
Public foundation 501(c)(3).

ELIGIBILITY:
Grants are made to senior scientists and postdoctoral students with professional qualifications and demonstrated capability in the area of human evolution. Graduate students must be advanced to candidacy (ABD) in order to be considered.

FINANCIAL DATA:
Amount of support per award: General Research Grants are awarded up to $15,000 for Ph.D. candidate students (ABD), and up to $25,000 for senior scientists and postdoctoral students.

Total amount of support: Approximately $1,000,000 per year.

NO. AWARDS: Approximately 40 to 60 per year.

APPLICATION INFO:
Guidelines and application forms are available on the Foundation's web site. Applications are submitted and accepted online only.

All applications must be for research projects related to understanding human evolution.

Duration: One year.

Deadline: Session One (Fall): July 15, with notification in mid-December. Session Two (Spring): January 10, with notification in May.

PUBLICATIONS:
Application guidelines; newsletter.

IRS I.D.: 95-2536475

ADDRESS INQUIRIES TO:
See e-mail address above.

NATIONAL SCIENCE FOUNDATION   [1841]

2415 Eisenhower Avenue
Alexandria, VA 22314
(703) 292-7315
Fax: (703) 292-9068
E-mail: jmantz@nsf.gov
Web Site: www.nsf.gov

FOUNDED: 1950

AREAS OF INTEREST:
Scientific research on the causes and consequences of human social and cultural variability.

NAME(S) OF PROGRAMS:
- **Cultural Anthropology Program**

TYPE:
Conferences/seminars; Grants-in-aid; Project/program grants; Research grants. The program supports a broad portfolio of research by both senior scholars and by graduate students.

YEAR PROGRAM STARTED: 1952

PURPOSE:
To support basic scientific research on the causes, consequences, and complexities of human social and cultural variability.

LEGAL BASIS:
National Science Foundation Act of 1950.

ELIGIBILITY:
The program does not fund research that takes as its primary goal improved clinical practice or applied policy.

Applicants may be colleges and universities on behalf of their staff members, nonprofit, U.S. nonacademic research institutions, such as independent museums, observatories, research laboratories, stock centers and similar organizations, private profit organizations, in exceptional circumstances, rarely, foreign institutions utilizing U.S. currency, and under special circumstances, unaffiliated U.S. scientists.

FINANCIAL DATA:
Support may cover salaries, research assistantships, staff benefits related directly to purpose, permanent equipment, travel, publication costs, computer costs and certain other direct and indirect costs.

Amount of support per award: $5,000 to $300,000; average $150,000.

Total amount of support: Approximately $4,000,000.

NO. AWARDS: 30 to 40.

APPLICATION INFO:
Application must be submitted online at FastLane or Grants.gov.

Duration: Up to 60 months, depending on the scientific merit and requirements of the project.

Deadline: August 15 and January 15.

STAFF:
Jeffrey Mantz, Program Director

ADDRESS INQUIRIES TO:
Jeffrey Mantz, Program Director
(See address above.)

NATIONAL SCIENCE FOUNDATION   [1842]

Division of Behavioral and Cognitive Sciences
2415 Eisenhower Avenue
Alexandria, VA 22314
(703) 292-8759
E-mail: jyellen@nsf.gov
Web Site: www.nsf.gov

NAME(S) OF PROGRAMS:
- **Archaeology Program**
- **Archaeometry Program**

TYPE:
Conferences/seminars; Research grants. The programs provide support for anthropologically relevant archaeological research at both a "senior" and doctoral-dissertation level. It also funds anthropologically significant archaeometric research and high-risk exploratory research proposals.

FINANCIAL DATA:
Maximum of $20,000 in direct costs to meet expenses associated with doctoral dissertation research.

Amount of support per award: Varies.

Total amount of support: Approximately $7,200,000 for the year 2018.

APPLICATION INFO:
Instructions and application form are available on the web site above.

Duration: One to five years.

Deadline: Target dates: Archaeology: July 1 and December 20; Archaeometry: December 1. Dissertations may be submitted at any time.

STAFF:
Dr. John E. Yellen, Program Director

ADDRESS INQUIRIES TO:
Dr. John E. Yellen, Program Director
(See address above.)

*PLEASE NOTE:
All proposals must be submitted online.

SCHOOL FOR ADVANCED RESEARCH   [1843]

P.O. Box 2188
Santa Fe, NM 87504-2188
(505) 954-7237
Fax: (505) 954-7214
E-mail: scholar@sarsf.org
seminar@sarsf.org
Web Site: sarweb.org

FOUNDED: 1907

AREAS OF INTEREST:
Anthropology and allied disciplines in the humanities and social sciences.

NAME(S) OF PROGRAMS:
- **Advanced Seminar Program**
- **Resident Scholar Fellowships**

TYPE:
Conferences/seminars; Fellowships; Residencies. Advanced Seminars promote in-depth communication among scholars who are at a critical stage of research on a common topic and whose interaction has the potential to move the discipline of anthropology forward with new insights into human evolution, behavior, culture or society, including critical contemporary issues. Each consists of up to 10 scholars who meet at SAR's Santa Fe campus for five days of intense discussion on a topic that provides new insights into human evolution, behavior, society or culture. Support is also available for two- and three-day short seminars, including a program funded by the National Science Foundation for research team seminars. Participants appraise ongoing research, assess recent innovations in theory and methods, and share data relevant to broad problems in anthropology and related disciplines.

Resident Scholar Fellowships are awarded each year to scholars in anthropology and related disciplines who have completed their research and who need time to prepare book-length manuscripts or doctoral dissertations on topics important to the understanding of humankind.

YEAR PROGRAM STARTED: 1973

PURPOSE:
To support advanced research in anthropology and related disciplines.

LEGAL BASIS:
Private, nonprofit.

ELIGIBILITY:
Proposals are sought for the Advanced Seminar Program.

Resident Scholar Program: Applications are evaluated on the basis of the overall excellence and significance of the proposed project, clarity of presentation and the applicant's academic accomplishments relative to subdiscipline and career stage. The program supports scholars whose work is broad, synthetic and interdisciplinary and promises to yield significant advances in understanding human culture, behavior, evolution or critical contemporary issues. Projects that are narrowly focused geographically and theoretically or that are primarily methodological seldom receive strong consideration. Each year the program supports a mix of scholars with scientific and humanistic orientations. Preference is given to applicants whose research and analysis are complete and who need time to prepare manuscripts. Applicants for postdoctoral fellowships must have their Ph.D. in hand at time of application. Immediate dissertation rewrites are not encouraged.

FINANCIAL DATA:
Advanced Seminars: SAR provides round-trip coach airfare within the U.S., lodging and all meals. Overseas airfare for up to two participants may also be offered.

Resident scholars are provided with an office, low-cost housing, a stipend, library assistance and other benefits during a nine-month tenure, from September through the following May. Books written by scholars may be considered for publication by SAR Press.

Amount of support per award: Resident Scholar Program: Maximum stipend up to $50,000.

Total amount of support: Varies.

CO-OP FUNDING PROGRAMS: Funding for the Resident Scholar Program is provided by the Weatherhead Foundation, the Katrin H. Lamon Endowment for Native American Art and Education, the Andrew H. Mellon Foundation and the Vera R. Campbell Foundation.

NO. MOST RECENT APPLICANTS: 200 for the year 2018.

NO. AWARDS: Advanced Seminars: 1 to 2 seminars annually (10 per seminar); Resident Scholar Fellowships: 5 to 6 annually.

APPLICATION INFO:
Submissions must be made via online application process. Guidelines and application form are available on the web site.

Duration: Advanced Seminars: Five days; Resident Scholar Fellowships: Nine months, September 1 through May 31.

Deadline: Resident Scholar Program: November 1. Announcement in April.

PUBLICATIONS:
Application guidelines.

OFFICERS:
Dr. Michael Brown, President and Chief Executive Officer
Paul Ryer, Director of Scholar Programs

ADDRESS INQUIRIES TO:
Maria Spray, Program Coordinator
(See address above.)

SCHOOL FOR ADVANCED RESEARCH [1844]
P.O. Box 2188
Santa Fe, NM 87504-2188
(505) 954-7237
Fax: (505) 954-7214
E-mail: staley@sarsf.org
Web Site: sarweb.org

FOUNDED: 1907

AREAS OF INTEREST:
Anthropology and related disciplines in the humanities and social sciences.

NAME(S) OF PROGRAMS:
● **J.I. Staley Prize**

TYPE:
Awards/prizes. Prize awarded annually to a living author of a ground-breaking book that exemplifies outstanding scholarship and writing in anthropology. The award recognizes innovative works that add new dimensions to the understanding of the human species.

YEAR PROGRAM STARTED: 1988

PURPOSE:
To acknowledge those innovative works that have gone beyond traditional frontiers and dominant schools of thought in anthropology and given new dimensions to our understanding of the human species; to honor books that cross subdisciplinary boundaries within anthropology and reach out in new and expanded interdisciplinary directions.

LEGAL BASIS:
Private, nonprofit.

ELIGIBILITY:
To be considered, a book must be currently in print and must have been in publication at least two years, but not more than eight years. Co-authored books may be nominated, but edited volumes and textbooks may not. The nomination must clearly be for a single book. The award is for one outstanding and influential publication, not for an author's lifetime achievement.

Nominated books are evaluated according to the following criteria:
(1) significant contribution to our understanding of humankind;
(2) innovative and rigorous thinking in terms of theory, research methods and/or application of findings;
(3) superior integration of subdisciplinary and/or interdisciplinary perspectives;
(4) exemplary writing and clarity of expression and;
(5) demonstrated or anticipated impact on the field of anthropology.

FINANCIAL DATA:
Amount of support per award: Cash award of $7,500.

Total amount of support: $7,500.

NO. MOST RECENT APPLICANTS: 10 for the year 2018.

NO. AWARDS: 1 annually.

APPLICATION INFO:
Detailed information is available on the web site.

Duration: One-time award.

Deadline: Nominations may be submitted at any time throughout the year. Nominations received by October 1 will be considered for next year's prize.

OFFICERS:
Dr. Michael Brown, President and Chief Executive Officer
Paul Ryer, Director of Scholar Programs

ADDRESS INQUIRIES TO:
Maria Spray, Program Coordinator
(See address above.)

THE AMAURY TALBOT FUND [1845]
Royal Anthropological Institute
50 Fitzroy Street
London W1T 5BT England
(44) 020 7387 0455
Fax: (44) 020 7388 8817
E-mail: admin@therai.org.uk
Web Site: www.therai.org.uk/awards/prizes/the-amaury-talbot-prize-for-african-anthropology/

FOUNDED: 1948

AREAS OF INTEREST:
Nigeria or West Africa.

NAME(S) OF PROGRAMS:
● **Amaury Talbot Prize for African Anthropology**

TYPE:
Awards/prizes. Prize for a significant book, article or work of anthropological research relating to West Africa.

YEAR PROGRAM STARTED: 1948

PURPOSE:
To recognize and support valuable works dealing with African anthropological research.

LEGAL BASIS:
Created under the terms of the will of Mrs. Miriam Winifred Florence Talbot.

ELIGIBILITY:
Works of anthropological research concerning Africa which were published during a calendar year, to be received no later than March 31 in succeeding year, are eligible for the prize. Although works relating to any region of Africa may be submitted, preference is given first to works focusing on Nigeria, then to those dealing with any other section of West Africa or to publications relating to West Africa in general.

FINANCIAL DATA:
The amount of the prize is determined by income from investments and is therefore not constant.

Amount of support per award:
Approximately GBP 750 per annum.

NO. MOST RECENT APPLICANTS: 10.

NO. AWARDS: 1.

APPLICATION INFO:
No official application form is required, but copies of the prospectus are available upon request to the Coordinator at the address above. Entries must be accompanied by three copies of the book, article or work in question. Entries will not be returned.

Deadline: March 31 in the year following publication.

ADDRESS INQUIRIES TO:
Amaury Talbot Prize Coordinator
Royal Anthropological Institute
(See address above.)

WENNER-GREN FOUNDATION FOR ANTHROPOLOGICAL RESEARCH, INC.   [1846]

655 3rd Avenue, 23rd Floor
New York, NY 10017
(212) 683-5000
E-mail: inquiries@wennergren.org
Web Site: www.wennergren.org

FOUNDED: 1941

AREAS OF INTEREST:
All branches of anthropology, including cultural/social anthropology, ethnology, biological/physical anthropology, archaeology and anthropological linguistics, and closely related disciplines concerned with human origins, development and variation.

NAME(S) OF PROGRAMS:
● **Individual Research Grants**

TYPE:
Awards/prizes; Research grants. The Foundation offers Dissertation Fieldwork Grants, Post-Ph.D. Research Grants, and Hunt Postdoctoral Fellowships. Awards are available for basic research in all branches of anthropology. Grants are made to cover expenses or phases of a research project. The Foundation particularly invites projects employing comparative perspectives or integrating two or more subfields of anthropology.

The Hunt Postdoctoral Fellowship is awarded to scholars within 10 years of receipt of the Doctorate to aid the write-up of research results for publication.

Dissertation Fieldwork Grants are awarded to individuals to aid doctoral dissertation or thesis research.

Post-Ph.D. Research Grants are awarded to individual scholars holding the Doctorate or equivalent qualification in anthropology or a related discipline.

YEAR PROGRAM STARTED: 1941

PURPOSE:
To support anthropological research.

LEGAL BASIS:
Private operating foundation.

ELIGIBILITY:
Qualified scholars are eligible without regard to nationality or institutional affiliation for Dissertation Fieldwork, Post-Ph.D. Research Grants and Hunt Postdoctoral Fellowships.

Application for grants may be made by the scholar. Predoctoral grants application must be made jointly with a thesis advisor.

Dissertation Fieldwork Grants are for individuals enrolled in a doctoral program. These grants are contingent upon the applicant's successful completion of all requirements for the degree other than the dissertation/thesis.

Post-Ph.D. Research Grants are for individual scholars holding the Doctorate or equivalent qualification in anthropology or a related discipline.

Hunt Postdoctoral Fellowships are available to all scholars regardless of institutional affiliation and nationality. Applicants must have their Ph.D. in hand to apply and be within 10 years of receipt of their Doctorate.

FINANCIAL DATA:
Individual Research Grants, except for the Hunt Fellowship, are primarily for basic research. Grants cover research expenses directly related and essential to the project (i.e., travel, living expenses during fieldwork, equipment, supplies, research assistance and other relevant expenditures). Aid is not provided for salary and/or fringe benefits of applicant, tuition, nonproject personnel, travel to meetings, institutional overhead or institutional support. Expenses incurred prior to the effective date of an award will not be covered.

Amount of support per award: Dissertation Fieldwork Grants and Post Ph.D. Research Grants: Up to $20,000; May apply for a supplementary award, maximum $5,000. Hunt Fellowship: $40,000.

Total amount of support: Approximately $5,000,000.

APPLICATION INFO:
Applicants are required to submit a formal application. Application forms must be submitted online through the Foundation's web site beginning three months prior to the application deadline.

Duration: Hunt Postdoctoral Fellowship: Up to one year (12 continuous months of full-time writing). Nonrenewable; Research Grants: Duration of the project.

Deadline: May 1 for funding during first half of the year. November 1 for projects scheduled to begin July or later.
Announcement within six to eight months.

PUBLICATIONS:
Program announcement.

IRS I.D.: 13-1813827

WENNER-GREN FOUNDATION FOR ANTHROPOLOGICAL RESEARCH, INC.   [1847]

655 3rd Avenue, 23rd Floor
New York, NY 10017
(212) 683-5000
E-mail: lobbink@wennergren.org
Web Site: www.wennergren.org

FOUNDED: 1941

AREAS OF INTEREST:
All branches of anthropology, including cultural/social anthropology, ethnology, biological/physical anthropology, archaeology, anthropological linguistics, and closely related disciplines concerned with human origins, development and variation.

NAME(S) OF PROGRAMS:
● **Conference and Workshop Grants**
● **Wenner-Gren Symposium Program**

TYPE:
Conferences/seminars. Workshops.

PURPOSE:
To support anthropological research.

LEGAL BASIS:
Private operating foundation.

ELIGIBILITY:
The Foundation provides conference support in two forms. Conference and workshop grants are made to the organizer(s). Priority is given to public conferences sponsored by international scholarly organizations (e.g., the IUAES and EASA) that serve as their annual or periodic meetings and to working conferences that address broad research issues in anthropology and provide for intensive interaction among participants. Funds are not normally provided for panels or sessions that are part of larger meetings.

The Foundation also sponsors and directly administers a limited number of conferences each year under the Wenner-Gren Symposium Program. These symposia are intended for topics of broad significance for anthropology. They are planned jointly by the organizer(s) and the Foundation president and follow a specific format developed by the Foundation.

Requests by individuals to support their own travel to meetings are not accepted.

FINANCIAL DATA:
The Foundation pays all costs related to the Wenner-Gren Symposium and actively manages it, including sending out invitations and making travel arrangements.

Amount of support per award: Conference and Workshop Grants: $20,000.

Total amount of support: Varies.

NO. MOST RECENT APPLICANTS: 65.

NO. AWARDS: 30.

APPLICATION INFO:
Procedures are available on the Foundation web site.

Duration: Length of particular conference.

Deadline: Conference and Workshop Grants: June 1 and December 1.

PUBLICATIONS:
Annual report.

IRS I.D.: 13-1813827

ADDRESS INQUIRIES TO:
Laurie Obbink
Conference Program Associate
(See address above.)

PHYSICAL SCIENCES

Physical sciences (general)

AMERICAN CHEMICAL SOCIETY　　[1848]

1155 16th Street, N.W.
Washington, DC 20036
(202) 872-6092
(800) 227-5558
Fax: (202) 872-6319
E-mail: prfinfo@acs.org
Web Site: www.acsprf.org

FOUNDED: 1944

AREAS OF INTEREST:
Fundamental research in chemistry, engineering and geology which may impact the petroleum field.

NAME(S) OF PROGRAMS:
- The Petroleum Research Fund

TYPE:
Grants-in-aid; Research grants. The project may be in any field of pure science which may afford a basis for subsequent research directly connected with the petroleum field.

YEAR PROGRAM STARTED: 1944

PURPOSE:
To support advanced scientific education and fundamental research in the petroleum field.

LEGAL BASIS:
Private trust established in 1944 with contributions of seven petroleum companies.

ELIGIBILITY:
Grants are made to nonprofit scientific or educational institutions, such as universities, on behalf of projects of their regularly appointed faculty.

FINANCIAL DATA:
Amount of support per award: Up to $110,000, depending upon the grant program.
Total amount of support: Varies.
Matching fund requirements: Varies.

APPLICATION INFO:
Application information is available on the web site.
Duration: Up to three years.
Deadline: Approximately six months prior to each scheduled meeting. Specific deadlines are posted on the Society's web site.

PUBLICATIONS:
Annual report.

ADDRESS INQUIRIES TO:
Nancy Jensen, Interim Assistant Director
(See address above.)

AMERICAN SOCIETY FOR MASS SPECTROMETRY　　[1849]

2019 Galisteo Street
Building I-1
Santa Fe, NM 87505
(505) 989-4517
Fax: (505) 989-1073
E-mail: info@asms.org
Web Site: www.asms.org

FOUNDED: 1969

AREAS OF INTEREST:
Mass spectrometry.

NAME(S) OF PROGRAMS:
- ASMS Research Awards in Mass Spectrometry

TYPE:
Project/program grants; Research grants.

YEAR PROGRAM STARTED: 1985

PURPOSE:
To promote academic research in mass spectrometry by young scientists.

LEGAL BASIS:
Nonprofit corporation.

ELIGIBILITY:
Grant applicants must be academic scientists within four years of joining the tenure track faculty or equivalent in a North American university for research in mass spectrometry.

Applicants must be members of ASMS.

GEOG. RESTRICTIONS: North America.

FINANCIAL DATA:
Grants are made to the university in the name of the selected individual.
Amount of support per award: $35,000.
Total amount of support: $70,000 annually.

NO. MOST RECENT APPLICANTS: 15.

NO. AWARDS: 2.

APPLICATION INFO:
Applicants should submit applications electronically in a PDF format including a curriculum vitae, list of current research support, three-page proposal, one-page fiscal proposal and justification, and two letters of recommendation. Proposals are ranked primarily on scientific merit and secondarily on effectiveness of proposed use of funds.
Duration: Varies.
Deadline: November 30.

IRS I.D.: 23-7050068

ADDRESS INQUIRIES TO:
See e-mail address above.

AMERICAN SOCIETY OF NAVAL ENGINEERS (ASNE)

1452 Duke Street
Alexandria, VA 22314-3458
(703) 836-6727
Fax: (703) 836-7491
E-mail: scholarships@navalengineers.org
Web Site: www.navalengineers.org

TYPE:
Scholarships. Stipend for tuition, fees and expenses to follow a full-time or co-op program of study that applies to naval engineering, such as naval architecture, marine engineering, ocean engineering, mechanical engineering, structural engineering, electrical engineering, electronic engineering and the physical sciences, as well as other programs leading to careers with civilian and military maritime organizations supporting and developing work and life at sea.

See entry 2428 for full listing.

ASPRS - THE IMAGING AND GEOSPATIAL INFORMATION SOCIETY　　[1850]

425 Barlow Place
Suite 210
Bethesda, MD 20814-2160
(301) 493-0290
Fax: (225) 408-4422
E-mail: office@asprs.org
Web Site: www.asprs.org

FOUNDED: 1934

AREAS OF INTEREST:
Geospatial sciences, photogrammetry, remote sensing, geographic information systems (GIS), unmanned autonomous systems (UAS), and Lidar supporting technologies.

NAME(S) OF PROGRAMS:
- **Robert E. Altenhofen Memorial Scholarship**
- **Abraham Anson Memorial Scholarship**
- **John O. Behrens Institute for Land Information (ILI) Memorial Scholarship**
- **Robert N. Colwell Memorial Fellowship**
- **William A. Fischer Memorial Scholarship**
- **Ta Liang Memorial Award**
- **Francis H. Moffitt Memorial Scholarship**
- **The Kenneth J. Osborn Memorial Scholarship**
- **Paul R. Wolf Memorial Scholarship**

TYPE:
Assistantships; Awards/prizes; Fellowships; Internships; Scholarships; Travel grants.
Robert E. Altenhofen Memorial Scholarship is for undergraduate or graduate study in photogrammetry.

Abraham Anson Memorial Scholarship is designed to encourage undergraduate students who have an exceptional interest in pursuing scientific research or education in geospatial science or technology related to photogrammetry, remote sensing, surveying and mapping to enter a professional field where they can use the knowledge of their discipline to excel in their profession.

John O. Behrens Institute for Land Information (ILI) Memorial Scholarship is an undergraduate award established by the Institute for Land Information to encourage those who have an exceptional interest in pursuing scientific research or education in geospatial science or technology or land information systems/records to enter a professional field where they can use the knowledge of this discipline.

Robert N. Colwell Memorial Fellowship is made to a graduate student (Master's or Ph.D. level) currently enrolled or intending to enroll in a college or university in the U.S. or Canada, who is pursuing a program of study aimed at starting a professional career where expertise is required in remote sensing or other related geospatial information technologies.

William A. Fischer Memorial Scholarship facilitates graduate-level studies and career goals adjudged to address new and innovative uses of remote sensing data/techniques that relate to the natural, cultural or agricultural resources of the Earth.

Ta Liang Memorial Award facilitates research-related travel by outstanding graduate students in remote sensing. Such travel includes field investigations, agency visits, participation in conferences, or any travel that enhances or facilitates a graduate research program.

Francis H. Moffitt Memorial Scholarship is for students currently enrolled or intending to enroll in a college or university in the U.S. or Canada, who are pursuing a program of study in surveying or photogrammetry leading to a career in the geospatial mapping profession.

The Kenneth J. Osborn Memorial Scholarship is made to an undergraduate student currently enrolled or intending to enroll in a college or university in the U.S., who is pursuing a program of study in preparation for entering the profession in the general area of surveying, mapping, photogrammetry or geospatial information and technology, and shows good collaboration skills.

The Paul R. Wolf Memorial Scholarship is designed for prospective teachers in the general area of surveying, mapping or photogrammetry.

PURPOSE:
To advance knowledge and improve understanding of mapping sciences; to promote the responsible applications of photogrammetry, remote sensing, geographic information systems (GIS) and supporting technologies.

LEGAL BASIS:
501(c)(3) organization.

ELIGIBILITY:
Requirements vary with the program. Applicant must be enrolled in an accredited college or university and in most cases be an active or student member of ASPRS.

FINANCIAL DATA:
Amount of support per award: Altenhofer, Anson, Behrens, Fischer, Liang and Osborn Scholarship: $2,000; Colwell Memorial Fellowship and Moffitt Memorial Scholarship: $7,000; Wolf Scholarship: $4,000.

NO. MOST RECENT APPLICANTS: 100.

NO. AWARDS: 1 for each award.

APPLICATION INFO:
Application information is available on the web site. All complete applications, including reference letters and transcripts, must be submitted electronically.
Duration: One year.
Deadline: Contact the Society for dates.

PUBLICATIONS:
ASPRS Awards and Scholarships booklet (including application form).

STAFF:
Jesse Winch, Acting Executive Director

ADDRESS INQUIRIES TO:
Awards and Scholarships
(See address and e-mail above.)

COOPERATIVE INSTITUTE FOR RESEARCH IN ENVIRONMENTAL SCIENCES (CIRES)

CIRES Building, Room 318
University of Colorado
Boulder, CO 80309-0216
(303) 497-3584
Fax: (303) 492-1149
E-mail: christine.wiedinmyer@colorado.edu
Web Site: cires.colorado.edu

TYPE:
Fellowships. The program provides opportunities for interactions between CIRES scientists and visiting fellows to pursue common research interests. CIRES research includes theoretical studies, laboratory experimentation, and field investigations which may affect the enhancement of air and water quality and prediction of weather climate fluctuations.

See entry 1990 for full listing.

JILA   [1851]

440 UCB
University of Colorado at Boulder
Boulder, CO 80309-0440
(303) 492-7789
Fax: (303) 492-5235
E-mail: kim.monteleone@jila.colorado.edu
Web Site: jila.colorado.edu

FOUNDED: 1962

AREAS OF INTEREST:
Atomic and molecular physics, chemical physics, laser physics, astrophysics, optical physics, precision measurements, geophysical measurement and other closely related areas.

NAME(S) OF PROGRAMS:
● **Postdoctoral Research Associateships**
● **Visiting Fellowships**

TYPE:
Assistantships; Fellowships. Postdoctoral Research Associateships provide advanced research experience in the years immediately after the Ph.D. degree. Visiting Fellowships support research and study for experienced scientists.

YEAR PROGRAM STARTED: 1963

PURPOSE:
To further scientific exchange.

LEGAL BASIS:
Jointly sponsored by the University of Colorado at Boulder and the National Institute of Standards and Technology.

ELIGIBILITY:
Postdoctoral Research Associateships are awarded on the basis of the applicants' scholarly qualifications, promise as research scientists, and research interests and experience in relation to those specific ongoing research programs for which financial support is available. There are no restrictions as to citizenship except as may be imposed by conditions of individual contracts. Ph.D. required.

Visiting Fellowships are available to scientists with extensive research experience beyond the doctoral degree, although younger persons with significant scientific achievements are also encouraged to apply. Awards are based on the fields of scientific interest and the scholarly achievements or promise of the applicants. There are no restrictions as to citizenship.

FINANCIAL DATA:
Amount of support per award: Varies.
Total amount of support: Varies.

APPLICATION INFO:
Application information is available on the web site.
Deadline: Varies.

ADDRESS INQUIRIES TO:
Kim Monteleone, Coordinator
Visiting Scientists Program
(See address above.)

LINK FOUNDATION   [1852]

c/o Binghamton University Foundation
P.O. Box 6005
Binghamton, NY 13902-6005
(607) 777-2210
Fax: (607) 777-2533
Web Site: www.linkfoundation.org

FOUNDED: 1953

AREAS OF INTEREST:
Energy, oceanographic, aerospace simulation research and fellowships.

NAME(S) OF PROGRAMS:
● **Energy Fellowship Program**
● **Oceanography Engineering Fellowship Program**
● **Simulation Fellowship Program**

TYPE:
Fellowships. Grants for research, development and training related to the mastery of air, sea and energy resources.

YEAR PROGRAM STARTED: 1953

PURPOSE:
To promote the general welfare through the advancement of scientific, technological and general educational projects.

ELIGIBILITY:
Nonprofit educational institutions and organizations with appropriate interests are eligible to apply. Grants are not awarded directly to individuals.

FINANCIAL DATA:
Amount of support per award: $6,000 to $30,000 for the year 2020-21.

APPLICATION INFO:
Information on applying for fellowships may be obtained from the administrators for the individual programs. Proof of an organization's tax-exempt status must accompany the application if not listed in the publication Cumulative List of Organizations described in Section 170(c) of the Internal Revenue Code.

The following documents must be submitted in the order indicated or they will not be accepted:
(1) cover sheet specific to the individual program;
(2) 500-word description of the project that places the research in the context of current activities in the field;
(3) two letters of recommendation, as specified for the individual program;
(4) two additional letters of reference (professional or educational);
(5) project objectives, timeline and projected budget (projected budget only for Energy Program) and;
(6) current resume.
Duration: Subject to annual review.
Deadline: January 15.

TRUSTEES:
Dr. Thomas F. Kelly, Chairman
Douglas R. Johnson, Treasurer
Jimmie Anne Haisley, Secretary
Dr. Andrew M. Clark
David Gdovin

ADDRESS INQUIRIES TO:
Dr. Thomas F. Kelly, Chairman
(See address above.)

THE NATIONAL ACADEMIES OF SCIENCES, ENGINEERING, AND MEDICINE   [1853]

500 Fifth Street, N.W.
Washington, DC 20001
(202) 334-2760
E-mail: rap@nas.edu
Web Site: www.nationalacademies.org/rap

AREAS OF INTEREST:
All fields in science and engineering.

NAME(S) OF PROGRAMS:
● **NRC Research Associateship Programs**

TYPE:
Research scientists. Fellowships at the graduate, postdoctoral and senior levels for research-in-residence at U.S. federal laboratories and affiliated institutions.

YEAR PROGRAM STARTED: 1954

PURPOSE:
To provide research opportunities for qualified personnel.

LEGAL BASIS:
Not-for-profit agency.

ELIGIBILITY:
In most instances, applicants must be U.S. citizens. U.S. permanent residents and non-U.S. citizens are eligible to apply at select laboratories. Must have or expect to receive Ph.D., Sc.D. or other earned equivalent research Doctorate. Program also available for graduate-level applicants.

Awards are tenable only at participating U.S. federal laboratories and affiliated institutions.

GEOG. RESTRICTIONS: United States.

FINANCIAL DATA:
NRC Research Associateship awards include stipend, support for relocation, if eligible, and professional travel and health insurance.
Amount of support per award: Annual stipend for recent Ph.D. recipients: $45,000 to $80,000, with higher stipend for additional experience.
Total amount of support: Varies.

NO. MOST RECENT APPLICANTS: Approximately 500.

NO. AWARDS: Approximately 200 for the year 2018.

APPLICATION INFO:
Application information is available on the web site.
Duration: One to three years.
Deadline: February 1, May 1, August 1 and November 1.

STAFF:
Dr. H. Ray Gamble, Director of Fellowships and Associateships

ADDRESS INQUIRIES TO:
NRC Research Associateship Programs
(See address above.)

NATIONAL INSTITUTE OF STANDARDS AND TECHNOLOGY, FIRE RESEARCH DIVISION [1854]

100 Bureau Drive, Stop 8660
Gaithersburg, MD 20899-8660
(301) 975-6689
Fax: (301) 975-4052
E-mail: nelson.bryner@nist.gov
Web Site: www.nist.gov/el/fire-research-division-73300

FOUNDED: 1974

AREAS OF INTEREST:
Exploratory fire research, furnishing flammability, fire performance and validation, smoke hazard calculation, fire growth and extinction, compartment fire models and fire safety performance.

NAME(S) OF PROGRAMS:
• **Fire Research Grants Program**

TYPE:
Research grants. The program includes the following: Fire Fighting Technology Group,

Engineered Fire Safety Group, Flammability Reduction Group, Wildland Urban Interface Fire Group and National Fire Research Laboratory.

YEAR PROGRAM STARTED: 1981

PURPOSE:
To conduct research in the areas of fire analysis and prediction, fire metrology, fire fighting technology, integrated performance assessment, and materials and products.

LEGAL BASIS:
Public Law 93-498; Section 18.

ELIGIBILITY:
Institutions of higher education, hospitals, nonprofit organizations, commercial organizations, state, local, and Indian tribal governments, foreign governments, organizations under the jurisdiction of foreign governments, and international organizations are eligible. Joint programs with participation by more than one eligible entity are possible.

GEOG. RESTRICTIONS: United States.

FINANCIAL DATA:
Amount of support per award: Typically $50,000 to $100,000 per award.

NO. MOST RECENT APPLICANTS: 30.

NO. AWARDS: 3 to 5 annually.

APPLICATION INFO:
Prospective proposers are encouraged to contact the appropriate research group to determine the extent of interest prior to preparation of a detailed proposal. Electronic filing is accepted through www.grants.gov.
Duration: Up to three years.
Deadline: As listed in *Federal Register* notice.

NATIONAL SCIENCE FOUNDATION [1855]

Division of Atmospheric and Geospace Sciences
2415 Eisenhower Avenue
Alexandria, VA 22314
(703) 292-8520
E-mail: trozell@nsf.gov
Web Site: www.nsf.gov

FOUNDED: 1950

AREAS OF INTEREST:
The Atmospheric Sciences program supports research to add new understanding of the behavior of the Earth's atmosphere and its interactions with the Sun. Included are studies of the physics, chemistry and dynamics of the Earth's upper and lower atmosphere and its space environment, research on climate processes and variations and studies to understand the natural global cycles of gases and particles in the Earth's atmosphere.

TYPE:
Conferences/seminars; Research grants.

YEAR PROGRAM STARTED: 1962

PURPOSE:
To continue to build a base of fundamental knowledge of the atmospheres of the Earth and other planets and of the Sun.

LEGAL BASIS:
Government agency.

ELIGIBILITY:
Proposals may be submitted by academic institutions, nonacademic and nonprofit research organizations, profitmaking and

private research organizations and individuals. Occasionally, NSF sponsors efforts by other government agencies, particularly for field programs.

GEOG. RESTRICTIONS: United States and its territories.

FINANCIAL DATA:
Amount of support per award: Varies.
Total amount of support: Varies.

APPLICATION INFO:
Application information is available on the web site.
Duration: Varies.
Deadline: Varies.

PUBLICATIONS:
NSF Guide to Programs.

ADDRESS INQUIRIES TO:
Tracy L. Rozell, Program Support Manager
(See address above.)

OAK RIDGE INSTITUTE FOR SCIENCE AND EDUCATION (ORISE)

100 ORAU Way
Oak Ridge, TN 37830
(865) 574-1751
E-mail: science.education@orau.org
Web Site: orise.orau.gov/science-education

TYPE:
Fellowships; Internships; Scholarships. ORISE administers a broad range of internships, scholarships, fellowships and research experiences. ORISE programs include research experiences at Department of Energy national laboratories as well as other federal agencies with research facilities located across the country as well as some positions outside the U.S.

See entry 2444 for full listing.

RESEARCH CORPORATION FOR SCIENCE ADVANCEMENT [1856]

4703 East Camp Lowell Drive
Suite 201
Tucson, AZ 85712-1281
(520) 571-1111
Fax: (520) 571-1119
E-mail: awards@rescorp.org
Web Site: www.rescorp.org

FOUNDED: 1912

AREAS OF INTEREST:
University research and education in physics, chemistry and astronomy.

NAME(S) OF PROGRAMS:
• **Cottrell Scholar Awards**
• **Scialog Awards**

TYPE:
Awards/prizes; Conferences/seminars; Research grants; Seed money grants. Cottrell Scholar Awards recognize early-career faculty in Ph.D.-granting universities and in primarily undergraduate institutions.

Scialog Awards provide seed funding for early-career academic scientists that work in highly innovative cross-disciplinary teams. Programs have included solar energy conversion research and cell biology and theoretical physics collaborations.

PURPOSE:
To promote excellence in both research and teaching in science departments in colleges and universities.

LEGAL BASIS:
Operating foundation.

ELIGIBILITY:
Cottrell Scholar Awards: Applicants must be tenure-track assistant professors in a Ph.D.-granting or primarily undergraduate institution in a department of astronomy, chemistry or physics. Additionally, they must be in their third academic year during the calendar year of application.

Scialog: Faculty in U.S. and Canadian colleges and universities may apply.

FINANCIAL DATA:
Cottrell Scholar and Scialog Awards: Grant awards can be used at discretion of awardee for most direct costs.

Amount of support per award: Cottrell Scholar Award: $100,000; Scialog: Varies, with typical award $100,000 per team of two to three members.

Total amount of support: Varies.

NO. MOST RECENT APPLICANTS: Varies.

NO. AWARDS: Cottrell Scholars Awards: Approximately 30; Scialog Awards: Varies with number of conferences.

APPLICATION INFO:
Application information is available on the web site.

Duration: Cottrell Scholars Awards: Three years; Scialog Awards: Varies.

Deadline: Varies.

PUBLICATIONS:
Annual report; newsletter; occasional publications and guidelines.

IRS I.D.: 13-1963407

STAFF:
Silvia Ronco, Ph.D., Senior Program Director, Cottrell Scholar Awards
Richard Wiener, Ph.D., Senior Program Director, Scialog Awards

BOARD OF DIRECTORS:
Daniel Linzer, Ph.D., President
Lars Bildsten, Ph.D.
G. Scott Clemons
Danielle Dana
James De Naut
Peter K. Dorhout, Ph.D.
Eugene Flood, Jr., Ph.D.
Nancy Haegel, Ph.D.
Brent L. Iverson, Ph.D.
Kristine Lipscomb
Catherine J. Murphy, Ph.D.
Joan B. Woodard, Ph.D.

ALFRED P. SLOAN FOUNDATION   [1857]
630 Fifth Avenue
Suite 2200
New York, NY 10111
(212) 649-1649
E-mail: researchfellows@sloan.org
Web Site: sloan.org/fellowships

FOUNDED: 1934

AREAS OF INTEREST:
Science, technology, mathematics, computer science, economics, ocean sciences, neuroscience, physics, chemistry and computational and evolutionary molecular biology.

NAME(S) OF PROGRAMS:
• **Sloan Research Fellowships**

TYPE:
Awards/prizes; Fellowships. Research fellowships are awarded to young scholars in chemistry, computational and evolutionary molecular biology, computer science, economics, mathematics, neuroscience, physics, and ocean sciences. The Fellow need not pursue a specified research project and is free to change the direction of his or her research at any time.

YEAR PROGRAM STARTED: 1955

PURPOSE:
To identify and support promising young scientists at an early stage.

LEGAL BASIS:
Private foundation.

ELIGIBILITY:
Candidates are required to hold a Ph.D. (or equivalent) in chemistry, physics, mathematics, computer science, economics, computational and evolutionary molecular biology, neuroscience, ocean sciences, or a related field, and must be members of the regular faculty of a U.S. or Canadian college or university.

Applicant must be employed at a U.S. or Canadian institution.

GEOG. RESTRICTIONS: United States and Canada.

FINANCIAL DATA:
Each fellowship is administered by the Fellow's institution and is designed to allow the greatest possible freedom and flexibility in its use. The award may be used for equipment, technical assistance, professional travel, or any other activity directly related to the Fellow's research.

Amount of support per award: $75,000 over a two-year period.

Total amount of support: $9,450,000 for fiscal year 2020.

NO. MOST RECENT APPLICANTS: Over 1,100.

NO. AWARDS: 126 fellowships: 23 for physics, 23 for chemistry, 20 for mathematics, 16 for neuroscience, 20 for computer science, 8 for economics, 8 for earth system science, and 8 for computational and evolutionary molecular biology.

APPLICATION INFO:
Candidates may not apply directly, but must be nominated by a department head or other senior researcher. The nominator should submit a letter describing the candidate's qualifications and must see that the Foundation receives three supporting letters directly from other researchers, preferably not all from the same institution. A curriculum vitae, a list of scientific publications plus one copy of two representative publications, and a one-page statement by the candidate describing his or her significant scientific work and immediate research plans should accompany the nomination form and letter. Strong evidence in submitted publications and supporting letters of the nominee's independent creativity is one of the most important considerations in the review process.

Duration: Two years. One two-year extension is permitted on request.

Deadline: Selections are announced in February. Nominations must be received no later than September 15 for awards to begin the following September.

PUBLICATIONS:
Brochure; annual report.

ADMINISTRATIVE OFFICERS AND STAFF:
Adam F. Falk, President
Leisle Lin, Senior Vice President, Finance and Operations/Treasurer
Michelle Tepper, Controller

ADDRESS INQUIRIES TO:
Lauren von Eckartsberg
Grants Coordinator
(See e-mail address above.)

SOCIETY FOR THE STUDY OF AMPHIBIANS AND REPTILES   [1858]
Department of Biology
Carroll University
Waukesha, WI 53186
(262) 951-3295
E-mail: rbrenes@carrollu.edu
Web Site: www.ssarherps.org

AREAS OF INTEREST:
Herpetology.

NAME(S) OF PROGRAMS:
• **Roger Conant Grants in Herpetology**

TYPE:
Awards/prizes; Research grants. Awards are given in six categories: Conservation of Amphibians and/or Reptiles, Field Research, Laboratory Research, Herpetological Education, Travel and International Research.

PURPOSE:
To advance research, conservation, and education concerning amphibians and reptiles; to provide financial support for deserving individuals or organizations involved in herpetological research, education, or conservation.

ELIGIBILITY:
Applicants applying for the International category must be students. Membership in SSAR is not required.

FINANCIAL DATA:
Amount of support per award: $500.
Total amount of support: $6,000 to $7,000 annually.

NO. MOST RECENT APPLICANTS: 52 for the year 2019.

NO. AWARDS: 12 to 14.

APPLICATION INFO:
Applicants may only apply for one category and must designate to which of the six their proposal is submitted. Each proposal must include the following:
(1) title page;
(2) background and objects of the proposed project;
(3) methods of carrying out the project;
(4) complete project budget;
(5) brief resume or curriculum vitae of the applicant or project coordinator and;
(6) letter of support.

Duration: One-time award.
Deadline: December 15.

ADDRESS INQUIRIES TO:
Dr. Roberto Brenes, Chairperson
(See address above.)

WILLIAM P. WHARTON TRUST   [1859]
c/o Choate, Hall & Stewart
2 International Place
Boston, MA 02110
E-mail: williamwhartontrust@choate.com
Web Site: www.williamwharton.org

AREAS OF INTEREST:
Conservation and nature.

TYPE:
Project/program grants.

YEAR PROGRAM STARTED: 1976

PURPOSE:
To support projects that directly promote the study, conservation and appreciation of nature.

ELIGIBILITY:
Organizations must be 501(c)(3) tax-exempt. No funding for individuals.

GEOG. RESTRICTIONS: United States and Canada.

FINANCIAL DATA:
Amount of support per award: Up to $15,000.
Total amount of support: Approximately $175,000 annually.

NO. AWARDS: Approximately 17 for the year 2019.

APPLICATION INFO:
Complete application instructions are available on the Trust web site.
Duration: Varies.
Deadline: March 1 and September 15 for preliminary proposals. April 5 and October 31 for final proposals.

ADDRESS INQUIRIES TO:
See e-mail address above.

Astronomy and aerospace science

AMERICAN ASTRONOMICAL SOCIETY [1860]
1667 K Street, N.W.
Suite 800
Washington, DC 20006
(202) 328-2010
Fax: (202) 234-2560
E-mail: marvel@aas.org
Web Site: www.aas.org

FOUNDED: 1899

AREAS OF INTEREST:
The advancement of astronomy and closely related branches of science.

NAME(S) OF PROGRAMS:
● **Chrétien International Research Grant**

TYPE:
Research grants. Research grant(s) with preference given to individuals of high promise who are otherwise unfunded.

YEAR PROGRAM STARTED: 1982

PURPOSE:
To further international collaborative projects in observational astronomy, with emphasis on long-term international visits and the development of close working relationship with astronomers in other countries.

LEGAL BASIS:
Nonprofit, scientific corporation.

ELIGIBILITY:
Astronomers with a Ph.D. or equivalent are eligible. Graduate students are not eligible.

FINANCIAL DATA:
Amount of support per award: Up to $20,000.

Total amount of support: $20,000 each year.

NO. MOST RECENT APPLICANTS: 18.

NO. AWARDS: 1 or more individuals or groups.

APPLICATION INFO:
Application and all supporting materials should be submitted electronically to Sara Asfaw at grants@aas.org. Applications should include:
(1) a description of the research project (less than three pages in length), including an assessment of its importance to that particular subfield of astronomy and a statement enumerating all the aspects of international collaboration;
(2) a statement of the candidate's ability to do the proposed research, with special emphasis on international collaboration and foreign visits which have been arranged, including facilities available and observing time allocations, if any;
(3) the proposed budget, with brief justification for the amount requested;
(4) a description of other financial resources available;
(5) the candidate's curriculum vitae and bibliography of recent papers;
(6) two letters of reference from astronomers who know the candidate's work and;
(7) any special circumstances which might help in the decision process.
Duration: One year.
Deadline: Application due April 1. Announcement the following September.

ADDRESS INQUIRIES TO:
Sara Asfaw, Grants Contact
E-mail: grants@aas.org

AMERICAN ASTRONOMICAL SOCIETY [1861]
1667 K Street, N.W.
Suite 800
Washington, DC 20006
(202) 328-2010
Fax: (202) 234-2560
E-mail: kevin.marvel@aas.org
Web Site: www.aas.org/grants-and-prizes

FOUNDED: 1899

AREAS OF INTEREST:
Astronomy and closely related branches of science.

NAME(S) OF PROGRAMS:
● **Newton Lacy Pierce Prize in Astronomy**

TYPE:
Awards/prizes. Given to recognize outstanding achievement during the five years preceding the award in observational astronomical research based on measurements of radiation from an astronomical object. A monetary prize and certificate are awarded annually.

YEAR PROGRAM STARTED: 1974

LEGAL BASIS:
Nonprofit, scientific corporation.

ELIGIBILITY:
Applicants must be residents of North America (including Hawaii or Puerto Rico) or a member of a North American institution stationed abroad. Applicants should also be under 36 years of age.

FINANCIAL DATA:
Amount of support per award: $1,500.
Total amount of support: $1,500.

NO. AWARDS: 1.

APPLICATION INFO:
Contact the Society regarding application materials and requirements.
Deadline: Nomination due by June 30.

PUBLICATIONS:
Program announcement.

ASTRONOMICAL SOCIETY OF THE PACIFIC [1862]
390 Ashton Avenue
San Francisco, CA 94112
(415) 337-1100
Fax: (415) 337-5205
E-mail: awards@astrosociety.org
Web Site: www.astrosociety.org

FOUNDED: 1889

AREAS OF INTEREST:
Astronomy and science education.

NAME(S) OF PROGRAMS:
● **Maria and Eric Muhlmann Award**

TYPE:
Awards/prizes. Maria and Eric Muhlmann Award recognizes important research results based upon development of groundbreaking instruments and techniques.

YEAR PROGRAM STARTED: 1995

PURPOSE:
To improve significant observational research, possibly through advances in astronomical instrumentation, software or support infrastructure.

ELIGIBILITY:
Award is available to individuals. Applicants do not have to be U.S. citizens or residents.

FINANCIAL DATA:
Award includes travel reimbursement and hotel accommodations to Annual Awards Gala.
Amount of support per award: $500 and plaque.

NO. MOST RECENT APPLICANTS: Varies.

NO. AWARDS: 1.

APPLICATION INFO:
Sponsors should submit a two-page nomination giving strong support to the choice.
Duration: One-time award.
Deadline: March 1.

ADDRESS INQUIRIES TO:
Dr. Linda Shore, Chief Executive Officer (See address above.)

ASTRONOMICAL SOCIETY OF THE PACIFIC [1863]
390 Ashton Avenue
San Francisco, CA 94112
(415) 337-1100
Fax: (415) 337-5205
E-mail: awards@astrosociety.org
Web Site: www.astrosociety.org

AREAS OF INTEREST:
Astronomy.

NAME(S) OF PROGRAMS:
● **Klumpke-Roberts Award**

TYPE:
Awards/prizes.

PURPOSE:
To recognize outstanding contributions to the public understanding and appreciation of astronomy.

ELIGIBILITY:
There are no restrictions on nominations for this award. The contributions may be in the form of popular books and articles; lectures; radio, TV or movie productions; or service to public education in astronomy of any other nature.

FINANCIAL DATA:
Award includes travel reimbursement and hotel accommodation to Annual Awards Gala.

Amount of support per award: $500 and plaque.

NO. MOST RECENT APPLICANTS: Varies.

NO. AWARDS: 1.

APPLICATION INFO:
Nominations only. Self-nominations are not accepted.

Duration: One-time award.

Deadline: March 1.

ADDRESS INQUIRIES TO:
Dr. Linda Shore, Chief Executive Officer (See e-mail address above.)

ASTRONOMICAL SOCIETY OF THE PACIFIC [1864]

390 Ashton Avenue
San Francisco, CA 94112
(415) 337-1100
Fax: (415) 337-5205
E-mail: awards@astrosociety.org
Web Site: www.astrosociety.org

AREAS OF INTEREST:
Astronomy.

NAME(S) OF PROGRAMS:
● **Thomas J. Brennan Award**

TYPE:
Awards/prizes.

PURPOSE:
To recognize exceptional achievement related to the teaching of astronomy at the high school level.

ELIGIBILITY:
Nominees must reside in North America.

GEOG. RESTRICTIONS: North America.

FINANCIAL DATA:
Award includes travel reimbursement and hotel accommodation to attend the Annual Awards Gala.

Amount of support per award: $500 and plaque.

NO. MOST RECENT APPLICANTS: Varies.

NO. AWARDS: 1.

APPLICATION INFO:
Nominations must be made on the Brennan Award form, available on the web site. Neither self-nominations nor nomination by a family member will be accepted.

Duration: One-time award.

Deadline: March 1.

ADDRESS INQUIRIES TO:
Dr. Linda Shore, Chief Executive Officer (See e-mail address above.)

ASTRONOMICAL SOCIETY OF THE PACIFIC [1865]

390 Ashton Avenue
San Francisco, CA 94112
(415) 337-1100
Fax: (415) 337-5205
E-mail: awards@astrosociety.org
Web Site: www.astrosociety.org

AREAS OF INTEREST:
Astronomy and amateur astronomy.

NAME(S) OF PROGRAMS:
● **Amateur Achievement Award**
● **Las Cumbres Amateur Outreach Award**
● **The Gordon Myers Amateur Achievement Award**

TYPE:
Awards/prizes. Amateur Achievement Award recognizes significant observational or technical contributions to astronomy or amateur astronomy.

Las Cumbres Amateur Outreach Award honors outstanding educational outreach by an amateur astronomer to K-12 children and the interested lay public.

The Gordon Myers Amateur Achievement Award recognizes significant observational or technological contributions to astronomy or amateur astronomy by an individual not employed in the field of astronomy in a professional capacity.

PURPOSE:
To award outstanding contribution or educational outreach in the field of astronomy or amateur astronomy.

ELIGIBILITY:
Amateur Achievement Award: Nominees must not be employed as professional astronomers.

Las Cumbres Amateur Outreach Award: Nominee must not receive compensation (other than expenses) for their activitiy and not receive the majority of their income from a profession in astronomy.

FINANCIAL DATA:
Awards include travel reimbursement and hotel accommodation to Annual Awards Gala.

Amount of support per award: $500 and plaque.

NO. MOST RECENT APPLICANTS: Varies.

NO. AWARDS: 1 per award.

APPLICATION INFO:
Nominations are made from the ASP Amateur Advisory Committee and by members of the astronomical community. Self-nominations or nomination by a family member will not be accepted. Letters of support are required.

Duration: One-time award.

Deadline: March 1.

ADDRESS INQUIRIES TO:
Dr. Linda Shore, Chief Executive Officer (See e-mail address above.)

ASTRONOMICAL SOCIETY OF THE PACIFIC [1866]

390 Ashton Avenue
San Francisco, CA 94112
(415) 337-1100
Fax: (415) 337-5205
E-mail: awards@astrosociety.org
Web Site: www.astrosociety.org

FOUNDED: 1889

AREAS OF INTEREST:
Astronomy and science education.

NAME(S) OF PROGRAMS:
● **Arthur B.C. Walker II Award**

TYPE:
Awards/prizes.

PURPOSE:
To improve significant observational research, possibly through advances in astronomical instrumentation, software or support infrastructure.

ELIGIBILITY:
Nominees can include a broad range of individuals of African descent from the U.S. or any country who are astronomers or space scientists whose research and educational efforts are of note in their field. Nominees must demonstrate a commitment to increasing the participation of underrepresented groups in STEM areas, especially astronomy and space science.

FINANCIAL DATA:
Amount of support per award: $500 and plaque.

NO. AWARDS: 1.

APPLICATION INFO:
Nominations are solicited from anyone familiar with or knowledgeable of the nominee's achievements. Self-nominations are not accepted. The nominator should submit a resume or curriculum vitae of the nominee, along with a letter of no more than two pages explaining in detail the specific contributions and achievements of the nominee that merit the Award. In addition to the nomination letter, two independent letters of support (no more than two pages each) must be submitted.

Deadline: March 1.

ADDRESS INQUIRIES TO:
See e-mail address above.

ASTRONOMICAL SOCIETY OF THE PACIFIC [1867]

390 Ashton Avenue
San Francisco, CA 94112
(415) 337-1100
Fax: (415) 337-5205
E-mail: awards@astrosociety.org
Web Site: www.astrosociety.org

FOUNDED: 1889

AREAS OF INTEREST:
Astronomy and science education.

NAME(S) OF PROGRAMS:
● **Richard H. Emmons Award**

TYPE:
Awards/prizes.

YEAR PROGRAM STARTED: 2006

PURPOSE:
To improve significant observational research, possibly through advances in astronomical instrumentation, software or support infrastructure.

ELIGIBILITY:
Nominees must be teachers of college-level introductory astronomy for non-science majors.

FINANCIAL DATA:
Amount of support per award: $500 and plaque.

NO. AWARDS: 1.

APPLICATION INFO:
Nominations are solicited from colleagues, students or others familiar with or knowledgeable of the nominee's achievements. Nominations may be made by anyone except the nominee or someone from the nominee's family. The nominator should submit a resume or curriculum vitae of the nominee, along with a letter of no more than two pages explaining in detail the specific contributions and achievements of the nominee that merit the Award. In addition to the nomination letter, two independent letters of support (no more than two pages each) must be submitted.

Deadline: March 1.

ADDRESS INQUIRIES TO:
See e-mail address above.

LUNAR AND PLANETARY INSTITUTE [1868]

3600 Bay Area Boulevard
Houston, TX 77058
(281) 486-2159
Fax: (281) 486-2127
E-mail: internprogram@lpi.usra.edu
Web Site: www.lpi.usra.edu

FOUNDED: 1968

AREAS OF INTEREST:
Study of lunar exploration, planetary remote sensing and spectroscopy, image processing, planetary geology and surface processes, impact studies, geophysical data analysis and modeling, physics and chemistry of planetary atmospheres, meteorites and sample analysis, interplanetary dust and presolar grains, minerology/petrology and astrobiology.

NAME(S) OF PROGRAMS:
● **LPI Summer Intern Program in Planetary Science**

TYPE:
Conferences/seminars; Internships; Scholarships; Travel grants.

YEAR PROGRAM STARTED: 1969

PURPOSE:
To promote and assist in the analysis and interpretation of lunar and planetary data.

ELIGIBILITY:
College undergraduates with at least 50 semester hours of credit interested in pursuing a career in the sciences are eligible. Applicants will be considered for appointment without regard to race, creed, color, sex, national origin, age, handicap status or other non-merit factors.

Due to security issues, citizens of U.S. State Department designated countries are not eligible. See link under "ECP Notices" at oiir.hq.nasa.gov/nasaecp.

FINANCIAL DATA:
In addition to the stipend, financial support up to $1,000 is offered to interns who submit an accepted abstract as first author to the upcoming Lunar and Planetary Science Conference.

Amount of support per award: Selected interns will receive a $7,300 stipend to cover the costs associated with being in Houston for the duration of the program.

Total amount of support: Varies.

NO. AWARDS: 14 to 16.

APPLICATION INFO:
Applications are only accepted using the electronic application form found on the Institute web site.

Duration: 10-week program, June to August.

Deadline: January.

ADDRESS INQUIRIES TO:
See e-mail address above.

NATIONAL CENTER FOR ATMOSPHERIC RESEARCH [1869]

High Altitude Observatory
P.O. Box 3000
Boulder, CO 80307-3000
(303) 497-1598
Fax: (303) 497-1589
E-mail: cquinn@ucar.edu
Web Site: www2.hao.ucar.edu

FOUNDED: 1940

AREAS OF INTEREST:
Solar physics, solar-terrestrial physics and related astrophysics. Specific research interests include coronal and interplanetary physics, solar activity and magnetic fields, the solar interior and terrestrial interactions.

NAME(S) OF PROGRAMS:
● **Newkirk Graduate Research Fellowship**

TYPE:
Fellowships.

PURPOSE:
To promote cooperative research between HAO and academic institutions by providing support for aspiring young scientists at formative stages in their careers.

ELIGIBILITY:
Applicants must be full-time graduate students enrolled in a university program leading to the Ph.D. Students must declare their intention of working on their thesis in cooperation with an HAO staff member and should expect to spend a significant fraction of their time in residence at HAO.

FINANCIAL DATA:
Amount of support per award: Varies.
Total amount of support: Varies.

APPLICATION INFO:
Application includes transcripts of undergraduate and graduate courses, brief statement of goals and three letters of recommendation.

Duration: One-year term with possibility of renewals until completion of the Ph.D. degree.

PUBLICATIONS:
Brochure.

ADDRESS INQUIRIES TO:
Caitlyn Quinn Erdesz
HAO Visitor Committee
(See address above.)

*PLEASE NOTE:
Fellowship award is dependent upon funding.

NATIONAL RADIO ASTRONOMY OBSERVATORY [1870]

520 Edgemont Road
Charlottesville, VA 22903-2475
(434) 296-0237
Fax: (434) 296-0278
E-mail: jutley@nrao.edu
Web Site: www.nrao.edu

FOUNDED: 1957

AREAS OF INTEREST:
Ground-based radio astronomy. Current areas of research include cosmology, theoretical and observational studies of radio sources, the interstellar and intergalactic medium, structure and dynamics of galactic and extragalactic sources, physics of HII regions, stars, solar system objects and astrometry.

NAME(S) OF PROGRAMS:
● **Jansky Fellowships at the NRAO**

TYPE:
Fellowships. Research appointments. Postdoctoral appointments with liberal support for research travel, data reduction and publication. Jansky Fellows may or may not be residents at NRAO sites.

YEAR PROGRAM STARTED: 1960

LEGAL BASIS:
Federally funded research organization.

ELIGIBILITY:
Fellows must have received their Ph.D. prior to beginning the appointment. Preference is given to recent Ph.D. recipients.

FINANCIAL DATA:
Vacation accrual, health insurance, a moving allowance and other benefits available.

Amount of support per award: Annual salary $67,500, plus $17,000 travel budget per year.

NO. MOST RECENT APPLICANTS: 52.

NO. AWARDS: 5 for the year 2020-21.

APPLICATION INFO:
Application should include a curriculum vitae and a statement of the type of research activity to be undertaken at the NRAO. The applicant should request letters of recommendation from three references. These letters should be sent directly to the NRAO.

Duration: Two years. Possibility of renewal for a third year if mutually agreeable.

Deadline: On or around November 1 of each year.

PUBLICATIONS:
Program announcement.

ADDRESS INQUIRIES TO:
Jessica Utley
Science Support and Research
(See address above.)

NATIONAL SCIENCE FOUNDATION [1871]

Division of Astronomical Sciences
2415 Eisenhower Avenue
Alexandria, VA 22314
(703) 292-8820
Fax: (703) 292-9452
E-mail: jneff@nsf.gov
Web Site: www.nsf.gov

FOUNDED: 1950

AREAS OF INTEREST:
Astronomical sciences.

NAME(S) OF PROGRAMS:
● **Astronomy and Astrophysics Research Grants**

TYPE:
Awards/prizes; Challenge/matching grants; Conferences/seminars; Fellowships; Project/program grants; Research grants; Seed money grants; Travel grants; Research contracts. Broad base of support for fundamental research directed at explaining celestial objects and the cosmos in terms of physical principles.

Basic research support is provided under the following grant programs:

Planetary Astronomy - Objects studied in this program include the planets and their satellites, the asteroids and the comets. Ground-based observations are indispensable to the complete understanding of their structure, composition and origin.

Stellar Astronomy and Astrophysics - This program supports studies of the physical and chemical characteristics of the Sun and other stars, especially as they relate to the stars' past and future evolution. These studies make use of observations at many wavelengths, as well as laboratory measurements and theoretical modeling.

Galactic Astronomy - The topics studied in this program are the spatial and kinematics characteristics of the stars in our galaxy and the properties and distribution of the interstellar medium.

Extragalactic Astronomy and Cosmology - The objective of this program is the description of the nature, structure and evolution of external galaxies and quasars, as well as the implications of these data for the birth, expansion rate and future of the universe.

Advanced Technologies and Instrumentation - This program provides support for development of astronomical equipment at universities. In addition to supporting the acquisition of telescopes and auxiliary instrumentation, this program also supports the reduction of astronomical data by providing funds for minicomputers. Particular emphasis is being placed on the use of advanced technology detectors at radio, infrared and optical wavelengths.

PURPOSE:
To support research and education in astronomy and astrophysics.

LEGAL BASIS:
Government agency.

ELIGIBILITY:
NSF eligibility criteria apply.

GEOG. RESTRICTIONS: United States.

FINANCIAL DATA:
Amount of support per award: Varies.

Total amount of support: Estimated $48,500,000 for fiscal year 2019.

NO. AWARDS: Approximately 100 for fiscal year 2019.

APPLICATION INFO:
Application information is available on the Foundation web site.

Duration: Varies.

Deadline: November 15.

PUBLICATIONS:
Guide to Programs; *Grants for Scientific and Engineering Research.*

ADDRESS INQUIRIES TO:
James E. Neff, Program Director
(See address and e-mail above.)

SMITHSONIAN ASTROPHYSICAL OBSERVATORY   [1872]
60 Garden Street
Mail Stop 67
Cambridge, MA 02138
(617) 495-7103
Fax: (617) 496-7589
E-mail: predoc@cfa.harvard.edu
Web Site: www.cfa.harvard.
edu/opportunities/fellowships/predoc

FOUNDED: 1890

AREAS OF INTEREST:
Astrophysical research, including the fields of astronomy, astrophysics and planetary sciences.

NAME(S) OF PROGRAMS:
● **Predoctoral Research Fellowships**

TYPE:
Exchange programs; Fellowships; Internships. Predoctoral fellowships for thesis research. Fellowships are designed to allow students from other institutions throughout the world to do all or part of their thesis research at the Observatory. A wide variety of research projects may be proposed. About 300 scientific staff conduct research in observation, theory and instrumentation, and in nearly all areas related to astronomy.

YEAR PROGRAM STARTED: 1985

ELIGIBILITY:
Applicants must be enrolled in a Ph.D. program in appropriate fields (i.e., astronomy or astrophysics) and have completed all course work and examinations.

Applicants must be ready to begin dissertation research at the time of the award. They must have the approval of their department head at their home institution to conduct their thesis research at the Observatory. Students from any country are eligible.

FINANCIAL DATA:
Some funds may be available for relocation, travel and other expenses.

Amount of support per award: $37,932 for the year 2020.

NO. MOST RECENT APPLICANTS: 30 for the year 2019.

NO. AWARDS: 16 for the year 2019.

APPLICATION INFO:
Application forms are available on the web site.

Duration: Six months. Renewable up to three years.

Deadline: Proposals are reviewed on an ongoing basis.

STAFF:
Charles R. Alcock, Director

ADDRESS INQUIRIES TO:
Christine A. Crowley
Fellowship Programs Coordinator
(See address above.)

SMITHSONIAN ASTROPHYSICAL OBSERVATORY   [1873]
60 Garden Street
Mail Stop 67
Cambridge, MA 02138
(617) 495-7103
Fax: (617) 496-7589
E-mail: postdoc@cfa.harvard.edu
Web Site: www.cfa.harvard.
edu/opportunities/postdocs.html

FOUNDED: 1973

AREAS OF INTEREST:
Astrophysics, including the areas of theory, observation, instrumentation and/or laboratory research. Research programs at the Center are organized into seven divisions including atomic and molecular physics, high energy astrophysics, optical and infrared astronomy, radio and geoastronomy, solar, stellar and planetary sciences, theoretical astrophysics, and science education.

NAME(S) OF PROGRAMS:
● **Clay Postdoctoral Fellowship**

TYPE:
Fellowships. Postdoctoral fellowships for research in the Center's areas of interest.

YEAR PROGRAM STARTED: 1974

ELIGIBILITY:
Open to recent Ph.D. recipients with interests in any of the areas above.

FINANCIAL DATA:
Amount of support per award: Stipends of approximately $69,500; annual research budget of approximately $16,000 per appointee for the year 2019-20.

NO. MOST RECENT APPLICANTS: 251.

NO. AWARDS: 1.

APPLICATION INFO:
Application forms are available online.
Duration: Four years. Renewal possible for a fifth year.
Deadline: October 30.

PUBLICATIONS:
Observatory reports issue of the *Bulletin of the American Astronomical Society.*

STAFF:
Charles R. Alcock, Director

ADDRESS INQUIRIES TO:
Christine A. Crowley
Fellowship Programs Coordinator
(See address above.)

SPACE TELESCOPE SCIENCE INSTITUTE   [1874]
3700 San Martin Drive
Baltimore, MD 21218
(410) 338-2474
E-mail: nhfp@stsci.edu
Web Site: www.stsci.edu

FOUNDED: 1990

AREAS OF INTEREST:
Astronomy, astrophysics and related disciplines.

NAME(S) OF PROGRAMS:
● **NASA Hubble Fellowship Program**

TYPE:
Fellowships. Provides a limited number of recent postdoctoral scientists of unusual promise and ability with the opportunity to

pursue research of their choice at a participating U.S. astronomical institution designated as host institution by the scientist.

YEAR PROGRAM STARTED: 1990

PURPOSE:
To expand and strengthen the research work of the astronomical community.

ELIGIBILITY:
Applicants must have earned a Doctorate degree, up to three years prior to application, in physics, astronomy or a related discipline. Applicants can be any nationality. Candidates are selected on the basis of their research proposal, publications and academic achievement. No more than one fellow per year is approved for any one academic location.

Fellowships must be held at U.S. institutions.

FINANCIAL DATA:
Amount of support per award: Annual stipend of approximately $70,500, plus $16,000 per year for research expenses, and up to $20,000 for health insurance.
Total amount of support: Varies.

CO-OP FUNDING PROGRAMS: NASA Exoplanet Science Institute and the Chandra X-ray Center.

NO. MOST RECENT APPLICANTS: 350 for the year 2020.

NO. AWARDS: Up to 24.

APPLICATION INFO:
Application information is available on the web site.
Duration: One year and two annual renewals contingent on satisfactory performance and availability of NASA funds.
Deadline: First week in November.

ADDRESS INQUIRIES TO:
NASA Hubble Fellowship Program Coordinator
(See address above.)

ZONTA INTERNATIONAL FOUNDATION   [1875]
1200 Harger Road, Suite 330
Oak Brook, IL 60523
(630) 928-1400
Fax: (630) 928-1559
E-mail: programs@zonta.org
Web Site: www.zonta.org

FOUNDED: 1919

AREAS OF INTEREST:
Aerospace-related sciences or aerospace-related engineering.

NAME(S) OF PROGRAMS:
● **Amelia Earhart Fellowship**

TYPE:
Fellowships. Awarded annually to women for graduate study in aerospace-related sciences or aerospace-related engineering at any university or college offering accredited graduate courses and degrees.

YEAR PROGRAM STARTED: 1938

PURPOSE:
To encourage and support the study and research of women scientists and engineers throughout the world and to improve the status of women.

LEGAL BASIS:
Incorporated in the state of Illinois as a nonprofit organization.

ELIGIBILITY:
Women of any nationality pursuing a Ph.D./doctoral degree who demonstrate a superior academic record in the field of aerospace-related sciences or aerospace-related engineering are eligible. Students must be registered in a full-time Ph.D./doctoral program and have completed at least one year of that program or have received a Master's degree in an aerospace-related field at the time the application is submitted. Applicants must not graduate from their Ph.D. or doctoral program before April 2022.

Postdoctoral research programs are not eligible for the fellowship. Members and employees of Zonta International or the Zonta International Foundation are also not eligible to apply for the fellowship. Previous Amelia Earhart Fellows are not eligible to apply to renew the fellowship for a second year.

FINANCIAL DATA:
Fellowship awards may be used for tuition, books, fees or living expenses.
Amount of support per award: $10,000 annually.
Total amount of support: Up to $350,000.

NO. MOST RECENT APPLICANTS: 145.

NO. AWARDS: Up to 35.

APPLICATION INFO:
Applications may be submitted at zontainternational.awardspring.com and must include the following:
(1) biographical information;
(2) plan for intended study;
(3) list of schools attended, including official detailed transcripts of grades or equivalent records from all universities, colleges, or institutions attended, including undergraduate institutions and degrees received;
(4) scholarships, fellowships and honors received, if any;
(5) previous publications, if any;
(6) employment history;
(7) essay on academic program and professional goals and;
(8) three recommendations from university professors or supervisors who can assess applicant's ability to succeed in the program.
Duration: One academic year. Nonrenewable.
Deadline: November 15.

ADDRESS INQUIRIES TO:
Program Coordinator
(See address above.)

Chemistry

AMERICAN CHEMICAL SOCIETY   [1876]
1155 16th Street, N.W.
Washington, DC 20036-4800
(202) 872-4575
Fax: (202) 776-8008
E-mail: awards@acs.org
Web Site: www.acs.org/nationalawards

FOUNDED: 1876

AREAS OF INTEREST:
Chemical.

CONSULTING OR VOLUNTEER SERVICES:
Volunteer services.

NAME(S) OF PROGRAMS:
● **Nakanishi Prize**

TYPE:
Awards/prizes. Award presented in the U.S. in odd years and Japan in even years.

YEAR PROGRAM STARTED: 1995

PURPOSE:
To recognize and stimulate significant work that extends chemical and spectroscopic methods to the study of important biological phenomena.

LEGAL BASIS:
Nonprofit association.

ELIGIBILITY:
Individuals can apply. There are no limits on age or nationality.

FINANCIAL DATA:
Amount of support per award: $5,000, plus up to $2,500 travel allowance, medallion with presentation box and certificate.

NO. AWARDS: 1.

APPLICATION INFO:
Application procedures are available online.
Duration: Nomination renewable.
Deadline: November 1.

ADDRESS INQUIRIES TO:
Awards Office
(See address above.)

*SPECIAL STIPULATIONS:
Special consideration will be given for work that has contributed broadly on an international scope.

AMERICAN CHEMICAL SOCIETY   [1877]
1155 16th Street, N.W.
Washington, DC 20036-4800
(202) 872-4575
Fax: (202) 776-8008
E-mail: awards@acs.org
Web Site: www.acs.org/awards

FOUNDED: 1876

AREAS OF INTEREST:
Research in industrial and engineering chemistry and chemical engineering principles.

NAME(S) OF PROGRAMS:
● **E.V. Murphree Award in Industrial and Engineering Chemistry**

TYPE:
Awards/prizes.

YEAR PROGRAM STARTED: 1955

PURPOSE:
To stimulate fundamental research in industrial and engineering chemistry, the development of chemical engineering principles and their application to industrial processes.

LEGAL BASIS:
Nonprofit association.

ELIGIBILITY:
Individuals can apply. Nominee must have accomplished outstanding research of theoretical or experimental nature in fields of industrial chemistry or chemical engineering. There are no limits on age or nationality.

FINANCIAL DATA:
Amount of support per award: $5,000, certificate, and up to $1,000 travel expenses.

NO. AWARDS: 1.

APPLICATION INFO:
Application procedures are available online.
Duration: One year. Nominations renewable.
Deadline: November 1.

ADDRESS INQUIRIES TO:
Awards Office
(See address above.)

AMERICAN CHEMICAL SOCIETY [1878]

Office of Research Grants
1155 16th Street, N.W.
Washington, DC 20036
(202) 872-4600
(202) 872-6207
(800) 227-5558
E-mail: a_fahr@acs.org
Web Site: www.acs.org/content/acs/en/funding-and-awards.html

AREAS OF INTEREST:
Biology-chemistry interface.

NAME(S) OF PROGRAMS:
- **Irving S. Sigal Postdoctoral Fellowship**

TYPE:
Fellowships. The Sigal Fellowship is awarded every two years to a Ph.D. candidate who will pursue research at the chemistry and biology interface.

PURPOSE:
To advance research at the chemistry and biology interface.

ELIGIBILITY:
Nominee must be a scientist who has earned or will earn a doctoral degree in chemistry during the academic year of the competition or the preceding year in a graduate chemistry department within the U.S. Nominee must intend to pursue chemistry postdoctoral research at the biology-chemistry interface. There are no restrictions on the age or nationality of the fellow.

FINANCIAL DATA:
Amount of support per award: $60,000 per year.

NO. AWARDS: 1.

APPLICATION INFO:
Candidates are nominated by chairs of Ph.D.-granting Chemistry Departments in the U.S. During a competition, approximately one-fifth of the U.S. doctoral chemistry departments are invited to nominate one candidate for the Sigal Fellowship.

Individuals are not able to submit an application without being nominated.
Duration: Two years.

ADDRESS INQUIRIES TO:
E-mail: sigalinfo@acs.org or
Dr. Askar Fahr, Program Manager
(See e-mail address above.)

AMERICAN CHEMICAL SOCIETY [1879]

Office of Research Grants
1155 16th Street, N.W.
Washington, DC 20036
(202) 872-4600
(202) 872-6186
(800) 227-5558
E-mail: n_jensen@acs.org
Web Site: www.acs.org/content/acs/en/funding-and-awards.html

AREAS OF INTEREST:
Organic and medicinal chemistry.

NAME(S) OF PROGRAMS:
- **Teva Pharmaceuticals Marc A. Goshko Memorial Grant Program**

TYPE:
Research grants.

PURPOSE:
To support academic researchers in the fields of organic and medicinal chemistry.

ELIGIBILITY:
Applicant must be a recently-tenured faculty member of a Ph.D.-granting department in the U.S.

Proposed research must be in the area of organic chemistry, with potential or direct connections with medicinal or pharmaceutical chemistry, such that the successful results would be of potential practical benefit to the discovery of organic compounds useful as human medicines. Proposals are evaluated on scientific merit, creativity and novelty. Proposal must address unexplored fields in organic and/or medicinal chemistry.

FINANCIAL DATA:
Amount of support per award: $100,000.

CO-OP FUNDING PROGRAMS: Teva Pharmaceuticals.

NO. AWARDS: 1.

APPLICATION INFO:
Application must include a budget in the amount of $100,000 for each of the three years with the following categories:
(1) personnel;
(2) reagents and expendables;
(3) permanent equipment and;
(4) travel.

A brief budget explanation should be part of the proposal.
Duration: Three years.
Deadline: Submission window will be posted online in the winter of 2020.

ADDRESS INQUIRIES TO:
Dr. Nancy Jensen, Program Manager
(See e-mail address above.)

*SPECIAL STIPULATIONS:
At the end of each grant year, the grantee will submit a financial report and a scientific progress report.

AMERICAN CHEMICAL SOCIETY [1880]

1155 16th Street, N.W.
Washington, DC 20036
(800) 227-5558 ext. 6250
Fax: (202) 872-4361
E-mail: scholars@acs.org
Web Site: www.acs.org/content/acs/en/funding-and-awards.html

AREAS OF INTEREST:
Chemistry-related disciplines.

NAME(S) OF PROGRAMS:
- **ACS Scholars Program**

TYPE:
Scholarships.

PURPOSE:
To support the advancement of the chemical sciences through research, education, and community projects.

ELIGIBILITY:
To be considered for a scholarship, candidate must:
(1) be a U.S. citizen or legal permanent resident of the U.S.;
(2) be African-American/Black, Hispanic/Latino, or American Indian;
(3) be a graduating high school senior or college freshman, sophomore or junior. Seniors can apply for their fifth year;
(4) intend to major or already major in chemistry, biochemistry, chemical engineering, chemical technology, or another chemistry-related science and plan to pursue a career in a chemistry-related science;
(5) be a full-time student at a high school or accredited college, university or community college and;
(6) demonstrate high academic achievement in chemistry or science with a grade point average 3.0 or higher.

FINANCIAL DATA:
Amount of support per award: $2,500 for freshmen, $3,000 for sophomores, and $5,000 for juniors and seniors.
Total amount of support: Approximately $900,000 annually.

NO. AWARDS: 350 annually.

APPLICATION INFO:
Application must include fall semester grades or college transcripts. These must be sent directly from the school either in a sealed envelope or by transcript clearinghouse to the address or e-mail listed above.

Two letters of recommendation are required. One letter must be from a chemistry, science, or math teacher or research advisor.

Applicant must also submit the Student Aid Report (SAR) for the upcoming academic year, after submission of the FAFSA form. SAR must be sent to the e-mail address listed above.
Duration: One year. Renewable.
Deadline: March 1.

ADDRESS INQUIRIES TO:
Mahalia Randle, Program Manager
(See address and e-mail above.)

AMERICAN NUCLEAR SOCIETY (ANS) [1881]

555 North Kensington Avenue
LaGrange Park, IL 60526
(708) 352-6611
Fax: (708) 352-0499
E-mail: scholarships@ans.org
Web Site: www.ans.org

FOUNDED: 1954

AREAS OF INTEREST:
Radioanalytical chemistry or analytical applications of nuclear science.

NAME(S) OF PROGRAMS:
- **James R. Vogt Radiochemistry Scholarship**

TYPE:
Scholarships. Scholarship award to recognize one outstanding undergraduate student or one graduate student pursuing a career in radioanalytical chemistry or analytical applications of nuclear science.

YEAR PROGRAM STARTED: 1987

ELIGIBILITY:
U.S. and non-U.S. applicants must be ANS student members. Applicants must have completed a minimum of two years in an accredited undergraduate program and be enrolled in a four-year college or university in the U.S. Undergraduates in their junior

and senior years are eligible to apply as are graduate students in their first or second year of graduate study.

Student must be engaged in proposing to undertake graduate or undergraduate research in radioanalytical chemistry or its applications.

Applicants must be U.S. citizens or hold permanent resident visa at the time of application.

FINANCIAL DATA:
Scholarship funds may be used by the student to defray any bona fide education costs including tuition, fees, books, room and board.
Amount of support per award: $3,000.

NO. AWARDS: 1 annually.

APPLICATION INFO:
Applications must be submitted online. Applicant should include interest in radioanalytical chemistry and its applications in their Personal Statement of Future Plans.
Duration: One year. Nonrenewable.
Deadline: February 1.

ADDRESS INQUIRIES TO:
Scholarship Coordinator
(See address above.)

*PLEASE NOTE:
Scholarships are only offered to ANS student members.

AMERICAN OIL CHEMISTS SOCIETY (AOCS) [1882]
2710 South Boulder Drive
Urbana, IL 61802-6996
(217) 693-4821
Fax: (217) 693-4865
E-mail: awards@aocs.org
Web Site: www.aocs.org/awards

FOUNDED: 1909

AREAS OF INTEREST:
Oils, fats, proteins, surfactants, lipid chemistry, biochemistry, sterols and related materials.

NAME(S) OF PROGRAMS:
- **Alton E. Bailey Award**
- **Stephen S. Chang Award**
- **Corporate Achievement Award**
- **Schroepfer Medal**
- **Supelco AOCS Research Award**
- **Young Scientist Research Award**

TYPE:
Awards/prizes.

YEAR PROGRAM STARTED: 1982

PURPOSE:
To annually recognize scientists, technologists or engineers who have made substantial accomplishments in lipid chemistry, either by one major breakthrough or by an accumulation of publications.

LEGAL BASIS:
Professional society.

ELIGIBILITY:
Nominations are accepted. Preference shall be given to individuals who are actively associated with research and who have made discoveries that have influenced their fields of endeavor.

FINANCIAL DATA:
Amount of support per award: Varies.
Total amount of support: Varies.

NO. MOST RECENT APPLICANTS: 20.

NO. AWARDS: Bailey Award, Chang Award, Supelco AOCS Research Award and Young Scientist Research Award: 1 of each annually. Corporate Achievement Award and Schroepfer Medal: 1 of each biennially in odd-numbered years.

APPLICATION INFO:
Nominations for the Chang Award must include a letter from the nominator describing the nominee's distinguished accomplishments in basic research and how they have been utilized by industry to help improve or develop products related to lipids. The nomination must include at least three letters of recommendation and biographical information, including the curriculum vitae.

Nominations for the Schroepfer Medal should include a 300- to 1,000-word summary describing the significance of the nominee's accomplishments in the steriod field, a current curriculum vitae including a full list of publications, and two supporting letters.
Duration: One-time awards.
Deadline: August 1.

PUBLICATIONS:
INFORM: International News on Fats, Oils, and Related Materials; *JAOCS: Journal of the American Oil Chemists' Society*; *Lipids*; *Journal of Surfactants and Detergents*.

ADDRESS INQUIRIES TO:
Victoria Santo, AOCS Program Manager Membership Recognition
E-mail: victoria@aocs.org

CANADIAN SOCIETY FOR CHEMICAL TECHNOLOGY [1883]
222 Queen Street
Suite 1900
Ottawa ON K1P 5V9 Canada
(613) 232-6252
Fax: (613) 232-5862
E-mail: awards@cheminst.ca
Web Site: www.cheminst.ca/awards

AREAS OF INTEREST:
Chemistry, biochemistry, chemical engineering technology or chemical technology.

NAME(S) OF PROGRAMS:
- **Norman and Marion Bright Memorial Award**

TYPE:
Awards/prizes.

YEAR PROGRAM STARTED: 1980

PURPOSE:
To reward an individual who has made an outstanding contribution in Canada to the furtherance of chemical technology.

ELIGIBILITY:
The person honored must be either a chemical sciences technologist or a person from outside the field who had made a significant or noteworthy contribution to its advancement.

GEOG. RESTRICTIONS: Canada.

FINANCIAL DATA:
Amount of support per award: $500.

NO. AWARDS: 1.

APPLICATION INFO:
Applicants must complete a nomination form.
Deadline: December 1.

ADDRESS INQUIRIES TO:
Awards Manager
(See address above.)

CANADIAN SOCIETY FOR CHEMISTRY [1884]
222 Queen Street
Suite 1900
Ottawa ON K1P 5V9 Canada
(613) 232-6252
Fax: (613) 232-5862
E-mail: awards@cheminst.ca
Web Site: www.cheminst.ca/awards

AREAS OF INTEREST:
Biochemistry, organic and bioorganic chemistry.

NAME(S) OF PROGRAMS:
- **CCUCC Chemistry Doctoral Award**

TYPE:
Awards/prizes. CCUCC Chemistry Doctoral Award recognizes outstanding achievement and potential in research by a graduate student.

PURPOSE:
To recognize outstanding contributions by chemists for their research in a wide variety of fields.

ELIGIBILITY:
CCUCC Chemistry Doctoral Award is intended to recognize outstanding achievement and potential in research by a graduate student whose Ph.D. thesis in chemistry was formally accepted by a Canadian university in the 12-month period preceding the nomination deadline.

FINANCIAL DATA:
Amount of support per award: $2,000.

NO. AWARDS: 1.

APPLICATION INFO:
Nominations must include:
(1) letter of support by nominator;
(2) curriculum vitae (using NSERC guidelines);
(3) thesis synopsis;
(4) statement of merit and;
(5) one representative publication.
Deadline: September 15.

PUBLICATIONS:
Program announcement.

ADDRESS INQUIRIES TO:
Awards Manager
(See address above.)

GEORGETOWN UNIVERSITY [1885]
Department of Chemistry
Box 571227
Washington, DC 20057-1227
(202) 687-6073
Fax: (202) 687-6209
E-mail: chemad@georgetown.edu
Web Site: chemistry.georgetown.edu

FOUNDED: 1789

AREAS OF INTEREST:
Graduate education in chemistry.

NAME(S) OF PROGRAMS:
- **Doctoral Program in Chemistry**

TYPE:
Assistantships; Awards/prizes; Conferences/seminars; Exchange programs; Fellowships; General operating grants; Professorships; Research grants; Scholarships; Visiting scholars.

YEAR PROGRAM STARTED: 1924

PURPOSE:
To enable graduate students to earn a Ph.D. degree in chemistry, inorganic, organic, analytical, physical or theoretical chemistry, organometallic, synthetic, or nano-chemistry, biochemistry, or structural crystallography.

LEGAL BASIS:
University.

ELIGIBILITY:
Fellowships are open to nationals of any country. Bachelor's degree or the equivalent is required.

FINANCIAL DATA:
Amount of support per award: $32,760 stipend, full-time tuition coverage and comprehensive individual medical insurance.

NO. MOST RECENT APPLICANTS: 95.

NO. AWARDS: 10.

APPLICATION INFO:
Application information is available on the web site.
Duration: Nine months to one year. Renewable for as long as student continues good progress toward the degree.
Deadline: January 15.

PUBLICATIONS:
Graduate Studies in Chemistry, booklet.

ADDRESS INQUIRIES TO:
Dr. Timothy H. Warren
Professor and Chairperson
(See address above.)

NATIONAL MOLE DAY FOUNDATION [1886]
3896 Leaman Court
Freeland, MI 48623
(989) 964-8020
E-mail: moleday@hotmail.com
Web Site: www.moleday.org

FOUNDED: 1991

AREAS OF INTEREST:
Chemistry education.

NAME(S) OF PROGRAMS:
- **The George Hague Memorial Travel Award**
- **National Mole of the Year Award (MOTY)**

TYPE:
Grants-in-aid. The George Hague Memorial Travel Award is given to financially support a young chemistry instructor (with two to five years of chemistry experience) in attending a biennial ChemEd conference.

The National Mole of the Year Award (MOTY) is given to a member of the National Mole Day Foundation who has contributed the most to furthering the cause of Mole Day and chemistry education.

PURPOSE:
To support Mole Day activities in classrooms, schools or communities.

ELIGIBILITY:
Must be a member of the National Mole Day Foundation and be involved with chemical education. Those receiving grants are not eligible again for the following three years.

FINANCIAL DATA:
Amount of support per award: The George Hague Memorial Travel Award: Up to $750; National Mole of the Year Award (MOTY): $250.

APPLICATION INFO:
Application information is available on the web site.
Deadline: March 1 of odd-numbered years.

ADDRESS INQUIRIES TO:
Rebecca Logan, Executive Director
(See address above.)

THE UNIVERSITY OF SYDNEY [1887]
Scholarships Office
Level 4, Jane Foss Russell Building G02
The University of Sydney N.S.W. 2006
Australia
61 (02) 8627 1444
E-mail: scholarships.officer@sydney.edu.au
Web Site: www.sydney.edu.au/scholarships

FOUNDED: 1850

AREAS OF INTEREST:
Chemistry in relation to agriculture and industry.

NAME(S) OF PROGRAMS:
- **Henry Bertie and Florence Mabel Gritton Postgraduate Research Scholarships**

TYPE:
Scholarships. Scholarships are awarded for research leading to a higher degree.

PURPOSE:
To promote the knowledge and study of chemistry in relation to industry and agriculture, including chemistry connected with electrical engineering, metallurgical chemistry and chemistry in its application to mining and the winning and treatment of minerals and natural products of the soil.

LEGAL BASIS:
University.

ELIGIBILITY:
Open to graduates of universities which are members of the Association of Commonwealth Universities, graduates of any country who are citizens of a Commonwealth country, or Australian permanent residents. Candidates for scholarships must hold at least a first class honours degree.

Tenable at the University of Sydney.

FINANCIAL DATA:
Scholarship does not cover tuition fees payable by international students.
Amount of support per award: $35,000 AUD per annum for the year 2020.

APPLICATION INFO:
Application information is available on the web site.
Duration: Two years for a Master's research degree and three years for a Ph.D.
Deadline: September.

THE ROBERT A. WELCH FOUNDATION [1888]
5555 San Felipe
Suite 1900
Houston, TX 77056-2730
(713) 961-9884
Fax: (713) 961-5168
E-mail: info@welch1.org
Web Site: www.welch1.org

FOUNDED: 1954

AREAS OF INTEREST:
Basic research in chemistry.

NAME(S) OF PROGRAMS:
- **Departmental Grants**
- **Research Grants**
- **Welch Summer Scholar Program**

TYPE:
Research grants. Grants to support long-range fundamental research in the broad domain of chemistry.

The Welch Foundation supports chemical research at educational institutions within the state of Texas.

LEGAL BASIS:
Corporate.

ELIGIBILITY:
Full-time regular faculty members at Texas colleges or universities, who are tenured or on the tenured track, are eligible to apply for research grants.

GEOG. RESTRICTIONS: Texas.

FINANCIAL DATA:
Amount of support per award: Minimum $80,000 research grant per year.
Total amount of support: Varies.

NO. AWARDS: Varies.

APPLICATION INFO:
Application information is available on the web site.
Duration: Three years. Renewable.
Deadline: Departmental Grants: September 15; Research Grants: Last business day of January.

IRS I.D.: 76-0343128

ADDRESS INQUIRIES TO:
See e-mail address above.

Earth sciences

THE AMERICAN ASSOCIATION OF GEOGRAPHERS [1889]
1710 16th Street, N.W.
Washington, DC 20009
(202) 234-1450
Fax: (202) 234-2744
E-mail: grantsawards@aag.org
Web Site: www.aag.org

FOUNDED: 1904

NAME(S) OF PROGRAMS:
- **AAG Research Grant**

TYPE:
Research grants. Small grant to support research and fieldwork.

PURPOSE:
To support research and fieldwork proposals which offer the prospect of obtaining substantial subsequent support from private foundations or federal agencies and that address questions of major importance to the discipline.

ELIGIBILITY:
Must be an AAG member for at least two years at the time of application. Grants can be used only for direct expenses of research; salary and overhead costs are not allowed. The committee will not approve awards for Master's or doctoral dissertation research.

FINANCIAL DATA:
Amount of support per award: Up to $500.

APPLICATION INFO:
Digital submissions are required.
Deadline: December 31.

ADDRESS INQUIRIES TO:
See e-mail address above.

THE AMERICAN ASSOCIATION OF GEOGRAPHERS [1890]

1710 16th Street, N.W.
Washington, DC 20009
(202) 234-1450
Fax: (202) 234-2744
E-mail: grantsawards@aag.org
Web Site: www.aag.org

FOUNDED: 1904

NAME(S) OF PROGRAMS:
• **AAG Dissertation Research Grants**

TYPE:
Research grants.

PURPOSE:
To provide financial assistance to candidates preparing doctoral dissertations in geography.

ELIGIBILITY:
Applicant must:
(1) be an AAG member for at least one year at the time of application;
(2) not have a Doctorate at the time of the award and;
(3) have completed all Ph.D. requirements except the dissertation by the end of the semester or term following approval of the award. Dissertation supervisor must certify eligibility.

FINANCIAL DATA:
Amount of support per award: Up to $1,000.

APPLICATION INFO:
Digital submissions are required.
Deadline: December 31.

THE AMERICAN ASSOCIATION OF GEOGRAPHERS [1891]

1710 16th Street, N.W.
Washington, DC 20009
(202) 234-1450
Fax: (202) 234-2744
E-mail: grantsawards@aag.org
Web Site: www.aag.org

FOUNDED: 1904

NAME(S) OF PROGRAMS:
• **AAG Globe Book Award for Public Understanding of Geography**
• **AAG Meridian Book Award for the Outstanding Scholarly Work in Geography**

TYPE:
Awards/prizes. AAG Globe Book Award is awarded annually to a book that conveys most powerfully the nature and importance of geography to the nonacademic world.

AAG Meridian Book Award is awarded annually to a book that makes an unusually important contribution to advancing the science and art of geography.

PURPOSE:
To award outstanding geographic authors.

ELIGIBILITY:
Books must be written or co-authored by a geographer. Books published in the previous calendar year are eligible.

FINANCIAL DATA:
Amount of support per award: $1,000.

APPLICATION INFO:
Nomination statements (two-page maximum) should provide full contact information for the author(s) and the nominator(s), including e-mail addresses, and should document the ways the nominated work conveys the nature and importance of geography to the nonacademic world (Globe Book Award) or contributes to advancing the science and art of geography (Meridian Book Award). Nomination statements and four copies of each nominated book should be submitted.
Deadline: December 31.

ADDRESS INQUIRIES TO:
Attn: Globe Book Award or
Attn: Meridian Book Award
(See address and e-mail above.)

AMERICAN ASSOCIATION OF PETROLEUM GEOLOGISTS FOUNDATION [1892]

1444 South Boulder Avenue
Tulsa, OK 74119
(855) 302-2743
Fax: (918) 560-2642
E-mail: foundation@aapg.org
Web Site: foundation.aapg.org

FOUNDED: 1917

AREAS OF INTEREST:
The science of geology, especially as it relates to the search and development of hydrocarbons and economic sedimentary minerals and/or to environmental geology as it pertains to the petroleum industry.

NAME(S) OF PROGRAMS:
• **AAPG Foundation Grants-in-Aid**

TYPE:
Grants-in-aid; Research grants.

YEAR PROGRAM STARTED: 1956

PURPOSE:
To foster research in the geosciences by providing support to graduate students in the earth sciences whose research has application to the search for and development of petroleum and energy mineral resources, and to related environmental geology issues.

LEGAL BASIS:
Special-interest foundation.

ELIGIBILITY:
Graduate students in the geological sciences are eligible to apply. Factors weighed in selection of successful applicants include qualifications of the applicant as indicated by past performance, originality and imagination of the proposed project, support of the department in which the work is being done and perceived significance of the project to science and industry. The program focuses on support of qualified Master's candidates. Qualified doctoral candidates with expenses outside the usual scope of funding by other agencies are also encouraged to apply.

Grants are based on merit and, in part, on the financial needs of the applicant.

Applicants are eligible to receive awards twice as long as they remain qualified graduate students.

FINANCIAL DATA:
Grants are to be applied to selected expenses of graduate study such as a summer of field work, etc. Funds may not be used for tuition, room and board, capital expenses, to pay salaries or attend conferences.

Amount of support per award: Grants not to exceed $3,000.
Total amount of support: $299,000 for fiscal year 2019.

NO. MOST RECENT APPLICANTS: Over 350 for fiscal year 2019.

NO. AWARDS: 114 for fiscal year 2019.

APPLICATION INFO:
Applications, guidelines and restrictions can be found on the Foundation web site. Applications are submitted electronically and must include the following:
(1) applicant name and contact information;
(2) academic and employment history;
(3) a project summary;
(4) description of the research project (limited to 300 words);
(5) project budget and funding request;
(6) disclose if applicant has been a previous recipient of an AAPG Foundation grant;
(7) name and e-mail address for two separate references qualified to endorse the applicant and project and;
(8) official academic transcripts from the last two years (or equivalent).
Duration: One year.
Deadline: December 3.

PUBLICATIONS:
Explorer, magazine; annual report; application guidelines.

IRS I.D.: 73-1298684

EXECUTIVE DIRECTOR:
David Curtiss

ADDRESS INQUIRIES TO:
Grants-in-Aid Program Coordinator
E-mail: GIA@aapg.org
(See address above.)

*PLEASE NOTE:
This program is intended for support of individuals only in earth sciences related to the petroleum industry.

THE AMERICAN GEOSCIENCES INSTITUTE (AGI) [1893]

4220 King Street
Alexandria, VA 22302-1502
(703) 379-2480
Fax: (703) 379-7563
E-mail: wallacescholarship@agiweb.org
Web Site: www.americangeosciences.
org/workforce/harriet-evelyn-wallace-scholarship

FOUNDED: 1948

AREAS OF INTEREST:
Major study in the fields of geology, geophysics, geochemistry, hydrology, meteorology, physical oceanography, planetary geology and earth-science education.

NAME(S) OF PROGRAMS:
• **Harriet Evelyn Wallace Scholarship**

TYPE:
Scholarships. Open to all women pursuing a Master's or Doctorate degree in geosciences at an accredited institution of higher education in a recognized geoscience program.

YEAR PROGRAM STARTED: 2013

PURPOSE:
To increase the participation of female students in the geosciences by providing financial support.

LEGAL BASIS:
Nonprofit, tax-exempt scientific federation.

ELIGIBILITY:
The successful applicant will be a thesis-based, full-time student and must be a U.S. citizen or permanent resident. Applicants will be evaluated on their probability of successfully completing a geoscience graduate program and transitioning into the geoscience profession following graduation. The successful applicant will have an undergraduate grade point average of 3.25 or higher and a graduate grade point average of 3.0 or higher. In addition, all applicants must be active members of at least one of AGI's professional member societies.

GEOG. RESTRICTIONS: United States.

FINANCIAL DATA:
Amount of support per award: $5,000 per year.

CO-OP FUNDING PROGRAMS: Funding for the Wallace Scholarship is from a bequest by Harriet Evelyn Wallace, a founding member of the Geoscience Information Society of AGI.

NO. AWARDS: 2 per year.

APPLICATION INFO:
Applications may be submitted beginning October. Applicants must submit unofficial Graduate Record Examination scores, all postsecondary unofficial academic transcripts, unofficial graduate academic transcripts (if applicable), curriculum vitae or resume, and a 500-word abstract about their research interests. If the applicant is intending on pursuing graduate school, she will need to send proof of acceptance in the program before the award is funded.

Duration: Up to two years.

Deadline: January 4.

ADDRESS INQUIRIES TO:
Workforce Development, Education, Outreach and Scholarship Coordinator
The American Geosciences Institute (AGI)
(See address above.)

AMERICAN METEOROLOGICAL SOCIETY

45 Beacon Street
Boston, MA 02108-3693
(617) 227-2426 ext. 3907
Fax: (617) 742-8718
E-mail: dfernandez@ametsoc.org
Web Site: www.ametsoc.org

TYPE:
Fellowships; Scholarships. AMS Freshman Undergraduate Scholarship Program awards funding to high school seniors entering their freshman year of undergraduate study in the fall.

AMS Graduate Fellowship in the History of Science is awarded to a student wishing to complete a dissertation on the history of the atmospheric and related oceanic or hydrologic sciences.

AMS Graduate Fellowships are designed to attract students entering their first year of graduate study in the fall who wish to pursue advanced degrees in the atmospheric and related oceanic and hydrologic sciences.

AMS Minority Scholarship awards funding to high school minority students entering freshman year of undergraduate study in the fall who have been traditionally underrepresented in the sciences, especially Hispanic, Native American and Black/African American students.

AMS Senior Named Scholarships are directed to students entering their final year of undergraduate study in the fall.

The Father James B. Macelwane Annual Awards in Meteorology is intended to stimulate interest in meteorology among college students through the submission of original student papers concerned with some phase of the atmospheric sciences. The student must be enrolled as an undergraduate at the time the paper was written.

See entry 2407 for full listing.

THE GEOLOGICAL SOCIETY OF AMERICA, INC.   [1894]

3300 Penrose Place
Boulder, CO 80301-9140
(303) 357-1025
(888) 443-4472
Fax: (303) 357-1070
E-mail: researchgrants@geosociety.org
Web Site: www.geosociety.org

FOUNDED: 1888

AREAS OF INTEREST:
Geoscience.

NAME(S) OF PROGRAMS:
• GSA Research Grants

TYPE:
Grants-in-aid; Project/program grants; Research grants. Grants for projects contributing to the science of geology.

YEAR PROGRAM STARTED: 1933

PURPOSE:
To provide partial support of Master's and doctoral thesis research in earth science for graduate students.

LEGAL BASIS:
Private membership association.

ELIGIBILITY:
Qualified investigators with appropriate interests are eligible to apply. Graduate students apply for support of Master's or doctoral thesis work. The GSA strongly encourages women, minorities and persons with disabilities to participate in this grants program.

Applicants must be members of GSA.

GEOG. RESTRICTIONS: North and Central America.

FINANCIAL DATA:
Funds are intended as an aid to the research project and not to sustain entire research costs.
Amount of support per award: Generally $500 to $2,500.

NO. MOST RECENT APPLICANTS: 750.

NO. AWARDS: 395.

APPLICATION INFO:
Official application materials are available online.
Duration: One year.
Deadline: Applications must be submitted electronically by February 1 for consideration at the spring review meeting.

PUBLICATIONS:
Annual report; application guidelines.

OFFICERS:
Vicki McConnell, Executive Director

ADDRESS INQUIRIES TO:
Program Manager, Research Grants
(See address above.)

INTERNATIONAL WOMEN'S FISHING ASSOCIATION SCHOLARSHIP TRUST   [1895]

P.O. Box 460387
Fort Lauderdale, FL 33346-0387
E-mail: scholarshiptrust@iwfa.org
Web Site: www.iwfa.org/scholarship

FOUNDED: 1965

AREAS OF INTEREST:
Marine science.

NAME(S) OF PROGRAMS:
• IWFA Scholarship Trust

TYPE:
Scholarships. For postgraduate educational expense including tuition, supplies and books.

YEAR PROGRAM STARTED: 1965

PURPOSE:
To aid needy students who are seeking postgraduate degrees in marine science.

LEGAL BASIS:
501(c)(3) nonprofit organization.

ELIGIBILITY:
Applicant must be a graduate student in marine science. Student must be matriculated at a school in the U.S.

FINANCIAL DATA:
Amount of support per award: Up to $2,000.
Total amount of support: $36,000 for the year 2017.

NO. AWARDS: 23.

APPLICATION INFO:
Application must be entered electronically.
Duration: One year.
Deadline: March 1.

ADDRESS INQUIRIES TO:
Chairman, IWFA Scholarship Trust
(See address above.)

*SPECIAL STIPULATIONS:
For graduate students in the Marine Science field only.

LUNAR AND PLANETARY INSTITUTE

3600 Bay Area Boulevard
Houston, TX 77058
(281) 486-2159
Fax: (281) 486-2127
E-mail: internprogram@lpi.usra.edu
Web Site: www.lpi.usra.edu

TYPE:
Conferences/seminars; Internships; Scholarships; Travel grants.

See entry 1868 for full listing.

THE MINERALOGICAL SOCIETY OF AMERICA   [1896]

3635 Concorde Parkway, Suite 500
Chantilly, VA 20151-1110
(703) 652-9950
Fax: (703) 652-9951
E-mail: jaspeer@minsocam.org
abenbow@minsocam.org
Web Site: www.minsocam.org

FOUNDED: 1919

AREAS OF INTEREST:
Crystallography, mineralogy and petrology.

NAME(S) OF PROGRAMS:
- **Research Grant in Crystallography, Mineral Physics or Chemistry and Mineralogy**
- **Student Research Grant in Mineralogy and Petrology**

TYPE:
Research grants. Grants supported through endowment funds.

YEAR PROGRAM STARTED: 1973

PURPOSE:
To encourage research in mineralogy, crystallography, geochemistry, and petrology.

LEGAL BASIS:
501(c)(3) organization and Virginia corporation.

ELIGIBILITY:
Crystallography grant is open to students, as well as beginners, faculty and young researchers. The mineralogy/petrology grant is limited to students.

FINANCIAL DATA:
The grant is for research-related expenses only. Travel to meetings, conferences, short courses, nonresearch field trips, tuition, nonresearch living (room and board) expenses, etc., are not suitable uses of the money. Neither should the money be used for salary or wages for the researcher.
Amount of support per award: $5,000.
Total amount of support: $15,000.

NO. MOST RECENT APPLICANTS: 50 to 60 annually.

NO. AWARDS: 3.

APPLICATION INFO:
Proposal submissions are to be made online.
Duration: One year.
Deadline: March 1.

PUBLICATIONS:
American Mineralogist; Reviews in Mineralogy and Geochemistry; Elements.

IRS I.D.: 52-6044250

ADDRESS INQUIRIES TO:
Dr. J. Alex Speer, Executive Director
(See address above.)

NATIONAL ASSOCIATION OF GEOSCIENCE TEACHERS [1897]
c/o Science Education Resource Center
200 Division Street, Suite 210
Northfield, MN 55057
(507) 222-5634
(507) 222-7096
Fax: (507) 222-5175
E-mail: nagtservice@nagt.org
acollette@carleton.edu
Web Site: www.nagt.org

FOUNDED: 1938

AREAS OF INTEREST:
Earth sciences.

NAME(S) OF PROGRAMS:
- **Scholarships for Field Study**
- **Dottie Stout Professional Development Grants**

TYPE:
Development grants; Scholarships.
Scholarships for Field Study: Cash award to undergraduate students to facilitate their study of field geoscience.

Dottie Stout Professional Development Grants will be awarded in support of the following activities:
(1) participation in earth science classes or workshops;
(2) attendance at professional scientific or science education meetings;
(3) participation in earth science field trips and;
(4) purchase of earth science materials for classroom use.

YEAR PROGRAM STARTED: 1970

PURPOSE:
To further geological education at the undergraduate level.

LEGAL BASIS:
Tax-exempt corporation.

ELIGIBILITY:
Scholarships for Field Study: Applicants must be full-time students with a geology major. The chief criterion for selection is advanced students with distinguished academic records within the major.

Dottie Stout Professional Development Grants: Community college faculty and K-12th grade teachers who teach one or more earth science courses and community college students actively pursuing a career in the earth sciences are encouraged to apply for these awards.

FINANCIAL DATA:
Amount of support per award: Scholarships for Field Study: $750; Dottie Stout Professional Development Grants: $750 each to a community college faculty member, a community college student and a K-12th grade educator.
Total amount of support: Varies.

NO. MOST RECENT APPLICANTS: Scholarships for Field Study: 80; Dottie Stout Professional Development Grants: 10.

NO. AWARDS: Scholarships for Field Study: 18; Dottie Stout Professional Development Grants: 3.

APPLICATION INFO:
Application information is available at the web site.
Deadline: Scholarships for Field Study: February 14; Dottie Stout Professional Development Grants: April 15.

PUBLICATIONS:
Journal of Geoscience Education; In The Trenches, magazine.

IRS I.D.: 74-6068050

OFFICERS:
David McConnell, President

NATIONAL CENTER FOR ATMOSPHERIC RESEARCH
1850 Table Mesa Drive
Boulder, CO 80305
(303) 497-1607
Fax: (303) 497-1646
E-mail: sbriggs@ucar.edu
Web Site: www.asp.ucar.edu

TYPE:
Fellowships. The fellowships cover a year's appointment, with a likely extension to two years, at NCAR to take advantage of its educational programs and/or research facilities in the broad field of atmospheric sciences.

See entry 1661 for full listing.

NATIONAL GEOGRAPHIC SOCIETY [1898]
Committee for Research and Exploration
1145 17th Street, N.W.
Washington, DC 20036
(202) 857-7000
E-mail: grantsinfo@ngs.org
cre@ngs.org
Web Site: www.nationalgeographic.org/grants

FOUNDED: 1888

AREAS OF INTEREST:
Conservation, education, research, storytelling and technology.

NAME(S) OF PROGRAMS:
- **National Geographic Society Committee for Research and Exploration**

TYPE:
Grants-in-aid; Research grants; Seed money grants. Grants-in-aid for basic research in the sciences pertinent to geography (including, but not limited to, projects in geography). Support may also be provided for projects in these fields that depend on exploration. The Society is currently emphasizing multidisciplinary projects that address environmental issues.

YEAR PROGRAM STARTED: 1890

PURPOSE:
To further understanding of our planet and empower the global community to generate solutions for a healthier and more sustainable future.

LEGAL BASIS:
Nonprofit.

ELIGIBILITY:
Applicants are expected to have advanced degrees (Ph.D. or equivalent) and be associated with an educational organization or institution. Independent researchers or those pursuing a Ph.D.-level degree may apply, but competition is keen and awards to non-Ph.D. applicants are rare. As a general rule, all applicants are expected to have published a minimum of three articles in peer-reviewed scientific journals. Individuals between the ages of 18 and 25 are invited to apply to the Young Explorers Program. These applicants are not expected to have advanced degrees but should have a record of prior experience as it pertains to their proposed project. Citizens of any country are eligible.

Grants normally are made only for field research. Laboratory work is supported only to the extent that it may be a necessary follow-up to Society-funded field research.

Grants are awarded on the basis of the project's scientific merit. All proposed projects must have both a geographical dimension and relevance to other scientific fields and be of broad scientific interest. The Committee pays special attention to the significance of the research proposal in terms of its relationship to major scientific questions or problems. The Committee's priorities favor research that relates to environmental concerns and has relevance to global geographic issues.

FINANCIAL DATA:
Society funds may be used for transportation, supplies, and daily subsistence. Capital equipment (generally defined as any item costing more than U.S. $500) must be

individually justified. Laboratory expenses are acceptable, provided the laboratory work is a logical extension of the field research.

Amount of support per award: Early Career Grants: $5,000 to $10,000; Exploration Grants: $10,000 to $30,000.

Total amount of support: $12,000,000 budgeted for research program annually.

Matching fund requirements: National Geographic Society funds are intended to function as complementary support. The committee strongly encourages applicants to seek additional, concurrent funding from other agencies.

NO. MOST RECENT APPLICANTS: 7,000.

NO. AWARDS: Approximately 600 per year.

APPLICATION INFO:
Project leader must submit a proposal using the online application in the Grants Portal. All application material must be in English.

To prepare the proposal, applicant will need:
(1) a primary project focus;
(2) curriculum vitae or resume, in English;
(3) a budget and;
(4) a list of the name, e-mail address, project role, affiliate organization, highest degree earned, and country of primary residence for all members of the project team. If applicant plans to work outside their home country, at least one local collaborator on the project team must be included. Early Career Grant applicants need to include the name and contact information of one advisor, mentor or supervisor.

Early Career Grant applicants must also submit a two-minute video that will be used to help evaluate the proposal. Applicant may speak in their primary language, but if that is not English, then it must include English subtitles or an English video transcript.

Duration: One year.

Deadline: At least six months in advance of anticipated project start date. Board meets quarterly in January, April, July and October.

PUBLICATIONS:
Program description; National Geographic Index 1888-1988.

*PLEASE NOTE:
Applicants are encouraged to confirm program online for recent changes.

NATIONAL OCEANIC AND ATMOSPHERIC ADMINISTRATION [1899]

1315 East West Highway, 12th Floor
Silver Spring, MD 20910-5603
(301) 734-1206
Fax: (301) 713-0517
E-mail: cpograms@noaa.gov
diane.brown@noaa.gov
Web Site: www.cpo.noaa.gov

FOUNDED: 1966

AREAS OF INTEREST:
Climate and atmospheric research.

NAME(S) OF PROGRAMS:
• **Climate Program**

TYPE:
Challenge/matching grants;
Conferences/seminars; Formula grants. Grant activities are organized within four programs:
(1) Climate Observation Division designs, deploys, and maintains an integrated global in situ network of oceanic and atmospheric

observing instruments to produce continuous records and analyses of a range of ocean and atmosphere parameters. Climate Observation coordinates observing efforts across NOAA, collaborates with federal agencies, and has strong international partnerships.
(2) Earth System Science (ESS) Program aims to provide process-level understanding of the climate system through observation, modeling, research analysis and field studies to support the development of improved climate models and predictions in support of NOAA's mission. ESS-sponsored research is carried out at NOAA and other federal laboratories, NOAA Cooperative Institutes, and academic institutions and is coordinated with major national and international scientific bodies including the World Climate Research Programme, the International Geosphere-Biosphere Programme, and the U.S. Global Change Research Program.
(3) Modeling, Analysis, Predictions, and Projections (MAPP) Program aims to enhance the Nation's capability to predict variability and changes in Earth's climate system. The MAPP Program focuses on the coupling, integration, and application of Earth system models and analyses across NOAA, among partner agencies, and with the external research community. The MAPP Program includes targeted infrastructure support, competitive grants programs, and mechanisms to support transferring research findings into NOAA's operations.
(4) Climate and Societal Interactions (CSI) Program provides leadership and support for research, assessments and climate services development activities designed to bring sound, interdisciplinary science to bear on climate-sensitive resource management and adaptation challenges in key sectors and regions.

PURPOSE:
To develop the knowledge required to establish a predictive capability for short- and long-term climate fluctuations and trends.

LEGAL BASIS:
Government agency.

ELIGIBILITY:
Applicants may be institutions of higher education, other nonprofits, commercial organizations, international organizations, state, local and Indian tribal governments. Federal agencies or institutions are ineligible.

FINANCIAL DATA:
Grants may be used for research and development, advisory services and operational systems as they relate to specific programs.

Amount of support per award: $50,000 to $300,000.

Total amount of support: Approximately $11,250,000 for the year 2019.

NO. AWARDS: Approximately 90 new awards for the year 2019.

APPLICATION INFO:
Applications are to be submitted through grants.gov.

Duration: One to three years.

Deadline: Varies.

ADDRESS INQUIRIES TO:
Diane Brown
Grants Administration Team Leader
Climate Program Office
(See address above.)

NATIONAL OCEANIC AND ATMOSPHERIC ADMINISTRATION [1900]

National Marine Fisheries Service
263 13th Avenue South
St. Petersburg, FL 33701
(727) 824-5324
Fax: (727) 824-5364
E-mail: dax.ruiz@noaa.gov
kelly.donnelly@noaa.gov
Web Site: www.fisheries.noaa.gov/funding-opportunities

AREAS OF INTEREST:
Southeast region.

NAME(S) OF PROGRAMS:
• **Bluefin Tuna Research Program Grants**
• **Cooperative Research Program Grants**
• **Marine Fisheries Initiative Grants**

TYPE:
Development grants; Research grants.

YEAR PROGRAM STARTED: 2003

PURPOSE:
To support research and development.

ELIGIBILITY:
Bluefin Tuna Research Program Grants are available to institutions of higher education, nonprofits, commercial organizations, individuals, and state, local, and Indian tribal governments. Federal agencies or institutions are not eligible.

Cooperative Research Program Grants: Applicants who are not commercial or recreational fishermen must have commercial or recreational fishermen participating in their project. There must be a written agreement with a fisherman describing the involvement in the project activity. Eligible applicants include institutions of higher education, other nonprofits, commercial organizations, state, local and Indian tribal governments and individuals. Federal agencies or institutions are not eligible.

Marine Fisheries Initiative Grants are available to institutions of higher education, other nonprofits, commercial organizations, state, local and Indian tribal governments. Federal agencies or institutions are not eligible.

Foreign governments, organizations under the jurisdiction of foreign governments, and international organizations are excluded for purposes of these solicitations since the objective of these programs is to optimize research and development benefits from U.S. marine fishery resources.

FINANCIAL DATA:
Amount of support per award: Bluefin Tuna: $25,000 to $600,000; CRP: $25,000 to $250,000; MARFIN: Up to $525,000.

Total amount of support: Bluefin Tuna: Approximately $600,000; CRP: Approximately $1,500,000 for the year 2020.

Matching fund requirements: Cost sharing is not required.

NO. MOST RECENT APPLICANTS: Bluefin Tuna: 7; CRP: 30, MARFIN: 30.

NO. AWARDS: Bluefin Tuna: 5; CRP: Approximately 8; MARFIN: 5.

APPLICATION INFO:
Applications are available on grants.gov. New applicants should contact the National Marine Fisheries Service Office.

Duration: Bluefin Tuna Research Program Grants and Cooperative Research Program Grants: One year; Marine Fisheries Initiative Grants: One to three years.

Deadline: Announced in NOAA solicitation and grant opportunities index.

PUBLICATIONS:
Annual report.

ADDRESS INQUIRIES TO:
Cooperative Research Program Grants:
Dax Ruiz, Federal Grants Program Officer

Marine Fisheries Initiative Grants:
Kelly Donnelly
Federal Grants Program Manager
(See address above.)

NATIONAL OCEANIC AND ATMOSPHERIC ADMINISTRATION [1901]

Ocean Exploration and Research Program
SSMC3, R/OER, Room 10210
1315 East-West Highway
Silver Spring, MD 20910
(301) 734-1014
(301) 734-1017
Fax: (301) 713-1967
E-mail: frank.cantelas@noaa.gov
oceanexplorer@noaa.gov
Web Site: oceanexplorer.noaa.gov

AREAS OF INTEREST:
Marine research.

NAME(S) OF PROGRAMS:
- **Ocean Exploration and Research Program**

TYPE:
Project/program grants; Research grants.

ELIGIBILITY:
Eligible applicants are U.S. institutions of higher education, not-for-profit institutions, and federal, state, and local governments. Federal agencies may not charge salary or overhead.

GEOG. RESTRICTIONS: United States.

FINANCIAL DATA:
Amount of support per award: $10,000 to $750,000 projected for fiscal year 2020.

Total amount of support: Approximately $3,000,000 projected for fiscal year 2020.

NO. AWARDS: Approximately 10 for the year 2020.

APPLICATION INFO:
Each National Undersea Research Center has its own proposal forms and guidelines. Specific locations and instructions are available online.

Duration: Up to two years.

Deadline: Varies by Center.

ADDRESS INQUIRIES TO:
Frank Cantelas, Deputy Director
(See address above.)

NATIONAL SCIENCE FOUNDATION [1902]

Division of Earth Sciences
2415 Eisenhower Avenue
Alexandria, VA 22314
(703) 292-8550
Fax: (703) 292-9025
Web Site: www.nsf.gov

FOUNDED: 1950

AREAS OF INTEREST:
Earth sciences.

TYPE:
Research grants. The Division of Earth Sciences supports proposals for research geared toward improving the understanding of the structure, composition, and evolution of the Earth and the processes that govern the formation and behavior of the Earth's materials.

YEAR PROGRAM STARTED: 1950

PURPOSE:
To create a better understanding of the Earth's changing environments and the natural distribution of its mineral, water and energy resources; to provide methods for predicting and mitigating the effects of geologic hazards such as earthquakes, volcanic eruptions, floods and landslides.

LEGAL BASIS:
Federal agency.

ELIGIBILITY:
Scientists and engineers, especially college and university faculty members, are eligible to apply.

GEOG. RESTRICTIONS: United States and its territories.

FINANCIAL DATA:
Amount of support per award: Varies.

Total amount of support: Varies.

NO. MOST RECENT APPLICANTS: 1,600.

NO. AWARDS: 500.

APPLICATION INFO:
Application information is available on the web site.

Duration: One to five years.

PUBLICATIONS:
Grant proposal guide (NSF 04-23).

NATIONAL SCIENCE FOUNDATION [1903]

Division of Ocean Sciences
2415 Eisenhower Avenue
Alexandria, VA 22314
(703) 292-8580
Fax: (703) 292-9449
E-mail: tquinn@nsf.gov
Web Site: www.nsf.gov

FOUNDED: 1950

AREAS OF INTEREST:
Biological, chemical and physical processes in the ocean.

NAME(S) OF PROGRAMS:
- **Ocean Section**

TYPE:
Research grants. Support for fundamental research in marine science, including physical oceanography and limnology, chemical oceanography, biological oceanography and marine geology, geophysics and ocean technology, with the objective of increasing knowledge and enhancing our understanding of the marine environment.

Most of the research supported is basic in character, although some applied research is also supported. This program also supports research workshops, symposia and conferences and purchases of scientific equipment related to projects supported.

YEAR PROGRAM STARTED: 1980

PURPOSE:
To improve understanding of the nature of the ocean and its influence on human activities and of human impacts on the marine environment.

LEGAL BASIS:
Government agency.

ELIGIBILITY:
Program is primarily for support of scientists in basic research in ocean sciences and instrumentation and the facilities to support it.

FINANCIAL DATA:
Amount of support per award: Varies.

Total amount of support: Varies.

APPLICATION INFO:
Application information is available at the web site.

Duration: Varies.

Deadline: Proposals may be submitted at any time. Approximately six months are required for review and processing. Target dates are February 15 and August 15.

STAFF:
Terrence M. Quinn, Division Director
Michael Sieracki, Program Director, Biological and Physical Oceanography

ADDRESS INQUIRIES TO:
Division of Ocean Sciences
(See address above.)

NATIONAL SOCIETY OF PROFESSIONAL SURVEYORS (NSPS)

5119 Pegasus Court
Suite Q
Frederick, MD 21704
(240) 439-4615 ext. 105
Fax: (240) 439-4952
E-mail: trisha.milburn@nsps.us.com
Web Site: www.nsps.us.com

TYPE:
Scholarships. Berntsen International Scholarship in Surveying: Annual scholarship award for undergraduate study in four-year degree programs in surveying or in closely related degree programs such as geomatics or surveying engineering.

Berntsen International Scholarship in Surveying Technology: For students enrolled in two-year degree programs in surveying technology. Scholarship awarded in even years only.

See entry 2441 for full listing.

NATIONAL SOCIETY OF PROFESSIONAL SURVEYORS (NSPS)

5119 Pegasus Court
Suite Q
Frederick, MD 21704
(240) 439-4615 ext. 105
Fax: (240) 439-4952
E-mail: trisha.milburn@nsps.us.com
Web Site: www.nsps.us.com

TYPE:
Scholarships. For students enrolled in four-year degree programs in surveying or in closely related degree programs such as geomatics or surveying engineering.

See entry 2439 for full listing.

NATIONAL SOCIETY OF PROFESSIONAL SURVEYORS (NSPS)

5119 Pegasus Court
Suite Q
Frederick, MD 21704
(240) 439-4615 ext. 105
Fax: (240) 439-4952
E-mail: trisha.milburn@nsps.us.com
Web Site: www.nsps.us.com

TYPE:
Scholarships.

See entry 2440 for full listing.

NATIONAL SOCIETY OF PROFESSIONAL SURVEYORS (NSPS) AMERICAN ASSOCIATION FOR GEODETIC SURVEYING (AAGS)

5119 Pegasus Court
Suite Q
Frederick, MD 21704
(240) 439-4615 ext. 105
Fax: (240) 439-4952
E-mail: trisha.milburn@nsps.us.com
Web Site: www.aagsmo.org
www.nsps.us.com

TYPE:
Fellowships. Annual fellowship award to support graduate study in a program with a significant focus on geodetic surveying or geodesy at a school of the recipient's choice.

See entry 2442 for full listing.

NATIONAL SOCIETY OF PROFESSIONAL SURVEYORS (NSPS) AMERICAN ASSOCIATION FOR GEODETIC SURVEYING (AAGS)

5119 Pegasus Court
Suite Q
Frederick, MD 21704
(240) 439-4615 ext. 105
Fax: (240) 439-4952
E-mail: trisha.milburn@nsps.us.com
Web Site: www.aagsmo.org
www.nsps.us.com

TYPE:
Scholarships. The award is intended for students enrolled in four-year degree programs in surveying or in closely related degree programs.

See entry 2443 for full listing.

V. KANN RASMUSSEN FOUNDATION   [1904]

475 Riverside Drive, Suite 900
New York, NY 10115
(212) 812-4271
Web Site: www.vkrf.org

FOUNDED: 1991

AREAS OF INTEREST:
Climate change and unsustainable consumption.

TYPE:
Project/program grants.

PURPOSE:
To support the transition to a more environmentally resilient, stable and sustainable planet.

LEGAL BASIS:
Private foundation.

ELIGIBILITY:
Eligible organizations must be IRS 501(c)(3) tax-exempt. Only projects that are global in scope will be considered.

GEOG. RESTRICTIONS: United States.

FINANCIAL DATA:
Amount of support per award: Varies.

APPLICATION INFO:
Application procedures can be found on the Foundation web site.
Duration: One to two years.
Deadline: Varies.

IRS I.D.: 22-3101266

STAFF:
Irene Krarup, Executive Director and Head of Programs

ADDRESS INQUIRIES TO:
Irene Krarup, Executive Director and Head of Programs
(See address above.)

THE PERCY SLADEN MEMORIAL FUND

c/o The Linnean Society of London
Burlington House, Piccadilly
London W1J 0BF England
(44) 020 7434 4479
Fax: (44) 020 7287 9364
E-mail: info@linnean.org
gina@linnean.org
Web Site: www.linnean.org

TYPE:
Awards/prizes; Project/program grants; Research grants; Travel grants. Field work grants in life and earth sciences (excludes any projects which are part of further education, e.g., a Doctorate or a Master's course).

See entry 1927 for full listing.

SOCIETY OF EXPLORATION GEOPHYSICISTS   [1905]

8801 South Yale Avenue
Suite 500
Tulsa, OK 74137
(918) 497-4630
Fax: (918) 497-5560
E-mail: scholarships@seg.org
Web Site: www.seg.org/foundation
www.seg.org/scholarships

FOUNDED: 1956

AREAS OF INTEREST:
Applied geophysics.

NAME(S) OF PROGRAMS:
● SEG Scholarship Program

TYPE:
Scholarships. Undergraduate and graduate scholarships for the study of geophysics.

YEAR PROGRAM STARTED: 1956

PURPOSE:
To assist young people in pursuing careers in the field of applied geophysics.

LEGAL BASIS:
Nonprofit society.

ELIGIBILITY:
Applicant must intend to pursue a college course directed toward a career in applied geophysics and must have an interest in and

aptitude for physics, mathematics, and geology. Applicant must be:
(1) a high school student with above-average grades planning to enter college the next fall term;
(2) an undergraduate college student whose grades are above average or;
(3) a graduate college student whose studies are directed toward a career in applied geophysics in operations, teaching or research.

FINANCIAL DATA:
Amount of support per award: $500 to $10,000 per academic year, averaging $3,500 per academic year.
Total amount of support: $578,000 for the academic year 2019.

NO. MOST RECENT APPLICANTS: 428.

NO. AWARDS: 140 for the academic year 2019.

APPLICATION INFO:
Application must be submitted electronically. Transcripts and letters of recommendation may be submitted online or sent via regular mail. Results of aptitude tests are not required but should be included if taken.
Duration: One year. Renewable at the discretion of the SEG Scholarship Committee, subject to student's maintenance of satisfactory grades, funds available and continued study leading to a career in geophysics.
Deadline: March 1.

ADDRESS INQUIRIES TO:
Scholarship Administrator
(See address above.)

*SPECIAL STIPULATIONS:
Certain scholarships carry additional qualifications specified by the scholarships' donors.

THE UNIVERSITY OF CALGARY   [1906]

Faculty of Graduate Studies
Earth Sciences Building, Room 1010
2500 University Drive, N.W.
Calgary AB T2N 1N4 Canada
(403) 220-4938
Fax: (403) 289-7635
E-mail: gsaward@ucalgary.ca
Web Site: grad.ucalgary.ca/awards

NAME(S) OF PROGRAMS:
● Harry and Laura Jacques Graduate Scholarship

TYPE:
Scholarships.

ELIGIBILITY:
Open to students registered full-time in a thesis-based graduate program at the University of Calgary.

FINANCIAL DATA:
Amount of support per award: $5,200.
Total amount of support: $5,200.

NO. AWARDS: 1.

APPLICATION INFO:
Students should consult the Graduate Award Competition Guidelines and Application available at the web site.
Duration: One year.
Deadline: February 1 to the candidate's graduate program office, unless the program has an earlier deadline.

ADDRESS INQUIRIES TO:
Graduate Scholarship Office
(See address above.)

Mathematics

THE ACTUARIAL FOUNDATION [1907]

475 North Martingale Road
Suite 600
Schaumburg, IL 60173-2226
(847) 706-3535
E-mail: Scholarships@ActFnd.org
Web Site: www.actuarialfoundation.org

FOUNDED: 1994

AREAS OF INTEREST:
Actuarial science, a branch of mathematics based on calculus, probability and statistics, as well as business economics.

NAME(S) OF PROGRAMS:
• **Actuarial Diversity Scholarship**

TYPE:
Scholarships. This scholarship promotes diversity in the profession through an annual scholarship program for Black/African American, Hispanic, Native North American and Pacific Islander students. The scholarship award recognizes and encourages academic achievements by awarding scholarships to full-time undergraduate students pursuing a degree that may lead to a career in the actuarial profession.

YEAR PROGRAM STARTED: 2009

PURPOSE:
To promote diversity in the actuarial profession.

LEGAL BASIS:
Private- and corporate-funded.

ELIGIBILITY:
Each applicant must fulfill all of the following requirements:
(1) must have at least one birth parent who is a member of one of the following minority groups: Black/African American, Hispanic, Native North American, or Pacific Islander;
(2) enrolled as a full-time undergraduate student at a U.S.-accredited educational institution during the application academic year;
(3) minimum grade point average of 3.0 (on a 4.0 scale), emphasis on math or actuarial courses;
(4) entering college freshmen must have a minimum ACT math score of 28 or SAT math score of 620 and;
(5) intent on pursuing a career in the actuarial profession.

GEOG. RESTRICTIONS: United States.

FINANCIAL DATA:
Amount of support per award: $1,000 to $4,000.
Total amount of support: Approximately $186,000 for the year 2019.

NO. AWARDS: 77 for the year 2019.

APPLICATION INFO:
Applications are posted in early November. Application and guidelines are available online.
Duration: One academic year. Renewable based on academic performance.
Deadline: March 15.

IRS I.D.: 36-2136422

ADDRESS INQUIRIES TO:
Scholarship Coordinator
(See address above.)

*PLEASE NOTE:
Applicants must intend to pursue a career in the actuarial profession.

THE ACTUARIAL FOUNDATION [1908]

475 North Martingale Road
Suite 600
Schaumburg, IL 60173-2226
(847) 706-3535
E-mail: Scholarships@ActFnd.org
Web Site: www.actuarialfoundation.org

FOUNDED: 1994

AREAS OF INTEREST:
Actuarial science.

NAME(S) OF PROGRAMS:
• **Actuary of Tomorrow - Stuart A. Robertson Memorial Scholarship**

TYPE:
Scholarships.

YEAR PROGRAM STARTED: 2006

PURPOSE:
To recognize and encourage the academic achievements of undergraduate students pursuing a career in actuarial science.

ELIGIBILITY:
Applicant must:
(1) be a full-time undergraduate student entering as a sophomore, junior or senior in the fall term;
(2) have a minimum cumulative grade point average of 3.0 (on a 4.0 scale) and;
(3) have successfully completed two actuarial exams.

GEOG. RESTRICTIONS: United States.

FINANCIAL DATA:
Amount of support per award: Up to $9,000.

NO. AWARDS: 3 for the year 2019.

APPLICATION INFO:
Application is available online. Applicant should:
(1) attach a current unofficial copy of transcripts from attending college/university;
(2) provide a letter of recommendation supporting academic achievement, leadership and communication skills from professor or advisor;
(3) provide a letter of recommendation from an employer or previous employer and;
(4) submit a personal essay of approximately 500 words, focusing on why you want to be an actuary.
Deadline: June 1. Notification by e-mail after August 1.

ADDRESS INQUIRIES TO:
Scholarship Coordinator
(See address and e-mail above.)

*SPECIAL STIPULATIONS:
Scholarships are awarded directly to the college/university of choice in the recipients' name.

THE ACTUARIAL FOUNDATION [1909]

475 North Martingale Road
Suite 600
Schaumburg, IL 60173-2226
(847) 706-3535
E-mail: Scholarships@ActFnd.org
Web Site: www.actuarialfoundation.org

FOUNDED: 1994

AREAS OF INTEREST:
Actuarial science, mathematics and statistics.

NAME(S) OF PROGRAMS:
• **Curtis E. Huntington Memorial Scholarship**

TYPE:
Scholarships. Originally named the John Culver Wooddy Scholarship, the Curtis E. Huntington Memorial Scholarship is awarded annually to undergraduate seniors enrolled as full-time students at an accredited U.S. educational institution.

YEAR PROGRAM STARTED: 2014

PURPOSE:
To recognize the remarkably positive impact Curtis E. Huntington had on the actuarial profession.

ELIGIBILITY:
Undergraduate seniors who are enrolled as full-time students at an accredited U.S. educational institution may apply. Student must have successfully completed at least one actuarial examination, have a minimum 3.0 grade point average on a 4.0 scale, and must be nominated by a professor at their school.

U.S. citizenship or permanent residency is required.

FINANCIAL DATA:
Amount of support per award: $2,000.
Total amount of support: $18,000 for the year 2019.

NO. AWARDS: 9 for the year 2019.

APPLICATION INFO:
Student must be nominated by a professor at their school.
Deadline: April 1.

ADDRESS INQUIRIES TO:
Scholarship Coordinator
(See address and e-mail above.)

AMERICAN MATHEMATICAL SOCIETY [1910]

201 Charles Street
Providence, RI 02904-2213
(800) 321-4267 ext. 4096
(401) 455-4096
Fax: (401) 455-4004
E-mail: prof-serv@ams.org
Web Site: www.ams.org

FOUNDED: 1888

AREAS OF INTEREST:
Research mathematics.

NAME(S) OF PROGRAMS:
• **American Mathematical Society Centennial Fellowship**

TYPE:
Fellowships. The AMS Centennial Research Fellowship Program makes awards annually to outstanding mathematicians to help further their careers in research.

YEAR PROGRAM STARTED: 1974

PURPOSE:
To help outstanding mathematicians further their careers in research.

LEGAL BASIS:
Nonprofit corporation.

ELIGIBILITY:
The primary selection criterion for the Centennial Fellowship is the excellence of the candidate's research. Preference will be given to candidates who have not had extensive fellowship support in the past. Recipients may not hold the Centennial

Fellowship concurrently with another research fellowship such as a Sloan Fellowship, NSF Postdoctoral Fellowship, or Career Award. Under normal circumstances, the fellowship cannot be deferred. A recipient of the fellowship shall have held his or her doctoral degree for at least three years and not more than 12 years at the inception of the award. Applications will be accepted from those currently holding a tenured, tenure-track, postdoctoral, or comparable (at the discretion of the selection committee) position at an institution in North America.

GEOG. RESTRICTIONS: North America.

FINANCIAL DATA:
Amount of support per award: $50,000 for the academic year 2021-22.

CO-OP FUNDING PROGRAMS: The Society has a matching program so that funds for at least one fellowship are guaranteed.

NO. AWARDS: Usually 1 per academic year.

APPLICATION INFO:
Applications should include a cogent plan indicating how the fellowship will be used. The plan should include travel to at least one other institution and should demonstrate that the fellowship will be used for more than reduction of teaching at the candidate's home institution. The selection committee will consider the plan in addition to the quality of the candidate's research, and will try to award the fellowship to those for whom the award would make a real difference in the development of their research careers. Work in all areas of mathematics, including interdisciplinary work, is eligible.

Application forms can be accessed at the web site.
Duration: One year. Nonrenewable.
Deadline: December 1. Announcement in February.

PUBLICATIONS:
Application guidelines.

STAFF:
Kim Kuda, Senior Program Coordinator

ADDRESS INQUIRIES TO:
See e-mail address above.

*SPECIAL STIPULATIONS:
Acceptance of the Fellowship cannot be postponed.

CONFERENCE BOARD OF THE MATHEMATICAL SCIENCES   [1911]
1600 Grand Avenue
St. Paul, MN 55105
(651) 696-6559
E-mail: bressoud@macalester.edu
Web Site: www.cbmsweb.org

FOUNDED: 1960

AREAS OF INTEREST:
Mathematical sciences.

NAME(S) OF PROGRAMS:
● **NSF-CBMS Regional Conferences in the Mathematical Sciences**

TYPE:
Conferences/seminars. Grants given by NSF for five-day conferences in the mathematical sciences.

YEAR PROGRAM STARTED: 1969

PURPOSE:
To stimulate interest and activity in mathematical sciences research.

LEGAL BASIS:
A nonprofit professional society.

ELIGIBILITY:
Proposals may only be submitted by the following:
(1) Two- and four-year institutions of higher education accredited in, and having a campus located in the U.S., acting on behalf of their faculty members and;
(2) Nonprofit, non-academic organizations, independent museums, observatories, research labs, professional societies and similar organizations in the U.S. associated with educational or research activities.

FINANCIAL DATA:
Grants may include travel and lodging costs, director's and secretary's salaries, announcement costs and other miscellaneous expenses.
Amount of support per award: $35,000 per conference.

NO. AWARDS: Up to 10.

APPLICATION INFO:
Proposals must be submitted electronically via Fastlane to the Division of Mathematical Sciences (DMS) at NSF.
Duration: Five days during the summer or during a recess in the academic year.
Deadline: Last Friday in April.
Announcement in October.

PUBLICATIONS:
Monographs of the conferences are available from the American Mathematical Society, the Society for Industrial and Applied Mathematics, the Institute of Mathematical Statistics and the American Statistical Association.

ADDRESS INQUIRIES TO:
Swatee Naik
Tel: (703) 292-4876
E-mail: snaik@nsf.gov

IBM THOMAS J. WATSON RESEARCH CENTER   [1912]
Department of Mathematical Sciences
1101 Kitchawan Road
Yorktown Heights, NY 10598
E-mail: gldpost2@us.ibm.com
Web Site: www.research.ibm.com/goldstine

AREAS OF INTEREST:
Research in pure and applied mathematics and in theoretical and exploratory computer science.

NAME(S) OF PROGRAMS:
● **IBM Herman Goldstine Memorial Postdoctoral Fellowship for Research in Mathematical and Computer Sciences**

TYPE:
Fellowships.

YEAR PROGRAM STARTED: 1972

PURPOSE:
To provide scientists of outstanding ability an opportunity to advance their scholarship as resident department members at the IBM Thomas J. Watson Research Center.

ELIGIBILITY:
Applicant must have a Ph.D. in science, engineering or mathematics received within the last five years, or must expect to receive one before the fellowship commences in the second half of the year (usually in September).

FINANCIAL DATA:
Allowance provided for moving expenses.

Amount of support per award:
Approximately $130,000 to $150,000 per year, depending on the length of experience.

NO. AWARDS: Up to 2 per year.

APPLICATION INFO:
Applicants are required to complete an online form and provide their full curriculum vitae, Ph.D. dissertation abstract, a two- to three-page research statement describing current research and the research they plan to pursue if offered the fellowship, and three or more letters of recommendation, including one from their thesis advisor.
Duration: One year. Renewable for a second year if of mutual interest.
Deadline: Applications accepted November to January (exact dates vary).

ADDRESS INQUIRIES TO:
See e-mail address above.

MICRON TECHNOLOGY FOUNDATION, INC.   [1913]
P.O. Box 6
Boise, ID 83707-0006
(208) 363-3675
Fax: (208) 368-4435
E-mail: mtf@micron.com
Web Site: www.micron.com/foundation

FOUNDED: 1999

AREAS OF INTEREST:
Education with an emphasis on STEM (science, technology, engineering and mathematics).

TYPE:
Matching gifts; Professorships; Project/program grants; Research grants.

YEAR PROGRAM STARTED: 2000

PURPOSE:
To advance education and local communities; to partner with educators to spark a passion in youth for science, technology, engineering and mathematics; to engineer the future for students; to enrich the communities through strategic giving where team members live, work and volunteer.

LEGAL BASIS:
Private corporate foundation.

ELIGIBILITY:
Micron will consider projects or programs which:
(1) address an educational need, especially those which advance math and science;
(2) impact basic human needs for a large number of people;
(3) have long-term benefits and;
(4) are in a geographic area where Micron has operations.

Micron generally does not address individual sponsorships or donations, requests for assistance with travel or lodging expenses, religious organizations requesting funds for purposes other than nondenominational education or organizations located in areas where Micron has no operations.

GEOG. RESTRICTIONS: Boise, Idaho and Manassas, Virginia.

FINANCIAL DATA:
Amount of support per award: Varies.
Total amount of support: Varies.

Matching fund requirements: Micron may match employee donations at a 1:1 ratio, K-12 and higher education organizations up to $2,000 per employee per calendar year to qualified educational institutions.

NO. AWARDS: Varies.

REPRESENTATIVE AWARDS:
Boise State University; Leadership Prince William; Rochester Institute of Technology; Stanford University.

APPLICATION INFO:
Paper applications are no longer accepted. Applicants for K-12 grants and nonprofit community grants must apply online on the web site.

Higher education grants by invitation only.
Duration: Varies.

IRS I.D.: 82-0516178

ADDRESS INQUIRIES TO:
Micron Technology Foundation, M/S 407 Community and Academic Relations 8000 South Federal Way, P.O. Box 6 Boise, ID 83707-0006

SOCIETY OF ACTUARIES (SOA) [1914]
475 North Martingale Road
Suite 600
Schaumburg, IL 60173-2226
(847) 706-3509
Fax: (847) 273-8605
E-mail: ttatsumi@soa.org
Web Site: www.soa.org/doctoral-stipend

FOUNDED: 1949

AREAS OF INTEREST:
Actuarial science, a branch of mathematics based on calculus, probability and statistics, as well as business economics.

NAME(S) OF PROGRAMS:
● **Society of Actuaries' James C. Hickman Scholar Doctoral Stipend Program**

TYPE:
Awards/prizes; Scholarships. Society of Actuaries' James C. Hickman Scholar Doctoral Stipend Program is designed to provide stipends to doctoral students who will, through their studies, address research and education needs of the profession, including both the theoretical and practical aspects.

YEAR PROGRAM STARTED: 2009

PURPOSE:
To increase the number of academic actuaries who hold a Ph.D. and an actuarial designation, and who intend to pursue academic careers in the U.S. or Canada.

LEGAL BASIS:
Society-funded.

ELIGIBILITY:
Individuals who meet the following requirements may apply:
(1) enrolled full-time, have recently been admitted or are currently applying to a qualifying doctoral program in the U.S. or Canada; a qualifying doctoral program is one in actuarial science or a field related to actuarial science (e.g., business, demography, economics, financial economics, insurance, mathematics, risk management, statistics); applicants may apply at the same time they are applying for a doctoral program; if selected, these applicants will be awarded the

stipend conditional upon enrollment in a qualifying doctoral program;
(2) hold a fellowship-level actuarial credential or are pursuing Associateship or Fellowship membership of an accrediting actuarial organization (i.e., AI, CAS, CIA, IFoA, SOA); applicants who are already Associate members (including those awarded the CERA designation) will be expected to pursue a Fellowship credential and;
(3) all applicants must have at least two actuarial exams passed.

While U.S. or Canadian citizenship is not expressly required, the applicant will attest to citizenship status on the application. An applicant's citizenship status may be used to evaluate the likelihood that the applicant will pursue an academic career in the U.S. or Canada.

FINANCIAL DATA:
The stipend is to be used at the discretion of the Ph.D. candidate for appropriate expenses related to the completion of the Ph.D. and the actuarial credential if not yet attained. Applicants should be aware that stipend funds are provided for qualified expenses (tuition, books, fees, etc.). Qualified expenses do not include room and board. Stipend funds not used for qualified expenses may be taxable. Please consult one's tax advisor if one has any questions.
Amount of support per award: Generally $20,000 per academic year.
Total amount of support: Varies.

NO. MOST RECENT APPLICANTS: 27.

NO. AWARDS: Varies.

APPLICATION INFO:
Applicants must submit an application and supporting documentation that includes the following:
(1) Applicants currently applying to doctoral programs must provide the names of the schools/programs to which they have applied, and the intended field of study in each school/program. (If a stipend is awarded, it will be conditional on enrollment in the specified program and for the field of study proposed in the application.);
(2) Applicants already enrolled in a doctoral program will indicate how many years they have been studying, and approximately how many more years they believe they need to complete their Doctorate. They will also provide a statement from their supervisor or program director attesting to progess in their doctoral program and;
(3) Applicant must submit a Statement of Interest. This may be the same statement submitted for the doctoral program, but additional language should be added for this application to clearly explain their goals regarding teaching, research and contributions to the actuarial profession.
Duration: One academic year. Renewable up to four times based on satisfactory progress.
Deadline: Completed application forms and supporting materials must be received at the Society no later than February 15. Recipients will be announced April 15. Recipients must notify the Society of acceptance of the stipend by May 15.

PUBLICATIONS:
Application guidelines.

ADDRESS INQUIRIES TO:
SOA James C. Hickman Scholar Doctoral Stipend Program (See address above.)

SOCIETY OF ACTUARIES (SOA) [1915]
475 North Martingale Road
Suite 600
Schaumburg, IL 60173-2226
(847) 706-3509
Fax: (847) 273-8605
E-mail: ttatsumi@soa.org
Web Site: www.soa.org/education/resources/edu-institution-grant/default.aspx

FOUNDED: 1949

AREAS OF INTEREST:
Actuarial science, a branch of mathematics based on calculus, probability and statistics, as well as business economics.

NAME(S) OF PROGRAMS:
● **Society of Actuaries Educational Institution Grant**

TYPE:
Awards/prizes; Development grants; General operating grants; Project/program grants; Research grants; Scholarships; Travel grants. Grants to educational institutions.

YEAR PROGRAM STARTED: 1991

PURPOSE:
To provide financial support for the promotion and development of educational and research programs in actuarial science; to recognize the added value professional actuarial qualifications offer to actuarial teaching and research.

LEGAL BASIS:
Society-funded.

ELIGIBILITY:
A full-time faculty member at the applying institution must attain Associateship (ASA) status or Fellowship (FSA) status to qualify the institution for a grant.

Full-time faculty are defined as individuals employed by a college or university who are considered to be full-time members of the regular faculty by their employer. This does not include visiting faculty, adjuncts, graduate students or teaching assistants.

The institution must appear on the Universities and Colleges Actuarial Programs (UCAP) list at the time the ASA or FSA designation is earned, or within one year from the date the designation is earned, and must continue on the list through the time of application.

FINANCIAL DATA:
Amount of support per award: $5,000 one-time grant to an educational institution when a full-time faculty member attains ASA status; $7,500 one-time grant to an educational institution when a full-time faculty member attains FSA status.
Total amount of support: Varies.

NO. MOST RECENT APPLICANTS: 9.

NO. AWARDS: Varies.

APPLICATION INFO:
Application form and details are available online.
Deadline: Applications for institution grants must be received within three years of the date the faculty member attains FSA or ASA status as indicated on the FSA or ASA diploma.

PUBLICATIONS:
Application guidelines.

ADDRESS INQUIRIES TO:
Educational Institution Grants (ASA/FSA Grants)
(See address above.)

Physics

AMERICAN INSTITUTE OF PHYSICS [1916]

One Physics Ellipse
College Park, MD 20740-3843
(301) 209-3090
(301) 209-3092
E-mail: writing@aip.org
Web Site: www.aip.org/aip/awards/science-communication

FOUNDED: 1931

AREAS OF INTEREST:
The advancement and diffusion of the knowledge of physics and its application to human welfare.

NAME(S) OF PROGRAMS:
- **American Institute of Physics Science Communication Awards**

TYPE:
Awards/prizes. Four writing awards, one to a physicist, astronomer or member of an AIP society, one to a journalist for noteworthy writing about physics and astronomy in the print media, one to a journalist for noteworthy writing about physics and astronomy for broadcast media, and one for science writing aimed at children.

PURPOSE:
To stimulate distinguished reporting and writing that will improve public appreciation of the physical sciences, astronomy, math and related science fields.

ELIGIBILITY:
Entries must have been printed in any recognized international, national or local medium of communication such as newspapers, magazines or books. The media should normally be available to, and intended for, the general public. Purely scientific, technical and trade publications are excluded.

Entries must have been published or translated into English during the period one year immediately prior to the deadline date. No more than three entries may be submitted by any one individual. Persons other than the author may submit entries on behalf of an author in accordance with the rules.

FINANCIAL DATA:
Amount of support per award: $3,000.
Total amount of support: $12,000.

NO. AWARDS: 4.

APPLICATION INFO:
Application information is available on the web site.
Deadline: March 31.

OFFICERS AND STAFF:
Michael H. Moloney, Chief Executive Officer
Gigi Swartz, Chief Financial Officer
John Hayes, Chief Executive Officer, Publishing
Naomi Schmuckler, Senior Director, Human Resources

ADDRESS INQUIRIES TO:
Marissa Nielsen, Programs Coordinator
(See address above.)

AMERICAN VACUUM SOCIETY (AVS) [1917]

125 Maiden Lane, Suite 15B
New York, NY 10038-4714
(212) 248-0200
Fax: (212) 248-0245
E-mail: avsnyc@avs.org
Web Site: avs.org

FOUNDED: 1953

AREAS OF INTEREST:
Vacuum science and technology, thin film research, vacuum metallurgy, surface physics, electronic materials and processing, plasma science and technology and applied surface science.

NAME(S) OF PROGRAMS:
- **Graduate Research Awards**
- **Russell and Sigurd Varian Award**
- **Nellie Yeoh Whetten Award**

TYPE:
Awards/prizes; Fellowships. Cash awards and a one-year fellowship in recognition of scientific promise or excellence in graduate studies in vacuum science.

The Whetten Award is offered to encourage and recognize participation by women in science and engineering.

PURPOSE:
To recognize and encourage excellence in graduate studies in the sciences and technologies of interest to the Society.

LEGAL BASIS:
Nonprofit 501(c)(3) organization.

ELIGIBILITY:
All awards are open to students engaged in graduate studies in major fields of the organization's interest at accredited graduate schools in North America.

For the Whetten Award, the nominee must be a registered female graduate student in an accredited academic institution at the time when the applications are due. Criteria for selection of the awardee are research and academic excellence.

FINANCIAL DATA:
Amount of support per award: Graduate Research Awards: $1,000 per award; $1,500 each for the Whetten Award and for the Varian Award, plus reimbursed travel support (up to $750 maximum) to attend the International Symposium.
Total amount of support: Varies.

NO. MOST RECENT APPLICANTS: 11.

NO. AWARDS: Graduate Research Awards: Approximately 3 annually; Varian Award and Whetten Award: 1 each per year.

APPLICATION INFO:
Deadline: May 1.

ADDRESS INQUIRIES TO:
Angela Klink, Program Administrator
E-mail: angela@avs.org

NATIONAL SCIENCE FOUNDATION [1918]

Division of Physics
2415 Eisenhower Avenue
Alexandria, VA 22314
(703) 292-8890
Fax: (703) 292-9078
E-mail: info@nsf.gov
Web Site: www.nsf.gov

AREAS OF INTEREST:
Nuclear, theoretical, atomic and molecular, gravitational, and elementary particles, education and interdisciplinary research, physics of living systems, particle and nuclear astrophysics.

NAME(S) OF PROGRAMS:
- **Investigator-Initiated Research Projects**

TYPE:
Research grants.

PURPOSE:
To support physics research and the preparation of future scientists in U.S. colleges and universities across a broad range of physics disciplines.

ELIGIBILITY:
As specified in the NSF Grant Proposal Guidelines.

FINANCIAL DATA:
Amount of support per award: Varies.
Total amount of support: Approximately $90,000,000 in new awards annually, pending availability of funds.

NO. AWARDS: Approximately 300.

APPLICATION INFO:
Proposals must be submitted through FastLane or grants.gov.
Duration: Typically one to five years. Renewals by reapplication.
Deadline: Varies according to program.

ADDRESS INQUIRIES TO:
Cognizant Program Director
Division of Physics
(See address above.)

SOCIETY OF PHYSICS STUDENTS [1919]

American Institute of Physics
One Physics Ellipse
College Park, MD 20740
(301) 209-3007
Fax: (301) 209-0839
E-mail: sps@aip.org
Web Site: www.spsnational.org/programs/awards/research.htm

AREAS OF INTEREST:
Physics.

NAME(S) OF PROGRAMS:
- **SPS Award for Outstanding Undergraduate Research**

TYPE:
Awards/prizes.

PURPOSE:
To promote interest in physics among students and the general public.

LEGAL BASIS:
Not-for-profit, 501(c)(3).

ELIGIBILITY:
Must participate in annual competition and must be SPS national member. Applicants must be undergraduate students at the time the application is due. Winners are chosen based on their research, letters of recommendation and SPS participation from among qualified applicants.

FINANCIAL DATA:
Amount of support per award: $500 honorarium for winner and $500 for the SPS chapter.
Total amount of support: Varies.

NO. MOST RECENT APPLICANTS: 9.

NO. AWARDS: 2 winners and 1 runner-up.

APPLICATION INFO:
Consult the web site.
Duration: One year.
Deadline: March 15.

STAFF:
Mikayla Cleaver, Program Coordinator

ADDRESS INQUIRIES TO:
Mikayla Cleaver, Program Coordinator
(See address above.)

SOCIETY OF PHYSICS STUDENTS   [1920]
One Physics Ellipse
College Park, MD 20740
(301) 209-3007
Fax: (301) 209-0839
E-mail: sps@aip.org
Web Site: www.spsnational.org

FOUNDED: 1968

AREAS OF INTEREST:
Physics.

NAME(S) OF PROGRAMS:
● **Future Faces of Physics Awards**

TYPE:
Awards/prizes.

YEAR PROGRAM STARTED: 2011

PURPOSE:
To promote interest in physics across cultures.

LEGAL BASIS:
Not-for-profit, 501(c)(3).

ELIGIBILITY:
Applicant must be a Society of Physics Students member.

FINANCIAL DATA:
Amount of support per award: Up to $500.

NO. MOST RECENT APPLICANTS: 11.

NO. AWARDS: 8.

APPLICATION INFO:
Application information is available on the web site.
Duration: One year.
Deadline: November 15.

STAFF:
Mikayla Cleaver, Program Coordinator

ADDRESS INQUIRIES TO:
Mikayla Cleaver, Program Coordinator
(See address above.)

*SPECIAL STIPULATIONS:
Only one proposal may be submitted by an SPS chapter.

SOCIETY OF PHYSICS STUDENTS   [1921]
One Physics Ellipse
College Park, MD 20740
(301) 209-3007
Fax: (301) 209-0839
E-mail: sps@aip.org
Web Site: www.spsnational.org/awards

FOUNDED: 1968

AREAS OF INTEREST:
Physics.

NAME(S) OF PROGRAMS:
● **Marsh W. White Awards**

TYPE:
Awards/prizes.

YEAR PROGRAM STARTED: 1975

PURPOSE:
To support projects by SPS chapters that promote interest in physics among students and the general public.

LEGAL BASIS:
Not-for-profit, 501(c)(3).

ELIGIBILITY:
Applicants must be SPS chapters in good standing with the SPS national organization. The project leader must be a student that is a member of the SPS national organization.

FINANCIAL DATA:
Amount of support per award: Up to $500.

NO. MOST RECENT APPLICANTS: 16.

NO. AWARDS: 15.

APPLICATION INFO:
Consult the web site.
Duration: One year.
Deadline: November 15.

STAFF:
Mikayla Cleaver, Program Coordinator

ADDRESS INQUIRIES TO:
Mikayla Cleaver, Program Coordinator
(See address above.)

*SPECIAL STIPULATIONS:
Only one proposal may be submitted by an SPS chapter.

SOCIETY OF PHYSICS STUDENTS
One Physics Ellipse
College Park, MD 20740-3843
(301) 209-3007
Fax: (301) 209-0839
E-mail: sps@aip.org
Web Site: www.spsnational.org

TYPE:
Scholarships.

See entry 1593 for full listing.

LIFE SCIENCES

Life sciences (general)

DJ & T FOUNDATION [1922]
P.O. Box 5109
West Hills, CA 91308
(323) 819-9295
Fax: (323) 446-7187
E-mail: will@prappascompany.com
Web Site: www.djtfoundation.org

FOUNDED: 1995

AREAS OF INTEREST:
Animal population control.

TYPE:
Grants-in-aid. Fund grants to organizations
that operate low-cost spay/neuter clinics.

YEAR PROGRAM STARTED: 1995

PURPOSE:
To fund nonprofit, low-cost spay and neuter
clinics.

LEGAL BASIS:
Private foundation.

ELIGIBILITY:
Eligible organizations must be IRS 501(c)(3)
tax-exempt.

GEOG. RESTRICTIONS: United States.

FINANCIAL DATA:
Amount of support per award: Varies.
Total amount of support: Varies.

NO. MOST RECENT APPLICANTS: Approximately
80.

NO. AWARDS: 40 to 50.

APPLICATION INFO:
Applications are available at the web site and
must include a copy of the IRS tax
determination letter.
Duration: Varies.

ADDRESS INQUIRIES TO:
DJ & T Foundation
(See address above.)

THE HASTINGS CENTER [1923]
21 Malcolm Gordon Road
Garrison, NY 10524
(845) 424-4040
Fax: (845) 424-4545
E-mail: visitors@thehastingscenter.org
Web Site: www.thehastingscenter.org

FOUNDED: 1969

AREAS OF INTEREST:
Ethical issues in medicine, health care and
the life sciences. Recent research topics
include biotechnology, death and dying,
aging, neonatal care, allocation of resources,
occupational health, health
professional-patient relationships, chronic
illness, rehabilitation medicine, AIDS,
surrogate motherhood and artificial
reproduction, organ transplantation,
prospective payment systems,
deinstitutionalization, nursing homes, animal
experimentation, environmental protection,
civic education and the professions and the
public good.

NAME(S) OF PROGRAMS:
● **Visiting Scholars Program**

TYPE:
Residencies; Visiting scholars. Independent
study.

YEAR PROGRAM STARTED: 1969

PURPOSE:
To permit scholars and practitioners in the
humanities or the sciences to conduct
productive research on ethical issues in
medicine, the life sciences and the
professions.

LEGAL BASIS:
Nonprofit independent research association.

ELIGIBILITY:
Visiting Scholars Program is open to persons
with a degree in the humanities, sciences,
law or medicine and that are prepared to
pursue their own independent research
project in the Center's areas of interest.

NO. MOST RECENT APPLICANTS: Varies.

NO. AWARDS: Varies.

APPLICATION INFO:
Application information is available on the
web site.
Duration: Two to eight weeks.

PUBLICATIONS:
Annual report; application guidelines;
*Hastings Center Report; Hastings Center
Books in Print; IRB: Ethics and Human
Research; Bioethics Forum.*

ADDRESS INQUIRIES TO:
Visiting Scholars Program
(See address above.)

THOMAS F. AND KATE MILLER JEFFRESS MEMORIAL TRUST [1924]
Bank of America-Private Bank of America
DC1-842-0501
1800 K Street, N.W., Fifth Floor
Washington, DC 20006
(202) 442-7460
E-mail: dc.grantmaking@bofa.com
lee.parker@bofa.com
Web Site: hria.org/tmf/jeffress

FOUNDED: 1981

AREAS OF INTEREST:
Astronomy, biosciences, chemistry, computer
sciences, engineering, environmental
sciences, material science, mathematics and
physics.

NAME(S) OF PROGRAMS:
● **Jeffress Trust Awards Program in
Interdisciplinary Research**

TYPE:
Seed money grants. Administered by The
Medical Foundation, this awards program
supports high-impact, innovative one-year
projects that integrate computational and
quantitative scientific methodologies across a
broad range of scientific disciplines.

YEAR PROGRAM STARTED: 1982

PURPOSE:
To support basic research in chemical,
medical, or other scientific fields at
educational and research institutions in the
Commonwealth of Virginia.

LEGAL BASIS:
Trust.

ELIGIBILITY:
Grants are made to tax-exempt institutions
and organizations which are operated
exclusively for charitable, scientific purposes.
Grants are not made to private foundations.

GEOG. RESTRICTIONS: Virginia.

FINANCIAL DATA:
Amount of support per award: $100,000.

Total amount of support: Up to $1,000,000.

NO. MOST RECENT APPLICANTS: 24 for the year
2019.

NO. AWARDS: Up to 12 annually.

APPLICATION INFO:
Grant procedures and guidelines are available
at the web site above.
Duration: One year.
Deadline: Dates are posted on the Trust web
site.

PUBLICATIONS:
Guidelines.

ADDRESS INQUIRIES TO:
Jeanne Brown, Program Officer
E-mail: jbrown@hria.org
Tel: (617) 279-2240 ext. 709

*PLEASE NOTE:
The Trust grants funds only in Virginia.

THE NATIONAL ACADEMIES OF SCIENCES, ENGINEERING, AND MEDICINE
500 Fifth Street, N.W.
Washington, DC 20001
(202) 334-2760
E-mail: rap@nas.edu
Web Site: www.nationalacademies.org/rap

TYPE:
Research scientists. Fellowships at the
graduate, postdoctoral and senior levels for
research-in-residence at U.S. federal
laboratories and affiliated institutions.

See entry 1853 for full listing.

NATIONAL DAIRY COUNCIL
10255 West Higgins Road
Suite 900
Rosemont, IL 60018-5616
(847) 803-2000
Fax: (847) 803-2077
E-mail: nutritionresearch@rosedmi.com
Web Site: researchsubmission.
nationaldairycouncil.org

TYPE:
Research contracts. The National Dairy
Council is the nutrition research, education
and communications arm of Dairy
Management Inc. On behalf of U.S. dairy
farmers, the National Dairy Council provides
science-based nutrition information to, and in
collaboration with, a variety of stakeholders
committed to fostering a healthier society,
including health professionals, educators,
school nutrition directors, academia, industry,
consumers and media. The National Dairy
Council comprises a staff of nutrition science
researchers, registered dietitians and
communications experts dedicated to
educating the public on the health benefits of
consuming milk and milk products
throughout a person's lifespan.

See entry 2460 for full listing.

NATIONAL EYE INSTITUTE
National Institutes of Health
6700B Rockledge Drive, MSC 6914
Bethesda, MD 20817
(301) 451-2020
E-mail: wujekjer@nei.nih.gov
Web Site: www.nei.nih.gov

TYPE:
Conferences/seminars; Fellowships; Research
grants; Training grants. Research Project

Grants support individual investigators whose work is aimed at discovering means of improving the prevention, diagnosis and treatment of blinding and disabling eye and vision disorders.

Small Business Innovation Research Awards aim to stimulate technological innovations, to use small business to meet federal research-development needs that may ultimately lead to commercial products or services and to foster and encourage participation by minority and disadvantaged persons in technological innovations.

Areas of study include vision research, retinal diseases, corneal diseases, cataract, glaucoma, low vision and blindness rehabilitation, visual impairment and its rehabilitation, strabismus, amblyopia and visual processing.

See entry 2316 for full listing.

NATIONAL EYE INSTITUTE
National Institutes of Health
6700B Rockledge Drive, Suite 3400
Bethesda, MD 20817
(301) 451-2020
Fax: (301) 402-0528
E-mail: esl@nei.nih.gov
Web Site: www.nei.nih.gov

TYPE:
Research grants.

See entry 2315 for full listing.

PFD RESEARCH FOUNDATION   [1925]
1100 Wayne Avenue
Suite 825
Silver Spring, MD 20910
(301) 273-0570
Fax: (301) 273-0778
E-mail: info@augs.org
Web Site: www.pfdresearch.org

AREAS OF INTEREST:
Incontinence and pelvic floor dysfunctions.

NAME(S) OF PROGRAMS:
● **PFD Research Foundation Grants Program**

TYPE:
Research grants.

PURPOSE:
To provide research training and experience for a candidate who exhibits significant evidence of talent and dedication to research.

ELIGIBILITY:
Applicant must:
(1) be an active, life, honorary or allied health member of the PFD Research Foundation;
(2) be a current fellow in either an accredited or nonaccredited fellowship program;
(3) have a senior research mentor or mentoring team. Mentors or co-investigators need not be members of the PFD Research Foundation and;
(4) funding must remain at the same institution for the period of the research project.

FINANCIAL DATA:
The award may be used for purchases of equipment and supplies, laboratory tests, technician/research assistant salaries, Institutional Review Board costs, and/or statistical report. Salary support for the applicant is not allowed.

Amount of support per award: Up to $25,000.

Total amount of support: Up to $75,000.

NO. MOST RECENT APPLICANTS: Average 20 per year.

NO. AWARDS: Up to 3.

APPLICATION INFO:
Application requirements are available online.

Duration: Two years.

Deadline: March 1.

ADDRESS INQUIRIES TO:
Tristan Wood, Director of Marketing and Membership
(See e-mail address above.)

KENNETH A. SCOTT CHARITABLE TRUST   [1926]
c/o KeyBank Nonprofit Services
100 Public Square, Suite 600
Cleveland, OH 44113
E-mail: director@kennethscottcharitabletrust.org
Web Site: www.kennethscottcharitabletrust.org

FOUNDED: 1995

AREAS OF INTEREST:
Animal welfare.

TYPE:
Project/program grants. Grants are available for projects of shelters and humane groups in Ohio and other Great Lakes states in the U.S.

YEAR PROGRAM STARTED: 1995

PURPOSE:
To prevent cruelty to animals and promote the humane treatment of animals, particularly companion animals (dogs, cats) and other species commonly kept as household pets. Requests related to wildlife and animals in other settings may also be considered.

LEGAL BASIS:
Private foundation.

ELIGIBILITY:
Eligible organizations must be IRS 501(c)(3) tax-exempt. No grants to individuals.

GEOG. RESTRICTIONS: Ohio. Some grants in other Great Lakes states.

FINANCIAL DATA:
Amount of support per award: $10,000 to $50,000.

Total amount of support: $801,725 for the year 2019.

NO. AWARDS: 58 for the year 2019.

APPLICATION INFO:
A letter of inquiry, e-mail or phone call to the Trust is required before submitting the application.

Duration: One year.

Deadline: April 15, August 15 and December 15 for proposals.

IRS I.D.: 34-7034544

ADDRESS INQUIRIES TO:
Dr. H. Richard Obermanns
Executive Director
(See address above.)

THE PERCY SLADEN MEMORIAL FUND   [1927]
c/o The Linnean Society of London
Burlington House, Piccadilly
London W1J 0BF England
(44) 020 7434 4479
Fax: (44) 020 7287 9364
E-mail: info@linnean.org
gina@linnean.org
Web Site: www.linnean.org

FOUNDED: 1904

AREAS OF INTEREST:
Natural sciences, with a focus of support on field work in the life and earth sciences, both through expeditions and individual research projects overseas.

NAME(S) OF PROGRAMS:
● **Percy Sladen Memorial Fund Grants**

TYPE:
Awards/prizes; Project/program grants; Research grants; Travel grants. Field work grants in life and earth sciences (excludes any projects which are part of further education, e.g., a Doctorate or a Master's course).

YEAR PROGRAM STARTED: 1904

PURPOSE:
To support field work in life and earth sciences away from usual country of residence.

LEGAL BASIS:
Registered charity.

ELIGIBILITY:
There are no restrictions in award of grants based on nationality, age, sex or prior qualifications. No grants for field work undertaken as part of a higher degree or general support for undergraduate expeditions.

FINANCIAL DATA:
Grants may be used toward a portion of total costs or for specific items of equipment.

Amount of support per award: Up to GBP 1,500; generally less than GBP 1,000.

Total amount of support: Approximately GBP 19,000 annually.

NO. MOST RECENT APPLICANTS: 44.

NO. AWARDS: 27.

APPLICATION INFO:
Application form and referees reports are available from the Secretary to the Trustees at the address above.

Duration: Grant must be taken up within one year of receipt.

Deadline: January 30 and September 30.

ADDRESS INQUIRIES TO:
Gina Douglas
Secretary to the Trustees
(See address above.)

*SPECIAL STIPULATIONS:
No support for course work. No undergraduate expeditions. No grants for field work for completion of dissertations or higher degrees.

SOCIETY FOR THE STUDY OF AMPHIBIANS AND REPTILES
Department of Biology
Carroll University
Waukesha, WI 53186
(262) 951-3295
E-mail: rbrenes@carrollu.edu
Web Site: www.ssarherps.org

TYPE:
Awards/prizes; Research grants. Awards are given in six categories: Conservation of Amphibians and/or Reptiles, Field Research, Laboratory Research, Herpetological Education, Travel and International Research.

See entry 1858 for full listing.

ROB AND BESSIE WELDER WILDLIFE FOUNDATION [1928]

10429 Welder Wildlife
Sinton, TX 78387
(361) 364-2643
Fax: (361) 364-2650
E-mail: tblankenship@welderwildlife.org
Web Site: www.welderwildlife.org

FOUNDED: 1954

AREAS OF INTEREST:
Wildlife conservation, wildlife ecology, wildlife science and higher education (graduate level only).

TYPE:
Fellowships. Graduate research fellowships only in fields of wildlife ecology and management.

YEAR PROGRAM STARTED: 1956

PURPOSE:
To encourage and sponsor wildlife research and education.

LEGAL BASIS:
Private, nonprofit foundation.

ELIGIBILITY:
Graduate students at accredited universities seeking advanced degrees in the above-designated fields are eligible to apply. Undergraduates need not apply.

GEOG. RESTRICTIONS: Continental United States.

FINANCIAL DATA:
Fellowships are generally $1,800 (M.S.) to $2,000 (Ph.D.) per month, plus some funds for field supplies and travel. Living quarters are available for students doing research on the Foundation's refuge area near Sinton, TX, including utilities.
Amount of support per award: Normally $25,000 per calendar year.
Total amount of support: $140,000 available for the year 2020.

CO-OP FUNDING PROGRAMS: The Foundation participates in cooperative funding for approvable proposals not adequately financed through other sources, if and when surplus funds are available.

NO. MOST RECENT APPLICANTS: Over 20.

NO. AWARDS: 5 to 6.

APPLICATION INFO:
Initial contact with the Foundation may be submitted in an abbreviated outline of the research problem, a preliminary estimate of expenses, and letter signed by a qualified member of the faculty at the parent university. If the Foundation staff thereafter entertains the matter further, a more complete proposal will be requested along with material concerning the proposed fellowship recipient.
Duration: One year. May be renewed if progress is satisfactory.
Deadline: October 1.

PUBLICATIONS:
Biennial report of staff and student activities.

IRS I.D.: 74-1381321

OFFICERS:
Terry Blankenship, Ph.D., Director
Selma Glasscock, Ph.D., Assistant Director

TRUSTEES:
Hughes C. Thomas
H.C. Weil
John J. Welder, V

ADDRESS INQUIRIES TO:
Terry Blankenship, Ph.D., Director
(See address above.)

*SPECIAL STIPULATIONS:
Priority will be given to research proposals involving studies on the Foundation's refuge area and/or in south Texas.

THE WILEY FOUNDATION, INC. [1929]

111 River Street
Hoboken, NJ 07030-5774
(201) 748-6000
E-mail: wileyfoundation@wiley.com
Web Site: www.wileyfoundation.org

FOUNDED: 2001

AREAS OF INTEREST:
Biomedical sciences.

NAME(S) OF PROGRAMS:
● **Wiley Prize in Biomedical Sciences**

TYPE:
Awards/prizes. The annual Wiley Prize in Biomedical Sciences has recognized breakthrough research in pure or applied life science research.

YEAR PROGRAM STARTED: 2002

PURPOSE:
To honor research that is distinguished by its excellence, originality and impact on the understanding of biological systems and processes.

ELIGIBILITY:
The Foundation invites the nomination of exceptional scientists or research teams whose work has achieved an impressive level of excellence in pure or applied life science research.

The Foundation encourages international nominations.

FINANCIAL DATA:
Amount of support per award: $50,000 prize and a luncheon in honor of the recipient.

NO. AWARDS: Varies.

APPLICATION INFO:
Each nomination should be submitted by someone other than the nominee. More than one nomination can be made from the same organization.
Duration: Annual award.
Deadline: September 30.

Agriculture, land resources, rural development

AGRICULTURAL HISTORY SOCIETY

Mount Royal University
Faculty of Arts
4825 Mount Royal Gate, S.W.
Calgary AB T3E 6K6 Canada
(403) 440-8796
E-mail: aghistorysociety@gmail.com
Web Site: www.aghistorysociety.org

TYPE:
Awards/prizes. The Everett E. Edwards Award is presented to the graduate student who submits the best manuscript on any aspect of agricultural history and rural studies during the current calendar year.

The Gilbert C. Fite Dissertation Award will be presented to the author of the best dissertation on any aspect of agricultural history completed during the current calendar year.

The Wayne D. Rasmussen Award is given to the author of the best article on agricultural history published by a journal other than *Agricultural History* during the current calendar year.

The Theodore Saloutos Book Award is presented to the author of a book on any aspect of agricultural history in the U.S. within the current year, broadly interpreted.

The Henry A. Wallace Award is presented to the author of a book on any aspect of agricultural history outside of the U.S. within the current year, broadly interpreted.

See entry 531 for full listing.

THE AMERICAN CHESTNUT FOUNDATION [1930]

50 North Merrimon Avenue
Suite 115
Asheville, NC 28804
(828) 281-0047
Fax: (828) 253-5373
E-mail: samantha.bowers@acf.org
Web Site: www.acf.org

FOUNDED: 1983

AREAS OF INTEREST:
Chestnut research.

TYPE:
Research grants.

YEAR PROGRAM STARTED: 1983

PURPOSE:
To restore the American chestnut to Eastern forests.

ELIGIBILITY:
Grants are reviewed on a case-by-case basis.

GEOG. RESTRICTIONS: United States.

FINANCIAL DATA:
Amount of support per award: $1,000 to $10,000.
Total amount of support: Approximately $30,000 for the year 2019.

NO. MOST RECENT APPLICANTS: 10.

NO. AWARDS: 5.

APPLICATION INFO:
Send a letter of inquiry letter form, outlining the goal and purpose, the intended use, and amount of the grant requested.

Duration: Up to one year.

Deadline: Varies.

ADDRESS INQUIRIES TO:
Samantha Bowers, Grants Manager
(See address above.)

AMERICAN FARM BUREAU FOUNDATION FOR AGRICULTURE   [1931]

600 Maryland Avenue, S.W.
Suite 1000 West
Washington, DC 20024
(800) 443-8456
Fax: (202) 406-3600
E-mail: foundation@fb.org
Web Site: www.agfoundation.org

AREAS OF INTEREST:
Agricultural, consumer education, classroom, consumer and farm safety programs.

NAME(S) OF PROGRAMS:
● **White-Reinhardt Fund for Education**

TYPE:
Conferences/seminars; Project/program grants; Research contracts. Teacher Scholarships to National Conference.

YEAR PROGRAM STARTED: 1967

PURPOSE:
To provide travel expense funds to educators employed by a school system or to active agricultural literacy volunteers to attend the national conference; to provide funds for projects that will increase agricultural literacy in students grades K-12.

GEOG. RESTRICTIONS: United States.

FINANCIAL DATA:
Amount of support per award: Mini-Grant: Up to $1,000; Scholarship: Up to $1,500 for reimbursement of expenses not covered by other funding source.

Total amount of support: Varies.

APPLICATION INFO:
Mini-grant applications must be completed and submitted to the State Farm Bureau president, Agriculture in the Classroom coordinator or administrator for signature. All applications will be pre-screened for compliance with grant proposal guidelines. Any grant not meeting guidelines will be eliminated from the judging process prior to examination by judges.

Duration: One year.

Deadline: Mini-Grant: April 15 and October 15. Scholarship: October 15.

ADDRESS INQUIRIES TO:
Sydney Andrews, Assistant Director of Education Outreach
(See address above.)

AMERICAN FLORAL ENDOWMENT   [1932]

1001 North Fairfax Street
Suite 201
Alexandria, VA 22314
(703) 838-5211
Fax: (703) 838-5212
E-mail: afe@endowment.org
Web Site: endowment.org

FOUNDED: 1961

AREAS OF INTEREST:
Floricultural/environmental horticulture research and development funding in the U.S.

TYPE:
Internships; Project/program grants; Research grants; Scholarships. The Endowment funds research and educational development in floriculture and environmental horticulture designed to produce solutions to industry needs and promote the growth and improvement of the floral industry for the benefit of the grower, wholesale, retail, allied segments and the general public.

The Endowment supports educational programs focused on attracting young people to the industry, and educational endeavors to identify and solve industry needs and/or challenges. The programs are divided into two major areas:
(1) paid floriculture internships/scholarships for full-time college students and;
(2) general educational grants to national programs.

YEAR PROGRAM STARTED: 1961

PURPOSE:
To further the advancement of education and science in the field of floriculture through funding research and studies in the floriculture field, the results of which will be published; to finance scholarships and internships to students interested in floriculture.

LEGAL BASIS:
Not-for-profit, nongovernmental organization.

GEOG. RESTRICTIONS: United States.

FINANCIAL DATA:
Amount of support per award: Varies.
Total amount of support: Varies.

APPLICATION INFO:
Contact the Endowment.

Duration: Typically one year; research grants can be multiyear.

Deadline: Varies.

PUBLICATIONS:
Update, quarterly newsletter; annual report.

AMERICAN SOCIETY FOR ENOLOGY AND VITICULTURE   [1933]

1724 Picasso Avenue, Suite E
Davis, CA 95618-0551
(530) 753-3142
Fax: (530) 753-3318
E-mail: info@asev.org
Web Site: www.asev.org

FOUNDED: 1951

AREAS OF INTEREST:
A scientific society of enologists, viticulturists and others in the fields of wine and grape production, promoting technical advancement and integrated research in science and industry.

TYPE:
Scholarships. Awards for undergraduate or graduate students enrolled in enology or viticulture or in a curriculum which emphasizes a science basic to the wine and grape industry and who intend to pursue a career in research for the wine or grape industry after graduation from college or university.

PURPOSE:
To support education and research in enology, viticulture or related fields.

LEGAL BASIS:
Professional, scientific association.

ELIGIBILITY:
Undergraduate and graduate students who have been accepted at an accredited college or university in North America, are enrolled in an appropriate field of study and reside in North America may apply. Applicants must be at least junior level in academic status (60 quarter units or 45 semester units). Undergraduate students must have a minimum 3.0 overall grade point average on a scale of 4.0. Graduate students must have a minimum 3.2 overall grade point average on a scale of 4.0.

FINANCIAL DATA:
Amount of support per award: Varies each academic year.

Total amount of support: Varies each academic year.

APPLICATION INFO:
Applications can be downloaded from the web site.

Duration: One academic year. Renewable in open competition.

Deadline: All completed forms, letters and transcripts must be received by March 1.

ADDRESS INQUIRIES TO:
Scholarship Committee
P.O. Box 1855
Davis, CA 95617-1855

CENTER FOR PLANT CONSERVATION   [1934]

15600 San Pasqual Valley Road
Escondido, CA 92027-7000
(760) 796-5686
E-mail: info@saveplants.org
Web Site: saveplants.org

FOUNDED: 1984

AREAS OF INTEREST:
Education.

NAME(S) OF PROGRAMS:
● **Catherine H. Beattie Fellowship for Conservation Horticulture**

TYPE:
Fellowships.

YEAR PROGRAM STARTED: 1984

PURPOSE:
To promote conservation of rare and endangered flora in the U.S.

LEGAL BASIS:
501(c)(3) nonprofit organization.

ELIGIBILITY:
Open to graduate students in biology, horticulture, or a related field. Preference is given to students whose projects focus on the endangered flora of the Carolinas and southeastern U.S.

FINANCIAL DATA:
Amount of support per award: Up to $4,500.

NO. MOST RECENT APPLICANTS: 10.

NO. AWARDS: 1.

APPLICATION INFO:
Applicants should submit the following:
(1) a two- to three-page proposal, which includes a description of the research project and how it relates to the student's academic and professional development;
(2) an itemized budget for the funds requested;

(3) a current resume;

(4) a letter of endorsement by an academic advisor from the institution where the student is pursuing graduate studies;

(5) the names of three additional persons qualified to describe the student's character and ability and;

(6) official transcripts for both undergraduate and graduate academic records.

Applicant should be prepared to write an article for CPC Newsletter, *Plant Conservation.*

Duration: Varies.

Deadline: December 15. Notification by mid-February.

PUBLICATIONS:
Plant Conservation, newsletter.

THE CH FOUNDATION [1935]

6102 82nd Street
Suite 8A
Lubbock, TX 79424
(806) 792-0448
Fax: (806) 792-7824
E-mail: hhocker@chfoundation.com
Web Site: www.chfoundationlubbock.com

FOUNDED: 1976

AREAS OF INTEREST:
Agriculture, arts, community development, cultural education, health, ranching, research, social services and youth.

TYPE:
Capital grants; Project/program grants.

YEAR PROGRAM STARTED: 1991

PURPOSE:
To support programs that meet the needs of and improve the quality of life.

ELIGIBILITY:
Grants are limited to organizations whose services benefit the Lubbock area of Texas. Grants are made to organizations that have tax-exempt status under Section 501(c)(3) of the Internal Revenue Code. No grants are made to individuals or political organizations.

GEOG. RESTRICTIONS: Lubbock, Texas and surrounding counties.

APPLICATION INFO:
Contact the Foundation to determine the interest and appropriateness of a full proposal. Funding guidelines are available online.

Duration: One year. Renewal possible.

Deadline: May 1. Disbursements are made in December.

PUBLICATIONS:
Application guidelines.

IRS I.D.: 75-1534816

ADDRESS INQUIRIES TO:
Heather Hocker, Grants Administrator
(See address above.)

FARM AID [1936]

501 Cambridge Street
Third Floor
Cambridge, MA 02141
(617) 354-2922
Fax: (617) 354-6992
E-mail: grants@farmaid.org
Web Site: www.farmaid.org

FOUNDED: 1985

AREAS OF INTEREST:
Supporting organizations that help farm families stay on their land, build local markets, confront the threat of corporate control of agriculture, train new farmers and support farmer-to-farmer programs for more sustainable agricultural practices. Emergency and disaster assistance for farm families.

TYPE:
General operating grants; Project/program grants. Grants fall within three broad categories which make it possible for organizations to build long-term solutions to the problems farmers face.

(1) Growing the Good Food Movement: These grants fund organizations or projects that seek to strengthen what Farm Aid calls the Good Food Movement, the growing number of Americans reaching for and demanding family farm-identified, local, organic or humanely raised food. These grants build connections between farmers and consumers, creating new markets for family farmers.

(2) Helping Farmers Thrive: These grants fund organizations or projects that assist farmers in transitioning to more sustainable and profitable farming practices, finding alternative markets, or starting a new farming operation as well as providing support services to farm families in crisis. These organizations are the core of the Farmer Resource Network which responds to individual farmers as well as regional events such as natural disasters. (See www.farmaid.org/ideas.)

(3) Taking Action to Change the System: These grants fund organizations or projects that promote fair farm policies and organize grassroots campaigns to defend and bolster family farm-centered agriculture. These grants enable advocates to strengthen the voices of family farmers and promote their interests on a local, regional and national level.

YEAR PROGRAM STARTED: 1985

LEGAL BASIS:
Tax-exempt, charitable and educational organization.

ELIGIBILITY:
Applicants must be IRS 501(c)(3) nonprofit organizations and include a copy of their IRS 501(c)(3) tax-exempt verification letter. If organization does not have 501(c)(3) status, it must include the IRS 501(c)(3) letter and authorization from the organization acting as its fiscal agent.

The following types of projects are not eligible for Farm Aid funding:

(1) grants or loans to individuals;

(2) grants or loans to support commercial operation of a farming enterprise;

(3) production of book, film, television or radio projects;

(4) projects outside the U.S.;

(5) projects directed or substantially funded by government bodies (federal, state or local), including Resource Conservation & Development Councils (RC & Ds);

(6) legal defense funds;

(7) capital campaigns, equipment purchases, endowments or deficit financing;

(8) historic preservation of farmland or buildings;

(9) lobbying to influence elections or legislation and;

(10) conferences, publications or research projects unless they are directly connected to ongoing program activities.

GEOG. RESTRICTIONS: United States.

FINANCIAL DATA:
Amount of support per award: $3,000 to $30,000 for the year 2019.

Total amount of support: Varies.

NO. AWARDS: 95 for the year 2019.

APPLICATION INFO:
Up-to-date application information is available on the web site.

Deadline: August 1. Grants are awarded in December.

PUBLICATIONS:
Newsletter.

IRS I.D.: 36-3383233

ADDRESS INQUIRIES TO:
Grant Program
(See address above.)

THE GARDEN CLUB OF AMERICA [1937]

14 East 60th Street, Third Floor
New York, NY 10022
(212) 753-8287
Fax: (212) 753-0134
E-mail: scholarshipapplications@gcamerica.org
Web Site: www.gcamerica.org/scholarships

FOUNDED: 1913

AREAS OF INTEREST:
Public horticulture.

NAME(S) OF PROGRAMS:
- **The Garden Club of America Hope Goddard Iselin Fellowship in Public Horticulture**

TYPE:
Fellowships. Garden Club of America Hope Goddard Iselin Fellowship in Public Horticulture: Funds one or more students annually for practical research and training at a recognized public garden, botanic garden, arboretum or other institution directly engaged with connecting people, plants and gardening within the U.S.

YEAR PROGRAM STARTED: 2013

PURPOSE:
To further the study of public horticulture through experiential learning that takes place at a recognized public garden, botanic garden, arboretum or other closely aligned public horticulture institution within the U.S.

LEGAL BASIS:
Nonprofit national organization.

ELIGIBILITY:
Open to students enrolled in a graduate-level university program to study public horticulture. Student applicant must confirm ability to conduct research or otherwise utilize facility where study will be undertaken.

FINANCIAL DATA:
Amount of support per award: $5,000.

NO. AWARDS: 1 or more.

APPLICATION INFO:
Applications are available online and must be sent to the American Public Gardens Association (see address below).

Duration: One year.

Deadline: February 1 preceding the period of study.

PUBLICATIONS:
Program announcement.

ADDRESS INQUIRIES TO:
Ms. Kate Tyrawski
American Public Gardens Association
351 Longwood Road
Kennett Square, PA 19348
Tel: (610) 708-3010
E-mail: ktyrawski@publicgardens.org
Web Site: www.publicgardens.org

*PLEASE NOTE:
Only one GCA scholarship, fellowship or
award may be applied for annually.

THE GARDEN CLUB OF
AMERICA   [1938]
14 East 60th Street, Third Floor
New York, NY 10022
(212) 753-8287
Fax: (212) 753-0134
E-mail: scholarshipapplications@gcamerica.org
Web Site: www.gcamerica.org/scholarships

FOUNDED: 1913

AREAS OF INTEREST:
Botany.

NAME(S) OF PROGRAMS:
● **The Garden Club of America Summer
Scholarship in Field Botany**

TYPE:
Scholarships. Summer Scholarship in Field
Botany offers students the opportunity to
gain knowledge and experience beyond the
regular course of study.

YEAR PROGRAM STARTED: 2000

PURPOSE:
To support student's field studies.

LEGAL BASIS:
Nonprofit national organization.

ELIGIBILITY:
Open to undergraduate and Master's degree
students. Research must be conducted in the
Western Hemisphere. Eligibility is open to
U.S. citizens and permanent residents who
are enrolled in a U.S.-based institution.

FINANCIAL DATA:
Amount of support per award: $3,000.

NO. AWARDS: 1.

APPLICATION INFO:
Application and instructions are available
online.
Deadline: February 1.

ADDRESS INQUIRIES TO:
See e-mail address above.

THE GARDEN CLUB OF
AMERICA   [1939]
14 East 60th Street, Third Floor
New York, NY 10022
(212) 753-8287
Fax: (212) 753-0134
E-mail: scholarshipapplications@gcamerica.org
Web Site: www.gcamerica.org/scholarships

FOUNDED: 1913

AREAS OF INTEREST:
Medicinal botany.

NAME(S) OF PROGRAMS:
● **The Zeller Summer Scholarship in
Medicinal Botany**

TYPE:
Scholarships. Zeller Scholarship encourages
undergraduates to expand their knowledge of
medicinal botany by pursuing summer study
through coursework or internships.

YEAR PROGRAM STARTED: 2003

LEGAL BASIS:
Nonprofit national organization.

ELIGIBILITY:
Open to undergraduate students enrolled in
an accredited U.S. college or university for
study or work during the summer following
the freshman, sophomore, junior or senior
year. Applicant must be a U.S. citizen or
permanent resident.

FINANCIAL DATA:
Amount of support per award: $3,000.

NO. AWARDS: 1.

APPLICATION INFO:
Application and instructions are available
online.
Deadline: February 1.

ADDRESS INQUIRIES TO:
See e-mail address above.

THE GARDEN CLUB OF
AMERICA   [1940]
14 East 60th Street, Third Floor
New York, NY 10022
(212) 753-8287
Fax: (212) 753-0134
E-mail: scholarshipapplications@gcamerica.org
Web Site: www.gcamerica.org/scholarships

FOUNDED: 1913

AREAS OF INTEREST:
Botany.

NAME(S) OF PROGRAMS:
● **The Joan K. Hunt and Rachel M. Hunt
Summer Scholarship in Field Botany**

TYPE:
Scholarships. Hunt Summer Scholarship
offers an opportunity to gain knowledge and
experience in the field beyond the regular
course of study.

YEAR PROGRAM STARTED: 2003

PURPOSE:
To promote the importance of botany to
horticulture by encouraging students to study
field botany in the U.S.

LEGAL BASIS:
Nonprofit national organization.

ELIGIBILITY:
Open to undergraduate and graduate students
up to the Master's degree level, with
preference given to undergraduate students.
Applicant must be a U.S. citizen or
permanent resident enrolled in a U.S.-based
institution.

FINANCIAL DATA:
Amount of support per award: $3,500.

NO. AWARDS: 1.

APPLICATION INFO:
Application and instructions are available
online.
Deadline: February 1.

ADDRESS INQUIRIES TO:
See e-mail address above.

THE GARDEN CLUB OF
AMERICA   [1941]
14 East 60th Street, Third Floor
New York, NY 10022
(212) 753-8287
Fax: (212) 753-0134
E-mail: scholarshipapplications@gcamerica.org
Web Site: www.gcamerica.org/scholarships

FOUNDED: 1913

AREAS OF INTEREST:
Garden history and design.

NAME(S) OF PROGRAMS:
● **The Garden Club of America
Internship in Garden History and
Design**

TYPE:
Internships. Internship supports independent
study in the field of landscape history and
design.

YEAR PROGRAM STARTED: 1997

PURPOSE:
To encourage the study of garden history and
design.

LEGAL BASIS:
Nonprofit national organization.

ELIGIBILITY:
Open to graduate students in museum
studies, public history, or information studies
with courses in collections management for
archives and museums. Eligibility is open to
U.S. citizens and permanent residents who
are enrolled in a U.S.-based institution.

FINANCIAL DATA:
Amount of support per award: Up to $4,000.

NO. AWARDS: 1 or more.

APPLICATION INFO:
Application and instructions are available
online. Applicants interested in applying for
work at the Smithsonian's AAG must file an
additional application with the Smithsonian.
Duration: 10 weeks.
Deadline: Winter and Spring: December 1.
Summer: February 1. Fall: July 1.

ADDRESS INQUIRIES TO:
See e-mail address above.

THE GARDEN CLUB OF
AMERICA   [1942]
14 East 60th Street, Third Floor
New York, NY 10022
(212) 753-8287
Fax: (212) 753-0134
E-mail: scholarshipapplications@gcamerica.org
Web Site: www.gcamerica.org/scholarships

FOUNDED: 1913

AREAS OF INTEREST:
Horticulture.

NAME(S) OF PROGRAMS:
● **The Corliss Knapp Engle Scholarship
in Horticulture**

TYPE:
Scholarships. Corliss Knapp Engle
Scholarship encourages the development of
research, documentation and teaching skills
in the field of horticulture.

YEAR PROGRAM STARTED: 2010

PURPOSE:
To support study at an accredited college,
university, or major botanic garden or
arboretum.

LEGAL BASIS:
Nonprofit national organization.

ELIGIBILITY:
Project may include, but are not restricted to,
plant propagation, photographic
documentation of studies and research

projects, the acquisition of skills for working with horticulture collections, and research in horticulture in the broadest sense.

FINANCIAL DATA:
Amount of support per award: $3,000.

NO. AWARDS: 1 or more.

APPLICATION INFO:
Application and instructions are available online.
Deadline: February 1.

ADDRESS INQUIRIES TO:
See e-mail address above.

THE GARDEN CLUB OF AMERICA   [1943]

14 East 60th Street, Third Floor
New York, NY 10022
(212) 753-8287
Fax: (212) 753-0134
E-mail: scholarshipapplications@gcamerica.org
Web Site: www.gcamerica.org/scholarships

FOUNDED: 1913

AREAS OF INTEREST:
Horticulture, particularly native plants.

NAME(S) OF PROGRAMS:
● **The Garden Club of America Motine M. Freeman Scholarship in Native Plants**

TYPE:
Scholarships. Freeman Scholarship encourages the understanding, development and use of underutilized native plants.

YEAR PROGRAM STARTED: 2017

PURPOSE:
To encourage the development of research, documentation and teaching skills in the field of horticulture.

LEGAL BASIS:
Nonprofit national organization.

ELIGIBILITY:
Open to college undergraduate and graduate students, advanced degree candidates, or non-degree seeking applicants above the high school level. Applicant must be a U.S. citizen or permanent resident enrolled in a U.S.-based institution.

Projects may include, but are not restricted to, plant propagation and the acquisition of skills for working with native plant collections, including techniques for incorporating them in managed landscapes. Photographic and written documentation of studies and research projects may be considered.

FINANCIAL DATA:
Amount of support per award: $3,000 minimum.

NO. AWARDS: 1 or more.

APPLICATION INFO:
Application and instructions are available online.
Deadline: February 1.

ADDRESS INQUIRIES TO:
See e-mail address above.

THE FRED C. GLOECKNER FOUNDATION, INC.   [1944]

550 Mamaroneck Avenue
Suite 510
Harrison, NY 10528-1609
(914) 698-2300
Fax: (914) 698-0848
E-mail: jsimone@fredgloeckner.com
Web Site: www.gloecknerfoundation.org

FOUNDED: 1960

AREAS OF INTEREST:
Floriculture and related fields such as plant pathology, plant breeding, agricultural engineering, agricultural economics, entomology and plant physiology related to floriculture.

TYPE:
Assistantships; Project/program grants; Research grants.

YEAR PROGRAM STARTED: 1961

PURPOSE:
To support floriculture research and education.

LEGAL BASIS:
Nonprofit educational corporation.

ELIGIBILITY:
Grants are awarded to nonprofit institutions, primarily colleges and universities, for research and education projects in the above fields. Research in basic plant physiology unrelated to floriculture is not considered. Grants may include assistantships for qualified graduate students seeking an M.S. or Ph.D. in the above fields. Grants are not made directly to students.

GEOG. RESTRICTIONS: United States.

FINANCIAL DATA:
Amount of support per award: $2,000 to $20,000.
Total amount of support: Varies.

NO. MOST RECENT APPLICANTS: 40 to 50.

NO. AWARDS: 14 for the year 2018.

REPRESENTATIVE AWARDS:
$13,000 to K. Nemali, Purdue University, for smartphone-based rapid, inexpensive, and accurate estimation of plant nitrogen status in floriculture production; $11,000 to B. Jackson, North Carolina University, for in situ, quantitative analysis of substrate rooting effects of poinsettia by x-ray microtomography; $10,000 to T. Colquhoun, University of Florida, for augmenting cut flowers with LEDs.

APPLICATION INFO:
Applications are available from the Foundation office, or can be downloaded from the web site.
Duration: One year. Renewals possible.
Deadline: April 1.

PUBLICATIONS:
Annual report; application guidelines.

OFFICERS:
Dr. Richard Craig, President
Dr. Paul Allen Hammer, Vice President
Martin D. Kortjohn, Treasurer
Joseph A. Simone, Secretary

DIRECTORS:
Dr. David G. Clark
Dr. Richard Craig
Margery Daughtery
Dr. Paul Allen Hammer
Shayne Johnson
J. Michael Klesa

Martin D. Kortjohn
Andrew Lee
Jay Sheely
Joseph A. Simone

ADDRESS INQUIRIES TO:
Joseph A. Simone, Secretary
(See e-mail address above.)

THE HERB SOCIETY OF AMERICA, INC.   [1945]

9019 Kirtland Chardon Road
Kirtland, OH 44094
(440) 256-0514
Fax: (440) 256-0541
E-mail: director@herbsociety.org
Web Site: www.herbsociety.org

FOUNDED: 1933

AREAS OF INTEREST:
Furthering the knowledge and use of herbs and contributing the results of the experience and research of its members to the records of horticulture, science, literature, history, art or economics.

CONSULTING OR VOLUNTEER SERVICES:
Volunteer services including maintenance of public gardens and workshops.

NAME(S) OF PROGRAMS:
● **HSA Research Grant**

TYPE:
Research grants.

YEAR PROGRAM STARTED: 1971

PURPOSE:
To promote the knowledge, use and delight of herbs through educational programs, research, and sharing the experiences of its members with the community.

LEGAL BASIS:
Tax-exempt, nonprofit corporation under IRS 501(c)(3).

ELIGIBILITY:
Students, professionals and individuals engaged in research on the horticultural, scientific and/or social applications or use of herbs throughout history.

Funding does not cover indirect costs, purchase or maintenance of durable computer, laboratory or office equipment, expenses related to tuition, textbooks, or conference attendance, private garden development, or travel to/from research site.

Only U.S. residents may apply.

FINANCIAL DATA:
Amount of support per award: $5,000.
Total amount of support: $5,000.

NO. MOST RECENT APPLICANTS: 30.

NO. AWARDS: 1.

APPLICATION INFO:
Applications should include the following:
(1) application form;
(2) professional vitae, not to exceed two pages, listing qualifications for the project, academic degrees and honors;
(3) explanation, not to exceed 500 words, describing how the project will be completed, where the work will be done, and what facilities and equipment are available;
(4) detailed listing of all anticipated costs and;
(5) specific timeline for the project.

Successful applicants will be required to sign a Grant Acceptance Form prior to the award of a grant.

Duration: One year. No renewals.

Deadline: January 31. Announcement May 1.

PUBLICATIONS:
The Herbarist; newsletter; grant guidelines.

IRS I.D.: 34-1596261

*SPECIAL STIPULATIONS:
Under the terms of the grant, periodic progress reports are to be sent to the Research Grant Chairman. At the termination of the project, The Herb Society expects a complete copy of the finished product for the Herb Society Library and a summary of the work for publication in the Society's publication, *The Herbarist*. The Society reserves the right to reject or accept credit in any publication resulting from the grant.

HORTICULTURAL RESEARCH INSTITUTE, INC. [1946]

2130 Stella Court
Columbus, OH 43215
(614) 487-1117
Fax: (614) 487-1216
E-mail: jenniferg@americanhort.org
Web Site: www.hriresearch.org

FOUNDED: 1962

AREAS OF INTEREST:
Nursery and landscape research.

NAME(S) OF PROGRAMS:
- **HRI Competitive Research Grant Program**

TYPE:
Grants-in-aid; Research grants; Scholarships; Seed money grants; Research contracts.

YEAR PROGRAM STARTED: 1974

PURPOSE:
To direct, fund, promote and communicate research which increases the quality and value of plants, improves the productivity and profitability of the nursery and landscape industry and protects and enhances the environment.

LEGAL BASIS:
501(c)(3).

ELIGIBILITY:
Proposals are evaluated on the basis of their relevance to the nursery industry.

GEOG. RESTRICTIONS: North America.

FINANCIAL DATA:
Amount of support per award: $5,000 to $35,000 for the year 2019.
Total amount of support: Varies.
Matching fund requirements: Not required, but preferred.

NO. MOST RECENT APPLICANTS: 65.

NO. AWARDS: 12 for the year 2019.

APPLICATION INFO:
Completed proposals must be submitted using HRI's online application process. No hard copies or e-mailed applications will be accepted.
Deadline: May 31. Announcement in late January/early February.

PUBLICATIONS:
Application guidelines.

IRS I.D.: 52-1052547

ADDRESS INQUIRIES TO:
Jennifer Gray
Research Programs Administrator
(See address above.)

HORTICULTURAL RESEARCH INSTITUTE, INC.

2130 Stella Court
Columbus, OH 43215
(614) 487-1117
Fax: (614) 487-1216
E-mail: jenniferg@americanhort.org
Web Site: www.hriresearch.org

TYPE:
Scholarships.

See entry 1531 for full listing.

LAND O'LAKES FOUNDATION

4001 Lexington Avenue North
Arden Hills, MN 55126
(651) 375-2470
E-mail: landolakesfoundation@landolakes.com
Web Site: www.landolakesinc.com/responsibility

TYPE:
Scholarships. John Brandt Memorial Scholarship Program is a $5,000 scholarship available to graduate students pursuing dairy-related degrees. One or two scholarships are awarded annually to deserving candidates who have demonstrated exceptional commitment and aptitude toward their field of study.

See entry 183 for full listing.

NATIONAL ASSOCIATION OF FARM BROADCASTING FOUNDATION

1100 Platte Falls Road
Platte City, MO 64079
(816) 431-4032
Fax: (816) 431-4087
E-mail: susan@nafb.com
Web Site: www.nafbfoundation.com

TYPE:
Scholarships. Since 1977, the NAFB Foundation has provided financial support and educational opportunities in the form of college scholarships to assist students in pursuit of careers in agricultural communications. Currently the NAFB Foundation offers three annual college scholarships. These scholarships are recognized at the National NAFB Convention.

See entry 1771 for full listing.

NATIONAL CATTLEMAN'S BEEF ASSOCIATION

9110 East Nichols Avenue
Suite 300
Centennial, CO 80112-3450
(303) 694-0305
Fax: (303) 694-2851
E-mail: beefresearch@beef.org
Web Site: www.ncba.org
www.beefresearch.org

TYPE:
Grants-in-aid; Research grants; Research contracts. Research contracts and grants-in-aid for experimental projects in the areas of:
(1) beef as part of a balanced diet;
(2) parity studies;
(3) health benefits of beef lipids and;
(4) contribution of beef nutrients to total diet.

Proposals solicited via specific RFPs (request for proposals).

See entry 2459 for full listing.

NATIONAL DAIRY SHRINE [1947]

P.O. Box 68
Fort Atkinson, WI 53538
(920) 542-1003
E-mail: info@dairyshrine.org
Web Site: www.dairyshrine.org

FOUNDED: 1949

AREAS OF INTEREST:
Dairy production, research, milk products, milk marketing, genetics and education.

NAME(S) OF PROGRAMS:
- **National Dairy Shrine Student Recognition Program**
- **NDS/DMI Education and Communication Scholarship**
- **NDS/DMI Milk Marketing Scholarships**
- **NDS/Iager Scholarship**
- **NDS/Kildee Scholarships**
- **NDS/Lancaster Sophomore Scholarship**
- **NDS/Maurice E. Core Scholarship**
- **NDS/McCullough Scholarships**
- **NDS/Sowerby Junior Merit Scholarship**

TYPE:
Project/program grants; Scholarships. Awards made annually to students interested in careers in the dairy industry. Majors can include dairy science, animal science, agricultural economics, agricultural communications, agriculture education, agricultural marketing and sales, food and nutrition.

YEAR PROGRAM STARTED: 1951

PURPOSE:
To encourage students to pursue careers in the dairy industry.

LEGAL BASIS:
Nonprofit corporation.

ELIGIBILITY:
National Dairy Shrine Student Recognition Program: Graduating seniors planning a career related to dairy-production agriculture who have demonstrated leadership skills, academic ability and interest in dairy cattle.

NDS/DMI Education and Communication Scholarship: Available to undergraduate students (except previous winners) during his or her sophomore or junior year with an explicit interest in dairy products marketing. The applicants must have at least a cumulative 2.5 grade point average on a 4.0 scale.

NDS/DMI Milk Marketing Scholarships: Available to undergraduate students (except previous winners) during his or her sophomore or junior year with an explicit interest in dairy products marketing. The applicants must have at least a cumulative 2.5 grade point average on a 4.0 scale.

NDS/Iager Scholarship: Open to outstanding second-year college dairy students in a two-year agricultural college.

NDS/Kildee Scholarships: Applicants must have placed in Top 25 at National Intercollegiate or National 4-H Dairy Judging Contests. Platinum winners in the last three National Dairy Challenge Contests may apply for Kildee Graduate Study Scholarships.

NDS/Lancaster Sophomore Merit Scholarship: Applicants must be outstanding sophomore college students at a four-year agricultural college in a dairy related field.

NDS/Maurice E. Core Scholarship: Applicants must be outstanding freshman college students at a four-year agricultural college in a dairy related field.

NDS/McCullough Scholarships: The applicant must be a freshman in college with intent to major in Dairy/Animal Science with a Communications emphasis or Agricultural Journalism with a Dairy/Animal Science emphasis and be a U.S. citizen.

NDS/Sowerby Junior Merit Scholarship: Applicants must be outstanding junior college students at a four-year agricultural college in a dairy related field.

GEOG. RESTRICTIONS: United States.

FINANCIAL DATA:
Amount of support per award: National Dairy Shrine Student Recognition Program: $2,000, $1,500 and $1,000; NDS/DMI Education and Communication Scholarships, NDS/DMI Milk Marketing Scholarships, NDS/Lancaster Sophomore Scholarships and NDS/Sowerby Junior Scholarships: $1,500 and $1,000; NDS/Iager Scholarship, NDS/Maurice E. Core Scholarship and NDS/McCullough Scholarships: $1,000; NDS/Kildee Scholarships: $3,000.

Total amount of support: Over $45,000.

NO. MOST RECENT APPLICANTS: 110.

NO. AWARDS: National Dairy Shrine Student Recognition Program: 7 to 10; NDS/DMI Education and Communication Scholarships, NDS/DMI Milk Marketing Scholarships, NDS/Lancaster Sophomore Scholarships and NDS/Sowerby Junior Scholarships: 3 or 7 awards of $1,000 and 1 award of $1,500; NDS/Iager Scholarship: 2 or more; NDS/Kildee and NDS/McCullough Scholarships: 2; NDS/Maurice E. Core Scholarship: 2 to 5.

APPLICATION INFO:
All NDS scholarships and awards require the submission of a completed application form with additional requirements for some scholarships. Forms are available at the web site above. All requirements for the scholarship application and submission deadlines must be followed.

Duration: One year.

Deadline: Applications accepted March 1 to April 15 (postmarked). Announcements by July 1.

EXECUTIVE DIRECTOR:
Mike Opperman

ADDRESS INQUIRIES TO:
Mike Opperman, Executive Director
(See address above.)

*SPECIAL STIPULATIONS:
The second half of each scholarship will be awarded after successful completion of next year. Recipients will be asked to submit their most recent grade transcript and proof of enrollment in the first term of the following year.

NATIONAL FARMER'S ORGANIZATION [1948]
528 Billy Sunday Road
Suite 100
Ames, IA 50010
(515) 292-2000
Fax: (866) 629-4853
E-mail: nfo@nfo.org
Web Site: www.nfo.org

AREAS OF INTEREST:
Agricultural careers.

NAME(S) OF PROGRAMS:
● **Farm Kids for College Scholarships**

TYPE:
Scholarships.

PURPOSE:
To assist students planning careers in agriculture and farming.

ELIGIBILITY:
Must be a high school senior that will major in an agricultural field at an accredited college or university.

GEOG. RESTRICTIONS: United States.

FINANCIAL DATA:
Amount of support per award: $1,000.
Total amount of support: $3,000.

NO. AWARDS: 3.

APPLICATION INFO:
Application information is available on the web site.
Duration: One year.
Deadline: Late February to early March.

ADDRESS INQUIRIES TO:
Helene Bergren
National Scholarship Coordinator
(See address above.)

NORTHEAST AGRICULTURAL EDUCATION FOUNDATION [1949]
220 South Warren Street
9th Floor
Syracuse, NY 13202
(315) 671-0588
Fax: (315) 671-0589
E-mail: info@northeastagriculture.org
Web Site: www.northeastagriculture.org

FOUNDED: 1966

AREAS OF INTEREST:
Agriculture, civic and community.

TYPE:
Project/program grants.

PURPOSE:
To support nonprofit organizations dedicated to serving the interests of farmers and rural communities in the Northeast.

LEGAL BASIS:
Private foundation.

ELIGIBILITY:
Grants are made to nonprofit organizations that have tax-exempt status under Section 501(c)(3) of the Internal Revenue Code. No grants are made to individuals.

GEOG. RESTRICTIONS: Primarily northeastern United States.

FINANCIAL DATA:
Amount of support per award: $1,000 to $10,000.
Total amount of support: Varies.

NO. AWARDS: 25 to 30 annually.

APPLICATION INFO:
Applicants to the Foundation should include the following materials in their submissions: (1) Grant Summary Sheet, which can be downloaded with the Grant Guidelines (PDF); (2) a letter, no longer than two pages, describing the organization, the proposed program or activity, the funding amount requested, and an evaluation methodology; (3) most recent audited annual financial report; (4) current operating budget summary, including fund-raising goals and a current donor list; (5) detailed budget summary for the proposed project or program, indicating what portion would be funded by the grant request; (6) current Board of Directors roster, including their affiliations; (7) copy of the Section 501(c)(3) letter from the IRS; (8) a statement of affiliation with the United Way or other federated fund-raising campaigns and; (9) additional information about the organization and/or project.
Duration: Varies.
Deadline: May 1.

PUBLICATIONS:
Background and application guidelines; application requirements; grant request summary.

ADDRESS INQUIRIES TO:
Craig Buckhout, Administrator
(See address above.)

*SPECIAL STIPULATIONS:
The Foundation does not fund recurring operating costs unless it is for programmatic start-up.

NORTHEASTERN LOGGERS' ASSOCIATION, INC. [1950]
3311 State Route 28
Old Forge, NY 13420-0069
(315) 369-3078
Fax: (315) 369-3736
E-mail: mona@northernlogger.com
Web Site: northernlogger.com

FOUNDED: 1952

AREAS OF INTEREST:
Forestry, wood science and technology.

NAME(S) OF PROGRAMS:
● **NELA Annual Scholarship Contest**

TYPE:
Scholarships. Essay scholarship contest.

YEAR PROGRAM STARTED: 1975

PURPOSE:
To provide support for students and employees of members.

LEGAL BASIS:
501(c)(6) giving program.

ELIGIBILITY:
Scholarships are available to the immediate families of individual members, or the immediate families of employees of Industrial and Associate Members of the Northeastern Loggers' Association. Applicants must be bound for or engaged in post-high school education and must be either seniors in high school graduating in the current year, students in two-year Associate's degree or technical school programs or juniors/seniors in four-year Bachelor's degree programs.

GEOG. RESTRICTIONS: United States.

FINANCIAL DATA:
Amount of support per award: $500 to
$1,000.
Total amount of support: $6,000 for the year
2016-17.

NO. MOST RECENT APPLICANTS: 17.

NO. AWARDS: Up to 8 annually.

APPLICATION INFO:
Applicants must prepare a 1,000-word essay,
a captioned photo-essay, a seven-minute
audio essay, or a seven-minute video essay
presentation on the topic: "Why the Forest
Products Industry is Important To Us All."
Submit with completed application form and
grade transcript.
Duration: One year.
Deadline: March 31. Notification in May.

ADDRESS INQUIRIES TO:
Mona Lincoln, Bookkeeper
(See address and e-mail above.)

RURAL HOUSING
SERVICE   [1951]

1400 Independence Avenue, S.W.
Room 5014, Stop 0701
Washington, DC 20250-0701
(202) 692-0268
Web Site: www.rd.usda.gov

FOUNDED: 1949

AREAS OF INTEREST:
Rural development.

NAME(S) OF PROGRAMS:
• **Rural Housing Grants (Section 504)**

TYPE:
Grants-in-aid; Project/program grants. Grants
to assist elderly, very low-income
owner-occupants in rural areas to repair or
improve their dwellings to make such
dwellings safe and sanitary and remove
hazards.

RHS is the credit agency for rural
development in USDA. RHS has offices at
the state, district and county levels which
serve every county or parish in the 50 states,
plus the western Pacific areas, Guam, Puerto
Rico and the Virgin Islands.

YEAR PROGRAM STARTED: 1961

PURPOSE:
To assist applicants who are unable to repay
a loan amortized at one percent over 20
years.

LEGAL BASIS:
42 U.S.C. 1474.

ELIGIBILITY:
Open to counties and towns or places of
10,000 or less within SMA's and towns or
places of up to 20,000 outside SMA's. Areas
classified as rural prior to October 1, 1990,
with a population in excess of 10,000 are
eligible if the area population is 25,000 or
less.

Applicants must own and occupy houses in
rural areas that need repair to remove health
or safety hazards. Grant recipients must be
62 years of age or older, very low-income
households (under 50% of median income)
owner-occupants, and unable to pay for that
cost of repair with a loan.

FINANCIAL DATA:
Amount of support per award: Lifetime
assistance cannot exceed $7,500.

Total amount of support: $30,000,000 for the
year 2018.

NO. AWARDS: 4,765 for the year 2017.

APPLICATION INFO:
Applicants must apply at the local county
Rural Development (RD) office. Awards are
approved by Community Development
Manager.

TREE RESEARCH &
EDUCATION ENDOWMENT
FUND (TREE FUND)   [1952]

552 South Washington Street
Suite 109
Naperville, IL 60540
(630) 369-8300
Fax: (630) 369-8382
E-mail: treefund@treefund.org
Web Site: www.treefund.org

FOUNDED: 1975

AREAS OF INTEREST:
Research in areas of urban tree care,
preservation and arboriculture education.

NAME(S) OF PROGRAMS:
• **Bonnie Appleton Memorial Scholarship**
• **Barborinas Family Fund Grant**
• **John Duling Grant**
• **Robert Felix Memorial Scholarship**
• **Hyland Johns Grant**
• **Jack Kimmel International Grant**
• **Ohio Chapter ISA Education Grant**
• **Safe Arborist Techniques Fund Grant**
• **Bob Skiera Memorial Fund Building
  Bridges Initiative Grant**
• **Utility Arborist Research Fund Grant
  Program**
• **Fran Ward Women in Arboriculture
  Scholarship**
• **John Wright Memorial Scholarship**

TYPE:
Fellowships; Research grants; Scholarships;
Seed money grants. Grants to further
research relating to arboriculture.
Scholarships are for arboriculture and
horticulture students.

YEAR PROGRAM STARTED: 1976

PURPOSE:
To sustain the world's urban forests by
providing funding for scientific research,
education programs and scholarships related
to arboriculture and urban forestry.

LEGAL BASIS:
Tax-exempt public-supported corporation,
501(c)(3) classification.

ELIGIBILITY:
Qualified persons who have a B.S. degree
and are planning on graduate study for a
Master's or Doctorate in a related field are
eligible to apply for scholarship program.
Scholarships available for undergraduate
study focusing on arboriculture or
horticulture.

GEOG. RESTRICTIONS: Scholarships: United
States.

FINANCIAL DATA:
Institutional overhead costs are capped at
10% of total grant value.
Amount of support per award: Appleton,
Felix, Ward and Wright Scholarships: $5,000;
Barborinas Family Fund Grant and Jack
Kimmel International Grant: Up to $10,000;
John Duling and Hyland Johns Grant: Up to
$25,000; Ohio Chapter ISA Education Grant:
Up to $5,000; Safe Arborist Techniques Fund

Grant: Up to $15,000; Bob Skiera Memorial
Fund Grant: Up to $30,000; Utility Arborist
Research Fund Grant: Up to $50,000.
Matching fund requirements: 10% match or
in-kind.

NO. MOST RECENT APPLICANTS: Varies.

NO. AWARDS: Varies.

APPLICATION INFO:
Applications are to be completed online.
Before applying for a grant, carefully read
the Grant Guidelines. Applications that do
not contain all the requested information may
be denied.
Duration: Ohio Education Grants: One year.
All other grants: Multiyear. Scholarships:
Two years.
Deadline: Barborinas, John Duling, Jack
Kimmel, Safe Arborist Techniques Fund, Bob
Skiera and Utility Arborist Research Grants:
October 1; Hyland Johns Grant and Ohio
Education Grant: March 15; Scholarships:
March 15.

PUBLICATIONS:
Application guidelines.

IRS I.D.: 37-1018692

STAFF:
J. Eric Smith, President and Chief Executive
Officer
Monika Otting, Business Relations Manager
Teresa Recchia, Communications Manager
Maggie Harthoorn, Community Engagement
Manager
Barbara Duke, Grants and Operations
Manager

ADDRESS INQUIRIES TO:
Barbara Duke, Grants and
Operations Manager
E-mail: bduke@treefund.org

*SPECIAL STIPULATIONS:
No part of grant can be used for overhead
expenses.

U.S. DEPARTMENT OF
AGRICULTURE

1400 Independence Avenue, S.W.
Stop 0513
Washington, DC 20250-0510
(202) 720-6221
Fax: (202) 720-4619
E-mail: shanita.landon@usda.gov
Web Site: www.fsa.usda.gov

TYPE:
Grants-in-aid. Cost-share assistance with
agricultural producers to rehabilitate
agricultural lands damaged by natural
disasters. Assistance may also be provided
for carrying out emergency water
conservation measures during periods of
severe drought.

See entry 2015 for full listing.

U.S.-ISRAEL BINATIONAL
AGRICULTURE RESEARCH AND
DEVELOPMENT FUND
(BARD)   [1953]

P.O. Box 15159
Rishon LeZion 7505101 Israel
(972) 3-968-3834
(972) 3-968-3980
Fax: (972) 3-966-2506
E-mail: nitsan@bard-isus.com
Web Site: www.bard-isus.com

FOUNDED: 1977

AREAS OF INTEREST:
Agriculture.

NAME(S) OF PROGRAMS:
- **Graduate Student Fellowship Program**
- **Senior Research Fellowship Program**
- **Vaadia-BARD Postdoctoral Fellowship Program**

TYPE:
Fellowships; Research grants; Visiting scholars.

YEAR PROGRAM STARTED: 1977

PURPOSE:
To promote cooperative agriculture research between the U.S. and Israel; to provide BARD with input into new research areas; to enhance scientific competence in these areas.

LEGAL BASIS:
Nonprofit organization. Governmental Associations in U.S. and Israel.

ELIGIBILITY:
Citizens of the U.S. or Israel who are established research scientists, Ph.D. students and young scientists from American or Israeli nonprofit research institutions, universities, or federal or state agencies are eligible.

GEOG. RESTRICTIONS: United States and Israel.

FINANCIAL DATA:
Amount of support per award: Graduate Student Fellowship: $1,500 per month, plus $2,000 to cover travel costs. Postdoctoral Fellowship: $40,000, plus $9,000 for fellows with dependents. Research Grant: Approximately $310,000 over three years. Senior Research Fellowship: $3,000 per month, plus one-time allocation of $2,000 for travel.
Total amount of support: $7,000,000 for the year 2019.

NO. MOST RECENT APPLICANTS: 100.

NO. AWARDS: 37 for the year 2019.

APPLICATION INFO:
Guidelines and application forms are available online.
Duration: Graduate Student Fellowship: Two to six months. Postdoctoral Fellowship: One year; second year possible with agreement from mentor and shared on a matching basis between BARD and host lab. Research awards: Three years. Senior Research Fellowship: Two to 12 months.
Deadline: Research awards: Mid-September. Postdoctoral Fellowship, Senior Fellowship Program, and Graduate Student Fellowship Program: Mid-January.

PUBLICATIONS:
Application guidelines.

OFFICERS:
Yoram Kapulnik, Executive Director
Miriam Green, Controller

THE UNIVERSITY OF SYDNEY [1954]
Scholarships Office
Level 4, Jane Foss Russell Building G02
The University of Sydney N.S.W. 2006
Australia
61 (02) 8627 1444
E-mail: scholarships.officer@sydney.edu.au
Web Site: www.sydney.edu.au/scholarships

FOUNDED: 1850

AREAS OF INTEREST:
Veterinary science.

NAME(S) OF PROGRAMS:
- **F.H. Loxton Postgraduate Studentships**

TYPE:
Scholarships. Awarded for research leading to a higher degree. Tenable at the University of Sydney.

PURPOSE:
To enable a male graduate of any university to engage in postgraduate research at the University of Sydney, within the Faculty of Veterinary Science.

LEGAL BASIS:
University.

ELIGIBILITY:
Open only to male graduates of any university enrolled in a higher degree by research in the Faculty of Veterinary Science.

FINANCIAL DATA:
Award does not cover tuition fees payable by international students. Relocation allowance within Australia and thesis allowance available.
Amount of support per award: $35,000 AUD per annum for the year 2020.

NO. AWARDS: Offered as vacancies occur. Awarded annually depending on the availability of funds in the area of Agriculture and Environment.

APPLICATION INFO:
Particulars are available from the Faculty of Veterinary Science, The University of Sydney.
Duration: Master's research degree: Two years; Ph.D. degree: Three years.
Deadline: Varies.

ADDRESS INQUIRIES TO:
The Faculty of Veterinary Science
The University of Sydney
N.S.W. 2006 Australia
E-mail: vetsci.education@sydney.edu.au

USDA - RURAL UTILITIES SERVICE [1955]
1400 Independence Avenue, S.W.
Stop 1548, Room 5143
Washington, DC 20250
(202) 720-0986
Web Site: www.rd.usda.gov

FOUNDED: 1935

AREAS OF INTEREST:
Rural areas and towns that have a population of up to 10,000.

NAME(S) OF PROGRAMS:
- **Water and Waste Disposal Systems for Rural Communities**

TYPE:
Capital grants; Development grants; Project/program grants. Loans. Provides funding for clean and reliable drinking water systems, sanitary sewage disposal, sanitary solid waste disposal, and storm water drainage to households and businesses in eligible rural areas.

YEAR PROGRAM STARTED: 1965

PURPOSE:
To provide financial assistance for water and waste disposal facilities in rural areas and towns.

LEGAL BASIS:
Government agency.

ELIGIBILITY:
Only rural areas and cities and towns with populations under 10,000 are eligible.

Applicants must:
(1) be a public entity, nonprofit corporation or Indian tribe;
(2) be unable to obtain needed funds from other sources at reasonable rates and terms;
(3) have legal capacity and;
(4) have adequate security for loans.

FINANCIAL DATA:
Amount of support per award: Varies.

CO-OP FUNDING PROGRAMS: Can cooperate with any other federal, state, local or private credit source.

APPLICATION INFO:
Applications must be filed electronically through RD Apply.
Deadline: Varies.

ADDRESS INQUIRIES TO:
Edna Primrose
Assistant Administrator
Water and Environmental Programs
(See address above.)

WOMAN'S NATIONAL FARM & GARDEN ASSOCIATION, INC. [1956]
2729 Red Fox Trail
Troy, MI 48098
E-mail: info@wnfga.org
Web Site: www.wnfga.org

FOUNDED: 1914

AREAS OF INTEREST:
Agriculture, horticulture, and related fields.

NAME(S) OF PROGRAMS:
- **Sarah Bradley Tyson Memorial Fellowship**

TYPE:
Fellowships; Internships; Scholarships. Awards for advanced study in the fields of agriculture, horticulture and allied subjects.

YEAR PROGRAM STARTED: 1928

PURPOSE:
To encourage better living around the world.

ELIGIBILITY:
Open to properly qualified young women (now including men) who have proven their ability by several years of experience. Awards have been made in recognition of leadership in cooperative extension work and initiative in scientific research.

The Fellowship is to be used for advanced study (Master's or Doctorate) at an educational institution of recognized standing within the U.S. It is to be chosen by the candidate and with the approval of the Fellowship Committee.

FINANCIAL DATA:
Amount of support per award: $1,000 to $3,000.

APPLICATION INFO:
There are no application forms. The e-mail letter of application should contain:
(1) an account of the applicant's educational training;
(2) a statement, in full, of the object in view and the plan of study;
(3) a certificate (transcript) from the registrar of the school, college or university awarding the degree or degrees received by the applicant;
(4) testimonials as to character, ability, personality and scholarship and;
(5) theses, papers or reports of investigations,

published or unpublished, if available and; confidential letters sent to the Committee are retained.

Duration: One year.

Deadline: Applications and recommendations for the Fellowship must be received not later than March 15 of the year to be awarded.

IRS I.D.: 52-6073829

OFFICERS:
Rita Urbanski, President
Mary Pat Ford, President Elect
Mary Schwark, Vice President
Lenore Treba, A and O Treasurer
Kathy Beveridge, E and C Treasurer
Audrey Ehrler, Corresponding Secretary
Fran Ralstrom, Recording Secretary
Molly Hammerle, Advisor

ADDRESS INQUIRIES TO:
Cindy Nuss, Chairman
Fellowship Committee
Woman's National Farm &
Garden Association, Inc.
3274 Susquehanna Road
Dresher, PA 19025
Tel: (215) 576-6524
E-mail: nussci56@gmail.com

*SPECIAL STIPULATIONS:
The acceptance of the Fellowship implies the obligation on the part of the student to devote herself or himself unreservedly to study or research as outlined in her or his application, and to submit any proposed change in her or his plan to the Chairman for approval.

Biology

THE ACADEMY OF NATURAL SCIENCES OF PHILADELPHIA [1957]

1900 Benjamin Franklin Parkway
Philadelphia, PA 19103-1195
(215) 299-1065
Fax: (215) 299-1079
E-mail: kepics@ansp.org
Web Site: ansp.org/research/fellowships-endowments/jessup-mchenry

FOUNDED: 1812

AREAS OF INTEREST:
Research, exhibition and education in natural sciences.

NAME(S) OF PROGRAMS:
• Jessup Fellowship
• McHenry Fellowship

TYPE:
Fellowships. The Jessup Fellowship is for research support in any specialty in which the curatorial staff of the Academy have expertise. The McHenry Fellowship is for botanical research support.

PURPOSE:
To promote research in the natural sciences.

ELIGIBILITY:
Jessup funds are awarded competitively to students wishing to conduct studies at the postgraduate, doctoral and postdoctoral levels under the supervision or sponsorship of a member of the curatorial staff of the Academy. The Fellowships are not available for undergraduate study. These Fellowships are restricted to those who wish to conduct

their study at the Academy and are intended to assist predoctoral and postdoctoral students within several years of receiving their Ph.Ds.

FINANCIAL DATA:
Costs for round-trip travel, lodging, scientific supplies, and equipment are negotiable and should be included in the application materials.

APPLICATION INFO:
Applicant is responsible to submit his or her application in time and to be sure that the three letters of recommendation also reach the Fund Chairman in time. One of these letters of recommendation must be from the Academy curator overseeing or sponsoring the student.

Duration: Two to 16 weeks.

Deadline: Applications for grants will be considered in March and October of each year. Applicants wishing to do their research between April 1 and October 31 should apply by March 1; those wishing to work between November 1 and March 31 should apply by October 1.

ADDRESS INQUIRIES TO:
Kristen Kepics, Department Administrator
(See e-mail address above.)

*SPECIAL STIPULATIONS:
Fellowship awardees are expected to give a seminar after their arrival and are encouraged to publish at least some of their work accomplished at the Academy.

AMERICAN ASSOCIATION OF ZOO KEEPERS [1958]

8476 East Speedway
Suite 204
Tucson, AZ 85710-1728
(520) 298-9688
Fax: (520) 298-9688
E-mail: ed.hansen@aazk.org
Web Site: www.aazk.org

FOUNDED: 1968

AREAS OF INTEREST:
Animal care and the promotion of animal keeping as a profession.

NAME(S) OF PROGRAMS:
• **Bowling for Rhinos Conservation Resource Grant (BFR CRG)**
• **Conservation, Preservation and Restoration (CPR) Grant**
• **Latin American Professional AAZK Travel Grant**
• **Professional Development Grants**
• **Research Grant**
• **Trees for You and Me (TFYM) Reforestation Grant**

TYPE:
Challenge/matching grants; Conferences/seminars; Grants-in-aid; Research grants; Scholarships; Training grants; Travel grants. Grants in the area of zoology, with emphasis on contributions to improving animal management.

YEAR PROGRAM STARTED: 1980

PURPOSE:
To provide funds for original keeper-initiated research of behavioral and/or biomedical topics and general zoological park management principles.

LEGAL BASIS:
Nonprofit corporation.

ELIGIBILITY:
Candidates must be full-time, permanent keepers in the zoo and aquarium profession and must be AAZK professional members in good standing.

GEOG. RESTRICTIONS: United States and Canada.

FINANCIAL DATA:
Amount of support per award: BFR CRG Grant: $12,000; CPR Grant and Research Grant: Up to $1,000; Latin American Professional AAZK Travel Grant: $2,000; Professional Development Grants: Maximum $2,500; TFYM Reforestation Grant: Up to $20,000.

Total amount of support: Approximately $40,000.

NO. MOST RECENT APPLICANTS: 20.

NO. AWARDS: Professional Development Grants: 4; All others: Varies.

APPLICATION INFO:
Applications consist of an application form, brief research proposal and resume. Application materials and further information are available from the Committee chairperson or can be downloaded from the web site.

Duration: CPR Grant and Research Grant: One year. One-year extension is possible with status report and Committee approval.

Deadline: March 1. Successful applicants are notified within three months of the deadline.

PUBLICATIONS:
Application guidelines.

IRS I.D.: 23-7274856

BOARD OF DIRECTORS:
Bethany Bingham, President
Mary Ann Cisneros, Vice President
Paul Brandenburger
Hardy Kern
Nicole Pepo
Bill Steele
Ellen Vossekuil

ADDRESS INQUIRIES TO:
Ed Hansen, Chief Executive Officer/Chief Financial Officer
(See address above.)

*SPECIAL STIPULATIONS:
Noninvasive research results must be presented to the AAZK membership by either an oral presentation at an AAZK conference, a paper published in *Animal Keepers' Forum* or a research summary report published in *Animal Keepers' Forum*.

THE AMERICAN MUSEUM OF NATURAL HISTORY [1959]

Richard Gilder Graduate School
Central Park West at 79th Street
New York, NY 10024-5192
(212) 769-5017
Fax: (212) 769-5257
E-mail: assistantdirector-rggs@amnh.org
fellowships-rggs@amnh.org
Web Site: www.amnh.org/our-research/richard-gilder-graduate-school

FOUNDED: 1869

AREAS OF INTEREST:
Education of Ph.D. candidates in scientific disciplines.

NAME(S) OF PROGRAMS:
• **Graduate Student Fellowship Program**

TYPE:

Fellowships. An educational partnership with selected universities dedicated to the training of Ph.D. candidates. The university exercises educational jurisdiction over the program and awards the degree. The museum curator serves as a graduate advisor, co-major professor, or major professor. The student benefits by having the staff and facilities of both the university and the museum in order to carry on his or her training and research programs. Joint programs are with the following universities:
(1) Columbia University in astronomy, earth and planetary sciences, ecology, evolutionary and environmental biology;
(2) Cornell University in entomology;
(3) The Graduate Center of the City University of New York in earth and planetary sciences and evolutionary biology;
(4) New York University in molecular biology and;
(5) Stony Brook University in astronomy and astrophysics.

PURPOSE:

To encourage bright and promising students to enter the fields of science in which the museum participates.

ELIGIBILITY:

Applicants must have a Bachelor's degree and be able to fulfill university admission requirements, including TOEFL and Graduate Record Examinations. The program is not open to candidates for the Master's degree.

FINANCIAL DATA:

Fellowships cover stipend, tuition and health insurance.

Amount of support per award: Varies.

Total amount of support: Varies.

NO. MOST RECENT APPLICANTS: 40.

NO. AWARDS: 2.

APPLICATION INFO:

All applications are to be completed online only. All materials, including reference letters, must be submitted electronically, using the forms provided on the web site. Complete instructions are available on the web site.

Duration: One year. Renewable annually for up to four years.

Deadline: December 15.

PUBLICATIONS:

Program announcement; application.

ADDRESS INQUIRIES TO:

Maria Rios, Assistant Director
Fellowships and Student Affairs
(See address above.)

AMERICAN ORCHID
SOCIETY   [1960]

Fairchild Tropical Botanic Garden
10901 Old Cutler Road
Coral Gables, FL 33156
(305) 740-2010
E-mail: theaos@aos.org
Web Site: www.aos.org

FOUNDED: 1921

AREAS OF INTEREST:
Orchid research.

NAME(S) OF PROGRAMS:
- **American Orchid Society Grants for Orchid Research**

TYPE:

Awards/prizes; Block grants; Capital grants; Development grants; Grants-in-aid; Research grants. Grants and research contracts for experimental projects and applied and fundamental research pertaining to orchids and grants-in-aid to graduate students engaged in research on orchids. Support is given in such areas relevant to orchids as biological research (including taxonomy, anatomy, genetics, physiology development, tissue culture and pathology), conservation and education.

YEAR PROGRAM STARTED: 1966

PURPOSE:

To advance the scientific study of orchids in every aspect; to assist in the publication of scholarly and popular scientific literature on orchids.

LEGAL BASIS:
Corporation.

ELIGIBILITY:

Qualified personnel associated with accredited institutions or appropriate institutes or organizations may apply for grants. Support is not restricted to individuals or institutions within the U.S. The salaries of established scientists is not supported. Qualified graduate students with appropriate interests may apply for grants in support of their research.

In general, travel to collect orchids is not supported. Other types of travel may be supported on a case-by-case basis. Projects that involve commercial sales of plants are generally not supported.

FINANCIAL DATA:

Amount of support per award: Generally $1,000 to $10,000.

Total amount of support: $20,000 budgeted.

NO. MOST RECENT APPLICANTS: 21 for the year 2018.

NO. AWARDS: 4 for the year 2018.

APPLICATION INFO:

Detailed instructions are available on the Society's web site.

Duration: Although the duration of each grant depends upon the particular project, most grants are awarded for one year with the possibility of renewal.

Deadline: March 1.

PUBLICATIONS:
Application guidelines.

ADDRESS INQUIRIES TO:
Ron McHatton, Chief Education and Science Officer
(See address above.)

*SPECIAL STIPULATIONS:
Research application must involve orchids.

AMERICAN SOCIETY FOR
MICROBIOLOGY   [1961]

Education Department
1752 N Street, N.W.
Washington, DC 20036
(202) 942-9282
Fax: (202) 942-9329
E-mail: fellowships@asmusa.org
Web Site: www.asm.org

FOUNDED: 1899

AREAS OF INTEREST:
Biological research.

NAME(S) OF PROGRAMS:
- **Research Capstone Fellowship**
- **Undergraduate Research Fellowship**

TYPE:

Fellowships. Research Capstone Fellowship provides funding for professional development and career networking to underrepresented minority students.

Undergraduate Research Fellowships provide undergraduate, community college and post-Baccalaureate students the opportunity to perform summer research with an ASM faculty member, in addition to receiving professional development training at the Microbe Academy for Professional Development (MAPD).

PURPOSE:

To promote study and research in microbiology; to fulfill the later stages of undergraduate professional development for underrepresented minority students completing doctoral degrees in microbiology.

LEGAL BASIS:
Private, nonprofit science organization.

ELIGIBILITY:

Research Capstone Fellowship applicant must meet the following criteria:
(1) be an ASM member;
(2) be a U.S. citizen, permanent resident, or DACA eligible;
(3) be from an underrepresented minority group;
(4) have conducted research in the microbiological sciences;
(5) have submitted an abstract for presentation at ASM Microbe and;
(6) have a research mentor that is an ASM member (does not apply to the community college, undergraduate and post-Baccalaureate track).

To quality for consideration for the Undergraduate Research Fellowship, applicant must:
(1) be an ASM member;
(2) be a U.S. citizen, permanent resident, or DACA eligible;
(3) be erolled as a full-time matriculating undergraduate student during the 2019-20 academic year at an accredited U.S. institution;
(4) be involved in a research project;
(5) have an ASM member at applicant's home institution wiling to serve as a mentor and;
(6) not be receiving other financial support for research during the fellowship.

GEOG. RESTRICTIONS: United States.

FINANCIAL DATA:

Amount of support per award: Research Capstone Fellowship: Up to $2,000 to attend and present at the ASM Microbe Academy for Professional Development and the ASM Microbe Meeting (contingent upon abstract acceptance). Doctoral candidates receive up to $2,000 in additional funding during years two and three of the fellowship to participate in professional development; Undergraduate Research Fellowship: Up to $4,000 stipend and $2,000 in travel funds to attend the MAPD.

Total amount of support: Varies.

APPLICATION INFO:

Applicants must submit:
(1) online application;
(2) letter of recommendation and;
(3) personal statement and research experience.

Undergraduate Research Fellowship applicants must also provide a research project overview.

Duration: Research Capstone Fellowship: Up to three years; Undergraduate Research Fellowship: 10 to 12 weeks.

Deadline: Research Capstone Fellowship: March 15; Undergraduate Research Fellowship: February 15.

PUBLICATIONS:
Application guidelines.

ADDRESS INQUIRIES TO:
See e-mail address above.

AMERICAN SOCIETY FOR MICROBIOLOGY   [1962]
Education Board
1752 N Street, N.W.
Washington, DC 20036
E-mail: education@asmusa.org
Web Site: www.asm.org

FOUNDED: 1899

AREAS OF INTEREST:
Microbiology.

NAME(S) OF PROGRAMS:
● **Career Development Grants for Postdoctoral Women (CDGPW)**

TYPE:
Travel grants. Career Development Grants for Postdoctoral Women are given to support the career development of the candidate by providing funds to travel to a meeting, visit another laboratory, take a course in a geographically distant place, or for other travel to advance the candidate's career. The fields covered by the award are any of those represented by Divisions of the American Society for Microbiology.

PURPOSE:
To support career development of postdoctoral women.

LEGAL BASIS:
Private, nonprofit science organization.

ELIGIBILITY:
Grants will be awarded to enhance the careers of postdoctoral women with outstanding scientific accomplishments and potential for significant research in the area of microbiology. Candidates must:
(1) be a woman scientist;
(2) have a doctoral degree;
(3) have no more than five years of cumulative postdoctoral experience;
(4) perform postdoctoral work in microbiology at an institution in the U.S. and;
(5) be an ASM member.

GEOG. RESTRICTIONS: United States.

FINANCIAL DATA:
Amount of support per award: $1,500.
Total amount of support: Up to $6,000.

NO. AWARDS: Up to 4.

APPLICATION INFO:
Candidates must be nominated. Details are available on the ASM web site.
Duration: Must be used within one year.
Deadline: January 15.

PUBLICATIONS:
Application guidelines.

ADDRESS INQUIRIES TO:
See e-mail address above.

ATLANTIC SALMON FEDERATION   [1963]
P.O. Box 5200
St. Andrews NB E5B 3S8 Canada
(506) 529-1062
Fax: (506) 529-1028
E-mail: emansfield@asf.ca
Web Site: www.asf.ca

FOUNDED: 1948

AREAS OF INTEREST:
Conservation of Atlantic salmon and its habitat through programs in education, research, enhancement, restoration and international cooperation.

NAME(S) OF PROGRAMS:
● **Olin Fellowships**

TYPE:
Awards/prizes; Block grants; Capital grants; Demonstration grants; Fellowships; General operating grants; Grants-in-aid; Internships; Project/program grants; Research grants; Scholarships; Training grants; Travel grants; Visiting scholars; Work-study programs. Fellowships are offered to individuals seeking to improve their knowledge or skills in advanced fields while looking for solutions to current problems in Atlantic salmon biology, management or conservation.

YEAR PROGRAM STARTED: 1971

PURPOSE:
To further salmon conservation.

LEGAL BASIS:
Tax-exempt, nonprofit organization.

ELIGIBILITY:
Applicants must be legal residents of the U.S. or Canada. The Fellowships are tenable at any accredited university or research laboratory or in an active management program and may be applied toward a wide range of endeavors including salmon management, graduate study and research. Applicants need not be enrolled in a degree program.

FINANCIAL DATA:
Amount of support per award: $1,000 to $3,000.
Total amount of support: Varies.

NO. AWARDS: Up to 3.

APPLICATION INFO:
Information and application forms may be obtained from the address above, from Atlantic Salmon Federation, P.O. Box 807, Calais, ME 04619 or from the web site.
Duration: One year. May be renewed.
Deadline: Applications must be received at the St. Andrews office by March 15. Applicants will be advised of awards by May 15.

PUBLICATIONS:
Atlantic Salmon Journal; annual report.

OFFICERS:
Bill Taylor, President
Alan Graham, Q.C., Chairman, ASF (Canada)
John Dillan, Chairman, ASF (U.S.)

ADDRESS INQUIRIES TO:
Ellen Mansfield, Office Manager
Research and Environment
(See address above.)

CALIFORNIA ACADEMY OF SCIENCES   [1964]
55 Music Concourse Drive
San Francisco, CA 94118
(415) 379-8000
E-mail: ssi-bi@calacademy.org
Web Site: www.calacademy.org/scientists
www.calacademy.org/summer-systematics-institute

FOUNDED: 1853

AREAS OF INTEREST:
Biology, anthropology, aquatic biology, botany, entomology, geology, herpetology, ichthyology, invertebrate zoology, mammalogy, ornithology and paleontology.

NAME(S) OF PROGRAMS:
● **Summer Systematics Institute**

TYPE:
Internships. Matches students with Academy scientists to work on specific research projects. May include laboratory and molecular components.

YEAR PROGRAM STARTED: 1995

PURPOSE:
To allow students to gain hands-on experience in the labs and collections archive.

ELIGIBILITY:
Applicants must be undergraduates who are U.S. citizens or alien residents with an excellent academic record and demonstrated participation in a wide range of campus activities.

FINANCIAL DATA:
Travel costs to and from San Francisco will be provided. Housing will be provided in dormitories in San Francisco, with details to be disclosed upon selection of interns.
Amount of support per award: $5,175 stipend for the internship period.
Total amount of support: Varies.

NO. MOST RECENT APPLICANTS: 150.

NO. AWARDS: 7 to 10.

APPLICATION INFO:
Application information is available online.
Duration: Full-time (40 hours per week) for nine weeks (mid-June to mid-August).
Deadline: February.

PUBLICATIONS:
Program announcement.

IRS I.D.: 94-1156258

ADDRESS INQUIRIES TO:
Dr. Lauren Esposito, REU Site Director or Dr. Rebecca Johnson, REU Site Director
(See address above.)

COLUMBIA UNIVERSITY   [1965]
Irving Medical Center, Vagelos College of Physicans and Surgeons
630 West 168th Street, Box 37b
New York, NY 10032
(212) 305-7970
E-mail: horwitzprize@columbia.edu
Web Site: www.cuimc.columbia.edu/research/louisa-gross-horwitz-prize

FOUNDED: 1754

AREAS OF INTEREST:
Biology and biochemistry.

NAME(S) OF PROGRAMS:
● **The Louisa Gross Horwitz Prize**

TYPE:
Awards/prizes. An annual prize designed to honor a major scientific contribution in basic research to the fields of biology or biochemistry.

YEAR PROGRAM STARTED: 1967

PURPOSE:
To honor a scientific investigator, or group of investigators, whose contributions to knowledge in either of these fields are deemed worthy of special recognition.

ELIGIBILITY:
The prize is open to scientists for outstanding basic research in the fields of biology or biochemistry.

NO. AWARDS: 3.

APPLICATION INFO:
Nomination must include the name, title, mailing address and e-mail address of the nominee and nominator, along with the following supporting documents:
(1) curriculum vitae;
(2) biographical sketch;
(3) 500-word research summary;
(4) 500-word research significance and;
(5) key publications list (up to 10).
Deadline: January 31.

ADDRESS INQUIRIES TO:
See e-mail address above.

HUMAN FRONTIER SCIENCE PROGRAM ORGANIZATION [1966]

12 Quai St. Jean
67000 Strasbourg France
(33) 3-88-21-51-26 (Grants)
(33) 3-88-21-51-27 (Fellowships)
Fax: (33) 3-88-32-88-97
E-mail: grant@hfsp.org
fellow@hfsp.org
Web Site: www.hfsp.org

FOUNDED: 1989

AREAS OF INTEREST:
Interdisciplinary research into the complex mechanisms of biological functions.

NAME(S) OF PROGRAMS:
● **Cross-Disciplinary Fellowships**
● **Long-Term Fellowships**
● **Program Grants**
● **Young Investigator Grants**

TYPE:
Fellowships; Project/program grants; Research grants. Long-Term Fellowships are for young scientists within three years of obtaining their Ph.D. who wish to broaden their scientific experience in a foreign laboratory.

Cross-Disciplinary Fellowships are modeled on the Long-Term Fellowships but are specifically for scientists with Ph.Ds. in nonbiological disciplines who seek training in the life sciences.

Program Grants are collaborative research projects for interdisciplinary teams of researchers in different countries at any stage of their career.

Young Investigator Grants are collaborative research projects for interdisciplinary teams of young researchers who are within the first five years of their first independent positions and located in different countries.

YEAR PROGRAM STARTED: 1989

PURPOSE:
To foster international collaboration and postdoctoral training at the frontiers of the life sciences.

LEGAL BASIS:
Not-for-profit association.

ELIGIBILITY:
Scientists from all countries can apply, but with some restrictions. The principal applicant of grants must be from a member country. Fellowship candidates from nonmember countries can only apply to work in a member country.

FINANCIAL DATA:
Amount of support per award: Varies, depending upon the size of the grant team or the host country of the fellowship.

NO. MOST RECENT APPLICANTS:
Cross-Disciplinary Fellowships and Long-Term Fellowships: 661; Young Investigator Grants and Program Grants: 814 letters of intent, 84 full applications.

NO. AWARDS: Cross-Disciplinary Fellowships: 10; Long-Term Fellowships: 79; Program Grants: 25; Young Investigator Grants: 9.

APPLICATION INFO:
Application information is available on the web site.
Duration: Up to three years.

PUBLICATIONS:
Annual report.

ADDRESS INQUIRIES TO:
For fellowships: fellow@hfsp.org
For grants: grant@hfsp.org

INTERNATIONAL CRANE FOUNDATION, INC. [1967]

E-11376 Shady Lane Road
Baraboo, WI 53913
(608) 356-9462
Fax: (608) 356-9465
E-mail: info@savingcranes.org
Web Site: www.savingcranes.org

FOUNDED: 1973

AREAS OF INTEREST:
Aviculture, crane ecology and conservation education.

CONSULTING OR VOLUNTEER SERVICES:
Work with individuals who have specific questions regarding crane propagation, restoration of natural habitats, or conservation education on an informal basis and as the need arises.

TYPE:
Internships. Formal stipended internship programs in the fields of aviculture, crane ecology and conservation education.

YEAR PROGRAM STARTED: 1980

PURPOSE:
To act as the world center for the study and preservation of cranes and their natural habitats.

LEGAL BASIS:
Nonprofit corporation.

ELIGIBILITY:
College sophomores through recent college graduates in biology, zoology, botany or education who have a willingness to work at a variety of tasks and can work in a self-directed manner.

FINANCIAL DATA:
Amount of support per award: $567 stipend per month, plus housing.

NO. AWARDS: 4 for the year 2019.

APPLICATION INFO:
Letter of application indicating interest, relevant coursework and experience, plus three references. An interview will be required, although a phone interview may suffice.
Duration: Six to eight months. Must submit additional application for renewal.

IRS I.D.: 39-1187711

ADDRESS INQUIRIES TO:
See e-mail address above.

LIFE SCIENCES RESEARCH FOUNDATION (LSRF) [1968]

Lewis Thomas Laboratory
Princeton University
Washington Road
Princeton, NJ 08544
E-mail: direnzo@lsrf.org
Web Site: www.lsrf.org

FOUNDED: 1984

AREAS OF INTEREST:
Biological sciences.

NAME(S) OF PROGRAMS:
● **Three-Year Postdoctoral Fellowships**

TYPE:
Fellowships.

YEAR PROGRAM STARTED: 1984

PURPOSE:
To offer research support for aspiring scientists.

LEGAL BASIS:
Private organization.

ELIGIBILITY:
Individuals who have held a Ph.D. or M.D. degree for more than five years at the time of application are not eligible for an LSRF fellowship.

FINANCIAL DATA:
Stipend includes salary, fringe benefits, travel to the host institution and to the annual meeting and research expenses.
Amount of support per award: $62,000 per year.

NO. MOST RECENT APPLICANTS: Over 1,000.

NO. AWARDS: 15 to 25.

APPLICATION INFO:
Applications are to be completed online and must contain all three components: Application Info, Research Proposal, and Letters of Reference and Support.
Duration: Three years.
Deadline: October 1.

ADDRESS INQUIRIES TO:
Susan DiRenzo, Assistant Director
(See address above.)

MARINE BIOLOGICAL LABORATORY [1969]

7 MBL Street
Woods Hole, MA 02543
(508) 289-7173
Fax: (508) 289-7934
E-mail: researchprograms@mbl.edu
Web Site: www.mbl.edu

FOUNDED: 1888

AREAS OF INTEREST:
Cellular and molecular physiology, molecular biology, developmental biology, neurobiology, innate immunity, ecology, parasitology, microbiology, pharmacology, toxicology, cancer biology, regenerative biology, aging, molecular evolution, microbial biology, sensory physiology, aquaculture, metabolic diseases, environmental science, climate change, and plant physiology.

NAME(S) OF PROGRAMS:
- **Marine Biological Laboratory Research Awards**

TYPE:
Research grants.

PURPOSE:
To provide funding to scientists interested in conducting research projects in various scientific areas.

LEGAL BASIS:
Nonprofit organization.

ELIGIBILITY:
Applicants must be independent investigators. Working scientists must be willing to come to the Laboratory for a minimum six-week stay to conduct independent research in areas of interest to the Laboratory. Sabbaticals are encouraged.

FINANCIAL DATA:
Amount of support per award: Varies.
Total amount of support: Varies.
Matching fund requirements: Strongly encouraged from home institution.

CO-OP FUNDING PROGRAMS: APA, ASCB and HHMI.

NO. AWARDS: Varies.

APPLICATION INFO:
Application information is available on the web site.
Duration: Varies.
Deadline: Varies.

IRS I.D.: 04-2104690

ADDRESS INQUIRIES TO:
Diane Cook, Senior Grants and Contracts Administrator
(See address above.)

MICROSCOPY SOCIETY OF AMERICA [1970]
11130 Sunrise Valley Drive
Suite 350
Reston, VA 20191
(703) 234-4115
E-mail: associationmanagement@microscopy.org
Web Site: www.microscopy.org/awards

FOUNDED: 1942

AREAS OF INTEREST:
Microscopy.

NAME(S) OF PROGRAMS:
- **MSA Professional Technical Staff Awards**

TYPE:
Travel grants.

PURPOSE:
To stimulate attendance for those who ordinarily might not participate; to encourage supervisors to support their staff in professional activities.

LEGAL BASIS:
Special interest society.

ELIGIBILITY:
Applicants must be regular, current members of MSA at the time of submission. Awards are based on the quality of the paper submitted for presentation at the meeting. Abstracts will be judged by the MSA Technologist's Forum. The applicant must be the first author of the submitted paper.

Successful applicants must present their papers personally at the meeting in order to receive the award. They are expected to attend and participate in the entire meeting. Former winners will not be eligible for another award.

FINANCIAL DATA:
Amount of support per award: The award consists of complimentary full registration for the Microscopy and Microanalysis meeting including proceedings and the social event ticket. In addition, MSA will reimburse awardees up to $1,000 for travel, lodging and meeting expenses.
Total amount of support: Varies.

NO. AWARDS: Up to 4.

APPLICATION INFO:
Applications shall consist of a copy of the abstract and data form to be sent to the Technologist's Forum Committee and a supporting letter from the applicant's employer, manager or supervisor, attesting to the applicant's status as a full-time, professional staff member.
Duration: One-time award.
Deadline: February 8.

STAFF:
Ashley Carey, Managing Director

ADDRESS INQUIRIES TO:
See e-mail address above.

MUSEUM OF COMPARATIVE ZOOLOGY [1971]
Harvard University
26 Oxford Street
Cambridge, MA 02138
(617) 495-2460
E-mail: grants@oeb.harvard.edu
Web Site: www.mcz.harvard.edu/ernst-mayr-travel-grants

FOUNDED: 1858

AREAS OF INTEREST:
Comparative zoology.

NAME(S) OF PROGRAMS:
- **Ernst Mayr Grants in Animal Systematics**

TYPE:
Awards/prizes; Research grants; Travel grants.

YEAR PROGRAM STARTED: 1984

PURPOSE:
To enable animal systematists to make short visits to museums for research needed to complete taxonomic revisions and monographs; to stimulate taxonomic work on neglected taxa, including those with numerous poorly described species, genera and families known to have many undescribed species in institutional collections, taxa for which it is unknown what proportion of the nominal species are synonyms, and difficult genera without keys.

ELIGIBILITY:
Preference is given to studies that use the Museum of Comparative Zoology collections, although applications to work at other museums also will be considered.

FINANCIAL DATA:
Grants may cover travel, lodging and meals for up to a few months while conducting research at the museums, services purchased from the host institution, research supplies, etc.
Amount of support per award: Up to $1,500. Average grant is $1,000.
Total amount of support: Varies.

NO. AWARDS: Approximately 20.

APPLICATION INFO:
Proposals should consist of an application form which includes a short project description and explicit statement of the goals of the research, itinerary and budget, a curriculum vitae, and three letters of support. All applications should be written in English. Proposals may be submitted through standard mail to the address above or electronically to the e-mail listed above. Submissions through standard mail must include five copies of the proposal materials and must be received by the deadline.
Duration: Must be used within one year.
Deadline: April 1 and October 15. Announcements typically within two months following the application deadline.

STAFF:
Melissa Aja, Museum Projects Coordinator

ADDRESS INQUIRIES TO:
Melissa Aja
Museum Projects Coordinator
(See address and e-mail above.)

*SPECIAL STIPULATIONS:
Each grantee is required to submit a written report summarizing the scientific accomplishments achieved with the award within one month of travel completion.

MYCOLOGICAL SOCIETY OF AMERICA [1972]
2424 American Lane
Madison, WI 53704
(608) 443-2468 ext. 162
(608) 443-2468 ext. 136
Fax: (608) 443-2474
E-mail: msafungi@reesgroupinc.com
Web Site: msafungi.org/msa-awards-chart

FOUNDED: 1932

AREAS OF INTEREST:
The study of fungi.

NAME(S) OF PROGRAMS:
- **Backus Award**
- **Salomon Bartnicki-Garcia Award**
- **Forest Fungal Ecology Awards**
- **International Travel Awards**
- **Martin-Baker Research Awards**
- **Mentor Student Travel Awards**
- **MSA Graduate Fellowship**
- **NAMA Memorial Fellowship**
- **John W. Rippon Research Award**
- **Clark T. Rogerson Research Award**
- **Alexander H. and Helen V. Smith Research Fund**
- **Undergraduate Research Award**

TYPE:
Awards/prizes; Conferences/seminars; Fellowships; Travel grants. Supplementary grant for an outstanding candidate awarded in addition to any fellowship, scholarship or

assistantship support from other sources to further undergraduate and graduate studies in the field of mycology.

LEGAL BASIS:
Nonprofit organization.

ELIGIBILITY:
Applicants must be student members of the Mycological Society of America. In selecting the recipient of the Fellowship, consideration is given to scholastic merit, research ability and promise shown as a future mycologist.

FINANCIAL DATA:
Amount of support per award: Backus and Rogerson Research Awards: $1,000; Bartnicki-Garcia, Rippon Research and Undergraduate Research Awards: $500; Forest Fungal Ecology Awards: $1,250 to $2,500; International Travel Awards: $1,500 to $2,500; Martin Baker Research Award: $3,000; Mentor Student Travel Awards: Varies; MSA Graduate Fellowship and NAMA Memorial Fellowship: $2,000.
Total amount of support: Approximately $15,000 annually.

NO. AWARDS: 71.

APPLICATION INFO:
Application information is available on the web site.
Duration: One year. Nonrenewable.
Deadline: February 15.

PUBLICATIONS:
Mycologia, research journal; *Inoculum*, newsletter.

ADDRESS INQUIRIES TO:
Backus Award, MSA Graduate and NAMA Memorial Fellowships, and Undergraduate Research Award:
Dr. Heather Hallen-Adams, Chairperson Student Awards Committee
E-mail: hhallen-adams2@unl.edu

Bartnicki-Garcia and
Forest Fungal Ecology Awards,
Martin-Baker Research,
John W. Rippon Research,
Clark T. Rogerson Research Awards, and
Smith Research Fund:
Dr. Jolanta Miadlikowska, Chairperson
Research Awards Committee
E-mail: jolantam@duke.edu

International Travel Awards:
Dr. Maria P. Martin-Esteban, Chairperson
International Committee
E-mail: maripaz@rjb.csic.es

Mentor Student Travel Awards:
Dr. Mahajabeen Padamsee, Chairperson
Mentor Travel Awards Committee
E-mail: padamseem@landcareresearch.co.nz

NATIONAL ALOPECIA AREATA FOUNDATION   [1973]
65 Mitchell Boulevard
Suite 200-B
San Rafael, CA 94903
(415) 472-3780
Fax: (415) 480-1800
E-mail: info@naaf.org
abby@naaf.org
Web Site: www.naaf.org

FOUNDED: 1981

AREAS OF INTEREST:
Baldness, hair loss and alopecia areata.

TYPE:
Research grants.

YEAR PROGRAM STARTED: 1985

PURPOSE:
To support research to find an acceptable treatment and studies that will lead to an eventual cure for alopecia areata.

ELIGIBILITY:
Must be an Institute Review Board-approved researcher who has submitted a proposal about alopecia areata or hair biology. No funding for established investigators.

FINANCIAL DATA:
Salaries only fellows, assistants, residents and technicians.
Amount of support per award: $1,000 to $50,000.
Total amount of support: Over $5,700,000 since inception of program.

CO-OP FUNDING PROGRAMS: Joint grants with other organizations.

NO. MOST RECENT APPLICANTS: Varies.

NO. AWARDS: Varies.

APPLICATION INFO:
Contact the Foundation for application procedures.
Duration: One year.

ADDRESS INQUIRIES TO:
Abby Ellison, Director of Research
(See address above.)

NATIONAL SCIENCE FOUNDATION   [1974]
Division of Molecular and Cellular Biosciences
2415 Eisenhower Avenue
Alexandria, VA 22314
(703) 292-8440
Fax: (703) 292-9459
E-mail: bnikolau@nsf.gov
Web Site: www.nsf.gov

FOUNDED: 1950

AREAS OF INTEREST:
Molecular biophysics, cellular dynamics and function, genetic mechanisms, and systems and synthetic biology.

NAME(S) OF PROGRAMS:
● **Division of Molecular and Cellular Biosciences Programs**

TYPE:
Conferences/seminars; Project/program grants; Research grants; Seed money grants. The Division of Molecular and Cellular Biosciences at the National Science Foundation has the following clusters:

Molecular Biophysics, which encourages proposals such as the following areas of research:
(1) general principles of the relationship between structure, dynamics and function of biomolecules and;
(2) fundamental principles governing biomolecular interactions and mechanisms.

Cellular Dynamics and Function, which encourages proposals such as the following areas of research:
(1) predictive understanding of the behavior of living cells through integration of modeling and experimentation;
(2) integrative cellular function across broad spatiotemporal scales, from single molecules to whole cells and;
(3) origin, evolution and function of cells, organelles and microcompartments.

Genetic Mechanisms, which encourages proposals such as the following areas of research:
(1) gene expression, including epigenetics and RNA-mediated regulation;
(2) chromosome dynamics, DNA replication, repair, recombination and inheritance and;
(3) evolution of genes and genomes.

Systems and Synthetic Biology, which encourages proposals such as the following areas of research:
(1) systems-level, theory-driven analysis of regulatory, signaling and metabolic networks;
(2) synthetic biology to address fundamental biological questions including the origin of life, minimal cell, emergent behavior in complex systems, robustness in design and organization and;
(3) tool development to facilitate systems and synthetic biology studies.

YEAR PROGRAM STARTED: 1992

PURPOSE:
To increase our store of knowledge in these fields and enhance our understanding of the scientific aspects of major problems confronting the nation.

LEGAL BASIS:
National Science Foundation Act of 1950, Public Law 81-507, as amended.

ELIGIBILITY:
The principal recipients of scientific research project support are academic institutions and nonprofit research institutions. Grants may also be awarded to other types of institutions and to individuals. In these cases, preliminary inquiry should be made to the cognizant program officer before a proposal is submitted. Support may be provided to projects involving a single scientist or to projects covering the activities of a number of scientists. Awards are made for projects confined to a single disciplinary area and for projects which cross or merge disciplinary interests. Clinically oriented research is not supported.

FINANCIAL DATA:
Amount of support per award: Varies.
Total amount of support: Varies.

APPLICATION INFO:
Application information is available on the web site.
Duration: Varies.
Deadline: Contact Foundation for specific dates.

PUBLICATIONS:
Brochures.

DIRECTORS:
Bassilios Nikolau, Division Director

ADDRESS INQUIRIES TO:
Cognizant Program Officer

NATIONAL SCIENCE FOUNDATION   [1975]
Division of Environmental Biology
2415 Eisenhower Avenue
Alexandria, VA 22314
(703) 292-8480
Fax: (703) 292-9064
E-mail: shampton@nsf.gov
Web Site: www.nsf.gov/bio/deb/about.jsp

FOUNDED: 1950

AREAS OF INTEREST:
Population and community, ecology, ecosystem science, population and systematic biology, biodiversity inventories cluster and evolution processes.

NAME(S) OF PROGRAMS:
- **Division of Environmental Biology**

TYPE:
Conferences/seminars; Research grants; Training grants; Travel grants.

PURPOSE:
To increase our store of knowledge in these fields and enhance our understanding of the scientific aspects of major problems confronting the nation.

LEGAL BASIS:
National Science Foundation Act of 1950, Public Law 81-507, as amended.

ELIGIBILITY:
The principal recipients of scientific research project support are academic institutions and nonprofit research institutions. Grants may also be awarded to other types of institutions and to individuals. In these cases, preliminary inquiry should be made to the cognizant program officer before a proposal is submitted. Support may be provided to projects involving a single scientist or to projects covering the activities of a number of scientists. Awards are made for projects confined to a single disciplinary area and for projects which cross or merge disciplinary interests.

FINANCIAL DATA:
Amount of support per award: $108,000 average.

NO. MOST RECENT APPLICANTS: 2,500.

NO. AWARDS: 500.

APPLICATION INFO:
Application information is available on the web site.
Duration: 12 to 60 months, depending on the scientific merit and requirements of the project.

PUBLICATIONS:
Awards list; program description.

ADDRESS INQUIRIES TO:
Stephanie Hampton, Division Director
(See address above.)

SOCIETY FOR DEVELOPMENTAL BIOLOGY [1976]

6120 Executive Boulevard
Suite 725
Rockville, MD 20852
(301) 634-7815
E-mail: sdb@sdbonline.org
Web Site: www.sdbonline.org

FOUNDED: 1939

AREAS OF INTEREST:
Developmental biology.

NAME(S) OF PROGRAMS:
- **Edwin G. Conklin Medal**
- **Developmental Biology-SDB Lifetime Achievement Award**
- **John Doctor Best Education Award**
- **Viktor Hamburger Outstanding Educator Prize**
- **Elizabeth D. Hay New Investigator Award**
- **SDB Boot Camp for New Faculty**
- **SDB Education Activities Grant**

- **SDB Emerging Models Grant**
- **SDB Innovation Grant**
- **SDB International Scholarships**
- **SDB Meeting Grants**
- **SDB Trainee Science Communication Award**
- **SDB Travel Awards**
- **Teaching and Junior Faculty Travel Grants**

TYPE:
Awards/prizes; Conferences/seminars; Scholarships.

PURPOSE:
To further the study of development in all organisms and at all levels; to represent and promote communication among students of development; to promote the field of developmental biology.

ELIGIBILITY:
Must be a student or investigator studying in the field of developmental biology.

FINANCIAL DATA:
Amount of support per award: John Doctor Best Education Award: $1,000; SDB International Scholarships: $2,000; Student/Postdoctoral Travel Awards: Varies; Teaching and Junior Faculty Travel Grants: $700.
Total amount of support: Varies.

NO. MOST RECENT APPLICANTS: 114 for Student/Postdoctoral Travel Awards.

NO. AWARDS: 86 Student/Postdoctoral Travel Awards.

APPLICATION INFO:
Nomination instructions and application guidelines may be obtained from the Society's web site.
Duration: One-time award. Reapplication possible for grants and scholarships.
Deadline: Varies.

ADDRESS INQUIRIES TO:
Ida Chow, Executive Director
(See address above.)

SOCIETY FOR THE STUDY OF AMPHIBIANS AND REPTILES

Department of Biology
Carroll University
Waukesha, WI 53186
(262) 951-3295
E-mail: rbrenes@carrollu.edu
Web Site: www.ssarherps.org

TYPE:
Awards/prizes; Research grants. Awards are given in six categories: Conservation of Amphibians and/or Reptiles, Field Research, Laboratory Research, Herpetological Education, Travel and International Research.

See entry 1858 for full listing.

THE UNIVERSITY OF CALGARY

Faculty of Graduate Studies
Earth Sciences Building, Room 1010
2500 University Drive, N.W.
Calgary AB T2N 1N4 Canada
(403) 220-4938
Fax: (403) 289-7635
E-mail: gsaward@ucalgary.ca
Web Site: grad.ucalgary.ca/awards

TYPE:
Awards/prizes; Scholarships. Award for study in the fields of cellular, molecular, microbial

or biochemical biology. Tenable at The University of Calgary, Department of Biological Sciences.

See entry 1618 for full listing.

THE WETLANDS INSTITUTE [1977]

1075 Stone Harbor Boulevard
Stone Harbor, NJ 08247-1424
(609) 368-1211
Fax: (609) 368-3871
E-mail: research@wetlandsinstitute.org
Web Site: www.wetlandsinstitute.org

FOUNDED: 1969

AREAS OF INTEREST:
Environmental education and conservation research.

NAME(S) OF PROGRAMS:
- **Coastal Conservation Research Program**
- **Environmental Education Internship**

TYPE:
Internships. Coastal Conservation Research Program offers 10-week summer internships for field research on mid-Atlantic coastal organisms and environments at the Wetlands Institute.

Environmental Education Internships are for undergraduate students with an interest in environmental or outdoor education and/or classroom science education.

YEAR PROGRAM STARTED: 1969

PURPOSE:
To involve undergraduate students in a wide variety of research projects pertaining to the environment.

LEGAL BASIS:
Nonprofit organization that conducts research and education.

ELIGIBILITY:
Coastal Conservation Research Program applicants should be completing their sophomore, junior or senior year at a college or university and be interested in biological research as a career.

Environmental Education Internship applicants must have completed at least two years of college.

A science or education major is desired, but not required.

GEOG. RESTRICTIONS: United States.

FINANCIAL DATA:
Amount of support per award: Varies with project.
Total amount of support: Varies.

NO. MOST RECENT APPLICANTS: Over 100.

NO. AWARDS: 10.

APPLICATION INFO:
Contact the Institute for guidelines.
Duration: Late May to early August.
Deadline: March 1.

IRS I.D.: 23-7046783

ADDRESS INQUIRIES TO:
Coastal Conservation Research Program
E-mail: research@wetlandsinstitute.org

Environmental Education Internship
E-mail: education@wetlandsinstitute.org

WHITEHALL FOUNDATION, INC. [1978]

125 Worth Avenue
Suite 220
Palm Beach, FL 33480
(561) 655-4474
Fax: (561) 655-1296
E-mail: email@whitehall.org
Web Site: www.whitehall.org

FOUNDED: 1937

AREAS OF INTEREST:
Exclusive focus on assisting basic research in vertebrate (excluding clinical) and invertebrate neurobiology in the U.S.

TYPE:
Grants-in-aid; Research grants. Grants are available to established scientists of all ages working at accredited institutions in the U.S.

YEAR PROGRAM STARTED: 1937

PURPOSE:
To assist scholarly research in the life sciences; to assist those dynamic areas of basic biological research that are not heavily supported by federal agencies or other foundations with specialized missions.

LEGAL BASIS:
Not-for-profit corporation.

ELIGIBILITY:
Applications will be judged on the scientific merit and innovative aspects of the proposal, as well as on past performance and evidence of the applicant's continued productivity.

The Foundation does not award funds to investigators who have substantial existing or potential support (even if it is for an unrelated purpose), and applications may be held in abeyance until the results of other funding decisions are determined. In general, the Foundation currently defines "substantial" as approximately $200,000 per year (including both direct and indirect expense but excluding the principal investigator's salary). The principal investigator must hold no less than the position of assistant professor, or the equivalent, in order to make application.

GEOG. RESTRICTIONS: United States.

FINANCIAL DATA:
Amount of support per award: Research Grants: Up to $75,000 per year; Grants-in-aid: Up to $30,000.

APPLICATION INFO:
Application information is available on the Foundation web site.
Duration: Grants-in-aid: One year. Research Grants: Up to three years; a renewal grant with a maximum of two years is possible, but it will be awarded on a competitive basis.
Deadline: Dates are posted on the Foundation web site.

IRS I.D.: 13-5637595

ADDRESS INQUIRIES TO:
See e-mail address above.

*PLEASE NOTE:
The Foundation encourages the use of electronic mail. All correspondence and reports should be sent to the e-mail address above. The Letter of Intent must be submitted in hard copy on institutional letterhead.

THE WILEY FOUNDATION, INC.

111 River Street
Hoboken, NJ 07030-5774
(201) 748-6000
E-mail: wileyfoundation@wiley.com
Web Site: www.wileyfoundation.org

TYPE:
Awards/prizes. The annual Wiley Prize in Biomedical Sciences has recognized breakthrough research in pure or applied life science research.
See entry 1929 for full listing.

WILSON ORNITHOLOGICAL SOCIETY [1979]

Museum of Zoology
University of Michigan
3600 Varsity Drive
Ann Arbor, MI 48108
(734) 764-0457
E-mail: wos@salve.edu
Web Site: wilsonsociety.org/awards

FOUNDED: 1888

AREAS OF INTEREST:
Ornithology.

NAME(S) OF PROGRAMS:
- **Louis Agassiz Fuertes Grant**
- **George A. Hall/Harold F. Mayfield Grant**
- **Research Grants**
- **Paul A. Stewart Grants**
- **Student Travel Awards**
- **Alexander Wilson Prize**

TYPE:
Grants-in-aid; Research grants. Fuertes, Hall/Mayfield and Stewart Grants provide for the promotion and encouragement of field research on birds. A research proposal is required.

Student Travel Awards provide funds for students to attend the annual meeting.

Alexander Wilson Prize is given to the best student paper presented at the annual meeting.

YEAR PROGRAM STARTED: 1947

PURPOSE:
To promote the scientific study of birds.

LEGAL BASIS:
Corporation.

ELIGIBILITY:
Each award requires a willingness of the awardee to report results of the research as an oral or poster paper at an annual meeting of the Wilson Ornithological Society.

Louis Agassiz Fuertes Grant: Available to all ornithologists, although graduate students and young professionals are preferred. Any avian research is eligible.

George A. Hall/Harold F. Mayfield Grant: Limited to independent researchers without access to funds and facilities available at colleges, universities or governmental agencies, and is restricted to nonprofessionals, including high school students. Any kind of avian research is eligible.

Research Grants are limited to research by Master's students for work in any area of ornithology.

Paul A. Stewart Grants: Preference will be given to proposals for studies of bird movements based on banding, analysis of recoveries and returns of banded birds, with an emphasis on economic ornithology.

Student Travel Awards: Students presenting an oral paper or poster at WOS Annual Meeting are invited to apply.

FINANCIAL DATA:
Amount of support per award: Fuertes Grant: $2,500; Hall/Mayfield Grant and Stewart Grant: $1,000; Research Grants: $1,500.

NO. MOST RECENT APPLICANTS: Approximately 100.

NO. AWARDS: Fuertes Grant: Up to 2; Hall/Mayfield Grant: 1; Research Grants and Stewart Grant: Up to 4.

APPLICATION INFO:
Requirements and application instructions are available on the Society web site.
Duration: One-time grant. Nonrenewable.
Deadline: February 1.

PUBLICATIONS:
Wilson Journal of Ornithology; Wilson Bulletin; Guide to Graduate Programs in Ornithology; Manual of Ornithology.

Environment

ACORN FOUNDATION [1980]

c/o Common Counsel Foundation
1624 Franklin Street, Suite 1022
Oakland, CA 94612
(510) 834-2995
Fax: (510) 834-2998
E-mail: info@commoncounsel.org
grantsadmin@commoncounsel.org
Web Site: www.commoncounsel.org

FOUNDED: 1978

AREAS OF INTEREST:
A sustainable ecological future and a healthy global environment.

TYPE:
General operating grants.

YEAR PROGRAM STARTED: 1978

PURPOSE:
To advance community-based organizations working for environmental conservation, sustainability and environmental justice.

ELIGIBILITY:
The Foundation makes grants to grassroots organizations. Organizational budget must be $600,000 or less. The Foundation is particularly interested in small and innovative community-based projects that engage in community organizing in order to:
(1) preserve and restore habitats supporting biological diversity and wildlife;
(2) advocate for environmental justice, particularly in low-income and indigenous communities and;
(3) prevent or remedy toxic pollution.

GEOG. RESTRICTIONS: Western and southern United States and Appalachia.

FINANCIAL DATA:
Amount of support per award: $5,000 to $10,000.

NO. MOST RECENT APPLICANTS: More than 100.

NO. AWARDS: 10 to 14 per year.

APPLICATION INFO:
Organizations that meet the eligibility and funding criteria are encouraged to submit a letter of inquiry form.
Duration: 12 months.

Deadline: January 15 and June 15 for spring and fall grantmaking meetings.

ADDRESS INQUIRIES TO:
Grants Administrator
(See address above.)

ALASKA CONSERVATION FOUNDATION [1981]

1227 West Ninth Avenue
Suite 300
Anchorage, AK 99501
(907) 276-1917
Fax: (907) 274-4145
E-mail: grants@alaskaconservation.org
Web Site: www.alaskaconservation.org

AREAS OF INTEREST:
Conservation, ecosystem and lands protection, marine conservation, linking conservation with the economy and organizational effectiveness.

NAME(S) OF PROGRAMS:
● **Rapid Response Grant**

TYPE:
Awards/prizes; General operating grants; Internships; Project/program grants.

YEAR PROGRAM STARTED: 1977

PURPOSE:
To allow for a timely response to fast-breaking, unforeseen environmental threats of statewide or national significance.

ELIGIBILITY:
Applicants for Rapid Response Grants must meet the following criteria:
(1) be a nonprofit organization engaged in Alaska conservation advocacy;
(2) be based in Alaska, or have an Alaska-based program;
(3) if a current ACF grantee, be in good standing with required grants reports;
(4) grant must address an unforeseen opportunity for action and;
(5) issue must be a statewide concern or have statewide impact.

GEOG. RESTRICTIONS: Alaska.

FINANCIAL DATA:
Amount of support per award: $2,500 to $10,000.

APPLICATION INFO:
Applicants should carefully review the Rapid Response Grant Guidelines before starting the application process. E-mail adalton@alaskaconservation.org or phone (907) 433-8213 prior to applying to ensure your project is eligible.
Duration: Up to six months.

EXECUTIVE DIRECTOR:
Michael Barber

ADDRESS INQUIRIES TO:
See e-mail address above.

ALASKA CONSERVATION FOUNDATION [1982]

1227 West Ninth Avenue
Suite 300
Anchorage, AK 99501
(907) 276-1917
Fax: (907) 274-4145
E-mail: grants@alaskaconservation.org
Web Site: www.alaskaconservation.org

FOUNDED: 1980

AREAS OF INTEREST:
Conservation, ecosystem and lands protection, marine conservation, linking conservation with the economy and organizational effectiveness.

NAME(S) OF PROGRAMS:
● **Alaska Defense Fund**
● **Discovery Grants Program**

TYPE:
General operating grants; Internships; Project/program grants.

YEAR PROGRAM STARTED: 1980

PURPOSE:
To build strategic leadership and support for Alaskan efforts to take care of wild lands, water and wildlife, which sustain diverse cultures, healthy communities and prosperous economies.

LEGAL BASIS:
501(c)(3) public foundation.

ELIGIBILITY:
Incorporate, tax-exempt organizations and non-incorporated organizations may apply according to program guidelines.

GEOG. RESTRICTIONS: Alaska.

FINANCIAL DATA:
Amount of support per award: Alaska Defense Fund: Varies; Discovery Grants: $500 to $2,000.
Total amount of support: $1,260,000 for the year 2019.

NO. AWARDS: 81 for the year 2019.

APPLICATION INFO:
Alaska Defense Fund: Applications are accepted by invitation only. Discovery Grant applications must be submitted online.
Duration: Varies.
Deadline: Varies.

IRS I.D.: 92-0061466

EXECUTIVE DIRECTOR:
Michael Barber

ADDRESS INQUIRIES TO:
See e-mail address above.

*SPECIAL STIPULATIONS:
ACF funds only in Alaska.

AMERICAN ACADEMY IN ROME [1983]

7 East 60th Street
New York, NY 10022
(212) 751-7200
Fax: (212) 751-7220
E-mail: info@aarome.org
Web Site: www.aarome.org

FOUNDED: 1894

AREAS OF INTEREST:
Landscape architecture.

NAME(S) OF PROGRAMS:
● **The Rome Prize Fellowship in Landscape Architecture**

TYPE:
Awards/prizes; Fellowships; Residencies. Provides a residential year at the American Academy in Rome for an American landscape architect for advanced study, travel and association with other fellows in the arts and humanities.

YEAR PROGRAM STARTED: 1920

PURPOSE:
To provide American landscape architects with a special opportunity for advanced study in Rome.

LEGAL BASIS:
Nonprofit, national organization.

ELIGIBILITY:
Applicants must hold an accredited degree in landscape architecture, or equivalent experience.

GEOG. RESTRICTIONS: United States.

FINANCIAL DATA:
Award consists of stipend, plus housing and meals allowance.
Amount of support per award: $16,000 for half-term fellowship; $28,000 for full-term fellowship.

NO. MOST RECENT APPLICANTS: 25.

NO. AWARDS: 2 annually.

APPLICATION INFO:
Applications are submitted electronically.
Duration: Five and one-half months or 11 months.
Deadline: November 1. Announcement in April.

PUBLICATIONS:
Program announcement.

STAFF:
Mark Robbins, President
Shawn Miller, Program Director

ADDRESS INQUIRIES TO:
Program Director
(See address above.)

AMERICAN ALPINE CLUB [1984]

710 10th Street
Suite 100
Golden, CO 80401
(303) 384-0110
E-mail: grants@americanalpineclub.org
Web Site: americanalpineclub.org

FOUNDED: 1902

AREAS OF INTEREST:
Mountaineering, mountain environment and polar regions.

NAME(S) OF PROGRAMS:
● **Copp-Dash Inspire Award**
● **Cornerstone Conservation Grant**
● **Cutting Edge Grant**
● **Jones Back Country Adventure Grant**
● **Live Your Dream Grant**
● **Zack Martin Breaking Barriers Grant**
● **McNeill-Nott Climbing Award**
● **Mountaineering Fellowship**
● **Research Grants**

TYPE:
Project/program grants; Research grants; Travel grants. Grants to support research in Arctic and alpine environments. Funds may also be used to assist in publication or other dissemination of the results of such research.

Cornerstone Conservation Grant aims to create healthy climbing landscape, promote respect for places to climb, and empowers local climbing communities.

Cutting Edge Grant supports advanced, seasoned climbers undertaking high-level climbing and mountaineering objectives.

Jones Backcountry Adventure Grant supports a multiday splitboarding expedition with a strong exploratory and adventure component. The project objective may focus on a single descent/summit or a tour/traverse of a region.

Live Your Dream Grant supports everyday adventurers looking to take their abilities to the next level, regardless of age, experience, or discipline.

Zack Martin Breaking Barriers Grant is a dual-purpose grant that focuses on projects with a humanitarian objective and an objective involving alpinism, iceclimbing, rock climbing or bouldering.

McNeill-Nott Award seeks to preserve the spirit of Sue Nott and her partner, Karen McNeill, by giving grants to amateur climbers exploring new routes or unclimbed peaks with small and lightweight teams.

Mountaineering Fellowship grants encourage American climbers age 25 years and younger to go into remote areas and seek out climbs more difficult than they might ordinarily be able to do.

Research Grants support scientific endeavors in mountains and crags around the world. ACC funds projects that contribute vital knowledge to the climbing environment, enrich understanding of global climber impacts, and support and improve the health and sustainability of mountain environments and habitats.

YEAR PROGRAM STARTED: 1945

PURPOSE:
To encourage and broaden scientific research in mountains and the polar regions.

LEGAL BASIS:
Membership organization.

ELIGIBILITY:
Individuals engaged in appropriate research are eligible to apply.

FINANCIAL DATA:
Amount of support per award: Cornerstone Conservation Grant: $1,000 to $8,000; Cutting Edge Grant: $5,000 to $15,000; Jones Grant: $1,500 plus a Jones splitboard, skins and backpack; Live Your Dream Grant: $200 to $1,000; McNeill-Nott Award: Up to $5,000; Mountaineering Fellowship: $300 to $800; Research Grants: Varies.
Total amount of support: Over $130,000 annually.

APPLICATION INFO:
Application information is available on the web site.
Duration: One-time grant. New application required for ongoing projects.
Deadline: Copp-Dash Inspire Award: September 1. Cornerstone Conservation Grant: August 15. Cutting Edge Grant and Jones Grant: November 30. Live Your Dream Grant: March 31. Zack Martin Grant: April 15. McNeill-Nott Climbing Award: January 1. Mountaineering Fellowship: April 1 and November 1. Research Grants: January 15.

PUBLICATIONS:
Application guidelines.

ADDRESS INQUIRIES TO:
Caroline Bridges, Grants Manager
(See e-mail address above.)

AMERICAN WATER RESOURCES ASSOCIATION   [1985]
P.O. Box 2663
Woodbridge, VA 22195
(540) 687-8390
Fax: (540) 687-8395
E-mail: info@awra.org
Web Site: www.awra.org

FOUNDED: 1964

AREAS OF INTEREST:
Water resources.

NAME(S) OF PROGRAMS:
● **Richard A. Herbert Memorial Scholarship**

TYPE:
Scholarships.

YEAR PROGRAM STARTED: 1980

PURPOSE:
To advance multidisciplinary water resources management and research.

ELIGIBILITY:
Applicant must be a national AWRA member who is enrolled in a program related to water resources. May be a full-time undergraduate student working towards an undergraduate degree or a full-time graduate student.

The undergraduate scholarship will be awarded to the student most qualified by academic performance. The graduate scholarship will be awarded to the student most qualified by academic and/or research performance. Measures of academic performance include the cumulative grade point average, relevance of the student's curriculum to water resources, and leadership in extracurricular activities related to water resources.

FINANCIAL DATA:
Amount of support per award: $2,000.
Total amount of support: $8,000.

NO. MOST RECENT APPLICANTS: 40 undergraduate and 20 graduate applications.

NO. AWARDS: 4.

APPLICATION INFO:
Application must be submitted electronically as one document to the e-mail listed above. File cannot be greater that 10 MB in size to ensure delivery. A complete application includes:
(1) a title page;
(2) a two-page summary of academic interests and achievements, extracurricular interests, and career goals as they relate to the selection criteria;
(3) resume or curriculum vitae;
(4) three signed letters of reference from professors and/or advisors and;
(5) transcripts of all college courses (undergraduate and graduate).
Duration: One year.
Deadline: April.

ADDRESS INQUIRIES TO:
AWRA Scholarship Coordinator
(See e-mail address above.)

BEN & JERRY'S FOUNDATION
30 Community Drive
South Burlington, VT 05403-6828
(802) 846-1500
E-mail: info@benandjerrysfoundation.org
Web Site: www.benandjerrysfoundation.org

TYPE:
General operating grants; Project/program grants. Grants to nonprofit organizations which facilitate progressive social change by addressing the underlying conditions of societal and/or environmental problems using organizing as a strategy to create change.

See entry 901 for full listing.

BONNEVILLE ENVIRONMENTAL FOUNDATION   [1986]
1500 S.W. 1st Avenue
Suite 885
Portland, OR 97201
(503) 248-1905
Fax: (503) 248-1908
E-mail: info@b-e-f.org
Web Site: www.b-e-f.org

FOUNDED: 1998

AREAS OF INTEREST:
Environmental conservation and the development of new sources of renewable energy.

NAME(S) OF PROGRAMS:
● **Model Watershed Program**
● **Renewable Energy Program**

TYPE:
Grants-in-aid. Model Watershed Program is intended to restore ecological integrity and native fish populations in watersheds across the western U.S.

Renewable Energy Program supports school solar projects and other renewable energy technologies that are taken up by utility and community-based renewable energy projects.

PURPOSE:
To support watershed restoration programs; to develop new sources of renewable energy.

ELIGIBILITY:
The Foundation does not fund residential projects.

FINANCIAL DATA:
Amount of support per award: Varies.
Total amount of support: Varies.

APPLICATION INFO:
Complete application information is available on the Foundation web site.
Duration: Varies.

STAFF:
Dick Wanderscheid, Vice President for Renewable Energy Program
Todd Reeve, Chief Executive Officer
Robert Warren, Director, Model Watershed Program

BRUNSWICK PUBLIC FOUNDATION   [1987]
26125 North Riverwoods Boulevard
Suite 500
Mettawa, IL 60045
(847) 735-4344
Fax: (847) 735-4765
E-mail: services@brunswick.com
Web Site: www.brunswick.com

FOUNDED: 1998

AREAS OF INTEREST:
Environmental waterways.

TYPE:
Project/program grants.

PURPOSE:
To support community development primarily through contributions to preselected local United Way organizations; to support organizations that enhance the country's water resources for the recreational use by the public through proposals invited by the Foundation trustees.

ELIGIBILITY:
Grants are made to organizations that have tax-exempt status under Section 501(c)(3) of the Internal Revenue Code. Nonsectarian religious programs may apply. No grants are made to individuals.

FINANCIAL DATA:
Amount of support per award: $5,000 to $80,000.

Total amount of support: Approximately $350,000.

NO. AWARDS: 10.

APPLICATION INFO:
Contact the Foundation for guidelines.
Duration: One year.
Deadline: March 15, July 15 and October 15.

IRS I.D.: 36-4195390

STAFF:
Lisa DeBartolo, Coordinator

BOARD OF DIRECTORS:
Jim Baugh
Kevin Grodzki
Jim Hubbard
Sarah Humphries

ADDRESS INQUIRIES TO:
Lisa DeBartolo, Coordinator
(See address above.)

*SPECIAL STIPULATIONS:
By invitation only.

THE BULLITT FOUNDATION [1988]

1501 East Madison, Suite 600
Seattle, WA 98122
(206) 343-0807
E-mail: grants@bullitt.org
Web Site: www.bullitt.org

FOUNDED: 1952

AREAS OF INTEREST:
Environment.

NAME(S) OF PROGRAMS:
- **Deep Green Buildings**
- **Energy, Climate and Materials**
- **Regional Ecosystem Health**
- **Resilient Cities, Healthy Communities**
- **Thought Leadership and Innovation**

TYPE:
Awards/prizes; Matching gifts; Project/program grants.

YEAR PROGRAM STARTED: 1952

PURPOSE:
To safeguard the natural environment by promoting responsible human activities and sustainable communities in the Pacific Northwest.

LEGAL BASIS:
Private foundation.

ELIGIBILITY:
Applicants must be organizations that have nonprofit tax status with clear, significant and achievable goals, as well as a cogent strategy to realize them. The trustees favor projects that avoid excessive reliance on any one source of funding. The Foundation cannot fund political elections or lobbying activities involving specific legislation. The Foundation does not fund university overhead costs or capital projects.

GEOG. RESTRICTIONS: Emerald Corridor: Vancouver, British Columbia to Portland, Oregon.

FINANCIAL DATA:
Amount of support per award: Grants: $5,000 to $100,000; $35,000 average.

Matching fund requirements: Employee and trustee donations will be matched.

NO. MOST RECENT APPLICANTS: 200.

NO. AWARDS: Approximately 125 annually.

REPRESENTATIVE AWARDS:
$50,000 to Justice Alliance Education Fund; $100,000 to Climate Solutions; $30,000 to Duwamish River Cleanup Coalition; $25,000 to Ecotrust.

APPLICATION INFO:
An organization must first submit a proposal inquiry via the web site. Complete application information is available online.
Duration: One year.
Deadline: Proposal inquiry: March 15 and September 15.

PUBLICATIONS:
Guidelines.

IRS I.D.: 91-6027795

TRUSTEES AND OFFICERS:
Rod Brown, Chairperson
Bill Ruckelshaus, Vice Chairperson
Sally Anderson, Treasurer
Jessie Woolley-Wilson, Secretary
Harriett Bullitt
Maud Daudon
Mark Edlen
Erin Gomez
Lisa Graumlich
Frank Greer
Denis Hayes
Martha Kongsgaard

ADDRESS INQUIRIES TO:
See e-mail address above.

LIZ CLAIBORNE ART ORTENBERG FOUNDATION [1989]

1385 Broadway
23rd Floor
New York, NY 10018
(212) 333-2536
E-mail: lcaof@lcaof.org
Web Site: www.lcaof.org

FOUNDED: 1984

AREAS OF INTEREST:
Integration of conservation and development in the rural landscape.

TYPE:
Challenge/matching grants; Development grants; General operating grants; Project/program grants; Research grants; Seed money grants.

PURPOSE:
To conserve nature and relieve human distress; to redress the breakdown in the processes linking nature and humanity.

ELIGIBILITY:
The Foundation funds modest, carefully designed field projects, primarily in developing countries. No funding for general support or to underwrite institutional overhead. Local people should have a substantial proprietary interest in the project.

GEOG. RESTRICTIONS: Northern Rockies region of the United States.

FINANCIAL DATA:
Amount of support per award: $10,000 to $100,000.

Total amount of support: $4,000,000 for fiscal year 2017.

REPRESENTATIVE AWARDS:
$142,000 to African Conservation Centre for Amboseli Research and Conservation Program in Kenya and Tanzania; $49,030 to Wildlife Conservation Society for Tiger Conservation Program in Cambodia; $90,000 to Panthera Corporation for Jaguar Conservation Program in Brazil.

APPLICATION INFO:
Contact the Foundation for guidelines. Applications are accepted by invitation only.
Duration: One year.

PUBLICATIONS:
The View from Airlie; MONTANA: *People and the Economy*; brochure; *Next Year Country-View from Red Lodge*; *9 Case Studies on the Interior West of U.S.*

TRUSTEES:
Victor Kovner
Alison Richard

DIRECTORS:
Douglas Chadwick
William Conway
William deBuys
Ullas Karanth
Grant Parker
David Western

ADDRESS INQUIRIES TO:
Kent Wommack, Executive Director
Lori Cohen, Administrative Coordinator
(See address above.)

*PLEASE NOTE:
The Foundation is not accepting unsolicited proposals at this time.

COLUMBIA JOURNALISM SCHOOL

2950 Broadway
New York, NY 10027
(212) 854-6468
Fax: (212) 854-3148
E-mail: cm3443@columbia.edu
Web Site: journalism.columbia.edu/oakes

TYPE:
Awards/prizes. Awarded for distinguished excellence in environmental journalism.

See entry 1753 for full listing.

COOPERATIVE INSTITUTE FOR RESEARCH IN ENVIRONMENTAL SCIENCES (CIRES) [1990]

CIRES Building, Room 318
University of Colorado
Boulder, CO 80309-0216
(303) 497-3584
Fax: (303) 492-1149
E-mail: christine.wiedinmyer@colorado.edu
Web Site: cires.colorado.edu

FOUNDED: 1967

AREAS OF INTEREST:
Physics, chemistry and dynamics of the earth system; global and regional environmental change; climate system monitoring, diagnostics, and modeling; development and application of remote sensing and in-situ measurement techniques for the earth and its atmosphere, cryosphere, ecosystems, and oceans.

NAME(S) OF PROGRAMS:
- **CIRES Visiting Fellowship Program in Environmental Sciences**

TYPE:
Fellowships. The program provides opportunities for interactions between CIRES scientists and visiting fellows to pursue common research interests. CIRES research includes theoretical studies, laboratory experimentation, and field investigations which may affect the enhancement of air and water quality and prediction of weather climate fluctuations.

YEAR PROGRAM STARTED: 1968

PURPOSE:
To provide support for scientists from around the world to visit CIRES and collaborate in a variety of research projects.

LEGAL BASIS:
Sponsored jointly by the University of Colorado and National Oceanic and Atmospheric Administration.

ELIGIBILITY:
Applicants must be Ph.D. scientists at all levels; faculty planning sabbatical leave and recent Ph.D. recipients are especially encouraged to apply. Priority is given to candidates with research experience at institutions outside the Boulder scientific community. The program is open to scientists of all countries. The University of Colorado is committed to diversity and equality in education and employment.

FINANCIAL DATA:
Amount of support per award: Stipend is flexible based on research experience.

NO. AWARDS: Up to 10.

APPLICATION INFO:
Applicant must send a resume, publications list and a brief (two- to four-page) description of the proposed research. In addition, candidates should request three letters of recommendation, to be sent directly to CIRES, from persons familiar with their qualifications. Postdoctoral-level applicants must also submit undergraduate and graduate transcripts.
Duration: Postdoctoral: Two years. Senior Scientist: Three to 12 months.
Deadline: January 3. Selection the following March.

ADDRESS INQUIRIES TO:
Christine Wiedinmyer
Associate Director for Science
(See address above.)

THE ENERGY FOUNDATION [1991]
301 Battery Street, 5th Floor
San Francisco, CA 94111
(415) 561-6700
Fax: (415) 561-6709
E-mail: grants@ef.org
Web Site: www.ef.org

FOUNDED: 1991

AREAS OF INTEREST:
Energy efficiency and renewable energy.

NAME(S) OF PROGRAMS:
- **Buildings Program**
- **Climate Program**
- **Energy Foundation China**
- **Power Program**
- **Public Engagement Program**
- **Transportation Program**

TYPE:
Project/program grants. Promotes energy efficiency and renewable energy.

Buildings Program supports policies to increase the efficiency of U.S. homes and businesses and to reduce carbon emissions and utility bills.

Climate Program has a goal of putting the U.S. on a path to meet or exceed its stated target of reducing greenhouse gas emissions by 17 percent below 2005 levels by 2020.

Energy Foundation China, with an emphasis on both national policy and regional implementation, assists agencies, experts and entrepreneurs in solving that country's energy challenges.

Power Program seeks to move the U.S. toward cleaner, more affordable sources of energy.

Public Engagement Program seeks to build national and state support for clean energy and strong climate policies.

Transportation Program works to reduce energy use and carbon pollution through policies that improve vehicle efficiency and promote clean fuels.

YEAR PROGRAM STARTED: 1991

PURPOSE:
To assist in a national, and ultimately a global, transition to a sustainable future by promoting energy efficiency and renewable energy.

LEGAL BASIS:
Public charity 501(c)(3).

ELIGIBILITY:
501(c)(3) organizations only. No grants to individuals or for-profit organizations. Projects must have broad regional or national implications. No grants to religious organizations, political parties or for development of technology. No research and development or demonstration grants.

GEOG. RESTRICTIONS: United States and China.

FINANCIAL DATA:
Amount of support per award: Varies.
Total amount of support: Approximately $60,000,000 in grant payments for the year 2017.

APPLICATION INFO:
Program officers identify funding opportunities in accordance with program strategies. The Foundation does not accept unsolicited proposals or letters of inquiry.
Duration: Typically one year. Renewal possible.

PUBLICATIONS:
Annual report.

IRS I.D.: 94-3126848

BOARD OF DIRECTORS:
Bill Ritter, Jr., Chairperson
Melanie Audette
Robert Crane
Don Cravins, Jr.
Carlos Curbelo
Stephen Harper
Jason Mark
Kris Mayes
Gina McCarthy
Rose McKinney-James
Nicole Systrom
Sue Tierney

ADDRESS INQUIRIES TO:
Jason Mark, Chief Executive Officer
(See address above.)

ENVIRONMENTAL LAW INSTITUTE
1730 M Street, N.W.
Suite 700
Washington, DC 20036
(202) 939-3800
Fax: (202) 939-3868
E-mail: law@eli.org
Web Site: www.eli.org

TYPE:
Scholarships. Scholarships to annual Environmental Law Course.

See entry 1800 for full listing.

FISHAMERICA FOUNDATION [1992]
1001 North Fairfax Street, Suite 501
Alexandria, VA 22314
(703) 519-9691
Fax: (703) 519-1872
E-mail: fafgrants@asafishing.org
Web Site: www.fishamerica.org

FOUNDED: 1983

AREAS OF INTEREST:
Environment and conservation.

NAME(S) OF PROGRAMS:
- **Fisheries Conservation and Research Projects**

TYPE:
Challenge/matching grants; Project/program grants; Research grants; Seed money grants.

YEAR PROGRAM STARTED: 1983

PURPOSE:
To provide funding for on-the-ground projects aimed at enhancing fish populations, restoring fish habitat, improving water quality and advancing fisheries research to improve sportfishing success.

LEGAL BASIS:
Public foundation, 501(c)(3).

ELIGIBILITY:
Any nonprofit tax-exempt organization including conservation organizations, sporting clubs, civic groups, and local and state agencies can apply.

GEOG. RESTRICTIONS: United States and Canada.

FINANCIAL DATA:
Amount of support per award: Average $15,000 per grant.
Matching fund requirements: 1:1.

NO. MOST RECENT APPLICANTS: 162.

NO. AWARDS: 22.

REPRESENTATIVE AWARDS:
$20,000 to Mississippi Fish and Wildlife Foundation to improve water quality within the Bayou Pierre River and its tributaries; $50,000 to Toe River Valley Watch to implement the stream restoration project and greenway along Grassy Creek; $5,000 to New Hampshire B.A.S.S. Nation for the bass research project.

APPLICATION INFO:
Applicants should submit application, letter of support from the appropriate state resource agency biologist, and evidence of nonprofit status.
Duration: One year.

PUBLICATIONS:
Guidelines and application.

IRS I.D.: 36-3219015

BOARD OF DIRECTORS:
Chris Megan, Chairman
Zack Swanson, Vice Chairman
Jim Hubbard, Treasurer
Louis Chemi, Secretary
Bruce Akin
Dale Barnes
Ed Carter
Thomas Dammrich
Dan Ferris
Peter Foley
Patrick M. Gill
Kirk Immens
Carl Liederman
Dave J. Pfeiffer
Jesse Simpkins
Steve Smits

ADDRESS INQUIRIES TO:
Grants Manager
(See address above.)

THE GARDEN CLUB OF AMERICA [1993]

14 East 60th Street, Third Floor
New York, NY 10022
(212) 753-8287
Fax: (212) 753-0134
E-mail: scholarshipapplications@gcamerica.org
Web Site: www.gcamerica.org/scholarships

FOUNDED: 1913

AREAS OF INTEREST:
Horticulture, botany, landscape architecture and environmental studies.

NAME(S) OF PROGRAMS:
- **The GCA and The Royal Horticultural Society Interchange Fellowships**

TYPE:
Exchange programs; Fellowships. A graduate academic year in the U.S. for a British student and a work-study program for an American at universities and botanical gardens in the U.K. in fields related to horticulture, botany and landscape design.

YEAR PROGRAM STARTED: 1948

PURPOSE:
To foster British-American relations through the interchange of scholars in horticulture, botany, landscape architecture and environmental studies.

LEGAL BASIS:
Nonprofit, national organization.

ELIGIBILITY:
GCA Fellowship is open to a British university graduate with a degree in horticulture, landscape architecture, botany, or environmental studies, or to a British student horticulturist with a recognized horticultural qualification.

RCA Fellowship is open to a single, unaccompanied American college graduate who has earned a B.A. or B.S. degree in horticulture, landscape architecture, or a related degree.

GEOG. RESTRICTIONS: United Kingdom and United States.

FINANCIAL DATA:
The Fellowship covers the cost of tuition, travel expenses, board, lodging and incidental college expenses. It also provides an allowance for personal needs.

Amount of support per award: Varies.

CO-OP FUNDING PROGRAMS: Sponsored jointly by The Garden Club of America and The Royal Horticultural Society.

NO. AWARDS: 2 annually.

APPLICATION INFO:
Guidelines and application forms are available online.
Duration: 10-month program.
Deadline: American scholars to the U.K.: January 15. British scholars to the U.S.: October 1.

PUBLICATIONS:
Program announcement.

ADDRESS INQUIRIES TO:
The Garden Club of America
Camila Bustos, Administrator
GCA/RHS Interchange Fellowships
(See address above.)

THE GARDEN CLUB OF AMERICA [1994]

14 East 60th Street, Third Floor
New York, NY 10022
(212) 753-8287
Fax: (212) 753-0134
E-mail: scholarshipapplications@gcamerica.org
Web Site: www.gcamerica.org/scholarships

FOUNDED: 1913

AREAS OF INTEREST:
Native bird habitat.

NAME(S) OF PROGRAMS:
- **The Frances M. Peacock Scholarship for Native Bird Habitat**

TYPE:
Research grants. Financial assistance to college seniors and graduate students to study habitat-related issues that will benefit threatened or endangered bird species and lend useful information for land management decisions.

YEAR PROGRAM STARTED: 1994

PURPOSE:
To study areas in the U.S. that provide seasonal habitat for threatened or endangered native birds and to tend useful information for land-management decisions.

LEGAL BASIS:
Nonprofit, national organization.

ELIGIBILITY:
College seniors and graduate students only. (Second-semester juniors may apply for their senior year.)

GEOG. RESTRICTIONS: United States.

FINANCIAL DATA:
Amount of support per award: $4,500 annually. In special instances, because of two unusually fine candidates or two candidates working on one project, the award may be divided between two candidates.

NO. AWARDS: 1 to 2.

APPLICATION INFO:
Guidelines and application form are available online.
Duration: One year.
Deadline: January 15 preceding the proposed period of study.

PUBLICATIONS:
Program announcement.

STAFF:
Camila Bustos, Administrator

ADDRESS INQUIRIES TO:
Frances M. Peacock Scholarship:
Prof. Irby Lovette
Cornell Lab of Ornithology
159 Sapsucker Woods Road
Ithaca, NY 14850-1999
E-mail: ijl2@cornell.edu
Web Site: www.birds.cornell.edu

*PLEASE NOTE:
Only one GCA scholarship, fellowship or award may be applied for annually.

THE GARDEN CLUB OF AMERICA [1995]

14 East 60th Street, Third Floor
New York, NY 10022
(212) 753-8287
Fax: (212) 753-0134
E-mail: scholarshipapplications@gcamerica.org
Web Site: www.gcamerica.org/scholarships

FOUNDED: 1913

AREAS OF INTEREST:
Conservation, historic preservation and plant conservation, and tropical plant study.

NAME(S) OF PROGRAMS:
- **The Garden Club of America Award in Coastal Wetland Studies**

TYPE:
Fellowships. Funds one graduate student annually to support field-based wetlands research. A student may propose a wetlands program of his or her choice at a leading educational institution within the U.S. that specializes in wetlands studies. For the purposes of this scholarship, coastal wetlands are defined as those tidal or nontidal wetlands found within coastal states, including the Great Lakes.

YEAR PROGRAM STARTED: 1983

PURPOSE:
To promote wetlands conservation through the support of young scientists in their field work and research.

LEGAL BASIS:
Nonprofit, national organization.

ELIGIBILITY:
Graduate students pursuing advanced degrees in coastal wetlands science may apply. Applicant must be a U.S. citizen or permanent resident enrolled in a U.S.-based institution.

GEOG. RESTRICTIONS: United States.

FINANCIAL DATA:
Amount of support per award: $5,000.

NO. AWARDS: 1 annually.

APPLICATION INFO:
Guidelines and application form are available online.
Duration: One year.
Deadline: January 15 preceding the year of study.

PUBLICATIONS:
Program announcement.

ADDRESS INQUIRIES TO:
Camila Bustos, Administrator
The Garden Club of America
(See address above.)

*PLEASE NOTE:
Only one GCA scholarship, fellowship or award may be applied for annually.

THE GARDEN CLUB OF AMERICA [1996]

14 East 60th Street, Third Floor
New York, NY 10022
(212) 753-8287
Fax: (212) 753-0134
E-mail: scholarshipapplications@gcamerica.org
Web Site: www.gcamerica.org/scholarships

FOUNDED: 1913

AREAS OF INTEREST:
Conservation, historic preservation and plant conservation.

NAME(S) OF PROGRAMS:
● **GCA Awards for Summer Environmental Studies**

TYPE:
Scholarships.

YEAR PROGRAM STARTED: 1964

PURPOSE:
To encourage studies and careers in the environmental field.

LEGAL BASIS:
Nonprofit, national organization.

ELIGIBILITY:
Open to qualified undergraduates entering a summer program following their freshman, sophomore, or junior year.

FINANCIAL DATA:
Amount of support per award: $3,000.

NO. AWARDS: 1 or more.

APPLICATION INFO:
Application guidelines and form are available online.
Deadline: February 5.

PUBLICATIONS:
Program announcement.

ADDRESS INQUIRIES TO:
Camila Bustos, Administrator
(See address above.)

GREAT LAKES PROTECTION FUND [1997]

1560 Sherman Avenue
Suite 1370
Evanston, IL 60201
(847) 425-8150
Fax: (847) 424-9832
E-mail: info@glpf.org
Web Site: www.glpf.org

FOUNDED: 1989

AREAS OF INTEREST:
To identify, demonstrate and promote regional action to enhance the health of the Great Lakes ecosystem.

NAME(S) OF PROGRAMS:
● **Great Lakes Protection Fund**

TYPE:
Demonstration grants; Development grants; Seed money grants.

YEAR PROGRAM STARTED: 1990

PURPOSE:
To support projects that identify, demonstrate and promote regional action to enhance the health of the Great Lakes ecosystem.

LEGAL BASIS:
Nonprofit, multi-state endowment.

ELIGIBILITY:
The Great Lakes Protection Fund can support a wide variety of applicants. Nonprofit organizations (including environmental organizations, trade associations, and universities), for-profit businesses, government agencies, and individuals are eligible for Fund support. Successful applicants must maintain open access to certain project data, records and information.

All applicants must comply with the Fund's guidelines, show that the proposed work has clear public benefit to the Great Lakes basin, and that any related financial benefits will accrue to the public good. Government agencies must show that Fund support is not being used to replace or duplicate public funds.

FINANCIAL DATA:
Since inception, the Great Lakes Protection Fund has awarded more than $73,000,000 to support 260 projects with the goal of improving the health of the Great Lakes ecosystem.
Amount of support per award: Varies.
Total amount of support: Varies.

REPRESENTATIVE AWARDS:
$435,000 over 24 months to the Delta Institute to develop a series of tools to track and measure the full extent of the environmental impacts associated with specific reduction actions. Working with 13 facilities in Michigan, the team expects to reduce water use by over 15 million gallons per day, to eliminate almost 3 million tons of solid waste, reduce CO_2 emissions by over 11,000 tons, reduce emissions of criteria air pollutants by 150,000 pounds, and reduce hazard chemical use by over 200,000 gallons each year. The tools developed will provide a more accurate account of how on-site energy efficiency actions translate into "real" air pollutant reductions at a power generating facility. In conjunction with a panel of Sustainability Institute Fellows, the team will verify these ecosystem impacts and identify third-party transactions to retire the benefits.

APPLICATION INFO:
The first step is the submission of a brief proposal that summarizes the proposed project. The following documents must be included:
(1) completed applicant cover sheet;
(2) preproposal document, no more than three pages, describing the environmental outcome, proposed work, key personnel and financial plan and;
(3) a resume of the project's manager (no more than two pages).

Preproposal documents can be submitted by e-mail to preproposal@glpf.org or send six copies addressed to Preproposal Application, Great Lakes Protection Fund, at the address above.
Duration: Multiyear.

PUBLICATIONS:
Annual report; guidelines for funding; summary papers.

STAFF:
J. David Rankin, Executive Director
Drew Pfeifer, Vice President of Operations
Steve Cole, Vice President of Programs
Amy Elledge, Communications Manager
Shannon Donley, Project Implementation Manager
Janis Post, Business Manager

BOARD MEMBERS:
Kate Bartter
Timothy Bruno
Vita DeMarchi
Kendra Fogarty
Patricia Glaza
Peter Gove
Richard Hylant
Jill Jedlicka
Andrew McElwaine
Mark Meijer
Don Ness
Kevin Shafer
Debra Shore

ADDRESS INQUIRIES TO:
E-mail: startaconversation@glpf.org (initial inquiry)
preproposal@glpf.org (preproposal submission)

THE JACOB AND TERESE HERSHEY FOUNDATION [1998]

3212 Smith Street
Suite 202
Houston, TX 77006-6622
(713) 529-7611
E-mail: judithboyce@jthershey.org
Web Site: www.jthershey.org

FOUNDED: 1961

AREAS OF INTEREST:
Care facilities for domestic and wild animals, natural resources conservation, environmental preservation, parks and open space for public use, environmental education, land conservation, and reproductive rights, women's health, family planning and sex education.

TYPE:
Conferences/seminars; General operating grants; Matching gifts; Project/program grants; Seed money grants.

YEAR PROGRAM STARTED: 1961

PURPOSE:
To promote preservation and conservation of land, forests, streams, wetlands and habitat existing in a natural state and the defense of such resources; to establish, conserve and preserve parks and open space for public use; to help provide care facilities for animals and birds, both domestic and wild; to aid education efforts to promote environmental literacy and comprehension of the complexities of the web of life, particularly in museums and through citizen nonprofit organizations with similar purpose; to promote efforts toward population control.

LEGAL BASIS:
Private foundation.

ELIGIBILITY:
Grants are made to organizations that have tax-exempt status under Section 501(c)(3) of the Internal Revenue Code. Grants are not made to individuals, or for galas or fundraisers.

GEOG. RESTRICTIONS: Southwestern Colorado; Austin and Houston, Texas areas.

FINANCIAL DATA:
Amount of support per award: $2,000 to $50,000.
Total amount of support: $2,371,178 for the year 2019.

NO. MOST RECENT APPLICANTS: 72.

NO. AWARDS: 66.

APPLICATION INFO:
Guidelines are available on the Foundation web site.
Duration: One year. May reapply.
Deadline: Varies.

IRS I.D.: 74-6039126

EXECUTIVE DIRECTOR:
Judith Boyce

ADDRESS INQUIRIES TO:
Judith Boyce, Executive Director
(See address above.)

THE HUDSON RIVER FOUNDATION [1999]

17 Battery Place, Suite 915
New York, NY 10004
(212) 483-7667
Fax: (212) 924-8325
E-mail: info@hudsonriver.org
Web Site: www.hudsonriver.org

FOUNDED: 1981

AREAS OF INTEREST:
Environmental, ecological and public policy
aspects of the Hudson River estuary.

NAME(S) OF PROGRAMS:
- **Hudson River Fund**
- **Hudson River Improvement Fund**
- **New York City Environmental Fund**
- **New York-New Jersey Harbor & Estuary Program**

TYPE:
Capital grants; Fellowships; Research grants;
Travel grants. The Hudson River Fund was
created to meet the critical need for an
independent institution to sponsor scientific
research programs that would contribute to
the development of sound public policy
concerning the River's ecological system.
The Hudson River Fund makes grants in five
categories: Hudson River Research Grants,
Travel Grants, Expedited Grants, Mark B.
Baine Graduate Fellowship, and Tibor T.
Polgar Fellowships.

The Hudson River Improvement Fund
supports projects to enhance public use and
enjoyment of the Hudson River's natural,
scenic and cultural resources. The emphasis
of the Improvement Fund is on physical
projects requiring capital construction,
development, or improvement.

The New York City Environmental Fund
proposes to foster "restoration, care, public
enjoyment of, and education about New York
City's natural resources."

YEAR PROGRAM STARTED: 1983

PURPOSE:
To make science integral to decision-making
with regard to the Hudson River and its
watershed; to support competent stewardship
of this extraordinary resource.

LEGAL BASIS:
Private foundation.

ELIGIBILITY:
Research must be focused on Hudson River.

FINANCIAL DATA:
Amount of support per award: Graduate
Fellowships: Up to $11,000 for one year,
plus up to $1,000 toward supplies (Master's
students); up to $15,000 for one year, plus up
to $1,000 for supplies (doctoral students).
Polgar Fellowships: $3,800, plus $1,000 for
equipment and supplies.
Total amount of support: Varies.

NO. MOST RECENT APPLICANTS: 60 for research
grants.

NO. AWARDS: 15.

APPLICATION INFO:
Guidelines are available online.

Duration: Hudson River Fund Research
Fellowship: One to two years; Baine
Graduate Fellowship: One year; Polgar
Fellowship: One summer.
Deadline: Contact the Foundation.

PUBLICATIONS:
Annual Program Plan; *Hudson River Fund:
Call for Proposals.*

EXECUTIVE DIRECTOR:
Clay Hiles

ILLINOIS CLEAN ENERGY COMMUNITY FOUNDATION [2000]

2 North LaSalle Street, Suite 1140
Chicago, IL 60602
(312) 372-5191
Fax: (312) 372-5190
E-mail: dobrien@illinoiscleanenergy.org
Web Site: www.illinoiscleanenergy.org

FOUNDED: 1999

AREAS OF INTEREST:
Improving the environmental quality of life
in the state of Illinois and natural habitat
preservation.

TYPE:
Grants-in-aid; Project/program grants. The
Foundation provides financial support in two
principal ways:
(1) Grantmaking: The Foundation provides
grants on a competitive basis, in response to
proposals submitted by organizations in
accord with the Foundation's announced
strategic priorities and the application process
described below. The Foundation can provide
several different types of financial support,
including grants.
(2) Direct Initiatives: The Foundation
identifies strategic opportunities to undertake
large-scale, high-impact projects and special
initiatives that further its program objectives
in energy efficiency, renewable energy and
natural areas conservation.

YEAR PROGRAM STARTED: 2001

PURPOSE:
To invest in clean energy development and
land preservation efforts, working with
communities and citizens to improve
environmental quality in Illinois.

LEGAL BASIS:
Independent, nonprofit grantmaking
institution.

ELIGIBILITY:
The Foundation provides funding to
tax-exempt organizations, including
governmental entities. The Foundation will
not provide funding for remediation of
environmentally impaired properties,
technology research, promotion of proprietary
products, reoccurring operating costs,
political campaigns or lobbying, capital
campaigns or support for an organization's
endowment, or projects undertaken by
individuals.

GEOG. RESTRICTIONS: Illinois.

FINANCIAL DATA:
Amount of support per award: Varies.
Matching fund requirements: Approximately
$13,000,000 in total grants awarded for the
year 2017.

APPLICATION INFO:
Guidelines are available on the Foundation
web site.
Duration: One to two years.

ADDRESS INQUIRIES TO:
Gabriela Martin, Program Director
(See address above.)

INTERNATIONAL CRANE FOUNDATION, INC.

E-11376 Shady Lane Road
Baraboo, WI 53913
(608) 356-9462
Fax: (608) 356-9465
E-mail: info@savingcranes.org
Web Site: www.savingcranes.org

TYPE:
Internships. Formal stipended internship
programs in the fields of aviculture, crane
ecology and conservation education.

See entry 1967 for full listing.

LANDSCAPE ARCHITECTURE FOUNDATION [2001]

1200 17th Street, N.W.
Suite 210
Washington, DC 20036
(202) 331-7070 ext. 14
E-mail: scholarships@lafoundation.org
Web Site: www.lafoundation.org/scholarship

FOUNDED: 1966

AREAS OF INTEREST:
The profession of landscape architecture.

NAME(S) OF PROGRAMS:
- **ASLA Council of Fellows Scholarship**
- **ASLA-NY Designing in the Public Realm Scholarship**
- **EDSA Minority Scholarship**
- **Steven G. King Play Environments Scholarship**
- **LAF Honor Scholarship in Memory of Joe Lalli, FASLA**
- **Landscape Forms Scholarship in Memory of Peter Schaudt, FASLA**
- **Courtland Paul Scholarship**
- **Peridian International Inc./Rae L. Price, FASLA Scholarship**
- **Rain Bird Intelligent Use of Water Scholarship**
- **Douglas Dockery Thomas Fellowship in Garden History and Design**

TYPE:
Fellowships; Scholarships. Awards for
undergraduate and graduate students pursuing
an education in landscape architecture.

PURPOSE:
To assist students enrolled in programs of
landscape architecture.

LEGAL BASIS:
Nonprofit, tax-exempt foundation.

ELIGIBILITY:
Open to undergraduate and graduate students
currently enrolled in a professional degree
program in landscape architecture. Available
to students in financial need who show
promise and commitment to the profession.

GEOG. RESTRICTIONS: United States and
Canada.

FINANCIAL DATA:
Amount of support per award: LAF Honor
Scholarship in Memory of Joe Lalli, FASLA:
$20,000 annually. All others: $2,000 to
$5,000.
Total amount of support: Over $80,000
annually.

NO. MOST RECENT APPLICANTS: Varies.

NO. AWARDS: Varies.

APPLICATION INFO:
Application information is available on the web site.
Duration: One academic year.
Deadline: February 1.

PUBLICATIONS:
Guidelines.

ADDRESS INQUIRIES TO:
Program Manager
(See address and e-mail above.)

THE LEF FOUNDATION
P.O. Box 382066
Cambridge, MA 02238-2066
(617) 492-5333
Fax: (617) 868-5603
E-mail: gen@lef-foundation.org
Web Site: lef-foundation.org

TYPE:
The Foundation gives grants for preproduction, production and post production of nonfiction film and video.

See entry 382 for full listing.

MARSHALL COMMUNITY FOUNDATION
614 Homer Road
Marshall, MI 49068
(269) 781-2273
Fax: (269) 781-9747
E-mail: info@marshallcf.org
Web Site: www.marshallcf.org

TYPE:
Project/program grants; Scholarships.

See entry 1423 for full listing.

NATIONAL FISH AND WILDLIFE FOUNDATION (NFWF)   [2002]
1133 15th Street, N.W.
Suite 1000
Washington, DC 20005
(202) 857-0166
Fax: (202) 857-0162
E-mail: info@nfwf.org
Web Site: www.nfwf.org

FOUNDED: 1984

AREAS OF INTEREST:
Sustaining, restoring and enhancing the nation's fish, wildlife, plants and habitats for current and future generations.

TYPE:
Challenge/matching grants; Project/program grants.

YEAR PROGRAM STARTED: 1986

PURPOSE:
To conserve natural resources through habitat protection, environmental education, natural resource management, species conservation and leadership training for conservation professionals.

LEGAL BASIS:
Private 501(c)(3) organization.

ELIGIBILITY:
Must be a 501(c)(3) organization. No grants to individuals.

GEOG. RESTRICTIONS: Primarily United States.

FINANCIAL DATA:
Amount of support per award: Varies.

Total amount of support: Approximately $375,000,000 in on-the-ground conservation impact.

Matching fund requirements: At least 1:1, preference for higher leverage.

NO. MOST RECENT APPLICANTS: Varies.

NO. AWARDS: Varies.

REPRESENTATIVE AWARDS:
$100,000 to Iowa Department of Natural Resources to restore 1,254 acres of bottomland hardwood forest in northeast Iowa on former agricultural lands. The project is working to reduce forest fragmentation, enhance water quality, and improve critical habitat for neo-tropical birds and other wildlife; $400,000 to Conservation Fund to reduce nutrient and sediment runoff entering Rockymarsh Run – a tributary to the Potomac River and ultimately the Chesapeake Bay.

APPLICATION INFO:
Application information may be obtained online.

Duration: Support usually lasts for one year. Renewals are on a case-by-case basis.

PUBLICATIONS:
Annual report; application guidelines.

IRS I.D.: 52-1384129

STAFF:
Jeff Trandahl, Executive Director/Chief Executive Officer
Lila Helms, Executive Vice President, External Affairs
Holly Bamford, Chief Conservation Officer
Tokunbo Falayi, Chief Financial Officer

BOARD OF DIRECTORS:
Edwin R. Rodriguez, Jr., Chairman
Sydney McNiff Johnson, Vice Chairperson
Reuben Mark, Vice Chairperson
Michael L. Campbell
Max C. Chapman, Jr.
J. Michael Cline
Bruce Culpepper
John Dane, III
John V. Faraci, Jr.
Blas Fonalledas
Tim Gallaudet
Harold Hamm
J.J. Healy
Paul Tudor Jones, II
Eaddo H. Kiernan
Jim Kurth
Ryan Lance
Charles D. McCrary
Don J. McGrath
R. King Milling
Jennifer Mull Neuhaus
Trina Overlock
Chad Pike
Thomas L. Strickland
Federico Stubbe
John A. Tomke
Victoria J. Tschinkel
Mark J. Vallely
K.C. Walsh

ADDRESS INQUIRIES TO:
Appropriate Partnership Office Director
(See address above.)

NATIONAL INSTITUTE OF ENVIRONMENTAL HEALTH SCIENCES   [2003]
Division of Extramural Research and Training
MD K3-05
111 T.W. Alexander Drive
Research Triangle Park, NC 27709
(984) 287-3285
Fax: (919) 541-3976
E-mail: mastin@niehs.nih.gov
Web Site: www.niehs.nih.gov

FOUNDED: 1966

AREAS OF INTEREST:
Research on environmental agents and chemicals and their effects on human health.

NAME(S) OF PROGRAMS:
● **Environmental Health Sciences Research and Training Grants**

TYPE:
Conferences/seminars; Demonstration grants; Development grants; Fellowships; Project/program grants; Research grants; Training grants. NIEHS pursues its mission by supporting basic and applied research on the consequences of the exposure of humans to potentially toxic or harmful agents in the environment.

Research of interest encompasses studies that relate to the biological effects of environmental chemicals and physical factors including such agents as hazardous gases, suspended particles, aerosols, industrial by-products and intermediates, heavy metals, trace elements, food additives, adulterants and pesticides.

Research Training Programs support individuals at both the predoctoral and postdoctoral levels in the areas of environmental toxicology, environmental pathology, environmental mutagenesis and environmental epidemiology.

YEAR PROGRAM STARTED: 1966

PURPOSE:
To support research and research training in environmental health.

LEGAL BASIS:
Government agency authorized under Section 301(d), Public Health Services Act; 42 U.S.C. 241; 42 C.F.R. 52.

ELIGIBILITY:
Universities, research institutes and other public or private institutions may apply on behalf of qualified researchers. Small businesses may apply for SBIR grants.

GEOG. RESTRICTIONS: United States.

FINANCIAL DATA:
Funds are provided, as available, for all allowable expenses associated with approved research projects.
Amount of support per award: Varies.
Total amount of support: Varies.

NO. AWARDS: Approximately 1,150.

APPLICATION INFO:
Guidelines are available on the web site.

Duration: Total grant project periods may not exceed five years and are renewable on a competitive basis at the end of the project period. Average project period length is currently four years.

Deadline: Varies with the specific grant.

PUBLICATIONS:
Fact book; special announcements.

ADDRESS INQUIRIES TO:
J. Patrick Mastin, Ph.D.
Deputy Director
(See address above.)

NATIONAL WILDLIFE
FEDERATION   [2004]

11100 Wildlife Center Drive
Reston, VA 20190-5362
(703) 438-6265
Fax: (703) 438-6468
E-mail: fellows@nwf.org
ecoleaders@nwf.org
Web Site: www.nwf.org
www.nwfecoleaders.org

FOUNDED: 1936

AREAS OF INTEREST:
Environment, conservation and sustainability.

NAME(S) OF PROGRAMS:
• **NWF EcoLeaders Fellowships**

TYPE:
Fellowships.

YEAR PROGRAM STARTED: 2014

PURPOSE:
To give well-qualified and highly motivated
individuals substantive practical experience.

LEGAL BASIS:
Nonprofit organization able to carry on a
defined amount of lobbying.

ELIGIBILITY:
Graduate students from any college or
university within the U.S. may apply.
Applications are invited from students in all
disciplines and are not limited to
environmental studies majors.

Current and former employees of National
Wildlife Federation and former NWF
Campus Ecology Fellows are ineligible to
apply. Former NWF interns are eligible to
apply following one year from their final
work date.

Applicant must be enrolled in school through
the duration of the four-month grant period.

GEOG. RESTRICTIONS: United States.

FINANCIAL DATA:
Amount of support per award: Up to $5,000.
Total amount of support: Varies.

NO. MOST RECENT APPLICANTS: Approximately
400.

NO. AWARDS: Varies.

APPLICATION INFO:
Information is available on the web site.
Duration: Four months.
Deadline: Varies.

PUBLICATIONS:
Program description.

OFFICERS:
Collin O'Mara, President and Chief
Executive Officer

ADDRESS INQUIRIES TO:
E-mail: fellows@nwf.org

NEW YORK SEA GRANT   [2005]

125 Nassau Hall
SUNY at Stony Brook
Stony Brook, NY 11794-5001
(631) 632-6905
Fax: (631) 632-6917
E-mail: nyseagrant@stonybrook.edu
Web Site: nyseagrant.org

FOUNDED: 1971

AREAS OF INTEREST:
Coastal resource management, fisheries
biology, contaminants and environmental
quality, environmental processes and marine
economics, seafood use and technology,
recreation and tourism, human dimensions,
marine aquaculture, youth education, biotech,
and coastal processes.

TYPE:
Awards/prizes; Conferences/seminars;
Development grants; Endowments;
Fellowships; Internships; Project/program
grants; Research grants; Scholarships;
Technical assistance; Travel grants.
Principally grants for laboratory and field
studies, publications and communication and
curriculum development.

YEAR PROGRAM STARTED: 1971

PURPOSE:
To foster the wise use and development of
coastal resources through research, education
and training.

LEGAL BASIS:
A cooperative research and education activity
of the State University of New York and
Cornell University, as well as NOAA's
National Sea Grant College Program.

ELIGIBILITY:
Applicant must be a member of the faculty
of an institution of higher learning or of a
nonprofit organization. Projects must address
issues relevant to New York state. In most
cases, applicants are affiliated with New York
institutions.

FINANCIAL DATA:
Amount of support per award: Varies.
Total amount of support: $1,000,000.
Matching fund requirements: 50% of funds
requested must be provided by applicant
from non-federal sources.

NO. MOST RECENT APPLICANTS: Around 100 for
most biennial solicitations.

NO. AWARDS: Approximately 10 per year.

APPLICATION INFO:
Application information is available on the
web site.
Duration: One or two years. Continuation
possible.
Deadline: Biennial with occasional
out-of-cycle.

ADDRESS INQUIRIES TO:
Lane Smith, Research Coordinator
E-mail: lane.smith@stonybrook.edu

JESSIE SMITH NOYES
FOUNDATION   [2006]

122 East 42nd Street
Suite 2501
New York, NY 10168
(212) 684-6577
Fax: (212) 689-6549
E-mail: noyes@noyes.org
Web Site: noyes.org

FOUNDED: 1947

AREAS OF INTEREST:
Racial justice, environmental justice, and
gender equity.

TYPE:
General operating grants; Project/program
grants.

PURPOSE:
To support people-powered organizations
participating in intersecting social-justice
movements across the U.S.

LEGAL BASIS:
Family foundation.

ELIGIBILITY:
The Foundation makes grants to tax-exempt
organizations with 501(c)(3) classification
from the IRS for work within the U.S. It will
not consider requests for endowments, capital
construction, or deficit financing.

GEOG. RESTRICTIONS: United States.

FINANCIAL DATA:
Amount of support per award: Typically,
$25,000 to $50,000.

NO. AWARDS: 18 for the year 2018.

REPRESENTATIVE AWARDS:
$50,000 to Common Counsel Foundation,
Oakland, CA; $53,000 to JustFund,
Washington, DC; $20,000 to White Earth
Land Recovery, Callaway, MN.

APPLICATION INFO:
The Foundation does not accept unsolicited
proposals.
Duration: Varies.
Deadline: Most grants approved during
spring, summer and fall Board meetings.

IRS I.D.: 13-5600408

STAFF:
Rini Banerjee, President
Kolu Zigbi, Program Director
Gabby Dizon, Grants and Operations
Manager

ADDRESS INQUIRIES TO:
Gabby Dizon
Grants and Operations Manager
(See address above.)

PATAGONIA INC.   [2007]

259 West Santa Clara Street
Ventura, CA 93001
(805) 643-8616
E-mail: grants@patagonia.com
Web Site: www.patagonia.com/how-we-fund

AREAS OF INTEREST:
Preservation and protection of the natural
environment.

NAME(S) OF PROGRAMS:
• **Environmental Grant Program**

TYPE:
General operating grants; Product donations;
Project/program grants. Funds to help local
groups working to protect local habitats and
to force the government to abide by its own
laws in regards to biodiversity and ecosystem
protection.

YEAR PROGRAM STARTED: 1987

PURPOSE:
To assist groups who strive to preserve and
restore the natural environment.

LEGAL BASIS:
Private corporation giving program.

ELIGIBILITY:
Applicants must be 501(c)(3) tax-exempt
organizations. Support is given to small,
grassroots, activist organizations with
provocative direct-action agendas, working on
multipronged campaigns to preserve and
protect the environment. No grants for more
general environmental education efforts.
Contact Patagonia Inc. for complete details.

GEOG. RESTRICTIONS: Argentina, Australia, Austria, Belgium, Canada, Chile, Czechia, Denmark, France, Germany, Ireland, Italy, Japan, Korea, Luxembourg, The Netherlands, Norway, Spain, Sweden, Switzerland, United Kingdom and United States.

FINANCIAL DATA:
Company pledges one percent of sales to grassroots environmental groups.
Amount of support per award: $5,000 to $20,000.

NO. AWARDS: 954 grants to environmental groups in fiscal year 2017.

APPLICATION INFO:
Application information is available on the web site.
Duration: One year. Applicants must reapply for continued funding.
Deadline: Varies by program.

PUBLICATIONS:
Program guidelines.

ADDRESS INQUIRIES TO:
Lisa Myers
Senior Manager of Environmental Grants
(See address above.)

*PLEASE NOTE:
Phone calls are discouraged.

RESOURCES FOR THE FUTURE   [2008]
1616 P Street, N.W., Suite 600
Washington, DC 20036-1436
(202) 328-5000
Fax: (202) 939-3460
E-mail: info@rff.org
Web Site: www.rff.org

AREAS OF INTEREST:
Economics, policy sciences or issues relating to the environment and natural resources of energy.

NAME(S) OF PROGRAMS:
● **Summer Research Internship**

TYPE:
Awards/prizes; Internships. The Summer Research Internship is a paid internship for advanced graduates, graduates and early career professionals to prepare for careers that engage in academic and policy-relevant research.

PURPOSE:
To offer students and recent graduates the opportunity to experience working in a world renowned center for environmental and energy research.

ELIGIBILITY:
Candidates should display strong writing skills and a desire to understand complex environmental policy problems amenable to interdisciplinary methods. The ability to work without supervision in a careful and conscientious manner is essential. Highly motivated candidates in the social and natural sciences with training in economics and quantitative methods, or with keen interest in public policy, are encouraged to apply.

Priority consideration is given to graduate students.

FINANCIAL DATA:
Amount of support per award: $525 stipend per week. No housing assistance is provided.

APPLICATION INFO:
All applications must be submitted electronically. Completed application,

supplemental questions and the following materials must be uploaded:
(1) a cover letter that explains applicant's interest in and how their qualifications match to a specific opening;
(2) resume summarizing applicant's qualifications for the position;
(3) copy of postsecondary academic transcripts (unofficial transcripts are acceptable at this stage);
(4) a writing sample of three to fives pages from a recent paper (excerpts are acceptable) and;
(5) the name, address, telephone number and e-mail information for two references.
Duration: 10 weeks during the summer.

THE RUSSELL FAMILY FOUNDATION   [2009]
3025 Harborview Drive
Gig Harbor, WA 98335
(253) 858-5050
Fax: (253) 851-0460
E-mail: info@trff.org
Web Site: www.trff.org

FOUNDED: 1999

AREAS OF INTEREST:
Environmental sustainability.

NAME(S) OF PROGRAMS:
● **Environmental Education Fund**

TYPE:
General operating grants; Project/program grants. Grants focused on environmental education for grades five to 12 in Jefferson, King, Kitsap, Pierce and Thurston counties.

YEAR PROGRAM STARTED: 2001

PURPOSE:
To implement strategies that raise awareness and understanding of our environment and the importance of protecting it.

ELIGIBILITY:
Organizations must be 501(c)(3) or nonprofit entities such as public schools and school districts, and must be located in and/or provide services within the Puget Sound region. No grants to individuals.

GEOG. RESTRICTIONS: Western Washington state (Jefferson, King, Kitsap, Pierce and Thurston counties).

FINANCIAL DATA:
Amount of support per award: $10,000 to $40,000. Average grant: $25,000.

APPLICATION INFO:
Submit letter of inquiry through Foundation's online grantmaking system. Full proposals are accepted by invitation only.
Duration: One year. Renewal by reapplication.
Deadline: October.

ADDRESS INQUIRIES TO:
Linsey Sauer, Grants Manager
(See address above.)

SMITHSONIAN ENVIRONMENTAL RESEARCH CENTER (SERC)   [2010]
647 Contees Wharf Road
Edgewater, MD 21037
(443) 482-2217
Fax: (443) 482-2380
E-mail: gustafsond@si.edu
Web Site: serc.si.edu

FOUNDED: 1965

AREAS OF INTEREST:
Environmental research and education.

NAME(S) OF PROGRAMS:
● **Professional Training**

TYPE:
Fellowships; Internships. The Internship Program enables undergraduates, recent graduates and graduate students to work on specific projects under the direction of the Center's professional staff and is tailored to provide the maximum educational benefit to each participant. Graduate students and undergraduates may conduct independent projects with the approval of the staff member with whom they plan to study.

Subject matter of the projects includes terrestrial and estuarine environmental research within the disciplines of mathematics, chemistry, microbiology, botany, zoology, and environmental education.

Fellowships are offered annually at the postdoctoral, predoctoral and graduate levels.

Internships are offered three times per year at the undergraduate levels, recent graduate, or beginning Master's student.

YEAR PROGRAM STARTED: 1972

PURPOSE:
To offer undergraduate and graduate-level students a unique opportunity to gain exposure to and experience in environmental research.

LEGAL BASIS:
Research unit of the Smithsonian Institution.

ELIGIBILITY:
Applicants must be qualified students from academic institutions in the U.S. or abroad. The SERC will accept applications from interested individuals who are in a position to commit themselves fully to the completion of a project. Selection is based upon the student's academic credentials, extent of relevant training or experience, letters of recommendation and the congruence of the student's expressed goals with those of the Professional Training Program.

FINANCIAL DATA:
Dorm space is available for $105 per week and does not include board. Space is limited.
Amount of support per award: Interns receive $550 per week.
Total amount of support: $50,400 postdoctoral/senior stipend; $36,000 predoctoral stipend; $7,500 graduate student; research allowances are additional.

NO. MOST RECENT APPLICANTS: 49 fellowship applicants and 460 internship applicants for the year 2019.

NO. AWARDS: 1 to 3 fellowships and 35 to 50 internships for the year 2019.

APPLICATION INFO:
Application materials and additional information regarding fellowships can be obtained from the Smithsonian Institution Office of Fellowships and Grants, E-mail: siofg@ofg.si.edu.

Applicants must use the Smithsonian On-Line Academic Appointment (SOLAA) web site for application submittal:
https://solaa.si.edu/solaa/solaahome.html.
Duration: Intern Appointments: Generally 10 to 16 weeks; Fellowships: One year, with renewal.

Deadline: November 1 for most fellowships; James Smithson Fellowship: January 15. Internships: November 15 for Winter/Spring Session; February 15 for Summer Session; June 1 for Fall Session.

PUBLICATIONS:
Application guidelines.

STAFF:
Anson H. Hines, Director
Patrick Megonigal, Associate Director of Research
Daniel E. Gustafson, Jr., Professional Training Coordinator

ADDRESS INQUIRIES TO:
Daniel E. Gustafson, Jr.
Professional Training Coordinator
(See address and e-mail above.)

SOIL AND WATER CONSERVATION SOCIETY [2011]

945 S.W. Ankeny Road
Ankeny, IA 50023-9723
(515) 289-2331
E-mail: awards@swcs.org
Web Site: www.swcs.org

AREAS OF INTEREST:
Soil, water and related natural resource management.

NAME(S) OF PROGRAMS:
● **Kenneth E. Grant Research Scholarship**

TYPE:
Research grants. Provides financial aid to members of the Society for graduate-level research on a specific conservation topic that will help the Society carry out its mission of fostering the science and the art of soil, water, and related natural resource management to achieve sustainability.

YEAR PROGRAM STARTED: 1978

PURPOSE:
To foster the science and the art of soil, water and related natural resource management to achieve sustainability; to promote and practice an ethic recognizing the interdependence of people and the environment.

ELIGIBILITY:
Open to members of the Society who have demonstrated integrity, ability and competence to complete the specified study topic. Applicants must be eligible for graduate work at an accredited institution and show reasonable need for financial assistance. Must be members of the Society for at least one year.

FINANCIAL DATA:
Amount of support per award: $300 to $500 for the year 2018.

NO. AWARDS: 1.

APPLICATION INFO:
Applicants must provide responses to questions in the online application. The following supplemental materials can be uploaded during the application process:
(1) a proposal (three pages maximum) that supports completing a specified research project related to this year's research and;
(2) budget for the project.
Included in the proposal should be material supporting the applicant's ability to meet the eligibility requirements outlined above.

Scholarship application can be completed and submitted electronically.

Duration: One year.
Deadline: April 24.

ADDRESS INQUIRIES TO:
Tel: (515) 289-2331, ext. 112
(See e-mail address above.)

SOIL AND WATER CONSERVATION SOCIETY [2012]

945 S.W. Ankeny Road
Ankeny, IA 50023-9723
(515) 289-2331
E-mail: awards@swcs.org
Web Site: www.swcs.org

AREAS OF INTEREST:
Soil, water and related natural resource management.

NAME(S) OF PROGRAMS:
● **Melvin H. Cohee Student Leader Conservation Scholarship**

TYPE:
Scholarships. The Cohee Scholarship provides financial assistance to Society members who are in their junior or senior year of full-time undergraduate study or are pursuing graduate level studies with a natural resource conservation orientation at a properly accredited college or university.

PURPOSE:
To foster the science and the art of soil, water and natural resource management to achieve sustainability.

ELIGIBILITY:
Applicant must:
(1) be a member of SWCS for at least one year prior to the application deadline;
(2) be in their junior or senior year of full-time undergraduate study in fall of 2020 or pursuing graduate level studies in a natural resource field and;
(3) show a reasonable need for financial assistance.

Members of the SWCS Awards Committee and their immediate families are not eligible.

FINANCIAL DATA:
Amount of support per award: Up to $500.

NO. AWARDS: 1.

APPLICATION INFO:
Application form must be submitted electronically. All supporting materials are to be uploaded in the online application.
Duration: One year.
Deadline: April 24.

ADDRESS INQUIRIES TO:
Tel: (515) 289-2331, ext. 112
(See e-mail address above.)

SOIL AND WATER CONSERVATION SOCIETY [2013]

945 S.W. Ankeny Road
Ankeny, IA 50023-9723
(515) 289-2331
E-mail: awards@swcs.org
Web Site: www.swcs.org

AREAS OF INTEREST:
Soil, water and related natural resource management.

NAME(S) OF PROGRAMS:
● **Donald A. Williams Soil Conservation Scholarship**

TYPE:
Scholarships. The Williams Scholarship provides financial assistance to Society members who are currently employed, but who wish to improve their technical or administrative competence in a conservation-related field through course work at an accredited college or through a program of special study.

PURPOSE:
To foster the science and the art of soil, water and natural resource management to achieve sustainability.

ELIGIBILITY:
Applicant must:
(1) be a member of SWCS for at least one year prior to the application deadline;
(2) have demonstrated integrity, ability, and competence in his or her work and possess skills gained through training or experience;
(3) have completed at least one year of full-time employment in a natural resource conservation endeavor;
(4) be currently employed in a natural resource-related field and;
(5) show reasonable financial need.

Members of the SWCS Awards Committee and their immediate families are not eligible.

FINANCIAL DATA:
Amount of support per award: $1,000.

NO. AWARDS: 1.

APPLICATION INFO:
Application form is to be submitted electronically. All supporting materials must be uploaded in the online application.
Deadline: April 24.

ADDRESS INQUIRIES TO:
Tel: (515) 289-2331, ext. 112
(See e-mail address above.)

THE ROBERT & PATRICIA SWITZER FOUNDATION [2014]

P.O. Box 293
Belfast, ME 04915-0293
(207) 338-5654
Fax: (207) 338-5655
E-mail: erin@switzernetwork.org
Web Site: www.switzernetwork.org

FOUNDED: 1987

AREAS OF INTEREST:
Environment.

NAME(S) OF PROGRAMS:
● **Switzer Environmental Fellowship Program**

TYPE:
Fellowships; Project/program grants. Annual fellowship to recognize environmental leaders who have the ability and determination to make a significant impact on environmental quality.

YEAR PROGRAM STARTED: 1987

PURPOSE:
To support highly talented graduate students in California and New England whose studies are directed toward improving environmental quality and who demonstrate leadership in their field.

ELIGIBILITY:
Applicants must meet the following criteria:
(1) be a U.S. citizen;
(2) be enrolled in an accredited institution in California or New England and;
(3) have strong academic qualifications.

Master's degree candidates must have completed at least one semester of course work.

Ph.D. candidates must have completed at least three years of doctoral work or passed their qualifying exams.

GEOG. RESTRICTIONS: California and New England.

FINANCIAL DATA:
Amount of support per award: $15,000, paid in two equal installments, the first in June and the second in late January or early February.
Total amount of support: $300,000.

NO. MOST RECENT APPLICANTS: 300.

NO. AWARDS: 20 annually; 10 in California and 10 in New England.

APPLICATION INFO:
Application information is available on the web site.
Duration: One year.
Deadline: Early January.

ADDRESS INQUIRIES TO:
Erin Lloyd, Program Director
(See address above.)

U.S. DEPARTMENT OF
AGRICULTURE   [2015]
1400 Independence Avenue, S.W.
Stop 0513
Washington, DC 20250-0510
(202) 720-6221
Fax: (202) 720-4619
E-mail: shanita.landon@usda.gov
Web Site: www.fsa.usda.gov

FOUNDED: 1933

AREAS OF INTEREST:
The conservation of the nation's soil, forest and water resources.

CONSULTING OR VOLUNTEER SERVICES:
Technical assistance is provided by federal and state agencies cooperating with this program.

NAME(S) OF PROGRAMS:
● **Emergency Conservation Program (ECP)**

TYPE:
Grants-in-aid. Cost-share assistance with agricultural producers to rehabilitate agricultural lands damaged by natural disasters. Assistance may also be provided for carrying out emergency water conservation measures during periods of severe drought.

YEAR PROGRAM STARTED: 1957

PURPOSE:
To provide emergency funding and technical assistance for farmers and ranchers to rehabilitate farmland damaged by natural disasters and for carrying out emergency water conservation measures in periods of severe drought.

LEGAL BASIS:
Government agency, authorized by P.L. 95-334, August 1978.

ELIGIBILITY:
Applicants are limited to agricultural producers, such as owners, landlords, tenants or sharecroppers of farms or ranches used to produce grains, row crops, livestock, vegetables, hay, orchards, vineyards, seed crops or other agricultural commodities commercially.

All landowners, regardless of race, sex, religion, marital status, disability, color, age or national origin, may apply for cost-sharing.

GEOG. RESTRICTIONS: United States.

FINANCIAL DATA:
Amount of support per award: Maximum of $200,000 per person per disaster.
Matching fund requirements: Producers are required to contribute the difference between the cost-share amount and the total cost of each ECP practice.

ADDRESS INQUIRIES TO:
Contact the nearest FSA County Office where your land is located.

U.S. ENVIRONMENTAL
PROTECTION AGENCY   [2016]
Office of Superfund Remediation and Technology Innovation (5202P)
1200 Pennsylvania Avenue, N.W.
Washington, DC 20460
(703) 603-8714
E-mail: fine.ellyn@epa.gov
Web Site: www.epa.gov/superfund

FOUNDED: 1970

AREAS OF INTEREST:
Cleanup of hazardous waste releases into the environment.

NAME(S) OF PROGRAMS:
● **Superfund State and Indian Tribe Core Program Cooperative Agreements**
● **Superfund State, Political Subdivision, and Indian Tribe Site-Specific Cooperative Agreements**

TYPE:
Project/program grants. Superfund State and Indian Tribe Core Program Cooperative Agreements: This program seeks to effectively implement the statutory requirements of the Comprehensive Environmental Response, Compensation, and Liability Act (CERCLA), Section 121(f) for state involvement. It is intended to provide funds to conduct CERCLA activities which are not assignable to specific sites, but support a recipient's site-specific response program.

Superfund State, Political Subdivision, and Indian Tribe Site-Specific Cooperative Agreements: This program proposes to:
(1) conduct site characterization activities at potential or confirmed hazardous waste sites;
(2) undertake response planning and implementation actions at sites on the National Priorities List (NPL) to clean up the hazardous waste sites that are found to pose hazards to human health and;
(3) effectively implement the statutory requirements of CERCLA 121(f) which mandates substantial and meaningful state involvement.

YEAR PROGRAM STARTED: 1981

PURPOSE:
To undertake removal actions at NPL and non-NPL sites to protect the public from the release of hazardous materials; to conduct preremedial activities to determine if sites require listing on the NPL; to perform remedial planning and remedial implementation actions in response to releases on the NPL; to clean up the hazardous waste sites that are found to pose

the most imminent threat to human health; to support state involvement in the Superfund program.

LEGAL BASIS:
Comprehensive Environmental Response, Compensation and Liability Act of 1980 (Superfund) (P.L. 96-510), as amended by The Superfund Amendments and Reauthorization Act of 1986 (SARA) (P.L. 99-499), The Small Business Liability Relief and Brown Fields Revitalization Act (PL 107-118).

ELIGIBILITY:
States (and political subdivisions thereof), commonwealths, U.S. territories and possessions, and federally recognized Indian tribal governments, including intertribal consortia.

GEOG. RESTRICTIONS: United States and its territories.

FINANCIAL DATA:
Amount of support per award: Varies.

ADDRESS INQUIRIES TO:
Ellyn Fine, State Coordinator
(See address above.)

U.S. SOCIETY ON DAMS
9975 Wadsworth Parkway
Suite K-2, 145
Westminster, CO 80021
(303) 792-8753
Fax: (303) 792-8782
E-mail: info@ussdams.org
Web Site: www.ussdams.org

TYPE:
Awards/prizes; Scholarships.
See entry 2451 for full listing.

UNIVERSITY OF
PITTSBURGH   [2017]
Pymatuning Laboratory of Ecology
13142 Hartstown Road
Linesville, PA 16424
(814) 273-0416
Fax: (814) 683-2302
E-mail: pymlab@pitt.edu
Web Site: www.biology.pitt.
edu/facilities/pymatuning

FOUNDED: 1949

AREAS OF INTEREST:
Ecology research.

NAME(S) OF PROGRAMS:
● **Leasure K. Darbaker Prize in Botany**
● **McKinley Research Fund**
● **Pape Research Fund**

TYPE:
Research grants. The Leasure K. Darbaker Prize in Botany is an annual award available for support of botanically related studies at the graduate or postdoctoral level.

The G. McKinley Research Fund and the Pape Research Fund of the Pittsburgh Foundation provide grants for support of graduate and postdoctoral research in ecology. Several are awarded each summer.

LEGAL BASIS:
Department of the University of Pittsburgh.

ELIGIBILITY:
Proposals are welcome at all academic graduate and postdoctoral levels for research in any area of ecology.

Awards are granted for work to be carried out at the facility in northwestern Pennsylvania.

FINANCIAL DATA:
Funds for travel, equipment, supplies, assistants and room and board at the laboratory may be included.

Amount of support per award: Up to $3,500 per award.

Total amount of support: Approximately $14,000 annually.

APPLICATION INFO:
Application information can be found at the web site.

Deadline: February 19.

PUBLICATIONS:
Application guidelines.

ADDRESS INQUIRIES TO:
Chris Davis, Assistant Director
(See address above.)

THE UNIVERSITY OF SYDNEY [2018]
Scholarships Office
Level 4, Jane Foss Russell Building G02
The University of Sydney N.S.W. 2006
Australia
61 (02) 8627 1444
E-mail: scholarships.officer@sydney.edu.au
Web Site: www.sydney.edu.au/scholarships

FOUNDED: 1850

AREAS OF INTEREST:
Water conservation.

NAME(S) OF PROGRAMS:
● **Richard Claude Mankin Scholarship**

TYPE:
Scholarships. Postdoctoral award for research and postgraduate for research leading to a higher degree. Tenable at the University of Sydney.

YEAR PROGRAM STARTED: 1973

PURPOSE:
To promote research related to water conservation at the University of Sydney.

LEGAL BASIS:
University.

ELIGIBILITY:
Candidates may be of postgraduate or postdoctoral standing at the University of Sydney.

FINANCIAL DATA:
The scholarship does not cover tuition fees payable by international students.

Amount of support per award: $35,000 AUD per annum for the year 2020.

NO. AWARDS: 1 offered as vacancy occurs and funds are available.

APPLICATION INFO:
Application information is available on the web site.

Duration: Two years for Master's candidate. Up to three years for Ph.D. candidate. In extraordinary circumstances, an additional six months may be granted to Ph.D. candidates.

VIRGINIA ENVIRONMENTAL ENDOWMENT [2019]
919 East Main Street, Suite 1070
Richmond, VA 23219
(804) 644-5000
Fax: (804) 644-0603
E-mail: info@vee.org
Web Site: www.vee.org

FOUNDED: 1977

AREAS OF INTEREST:
Environmental improvement.

NAME(S) OF PROGRAMS:
● **James River Water Quality Improvement Program**
● **Kanawha and Ohio River Valleys Program**
● **Virginia Program**

TYPE:
Challenge/matching grants; Demonstration grants; Project/program grants; Research grants; Seed money grants; Research contracts. Provides grants to projects that demonstrate feasibility, innovation and appropriateness to the Endowment's purpose and priorities. Improvement of the quality of the environment in the Commonwealth of Virginia, especially water quality research and monitoring; land conservation; Chesapeake Bay conservation, research and education; and environmental education. Programs addressing water quality and the effects of water pollution on public health and the environment in the Kanawha River and Ohio River valleys of Kentucky and West Virginia.

YEAR PROGRAM STARTED: 1977

PURPOSE:
To improve the quality of the environment by using its capital, expertise and resources to encourage all sectors to work together to prevent pollution, conserve natural resources and promote environmental literacy.

LEGAL BASIS:
Tax-exempt, grantmaking organization 501(c)(4).

ELIGIBILITY:
The Endowment makes grants to nonprofit, tax-exempt, charitable organizations and institutions, and governmental agencies. It encourages requests for specific projects that promise measurable results to improve the environment. Applicants should describe specifically how they propose to measure the success of a grant project. Grant funds are not provided for general support, overhead, indirect costs, capital projects, land purchases, building construction or renovation, endowments, lawsuits or to individuals.

GEOG. RESTRICTIONS: The state of Virginia and the Kanawha and Ohio River valleys of Kentucky and West Virginia.

FINANCIAL DATA:
Reviewed asset value: $38,636,833 as of March 31, 2018.

Amount of support per award: Varies.
Total amount of support: $542,970 for fiscal year ended March 31, 2018.

Matching fund requirements: At least a 1:1 match is normally required.

CO-OP FUNDING PROGRAMS: The Endowment welcomes opportunities for collaboration.

NO. MOST RECENT APPLICANTS: 70 for fiscal year 2018.

NO. AWARDS: 29 for fiscal year ended March 31, 2018.

APPLICATION INFO:
Two copies of the complete proposal, signed by the organization's chief executive officer or board chairman, must be received by the deadline date. The Endowment does not review or comment on preliminary proposals.

Each proposal must include the following information:
(1) a cover letter identifying the applicant,

project title, grant request, matching funds, project schedule, and whether the proposal is being submitted to the Virginia Program, the James River Water Quality Improvement Program, or the Kanawha and Ohio River Valleys Program;
(2) a project description, limited to five pages, clearly stating the need for the project, goals and objectives and how they will be achieved, how project results will be measured, and relationship to other work being done in the field;
(3) a description of the organization, names and qualifications of key project staff, a list of the members of the governing board, the current operating budget, and a copy of the current tax-exempt ruling from the IRS, if applicable;
(4) a line-item budget for the proposed project showing total project costs, the amount and proposed allocation of grant funds requested from the Endowment, and all sources and amounts of matching funds, which must equal or exceed the requested grant;
(5) the project schedule, with specific beginning and ending dates for requested grant support and;
(6) a detailed plan for evaluating and disseminating project results, for continuing project activities, and for raising future financial support.

For delivery by U.S. Mail, address to Joseph Maroon, Executive Director, Virginia Environmental Endowment, P.O. Box 790, Richmond, VA 23218-0790.

The complete list of priorities, grant criteria and required documentation is available on the Endowment's web site listed above.

Duration: Stipulated with specific projects. One year preferred.

Deadline: James River Water Quality Improvement Program: June 15; Kanawha and Ohio River Valleys Program: December 1; Virginia Program: June 15 and December 1.

PUBLICATIONS:
Annual report, including guidelines.

IRS I.D.: 54-1041973

STAFF:
Joseph Maroon, Executive Director

DIRECTORS:
Robin D. Baliles
Dixon M. Butler
Lawrence Kochard
Nina Randolph
Nancy N. Rogers
Robert B. Smith, Jr.
Blair Winbush

ADDRESS INQUIRIES TO:
Joseph Maroon, Executive Director
(See address above.)

*SPECIAL STIPULATIONS:
No preliminary proposal reviews are provided; full proposals are required.

WEEDEN FOUNDATION [2020]
P.O. Box 606
Bedford Hills, NY 10507-0606
(914) 864-1375
Fax: (914) 864-1377
E-mail: info@weedenfoundation.org
Web Site: www.weedenfoundation.org

FOUNDED: 1963

AREAS OF INTEREST:
Biodiversity, population and environment, natural resource conservation and consumption.

NAME(S) OF PROGRAMS:
- **Consumption**
- **Domestic Biodiversity**
- **International Biodiversity**
- **Population**

TYPE:
General operating grants; Project/program grants.

YEAR PROGRAM STARTED: 1963

PURPOSE:
To embrace the protection of biodiversity.

LEGAL BASIS:
Nonprofit, family foundation.

ELIGIBILITY:
Applicants must be nonprofit, tax-exempt organizations with 501(c)(3) status or international equivalent.

GEOG. RESTRICTIONS: Chile, Northern California and the High Divide.

FINANCIAL DATA:
Amount of support per award: Average: $15,000 to $20,000.
Total amount of support: Varies.

NO. MOST RECENT APPLICANTS: 76 for the year 2019.

NO. AWARDS: 64 for the year 2019.

APPLICATION INFO:
Applications are submitted through the Foundation web site.
Duration: One year. Renewal possible.
Deadline: Varies.

IRS I.D.: 94-6109313

STAFF:
Donald A. Weeden, Executive Director
Peggy Kennedy, Research Assistant

BOARD OF DIRECTORS:
Norm Weeden, Ph.D., President
John D. Weeden, Vice President
Bob Weeden, Treasurer
Leslie Weeden, Secretary
Barbara Daugherty
Nicholas Leibowitz
Malcolm Roux
Alan Weeden
William Weeden

ADDRESS INQUIRIES TO:
Donald A. Weeden, Executive Director
(See address above.)

THE DEAN WITTER FOUNDATION

57 Post Street, Suite 510
San Francisco, CA 94104
(415) 981-2966
Fax: (415) 981-5218
E-mail: admin@deanwitterfoundation.org
Web Site: www.deanwitterfoundation.org

TYPE:
Challenge/matching grants; Fellowships; General operating grants; Internships; Matching gifts; Professorships; Project/program grants; Research grants; Scholarships; Seed money grants.

See entry 1746 for full listing.

Medicine (multiple disciplines)

A-T CHILDREN'S PROJECT [2021]

6810 State Road 7
Suite 125
Coconut Creek, FL 33073
(954) 481-6611
E-mail: grants@atcp.org
Web Site: www.atcp.org

FOUNDED: 1993

AREAS OF INTEREST:
Projects that, while drawing on basic discoveries, apply innovative and novel strategies for suggesting, developing and evaluating specific disease-modifying and symptomatic interventions for ataxia-telangiectasia (A-T); clinical studies for A-T.

NAME(S) OF PROGRAMS:
- **A-T Postdoctoral Fellowship Award**
- **A-T Research Grant Program**

TYPE:
Research grants.

YEAR PROGRAM STARTED: 1993

PURPOSE:
To accelerate first-rate, international scientific research in an attempt to help find a cure or life-improving therapies for children with ataxia-telangiectasia.

ELIGIBILITY:
Open to all ages and nationalities. Proposal for grant must have direct relevance to ataxia-telangiectasia.

Applicants should be aware that meritorious proposals may be rejected if:
(1) the proposed research is too far from being relevant to a therapeutic intervention;
(2) the A-T Children's Project's scientific advisors find the research redundant and in no need of validation;
(3) the proposed research is likely to happen anyway, without the A-T Children's Project's support and;
(4) the research cannot realistically be achieved with the proposed budget.

FINANCIAL DATA:
Amount of support per award: A-T Postdoctoral Fellowship: $30,000 to $40,000 over two years; A-T Research Grant: Up to $75,000 per year.
Total amount of support: Varies.

APPLICATION INFO:
Detailed information can be found on the organization web site. A Letter of Intent (LOI) is required prior to submission of a full-length proposal. An LOI form can be downloaded from the web site.
Duration: One to two years.
Deadline: Letter of Intent: August 1 for September 1 deadline and February 1 for March 1 deadline. Full proposal: March 1 and September 1.

ADDRESS INQUIRIES TO:
Dr. Cynthia Rothblum-Oviatt
Science Coordinator
E-mail: cynthia@atcp.org

THE JOHN W. ALDEN TRUST

c/o Emma M. Greene, Senior V.P.
Philanthropic Client Dir., U.S. Trust
Bank of America Private Wealth Management
225 Franklin Street, MA1-225-04-02
Boston, MA 02110
(617) 951-1108
E-mail: susan.t.monahan@gmail.com
Web Site: www.cybergrants.com/alden

TYPE:
Capital grants; Challenge/matching grants; Conferences/seminars; Demonstration grants; Development grants; Matching gifts; Project/program grants; Research grants; Seed money grants; Technical assistance; Training grants.

See entry 1008 for full listing.

ALZHEIMER'S DRUG DISCOVERY FOUNDATION [2022]

57 West 57th Street
Suite 904
New York, NY 10019
(212) 901-8000
Fax: (212) 901-8010
E-mail: info@alzdiscovery.org
grants@alzdiscovery.org
Web Site: www.alzdiscovery.org

FOUNDED: 2004

AREAS OF INTEREST:
Drug discovery and development for Alzheimer's disease, related dementias and cognitive decline.

NAME(S) OF PROGRAMS:
- **ADDF/NIH**
- **Biomarkers Development**
- **Drug Development**
- **Prevention Beyond the Pipeline**
- **Program to Accelerate Clinical Trials (PACT)**

TYPE:
Awards/prizes; Conferences/seminars; Research grants.

PURPOSE:
To promote the research and development of therapies to identify, treat and prevent cognitive decline, Alzheimer's disease and related dementias.

LEGAL BASIS:
Nonprofit Delaware corporation 501(c)(3) public charity.

ELIGIBILITY:
Applicant must be a university medical center or early-stage biotechnology company.

FINANCIAL DATA:
Amount of support per award: ADDF/NIH: Varies; Biomarkers Development and Drug Development: Up to $600,000; Prevention Beyond the Pipeline: $50,000 to $100,000; Budget requests up to $3,000,000 are accepted for clinical trial submissions.
Total amount of support: Varies.

NO. MOST RECENT APPLICANTS: Approximately 450 for the year 2017.

APPLICATION INFO:
Complete instructions are available on the Foundation web site.
Duration: One to two years.
Deadline: Letters of intent accepted on an ongoing basis. Applications due quarterly.

ADDRESS INQUIRIES TO:
Dan Teng, Grants Manager
(See address above.)

AMERICAN ASSOCIATION FOR HAND SURGERY [2023]

500 Cummings Center
Suite 4400
Beverly, MA 01915
(978) 927-8330
Fax: (978) 524-0498
E-mail: contact@handsurgery.org
Web Site: www.handsurgery.org

FOUNDED: 1970

AREAS OF INTEREST:
Hand surgery and hand therapy.

TYPE:
Research grants. International hand therapy outreach.

YEAR PROGRAM STARTED: 1970

PURPOSE:
To promote education and research; to foster creativity and innovation in basic and/or clinical research in all areas pertinent to hand surgery and hand therapy.

ELIGIBILITY:
Applications are open to AAHS members and candidates for membership. Residents and fellows sponsored by an AAHS member are also eligible to apply. One of the co-investigators must be an Active or Affiliate AAHS member. AAHS therapist and surgeon members are eligible to apply for the Vargas International Hand Therapy Teaching Award.

FINANCIAL DATA:
Amount of support per award: AAHS/PSF Combined Pilot Research Grant and AAHS Research Grant: $10,000; Vargas International Hand Therapy Teaching Award: Up to $5,000 in reimbursement for mission expenses.

CO-OP FUNDING PROGRAMS: Match grant with Plastic Surgery Foundation.

APPLICATION INFO:
Application information is available on the web site.
Duration: One year.

ADDRESS INQUIRIES TO:
See e-mail address above.

AMERICAN COLLEGE OF LEGAL MEDICINE [2024]

1061 East Main Street
Suite 300
East Dundee, IL 60118
(847) 752-5355
E-mail: info@aclm.org
Web Site: www.aclm.org

FOUNDED: 1960

AREAS OF INTEREST:
Legal medicine.

NAME(S) OF PROGRAMS:
● **American College of Legal Medicine's Student Writing Competition in Law, Medicine and Bioethics**

TYPE:
Awards/prizes. The Hirsh Award is awarded to a law, dentistry, podiatry, nursing, pharmacy, health science, health care administration, or public health student.

PURPOSE:
To promote interdisciplinary cooperation and an understanding of issues where law and medicine converge.

ELIGIBILITY:
Must be a student at an accredited school of law, medicine, dentistry, podiatry, nursing, pharmacy, health science, health care, administration, or public health that has written an outstanding original paper on Legal Medicine.

FINANCIAL DATA:
Amount of support per award: Hirsh Award: $1,000 first prize, $500 second prize and $250 third prize.
Total amount of support: $1,750.

NO. MOST RECENT APPLICANTS: 12 to 14.

NO. AWARDS: 3.

APPLICATION INFO:
Contact the College.
Deadline: January 15.

ADDRESS INQUIRIES TO:
Gina Baxter, Associate Director
(See address above.)

AMERICAN FEDERATION FOR AGING RESEARCH (AFAR) [2025]

55 West 39th Street
16th Floor
New York, NY 10018
(212) 703-9977
(888) 582-2327
Fax: (212) 997-0330
E-mail: grants@afar.org
Web Site: www.afar.org

FOUNDED: 1981

AREAS OF INTEREST:
Biomedical aging research.

NAME(S) OF PROGRAMS:
● **Glenn Foundation for Medical Research Postdoctoral Fellowships in Aging Research**

TYPE:
Fellowships; Research grants; Training grants. Glenn Foundation for Medical Research Postdoctoral Fellowships in Aging Research support basic and translational research that builds on early discoveries that show translational potential for clinical relevant strategies. In partnership with the American Federation for Aging Research (AFAR), these fellowships aim to encourage and further the careers of postdoctoral fellows who are conducting research in the basic biology of aging, as well as translating advances in basic research from the laboratory to the clinic. The award is intended to provide significant research and training support to permit these postdoctoral fellows to become established in the field of aging.

PURPOSE:
To support basic biomedical research that promotes healthier aging and advances the understanding of the aging process and its associated diseases and disorders.

LEGAL BASIS:
Private foundation.

ELIGIBILITY:
Applicant must be a postdoctoral fellow (M.D. and/or Ph.D. or equivalent) at the start date of the award. Applicants whose total postdoctoral training period is great than five years must provide a justification for the additional training period.

The proposed research must be conducted at a qualified not-for-profit setting in the U.S.

Individuals who are employees in the NIH intramural program and individuals who are currently receiving financial support at a Paul F. Glenn Center for Biology of Aging Research are not eligible.

Fellows may not hold any concurrent not-for-profit or government funding for the same research project.

Applications from underrepresented groups in the biomedical sciences are encouraged.

GEOG. RESTRICTIONS: United States.

FINANCIAL DATA:
Amount of support per award: $60,000.

NO. AWARDS: Up to 10.

APPLICATION INFO:
Duration: One year.
Deadline: Letter of Inquiry: January. Invited Application: Mid-May.

PUBLICATIONS:
Program announcement.

STAFF:
Stephanie Lederman, Executive Director
Odette van der Willik, Director, Grant Programs
Hattie Herman, Program Officer
Catherine Cullar, Administrative Manager

ADDRESS INQUIRIES TO:
Hattie Herman, Program Officer
(See address above.)

AMERICAN FEDERATION FOR AGING RESEARCH (AFAR) [2026]

55 West 39th Street
16th Floor
New York, NY 10018
(212) 703-9977
(888) 582-2327
Fax: (212) 997-0330
E-mail: grants@afar.org
Web Site: www.afar.org

FOUNDED: 1981

AREAS OF INTEREST:
Biomedical aging research.

NAME(S) OF PROGRAMS:
● **Paul Beeson Career Development Awards in Aging Research Program**
● **Glenn Foundation for Medical Research and AFAR Grants for Junior Faculty**
● **Glenn Foundation for Medical Research Breakthroughs in Gerontology (BIG) Awards**
● **Diana Jacobs Kalman/AFAR Scholarships for Research in the Biology of Aging**
● **Medical Student Training in Aging Research Program (MSTAR)**

TYPE:
Fellowships; Research grants; Scholarships; Training grants. The Paul Beeson Career Development Awards in Aging Research Program is intended to bolster the current and severe shortage of academic physicians who have the combination of medical, academic and scientific training relative to caring for older people.

The Glenn Foundation for Medical Research and AFAR Grants for Junior Faculty are given to provide one to two years of support for junior faculty to do research that will serve as the basis for longer-term research efforts.

The Glenn Foundation for Medical Research Breakthroughs in Gerontology Awards are to provide timely support to a small number of pilot research programs that may be of relatively high risk but which offer significant promise of yielding transforming discoveries in the fundamental biology of aging.

The Diana Jacobs Kalman/AFAR Scholarships for Research in the Biology of Aging aims to attract new generations of talented investigators to the field of aging research.

Medical Student Training in Aging Research Program (MSTAR) provides medical students, early in their training, with an enriching experience in aging-related research and geriatrics, under the mentorship of top experts in the field. Students participate in an eight- to 12-week structured research, clinical and didactic program in geriatrics.

PURPOSE:
To support basic biomedical research that promotes healthier aging and advances the understanding of the aging process and its associated diseases and disorders; to encourage the training of new scientists and physicians in geriatric research and in the practice of geriatric medicine.

LEGAL BASIS:
Private foundation.

ELIGIBILITY:
Paul Beeson Career Development Awards in Aging Research Program applicants are clinically trained individuals who are pursuing research careers in aging.

For the Glenn Foundation for Medical Research and AFAR Grants for Junior Faculty, applicants must be junior faculty (M.Ds. and Ph.Ds.).

For the Glenn Foundation for Medical Research Breakthroughs in Gerontology Awards, qualified applicants must be full-time faculty members at the rank of assistant professor or higher who can demonstrate a strong record of independence.

For the Diana Jacobs Kalman/AFAR Scholarships for Research in the Biology of Aging, student must be enrolled in an M.D., D.O., Ph.D., or combined-degree program.

The Medical Student Training in Aging Research Program (MSTAR) is intended for medical students and is built on the Medical Student Geriatric Scholars Program.

GEOG. RESTRICTIONS: United States.

FINANCIAL DATA:
Amount of support per award: Paul Beeson Career Development Awards in Aging Research: $200,000 per year; Glenn Foundation/AFAR Grants: Up to $100,000; Glenn Foundation for Medical Research BIG Awards: Up to $300,000; Diana Jacobs Kalman/AFAR Scholarships: $5,000.

NO. MOST RECENT APPLICANTS: Paul Beeson Career Development Awards in Aging Research: Varies; Glenn Foundation/AFAR Grants: 148; Glenn Foundation for Medical Research BIG Awards: 68.

NO. AWARDS: Paul Beeson Career Development Awards in Aging Research, Glenn Foundation/AFAR Grants and Diana Jacobs Kalman/AFAR Scholarships: Up to 10; Glenn Foundation for Medical Research BIG Awards: 2.

APPLICATION INFO:
Required application form is available on the web site.

Duration: Beeson Career Development Awards in Aging Research: Up to five years. Glenn Foundation/AFAR Grants: One to two years. Glenn Foundation for Medical Research BIG Awards: Three years. Diana Jacobs Kalman/AFAR Scholarships: Three to six months.

Deadline: Glenn Foundation/AFAR Grants and Glenn Foundation for Medical Research BIG Awards: Mid-December. Paul Beeson: Varies.

PUBLICATIONS:
Program announcement.

STAFF:
Stephanie Lederman, Executive Director
Odette van der Willik, Director, Grant Programs
Hattie Herman, Program Officer
Catherine Cullar, Administrative Manager

ADDRESS INQUIRIES TO:
Hattie Herman, Program Officer
(See address above.)

AMERICAN KIDNEY FUND [2027]

11921 Rockville Pike, Suite 300
Rockville, MD 20852
(800) 638-8299
(866) 300-2900 (Spanish/English HelpLine)
Fax: (301) 881-0898
E-mail: helpline@kidneyfund.org
Web Site: www.kidneyfund.org

FOUNDED: 1971

AREAS OF INTEREST:
Treatment, prevention and cure of kidney disease.

NAME(S) OF PROGRAMS:
● **Clinical Scientist in Nephrology (CSN)**

TYPE:
Fellowships.

YEAR PROGRAM STARTED: 1988

PURPOSE:
To improve the quality of care provided to kidney patients; to promote clinical research in nephrology.

ELIGIBILITY:
Applicant must be a nephrologist in a current academic setting.

GEOG. RESTRICTIONS: United States and its territories.

FINANCIAL DATA:
Amount of support per award: Up to $80,000 per year.
Total amount of support: Up to $160,000.

NO. MOST RECENT APPLICANTS: 10.

NO. AWARDS: 1 to 2.

APPLICATION INFO:
Complete application information may be found on the web site.
Duration: One to two years.
Deadline: December 1.

ADDRESS INQUIRIES TO:
Michael Spigler, Vice President of Patient Services and
Kidney Disease Education
(See address above.)

AMERICAN KIDNEY FUND [2028]

11921 Rockville Pike, Suite 300
Rockville, MD 20852
(800) 638-8299
(866) 300-2900 (Spanish/English HelpLine)
Fax: (301) 881-0898
E-mail: patientservice@kidneyfund.org
Web Site: www.kidneyfund.org

FOUNDED: 1971

AREAS OF INTEREST:
Treatment, prevention and cure of kidney disease.

NAME(S) OF PROGRAMS:
● **Patient Services Grants: Safety Net Grant Program**

TYPE:
Grants-in-aid. Medical Grants. Provides financial assistance to qualified dialysis patients who are referred by their physicians and social workers for treatment-specific expenses such as transportation, over-the-counter medicines, medication co-payments, kidney donor expenses, mobility aids and nutritional supplements.

YEAR PROGRAM STARTED: 1971

PURPOSE:
To provide aid in the treatment, prevention, and cure of kidney disease.

ELIGIBILITY:
Based on financial need. Kidney dialysis and transplant patients living in the U.S. are eligible. Additional requirements are available online.

GEOG. RESTRICTIONS: United States and its territories.

FINANCIAL DATA:
Amount of support per award: $100 per year.

APPLICATION INFO:
Applications must be submitted online via Grants Management System. Applications must be completed by the patient and a dialysis or transplant renal professional. Paper applications will no longer be accepted.
Duration: Renewable 12 months from the check date of the last grant.

IRS I.D.: 23-7124261

ADDRESS INQUIRIES TO:
Patient Services Department
Tel: (800) 795-3226
(See address above.)

AMERICAN MEDICAL ASSOCIATION FOUNDATION

330 North Wabash Avenue
Suite 39300
Chicago, IL 60611-5885
(312) 464-4200
Fax: (312) 464-4142
E-mail: amafoundation@ama-assn.org
Web Site: www.amafoundation.org

TYPE:
Awards/prizes; Project/program grants; Scholarships. Excellence in Medicine Awards are given to recognize physicians and medical students who are improving the health of their communities and the lives of those who are most in need.

The Joan F. Giambalvo Memorial Scholarship is presented in conjunction with the AMA's Women Physicians Congress to provide a research grant to help researchers advance the progress of women in the medical profession and identify and address the needs of women physicians and medical students.

The Physicians of Tomorrow Scholarships are awarded to rising fourth-year medical students based on financial need and academic excellence.

See entry 1500 for full listing.

AMERICAN MEDICAL WOMEN'S ASSOCIATION, INC. [2029]

1100 East Woodfield Road
Suite 350
Schaumburg, IL 60173
(847) 517-2801
Fax: (847) 517-7229
E-mail: associatedirector@amwa-doc.org
Web Site: www.amwa-doc.org

FOUNDED: 1915

AREAS OF INTEREST:
Women physicians, women medical students and women's health.

NAME(S) OF PROGRAMS:
● **American Women's Hospitals Service (AWHS)**

TYPE:
Awards/prizes; Conferences/seminars; General operating grants; Project/program grants; Training grants; Travel grants. Support for clinics serving the poor in medically underserved areas, scholarships and loans to qualifying women medical students, and continuing medical education for physicians in areas related to women's health.

YEAR PROGRAM STARTED: 1915

PURPOSE:
To advance women in medicine and improve women's health through advocacy, leadership, education, expertise and mentoring, and strategic alliances.

LEGAL BASIS:
AMWA: 501(c)(6) corporation. AWHS: 501(c)(3) foundation.

ELIGIBILITY:
Open to women who are enrolled in accredited medical schools in the U.S.

GEOG. RESTRICTIONS: United States.

FINANCIAL DATA:
Amount of support per award: Overseas Clinic Support Grants: $2,000 to $3,500; Overseas Travel and Community Project Grants: $500 to $1,000.

NO. MOST RECENT APPLICANTS: Overseas Clinic Support Grants: 3; Overseas Travel and Community Project Grants: 11.

NO. AWARDS: Overseas Clinic Support Grants: 3; Overseas Travel and Community Project Grants: 7.

APPLICATION INFO:
Duration: Overseas Clinic Support Grants: One year; Overseas Travel and Community Project Grants: One trip minimum four weeks or one project.
Deadline: Overseas Clinic Support Grants: July 5. Overseas Travel and Community Project Grants: January 5, May 5 and September 5.

OFFICER:
Roberta Gebhard, D.O., President

ADDRESS INQUIRIES TO:
Danielle Carrier, Associate Director
(See address above.)

THE AMERICAN PORPHYRIA FOUNDATION [2030]

4915 St. Elmo Avenue
Suite 105
Bethesda, MD 20814
(301) 347-7166
(866) 273-3635
E-mail: porphyrus@porphyriafoundation.com
Web Site: www.porphyriafoundation.com

AREAS OF INTEREST:
Porphyria.

TYPE:
Research grants.

PURPOSE:
To improve the health and well-being of individuals and families affected by porphyria.

ELIGIBILITY:
Qualified investigators involved in porphyria research.

FINANCIAL DATA:
Amount of support per award: $5,000 to $10,000.
Total amount of support: Varies.

APPLICATION INFO:
Send a two-page summary of proposed research and research experience to the Foundation.
Duration: Typically one year.

PUBLICATIONS:
Newsletters.

ADDRESS INQUIRIES TO:
Desiree H. Lyon, Executive Director
(See address above.)

AMERICAN ROENTGEN RAY SOCIETY [2031]

44211 Slatestone Court
Leesburg, VA 20176-5109
(703) 729-3353
Fax: (703) 729-4839
E-mail: scholarships@arrs.org
Web Site: www.arrs.org

FOUNDED: 1900

AREAS OF INTEREST:
Diagnostic radiology.

NAME(S) OF PROGRAMS:
● **ARRS Annual Scholarship Program**

TYPE:
Scholarships.

YEAR PROGRAM STARTED: 1992

PURPOSE:
To provide resources needed to acquire knowledge, skills and training in areas that are vital to radiology but have traditionally been outside the scope of diagnostic radiology.

ELIGIBILITY:
Candidates must have earned an M.D. or D.O. from an accredited institution and must have completed all residencies or fellowship training or equivalent.

Candidate must be a member of ARRS at the time the application is submitted and for the duration of the award.

FINANCIAL DATA:
Funds distributed to individual's institution.
Amount of support per award: ARRS Scholarship: $140,000; ARRS Berlin Scholarship in Medical Professionalism: $100,000 over one or two years.
Total amount of support: Varies.

NO. AWARDS: 1 per award.

APPLICATION INFO:
Submission of a curriculum vitae, summary of qualifications, goals and purposes of the study, estimated budget, and a statement from department regarding applicant's goals and commitment ensuring applicant's return to faculty upon completion.

Applications are to be submitted to scholarships@arrs.org with required documents attached.
Duration: One or two years.
Deadline: October.

ADDRESS INQUIRIES TO:
See e-mail address above.

AMERICAN SOCIETY OF HEMATOLOGY [2032]

2021 L Street, N.W.
Suite 900
Washington, DC 20036
(202) 776-0544
E-mail: awards@hematology.org
Web Site: www.hematology.org

AREAS OF INTEREST:
Hematology.

NAME(S) OF PROGRAMS:
● **Physician-Scientist Career Development Award**
● **Research Training Award for Fellows**

TYPE:
Awards/prizes. Physician-Scientist Career Development Award allows medical students to gain knowledge and perform research in between their first, second and third year of school.

Research Training Award for Fellows allows protected time for research.

PURPOSE:
To help medical students gain experience in hematology research; to encourage research in hematology, hematology/oncology, or other hematology-related training programs.

ELIGIBILITY:
Physician-Scientist Career Development Award applicant must:
(1) be a medical student member of ASH;
(2) be a first-, second- or third-year medical student actively enrolled in an M.D. or D.O. medical program in an LCME or AOA COCA (or its equivalent) accredited medical school in the U.S. or Canada. Applicant must be in good standing relative to their course work at the time of application and be between their first and second, second and third, or third and fourth year of medical school at the time the research is done;
(3) not be currently enrolled in a combined M.D.-Ph.D. program;
(4) be planning an investigative career in laboratory, translational, or clinical hematology research;
(5) have a mentor who is an active ASH member at the time of application and;
(6) not have any other concurrent funding for a similar experience.

Research Training Award for Fellows applicant must be a second-, third-, fourth- or fifth-year student at the time of the award, who is not yet eligible for the ASH Scholar Awards. Applicant must:
(1) possess an M.D. or D.O.;
(2) continue to maintain ASH membership and remain a member in good standing for the duration of the award term;
(3) plan to pursue an investigative career in hematology research;
(4) have a mentor who is an ASH member at the time the application is submitted and;
(5) not hold a position as an Assistant Professor.

FINANCIAL DATA:
Amount of support per award: Physician-Scientist Award: $42,000; Research Training Award: $70,000.

NO. AWARDS: Physician-Scientist Award: Up to 5; Research Training Award: Up to 6.

APPLICATION INFO:
Guidelines are available on the Society's web site.
Duration: One year.
Deadline: Physician-Scientist Award: January; Research Training Award: Mid-January.

ADDRESS INQUIRIES TO:
Allie Samis, Awards Program Specialist
(See address above.)

AMERICAN SOCIETY OF HEMATOLOGY   [2033]
2021 L Street, N.W.
Suite 900
Washington, DC 20036
(202) 776-0544
E-mail: awards@hematology.org
Web Site: www.hematology.org

FOUNDED: 1985

AREAS OF INTEREST:
Hematology, basic and clinical/translational research.

NAME(S) OF PROGRAMS:
● **Fellow Scholar Award**
● **Fellow to Faculty Scholar Award**
● **Junior Faculty Scholar Award**

TYPE:
Awards/prizes; Fellowships; Research grants; Scholarships.

PURPOSE:
To support hematologists who have chosen a career in research.

ELIGIBILITY:
Applicants must be a citizen of, or hold a visa in, the U.S. or Canada. Research must be conducted within the U.S. and Canada. Applicants are required to be members of ASH in good standing at the time of the Letter of Intent submission, and for the duration of the Scholar Award Program. Consideration will be given if membership application is pending at the time of the application deadline.

For the Fellow Scholar Award, Ph.D. or M.D./Ph.D. applicants must have fewer than five years of research experience after completion of their Ph.D. (including research performed during fellowship, but excluding clinical fellowship time). M.D. applicants should have more than three but fewer than five years of research experience (including research performed during fellowship, but

excluding clinical fellowship time). M.D. applicants with fewer than three years research experience (inclusive of fellowship research time) should consider applying for the Senior RTAF award.

For the Junior Faculty Scholar Awards, applicant must hold an M.D., Ph.D. or M.D./Ph.D. and have more than five but fewer than 10 years of research experience after completion of their Ph.D. (including research performed during fellowship, but excluding clinical fellowship time).

Applicants with the title of Assistant Professor or equivalent must apply for the Junior Faculty Award, regardless of research experience.

GEOG. RESTRICTIONS: United States and Canada.

FINANCIAL DATA:
Amount of support per award: $150,000 for a Junior Faculty Scholar Award, $125,000 for a Fellow to Faculty Award or $100,000 for a Fellow Scholar Award. These awards can be spread over two or three years with an annual maximum not to exceed $75,000 for junior faculty, $62,500 for fellow to faculty and $50,000 for fellows.
Total amount of support: Approximately $3,800,000.

NO. MOST RECENT APPLICANTS: 198.

NO. AWARDS: 30.

APPLICATION INFO:
A letter of intent is required before submission of full proposal. Contact the Society for details.
Duration: Two to three years.
Deadline: Mandatory Letter of Intent: May 1.

ADDRESS INQUIRIES TO:
Vonnie Calemine
Awards Program Specialist
(See address above.)

AMERICAN SOCIETY OF HEMATOLOGY   [2034]
2021 L Street, N.W.
Suite 900
Washington, DC 20036
(202) 776-0544
E-mail: awards@hematology.org
Web Site: www.hematology.org

AREAS OF INTEREST:
Hematology.

NAME(S) OF PROGRAMS:
● **HONORS (Hematology Opportunities for the Next Generation of Research Scientists)**

TYPE:
Awards/prizes. Each scholarship provides the medical school with funds to cover the expenses for students to complete a program and travel support for students to attend the ASH annual meetings.

PURPOSE:
To provide medical students and residents with an introduction to the specialty of hematology by encouraging them to take time during their medical school curriculum to work on a project with a hematologist.

ELIGIBILITY:
Medical students and residents in the U.S., Mexico and Canada.

GEOG. RESTRICTIONS: United States, Mexico and Canada.

FINANCIAL DATA:
Amount of support per award: $5,000 cash award and $1,000 travel stipend for each of the two annual meetings.
Total amount of support: Varies.

APPLICATION INFO:
The institution is responsible for selecting student participants. Contact the Society for additional application information.
Duration: Varies.
Deadline: Mid-February.

ADDRESS INQUIRIES TO:
Allie Samis, Awards Program Specialist
(See address above.)

AMERICAN SOCIETY OF REGIONAL ANESTHESIA AND PAIN MEDICINE
3 Penn Center West
Suite 224
Pittsburgh, PA 15276
(412) 471-2718
Fax: (412) 471-7503
E-mail: asraassistant@asra.com
Web Site: www.asra.com

TYPE:
Research grants.

See entry 2332 for full listing.

AMERICAN SOCIETY OF REGIONAL ANESTHESIA AND PAIN MEDICINE   [2035]
3 Penn Center West
Suite 224
Pittsburgh, PA 15276
(412) 471-2718
Fax: (412) 471-7503
E-mail: asraassistant@asra.com
Web Site: www.asra.com

AREAS OF INTEREST:
Regional anesthesia and pain medicine.

NAME(S) OF PROGRAMS:
● **ASRA Early-Career Investigator Award**
● **ASRA Graduate Student Award**

TYPE:
Research grants.

PURPOSE:
To support research related to any aspect of regional anesthesia, acute and chronic pain medicine and their application to surgery, obstetrics and pain control; to encourage anesthesiologists and other researchers who are interested in the field.

ELIGIBILITY:
Applicant and co-investigators must be North Americans and members of ASRA.

For the Early-Career Investigator Award, the primary applicant must be an M.D. or D.O. within five years of graduating from a residency or fellowship program.

For the Graduate Student Award, the applicant must be a graduate or medical student.

FINANCIAL DATA:
Amount of support per award: Early-Career Investigator Award: Up to $30,000; Graduate Student Award: Up to $10,000.

NO. MOST RECENT APPLICANTS: 5.

NO. AWARDS: 1 per award.

APPLICATION INFO:
The application, which must be written by the applicant, should be accompanied by a complete narrative research protocol. The research proposal must be concerned with an original idea or concept. The research must be carried out primarily by the applicant.

Duration: Up to two years.

Deadline: Specific deadlines are posted on the ASRA web site.

ADDRESS INQUIRIES TO:
Angie Stengel, Executive Director
(See address above.)

AMERICAN VETERINARY MEDICAL ASSOCIATION   [2036]
AVMA Government Relations Division
1910 Sunderland Place, N.W.
Washington, DC 20036
(202) 289-3207
Fax: (202) 842-4360
E-mail: fellowship@avma.org
Web Site: www.avma.org/fellowship

AREAS OF INTEREST:
Veterinary medicine.

NAME(S) OF PROGRAMS:
● **AVMA Fellowship**

TYPE:
Fellowships.

YEAR PROGRAM STARTED: 1988

PURPOSE:
To support AVMA members to serve as a congressional fellow for one year in a personal or committee office of the U.S. Congress.

LEGAL BASIS:
Association.

ELIGIBILITY:
Applicants must be AVMA members and U.S. citizens who demonstrate special competence in an area of veterinary medicine, possess a broad professional background and exhibit an interest in applying scientific knowledge to solve societal/public policy problems.

Applicants must be articulate, literate, adaptable and capable of working on a wide range of policy issues.

Fellows must serve in Washington, DC.

FINANCIAL DATA:
Amount of support per award: Approximately $91,232.

NO. AWARDS: 2 for the year 2018-19.

APPLICATION INFO:
Applicants must submit:
(1) a letter of intent;
(2) a curriculum vitae;
(3) two letters of reference from professional colleagues;
(4) a letter of support from the applicant's local, state, specialty or allied veterinary medical organization and;
(5) a personal statement (not to exceed 750 words) describing the applicant's qualifications, commitment to veterinary medicine and why the fellowship is desired.

Duration: One year.

Deadline: Usually second Friday in February.

PUBLICATIONS:
Program announcement.

IRS I.D.: 36-6117739

ADDRESS INQUIRIES TO:
See e-mail address above.

ANIMAL ASSISTANCE FOUNDATION   [2037]
405 Urban Street
Suite 340
Lakewood, CO 80228
(303) 744-8396
E-mail: info@aaf-fd.org
Web Site: www.aaf-fd.org

FOUNDED: 1975

AREAS OF INTEREST:
Companion animal overpopulation, operational optimization, adoption and permanent homes, cruelty prevention and intervention, innovation and ingenuity and companion animals and unwanted horse issues.

TYPE:
Capital grants; General operating grants; Project/program grants. Operating and service grants. The Foundation offers charitable support through its grantmaking program to organizations located within the state of Colorado or an agency that has a direct impact on animals and their owners in Colorado. Direct impact on animals and their owners in Colorado applies to institutions conducting studies that result in new science, practice or knowledge significantly affecting animals living in Colorado.

YEAR PROGRAM STARTED: 1975

PURPOSE:
To provide leadership and support to make Colorado the Model State for animal welfare through philanthropy toward animals.

LEGAL BASIS:
Private foundation.

ELIGIBILITY:
Requirements vary by program and are outlined on the Foundation web site.

GEOG. RESTRICTIONS: Colorado.

FINANCIAL DATA:
Amount of support per award: Varies.

Total amount of support: More than $1,000,000 in grants for the year 2019.

Matching fund requirements: Varies.

NO. MOST RECENT APPLICANTS: 100.

NO. AWARDS: Approximately 60.

REPRESENTATIVE AWARDS:
$5,000 to Fort Collins Cat Rescue; $10,000 to Humane Society of Weld County.

APPLICATION INFO:
Application information is available on the Foundation web site.

Duration: One to two years. Renewable with reapplication.

Deadline: Letter of Intent: June 1 to August 1. Application (for approved LOIs): September 15.

IRS I.D.: 84-0715412

STAFF:
Katie Parker, Executive Director

ADDRESS INQUIRIES TO:
Rachel Gonzales, Program Director
E-mail: rgonzales@aaf-fd.org
(See address above.)

APLASTIC ANEMIA AND MDS INTERNATIONAL FOUNDATION   [2038]
4330 East West Highway
Suite 230
Bethesda, MD 20814
(301) 279-7202
(800) 747-2820
Fax: (240) 534-2231
E-mail: help@aamds.org
Web Site: aamds.org

FOUNDED: 1983

AREAS OF INTEREST:
Aplastic anemia, myelodysplastic syndrome (MDS) and paroxysmal nocturnal hemoglobinuria (PNH).

NAME(S) OF PROGRAMS:
● **AA&MDSIF Research Grant Program**

TYPE:
Research grants.

YEAR PROGRAM STARTED: 1989

PURPOSE:
To support research related to aplastic anemia, myelodysplastic syndrome (MDS) and paroxysmal nocturnal hemoglobinuria (PNH).

ELIGIBILITY:
Qualified investigators affiliated with appropriate institutions are eligible to apply.

FINANCIAL DATA:
Amount of support per award: $30,000 per year.

Total amount of support: $60,000.

NO. AWARDS: 2 for the year 2019.

APPLICATION INFO:
Letter of Intent is required prior to submitting a full application. Applicants will be invited to submit the full application based on their Letter of Intent.

Duration: Two years. Second-year funding pending approval by Medical Board.

Deadline: Letter of Intent: May 29. Full Application: September 30. Notification: December 1.

STAFF:
Alice Houk, Senior Director of Health Professional Programs

ADDRESS INQUIRIES TO:
Alice Houk, Senior Director of Health Professional Programs
(See address above.)

ARTHRITIS NATIONAL RESEARCH FOUNDATION (ANRF)   [2039]
19200 Von Karman Avenue
Suite 350
Irvine, CA 92612
(800) 588-2873
(562) 437-6808
E-mail: grants@curearthritis.org
Web Site: www.curearthritis.org

FOUNDED: 1952

AREAS OF INTEREST:
Research related to arthritis.

NAME(S) OF PROGRAMS:
● **ANRF Arthritis Research Grants**

TYPE:
Research grants; Travel grants. ANRF Arthritis Research Grants are intended to support basic and clinical research focusing

on rheumatic and related autoimmune diseases, such as osteoarthritis and rheumatoid arthritis.

YEAR PROGRAM STARTED: 1952

PURPOSE:
To support basic and clinical research related to arthritis.

ELIGIBILITY:
Applicants must hold an M.D. and/or Ph.D. degree or equivalent. Applicants need not be U.S. citizens, but must conduct their research at U.S. nonprofit institutions.

FINANCIAL DATA:
No overhead expenses funded.
Amount of support per award: Up to $100,000.
Total amount of support: $1,600,000 for fiscal year 2018-19.

CO-OP FUNDING PROGRAMS: American Federation for Aging Research (AFAR) and National Psoriasis Foundation.

NO. AWARDS: 10 to 20 annually.

REPRESENTATIVE AWARDS:
$100,000 to study the role of autoantibodies in pulmonary manifestations of inflammatory arthritis.

APPLICATION INFO:
A standard cover sheet and budget page are required and provided on the Foundation's web site. Application must be submitted online. Hard copies are not accepted.
Duration: One year. May apply for second year of funding.
Deadline: January 15 or next business day.

IRS I.D.: 95-6043953

ADDRESS INQUIRIES TO:
See e-mail address above.

ASCP [2040]
33 West Monroe, Suite 1600
Chicago, IL 60603
(312) 541-4110
E-mail: membership@ascp.org
Web Site: www.ascp.org/foundation

FOUNDED: 1922

AREAS OF INTEREST:
Laboratory medicine.

TYPE:
Development grants; Fellowships; Scholarships; Travel grants. American Society for Clinical Pathology (ASCP) and the ASCP Foundation offer a number of grants, scholarships and fellowships to pathologists, pathology residents, medical students, laboratory professionals, and laboratory science students.

PURPOSE:
To support outstanding pathology residents and laboratory science students as they expand their knowledge, skills and professional networks.

LEGAL BASIS:
Professional society.

ELIGIBILITY:
Criteria vary per award. Details are available on the ASCP web site.

GEOG. RESTRICTIONS: United States.

FINANCIAL DATA:
Amount of support per award: Varies.
Total amount of support: Varies.

NO. AWARDS: Varies.

APPLICATION INFO:
Application form required. Contact ASCP.
Duration: Varies.
Deadline: Varies.

PUBLICATIONS:
Announcement.

ADDRESS INQUIRIES TO:
Angela Collier, Manager, Membership
(See address above.)

AUTISM SPEAKS INC. [2041]
1060 State Road, 2nd Floor
Princeton, NJ 08540
(609) 228-7313
E-mail: jnew@autismspeaks.org
Web Site: www.autismspeaks.org

FOUNDED: 1994

AREAS OF INTEREST:
Autism.

NAME(S) OF PROGRAMS:
• **Non-Science Providers Grants**

TYPE:
Project/program grants; Research grants. Research grants that are in line with Autism Speaks research priorities.

YEAR PROGRAM STARTED: 2005

PURPOSE:
To promote solutions, across the spectrum and throughout the lifespan, for the needs of individuals with autism and their families through advocacy and support; to increase understanding and acceptance of people with autism spectrum disorder; to advance research into causes and better interventions for autism spectrum disorder and related conditions.

LEGAL BASIS:
National nonprofit, tax-exempt organization.

ELIGIBILITY:
Open to investigators at established research institutions.

GEOG. RESTRICTIONS: Non-Science Providers Grants: United States.

FINANCIAL DATA:
Amount of support per award: Varies.
Total amount of support: Varies.

NO. AWARDS: Varies.

APPLICATION INFO:
Applications are available online.
Duration: Varies.
Deadline: Varies.

IRS I.D.: 20-2329938

ADDRESS INQUIRIES TO:
Joan New, Grants Manager
(See address above.)

Non-Science Providers:
Serena Selkin, Grants Manager
E-mail: sselkin@autismspeaks.org

BATTEN DISEASE SUPPORT AND RESEARCH ASSOCIATION [2042]
2780 Airport Drive
Suite 342
Columbus, OH 43219
(800) 448-4570
Fax: (866) 648-8718
E-mail: tkirby@bdsra.org
Web Site: www.bdsra.org

FOUNDED: 1987

AREAS OF INTEREST:
Batten Disease research.

NAME(S) OF PROGRAMS:
• **Batten Disease Research Grant**

TYPE:
Fellowships; Research grants; Seed money grants.

YEAR PROGRAM STARTED: 1994

PURPOSE:
To further Batten Disease basic and translational research.

ELIGIBILITY:
Applications will be reviewed based upon the quality of the proposed science, the probability of achieving the specific aims proposed and the likelihood of securing federal funding for continued research.

APPLICATION INFO:
Guidelines are available on the Foundation web site.
Duration: One year.

IRS I.D.: 91-1397792

STAFF:
Noreen Murphy, Grants Administrator

ADDRESS INQUIRIES TO:
Noreen Murphy, Grants Administrator
(See address above.)

*SPECIAL STIPULATIONS:
Grants must not be used to cover indirect or overhead costs.

BRIGHAM AND WOMEN'S HOSPITAL
75 Francis Street
Boston, MA 02115
(617) 732-5500
Fax: (617) 582-6112
E-mail: bwhdeland@partners.org
Web Site: www.brighamandwomens.org

TYPE:
Fellowships.

See entry 1297 for full listing.

BURROUGHS WELLCOME FUND [2043]
21 T.W. Alexander Drive
Research Triangle Park, NC 27709
(919) 991-5100
Fax: (919) 991-0695
E-mail: info@bwfund.org
Web Site: www.bwfund.org

FOUNDED: 1955

AREAS OF INTEREST:
Biomedical research.

NAME(S) OF PROGRAMS:
• **Career Awards at the Scientific Interface**
• **Career Awards for Medical Scientists**
• **Investigators in the Pathogenesis of Infectious Disease**
• **Preterm Birth Initiative**

TYPE:
Awards/prizes; Conferences/seminars; Research grants. Career Awards at the Scientific Interface bridge advanced postdoctoral training and the first three years of faculty service. These awards are intended to foster the early career development of

researchers with backgrounds in the physical/mathematical/computational sciences whose work addresses biological questions.

Career Awards for Medical Scientists provide funds to bridge advanced postdoctoral/fellowship training and the early years of faculty service. This award addresses the ongoing problem of increasing the number of physician scientists and will help facilitate the transition to a career in research.

Investigators in the Pathogenesis of Infectious Disease provides awards for opportunities for accomplished investigators at the assistant professor level to study pathogenesis, with a focus on the intersection of human and microbial biology. The program is intended to shed light on the overarching issues of how human hosts handle infectious challenge.

Preterm Birth Initiative brings together a diverse interdisciplinary group with expertise in genetics/genomics, immunology, microbiology and proteomics along with the more traditional areas of parturition research such as maternal fetal medicine, obstetrics and pediatrics to address the scientific issues related to preterm birth.

PURPOSE:
To advance the biomedical sciences by supporting research and other scientific and educational activities; to help scientists early in their careers develop as independent investigators; to advance fields in the basic biomedical sciences that are undervalued or in need of particular encouragement.

LEGAL BASIS:
Private foundation.

GEOG. RESTRICTIONS: United States and Canada.

FINANCIAL DATA:
Amount of support per award: Career Awards at the Scientific Interface and Investigators in Pathogenesis of Infectious Disease: $500,000; Career Awards for Medical Scientists: $700,000; Preterm Birth Initiative: Up to $500,000.

Total amount of support: Approximately $25,000,000 in grants awarded annually.

APPLICATION INFO:
Contact the Fund.

Duration: Preterm Birth Initiative: Four years. All others: Five years.

Deadline: Varies.

PUBLICATIONS:
FOCUS, newsletter; *Career Development Guides,* annual report.

IRS I.D.: 23-7225395

ADDRESS INQUIRIES TO:
Burroughs Wellcome Fund
P.O. Box 13901
Research Triangle Park, NC 27709-3901

CANADIAN BLOOD SERVICES   [2044]

1800 Alta Vista Drive
Ottawa ON K1G 4J5 Canada
(613) 739-2496
Fax: (613) 739-2201
E-mail: centreforinnovation@blood.ca
Web Site: blood.ca

AREAS OF INTEREST:
Research in transfusion science.

NAME(S) OF PROGRAMS:
● **Canadian Blood Services Graduate Fellowship Program**
● **Canadian Blood Services Postdoctoral Fellowship Program**

TYPE:
Fellowships.

PURPOSE:
To attract and support young investigators to initiate or continue training in the field of transfusion science; to foster careers related to transfusion science in Canada.

ELIGIBILITY:
Graduate Fellowship: Applicants must be engaged in full-time training research in a graduate program at a Canadian university leading to a Ph.D. or combined health professional Ph.D. program. While priority will be given to applicants enrolled in a Ph.D. program, applications from applicants enrolled in an M.Sc. program will be considered. Applicants must not hold another stipend award at the same time as the Canadian Blood Services Graduate Fellowship.

Postdoctoral Fellowship: Applicants must hold a relevant prerequisite degree (Ph.D., M.D., D.D.S., or D.V.M.) from a recognized academic institution. Applicants must be within five years of completing their prerequisite degree. Applicants must secure the sponsorship of a primary academic supervisor who is either a Canadian Blood Services Scientist/Investigator, a Canadian Blood Services Adjunct Scientist, or a Medical Officer/Director. Applicants must not hold another salary or stipend award at the same time as the Postdoctoral Fellowship.

GEOG. RESTRICTIONS: Canada.

FINANCIAL DATA:
Fellowship offers one-time research allowance of $20,000.

Amount of support per award: Graduate Fellowship: $25,000 per annum (CIHR guidelines); Postdoctoral Fellowship: $21,000 to $50,000 per annum based on degree, licensure and experience.

Total amount of support: Graduate Fellowship: Approximately $300,000; Postdoctoral Fellowship: Approximately $200,000.

NO. AWARDS: 4 new Graduate Fellowships and 2 new Postdoctoral Fellowships for the year 2017.

APPLICATION INFO:
Competition guidelines are posted on the web site.

Duration: Two years. Renewal to maximum of four years for Graduate Fellowship and three years for Postdoctoral Fellowship.

Deadline: Graduate Fellowship Program: Spring and fall; Postdoctoral Fellowship: Summer.

ADDRESS INQUIRIES TO:
Everad Tilokee, Manager
Research and Training Programs
Centre for Innovation
(See e-mail address above.)

*SPECIAL STIPULATIONS:
Awards must be held in Canada.

CANADIAN BLOOD SERVICES   [2045]

1800 Alta Vista Drive
Ottawa ON K1G 4J5 Canada
(613) 739-2496
Fax: (613) 739-2201
E-mail: centreforinnovation@blood.ca
Web Site: blood.ca

AREAS OF INTEREST:
Research in transfusion science.

NAME(S) OF PROGRAMS:
● **Transfusion Medicine Research Program Support Award**

TYPE:
Project/program grants; Research grants. Program Support Award provides funding to research groups that constitute centers of excellence in transfusion research in Canada to enable the development of research activities and to foster collaboration and knowledge dissemination within a center and across the Canadian transfusion community.

YEAR PROGRAM STARTED: 2017

PURPOSE:
To promote national excellence in transfusion science and medicine in service of Canadian patients.

ELIGIBILITY:
Priority will be given to research groups that conduct transfusion research to inform evidence-based clinical practice and that promote the uptake of research findings by the transfusion community through changes in policy or practice. The award is not intended to provide operating funds for individual research projects; rather it is intended to fund activities and resources to promote the success of the group's transfusion research strategy.

The primary applicant must have a senior leadership role (Program Director or equivalent) within the research group and must be affiliated with a Canadian academic program as a faculty member. The research group must be based at a Canadian university or hospital. The group must have an established research program in transfusion science and medicine with a clearly articulated transfusion research strategy. Group investigators must be affiliated with an academic program as faculty members. There is no restriction on the number of investigators. However, all identified investigators must have a defined role in the delivery of the research program, and their expertise must be clearly required to adequately address the proposed goals.

GEOG. RESTRICTIONS: Canada.

FINANCIAL DATA:
Amount of support per award: Up to $230,000 per year.

Total amount of support: $2,300,000 over five years.

NO. AWARDS: 2 for the year 2017.

APPLICATION INFO:
Candidates must complete the Transfusion Medicine Research Program Support Award Registration Form as per the instructions. Registration Form must be submitted to the Centre for Innovation at the e-mail address listed above. After administrative review, Canadian Blood Services will contact all registrants and provide the full application form to those who meet the basic eligibility criteria. No feedback on the proposal will be provided to the registrants.

Unsolicited applications will not be accepted.

Duration: Up to five years, with a requirement for successful renewal at three years.

ADDRESS INQUIRIES TO:
Centre for Innovation
Tel: (613) 739-6480
(See e-mail address above.)

*SPECIAL STIPULATIONS:
Awards must be held in Canada.

CANADIAN BLOOD SERVICES [2046]
1800 Alta Vista Drive
Ottawa ON K1G 4J5 Canada
(613) 739-2496
Fax: (613) 739-2201
E-mail: centreforinnovation@blood.ca
Web Site: blood.ca

AREAS OF INTEREST:
Research in transfusion science.

NAME(S) OF PROGRAMS:
● **Intramural Research Grant Program**

TYPE:
Research grants.

PURPOSE:
To advance knowledge in blood product utilization, supply, transfusion and quality; to replace or improve blood products through new therapies or technologies.

ELIGIBILITY:
The principal investigator must be affiliated with Canadian Blood Services as a Canadian Blood Services scientist, medical officer/director/consultant, or adjunct scientist. The research team must include at least two investigators, including the principal investigator. All investigators must have a defined role in the project, and their expertise must be clearly required to adequately address the project goals. All investigators must be affiliated with a Canadian academic program as faculty members.

Proposals must be aligned with one or more of the research priorities identified. Proposals that are not relevant to any of these priorities will not be considered for funding.

GEOG. RESTRICTIONS: Canada.

FINANCIAL DATA:
Amount of support per award: Up to $200,000 per year.
Total amount of support: $1,200,000 for the year 2020.

NO. AWARDS: Up to 3 for the year 2020.

APPLICATION INFO:
Candidate must complete the Canadian Blood Services Intramural Research Grant Registration Form as per the instructions. Registration Form must be submitted to the Centre for Innovation at the e-mail address listed above. After administrative review, Canadian Blood Services will contact all registrants and provide the full application form to those who meet the basic eligibility criteria. No feedback on the proposed project will be provided to the registrants.

Unsolicited applications will not be accepted.
Duration: Two years.
Deadline: April.

ADDRESS INQUIRIES TO:
Centre for Innovation
Tel: (613) 739-2564
(See e-mail address above.)

*SPECIAL STIPULATIONS:
Awards must be held in Canada.

CANADIAN BLOOD SERVICES [2047]
1800 Alta Vista Drive
Ottawa ON K1G 4J5 Canada
(613) 739-2496
Fax: (613) 739-2201
E-mail: centreforinnovation@blood.ca
Web Site: blood.ca

AREAS OF INTEREST:
Research in transfusion science.

NAME(S) OF PROGRAMS:
● **Kenneth J. Fyke Award**

TYPE:
Project/program grants; Research grants. In order to honor the contributions of Kenneth J. Fyke to Canada's health care system, the Kenneth J. Fyke Award was established in his name. This competition supports one health services or policy research project for a period of one year. The competition is held on a biennial basis.

PURPOSE:
To support health services and policy research in order to promote the development of evidence-based Canadian practices and policies in blood transfusion, blood stem cell transplantation, and organ and tissue donation and transplantation for the benefit of Canadian patients.

ELIGIBILITY:
Applicants must be Canadian researchers affiliated with a Canadian academic program related to health services or health policy, or transfusion medicine, stem cell transplantation, or organ/tissue donation and transplantation medicine. Priority will be given to applicants that are not employees of or contracted to Canadian Blood Services at the time of application. Priority will also be given to projects that are collaborative in nature and, when relevant, include team members from different disciplines.

GEOG. RESTRICTIONS: Canada.

FINANCIAL DATA:
Amount of support per award: Up to $100,000.
Total amount of support: Up to $100,000.

NO. AWARDS: 1.

APPLICATION INFO:
Application form and supporting documents must be submitted to the Centre for Innovation at the e-mail address listed above.
Duration: One year.
Deadline: Fall of even-numbered years.

ADDRESS INQUIRIES TO:
Centre for Innovation
(See telephone and e-mail address above.)

*SPECIAL STIPULATIONS:
Awards must be held in Canada.

CANADIAN BLOOD SERVICES [2048]
1800 Alta Vista Drive
Ottawa ON K1G 4J5 Canada
(613) 739-2496
Fax: (613) 739-2201
E-mail: centreforinnovation@blood.ca
Web Site: blood.ca

AREAS OF INTEREST:
Research in transfusion science.

NAME(S) OF PROGRAMS:
● **James Kreppner Award**

TYPE:
Project/program grants; Research grants. In order to honor the contributions of James Kreppner to Canada's blood system, the James Kreppner Award was established in his name. The competition supports one legal research project for a period of one year. Research priorities include the legal and regulatory aspects of donation, collection, storage, and use of blood, blood products, and hematopoietic stem cells, and organ and tissue donation and transplantation.

PURPOSE:
To support legal research relevant to Canadian Blood Services' priorities.

ELIGIBILITY:
Applicant must be a Canadian legal researcher affiliated with a Canadian academic program as a faculty member. There is no restriction on the number of team members. However, all team members must have a defined role in the project, and their expertise must be clearly required to adequately address the project goals. The project must have a clear plan with defined goals and deliverables that will be completed within the term of the award and that are aligned with the research priorities. Priority will be given to projects that are collaborative in nature and, when relevant, include team members from different disciplines.

GEOG. RESTRICTIONS: Canada.

FINANCIAL DATA:
Amount of support per award: Up to $50,000.
Total amount of support: Up to $50,000.

NO. AWARDS: 1.

APPLICATION INFO:
Application form and supporting documents must be submitted to the Centre for Innovation at the e-mail address listed above.
Duration: One year.
Deadline: Fall.

ADDRESS INQUIRIES TO:
Everad Tilokee, Manager
Research and Training Programs
Centre for Innovation
(See e-mail address above.)

*SPECIAL STIPULATIONS:
Awards must be held in Canada.

CANADIAN BLOOD SERVICES [2049]
1800 Alta Vista Drive
Ottawa ON K1G 4J5 Canada
(613) 739-2496
Fax: (613) 739-2201
E-mail: centreforinnovation@blood.ca
Web Site: blood.ca

AREAS OF INTEREST:
Research in transfusion science.

NAME(S) OF PROGRAMS:
● **BloodTechNet Award Program**

TYPE:
Project/program grants.

PURPOSE:
To support the development of innovative educational projects that network the transfusion, cellular therapy and transplantation communities in Canada.

ELIGIBILITY:
The primary applicant must be a health professional belonging to the transfusion, cellular therapy and/or transplantation communities in Canada. This program is targeted towards medical lab technologists, nurses and physicians. There is no restriction on the number of team members. However, all team members must have a defined role in the project, and their expertise must be clearly required to adequately address the project goals. The project must have a clear plan with defined educational goals and deliverables that will be completed within the term of the award. Priority will be given to projects that are collaborative in nature and, when relevant, include team members from a variety of health care professions, departments, organizations and/or jurisdictions.

GEOG. RESTRICTIONS: Canada.

FINANCIAL DATA:
Amount of support per award: $10,000 to $50,000.
Total amount of support: $50,000 for the year 2019.

NO. AWARDS: Varies depending on the requested budgets.

APPLICATION INFO:
Application package must be submitted to the Centre for Innovation at the e-mail address listed above.
Duration: One year.
Deadline: Fall 2020.

ADDRESS INQUIRIES TO:
Everad Tilokee, Manager
Research and Training Programs
Centre for Innovation
(See e-mail address above.)

*SPECIAL STIPULATIONS:
Awards must be held in Canada.

CANADIAN BLOOD SERVICES   [2050]
1800 Alta Vista Drive
Ottawa ON K1G 4J5 Canada
(613) 739-2496
Fax: (613) 739-2201
E-mail: centreforinnovation@blood.ca
Web Site: blood.ca

AREAS OF INTEREST:
Research in transfusion science.

NAME(S) OF PROGRAMS:
● **MSM Research Grant Program**

TYPE:
Research grants.

YEAR PROGRAM STARTED: 2017

PURPOSE:
To ensure the generation of adequate evidence-based research for alternative screening approaches for blood or plasma donors, which could evolve the current deferral policy for men who have sex with men (MSM), while maintaining the safety of the blood supply.

ELIGIBILITY:
The principal investigator must be affiliated with a Canadian academic program as a

faculty member or with Canadian Blood Services or Hema-Quebec. There is no restriction on the number of team members. However, all team members must have a defined role in the project, and their expertise must be clearly required to adequately address the project goals. Co-investigators must be affiliated with an academic program as faculty members or with a blood operator. Co-investigators are eligible for project funding.

MSM Research Grant proposals must be aligned with the program objective and one or more of the research priorities.

GEOG. RESTRICTIONS: Canada.

FINANCIAL DATA:
Amount of support per award: Small projects: Up to $50,000; Large projects: Up to $300,000.
Total amount of support: $850,000 for the year 2018.

NO. AWARDS: 15 new and continued for the year 2018.

APPLICATION INFO:
Candidate must complete the Canadian Blood Services MSM Research Grant Registration Form as per the instructions. Registration Form must be submitted to the Centre for Innovation at the e-mail address listed above. After administrative review, Canadian Blood Services will contact all registrants and provide the full application form to those who meet the basic eligibility criteria. No feedback on the proposed project will be provided to registrants.

Unsolicited applications will not be accepted.
Duration: Up to two years.
Deadline: Registration: April 15.
Application: June 30.

ADDRESS INQUIRIES TO:
Everad Tilokee, Manager
Research and Training Programs
Centre for Innovation
(See e-mail address above.)

*SPECIAL STIPULATIONS:
Awards must be held in Canada.

CANADIAN LIVER FOUNDATION
3100 Steeles Avenue East
Suite 801
Markham ON L3R 8T3 Canada
(416) 491-3353
(800) 563-5483 (within Canada and U.S.)
Fax: (905) 752-1540
E-mail: clf@liver.ca
Web Site: www.liver.ca

TYPE:
Scholarships. One graduate studentship may be awarded to a student in Alberta whose research project is related to hepatobiliary research and two graduate studentships may be awarded to students in Canada whose research projects are related to hepatitis B.

See entry 2205 for full listing.

CANADIAN LIVER FOUNDATION   [2051]
3100 Steeles Avenue East
Suite 801
Markham ON L3R 8T3 Canada
(416) 491-3353
(800) 563-5483 (within Canada and U.S.)
Fax: (905) 752-1540
E-mail: clf@liver.ca
Web Site: www.liver.ca

FOUNDED: 1969

AREAS OF INTEREST:
Research and education into the causes, diagnosis, prevention and treatment of diseases of the liver.

NAME(S) OF PROGRAMS:
● **Summer Studentships**

TYPE:
Scholarships. One summer studentship grant may be awarded to a student in Canada whose research project is related to hepatobiliary research. Two summer studentship grants may be awarded to students in Canada whose research projects are related to liver cancer. One Raj Bhargava Memorial Summer Studentship may be awarded to a student enrolled at the University of Alberta whose research project is related to radiology of liver disease.

PURPOSE:
To provide an opportunity for a limited number of well-motivated students with records of strong academic performance to participate in liver-related research in Canada.

LEGAL BASIS:
Registered Canadian charity.

ELIGIBILITY:
Applicants must be registered at a Canadian institution in an undergraduate degree program.

Canadian citizens, landed immigrants, and permanent residents will receive first consideration.

GEOG. RESTRICTIONS: Canada.

FINANCIAL DATA:
Amount of support per award: $3,500 stipend plus $500 for supplies.

NO. AWARDS: 4 for the year 2020.

APPLICATION INFO:
A single PDF file of the entire grant application, one reference letter from someone other than the applicant's supervisor, and a scanned copy of the applicant's academic transcript must be submitted by e-mail to researchgrants@liver.ca by the deadline.
Duration: Any three summer months (May to August).
Deadline: February 24, for awards to become tenable the following June 1.

PUBLICATIONS:
Program description and guidelines.

STAFF:
Nem Maksimovic, Manager, National Health Promotion and Education

ADDRESS INQUIRIES TO:
Nem Maksimovic, Manager
National Health Promotion
and Education
(See address above.)

*SPECIAL STIPULATIONS:
At the conclusion of the award period, a written report of approximately 1,000 words

must be submitted to the CLF National Office giving an overview of the summer's work, including methods used, an evaluation of the results with a discussion of their significance, and an evaluation of the experience gained.

CANADIAN LIVER FOUNDATION

3100 Steeles Avenue East
Suite 801
Markham ON L3R 8T3 Canada
(416) 491-3353
(800) 563-5483 (within Canada and U.S.)
Fax: (905) 752-1540
E-mail: clf@liver.ca
Web Site: www.liver.ca

TYPE:
Research grants. Operating grants may be offered to one researcher in Canada whose research project is related to hepatobiliary research, one researcher in Canada whose research project is related to hepatitis B, and one researcher in Canada whose research project is related to liver cancer.

See entry 2206 for full listing.

CHINESE AMERICAN MEDICAL SOCIETY [2052]

11 East Broadway, Unit 4-C
New York, NY 10038
(212) 334-4760
Fax: (646) 304-6373
E-mail: jlove@camsociety.org
Web Site: www.camsociety.org

FOUNDED: 1963

AREAS OF INTEREST:
Medicine.

NAME(S) OF PROGRAMS:
● **CAMS Scholarship Program**
● **Medical Student Summer Research Fellowship**

TYPE:
Fellowships; Scholarships.

YEAR PROGRAM STARTED: 1973

PURPOSE:
To promote the scientific association of medical professionals of Chinese descent; to advance medical knowledge and scientific research with emphasis on aspects unique to the Chinese; to establish scholarships to medical and dental students and to provide endowments to medical schools and hospitals of good standing; to promote the health status of Chinese Americans.

LEGAL BASIS:
A nonprofit, charitable, educational, and scientific society.

ELIGIBILITY:
Candidates must currently be in their first, second or third year of medical or dental school in a U.S.-accredited medical or dental school when applying. Candidates must reside in the U.S. at the time of application either as an alien student or citizen of the U.S. Students who have just been accepted into medical or dental school at the time of application are not eligible.

FINANCIAL DATA:
Amount of support per award: Scholarships: $5,000; Research Fellowships: $3,200 to $4,000.
Total amount of support: $10,000 to $15,000.

NO. AWARDS: Scholarships: 4; Research Fellowships: Up to 3.

APPLICATION INFO:
Contact the Society.
Duration: One-time award.
Deadline: March 31.

STAFF:
Ms. Jamie Love, Administrator

ADDRESS INQUIRIES TO:
Warren W. Chin, M.D.
Executive Director
(See address above.)

COLLEGE OF PHYSICIANS OF PHILADELPHIA

Francis Clark Wood Institute
for the History of Medicine
19 South 22nd Street
Philadelphia, PA 19103-3097
(215) 399-2301
Fax: (215) 569-0356
E-mail: travelgrants@collegeofphysicans.org
Web Site: www.collegeofphysicians.
org/library/wood-institute

TYPE:
Travel grants; Visiting scholars. This program allows scholars to conduct short-term research in the College's Library and/or Mutter Museum.

See entry 539 for full listing.

CUREPSP FOUNDATION FOR PSP/CBD AND RELATED BRAIN DISEASES

1216 Broadway, Second Floor
New York, NY 10001
(347) 294-2871
Fax: (410) 785-7009
E-mail: info@curepsp.org
Web Site: www.curepsp.org

TYPE:
Research grants.

See entry 2249 for full listing.

THE DANA FOUNDATION [2053]

505 Fifth Avenue, Sixth Floor
New York, NY 10017
(212) 223-4040
Fax: (212) 317-8721
E-mail: danainfo@dana.org
Web Site: www.dana.org

FOUNDED: 1950

AREAS OF INTEREST:
Science, health and education, with a current focus on neuroscience research.

NAME(S) OF PROGRAMS:
● **Clinical Neuroscience Research Program**
● **David Mahoney Neuroimaging Program**

TYPE:
Awards/prizes; Research grants. The Foundation focuses on brain research. Grants in these areas are made principally through competitive Clinical Hypotheses Programs in immuno-imaging, neuroimaging and brain-cardiovascular system interactions. These competitive grants programs support pilot testing of experimental and innovative ideas that in immunology and neuroscience research have the potential of advancing clinical applications. The Foundation also

supports an invitational program in which leading scientists are invited to compete for research grants designed to improve immune system responses to biological agents.

The Foundation has supported advances in education throughout its history. Its current interest is focused primarily on professional development programs that foster improved teaching of the performing arts in public schools. Programs emphasize innovative training projects that are exported from, or imported to, New York City, Washington, DC, Los Angeles and their surrounding areas.

YEAR PROGRAM STARTED: 1950

PURPOSE:
To strengthen and improve the quality of science, health and education.

LEGAL BASIS:
Private, independent philanthropic foundation.

ELIGIBILITY:
The Foundation, in general, makes its grants in accordance with the following policies: (1) it supports programs in science, health and education; carefully defined objectives in each field guide its grantmaking; (2) in many cases, it requires grantee institutions to share the cost of a project; (3) it makes no grants directly to individuals; (4) it does not support annual operating budgets of organizations, deficit reduction, capital campaigns or individual sabbaticals and; (5) it does not schedule meetings with applicants, other than by specific invitation initiated by the Foundation.

GEOG. RESTRICTIONS: United States.

FINANCIAL DATA:
Amount of support per award: Clinical Neuroscience Research Program: $100,000 to $300,000; David Mahoney Neuroimaging Program: $100,000 to $200,000 per institution.
Total amount of support: Varies by program.

NO. MOST RECENT APPLICANTS: 120.

NO. AWARDS: Varies.

APPLICATION INFO:
Application details can be found on the web site.
Duration: Up to three years. Renewals are rare.
Deadline: Clinical Neuroscience Research Program applications are accepted on a rolling basis.

PUBLICATIONS:
Annual report; *Dana Report*, newsletter; application guidelines.

IRS I.D.: 06-6036761

BOARD OF DIRECTORS:
Steven E. Hyman, M.D., Chairman
Edward Bleier
Wallace L. Cook
Charles A. Dana, III
Hildegarde E. Mahoney
Ann McLaughlin-Korologos
Peter A. Nadosy
Herbert J. Siegel

ADMINISTRATION:
Burton M. Mirsky, President and Treasurer
Barbara E. Gill, Executive Vice President, Public Affairs

ADDRESS INQUIRIES TO:
Celina Sooksatan, Grants Associate
(See address above.)

DERMATOLOGY FOUNDATION [2054]

1560 Sherman Avenue
Suite 500
Evanston, IL 60201-4808
(847) 328-2256
Fax: (847) 328-0509
E-mail: dfgen@dermatologyfoundation.org
Web Site: www.dermatologyfoundation.org

FOUNDED: 1964

AREAS OF INTEREST:
Cancer and other diseases of the skin, hair and nails.

TYPE:
Fellowships; Research grants. Research funding in the form of career development grants, fellowships, and research grants for academic investigators in the early stages of their careers.

There are 12 research award categories. Career development awards include Physician Scientist, Dermatologic Surgery, Public Health, Medical Dermatology, Science of Human Appearance and Women's Health. Dermatologist Investigator Fellowships. Various Patient-Directed and Research Grants available.

YEAR PROGRAM STARTED: 1964

PURPOSE:
To advance the research careers of young individuals in dermatology and cutaneous biology, with the emphasis on research benefiting the dermatology community at large.

LEGAL BASIS:
Nonprofit charitable organization.

GEOG. RESTRICTIONS: United States.

FINANCIAL DATA:
Amount of support per award: Career development awards: Average $55,000; Fellowships: Average $30,000; Grants: Average $20,000. Stiefel Scholar Award and Sun Pharma Research Award: $100,000.
Total amount of support: $2,600,000 in research funding for the year 2018.

NO. AWARDS: 58 for the year 2018.

APPLICATION INFO:
Forms are available only on the Foundation web site.
Duration: Most awards are for one year. Stiefel Scholar Award and Sun Pharma Research Award: Up to two years. Renewal possibilities vary.
Deadline: October 15. Announcement midwinter at the annual meeting of the American Academy of Dermatology.

PUBLICATIONS:
Annual report; *Dermatology Focus*, scientific publication.

IRS I.D.: 04-6115524

OFFICERS:
Bruce U. Wintroub, M.D., Chairman, Board of Trustees
Janet A. Fairley, M.D., President
Stuart R. Lessin, M.D., Vice President
Elizabeth I. McBurney, M.D., Secretary/Treasurer

ADDRESS INQUIRIES TO:
Sandra R. Benz, Executive Director
(See address above.)

THE EDUCATIONAL AND RESEARCH FOUNDATION FOR THE AMERICAN ACADEMY OF FACIAL PLASTIC AND RECONSTRUCTIVE SURGERY (AAFPRS FOUNDATION) [2055]

310 South Henry Street
Alexandria, VA 22314
(703) 650-9226
Fax: (703) 299-8284
E-mail: ksloat@aafprs.org
Web Site: www.aafprs.org

FOUNDED: 1964

AREAS OF INTEREST:
Facial plastic and reconstructive surgery.

CONSULTING OR VOLUNTEER SERVICES:
Combined Otolaryngology Research Efforts (C.O.R.E.).

NAME(S) OF PROGRAMS:
● **Leslie Bernstein Resident Research Grants**

TYPE:
Research grants; Seed money grants. Research supported by this grant should be specifically directed toward the advancement of the state of knowledge in the theory, techniques, and application of facial plastic and reconstructive surgery.

YEAR PROGRAM STARTED: 1983

PURPOSE:
To stimulate resident research in facial plastic and reconstructive surgery projects that are well conceived and scientifically valid.

LEGAL BASIS:
Professional association of independent members.

ELIGIBILITY:
Applicant must be an AAFPRS member. Residents at any level may apply, even if the research work will be done during their fellowship year.

FINANCIAL DATA:
Grant money must be used for direct costs; only 10% of monies can be used for indirect cost.
Amount of support per award: $5,000.
Total amount of support: $5,000.

NO. MOST RECENT APPLICANTS: 5.

NO. AWARDS: 1.

APPLICATION INFO:
Applicants must submit a letter of intent. Guidelines are available from AAFPRS.
Duration: Two years. Nonrenewable.
Deadline: January 15. Announcement in August.

PUBLICATIONS:
Guidelines; application form.

IRS I.D.: 36-2952891

ADDRESS INQUIRIES TO:
Karen Sloat, Senior Project Consultant
(See e-mail address above.)

THE EDUCATIONAL AND RESEARCH FOUNDATION FOR THE AMERICAN ACADEMY OF FACIAL PLASTIC AND RECONSTRUCTIVE SURGERY (AAFPRS FOUNDATION) [2056]

310 South Henry Street
Alexandria, VA 22314
(703) 650-9226
Fax: (703) 299-8284
E-mail: ksloat@aafprs.org
Web Site: www.aafprs.org

FOUNDED: 1964

AREAS OF INTEREST:
Physician education in cosmetic and reconstructive surgery of the face, head and neck.

CONSULTING OR VOLUNTEER SERVICES:
Combined Otolaryngology Research Efforts (C.O.R.E.).

NAME(S) OF PROGRAMS:
● **Leslie Bernstein Investigator Development Grant**

TYPE:
Project/program grants; Research grants; Seed money grants. Support for the work of a young faculty member conducting significant clinical or laboratory research in facial plastic surgery and training resident surgeons in research. Funded by a donation from Leslie Bernstein, M.D., D.D.S., to the AAFPRS Foundation.

YEAR PROGRAM STARTED: 1983

PURPOSE:
To support work of a young faculty member in Facial Plastic Surgery conducting significant clinical or laboratory research and involved in the training of resident surgeons in research.

LEGAL BASIS:
Professional association of independent members.

ELIGIBILITY:
Applicants must be Academy members. Research proposals are subject to the following conditions:
(1) a sponsor, either an Academy Fellow or the investigator's department chairman, is required;
(2) the parent institution must provide professional support and;
(3) the research plan must incorporate a resident or residents in the research activities.

FINANCIAL DATA:
Grant monies must be used for direct costs; only 10% can be used for indirect cost.
Amount of support per award: $15,000.
Total amount of support: $15,000.

NO. MOST RECENT APPLICANTS: 2.

APPLICATION INFO:
Applicants must submit a letter of intent. The official entry form must be completed and submitted with the proposal. Failure to comply with the particular requirements and format outlined in the guidelines may result in disqualification.
Duration: Three years.
Deadline: January 15 each year. Announcement in August.

PUBLICATIONS:
Grants and awards brochure.

IRS I.D.: 36-2952891

ADDRESS INQUIRIES TO:
Karen Sloat, Senior Project Consultant
(See e-mail address above.)

THE EDUCATIONAL AND RESEARCH FOUNDATION FOR THE AMERICAN ACADEMY OF FACIAL PLASTIC AND RECONSTRUCTIVE SURGERY (AAFPRS FOUNDATION)   [2057]

310 South Henry Street
Alexandria, VA 22314
(703) 650-9226
Fax: (703) 299-8284
E-mail: ksloat@aafprs.org
Web Site: www.aafprs.org

FOUNDED: 1964

AREAS OF INTEREST:
Physician education in cosmetic and reconstructive surgery of the face, head and neck.

CONSULTING OR VOLUNTEER SERVICES:
Combined Otolaryngology Research Efforts (C.O.R.E.).

NAME(S) OF PROGRAMS:
● **Leslie Bernstein Research Grant**

TYPE:
Project/program grants; Research grants; Seed money grants. Research award for Academy members, funded by income from a donation by Leslie Bernstein, M.D., D.D.S., to the Academy's Foundation.

YEAR PROGRAM STARTED: 1988

PURPOSE:
To support and encourage original research projects which will advance facial plastic and reconstructive surgery.

LEGAL BASIS:
Professional association of independent members.

ELIGIBILITY:
Applicants must be AAFPRS members undertaking research that will advance facial plastic and reconstructive surgery. The primary criteria are that the research be original and have direct application to facial plastic surgery.

FINANCIAL DATA:
Grants monies must be used for direct costs; only 10% can be used for indirect costs.
Amount of support per award: $25,000.

NO. MOST RECENT APPLICANTS: 3.

APPLICATION INFO:
Proposals should be typed (double-spaced) and include the following information:
(1) investigator's curriculum vitae;
(2) brief statement of the specific aims of the investigator's research project, not to exceed 150 words;
(3) brief review of the significance of the work performed by the investigator and/or others, not to exceed two pages;
(4) a detailed description of research procedures including the experimental design, justification of sample size, outcome measures and methods of analysis including justification of each item;
(5) budget for the research award;
(6) description of facilities;
(7) certification of institutional conformity to the U.S. Government Guidelines for Human and Animal Experimentation and;
(8) application must be submitted through C.O.R.E. program.

Duration: Three years.
Deadline: January 15 for review. Announcement in August.

PUBLICATIONS:
Grants and awards brochure.

IRS I.D.: 36-2952891

ADDRESS INQUIRIES TO:
Karen Sloat, Senior Project Consultant
(See e-mail address above.)

THE EDUCATIONAL AND RESEARCH FOUNDATION FOR THE AMERICAN ACADEMY OF FACIAL PLASTIC AND RECONSTRUCTIVE SURGERY (AAFPRS FOUNDATION)   [2058]

310 South Henry Street
Alexandria, VA 22314
(703) 299-9291 ext. 234
Fax: (703) 299-8898
E-mail: info@aafprs.org
Web Site: www.aafprs.org

AREAS OF INTEREST:
Facial plastic and reconstructive surgery.

NAME(S) OF PROGRAMS:
● **Community Service Award**
● **John Dickinson Teacher of the Year Award**
● **Sir Harold Delf Gillies Award**
● **F. Mark Rafaty Memorial Award**
● **Residency Travel Award**
● **John Orlando Roe Award**
● **Ben Shuster Memorial Award**
● **Ira Tresley Research Award**
● **William K. Wright Award**

TYPE:
Awards/prizes; Fellowships; Travel grants. Community Service Award may be presented annually to an AAFPRS member who has distinguished himself/herself by providing and/or making possible free medical service to the poor in his or her community.

John Dickinson Teacher of the Year Award honors an AAFPRS fellow member for sharing knowledge about facial plastic and reconstructive surgery with the effective use of audiovisuals in any one year.

Sir Harold Delf Gillies Award is presented each year to the graduate fellow who submits the best basic science research paper written during fellowship.

The F. Mark Rafaty Memorial Award may be presented each year to an AAFPRS member who has made outstanding contributions to facial plastic and reconstructive surgery.

The Residency Travel Award is presented to the most outstanding paper in facial plastic and reconstructive surgery, primarily authored by a resident or medical student in training. The paper must be submitted by February 1 for consideration, and to be presented at the Annual Fall Meeting.

The John Orlando Roe Award is presented each year to the graduate fellow who submits the best clinical research paper written during fellowship.

The Ben Shuster Memorial Award is presented for the most outstanding research paper by a resident or fellow in training on any clinical work or research in facial plastic and reconstructive surgery delivered at a national meeting (or its equivalent) between

March 1 and the following February 28. Each entrant must be the sole or senior author and an AAFPRS member.

The Ira Tresley Research Award recognizes the best original research in facial plastic surgery by an AAFPRS member who has been board-certified for at least three years. Papers presented at a national meeting (or its equivalent) between March 1 and the following February 28 are eligible for this award.

William Wright Award may be presented each year to an AAFPRS member who has made outstanding contributions to facial plastic and reconstructive surgery.

PURPOSE:
To support research in facial and reconstructive plastic surgery.

LEGAL BASIS:
Foundation.

ELIGIBILITY:
Applicants must be AAFPRS members, except medical students may apply for Resident Travel Award.

GEOG. RESTRICTIONS: United States.

FINANCIAL DATA:
Amount of support per award: $1,000;
Residency Travel Award: $500.
Total amount of support: $5,000.

NO. AWARDS: Residency Travel Award: Up to 2; All others: 1.

APPLICATION INFO:
Contact AAFPRS for application information.
Deadline: June 1.

PUBLICATIONS:
Application form.

STAFF:
Steven J. Jurich, Executive Vice President
Rita Magness, Director, Industry Relations and Communications
Ada Phillips, Director, Meetings
Jenn Waugh, Director, Operations
Fatima Porter El Mitchell, Manager, Fellowship Programs

ADDRESS INQUIRIES TO:
Awards Coordinator
(See address above.)

THE EDUCATIONAL AND RESEARCH FOUNDATION FOR THE AMERICAN ACADEMY OF FACIAL PLASTIC AND RECONSTRUCTIVE SURGERY (AAFPRS FOUNDATION)   [2059]

310 South Henry Street
Alexandria, VA 22134
(703) 650-9226
Fax: (703) 299-8284
E-mail: ksloat@aafprs.org
Web Site: www.aafprs.org

FOUNDED: 1964

AREAS OF INTEREST:
Facial plastic and reconstructive surgery.

CONSULTING OR VOLUNTEER SERVICES:
Combined Otolaryngology Research Efforts (C.O.R.E.)

NAME(S) OF PROGRAMS:
● **AAFPRS Clinical Research Scholarship**
● **AAFPRS Research Scholar Award**
● **AAFPRS Wally K. Dyer Award**

TYPE:
Project/program grants; Research grants; Scholarships. AAFPRS Clinical Research Scholarship is intended to provide financial support to AAFPRS members to pursue academic training in the principles of clinical research design, data management, statistical analysis, and manuscript and grant preparation.

AAFPRS Research Scholar Award aims to support and encourage original work of an AAFPRS member undertaking research that will advance facial plastic and reconstructive surgery. The grant is supported by funds from The Many Faces of Generosity capital campaign and may be used as seed money for larger research projects.

AAFPRS Wally K. Dyer Award is intended to provide funding to AAFPRS members who do not normally participate in research pojrects but demonstrate an interest in furthering the profession. These grants are meant to foster career development and provide mentorship to members.

PURPOSE:
To encourage and support research projects which will advance facial plastic and reconstructive surgery.

LEGAL BASIS:
Professional association of independent members.

ELIGIBILITY:
Applicants must be AAFPRS members undertaking research that will advance facial plastic and reconstructive surgery.

AAFPRS Research Scholar Award: Candidates must reside in the U.S. or Canada and be a physician (M.D.) who is an AAFPRS member in good standing. Fellows and residents are not eligible to apply.

FINANCIAL DATA:
AAFPRS Clinical Research Scholarship: Applicant must have a Letter of Acceptance from their institution of choice before funds will be disbursed. If an applicant has already been accepted, they may apply for reimbursement of expenses up to the maximum of the scholarship. Funds cannot be applied retroactively.

AAFPRS Research Scholar Award: All research grant monies are provided to fund direct costs related to the research; no more than 10% can be applied for indirect costs.

AAFPRS Wally K. Dyer Award: The Academy reserves the right to withhold up to 10% of the grant until such time that the research project is completed and all requirements have been met.

Amount of support per award: AAFPRS Clinical Research Scholarship: $15,000; AAFPRS Research Scholar Award: $30,000; AAFPRS Wally K. Dyer Award: $2,500.

NO. MOST RECENT APPLICANTS: AAFPRS Research Scholar Award: 4; AAFPRS Wally K. Dyer Award: 2.

NO. AWARDS: AAFPRS Research Scholar Award: 1.

APPLICATION INFO:
AAFPRS Clinical Research Scholarship and AAFPRS Wally K. Dyer Award: Applicants must complete the corresponding application. In addition, the individual must submit supporting documentation, including their curriculum vitae and two letters of support.

AAFPRS Research Scholar Award: Applications are in similar format to the National Institutes of Health. All applications must be completed and submitted online through proposalCENTRAL.

Duration: AAFPRS Clinical Research Scholarship: One year; to receive funding for a second-year degree program, the recipient must demonstrate satisfactory progress during the first year of the course. AAFPRS Research Scholar Award: Up to three years; no-cost extensions are available upon written request.

Deadline: January 15. Announcement in August.

PUBLICATIONS:
Grants and awards brochure.

IRS I.D.: 36-2952891

ADDRESS INQUIRIES TO:
Karen Sloat, Senior Project Consultant
(See e-mail address above.)

*SPECIAL STIPULATIONS:
Dyer Award recipients are expected to write a paper that is suitable for publishing in the Academy's journal or web site within one year of receiving the award.

EMERGENCY MEDICINE FOUNDATION   [2060]
4950 West Royal Lane
Irving, TX 75063-2524
(469) 499-0297
(800) 798-1822 ext. 3217
Fax: (972) 580-2816
E-mail: csingh@acep.org
Web Site: www.emfoundation.org

FOUNDED: 1972

AREAS OF INTEREST:
Emergency medicine research.

NAME(S) OF PROGRAMS:
● **Emergency Medicine Research**

TYPE:
Research grants; Technical assistance. Policy-based research awards in emergency medicine.

YEAR PROGRAM STARTED: 1972

PURPOSE:
To promote education and research in emergency medicine.

LEGAL BASIS:
501(c)(3) nonprofit.

ELIGIBILITY:
Must be an emergency medicine researcher.

GEOG. RESTRICTIONS: United States.

FINANCIAL DATA:
Amount of support per award: $5,000 to $250,000.
Total amount of support: Varies.

NO. AWARDS: 22 for the year 2019-20.

APPLICATION INFO:
Contact the Foundation.
Deadline: Varies.

IRS I.D.: 75-2331221

STAFF:
Peggy Brock, Executive Director

ADDRESS INQUIRIES TO:
Cynthia Singh
Director of Grant Development
(See address above.)

FOUNDATION FOR ANESTHESIA EDUCATION AND RESEARCH   [2061]
1061 American Lane
Schaumburg, IL 60173-4973
(630) 912-2554
Fax: (847) 825-2085
E-mail: FAER@faer.org
Web Site: www.asahq.org/faer

AREAS OF INTEREST:
Anesthesiology, critical care, pain, and all areas of perioperative medicine.

NAME(S) OF PROGRAMS:
● **FAER Mentored Research Training Grant**
● **FAER Research Fellowship Grant**
● **FAER Research in Education Grant**
● **FAER Transition to Independence Grant**

TYPE:
Fellowships; Research grants; Training grants. These grants are designed to create opportunities for physicians to excel in an exceedingly competitive environment and to eventually acquire NIH funding.

PURPOSE:
To provide research grant funding for promising investigators to train in clinical, basic science and translational anesthesiology research.

ELIGIBILITY:
FAER Mentored Research Training Grant: Applicants must be instructors or assistant professors who are within 10 years of their initial appointment.

FAER Research Fellowship Grant: Open to anesthesiology residents after CA-1 training and six months of clinical scientist track.

FAER Research in Education Grant: Open to anesthesiology residents or faculty.

A 20-member committee consisting of both clinical and basic science anesthesiologists reviews proposals. Clinical and outcomes projects are encouraged.

GEOG. RESTRICTIONS: United States.

FINANCIAL DATA:
Amount of support per award: $75,000 to $250,000.
Total amount of support: $3,100,000 annually.

NO. MOST RECENT APPLICANTS: 30.

NO. AWARDS: Average 15 per year.

APPLICATION INFO:
Contact the Foundation.
Duration: One to two years.
Deadline: February 15 and August 15.

IRS I.D.: 52-1494164

ADDRESS INQUIRIES TO:
Maggie Voes, Coordinator
(See address above.)

THE FOUNDATION OF THE AMERICAN SOCIETY OF NEURORADIOLOGY   [2062]
800 Enterprise Drive, Suite 205
Oak Brook, IL 60523
(630) 574-0220
Fax: (630) 574-0661
E-mail: rbhala@asnr.org
Web Site: foundation.asnr.org

FOUNDED: 1995

AREAS OF INTEREST:
Neuroradiology.

TYPE:
Research grants.

PURPOSE:
To promote education and research in the field of neuroradiology and the development of new ideas for clinical practice.

ELIGIBILITY:
Applicant must be a member in good standing of the American Society of Neuroradiology with an M.D., D.O. or Ph.D. degree and must be board-certified or board-eligible in radiology by the American Board of Radiology or the Royal College of Physicians and Surgeons of Canada.

FINANCIAL DATA:
Amount of support per award: Up to $60,000.
Total amount of support: Approximately $300,000 in grants annually.

NO. AWARDS: Varies.

APPLICATION INFO:
Award prospectus and information on applying is posted on the Foundation web site in October. Applicants must submit a letter of intent and a one-page abstract of the research proposal. Those selected will receive a follow-up e-mail invitation.
Duration: One year. Some renewals.
Deadline: Varies.

PUBLICATIONS:
American Journal of Neuroradiology.

ADDRESS INQUIRIES TO:
Rahul Bhala, Director of Research
(See address above.)

THE MICHAEL J. FOX FOUNDATION FOR PARKINSON'S RESEARCH [2063]

Grand Central Station
P.O. Box 4777
New York, NY 10163-4777
(212) 509-0995
(800) 708-7644
Fax: (212) 509-2390
E-mail: research@michaeljfox.org
Web Site: www.michaeljfox.org

FOUNDED: 2000

AREAS OF INTEREST:
Medical research and Parkinson's disease.

TYPE:
Conferences/seminars; Research grants.

YEAR PROGRAM STARTED: 2000

PURPOSE:
To find a cure for Parkinson's disease through an aggressively funded research agenda; to ensure the development of improved therapies for those living with Parkinson's today.

LEGAL BASIS:
501(c)(3).

ELIGIBILITY:
Varies depending on research program.

FINANCIAL DATA:
Amount of support per award: Varies.
Total amount of support: Varies.

APPLICATION INFO:
The Foundation has implemented an electronic grant submission and review system that will enable research to be funded

quickly and efficiently. Applicants should consult the Foundation web site for information.
Duration: Varies.
Deadline: Varies.

PUBLICATIONS:
The Fox Focus, newsletter; annual report; progress report.

IRS I.D.: 13-4141945

STAFF:
Deborah W. Brooks, Co-Founder and Executive Vice Chairman
Todd Sherer, Ph.D., Chief Executive Officer
Sohini Chowdhuri, Deputy Chief Executive Officer
Brian Fiske, Senior Vice President of Research Programs
Mark Frasier, Senior Vice President of Research Programs

ADDRESS INQUIRIES TO:
Brian Fiske, Senior Vice President of Research Programs
(See address above.)

THE PARKER B. FRANCIS FELLOWSHIP PROGRAM [2064]

UVMMC, 111 Colchester Avenue
Fletcher 311
Burlington, VT 05401
(802) 847-2550
Fax: (802) 847-5368
E-mail: polly.parsons@uvmhealth.org
Web Site: www.francisfellowships.org

FOUNDED: 1951

AREAS OF INTEREST:
Research related to lung biology, critical illness and control of breathing.

TYPE:
Fellowships. Awarded to scientists embarking on careers in clinical, laboratory or translational science in pulmonary, critical care and sleep medicine.

YEAR PROGRAM STARTED: 1975

PURPOSE:
To exert a favorable and lasting influence on the field of pulmonary medicine by providing the means to support promising young physicians and scientists for a period of training in research.

LEGAL BASIS:
Private foundation.

ELIGIBILITY:
Evaluation criteria and eligibility requirements can be found on the Foundation's web site.

GEOG. RESTRICTIONS: United States and Canada.

FINANCIAL DATA:
Funds to be used for stipends and fringe benefits, with up to $2,000 per year as a travel allowance.
Amount of support per award: $225,000 over three years.

NO. AWARDS: 10 to 14.

APPLICATION INFO:
Contact the Program.
Duration: Three years.
Deadline: October of each year.

STAFF:
Laurie St. Gelais, Administrator

ADDRESS INQUIRIES TO:
Laurie St. Gelais
PBF Fellowship Program Administrator
(See e-mail address above.)

FRAXA RESEARCH FOUNDATION [2065]

10 Prince Place
Suite 203
Newburyport, MA 01950
(978) 462-1866
E-mail: info@fraxa.org
Web Site: www.fraxa.org

FOUNDED: 1994

AREAS OF INTEREST:
Medical research aimed at the treatment of Fragile X Syndrome.

NAME(S) OF PROGRAMS:
● **FRAXA Grants and Fellowships**

TYPE:
Fellowships; Research grants; Research contracts.

YEAR PROGRAM STARTED: 1994

PURPOSE:
To promote research aimed at finding a specific treatment for Fragile X Syndrome; to provide funds for postdoctoral fellowships and investigator-initiated grants.

FINANCIAL DATA:
Amount of support per award: Up to $45,000 per year for fellowships. No limit on grants.

APPLICATION INFO:
Application form, plus a one-page initial inquiry letter.
Duration: Fellowships: Up to two years. Second year contingent upon successful progress and timely submission of renewal application.
Deadline: Fellowships: February 1.

PUBLICATIONS:
Newsletter; e-mail updates.

IRS I.D.: 04-3222167

OFFICER:
Katherine Clapp, President

ADDRESS INQUIRIES TO:
Michael Tranfaglia, Chief Scientific Officer
E-mail: mtranfaglia@fraxa.org and
Katherine Clapp, President
E-mail: kclapp@fraxa.org

FSHD SOCIETY, INC. [2066]

450 Bedford Street
Lexington, MA 02420
(781) 301-6060
Fax: (781) 862-1116
E-mail: daniel.perez@fshsociety.org
Web Site: www.fshsociety.org

FOUNDED: 1991

AREAS OF INTEREST:
Facioscapulohumeral Muscular Dystrophy.

TYPE:
Conferences/seminars; Project/program grants; Research grants.

YEAR PROGRAM STARTED: 1998

PURPOSE:
To promote research on and disperse information on Facioscapulohumeral Muscular Dystrophy.

LEGAL BASIS:
501(c)(3) organization.

ELIGIBILITY:
Preference will be given to postdoctoral trainees, clinical fellows and younger faculty establishing their first independent laboratory (less than five years). More established researchers should allow their postdoctoral trainees and fellows apply for these awards directly, while providing mentorship and guidance for a successful outcome to the proposal.

FINANCIAL DATA:
Amount of support per award: $5,000 to $100,000 per year.
Total amount of support: $1,037,579 for the year 2018.

NO. MOST RECENT APPLICANTS: 17 for the year 2018.

NO. AWARDS: 6 for the year 2018.

APPLICATION INFO:
Contact the Society.
Duration: Up to two years.
Deadline: February 28 and August 31.

PUBLICATIONS:
FSH Watch Newsletter; patient information on FSHD (English and Spanish).

IRS I.D.: 52-1762747

STAFF:
Mark A. Stone, Chief Executive Officer
June Kinoshita, Director of Research and Patient Engagement
Daniel Paul Perez, Co-Founder

ADDRESS INQUIRIES TO:
Daniel Paul Perez, Co-Founder
(See address above.)

GLAUCOMA RESEARCH FOUNDATION

251 Post Street, Suite 600
San Francisco, CA 94108
(415) 986-3162
Fax: (415) 986-3763
E-mail: research@glaucoma.org
Web Site: www.glaucoma.org

TYPE:
Research grants.

See entry 2311 for full listing.

THE GRAYSON-JOCKEY CLUB RESEARCH FOUNDATION [2067]

821 Corporate Drive
Lexington, KY 40503
(859) 224-2850
Fax: (859) 224-2853
E-mail: jhaydon@jockeyclub.com
Web Site: www.grayson-jockeyclub.org

FOUNDED: 1940

AREAS OF INTEREST:
Race horses, veterinary medicine and research for all horses.

TYPE:
Fellowships; Project/program grants; Research grants. Supports research relevant to equine health and performance.

YEAR PROGRAM STARTED: 1940

PURPOSE:
To promote research in veterinary medicine and in the breeding, raising and handling of horses.

LEGAL BASIS:
Nonprofit foundation.

ELIGIBILITY:
The principal investigator should have some professional rank and salary from the institution involved, or hold some grade of Research Professorship with salary from the institution. Research interest must be relevant to the equine, particularly in regard to, but not limited to, cardiopulmonary disorders, infectious diseases, musculoskeletal disorders, and reproduction.

FINANCIAL DATA:
Amount of support per award: Average $75,000.
Total amount of support: Approximately $1,000,000 annually.

NO. MOST RECENT APPLICANTS: Approximately 55.

NO. AWARDS: 19 for the year 2019.

APPLICATION INFO:
The Foundation will only accept the online application. Complete information is available on the Foundation web site.
Duration: One or two years.
Deadline: October 1. Announcement April 1.

PUBLICATIONS:
Application; guidelines; *Research Today,* newsletter.

IRS I.D.: 61-6031750

OFFICERS:
Dell Hancock, Chairman
Kevin Lavin, D.V.M., Vice Chairman
Jamie Haydon, President
Laura Barillaro, Treasurer
Resia Ayres, Secretary

STAFF:
Holly E. White, Director of Development
Shannon Kelly, Development Manager
Resia Ayres, Operations Manager

HEALTH RESOURCES AND SERVICES ADMINISTRATION [2068]

Bureau of Health Workforce
Division of Medicine and Dentistry
5600 Fishers Lane, Room 9A-27
Rockville, MD 20857
(301) 443-8437
E-mail: aanyanwu@hrsa.gov
Web Site: bhw.hrsa.gov/grants/medicine

NAME(S) OF PROGRAMS:
● **Primary Care Training and Enhancement (PCTE)**

TYPE:
Residencies; Training grants. Grants to strengthen the primary care workforce by supporting enhanced training for future primary care clinicians, teachers, and researchers and promoting primary care practice in rural and underserved areas. This grant focuses on producing primary care providers who will be well prepared to practice in and lead transforming health care systems aimed at improving access, quality of care, and cost effectiveness.

YEAR PROGRAM STARTED: 1972

PURPOSE:
To improve and expand access to quality health care for all.

LEGAL BASIS:
Section 747(a) of the PHS Act, as amended by the Health Professions Education Extension Amendments of 1992, Public Law 102-408.

ELIGIBILITY:
Applicants for the PCTE program must focus on training for transforming health care systems, particularly enhancing the clinical training experience of trainees.

Eligible applicants are accredited health professions schools and programs, including schools of allopathic or osteopathic medicine, academically affiliated physician assistant training programs, accredited public or nonprofit private hospitals, and public or nonprofit private entity capable of carrying out the grant.

GEOG. RESTRICTIONS: United States.

NO. AWARDS: Varies.

APPLICATION INFO:
Applicants are required to apply for this funding opportunity electronically through www.grants.gov.

All applications are competitively reviewed and evaluated.
Duration: Five years.

THE LARRY L. HILLBLOM FOUNDATION, INC. [2069]

755 Baywood Drive, Suite 180
Petaluma, CA 94954
(707) 762-6691
Fax: (707) 762-6694
E-mail: petaluma@llhf.org
Web Site: www.llhf.org

FOUNDED: 1996

AREAS OF INTEREST:
Medical research on diabetes mellitus and diseases associated with aging.

NAME(S) OF PROGRAMS:
● **Fellowship Research Grants**
● **Network Grants**
● **Start-Up Research Grants**

TYPE:
Assistantships; Block grants; Endowments; Fellowships. Fellowship Research Grants are intended to enable qualified institutions to provide postdoctoral research fellowship training to qualified applicants in one of the two areas of stated interest to the Foundation.

Network Grants facilitate interaction between a network of researchers. It is anticipated these investigators will be independently funded and have demonstrated productivity in their own field.

Start-Up Research Grants are offered to qualified institutions to enable them to select and assist qualified researchers to initiate independent research careers.

YEAR PROGRAM STARTED: 2000

PURPOSE:
To provide philanthropic support exclusively for charitable, religious, scientific, literary and educational purposes.

ELIGIBILITY:
Eligible organizations must have 501(c)(3) status.

GEOG. RESTRICTIONS: Primarily, California.

FINANCIAL DATA:
Amount of support per award: Fellowship Grants: Up to $65,000 per year; Network Grants: $300,000 per year; Start-Up Grants: $70,000 per year.
Total amount of support: Varies.

NO. MOST RECENT APPLICANTS: Varies.

NO. AWARDS: Varies.

APPLICATION INFO:
Contact the Foundation.

Duration: Fellowship Grants and Start-Up Grants: Up to three years; Network Grants: Four years.

Deadline: Fellowship Grants and Start-Up Grants: January. Notification by June. Network Grants: January 31 for Letters of Inquiry; July 31 for full application.

HIMSS FOUNDATION [2070]
33 West Monroe Street, Suite 1700
Chicago, IL 60603-5616
(312) 915-9289
Fax: (312) 664-6143
E-mail: scholarships@himss.org
Web Site: www.himss.org/health-it.education/scholarships

FOUNDED: 1961

AREAS OF INTEREST:
Health care information and management systems.

NAME(S) OF PROGRAMS:
- **HIMSS Foundation Scholarship Program**

TYPE:
Awards/prizes; Conferences/seminars; Fellowships; Internships; Research grants; Scholarships.

YEAR PROGRAM STARTED: 1986

PURPOSE:
To recognize students who have the potential to be future leaders in the health care information management systems industry.

ELIGIBILITY:
For scholarship consideration, nominees must meet the following criteria:
(1) The primary occupation of the applicant at the time the scholarship is awarded must be that of student in an accredited undergraduate, graduate, or doctoral program related to the health information or management systems field. The specific degree program is not a critical factor, although it is expected that programs similar to those in industrial engineering, operations research, bioinformatics, health informatics, computer science and information systems, mathematics, and quantitative programs in business administration, clinical disciplines, and health administration will predominate;
(2) Undergraduate applicants must be at least a first-term junior when the scholarship is awarded;
(3) Current member in good standing of HIMSS;
(4) Not currently serving on one of HIMSS boards (HIMSS NA, HIMSS Analytics, PCHAlliance) and;
(5) Cannot be currently employed by HIMSS, nor engaged in a consulting contract with any component of HIMSS.

Award judges and previous Foundation Scholarship recipients are ineligible.

FINANCIAL DATA:
An all-expense-paid trip to the HIMSS global conference is awarded in addition to grant.

Amount of support per award: $5,000 and $200 honorarium.

Total amount of support: Varies.

NO. MOST RECENT APPLICANTS: 125.

NO. AWARDS: 8 for the year 2018.

APPLICATION INFO:
Application may be requested by e-mail and is also posted on the Foundation web site in early August.

Duration: One year.

Deadline: September 23.

ADDRESS INQUIRIES TO:
See e-mail address above.

THE MAXIMILIAN E. & MARION O. HOFFMAN FOUNDATION, INC. [2071]
970 Farmington Avenue, Suite 203
West Hartford, CT 06107
(860) 521-2949
Fax: (860) 561-5082

AREAS OF INTEREST:
Education, medicine and the arts.

TYPE:
Project/program grants.

PURPOSE:
To provide funding to 501(c)(3) nonprofits conducting projects in education, medicine, and the arts.

LEGAL BASIS:
Nonprofit private foundation.

ELIGIBILITY:
Applicants must be 501(c)(3). No grants to individuals.

GEOG. RESTRICTIONS: United States, with preference to Connecticut.

FINANCIAL DATA:
Amount of support per award: Varies depending on needs and nature of the request.

APPLICATION INFO:
Submit Letter of Inquiry with copy of 501(c)(3).

Duration: One year. Some multiyear grants. Renewal possible by reapplication.

Deadline: The Board of Directors meets four to six times a year to consider requests.

PUBLICATIONS:
Application form.

IRS I.D.: 22-2648036

ADDRESS INQUIRIES TO:
Marion Barrak, President
(See address above.)

HOWARD HUGHES MEDICAL INSTITUTE [2072]
Medical Research Fellows Program
4000 Jones Bridge Road
Chevy Chase, MD 20815
(800) 448-4882 ext. 6708
Fax: (240) 497-2314
E-mail: medfellows@hhmi.org
Web Site: www.hhmi.org/medfellowships

FOUNDED: 1953

AREAS OF INTEREST:
Fundamental biomedical research.

NAME(S) OF PROGRAMS:
- **Medical Research Fellows Program**

TYPE:
Fellowships.

YEAR PROGRAM STARTED: 1989

PURPOSE:
To strengthen and expand the pool of medically trained researchers.

LEGAL BASIS:
Medical research organization.

ELIGIBILITY:
Applicant must attend a medical, dental or veterinary school located in the U.S., not in a Ph.D. or M.D./Ph.D. or other combined professional degree/Ph.D. program. Applicant must have laboratory research experience and plan to spend a year full-time in fundamental biomedical research.

FINANCIAL DATA:
Amount of support per award: $32,000 stipend, $5,500 research allowance, and $5,500 Fellow's allowance.

NO. MOST RECENT APPLICANTS: 174 for the year 2018.

NO. AWARDS: 72 for the year 2017.

APPLICATION INFO:
Online application requires the following information:
(1) educational background;
(2) prior research experience;
(3) research plan and;
(4) mentor's endorsement and reference letters.

Duration: One year.

Deadline: January 11. Announcement mid-March.

IRS I.D.: 59-0735717

ADDRESS INQUIRIES TO:
Melanie Daub, Program Officer
(See e-mail address above.)

IMMUNE DEFICIENCY FOUNDATION
110 West Road
Suite 300
Towson, MD 21204
(410) 321-6647
Fax: (410) 321-9165
E-mail: jmagnusson@primaryimmune.org
Web Site: usidnet.org
primaryimmune.org

TYPE:
Travel grants; Visiting scholars.

See entry 2130 for full listing.

INTERNATIONAL ANESTHESIA RESEARCH SOCIETY (IARS) [2073]
90 New Montgomery Street
Suite 412
San Francisco, CA 94104
(415) 296-6905
Fax: (415) 296-6901
E-mail: awards@iars.org
Web Site: www.iars.org

FOUNDED: 1922

AREAS OF INTEREST:
Anesthesia.

NAME(S) OF PROGRAMS:
- **Frontiers in Anesthesia Research Award**
- **IARS Mentored Research Awards**

TYPE:
Research grants. Education awards.

YEAR PROGRAM STARTED: 1983

ELIGIBILITY:
Applicant must be a member of the IARS.

FINANCIAL DATA:
Amount of support per award: Frontiers in Anesthesia Research Award: $750,000, in

three annual installments; IARS Mentored Research Awards: $175,000; Innovation in Education grant: $15,000.

NO. MOST RECENT APPLICANTS: Frontiers in Anesthesia Research Award: 30; IARS Mentored Research Awards: Average 30.

NO. AWARDS: Frontiers in Anesthesia Research Award: 1 triennially; IARS Mentored Research Awards: 4 annually.

APPLICATION INFO:
Interested applicants should visit the IARS web site. Applications can be submitted online.
Duration: Frontiers in Anesthesia Research Award: Three years; IARS Mentored Research Awards: Two years.
Deadline: Contact IARS for exact date.

PUBLICATIONS:
Anesthesia & Analgesia, journal; *Anesthesia & Analgesia Case Reports,* online journal.

ADDRESS INQUIRIES TO:
See e-mail address above.

INTERNATIONAL COLLEGE OF SURGEONS (ICS)   [2074]
1516 North Lakeshore Drive
Chicago, IL 60610-1694
(312) 560-5006
Fax: (312) 787-1683
E-mail: max@icsglobal.org
Web Site: www.icsglobal.org

AREAS OF INTEREST:
Medical research and surgery.

NAME(S) OF PROGRAMS:
● **ICS Scholarship**

TYPE:
Scholarships. ICS makes grants available to surgeons who wish to enhance their surgical skills through postgraduate training.

PURPOSE:
To support education and research.

ELIGIBILITY:
Open to surgeons around the world traveling to developed countries to further their education.

FINANCIAL DATA:
Amount of support per award: Varies.
Total amount of support: Varies.

NO. MOST RECENT APPLICANTS: Varies.

NO. AWARDS: Varies.

APPLICATION INFO:
Send request to ICS.
Duration: Varies.

ADDRESS INQUIRIES TO:
Max C. Downham, Executive Director
(See address above.)

INTERNATIONAL MYELOMA FOUNDATION (IMF)   [2075]
12650 Riverside Drive, Suite 206
North Hollywood, CA 91607-3421
(818) 487-7455
Fax: (818) 487-7454
E-mail: theimf@myeloma.org
Web Site: www.myeloma.org

FOUNDED: 1990

AREAS OF INTEREST:
Myeloma.

NAME(S) OF PROGRAMS:
● **Brian D. Novis Research Grants**

TYPE:
Internships; Research grants; Travel grants.

YEAR PROGRAM STARTED: 1995

PURPOSE:
To promote research into better treatments, management, prevention and a cure for myeloma.

LEGAL BASIS:
Nonprofit organization.

ELIGIBILITY:
Open to junior researchers or senior researchers working in the field of multiple myeloma. Junior researchers must have completed postdoctoral studies or clinical fellowships no later than August 1 of the application year and must have the ability to devote a minimum of 50% of his or her time to research during the award year. Also, must provide a completed application with evidence of a meritorious research project.

FINANCIAL DATA:
Amount of support per award: Junior researchers: $50,000; Senior researchers: $80,000.
Total amount of support: Varies each year.

APPLICATION INFO:
Applications can be downloaded from the Foundation's web site.
Duration: One year. Renewable upon reapplication.
Deadline: August 1 (postmarked) for the following year's program.

PUBLICATIONS:
Myeloma Today, newsletter.

IRS I.D.: 95-4296919

STAFF:
Susie Durie, President
Lisa Paik, Senior Vice President of Clinical Education and Research Initiatives

ADDRESS INQUIRIES TO:
Lisa Paik, Senior Vice President of Clinical Education and Research Initiatives or
Amirah Limayo, Research Project Coordinator
(See address above.)

ROBERT WOOD JOHNSON FOUNDATION   [2076]
50 College Road East
Princeton, NJ 08540
(877) 843-7953
Fax: (609) 627-5985
E-mail: lryba@rwjf.org
Web Site: www.rwjf.org

FOUNDED: 1972

AREAS OF INTEREST:
Health leadership, healthy children and families, healthy communities, and transforming health/healthcare systems.

TYPE:
Research grants. Program contracts; Evaluations.

YEAR PROGRAM STARTED: 1972

PURPOSE:
To build a national culture of health; to raise the health of everyone in the U.S. to the level a great nation deserves by placing well-being at the center of every aspect of life.

LEGAL BASIS:
Private foundation.

ELIGIBILITY:
Preference is given to tax-exempt, public agencies under Section 501(c)(3). The Foundation does not fund general operating expenses or existing deficits, endowments or capital costs, basic biomedical research, drug therapies or devices research, direct support of individuals, or lobbying of any kind.

Additionally, the Foundation rarely makes grants for conferences, unless they relate clearly to the Foundation's goals, or for publications and media projects, except those that grow out of one of the Foundation's grant programs.

GEOG. RESTRICTIONS: United States.

FINANCIAL DATA:
Amount of support per award: Most grants average $535,000.
Total amount of support: $415,856,067 for the year 2019.
Matching fund requirements: Varies; only a limited number of awards include matching fund requirements.

NO. AWARDS: 774 for the year 2019.

REPRESENTATIVE AWARDS:
$250,000 to Children's Hospital Medical Center, Cincinnati, OH, for identifying and testing systems solutions to barriers to enrollment in early care and education programs in Cincinnati; $200,000 to Kentucky Coalition, Inc., London, KY, for general operating support; $368,752 to Milken Institute School of Public Health at George Washington University, Washington, DC, for building a platform to evaluate how media affects human attitudes, perceptions, and behavior change on climate change to motivate public action.

APPLICATION INFO:
Funding is awarded through targeted calls for proposals. The Foundation will accept brief proposals for funding of new and creative approaches to building a culture of health.
Duration: Varies.
Deadline: Varies.

STAFF:
Richard E. Besser, President and Chief Executive Officer
Katherine Hatton, J.D., Vice President, General Counsel and Secretary
Pat A. McFadzean, Vice President, Human Resources and Administration
Margaret Einhorn, MBA, Chief Financial Officer
Brian S. O'Neil, MBA, C.F.A., Chief Investment Officer

ADDRESS INQUIRIES TO:
Lydia Ryba, Senior Manager
Office of Proposal Management
(See address above.)

THE JACOB AND VALERIA LANGELOTH FOUNDATION   [2077]
275 Madison Avenue
Suite 2102
New York, NY 10016
(212) 687-1133
E-mail: info@langeloth.org
Web Site: www.langeloth.org

AREAS OF INTEREST:
Social justice, criminal justice system, safe and healthy communities, and health care policy.

NAME(S) OF PROGRAMS:
- **Criminal Justice Reform**
- **Safe and Healthy Communities**

TYPE:
Demonstration grants; Project/program grants; Research grants.

PURPOSE:
To promote and support effective and creative programs, practices and policies related to healing from illness, accident, physical, social or emotional trauma; to extend the availability of programs that promote healing to underserved populations.

ELIGIBILITY:
Grants are made to organizations that have tax-exempt status under Section 501(c)(3) of the Internal Revenue Code and that are health care providers, academic research institutions or community-based organizations. Grants are made nationwide, with a specific interest in New York state.

GEOG. RESTRICTIONS: Primarily New York state.

FINANCIAL DATA:
$88,308,586 in assets (unaudited) for fiscal year ended December 31, 2018.
Amount of support per award: Varies.
Total amount of support: Approximately $6,800,000 for the year 2018.

NO. AWARDS: 15.

APPLICATION INFO:
Letter of intent and proposal submissions are by invitation only. Interested organizations must first register their project for review.
Duration: Up to three years.
Deadline: June and December.

STAFF:
Scott Moyer, President
Andrea Fionda, Program Officer
Melissa Houston, Grants and Office Administrator

*SPECIAL STIPULATIONS:
Foundation does not accept unsolicited proposals.

LEUKEMIA RESEARCH FOUNDATION

191 Waukegan Road
Suite 105
Northfield, IL 60093
(847) 424-0600
Fax: (847) 424-0606
E-mail: info@lrfmail.org
Web Site: www.allbloodcancers.org

TYPE:
Research grants. The goal of the grant program is to support new investigators. It funds scientists and physicians around the world.

See entry 2232 for full listing.

LOVELACE RESPIRATORY RESEARCH INSTITUTE

2425 Ridgecrest Drive, S.E.
Albuquerque, NM 87108
(505) 348-9400
Fax: (505) 348-8567
E-mail: info@lrri.org
Web Site: lrri.org

TYPE:
Fellowships. Training program in respiratory tract disease caused by environmental agents.

See entry 2131 for full listing.

LOWE SYNDROME ASSOCIATION   [2078]

P.O. Box 417
Chicago Ridge, IL 60415
(216) 630-7723
E-mail: info@lowesyndrome.org
jgkubicki@gmail.com
Web Site: www.lowesyndrome.org

FOUNDED: 1982

AREAS OF INTEREST:
Medical research pertaining to Lowe Syndrome.

NAME(S) OF PROGRAMS:
- **The Leland McSpadden Memorial Fund for Medical and Scientific Research**

TYPE:
Research grants. Supports research leading to a better understanding of the metabolic basis of Lowe Syndrome, to better treatments of the major complications of Lowe Syndrome, to the prevention of Lowe Syndrome, and/or to a cure for Lowe Syndrome.

YEAR PROGRAM STARTED: 1983

PURPOSE:
To improve the lives of persons with Lowe Syndrome and their families through fostering communication, providing education and supporting research so that individuals can attain their highest potential.

ELIGIBILITY:
Researchers of all types are invited to send applications, including but not limited to, universities, hospitals, and other nonprofit organizations with interest in research in areas specified by the Association.

FINANCIAL DATA:
Amount of support per award: Varies.
Total amount of support: Varies.

NO. MOST RECENT APPLICANTS: Varies.

NO. AWARDS: Varies.

APPLICATION INFO:
Contact the Association.
Duration: One year.
Deadline: Varies.

ADDRESS INQUIRIES TO:
Lisa Waldbaum, President
(See address above.)

LUPUS FOUNDATION OF AMERICA, INC.   [2079]

2121 K Street, N.W., Suite 200
Washington, DC 20037
(202) 349-1150
(800) 875-2562 (customer support)
Fax: (202) 349-1156
E-mail: marion@lupus.org
Web Site: www.lupus.org/finzifellowships

FOUNDED: 1977

AREAS OF INTEREST:
Lupus research.

NAME(S) OF PROGRAMS:
- **Gina M. Finzi Memorial Student Summer Fellowship Program**

TYPE:
Summer Fellowship. The Gina M. Finzi Memorial Student Summer Fellowship Program proposes to foster an interest among students in the areas of basic, clinical, translational, epidemiological or behavioral research relevant to lupus under the sponsorship and supervision of an established, tenure-track Principal Investigator who directs a laboratory dedicated at least in part to the investigation of lupus at a U.S. or Canadian academic, medical or research institution.

YEAR PROGRAM STARTED: 1984

ELIGIBILITY:
Institution must be in the U.S., Canada, or Mexico.

FINANCIAL DATA:
The Finzi Student Summer Fellowship provides financial support for a summer research project, opportunities for professional training, enrichment and mentorship, lifetime professional association with LFA network, and access to LFA professional resources.
Amount of support per award: $4,000.

NO. MOST RECENT APPLICANTS: 17.

NO. AWARDS: 6.

APPLICATION INFO:
Grant applicants must submit their full application package through Altum's proposalCENTRAL online system. Paper applications will not be accepted.
Duration: One summer.
Deadline: April 17.

ADDRESS INQUIRIES TO:
Ashley Marion, Research and Grants Senior Coordinator
(See e-mail address above.)

JOSIAH MACY JR. FOUNDATION   [2080]

44 East 64th Street
New York, NY 10065
(212) 486-2424
Fax: (212) 644-0765
E-mail: info@macyfoundation.org
Web Site: www.macyfoundation.org

FOUNDED: 1930

AREAS OF INTEREST:
Health care, health professions and medical education.

NAME(S) OF PROGRAMS:
- **Board Grants**
- **Macy Faculty Scholars**
- **President's Grants**

TYPE:
Conferences/seminars; Demonstration grants; Development grants; Matching gifts; Project/program grants. Major interest in education for careers in medicine or medical science. Special programs on preparation of minority groups for health professions and teamwork among and between health professions.

YEAR PROGRAM STARTED: 1930

PURPOSE:
To promote diversity, equity and belonging; to increase collaboration among future health professionals; to prepare future health professionals to navigate ethical dilemmas.

LEGAL BASIS:
Private foundation.

ELIGIBILITY:
Applicants must be qualified not-for-profit institutions with appropriate interests. No

grants are made directly to individuals, nor for building, annual fund appeals or medical research.

GEOG. RESTRICTIONS: United States.

FINANCIAL DATA:
Amount of support per award: Board Grants and Macy Faculty Scholars: Varies based on need; President's Grants: Up to $25,000, including overhead.

Total amount of support: Varies.

Matching fund requirements: Foundation matches gifts from full-time employees, directors and officers only to charitable organizations.

NO. AWARDS: Up to 40 annually.

APPLICATION INFO:
Complete application information can be found on the Foundation web site.

Duration: Board Grants: One to three years. President's Grants: Up to one year.

PUBLICATIONS:
Annual report; conference proceedings.

STAFF:
Holly J. Humphrey, M.D., M.A.C.P., President
Peter Goodwin, MBA, Chief Operating Officer and Treasurer
Karen Butler, Assistant Treasurer
Yasmine R. Legendre, MPA, Program Associate
Heather Snijdewind, Program Assistant, Macy Faculty Scholars Program
Stephen C. Schoenbaum, M.D., M.P.H., Special Advisor to the President

BOARD OF DIRECTORS:
William H. Wright, II, Chairman
Holly J. Humphrey, M.D., M.A.C.P., President
David Blumenthal, M.D., M.P.P.
George Campbell, Jr., Ph.D.
Francisco G. Cigarroa, M.D.
Linda Cronenwett, Ph.D., R.N.
Linda P. Fried, M.D., M.P.H.
Terry Fulmer, Ph.D., R.N.
Meredith B. Jenkins
Howard K. Koh, M.D., M.P.H.
Valerie Montgomery Rice, M.D.
Steven M. Safyer, M.D.
Mary K. Wakefield
Gregory H. Warner, MBA

ADDRESS INQUIRIES TO:
See e-mail address above.

MARCH OF DIMES   [2081]
1550 Crystal Drive, Suite 1300
Arlington, VA 22202
(914) 997-4563
E-mail: researchgrantssupport@marchofdimes. org
Web Site: www.marchofdimes.org
modresearchgrants.aibs-scores.org (online application system)

FOUNDED: 1938

AREAS OF INTEREST:
Prevention of birth defects, premature birth, infant mortality, and maternal morbidity and mortality.

NAME(S) OF PROGRAMS:
● **Basil O'Connor Starter Scholar Research Award**

TYPE:
Research grants. Basil O'Connor Starter Scholar Research Awards (BOC) support young physicians/scientists committed to the

mission of the March of Dimes. March of Dimes leads the fight for the health of all moms and babies.

YEAR PROGRAM STARTED: 1973

PURPOSE:
To support young scientists just embarking on their independent research careers.

LEGAL BASIS:
Tax-exempt 501(c)(3) organization.

ELIGIBILITY:
Award is intended to be an initial independent grant to young investigators. Eligibility is thus restricted.

Each application should be accompanied by a Letter of Support from a Nominator. The Nominator should first vouch for a candidate's having an unrestricted faculty position and lab space. Ph.D. applicants should be no more than eight years past their degree. Successful applicants have traditionally had four to six years of postdoctoral training or other faculty-mentored work, but not more than eight years. For M.D. or M.D./Ph.D. applicants, the same four- to eight-year timeline applies, but begins upon completion of the last year of clinical training required for medical specialty board certification. Requests for exceptions (e.g., pregnancy and maternity leave) should be directed to the Senior Vice President for Research and Global Programs.

March of Dimes takes into account the purpose of the research program and plan submitted, qualifications, experience and abilities of the persons who are to supervise and participate in the proposed program and the facilities available.

FINANCIAL DATA:
The budget covers salary support for technical help and a portion of the Principal Investigator's salary, which may not exceed 10% of the NIH salary cap.

Amount of support per award: $75,000 per year for two years.

NO. MOST RECENT APPLICANTS: 54 for the year 2019.

NO. AWARDS: 4 for the year 2019.

REPRESENTATIVE AWARDS:
$150,000 to Prasanna Jagannathan, M.D., Stanford University, for "Identifying Novel Immunologic Targets to Reduce the Burden of Malaria during Pregnancy and Infancy;" $150,000 to Ethan Goldberg, M.D., Ph.D., The Children's Hospital of Philadelphia, for "Investigating the Mechanism of a Novel Cause of Congenital Brain Malformation;" $150,000 to Eliezer Calo, Ph.D., Massachusetts Institute of Technology, for "Elucidating Mechanisms Underlying Phenotypic Variation in Childhood Disorders."

APPLICATION INFO:
The entire process must be completed online via the March of Dimes online application system.

The following information is required from the candidate:
(1) Letter of Intent (template provided) for the proposed research.

This Letter of Intent must include the following information in this order:
(a) title of proposal;
(b) hypothesis;
(c) preliminary data;

(d) specific aims and a brief summary of the methods proposed and;
(e) current financial support: list all current financial support; if there is no other support, state "NONE."
NOTE: Items a-e should not exceed three pages.
(2) candidate's biographical sketch and;
(3) candidate's facilities available.

Information required from the Nominator: Deans, Chairpersons of Departments or Directors of Institutes/Centers may submit nominations for this award, addressed to the Chief Scientific Officer. Included should be the Nominator's name, academic appointment, mailing address, telephone and e-mail address. The Letter of Nomination should be submitted via the online application system. The nomination letter should vouch for the candidate's having an unrestricted faculty position and dedicated lab/clinical research space. Information provided should explicitly include details concerning the candidate's faculty appointment, independence, laboratory space (assigned to the candidate), startup package, and access to core facilities. This information will be scrutinized closely.

Duration: Awards are approved for two years.

Deadline: Nominations: July 17. Proposals: By December 5. Reviewed in April for July 1 funding cycle.

PUBLICATIONS:
Program announcement and grants list.

NATIONAL OFFICERS:
Gary Dixon, Chairperson
Monica Luechtefeld, M.D., Vice Chairperson and Treasurer
John Rainey, Secretary
Donald Germano, Vice Chairperson
John Spector, Vice Chairperson

ADDRESS INQUIRIES TO:
Rachel Hauser
Research Grants Administrator
E-mail: rhauser@marchofdimes.org

*PLEASE NOTE:
The Foundation does not accept applications dealing with infertility.

*SPECIAL STIPULATIONS:
Basil O'Connor applicants may not be recipients of a major grant (e.g., an R01, or other grant exceeding $200,000 a year) at the time of the application. If an application for such other grant is under review, eligibility for Basil O'Connor remains so long as it has not been awarded at the time of March of Dimes review. Applicants who have transition faculty-mentored awards (e.g., K99/R00) are welcome, if they have completed the mentored portion. If not, application should be deferred. Candidates may not simultaneously submit an application for any other March of Dimes research program. Those who have previously submitted an application to the March of Dimes are not eligible for a Basil O'Connor Award unless permission has been explicitly given; however, application for a regular research grant is welcomed.

MARCH OF DIMES   [2082]

1550 Crystal Drive, Suite 1300
Arlington, VA 22202
(914) 997-4563
E-mail: researchgrants@marchofdimes.org
Web Site: www.marchofdimes.org
modresearchgrants.aibs-scores.org (online
application system)

FOUNDED: 1938

AREAS OF INTEREST:
Prevention of birth defects, premature birth,
infant mortality, and maternal morbidity and
mortality.

NAME(S) OF PROGRAMS:
● **Research Grants Program**

TYPE:
Research grants. Clinical and social science
challenge grants; Innovative challenge grants;
Novel discovery grants. Research grants in
the areas of pregnancy-related disorders,
genetic and environmentally-induced birth
defects, opioid exposure and dependency, and
health disparities surrounding each of these
areas.

March of Dimes is looking for proposals that
involve translational and actionable science
that will lead directly to interventions or
preventions. These should include human
studies or studies with human tissue. Model
systems research is discouraged, but mouse
studies are eligible if they are to validate
novel human disease processes. These studies
may also involve information and
communications technology innovations. The
goal is to turn observations in the laboratory
and clinic into interventions, drugs and
devices that improve the health of moms and
babies.

YEAR PROGRAM STARTED: 1974

PURPOSE:
To support programs designed to gain new
knowledge about the mechanisms that cause
birth defects and to find ways of controlling
or preventing them.

LEGAL BASIS:
Tax-exempt 501(c)(3) organization.

ELIGIBILITY:
March of Dimes invites health professionals,
health researchers, epidemiologists and social
scientists with doctoral or Master's-level
academic degrees and either a faculty
appointment or equivalent at academic
universities, hospital and research institutions;
or employees of small businesses, startup
companies, nonprofit organizations or
pharmaceutical companies committed to
research in the area of maternal and child
health.

These applications are not limited to U.S.
citizens and are open to global applicants.

Applicants may not hold any other
concurrent March of Dimes grants when
applying.

FINANCIAL DATA:
The budget covers salary support for
technical help and a portion of the Principal
Investigator's salary, which may not exceed
10% of the NIH salary cap.

Amount of support per award: Clinical and
Social Science Challenge Grants: $50,000 to
$100,000 for the first six months with clear
cut deliverables defined in the application;
Innovative Challenge Grants: $50,000 for the
first six months with clear cut deliverables
defined in the application; Novel Discovery
Grants: $50,000 to $100,000.

NO. MOST RECENT APPLICANTS: 63 for the year
2019.

NO. AWARDS: 14 for the year 2019.

REPRESENTATIVE AWARDS:
Rupsa Boelig, M.D., Thomas Jefferson
University, for "Aspirin Prevention of
Preeclampsia: Individual Determinants of
Platelet Response and Pregnancy Outcomes;"
Jennifer Condon, Ph.D., Wayne State
University, for "A Novel Uterine Secretome
Generated by Gestational Preconditioning
Acts to Mitigate Preterm Birth;" Dean
Carson, Ph.D., Katana Pharmaceuticals, for
"Development of a preservative free oxytocin
formulation and pediatric nasal delivery
device for the treatment of neonatal
abstinence syndrome."

APPLICATION INFO:
The entire process must be completed online
via the March of Dimes online application
system. Applicants may only submit one
Letter of Intent to one of the research grant
categories.

Applicants must provide:
(1) Letter of Intent for the proposed research
(template provided), which must include the
following information in this order:
(a) title of proposal;
(b) hypothesis;
(c) preliminary data;
(d) statement of specific aims and methods of
procedure and;
(e) current financial support; list each current
grant or contract for the conduct of this
research. If there is no current support, state
"NONE."
Items a-e may not exceed three pages.
(2) candidate's biographical sketch and;
(3) facilities available.
Duration: Clinical and Social Science
Challenge Grants and Innovative Challenge
Grants: Six months with the option of
another 12 months of support if significant
progress is made. Novel Discovery Grants:
One year. Renewable for another 12 months
if significant progress is made.
Deadline: The online Letter of Intent process
must be completed by April 19. The
scientific advisory committee's selection will
be transmitted by July 30. Complete
application (from those selected): September
4. Applicants will be informed of the
decisions regarding these applications by
December 16. Funding initiated January 1.

PUBLICATIONS:
Program announcement; grants list.

ADDRESS INQUIRIES TO:
Rachel Hauser
Research Grants Administrator
E-mail: rhauser@marchofdimes.org

*PLEASE NOTE:
The Foundation does not accept applications
dealing with infertility.

Please adhere to the instructions precisely.
Any letter that does not follow this precise
format will not be included in the review
process.

MAYO CLINIC   [2083]

Mayo School of Graduate Medical Education
200 First Street, S.W.
Rochester, MN 55905
(507) 538-6453
Fax: (507) 538-3267
E-mail: pathologyeducation@mayo.edu
Web Site: www.mayo.edu/msgme

AREAS OF INTEREST:
Surgical and medical pathology, including
bone and soft tissue pathology, cardiovascular
pathology, cytopathology, GI/liver pathology,
breast pathology, and renal pathology.

NAME(S) OF PROGRAMS:
● **Surgical Pathology Fellowships**

TYPE:
Fellowships. Available subspecialty
fellowships include bone and soft tissue
pathology, breast pathology, cardiovascular
pathology, cytopathology, gastrointestinal
pathology, hematopathology, molecular
genetic pathology, neuropathology,
pulmonary pathology, renal pathology, special
coagulation, and surgical pathology. Each
fellowship will give ample opportunity to
diagnose and work with a large diverse
volume of tissue specimens. Fellows will
assist Mayo's staff consultants with projects
and will be encouraged to initiate and
participate in clinical pathology and basic
research studies for publication and
presentation at national meetings. Fellows
will also develop and present studies at
conferences and seminars and may assist in
teaching pathology residents, medical
students and fellows from other departments.
Each specialty fellowship consists of a
one-year program except neuropathology,
which is a two-year appointment. Combined
fellowships are also possible.

PURPOSE:
To promote the belief that physicians need to
work together, teach and learn from others
and conduct research to provide sustained,
excellent patient care.

LEGAL BASIS:
Hospital.

ELIGIBILITY:
Applicants must have a medical degree with
U.S. or Canadian specialty training in
anatomic pathology for all specialty
fellowships.

FINANCIAL DATA:
Fellows will be permitted 15 days each year
for vacation. Fellows will also receive a
stipend and benefits package including a
comprehensive medical care plan, short-term
disability insurance, voluntary family life
insurance, dental assistance plan, professional
liability coverage and excess personal
liability insurance.

Amount of support per award: Varies
depending on experience and fellowship.

NO. AWARDS: 1 in each specialty except for
surgical pathology, which has 9 fellows.

APPLICATION INFO:
Applications are to be submitted through the
Apply Yourself application service.
Completed online application must include:
(1) three letters of recommendation (one
must be from applicant's current program
director or supervisor);
(2) curriculum vitae;
(3) personal statement of professional goals;
(4) copy of graduate school and/or medical
school diploma;
(5) dean's letter;
(6) official final transcripts;
(7) official test transcripts for all applicable
examinations (USMLE, LMCC, COMLEX,
NBOME, FMGEMS, FLEX, NBME);
(8) valid ECFMG certificate (if applicable)
and;

(9) copy of completion certification from each of applicant's prior residency and/or fellowship training programs.

There is a $15 application fee.

If an applicant is considered for an appointment, they will be asked to visit Mayo Clinic Rochester for an interview with the program director and selected faculty. Interviews are conducted September and October of each year.

Duration: One year.

Deadline: July 1 of the year preceding appointment.

BENJAMIN AND MARY SIDDONS MEASEY FOUNDATION [2084]

P.O. Box 258
Media, PA 19063
(610) 566-5800
Fax: (610) 566-8197
E-mail: admin@measeyfoundation.org
Web Site: measeyfoundation.org

FOUNDED: 1958

AREAS OF INTEREST:
Medical education in Philadelphia area processed through Philadelphia medical schools only.

NAME(S) OF PROGRAMS:
• **Medical Education Grants**

TYPE:
Challenge/matching grants; Fellowships; Grants-in-aid.

YEAR PROGRAM STARTED: 1958

PURPOSE:
To advance medical education of physicians.

LEGAL BASIS:
1958 Trust Document.

ELIGIBILITY:
Grants are made through accredited medical schools in the immediate Philadelphia, PA area. Individual applications are not accepted by the Foundation; institutions only.

GEOG. RESTRICTIONS: Philadelphia, Pennsylvania area.

FINANCIAL DATA:
Amount of support per award: $7,500 to $500,000.
Total amount of support: $2,000,000.

NO. MOST RECENT APPLICANTS: 10.

APPLICATION INFO:
Application is by letter. Organizations must provide 501(c)(3) tax-exempt information.
Duration: One year. Nonrenewable.
Deadline: One month prior to quarterly meetings held in March, June, September and December.

IRS I.D.: 23-6298781

STAFF:
James C. Brennan, Esq., Manager
M.S. Donaldson, Esq., Secretary

ADDRESS INQUIRIES TO:
James C. Brennan, Esq., Manager and Counsel
(See address above.)

*SPECIAL STIPULATIONS:
No applications to Foundation directly.

MEDICAL LIBRARY ASSOCIATION

225 West Wacker Drive
Suite 650
Chicago, IL 60606
(312) 419-9094
E-mail: awards@mail.mlahq.org
Web Site: www.mlanet.org

TYPE:
Fellowships; Scholarships. Awarded for study and doctoral work in health sciences librarianship.

See entry 680 for full listing.

NATIONAL ALOPECIA AREATA FOUNDATION

65 Mitchell Boulevard
Suite 200-B
San Rafael, CA 94903
(415) 472-3780
Fax: (415) 480-1800
E-mail: info@naaf.org
abby@naaf.org
Web Site: www.naaf.org

TYPE:
Research grants.

See entry 1973 for full listing.

NATIONAL HEART, LUNG AND BLOOD INSTITUTE (NHLBI)

Division of Extramural Research
Rockledge II, Room 7160
6701 Rockledge Drive, MSC 7926
Bethesda, MD 20892-7926
(301) 435-0166
Fax: (301) 451-5462
E-mail: lombardr@nhlbi.nih.gov
Web Site: www.nhlbi.nih.gov

TYPE:
Conferences/seminars; Fellowships; Project/program grants; Research grants; Training grants; Loan forgiveness programs. Career awards and other grant mechanisms to foster research on heart, vascular and lung diseases, and to develop scientists in these areas. Also, small business grants. Loan forgiveness programs are for research.

See entry 2186 for full listing.

THE NATIONAL HEMOPHILIA FOUNDATION [2085]

7 Penn Plaza
370 Seventh Avenue, Suite 1204
New York, NY 10001
(212) 328-3700
(800) 424-2634
Fax: (212) 328-3777
E-mail: mwitkop@hemophilia.org
Web Site: www.hemophilia.org/Researchers-Healthcare-Providers/Research-Grant-Programs

FOUNDED: 1948

AREAS OF INTEREST:
Biochemistry, genetics, hematology, microbiology, orthopedics, psychiatry and other disciplines related to hemophilia and other bleeding disorders.

NAME(S) OF PROGRAMS:
• **Bridge Award**
• **Innovative Investigator Award**

• **NHF/Novo Nordisk Career Development Award**
• **Judith Graham Pool Postdoctoral Research Fellowships in Bleeding Disorders**

TYPE:
Development grants; Fellowships; Research grants. Support for research in clinical and/or basic sciences in areas relating to problems in hemophilia and other bleeding disorders.

Bridge Award assists hematology investigators to continue their critical research into inherited bleeding disorders.

Innovative Investigator Award and NHF/Novo Nordisk Career Development Award fund innovative projects that promote the development of novel technologies and/or therapies to advance the field of bleeding disorder research.

Judith Graham Pool Postdoctoral Research Fellowships are designed to support research studies of high scientific merit and relevance to bleeding disorders. They are awarded through professional and graduate schools, or research institutions.

YEAR PROGRAM STARTED: 1972

PURPOSE:
To encourage and support hemophilia-related and other bleeding disorders research.

LEGAL BASIS:
Voluntary, nonprofit health organization.

ELIGIBILITY:
Applicants must have completed doctoral training and must enter the fellowship program from a doctoral, postdoctoral, internship or residency training program.

Individuals with more than six years of experience since completing doctoral training are not eligible to apply. Established investigators or faculty members are also not eligible.

Bridge Award seeks applications from hematology investigators who have submitted to the NIH an R01 or R01-equivalent application with the past 18 months that was scored but not funded. Applicant must be the principal investigator on the submission.

Innovative Investigator Award seeks research grant applications from any multidisciplinary team member within the federally funded Hemophilia Treatment Center (HTC) network for innovative-investigator research (IIR) projects that demonstrate a commitment to the bleeding disorders community.

NHF/Novo Nordisk Career Development Award seeks research grant applications from established investigators, preferably at the assistant professor level or above, who have demonstrated a commitment to bleeding disorders research.

GEOG. RESTRICTIONS: United States.

FINANCIAL DATA:
Amount of support per award: Bridge Award: Up to $125,000; Innovative Investigator Award: Up to $60,000; NHF/Novo Nordisk Career Development Award: Up to $70,000; Judith Graham Pool Postdoctoral Research Fellowship: Up to $52,000 per year.
Total amount of support: Varies.

NO. AWARDS: NHF/Novo Nordisk Award: 1 every other year; All others: Varies.

APPLICATION INFO:
Interested candidates must submit a Letter of Intent. This should be a brief letter

identifying the researcher, their mentor, institution, and a description of the proposed research project. Letters of Intent should include an NIH-style curriculum vitae or biosketch for both candidate and mentor. After review, candidates may be invited to submit a full application.

Duration: Bridge Award: One year; Innovative Investigator Award: 12 to 18 months. Continuation for second year is based upon progress report and continuation application; NHF/Novo Nordisk Career Development Award: Up to three years. Continuation for second and third year is based upon progress report and continuation application; Judith Graham Pool Postdoctoral Research Fellowships: Up to two years. Continuation for second year is based upon progress report and continuation application.

Deadline: Usually March. Check web site for current information.

ADDRESS INQUIRIES TO:
Michele Witkop, Head of Research
(See e-mail address above.)

NATIONAL INSTITUTE OF ENVIRONMENTAL HEALTH SCIENCES

Division of Extramural Research and Training
MD K3-05
111 T.W. Alexander Drive
Research Triangle Park, NC 27709
(984) 287-3285
Fax: (919) 541-3976
E-mail: mastin@niehs.nih.gov
Web Site: www.niehs.nih.gov

TYPE:
Conferences/seminars; Demonstration grants; Development grants; Fellowships; Project/program grants; Research grants; Training grants. NIEHS pursues its mission by supporting basic and applied research on the consequences of the exposure of humans to potentially toxic or harmful agents in the environment.

Research of interest encompasses studies that relate to the biological effects of environmental chemicals and physical factors including such agents as hazardous gases, suspended particles, aerosols, industrial by-products and intermediates, heavy metals, trace elements, food additives, adulterants and pesticides.

Research Training Programs support individuals at both the predoctoral and postdoctoral levels in the areas of environmental toxicology, environmental pathology, environmental mutagenesis and environmental epidemiology.

See entry 2003 for full listing.

NATIONAL INSTITUTE OF GENERAL MEDICAL SCIENCES [2086]

National Institutes of Health
45 Center Drive, MSC 6200
Bethesda, MD 20892-6200
(301) 496-7301
Fax: (301) 402-0224
E-mail: info@nigms.nih.gov
Web Site: www.nigms.nih.gov

FOUNDED: 1962

AREAS OF INTEREST:
Basic biomedical research and research training.

TYPE:
Fellowships; Research grants; Training grants; Research contracts. Capacity building. The National Institute of General Medical Sciences (NIGMS) supports basic research that increases understanding of biological processes and lays the foundation for advances in disease diagnosis, treatment and prevention. NIGMS-funded scientists investigate how living systems work at a range of levels, from molecules and cells to tissues, whole organisms and populations. The Institute also supports research in certain clinical areas, primarily those that affect multiple organ systems. To assure the vitality and continued productivity of research enterprise, NIGMS provides leadership in training the next generation of scientists, in enhancing the diversity of scientific workforce, and in developing research capacities throughout the country.

YEAR PROGRAM STARTED: 1962

PURPOSE:
To support basic biomedical research that lays the foundation for advances in disease diagnosis, treatment, and prevention; to help provide the most critical element of good research: well-prepared scientists.

LEGAL BASIS:
Part of a government agency under the PHS Act, various sections, and various public laws.

ELIGIBILITY:
For Research Grants, applicants must be academic institutions, teaching hospitals, public agencies, nonprofit organizations and for-profit corporations.

National Research Service Awards for the above areas may be made to individuals for postdoctoral training or nonprofit institutions for the training of individuals at the predoctoral and postdoctoral level.

For Small Business Innovative Research Program, applicants must be qualified small businesses to stimulate technological innovation in areas of interest to the Institute.

FINANCIAL DATA:
Amount of support per award: Varies by program.

Total amount of support: $2.872 billion for fiscal year 2019.

NO. AWARDS: 5,313 NIGMS-funded research grants for fiscal year 2019.

APPLICATION INFO:
Instructions vary by program. Application materials are available on the NIMH web site.

Duration: Varies.

Deadline: Varies by program.

STAFF:
Stephanie Older, Chief, Office of Communications and Public Liaison

ADDRESS INQUIRIES TO:
Office of Communications and Public Liaison
(See address above.)

NATIONAL INSTITUTE OF GENERAL MEDICAL SCIENCES [2087]

Center for Research Capacity Building
45 Center Drive, Room 2AS-43
Bethesda, MD 20892
(301) 594-3900
Fax: (301) 480-2753
E-mail: irina.krasnova@nih.gov
Web Site: www.nigms.nih.gov

FOUNDED: 1972

NAME(S) OF PROGRAMS:
● **Support of Competitive Research Awards**

TYPE:
Development grants; Research grants. Grants to assist eligible institutions to strengthen the institutions' biomedical research capabilities and provide opportunities to students to engage in biomedical or behavioral research and other activities in preparation for Ph.D. training in these areas.

YEAR PROGRAM STARTED: 1972

PURPOSE:
To increase the number of faculty, students, and investigators who are members of groups underrepresented in the biomedical and behavioral sciences who are engaged in research in these fields.

LEGAL BASIS:
Public Health Service Act of 1944 as amended, Section 301(c); U.S.C. 241.d.

ELIGIBILITY:
Applicant must be located in a state, the District of Columbia or a U.S. territory, and be a public or private university, four-year college or other institution offering undergraduate, graduate or health professional degrees with more than 50% minority enrollment, a public or private nonprofit four-year college or other institution offering undergraduate, graduate or health professional degrees, with a significant enrollment (but not necessarily more than 50%) derived from ethnic minorities, if the secretary of DHHS determines that the institution is committed to encouragement and assistance to ethnic minority faculty, students and investigators, or an Indian tribe with a recognized governing body which performs substantial government functions or an Alaska Regional Corporation (ARC) as defined in the Alaska Native Claims Settlement Act and located in a state, the District of Columbia, Puerto Rico, the Virgin Islands, the Canal Zone, Guam, American Samoa or the Trust Territory of the Pacific Islands.

GEOG. RESTRICTIONS: United States and its territories.

FINANCIAL DATA:
Amount of support per award: $75,000 to $250,000 direct costs.

CO-OP FUNDING PROGRAMS: Co-funding with other NIH Institutes.

APPLICATION INFO:
Detailed information is available from the Branch Chief.

Duration: Typically three to four years.

ADDRESS INQUIRIES TO:
Dr. Irina N. Krasnova, Program Director
(See address above.)

NATIONAL INSTITUTE OF GENERAL MEDICAL SCIENCES [2088]

Natcher Building, MSC 6200
45 Center Drive, 2AS-13C
Bethesda, MD 20892-6200
(301) 594-0943
Fax: (301) 480-2004
E-mail: stefan.maas@nih.gov
Web Site: www.nigms.nih.gov

AREAS OF INTEREST:
Basic biomedical research.

NAME(S) OF PROGRAMS:
● **Medical Scientist Training Program**

TYPE:
Grants-in-aid; Training grants. The goal of this program is to prepare its graduates to function independently in both clinical practice and scientific research. MSTP has 50 participating programs.

YEAR PROGRAM STARTED: 1964

PURPOSE:
To support research training leading to the combined M.D.-Ph.D. degree.

ELIGIBILITY:
Applicants must be U.S. domestic institutions.

GEOG. RESTRICTIONS: United States.

FINANCIAL DATA:
Many institutions supplement the basic stipend provided by the MSTP grant. Trainees incur no payback obligation.
Amount of support per award: $24,816 stipend, plus tuition allowance of up to $21,000, travel allowance of $300, and $4,200 for equipment, supplies and health care for the year 2019.
Total amount of support: Varies.

NO. AWARDS: Approximately 970.

APPLICATION INFO:
Individuals who wish to enter the program should contact the program office at the participating institution(s) of their choice directly for curriculum information and admission requirements. Interested institutions should contact the NIGMS program director. Institutions should include the standard Form 424.

Applications guidelines are available online.
Duration: Up to five years, although the course of study for the combined degree may take longer. Continued support conditional upon annual review and availability of funds to the institution.
Deadline: January 25, May 25 and September 25. Grant awarded only once per year.

NATIONAL INSTITUTES OF HEALTH [2089]

6705 Rockledge 1
Bethesda, MD 20817
(301) 945-7573
TTY: (301) 451-5936
E-mail: grantsinfo@nih.gov
oer@od.nih.gov
Web Site: grants.nih.gov/grants/oer.htm

FOUNDED: 1930

AREAS OF INTEREST:
Biomedical research and improvement of human health.

NAME(S) OF PROGRAMS:
● **Ruth L. Kirschstein National Research Service Awards (NRSA) for Individual Postdoctoral Fellows (Parent F32)**

TYPE:
Fellowships; Research grants; Training grants. This individual postdoctoral research training fellowship is to enhance training of promising postdoctoral candidates who have the potential to become productive, independent investigators in scientific health-related research fields relevant to the missions of the participating NIH Institutes and Centers.

PURPOSE:
To help ensure that a diverse pool of highly trained scientists is available in appropriate scientific disciplines to address the nation's biomedical, behavioral and clinical research needs.

ELIGIBILITY:
Eligible organizations: Higher education institutions, nonprofits other than institutions of higher education, for-profit organizations, governments and other (non-U.S.) entities.

Eligible Individuals: Applicant - Project Director/Principal Investigator (PD/PI) - must be a citizen or a permanent resident of the U.S. and must have received a research doctoral degree from an accredited domestic or foreign institution.

Before the award can be activated, the candidate must have received a Ph.D., M.D., D.O., D.C., D.D.S., D.V.M., O.D., D.P.M., Sc.D., Eng.D., Dr.P.H., DNSc., N.D., Pharm.D., D.S.W., Psy.D., or equivalent doctoral degree from an accredited domestic or foreign institution.

GEOG. RESTRICTIONS: United States and its territories.

FINANCIAL DATA:
Award budgets are composed of stipends, tuition and fees, and institutional allowance. NIH does not separately reimburse indirect costs (also known as Facilities and Administrative - or F and A - Costs) for fellowships. Costs for administering fellowships are part of institutional allowance.

NO. AWARDS: Varies.

APPLICATION INFO:
Guidelines and detailed information are available on the NIH web site. Applicants are encouraged to apply early to allow adequate time to make any corrections to errors found in the application during the submission process by the due date. Paper applications will not be accepted.

Applicants are strongly urged to check the NIH web site for the most up-to-date information.
Duration: Varies; up to three years for individuals.

*SPECIAL STIPULATIONS:
Conformance to all requirements (both in the Application Guide and the Funding Opportunity Announcement (FOA)) is required and strictly enforced.

At the time of award, individuals are required to pursue their research training on a full-time basis, normally defined as 40 hours per week or as specified by the sponsoring institution in accordance with its own policies.

NATIONAL INSTITUTES OF HEALTH [2090]

6705 Rockledge 1
Bethesda, MD 20817
(301) 945-7573
TTY: (301) 451-5936
E-mail: grantsinfo@nih.gov
oer@od.nih.gov
Web Site: grants.nih.gov/grants/oer.htm

FOUNDED: 1887

AREAS OF INTEREST:
Biomedical and behavioral research and improvement of human health.

NAME(S) OF PROGRAMS:
● **Mentored Clinical Scientist Research Career Development Award (Parent K08)**

TYPE:
Research grants. This program prepares qualified individuals for careers that have a significant impact on the health-related research needs of the nation.

PURPOSE:
To help ensure that a diverse pool of highly trained scientists are available in appropriate scientific disciplines to address the nation's biomedical, behavioral and clinical research needs.

LEGAL BASIS:
Public Health Service Act, Section 301(c).

ELIGIBILITY:
Eligible organizations include higher education institutions, nonprofits other than institutions of higher education, for-profit organizations, different domestic levels of government, Native American tribal organizations and faith-based or community-based organizations.

Eligible individuals (program director/principal investigator) must be a citizen or a noncitizen national of the U.S. or have been lawfully admitted for permanent residence. They must have a clinical doctoral degree (e.g., M.D., D.D.S., D.M.D., D.O., D.C., O.D., N.D., D.V.M., Pharm.D., or, in certain clinical disciplines, Ph.D.). The K08 award may be used by candidates with different levels of prior research training and at different stages in their mentored career development.

GEOG. RESTRICTIONS: United States.

NO. AWARDS: Varies.

APPLICATION INFO:
Applications must be submitted electronically. Paper applications will not be accepted.

Applicants are strongly urged to check the NIH web site for the most up-to-date information.
Duration: Up to five years.

NATIONAL INSTITUTES OF HEALTH [2091]

6705 Rockledge 1
Bethesda, MD 20817
(301) 945-7573
TTY: (301) 451-5936
E-mail: grantsinfo@nih.gov
oer@od.nih.gov
Web Site: grants.nih.gov/grants/oer.htm

FOUNDED: 1930

AREAS OF INTEREST:
Biomedical research and improvement of human health.

NAME(S) OF PROGRAMS:
- **Ruth L. Kirschstein National Research Service Awards (NRSA) for Individual Senior Fellows (Parent F33)**

TYPE:
Fellowships. This program awards senior individual research training fellowships to experienced scientists who wish to make major changes in the direction of their research careers or who wish to broaden their scientific background by acquiring new research capabilities as independent investigators in research fields relevant to the missions of the participating NIH Institutes and Centers.

PURPOSE:
To help ensure that a diverse pool of highly trained scientists is available in appropriate scientific disciplines to address the nation's biomedical, behavioral and clinical research needs.

LEGAL BASIS:
An agency of the U.S. Public Health Service.

ELIGIBILITY:
Eligible organizations include higher education institutions, nonprofits other than institutions of higher education, for-profit organizations, governments and other (non-U.S.) entities.

The Project Director/Principal Investigator must have had at least seven subsequent years of relevant research or professional experience and will have established an independent research career. By the time of the award, that individual must be a citizen or permanent resident of the U.S.

GEOG. RESTRICTIONS: United States.

FINANCIAL DATA:
Award budgets are composed of stipends, tuition and fees, and institutional allowance. NIH does not separately reimburse indirect costs (also known as Facilities and Administrative - or F and A - Costs) for fellowships. Costs for administering fellowships are part of institutional allowance.

NO. AWARDS: Varies.

APPLICATION INFO:
Guidelines and detailed information are available on the NIH web site. Applicants are encouraged to apply early to allow adequate time to make any corrections to errors found in the application during the submission process by the due date. Paper applications will not be accepted.

Applicants are strongly urged to check the NIH web site for the most up-to-date information.

Duration: Typically, up to two years.

*SPECIAL STIPULATIONS:
Conformance to all requirements (both in the Application Guide and the Funding Opportunity Announcement (FOA)) is required and strictly enforced.

At the time of award, individuals are required to pursue their research training on a full-time basis, normally defined as 40 hours per week or as specified by the sponsoring institution in accordance with its own policies.

NATIONAL INSTITUTES OF HEALTH [2092]
Office of Research Infrastructure Programs
One Democracy Plaza, Room 966
6701 Democracy Boulevard, MSC 4877
Bethesda, MD 20892-4877
(301) 435-0772
Fax: (301) 480-3819
E-mail: sig@mail.nih.gov
Web Site: orip.nih.gov/construction-and-instruments

FOUNDED: 1930

AREAS OF INTEREST:
Biomedical research and improvement of human health.

NAME(S) OF PROGRAMS:
- **Shared Instrumentation Grant Program**

TYPE:
Project/program grants.

YEAR PROGRAM STARTED: 1982

PURPOSE:
To provide research institutions the opportunity to obtain expensive (over $50,000 per item) commercially available instruments to be shared by groups of NIH-funded investigators.

LEGAL BASIS:
An agency of the U.S. Public Health Service.

ELIGIBILITY:
Federal agencies, foreign institutions and for-profit institutions are not eligible.

GEOG. RESTRICTIONS: United States.

FINANCIAL DATA:
Amount of support per award: Maximum award is $600,000.

Total amount of support: $35,000,000 for fiscal year 2020.

NO. AWARDS: Approximately 75.

APPLICATION INFO:
Contact the National Institutes of Health.

Duration: One year. No renewals.

Deadline: May 31.

ADDRESS INQUIRIES TO:
Shared Instrumentation Grant Program
(See address above.)

NATIONAL INSTITUTES OF HEALTH [2093]
6705 Rockledge 1
Bethesda, MD 20817
(301) 945-7573
E-mail: grantsinfo@nih.gov
oer@od.nih.gov
Web Site: grants.nih.gov/grants/oer.htm

NAME(S) OF PROGRAMS:
- **Research Project Grant Program (R01)**

TYPE:
Project/program grants; Research grants. Research Project Grant (R01) is an award made to support a discrete, specified, circumscribed project to be performed by the named investigator(s) in an area representing the investigator's specific interest and competencies, based on the mission of the NIH. The Research Project Grant (R01) is the original and historically oldest grant mechanism used by NIH. The R01 provides support for health-related research and development based on the mission of the NIH.

PURPOSE:
To provide support for health-related research and development.

LEGAL BASIS:
Government agency.

FINANCIAL DATA:
The following are allowable costs:
(1) salary and fringe benefits for Principal Investigator, key personnel and other essential personnel;
(2) equipment and supplies;
(3) consultant costs;
(4) alterations and renovations;
(5) publications and miscellaneous costs;
(6) contract services;
(7) consortium costs;
(8) facilities and administrative costs (indirect costs) and;
(9) travel expenses.

Amount of support per award: Varies.

NO. AWARDS: Contingent upon appropriations and submission of a sufficient number of meritorious applications.

APPLICATION INFO:
Applicants may find it helpful to seek advice from an experienced investigator and to contact the Institute or Center most likely to fund their application.

Applicants are strongly urged to check the NIH web site for the most up-to-date information.

Duration: Generally three to five years.

Deadline: Varies.

NATIONAL INSTITUTES OF HEALTH [2094]
6705 Rockledge 1
Bethesda, MD 20817
(301) 945-7573
E-mail: grantsinfo@nih.gov
oer@od.nih.gov
Web Site: grants.nih.gov/grants/oer.htm

NAME(S) OF PROGRAMS:
- **Small Research Grant Program (Parent R03)**

TYPE:
Research grants. This program supports different types of projects including pilot and feasibility studies; secondary analysis of existing data; small, self-contained research projects; development of research methodology; and development of new research technology.

PURPOSE:
To support small research projects that can be carried out in a short period of time with limited resources.

ELIGIBILITY:
The Small Research Grant Program supports discrete, well-defined projects that realistically can be completed in two years and that require limited levels of funding.

Higher education institutions, other nonprofits, for-profit organizations, governments, other institutions, and foreign institutions are eligible to apply.

Any individual(s) with the skills, knowledge and resources necessary to carry out the proposed research as the Program Director(s)/Principal Investigator(s) (PD(s)/PI(s)) is invited to work with his or her organization to develop an application for support. Individuals from underrepresented racial and ethnic groups as well as individuals with disabilities are always encouraged to apply for NIH support.

FINANCIAL DATA:
This grant support mechanism provides money, property or both to an eligible entity to carry out an approved project or activity.

Amount of support per award: Up to $50,000 in direct costs per year.

NO. AWARDS: Varies depending on NIH appropriations and the submission of a sufficient number of meritorious applications.

APPLICATION INFO:
Duration: Up to two years.

ADDRESS INQUIRIES TO:
See e-mail addresses above.

NATIONAL INSTITUTES OF HEALTH [2095]

Office of Research Infrastructure Programs
One Democracy Plaza, Suite 902
6701 Democracy Boulevard, MSC 4877
Bethesda, MD 20892-4877
(301) 435-0772
Fax: (301) 480-3819
E-mail: hei@mail.nih.gov
Web Site: dpcpsi.nih.
gov/orip/diic/shared_instrumentation

FOUNDED: 1930

AREAS OF INTEREST:
Biomedical research and improvement of human health.

NAME(S) OF PROGRAMS:
● **High-End Instrumentation (HEI) Grant Program**

TYPE:
Project/program grants.

YEAR PROGRAM STARTED: 1982

PURPOSE:
To provide research institutions the opportunity to obtain expensive (over $600,001 per item) commercially available instruments to be shared by groups of NIH-funded investigators.

LEGAL BASIS:
An agency of the U.S. Public Health Service.

ELIGIBILITY:
High-End Instrumentation Grant Program encourages applications from groups of NIH-supported investigators to purchase or upgrade a single item of expensive, specialized, commercially available instruments or integrated systems. Types of instruments supported include, but are not limited to, X-ray diffraction systems, nuclear magnetic resonance (NMR) and mass spectrometers, DNA and protein sequencers, biosensors, electron and confocal microscopes, cell-sorters, and biomedical imagers.

GEOG. RESTRICTIONS: United States.

FINANCIAL DATA:
Amount of support per award: $600,001 to $2,000,000.

Total amount of support: Approximately $30,000,000 for fiscal year 2020.

NO. AWARDS: Varies.

APPLICATION INFO:
Contact the National Institutes of Health.
Duration: One year. No renewals.
Deadline: June 1.

ADDRESS INQUIRIES TO:
Shared Instrumentation Grant Program
(See address above.)

NATIONAL MEDICAL FELLOWSHIPS, INC. [2096]

12 East 46th Street
Suite 5E
New York, NY 10017
(212) 483-8880
Fax: (212) 483-8897
E-mail: scholarships@nmfonline.org
Web Site: www.nmfonline.org

FOUNDED: 1946

AREAS OF INTEREST:
Underrepresented minority students in medicine and the health professions and the health care of low-income and minority communities.

NAME(S) OF PROGRAMS:
● **Aetna/NMF Rural Health Scholars Program at Morehouse**
● **Alliant Health Solutions/NMF Alzheimer's or Related Dementia Care Scholarship**
● **Anarcha, Betsy, and Lucy Memorial Scholarship Award**
● **Hugh J. Andersen Memorial Scholarship Program**
● **Association of American Medical Colleges (AAMC)/Darrell G. Kirch, M.D. Scholarship**
● **Wayne Anthony Butts Scholarship**
● **William and Charlotte Cadbury Award**
● **Dr. Thelma Jan Caison-Sorey Scholarship**
● **Mary Ball Carrera Scholarship**
● **Dr. Randolph Chase Memorial Scholarship**
● **Colgate-Palmolive/NMF Dental Leadership Program**
● **Drs. Ludlow & Ruth Creary Family Foundation Scholarship**
● **Dr. James Curtis Scholarship**
● **CVS Health/NMF Pharm.D. Scholarship**
● **Emergency Scholarship Fund Program**
● **Empire State Medical Association Scholarship Award**
● **Fitzbutler Jones Scholarship**
● **Dr. Herman Gray/Skillman Scholarship**
● **Genita Evangelista Johnson Endowed Scholarship**
● **Dr. Marc Keshisian Scholarship**
● **Don Levin Trust Scholarship**
● **Josiah Macy Jr. Foundation Scholarship**
● **Manhattan Central Medical Society Scholarship**
● **Dr. David Kearney McDonogh Scholarship in Ophthalmology/ENT**
● **Franklin C. McLean Award**
● **Michigan Scholarship Fund**
● **Dr. Theodore Quincy Miller Scholarship**
● **New York Community Trust/NMF Medical Research Scholarships**
● **NMA Diversity Innovation Fellows**
● **NMA Emerging Scholars Awards**
● **NMA Emerging Scholars Infectious Diseases Research Awards**
● **NMF National Alumni Council Scholarship Program**
● **NMF Primary Care Leadership Program**
● **Dr. Fred Parrott Scholarship**
● **Dr. Muriel Petioni Scholarship: Collegiate Student Award**

● **Dr. Muriel Petioni Scholarship: Medical Student Award**
● **Dr. Pinnock/Byrd Foundation Scholarship**
● **Victor Grifols Roura Scholarship**
● **Dr. James McCune Smith Medical Student Award**
● **United Health Foundation/NMF Diverse Medical Scholars Program**
● **Dr. Felecia Williams Scholarship**
● **Zimmer Biomet/NMF Orthopaedic Scholarship**

TYPE:
Awards/prizes; Project/program grants; Scholarships. Service learning. NMF supports underrepresented minority medical students and health professions students enrolled in U.S. accredited programs as they matriculate. Awards are available to students M1 to M4/5. In addition to financial support, NMF provides opportunities for aspiring doctors to take their learning into the community.

YEAR PROGRAM STARTED: 1946

PURPOSE:
To improve the health of low-income and minority communities by increasing the number of minority physicians and addressing the special needs of these communities.

LEGAL BASIS:
Nonprofit corporation.

ELIGIBILITY:
Varies by program. Scholarship applicants must be U.S. citizens or have Deferred Action for Childhood Arrivals (DACA) approval.

FINANCIAL DATA:
Amount of support per award: Varies.

Total amount of support: Varies.

NO. MOST RECENT APPLICANTS: Varies.

NO. AWARDS: Varies.

APPLICATION INFO:
Guidelines and official application materials are available on the organization web site.

Duration: Varies by program.

Deadline: Varies by program.

BOARD OF DIRECTORS AND OFFICERS:
Sandra B. Nichols, M.D., Chairman
Ester R. Dyer, M.L.S., D.L.S., President and Chief Executive Officer
Stephen N. Keith, M.D., M.S.P.H., Treasurer and Secretary
Rahn K. Bailey, M.D.
Neal Ball
Bryan P. Baugh, M.D.
Lloyd C. Bishop
Cedric M. Bright, M.D., FACP
Castulo de la Rocha, J.D.
H. Jack Geiger, M.D.
Larry J. Harrison, M.P.H., MBA
Emil Hill
Darrell G. Kirch, M.D.
Pamela T. Miller, Esq.
Denise Powell, M.D.
Carmen Sachiko Villar
Calvin Wheeler, M.D.

ADDRESS INQUIRIES TO:
Franca Gaudio, Chief Operating Officer
Ali Gemma, Program Manager
(See address above.)

THE NATIONAL ORGANIZATION FOR RARE DISORDERS (NORD)   [2097]

55 Kenosia Avenue
Danbury, CT 06810
(203) 744-0100
Fax: (203) 263-9938
E-mail: research@rarediseases.org
Web Site: www.rarediseases.org

FOUNDED: 1983

AREAS OF INTEREST:
Rare "orphan" disease.

NAME(S) OF PROGRAMS:
- **Rare Disease Research Grant Program**

TYPE:
Research grants; Seed money grants. The
Rare Disease Research Grant Program
provides seed money grants to academic
scientists and clinicians for translational or
clinical studies related to development of
potential new diagnostics or treatments for
rare disease.

YEAR PROGRAM STARTED: 1989

PURPOSE:
To provide small seed grants to scientists and
clinicians performing basic translational
sciences, studying new treatments, or
developing diagnostic tests for rare diseases.

ELIGIBILITY:
For each grant, the principal investigator
must have sufficient education and experience
to demonstrate subject matter expertise.
Strong preference is given to researchers
holding a faculty-level appointment or senior
scientific position at an academic or nonprofit
institution or foundation. Grants are available
to researchers both within the U.S. and
internationally.

FINANCIAL DATA:
Overhead and indirect costs are not awarded.
Amount of support per award: Minimum
$30,000.
Total amount of support: Varies.

NO. MOST RECENT APPLICANTS: Approximately
40.

NO. AWARDS: Varies.

APPLICATION INFO:
Submit a letter of intent, curriculum vitae,
one-page abstract, and a brief budget. Full
proposals by invitation only. Requests for
proposals announcements typically posted
online.
Duration: One to two years.
Deadline: Varies.

ADDRESS INQUIRIES TO:
Research Program Administrator
(See address above.)

*SPECIAL STIPULATIONS:
Reports and communication must be written
in English and adhere to the most recent
guidelines set forth by the National Institutes
of Health.

NATIONAL SOCIETY DAUGHTERS OF THE AMERICAN REVOLUTION [2098]

1776 D Street, N.W.
Washington, DC 20006-5303
(202) 879-3263
E-mail: nsdarscholarships@nsdar.org
Web Site: www.dar.org

FOUNDED: 1895

AREAS OF INTEREST:
Medicine and psychiatric nursing.

NAME(S) OF PROGRAMS:
- **Irene and Daisy MacGregor Memorial Scholarship**

TYPE:
Scholarships.

YEAR PROGRAM STARTED: 1991

PURPOSE:
To provide ways and means to aid students
in attaining higher education.

LEGAL BASIS:
Incorporated historical society.

ELIGIBILITY:
Scholarships are awarded without regard to
race, religion, sex or national origin. All
four-year scholarships must be for
consecutive years and are renewable only
upon review and approval of annual
transcript. Candidates must be U.S. citizens
and must attend or plan to attend an
accredited college or university in the U.S.
No affiliation or relationship to DAR is
required for qualification. Awards are judged
on the basis of academic excellence,
commitment to field of study, as required,
and financial need.

The MacGregor Memorial Scholarship is
awarded to students of high scholastic
standing and character who have been
accepted into or are pursuing an approved
course of study to become a medical doctor
(not pre-med) at an approved, accredited
medical school.

This MacGregor Memorial Scholarship is
also available to students who have been
accepted into or who are pursuing an
approved course of study in the field of
psychiatric nursing, graduate level, at medical
schools, colleges or universities. There is a
preference to females "if equally qualified."

GEOG. RESTRICTIONS: United States.

FINANCIAL DATA:
Amount of support per award: $5,000
annually.

NO. AWARDS: 2.

APPLICATION INFO:
Applicants must use the DAR Scholarship
Committee's online submission process found
on the DAR public web site. Once applicants
have set up their scholarship profile, they will
be able to complete the application. If
necessary, applicants will be able to provide
access to individuals wishing to submit
confidential letters of recommendations or
school transcripts.
Duration: Up to four consecutive years
possible, depending upon availability of
funds. Annual transcript review required for
renewal and award.
Deadline: February 15.

PUBLICATIONS:
American Spirit, magazine.

ADDRESS INQUIRIES TO:
National Vice Chairman
E-mail: macgregorscholarship@nsdar.org

NORTH AMERICAN SPINE SOCIETY (NASS)   [2099]

8320 St. Moritz Drive
Spring Grove, IL 60081
(630) 230-3691
Fax: (630) 230-3791
E-mail: kjames@spine.org
Web Site: www.spine.org

FOUNDED: 1985

AREAS OF INTEREST:
Disorders and functions of the human spine.

NAME(S) OF PROGRAMS:
- **Clinical Traveling Fellowship**
- **Research Grant**
- **Research Traveling Fellowship**
- **Young Investigator Grants**

TYPE:
Awards/prizes; Fellowships; Research grants.
Clinical Traveling Fellowship: At least one
month to be spent in three to five different
medical centers studying spine techniques.

Research Traveling Fellowship: At least five
months at one medical center, other than the
one in which the applicants currently
practice. This Fellowship primarily covers the
cost of travel and housing.

Research Grant: This grant is for
investigative, basic, clinical and translational
research on the spine.

Young Investigator Grant: This grant is for
projects in basic science, clinical or
translational.

YEAR PROGRAM STARTED: 1989

PURPOSE:
To advance quality spine care through
education, research and advocacy; to
encourage and support basic and clinical
science that is performed with integrity and
with a goal towards improving quality spine
care for patients and understanding
underlying disorders.

ELIGIBILITY:
Qualified investigators are eligible to apply.

FINANCIAL DATA:
Amount of support per award: $50,000.
Total amount of support: Varies.

NO. MOST RECENT APPLICANTS: 166.

APPLICATION INFO:
Contact the Organization for application
procedures. Budget restrictions are available
when requesting an application.
Duration: Two years.
Deadline: Letters of Proposals for Grants:
Second week in February. Invited Grants and
Fellowships: Second week in May.

ADDRESS INQUIRIES TO:
Karen James, Manager of Research and
Quality Improvement
(See address above.)

ORTHOPAEDIC RESEARCH AND EDUCATION FOUNDATION   [2100]

9400 West Higgins Road
Suite 215
Rosemont, IL 60018-4975
(847) 698-9980
Fax: (847) 698-7806
E-mail: grants@oref.org
Web Site: www.oref.org

FOUNDED: 1955

AREAS OF INTEREST:
Orthopaedic research.

NAME(S) OF PROGRAMS:
- **Career Development Grant Award**

TYPE:
Research grants. Grants for scientific research in orthopaedic surgery.

YEAR PROGRAM STARTED: 1984

PURPOSE:
To encourage a commitment to scientific research in orthopaedic surgery.

LEGAL BASIS:
501(c)(3) special-interest foundation.

ELIGIBILITY:
Candidates must have completed residency in orthopaedic surgery and have demonstrated a sustained interest in research, as well as excellence in clinical training. Letters of nomination and support must offer convincing evidence of the candidate's potential to develop as an investigator.

GEOG. RESTRICTIONS: United States.

FINANCIAL DATA:
Amount of support per award: $225,000.
Total amount of support: $225.000.

NO. AWARDS: 1.

APPLICATION INFO:
Contact the Foundation.
Duration: Up to three years, conditional upon annual review.
Deadline: Letter of Intent: October 4.

PUBLICATIONS:
Annual report; application guidelines.

ADDRESS INQUIRIES TO:
See e-mail address above.

*SPECIAL STIPULATIONS:
Applicant must be working in the U.S. only.

ORTHOPAEDIC RESEARCH AND EDUCATION FOUNDATION   [2101]
9400 West Higgins Road
Suite 215
Rosemont, IL 60018-4975
(847) 698-9980
Fax: (847) 698-7806
E-mail: grants@oref.org
Web Site: www.oref.org

FOUNDED: 1955

AREAS OF INTEREST:
Orthopaedic surgery research.

NAME(S) OF PROGRAMS:
● **Resident Clinician Scientist Training Grant**

TYPE:
Research grants. Grants to prepare residents for a career with research as a major component.

YEAR PROGRAM STARTED: 1961

PURPOSE:
To encourage the research interests and meritorious projects of residents and fellows in approved orthopaedic programs.

LEGAL BASIS:
501(c)(3) special-interest foundation.

ELIGIBILITY:
Candidates must be residents or fellows in approved orthopaedic programs.

GEOG. RESTRICTIONS: United States.

FINANCIAL DATA:
Grants provide funds for supplies and expenses, but not for resident salary or travel.
Amount of support per award: $20,000.

Total amount of support: Varies.

APPLICATION INFO:
Applications are available on the web site.
Duration: One year.

PUBLICATIONS:
Annual report; application guidelines.

ADDRESS INQUIRIES TO:
See e-mail address above.

*SPECIAL STIPULATIONS:
Resident must be working in the U.S.

ORTHOPAEDIC RESEARCH AND EDUCATION FOUNDATION   [2102]
9400 West Higgins Road
Suite 215
Rosemont, IL 60018-4975
(847) 430-5109
Fax: (847) 698-7806
E-mail: grants@oref.org
Web Site: www.oref.org

FOUNDED: 1955

AREAS OF INTEREST:
Musculoskeletal research.

NAME(S) OF PROGRAMS:
● **OREF Clinical Research Award**

TYPE:
Awards/prizes.

YEAR PROGRAM STARTED: 1996

PURPOSE:
To award outstanding research related to clinical musculoskeletal disease or injury.

LEGAL BASIS:
Special-interest foundation, 501(c)(3).

ELIGIBILITY:
Individual applicants must be members of the AAOS, ORS, Canadian Orthopaedic Association, Canadian ORS or sponsored by a member.

FINANCIAL DATA:
Amount of support per award: $20,000.
Total amount of support: $20,000.

NO. AWARDS: 1.

APPLICATION INFO:
Submission guidelines are available on the web site.
Duration: One-time award.
Deadline: July 1.

PUBLICATIONS:
Annual report; application guidelines.

ADDRESS INQUIRIES TO:
See e-mail address above.

OSTEOGENESIS IMPERFECTA FOUNDATION   [2103]
804 West Diamond Avenue
Suite 210
Gaithersburg, MD 20878
(301) 947-0083
(844) 889-7579
Fax: (301) 947-0456
E-mail: bonelink@oif.org
Web Site: www.oif.org

FOUNDED: 1970

AREAS OF INTEREST:
Osteogenesis imperfecta medical research.

NAME(S) OF PROGRAMS:
● **Michael Geisman Fellowships**

TYPE:
Fellowships.

YEAR PROGRAM STARTED: 1970

PURPOSE:
To expand understanding and identify improved treatments for osteogenesis imperfecta.

LEGAL BASIS:
Nonprofit organization.

ELIGIBILITY:
Applicants for the fellowship must be postdoctoral fellows in academic institutions and the work must be done under the supervision of a mentor with appropriate training and experience in osteogenesis imperfect (OI) or related field.

FINANCIAL DATA:
Amount of support per award: Up to $50,000 per year ($35,000 toward the investigator's salary and up to $15,000 per year for supplies).

APPLICATION INFO:
Applicants should submit an original application with 10 copies. The application should include an abstract for a lay audience, budget, education, previous research experience, professional training, publications and a research plan. Electronic submissions are accepted.
Duration: One year with possible renewal.
Deadline: December 1.

PUBLICATIONS:
Annual report; application guidelines; bimonthly newsletter.

IRS I.D.: 23-7076021

ADDRESS INQUIRIES TO:
OIF Research Department
(See address above.)

OXALOSIS AND HYPEROXALURIA FOUNDATION   [2104]
579 Albany Post Road
New Paltz, NY 12561
(212) 777-0470
(800) 643-8699
Fax: (212) 777-0471
E-mail: info@ohf.org
kimh@ohf.org
Web Site: www.ohf.org

FOUNDED: 1989

AREAS OF INTEREST:
Hyperoxaluria and oxalosis.

NAME(S) OF PROGRAMS:
● **OHF Research Grant**

TYPE:
Research grants. The Research Grant program assists investigators, new or established, who have research projects for which they need support.

PURPOSE:
To support research that will ultimately lead to new diagnostics, treatments and a cure for primary hyperoxaluria and related hyperoxaluria conditions.

ELIGIBILITY:
Applicants must hold an M.D., Ph.D. or equivalent degree by the start of the funding period and have an appointment at an academic institution. Compliance with local and federal statutes and regulations of the country of origin must be met.

FINANCIAL DATA:
Funds may be used for salaries for the investigators, technical assistance, special equipment, animals, supplies and travel.
Amount of support per award: Up to $200,000.
Total amount of support: Varies.

APPLICATION INFO:
All completed applications must be submitted electronically to grantapp@ohf.org in Word or PDF format. Late applications will not be accepted. Applications must be typed, single-spaced, 11-point Times New Roman with at least one-inch margins. A short paragraph should be included in the General Objectives and Rationale section describing the relevance of the proposed research to the goals of the OHF.
Duration: Up to two years.
Deadline: December 15.

ADDRESS INQUIRIES TO:
Kim Hollander, Executive Director
(See address above.)

OXNARD FOUNDATION   [2105]
5 Royal St. George Road
Newport Beach, CA 92660
(949) 644-4160
Fax: (949) 644-4171
E-mail: covlineage@gmail.com

AREAS OF INTEREST:
General medical research.

TYPE:
Matching gifts; Research grants.

PURPOSE:
To help continue medical research in the areas of concern for the Foundation.

ELIGIBILITY:
IRS 501(c)(3) tax-exempt organizations, schools and hospitals.

GEOG. RESTRICTIONS: California, Florida, New Mexico and Tennessee.

FINANCIAL DATA:
Amount of support per award: $35,000 to $50,000.
Total amount of support: Varies.

APPLICATION INFO:
Applicants should first send a letter and include a copy of the IRS tax determination letter.
Duration: One to three years.
Deadline: Applications are reviewed at Board meetings in February, June and November.

IRS I.D.: 23-7323007

ADDRESS INQUIRIES TO:
Christopher Veitch, President
(See address above.)

PHARMACEUTICAL RESEARCH AND MANUFACTURERS OF AMERICA FOUNDATION, INC.   [2106]
950 F Street, N.W.
Suite 300
Washington, DC 20004
(202) 572-7756
E-mail: foundation@phrma.org
Web Site: www.phrmafoundation.org

FOUNDED: 1965

AREAS OF INTEREST:
Biology, biomedical engineering, biotechnology, clinical outcomes assessment, drug delivery, drug discovery, genetics, health outcomes, medical research, pharmaceutical biotechnology, pharmaceutics, pharmacology and toxicology.

NAME(S) OF PROGRAMS:
- **Postdoctoral Fellowship in Drug Delivery**
- **Postdoctoral Fellowship in Drug Discovery**
- **Postdoctoral Fellowship in Health Outcomes Research**
- **Postdoctoral Fellowship in Translational Medicine**

TYPE:
Fellowships. This program provides stipend to well-trained graduates from Pharm.D., M.D., and Ph.D. programs who seek to further develop and refine research skills through formal postdoctoral training.

PURPOSE:
To encourage graduates from Ph.D. programs in drug delivery, drug discovery and translational medicine to continue their research skills through formal postdoctoral training.

LEGAL BASIS:
501(c)(3) organization.

ELIGIBILITY:
Applicant must live in the U.S. and attend a university or research institution in the U.S.

Postdoctoral Fellowship in Drug Delivery and Drug Discovery applicants must have a firm commitment from a sponsor/mentor at an accredited U.S. university. The award supports candidates proposing to gain new skills in drug delivery or drug discovery research. Ideal applicants will be within their first two years of postdoctoral study. Applicants must hold a Ph.D. or appropriate terminal research doctoral in a field related to the proposed postdoctoral activities or expect to receive such a degree before activating the award.

Postdoctoral Fellowship in Health Outcomes Research applicants must be attending schools of medicine, pharmacy, public health, nursing or dentistry. Applicants must hold a Ph.D. degree or appropriate terminal research doctoral in a field of study logically or functionally related to the proposed postdoctoral activities or expect to receive the Ph.D. before activating the award.

Eligible candidates for the Postdoctoral Fellowship in Translational Medicine will have doctoral degrees, e.g., Ph.D., D.Sc., D.Eng., M.D., before award activation and seek to further develop and refine their skills and understanding of translational medicine through postdoctoral training.

GEOG. RESTRICTIONS: United States.

FINANCIAL DATA:
Stipend support only. Funds may not be used for travel, tuition, indirect costs or fringe benefits. The award is made to the university on behalf of the fellow and provides a stipend, payable quarterly. This award is intended solely as a stipend and may not be used otherwise. If necessary, the institution may supplement the award to a level that is consistent with other postdoctoral fellowships it offers. An individual may not simultaneously hold or interrupt any other fellowship providing stipend support while the PhRMA Foundation Fellowship is active.

These funds are nontransferable. Unspent funds will be returned to the PhRMA Foundation upon the fellowship's conclusion.
Amount of support per award: Drug Delivery and Drug Discovery: $50,000 stipend per year; Health Outcomes: $55,000 stipend per year; Translational Medicine: $60,000 stipend per year.
Total amount of support: Varies.

NO. MOST RECENT APPLICANTS: Varies.

NO. AWARDS: Varies.

APPLICATION INFO:
Applications should be submitted on the Foundation web site.
Duration: Two years. Funding beyond the first year is contingent upon a ten-month progress report approved by the PhRMA Foundation and a first year financial report.
Deadline: Drug Delivery and Drug Discovery: Letter of Intent due May 15. Selected submissions will be notified by July 1 to submit a full application. Health Outcomes and Translational Medicine: February 1. Announcement April 15.

PUBLICATIONS:
Brochure.

IRS I.D.: 52-6063009

ADDRESS INQUIRIES TO:
See e-mail address above.

*SPECIAL STIPULATIONS:
Funds are not to be used for fringe benefits, indirect costs to the institution, travel or tuition.

PHARMACEUTICAL RESEARCH AND MANUFACTURERS OF AMERICA FOUNDATION, INC.
950 F Street, N.W.
Suite 300
Washington, DC 20004
(202) 572-7756
E-mail: foundation@phrma.org
Web Site: www.phrmafoundation.org

TYPE:
Project/program grants; Research grants; Seed money grants. Starter grants to support research in the fields of biology, biomedical engineering, biopharmaceutics, clinical outcomes assessment, disease modeling, drug delivery, drug discovery, genetics, health outcomes, molecular epidemiology, pharmaceutics, pharmaceutical biotechnology, pharmaceutical engineering, pharmacology and toxicology. The grants offer financial support to individuals beginning independent research careers at the faculty level.

See entry 2333 for full listing.

PHARMACEUTICAL RESEARCH AND MANUFACTURERS OF AMERICA FOUNDATION, INC.   [2107]
950 F Street, N.W.
Suite 300
Washington, DC 20004
(202) 572-7756
E-mail: foundation@phrma.org
Web Site: www.phrmafoundation.org

FOUNDED: 1965

AREAS OF INTEREST:
Biology, biomedical engineering, biopharmaceutics, chemistry, drug delivery, drug discovery, health outcomes research,

medical research, pharmaceutical biotechnology, pharmaceutics, pharmacology and toxicology.

NAME(S) OF PROGRAMS:
- **Predoctoral Fellowship in Drug Delivery**
- **Predoctoral Fellowship in Drug Discovery**
- **Predoctoral Fellowship in Health Outcomes Research**

TYPE:
Fellowships. Stipend support for full-time students in the areas of drug delivery, drug discovery and health outcomes research during their thesis research.

PURPOSE:
To support promising students during their advanced stages of training and thesis research.

LEGAL BASIS:
501(c)(3) organization.

ELIGIBILITY:
Applicant must live in the U.S. and attend a university or research institution in the U.S.

In the areas of drug delivery and drug discovery, applicant must hold a B.S., M.S. or Pharm.D. degree from an accredited school in pharmacy or a related area. Applicants must expect to complete the requirements for a Ph.D. in two years or less from the time the fellowship begins.

In the area of health outcomes research, applicants must be attending schools of medicine, pharmacy, public health, nursing or dentistry. This program supports full-time, in-residence students who will have completed most of their pre-thesis requirements (at least two years of study) and be engaged in thesis research as Ph.D. candidates by the time the award is active.

GEOG. RESTRICTIONS: United States.

FINANCIAL DATA:
Award is made to the university on behalf of the fellow. Annual stipend payable quarterly, which includes $1,000 per year for incidentals directly associated with thesis research preparation.
Amount of support per award: Maximum $50,000 ($25,000 per year).
Total amount of support: Varies.

NO. MOST RECENT APPLICANTS: Varies.

NO. AWARDS: Varies.

APPLICATION INFO:
Applications should be submitted on the Foundation web site.
Duration: 12, 18 or 24 months. Funding beyond the first 12 months is contingent upon a ten-month progress report approved by the PhRMA Foundation and a first year financial report.
Deadline: Drug Delivery and Drug Discovery: Letter of Intent due May 15. Selected submissions will be notified by July 1 to submit a full application. Health Outcomes Research: February 1. Announcement April 15.

PUBLICATIONS:
Brochure.

IRS I.D.: 52-6063009

STAFF:
Eileen Cannon, President
Joanne Westphal, Director of Development

BOARD OF DIRECTORS:
Alfred Sandrock, M.D., Ph.D., Chairman

Andrew Plump, M.D., Ph.D., Treasurer
Mikael Dolsten, M.D., Ph.D.
Iris Loew-Friedrich, M.D.
Aran Maree, M.B., B.Ch.
Joseph P. Miletich, M.D., Ph.D.
Richard Moscicki, M.D.
John C. Reed, M.D., Ph.D.
Daniel Skovronsky, M.D., Ph.D.
Rupert Vessey, FRCP, D.Phil.

ADVISORY COMMITTEE:
Terry L. Bowlin, Ph.D.
Michael J. Hageman, Ph.D.
Michael N. Liebman, Ph.D.
Bryan R. Luce, Ph.D., MBA
Richard Moscicki, M.D.
Nancy C. Santanello, M.D., M.S.

ADDRESS INQUIRIES TO:
See e-mail address above.

*SPECIAL STIPULATIONS:
Funds are not to be used for fringe benefits, indirect costs to the institution, travel or tuition.

PHARMACEUTICAL RESEARCH AND MANUFACTURERS OF AMERICA FOUNDATION, INC.   [2108]
950 F Street, N.W.
Suite 300
Washington, DC 20004
(202) 572-7756
E-mail: foundation@phrma.org
Web Site: www.phrmafoundation.org

FOUNDED: 1965

AREAS OF INTEREST:
Clinical sciences, health care evaluation, health economics, outcomes research and value assessment.

NAME(S) OF PROGRAMS:
- **Value Assessment Challenge Awards**
- **Value Assessment Research Award**

TYPE:
Awards/prizes; Project/program grants. The PhRMA Foundation, through the Value Assessment Challenge Awards, seeks papers that describe solutions to a pressing question related to value assessment in health care. Each year the question is updated.

The PhRMA Foundation, through the Value Assessment Research Award, seeks transformative, multi-stakeholder driven solutions to address challenges in assessing the value of medicines and health care services to improve patient outcomes and reduce inefficiency.

PURPOSE:
To address challenges in assessing the value of medicines and health care services to improve patient outcomes and reduce inefficiency.

LEGAL BASIS:
501(c)(3) organization.

ELIGIBILITY:
Award opportunities are open to all individuals and organizations with training in health economics, outcomes research, clinical sciences or health care evaluation. Eligible applicants should have an advanced degree in a field of study logically or functionally related to the proposed activities, such as a Ph.D. or equivalent. Interdisciplinary collaboration is highly encouraged.

For the Value Assessment Research Award, at least one collaborator must also have a firm commitment from an accredited U.S. university or research organization.

FINANCIAL DATA:
Value Assessment Research Award: Level of funding will depend on the scope of proposed activities. A maximum of 20% of the award may be used for indirect institutional costs and/or fringe benefits. Funding may not be used for tuition assistance.
Amount of support per award: Value Assessment Challenge Awards: $50,000 for first place, $25,000 for second place, $5,000 for third and fourth place; Value Assessment Research Award: Up to $100,000.

NO. MOST RECENT APPLICANTS: Varies.

NO. AWARDS: Value Assessment Challenge Awards: 4 budgeted; Value Assessment Research Award: 3 budgeted.

APPLICATION INFO:
Applications should be submitted on the Foundation web site.
Duration: Value Assessment Challenge Awards: One-time award; Value Assessment Research Award: One year.
Deadline: Letter of Intent: July 15. Selected submissions will be notified by August 10 to submit a full application.

PUBLICATIONS:
Brochure.

IRS I.D.: 52-6063009

ADDRESS INQUIRIES TO:
See e-mail address above.

*PLEASE NOTE:
Value Assessment Research Award recipient must submit a final progress report and financial report upon the conclusion of the grant.

DR. AND MRS. ARTHUR WILLIAM PHILLIPS CHARITABLE TRUST   [2109]
P.O. Box 316
Oil City, PA 16301-0316
(814) 676-2736
Fax: (814) 676-2736
E-mail: bwinters_pct@comcast.net
Web Site: phillipscharitabletrust.communityforce.com

FOUNDED: 1979

AREAS OF INTEREST:
Primarily medical centers, research and education.

TYPE:
Project/program grants; Scholarships.

PURPOSE:
To support many varied projects.

ELIGIBILITY:
Organizations must be:
(1) IRS 501(c)(3) tax-exempt;
(2) located in northwestern Pennsylvania;
(3) able to raise the balance of necessary funding from other sources and;
(4) able to show evidence of financial responsibility that will insure the completion and success of the project.

GEOG. RESTRICTIONS: Northwestern Pennsylvania.

FINANCIAL DATA:
Amount of support per award: Varies.
Total amount of support: Approximately $652,000.

NO. MOST RECENT APPLICANTS: 37.

NO. AWARDS: 28.

APPLICATION INFO:
Applicants must follow directions and file electronically at phillipscharitabletrust.communityforce.com.

Duration: Typically one year.

Deadline: March 15 for spring meeting; July 31 for fall meeting.

IRS I.D.: 25-6201015

ADDRESS INQUIRIES TO:
Robert W. McFate, Trustee
(See address above.)

PLASTIC SURGERY FOUNDATION (PSF)   [2110]
ASPS/PSF
444 East Algonquin Road
Arlington Heights, IL 60005
(847) 228-9900
E-mail: research@plasticsurgery.org
Web Site: www.thepsf.org/research/grants-program

AREAS OF INTEREST:
Basic/translational research, clinical, or health services research.

NAME(S) OF PROGRAMS:
- **ASE/PSF Combined Research Grant**
- **Combined Pilot Research Grants**
- **Innovation in Wound Care Research and Academic Development Fellowship**
- **National Endowment for Plastic Surgery**
- **Pilot Research Grants**
- **PSF Directed Research Grant - Breast Implant Safety**
- **The PSF Translational and Innovation Research Grant**
- **The PSF/MTF Biologics Allograft Tissue Research Grant**
- **Research Fellowships**
- **Scott Spear Innovation in Breast Reconstruction Research Fellowship**

TYPE:
Awards/prizes. ASE/PSF Combined Research Grant: The PSF and the Association for Surgical Education (ASE) recognize the importance of fostering the development of surgeon scientists that yield improvements in patient care in surgery. The ASE/PSF Combined Research Grant is intended to fund a research project that will advance the scientific knowledge and aims to develop and validate new methods of surgical care.

Combined Pilot Research Grants: The PSF, along with the AHS, AAPPS, AAPS, ACAPS, ASMS, ASPN, ASRM and PSRC, recognizes the importance of promoting innovative research in hand surgery, academic plastic surgery related to research, peripheral nerve research, microsurgery and stimulating fundamental research in plastic surgery. Together, these subspecialty organizations are dedicated to fostering the development of surgeon scientists and are committed to increasing the amount of research dollars, in order to fund pilot research studies that set the stage for investigators to apply to larger funding agencies.

Innovation in Wound Care Research and Academic Development Fellowship: This grant is to promote and support the career development of junior surgeon-scientists who are focused on advancing wound healing patient care through research and are interested in building a competitive research lab.

National Endowment for Plastic Surgery: This grant is intended to support research projects which translate clinical or basic science research findings into clinically relevant advancements or tools with a high likelihood of impacting daily practice and patient care within the next few years.

Pilot Research Grants are intended to support residents and junior faculty in their efforts to address focused research questions, obtain preliminary data to support larger grant proposals in the future, and develop a line of research that can be carried forward into an academic career. This grant supports the preliminary or pilot phase of these research projects.

PSF Directed Research Grant: Studies designed to assess breast implant safety, including local and systemic complications and illnesses related to breast implants, will be considered. Proposals that examine implant surveillance techniques and imaging are also invited. Basic, translational and clinical research studies are all within scope.

The PSF Translational and Innovation Research Grant aims to accelerate the translation of scientific discoveries and technical developments into practical solutions that improve human health through innovative funding, and to encourage collaborative, transdisciplinary work to accelerate the translation of medical discoveries into improved health. These seed grants will be awarded in the areas of medical technology, therapeutics, diagnostics, population health sciences and community engagement.

The PSF/MTF Biologics Allograft Tissue Research Grant: The PSF and MTF Biologics offer research grants to investigators studying allograft tissue transplantation in plastic and reconstructive surgery. These grants are intended to provide support for research projects focused on biologic reconstruction with a strong clinical translation component that utilize dermal, adipose, placental or other allograft transplant technologies. Grants are offered to projects with a high likelihood of impact on scientific discipline and/or on patient care. Both clinical and basic science research projects will be considered.

Research Fellowships support investigators from the beginning of their careers, during residence and as they advance to becoming experienced and well-established plastic surgeons. The purpose is to encourage research and academic career development in plastic surgery. This grant is for salary support only for a resident or fellow to obtain training and experience in research, under the guidance of an experienced mentor.

The Scott Spear Innovation in Breast Reconstruction Research Fellowship aims to nurture and grow the training and expertise of young academicians considering a career in breast reconstruction and patient care. The fellowship provides salary support to residents and fellows to undertake a research project under the guidance of an experienced mentor. The research project must be focused on breast cancer or breast reconstruction.

ELIGIBILITY:
ASE/PSF Combined Research Grant: Applicants must be M.D., D.O. or Ph.D. and hold a full-time clinical or research position in a U.S. or Canadian institution where the research will be conducted. Applicants must be an active or candidate member of ASPS or obtain sponsorship from an active ASPS member at one's institution. Additional eligibility criteria may apply.

Combined Pilot Research and Pilot Research Grants: Applicants must be M.D., D.O. or Ph.D. and hold a full-time clinical or research position in a U.S. or Canadian institution where the research will be conducted. Applicants must be an active or candidate member of ASPS or obtain sponsorship from an active ASPS member at one's institution. Additional eligibility criteria may apply for the Combined Pilot Research Grant.

Innovation in Wound Care Research and Academic Development Fellowship: Eligible applicants must be plastic surgeons within the first five years of entering practice and interested in establishing an academic research career with a clinical focus in wound care. Competitive applications must describe a multiyear structured research plan that includes conduct of basic and/or clinical research with emphasis on biochemical and molecular biologic mechanisms of wound healing and/or clinical innovation.

National Endowment for Plastic Surgery: Applicants must be M.D., D.O. or Ph.D. and hold a full-time clinical or research position in a U.S. or Canadian institution where the research will be conducted. Applicants must be an active or candidate member of ASPS or obtain sponsorship from an active ASPS member at one's institution.

The PSF/MTF Allograft Tissue Research Grant: Applicants must be an M.D., D.O. or Ph.D. and hold a full-time clinical or research position in a U.S. or Canadian institution where the research will be conducted. Applicants must be an active or candidate member of ASPS or obtain sponsorship from an active ASPS member at one's institution.

Research Fellowship: Applicants must be an M.D. or D.O. and hold a full-time clinical or research position in a U.S. or Canadian institution where the research will be conducted. Applicants must be a resident or within five years of an initial faculty appointment and must be an active or candidate member of ASPS or obtain sponsorship from an active ASPS member at one's institution.

FINANCIAL DATA:
Amount of support per award: ASE/PSF Combined Research Grant: Up to $15,000; Combined Pilot Research Grants and Pilot Research Grants: Up to $10,000; Innovation in Wound Care Research and Academic Development Fellowship: Up to $150,000; National Endowment for Plastic Surgery Grant, PSF Directed Research Grant, The PSF Translational and Innovation Research Grant and Research Fellowship: Up to $50,000; PSF/MTF Biologics Allograft Tissue Research Grant: Up to $100,000; Scott Spear Innovation in Breast

Reconstruction Research Fellowship: Up to $72,500 for one-year projects ($50,000 salary support and $22,500 for research).

Total amount of support: The Foundation awarded $891,274 in grant funding in 2019.

NO. MOST RECENT APPLICANTS: 146 for the 2018 cycle.

NO. AWARDS: 33 research grants for the 2019 cycle.

APPLICATION INFO:
Application instructions can be found on the Foundation web site.

Duration: One to two years.

Deadline: Approximately December 1.

ADDRESS INQUIRIES TO:
Mary Ruth Arway
Research Grants Project Manager
E-mail: rarway@plasticsurgery.org

POST-POLIO HEALTH INTERNATIONAL   [2111]

50 Crestwood Executive Center
Suite 440
St. Louis, MO 63126
(314) 534-0475
Fax: (314) 534-5070
E-mail: director@post-polio.org
Web Site: www.post-polio.org

FOUNDED: 1995

AREAS OF INTEREST:
Neuromuscular respiratory diseases and post-poliomyelitis.

NAME(S) OF PROGRAMS:
● **The Research Fund**

TYPE:
Research grants; Seed money grants. The Research Fund supports the work of researchers investigating the late effects of poliomyelitis and/or neuromuscular respiratory disease through one of two grants:

The Thomas Wallace Rogers Memorial Respiratory Research Grant: To study the cause(s) and treatment of neuromuscular respiratory insufficiency and the effects of long-term home mechanical ventilation.

The Post-Poliomyelitis Research Grant: This grant is to study the cause(s), treatment and management of the problem of the late effects of polio.

YEAR PROGRAM STARTED: 2000

PURPOSE:
To help support researchers, scientists, and clinicians worldwide to investigate the cause, treatment, and management of post-poliomyelitis and neuromuscular respiratory disease; to seek scientific information leading to eventual amelioration of the consequences of poliomyelitis and/or neuromuscular respiratory diseases.

LEGAL BASIS:
Not-for-profit organization.

ELIGIBILITY:
Applicants must be affiliated with an institution or organization. Citizens of all countries may apply. Applications, however, must be in English. Proposals will not be accepted via fax. The research may be quantitative and/or qualitative and follow sound and appropriate research standards relevant to the subject matter. The research findings must relate to improving the quality

of life for people with disabilities. Preference will be given to innovative or original research.

FINANCIAL DATA:
Amount of support per award: $50,000 per year; maximum $100,000.

NO. MOST RECENT APPLICANTS: 11.

NO. AWARDS: 1.

APPLICATION INFO:
Contact the organization.

Duration: Up to two years.

IRS I.D.: 34-0961952

ADDRESS INQUIRIES TO:
Brian Tiburzi, Executive Director
(See address above.)

PULMONARY FIBROSIS FOUNDATION   [2112]

230 East Ohio Street
Suite 500
Chicago, IL 60611
(888) 733-6741
Fax: (866) 587-9158
E-mail: grants@pulmonaryfibrosis.org
Web Site: www.pulmonaryfibrosis.org

AREAS OF INTEREST:
Research of and treatment for pulmonary fibrosis.

NAME(S) OF PROGRAMS:
● **PFF Scholars Program**

TYPE:
Matching gifts; Research grants. Supports early career investigators in their emerging research in the field of pulmonary fibrosis.

YEAR PROGRAM STARTED: 2000

PURPOSE:
To support projects that offer a high likelihood of improving the understanding of pulmonary fibrosis in the areas of basic science, translational research, clinical medicine and research, social sciences, and quality of life.

ELIGIBILITY:
Junior investigators who are within five years of formal training are eligible to apply. Established investigators who are over five years beyond their formal training may also apply.

FINANCIAL DATA:
Amount of support per award: $50,000 over a two-year period.

Total amount of support: Varies.

NO. AWARDS: 6 for the year 2019.

APPLICATION INFO:
Letter of Intent must be submitted between October and the November deadline. Full proposals are by invitation only.

Duration: Two years, with six-month and annual deliverables.

Deadline: Letter of Intent: November. Full proposal: February or March. Notification in May or June.

IRS I.D.: 84-1558631

ADDRESS INQUIRIES TO:
Zoe Dirks Bubany, Vice President of Board and External Relations
(See address above.)

RADIOLOGICAL SOCIETY OF NORTH AMERICA RESEARCH AND EDUCATION FOUNDATION   [2113]

820 Jorie Boulevard, Suite 200
Oak Brook, IL 60523-2251
(630) 571-7816
E-mail: kosley@rsna.org
Web Site: www.rsna.org/re-foundation

FOUNDED: 1984

AREAS OF INTEREST:
Radiology.

NAME(S) OF PROGRAMS:
● **Research Seed Grant**

TYPE:
Seed money grants. Research Seed Grant support is available for any area of research related to the radiologic sciences.

PURPOSE:
To enable investigators to gain experience in defining objectives and testing hypotheses in preparation for major grant applications to corporations, foundations and governmental agencies.

ELIGIBILITY:
Applications are accepted from individuals throughout the world. Applicants must be RSNA members at the time of application. Contact the Foundation for full details.

FINANCIAL DATA:
Research Seed Grant is to support the preliminary or pilot phase of scientific projects, not to supplement major funding already secured. No salary support for the principal investigator will be provided.
Amount of support per award: Up to $40,000.

Total amount of support: Varies.

NO. MOST RECENT APPLICANTS: Foundation generally funds approximately 25% of the applications received.

NO. AWARDS: 6 for the year 2018.

APPLICATION INFO:
Applications are completed using the online Grant Application System.

Duration: One year.

Deadline: January 15.

ADDRESS INQUIRIES TO:
Keshia Osley
Assistant Director, Grant Administration
(See address above.)

RADIOLOGICAL SOCIETY OF NORTH AMERICA RESEARCH AND EDUCATION FOUNDATION   [2114]

820 Jorie Boulevard, Suite 200
Oak Brook, IL 60523-2251
(630) 571-7816
E-mail: kosley@rsna.org
Web Site: www.rsna.org/re-foundation

FOUNDED: 1984

AREAS OF INTEREST:
Radiology.

NAME(S) OF PROGRAMS:
● **Research Medical Student Grant**

TYPE:
Research grants. Research Medical Student Grant is for any area of research related to the radiologic sciences.

PURPOSE:
To make radiology research opportunities possible for medical students and to

encourage them, early in their medical careers, to consider academic radiology as an important option for their future.

ELIGIBILITY:
Applicants must be RSNA members at the time of application and be full-time medical students at an accredited North American medical school. The scientific advisor or one of the co-investigators must also be a dues-paying RSNA member. Contact the Foundation for full details.

FINANCIAL DATA:
Funds are intended to secure protected time for the recipient and may not be used for nonpersonnel research expenses.
Amount of support per award: $3,000 stipend.
Total amount of support: Approximately $75,000.
Matching fund requirements: $3,000 to be matched by the sponsoring department ($6,000 total) as a stipend for the medical student.

NO. AWARDS: 21 for the year 2018.

APPLICATION INFO:
Applications are completed using the online Grant Application System.
Duration: 10 weeks full-time (or equivalent).
Deadline: February 1.

ADDRESS INQUIRIES TO:
Keshia Osley
Assistant Director, Grant Administration
(See address above.)

RADIOLOGICAL SOCIETY OF NORTH AMERICA RESEARCH AND EDUCATION FOUNDATION   [2115]
820 Jorie Boulevard, Suite 200
Oak Brook, IL 60523-2251
(630) 571-7816
E-mail: kosley@rsna.org
Web Site: www.rsna.org/re-foundation

FOUNDED: 1984

AREAS OF INTEREST:
Radiology.

NAME(S) OF PROGRAMS:
● **Education Scholar Grant**

TYPE:
Training grants. Any area of education related to the radiologic sciences.

PURPOSE:
To fund individuals in radiology or related disciplines who are seeking an opportunity to develop their expertise in radiologic education; to develop teachers in radiology who can share their knowledge with the radiology community.

ELIGIBILITY:
Applications are accepted from individuals throughout the world. Applicants must be RSNA members (at any level) at the time of application. Contact the Foundation for full details.

FINANCIAL DATA:
Education Scholar Grant to be used for salary support and/or other project costs.
Amount of support per award: Up to $75,000.

NO. MOST RECENT APPLICANTS: Foundation generally funds approximately 25% of the applications received.

NO. AWARDS: 1 for the year 2019.

APPLICATION INFO:
Applications are completed using the online Grant Application System.
Duration: One year. In exceptional cases, grants for up to two years will be considered.
Deadline: January 15.

ADDRESS INQUIRIES TO:
Keshia Osley
Assistant Director, Grant Administration
(See address above.)

RADIOLOGICAL SOCIETY OF NORTH AMERICA RESEARCH AND EDUCATION FOUNDATION   [2116]
820 Jorie Boulevard, Suite 200
Oak Brook, IL 60523-2251
(630) 571-7816
E-mail: kosley@rsna.org
Web Site: www.rsna.org/re-foundation

FOUNDED: 1984

AREAS OF INTEREST:
Radiology.

NAME(S) OF PROGRAMS:
● **RSNA/AUR/APDR/SCARD Radiology Education Research Development Grant**

TYPE:
Research grants.

PURPOSE:
To encourage innovation and improvement in health sciences education by providing research opportunities to individuals in pursuit of advancing the science of radiology education; to help in building a critical mass of radiology education researchers and promote the careers of persons advancing the science of radiology education.

ELIGIBILITY:
Applications are accepted from individuals throughout the world. Grants are awarded to any person, at any level of career development, who have a primary appointment in a radiology department. Applicants must be members of one or more of the sponsoring organizations. Contact the Foundation for full details.

FINANCIAL DATA:
Grants can be used to help cover the costs of research materials, research assistant support and limited primary investigator salary support (no more than half of grant award).
Amount of support per award: Up to $10,000.
Total amount of support: Varies.

CO-OP FUNDING PROGRAMS: Co-sponsored by the Radiological Society of North America (RSNA), Association of University Radiologists (AUR), Association of Program Directors in Radiology (APDR), and Society of Chairmen of Academic Radiology Departments (SCARD).

NO. MOST RECENT APPLICANTS: Foundation generally funds approximately 25% of the applications received.

NO. AWARDS: 2 for the year 2018.

APPLICATION INFO:
Applications must be submitted online.
Duration: One year.
Deadline: January 10.

ADDRESS INQUIRIES TO:
Keshia Osley
Assistant Director, Grant Administration
(See address above.)

RADIOLOGICAL SOCIETY OF NORTH AMERICA RESEARCH AND EDUCATION FOUNDATION   [2117]
820 Jorie Boulevard, Suite 200
Oak Brook, IL 60523-2251
(630) 571-7816
E-mail: kosley@rsna.org
Web Site: www.rsna.org/re-foundation

FOUNDED: 1984

AREAS OF INTEREST:
Radiology.

NAME(S) OF PROGRAMS:
● **RSNA Research Scholar Grant**

TYPE:
Research grants.

PURPOSE:
To support junior faculty members who have completed the conventional resident/fellowship training programs but have not yet been recognized as independent investigators.

ELIGIBILITY:
Any area of research related to the radiologic sciences is eligible for Research Scholar Grant support. Applicants must be nominated by their department chair (one new application per department per year). Contact the Foundation for full details.

GEOG. RESTRICTIONS: North America.

FINANCIAL DATA:
Amount of support per award: $150,000 ($75,000 per year).
Total amount of support: Varies.

NO. MOST RECENT APPLICANTS: Foundation generally funds approximately 25% of the applications received.

NO. AWARDS: 5 for the year 2019.

APPLICATION INFO:
Applications must be submitted online.
Duration: Two years.
Deadline: January 15.

ADDRESS INQUIRIES TO:
Keshia Osley
Assistant Director, Grant Administration
(See address above.)

*SPECIAL STIPULATIONS:
Applicant must commit to devoting 40% of time to granted project.

RADIOLOGICAL SOCIETY OF NORTH AMERICA RESEARCH AND EDUCATION FOUNDATION   [2118]
820 Jorie Boulevard, Suite 200
Oak Brook, IL 60523-2251
(630) 571-7816
E-mail: kosley@rsna.org
Web Site: www.rsna.org/re-foundation

FOUNDED: 1984

AREAS OF INTEREST:
Radiology.

NAME(S) OF PROGRAMS:
● **Research Resident/Fellow Grant**

TYPE:
Research grants. Grants will be awarded for diverse types of projects in the radiologic sciences including basic science and clinical research studies. This program is not intended to fund Ph.D. postdoctoral projects, nor to support those whose primary aim is to obtain practical experience in clinical radiology.

PURPOSE:
To provide young investigators not yet professionally established in the radiologic sciences an opportunity to gain further insight into scientific investigation and to develop competence in research techniques and methods.

ELIGIBILITY:
At the time of application, the applicant must:
(1) be an RSNA member (at any level);
(2) be (if an applicant within North American educational institutions) a resident or fellow in a department of radiology, radiation oncology or nuclear medicine; applicants from outside North America must already be accepted into a one- or two-year Fellowship position at a North American education institution at the time of the grant application;
(3) have completed the internship year (PGY-1) and at least six months of specialty training in the radiologic sciences (PGY-2) for the resident grant, or be in the last year of, or have completed, the prescribed residency training for the fellow grant. (If awarded the latter, recipient must be in a fellowship position during the period of grant support);
(4) be certified by the American Board of Radiology, or on track for certification;
(5) not have been principal investigator on external/extramural grant/contract amounts totaling more than $60,000 in a single calendar year (includes support from single or combined grants or contracts from any source including government, private or industrial/commercial sources);
(6) not be agent(s) of any for-profit, commercial company in the radiologic sciences (applies to applicant/co-principal investigator);
(7) not submit more than one research or education grant application to the RSNA Research and Education Foundation per year;
(8) not have concurrent RSNA grants and;
(9) devote at least 50% of applicant's time to granted project under the guidance of a scientific advisor/mentor.

Supplementation of funding from other grant sources must be approved by Foundation staff if not described in the original research plan. Awards from other sources may be approved by Foundation staff if the investigator submits a satisfactory plan to address any budgetary overlap.

Contact the Foundation for full details.

FINANCIAL DATA:
Funds may be used for salary and/or nonpersonnel research expenses.
Amount of support per award: $50,000 salary support for one-year Research Fellow project or $30,000 salary support for one-year Research Resident project.
Total amount of support: Varies.

NO. MOST RECENT APPLICANTS: Foundation generally funds approximately 25% of the applications received.

NO. AWARDS: Research Fellow Grant: 8; Resident Research Grant: 51 for the year 2019.

APPLICATION INFO:
Applications are completed online using the Online Grant Application System.
Duration: One year; however, residents may opt for a six-month, full-time research project.
Deadline: January 15.

ADDRESS INQUIRIES TO:
Keshia Osley
Assistant Director, Grant Administration
(See address above.)

SAVOY FOUNDATION   [2119]
230 Foch Street
St.-Jean-sur-Richelieu QC J3B 2B2 Canada
(450) 358-9779
Fax: (450) 346-1045
E-mail: epilepsy@savoy-foundation.ca
Web Site: savoy-foundation.ca

FOUNDED: 1971

AREAS OF INTEREST:
Epilepsy and medical research.

TYPE:
Fellowships; Research grants; Scholarships.

PURPOSE:
To promote research on epilepsy.

ELIGIBILITY:
Studentships will be awarded to meritorious applicants wishing to acquire training and pursue research in a biomedical discipline, the health sciences or social sciences related to epilepsy. To be eligible, the candidate must have a good university record (B.Sc., M.D. or equivalent diploma) and have ensured that a qualified researcher affiliated to a university and/or hospital will supervise his or her work. Concomitant registration in a graduate program (M.Sc. or Ph.D.) is encouraged.

Post-Doctoral and Clinical Research Fellowships will be awarded to scientists or medical specialists (Ph.D. or M.D.) wishing to carry out a full-time research project in the field of epilepsy.

Research Grants are available to clinicians and/or established scientists working on epilepsy or related subjects.

Studentships, fellowships, and grants are available to Canadian researchers, to foreign nationals or for projects conducted in Canada.

FINANCIAL DATA:
Amount of support per award: Studentships: $17,000 (CAN) per year. Postdoctoral and Clinical Research Fellowships: $35,000. Research Grants: Up to $25,000.
Total amount of support: More than $320,000 (CAN) per year.

NO. MOST RECENT APPLICANTS: 63 for the year 2019-20.

NO. AWARDS: 15 for the year 2019-20.

APPLICATION INFO:
Application information is available on the web site.
Duration: Studentships: One year. Renewable for a maximum duration of four years; Post-Doctoral, Clinical Research Fellowships and Research Grants: One year. Nonrenewable.

Deadline: January 15 (postmark). If January 15 falls on a weekend or holiday, the Foundation will consider the next working day as the deadline.

EXECUTIVE COMMITTEE:
George M. Savoy, President
Caroline Savoy, Vice President/Secretary
Alain Barbeau, Secretary and Treasurer

ADDRESS INQUIRIES TO:
Caroline Savoy, Secretary
(See address above.)

SCLERODERMA
FOUNDATION   [2120]
300 Rosewood Drive, Suite 105
Danvers, MA 01923
(978) 463-5843
(800) 722-4673
Fax: (978) 777-1313
E-mail: research@scleroderma.org
Web Site: www.scleroderma.org

FOUNDED: 1998

AREAS OF INTEREST:
Scleroderma.

NAME(S) OF PROGRAMS:
● **Scleroderma Foundation Research Grants**

TYPE:
Research grants.

YEAR PROGRAM STARTED: 1998

PURPOSE:
To support research in the area of scleroderma.

ELIGIBILITY:
Applicants must be principal investigators.

GEOG. RESTRICTIONS: United States for new and established investigators; international for established investigators only.

FINANCIAL DATA:
Amount of support per award: $150,000.
Total amount of support: Average $1,000,000 annually.

NO. AWARDS: Average 7 annually.

APPLICATION INFO:
Applicants must use the application form following NIH guidelines which is available, along with other pertinent information, on the Foundation's web site.
Duration: Established investigators: Two years; New investigators: Three years.
Deadline: September 15 annually. Deadline is subject to change. Call or visit the web site to verify deadline date.

PUBLICATIONS:
Quarterly magazine; literature.

IRS I.D.: 52-1375827

ADDRESS INQUIRIES TO:
Research Department
(See e-mail address above.)

SMITH FAMILY AWARDS
PROGRAM FOR EXCELLENCE
IN BIOMEDICAL
RESEARCH   [2121]
2 Boylston Street, 4th Floor
Boston, MA 02116
E-mail: lphelan@hria.org
Web Site: hria.org/tmf/smith

FOUNDED: 1991

AREAS OF INTEREST:
Basic biomedical science including physics, chemistry and engineering with a focus on biomedical research.

TYPE:
Research grants.

YEAR PROGRAM STARTED: 1991

PURPOSE:
To provide research grants for newly independent junior faculty.

ELIGIBILITY:
Detailed information is available on the web site.

GEOG. RESTRICTIONS: Massachusetts, Yale University and Brown University.

FINANCIAL DATA:
Amount of support per award: $300,000 over three years.
Total amount of support: $1,800,000 in new awards for the year 2019.

CO-OP FUNDING PROGRAMS: Funding provided by the Richard and Susan Smith Family Foundation.

NO. MOST RECENT APPLICANTS: 39 for the year 2019.

NO. AWARDS: 6 for the funding cycle 2019-22.

REPRESENTATIVE AWARDS:
"Maintenance of Genome Stability by the Hippo Tumor Suppressor Pathway;" "Neuro-molecular Mechanisms Underlying Alcoholism;" "Micro-Environmental Regulation of Network State and Drug Sensitivity in Triple-Negative Breast Cancer."

APPLICATION INFO:
Information and forms are available on the web site.
Duration: Three years. Nonrenewable.
Deadline: July.

PUBLICATIONS:
Application guidelines; directory of grant recipients (online); summaries of current and previous funded projects.

ADDRESS INQUIRIES TO:
Grants Officer
(See address above.)

THE SOCIETY FOR INVESTIGATIVE DERMATOLOGY [2122]

526 Superior Avenue East
Suite 340
Cleveland, OH 44114-1999
(216) 579-9300
Fax: (216) 579-9333
E-mail: sid@sidnet.org
Web Site: www.sidnet.org

FOUNDED: 1938

AREAS OF INTEREST:
Skin biology, skin disease, and publication and results of skin research.

CONSULTING OR VOLUNTEER SERVICES:
Advocacy for biomedical research.

NAME(S) OF PROGRAMS:
● **Albert M. Kligman Fellowship Fund Award**

TYPE:
Awards/prizes; Conferences/seminars; Fellowships; Research grants; Travel grants. Awards will be used to support resident,

fellow and medical student travel to the Society's annual meetings to present their scientific work.

YEAR PROGRAM STARTED: 1973

PURPOSE:
To encourage trainees to become skin scientists; to encourage the best and brightest young scholars to become members of the research community in dermatology and to participate in the activities of the Society; to advance and promote the sciences relevant to skin health and diseases through education, advocacy and scholarly exchange of scientific information.

LEGAL BASIS:
Tax-exempt.

ELIGIBILITY:
Applicants must hold the M.D. or Ph.D. Project must be skin-/skin disease-related. Preceptor is required. One year of work minimum.

FINANCIAL DATA:
No indirect costs.
Amount of support per award: $25,000.

NO. AWARDS: Approximately 20.

APPLICATION INFO:
Information on application can be obtained from the address above.
Duration: One year.
Deadline: Contact the Society for exact dates.

IRS I.D.: 23-1361165

OFFICERS:
Ponciano Cruz, M.D., President
Sarah Millar, Ph.D., Vice President

SOCIETY OF CARDIOVASCULAR ANESTHESIOLOGISTS

8735 West Higgins Road
Suite 300
Chicago, IL 60631
(855) 658-2828
Fax: (847) 375-6323
E-mail: info@scahq.org
Web Site: www.scahq.org

TYPE:
Research grants.

See entry 2190 for full listing.

SOCIETY OF CRITICAL CARE MEDICINE [2123]

500 Midway Drive
Mount Prospect, IL 60056
(847) 827-6888
Fax: (847) 439-7226
E-mail: vkumar@sccm.org
Web Site: www.sccm.org

AREAS OF INTEREST:
Critical care medicine.

NAME(S) OF PROGRAMS:
● **SCCM-Weil Research Grant**

TYPE:
Research grants. Recipients receive financial rewards, prestige and recognition within the field of critical care medicine.

PURPOSE:
To promote excellence in critical care teaching and research for the improved care of the critically ill and injured.

ELIGIBILITY:
SCCM membership is required for research grants. Entries are judged by a committee with expertise in the field.

FINANCIAL DATA:
Amount of support per award: $50,000.
Total amount of support: $100,000.

NO. AWARDS: 2.

APPLICATION INFO:
Contact the Society for guidelines.

ADDRESS INQUIRIES TO:
Vishakha Kumar, Senior Manager, Research
(See e-mail address above.)

TASTE AND SMELL CLINIC [2124]

Center for Molecular Nutrition and Sensory Disorders
5125 MacArthur Boulevard, N.W., Suite 20
Washington, DC 20016
(202) 364-4180
Fax: (202) 364-9727
E-mail: doc@tasteandsmell.com
Web Site: www.tasteandsmell.com

FOUNDED: 1969

AREAS OF INTEREST:
Taste and smell, clinical treatment of patients with taste and smell disorders, growth factors in relationship to stem cell maturation and development, saliva, salivary diagnostics, salivary proteins, functional magnetic imaging of the brain, transcranial magnetic stimulation of the brain, nasal mucus physiology and pathology, and nasal mucus diagnostics.

CONSULTING OR VOLUNTEER SERVICES:
The Taste and Smell Dysfunction Foundation.

NAME(S) OF PROGRAMS:
● **Taste and Smell Disorders Internship Program**

TYPE:
Internships; Training grants. The Taste and Smell Disorders Internship Program is offered to provide internships and programs to evaluate and treat patients with taste and smell dysfunctions.

YEAR PROGRAM STARTED: 1975

PURPOSE:
To provide internships and other programs to evaluate and treat patients with taste and smell dysfunctions; to study salivary and nasal mucus proteins; to support biochemists and physicians interested in cognitive neurology who want to come work with the clinic.

LEGAL BASIS:
Private organization.

ELIGIBILITY:
Preference to individuals from the Washington, DC metropolitan area.

GEOG. RESTRICTIONS: Washington, DC region.

FINANCIAL DATA:
Stipend commensurate with best academic and/or clinical achievement.
Amount of support per award: Varies depending on need and tasks required.
Total amount of support: $20,000 to $60,000 per year.

CO-OP FUNDING PROGRAMS: Taste and Smell Dysfunction Foundation.

NO. MOST RECENT APPLICANTS: 3.

NO. AWARDS: 1.

APPLICATION INFO:
Resume and three letters of recommendation from scientific mentors are required.
Duration: One year. Renewable for second and third year.
Deadline: June 30.

STAFF:
R.I. Henkin, Director
S. Holen, Staff Scientist
S.J. Potolicchio, Senior Scientist in Neurology

ADDRESS INQUIRIES TO:
R.I. Henkin, Director
(See address above.)

*SPECIAL STIPULATIONS:
Work limited to Washington, DC region.

U.S. DEPARTMENT OF THE NAVY [2125]
Navy Bureau of Medicine and Surgery
NM Accessions Department
8955 Wood Road, Room 13132
Bethesda, MD 20889-5628
(301) 319-4059
(301) 295-9950
E-mail: usn.ohstudent@mail.mil
Web Site: www.med.navy.
mil/Accessions/Pages/default.aspx

FOUNDED: 1972

AREAS OF INTEREST:
Medicine, dentistry, optometry, and clinical psychology.

CONSULTING OR VOLUNTEER SERVICES:
Navy Recruiting Command.

NAME(S) OF PROGRAMS:
● **Navy Health Professions Scholarship Program (HPSP)**

TYPE:
Scholarships. This is an educational support program for individuals pursuing graduate degrees in professional medical programs and who have a desire to serve in the U.S. Navy following graduation.

YEAR PROGRAM STARTED: 1972

PURPOSE:
To provide officers for the Navy who are trained in these disciplines.

LEGAL BASIS:
Authorized by Public Law 92-426.

ELIGIBILITY:
Applicants must be:
(1) U.S. citizens (dual citizenship not permitted);
(2) physically qualified for a commission as a U.S. Navy officer and;
(3) accepted into or enrolled in an AMA or AOA school of medicine, an ADA school of dentistry, an accredited optometry or physician assistant Masters' program, or in the first year of didactic education for a Ph.D. or Psy.D. in clinical psychology from an APA accredited school. School must be located in the U.S. or Puerto Rico.

Applicant must not have reached the age of 42 at the time of entry into active duty following completion of their education.

GEOG. RESTRICTIONS: United States and Puerto Rico.

FINANCIAL DATA:
Amount of support per award: Scholarship includes full tuition (no upper limit) and allowable fees, reimbursement for all

required books, supplies and equipment (some limits apply), $20,000 signing bonus (medicine and dentistry only), monthly stipend of $2,330 (taxable), full pay and allowances of an ensign (O-1) for 45 days per year (about $4,500), and reimbursement for student's health insurance if required by school.
Total amount of support: Over $125,000,000 in tuition and stipends. Part of annual Congressional appropriation.

NO. MOST RECENT APPLICANTS: 500 for medical; 200 for dental.

NO. AWARDS: 330.

APPLICATION INFO:
Must apply through Navy Recruiting Command.
Duration: Two to four years, according to year level upon entry. Acceptance of the program requires continuous participation until graduation. Dental scholarships are the same as medical scholarships.
Deadline: Rolling acceptance for medical, dental and optometry. Clinical psychology applications: January.

ADDRESS INQUIRIES TO:
See e-mail address above.

*SPECIAL STIPULATIONS:
For Scholarship awardees, one year of active duty (not in training) is required for each year of the Scholarship, with a three-year minimum.

THE UNIVERSITY OF CALGARY
Faculty of Graduate Studies
Earth Sciences Building, Room 1010
2500 University Drive, N.W.
Calgary AB T2N 1N4 Canada
(403) 220-4938
Fax: (403) 289-7635
E-mail: gsaward@ucalgary.ca
Web Site: grad.ucalgary.ca/awards

TYPE:
Awards/prizes; Scholarships. Awards for study in the medical sciences. Tenable at The University of Calgary. Award endowed through a bequest of the late William H. Davies.

See entry 1616 for full listing.

THE UNIVERSITY OF SYDNEY [2126]
Scholarships Office
Level 4, Jane Foss Russell Building G02
The University of Sydney N.S.W. 2006
Australia
61 (02) 8627 1444
E-mail: scholarships.officer@sydney.edu.au
Web Site: www.sydney.edu.au/scholarships

FOUNDED: 1850

AREAS OF INTEREST:
Medicine.

NAME(S) OF PROGRAMS:
● **Sydney Medical School Postgraduate Research Scholarships**

TYPE:
Scholarships. For research leading to a higher degree. Tenable in the Sydney Medical School at the University of Sydney.

PURPOSE:
To promote and encourage research in the medical sciences at the University of Sydney.

LEGAL BASIS:
University.

ELIGIBILITY:
Available to full-time research candidates, normally Ph.D., in any department or research unit associated with the Sydney Medical School at the University of Sydney. Applicants must be either Australian or New Zealand citizens or permanent residents of Australia.

Scholarships are awarded on the basis of academic merit and any other criteria stipulated for individual scholarships.

FINANCIAL DATA:
Amount of support per award: Varies.

NO. AWARDS: Varies according to availability of funds.

APPLICATION INFO:
Contact the University for guidelines.
Duration: Varies.

ADDRESS INQUIRIES TO:
Scholarships Officer
Sydney Medical School
Edward Ford Building (A27)
Fisher Road
The University of Sydney
N.S.W. 2006 Australia
(See e-mail address above.)

*PLEASE NOTE:
Very few awards are available and competition for them is extremely keen. They are awarded strictly on academic merit and only graduates with First Class Honours or equivalent qualifications (e.g., graduation magna cum laude) will be considered.

THE VALLEY FOUNDATION [2127]
999 West Taylor Street
Suite A
San Jose, CA 95126
E-mail: info@valley.org
Web Site: www.valley.org

FOUNDED: 1984

AREAS OF INTEREST:
Medical services and health care for lower-income households, the arts, senior citizens, education and research.

TYPE:
Project/program grants.

YEAR PROGRAM STARTED: 1984

PURPOSE:
To provide funding for nonprofit organizations, with an emphasis in the medical field.

LEGAL BASIS:
Nonprofit foundation.

ELIGIBILITY:
Qualified 501(c)(3) charitable organizations. No individuals or political organizations.

GEOG. RESTRICTIONS: United States.

FINANCIAL DATA:
The Foundation prefers to avoid grants which provide more than one-half of an organization's total budget in a 12-month period, usually expecting community and applicant commitment to a project through local cost sharing.
Amount of support per award: $5,000 to $1,000,000.

APPLICATION INFO:
Guidelines are available on the Foundation web site.

Duration: Varies, but multiple-year requests are discouraged. Organizations which have received funding must wait at least one full year before submitting another application. Organizations that did not make it to the full LOI full proposal cycle can reapply on the anniversary of their first LOI submission.

Deadline: February 20, May 20, August 20 and November 20.

PUBLICATIONS:
Application guidelines.

IRS I.D.: 94-1584547

BOARD OF TRUSTEES:
Phillip R. Boyce, Chairman
Richard Sieve, M.D., Vice Chairman
Robert Lee, C.P.A., Secretary

ADDRESS INQUIRIES TO:
See e-mail address above.

Allergy, immunology, infectious diseases

AMERICAN ACADEMY OF ALLERGY ASTHMA & IMMUNOLOGY [2128]
555 East Wells Street, Suite 1100
Milwaukee, WI 53202-3823
(414) 272-6071
Fax: (414) 272-6070
E-mail: info@aaaai.org
Web Site: www.aaaai.org

FOUNDED: 1943

AREAS OF INTEREST:
Allergy and immunology.

NAME(S) OF PROGRAMS:
● **Domestic Fellow-In-Training Travel Scholarship**

TYPE:
Travel grants. Travel scholarships to attend the AAAAI Annual Meeting.

PURPOSE:
To advance the knowledge and practice of allergy by discussion at meetings, by fostering the education of students and the public, by encouraging union and cooperation among those engaged in this field and by promoting and stimulating research and study in allergy.

LEGAL BASIS:
Nonprofit.

ELIGIBILITY:
Travel grants for the annual meeting are awarded to member fellows-in-training in the field of allergy and immunology. The grants will be awarded on the basis of merit as judged by the committee. Individuals with a faculty appointment will not be considered.

GEOG. RESTRICTIONS: United States and Canada.

FINANCIAL DATA:
Amount of support per award: Maximum of $800 for first- or second-year Fellow-In-Training who apply for a travel scholarship without an accepted abstract or case report for presentation; Maximum of $650 for third-, fourth- or fifth-year Fellow-In-Training who apply for a travel scholarship without an accepted abstract for presentation; Maximum of $1,100 to Fellow-In-Training who applies for a travel scholarship and is the first author of an

accepted abstract for presentation or is the first author Fellow-In-Training with a Case Report (candidate must present their abstract or case report at the Annual Meeting in order to be eligible).

Total amount of support: Varies.

NO. MOST RECENT APPLICANTS: 232.

NO. AWARDS: 231.

APPLICATION INFO:
Application information is available online.
Deadline: November 2021.

ADDRESS INQUIRIES TO:
Mari Duran, Program Manager
E-mail: mduran@aaaai.org

ARTHRITIS NATIONAL RESEARCH FOUNDATION (ANRF)
19200 Von Karman Avenue
Suite 350
Irvine, CA 92612
(800) 588-2873
(562) 437-6808
E-mail: grants@curearthritis.org
Web Site: www.curearthritis.org

TYPE:
Research grants; Travel grants. ANRF Arthritis Research Grants are intended to support basic and clinical research focusing on rheumatic and related autoimmune diseases, such as osteoarthritis and rheumatoid arthritis.

See entry 2039 for full listing.

CANCER RESEARCH INSTITUTE
29 Broadway, 4th Floor
New York, NY 10006
(212) 688-7515
(800) 992-2623
Fax: (212) 832-9376
E-mail: grants@cancerresearch.org
Web Site: www.cancerresearch.org

TYPE:
Fellowships; Research grants; Training grants.

See entry 2224 for full listing.

DYSTROPHIC EPIDERMOLYSIS BULLOSA RESEARCH ASSOCIATION OF AMERICA, INC. (DEBRA) [2129]
75 Broad Street
Suite 300
New York, NY 10004
(212) 868-1573 ext. 110
Fax: (212) 868-9296
E-mail: staff@debra.org
Web Site: www.debra.org

FOUNDED: 1980

AREAS OF INTEREST:
Research into the causes, treatment and cure of EB and other genetic disorders of the skin.

NAME(S) OF PROGRAMS:
● **debra International Research Grants**

TYPE:
Research grants. Financial aid for EB families in crisis.

YEAR PROGRAM STARTED: 1980

PURPOSE:
To provide opportunity to advance research into the effects, causes, treatments and cure for epidermolysis bullosa.

ELIGIBILITY:
Peer-reviewed grants made to full-time or part-time researchers.

FINANCIAL DATA:
Amount of support per award: Varies.
Total amount of support: Varies.

APPLICATION INFO:
Guidelines may be obtained from the organization at the address above.
Duration: One to three years.

IRS I.D.: 11-2519726

ADDRESS INQUIRIES TO:
Brett Kopelan, Executive Director
(See address above.)

IMMUNE DEFICIENCY FOUNDATION [2130]
110 West Road
Suite 300
Towson, MD 21204
(410) 321-6647
Fax: (410) 321-9165
E-mail: jmagnusson@primaryimmune.org
Web Site: usidnet.org
primaryimmune.org

AREAS OF INTEREST:
Primary immunodeficiency diseases.

NAME(S) OF PROGRAMS:
● **U.S. Immunodeficiency Network**

TYPE:
Travel grants; Visiting scholars.

YEAR PROGRAM STARTED: 2003

PURPOSE:
To improve the diagnosis and treatment of patients with primary immunodeficiency diseases through research and education.

ELIGIBILITY:
Open to medical students, residents and fellows who are interested in immunology and want to increase their knowledge of clinical diagnoses and treatments of primary immunodeficiency diseases.

GEOG. RESTRICTIONS: United States.

FINANCIAL DATA:
Amount of support per award: Generally up to $2,400.
Total amount of support: $15,000 annually.

NO. MOST RECENT APPLICANTS: 6.

NO. AWARDS: 4 to 5 per year.

APPLICATION INFO:
Contact USIDNET for guidelines.
Duration: Travel grants (reimbursement) for one- to two-week training visits.
Deadline: Applications accepted on a rolling basis.

ADDRESS INQUIRIES TO:
Julieann Magnusson
USIDNET Program Manager
(See address above.)

MAGIC JOHNSON FOUNDATION
9100 Wilshire Boulevard
Suite 700, East Tower
Beverly Hills, CA 90212
(310) 246-4400
Fax: (310) 786-8796
Web Site: magicjohnson.org

TYPE:
Project/program grants; Technical assistance.

See entry 156 for full listing.

LOVELACE RESPIRATORY RESEARCH INSTITUTE   [2131]
2425 Ridgecrest Drive, S.E.
Albuquerque, NM 87108
(505) 348-9400
Fax: (505) 348-8567
E-mail: info@lrri.org
Web Site: lrri.org

FOUNDED: 1947

AREAS OF INTEREST:
Respiratory diseases.

NAME(S) OF PROGRAMS:
● **Postdoctoral Training Program**

TYPE:
Fellowships. Training program in respiratory tract disease caused by environmental agents.

YEAR PROGRAM STARTED: 1947

PURPOSE:
To provide research into prevention, treatment and cure of respiratory disease.

LEGAL BASIS:
Private biomedical research organization.

ELIGIBILITY:
Programs are tailored to individuals. Laboratory research or pathogenesis of disease can focus on one of several disciplinary areas, including cell biology, molecular biology, biochemistry, immunology, pathology, physiology, radiobiology or aerosol science, depending on interests and qualifications. Applicants must be U.S. citizens or permanent residents or eligible for a visa.

GEOG. RESTRICTIONS: United States.

FINANCIAL DATA:
Fellowship includes stipend and health insurance, relocation allowance, tuition and fees.
Amount of support per award: Varies.
Total amount of support: Varies.

NO. AWARDS: Varies.

APPLICATION INFO:
Application form required. Contact Institute for application guidelines.
Duration: One year. Renewable for second and third year.
Deadline: Varies.

ROBERT MAPPLETHORPE FOUNDATION, INC.
477 Madison Avenue, 15th Floor
New York, NY 10022-5835
(212) 755-3025
Fax: (212) 941-4764
E-mail: joree@mapplethorpe.org
info@mapplethorpe.org
Web Site: www.mapplethorpe.org

TYPE:
Project/program grants. Funds medical research in the fight against AIDS and HIV infection and supports the promotion of photography as a fine art, embracing exhibitions, acquisitions, and publications.

See entry 432 for full listing.

Dentistry

THE AMERICAN ACADEMY OF ESTHETIC DENTISTRY   [2132]
225 West Wacker Drive
Suite 650
Chicago, IL 60606
(312) 981-6770
Fax: (312) 265-2908
E-mail: info@estheticacademy.org
Web Site: www.estheticacademy.org

FOUNDED: 1975

AREAS OF INTEREST:
Dentistry.

NAME(S) OF PROGRAMS:
● **AAED Esthetic Dentistry Research Grants**

TYPE:
Research grants.

YEAR PROGRAM STARTED: 1993

PURPOSE:
To promote the integration of dental esthetics into the total spectrum of oral health care.

ELIGIBILITY:
Applicant must be a graduate student or young untenured faculty at the instructor or assistant professor level at an accredited dental school.

GEOG. RESTRICTIONS: United States, Canada and Puerto Rico.

FINANCIAL DATA:
Amount of support per award: Up to $3,000.

NO. AWARDS: 1 per year.

APPLICATION INFO:
Contact the Academy for application procedures.
Duration: One year.
Deadline: End of May.

ADDRESS INQUIRIES TO:
Joe Jackson, Executive Director
(See address above.)

AMERICAN ACADEMY OF IMPLANT DENTISTRY (AAID) FOUNDATION   [2133]
211 East Chicago Avenue
Suite 1100
Chicago, IL 60611
(312) 335-1550
Fax: (312) 335-9090
E-mail: barb@aaid.com
Web Site: www.aaid.com

FOUNDED: 1979

AREAS OF INTEREST:
Dental implant research.

NAME(S) OF PROGRAMS:
● **Humanitarian Project Support**
● **Research Award**
● **Student Research Grant**
● **Wish a Smile**

TYPE:
Awards/prizes; Project/program grants; Research grants. Research Award provides limited support for meritorious dental implant research projects which determine the feasibility of a larger research project. This may be described as the conduct of pilot studies or venture research to develop and test new techniques and procedures, to carry out a small clinical or animal research project and to analyze existing data.

Student Research Grant is available for all graduate dental students. Research must be related to dental implant.

Wish a Smile, a partnership between the AAID Foundation, Dental Lifeline Network, Implant and Bone Grafting corporate sponsors and volunteer dentists, aims to provide free dental service to patients who have congenitally missing teeth and are financially disadvantaged, disabled veterans with congenitally missing teeth, and disabled veterans with no teeth remaining requiring implants to retain a denture. The AAIDF and DLN would seek to get all needed restorative supplies and services donated in addition to implant.

YEAR PROGRAM STARTED: 1981

PURPOSE:
To provide limited support for meritorious dental implant research projects; to provide a humanitarian service to the public; to increase public awareness of the AAID Foundation, AAID, AAID's members and Dental Lifeline Network.

LEGAL BASIS:
Research foundation.

ELIGIBILITY:
Investigators from any scientific discipline and at any stage of their career may apply for a Research Award. These awards are appropriated for new investigators and those changing areas of research or resuming research careers.

Student Research Grant is available to postgraduate dental students for implant-related research studies.

Wish a Smile requires applicants to meet the following criteria:
(1) be 17 years of age or older at the time of application;
(2) be congenitally missing one to three teeth with no more than three teeth requiring replacement;
(3) be medically healthy and a nonsmoker and;
(4) have a patient or family gross income (if patient is a dependent minor) that is low or displays significant need.

FINANCIAL DATA:
Grants may be used for supplies, small items of equipment and salary for technical and support personnel.
Amount of support per award: Humanitarian Project Support: Varies; Small Research Award: Up to $25,000 (total project costs); Student Research Grant: Up to $2,500 per year.
Total amount of support: $100,000.

NO. MOST RECENT APPLICANTS: 36.

NO. AWARDS: Research Award: 4; Student Research Grant: Up to 8.

APPLICATION INFO:
Required documentation includes abstract of research plan, budget estimate, explanation of the project, including its specific aims, significance, experimental design and methods, sequence of events and time schedule and a complete bibliography, curriculum vitae and a list of all co-investigators and consultants.
Duration: Student Research Grant: Up to two years. Nonrenewable.
Deadline: Research Award: August 1. Student Research Grant: June 15.

PUBLICATIONS:
Guidelines.

OFFICERS:
James L. Bush, Chairman
Richard Mercurio, D.D.S., Vice Chairman

ADDRESS INQUIRIES TO:
E-mail: foundation@aaid.com

AMERICAN ASSOCIATION FOR DENTAL RESEARCH   [2134]

1619 Duke Street
Alexandria, VA 22314-3406
(703) 548-0066
Fax: (703) 548-1883
E-mail: sherren@iadr.org
Web Site: www.aadr.org

AREAS OF INTEREST:
Dental research.

NAME(S) OF PROGRAMS:
● **AADR Hatton Competition**

TYPE:
Awards/prizes. For junior investigators
(junior, senior and postdoctoral) who exhibit
potential for a productive career in dental
research.

PURPOSE:
To advance research and increase knowledge
for the improvement of oral health; to
support and represent the oral health research
community; to facilitate the communication
and application of research findings.

ELIGIBILITY:
Applicants must be U.S. citizens or
noncitizen nationals of the U.S. (or who have
been lawfully admitted for permanent
residence at the time of submission of the
abstract - those with a "green card") or
persons of other nationalities whose research
is performed in the U.S. Must be an AADR
member. There is no age limit for entrants in
the AADR competition.

FINANCIAL DATA:
Amount of support per award: First prize:
$1,000; Second prize: $500.
Total amount of support: $4,500.

NO. MOST RECENT APPLICANTS: Over 200.

NO. AWARDS: 3 First Prizes and 3 Second
Prizes.

APPLICATION INFO:
Details of the abstract to be submitted are
available on the web site.
Deadline: October 19.

ADDRESS INQUIRIES TO:
Sheri S. Herren
Assistant Director of Strategic Programs
(See address above.)

AMERICAN ASSOCIATION FOR DENTAL RESEARCH   [2135]

1619 Duke Street
Alexandria, VA 22314-3406
(703) 548-0066
Fax: (703) 548-1883
E-mail: sherren@iadr.org
Web Site: www.aadr.org

AREAS OF INTEREST:
Basic and clinical research related to oral
health.

NAME(S) OF PROGRAMS:
● **Student Research Fellowships**

PURPOSE:
To advance research and increase knowledge
for the improvement of oral health; to
support and represent the oral health research
community; to facilitate the communication
and application of research findings.

ELIGIBILITY:
Applicant must be enrolled in an accredited
D.D.S./D.M.D. or hygiene program in a
dental institution and must be sponsored by a
faculty member. Students should not have
received their degree, nor should they in the
year of award. Applicant may have an
advanced degree in a basic science subject.
Must be an AADR member.

GEOG. RESTRICTIONS: United States.

FINANCIAL DATA:
Amount of support per award: $2,700.

Total amount of support: Varies.

NO. MOST RECENT APPLICANTS: 100.

NO. AWARDS: 16 for the year 2020.

APPLICATION INFO:
Proposals will follow the general format of
the Public Health Service Grant Application
Form PHS 398, which is to be used only as a
guideline. Each proposal must include the
following:
(1) objectives, describing what the research is
intended to accomplish and the hypothesis to
be tested;
(2) research strategy, including significance,
innovation and approach;
(3) facilities and equipment to be used for
the research project;
(4) other support for applicant and sponsor
and;
(5) for those projects involving Recombinant
DNA/Recombinant DNA Molecules, an
indication that the project adheres to the
current NIH Guidelines for Research
Involving Recombinant DNA Molecules.

The following documents must also be
included:
(1) cover letter from the applicant's sponsor,
indicating the dental school's and the
sponsor's support of the proposed research;
(2) cover letter from the applicant explaining
student's motivations and reasons to have the
Fellowship experience and what plans are
after completion of this phase of their
education;
(3) curriculum vitae, not to exceed two
pages, outlining the student's career up to the
time of application;
(4) sponsor's biographical sketch in NIH
format, not to exceed two pages;
(5) literature cited and;
(6) documentation that the project has been
approved by the Institutional Review Board
for projects involving human subjects or
vertebrate animals.

Proposals longer than four pages (PDF)
and/or 1,400 words will not be considered.

Deadline: January 18, 2021.

ADDRESS INQUIRIES TO:
Sheri S. Herren
Assistant Director of Strategic Programs
(See address above.)

AMERICAN ASSOCIATION FOR DENTAL RESEARCH   [2136]

1619 Duke Street
Alexandria, VA 22314-3406
(703) 548-0066
Fax: (703) 548-1883
E-mail: sherren@iadr.org
Web Site: www.aadr.org

AREAS OF INTEREST:
Clinical research in periodontology.

NAME(S) OF PROGRAMS:
● **William B. Clark Fellowship in Clinical Research**

TYPE:
Fellowships.

PURPOSE:
To advance research and increase knowledge
for the improvement of oral health; to
support and represent the oral health research
community; to facilitate the communication
and application of research findings.

ELIGIBILITY:
Applicant must have completed first
professional degree, should be appointed at
an accredited dental school or academic
research center in U.S., and must be a
member of AADR.

GEOG. RESTRICTIONS: United States.

FINANCIAL DATA:
Amount of support per award: $5,000.
Total amount of support: $5,000.

NO. MOST RECENT APPLICANTS: 1.

NO. AWARDS: 1.

APPLICATION INFO:
Applicants must submit the following:
(1) letter stating their interest in applying for
the award;
(2) curriculum vitae;
(3) three- to four-page (double-spaced)
overview of their proposed areas of training,
including how the experience will affect
future research to be conducted by the
applicant;
(4) brief description of the facility which will
provide the training and;
(5) letter of support from the proposed
mentor.
Deadline: October 19.

ADDRESS INQUIRIES TO:
Sheri S. Herren
Assistant Director of Strategic Programs
(See address above.)

AMERICAN ASSOCIATION FOR DENTAL RESEARCH   [2137]

1619 Duke Street
Alexandria, VA 22314-3406
(703) 548-0066
Fax: (703) 548-1883
E-mail: sherren@iadr.org
Web Site: www.aadr.org

AREAS OF INTEREST:
Dental research.

NAME(S) OF PROGRAMS:
● **William J. Gies Award**

TYPE:
Awards/prizes. For the best paper published
in the *Journal of Dental Research* during the
preceding year.

PURPOSE:
To advance research and increase knowledge
for the improvement of oral health; to

support and represent the oral health research community; to facilitate the communication and application of research findings.

FINANCIAL DATA:
Amount of support per award: $1,000.

Total amount of support: $3,000.

NO. MOST RECENT APPLICANTS: More than 10 nominations.

NO. AWARDS: 3.

APPLICATION INFO:
Information on the nomination process is available on the web site.

Deadline: October 19.

ADDRESS INQUIRIES TO:
Sheri S. Herren
Assistant Director of Strategic Programs
(See address above.)

AMERICAN ASSOCIATION OF WOMEN DENTISTS   [2138]

7794 Grow Drive
Pensacola, FL 32514
(850) 484-9987
(800) 920-2293
Fax: (850) 484-8762
E-mail: info@aawd.org
Web Site: www.aawd.org

FOUNDED: 1921

AREAS OF INTEREST:
Dentistry.

NAME(S) OF PROGRAMS:
● **Eleanor Bushee Award**
● **Lucy Hobbs Taylor Award**

TYPE:
Awards/prizes; Scholarships. The Eleanor Bushee Award honors senior dental students who have achieved academic excellence and have demonstrated outstanding leadership.

Lucy Hobbs Taylor Award is presented to a woman dentist who has made outstanding individual achievements in civic, cultural, academic and professional areas and exhibits role model qualities that positively reflect the image of women dentists and commitment to the profession.

PURPOSE:
To encourage women dental students who contribute to the school, to dentistry or dental health who are in need of financial assistance.

ELIGIBILITY:
Applicants must be dentists or junior/senior dental students. Lucy Hobbs Taylor Award applicant must be an AAWD member in good standing.

FINANCIAL DATA:
Amount of support per award: Varies.

Total amount of support: Varies.

APPLICATION INFO:
Contact the Association for detailed guidelines.

Duration: One year.

Deadline: Varies.

PUBLICATIONS:
Chronicle; Women's Dental Journal.

AMERICAN DENTAL ASSISTANTS ASSOCIATION   [2139]

140 North Bloomingdale Road
Bloomingdale, IL 60108
(630) 994-4247
Fax: (630) 351-8490
E-mail: jaykasper@adaausa.org
Web Site: www.adaausa.org

FOUNDED: 1924

AREAS OF INTEREST:
Dental assisting.

NAME(S) OF PROGRAMS:
● **Juliette A. Southard Scholarship Program**

TYPE:
Scholarships. Tuition scholarships awarded to dental professional students interested in furthering their education.

YEAR PROGRAM STARTED: 1924

PURPOSE:
To provide financial assistance for highly qualified applicants pursuing dental professional education.

LEGAL BASIS:
Nonprofit professional organization.

ELIGIBILITY:
Applicants must be high school graduates or equivalent and enrolled in a dental professional program. Candidates will be considered on the basis of academic achievement, ability, interest in dentistry and personal attributes. Must be a member of the ADAA.

GEOG. RESTRICTIONS: United States.

FINANCIAL DATA:
Amount of support per award: Up to $750, a congratulatory letter and one year active membership with the ADAA.

NO. MOST RECENT APPLICANTS: 9 for the year 2018.

NO. AWARDS: 5 for the year 2018.

APPLICATION INFO:
Applicants must submit academic transcripts (high school and/or college), proof of acceptance into an accredited program and a letter of intent to pursue a long-range career in dental profession. Two letters of reference are also required.

Duration: One year.

Deadline: March 15.

STAFF:
John Kasper, Executive Director
Jay Kasper, Associate Executive Director

ADDRESS INQUIRIES TO:
Scholarship Committee
(See address above.)

AMERICAN DENTAL HYGIENISTS' ASSOCIATION INSTITUTE FOR ORAL HEALTH   [2140]

444 North Michigan Avenue
Suite 400
Chicago, IL 60611
(312) 440-8900 ext. 244
E-mail: institute@adha.net
Web Site: www.adha.org/institute-for-oral-health

FOUNDED: 1927

AREAS OF INTEREST:
Dental hygiene.

NAME(S) OF PROGRAMS:
● **ADHA Institute for Oral Health Dental Hygiene Scholarships**

TYPE:
Scholarships. The Graduate Scholarship Program awards licensed dental hygienists who are, or will be, enrolled as graduate students in a program leading to a Master's or doctoral degree in dental hygiene or dental hygiene education. There is also an undergraduate scholarship program.

YEAR PROGRAM STARTED: 1986

PURPOSE:
To invest in the future careers of dental hygiene students by ensuring that they will be of exceptional quality and dedication.

LEGAL BASIS:
501(c)(3) public charity, as described in Sections 509(1)(1)-170(b)(1)(A)(vi) of the Internal Revenue Code.

ELIGIBILITY:
Applicant must be an undergraduate or graduate student in an accredited dental hygiene program in the U.S and an active member of the American Dental Hygienists' Association.

GEOG. RESTRICTIONS: United States.

FINANCIAL DATA:
Amount of support per award: Varies.
Total amount of support: Varies.

NO. MOST RECENT APPLICANTS: 50 to 100.

NO. AWARDS: 25 to 35.

APPLICATION INFO:
Application is available on October 1 and can only be downloaded from the web site.
Duration: Scholarships are awarded for a period of one academic year.
Deadline: February 1.

PUBLICATIONS:
Annual report.

ADDRESS INQUIRIES TO:
Joan Brazas, IOH Development Manager
(See e-mail address above.)

HISPANIC DENTAL ASSOCIATION FOUNDATION   [2141]

17225 El Camino Real
Houston, TX 77058
(317) 714-0037
E-mail: hdafoundationscholarships@gmail.com
Web Site: hdassoc.org

FOUNDED: 1990

AREAS OF INTEREST:
Oral health careers.

NAME(S) OF PROGRAMS:
● **A-dec Scholarship**
● **Colgate-Palmolive Dental Residency or Specialty Program Scholarship**
● **Colgate-Palmolive Scholarship for Dental Students and Dental Hygiene Students**
● **Procter & Gamble Scholarship**
● **Dr. Esperanza Rodriguez Scholarship**
● **Dr. Juan D. Villarreal Scholarship**

TYPE:
Awards/prizes; Conferences/seminars; Internships; Product donations; Scholarships.

YEAR PROGRAM STARTED: 1990

PURPOSE:
To encourage entry of Hispanics into oral health careers.

ELIGIBILITY:
Students must have permanent resident status in the U.S., be current student members of the Hispanic Dental Association, and attending U.S. dental schools.

A-dec Scholarship is open to third- or fourth-year dental students.

Colgate-Palmolive Dental Residency or Specialty Program Scholarships are open to student members of the Association who have been accepted into or are currently enrolled in an accredited residency program in a dentistry-related field. Students must have an undergraduate or graduate degree in an oral health-related field (dental hygienist, dentistry, etc.) from the U.S. or abroad.

Colgate-Palmolive Scholarship for Dental Students and Dental Hygiene Students are awarded to students enrolled in an accredited dental or dental hygiene program.

Procter & Gamble Scholarship is open to first- to fourth-year dental students and first- and second-year dental hygiene and dental assisting students.

Dr. Esperanza Rodriguez Scholarship is open to first-, second- or third-year dental students.

Dr. Juan D. Villarreal Scholarships are open to student members of the Association who have been accepted into or are currently enrolled in an accredited dental school or dental hygiene program in the state of Texas. The student may be at any stage of the undergraduate program, first through fourth years.

GEOG. RESTRICTIONS: Dr. Juan D. Villareal Scholarship: Texas; United States for all others.

FINANCIAL DATA:
Amount of support per award: A-dec Scholarship: $4,000; Colgate-Palmolive Dental Residency or Specialty Program Scholarship: $5,000; Colgate-Palmolive Scholarship for Dental Students and Dental Hygiene Students: $4,000 for Dental students and $2,000 for Dental Hygiene students; Procter & Gamble Scholarships: $2,000 to $4,000; Dr. Esperanza Rodriguez Scholarship and Dr. Juan D. Villarreal Scholarship: $2,000.

Total amount of support: Varies.

NO. MOST RECENT APPLICANTS: Approximately 90.

NO. AWARDS: A-dec Scholarship: 2; Colgate-Palmolive Scholarships: 4 Resident, 6 Dental students and 2 Hygiene students; Procter & Gamble Scholarships: 9; Dr. Esperanza Rodriguez Scholarships: 1; Dr. Juan D. Villarreal Scholarships: 2 for Dental students and 1 for Dental Hygiene student.

APPLICATION INFO:
Application can be downloaded from the web site.

Duration: One year. Renewal possible by reapplication.

Deadline: July 1.

STAFF:
Jen Blake, Director

ADDRESS INQUIRIES TO:
See e-mail address above.

INTERNATIONAL ASSOCIATION FOR DENTAL RESEARCH (IADR) [2142]

1619 Duke Street
Alexandria, VA 22314-3406
(703) 548-0066
Fax: (703) 548-1883
E-mail: sherren@iadr.org
Web Site: www.iadr.org

AREAS OF INTEREST:
Original research in the area of oral health, basic, clinical and applied studies.

NAME(S) OF PROGRAMS:
- **IADR Colgate Research in Prevention Travel Awards**

TYPE:
Awards/prizes; Travel grants. These Awards are for young investigators who have submitted an abstract which has a preventive component for a travel award to support their attendance at the IADR General Session.

Contact IADR for the full range of awards.

PURPOSE:
To advance research and increase knowledge for the improvement of oral health; to support and represent the oral health research community; to facilitate the communication and applications of research findings.

ELIGIBILITY:
Applicants must be IADR members. Young investigators (up to five years postgraduation from dental, dental hygiene, specialty training or pre-Ph.D.) are eligible to apply for a travel award. (No persons who have already obtained a Ph.D. are eligible to apply.) Entrants must provide a verification letter of their educational status and can only receive this Award once.

FINANCIAL DATA:
Amount of support per award: $2,000.
Total amount of support: $2,000.

NO. MOST RECENT APPLICANTS: 16.

NO. AWARDS: At least 1 for North America (Canada, U.S. and Mexico). There are also Awards for other geographic regions.

APPLICATION INFO:
In applying for this Award, candidates must submit their abstract as well as a separate and more detailed overview of their projects (two pages, double-spaced). This overview must include brief details of their material and methods, the results of the research including details of statistical analysis and a brief discussion including how the research will affect the prevention of the condition stated.

Deadline: January 14.

ADDRESS INQUIRIES TO:
Sheri S. Herren
Strategic Programs Manager
(See e-mail address above.)

NATIONAL INSTITUTE OF DENTAL AND CRANIOFACIAL RESEARCH (NIDCR) [2143]

National Institutes of Health
6701 Democracy Boulevard, Room 688
Bethesda, MD 20892
(301) 496-4263
E-mail: leslie.frieden@nih.gov
Web Site: www.nidcr.nih.gov/careers-training

FOUNDED: 1948

AREAS OF INTEREST:
Dental, craniofacial health and research.

NAME(S) OF PROGRAMS:
- **Individual NRSA Postdoctoral Fellowships (F-32)**

TYPE:
Fellowships. Provides up to three years of support for trainees at academic institutions to broaden their scientific background or extend their potential for research in health-related areas.

YEAR PROGRAM STARTED: 1974

PURPOSE:
To develop individuals for careers in oral health research.

LEGAL BASIS:
Public Health Service Act as amended, Section 301c; 42 CFR 61; 42 U.S.C. 288a.

ELIGIBILITY:
Applicants must be citizens, non-citizen nationals or permanent residents of the U.S. at the time of the award and have a Ph.D., M.D., D.D.S., D.O., D.V.M. or equivalent degree prior to the beginning date of the proposed fellowship.

GEOG. RESTRICTIONS: United States.

FINANCIAL DATA:
Stipend level is based on number of years of postdoctoral experience and at NRSA level. Additional funds are available for other training-related expenses.

Total amount of support: Varies.

APPLICATION INFO:
Detailed information can be obtained from the Institute.

Duration: One, two or three years.

Deadline: April 8, August 8 and December 8.

ADDRESS INQUIRIES TO:
Leslie Frieden
Extramural Training Officer
(See address above.)

NATIONAL INSTITUTE OF DENTAL AND CRANIOFACIAL RESEARCH (NIDCR) [2144]

National Institutes of Health
31 Center Drive, Room 5B-55
MSC 2190
Bethesda, MD 20892-2190
(301) 496-4261
E-mail: nidcrinfo@mail.nih.gov
Web Site: www.nidcr.nih.gov

FOUNDED: 1948

AREAS OF INTEREST:
Multiple areas of research with the goal of improving dental, oral and craniofacial health.

NAME(S) OF PROGRAMS:
- **Behavioral & Social Science Research**
- **Clinical & Practice-Based Research**
- **Clinical Research & Clinical Technologies**
- **Clinical Trials**
- **Data Science, Computational Biology & Bioinformatics**
- **Dental Materials & Biomaterials**
- **Developmental Biology and Genetics**
- **Health Disparities**
- **HIV/AIDS & Oral Health**
- **Microbiology**
- **Mineralized Tissue Physiology**

- **Neuroscience of Orofacial Pain & Temporomandibular Disorders**
- **Oral & Salivary Cancer Biology**
- **Research Training & Career Development**
- **Salivary Biology & Immunology**
- **Small Business Innovation/Small Business Technology Transfer (SBIR/STTR)**
- **Tissue Engineering and Regenerative Medicine**
- **Translational Genetics & Genomics**

TYPE:
Conferences/seminars; Project/program grants; Research grants; Research contracts. Grants for the support of basic and clinical research.

YEAR PROGRAM STARTED: 1948

PURPOSE:
To develop methods for preventing and treating oral diseases and conditions through research related to oral and craniofacial health.

LEGAL BASIS:
Public Health Service Act as amended, Section 301c; 42 CFR 61; 42 U.S.C. 288a.

ELIGIBILITY:
Open to scientists at universities, hospitals, laboratories and other public, nonprofit or profit institutions. Applications are competitively rated on the basis of scientific merit and grants must be approved by the National Advisory Dental and Craniofacial Research Council.

FINANCIAL DATA:
Amount of support per award: Varies.

APPLICATION INFO:
Varies by program. Visit the NIDCR web site above for detailed information.
Duration: Varies.

NATIONAL INSTITUTE OF DENTAL AND CRANIOFACIAL RESEARCH (NIDCR)   [2145]
National Institutes of Health
6701 Democracy Boulevard, Room 688
Bethesda, MD 20892
(301) 496-4263
E-mail: leslie.frieden@nih.gov
Web Site: www.nidcr.nih.gov/careers-training

FOUNDED: 1948

AREAS OF INTEREST:
Biomedical and behavioral research.

NAME(S) OF PROGRAMS:
- **Individual NRSA Senior Fellowship Award (F-33)**

TYPE:
Fellowships. Provides health research training for experienced scientists, enabling them to update their skills or make changes in the direction of their career.

YEAR PROGRAM STARTED: 1979

PURPOSE:
To provide opportunities for experienced scientists to make major changes in the direction of their research careers, to enlarge their scientific background, to acquire new research capabilities, or to enlarge their command of an allied research field.

LEGAL BASIS:
Section 472 of the Public Health Service Act as amended (42 U.S.C. 2981-1).

ELIGIBILITY:
Applicants must be citizens, non-citizen nationals or permanent residents of the U.S. at the time of the award. Applicants must be at least seven years beyond the qualifying doctoral degree and have a sponsoring institution and mentor.

GEOG. RESTRICTIONS: United States.

FINANCIAL DATA:
A stipend is provided. Additional funds are available for other training-related expenses.
Amount of support per award: Varies based on experience.
Total amount of support: Varies.

NO. AWARDS: 3.

APPLICATION INFO:
Detailed information can be obtained from the Institute.
Duration: Up to two years.
Deadline: April 8, August 8 and December 8.

ADDRESS INQUIRIES TO:
Leslie Frieden
Extramural Training Officer
(See address above.)

Internal medicine

A.S.P.E.N. RHOADS RESEARCH FOUNDATION
8401 Colesville Road
Suite 510
Silver Spring, MD 20910
(301) 587-6315
Fax: (301) 587-2365
E-mail: aspen@nutritioncare.org
Web Site: www.nutritioncare.org

TYPE:
Research grants. Annual support for nutritional research.

See entry 2191 for full listing.

AMERICAN SOCIETY OF HEMATOLOGY   [2146]
2021 L Street, N.W.
Suite 900
Washington, DC 20036
(202) 776-0544
E-mail: ashabstracts@hematology.org
Web Site: www.hematology.org

AREAS OF INTEREST:
Scientific abstracts.

NAME(S) OF PROGRAMS:
- **Abstract Achievement Award**
- **Outstanding Abstract Achievement Award**

TYPE:
Awards/prizes; Travel grants.

PURPOSE:
To offer need- and merit-based awards to select individuals in order to help defray annual meeting travel expenses.

ELIGIBILITY:
Abstract Achievement Award: Applicants must be undergraduate students, medical students, graduate students, resident physicians, and postdoctoral fellows who are both first author and presenter of an abstract.

Outstanding Abstract Achievement Award: Awards are offered to the first authors/presenters of abstracts that receive the highest score in the categories of undergraduate student, medical student, graduate student, resident physician, and postdoctoral fellow (M.D. or Ph.D.).

FINANCIAL DATA:
Amount of support per award: Abstract Achievement Award: $500; Outstanding Abstract Achievement Award: $2,000.
Total amount of support: Varies.

APPLICATION INFO:
Contact the Society for application procedures.
Duration: One-time award.
Deadline: Early August.

ADDRESS INQUIRIES TO:
Vonnie Calemine
Awards Program Specialist
(See address above.)

AMERICAN SOCIETY OF NEPHROLOGY   [2147]
1510 H Street, N.W.
Suite 800
Washington, DC 20005
(202) 640-4660
Fax: (202) 478-2117
E-mail: grants@asn-online.org
Web Site: www.asn-online.org

AREAS OF INTEREST:
Nephrology.

NAME(S) OF PROGRAMS:
- **William and Sandra Bennett Clinical Scholars Program**
- **OHF - ASN Foundation for Kidney Research Grant**

TYPE:
Project/program grants; Research grants. William and Sandra Bennett Clinical Scholars Program supports aspiring nephrology educators to conduct a project to advance all facets of nephrology education and teaching.

OHF - ASN Foundation for Kidney Research Grant supports research on topics relevant to oxalosis, primary hyperoxaluria and related stone diseases.

PURPOSE:
To enhance and assist the study and practice of nephrology; to provide a forum for the promulgation of research; to meet the professional and continuing education needs of its members.

FINANCIAL DATA:
Amount of support per award: William and Sandra Bennett Clinical Scholars Program: $50,000 annually; OHF - ASN Foundation for Kidney Research Grant: $100,000 annually.

NO. AWARDS: 1 of each award annually.

APPLICATION INFO:
Only online applications will be accepted.
Duration: Two years.
Deadline: Mid-December.

ADDRESS INQUIRIES TO:
E-mail: grants@asn-online.org

AMERICAN SOCIETY OF NEPHROLOGY [2148]

1510 H Street, N.W.
Suite 800
Washington, DC 20005
(202) 640-4660
Fax: (202) 478-2117
E-mail: grants@asn-online.org
Web Site: www.asn-online.org

AREAS OF INTEREST:
Nephrology.

NAME(S) OF PROGRAMS:
- **Carl W. Gottschalk Research Scholar Grant**
- **John Merrill Grant in Transplantation**
- **Norman Siegel Research Scholar Grant**

TYPE:
Research grants. The Gottschalk, Merrill and Siegel Grants are part of the Transition to Independent Grants program.

PURPOSE:
To enhance and assist the study and practice of nephrology; to provide a forum for the promulgation of research; to meet the professional and continuing education needs of its members; to foster the independent careers of young investigators in biomedical research related to nephrology and transplantation.

ELIGIBILITY:
Merrill and Gottschalk Grants: Applicants must be active ASN members and hold an M.D., Ph.D., or equivalent degree. At the time of submission, the applicant's membership must be current and their dues paid. Appointment to full-time faculty must be confirmed in writing by the department chair, indicating the date of first full-time faculty appointment, and providing assurance that the department will provide needed resources for conducting independent research. Additionally, applicants will be considered ineligible should they submit more than one ASN grant application during any particular grants cycle.

GEOG. RESTRICTIONS: North America.

FINANCIAL DATA:
Amount of support per award: $100,000 per year.

APPLICATION INFO:
Only online applications will be accepted.
Duration: Two years.
Deadline: Mid-December.

ADDRESS INQUIRIES TO:
See e-mail address above.

AMERICAN SOCIETY OF NEPHROLOGY [2149]

1510 H Street, N.W.
Suite 800
Washington, DC 20005
(202) 640-4660
Fax: (202) 478-2117
E-mail: grants@asn-online.org
Web Site: www.asn-online.org

AREAS OF INTEREST:
Nephrology.

NAME(S) OF PROGRAMS:
- **ASN Research Fellowships**

TYPE:
Fellowships. ASN Research Fellowships: The Society especially encourages applications from women and members of underrepresented minorities.

PURPOSE:
To fund fellows to conduct original, meritorious research projects, fostering, under the direction of a sponsor, the training of fellows who are highly motivated to make contributions to the understanding of kidney biology and disease.

ELIGIBILITY:
To apply for an ASN Research Fellowship, a candidate:
(1) must hold an M.D., D.O., Ph.D. or the equivalent degree;
(2) may not have completed more than three years of research training after the completion of the M.D. or D.O. degree or equivalent, or one year of postdoctoral research training after the Ph.D. degree (at the time of the activation of the award);
(3) cannot have or have had at any time a faculty position at any academic institution;
(4) must complete research under the direction and mentorship of a sponsor;
(5) must be a member of ASN at the time of the fellowship application; the sponsor of the candidate must also be an ASN member at the time of the fellowship application;
(6) cannot hold another full fellowship award such as another foundation fellowship or grant or a postdoctoral research fellowship from the National Institutes of Health; however, a candidate's institutions may supplement the support provided by ASN;
(7) must be working in North or Central America during the fellowship period and;
(8) must commit a minimum of 75% time to research during the fellowship period.

GEOG. RESTRICTIONS: North America.

FINANCIAL DATA:
Funds must be used for salary support (including fringe benefits) and cannot be used for project costs, travel expenses or overhead costs.
Amount of support per award: $50,000 per year for up to two years.
Total amount of support: Varies.

NO. AWARDS: Approximately 10.

APPLICATION INFO:
Only online applications will be accepted.
Duration: Up to two years. Second-year funding is contingent on a satisfactory progress report.
Deadline: Mid-December.

ADDRESS INQUIRIES TO:
See e-mail address above.

CANCER FEDERATION, INC. [2150]

711 West Ramsey Street
Banning, CA 92220
(951) 849-4325
E-mail: info@cancerfed.org
Web Site: cancerfed.org

FOUNDED: 1977

AREAS OF INTEREST:
Cancer.

TYPE:
Awards/prizes; Research grants; Scholarships; Seed money grants.

YEAR PROGRAM STARTED: 1977

PURPOSE:
To fund research in cancer immunology and scholarships.

LEGAL BASIS:
501(c)(3) tax-exempt.

ELIGIBILITY:
Candidates must major in biology, microbiology, oncology, hematology, psychiatry, psychology or natural sciences.

FINANCIAL DATA:
Total amount of support: Varies.

NO. AWARDS: Varies.

APPLICATION INFO:
Scholar is chosen by institution.
Duration: One year. Renewal possible by reapplication. Scholarships are one-time only.
Deadline: Varies according to sponsoring institution.

PUBLICATIONS:
Challenge, magazine; *CF Newsletter*; *Four Women Against Cancer*; and several others.

IRS I.D.: 95-3133568

ADDRESS INQUIRIES TO:
Lya Cole, Executive Director
P.O. Box 1298
Banning, CA 92220

CHILDREN'S TUMOR FOUNDATION [2151]

370 Lexington Avenue
Suite 2100
New York, NY 10017
(212) 344-6633
Fax: (212) 747-0004
E-mail: slarosa@ctf.org
Web Site: www.ctf.org

AREAS OF INTEREST:
Neurofibromatosis research.

NAME(S) OF PROGRAMS:
- **Clinical Research Awards**
- **Drug Discovery Initiative Registered Reports (DDI-RR)**
- **NF Clinic Network (CTF-NFCN)**
- **Young Investigator Awards**

TYPE:
Conferences/seminars; Research grants; Seed money grants; Travel grants; Research contracts. Clinic support grants.

PURPOSE:
To improve the health and well-being of individuals and families affected by neurofibromatosis.

ELIGIBILITY:
Clinical Research Award: Preclinical/clinical collaborative studies, pilot clinical trials, and clinical enabling studies are considered for support.

Drug Discovery Initiative Registered Reports: Applicants should have an M.D., Ph.D., or equivalent degree and access to all resources needed. Applicants from academia and the private sector are welcome, and partnerships between the two are encouraged.
Applications are welcomed from all qualified individuals worldwide.

NF Clinic Network: Any clinic in the U.S. that sees NF patients may apply to be a CTF-NFCN Affiliate Clinic.

Young Investigator Award: Open to graduate students, postdoctoral fellows and young investigators no more than seven years past completion of their M.D./Ph.D. training. The Investigator can be a graduate student or postdoctoral fellow associated with the laboratory of a more senior researcher, who acts as the research sponsor.

FINANCIAL DATA:
   Amount of support per award: Clinical Research Award: Up to $150,000; Drug Discovery Initiative Registered Reports: Up to $85,000 for in vivo studies and up to $40,000 for in vitro studies; NF Clinic Network: Up to $6,000 per year; Young Investigator Award: Commensurate with experience.

   Total amount of support: Young Investigator Award: $64,000 to $110,000.

NO. MOST RECENT APPLICANTS: Clinical Research Award: 10; Drug Discovery Initiative Registered Reports: 10 to 15; NF Clinic Network: Approximately 50 annually; Young Investigator Award: Approximately 25.

NO. AWARDS: Clinical Research Award: 2; Drug Discovery Initiative Registered Reports: 3; Young Investigator Award: 5.

APPLICATION INFO:
   Application information is available on the web site. Applications may be submitted online.

   Clinical Research Award: Letter of Inquiry required. Based on review, applicant may be invited to submit full application.

   Duration: Clinical Research Award: 18 to 24 months; Drug Discovery Initiative and NF Clinic Network: One year; Young Investigator Award: Up to two years.

   Deadline: Drug Discovery Initiative Registered Reports: September to October. NF Clinic Network: October. Young Investigator Award: January to February.

IRS I.D.: 13-2298956

STAFF:
   Vidya Browder, Basic Science Senior Manager

ADDRESS INQUIRIES TO:
   Salvatore La Rosa
   Chief Scientific Officer
   (See address above.)

CYSTIC FIBROSIS CANADA   [2152]
2323 Yonge Street
Suite 800
Toronto ON M4P 2C9 Canada
(416) 485-9149
(800) 378-2233 (Canada only)
E-mail: research@cysticfibrosis.ca
Web Site: www.cysticfibrosis.ca

FOUNDED: 1960

AREAS OF INTEREST:
   Cystic fibrosis.

NAME(S) OF PROGRAMS:
   ● **Early Career Investigator**

TYPE:
   Awards/prizes; Fellowships; General operating grants; Grants-in-aid; Research grants; Training grants; Travel grants. Studentships; Summer studentships.

   A limited number of competitive fellowships are offered by the Organization each year for basic or clinical research training in areas of the biomedical or behavioral sciences pertinent to cystic fibrosis.

   Research grants are intended to facilitate the scientific investigation of all aspects of cystic fibrosis.

Early Career Investigator awards provide salary support for a limited number of exceptional investigators, offering them an opportunity to develop outstanding cystic fibrosis research programs, unhampered by heavy teaching or clinical loads.

   A limited number of competitive studentships are offered by the Organization each year to: (1) highly qualified graduate students who are registered for a higher degree, and who are undertaking full-time research training in areas of the biomedical or behavioral sciences relevant to cystic fibrosis or; (2) highly qualified students who are registered in a joint M.D./M.Sc. or M.D./Ph.D. program.

YEAR PROGRAM STARTED: 1961

PURPOSE:
   To further research on cystic fibrosis.

LEGAL BASIS:
   Nonprofit organization.

ELIGIBILITY:
   Requirements for Early Career Investigator awards, fellowships, research grants and studentships are available on the web site.

GEOG. RESTRICTIONS: Canada.

FINANCIAL DATA:
   Fellowship and Studentship awards follow prevailing Canadian rates.

   Amount of support per award: Varies.

   Total amount of support: Varies.

CO-OP FUNDING PROGRAMS: CIHR Partnerships, CFC-SMH Adult CF Research Chair.

APPLICATION INFO:
   Forms are available online.
   Duration: Varies.
   Deadline: Varies.

PUBLICATIONS:
   Annual report; *Grants and Awards Guide*, English/French booklet; application guidelines.

ADDRESS INQUIRIES TO:
   See e-mail address above.

CYSTIC FIBROSIS CANADA   [2153]
2323 Yonge Street
Suite 800
Toronto ON M4P 2C9 Canada
(416) 485-9149
(800) 378-2233 (Canada only)
Fax: (416) 485-0960
E-mail: info@cysticfibrosis.ca
Web Site: www.cysticfibrosis.ca

FOUNDED: 1960

AREAS OF INTEREST:
   Cystic fibrosis.

NAME(S) OF PROGRAMS:
   ● **Clinic Incentive Grants**

TYPE:
   Grants-in-aid; Seed money grants. Clinic Incentive Grants are intended to enhance the standard of clinical care available to Canadians with cystic fibrosis, by providing funds to initiate a comprehensive program for cystic fibrosis patient care, research and teaching, or to strengthen an existing program.

YEAR PROGRAM STARTED: 1961

PURPOSE:
   To help establish a comprehensive program for patient care, research, and teaching in cystic fibrosis.

LEGAL BASIS:
   Nonprofit organization.

ELIGIBILITY:
   Grants may be made to medical schools or hospitals in Canada. Program potential, regional need, relative need of the institution for assistance and special medical and technical advantages will be considered.

GEOG. RESTRICTIONS: Canada.

FINANCIAL DATA:
   Grant payments will be made at the beginning of each quarter. Limited funding is available for related travel.

   Amount of support per award: Varies.

   Total amount of support: Varies.

NO. MOST RECENT APPLICANTS: 42.

NO. AWARDS: 42.

APPLICATION INFO:
   Application information is available on the web site.

   Duration: One year. Grants are to be renegotiated annually.

   Deadline: October 1.

ADDRESS INQUIRIES TO:
   Ian D. McIntosh
   Director, Healthcare
   (See address above.)

HISTIOCYTOSIS ASSOCIATION   [2154]
332 North Broadway
Pitman, NJ 08071
(856) 589-6606
Fax: (856) 589-6614
E-mail: grants@histio.org
Web Site: www.histio.org

FOUNDED: 1986

AREAS OF INTEREST:
   Histiocytosis, hemophagocytic lymphohistiocytosis, Langerhans cell histiocytosis, and histiocytic disorders.

NAME(S) OF PROGRAMS:
   ● **Research Grant Program**

TYPE:
   Project/program grants; Research grants; Seed money grants.

YEAR PROGRAM STARTED: 1989

PURPOSE:
   To fund worthy scientific research projects; to educate physicians and scientists; to encourage and support symposia into histiocytic disorders; to directly participate in research projects; to encourage publication of scientific information.

ELIGIBILITY:
   Applicants must be full-time faculty members at an academic institution.

FINANCIAL DATA:
   Amount of support per award: Up to $50,000 for one-year grants.

   Total amount of support: Varies.

NO. MOST RECENT APPLICANTS: 25.

NO. AWARDS: 6.

APPLICATION INFO:
   Application must be submitted online.
   Duration: Up to one year.
   Deadline: July 1.

IRS I.D.: 22-2827069

EXECUTIVE DIRECTOR:
Deanna Fournier

ADDRESS INQUIRIES TO:
Heather Fullerton
Research Grants Director
(See address above.)

THE LEUKEMIA & LYMPHOMA SOCIETY [2155]

3 International Drive
Suite 200
Rye Brook, NY 10573
(914) 949-5213
E-mail: James.Kasper@lls.org
researchprograms@lls.org
Web Site: www.lls.org

AREAS OF INTEREST:
Medicinal chemistry and/or drug target screening in hematological malignancies.

NAME(S) OF PROGRAMS:
● **Screen to Lead Program (SLP)**

TYPE:
Research grants. Research grant is for new laboratories/projects to participate in a model of collaboration whereby the Society, grantee, sponsoring institution and appropriate contract service organizations (CROs) or core facilities at academic institutions work together to develop compounds with the potential to change the standard of care for patients with blood cancer.

PURPOSE:
To provide drug discovery support specifically directed towards medicinal chemistry and/or drug target screening in hematological malignancies.

ELIGIBILITY:
Investigators at academic laboratories are eligible to apply. Projects previously funded through SLP are ineligible to apply. Investigators must demonstrate that their research environment is equipped and suitable for aspects of the work plan that would be carried out at their institution rather than at a CRO. Collaborations between multiple investigators to strengthen the work proposed will be considered favorably but are not a requirement. Applicants need not be U.S. citizens nor associated with a U.S.-based institution. Applicants should hold a Ph.D., M.D., D.V.M. or equivalent degree.

FINANCIAL DATA:
The budget ceiling includes all costs associated with the grant including CRO and indirects. For any budgeted line items that are specifically related to the Principal Investigator, for work conducted in their laboratory, indirect costs will be capped at 11.1%.
Amount of support per award: Up to $1,000,000 for the two years of the grant.

APPLICATION INFO:
Application may be obtained at the following web site: lls.fluxx.io under Screen to Lead Program.
Duration: One to two years. Second-year funding is contingent on demonstrating suitable progress toward the aims of the proposal, at the sole discretion of the Society.

ADDRESS INQUIRIES TO:
James Kasper, Senior Director
(See e-mail address above.)

*PLEASE NOTE:
This program is not offered on a regular basis.

THE LEUKEMIA & LYMPHOMA SOCIETY [2156]

3 International Drive
Suite 200
Rye Brook, NY 10573
(914) 821-8301
(914) 949-5213
E-mail: researchprograms@lls.org
Web Site: www.lls.org

AREAS OF INTEREST:
Leukemia, lymphoma and myeloma.

NAME(S) OF PROGRAMS:
● **Career Development Program**

TYPE:
Fellowships; Research grants; Scholarships. The Career Development Program provides awards intended to meet the specific needs of investigators at different stages of their research careers. The five awards, Fellow, Scholar, Scholar in Clinical Research, Special Fellow and Special Fellow in Clinical Research, provide stipends to investigators, allowing them to devote themselves to researching questions of direct relevance to hematological malignancies and/or relevant pre-malignant conditions.

YEAR PROGRAM STARTED: 1949

PURPOSE:
To cure leukemia, lymphoma, Hodgkin's disease and myeloma; to improve the quality of life of patients and their families; to support individuals pursuing careers in basic or clinical research in leukemia, lymphoma and myeloma.

ELIGIBILITY:
Qualified investigators affiliated with appropriate institutions are eligible to apply. Applicants must have the approval of the institution and recommendation of the department head where the research training will be conducted. Ph.D. or M.D. status is required.

FINANCIAL DATA:
Amount of support per award: Fellows: $60,000 per year; Scholars: $120,000; Scholars in Clinical Research: $125,000 per year; Special Fellows and Special Fellows in Clinical Research: $67,000 per year.

APPLICATION INFO:
The Society uses its own research portal for preliminary and full application submission. First-time users must register by sending an e-mail to the address listed above.
Duration: Renewable for up to five years at the level of Scholar and three years at the level of Special Fellow and Fellow.
Deadline: Eligibility: September 1. Abstracts: September 13. Reference Letters and Full Application: September 27.

ADDRESS INQUIRIES TO:
Senior Director of Research Administration
(See address above.)

THE LEUKEMIA & LYMPHOMA SOCIETY [2157]

3 International Drive
Suite 200
Rye Brook, NY 10573
(914) 821-8301
(914) 949-5213
E-mail: researchprograms@lls.org
Web Site: www.lls.org

AREAS OF INTEREST:
Leukemia, lymphoma and myeloma.

NAME(S) OF PROGRAMS:
● **Translational Research Program**

TYPE:
Research grants. Translational Research Program is intended to encourage and provide support for new and novel clinical research. The goal of the program is to accelerate transfer of findings from the laboratory to clinical application.

YEAR PROGRAM STARTED: 1996

PURPOSE:
To encourage and provide early-stage support for clinical research in leukemia, lymphoma, and myeloma, with the intention of developing innovative approaches to treatment, diagnosis or prevention; to support projects that translate laboratory findings to clinical application.

ELIGIBILITY:
Ph.D., M.D., or D.V.M. status is required. Candidates must be affiliated with a nonfederal public or private nonprofit institution engaged in cancer-related research.

FINANCIAL DATA:
Amount of support per award: $250,000 annually.

APPLICATION INFO:
Guidelines are available on the web site.
Duration: Three years. In special cases these may be renewed for two years.
Deadline: Letter of intent: August 31. Full application: October 31.

ADDRESS INQUIRIES TO:
See e-mail address above.

THE LEUKEMIA & LYMPHOMA SOCIETY [2158]

3 International Drive
Suite 200
Rye Brook, NY 10573
(914) 821-8301
(914) 949-5213
E-mail: researchprograms@lls.org
Web Site: www.lls.org

AREAS OF INTEREST:
Leukemia, lymphoma, Hodgkin's disease and myeloma.

NAME(S) OF PROGRAMS:
● **Specialized Center of Research Program**

TYPE:
Research grants. The core program intends to bring together distinguished investigators from one or several institutions to develop a focused research center, foster new interactions and cooperation, and enhance disciplinary research among the participants to understand the causes of hematological malignancies and ultimately develop effective treatments for cancer patients.

PURPOSE:
To support research programs that are focused on any aspect of leukemia, lymphoma, Hodgkin's disease and myeloma in order to foster interactions, cooperation, and to enhance interdisciplinary research among the participants.

ELIGIBILITY:
Applications may be submitted by individuals holding an M.D., Ph.D., D.V.M.or equivalent degree, working in domestic or foreign nonprofit organizations, such as universities, colleges, hospitals or laboratories.

Applications may be multi-institutional in nature. Applicants need not be U.S. citizens, and there are no restrictions on applicant age, race, gender or creed.

FINANCIAL DATA:
Expenses for administrative staff (including secretarial) costs cannot exceed one full-time equivalent for the Center per year. The aggregate of office supplies and telephone costs cannot exceed $6,000 per year for the Center.

Amount of support per award: Up to $1,000,000 annually.

APPLICATION INFO:
Guidelines are available on the web site.

Duration: Five years.

Deadline: Letter of Intent: October 1. Notification sent to those selected for full application submission by December 31. Application: March 15.

ADDRESS INQUIRIES TO:
See e-mail address above.

LYMPHOMA RESEARCH FOUNDATION   [2159]
Wall Street Plaza
88 Pine Street, Suite 2400
New York, NY 10005
(212) 349-2910
Fax: (212) 349-2886
E-mail: researchgrants@lymphoma.org
Web Site: lymphoma.org/grants

FOUNDED: 2001

AREAS OF INTEREST:
Lymphoma research.

CONSULTING OR VOLUNTEER SERVICES:
The LRF Ambassador program is comprised of individuals from around the country, each with a personal lymphoma story. The ambassadors represent several subtypes and treatment options for the disease. The group includes current patients, caregivers of patients and survivors. Ambassadors are able to share their individual stories and experiences navigating this diagnosis.

The LRF Advocacy Program offers volunteers a variety of opportunities, including attending in-person meetings with members of Congress and submitting letters to the editor and op-eds which cover issues important to the lymphoma community.

NAME(S) OF PROGRAMS:
● **Clinical Investigator Career Development Awards (CDA)**
● **Disease Focus Area Grants for Senior Investigators**
● **LRF Scientific Research Mentoring Program (LSRMP)**
● **Postdoctoral Fellowship Grants**

TYPE:
Fellowships; Research grants; Training grants.

YEAR PROGRAM STARTED: 1992

PURPOSE:
To support innovative lymphoma research in keeping with the Foundation's mission to eradicate lymphoma and serve those touched by this disease.

LEGAL BASIS:
Nonprofit organization.

ELIGIBILITY:
CDA: Advanced fellows or junior faculty with at least two years fellow/postdoctoral

experience and no more than five years beyond completion of fellowship/postdoctoral; 35 to 50% protected time for research; must be licensed physicians at a nonprofit clinical research institution.

Disease Focus Area Grants: Open to licensed senior researchers (usually Assistant, Associate or Full Professor or their equivalent) at accredited, nonprofit research institutions; other restrictions vary by individual RFP.

LSRMP Clinical Track: Applicant must hold an M.D. or equivalent degree within at least the second year of the fellowship or no more than four years in their first faculty position. LSRMP Translational Track: Applicant must hold a Ph.D. or equivalent degree with no more than seven years of postdoctoral work or no more than four years in instructor level position, or M.D. or equivalent in at least the second year of clinical fellowship or no more than four years in instructor level position.

Postdoctoral Fellowship Grants: Advanced clinical fellows or those with postdoctoral experience (with no more than five years fellow/postdoctoral experience). M.D. applicants must have completed at least two years of clinical fellowship work. Faculty are not eligible for this grant.

CDA, LSRMP and Postdoctoral Fellowship Grants are limited to applicants based at institutions in the U.S. or Canada for the duration of the grant. Citizenship is not required. For other programs, refer to RFP.

FINANCIAL DATA:
Amount of support per award: CDA: $225,000 total over three years, salary support and professional development expenses; Disease Focus Area Grants: Research expenses (personnel and nonpersonnel) vary by RFP; LSRMP: $10,000 total professional development expenses over two years plus travel to LSRMP workshops; Postdoctoral Fellowship Grants: $105,000 total over two years, salary support and professional development expenses.

Total amount of support: Varies.

NO. MOST RECENT APPLICANTS: 38.

NO. AWARDS: 16 grants in fiscal year 2020.

REPRESENTATIVE AWARDS:
$225,000 CDA to Anita Kumar, M.D., Memorial Sloan Kettering Cancer Center for "A Multicenter Phase I Study of Ibrutinib in Relapsed and Refractory T-cell Lymphoma;" $105,000 Fellowship to Andrea Rabellino, Ph.D., University of Texas - Southwestern Medical Center for "Role of PIAS1 in c-MYC-driven lymphomagenesis;" $100,000 Disease Focus Area Grant (in Adolescent/Young Adult Lymphoma Correlative Studies) to David Scott, M.D., MBChB of British Columbia Cancer Agency for "Biomarkers predicting early treatment response in advanced stage classical Hodgkin lymphoma."

APPLICATION INFO:
Application information is available online.

Duration: CDA: Three years. Disease Focus Area Grants: Varies by RFP (usually two to three years). LSRMP and Postdoctoral Fellowship Grants: Two years.

Deadline: CDA, Postdoctoral Fellowship Grants and LSRMP generally opens early June and closes early September. Disease Focus Area Grants: Varies by RFP.

IRS I.D.: 95-4335088

ADDRESS INQUIRIES TO:
Whitney Steen
(See e-mail address above.)

NATIONAL HEADACHE FOUNDATION   [2160]
820 North Orleans, Suite 201
Chicago, IL 60610-3132
(312) 274-2650
(888) 643-5552
Fax: (312) 640-9049
E-mail: info@headaches.org
Web Site: www.headaches.org

FOUNDED: 1970

AREAS OF INTEREST:
Headache and pain.

TYPE:
Research grants. Support for research in the field of headache and pain.

YEAR PROGRAM STARTED: 1970

PURPOSE:
To enhance the health care of individuals with headache; to provide a source of help to families, physicians and allied health care professionals who treat them, and to the public; to provide educational and informational resources, supporting headache research, and advocating for the understanding of headache as a legitimate neurobiological disease.

LEGAL BASIS:
Nonprofit organization.

ELIGIBILITY:
Investigators from departments of neurology and pharmacology are invited to apply. Submissions from other departments and individual investigators are also welcome. No funding for overhead, salaries, rent or indirect expenses. Grants may be used for data analysis, interpretation, reading of results, etc.

GEOG. RESTRICTIONS: United States.

FINANCIAL DATA:
Full or partial funding may be granted.
Amount of support per award: Varies depending on project.

NO. MOST RECENT APPLICANTS: Approximately 9.

NO. AWARDS: Approximately 2 when funding available.

APPLICATION INFO:
Applicants must submit abstract of research proposal on Foundation form as well as protocol and proposed budget. Proposed projects will be evaluated at the winter board meeting of the NHF.
Duration: One year.
Deadline: Varies.

PUBLICATIONS:
Program announcement.

ADDRESS INQUIRIES TO:
Mary A. Franklin, Executive Director
(See address above.)

NATIONAL HEART, LUNG AND BLOOD INSTITUTE (NHLBI) [2161]

Two Rockledge Center, Suite 9030
6701 Rockledge Drive, MSC 7950
Bethesda, MD 20892-7950
(301) 435-0080
Fax: (301) 480-0867
E-mail: hootswk@mail.nih.gov
Web Site: www.nhlbi.nih.gov

FOUNDED: 1948

AREAS OF INTEREST:
Research on the causes, prevention, and treatment of nonmalignant blood diseases, including anemias, sickle cell disease, and thalassemia; premalignant processes such as myelodysplasia and myeloproliferative disorders; hemophilia and other abnormalities of hemostasis and thrombosis; and immune dysfunction.

NAME(S) OF PROGRAMS:
● **Blood Diseases and Resources Research**

TYPE:
Conferences/seminars; Demonstration grants; Fellowships; Grants-in-aid; Project/program grants; Training grants; Research contracts. Funding encompasses a broad spectrum of research ranging from basic biology to medical management of blood diseases.

YEAR PROGRAM STARTED: 1972

PURPOSE:
To develop programs that will reduce the morbidity and mortality caused by blood diseases, lead to the primary prevention of these diseases and ensure the availability of adequate supplies of safe and efficacious blood products.

LEGAL BASIS:
Public Health Service Act, Section 301(e) and Section 412; Public Law 78-410, as amended; 42 U.S.C. 241; 42 U.S.C. 287a; Public Health Service Act, Section 472; Public Law 78-410, as amended; 42 U.S.C. 289 1-1.

ELIGIBILITY:
Any nonprofit organization engaged in biomedical research and institutions (or companies) organized for profit may apply for grants with the exception of National Research Service Awards. Only citizens and noncitizen nationals are eligible for support by research training and career development programs. Other mechanisms are not restricted.

FINANCIAL DATA:
Grants may support salaries, equipment, supplies, travel and patient hospitalization as required to perform the research effort.

Amount of support per award: Varies by the type of grant.

APPLICATION INFO:
Application information is available on the web site.
Duration: One to five years. Renewable through reapplication.
Deadline: Varies.

PUBLICATIONS:
Annual report.

DIRECTORS:
W. Keith Hoots, M.D., Director
Donna DiMichele, M.D., Deputy Director

RESEARCH STAFF:
Simone Glynn, M.D., M.Sc., M.P.H., Branch Chief, Blood Epidemiology and Clinical Therapeutics Branch
Traci Mondoro, Ph.D., Branch Chief, Translational Blood Science and Resources Branch
Yu-Chung Yang, Ph.D., Branch Chief, Molecular, Cellular and Systems Blood Science Branch

ADDRESS INQUIRIES TO:
Division of Blood Diseases and Resources
(See address above.)

Cardiovascular and pulmonary

AMERICAN COLLEGE OF CARDIOLOGY [2162]

2400 N Street, N.W.
Washington, DC 20037
(202) 375-6000
Fax: (202) 375-7000
E-mail: resource@acc.org
Web Site: www.acc.org

AREAS OF INTEREST:
Cardiology.

NAME(S) OF PROGRAMS:
● **ACCF/Merck Research Fellowships in Cardiovascular Disease**

TYPE:
Awards/prizes; Development grants; Endowments; Fellowships; Internships; Project/program grants; Research grants; Scholarships; Seed money grants; Technical assistance; Training grants; Travel grants; Visiting scholars; Work-study programs; Research contracts.

PURPOSE:
To advance research in cardiovascular disease.

ELIGIBILITY:
Anyone currently in an adult cardiology fellowship training program recognized by the Accreditation Council for Graduate Medical Education or the American Osteopathic Association and who has the recommendation and agreement of their training program director and institution is eligible to apply. Preference is given to individuals who have had no more than two years of prior full-time experience either in clinical or basic research.

GEOG. RESTRICTIONS: United States and Canada.

FINANCIAL DATA:
Fellowships must be used only for salary support.

Amount of support per award: $70,000.

NO. MOST RECENT APPLICANTS: 30.

NO. AWARDS: 2.

APPLICATION INFO:
Guidelines and application form are available online.
Duration: One year.
Deadline: September.

AMERICAN COLLEGE OF CARDIOLOGY [2163]

2400 N Street, N.W.
Washington, DC 20037
(202) 375-6000 ext. 6390
Fax: (202) 375-6842
E-mail: kroberts@acc.org
Web Site: www.acc.org

AREAS OF INTEREST:
Cardiology.

NAME(S) OF PROGRAMS:
● **ACC Young Investigators Awards Competition**

TYPE:
Awards/prizes. Awarded in three categories:
(1) Clinical Investigations;
(2) Basic and Translational Sciences and;
(3) Outcomes Research.

PURPOSE:
To encourage and recognize young scientific investigators of promise.

ELIGIBILITY:
Any physician or scientist presently in a residency or fellowship training program or who has been in such a program within the past three years, medical students, and Ph.D. candidates are eligible to apply.

FINANCIAL DATA:
Each candidate receives up to $1,500 reimbursement for travel to attend the annual meeting.
Amount of support per award: First Place: $2,000; Second Place: $1,000; Honorable Mention: $500.

NO. MOST RECENT APPLICANTS: 150.

NO. AWARDS: 18 awards; 6 awards per category.

APPLICATION INFO:
Guidelines and application form are available online.
Deadline: September.

ADDRESS INQUIRIES TO:
Kristen Robertson, Director
(See address above.)

AMERICAN COLLEGE OF CARDIOLOGY [2164]

2400 N Street, N.W.
Washington, DC 20037
(202) 375-6000
Fax: (202) 375-7000
E-mail: resource@acc.org
Web Site: www.acc.org

AREAS OF INTEREST:
Cardiology.

NAME(S) OF PROGRAMS:
● **ACCF/William F. Keating, Esq. Endowment Award for Hypertension and Peripheral Vascular Disease**

TYPE:
Awards/prizes; Research grants. This is a career development award.

PURPOSE:
To recognize and provide financial support for research efforts by outstanding young cardiovascular scholars; to encourage junior faculty in the early phases of their careers in the field of cardiology.

ELIGIBILITY:
The award recipient must meet the following qualifications:
(1) hold the rank of instructor or assistant professor at the time of the initiation of the award and have completed adult, pediatric, surgical cardiology fellowship training in a program approved by the Accreditation Council for Graduate Medical Education or the American Osteopathic Association;
(2) be a member or be eligible to become a member of the American College of Cardiology (ACC);
(3) be no more than five years out of training;
(4) have the recommendation and agreement of his or her division chief and his or her chief's assurance that the award's support will provide protected time for the applicant to pursue his or her research program and;
(5) have an agreement with his or her institution that the full amount of the award will be designated for the salary support.

GEOG. RESTRICTIONS: United States and Canada.

FINANCIAL DATA:
Award funds can only be used for salary support. They cannot be used for any institutional or indirect costs.
Amount of support per award: $70,000.

NO. MOST RECENT APPLICANTS: 20.

NO. AWARDS: 1 per year.

APPLICATION INFO:
Guidelines and application form are available online.
Duration: One year, beginning July 1 through June 30.
Deadline: September.

AMERICAN HEART ASSOCIATION   [2165]
AHA National Center
7272 Greenville Avenue
Dallas, TX 75231-4596
(214) 360-6107
E-mail: apply@heart.org
Web Site: professional.heart.org

FOUNDED: 1948

AREAS OF INTEREST:
All basic, clinical, translational, behavioral and population research broadly related to cardiovascular function and disease and stroke, or to related clinical, behavioral, basic science, bioengineering or biotechnology, and public health problems.

NAME(S) OF PROGRAMS:
● **Postdoctoral Fellowship**

TYPE:
Fellowships. Recognizing the unique challenges that clinicians, in particular, experience in balancing research and clinical activity, this award aims to be as flexible as possible to enable applicants to develop academic careers in research alongside fulfilling clinical service commitments.

PURPOSE:
To enhance the integrated research and clinical training of postdoctoral applicants who are not yet independent.

LEGAL BASIS:
Research association.

ELIGIBILITY:
Applicant must be an AHA Professional Member. Awards are open to the array of academic and health professionals. This includes, but is not limited to, all academic disciplines (biology, chemistry, mathematics, technology, physics, etc.) and all health-related professions (physicians, nurses, nurse practitioners, pharmacists, dentists, physical and occupational therapists, statisticians, nutritionists, etc.). Clinical, translational, population, and basic scientists are encouraged to apply.

AHA strongly encourages applications by women, underrepresented minorities in the sciences, and those who have experienced varied and nontraditional career trajectories.

At the time of award activation the candidate must:
(1) be a U.S. citizen, permanent resident, pending permanent resident, or have an E-3, F-1, H1-B, J-1, O-1, TN or G-4 visa;
(2) hold a post-Baccalaureate Ph.D degree or equivalant;
(3) have no more than five years of postdoctoral research training or experience and;
(4) not be pursuing a doctoral degree.

A postdoctoral fellowship applicant who is outside the U.S. at the time of application must provide visa documentation prior to award activation. Funding is prohibited for awards at non-U.S. institutions.

GEOG. RESTRICTIONS: United States.

FINANCIAL DATA:
Amount of support per award: Varies per initiative for each geographical area and years of experience.

APPLICATION INFO:
Guidelines and application form are available on the web site.
Duration: One or two years. May apply for second two-year award.
Deadline: July 12.

ADDRESS INQUIRIES TO:
See e-mail address above.

AMERICAN HEART ASSOCIATION   [2166]
AHA National Center
7272 Greenville Avenue
Dallas, TX 75231-4596
(214) 360-6107
E-mail: apply@heart.org
Web Site: professional.heart.org

FOUNDED: 1948

AREAS OF INTEREST:
Research broadly related to cardiovascular function and disease and stroke, or to related clinical, basic science, bioengineering or biotechnology, and public health problems, including multidisciplinary efforts.

NAME(S) OF PROGRAMS:
● **Predoctoral Fellowship**

TYPE:
Fellowships.

PURPOSE:
To enhance the integrated research and clinical training of promising students who are matriculated in predoctoral or clinical health professional degree training programs

and who intend careers as scientists, physicians-scientists or other clinician-scientists, or related careers aimed at improving global cardiovascular health.

LEGAL BASIS:
Research association.

ELIGIBILITY:
Applicant must be an AHA Professional Member. Proposals are encouraged from all basic, behavioral, epidemiological, and community and clinical investigations that bear on cardiovascular and stroke problems. Applicants must meet the following criteria:
(1) be a U.S. citizen, permanent resident, pending permanent resident, or have an E-3, F-1, H1-B, J-1, O-1, TN or G-4 visa;
(2) be post-Baccalaureate, predoctoral M.D., Ph.D., D.O., D.V.M. (or equivalent) student seeking research training with a sponsor/mentor prior to embarking on a research career and;
(3) be a full-time student working toward their degree.

GEOG. RESTRICTIONS: United States.

FINANCIAL DATA:
Amount of support per award: Stipend of $23,844, plus $1,000 per year for health insurance and $2,000 project support.

APPLICATION INFO:
Guidelines and application form are available on the web site.
Duration: One or two years.
Deadline: July 11.

ADDRESS INQUIRIES TO:
See e-mail address above.

AMERICAN HEART ASSOCIATION   [2167]
AHA National Center
7272 Greenville Avenue
Dallas, TX 75231-4596
(214) 360-6107
E-mail: apply@heart.org
Web Site: professional.heart.org

FOUNDED: 1948

AREAS OF INTEREST:
Research broadly related to cardiovascular function and disease and stroke, or to related clinical, basic science, bioengineering or biotechnology, and public health problems, including multidisciplinary efforts.

NAME(S) OF PROGRAMS:
● **Transformational Project Award**

TYPE:
Awards/prizes; Project/program grants.

PURPOSE:
To support independent investigators with innovative and advanced projects related to cardiovascular disease and stroke.

LEGAL BASIS:
Research association.

ELIGIBILITY:
Applicant must be an AHA Professional Member. Proposals are encouraged from all basic disciplines, as well as epidemiological, behavioral, community and clinical investigations that bear on cardiovascular and stroke problems.

At the time of application, the applicant must be a U.S. citizen, permanent resident, pending permanent resident or hold these visas: E-3, H1-B, J-1, O-1, TN or G-4.

At the time of activation, the candidate must hold a post-baccalaureate Ph.D. degree or equivalent, or a doctoral-level clinical degree, such as M.D., D.O., D.V.M., Pharm.D., or Ph.D. in nursing, public health, or other clinical health science.

No limit is placed on eligibility based on career state, academic rank or discipline. Evidence of employment at a qualified institution is required.

While no minimum percent effort is specified, the principal investigator must demonstrate that adequate time will be devoted to ensuring successful completion of the proposed project.

GEOG. RESTRICTIONS: United States.

FINANCIAL DATA:
Amount of support per award: $100,000 (including 10% indirect costs) per year.

APPLICATION INFO:
Guidelines and application form are available on the web site.
Duration: Three years.
Deadline: January 23.

ADDRESS INQUIRIES TO:
See e-mail address above.

AMERICAN HEART ASSOCIATION [2168]

AHA National Center
7272 Greenville Avenue
Dallas, TX 75231-4596
(214) 360-6107
E-mail: apply@heart.org
Web Site: professional.heart.org

FOUNDED: 1948

AREAS OF INTEREST:
Research broadly related to cardiovascular function and disease and stroke, or to related clinical, basic science, bioengineering or biotechnology, and public health problems, including multidisciplinary efforts.

NAME(S) OF PROGRAMS:
● **Innovative Project Award**

TYPE:
Research grants. Program funds ideas that may introduce new paradigms, challenge current paradigms, look at existing problems from new perspectives, or exhibit other uniquely creative qualities.

PURPOSE:
To support highly innovative, high-impact research that could ultimately lead to critical discoveries or major advancements that will accelerate the field of cardiovascular and stroke research.

LEGAL BASIS:
Research association.

ELIGIBILITY:
Applicant must be an AHA Professional Member. Proposals are encouraged from all basic, behavioral, epidemiological, and community and clinical investigations that bear on cardiovascular and stroke problems. At the time of application, the applicant must:
(1) hold a post-Baccalaureate Ph.D. degree or equivalent, or a doctoral-level clinical degree, such as M.D., D.O., D.V.M., Pharm.D., or Ph.D. in nursing, public health, or clinical health science and;
(2) be a U.S. citizen, permanent resident,

pending permanent resident, or have one of the following visas: E-3, H-1B, J-1, O-1, TN or G-4.

There is no limit on eligibility based on career stage, academic rank or discipline.

While no minimum percent effort is specified, the principal investigator must demonstrate that adequate time will be devoted to ensuring successful completion of the proposed project.

FINANCIAL DATA:
Amount of support per award: $100,000 per year (including 10% indirect costs).

APPLICATION INFO:
Guidelines and application form are available on the web site.
Duration: Two years.
Deadline: Letter of Intent: October 29.
Invited Proposal: January 17.

ADDRESS INQUIRIES TO:
See e-mail address above.

AMERICAN HEART ASSOCIATION [2169]

AHA National Center
7272 Greenville Avenue
Dallas, TX 75231-4596
(214) 360-6107
E-mail: apply@heart.org
Web Site: professional.heart.org

FOUNDED: 1948

AREAS OF INTEREST:
Research broadly related to cardiovascular function and disease and stroke, or to related clinical, translational, population or basic science, bioengineering or biotechnology, and public health problems, including multidisciplinary efforts.

NAME(S) OF PROGRAMS:
● **Established Investigator Award**

TYPE:
Research grants. Candidates for this award have a demonstrated commitment to cardiovascular or cerebrovascular science as indicated by prior publication history and scientific accomplishments. A candidate's career is expected to be in a rapid growth phase.

PURPOSE:
To support midcareer investigators with unusual promise and an established record of accomplishments.

LEGAL BASIS:
Research association.

ELIGIBILITY:
Applicant must be an AHA Professional Member. Proposals are encouraged from all basic disciplines as well as epidemiological, behavioral, community and clinical investigations that bear on cardiovascular and stroke problems.

At the time of application, the applicant must:
(1) have an M.D., Ph.D., D.O. or equivalent doctoral degree;
(2) be a faculty/staff member;
(3) have current national-level funding as a principal investigator (or co-PI) on an R01 grant or its equivalent and;
(4) be a U.S. citizen, permanent resident, pending permanent resident, or have an H1-B, J-1, O-1, TN or E3 visa.

At the time of award activation, the applicant must be at least four years, but no more than nine years, since the first faculty/staff appointment at the assistant professor level or equivalent (including, but not limited to, research assistant professor, research scientist, staff scientist, etc.). Instructor positions (or equivalent positions) do not count toward the four or nine years of eligibility.

FINANCIAL DATA:
Amount of support per award: $80,000 per year (including up to 10% indirect costs).

APPLICATION INFO:
Applicant must submit a Letter of Intent no more than three pages. AHA will contact applicants with the highest-rated LOIs and invite them to submit a full application. The LOI should briefly address the investigator's competitiveness in terms of:
(1) demonstrated commitment to cardiovascular or cerebrovascular diseases, and scientific innovation;
(2) independence as assessed by publications, research funding, and impact of scientific work as a principal investigator and;
(3) how the award will enhance the investigator's rapid growth phase.

In addition to the Letter of Intent, applicant must identify and list their 15 best papers (limited to two pages) and submit a biosketch (limited to five pages).

No reference letters are to be supplied with the initial LOI. Three references will be required from those selected to submit a full application.
Duration: Five years. No renewals.
Deadline: January 15.

ADDRESS INQUIRIES TO:
See e-mail address above.

AMERICAN HEART ASSOCIATION [2170]

AHA National Center
7272 Greenville Avenue
Dallas, TX 75231-4596
(214) 360-6107
E-mail: apply@heart.org
Web Site: professional.heart.org

FOUNDED: 1948

AREAS OF INTEREST:
Research broadly related to cardiovascular function and disease and stroke, or to related clinical, translational, population, basic science, bioengineering or biotechnology, and public health problems, including multidisciplinary efforts.

NAME(S) OF PROGRAMS:
● **Institutional Undergraduate Student Fellowship**

TYPE:
Fellowships. This is an institutional award, made to qualified research institutions that can offer a meaningful research experience that supports the mission of the American Heart Association to undergraduate college students. The institution must demonstrate the ability to provide a meaningful research experience to students during the allotted 10-week fellowship experience.

PURPOSE:
To encourage students from all disciplines to consider research careers.

LEGAL BASIS:
Research association.

ELIGIBILITY:

Research awards are limited to U.S.-based nonprofit institutions, including medical, osteopathic and dental schools, veterinary schools, schools of public health, pharmacy schools, nursing schools, universities and colleges, public and voluntary hospitals and other institutions that can demonstrate the ability to conduct the proposed research. Applications proposed by federal institutions or employees will not be accepted, except from Veterans Administrations employees.

The program director is the applicant for this award. At the time of application, the program director must:
(1) possess a demonstrated track record of providing mentoring to student researchers;
(2) be a full-time faculty member at the level of assistant professor or equivalent, or above and;
(3) be a U.S. citizen, permanent resident, pending permanent resident, or hold an E-3, H-1B, J-1, O-1, TN, or G-4 visa. Program director must maintain one of these designations throughout the duration of the award.

FINANCIAL DATA:
Amount of support per award: $4,000 per student for the 10-week research experience.

APPLICATION INFO:
Guidelines and application form are available on the web site.

Duration: Three years.

Deadline: July 18.

ADDRESS INQUIRIES TO:
See e-mail address above.

AMERICAN HEART ASSOCIATION   [2171]
AHA National Center
7272 Greenville Avenue
Dallas, TX 75231-4596
(214) 360-6107
E-mail: apply@heart.org
Web Site: professional.heart.org

FOUNDED: 1948

AREAS OF INTEREST:
Research broadly related to cardiovascular function and disease and stroke, or to related clinical, translational, population or basic science, bioengineering or biotechnology, and public health problems, including multidisciplinary efforts.

NAME(S) OF PROGRAMS:
● **AHA Institutional Research Enhancement Award (AIREA)**

TYPE:
Research grants. AIREA award supports any part of the full range of research and development from very basic to clinical. The goals of the program are to support meritorious research, expose students to research, and strengthen the research environment of the institution.

PURPOSE:
To support small-scale research projects related to cardiovascular diseases and stroke at educational institutions that provide Baccalaureate or advanced degrees but that have not been major recipients of NIH support.

LEGAL BASIS:
Research association.

ELIGIBILITY:
AHA awards are open to the array of academic and health professionals. Clinical, translational, population, and basic scientists are encouraged to apply. AHA strongly encourages applications by women, underrepresented minorities in the sciences, and those who have experienced varied and nontraditional career trajectories.

Institution must be a domestic accredited public or nonprofit institution of higher education. Federal government institutions are not eligible. The institution must grant Baccalaureate or advanced degrees in the biomedical or behavioral sciences. Institution may not have received more than $6,000,000 per year in NIH support in each of four of the last seven years.

Principal Investigator must have a primary appointment at an AREA-eligible institution. While no minimum percent effort is specified, the principal investigator must demonstrate that adequate time will be devoted to ensuring the successful completion of the proposed project. At the time of application, the principal investigator must be a U.S. citizen, permanent resident, pending permanent resident, or hold an E-3, H1-B, J-1, O-1, TN or G-4 visa. Awardee must maintain one of these designations throughout the duration of the award.

FINANCIAL DATA:
Amount of support per award: $77,000 per year (including up to 10% indirect costs).

APPLICATION INFO:
Guidelines and application form are available on the web site.

Duration: Two years.

Deadline: July 19. Notification in December.

ADDRESS INQUIRIES TO:
See e-mail address above.

AMERICAN HEART ASSOCIATION   [2172]
AHA National Center
7272 Greenville Avenue
Dallas, TX 75231-4596
(214) 360-6107
E-mail: apply@heart.org
Web Site: professional.heart.org

FOUNDED: 1948

AREAS OF INTEREST:
Research broadly related to cardiovascular function and disease and stroke, or to related clinical, basic science, bioengineering or biotechnology, and public health problems, including multidisciplinary efforts.

NAME(S) OF PROGRAMS:
● **Merit Award**

TYPE:
Research grants. Merit Award supports individual scientists with a trajectory of success, who propose novel approaches to major research challenges in the areas of cardiovascular disease and stroke that have the potential to produce unusually high impact. This competition will enable AHA to further develop and strengthen the community of cardiovascular and stroke researchers and bring innovative approaches to basic, clinical, population and translational studies through funding a variety of disciplines.

PURPOSE:
To fund highly promising investigators with stellar track records of accomplishment who have the potential to move a field of science forward with creative approaches that are aligned with the mission of the American Heart Association.

LEGAL BASIS:
Research association.

ELIGIBILITY:
Applicant must be an AHA Professional Member. Applications are encouraged from all basic disciplines as well as epidemiological, behavioral, community and clinical investigations that bear on cardiovascular and stroke problems, and must describe the capacity of the investigator's work to transform public health policy. This award will be given to applicants with the following or equivalent credentials:
(1) have a Ph.D., M.D., or the equivalent;
(2) hold a tenured or tenure-track position as associate professor or higher academic rank at an eligible nonprofit U.S. institution or, if at an eligible institution that has no tenure track, hold an appointment that reflects a significant institutional commitment at the time of the application deadline and;
(3) be the principal investigator on multiple active, national peer-reviewed research awards of at least three years' duration. Mentored awards, career development and training grants do not qualify.

Federal government employees are not eligible.

At the time of application, the principal investigator must be a U.S. citizen, permanent resident, pending permanent resident, or hold a H1-B, J-1, O-1, G-4, TN or E-3 visa. Awardee must meet AHA citizenship criteria throughout the duration of the award.

FINANCIAL DATA:
Amount of support per award: $200,000 per year.

NO. AWARDS: 2 for the year 2019.

APPLICATION INFO:
A Letter of Intent (LOI), limited to three pages, will be required. AHA will contact applicants with the highest-rated LOIs and invite them to submit a full application.

Duration: Five years.

Deadline: Letter of Intent: July 26.

ADDRESS INQUIRIES TO:
See e-mail address above.

AMERICAN HEART ASSOCIATION   [2173]
AHA National Center
7272 Greenville Avenue
Dallas, TX 75231-4596
(214) 360-6107
E-mail: apply@heart.org
Web Site: professional.heart.org

FOUNDED: 1948

AREAS OF INTEREST:
Research broadly related to cardiovascular function, cardiovascular disease and stroke, or to related clinical, basic science, bioengineering, biotechnology, or public health problems.

NAME(S) OF PROGRAMS:
● **Collaborative Sciences Award**

TYPE:
Research grants. Award is intended to foster collaboration between established and early- or midcareer investigators.

PURPOSE:
To foster innovative collaborative approaches to research projects that propose novel pairing of investigators from at least two broadly disparate disciplines.

LEGAL BASIS:
Research association.

ELIGIBILITY:
Each applicant must be an AHA Professional Member. Proposal must focus on the collaborative relationship, such that the scientific objectives could not be achieved without the efforts of at least two co-principal investigators and their respective disciplines. The combination and integration of studies may be inclusive of basic, clinical, population, behavioral, and/or translational research. Project must include at least one co-principal investigator from a field outside cardiovascular disease and stroke. Applications by existing collaborators are permitted, provided that the proposal is for a new and novel idea or approach that has not been funded before.

While no minimum percent effort is specified, the co-principal investigators must demonstrate that adequate time will be devoted to ensuring successful completion of the proposed project.

At the time of application, each co-principal investigator must be a U.S. citizen, permanent resident, pending permanent resident, or hold an E-3, H1-B, F-1, J-1, O-1, TN or G-4 visa. Awardee must meet AHA citizenship criteria throughout the duration of the award.

Sponsoring institution must be a U.S.-based nonprofit institution, including medical, osteopathic and dental schools, veterinary schools, schools of public health, pharmacy schools, nursing schools, universities and colleges, public and voluntary hospitals and others that can demonstrate the ability to conduct the proposed research. Applications will not be accepted for work with funding to be administered through any federal institution or work to be performed by a federal employee, except for Veterans Administration employees.

FINANCIAL DATA:
Amount of support per award: $250,000 per year (including 10% institutional indirect costs).

NO. AWARDS: Up to 6 for the year 2018.

APPLICATION INFO:
A Letter of Intent is required to ensure responsiveness to the novel, collaborative nature of this program. Only those applicants who submit a Letter of Intent and are invited to apply may submit a full application.

Duration: Three years.

Deadline: Letter of Intent: October 9. Full application: January 31.

ADDRESS INQUIRIES TO:
See e-mail address above.

AMERICAN HEART ASSOCIATION [2174]

AHA National Center
7272 Greenville Avenue
Dallas, TX 75231-4596
(214) 360-6107
E-mail: apply@heart.org
Web Site: professional.heart.org

FOUNDED: 1948

AREAS OF INTEREST:
Research broadly related to cardiovascular function and disease and stroke, or to related clinical, translational, behavioral, population or basic science, bioengineering or biotechnology, and public health problems, including multidisciplinary efforts.

NAME(S) OF PROGRAMS:
● **Career Development Award**

TYPE:
Awards/prizes; Development grants; Research grants. Career Development Award is intended to develop the research skills to support and greatly enhance the awardee's chances to obtain and retain a high quality cardiovascular and/or stroke career position.

YEAR PROGRAM STARTED: 1997

PURPOSE:
To support promising health care and academic professionals in the early years of their first professional appointment; to explore innovative questions or pilot studies that will provide preliminary data and training necessary to ensure future success as a research scientist in the field of cardiovascular and stroke research.

LEGAL BASIS:
Research association.

ELIGIBILITY:
Applicant must be an AHA Professional Member and a U.S. citizen or permanent resident. At the time of application, the applicant must hold an M.D., Ph.D., D.O., D.V.M., D.D.S., or equivalent post-Baccalaureate doctoral degree.

At the time of award activation, candidate must hold a faculty/staff position up to and including the rank of assistant professor (or equivalent). No more than four years may have elapsed since the first faculty/staff appointment at the assistant professor level or equivalent. Applications may be submitted for review in the final year of a postdoctoral research fellowship or in the initial years of the first faculty/staff appointment. While no minimum percent effort is required, the applicant must demonstrate that adequate time will be devoted to ensuring successful completion of the project.

GEOG. RESTRICTIONS: United States.

FINANCIAL DATA:
Amount of support per award: $77,000 per year, including 10% institutional indirect costs.

APPLICATION INFO:
Guidelines and application form are available on the web site.

Duration: Three years. Nonrenewable.

Deadline: October 17.

ADDRESS INQUIRIES TO:
See e-mail address above.

AMERICAN LUNG ASSOCIATION [2175]

55 West Wacker Drive
Suite 1150
Chicago, IL 60601
E-mail: research@lung.org
Web Site: www.lung.org/research

FOUNDED: 1904

AREAS OF INTEREST:
Adult pulmonary medicine, lung biology, pediatric pulmonary medicine, and research and education for the prevention and control of lung disease.

NAME(S) OF PROGRAMS:
● **Catalyst Award**

TYPE:
Training grants. American Lung Association Catalyst Award is a mentored award meant to support outstanding investigators on the path to independence for research into the mechanisms of lung disease and general lung biology.

YEAR PROGRAM STARTED: 1948

PURPOSE:
To prevent lung disease and promote lung health through research, education and advocacy.

LEGAL BASIS:
Nonprofit foundation.

ELIGIBILITY:
At the time of application, candidates must be U.S. citizens or foreign nationals holding green card, J-1, H-1B, TN, E-3 or O-1 visa immigration status. At the time of application and throughout the award, an applicant must be employed by a U.S. institution.

Applicant must hold a doctoral degree and have a faculty appointment or equivalent with demonstrated institutional commitment (salary support and research space) in a recognized academic or other not-for-profit institution.

Preference is given to projects that are novel, innovative in design and approach, utilize modern technologies, and incorporate a multidisciplinary collaborative training plan.

Medical residents, those presently enrolled in a degree program, and established investigators are not eligible to apply.

GEOG. RESTRICTIONS: United States.

FINANCIAL DATA:
Amount of support per award: $50,000 per year.

APPLICATION INFO:
Application information is available on the web site.

Duration: Up to two years.

Deadline: December 12. Notification in June.

PUBLICATIONS:
Program announcement.

ADDRESS INQUIRIES TO:
See e-mail address above.

AMERICAN LUNG ASSOCIATION [2176]

55 West Wacker Drive
Suite 1150
Chicago, IL 60601
E-mail: research@lung.org
Web Site: www.lung.org/research

FOUNDED: 1904

AREAS OF INTEREST:
Research and education for the prevention and control of lung disease.

NAME(S) OF PROGRAMS:
- **Innovation Award**

TYPE:
Seed money grants. The aim of this award is to support promising independent investigators who are leveraging their existing body of work to conduct basic science, behavioral, clinical, or translational research for lung health.

YEAR PROGRAM STARTED: 1921

PURPOSE:
To prevent lung disease and promote lung health through research, education and advocacy.

LEGAL BASIS:
Nonprofit foundation.

ELIGIBILITY:
Intended for junior investigators researching the mechanisms of lung disease and general lung biology. At the time of application, candidates must:
(1) be U.S. citizens or foreign nationals;
(2) be employed by a U.S. institution;
(3) hold a doctoral degree;
(4) have a faculty appointment or equivalent with demonstrated institutional commitment in a recognized academic or other not-for-profit research institute and;
(5) have held a K or R level grant in the three years prior to the application.

FINANCIAL DATA:
Amount of support per award: $75,000 per year.

APPLICATION INFO:
Application information is available on the web site.
Duration: Up to two years.
Deadline: December 12. Announcement in June.

PUBLICATIONS:
Program announcement.

ADDRESS INQUIRIES TO:
See e-mail address above.

AMERICAN LUNG ASSOCIATION   [2177]
55 West Wacker Drive
Suite 1150
Chicago, IL 60601
E-mail: research@lung.org
Web Site: www.lung.org/research

FOUNDED: 1904

AREAS OF INTEREST:
Research and education for the prevention and control of lung disease.

NAME(S) OF PROGRAMS:
- **Allergic Respiratory Diseases Research Award**

TYPE:
Research grants. The American Lung Association and the American Academy of Allergy, Asthma & Immunology Allergic Respiratory Diseases Research Award represents a joint effort to encourage and support early-stage investigators with a primary faculty appointment in an allergy/immunology division or section conducting research into advancing the understanding of allergic respiratory disease.

One of the goals of this collaboration is to fund researchers at important crossroads of their careers.

PURPOSE:
To encourage and support research into advancing the understanding of allergic respiratory disease.

LEGAL BASIS:
Nonprofit organization.

ELIGIBILITY:
At the time of application, candidates must be U.S. citizens or foreign nationals holding a green card, J-1, H-1B, TN, E-3 or O-1 visa immigration status. At the time of application and throughout the award, an applicant must be employed by a U.S. institution.

Applicant must hold a doctoral degree and have a primary faculty appointment in a Clinical Allergy and Immunology division or section of an academic institution. Applicants from outside of an Allergy and Immunology Division will not be considered.

Applicant must be undertaking a project related to allergic respiratory disease, have completed training, and be an independent and self-directed researcher for whom their institution must provide space and other resources customary for independent investigators. Applicant may be at any level of research experience, but priority will be given to applicants below the rank of associate professor who have not received more than one R award.

GEOG. RESTRICTIONS: United States.

FINANCIAL DATA:
No more than 75% of the requested budget may be used for an awardee's salary and/or fringe benefits. No more than 30% of the total award budget may be used to fund the purchase of permanent equipment. Grant funds may be used for the salary and fringe benefit costs of personnel other than the applicant.
Amount of support per award: $75,000 per year.

NO. MOST RECENT APPLICANTS: 15.

NO. AWARDS: 1.

APPLICATION INFO:
Application information is available on the web site.
Duration: Up to two years.
Deadline: December 12. Notification in June.

ADDRESS INQUIRIES TO:
See e-mail address above.

AMERICAN LUNG ASSOCIATION   [2178]
55 West Wacker Drive
Suite 1150
Chicago, IL 60601
E-mail: research@lung.org
Web Site: www.lung.org/research

FOUNDED: 1904

AREAS OF INTEREST:
Research and education for the prevention and control of lung disease.

NAME(S) OF PROGRAMS:
- **Dalsemer Research Grant**

TYPE:
Seed money grants. This mentored award provides seed money to junior investigators for researching the mechanisms and biology of interstitial lung disease.

PURPOSE:
To support research in interstitial lung disease.

LEGAL BASIS:
Nonprofit.

ELIGIBILITY:
At the time of application, applicant must:
(1) hold a doctoral degree and be assured of a faculty appointment or equivalent with demonstrated institutional commitment (salary support, research space) by the start of the award;
(2) have completed two years of postdoctoral research training;
(3) be U.S. citizens or foreign nationals holding one of the following visa immigration statuses: permanent resident (Green Card), exchange visitor (J-1), temporary worker in a specialty occupation (H-1, H-1B), Canadian or Mexican citizen engaging in professional activities (TC or TN), or temporary worker with extraordinary abilities in the sciences (O-1). Non-citizens must submit a notarized copy of proof of visa immigration status and;
(4) be employed by a U.S. institution.

Grantee organizations must be recognized academic or other nonprofit research entities.

Medical residents, those presently enrolled in a degree program (e.g., graduate students), and established investigators are not eligible to apply.

FINANCIAL DATA:
No more than 75% of the requested budget may be used for the awardee's salary and/or fringe benefits. No more than 30% of the total award budget may be used to fund the purchase of permanent equipment. Grant funds may be used for the salary and fringe benefit costs of personnel other than the applicant.
Amount of support per award: $50,000 per year.

NO. AWARDS: 1 to 2.

APPLICATION INFO:
Applications are accepted through proposalCENTRAL.
Duration: Up to two years.
Deadline: December 12. Announcement in June.

PUBLICATIONS:
Program announcement.

ADDRESS INQUIRIES TO:
See e-mail address above.

AMERICAN LUNG ASSOCIATION   [2179]
55 West Wacker Drive
Suite 1150
Chicago, IL 60601
E-mail: research@lung.org
Web Site: www.lung.org/research

FOUNDED: 1904

AREAS OF INTEREST:
Research and education for the prevention and control of lung disease.

NAME(S) OF PROGRAMS:
- **Public Policy Research Award**

TYPE:
Research grants. Public Policy Research Award is intended to support research on and evaluation of existing public policy and programs, as well as pilot and demonstration

projects that inject innovative ideas and provide evidence for the development of new public policies impacting lung health.

PURPOSE:
To help stimulate and inform important public policy debates around healthy air and lung disease; to support research on and evaluation of existing public policy and programs, as well as projects that inject innovative ideas into public policies impacting lung health.

LEGAL BASIS:
Nonprofit foundation.

ELIGIBILITY:
At the time of application, candidates must be U.S. citizens or foreign nationals holding a green card, J-1, H-1B, TN, E-3 or O-1 visa status. Applicant must be employed by a U.S. institution at the time of application and throughout the award period.

Applicant must hold a doctoral degree or relevant terminal professional degree such as an M.P.H. and have a faculty appointment or equivalent with demonstrated institutional commitment in a recognized academic institution or established not-for-profit research entity.

Applicants should be on-track to pursue a career in public policy research. The application is open to researchers in public policy, economics, political science, sociology, law, and related disciplines.

GEOG. RESTRICTIONS: United States.

FINANCIAL DATA:
No more than 50% of the requested budget may be used for an awardee's salary and/or fringe benefits. No more than 30% of the total award budget may be used to fund the purchase of permanent equipment. Grant funds may be used for the salary and fringe benefit costs of personnel other than the applicant.

Amount of support per award: $50,000 per year.

APPLICATION INFO:
Proposal should include the following information:
(1) lay summary;
(2) curriculum vitae for the Principal Investigator and team;
(3) information on the project;
(4) study design and methods, including statistical analysis;
(5) plan for dissemination and translation;
(6) itemized project budget and;
(7) references.

The application must include a letter from the applicant's chair or institutional equivalent that conveys the commitment of the institution to the applicant and the proposed research activities.

Duration: Up to two years. Second year of funding is based on demonstrating satisfactory progress and availability of funding.

Deadline: December 12. Notification in June.

PUBLICATIONS:
Program announcement.

ADDRESS INQUIRIES TO:
See e-mail address above.

AMERICAN LUNG ASSOCIATION [2180]
55 West Wacker Drive
Suite 1150
Chicago, IL 60601
E-mail: research@lung.org
Web Site: www.lung.org/research

FOUNDED: 1904

AREAS OF INTEREST:
Research and education for the prevention and control of lung disease.

NAME(S) OF PROGRAMS:
● **Lung Cancer Discovery Awards**

TYPE:
Research grants. The objective of these awards is to support independent investigators conducting clinical, laboratory, epidemiological or any groundbreaking project aimed at revolutionizing our current understanding of lung cancer and improving diagnostic, clinical and treatment methods.

PURPOSE:
To support research to find better methods of detection, treatment and cures for all lung diseases.

LEGAL BASIS:
Nonprofit foundation.

ELIGIBILITY:
At the time of application, candidates must be U.S. citizens or foreign nationals holding a green card, J-1, H-1B, TN, E-3 or O-1 visa status. Applicant must be employed by a U.S. institution at the time of application and throughout the award period.

Applicant must hold a doctoral degree, have a faculty appointment at an academic institution (including research institutions not formally associated with a university), and have completed a training fellowship. Applicants may be at any level of research experience.

Applicants must be independent, self-directed researchers for whom their institution must provide space and other resources customary for independent investigators. The application must convey the commitment of the institution to the applicant and the proposed research activities.

GEOG. RESTRICTIONS: United States.

FINANCIAL DATA:
Grant funds may be used for the salary and fringe benefit costs of personnel other than the applicant. No more than 75% of the requested budget may be used for an awardee's salary and/or fringe benefits and no more than 30% of the total award budget may go to fund the purchase of permanent equipment.

Amount of support per award: $100,000 per year.

NO. MOST RECENT APPLICANTS: 46.

NO. AWARDS: 5.

APPLICATION INFO:
A Letter of Intent is required and must be submitted through proposalCENTRAL. Outcome notifications of the first stage of the application process will be e-mailed to applicants. Those applicants selected to go forward will be asked to submit a full proposal.

Duration: Up to two years.

Deadline: Letter of Intent: October 3. Application: January 23. Announcement in June.

PUBLICATIONS:
Program announcement.

ADDRESS INQUIRIES TO:
See e-mail address above.

THE CANADIAN LUNG ASSOCIATION (CLA)
885 Meadowlands Drive
Suite 502
Ottawa ON K2C 3N2 Canada
(613) 569-6411 ext. 262
(888) 566-5864 (within Canada)
Fax: (613) 569-8860
E-mail: research@lung.ca
Web Site: www.lung.ca

TYPE:
Fellowships; Research grants. Fellowships are offered to registered nurses pursuing postgraduate education with a major component of the program involving respiratory nursing practice, physiotherapists pursuing postgraduate training with respiratory research as the major component, and respiratory therapists pursuing postgraduate education with a major component of the program involving respiratory therapy practice.

Grants for research and feasibility studies are offered to registered nurses undertaking research investigations related to nursing management of patients with respiratory disease and symptoms. Grants are also offered to physiotherapists undertaking investigations related to management of patients with respiratory disease. Respiratory therapists undertaking research investigations related to the management of patients with respiratory disease and symptoms may also qualify.

See entry 2278 for full listing.

THE CANADIAN LUNG ASSOCIATION (CLA) [2181]
885 Meadowlands Drive
Suite 502
Ottawa ON K2C 3N2 Canada
(613) 569-6411 ext. 262
(888) 566-5864 (within Canada)
Fax: (613) 569-8860
E-mail: research@lung.ca
Web Site: www.lung.ca

FOUNDED: 1958

AREAS OF INTEREST:
Prevention and control of lung disease including asthma, emphysema, chronic bronchitis, tuberculosis and lung cancer; air pollution and smoking.

NAME(S) OF PROGRAMS:
● **Breathing as One: Research Fellowships and Studentships**

TYPE:
Fellowships. The Lung Association - National Office - offers two types of research trainee awards to the medical and scientific community: postdoctoral fellowships and Ph.D. graduate studentships.

YEAR PROGRAM STARTED: 1959

PURPOSE:
To build Canadian research capacity that contributes to the field of respiratory health in Canada.

LEGAL BASIS:
Not-for-profit, incorporated.

ELIGIBILITY:
Open to members and non-members of CTS and CRHP who are conducting lung research that aligns with the Lung Association mandate. To be eligible for a Breathing as One Fellowship or Studentship Award the following criteria apply:
(1) Studentship applicants should be enrolled or accepted in a graduate (thesis-based) program at the doctoral level at a Canadian academic institution. Individuals who have applied to a graduate program but have not received acceptance may apply for a Studentship award. The award, however, will be conditional on acceptance into the program;
(2) Fellowship applicants should be working under supervision of a faculty member at an accredited Canadian academic institution. Under special circumstances, an applicant may pursue a fellowship in another country; however, the applicant must justify why they could not find the same kind of training in Canada and must have plans to pursue a career in research in Canada;
(3) Awardee may not be in receipt of another major award at the same time as holding a Fellowship or Studentship Award from the Lung Association - National Office and;
(4) Applicant must be pursuing a research study with respiratory health as the major focus.

FINANCIAL DATA:
Amount of support per award: Fellowships: $45,000 to $55,000 (CAN) per year; Studentships: $21,000 (CAN) per year.
Total amount of support: Varies.

CO-OP FUNDING PROGRAMS: Partnerships include CIHR and the pharmaceutical industry (peer review only).

NO. AWARDS: Approximately 6 each year.

APPLICATION INFO:
Forms may be downloaded from the Lung Association web site. Applicant must upload one copy of the completed application and all relevant documents.
Duration: One to two years. Competitive renewal.
Deadline: May 17.

PUBLICATIONS:
Canadian Respiratory Journal.

ADDRESS INQUIRIES TO:
Fatima Kazoun, Manager
National Research Programs
(See address above.)

THE CHEST FOUNDATION [2182]
2595 Patriot Boulevard
Glenview, IL 60026
(224) 521-9527
Fax: (224) 521-9801
E-mail: chestfoundation@chestnet.org
Web Site: foundation.chestnet.org

FOUNDED: 1935

AREAS OF INTEREST:
All aspects of chest medicine and surgery.

NAME(S) OF PROGRAMS:
- **CHEST Foundation and the Alpha-1 Foundation Research Grant in Alpha-1 Antitrypsin Deficiency**
- **CHEST Foundation Research Grant in Chronic Obstructive Pulmonary Disease**
- **CHEST Foundation Research Grant in Cystic Fibrosis**
- **CHEST Foundation Research Grant in Lung Cancer**
- **CHEST Foundation Research Grant in Nontuberculous Mycobacteria Diseases**
- **CHEST Foundation Research Grant in Pulmonary Arterial Hypertension**
- **CHEST Foundation Research Grant in Pulmonary Fibrosis**
- **CHEST Foundation Research Grant in Sarcoidosis**
- **CHEST Foundation Research Grant in Severe Asthma**
- **CHEST Foundation Research Grant in Sleep Medicine**
- **CHEST Foundation Research Grant in Venous Thromboembolism**
- **CHEST Foundation Research Grant in Women's Lung Health**
- **Community Service Grant Honoring D. Robert McCaffree, M.D., Master FCCP**
- **GlaxoSmithKline Distinguished Scholar in Respiratory Health**

TYPE:
Research grants. Medical research grants; community service grants.

YEAR PROGRAM STARTED: 1996

PURPOSE:
To provide resources to advance the prevention and treatment of diseases of the chest: asthma, tuberculosis, end-of-life issues, smoking prevention and chronic obstructive pulmonary disease.

LEGAL BASIS:
Supporting organization.

ELIGIBILITY:
Applicant must be a CHEST member to apply for CHEST Foundation grants. For a community service grant, applicant or sponsor must be a current member of CHEST.

Special consideration will be given to applicants who are within five years of completing an advanced training program or equivalent experience.

FINANCIAL DATA:
Amount of support per award: Varies by program.
Total amount of support: Over $500,000 for the year 2017.

CO-OP FUNDING PROGRAMS: Actelion Pharmaceuticals, US, Inc.; Alpha-1 Foundation; The American Society of Transplantation; Astra Zeneca; Daiichi Sankyo; Genentech Inc.; Insmed.

APPLICATION INFO:
Application guidelines can be found on the Foundation web site.
Duration: One to three years.
Deadline: Generally early May.

PUBLICATIONS:
Call for Abstracts, brochure; also in *Ads in CHEST*, monthly publication of The American College of Chest Physicians (ACCP).

IRS I.D.: 36-3286520

ADDRESS INQUIRIES TO:
E-mail: grants@chestnet.org

GREENBURG-MAY FOUNDATION
280 Park Avenue, 41st Floor
New York, NY 10017
(212) 451-3200
E-mail: pmay@trianpartners.com

TYPE:
Development grants; Research grants. Social services.

See entry 2230 for full listing.

HEART AND STROKE FOUNDATION OF CANADA [2183]
1525 Carling Avenue
Suite 110
Ottawa ON K1Z 8R9 Canada
(613) 691-4042
Fax: (613) 727-1895
E-mail: research@heartandstroke.ca
Web Site: www.heartandstroke.ca/research

FOUNDED: 1956

AREAS OF INTEREST:
Cardiovascular/cerebrovascular research.

NAME(S) OF PROGRAMS:
- **Grant-in-Aid**

TYPE:
Grants-in-aid. Grant-in-Aid program provides operating funds to support important, pertinent, novel research in the areas of heart disease and stroke. Funding promotes research discovery, exploration and innovation across all health research themes. Knowledge gained from scientific findings contributes to the cardiovascular and cerebrovascular health of Canadians through prevention, treatment and recovery.

YEAR PROGRAM STARTED: 1958

PURPOSE:
To reduce the morbidity and mortality from cardiovascular/cerebrovascular disease in Canada.

LEGAL BASIS:
Nonprofit.

ELIGIBILITY:
Researchers at all career stages are encouraged to apply. Principal Investigators must have a full-time academic or faculty appointment in Canada at the time of application.

GEOG. RESTRICTIONS: Canada.

FINANCIAL DATA:
Amount of support per award: Varies, depending upon the needs and nature of the request.

APPLICATION INFO:
Applications will be completed online using Heart and Stroke's online system, CIRCUlink. A scanned copy of the original signature and electronic signatures will be accepted. Applicants need not send an original copy of the signature page to the Foundation.

Due to conflict of interest, letters of support from the Foundation are not permitted as part of any application to any Heart and Stroke research competition.

Applicants are required to attach a detailed research proposal, which must include:
(1) hypothesis to be tested;
(2) knowledge to date;
(3) methods to be used;
(4) anticipated results and conclusions;
(5) possible problems and;
(6) pertinent references.
Research proposal should be predominantly text and is limited to ten pages.
Duration: One to three years.

Deadline: Applications must be submitted online by the submission deadline (listed online) for funding to become effective on July 1 of the following year.

ADDRESS INQUIRIES TO:
Research Department
(See e-mail address above.)

HEART AND STROKE FOUNDATION OF CANADA [2184]

1525 Carling Avenue
Suite 110
Ottawa ON K1Z 8R9 Canada
(613) 691-4042
Fax: (613) 727-1895
E-mail: research@heartandstroke.ca
Web Site: www.heartandstroke.ca/research

FOUNDED: 1956

AREAS OF INTEREST:
Cardiovascular and cerebrovascular research.

NAME(S) OF PROGRAMS:
● **National New Investigator**

TYPE:
Awards/prizes; Scholarships. National New Investigator program is a salary award to support new investigators who have demonstrated excellence in their doctoral and postdoctoral training and wish to establish their own independent research career. Salary support opportunities of this kind provide an added incentive for researchers to continue or begin their program of research within Canada.

YEAR PROGRAM STARTED: 1958

PURPOSE:
To reduce the morbidity and mortality from cardiovascular disease in Canada.

LEGAL BASIS:
Nonprofit.

ELIGIBILITY:
At the time of submission, applicant must have a full-time appointment at the assistant professor level or above in Canada. The candidate should clearly demonstrate the potential to become an independent investigator. No more than five years may have passed since the date of the first faculty appointment.

Applicant must have an M.D., Ph.D. or equivalent degree.

Applications for this award must be supported by the university or institution at which the applicant will conduct the proposed research program. The university or institution is expected to guarantee the applicant appropriate academic rank and to provide adequate space and facilities for the investigator's research, commensurate with the status of the individual's experience and level of support by the Heart and Stroke Foundation.

GEOG. RESTRICTIONS: Canada.

FINANCIAL DATA:
Amount of support per award: $65,000 (CAN) including employer's portion of fringe benefits.

APPLICATION INFO:
Complete application must include:
(1) a six-page detailed description of the proposed research program, which includes identification of the applicant's role and how the execution of the research plan contributes to the applicant's development as an independent researcher;
(2) an institutional statement completed by the Dean and Department Head (or institutional equivalents) confirming that the applicant will have 75% of their time allocated to the proposed research program;
(3) three letters of recommendation in sealed envelopes with the signature of the referee across the seal;
(4) an executive summary of the proposed research;
(5) sex and gender considerations;
(6) a complete structured lay summary with a clear explanation of how the proposed research is directly relevant to heart disease and/or stroke and what is the impact of the proposed research to heart disease and/or stroke;
(7) a completed copy of the applicant's common curriculum vitae (HSFC version only) and;
(8) original signatures, a scanned copy of the original signatures, or electronic signatures.
Duration: Maximum four years.
Deadline: September 5, to become tenable July 1 of the following year.

ADDRESS INQUIRIES TO:
Research Department
(See e-mail address above.)

NATIONAL BLOOD FOUNDATION, A PROGRAM OF AABB [2185]

4550 Montgomery Avenue
Suite 700, North Tower
Bethesda, MD 20814-2749
(301) 215-6552
Fax: (301) 686-7865
E-mail: nbf@aabb.org
Web Site: www.aabb.org/nbf

FOUNDED: 1983

AREAS OF INTEREST:
Blood banking, blood safety, transfusion medicine, tissue transplantation, cellular therapy, and patient blood management.

NAME(S) OF PROGRAMS:
● **Early-Career Scientific Research Grants Program**

TYPE:
Awards/prizes; Development grants; Research grants; Seed money grants. Basic medical research grants.

The focus of the NBF's Scientific Research Grants Program is to support early career researchers in the field of transfusion medicine, to include aspects of immunology, hematology, tissue and transplantation medicine, cellular therapies, emerging infectious disease, immunohematology, donor health and recruitment and retention, implementation of technological advances, and patient blood management. Priority is given to early-stage investigators and innovative new projects with the potential to have a practical impact on patients and donors in transfusion medicine and biotherapies.

YEAR PROGRAM STARTED: 1985

PURPOSE:
To actively support the leadership role of the AABB in establishing and promoting the highest standards of care for patients and donors by funding basic and applied scientific research, administrative research/projects, professional education in all aspects of blood banking, transfusion medicine, cellular therapies and patient blood management.

LEGAL BASIS:
Nonprofit association.

ELIGIBILITY:
An applicant must be a doctor (M.D or Ph.D.), medical technologist, transfusion medicine or cellular therapies professional. All applicants will be considered regardless of age, race, gender, national origin or religion.

The NBF accepts national and international early-career applicants. The NBF intends to fund researchers on a path towards independence. No candidate is eligible to receive more than one NBF grant over the course of their career. No particular project can be funded more than once. Applications for research into innovative and new projects are a priority.

Awards will not be made to increase the funding available for currently funded research projects. NBF grants are intended to provide "seed" funding that allows the principal investigator to enhance preliminary data. This data may be useful in applying for larger grants.

FINANCIAL DATA:
Grant awards may not cover indirect costs. Equipment expenditures cannot exceed $8,000 per grant.
Amount of support per award: Up to $75,000.
Total amount of support: $450,000.

NO. MOST RECENT APPLICANTS: 20.

NO. AWARDS: 8.

APPLICATION INFO:
Required application forms are available from the Foundation and must be submitted electronically. Application fee of $160 if applicant is not an AABB Individual Healthcare Professional or Physician in Residency member.
Duration: One to two years.
Deadline: December 1. Announcement in June for funds to be distributed in July.

PUBLICATIONS:
Application; program announcement.

IRS I.D.: 36-2384118

ADDRESS INQUIRIES TO:
Amy Quiggins, Director
(See address above.)

NATIONAL HEART, LUNG AND BLOOD INSTITUTE (NHLBI) [2186]

Division of Extramural Research
Rockledge II, Room 7160
6701 Rockledge Drive, MSC 7926
Bethesda, MD 20892-7926
(301) 435-0166
Fax: (301) 451-5462
E-mail: lombardr@nhlbi.nih.gov
Web Site: www.nhlbi.nih.gov

FOUNDED: 1948

AREAS OF INTEREST:
Diseases of the heart, blood vessels, lung and blood, sleep disorders, clinical use of blood and blood resources, and transfusion medicine.

TYPE:
Conferences/seminars; Fellowships; Project/program grants; Research grants; Training grants; Loan forgiveness programs. Career awards and other grant mechanisms to foster research on heart, vascular and lung diseases, and to develop scientists in these areas. Also, small business grants. Loan forgiveness programs are for research.

YEAR PROGRAM STARTED: 1948

PURPOSE:
To support research into the causes, improved diagnosis, treatment and prevention of cardiovascular diseases in arteriosclerosis, hypertension, cardiovascular disease, coronary heart disease, peripheral vascular disease, arrhythmias, heart failure and shock, congenital and rheumatic heart disease, cardiomyopathies and infections of the heart, circulatory assistance and AIDS.

LEGAL BASIS:
Public Health Service Act, Sections 301(c), 412 and 472.

ELIGIBILITY:
Any nonprofit or for-profit organization engaged in biomedical research may apply. An individual may apply for a fellowship award. Some restrictions may apply to foreign grantee institutions.

FINANCIAL DATA:
Amount of support per award: Varies by type of award.

APPLICATION INFO:
Application information is available on the web site.
Duration: Varies.
Deadline: Varies.

PUBLICATIONS:
NHLBI Fact Book; Annual Report of Director, NHLBI.

OFFICER:
Ryan Lombardi, Director, Office of Grants Management

ADDRESS INQUIRIES TO:
Ryan Lombardi, Director
Office of Grants Management
(See address above.)

NATIONAL HEART, LUNG AND BLOOD INSTITUTE (NHLBI)   [2187]
Two Rockledge Center, Suite 10042
6701 Rockledge Drive, MSC 7952
Bethesda, MD 20892-7952
(301) 435-0202
Fax: (301) 480-3547
E-mail: nhlbiinfo@nhlbi.nih.gov
Web Site: www.nhlbi.nih.gov

FOUNDED: 1948

AREAS OF INTEREST:
Pulmonary research, prevention, education and training programs in pulmonary diseases.

NAME(S) OF PROGRAMS:
● **Lung Diseases Research**

TYPE:
Project/program grants. Cooperative agreements.

YEAR PROGRAM STARTED: 1970

PURPOSE:
To use available knowledge and technology to solve specific disease problems of the lungs; to promote further studies on the

structure and function of the lung; to achieve improvement in the prevention and treatment of lung diseases.

LEGAL BASIS:
Public Health Service Act, Section 301, 422 and 487, as amended, Public Laws 78-410 and 99-158, 42 U.S.C. 241, 42 U.S.C. 285, and 42 U.S.C. 288, as amended.

ELIGIBILITY:
Any nonprofit or for-profit organization engaged in biomedical research may apply for grants with the exception of NRSAs. An individual may apply for an NRSA or, in some cases, may qualify for a research grant if adequate facilities in which to perform the research are available.

Some grants are available to U.S. citizens or institutions only.

FINANCIAL DATA:
Grants may support salaries, equipment, supplies, travel, and patient hospitalization as required to perform the research effort.

APPLICATION INFO:
Funding opportunities and award policies are posted online.
Duration: One to five years. Renewable.

PUBLICATIONS:
Annual Program Report.

STAFF:
James P. Kiley, Ph.D., Director, Division of Lung Diseases
Gail Weinmann, M.D., Deputy Director

ADDRESS INQUIRIES TO:
James P. Kiley, Ph.D., Director
Division of Lung Diseases
(See address above.)

THE POTTS MEMORIAL FOUNDATION   [2188]
P.O. Box 1015
Hudson, NY 12534
(518) 851-2292
E-mail: pottsfoundation@outlook.com

FOUNDED: 1922

AREAS OF INTEREST:
Tuberculosis.

TYPE:
Fellowships; Grants-in-aid; Research grants; Seed money grants. At present, the program allows the Foundation to provide for the care, treatment and rehabilitation of persons afflicted with tuberculosis by methods selected by the trustees. This may include maintenance, operation of hospitals, research, vocational counseling and guidance, scholarships, subsidies for education and training, job placement, grants to hospitals and charitable institutions and the operation of sheltered workshops.

YEAR PROGRAM STARTED: 1922

PURPOSE:
To help people who are battling tuberculosis.

LEGAL BASIS:
Nonprofit corporation.

FINANCIAL DATA:
Amount of support per award: $1,000 to $50,000.

NO. MOST RECENT APPLICANTS: Under 50.

NO. AWARDS: 10 to 15.

APPLICATION INFO:
A letter of request and proposal should be furnished in as much detail as possible,

including a detailed budget, to the Foundation. Eight (8) copies would be appreciated.
Duration: One year.
Deadline: 30 days prior to May 15 and October 15.

IRS I.D.: 14-1347714

OFFICERS:
Kathleen A. McDonough, Ph.D., President
John Chan, M.D., Vice President
Sidney D. Richter, Treasurer
Donna D. Klose, Secretary

TRUSTEES:
Richard Gullot, M.D.
Anthony Malanga, M.D.
Donna O'Hare, M.D.
Martin S. Pavelka, Jr., Ph.D.
Ananthakrishnan Ramani, M.D.

ADDRESS INQUIRIES TO:
Donna D. Klose, Secretary
(See address above.)

SALON NATIONAL LA BOUTIQUE
P.O. Box 1108
Lake Dallas, TX 75065-1108
(940) 230-0919
Fax: (940) 497-3044
E-mail: lasecretaire@8and40.org
Web Site: www.8and40.org

TYPE:
Scholarships. Grants for registered nurses.

See entry 2286 for full listing.

THE SARNOFF CARDIOVASCULAR RESEARCH FOUNDATION   [2189]
731 Walker Road
Suite G2
Great Falls, VA 22066
(703) 759-7600
E-mail: dboyd@sarnofffoundation.org
Web Site: www.sarnofffoundation.org

FOUNDED: 1981

AREAS OF INTEREST:
Cardiovascular research.

NAME(S) OF PROGRAMS:
● **Sarnoff Fellowship Program**
● **Sarnoff Scholar Award**

TYPE:
Awards/prizes; Fellowships. Research Fellowship and Award.

PURPOSE:
To give medical students the opportunity to spend a year conducting intensive work in a biomedical research laboratory; to provide financial support to former Sarnoff Fellows committed to pursuing a career in cardiovascular research.

ELIGIBILITY:
Sarnoff Fellowship Program is for medical students enrolled in any accredited medical school in the U.S. Applications are encouraged from second- and third-year medical students. Fourth-year medical students are required to submit an official letter from their medical schools granting graduation deferment. There are no citizenship requirements for application, but those who are not U.S. citizens must have and maintain an appropriate visa. Applicants enrolled in an M.D./Ph.D. program are ineligible. The Foundation strongly

encourages applicants from members of underrepresented or historically disadvantaged backgrounds.

Sarnoff Scholar Award applicant must be a former Sarnoff Fellow pursuing a career in cardiovascular research. Applicants may apply during the second half of their post-residency training/fellowship program and/or overlapping with the first two junior faculty years.

FINANCIAL DATA:
Amount of support per award: Fellowship: $32,000 stipend and up to $8,000 allowance for moving expenses, health insurance, financial support to attend the Sarnoff Annual Scientific Meeting and American Heart Association Scientific Sessions, and travel to present a paper, based on Fellowship research, at two national conferences.

Scholar: $90,000 stipend; up to $12,000 for laboratory supplies and professional journal subscriptions; up to $1,500 annually to defray the cost of health insurance; travel funds up to $1,500 to enable the Scholar to present a paper at a national conference; and maximum of 10% indirect costs paid to the institution for handling the award.

NO. AWARDS: Fellowship: Up to 18 annually; Scholar: 1 to 2 annually.

APPLICATION INFO:
Applicants to the Fellowship Program must submit the following:
(1) one-page personal statement describing scholarly interests and career plans;
(2) three-page essay on the applicant's cardiovascular topic of interest;
(3) completed application form and signed statement of confidentiality;
(4) official medical school transcript;
(5) curriculum vitae;
(6) recommendation from the applicant's sponsor;
(7) two additional recommendations and;
(8) any other material that the applicant determines is appropriate to support the application.
Duration: Fellowship: One year; Scholar: Two years.
Deadline: January 10.

ADDRESS INQUIRIES TO:
Dana Quinn Boyd, Executive Director
(See address above.)

SOCIETY OF CARDIOVASCULAR ANESTHESIOLOGISTS [2190]

8735 West Higgins Road
Suite 300
Chicago, IL 60631
(855) 658-2828
Fax: (847) 375-6323
E-mail: info@scahq.org
Web Site: www.scahq.org

AREAS OF INTEREST:
Cardiothoracic and vascular anesthesia.

NAME(S) OF PROGRAMS:
● **SCA Starter Grants**
● **SCA-IARS Mid-Career Grant**

TYPE:
Research grants.

PURPOSE:
To promote excellence in patient care through education and research in perioperative care for patients undergoing cardiothoracic and vascular procedures.

ELIGIBILITY:
Grant applicants must be a member of Society of Cardiovascular Anesthesiologists and hold an M.D. or Ph.D. degree.

No part of the grant may be used for salary support of the principal investigator (or fellows or residents), travel or tuition expenses of the principal investigator, patient costs (except to pay for pertinent laboratory studies), consultant costs, alterations or renovations.

FINANCIAL DATA:
Amount of support per award: Mid-Career Grant: Up to $50,000 per year; Starter Grant: Up to $25,000 per year.
Total amount of support: Up to $100,000 per recipient, depending on which grant is applied for.

NO. MOST RECENT APPLICANTS: 21.

NO. AWARDS: Maximum of 5 each year.

APPLICATION INFO:
Application information is available on the web site.
Duration: Up to two years.
Deadline: Varies.

IRS I.D.: 72-0863580

ADDRESS INQUIRIES TO:
See e-mail address above.

Metabolism, gastroenterology, nephrology

A.S.P.E.N. RHOADS RESEARCH FOUNDATION [2191]

8401 Colesville Road
Suite 510
Silver Spring, MD 20910
(301) 587-6315
Fax: (301) 587-2365
E-mail: aspen@nutritioncare.org
Web Site: www.nutritioncare.org

FOUNDED: 1975

AREAS OF INTEREST:
Metabolic issues and nutrition support therapy.

TYPE:
Research grants. Annual support for nutritional research.

YEAR PROGRAM STARTED: 1992

PURPOSE:
To support the personal and professional development of nutrition researchers throughout their careers.

LEGAL BASIS:
Nonprofit foundation.

ELIGIBILITY:
Applicants are encouraged from the fields of medicine, dietetics, nursing and pharmacy. Grants are only given to individuals. There are no citizenship requirements. Preference is given to individuals who are active in developing a career in nutritional research. A.S.P.E.N. membership is required.

FINANCIAL DATA:
Amount of support per award: Up to $25,000.

Total amount of support: Up to $120,000 annually.

NO. AWARDS: Up to 4 at $25,000; 2 at $10,000.

APPLICATION INFO:
Application form required. Contact the Foundation for additional information.
Duration: One year. Renewal possible up to two years.
Deadline: June 10. See program announcement to confirm date.

PUBLICATIONS:
Application guidelines.

ADDRESS INQUIRIES TO:
Michelle Spangenburg
Director of Education and Research
(See address above.)

AMERICAN DIABETES ASSOCIATION [2192]

2451 Crystal Drive
Suite 900
Arlington, VA 22202
(703) 549-1500 ext. 5532
Fax: (703) 621-3759
E-mail: grantquestions@diabetes.org
Web Site: www.professional.diabetes.org/grants

FOUNDED: 1940

AREAS OF INTEREST:
Programs serving the needs of people with diabetes, their families, researchers, clinicians and health care professionals.

CONSULTING OR VOLUNTEER SERVICES:
Various support and education programs carried out at affiliate level. Research program on national level.

NAME(S) OF PROGRAMS:
● **Innovative Basic Science Award (IBS)**
● **Innovative Clinical or Translational Science Award (ICTS)**
● **Junior Faculty Development Award (JFD)**
● **Minority Junior Faculty Development Award (JDFM)**
● **Minority Postdoctoral Fellowship**
● **Minority Undergraduate Internship (MUI)**
● **Postdoctoral Fellowship (PDF)**

TYPE:
Fellowships; Research grants; Training grants.

YEAR PROGRAM STARTED: 1952

PURPOSE:
To aid in the search for a cure and prevention of diabetes; to help those with diabetes complications.

LEGAL BASIS:
Nonprofit voluntary health organization.

ELIGIBILITY:
Applicants must have a Ph.D., M.D., Pharm.D., D.O. or D.P.M. degree or appropriate health or science-related degrees and must hold full-time faculty position or the equivalent at university-affiliated institutions within the U.S. or its possessions. Postdoctoral Fellowship applicants must hold a full-time postdoctoral fellowship or the equivalent.

All investigators must be legally authorized to work in the U.S. Institutional certification of work permission will be required for all funded awards.

For the Junior Faculty Development Award, applicants can have any level of faculty appointment up to and including Assistant Professor and have no more than 10 years of research experience following receipt of their terminal degree.

For the Minority Junior Faculty Development and the Minority Postdoctoral Awards, underrepresented minorities are defined as the minority groups that are underrepresented in the area of biomedical and behavioral research: African American or Black, Hispanic/Spanish/Latino, American Indian/Alaskan Native, and Native Hawaiian or other Pacific Islander descent.

GEOG. RESTRICTIONS: United States.

FINANCIAL DATA:
Amount of support per award: Innovative Basic Science Award: Up to $115,000 per year; Innovative Clinical or Translational Science Award: Up to $200,000 per year; Junior Faculty Development Award and Minority Junior Faculty Development Award: $138,000 per year, plus optional student loan repayment of $10,000 per year; Minority Postdoctoral Fellowship and Postdoctoral Fellowship: $47,484 to $55,581 per year salary, plus $5,000 per year research and $5,000 per year fringe allowances; Minority Undergraduate Internship: $3,000 stipend.

NO. MOST RECENT APPLICANTS: 1,000.

APPLICATION INFO:
Applicants for all grants must submit application forms, a nontechnical description of the research project of less than 200 words and a scientific abstract of the proposal of no more than 200 words.
Duration: Innovative Basic Science Award, Innovative Clinical or Translational Science Award, Minority Postdoctoral Fellowship and Postdoctoral Fellowship: Up to three years; Junior Faculty Development Award and Minority Junior Faculty Development Award: Two to four years, dependent on previous career development funding; Minority Undergraduate Internship: Up to one year.
Deadline: July 15.

PUBLICATIONS:
Annual reports.

ADDRESS INQUIRIES TO:
Magda Galindo, Director Research and Community Programs
(See address above.)

AMERICAN GASTROENTEROLOGICAL ASSOCIATION (AGA)   [2193]
4930 Del Ray Avenue
Bethesda, MD 20814
(301) 654-2055
Fax: (301) 654-5920
E-mail: awards@gastro.org
Web Site: www.gastro.org/research-and-awards

FOUNDED: 1990

AREAS OF INTEREST:
Gastroenterology and related fields.

NAME(S) OF PROGRAMS:
● **AGA-R. Robert and Sally D. Funderburg Research Award in Gastric Cancer**

TYPE:
Research grants. Research award supporting an established investigator in the field of gastric cancer research working to enhance

our fundamental understanding of gastric cancer pathobiology or approaches to prevent, treat or cure gastric cancer.

YEAR PROGRAM STARTED: 1990

PURPOSE:
To support an established investigator in the field of gastric biology which enhances our fundamental understanding of gastric cancer pathobiology in order to prevent or develop a cure for the disease.

LEGAL BASIS:
Nonprofit foundation.

ELIGIBILITY:
Candidates must hold faculty positions at accredited North American institutions and be established as an independent investigator in the field of gastric biology. Applicant must also be a member of the AGA. Women and minorities are strongly encouraged to apply.

The recipient will be selected based on significance, investigator, innovation, approach, environment, evidence of institutional commitment, and relevance to AGA's mission. Preference will be given to novel approaches.

GEOG. RESTRICTIONS: North America.

FINANCIAL DATA:
Funds are to be used for the salary, support, equipment and supplies of the investigator, to promote his or her involvement in the field. No indirect costs will be allowed.
Amount of support per award: $50,000 per year.
Total amount of support: $100,000.

NO. AWARDS: 1.

APPLICATION INFO:
Application information is available online.
Duration: Two years.
Deadline: July 29.

PUBLICATIONS:
Announcements.

ADDRESS INQUIRIES TO:
See e-mail address above.

AMERICAN GASTROENTEROLOGICAL ASSOCIATION (AGA)   [2194]
4930 Del Ray Avenue
Bethesda, MD 20814
(301) 654-2055
Fax: (301) 654-5920
E-mail: awards@gastro.org
Web Site: www.gastro.org/research-and-awards

FOUNDED: 1990

AREAS OF INTEREST:
Gastroenterology and related fields.

NAME(S) OF PROGRAMS:
● **AGA-Takeda Pharmaceuticals Research Scholar Award in Inflammatory Bowel Disease**

TYPE:
Research grants. Research award for early career faculty working toward independent careers in inflammatory bowel disease research.

YEAR PROGRAM STARTED: 1990

PURPOSE:
To support young gastroenterologists working toward independent and productive research careers in irritable bowel disease.

LEGAL BASIS:
Nonprofit foundation.

ELIGIBILITY:
The applicant must hold an M.D., Ph.D. or equivalent degree, and a full-time faculty position at a North American institution by the start of this award. Applicant must also be a member of the AGA in good standing. The award is not intended for fellows, but for young faculty who have demonstrated exceptional promise and have some record of accomplishment in research. Candidates should be early in their careers; therefore, established investigators are not appropriate candidates. Women, minorities and physician/scientist investigators are strongly encouraged to apply. Applicants working in a nonprofit institution in North America are eligible for this award (U.S. citizenship is not required). For M.D. applicants, no more than seven years shall have elapsed following the completion of clinical training (GI fellowship or its equivalent) at the start date of the award. For Ph.D. applicants, no more than seven years shall have elapsed following the awarding of the applicant's Ph.D. and the start date of the award. An appropriately documented parental leave of absence will not be counted toward the seven-year eligibility criteria. Exceptional circumstances may also be considered.

Applicants cannot hold or have held, prior to receiving the first payment of this award, an R01, R29, K-series award, VA career development award, or any award with similar objectives from non-federal sources. However, awards or grants obtained after receipt of the Research Scholar Award support by the RSA would be required to forfeit the remaining balance of award.

GEOG. RESTRICTIONS: North America.

FINANCIAL DATA:
Amount of support per award: $300,000 ($100,000 per year).

CO-OP FUNDING PROGRAMS: Jointly sponsored by the American Gastroenterological Association and Takeda Pharmaceuticals.

NO. AWARDS: 1.

APPLICATION INFO:
Applications must be submitted through the AGA Grants Management System. Materials will not be accepted via mail, fax or e-mail.
Duration: Three years.
Deadline: November 9.

ADDRESS INQUIRIES TO:
See e-mail address above.

AMERICAN GASTROENTEROLOGICAL ASSOCIATION (AGA)   [2195]
4930 Del Ray Avenue
Bethesda, MD 20814
(301) 654-2055
Fax: (301) 654-5920
E-mail: awards@gastro.org
Web Site: www.gastro.org/research-and-awards

FOUNDED: 1990

AREAS OF INTEREST:
Gastroenterology and related fields.

NAME(S) OF PROGRAMS:
● **AGA Pilot Research Award**

TYPE:
Research grants. Research awards for one-year projects for independent

investigators at any career stage performing research in gastroenterology- or hepatology-related areas.

YEAR PROGRAM STARTED: 1990

PURPOSE:
To provide funds to early career investigators to help them establish their independence; to support pilot projects that represent new research directions for established investigators.

LEGAL BASIS:
Nonprofit foundation.

ELIGIBILITY:
Open to investigators with M.Ds. or Ph.Ds. (or equivalent), who must hold full-time faculty positions at accredited North American institutions. Applicant must also be a member of the AGA. Women and minorities are strongly encouraged to apply.

The recipient will be selected based on significance, investigator, innovation, approach, environment, relevance to AGA's mission, evidence of institutional commitment, and the overall likelihood that the project will lead to subsequent, more substantial grants.

GEOG. RESTRICTIONS: North America.

FINANCIAL DATA:
Funds may be used for salary (for lab personnel and technicians only), supplies or equipment. Indirect costs are not allowed.
Amount of support per award: $30,000.

NO. AWARDS: 3.

APPLICATION INFO:
Applications must be submitted through the AGA Grants Management System. Materials will not be accepted via mail, fax or e-mail.
Duration: One year.
Deadline: September 2.

ADDRESS INQUIRIES TO:
See e-mail address above.

AMERICAN GASTROENTEROLOGICAL ASSOCIATION (AGA) [2196]
4930 Del Ray Avenue
Bethesda, MD 20814
(301) 654-2055
Fax: (301) 654-5920
E-mail: awards@gastro.org
Web Site: www.gastro.org/research-and-awards

AREAS OF INTEREST:
Gastroenterology and related fields.

NAME(S) OF PROGRAMS:
● **AGA Student Abstract Award**

TYPE:
Awards/prizes; Travel grants. Awards for graduate students, medical students and residents presenting an abstract chosen by AGA for presentation during Digestive Disease Week (DDW).

PURPOSE:
To stimulate interest in gastroenterology/hepatology research careers through competition and recognition.

LEGAL BASIS:
Nonprofit foundation.

ELIGIBILITY:
Applicant must be high school, undergraduate, graduate or medical student or medical resident (up to and including postgraduate year three) who has performed

original research related to diseases, structure or functioning of the digestive system. The applicant's sponsor must be a member of AGA. Applicants may only submit one abstract for consideration and must be the designated presenter or first author of the abstract. Women and minority students are strongly encouraged to apply. Awardees will be selected based on novelty, significance of the proposal, clarity of the abstract and contribution of the student.

Postdoctoral fellows, technicians, visiting scientists and M.D. research fellows are not eligible.

GEOG. RESTRICTIONS: North America.

FINANCIAL DATA:
Amount of support per award: Travel Award: $500; Student Abstract of the Year: $1,000.

NO. AWARDS: 24.

APPLICATION INFO:
Applications must be submitted through the AGA Grants Management System. Materials will not be accepted by mail, fax or e-mail.
Deadline: February 24, 2021.

ADDRESS INQUIRIES TO:
See e-mail address above.

AMERICAN GASTROENTEROLOGICAL ASSOCIATION (AGA) [2197]
4930 Del Ray Avenue
Bethesda, MD 20814
(301) 654-2055
Fax: (301) 654-5920
E-mail: awards@gastro.org
Web Site: www.gastro.org/research-and-awards

AREAS OF INTEREST:
Gastroenterology and related fields.

NAME(S) OF PROGRAMS:
● **AGA-Moti L. and Kamla Rustgi International Travel Awards**

TYPE:
Awards/prizes; Travel grants. Awards for young basic, translational and clinical investigators residing outside North America to offset travel expenses to attend Digestive Disease Week (DDW).

PURPOSE:
To enable young investigators outside of North American institutions to attend DDW and encourage them to maintain a commitment to digestive disease research.

LEGAL BASIS:
Nonprofit foundation.

ELIGIBILITY:
The applicant must hold an M.D. or Ph.D. degree or a non-U.S. equivalent degree, be 35 years of age or younger at the time of DDW and be fluent in English. The applicant must be an AGA member, who is sponsored by an international AGA member. The applicant must be the first author of an abstract accepted by the AGA for presentation at DDW and provide evidence of abstract acceptance. Applicants must only submit one abstract for consideration.

Awardees will be selected based on the applicant's credentials and achievements as documented in their application.

FINANCIAL DATA:
Amount of support per award: $750.

NO. AWARDS: 2.

APPLICATION INFO:
Applications must be submitted through the AGA Grants Management System. Materials will not be accepted by mail, fax or e-mail.
Deadline: February 24, 2021.

ADDRESS INQUIRIES TO:
See e-mail address above.

AMERICAN GASTROENTEROLOGICAL ASSOCIATION (AGA) [2198]
4930 Del Ray Avenue
Bethesda, MD 20814
(301) 654-2055
Fax: (301) 654-5920
E-mail: awards@gastro.org
Web Site: www.gastro.org/research-and-awards

AREAS OF INTEREST:
Gastroenterology and related fields.

NAME(S) OF PROGRAMS:
● **AGA Fellow Abstract Award**

TYPE:
Awards/prizes; Travel grants. Awards to support recipients who are M.D., Ph.D. or equivalent fellows giving abstract-based oral or poster presentations at Digestive Disease Week (DDW).

PURPOSE:
To stimulate interest in gastroenterology and hepatology research careers.

LEGAL BASIS:
Nonprofit foundation.

ELIGIBILITY:
Applicants must be M.D. and/or Ph.D. postdoctoral fellows who are active or trainee members of AGA, and must be sponsored by a member of AGA. Applicants must be first author of an abstract accepted by AGA for oral or poster presentation, and must provide confirmation of AGA abstract acceptance.

GEOG. RESTRICTIONS: North America.

FINANCIAL DATA:
Amount of support per award: Travel Award: $500; Fellow Abstract of the Year: $1,000.

NO. AWARDS: 24.

APPLICATION INFO:
Applications must be submitted through the AGA Grants Management System. Materials will not be accepted by mail, fax or e-mail.
Deadline: February 24, 2021.

ADDRESS INQUIRIES TO:
See e-mail address above.

AMERICAN GASTROENTEROLOGICAL ASSOCIATION (AGA) [2199]
4930 Del Ray Avenue
Bethesda, MD 20814
(301) 654-2055
Fax: (301) 654-5920
E-mail: awards@gastro.org
Web Site: www.gastro.org/research-and-awards

AREAS OF INTEREST:
Gastroenterology and related fields.

NAME(S) OF PROGRAMS:
● **AGA-Caroline Craig Augustyn and Damian Augustyn Award in Digestive Cancer**

TYPE:
Research grants. Award for an early career investigator who currently holds a federal or

non-federal career development award devoted to conducting research related to digestive cancer.

PURPOSE:
To support early career investigators conducting research relevant to the pathogenesis, prevention, diagnosis, or treatment of digestive cancer; to supplement existing career development funding.

LEGAL BASIS:
Nonprofit foundation.

ELIGIBILITY:
Candidates must hold an M.D., Ph.D. or equivalent degree and a full-time position at a North American institution. Research must be conducted at a North American institution. Candidates must also be members of AGA. Candidates must hold an NIH K series or other federal or non-federal career development award of at least four years duration. There must be at least one remaining year on the award by the start date of this award. Women and underrepresented minority applicants are strongly encouraged to apply. Physician/scientist investigators and candidates interested in translational research are especially encouraged to apply. Awardees will be selected based on qualifications of the candidate, the novelty, feasibility and significance of their research and the potential for a future independent research career.

M.D. applicants: no more than seven years shall have elapsed following the completion of clinical training (GI fellowship or its equivalent) and the start date of this award. Ph.D. applicants: no more than seven years shall have elapsed following the awarding of the Ph.D. and the start date of this award. An appropriately documented parental leave of absence will not be counted toward the seven-year eligibility criteria. Exceptional circumstances may also be considered.

Candidates may not hold an R01 or equivalent, such as a VA Merit award; therefore, established investigators will not be considered for this award.

FINANCIAL DATA:
Funds are to be used to support direct research-related activities and may be used to support a new endeavor or an ongoing basic or clinical project. Funds may also be used for equipment, supplies, animal costs and other materials. No indirect costs will be allowed.
Amount of support per award: $40,000.

NO. AWARDS: 1.

APPLICATION INFO:
Applications must be submitted through the AGA Grants Management System. Materials will not be accepted by mail, fax or e-mail.
Duration: One year.
Deadline: July 29.

ADDRESS INQUIRIES TO:
See e-mail address above.

AMERICAN GASTROENTEROLOGICAL ASSOCIATION (AGA) [2200]
4930 Del Ray Avenue
Bethesda, MD 20814
(301) 654-2055
Fax: (301) 654-5920
E-mail: awards@gastro.org
Web Site: www.gastro.org/research-and-awards

AREAS OF INTEREST:
Gastroenterology and related fields.

NAME(S) OF PROGRAMS:
● **AGA-Gastric Cancer Foundation Ben Feinstein Memorial Research Scholar Award in Gastric Cancer**

TYPE:
Awards/prizes. Scholar award for early career faculty working toward an independent career in gastric cancer research.

PURPOSE:
To support young gastroenterologists working toward independent and productive research careers in digestive diseases.

LEGAL BASIS:
Nonprofit foundation.

ELIGIBILITY:
Candidate must hold an M.D., Ph.D. or equivalent degree and a full-time faculty position at a North American institution by the start date of the award. Proposals spanning the research spectrum, from basic to clinical science, are eligible.

Candidate must be an AGA member in good standing at the time of application submission.

Women, minorities and physician-scientist investigators are strongly encouraged to apply.

GEOG. RESTRICTIONS: North America.

FINANCIAL DATA:
Amount of support per award: $100,000.
Total amount of support: $300,000.

NO. AWARDS: 1.

APPLICATION INFO:
Applications must be submitted through the AGA Grants Management System. Materials will not be accepted via mail, fax or e-mail.
Duration: Three years.
Deadline: December 16.

ADDRESS INQUIRIES TO:
Nick Tomeo, Manager, Research Affairs (See address above.)

*SPECIAL STIPULATIONS:
AGA membership must be maintained throughout the three-year duration of the award.

AMERICAN GASTROENTEROLOGICAL ASSOCIATION (AGA) [2201]
4930 Del Ray Avenue
Bethesda, MD 20814
(301) 654-2055
Fax: (301) 654-5920
E-mail: awards@gastro.org
Web Site: www.gastro.org/research-and-awards

FOUNDED: 1990

AREAS OF INTEREST:
Gastroenterology and related fields.

NAME(S) OF PROGRAMS:
● **AGA Research Scholar Award**

TYPE:
Research grants. Research Scholar Award provides funding to early career faculty working toward an independent career in digestive disease research.

PURPOSE:
To support young gastroenterologists working toward independent and productive research

careers in digestive diseases by ensuring that a major proportion of their time is protected for research.

LEGAL BASIS:
Nonprofit foundation.

ELIGIBILITY:
Candidate must hold an M.D., Ph.D. or equivalent degree and a full-time faculty position at a North American institution by the start of the award. No more than seven years shall have passed following the completion of clinical training. At the time of application submission, candidate may not hold, or have held, an NIH K01, K08, K23, K99, R00, R01, R21, R29, Veterans Affairs Career Development Award or any award with similar objectives from non-federal sources. Candidates with an active K12 may apply.

Proposals spanning the research spectrum, from basic to clinical science, are eligible.

Candidate must be an AGA member in good standing at the time of application submission.

Women, underrepresented minorities, and physician/scientist investigators are strongly encouraged to apply.

GEOG. RESTRICTIONS: North America.

FINANCIAL DATA:
Amount of support per award: $300,000 ($100,000 per year).

NO. AWARDS: 5.

APPLICATION INFO:
Applications must be submitted through the AGA Grants Management System. Application materials will not be accepted via mail, fax or e-mail.
Duration: Three years.
Deadline: November 9.

PUBLICATIONS:
Announcements.

ADDRESS INQUIRIES TO:
See e-mail address above.

AMERICAN GASTROENTEROLOGICAL ASSOCIATION (AGA) [2202]
4930 Del Ray Avenue
Bethesda, MD 20814
(301) 654-2055
Fax: (301) 654-5920
E-mail: awards@gastro.org
Web Site: www.gastro.org/research-and-awards

FOUNDED: 1990

AREAS OF INTEREST:
Gastroenterology and related fields.

NAME(S) OF PROGRAMS:
● **AGA-Takeda Pharmaceuticals Research Scholar Awards in Celiac Disease**

TYPE:
Research grants. Research award for early career faculty working toward independent careers in celiac disease research.

PURPOSE:
To support early career investigators working toward independent and productive research careers in digestive diseases.

ELIGIBILITY:
Applicants must hold an M.D., Ph.D. or equivalent degree and a full-time faculty or equivalent position at an institution in North America. Applicants performing any type of

research relevant to celiac disease are eligible to apply. Studies of non-celiac gluten sensitivity will be considered if their contribution to the overall understanding of celiac disease is clearly justified in the application.

AGA membership is required at the time of application submission.

Applicants who are physician-scientists, female or from racial/ethnic groups underrepresented in biomedical research are strongly encouraged to apply.

GEOG. RESTRICTIONS: North America.

FINANCIAL DATA:
Amount of support per award: $300,000 (100,000 per year).

NO. AWARDS: 1.

APPLICATION INFO:
Applications must be submitted through the AGA Grants Management System. Materials will not be accepted via mail, fax or e-mail.
Duration: Three years.
Deadline: November 9.

ADDRESS INQUIRIES TO:
See e-mail address above.

AMERICAN GASTROENTEROLOGICAL ASSOCIATION (AGA) [2203]

4930 Del Ray Avenue
Bethesda, MD 20814
(301) 654-2055
Fax: (301) 654-5920
E-mail: awards@gastro.org
Web Site: www.gastro.org/research-and-awards

FOUNDED: 1990

AREAS OF INTEREST:
Gastroenterological and related fields.

NAME(S) OF PROGRAMS:
* **AGA-Medtronic Pilot Research Award in Technology Innovation**

TYPE:
Research grants. Research award for independent investigators at any career stage to support the research and development of novel devices or technologies that will potentially impact the diagnosis or treatment of digestive disease.

PURPOSE:
To provide funds to early career investigators to help establish their research careers or to support projects that represent new research directions for established investigators.

ELIGIBILITY:
Applicants must hold an M.D., Ph.D. or equivalent degree and a full-time faculty or equivalent position at an institution in North America. AGA membership is required at the time of application submission.

Applicants performing any type of research relevant to digestive disorders are eligible to apply. Projects must focus on designing and/or testing improvements to existing technology, developing a new device, diagnostic, research method technology, and/or investigating the application of nanotechnology or methodologies such as computational biology to gastroenterology- or hepatology-related areas.

Applicants who are physician-scientists, female, or from racial/ethnic groups underrepresented in biomedical research are strongly encouraged to apply.

GEOG. RESTRICTIONS: North America.

FINANCIAL DATA:
Amount of support per award: $30,000.

NO. AWARDS: 1.

APPLICATION INFO:
Applications must be submitted through the AGA Grants Management System. Materials will not be accepted via mail, fax or e-mail.
Duration: One year.
Deadline: September 2.

ADDRESS INQUIRIES TO:
See e-mail address above.

AMERICAN GASTROENTEROLOGICAL ASSOCIATION (AGA) [2204]

4930 Del Ray Avenue
Bethesda, MD 20814
(301) 654-2055
Fax: (301) 654-5920
E-mail: awards@gastro.org
Web Site: www.gastro.org/research-and-awards

FOUNDED: 1990

AREAS OF INTEREST:
Gastroenterology and related fields.

NAME(S) OF PROGRAMS:
* **AGA-Pfizer Pilot Research Award in Inflammatory Bowel Disease**

TYPE:
Research grants. Research award for independent investigators at any career stage to support research focused on improving the diagnosis and treatment of inflammatory bowel disease.

PURPOSE:
To provide funds for early career investigators to help establish their careers or to support projects that represent new research directions for established investigators.

ELIGIBILITY:
Applicants must hold an M.D., Ph.D. or equivalent degree and a full-time faculty position or equivalent at an institution in North America. AGA membership is required at the time of application submission.

Applicants performing any type of research relevant to digestive disorders are eligible to apply. Projects must focus on new research areas that could improve the diagnosis and treatment of inflammatory bowel disease (IBD).

Applicants who are physician-scientists, female or from racial/ethnic groups underrepresented in biomedical research are strongly encouraged to apply.

GEOG. RESTRICTIONS: North America.

FINANCIAL DATA:
Amount of support per award: $30,000.

NO. AWARDS: 1.

APPLICATION INFO:
Applications must be submitted through the AGA Grants Management System. Materials will not be accepted via mail, fax or e-mail.
Duration: One year.
Deadline: September 2.

ADDRESS INQUIRIES TO:
See e-mail address above.

CANADIAN LIVER FOUNDATION

3100 Steeles Avenue East
Suite 801
Markham ON L3R 8T3 Canada
(416) 491-3353
(800) 563-5483 (within Canada and U.S.)
Fax: (905) 752-1540
E-mail: clf@liver.ca
Web Site: www.liver.ca

TYPE:
Scholarships. One summer studentship grant may be awarded to a student in Canada whose research project is related to hepatobiliary research. Two summer studentship grants may be awarded to students in Canada whose research projects are related to liver cancer. One Raj Bhargava Memorial Summer Studentship may be awarded to a student enrolled at the University of Alberta whose research project is related to radiology of liver disease.

See entry 2051 for full listing.

CANADIAN LIVER FOUNDATION [2205]

3100 Steeles Avenue East
Suite 801
Markham ON L3R 8T3 Canada
(416) 491-3353
(800) 563-5483 (within Canada and U.S.)
Fax: (905) 752-1540
E-mail: clf@liver.ca
Web Site: www.liver.ca

FOUNDED: 1969

AREAS OF INTEREST:
Research and education into the causes, diagnosis, prevention and treatment of diseases of the liver.

NAME(S) OF PROGRAMS:
* **Graduate Studentships**

TYPE:
Scholarships. One graduate studentship may be awarded to a student in Alberta whose research project is related to hepatobiliary research and two graduate studentships may be awarded to students in Canada whose research projects are related to hepatitis B.

PURPOSE:
To enable academically superior students to undertake full-time studies in a Canadian university in a discipline relevant to the objectives of the Foundation.

LEGAL BASIS:
Registered Canadian charity.

ELIGIBILITY:
Applicants must be accepted into a full-time university graduate science program in a medically-related discipline related to a Master's or doctoral degree and hold a record of superior academic performance in studies relevant to the proposed training.

Canadian citizens, landed immigrants, and permanent residents will receive first consideration.

Applicants must be sponsored by a faculty supervisor with a record of productive medical research and sufficient competitively acquired research funding to ensure the satisfactory conduct of the student's research during the term of the award. The supervisor's publication record should indicate significant contribution to liver related studies. The supervisor must agree to provide personal, direct and continuing supervision of the student and must be a member of the Canadian Association for the Study of the Liver.

GEOG. RESTRICTIONS: Canada.

FINANCIAL DATA:
Amount of support per award: $20,000 (CAN) per year paid in quarterly installments.

NO. AWARDS: 3 for the year 2020.

APPLICATION INFO:
A single PDF file of the entire grant application, a Referee's Assessment Form completed by three referees, and a scanned copy of the official transcript must be submitted by e-mail to researchgrants@liver.ca by the deadline.
Duration: Two years.
Deadline: March 31.

PUBLICATIONS:
Program description and guidelines.

STAFF:
Nem Maksimovic, Manager, National Health Promotion and Education

ADDRESS INQUIRIES TO:
Nem Maksimovic, Manager
National Health Promotion
and Education
(See address above.)

CANADIAN LIVER FOUNDATION [2206]

3100 Steeles Avenue East
Suite 801
Markham ON L3R 8T3 Canada
(416) 491-3353
(800) 563-5483 (within Canada and U.S.)
Fax: (905) 752-1540
E-mail: clf@liver.ca
Web Site: www.liver.ca

FOUNDED: 1969

AREAS OF INTEREST:
Research and education into the causes, diagnosis, prevention and treatment of diseases of the liver.

NAME(S) OF PROGRAMS:
● **Canadian Liver Foundation Operating Grant**

TYPE:
Research grants. Operating grants may be offered to one researcher in Canada whose research project is related to hepatobiliary research, one researcher in Canada whose research project is related to hepatitis B, and one researcher in Canada whose research project is related to liver cancer.

YEAR PROGRAM STARTED: 1970

PURPOSE:
To support research projects directed towards a defined objective, conducted by an investigator working alone or in collaboration with others.

LEGAL BASIS:
Registered Canadian charity.

ELIGIBILITY:
Investigators with primary research interest in liver disease who hold an academic appointment in a Canadian university or affiliated institution are eligible to apply. Clinical investigators and basic scientists will be considered. Applicants for operating grants must be members of the Canadian Association for the Study of the Liver.

Canadian citizens, landed immigrants, and permanent residents will receive first consideration.

GEOG. RESTRICTIONS: Canada.

FINANCIAL DATA:
Amount of support per award: $60,000 (CAN) per year.
Total amount of support: Varies depending on the number of suitable candidates and the funds available.

NO. AWARDS: 3 for the year 2020.

APPLICATION INFO:
A single PDF of the entire grant application, including curriculum vitae and other attachments, should be sent by e-mail to researchgrants@liver.ca by the deadline.
Duration: Two years.
Deadline: March 31, for awards to become tenable the following September 1.

PUBLICATIONS:
Program description and guidelines.

STAFF:
Nem Maksimovic, Research Grants Administrator

ADDRESS INQUIRIES TO:
Nem Maksimovic
Research Grants Administrator
(See address above.)

COOLEY'S ANEMIA FOUNDATION, INC. [2207]

330 7th Avenue
Suite 200
New York, NY 10001-5264
(212) 279-8090 ext. 201
Fax: (212) 279-5999
E-mail: info@thalassemia.org
Web Site: www.thalassemia.org

FOUNDED: 1954

AREAS OF INTEREST:
Cooley's anemia and all thalassemias.

TYPE:
Fellowships; Research grants. Clinical grants. Research, public and professional education, patient care and public information. Basic and clinical research and fellowships.

YEAR PROGRAM STARTED: 1954

PURPOSE:
To provide impetus to benefit the advancement of knowledge and the quality of care in Cooley's anemia and other thalassemias.

LEGAL BASIS:
Federal tax-exempt, nonprofit, voluntary health agency.

ELIGIBILITY:
Medical researchers who are interested in initiating a thalassemia related project or who have an existing project that requires additional funding may apply.

FINANCIAL DATA:
Amount of support per award: Fellowships: $50,000; Clinical grants: Up to $50,000.
Total amount of support: $250,000 for the year 2020.

NO. MOST RECENT APPLICANTS: 30.

APPLICATION INFO:
Applications are available on the Foundation web site.
Duration: One year. Possibility for renewal for second year.

Deadline: First Monday in February.

PUBLICATIONS:
Lifeline Newsletter; screening material; educational pamphlets.

IRS I.D.: 11-1971539

OFFICERS:
Peter Chieco, President

ADDRESS INQUIRIES TO:
Craig Butler, National Executive Director
(See address above.)

CROHN'S AND COLITIS FOUNDATION [2208]

733 Third Avenue, Suite 510
New York, NY 10017
(646) 943-7505
(800) 932-2423
E-mail: grant@crohnscolitisfoundation.org
Web Site: www.crohnscolitisfoundation.org

FOUNDED: 1967

AREAS OF INTEREST:
Research and education in inflammatory bowel disease (Crohn's disease and ulcerative colitis).

CONSULTING OR VOLUNTEER SERVICES:
Medical committees (consisting of physician volunteers) provide services in the areas of patient and professional education, research development, grants review, etc.

NAME(S) OF PROGRAMS:
● **Career Development Award**
● **Research Fellowship Award**
● **Research Initiative**
● **Senior Research Award**
● **Student Research Fellowship Awards**

TYPE:
Awards/prizes; Conferences/seminars; Fellowships; Project/program grants; Research grants; Scholarships; Training grants; Visiting scholars. Career Development Awards prepare potential basic/translational researchers to transition to a career of independent investigation and research.

Research Fellowship Awards support postdoctoral individuals in developing skills related to basic and/or clinical investigation into IBD.

Research Initiative program provides support for cutting-edge translational studies focused on the priority areas to address unmet clinical needs in IBD.

Senior Research Award provides funding for established basic/translational researchers so they are able to generate enough preliminary data to be competitive for additional funding.

Student Research Fellowship Awards are available for undergraduate, graduate, and medical students to support their IBD-related research.

YEAR PROGRAM STARTED: 1967

PURPOSE:
To fund research leading to understanding of and ultimate cure for Crohn's disease and ulcerative colitis.

LEGAL BASIS:
Nonprofit, special-interest foundation.

ELIGIBILITY:
For Career Development Awards, candidates must have at least five years of relevant postdoctoral experience prior to the beginning date of the awards and not in excess of 10 years beyond the attainment of their Doctorate degrees.

For Research Fellowship Awards, candidates must have two years of relevant postdoctoral experience prior to the beginning date of the award.

For Research Training Awards, candidates must be sponsored by a public or private nonprofit institution or a government institution engaged in health care and health-related research within the U.S. and its possessions. Individuals who already are well established in the field are not considered eligible for these awards. Applicants must hold M.D. or Ph.D. degrees and be employed within the U.S. at the time of submission. Eligibility is not restricted by citizenship.

For Senior Research Awards, applicants must be established researchers in the field of inflammatory bowel disease.

FINANCIAL DATA:
Amount of support per award: Career Development Award: $90,000 per year; Research Fellowship Award: $58,250 per year; Senior Research Award: $115,830 per year; Student Research Fellowship Award: Up to $2,500.

Total amount of support: Approximately $28,000,000 annually.

CO-OP FUNDING PROGRAMS:
NASPGHAN/CDHNF.

NO. MOST RECENT APPLICANTS: 500 to 600.

NO. AWARDS: 200.

APPLICATION INFO:
Before submitting a Letter of Intent or Full Proposal, applicants are urged to view the online policies and instructions. After the Letter of Intent is submitted and approved, Research Grants Administration will send an e-mail to the applicant with a link to complete and submit a Full Proposal.

Duration: Career Development Award, Research Fellowship Award and Senior Research Award: One to three years.

Deadline: Career Development Award, Research Fellowship Award and Senior Research Award: Letter of Intent due November 8 for Spring/Summer and May 5 for Fall/Winter. Online Application due January 28 for Spring/Summer and July 20 for Fall/Winter. Decision June and December, respectively; Student Research Fellowship Awards: March 15. Awards begin on or about June 15.

PUBLICATIONS:
Annual report; *Inflammatory Bowel Diseases*; *Foundation Focus*; brochures.

IRS I.D.: 13-6193105

STAFF:
Michael Osso, President and Chief Executive Officer

FOUNDERS:
Henry D. Janowitz, M.D.
William D. Modell
Irwin M. Rosenthal

ADDRESS INQUIRIES TO:
Orlando Green, Senior Manager
(See address above.)

CYSTIC FIBROSIS FOUNDATION [2209]
4550 Montgomery Avenue
Suite 1100 N
Bethesda, MD 20816
(301) 841-2614
(800) 344-4823
E-mail: grants@cff.org
Web Site: www.cff.org
FOUNDED: 1955

AREAS OF INTEREST:
Research, care and education programs to benefit patients with cystic fibrosis.

NAME(S) OF PROGRAMS:
- **CFF/NIH Unfunded Grants**
- **Clinical Fellowship Awards**
- **Clinical Pilot and Feasibility Awards**
- **Clinical Research Awards**
- **Leroy Matthews Physician/Scientist Award**
- **Pilot and Feasibility Awards**
- **Postdoc-to-Faculty Transition Awards**
- **Postdoctoral Research Fellowship Award**
- **Research Grants**
- **Harry Shwachman Clinical Investigator Award**

TYPE:
Fellowships; Research grants; Training grants. CFF/NIH Unfunded Grants support excellent cystic fibrosis-related research projects that have been submitted to and approved by the National Institute of Health, but cannot be supported by available NIH funds.

Clinical Fellowship Awards encourage specialized training early in a physicians career and prepare candidates for careers in academic medicine.

Clinical Pilot and Feasibility Awards are intended to support projects involving human subjects or samples that will develop and test new hypotheses and/or new methods in research areas relevant to cystic fibrosis.

Clinical Research Awards provide support for generating clinical data that will make future award applications competitive upon submission to the NIH. Projects may address diagnostic or therapeutic methods related to cystic fibrosis or the pathophysiology of CF, and applicants must demonstrate access to a sufficient number of CF patients from CF Foundation-accredited care.

The Leroy Matthews Physician-Scientist Award encourages outstanding newly trained pediatricians and internists to enhance clinical proficiency in cystic fibrosis-related subspecialties and to develop the necessary research capabilities.

Pilot and Feasibility Awards are intended to support basic science research studies focused on developing and testing new hypothesis in areas relevant to cystic fibrosis.

The Postdoc-to-Faculty Transition Awards are designed to support postdoctoral research fellows during their cystic fibrosis fellowship and aid in their transition to an independent research faculty position.

Postdoctoral Research Fellowship Awards are offered to M.D.s, Ph.Ds, and M.D./Ph.D.s who are interested in conducting basic or clinical research related to cystic fibrosis.

Research Grants are intended to encourage the development of new information that contributes to the understanding of the basic etiology and pathogenesis of cystic fibrosis.

The Harry Shwachman Clinical Investigator Award provides the opportunity for clinically-trained physicians to develop into independent biomedical research investigators who are actively involved in cystic fibrosis-related areas. .

YEAR PROGRAM STARTED: 1955

PURPOSE:
To encourage clinical research into the cause, care and treatment of cystic fibrosis; to train specialists for careers in academic medicine.

LEGAL BASIS:
501(c)(3) organization, incorporated as a nonprofit, tax-exempt organization.

ELIGIBILITY:
Contact the Foundation for specific eligibility details for the various grant programs.

FINANCIAL DATA:
Amount of support per award: CFF/NIH Unfunded Grants: Up to $125,000 per year; Clinical Fellowship Awards: Up to $80,000 stipend and $20,000 for research cost; Clinical Pilot and Feasibility Awards: $80,000 annually; Clinical Research Awards: Up to $150,000 per year (single-center) and up to $350,000 per year (multicenter); Leroy Matthews Physician/Scientist Award: $70,000 for year one to $130,000 for year six; Pilot Feasibility Awards: $50,000 per year; Postdoc-to-Faculty Transition Awards: $58,850 to $70,500 stipend, plus $10,000 research support, based on years of postdoctoral experience; Postdoctoral Research Fellowship Award: $58,850 salary and fringe, plus $1,250 travel and $3,000 research support for year one, $61,200 salary and fringe, plus $1,250 travel and $3,000 research support for year two; Research Grants: $125,000 per year; Harry Shwachman Clinical Investigator Award: $100,000 per year, plus $30,000 for supplies.

APPLICATION INFO:
Detailed information can be obtained from the CFF Grants and Contracts Office.

Duration: CFF/NIH Unfunded Grants, Clinical Pilot and Feasibility Awards, Pilot and Feasibility Awards and Research Grants: Up to two years; Clinical Fellowship Awards: Three to five years; Clinical Research Awards: Three years maximum; Leroy Matthews Physician/Scientist Award: Up to six years; Postdoc-to-Faculty Transition Awards: Up to five years; Postdoctoral Research Fellowship Award: Two years; Harry Shwachman Clinical Investigator Award: Three years.

Deadline: Varies. Consult web site for exact dates.

PUBLICATIONS:
Annual report; application form; guidelines.

IRS I.D.: 13-1930701

STAFF:
Michael P. Boyle, M.D., President and Chief Executive Officer
Marc S. Ginsky, Executive Vice President and Chief Operating Officer
Vera H. Twigg, Executive Vice President and Chief Financial Officer
William Skach, M.D., Executive Vice President and Chief Scientific Officer
Marybeth McMahon, Ph.D., Chief of Staff

ADDRESS INQUIRIES TO:
Grants and Contracts Manager
(See address above.)

DIABETES CANADA   [2210]

522 University Avenue
Suite 1300
Toronto ON M5G 2R5 Canada
(416) 363-3373
Fax: (416) 363-7465
E-mail: research@diabetes.ca
Web Site: www.diabetes.ca

FOUNDED: 1953

AREAS OF INTEREST:
Medical research into the causes and cure of diabetes.

NAME(S) OF PROGRAMS:
● **Charles H. Best Research Fund**

TYPE:
Fellowships; General operating grants; Research grants; Training grants. Scholar awards. Support for new and ongoing research into better ways to prevent, treat, and manage diabetes and to ultimately find a cure.

YEAR PROGRAM STARTED: 1975

PURPOSE:
To promote the health of Canadians through diabetes research, education, service, and advocacy.

LEGAL BASIS:
Nonprofit.

ELIGIBILITY:
Individuals and groups may apply for research programs in Canada only.

GEOG. RESTRICTIONS: Canada.

FINANCIAL DATA:
Total amount of support: Varies.

NO. MOST RECENT APPLICANTS: 200.

APPLICATION INFO:
Guidelines and application form are available on the web site.
Duration: One to five years, depending on the type of grant/award.

ADDRESS INQUIRIES TO:
Research and Education
(See e-mail address above.)

JDRF INTERNATIONAL   [2211]

200 Vesey Street
28th Floor
New York, NY 10281
(212) 785-9500
(800) 533-2873
Fax: (212) 785-9595
E-mail: info@jdrf.org
preawardsupport@jdrf.org
Web Site: www.jdrf.org

FOUNDED: 1970

AREAS OF INTEREST:
To support research into the causes, treatment, prevention and cure of diabetes and its complications.

NAME(S) OF PROGRAMS:
● **Strategic Research Agreements: Project Concept Call**

TYPE:
Project/program grants; Research grants; Training grants. Support for a variety of needs, such as salaries for technical assistance, special equipment, animals and supplies for scientific investigations related to diabetes.

YEAR PROGRAM STARTED: 1973

PURPOSE:
To support scientific investigations of diabetes.

LEGAL BASIS:
Incorporated not-for-profit voluntary health agency.

ELIGIBILITY:
Applicants must hold an M.D., D.M.D., D.V.M., Ph.D., or equivalent and have a faculty position or equivalent at a college, university, medical school, company, or other research facility. Applications may be submitted by domestic and foreign nonprofit organizations, public and private, such as colleges, universities, hospitals, laboratories, units of state and local governments, and eligible agencies of the federal government. Ordinarily, for-profit organizations will not be considered, except under special circumstances.

There are no citizenship requirements for this program. To assure continued excellence and diversity among applicants and awardees, JDRF welcomes applications from all qualified individuals and encourages applications from persons with disabilities, women, and members of minority groups underrepresented in the sciences.

Project Concepts are selected on the basis of programmatic fit and robustness of the concept. In addition, projects that hold a prospect for transformative breakthroughs that prevent, treat or cure Type 1 diabetes will be given top priority.

FINANCIAL DATA:
Salary support plus fringe benefits for the principal investigator may not exceed his or her percentage effort on the project multiplied by institutional base salary. Indirect costs (excluding equipment) may not exceed 10% of the total direct costs. Funds may be used for salaries for key project personnel, other costs, travel, supplies, equipment, and subcontract costs.

Amount of support per award: Varies.

Total amount of support: Varies.

APPLICATION INFO:
An investigator interested in pursuing a research opportunity with JDRF must submit a Project Concept through JDRF's Project Concept Call in RMS360 (jdrf.smartsimple.us). Applicants must submit an application that outlines the rationale for the request, a proposed budget, and the principal investigator's other support (current and pending) and curriculum vitae. Only those Project Concepts approved by JDRF will be asked to submit a full research application.

Duration: Up to three years.

Deadline: Project Concepts are due by 5 P.M. on February 4, August 1 and November 1. No extensions will be granted. Notification in March, September and December, respectively.

PUBLICATIONS:
Annual report; policy statement; research appropriations sheet; *Countdown Magazine.*

ADDRESS INQUIRIES TO:
Director, Operations and Administration
(See address above.)

JDRF INTERNATIONAL   [2212]

200 Vesey Street
28th Floor
New York, NY 10281
(212) 785-9500
(800) 533-2873
Fax: (212) 785-9595
E-mail: info@jdrf.org
Web Site: www.jdrf.org

FOUNDED: 1970

AREAS OF INTEREST:
To support research into the causes, treatment, prevention and cure of diabetes and its complications.

NAME(S) OF PROGRAMS:
● **Postdoctoral Fellowships**

TYPE:
Fellowships. Postdoctoral fellowships to attract qualified and promising scientists entering their professional career into fields of research in diabetes. The applicant is required to work with a sponsor who can provide a training environment most conducive to beginning a career in diabetes-relevant research. Fellowship research may be conducted at foreign and domestic, for-profit and nonprofit, public and private organizations such as universities, colleges, hospitals, laboratories, units of state and local governments, and eligible agencies of the federal government.

YEAR PROGRAM STARTED: 1973

PURPOSE:
To support advanced training in fields of research directly related to diabetes.

LEGAL BASIS:
Incorporated not-for-profit voluntary health agency.

ELIGIBILITY:
By the beginning of the period of support sought, the applicant must have a doctoral degree (M.D., D.M.D., D.V.M., Ph.D. or the equivalent) for no more than five years before the fellowship and may not have a faculty appointment. Each applicant must be sponsored by a scientist who is affiliated full-time with an accredited institution and who agrees to supervise that individual's training. JDRF welcomes applications from persons with disabilities, women and members of minority groups underrepresented in the sciences.

The applicant is responsible for selecting a research mentor and for making arrangements to work in this person's laboratory. The designated mentor must be the senior scientist who will directly supervise the proposed research.

FINANCIAL DATA:
The stipend is dependent on the number of years of relevant experience.

Amount of support per award: Varies.

APPLICATION INFO:
Application forms are available from the address above. Applicants must submit a signed original with 15 copies. The applicant must include three letters of reference assessing the scientific abilities and potential of the applicant and a statement of career goals with the relevance to diabetes-related research. The sponsor must outline a specific training program, confirm the space and facilities for the research project, provide information on all sources of grant support (current or pending, federal or nonfederal)

and must include the title, amounts, funding periods and abstract pages of all current and pending support.

Duration: Three years.

Deadline: Contact JDRF for up-to-date details.

PUBLICATIONS:
Annual report; policy statement; research appropriations sheet; *Countdown Magazine.*

ADDRESS INQUIRIES TO:
E-mail: preawardsupport@jdrf.org

*SPECIAL STIPULATIONS:
Awardees will be required to produce a progress report at the end of each funding year. Awardees must spend at least 75% of time and effort on the research project during the period of the award.

JDRF INTERNATIONAL [2213]
200 Vesey Street
28th Floor
New York, NY 10281
(212) 785-9500
(800) 533-2873
Fax: (212) 785-9595
E-mail: info@jdrf.org
Web Site: www.jdrf.org

FOUNDED: 1970

AREAS OF INTEREST:
Prevention and treatment of type I diabetes and its complications.

NAME(S) OF PROGRAMS:
● **Career Development Awards**

TYPE:
Development grants; Research grants; Training grants. Grants are awarded to promising scientists entering their professional career in the diabetes research field. In the five-year term, awardees will focus their research efforts in a subject directly related to JDRF's research mission goals and position themselves to work at the leading edge of diabetes research.

YEAR PROGRAM STARTED: 1979

PURPOSE:
To attract qualified and promising scientists early in their faculty careers and to give them the opportunity to establish themselves in areas that reflect the JDRF research mission goals.

LEGAL BASIS:
Charitable foundation.

ELIGIBILITY:
The individuals must be in a relatively early stage of their career who have demonstrated superior scholarship and show the greatest promise for future achievement in research, including either clinically relevant research or basic research. Ordinarily, their first degree (M.D., Ph.D., D.M.D., D.V.M. or equivalent) will have been received at least three, but not more than seven, years before the award. The applicant must hold an academic faculty-level position (including assistant professor or equivalent) at the time of the proposal, at a university, health science center or comparable institution with strong, well-established research and training programs for the chosen area of interest.

FINANCIAL DATA:
Indirect costs cannot exceed 10% of subtotal direct costs.

Amount of support per award: Up to $150,000 per year, including indirect costs; these funds may be used for a research allowance, which can include a technician, supplies, equipment and travel up to $2,000 per year. Salary for additional research personnel is permitted. Requests for equipment, in years other than the first year, must be strongly justified. Salary requests must be consistent with the established salary structure of the applicant's institution.

APPLICATION INFO:
Application forms are available from the address above. Applicants must submit a signed original with 15 copies and include three letters of reference assessing the candidate's scientific abilities, assurance from the university of an academic commitment to the applicant and the research project, all other sources of funding (current, federal and nonfederal), with the title, abstract, annual and total amount of support and inclusive funding periods of all current and pending grants.

Duration: Up to five years.

Deadline: Contact JDRF for up-to-date details.

PUBLICATIONS:
Annual report; policy statement; research appropriations sheet; *Countdown Magazine.*

ADDRESS INQUIRIES TO:
E-mail: preawardsupport@jdrf.org

THE KIDNEY FOUNDATION OF CANADA [2214]
5160 Decarie Boulevard, Suite 310
Montreal QC H3X 2H9 Canada
(514) 369-4806
Fax: (514) 369-2472
E-mail: christine.marquis@kidney.ca
Web Site: www.kidney.ca

FOUNDED: 1964

AREAS OF INTEREST:
Research that may further the current knowledge pertaining to the kidney.

NAME(S) OF PROGRAMS:
● **Kidney Health Research Grants**

TYPE:
Research grants. Provides funds to defray the cost of research, including the purchase of materials, supplies and equipment and the payment of laboratory assistants.

YEAR PROGRAM STARTED: 1972

PURPOSE:
To acquire a greater understanding of kidney diseases and the importance of the role of the kidneys in the human body.

LEGAL BASIS:
Corporation.

ELIGIBILITY:
Applicants must be Canadian citizens or permanent residents. Research must be conducted within Canada and funding is limited to individuals holding staff appointments at Canadian universities or other recognized Canadian academic institutions.

Grant applications for equipment only will not be considered.

GEOG. RESTRICTIONS: Canada.

FINANCIAL DATA:
Amount of support per award: Maximum $60,000 (CAN) per year.

APPLICATION INFO:
All forms, guidelines and procedures can be found on the proposalCENTRAL web site.

Duration: Up to three years. Grants run from July 1 to June 30.

Deadline: Registration: September 1; Full application: October 1.

ADDRESS INQUIRIES TO:
Christine Marquis, Research Grants and Awards Manager
(See e-mail address above.)

THE KIDNEY FOUNDATION OF CANADA [2215]
5160 Decarie Boulevard, Suite 310
Montreal QC H3X 2H9 Canada
(514) 369-4806
Fax: (514) 369-2472
E-mail: christine.marquis@kidney.ca
Web Site: www.kidney.ca

FOUNDED: 1964

AREAS OF INTEREST:
Research that may further the current knowledge pertaining to the kidney.

NAME(S) OF PROGRAMS:
● **Allied Health Kidney Research Grant**

TYPE:
Research grants. Funds allocated to assist in defraying the cost of research, including the purchase and maintenance of experimental animals, the purchase of materials, supplies and equipment and the payment of laboratory assistants. Travel assistance is also available.

YEAR PROGRAM STARTED: 1972

PURPOSE:
To foster and encourage research relevant to clinical practice in the area of nephrology and organ donation.

LEGAL BASIS:
Corporation.

ELIGIBILITY:
Funds are available for research conducted in Canada related to clinical practice in nephrology or organ donation and relevant to the mission of the Foundation. The principal applicant must be an allied health professional, including but not limited to, nurses, psychologists, social workers, technicians, biomedical engineers, dietitians, physiotherapists, pharmacists and occupational therapists.

GEOG. RESTRICTIONS: Canada.

FINANCIAL DATA:
Amount of support per award: Up to $60,000 (CAN) per year.

NO. AWARDS: 2 for the year 2018.

APPLICATION INFO:
All forms, policies and procedures can be found on the proposalCENTRAL web site.

Duration: Up to two years. Grants run from July 1 to June 30.

Deadline: March 1. Decision in May.

ADDRESS INQUIRIES TO:
Christine Marquis, Research Grants and Awards Manager
(See e-mail address above.)

THE KIDNEY FOUNDATION OF CANADA   [2216]

5160 Decarie Boulevard, Suite 310
Montreal QC H3X 2H9 Canada
(514) 369-4806
Fax: (514) 369-2472
E-mail: christine.marquis@kidney.ca
Web Site: www.kidney.ca/krescent

FOUNDED: 1964

AREAS OF INTEREST:
Kidney biology, genetics and development,
transplantation, and organ donation.

NAME(S) OF PROGRAMS:
● **KRESCENT: Kidney Research
  Scientist Core Education and National
  Training Program**

TYPE:
Awards/prizes; Fellowships. Salary awards.
The KRESCENT program is comprised of
three components: Allied Health Kidney
Doctoral Award, New Investigator Awards
and Postdoctoral Fellowships.

YEAR PROGRAM STARTED: 2005

PURPOSE:
To build capacity in the kidney research field;
to train an increased number of highly skilled
scientists, with a focus on the prevention of
end-state renal disease and new treatments to
improve health of individuals affected by
kidney disease.

LEGAL BASIS:
Corporation.

ELIGIBILITY:
Applicants must be Canadian citizens,
permanent residents or landed immigrants at
the time of submission of their application.
For New Investigator Awards, applicants
must apply through a university department
or affiliated institution offering the faculty
appointment. For the Postdoctoral
Fellowship, applicants must apply through a
university department or affiliated institution
that has been accepted as suitable for
research training by the KRESCENT
program. Institutions eligible to host a
KRESCENT Fellow include Canadian or
foreign universities, affiliated research
hospitals, and colleges with a strong research
mandate and capacity.

FINANCIAL DATA:
Amount of support per award: Allied Health
Kidney Doctoral Award: Maximum $31,000
per year; New Investigator Awards: $65,000
to $70,000 per year; Postdoctoral
Fellowships: $55,000 to $65,000 per year.

NO. AWARDS: 8 for the year 2019.

APPLICATION INFO:
All forms, guidelines and procedures can be
found on the proposalCENTRAL web site.

Duration: Two to three years.

Deadline: February 1.

PUBLICATIONS:
Guidelines; application form; annual report.

ADDRESS INQUIRIES TO:
Christine Marquis, Research Grants and
Awards Manager
(See e-mail address above.)
Stephanie Lord-Fontaine
National Director of Research
(See address above.)

THE KIDNEY FOUNDATION OF CANADA   [2217]

5160 Decarie Boulevard, Suite 310
Montreal QC H3X 2H9 Canada
(514) 369-4806
Fax: (514) 369-2472
E-mail: christine.marquis@kidney.ca
Web Site: www.kidney.ca

AREAS OF INTEREST:
Research into the incidence and cure of
kidney disease, organ donation, patient
services and public education.

NAME(S) OF PROGRAMS:
● **Allied Health Kidney Doctoral
  Fellowship**
● **Allied Health Kidney Scholarship**

TYPE:
Fellowships; Scholarships. These programs
aim to promote and enhance the development
of nephrology/organ donation allied health
investigators in Canada.

YEAR PROGRAM STARTED: 1991

PURPOSE:
To promote and enhance the development of
allied health investigators in Canada in the
field of nephrology and organ donation.

LEGAL BASIS:
Corporation.

ELIGIBILITY:
Allied Health Kidney Doctoral Fellowship:
Preference will be given to applications
submitted by allied health professionals,
including but not limited to, nurses,
psychologists, social workers, technicians,
biomedical engineers, dietitians, pharmacists,
physiotherapists and occupational therapists.
Applicants must meet the following
eligibility requirements:
(1) have Canadian citizenship or landed
immigrant status;
(2) have a demonstrated commitment to the
area of nephrology or organ donation, with a
focus on increasing the number of kidneys
available for transplantation, in either direct
clinical practice or research experience.
Preference will be given to applicants with a
minimum of two years full-time equivalent
experience;
(3) be accepted in proposed course of
full-time study and;
(4) have the intention to return to Canada, if
studies are outside the country.

Allied Health Kidney Scholarship: Applicants
must meet the following eligibility
requirements:
(1) serve as a nephrology nurse or technician,
social worker, pharmacist, dietitian, transplant
coordinator or other allied health
professional;
(2) have a demonstrated commitment to the
area of nephrology or organ donation with an
interest in kidney research;
(3) have Canadian citizenship or landed
immigrant status and;
(4) be accepted in proposed course of
full-time or part-time study.
Preference will be given to applicants with a
minimum of two years full-time equivalent
experience.

FINANCIAL DATA:
Amount of support per award: Allied Health
Kidney Doctoral Fellowship: $25,000 to
$31,000 per year; Allied Health Kidney
Scholarship: Up to $5,000 per year for
full-time studies and $2,500 per year for
part-time studies up to a maximum of
$10,000 (CAN).

NO. AWARDS: Varies depending on funding.

APPLICATION INFO:
Allied Health Kidney Doctoral Fellowship:
All forms, policies and procedures can be
found on the proposalCENTRAL web site;
Allied Health Kidney Scholarship: All
applications must be submitted by e-mail.

Duration; Allied Health Kidney Doctoral
Fellowship: Two years. Must reapply for
third and fourth year of funding; Allied
Health Kidney Scholarship: One year. Must
reapply for second year of funding.

Deadline: March 1.

PUBLICATIONS:
Guidelines; application forms; annual report.

ADDRESS INQUIRIES TO:
Christine Marquis, Research Grants and
Awards Manager
(See e-mail address above.)

NATIONAL KIDNEY FOUNDATION   [2218]

30 East 33rd Street
New York, NY 10016
(212) 889-2210
(800) 622-9010
Fax: (212) 889-4287
E-mail: research@kidney.org
Web Site: www.kidney.
org/professionals/research/awards

AREAS OF INTEREST:
Improvement in the treatment and prevention
of kidney disease.

NAME(S) OF PROGRAMS:
● **Young Investigator Grant Program**

TYPE:
Development grants; Project/program grants;
Research grants; Seed money grants.

YEAR PROGRAM STARTED: 1987

PURPOSE:
To support research in the fields of
nephrology, urology and related disciplines
by individuals who have completed
fellowship training and who hold junior
faculty positions at university-affiliated
medical centers in the U.S.

LEGAL BASIS:
Voluntary health agency.

ELIGIBILITY:
Applications will be considered from
individuals who will have completed research
training in nephrology or closely related
fields prior to the start of the grant award and
who intend to pursue research directly related
to these areas. At the time funding begins
(July 1), the applicant must hold a full-time
appointment to a faculty position at a
university or an equivalent position as a
scientist on the staff of a research-oriented
institution, e.g., National Institutes of Health
(NIH) or other research organization, in the
U.S. Customarily, the appropriate faculty
rank is that of Assistant Professor. (In some
institutions a title other than Assistant
Professor, e.g., Instructor, is used to
designate junior faculty status; individuals at
that rank in such institutions are eligible to
apply for a Young Investigator Grant).
Qualifications should be documented in the
bio-sketch (maximum four pages).

Young Investigator Grants will be awarded to
individuals no later than four years after
initial appointment to a faculty (or
equivalent) position or after appointment to a

staff scientist (or equivalent) position in a research organization. It is the responsibility of the applicant to demonstrate that he or she satisfies the eligibility requirements for a Young Investigator Grant. Eligibility rules will be strictly enforced. Anyone who may not be certain as to his or her eligibility should request an advisory opinion from NKF staff before submitting an application.

Young Investigator Grants are primarily intended to support research by individuals holding M.D. or Ph.D. degrees who are commencing careers on the faculty of medical schools or research institutions. In all cases, the applicant's research and career goals must be directed to the study of normal or abnormal kidney function or of diseases of the kidney and urinary tract. Only one investigator in an institution will be supported in any funding cycle by a Young Investigator Grant. Since the NKF research support program is an integral part of the Foundation's overall scientific mission, it is expected that candidates for support pursuant to this funding mechanism participate as dues-paying professional members of the National Kidney Foundation, Inc.

GEOG. RESTRICTIONS: United States.

FINANCIAL DATA:
Amount of support per award: $35,000.

NO. MOST RECENT APPLICANTS: 12.

NO. AWARDS: 3 to 5.

APPLICATION INFO:
Application form, letter of commitment from the applicant's department and three letters of recommendation are required.
Duration: One year, with the opportunity to apply for a second year of funding.
Deadline: Second Monday in February.

PUBLICATIONS:
Program announcement.

STAFF:
Kerry Willis, Chief Scientific Officer
Jessica Joseph, Senior Vice President, Scientific Operations
Kiley Thornton, Director, Professional Membership

ADDRESS INQUIRIES TO:
Kiley Thornton
Director, Professional Membership
(See address above.)

Oncology

AMERICAN ASSOCIATION FOR CANCER RESEARCH   [2219]
615 Chestnut Street, 17th Floor
Philadelphia, PA 19106
(215) 440-9300
Fax: (267) 825-9550
E-mail: grants@aacr.org
Web Site: www.aacr.org

FOUNDED: 1907

AREAS OF INTEREST:
Cancer.

NAME(S) OF PROGRAMS:
- **AACR Independent Investigator Grants**
- **AACR NextGen Grants for Transformative Cancer Research**
- **AACR Team Science Grants**
- **Career Development Awards**
- **Research Grants and Fellowships**
- **Scholar-in-Training Awards**

TYPE:
Awards/prizes; Fellowships; Research grants; Travel grants. AACR Independent Investigator Grants support research by junior and senior investigators. These grants provide funding for investigators to develop and study new ideas and innovative approaches to cancer research.

AACR NextGen Grants for Transformative Cancer Research support early-career scientists within the first three years of a tenure-eligible faculty appointment. These grants are intended to promote and support creative, paradigm-shifting cancer research that may not be funded through conventional channels.

AACR Team Science Grants provide support for multi-institutional teams conducting innovative, collaborative cancer research.

Career Development Awards in Cancer Research support research by junior investigators. These awards provide an important source of support for direct research expenses as researchers embark on their independent research careers.

Research Fellowships in Basic, Clinical and Translational Research foster cancer research throughout the world by scientists currently at the postdoctoral or clinical research fellow level.

Scholar-in-Training Awards enhance the education and training of graduate students, medical students and residents, clinical fellows or equivalent, and postdoctoral fellows by facilitating their attendance at the Annual Meeting and Special Conferences of the American Association for Cancer Research. These awards are presented to scientists in training who are presenters of abstracts that have been highly rated by AACR.

PURPOSE:
To facilitate communication and dissemination of knowledge among scientists and others dedicated to the cancer problem; to foster research in cancer and related biomedical sciences; to encourage presentation and discussion of new and important observations in the field; to foster public education, science education and training; to advance the understanding of cancer etiology, prevention, diagnosis and treatment throughout the world.

LEGAL BASIS:
Not-for-profit society.

ELIGIBILITY:
Grants are given to individuals. For some programs, applicants must be working at an academic institution in the U.S. No grants to religious organizations. Associate Members of AACR are eligible for awards.

Career Development Award candidates must be full-time, junior faculty at the time the grant term begins. Candidates must also have completed productive postdoctoral research and demonstrated independent, investigator-initiated research. Employees of a national government and employees of private industry are not eligible. Candidates must be nominated by a member of AACR and must be an AACR member or apply for membership by the time the application is submitted. AACR Associate Members may not serve as nominators.

Fellowship candidates must have completed a Ph.D., M.D., or other doctoral degree. Candidates must be working as a postdoctoral or clinical research fellow at an academic facility, teaching hospital, or research institution, and must be in their second, third, or fourth year of a cancer research fellowship at the beginning of the award year. Academic faculty holding the rank of adjunct professor, associate professor, assistant professor, or higher, graduate or medical students, medical residents, permanent national government employees, and employees of private industry are not eligible. Candidates must be nominated by a member of AACR and must be an AACR member or apply for membership by the time the fellowship application is submitted. AACR Associate Members may not serve as nominators.

Independent Investigator Grant candidates must be full-time faculty at the time the grant term begins. These grants are open to faculty members at all career stages. Employees of a national government and employees of private industry are not eligible.

NextGen Grants for Transformative Cancer Research candidates must be in a full-time, tenure-eligible faculty position for no more than three years at the time the grant term begins. Candidates must also have completed productive postdoctoral research and demonstrated independent, investigator-initiated research. Employees of a national government and employees of private industry are not eligible. Candidates must be nominated by a member of AACR and must be an AACR member or apply for membership by the time the application is submitted. AACR Associate Members may not serve as nominators.

FINANCIAL DATA:
Amount of support per award: Career Development Awards: $75,000 to $100,000 per year; Fellowships: $50,000 to $100,000 salary support per year; Independent Investigators Grants: $100,000 to $200,000 per year; NextGen Grants: $150,000 per year; Team Science Grants: $300,000 to $500,000 per year.

Total amount of support: Varies.

NO. MOST RECENT APPLICANTS: Over 600.

NO. AWARDS: Scholar-in-Training: Approximately 250 per year; Awards and Fellowships: More than 70 per year.

APPLICATION INFO:
Application form is available online.

Duration: Career Development Awards and Independent Investigators Grants: Two to three years. Fellowships: One to three years; NextGen Grants and Team Science Grants: Three years; Scholar-in-Training Awards: One year.

Deadline: Scholar-in-Training: November of each year for Annual Meeting Awards, with notification the following February; Fellowships and Awards: Fall of each year, with notification the following February.

PUBLICATIONS:
Cancer Research, scientific journal; *Clinical Cancer Research*, journal; *Cell Growth and Differentiation*, journal; *Cancer Epidemiology, Biomarkers and Prevention*, journal.

ADDRESS INQUIRIES TO:
Scientific Review and
Grants Administration Department
(See e-mail address above.)

AMERICAN BRAIN TUMOR ASSOCIATION

8550 West Bryn Mawr Avenue
Suite 550
Chicago, IL 60631
(773) 577-8750
Fax: (773) 577-8738
E-mail: grants@abta.org
Web Site: www.abta.org/research

TYPE:
Fellowships; Seed money grants; Training
grants. Medical Student Summer Fellowships
support a 10- to 12-week summer laboratory
experience.

See entry 2244 for full listing.

AMERICAN CANCER SOCIETY, INC.   [2220]

250 Williams Street, N.W.
6th Floor
Atlanta, GA 30303-1002
(404) 329-7558
Fax: (404) 417-5974
E-mail: grants@cancer.org
Web Site: www.cancer.org/research

FOUNDED: 1946

AREAS OF INTEREST:
All forms of cancer and their cures.

NAME(S) OF PROGRAMS:
● **Postdoctoral Fellowship**

TYPE:
Fellowships.

YEAR PROGRAM STARTED: 1946

PURPOSE:
To speed the conquest of cancer by training
and supporting personnel for cancer research.

LEGAL BASIS:
Nonprofit corporation.

ELIGIBILITY:
Applicants must be U.S. citizens or legal
permanent residents. The latter must provide
notarized evidence of their legal resident
alien status. Applicants who hold doctoral
degrees in appropriate disciplines are eligible
to apply. Applicant shall have been awarded
a doctoral degree prior to the activation of
the grant.

GEOG. RESTRICTIONS: United States.

FINANCIAL DATA:
Amount of support per award: Award
includes an annual stipend of $48,000 in the
first year, $50,000 in the second and $52,000
in the third. Relocation travel expenses for
fellow only and a fellowship allowance of up
to $4,000 per year.

APPLICATION INFO:
Official application materials are available on
the Society's web site.

Duration: Up to three years.

Deadline: For receipt of completed materials:
April 1, for approved grants to be activated
on or after January 1; and October 15, for
approved grants to be activated on July 1.

ADDRESS INQUIRIES TO:
Shannon Pair
Operations Systems Specialist
(See address above.)

AMERICAN CANCER SOCIETY, INC.   [2221]

250 Williams Street, N.W.
6th Floor
Atlanta, GA 30303-1002
(404) 329-7558
Fax: (404) 417-5974
E-mail: grants@cancer.org
Web Site: www.cancer.org/research

FOUNDED: 1946

AREAS OF INTEREST:
Cancer and its cures.

NAME(S) OF PROGRAMS:
● **Institutional Research Grants**

TYPE:
Block grants. Grants for institutional cancer
research projects. Support is available for
integration of varied efforts in cancer
research within the institution and
preliminary testing of new and venturesome
ideas for research on cancer by junior
investigators without other national research
support.

YEAR PROGRAM STARTED: 1957

PURPOSE:
To eliminate cancer as a major health
problem by preventing cancer, saving lives
and diminishing suffering from cancer
through research, education, advocacy and
service.

LEGAL BASIS:
Nonprofit corporation.

ELIGIBILITY:
Institutions of higher learning in the U.S. and
its territories are eligible to apply for support
of appropriate research to be conducted by
qualified investigators.

GEOG. RESTRICTIONS: United States.

FINANCIAL DATA:
Amount of support per award: Average
$120,000 per year.

APPLICATION INFO:
Grant application materials become available
January 1 and are accessible on the Society's
web site.

Duration: One to three years. Renewable
upon reapplication.

Deadline: April 1.

ADDRESS INQUIRIES TO:
Shannon Pair
Operations Systems Specialist
(See address above.)

AMERICAN GASTROENTEROLOGICAL ASSOCIATION (AGA)

4930 Del Ray Avenue
Bethesda, MD 20814
(301) 654-2055
Fax: (301) 654-5920
E-mail: awards@gastro.org
Web Site: www.gastro.org/research-and-awards

TYPE:
Research grants. Research award supporting
an established investigator in the field of
gastric cancer research working to enhance
our fundamental understanding of gastric
cancer pathobiology or approaches to
prevent, treat or cure gastric cancer.

See entry 2193 for full listing.

AMERICAN INSTITUTE FOR CANCER RESEARCH   [2222]

1560 Wilson Boulevard
Suite 1000
Arlington, VA 22209
(202) 600-3004
Fax: (703) 527-8264
E-mail: research@aicr.org
Web Site: www.aicr.org

FOUNDED: 1982

AREAS OF INTEREST:
Food, nutrition, physical activity and the
prevention and treatment of cancer; food,
nutrition, physical activity and cancer
survivorship.

NAME(S) OF PROGRAMS:
● **Investigator Initiated Grants (IIG)**

TYPE:
Research grants. The Investigator Initiated
Research Grant program is open to
researchers at not-for-profit universities,
hospitals or research centers. The Institute
encourages new research on dietary means of
preventing and treating cancer, or improving
the life of the cancer patient or survivor.

YEAR PROGRAM STARTED: 1983

PURPOSE:
To foster research on diet, nutrition, physical
activity and cancer and educate the public
about the results.

ELIGIBILITY:
Institutions: Research grants are awarded to
nonprofit institutions in the Americas. Grant
applications will not be accepted from
agencies of the federal government or
agencies supported entirely by the federal
government of any country. Proof of
nonprofit status of the institution must be
submitted with the grant application.

Investigators: The Principal Investigator must
have a Ph.D. or equivalent degree or M.D.
degree and be a research staff or faculty
member at a nonprofit academic or research
institution at the minimum level of an
assistant professor (or its equivalent) or
higher. The Principal Investigator at an
institution in the U.S. must be a citizen of
the U.S. or foreign national with a permanent
residence visa that is valid for the duration of
the grant award. In other countries, the
Principal Investigator must meet the
requirements of that country for permanent
residency and employment.

GEOG. RESTRICTIONS: North, Central and South
America and the Caribbean.

FINANCIAL DATA:
Amount of support per award: Up to $75,000
per year, plus 10% direct and indirect costs.

Total amount of support: $165,000 to
$247,500.

APPLICATION INFO:
Online application is required. There are two
stages to the application process. Letter of
Intent is required before full application
invitation.

Duration: One to three years.

PUBLICATIONS:
Grant application package; recipients list.

ADDRESS INQUIRIES TO:
Research Department
(See address above.)

CANADIAN CANCER SOCIETY [2223]

55 St. Clair Avenue West
Suite 300
Toronto ON M4V 2Y7 Canada
(416) 961-7223
Fax: (416) 961-4189
E-mail: research@cancer.ca
Web Site: www.cancer.ca/research

FOUNDED: 1947

AREAS OF INTEREST:
Cancer research.

TYPE:
General operating grants; Research grants; Travel grants. Innovation grants. Grants for support of clinical cancer research and basic research projects related to the problem of cancer.

PURPOSE:
To stimulate Canadian investigators in a very broad spectrum of cancer research, not limited to but including biological, chemical, physical, clinical and population health sciences.

LEGAL BASIS:
Registered charity.

ELIGIBILITY:
Applicants must be persons holding eligible appointments at Canadian universities or other recognized Canadian institutions. Basic equipment and research facilities and necessary administrative services must be available at the institution concerned.

GEOG. RESTRICTIONS: Canada.

FINANCIAL DATA:
Grants may be used for the purchase and maintenance of animals, for expendable supplies and minor items of equipment and for payment of graduate students, postdoctoral fellows and technical and professional assistants, but do not include personal support for the grantee.

Amount of support per award: Varies.

Total amount of support: Approximately $40,000,000 (CAN) for fiscal year ended January 2019.

NO. MOST RECENT APPLICANTS: Over 750.

NO. AWARDS: 340 new and continuing grants/awards for the fiscal year ended January 2017.

APPLICATION INFO:
Applications must be made via online application system available on Institute web site.

Duration: Up to five years.

Deadline: Varies.

PUBLICATIONS:
Research report/impact report.

BOARD OF DIRECTORS:
Robert Lawrie, Chairperson

ADDRESS INQUIRIES TO:
See e-mail address above.

CANCER RESEARCH INSTITUTE [2224]

29 Broadway, 4th Floor
New York, NY 10006
(212) 688-7515
(800) 992-2623
Fax: (212) 832-9376
E-mail: grants@cancerresearch.org
Web Site: www.cancerresearch.org

FOUNDED: 1953

AREAS OF INTEREST:
Tumor immunology.

NAME(S) OF PROGRAMS:
● **Cancer Research Institute Irvington Postdoctoral Fellowship**

TYPE:
Fellowships; Research grants; Training grants.

YEAR PROGRAM STARTED: 1971

PURPOSE:
To offer postdoctoral fellowships to qualified individuals in the formative stages of their career who wish to receive training in cancer immunology.

LEGAL BASIS:
Private, nonprofit organization.

ELIGIBILITY:
Applicants must have a doctoral degree and must conduct research under a sponsor who holds a formal appointment at the sponsoring institution. There are no nationality restrictions. Work may be carried out in the U.S. or abroad at nonprofit institutions and medical centers. Fellows with five or more years of postdoctoral experience are ineligible.

FINANCIAL DATA:
Amount of support per award: $55,000 stipend for the first year, $57,000 for the second year, and $59,000 for the third year. An institutional allowance of $1,500 is provided for the host institution to cover laboratory supplies, scientific travel and health insurance on behalf of the fellow.

Total amount of support: Approximately $5,265,000 for the year 2018.

NO. MOST RECENT APPLICANTS: Approximately 350 for the year 2018.

NO. AWARDS: Average 26 annually.

APPLICATION INFO:
Paper applications will not be accepted. Applicants must complete an electronic application form to be submitted with the following attachments:
(1) scanned copy of paper application form with signatures of certifying officers;
(2) brief description of the applicant's background;
(3) list of other funding sources to which applications have been submitted;
(4) applicant's curriculum vitae and bibliography;
(5) brief summary of project with description of how the proposed research is relevant to cancer immunology;
(6) abstract of research in nontechnical English;
(7) concise research proposal, not to exceed six pages;
(8) letter of introduction from sponsor;
(9) sponsor's curriculum vitae, bibliography and current support and;
(10) letters of reference from two individuals acquainted with applicant's work.

Duration: Up to three years.

Deadline: April 1 and October 1. Notification eight to 10 weeks after the deadline.

PUBLICATIONS:
Annual report; application guidelines.

IRS I.D.: 13-1837442

STAFF:
Jill O'Donnell-Tormey, Chief Executive Officer and Director, Scientific Affairs
Lynne Harmer, Director of Grants Administration

ADDRESS INQUIRIES TO:
Ryan Godfrey, Grants Administrator
(See address above.)

CANCER RESEARCH INSTITUTE [2225]

29 Broadway, 4th Floor
New York, NY 10006
(212) 688-7515
Fax: (212) 832-9376
E-mail: grants@cancerresearch.org
Web Site: www.cancerresearch.org

FOUNDED: 1953

AREAS OF INTEREST:
Tumor immunology.

NAME(S) OF PROGRAMS:
● **Clinic and Laboratory Integration Program (CLIP)**

TYPE:
Awards/prizes; Research grants. This Program awards investigators at tenure-track assistant professor level or higher seeking to answer clinically relevant questions aimed at improving the effectiveness of cancer immunotherapies.

YEAR PROGRAM STARTED: 2011

PURPOSE:
To support qualified scientists who are working to explore clinically relevant questions aimed at improving the effectiveness of cancer immunotherapies; to support basic, preclinical and translational research, which will provide information that can be directly applied to optimizing cancer immunotherapy in the clinic.

ELIGIBILITY:
Investigators must be tenure-track assistant professors or higher when award activates. Eligible organizations must have IRS 501(c)(3) not-for-profit status. Grants are not made to religious organizations.

FINANCIAL DATA:
The award can be used at the recipient's discretion for salary, technical assistance, supplies and/or equipment.

Amount of support per award: Up to $100,000 per year for two years.

NO. MOST RECENT APPLICANTS: 200.

NO. AWARDS: 10.

APPLICATION INFO:
Letters of Intent are accepted November 1 annually. Candidates will be notified by December 15 whether or not they have been invited to submit a full grant proposal. An application form needs to be completed.

Duration: Up to two years. Grant is not renewable.

Deadline: Letters of Intent: November 1 annually. Full application: February 1.

ADDRESS INQUIRIES TO:
Ryan Godfrey, Grants Administrator
Cancer Research Institute
(See address above.)

CANCER RESEARCH SOCIETY [2226]

625 President Kennedy Avenue
Suite 402
Montreal QC H3A 3S5 Canada
(514) 861-9227
E-mail: grants@src-crs.ca
Web Site: www.src-crs.ca

FOUNDED: 1945

AREAS OF INTEREST:
Cancer research.

NAME(S) OF PROGRAMS:
● **Scholarship for the Next Generation of Scientists**

TYPE:
Fellowships; Research grants. One year of salary award as a senior postdoctoral fellow and two-year operating grant available when the awardee secures an academic appointment in a Canadian accredited institution.

YEAR PROGRAM STARTED: 2013

PURPOSE:
To support the future generation of Canadian researchers in the field of cancer research.

LEGAL BASIS:
Nonprofit registered fund-raising corporation.

ELIGIBILITY:
Applicants must be holders of a Ph.D. or a professional diploma (M.D., D.M.V.) obtained within the last six years and undergoing an additional postdoctoral training since a minimum of two years, each one of these two years having been completed uninterrupted, with at least 75% of the time devoted to research.

In order to receive the operating grant attached to the award, the awardee must obtain an academic appointment in a Canadian university or accredited institution and must begin his or her functions with 18 months of the start of the fellowship award.

FINANCIAL DATA:
Amount of support per award: $50,000 for the first year (fellowship) and $60,000 for the second and third year (operating grant).

NO. MOST RECENT APPLICANTS: Approximately 30.

NO. AWARDS: 3 to 4.

APPLICATION INFO:
Application information is available on the web site.
Duration: Three years. No renewal possible.
Deadline: Late April.

ADDRESS INQUIRIES TO:
Dajan O'Donnell, Ph.D.
Director of Scientific Affairs
and Partnerships
(See address above.)

CANCER RESEARCH SOCIETY [2227]

625 President Kennedy Avenue
Suite 402
Montreal QC H3A 3S5 Canada
(514) 861-9227
E-mail: grants@src-crs.ca
Web Site: www.src-crs.ca

FOUNDED: 1945

AREAS OF INTEREST:
Cancer research.

NAME(S) OF PROGRAMS:
● **Grants for Cancer Research**

TYPE:
General operating grants.

YEAR PROGRAM STARTED: 1946

PURPOSE:
To find the cause, cure and prevention of cancer.

LEGAL BASIS:
Nonprofit registered fund-raising corporation.

ELIGIBILITY:
Any qualified researcher who is associated with a Canadian accredited institution may apply, provided the research is done in Canada.

GEOG. RESTRICTIONS: Canada.

FINANCIAL DATA:
Amount of support per award: $60,000 per year.
Total amount of support: $8,900,000 in grants budgeted for the year 2019.

CO-OP FUNDING PROGRAMS: Funding through different partnerships available for several of the operating grants.

NO. MOST RECENT APPLICANTS: Approximately 400.

NO. AWARDS: 60 to 70.

APPLICATION INFO:
Application information is available on the web site.
Duration: Two years. Renewal possible.
Deadline: Mid-February.

OFFICERS AND DIRECTORS:
Francois Painchaud, President
Heidi Lange, C.R.H.A., Vice President and Secretary
Marie Valcourt, C.P.A., Treasurer
Ghassan Deko
Benoit Durocher
Annie Lemieux
Peter McCarthy
Monique Mercier
Sean O'Brien
Dorothy Quann
Joanna Wilson
George Zogopoulos, M.D., Ph.D.

ADDRESS INQUIRIES TO:
Dajan O'Donnell, Ph.D.
Director of Scientific Affairs
and Partnerships
(See address above.)

CANCER RESEARCH UK [2228]

Research Funding
Angel Building
407 St. John Street
London EC1V 4AD England
(44) 020 7242 0200
(44) 020 3469 5452 (grants helpline)
Fax: (44) 020 3469 6400
E-mail: grants.helpline@cancer.org.uk
Web Site: www.cancerresearchuk.org/funding-for-researchers

FOUNDED: 2002

AREAS OF INTEREST:
Research into the causes, diagnosis, treatment and prevention of cancer.

TYPE:
Fellowships; Project/program grants; Research grants; Training grants; Travel grants. There are various grant programs for cancer research including clinical trials. Funding includes research groups, fellowships, programs and project grants.

YEAR PROGRAM STARTED: 2002

PURPOSE:
To carry out world-class research to improve understanding of cancer and find out how to prevent, diagnose and treat different kinds of cancer; to ensure that the findings are used to improve the lives of all cancer patients; to help people to understand cancer, the progress being made and the choices each person can make; to work in partnership with others to achieve the greatest impact in the fight against cancer.

LEGAL BASIS:
Charity (public-funded).

ELIGIBILITY:
Research should be conducted in the U.K. Awards are made to researchers in universities, medical schools and independent research organizations.

GEOG. RESTRICTIONS: United Kingdom.

FINANCIAL DATA:
Amount of support per award: Varies.
Matching fund requirements: Varies.

NO. MOST RECENT APPLICANTS: Over 800.

NO. AWARDS: Over 1,100 projects supported.

APPLICATION INFO:
Contact a member of Research Funding for a discussion prior to sending an application. Applications for funding must be made using the electronic Grants Management System (eGMS).
Duration: Two to six years (longer for clinical trials).
Deadline: Varies.

PUBLICATIONS:
Scientific Yearbook; Annual Review.

THE JANE COFFIN CHILDS MEMORIAL FUND FOR MEDICAL RESEARCH [2229]

333 Cedar Street
New Haven, CT 06510
(203) 785-4612
Fax: (203) 785-3301
E-mail: jccfund@yale.edu
Web Site: www.jccfund.org

FOUNDED: 1937

AREAS OF INTEREST:
Cancer-related research.

TYPE:
Fellowships. Postdoctoral fellowships for studies in the medical and related sciences bearing on cancer.

YEAR PROGRAM STARTED: 1944

PURPOSE:
To further research into the causes, origins and treatment of cancer.

LEGAL BASIS:
Private foundation.

ELIGIBILITY:
Applicants must be U.S. or foreign citizens holding the M.D. or Ph.D. degree in the proposed field of study (or the equivalent in training and experience) and have no more than one year postdoctoral experience. The prior sponsorship of the laboratory at which they promise to work must be obtained.

Awards to foreign nationals will be made only for work in the U.S., whereas fellowships to American citizens are tenable in the U.S. or any foreign country.

FINANCIAL DATA:
Amount of support per award: $52,000 for year one, $54,000 for year two and $56,000 for year three. A grant of $2,000 per year to be applied toward the cost of research is usually made available to the sponsoring laboratory each year.
Total amount of support: $4,000,000.

NO. MOST RECENT APPLICANTS: 434.

NO. AWARDS: 25 to 30.

APPLICATION INFO:
Official application materials are available online.
Duration: Three years.
Deadline: February 1 to be considered at late spring meetings.

IRS I.D.: 06-6034840

OFFICERS:
James E. Childs, Chairman
Bronwen Childs, Treasurer

STAFF:
Stephen Elledge, Science Director
Kim Roberts, Administrative Director

ADDRESS INQUIRIES TO:
Kim Roberts, Administrative Director
(See address above.)

GREENBURG-MAY FOUNDATION [2230]
280 Park Avenue, 41st Floor
New York, NY 10017
(212) 451-3200
E-mail: pmay@trianpartners.com

FOUNDED: 1947

AREAS OF INTEREST:
Medical research, Parkinson's disease, with primary focus on research in cancer and heart disease, the aged, and Jewish institutions.

TYPE:
Development grants; Research grants. Social services.

PURPOSE:
To improve health conditions and expedite cures in many diseases through research.

ELIGIBILITY:
Eligible organizations must be IRS 501(c)(3) tax-exempt and be located in Florida or New York. No funding to individuals.

GEOG. RESTRICTIONS: Florida and New York.

FINANCIAL DATA:
Amount of support per award: Varies depending on project.
Total amount of support: Varies.

APPLICATION INFO:
Applicants must submit a copy of their tax-exempt determination letter. Contact the Foundation for further guidelines.

ADDRESS INQUIRIES TO:
Isabel May, President
(See address above.)

SUSAN G. KOMEN [2231]
5005 LBJ Freeway
Suite 526
Dallas, TX 75244
(972) 855-4390
(877) 465-6636
E-mail: helpdesk@komengrantsaccess.org
Web Site: www.komen.org

FOUNDED: 1982

AREAS OF INTEREST:
Breast cancer research.

CONSULTING OR VOLUNTEER SERVICES:
Through a Komen Affiliate; find a Komen Affiliate on the Organization's web site.

NAME(S) OF PROGRAMS:
● **Career Catalyst Research Grants (CCR)**
● **Global Grants**
● **Graduate Training in Disparities Research (GTDR)**
● **Investigator-Initiated Research (IIR)**
● **Komen Scholar Grants**
● **Postdoctoral Fellowship (PDF)**
● **Promise Grants**

TYPE:
Fellowships; Research grants; Training grants.

YEAR PROGRAM STARTED: 1982

PURPOSE:
To support breast cancer research and awareness.

LEGAL BASIS:
Texas nonprofit corporation.

ELIGIBILITY:
Varies with each award or grant.

FINANCIAL DATA:
Amount of support per award: CCR: Up to $150,000 per year; GTDR: $135,000 per year; IIR: Up to $1,000,000; PDF: $60,000 per year; Promise Grants: Up to $7,500,000.
Total amount of support: Varies per program.

APPLICATION INFO:
Application information is available on the web site.
Duration: CCR and PDF: Two or three years; GTDR: Up to three years; IIR: Three or four years; Promise Grants: Three to five years.

PUBLICATIONS:
Annual report.

IRS I.D.: 75-1835298

LEUKEMIA RESEARCH FOUNDATION [2232]
191 Waukegan Road
Suite 105
Northfield, IL 60093
(847) 424-0600
Fax: (847) 424-0606
E-mail: info@lrfmail.org
Web Site: www.allbloodcancers.org

FOUNDED: 1946

AREAS OF INTEREST:
Curing all blood cancers.

NAME(S) OF PROGRAMS:
● **New Investigator Awards**

TYPE:
Research grants. The goal of the grant program is to support new investigators. It funds scientists and physicians around the world.

YEAR PROGRAM STARTED: 1946

PURPOSE:
To conquer all blood cancers by funding research into their causes and cures; to enrich the quality of life of those touched by these diseases.

ELIGIBILITY:
Preference will be given to applicants proposing new lines of investigation.

FINANCIAL DATA:
Amount of support per award: Up to $100,000.
Total amount of support: More than $1,000,000 annually.

NO. AWARDS: Varies.

APPLICATION INFO:
Applications will only be accepted electronically and should be e-mailed to grants@lrfmail.org. All applicants will receive a receipt via e-mail when their application is received. Hard copies of grant applications will not be accepted. Full application is by invitation only.
Duration: One year. Funding cycle begins July 1.
Deadline: Letter of Intent: Mid-February. Full application: Mid-March.

IRS I.D.: 36-6102182

ADDRESS INQUIRIES TO:
Linda Kabot
Research Grants Administrator
(See address above.)

ONCOLOGY NURSING FOUNDATION [2233]
125 Enterprise Drive
Pittsburgh, PA 15275-1214
(866) 257-4667 (option 4)
E-mail: grants@onfgivesback.org
Web Site: www.onfgivesback.org

FOUNDED: 1981

AREAS OF INTEREST:
Oncology nursing.

TYPE:
Awards/prizes; Research grants; Scholarships.

YEAR PROGRAM STARTED: 1984

PURPOSE:
To provide opportunity for oncology nurses through education, research and leadership to pursue their career goals.

LEGAL BASIS:
National public, nonprofit, charitable organization.

ELIGIBILITY:
Applicant must be a registered nurse actively pursuing a career in some aspect of cancer patient care, education or research, and be a Ph.D. student. Funding preference is given to projects that promote theoretically based oncology practice.

FINANCIAL DATA:
Amount of support per award: Varies.
Total amount of support: Over $700,000 for the year 2019.

NO. AWARDS: Varies.

APPLICATION INFO:
Letters of Intent and applications must be submitted online.
Duration: Research Grant: Up to two years.
Deadline: Varies.

PUBLICATIONS:
Program announcement; applications; guidelines; *Recognition of Achievement: Awards, Grants, Honors, Scholarships.*

THE ELSA U. PARDEE FOUNDATION   [2234]

P.O. Box 2767
Midland, MI 48641-2767
(989) 832-3691
E-mail: kmcdonald@pardeefoundation.org
Web Site: www.pardeefoundation.org

FOUNDED: 1944

AREAS OF INTEREST:
Research for control and cure of cancer.

TYPE:
Research grants. Grants for research projects relating to the cure and control of cancer and for the treatment needs of cancer victims.

The Foundation supports activities in two major areas:
(1) innovative and new approaches to cancer research and;
(2) Pardee Cancer Treatment Funds in six counties in central Michigan and one Texas county. The Treatment Funds assist cancer patients, who are residents of those counties, with their treatment expenses.

PURPOSE:
To promote the control and cure of cancer.

LEGAL BASIS:
Private foundation.

ELIGIBILITY:
Grants are limited under the terms of the charter to the cure and control of cancer, and in general do not provide for building funds, equipment (except that used in a specific project), fellowships or fund-raising campaign contributions.

Priority is given to researchers at nonprofit institutions in the U.S. who are new to the field of cancer research, or to established research investigators examining new approaches to cancer cure.

FINANCIAL DATA:
The Foundation has provided more than $146,500,000 since 1944 to support its purpose. Generally, two-thirds of the Foundation's annual gift giving is directed toward research.
Amount of support per award: Grants vary in amount, depending upon the needs and nature of the request.
Total amount of support: $2,523,717 for the year 2019.

NO. MOST RECENT APPLICANTS: 298 for the year 2019.

NO. AWARDS: 17 for the year 2019.

REPRESENTATIVE AWARDS:
$138,939 to the University of Alabama, Birmingham for the study of targeting ncRNA as a curative therapy for metastatic breast cancer; $99,876 to Memorial Sloan Kettering Cancer Center for exercise therapy in lung cancer prevention and treatment; $152,174 to Northwestern University for novel targeted combination therapies based on PIM kinase inhibition.

APPLICATION INFO:
Grant applications are required to be submitted online at the Foundation web site.
Duration: Typically one year.

Deadline: Grant applications are reviewed by the Medical Committee in April, August and December, with final approval occurring at the Board of Trustees meetings in September, December and May, respectively.

PUBLICATIONS:
Annual report; application guidelines.

OFFICERS AND TRUSTEES:
Gail E. Lanphear, President
Lisa J. Gerstacker, Vice President and Assistant Treasurer
William C. Lauderbach, Treasurer
Laurie G. Bouwman, Secretary
W. James Allen, Trustee
Alan W. Ott, Trustee
Bill Schuette, Trustee
William G. Schuette, Trustee
Andreas Teich, Trustee

PREVENT CANCER FOUNDATION   [2235]

1600 Duke Street, Suite 500
Alexandria, VA 22314
(703) 836-4412
Fax: (703) 836-4413
E-mail: ximena.marquez@preventcancer.org
Web Site: www.preventcancer.org

FOUNDED: 1985

AREAS OF INTEREST:
Cancer prevention and cancer early detection.

TYPE:
Fellowships; Research grants.
Grants/Fellowships are given for prevention and early detection of cancer through scientific research and education.

PURPOSE:
To support innovative projects in prevention and early detection of cancer through scientific research.

ELIGIBILITY:
Fellowships: Citizenship is unrestricted, but research must be conducted primarily in the U.S. Postdoctoral Fellows (graduate students who will have their doctoral degrees before the project start date) are eligible to apply. Individuals with academic or professional degrees (e.g., M.D., Phar.D., Ph.D.) who are conducting cancer prevention research under the guidance of a mentor are also eligible.

Grants: Citizenship is unrestricted, but research must be conducted primarily in the U.S. Researchers at the instructor or assistant professor level with relevant academic or professional degrees (e.g., M.D., Phar.D., Ph.D.) who are conducting cancer prevention research and researchers who are farther along in their careers and who are shifting their focus to cancer prevention are eligible to apply.

GEOG. RESTRICTIONS: United States.

FINANCIAL DATA:
Indirect costs will not be covered.
Amount of support per award: $50,000 per year.
Total amount of support: Varies.

NO. MOST RECENT APPLICANTS: 56.

APPLICATION INFO:
Application process begins on May 18. Applicants must submit proposals electronically through proposalcentral.altrum.com.
Duration: Two years.
Deadline: June 24.

ADDRESS INQUIRIES TO:
Ximena Marquez, Grants Manager
(See e-mail address above.)

DAMON RUNYON CANCER RESEARCH FOUNDATION [2236]

One Exchange Plaza
55 Broadway, Suite 302
New York, NY 10006-3720
(212) 455-0520
Fax: (212) 455-0529
E-mail: awards@damonrunyon.org
shannon.donovan@damonrunyon.org
Web Site: www.damonrunyon.org

FOUNDED: 1946

AREAS OF INTEREST:
All theoretical and experimental research that is relevant to the study of cancer and the search for cancer causes, mechanisms, therapies and prevention.

NAME(S) OF PROGRAMS:
● **Damon Runyon Clinical Investigator Award**
● **Damon Runyon Dale F. Frey Award for Breakthrough Scientists**
● **Damon Runyon Fellowship Award**
● **Damon Runyon Physician-Scientist Training Award**
● **Damon Runyon-Rachleff Innovation Award**
● **Damon Runyon-Sohn Pediatric Cancer Fellowship Award**

TYPE:
Fellowships; Project/program grants; Research grants; Training grants. The Damon Runyon Clinical Investigator Award supports early career physician-scientists conducting patient-oriented research. The goal of this innovative program is to increase the number of physicians capable of moving seamlessly between the laboratory and the patient's bedside in search of breakthrough treatments.

Damon Runyon Dale F. Frey Award for Breakthrough Scientists provides additional funding to scientists completing a Damon Runyon Fellowship who are most likely to make paradigm-shifting breakthroughs. This funding is to accelerate their path to independence and their impact on cancer.

The Damon Runyon Fellowship Award supports the training of the brightest postdoctoral scientists as they embark upon their research careers. This funding enables them to be trained by established investigators in leading research laboratories across the country.

The Damon Runyon Physician-Scientist Training Award is designed to encourage outstanding physicians to pursue cancer research careers by providing them with the opportunity for a protected research training experience under the mentorship of a highly qualified and gifted mentor.

The Damon Runyon-Rachleff Innovation Award supports the next generation of exceptionally creative thinkers with high-risk/high-reward ideas that have the potential to significantly impact our understanding of and/or approaches to the prevention, diagnosis or treatment of cancer, but lack sufficient preliminary data to obtain traditional funding.

The Damon Runyon-Sohn Pediatric Cancer Fellowship Award provides funding to basic scientists and clinicians who conduct research with the potential to significantly impact the prevention, diagnosis, or treatment of one or more pediatric cancers.

YEAR PROGRAM STARTED: 1947

PURPOSE:
To advance cancer research through supporting the development of the most promising young talent in cancer research.

LEGAL BASIS:
501(c)(3) organization, classified as a publicly supported organization and not as a private foundation under Section 509(a)(1) of the IRS, incorporated in New York.

ELIGIBILITY:
Clinical Investigator Award: Each applicant must be nominated by his or her institution. Applicants must be conducting independent research at a U.S. research institution and be within the first four years of his or her initial full faculty appointment.

For the Fellowship Award, applicants must have completed one or more of the following degrees or its equivalent: M.D., M.D./Ph.D., Ph.D., D.D.S., D.V.M.

Level I Funding is for basic and physician scientist applicants who must have received their degrees within the year prior to the FAC meeting at which their applications are to be considered.

Level II Funding is for physician scientists (M.D.) and clinical scientists (M.D., M.D./Ph.D., D.D.S., D.V.M. or the equivalent) who have completed their residencies and clinical fellowship training, are board-eligible, and have not yet been appointed Assistant Professor (or equivalent).

The proposed investigation must be conducted at a university, hospital, or research institution. Foreign candidates may only apply to do research in the U.S.

Only candidates who are beginning their first full-time postdoctoral research fellowship are eligible.

Frey Award: Damon Runyon Fellows are eligible to apply in the fourth year of their Fellowship.

Innovation Award: Institutional nominations are not required and there is no limit to the number of applications that can be received from a particular institution. Applicants (including non-U.S. citizens) must be conducting independent research at a U.S. research institution.

Physician-Scientist Training Award: Applicant must have an M.D. degree. Applicants must have completed their residencies and clinical training and be U.S. Specialty Board eligible at the time of application.

FINANCIAL DATA:
Awards are made to institutions for the support of the Damon Runyon scientist, pursuant to the requirements of the specific award.

Amount of support per award: Clinical Investigator Awards: $200,000 per year. In addition, awardees may be eligible to retire up to $100,000 of their medical school debt; Dale F. Frey Award: $100,000; Fellowship Award: $223,000 over four years; Innovation Award: $200,000 per year; Physician-Scientist Training Award: $460,000 over four years. A sum of $2,000 is awarded each year to the laboratory in which the Fellow is working, and can be used by the

Fellow for his or her educational and scientific expenses. Additionally, the Foundation also provides a Dependent Child Allowance of $1,000 per child per year. There is no allowance for a spouse.

Total amount of support: Approximately $3,000,000 in Clinical Investigator Awards; approximately $7,600,000 in Fellowship Awards; $600,000 in Dale F. Frey Awards; approximately $2,000,000 in Innovation Awards; approximately $2,800,000 in Physician-Scientist Training Awards; $924,000 in Sohn Pediatric Fellowship Awards.

NO. MOST RECENT APPLICANTS: Clinical Investigator Awards: 52; Fellowship Awards: 295; Frey Awards: 14; Innovation Awards: 110; Physician-Scientist Awards: 17; Sohn-Pedriatic Fellowship Awards: 16.

NO. AWARDS: Clinical Investigator Awards: 5 new, 19 renewals; Fellowship Awards: 33 new, 97 renewals; Frey Awards: 6 new, 6 renewals; Innovation Awards: 5 new, 15 renewals; Physician-Scientist Awards: 6 new, 11 renewals; Sohn-Pedriatic Fellowship Awards: 4 new, 11 renewals.

REPRESENTATIVE AWARDS:
Damon Runyon Clinical Investigator Award: Carey K. Anders, M.D., "mTOR inhibition in the treatment of HER2-positive breast cancer brain metastases," with Lisa A. Carey, M.D., and Charles M. Peron, Ph.D., University of North Carolina, Chapel Hill, NC; Damon Runyon Postdoctoral Fellowship: Douglas H. Phanstiel, Ph.D., "Exploring the regulatory role of long-range chromatin interactions," with Michael P. Snyder, Ph.D., Stanford University School of Medicine, Stanford, CA.

APPLICATION INFO:
The following requirements apply:
(1) online At-a-Glance form; the information submitted here must match one's application; therefore, bookmark the "Edit your response" link in case one needs to make changes;
(2) application cover sheet; applicants must submit a hard copy of the cover sheet with all required signatures; signatures can be ink or electronic, or a mix of the two; electronic signatures are acceptable but not required for the USB copy; (if applying under the mentorship of two sponsors, one's second sponsor must fill out the co-sponsor cover sheet;)
(3) sponsor's biographical sketch in NIH format and a list of current funding; do not include sponsor's full bibliography; (if applying under the mentorship of two sponsors, co-Sponsor must also submit a biosketch;)
(4) sponsor's letter including: description of training plan for the candidate; and numerical percentage (_%) of proposal written by the candidate (if applying under the mentorship of two sponsors, the training plan for the candidate must be written jointly and each co-sponsor must submit his or her individual track record of mentorship with list of graduate and postdoctoral fellows trained;)
(5) sponsor's mentorship track record with names and current positions of graduate and postdoctoral trainees from the past 10 years;
(6) applicant's curriculum vitae, including a bibliography of all published works;
(7) applicant's letter of approximately two pages including: description of previous research and teaching experience; statement on the transformative impact he or she had on his or her field of research as a graduate student; if applicant is training at the same

institution in which he or she received his or her degree, an explanation of the reasons(s) for remaining at the same institution (can be copied for page 2 of cover sheet);
(8) statement of applicant's long-term commitment to a career in cancer research; this statement should be no longer than one paragraph and indicate what applicant plans to do after completing his or her postdoctoral experience;
(9) research proposal, not to exceed five pages of single-spaced, 12-point type with at least 1/2-inch margins; in the proposal, the applicant should: provide a summary of the research proposed (this is in addition to the required summary form); provide a brief background to the proposed research; state specific research objectives/aims; describe concisely the method of approach for the proposed research; explain the significance of the proposed research to the Foundation's goals: understanding the causes and mechanisms of cancer and developing more effective cancer therapies and prevention; demonstrate the relevance of his or her own background and the background and previous work of the Sponsor and any other investigators to the proposed research; list references including the full title of each work cited - references are not included in the five-page limit; figures or tables may be appended or incorporated into the text (not to exceed two extra pages); if the figures are incorporated into the text, the proposal may be up to seven pages;
(10) copy of the applicant's degree certificate; applicants who have not yet received their Ph.D. diploma but have successfully completed all Ph.D. requirements, including Ph.D. defense, may submit a letter from their graduate school explicitly stating such, with the dates of the Ph.D. defense and degree conferral;
(11) summary of Research Form, not to exceed one page - no attachments;
(12) if available, PDFs of up to three of applicant's published papers (no submitted manuscripts, no hard copies); and
(13) if applicable, up to two letters from collaborators indicating their willingness to contribute equipment, materials or expertise (not reference letters).

Duration: Clinical Investigator Award: Three years. Awardees can apply for a two-year continuation grant. Damon Runyon-Sohn Fellowship, Fellowship Award and Physician-Scientist Training Award: Four years. Frey Award: Up to two years. Innovation Award: Two years with the possibility of two years additional funding.

Deadline: Clinical Investigator Award: February 1; Damon Runyon-Sohn Fellowship Award: March 15; Fellowship Award: March 15 and August 15; Frey Award: July 17; Innovation Award: July 6; Physician-Scientist Training Award: December 1.

PUBLICATIONS:
Annual report; award brochures.

ADDRESS INQUIRIES TO:
Clare M. Cahill, Chief Administrative Officer
(See address above.)

THE SKIN CANCER FOUNDATION [2237]

205 Lexington Avenue, 11th Floor
New York, NY 10016
(212) 725-5176
Fax: (212) 725-5751
E-mail: spierson@skincancer.org
Web Site: www.skincare.org/about-us/research-grants

FOUNDED: 1979

AREAS OF INTEREST:
Basic and clinical studies that address improved methods of prevention, detection and treatment of skin cancer.

NAME(S) OF PROGRAMS:
- **The Big See**
- **Destination: Healthy Skin**
- **Heads Up**
- **Research Grants Program**
- **Sun Smart U**

TYPE:
Awards/prizes; Research grants; Seed money grants.

YEAR PROGRAM STARTED: 1981

PURPOSE:
To reduce the incidence, morbidity, and mortality of skin cancer.

LEGAL BASIS:
Nonprofit foundation.

ELIGIBILITY:
Applications must be for research conducted by dermatology residents, fellows, or junior investigators (five to 10 years past first academic appointment) from institutions within the U.S. and Canada. Preference is given to projects that address, at the basic science and clinical level, improved methods of prevention, detection and treatment of skin cancers.

GEOG. RESTRICTIONS: United States and Canada.

FINANCIAL DATA:
Amount of support per award: $25,000 to $50,000.
Total amount of support: $125,000 annually.

NO. MOST RECENT APPLICANTS: 41.

NO. AWARDS: Research Grant: 3.

APPLICATION INFO:
Application information is available on the web site.
Duration: One year.
Deadline: Research Grant: Mid-October.

IRS I.D.: 13-2948778

BOARD OF DIRECTORS AND OFFICERS:
Perry Robins, M.D., Chairman
Deborah S. Sarnoff, M.D., President
Rex A. Amonette, M.D., Senior Vice President
Elizabeth K. Hale, M.D., Senior Vice President
C. William Hanke, M.D., Senior Vice President
Ronald L. Moy, M.D., Senior Vice President
Maritza Perez, M.D., Senior Vice President
Leonard H. Goldberg, M.D., Vice President
Allan C. Halpern, M.D., Vice President
Mark A. Corrado, C.P.A., Treasurer
Elizabeth Robins, Esq., Secretary
Bennet Weiner, Esq., General Counsel

ADDRESS INQUIRIES TO:
Staci Pierson, Director of Development
(See address above.)

*SPECIAL STIPULATIONS:
E-mail applications are not accepted. Because the amounts of the grants are small, the Foundation does not fund overhead or indirect costs.

LADY TATA MEMORIAL TRUST [2238]

c/o Mr. F.H. Parekh
Tata Limited
18 Grosvenor Place
London SW1X 7HS England
(44) 020 7235 8281
Fax: (44) 020 7259 5996
E-mail: sonia@tata.co.uk
pam@tata.co.uk
Web Site: www.ladytatatrust.org

FOUNDED: 1933

AREAS OF INTEREST:
Leukemia research.

TYPE:
Fellowships. Studentships (Ph.D.). Annual awards for postgraduate scientists of any nationality to support programs of research likely to throw light on the nature of leukemia. One or more grants of a studentship for a student entering an M.Phil./Ph.D. program is available. The Trustees especially wish to encourage studies on the leukaemogenic agents and on the epidemiology, pathogenesis, immunology and genetic basis of leukemia. The work may be done in any country or in an institution where the candidate has been accepted.

YEAR PROGRAM STARTED: 1933

PURPOSE:
To support research in leukemia.

LEGAL BASIS:
Registered charity.

ELIGIBILITY:
Suitably qualified medical or science graduates of any nationality, who are accepted in the institution where the work is to be undertaken, may apply.

FINANCIAL DATA:
Stipends are paid in quarterly installments. Since amounts vary according to age, qualifications, experience and the scales appropriate to the institution where the applicant has been accepted, intending applicants should try to find out the range of salary that would be appropriate before they apply.
Amount of support per award: GBP 25,000 to 35,000 per annum.
Total amount of support: GBP 350,000 per year.

NO. MOST RECENT APPLICANTS: 40 to 50.

NO. AWARDS: Approximately 12 per year.

APPLICATION INFO:
Applications are only accepted online during the current year schedule.
Duration: All awards are tenable for one academic year, October to September. Awards for two years may be given if considered by the Trust to be in best interests of a particular project.
Deadline: March 15. Announcements June 18.

OFFICERS:
Prof. Brian Huntly, Chairperson, Scientific Advisory Board
Prof. Nicholas Cross, Secretary

ADDRESS INQUIRIES TO:
Professor Brian Huntly, Chairperson
c/o Mr. F.H. Parekh
(See address above.)

*SPECIAL STIPULATIONS:
Holders of awards are expected to submit yearly reports on their progress to the Scientific Advisory Committee and to acknowledge the support of the Trust in their publication.

UNION FOR INTERNATIONAL CANCER CONTROL (UICC) [2239]

31-33 Avenue Giuseppe Motta
1202 Geneva Switzerland
(41) 22 809 1811
Fax: (41) 22 809 1810
E-mail: fellows@uicc.org
Web Site: www.uicc.org/what-we-do/capacity-building

FOUNDED: 1933

AREAS OF INTEREST:
Cancer research, clinical oncology, oncology nursing and voluntary cancer societies.

NAME(S) OF PROGRAMS:
- **Bourses pour L'Afrique Francophone (BAF)**
- **UICC Technical Fellowhips (UICC-TF)**
- **Yamagiwa-Yoshida Memorial International Study Grants (YY)**

TYPE:
Fellowships. The UICC Fellowships Programme provides long-, medium- and short-term fellowships abroad to qualified investigators, clinicians, and nurses, who are actively engaged in cancer research, clinical oncology, or oncology nursing. Short-term scheme offers nonmedical training opportunities in the Asia-Pacific region.

YEAR PROGRAM STARTED: 1933

PURPOSE:
To enable qualified cancer investigators, doctors, nurses, cancer society staff or accredited volunteers to carry out specific research and clinical projects, or to obtain training in cancer society work in appropriate organizations abroad.

ELIGIBILITY:
Candidates must:
(1) possess appropriate professional qualifications and experience according to the specific fellowship applied for;
(2) be currently engaged in cancer research, clinical oncology practice, oncology nursing, or cancer society work;
(3) be on the staff payroll of a university, research laboratory or institute, hospital, oncology unit, or voluntary cancer society (or be accredited volunteers of such societies) to where they will return at the end of a fellowship and;
(4) have adequate fluency in a language that will permit effective communication at the host institute.
Candidates may submit application for only one fellowship scheme at a time. Applicants who have already obtained a UICC fellowship in the past may apply for further UICC awards only if they are members of the Association of UICC Fellows.

No distinction will be made among candidates on the basis of gender, ethnic origin, religious or political beliefs. Awards are made on the basis of scientific and expert evaluation of the application and the proposed work as set out by the candidate in the project description by reviewers of the highest international standing in their respective fields. Decisions are final and cannot be appealed.

Fellowships are conditional on Fellows returning to the home institutes at the end of the fellowship period. Awards are not granted for basic training courses, lectures, meetings, conferences, congresses or for visiting institutes. They cannot prolong or run concurrently with other awards and cannot be granted to candidates who are already physically present at the proposed host institute while their applications are under consideration.

FINANCIAL DATA:
Amount of support per award: BAF: $2,000 to $3,400; UICC-TF: Up to $3,400; YY: $10,000 average.

NO. AWARDS: BAF: 9 for the year 2018; UICC-TF: 50 to 60; YY: 6 to 8.

APPLICATION INFO:
Applications and all supporting documentation must be submitted in English. Applications may be submitted using the online grant system and will be acknowledged promptly. Candidates will be advised if items are missing. Those proposals that have undergone a review and selection process and were not approved for funding cannot be resubmitted. However, candidates are encouraged to submit new applications for new work programs.
Duration: BAF and UICC-TF: One month. YY: Three months.
Deadline: BAF and UICC-TF: Applications are accepted at any time; YY: October.

ADDRESS INQUIRIES TO:
UICC Fellowships Department
(See address above.)

*SPECIAL STIPULATIONS:
UICC requires an end-of-the-project report in English within one month of the end of the project.

Rheumatology

ARTHRITIS FOUNDATION [2240]
1355 Peachtree Street
Suite 600
Atlanta, GA 30309
(404) 872-7100
(844) 571-4357 (Helpline)
E-mail: AFScience@arthritis.org
Web Site: www.arthritis.org/science

FOUNDED: 1948

AREAS OF INTEREST:
Quality of care, juvenile arthritis, osteoarthritis and rheumatology.

TYPE:
Awards/prizes; Research contracts. Deliverable-based contracts.

YEAR PROGRAM STARTED: 1951

PURPOSE:
To support scientific projects that show promise to achieve a faster cure for types of arthritis. The Arthritis Foundation Scientific Strategy 2015-20: To prioritize expediting scientific discoveries to reach the point of care for improving clinical decision-making and health outcomes among people with arthritis.

LEGAL BASIS:
Nonprofit organization.

ELIGIBILITY:
The Foundation will post descriptions of opportunities and initiatives on the web site when actively seeking applicants.

FINANCIAL DATA:
Amount of support per award: Varies.
Total amount of support: Varies.

NO. AWARDS: Varies.

APPLICATION INFO:
Official application materials are available from the Foundation.
Duration: One to three years.

OFFICERS:
Laurie Stewart, Chairperson
Anna M. Palmer, President

ADDRESS INQUIRIES TO:
Science Department
(See address above.)

THE ARTHRITIS SOCIETY [2241]
393 University Avenue, Suite 1700
Toronto ON M5G 1E6 Canada
(416) 979-7228
Fax: (416) 979-1149
E-mail: research@arthritis.ca
Web Site: arthritis.ca

FOUNDED: 1948

AREAS OF INTEREST:
Arthritis medical and scientific research.

NAME(S) OF PROGRAMS:
- **CRA (CIORA) AS New Clinical Investigator Grant**
- **Graduate Ph.D. Award**
- **Postdoctoral Fellowship Award**

- **Stars Career Development Award**
- **Strategic Operating Grants**

TYPE:
General operating grants; Research grants; Scholarships. Salary awards.

PURPOSE:
To invest in cutting-edge research, proactive advocacy and innovative solutions that will deliver better health outcomes and an improved quality of life for people affected with arthritis.

LEGAL BASIS:
Registered charity.

ELIGIBILITY:
Applicants are restricted to Canadian citizens and permanent residents of Canada. Applicants for research grants must hold faculty appointments at Canadian medical schools. Specific requirements vary by program.

GEOG. RESTRICTIONS: Canada.

FINANCIAL DATA:
Amount of support per award: Varies.
Total amount of support: Varies.

APPLICATION INFO:
Application to any program must be submitted through the Society's online grant management system.
Duration: Varies by program.
Deadline: Varies by program.

PUBLICATIONS:
Annual report; regulations.

BOARD MEMBERS:
Kenneth Smith, Chairperson
Duncan Mathieson, Vice Chairperson and Treasurer
Trish Barbato, President and Chief Executive Officer
Mary E. Hofstetter, C.M., Chairperson, Governance and Nominating Committee
Dr. Giovanni Di Battista, Director
Ingrid Gutzmann, Director
Nancy Hopkins, Director
Lisa Hryniw, Director
Thomas Jedrej, Director
Jennifer LaPlante, Director
Drew McArthur, Director
Lynne McCarthy, Director
Cathy McIntyre, Director
Neal Oswald, Director
Anne-Marie Renaud, Director
Bill Stewart, Director
Dr. Evelyn Sutton, Director
Michele Walsh, Director

ADDRESS INQUIRIES TO:
The Research Department
(See e-mail address above.)

LUPUS FOUNDATION OF AMERICA, INC.
2121 K Street, N.W., Suite 200
Washington, DC 20037
(202) 349-1150
(800) 875-2562 (customer support)
Fax: (202) 349-1156
E-mail: marion@lupus.org
Web Site: www.lupus.org/finzifellowships

TYPE:
Summer Fellowship. The Gina M. Finzi Memorial Student Summer Fellowship Program proposes to foster an interest among students in the areas of basic, clinical, translational, epidemiological or behavioral research relevant to lupus under the sponsorship and supervision of an

established, tenure-track Principal Investigator who directs a laboratory dedicated at least in part to the investigation of lupus at a U.S. or Canadian academic, medical or research institution.

See entry 2079 for full listing.

Neurology

THE ALS ASSOCIATION   [2242]
National Headquarters
1300 Wilson Boulevard, Suite 600
Arlington, VA 22209
(202) 407-8580
E-mail: researchgrants@alsa-national.org
Web Site: www.alsa.org

FOUNDED: 1985

AREAS OF INTEREST:
Amyotrophic lateral sclerosis (ALS) programs include research grants, patient services, public education and awareness, local chapter development, and advocacy.

NAME(S) OF PROGRAMS:
● **Research Grant Program**

TYPE:
Awards/prizes; Conferences/seminars; Fellowships; Project/program grants; Research grants; Technical assistance; Research contracts. Grants, for a specified number of years, to neuroscientific researchers to pursue a project of relevance to Amyotrophic Lateral Sclerosis. Both basic and clinical research supported (including postdoctoral fellowships). The ALS Association forms partnerships on clinical trials.

YEAR PROGRAM STARTED: 1985

PURPOSE:
To direct, encourage, identify, fund and monitor relevant and cutting-edge research into the cause, treatment, prevention and cure for amyotrophic lateral sclerosis.

LEGAL BASIS:
Nonprofit voluntary health agency under IRS 501(c)(3).

ELIGIBILITY:
All nationalities are welcome to apply. Applicant should be a faculty member at a reputable scientific facility.

FINANCIAL DATA:
Amount of support per award: Multiyear grants: Maximum $100,000 per year; Starter grants: Maximum $50,000; Postdoctoral fellows: Maximum $50,000 per year.
Total amount of support: Varies.

NO. MOST RECENT APPLICANTS: Over 300.

NO. AWARDS: 70.

REPRESENTATIVE AWARDS:
$50,000 to Thomas Gaj, Ph.D., Board of Trustees of the University of Illinois; $100,000 to Paul McKeever, B.Sc., Ph.D., The Governing Council of the University of Toronto; $300,000 to Meredith Jackrel, Ph.D., Washington University in St. Louis; $499,413 to Kuti Baruch, Ph.D., ImmunoBrain Checkpoint, Inc.; $200,000 to Dexter Ang, Pison Technology, Inc.

APPLICATION INFO:
Detailed information can be found on the Foundation web site.

Duration: Managing ALS and Postdoctoral fellows: Two years. Multiyear grants: Up to three years. Starter grants: One year.
Deadline: Information available upon request to the e-mail address above.

PUBLICATIONS:
Research ALS Today, newspaper; miscellaneous ALS information and patient care brochures; *ALS Journal News*, monthly.

IRS I.D.: 13-3271855

STAFF:
Kuldip Dave, Ph.D., Vice President, Research

ADDRESS INQUIRIES TO:
See e-mail address above.

ALZHEIMER'S ASSOCIATION   [2243]
225 North Michigan Avenue, Suite 18
Chicago, IL 60601-7633
(312) 335-5747
E-mail: grantsapp@alz.org
Web Site: www.alz.org

FOUNDED: 1980

AREAS OF INTEREST:
Basic biology; clinical, adoptive technology, social/behavioral and cognitive/functional.

NAME(S) OF PROGRAMS:
● **Alzheimer's Association Clinician Scientist Fellowship (AACSF)**
● **Alzheimer's Association Clinician Scientist Fellowship to Promote Diversity (AACSF-D)**
● **Alzheimer's Association Research Fellowship (AARF)**
● **Alzheimer's Association Research Fellowship to Promote Diversity (AARF-D)**
● **Alzheimer's Association Research Grant (AARG)**
● **Alzheimer's Association Research Grant to Promote Diversity (AARG-D)**
● **Zenith Fellows Award (ZNTH)**

TYPE:
Fellowships; Research grants; Seed money grants. International Research Grant Program funds investigations that advance our understanding of Alzheimer's disease, help identify new treatment strategies, provide information to improve care for people with dementia, and further our knowledge of brain health and disease prevention. Awards support investigators at every professional stage and always include categories specifically designed to help talented young scientists establish careers in Alzheimer's research. The Association's entire grant portfolio is structured to meet the needs of the field and to nurture fresh ideas.

YEAR PROGRAM STARTED: 1982

PURPOSE:
To accelerate the global effort to eliminate Alzheimer's disease; to connect with scientific, academic, government and industry thought-leaders and key stakeholders worldwide; to become a catalyst toward the time when there will be disease-modifying treatments, preventive strategies and gold-standard care for all people affected by Alzheimer's disease.

LEGAL BASIS:
Voluntary health association, not-for-profit 501(c)(3).

ELIGIBILITY:
Each program has specific requirements. Therefore, contact the Association for additional information.

FINANCIAL DATA:
Amount of support per award: AACSF, AACSF-D, AARF and AARF-D: $175,000; AARG and AARG-D: $150,000; ZNTH: $450,000.
Total amount of support: Approximately $25,000,000 for the year 2017.

NO. MOST RECENT APPLICANTS: 700 for the year 2017.

NO. AWARDS: 120 for the year 2017.

APPLICATION INFO:
The first step in applying for any research grant is to submit a Letter of Intent (LOI) through the proposalCENTRAL online application system at proposalcentral.altum.com. Applications will not be accepted without an approved LOI. The Association requires all applicants be registered as a reviewer with the Association to submit an LOI. Additionally, it is required that the applicant review at least one grant proposal within their area of expertise, outside the grant competition to which they are applying.

LOI and completed application must be submitted by a single Principal Investigator. A PI cannot submit an LOI that had been approved or rejected during a previous grant cycle. All LOIs must be approved or rejected in the current grant cycle.

Applicants are responsible for adhering to the space limitations, as outlined in the Program Announcement.

Hard copies of the LOI will not be accepted. LOIs will not be accepted after the deadline date.
Duration: Up to three years.
Deadline: Varies per grant cycle.

PUBLICATIONS:
Annual report; application guidelines.

ADDRESS INQUIRIES TO:
E-mail: grantsapp@alz.org

AMERICAN BRAIN TUMOR ASSOCIATION   [2244]
8550 West Bryn Mawr Avenue
Suite 550
Chicago, IL 60631
(773) 577-8750
Fax: (773) 577-8738
E-mail: grants@abta.org
Web Site: www.abta.org/research

AREAS OF INTEREST:
Brain tumor research.

NAME(S) OF PROGRAMS:
● **ABTA Research Collaboration Grant**
● **Basic Research Fellowship Awards**
● **Discovery Grants**
● **Medical Student Summer Fellowships**

TYPE:
Fellowships; Seed money grants; Training grants. Medical Student Summer Fellowships support a 10- to 12-week summer laboratory experience.

PURPOSE:
To encourage talented scientists early in their careers to enter, or remain in, the field of brain tumor research; to facilitate the development of potentially important research studies; to support innovative brain tumor research.

ELIGIBILITY:
Varies by grant mechanism.

GEOG. RESTRICTIONS: Medical Student Summer Fellowship: United States and Canada.

FINANCIAL DATA:
Amount of support per award: ABTA Research Collaboration Grant: $200,000; Discovery Grants: $50,000; Medical Student Summer Fellowships: $3,000; Research Fellowships: $100,000.

NO. MOST RECENT APPLICANTS: Varies by grant mechanism.

NO. AWARDS: Varies.

APPLICATION INFO:
Details are available on the Association web site.

Duration: ABTA Research Collaboration Grant and Research Fellowships: Two years; Discovery Grants: One year; Medical Student Summer Fellowships: 10 to 12 weeks over the summer.

Deadline: Current deadlines are posted on the Association web site.

ADDRESS INQUIRIES TO:
Research Grants Manager
(See e-mail address above.)

AMERICAN EPILEPSY SOCIETY (AES) [2245]

135 South LaSalle Street
Suite 2850
Chicago, IL 60603
(312) 883-3800
Fax: (312) 896-5784
E-mail: info@aesnet.org
Web Site: www.aesnet.org

FOUNDED: 1936

AREAS OF INTEREST:
Study and acquisition, dissemination and application of knowledge concerning epilepsy in all its phases including biological, clinical and social.

NAME(S) OF PROGRAMS:
- **Junior Investigator Awards**
- **Postdoctoral Research Fellowship**
- **Predoctoral Research Fellowship**
- **Research and Training Workshops**
- **Seed Grants**
- **Susan S. Spencer Clinical Research Training Fellowship in Epilepsy**

TYPE:
Awards/prizes; Fellowships; Seed money grants. The American Epilepsy Society is one of the oldest neurological professional organizations in the U.S. The Society, in partnership with other organizations, funds Grants and Fellowships that are awarded to individuals with a professional degree whose research impacts an aspect of the study of, and work toward the cure for, epilepsy. Some funding programs are for Society members only.

Junior Investigator Awards support research by recently independent investigators with the intent to facilitate successful competition for subsequent longer-term support from the NIH or other sources. Proposals are welcome across the spectrum of basic, translational, and clinical epilepsy research, including studies of disease mechanisms or treatments, epidemiologic or behavioral studies, the development of new technologies, and health services and outcomes research.

Postdoctoral Research Fellowship: This one-year fellowship, administered by AES, is available to physicians or Ph.D. neuroscientists who desire postdoctoral research experience.

Predoctoral Research Fellowship: This one-year fellowship, administered by AES, is offered to graduate students matriculating in a full-time doctoral (Ph.D.) program with an academic career focus, with dissertation research related to epilepsy.

Research and Training Workshops: The Society, through the Research and Training Committee, provides funding for targeted workshops, intended for clinical or scientific audiences and on specific collaborative topics in neuroscience.

Seed Grants: This grant is to foster collaborative interactions between two or more established investigators to make future grants related to epilepsy more competitive for larger awards and to fuel multi-investigator projects.

Susan S. Spencer Clinical Research Training Fellowship in Epilepsy: A two-year fellowship, administered by the American Academy of Neurology, to support clinical research training in the field of epilepsy.

YEAR PROGRAM STARTED: 1970

PURPOSE:
To promote interdisciplinary communications, scientific investigation and exchange of clinical information about epilepsy; to improve the quality of life for people with epilepsy; to provide those engaged in research with information and assistance of potential benefit in advancing their work.

LEGAL BASIS:
501(c)(3) organization.

ELIGIBILITY:
Details for the different programs can be found online.

FINANCIAL DATA:
Amount of support per award: Varies by mechanism.
Total amount of support: Varies.

CO-OP FUNDING PROGRAMS: The Society has formed alliances with other organizations that provide research funding, including the Grass Foundation, Epilepsy Foundation and other funding sources.

Susan S. Spencer Clinical Research Training Fellowship in Epilepsy is supported by the AAN Foundation, the American Epilepsy Society and the Epilepsy Foundation.

NO. MOST RECENT APPLICANTS: Varies.

NO. AWARDS: Varies.

APPLICATION INFO:
Application information is available on the web site.
Duration: One to two years.
Deadline: Varies.

IRS I.D.: 04-6112600

AMERICAN PARKINSON DISEASE ASSOCIATION, INC. [2246]

135 Parkinson Avenue
Staten Island, NY 10305
(718) 981-8491
(800) 223-2732
Fax: (718) 981-4399
E-mail: hgray@apdaparkinson.org
Web Site: www.apdaparkinson.org

FOUNDED: 1961

AREAS OF INTEREST:
Parkinson's disease, medical neurology and neuropathology.

NAME(S) OF PROGRAMS:
- **Post-Doctoral Research Fellowships**

TYPE:
Fellowships.

PURPOSE:
To support postdoctoral trainees at U.S. research institutions whose research training focuses on new insights into the pathophysiology, etiology, and/or treatment of Parkinson's disease.

LEGAL BASIS:
Not-for-profit organization.

ELIGIBILITY:
Applicants must have completed their M.D., Ph.D., M.D./Ph.D. or clinical residency program within two years of the onset of the proposed award.

Funding is not to be used for indirect costs, institutional overhead, travel expenses, publication costs higher than $1,000 or equipment costs higher than $8,000.

GEOG. RESTRICTIONS: United States.

FINANCIAL DATA:
Amount of support per award: Maximum $50,000.

APPLICATION INFO:
Completed application must be uploaded as one PDF document. Description of the research proposal should not exceed three pages and should consist of background, specific aims, research design, and a statement of significance for Parkinson's disease research. The applicant's NIH biosketch, the mentor's NIH biosketch, as well as a letter of reference from the mentor and any other key collaborators should be included. The applicant should list all current and pending support, including sponsoring agency, amount and dates for awards. The application should indicate how other sponsored research complements or supplements the present proposal.

The three page limit only applies to the length of the proposal, not the entire application.
Duration: One year. Nonrenewable.
Deadline: March 12. Notification in July.

PUBLICATIONS:
Program announcement; guidelines.

ADDRESS INQUIRIES TO:
Heather Gray, Programs and Research Manager
(See address above.)

BENIGN ESSENTIAL BLEPHAROSPASM RESEARCH FOUNDATION INC.

755 South 11th Street
Suite 211
Beaumont, TX 77701
(409) 832-0788
Fax: (409) 832-0890
E-mail: bebrf@blepharospasm.org
Web Site: www.blepharospasm.org

TYPE:
Project/program grants; Research grants; Seed money grants.

See entry 2304 for full listing.

BRIGHT FOCUS FOUNDATION [2247]

22512 Gateway Center Drive
Clarksburg, MD 20871
(301) 948-3244
(800) 437-2423
Fax: (301) 948-4403
E-mail: researchgrants@brightfocus.org
Web Site: www.brightfocus.org

FOUNDED: 1973

AREAS OF INTEREST:
Alzheimer's disease research.

NAME(S) OF PROGRAMS:
• **Alzheimer's Disease Research**

TYPE:
Research grants. Awards for basic research into the causes and treatment of Alzheimer's.

YEAR PROGRAM STARTED: 1985

PURPOSE:
To develop treatments, preventions and cures for Alzheimer's disease.

LEGAL BASIS:
Nonprofit foundation.

ELIGIBILITY:
Grants are awarded on the basis of the proposal's scientific merit and its relevance to understanding the disease studied. No funds for large equipment, institutional overhead costs, construction or building expenses.

Fellowships are limited to researchers within five years of doctoral degree conferral.

FINANCIAL DATA:
Amount of support per award: $100,000 per year.
Total amount of support: Varies.

NO. AWARDS: 43 for fiscal year 2019.

APPLICATION INFO:
Applications are submitted through ProposalCentral.
Duration: Three-year projects and two-year research fellowships.
Deadline: Contact the Foundation for exact dates.

PUBLICATIONS:
Annual report; clinical brochures; newsletters.

ADDRESS INQUIRIES TO:
Kara Summers, Program Officer
(See e-mail address above.)

CEREBRAL PALSY FOUNDATION [2248]

3 Columbus Circle, 15th Floor
New York, NY 10019
(212) 520-1686
E-mail: rebecca.lam@yourcpf.org
info@yourcpf.org
Web Site: www.yourcpf.org

FOUNDED: 1955

NAME(S) OF PROGRAMS:
• **Research Grants**

TYPE:
Research grants. Grants are awarded for pilot studies in areas which have a relationship to cerebral palsy. While most research in the central nervous system may be useful, the Foundation requires that research proposals define clear and direct relevance to cerebral palsy. Currently, high priority is assigned to prevention of prematurity, decrease of perinatal neurologic morbidity, prevention of central nervous system infections of the newborn and to medical, surgical and bioengineering methods that may improve the functioning of persons with cerebral palsy, addressing issues such as impaired mobility, impaired communication skills, swallowing, drooling and effects of aging on further diminution of function. However, any proposal designed to prevent cerebral palsy or to improve its treatment and management will be considered.

YEAR PROGRAM STARTED: 1955

PURPOSE:
To support research pilot studies in areas of etiology, pathology, prevention and therapy bearing directly on cerebral palsy and the disabilities associated with it.

LEGAL BASIS:
Private foundation.

ELIGIBILITY:
Tax-exempt universities and other organizations are eligible to apply on behalf of qualified individuals.

FINANCIAL DATA:
Amount of support per award: Up to $50,000 for one year; total of $100,000 for two years including indirect costs not in excess of 10% of each budgetary item, except for equipment.
Total amount of support: Approximately $700,000.

NO. MOST RECENT APPLICANTS: 35.

NO. AWARDS: 7.

APPLICATION INFO:
Application form required. The grant review process usually takes about three months.
Duration: Up to two years.
Deadline: March 1.

IRS I.D.: 13-6093337

STAFF:
Richard Ellenson, President and Chief Executive Officer
Rebecca Lam, Director of Administration

ADDRESS INQUIRIES TO:
Rebecca Lam
Director of Administration
(See address above.)

CUREPSP FOUNDATION FOR PSP/CBD AND RELATED BRAIN DISEASES [2249]

1216 Broadway, Second Floor
New York, NY 10001
(347) 294-2871
Fax: (410) 785-7009
E-mail: info@curepsp.org
Web Site: www.curepsp.org

FOUNDED: 1990

AREAS OF INTEREST:
Progressive supranuclear palsy and corticobasal degeneration.

TYPE:
Research grants.

YEAR PROGRAM STARTED: 1997

PURPOSE:
To provide support for basic and clinical research in progressive supranuclear palsy and corticobasal degeneration.

ELIGIBILITY:
Qualified investigators affiliated with appropriate institutions are eligible to apply. Applicants must have the approval of the institution where the research training will be conducted. Ph.D. or M.D. status is required.

FINANCIAL DATA:
Amount of support per award: Varies.
Total amount of support: $100,000.

APPLICATION INFO:
Application information is available on the web site.
Duration: Varies.
Deadline: July 15 and November 15.

ADDRESS INQUIRIES TO:
Joanna Teters
E-mail: teters@curepsp.org

DYSAUTONOMIA FOUNDATION, INC. [2250]

315 West 39th Street
Suite 701
New York, NY 10018
(212) 279-1066
Fax: (212) 279-2066
E-mail: info@famdys.org
Web Site: www.familialdysautonomia.org

FOUNDED: 1951

AREAS OF INTEREST:
Familial dysautonomia.

CONSULTING OR VOLUNTEER SERVICES:
Dysautonomia Treatment and Evaluation Center at New York University Medical Center, 530 First Avenue, Suite 9Q, New York, NY 10016, under the direction of Felicia B. Axelrod, M.D.

NAME(S) OF PROGRAMS:
• **Dysautonomia Research Program**

TYPE:
Project/program grants; Research grants; Seed money grants. In addition to support for research and clinical study, the Foundation also provides financial support to the Dysautonomia Treatment and Evaluation Center at NYU and the Israeli FD Center in Tel Aviv.

YEAR PROGRAM STARTED: 1955

PURPOSE:
To fund research for treatment and/or cure for familial dysautonomia; to stimulate and promote medical research into familial dysautonomia (an inherited disease of the autonomic nervous system); to provide information to lay and medical public.

LEGAL BASIS:
Nonprofit, tax-exempt corporation.

ELIGIBILITY:
Researcher connected with a recognized medical and/or teaching institution may apply.

FINANCIAL DATA:
Amount of support per award: Varies, depending upon the needs and nature of the request.
Total amount of support: Varies.

APPLICATION INFO:
Application forms are supplied upon request. Researchers must check online to see if the Foundation is soliciting research application before submitting.
Duration: One year with option to apply for ongoing research and/or renewal. Renewal application (with progress report) is required each year.
Deadline: Contact the Foundation.

IRS I.D.: 13-6145280

EXECUTIVE DIRECTOR:
Lanie Etkind

DYSTONIA MEDICAL RESEARCH FOUNDATION [2251]

One East Wacker Drive
Suite 1730
Chicago, IL 60601-1980
(312) 755-0198
Fax: (312) 803-0138
E-mail: dystonia@dystonia-foundation.org
Web Site: www.dystonia-foundation.org

FOUNDED: 1976

AREAS OF INTEREST:
Dystonia.

NAME(S) OF PROGRAMS:
• **Research Grants**

TYPE:
Project/program grants; Research grants.
Research Grants to be used for
hypothesis-driven dystonia relevant research.

YEAR PROGRAM STARTED: 1976

PURPOSE:
To fund research into the cause of, treatments
and a cure for, dystonia.

LEGAL BASIS:
Private foundation.

ELIGIBILITY:
For all programs, all nonprofit institutions or
organizations within the U.S., Canada and
those foreign countries where supervision of
grant administration is possible are eligible.
For all investigations involving humans,
approval by the institution's human subject
protection committee is necessary. No
support for medical care of dystonia patients,
construction or alterations. Investigators must
have M.D. or Ph.D. degrees.

FINANCIAL DATA:
Support cannot be used for indirect costs,
new construction or renovation of existing
facilities, consultant fees or travel costs
unless specified in the original grant
application.
Amount of support per award: Average
$65,000.
Total amount of support: Varies.

APPLICATION INFO:
Application form required for all programs.
Duration: Up to two years.

PUBLICATIONS:
Guidelines.

IRS I.D.: 95-3378526

ADDRESS INQUIRIES TO:
Jody Roosevelt, Grants Manager
(See address above.)

EPILEPSY FOUNDATION OF AMERICA [2252]

8301 Professional Place, Suite 200
Landover, MD 20785-2353
(800) 332-1000
Fax: (301) 577-4941
E-mail: grants@efa.org
research.department@efa.org
Web Site: www.epilepsy.com

FOUNDED: 1968

AREAS OF INTEREST:
Epilepsy research and training.

NAME(S) OF PROGRAMS:
• **AES/EF Clinical Research and Training Fellowship Award**
• **AES/EF Junior Investigator Research Award**
• **Cannabinoids and Epilepsy**
• **My Seizure Gauge**
• **New Therapy Commercialization Grants**
• **Shark Tank Awards**
• **SUDEP Biomarker Challenge**

TYPE:
Fellowships; Research grants; Seed money
grants. Commercialization grants; Innovation
grants. Seed grants are awarded to clinical
investigators or basic scientists for support of
biological or behavioral research which will
advance the understanding, treatment and
prevention of epilepsy.

PURPOSE:
To provide funding for investigators in the
early stages of their careers.

LEGAL BASIS:
Private foundation.

ELIGIBILITY:
Criteria varies per initiative.

GEOG. RESTRICTIONS: United States.

FINANCIAL DATA:
Amount of support per award: AES/EF
Clinical Research and Training Fellowship
Award, AES/EF Junior Investigator Research
Award and Cannabinoids and Epilepsy: Up to
$50,000; My Seizure Gauge: $1,000,000;
New Therapy Commercialization Grants: Up
to $200,000; Shark Tank Awards: Up to
$150,000; SUDEP Biomarker Challenge: Up
to $800,000 prize.

APPLICATION INFO:
Application forms and guidelines are
available on the Foundation's web site.
Duration: One to two years.
Deadline: Varies.

ADDRESS INQUIRIES TO:
E-mail: grants@efa.org

THE GRASS FOUNDATION [2253]

P.O. Box 11342
Tacoma Park, MD 20913
(443) 562-9693
Fax: (310) 986-2252
E-mail: info@grassfoundation.org
Web Site: www.grassfoundation.org

FOUNDED: 1955

AREAS OF INTEREST:
Research and education in neuroscience.

NAME(S) OF PROGRAMS:
• **Grass Fellowships in Neuroscience**

TYPE:
Fellowships; Research grants. Summer
research support for independent research
projects in neuroscience at the Marine
Biological Laboratories, Woods Hole, MA.

YEAR PROGRAM STARTED: 1955

PURPOSE:
To encourage young investigators in the field
of neuroscience.

LEGAL BASIS:
Private foundation.

ELIGIBILITY:
Applicants must be late predoctoral,
postdoctoral, or early independent
investigators. Fellow must be a U.S. citizen,
permanent resident, or have proper visa.

FINANCIAL DATA:
The Grass Foundation pays traveling
expenses, reasonable living expenses while at
MBL and certain laboratory costs. There is a
modest drawing account for personal
expenses. Expenses of the spouse or
domestic partner and dependent children are
likewise paid.
Amount of support per award: Varies.
Total amount of support: Varies.

NO. AWARDS: 10 to 12.

APPLICATION INFO:
Application materials may be obtained from
the Foundation's web site.
Duration: 14 weeks.
Deadline: December 5. Announcement in
January.

TRUSTEES:
Andrew Blum, M.D., Ph.D.
Catherine E. Carr, Ph.D.
Victor Chin, C.F.A.
Elva Diaz, Ph.D.
Andre Fenton, Ph.D.
Bernice Grafstein, Ph.D.
Henry J. Grass, M.D.
Joshua Grass, Ph.D.
Ronald R. Hoy, Ph.D
Kamran Khodakhah, Ph.D.
Matt McFarlane, Ph.D., J.D.
Vanessa Ruta, Ph.D.
Felix E. Schweizer, Ph.D
Steven J. Zottoli, Ph.D

ADDRESS INQUIRIES TO:
Executive Assistant
(See address above.)

HUNTINGTON'S DISEASE SOCIETY OF AMERICA, INC. [2254]

505 Eighth Avenue, Suite 902
New York, NY 10018
(212) 242-1968
Fax: (212) 239-3430
E-mail: lfox@hdsa.org
Web Site: www.hdsa.org

FOUNDED: 1967

AREAS OF INTEREST:
Research into Huntington's disease.

NAME(S) OF PROGRAMS:
• **HD Human Biology Project**
• **HDSA Berman-Topper Family Huntington's Disease Career Development Fellowship**
• **Donald King Summer Research Fellowship**

TYPE:
Fellowships; Research grants.

YEAR PROGRAM STARTED: 1986

PURPOSE:
To support and stimulate research into the
cause, prevention and treatment of
Huntington's disease.

LEGAL BASIS:
Nonprofit, tax-exempt voluntary health
agency.

FINANCIAL DATA:
Amount of support per award: HDSA
Berman-Topper Fellowship: $80,000 per
year; Human Biology Project: $75,000 per
year; Summer Research Fellowship: $4,000.
Total amount of support: Varies.

APPLICATION INFO:
Application information is available on the
web site.

Duration: HDSA Berman-Topper Family Fellowship: Up to three years. Human Biology Project: One or two years. Nonrenewable. Summer Research Fellowship: 10 weeks.

Deadline: HDSA Berman-Topper Family Fellowship: March. Human Biology Project: Letter of Intent must be received by May; full application deadline is July. Summer Research Fellowship: March.

PUBLICATIONS:
Annual report; application guidelines; *Toward a Cure*; *The Marker*.

IRS I.D.: 13-3349872

ADDRESS INQUIRIES TO:
George Yohrling, Ph.D.
Senior Director, Mission and Scientific Affairs
(See address above.)

THE MCKNIGHT ENDOWMENT FUND FOR NEUROSCIENCE   [2255]

The McKnight Foundation
710 South Second Street, Suite 400
Minneapolis, MN 55401
(612) 333-4220
E-mail: info@mcknight.org
Web Site: www.mcknight.org

FOUNDED: 1986

AREAS OF INTEREST:
Neuroscience.

NAME(S) OF PROGRAMS:
● **McKnight Neuroscience Scholar Award**

TYPE:
Awards/prizes; Research grants.

PURPOSE:
To encourage neuroscientists in the early stages of their careers to focus on disorders of learning and memory.

LEGAL BASIS:
Nonprofit.

ELIGIBILITY:
Applicants must hold an M.D. and/or Ph.D. degree, have completed formal postdoctoral training and be in the early stages of an independent research career. Applicants should show evidence of a commitment to a continuing career in neuroscience and be in a tenured or tenure-track position.

GEOG. RESTRICTIONS: United States.

FINANCIAL DATA:
Awards are made to the sponsoring institution.
Amount of support per award: $75,000 per year.

NO. MOST RECENT APPLICANTS: 55.

NO. AWARDS: Up to 6 annually.

APPLICATION INFO:
Application forms and guidelines are available in September.
Duration: Three years.
Deadline: Early January. Announcement by late May.

ADDRESS INQUIRIES TO:
Eileen Maler, Program Manager
(See address above.)

MULTIPLE SCLEROSIS SOCIETY OF CANADA   [2256]

250 Dundas Street West
Suite 500
Toronto ON M5T 2Z5 Canada
(416) 922-6065
(866) 922-6065
Fax: (416) 922-7538
E-mail: msresearchgrants@mssociety.ca
Web Site: mssociety.ca

FOUNDED: 1948

AREAS OF INTEREST:
Neurology, immunology, virology, pathology and biochemistry, fields of biomedical research, and clinical and population health research.

NAME(S) OF PROGRAMS:
● **endMS Doctoral Studentship Award**
● **endMS Master's Studentship Award**

TYPE:
Research grants. Studentships offered at the Master's and Ph.D. levels.

PURPOSE:
To find the cause and cure of multiple sclerosis.

LEGAL BASIS:
Charitable organization.

ELIGIBILITY:
Applicant must be a Canadian citizen, landed immigrant, or person holding a Canadian student visa who is going to school at a recognized Canadian research institute, or a Canadian citizen or landed immigrant who is going to school at a recognized foreign research institute.

FINANCIAL DATA:
Amount of support per award: Master's: $20,000 (CAN) per year; Ph.D.: $22,000 (CAN) per year; Ph.D. (who hold an M.D.): $50,500 (CAN) per year.
Total amount of support: Varies.

NO. AWARDS: 11 Master's Studentships and 23 Doctoral Studentships for the year 2018-19.

APPLICATION INFO:
The Society uses an online research grants and awards management system that enables researchers to submit and review applications on the Web. The system is called Easygrants and can be accessed through www.mscanadagrants.ca.
Duration: endMS Master's Studentships: Up to two years. No renewals; endMS Doctoral Studentships: Up to four years. No renewals.
Deadline: October 1. Announcement the following March 1 to begin July 1.

ADDRESS INQUIRIES TO:
Research and Programs Department
(See e-mail address above.)

MULTIPLE SCLEROSIS SOCIETY OF CANADA   [2257]

250 Dundas Street West
Suite 500
Toronto ON M5T 2Z5 Canada
(416) 922-6065
(866) 922-6065
Fax: (416) 922-7538
E-mail: msresearchgrants@mssociety.ca
Web Site: mssociety.ca

FOUNDED: 1948

AREAS OF INTEREST:
Neurology, immunology, virology, pathology and biochemistry.

NAME(S) OF PROGRAMS:
● **Clinical and Population Health Pilot Grant**
● **Operating Grants**

TYPE:
Research grants.

PURPOSE:
To find the cause and cure of multiple sclerosis.

LEGAL BASIS:
Charitable organization.

ELIGIBILITY:
Applicants must carry out research at a recognized Canadian research institute (e.g., university or hospital).

FINANCIAL DATA:
Amount of support per award: Clinical and Population Health Pilot Grant: Approximately $50,000 for up to two years; Operating Grants: Up to $100,000 (CAN) per year.
Total amount of support: Varies.

APPLICATION INFO:
The Society uses an online research grants and awards management system that enables researchers to submit and review applications on the Web. The system is called Easygrants and can be accessed through www.mscanadagrants.ca.
Duration: Clinical and Population Health Pilot Grant: Up to two years; Operating Grants: Up to three years.
Deadline: October 1, with announcement the following March.

ADDRESS INQUIRIES TO:
Research and Programs Department
(See e-mail address above.)

MULTIPLE SCLEROSIS SOCIETY OF CANADA   [2258]

250 Dundas Street West
Suite 500
Toronto ON M5T 2Z5 Canada
(416) 922-6065
(866) 922-6065
Fax: (416) 922-7538
E-mail: msresearchgrants@mssociety.ca
Web Site: mssociety.ca

FOUNDED: 1948

AREAS OF INTEREST:
Neurology, immunology, virology, pathology and biochemistry, fields of biomedical research, and clinical and population health research.

NAME(S) OF PROGRAMS:
● **endMS Postdoctoral Fellowship**

TYPE:
Fellowships. The program is intended to support research for training of postdoctoral fellows in studies related to MS.

PURPOSE:
To find the cause and cure of multiple sclerosis.

LEGAL BASIS:
Charitable organization.

ELIGIBILITY:
Applicant must be a Canadian citizen, landed immigrant or person holding a Canadian student visa who is working at a recognized Canadian research institute, or a Canadian citizen or landed immigrant who is working at a recognized foreign research institute. Applicant must have completed their doctoral degree within the last three years by the time of the competition deadline.

FINANCIAL DATA:
Amount of support per award: Postdoctoral Fellows: $41,000 (CAN) per year; Postdoctoral Fellows (for those who hold an M.D.): $50,500 (CAN) per year.
Total amount of support: Varies.

NO. AWARDS: 13 for the year 2018-19.

APPLICATION INFO:
The Society uses an online research grants and awards management system that enables researchers to submit and review applications on the Web. The system is called Easygrants and can be accessed through www.mscanadagrants.ca.
Duration: Up to three years. No renewals.
Deadline: October 1. Announcement the following March to begin July 1.

ADDRESS INQUIRIES TO:
Research and Programs Department (See e-mail address above.)

MUSCULAR DYSTROPHY ASSOCIATION   [2259]
161 North Clark Street
Suite 3550
Chicago, IL 60601
(312) 254-0632
E-mail: grants@mdausa.org
ksmith@mdausa.org
Web Site: www.mda.org

FOUNDED: 1950

AREAS OF INTEREST:
Research into diseases of the neuromuscular system.

NAME(S) OF PROGRAMS:
● **Neuromuscular Disease Research**

TYPE:
Research grants; Training grants. Translational Research Grants. Basic scientific and clinical research grants are offered.

MDA supports research into diseases of the neuromuscular system to develop effective treatments for the muscular dystrophies and related diseases which include spinal muscular atrophy and other motor neuron diseases, inflammatory myopathies, metabolic myopathies, diseases of the neuromuscular junction, certain peripheral neuropathies and basic research increasing general knowledge in the neuromuscular field.

YEAR PROGRAM STARTED: 1950

PURPOSE:
To find the causes of, and treatments for, neuromuscular diseases.

LEGAL BASIS:
Nonprofit, voluntary health agency.

ELIGIBILITY:
An applicant must be a professional or faculty member at an appropriate educational, medical or research institution and be qualified to conduct and supervise a program of original research, have access to institutional resources necessary to conduct the proposed research project and hold a Doctor of Medicine, Doctor of Philosophy, Doctor of Science or equivalent degree.

Proposals from applicants outside the U.S. will be considered only for projects of highest priority to MDA and when, in addition to the applicant's having met the eligibility requirements noted above, one or more of the following conditions exist: the applicant's country of residence has inadequate sources of financial support for biomedical research, collaboration with an MDA-supported U.S. investigator is required to conduct the project, or an invitation to submit an application has been extended by MDA.

FINANCIAL DATA:
Amount of support per award: Primary Research Grants: $100,000 per year including indirect costs. Overhead limited to a maximum of 10% of the total direct costs of the grant requested; Development Grants: Up to $70,000 per year.

NO. MOST RECENT APPLICANTS: 612.

NO. AWARDS: Approximately 90.

APPLICATION INFO:
Guidelines are available on the web site.
Duration: One, two or three years.
Deadline: For Neuromuscular Disease Research, applications must be requested by December 15 and submitted by January 30 for funding to commence the following August 1. Applications must be requested by June 15 and submitted by July 15 for funding to commence the following February 1.

STAFF:
Lynn O'Connor Vos, President and Chief Executive Officer
Michael J. Kennedy, MBA, C.P.A., Executive Vice President and Chief Financial Officer

ADDRESS INQUIRIES TO:
See e-mail address above.

MYASTHENIA GRAVIS FOUNDATION OF AMERICA, INC.   [2260]
355 Lexington Avenue
15th Floor
New York, NY 10017
(800) 541-5454
Fax: (212) 297-2159
E-mail: mgfa@myasthenia.org
Web Site: www.myasthenia.org

FOUNDED: 1952

AREAS OF INTEREST:
Myasthenia gravis and related neuromuscular conditions.

CONSULTING OR VOLUNTEER SERVICES:
Nationwide Support Group Network.

NAME(S) OF PROGRAMS:
● **Nursing Research Grant**

TYPE:
Research grants. Awards for research pertaining to problems faced by myasthenia gravis patients.

YEAR PROGRAM STARTED: 1988

PURPOSE:
To create an effective communications, service and human relations network for myasthenics, their families and friends; to educate both the lay and professional community about myasthenia gravis; to stimulate and support scientific inquiry, interchange and research in the quest for improved treatment techniques and a cure.

LEGAL BASIS:
Nonprofit corporate foundation.

ELIGIBILITY:
Candidates must be currently licensed as registered professional nurses. Fellowships are limited to U.S. or Canadian citizens or holders of bona fide permanent visas for training in U.S. institutions.

FINANCIAL DATA:
Amount of support per award: Up to $5,000.

NO. MOST RECENT APPLICANTS: 1.

NO. AWARDS: 1.

APPLICATION INFO:
Candidates should submit four copies of cover letter stating that he or she is applying for the Nursing Research Grant, proposed budget, curriculum vitae, research proposal and letters of approval to conduct research by appropriate parties (i.e., institution, physicians and educational facilities).
Duration: One year.
Deadline: September 1.

PUBLICATIONS:
Guidelines.

IRS I.D.: 13-5672224

ADDRESS INQUIRIES TO:
Anne Williams, R.N.
E-mail: annewilliams515@yahoo.com

NATIONAL ATAXIA FOUNDATION   [2261]
600 Highway 169 South
Suite 1725
Minneapolis, MN 55426
(763) 553-0020
Fax: (763) 553-0167
E-mail: kelsey@ataxia.org
Web Site: www.ataxia.org

FOUNDED: 1957

AREAS OF INTEREST:
Cause and treatment of ataxia.

NAME(S) OF PROGRAMS:
● **National Ataxia Foundation Pioneer SCA3/MJD Translational Research Award**
● **National Ataxia Foundation Postdoctoral Fellowship Award**
● **National Ataxia Foundation Seed Money Research Grant**
● **National Ataxia Foundation Young Investigator Award**

TYPE:
Fellowships; Seed money grants. Young investigator award. Translation research awards.

YEAR PROGRAM STARTED: 1978

PURPOSE:
To support research into hereditary and sporadic ataxia, as well as treatment, services, and education of the disorder.

LEGAL BASIS:
Nonprofit 501(c)(3) organization.

ELIGIBILITY:
Individuals and organizations, including religious, can apply.

FINANCIAL DATA:
Amount of support per award: Pioneer SCA3/MJD Translational Research Award: $100,000; Postdoctoral Fellowship Award: Up to $35,000; Research Seed Money Grant and Young Investigator Award: Up to $50,000.

Total amount of support: Approximately $1,000,000 for the year 2020-21.

NO. MOST RECENT APPLICANTS: 66.

NO. AWARDS: 25 for the year 2020-21.

APPLICATION INFO:
Letter of Intent must be submitted one month prior to application deadlines.

Duration: Pioneer SCA3/MJD Translational Award and Young Investigator Award: One year. Seed Money Research Grant and Research Fellowship: One year. Renewals by reapplication each year for continuing support.

Deadline: Letters of Intent: September 21 for Seed Money Grant; September 28 for Young Investigator Award; October 5 for Pioneer SCA3/MJD Translational Award and Postdoctoral Fellowship Award. Full Proposals: October 19 for Seed Money Grant; October 26 for Young Investigator Award; November 2 for Pioneer SCA3/MJD Translation Award and Postdoctoral Fellowship Award.

PUBLICATIONS:
Annual report; application guidelines.

IRS I.D.: 41-0832903

ADDRESS INQUIRIES TO:
Kelsey Trace, Research Manager
(See address and e-mail above.)

NATIONAL HEADACHE FOUNDATION

820 North Orleans, Suite 201
Chicago, IL 60610-3132
(312) 274-2650
(888) 643-5552
Fax: (312) 640-9049
E-mail: info@headaches.org
Web Site: www.headaches.org

TYPE:
Research grants. Support for research in the field of headache and pain.

See entry 2160 for full listing.

NATIONAL INSTITUTE OF NEUROLOGICAL DISORDERS AND STROKE   [2262]

Building 31, Room 8A34
31 Center Drive, MSC 2540
Bethesda, MD 20892
(301) 496-4927
E-mail: quynh.ly@nih.gov
Web Site: www.ninds.nih.gov

FOUNDED: 1950

AREAS OF INTEREST:
Neurological disorders, including multiple sclerosis and amyotrophic lateral sclerosis, movement disorders, such as the dystonias and Tourette's syndrome and degenerative and dementing disorders such as Parkinson's, Huntington's and Alzheimer's diseases, stroke, spinal cord injury, neural regeneration and plasticity, coma, chronic pain, head injury, traumatic brain injury, peripheral nerve injury, tumors of the nervous system, brain edema and manipulative therapy, and convulsive, developmental and neuromuscular disorders.

TYPE:
Assistantships; Conferences/seminars; Fellowships; Project/program grants; Research grants; Training grants; Research contracts. Support for research, including neurological science basic research, which explores the fundamental structure and function of the brain and the nervous system, research to understand the causes and origins of pathological conditions of the nervous system with the goal of prevention of these disorders, research on the natural course of neurological disorders, research training in the basic neurological sciences and mechanisms associated with stroke and other cerebrovascular disorders, effects of trauma to the nervous system, neuroplasticity and regeneration and tumors of neural and sensory tissues.
Research may include:
(1) improved methods of disease prevention;
(2) new methods of diagnosis and treatment;
(3) clinical trials;
(4) drug development;
(5) development of neural prostheses for stroke and paraplegia;
(6) epidemiological research and;
(7) research training in the clinical sciences.

PURPOSE:
To support research on neurological diseases and stroke.

LEGAL BASIS:
PHS Act, Section 301, Section 431 and Section 433; Public Law 78-410, as amended; (42 U.S.C. 241), (42 U.S.C. 289C). PHS Act, Section 472; Public Law 78-410, as amended; (42 U.S.C. 289L-1).

ELIGIBILITY:
Research grants are available to any public or private nonprofit university, college, hospital, laboratory, or other institution, including state and local units of government, or to any individual. National Research Service Awards for the above areas may be made to individuals or to nonfederal public and private nonprofit institutions for the training of individuals at the pre- and postdoctoral levels.

FINANCIAL DATA:
Grants may be used for any usual research expenses including salaries, equipment supplies, travel to scientific meetings, patient care, publications, etc.

Amount of support per award: Approximately $380,000.

Total amount of support: $2.2 billion appropriated for fiscal year 2019.

APPLICATION INFO:
Application forms may be requested from the Division of Research Grants, National Institutes of Health, Bethesda, MD 20892.

Duration: One to five years. Renewal applications may be submitted.

Deadline: November 1, March 1, and July 1. Awards are announced throughout the year.

ADDRESS INQUIRIES TO:
Director, Division of Extramural Activities
NINDS, NIH MSC 9531
6001 Executive Boulevard
Rockville, MD 20892

NATIONAL MULTIPLE SCLEROSIS SOCIETY   [2263]

733 Third Avenue, 3rd Floor
New York, NY 10017-3288
(212) 476-0475
Fax: (212) 986-7981
E-mail: elisabeth.mari@nmss.org
Web Site: www.nationalmssociety.org

FOUNDED: 1946

AREAS OF INTEREST:
Multiple sclerosis.

NAME(S) OF PROGRAMS:
● **Postdoctoral Fellowships Program in Multiple Sclerosis Research**

TYPE:
Fellowships. Postdoctoral fellowships for training leading to an academic career involving clinical or basic research in multiple sclerosis.

YEAR PROGRAM STARTED: 1955

PURPOSE:
To support investigators for whom further assistance may be critical in obtaining the training required for a research or academic career, or for whom the additional training will increase research or teaching potential in areas related to multiple sclerosis.

LEGAL BASIS:
Voluntary health agency, tax status 501(c)(3).

ELIGIBILITY:
Qualified investigators holding a doctoral-level degree in medicine or appropriate biological fields are eligible to apply. Candidates must select their own training institutions and make all necessary arrangements for the conduct of proposed training or study program. Awards are based upon the applicant's professional status, training and experience.

FINANCIAL DATA:
Candidates must request all funds required.
Amount of support per award: Varies.
Total amount of support: Varies.

NO. MOST RECENT APPLICANTS: Varies.

NO. AWARDS: Varies.

APPLICATION INFO:
Instructions for completing the pre-application and full application are available on the Society's web site.

Duration: Up to three years.

Deadline: Mid-August. Pre-application one week prior to full application deadline.

OFFICERS OF THE BOARD:
Peter A. Galligan, Chairman
Cynthia Zagieboylo, President and Chief Executive Officer
Peter Porrino, Treasurer
Linda J. McAleer, Secretary

ADDRESS INQUIRIES TO:
Elisabeth R. Mari, Ph.D.
Director of Biomedical Programs
(See telephone and e-mail address above.)

NATIONAL MULTIPLE SCLEROSIS SOCIETY   [2264]

Research Programs
733 Third Avenue, 3rd Floor
New York, NY 10017-3288
(212) 476-0451
Fax: (212) 986-7981
E-mail: cathy.carlson@nmss.org
Web Site: www.nationalmssociety.org

FOUNDED: 1946

AREAS OF INTEREST:
Multiple sclerosis.

NAME(S) OF PROGRAMS:
- **National Multiple Sclerosis Society Research Grants Program**

TYPE:
Awards/prizes; Fellowships; Research grants; Research contracts. Pilot grants; Training/early career awards. Grants for fundamental or applied research in scientific areas pertinent to multiple sclerosis. Grants are available for clinical or nonclinical studies, providing they show relevance to the Society's research priorities.

YEAR PROGRAM STARTED: 1947

PURPOSE:
To support research into the cause, prevention, alleviation and cure of multiple sclerosis.

LEGAL BASIS:
Voluntary health agency, tax status 501(c)(3).

ELIGIBILITY:
Qualified investigators affiliated with appropriate institutions are eligible to apply. Institutions are the official recipients of grants. Some commercial partnerships supported.

FINANCIAL DATA:
The principal investigator and the grantee institution will be advised of the exact amount and duration of the grant award. Grant funds may be requested for professional and nonprofessional personnel, consumable supplies, travel and other expenditures and indirect costs.
Amount of support per award: Varies.
Total amount of support: Varies.

NO. MOST RECENT APPLICANTS: 613 for the year 2019.

NO. AWARDS: 110 for the year 2019.

APPLICATION INFO:
Before submitting a proposal for research support, investigators must submit preapplication online to determine whether the research plan is appropriate and relevant to the Society's goals.
Duration: Maximum of five years.
Deadline: February and August for research grants. Usually January, May and September for pilot research grants. Specific dates are posted online.

OFFICERS OF THE BOARD:
Richard Knutson, Chairman
Cynthia Zagieboylo, President and Chief Executive Officer
Peter Porrino, Treasurer
Linda J. McAleer, Secretary

ADDRESS INQUIRIES TO:
See e-mail address above.

THE NEURO [2265]

3801 University Street
Room 636
Montreal QC H3A 2B4 Canada
(514) 398-1238
Fax: (514) 398-8248
E-mail: john.mccall@mcgill.ca
Web Site: mcgill.ca/neuro

FOUNDED: 1934

AREAS OF INTEREST:
Neurology, neurosurgery and neuroscience.

NAME(S) OF PROGRAMS:
- **Jeanne Timmins Costello Fellowships**
- **Preston Robb Fellowship**

TYPE:
Exchange programs; Fellowships. Awards for research and study in the fields of clinical and basic neurosciences.

PURPOSE:
To provide the recipient with the experience of going from laboratory bench to the patient's bedside by exploiting the strengths of the Institute in basic and clinical science.

LEGAL BASIS:
University, research institute.

ELIGIBILITY:
For the Costello Fellowship, candidates must have an M.D. or Ph.D. degree. Those candidates with M.D. degrees will ordinarily have completed clinical studies in neurology or neurosurgery. Research themes at the MNI include neuroanatomy, neurochemistry, neurogenetics, molecular genetics, neuroimaging, neuroimmunology, epilepsy, neuromuscular disease, neuro-oncology, molecular and cellular biology and neuropsychology.

For the Robb Fellowship, candidates must have an M.D. degree with clinical studies in neurology or neurosurgery.

FINANCIAL DATA:
Amount of support per award: $40,000 per year.

NO. AWARDS: Jeanne Timmins Costello Fellowships: 4; Preston Robb Fellowship: 1.

APPLICATION INFO:
Application form and guidelines are available online from August 1 to October 31.
Duration: One year. Renewal possible for one additional year.
Deadline: October 31.

PUBLICATIONS:
Annual report.

ADDRESS INQUIRIES TO:
Fellowship Committee
E-mail: fellowships.mni@mcgill.ca

NEUROSURGERY RESEARCH AND EDUCATION FOUNDATION [2266]

5550 Meadowbrook Drive
Rolling Meadows, IL 60008-3852
(847) 378-0500
Fax: (847) 378-0600
E-mail: info@nref.org
Web Site: www.nref.org

FOUNDED: 1982

AREAS OF INTEREST:
Neurosurgery.

NAME(S) OF PROGRAMS:
- **Research Fellowships**
- **Young Clinician Investigator Award**

TYPE:
Awards/prizes; Fellowships; Research grants.

YEAR PROGRAM STARTED: 1983

PURPOSE:
To advance the neurosciences.

LEGAL BASIS:
Private foundation.

ELIGIBILITY:
Applicants for the Research Fellowship must be physicians who have been accepted into or who are in an approved residency training program in neurological surgery in North America.

Applicants for the Young Clinician Investigator Award must be neurosurgeons, no more than two years from having completed their neurosurgical residency training and/or clinical fellowship, who are full-time faculty in North American teaching institutions.

Those who accept grants from other sources for the same project are ineligible.

GEOG. RESTRICTIONS: North America.

FINANCIAL DATA:
Amount of support per award: Up to $50,000.

NO. AWARDS: 12 for the year 2019-20.

APPLICATION INFO:
Applications are only available online through the application portal on the NREF web site.
Duration: One year.
Deadline: November 1. Announcement no later than February 15.

ADDRESS INQUIRIES TO:
E-mail: grants@nref.org.

PARKINSON'S FOUNDATION [2267]

1359 Broadway, Suite 1509
New York, NY 10018
(212) 923-4700
(800) 457-6676
E-mail: bvernaleo@parkinson.org
grants@parkinson.org
Web Site: www.parkinson.org

FOUNDED: 1957

AREAS OF INTEREST:
Basic and clinical research toward finding the cause and cure for Parkinson's disease.

CONSULTING OR VOLUNTEER SERVICES:
Information and referral service to Parkinson's disease patients and caregivers; counseling.

NAME(S) OF PROGRAMS:
- **Conference Awards**

TYPE:
Conferences/seminars.

PURPOSE:
To support the gathering of experts in the field working to address unsolved clinical or basic science problems relevant to Parkinson's disease.

ELIGIBILITY:
Open to independent investigators, both nationally and internationally, possessing postdoctoral training or a medical degree (or the equivalent). The Award supports gatherings of experts in the field in order to address emerging clinical or basic science questions about Parkinson's. Award is not open to postdoctoral researchers or fellows.

FINANCIAL DATA:
Amount of support per award: Average award $10,000, with a maximum of $15,000.

NO. AWARDS: 3 to 4.

APPLICATION INFO:
All applications must be submitted online. Paper copies will not be accepted.
Duration: Up to one year.

Deadline: Applications will be accepted anytime, as long as they are submitted at least 90 days prior to proposed conference start date; award notification four to six weeks after application submission.

ADDRESS INQUIRIES TO:
Beth A. Vernaleo, Ph.D.
Senior Director of Research Programs or James Beck, Ph.D., Chief Scientific Officer
(See address above.)

PARKINSON'S FOUNDATION [2268]

1359 Broadway, Suite 1509
New York, NY 10018
(212) 923-4700
(800) 457-6676
E-mail: bvernaleo@parkinson.org
grants@parkinson.org
Web Site: www.parkinson.org

FOUNDED: 1957

AREAS OF INTEREST:
Basic and clinical research toward finding the cause and cure for Parkinson's disease.

NAME(S) OF PROGRAMS:
• **Stanley Fahn Faculty Scholar Award**

TYPE:
Research grants. Stanley Fahn Faculty Scholar Award provides investigators - in conjunction with their institution's commitment - with the support necessary to develop their own independent funding source (such as an NIH R01 award) and stay in the field of Parkinson's disease research.

PURPOSE:
To act as a bridge to ensure that promising early career scientists stay in the field of Parkinson's research and help solve, treat and end the disease; to stem the loss of talent from Parkinson's research.

ELIGIBILITY:
Faculty members possessing a Ph.D., M.D. or equivalent are eligible to apply. Applicants must generally meet the NIH definition of a "new investigator." The Foundation anticipates the typical applicant will hold an assistant professor-level position with up to several years of experience. Earlier-stage faculty and those with more experience will be considered provided that the above eligibility criteria are met.

This Award is open to applicants, regardless of citizenship, who reside in the U.S. and are faculty members of U.S. institutions.

Applicants from Foundation Research Centers are eligible to apply. A letter of support from the applicant's department chair will be required to demonstrate level of institutional commitment to the applicant.

This program is restricted to full-time faculty members of U.S. institutions with a current post of instructor or assistant professor. As a career development initiative, the program is not open to current or prior holders of NIH R01 awards or their equivalent. In principle, only one award will be made per institution in a given year, but special exceptions may be considered.

FINANCIAL DATA:
Amount of support per award: $300,000 in total costs. Indirect costs, not exceeding 10% of direct costs, may be deducted from the total. Applicant salary support is permitted up to 40% of total salary.
Total amount of support: $900,000.

NO. MOST RECENT APPLICANTS: 39 for the year 2019.

NO. AWARDS: 3.

APPLICATION INFO:
Application process is divided into two parts. Applicants first submit a letter of intent (LOI). Second, based on favorable peer review, applicants may then be invited to submit a full application, also for peer review. All materials must be submitted online at grants.pdf.org.
Duration: Three years, subject to review of annual progress. Submission of an NIH R01 or equivalent is a required milestone of this Award and upon which third year of funding is contingent.
Deadline: Letter of Intent: November 15. Invited full application: February 18. Award notification late April.

ADDRESS INQUIRIES TO:
Beth A. Vernaleo, Ph.D.
Senior Director of Research Programs
(See address above.)

PARKINSON'S FOUNDATION [2269]

1359 Broadway, Suite 1509
New York, NY 10018
(212) 923-4700
(800) 457-6676
E-mail: bvernaleo@parkinson.org
grants@parkinson.org
Web Site: www.parkinson.org

FOUNDED: 1957

AREAS OF INTEREST:
Basic and clinical research toward finding the cause and cure for Parkinson's disease.

NAME(S) OF PROGRAMS:
• **Visiting Scholar Award**

TYPE:
Visiting scholars. Visiting Scholar Award provides graduate students with opportunities for expanding their existing skillset to benefit their Parkinson's research.

PURPOSE:
To seek the cause and cure of Parkinson's disease.

ELIGIBILITY:
Ph.D. students and postdoctoral fellows conducting Parkinson's research for their thesis are eligible for this program. The program is open to applicants regardless of nationality or location. Each applicant must identify a mentor with whom he or she will conduct the proposed project. Students must be in their second year or later, and have an expected graduation date no sooner than six months after the end of the summer project.

FINANCIAL DATA:
Award is to be used at the scholar's discretion to supplement research costs or travel and housing costs while visiting the host laboratory.
Amount of support per award: $4,000 stipend plus up to $1,000 travel to a related scientific conference to present their research.
Total amount of support: $40,000.

NO. MOST RECENT APPLICANTS: 12.

NO. AWARDS: 8.

APPLICATION INFO:
Applications must be submitted online. No paper copies will be accepted.
Duration: Generally three months.

Deadline: Cycle 1: Application due November 4. Cycle 2: Application due April 1. Award starts within six months of award notification.

PARKINSON'S FOUNDATION [2270]

1359 Broadway, Suite 1509
New York, NY 10018
(212) 923-4700
(800) 457-6676
E-mail: bvernaleo@parkinson.org
grants@parkinson.org
Web Site: www.parkinson.org

FOUNDED: 1957

AREAS OF INTEREST:
Basic and clinical research toward finding the cause and cure for Parkinson's disease.

CONSULTING OR VOLUNTEER SERVICES:
Information and referral service to Parkinson's disease patients and caregivers; counseling.

NAME(S) OF PROGRAMS:
• **Parkinson's Foundation-PSG Mentored Clinical Research Award**

TYPE:
Research grants.

PURPOSE:
To seek the cause and cure of Parkinson's disease.

LEGAL BASIS:
Nonprofit organization.

ELIGIBILITY:
Clinicians and scientists who are within five years of having completed formal training may apply. Applicants must identify an appropriate mentor or mentors with extensive research experience. Either the applicant or the mentor must be a member of the PSG.

FINANCIAL DATA:
Amount of support per award: $50,000 per year.

CO-OP FUNDING PROGRAMS: Research Award is funded by a grant from the PDF to the Parkinson Study Group (PSG).

NO. AWARDS: 1.

APPLICATION INFO:
This is a collaborative fellowship and, for this program, applicants cannot use the Parkinson's Foundation online grant management system. Instead, applicants should submit an electronic copy of the proposal in Word or PDF format to the Parkinson Study Group to roseanna.battista@chet.rochester.edu with a cover note that includes the candidate's name and the title of the proposal. Visit the Parkinson Study Group web site (www.parkinson-study-group.org/award-announcements) for more award details.
Duration: One year.
Deadline: January 10. Award notification March 2.

PUBLICATIONS:
Annual reports; research reports; application guidelines and forms.

ADDRESS INQUIRIES TO:
Beth A. Vernaleo, Ph.D.
Senior Director of Research Programs or James Beck, Ph.D., Chief Scientific Officer
(See address above.)

PARKINSON'S FOUNDATION [2271]

1359 Broadway, Suite 1509
New York, NY 10018
(212) 923-4700
(800) 457-6676
E-mail: bvernaleo@parkinson.org
grants@parkinson.org
Web Site: www.parkinson.org

FOUNDED: 1957

AREAS OF INTEREST:
Basic and clinical research toward finding the cause and cure for Parkinson's disease.

CONSULTING OR VOLUNTEER SERVICES:
Information and referral service to Parkinson's disease patients and caregivers; counseling.

NAME(S) OF PROGRAMS:
- **Clinical Research Award**

TYPE:
Research grants. Research award for clinician-scientists to conduct patient-oriented research in Parkinson's disease.

PURPOSE:
To seek the cause and cure of Parkinson's disease.

LEGAL BASIS:
Nonprofit organization.

ELIGIBILITY:
Any clinician-scientist licensed to care for patients regardless of nationality or location may apply. Physicians must have completed a residency in neurology or be able to justify the relevance of their training pathway is of benefit to people with pulmonary disease. Allied health professionals must hold an advanced research degree, typically a Ph.D. All applicants must demonstrate a significant research focus on pulmonary disease.

Preference will be given to early career scientists.

FINANCIAL DATA:
Amount of support per award: $200,000 in total costs. Indirect costs, not exceeding 10% of direct costs, may be deducted from the total. Applicant salary support is permitted up to 40% of total salary.

Total amount of support: $600,000.

NO. MOST RECENT APPLICANTS: 29 for the year 2019.

NO. AWARDS: 2 to 3.

APPLICATION INFO:
Application information is available on the web site.

Duration: Two years.

Deadline: Letter of Intent: January 21. Invited Full Application: April 10.

PUBLICATIONS:
Annual reports; research reports; application guidelines and forms.

ADDRESS INQUIRIES TO:
Beth A. Vernaleo, Ph.D.
Senior Director of Research Programs or James Beck, Ph.D.
Chief Scientific Officer
(See address above.)

PARKINSON'S FOUNDATION [2272]

1359 Broadway, Suite 1509
New York, NY 10018
(212) 923-4700
(800) 457-6676
E-mail: bvernaleo@parkinson.org
grants@parkinson.org
Web Site: www.parkinson.org

FOUNDED: 1957

AREAS OF INTEREST:
Basic and clinical research toward finding the cause and cure for Parkinson's disease.

CONSULTING OR VOLUNTEER SERVICES:
Information and referral service to Parkinson's disease patients and caregivers.

NAME(S) OF PROGRAMS:
- **Postdoctoral Fellowship**

TYPE:
Fellowships. The Postdoctoral Fellowship program has two distinct components: (1) Postdoctoral Fellowship for Basic Scientists and (2) Postdoctoral Fellowship for Neurologists.

YEAR PROGRAM STARTED: 1990

PURPOSE:
To provide support and training for Parkinson's disease researchers at early stages in their careers.

LEGAL BASIS:
Nonprofit organization.

ELIGIBILITY:
Postdoctoral Fellowship for Basic Scientists: The applicant must be within five years of receiving his or her Ph.D., and must identify an individual who will serve as his or her mentor and supervisor of the research.

Postdoctoral Fellowship for Neurologists: Applicants seeking a Postdoctoral Fellowship for Neurologists must possess an M.D. or equivalent and be within three years of having completed a residency in neurology. Applicants may not have their own lab and must identify an individual who will serve as his or her mentor and supervisor of their research.

FINANCIAL DATA:
The Postdoctoral Fellowship does not pay indirect or overhead costs and requires the grant recipient to account for all expenditures. The second year's funding is dependent upon submission of a satisfactory report covering the first year's work.

Amount of support per award: Postdoctoral Fellowship for Basic Scientists: Up to $55,000, plus $5,000 research allowance. Postdoctoral Fellowship for Neurologists: Up to $65,000, plus $5,000 research allowance.

Total amount of support: $600,000.

NO. MOST RECENT APPLICANTS: 76.

NO. AWARDS: 5.

APPLICATION INFO:
Applications must be submitted online. Applicants for the Postdoctoral Fellowship must also submit the investigator's curriculum vitae, an outline of work to be undertaken and a detailed budget.

Duration: Two years.

Deadline: Letter of Intent: November 12. Invited Full Application: February 18. Award notification in late April.

PUBLICATIONS:
Annual reports; research reports; application guidelines.

ADDRESS INQUIRIES TO:
Research
(See address above.)

PARKINSON'S FOUNDATION [2273]

1359 Broadway, Suite 1509
New York, NY 10018
(212) 923-4700
(800) 457-6676
E-mail: bvernaleo@parkinson.org
grants@parkinson.org
Web Site: www.parkinson.org

FOUNDED: 1957

AREAS OF INTEREST:
Basic and clinical research toward finding the cause and cure for Parkinson's disease.

CONSULTING OR VOLUNTEER SERVICES:
Information and referral service to Parkinson's disease patients and caregivers; counseling.

NAME(S) OF PROGRAMS:
- **Parkinson's Foundation Summer Student Fellowship**

TYPE:
Fellowships. Supports medical students and undergraduates for study under the supervision of an established investigator.

YEAR PROGRAM STARTED: 2002

PURPOSE:
To seek the cause and cure of Parkinson's disease.

LEGAL BASIS:
Nonprofit organization.

ELIGIBILITY:
Undergraduate and medical students are eligible.

FINANCIAL DATA:
Amount of support per award: $4,000 stipend, plus up to $1,000 travel to a PD-related conference to present summer project data.

Total amount of support: $40,000.

NO. MOST RECENT APPLICANTS: 26.

NO. AWARDS: 8.

APPLICATION INFO:
Application information is available on the web site.

Duration: 10 weeks.

Deadline: December 2. Award notification by March 2.

PUBLICATIONS:
Annual reports; research reports; application guidelines and forms.

STAFF:
John L. Lehr, President and Chief Executive Officer
Veronica Todaro, Executive Vice President and Chief Operating Officer
James Beck, Ph.D., Senior Vice President and Chief Scientific Officer
Curt De Greff, Senior Vice President and Chief Financial Officer

ADDRESS INQUIRIES TO:
Beth A. Vernaleo, Ph.D.
Senior Director of Research Programs or James Beck, Ph.D.
Chief Scientific Officer
(See address above.)

TOURETTE ASSOCIATION OF AMERICA, INC.   [2274]
42-40 Bell Boulevard
Suite 205
Bayside, NY 11361-2820
(718) 224-2999
Fax: (718) 279-9596
E-mail: support@tourette.org
Web Site: www.tourette.org

FOUNDED: 1972

AREAS OF INTEREST:
Education, research and services relating to Tourette Syndrome and relevant scientific fields, such as biochemistry, neuroanatomy, neurophysiology, genetics, molecular biology, epidemiology, psychiatry, psychology, neuropsychology, neurology, neuroimaging, neuropathology, pharmacology and/or animal models.

NAME(S) OF PROGRAMS:
• **Young Investigator Program**

TYPE:
Fellowships; General operating grants; Research grants; Seed money grants; Technical assistance. Research grants available for Ph.D. and M.D. researchers in the following categories:
(1) proposals in basic neuroscience specifically relevant to Tourette Syndrome and;
(2) clinical studies related to the etiology, pathophysiology and treatment of Tourette Syndrome.

Fellowships provide one-year postdoctoral training.

YEAR PROGRAM STARTED: 1984

PURPOSE:
To support significant basic and clinical research in Tourette Syndrome.

LEGAL BASIS:
Not-for-profit organization.

ELIGIBILITY:
Open to Ph.D. and M.D. investigators from all areas of science who can contribute to the understanding of the genetics, pathogenesis, pathophysiology and the treatment of Tourette Syndrome. Investigators already studying Tourette Syndrome and those currently working in areas of science that can be applied to the problems of Tourette Syndrome are invited to apply.

FINANCIAL DATA:
These designated award levels can include indirect costs no greater than 10%. However, the total grant award cannot exceed $80,000 for a one-year research grant or $160,000 for a two-year award.
Amount of support per award: $80,000 per year.
Total amount of support: Varies.

REPRESENTATIVE AWARDS:
$150,000 to Deanna Greene, Ph.D., Washington University School of Medicine, St. Louis, MO, for "Network Architecture of the Brain in Tourette Syndrome and in Phenotypic Sub-Groups;" $150,000 to Izhar Bar-Gad, Ilan University, Ramat-Gan, Israel, for "Interaction of the Dopaminergic and GABAergic Systems in the Formation of Tics."

APPLICATION INFO:
Application information is available on the web site.

For preliminary screening, a preproposal is required. The approximate project funding level should be included. Inquirers will be informed as to whether to proceed with a full application.
Duration: One or two years.
Deadline: Preproposals are due December 5 each year. Final proposals are due in March each year. Awards are announced in July.

PUBLICATIONS:
Brochure.

ADDRESS INQUIRIES TO:
Leo Neuringer, Program Assistant
Research and Medical Programs
(See address above.)

*PLEASE NOTE:
The Scientific Advisory Board guides the Tourette Association of America in defining the strategic direction for grant funding. Ultimately, the Scientific Advisory Board makes recommendations for grant funding to the TAA's Board of Directors.

Nursing

AMERICAN ASSOCIATION FOR THE HISTORY OF NURSING, INC.   [2275]
P.O. Box 7
Mullica Hill, NJ 08062
(609) 519-9689
E-mail: grants@aahn.org
Web Site: www.aahn.org

FOUNDED: 1978

AREAS OF INTEREST:
Nursing historical research.

NAME(S) OF PROGRAMS:
• **Competitive Student Research H-31 Predoctoral Grant**
• **H-15 Grant for Faculty Members or Independent Researchers**

TYPE:
Awards/prizes; Research grants. Research awards.

YEAR PROGRAM STARTED: 2008

PURPOSE:
To encourage and support research in nursing history.

ELIGIBILITY:
Competitive Student Research H-31 Predoctoral Grant: Student must be an AAHN member enrolled in an accredited Master's or doctoral program. Proposals must focus on a significant question in the history of nursing and the research advisor will be doctorally prepared with scholarly activity in the field of nursing history and prior experience in guidance of research training.

H-15 Grant: Applicant must be an AAHN member with a doctoral degree. Proposals must outline a historical research project and will be judged for scholarly merit and significance to the field of nursing history.

FINANCIAL DATA:
Amount of support per award: Competitive Student Research H-31 Predoctoral Grant: $2,000; H-15 Grant: $3,000, including eight percent indirect costs for facilities and administration fees.
Total amount of support: $5,000.

NO. MOST RECENT APPLICANTS: 8 to 12.

NO. AWARDS: 1 per award.

APPLICATION INFO:
Contact the Association.
Deadline: April 1.

ADDRESS INQUIRIES TO:
Brian Riggs, Executive Director
(See address above.)

AMERICAN NURSES FOUNDATION   [2276]
8515 Georgia Avenue
Suite 400
Silver Spring, MD 20910
(301) 628-5227
Fax: (301) 628-5354
E-mail: givetonursing@ana.org
Web Site: www.nursingworld.org/foundation

FOUNDED: 1955

AREAS OF INTEREST:
Nursing research.

NAME(S) OF PROGRAMS:
• **Nursing Research Grants**

TYPE:
Research grants.

YEAR PROGRAM STARTED: 1955

PURPOSE:
To encourage the research career development of nurses.

LEGAL BASIS:
Not-for-profit corporation under Section 501(c)(3) of the Internal Revenue Code.

ELIGIBILITY:
Nurse researchers at all levels and expertise both in academia and in clinical settings are encouraged to apply. Funding is considered towards all studies that contribute to the advancement of nursing science and the enhancement of patient care.

FINANCIAL DATA:
Total funding is dependent, in part, on the participation of external sponsors.
Amount of support per award: Varies.
Total amount of support: Varies.

NO. MOST RECENT APPLICANTS: Varies.

NO. AWARDS: Varies.

APPLICATION INFO:
The application packet is available online beginning February 1.
Duration: One year.
Deadline: May 1. Award announcement: Fall.

PUBLICATIONS:
Annual report; newsletter; research publications.

BOARD OF TRUSTEES:
Timothy Porter-O'Grady, Chairperson
Joyce Fitzpatrick, Vice Chairperson

ADDRESS INQUIRIES TO:
Patrick Giblin, Development Associate
(See address above.)

*PLEASE NOTE:
Some of the grants are restricted to a particular field of study.

ASSOCIATION OF WOMEN'S HEALTH, OBSTETRIC AND NEONATAL NURSES (AWHONN) [2277]

1800 M Street, N.W.
Suite 740 South
Washington, DC 20036
(202) 261-2400
Fax: (202) 728-0575
E-mail: researchprograms@awhonn.org
Web Site: www.awhonn.org

FOUNDED: 1969

AREAS OF INTEREST:
Women's health, obstetrics, neonatal nursing, newborns, nursing profession, advocacy, research and clinical resources for nurses.

NAME(S) OF PROGRAMS:
● **AWHONN Research Grants Program**

TYPE:
Research grants.

YEAR PROGRAM STARTED: 1993

PURPOSE:
To promote the advancement of nursing research among members.

ELIGIBILITY:
Applicant must be a full member at the time of application and at time of selection and funding. Researchers who are currently principal investigators on a federally funded grant, or who have received an AWHONN-funded research grant within the past five years are ineligible to apply.

GEOG. RESTRICTIONS: United States and its territories.

FINANCIAL DATA:
Amount of support per award: $5,000 to $15,000.
Total amount of support: $37,000 for the year 2020.

NO. AWARDS: 5 for the year 2020.

APPLICATION INFO:
Application information is available on the web site.
Duration: One year.
Deadline: December 1.

PUBLICATIONS:
Journal of Obstetric, Gynecologic and Neonatal Nursing; Nursing for Women's Health.

ADDRESS INQUIRIES TO:
Research Programs
(See e-mail address above.)

THE CANADIAN LUNG ASSOCIATION (CLA) [2278]

885 Meadowlands Drive
Suite 502
Ottawa ON K2C 3N2 Canada
(613) 569-6411 ext. 262
(888) 566-5864 (within Canada)
Fax: (613) 569-8860
E-mail: research@lung.ca
Web Site: www.lung.ca

FOUNDED: 1959

AREAS OF INTEREST:
Respiratory health.

NAME(S) OF PROGRAMS:
● **Breathing as One: Allied Health Research Fellowships**
● **Breathing as One: Allied Health Research Grants**

TYPE:
Fellowships; Research grants. Fellowships are offered to registered nurses pursuing postgraduate education with a major component of the program involving respiratory nursing practice, physiotherapists pursuing postgraduate training with respiratory research as the major component, and respiratory therapists pursuing postgraduate education with a major component of the program involving respiratory therapy practice.

Grants for research and feasibility studies are offered to registered nurses undertaking research investigations related to nursing management of patients with respiratory disease and symptoms. Grants are also offered to physiotherapists undertaking investigations related to management of patients with respiratory disease. Respiratory therapists undertaking research investigations related to the management of patients with respiratory disease and symptoms may also qualify.

PURPOSE:
To promote research in areas that contribute to the field of respiratory health in Canada; to build research capacity within the respiratory health professional community; to support respiratory health professionals completing postgraduate studies in the completion of thesis-based programs.

LEGAL BASIS:
Not-for-profit, incorporated.

ELIGIBILITY:
To be eligible for a Breathing as One: Allied Health Fellowship Award the applicant must be:
(1) a Canadian citizen, Canadian resident or landed immigrant;
(2) a respiratory health professional from a recognized clinically based discipline (e.g., registered nurse, nurse practitioner, physiotherapist, respiratory therapist, pharmacist, cardiopulmonary technologist, polysomnographic technologist, kinesiologist, dietician, occupational therapist, social worker, or psychologist). M.Ds. are not eligible for support;
(3) enrolled in a graduate (thesis-based) program at the Master's or doctoral level during the funding period. Individuals who have applied to a graduate program but have not received acceptance may apply for a Fellowship. The award, however, will be conditional on acceptance into the program and;
(4) pursuing a research study with respiratory health as the major focus.

To be eligible for a Breathing as One: Allied Health Research Grant the principle applicant must be:
(1) a Canadian citizen, permanent Canadian resident or landed immigrant;
(2) a respiratory health professional from a recognized clinically based discipline (e.g., registered nurse, nurse practitioner, physiotherapist, respiratory therapist, pharmacist, cardiopulmonary technologist, polysomnographic technologist, kinesiologist, dietician, occupational therapist, social worker, or psychologist). M.Ds. are not eligible for support as a principal investigator;
(3) affiliated with a health care organization, an educational institution or any other Canadian institution that can manage funds in

the approved way and;
(4) pursuing a research study with respiratory health as the major focus.

FINANCIAL DATA:
Amount of support per award: Research Fellowship: $10,000 maximum for full-time and $5,000 for part-time students; Research Grant: Up to $20,000.
Total amount of support: Varies.

NO. MOST RECENT APPLICANTS: Approximately 12.

NO. AWARDS: Approximately 8 each year.

APPLICATION INFO:
Forms may be downloaded from the Lung Association web site. Applicant must upload one copy of the completed application and all relevant documents.
Duration: One year.
Deadline: May 17.

PUBLICATIONS:
Brochure; newsletters.

ADDRESS INQUIRIES TO:
Fatima Kazoun, Manager
National Research Programs
(See address above.)

FOUNDATION FOR NEONATAL RESEARCH AND EDUCATION (FNRE) [2279]

200 East Holly Avenue
Sewell, NJ 08080
(856) 256-2343
Fax: (856) 589-7463
E-mail: contact@fnre.com
Web Site: www.ajj.com/fnre

FOUNDED: 1992

AREAS OF INTEREST:
Neonatal nursing.

TYPE:
Research grants; Scholarships.

YEAR PROGRAM STARTED: 1992

PURPOSE:
To support research and education in neonatal nursing; to promote the development of expertise in the neonatal profession; to raise awareness of the general public as consumers of neonatal services.

LEGAL BASIS:
Nonprofit.

ELIGIBILITY:
Members of the FNRE Research Review Committee and the FNRE Board members are not eligible to apply.

All grant applicants must be professionally active neonatal nurses. Applicant must be principal investigator of the project. If the principal investigator has limited research experience, it is expected that the application will reflect appropriate nursing research consultation.

Scholarship applicants must:
(1) be officially admitted to a college or school of higher education for Bachelor of Science in Nursing, Master in Science in Nursing for Advance Practice in Neonatal Nursing, Doctoral degree in Nursing, or Master's or Post-Master degree in Nursing Administration or Business Management;
(2) have a 3.0 grade point average or higher;
(3) be a professionally active neonatal nurse and;
(4) not have received a FNRE scholarship or grant in the past five years.

GEOG. RESTRICTIONS: United States.

FINANCIAL DATA:

Amount of support per award: Grants: Up to $5,000 per project.

Total amount of support: Varies.

NO. AWARDS: 1 to 2.

APPLICATION INFO:

Grant applicants must submit:
(1) a research plan addressing the problem or significance of the project, literature review (five-page maximum), methodology, data collection instruments, data analysis and completion schedule;
(2) Institutional Review Board approval;
(3) documentation verifying that research procedures meet federal guidelines for animal protection if animals are to be used;
(4) detailed budget;
(5) one-page curriculum vitae of each principal investigator, co-investigator and support person;
(6) a conflict of interest disclosure and;
(7) the signature of their major advisor or dissertation/thesis/project committee chairperson.

Duration: One year. Extensions requested in writing may be granted.

Deadline: May 1. Award notifications will be mailed by September.

FOUNDATION OF THE NATIONAL STUDENT NURSES' ASSOCIATION, INC. [2280]

45 Main Street
Suite 606
Brooklyn, NY 11201-1075
(718) 210-0705
Fax: (718) 797-1186
E-mail: lauren@nsna.org
fnsna@forevernursing.org
Web Site: www.forevernursing.org

FOUNDED: 1969

AREAS OF INTEREST:
Nursing education.

TYPE:
Scholarships. General Scholarship Program awards funds based on a set of criteria established by the sponsor of the scholarship. These scholarships typically reflect a specific area of specialization within the nursing profession such as oncology, critical care, or emergency nursing or a certain population of the nursing profession that is often underrepresented.

PURPOSE:
To provide aid to nursing students.

LEGAL BASIS:
501(c)(3) charitable foundation.

ELIGIBILITY:
Applicants must be U.S. citizens or students with an Alien Registration number. They must also be currently enrolled in state-approved schools of nursing or pre-nursing in Associate degree, Baccalaureate, diploma, generic Doctorate, generic Master's and 16- to 18-month accelerated programs. Funds are not available for graduate study unless it is for a first degree in nursing. Graduating high school seniors are not eligible. Monies are awarded in the spring to be used in the next academic year and summer school. Monies can only be used for nursing or pre-nursing in one of the above-mentioned programs. No monies can be used for graduate education unless leading to a first degree in nursing. If applicant is matriculating into a nursing program, letter of acceptance must accompany this application. Proof of enrollment will be required at time of award. Current Association Board of Directors and Association Nominating and Elections Committee members are not eligible.

FINANCIAL DATA:
Amount of support per award: Scholarships: $1,000 to $7,500.

Total amount of support: Over $250,000 annually in the general scholarship program.

NO. AWARDS: 99 for the 2020-21 academic year.

APPLICATION INFO:
Applications can be completed online at the NSNA web site from August until the following January.

Applicants must submit a copy of their recent nursing school and college transcripts, or grade report. NSNA members must submit proof of their membership. Registered nurses in Baccalaureate programs and licensed practical/vocational nurses in programs leading to registered nurse licensure must submit a copy of their license to be considered for the Career Mobility Scholarships.

Duration: One year. Scholarships are awarded in the spring for use in the upcoming academic year.

Deadline: January.

ADDRESS INQUIRIES TO:
Lauren Sperle
Scholarship Program Committee
(See address above.)

*PLEASE NOTE:
The scholarships are based on academic achievement, financial need, and involvement in nursing student organizations and community activities related to health care. Additional criteria may be required by some sponsors.

MYASTHENIA GRAVIS FOUNDATION OF AMERICA, INC.

355 Lexington Avenue
15th Floor
New York, NY 10017
(800) 541-5454
Fax: (212) 297-2159
E-mail: mgfa@myasthenia.org
Web Site: www.myasthenia.org

TYPE:
Research grants. Awards for research pertaining to problems faced by myasthenia gravis patients.

See entry 2260 for full listing.

NATIONAL BLACK NURSES ASSOCIATION, INC. [2281]

8630 Fenton Street
Suite 910
Silver Spring, MD 20910
(301) 589-3200
Fax: (301) 589-3223
E-mail: info@nbna.org
Web Site: www.nbna.org

AREAS OF INTEREST:
HIV/AIDS, cardiovascular disease, women and children's health, cancer, substance abuse, diabetes, obesity, and violence in African American communities.

NAME(S) OF PROGRAMS:
- **Childrens Mercy Kansas City Scholarship**
- **Dr. Martha A. Dawson Genesis Nurse Leader Scholarship**
- **Maria Dudley Scholarship**
- **Martha Dudley Scholarship**
- **Lynne Edwards Research Scholarship**
- **Dr. Millicent Gorham Scholarship**
- **George McGuire Memorial Scholarship**
- **Rita E. Miller Scholarship**
- **NBNA Board of Directors Scholarship**
- **Margaret Pemberton Scholarship**
- **Iona Princess Pierre Memorial Scholarship**
- **Dr. Lauranne Sams Scholarship**
- **VITAS Healthcare/Esther Colliflower Scholarship**
- **Dr. Eric J. Williams Scholarship**

TYPE:
Scholarships.

PURPOSE:
To advance nursing practice, improve health care for all Americans, particularly the unserved and the underserved, and shape health policy for the access and delivery of health care services.

LEGAL BASIS:
Nonprofit professional association.

ELIGIBILITY:
Awards are given primarily to African Americans enrolled at any level in a nursing program (AD, BSN or LPN/LVN). Applicant must be in good standing at the time of application and be a member of NBNA.

GEOG. RESTRICTIONS: United States.

FINANCIAL DATA:
Amount of support per award: $1,000 to $5,000.

NO. MOST RECENT APPLICANTS: 63.

NO. AWARDS: 25.

APPLICATION INFO:
Applicant must provide:
(1) official transcript from an accredited school of nursing;
(2) two-page written essay;
(3) two letters of recommendation (one from applicant's school of nursing and one from the local chapter, or a nurse in the area if a local chapter does not exist). Letters of recommendation and essay must be attached to the application and;
(4) a clean/clear professional headshot.

Additional items to accompany the application in support of the candidate's eligibility and desirability may include documented evidence of participation in student nurse activities and involvement in the African American community, i.e., letters, news clippings, awards, certificates, etc.

Completed application and all supporting documents are to be sent via e-mail to charold@nbna.org. Scholarship applications will not be accepted by mail.

Duration: One year. May reapply.

Deadline: April 15. Awards are presented at the July/August conference.

BOARD OF DIRECTORS:
Dr. Martha A. Dawson, President

ADDRESS INQUIRIES TO:
Scholarships Committee
(See address above.)

NATIONAL INSTITUTE OF NURSING RESEARCH [2282]

Building 31, Room B1-B55
31 Center Drive
Bethesda, MD 20892-2178
(301) 496-0207
Fax: (301) 480-4969
E-mail: info@ninr.nih.gov
Web Site: www.ninr.nih.gov

FOUNDED: 1986

AREAS OF INTEREST:
Health of individuals, families, communities and populations.

CONSULTING OR VOLUNTEER SERVICES:
For potential principal investigators.

NAME(S) OF PROGRAMS:
- **Career Development Grants**
- **Research Grants**
- **Research Training Grants**
- **Small Business Innovation Research Grants**

TYPE:
Fellowships; Project/program grants; Research grants; Training grants. Funds may be used for salaries, consultation, equipment, travel and other usual costs, subject to federal regulations applicable to the grant. Fellowships are for postdoctoral research training; predoctoral support is also available.

YEAR PROGRAM STARTED: 1986

PURPOSE:
To support nursing research, research training at pre- and postdoctoral levels, and research related to patient care, the promotion of health, the prevention of disease and the mitigation of the effects of acute and chronic illnesses and disabilities.

LEGAL BASIS:
Public Health Service Act, Sections 301, 483, 484, and 487, as amended by Public Law 99-158.

ELIGIBILITY:
Applicant may be a for-profit organization, a nonprofit organization, a public or private institution such as a university, college, hospital and laboratory, a unit of state government, a unit of local government, an eligible agency of the federal government, a foreign institution, a domestic institution, a faith-based or community-based organization, an Indian/Native American tribal government (federally recognized), an Indian/Native American tribal government (other than federally recognized), or an Indian/Native American tribally designated organization.

FINANCIAL DATA:
Amount of support per award: Varies based on type of grant and duration.
Total amount of support: Varies.

CO-OP FUNDING PROGRAMS: Co-funding of research project grants with other NIH Institutes and Centers.

APPLICATION INFO:
With few exceptions, all types of grant applications are electronic. When determining which form to submit, applicants are encouraged to read the funding opportunity announcement.
Duration: Varies.
Deadline: Applications are accepted at any time for inclusion in one of the three annual review cycles (depending on the activity code).

PUBLICATIONS:
Investigators' publications.

ADDRESS INQUIRIES TO:
Melissa Barrett, Chief, Office of Communications and Public Liaison
(See address above.)

NATIONAL SOCIETY DAUGHTERS OF THE AMERICAN REVOLUTION [2283]

1776 D Street, N.W.
Washington, DC 20006-5303
(202) 879-3263
E-mail: nsdarscholarships@nsdar.org
Web Site: www.dar.org

FOUNDED: 1895

AREAS OF INTEREST:
Nursing.

NAME(S) OF PROGRAMS:
- **Madeline Pickett (Halbert) Cogswell Nursing Scholarship**
- **District of Columbia Nursing Scholarship**
- **Caroline E. Holt Nursing Scholarship**

TYPE:
Scholarships. Awarded to students who are enrolled or currently attending an accredited school of nursing.

PURPOSE:
To provide ways and means to help students to attain higher education; to perpetuate the memory and spirit of men and women who achieved American Independence by acquisition and protection of historical spots and erection of monuments; to carry out injunction of Washington in his farewell address to the American people; to maintain institutions of American Freedom; to aid liberty.

LEGAL BASIS:
Incorporated historical society.

ELIGIBILITY:
Scholarships are awarded without regard to race, religion, sex or national origin. Candidates must be U.S. citizens and must attend an accredited college or university in the U.S. Awards are judged on the basis of academic excellence, commitment to field of study, as required, and financial need.

Applicants for the Cogswell Nursing Scholarship must be members, descendants of members or eligible for membership in NSDAR. DAR member number must be on the application.

The District of Columbia Nursing Scholarship is intended for minority students in need who are enrolled in or attending the University of the District of Columbia.

No affiliation or relationship to DAR is required for qualification for the Holt Nursing Scholarship.

GEOG. RESTRICTIONS: United States.

FINANCIAL DATA:
Amount of support per award: $2,500.
Total amount of support: Cogswell and District of Columbia Scholarships: $5,000; Holt Scholarship $7,500.

NO. AWARDS: Cogswell and District of Columbia Scholarship: 2; Holt Scholarship: 3.

APPLICATION INFO:
Applicants must use the DAR Scholarship Committee's online submission process found on the DAR public web site. Once applicants have set up their scholarship profile, they will be able to complete the application. If necessary, applicants will be able to provide access to individuals wishing to submit confidential letters of recommendations or school transcripts.
Duration: One academic year. Nonrenewable.
Deadline: February 15.

PUBLICATIONS:
American Spirit, magazine.

ADDRESS INQUIRIES TO:
National Vice Chairman
E-mail:
mphcogswellnursingscholarship@nsdar.org,
dcscholarship@nsdar.org or
carolineeholtscholarship@nsdar.org

*PLEASE NOTE:
Awards are placed on deposit with the college or university. Any unused portion shall be returned to the National Society.

NATIONAL SOCIETY DAUGHTERS OF THE AMERICAN REVOLUTION

1776 D Street, N.W.
Washington, DC 20006-5303
(202) 879-3263
E-mail: nsdarscholarships@nsdar.org
Web Site: www.dar.org

TYPE:
Scholarships.

See entry 2098 for full listing.

NURSES' EDUCATIONAL FUNDS, INC. [2284]

137 Montague Street, Suite 144
Brooklyn, NY 11201
(917) 524-8051
E-mail: info@n-e-f.org
Web Site: www.n-e-f.org

FOUNDED: 1912

AREAS OF INTEREST:
Graduate nursing education.

TYPE:
Scholarships. Scholarships for registered nurses seeking Master's and Doctorate degrees in nursing.

YEAR PROGRAM STARTED: 1912

PURPOSE:
To increase the number of graduate prepared nurses in leadership positions in nursing education, research, clinical care, academic and health care administrative positions.

LEGAL BASIS:
Nonprofit organization; 501(c)(3) corporation.

ELIGIBILITY:
Registered nurses with proof of current citizenship or legal residence status, such as U.S. passport (biographic page), birth certificate, naturalization certificate from the USCIS, or permanent resident (Green Card) are eligible to apply if they are enrolled full- or part-time in a Master's or doctoral program that is a professionally accredited nursing program (i.e., Accreditation Commission for Education in Nursing, ACEN, or Commission on Collegiate Nursing Education). Applicants must be able to present proof of membership in a national professional nursing association.

GEOG. RESTRICTIONS: United States.

FINANCIAL DATA:
Amount of support per award: Scholarships vary in amount, according to the funds available.
Total amount of support: Varies.

NO. MOST RECENT APPLICANTS: 200 to 500 annually.

NO. AWARDS: 23 to 29 annually.

APPLICATION INFO:
Applications are submitted online.
Duration: One academic year. Can reapply for one additional year provided two semesters remain before graduation.
Deadline: February 1 annually.

IRS I.D.: 13-6122744

BOARD OF DIRECTORS:
Joan M. Marren, M.Ed., R.N., President
Cynthia Sculco, Ed.D., R.N., Vice President
Joan Arnold, Ph.D., R.N., Treasurer
Rebecca R. Eddy, MBA, PDDM, Secretary
Allison Adams, B.S., B.A.
Karen A. Ballard, M.A., R.N.
Vincent Batyr, C.P.A.
Susan Bowar-Ferres, Ph.D., R.N.
Kathleen M. Dirschel, Ph.D., R.N.
Craig Donner
Sarah Garrity
Carl A. Kirton, D.N.P., R.N.
Mathy Mezey, Ed.D., R.N.
Rosanne Raso, M.S., R.N.
Thelma Schoor, B.S.N., R.N.
Lawrence J. Siegel, MBA, J.D.
Roy L. Simpson, D.N.P., R.N.
Henry B. Spencer
Gerhard Stubi
Madeleine S. Sugimoto, M.Ed., R.N.
Edwidge Thomas, D.N.P.
Judith Ann Vessey, Ph.D., R.N.

ADDRESS INQUIRIES TO:
Jerelyn Weiss, Executive Director
(See e-mail address above.)

REHABILITATION NURSING FOUNDATION (RNF) [2285]
8735 West Higgins Road
Suite 300
Chicago, IL 60631
(800) 229-7530
Fax: (847) 375-6481
E-mail: info@rehabnurse.org
Web Site: www.rehabnurse.org

FOUNDED: 1976

AREAS OF INTEREST:
Rehabilitation nursing.

NAME(S) OF PROGRAMS:
● ARN/RNF Grant

TYPE:
Project/program grants; Research grants.

YEAR PROGRAM STARTED: 1988

PURPOSE:
To promote and advance professional rehabilitation nursing practice through education, advocacy, collaboration, and research to enhance the quality of life for those affected by disability and chronic illness.

ELIGIBILITY:
The principal investigator for the research project must be a registered nurse who is active in rehabilitation or who demonstrates interest in and significant contributions to rehabilitation nursing. Graduate student researchers may be eligible for funding.

FINANCIAL DATA:
Amount of support per award: Up to $30,000.

NO. MOST RECENT APPLICANTS: 3.

NO. AWARDS: 1.

APPLICATION INFO:
Proposals must be typed and electronically submitted to the e-mail address above. All applicants must:
(1) complete a Summary Data Form;
(2) submit a typed, 250- to 350-word abstract;
(3) have the institution or agency named in the proposal complete the Administrative Approval Form to indicate acknowledgment and approval and;
(4) complete the Grant Contact Form regarding the contact person for the grant funding agreement and disbursement of funds should application be selected.

All forms and instructions can be downloaded from the web site.
Deadline: March 1 in even-numbered years.

ADDRESS INQUIRIES TO:
Melissa Bellows, Operations Manager
(See e-mail address above.)

SALON NATIONAL LA BOUTIQUE [2286]
P.O. Box 1108
Lake Dallas, TX 75065-1108
(940) 230-0919
Fax: (940) 497-3044
E-mail: lasecretaire@8and40.org
Web Site: www.8and40.org

FOUNDED: 1919

NAME(S) OF PROGRAMS:
● Eight and Forty Lung and Respiratory Disease Nursing Scholarship Fund

TYPE:
Scholarships. Grants for registered nurses.

YEAR PROGRAM STARTED: 1957

PURPOSE:
To allow registered nurses to further their education at the graduate level in the area of pediatric lung and respiratory diseases.

ELIGIBILITY:
Applicant must be a registered nurse, in adequate health and a U.S. citizen. Applicant must also have freedom to pursue full-time employment, have qualities of leadership and be able to attend classes full- or part-time at an accredited school of nursing.

FINANCIAL DATA:
Amount of support per award: Up to $3,000.

NO. MOST RECENT APPLICANTS: 43.

APPLICATION INFO:
Application forms may be obtained from the address above.
Duration: One school year.
Deadline: May 15. Announcement July 1.

PUBLICATIONS:
Brochure.

ADDRESS INQUIRIES TO:
Eight and Forty Scholarships
(See address above.)

SIGMA THETA TAU INTERNATIONAL [2287]
Honor Society of Nursing
550 West North Street
Indianapolis, IN 46202
(317) 634-8171 (Local)
(888) 634-7575 (U.S./Canada)
Fax: (317) 634-8188
E-mail: research@sigmanursing.org
Web Site: sigmanursing.org

FOUNDED: 1922

AREAS OF INTEREST:
Nursing.

NAME(S) OF PROGRAMS:
● Rosemary Berkel Crisp Research Award
● Doris Bloch Research Award
● Virginia Henderson Clinical Research Grant
● Small Grants
● Joan K. Stout, R.N., Research Grant

TYPE:
Research grants.

YEAR PROGRAM STARTED: 1936

PURPOSE:
To encourage qualified nurses to contribute to the advancement of nursing through research.

LEGAL BASIS:
Incorporated.

ELIGIBILITY:
Applicants must meet the following requirements:
(1) be a registered nurse with a current license;
(2) hold a Master's or doctoral degree or be enrolled in a doctoral program;
(3) be ready to implement research project when funding is received and;
(4) complete the project within one year of funding.

For the Rosemary Berkel Crisp Research Award, applicant must be a member of Sigma Theta Tau International. Some preference will be given to applicants residing in Arkansas, Illinois, Kentucky, Missouri and Tennessee.

For the Virginia Henderson Clinical Research Grant, applicant must be a member of Sigma Theta Tau International and be actively involved in some aspect of health care delivery, education or research in a clinical setting.

FINANCIAL DATA:
Amount of support per award: $5,000 maximum.

NO. AWARDS: Small Grants: 10 to 15; All others: 1 per award or grant.

APPLICATION INFO:
Application information is available on the web site.
Duration: For approved research time.
Deadline: Varies.

PUBLICATIONS:
Guidelines; applications.

ADDRESS INQUIRIES TO:
Grants Coordinator
(See address above.)

U.S. DEPARTMENT OF HEALTH AND HUMAN SERVICES [2288]

HRSA/BHW, Division of Nursing and Public Health
11N Parklawn Building, Room 9-89
5600 Fishers Lane
Rockville, MD 20857
(301) 443-0856
Fax: (301) 443-0791
E-mail: mmccalla@hrsa.gov
Web Site: bhw.hrsa.gov/grants/nursing

AREAS OF INTEREST:
Nursing education and practice.

TYPE:
Project/program grants; Training grants.

YEAR PROGRAM STARTED: 1965

PURPOSE:
To improve nursing practice and education through projects that increase the knowledge and skills of nursing personnel, enhance their effectiveness in primary care delivery, increase the number of qualified professional nurses and increase nursing workforce diversity.

LEGAL BASIS:
Amendment to Public Health Service Act, Title VIII, Section 820 by "The Health Professions Education Partnership Act of 1998" Public Law 105-392, Subtitle B.

ELIGIBILITY:
Eligible entities are schools of nursing, nursing centers, academic health centers, state or local governments, and other public or private nonprofit entities appropriate by the Secretary that submit an application in accordance with Section 802.

GEOG. RESTRICTIONS: United States.

FINANCIAL DATA:
Amount of support per award: Grants vary in amount, depending on the needs and nature of the project.
Total amount of support: Varies.

APPLICATION INFO:
Contact the U.S. Department of Health and Human Services.
Duration: Varies according to project.

ADDRESS INQUIRIES TO:
Division of Nursing and Public Health, BHW/HRSA
Nursing Education Practice Quality and Retention Branch
(See address above.)

VIRGINIA DEPARTMENT OF HEALTH [2289]

Office of Health Equity
109 Governor Street, Seventh Floor
Suite 714 West
Richmond, VA 23219
(804) 864-7422
Fax: (804) 864-7440
E-mail: incentiveprograms@vdh.virginia.gov
Web Site: www.vdh.virginia.gov/health-equity

NAME(S) OF PROGRAMS:
- **Commonwealth of Virginia Nurse Educator Scholarship Program**
- **Mary Marshall Nursing Scholarship/Practical Nurse Program**
- **Mary Marshall Nursing Scholarship/Registered Nurse Program**
- **Nurse Practitioner/Nurse Midwife Scholarship Program**

TYPE:
Awards/prizes; Challenge/matching grants; Scholarships; Technical assistance; Loan forgiveness programs. Awarded to eligible students enrolled in undergraduate or graduate nursing programs at schools of nursing approved by the Virginia State Board of Nursing to assist with their professional education.

Undergraduate nursing programs are defined as those leading to a licensed practical nurse, an Associate degree, diploma, or Baccalaureate degree in nursing.

YEAR PROGRAM STARTED: 1950

PURPOSE:
To provide the citizens of the state with more skilled and greater nursing care coverage.

LEGAL BASIS:
Funding is appropriated by the General Assembly of Virginia under code 23-35.9-23-35.13; code 32.1-122.6-01; and Title 32.1, Chapter 6, 32.1-122.6-02.

ELIGIBILITY:
Criteria vary for the different scholarships. Because of the strict nature of these criteria, it is vital that the applicant contact the Department for full particulars.

GEOG. RESTRICTIONS: Virginia.

FINANCIAL DATA:
Amount of scholarships varies, depending upon amount appropriated by the General Assembly, amount collected by the Board of Nursing and the number of qualified applicants. There are strict conditions attached to these scholarships. (They are not outright gifts; require service in the Commonwealth of Virginia.)
Amount of support per award: Varies each year.
Total amount of support: Varies each year.

NO. AWARDS: Varies each year.

APPLICATION INFO:
Applications are available online. Required data for application include most current transcript of grades (or last school attended if not currently enrolled), verification of need from the Financial Aid Officer and recommendation of the Director of the School of Nursing.
Duration: Each scholarship is awarded for a single year. Upon reapplication, scholarships may be awarded for succeeding years to a maximum of four years.

PUBLICATIONS:
Guidelines.

OFFICER:
Olivette Burroughs, Health Workforce Specialist

ADDRESS INQUIRIES TO:
Nursing Scholarships
(See address above.)

Obstetrics and gynecology

CENTRAL ASSOCIATION OF OBSTETRICIANS AND GYNECOLOGISTS [2290]

15 North Main
Minot, ND 58703
(701) 838-8323
Fax: (701) 852-8733
E-mail: rhickel@caog.org
Web Site: www.caog.org

FOUNDED: 1929

AREAS OF INTEREST:
Obstetrics and gynecology, including investigative and/or clinical work.

NAME(S) OF PROGRAMS:
- **Annual Central Prize Award**
- **Central Poster Award**
- **Community Hospital Award**
- **FAR Research Network Award**
- **President's Certificate of Merit Award**
- **Young Investigator's Award**

TYPE:
Awards/prizes. The Annual Central Prize Award, President's Certificate of Merit Award and Central Poster Awards are presented annually for manuscripts demonstrating outstanding investigative or clinical work in the field of obstetrics and gynecology.

The Community Hospital Award is presented annually for clinical study or research in the field of obstetrics and gynecology to members located in community hospitals who are not full-time faculty in medical schools. Preference for this award will be given to papers concerning gynecologic endoscopy or any other diagnostic or therapeutic procedures which enhance the quality of care of gynecologic or obstetric patients.

The Young Investigator's Award is presented annually for clinical study or research in the field of obstetrics and gynecology to residents, fellows, and clinicians residing in the geographic confines of the Central Association.

YEAR PROGRAM STARTED: 1929

PURPOSE:
To encourage original work in obstetrics and gynecology.

LEGAL BASIS:
Nonprofit medical organization.

ELIGIBILITY:
Those eligible to compete are accredited physicians, teachers, research workers and medical students whose work was done within the geographic area of the Association.

For the Community Hospital Award, at least one author must be a member of the Central Association. Manuscripts must be written expressly for this competition and they must be original, not having been previously presented or published. Manuscripts will be considered for both the general program and the award unless the author specifically requests otherwise in writing.

GEOG. RESTRICTIONS: Alabama, Arizona, Arkansas, Colorado, Idaho, Illinois, Indiana, Iowa, Kansas, Kentucky, Louisiana, Michigan, Minnesota, Mississippi, Missouri, Montana, Nebraska, Nevada, New Mexico,

North Dakota, Ohio, Oklahoma, South Dakota, Tennessee, Texas, Utah, West Virginia, Wisconsin and Wyoming.

FINANCIAL DATA:
Amount of support per award: Annual Central Prize Award: $2,000; Central Poster Award: $500 each; Community Hospital Award and FAR Research Network Award: $1,000; President's Certificate of Merit Award: $1,500; Young Investigator's Award: $750.

NO. MOST RECENT APPLICANTS: 50.

NO. AWARDS: Annual Central Prize Award, Community Hospital Award, FAR Research Network Award, President's Certificate of Merit, and Young Investigator's Award: 1 of each annually. Central Poster Award: 2 annually.

APPLICATION INFO:
For consideration for these awards, an online abstract must be submitted. The abstract maximum length is 800 words.

Duration: One year. Nonrenewable.

Deadline: Late April. Award winners notified early May.

OFFICERS AND TRUSTEES:
David F. Lewis, M.D., President
Lee P. Shulman, M.D., President Elect I
Vanessa M. Barnabei, M.D., Ph.D., President Elect II
A. Michael Drachler, M.D., Vice President
Suneet P. Chauhan, M.D., Secretary-Treasurer
Thomas F. Arnold, M.D.
Pamela R. Midboe-Penn, M.D.
Susan M. Mou, M.D.
Michelle Y. Owens, M.D.
Roger P. Smith, M.D.
William J. Todia, M.D.
James W. Van Hook, M.D.

ADDRESS INQUIRIES TO:
Rochelle Hickel, Executive Director
(See address above.)

THE LALOR FOUNDATION, INC. [2291]
c/o GMA Foundations
2 Liberty Square, Suite 500
Boston, MA 02109
(617) 426-7080
(617) 391-3088
Fax: (617) 426-7087
E-mail: fellowshipmanager@gmafoundations.com
Web Site: lalorfound.org

FOUNDED: 1935

AREAS OF INTEREST:
Sexual and reproductive health, contraception and pregnancy termination.

NAME(S) OF PROGRAMS:
● **The Anna Lalor Burdick Program**

TYPE:
Project/program grants.

PURPOSE:
To empower young women through education about healthy reproduction in order to broaden and enhance their options in life.

LEGAL BASIS:
Tax-exempt philanthropic foundation.

ELIGIBILITY:
Applicants must be tax-exempt under Section 501(c)(3) of the Internal Revenue Code and defined as "not a private foundation" under

Section 509(a). Projects may take place outside of the U.S., but organization must be based in the U.S.

Grants are not normally made to individuals, research projects and scholarships, requests for endowment or major capital support, or general operating support for ongoing programs.

FINANCIAL DATA:
Amount of support per award: $10,000 to $35,000.

Total amount of support: $205,750 for fiscal year 2016.

NO. AWARDS: 8 for the year 2017.

APPLICATION INFO:
Applicant must submit a Concept Paper online. Full application information is available on the web site.

Duration: One year.

Deadline: Concept Paper: May 1 and November 1. Invitation for full proposals six to eight weeks later.

IRS I.D.: 51-6000153

OFFICERS:
Cynthia B. Patterson, President
Christopher Burdick, Vice President
Lalor Burdick, Secretary and Treasurer

BOARD OF TRUSTEES:
Christopher Burdick
Lalor Burdick
Carol Chandler, Esq.
Marnie Cochran
Cynthia B. Patterson
Sally H. Zeckhauser

ADDRESS INQUIRIES TO:
Fellowship Manager
(See address above.)

REPRODUCTIVE SCIENTIST DEVELOPMENT PROGRAM (RSDP) [2292]
University of Missouri
Department of Obstetrics, Gynecology and Women's Health
500 North Keene, Suite 203
Columbia, MO 65201
(573) 817-3114
E-mail: heflina@missouri.edu
Web Site: www.rsdprogram.org

FOUNDED: 1986

AREAS OF INTEREST:
Obstetric-gynecologic academic investigative careers in fundamental biomedical science.

TYPE:
Research grants. National career development program grant for full-time basic research under the mentorship of internationally recognized senior scientists.

YEAR PROGRAM STARTED: 1988

PURPOSE:
To train obstetrician-gynecologists committed to academic investigative careers in fundamental biomedical science.

ELIGIBILITY:
Candidates must be seeking a career in academic obstetrics and gynecology research and meet the following criteria:
(1) possess M.D. or D.O. degree;
(2) be a U.S. citizen, noncitizen national, verification as a permanent citizen at time of award;
(3) have completed a four-year internship and residency in obstetrics-gynecology approved

by the Accreditation Council for Graduate Medical Education or the Royal College of Physicians and Surgeons of Canada and; (4) submit a research proposal as part of application.

GEOG. RESTRICTIONS: United States.

FINANCIAL DATA:
Amount of support per award: Up to $125,000 for salary plus fringes and up to $25,000 for research support may be provided from NICHD funds for Phase I scholars.

Up to $100,000 for salary plus fringes and up to $25,000 for research support may be provided from NICHD funds for Phase II scholars. Phase II Scholars are also eligible to receive support from program sponsors of the RSDP Program. Award amounts vary.

NO. MOST RECENT APPLICANTS: 6.

NO. AWARDS: Up to 2 new positions are available each year.

APPLICATION INFO:
Applicant must submit a Letter of Intent to the RSDP office indicating the name of the Department of Ob/Gyn sponsor, name and address of proposal scientific mentor, and a brief description of the research project. This will be reviewed by the Executive Committee for appropriateness, and feedback will be provided to potential applicants.

Duration: Two to four years of support is available.

Deadline: Letter of Intent: August 15. Application: October 1.

ADDRESS INQUIRIES TO:
Amanda Heflin, MBA
Program Administrator
Tel: (618) 977-8070
(See address above.)

U.S. DEPARTMENT OF HEALTH AND HUMAN SERVICES [2293]
Maternal and Child Health Bureau
Parklawn Building, Room 5C 26
5600 Fishers Lane
Rockville, MD 20857
(301) 443-2204
Fax: (301) 443-9354
E-mail: CallCenter@hrsa.gov (grants information)
Web Site: mchb.hrsa.gov

FOUNDED: 1936

AREAS OF INTEREST:
Health of mothers and children.

NAME(S) OF PROGRAMS:
● **Maternal and Child Health Services Block Grant**

TYPE:
Block grants. The Title V Block Grant Program has as a general purpose the improvement of the health of all mothers and children in the nation. The Block Grant Program has three components: Formula Block Grants to 59 states and other political jurisdictions, Special Projects of Regional and National Significance (SPRANS), and Community Integrated Service Systems (CISS) Grants.

PURPOSE:
To improve the health of all mothers and children; to create federal-state partnerships to develop service systems in U.S. communities that can meet the critical challenges facing maternal and child health.

LEGAL BASIS:
Title V, Section 501, of the Social Security Act, as amended by Public Law 101-239.

ELIGIBILITY:
State health agencies.

GEOG. RESTRICTIONS: United States and its territories.

FINANCIAL DATA:
Amount of support per award: Grants vary in amount, depending upon the number of children at the poverty level in the state.

Total amount of support: Varies.

Matching fund requirements: The Title V Block Grant Program requires that every four dollars of federal Title V money must be matched by at least three dollars of state and local money.

CO-OP FUNDING PROGRAMS: NICHD, CDC, Department of Education, ADAMHA and other inter-agency agreements.

NO. AWARDS: 59.

APPLICATION INFO:
Instructions available at grants.gov.

Duration: One to two years. Must reapply annually.

Deadline: July 15.

ADDRESS INQUIRIES TO:
Maternal and Child Health Bureau
(See address above.)

Ophthalmology and otolaryngology

THE ALCON FOUNDATION, INC. [2294]

6201 South Freeway
Fort Worth, TX 76134-2099
(817) 293-0450
E-mail: alcon.foundation@alcon.com
Web Site: www.alcon.com

AREAS OF INTEREST:
Ophthalmology and vision care.

TYPE:
Project/program grants.

YEAR PROGRAM STARTED: 1962

PURPOSE:
To support programs that improve the quality of eye care services and patient access to care, as well as programs that promote the advancement of eye health education, training and skills-transfer; to support select cultural, humanitarian and community development programs that meaningfully enhance quality of life in the communities where Alcon has a U.S. facility.

LEGAL BASIS:
Corporate foundation.

ELIGIBILITY:
Eligible organizations must be 501(c)(3) nonprofit entities. The Foundation accepts charitable monetary donation applications from 501(c)(3) charities with high-quality programs and services, well-defined goals, a commitment to maximizing available resources, a reputation for meeting results, and the ability to report results.

GEOG. RESTRICTIONS: For cultural, humanitarian and community development programs: Irvine and Lake Forest, CA; Johns Creek, GA; Sinking Spring, PA; Fort Worth and Houston, TX; and Huntington, WV.

APPLICATION INFO:
Only online application will be accepted.

Duration: One year.

Deadline: July 31 for requests larger than $10,000.

ADDRESS INQUIRIES TO:
Melissa Thompson, President
(See address above.)

AMERICAN ACADEMY OF OPTOMETRY FOUNDATION [2295]

2909 Fairgreen Street
Orlando, FL 32803
(321) 319-4858
Fax: (407) 893-9890
E-mail: helenv@aaoptom.org
Web Site: www.aaopt.org/home/aaof/programs

FOUNDED: 1922

AREAS OF INTEREST:
Vision science and vision care.

NAME(S) OF PROGRAMS:
• **Julius F. Neumueller Award in Optics**

TYPE:
Awards/prizes.

YEAR PROGRAM STARTED: 1969

PURPOSE:
To advance optometric education in optics.

LEGAL BASIS:
Tax-exempt corporation.

ELIGIBILITY:
Applicant must be a student pursuing an O.D. degree in a school of optometry recognized by the AOA Council on Optometric Education.

GEOG. RESTRICTIONS: Primarily United States and Canada.

FINANCIAL DATA:
Amount of support per award: Approximately $750.

Total amount of support: Approximately $750 annually.

NO. MOST RECENT APPLICANTS: 2.

NO. AWARDS: 2.

APPLICATION INFO:
Applicant must submit a paper, not to exceed 3,000 words, on Geometrical Optics, Physical Optics, Ophthalmic Optics or Optics of the Eye. Each school may submit two papers each year to the Chairman of the Awards Committee, which are judged by selected members of the American Academy of Optometry.

Duration: One-time award.

Deadline: April 1. Award announcement July 1.

ADDRESS INQUIRIES TO:
Helen Viksnins
Senior Director of Programs
(See address above.)

AMERICAN ACADEMY OF OPTOMETRY FOUNDATION [2296]

2909 Fairgreen Street
Orlando, FL 32803
(321) 319-4870
Fax: (407) 893-9890
E-mail: aaof@aaoptom.org
Web Site: www.aaopt.org/home/aaof/programs

FOUNDED: 1947

AREAS OF INTEREST:
Optometric research and education.

NAME(S) OF PROGRAMS:
• **J. Pat Cummings Scholarships**
• **VSP and AAOF Practice Excellence Scholarships**
• **VSP and FYidoctors - AAOF Practice Excellence Scholarships**

TYPE:
Scholarships; Travel grants. In collaboration with Johnson & Johnson Vision, the Pat Cummings Scholarships are bestowed annually to second- or third-year optometry students who best demonstrate the ideal eye care standards of practice, achievement in both academic performance and extracurricular activities, and participation with other professional pursuits such as involvement with patients through internships, community service, and other volunteer activities.

VSP and AAOF Practice Excellence Scholarships are awarded to optometry students at every school and college of optometry in the U.S. and Puerto Rico. The travel grant will enable outstanding students to attend a premier education opportunity in primary eye care, as well as attend a reception co-hosted by VSP Global and AAOF to help foster networking opportunities and teach the importance of Academy Fellowship.

VSP and FYidoctors - AAOF Practice Excellence Scholarships are awarded to optometry students at two schools of optometry in Canada. The travel grant will enable outstanding students to attend a premier education opportunity in primary eye care, as well as attend a reception co-hosted by VSP and the AAOF to help foster networking opportunities and teach the importance of Academy Fellowship.

YEAR PROGRAM STARTED: 1952

PURPOSE:
To encourage careers in optometry and to further vision research, both basic and clinical.

LEGAL BASIS:
IRS tax status 501(c)(3).

ELIGIBILITY:
Student must be a member of the American Academy of Optometry.

VSP and AAOF Practice Excellence Scholarship and VSP and FYidoctors - AAOF Practice Excellence Scholarship Programs: Candidate must excel in primary eye care services to clinical patients and must have a grade point average that ranks in the top half of the class. Student should have a commitment to enter the practice of optometry. Participation in the private practice or practice management club on campus is recommended, with special consideration given to students who have served a leadership role.

GEOG. RESTRICTIONS: Canada, Puerto Rico and
United States.

FINANCIAL DATA:
Amount of support per award: Cummings
Scholarships: $875; VSP and AAOF
Scholarships: $4,000, including $750 travel
support; VSP and FYidoctors - AAOF
Scholarships: $6,000 total among four
students, plus $750 travel support to attend
the AAO Annual Meeting.

Total amount of support: Varies.

NO. AWARDS: Cummings Scholarships: 23; VSP
and AAOF Scholarships: 42; VSP and
FYidoctors - AAOF Scholarships: 4.

APPLICATION INFO:
The J. Pat Cummings Nomination Form and
a copy of the appropriate IRS tax form are
provided directly to institution contacts via
e-mail prior to the opening of the submission
window. The appropriate award selection
committee at each school or college of
optometry will select the one student who
meets the eligibility requirements and best
demonstrates the detailed qualities. The
AAOF will not accept applications directly
from students. Interested students should
relay their desire for consideration to the
award chair or financial aid representative at
their institution.

VSP and AAOF Practice Excellence
Scholarships and VSP and FYidoctors -
AAOF Practice Excellence Scholarships:
Each institution's Awards and Scholarship
committee is tasked with selecting a pool of
five business-minded students who meet the
clinical and academic standards and then
choose two scholarship recipients. The
AAOF will not accept applications directly
from students for this program. AAOF will
notify institutional contacts that the
submission window is open for nominations.

Duration: Fellowships are awarded for a
period of one year.

Deadline: Cummings Scholarships:
September 15; VSP and AAOF Scholarships
and VSP and FYidoctors - AAOF
Scholarships: August 15.

PUBLICATIONS:
Application guidelines/criteria.

STAFF:
Peter Scott, C.A.E., MBA, Executive Director
Bob Gray, Development Director
Jennifer Rubin, Foundation Program Manager

BOARD OF DIRECTORS AND OFFICERS:
Peter Kollbaum, O.D., Ph.D., President
Wendy Harrison, O.D., Ph.D., President-Elect
Dr. Rachel A. Coulter, O.D., M.S.,
Secretary-Treasurer
Kerry Giedd, O.D., M.S.
April Jasper, O.D.
David G. Kirschen, O.D., Ph.D.
Kathryn L. Richdale, O.D., Ph.D.
David G. Sattler
Valerie L. Sharpe, O.D.
Loretta Szczotka-Flynn, O.D., Ph.D.
Danne Ventura
Jeffrey Walline, O.D., Ph.D.

ADDRESS INQUIRIES TO:
Jennifer Rubin, Foundation Program Manager
(See e-mail address above.)

AMERICAN ACADEMY OF OPTOMETRY FOUNDATION [2297]

2909 Fairgreen Street
Orlando, FL 32803
(321) 319-4870
Fax: (407) 893-9890
E-mail: aaof@aaoptom.org
Web Site: www.aaopt.org/home/aaof/programs

FOUNDED: 1947

AREAS OF INTEREST:
Vision science and vision education.

NAME(S) OF PROGRAMS:
● **Joseph T. Barr Early Cornea and
Contact Lens Research Award**

TYPE:
Awards/prizes; Seed money grants.

YEAR PROGRAM STARTED: 2012

PURPOSE:
To advance optometric education in
cornea/ocular surface or contact lenses.

LEGAL BASIS:
Tax-exempt corporation.

ELIGIBILITY:
Applicant must be a student member of the
American Academy of Optometry. Applicant
must be an entering first- or second-year
M.S. or Ph.D. vision science or physiological
optics student attending a North American
school or college of optometry. Applicant can
be in a graduate program alone or combined
with professional/residence program.

To receive this award, applicant must not
have applied during the same application
year nor previously received an Ezell
Fellowship.

GEOG. RESTRICTIONS: Primarily United States
and Canada.

FINANCIAL DATA:
Amount of support per award: $2,000, plus
$750 travel funding to attend the AAO
Annual Meeting.

NO. AWARDS: 1.

APPLICATION INFO:
The following documents must be submitted
in PDF format to Jennifer Rubin, Foundation
Program Manager, at jenniferr@aaoptom.org:
(1) a copy of a current curriculum vitae or
resume;
(2) a one-page statement describing past and
present educational and research
achievements, future educational objectives,
and long-term career goals in the areas of
cornea and contact lens research;
(3) an up to two-page summary of the
proposed research project including a
summary of the relevant background and
hypotheses, purpose, methods and budget;
(4) up to three best representations of
students submitted or published papers, if
applicable;
(5) a letter from the Dean, Associate Dean
for Research, or authorized official stating
that the applicant has been accepted into or is
currently enrolled in a Vision
Science/Physiological Optics M.S. or Ph.D.
program at a school or college of optometry
and that any funds received from the AAOF
will go only in support of the proposed
project and not decrease any academic
financial support and;
(6) a letter from a research supervisor or
mentor describing their support of the
described project and education advancement
of the applicant during the award period.

Duration: One-time renewal possible.
Deadline: April 1.

ADDRESS INQUIRIES TO:
Jennifer Rubin, Foundation Program Manager
(See e-mail address above.)

*SPECIAL STIPULATIONS:
Recipient must attend the Annual Meeting of
the American Academy of Optometry and
attend the AAOF Celebration Luncheon to
receive their award. The recipient is also
required to perform volunteer service at the
AAOF Booth.

AMERICAN ACADEMY OF OPTOMETRY FOUNDATION [2298]

2909 Fairgreen Street
Orlando, FL 32803
(321) 319-4870
Fax: (407) 893-9890
E-mail: aaof@aaoptom.org
Web Site: www.aaopt.org/home/aaof/programs

FOUNDED: 1947

AREAS OF INTEREST:
Vision science and vision care.

NAME(S) OF PROGRAMS:
● **Bert C. and Lydia M. Corwin Contact
Lens Residency Award**
● **Douglas W. Hopkins Primary Care
Residency Award**
● **Terrance N. Ingraham Pediatric
Optometry Residency Award**
● **Alfred A. Rosenbloom, Jr. Low Vision
Residency Award**
● **Sheldon Wechsler and George Mertz
Contact Lens Residency Award**

TYPE:
Residencies; Training grants. The Bert C. and
Lydia M. Corwin Contact Lens Residency
Award is intended to promote the practice
and development of the field of contact
lenses by providing incentive and support to
talented optometric residents who
demonstrate a passion and commitment to
practice, research and education.

The Douglas Hopkins Primary Care
Residency Award is intended to promote the
practice and development of the field of
primary care optometry by providing
incentive and support to talented optometric
residents who demonstrate a passion and
commitment to practice, research and
education in primary care.

The Terrance N. Ingraham Pediatric
Optometry Residency Program, funded by
Johnson & Johnson Vision, is intended to
promote the practice and development of the
field of pediatric optometry by providing
incentive and support to sustain talented
optometric residents who demonstrate a
passion and commitment to practice, research
and education in the field of children's
vision. A goal of this program is to invest in
the evolution of the field of pediatric
optometry, particularly but not limited to the
application of soft contact lenses for
children's vision disorders, by providing
opportunities for future practitioners,
educators and researchers.

The Alfred A. Rosenbloom, Jr. Residency
Award is intended to promote the practice
and development of the field of low vision by
providing incentive and support to sustain
talented optometric residents who
demonstrate a passion and commitment to
practice, research, and education.

The Sheldon Wechsler and George Mertz Contact Lens Residency Programs, which are funded by Johnson & Johnson Vision, are intended to promote the practice and development of the field of contact lenses by providing incentive and support to sustain talented optometric residents who demonstrate a passion and commitment to practice, research and education.

PURPOSE:
To advance optometric education.

LEGAL BASIS:
Tax-exempt corporation.

ELIGIBILITY:
Applicant must be a student member of the American Academy of Optometry.

Corwin Contact Lens Residency Award: Any optometrist currently serving in a 2020-21 academic year calendar contact lens residency through a North American school or college of optometry is eligible to apply.

Hopkins Primary Care Residency Award: Any optometrist currently serving in a 2020-21 academic year calendar primary care/family practice residency through a North American school or college of optometry or veterans administration facility is eligible to apply.

Ingraham Pediatric Optometry Residency Award: Optometrists currently serving in a 2020-21 academic year calendar advanced practice pediatric/vision therapy residency program through a North American school or college of optometry may apply.

Rosenbloom, Jr. Low Vision Residency Award: Any optometrist currently serving in a 2020-21 academic year calendar advanced practice low vision residency program through a North American school or college of optometry may apply.

Wechsler and Mertz Contact Lens Residency Award: Optometrists currently serving in a 2020-21 academic year calendar advanced practice contact lens residency program through a North American school or college of optometry may apply.

For all awards, anyone who has yet to begin a residency for the 2020-21 academic year calendar is ineligible.

GEOG. RESTRICTIONS: Primary United States and Canada.

FINANCIAL DATA:
Amount of support per award: $2,000, plus $750 travel fellowship to attend the AAO Annual Meeting.

NO. AWARDS: Corwin, Hopkins, Ingraham and Rosenbloom, Jr. Residency Award: 1; Wechsler and Mertz Residency Award: 2.

APPLICATION INFO:
Applicant must be a member of the American Academy of Optometry, whether as a student, candidate or fellow at the time of acceptance of any award. Application must include:
(1) a cover page that lists the applicant's name, any degrees, residency facility, the residency's host optometric institution, current and permanent address information, e-mail and phone contact information;
(2) applicant's education, clinical, research and teaching experience, typically in the form of a curriculum vitae;
(3) a brief description of the residency program and the names and e-mail addresses of the three people applicant has contacted to

submit letters of recommendation;
(4) a one-page statement of career goals and;
(5) three letters of recommendation from persons qualified to comment on the applicant's educational qualifications, research abilities and potential. One must be from the Residency Director or Program Coordinator of the host optometric institution. These letters should be e-mailed separately by the recommender.

Applications and letters of recommendation must be submitted electronically to the Foundation at the e-mail address listed above. Include the residency name and applicant's last name in the subject line.
Duration: One-time award.
Deadline: June 1.

ADDRESS INQUIRIES TO:
Jennifer Rubin, Foundation Program Manager (See e-mail address above.)

AMERICAN ACADEMY OF OPTOMETRY FOUNDATION [2299]
2909 Fairgreen Street
Orlando, FL 32803
(321) 319-4870
Fax: (407) 893-9890
E-mail: aaof@aaoptom.org
Web Site: www.aaopt.org/home/aaof/programs

FOUNDED: 1947

AREAS OF INTEREST:
Vision science and vision care.

NAME(S) OF PROGRAMS:
- **Beta Sigma Kappa (BSK) Student Travel Fellowship**
- **Elmer H. Eger Memorial Student Travel Fellowship**
- **N. Rex Ghormley Student Travel Fellowship**
- **Kirschen Family Student Travel Fellowship**

TYPE:
Fellowships; Travel grants. The BSK Student Travel Fellowship gives an optometry student the opportunity to engage in cutting edge learning, participate in hands on workshops, and experience an amazing exhibit hall at the annual Academy meeting.

The Eger Memorial Student Travel Fellowship is designed to support students whose professional goal is to be in private practice. It is also designed to encourage optometry students to attend key national meetings and exchange scientific ideas and research for use in an everyday clinical environment.

Ghormley Student Travel Fellowship is designed to encourage optometry students to attend key national meetings and exchange scientific ideas and research for use in an everyday clinical environment.

The Kirschen Family Student Travel Fellowship encourages optometry students to come to the annual meeting and become fellows in the Academy.

PURPOSE:
To advance optometric education.

LEGAL BASIS:
Tax-exempt corporation.

ELIGIBILITY:
Student must be a member of the American Academy of Optometry.

BSK Student Travel Fellowship: Optometry students who are currently enrolled full-time as second-, third- or fourth-year students may apply.

Eger Memorial Student Travel Fellowship: Schools will follow a rotation schedule which gives eight schools each year the opportunity to submit a nominee. Nominee must be pursuing a career in private practice and must be a third- or fourth-year student. Postdoctoral students and residents are not eligible.

The Ghormley Student Travel Fellowship: Optometry students who are currently enrolled full-time or have graduated within a year of the meeting are eligible to apply. Applicant must have had an abstract accepted as a first presenter/author of a paper or poster. Postdoctoral students and residents are not eligible. Fellowship will be awarded primarily for accomplishment and potential in optometric research and education. Academic abilities, including clinical abilities if relevant, are considered.

Kirschen Family Student Travel Fellowship is available to students currently in their third or fourth year of optometry school, who are in good academic standing and plan to pursue a career in private practice. Presentation of a paper or poster is desired, but not a requirement for this award.

GEOG. RESTRICTIONS: Primarily United States and Canada.

FINANCIAL DATA:
Amount of support per award: $750.

NO. AWARDS: 1 per award.

APPLICATION INFO:
BSK Student Travel Fellowship applicant must submit a short essay (300 to 500 words) on the subject "Why I want to attend the AAO meeting and how it will help me contribute to the professional in the future." Being a presenter of a paper or poster is desired, but not required. If applicable, submit a copy of the accepted paper or poster.

Eger Memorial Student Travel Fellowship: Student must submit a one-page statement describing why they want to pursue a career in private practice.

Ghormley Student Travel Fellowship: Student must submit a one-page statement which includes their commitment and interest in optometric research and/or education, their short- and long-term career goals, previous research training talks, papers and posters, summary of academic training (including honors), and demonstrated potential for self-motivation, independence and leadership. Also include a copy of the abstract of paper or poster that has been accepted and a recommendation letter from faculty.

Kirschen Family Student Travel Fellowship: Applicant must submit a one-page statement about themselves and why they are choosing private practice. One letter of recommendation is required.
Duration: One-time award.
Deadline: July 31.

ADDRESS INQUIRIES TO:
Jennifer Rubin, Foundation Program Manager (See e-mail address above.)

AMERICAN ACADEMY OF OPTOMETRY FOUNDATION [2300]

2909 Fairgreen Street
Orlando, FL 32803
(321) 319-4870
Fax: (407) 893-9890
E-mail: aaof@aaoptom.org
Web Site: www.aaopt.org/home/aaof/programs

FOUNDED: 1947

AREAS OF INTEREST:
Vision science and vision care.

NAME(S) OF PROGRAMS:
- **Allergan Foundation Research Grant**
- **Award of Excellence in Contact Lens Patient Care Grant**
- **Korb-Exford Dry Eye Career Development Grant**
- **Fredric Rosemore Low Vision Educational Grants**

TYPE:
Development grants; Project/program grants; Research grants. Allergan Foundation Research Grant supports talented optometry and vision science faculty and researchers in the area of glaucoma or the anterior segment.

Award of Excellence in Contact Lens Patient Care Grant, sponsored by Johnson & Johnson Vision, recognizes outstanding fourth-year student clinicians who have demonstrated excellence in contact lens patient care during their optometric education.

The Korb-Exford Dry Eye Career Development Grant is designed to support an individual to further their knowledge in the broad area of dry eye.

The Rosemore Low Vision Educational Grants are intended to increase and reward excellence in the field of low vision for faculty at North American schools and colleges of optometry.

PURPOSE:
To advance optometric education.

LEGAL BASIS:
Tax-exempt corporation.

ELIGIBILITY:
Allergan Foundation Research Grant is open to all faculty and researchers in optometry and vision science. Preference will be given to North American applicants. The Principal Investigator must be a member of the American Academy of Optometry. It is also encouraged that the co-investigator be a member.

Award of Excellence nominee must be a fourth-year student and a student member of the American Academy of Optometry. Nominee must represent outstanding clinical patient care as demonstrated by the student's overall knowledge in the contact lens field and skillful, considerate and professional care of their contact lens patients.

Korb-Exford Development Grant applicant must possess an O.D. or relevant graduate degree and must be a member of the American Academy of Optometry as a student, candidate or fellow at the time of applying for the award. The successful individual must have a demonstrable interest in either a clinical or basic science area of dry eye and may be a clinician, educator, researcher or student. Funds from this award may not be used to purchase major equipment for an institution for dry eye research.

Fredric Rosemore Educational Grants applicant must be a member of the American Academy of Optometry as a student, candidate or fellow at the time of acceptance of this award. Grant may be used to provide care, to support personnel, to provide equipment, or to fill any other need in the field of low vision as identified by the institution and consistent with the AAOF mission.

FINANCIAL DATA:
Amount of support per award: Allergan Grant: $60,000; Award of Excellence: $500; Korb-Exford Development Grant: $25,000; Rosemore Educational Grants: $1,000.

NO. AWARDS: Allergan Grant, Korb-Exford Development Grant and Rosemore Educational Grants: 1; Award for Excellence: 23 for the year 2018.

APPLICATION INFO:
Allergan Foundation Research Grant proposal must contain the following components:
(1) a cover page, including project title, institution and address, name and titles for principal investigator and a maximum of three co-investigators with contact information;
(2) an introduction including background and significance, specific aims, preliminary studies, and study design and methods (no more than five pages);
(3) references (maximum one page);
(4) budget and budget justification;
(5) biographical sketch of principal investigator and up to three co-investigators (maximum two pages for each investigator) and;
(6) a signed Letter of Assurance by the Dean or President indicating that the proposal has been reviewed and meets with the standards of the institution and, if warranted, observes all rules and regulations regarding compliance with research on human or animal subjects.

Award of Excellence: Institutions will be contacted directly via e-mail as to the opening of the submission window. The appropriate grant selection committee at each school or college of optometry will select the one student who best demonstrates the qualities outlined for this award.

The Korb-Exford Dry Eye Career Development Grant application must begin with a cover letter consisting of full contact information including how the applicant's degree should appear in reports and/or news items. The applicant must submit a two-page description of how the "Dry Eye Grant" will be used, the exceptional opportunity that it will provide, and the impact it will have on the applicant's career. Curriculum vitae of no more than three pages should accompany the application.

Fredric Rosemore Low Vision Educational Grants application should include:
(1) a curriculum vitae with applicant's education, clinical, research and employment experience;
(2) a proposal and budget and;
(3) a letter of endorsement by the Dean, President or Director of the school or college (optional).

Duration: One year.

Deadline: Allergan Grant: July 15. Award of Excellence: April 1. Korb-Exford Development Grant: July 1. Rosemore Educational Grants: June 1.

ADDRESS INQUIRIES TO:
Jennifer Rubin, Foundation Program Manager
(See e-mail address above.)

AMERICAN ACADEMY OF OPTOMETRY FOUNDATION [2301]

2909 Fairgreen Street
Orlando, FL 32803
(321) 319-4870
Fax: (407) 893-9890
E-mail: aaof@aaoptom.org
Web Site: www.aaopt.org/home/aaof/programs

FOUNDED: 1947

AREAS OF INTEREST:
Vision science and vision care.

NAME(S) OF PROGRAMS:
- **Beta Sigma Kappa Research Fellowships**
- **William C. Ezell Fellowship**
- **David and Diane Goss Optometry History Fellowship**

TYPE:
Fellowships. The Beta Sigma Kappa Research Fellowships support new optometric and vision science faculty research and optometric resident research. The funding is designed to benefit individuals early in their careers whose academic curiosity leads them to seek answers to a vast variety of professionally-based questions covering a wide area of vision science, clinical practice or eye-related public health.

William C. Ezell Fellowship aims to encourage talented persons to pursue full-time careers in optometric research and education in a school or college of optometry. These fellowships provide support to graduate students enrolled in a full-time program of study and training in vision-related research that leads to a Master's or Ph.D. degree.

The David and Diane Goss Optometry History Fellowship, awarded biennially, provides support to an individual pursuing research in optometric history. Researcher or student may use the funds to visit a library, archives or museum to conduct research.

PURPOSE:
To advance optometric education.

LEGAL BASIS:
Tax-exempt corporation.

ELIGIBILITY:
Applicant must be a member of the American Academy of Optometry.

Beta Sigma Kappa Research Fellowships: All optometric-related faculty, including adjunct faculty, within three years of faculty appointment, optometric residents, and Advanced Practice Fellows at any school or college of optometry, irrespective of membership in BSK, are eligible to apply.

William C. Ezell Fellowship focuses on specialized areas of research, such as glaucoma, cornea and contact lenses, and binocular vision and pediatrics. Preference will be given to first-time awardees. Previous Ezell fellows are eligible to apply, although the maximum number of years an individual can be awarded this fellowship is two years. Applicant must be a graduate student enrolled in a full-time program of study and training in vision-related research that leads to a Master's or Ph.D. degree. Completion of the degree program cannot be within the calendar years of the award competition.

David and Diane Goss Optometry History Fellowship applicants may be optometrists or optometry students, but may also be individuals outside the field of optometry, such as a historian or librarian, and may be at any career stage from student to retirement.

GEOG. RESTRICTIONS: Primarily United States and Canada.

FINANCIAL DATA:
Amount of support per award: Beta Sigma Kappa Research Fellowships: $4,000; Ezell Fellowship: $8,000; Goss Fellowship: $1,000.

NO. MOST RECENT APPLICANTS: Ezell Fellowship: Approximately 40.

NO. AWARDS: Beta Sigma Kappa Research Fellowships: 1; Ezell Fellowship: 9 to 11; Goss Fellowship: 1 biennially.

APPLICATION INFO:
Beta Sigma Kappa Research Fellowships: Applications should consist of six pages or less and contain the following:
(1) a cover page with project title, institution and address, name (including degrees) and title for faculty member with contact information;
(2) research plan;
(3) budget explanation;
(4) Helsinki Declaration (required only if human subjects are involved) and;
(5) letter of endorsement by Faculty Advisor, Dean or President/Director of the school or college that also indicates the proposal was reviewed and meets with the standards of the institution.

William C. Ezell Fellowship: Applicant must upload the "non-fellowship" NIH formatted bio sketch, their published works bibliography submitted as a URL link, and three letters of recommendation from persons qualified to comment on the applicant's educational qualifications, research abilities and potential, and future teaching capabilities and potential.

David and Diane Goss Optometry History Fellowship applicants must include the following:
(1) a cover letter consisting of full contact information including how the applicant's degree should appear in reports and/or news items;
(2) a two-page description of how the fellowship will be used, the opportunity that it will provide and the impact it will have on the applicant's career and;
(3) a curriculum vitae (no more than three pages).

Duration: Beta Sigma Kappa Research Fellowships: Up to one year; Ezell Fellowship: One year.

Deadline: Beta Sigma Kappa Research Fellowships and Goss Fellowship: August 1. Ezell Fellowship: February 1.

ADDRESS INQUIRIES TO:
Jennifer Rubin, Foundation Program Manager (See e-mail address above.)

*SPECIAL STIPULATIONS:
One year after the award is made, the Goss Fellowship recipient must submit a progress report suitable for publication in *Hindsight*, the Optometric Historical Society's quarterly publication.

AMERICAN DIABETES ASSOCIATION
2451 Crystal Drive
Suite 900
Arlington, VA 22202
(703) 549-1500 ext. 5532
Fax: (703) 621-3759
E-mail: grantquestions@diabetes.org
Web Site: www.professional.diabetes.org/grants

TYPE:
Fellowships; Research grants; Training grants.

See entry 2192 for full listing.

AMERICAN OTOLOGICAL SOCIETY RESEARCH FOUNDATION [2302]
Administrative Office
5830 1st Street North
St. Petersburg, FL 33703
(217) 638-0801
Fax: (727) 800-9428
E-mail: administrator@
americanotologicalsociety.org
Web Site: www.americanotologicalsociety.org

FOUNDED: 1868

AREAS OF INTEREST:
Research related to any aspects of the ear, hearing and balance disorders.

NAME(S) OF PROGRAMS:
• **Clinical Investigations Grant**
• **Clinician-Scientist Award**
• **Fellowship Grant**
• **Research Grant**

TYPE:
Fellowships; Research grants. Clinical Investigations Grant: Intended to encourage and support academic research in sciences related to the ear.

Clinician-Scientist Award: For salary and research support of a new academic clinician-scientist, at the Assistant Professor level, in order to facilitate development into an independent otologic investigator. Department chair guarantees at least 50% time commitment in research.

Fellowship Grant: For clinical fellows, residents, medical students postdoctoral fellows and graduate students, to support full-time research conducted outside of residency training.

Research Grant: Research on any topic related to ear disorders.

YEAR PROGRAM STARTED: 1926

PURPOSE:
To encourage and support academic research in sciences related to the ear.

LEGAL BASIS:
Private foundation.

ELIGIBILITY:
Clinical Investigations Grant: Grant awards may involve research on any topic related to ear disorders. The research need not be directly on an otological disease but may explore normal functions of the cochlea, labyrinth or central auditory or vestibular systems. However, the applicant must describe how the proposed research will benefit the understanding, diagnosis or treatment of otological disorders. The Research Foundation Advisory Board will review applications that propose, as a central focus, a clinical trial or other "hands-on"

patient clinical investigative study. Applicants should follow general guidelines for research proposals and also include information about the clinical study design and ethical requirements regarding human research subject participation. Grants are available to physician or doctoral-level investigators in the U.S. and Canada only.

For the Clinician-Scientist Award, the applicant must:
(1) hold or be approved for a full-time university faculty appointment at the rank of Assistant Professor in a department or division of Otolaryngology - Head and Neck Surgery;
(2) be citizens of the U.S., or have been lawfully admitted for permanent U.S. residency at the time of application;
(3) hold a Doctor of Medicine (M.D.) or equivalent degree from an accredited institution awarded within the last 10 years;
(4) have completed an ACGME-approved otolaryngology residency program and;
(5) have demonstrated the capacity or potential for a highly productive, independent research career with an emphasis in otology/neurotology.
Preference will be given to candidates who are currently enrolled in or have completed (within the preceding three years) a two-year otology/neurotology fellowship program.

Fellowship Grant: Research must be conducted in U.S. or Canadian institutions. Applicants must be medical students, residents or fellows (not nonmedical postgraduate researchers). Recipients must be relieved of all clinical duties during the fellowship period.

Research Grants are available to physician or doctoral-level investigators in the U.S. and Canada only.

FINANCIAL DATA:
Amount of support per award: Clinical Investigations Grant: Up to $66,000 per year, including indirect costs (overhead); indirect costs not to exceed 10% of direct costs; Clinician-Scientist Award: Up to $80,000 for salary and research support; Fellowship Grant: $44,000 stipend including $5,000 for supplies and $4,000 indirect costs; Research Grant: $55,000 maximum per year, including indirect costs.

Total amount of support: $350,000.

NO. MOST RECENT APPLICANTS: Approximately 35 applicants and 20 invitations.

NO. AWARDS: 6 to 8.

APPLICATION INFO:
Clinical Investigations Grant uses a simplied version of the NIDCD Early Career Research Award (R21) application. The Clinician-Scientist Award uses a simplified version of the NIDCD Early Career Research Award (K08/K23) application. The Fellowship Grant uses a simplfied version of the NIH NRSA Individual Postdoctoral Fellowship (F32) application. The Research Grant uses a simplified version of the NIDCD Early Career Research Award (R21) application.

For all awards, there are no forms to fill out. All applications must be formatted using 11-point Arial font, with page margins set to be 0.5 inches circumferentially. The Principal Investigator's name must appear on each page. The completed application should be submitted in PDF format. Applications must meet the formatting rules to be considered.

Duration: Clinical Investigations Grant: One year. Clinician-Scientist Award: Up to three years. Renewable annually. Fellowship Grant and Research Grant: One year. Non-renewable.

Deadline: Letter of Intent: November 1. Invited applications: January 31.

STAFF:
John S. Oghalai, M.D., Executive Secretary

ADDRESS INQUIRIES TO:
Kristen Bordignon, Executive Administrator
American Otological Society
Research Foundation
(See e-mail address above.)

AMERICAN SPEECH-LANGUAGE-HEARING FOUNDATION   [2303]

2200 Research Boulevard
Rockville, MD 20850-3289
(301) 296-8703
Fax: (301) 296-8567
E-mail: foundationprograms@asha.org
Web Site: www.ashfoundation.org

FOUNDED: 1946

AREAS OF INTEREST:
Communication sciences and disorders.

NAME(S) OF PROGRAMS:
- **Clinical Research Grant**
- **Louis M. DiCarlo Award for Recent Clinical Achievement**
- **Graduate Student Scholarship for International/Minority Students**
- **Graduate Student Scholarship for Minority Students**
- **Graduate Student Scholarship for NSSLHA Members**
- **Graduate Student Scholarship for Students with a Disability**
- **Graduate Student Scholarships**
- **Frank R. Kleffner Clinical Career Award**
- **New Century Scholars Doctoral Scholarship**
- **New Century Scholars Research Grant**
- **New Investigators Research Grant**
- **Speech Science Research Grant**
- **Student Research Grant in Audiology**
- **Student Research Grant in Early Childhood Language**
- **Rolland J. Van Hattum Award for Contribution in the Schools**

TYPE:
Research grants; Scholarships. Clinical achievement awards. Clinical Research Grants are awarded to researchers to advance knowledge of the efficacy of treatment and assessment practices in communication sciences and disorders.

Louis M. DiCarlo Award for Clinical Achievement recognizes individuals demonstrating outstanding achievement in the advancement of knowledge in clinical practice within the past three years.

Graduate Student Scholarships are available to students demonstrating outstanding academic achievement in communication sciences and disorders. These include general scholarships, scholarships for students with disabilities, scholarships for international and minority students, and scholarships for NSSLHA members.

Frank R. Kleffner Clinical Career Award recognizes outstanding lifetime achievement in clinical science and practice.

New Century Scholars Doctoral Scholarships are available to students enrolled in a research doctoral program (Ph.D. or equivalent) in communication sciences and disorders.

New Century Scholars Research Grants are awarded to individuals committed to teacher-investigator careers in the university or college environment or in external research institutes or laboratories.

New Investigators Research Grants are awarded to new scientists to pursue research in audiology or speech-language pathology.

Speech Science Research Grants are awarded to new investigators to encourage research activities in the area of speech science.

Student Research Grant in Audiology supports a proposed one-year study to conduct research in audiology.

Student Research Grant in Early Childhood Language supports a proposed one-year study to conduct research in early childhood language development.

Rolland J. Van Hattum Award for Contribution in the Schools recognizes professionals demonstrating significant contribution to the delivery of audiology and/or speech pathology services in the schools.

YEAR PROGRAM STARTED: 1979

PURPOSE:
To further education in speech, language and hearing through the provision of financial assistance; to recognize and support research and similar endeavors which contribute to the advancement of knowledge and improvement of practice in serving children and adults with speech, language, or hearing disorders; to identify and facilitate new directions in the field of communication sciences and disorders through support of such vehicles as conferences, publications and other activities.

LEGAL BASIS:
501(c)(3) association.

FINANCIAL DATA:
Amount of support per award: Research Grants: $2,000 to $75,000, depending on grant type; Scholarships: $5,000 to $10,000.
Total amount of support: Varies.

NO. MOST RECENT APPLICANTS: Approximately 300 for all programs.

NO. AWARDS: 82.

APPLICATION INFO:
Guidelines are available from the ASH Foundation web site. Required documentation for scholarships includes application form, academic documentation, faculty recommendation committee report, and student essay. Research grant submissions require a research proposal.
Duration: One year. Nonrenewable.
Deadline: Usually April or May. Awards presented in November.

PUBLICATIONS:
Annual report; program and application guidelines; fact sheet.

IRS I.D.: 52-6055761

BOARD OF TRUSTEES:
Allan O. Diefendorf, President

ADDRESS INQUIRIES TO:
Program Administrator
(See address above.)

BENIGN ESSENTIAL BLEPHAROSPASM RESEARCH FOUNDATION INC.   [2304]

755 South 11th Street
Suite 211
Beaumont, TX 77701
(409) 832-0788
Fax: (409) 832-0890
E-mail: bebrf@blepharospasm.org
Web Site: www.blepharospasm.org

FOUNDED: 1981

AREAS OF INTEREST:
Benign essential blepharospasm, Meige syndrome, hemifacial spasm and related disorders and infirmities of the facial musculature.

TYPE:
Project/program grants; Research grants; Seed money grants.

YEAR PROGRAM STARTED: 1985

PURPOSE:
To undertake, promote, develop and carry on the search for the cause and cure for benign essential blepharospasm and other related disorders and infirmities of the facial musculature.

LEGAL BASIS:
Foundation.

ELIGIBILITY:
Research proposals must relate specifically to benign essential blepharospasm and Meige to include new treatments, pathophysiology and genetics, photophobia and dry eye.

FINANCIAL DATA:
Amount of support per award: $10,000 to $100,000.

Total amount of support: $100,000 for the year 2018.

NO. MOST RECENT APPLICANTS: 9 for the year 2018.

NO. AWARDS: 1 for the year 2018.

APPLICATION INFO:
Application information is available on the web site or by sending an e-mail to the address above.
Duration: One to two years. Extensions have been granted.
Deadline: August 31.

PUBLICATIONS:
Program announcement; application guidelines; brochure.

IRS I.D.: 74-2193322

BOARD OF DIRECTORS:
Nilda Rendino, President
Linda Peterson, First Vice President
Peter Bakalor, Treasurer
Charlene Hudgins, Executive Director and Secretary
Barbara Benton
Jane Boyd
Tishana Cundiff
Deborah H. Drago
Jonathan Healy, Esq.
Dee Linde

ADDRESS INQUIRIES TO:
Charlene Hudgins, Executive Director
E-mail: charlene@blepharospasm.org

BRIGHT FOCUS FOUNDATION
22512 Gateway Center Drive
Clarksburg, MD 20871
(301) 948-3244
(800) 437-2423
Fax: (301) 948-4403
E-mail: researchgrants@brightfocus.org
Web Site: www.brightfocus.org

TYPE:
Research grants.

See entry 1298 for full listing.

BRIGHT FOCUS FOUNDATION [2305]
22512 Gateway Center Drive
Clarksburg, MD 20871
(301) 948-3244
(800) 437-2423
Fax: (301) 948-4403
E-mail: researchgrants@brightfocus.org
Web Site: www.brightfocus.org

FOUNDED: 1978

AREAS OF INTEREST:
Glaucoma research.

NAME(S) OF PROGRAMS:
- **National Glaucoma Research Program**

TYPE:
Research grants. Support for basic research into the causes and potential treatments of glaucoma.

YEAR PROGRAM STARTED: 1978

PURPOSE:
To develop treatments, preventions and cures for glaucoma.

LEGAL BASIS:
Nonprofit foundation.

ELIGIBILITY:
Grants are awarded on the basis of the proposal's scientific merit and its relevance to understanding the disease studied. No funds for large equipment, institutional overhead costs, construction or building expenses.

FINANCIAL DATA:
Amount of support per award: Up to $100,000 per year.
Total amount of support: Varies.

NO. AWARDS: 13 for the year 2019.

APPLICATION INFO:
Applications are submitted through ProposalCentral.
Duration: Up to two years.

PUBLICATIONS:
Annual report; newsletters; clinical brochures.

ADDRESS INQUIRIES TO:
Kara Summers, Program Officer
(See e-mail address above.)

CANADIAN NATIONAL INSTITUTE FOR THE BLIND [2306]
1929 Bayview Avenue
Toronto ON M4G 3E8 Canada
(416) 486-2500
Fax: (416) 480-7700
E-mail: info@cnib.ca
Web Site: www.cnib.ca

FOUNDED: 1918

AREAS OF INTEREST:
Ophthalmic subspecialties, vision research and macular degeneration.

NAME(S) OF PROGRAMS:
- **CNIB Barbara Tuck MacPhee Award in Macular Degeneration**

TYPE:
Research grants. Award supports researchers in the field of macular degeneration.

YEAR PROGRAM STARTED: 1961

PURPOSE:
To conduct research focused on better serving and improving the quality of life for people with vision loss; to fund cutting-edge medical research aimed at improving our understanding of how to prevent, diagnose and treat eye disease.

LEGAL BASIS:
Registered charity.

ELIGIBILITY:
Applicants must be residents of Canada and research must be conducted primarily in Canada.

FINANCIAL DATA:
Amount of support per award: Up to $25,000.
Total amount of support: Varies.

NO. AWARDS: 1 per year.

APPLICATION INFO:
Applications must be submitted online.
Duration: One year.
Deadline: January 15. Decision by March 31.

PUBLICATIONS:
Guidelines.

ADDRESS INQUIRIES TO:
Grants Administrator
(See address above.)

EYE BANK ASSOCIATION OF AMERICA [2307]
1101 17th Street, N.W.
Suite 400
Washington, DC 20036
(202) 775-4999
Fax: (202) 429-6036
E-mail: info@restoresight.org
Web Site: www.restoresight.org

FOUNDED: 1961

AREAS OF INTEREST:
Restoration of sight through eye banks.

NAME(S) OF PROGRAMS:
- **Richard Lindstrom Research Grant**
- **Networking Grants**

TYPE:
Research grants; Travel grants.

PURPOSE:
To promote scientific research in the fields of eye banking and corneal transplantation; to promote collaboration between eye banks.

ELIGIBILITY:
Lindstrom Grant applicant must be a physician, including corneal surgeon and other eye care specialist, basic scientist, including biomedical and social scientists, or eye-bank technician, nurse, fellow, ophthalmology fellow or medical student that is supervised by a physician.

FINANCIAL DATA:
Amount of support per award: Lindstrom Grant: Maximum $7,500; Networking Grants: $1,500.
Total amount of support: Varies.

NO. AWARDS: Lindstrom Grant: 7 for the year 2019; Networking Grants: 2 annually.

APPLICATION INFO:
Application information is available on the EBAA web site.
Duration: Lindstrom Grant: One year.
Deadline: Lindstrom Grant: March 25. Networking Grants: April 15.

ADDRESS INQUIRIES TO:
Stacey Gardner, Director of Education
(See address above.)

FIGHT FOR SIGHT, INC. [2308]
381 Park Avenue South
Suite 1119
New York, NY 10016
(212) 679-6060
Fax: (212) 679-4466
E-mail: arthur@fightforsight.org
janice@fightforsight.org
Web Site: www.fightforsight.org

FOUNDED: 1946

AREAS OF INTEREST:
Ophthalmology and visual sciences.

NAME(S) OF PROGRAMS:
- **Research Awards Program**

TYPE:
Fellowships; Grants-in-aid; Research grants. Fight for Sight primarily supports new investigators, promoting the development of scientific findings and pilot studies necessary to successfully apply for more substantial federal and private funding such as that provided by the National Eye Institute and other divisions of the NIH.

YEAR PROGRAM STARTED: 1946

PURPOSE:
To support and inspire eye and vision research by funding promising young scientists early in their careers.

LEGAL BASIS:
501(c)(3) corporation.

ELIGIBILITY:
Grants-in-Aid are available for academic researchers within the first three years of their academic appointments.

Summer Fellowships are open to undergraduate, graduate and medical students from the U.S. who are interested in pursuing eye-related clinical or basic research.

GEOG. RESTRICTIONS: United States and Canada.

FINANCIAL DATA:
Amount of support per award: Grants-in-Aid: Up to $22,500; Summer Fellowship: $2,500.
Total amount of support: Varies.

NO. MOST RECENT APPLICANTS: 90.

NO. AWARDS: 3 to 4.

APPLICATION INFO:
Application guidelines are available on the web site.
Duration: Grants-in-Aid: One year; Summer Fellowships: Eight to 12 weeks.
Deadline: Grants-in-Aid: November 15. Start date between July 1 and September 1. Summer Fellowship: February 15.

PUBLICATIONS:
Brochure.

ADDRESS INQUIRIES TO:
Arthur Makar, Executive Director
(See address above.)

FIGHT FOR SIGHT, INC.   [2309]

381 Park Avenue South
Suite 1119
New York, NY 10016
(212) 679-6060
Fax: (212) 679-4466
E-mail: arthur@fightforsight.org
janice@fightforsight.org
Web Site: www.fightforsight.org

FOUNDED: 1946

AREAS OF INTEREST:
Ophthalmology and visual sciences.

NAME(S) OF PROGRAMS:
● **Fight for Sight Postdoctoral Fellowship**

TYPE:
Fellowships. Stipend to support individuals
with a Doctorate who are interested in
academic careers involving basic or clinical
research in ophthalmology or visual sciences.

YEAR PROGRAM STARTED: 1953

PURPOSE:
To assist research and treatment aimed at
eliminating blinding eye diseases and sight
impairment.

LEGAL BASIS:
501(c)(3) corporation.

ELIGIBILITY:
Physicians or scientists holding a Doctorate
and who are interested in academic careers
involving fundamental or clinical research in
ophthalmology or its related sciences are
eligible to apply. If at the time of filing the
applicant does not as yet have a Doctorate, it
is required that a cover letter be submitted
together with the application advising that the
Doctorate will be conferred by the designated
commencement date.

GEOG. RESTRICTIONS: United States and
Canada.

FINANCIAL DATA:
Funds are to be used to defray costs of
equipment, consumable supplies and
personnel (excluding applicant).
Amount of support per award: Stipend up to
$22,500.

NO. MOST RECENT APPLICANTS: 130.

NO. AWARDS: Approximately 15.

APPLICATION INFO:
Applications are available online. Completed
applications should include:
(1) application face pages and related
information completed online and including
information about the applicant, his or her
education and training, institution and
sponsor;
(2) a research proposal of no more than eight
single-spaced pages, not including references;
(3) a letter of support from a sponsor or
departmental chair. The letter should include
an evaluation of the student, the role of the
mentor in advising the applicant during the
project, the training plan, any extracurricular
training the student will receive and other
information helpful to the committee in
evaluating the mentor, the laboratory and the
institutional resources in support of a FFS
Postdoctoral Award. They should specifically
address the suitability of the applicant's
training, his or her academic achievements
and, most importantly, his or her potential to
develop into an independent eye and vision
researcher and/or leader in academic
ophthalmology;
(4) curriculum vitae and NIH-style biosketch
of the applicant and sponsor;

(5) supplemental information, including
relevant awards, previous research experience
and academic or career goals and;
(6) a cover letter.
Duration: One year.
Deadline: November 15. Start date is
between July 1 and September 1.

PUBLICATIONS:
Brochure.

IRS I.D.: 23-7085732

ADDRESS INQUIRIES TO:
Janice Benson, Associate Director
(See address above.)

*SPECIAL STIPULATIONS:
Research work to be performed in the U.S.
or Canada.

THE GLAUCOMA FOUNDATION   [2310]

80 Maiden Lane, Suite 700
New York, NY 10038-4778
(212) 285-0080
Fax: (212) 651-1888
E-mail: info@glaucomafoundation.org
Web Site: www.glaucomafoundation.org

FOUNDED: 1984

AREAS OF INTEREST:
Glaucoma.

TYPE:
Research grants.

PURPOSE:
To fund research to determine the causes of
glaucoma; to improve methods of treatment,
and ultimately to develop cures for the
various kinds of glaucoma.

ELIGIBILITY:
Applicants must have a full-time faculty
position or the equivalent. Applicant must
also demonstrate the Principal Investigator's
understanding of glaucoma or his or her
collaboration with an investigator who has
experience in glaucoma research. If
collaboration is warranted, a letter of support
from the glaucoma researcher must be
included in the application.

FINANCIAL DATA:
Amount of support per award: Up to
$60,000.
Total amount of support: Varies.

NO. MOST RECENT APPLICANTS: 20.

APPLICATION INFO:
Grant application and instructions are posted
on the Foundation web site.
Duration: One year. Renewable.
Deadline: Varies.

GLAUCOMA RESEARCH FOUNDATION   [2311]

251 Post Street, Suite 600
San Francisco, CA 94108
(415) 986-3162
Fax: (415) 986-3763
E-mail: research@glaucoma.org
Web Site: www.glaucoma.org

FOUNDED: 1978

AREAS OF INTEREST:
Research and education pertaining to
glaucoma.

NAME(S) OF PROGRAMS:
● **Shaffer Fund for Innovative Glaucoma
Research**

TYPE:
Research grants.

PURPOSE:
To cure glaucoma and restore vision through
innovative research.

ELIGIBILITY:
Applicants must hold a graduate degree.

FINANCIAL DATA:
Amount of support per award: $50,000.
Total amount of support: Typically $400,000.

NO. MOST RECENT APPLICANTS: 50.

NO. AWARDS: 8.

APPLICATION INFO:
Preliminary proposals are accepted annually
between June 1 and July 15, when a link to
the online application will be available on the
GRF web site. A link to the full online grant
application will be e-mailed to those whose
preliminary proposals meet the required
criteria.

Applications received by mail will not be
reviewed or returned.
Duration: One year.
Deadline: Preliminary proposals: June 1 to
July 15. Full grant application: September 1
to September 30.

IRS I.D.: 94-2495035

ADDRESS INQUIRIES TO:
Catalina San Agustin, Director of Operations
(See e-mail address above.)

HEARING HEALTH FOUNDATION   [2312]

575 Eighth Avenue
Suite 1201
New York, NY 10018
(212) 257-6140
Fax: (212) 257-6139
E-mail: info@hhf.org
grants@hhf.org
Web Site: hearinghealthfoundation.org

FOUNDED: 1958

AREAS OF INTEREST:
Research concerning the causes, treatment
and prevention of hearing loss and related ear
and balance disorders.

NAME(S) OF PROGRAMS:
● **Emerging Research Grants (ERG)**
● **Hearing Restoration Project (HRP)**

TYPE:
Research grants. Limited in amount and term,
Emerging Research Grants are awarded as
seed funding in support of projects directed
by early career and senior investigators or for
promising new studies in areas of
demonstrable basic science or clinical
importance.

Specifically, applications will be considered
for research directed to any aspect of the ear;
that is, investigation of the function,
physiology, biochemistry, genetics, anatomy
or pathology. Basic and applied research is
welcome.

Through the Hearing Restoration Project
(HRP), the Foundation is striving toward a
cure for hearing loss and tinnitus, a promise
that is very real. Underlying that promise is
the discovery that chickens have the ability to
spontaneously restore their hearing and the
HRP is aiming to enable just that in humans.

YEAR PROGRAM STARTED: 1958

PURPOSE:
To prevent and cure hearing loss through groundbreaking research.

LEGAL BASIS:
Nonprofit public voluntary organization.

ELIGIBILITY:
ERG Program: Applications are accepted from all U.S. institutions, including universities, hospitals and nonprofit tax-exempt institutions, public or private.

The HHF's Scientific Review Committee will consider the subject of the research, the quality of its design, its potential for significant advance in basic knowledge or clinical application, the available facilities and personnel at the institution in which the research will be carried out and the qualifications of the investigators.

In accepting a research grant, the institution and the principal investigator are responsible for using grant funds only for those purposes set forth in the application and approved in the HHF award letter.

GEOG. RESTRICTIONS: United States.

FINANCIAL DATA:
Grant funds may be budgeted and used for direct costs of carrying out approved projects, including equipment purchases and supplies. Grant funds may not be used for the salary of principal investigator, travel, living expenses, printing costs, overhead costs exceeding 10% of project costs or public information/education programs.

Amount of support per award: Grant amount is determined at the discretion of the Foundation. Regardless of the indirect amount, the HHF award will not exceed $50,000.

Total amount of support: Varies.

NO. MOST RECENT APPLICANTS: 47 for the year 2020.

NO. AWARDS: ERG: 15 for the year 2019.

APPLICATION INFO:
New project applications and renewal applications must be submitted using the current forms available on the web site.

Duration: One calendar year, October 1 to September 30. Grants are eligible for renewal for an additional year.

Deadline: ERG: Mid-February. Principal investigators are notified in late spring.

PUBLICATIONS:
Hearing Health Magazine.

IRS I.D.: 13-1882107

STAFF:
Timothy L. Higdon, Chief Executive Officer

ADDRESS INQUIRIES TO:
Christopher Geissler, Ph.D.
Director of Program and Research Support
(See address above.)

HEED OPHTHALMIC FOUNDATION [2313]
655 Beach Street
San Francisco, CA 94109
(415) 447-0249
Fax: (415) 561-8531
E-mail: heed@aao.org
Web Site: www.heed.org

AREAS OF INTEREST:
Diseases and surgery of the eye or research in opthalmology.

NAME(S) OF PROGRAMS:
● **Heed Fellowship**

TYPE:
Fellowships.

YEAR PROGRAM STARTED: 1947

PURPOSE:
To provide assistance to ophthalmology residents and fellows who desire to further their education or to conduct research in ophthalmology.

ELIGIBILITY:
Graduates who are U.S. citizens from accredited medical schools, schools of osteopathic medicine, or hold an ECEMG certificate are eligible.

FINANCIAL DATA:
Amount of support per award: $10,000.
Total amount of support: $240,000 for the year 2019-20.

NO. MOST RECENT APPLICANTS: 101.

NO. AWARDS: 24 for the year 2019-20.

APPLICATION INFO:
Applicants are required to submit:
(1) a one-page statement setting forth the applicant's major ophthalmic interest, professional aims and objectives, and noting qualifications deserving of particular consideration;
(2) a letter of recommendation from the Chair of Ophthalmology who supervised residency training;
(3) a letter from the preceptor of the applicant's fellowship program describing the program, including a statement that a minimum of 20% of the fellowship will be spent in research;
(4) two additional letters of recommendation from physicians who have supervised the applicant;
(5) a letter of acceptance of the applicant at the institution where the fellowship is to be taken (this may be a copy of the applicant's match letter) and;
(6) a letter of recommendation from the Chairman of the department who has offered an academic appointment (optional).

Do not send curriculum vitae.

Duration: One year. Nonrenewable.
Deadline: March 1.

ADDRESS INQUIRIES TO:
Lisa Brown
Heed Administrator
(See e-mail address above.)

THE MARFAN FOUNDATION [2314]
22 Manhasset Avenue
Port Washington, NY 11050
(516) 883-8712 ext. 117
Fax: (516) 883-8040
E-mail: research@marfan.org
Web Site: www.marfan.org

FOUNDED: 1981

AREAS OF INTEREST:
Research relating to Marfan syndrome and related disorders.

NAME(S) OF PROGRAMS:
● **Clinical Research Program**
● **Early Investigator Grant Program**
● **Faculty Grant Program**
● **Victor A. McKusick Fellowship Program**

TYPE:
Fellowships; Research grants. Basic, translational and clinical research related to the Marfan syndrome and related connective tissue conditions. Specific areas of specialty include genetics, cardiology, ophthalmology and orthopedic issues of the Marfan syndrome.

YEAR PROGRAM STARTED: 1986

PURPOSE:
To provide financial support for investigators, scientists and physicians studying any or all disciplines involved in Marfan syndrome research.

ELIGIBILITY:
The principal investigator must hold an M.D., D.O., Ph.D., Sc.D., D.D.S., D.V.M. or equivalent degree. The investigator must have proven ability to pursue independent research publications in peer-reviewed journals.

FINANCIAL DATA:
Amount of support per award: Clinical Research $25,000 to $50,000 per year; Early Investigator: $37,500; Faculty: $50,000; Fellowship: $50,000 to $75,000.
Total amount of support: Varies.

NO. MOST RECENT APPLICANTS: 25 for the year 2019.

NO. AWARDS: 3 Faculty, 2 Clinical Investigator and 2 Fellowship Awards for the year 2018.

APPLICATION INFO:
Application information is available on the web site.
Duration: Up to two years.
Deadline: Early Investigator and Fellowship: February; Clinical and Faculty: April.

ADDRESS INQUIRIES TO:
Josephine Grima, Ph.D.
Chief Science Officer
(See address above.)

NATIONAL EYE INSTITUTE [2315]
National Institutes of Health
6700B Rockledge Drive, Suite 3400
Bethesda, MD 20817
(301) 451-2020
Fax: (301) 402-0528
E-mail: esl@nei.nih.gov
Web Site: www.nei.nih.gov

AREAS OF INTEREST:
Vision research, cooperative clinical trials for evaluation, diagnosis and therapy of ocular diseases, and epidemiologic and risk factor studies of ocular diseases.

NAME(S) OF PROGRAMS:
● **Center Core Grants**

TYPE:
Research grants.

PURPOSE:
To support centralized resources and facilities shared by investigators with existing NEI-funded research projects; to enrich the effectiveness of ongoing research; to promote new research directions.

FINANCIAL DATA:
Amount of support per award: Applicants may request up to $400,000 for less than 20 R01s or up to $500,000 for 20 or more R01s per year in direct costs.
Total amount of support: Varies depending on the indirect costs at the institution.

Matching fund requirements: Cost sharing is not required to be eligible for this program. However, it is strongly encouraged for applicant organizations to make appropriate and needed commitments to the Center in order to maximize the effectiveness and utility of the shared resources.

NO. AWARDS: Approximately 40.

APPLICATION INFO:
Contact NEI for details.
Duration: Maximum project period of five years.
Deadline: September 18.

ADDRESS INQUIRIES TO:
Ellen S. Liberman, Ph.D.
(See address above.)

NATIONAL EYE INSTITUTE   [2316]
National Institutes of Health
6700B Rockledge Drive, MSC 6914
Bethesda, MD 20817
(301) 451-2020
E-mail: wujekjer@nei.nih.gov
Web Site: www.nei.nih.gov

FOUNDED: 1968

AREAS OF INTEREST:
Vision research, cooperative clinical trials for evaluation, diagnosis and therapy of ocular diseases, and epidemiologic and risk factor studies of ocular diseases.

NAME(S) OF PROGRAMS:
- **Cooperative Clinical Research Grants**
- **Small Business Innovation Research Awards**

TYPE:
Conferences/seminars; Fellowships; Research grants; Training grants. Research Project Grants support individual investigators whose work is aimed at discovering means of improving the prevention, diagnosis and treatment of blinding and disabling eye and vision disorders.

Small Business Innovation Research Awards aim to stimulate technological innovations, to use small business to meet federal research-development needs that may ultimately lead to commercial products or services and to foster and encourage participation by minority and disadvantaged persons in technological innovations.

Areas of study include vision research, retinal diseases, corneal diseases, cataract, glaucoma, low vision and blindness rehabilitation, visual impairment and its rehabilitation, strabismus, amblyopia and visual processing.

YEAR PROGRAM STARTED: 1968

PURPOSE:
To gain new knowledge about normal and abnormal functioning of the eye and visual system; to support research aimed at improving the prevention, diagnosis and treatment of eye disease and disorders of vision. These are essential for progress against the major causes of blindness and visual disability.

ELIGIBILITY:
Research grants are available to any public or private university, college, hospital, laboratory, or other institution, including state and local units of government and federal institutions; eligibility is no longer restricted to nonprofit organizations.

GEOG. RESTRICTIONS: Cooperative Clinical Research Grants: Primarily United States; Small Business Innovation Research Awards: United States.

FINANCIAL DATA:
Amount of support per award: Grants vary in amount, depending upon the needs and nature of the request and the limitations of the program.

APPLICATION INFO:
Those interested in applying are encouraged to contact the NEI staff prior to submitting applications.
Duration: Cooperative Clinical Research Grants: Up to five years; Small Business Innovation Research Award: Six months to two years.
Deadline: Varies according to award.

IRS I.D.: 52-0858115

STAFF:
Michael A. Steinmetz, Ph.D., Director

ADDRESS INQUIRIES TO:
Jerome Wujek, Ph.D.
Research Resources Officer
(See address above.)

Osteopathy

AMERICAN OSTEOPATHIC FOUNDATION   [2317]
142 East Ontario Street, Suite 1450
Chicago, IL 60611-2864
(312) 202-8235
Fax: (312) 202-8216
E-mail: info@aof.org
Web Site: www.aof.org

FOUNDED: 1949

AREAS OF INTEREST:
Osteopathic medical education, research and international humanitarian outreach.

TYPE:
Awards/prizes; Scholarships. Research, community service and international outreach grants.

PURPOSE:
To support programs and services that promote osteopathic medicine and enhance patient-centered care.

LEGAL BASIS:
Public charity.

ELIGIBILITY:
Specific requirements can be found on the Foundation web site.

FINANCIAL DATA:
Amount of support per award: $500 to $25,000.
Total amount of support: Varies.

NO. MOST RECENT APPLICANTS: More than 400.

NO. AWARDS: 130.

APPLICATION INFO:
Applications or nomination forms are available at various times throughout the year on the AOF web site.
Duration: Varies.
Deadline: Varies.

PUBLICATIONS:
Application; brochure.

IRS I.D.: 36-6056120

ADDRESS INQUIRIES TO:
Rita Forden, Chief Executive Offcer
(See address above.)

FOUNDATION FOR OSTEOPATHIC EMERGENCY MEDICINE   [2318]
142 East Ontario Street
Suite 1500
Chicago, IL 60611
(312) 445-5704
Fax: (312) 587-9951
E-mail: lroden@acoep.org
Web Site: www.foem.org

FOUNDED: 1998

AREAS OF INTEREST:
Osteopathic emergency medicine.

NAME(S) OF PROGRAMS:
- **Benjamin J. Field, D.O., FACOEP Medical Education Grant**
- **Investigator Research Grant**
- **David A. Kuchinski Memorial Research Grant**
- **Resident Research Grant**
- **Young Investigator Research Grant**

TYPE:
Awards/prizes; Research grants.

YEAR PROGRAM STARTED: 1998

PURPOSE:
To improve patient care through quality research and education in osteopathic emergency medicine.

LEGAL BASIS:
501(c)(3).

ELIGIBILITY:
Grants are made to individuals or organizations that have tax-exempt status under Section 501(c)(3) of the Internal Revenue Code.

GEOG. RESTRICTIONS: United States.

FINANCIAL DATA:
Amount of support per award: Investigator Grant and Young Investigator Grant: $1,000 to $3,000; Kuchinski Memorial Research Grant: Varies; Resident Research Grant: $500 to $2,000.
Total amount of support: Varies.

NO. AWARDS: 1 per award.

APPLICATION INFO:
Contact the Foundation for application procedures.
Duration: One-time grants.
Deadline: Postmarked by July 31. Reviewed in April, July and October.

PUBLICATIONS:
Research Beacon.

MAINE OSTEOPATHIC ASSOCIATION   [2319]
29 Association Drive
Manchester, ME 04351
(207) 623-1101
Fax: (207) 623-4228
E-mail: info@mainedo.org
Web Site: www.mainedo.org

FOUNDED: 1912

AREAS OF INTEREST:
Osteopathic medicine.

NAME(S) OF PROGRAMS:
- **Maine Osteopathic Association Scholarship**

TYPE:
Scholarships. The program is a tuition subsidy for eligible students who enroll in a qualifying medical school program.

LEGAL BASIS:
Nonprofit physician membership organization.

ELIGIBILITY:
Any Maine resident who will enroll in a participating accredited college of osteopathic medicine. School does not have to be located in Maine.

FINANCIAL DATA:
Amount of support per award: $1,000.
Total amount of support: Varies.

NO. AWARDS: Varies.

APPLICATION INFO:
Application is available online or by contacting the Association directly.
Duration: One year.
Deadline: June 30.

ADDRESS INQUIRIES TO:
Amanda Richards, Executive Director
(See address above.)

NEW JERSEY OSTEOPATHIC EDUCATION FOUNDATION [2320]

666 Plainsboro Road
Suite 356
Plainsboro, NJ 08536
(732) 940-9000 ext. 303
Fax: (732) 940-8899
E-mail: info@njosteo.com
Web Site: www.njosteo.com

FOUNDED: 1901

AREAS OF INTEREST:
Osteopathic education.

TYPE:
Scholarships. For students pursuing osteopathic medical education. A first-year scholarship will be awarded to New Jersey residents accepted to the fall class of any approved college of osteopathic medicine.

YEAR PROGRAM STARTED: 1965

PURPOSE:
To provide the means to promote education in the field of osteopathic medicine.

LEGAL BASIS:
Not-for-profit corporation.

ELIGIBILITY:
Applicants must be residents of New Jersey having completed four years of pre-medical education and entering their first year in an osteopathic college. Applicants must have a 3.0 grade point average on a 4.0 scale or be in the upper 25% of his or her class. Selections are based on class standing, financial need, high motivation and professional promise. Students accepting scholarships must agree to become members of the New Jersey Association of Osteopathic Physicians and Surgeons and the American Osteopathic Association.

GEOG. RESTRICTIONS: New Jersey.

FINANCIAL DATA:
The scholarship sum will be paid directly to the college to cover part of the first year's tuition.

Amount of support per award: $4,000 to $7,000.
Total amount of support: $27,000.

NO. MOST RECENT APPLICANTS: 20.

NO. AWARDS: 10.

APPLICATION INFO:
To apply for a scholarship, qualified students must:
(1) submit a completed NJOEF scholarship application;
(2) provide four named references, at least one of whom is an osteopathic physician;
(3) provide four completed reference evaluation forms;
(4) supply MCAT scores with confirmation code;
(5) supply pre-med college transcripts directly from the college;
(6) supply copy of medical school acceptance letter;
(7) compose an essay sharing his or her desire to become an osteopathic physician (why osteopathic medicine?) and;
(8) supply the prior year's tax return or that of the parent/guardian, if the student is claimed as a dependent.
Duration: One year.
Deadline: June 15.

IRS I.D.: 22-6088562

ADDRESS INQUIRIES TO:
Scholarship Program
(See address above.)

Pediatrics

ACADEMIC PEDIATRIC ASSOCIATION (APA) [2321]

6728 Old McLean Village Drive
McLean, VA 22101
(703) 556-9222
Fax: (703) 556-8729
E-mail: info@academicpeds.org
Web Site: www.academicpeds.org

FOUNDED: 1960

AREAS OF INTEREST:
General pediatrics and pediatric hospitalist medicine.

NAME(S) OF PROGRAMS:
- **APA Young Investigator Awards Program**

TYPE:
Research grants.

YEAR PROGRAM STARTED: 1994

PURPOSE:
To assist pediatric clinician-educators and clinician-researches in developing themselves as fulfilled faculty members engaged in important and exciting research and to increase the quality and breadth of child health research.

ELIGIBILITY:
The principal investigator of any proposal submitted must be a member of the APA or have submitted an application for membership. Preference will be given to new investigators, including those in training. Preference will be given to proposals that have the potential of leading to projects of a larger or longer-term nature.

FINANCIAL DATA:
Amount of support per award: Up to $10,000.
Total amount of support: $60,000.

NO. MOST RECENT APPLICANTS: 32 for the year 2020.

NO. AWARDS: 6 for the year 2020.

APPLICATION INFO:
Applicants must submit a two-page proposal. Only electronic submissions as an e-mail attachment are accepted. The proposals should contain a brief overview of the project including purpose, methods, evaluation and estimated budget. A curriculum vitae for the principal investigator must also be included with the proposal. Budget requests should not include overhead or salary for the principal investigator if they are full-time faculty. The review panel will identify those that warrant further elaboration. Re-submitted proposals can be no more than 10 pages in length including tables and appendices. They must contain background, hypothesis, description of key personnel, detailed budget with justification and methods.
Duration: One year. Award recipients can request up to a 12-month no-cost extension.
Deadline: Fall.

ADDRESS INQUIRIES TO:
See address and e-mail above.

*SPECIAL STIPULATIONS:
The applicant must be a member of the APA or have submitted an application for membership.

AMERICAN ACADEMY OF PEDIATRICS [2322]

345 Park Boulevard
Itasca, IL 60143
(847) 434-4000
(800) 433-9016 ext. 6134
Fax: (847) 434-8000
E-mail: kvandenbrook@aap.org
Web Site: www.aap.org/sopt

FOUNDED: 1930

AREAS OF INTEREST:
Pediatric training.

NAME(S) OF PROGRAMS:
- **American Academy of Pediatrics Hardship Scholarship Program**

TYPE:
Residencies; Scholarships. Stipend for the support of pediatric residents and fellowship trainees.

YEAR PROGRAM STARTED: 1982

PURPOSE:
To enable young physicians to complete their pediatric training.

LEGAL BASIS:
Nonprofit organization.

ELIGIBILITY:
Applicant must have completed, or will have completed by July 1, a qualifying approved internship (PL-0) and have a definite commitment for a first-year pediatric residency (PL-1) accredited by the Residency Review Committee for Pediatrics. In addition, applicant must be a pediatric resident or chief resident (categorical pediatrics or combined-training program) in a training program and have made a definite commitment for another year of residency (not fellowship) in a U.S. or Canadian

program accredited by the Residency Review Committee for Pediatrics, as well as have a substantial need for financial assistance.

GEOG. RESTRICTIONS: United States and Canada.

FINANCIAL DATA:
Amount of support per award: $1,000 to $5,000.
Total amount of support: Varies.

APPLICATION INFO:
Official application materials are available upon request in December. Applications must be supported by a form from the Department Head or the Chief of Service or the Residency Program Director addressing the financial need, commitment to pediatrics and performance in the program.
Duration: One year. Possible renewals.
Deadline: Last day in February.

ADDRESS INQUIRIES TO:
Kimberley VandenBrook
Member Engagement Specialist
(See address above.)

CEREBRAL PALSY FOUNDATION
3 Columbus Circle, 15th Floor
New York, NY 10019
(212) 520-1686
E-mail: rebecca.lam@yourcpf.org
info@yourcpf.org
Web Site: www.yourcpf.org

TYPE:
Research grants. Grants are awarded for pilot studies in areas which have a relationship to cerebral palsy. While most research in the central nervous system may be useful, the Foundation requires that research proposals define clear and direct relevance to cerebral palsy. Currently, high priority is assigned to prevention of prematurity, decrease of perinatal neurologic morbidity, prevention of central nervous system infections of the newborn and to medical, surgical and bioengineering methods that may improve the functioning of persons with cerebral palsy, addressing issues such as impaired mobility, impaired communication skills, swallowing, drooling and effects of aging on further diminution of function. However, any proposal designed to prevent cerebral palsy or to improve its treatment and management will be considered.

See entry 2248 for full listing.

CHILDREN'S LEUKEMIA RESEARCH ASSOCIATION [2323]
585 Stewart Avenue
Suite 520
Garden City, NY 11530
(516) 222-1944
Fax: (516) 222-0457
E-mail: info@childrensleukemia.org
Web Site: www.childrensleukemia.org

FOUNDED: 1965

AREAS OF INTEREST:
Leukemia.

NAME(S) OF PROGRAMS:
● **Children's Leukemia Research Grants**

TYPE:
Research grants. Support for research efforts into the causes and cure of leukemia. Patient aid to families in need while meeting the expenses incurred in leukemia treatment.

YEAR PROGRAM STARTED: 1965

PURPOSE:
To work towards a cure for leukemia; to provide patient aid.

ELIGIBILITY:
Any doctor at the Ph.D. or M.D. level who is involved in research towards finding the causes and cure for leukemia may apply.

FINANCIAL DATA:
Amount of support per award: Up to $30,000 per year.

APPLICATION INFO:
Information is available on the Association's web site.
Duration: One year. Renewal for a second year is considered if other funding for promising projects has not been obtained.
Deadline: June 30.

ADDRESS INQUIRIES TO:
Anthony R. Pasqua, President
(See address above.)

DYSAUTONOMIA FOUNDATION, INC.
315 West 39th Street
Suite 701
New York, NY 10018
(212) 279-1066
Fax: (212) 279-2066
E-mail: info@famdys.org
Web Site: www.familialdysautonomia.org

TYPE:
Project/program grants; Research grants; Seed money grants. In addition to support for research and clinical study, the Foundation also provides financial support to the Dysautonomia Treatment and Evaluation Center at NYU and the Israeli FD Center in Tel Aviv.

See entry 2250 for full listing.

CHARLES H. HOOD FOUNDATION, INC. [2324]
2 Boylston Street, 4th Floor
Boston, MA 02116
(617) 695-9439
E-mail: cmancusi@hria.org
Web Site: charleshoodfoundation.org

FOUNDED: 1942

AREAS OF INTEREST:
Child health research.

NAME(S) OF PROGRAMS:
● **Child Health Research Awards Program**

TYPE:
Research grants. Medical research grants that are relevant to child health. Projects must be hypothesis-driven clinical, basic science, public health, health services research or epidemiology.

YEAR PROGRAM STARTED: 1942

PURPOSE:
To improve the health and quality of life for children through grant support of New England-based pediatric researchers.

LEGAL BASIS:
Private family foundation.

ELIGIBILITY:
Investigators working in tax-exempt academic, medical and research institutions in New England are eligible. Grants must

have relevance to child health. Investigators must be within five (Ph.D. scientists) or seven (physician-scientists) years of their first faculty appointment. In addition to basic science research, grants are also given to researchers in public health, epidemiology, clinical research and health services research.

GEOG. RESTRICTIONS: New England.

FINANCIAL DATA:
Amount of support per award: $82,500 per year for two years (inclusive of 10% overhead).

NO. MOST RECENT APPLICANTS: 42 for the year 2019.

NO. AWARDS: 10 new grants for the year 2019.

APPLICATION INFO:
Application guidelines, instructions and forms are available on the web site.
Duration: Two years.
Deadline: Spring and Fall for Child Health Research Grants. Funding begins on July 1 and January 1. Deadlines and guidelines change each cycle.

PUBLICATIONS:
Application guidelines; alumni directory; summaries of current and previous funded projects.

IRS I.D.: 04-3507847

OFFICERS:
Neil Smiley, President and Treasurer
John Parker, Jr., Vice President and Clerk

TRUSTEES:
Robert Boutwell
Barbara Bula
Brendon Bula
Elizabeth Hood

ADDRESS INQUIRIES TO:
See e-mail address above.

HUMAN GROWTH FOUNDATION [2325]
997 Glen Cove Avenue, Suite 5
Glen Head, NY 11545
(516) 671-4041
(800) 451-6434
Fax: (516) 671-4055
E-mail: hgf1@hgfound.org
Web Site: www.hgfound.org

FOUNDED: 1965

AREAS OF INTEREST:
Growth disorders and pediatrics.

NAME(S) OF PROGRAMS:
● **Small Grants for Research in Field of Short Stature**

TYPE:
Research grants.

YEAR PROGRAM STARTED: 1965

PURPOSE:
To help medical science better understand the process of growth and to help individuals with growth-related disorders, their families and health care professionals through education, research and advocacy.

ELIGIBILITY:
Applicants must be involved in research of the human growth process. Special consideration will be given to young investigators and to projects dealing with psychological, social, and educational aspects of dwarfism and its treatment and to new approaches to diagnosis and management, as well as clinical and basic research in the

mechanisms of statural growth disorders of children including chondrodystrophies, genetic, or psychological causes.

FINANCIAL DATA:
Amount of support per award: Average: $10,000 to $15,000.

NO. MOST RECENT APPLICANTS: Over 40.

NO. AWARDS: Up to 3.

APPLICATION INFO:
Application and guidelines are available from the Foundation. Applicants must first provide a Letter of Intent. Grant applications must be in NIH format.
Duration: One-time funding.
Deadline: Letter of Intent: May 15. Final application: September 1.

ADDRESS INQUIRIES TO:
Patricia D. Costa, Executive Director
(See address above.)

SICKKIDS FOUNDATION
525 University Avenue, Suite 835
Toronto ON M5G 2L3 Canada
(416) 813-8104
(800) 661-1083 ext. 2354
E-mail: national.grants@sickkidsfoundation.com
Web Site: www.sickkidsfoundation.com/about-us/grants

TYPE:
Awards/prizes; Conferences/seminars; Project/program grants; Research grants. Community Conference Grants program brings together families with researchers and clinicians for medical presentations and family-oriented discussions. It helps ensure knowledge exchange with families so that they are able to access the most up-to-date information about their children's health.

New Investigator Research Grants program focus is to ensure that there continues to be well-trained researchers across the country working to address the most pressing childhood diseases and conditions.

See entry 1336 for full listing.

SOCIETY FOR PEDIATRIC DERMATOLOGY [2326]
8365 Keystone Crossing, Suite 107
Indianapolis, IN 46240
(317) 202-0224
Fax: (317) 205-9481
E-mail: info@pedsderm.net
Web Site: www.pedsderm.net/grants-awards

FOUNDED: 1975

AREAS OF INTEREST:
Pediatric dermatology.

NAME(S) OF PROGRAMS:
● **Pilot Project Grants**
● **Team Grants**
● **Weston Pediatric Dermatology Career Development Award (CDA)**

TYPE:
Research grants; Seed money grants. Research grants for investigators on the faculty and postdoctoral levels.

PURPOSE:
To foster research in pediatric dermatology.

LEGAL BASIS:
Medical society.

ELIGIBILITY:
Applicants must have completed training in pediatrics or dermatology and be active in

the investigation of pediatric dermatology. Importance of the project and feasibility within the timeframe available are selection criteria.

FINANCIAL DATA:
Amount of support per award: Pilot Project Grants: Up to $7,500; Team Grants: Up to $25,000. Weston Pediatric Dermatology Career Development Award: $40,000.
Total amount of support: Pilot Project Grants and Team Grants: Up to $97,600.

NO. AWARDS: Pilot Project Award: Varies. Weston Pediatric Dermatology Career Development Award: 1 given every other (odd-numbered) year.

APPLICATION INFO:
Application information is available on the Society's website.
Duration: Weston Pediatric Dermatology Career Development Award: One year.
Deadline: First cycle: May 1. Notification in June. Second cycle: December 1. Notification the following February.

ADDRESS INQUIRIES TO:
Awards and Goals Committee
(See address above.)

*SPECIAL STIPULATIONS:
Research funds may not be used for investigator travel expenses to attend meetings or to present their work.

THRASHER RESEARCH FUND [2327]
68 South Main Street, Suite 400
Salt Lake City, UT 84101
(801) 240-4753
Fax: (801) 240-1625
E-mail: martinezaf@thrasherresearch.org
Web Site: www.thrasherresearch.org

FOUNDED: 1977

AREAS OF INTEREST:
Pediatric medical research, with emphasis on clinical/translational research with potential findings that would be clinically applicable in a short period of time in the prevention, diagnosis and/or treatment of pediatric medical problems.

TYPE:
Research grants. Grants for support of research that addresses problems in children's health in areas of critical illnesses that have been insufficiently researched or investigated. The Fund assumes that significant solutions to children's health problems remain undiscovered and invites a broad array of applications designed to remedy these deficiencies.

YEAR PROGRAM STARTED: 1977

PURPOSE:
To provide grants for pediatric medical research that addresses problems in children's health that are significant in terms of either magnitude or severity.

LEGAL BASIS:
Private organization.

ELIGIBILITY:
The Fund supports medical research that seeks to prevent or cure children's critical illnesses, injuries and disabilities. Projects should:
(1) be scientifically sound and culturally appropriate;
(2) document methods and practices that have sustainable benefits;

(3) have specific aims and a well-designed methodology and;
(4) evaluate the significance of impact on children's health.

Funding is limited to research. The Fund does not award grants for general operations, construction or renovation of buildings or facilities, nor does the Fund award grants for general donations, loans, student aid, scholarships, educational programs or support of other funds or institutions.

The Fund excludes research using human fetal tissue, stem cell research, or behavioral science research.

FINANCIAL DATA:
Support may be provided for supplies, minor equipment and technical personnel assistance related to a specific Fund-sponsored project. Principal investigators in need of salary support for a specific project may apply for 20% support, based on federal guidelines.
Amount of support per award: $25,000 to $500,000. Typically $250,000 to $350,000.
Total amount of support: Varies.

NO. MOST RECENT APPLICANTS: 100.

NO. AWARDS: 25.

APPLICATION INFO:
Application guidelines are available on the Fund's web site. Potential applicants are encouraged to contact Fund staff prior to a formal submission to determine the potential fit of a project with current Fund interests.
Duration: Up to three years.

PUBLICATIONS:
Brochure; application information.

STAFF:
R. Justin Brown, M.P.H., President
Aaron V. Pontsler, M.S., MBA, Research Manager
Brittni Smith, Ph.D., Research Manager

U.S. DEPARTMENT OF HEALTH AND HUMAN SERVICES
Maternal and Child Health Bureau
Parklawn Building, Room 5C 26
5600 Fishers Lane
Rockville, MD 20857
(301) 443-2204
Fax: (301) 443-9354
E-mail: CallCenter@hrsa.gov (grants information)
Web Site: mchb.hrsa.gov

TYPE:
Block grants. The Title V Block Grant Program has as a general purpose the improvement of the health of all mothers and children in the nation. The Block Grant Program has three components: Formula Block Grants to 59 states and other political jurisdictions, Special Projects of Regional and National Significance (SPRANS), and Community Integrated Service Systems (CISS) Grants.

See entry 2293 for full listing.

Pharmacology

AMERICAN ASSOCIATION OF COLLEGES OF PHARMACY [2328]

1400 Crystal Drive
Suite 300
Arlington, VA 22202
(703) 739-2330
Fax: (703) 836-8982
E-mail: nia@aacp.org
Web Site: www.aacp.org

FOUNDED: 1900

AREAS OF INTEREST:
Pharmaceutical education.

NAME(S) OF PROGRAMS:
- **New Investigator Award**

TYPE:
Research grants.

YEAR PROGRAM STARTED: 1985

PURPOSE:
To provide start-up funds for new faculty members to assist in establishing a research program; to assist new faculty in establishing themselves as independent investigators.

LEGAL BASIS:
Nonprofit foundation, tax-exempt under the IRS Code.

ELIGIBILITY:
Applicants must have earned terminal degrees in their disciplines (Pharm.D., Ph.D.), hold a regular full-time academic faculty appointment in a college or school of pharmacy, hold the rank of assistant professor, and be in the first to fifth year of their academic appointment. The applicant must be a current individual member of AACP. Only one application per investigator will be accepted for review.

A faculty member who has been a principle investigator on an AACP NIA or equivalent starter grant, on a professional (e.g., ACCP, ASHP, AAPS, PhRMA, etc.), organizational (e.g., American Heart or American Cancer) or federal grant (e.g., NIH, NSF, AHRQ, DOD, CDC, etc.) is not eligible to apply.

Intramural university or college/school start-up support may be used for supplementing the proposed research.

GEOG. RESTRICTIONS: United States.

FINANCIAL DATA:
No overhead allowed. In addition to grant monies, each award winner will receive $1,000 for required travel to the AACP Annual Meeting.
Amount of support per award: $10,000 maximum.

NO. MOST RECENT APPLICANTS: 138.

NO. AWARDS: Up to 16.

APPLICATION INFO:
Application specifics are available on the AACP web site.
Duration: One year.
Deadline: Letter of Intent: July 31. Full Proposal: September 18.

PUBLICATIONS:
Program announcement.

OFFICERS:
Lucinda Maine, Executive Vice President and Chief Executive Officer

ADDRESS INQUIRIES TO:
See e-mail address above.

AMERICAN FOUNDATION FOR PHARMACEUTICAL EDUCATION (AFPE) [2329]

6076 Franconia Road, Suite C
Alexandria, VA 22310-1758
(703) 875-3095
Fax: (703) 875-3098
E-mail: hardimon@afpepharm.org
Web Site: afpepharm.org

FOUNDED: 1942

AREAS OF INTEREST:
Pharmaceutical education.

NAME(S) OF PROGRAMS:
- **Phi Lambda Sigma-AFPE First Year Graduate Fellowship**
- **Rho Chi-AFPE First Year Graduate Fellowship**

TYPE:
Fellowships. Phi Lambda Sigma-AFPE First Year Graduate Fellowship encourages outstanding Phi Lambda Sigma members to pursue the Ph.D. in a college or school of pharmacy graduate program.

Rho Chi-AFPE First Year Graduate Fellowship encourages outstanding Rho Chi Honor Society members to pursue the Ph.D. in a college of pharmacy graduate program.

YEAR PROGRAM STARTED: 1985

PURPOSE:
To encourage outstanding Rho Chi and Phi Lambda Sigma members to continue their education in a graduate program for the Ph.D. in a college of pharmacy.

LEGAL BASIS:
Nonprofit foundation, tax-exempt under the IRS Code.

ELIGIBILITY:
Phi Lambda Sigma-AFPE Fellowship: Applicant must be a member of Phi Lambda Sigma and a pharmacy Pharm.D. degree student in the final year of professional studies who is planning to enroll full-time for the Ph.D. degree in the pharmaceutical sciences after graduation in a Ph.D. degree program at or affiliated with an accredited U.S. school/college of pharmacy or be a pharmacy Pharm.D. degree student in the final year of professional studies who is currently enrolled in a joint Pharm.D./Ph.D. degree program at or affiliated with an accredited U.S. school or college of pharmacy who will pursue full-time graduate study in the year the award is made. U.S. citizenship or permanent resident status is required.

Rho Chi-AFPE Fellowship: Applicants must be members of the Rho Chi Honor Society. Applicants must be a pharmacy student in the final year of professional studies or a professional pharmacy degree program graduate entering a pharmaceutical sciences (including social/administrative sciences) Ph.D. program in an accredited U.S. school or college of pharmacy as a full-time student. Pharmacy students who have initiated graduate work through a dual Pharm.D./Ph.D. degree pathway are eligible if they have completed their professional degree and will be pursuing full-time graduate study in the year the award is made. Applicants must be a U.S. citizen or permanent resident.

GEOG. RESTRICTIONS: United States.

FINANCIAL DATA:
Phi Lambda Sigma-AFPE: The scholarship may be used for any purpose decided by the awardee and faculty sponsor that will enable the student to have a successful program, i.e., student stipend, laboratory supplies, books, materials, travel, etc., related to the program of graduate study. None of the funds shall be used for indirect costs by the institution.

Amount of support per award: $7,500.

Total amount of support: $15,000.

NO. MOST RECENT APPLICANTS: 12.

NO. AWARDS: 1 of each.

APPLICATION INFO:
For the Phi Lambda Sigma-AFPE Fellowship, the following information should be sent to exec_director@philambdasigma.org:
(1) letters of recommendation from two college faculty members who are acquainted with the student and his or her potential for graduate study;
(2) name of the graduate school the student plans to attend (if known);
(3) a one- to two-page statement by applicant elaborating reasons for wishing to attend graduate school;
(4) a list of special honors, awards and accomplishments in high school and college reflecting achievement and ability to succeed in graduate school and;
(5) an official transcript of all collegiate grades and copies of GRE, SAT and other national achievement test scores.

For the Rho Chi Fellowship, application forms are available from Rho Chi Faculty Advisors or the Secretary of Rho Chi. Required information should be sent to: The Rho Chi Society National Office, UNC Eshelman School of Pharmacy, 3210 Kerr Hall, CB No. 7569, Chapel Hill, NC 27599-7569; Tel: (919) 843-9001; E-mail: rhochi@unc.edu. The packet should include the following:
(1) a completed application form;
(2) a one-page description of present academic status including all previous scholarships and fellowships and memberships in professional, scientific, scholastic and honor societies;
(3) a one-page account of involvement in professional and extracurricular activities, list of proposed expenses for the year; if married, include spouse and family expenses; list all sources and amounts of income;
(4) name of university to be attended and planned field of study;
(5) graduate record examination scores;
(6) a one- to two-page statement describing career goals;
(7) official transcripts from all colleges or universities attended and;
(8) letters of reference from three individuals who are directly familiar with the applicant and can speak specifically to educational achievements and capacity for graduate study.

Duration: One academic year.

Deadline: Phi Lambda Sigma-AFPE Fellowship: May 15. Rho Chi Fellowship: May 1.

PUBLICATIONS:
Program announcement.

OFFICERS:
Ellen L. Woods, President and Secretary

AMERICAN FOUNDATION FOR PHARMACEUTICAL EDUCATION (AFPE) [2330]

6076 Franconia Road, Suite C
Alexandria, VA 22310-1758
(703) 875-3095
Fax: (703) 875-3098
E-mail: hardimon@afpepharm.org
Web Site: afpepharm.org

FOUNDED: 1942

AREAS OF INTEREST:
Pharmaceutical education.

NAME(S) OF PROGRAMS:
● **Kappa Epsilon-AFPE-Nellie Wakeman First Year Graduate Fellowship**

TYPE:
Fellowships.

PURPOSE:
To encourage an outstanding pharmacy school graduate to pursue an advanced degree in the pharmaceutical sciences.

ELIGIBILITY:
An applicant must be in the final year of the Pharm.D. program or have completed a pharmacy degree. Consideration is given to those who need financial assistance to further their education in pharmacy. At the time of application, the Kappa Epsilon member must be in good financial standing with the KE Fraternity and planning to pursue a Doctor of Philosophy (Ph.D.) degree, a Master's degree, or a combined Residency/Master's degree program at a U.S. college or school of pharmacy.

FINANCIAL DATA:
The funds may be used for any purpose decided by the awardee and faculty sponsor that will enable the student to have a successful program, e.g., student stipend, laboratory supplies, books, materials, travel related to the program of study. None of the funds shall be used for indirect costs by the institution.

Amount of support per award: $7,500.

Total amount of support: $7,500.

NO. AWARDS: 1.

APPLICATION INFO:
Applications can be downloaded from the web site. Applications must include:
(1) a completed application form (application and reference forms available from a Kappa Epsilon faculty advisor or the Kappa Epsilon Executive Office, Tel: (913) 262-2749);
(2) a letter of recommendation from the faculty advisor and one other faculty member familiar with the applicant (both faculty members are to complete a letter of reference form) and;
(3) official transcripts of all collegiate grades, undergraduate and graduate.
Applications should be sent to the Kappa Epsilon Executive Office: 7700 Shawnee Mission Parkway, Suite 201, Overland Park, KS 66202.

Duration: One year.

Deadline: All application materials must be received by February 1. Notification end of April.

AMERICAN INSTITUTE OF THE HISTORY OF PHARMACY [2331]

University of Wisconsin School of Pharmacy
Rennebohm Hall
777 Highland Avenue
Madison, WI 53705-2222
(608) 262-5378
E-mail: aihp@aihp.org
Web Site: www.aihp.org

FOUNDED: 1941

AREAS OF INTEREST:
History of pharmacy.

NAME(S) OF PROGRAMS:
● **Fischelis Grants for Research in the History of American Pharmacy**
● **History of Pharmacy Thesis Research Grants-in-Aid**

TYPE:
Grants-in-aid; Research grants.

PURPOSE:
To contribute to the understanding of the development of civilization by fostering the creation, preservation and dissemination of knowledge concerning the history and related humanistic aspects of the pharmaceutical field.

ELIGIBILITY:
For grants-in-aid, applicants must be Ph.D. students in good standing at an institution of the U.S. Students need not be American citizens, nor does the research topic have to be related to American history. Thesis research must be clearly related to some aspect of pharmaceutical history or some other humanistic investigation that utilizes a pharmaco-historical approach.

For Fischelis Grants, applicants do not have to be U.S. citizens, but must attend American institutions.

FINANCIAL DATA:
Grants-in-Aid only cover direct costs of research attributable to supplies and other expenses that cannot be reimbursed by the degree-granting institution itself. These can include computer time and programming, obtaining a photocopy or microform of essential sources, travel and maintenance at a site away from the home university. Ineligible expenses include routine typing of the manuscript, living expenses at the home university, publication of research results or routine illustrations for the manuscript.

Amount of support per award: Fischelis Grants: Varies; Grants-in-Aid: Up to $2,000.

APPLICATION INFO:
Application forms required for both programs. For Grants-in-Aid, application must be no longer than four pages and must include identifying information of the graduate student, educational background, faculty reference information, thesis topic and description, estimate of expenses, statement of other financial support applied for and other information considered important to the proper consideration of the application.

Deadline: February 1.

ADDRESS INQUIRIES TO:
Beth D. Fisher
Director of Curatorial Affairs
(See address above.)

AMERICAN SOCIETY OF REGIONAL ANESTHESIA AND PAIN MEDICINE [2332]

3 Penn Center West
Suite 224
Pittsburgh, PA 15276
(412) 471-2718
Fax: (412) 471-7503
E-mail: asraassistant@asra.com
Web Site: www.asra.com

AREAS OF INTEREST:
Regional anesthesia and pain medicine.

NAME(S) OF PROGRAMS:
● **ASRA Carl Koller Memorial Research Grant**
● **ASRA Chronic Pain Research Grant**

TYPE:
Research grants.

PURPOSE:
To support research related to any aspect of regional anesthesia, acute and chronic pain medicine and their application to surgery, obstetrics and pain control; to encourage anesthesiologists and other researchers who are interested in the field.

ELIGIBILITY:
Applicant must be North American and a member of the ASRA.

FINANCIAL DATA:
Amount of support per award: $10,000 to $200,000.

Total amount of support: Up to $200,000 biennially.

NO. MOST RECENT APPLICANTS: 17.

NO. AWARDS: 1 every other year per award.

APPLICATION INFO:
The application, which must be written by the applicant, should be accompanied by a complete narrative research protocol. The research proposal must be concerned with an original idea or concept. The research must be carried out primarily by the applicant.

Deadline: Specific deadlines are posted on the ASRA web site.

ADDRESS INQUIRIES TO:
Angie Stengel, Executive Director
(See address above.)

AMERICAN SOCIETY OF REGIONAL ANESTHESIA AND PAIN MEDICINE

3 Penn Center West
Suite 224
Pittsburgh, PA 15276
(412) 471-2718
Fax: (412) 471-7503
E-mail: asraassistant@asra.com
Web Site: www.asra.com

TYPE:
Research grants.

See entry 2035 for full listing.

PHARMACEUTICAL RESEARCH AND MANUFACTURERS OF AMERICA FOUNDATION, INC. [2333]

950 F Street, N.W.
Suite 300
Washington, DC 20004
(202) 572-7756
E-mail: foundation@phrma.org
Web Site: www.phrmafoundation.org

FOUNDED: 1965

AREAS OF INTEREST:
Biology, biomedical engineering, biopharmaceutics, clinical outcomes assessment, disease modeling, drug delivery, drug discovery, genetics, health outcomes, molecular epidemiology, pharmaceutics, pharmaceutical biotechnology, pharmaceutical engineering, pharmacology and toxicology.

NAME(S) OF PROGRAMS:
- **Research Starter Grant in Drug Delivery**
- **Research Starter Grant in Drug Discovery**
- **Research Starter Grant in Health Outcomes Research**
- **Research Starter Grant in Translational Medicine**

TYPE:
Project/program grants; Research grants; Seed money grants. Starter grants to support research in the fields of biology, biomedical engineering, biopharmaceutics, clinical outcomes assessment, disease modeling, drug delivery, drug discovery, genetics, health outcomes, molecular epidemiology, pharmaceutics, pharmaceutical biotechnology, pharmaceutical engineering, pharmacology and toxicology. The grants offer financial support to individuals beginning independent research careers at the faculty level.

PURPOSE:
To help promising young scientists advance their research projects; to offer financial support to individuals beginning their independent research careers at the faculty level.

LEGAL BASIS:
501(c)(3) organization.

ELIGIBILITY:
Applicants must currently be in Ph.D. and/or M.S. degree granting institutions in the U.S. Those holding the academic rank of assistant professor (or research assistant professor) within a tenure track (or research track) appointment, or instructor, if eligible to apply for independent research funding by their institution, are eligible to apply for the Research Starter Grant in Drug Delivery or Research Starter Grant in Drug Discovery, providing their proposed research is neither directly nor indirectly already being subsidized to any significant degree by an extramural support mechanism. Individuals receiving only intramural funding or start-up funding from their institution may apply.

Applicants for the Research Starter Grant in Health Outcomes Research must be beginning independent research careers at the faculty level in schools of medicine, pharmacy, public health, nursing or dentistry. This program is not intended for individuals in postdoctoral training. However, those enrolled in postdoctoral training programs scheduled to conclude by July 1, who will hold an academic appointment by that time, may apply. Those holding academic rank of instructor or assistant professor, and investigators at the doctoral level with equivalent positions, are eligible to apply, provided the proposed research is neither directly nor indirectly subsidized to any significant degree by an extramural support mechanism.

Applicants for the Research Starter Grant in Translational Medicine must hold the academic rank of assistant professor (or research assistant professor) within a tenure track (or research track) appointment, or instructor, if eligible to apply for independent research funding by their institution, providing their proposed research is neither directly nor indirectly already being subsidized to any significant degree by an extramural support mechanism.

GEOG. RESTRICTIONS: United States.

FINANCIAL DATA:
Up to $1,500 may be used for travel to a scientific conference for the grantee. Funds may be budgeted for the hourly support of a technical assistant or graduate student. Funds may not be used for fringe benefits, indirect costs or tuition assistance. Up to 25% of the award may be used for the Research Starter Grant in Health Outcomes Research grantee's stipend.

Amount of support per award: $100,000 per award.

Total amount of support: Varies.

NO. MOST RECENT APPLICANTS: Varies.

NO. AWARDS: Varies.

APPLICATION INFO:
Applications should be submitted on the Foundation web site.

Duration: One year.

Deadline: Drug Delivery and Drug Discovery: Letter of Intent due May 15. Selected submissions will be notified by July 1 to submit a full application. Health Outcomes and Translational Medicine: February 1.

PUBLICATIONS:
Brochure.

IRS I.D.: 52-6063009

STAFF:
Eileen Cannon, President
Joanne Westphal, Director of Development

BOARD OF DIRECTORS:
Alfred Sandrock, M.D., Ph.D., Chairman
Andrew Plump, M.D., Ph.D., Treasurer
Mikael Dolsten, M.D., Ph.D.
Iris Loew-Friedrich, M.D.
Aran Maree, M.B., B.Ch.
Joseph P. Miletich, M.D., Ph.D.
Richard Moscicki, M.D.
John C. Reed, M.D., Ph.D
Daniel Skovronsky, M.D., Ph.D.
Rupert Vessey, FRCP, D.Phil.

ADVISORY COMMITTEE:
Terry L. Bowlin, Ph.D.
Michael J. Hageman, Ph.D.
Michael N. Liebman, Ph.D.
Bryan R. Luce, Ph.D., MBA
Richard Moscicki, M.D.
Nancy C. Santanello, M.D., M.S.

ADDRESS INQUIRIES TO:
See e-mail address above.

*PLEASE NOTE:
A final progress report and financial report are due upon the conclusion of the grant.

*SPECIAL STIPULATIONS:
Funds may not be used for fringe benefits, indirect costs, or tuition.

Physical medicine and rehabilitation

AMERICAN BURN ASSOCIATION [2334]
311 South Wacker Drive
Suite 4150
Chicago, IL 60606
(312) 642-9260
Fax: (312) 642-9130
E-mail: info@ameriburn.org
Web Site: ameriburn.org

AREAS OF INTEREST:
Thermal injury.

NAME(S) OF PROGRAMS:
- **Cheryl Jordan Scholarship Fund**

TYPE:
Exchange programs; Travel grants.

PURPOSE:
To support efforts that address the problems of burn injuries and burn victims; to provide care and rehabilitation to burn patients, conduct burn-related research, educate burn team members, develop and implement burn injury prevention programs, fight fires and address the psychosocial needs of burn victims.

ELIGIBILITY:
Applicant must be a non-physician burn team member.

GEOG. RESTRICTIONS: United States and Canada.

FINANCIAL DATA:
Amount of support per award: Varies.
Total amount of support: Varies.

NO. AWARDS: Varies.

APPLICATION INFO:
Application is submitted through the Association web site.

ADDRESS INQUIRIES TO:
Kimberly A. Hoarle, Executive Director
(See address above.)

AMERICAN GERIATRICS SOCIETY [2335]
40 Fulton Street, 18th Floor
New York, NY 10038
(212) 308-1414
Fax: (212) 832-8646
E-mail: info.amger@americangeriatrics.org
Web Site: www.americangeriatrics.org

AREAS OF INTEREST:
Problems of the aged.

NAME(S) OF PROGRAMS:
- **Clinical Student Research Award**
- **Clinician of the Year Award**
- **Health in Aging Foundation New Investigator Awards**
- **Edward Henderson Student Research Award**
- **Dennis W. Jahnigen Memorial Award**
- **Nascher/Manning Award**
- **Outstanding Junior Clinician Education Manuscript**
- **Outstanding Junior Clinician Educator of the Year**
- **Outstanding Junior Investigator of the Year**
- **Outstanding Junior Research Manuscript**
- **Outstanding Mid-Career Clinician Educator of the Year**

- **Scientist-in-Training Research Award**
- **Thomas and Catherine Yoshikawa Award for Outstanding Scientific Achievement in Clinical Investigation**

TYPE:
Awards/prizes. The AGS Student Research Award is presented to an undergraduate student in medicine, dentistry, nursing, social work, pharmacy, occupational therapy, or physical therapy for presenting at the AGS Annual Meeting.

Clinician of the Year Award was established to recognize the great contributions of practitioners for delivering quality health care for older people, as well as to showcase the importance of the geriatrics clinician in our health care system.

Health in Aging Foundation New Investigator Awards are presented to individuals whose original research, as presented in a submitted abstract, reflects new and relevant insights in geriatrics.

Edward Henderson Student Research Award is presented to a medical student interested in pursuing a career in geriatrics who has demonstrated excellence in the field.

Dennis W. Jahnigen Memorial Award is given annually to an AGS member who has provided leadership to train students in geriatrics and has contributed significantly to the progress of geriatrics education in health professions schools.

Nascher/Manning Award recognizes distinguished, lifelong achievement in clinical geriatrics, including medicine, psychiatry, and all other related disciplines.

Outstanding Junior Clinician Education Manuscript Award is given to a junior faculty member (Assistant Professor/Instructor) or an Associate Professor (having held the position for no more than three years) who has been first author on an important peer-reviewed clinical education article published in a scientific journal.

Outstanding Junior Clinician Educator of the Year Award is given to an outstanding clinician educator junior faculty member (Assistant Professor/Instructor) for an impressive body of work in geriatric education.

Outstanding Junior Investigator of the Year Award is given to an outstanding junior investigator for their body of work. The award takes into consideration independence of thought and originality in new and relevant research in geriatrics and gerontology.

Outstanding Junior Research Manuscript Award is given to a junior investigator (Assistant Professor/Instructor or equivalent) who has been first author on an important or interesting peer-reviewed geriatrics research article within the past year.

Outstanding Mid-Career Clinician Educator of the Year Award is given to an outstanding clinician educator midcareer faculty member (Associate Professor) for an impressive body of work in geriatric education.

Scientist-in-Training Research Award is presented to a predoctoral candidate from a range of disciplines, including psychology, gerontology, epidemiology, to celebrate the awardees promise as a geriatrics scientist.

Thomas and Catherine Yoshikawa Award for Outstanding Achievement in Clinical Investigation recognizes outstanding achievement in clinical research addressing health problems of older adults as evaluated by an investigator actively involved in direct patient care.

PURPOSE:
To encourage and promote the field of geriatrics and to stress the importance of medical research in the field of aging; to recognize individuals whose outstanding work in geriatrics education, research and clinical practice contribute to the delivery of high-quality care for older people.

FINANCIAL DATA:
Amount of support per award: Clinical Student Research Award, Edward Henderson Student Research Award and Scientist-in-Training Research Award: $500; Clinician of the Year and Thomas and Catherine Yoshikawa Award: $2,000; Health in Aging Foundation New Investigator Awards: $1,000; Dennis W. Jahnigen Memorial Award and Nascher/Manning Award: Travel expenses to attend the AGS meeting.

Total amount of support: Varies.

APPLICATION INFO:
Application is posted on the Society web site by mid-August.

Deadline: December 1.

ADDRESS INQUIRIES TO:
Dennise McAlpin, Assistant Director Professional Education and Special Projects (See address above.)

AMERICAN KINESIOTHERAPY ASSOCIATION, INC. [2336]
P.O. Box 24822
Richmond, VA 23224
(800) 296-2582
E-mail: info@akta.org
Web Site: www.akta.org

FOUNDED: 1946

AREAS OF INTEREST:
Kinesiotherapy, including adaptive physical education.

NAME(S) OF PROGRAMS:
- **AKTA Lou Montalvano Memorial Scholarship**

TYPE:
Scholarships. Award for students in AKTA-accredited kinesiotherapy programs.

PURPOSE:
To recognize academic excellence and career planning through funding for educational needs.

LEGAL BASIS:
Incorporated, nonprofit organization.

ELIGIBILITY:
Candidate must be currently enrolled in an AKTA-accredited kinesiotherapy program in a university and have definite intentions to pursue certification and a career in kinesiotherapy. Candidate must be a current member of the AKTA. Past AKTA scholarship winners are ineligible to apply for further AKTA scholarships.

FINANCIAL DATA:
Amount of support per award: $500.
Total amount of support: $500.

NO. AWARDS: 1 annually.

APPLICATION INFO:
Application process includes college transcripts and three letters of recommendation. Further information is available from the Association.

Duration: One year.

Deadline: August 31.

ADDRESS INQUIRIES TO:
Byron Washington
Scholarship Committee Chairman
E-mail: firstvp.akta@gmail.com

THE AMERICAN ORTHOPAEDIC SOCIETY FOR SPORTS MEDICINE (AOSSM) [2337]
9400 West Higgins Road
Suite 300
Rosemont, IL 60018
(877) 321-3500 (IL only)
(847) 292-4900
Fax: (847) 292-4905
E-mail: kevin@aossm.org
Web Site: www.sportsmed.org/research

FOUNDED: 1972

AREAS OF INTEREST:
Sports medicine.

NAME(S) OF PROGRAMS:
- **Steven P. Arnoczky Young Investigator Grant**

TYPE:
Awards/prizes; Research grants. Grant is intended to encourage early career researchers.

PURPOSE:
To increase the knowledge of and improve the care of sports-related injuries and disease.

ELIGIBILITY:
Grants will be awarded to the principal investigators who fulfill the following criteria:
(1) has not received any peer-reviewed external funding nor any external funding greater than $25,000;
(2) must be an early career orthopedic surgeon or sports medicine fellow who has graduated from an approved residency program;
(3) must document and play the primary role in the proposed investigation and;
(4) must stay at the parent institution while completing the project.

FINANCIAL DATA:
Amount of support per award: Up to $40,000 over a 24-month period.

NO. MOST RECENT APPLICANTS: 10 to 15.

NO. AWARDS: 1.

APPLICATION INFO:
Online submission only.

Duration: Two years.

Deadline: Pre-review (required) and final deadlines are posted online.

ADDRESS INQUIRIES TO:
Kevin Boyer, M.P.H., Director of Research (See address above.)

THE AMERICAN ORTHOPAEDIC SOCIETY FOR SPORTS MEDICINE (AOSSM)   [2338]
9400 West Higgins Road
Suite 300
Rosemont, IL 60018
(847) 292-4900
(877) 321-3500 (IL only)
Fax: (847) 292-4905
E-mail: kevin@aossm.org
Web Site: www.sportsmed.org/research

AREAS OF INTEREST:
Sports medicine.

NAME(S) OF PROGRAMS:
● **AOSSM Sandy Kirkley Clinical Outcome Research Grant**

TYPE:
Research grants. Research grant provides start-up seed or supplemental funding for an outcome research project or pilot study.

PURPOSE:
To support clinical outcome research that has the potential to inform evidence-based practice.

ELIGIBILITY:
Grants will be awarded to the principal investigators who fulfill the following criteria:
(1) must document and play the primary role in the proposed investigation and;
(2) must stay at the parent institution while completing the project.

FINANCIAL DATA:
Amount of support per award: Up to $20,000 over two years.

NO. MOST RECENT APPLICANTS: 8 to 10.

NO. AWARDS: 1.

APPLICATION INFO:
Online submission only.
Duration: Two years.
Deadline: Pre-review and final deadlines are posted online.

ADDRESS INQUIRIES TO:
Kevin Boyer, M.P.H.
Director of Research
(See address above.)

FOUNDATION FOR PHYSICAL THERAPY RESEARCH, INC.   [2339]
1111 North Fairfax Street
Alexandria, VA 22314-1488
(800) 875-1378
Fax: (703) 684-4083
E-mail: info@foundation4pt.org
Web Site: foundation4pt.org

FOUNDED: 1979

AREAS OF INTEREST:
Physical therapy research, investigative studies that add to or refine the body of clinical knowledge on which physical therapy practice is based, and intervention projects involving therapeutic procedures and modalities.

TYPE:
Research grants.

YEAR PROGRAM STARTED: 1998

PURPOSE:
To add to or refine the body of clinical knowledge on which physical therapy practice is based and to evaluate patient interventions.

LEGAL BASIS:
Foundation.

ELIGIBILITY:
Awards are made to qualified physical therapists and physical therapist assistants or groups of investigators. Must be a U.S. citizen or permanent resident. Projects must be sponsored by a U.S. institution or organization. No funds will be approved to finance cost overruns or deficits on existing projects or to finance projects already in progress.

GEOG. RESTRICTIONS: United States.

FINANCIAL DATA:
Amount of support per award: Maximum $40,000 to $360,000 depending upon grant.
Total amount of support: $1,063,000 for the year 2020.

NO. AWARDS: 30.

APPLICATION INFO:
Application guidelines and access to the online application system are available on the Foundation's web site.
Duration: One to two years.
Deadline: Proposals are due first week in August for most types of grants. Contact Foundation for details.

PUBLICATIONS:
Application guidelines.

IRS I.D.: 13-6161225

ADDRESS INQUIRIES TO:
Barbara Malm, Chief Executive Officer
(See address above.)

*PLEASE NOTE:
Applicants can only apply to one grant mechanism per cycle.

FOUNDATION FOR PHYSICAL THERAPY RESEARCH, INC.   [2340]
1111 North Fairfax Street
Alexandria, VA 22314-1488
(800) 875-1378
Fax: (703) 684-4083
E-mail: info@foundation4pt.org
Web Site: foundation4pt.org

FOUNDED: 1979

AREAS OF INTEREST:
Physical therapy.

NAME(S) OF PROGRAMS:
● **New Investigator Fellowship Training Initiative (NIFTI)**
● **Promotion of Doctoral Studies Scholarships (PODS)**

TYPE:
Fellowships; Scholarships. Fellowships for postdoctoral physical therapy research. Scholarships for physical therapists who intend to pursue physical therapy research as a career.

YEAR PROGRAM STARTED: 1979

PURPOSE:
To provide scholarships that support physical therapists who wish to continue their doctoral coursework and enter the dissertation phase; to provide fellowships that support developing researchers and improve their competitiveness in securing external funding for future research.

LEGAL BASIS:
Foundation.

ELIGIBILITY:
Must be U.S. citizen or permanent resident. Scholarship applicants must be physical therapists or physical therapist assistants pursuing a doctoral degree in physical therapy or a related field with a research focus related to the clinical practice of physical therapy. Applicants must demonstrate a commitment to research.

Fellowship applicants must be physical therapists or physical therapist assistants who have completed Doctorate, or the professional education degree in physical therapy for those already holding a post-professional doctoral degree in the last five years.

One year of teaching is expected for each year of support.

FINANCIAL DATA:
Amount of support per award: PODS I: $7,500; PODS II: $15,000; Fellowship: $100,000.

NO. AWARDS: 20 to 25.

APPLICATION INFO:
Applicants must check the online eligibility guidelines, review the application instructions, then submit the online application.
Duration: Scholarships: One year. Must reapply. Fellowships: Two years.
Deadline: Mid-January.

IRS I.D.: 13-6161225

ADDRESS INQUIRIES TO:
Barbara Malm, Chief Executive Officer
(See address above.)

INTERNATIONAL ORDER OF ALHAMBRA   [2341]
4200 Leeds Avenue
Baltimore, MD 21229-5496
(800) 478-2946
(410) 242-0660
Fax: (410) 536-5729
E-mail: salaam@orderofalhambra.org
Web Site: www.orderalhambra.org

FOUNDED: 1904

AREAS OF INTEREST:
Scholarships for those interested in teaching special education.

NAME(S) OF PROGRAMS:
● **Scholarship and Charity Fund**

TYPE:
Grants-in-aid; Scholarships.

YEAR PROGRAM STARTED: 1970

PURPOSE:
To further education in the field of the intellectually disabled.

LEGAL BASIS:
A nonprofit 501(c)(3) fraternal organization of Catholic men and women dedicated to assisting intellectually disabled persons.

ELIGIBILITY:
Applicant should be attending college or postgraduate study. Applicants must be majoring in special education, which involves the mentally, physically or emotionally handicapped person, and must be eligible to teach special education upon graduation.

GEOG. RESTRICTIONS: United States and Canada.

FINANCIAL DATA:
Amount of support per award: Varies depending on the level of education.

NO. AWARDS: Varies.

APPLICATION INFO:
Students may only apply for one semester per application. Call (800) 478-2946 for further information.
Duration: One semester. Renewable by reapplication.
Deadline: March 1.

*PLEASE NOTE:
Student is limited to two scholarships.

NATIONAL AMBUCS, INC. [2342]
4285 Regency Drive
Greensboro, NC 27410
(743) 223-1330
Fax: (336) 852-6830
E-mail: scholars@ambucs.org
Web Site: www.ambucs.org

FOUNDED: 1948

AREAS OF INTEREST:
Physical therapy, occupational therapy, speech-language pathology and hearing audiology.

NAME(S) OF PROGRAMS:
● **AMBUCS Scholars-Scholarships for Therapists**

TYPE:
Scholarships. AMBUCS Scholars is the largest private single source of educational grants for therapists in America. The goal of this program is to provide financial assistance to needy students studying therapy, which in return places trained individuals in the therapy community to help people with disabilities.

YEAR PROGRAM STARTED: 1955

PURPOSE:
To financially assist students studying for qualification in one of the therapy professions.

LEGAL BASIS:
Private nonprofit association.

ELIGIBILITY:
Applicant must be a citizen of the U.S., document financial need, document good scholastic standing and be accepted at the junior or senior undergraduate or graduate level in an accredited program by the appropriate health therapy profession authority in occupational therapy, physical therapy, speech-language pathology or hearing audiology.

GEOG. RESTRICTIONS: United States.

FINANCIAL DATA:
Amount of support per award: Average $757, plus one two-year scholarship (awarded annually) of $6,000.
Total amount of support: $201,300 for the year 2019.

CO-OP FUNDING PROGRAMS: Funding for this scholarship program is provided entirely by individual AMBUCS chapters and private donations.

NO. MOST RECENT APPLICANTS: 1,783.

NO. AWARDS: 266.

APPLICATION INFO:
Applications must be submitted electronically. If the student is being sponsored by a local chapter, the student should give the local chapter a copy of the completed application, along with the most current IRS Form 1040, a narrative statement, and enrollment certification.

Duration: One academic year.
Deadline: Applications accepted from March 5 to May 4 only.

ADDRESS INQUIRIES TO:
Alyssa Magalski
AMBUCS Scholarship Coordinator
AMBUCS Resource Center
P.O. Box 5127
High Point, NC 27262
E-mail: ambucs@ambucs.org

NATIONAL ASSOCIATION OF HEALTH SERVICES EXECUTIVES (NAHSE) [2343]
NAHSE National Office
1050 Connecticut Avenue, N.W.
5th Floor
Washington, DC 20036
(202) 772-1030
Fax: (202) 772-1072
E-mail: nahsehq@nahse.org
Web Site: www.nahse.org

FOUNDED: 1968

AREAS OF INTEREST:
Health care.

NAME(S) OF PROGRAMS:
● **The Ellis Bonner Award**
● **The Florence Gaynor Award**
● **The Haynes Rice Award**

TYPE:
Scholarships. The Ellis Bonner Award is a special scholarship to recognize the distinguished leadership and academic achievement among non-traditional graduate students who are striving to become future leaders in health care management and NAHSE.

The Florence Gaynor Award recognizes outstanding achievements among female graduate students who are striving to become future leaders in health care management and NAHSE.

The Haynes Rice Award is bestowed by NAHSE to outstanding graduate students who are striving to become future leaders in health care management and NAHSE.

PURPOSE:
To promote the advancement and development of Black health care leaders and elevate the quality of health care services rendered to minority and underserved communities.

ELIGIBILITY:
Applicant must:
(1) be either enrolled or accepted in an accredited college or university program, pursuing a B.S., M.S. or Doctorate degree, majoring in computer science, management of information technology or information management, or provide proof of intent to pursue a major in one of the above areas of study;
(2) be able to demonstrate financial need;
(3) be an active NAHSE member;
(4) have a minimum academic grade point average of 3.0 or above on a scale of 4.0 and;
(5) submit a position paper examining new information and technology trends and their effects on health care.

To retain the scholarship for the second year, the recipient must maintain a 3.0 grade point average and produce a position paper on new technologies and present the position paper to an FCG or NAHSE panel.

FINANCIAL DATA:
Amount of support per award: $2,500.
Total amount of support: $7,500.

NO. MOST RECENT APPLICANTS: 12.

NO. AWARDS: 3.

APPLICATION INFO:
Contact the Association for guidelines.
Duration: One year.
Deadline: May 30.

ADDRESS INQUIRIES TO:
Beverly Glover, Manager
(See address above.)

NATIONAL MULTIPLE SCLEROSIS SOCIETY
Research Programs
733 Third Avenue, 3rd Floor
New York, NY 10017-3288
(212) 476-0451
Fax: (212) 986-7981
E-mail: cathy.carlson@nmss.org
Web Site: www.nationalmssociety.org

TYPE:
Awards/prizes; Fellowships; Research grants; Research contracts. Pilot grants; Training/early career awards. Grants for fundamental or applied research in scientific areas pertinent to multiple sclerosis. Grants are available for clinical or nonclinical studies, providing they show relevance to the Society's research priorities.

See entry 2264 for full listing.

NATIONAL SOCIETY DAUGHTERS OF THE AMERICAN REVOLUTION [2344]
1776 D Street, N.W.
Washington, DC 20006-5303
(202) 879-3263
E-mail: nsdarscholarships@nsdar.org
Web Site: www.dar.org

FOUNDED: 1895

AREAS OF INTEREST:
Occupational and physical therapy.

NAME(S) OF PROGRAMS:
● **Occupational/Physical Therapy Scholarship**

TYPE:
Scholarships. Awarded to students who are in financial need and have been accepted or are attending an accredited school of occupational or physical therapy (including art, music, or physical therapy).

PURPOSE:
To provide ways and means to aid students in attaining higher education.

LEGAL BASIS:
Incorporated historical society.

ELIGIBILITY:
Scholarships are awarded without regard to race, religion, sex or national origin. Candidates must be U.S. citizens and must be enrolled in an accredited school of occupational or physical therapy in the U.S. No affiliation or relationship to DAR is required for qualification.

Candidate must be majoring in occupational therapy or physical therapy and must be in financial need.

Awards are judged on the basis of academic excellence, commitment to field of study, as required, and need.

GEOG. RESTRICTIONS: United States.

FINANCIAL DATA:
Amount of support per award: $2,000.
Total amount of support: $4,000.

NO. AWARDS: 2.

APPLICATION INFO:
Applicants must use the DAR Scholarship Committee's online submission process found on the DAR public web site. Once applicants have set up their scholarship profile, they will be able to complete the application. If necessary, applicants will be able to provide access to individuals wishing to submit confidential letters of recommendations or school transcripts.
Duration: One-time scholarship.
Deadline: February 15.

PUBLICATIONS:
American Spirit, magazine.

ADDRESS INQUIRIES TO:
National Vice Chairman
E-mail: occupationalphysicaltherapyscholar-ship@nsdar.org

PARALYZED VETERANS OF AMERICA RESEARCH AND EDUCATION FOUNDATIONS [2345]
801 Eighteenth Street, N.W.
Washington, DC 20006
(202) 416-7611
E-mail: lindsayp@pva.org
Web Site: www.pva.org/research-foundation

FOUNDED: 1976

AREAS OF INTEREST:
Basic and applied research in spinal cord injury and diseases.

TYPE:
Development grants; Fellowships; Project/program grants; Research grants. The PVA Research Foundation funds research projects and fellowships relevant to spinal cord injury and diseases, in addition to sponsoring basic research that will increase scientific knowledge leading to a cure for spinal cord injury. The Foundation also funds research that deals with applied medical, psychological and technological areas of importance to persons with spinal cord injury or disease.

YEAR PROGRAM STARTED: 1976

PURPOSE:
To support research projects designed to alleviate and eventually end the serious medical, rehabilitative, and psycho social consequences of spinal cord injury and/or disease.

LEGAL BASIS:
Tax-exempt corporation under Sections 170(c) and 501(c)(3) of the Internal Revenue Code. Incorporated in the District of Columbia as a nonprofit organization.

ELIGIBILITY:
All applications must be submitted by fiscally responsible organizational entities in the name of the Principal Investigator. Entities should be nonprofit academic institutions, health care providers, associations and/or organizations. Each application must include appropriate

endorsement of an official who is responsible for the administration of awarded funds (hereafter called the "Grant Administrator").

Grantee institutions must be located in the U.S. or Canada. However, investigators and fellows are not required to be U.S. or Canadian citizens. The Foundation does not fund undergraduate or predoctoral students. Postdoctoral students who received their Ph.D. or M.D. within four years or less should apply for a fellowship grant, and may not be proposed as a Principal Investigator if they have not held such a position under previous funding (from any source). However, if a postdoctoral student has completed a postdoctoral fellowship under any source (please document), they may apply as a Principal Investigator. The Foundation is concerned about any Principal Investigator committing 5% effort or less in a project, with project activities falling primarily on less experienced investigators. Foreign nationals who will serve as a grant's Project Director (PD), Principal Investigator (PI), Research Fellow (RF) or a Significant Project Staff member(s) (20% of time) must provide verification that their U.S. or Canadian visa is current and that the visa will allow sufficient in-country (U.S. or Canada) time to complete the approved and funded grant project or fellowship award. Visa verification can be accomplished by submitting a letter from the PDs, PIs, RFs or significant staff on the sponsoring institution's letterhead that identifies the individual's visa expiration date. The letter must bear the individual's signature and the signature of the institution's grant administrator. The PD, PI, RF or significant staff person may also submit a copy of his or her current visa that identifies the visa's expiration date.

GEOG. RESTRICTIONS: United States and Canada.

FINANCIAL DATA:
Fringe benefits limited to 40%. Indirect cost limited to eight percent.
Amount of support per award: Fellowships: Maximum $50,000 per year; Basic science, clinical, design development: Maximum $75,000 per year.
Total amount of support: Varies.

NO. MOST RECENT APPLICANTS: 79 for the year 2019.

NO. AWARDS: 6 for the year 2019.

APPLICATION INFO:
Before submitting a grant application, carefully read the Research Foundation's Policies and Procedures, as policies may change from year to year. Submission must be made through the link on the Foundation web site.
Duration: One or two years.
Deadline: July. Announcement in December.

PUBLICATIONS:
Annual report; application guidelines.

IRS I.D.: 52-1064398

EXECUTIVE COMMITTEE:
David Zurfluh, National President
Charles Brown, National Senior Vice President
Hack Albertson, National Vice President
Tammy Jones, National Vice President
Ken Ness, National Vice President
Robert Thomas, National Vice President
Tom Wheaton, National Treasurer

Marcus Murray, National Secretary
Carl Blake, Executive Director
Shaun Castle, Deputy Executive Director

ADDRESS INQUIRIES TO:
Rita Obi, Associate Director of Research and Education
(See address above.)

PHYSIOTHERAPY FOUNDATION OF CANADA [2346]
955 Green Valley Crescent
Suite 270
Ottawa ON K2C 3V4 Canada
(613) 564-5454
(800) 387-8679 ext. 253
Fax: (613) 564-1577
E-mail: foundation@physiotherapy.ca
Web Site: physiotherapy.ca/make-an-impact

FOUNDED: 1982

AREAS OF INTEREST:
Canadian research and scholarship in physiotherapy.

NAME(S) OF PROGRAMS:
• **Constance Beattie Memorial Fund Bursary Program**
• **Alun Morgan Memorial Research Grant in Orthopaedic Physiotherapy**
• **PFC Research Grants**
• **Ann Collins Whitmore Memorial Scholarship**

TYPE:
Research grants; Scholarships. Continuing education bursary. Beattie Memorial Fund Bursary Program is to provide support for continuing education courses that are relevant to applicants' career goals.

Alun Morgan Memorial Research Grant provides support for physiotherapy research projects that deal with the management of musculoskeletal problems in Canada.

PFC Research Grants seek to encourage the development of new technology and treatment methods, develop methods for the prevention and early recognition of physical disabilities, evaluate the effectiveness and efficiency of both new and existing treatment methods, and encourage epidemiological studies on the incidence and prevalence of physical disabilities.

Ann Collins Whitmore Memorial Scholarship are for physiotherapists enrolled in a Ph.D. or Master's program. Special consideration will be made for blind physiotherapists.

YEAR PROGRAM STARTED: 1983

PURPOSE:
To fund physiotherapy research and education in Canada to improve mobility, health and well-being.

LEGAL BASIS:
Public foundation.

ELIGIBILITY:
Applicant must be a member of the Canadian Physiotherapy Association.

GEOG. RESTRICTIONS: Canada.

FINANCIAL DATA:
$1,300,000 awarded since inception.
Amount of support per award: Beattie Memorial Fund Bursary Program: Up to $1,500; Morgan Memorial Research Grant: Up to $10,000; PFC Research Grants: $10,000; Whitmore Memorial Scholarship: Up to $4,000.

NO. MOST RECENT APPLICANTS: Varies.

NO. AWARDS: Beattie Memorial Fund Bursary Program: 1 biennially; Morgan Memorial Research Grant: 2 biennially; PFC Research Grants and Whitmore Memorial Scholarship: Varies.

APPLICATION INFO:
Applicant must use authorized application form.
Duration: One year. Renewal possible with reapplication.
Deadline: Mid-February.

GOVERNING BOARD:
Sandra Lamb, PFC Board Chairman

ADDRESS INQUIRIES TO:
Krissy Murphy
Chief Marketing and Membership Officer
(See address above.)

CHRISTOPHER & DANA REEVE FOUNDATION [2347]

636 Morris Turnpike, Suite 3A
Short Hills, NJ 07078
(973) 379-2690
(800) 225-0292
Fax: (973) 912-9433
E-mail: qol@christopherreeve.org
Web Site: www.christopherreeve.org

FOUNDED: 1982

AREAS OF INTEREST:
Improving the quality of life for individuals living with paralysis, as well as their families.

NAME(S) OF PROGRAMS:
• **Quality of Life Grants**

TYPE:
Project/program grants. Provide funding to organizations nationwide that help improve opportunities, access and day-to-day quality of life for individuals with paralysis. The program recognizes the unique and numerous needs of these individuals and the importance of providing services that enable them to participate in all areas of life. The awards fulfill a variety of needs for recipient organizations.

YEAR PROGRAM STARTED: 1999

PURPOSE:
To support exemplary organizations that provide valuable services to individuals with paralysis and their quality of life and health.

LEGAL BASIS:
Not-for-profit organization.

ELIGIBILITY:
Quality of Life Grants are awarded to 501(c)(3) organizations, as well as community parks, schools, veterans hospitals, tribal entities, etc.

Funds cannot be used to support food, grants to individuals, research, rehabilitative therapy, or new construction (although facility modifications to improve accessibility in existing structures is allowed).

GEOG. RESTRICTIONS: United States.

FINANCIAL DATA:
Amount of support per award: Direct Effect (Tier 1): Up to $25,000; Expanded Impact: Up to $100,000; High Impact: $30,000 for Tier 2, $40,000 for Tier 3, and $50,000 for Tier 4. High Impact Assistive Technology Grants: Up to $75,000.
Total amount of support: $4,074,152 for the year 2019.

Matching fund requirements: Although matching funds are not required, it is beneficial to seek funding from additional sources.

CO-OP FUNDING PROGRAMS: Quality of Life Grants are currently funded through a cooperative agreement with the Administration for Community Living (ACL).

NO. MOST RECENT APPLICANTS: Approximately 800.

NO. AWARDS: 164 for the year 2019.

APPLICATION INFO:
Guidelines are available on the Foundation web site. Applications are submitted through the online portal.
Duration: Generally one year or less.
Deadline: Varies. Schedule is posted on the Foundation web site.

PUBLICATIONS:
Guidelines; application questions; final report form; People First Language Guide; A Quick Guide to Establishing Evaluation Indicators.

IRS I.D.: 22-2939536

ADDRESS INQUIRIES TO:
Mark Bogosian, Director
Quality of Life Grants Program
(See address above.)

*SPECIAL STIPULATIONS:
Prior grant recipients must wait two years following the close of their grant to reapply for funding.

U.S. DEPARTMENT OF HEALTH AND HUMAN SERVICES [2348]

Administration for Community Living
300 C Street, S.W., Room 1317B
Washington, DC 20201
(202) 795-7356
(202) 401-4634
E-mail: robert.groenendaal@acl.hhs.gov
Web Site: acl.gov

FOUNDED: 1978

AREAS OF INTEREST:
Priorities are established annually for certain programs.

NAME(S) OF PROGRAMS:
• **Assistive Technology Programs**

TYPE:
Project/program grants. Assistive Technology Program provides states with financial assistance that supports programs designed to maximize the ability of individuals with disabilities and their family members, guardians, advocates, and authorized representatives to obtain assistive technology devices and assistive technology services.

YEAR PROGRAM STARTED: 1978

PURPOSE:
To support state efforts to improve the provision of assistive technology devices and services to individuals with disabilities of all ages through comprehensive statewide programs of technology-related assistance.

LEGAL BASIS:
Assistive Technology Act of 1998, as amended by Public Law 108-364.

ELIGIBILITY:
Requirements vary according to program. Full information is available on the Administration for Community Living web site.

FINANCIAL DATA:
Amount of support per award: Grants vary in amount depending on type of program.

APPLICATION INFO:
Guidelines are available online.
Duration: Annual formula grant awards.
Deadline: Varies.

ADDRESS INQUIRIES TO:
Robert Groenendaal
Assistive Technology Programs Manager
(See e-mail address above.)

Psychiatry, psychology, mental health

AMERICAN ACADEMY OF CHILD AND ADOLESCENT PSYCHIATRY [2349]

3615 Wisconsin Avenue, N.W.
Washington, DC 20016-3007
(202) 966-7300 ext. 117
Fax: (202) 966-5894
E-mail: aarcher@aacap.org
Web Site: www.aacap.org

FOUNDED: 1953

AREAS OF INTEREST:
Child and adolescent psychiatry.

NAME(S) OF PROGRAMS:
• **Jeanne Spurlock Minority Medical Student Research Fellowship in Substance Abuse and Addiction**
• **Summer Medical Student Fellowship**

TYPE:
Awards/prizes; Conferences/seminars; Fellowships; Research grants; Travel grants. Jeanne Spurlock Minority Medical Student Research Fellowship in Substance Abuse and Addiction provides support for research training in substance abuse and addiction under a mentor with experience in the type of research that is being proposed, and whose work includes children and adolescents participants.

Summer Medical Student Fellowship provides clinical or research training under a child and adolescent psychiatrist mentor.

YEAR PROGRAM STARTED: 1994

PURPOSE:
To increase the number of minority child and adolescent psychiatrists trained in research.

LEGAL BASIS:
Nonprofit organization.

ELIGIBILITY:
Spurlock Minority Medical Student Research Fellowship: Applications are considered from African American, Native American, Alaskan Native, Mexican American, Hispanic, Asian and Pacific Islander students in accredited U.S. medical schools or students whose research will focus on minorities.

GEOG. RESTRICTIONS: United States.

FINANCIAL DATA:
Amount of support per award: Spurlock Fellowship: Up to $4,000, plus travel support for AACAP's Annual Meeting; Summer Fellowship: $3,500, plus travel support for AACAP's Annual Meeting.
Total amount of support: All awards contingent upon available funding.

NO. MOST RECENT APPLICANTS: Spurlock Fellowship: 2 for the year 2018.

NO. AWARDS: Spurlock Fellowship: 3 for the year 2017.

APPLICATION INFO:
E-mail training@aacap.org to receive application materials.
Duration: 12 weeks.
Deadline: March.

PUBLICATIONS:
Program announcement; *Research Notes*, newsletter.

ADDRESS INQUIRIES TO:
Research, Grants and Workforce Department
E-mail: training@aacap.org

AMERICAN ACADEMY OF CHILD AND ADOLESCENT PSYCHIATRY　[2350]

3615 Wisconsin Avenue, N.W.
Washington, DC 20016-3007
(202) 966-7300 ext. 117
Fax: (202) 966-5894
E-mail: aarcher@aacap.org
Web Site: www.aacap.org

FOUNDED: 1953

AREAS OF INTEREST:
Child and adolescent psychiatry.

NAME(S) OF PROGRAMS:
● **Educational Outreach Program**
● **Paramjit Toor Joshi, M.D., International Scholar Awards**
● **Junior Investigator Award**
● **Life Members Mentorship Grant for Medical Students**
● **Pilot Awards**
● **Ülkü Ülgür, M.D., International Scholar Award**

TYPE:
Conferences/seminars; Fellowships; Research grants; Travel grants. Educational Outreach Program provides travel support for residents and CAP fellows to travel to the Annual Meeting and network with child and adolescent psychiatrists.

Joshi International Scholar Awards recognize midcareer international physicians who primarily work with children and adolescents providing mental health services outside the U.S.

Junior Investigator Award is offered for one child and adolescent psychiatry junior faculty to pursue innovative research. The research may be basic or clinical in nature but must be relevant to the understanding, treatment and prevention of child and adolescent mental health disorders. The award also includes the cost of attending AACAP's Annual Meeting for five days.

Life Members Mentorship Grant for Medical Students provides travel support for medical student recipients to receive a formal overview of child and adolescent psychiatry, establish mentor relationships with child and adolescent psychiatrists, and experience AACAP's Annual Meeting.

Pilot Awards are offered to members with a career interest in child and adolescent mental health research.

Ülgür International Scholar Award recognizes a child and adolescent psychiatrist or a physician in the international community who has made significant contributions to the enhancement of mental health services for children and adolescents.

PURPOSE:
To increase the number of minority child and adolescent psychiatrists trained in research.

LEGAL BASIS:
Nonprofit organization.

ELIGIBILITY:
Joshi International Scholar Awards: Qualified international physicians may include pediatricians, family medicine doctors, adult psychiatrists, child and adolescent psychiatrists and other physicians who primarily work with children and adolescents providing mental health services.

FINANCIAL DATA:
Amount of support per award: Educational Outreach Program and Life Members Mentorship Grant for Medical Students: Up to $1,000; Junior Investigator Award: Up to $30,000 per year; Pilot Awards: Up to $15,000. All awards are contingent upon available funding.

NO. MOST RECENT APPLICANTS: Educational Outreach Program: 136; Life Members Mentorship Grant for Medical Students: 56.

NO. AWARDS: Educational Outreach Program: 64; Joshi International Scholar Awards: 2; Junior Investigator Award: 1; Life Members Mentorship Grant for Medical Students: 13; Pilot Awards: 1; Ülgür International Scholar Award: 1.

APPLICATION INFO:
E-mail training@aacap.org to receive application materials.
Duration: Educational Outreach Program, Joshi International Scholar Awards, Life Members Mentorship Grant for Medical Students and Ülgür International Scholar Award: One week. Junior Investigator Award: Two years. Pilot Awards: Up to two years.
Deadline: Educational Outreach Program and Life Members Mentorship Grant: July. Joshi International and Ülgür Scholar Awards: May. Junior Investigator Award: March. Pilot Awards: April.

PUBLICATIONS:
Program announcement; *Research Notes*, newsletter.

ADDRESS INQUIRIES TO:
Research, Grants and Workforce Department
E-mail: training@aacap.org

AMERICAN ACADEMY OF CHILD AND ADOLESCENT PSYCHIATRY　[2351]

3615 Wisconsin Avenue, N.W.
Washington, DC 20016-3007
(202) 966-7300 ext. 117
Fax: (202) 966-5894
E-mail: aarcher@aacap.org
Web Site: www.aacap.org

FOUNDED: 1953

AREAS OF INTEREST:
Child and adolescent psychiatry.

NAME(S) OF PROGRAMS:
● **Marilyn B. Benoit, M.D., Child Maltreatment Mentorship Award**
● **Psychodynamic Faculty Training and Mentorship Initiative**

TYPE:
Project/program grants; Research grants; Travel grants. The Marilyn B. Benoit, M.D., Child Maltreatment Mentorship Award facilitates the completion of a project in which the applicant collaborates with a mentor specializing in the areas of child welfare, foster care, and/or children maltreatment prevention/intervention.

The Psychodynamic Faculty Training and Mentorship Initiative provides a reimbursable travel stipend to cover travel support for attending the required program events during AACAP's Annual Meeting.

PURPOSE:
To increase awareness and interest in the fields of child welfare, foster care, and/or child maltreatment prevention/intervention; to strengthen psychodynamic psychotherapy training in child and adolescent psychiatry residency programs through faculty development.

LEGAL BASIS:
Nonprofit organization.

ELIGIBILITY:
For the Marilyn B. Benoit, M.D., Child Maltreatment Mentorship Award, applicant must:
(1) be a current AACAP member or have a pending membership application submitted;
(2) be either a child and adolescent psychiatry fellow or early career psychiatrist within seven years of graduating a fellowship program and;
(3) have a mentor who has had experience in key issues in the areas of child welfare, foster care and/or child maltreatment prevention/intervention. It is preferred that the mentor's work include children and adolescents.

For the Psychodynamic Faculty Training and Mentorship Initiative, candidate must:
(1) have an M.D., D.O. or equivalent degree;
(2) teach in a child psychiatry, triple board or post-pediatric portal training program;
(3) be affiliated with an ACGME accredited training program and;
(4) be an active AACP member or have a membership application pending at the time of submission.

GEOG. RESTRICTIONS: United States.

FINANCIAL DATA:
Amount of support per award: Marilyn B. Benoit, M.D., Child Maltreatment Mentorship Award: Up to $8,000; Psychodynamic Faculty Training and Mentorship Initiative: $350.

Total amount of support: All awards are contingent upon available funding.

NO. AWARDS: Marilyn B. Benoit, M.D., Child Maltreatment Mentorship Award: 1 or 2; Psychodynamic Faculty Training and Mentorship Initiative: Up to 6.

APPLICATION INFO:
Requirements and application forms are available online.
Duration: Marilyn B. Benoit, M.D., Child Maltreatment Mentorship Award: 12 to 16 weeks; Psychodynamic Faculty Training and Mentorship Initiative: One year.
Deadline: Marilyn B. Benoit, M.D., Child Maltreatment Mentorship Award: April 15; Psychodynamic Faculty Training and Mentorship Initiative: May 1.

PUBLICATIONS:
Program announcement; *Research Notes*, newsletter.

ADDRESS INQUIRIES TO:
Research, Grants and Workforce Department
E-mail: training@aacap.org

AMERICAN PSYCHIATRIC ASSOCIATION [2352]

800 Maine Avenue, S.W.
Suite 900
Washington, DC 20024
(202) 559-3900
(800) 368-5777
Fax: (202) 403-3094
E-mail: lthompson@psych.org
Web Site: www.psychiatry.org

AREAS OF INTEREST:
Psychiatric research.

NAME(S) OF PROGRAMS:
- **Kempf Fund Award for Research Development in Psychobiological Psychiatry**

TYPE:
Awards/prizes; Research grants. The Award supports the research-career development of a young research psychiatrist working in a mentor-trainee relationship with the award winner on further research in the field of schizophrenia.

YEAR PROGRAM STARTED: 1988

PURPOSE:
To recognize a senior researcher who has made a significant contribution to research on the causes and treatment of schizophrenia as both a researcher and a mentor.

ELIGIBILITY:
Applicants must be psychiatrists, American Psychiatric Association members and citizens or permanent residents of the U.S. or Canada.

FINANCIAL DATA:
Amount of support per award: $1,500 award to the senior researcher and $20,000 for support of the research-career development of a young research psychiatrist working in a mentor-trainee relationship with the award winner on further research in this field.

APPLICATION INFO:
Applicants are required to submit their application to the e-mail address above with the subject of the e-mail entitled "Kempf Fund Award."
Duration: One year. Nonrenewable.
Deadline: August 15.

ADDRESS INQUIRIES TO:
Laura Thompson, M.S.
(See e-mail address above.)

AMERICAN PSYCHIATRIC ASSOCIATION [2353]

800 Maine Avenue, Suite 900
Washington, DC 20023
(202) 559-3900
(800) 368-5777
Fax: (202) 403-3094
E-mail: podai-afotey@psych.org
mfp@psych.org
Web Site: www.psychiatry.org/residents

AREAS OF INTEREST:
Psychiatric research and mental health disparities.

NAME(S) OF PROGRAMS:
- **American Psychiatric Leadership Fellowship**
- **APA Child & Adolescent Psychiatry Fellowship**
- **APA Public Psychiatry Fellowship**
- **APA SAMHSA Minority Fellowships**

TYPE:
Fellowships. American Psychiatric Leadership Fellowship: This two-year fellowship offers psychiatric residents, with exceptional leadership potential, many different experiences that prepare them for leadership roles. Only the Chair of the Department or the Director of the Training Program can nominate.

APA Child & Adolescent Psychiatry Fellowship: This fellowship is designed to promote interest among general psychiatry residents in pursuing careers in child and adolescent psychiatry. Fellows will learn about new clinical research, successful treatments for children and adolescents with mental disorders and many other issues associated with child and adolescent mental health.

APA Public Psychiatry Fellowship: This fellowship aims to create the next generation of leaders in public psychiatry. Fellows will participate in APA activities, plan workshops at IPS, and interact with thought leaders in the field of public psychiatry.

APA SAMHSA Minority Fellowships: These fellowships endeavor to eliminate racial and ethnic disparities in mental health and substance abuse care by providing specialized training to psychiatry residents and medical students interested in serving minority communities.

PURPOSE:
To promote psychiatric research.

ELIGIBILITY:
Applicant must be in a psychiatry residency training program.

FINANCIAL DATA:
Amount of support per award: APA SAMHSA Minority Fellowships: $25,000 to $28,000, based on postgraduate year.

NO. MOST RECENT APPLICANTS: 10 to 20 per fellowship.

NO. AWARDS: Varies pending funding.

APPLICATION INFO:
Applications must be submitted online.
Duration: American Psychiatric Leadership and APA Public Psychiatry Fellowships: Two years. APA SAMHSA Minority Fellowships: One year. Optional second year with reapplication.
Deadline: January 31.

ADDRESS INQUIRIES TO:
APA Fellowship Programs
(See address above.)

AMERICAN PSYCHIATRIC ASSOCIATION [2354]

800 Maine Avenue, Suite 900
Washington, DC 20023
(202) 559-3900
(800) 368-5777
Fax: (202) 403-3094
E-mail: dclarke@psych.org
podai-afotey@psych.org
Web Site: www.psychiatry.org/residents

AREAS OF INTEREST:
Psychiatric research.

NAME(S) OF PROGRAMS:
- **Psychiatric Research Fellowship**
- **Jeanne Spurlock, M.D. Congressional Fellowship**

TYPE:
Fellowships; Travel grants. Psychiatric Research Fellowship sponsors one postgraduate psychiatry trainee specifically to focus on research and personal scholarship.

Jeanne Spurlock, M.D. Congressional Fellowship provides a psychiatry resident or early career psychiatrist an opportunity to work in a congressional office on federal health policy, particularly policy related to child and/or minority issues.

ELIGIBILITY:
Applicant must be in a psychiatry residency training program or an early career psychiatrist.

FINANCIAL DATA:
Amount of support per award: Psychiatric Research Fellowship: $45,000 stipend; Spurlock Fellowship: $85,000 stipend.

NO. AWARDS: 1 per award.

APPLICATION INFO:
Applications must be submitted online.
Duration: Psychiatric Research Fellowship: Two years. Spurlock Fellowship: 10 months.
Deadline: January 31.

ADDRESS INQUIRIES TO:
APA Fellowship Programs
(See address above.)

AMERICAN PSYCHOLOGICAL ASSOCIATION [2355]

Minority Fellowship Program/APA
750 First Street, N.E.
Washington, DC 20002-4242
(202) 336-6127
Fax: (202) 336-6012
E-mail: mfp@apa.org
Web Site: www.apa.org/pi/mfp

FOUNDED: 1892

AREAS OF INTEREST:
Psychology.

NAME(S) OF PROGRAMS:
- **MFP Services for Transition Age Youth**

TYPE:
Fellowships.

YEAR PROGRAM STARTED: 2014

PURPOSE:
To support training of Master's level practitioners in mental health services.

LEGAL BASIS:
Nonprofit.

ELIGIBILITY:
Applicant must:
(1) be U.S. citizens, noncitizen nationals, or permanent residents;
(2) have a strong commitment to a career in mental health services with ethnic minority transition age youth and their families;
(3) be enrolled full-time in a terminal Master's program in psychology;
(4) be on track to graduate and/or receive the specialist/certificate portion of their Master's Program at any time during 2022 for the 2021 deadline and;
(5) be prepared to enter the field as a mental health practitioner immediately upon graduation.

It is not required for applicants to identify as ethnic minorities; however, African-Americans, Alaska Natives, American Indians, Asian-Americans, Hispanics/Latinos, Native Hawaiians and Pacific Islanders are especially encouraged to apply.

FINANCIAL DATA:
Amount of support per award: Up to
$10,000.

CO-OP FUNDING PROGRAMS: Funding for
services training is made available through
Substance Abuse and Mental Health Services
Administration allocations.

NO. AWARDS: 23.

APPLICATION INFO:
Applications are available mid-October to
January 15. Guidelines are available online.
Duration: One academic year, in last year of
Master's Program.
Deadline: January 15. Announcement by
April.

ADDRESS INQUIRIES TO:
Minority Fellowship Program
(See telephone and e-mail address above.)

AMERICAN PSYCHOLOGICAL
ASSOCIATION   [2356]
Government Relations Office
Public Interest Directorate
750 First Street, N.E.
Washington, DC 20002-4242
(202) 336-5931
Fax: (202) 336-6063
E-mail: gtwose@apa.org
Web Site: www.apa.org/about/gr/fellows/index.
aspx

FOUNDED: 1892

AREAS OF INTEREST:
Professional organization to advance
psychology as a science and profession and
as a means of promoting health, education
and human welfare.

NAME(S) OF PROGRAMS:
● **APA Congressional Fellowship
  Program**

TYPE:
Fellowships. Program provides trained
scientists and practitioners an opportunity for
enhanced understanding of and involvement
in the federal policymaking process by
serving as congressional staff in Washington,
DC.

YEAR PROGRAM STARTED: 1974

PURPOSE:
To provide an opportunity for psychologists
to participate in the policymaking process.

LEGAL BASIS:
Nonprofit professional organization.

ELIGIBILITY:
Doctoral degree in psychology and APA
membership required. Two years of
postdoctoral experience is preferred.
Individuals with sabbatical funds are eligible.
Must be U.S. citizen and willing to relocate
to Washington, DC.

GEOG. RESTRICTIONS: United States.

FINANCIAL DATA:
Amount of support per award: For the year
2019-20: $75,000 to $90,000, depending on
years of postdoctoral experience. Up to
$3,750 is allocated per Fellow for relocation
to the Washington, DC area and for travel
expenses during the year.
Total amount of support: Varies.

CO-OP FUNDING PROGRAMS: Fellowship is
sponsored by the APA in cooperation with
the American Association for the

Advancement of Science and with funds
from the American Psychological Foundation
Goldman Fellowship.

NO. AWARDS: Up to 2.

APPLICATION INFO:
Completed online application form,
curriculum vitae, three letters of reference
and a statement of interest are required.
Duration: September through August.
Nonrenewable.
Deadline: Early January. Announcement in
March.

STAFF:
Gabriel Twose, Program Director

ADDRESS INQUIRIES TO:
Gabriel Twose, Program Director
APA Congressional Fellowship Program
(See telephone and e-mail address above.)

AMERICAN PSYCHOLOGICAL
ASSOCIATION   [2357]
Minority Fellowship Program/APA
750 First Street, N.E.
Washington, DC 20002-4242
(202) 336-6127
Fax: (202) 336-6012
E-mail: mfp@apa.org
Web Site: www.apa.org/pi/mfp

FOUNDED: 1892

AREAS OF INTEREST:
Psychology.

NAME(S) OF PROGRAMS:
● **MFP Mental Health and Substance
  Abuse Services Fellowship**

TYPE:
Fellowships. Fellowship is geared to those
pursuing careers as practitioners specializing
in the delivery of behavioral health services
to ethnic minority populations. Students
specializing in clinical, school and counseling
psychology are encouraged to apply.

YEAR PROGRAM STARTED: 1974

PURPOSE:
To provide financial support, professional
development activities, and guidance to
promising doctoral students, postdoctoral
trainees and early career professionals with
the goals of promoting culturally competent
behavioral health services and increasing the
number of ethnic minority psychologists
providing behavioral health services to and
developing policy for ethnic minority
populations.

LEGAL BASIS:
Nonprofit.

ELIGIBILITY:
Applicants must:
(1) be citizens, noncitizen nationals, or
permanent residents of the U.S.;
(2) have a strong commitment to a career in
ethnic minority behavioral health services or
policy;
(3) be enrolled full-time in an
APA-accredited doctoral program during the
fall term immediately following the
application deadline and;
(4) not be interns.

It is not required for applicants to identify as
ethnic minorities; however,
African-Americans, Alaska Natives,
American Indians, Asian-Americans,
Hispanics/Latinos, Native Hawaiians and
Pacific Islanders are especially encouraged to
apply.

FINANCIAL DATA:
Amount of support per award: Follows
NRSA guidelines.

CO-OP FUNDING PROGRAMS: Funding for
services training is made available through
the Substance Abuse and Mental Health
Services Administration allocations.

NO. MOST RECENT APPLICANTS: 145.

NO. AWARDS: Generally 5% to 7% acceptance
rate.

APPLICATION INFO:
Applications are available mid-October to
January 15. Guidelines are available online.
Duration: One academic year. Renewable for
up to two additional years.
Deadline: January 15. Announcement by
April.

ADDRESS INQUIRIES TO:
Minority Fellowship Program
(See telephone and e-mail address above.)

AMERICAN PSYCHOSOMATIC
SOCIETY   [2358]
6728 Old McLean Village Drive
McLean, VA 22101
(703) 556-9222
Fax: (703) 556-8729
E-mail: info@psychosomatic.org
Web Site: www.psychosomatic.org

FOUNDED: 1942

AREAS OF INTEREST:
Psychosomatic medicine.

NAME(S) OF PROGRAMS:
● **Patricia R. Barchas Award in
  Sociophysiology**

TYPE:
Awards/prizes.

YEAR PROGRAM STARTED: 1999

PURPOSE:
To further the field of sociophysiology, the
study of the reciprocal relationships that
could lead to long-term change both in social
behavior and in physiology.

ELIGIBILITY:
Applicant must have accomplished interesting
and exciting work to expand knowledge of
the interface of the social and psychological
worlds.

FINANCIAL DATA:
Amount of support per award: $1,500,
complimentary meeting registration and a
plaque, which is presented at the Annual
Meeting.

NO. AWARDS: 1.

APPLICATION INFO:
Nominations should include a 500- to
1,000-word justification for the nomination
and an updated curriculum vitae.
Duration: One-time award.
Deadline: November 1.

IRS I.D.: 11-1866747

ADDRESS INQUIRIES TO:
Awards Committee
(See address above.)

AMERICAN PSYCHOSOMATIC SOCIETY [2359]

6728 Old McLean Village Drive
McLean, VA 22101
(703) 556-9222
Fax: (703) 556-8729
E-mail: info@psychosomatic.org
Web Site: www.psychosomatic.org

FOUNDED: 1942

AREAS OF INTEREST:
Psychosomatic medicine.

NAME(S) OF PROGRAMS:
● **Distinguished Scientist Award**

TYPE:
Awards/prizes.

YEAR PROGRAM STARTED: 2012

PURPOSE:
To acknowledge senior scientists and physicians who have made an important and protracted contribution in the field of psychosomatic medicine.

ELIGIBILITY:
Recipients must be senior scientists and physicians who have made an important and protracted contribution in any research field within the Society's areas of interest. Nominees should be members of the Society and would be expected to have contributed substantially over the years to its aims and goals.

FINANCIAL DATA:
Amount of support per award: $1,500, a commemorative plaque and complimentary meeting registration.

NO. AWARDS: 1.

APPLICATION INFO:
Nominations should include a 500- to 1,000-word justification for the nomination and an updated curriculum vitae of the nominee.
Duration: One-time award.
Deadline: November 1.

ADDRESS INQUIRIES TO:
Award Committee
(See address above.)

AMERICAN PSYCHOSOMATIC SOCIETY [2360]

6728 Old McLean Village Drive
McLean, VA 22101
(703) 556-9222
Fax: (703) 556-8729
E-mail: info@psychosomatic.org
Web Site: www.psychosomatic.org

FOUNDED: 1942

AREAS OF INTEREST:
Psychosomatic medicine.

NAME(S) OF PROGRAMS:
● **Paul D. MacLean Award**

TYPE:
Awards/prizes. This award is intended to honor Dr. Paul D. MacLean and promote the line of research that he created on emotion, the brain and physical disease.

YEAR PROGRAM STARTED: 2010

PURPOSE:
To reward outstanding neuroscience research in psychosomatic medicine.

ELIGIBILITY:
Nominee must have performed outstanding neuroscientific research (human or animal)

that advances knowledge directly related to Dr. MacLean's hypothesis regarding altered cortical-subcortical interactions affecting physical disease outcomes or mediating processes (e.g., autonomic, neuroendocrine, immune) that can be directly linked to disease outcomes.

Individuals may self-nominate.

FINANCIAL DATA:
Amount of support per award: Up to $1,000 in travel expenses, complimentary meeting registration, a plaque and the opportunity to give a talk at the APS Annual Meeting.

NO. AWARDS: 1.

APPLICATION INFO:
Nominations should include a 500- to 1,000-word supporting statement, the nominee's curriculum vitae and three representative reprints.
Deadline: November 1.

IRS I.D.: 11-1866747

ADDRESS INQUIRIES TO:
Award Committee
(See address above.)

AMERICAN PSYCHOSOMATIC SOCIETY [2361]

6728 Old McLean Village Drive
McLean, VA 22101
(703) 556-9222
Fax: (703) 556-8729
E-mail: info@psychosomatic.org
Web Site: www.psychosomatic.org

FOUNDED: 1942

AREAS OF INTEREST:
Psychosomatic medicine.

NAME(S) OF PROGRAMS:
● **Herbert Weiner Early Career Award for Contributions to Psychosomatic Society**

TYPE:
Awards/prizes.

YEAR PROGRAM STARTED: 1991

PURPOSE:
To support individuals who show substantial promise in continuing study in psychosomatic medicine.

LEGAL BASIS:
Not-for-profit organization.

ELIGIBILITY:
Nominees must be fewer than 10 years past their final academic degree and must be members of the American Psychosomatic Society.

FINANCIAL DATA:
Amount of support per award: $1,000, plaque, complimentary meeting registration and an opportunity to present the research for which the award was given during the annual meeting of the Society.

NO. MOST RECENT APPLICANTS: 5.

NO. AWARDS: 1.

APPLICATION INFO:
Nominations must include a 500- to 1,000-word justification for the nomination, an updated curriculum vitae and reprints of the two to six publications of the work for which the nomination is being made.
Duration: One-time award.
Deadline: November 1.

PUBLICATIONS:
Award announcement.

IRS I.D.: 11-1866747

ADDRESS INQUIRIES TO:
Award Committee
(See address above.)

ANNA-MONIKA-FOUNDATION [2362]

Kieshecker Weg 240
D-40468 Duesseldorf Germany
(49) 211 437187 13
Fax: (49) 211 437187 23
E-mail: m.bommers@gospax.com
Web Site: anna-monika-stiftung.de

FOUNDED: 1965

AREAS OF INTEREST:
Biochemistry, neurophysiology, neuropathology, psychopharmacology, psychiatry, depression and psychosomatic illnesses.

NAME(S) OF PROGRAMS:
● **The Anna-Monika-Foundation Prize**

TYPE:
Awards/prizes. Prizes for research papers investigating the biological substrate and functional disturbances of depression. Prize-winning lectures will be published in *Pharmacopsychiatry*.

YEAR PROGRAM STARTED: 1966

PURPOSE:
To support international pioneering research in the area of depression research.

LEGAL BASIS:
Private foundation, authorized by the state of Nordrhein-Westfalen, Germany.

ELIGIBILITY:
As far as possible, the papers describing the studies should feature information about the recent advances and the knowledge that should be helpful in promoting treatment and open new paths of scientific progress in depression. Papers published in the last two years in an international scientific peer-reviewed journal may be submitted. Papers should be written in English.

FINANCIAL DATA:
Total amount of support: EUR 25,000.

NO. AWARDS: Maximum of 3 biennially in odd-numbered years.

APPLICATION INFO:
A maximum of three publications (in sets of four copies) plus a short summary (approximately 600 words) emphasizing the relevance and importance of the research are required. A curriculum vitae and summary of achievements in the field should be added; hitherto unpublished studies or papers published in an international professional journal within the past two years may also be submitted. Papers may be written in English and should be submitted to the Chairman of the Jury by e-mail to Rainer.Rupprecht@medbo.de.
Deadline: February 28.

ADDRESS INQUIRIES TO:
Michael Bommers, Managing Director
(See address above.)

ASSOCIATION FOR BEHAVIORAL AND COGNITIVE THERAPIES [2363]

305 Seventh Avenue
16th Floor
New York, NY 10001
(212) 647-1890
Fax: (212) 647-1865
E-mail: mjeimer@abct.org
Web Site: www.abct.org

AREAS OF INTEREST:
Behavior therapy and cognitive behavior therapy.

NAME(S) OF PROGRAMS:
● **Virginia Roswell Dissertation Award**

TYPE:
Awards/prizes.

PURPOSE:
To explore the application of behavioral and cognitive sciences to understanding human behavior, developing interventions to enhance the human condition, and promoting the appropriate utilization of these interventions.

ELIGIBILITY:
Applicant must be an AABT student member who has already had their dissertation proposal approved and be investigating an area of direct relevance to behavior therapy or cognitive behavior therapy.

FINANCIAL DATA:
Amount of support per award: $1,000.

NO. AWARDS: 1.

APPLICATION INFO:
All candidates must be nominated. Contact the Organization for nomination procedures.
Deadline: March.

ADDRESS INQUIRIES TO:
M.J. Eimer, Executive Director
(See address above.)

ASSOCIATION FOR BEHAVIORAL AND COGNITIVE THERAPIES [2364]

305 Seventh Avenue
16th Floor
New York, NY 10001
(212) 647-1890
Fax: (212) 647-1865
E-mail: mjeimer@abct.org
Web Site: www.abct.org

AREAS OF INTEREST:
Behavior therapy and cognitive sciences.

NAME(S) OF PROGRAMS:
● **President's New Researcher Award**

TYPE:
Awards/prizes.

PURPOSE:
To explore the application of behavioral and cognitive sciences to understanding human behavior, developing interventions to enhance the human condition, and promoting the appropriate utilization of these interventions.

ELIGIBILITY:
Must be authored by an individual with five years or less posttraining experience and have been published in the last two years or currently in press.

FINANCIAL DATA:
Amount of support per award: $500.

NO. AWARDS: 1.

APPLICATION INFO:
Contact the Organization for application procedures.
Deadline: March.

ADDRESS INQUIRIES TO:
M.J. Eimer, Executive Director
(See address above.)

AUTISM SPEAKS INC.

1060 State Road, 2nd Floor
Princeton, NJ 08540
(609) 228-7313
E-mail: jnew@autismspeaks.org
Web Site: www.autismspeaks.org

TYPE:
Project/program grants; Research grants. Research grants that are in line with Autism Speaks research priorities.

See entry 2041 for full listing.

BRAIN & BEHAVIOR RESEARCH FOUNDATION [2365]

747 Third Avenue, 33rd Floor
New York, NY 10017
(800) 829-8289
Fax: (646) 681-4891
E-mail: grants@bbrfoundation.org
Web Site: www.bbrfoundation.org

FOUNDED: 1987

AREAS OF INTEREST:
Mental health, brain and behavior disorders.

NAME(S) OF PROGRAMS:
● **NARSAD Distinguished Investigator Grant**
● **NARSAD Independent Investigator Grant**
● **NARSAD Young Investigator Grant**

TYPE:
Research grants. Distinguished Investigator Grant supports senior investigators (professor or equivalent level) who maintain a laboratory and who propose an innovative and new direction in their research with a one-year grant to encourage pursuit of innovative projects in schizophrenia, affective disorders, or other serious mental illnesses.

Independent Investigator Grant is intended for the scientist at the academic level of associate professor or equivalent, who has won national competitive support as a principal investigator. Assistant professors who have NIH R01s and equivalent are also eligible. The program is intended to facilitate innovative research opportunities.

Young Investigator Grant enables promising investigators to either extend their research fellowship training or to begin careers as independent research faculty.

PURPOSE:
To raise and distribute funds for scientific research into the causes, cures, treatments and prevention of severe psychiatric brain disorders.

LEGAL BASIS:
Private, not-for-profit organization.

ELIGIBILITY:
Applicant must hold a doctoral-level degree and be affiliated with a university or research institution.

For the Distinguished Investigator Grant, applicant must be a full professor (or professional equivalent) who maintains a laboratory.

For the Independent Investigator Grant, applicant must be at associate professor level with national competitive support as a principal investigator. Assistant professors who have NIH R01s and equivalent are also eligible.

For the Young Investigator Grant, applicant must be advanced postdoctoral fellow through assistant professor (or equivalent) to either extend research fellowship training or to begin career as independent research faculty. Basic and/or clinical investigators are supported, but research must be relevant to schizophrenia, major affective disorders or other serious mental illnesses.

FINANCIAL DATA:
Amount of support per award: Distinguished Investigator: $100,000; Independent Investigator: $50,000 per year for two years; Young Investigator: Up to $35,000 per year for up to two years.

NO. MOST RECENT APPLICANTS: Young Investigator: Over 900 for the year 2019.

NO. AWARDS: Distinguished Investigator: 15; Independent Investigator: 40; Young Investigator: 200 for the year 2019.

APPLICATION INFO:
Guidelines are available on the Foundation web site.
Duration: Distinguished Investigator Grant: One-year, one-time award; Independent Investigator Grant: Two-year, one-time award; Young Investigator Grant: One or two years. May not apply more than twice for initial grant and more than once for second grant.
Deadline: Varies.

IRS I.D.: 31-1020010

STAFF:
Jeff Borenstein, President and Chief Executive Officer
Lou Innamorato, Vice President, Finance and Chief Financial Officer
Lauren Duran, Vice President, Communications, Marketing and Public Relations
Faith Rothblatt, Vice President of Development
Sho Tin Chen, Director, Research Grants
Nieves Ortiz, Manager of Donor-based Management
Grace Nagaur, Manager, Research Grants
John Bayat, Senior Accountant
Mike Kirsic, Senior Accountant

ADDRESS INQUIRIES TO:
Grants Management
(See address above.)

JAMES MCKEEN CATTELL FUND [2366]

Duke University
Genome Sciences Research Building II, 3rd floor
572 Research Drive, Box 91050
Durham, NC 27708
(919) 660-5638
Fax: (919) 660-5726
E-mail: williams@psych.duke.edu
Web Site: www.cattell.duke.edu

FOUNDED: 1941

NAME(S) OF PROGRAMS:
● **James McKeen Cattell Fund Sabbatical Fellowships for Psychologists**

TYPE:
Fellowships. The fellowship provides funds to supplement the regular sabbatical allowance provided by the recipients' home institutions.

YEAR PROGRAM STARTED: 1942

PURPOSE:
To promote scientific research and the dissemination of knowledge with the object of obtaining results beneficial to the development of the science of psychology.

LEGAL BASIS:
Tax-exempt foundation.

ELIGIBILITY:
The awards are available to psychologists who are faculty members at colleges and universities in the U.S. and Canada and are eligible, according to the regulations of their own institutions, for a sabbatical leave or its equivalent.

GEOG. RESTRICTIONS: United States and Canada.

FINANCIAL DATA:
Amount of support per award: Up to $40,000.
Total amount of support: Varies.

NO. MOST RECENT APPLICANTS: 45 for the year 2019.

NO. AWARDS: 1 to 4 per year.

APPLICATION INFO:
Fellowship application is available at the Fund web site.
Duration: One academic year.
Deadline: January 15.

TRUSTEES AND OFFICERS:
Peter A. Ornstein, Managing Trustee
Christina L. Williams, Secretary-Treasurer
Robert W. Levenson
Scott E. Maxwell
Sharon Thompson-Schill

ADDRESS INQUIRIES TO:
Dr. Christina L. Williams
Secretary-Treasurer
(See address above.)

COUNCIL ON SOCIAL WORK EDUCATION
1701 Duke Street, Suite 200
Alexandria, VA 22314-3457
(703) 683-8080
Fax: (703) 683-8099
E-mail: dnguyen@cswe.org
Web Site: www.cswe.org

TYPE:
Fellowships. Awards for doctoral-level studies in social work, specializing in mental health and substance abuse-related education, research, policy and practice.

See entry 905 for full listing.

DEPARTMENT OF VETERANS AFFAIRS [2367]
Associated Health Education (10X1)
Office of Academic Affiliations
810 Vermont Avenue, N.W.
Washington, DC 20420
(202) 461-9877
E-mail: stacy.pommer@va.gov
Web Site: www.psychologytraining.va.gov

FOUNDED: 1946

AREAS OF INTEREST:
Veterans' mental health.

NAME(S) OF PROGRAMS:
● **VA Psychology Training Program**

TYPE:
Fellowships; Internships. Stipends for internship and postdoctoral training in clinical or counseling psychology. Provides one year of supervised training in the skills and techniques of these specialty areas. Participants have no obligation to remain with the VA after completion of training.

YEAR PROGRAM STARTED: 1946

PURPOSE:
To provide a source of highly qualified psychologists who are interested in the direct delivery of professional services in federal, state, and community facilities; to provide internship training to students enrolled in doctoral programs in clinical or counseling psychology from those schools accredited by the American Psychological Association (APA), Canadian Psychological Association (CPA), or Psychological Clinical Science Accreditation System (PCSAS); to provide postdoctoral fellowships to graduates of clinical or counseling psychology doctoral programs accredited by the APA, CPA, or PCSAS and internships that are accredited by APA or CPA.

LEGAL BASIS:
Federal agency.

ELIGIBILITY:
Applicant must be a U.S. citizen. Prospective intern must be enrolled in an academic graduate program leading to the doctoral degree in clinical or counseling psychology from an APA-, CPA-, or PCSAS-accredited program. Prospective postdoctoral fellow must have completed a doctoral program in clinical or counseling psychology from an APA-, CPA-, or PCSAS-accredited program and an internship accredited by APA or CPA.

FINANCIAL DATA:
Amount of support per award: Stipend of $26,166 to $31,589 for full-time interns and $46,102 to $58,665 for full-time postdoctoral fellows.
Total amount of support: Varies.

NO. AWARDS: 711 intern positions at 131 sites and 454 postdoctoral residency positions at 70 sites for academic year 2019-20.

APPLICATION INFO:
Interested persons should contact the Director of Psychology Training at the VA Medical Center they are interested in.
Duration: One year. Occasionally two years for postdoctoral residencies.
Deadline: November.

ADDRESS INQUIRIES TO:
Chief of Psychology Service or Director of Psychology Training at a local VA Medical Center

ALBERT ELLIS INSTITUTE [2368]
145 East 32nd Street, 9th Floor
New York, NY 10016
(212) 535-0822
Fax: (212) 249-3582
E-mail: krisdoyle@albertellis.org
Web Site: www.albertellis.org

FOUNDED: 1968

AREAS OF INTEREST:
Psychotherapy.

CONSULTING OR VOLUNTEER SERVICES:
Work-study positions offered.

NAME(S) OF PROGRAMS:
● **Postgraduate Clinical Fellowship Training Program at the Albert Ellis Institute**

TYPE:
Conferences/seminars; Fellowships; Internships; Work-study programs. Postdoctoral fellowships and internships in cognitive behavior therapy for a comprehensive program, featuring intensive supervision of individual and group clients seen at the Institute's clinic, seminars and workshops.

YEAR PROGRAM STARTED: 1969

PURPOSE:
To train professionals in cognitive behavioral and Rational Emotive Behavior Therapy.

LEGAL BASIS:
501(c)(3) nonprofit organization.

ELIGIBILITY:
Applicant must have a Ph.D. in psychology, M.D., M.S.W. or R.N.

NO. MOST RECENT APPLICANTS: 30.

NO. AWARDS: 6.

APPLICATION INFO:
Application form and information are available online.
Duration: One to two years.
Deadline: February 15.

ADDRESS INQUIRIES TO:
Dr. Kristene Doyle, Director
(See address above.)

*PLEASE NOTE:
Training takes place in New York City.

FONDATION DES ETATS-UNIS
15, boulevard Jourdan
75014 Paris France
(33) 1 53 80 68 80
Fax: (33) 1 53 80 68 99
E-mail: culture@feusa.org
Web Site: www.feusa.org/harriet-hale-woolley-scholarship

TYPE:
Awards/prizes; Development grants; Scholarships. Bequeathed to the Fondation des Etats-Unis, Cite Internationale Universitaire de Paris in the early 1930s, the Harriet Hale Woolley Scholarship is awarded annually to a select number of exceptional American artists and musicians who plan to pursue their studies in Paris.

A scholarship is also available to French, Swiss and American medical postgraduates specializing in psychiatry with an internship in a Parisian hospital.

The scholarship is not intended for research in art history or musicology, nor for dance or theater.

See entry 713 for full listing.

FOUNDATION FOR EDUCATION AND RESEARCH IN BIOFEEDBACK AND RELATED SCIENCES (FERB) [2369]

1230 South Federal Highway
Boynton Beach, FL 33435
(561) 742-7122
Fax: (561) 742-7452
E-mail: ferbfound@gmail.com
Web Site: www.aapb.org

FOUNDED: 1969

AREAS OF INTEREST:
Biofeedback and psychophysiology.

TYPE:
Travel grants.

PURPOSE:
To advance the development, dissemination and utilization of knowledge about applied psychophysiology and biofeedback to improve health and the quality of life through research, education and practice.

ELIGIBILITY:
Must be a full-time student pursuing a professional or doctoral degree in a health-related field.

FINANCIAL DATA:
Total amount of support: Varies.

NO. AWARDS: Varies.

APPLICATION INFO:
Contact the Organization for application procedures.
Deadline: February 20.

INTERNATIONAL OCD FOUNDATION [2370]

18 Tremont Street, Suite 308
Boston, MA 02108
(617) 973-5801
Fax: (617) 973-5803
E-mail: info@iocdf.org
Web Site: www.iocdf.org

FOUNDED: 1986

AREAS OF INTEREST:
Obsessive-compulsive disorders and obsessive compulsive spectrum disorder.

NAME(S) OF PROGRAMS:
● **Annual Conference**
● **Behavior Therapy Training Institute (BTTI)**
● **Research Awards**

TYPE:
Awards/prizes; Conferences/seminars; Research grants. The International OCD Foundation is committed to finding and promoting the most effective treatment methods for OCD and related disorders. Research is vital to better understanding OCD and related disorders, and improving treatment. To help achieve these goals, each year the IOCDF awards research grants to promising studies thanks to generous donors from within the OCD community. The IOCDF awards grants to investigators whose research focuses on the nature, causes, and treatment of OCD and related disorders.

YEAR PROGRAM STARTED: 1986

PURPOSE:
To increase access to effective treatment; to end the stigma associated with mental health issues; to foster a community for those affected by OCD and the professionals who treat them.

ELIGIBILITY:
Research Awards: Investigators whose research focuses on the nature, causes and treatment of OCD and related disorders are eligible to apply. Junior investigators are encouraged to apply. Senior investigators may also ask for grant funding for projects that would provide pilot data for future larger-scale federal grant applications.

FINANCIAL DATA:
Awards do not cover indirect or travel costs.
Amount of support per award: Varies.
Total amount of support: Varies.

NO. MOST RECENT APPLICANTS: Approximately 50.

NO. AWARDS: 3.

APPLICATION INFO:
Application information is available on the web site. Applicants can request application guidelines from the Foundation.
Duration: One to two years.
Deadline: January.

PUBLICATIONS:
OCD Newsletter.

IRS I.D.: 22-2894564

STAFF:
Jeff Szymanski, Ph.D., Executive Director
Melissa Smith, Event Manager

ADDRESS INQUIRIES TO:
See e-mail address above.

THE KLINGENSTEIN THIRD GENERATION FOUNDATION [2371]

80 8th Avenue
Suite 1400
New York, NY 10011
(332) 219-0601
E-mail: info@klingenstein.org
Web Site: www.ktgf.org

FOUNDED: 1993

AREAS OF INTEREST:
Child and adolescent depression and ADHD.

TYPE:
Fellowships; Research grants. The Foundation funds research and other programs related to childhood and adolescent ADHD and depression. All funding is directed towards three research fellowship programs (funding postdoctoral research in ADHD, depression and access to care) and the medical student training program. The Foundation does not accept general applications for project or research funding.

YEAR PROGRAM STARTED: 1993

PURPOSE:
To address the need for further research in pediatric ADHD and pediatric depression, and the need to cultivate more child and adolescent psychiatrists and psychologists.

LEGAL BASIS:
Family foundation.

ELIGIBILITY:
The Foundation makes fellowship grants to medical institutions that have nominated research projects led by outstanding postdoctoral candidates.

The Foundation is prohibited from making grants to political action groups and from lobbying the government, and makes no grants to individuals.

FINANCIAL DATA:
Amount of support per award: Fellowships: $30,000 per year.

NO. AWARDS: Fellowships: Up to 5.

APPLICATION INFO:
Applications must be submitted online.
Duration: Fellowships: Two years.
Deadline: Fellowship nominations: November 15.

ADDRESS INQUIRIES TO:
See e-mail address above.

*PLEASE NOTE:
The Foundation does not accept unsolicited applications.

DELLA MARTIN FOUNDATION [2372]

333 South Hope Street
43rd Floor
Los Angeles, CA 90071
(213) 617-4143
Fax: (213) 620-1398
E-mail: lgould@sheppardmullin.com

FOUNDED: 1975

AREAS OF INTEREST:
Mental health research.

TYPE:
Endowments; Fellowships; Professorships. Foundation has endowed four university chairs for mental health research and seven postdoctoral mental health research fellowships.

YEAR PROGRAM STARTED: 1975

PURPOSE:
To promote research into causes of and cures for mental illness.

LEGAL BASIS:
Nonprofit foundation.

ELIGIBILITY:
For southern California tax-exempt organizations only. No grants are made to individuals.

GEOG. RESTRICTIONS: Southern California.

FINANCIAL DATA:
Amount of support per award: Varies.
Total amount of support: $450,000 annually.
Matching fund requirements: Generally 1:1.

NO. MOST RECENT APPLICANTS: 20.

NO. AWARDS: 1 annually.

REPRESENTATIVE AWARDS:
$450,000 to California Institute of Technology for endowment of postdoctoral research fellowships.

APPLICATION INFO:
Send brief letter to the Foundation describing grant request.

IRS I.D.: 23-7444954

ADDRESS INQUIRIES TO:
Laurence K. Gould, Jr., Chairperson
(See address above.)

NATIONAL INSTITUTE OF MENTAL HEALTH [2373]

6001 Executive Boulevard, Room 6146
Bethesda, MD 20892
(301) 443-1368
E-mail: jnoronha@mail.nih.gov
Web Site: www.nimh.nih.gov

FOUNDED: 1948

AREAS OF INTEREST:
Basic neuroscience, genetics, basic behavioral science aimed at understanding mental disorders, research training, resource and technology development and drug discovery; translational research on the mechanisms of adult psychopathology and the development of novel treatment approaches for adult mental disorders; integrated research and research training that translates knowledge from basic/behavioral science into a better understanding of pediatric psychopathology and the development of novel treatment and prevention strategies; research on mechanisms and interventions on the interrelationship of physical and mental health; mental health research on AIDS that includes studies that range from the molecular and cellular basis of HIV/AIDS CNS infection to the domestic and international dissemination of effective preventative interventions; research that evaluates the effectiveness of treatment and preventive mental health interventions and mental health services research.

TYPE:
Development grants; Fellowships; Project/program grants; Research grants; Training grants; Research contracts.

YEAR PROGRAM STARTED: 1948

PURPOSE:
To support innovative science that will profoundly transform the diagnosis, treatment and prevention of mental disorders, paving the way for a cure; to reduce the burden of mental illness and behavioral disorders through research on mind, brain and behavior.

LEGAL BASIS:
Government agency.

ELIGIBILITY:
Public, private, profit or nonprofit agencies, including state and local government agencies, eligible Federal agencies, universities, colleges, hospitals, and academic or research institutions may apply for research grants. SBIR grants can be awarded only to domestic small businesses, and STTR grants can be awarded only to domestic small businesses which partner with a research institution in cooperative research and development.

An applicant for individual predoctoral fellowship support must be enrolled in a research doctoral degree program by the proposed activation date of the fellowship. A postdoctoral applicant must have received a Ph.D., Psy.D., M.D., D.D.S., Sc.D., D.N.S., D.O., D.S.W., or equivalent degree from an accredited institution to be eligible for an individual postdoctoral fellowship.

All research training awards are made to appropriate domestic research centers, medical schools, departments of psychiatry, nonmedical academic departments, psychiatric hospitals or hospitals with psychiatric services, community mental health centers, and biomedical research institutes on behalf of individuals who need the opportunity to realize research potential. Except for the NIH Pathway to Independence Award, the individuals must be citizens or nationals of the U.S. or have been lawfully admitted for permanent residence. NIH Pathway to Independence Award is open to both U.S. citizens and non-U.S. citizens. Individuals must qualify by scholastic degree and previous training and/or experience.

FINANCIAL DATA:
Amount of support per award: Grants and awards vary in amount, depending upon the program and type of funding mechanism.
Total amount of support: Varies.

APPLICATION INFO:
Application materials are available on NIMH web site. Prospective applicants should contact NIMH staff prior to submission to ensure the area of research that they investigate is within NIMH priorities.
Duration: Varies, with project periods ranging one to five years. Funding commitments are made annually.

ADDRESS INQUIRIES TO:
Dr. Jean Noronha, Director
Division of Extramural Activities
(See address above.)

NATIONAL INSTITUTE OF MENTAL HEALTH

Division of Translational Research (DTR)
6001 Executive Boulevard, Room 7111, MSC 9632
Bethesda, MD 20892-9632
(301) 443-9232
E-mail: ftuma@nih.gov
Web Site: www.nimh.nih.
gov/about/organization/dtr

TYPE:
Fellowships; Project/program grants; Research grants; Technical assistance; Training grants.

See entry 1692 for full listing.

NATIONAL SCIENCE FOUNDATION [2374]

Directorate for Social Behavorial and Economic Sciences
2415 Eisenhower Avenue
Alexandria, VA 22314
(703) 292-8728
Fax: (703) 292-9083
E-mail: sbreckle@nsf.gov
Web Site: www.nsf.gov

FOUNDED: 1950

AREAS OF INTEREST:
Human social behavior, including cultural differences and development over the lifespan.

NAME(S) OF PROGRAMS:
● **Social Psychology Program**

TYPE:
Project/program grants; Research grants; Training grants; Travel grants; Visiting scholars.

YEAR PROGRAM STARTED: 1972

PURPOSE:
To initiate and support scientific research and programs to strengthen research potential.

LEGAL BASIS:
National Science Foundation Act of 1950.

ELIGIBILITY:
Applicants may be colleges and universities on behalf of their staff members, nonprofit, nonacademic research institutions, such as independent museums, observatories, research laboratories, stock centers and similar organizations, private profit organizations, in exceptional circumstances, rarely, foreign institutions utilizing U.S. currency and, under special circumstances, unaffiliated U.S. scientists.

GEOG. RESTRICTIONS: United States.

FINANCIAL DATA:
Support may cover salaries, research assistantships, staff benefits if a direct cost, permanent equipment, travel, publication costs, computer costs and certain other direct and indirect costs.
Amount of support per award: Average $100,000 to $500,000.

NO. MOST RECENT APPLICANTS: Varies.

NO. AWARDS: Varies.

APPLICATION INFO:
Proposals must be submitted via FastLane or Grants.gov.
Duration: Research grants may be awarded for periods of up to five years. Most grants are for two or three years.
Deadline: Target dates are January 15 and July 15.

ADDRESS INQUIRIES TO:
Program Director
(See address above.)

NATIONAL SCIENCE FOUNDATION [2375]

Division of Behavioral and Cognitive Sciences
2415 Eisenhower Avenue
Alexandria, VA 22314
(703) 292-7238
Fax: (703) 292-9068
Web Site: www.nsf.gov

FOUNDED: 1950

AREAS OF INTEREST:
Human behavior.

NAME(S) OF PROGRAMS:
● **Perception, Action & Cognition Program**

TYPE:
Research grants. Supports research on perception, action and cognition. Emphasis is on research strongly grounded in theory. Research topics include vision, audition, haptics, attention, memory, reasoning, written and spoken discourse, motor control, and developmental issues in all topic areas. The program encompasses a wide range of theoretical perspectives such as symbolic

computation, connectionism, ecological, nonlinear dynamics, complex systems, and a variety of methodologies including both experimental studies and modeling. Research involving acquired or developmental deficits is appropriate if the results speak to basic issues of cognition, perception or action.

YEAR PROGRAM STARTED: 1976

PURPOSE:
To initiate and support scientific research and programs to strengthen research potential.

LEGAL BASIS:
National Science Foundation Act of 1950.

ELIGIBILITY:
Requirements vary according to program. Applicants should consult web site for current programs.

GEOG. RESTRICTIONS: United States.

FINANCIAL DATA:
Amount of support per award: Approximately $120,000 per year.
Total amount of support: Varies.

APPLICATION INFO:
Application should be submitted by FastLane, research.gov or through the Foundation's web site. Standard grant proposal guidelines apply.
Duration: 12 to 60 months, depending on the scientific merit and requirements of the project, and the type of program.

STAFF:
Betty Tuller, Ph.D., Program Director

ADDRESS INQUIRIES TO:
Betty Tuller, Ph.D., Program Director
(See address above.)

PARAPSYCHOLOGY FOUNDATION, INC. [2376]

P.O. Box 1562
New York, NY 10021-0043
(212) 628-1550
Fax: (212) 628-1559
E-mail: office@parapsychology.org
Web Site: parapsychology.org

AREAS OF INTEREST:
Parapsychology.

NAME(S) OF PROGRAMS:
● **Eileen J. Garrett Scholarship**

TYPE:
Scholarships. Assists students attending an accredited college or university in pursuing the academic study of the science of parapsychology.

PURPOSE:
To promote research in parapsychology.

ELIGIBILITY:
Open to nationals of any country.

FINANCIAL DATA:
Amount of support per award: $2,000.

NO. AWARDS: 1.

APPLICATION INFO:
Applicants must submit samples of writings on the subject with an application form from the Foundation. Letters of reference from three individuals who are familiar with the applicant's work and/or studies in parapsychology are required.
Duration: One year.
Deadline: July 1. Notification on August 1.

PARAPSYCHOLOGY FOUNDATION, INC. [2377]

P.O. Box 1562
New York, NY 10021-0043
(212) 628-1550
Fax: (212) 628-1559
E-mail: office@parapsychology.org
Web Site: parapsychology.org

AREAS OF INTEREST:
Parapsychology and psychic phenomena.

NAME(S) OF PROGRAMS:
● **Frances P. Bolton Fellowship**

TYPE:
Fellowships.

PURPOSE:
To further write up and polish the data amassed during the preparation of a doctoral dissertation/thesis.

ELIGIBILITY:
Awarded to a person who obtained their Ph.D. on the basis of a dissertation/thesis which dealt with some aspect of parapsychological phenomena.

FINANCIAL DATA:
Amount of support per award: $2,000.

NO. AWARDS: 1.

APPLICATION INFO:
Applications must be accompanied by a copy of the doctoral dissertation/thesis, three references, and a description of how the Fellowship will be utilized.
Deadline: November 1. Award notification January 1.

ADDRESS INQUIRIES TO:
Lisette Coly, Executive Director
(See address above.)

PARAPSYCHOLOGY FOUNDATION, INC. [2378]

P.O. Box 1562
New York, NY 10021-0043
(212) 628-1550
Fax: (212) 628-1559
E-mail: office@parapsychology.org
Web Site: parapsychology.org

AREAS OF INTEREST:
Parapsychology and psychic phenomena.

NAME(S) OF PROGRAMS:
● **Charles T. and Judith A. Tart Student Incentive Award**

TYPE:
Awards/prizes. Incentive award for research proposal.

YEAR PROGRAM STARTED: 2001

ELIGIBILITY:
Student must demonstrate a strong commitment to work within parapsychology. Open to undergraduate, graduate and postgraduate students who have in mind a specific research proposal which may be experimental, experiential, clinical, historical, survey- or questionnaire-based, archival, bibliographic, literary or any other type of investigation a student may propose.

FINANCIAL DATA:
Amount of support per award: $500.

APPLICATION INFO:
Application must be in English and should be accompanied by two letters of reference, a one- to two-page description of the project that includes purpose, method, materials and duration of the project, and a one-page budget.

Deadline: September 1. Award notification on or around October 1.

ADDRESS INQUIRIES TO:
Lisette Coly, Executive Director
(See address above.)

SCOTTISH RITE CHARITABLE FOUNDATION OF CANADA [2379]

4 Queen Street South
Hamilton ON L8P 3R3 Canada
(905) 522-0033
Fax: (905) 522-3716
E-mail: grantsandawards@srcf.ca
info@srcf.ca
Web Site: www.srcf.ca

FOUNDED: 1970

AREAS OF INTEREST:
Biomedical research into intellectual impairment.

NAME(S) OF PROGRAMS:
● **Scottish Rite Charitable Foundation Major Research Grants**

TYPE:
Research grants. SRCFC grants support biomedical research into Solving the Puzzles of the Mind focused on the following:
(1) the causes of Puzzles of the Mind, such as dyslexia and autism, especially as it affects children;
(2) the causes and eventual cure of cognitive impairments such as Alzheimer's disease and other neurodegenerative diseases and;
(3) research into other Puzzles of the Mind may be considered.

The focus of the research should be on the causes and cure of the disease as opposed to the active treatment or palliative care.

YEAR PROGRAM STARTED: 1970

PURPOSE:
To provide financial support to researchers studying developmental disabilities.

LEGAL BASIS:
Nonprofit.

ELIGIBILITY:
Applications are limited to researchers who have no more than five years experience as an independent investigator. A researcher who is designated as the Principal Investigator on the research grant must be based in, or formally affiliated with, an eligible Canadian host institution such as a university, research institute or health care agency. The Foundation does not consider trainees, including postdoctoral fellows, research assistants or research associates, to be eligible to apply as the Principal Investigator.

Research projects must be endorsed by the Research Services Department or equivalent of the university, hospital or research institute.

GEOG. RESTRICTIONS: Canada.

FINANCIAL DATA:
Amount of support per award: Up to $40,000 per year.

NO. AWARDS: Approximately 12 new and renewals per year.

APPLICATION INFO:
Application package consists of the Research Grant Form and Application Guide. All applicants must refer to the Application Guide when completing an application.

Duration: One, two or three years. Renewal contingent on a progress report of the work and research results.

Deadline: April 30 each year.

OFFICERS:
Gareth R. Taylor, President
Brian W. Gilkinson, Vice President
Duncan S. Skinner, Treasurer
Thomas E. Wills, Secretary

ADDRESS INQUIRIES TO:
The Awards Committee
(See address above.)

SOCIETY OF BIOLOGICAL PSYCHIATRY [2380]

5034A Thoroughbred Lane
Brentwood, TN 37027
(615) 432-0096
E-mail: sobp@sobp.org
Web Site: sobp.org

FOUNDED: 1945

AREAS OF INTEREST:
Biological psychiatry, neuropsychopharmacology and clinical neuroscience.

NAME(S) OF PROGRAMS:
● **A.E. Bennett Research Awards**

TYPE:
Awards/prizes. Awards for recent, unpublished research papers in the field of biological psychiatry.

YEAR PROGRAM STARTED: 1958

PURPOSE:
To promote research in biological psychiatry.

LEGAL BASIS:
Nonprofit foundation.

ELIGIBILITY:
Applicants must be qualified investigators with appropriate interests. Candidates shall either:
(1) have not passed their 45th birthday by January 1 for the year of the award or;
(2) have not been engaged in research for greater than 10 years following award of their terminal degree or the end of formal clinical/fellowship training, whichever is later.

Membership in the Society is not required. The prize will be awarded based on a body of work rather than a single paper.

FINANCIAL DATA:
Amount of support per award: $5,000 each for the best clinical paper and the best basic science paper submitted.

NO. AWARDS: 1 or 2 each year.

APPLICATION INFO:
Applications are submitted electronically.
Duration: One year.
Deadline: Nominations must be submitted online on or before September 30.

OFFICERS:
Mary Phillips, M.D., President
Trey Sunderland, Treasurer
Scott Rauch, M.D., Executive Secretary

SOCIETY OF BIOLOGICAL PSYCHIATRY [2381]

5034A Thoroughbred Lane
Brentwood, TN 37027
(615) 432-0096
E-mail: sobp@sobp.org
Web Site: sobp.org

FOUNDED: 1945

AREAS OF INTEREST:
Biological psychiatry, neuropsychopharmacology and clinical neuroscience.

NAME(S) OF PROGRAMS:
● **Ziskind-Somerfeld Research Award**

TYPE:
Awards/prizes. Award for recent, unsubmitted, unpublished research paper in the field of biological psychiatry.

YEAR PROGRAM STARTED: 1991

PURPOSE:
To stimulate investigations in biological psychiatry by senior investigators.

LEGAL BASIS:
Nonprofit.

ELIGIBILITY:
The award winner is the first author of the award paper. Special consideration is given to the originality of the approach and independence of thought in the archival report. The studies and the data must not have been published elsewhere.

FINANCIAL DATA:
Amount of support per award: $5,000.
Total amount of support: $5,000 annually.

NO. AWARDS: 1 each year.

APPLICATION INFO:
No application submission is required for the award. The Society provides a list of the top 15 articles to the Ziskind-Somerfeld Award Committee to review and make a final award selection.
Duration: One-time award.
Deadline: Announcement in May.

SUBSTANCE ABUSE AND MENTAL HEALTH SERVICES ADMINISTRATION, DISASTER TECHNICAL ASSISTANCE CENTER [2382]

5600 Fishers Lane
Rockville, MD 20857
(800) 308-3515
E-mail: dtac@samhsa.hhs.gov
Web Site: www.samhsa.gov/dtac

AREAS OF INTEREST:
Emergency mental health and crisis counseling.

NAME(S) OF PROGRAMS:
● **Crisis Counseling Assistance and Training Program**

TYPE:
Project/program grants. Grants to address the various dimensions of mental health crises affecting victims of presidentially declared major disasters. Support is available for development of training models and other psychological material for the delivery of crisis intervention services/outreach.

YEAR PROGRAM STARTED: 1974

PURPOSE:
To provide supplemental support to victims of major disasters and their families in emergency mental health and crisis intervention.

LEGAL BASIS:
Section 416 of The Robert T. Stafford Disaster Relief and Emergency Assistance Act (Public Law 100-707).

ELIGIBILITY:
Must be presidentially declared major disaster. U.S. territories and federally recognized tribes are also eligible.

FINANCIAL DATA:
Amount of support per award: Grants given according to justifiable need. Amounts vary in accordance with existing resources in stricken community.
Total amount of support: Varies.

CO-OP FUNDING PROGRAMS: Program funding is supplemental when existing programs are inadequate to meet the needs of the community.

NO. MOST RECENT APPLICANTS: 21 for the year 2017.

NO. AWARDS: 21 for the year 2017.

APPLICATION INFO:
Contact the organization for guidelines.
Duration: Nine months; renewal possible upon approval of CMHS and SAMHSA. Extension of grant possible in limited circumstances.
Deadline: 60 days following the disaster.

ADDRESS INQUIRIES TO:
Nikki Bellamy, Project Officer
SAMHSA/CMHS
(See address above.)

VAN AMERINGEN FOUNDATION, INC. [2383]

509 Madison Avenue
Room 2010
New York, NY 10022
(212) 758-6221
Fax: (212) 688-2105
E-mail: info@vanamfound.org
Web Site: www.vanamfound.org

FOUNDED: 1950

AREAS OF INTEREST:
Mental illness and mental health.

TYPE:
Demonstration grants; Development grants; General operating grants; Project/program grants; Research grants; Seed money grants. Grants for projects and activities in areas of social welfare, with particular emphasis on mental health.

YEAR PROGRAM STARTED: 1950

PURPOSE:
To promote mental health through preventive medicine, research, treatment and rehabilitation.

LEGAL BASIS:
Private foundation.

ELIGIBILITY:
Tax-exempt organizations with appropriate interests are eligible. No grants are made to individuals.

GEOG. RESTRICTIONS: Metropolitan New York area and Philadelphia, Pennsylvania.

FINANCIAL DATA:
Amount of support per award: $25,000 to $250,000, based on the needs and nature of the project.
Total amount of support: Approximately $5,000,000 for the year 2018.

NO. MOST RECENT APPLICANTS: Approximately 500.

NO. AWARDS: 50.

APPLICATION INFO:
Applicants must first complete a brief eligibility quiz. Those organizations that meet the basic eligibility requirements will then be able to register and submit a letter of inquiry through the grants application portal. Foundation staff will contact those organizations selected to submit a full proposal and schedule a site visit.

Deadline: Varies.

PUBLICATIONS:
Annual report; guidelines.

DIRECTORS:
Kenneth A. Kind, President and Treasurer
Maurizio Morello, Vice President and Secretary
Judith Beck
Alexandra Herzan

Christina K. Kind
Valerie Kind-Rubin
Andrew Kindfuller
Laura K. McKenna
Clarence Sundram
Henry van Ameringen

ADDRESS INQUIRIES TO:
Kenneth A. Kind, President
(See address above.)

TECHNOLOGY AND INDUSTRY

Technology and industry

AGC EDUCATION AND RESEARCH FOUNDATION
2300 Wilson Boulevard, Suite 300
Arlington, VA 22201
(703) 837-5342
Fax: (703) 837-5451
E-mail: patricianm@agc.org
Web Site: www.agcfoundation.org

TYPE:
Awards/prizes; Internships; Project/program grants; Scholarships. Allhands Essay Competition: Awarded to a student essay on a specific topic that is deemed to be beneficial to the advancement of technological, educational or vocational expertise in the construction industry.

Graduate Scholarship Program: Scholarships for students enrolled in ABET- or ACCE-accredited construction management or construction-related engineering programs.

Industry Case Studies: Commissioning case studies on industry scenarios.

Outstanding Educator Award: Awards to top competitors in essay competition for seniors and faculty nominated as outstanding educator.

Undergraduate Scholarship Program: Scholarships for students enrolled in ABET- or ACCE-accredited construction management or construction-related engineering programs.

Workforce Development Scholarship: Awarded for students entering craft training or technical programs.

See entry 2415 for full listing.

AIR & WASTE MANAGEMENT ASSOCIATION (A&WMA)   [2384]
Koppers Building
436 Seventh Avenue, Suite 2100
Pittsburgh, PA 15219
(412) 904-6006
Fax: (412) 232-3450
E-mail: sglyptis@awma.org
Web Site: www.awma.org

FOUNDED: 1907

AREAS OF INTEREST:
Air quality, waste management, environmental management/policy/law and sustainability research.

NAME(S) OF PROGRAMS:
● **Scholarship Endowment Trust Fund**

TYPE:
Scholarships.

PURPOSE:
To provide monies for students with interest in the area of air quality, waste management and/or environmental management/policy/law.

ELIGIBILITY:
Must be a full-time graduate student pursuing studies in the area of air quality, waste management and/or environmental management/policy/law.

FINANCIAL DATA:
Amount of support per award: Varies.
Total amount of support: Approximately $26,000 annually.

NO. MOST RECENT APPLICANTS: 50.

NO. AWARDS: Approximately 10.

APPLICATION INFO:
Applications must be completed online.
Duration: One year. Renewal possible by reapplying.
Deadline: January.

ADDRESS INQUIRIES TO:
Stephanie Glyptis, Executive Director
(See address above.)

AIR TRAFFIC CONTROL ASSOCIATION (ATCA)   [2385]
225 Reinekers Lane
Suite 400
Alexandria, VA 22314-2875
(703) 299-2430 ext. 309
Fax: (703) 299-2437
E-mail: jessica.morin@atca.org
Web Site: www.atca.org

FOUNDED: 1956

AREAS OF INTEREST:
Air traffic control and aviation.

TYPE:
Scholarships. Scholarships to promising young men and women enrolled in programs leading to careers in aviation or air traffic control and scholarships for dependents of air traffic controllers pursuing a degree.

PURPOSE:
To promote careers in air traffic control or aviation disciplines.

LEGAL BASIS:
Private, 501(c)(3) charity.

ELIGIBILITY:
Requirements vary per award category.

FINANCIAL DATA:
Amount of support per award: $2,000 to $10,000.
Total amount of support: Varies.

NO. MOST RECENT APPLICANTS: 300.

NO. AWARDS: 8 to 12.

APPLICATION INFO:
Application, with supporting documents, must be completed online.
Duration: One year.
Deadline: May 1.

ADDRESS INQUIRIES TO:
Jessica Morin, Membership Manager
(See address above.)

AMERICAN GROUND WATER TRUST   [2386]
50 Pleasant Street, Suite 2
Concord, NH 03301-4073
(603) 228-5444
Fax: (603) 228-6557
E-mail: trustinfo@agwt.org
Web Site: www.agwt.org

FOUNDED: 1986

AREAS OF INTEREST:
Groundwater education, sustainable management and protection.

NAME(S) OF PROGRAMS:
● **Baroid Scholarship**
● **Flexcon Industries Scholarship**
● **Thomas M. Stetson Scholarship**

TYPE:
Awards/prizes; Scholarships.

YEAR PROGRAM STARTED: 1986

PURPOSE:
To provide education outreach to inform the public about the optimal utilization and protection of groundwater for the benefit of mankind.

LEGAL BASIS:
501(c)(3) nonprofit organization.

ELIGIBILITY:
Applicants must be U.S. citizens, apply during their senior year in high school, and be enrolled the following year in an undergraduate program relevant to the groundwater industry.

GEOG. RESTRICTIONS: United States.

FINANCIAL DATA:
Amount of support per award: $1,000 to $2,000.

NO. MOST RECENT APPLICANTS: Approximately 40.

NO. AWARDS: 4.

APPLICATION INFO:
Applicant must submit only one application to be considered for all scholarships. Completed application form must be countersigned by a teacher at the applicant's high school and accompanied by two letters of recommendation. A 500-word essay and a 300-word description of the applicant's high school groundwater project and/or practical environmental work experience must accompany the application. Documentary evidence of scholastic achievements and references will be requested from finalists.
Duration: One academic year.
Deadline: June 1. The Trust will write to all applicants (successful and unsuccessful) at the end of August.

IRS I.D.: 23-7244958

EXECUTIVE DIRECTOR:
Andrew W. Stone

ADDRESS INQUIRIES TO:
Andrew W. Stone, Executive Director
(See address above.)

AMERICAN SOCIETY FOR ENOLOGY AND VITICULTURE
1724 Picasso Avenue, Suite E
Davis, CA 95618-0551
(530) 753-3142
Fax: (530) 753-3318
E-mail: info@asev.org
Web Site: www.asev.org

TYPE:
Scholarships. Awards for undergraduate or graduate students enrolled in enology or viticulture or in a curriculum which emphasizes a science basic to the wine and grape industry and who intend to pursue a career in research for the wine or grape industry after graduation from college or university.

See entry 1933 for full listing.

THE AMERICAN SOCIETY FOR NONDESTRUCTIVE TESTING, INC.   [2387]
1711 Arlingate Lane
Columbus, OH 43228-0518
(614) 274-6003
(800) 222-2768
Fax: (614) 274-6899
E-mail: james@asnt.org
Web Site: www.asnt.org

FOUNDED: 1941

AREAS OF INTEREST:
Nondestructive testing.

NAME(S) OF PROGRAMS:
- **ASNT Fellowship Award**

TYPE:
Fellowships. Nondestructive evaluation and testing (NDE/NDT) is the science of examining components and systems in a manner that does not impair their further usefulness. NDE/NDT is a complex, multidisciplinary field offering exciting career opportunities. Current areas for applying new and advanced nondestructive testing technology include power plant life extension, aging aircraft and deteriorating civil engineering structures.

YEAR PROGRAM STARTED: 1981

PURPOSE:
To provide assistance to university or college graduate students in defraying costs of their postgraduate research in NDT.

LEGAL BASIS:
Nonprofit organization.

ELIGIBILITY:
Academic institutions with graduate educational research in NDT related fields are eligible for this fellowship.

FINANCIAL DATA:
Amount of support per award: $20,000.
Total amount of support: Up to $100,000.

NO. AWARDS: Up to 5 per year.

APPLICATION INFO:
Guidelines and application are available online.
Duration: One year.
Deadline: October 15.

ADDRESS INQUIRIES TO:
Jessica Ames
ASNT Program Coordinator
(See address above.)

AWS FOUNDATION, INC. [2388]
8669 N.W. 36th Street
No. 130
Miami, FL 33166
(305) 443-9353 ext. 212
(800) 443-9353 ext. 212
E-mail: jdouglass@aws.org
Web Site: www.aws.org

FOUNDED: 1989

AREAS OF INTEREST:
Welding and materials joining.

NAME(S) OF PROGRAMS:
- **AWS National, District and Section Scholarships**

TYPE:
Scholarships.

YEAR PROGRAM STARTED: 1991

PURPOSE:
To promote education in the welding industry.

ELIGIBILITY:
Student must be enrolled or planning to enroll in a welding program or related field.

FINANCIAL DATA:
Amount of support per award: $500 to $6,500.
Total amount of support: $800,000.

NO. AWARDS: 675.

APPLICATION INFO:
Details are available on the Foundation web site.
Duration: One year.
Deadline: March 1.

ADDRESS INQUIRIES TO:
John Douglass, Associate Director
(See address above.)

AWS FOUNDATION, INC. [2389]
8669 N.W. 36th Street
No. 130
Miami, FL 33166
(305) 443-9353 ext. 212
(800) 443-9353 ext. 212
E-mail: jdouglass@aws.org
Web Site: www.aws.org

FOUNDED: 1989

AREAS OF INTEREST:
Welding and materials joining.

NAME(S) OF PROGRAMS:
- **Welding Workforce Grant**

TYPE:
Training grants.

PURPOSE:
To improve and expand training programs and institutions to increase the number of welding graduates across the country.

ELIGIBILITY:
Schools or training institutions must be AWS Educational Institution members and SENSE registered.

FINANCIAL DATA:
Amount of support per award: Up to $25,000.
Total amount of support: Up to $300,000 annually.

NO. AWARDS: 10 to 14.

APPLICATION INFO:
Application must be submitted on the AWS web site.
Duration: One year.
Deadline: April 1 and October 1.

ADDRESS INQUIRIES TO:
John Douglass, Associate Director
(See e-mail address above.)

AWS FOUNDATION, INC. [2390]
8669 N.W. 36th Street
No. 130
Miami, FL 33166
(305) 443-9353 ext. 212
(800) 443-9353 ext. 212
E-mail: jdouglass@aws.org
Web Site: www.aws.org

FOUNDED: 1989

AREAS OF INTEREST:
Welding and materials joining.

NAME(S) OF PROGRAMS:
- **Graduate Research Fellowship**

TYPE:
Fellowships.

PURPOSE:
To foster university research in joining; to recognize outstanding faculty and student talent.

ELIGIBILITY:
Fellowships are awarded to students for graduate research toward a Master's or Ph.D. degree under a sponsoring professor.

GEOG. RESTRICTIONS: North America.

FINANCIAL DATA:
Amount of support per award: Up to $30,000.
Total amount of support: $120,000.

NO. AWARDS: 4.

APPLICATION INFO:
Guidelines are available online.
Duration: One year. Renewal up to three years possible. Must reapply.
Deadline: August 31.

ADDRESS INQUIRIES TO:
John Douglass, Associate Director
(See address above.)

AWS FOUNDATION, INC. [2391]
8669 N.W. 36th Street
No. 130
Miami, FL 33166
(305) 443-9353 ext. 212
(800) 443-9353 ext. 212
E-mail: jdouglass@aws.org
Web Site: www.aws.org

FOUNDED: 1989

AREAS OF INTEREST:
Welding and materials joining.

NAME(S) OF PROGRAMS:
- **Welder Training Scholarship**

TYPE:
Scholarships.

PURPOSE:
To encourage education pertaining to welding and materials joining.

ELIGIBILITY:
Applicant must be planning to attend a trade school, community college, or other facility providing welder training.

FINANCIAL DATA:
Amount of support per award: $1,000.
Total amount of support: $550,000.

NO. MOST RECENT APPLICANTS: 1,600.

NO. AWARDS: 550.

APPLICATION INFO:
Applications must be submitted online.
Duration: One year.
Deadline: Applications are accepted on an ongoing basis.

ADDRESS INQUIRIES TO:
John Douglass, Associate Director
(See address above.)

CHARLES BABBAGE INSTITUTE [2392]
University of Minnesota
211 Elmer L. Anderson Library
222 21st Avenue South
Minneapolis, MN 55455
(612) 624-5050
E-mail: cbi@umn.edu
Web Site: www.cbi.umn.edu

FOUNDED: 1978

AREAS OF INTEREST:
History of computers and information technology.

NAME(S) OF PROGRAMS:
- **The Adelle and Erwin Tomash Fellowship in the History of Information Technology**

TYPE:
Fellowships.

YEAR PROGRAM STARTED: 1978

PURPOSE:
To advance the professional development of historians of information technology.

LEGAL BASIS:
University and research association.

ELIGIBILITY:
Open to graduate students whose dissertation addresses some aspect of the history of computers and information technology. Topics may be chosen from the technical history of hardware or software, economic or business aspects of the information technology industry or other topics in the social, institutional or legal history of computing. Theses that consider technical issues in their socio-economic context are especially encouraged.

Priority will be given to students who have completed all requirements for the doctoral degree except the research and writing of the dissertation.

The fellowship may be held at the home academic institution, the Babbage Institute or any other location where there are appropriate research facilities.

FINANCIAL DATA:
Amount of support per award: $14,000 stipend.
Total amount of support: $14,000.

NO. MOST RECENT APPLICANTS: 5.

NO. AWARDS: 1.

APPLICATION INFO:
Applicants should send biographical data and a research plan. The plan should contain a statement and justification of the research problem, a discussion of procedure for research and writing, information on availability of research materials and evidence of faculty support for the project. Applicants should arrange for three letters of reference and certified transcripts of college credits to be sent directly to the Institute. There is no special application form. A one-page flyer describing the fellowship is available.
Duration: One academic year.
Deadline: January 15.

PUBLICATIONS:
Newsletter.

ADDRESS INQUIRIES TO:
Jeffrey Yost, Director
Charles Babbage Institute
(See address above.)

COIN-OP CARES CHARITABLE AND EDUCATION FOUNDATION   [2393]
c/o Amusement & Music Operators Association
380 Terra Cotta Road, Suite F
Crystal Lake, IL 60012
(800) 937-2662
Fax: (815) 893-6248
E-mail: laura@amoa.com
Web Site: www.amoa.com

FOUNDED: 1948

AREAS OF INTEREST:
Higher education.

NAME(S) OF PROGRAMS:
● **Wayne E. Hesch Memorial Scholarships**

TYPE:
Scholarships. Designed to provide financial support to students who are, or plan or hope to be, engaged in the profession.

YEAR PROGRAM STARTED: 1985

PURPOSE:
To provide leadership for the amusement, music, entertainment and vending industry; to protect and promote the industry interests.

ELIGIBILITY:
Open to individuals in need of financial assistance who are attending or plan to attend an institution of higher education and have a 3.0 grade point average on a 4.0 scale.

FINANCIAL DATA:
Amount of support per award: $1,000 each.

APPLICATION INFO:
Applicant must call AMOA office to receive the form.
Duration: One year.
Deadline: February 13.

ADDRESS INQUIRIES TO:
AMOA Executive Office
(See address above.)

EARLY AMERICAN INDUSTRIES ASSOCIATION, INC.   [2394]
P.O. Box 524
Hebron, MD 21830-0524
(703) 967-9399
E-mail: executivedirector@eaiainfo.org
Web Site: www.eaiainfo.org

FOUNDED: 1933

AREAS OF INTEREST:
To encourage study and better understanding of early American industries in the home, shop, on the farm and the sea; to discover, identify, classify, preserve and exhibit obsolete tools, implements and mechanical devices used in early America, craft practices, and industrial technology.

NAME(S) OF PROGRAMS:
● **Research Grants Program**

TYPE:
Research grants. These are not scholarship or internship grants.

YEAR PROGRAM STARTED: 1977

PURPOSE:
To preserve and present historic trades, crafts and tools, and to interpret their impact on the present generation.

LEGAL BASIS:
Nonprofit corporation.

ELIGIBILITY:
Applicants may be sponsored by an institution or engaged in self-directed projects. Projects must relate to the purposes of the Association. Grants can supplement existing aid. These are not scholarship, fellowship or internship funds. A grant may not be used to pay for salaries, historical artifacts, software or equipment in whole or in part.

GEOG. RESTRICTIONS: United States.

FINANCIAL DATA:
Amount of support per award: Up to $3,000.

NO. MOST RECENT APPLICANTS: 7.

NO. AWARDS: 3.

APPLICATION INFO:
Application is available online, and must be completed and mailed to the above address.

Duration: One year. Nonrenewable.
Deadline: March 15 annually.
Announcements in April annually.

PUBLICATIONS:
The Chronicle, quarterly journal; *Shavings,* newsletter for members; application guidelines; E.A.I.A. brochure.

OFFICERS:
John H. Verrill, Executive Director

ADDRESS INQUIRIES TO:
John H. Verrill, Executive Director
(See address above.)

*PLEASE NOTE:
A project report, including a statement of expenditures, must be filed by recipients.

FEDERAL HIGHWAY ADMINISTRATION   [2395]
Center of Transportation Workforce Development
1200 New Jersey Avenue, S.E.
Washington, DC 20590
(703) 235-0538
E-mail: transportationedu@dot.gov
Web Site: www.fhwa.dot.gov/ugp

AREAS OF INTEREST:
Transportation-related disciplines.

NAME(S) OF PROGRAMS:
● **Dwight David Eisenhower Transportation Fellowship Program**

TYPE:
Fellowships; Internships; Research grants. Dwight David Eisenhower Transportation Fellowship Program's objectives are to attract the nation's brightest minds to the field of transportation, to enhance the careers of transportation professionals by encouraging them to seek advanced degrees, and to retain top talent in the transportation industry of the U.S. This Program encompasses all areas of transportation. The Program has seven award categories:
(1) Eisenhower Graduate (GRAD) Fellowships enable students to pursue Master's degrees or Doctorates in transportation-related fields at the university of their choice;
(2) Eisenhower Grants for Research (GRF) Fellowships acquaint undergraduate and graduate students with transportation research, development and technology-transfer activities at the U.S. Department of Transportation facilities;
(3) Eisenhower Historically Black Colleges and Universities (HBCU) Fellowships provide HBCU students with additional opportunities to enter careers in transportation. The Fellowships also serve as a feeder for other Eisenhower fellowships;
(4) Eisenhower Hispanic Serving Institutions (HSI) Fellowships provide HSI students with additional opportunities to enter careers in transportation. The Fellowships also serve as a feeder for other Eisenhower fellowships;
(5) Eisenhower Tribal College and Universities Fellowships (TCU) provides students with additional opportunities to enter careers in transportation. The Fellowships also serve as a feeder for other Eisenhower fellowships;
(6) Eisenhower Intern Fellowships (EIF) provides students with opportunities to perform a wide range of transportation-related activities at public and private-sector transportation organizations and;

(7) Eisenhower Community College Fellowships provide students at community colleges with opportunities to enter careers in transportation. The Fellowships also serve as a feeder for other Eisenhower fellowships.

YEAR PROGRAM STARTED: 1983

PURPOSE:
To attract the nation's brightest minds to the field of transportation; to enhance the careers of transportation professionals by encouraging them to seek advanced degrees; to retain top talent in the transportation industry of the U.S.

LEGAL BASIS:
Government agency.

ELIGIBILITY:
Applicants must be enrolled in transportation-related disciplines (e.g., engineering, computer science, physics, transportation planning) at accredited U.S. universities.

GEOG. RESTRICTIONS: United States.

FINANCIAL DATA:
Award may include an allowance for tuition, stipend and travel expenses for the student to attend the annual Transportation Research Board (TRB) conference held in Washington, DC every January.
Amount of support per award: $1,500 to $35,500.
Total amount of support: Varies.

NO. AWARDS: 150 to 200 annually.

APPLICATION INFO:
Undergraduate applicants must submit applications through their faculty advisors and be nominated for awards by their respective universities. Graduate applicants must apply to the Arlington, VA office. Further information is available from the Administration.
Duration: Minimum three months during the summer. Maximum three years of funding, with five years to complete the course.
Deadline: Annual notice of funding programs are published on www.grants.gov.

PUBLICATIONS:
Application guidelines; brochures.

ADDRESS INQUIRIES TO:
Ewa Flom, Program Manager
Universities and Grants Programs
(See address above.)

FOUNDATION FOR TECHNOLOGY AND ENGINEERING EDUCATION

1914 Association Drive
Suite 201
Reston, VA 20191-1539
(703) 860-2100
Fax: (703) 860-0353
E-mail: iteea@iteea.org
Web Site: www.iteea.org

TYPE:
Scholarships. The scholarship is for an undergraduate student majoring in technology and engineering education teacher preparation.

See entry 1524 for full listing.

FOUNDATION FOR TECHNOLOGY AND ENGINEERING EDUCATION

1914 Association Drive
Suite 201
Reston, VA 20191-1539
(703) 860-2100
Fax: (703) 860-0353
E-mail: iteea@iteea.org
Web Site: www.iteea.org

TYPE:
Scholarships.

See entry 1406 for full listing.

FOUNDATION FOR TECHNOLOGY AND ENGINEERING EDUCATION

1914 Association Drive
Suite 201
Reston, VA 20191-1539
(703) 860-2100
Fax: (703) 860-0353
E-mail: iteea@iteea.org
Web Site: www.iteea.org

TYPE:
Scholarships.

See entry 1525 for full listing.

THE FOUNDATION OF FLEXOGRAPHIC TECHNICAL ASSOCIATION   [2396]

3920 Veterans Memorial Highway, Suite 9
Bohemia, NY 11716
(631) 737-6020
Fax: (631) 737-6813
E-mail: srubin@flexography.org
Web Site: www.flexography.org

FOUNDED: 1958

AREAS OF INTEREST:
Flexographic printing.

NAME(S) OF PROGRAMS:
● **Flexographic Technical Association Scholarship**

TYPE:
Scholarships.

PURPOSE:
To support education in the study of flexography.

ELIGIBILITY:
Must be enrolled in a qualified school offering a study of flexography. Must have grade point average of 3.0 or better.

FINANCIAL DATA:
Amount of support per award: $3,000 per year.
Total amount of support: Varies.

NO. AWARDS: Varies.

APPLICATION INFO:
Contact the Organization for application procedures.
Duration: One year. Renewable upon reapplication.
Deadline: Usually March of each year.

ADDRESS INQUIRIES TO:
Shelley Rubin
Manager, Educational Services
(See address above.)

GREAT MINDS IN STEM   [2397]

2465 Whittier Boulevard
Suite 202
Montebello, CA 90640
(323) 262-0997
Fax: (323) 262-0946
E-mail: scholars@greatmindsinstem.org
Web Site: www.greatmindsinstem.org

FOUNDED: 1989

AREAS OF INTEREST:
Science, technology, computer science, engineering and math.

NAME(S) OF PROGRAMS:
● **GMiS Scholars Program**

TYPE:
Scholarships.

YEAR PROGRAM STARTED: 2000

PURPOSE:
To provide undergraduate and graduate scholarships to students majoring in science, technology, computer science, engineering and math.

ELIGIBILITY:
Applicants must be of Hispanic origin and/or must significantly participate in and promote organizations and activities in the Hispanic community. Applicants must be enrolled in an undergraduate or graduate engineering or science program at a college or university and must be planning to pursue a career in either area. Selection is based on academic standing, career potential and character.

GEOG. RESTRICTIONS: United States and Puerto Rico.

FINANCIAL DATA:
Amount of support per award: $500 to $10,000.
Total amount of support: Varies.

NO. MOST RECENT APPLICANTS: 1,200.

NO. AWARDS: 125 for the year 2019.

APPLICATION INFO:
All applications must be completed and submitted electonically. Absolutely no faxes will be accepted.
Duration: One academic year. Renewal possible.
Deadline: April 1.

STAFF:
Dr. Gary Cruz, Director of Academic Affairs
Sonia Martinez, Academic Officer

ADDRESS INQUIRIES TO:
GMiS Scholars Program
(See address above.)

HIMSS FOUNDATION

33 West Monroe Street, Suite 1700
Chicago, IL 60603-5616
(312) 915-9289
Fax: (312) 664-6143
E-mail: scholarships@himss.org
Web Site: www.himss.org/health-it.education/scholarships

TYPE:
Awards/prizes; Conferences/seminars; Fellowships; Internships; Research grants; Scholarships.

See entry 2070 for full listing.

IEEE HISTORY CENTER

Stevens Institute of Technology
Samuel C. Williams Library, Third Floor
One Castle Point Terrace
Hoboken, NJ 07030
(732) 562-5468
Fax: (732) 562-6020
E-mail: ieee-history@ieee.org
Web Site: www.ieee.org/history_center

TYPE:
Fellowships; Internships. Fellowship in the
History of Electrical and Computing
Technology: Award for one year of full-time
doctoral or postdoctoral work in the history
of electrical engineering and technology at a
college or university of recognized standing.

The Elizabeth and Emerson Pugh Young
Scholar in Residence: Two-month internship
for graduate research.

See entry 555 for full listing.

INSTITUTE OF FOOD TECHNOLOGISTS FOUNDATION [2398]

525 West Van Buren Street
Suite 1000
Chicago, IL 60607
(312) 782-8424
Fax: (312) 416-7919
E-mail: feedingtomorrow@ift.org
Web Site: www.ift.org/scholarships

FOUNDED: 1939

AREAS OF INTEREST:
Food science and technology.

NAME(S) OF PROGRAMS:
● **Freshman Scholarships**
● **Graduate Scholarships**
● **Undergraduate Scholarships**

TYPE:
Scholarships. Freshman Scholarships and
Undergraduate Scholarships encourage
undergraduate enrollment in food science and
technology. Graduate Scholarships support
advanced study in the field of food science
and technology.

YEAR PROGRAM STARTED: 1950

PURPOSE:
To encourage and support outstanding
research in food science/technology including
such areas as food packaging, flavor
chemistry, new food ingredients and
products; to recognize scholastic
achievement.

LEGAL BASIS:
Nonprofit 501(c)(3) foundation.

ELIGIBILITY:
Freshman scholarships are awarded to high
school seniors entering college for the first
time. Applicant must be a current high
school senior and accepted into an
IFT-approved undergraduate food science
program, have at least a 3.0 cumulative grade
point average, and become an IFT student
member.

Graduate scholarships are awarded to
outstanding M.S. and Ph.D. students pursuing
research and education in the field of food
science and technology. Student applicants
must be pursuing a graduate with an
emphasis in food science and related
disciplines. They must be able to understand
and appreciate the impact of their research on
the global food supply. Research in such
disciplines as genetics, horticulture, nutrition,

microbiology, biochemistry, engineering,
chemistry, etc. are not eligible unless it is
directly related to the student's research
program in food science, except as otherwise
noted. The school of enrollment can be any
educational institution conducting
fundamental investigations for the
advancement of food science and food
technology, unless there are stated exceptions
of scholarship criteria for sponsored
scholarships. Applicant must be enrolled as a
full-time M.S. or Ph.D. student, have at least
a 3.0 cumulative grade point average, and be
a student member of IFT at the time of
application.

Undergraduate scholarships are awarded to
sophomore, junior, and senior students
enrolled as a full-time student pursuing an
undergraduate degree in an IFT-approved
undergraduate food science program, have at
least a 3.0 cumulative grade point average,
and be a student member of IFT at the time
of application.

FINANCIAL DATA:
Amount of support per award: $1,000 to
$5,000.

Total amount of support: Varies.

CO-OP FUNDING PROGRAMS: The scholarships
are sponsored by Feeding Tomorrow donors.

NO. MOST RECENT APPLICANTS: Approximately
300.

NO. AWARDS: Approximately 75.

APPLICATION INFO:
Applications are available on the Institute's
web site.

Duration: One year.

Deadline: Varies.

ADDRESS INQUIRIES TO:
Jaime Gutshall, Coordinator
(See address and e-mail above.)

THE INTERNATIONAL EXECUTIVE HOUSEKEEPERS ASSOCIATION [2399]

1001 Eastwind Drive
Suite 302
Westerville, OH 43081-3361
(847) 982-0800 ext. 1377 or 1385
Fax: (614) 895-1248
E-mail: excel@ieha.org
Web Site: www.ieha.org

FOUNDED: 1930

AREAS OF INTEREST:
Directors, project managers, managers and
supervisors of environmental services or
housekeeping departments, facilities
management, and training.

NAME(S) OF PROGRAMS:
● **PECP Self Study Program**

TYPE:
Scholarships. The PECP Program is a
330-hour course.

YEAR PROGRAM STARTED: 1960

PURPOSE:
To provide a professional organization for
executive housekeepers, directors of
environmental services, managers within the
housekeeping or custodial activities, and
suppliers of custodial goods and services.

ELIGIBILITY:
Must be a member of IEHA and be working
towards any degree program at a university
or college, in a certification program or
engaged in self-study.

FINANCIAL DATA:
Amount of support per award: $1,000 to
$1,800 per year.

Total amount of support: Varies.

NO. MOST RECENT APPLICANTS: 5.

NO. AWARDS: Approximately 3.

APPLICATION INFO:
Application may be requested from the
e-mail address above.

Duration: One year.

Deadline: Must be postmarked by May 31.

ADDRESS INQUIRIES TO:
Michael Patterson, Executive Director
(See address above.)

INTERNATIONAL FOOD SERVICE EXECUTIVES ASSOCIATION, INC. (IFSEA) [2400]

9510 S.W. 70th Loop
Ocala, FL 34481
(855) 273-6379
E-mail: hq@ifsea.org
Web Site: www.ifsea.org

FOUNDED: 1901

AREAS OF INTEREST:
Food service field.

NAME(S) OF PROGRAMS:
● **Worthy Goal Scholarship**

TYPE:
Scholarships. Tuition scholarships.

YEAR PROGRAM STARTED: 1939

PURPOSE:
To give needed assistance to qualified young
people in furthering their careers in the food
service field.

LEGAL BASIS:
Nonprofit.

ELIGIBILITY:
Students must be enrolled as or accepted as a
full-time student in hospitality management
or a food service-related major at a two- or
four-year college/university.

GEOG. RESTRICTIONS: United States.

FINANCIAL DATA:
Amount of support per award: $500 to
$2,500.

Total amount of support: $25,000.

NO. MOST RECENT APPLICANTS: 17.

NO. AWARDS: 17.

APPLICATION INFO:
Scholarship application is available at the
Association web site.

Duration: One year. Renewable.

Deadline: March 20. The scholarship is
awarded every spring for the following fall
semester.

ADDRESS INQUIRIES TO:
Dr. Ernest Boger
Worthy Goal Scholarship Chairperson
E-mail: epboger@umes.edu

PRINT AND GRAPHICS SCHOLARSHIP FOUNDATION [2401]

P.O. Box 787
Warrendale, PA 15095
(412) 259-1740
(866) 556-7473
E-mail: bernie.eckert@pgsf.org
Web Site: pgsf.org

FOUNDED: 1956

AREAS OF INTEREST:
Graphic communications, printing technology, printing management and publishing.

TYPE:
Fellowships. For advanced study relating to the printing, publishing and packaging industries. Support is provided for research and study in engineering, chemistry, physics, mathematics, industrial education or such business technology areas as systems analysis, operations research and marketing research, provided the area of study has potential application in the printing, publishing and packaging industries.

YEAR PROGRAM STARTED: 1956

PURPOSE:
To strengthen the print and graphics industry through scholarship assistance.

LEGAL BASIS:
Nonprofit organization.

ELIGIBILITY:
Applicants must be students who plan to major and have a career in graphic communications, printing technology, printing management or publishing. Must have and maintain a 3.0 grade point average.

FINANCIAL DATA:
Amount of support per award: $1,000 to $5,000.

NO. MOST RECENT APPLICANTS: 10 to 15.

NO. AWARDS: Varies.

APPLICATION INFO:
Fellowship application is not available online. Contact the Foundation.
Duration: One academic year. Renewable.
Deadline: April 1.

ADDRESS INQUIRIES TO:
Bernadine Eckert, Administrator
(See address above.)

PRINT AND GRAPHICS SCHOLARSHIP FOUNDATION [2402]

P.O. Box 787
Warrendale, PA 15095
(412) 259-1740
(866) 556-7473
E-mail: bernie.eckert@pgsf.org
Web Site: pgsf.org

FOUNDED: 1956

AREAS OF INTEREST:
Graphic communications and graphic arts; printing technology and management.

TYPE:
Scholarships. Awarded to students who plan to major and have a career in graphic communications, printing technology, printing management or publishing.

YEAR PROGRAM STARTED: 1956

PURPOSE:
To encourage eligible students to enter the field of graphic communications in the printing and publishing industries.

LEGAL BASIS:
Nonprofit foundation.

ELIGIBILITY:
Applicant must:
(1) be a high school senior or a high school graduate;
(2) be pursuing a career in print technology, printing management, publishing, or graphic communications;
(3) be a full-time student enrolled in a printing or graphics program at a technical school, college or university within the U.S. and;
(4) be able to maintain a grade point average of 3.0 or higher.

GEOG. RESTRICTIONS: United States.

FINANCIAL DATA:
Awards are paid directly to colleges for payment of tuition, fees and other charges.
Amount of support per award: $1,000 to $5,000.

NO. MOST RECENT APPLICANTS: 400.

NO. AWARDS: 200.

APPLICATION INFO:
Applications and letters of recommendation must be submitted online.
Duration: Renewable for up to four years (unless otherwise specified).
Deadline: April 1. Decisions are announced in July.

PUBLICATIONS:
Annual reports; newsletter; career brochures.

IRS I.D.: 25-1668339

ADDRESS INQUIRIES TO:
Bernadine Eckert
Scholarship Administrator
(See address above.)

*SPECIAL STIPULATIONS:
Candidates must be pursuing a career in graphic communications or printing and must maintain a 3.0 grade point average.

SME-EF (SOCIETY OF MANUFACTURING ENGINEERS EDUCATION FOUNDATION) [2403]

1000 Town Center
Suite 1910
Southfield, MI 48075
(313) 425-3300
Fax: (313) 425-3410
E-mail: foundation@sme.org
Web Site: www.smeef.org

FOUNDED: 1932

AREAS OF INTEREST:
Manufacturing and industrial engineering technology, machining technology, robotics, automated systems and technology.

NAME(S) OF PROGRAMS:
- **Connie and Robert T. Gunter Scholarship**
- **Clinton J. Helton Manufacturing Scholarship**
- **Kalamazoo Chapter No. 116-Roscoe Douglas Scholarship**
- **Lucille B. Kaufman Women's Scholarship**
- **E. Wayne Kay Scholarships**

- **St. Louis Chapter No. 17 Scholarship**
- **Myrtle and Earl Walker Scholarship**
- **William E. Weisel Scholarship**

TYPE:
Scholarships. Support for full- or part-time students seeking careers in manufacturing or industrial engineering technology or closely related fields.

YEAR PROGRAM STARTED: 1982

LEGAL BASIS:
Professional society.

ELIGIBILITY:
Applicants must reside in the U.S. or Canada, be a full- or part-time student pursuing a degree in manufacturing engineering, manufacturing engineering technology, or a closely related engineering field of study, and must attend an accredited institution in the U.S. or Canada. Applicants must have a minimum 2.5 grade point average.

GEOG. RESTRICTIONS: United States and Canada.

FINANCIAL DATA:
Amount of support per award: Varies according to scholarship.
Total amount of support: Over $550,000 awarded annually.

NO. MOST RECENT APPLICANTS: Over 800 for the 2020-21 academic year.

NO. AWARDS: 242.

APPLICATION INFO:
Application must be completed online.
Duration: One year. Students may reapply for undergraduate scholarships.
Deadline: February 1. Announcements in May and June.

PUBLICATIONS:
Program announcement.

BOARD OF DIRECTORS:
Irving Pressley McPhail, Ed.D., President
Joe Kann, Vice President
John Miller, Secretary/Treasurer
Frank Ervin, III
Wayne Frost
Brian A. Ruestow
Pamela J. Ruschau, Esq.

ADDRESS INQUIRIES TO:
Kathy Carter, Senior Scholarship Officer
(See address above.)

TRANSPORTATION ASSOCIATION OF CANADA FOUNDATION [2404]

401-1111 Prince of Wales Drive
Ottawa ON K2C 3T2 Canada
(613) 736-1350
Fax: (613) 736-1395
E-mail: foundation@tac-atc.ca
Web Site: www.tac-foundation.ca

FOUNDED: 2003

AREAS OF INTEREST:
Transportation.

NAME(S) OF PROGRAMS:
- **TAC Foundation Scholarships and Bursaries**

TYPE:
Scholarships. Awards are provided for the study of road and transportation sciences, such as highway engineering, transport economics and administration.

YEAR PROGRAM STARTED: 2004

PURPOSE:
To encourage studies by Canadians in the field of transportation.

LEGAL BASIS:
Foundation.

ELIGIBILITY:
Applicants must be Canadian citizens or permanent residents in Canada who are enrolled in a university or college and pursuing studies full-time in some aspect of transportation. Student must have achieved an overall B average or equivalant in their previous academic year.

GEOG. RESTRICTIONS: Canada.

FINANCIAL DATA:
Amount of support per award: Scholarships: $2,500 to $6,000.

Total amount of support: $106,000 in scholarships for the year 2019.

NO. MOST RECENT APPLICANTS: Approximately 125.

NO. AWARDS: 23 for the year 2019.

APPLICATION INFO:
Full information is available on the Foundation web site.

Duration: One year. Applicants may apply at each level: college student, undergraduate and graduate.

Deadline: End of February.

ADDRESS INQUIRIES TO:
See e-mail address above.

THE UNIVERSITY OF CALGARY
Faculty of Graduate Studies
Earth Sciences Building, Room 1010
2500 University Drive, N.W.
Calgary AB T2N 1N4 Canada
(403) 220-4938
Fax: (403) 289-7635
E-mail: gsaward@ucalgary.ca
Web Site: grad.ucalgary.ca/awards

TYPE:
Awards/prizes; Scholarships. Graduate scholarship for study in all areas relevant to the petroleum industry. Tenable at The University of Calgary. Award endowed through a bequest of the late Corinne Patteson.

See entry 1615 for full listing.

Aeronautics and astronautics

AIRCRAFT ELECTRONICS ASSOCIATION (AEA) [2405]
3570 N.E. Ralph Powell Road
Lee's Summit, MO 64064
(816) 347-8400
E-mail: info@aea.net
Web Site: www.aea.net/educationalfoundation/scholarships.asp

FOUNDED: 1957

AREAS OF INTEREST:
Avionics and aircraft electronics.

NAME(S) OF PROGRAMS:
- **David Arver Memorial Scholarship**
- **Dutch and Ginger Arver Scholarship**
- **Gene Baker Memorial Scholarship**
- **Jim Cook Honorary Scholarship**
- **Johnny Davis Memorial Scholarship**
- **Duncan Aviation Scholarship**
- **Field Aviation Company Scholarship**
- **Chuck Freeland Memorial Scholarship for Flight Training**
- **Garmin - Jerry Smith Memorial Scholarship**
- **Garmin Scholarship**
- **Gogo Business Aviation Scholarship**
- **Leon Harris/Les Nichols Memorial Scholarship**
- **L-3 Avionics Systems Scholarship**
- **Mid-Continent Instrument Scholarship**
- **Monte Mitchell Scholarship**
- **Chuck Peacock Memorial Scholarship**
- **Stone Foundation Scholarship**
- **Lee Tarbox Memorial Scholarship**
- **Tom Taylor Memorial Scholarship**
- **Marshall Temple Memorial Scholarship**
- **Universal Avionics Systems Corporation Scholarship**

TYPE:
Scholarships.

PURPOSE:
To provide funding for students seeking higher education in the fields of avionics and aircraft electronics.

LEGAL BASIS:
Nonprofit.

ELIGIBILITY:
Applicants for the Arver Scholarship, Johnny Davis Memorial Scholarship, Duncan Aviation Scholarship, Field Aviation Scholarship, Garmin Scholarship, Garmin-Jerry Smith Scholarship, Gogo Business Aviation Scholarship, L-3 Aviation Products Scholarship, Mid-Continent Instruments Scholarship, Stone Foundation Scholarship, Lee Tarbox Memorial Scholarship, Chuck Peacock Memorial Scholarship, Marshall Temple Memorial Scholarship and Universal Avionics Systems Scholarship can be anyone who plans to or is enrolled in an avionics or aircraft maintenance program in an accredited U.S. or Canadian school.

Gene Baker Memorial Scholarship and Jim Cook Honorary Scholarship are available to AEA members, their children, grandchildren or dependents.

Monte Mitchell Scholarship applicant must be an AEA member employee exhibiting exemplary job performance and pursuit of professional development.

Leon Harris/Les Nichols Memorial Scholarship is awarded to an individual wanting to pursue an Associate degree in applied science in aviation electronics at the Spartan College of Aeronautics and Technology. The applicant cannot be enrolled currently in the avionics program at Spartan.

Tom Taylor Memorial Scholarship is awarded to an individual desiring to pursue an Associate degree in applied science or a diploma in aviation maintenance technology at the Spartan College of Aeronautics and Technology. The applicant cannot be enrolled currently in the AMT program at Spartan.

The Scholarships are not available to obtain pilot licenses.

GEOG. RESTRICTIONS: North America.

FINANCIAL DATA:
Amount of support per award: $1,000 to $35,000, depending on award.

Total amount of support: More than $100,000 in scholarships for the 2019-20 academic year.

NO. AWARDS: 22.

APPLICATION INFO:
Contact the Association.

Duration: One year.

Deadline: Approximately April 1.

ADDRESS INQUIRIES TO:
Educational Foundation
(See address above.)

THE AMERICAN HISTORICAL ASSOCIATION
400 A Street, S.E.
Washington, DC 20003
(202) 544-2422
Fax: (202) 544-8307
E-mail: awards@historians.org
Web Site: www.historians.org

TYPE:
Fellowships. The Association annually funds at least one fellow for a period of six to nine months, to undertake a proposed research project related to aerospace history. The Fellowship is supported by the National Aeronautics and Space Administration (NASA).

See entry 535 for full listing.

AMERICAN INSTITUTE OF AERONAUTICS AND ASTRONAUTICS [2406]
12700 Sunrise Valley Drive
Suite 200
Reston, VA 20191-5807
(800) 639-2422
E-mail: scholarships@aiaa.org
Web Site: www.aiaa.org

FOUNDED: 1977

AREAS OF INTEREST:
Arts, sciences, and technology of aeronautics and astronautics.

NAME(S) OF PROGRAMS:
- **American Institute of Aeronautics and Astronautics Undergraduate Scholarship Program**

TYPE:
Scholarships. Graduate financial awards. Program presents yearly scholarships to college sophomores, college juniors and college seniors. Graduate awards are also offered.

YEAR PROGRAM STARTED: 1977

PURPOSE:
To encourage original research; to further dissemination of new knowledge; to foster the professional development of those engaged in scientific and engineering activities; to improve public understanding of the profession and its contributions; to foster education in engineering and science; to promote communication among engineers and scientists and with other professional groups; to stimulate outstanding professional accomplishments.

ELIGIBILITY:
Applicants must meet the following eligibility requirements:
(1) be a current AIAA student member in good standing;
(2) have completed at least one academic semester of full-time college work;
(3) have a minimum cumulative grade point

average of 3.3 on a 4.0 scale and;
(4) be enrolled in an accredited college or university within the U.S. or U.S. territories.

Applicant's education plan shall be such as to provide entry into some field of science or engineering encompassed by the technical activities of AIAA.

FINANCIAL DATA:
Amount of support per award: Up to $10,000.

Total amount of support: Varies.

NO. MOST RECENT APPLICANTS: 150.

NO. AWARDS: Graduate Awards and Scholarships: 22.

APPLICATION INFO:
Award applications must be submitted online.

Duration: One year.

Deadline: Applications must be received by January 31.

ADDRESS INQUIRIES TO:
Michael Lagana
University Programs Coordinator
(See address above.)

AMERICAN METEOROLOGICAL SOCIETY [2407]
45 Beacon Street
Boston, MA 02108-3693
(617) 227-2426 ext. 3907
Fax: (617) 742-8718
E-mail: dfernandez@ametsoc.org
Web Site: www.ametsoc.org

FOUNDED: 1919

AREAS OF INTEREST:
Weather, water and climate.

NAME(S) OF PROGRAMS:
• **AMS Freshman Undergraduate Scholarship Program**
• **AMS Graduate Fellowship in the History of Science**
• **AMS Graduate Fellowships**
• **AMS Minority Scholarship**
• **AMS Senior Named Scholarships**
• **AMS Women in Science Scholarship**
• **The Father James B. Macelwane Annual Awards in Meteorology**

TYPE:
Fellowships; Scholarships. AMS Freshman Undergraduate Scholarship Program awards funding to high school seniors entering their freshman year of undergraduate study in the fall.

AMS Graduate Fellowship in the History of Science is awarded to a student wishing to complete a dissertation on the history of the atmospheric and related oceanic or hydrologic sciences.

AMS Graduate Fellowships are designed to attract students entering their first year of graduate study in the fall who wish to pursue advanced degrees in the atmospheric and related oceanic and hydrologic sciences.

AMS Minority Scholarship awards funding to high school minority students entering freshman year of undergraduate study in the fall who have been traditionally underrepresented in the sciences, especially Hispanic, Native American and Black/African American students.

AMS Senior Named Scholarships are directed to students entering their final year of undergraduate study in the fall.

The Father James B. Macelwane Annual Awards in Meteorology is intended to stimulate interest in meteorology among college students through the submission of original student papers concerned with some phase of the atmospheric sciences. The student must be enrolled as an undergraduate at the time the paper was written.

YEAR PROGRAM STARTED: 1965

PURPOSE:
To stimulate interest in meteorology among college students and to recognize academic excellence and achievement; to stimulate careers in atmospheric and related oceanic and hydrologic sciences.

LEGAL BASIS:
Nonprofit organization.

ELIGIBILITY:
Candidates must be U.S. citizens or hold permanent resident status.

AMS encourages applications from women, minorities and disabled students who are traditionally underrepresented in the atmospheric and related oceanic and hydrologic sciences.

AMS Freshman Undergraduate Scholarship Program makes awards on the basis of academic excellence.

AMS Graduate Fellowship in the History of Science: Candidate must be a graduate student in good standing who proposes to complete a dissertation on the history of the atmospheric, or related oceanic or hydrologic sciences.

AMS Graduate Fellowships: Applicants must be entering their first year of graduate study in the fall pursuing an advanced degree in the atmospheric and related oceanic and hydrologic sciences. Prospective candidates from the fields of chemistry, computer sciences, engineering, environmental sciences, mathematics or physics who intend to pursue careers in the atmospheric or related oceanic or hydrologic sciences are also encouraged to apply.

AMS Minority Scholarship: Funding to high school minority students who have been traditionally underrepresented in the sciences, especially Hispanic, Native American and Black/African American students. Minority students must be entering their freshman year of undergraduate study in the fall at a four-year U.S. accredited institution, and must plan to pursue a career in the atmospheric or related oceanic or hydrologic sciences.

AMS Senior Named Scholarships: Candidates must be entering their final undergraduate year in the fall and majoring in the atmospheric or related oceanic or hydrologic sciences and/or must show clear intent to make atmospheric or related sciences their career.

Father James B. Macelwane Annual Awards in Meteorology: Student must be enrolled as an undergraduate at the time the paper is written. No more than two students from any one institution may enter papers in any one contest.

GEOG. RESTRICTIONS: United States.

FINANCIAL DATA:
Amount of support per award: AMS Freshman Undergraduate Scholarship Program: $2,500 per year (freshman and sophomore years); AMS Graduate Fellowship

in the History of Science: $20,000 stipend; AMS Graduate Fellowships: $25,000 stipend; AMS Minority Scholarship: $3,000 per year (freshman and sophomore years); AMS Senior Named Scholarships: Up to $10,000; AMS Women in Science Scholarship: $10,000 for the senior year; Father James B. Macelwane Annual Awards in Meteorology: $1,000 stipend and partial travel support to the AMS Annual Meeting.

Total amount of support: Varies.

NO. MOST RECENT APPLICANTS: 340.

NO. AWARDS: 55.

APPLICATION INFO:
Those interested should apply online at the AMS web site. When writing for an application package, specify which application is being requested, and what year of academic study applicant will be entering in the fall. Submit a complete application form, written letters of reference and official transcripts.

Duration: AMS Freshman Undergraduate Scholarship Program: Up to two years; AMS Graduate History of Science Fellowship and AMS Women in Science Scholarship: One year; AMS Minority Scholarship: Two years; AMS Graduate Fellowships: Nine months.

Deadline: AMS Senior Named Scholarship: March. Graduate Fellowship: January. Graduate Fellowship in the History of Science: April. Father James B. Macelwane: Mid-June. All other programs: February.

PUBLICATIONS:
Program announcement.

OFFICERS:
Dr. Keith L. Seitter, Executive Director

ADDRESS INQUIRIES TO:
Donna Fernandez, Development and Student Programs Manager
(See address/phone/e-mail above) or

Stephanie Armstrong
Associate Executive Director
Tel: (617) 227-2426 ext. 3906
E-mail: armstrong@ametsoc.org

*SPECIAL STIPULATIONS:
Applicants must review program requirements before applying.

AVIATION DISTRIBUTORS AND MANUFACTURERS ASSOCIATION (ADMA) [2408]
P.O. Box 3948
Parker, CO 80134
(720) 249-0999
Fax: (720) 496-4974
E-mail: info@adma.org
Web Site: www.adma.org

FOUNDED: 1943

AREAS OF INTEREST:
Aviation and pilot education, mechanics and maintenance.

NAME(S) OF PROGRAMS:
• **ADMA Scholarship Programs**

TYPE:
Scholarships.

ELIGIBILITY:
Applicant must be one of following:
(1) third- or fourth-year B.S. candidate with Aviation Management major, emphasis in General Aviation, Airway Science Management, Aviation Maintenance or Airway Science Maintenance Management;
(2) third- or fourth-year B.S. candidate with

major in Professional Pilot with any of the following emphases: General Aviation, Flight Engineer, Airway Science A/C Systems Management or;
(3) second-year student in A/P education program (two-year accredited aviation technical school).

Applicant must also have 3.0 grade point average or higher.

GEOG. RESTRICTIONS: United States.

FINANCIAL DATA:
Amount of support per award: $1,500.
Total amount of support: $6,000 for the year 2019.

NO. MOST RECENT APPLICANTS: 25.

NO. AWARDS: 4 for the year 2019.

APPLICATION INFO:
Detailed information is available from the Association.
Duration: One year.
Deadline: Early April.

ADDRESS INQUIRIES TO:
Nicole Singleton, Executive Director
(See address above.)

AVIATION INSURANCE ASSOCIATION (AIA) [2409]
7200 West 75th Street
Overland Park, KS 66204
(913) 627-9632
E-mail: mandie@aiaweb.org
Web Site: www.aiaweb.org

FOUNDED: 2005

AREAS OF INTEREST:
Aviation insurance.

NAME(S) OF PROGRAMS:
• AIA Scholarship

TYPE:
Scholarships.

PURPOSE:
To help students with an interest in aviation insurance to continue on to higher education.

LEGAL BASIS:
Nonprofit association.

ELIGIBILITY:
Applicants must:
(1) be currently enrolled in an accredited undergraduate or graduate degree program;
(2) currently be an intern or recently completed an internship program within a facet of the aviation insurance industry;
(3) have completed at least 45 college credits and;
(4) have a minimum 2.5 grade point average on a 4.0 scale.

FINANCIAL DATA:
Amount of support per award: $2,500.

NO. AWARDS: 4.

APPLICATION INFO:
Applicants must submit the following documents to be considered a scholarship candidate:
(1) completed AIA Scholarship application;
(2) letter describing activities, indicating leadership qualities, goals, rolls and reason for applying;
(3) at least one letter of recommendation from a supervisor during the internship program and;
(4) latest transcript(s) from all universities and colleges attended.

Duration: One-time award.
Deadline: February 28.

ADDRESS INQUIRIES TO:
Mandie Loroff, Executive Director
(See address above.)

RTCA [2410]
1150 18th Street, N.W.
Suite 910
Washington, DC 20036
(202) 330-0680
Fax: (202) 833-9434
E-mail: khofmann@rtca.org
Web Site: www.rtca.org

FOUNDED: 1935

AREAS OF INTEREST:
Aviation electronics, telecommunications, and other closely allied fields such as determination of common operational requirements, state-of-the-art developments and applications, other problems associated with air traffic control, navigation, communications, and efficient utilization of airports and airspace.

CONSULTING OR VOLUNTEER SERVICES:
Federal Advisory Committee under Federal Advisory Committee Act (FACA).

NAME(S) OF PROGRAMS:
• The William E. Jackson Award

TYPE:
Awards/prizes. Award for a paper by an outstanding graduate student in aviation electronics or telecommunications, in memory of William E. Jackson, an outstanding pioneer in the development and implementation of the present airways, air traffic control, and aviation communication systems.

YEAR PROGRAM STARTED: 1975

PURPOSE:
To honor an outstanding graduate student in aviation electronics or telecommunications.

LEGAL BASIS:
Nonprofit, 501(c)(3) organization.

ELIGIBILITY:
Open to any graduate student earning a degree in the field of aviation electronics or telecommunication systems. There are no restrictions as to race, creed, color, religious affiliation, national origin or citizenship. The sole basis for selection will be the written report, which must be in English.

FINANCIAL DATA:
The recipient will travel at the expense of RTCA to the location of the award presentation. Complimentary registration for any RTCA business meeting taking place concurrently is also awarded.
Amount of support per award: $4,000.

NO. MOST RECENT APPLICANTS: 3.

NO. AWARDS: 1.

APPLICATION INFO:
Submissions must be in the form of a thesis, project report, or paper in a technical journal. The work must have been completed no earlier than three years before the submission deadline and only those in English and without publication restrictions will be considered. Joint authors may submit if both or all qualify as students and candidates for undergraduate or graduate degrees in this field. Joint authors would share the award. Additionally, candidates must submit a one-

to two-page summary of the written material, a biographical sketch of the candidate, and a letter of endorsement from the candidate's instructor, professor, or departmental head.

All materials must be submitted electronically.
Deadline: October 31.

OFFICERS:
Karan Hofmann, Program Director

ADDRESS INQUIRIES TO:
William E. Jackson Award Committee
(See address above.)

SMITHSONIAN NATIONAL AIR AND SPACE MUSEUM [2411]
P.O. Box 37012, MRC 312
Washington, DC 20013-7012
(202) 633-2648
E-mail: nasm-fellowships@si.edu
Web Site: airandspace.si.edu

FOUNDED: 1946

AREAS OF INTEREST:
Aeronautics.

NAME(S) OF PROGRAMS:
• Aviation Space Writers Foundation Award
• Guggenheim Fellowship
• Charles A. Lindbergh Chair in Aerospace History
• Postdoctoral Earth and Planetary Sciences Fellowship
• A. Verville Fellowship

TYPE:
Fellowships; Research grants. Aviation Space Writers Foundation Award, offered in even-numbered years, is intended to support research on aerospace topics.

The Guggenheim Fellowship is a competitive three- to 12-month in-residence fellowship for pre- or postdoctoral research in aviation and space history.

The Charles A. Lindbergh Chair in Aerospace History is a competitive 12-month fellowship.

Postdoctoral Earth and Planetary Sciences Fellowship supports scientific research in the area of earth and planetary sciences. Scientists in the Center for Earth and Planetary Studies concentrate on geologic and geophysical research of the earth and other terrestrial planets, using remote sensing data obtained from earth-orbiting and interplanetary spacecraft. Research also focuses on global environmental change.

The A. Verville Fellowship is a competitive nine- to 12-month in-residence fellowship intended for analysis of major trends, developments, and accomplishments in the history of aviation or space studies.

All candidates are encouraged to pursue programs of research and writing that support publication of works that are scholarly in tone and substance, and/or addressed to an audience with broad interests. Each fellow will work closely with staff members who share similar interests.

PURPOSE:
To promote research into, and writing about, the history of aviation and space flight.

ELIGIBILITY:
All applicants must be able to write and converse fluently in English. Additional information is available online.

Aviation Space Writers Foundation Award: The product created as a result of the grant must be in any form suitable for potential public dissemination in print, electronic, broadcast or other visual medium, including, but not limited to, a book manuscript, a video, or film script or monograph.

Guggenheim Fellowship: Predoctoral applicants should have completed preliminary course work and examinations and be engaged in dissertation research. Postdoctoral applicants should have received their Ph.D. within the past seven years.

Lindbergh Chair in Aerospace History: Open to senior scholars with distinguished records of publication who are at work on, or anticipate being at work on, books in aerospace history.

Verville Fellowship: Open to interested candidates with demonstrated skills in research and writing. Publishing experience should demonstrate either a mid-level academic record of accomplishment or proven ability to engage in a reliable manner broader audiences. An advanced degree in history or a related field is preferred but not a requirement.

FINANCIAL DATA:
Amount of support per award: Aviation Space Writers Foundation Award: Grant of $5,000; Guggenheim Fellowship: Annual stipend of $30,000 for predoctoral candidates and $45,000 for postdoctoral candidates; Lindbergh Chair in Aerospace History: Support is available for living expenses in the Washington, DC area up to a maximum of $100,000 a year; Postdoctoral Earth and Planetary Sciences Fellowship: Stipends are compatible with National Research Council postdoctoral fellowships in the applicant's field; Verville Fellowship: Annual stipend of $55,000 (for a 12-month fellowship tenure), with limited additional funds for travel and miscellaneous expenses.

NO. AWARDS: 1 each.

APPLICATION INFO:
All applications must be submitted electronically through the Smithsonian Online Academic Appointment System (SOLAA).

Duration: Guggenheim Fellowship: Three to 12 months; Lindbergh Chair in Aerospace History: Typically for an academic year (September through August); Postdoctoral Earth and Planetary Sciences Fellowship: Appointments can be made for one or more years; Verville Fellowship: Nine to 12 months.

Deadline: Postdoctoral Earth and Planetary Sciences Fellowship: November 1. All others: Application due December 1; Recommendation letters due December 15; Award presented mid-March.

PUBLICATIONS:
Brochure; application package.

ADDRESS INQUIRIES TO:
Aviation Space Writers Foundation Award:
Dr. Dominick A. Pisano
Aeronautics Department
National Air and Space Museum
E-mail: pisanod@si.edu

Guggenheim, Lindbergh and Verville Fellowships:
Collette Williams, Administrative Program Specialist
(See e-mail address above.)

Postdoctoral Earth and Planetary Sciences Fellowship: Rosemary Aiello
Center for Earth and Planetary Studies
National Air and Space Museum
Washington, DC 20560
Tel: (202) 633-2480
E-mail: aiellor@si.edu

*PLEASE NOTE:
Applicants are restricted to applying for a single National Air and Space Museum fellowship grant at a time. Proposals must reflect that the research to be undertaken is intended for publication in peer-reviewed books and journals.

SMITHSONIAN NATIONAL AIR AND SPACE MUSEUM [2412]
601 Independence Avenue, S.W.
Room 3762, MRC 305
Washington, DC 20560
(202) 633-2214
Fax: (202) 633-1957
E-mail: fay-lukic@si.edu
Web Site: airandspace.si.edu/support/get-involved/internships

FOUNDED: 1946

AREAS OF INTEREST:
Aeronautics.

NAME(S) OF PROGRAMS:
● **Summer Internship Program**

TYPE:
Internships. Full-time interns work 40 hours per week from approximately the first week in June until the second week in August.

PURPOSE:
To give interns a firsthand opportunity to learn about the historic artifacts and archival materials housed in the Museum and to study the scientific and technological advances they represent.

ELIGIBILITY:
Applicant must be a high school graduate and be enrolled in, or recently graduated from, a degree-granting undergraduate or graduate program at an accredited college or university. Applicant is expected to have a strong academic record.

Applicants from outside the U.S. are welcome. International applicants must have the appropriate J-1 visa and are responsible for any other necessary official documents.

FINANCIAL DATA:
Interns are responsible for locating and securing lodging.
Amount of support per award: $5,500.

NO. MOST RECENT APPLICANTS: 350 for the year 2020.

NO. AWARDS: 36 paid internships in 2018.

APPLICATION INFO:
Application information is available on the web site. Visit the Smithsonian Online Academic Appointment System (SOLAA) web site, which opens January 15, to apply.
Duration: 10 weeks during the summer; schedule is flexible.
Deadline: Applications are accepted from January 15 to February 15 during the calendar year of the internship. Interns are notified of the status of their application on or before April 1.

ADDRESS INQUIRIES TO:
E-mail: NASMInternships@si.edu

*SPECIAL STIPULATIONS:
A commitment of 10 weeks during the summer is required.

VERTICAL FLIGHT FOUNDATION [2413]
2701 Prosperity Avenue, Suite 210
Fairfax, VA 22031
(703) 684-6777
Fax: (703) 739-9279
E-mail: bchen@vtol.org
Web Site: www.vtol.org/vff

FOUNDED: 1967

AREAS OF INTEREST:
Support of scientific and educational activities related to VTOL (Vertical Take-Off and Landing) flight.

NAME(S) OF PROGRAMS:
● **Vertical Flight Foundation Engineering Scholarships**

TYPE:
Awards/prizes; Scholarships. Annual scholarships to undergraduate senior, Master's or Ph.D. students interested in pursuing careers in some technical aspect of helicopter or vertical flight engineering.

YEAR PROGRAM STARTED: 1967

PURPOSE:
To acquire the best technical experts for the vertical flight industry.

LEGAL BASIS:
Independent, charitable trust.

ELIGIBILITY:
Applicants must be full-time college students at an accredited school in a technical program. Technical disciplines relevant to complex aeronautics/aeronautics engineering or aviation systems, even if not directly considered vertical lift engineering, will receive equal consideration.

FINANCIAL DATA:
Amount of support per award: $3,000 to $6,000.

Total amount of support: $90,000 for the year 2018.

NO. AWARDS: Varies based on size of endowment.

APPLICATION INFO:
Detailed instructions are available at the web site. Professor's recommendation letter and transcripts must be submitted directly from the school. Submission by the student will not be accepted as valid documents.
Duration: One academic year.
Deadline: February 3, 2020. Postmark governs timeliness.

PUBLICATIONS:
Applications.

IRS I.D.: 23-6428319

ADDRESS INQUIRIES TO:
Betty Chen, Scholarship Coordinator
(See address above.)

Engineering

ADSC: THE INTERNATIONAL ASSOCIATION OF FOUNDATION DRILLING [2414]

8445 Freeport Parkway
Suite 325
Irving, TX 75063
(469) 359-6000
Fax: (469) 359-6007
E-mail: adsc@adsc-iafd.com
Web Site: www.adsc-iafd.com

FOUNDED: 1972

AREAS OF INTEREST:
Civil, geotechnical and structural engineering.

TYPE:
Scholarships.

PURPOSE:
To promote the foundation drilling and anchored earth retention industry.

ELIGIBILITY:
Must be a graduate student studying civil engineering.

GEOG. RESTRICTIONS: United States or Canada.

FINANCIAL DATA:
Amount of support per award: Maximum $3,000.
Total amount of support: Approximately $42,000 annually.

NO. AWARDS: Minimum of 17 per year.

APPLICATION INFO:
Applicants must submit a brief letter outlining personal goals, two letters of recommendation and a copy of their transcript with application. Further information and application may be obtained from the Association.
Duration: One year.
Deadline: Contact the Association for deadline.

ADDRESS INQUIRIES TO:
Emily Matthews, Director of Operations
(See address above.)

AGC EDUCATION AND RESEARCH FOUNDATION [2415]

2300 Wilson Boulevard, Suite 300
Arlington, VA 22201
(703) 837-5342
Fax: (703) 837-5451
E-mail: patricianm@agc.org
Web Site: www.agcfoundation.org

FOUNDED: 1968

AREAS OF INTEREST:
Construction and civic interest in improving the quality of educational programs for students specifically in the area of commercial construction and construction research.

NAME(S) OF PROGRAMS:
- **James L. Allhands Essay Competition**
- **Graduate Scholarship Program**
- **Industry Case Studies**
- **Outstanding Educator Award**
- **Undergraduate Scholarship Program**
- **Workforce Development Scholarship**

TYPE:
Awards/prizes; Internships; Project/program grants; Scholarships. Allhands Essay Competition: Awarded to a student essay on a specific topic that is deemed to be beneficial to the advancement of technological, educational or vocational expertise in the construction industry.
Graduate Scholarship Program: Scholarships for students enrolled in ABET- or ACCE-accredited construction management or construction-related engineering programs.
Industry Case Studies: Commissioning case studies on industry scenarios.
Outstanding Educator Award: Awards to top competitors in essay competition for seniors and faculty nominated as outstanding educator.
Undergraduate Scholarship Program: Scholarships for students enrolled in ABET- or ACCE-accredited construction management or construction-related engineering programs.
Workforce Development Scholarship: Awarded for students entering craft training or technical programs.

YEAR PROGRAM STARTED: 1968

PURPOSE:
To improve the science of construction through the funding of scholarships and construction research projects.

LEGAL BASIS:
501(c)(3).

ELIGIBILITY:
James L. Allhands Essay Competition is for seniors only in a four- or five-year ABET- or ACCE-accredited university construction management or construction-related engineering program.

Undergraduate scholarships are available to college sophomores and juniors enrolled or planning to enroll in a full-time, four- or five-year ABET- or ACCE-accredited construction or civil engineering program. High school seniors and college freshman are not eligible.

Graduate awards are available to college seniors enrolled in an undergraduate construction or civil engineering degree program, or others possessing an undergraduate degree in construction or civil engineering. The applicant must be enrolled, or planning to enroll, in a graduate-level construction or civil engineering degree program as a full-time student. All candidates must be U.S. citizens or permanent U.S. residents.

Workforce Development Scholarship is available to students already enrolled or planning to enroll in craft training or technical programs up to two years in length.

Contact the Foundation for details.

GEOG. RESTRICTIONS: United States.

FINANCIAL DATA:
Amount of support per award: Allhands Essay Competition: First Prize $1,000 and an expense-paid trip to the AGC Convention; Graduate Scholarships: Up to $7,500; Industry Case Studies: $9,000 grant; Outstanding Educator Award: $5,000 award and an expense-paid trip to the AGC Convention, plus two $2,500 scholarships for students of the educator; Undergraduate Scholarships: $2,500 per year renewable to a maximum of $7,500; Workforce Development Scholarship: $1,000 per year, renewable up to $2,000.
Total amount of support: $500,000 for all programs.

NO. AWARDS: First, second and third prizes awarded in Allhands Essay. Outstanding Educator: 1. Over 150 scholarships are awarded each year.

APPLICATION INFO:
Undergraduate and graduate applications are posted online after July 1. Online link: scholarship.agc.org. All other application links can be found at www.agcfoundation.org.
Duration: Varies.
Deadline: Allhands Essay Competition and Outstanding Educator Award: November 15; Graduate and Undergraduate Scholarships: Applications are accepted July 1 to November 1; Workforce Development Scholarship: Applications are accepted March 1 to June 1. Contact the Foundation for other deadlines.

IRS I.D.: 52-6083465

STAFF:
Melinda Patrician, Executive Director
Courtney Bishop, Associate Director

BOARD OF DIRECTORS:
Eric Wilson, President
Harry Mashburn, Vice President
Scott Holloway, Treasurer
Monique Ford, Secretary

ADDRESS INQUIRIES TO:
Courtney Bishop, Associate Director
Tel: (703) 837-5356
E-mail: courtney.bishop@agc.org
(See address above.)

AMERICAN CHEMICAL SOCIETY

1155 16th Street, N.W.
Washington, DC 20036-4800
(202) 872-4575
Fax: (202) 776-8008
E-mail: awards@acs.org
Web Site: www.acs.org/awards

TYPE:
Awards/prizes.

See entry 1877 for full listing.

AMERICAN INSTITUTE OF CHEMICAL ENGINEERS (AICHE) [2416]

120 Wall Street, Floor 23
New York, NY 10005-4020
(800) 242-4363
Fax: (646) 495-1503
E-mail: awards@aiche.org
Web Site: www.aiche.org

FOUNDED: 1908

AREAS OF INTEREST:
Chemical engineering.

NAME(S) OF PROGRAMS:
- **Minority Scholarship Awards for College Students**

TYPE:
Scholarships.

YEAR PROGRAM STARTED: 1994

PURPOSE:
To encourage minority undergraduate study of chemical engineering.

LEGAL BASIS:
Nonprofit.

ELIGIBILITY:
Applicants shall be required to be undergraduates in chemical engineering

during the current academic year and be members of a minority group that is under-represented in chemical engineering (African American, Hispanic, Native American, Alaskan Native and Pacific Islander).

FINANCIAL DATA:
Amount of support per award: $1,000.

NO. AWARDS: 8 for the year 2019.

APPLICATION INFO:
Contact the Institute.

Duration: One scholastic year. Renewable following year if student continues to meet eligibility requirements.

Deadline: Usually in summer.

PUBLICATIONS:
Awards nomination form.

AMERICAN NUCLEAR SOCIETY (ANS) [2417]
555 North Kensington Avenue
LaGrange Park, IL 60526
(708) 352-6611
Fax: (708) 352-0499
E-mail: scholarships@ans.org
Web Site: www.ans.org

FOUNDED: 1954

AREAS OF INTEREST:
Nuclear science, nuclear engineering or nuclear-related field.

NAME(S) OF PROGRAMS:
- **ANS Graduate Scholarships**
- **Everitt P. Blizard Memorial Scholarship**
- **Robert A. Dannels Memorial Scholarship**
- **James F. Schumar Scholarship**

TYPE:
Scholarships. Blizard Scholarship is for students pursuing graduate studies in the field of radiation protection and shielding.

Schumar Scholarship is for a student pursuing graduate studies in material science and technology for nuclear applications.

PURPOSE:
To support higher education in the field of nuclear science.

ELIGIBILITY:
U.S. and non-U.S. applicants must be ANS student members. Applicant must be a U.S. citizen or possess a permanent resident visa, be enrolled in a U.S. university and must be sponsored by an ANS local section, division, student branch, committee or organization member. More than one applicant can be sponsored by any of these organizations.

The Dannels Scholarship is for a graduate-level course of study leading toward a degree in mathematics and computation. Only U.S. citizens or persons possessing a permanent resident visa are eligible. Nomination of handicapped persons is encouraged.

GEOG. RESTRICTIONS: United States.

FINANCIAL DATA:
Scholarship funds may be used to defray any bona fide education costs including tuition, books, room and board.
Amount of support per award: ANS Graduate, Blizard and Schumar Scholarships: $3,000 each; Dannels Scholarship: $3,500.

NO. AWARDS: ANS Graduate Scholarships: Up to 5; Blizard, Dannels and Schumar Scholarships: 1 each.

APPLICATION INFO:
Applications must be submitted online.

Duration: One year. Nonrenewable.

Deadline: February 1.

ADDRESS INQUIRIES TO:
Scholarship Coordinator
(See address above.)

*PLEASE NOTE:
Scholarships are only offered to ANS student members.

AMERICAN NUCLEAR SOCIETY (ANS) [2418]
555 North Kensington Avenue
LaGrange Park, IL 60526
(708) 352-6611
Fax: (708) 352-0499
E-mail: scholarships@ans.org
Web Site: www.ans.org

FOUNDED: 1954

AREAS OF INTEREST:
Nuclear science, nuclear engineering and nuclear-related field.

NAME(S) OF PROGRAMS:
- **Pittsburgh Local Section Scholarship**

TYPE:
Scholarships. Two Pittsburgh Local Section Scholarships: one for a graduate student (studying nuclear science and technology) and one for an undergraduate student (studying nuclear science and technology) who either have some affiliation with western Pennsylvania or who attend school at a nearby university within the region.

PURPOSE:
To support higher education in nuclear science.

ELIGIBILITY:
Applicant must be a U.S. citizen or possess a permanent resident visa, be enrolled in a U.S. college or university, and must be sponsored by an ANS local section, division, student branch, committee or organization member. More than one applicant can be sponsored by any of these organizations.

GEOG. RESTRICTIONS: Western Pennsylvania.

FINANCIAL DATA:
Scholarship funds may be used to defray any bona fide education costs including tuition, books, room and board.
Amount of support per award:
Undergraduate: $2,000; Graduate: $3,500.

NO. AWARDS: Undergraduate and Graduate: 1 each.

APPLICATION INFO:
Applications must be submitted online.

Duration: One year. Nonrenewable.

Deadline: February 1.

ADDRESS INQUIRIES TO:
Scholarship Coordinator
(See address above.)

*PLEASE NOTE:
Scholarships are only offered to ANS student members.

AMERICAN NUCLEAR SOCIETY (ANS) [2419]
555 North Kensington Avenue
LaGrange Park, IL 60526
(708) 352-6611
Fax: (708) 352-0499
E-mail: scholarships@ans.org
Web Site: www.ans.org

FOUNDED: 1954

AREAS OF INTEREST:
Nuclear science, nuclear engineering or nuclear-related field.

NAME(S) OF PROGRAMS:
- **Delayed Education for Women Scholarship**
- **John and Muriel Landis Scholarships**

TYPE:
Scholarships. Delayed Education for Women Scholarship is designed for women in a nuclear-related field whose formal studies have been delayed or interrupted for at least one year.

Landis Scholarships are administered by the ANS NEED Committee, and are awarded to undergraduate and graduate students who have greater-than-average financial need.

PURPOSE:
To encourage mature women whose formal studies in the field of nuclear science, nuclear engineering, or a nuclear-related field have been delayed or interrupted for at least one year; to provide financial aid to students with greater-than-average need.

ELIGIBILITY:
Applicants must be ANS student members.

Delayed Education for Women Scholarship: Applicants must have experienced a minimum of a one-year delay or interruption of their undergraduate studies and must be entering a four-year curriculum. Those at graduate level of education can also apply. Applicants must also have proven academic ability as well as demonstrated financial need. An applicant must be a U.S. citizen or possess a permanent resident visa, be enrolled in a U.S. college or university, and must be sponsored by an ANS local section, division, student branch, committee or organization member. More than one applicant can be sponsored by any of these organizations. Those applying must be enrolled in a course of study relating to a degree in nuclear science or nuclear engineering in a U.S. institution. Applicants must be mature women whose undergraduate studies in nuclear science, nuclear engineering, or a nuclear-related field have been delayed.

Landis Scholarships: Applicants must be undergraduate or graduate students who have greater-than-average financial need. Consideration is given to conditions or experiences that render the student disadvantaged (poor high school/undergraduate preparation, etc.). Applicants should be planning a career in nuclear science, nuclear engineering, or a nuclear-related field and be enrolled or planning to enroll in a college or university located in the U.S. Applicants need not be U.S. citizens.

GEOG. RESTRICTIONS: United States.

FINANCIAL DATA:
Scholarship funds may be used by the student to defray any bona fide education costs including tuition, books, room and board.

Amount of support per award: $5,000.

CO-OP FUNDING PROGRAMS: Delayed Education for Women Scholarship: Sponsored jointly by the NEED and Professional Women in the ANS Committees.

NO. AWARDS: Delayed Education for Women Scholarship: 1; Landis Scholarships: Up to 5.

APPLICATION INFO:
Applications must be submitted online.
Duration: One year. Nonrenewable.
Deadline: February 1.

ADDRESS INQUIRIES TO:
Scholarship Coordinator
(See address above.)

*PLEASE NOTE:
Scholarships are only offered to ANS student members.

*SPECIAL STIPULATIONS:
Student may receive no more than three NEED scholarships over the course of their undergraduate and graduate studies.

AMERICAN NUCLEAR SOCIETY (ANS)   [2420]

555 North Kensington Avenue
LaGrange Park, IL 60526
(708) 352-6611
Fax: (708) 352-0499
E-mail: scholarships@ans.org
Web Site: www.ans.org

FOUNDED: 1954

AREAS OF INTEREST:
Nuclear science, nuclear engineering or nuclear-related fields.

NAME(S) OF PROGRAMS:
- **Decommissioning and Environmental Sciences (DESD) Undergraduate Scholarship**

TYPE:
Scholarships. For an undergraduate student pursuing a degree in engineering or science major with emphasis on decommissioning/decontamination, management/characterization of radioactive waste, restoration of the environment, or nuclear engineering.

YEAR PROGRAM STARTED: 2013

ELIGIBILITY:
Applicant must be at junior or senior undergraduate level and must be a U.S. citizen or permanent resident. He or she must be enrolled in a course of study relating to a degree in nuclear science or nuclear engineering in a U.S. institution. Additional criteria to be met include:
(1) the student must be enrolled in a curriculum of engineering or science that is associated either with decommissioning/decontamination of nuclear facilities, management/characterization of nuclear waste, restoration of the environment, or nuclear engineering;
(2) the scholarship is limited to U.S. citizens who are enrolled in U.S. schools;
(3) the student will join the American Nuclear Society (ANS);
(4) the student will designate the ANS DDR Division as one of his or her professional divisions and;
(5) he or she will commit to provide student support to the ANS DDR Division at the next ANS meeting after receipt of the scholarship award. (DDR will provide

funding for the student's travel to the ANS meeting, including student registration, reasonable transportation, food and lodging.)

FINANCIAL DATA:
Scholarship funds may be used by the student to defray any bona fide education costs including tuition, books, room and board.
Amount of support per award: $2,000.

NO. AWARDS: 1 annually.

APPLICATION INFO:
Applications must be submitted online.
Duration: One year. Nonrenewable.
Deadline: February 1.

ADDRESS INQUIRIES TO:
Scholarship Coordinator
(See address above.)

*PLEASE NOTE:
Scholarships are only offered to ANS student members.

AMERICAN NUCLEAR SOCIETY (ANS)   [2421]

555 North Kensington Avenue
LaGrange Park, IL 60526
(708) 352-6611
Fax: (708) 352-0499
E-mail: scholarships@ans.org
Web Site: www.ans.org

FOUNDED: 1954

AREAS OF INTEREST:
Nuclear science, nuclear engineering or nuclear-related field.

NAME(S) OF PROGRAMS:
- **Raymond DiSalvo Memorial Scholarship**
- **Robert T. Liner Memorial Scholarship**
- **Operations and Power Division Scholarship**
- **Charles (Tommy) Thomas Memorial Scholarship**

TYPE:
Scholarships. Award for a full-time undergraduate student in a program leading to a degree in nuclear science or nuclear engineering at an accredited institution in the U.S.

ELIGIBILITY:
U.S. and non-U.S. applicants must be ANS student members enrolled in an accredited institution in the U.S. Applicant must be a U.S. citizen or possess a permanent resident visa.

Academic accomplishments must be substantiated by transcript. Applicants must be sponsored by an ANS local section, division, student branch, committee or organization member.

Operations and Power Division Scholarship: Applicants must have completed a minimum of two complete academic years in a four-year nuclear science or engineering program.

Charles (Tommy) Thomas Memorial Scholarship: Undergraduate of at least junior-year status pursuing a degree in a discipline preparing them for a career dealing with the environmental aspects of nuclear science or nuclear engineering.

GEOG. RESTRICTIONS: United States.

FINANCIAL DATA:
Scholarship funds may be used by the student to defray any bona fide education costs including tuition, fees, books, room and board.
Amount of support per award: Raymond DiSalvo and Robert T. Liner Scholarship: $2,000; Charles (Tommy) Thomas Memorial Scholarship: $3,000; Operations and Power Division Scholarship: $2,500.

NO. AWARDS: Operations and Power Division Scholarship: 2; All others: 1 each.

APPLICATION INFO:
Applications must be submitted online.
Duration: One year. Nonrenewable.
Deadline: February 1.

ADDRESS INQUIRIES TO:
Scholarship Coordinator
(See address above.)

*PLEASE NOTE:
Scholarships are only offered to ANS student members.

AMERICAN NUCLEAR SOCIETY (ANS)

555 North Kensington Avenue
LaGrange Park, IL 60526
(708) 352-6611
Fax: (708) 352-0499
E-mail: scholarships@ans.org
Web Site: www.ans.org

TYPE:
Scholarships. Scholarship award to recognize one outstanding undergraduate student or one graduate student pursuing a career in radioanalytical chemistry or analytical applications of nuclear science.
See entry 1881 for full listing.

AMERICAN NUCLEAR SOCIETY (ANS)   [2422]

555 North Kensington Avenue
LaGrange Park, IL 60526
(708) 352-6611
Fax: (708) 352-0499
E-mail: scholarships@ans.org
Web Site: www.ans.org

FOUNDED: 1954

AREAS OF INTEREST:
Nuclear science, nuclear engineering or nuclear-related fields.

NAME(S) OF PROGRAMS:
- **ANS Undergraduate Scholarships**
- **Joseph R. Dietrich Memorial Scholarship**
- **Allan F. Henry/Paul A. Greebler Memorial Scholarship**
- **John R. Lamarsh Memorial Scholarship**

TYPE:
Scholarships.

ELIGIBILITY:
U.S. and non-U.S. applicants must be ANS student members enrolled in and attending an accredited institution in the U.S. Applicants must have completed a minimum of two complete academic years in a four-year nuclear engineering program and must be U.S. citizens or possess a permanent resident visa. Academic accomplishments must be substantiated by transcript. Applicant must be sponsored by an ANS local section, division, student branch, committee or organization member.

ANS Undergraduate Scholarships and Lamarsh Memorial Scholarship are open to full-time undergraduate students in a program leading to a degree in nuclear science or nuclear engineering at an accredited institution in the U.S.

Joseph R. Dietrich Scholarship is open to a full-time graduate student in a program leading to a degree in nuclear science or nuclear engineering at an accredited institution in the U.S.

Henry/Greebler Scholarship is open to a full-time graduate student of a North American university engaged in Master's or Ph.D. research in the area of nuclear reactor physics or radiation transport. Students of all nationalities are eligible.

FINANCIAL DATA:
Scholarship funds may be used by the student to defray any bona fide education costs including tuition, fees, room and board.
Amount of support per award: ANS Undergraduate, Joseph R. Dietrich Memorial and John R. Lamarsh Memorial Scholarships: $2,000; Alan F. Henry/Paul A. Greebler Memorial Scholarship: $3,500.

NO. AWARDS: ANS Undergraduate Scholarships: Up to 5; Dietrich, Greebler and Lamarsh Memorial Scholarships: 1 each.

APPLICATION INFO:
Applications must be submitted online.
Duration: One year. Nonrenewable.
Deadline: February 1.

ADDRESS INQUIRIES TO:
Scholarship Coordinator
(See address above.)

*PLEASE NOTE:
Scholarships are only offered to ANS student members.

AMERICAN PUBLIC POWER ASSOCIATION [2423]
2451 Crystal Drive
Suite 1000
Arlington, VA 22202
(202) 467-2900
(202) 467-2960
Fax: (202) 467-2910
E-mail: deed@publicpower.org
Web Site: www.publicpower.org/deed

FOUNDED: 1980

AREAS OF INTEREST:
Engineering, mathematics and computer science.

NAME(S) OF PROGRAMS:
● **DEED Interships**
● **Educational Scholarship**
● **Student Research Grant**
● **Technical Design Project**

TYPE:
Demonstration grants; Development grants; Internships; Project/program grants; Research grants; Scholarships.

YEAR PROGRAM STARTED: 1980

PURPOSE:
To promote the involvement of students studying in energy-related disciplines in the public power industry; to provide host utilities with technical assistance.

ELIGIBILITY:
Open to students conducting research on a project approved by the sponsoring utility who will then submit a final report on the

project, describing the activities, cost, bibliography, achievements, problems, results and recommendations. Applicants will not be discriminated against on the basis of sex, race, religion, national origin or citizenship.

Student must be accepted or enrolled in an accredited technical/trade/vocational school, community college, or four-year university in the U.S.

FINANCIAL DATA:
Amount of support per award: DEED Internships and Student Research Grant: $4,000; Educational Scholarship: $2,000; Technical Design Project: $5,000.
Total amount of support: Varies.

NO. MOST RECENT APPLICANTS: 37.

NO. AWARDS: 33.

APPLICATION INFO:
Applications must be sent from a DEED member utility and must be dated on the last page by an authorized individual at the utility.
Deadline: Spring cycle: Applications accepted December 1 to February 15; Fall cycle: Applications accepted August 1 to October 15.

ADDRESS INQUIRIES TO:
DEED Team
(See address above.)

AMERICAN SOCIETY FOR ENGINEERING EDUCATION [2424]
1818 N Street, N.W., Suite 600
Washington, DC 20036-2479
(202) 649-3831
Fax: (202) 265-8504
E-mail: ndsegf@sti-tec.com
Web Site: ndsegfellowship.org

FOUNDED: 1893

AREAS OF INTEREST:
STEM disciplines.

NAME(S) OF PROGRAMS:
● **Department of Defense National Defense Science and Engineering Graduate Fellowship Program (NDSEG)**

TYPE:
Fellowships.

YEAR PROGRAM STARTED: 1964

ELIGIBILITY:
For students at or near the beginning of their doctoral study in science or engineering. Field of study must fit under one of 15 supported STEM disciplines. Applicants must be citizens or nationals of the U.S.

FINANCIAL DATA:
Provides competitive stipend and full tuition.
Amount of support per award: Varies.
Total amount of support: Varies.

NO. AWARDS: Approximately 200 annually.

APPLICATION INFO:
Application guidelines are available online.
Deadline: Typically December. Applications open late summer/early fall.

ADDRESS INQUIRIES TO:
See e-mail address above.

AMERICAN SOCIETY FOR ENGINEERING EDUCATION [2425]
1818 N Street, N.W., Suite 600
Washington, DC 20036
(202) 350-5763
(202) 350-5757
Fax: (202) 463-1401
E-mail: postdocs@asee.org
Web Site: nrl.asee.org

FOUNDED: 1893

AREAS OF INTEREST:
Engineering education programs, scientific research in government, industry and the military.

NAME(S) OF PROGRAMS:
● **Naval Research Laboratory (NRL) Postdoctoral Fellowship Program**

TYPE:
Fellowships. Offered at Naval research and development centers and laboratories. NRL is charged with developing technologies that will support Naval Forces in meeting future operational needs. Scientists and fellows working at NRL pursue research on subjects including, but not limited to, processing, biomedicine, logistics, command control and intelligence, training and oceanography.

YEAR PROGRAM STARTED: 2002

PURPOSE:
To significantly increase the involvement of creative and highly trained scientists and engineers from academia and industry in scientific and technical areas of interest and relevance to the Navy.

LEGAL BASIS:
Special interest society.

ELIGIBILITY:
Applicants must be U.S. citizens and permanent residents and must be eligible for a Department of Defense security clearance of "Secret." In most cases, participants will be permitted to do research pending completion of the security clearance. All appointments are contingent upon fellows obtaining the appropriate level of security clearance. Prior to appointment, participants must present evidence of having received the Ph.D., Sc.D. or other earned research doctoral degree recognized in U.S. as equivalent to the Ph.D. within seven years of the date of application or must present acceptable evidence of having completed all formal academic requirements for one of these degrees. No support to applicants who received prior postdoctoral appointment under any program at the same Navy laboratory. No appointments or denials based on grounds of race, creed, color, national origin, age or sex.

GEOG. RESTRICTIONS: United States.

FINANCIAL DATA:
Awards include stipend, insurance, relocation expenses and travel.
Amount of support per award: Maximum stipend $79,720.
Total amount of support: Varies.

NO. AWARDS: Approximately 45 new appointments each year.

APPLICATION INFO:
Applicants should contact the research facility of interest to develop a suitable research proposal. Proposals developed closely with the proposed host facility stand the greatest chance of success in the selection process. A proposal should be no more than

10 pages, be concise, and address a problem of mutual interest to the applicant and Navy research facility.

Duration: One year. Renewable for a second and third year with satisfactory performance and availability of funds.

PUBLICATIONS:
Program announcement.

STAFF:
Shannon Becks, Program Director
Elisheba Wilson, Program Assistant

ADDRESS INQUIRIES TO:
NRL Postdoctoral Program
Contracts/Grants Office
(See address above.)

THE AMERICAN SOCIETY FOR NONDESTRUCTIVE TESTING, INC.

1711 Arlingate Lane
Columbus, OH 43228
(614) 274-6003
(800) 222-2768
Fax: (614) 274-6899
E-mail: james@asnt.org
Web Site: www.asnt.org

TYPE:
Scholarships.

See entry 1501 for full listing.

AMERICAN SOCIETY OF CIVIL ENGINEERS   [2426]

1801 Alexander Bell Drive
Reston, VA 20191-4400
(703) 295-6300 ext. 6382
(800) 548-2723
E-mail: awards@asce.org
Web Site: www.asce.org

FOUNDED: 1852

AREAS OF INTEREST:
Civil engineering.

NAME(S) OF PROGRAMS:
- **O.H. Ammann Research Fellowship in Structural Engineering**
- **CI Construction Engineering Scholarship and Student Prizes**
- **Lawrence W. and Francis W. Cox Scholarship**
- **Trent R. Dames and William W. Moore Fellowship**
- **Eugene C. Figg, Jr. Civil Engineering Scholarship**
- **Freeman Fellowship**
- **Jack E. Leisch Memorial National Graduate Fellowship**
- **John Lenard Civil Engineering Scholarship**
- **Robert B.B. and Josephine N. Moorman Scholarship**
- **J. Waldo Smith Hydraulic Fellowship**
- **Samuel Fletcher Tapman ASCE Student Chapter Scholarship**
- **Arthur S. Tuttle Memorial Fellowship**
- **Y.C. Yang Civil Engineering Scholarship**

TYPE:
Fellowships; Grants-in-aid; Research grants; Scholarships. Scholarships, fellowships and grants for research; undergraduate and graduate studies in civil engineering fields from ASCE endowments, operation or other funds.

Fellowships and scholarships are awarded annually.

YEAR PROGRAM STARTED: 1924

PURPOSE:
To aid and encourage education, research and studies in civil engineering.

LEGAL BASIS:
Nonprofit professional organization.

ELIGIBILITY:
Qualified engineers or engineering undergraduate or graduate students with appropriate interests are eligible to apply. Undergraduate students must be enrolled at an ABET-accredited university, be a member of an ASCE student chapter and also be a national student member in good standing. (A list of schools that have student chapters is available from the address above.)

FINANCIAL DATA:
Amount of support per award: Varies.

APPLICATION INFO:
Application forms are available at www.asce.org/student_resources.

Duration: One year.

Deadline: Majority due close of business February 10. O.H. Ammann Research Fellowship: November 1.

PUBLICATIONS:
Scholarships/Fellowships brochure.

OFFICERS:
Thomas Smith, Executive Director

ADDRESS INQUIRIES TO:
See e-mail address above.

*SPECIAL STIPULATIONS:
Requires ASCE membership of some kind.

THE AMERICAN SOCIETY OF MECHANICAL ENGINEERS AUXILIARY, INC.   [2427]

2 Park Avenue, MS-RB
New York, NY 10016-5990
(212) 591-7650
E-mail: bigleyr@asme.org
Web Site: go.asme.org/scholarships

FOUNDED: 1923

AREAS OF INTEREST:
Mechanical engineering students.

NAME(S) OF PROGRAMS:
- **Allen J. Baldwin Scholarship**
- **Berna Lou Cartwright Scholarship**
- **Carolyn and James M. Chenoweth Scholarship**
- **Lucy and Charles W.E. Clarke Scholarship**
- **Sylvia W. Farny Scholarship**
- **Agnes Malakate Kezios Scholarship**
- **Elisabeth M. and Winchell M. Parsons Scholarship**
- **Rice-Cullimore Scholarship**
- **Marjorie Roy Rothermel Scholarship**
- **Charles B. Scharp Scholarship**
- **Student Loan Fund**

TYPE:
Scholarships. Lucy and Charles W.E. Clarke Scholarship is for high school seniors participating on a FIRST team.

Baldwin, Cartwright, Chenoweth, Farny, Kezios and Scharp Scholarships are for undergraduate students in mechanical engineering.

Parsons and Rothermel Scholarships are for graduate students with a degree in mechanical engineering, to be used to pursue a Master's or Ph.D. degree in mechanical engineering.

Rice-Cullimore Scholarship is for foreign students at the graduate level.

Student Loan Fund is for juniors, seniors or graduate students enrolled as degree candidates in good standing.

YEAR PROGRAM STARTED: 1924

PURPOSE:
To give financial assistance to mechanical engineering students.

LEGAL BASIS:
Incorporated organization.

ELIGIBILITY:
Applicants must be U.S. citizens, enrolled in a degree program in a school with accredited mechanical engineering curriculum and members of the ASME for scholarships and student loans. Applicants must be foreign students, selected in their home country, who meet the requirements of the sponsor in their home country who holds a contract with the International Institute of Education for the Rice-Cullimore Scholarship.

FINANCIAL DATA:
Amount of support per award: Lucy and Charles W.E. Clarke Scholarship: $5,000. All other Scholarships: $3,000; Student Loans: $10,000 maximum.

Total amount of support: Varies.

NO. MOST RECENT APPLICANTS: Undergraduate Scholarships: 28; Parsons and Rothermel: 10.

NO. AWARDS: Undergraduate Scholarships: 8; Parsons Scholarship: 2; Rothermel Scholarship: 4 for the academic year 2020-21.

APPLICATION INFO:
For the Rice-Cullimore Scholarship, applications must be obtained from and filed with the local Institute of International Education (IIE) Office or the Education Officer at the U.S. Embassy in applicant's home country. For all other scholarships, contact the Society.

Duration: One year. Nonrenewable.

Deadline: Contact the Auxiliary for individual scholarship deadlines and notification dates.

PUBLICATIONS:
Application guidelines; scholarship forms; applications.

OFFICERS:
Sara Sahay, President
Ella Baldwin-Viereck, Executive Vice President
Stella Seiders, Treasurer
Ed Seiders, Student Loan Fund Treasurer
Vatsala Menon, Recording Secretary
Ada Ezekoye, Corresponding Secretary

ADDRESS INQUIRIES TO:
RuthAnn Bigley
Manager, Governance Programs
(See address above.)

AMERICAN SOCIETY OF NAVAL ENGINEERS (ASNE)   [2428]

1452 Duke Street
Alexandria, VA 22314-3458
(703) 836-6727
Fax: (703) 836-7491
E-mail: scholarships@navalengineers.org
Web Site: www.navalengineers.org

FOUNDED: 1888

AREAS OF INTEREST:

Naval Engineering includes all arts and sciences as applied in the research, development, design, construction, operation, maintenance and logistic support of surface and sub-surface ships and marine craft, naval maritime auxiliaries, aviation and space systems, combat systems, command control, electronics and ordnance systems, ocean structures and associated shore facilities, which are used by naval and other military forces and civilian maritime organizations for the defense and well-being of the Nation.

CONSULTING OR VOLUNTEER SERVICES:
Volunteer Services.

NAME(S) OF PROGRAMS:
● **ASNE Scholarship Program**

TYPE:

Scholarships. Stipend for tuition, fees and expenses to follow a full-time or co-op program of study that applies to naval engineering, such as naval architecture, marine engineering, ocean engineering, mechanical engineering, structural engineering, electrical engineering, electronic engineering and the physical sciences, as well as other programs leading to careers with civilian and military maritime organizations supporting and developing work and life at sea.

YEAR PROGRAM STARTED: 1979

PURPOSE:

To encourage college students to enter the field of naval engineering; to support naval engineers seeking advanced education in the field.

LEGAL BASIS:
Nonprofit professional society.

ELIGIBILITY:

Support will be limited to the last year of undergraduate education or one year of graduate education in an accredited college or university. Candidates must be U.S. citizens and must have demonstrated or expressed a genuine interest in a career in naval engineering. Graduate students must be members of ASNE or SNAME and may apply at time of application.

Selection criteria will be based on academic record, work history, professional promise and interest in naval engineering, extracurricular activities, recommendations of college faculty, employers and other character references. Demonstrated financial need is not a requirement, but it may be taken into consideration by the Scholarship Committee.

A scholarship will not be awarded to a doctoral candidate or to a person already having an advanced degree.

GEOG. RESTRICTIONS: United States.

FINANCIAL DATA:

The award will be in the form of a check for the first academic period payable jointly to the awardee and the college or university that the student will attend. Transcripts showing satisfactory performance constitute the basis for further awards for subsequent academic periods.

Amount of support per award: $4,000 per year.

NO. AWARDS: Varies.

APPLICATION INFO:

Application information is available on the Society's web site.

Duration: One year.

Deadline: February 28. Notification by early May.

PUBLICATIONS:
Naval Engineers Journal.

IRS I.D.: 53-0229465

EXECUTIVE DIRECTOR:
Dale Lumme

ADDRESS INQUIRIES TO:
ASNE Scholarship Committee
(See address above.)

AMERICAN SOCIETY OF SAFETY PROFESSIONALS [2429]

520 North Northwest Highway
Park Ridge, IL 60068
(847) 699-2929
Fax: (847) 296-9221
E-mail: copa@assp.org
Web Site: www.assp.org

FOUNDED: 1911

AREAS OF INTEREST:
Occupational safety and health.

NAME(S) OF PROGRAMS:
● **Safety Professional of the Year Award**

TYPE:
Awards/prizes. Cash honorarium to Society-selected award winners.

YEAR PROGRAM STARTED: 1980

PURPOSE:
To recognize exemplary achievements in Safety, Health and Environmental (SHE) Education.

LEGAL BASIS:
Not-for-profit professional society.

ELIGIBILITY:

Nominees must be active dues-paying professional members or members of the Society, domestic or international, and cannot have received this award within the past five years. The Society President is not eligible for the award until five years after he or she has left the Board of Directors. ASSE Fellows and members currently serving on the Society Technical and Professional Recognition Committee and/or the Board of Directors are ineligible.

FINANCIAL DATA:
Amount of support per award: $2,000 honorarium and an engraved statuette.

NO. MOST RECENT APPLICANTS: 9.

NO. AWARDS: 1 each year.

APPLICATION INFO:

Nominations must be submitted electronically. Individual members, chapters, regions, practice specialty, councils or the Society Board of Directors may submit them. Must be accompanied by a letter of endorsement from the nominating colleague (Chapter, Regional Operating Committees, Practice Specialty, Councils or the Society Board of Directors), as well as the immediate employment supervisor, a single-page resume, plus a petition listing the nominee's achievements.

Deadline: November 1. Award announcement in early May.

ADDRESS INQUIRIES TO:
Laura Clements
Director of External Affairs
(See address above.)

ASHRAE [2430]

180 Technology Parkway
Peachtree Corners, GA 30092
(404) 636-8400
Fax: (678) 539-2211
E-mail: mvaughn@ashrae.org
Web Site: www.ashrae.org

FOUNDED: 1894

AREAS OF INTEREST:
Engineering, environmental technology, technical assistance, public health and conservation.

CONSULTING OR VOLUNTEER SERVICES:
Cooperative research with government agencies and other organizations by supplying ASHRAE expertise, usually in the form of an advisory committee.

NAME(S) OF PROGRAMS:
● **ASHRAE Research Grants**

TYPE:
Research contracts. Institutional grants for basic research and technical studies concerned with the arts and sciences of heating, refrigeration, air conditioning and ventilation.

YEAR PROGRAM STARTED: 1912

PURPOSE:
To increase the amount and accuracy of fundamental information in the fields of heating, refrigeration, air conditioning/ventilation and related areas and to make this information available.

LEGAL BASIS:
Organization exempt under 501(c)(3) of the Internal Revenue Code.

ELIGIBILITY:
Private research firms and accredited institutions of higher learning may apply with appropriate proposals.

FINANCIAL DATA:
Amount of support per award: $5,000 to $250,000 per project.

Total amount of support: $2,500,000 to $3,000,000 annually.

Matching fund requirements: Although not required, matching funds could improve chances of award.

NO. MOST RECENT APPLICANTS: 60.

NO. AWARDS: Approximately 20 grants annually.

APPLICATION INFO:

Applications take the form of a proposal. Detailed information concerning its preparation is available upon request to the Manager of Research at the address above.

Duration: Up to three years, with the possibility of extension.

Deadline: Applications may be submitted throughout the year. Proposals are generally acted upon only in January and June.

ADDRESS INQUIRIES TO:
Michael R. Vaughn, Manager of Research and Technical Services
(See address above.)

ASHRAE [2431]

180 Technology Parkway
Peachtree Corners, GA 30092
(404) 636-8400
Fax: (678) 539-2211
E-mail: mvaughn@ashrae.org
Web Site: www.ashrae.org

FOUNDED: 1894

AREAS OF INTEREST:
Engineering, environmental technology, technical assistance, public health and conservation.

NAME(S) OF PROGRAMS:
- **ASHRAE Graduate Student Grant-in-Aid Program**

TYPE:
Grants-in-aid. Support for projects of original research concerned with the arts and sciences of heating, refrigeration, air-conditioning/ventilation and related areas.

YEAR PROGRAM STARTED: 1968

PURPOSE:
To stimulate interest in the areas of heating, refrigeration, air-conditioning and ventilation through the encouragement of original research in these fields.

LEGAL BASIS:
Organization exempt under 501(c)(3) of the Internal Revenue Code.

ELIGIBILITY:
Qualified graduate engineering students capable of carrying out appropriate and scholarly research are eligible to apply.

FINANCIAL DATA:
The awards are meant for students personal use while pursuing an HVAC&R related education. An award in the amount of $5,000 will be paid upon confirmation of enrollment. An additional $5,000 shall be paid upon receipt of a report prepared by the awardee documenting his or her attendance at one of the next three ASHRAE society meetings following the award; these funds will be retained by ASHRAE if attendee does not attend one of these meetings.

Amount of support per award: $10,000 with the opportunity to earn an additional $1,500 honorarium for presentation of an authored research paper at an ASHRAE meeting.

Total amount of support: Approximately $200,000 annually.

NO. MOST RECENT APPLICANTS: 60.

NO. AWARDS: Approximately 20 per year.

APPLICATION INFO:
Prospective applicants should complete the official Grant-in-Aid application containing the following:
(1) significance of proposed research;
(2) outline or plan of procedure;
(3) approximate budget and extent to which the applicant's institution will support the work;
(4) plans for seeking other funds for this or related work;
(5) anticipated plans for publication of research results;
(6) student's name and qualifications;
(7) faculty advisor's and institution's qualifications to do the work and;
(8) copy of official transcripts.

Duration: Grants are usually awarded for a maximum period of two years. Students who have previously received grants may not reapply; one grant per student.

Deadline: Applications should be submitted by or before March 1, for consideration at review meeting held in April.

OFFICERS:
Chuck Gulledge, President
Jeff Littleton, Executive Vice President and Secretary

ADDRESS INQUIRIES TO:
Michael R. Vaughn, Manager of Research and Technical Services
(See address above.)

ASM MATERIALS EDUCATION FOUNDATION

9639 Kinsman Road
Materials Park, OH 44073-0002
(440) 338-5151
(800) 336-5152
Fax: (440) 338-4634
E-mail: jeane.deatherage@asminternational.org
Web Site: www.asmfoundation.org

TYPE:
Scholarships.

See entry 2462 for full listing.

CANADIAN SOCIETY FOR CHEMICAL ENGINEERING [2432]

222 Queen Street
Suite 1009
Ottawa ON K1P 5V9 Canada
(613) 232-6252
Fax: (613) 232-5862
E-mail: awards@cheminst.ca
Web Site: www.cheminst.ca/awards

FOUNDED: 1945

AREAS OF INTEREST:
Chemical engineering.

NAME(S) OF PROGRAMS:
- **The CSChE Chemical Engineering Local Section Scholarships**
- **Hatch Plant Design Competition**

TYPE:
Scholarships. The CSChE Chemical Engineering Local Section Scholarships are offered to undergraduate students in chemical engineering about to enter the final year of studies at a Canadian university.

The Hatch Plant Design Competition is offered to students enrolled in undergraduate chemical engineering programs at Canadian universities.

PURPOSE:
To promote undergraduate study in chemical engineering and provide financial support for that study.

LEGAL BASIS:
Special interest society.

ELIGIBILITY:
Applicants for the CSChE Chemical Engineering Local Section Scholarships must be undergraduate students in chemical engineering entering their final year of studies at a Canadian university. The scholarship will look at academic performance, leadership qualities, and demonstrated contributions to the Society. Applicants must be paid undergraduate student members of the Canadian Society for Chemical Engineering.

Applicants for the Hatch Plant Design Competition must be individuals and groups of undergraduate students registered in chemical engineering programs in Canadian universities during the current academic year. To minimize the number of projects to be judged, each chemical engineering department may submit no more than two entries.

GEOG. RESTRICTIONS: Canada.

FINANCIAL DATA:
Amount of support per award: Chemical Engineering Local Section: $2,000; Hatch Plant Design Competition: $1,000 for first place, $500 for second place and $300 for third place teams.

NO. AWARDS: Local Section Scholarships: 2; Hatch Plant Design Competition: 3.

APPLICATION INFO:
For the CSChE Chemical Engineering Local Section Scholarships, application letters should document contributions to the Society. Applicant must provide a transcript of academic performance and two letters of support, along with the application letter. Applications must be submitted electronically.

Entries for the Hatch Plant Design Competition should contain copies of the following:
(1) a short summary, including a simplified flowsheet of the process;
(2) a copy of the final report submitted to the university at the end of the project;
(3) a list of students who performed the work, with their permanent addresses and phone numbers;
(4) the name of the collaborating organization and the engineers who assisted the students and;
(5) a brief description of the assistance provided by that organization.

The entry should be accompanied by a letter from the head of the department of chemical engineering indicating that the information is not confidential and that the summary may be published in *Canadian Chemical News*.

Deadline: Local Section Scholarships: April 30; Hatch Competition: June 30.

PUBLICATIONS:
Announcement.

ADDRESS INQUIRIES TO:
Awards Manager
(See address above.)

GEORGE WASHINGTON UNIVERSITY [2433]

Department of Electrical and Computer Engineering
Science and Engineering Hall
800 22nd Street N.W., Suite 5000
Washington, DC 20052
(202) 994-6083
Fax: (202) 994-0227
E-mail: ece@gwu.edu
Web Site: www.ece.seas.gwu.edu

FOUNDED: 1821

AREAS OF INTEREST:
Electrical engineering, computer engineering, and telecommunications.

NAME(S) OF PROGRAMS:
- **Graduate Teaching Assistantships**

TYPE:
Assistantships. Merit-based awards for graduate studies at George Washington University.

PURPOSE:
To attract high-quality graduate students.

LEGAL BASIS:
University.

ELIGIBILITY:
Usually for currently enrolled students. Some fellowships are limited to U.S. citizens. Must

have a grade point average of 3.5 on a possible scale of 4.0 and have taken the Graduate Record Examination.

GEOG. RESTRICTIONS: United States.

FINANCIAL DATA:
Amount of support per award: Varies.
Total amount of support: Varies.

APPLICATION INFO:
Graduate students should submit an application for admission to the School of Engineering and Applied Science.
Duration: One academic year. Must reapply for additional funding.

OFFICERS:
Suresh Subramanian, Department Chair

ADDRESS INQUIRIES TO:
Robert Baden
Department Operations Manager
Tel: (202) 994-5905
E-mail: robbaden@gwu.edu

GREAT MINDS IN STEM
2465 Whittier Boulevard
Suite 202
Montebello, CA 90640
(323) 262-0997
Fax: (323) 262-0946
E-mail: scholars@greatmindsinstem.org
Web Site: www.greatmindsinstem.org

TYPE:
Scholarships.

See entry 2397 for full listing.

INSTITUTE OF INDUSTRIAL AND SYSTEMS ENGINEERS (IISE)   [2434]
3577 Parkway Lane
Building 5, Suite 200
Norcross, GA 30092
(770) 449-0461
Fax: (770) 441-3295
E-mail: bcameron@iise.org
Web Site: www.iise.org

FOUNDED: 1948

AREAS OF INTEREST:
The design, improvement and installation of integrated systems of people, material, information, equipment and energy, incorporating specialized knowledge and skills from the mathematical, physical and social sciences, together with the principles and methods of engineering analysis and design to specify, predict and evaluate the results to be obtained from such systems.

NAME(S) OF PROGRAMS:
- **CISE Undergraduate Scholarship**
- **John S.W. Fargher Scholarship**
- **C.B. Gambrell Undergraduate Scholarship**
- **Dwight D. Garden Scholarship**
- **Gilbreth Memorial Fellowship**
- **IIE Council of Fellows Undergraduate Scholarship**
- **John L. Imhoff Scholarship**
- **Henry and Elisabeth Kroeze Memorial Scholarship**
- **Harold and Inge Marcus Scholarship**
- **Marvin Mundel Memorial Scholarship**
- **Presidents Scholarship**
- **A.O. Putnam Memorial Scholarship**
- **Vinod and Gail Sahney Scholarship**
- **E.J. Sierleja Memorial Fellowship**
- **Society for Health Systems Scholarship**

- **United Parcel Service Scholarship for Female Students**
- **United Parcel Service Scholarship for Minority Students**
- **Lisa Zaken Award of Excellence**

TYPE:
Fellowships; Scholarships. The Institute supports the advancement of engineering education and research through scholarships and fellowships to recognize and support these types of endeavors.

PURPOSE:
To recognize academic excellence and campus leadership.

LEGAL BASIS:
Nonprofit, international professional membership society.

ELIGIBILITY:
Candidates must be active Institute members enrolled full-time in graduate or undergraduate industrial engineering programs. The nominee's scholastic ability, character, leadership, service, and financial need are all considered.

Membership is not required for the Imhoff Scholarship.

FINANCIAL DATA:
Amount of support per award: Varies per award.

APPLICATION INFO:
Students may not apply directly for scholarships. They must be nominated by their department head or faculty advisor. Nominations must be mailed to the Institute. Call for nominations are sent out at the beginning of each school year in the fall.
Deadline: Vinod and Gail Sahney Scholarship: December 31. Society for Health Systems Scholarship: December 1. All others: November 15 (postmark).

STAFF:
Don Greene, Chief Executive Officer

ADDRESS INQUIRIES TO:
Bonnie Cameron
Headquarters Operations Administrator
(See address above.)

THE JAMES F. LINCOLN ARC WELDING FOUNDATION   [2435]
22801 St. Clair Avenue
Cleveland, OH 44117
(216) 481-8100
Fax: (216) 486-6476
E-mail: lori_hurley@lincolnelectric.com
Web Site: www.lincolnelectric.com
www.jflf.org

FOUNDED: 1936

AREAS OF INTEREST:
Engineering, welded design and fabrication.

NAME(S) OF PROGRAMS:
- **Awards for Achievement in Arc Welded Design, Engineering and Fabrication: College Division**

TYPE:
Awards/prizes. Awards to recognize and reward achievement by engineering and technology students (graduate and undergraduate) in solving design, engineering or fabricating problems involving the knowledge or application of arc welding.

YEAR PROGRAM STARTED: 1956

PURPOSE:
To recognize outstanding work in the welding design and fabrication field.

LEGAL BASIS:
Private corporate foundation.

ELIGIBILITY:
Graduate or undergraduate students enrolled in college or university programs leading to a Bachelor's, Master's or doctoral degree may submit papers completed within a one-year period, ending June 30 of the year of the contest. Papers should represent students' work on design, engineering or fabrication problems relating to any type of building, bridge or other generally stationary structure, any type of machine, product or mechanical apparatus or arc welding research, testing, procedure or process development.

Students to participate in the Undergraduate Division must be enrolled in a four-year or longer curriculum leading to a Bachelor's degree. Students to participate in the Graduate Division must be enrolled in a graduate program leading to a Master's or Doctorate degree. Qualified students may apply individually or jointly in groups of not more than five. Undergraduate students compete for 17 awards, and graduate students compete for 12 awards.

GEOG. RESTRICTIONS: United States.

FINANCIAL DATA:
Amount of support per award: $50 to $1,000.
Total amount of support: Varies.

NO. AWARDS: Varies.

APPLICATION INFO:
Official application materials are available upon request to the Secretary. Any number of entries may be submitted from one school, but no student may participate in more than one entry.
Deadline: June 30.

TRUSTEES:
Duane Miller

EXECUTIVE STAFF:
Leslie Brown, President
Jason Scales, Executive Director
Lori Hurley, Secretary

ADDRESS INQUIRIES TO:
Lori Hurley, Secretary
(See address above.)

LOS ALAMOS NATIONAL LABORATORY
P.O. Box 1663
MS-P290
Los Alamos, NM 87545
(505) 665-6406
E-mail: hrstaffing-postdocs@lanl.gov
Web Site: www.lanl.gov/science/postdocs

TYPE:
Fellowships. The Distinguished Postdoctoral Fellowships provide the opportunity for the recipients to collaborate with LANL scientists and engineers on staff-initiated research. Candidates for these awards must display extraordinary ability in scientific research and show clear and definite promise of becoming outstanding leaders in the research they pursue.

See entry 1658 for full listing.

NATIONAL ACTION COUNCIL FOR MINORITIES IN ENGINEERING, INC. (NACME) [2436]

One North Broadway
Suite 601
New York, NY 10601
(914) 539-4010
Fax: (914) 539-4032
E-mail: scholarships@nacme.org
Web Site: www.nacme.org

FOUNDED: 1974

AREAS OF INTEREST:
Engineering.

CONSULTING OR VOLUNTEER SERVICES:
NACME communicates and cooperates with the precollege, college and industry communities that are involved in the minority engineering effort.

NAME(S) OF PROGRAMS:
- **NACME Bridge Scholarship**
- **NACME Collegiate Scholarship**

TYPE:
Block grants; Scholarships. The NACME Bridge Scholarship program is designed to support students who have received and accepted freshman admission to an undergraduate engineering or computer science program at a NACME Partner Institution and have been invited to attend a residential academic program the summer prior to freshman matriculation. The scholarship covers the published cost of participation of the Bridge program.

The NACME Collegiate Scholarship provides support for qualified underrepresented students, Black/African American, Native/American Indian, and Laninx/Hispanic American, who have directly applied to an engineering or computer science undergraduate program at a NACME Partner Institution.

PURPOSE:
To enhance awareness of the engineering profession among students, parents, teachers, and guidance counselors; to recognize high school graduating seniors who have achieved exemplary academic performance and have decided to pursue an engineering education.

LEGAL BASIS:
Nonprofit organization incorporated in New York.

ELIGIBILITY:
For the NACME Bridge Scholarship, student must be a high school senior applying to an engineering or computer science program at a NACME Partner Institution. U.S. citizenship or permanent residency is required. Student must have a cumulative grade point average of 2.8.

To be eligible for the NACME Collegiate Scholarship, students must have a minimum cumulative grade point average of 3.0 and must verify, at the time of the award, Fall admission to an eligible full-time, on-campus program in an engineering or computer science major.

GEOG. RESTRICTIONS: United States.

FINANCIAL DATA:
Amount of support per award: NACME Collegiate Scholarship: Typically $1,500 to $4,000.

NO. MOST RECENT APPLICANTS: Varies.

NO. AWARDS: Varies.

APPLICATION INFO:
To apply for any NACME scholarship, block grant, bridge, corporate named scholarship or special named scholarship, an updated NACME common application must be on file.

Duration: NACME Bridge Scholarship: One-time award. NACME Collegiate Scholarship: One year. Renewable.

Deadline: NACME Bridge Scholarship: June 1. NACME Collegiate Scholarship: December 1.

STAFF:
Michele Lezama, President and Chief Executive Officer
Aisha Lawrey, Senior Director, Programs and Scholarships
Kevin G. Smith, Program Manager, Professional Development
Felisha Britton, Program Manager, Scholarships

ADDRESS INQUIRIES TO:
Felisha Britton
Program Manager, Scholarships
E-mail: scholars@nacme.org

NATIONAL ACTION COUNCIL FOR MINORITIES IN ENGINEERING, INC. (NACME) [2437]

One North Broadway
Suite 601
New York, NY 10601
(914) 539-4010
Fax: (914) 539-4032
E-mail: scholarships@nacme.org
Web Site: www.nacme.org

FOUNDED: 1974

AREAS OF INTEREST:
Engineering and computer science.

CONSULTING OR VOLUNTEER SERVICES:
NACME communicates and cooperates with the precollege, college and industry communities that are involved in the minority engineering effort.

NAME(S) OF PROGRAMS:
- **Americas Styrenics Scholarship**
- **Autodesk NACME Scholarship**
- **Bechtel Undergraduate Scholarship Award**
- **Bechtel Undergraduate Women in Engineering Scholarship**
- **Chevron Scholarship Program**
- **Sidney and Katherine Friend Scholarship**
- **William Randolph Hearst Endowment Scholarship**
- **Phillip D. Reed Undergraduate Endowment Fellowship**

TYPE:
Fellowships; Scholarships. Americas Styrenics Scholarship provides financial support that will promote high academic achievement, leadership qualities and commitment to excellence at Louisiana State University.

Autodesk NACME Scholarship is designed to provide financial support and work experience that will promote high academic achievement among underrepresented students enrolled in an undergraduate computer science or computer engineering program. The award is accompanied by a summer internship.

Bechtel Undergraduate Scholarship Award is a financial support program that encourages and recognizes high academic achievement of students interested in pursuing a corporate career in a construction-related engineering discipline. The award is accompanied by an internship and mentoring opportunities.

Bechtel Undergraduate Women in Engineering Scholarship is geared towards female students who are rising juniors or seniors.

Chevron Scholarship Program awards current matriculating students in engineering, specifically mechanical, chemical, electrical, civil and petroleum as well as computer science (and qualifying information technology programs), who have the potential to excel as scholars, leaders and potential contributors to Chevron Corporation. Assessment will be based on academic merit and leadership potential.

Sidney and Katherine Friend Scholarship is a joint endowment established between NACME and New York University, Tandon School of Engineering.

William Randolph Hearst Endowment Scholarship is supported by the William Randolph Hearst Foundation.

Phillip D. Reed Undergraduate Endowment Fellowship is made possible through an endowment from the Phillip D. Reed Foundation.

PURPOSE:
To increase the representation of underrepresented minorities in engineering and computer science.

LEGAL BASIS:
Nonprofit organization incorporated in New York.

ELIGIBILITY:
To be eligible for any NACME administered scholarship, students must be currently matriculating in an engineering or computer science program at a NACME Partner Institution, a U.S. citizen or permanent resident, and have a minimum high school cumulative grade point average of 2.8 (some named scholarships may have higher grade point average requirements).

Autodesk NACME Scholarship applicants must be enrolled full-time, on campus, and in good standing in an accredited computer engineering or computer science program, and have demonstrated financial need.

GEOG. RESTRICTIONS: United States.

FINANCIAL DATA:
Amount of support per award: Americas Styrenics: $6,000; Autodesk, Chevron and Reed: $5,000; Bechtel Undergraduate, Friend and Hearst: $2,500; Bechtel Women's: $10,000.

NO. AWARDS: Americas Styrenics, Friend and Reed: 1; Bechtel Undergraduate and Hearst: 2; All others: Varies.

APPLICATION INFO:
An updated NACME common application must be on file.

Duration: Americas Styrenics and Bechtel Undergraduate: Two years. Autodesk, Bechtel Women's and Chevron: One-time award. Friend: One year. Renewable up to five years. Hearst: One year. Renewable up to four years. Reed: One year. Renewable up to three years.

Deadline: Chevron: July 1. All others: November 15.

STAFF:
Michele Lezama, President and Chief
Executive Officer
Aisha Lawrey, Senior Director, Programs and
Scholarships
Kevin G. Smith, Program Manager,
Professional Development
Felisha Britton, Program Manager,
Scholarships

ADDRESS INQUIRIES TO:
Felisha Britton
Program Manager, Scholarships
E-mail: scholars@nacme.org

THE NATIONAL GEM CONSORTIUM

1430 Duke Street
Alexandria, VA 22314
(703) 562-3646
Fax: (202) 207-2518
E-mail: info@gemfellowship.org
Web Site: www.gemfellowship.org

TYPE:
Fellowships; Internships. All-expense
fellowship for graduate study (tuition and
stipend) and paid summer work experience in
a scientific or engineering environment.

See entry 920 for full listing.

NATIONAL RESEARCH COUNCIL OF CANADA

1200 Montreal Road, Building M-58
Room E-109
Ottawa ON K1A 0R6 Canada
(613) 949-4655
E-mail: info@nrc-cnrc.gc.ca
racoordinator.hrb@nrc-cnrc.gc.ca
Web Site: www.nrc-cnrc.gc.ca

TYPE:
Associateships. Research Associate Program
provides promising scientists and engineers
with the opportunity to work in a challenging
research environment during the early stages
of their career. Applicants will be selected
competitively and must demonstrate the
ability to perform original, high-quality
research in their chosen field.

Research Associates will be offered
appointments to the staff of the National
Research Council on a term basis and will be
offered salaries and benefits currently
available to Research Officers.

See entry 1664 for full listing.

NATIONAL SCIENCE FOUNDATION [2438]

Directorate for Engineering
Office of Assistant Director
2415 Eisenhower Avenue
Arlington, VA 22314
(703) 292-8300
Fax: (703) 292-9467
Web Site: www.nsf.gov

FOUNDED: 1950

AREAS OF INTEREST:
Chemical, biochemical and thermal
engineering, mechanics, structures and
materials engineering, electrical,
communications and systems engineering,
design, manufacturing and computer
engineering, emerging engineering systems,
cross-disciplinary research, engineering
research centers, civil and environment
engineering, earthquake engineering and
small business innovation research.

NAME(S) OF PROGRAMS:
● **Directorate for Engineering Grants Program**

TYPE:
Project/program grants; Research grants.

YEAR PROGRAM STARTED: 1984

PURPOSE:
To strengthen U.S. engineering education and
research; to focus on areas relevant to
national problems by supporting research
across the entire range of engineering
disciplines and by identifying areas where
results are expected to have timely
applications.

LEGAL BASIS:
Government agency.

ELIGIBILITY:
Proposals may be submitted by colleges,
universities, profit and nonprofit organizations
and by state, local or regional governments.
Industry, state and local governments and
other organizations are eligible to participate.
Joint proposals are encouraged.

NSF does not make loans or grants to
develop or promote any business venture,
technical assistance, pilot plant efforts,
research requiring security classification, the
development of products for commercial
marketing or market research for a particular
product or invention.

GEOG. RESTRICTIONS: United States and its
territories.

FINANCIAL DATA:
Amount of support per award: $2,000 to
$5,000,000. Average $63,000.
Total amount of support: Varies.

APPLICATION INFO:
Informal inquiry to the Directorate for
Engineering may be made to determine
whether or not a potential project would
qualify for support.
Duration: One to five years. Average is
approximately 30 months.
Deadline: Varies. Approximately six to eight
months are required for consideration of
formal proposals.

PUBLICATIONS:
Grants for Research and Education in
Science and Engineering; Guide to Programs.

STAFF:
Dawn Tilbury, Assistant Director,
Engineering

ADDRESS INQUIRIES TO:
Directorate for Engineering
(See address above.)

NATIONAL SOCIETY OF PROFESSIONAL SURVEYORS (NSPS) [2439]

5119 Pegasus Court
Suite Q
Frederick, MD 21704
(240) 439-4615 ext. 105
Fax: (240) 439-4952
E-mail: trisha.milburn@nsps.us.com
Web Site: www.nsps.us.com

AREAS OF INTEREST:
Surveying.

NAME(S) OF PROGRAMS:
● **The Schonstedt Scholarship in Surveying**

TYPE:
Scholarships. For students enrolled in
four-year degree programs in surveying or in
closely related degree programs such as
geomatics or surveying engineering.

PURPOSE:
To encourage and recognize students
committed to a career in surveying.

LEGAL BASIS:
Nonprofit educational organization.

ELIGIBILITY:
The Schonstedt Scholarship is for students
enrolled in four-year degree programs in
surveying or in closely related degree
programs such as geomatics or surveying
engineering. Preference will be given to
applicants with junior or senior standing.

GEOG. RESTRICTIONS: United States, Canada
and South America.

FINANCIAL DATA:
Amount of support per award: $1,500.
Total amount of support: $1,500 annually.

CO-OP FUNDING PROGRAMS: Scholarship is
made possible by a donation from the
Schonstedt Instrument Company of
Kearneysville, WV.

NO. MOST RECENT APPLICANTS: 32.

NO. AWARDS: 1 annually.

APPLICATION INFO:
Required documentation includes:
(1) a completed application form;
(2) proof of student membership in NSPS
(this will be checked);
(3) a brief yet complete statement indicating
educational objectives, future plans of study
or research, professional activities and
financial need;
(4) three letters of recommendation (at least
two from faculty members familiar with the
student's work) and;
(5) a complete original official transcript
through the end of the school year prior to
when the award will be presented; in
addition, send unofficial transcripts for the
fall semester when available.

Do not send applications by fax or e-mail.
Mail all documents in one envelope.
Incomplete or improperly completed
applications will be discarded.
Duration: One academic year.
Deadline: February 15.

ADDRESS INQUIRIES TO:
Patricia Milburn, Office Manager
(See telephone and e-mail address above.)

NATIONAL SOCIETY OF PROFESSIONAL SURVEYORS (NSPS) [2440]

5119 Pegasus Court
Suite Q
Frederick, MD 21704
(240) 439-4615 ext. 105
Fax: (240) 439-4952
E-mail: trisha.milburn@nsps.us.com
Web Site: www.nsps.us.com

FOUNDED: 1941

AREAS OF INTEREST:
Surveying.

NAME(S) OF PROGRAMS:
● **NSPS Board of Directors Scholarship**
● **The NSPS Scholarship**

TYPE:
Scholarships.

PURPOSE:
To recognize outstanding surveying students; to encourage qualified candidates to pursue an undergraduate degree in surveying.

LEGAL BASIS:
Nonprofit foundation.

ELIGIBILITY:
NSPS Board of Directors Scholarship applicants must be enrolled in studies in surveying or in closely related degree programs and entering their junior year of study in a four-year degree program of their choice (either full- or part-time) and must have maintained a minimum 3.0 grade point average.

The NSPS Scholarship is awarded in even-numbered years to students enrolled in four-year degree programs in surveying or in closely related degree programs such as geomatics or surveying engineering. The Scholarship is intended to recognize an outstanding student enrolled full-time in undergraduate surveying programs.

GEOG. RESTRICTIONS: United States.

FINANCIAL DATA:
Amount of support per award: $2,000 per scholarship.

NO. MOST RECENT APPLICANTS: 34.

NO. AWARDS: NSPS Board of Directors Scholarship: 1 (awarded in even-numbered years only); The NSPS Scholarship: 1.

APPLICATION INFO:
Applicants must submit (in the following order):
(1) a completed application form;
(2) proof of student membership in NSPS (this will be checked);
(3) a brief yet complete statement indicating educational objectives, future plans of study or research, professional activities and financial need;
(4) three letters of recommendation (at least two from faculty members familiar with the student's work) and;
(5) a complete original official transcript through the end of the school year prior to when the award will be presented; in addition, send unofficial transcripts for the fall semester when available.

Do not send applications by fax or e-mail. Mail all documents in one envelope. Incomplete or improperly completed applications will be discarded.
Duration: One academic year.
Deadline: February 15.

ADDRESS INQUIRIES TO:
Patricia Milburn, Office Manager
(See telephone and e-mail address above.)

NATIONAL SOCIETY OF PROFESSIONAL SURVEYORS (NSPS)   [2441]

5119 Pegasus Court
Suite Q
Frederick, MD 21704
(240) 439-4615 ext. 105
Fax: (240) 439-4952
E-mail: trisha.milburn@nsps.us.com
Web Site: www.nsps.us.com

FOUNDED: 1941

AREAS OF INTEREST:
Surveying and surveying technology.

NAME(S) OF PROGRAMS:
- **The Berntsen International Scholarship in Surveying**
- **The Berntsen International Scholarship in Surveying Technology**

TYPE:
Scholarships. Berntsen International Scholarship in Surveying: Annual scholarship award for undergraduate study in four-year degree programs in surveying or in closely related degree programs such as geomatics or surveying engineering.

Berntsen International Scholarship in Surveying Technology: For students enrolled in two-year degree programs in surveying technology. Scholarship awarded in even years only.

PURPOSE:
To provide financial assistance to students pursuing two- or four-year degree programs in surveying, surveying technology or closely related fields.

LEGAL BASIS:
Nonprofit, educational organization.

ELIGIBILITY:
The Berntsen International Scholarship in Surveying: Student applicants must be enrolled in four-year degree programs in surveying or in closely related degree programs such as geomatics or surveying engineering.

The Berntsen International Scholarship in Surveying Technology: Student applicants must be enrolled in two-year degree programs in surveying technology.

GEOG. RESTRICTIONS: United States.

FINANCIAL DATA:
Amount of support per award: $2,000.

CO-OP FUNDING PROGRAMS: Scholarships are made possible by Berntsen International, Inc., of Madison, WI.

NO. MOST RECENT APPLICANTS: Berntsen International Scholarship in Surveying: 34; Berntsen International Scholarship in Surveying Technology: 12.

NO. AWARDS: Berntsen International Scholarship in Surveying: 1 annually. Berntsen International Scholarship in Surveying Technology: 1 in even-numbered years.

APPLICATION INFO:
Required documentation includes:
(1) a completed application form;
(2) proof of student membership in NSPS (this will be checked);
(3) a brief yet complete statement indicating educational objectives, future plans of study or research, professional activities and financial need;
(4) three letters of recommendation (at least two from faculty members familiar with the student's work) and;
(5) a complete original official transcript through the end of the school year prior to when the award will be presented; in addition, send unofficial transcripts for the fall semester when available.

Do not send applications by fax or e-mail. Mail all documents in one envelope. Incomplete or improperly completed applications will be discarded.
Duration: One academic year.
Deadline: February 15.

ADDRESS INQUIRIES TO:
Patricia Milburn, Office Manager
(See telephone and e-mail address above.)

NATIONAL SOCIETY OF PROFESSIONAL SURVEYORS (NSPS) AMERICAN ASSOCIATION FOR GEODETIC SURVEYING (AAGS)   [2442]

5119 Pegasus Court
Suite Q
Frederick, MD 21704
(240) 439-4615 ext. 105
Fax: (240) 439-4952
E-mail: trisha.milburn@nsps.us.com
Web Site: www.aagsmo.org
www.nsps.us.com

FOUNDED: 1941

AREAS OF INTEREST:
Geodetic surveying.

NAME(S) OF PROGRAMS:
- **American Association for Geodetic Surveying (AAGS) Graduate Fellowship Award**

TYPE:
Fellowships. Annual fellowship award to support graduate study in a program with a significant focus on geodetic surveying or geodesy at a school of the recipient's choice.

PURPOSE:
To recognize outstanding graduate students committed to the pursuit of knowledge in geodetic surveying, thus enhancing the ability of the profession to better serve the needs of society.

LEGAL BASIS:
Nonprofit educational organization.

ELIGIBILITY:
Nominees must be members of the American Association for Geodetic Surveying (AAGS) and should be enrolled in or accepted by a graduate program in geodetic surveying or geodesy. Preference will be given to applicants having at least two years of employment experience in the surveying profession.

GEOG. RESTRICTIONS: United States, Canada and South America.

FINANCIAL DATA:
Amount of support per award: $2,000 and an appropriate citation to be presented at the annual meeting.

Total amount of support: $2,000 annually.

CO-OP FUNDING PROGRAMS: Provided by the American Association for Geodetic Surveying and administered by NSPS Foundation.

NO. MOST RECENT APPLICANTS: 4.

NO. AWARDS: 1 annually.

APPLICATION INFO:
Required documentation includes:
(1) a completed application form;
(2) proof of student membership in AAGS (this will be checked);
(3) a brief yet complete statement indicating educational objectives, future plans of study or research, professional activities and financial need;
(4) three letters of recommendation (at least two from faculty members familiar with the student's work) and;
(5) a complete original official transcript through the end of the school year prior to

when the award will be presented; in addition, send unofficial transcripts for the fall semester when available.

Do not send applications by fax or e-mail. Mail all documents in one envelope. Incomplete or improperly completed applications will be discarded.

Duration: One academic year.

Deadline: February 15.

PUBLICATIONS:
Surveying and Land Information Science Journal.

ADDRESS INQUIRIES TO:
Patricia Milburn, Office Manager
(See telephone and e-mail address above.)

NATIONAL SOCIETY OF PROFESSIONAL SURVEYORS (NSPS) AMERICAN ASSOCIATION FOR GEODETIC SURVEYING (AAGS)   [2443]

5119 Pegasus Court
Suite Q
Frederick, MD 21704
(240) 439-4615 ext. 105
Fax: (240) 439-4952
E-mail: trisha.milburn@nsps.us.com
Web Site: www.aagsmo.org
www.nsps.us.com

AREAS OF INTEREST:
Geodetic surveying.

NAME(S) OF PROGRAMS:
● **AAGS Joseph F. Dracup Scholarship Award**

TYPE:
Scholarships. The award is intended for students enrolled in four-year degree programs in surveying or in closely related degree programs.

PURPOSE:
To promote study in the surveying and mapping professions.

LEGAL BASIS:
Nonprofit educational organization.

ELIGIBILITY:
Nominees must be members of the National Society of Professional Surveyors. Student applicants must be enrolled in four-year degree programs in surveying or in closely related degree programs such as geomatics or surveying engineering. Preference will be given to applicants from programs with a significant focus on geodetic surveying.

GEOG. RESTRICTIONS: United States, Canada and South America.

FINANCIAL DATA:
Amount of support per award: $2,000 and an appropriate citation to be presented at the annual meeting.
Total amount of support: $2,000 annually.

CO-OP FUNDING PROGRAMS: Provided by the American Association for Geodetic Surveying and administered by NSPS.

NO. MOST RECENT APPLICANTS: 25.

NO. AWARDS: 1 annually.

APPLICATION INFO:
Required documentation includes:
(1) a completed application form;
(2) proof of student membership in AAGS (this will be checked);
(3) a brief yet complete statement indicating educational objectives, future plans of study

or research, professional activities and financial need;
(4) three letters of recommendation (at least two from faculty members familiar with the student's work) and;
(5) a complete original official transcript through the end of the school year prior to when the award will be presented; in addition, send unofficial transcripts for the fall semester when available.

Do not send applications by fax or e-mail. Mail all documents in one envelope. In addition, send unofficial transcripts for the fall semester when available. Incomplete or improperly completed applications will be discarded.

Duration: One academic year.

Deadline: February 15.

PUBLICATIONS:
Surveying and Land Information Science Journal.

ADDRESS INQUIRIES TO:
Patricia Milburn, Office Manager
(See telephone and e-mail address above.)

OAK RIDGE INSTITUTE FOR SCIENCE AND EDUCATION (ORISE)   [2444]

100 ORAU Way
Oak Ridge, TN 37830
(865) 574-1751
E-mail: science.education@orau.org
Web Site: orise.orau.gov/science-education

FOUNDED: 1946

AREAS OF INTEREST:
Energy-related disciplines and technologies.

TYPE:
Fellowships; Internships; Scholarships. ORISE administers a broad range of internships, scholarships, fellowships and research experiences. ORISE programs include research experiences at Department of Energy national laboratories as well as other federal agencies with research facilities located across the country as well as some positions outside the U.S.

YEAR PROGRAM STARTED: 1950

PURPOSE:
To provide hands-on research training for students seeking Associate, Baccalaureate, or graduate degrees in appropriate disciplines relating to science and engineering education, training and management systems, energy and environment systems.

LEGAL BASIS:
Government agency.

ELIGIBILITY:
ORISE programs are available to science and engineering students and educators at every academic level from K-12th grade, to college students and postdoctoral researchers, to university faculty members.

APPLICATION INFO:
Contact ORISE for general information and application guidelines.

PUBLICATIONS:
Program announcement; ORISE Resource Guide.

ADDRESS INQUIRIES TO:
Craig Layman, Associate Director
(See address above.)

PRECAST/PRESTRESSED CONCRETE INSTITUTE   [2445]

8770 West Bryn Mawr Avenue
Suite 1150
Chicago, IL 60631
(312) 786-0300
Fax: (312) 621-1114
E-mail: rbecker@pci.org
Web Site: www.pci.org

AREAS OF INTEREST:
Research, design and construction of buildings, bridges and other structures using precast/prestressed concrete.

NAME(S) OF PROGRAMS:
● **Daniel P. Jenny Research Fellowships**

TYPE:
Fellowships.

YEAR PROGRAM STARTED: 1972

PURPOSE:
To engage the interest of young engineering students in the precast concrete industry while providing a research experience of value to both the student and the Institute.

LEGAL BASIS:
Nonprofit trade association.

ELIGIBILITY:
Fellowship program is open to any university in North America with the facilities to conduct structural research. Students may be Ph.D. candidates, but Master's students are preferred.

GEOG. RESTRICTIONS: North America.

FINANCIAL DATA:
Amount of support per award: Varies.

NO. AWARDS: Varies.

APPLICATION INFO:
Application information is available online.
Duration: One to two years.
Deadline: January 14. Announcement by March 29.

ADDRESS INQUIRIES TO:
Roger Becker
Vice President Technical Services
(See address above.)

THE ROYAL SOCIETY OF EDINBURGH   [2446]

22-26 George Street
Edinburgh EH2 2PQ Scotland
(44) 0131 240 5000
Fax: (44) 0131 240 5024
E-mail: afraser@therse.org.uk
Web Site: www.rse.org.uk

AREAS OF INTEREST:
Science, technology, engineering and mathematics.

NAME(S) OF PROGRAMS:
● **John Moyes Lessells Travel Scholarships**

TYPE:
Scholarships; Travel grants; Visiting scholars. RSE John Moyes Lessells Scholarships support Scotland-based Honours Graduates in engineering who wish to study abroad.

YEAR PROGRAM STARTED: 1985

PURPOSE:
To enable engineers of promise to study some aspect of their profession in any other part of the world except the U.K.

ELIGIBILITY:
All branches of engineering are eligible for consideration, including computer and

software engineering. Applications from scholars seeking to study in Asia, Africa or South America are particularly welcomed.

Applicants must have graduated with an Honours or higher degree in engineering from a Scottish Higher Education Institution and/or be currently pursuing Ph.D. research in engineering at a Scottish HEI.

Funding cannot be used to cover the applicant's stipend.

FINANCIAL DATA:
Amount of support per award: Up to GBP 1,250 per month.

APPLICATION INFO:
Applicant must first register for an account. Application form and guidelines can then be downloaded from the "Apply For Funding" area once logged in.
Duration: Two to six months.
Deadline: March 4.

ADDRESS INQUIRIES TO:
E-mail: InternationalAwards@therse.org.uk

SNAME THE INTERNATIONAL COMMUNITY FOR MARITIME AND OCEAN PROFESSIONALS   [2447]
99 Canal Center Plaza, Suite 310
Alexandria, VA 22314
(703) 997-6701
E-mail: sname@sname.org
Web Site: www.sname.org

FOUNDED: 1893

AREAS OF INTEREST:
Naval architecture, marine engineering, ocean engineering or marine industry-related fields.

NAME(S) OF PROGRAMS:
- **Graduate Scholarships**
- **Undergraduate Scholarships**

TYPE:
Scholarships. SNAME annually awards both graduate and undergraduate scholarships to encourage study in naval architecture, marine engineering, ocean engineering, ship hydrodynamics and wave theory, ship and offshore structures, or marine industry-related fields.

Graduate Scholarships are made for one year of study leading to a Master's in naval architecture, marine engineering, ocean engineering or in fields directly related to the marine industry.

Undergraduate Scholarships are made for one year of study leading to a Bachelor of Science degree in naval architecture, marine engineering, ocean engineering, or in other fields directly related to the marine industry.

YEAR PROGRAM STARTED: 1933

PURPOSE:
To encourage young men and women to enter the fields of naval architecture, marine engineering, ocean engineering or marine industry-related fields as a career by aiding them to pursue courses of study in these specialties and to provide the incentive and attractions for such a career.

LEGAL BASIS:
Technical Society.

ELIGIBILITY:
SNAME scholarships are based solely on merit, not financial need.

Graduate Scholarships: Open to applicants worldwide that wish to pursue advanced studies in approved universities. SNAME membership is required to be in place at least four months prior to the application submission deadline (i.e., October 1). Awards are made for one year of study leading to a Master's degree in naval architecture, marine engineering, ocean engineering, ship hydrodynamics and wave theory, ship and offshore structures, or in other fields directly related to the marine industry. Almost all graduate scholarships can only be awarded to students who will receive their Master's degree after September 1 of the calendar year in which they are applying for their scholarship. The only exception is The John V. Wehausen graduate scholarship. Its applicants must receive their Master's degree after April 15 of the academic year they are applying for their scholarship.

Undergraduate Scholarships: Open to applicants worldwide, who are actively involved members of SNAME and committed to future membership. SNAME membership is required at least four months prior to the application submission deadline (i.e., February 1). Awards are made for one year of study leading to a Bachelor of Science degree in naval architecture, marine engineering, ocean engineering, or in other fields directly related to the marine industry. Applicants must not receive their Bachelor's degree prior to April 15 of the academic year they are applying for scholarship. Undergraduate scholarships may be awarded to an individual only once, and applicants remain eligible for a graduate scholarship.

FINANCIAL DATA:
Amount of support per award: Graduate Scholarships: Up to $20,000 per year; Undergraduate Scholarships: Up to $6,000.
Total amount of support: Varies.

NO. AWARDS: Varies.

APPLICATION INFO:
Application may be downloaded from the SNAME Scholarships web site. Application and supporting documents are to be submitted to scholarships@sname.org.
Duration: Graduate Scholarships: One year. No renewals. Undergraduate Scholarships: One year. Awardee may apply for a Graduate Scholarship.
Deadline: Graduate Scholarships: Application must be submitted prior to February 1; supporting documents by February 15. Selection made in April.

Undergraduate Scholarships: Application must be submitted prior to June 1; supporting documents by June 15. Selection made in July.

SCHOLARSHIP COMMITTEE:
David Chapman, Chairman

ADDRESS INQUIRIES TO:
E-mail: scholarships@sname.org

SOCIETY OF WOMEN ENGINEERS
130 East Randolph Street
Suite 3500
Chicago, IL 60601
(312) 596-5223
(877) 793-4636
Fax: (312) 312-9550
E-mail: scholarships@swe.org
Web Site: societyofwomenengineers.swe.org/scholarships

TYPE:
Awards/prizes; Conferences/seminars; Scholarships. Support for undergraduate and graduate engineering studies including women who have been out of the engineering job market and out of school for a minimum of two years and who will return to school for an engineering program.
See entry 998 for full listing.

SYSTEMS PLUS, INC.   [2448]
One Research Court
Suite 360
Rockville, MD 20850
(301) 948-4232
E-mail: afsffp.pmo@sysplus.com
Web Site: afsffp.sysplus.com

AREAS OF INTEREST:
Science, engineering and mathematics.

NAME(S) OF PROGRAMS:
- **USAF Summer Faculty Fellowship Program**

TYPE:
Fellowships. Research fellowship.

PURPOSE:
To complement research efforts and build critical links between Air Force scientists and counterparts in the academic community.

ELIGIBILITY:
Applicants must be citizens of the U.S. Applicants must currently hold a full-time appointment at an accredited Baccalaureate-granting U.S. college, university or technical institution, and have earned a Ph.D. in science or Air Force-relevant engineering discipline.

GEOG. RESTRICTIONS: United States.

FINANCIAL DATA:
Amount of support per award: Assistant Professor: $1,500 per week; Associate Professor: $1,700 per week; Full Professor: $1,900 per week.
Total amount of support: Varies.

NO. MOST RECENT APPLICANTS: 205.

NO. AWARDS: Up to 150.

APPLICATION INFO:
A complete application includes:
(1) a completed online application form, including citizenship, demographic, contact and employment information;
(2) an electronic copy of applicant's curriculum vitae uploaded in Adobe PDF format;
(3) complete contact information for three references, one of whom must be the applicant's department head or dean and;
(4) an electronic copy of the research proposal uploaded in Adobe PDF format. If the proposal includes using a graduate student in the research, their application must be included with the proposal.
Note: It is suggested that the applicant receive approval from the advisor of the program before uploading his or her proposal.
Duration: Eight to 12 weeks during the summer.
Deadline: Late November.

ADDRESS INQUIRIES TO:
AFSFFP Program Officer
(See address above.)

THE TAU BETA PI ASSOCIATION, INC.   [2449]
508 Dougherty Engineering Building
1512 Middle Drive - UTK
Knoxville, TN 37996-2215
(865) 546-4578
E-mail: tbp@tbp.org
fellowships@tbp.org
Web Site: www.tbp.org

FOUNDED: 1885

AREAS OF INTEREST:
Engineering.

NAME(S) OF PROGRAMS:
- **Raymond A. and Ina C. Best Fellowship for MBA at Rensselaer Polytechnic Institute**
- **Graduate Fellowship in Engineering**
- **Tau Beta Pi Undergraduate Scholarship**

TYPE:
Fellowships; Scholarships. Fellowship awards are for one academic year of study in engineering for qualified graduate students.

Scholarships are awarded for senior year of full-time undergraduate study.

YEAR PROGRAM STARTED: 1928

PURPOSE:
To support the advancement of engineering education and the profession.

LEGAL BASIS:
Corporation.

ELIGIBILITY:
Candidate must be a member of Tau Beta Pi.

Scholarship applicants must be planning to return to school for at least one semester, one trimester, or two quarters of full-time undergraduate study in engineering on campus in the upcoming academic year.

FINANCIAL DATA:
Fellows having other graduate study financial aid that is in excess of tuition may be awarded Tau Beta Pi Fellowships without stipend. Persons supported by a salary from industry, government or other sources may not be entitled to the stipend.
Amount of support per award: Fellowships: $10,000. Scholarships: $2,000 for full year, $1,000 for one semester, one trimester or two quarters.
Total amount of support: $700,000 to $820,000 per year.

NO. AWARDS: 25 fellowships and 272 scholarships for the academic year 2017-18.

APPLICATION INFO:
Application forms are available November 1 for fellowships and January 15 for scholarships for the following academic year.
Duration: One academic year. Fellowships and scholarships are not renewable.
Deadline: Fellowships: February 1. Scholarships: April 1.

PUBLICATIONS:
The Bent of Tau Beta Pi, quarterly magazine.

IRS I.D.: 62-0479545

OFFICERS:
Curtis D. Gomulinski, Executive Director
Sally J. Steadman, Ph.D., Director of Fellowships

EXECUTIVE COUNCIL:
Wayne B. Paugh, President
C. Craig Smith, Vice President
Stephen L. King-Monroe, Treasurer

Scott E. Fable, Secretary
Rachel K. Alexander, Councillor
George J. Morales, Ph.D., Councillor
Russ W. Pierce, Councillor
George Youssef, Councillor
Menna M. Youssef, Councillor

ADDRESS INQUIRIES TO:
Director of Fellowships
The Tau Beta Pi Association, Inc.
P.O. Box 2697
Knoxville, TN 37901-2697
E-mail: fellowships@tbp.org

U.S. DEPARTMENT OF ENERGY   [2450]
3610 Collins Ferry Road
P.O. Box 880
Morgantown, WV 26507-0880
(304) 285-4764
Fax: (304) 285-4403
Web Site: www.netl.doe.gov

FOUNDED: 1979

AREAS OF INTEREST:
Materials development to support direct power extraction and low-cost distributed sensing of fossil energy power systems.

NAME(S) OF PROGRAMS:
- **University Coal Research Program**

TYPE:
Assistantships; Project/program grants; Research grants. Topics change annually. In general, the program areas could include high performance materials, sensors and controls, simulation-based engineering, and water management research and development.

YEAR PROGRAM STARTED: 1980

PURPOSE:
To foster the highest quality fundamental research on coal at the university level; to ensure the continued training of researchers in the areas of fossil energy.

LEGAL BASIS:
Government agency.

ELIGIBILITY:
Open to U.S. colleges, universities and university-affiliated research institutions. Projects selected for an award must have a teaching professor as Principal Investigator or a Co-Principal Investigator.

GEOG. RESTRICTIONS: United States.

FINANCIAL DATA:
Amount of support per award: Maximum DOE funding for grant applications submitted by a U.S. college or university is up to $400,000 for a 36-month performance period.
Total amount of support: $3,825,000 for fiscal year 2020.
Matching fund requirements: No matching fund requirements; however, cost-sharing and/or industrial collaboration is encouraged.

NO. AWARDS: 7 for the year 2019.

APPLICATION INFO:
Funding opportunities are posted on the web site above.
Duration: Approximately 90 to 180 days. No renewals.
Deadline: Varies and subject to change. Check with contact person(s) listed on the Funding Opportunity Announcement.

U.S. SOCIETY ON DAMS   [2451]
9975 Wadsworth Parkway
Suite K-2, 145
Westminster, CO 80021
(303) 792-8753
Fax: (303) 792-8782
E-mail: info@ussdams.org
Web Site: www.ussdams.org

AREAS OF INTEREST:
Dams and water resources.

NAME(S) OF PROGRAMS:
- **USSD Scholarship Award**

TYPE:
Awards/prizes; Scholarships.

PURPOSE:
To advance the technology of dam engineering, construction, operation, maintenance and dam safety; to foster socially and environmentally responsible water resources projects; to promote awareness of the role of dams in the beneficial and sustainable development of the nation's water resources.

ELIGIBILITY:
Open to U.S. college or university graduate students whose research studies have a potential for developing practical solutions to design and construction problems and other dam-related issues. Applicants must be U.S. citizens or permanent residents enrolled full-time in U.S. academic institutions which have programs related to dams.

GEOG. RESTRICTIONS: United States.

FINANCIAL DATA:
Total amount of support: $20,000 for the year 2019.

NO. MOST RECENT APPLICANTS: 7 for the year 2019.

NO. AWARDS: 4 for the year 2019.

APPLICATION INFO:
Applicants must submit a proposal describing a specific research topic. The proposed research work should be original and innovative. The proposed research can be part of an ongoing research project. Applicants are encouraged to submit proposals in topics that are related to their graduate research work. The application package must include the application form, a description of the proposed research work, an official set of academic transcripts and two letters of recommendation, one of which must be from the applicant's academic advisor.

THE UNIVERSITY OF SYDNEY
Scholarships Office
Level 4, Jane Foss Russell Building G02
The University of Sydney N.S.W. 2006
Australia
61 (02) 8627 1444
E-mail: scholarships.officer@sydney.edu.au
Web Site: www.sydney.edu.au/scholarships

TYPE:
Scholarships. Awarded for research leading to a higher degree. Tenable at the University of Sydney.

See entry 1954 for full listing.

Home economics and nutrition

THE ACADEMY OF NUTRITION AND DIETETICS FOUNDATION [2452]

120 South Riverside Plaza
Suite 2190
Chicago, IL 60606
(800) 877-1600
E-mail: ereichling@eatright.org
Web Site: www.eatrightfoundation.org

FOUNDED: 1966

AREAS OF INTEREST:
Food, nutrition, dietetics and food service management.

TYPE:
Awards/prizes; Fellowships; Grants-in-aid; Research grants; Scholarships.

YEAR PROGRAM STARTED: 1966

PURPOSE:
To further progress in the educational and scientific advancement of dietetics.

LEGAL BASIS:
Public, not-for-profit foundation.

ELIGIBILITY:
Applicant must be a member of the Academy to qualify for its scholarships and (in general) for its awards as well.

GEOG. RESTRICTIONS: Primarily United States.

FINANCIAL DATA:
Amount of support per award: Awards: $150 to $30,000; Grants: $1,000 to $20,000; Scholarships: $500 to $10,000.
Total amount of support: Over $942,000.

CO-OP FUNDING PROGRAMS: Collaborative Consumer Research Program.

NO. MOST RECENT APPLICANTS: Scholarships: Over 1,100.

NO. AWARDS: Grants and Awards: 72; Scholarships: 234.

APPLICATION INFO:
One common application form is used for all scholarships. Scholarship applications are available online to Academy members.

Awards applications are available online.
Deadline: Awards, Fellowships and Grants: February 1, unless otherwise stated. Scholarships: April 20. Announcement in July.

PUBLICATIONS:
Annual report.

IRS I.D.: 36-6150906

ADDRESS INQUIRIES TO:
Elisha Reichling, Program Coordinator (See address above.)

AMERICAN ASSOCIATION OF FAMILY AND CONSUMER SCIENCES (AAFCS)

400 North Columbus Street
Suite 202
Alexandria, VA 22314-2752
(703) 706-4600
(800) 424-8080
Fax: (703) 706-4663
E-mail: awards@aafcs.org
Web Site: www.aafcs.org/resources/recognition

TYPE:
Fellowships. AAFCS awards fellowships to individuals who have exhibited the potential to make contributions to the family and consumer sciences profession.

See entry 878 for full listing.

AMERICAN ASSOCIATION OF FAMILY AND CONSUMER SCIENCES (AAFCS) [2453]

400 North Columbus Street
Suite 202
Alexandria, VA 22314-2752
(703) 706-4600
(800) 424-8080
Fax: (703) 706-4663
E-mail: awards@aafcs.org
Web Site: www.aafcs.org/resources/recognition

FOUNDED: 1909

AREAS OF INTEREST:
Family and consumer sciences.

NAME(S) OF PROGRAMS:
● **National Teacher of the Year Award**

TYPE:
Awards/prizes. Recognizes exemplary teachers who utilize cutting-edge methods, techniques and activities to provide the stimulus for and give visibility to family and consumer sciences elementary and secondary education.

YEAR PROGRAM STARTED: 1974

PURPOSE:
To provide leadership and support for professionals whose work assists individuals, families and communities in making informed decisions about their well-being, relationships and resources to achieve optimal quality of life.

LEGAL BASIS:
501(c)(3) nonprofit charity.

ELIGIBILITY:
Requirements vary from year to year.

FINANCIAL DATA:
Amount of support per award: A commemorative plaque and a $2,500 award, plus up to $1,000 of support for one year of AAFCS membership and participation in the AAFCS Annual Conference & Expo.

NO. MOST RECENT APPLICANTS: 10.

NO. AWARDS: Up to 3 merit finalists, from whom 1 National Teacher of the Year is selected.

APPLICATION INFO:
Detailed guidelines and instructions are available from the Association.
Deadline: Second Monday in January.

ADDRESS INQUIRIES TO:
See e-mail address above.

CANADIAN FOUNDATION FOR DIETETIC RESEARCH (CFDR) [2454]

c/o Dietitians of Canada
99 Yorkville Avenue, Second Floor
Toronto ON M5R 1C1 Canada
(416) 642-9309
Fax: (416) 596-0603
E-mail: info@cfdr.ca
Web Site: www.cfdr.ca

FOUNDED: 1991

AREAS OF INTEREST:
Applied research in food and nutrition/dietetic research.

NAME(S) OF PROGRAMS:
● **Research Grants in Dietetics**

TYPE:
Awards/prizes; Research grants.

YEAR PROGRAM STARTED: 1991

PURPOSE:
To promote and support dietetic research.

ELIGIBILITY:
For research awards, applicants must be practicing dietitians who are delivering direct/indirect client/patient public care or service. One of the investigators must be a member of the dietetic profession, as identified by membership in a professional association of dietitians and/or registration as a member of a Canadian dietetics regulatory body.

GEOG. RESTRICTIONS: Canada.

FINANCIAL DATA:
Amount of support per award: Maximum $20,000.
Total amount of support: $77,000 for the year 2019.

NO. AWARDS: 4 for the year 2019.

APPLICATION INFO:
Applicant must submit a Letter of Intent package. Full proposal by invitation only.
Duration: Up to two years.
Deadline: Research grant letters of intent: Mid-September. Full proposal: March 1. Announcement in June.

PUBLICATIONS:
Canadian Journal of Dietetic Practice and Research (Revue Canadienne de la Pratique et de la Recherche en Dietetique).

STAFF:
Janis Randall Simpson, Executive Director

ADDRESS INQUIRIES TO:
See e-mail address above.

CENTER FOR SCIENCE IN THE PUBLIC INTEREST [2455]

1220 L Street, N.W.
Suite 300
Washington, DC 20005
(202) 332-9110
Fax: (202) 265-4954
E-mail: hr@cspinet.org
Web Site: www.cspinet.org

FOUNDED: 1971

AREAS OF INTEREST:
Consumer advocacy on nutrition, diet and health, and food safety.

NAME(S) OF PROGRAMS:
● **Public Interest Internships**

TYPE:
Internships. These unpaid internships allow interns to work on specific projects under the direction of a Project Director or the Executive Director.

YEAR PROGRAM STARTED: 1978

PURPOSE:
To provide interns with direct, practical experience; to provide the Center with extra assistance.

LEGAL BASIS:
501(c)(3).

ELIGIBILITY:
Students in undergraduate, graduate, law and medical schools are eligible to apply. Requirements vary depending on specific internship applied for.

Must work out of the Washington, DC office.

NO. MOST RECENT APPLICANTS: 250.

NO. AWARDS: Varies.

APPLICATION INFO:
Cover letter should indicate preferred dates. Application materials should include the following:
(1) cover letter indicating issues of interest, future plans, and the dates that applicant is available;
(2) resume (experience with advocacy groups is not required, but would be advantageous) and;
(3) writing sample (a popularly written piece is preferred over a technical report).
Duration: 10 weeks. Renewal possible.
Deadline: Applicants are advised to follow the application guidelines and apply as soon as possible. Applications are taken on a rolling basis until all positions have been filled.

PUBLICATIONS:
Status report; general brochure; publications list; *Nutrition Action Healthletter*.

OFFICERS:
Dr. Peter Lurie, President and Executive Director

ADDRESS INQUIRIES TO:
Colleen O'Day, Human Resources Director
(See address above.)

DIETITIANS OF CANADA (DC)   [2456]
99 Yorkville Avenue
Second Floor
Toronto ON M5R 1C1 Canada
(416) 596-0857
Fax: (416) 596-0603
E-mail: contactus@dietitians.ca
Web Site: www.dietitians.ca

FOUNDED: 1935

AREAS OF INTEREST:
Dietetics and nutrition.

NAME(S) OF PROGRAMS:
● **Graduate Student Awards**
● **Undergraduate Student Awards**

TYPE:
Awards/prizes.

YEAR PROGRAM STARTED: 1966

PURPOSE:
To provide financial support to students in undergraduate and graduate levels of study.

LEGAL BASIS:
Incorporated under Canada Corporations Act.

ELIGIBILITY:
Applicants must be members of Dietitians of Canada and registered in a food and nutrition or related program.

GEOG. RESTRICTIONS: Canada.

FINANCIAL DATA:
Amount of support per award: $2,500 cash prize, plus $1,000 for travel support to attend the DC national conference.

NO. AWARDS: 3 for the year 2018.

APPLICATION INFO:
Completed online application, academic transcript, and names and contact information for two references are required.
Deadline: January 31.

ADDRESS INQUIRIES TO:
E-mail: centralinfo@dietitians.ca

FOOD AND DRUG LAW INSTITUTE (FDLI)
1155 15th Street, N.W., Suite 910
Washington, DC 20005-2706
(202) 371-1420
(800) 956-6293
Fax: (202) 371-0649
E-mail: info@fdli.org
Web Site: www.fdli.org/resources/career/austern-writing-competition

TYPE:
Awards/prizes. The subject matter of the competition is an in-depth analysis of a current issue relevant to the food and drug field, including a relevant case law, legislative history and other authorities, particularly where the U.S. Food and Drug Administration is involved.

See entry 1801 for full listing.

HANNAFORD CHARITABLE FOUNDATION
145 Pleasant Hill Road
Scarborough, ME 04074
E-mail: hannafordcharitablefoundation@hannaford.com
Web Site: www.hannaford.com

TYPE:
Capital grants; Project/program grants. Employee scholarships.

See entry 1409 for full listing.

ILLINOIS RESTAURANT ASSOCIATION EDUCATIONAL FOUNDATION
33 West Monroe, Suite 250
Chicago, IL 60603
(312) 787-4000
E-mail: kkramer@illinoisrestaurants.org
Web Site: www.illinoisrestaurants.org

TYPE:
Product donations; Scholarships.

See entry 1532 for full listing.

INTERNATIONAL ASSOCIATION FOR FOOD PROTECTION   [2457]
6200 Aurora Avenue
Suite 200W
Des Moines, IA 50322-2864
(515) 276-3344
(800) 369-6337
Fax: (515) 276-8655
E-mail: info@foodprotection.org
Web Site: www.foodprotection.org

FOUNDED: 1911

AREAS OF INTEREST:
Food science and research.

NAME(S) OF PROGRAMS:
● **Harold Barnum Industry Award**
● **Larry Beuchat Young Researcher Award**
● **Food Safety Innovation Award**
● **Harry Haverland Citation Award**

● **International Leadership Award**
● **Elmer Marth Educator Award**
● **Sanitarian Award**
● **Student Travel Scholarship Award**
● **Ewen C.D. Todd Control of Foodborne Illness Award**
● **Travel Award for Food Safety Professionals in a Country with a Developing Economy**
● **Travel Award for State or Provincial Health or Agricultural Department Employees**
● **Maurice Weber Laboratorian Award**

TYPE:
Awards/prizes; Travel grants. Cash awards and plaques to outstanding members.

YEAR PROGRAM STARTED: 1973

PURPOSE:
To provide food safety professionals worldwide with a forum to exchange information on protecting the food supply; to recognize and reward outstanding member contributions in the specified award area.

LEGAL BASIS:
Nonprofit, incorporated professional association.

ELIGIBILITY:
Nominees must be members of the International Association for Food Protection.

FINANCIAL DATA:
Amount of support per award: $1,500 to $2,500 and plaque or travel expense paid.

NO. AWARDS: Generally, 1 of each award annually. Travel awards: Multiple.

APPLICATION INFO:
Varies by award. Details are available on the Association web site.
Deadline: February 19.

IRS I.D.: 35-0894354

OFFICERS:
Tim Jackson, President
Kali Kniel, President-Elect
Roger Cook, Vice President
Ruth Petran, Secretary

EXECUTIVE DIRECTOR:
David W. Tharp

ADDRESS INQUIRIES TO:
David W. Tharp, Executive Director
(See address above.)

KAPPA OMICRON NU HONOR SOCIETY   [2458]
P.O. Box 798
Okemos, MI 48805-0798
(727) 940-2658 ext. 2003
E-mail: info@kon.org
Web Site: www.kon.org

FOUNDED: 1912

AREAS OF INTEREST:
Home economics, family and consumer sciences, and human sciences.

NAME(S) OF PROGRAMS:
● **Marjorie M. Brown Dissertation Fellowship**
● **Ruth E. Hawthorne Research Grant**
● **Kappa Omicron Phi/Hettie M. Anthony Fellowship**
● **The KON/GEICO LeaderShape Undergraduate Scholarship**
● **Eileen C. Maddex Fellowship**
● **Dorothy I. Mitstifer Scholarship**
● **National Alumni Chapter Fellowship**
● **National Alumni Chapter Grant**

- National Scholar Program
- New Initiatives Grant
- Omicron Nu Master's Fellowship
- Omicron Nu Research Fellowship
- Betty Jeanne Root Fellowship
- Undergraduate Research Award

TYPE:
Fellowships; Project/program grants; Research grants; Scholarships. Awarded to members for graduate or postgraduate study and research in human sciences or one of its specializations at colleges or universities with strong research programs and supporting disciplines for the chosen major or topic.

YEAR PROGRAM STARTED: 1969

PURPOSE:
To promote research and graduate study in human sciences by recognizing and encouraging scholastic excellence.

LEGAL BASIS:
Nonprofit corporation, 501(c)(3) status.

ELIGIBILITY:
Fellowships/Grants: Applicant must be a member of Kappa Omicron Nu who has demonstrated scholarship, research and leadership potential.

FINANCIAL DATA:
Amount of support per award: $150 to $10,000 per year.

Total amount of support: $40,000 for the year 2016.

NO. AWARDS: Doctoral Fellowships: 2 or 3; Master's Fellowships: 3; Scholar Grants: Varies; Marjorie M. Brown Dissertation Fellowship, Ruth E. Hawthorne Research Grant, Kappa Omicron Phi/Hettie M. Anthony Fellowship, Leadership Award, Dorothy I. Mitstifer Scholarship, National Alumni Chapter Grant, New Initiatives Grant and Betty Jeanne Root Fellowship: 1 per award or fellowship; KON/GEICO Scholarship: 2.

APPLICATION INFO:
Contact the Society.

Duration: One academic year. Nonrenewable.

Deadline: Research and Project Grants: February 15. Announcement April 15. Doctoral Fellowships: January 15. Announcement April 1. Master's Fellowships: April 1. Announcement May 15.

PUBLICATIONS:
Brochure.

IRS I.D.: 38-1245233

STAFF:
Ginger Phillips, Executive Director

BOARD OF DIRECTORS:
Bridget Clinton-Scott, Chairperson
Dr. Janelle Walter, Chairperson Elect
Dr. Amber Roth, First Vice Chairperson
Dr. Crystal Duncan Lane, Second Vice Chairperson
Dr. Denise Fisher, Secretary

ADDRESS INQUIRIES TO:
Ginger Phillips, Executive Director
(See address above.)

NATIONAL CATTLEMAN'S BEEF ASSOCIATION [2459]
9110 East Nichols Avenue
Suite 300
Centennial, CO 80112-3450
(303) 694-0305
Fax: (303) 694-2851
E-mail: beefresearch@beef.org
Web Site: www.ncba.org
www.beefresearch.org

FOUNDED: 1922

AREAS OF INTEREST:
Human nutrition, the relationship between nutrients in beef and health (including amino acids, vitamins and minerals), diet and health.

NAME(S) OF PROGRAMS:
- Human Nutrition Research

TYPE:
Grants-in-aid; Research grants; Research contracts. Research contracts and grants-in-aid for experimental projects in the areas of:
(1) beef as part of a balanced diet;
(2) parity studies;
(3) health benefits of beef lipids and;
(4) contribution of beef nutrients to total diet.

Proposals solicited via specific RFPs (request for proposals).

YEAR PROGRAM STARTED: 1923

PURPOSE:
To gain further knowledge of the value of beef in our diets; to develop research technology that can be applied to the areas noted above.

LEGAL BASIS:
Professional, nonprofit association.

ELIGIBILITY:
Open to qualified institutions (including universities, medical centers, nonprofit organizations and/or contract research laboratories) with appropriate interests.

GEOG. RESTRICTIONS: Primarily United States.

FINANCIAL DATA:
Amount of support per award: $20,000 to $50,000 for one year to $200,000 to $400,000 for multiyear awards. Most are $100,000 to $150,000.

Total amount of support: Varies.

CO-OP FUNDING PROGRAMS: Occasionally federally funded programs are under way that can be facilitated with other funds to expand the scope of the work.

APPLICATION INFO:
Official application materials are available upon request to NCBA at the address above, after it has been established that the proposal would be of mutual interest.

Duration: Support is provided for one to three years depending upon the project.

Deadline: Varies for RFPs.

PUBLICATIONS:
Annual research report.

ADDRESS INQUIRIES TO:
Shalene McNeill, Ph.D.
Executive Director, Nutrition Research
(See address above.)

NATIONAL DAIRY COUNCIL [2460]
10255 West Higgins Road
Suite 900
Rosemont, IL 60018-5616
(847) 803-2000
Fax: (847) 803-2077
E-mail: nutritionresearch@rosedmi.com
Web Site: researchsubmission.
nationaldairycouncil.org

FOUNDED: 1915

AREAS OF INTEREST:
Independent research to aid in the ongoing discovery of information about dairy foods' important role in a healthy lifestyle. This research provides insights to industry for new dairy product innovation.

NAME(S) OF PROGRAMS:
- Nutrition Research Program

TYPE:
Research contracts. The National Dairy Council is the nutrition research, education and communications arm of Dairy Management Inc. On behalf of U.S. dairy farmers, the National Dairy Council provides science-based nutrition information to, and in collaboration with, a variety of stakeholders committed to fostering a healthier society, including health professionals, educators, school nutrition directors, academia, industry, consumers and media. The National Dairy Council comprises a staff of nutrition science researchers, registered dietitians and communications experts dedicated to educating the public on the health benefits of consuming milk and milk products throughout a person's lifespan.

YEAR PROGRAM STARTED: 1915

PURPOSE:
To research and discover health benefits for dairy foods and ingredients and advance scientific understanding of these benefits; to increase demand for dairy.

LEGAL BASIS:
Nonprofit educational-scientific institution under IRS 501(c)(3).

ELIGIBILITY:
Qualified investigators associated with accredited institutions of higher learning are eligible for support. Applicants must hold a Ph.D., M.D., D.D.S., D.V.M. or other degree, with experience demonstrating ability to conduct the proposed research.

Funds are not available for alteration of facilities or purchase of permanent equipment.

FINANCIAL DATA:
Amount of support per award: Administered research contracts vary in amount, depending upon the needs and nature of the request.
Total amount of support: Varies.

CO-OP FUNDING PROGRAMS: If research interests of additional organizations coincide, cooperative projects are preferred to enhance efficiency of funds utilized and to benefit the researcher through a broader base of support.

NO. MOST RECENT APPLICANTS: 105 preproposals; approximately 17 selected for full proposal submission.

NO. AWARDS: Varies.

APPLICATION INFO:
The National Dairy Council invites submission of two-page preproposals in the beginning of each calendar year, typically

early July. Applications which meet the needs of the research program, which are stated in the guidelines for preproposal submission, will be reviewed. Approximately two to three weeks following the submission deadline, all applicants will receive notice of the outcome of this screening process. Applicants whose preproposals generated interest will receive further information and materials for submission of a detailed full research application to the program. Full proposals will be due approximately six to eight weeks later. All full proposals will be peer-reviewed for scientific merit by the Nutrition Research Scientific Advisory Committee, which is comprised of expert scientists from academia, government and industry. For information on the research program and research topics of interest in the next solicitation, please send a letter requesting the information and a self-addressed label to the address above or contact the NDC research office.

Duration: Projects supported on a yearly basis for up to three years.

Deadline: Preproposal: Early May, with decision made early June; Full Proposal: Early July, with decision made November or December.

PUBLICATIONS:
Guidelines for application and administration.

THE NATIONAL RESTAURANT ASSOCIATION EDUCATIONAL FOUNDATION [2461]

2055 L Street, N.W.
Washington, DC 20036
(202) 973-3672
E-mail: scholars@nraef.org
Web Site: www.chooserestaurants. org/scholarships

FOUNDED: 1987

AREAS OF INTEREST:
Foodservice education and training.

NAME(S) OF PROGRAMS:
● **National Restaurant Association Educational Foundation (NRAE) Scholarship Program**

TYPE:
Scholarships. Provides scholarships for students who are pursuing an education and career in the foodservice industry.

YEAR PROGRAM STARTED: 1987

PURPOSE:
To encourage and support students pursuing an education and career in the foodservice industry.

LEGAL BASIS:
Not-for-profit organization.

ELIGIBILITY:
Applicant must be a U.S. citizen or permanent resident alien who is accepted and/or enrolled in a foodservice-related postsecondary program.

GEOG. RESTRICTIONS: United States and its territories.

FINANCIAL DATA:
Amount of support per award: Undergraduate Scholarships: $2,500 to $10,000.

NO. MOST RECENT APPLICANTS: 700.

NO. AWARDS: Approximately 300.

APPLICATION INFO:
All applicants need:
(1) a valid e-mail address;
(2) at least two letters of recommendation (please note, applicant can either attach the letters of recommendation or contact their references via the application to request that they send letter(s) of recommendation);
(3) current resume;
(4) proof of enrollment;
(5) student transcripts that include a cumulative grade point average (official or unofficial) and;
(6) Student Aid Report (generated by FAFSA).

Duration: Varies depending upon the award.

Deadline: March 15.

PUBLICATIONS:
Awards brochure.

ADDRESS INQUIRIES TO:
Scholarships
(See address above.)

USDA FOOD AND NUTRITION SERVICE

Child Nutrition Service
3101 Park Center Drive, Room 628
Alexandria, VA 22302
(703) 305-2054
Fax: (703) 305-2879
Web Site: www.fns.usda.gov

TYPE:
Formula grants; Grants-in-aid; Project/program grants. Reimbursement for the support of food service in schools, child and adult care institutions to improve nutrition.

The Child and Adult Care Food Program helps child care facilities and institutions serve nutritious meals and snacks to preschool and school-age children. To participate, facilities and institutions must be licensed or approved to provide child care services. They must also meet certain other eligibility requirements. The program operates in nonresidential day care centers, settlement houses, outside-school-hours care centers, family day care homes, institutions providing day care for handicapped children and others. Participating facilities and institutions get cash assistance, USDA-donated foods and technical guidance. In child care centers, the amount of cash assistance varies according to the family size and income of children served. In day care homes, the amount of cash assistance is based on a food service payment rate. Similar benefits are also now available to adult day care centers which serve functionally impaired adults or persons 60 years of age or older.

The Fresh Fruit and Vegetable Program introduces school children to a variety of produce that they otherwise might not have the opportunity to sample. The goal is to improve children's overall diet and create healthier eating habits to impact their present and future health.

The National School Lunch Program makes well-planned nutritious meals available to school children. Any public or nonprofit private schools of high school grade or under and licensed public or nonprofit private residential child care institutions are eligible to participate in the National School Lunch and School Breakfast Programs. Schools that participate are required to provide free and

reduced-price meals to children unable to pay the full price. Eligibility is based on application information submitted by a parent or guardian. The household income limit for free lunches is set at or below 130% of the federal poverty level and for reduced price lunches household income must be above 130% or at or below 185% of the federal poverty level. Children from households not eligible for free or reduced-price meals must pay the school's full price charge for lunch. Cash and donated commodities are provided to participating schools and institutions according to the number of meals served.

The School Breakfast Program makes nutritious breakfasts available to school children under the same eligibility guidelines and general requirements as the National School Lunch Program.

The Special Milk Program makes it possible for all children attending a participating school or institution to purchase milk at a reduced price or receive it free, if they are eligible. Reimbursement is provided for each half-pint of milk served under the program. Schools and institutions that participate in other federal child nutrition programs authorized under the National School Lunch Act or the Child Nutrition Act of 1966 may not participate in the Special Milk Program, except for split-session kindergarten programs conducted in schools in which the children do not have access to the other meal program.

The Summer Food Service Program helps communities serve meals to needy children when school is not in session. The program is sponsored by public or private nonprofit school food authorities or local, municipal, county or state governments. Public or private nonprofit residential camps, other private nonprofit organizations, colleges and universities which participate in the National Youth Sports Program also may be sponsors. The program operates in areas in which at least 50% of the children meet the income criteria for free and reduced-price school meals. USDA reimburses sponsors for operating costs of food services up to a specified maximum rate for each meal served. In addition, sponsors receive some reimbursement for planning, operating and supervising expenses.

See entry 1050 for full listing.

Mining and metallurgy

ASM MATERIALS EDUCATION FOUNDATION [2462]

9639 Kinsman Road
Materials Park, OH 44073-0002
(440) 338-5151
(800) 336-5152
Fax: (440) 338-4634
E-mail: jeane.deatherage@asminternational.org
Web Site: www.asmfoundation.org

FOUNDED: 1913

AREAS OF INTEREST:
Materials science and engineering in related fields such as metallurgy, metallurgical engineering, polymeric engineering, ceramic engineering, advanced composites engineering and engineering of electronic materials.

NAME(S) OF PROGRAMS:
- **Acta Materialia Scholarships**
- **ASM Outstanding Scholars**
- **David J. Chellman Scholarship**
- **Edward J. Dulis Scholarship**
- **John M. Haniak Scholarship**
- **Ladish Co. Foundation Scholarships**
- **George A. Roberts Scholarship**
- **Lucille & Charles A. Wert Scholarship**
- **William Park Woodside Founder's Scholarship**

TYPE:
Scholarships.

YEAR PROGRAM STARTED: 1953

PURPOSE:
To encourage and support capable students with interest and potential in the field of metallurgy and materials science.

LEGAL BASIS:
501(c)(3) educational charity.

ELIGIBILITY:
Applicant must be a member of ASM International or Material Advantage student member. Additionally, the applicant must meet the following requirements:
(1) must have an intended or declared major in metallurgy or materials science engineering. Applicants majoring in related science or engineering disciplines will be considered if they demonstrate a strong academic emphasis and interest in materials science;
(2) must have completed at least one year of college and;
(3) must have junior or senior standing in the fall at a North American university. University must have an accredited science and engineering program leading to a Bachelor's degree.

All scholarships, except the ASM Outstanding Scholar Awards, are only awarded to students studying in North America who demonstrate financial need in addition to academic merit.

ASM Outstanding Scholar Awards are open to international students. Financial need is not considered.

GEOG. RESTRICTIONS: United States.

FINANCIAL DATA:
Most awards include a certificate of recognition and travel allowance for attendance to the awards ceremony.
Amount of support per award: Up to $10,000.

NO. AWARDS: Varies.

APPLICATION INFO:
To be considered, applicant must complete the online application and submit the following supporting papers by e-mail to ScholarshipsUG@asminternational.org:
(1) transcript;
(2) resume;
(3) photograph and;
(4) two letters of recommendation.

Applicant must forward the online Scholarships Recommendation Form to their references.
Duration: One academic year.
Deadline: Application and materials must be sent by May 1. Award winners will be notified by August 15.

IRS I.D.: 34-6541397

ADDRESS INQUIRIES TO:
ASM Foundation Undergraduate Scholarship Program
E-mail: foundation@asminternational.org

*SPECIAL STIPULATIONS:
Must have completed one year of undergraduate work.

INSTITUTE OF MATERIALS, MINERALS AND MINING   [2463]
The Boilerhouse
Springfield Business Park
Caunt Road
Grantham Lincs NG31 7FZ England
(44) 01476 513886
Fax: (44) 01476 513899
E-mail: anita.horton@iom3.org
Web Site: www.iom3.org

FOUNDED: 1892

AREAS OF INTEREST:
Mining and metallurgy.

NAME(S) OF PROGRAMS:
- **Centenary Scholarship**
- **Stanley Elmore Fellowship Fund**
- **G. Vernon Hobson Bequest**
- **Mining Club Award**
- **Edgar Pam Fellowship**
- **The Tom Seaman Travelling Scholarship**
- **Bosworth Smith Trust Fund**

TYPE:
Awards/prizes; Fellowships; Research grants; Scholarships; Training grants; Travel grants. The Centenary Scholarship is restricted to first- or second-year undergraduates in student membership of the Institute and will be awarded for projects, visits, etc., in furtherance of applicants' career development.

Stanley Elmore Fellowship Fund offers fellowships (normally two for one year) applicable at a U.K. university for research into all branches of extractive metallurgy and mineral processing and, in special cases, for expenditure related to such research.

The G. Vernon Hobson Bequest awards are given for the advancement of teaching and practice of geology as applied to mining. One or more awards may be made for travel, research or other objects in accordance with the terms of the Bequest.

The Mining Club Award will be offered to British subjects 21 to 35 years of age who are actively engaged (in full- or part-time postgraduate study or in employment) in the minerals industry, as defined by the Institute, for travel purposes (for example, to study mineral industry operations in the U.K. or overseas, to present a paper at an international minerals industry conference or to assist the applicant in attending a full-time course of study related to the minerals industry outside the U.K.), or for any other similar purpose that may be regarded as being within the spirit of the award.

The Edgar Pam Fellowship is awarded for postgraduate study in subjects within the Institute's fields of interest, which range from exploration geology to extractive metallurgy. Those eligible for the award are young graduates, domiciled in Australia, Canada, New Zealand, South Africa and the U.K., who wish to undertake advanced study or research in the U.K.

The Tom Seaman Travelling Scholarship is awarded annually to a member, not older than 35 years of age, who is training or has been trained for a career in mining and/or related technologies. The scholarship shall be to assist the study for an aspect of engineering in the minerals industry, with the intention of advancing the associated standards or techniques.

The Bosworth Smith Trust Fund is given for the assistance of postgraduate research in metal mining, non-ferrous extraction metallurgy or mineral dressing. Applications will be considered for grants towards working expenses, the cost of visits to mines and plants in connection with such research, and purchase of apparatus.

ELIGIBILITY:
Applicants should note that, in general, preference will be given to members of the Institution (student membership is required for the Centenary Scholarship). Recipients of the awards will be required to submit summary reports of the ways in which such awards have been used for publication.

In judging the applications received for each award, the Institute will take into account academic excellence and scholarship. The application must, therefore, specify academic ability. Candidates merely seeking assistance for financial hardship will not be considered.

Applicants for awards must ensure that the particular fund from which support is being sought is relevant to their field(s) of interest. Applications not in accordance with the specified terms and conditions of the various funds, those which are received after the deadline, and those for which the appropriate letters of support have not been received by that date will not be submitted to the awards committee.

FINANCIAL DATA:
Amount of support per award: Centenary Scholarship: GBP 500; Stanley Elmore Fellowship Fund: Up to GBP 14,000 distributed between one or two awardees; G. Vernon Hobson Bequest: Up to GBP 1,300; Mining Club Award: Up to GBP 1,500; Edgar Pam Fellowship: Maximum GBP 2,000; Tom Seaman Travelling Scholarship: Up to GBP 5,500; Bosworth Smith Trust Fund: Approximately GBP 5,000 in grants.

APPLICATION INFO:
Application form required. Applications not in accordance with the specified terms and conditions of the various funds, those which are received after the closing date each year, and those for which the appropriate levels of support have not been received by that date, will not be accepted for consideration.
Deadline: March 31.

PUBLICATIONS:
Guidelines.

ADDRESS INQUIRIES TO:
Anita Horton, Head of Governance
(See address above.)

INTERNATIONAL CENTRE FOR DIFFRACTION DATA   [2464]
12 Campus Boulevard
Newtown Square, PA 19073-3273
(610) 325-9814
Fax: (610) 325-9823
E-mail: info@icdd.com
Web Site: www.icdd.com

FOUNDED: 1991

AREAS OF INTEREST:
The science of crystallography.

NAME(S) OF PROGRAMS:
● **The Ludo Frevel Crystallography Scholarship Award**

TYPE:
Scholarships.

YEAR PROGRAM STARTED: 1991

PURPOSE:
To encourage promising graduate students to pursue crystallographically oriented research.

ELIGIBILITY:
Applicant should be a graduate student seeking a degree with major interest in crystallography, crystal structure analysis, crystal morphology, modulated structures, correlation of atomic structures with physical properties, systematic classification of crystal structures, phase identification and materials characterization. There are no restrictions on country, race, age or sex. Students with a graduation date prior to July 1 of the award year are not eligible.

Funds can be used for travel to conferences or for research-related purposes.

FINANCIAL DATA:
The scholarship stipend is to be used by the graduate student to help defray tuition and laboratory fees. A portion of the stipend may be applied to registration fees to accredited scientific meetings related to crystallography.
Amount of support per award: $2,000 to $2,500.

NO. MOST RECENT APPLICANTS: 59 for fiscal year 2019.

NO. AWARDS: 6 for fiscal year 2019.

APPLICATION INFO:
The following information must be prepared in advance of applying online:
(1) a description of the candidate's proposed research (limit two pages), including purpose and rationale for the research, proposed methodology to be used in the study, and references and/or descriptions of the scientific background for the proposed research and;
(2) a curriculum vitae, including educational preparation (institutions, dates, degrees obtained and in progress, and particularly pertinent coursework), awards/honors received, any research publications and/or

presentations given, any work experience (dates, employers, positions), and professional activities and memberships.
Duration: One year. Renewals possible. Renewal applications will be considered on a competitive basis in conjunction with all applications that have been submitted up to the closing date.
Deadline: October 17. Contact Centre for exact date.

ADDRESS INQUIRIES TO:
Stephanie Jennings, Conference Assistant
(See address above.)

MINERALOGICAL ASSOCIATION OF CANADA   [2465]

490, rue de la Couronne
Quebec QC G1K 9A9 Canada
(418) 653-0333
Fax: (418) 653-0777
E-mail: office@mineralogicalassociation.ca
Web Site: mineralogicalassociation.ca

FOUNDED: 1955

AREAS OF INTEREST:
Mineralogy.

NAME(S) OF PROGRAMS:
● **Leonard G. Berry Medal**
● **Hawley Medal**
● **MAC Foundation Scholarship**
● **MAC Student Travel/Research Grants**
● **Peacock Medal**
● **Pinch Medal**
● **Undergraduate Awards**
● **Young Scientist Award**

TYPE:
Awards/prizes; Grants-in-aid; Research grants; Scholarships; Travel grants.

PURPOSE:
To promote and advance the knowledge of mineralogy and the allied disciplines of crystallography, petrology, geochemistry and mineral deposits.

LEGAL BASIS:
Nonprofit scientific and charitable organization.

ELIGIBILITY:
The Leonard G. Berry Medal is awarded for distinguished service to the Mineralogical Association of Canada.

The Hawley Medal is presented to the author(s) of what is judged to be the best paper published in the preceding year's volume of *The Canadian Mineralogist*.

The MAC Foundation Scholarship is awarded to a graduate student involved in an M.Sc. or Ph.D. thesis program in the fields of mineralogy, crystallography, petrology, geochemistry or mineral deposits.

The MAC Student Travel/Research Grants are given to assist honours undergraduate and graduate students in the mineral sciences.

The Peacock Medal is awarded annually for excellence in research to a scientist who has made outstanding contributions to the mineralogical sciences in Canada.

The Pinch Medal is awarded every other year to recognize major and sustained contributions to the advancement of mineralogy by members of the collector-dealer community.

Undergraduate Awards are given to university students in mineralogy. The Association presents a MAC publication to the top student in the introductory mineralogy course at each Canadian university.

The Young Scientist Award is given to a young scientist who has made a significant international research contribution in a promising start to a scientific career.

FINANCIAL DATA:
Amount of support per award: Varies depending on award.
Total amount of support: $25,000.

NO. MOST RECENT APPLICANTS: MAC Travel/Research Grants: 23 for the year 2019.

NO. AWARDS: Varies.

APPLICATION INFO:
Contact the Association.
Duration: Varies.
Deadline: Varies.

PUBLICATIONS:
The Canadian Mineralogist.

STAFF:
Lee A. Groat, Editor

ADDRESS INQUIRIES TO:
Johanne Caron, Business Manager
(See address above.)

Indexes

Entry Listing by Chapter

MULTIPLE SPECIAL PURPOSE: 1-310

HUMANITIES (GENERAL): 311-373
Architecture: 374-389
Arts (multiple disciplines): 390-486
   Performing arts: 487-501
   Fine arts: 502-530
History: 531-602
Languages: 603-615
Literature: 616-660
Museums and libraries: 661-692
Music: 693-742
Religion and theology: 743-764

INTERNATIONAL AFFAIRS AND AREA STUDIES: 765-802
International studies and research abroad: 803-876
Programs for foreign scholars: 877-887
Technical assistance and cooperative research: 888-890

SPECIAL POPULATIONS: 891-937
African-American: 938-948
Native American: 949-971
Spanish-speaking: 972-976
Women: 977-1007

URBAN AND REGIONAL AFFAIRS: 1008-1381
Children and youth: 1008-1051
Community development and services: 1052-1287
Crime prevention: 1288-1292
Public health: 1293-1345
Social welfare: 1346-1381

EDUCATION: 1382-1636
Educational projects and research (general): 1382-1449
Elementary and secondary education: 1450-1462
Higher education projects and research: 1463-1492
Scholar aid programs (all disciplines): 1493-1636

SCIENCES (MULTIPLE DISCIPLINES): 1637-1677

SOCIAL SCIENCES (GENERAL): 1678-1717
Business and economics: 1718-1747
Communications: 1748-1792
Labor: 1793-1796
Law: 1797-1810
Political science: 1811-1839
Sociology and anthropology: 1840-1847

PHYSICAL SCIENCES (GENERAL): 1848-1859
Astronomy and aerospace science: 1860-1875
Chemistry: 1876-1888
Earth sciences: 1889-1906
Mathematics: 1907-1915
Physics: 1916-1921

LIFE SCIENCES (GENERAL): 1922-1929
Agriculture, land resources, rural development: 1930-1956
Biology: 1957-1979
Environment: 1980-2020
Medicine (multiple disciplines): 2021-2127
Allergy, immunology, infectious diseases: 2128-2131
Dentistry: 2132-2145
Internal medicine: 2146-2161
   Cardiovascular and pulmonary: 2162-2190
   Metabolism, gastroenterology, nephrology: 2191-2218
   Oncology: 2219-2239
   Rheumatology: 2240-2241
Neurology: 2242-2274
Nursing: 2275-2289
Obstetrics and gynecology: 2290-2293
Ophthalmology and otolaryngology: 2294-2316
Osteopathy: 2317-2320
Pediatrics: 2321-2327
Pharmacology: 2328-2333
Physical medicine and rehabilitation: 2334-2348
Psychiatry, psychology, mental health: 2349-2383

TECHNOLOGY AND INDUSTRY: 2384-2404
Aeronautics and astronautics: 2405-2413
Engineering: 2414-2451
Home economics and nutrition: 2452-2461
Mining and metallurgy: 2462-2465

Subject Index

Drugs. *See* Pharmacy and Pharmacology
Dysautonomia: 2250

E

Early Childhood Education: 197, 1009, 1042, 1051, 1088, 1241, 1372, 1451, 1461, 1626; *see also* Preschool Education and Care
Earth Sciences: 890, 1633, 1638, 1642, 1647, 1648, 1649, 1654, 1658, 1665, 1667, 1671, 1675, 1855, 1892, 1893, 1897, 1899, 1902, 1906, 1927, 1959, 1990; *see also* Atmospheric Sciences; Geology; Oceanography; Petroleum Sciences
Earthquake: 1990
East European Studies. *See* Slavic and East Europe
Eastern States: 303, 1531, 2053; *see also* states by name
Ecological Restoration: 1648, 1997
Ecology: 84, 841, 1638, 1647, 1648, 1649, 1668, 1928, 1967, 1969, 1975, 1977, 1980, 1986, 1989, 1996, 1999, 2002, 2007, 2010, 2015, 2016, 2017; *see also* Biological Sciences; Botany; Conservation; Environmental Studies
Ecology, Aquatic: 1430, 1663, 1668, 1900, 1901, 1963, 1975, 1992, 2002, 2005, 2019; *see also* Marine Biology
Economic Education: 1732
Economic Growth and Development: 18, 24, 27, 43, 50, 55, 69, 70, 72, 102, 112, 119, 123, 134, 136, 151, 158, 162, 188, 192, 209, 212, 217, 310, 394, 784, 790, 929, 946, 958, 970, 987, 1055, 1067, 1083, 1093, 1098, 1102, 1109, 1110, 1118, 1125, 1131, 1137, 1140, 1142, 1159, 1163, 1175, 1183, 1190, 1191, 1196, 1202, 1208, 1210, 1213, 1214, 1219, 1233, 1252, 1259, 1268, 1271, 1285, 1348, 1361, 1372, 1479, 1574, 1734, 1737, 1763; *see also* Developing Nations, Economic Growth
Economic History: 549, 596, 1726, 1822
Economic Justice: 126, 923, 981, 1162
Economic Policy: 19, 1093, 1695, 1817; *see also* Policy Analysis
Economics: 273, 286, 535, 548, 772, 778, 790, 802, 805, 970, 1106, 1362, 1473, 1610, 1684, 1685, 1695, 1732, 1739, 1756, 1824, 1914, 1915, 2008; *see also* Appraisal; Business; Finance; Labor, Economics; Management; Social Sciences
Economics, Education: 1420, 1471, 1510, 1582, 1624, 1633, 1693, 1723, 1737, 1741
Economics, International: 776, 777, 786, 870
Economics, Research: 867, 890, 1726, 1793, 1818
Ecuador: 1534
Education: 2, 3, 4, 5, 6, 7, 8, 11, 16, 17, 20, 21, 22, 23, 25, 26, 27, 28, 29, 30, 31, 33, 34, 36, 37, 38, 40, 41, 42, 43, 44, 45, 46, 47, 48, 53, 54, 55, 56, 57, 58, 61, 62, 63, 66, 67, 69, 70, 72, 75, 77, 78, 79, 81, 85, 86, 87, 89, 91, 93, 94, 95, 98, 99, 101, 102, 103, 105, 107, 108, 109, 111, 114, 115, 116, 119, 122, 123, 124, 125, 127, 128, 129, 132, 133, 136, 137, 138, 140, 141, 142, 143, 144, 145, 146, 147, 151, 154, 156, 158, 162, 163, 166, 169, 170, 172, 174, 175, 176, 185, 186, 187, 188, 192, 194, 195, 200, 201, 202, 203, 204, 210, 211, 213, 214, 216, 217, 218, 219, 222, 223, 224, 225, 226, 227, 228, 230, 232, 235, 236, 241, 243, 244, 245, 246, 247, 249, 250, 252, 253, 255, 256, 258, 260, 262, 263, 264, 265, 267, 269, 270, 272, 274, 275, 278, 279, 280, 282, 284, 285, 287, 288, 290, 294, 295, 297, 300, 307, 308, 309, 310, 337, 384, 394, 399, 403, 413, 420, 428, 452, 500, 538, 608, 625, 662, 663, 689, 753, 766, 784, 790, 802, 902, 906, 910, 911, 914, 929, 930, 934, 942, 971, 1009, 1013, 1014, 1018, 1019, 1020, 1021, 1023, 1024, 1028, 1029, 1030, 1032, 1041, 1042, 1044, 1051, 1053, 1055, 1057, 1058, 1059, 1060, 1062, 1063, 1064, 1069, 1070, 1071, 1074, 1075, 1076, 1078, 1079, 1084, 1085, 1086, 1089, 1090, 1091, 1092, 1093, 1094, 1098, 1100, 1102, 1103, 1104, 1107, 1109, 1110, 1111, 1114, 1115, 1117, 1118, 1119, 1124, 1125, 1126, 1127, 1128, 1129, 1132, 1133, 1134, 1137, 1138, 1139, 1141, 1144, 1145, 1146, 1147, 1148, 1150, 1152, 1153, 1154, 1155, 1158, 1159, 1160, 1161, 1164, 1165, 1166, 1167, 1168, 1170, 1171, 1172, 1173, 1174, 1175, 1176, 1177, 1178, 1179, 1180, 1182, 1183, 1186, 1187, 1195, 1196, 1197, 1202, 1203, 1205, 1206, 1207, 1208, 1210, 1211, 1212, 1213, 1216, 1222, 1224, 1227, 1228, 1231, 1232, 1233, 1234, 1238, 1239, 1241, 1243, 1244, 1245, 1246, 1247, 1250, 1253, 1256, 1257, 1258, 1259, 1261, 1265, 1266, 1267, 1269, 1271, 1276, 1277, 1279, 1281, 1282, 1283, 1285, 1286, 1296, 1302, 1334, 1338, 1339, 1344, 1348, 1353, 1365, 1371, 1375, 1379, 1382, 1383, 1384, 1385, 1386, 1393, 1394, 1395, 1397, 1399, 1400, 1406, 1409, 1410, 1411, 1413, 1417, 1419, 1425, 1433, 1436, 1439, 1450, 1451, 1454, 1456, 1460, 1461, 1470, 1474, 1485, 1492, 1495, 1499, 1524, 1525, 1527, 1544, 1552, 1569, 1572, 1591, 1592, 1628, 1632, 1633, 1646, 1685, 1737, 1738, 1793, 1898, 1905, 1913, 1967, 1977, 2010, 2071, 2098, 2109, 2280, 2461; *see also* Consumer Information and Education; Curriculum Development; entries beginning with Education and Educational; Equal Educational Opportunity; Faculty, Study and Research Programs; Instructional Materials;

International Study and Research Programs; Medical Education and Training; Nursing Education; Preschool Education and Care; Reading; Teaching, Outside U.S.; also specific professions and areas of study
Education, Adult: 1278, 1445, 1493, 1572, 1794; *see also* Education, Continuing
Education, Alternative Modes: 1491
Education, Comparative: 876
Education, Continuing: 988, 1458; *see also* Education, Adult
Education, Counseling and Guidance: 1486
Education, Developing Nations. *See* Developing Nations, Education
Education, Elementary: 301, 966, 1034, 1036, 1173, 1200, 1260, 1372, 1406, 1408, 1433, 1444, 1446, 1452, 1454, 1459, 1469, 1511, 1525
Education, Elementary and Secondary, Construction and Facilities Projects: 1284, 1655; *see also* Construction and Facilities Projects
Education, Government Policy and Legislation. *See* Education, Policy-Making
Education, Higher, Aid Programs for Undergraduate and Graduate Students in All Disciplines: 14, 175, 189, 271, 276, 277, 372, 375, 384, 429, 605, 653, 690, 835, 852, 854, 856, 869, 878, 885, 887, 893, 896, 900, 906, 907, 910, 912, 916, 919, 922, 925, 927, 938, 941, 943, 947, 948, 949, 950, 951, 953, 959, 960, 969, 971, 974, 975, 976, 980, 982, 983, 985, 988, 1000, 1001, 1022, 1035, 1119, 1141, 1149, 1160, 1187, 1198, 1307, 1387, 1393, 1398, 1403, 1404, 1405, 1406, 1435, 1438, 1442, 1463, 1465, 1469, 1482, 1488, 1490, 1493, 1494, 1495, 1496, 1497, 1499, 1501, 1502, 1504, 1506, 1508, 1509, 1512, 1513, 1514, 1515, 1516, 1517, 1518, 1519, 1520, 1521, 1522, 1523, 1524, 1525, 1526, 1527, 1528, 1529, 1530, 1532, 1533, 1534, 1537, 1538, 1539, 1540, 1541, 1542, 1543, 1544, 1547, 1548, 1549, 1550, 1552, 1553, 1554, 1555, 1556, 1557, 1558, 1559, 1562, 1563, 1564, 1565, 1566, 1567, 1568, 1569, 1570, 1571, 1572, 1573, 1574, 1575, 1576, 1577, 1578, 1579, 1580, 1583, 1585, 1586, 1588, 1589, 1590, 1591, 1593, 1594, 1595, 1596, 1597, 1598, 1599, 1600, 1601, 1602, 1603, 1604, 1605, 1606, 1607, 1608, 1609, 1610, 1611, 1612, 1613, 1614, 1615, 1617, 1620, 1622, 1625, 1627, 1630, 1631, 1634, 1635, 1636, 1655, 1718, 1719, 1720, 1721, 1722, 1727, 1747, 1791, 1824, 1839, 1850, 1881, 1985, 2001, 2014, 2083, 2131, 2138, 2150, 2280, 2320, 2331, 2340, 2343, 2385, 2386, 2393, 2397, 2399, 2403, 2405, 2409, 2414, 2418, 2419, 2420, 2421, 2422, 2428, 2434, 2436, 2437, 2440; *see also* specific disciplines
Education, Higher, Aid Programs for Undergraduate and Graduate Students in Surveying and Geomatics: 2439
Education, Higher, Aid Programs for Undergraduate Students in All Disciplines of Surveying: 2441
Education, Higher, Construction and Facilities Projects: 103, 107, 178, 190, 237, 281, 1492; *see also* Construction and Facilities Projects
Education, Higher, Research, Project, and General Support: 1, 10, 18, 39, 49, 51, 52, 63, 76, 82, 83, 88, 97, 104, 113, 117, 130, 131, 145, 155, 167, 187, 190, 196, 207, 220, 231, 234, 237, 238, 260, 266, 281, 283, 289, 291, 292, 299, 304, 333, 429, 596, 601, 602, 615, 699, 733, 764, 771, 797, 842, 906, 921, 944, 948, 979, 984, 1011, 1012, 1039, 1052, 1061, 1072, 1073, 1097, 1169, 1180, 1198, 1260, 1283, 1393, 1403, 1406, 1410, 1421, 1424, 1432, 1444, 1449, 1469, 1470, 1473, 1474, 1475, 1477, 1478, 1479, 1480, 1481, 1487, 1491, 1524, 1525, 1536, 1638, 1659, 1684, 1727, 1728, 1757, 1814, 1890, 2053, 2096, 2330, 2366, 2410, 2417, 2418, 2426
Education, Independent Schools: 948, 1255, 1437, 1455; *see also* Education, Secondary
Education, Learning Process. *See* Learning Process and Memory
Education, Legal. *See* Law, Education
Education, Loan Funds: 685, 688, 885, 1252, 1395, 1495, 1520, 1533, 1630, 2427
Education, Medical. *See* Medical Education and Training; Nursing Education
Education, Methods: 136, 1411, 1428, 1444, 1458, 1478; *see also* specific subjects of instruction
Education, Musical. *See* Music, Education
Education, Physical. *See* Physical Education
Education, Policy-Making: 5, 1411, 1444; *see also* Policy Analysis
Education, Preschool. *See* Preschool Education and Care
Education, Private Institutions: 49, 88, 264, 277, 749, 1266, 1512, 1596, 2053; *see also* Education, Higher, Research, Project, and General Support; Education, Secondary
Education, Professional. *See* specific professions
Education, Programs for Undergraduate and Graduate Students in the Field of Geodetic Surveying: 2442
Education, Publication. *See* Publication Prizes, Education
Education Reform: 52, 1180, 1478, 1817
Education, Religious. *See* Religious Education

Health Sciences, Education: 1, 205, 1031, 1333, 1345, 1412, 1571, 1596, 2080, 2091, 2181, 2278; *see also* Medical Education and Training
Health Services. *See* Medical and Health Services
Healthy Eating: 162, 962, 1312, 1409
Hearing Defects. *See* Deafness and Hearing Impairments
Heart Disease. *See* Cardiology and Cardiovascular Diseases
Heating: 2430, 2431
Hebrew Studies. *See* Judaism
Helicopter. *See* Aeronautics; Aviation
Hematology: 2032, 2033, 2034, 2044, 2045, 2046, 2047, 2048, 2049, 2050, 2085, 2146, 2161, 2185, 2207, 2238, 2323
Hemophilia: 2085
Hepatology: 2051, 2194, 2196, 2199, 2205, 2206
Herpetology: 1641
High School Seniors, Scholarships and Financial Aid: 392, 954, 1011, 1012, 1263, 1502, 1512, 1514, 1517, 1519, 1549, 1573, 1574, 1575, 1580, 1583, 1606, 1608, 1672; *see also* Education, Higher, Aid Programs for Undergraduate and Graduate Students in All Disciplines; Education, Loan Funds
Higher Education. *See* Education, Higher, Research, Project, and General Support
Hispanics: 894, 905, 909, 920, 925, 972, 973, 974, 975, 1178, 1276, 1404, 1724, 1807, 1907, 1961, 1969, 2141, 2355, 2357; *see also* Spanish-Speaking Americans
Histology: 2154
Historic Preservation and Restoration: 57, 64, 80, 99, 161, 222, 239, 241, 277, 342, 376, 380, 384, 387, 403, 552, 570, 572, 573, 576, 674, 753, 996, 1055, 1111, 1132, 1174, 1182, 1206, 1216
Historic Site Administration: 161, 572, 573, 596, 597; *see also* Museum Administration
History: 23, 51, 164, 165, 317, 320, 323, 325, 336, 337, 365, 368, 371, 408, 428, 533, 538, 539, 548, 554, 555, 562, 563, 564, 571, 572, 583, 585, 589, 598, 628, 772, 777, 800, 805, 952, 984, 1475, 1633, 1685, 1819, 2392; *see also* Area Studies, also area studies by name; Classical Studies; Ethnology; Humanities; Labor, History; Law, History; Medicine, History; Medieval Studies; Military History; Political History; Religion, History; Renaissance Studies; Sciences, History; Social History; Social Sciences; Technology, History; Theatre, History; also specific disciplines which lend themselves to an historical approach
History, African: 362, 533
History, American: 313, 337, 339, 354, 357, 531, 532, 533, 534, 540, 547, 548, 549, 550, 551, 558, 559, 560, 561, 567, 568, 569, 570, 572, 574, 575, 585, 587, 588, 590, 591, 592, 596, 599, 600, 1671, 1693, 1816, 1818, 1819, 1820, 1837
History, American–Colonial: 312, 359, 537, 567, 578, 579, 580
History, American–Contemporary: 1826, 1838
History, Asian: 533
History, Canadian: 533, 589, 1669
History, English: 339, 360, 373, 439, 533
History, European: 360, 532, 533, 549, 579, 595, 769, 850, 851, 864, 995
History, Latin American: 533, 537, 540
History, Publication: 410, 532, 533, 536, 540, 547, 550, 554, 557, 565, 567, 568, 581, 645, 1392, 2331; *see also* Publication Prizes, History and Humanities
History, Research and Study: 316, 324, 330, 335, 339, 349, 352, 354, 357, 359, 360, 362, 534, 535, 537, 539, 546, 549, 552, 574, 575, 577, 578, 579, 580, 582, 583, 585, 591, 594, 596, 597, 599, 995, 1582
History, Research and Study Abroad: 318, 340, 366, 367, 395, 556, 589, 595, 804, 817, 819, 821, 823, 827, 828, 868
History, Teaching Methods: 597
Home Economics: 878, 2453, 2458; *see also* Food Technology; Housing; Nutrition; Technology
Homelessness: 176, 304, 1029, 1036, 1088, 1116, 1188, 1213, 1357; *see also* Disadvantaged; Poverty Programs; Urban Affairs
Horticulture: 1531, 1930, 1932, 1937, 1940, 1941, 1942, 1943, 1945, 1946, 1952, 1956, 1960, 1993, 1995; *see also* Arboriculture; Botany; Floriculture
Hospice: 1309
Hospital Administration. *See* Health Administration
Hospitality Management: 1427
Hospitals: 1, 83, 97, 201, 215, 240, 264, 279, 303, 1084, 1151, 1160, 1300, 1305, 2068, 2083; *see also* Health Care Facilities; Medical and Health Services; Medicine
Hospitals, Construction and Facilities Projects: 178, 275, 281, 1169; *see also* Construction and Facilities Projects
Hotel Management: 2399
Housing and Shelter: 72, 100, 108, 151, 210, 212, 227, 255, 576, 1022, 1082, 1088, 1093, 1129, 1175, 1181, 1188, 1189, 1211, 1214, 1223, 1239, 1247, 1271, 1273, 1282, 1334, 1339, 1358, 1439, 1763, 1951; *see also* Community Development; Homelessness; Poverty Programs; Social Welfare; Urban Affairs; Urban and Regional Planning

Human Relations: 131; *see also* Race Relations
Human Rights: 74, 116, 126, 152, 322, 799, 868, 902, 943, 963, 1093, 1346, 1380, 1763, 1817
Human Sciences: 2458
Human Values: 1411, 1636, 1666, 1697, 2374; *see also* Ethics
Humanities: 7, 12, 13, 21, 48, 67, 103, 117, 133, 146, 151, 170, 171, 198, 207, 231, 258, 267, 275, 284, 332, 333, 336, 338, 342, 344, 345, 364, 368, 371, 403, 551, 595, 772, 841, 964, 1064, 1090, 1154, 1159, 1232, 1251, 1259, 1365, 1370, 1375, 1394, 1464, 1507, 1669, 1682, 1699, 1702, 1775, 1792, 1823, 1830; *see also* Arts; Social Sciences; specific disciplines
Humanities, Curriculum Development 331, 468
Humanities, International Cooperative Programs: 786
Humanities, Publication, Exhibition, and Public Information Projects: 331, 338, 341, 1260, 1679; *see also* Publication Prizes, History and Humanities
Humanities, Related to Other Disciplines: 314, 333, 369, 1666
Humanities, Research and Study: 312, 314, 326, 327, 328, 329, 330, 333, 339, 343, 344, 346, 347, 348, 349, 350, 351, 352, 353, 354, 355, 356, 357, 358, 359, 360, 361, 362, 363, 369, 370, 537, 577, 765, 792, 917, 964, 1333, 1507, 1623, 1634, 1636, 1698, 1699, 1700, 1701, 1702, 1792, 1843
Humanities, Research and Study Abroad 322, 334, 340, 793, 804, 806, 809, 815, 817, 828, 836, 838, 839, 862, 1472, 1510
Humanities, Workshops and Seminars: 315, 333, 347, 356
Humor: 629
Hunger: 176, 177, 182, 1070, 1115, 1201, 1205, 1362, 1363, 1376; *see also* Disadvantaged; Poverty Programs, Social Welfare
Huntington's Disease: 2254, 2262; *see also* Neuromuscular Disorders
Hydrology: 1902, 1999, 2010, 2407

I

Iberia: 605; *see also* Europe; specific nations
Iceland: 818
Ichthyology: 1641, 1964
Idaho: 148, 219, 421, 924, 1378, 1597, 1598, 1986
Illinois: 1, 32, 66, 92, 107, 110, 122, 193, 244, 252, 271, 293, 299, 422, 754, 928, 1078, 1079, 1100, 1222, 1532, 1540, 1655, 1680, 2000
Illustration: 218, 469, 652, 656; *see also* Graphic Arts
Immigrant Resettlement: 194, 1088, 1162, 1257
Immigration: 262
Immigration Studies. *See* Ethnology
Immunology: 156, 912, 1853, 1974, 2120, 2128, 2130, 2131, 2144, 2224, 2225, 2238; *see also* Microbiology
In-Service Training Projects: 666, 790, 909, 1644, 1760, 1766, 1784, 1795, 2368, 2452; *see also* specific disciplines
India: 604, 812, 832, 863, 1476, 1485
Indiana: 27, 187, 423, 677, 1146, 1274, 1533, 1680, 1937
Industrial Arts and Education: 2401, 2402, 2434; *see also* Education, Technical; Education, Vocational
Industrial Design: 1584
Industrial Development: 2394
Industry and Industrial Research: 1882, 1887; *see also* Technology, Industrial
Infectious Diseases: 2327; *see also* Immunology; Microbiology
Information Sciences: 213, 666, 667, 668, 669, 680, 684, 802, 1289, 1728, 1750, 2070, 2392; *see also* Communications; Computer Sciences; Educational Media; Libraries and Librarianship
Inner-City: 29, 122, 280, 1046, 1188, 1239; *see also* Community Development; Urban Affairs
Instructional Materials: 801, 1458; *see also* Communications; Curriculum Development; Education; Educational Media
Instrumentation, Biomedical: 2092, 2095
Insurance: 1730, 1907; *see also* Business; Finance
Interdisciplinary Research and Study: 329, 778, 779, 1666, 1918; *see also* Humanities, Related to Other Disciplines; Medicine, Related to Other Disciplines; Sciences, Related to Other Disciplines
Interior Design: 376, 439
Internal Medicine. *See* Medicine, Internal
International Development: 781, 790, 868, 870, 1192, 1193, 1194, 1817; *see also* Developing Nations
International Education. *See* Education, Comparative
International Exchange. *See* Cultural Exchange Programs; Educational Exchange Programs; International Study and Research Programs
International Law. *See* Law, International
International Market. *See* Trade

Organization and Program Index

The Organization and Program Index alphabetically lists grant programs in upper-lower case and funding organizations in upper case. In addition, programs also are listed following the organizations which sponsor them.

HOBLITZELLE FOUNDATION: 144
Hobson (G. Vernon) Bequest: 2463
Hoffberger (LeRoy E.) School of Painting (MFA): 516
HOFFMAN (THE MAXIMILIAN E. & MARION O.) FOUNDATION, INC.: 2071
Hollinshead (Marilyn) Fellowship: 469
Holmes/D'Accone Dissertation Fellowship in Opera Studies: 699
Hologgitas (Joanne V.) Ph.D., Past Grand President, Scholarship (Undergraduate): 985
Holt (Caroline E.) Nursing Scholarship: 2283
HOME DEPOT FOUNDATION (THE)
    Community Impact Grants Program: 1188
    Disaster Relief Program: 1188
    National Partner Grants Program: 1188
    Team Depot: 1188
    Veteran Housing Grants Program: 1188
HONIG (VICTOR AND LORRAINE) FUND: 1356
HONOR SOCIETY OF PHI KAPPA PHI (THE)
    Phi Kappa Phi Fellowship (The): 1530
HONORS (Hematology Opportunities for the Next Generation of Research Scientists): 2034
HOOD (CHARLES H.) FOUNDATION, INC.
    Child Health Research Awards Program: 2324
Hooper Memorial Scholarship: 1735
Hoover (Herbert) Presidential Travel Grant Program: 1822
HOOVER PRESIDENTIAL FOUNDATION
    Hoover (Herbert) Presidential Travel Grant Program: 1822
Hopewell Agave Chapter #224 Scholarship (Undergraduate): 985
Hopkins (Douglas W.) Primary Care Residency Award: 2298
Hopscotch House Artist Retreat Center: 989
Horizons Foundation Scholarship Program: 1002
Hornback (Miriam L.) Scholarship: 1465
HOROWITZ FOUNDATION FOR SOCIAL POLICY (THE): 1684
HORTICULTURAL RESEARCH INSTITUTE, INC.
    Akehurst (Carville M.) Memorial Scholarship: 1531
    Bigelow (Timothy) and Palmer W. Bigelow, Jr. Scholarship: 1531
    Champion (Bryan A.) Memorial Scholarship: 1531
    HRI Competitive Research Grant Program: 1946
    Muggets Scholarship: 1531
    Spring Meadow Nursery Scholarship: 1531
    Usrey Family Scholarship: 1531
    Usrey (Susie and Bruce) Education Scholarship: 1531
Horton Fellowship: 519
Horton-Hallowell Fellowship: 1000
Horwitz (The Louisa Gross) Prize: 1965
Housing: 1088
HOUSING EDUCATION AND RESEARCH ASSOCIATION (HERA)
    Agan (Tessie) Award Competition: 1189
HOUSTON ENDOWMENT INC.: 145
HOWARD (THE GEORGE A. AND ELIZA GARDNER) FOUNDATION: 1475
Howard (Peggy) Fellowship in Economics: 1000
Hoy (Christopher J.)/ERT Scholarship: 1465
HRI Competitive Research Grant Program: 1946
HRL Initiative on Religion in International Affairs: 191
HSA Research Grant: 1945
Hubbard Scholarship: 675
HUDSON RIVER FOUNDATION (THE)
    Hudson River Fund: 1999
    Hudson River Improvement Fund: 1999
    New York City Environmental Fund: 1999
    New York-New Jersey Harbor & Estuary Program: 1999
Hudson River Fund: 1999
Hudson River Improvement Fund: 1999
HUDSON-WEBBER FOUNDATION: 1190
HUEBNER (THE S.S.) FOUNDATION FOR INSURANCE EDUCATION: 1730
HUGHES (HOWARD) MEDICAL INSTITUTE
    Medical Research Fellows Program: 2072
HUGHES (MABEL Y.) CHARITABLE TRUST: 146
HUGOTON FOUNDATION: 1316
Human-Centered Artificial Intelligence (HAI): 770
HUMAN FRONTIER SCIENCE PROGRAM ORGANIZATION
    Cross-Disciplinary Fellowships: 1966
    Long-Term Fellowships: 1966
    Program Grants: 1966
    Young Investigator Grants: 1966
HUMAN GROWTH FOUNDATION
    Small Grants for Research in Field of Short Stature: 2325
Human Nutrition Research: 2459

Human Rights Program: 152
Human Service: 1238
Humane Studies Fellowships: 1823
Humanitarian Project Support: 2133
HUMANITIES NEW YORK
    Action Grants: 338
    Community Conversations Program: 338
    Reading and Discussion Program: 338
    Vision Grants: 338
Humanities Program: 334
HUMBOLDT AREA FOUNDATION
    Community Grants: 1191
    Consulting Grant: 1191
    Field of Interest Grant Program: 1191
    Grassroots Grant Program: 1191
    Native Cultures Fund: 1191
    Rapid Response Grants: 1191
    School Enrichment Grant Program: 1191
    Summer Youth Program: 1191
Humboldt Research Award Programme: 1498
Humboldt Research Fellowship for Experienced Researchers: 808
Humboldt Research Fellowship for Postdoctoral Researchers: 1464
Hunt (The Joan K.) and Rachel M. Hunt Summer Scholarship in Field Botany: 1940
HUNTER (A.V.) TRUST, INC.
    Direct Operating Grants: 1357
    Funds for One: 1357
Hunter (Amy Louise) Fellowship: 598
Huntington (Curtis E.) Memorial Scholarship: 1909
HUNTINGTON (HENRY E.) LIBRARY AND ART GALLERY
    Research Awards at the Huntington Library and Art Gallery: 339
HUNTINGTON'S DISEASE SOCIETY OF AMERICA, INC.
    HD Human Biology Project: 2254
    HDSA Berman-Topper Family Huntington's Disease Career Development Fellowship: 2254
    King (Donald) Summer Research Fellowship: 2254
HURI Research Fellowships in Ukrainian Studies (The): 367
Hursky Fellowship: 1602
HUSTON (THE STEWART) CHARITABLE TRUST: 753
HUTCHINSON COMMUNITY FOUNDATION: 420
HYAMS FOUNDATION, INC. (THE): 1358
HYDE AND WATSON FOUNDATION (THE): 147

I

I Tatti Fellowship: 871
I Tatti/Museo Nacional del Prado Joint Fellowship: 874
IADR Colgate Research in Prevention Travel Awards: 2142
IAICDV Annual Scholarship: 1414
IAPA Scholarship Fund: 1764
IARS Mentored Research Awards: 2073
IASA Memorial Fellowship: 557
IBM Herman Goldstine Memorial Postdoctoral Fellowship for Research in Mathematical and Computer Sciences: 1912
IBM THOMAS J. WATSON RESEARCH CENTER
    IBM Herman Goldstine Memorial Postdoctoral Fellowship for Research in Mathematical and Computer Sciences: 1912
ICS Scholarship: 2074
IDA Documentary Awards: 424
IDA/David L. Wolper Student Documentary Achievement Award: 424
IDAHO COMMISSION ON THE ARTS
    Arts Education Projects: 421
    Directory of Teaching Artists: 421
    Entry Track: 421
    Fellowships: 421
    Public Programs in the Arts: 421
    Quick Funds: 421
    Traditional Arts Apprenticeship Program: 421
    Writer-in-Residence Program: 421
IDAHO COMMUNITY FOUNDATION
    Bistline (The F.M., Anne G., and Beverly B.) Foundation Fund: 148
    Bonner County Fund for Arts Enhancement: 148
    Bonner County Human Rights Task Force Fund: 148
    CenturyLink Middle School Philanthropy Program: 148
    Garnier (Junior) and Bud Ashford Military Veterans Fund: 148
    Idaho Future Fund: 148
    Lassahn-Worrell Fund for Community Support Services: 148
    Ifft Foundation Fund: 148
    North Idaho Action Fund: 148

ROCKEFELLER FAMILY FUND
  Economic Justice for Women: 257
  Environment: 257
  Institutional Accountability and Individual Liberty: 257
ROCKWELL FUND, INC.
  Capacity Building Grants: 258
  Operating Funds: 258
  Program/Project Support: 258
Rodgers (Earlene S.) Student Teaching Stipend for Minorities: 1533
Rodgers (The Richard) Awards: 694
Rodriguez (Dr. Esperanza) Scholarship: 2141
Roe (John Orlando) Award: 2058
Rogers (Frank Bradway) Information Advancement Award: 681
Rogerson (Clark T.) Research Award: 1972
Rolex Awards for Enterprise Program: 259
ROLEX SA
  Rolex Awards for Enterprise Program: 259
Romanell-Phi Beta Kappa Professorship in Philosophy (The): 1581
Romani (The George T. and Margaret W.) Fellowship: 325
Romanowski (The Miroslaw) Medal: 1669
Rome Prize Fellowship in Landscape Architecture (The): 1983
Rome Prize Fellowships: 311
RONALD MCDONALD HOUSE CHARITIES
  Africa and South Asia: Child and Maternal Health: 1040
  U.S. Grants: Children's Oral Health Care: 1040
ROOSEVELT (FRANKLIN D.) LIBRARY AND MUSEUM
  Roosevelt Institute Research Grants: 587
Roosevelt Institute Research Grants: 587
Roosevelt (Theodore) Memorial Grants: 1641
Root (Betty Jeanne) Fellowship: 2458
ROSE COMMUNITY FOUNDATION: 1241
Rose Hills Ph.D. Fellowship: 1628
Rose Hills Summer Research Fellowships: 1629
Rosemore (Fredric) Low Vision Educational Grants: 2300
Rosenberg (The Dorothy) Prize: 533
ROSENBERG (HENRY AND RUTH BLAUSTEIN) FOUNDATION:
  1242
Rosenblith (Walter A.) New Investigator Award: 1310
Rosenbloom (Alfred A.), Jr. Low Vision Residency Award: 2298
Rosewood Family Scholarship Program: 941
ROSS FOUNDATION: 1243
Rossiter (Margaret W.) History of Women in Science Prize: 554
ROSWELL ARTIST-IN-RESIDENCE PROGRAM: 522
Roswell (Virginia) Dissertation Award: 2363
ROTARY CLUB OF BRYN MAWR (THE)
  Cabell (Harry H.) Scholarship Program: 1590
ROTARY FOUNDATION OF ROTARY INTERNATIONAL (THE)
  Rotary Peace Fellowships: 860
Rotary Peace Fellowships: 860
Rotch Travelling Scholarship: 385
ROTCH TRAVELLING SCHOLARSHIP IN ARCHITECTURE
  Rotch Travelling Scholarship: 385
Roth (Lois) Award for a Translation of a Literary Work: 608
Roth (Richard J.) Journalism Fellowship: 1830
Rothermel (Marjorie Roy) Scholarship: 2427
Roura (Victor Grifols) Scholarship: 2096
Rowe (The Leo S.) Pan American Fund: 885
ROYAL INSTITUTE OF BRITISH ARCHITECTS
  RIBA Research Fund: 386
ROYAL SOCIETY OF CANADA (THE)
  Allaire (Yvan) Medal: 1669
  Bancroft Award (The): 1669
  Chauveau (The Pierre) Medal: 1669
  Dawson (The Sir John William) Medal: 1669
  Flavelle Medal (The): 1669
  Franklin (Ursula) Award in Gender Studies: 1669
  Hannah (The Jason A.) Medal: 1669
  Innis-Gérin Medal (The): 1669
  McLaughlin Medal (The): 1669
  Miller (Willet G.) Medal: 1669
  Pierce (The Lorne) Medal: 1669
  Romanowski (The Miroslaw) Medal: 1669
  Rutherford Memorial Medals (The): 1669
  Synge (The John L.) Award: 1669
  Tory (The Henry Marshall) Medal: 1669
  Tyrrell (The J.B.) Historical Medal: 1669
ROYAL SOCIETY OF EDINBURGH (THE)
  Lessells (John Moyes) Travel Scholarships: 2446
ROYAL TOWN PLANNING INSTITUTE (THE)
  Pepler (George) International Award: 1696

Rozkuszka (W. David) Scholarship: 1465
RRF FOUNDATION FOR AGING
  Organizational Capacity Building: 928
  Responsive Grants: 928
RSNA Research Scholar Grant: 2117
RSNA/AUR/APDR/SCARD Radiology Education Research Development
  Grant: 2116
RTCA
  Jackson (The William E.) Award: 2410
Ruggles (The William B.) Journalist Scholarship: 1776
Runaway and Homeless Youth (RHY) Programs: 1048
RUNNING STRONG FOR AMERICAN INDIAN YOUTH: 965
RUNYON (DAMON) CANCER RESEARCH FOUNDATION
  Runyon (Damon) Clinical Investigator Award: 2236
  Runyon (Damon) Dale F. Frey Award for Breakthrough Scientists: 2236
  Runyon (Damon) Fellowship Award: 2236
  Runyon (Damon) Physician-Scientist Training Award: 2236
  Runyon (Damon)-Rachleff Innovation Award: 2236
  Runyon (Damon)-Sohn Pediatric Cancer Fellowship Award: 2236
Runyon (Damon) Clinical Investigator Award: 2236
Runyon (Damon) Dale F. Frey Award for Breakthrough Scientists: 2236
Runyon (Damon) Fellowship Award: 2236
Runyon (Damon) Physician-Scientist Training Award: 2236
Runyon (Damon)-Rachleff Innovation Award: 2236
Runyon (Damon)-Sohn Pediatric Cancer Fellowship Award: 2236
Rural Arts Access Grants: 486
Rural Housing Grants (Section 504): 1951
RURAL HOUSING SERVICE
  Rural Housing Grants (Section 504): 1951
RUSSELL FAMILY FOUNDATION (THE)
  Environmental Education Fund: 2009
  Jane's Fellowship Program: 1244
RUSSELL (JOSEPHINE G.) TRUST: 1334
Russell (Kenneth W.) Fellowship: 806
Rutherford Memorial Medals (The): 1669

S

Sacred Sites Program: 576
SAE-CES Pre-Dissertation Research Fellowships: 772
Safe and Healthy Communities: 2077
Safe Arborist Techniques Fund Grant: 1952
Safety Professional of the Year Award: 2429
SAGE (RUSSELL) FOUNDATION: 1697
SAGES Program (The): 1714
SAGINAW COMMUNITY FOUNDATION: 1245
SAH Prize for Historical Fiction: 590
Sahney (Vinod and Gail) Scholarship: 2434
SAIGH FOUNDATION (THE): 1041
SAILORS' SNUG HARBOR OF BOSTON: 1374
ST. ANDREW'S SOCIETY OF THE STATE OF NEW YORK
  Scholarship Program for Graduate Study in Scotland: 861
ST. CROIX VALLEY FOUNDATION
  Health and Wellness Grant: 1246
  Music Education Grant: 1246
  Valley Arts Initiative Grant: 1246
SAINT-GOBAIN CORPORATION FOUNDATION
  Direct Grants Program: 1247
St. Louis Chapter No. 17 Scholarship: 2403
SALISBURY-ROWAN COMMUNITY FOUNDATION: 260
Salivary Biology & Immunology: 2144
SALON NATIONAL LA BOUTIQUE
  Eight and Forty Lung and Respiratory Disease Nursing Scholarship
    Fund: 2286
Saloutos (Theodore) Book Award: 531
SAMLA Studies Award: 611
Sams (Dr. Lauranne) Scholarship: 2281
SAMUELS (THE FAN FOX AND LESLIE R.) FOUNDATION, INC.
  Healthy Aging Program: 261
  Performing Arts: 261
Samuelson (Orion) Scholarship: 1771
SAN ANGELO AREA FOUNDATION: 1248
San Antonio Area African-American Community Fund: 1249
SAN ANTONIO AREA FOUNDATION
  Annual Responsive Grants: 1249
  San Antonio Area African-American Community Fund: 1249
  Special and Urgent Needs: 1249
  Women and Girls Development Fund: 1249
SAN DIEGO ART INSTITUTE
  Mahoney (Matthew J.) Artist-in-Residence Program: 523

Seattle ASWA Chapter Scholarship: 1727
SEATTLE FOUNDATION
    Center for Community Partnerships: 267
SEAVER INSTITUTE (THE): 268
SEAY (GEORGE J. AND EFFIE L.) MEMORIAL TRUST: 1375
Seed Grants: 2245
SEG Scholarship Program: 1905
SELF FAMILY FOUNDATION (THE): 1255
Seminar and Conference Support: 811
Seminars and Institutes Program: 347
Senate Fellowship Program: 1814
Senior Adult Scholarship Program: 1493
Senior Companion Program: 1354
Senior Fellowship: 811
Senior Fellowships: 383
Senior Living Initiative: 1129
Senior Research Award: 2208
Senior Research Fellowship Program: 1953
Sessa (Frank B.) Scholarship for Continuing Professional Education of
    Beta Phi Mu Members: 669
SEYBERT FOUNDATION (THE): 1043
SFU Graduate Fellowships: 1743
Shackford (M.A. Cartland) Medical Fellowship: 1001
Shaffer Fund for Innovative Glaucoma Research: 2311
Shankar-Spiegel Award for the Best Dissertation Proposal in
    Direct/Interactive Marketing: 1736
SHARE OUR STRENGTH
    No Kid Hungry: 1376
Shared Instrumentation Grant Program: 2092
Shark Tank Awards: 2252
SHASTA REGIONAL COMMUNITY FOUNDATION
    McConnell Fund (The): 1256
    Redding Rancheria Community Fund: 1256
SHASTRI INDO-CANADIAN INSTITUTE (SICI): 863
Shaughnessy (Mina P.) Prize: 607
Shaw (Harriet A.) Fellowship: 1000
Shaw (The Peter) Memorial Award: 1480
Shea (The John Gilmary) Prize: 746
Sheeler (Harva L.) Excavation Fellowships: 828
Sheltering Arms Fund: 1107
Shelton (Perc H.) and Gladys A. Pospisil Foundation Advised Fund: 148
Short-term Fellowship: 370
Short-Term Research Fellowship: 563
Short-Term Research Fellowships: 326
SHRIVER (EUNICE KENNEDY) NATIONAL INSTITUTE OF CHILD
    HEALTH AND HUMAN DEVELOPMENT
    Child Development and Behavior Branch (CDBB): 1335
    Contraception Research Branch (CRB): 1335
    Developmental Biology and Structural Variation Branch (DBSVB):
        1335
    Fertility and Infertility (FI) Branch: 1335
    Gynecologic Health and Disease Branch (GHDB): 1335
    Intellectual and Developmental Disabilities Branch (IDDB): 1335
    Maternal and Pediatric Infectious Disease Branch (MPIDB): 1335
    Obstetric and Pediatric Pharmacology and Therapeutics Branch
        (OPPTB): 1335
    Pediatric Growth and Nutrition Branch (PGNB): 1335
    Pediatric Trauma and Critical Illness Branch (PTCIB): 1335
    Population Dynamics Branch (PDB): 1335
    Pregnancy and Perinatology Branch (PPB): 1335
SHUBERT FOUNDATION, INC. (THE): 500
Shuster (Ben) Memorial Award: 2058
Shwachman (Harry) Clinical Investigator Award: 2209
Sibley (Mary Isabel) Fellowship: 995
SICKKIDS FOUNDATION
    Community Conference Grants Program: 1336
    New Investigator Research Grants: 1336
Sidney Awards: 1763
Siegel (Norman) Research Scholar Grant: 2148
Sierleja (E.J.) Memorial Fellowship: 2434
SIERRA HEALTH FOUNDATION
    Conference and Education Center: 1377
    Health Leadership Program: 1377
    Healthy Sacramento Coalition: 1377
    Nonprofit Event Sponsorships: 1377
    Responsive Grants Program: 1377
Sigal (Irving S.) Postdoctoral Fellowship: 1878
SIGMA ALPHA IOTA PHILANTHROPIES, INC.
    Inter-American Music Awards: 737

SIGMA THETA TAU INTERNATIONAL
    Berkel Crisp (Rosemary) Research Award: 2287
    Bloch (Doris) Research Award: 2287
    Henderson (Virginia) Clinical Research Grant: 2287
    Small Grants: 2287
    Stout (Joan K.), R.N., Research Grant: 2287
SIGMA XI: THE SCIENTIFIC RESEARCH HONOR SOCIETY
    Grants in Aid of Research: 1670
SILICON VALLEY COMMUNITY FOUNDATION: 1257
SILICON VALLEY CREATES
    Artist Laureates: 461
    Local Arts Grants: 461
SIMMONS FAMILY FOUNDATION: 269
Simmons (The John) Short Fiction Award: 655
SIMON FRASER UNIVERSITY
    SFU Graduate Fellowships: 1743
Simpson (Carole) Scholarship: 1786
SIMS (J. MARION) FOUNDATION, INC.: 270
Simulation Fellowship Program: 1852
SIRAGUSA FAMILY FOUNDATION (THE): 271
Sister Cities Grant: 409
SISTERS OF ST. JOSEPH HEALTHCARE FOUNDATION: 1337
SKELLY (GERTRUDE E.) CHARITABLE FOUNDATION: 1484
Skiera (Bob) Memorial Fund Building Bridges Initiative Grant: 1952
SKILLBUILDERS FUND: 997
SKILLMAN FOUNDATION (THE): 272
SKIN CANCER FOUNDATION (THE)
    Big See (The): 2237
    Destination: Healthy Skin: 2237
    Heads Up: 2237
    Research Grants Program: 2237
    Sun Smart U: 2237
SKOWHEGAN SCHOOL OF PAINTING AND SCULPTURE: 525
SLADEN (THE PERCY) MEMORIAL FUND
    Sladen (Percy) Memorial Fund Grants: 1927
Sladen (Percy) Memorial Fund Grants: 1927
Slim (H. Colin) Award: 698
SLOAN (ALFRED P.) FOUNDATION: 273
    Sloan Research Fellowships: 1857
Sloan Research Fellowships: 1857
Small Business Innovation Research Awards: 2316
Small Business Innovation Research Grants: 2282
Small Business Innovation Research Program: 1329
Small Business Innovation/Small Business Technology Transfer
    (SBIR/STTR): 2144
Small Grant Support: 453
Small Grant Support for Schools: 453
Small Grants: 2287
Small Grants for Research in Field of Short Stature: 2325
Small Impact Building Grants: 1252
Small Operating Grants: 454
Small Research Grant Program: 1813
Small Research Grant Program (Parent R03): 2094
Small Research Grants: 1440
Small-Scale Events Advancing SPSSI (SEAS) Grants: 1708
SmART Initiative: 450
SME-EF (SOCIETY OF MANUFACTURING ENGINEERS
    EDUCATION FOUNDATION)
    Gunter (Connie and Robert T.) Scholarship: 2403
    Helton (Clinton J.) Manufacturing Scholarship: 2403
    Kalamazoo Chapter No. 116-Roscoe Douglas Scholarship: 2403
    Kaufman (Lucille B.) Women's Scholarship: 2403
    Kay (E. Wayne) Scholarships: 2403
    St. Louis Chapter No. 17 Scholarship: 2403
    Walker (Myrtle and Earl) Scholarship: 2403
    Weisel (William E.) Scholarship: 2403
SMITH (A.O.) FOUNDATION: 274
Smith (Alexander H. and Helen V.) Research Fund: 1972
Smith (Alice E.) Fellowship: 598
Smith (Bosworth) Trust Fund: 2463
Smith (Dr. James McCune) Medical Student Award: 2096
SMITH (THE ETHEL SERGEANT CLARK) MEMORIAL FUND: 275
SMITH FAMILY AWARDS PROGRAM FOR EXCELLENCE IN
    BIOMEDICAL RESEARCH: 2121
SMITH (HORACE) FUND: 1591
Smith (J. Waldo) Hydraulic Fellowship: 2426
Smith (Nila Banton) Teacher as Researcher Grant: 1415
Smith (W. Eugene) Grant in Humanistic Photography: 526
SMITH (W. EUGENE) MEMORIAL FUND
    Smith (W. Eugene) Grant in Humanistic Photography: 526

UDALL (THE MORRIS K.) AND STEWART L. UDALL
  FOUNDATION
    Congressional Internships: 968
    Udall Scholarship: 1610
Udall Scholarship: 1610
UICC Technical Fellowhips (UICC-TF): 2239
UKRAINIAN RESEARCH INSTITUTE AT HARVARD UNIVERSITY
    HURI Research Fellowships in Ukrainian Studies (The): 367
    Jacyk (Petro) Distinguished Fellowship in Ukrainian Studies: 366
    Mihaychuk (Jaroslaw and Nadia) Postdoctoral Research Fellowships in
      Ukrainian Studies (The): 367
Ülgür (Ülkü), M.D., International Scholar Award: 2350
Undergraduate Achievement Scholarship: 1527
Undergraduate Awards: 2465
Undergraduate Essay Award: 611
Undergraduate International Studies and Foreign Language Program: 1487
Undergraduate Research Award: 1972, 2458
Undergraduate Research Fellowship: 1961
Undergraduate Research Initiative: 811
Undergraduate Research Scholarship Program: 1659
Undergraduate Scholarship Program: 2415
Undergraduate Scholarships: 2398, 2447
Undergraduate Session Assistants Program: 1831
Undergraduate Student Awards: 2456
Undergraduate Student Poster Contest: 393
Undergraduate Transfer Scholarship: 1516
Understanding Dynamic and Multi-Scale Systems: 199
Understanding Human Cognition: 199
UNICO NATIONAL, INC.
    Alessio (Maria and Paolo) Southern Italy Scholarship: 1611
    Basilone (Sargeant John) Memorial Graduate Scholarship: 1611
    Cottone Postgraduate Scholarship (Medical Only): 1611
    Davini (William C.) Scholarship: 1611
    DiMattio Celli Undergraduate Study Abroad Program: 1611
    Gentile (Major Don S.) Scholarship: 1611
    Grasso (Ella) Literary Scholarship: 1611
    Inserra Scholarships: 1611
    Marconi (Guglielmo) Engineering Scholarship: 1611
    Mazza (Theodore) Scholarship: 1611
    Miele (Alphonse A.) Scholarship: 1611
    Tarte (Robert J.) Scholarship for Italian Studies: 1611
    Torraco (Bernard and Carolyn) Nursing Scholarships: 1611
    Torraco (Louise) Memorial Scholarship for Science: 1611
    Torraco (Ralph J.) Fine Arts Scholarship: 1611
    Torraco (Ralph J.) Scholarship: 1611
    Torraco (Ralph J.) Scholarship for Special Education: 1611
    Torraco (Ralph J.) Scholarship for Therapy Sciences: 1611
UNION FOR INTERNATIONAL CANCER CONTROL (UICC)
    Bourses pour L'Afrique Francophone (BAF): 2239
    UICC Technical Fellowhips (UICC-TF): 2239
    Yamagiwa-Yoshida Memorial International Study Grants (YY): 2239
UNION PACIFIC FOUNDATION: 298
UNITARIAN UNIVERSALIST ASSOCIATION OF CONGREGATIONS
    Stanfield and D'Orlando Art Scholarships: 467
UNITED ARTS COUNCIL OF RALEIGH AND WAKE COUNTY, INC.
    Artists-in-Schools Grants Program: 468
    Professional Development Grants for Artists: 468
    Program Support Grants: 468
United Health Foundation/NMF Diverse Medical Scholars Program: 2096
UNITED HOSPITAL FUND OF NEW YORK
    Health Care Improvement Grant Program: 1342
UNITED JEWISH APPEAL-FEDERATION OF JEWISH
  PHILANTHROPIES OF NEW YORK: 763
UNITED METHODIST COMMUNICATIONS
    Perryman (The Leonard M.) Communications Scholarship for Ethnic
      Minority Students: 932
    Stoody-West Fellowship (The): 1789
UNITED METHODIST HEALTH MINISTRY FUND
    Access to Health Care-System Change and Advocacy: 1381
    Early Childhood Development: 1381
    Healthy Congregations Program: 1381
UNITED NEGRO COLLEGE FUND (UNCF): 948
United Parcel Service Scholarship for Female Students: 2434
United Parcel Service Scholarship for Minority Students: 2434
UNITED SOUTH AND EASTERN TRIBES, INC.: 969
UNITED STATES HOLOCAUST MEMORIAL MUSEUM - JACK,
  JOSEPH AND MORTON MANDEL CENTER FOR ADVANCED
  HOLOCAUST STUDIES
    International Academic Programs: 595

UNITED STATES-JAPAN FOUNDATION
    Grants: 801
    Heinz (Elgin) Outstanding Teacher Award: 801
    U.S.-Japan Leadership Program: 801
United Way Match Program: 50
United Way Program: 34
UNITY FOUNDATION OF LAPORTE COUNTY (THE)
    Community Fund: 1274
Universal Avionics Systems Corporation Scholarship: 2405
University Coal Research Program: 2450
University Distinguished Fellowships: 916
University Enrichment Fellowships: 916
UNIVERSITY FILM AND VIDEO ASSOCIATION
    Fielding (Carole) Student Grants: 1790
UNIVERSITY OF ARIZONA SCHOOL OF INFORMATION: 691
UNIVERSITY OF BRISTOL
    Postgraduate Research Scholarships: 866
UNIVERSITY OF BRITISH COLUMBIA (THE)
    Affiliated Fellowships: 1612
    Four Year Doctoral Fellowships: 1613
    Graduate Support Initiative: 1614
UNIVERSITY OF CALGARY (THE)
    Bahlsen (Bettina) Memorial Graduate Scholarship: 1618
    Cairns (The A.T.J.) Memorial Scholarship: 1621
    Canadian Natural Resources Limited Graduate Scholarship: 1624
    Cogeco Inc. Graduate Scholarship: 1791
    Craigie (Peter C.) Memorial Scholarship: 1623
    Davies (William H.) Medical Research Scholarships: 1616
    Dingman (The Archibald Waynne) Memorial Graduate Scholarship:
      1615
    Faculty of Law Graduate Scholarship: 1625
    Graduate Faculty Council Scholarship: 1622
    Jacques (Harry and Laura) Graduate Scholarship: 1906
    Killam (Izaak Walton) Doctoral Scholarships: 1617
    Labatt (John) Limited Scholarship: 1619
    McDermid (The Honourable N.D.) Graduate Scholarship in Law: 1810
    ScotiaMcLeod Scholarship: 1619
    University of Calgary Silver Anniversary Graduate Fellowships (The):
      1620
    Willson (Robert A.) Doctoral Management Scholarship: 1488
University of Calgary Silver Anniversary Graduate Fellowships (The):
  1620
UNIVERSITY OF CALIFORNIA
    University of California President's Postdoctoral Fellowship Program:
      933
University of California President's Postdoctoral Fellowship Program: 933
UNIVERSITY OF CALIFORNIA, LOS ANGELES
    Ethnic Studies Fellowships: 934
    Institute of American Cultures Grant: 970
UNIVERSITY OF DELAWARE-HAGLEY GRADUATE PROGRAM
  (THE): 596
UNIVERSITY OF DELAWARE, DEPARTMENT OF HISTORY
    Stewart (E. Lyman) Fellowship: 597
UNIVERSITY OF ILLINOIS AT URBANA-CHAMPAIGN
    Kinley (Kate Neal) Memorial Fellowship: 529
UNIVERSITY OF IOWA (THE)
    Iowa Short Fiction Award (The): 655
    Simmons (The John) Short Fiction Award: 655
UNIVERSITY OF KANSAS CHILD LANGUAGE DOCTORAL
  PROGRAM
    Child Language Doctoral Program: 1626
UNIVERSITY OF MANCHESTER (THE)
    British Marshall Scholarships: 867
    Fulbright - University of Manchester Award: 867
    North American Foundation Awards: 867
    President's Doctoral Scholar Award: 867
UNIVERSITY OF MANITOBA
    University of Manitoba Graduate Fellowships: 1448
University of Manitoba Graduate Fellowships: 1448
UNIVERSITY OF MICHIGAN
    Knight-Wallace Fellowships for Journalists: 1792
UNIVERSITY OF MINNESOTA
    Hollinshead (Marilyn) Fellowship: 469
    Keats (The Ezra Jack)/Kerlan Memorial Fellowship: 656
UNIVERSITY OF NEBRASKA AT OMAHA
    UNO Graduate Assistantships: 1745
UNIVERSITY OF OSLO INTERNATIONAL SUMMER SCHOOL: 868
UNIVERSITY OF PITTSBURGH
    Darbaker (Leasure K.) Prize in Botany: 2017
    McKinley Research Fund: 2017
    Pape Research Fund: 2017

W

Geographical Index

Center for Hellenic Studies: 324
Center for Science in the Public Interest: 2455
Children's Bureau: 1016
Congressional Black Caucus Foundation, Inc.: 938, 939, 940
Congressional Hispanic Caucus Institute: 972, 973
Cooperative Development Foundation: 1142
Corporation for National and Community Service: 1143, 1354
Council of American Overseas Research Centers (CAORC): 836
Daughters of Penelope Foundation, Inc.: 907, 985
Department of Veterans Affairs: 2367
District of Columbia Commission on the Arts and Humanities: 409
Dumbarton Oaks: 335
Eisenhower Institute at Gettysburg College (The): 780
Embassy of France in the U.S., SCAC: 841
Environmental Law Institute: 1800
Eye Bank Association of America: 2307
Federal Highway Administration: 2395
Food and Drug Law Institute (FDLI): 1801
Foundation for Advancement in Conservation (FAIC) (The): 674
Freer Gallery of Art and Arthur M. Sackler Gallery: 414
Fund for American Studies (The): 1821
Fund for Investigative Journalism: 1761
George Washington University: 2433
Georgetown University: 1885
German Historical Institute: 548
Gwathmey Memorial Trust (The): 337
Hispanic Bar Association of D.C. Foundation (The): 1806
Hispanic National Bar Foundation (The): 1807
Institute of Current World Affairs: 782
Institute of International Education: 783
Institute of International Education/Council for International Exchange of
    Scholars: 1476
Institute of Museum and Library Services: 678, 679
International Research & Exchanges Board (IREX): 845
Jack and Jill of America Foundation (The): 942
Japan-U.S. Friendship Commission: 786
Japanese American Citizens League (JACL) (The): 1538, 1825, 787
Jeffress (Thomas F. and Kate Miller) Memorial Trust: 1924
Kennedy (Robert F.) Human Rights: 627
Landscape Architecture Foundation: 2001
Lupus Foundation of America, Inc.: 2079
Marshall (Thurgood) College Fund (TMCF): 1549
McNamara (The Margaret) Education Grants (MMEG): 203
Meyer (Eugene and Agnes E.) Foundation: 1211
Morgan (Marietta McNeill) and Samuel Tate Morgan, Jr. Trust: 1365
Morris (William) Society in the U.S.: 439
National Academies of Sciences, Engineering, and Medicine (The): 1853,
    917
National Academy of Education (The): 1425
National Association for Equal Opportunity in Higher Education
    (NAFEO): 944
National Association of Black Social Workers (The): 945
National Association of Health Services Executives (NAHSE): 2343
National Association of Hispanic Journalists: 918
National Center for Learning Disabilities: 1426
National Council for Eurasian and East European Research (The): 788
National Endowment for Democracy: 1827
National Endowment for the Arts: 440
National Endowment for the Humanities: 1775, 344, 345, 346, 347, 348
National Fish and Wildlife Foundation (NFWF): 2002
National Geographic Society: 1898
National Historical Publications and Records Commission: 568
National Institute of Justice, U.S. Department of Justice: 1289
National Italian American Foundation (The): 1556
National Press Foundation: 1777
National Restaurant Association Educational Foundation (The): 1740,
    2461
National Security Education Program: 857, 858
National Society Daughters of the American Revolution: 1558, 1559,
    1693, 2098, 2283, 2344, 384, 569
National Trust for Historic Preservation: 570
NEA Foundation (The): 1432, 1433
NewsGuild-CWA (TNG-CWA) (The): 1778, 1779
NICSA: 1435
Organization of American States: 790, 885
Paralyzed Veterans of America Research and Education Foundations: 2345
Patterson (The Alicia) Foundation: 1783
PEN/Faulkner Foundation: 647
Pharmaceutical Research and Manufacturers of America Foundation, Inc.:
    2106, 2107, 2108, 2333

Phi Beta Kappa Society (The): 1581, 1694, 649, 859, 995
President's Commission on White House Fellowships: 1833
Public Welfare Foundation, Inc.: 248
Radio Television Digital News Association Foundation: 1786
Replogle (Luther I.) Foundation: 1239
Reporters Committee for Freedom of the Press: 1787
Resources for the Future: 2008
RTCA: 2410
Rural Housing Service: 1951
Schork (Kurt) Memorial Fund: 1788
Scoville (Herbert, Jr.) Peace Fellowship: 791
Share Our Strength: 1376
Smithsonian Institution: 1671
Smithsonian National Air and Space Museum: 2411, 2412
Society for Science and the Public: 1672
Society for the Psychological Study of Social Issues (SPSSI) (The): 1703,
    1704, 1705, 1706, 1707, 1708, 1709, 1710, 1711, 1712, 1713, 1714,
    1715, 1716, 1836
Sons of Italy Foundation: 930
Subcommittee on Catholic Home Missions: 762
Swann Foundation for Caricature and Cartoon: 365
Taste and Smell Clinic: 2124
Truman (The Harry S.) Scholarship Foundation: 1839
U.S. Army Center of Military History: 593
U.S. Department of Agriculture: 2015
U.S. Department of Education: 1444, 1445, 1446, 1486, 1487, 1606, 1607,
    1608, 1609, 1744, 612, 613, 614, 615, 797, 865, 966
U.S. Department of Health and Human Services: 1047, 1048, 1049, 1272,
    2348, 967
U.S. Department of Health and Human Services/Administration for
    Children and Families/Office of Family Assistance: 1794
U.S. Department of Housing and Urban Development: 1273
U.S. Department of Justice: 1290, 1291, 1292
U.S. Department of Labor: 1795
U.S. Department of State, Fulbright Teacher Exchanges: 1447
U.S. Environmental Protection Agency: 2016
U.S. Institute of Peace: 798, 799, 800
United Negro College Fund (UNCF): 948
United States Holocaust Memorial Museum - Jack, Joseph and Morton
    Mandel Center for Advanced Holocaust Studies: 595
USDA - Rural Utilities Service: 1955
Wilson (Woodrow) International Center for Scholars: 369
Women's Congressional Policy Institute (WCPI): 1004
Word Works, Inc. (The): 659, 660
World Learning Inc.: 802
Youth For Understanding USA: 876

Florida

A-T Children's Project: 2021
Able Trust (The): 891
American Academy of Optometry Foundation: 2295, 2296, 2297, 2298,
    2299, 2300, 2301
American Association of Women Dentists: 2138
American Orchid Society: 1960
American Otological Society Research Foundation: 2302
AWS Foundation, Inc.: 2388, 2389, 2390, 2391
Broward Education Foundation: 1393
Bush (Edyth) Charitable Foundation, Inc.: 46
Chatlos Foundation, Inc. (The): 749
Chopin Foundation of the U.S.: 705
Cintas Foundation: 401
Community Foundation for Northeast Florida (The): 1112
Community Foundation for Palm Beach and Martin Counties: 1115
Community Foundation of Collier County: 1118
Davis (The Arthur Vining) Foundations: 88
Dunspaugh Dalton Foundation: 98
duPont (Jessie Ball) Fund: 99
Florida Department of Education: 1522, 1523, 941, 974
Florida Department of State, Division of Cultural Affairs: 411
Florida Education Fund: 1404
Foundation for Education and Research in Biofeedback and Related
    Sciences (FERB): 2369
Foundation for Science and Disability: 908
Gulf Coast Community Foundation: 1183
Health Foundation of South Florida: 1312
Inter American Press Association (IAPA): 1764
International Food Service Executives Association, Inc. (IFSEA): 2400
International Women's Fishing Association Scholarship Trust: 1895
Jacksonville Jaguars Foundation: 153
Knight (John S. and James L.) Foundation: 173

Koch Foundation, Inc.: 755
Macdonald (The Dr. John T.) Foundation, Inc.: 1031
Miami Foundation (The): 212
National Oceanic and Atmospheric Administration: 1900
National YoungArts Foundation: 441
Order Sons of Italy in America, Grand Lodge of Florida: 1579
Orlando Magic Youth Foundation: 1036
Peacock Foundation, Inc.: 240
Phi Alpha Theta History Honor Society: 581, 582, 583
Planning and Visual Education Partnership (The): 1584
Quantum Foundation: 1332
Radiant Peace Foundation International, Inc. (The): 1459
Skelly (Gertrude E.) Charitable Foundation: 1484
Southwest Florida Community Foundation: 1258
State Library and Archives of Florida: 689
Swedish Women's Educational Association Inc.: 795
Whitehall Foundation, Inc.: 1978

Georgia

American Academy of Religion: 743, 744
American Cancer Society, Inc.: 2220, 2221
Arthritis Foundation: 2240
ASHRAE: 2430, 2431
Callaway Foundation, Inc.: 1089
Children's Literature Association: 623, 624
Coca-Cola Foundation, Inc. (The): 1397
Coca-Cola Scholars Foundation: 1514
Community Foundation for Greater Atlanta, Inc.: 1108
Community Foundation for Northeast Georgia: 1113
Costume Society of America: 406
Georgia Council for the Arts: 415
Georgia Library Association: 675
Georgia-Pacific Foundation: 127
Golden Key International Honour Society, Inc.: 1527
Hambidge: 417
Home Depot Foundation (The): 1188
Huebner (The S.S.) Foundation for Insurance Education: 1730
Institute of Industrial and Systems Engineers (IISE): 2434
National Black MBA Association: 1219, 946
South Atlantic Modern Language Association: 611
SunTrust Foundation: 285
Tull Charitable Foundation, Inc.: 297
Whitehead (Joseph B.) Foundation: 1051
Woodruff (The Robert W.) Foundation: 309

Hawaii

Castle (Harold K.L.) Foundation: 54
Castle (Samuel N. and Mary) Foundation: 1451
East-West Center (The): 778, 779
Hawaii Community Foundation: 1186
Hawaii State Foundation on Culture and the Arts: 418

Idaho

Idaho Commission on the Arts: 421
Idaho Community Foundation: 148
Micron Technology Foundation, Inc.: 1913
State of Idaho Board of Education: 1597, 1598

Illinois

Abbott Fund: 1
Academy of Nutrition and Dietetics Foundation (The): 2452
Actuarial Foundation (The): 1907, 1908, 1909
Allstate Foundation (The): 1349
Alzheimer's Association: 2243
American Academy of Esthetic Dentistry (The): 2132
American Academy of Implant Dentistry (AAID) Foundation: 2133
American Academy of Pediatrics: 2322
American Association of Law Libraries: 662, 663
American Association of School Librarians: 664, 665
American Bandmasters Association (The): 696
American Bar Foundation: 1797, 892
American Brain Tumor Association: 2244
American Burn Association: 2334
American College of Legal Medicine: 2024
American Dental Assistants Association: 2139
American Dental Hygienists' Association Institute for Oral Health: 2140
American Epilepsy Society (AES): 2245

American Institute of Indian Studies: 604, 812
American Library Association (ALA): 1465, 666
American Lung Association: 2175, 2176, 2177, 2178, 2179, 2180
American Medical Association Foundation: 1500
American Medical Women's Association, Inc.: 2029
American Nuclear Society (ANS): 1881, 2417, 2418, 2419, 2420, 2421, 2422
American Oil Chemists Society (AOCS): 1882
American Orthopaedic Society for Sports Medicine (AOSSM) (The): 2337, 2338
American Osteopathic Foundation: 2317
American Planning Association: 1060, 894
American Society of Safety Professionals: 2429
Appraisal Institute of Professional Resources: 1723
Argonne National Laboratory: 1644, 1645
ASCP: 2040
Baxter International Foundation (The): 32
Benton Foundation: 1750
Blair (William) and Company Foundation: 1078
Blowitz-Ridgeway Foundation: 1079
Brunswick Foundation, Inc.: 1085
Brunswick Public Foundation: 1987
Caterpillar Foundation: 1092
Charleston Area Charitable Foundation: 1097
CHEST Foundation (The): 2182
Chicago Board of Trade Foundation: 1302
Chicago Community Trust (The): 1100
Civic Orchestra of Chicago: 706
Coin-Op Cares Charitable and Education Foundation: 2393
Coleman Foundation, Inc. (The): 66
Community Foundation of the Fox River Valley: 1133
Crossroads Fund: 1680
Dermatology Foundation: 2054
Dirksen Congressional Center (The): 1816
Donnelley (Gaylord and Dorothy) Foundation: 92
Dystonia Medical Research Foundation: 2251
Exelon Corporation: 107
Federation of American Consumers and Travelers: 1403, 1729
Field Foundation of Illinois: 110
Foundation for Anesthesia Education and Research: 2061
Foundation for Osteopathic Emergency Medicine: 2318
Foundation of the American College of Healthcare Executives (The): 1307
Foundation of the American Society of Neuroradiology (The): 2062
Fry (Lloyd A.) Foundation: 122
Graham Foundation for Advanced Studies in the Fine Arts: 381
Great Lakes Protection Fund: 1997
HIMSS Foundation: 2070
Illinois Arts Council Agency: 422
Illinois Clean Energy Community Foundation: 2000
Illinois Restaurant Association Educational Foundation: 1532
Illinois State Academy of Science: 1655
Immanuel Bible Foundation: 754
Institute for the International Education of Students (IES): 1534
Institute of Food Technologists Foundation: 2398
International College of Surgeons (ICS): 2074
International Foundation for Ethical Research, Inc. (IFER): 1656
Jewish Federation of Metropolitan Chicago Academic Scholarship Program: 1540
Journal of the American Medical Association: 1766
Joyce Foundation (The): 158
Kobe College Corporation-Japan Education Exchange: 849
Kraft Heinz Company Foundation (The): 177
Leukemia Research Foundation: 2232
Lowe Syndrome Association: 2078
MacArthur (John D. and Catherine T.) Foundation: 193
McCormick (Robert R.) Foundation: 197
Medical Library Association: 205, 680, 681, 884, 915
Millard (Adah K.) Charitable Trust: 215
Muscular Dystrophy Association: 2259
National Council of Teachers of English Research Foundation: 1428
National Dairy Council: 2460
National Headache Foundation: 2160
Neurosurgery Research and Education Foundation: 2266
Newberry Library (The): 350, 351, 352, 353, 354, 355, 356, 357, 358, 359, 360, 361, 577, 964
North American Spine Society (NASS): 2099
Northern Trust Corporation: 1222
Orthopaedic Research and Education Foundation: 2100, 2101, 2102
Pick (The Albert, Jr.) Fund: 244
Plastic Surgery Foundation (PSF): 2110

Precast/Prestressed Concrete Institute: 2445
Pulmonary Fibrosis Foundation: 2112
Radiological Society of North America Research and Education
    Foundation: 2113, 2114, 2115, 2116, 2117, 2118
Ragdale Foundation: 457
Regenstein Foundation (The): 252
Rehabilitation Nursing Foundation (RNF): 2285
Rock Island Arsenal Museum: 585
Ronald McDonald House Charities: 1040
Rotary Foundation of Rotary International (The): 860
RRF Foundation for Aging: 928
Scholl (Dr.) Foundation: 264
Siragusa Family Foundation (The): 271
Society of Actuaries (SOA): 1914, 1915
Society of Architectural Historians: 388
Society of Cardiovascular Anesthesiologists: 2190
Society of Critical Care Medicine: 2123
Society of Women Engineers: 998
Spencer Foundation: 1440
Stone (W. Clement & Jessie V.) Foundation: 1461
Tree Research & Education Endowment Fund (TREE Fund): 1952
University of Illinois at Urbana-Champaign: 529
USG Foundation, Inc.: 299
Woods Fund Chicago: 1287
Zonta International Foundation: 1007, 1747, 1875

Indiana

Ball Brothers Foundation: 27
Ball (George and Frances) Foundation: 28
Central Indiana Community Foundation: 1094
Community Foundation of Saint Joseph County: 1129
Contemporary Music Festival: 708
Cummins Foundation, Inc. (The): 85
Cushwa Center for the Study of American Catholicism: 542, 543, 544,
    545
Dearborn Community Foundation, Inc.: 1146
DePauw University Key Club International Bonner Scholarship: 1149
Health Foundation of Greater Indianapolis, Inc. (The): 1311, 1355
History of Science Society: 553, 554
Indiana Arts Commission: 423
Indiana Commission for Higher Education, Division of Student Financial
    Aid: 1533
Indiana Library Federation: 677
Lawrence County Community Foundation: 1202
Lilly Endowment Inc.: 187
Lincoln Financial Foundation: 188
Lumina Foundation: 1478
National Federation of Music Clubs: 723, 724, 725
Percussive Arts Society: 731
Pulliam Journalism Fellowship: 1784
Sigma Theta Tau International: 2287
Society for Pediatric Dermatology: 2326
Unity Foundation of LaPorte County (The): 1274
Wabash Center for Teaching and Learning in Theology and Religion
    (The): 764

Iowa

Carver (Roy J.) Charitable Trust: 1469
DuPont Pioneer: 1021
Greater Cedar Rapids Community Foundation (The): 1174
Hoover Presidential Foundation: 1822
International Association for Food Protection: 2457
Iowa Arts Council: 425
McElroy (R.J.) Trust: 1032
National Farmer's Organization: 1948
P.E.O. Sisterhood: 886
Principal Financial Group Foundation Inc.: 247
Quill and Scroll Foundation: 1785
Soil and Water Conservation Society: 2011, 2012, 2013
University of Iowa (The): 655

Kansas

Aviation Insurance Association (AIA): 2409
Eisenhower Foundation (The): 1818
Hutchinson Community Foundation: 420
Jellison Benevolent Society: 1417
Kansas Board of Regents: 1541
Kansas Health Foundation: 1321

Pi Gamma Mu, International Honor Society in Social Science: 1582
SkillBuilders Fund: 997
United Methodist Health Ministry Fund: 1381
University of Kansas Child Language Doctoral Program: 1626
Wichita Community Foundation: 1284

Kentucky

Brown (James Graham) Foundation, Inc.: 43
Community Foundation of Louisville, Inc. (The): 403
Cooke (V.V.) Foundation: 77
Foundation for the Tri-State Community, Inc.: 1167
Gheens Foundation, Inc. (The): 128
Grayson-Jockey Club Research Foundation (The): 2067
Kentucky Arts Council: 427
Kentucky Foundation for Women: 989
Kentucky Higher Education Assistance Authority (KHEAA): 1542, 1543
Kentucky Historical Society: 558
Presbyterian Church (U.S.A.): 1585, 1586, 760

Louisiana

Baton Rouge Area Foundation: 399
Booth-Bricker Fund (The): 42
Brown (The Joe W. and Dorothy Dorsett) Foundation: 44
Greater New Orleans Foundation (The): 1181
Historic New Orleans Collection (The): 550, 551
Honor Society of Phi Kappa Phi (The): 1530
Louisiana Division of the Arts, Department of Culture, Recreation and
    Tourism: 429
Zigler (Fred B. and Ruth B.) Foundation: 1449

Maine

Burnham (The Margaret E.) Charitable Trust: 45
Central Maine Power Company: 55
Hannaford Charitable Foundation: 1409
Haystack Mountain School of Crafts: 419
King (Stephen and Tabitha) Foundation: 169
Libra Foundation: 186
Libra Future Fund: 1734
Maine Arts Commission: 431
Maine Initiatives: 1362
Maine Osteopathic Association: 2319
Morton-Kelly Charitable Trust (The): 1216
Mulford (The Clarence E.) Trust: 218
Oak Grove School Foundation: 1437
Switzer (The Robert & Patricia) Foundation: 2014

Maryland

A.S.P.E.N. Rhoads Research Foundation: 2191
Abell Foundation, Inc. (The): 2
Agency for Healthcare Research and Quality (AHRQ): 1294
American Catholic Historical Association: 532, 745, 746, 747, 748
American Gastroenterological Association (AGA): 2193, 2194, 2195,
    2196, 2197, 2198, 2199, 2200, 2201, 2202, 2203, 2204
American Institute of Physics: 1916
American Kidney Fund: 2027, 2028
American Nurses Foundation: 2276
American Porphyria Foundation (The): 2030
American Speech-Language-Hearing Foundation: 2303
Ames (The Kathryn) Foundation: 766
AMVETS: 1502
Aplastic Anemia and MDS International Foundation: 2038
ASPRS - The Imaging and Geospatial Information Society: 1850
Association of Writers & Writing Programs (The): 619
Association on American Indian Affairs: 953
Bainum Family Foundation: 1009
Baker (The William G., Jr.) Memorial Fund: 398
Baltimore Community Foundation: 29
Blaustein (Jacob and Hilda) Foundation: 902
Bright Focus Foundation: 1298, 2247, 2305
Campbell Foundation, Inc.: 1014
Carson Scholars Fund, Inc. (The): 1511
Community Foundation of Frederick County, MD, Inc. (The): 1120
Community Foundation of the Eastern Shore: 1132
Cystic Fibrosis Foundation: 2209
Early American Industries Association, Inc.: 2394
Epilepsy Foundation of America: 2252
Foundation for Spirituality and Medicine (The): 1306

Michigan

Albion Community Foundation: 1054
Alger Regional Community Foundation: 1056
Allegan County Community Foundation: 1057
American Oriental Society: 503
Ann Arbor Area Community Foundation: 1066
Baraga County Community Foundation: 1072
Battle Creek Community Foundation: 31
Berrien Community Foundation: 37
Binc Foundation: 39
Capital Region Community Foundation: 1090
Community Foundation for Northeast Michigan: 1114
Community Foundation for Southeast Michigan: 70
Community Foundation of Greater Rochester: 1124
Community Foundation of the Holland/Zeeland Area (The): 72
Consumers Energy Foundation: 76
Cook Family Foundation: 1141
Dickinson Area Community Foundation: 1150
Ford (Gerald R.) Presidential Library: 1819, 1820
Ford Motor Company Fund and Community Services: 117
Frey Foundation: 120
Gerber Foundation (The): 1025
Grand Haven Area Community Foundation: 1173
Grand Rapids Community Foundation: 134
Great Lakes Colleges Association New Writers Awards: 625
Greater Lansing Foundation (The): 1179
Hess (Myrtle E. and William G.) Charitable Trust: 911
Hess (William G. and Myrtle E.) Charitable Trust: 1413
Hillsdale County Community Foundation: 1187
Hudson-Webber Foundation: 1190
Kantzler Foundation (The): 1196
Kappa Omicron Nu Honor Society: 2458
Kellogg (W.K.) Foundation: 162
Keweenaw Community Foundation: 1199
Kresge Foundation (The): 178
Livingston Awards: 1768
M & M Area Community Foundation: 1206
Marshall Community Foundation: 1423
McGregor Fund: 200
Michigan Council for Arts and Cultural Affairs: 434
Michigan Gateway Community Foundation: 1212
Michigan Society of Fellows: 343
Michigan State University: 856
Michigan State University, The Graduate School: 916
Michigan Women Forward: 991
Monroe-Brown Foundation: 1479
Mott (Charles Stewart) Foundation: 1217
National Mole Day Foundation: 1886
Pardee (The Elsa U.) Foundation: 2234
Parents Without Partners: 1438
Petoskey-Harbor Springs Area Community Foundation: 1231
Roberts (Forest) Theatre: 499
Saginaw Community Foundation: 1245
Skillman Foundation (The): 272
SME-EF (Society of Manufacturing Engineers Education Foundation): 2403
State of Michigan Department of Treasury: 1599, 1600
Steelcase Foundation: 282
Towsley (The Harry A. and Margaret D.) Foundation: 295
University of Michigan: 1792
Upjohn (W.E.) Institute for Employment Research: 1796
Wege Foundation: 1281
Wilson (Matilda R.) Fund: 308
Wilson Ornithological Society: 1979
Woman's National Farm & Garden Association, Inc.: 1956

Minnesota

American Swedish Institute (The): 829
Andersen Corporate Foundation (The): 1062
Andersen (Fred C. and Katherine B.) Foundation: 1063
Andersen (Hugh J.) Foundation: 1064
Arts Midwest: 490
Athwin Foundation: 21
Babbage (Charles) Institute: 2392
Bremer (Otto) Trust: 1083
Butler (Patrick and Aimee) Family Foundation: 1087
CommunityGiving: 1139
Conference Board of the Mathematical Sciences: 1911
Dell (Roger L. and Agnes C.) Charitable Trust: 1148

Deluxe Corporation Foundation: 89
Duluth Superior Area Community Foundation: 1153
Ecolab Foundation: 1158
Edwards (Ray) Memorial Trust: 1305
Forecast Public Art: 412
Fuller (H.B.) Company Foundation: 1024
Graco Foundation (The): 1172
Hallett Charitable Trusts (The): 1473
Jerome Foundation, Inc.: 426
Land O'Lakes Foundation: 182, 183
Marbrook Foundation: 194
Mayo Clinic: 2083
McKnight Endowment Fund for Neuroscience (The): 2255
McKnight Foundation (The): 1364
Medtronic Foundation: 206
Minneapolis Foundation (The): 1213
Minnesota Department of Education: 683
National Association of Geoscience Teachers: 1897
National Ataxia Foundation: 2261
National Council on Family Relations: 1368
Northwest Minnesota Foundation (The): 1223
Ordean Foundation (The): 1227
Phillips (Jay and Rose) Family Foundation of Minnesota: 1371
Playwrights' Center (The): 651
Porter (Irwin Andrew) Foundation: 245
RBC Foundation - U.S.A.: 1237
Rochester Area Foundation: 1240
3M Foundation, Inc.: 291
U.S. Bancorp Foundation: 1271
University of Minnesota: 469, 656
University of Oslo International Summer School: 868
Wasie Foundation (The): 302
Women's Foundation of Minnesota: 1005
Xcel Energy Foundation: 310

Mississippi

Foundation for the Mid South: 1166
Hardin (The Phil) Foundation: 1411
University of Southern Mississippi (The): 657

Missouri

Aircraft Electronics Association (AEA): 2405
Bayer Fund: 1075
BlueScope Foundation North America (The): 41
Caleres Cares Charitable Trust (The): 49
Community Foundation of the Ozarks: 1134
Consortium for Graduate Study in Management (The): 1724
Emerson: 104
Greater Kansas City Community Foundation and Affiliated Trusts (The): 1178
Hall Family Foundation: 137
Investigative Reporters and Editors: 1765
Kappa Tau Alpha: 1767
Knights of Columbus Vatican Film Library at St. Louis University: 628
Lutheran Foundation of St. Louis: 756
McDonnell (James S.) Foundation: 199
Mid-America Arts Alliance: 435
Missouri Department of Higher Education and Workforce Development: 1553, 1554
National Association of Farm Broadcasting Foundation: 1771
Post-Polio Health International: 2111
Press Club of St. Louis Charitable Fund - St. Louis Press Club (The): 1587
Reproductive Scientist Development Program (RSDP): 2292
Saigh Foundation (The): 1041
Sunnen Foundation: 1380
Truman (Harry S.) Library Institute: 1838
Veterans of Foreign Wars Auxiliary: 474
Washington University: 1633, 1634, 389
Whitaker Foundation: 480

Montana

Housing Education and Research Association (HERA): 1189
Montana Community Foundation: 1215
National Taxidermists Association: 922
Washington (Dennis & Phyllis) Foundation: 1279

Nebraska

Abel Foundation: 1052
Cooper Foundation: 78
Heuermann (B. Keith & Norma F.) Foundation: 141
Mid-Nebraska Community Foundation, Inc.: 214
Nebraska Arts Council: 442
Nebraska's Coordinating Commission for Postsecondary Education: 1564
Omaha Community Foundation: 229
Sowers Club of Nebraska Foundation: 278
Union Pacific Foundation: 298
University of Nebraska at Omaha: 1745
Woods Charitable Fund, Inc.: 1286

Nevada

Davidson Institute: 1518
Nevada Arts Council: 443
Redfield (The Nell J.) Foundation: 250
Wiegand (E. L.) Foundation: 307

New Hampshire

American Ground Water Trust: 2386
Bean (Norwin S. and Elizabeth N.) Foundation: 1076
Dartmouth College: 906
Lindsay (The Agnes M.) Trust: 1029
MacDowell: 430
New Hampshire Library Association: 685
New Hampshire State Council on the Arts: 445

New Jersey

American Accordion Musicological Society: 695
American Association for the History of Nursing, Inc.: 2275
American School of Classical Studies at Athens: 395, 819, 820, 821, 822, 823, 824, 825, 826, 827
Atran Foundation, Inc.: 23
Autism Speaks Inc.: 2041
Berkshire Conference of Women Historians: 536
Campbell Soup Foundation: 50
Capezio/Ballet Makers Dance Foundation, Inc.: 492
Darrin (Margaret A.) Charitable Trust: 87
Davis (Shelby Cullom) Center for Historical Studies: 546
Dodge (Geraldine R.) Foundation: 90
Dow Jones News Fund (The): 1760
Educational Testing Service: 1402
Electrochemical Society (The): 1650, 1651
Foundation for Neonatal Research and Education (FNRE): 2279
General Commission on Archives and History of The United Methodist Church: 752
Graduate Women in Science: 1653
Higher Education Student Assistance Authority (The): 1528, 1529
Histiocytosis Association: 2154
Horowitz Foundation for Social Policy (The): 1684
Hyde and Watson Foundation (The): 147
IEEE History Center: 555
Institute for Advanced Study: 1685
International Foundation (The): 784
Johnson & Johnson Family of Companies: 154
Johnson (Robert Wood) Foundation: 2076
Kirby (F.M.) Foundation, Inc.: 170
KPMG Foundation: 1733
Laurie (The Blanche and Irving) Foundation: 185
Life Sciences Research Foundation (LSRF): 1968
MCJ Amelior Foundation (The): 1033
National Poetry Series (The): 631
New Jersey Department of Military and Veterans Affairs: 1565, 1566
New Jersey Historic Trust: 572, 573
New Jersey Historical Commission: 574, 575
New Jersey Library Association: 686
New Jersey Office of the Secretary of Higher Education (OSHE): 1567
New Jersey Osteopathic Education Foundation: 2320
New Jersey State Council on the Arts: 446
Newcombe (The Charlotte W.) Foundation: 1572
Princeton Area Community Foundation: 1234
Reeve (Christopher & Dana) Foundation: 2347
Schumann Fund for New Jersey (The): 1042
Subaru of America Foundation, Inc.: 1441
Turrell Fund: 1046
UNICO National, Inc.: 1611

Verizon Foundation: 300
Victoria Foundation, Inc.: 1277
Wetlands Institute (The): 1977
Wiley Foundation, Inc. (The): 1929
Wilson (The Woodrow) National Fellowship Foundation: 1636

New Mexico

Albuquerque Community Foundation: 1055
American Indian Graduate Center: 950
American Society for Mass Spectrometry: 1849
Bynner (The Witter) Foundation for Poetry, Inc.: 621
Catching the Dream: 960
Frost Foundation, Ltd. (The): 121
Los Alamos National Laboratory: 1658
Lovelace Respiratory Research Institute: 2131
New Mexico Arts: 447
New Mexico Foundation: 1221
New Mexico Library Association: 687
NewMexicoWomen.org: 923
Roswell Artist-in-Residence Program: 522
Santa Fe Community Foundation: 929
School for Advanced Research: 1843, 1844
Wurlitzer (The Helene) Foundation of New Mexico: 485

New York

Achelis and Bodman Foundation (The): 5
Adams (Emma J.) Memorial Fund, Inc.: 1347
AFS Intercultural Programs/USA: 803
Alliance for Young Artists & Writers (The): 392
Altman Foundation: 1058
Alzheimer's Drug Discovery Foundation: 2022
America-Israel Cultural Foundation: 877
American Academy in Rome: 1983, 311
American Academy of Arts and Letters: 694
American Council of Learned Societies: 314
American Federation for Aging Research (AFAR): 2025, 2026
American Foundation for Suicide Prevention (The): 1382, 1383, 1384, 1385
American Geriatrics Society: 2335
American Institute of Chemical Engineers (AIChE): 1640, 2416
American Jewish Joint Distribution Committee (The): 813
American Museum of Natural History (The): 1641, 1642, 1959
American Musicological Society: 698, 699
American Numismatic Society (The): 315
American Parkinson Disease Association, Inc.: 2246
American-Scandinavian Foundation (The): 1466, 616, 818
American Society of Mechanical Engineers Auxiliary, Inc. (The): 2427
American Vacuum Society (AVS): 1917
Andrus Family Fund: 1065
Architectural League of New York: 377, 378
Armenian General Benevolent Union: 1504
ASCAP Foundation (The): 617, 701
Asian American Writers' Workshop: 618
Asian Cultural Council: 397
Association for Behavioral and Cognitive Therapies: 2363, 2364
Astraea Lesbian Foundation for Justice: 897, 898, 899
Baseball Tomorrow Fund: 1010
Bibliographical Society of America: 1392
Brain & Behavior Research Foundation: 2365
Brookhaven Women in Science: 982
Brooks (Gladys) Foundation: 1084
Cancer Research Institute: 2224, 2225
Carnegie Corporation of New York: 52
Carnegie Fund for Authors: 622
Carvel (Thomas and Agnes) Foundation: 1015
Center for LGBTQ Studies (The): 904
Center for Photography at Woodstock (The): 505
Central New York Community Foundation: 1095
Cerebral Palsy Foundation: 2248
Chamber Music America: 703, 704
Chapin (Harry) Foundation: 1096
Chautauqua Region Community Foundation (The): 1098
Children's Leukemia Research Association: 2323
Children's Tumor Foundation: 2151
Chinese American Medical Society: 2052
Churchill (Winston) Foundation of the United States: 834
City of New York: 1815
Claiborne (Liz) Art Ortenberg Foundation: 1989
Clark (Edna McConnell) Foundation: 60

Oklahoma

American Association of Petroleum Geologists Foundation: 1892
American Fidelity Foundation: 394
Bernsen (The Grace and Franklin) Foundation: 36
Cherokee Nation: 961
Kerr Foundation, Inc. (The): 166
Noble (The Samuel Roberts) Foundation: 1481
Oklahoma Arts Council: 453
Oklahoma City Community Foundation, Inc.: 1225
Sarkeys Foundation: 263
Schusterman (Charles and Lynn) Family Foundation: 1253
Society of Exploration Geophysicists: 1905
Stacey (The John F. and Anna Lee) Scholarship Fund: 527

Oregon

Bonneville Environmental Foundation: 1986
Carpenter Foundation (The): 1091
Collins Foundation (The): 67
Jackson Foundation (The): 151
Lamb Foundation: 181
McDowell (Verne Catt) Corporation: 758
Meyer Memorial Trust: 210
MRG Foundation: 1366
Oregon Arts Commission: 454
Oregon Community Foundation (The): 1228

Pennsylvania

Academy of Natural Sciences of Philadelphia (The): 1637, 1957
Air & Waste Management Association (A&WMA): 2384
Albright Institute of Archaeological Research (AIAR): 804
Alcoa Foundation: 9
Allegheny Foundation: 11
Alternatives Research and Development Foundation: 1639
American Association for Cancer Research: 2219
American Philosophical Society: 12, 13, 316, 952
American Research Institute in Turkey, Inc.: 815, 816, 817
American Society of Regional Anesthesia and Pain Medicine: 2035, 2332
Ampco-Pittsburgh Charitable Foundation: 1061
Barra Foundation: 30
Bayer USA Foundation: 1646
Berks County Community Foundation: 1077
Berwind Corporation: 38
Beta Phi Mu: 669
BNY Mellon Foundation of Southwestern Pennsylvania (The): 1081
Buhl Foundation (The): 1086
Chatham University: 1512
Chester County Community Foundation: 1099
College of Physicians of Philadelphia: 539
Connelly Foundation (The): 75
Curtis Institute of Music (The): 710
Douty Foundation (The): 93
Drexel University College of Medicine: 986
Duquesne University, Department of Philosophy: 336
Fels (Samuel S.) Fund: 1162
First Community Foundation Partnership of Pennsylvania: 112
Foundation for Enhancing Communities (The): 1164
Grundy Foundation (The): 1182
Hamilton Family Charitable Trust: 1408
Huston (The Stewart) Charitable Trust: 753
Independence Foundation: 149
International Centre for Diffraction Data: 2464
Jewish Healthcare Foundation of Pittsburgh (The): 1319
Katz (Herbert D.) Center for Advanced Judaic Studies: 848
Kazanjian (The Calvin K.) Economics Foundation, Inc.: 1732
Kline (Josiah W. and Bessie H.) Foundation, Inc.: 172
Leeway Foundation (The): 990
Lehigh Valley Community Foundation: 428
Library Company of Philadelphia: 559
McLean Contributionship (The): 201
Measey (Benjamin and Mary Siddons) Foundation: 2084
Mellon (Richard King) Foundation: 1210
National Federation of State Poetry Societies, Inc.: 630
NEED: 947
Oncology Nursing Foundation: 2233
Penn (The William) Foundation: 241
Pennsylvania Council on the Arts: 455
Pennsylvania Higher Education Assistance Agency: 1580
Pew Fellowships at the Pew Center for Arts & Heritage: 520

Philadelphia Foundation (The): 1232
Phillips (Dr. and Mrs. Arthur William) Charitable Trust: 2109
Pitt Poetry Series: 650
Pittsburgh Foundation (The): 1233
Pittsburgh New Music Ensemble, Inc. (The): 732
Pool (The Dorothy Rider) Health Care Trust: 1331
PPG Industries Foundation: 246
Presser Foundation: 733
Print and Graphics Scholarship Foundation: 2401, 2402
Quaker Chemical Foundation (The): 249
Rotary Club of Bryn Mawr (The): 1590
Saint-Gobain Corporation Foundation: 1247
Scaife (Sarah) Foundation, Inc.: 1835
Scranton Area Foundation: 1254
Seybert Foundation (The): 1043
Smith (The Ethel Sergeant Clark) Memorial Fund: 275
Smith (The W.W.) Charitable Trust: 276
Society for the Scientific Study of Sexuality (The): 1673
Templeton (John) Foundation: 289
U.S. Army Military History Institute: 594
University of Pittsburgh: 2017
West (Herman O.) Foundation: 305
Widener Memorial Foundation in Aid of Handicapped Children: 936
Wolf Humanities Center: 371

Rhode Island

American Mathematical Society: 1910
Brown (John Carter) Library: 537
Champlin Foundation (The): 57
Council on Technology and Engineering Teacher Education (CTETE): 1400
Hasbro Children's Fund: 1027
Howard (The George A. and Eliza Gardner) Foundation: 1475
Rhode Island Foundation/Rhode Island Community Foundation (The): 255
Rhode Island State Council on the Arts: 458
Rhode Island State Government Internship Program: 1834

South Carolina

Abney Foundation (The): 3
Ashburn Institute Inc.: 768
Coastal Community Foundation of South Carolina: 1103
Community Foundation of the Lowcountry, Inc.: 1399
Self Family Foundation (The): 1255
Sims (J. Marion) Foundation, Inc.: 270
South Carolina Arts Commission: 462
South Carolina Higher Education Tuition Grants Commission: 1595

South Dakota

Native American Community Board (NACB): 1431, 963
South Dakota Arts Council: 463

Tennessee

Assisi Foundation of Memphis Inc.: 20
Community Foundation of Greater Chattanooga, Inc. (The): 1121, 1122
Community Foundation of Greater Memphis: 71
East Tennessee Foundation: 1022
First Horizon Foundation: 1163
Frist Foundation (The): 1168
General Board of Higher Education and Ministry, The United Methodist Church: 751
Lyndhurst Foundation: 192
Oak Ridge Institute for Science and Education (ORISE): 2444
Plough Foundation: 1372
Society of Biological Psychiatry: 2380, 2381
Stokely (The William B., Jr.) Foundation: 283
Symphony of the Mountains: 738
Tau Beta Pi Association, Inc. (The): 2449
Tennessee Arts Commission: 465
Tennessee Student Assistance Corporation: 1603
United Methodist Communications: 1789, 932
United South and Eastern Tribes, Inc.: 969

Texas

ADSC: The International Association of Foundation Drilling: 2414
Alcon Foundation, Inc. (The): 2294
Amarillo Area Foundation: 1059

American Heart Association: 2165, 2166, 2167, 2168, 2169, 2170, 2171, 2172, 2173, 2174
Austin Community Foundation (The): 1069
Bat Conservation International: 1390
Benign Essential Blepharospasm Research Foundation Inc.: 2304
BNSF Railway Foundation: 954
Boy Scouts of America, National Eagle Scout Association (The): 1011, 1012
Brown Foundation, Inc. (The): 1394
Carter (Amon G.) Foundation: 53
CH Foundation (The): 1935
Coastal Bend Community Foundation: 62
Cockrell Foundation (The): 63
Communities Foundation of Texas, Inc.: 68
Community Foundation of Abilene: 1117
Community Foundation of the Texas Hill Country: 1135
Community Foundation of West Texas: 1136
Cullen Foundation (The): 83
Cullen Trust for Health Care (The): 1304
Dallas Foundation (The): 1144
Dallas Museum of Art: 506, 507, 508
Dell (Michael and Susan) Foundation: 1019, 1519
East Texas Communities Foundation: 1156
El Paso Community Foundation: 1159
Emergency Medicine Foundation: 2060
Halliburton Foundation, Inc.: 1474
Hershey (The Jacob and Terese) Foundation: 1998
Hispanic Dental Association Foundation: 2141
Hoblitzelle Foundation: 144
Houston Endowment Inc.: 145
Johnson (The Lyndon Baines) Foundation: 1826
Joslyn (The Carl W. and Carrie Mae) Charitable Trust: 1360
Kempner (Harris and Eliza) Fund: 163
Kimberly-Clark Foundation, Inc.: 168
Kleberg (Robert J., Jr.) and Helen C. Kleberg Foundation: 171
Komen (Susan G.): 2231
Kronkosky (Albert and Bessie Mae) Charitable Foundation: 179
Learning for Life: 1422
Lunar and Planetary Institute: 1868
Maytag (Freda)-Grace Crawford Trust: 1324
Meadows Foundation, Inc.: 204
Moody Foundation (The): 217
National Foster Parent Association: 1035
National Jewish Committee on Scouting: 1557
National Opera Association, Inc.: 726
Permian Basin Area Foundation: 1230
Phi Chi Theta Educational Foundation: 1741
Piper (Minnie Stevens) Foundation: 1583
Prospanica: 925
Richardson (Sid) Memorial Fund: 1589
Richardson (Sid W.) Foundation: 256
Rockwell Fund, Inc.: 258
Salon National La Boutique: 2286
San Angelo Area Foundation: 1248
San Antonio Area Foundation: 1249
Sons of the Republic of Texas (The): 591, 592
Sturgis (Roy and Christine) Charitable and Educational Trust: 284
Summerlee Foundation (The): 1264
Sumners (Hatton W.) Foundation: 1837
Texas Commission on the Arts: 466
Texas Instruments Foundation: 290
Texas Library Association: 690
Texas Women's Foundation: 999
Topfer Family Foundation: 293
Total USA Foundation: 294
Trull Foundation (The): 1270
University of Texas at Austin (The): 1489, 470
Violin Society of America (The): 740
Waco Foundation (The): 1278
Welch (The Robert A.) Foundation: 1888
Welder (Rob and Bessie) Wildlife Foundation: 1928

Utah

McCarthey Dressman Education Foundation: 1456
Simmons Family Foundation: 269
Thrasher Research Fund: 2327
Utah Division of Arts & Museums: 471

Vermont

Ben & Jerry's Foundation: 901
Bread Loaf Writers' Conference: 620
Francis (The Parker B.) Fellowship Program: 2064
Vermont Arts Council: 473
Vermont Student Assistance Corporation: 1630

Virgin Islands

Virgin Islands Council on the Arts: 475

Virginia

Academic Pediatric Association (APA): 2321
AGC Education and Research Foundation: 2415
Air Traffic Control Association (ATCA): 2385
ALS Association (The): 2242
American Association for Dental Research: 2134, 2135, 2136, 2137
American Association of Colleges of Pharmacy: 2328
American Association of Family and Consumer Sciences (AAFCS): 2453, 878
American Center of Oriental Research: 806
American Council for Polish Culture (ACPC): 1496
American Council of the Blind: 1497
American Diabetes Association: 2192
American Floral Endowment: 1932
American Foundation for Pharmaceutical Education (AFPE): 1463, 2329, 2330
American Geosciences Institute (AGI) (The): 1893
American Institute for Cancer Research: 2222
American Institute of Aeronautics and Astronautics: 2406
American Kinesiotherapy Association, Inc.: 2336
American Psychosomatic Society: 2358, 2359, 2360, 2361
American Public Power Association: 2423
American Research Center in Egypt, Inc.: 814
American Roentgen Ray Society: 2031
American Schools of Oriental Research (ASOR): 828
American Society of Civil Engineers: 2426
American Society of Naval Engineers (ASNE): 2428
American Tinnitus Association (ATA): 1643
American Water Resources Association: 1985
Bureau of Indian Education: 959
Catholic Charities USA: 1350
Community Foundation for a greater Richmond: 1107, 69
Cooke (Jack Kent) Foundation: 1516
Council on Social Work Education: 905
Cyprus American Archaeological Research Institute: 838, 839
DECA Inc.: 1725
Dominion Energy Charitable Foundation: 91
Educational and Research Foundation for the American Academy of Facial Plastic and Reconstructive Surgery (AAFPRS Foundation) (The): 2055, 2056, 2057, 2058, 2059
Fats and Proteins Research Foundation, Inc.: 1652
FEEA Scholarship Program: 1521
FishAmerica Foundation: 1992
Foundation for Physical Therapy Research, Inc.: 2339, 2340
Foundation for Technology and Engineering Education: 1406, 1524, 1525
Freedom Alliance: 1526
Gannett Foundation: 123
Graham Holdings Company: 132
Graham (Philip L.) Fund: 133
Hampton Roads Community Foundation (The): 1185
Imagine America Foundation: 1793
Institute for Humane Studies (IHS): 1823
International Association for Dental Research (IADR): 2142
International Association of Fire Chiefs Foundation, Inc.: 1535
International Road Federation: 881
Jenkins Foundation (The): 1318
Koch (Charles G.) Charitable Foundation: 1420
Madison (James) Memorial Fellowship Foundation: 560
March of Dimes: 2081, 2082
Marine Corps Scholarship Foundation, Inc.: 1548
Microscopy Society of America: 1659, 1660, 1970
Mineralogical Society of America (The): 1896
Mitsubishi Electric America Foundation: 1457
Mustard Seed Foundation (The): 1424
National Coalition of Black Meeting Planners (NCBMP): 1427
National Federation of Republican Women: 994
National GEM Consortium (The): 920
National Institute for Labor Relations Research: 1555, 1776

Personnel Index

References in index are to entry numbers.

Sanders, Carolanne: 1378
Sandorf, Julie: 253
Sandoval, Lester, Dr.: 960
Sandrock, Alfred, M.D., Ph.D.: 2107, 2333
Sandy, Heather Moulaison: 667, 668
Sanford, Shelton: 753
Sani, Nicola: 693
Sankey, C. Patrick: 881
Sant, Vickie A.: 175
Santana, Miguel A.: 304, 1088
Santanello, Nancy C., M.D., M.S.: 2107, 2333
Santino, Alyssa: 95
Santora, Kenneth, Ph.D.: 1327
Santucci, Marryn D.: 234
Sanzio, Anthony: 50
Sapon, Anne: 1055
Saran, Sally: 1347
Sardone, Frank J.: 1796
Sargeant, Geoffrey: 701
Sargent, Jocelyn: 1358
Sarnoff, Deborah S., M.D.: 2237
Sarofim, Louisa: 1394
Sasser, Barbara W.: 163
Sasser, Emily: 163
Sattler, David G.: 2296
Sauls, Shanaysha M.: 29
Sauvayre, Sara Chubb: 1277
Savage, Barbara D.: 1846
Savage, Eleanor: 426
Saville, Bei: 1277
Savoy, Caroline: 2119
Savoy, George M.: 2119
Sawyer, Raymond T., Esq.: 65
Sayer, Doug: 1598
Scace, Barbara: 241
Scalan, Jenna: 993
Scales, Jason: 2435
Scantlebury, Joseph: 162
Scarola, Albert: 1214
Schakelford, Marcia: 1234
Schatz, Edward: 788
Scheid, Randy: 1332
Scherago, Nina: 513
Scherer, Carol: 805
Scherer, Thomas: 349
Scherzer, Mitchell: 1762
Schieber-Acker, Traude: 769
Schiff, Stacy: 135
Schisler, Kurt E.: 175
Schlack, Marilyn: 1796
Schlessinger, Evan: 1195
Schlonsky, Michael: 1105
Schmeerbauch, Aaron L.: 756
Schmid, Kate: 134
Schmidt, Cade: 910
Schmidt, Oscar: 209
Schmidt, Paul: 1760
Schmuckler, Naomi: 1916
Schnaars, Donna: 876
Schnabel, Rockwell, Hon.: 1477
Schnarr, Laura: 1587
Schneider, Eric C., M.D.: 1352
Schneider-Salomon, Susanne: 843
Schnur, Eric R.: 190
Schoeler, Martina: 843
Schoenbaum, Stephen C., M.D., M.P.H.: 2080
Schoenhoff, Katie: 1381
Schoenmann, Charlotte: 1055
Scholl, Barry A.: 1352
Scholl, Pamela: 264
Scholnick, Lynn Okon, Ms.: 960
Schooley, Susan, M.D.: 200
Schoor, Thelma, B.S.N., R.N.: 2284
Schoppa, Leonard J., Jr., Dr.: 786
Schotland, Marvin I.: 1195
Schramling, Shaine: 1200
Schrantz, Jacob S.: 1098
Schroeder, Lisa: 1233
Schubach, Carolyn: 1456
Schuette, Bill: 2234

Schuette, William G.: 2234
Schultz, Jonathan D.: 756
Schultz, Tim: 1303
Schultz, Timothy: 402
Schwab, Charles R.: 265
Schwab, Helen O.: 265
Schwamborn, Laura: 1109
Schwark, Mary: 1956
Schwartz, Alan: 1534
Schwartz, Eric: 135
Schwartz, Mark: 1195
Schwartz, Mike: 48
Schwartz, Stephen: 701
Schwartz, Susan: 1396
Schwartz, Timothy J.: 1816
Schwarz, Colleen, MBA: 1303
Schweizer, Felix E., Ph.D: 2253
Schwenn, Carolyn: 1022
Schwister, Ann: 1175
Sciarra, Lorraine: 1847
Sconiers, Rose H., Hon.: 1109
Scott, Elizabeth H.J.: 1347
Scott, F. Laurence, Jr.: 26
Scott, Frank L.: 26
Scott, Joshua: 234
Scott, Lauren E.: 163
Scott, Patrick: 1456
Scott, Peter, C.A.E., MBA: 2296
Scott, Rick: 426
Scott, Rita: 1526
Sculco, Cynthia, Ed.D., R.N.: 2284
Sealey, Michelle: 258
Seals, Carol E.: 28
Searles, Simonne: 272
Sears, Suzanne Harte: 303
Seaver, Carlton: 268
Seaver, Christopher: 268
Seaver, Martha: 268
Seaver, Patrick: 268
Sedmak, Rich: 1043
Sedonaen, Maureen: 195
Seelbach, William R.: 65
Segal, Susan: 1005
Segal, Susan L.: 796
Segarra, Tere: 234
Seiden, Michael V., M.D., Ph.D.: 2236
Seiders, Ed: 2427
Seiders, Stella: 2427
Seides, Ted: 1846
Seidler, Lee J.: 500
Seitter, Keith L., Dr.: 2407
Seitz, Karen D.: 2236
Self, Furman C.: 1255
Self, J.C., III: 1255
Self, Sally E., M.D.: 1255
Self, W.M.: 1255
Self, W.M., Jr.: 1255
Sells, Marcia Lynn: 253
Semelsberger, Ken: 101
Sen, Rinku: 993
Senchak, Andrew: 430
Serio, Matt: 455
Sevillano, Lina M.: 885
Sewill, Ann: 1088
Seymour, Peter: 363
Shafer, Kevin: 1997
Shah, Nirav R.: 139
Shaheen, Tim N.: 234
Shane, David N.: 187
Shang, Ruby: 397
Shank, Suzanne: 272
Shanley, Claudia: 1632
Shanley, Frank E.: 1013
Shannon, Kathleen T.: 1330
Shapira, Edith L., M.D.: 1233
Shapiro, Adina: 25
Shapiro, Alex: 701
Sharma, Prakash, Dr.: 1638
Sharpe, Dan A.: 1104
Sharpe, Valerie L., O.D.: 2296

Sharples, Amber: 453
Shaughnessy, Sandy: 411
Shaw, Kathleen: 1112
Shaw, Minor M.: 97
Shaw, Ruth: 1165
Shearer, Chad: 1342
Sheehan, Mary: 1109
Sheely, Jay: 1944
Shelby, Tommy: 1757
Shelden, William W., Jr.: 200
Shelnitz, Mark A.: 131
Shelters, Sarah M.: 1098
Shenk, Janet: 19
Sheppard, Eileen D.: 2372
Sherer, Todd, Ph.D.: 2063
Sheridan, R. Kelly: 57
Sheriff, Edd: 3
Sherman, Cindy: 135
Sherman, Cynthia: 619
Sherman, Marny: 1838
Sherman, Sandra Brown: 170
Sherry, Andrew: 173
Shih, Anthony, M.D., M.P.H.: 1342
Shockley, Linda: 1760
Shockley, Scott E.: 27
Shore, Debra: 1997
Shorris, Anthony: 1342
Shragge, Katie: 253
Shrut, Arlene: 742
Shuford, Alex: 92
Shuford, Karen L.: 144
Shulman, Lee P., M.D.: 2290
Shulman, Randy: 339
Sidell, Sydney: 122
Siegel, Herbert J.: 2053
Siegel, Lawrence J., MBA, J.D.: 2284
Sieger, Diana R.: 134
Sieghart, Mary Ann: 882
Siegler, Julie A.: 187
Sieracki, John: 341
Sieracki, Michael: 1903
Sieve, Richard, M.D.: 2127
Sifferlin, Elena Brito: 1005
Silvers, Sam: 1471
Simmelink, Laura: 1118
Simmons, Omar: 1358
Simms-Mackey, Pamela J., Dr.: 1301
Simon, Renee B., M.S., M.L.S., Hon.: 1295
Simoncini, Matthew: 1190
Simonds, Joshua: 731
Simone, Joseph A.: 1944
Simonian, Nancy, M.D.: 2236
Simons, John C.: 1342
Simpkins, Jesse: 1992
Simpkins, Nancy K.: 2371
Simpson, Janis Randall: 2454
Simpson, Judy: 1453
Simpson, Megan: 1177
Simpson, Roy L., D.N.P., R.N.: 2284
Simpson, Valerie: 701
Simril, Renata: 1322
Singh, Sarah: 142
Sion, L. Gilles: 830
Siragusa, Alexander C.: 271
Siragusa, Isabel: 271
Siragusa, John R., III: 271
Siragusa, Marco: 271
Siragusa, Philip: 271
Siragusa, Ross D., III: 271
Siragusa, Sinclair C.: 271
Sit, Roger: 1364
Sittler, Hana: 769
Sjoquist, Gregg D.: 302
Skach, William, M.D.: 2209
Skaff, Daniel: 195
Skahen, Venetia: 51
Skinner, Duncan S.: 2379
Skovronsky, Daniel, M.D., Ph.D.: 2107, 2333
Skrzesz, Ken: 433
Skulimowski, Marek: 717, 850, 851, 852, 1545, 1546